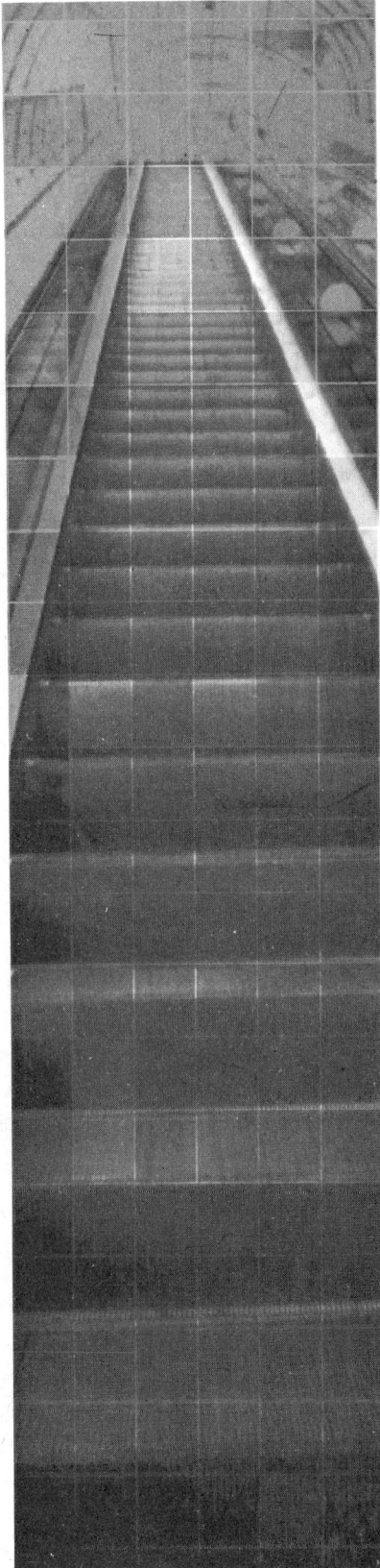

FINANCIAL MANAGEMENT

NINTH EDITION

By the Same Author:

- Capital Structure and the Cost of Capital
- Management Accounting
- Essentials of Management Accounting
- Essentials of Financial Management

FINANCIAL MANAGEMENT

NINTH EDITION

I M PANDEY

Professor of Finance
Indian Institute of Management, Ahmedabad

VIKAS®

VIKAS® PUBLISHING HOUSE PVT LTD

VIKAS® PUBLISHING HOUSE PVT LTD

A-22, Sector-4, Noida-201301 (UP)
Phone: 0120-4078900 • Fax: 4078999
VIKAS®   Regd. Office: 576, Masjid Road, Jangpura, New Delhi-110 014

• First Floor, N.S. Bhawan, 4th Cross, 4th Main, Gandhi Nagar,
  Bangalore-560 009 • Phone: 080-22204639, 22281254
• Damodhar Centre, New No. 62, Old No. 59, Nelson Manickam Road,
  Aminjikarai, **Chennai**-600 029 • Phone: 044-23744547, 23746090
• P-51/1, CIT Road, Scheme - 52, **Kolkata**-700014
  • Ph. 033-22866995, 22866996
• 67/68, 3rd Floor, Aditya Industrial Estate, Chincholi Bunder, Malad (West),
  Mumbai-400 064 • Ph. 022-28772545, 28768301

Distributors:

UBS PUBLISHERS' DISTRIBUTORS PVT LTD

5, Ansari Road, **New Delhi**-110 002
  • Ph. 011-23273601, 23266646 • Fax: 23276593, 23274261
• 10, First Main Road, Gandhi Nagar, **Bangalore**-560 009 • Ph. 080-22253903
• Z-18, M P Nagar, Zone-1, **Bhopal**-462 011 • Ph. 0755-4203183, 4203193
• Ist Floor 145, Cuttack Road, **Bhubaneshwar**-751 006
• 60, Nelson Manickam Road, Aminjikarai, **Chennai**-600 029 • Ph. 044-23746222
• 40/7940, Convent Road, **Ernakulam**-682 035 • Ph. 0484-2353901, **2363905**
• 3rd Floor, Alekhya Jagadish Chambers, H. No. 4-1-1058, Boggulkunta, Tilak Road,
  Hyderabad-500 001 • Ph. 040-24754472 / 73 / 74
• 8/1-B, Chowringhee Lane, **Kolkata**-700 016 • Ph. 033-22521821, 22522910
• 9 Ashok Nagar, Near Pratibha Press, Gautam Buddha Marg, Latush Road,
  Lucknow-226 001 • Ph. 0522-2294134, 3014010
• 2nd Floor, Apeejay Chambers, 5 Wallace Street, Fort, **Mumbai**-400 001
  • Ph. 022-66376922-3, 66102069 • Fax: 66376921
• GF, Western Side, Annapoorna Complex, Naya Tola, **Patna**-800 004
  • Ph. 0612-2672856, 2673973
• 680 Budhwar Peth, 2nd Floor, Appa Balwant Chowk, **Pune**-411 002
  • Ph. 020-24461653, 24433976

Ninth Edition 2005
Reprint 2009

VIKAS® is the registered trademark of Vikas Publishing House Pvt Ltd
Copyright © I M Pandey, 1978, 2005

Printed at International Print-o-Pac Ltd.,NOIDA-201 305

To
Meena

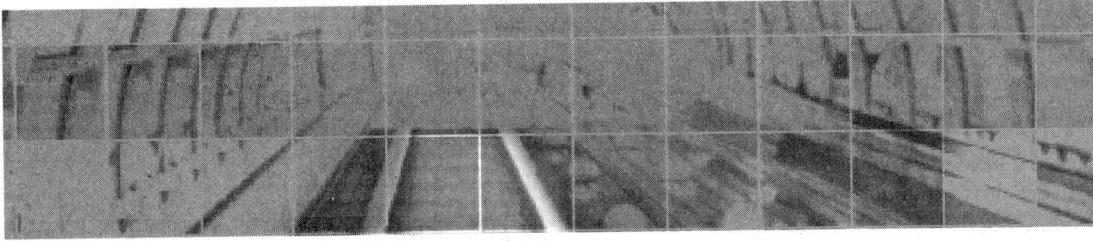

Preface

About three decades ago, the scope of financial management was confined to raising of funds, and little significance was attached to the analytical thinking in financial decision-making and problem solving. As a consequence, the finance text-books earlier were structured around this theme and contained description of the instruments and institutions of raising funds and of the major events, like promotion, reorganisation, readjustment, merger, consolidation etc., when funds were raised. In the mid-fifties, the emphasis shifted to the judicious utilisation of funds. The modern thinking in financial management accords a far greater importance to management decision-making and policy. Today, financial managers do not perform the passive role of scorekeepers of financial data and information, and arranging funds, whenever directed to do so. Rather, they occupy key positions in top management areas and play a dynamic role in solving complex management problems. They are now responsible for shaping the fortunes of the enterprise and are involved in the most vital management decision of allocation of capital. It is their duty to ensure that the funds are raised most economically and used in the most efficient and effective manner. Because of this change in emphasis, the descriptive treatment of the subject of financial management is being replaced by growing analytical content and sound theoretical underpinnings. This is the approach adopted by this book – *Financial Management*.

Focus of the Book

I wrote the first edition of *Financial Management* in 1978 with the following objectives which remain unchanged in the ninth edition of the book in 2005:

1. To demonstrate to readers that the subject of finance is simple to understand, relevant in practice and interesting to learn.

2. To help managers appreciate the logic for making better financial decisions.

3. To explain the concepts and theories of finance in a simple way so readers could grasp them very easily and be able to put them into practice.

4. To provide a book that has a comprehensive coverage for MBA and other post-graduate courses.

5. To create a book that differentiates itself from other text-books in terms of coverage, presentation, and with an equal focus on theory and practice with real life examples.

Financial Management combines theory with practical applications. It begins with the discussion of fundamental concepts of value and return, the risk and return relationship and the valuation of shares and bonds. With this foundation, readers can easily understand the theories and methods, decision criteria, and financial policies and strategies necessary to manage funds and create and enhance the value of the firm.

Financial Management in its ninth edition, like in its previous editions, highlights the "modern", analytical approach to corporate finance decision-making. The text material has been structured to focus on finance theory and its implications in the financial decision-making process and policy. The book discusses the theories, concepts, assumptions, and mechanics underlying financial decisions, viz., investment, financing, dividend, and working capital management. It also discusses sources and instruments of short-term and long-term finances, mergers and acquisitions, international financial management and the interface between financial and corporate policies. Importantly, the book helps students to relate theories and concepts to practice.

Features of the Book

Financial Management aims to assist the reader to develop a thorough understanding of the concepts and theories underlying financial management in a systematic way. To accomplish this purpose, the recent thinking in the field of finance has been presented in a most lucid, simple, unambiguous and precise manner.

The book contains a comprehensive treatment of topics on valuation, risk and return, options, capital budgeting, capital structure, dividend decisions, working capital management, mergers and acquisitions, shareholder value, corporate governance and international financial management with a view that readers understand these financial decisions thoroughly well and are able to evaluate their implications for shareholders and the company. The financial analysis, planning and modelling techniques are also discussed in detail for the benefit of those readers who have not been exposed to these topics earlier.

In all its previous editions, the book has stressed the analytical approach for solving financial problems. Concepts are made clear in simple language before introducing complicated and sophisticated techniques and theories. For a better and easy comprehension of the concepts and theories, the book contains a number of real life financial problems and cases in the Indian context in addition to examples and illustrative problems. Each chapter contains a summary of the key points as well as a list of key concepts. At the end of each chapter, review questions and problems, a number of them based on professional courses and examinations have been added. Review questions can be used for discussions in the class by teachers. Problems have been included to help readers apply the concepts discussed in the chapter. Review questions and problems illustrate the key points in the text. Some questions and problems require readers to evaluate a situation or critically examine and analyse it. It is hoped that this will facilitate a better understanding of the subject matter.

The main features of the book may be summarised as follows:

1. **Excel applications** Proficiency with spreadsheets and Excel is a great advantage to financial analysts and managers and a necessity for all the post-graduate management, commerce and accounting courses students. With this in mind, at appropriate places, we created Excel Applications showing how spreadsheets with the help of Excel could be used to solve finance problems and decisions. These have also been identified in the list of Contents.

2. **Web links for financial data** Students, who are future managers, must know how to access financial data and information on the Internet. With this in mind, we have created a list of useful web links to help readers retrieve useful financial information.

3. **Illustrative problems** Finance decisions involve solving problems using the theoretical concepts. The book contains solved illustrations showing readers how concepts could be used to solve problems and take decisions.

4. **Real life examples** The book contains a large number of real life cases and examples to illustrate the practical applications of the finance theories and concepts.

5. **Mini cases** Most chapters include mini cases that reflect the applications of the conceptual material in the chapters. This is a new feature of the ninth edition of the book.

6. **Key concepts** For the benefits of readers, the key concepts of each chapter have been listed at the end of the chapter.

Beta calculation in practice Over the past few years, the use of beta in decision-making has increased in India. The National Stock Exchange (www.nse-india.com) gives beta based on daily share prices for one-year period for a number of companies. This information may not be useful when we require beta based on a longer time period or for different time periods. Chapter 6 shows how beta can be calculated for a real company in practice. We demonstrate how the 'Regression function' of Excel can be used to calculate beta.

Valuation and governance Managers are required to maximise shareholder value. This needs a clear understanding of cash flows and discount rate and the financing impact. In practice, a number of managers are not able to understand the inter-relationships. We have introduced a new chapter (Chapter 16) that integrates cash flows, discount rate, financing and valuation. This material is further extended to shareholder value and corporate governance in Chapter 35.

Cost of capital The cost of capital is a contentious topic in finance. Its calculation could be quite tedious in practice. With the help of real world company, we have demonstrated its calculation in Chapter 9. In Chapter 16, we have analysed the effect of changes in capital structure on beta and the cost of capital.

Instructional Material for Teachers and Students

The following material is available for students and teachers:

1. **Student's CD** In the ninth edition of Financial Management, we have included a student's CD. The CD includes:
   (a) **Power point presentation of each chapter**

   (b) **Data of companies for analysing their financial performance and management**
   (c) **Excel problems to practice the use of spreadsheets and Excel functions in finance**
   (d) **Key definitions and formulae**
   (e) **Time value tables**
   (f) **Web links**

2. **Student's Guide** A guide illustrating the answers of Review Questions and Problems is available for students. In addition, a separate book containing professional examinations' problems with solution will also be available for students.

3. **Teacher's Manual** To help teachers teaching from the book and design their finance courses, a Teacher's Manual is available.

Changes in the Ninth Edition

The ninth edition is a thoroughly revised edition. The new topics added in this edition include:

- *Real Options*
- *Valuation and Financing*
- *Corporate Governance*
- *Balanced Scorecard*
- *Valuation of the Firm*
- *Beta Estimation in Real World*
- *Divisional Cost of Capital*
- *Financial Modelling*
- *Derivatives and Financial Risk Management*
- *Financial Management in Government Companies*

Most chapters have been updated with new material. A number of new real-life examples of companies have been included. Readers may notice that some real life cases and other materials have been provided in Exhibits (boxes) to draw their attention. These have also been identified in the list of Contents. Particular care has been taken to ensure the correctness of equations and formulae and solved problems and illustrations.

Audience of the Book

Financial Management is designed for use in MBA, M Com, Chartered Accountancy, Cost Accountancy, and Company Secretary courses. It will also be useful for financial executives who want to update their knowledge about the recent thinking in financial management and who wish to improve their ability in making financial decisions. To cater to the needs of both students and financial executives, the subject matter has been discussed in a conceptual-cum-analytical manner. It is the aim of the book to help readers develop skill to understand, analyse and interpret financial problems and data to make good financial decisions.

I M PANDEY
Indian Institute of Management
Vastrapur, Ahmedabad 380015, India
impandey@iimahd.ernet.in
1 January, 2005

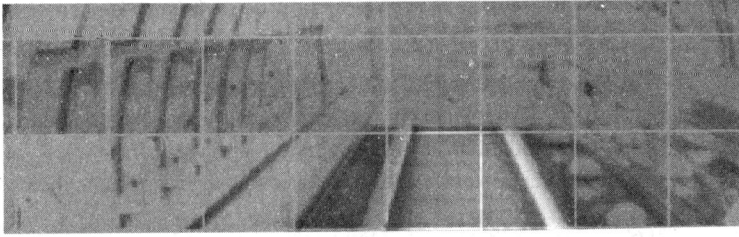

Acknowledgements

A large number of individuals have contributed in creating this book, *Financial Management*. I am thankful to all of them for their help and encouragement. Like most text-books, this book has also drawn from the works of a large number of researchers and authors in the field of finance. My writing in this book has also been influenced by a number of standard and popular text-books in the field. As far as possible, they have been fully acknowledged at the appropriate places. I express my gratitude to all of them. A number of problems, illustrations and exercises in the book have been drawn from or are based on the examinations of Universities and management institutes in India as well as the public examinations of the professional bodies in India, the UK and the USA such as the Institute of Chartered Accountants of India, the Institute of Cost and Works Accountants of India, the Institute of Certified Public Accountants (CPA), USA, National Association of Accountants (NAA), USA, the Institute of Cost and Management Accounting (ICMA), UK. I have tried to give credit to all sources from where I have drawn material in this book. Still there may have remained unintended errors. I shall feel obliged if they are brought to my notice. I have also used published data of a number of companies in India. I am thankful to those companies also.

I express my gratitude to all my colleagues from Universities, management schools and professional institutes in India and abroad for adopting the book, or for making suggestions for the improvement of the book, or for extending their support and encouragement. I have mentioned the names of friends who have been a source of motivation to me, and some adopters of the book.

R B Agadi, Gulburga University, Andhra Pradesh
J D Agarwal, Indian Institute of Finance, Delhi
Anup Agrawal, North Carolina State University, USA
K Ashok Anand, PES Institute of Technology, Bangalore
S Anand, J N N College of Engineering, Shimoga
M A Ansari, Banaras Hindu University, Varanasi
Deepika Arora, Rai Business School, New Delhi
T Asokan, Kannur University, Kannur
Alok Awtans, Amity School of Distance Learning, NOIDA
Abdul Azeez, P A College of Engineering, Mangalore
Balasubramanian, ICFAI University, Hyderabad
Basavacharya, Oxford College of Engineering, Bangalore
B K Basu, Calcutta University, Kolkata
Susanta K Basu, National Institute of Management, Kolkata
U K Basu, Institute of Modern Management, Kolkata
Gurdeep Singh Batra, Punjab University, Patiala
Ramesh Bhat, Indian Institute of Management, Ahmedabad
Ashis K Bhattacharya, Indian Institute of Management, Kolkata
Hrishikesh Bhattacharya, Indian Institute of Management, Kolkata
S K Bose, Birla Institute of Technology, Ranchi
B Bramhaiah, JNIDB, Hyderabad
Alok Chakraborty, Institute of Cost and Works Accountants of India, Kolkata
K S Hema Chandra, Acharaya Institute of Technology, Bangalore
Pareshnath Chattopadhyay, National Institute of Management, Kolkata
S N Chaturvedi, Institute of Management and Technology, Gorakhpur
M Chitale, Pune University, Pune
T Chotigeat, Nicholls State University, USA
Sumedha Datta, NIILM, New Delhi
Paul Draper, Strathclyde University, UK
Eresi, AES National College, Gauribidanur
Anne Gagenzel, Graduate Management Schools, ESCP, Paris, France
Dev Gandhi, University of Ottawa, Canada
Y S Ganesh, SJCE, Mysore
S K Ganguly, Institute of Cost and Works Accountants of India, Kolkata
Anil Gautam, Rashsri School of Management & Technology, Varanasi
N Gautam, Shiva Institute of Management, Ghaziabad
Debashish Ghosh, Nirma Institute of Management, Ahmedabad
Patrick Guegon, Graduate Management School, ESCP, Paris, France
G S Gupta, (formerly with) Indian Institute of Management, Ahmedabad
J L Gupta, (formerly with) Shri Ram College of Commerce, University of Delhi, Delhi
Jyoti P Gupta, Graduate Management School, ESCP, Paris, France
Ramesh Gupta, Indian Institute of Management, Ahmedabad
S Gupta, Institute of Chartered Accountants of India, Kolkata
Shipra Gupta, Rashsri School of Management & Technology, Varanasi
P Haridas, College of Engineering, Trivandrum
S Hariharan, Pondicherry University, Pondicherry
Niam Hasan, University of Birmingham, UK
Georges Hirsch, French-Vietnam Management School, Hanoi, Vietnam
Hugar, Karnataka University, Bangalore
Jamil, Institute of Productivity and Management, Gomatinagar, Lucknow
V K Janardhanan, Calicut University, Calicut
Hemant Joshi, VES's Institute of Management, Mumbai
P L Joshi, University of Bahrain, Kingdom of Bahrain
Jimmy M Kapadia, S R Luthra Institute of Management, Surat
Sanjay S Kaptan, Amravati University, Amravati

Mohindra N Kaura (late), (formerly with) Administrative Staff College of India, Hyderabad

Bhagwan Khanna, Wellington University, New Zealand.

Sunder Ram Korivi, Narsee Monjee Institute of Management Studies, Mumbai

Kotaresh, Manasagangothri University, Mysore

M G Krishnamurthy, J N N College of Engineering, Shimoga

Shilpa Kulkarni, JDC Bitco Institute of Management Studies and Research, Nasik

Ajoy Kumar, SIT, Tumkur

K M Suresh Kumar, Dr Ambedkar Institute of Technology, Bangalore

Rekha Arun Kumar, Bapuji Institute of Engineering and Technology, Davangere

Ashok Lahiri, Chief Economic Advisor, Government of India, New Delhi

R K Lele (late), (formerly with) Delhi School of Economics, University of Delhi, Delhi

Shyam Lodha, Southern Connecticut University, USA

Madhe Gowda, Kuvempu University, Shimoga

B B Maharana, Utkal University, Bhubaneswar

Manoj Rawal, Symbiosis Institute of Business Management, Pune

Mary Jessica, University of Hyderabad, Hyderabad

M R Mayya, (formerly with) Bombay Stock Exchange, Mumbai

Shabana Mazhar, Allahabad Agricultural Institute, Allahabad

Utkarsh Mazumdar, (formerly with) Indian Institute of Management, Lucknow

Sanjay Medhavi, Lucknow University, Lucknow

Anil Mishra, Jaipuri Institute of Management, Gomatinagar, Lucknow

Bishnupriya Mishra, Regional College of Management, Bhubaneswar

D P Mishra, Lucknow Univeristy, Lucknow

Dheeraj Mishra, Jaipuria Institute of Management, Lucknow

R K Mishra, Dean, Institute of Public Enterprises, Hyderabad

J K Misra, Institute of Professional Studies and Research, Cuttack

R K Misra, Institute of Public Enterprise, Hyderabad

Mohan B, Sri Venkateswara University, Tirupati

Hare Ram Mohanty, Institute of Business Administration and Training, Bhubaneswar

M S Moodithaya, NMAM, Nitte

B K Mukherjee, S A Jaipuria College, Kolkata

Alka Munjal, Amity Business School, NOIDA

B E V V N Murthy, Sri Venkateswara Univesity, Tirupati

B Diwakar Naidu, MVJ College of Engineering, Bangalore

Salya Nandini, BMS College of Engineering, Bangalore

M S Narasimhan, Institute of Financial & Management Research, Chennai

B M L Nigam, (formerly with) Delhi School of Economics, University of Delhi, Delhi

S Nigam, NIILM, New Delhi

A R Parshuraman, SOES's Institute of Management, Navi Mumbai, Mumbai

P B Patel, CSIBER, Kolhapur

V S Patil, Shivaji Univesity, Kolhapur

B A Prajapati, North Gujarat University, Patan

P K Priyan, Sardar Patel University, Vallabh Vidya Nagar, Gujarat

V M Purushothaman, M G University, Kottayam

Anand Rai, Harward Institute of Technology & Management, Greater Noida

J Rajan, Kerala University, Trivandrum

Y Rajaram, AES National College, Gauribidanur

Rajkumar, Banaras Hindu University, Varanasi

N Ramachandran, Indian Institute of Management, Kolkata

B Appa Rao, Andhra University, Vishakapatnam.

B. Parvatheswara Rao, Andhra University, Vishakapatnam

G V Keshava Rao, BMS College of Engineering, Bangalore

M Gangadhara Rao, Gandhi Institute of Technology Management Studies (GITAM), Vishakapatnam

P S Rao, KLE IMSR, Hubli

R Hanumanth Rao, Osmania University, Hyderabad

Bratati Ray, S A Jaipuria College, Kolkata

B Ramachandra Reddy, Sri Venkateswara Univesity, Tirupati

C Sivarami Reddy, Sri Venkateswara University, Tirupati

M S Reddy, Sri Venkateswara University, Tirupati

K.T. Rengamani, Vellore Institute of Technology, Vellore

Indrani Saha, Shree Shikshayatan College, Kolkata

P K Sahu, Utkal University, Bhubaneswar

Saritha Rani, Dr Ambadkar Institute of Technology, Bangalore

LVLN Sarma, Multimedia University, Malaysia

Y M Satish, M S Ramaiah Institute of Technology, Bangalore

G Sethu, UTI Institute of Capital Markets, Mumbai

A K Sharma, National Institute of Financial Management, Faridabad

J K Sharma, University of Lucknow, Lucknow

N R Sharma, North Maharashtra University, Jalgaon

Shekhar, Osmania University, Hyderabad

V Shivakumaran, SP Jain Institute of Management Studies, Mumbai

M S Shubash, Kousali Institute of Management Studies, Dharwad

Lomesh Shukla, Lucknow University, Lucknow

Shyam Sunder, University of Yale, USA.

Sidharth Sinha, Indian Institute of Management, Ahmedabad, India.

Amiya Shahu, S K Patel Institute of Management, Gandhi Nagar

Harpreet Singh, Panjabi University, Patiala

Inderjeet Singh, Panjabi University, Patiala

J P Singh, Banaras Hindu University, Varanasi

Sampat P Singh, (formerly with) National Institute of Management, Pune, India.

Phillipe Spisier, Graduate Management School, ESCP, Paris, France.

Srinivasan, Arora P G College, Hyderabad

Rakesh Srivastava, United College of Engineering, UPSIDC Industrial Area, Naini, Allahabad

Swagata Sengupta, Heritage Institute of Technology, Kolkata

S K Syan, MS University of Baroda, Vadodara

R Thenmozhi, University of Madras, Chennai

M Thiripalraju, Security and Exchange Board of India, Mumbai

R K Tripathi, Lucknow University, Lucknow

K Vashisth, University Business School, Chandigarh

N M Vechalkar, STES's Sinhgad Institute of Management, Pune
P Viswanadham, Andhra University, Vishakapatnam
S Yuvaraj, University of Madras, Chepauk, Chennai

My special thanks to Dr R K Mishra and Dr P L Joshi for contributing Chapter 36 on Financial Management in Government Companies.

I would very much appreciate and sincerely acknowledge suggestions from academic colleagues and readers for improving the quality of the book. I shall be happy to acknowledge the support of the adopters of the book.

The book is dedicated to my wife, Meena, who has always been a source of incessant motivation and encouragement to me and who has always extended her unstinted support to me in writing this book. I am thankful to my wife as well as my daughter, Ruchika and son, Abhishek, for their endurance through several months that I spent in writing this book.

I M PANDEY
Ahmedabad

About the Author

I M PANDEY holds a PhD (1977) from Delhi School of Economics, University of Delhi. He joined Indian Institute of Management, Ahmedabad (IIMA) in 1980 where he is currently a Professor of Finance. He has also taught at the School of Management, Asian Institute of Technology, Bangkok, Thailand (1994-96); College of Business Administration, Kansas State University, Kansas, USA (1984-85); Paris School of Management, ESCP, Paris, France; and Graduate School of Management, ESSEC, Cergy, France. He was also a visiting scholar at the Department of Finance, University of Birmingham, UK.

His research interests are focused on strategic financial management, financial decision-making processes, comparative financial systems, capital markets and financial services, with a focus on emerging markets. He is the author/co-author of ten books, five monographs and more than 100 articles and management cases. He is the Editor of IIMA's journal: *Vikalpa: The Journal for Decision-Makers* and is on the editorial board of several Indian and international finance journals.

Professor Pandey has conducted several management development programmes for practising executives and administrators. He has also undertaken consulting assignments for several organisations including the Asian Development Bank, World Bank, and the European Union.

At IIMA, he was Dean (1991-94), Chairman of Fellow (doctoral) programme (1988-90) and Chairman of the Finance & Accounting Area (1982-93 and 1986-88). He has also held a number of academic positions at different institutions.

Professor Pandey is currently member on the Boards of Directors of Industrial Finance Corporation of India and Cochin Shipyard Company. He served as member of the Controller of Capital Issues (CCI), Advisory Committee, Government of India (1988-90), member, IDBI Western Region Advisory Board, member on the Board of IDBI-Principal Company and as member, Board of Governors, National Institute of Management (1994-96). He was also member on the board of Ahmedabad Stock Exchange.

Professor Pandey was awarded the Best Case-writer of the Year 1996 in the First Asian Conference on Management Education and Case Research USM, Malaysia, August 1996; the Teacher of the Year 1996 Award, School of Management, Asian Institute of Technology, Thailand and the Best Course (Strategic Financial Management) and Teacher Award, 1986, Indian Institute of Management, Ahmedabad, India.

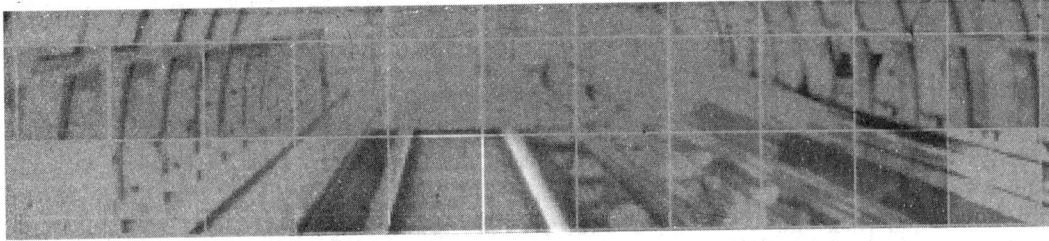

Contents

PART 1 Valuation

⊠ = Excel Applications.

PART 3 Financing and Dividend Decisions

PART 4 Long-Term Financing

PART 5 Financial and Profit Analysis

PART 6 Working Capital Management

PART 7 Managing Value and Risk

PART 8 Annexure

PART 1

Valuation

Nature of Financial Management

CHAPTER OBJECTIVES

- Explain the nature of finance and its interaction with other management functions
- Review the changing role of the finance manager and his/her position in the management hierarchy
- Focus on the shareholders' wealth maximisation (SWM) principle as an operationally desirable finance decision criterion
- Discuss agency problems arising from the relationship between shareholders and managers
- Illustrate organisation of finance function

INTRODUCTION

Financial management is that managerial activity which is concerned with the planning and controlling of the firm's financial resources. It was a branch of economics till 1890, and as a separate discipline, it is of recent origin. Still, it has no unique body of knowledge of its own, and draws heavily on economics for its theoretical concepts even today.

The subject of financial management is of immense interest to both academicians and practising managers. It is of great interest to academicians because the subject is still developing, and there are still certain areas where controversies exist for which no unanimous solutions have been reached as yet. Practising managers are interested in this subject because among the most crucial decisions of the firm are those which relate to finance, and an understanding of the theory of financial management provides them with conceptual and analytical insights to make those decisions skilfully.

SCOPE OF FINANCE

What is finance? What are a firm's financial activities? How are they related to the firm's other activities? Firms create manufacturing capacities for production of goods; some provide services to customers. They sell their goods or services to earn profit. They raise funds to acquire manufacturing and other facilities. Thus, the three most important activities of a business firm are:

- production
- marketing
- finance

A firm secures whatever capital it needs and employs it (finance activity) in activities, which generate returns on invested capital (production and marketing activities).

Real and Financial Assets

A firm requires real assets to carry on its business. **Tangible real assets** are physical assets that include plant, machinery, office, factory, furniture and building. **Intangible real assets** include technical know-how, technological collaborations, patents and copyrights. **Financial assets,** also called securities, are financial papers or instruments such as shares and bonds or debentures. Firms issue securities to investors in the **primary capital markets** to raise necessary funds. The securities issued by firms are traded – bought and sold – by investors in the **secondary capital markets**, referred to as stock exchanges. Financial assets also include lease obligations and borrowing from banks, financial institutions and other sources. In a **lease**, the lessee obtains a right to use the lessor's asset for an agreed amount of rental over the period of lease. Funds applied to assets by the firm are called capital expenditures or investment. The firm expects to receive return on investment and might distribute return (or profit) as dividends to investors.

Equity and Borrowed Funds

There are two types of funds that a firm can raise: equity funds (simply called equity) and borrowed funds (called debt). A firm sells shares to acquire equity funds. **Shares** represent ownership rights of their holders. Buyers of shares are called shareholders (or stockholders), and they are the legal owners of the firm whose shares they hold. Shareholders invest their money in the shares of a company in the expectation of a return on their invested capital. The return of shareholders consists of dividend and capital gain. Shareholders make capital gains (or loss) by selling their shares.

Shareholders can be of two types: ordinary and preference. **Preference shareholders** receive dividend at a fixed rate, and they have a priority over **ordinary shareholders**. The dividend rate for ordinary shareholders is not fixed, and it can vary from year to year depending on the decision of the board of directors. The payment of dividends to shareholders is not a legal obligation; it depends on the discretion of the board of directors. Since ordinary shareholders receive dividend (or repayment of invested capital, only when the company is wound up) after meeting the obligations of others, they are generally called owners of residue. Dividends paid by a company are not deductible expenses for calculating corporate income taxes, and they are paid out of profits after corporate taxes. As per the current laws in India, a company is required to pay 12.5 per cent tax on dividends.

A company can also obtain equity funds by retaining earnings available for shareholders. Retained earnings, which could be referred to as internal equity, are undistributed profits of equity capital. The retention of earnings can be considered as a form of raising new capital. If a company distributes all earnings to shareholders, then, it can reacquire new capital from the same sources (existing shareholders) by issuing new shares called **rights shares.** Also, a **public issue** of shares may be made to attract new (as well as the existing) shareholders to contribute equity capital.

Another important source of securing capital is **creditors** or **lenders.** Lenders are not the owners of the company. They make money available to the firm as loan or debt and retain title to the funds lent. Loans are generally furnished for a specified period at a fixed rate of interest. For lenders, the return on loans or debt comes in the form of **interest** paid by the firm. Interest is a cost of debt to the firm. Payment of interest is a legal obligation. The amount of interest paid by a firm is a deductible expense for computing corporate income taxes. Thus, interest provides **tax shield** to a firm. The **interest tax shield** is valuable to a firm. The firm may borrow funds from a large number of sources, such as banks, financial institutions, public or by issuing bonds or debentures. A **bond** or a **debenture** is a certificate acknowledging the amount of money lent by a bondholder to the company. It states the amount, the rate of interest and the maturity of the bond or debenture. Since bond or debenture is a financial instrument, it can be traded in the secondary capital markets.

Finance and Management Functions

There exists an inseparable relationship between finance on the one hand and production, marketing and other functions on the other. Almost all business activities, directly or indirectly, involve the acquisition and use of funds. For example, recruitment and promotion of employees in production is clearly a responsibility of the production department; but it requires payment of wages and salaries and other benefits, and thus, involves finance. Similarly, buying a new machine or replacing an old machine for the purpose of increasing productive capacity affects the flow of funds. Sales promotion policies come within the purview of marketing, but advertising and other sales promotion activities require outlays of cash and therefore, affect financial resources.

Where is the separation between production and marketing functions on the one hand and the finance function of making money available to meet the costs of production and marketing operations on the other hand? Where do the production and marketing functions end and the finance function begin? There are no clear-cut answers to these questions. The finance function of raising and using money although has a significant effect on other functions, yet it needs not necessarily limit or constraint the general running of the business. A company in a tight financial position will, of course, give more weight to financial considerations, and devise its marketing and production strategies in the light of the financial constraint. On the other hand, management of a company, which has a reservoir of funds or a regular supply of funds, will be more flexible in formulating its production and marketing policies. In fact, financial policies will be devised to fit production and marketing decisions of a firm in practice.

FINANCE FUNCTIONS

It may be difficult to separate the finance functions from production, marketing and other functions, but the functions themselves can be readily identified. The functions of raising funds, investing them in assets and distributing returns earned from assets to shareholders are respectively known as *financing decision, investment decision and dividend decision.* A firm attempts to balance cash inflows and outflows while performing these functions. This is called *liquidity decision,* and we may add it to the list of important finance decisions or functions. Thus finance functions include:

- Long-term asset-mix or investment decision
- Capital-mix or financing decision
- Profit allocation or dividend decision
- Sort-term asset-mix or liquidity decision

A firm performs finance functions simultaneously and continuously in the normal course of the business. They do not necessarily occur in a sequence. Finance functions call for skilful planning, control and execution of a firm's activities.

Let us note at the outset that shareholders are made better off by a financial decision that increases the value of their shares. Thus while performing the finance functions, the financial manager should strive to maximise the market value of shares. This point is elaborated in detail later on in the chapter.

Investment Decision (1)

A firm's investment decisions involve capital expenditures. They are, therefore, referred as capital budgeting decisions. A **capital budgeting decision** involves the decision of allocation of capital or commitment of funds to long-term assets that would yield benefits (cash flows) in the future. Two important aspects of investment decisions are: (*a*) the evaluation of the prospective profitability of new investments, and (*b*) the measurement of a **cut-off rate** against that the prospective return of new investments could be compared. Future benefits of investments are difficult to measure and cannot be predicted with certainty. **Risk** in investment arises because of the uncertain returns. Investment proposals should, therefore, be evaluated in terms of both **expected return** and risk. Besides the decision to commit funds in new investment proposals, capital budgeting also involves **replacement decisions,** that is, decision of recommitting funds when an asset becomes less productive or non-profitable.

There is a broad agreement that the correct cut-off rate or the **required rate of return** on investments is the opportunity cost of capital.[1] The **opportunity cost of capital** is the expected rate of return that an investor could earn by investing his or her money in financial assets of equivalent risk. However, there are problems in computing the opportunity cost of capital in practice from the available data and information. A decision maker should be aware of these problems.

Financing Decision (2)

Financing decision is the second important function to be performed by the financial manager. Broadly, he or she must decide when, where from and how to acquire funds to meet the firm's investment needs. The central issue before him or her is to determine the appropriate proportion of equity and debt. The mix of debt and equity is known as the firm's **capital structure**. The financial manager must strive to obtain the best financing mix or the **optimum capital structure** for his or her firm. The firm's capital structure is considered optimum when the market value of shares is maximised.

In the absence of debt, the shareholders' return is equal to the firm's return. The use of debt affects the return and risk of shareholders; it may increase the return on equity funds, but it always increases risk as well. The change in the shareholders' return caused by the change in the profits is called the **financial leverage.** A proper balance will have to be struck between return and risk. When the shareholders' return is maximised with given risk, the market value per share will be maximised and the firm's capital structure would be considered optimum. Once the

financial manager is able to determine the best combination of debt and equity, he or she must raise the appropriate amount through the best available sources. In practice, a firm considers many other factors such as control, flexibility, loan covenants, legal aspects etc. in deciding its capital structure.

Dividend Decision (3)

Dividend decision is the third major financial decision. The financial manager must decide whether the firm should distribute all profits, or retain them, or distribute a portion and retain the balance. The proportion of profits distributed as dividends is called the **dividend-payout ratio** and the retained portion of profits is known as the **retention ratio.** Like the debt policy, the dividend policy should be determined in terms of its impact on the shareholders' value. The **optimum dividend policy** is one that maximises the market value of the firm's shares. Thus, if shareholders are not indifferent to the firm's dividend policy, the financial manager must determine the optimum dividend-payout ratio. Dividends are generally paid in cash. But a firm may issue bonus shares. **Bonus shares** are shares issued to the existing shareholders without any charge. The financial manager should consider the questions of dividend stability, bonus shares and cash dividends in practice.

Liquidity Decision (4)

Investment in current assets affects the firm's profitability and liquidity. Current assets management that affects a firm's liquidity is yet another important finance function. Current assets should be managed efficiently for safeguarding the firm against the risk of illiquidity. Lack of liquidity (or illiquidity) in extreme situations can lead to the firm's insolvency. A conflict exists between profitability and liquidity while managing current assets. If the firm does not invest sufficient funds in current assets, it may become illiquid and therefore, risky. But it would lose profitability, as idle current assets would not earn anything. Thus, a proper trade-off must be achieved between profitability and liquidity. The **profitability-liquidity trade-off** requires that the financial manager should develop sound techniques of managing current assets. He or she should estimate firm's needs for current assets and make sure that funds would be made available when needed.

In sum, financial decisions directly concern the firm's decision to acquire or dispose off assets and require commitment or recommitment of funds on a continuous basis. It is in this context that finance functions are said to influence production, marketing and other functions of the firm. Hence finance functions may affect the size, growth, profitability and risk of the firm, and ultimately, the value of the firm. To quote Ezra Solomon:[2]

> ... The function of financial management is to review and control decisions to commit or recommit funds to new or ongoing uses. Thus, in addition to raising funds, financial

---

1. Robichek, A., *Financial Research and Management Decision*, John Wiley, 1967, p. 6.
2. Solomon, Ezra, *The Theory of Financial Management*, Columbia University Press, 1969, p. 3.

management is directly concerned with production, marketing and other functions, within an enterprise whenever decisions are made about the acquisition or distribution of assets.

Financial Procedures and Systems

For the effective execution of the finance functions, certain other functions have to be routinely performed. They concern procedures and systems and involve a lot of paper work and time. They do not require specialised skills of finance. Some of the important routine finance functions are:

* supervision of cash receipts and payments and safeguarding of cash balances
* custody and safeguarding of securities, insurance policies and other valuable papers
* taking care of the mechanical details of new outside financing
* record keeping and reporting

The finance manager in the modern enterprises is mainly involved in the managerial finance functions; executives at lower levels carry out the routine finance functions. Financial manager's involvement in the routine functions is confined to setting up of rules of procedures, selecting forms to be used, establishing standards for the employment of competent personnel and to check up the performance to see that the rules are observed and that the forms are properly used.

The involvement of the financial manager in the managerial financial functions is recent. About three decades ago, the scope of finance functions or the role of the financial manager was limited to routine activities. How the scope of finance function has widened or the role of the finance manager has changed is discussed in the following section.

FINANCIAL MANAGER'S ROLE

Who is a financial manager?[1] What is his or her role? A **financial manager** is a person who is responsible, in a significant way, to carry out the finance functions. It should be noted that, in a modern enterprise, the financial manager occupies a key position. He or she is one of the members of the top management team, and his or her role, day-by-day, is becoming more pervasive, intensive and significant in solving the complex funds management problems. Now his or her function is not confined to that of a scorekeeper maintaining records, preparing reports and raising funds when needed, nor is he or she a staff officer–in a passive role of an adviser. The finance manager is now responsible for shaping the fortunes of the enterprise, and is involved in the most vital decision of the allocation of capital. In his or her new role, he or she needs to have a broader and far-sighted outlook, and must ensure that the funds of the enterprise are utilised in the most efficient manner. He or she must realise that his or her actions have far-reaching consequences for the firm because they influence the size, profitability, growth, risk

and survival of the firm, and as a consequence, affect the overall value of the firm. The financial manager, therefore, must have a clear understanding and a strong grasp of the nature and scope of the finance functions.

The financial manager has not always been in the dynamic role of decision-making. About three decades ago, he or she was not considered an important person, as far as the top management decision-making was concerned. He or she became an important management person only with the advent of the modern or contemporary approach to the financial management. What are the main functions of a financial manager?

Funds Raising

The traditional approach dominated the scope of financial management and limited the role of the financial manager simply to funds raising. It was during the major events, such as promotion, reorganisation, expansion or diversification in the firm that the financial manager was called upon to raise funds. In his or her day-to-day activities, his or her only significant duty was to see that the firm had enough cash to meet its obligations. Because of its central emphasis on the procurement of funds, the finance textbooks, for example, in the USA, till the mid1950s covered discussion of the instruments, institutions and practices through which funds were obtained. Further, as the problem of raising funds was more intensely felt in the special events, these books also contained detailed descriptions of the major events like mergers, consolidations, reorganisations and recapitalisations involving **episodic financing.**[2] The finance books in India and other countries simply followed the American pattern. The notable feature of the traditional view of financial management was the assumption that the financial manager had no concern with the decision of allocating the firm's funds. These decisions were assumed as given, and he or she was required to raise the needed funds from a combination of various sources.

The traditional approach did not go unchallenged even during the period of its dominance. But the criticism related more to the treatment of various topics rather than the basic definition of the finance function. The traditional approach has been criticised because it failed to consider the day-to-day managerial problems relating to finance of the firm. It concentrated itself to looking into the problems from management's–*the insider's point of view.*[3] Thus the traditional approach of looking at the role of the financial manager lacked a conceptual framework for making financial decisions, misplaced emphasis on raising of funds, and neglected the real issues relating to the allocation and management of funds.

Funds Allocation

The traditional approach outlived its utility in the changed business situation particularly after the mid-1950s. A number of economic and environmental factors, such as the increasing pace of industrialisation, technological innovations and inventions,

---

1. Different titles are used for the persons performing the finance functions. The title, financial manager, is more popular and easily understood. A discussion of the labels of financial executives follows later in this chapter.
2. For a detailed discussion, see Archer, S.M. and D'Ambrosio; S.A., *Business Finance: Theory and Practice,* Macmillan, 1966, Chapter 1.
3. Solomon, *op. cit.,* p. 5.

intense competition, increasing intervention of government on account of management inefficiency and failure, population growth and widened markets, during and after mid-1950s, necessitated efficient and effective utilisation of the firm's resources, including financial resources. The development of a number of management skills and decision-making techniques facilitated the implementation of a system of optimum allocation of the firm's resources. As a result, the approach to, and the scope of financial management, also changed. The emphasis shifted from the episodic financing to the financial management, from raising of funds to efficient and effective use of funds. The new approach is embedded in sound conceptual and analytical theories.

The new or modern approach to finance is an analytical way of looking into the financial problems of the firm. Financial management is considered a vital and an integral part of overall management. To quote Ezra Solomon:[1]

> In this broader view the central issue of financial policy is the wise use of funds, and the central process involved is a rational matching of advantages of potential uses against the cost of alternative potential sources so as to achieve the broad financial goals which an enterprise sets for itself.

Thus, in a modern enterprise, the basic finance function is to decide about the expenditure decisions and to determine the demand for capital for these expenditures. In other words, the financial manager, in his or her new role, is concerned with the **efficient allocation of funds.** The allocation of funds is not a new problem, however. It did exist in the past, but it was not considered important enough in achieving the firm's long run objectives.

In his or her new role of using funds wisely, the financial manager must find a rationale for answering the following three questions:[2]

- How large should an enterprise be, and how fast should it grow?
- In what form should it hold its assets?
- How should the funds required be raised?

As discussed earlier, the questions stated above relate to three broad decision areas of financial management: investment (including both long and short-term assets), financing and dividend. The "modern" financial manager has to help making these decisions in the most rational way. They have to be made in such a way that the funds of the firm are used optimally. We have referred to these decisions as managerial finance functions since they require special care and extraordinary managerial ability.

As discussed earlier, the financial decisions have a great impact on all other business activities. The concern of the financial manager, besides his traditional function of raising money, will be on determining the size and technology of the firm, in setting the pace and direction of growth and in shaping the profitability and risk complexion of the firm by selecting the best asset mix and financing mix.

Profit Planning

The functions of the financial manager may be broadened to include profit-planning function. **Profit planning** refers to the operating decisions in the areas of pricing, costs, volume of output and the firm's selection of product lines. Profit planning is, therefore, a prerequisite for optimising investment and financing decisions.[3] The cost structure of the firm, i.e. the mix of fixed and variable costs has a significant influence on a firm's profitability. **Fixed costs** remain constant while **variable costs** change in direct proportion to volume changes. Because of the fixed costs, profits fluctuate at a higher degree than the fluctuations in sales. The change in profits due to the change in sales is referred to as **operating leverage**. Profit planning helps to anticipate the relationships between volume, costs and profits and develop action plans to face unexpected surprises.

Understanding Capital Markets

Capital markets bring investors (lenders) and firms (borrowers) together. Hence the financial manager has to deal with capital markets. He or she should fully understand the operations of capital markets and the way in which the capital markets value securities. He or she should also know-how risk is measured and how to cope with it in investment and financing decisions. For example, if a firm uses excessive debt to finance its growth, investors may perceive it as risky. The value of the firm's share may, therefore, decline. Similarly, investors may not like the decision of a highly profitable, growing firm to distribute dividend. They may like the firm to reinvest profits in attractive opportunities that would enhance their prospects for making high capital gains in the future. Investments also involve risk and return. It is through their operations in capital markets that investors continuously evaluate the actions of the financial manager.

FINANCIAL GOAL: PROFIT MAXIMISATION VERSUS WEALTH MAXIMISATION

The firm's investment and financing decisions are unavoidable and continuous. In order to make them rationally, the firm must have a goal. It is generally agreed in theory that the financial goal of the firm should be **shareholders' wealth maximisation** (SWM), as reflected in the market value of the firm's shares. In this section, we show that the shareholders' wealth maximisation is theoretically logical and operationally feasible **normative goal** for guiding the financial decision-making.

Profit Maximisation

Firms, producing goods and services, may function in a market economy, or in a government-controlled economy. In a market economy, prices of goods and services are determined in competitive markets. Firms in the market economy are expected to produce goods and services desired by society as efficiently as possible.

1. *Ibid*, p. 2,
2. Solomon, *op. cit.*, pp. 8–9.
3. Mao, James C.T., *Quantitative Analysis of Financial Decisions*, Macmillan, 1969, p. 4.

Price system is the most important organ of a market economy indicating what goods and services society wants. Goods and services in great demand command higher prices. This results in higher profit for firms; more of such goods and services are produced. Higher profit opportunities attract other firms to produce such goods and services. Ultimately, with intensifying competition, an equilibrium price is reached at which demand and supply match. In the case of goods and services, which are not required by society, their prices and profits fall. Producers drop such goods and services in favour of more profitable opportunities.[1] Price system directs managerial efforts towards more profitable goods or services. Prices are determined by the demand and supply conditions as well as the competitive forces, and they guide the allocation of resources for various productive activities.[2]

A legitimate question may be raised: Would the price system in a free market economy serve the interests of the society? Adam Smith has given the answer many years ago. According to him:[3]

> (The businessman), by directing...industry in such a manner as its produce may be of greater value...intends only his own gain, and he is in this, as in many other cases, led by an invisible hand to promote an end which was not part of his intention...pursuing his own interest he frequently promotes that of society more effectually than he really intends to promote it.

Following Smith's logic, it is generally held by economists that under the conditions of free competition, businessmen pursuing their own self-interests also serve the interest of society. It is also assumed that when individual firms pursue the interest of maximising profits, society's resources are efficiently utilised.

In the economic theory, the behaviour of a firm is analysed in terms of profit maximisation. **Profit maximisation** implies that a firm either produces maximum output for a given amount of input, or uses minimum input for producing a given output. The underlying logic of profit maximisation is **efficiency.** It is assumed that profit maximisation causes the efficient allocation of resources under the competitive market conditions, and profit is considered as the most appropriate measure of a firm's performance.

Objections to Profit Maximisation

The profit maximisation objective has been criticised. It is argued that profit maximisation assumes perfect competition, and in the face of imperfect modern markets, it cannot be a legitimate objective of the firm. It is also argued that profit maximisation, as a business objective, developed in the early 19th century when the characteristic features of the business structure were self-financing, private property and single entrepreneurship. The only aim of the single owner then was to enhance his or her individual wealth and personal power, which could easily be satisfied by the profit maximisation objective.[4] The modern business environment is characterised by limited liability and a divorce between management and ownership. Shareholders and lenders today finance the business firm but it is controlled and directed by professional management. The other important **stakeholders** of the firm are customers, employees, government and society. In practice, the objectives of these stakeholders or constituents of a firm differ and may conflict with each other. The manager of the firm has the difficult task of reconciling and balancing these conflicting objectives. In the new business environment, profit maximisation is regarded as unrealistic, difficult, inappropriate and immoral.[5]

It is also feared that profit maximisation behaviour in a market economy may tend to produce goods and services that are wasteful and unnecessary from the society's point of view. Also, it might lead to inequality of income and wealth. It is for this reason that governments tend to intervene in business. The price system and therefore, the profit maximisation principle may not work due to imperfections in practice. Oligopolies and monopolies are quite common phenomena of modern economies. Firms producing same goods and services differ substantially in terms of technology, costs and capital. In view of such conditions, it is difficult to have a truly competitive price system, and thus, it is doubtful if the profit-maximising behaviour will lead to the optimum social welfare. However, it is not clear that abandoning profit maximisation, as a decision criterion, would solve the problem. Rather, government intervention may be sought to correct market imperfections and to promote competition among business firms. A market economy, characterised by a high degree of competition, would certainly ensure efficient production of goods and services desired by society.[6]

Is profit maximisation an operationally feasible criterion? Apart from the aforesaid objections, profit maximisation fails to serve as an operational criterion for maximising the owner's economic welfare. It fails to provide an operationally feasible measure for ranking alternative courses of action in terms of their economic efficiency. It suffers from the following limitations:[7]

- It is vague
- It ignores the timing of returns
- It ignores risk.

Definition of profit: The precise meaning of the profit maximisation objective is unclear. The definition of the term profit is ambiguous. Does it mean short- or long-term profit? Does it refer to profit before or after tax? Total profits or profit per share? Does it mean total operating profit or profit accruing to shareholders?

1. Solomon, Ezra and Pringle John J., *An Introduction to Financial Management,* Prentice-Hall of India, 1978, pp. 6–7.
2. *Ibid.*
3. Adam Smith, *The Wealth of Nations,* Modern Library, 1937, p. 423, quoted in Solomon and Pringle, *op. cit.*
4. Solomon, *op. cit.*
5. Anthony, Robert B., The Trouble with Profit Maximization, *Harvard Business Review,* 38, (Nov.–Dec. 1960), pp. 126–34.
6. Solomon and Pringle, *op. cit.,* pp. 8–9.
7. Solomon, *op. cit.,* p. 19.

Time value of money: The profit maximisation objective does not make an explicit distinction between returns received in different time periods. It gives no consideration to the time value of money, and it values benefits received in different periods of time as the same.

Uncertainty of returns: The streams of benefits may possess different degree of certainty. Two firms may have same total expected earnings, but if the earnings of one firm fluctuate considerably as compared to the other, it will be more risky. Possibly, owners of the firm would prefer smaller but surer profits to a potentially larger but less certain stream of benefits.

Maximising Profit After Taxes

Let us put aside the first problem mentioned above, and assume that maximising profit means maximising profits after taxes, in the sense of net profit as reported in the profit and loss account (income statement) of the firm. It can easily be realised that maximising this figure will not maximise the economic welfare of the owners. It is possible for a firm to increase profit after taxes by selling additional equity shares and investing the proceeds in low-yielding assets, such as the government bonds. Profit after taxes would increase but **earnings per share** (EPS) would decrease. To illustrate, let us assume that a company has 10,000 shares outstanding, profit after taxes of Rs 50,000 and earnings per share of Rs 5. If the company sells 10,000 additional shares at Rs 50 per share and invests the proceeds (Rs 500,000) at 5 per cent after taxes, then the total profits after taxes will increase to Rs 75,000. However, the earnings per share will fall to Rs 3.75 (i.e., Rs 75,000/20,000). This example clearly indicates that maximising profits after taxes does not necessarily serve the best interests of owners.

Maximising EPS

If we adopt maximising EPS as the financial objective of the firm, this will also not ensure the maximisation of owners' economic welfare. It also suffers from the flaws already mentioned, i.e. it ignores timing and risk of the expected benefits. Apart from these problems, maximisation of EPS has certain deficiencies as a financial objective. For example, note the following observation:[1]

> ... For one thing, it implies that the market value of the company's shares is a function of earnings per share, which may not be true in many instances. If the market value is not a function of earnings per share, then maximisation of the latter will not necessarily result in the highest possible price for the company's shares. Maximisation of earnings per share further implies that the firm should make no dividend payments so long as funds can be invested internally at any positive rate of return, however small. Such a dividend policy may not always be to the shareholders' advantage.

It is, thus, clear that maximising profits after taxes or EPS as the financial objective fails to maximise the economic welfare of owners. Both methods do not take account of the timing and uncertainty of the benefits. An alternative to profit maximisation, which solves these problems, is the objective of **wealth maximisation.** This objective is also considered consistent with the survival goal and with the personal objectives of managers such as recognition, power, status and personal wealth.

Shareholders' Wealth Maximisation (SWM)

What is meant by shareholders' wealth maximisation (SWM)? SWM means maximising the net present value of a course of action to shareholders. **Net present value** (NPV) or wealth of a course of action is the difference between the present value of its benefits and the present value of its costs.[2] A financial action that has a positive NPV creates wealth for shareholders and, therefore, is desirable. A financial action resulting in negative NPV should be rejected since it would destroy shareholders' wealth. Between **mutually exclusive projects** the one with the highest NPV should be adopted. NPVs of a firm's projects are addititive in nature. That is

$$\text{NPV}(A) + \text{NPV}(B) = \text{NPV}(A+B)$$

This is referred to as the **principle of value-additivity.** Therefore, the wealth will be maximised if NPV criterion is followed in making financial decisions.[3]

The objective of SWM takes care of the questions of the timing and risk of the expected benefits. These problems are handled by selecting an appropriate rate (the shareholders' opportunity cost of capital) for discounting the expected flow of future benefits. *It is important to emphasise that benefits are measured in terms of cash flows.* In investment and financing decisions, it is the flow of cash that is important, not the accounting profits.

The objective of SWM is an appropriate and operationally feasible criterion to choose among the alternative financial actions. It provides an unambiguous measure of what financial management should seek to maximise in making investment and financing decisions on behalf of shareholders.[4]

---

1. Porterfield, James C.T., *Investment Decision and Capital Costs,* Prentice-Hall, 1965.
2. Solomon, *op. cit.,* p. 22.
3. The net present value or wealth can be defined more explicitly in the following way:

$$\text{NPV} = W = \frac{C_1}{(1+k)} + \frac{C_2}{(1+k)^2} + \dots \frac{C_n}{(1+k)^n} - C_0 = \sum_{t-1}^{n} \frac{C_t}{(1+k)^t} - C_0$$

where C_1, C_2 ... represent the stream of cash flows (benefits) expected to occur if a course of action is adopted, C_0 is the cash outflow (cost) of that action and k is the appropriate discount rate (opportunity cost of capital) to measure the quality of C's; k reflects both timing and risk of benefits, and W is the net present value or wealth which is the difference between the present value of the stream of benefits and the initial cost. The firm should adopt a course of action only when W is positive, i.e. when there is net increase in the wealth of the firm. This is a very simple model of expressing wealth maximisation principle. A complicated model can assume capital investments to occur over a period of time and k to change with time. The detailed discussion of the present value concept follows in Chapters 7 to 11.

4. Solomon, *op. cit.,* p. 20.

Maximising the shareholders' economic welfare is equivalent to maximising the utility of their consumption over time. With their wealth maximised, shareholders can adjust their cash flows in such a way as to optimise their consumption. From the shareholders' point of view, the wealth created by a company through its actions is reflected in the market value of the company's shares. Therefore, the wealth maximisation principle implies that the *fundamental objective of a firm is to maximise the market value of its shares*. The value of the company's shares is represented by their market price that, in turn, is a reflection of shareholders' perception about quality of the firm's financial decisions. The market price serves as the firm's performance indicator. How is the market price of a firm's share determined?

Need for a Valuation Approach

SWM requires a valuation model. The financial manager must know or at least assume the factors that influence the market price of shares, otherwise he or she would find himself or herself unable to maximise the market value of the company's shares. What is the appropriate share valuation model? In practice, innumerable factors influence the price of a share, and also, these factors change very frequently. Moreover, these factors vary across shares of different companies. For the purpose of the financial management problem, we can phrase the crucial questions normatively: How much *should* a particular share be worth? Upon what factor or factors *should* its value depend? Although there is no simple answer to these questions, it is generally agreed that the value of an asset depends on its risk and return.

Risk-return Trade-off

Financial decisions incur different degree of risk. Your decision to invest your money in government bonds has less risk as interest rate is known and the **risk of default** is very less. On the other hand, you would incur more risk if you decide to invest your money in shares, as return is not certain. However, you can *expect* a lower return from government bond and higher from shares. Risk and expected return move in tandem; the greater the risk, the greater the expected return. Figure 1.1 shows this **risk-return relationship.**

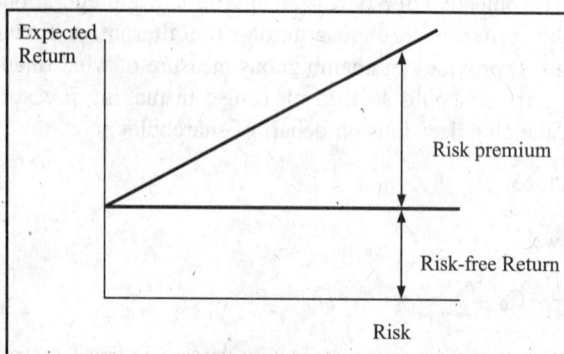

Figure 1.1: The risk-return relationship

Financial decisions of the firm are guided by the **risk-return trade-off.** These decisions are interrelated and jointly affect the market value of its shares by influencing return and risk of the

firm. The relationship between return and risk can be simply expressed as follows:

$$\text{Return} = \text{Risk-free rate} + \text{Risk premium} \qquad (1)$$

Risk-free rate is a rate obtainable from a default-risk free government security. An investor assuming risk from her investment requires a **risk premium** above the risk-free rate. Risk-free rate is a compensation for time and risk premium for risk. Higher the risk of an action, higher will be the risk premium leading to higher required return on that action. A proper balance between return and risk should be maintained to maximise the market value of a firm's shares. Such balance is called risk-return trade-off, and every financial decision involves this trade-off. The interrelation between market value, financial decisions and risk-return trade-off is depicted in Figure 1.2. It also gives an overview of the functions of financial management.

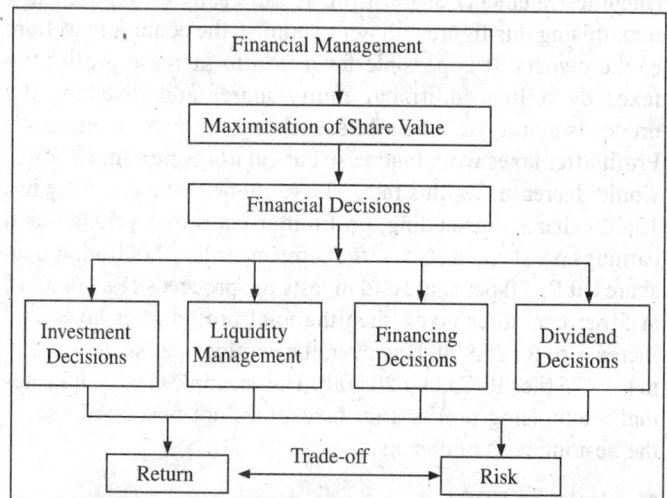

Figure 1.2: An overview of financial management

The financial manager, in a bid to maximise shareholders' wealth, should strive to maximise returns in relation to the given risk; he or she should seek courses of actions that avoid unnecessary risks. To ensure maximum return, funds flowing in and out of the firm should be constantly monitored to assure that they are safeguarded and properly utilised. The financial reporting system must be designed to provide timely and accurate picture of the firm's activities.

AGENCY PROBLEMS: MANAGERS VERSUS SHAREHOLDERS GOALS

In large companies, there is a divorce between management and ownership. The decision-taking authority in a company lies in the hands of managers. Shareholders as owners of a company are the principals and managers are their agents. Thus there is a **principal-agent relationship** between shareholders and managers. In theory, managers should act in the best interests of shareholders; that is, their actions and decisions should lead to SWM. In practice, managers may not necessarily act in the best interest of shareholders, and they may pursue their own personal goals. Managers may maximise their own wealth (in the form of high salaries and perks) at the cost of shareholders, or may play safe and create satisfactory wealth for shareholders than the maximum. They may avoid taking high investment and financing risks that may otherwise be needed to maximise shareholders' wealth. Such "satisficing" behaviour of managers will frustrate the objective of SWM as a *normative guide*. It is in the interests of managers that the firm survives over the long run. Managers also wish to enjoy independence and freedom from outside interference, control and monitoring. Thus their actions are very likely to be directed towards the goals of survival and self-sufficiency[1]. Further, a company is a complex organisation consisting of multiple stakeholders such as employees, debt-holders, consumers, suppliers, government and society. Managers in practice may, thus, perceive their role as reconciling conflicting objectives of stakeholders. This stakeholders' view of managers' role may compromise with the objective of SWM.

Shareholders continuously monitor modern companies that would help them to restrict managers' freedom to act in their own self-interest at the cost of shareholders. Employees, creditors, customers and government also keep an eye on managers' activities. Thus the possibility of managers pursuing *exclusively* their own personal goals is reduced. Managers can survive only when they are successful; and they are successful when they manage the company better than someone else. Every group connected with the company will, however, evaluate management success from the point of view of the fulfilment of its own objective. The survival of management will be threatened if the objective of any of these groups remains unfulfilled. In reality, the wealth of shareholders in the long run could be maximised only when customers and employees, along with other stakeholders of a firm, are fully satisfied. The wealth maximisation objective may be generally in harmony with the interests of the various groups such as owners, employees, creditors and society, and thus, it may be consistent with the management objective of survival[2]. There can, however, still arise situations where a conflict may occur between the shareholders' and managers' goals. Finance theory prescribes that under such situations, shareholders wealth maximisation goal should have precedent over the goals of other stakeholders.

The conflict between the interests of shareholders and managers is referred to as **agency problem** and it results into agency costs. **Agency costs** include the less than optimum share value for shareholders and costs incurred by them to monitor the actions of managers and control their behaviour. The agency problems vanish when managers own the company. Thus one way to mitigate the agency problems is to give ownership rights through stock options to managers. Shareholders can also offer attractive monetary and non-monetary incentives to managers to act in their interests. A close monitoring by other stakeholders, board of directors and outside analysts also may help in reducing the agency problems. In more capitalistic societies such as USA and UK, the takeovers and acquisitions are used as means of disciplining managers.

FINANCIAL GOAL AND FIRM'S MISSION AND OBJECTIVES

In SWM, wealth is defined in terms of wealth or value of the shareholders' equity. This basis of the theory of financial management is same as that of the classical theory of the firm: maximisation of owners' welfare. In the professionally managed firms of our times, managers are the agents of owners and act on their behalf.

SWM is a criterion for financial decisions, and therefore, valuation models provide the basic theoretical and conceptual framework. Is wealth maximisation the *objective of the firm?* Does a firm exist with the sole objective of serving the interests of owners? Firms do exist with the primary objective of maximising the welfare of owners, but, in operational terms, they always focus on the satisfaction of its customers through the production of goods and services needed by them. As Drucker puts it:[3]

> What is our business is not determined by the producer, but by the consumer. It is not defined by the company's name, statutes or articles of incorporation, but by the want the consumer satisfies when he buys a product or a service. The question can therefore be answered only by looking at the business from the outside, from the point of view of the customer and the market.

Firms in practice state their vision, mission and values in broad terms, and are also concerned about technology, leadership, productivity, market standing, image, profitability, financial resources, employees' satisfaction etc. For example, BHEL, a large Indian company with sales of Rs 72.87 billion (Rs 7,287 crore),[4] net assets of Rs 92.97 billion (Rs 9,297 crore) and a profit after tax of Rs 4.68 billion (Rs 468 crore) for the year 2001–02 and employing 47,729 employees states its multiple objectives in terms of leadership, growth, profitability, consumer satisfaction, employees needs, technology and image (see Exhibit 1.1). The stated financial goals of the firm are: (*a*) sales growth; (*b*) reasonable return on capital; and (*c*) internal financing.

Objectives vs. decision criteria Objectives and decision criteria should be distinguished. Wealth maximisation is more appropriately a *decision criterion,* rather than an *objective or a goal*.[5] **Goals** or **objectives** are missions or basic purposes – raison deter of a firm's existence. They direct the firm's actions. A firm may consider itself a provider of high technology, a builder of electronic base, or a provider of best and cheapest transport services. The firm designs its **strategy** around such basic objectives and accordingly, defines its markets, products and technology. To support its strategy, the firm lays down **policies** in the areas of production, purchase, marketing, technology, finance and so on.[6]

---

1. Donaldson, G., *Managing Corporate Wealth: The Operations of a Comprehensive Financial Goals System,* New York : Praeger, 1984.
2. For a detailed discussion, see Solomon, *op. cit.*
3. Drucker, Peter, *The Practice of Management,* Pan Books, 1968, p. 67.
4. 1 crore = 10 million; 10 lakh = 1 million; 1 lakh = 100 thousand.
5. Some people make a difference between objectives and goals. We use them interchangeably here.
6. Solomon and Pringle, *op. cit.*

EXHIBIT 1.1: BHEL'S MISSION AND OBJECTIVES

BHEL defines its vision, mission, values and objectives as follows:

- *Vision* To become a world class, innovative, competitive and profitable engineering enterprise providing total business solutions.
- *Business mission* To be the leading Indian engineering enterprise providing quality products, systems and services in the fields of energy, transportation, industry, infrastructure and other potential areas.
- *Values*
  - Meeting commitments made to external and internal customers.
  - Fostering learning, creativity and speed of response.
  - Respect for dignity and potential of individuals.
  - Loyalty and pride in the company.
  - Team playing.
  - Zeal to excel.
  - Integrity and fairness in all matters.
- *Objectives* BHEL defines its objectives as follows:
  - *Growth* To ensure a steady growth by enhancing the competitive edge of BHEL in existing business, new areas and international operations so as to fulfil national expectations for BHEL.
  - *Profitability* To provide a reasonable and adequate return on capital employed, primarily through improvements in operational efficiency, capacity utilisation and productivity, and generate adequate internal resources to finance the company's growth.
  - *Customer focus* To build a high degree of customer confidence by providing increased value for his money through international standards of product quality, performance and superior customer service.
  - *People orientation* To enable each employee to achieve his potential, improve his capabilities, perceive his role and responsibilities and participate and contribute positively to the growth and success of the company. To invest in human resources continuously and be alive to their needs.
  - *Technology* To achieve technological excellence in operations by development of indigenous technologies and efficient absorption and adaptation of imported technologies to sustain needs and priorities, and provide a competitive advantage to the company.
  - *Image* To fulfil the expectations which shareholders like government as owner, employees, customers and the country at large have from BHEL.

Source : BHEL's Annual Reports.

The first step in making a decision is to see that it is consistent with the firm's strategy and passes through the policy screening. The shareholders' wealth maximisation is the second-level criterion ensuring that the decision meets the minimum standard of the economic performance. It is important to note that the management is not only the *agent* of owners, but also *trustee* for various stakeholders (constituents) of an economic unit. It is the responsibility of the management to harmonise the interests of owners with that of the employees, creditors, government, or society. In the final decision-making, the judgment of management plays the crucial role. The wealth maximisation criterion would simply indicate whether an action is economically viable or not.

ORGANISATION OF THE FINANCE FUNCTIONS

The vital importance of the financial decisions to a firm makes it imperative to set up a sound and efficient organisation for the finance functions. The ultimate responsibility of carrying out the finance functions lies with the top management. Thus, a department to organise financial activities may be created under the direct control of the board of directors. The board may constitute a finance committee. The executive heading the finance department is the firm's **chief finance officer** (CFO), and he or she may be known by different designations. The finance committee or CFO will decide the major financial policy matters, while the routine activities would be delegated to lower levels. For example, at BHEL a director of finance at the corporate office heads the finance function. He is a member of the board of directors and reports to the chairman and managing director (CMD). An executive director of finance (EDF) and a general manager of finance (GMF) assist the director of finance. EDF looks after funding, budgets and cost, books of accounts, financial services and cash management. GMF is responsible for internal audit and taxation.

The reason for placing the finance functions in the hands of top management may be attributed to the following factors: *First,* financial decisions are crucial for the survival of the firm. The growth and development of the firm is directly influenced by the financial policies. *Second,* the financial actions determine solvency of the firm. At no cost can a firm afford to threaten its solvency. Because solvency is affected by the flow of funds, which is a result of the various financial activities, top management being in a position to coordinate these activities retains finance functions in its control. *Third,* centralisation of the finance functions can result in a number of economies to the firm. For example, the firm can save in terms of interest on borrowed funds, can purchase fixed assets economically or issue shares or debentures efficiently.

Status and Duties of Finance Executives

The exact organisation structure for financial management will differ across firms. It will depend on factors such as the size of the firm, nature of the business, financing operations, capabilities of the firm's financial officers and most importantly, on the financial philosophy of the firm. The designation of the chief financial officer (CFO) would also differ within firms. In some firms, the financial officer may be known as the financial manager, while in others as the vice-president of finance or the director of finance or the financial controller. Two more officers—**treasurer** and **controller**—may be appointed under the direct supervision of CFO to assist him or her. In larger companies, with modern management, there may be vice-president or director of finance, usually with both controller and treasurer reporting to him.[1]

Figure 1.3 illustrates the financial organisation of a large (hypothetical) business firm. It is a simple organisation chart, and as stated earlier, the exact organisation for a firm will depend on its circumstances. Figure 1.3 reveals that the finance function is one of the major functional areas, and the financial manager or director is under the control of the board of directors. Figure 1.4 shows the organisation for the finance function of a large, multi-divisional Indian company.

CFO has both line and staff responsibilities. He or she is directly concerned with the financial planning and control. He or she is a member of the top management, and he or she is closely associated with the formulation of policies and making decisions for the firm. The treasurer and controller, if a company has these executives, would operate under CFO's supervision. He or she must guide them and others in the effective working of the finance department.

The main function of the treasurer is to manage the firm's funds. His or her major duties include forecasting the financial needs, administering the flow of cash, managing credit, floating securities, maintaining relations with financial institution and protecting funds and securities. On the other hand, the functions of the controller relate to the management and control of assets. His or her duties include providing information to formulate accounting and costing policies, preparation of financial reports, direction of internal auditing, budgeting, inventory control, taxes etc. It may be stated that the controller's functions concentrate the asset side of the balance sheet, while treasurer's functions relate to the liability side.

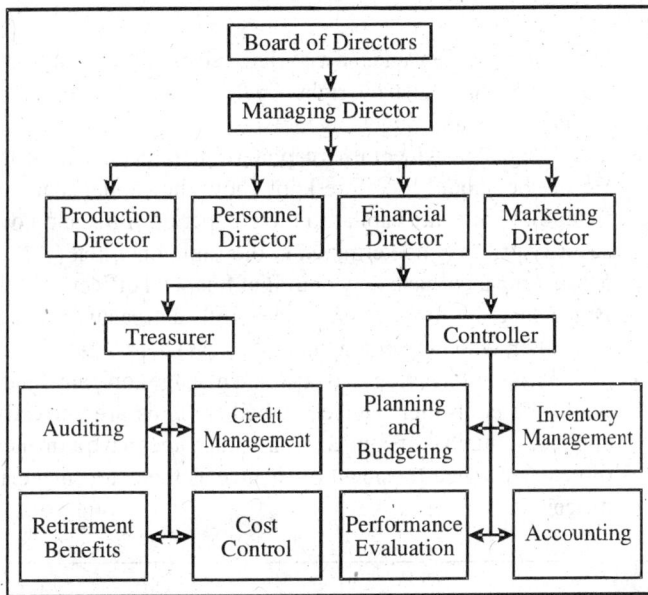

Figure 1.3: Organisation for finance function

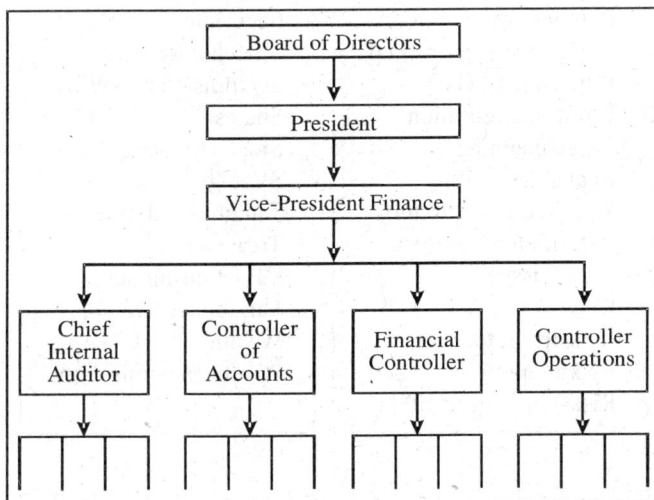

Figure 1.4: Organisation for finance function in a multi-divisional company

Controller's and Treasurer's Functions in the Indian Context

The controller and the treasurer are essentially American terms. Generally speaking, the American pattern of dividing the financial executive's functions into controllership and treasurership functions is not being widely followed in India. We do have a number of companies in India having officers with the designation of the controller, or the financial controller. The controller or the financial controller in India, by and large, performs the functions of a chief accountant or management accountant. The officer with the title of treasurer can also be found in a few companies in India.

The controllership functions, as stated by the Financial Executives' Institute of the USA, can prove to be useful under the Indian context. But presently the **company secretary** in India performs some of these duties. His or her duties, for example, include asset control and protection, maintaining records and preparing reports and government reporting. The economic appraisal function is generally performed at the top level in India. Some companies do have separate economics and statistical departments for this purpose. Some other functions, such as internal audit, can be brought within the fold of the controllership functions, if this concept is developed in the Indian context.

It should be realised that the financial controller *does not* control finances; he or she develops, uses and interprets information—some of which will be financial in nature—for management control and planning. For this reason, the financial controller may simply be called as the controller. Management of finance or money is a separate and important activity. Traditionally, the accountants have been involved in managing

---

1. Cohen, J.B. and Robbins, S.M., *The Financial Manager,* Harper and Row, 1966, pp. 11–12.

money in India. But the difference in managing money resources and information resources should be appreciated.

In the American business, the management of finance is treated as a separate activity and is being performed by the treasurer. The title of the treasurer has not found favour in India to the extent the controller has. The company secretary in India discharges some of the functions performed by the treasurer in the American context. Insurance coverage is an example in this regard. The function of maintaining relations with investors (particularly shareholders) may now assume significance in India because of the development in the Indian capital markets and the increasing awareness among investors.

The general title, financial manager or finance director, seems to be more popular in India. This title is also better than the title of treasurer since it conveys the functions involved. The main function of the financial manager in India should be the management of the company's funds. The financial duties may often be combined with others. But the significance of not combining the financial manager's duties with others should be realised. The managing of funds—a very valuable resource—is a business activity requiring extraordinary skill on the part of the financial manager. He or she should ensure the optimum use of money under various constraints. He or she should, therefore, be allowed to devote his or her full energy and time in managing the money resources only.

SUMMARY

- ❖ The finance functions can be divided into three broad categories: (1) investment decision, (2) financing decision, and (3) dividend decision. In other words, the firm decides how much to invest in short-term and long-term assets and how to raise the required funds.
- ❖ In making financial decisions, the financial manager should aim at increasing the value of the shareholders' stake in the firm. This is referred to as the principle of shareholders' wealth maximisation (SWM).
- ❖ Wealth maximisation is superior to profit maximisation since wealth is precisely defined as net present value and it accounts for time value of money and risk.
- ❖ Shareholders and managers have the principal-agent relationship. In practice, there may arise a conflict between the interests of shareholders and managers. This is referred to

- the agency problem and the associated costs are called agency costs. Offering ownership rights (in the form of stock options) to managers can mitigate agency costs.
- ❖ The financial manager raises capital from the capital markets. He or she should therefore know-how the capital markets function to allocate capital to the competing firms and how security prices are determined in the capital markets.
- ❖ Most companies have only one chief financial officer (CFO). But a large company may have both a treasurer and a controller, who may or may not operate under CFO.
- ❖ The treasurer's function is to raise and manage company funds while the controller oversees whether funds are correctly applied. A number of companies in India either have a finance director or a vice-president of finance as the chief financial officer.

KEY CONCEPTS

Agency costs	Financial asset	Owners of residue	Secondary markets
Assets	Financial leverage	Policies	Securities
Bond	Financing decision	Preference share capital	Shareholders' wealth
Bonus shares	Fixed costs	Primary markets	maximisation (SWM)
Capital expenditure	Goals	Profit maximisation	Shares
Capital markets	Intangible real assets	Profit planning	Stock dividend
Capital structure	Interest tax shield	Real assets	Strategy
Controller	Investment decision	Required rate of return	Tangible real assets
Cut-off rate	Liquidity decision	Return on investment	Treasurer
Debenture	Net present value	Rights issue	Valuation model
Dividend decision	Objectives	Risk	Variable costs
Dividend payout	Opportunity cost of capital	Risk-free rate	Wealth
Earnings per share (EPS)	Operating leverage	Risk premium	Wealth maximisation
Episodic financing	Optimum capital structure	Risk-return trade-off	

REVIEW QUESTIONS

1. Define the scope of financial management. What role should the financial manager play in a modern enterprise?
2. How does the "modern" financial manager differ from

the "traditional" financial manager? Does the "modern" financial manager's role differ for the large diversified firm and the small to medium size firm?

3. "... the function of financial management is to review and

control decisions to commit or recommit funds to new or ongoing uses. Thus, in addition to raising funds, financial management is directly concerned with production, marketing, and other functions within an enterprise whenever decisions are made about the acquisition or destruction of assets" (Ezra Solomon). Elucidate.

4. What are the basic financial decisions? How do they involve risk-return trade-off?

5. "The profit maximisation is not an operationally feasible criterion". Do you agree? Illustrate your views.

6. In what ways is the wealth maximisation objective superior to the profit maximisation objective? Explain.

7. "The basic rationale for the objective of shareholders' wealth maximisation is that it reflects the most efficient use of society's economic resources and thus leads to a maximisation of society's economic wealth" (Ezra Solomon). Comment critically.

8. How should the finance function of an enterprise be organised? What functions do the financial officer perform?

9. Should the titles of controller and treasurer be adopted under Indian context? Would you like to modify their functions in view of the company practices in India? Justify your opinion.

10. When can there arise a conflict between shareholders' and managers' goals? How does wealth maximisation goal take care of this conflict?

CASES

Case 1.1: The Anandnagar Electricity Company

The Anandnagar Electricity Board (AEB) has been operating under the ownership and control of the state of Anandnagar since the creation of the state in 1961. The state government privatised AEB in 2000 by selling it to a local business house that has interests in pharmaceutical, financial service and energy. AEB came to be known as the Anandnagar Electricity Company (AEC). Privatisation was intended to pave way to the company to improve performance and raise much needed finances from the capital market. The demand for electricity has always exceeded the supply, as the state government did not have enough funds to spend on capital expenditure to create the required power generation capacities. AEC would be now required to make sufficient investments to increase power generation capacity in order to meet ever-increasing demand for electricity. AEC management stated that being a private sector company, it shall maximise shareholders' return.

At the time of its privatisation, a large private sector financial institution valued the company at Rs 4,000 million. The issue of ordinary shares raised this money. The merchant bank division of the financial institution helped the public issue of ordinary shares, par value Rs 10 each, sold at a premium of 100 per cent for Rs 20 each. The issue was oversubscribed, and on the very first day of trading, the market price of share reached a value of Rs 35.

AEC has been in operation for three years as a private sector company. The Table 1.1.1 below provides select financial and operating data of the company's operations for the period 2001–2004. The financial data for 2001 are for the last year of the government ownership of the company. As a private sector company, AEC has paid dividend in accordance with the policy stated in the prospectus.

The Central Electricity Board regulates the prices and oversees the activities of the privatised electricity companies.

Table 1.1.1: The Anandnagar Electricity Company: Key Financial and Operating Data for Year ending 31 March *(Rs in million)*

	2001 Pub. Sector	2002 Pvt. Sector	2003 Pvt. Sector	2004 Pvt. Sector
Revenues	13,500	14,250	17,500	19,500
Operating profit	810	1,100	1,790	2,730
Taxes	160	200	300	400
Profit before depreciation & tax	900	960	1,030	1,190
Profit after tax	650	900	1,490	2,330
Dividends	200	320	600	900
Wages and salaries	3,000	3,000	2,700	2,600
Total assets	3,000	3,600	4,500	5,750
Capital expenditure	500	900	1,750	2,250
Debtors	6,000	3,200	3,000	3,600
Creditors	4,500	2,400	2,300	2,400
Directors' emoluments	30	70	80	100
Employees (number)	32,000	31,400	30,500	30,100
P/E ratio	—	10.5	12.0	11.5
Consumer price index	100	102.7	105.8	107.4

The demand for electricity in Anandnagar has grown at the rate of 4 per cent per annum.

Discussion Questions

1. What changes, if any, do you expect in the objectives of the company after privatisation and why?
2. Who are the company's stakeholders? Has the company been able to fulfil their objectives? State the additional information that you may need to answer this question.

Case 1.2: Bharat Heavy Electricals Limited (BHEL)

BHEL is the largest engineering company in India. It provides total systems to the core sectors of the Indian economy – power, industry and transportation. About two-thirds of the company's business is in power sector. It is a technology-intensive company having collaborations with reputed international companies. It ranks among "Fortune 500" biggest industrial giants. Its operations are spread over 13 manufacturing plants and eight service centres in India. BHEL employs about 46,050 persons, including nearly 10,000 executives. The company was initially a totally public sector company. It has been partially privatised now.

The company is committed to quality. It receives orders from several countries for industrial equipments, including complete power stations, consultancy services and providing technical manpower. These countries include USA, UK, West Germany, Russia, New Zealand, Indonesia, Thailand, Malaysia, Saudi Arabia, Libya, and Turkey etc. BHEL is recognized in the world market as a renovation, services and maintenance expert. A number of old boilers and TG sets from renowned international suppliers are being entrusted to BHEL for renovation.

BHEL produces a wide variety of products in core sectors of the economy. The characteristics of those products vary significantly. A number of its products such as hydro and thermal sets, boilers, boiler auxiliaries, compressors, industrial turbo sets and oilrigs are long production cycles items. BHEL has defined its objectives as follows:

Growth To ensure a steady growth by enhancing the competitive edge of BHEL in existing business, new areas and international operations so as to fulfil national expectations for BHEL.

Profitability To provide a reasonable and adequate return on capital employed, primarily through improvements in operational efficiency, capacity utilisation and productivity, and generate adequate internal resources to finance the company's growth.

Customer focus To build a high degree of customer confidence by providing increased value for his money through international standards of product quality, performance and superior customer service.

People orientation To enable each employee to achieve his potential, improve his capabilities, perceive his role and responsibilities and participate and contribute positively to the growth and success of the company. To invest in human resources continuously and be alive to their needs

Technology To achieve technological excellence in operations by development of indigenous technologies and efficient absorption and adaptation of imported technologies to sustain needs and priorities, and provide a competitive advantage to the company.

Image To fulfil the expectations which shareholders like government as owner, employees, customers and the country at large have from BHEL.

Discussion Question

1. Critically evaluate BHEL's objectives from the perspectives of financial management, in general and shareholders in particular.

CHAPTER 2

Concepts of Value and Return

CHAPTER OBJECTIVES

- Understand what gives money its time value
- Explain the methods of calculating present and future values
- Highlight the use of present value technique (discounting) in financial decisions
- Introduce the concept of internal rate of return

INTRODUCTION

Most financial decisions, such as the purchase of assets or procurement of funds, affect the firm's cash flows in different time periods. For example, if a fixed asset is purchased, it will require an immediate cash outlay and will generate cash inflows during many future periods. Similarly, if the firm borrows funds from a bank or from any other source, it receives cash now and commits an obligation to pay cash for interest and repay principal in future periods. The firm may also raise funds by issuing equity shares. The firm's cash balance will increase at the time shares are issued, but, as the firm pays dividends in future, the outflow of cash will occur. Sound decision-making requires that the cash flows, which a firm is expected to receive or give up over a period of time, should be logically comparable. In fact, the absolute cash flows, which differ in *timing* and *risk,* are not directly comparable. Cash flows become logically comparable when they are appropriately adjusted for their differences in timing and risk.

The recognition of the **time value of money** and **risk** is extremely vital in financial decision-making. If the timing and risk of cash flows is not considered, the firm may make decisions that may allow it to miss its objective of maximising the owners' welfare. The welfare of owners would be maximised when **wealth** or **net present value** is created from making a financial decision. What is net present value? How is it computed?

TIME PREFERENCE FOR MONEY

If an individual behaves rationally, he or she would not value the opportunity to receive a specific amount of money now equally with the opportunity to have the same amount at some future date. Most individuals value the opportunity to receive money now higher than waiting for one or more periods to receive the same amount. **Time preference for money** is an individual's preference for possession of a given amount of money *now,* rather than the same amount at some future time.

Three reasons may be attributed to the individual's time preference for money:[1]

- risk
- preference for consumption
- investment opportunities

We live under risk or uncertainty.[2] As an individual is not certain about future cash receipts, he or she prefers receiving cash now. Most people have subjective *preference for present consumption* over future consumption of goods and services either because of the urgency of their present wants or because of the risk of not being in a position to enjoy future consumption that may be caused by illness or death, or because of inflation. As money is the means by which individuals acquire most goods and services, they may prefer to have money now. Further, most individuals prefer present cash to future cash because of the available *investment*

---

1. Bierman, H. Jr., *The Capital Budgeting Decisions,* Macmillan, 1975, pp. 69–72.
2. The terms risk and uncertainty are used here interchangeably.

opportunities to which they can put present cash to earn additional cash. For example, an individual who is offered Rs 100 now or Rs 100 one year from now would prefer Rs 100 now as he could earn on it an interest of, say, Rs 5 by putting it in the savings account in a bank for one year. His total cash inflow in one year from now will be Rs 105. Thus, if he wishes to increase his cash resources, the opportunity to earn interest would lead him to prefer Rs 100 now, not Rs 100 after one year.

In case of the firms as well as individuals, the justification for time preference for money lies simply in the availability of investment opportunities.[1] In financial decision-making under certainty, the firm has to determine whether one alternative yields more cash or the other. In case of a firm, which is owned by a large number of individuals (shareholders), it is neither needed nor is it possible to consider the consumption preferences of owners. The uncertainty about future cash flows is also not a sufficient justification for time preference for money. We are not certain even about the usefulness of the present cash held; it may be lost or stolen. In investment and other decisions of the firm what is needed is the search for methods of improving decision-maker's knowledge about the future. In the firm's investment decision, for example, certain statistical tools such as probability theory, or decision tree could be used to handle the uncertainty associated with cash flows.

Required Rate of Return

The time preference for money is generally expressed by an interest rate. This rate will be positive even in the absence of any risk. It may be therefore called the **risk-free rate.** For instance, if time preference rate is 5 per cent, it implies that an investor can forego the opportunity of receiving Rs 100 if he is offered Rs 105 after one year (i.e. Rs 100 which he would have received now *plus* the interest which he could earn in a year by investing Rs 100 at 5 per cent). Thus, the individual is indifferent between Rs 100 and Rs 105 a year from now as he considers these two amounts equivalent in value. In reality, an investor will be exposed to some degree of risk. Therefore, he would require a rate of return, called **risk premium,** from the investment, which compensates him for both time and risk. Thus the **required rate of return** will be

Required rate of return = Risk-free rate + Risk premium   (1)

The risk-free rate compensates for time while risk premium compensates for risk. The required rate of return may also be called the **opportunity cost of capital** of comparable risk.[2] It is called so because the investor could invest his money in assets or securities of equivalent risk. Like individuals, firms also have required rates of return and use them in evaluating the desirability of alternative financial decisions. The interest rates account for the time value of money, irrespective of an individual's preferences and attitudes.[3]

How does knowledge of the required rate of return (or simply called the interest rate) help an individual or a firm in making

investment decision? It permits the individual or the firm to convert different cash flows occurring at different times to *amounts of equivalent value in the present,* that is, a common point of reference. Let us consider an example.

Let us assume an individual with a required interest rate of 10 per cent. If she is offered Rs 115.50 one year from now in exchange for Rs 100 which she should give up today, should she accept the offer? The answer in this particular case is that she should accept the offer. When her interest rate is 10 per cent, this implies that she is indifferent between any amount today and 110 per cent of that amount one year hence. She would obviously favour more than 110 per cent of the amount (i.e. more than Rs 110 in the example) one year from now; but if the amount offered one year from now were less than 110 per cent of the immediate payment, she would retain the immediate payment. She would accept Rs 115.50 after a year since it is more than 110 per cent of Rs 100, which she is required to sacrifice today.

We can ask a different question. Between what amount today and Rs 115.50 one year from now would our investor be indifferent? The answer is that amount of which Rs 115.50 is exactly 110 per cent. Dividing Rs 115.50 by 110 per cent or 1.10, we get

$$\frac{\text{Rs } 115.50}{1.10} = \text{Rs } 105$$

This amount is larger than what the investor has been asked to give up today. She would, therefore, accept the offer. This simple example illustrates two most common methods of adjusting cash flows for time value of money: **compounding** — the process of calculating future values of cash flows and **discounting**—the process of calculating present values of cash flows.

FUTURE VALUE

We just developed logic for deciding between cash flows that are separated by one period, such as one year. But most investment decisions involve more than one period. To solve such multi-period investment decisions, we simply need to extend the logic developed above. Let us assume that an investor requires 10 per cent interest rate to make him indifferent to cash flows one year apart. The question is: How should he arrive at comparative values of cash flows that are separated by two, three or any number of years?

Once the investor has determined his interest rate, say, 10 per cent, he would like to receive at least Rs 1.10 after one year or 110 per cent of the original investment of Re 1 today. A two-year period is two successive one-year periods. When the investor invested Re 1 for one year, he must have received Rs 1.10 back at the end of that year in exchange for the original Re 1. If the total amount so received (Rs 1.10) were reinvested, the investor would expect 110 per cent of that amount, or Rs 1.21 = Re 1 × 1.10 × 1.10 at the end of the second year. Notice that for any time after the first year, he will insist on receiving interest on the

1. *Ibid.*
2. Brealey, R. and Myers, S. *Principles of Corporate Finance,* McGraw Hill, 1991, p. 13.
3. Fisher, I., *The Theory of Interest,* McMillan, 1965.

first year's interest as well as interest on the original amount (principal). **Compound interest** is the interest that is received on the original amount (principal) as well as on any interest earned but not withdrawn during earlier periods. **Compounding** is the process of finding the future values of cash flows by applying the concept of compound interest. **Simple interest** is the interest that is calculated only on the original amount (principal), and thus, no compounding of interest takes place.

Future Value of a Single Cash Flow

Suppose your father gave you Rs 100 on your eighteenth birthday. You deposited this amount in a bank at 10 per cent rate of interest for one year. How much future sum would you receive after one year? You would receive Rs 110:

Future sum = Principal + Interest
$$= 100 + (0.10 \times 100) = 100 \times (1.10) = \text{Rs } 110$$

What would be the future sum if you deposited Rs 100 for two years? You would now receive interest on interest earned after one year:

Future sum $= [100 + (0.10 \times 100)] + 0.10[100 + (0.10 \times 100)]$
$$= 100 \times 1.10 \times 1.10 = \text{Rs } 121$$

You could similarly calculate future sum for any number of years. We can express this procedure of calculating compound, or future, value in formal terms.

Let i represent the interest rate per period, n the number of periods before pay-off, and F the **future value**, or **compound value**. If the present amount P is invested at i rate of interest for one year, then the future value F_1 (*viz.*, principal plus interest) at the end of one year will be

Future sum = Principal + Interest on principal
$$F_1 = P + P \times i = P(1 + i)$$

The outstanding amount at the beginning of second year is: $F_1 = P(1 + i)$. The compound sum at the end of second year will be:

$$F_2 = F_1 + F_1 i = F_1(1 + i)$$
$$F_2 = P(1 + i)(1 + i) = P(1 + i)^2$$

Similarly, $F_3 = F_2(1 + i) = P(1 + i)^3$ and so on. The general form of equation for calculating the future value of a lump sum after n periods may, therefore, be written as follows:

$$F_n = P(1 + i)^n \qquad (2)$$

The term $(1 + i)^n$ is the **compound value factor** (CVF) of a lump sum of Re 1, and it always has a value greater than 1 for positive i, indicating that CVF increases as i and n increase.

The compound value can be computed for any lump sum amount at i rate of interest for n number of years, using Equation

Illustration 2.1: Future Value of a Lump Sum

Suppose that Rs 1,000 are placed in the savings account of a bank at 5 per cent interest rate. How much shall it grow at the end of three years? It will grow as follows:

$$F_1 = 1,000.00 + 1,000.00 \times 5\%$$
$$= 1,000.00 + 50.00 = \text{Rs } 1,050.00$$

$$F_2 = 1,050.00 + 1,050.00 \times 5\%$$
$$= 1,050.00 + 52.50 = \text{Rs } 1,102.50$$
$$F_3 = 1,102.50 + 1,102.50 \times 5\%$$
$$= 1,102.50 + 55.10 = \text{Rs } 1,157.60$$

Notice that the amount of Rs 1,000 will earn interest of Rs 50 and will grow to Rs 1,050 at the end of the first year. The outstanding balance of Rs 1,050 in the beginning of the second year will earn interest of Rs 52.50, thus making the outstanding amount equal to Rs 1,102.50 at the beginning of the third year. Future or compound value at the end of third year will grow to Rs 1,157.60 after earning interest of Rs 55.10 on Rs 1,102.50. In compounding, interest on interest is earned. Thus the compound value of Rs 1,000 in the example can also be calculated as follows:

$$F_1 = 1,000 \times 1.05 = \text{Rs } 1,050$$
$$F_2 = 1,000 \times [1.05 \times 1.05] = 1,000 \times 1.05^2$$
$$= 1,000 \times 1.1025 = \text{Rs } 1,102.50$$
$$F_3 = 1,000 \times [1.05 \times 1.05 \times 1.05] = 1,000 \times 1.05^3$$
$$= 1,000 \times 1.1576 = \text{Rs } 1,157.60$$

We can see that the compound value factor (CVF) for a lump sum of one rupee at 5 per cent for one year is 1.05, for two years 1.1025 and for three years 1.1576.

In Figure 2.1 we show the future values of Re 1 for different interest rates. You can see from the figure that as the interest rate increases, the compound value of Re 1 increases appreciably.

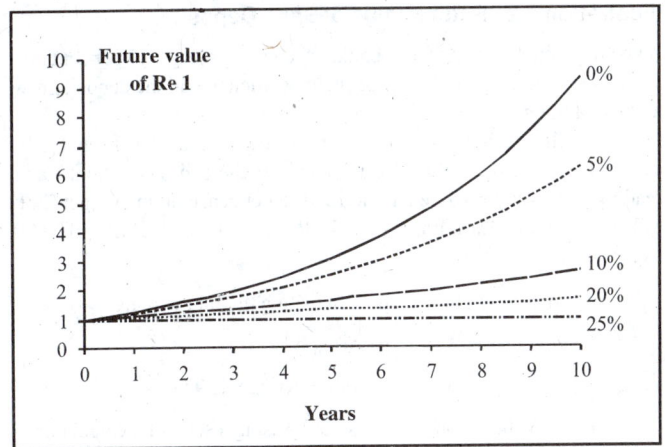

Figure 2.1: Future values with different interest rates

(2). With the help of a scientific calculator, the simple method of calculating future value is to use the power function. Suppose you have to calculate future value of Rs 1,000 for 5 years at 10 per cent rate of interest. In the calculator, you enter: 1.10, press the y^x key, press 5 and then the equal to key =. You shall obtain 1.611. This is CVF of Re 1 at 10 per cent for 5 years. Multiplying this factor by Rs 1,000, you get the future value of Rs 1,000 as Rs 1,000 × 1.611 = Rs 1,611. However, without a calculator, calculations of compound value will become very difficult if the amount is invested for a very long period. A table of future values, such as Table 2.1, can be used. Table A, given at the end of this book, is a more comprehensive table of future values.

To compute the future value of a lump sum amount, we should simply multiply the amount by compound value factor (CVF) for the given interest rate, i and the time period, n from Table A. Equation (2) can be rewritten as follows:

Table 2.1: Compound Value Factor of a Lump Sum of Re 1

					Interest Rate					
Period	*1%*	*2%*	*3%*	*4%*	*5%*	*10%*	*15%*	*20%*	*25%*	*30%*
1	1.010	1.020	1.030	1.040	1.050	1.100	1.150	1.200	1.250	1.300
2	1.020	1.040	1.061	1.082	1.103	1.210	1.323	1.440	1.563	1.690
3	1.030	1.061	1.093	1.125	1.158	1.331	1.521	1.728	1.953	2.197
4	1.041	1.082	1.126	1.170	1.216	1.464	1.749	2.074	2.441	2.856
5	1.051	1.104	1.159	1.217	1.276	1.611	2.011	2.488	3.052	3.713
6	1.062	1.126	1.194	1.265	1.340	1.772	2.313	2.986	3.815	4.827
7	1.072	1.149	1.230	1.316	1.407	1.949	2.660	3.583	4.768	6.275
8	1.083	1.172	1.267	1.369	1.477	2.144	3.059	4.300	5.960	8.157
9	1.094	1.195	1.305	1.423	1.551	2.358	3.518	5.160	7.451	10.604
10	1.105	1.219	1.344	1.480	1.629	2.594	4.046	6.192	9.313	13.786

$$F_n = P \times CVF_{n,i} \qquad (3)$$

F_n is the future or compound value after n number of periods, and $CVF_{n,i}$ the compound value factor for n periods at i rate of interest. As stated earlier, the compound value factor is always greater than 1.0 for positive interest rates, indicating that present value will always grow to a larger compound value.

Illustration 2.2: Future Value of Bank Deposit

If you deposited Rs 55,650 in a bank, which was paying a 15 per cent rate of interest on a ten-year time deposit, how much would the deposit grow at the end of ten years?

We will first find out the compound value factor at 15 per cent for 10 years. Referring to Table 2.1 (or Table A at the end of the book) and reading tenth row for 10-year period and 15 per cent column, we get CVF of Re 1 as 4.046. Multiplying 4.046 by Rs 55,650, we get Rs 225,159.90 as the compound value.

We can use Equation (3) for calculating the future value:

$$FV = 55,650 \times CVF_{10, 0.12}$$
$$= 55,650 \times 4.046 = Rs\ 225,159.90$$

We could obtain the same answer by using a scientific calculator

$$F_{10} = 55,650 \times 1.15^{10} = 55,650 \times 4.046 = Rs\ 225,159.90$$

Future Value of an Annuity

Annuity is a fixed payment (or receipt) each year for a *specified* number of years. If you rent a flat and promise to make a series of payments over an agreed period, you have created an annuity. The equal instalments loans from the house financing companies or employers are common examples of annuities. The compound value of an annuity cannot be computed directly from Equation (2). Let us illustrate the computation of the compound value of an annuity.

Suppose a constant sum of Re 1 is deposited in a savings account at the *end* of each year for four years at 6 per cent interest. This implies that Re 1 deposited at the end of the first year will grow for 3 years, Re 1 at the end of second year for 2 years, Re 1 at the end of the third year for 1 year and Re 1 at the end of the fourth year will not yield any interest. Using the concept of the compound value of a lump sum, we can compute the value of

Excel Application 2.1:
Future Value of a Single Cash Flow

We can use the Excel built-in function, *FV*, to find out the future value of a single cash flow. *FV* function is given as follows:

FV (RATE, NPER, PMT, PV, TYPE)

RATE is the discount or the interest rate for a period. NPER is the number of periods. *PV* is the present value. PMT is the equal payment (annuity) each period and TYPE indicates the timing of cash flow, occurring either in the beginning or at the end of the period. PMT and TYPE parameters are used while dealing with annuities. In the calculation of the future value of a single cash flow, we will set them to 0.

In the worksheet below, we use the values of parameters as given in Illustration 2.2. You can find the future value in C5 by entering the formula: *FV* (C4, C3, 0, –C2, 0). We get the same result as in Illustration 2.2. We enter negative sign for *PV*; that is –C2. If we do not do so, we shall obtain negative value for *FV*. You can also find the future value if you write the formula for Equation (2) as given in column C10.

	A	B	C	D
1		FUTURE VALUE OF SINGLE CASH FLOW		
2	Present value (PV)		55,650	
3	Years (NPER)		10	
4	Interest Rate (RATE)		15%	
5	Future value (FV)	Excel function	*225,135*	
6				
7	=FV(RATE,NPER,PMT,PV,TYPE)		=FV(C4,C3,0,-C2,0)	
8				
9				
10	Future value (FV)	Eq.(2)	*225,135*	
11				
12	$FV = PV \times (1+i)^n$		=C2*(1+C4)^C3	
13				

annuity. The compound value of Re 1 deposited in the first year will be: $1 \times 1.06^3 = Rs\ 1.191$, that of Re 1 deposited in the second year will be: Re $1 \times 1.06^2 = Rs\ 1.124$ and Re 1 deposited at the end of third year will grow to: Re 1×1.06^1 = Rs 1.06 and Re 1 deposited at the end of fourth year will remain Re 1. The aggregate compound value of Re 1 deposited at the end of each year for four years would be: 1.191 + 1.124 + 1.060 + 1.00 = Rs 4.375. This is the compound value of an annuity of Re 1 for four years at 6 per cent rate of interest. The graphic presentation of the compound value of an annuity of Re 1 is shown in Figure 2.2. It can be seen that for a given interest rate, the compound value increases over a period.

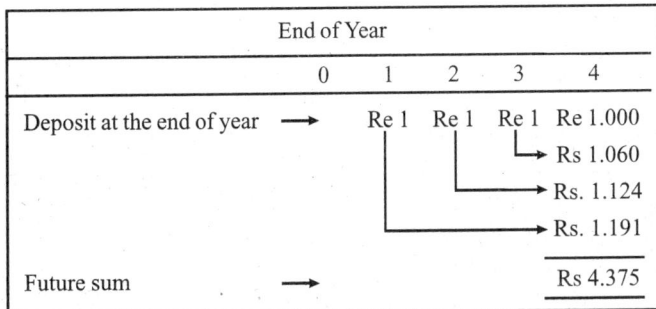

Figure 2.2: Graphic representation of compound value of an annuity of Re 1

The computations shown in Figure 2.2 can be expressed as follows:

$$F_4 = A(1+i)^3 + A(1+i)^2 + A(1+i) + A$$
$$F_4 = A[(1+i)^3 + (1+i)^2 + (1+i) + 1] \qquad (4)$$

In Equation (4) A is the annuity. We can extend Equation (4) for n periods and rewrite it as follows:

$$F_n = A\left[\frac{(1+i)^n - 1}{i}\right] \qquad (5)$$

The term within brackets is the **compound value factor for an annuity** of Re 1, which we shall refer as CVFA. Consider an example.

Suppose Rs 100 are deposited at the end of each of the next three years at 10 per cent interest rate. With a scientific calculator, the compound value, using Equation (5) is calculated as follows:

$$F = 100\left[\frac{(1.10)^3 - 1}{0.10}\right] = 100 \times 3.31 = \text{Rs } 331$$

It would be quite difficult to solve Equation (5) manually if n is very large. Either using a scientific calculator or a table, like Table 2.2, of pre-calculated compound values of an annuity of Re 1 can facilitate our calculations. Table B at the end of this book gives compound value factors for an annuity of Re 1 for a large combinations of time periods (n) and rates of interest (i). Table B is constructed under the assumption that the funds are deposited at the *end* of a period. CVFA should be ascertained from the table to find out the future value of the annuity. We can also write Equation (5) as follows:

Future value = Annuity cash flow × Compound value factor for annuity of Re 1

$$F_n = A \times \text{CVFA}_{n,i} \qquad (6)$$

$\text{CVFA}_{n,i}$ is the compound value factor of an annuity of Re 1 for n number of years at i rate of interest.

Illustration 2.3: Future Value of an Annuity

Suppose that a firm deposits Rs 5,000 at the end of each year for four years at 6 per cent rate of interest. How much would this annuity accumulate at the end of the fourth year? From Table B, we find that fourth year row and 6 per cent column give us a CVFA of 4.3746. If we multiply 4.375 by Rs 5,000, we obtain a compound value of Rs 21,875:

$$F_4 = 5{,}000(\text{CVFA}_{4,0.06}) = 5{,}000 \times 4.3746 = \text{Rs } 21{,}873$$

Sinking Fund

Suppose that we want to accumulate Rs 21,875 at the end of four years from now. How much should we deposit each year at an interest rate of 6 per cent so that it grows to Rs 21,875 at the end of fourth year? We know from Illustration 2.3 that the answer is Rs 5,000 each year. The problem posed is the reversal of the situation in Illustration 2.3; we are given the future amount and we have to calculate the annual payments. **Sinking fund** is a

Table 2.2: Compound Value Factor of an Annuity (CVFA) of Re 1

Period	\multicolumn{10}{c}{*Interest Rate*}									
	1%	*2%*	*3%*	*4%*	*5%*	*10%*	*15%*	*20%*	*25%*	*30%*
1	1.000	1.000	1.000	1.000	1.000	1.000	1.000	1.000	1.000	1.000
2	2.010	2.020	2.030	2.040	2.050	2.100	2.150	2.200	2.250	2.300
3	3.030	3.060	3.091	3.122	3.153	3.310	3.473	3.640	3.813	3.990
4	4.060	4.122	4.184	4.246	4.310	4.641	4.993	5.368	5.766	6.187
5	5.101	5.204	5.309	5.416	5.526	6.105	6.742	7.442	8.207	9.043
6	6.152	6.308	6.468	6.633	6.802	7.716	8.754	9.930	11.259	12.756
7	7.214	7.434	7.662	7.898	8.142	9.487	11.067	12.916	15.073	17.583
8	8.286	8.583	8.892	9.214	9.549	11.436	13.727	16.499	19.842	23.858
9	9.369	9.755	10.159	10.583	11.027	13.579	16.786	20.799	25.802	32.015
10	10.462	10.950	11.464	12.006	12.578	15.937	20.304	25.959	33.253	42.619

Excel Application 2.2: Future Value of an Annuity

The Excel *FV* function for an annuity is the same as for a single cash flow. Here we are given value for PMT instead of *PV*. We will set a value with negative sign for PMT (annuity) and a zero value for *PV*. We use the values for the parameters as given in Illustration 2.3. In column C5 we write the formula: *FV* (C3, C4, -C2, 0, 0). *FV* of Rs 21,873 is the same as in Illustration 2.3.

Instead of the built-in Excel function, we can directly use Equation (5) to find the future value. We can enter formula for Equation (5) and find the future value. We will get the same result. You can enter the formula in column C10 and verify the RESULT.

	A	B	C	D
		FUTURE VALUE OF ANNUITY		
1	Present value (PV)		0	
2	Payment (PMT)		5,000	
3	Interest Rate (RATE)		6%	
4	Years (NPER)		4	
5	Future value (FV)	Excel function	21,873	
6				
7	=FV(RATE,NPER,PMT,PV,TYPE)		=FV(C3,C4,-C2,0,0)	
8				
9				
10	Future value (FV)	Eq. (5)	21,873	
11				
12	$FV_A = A \times \left[\dfrac{(1+i)^n - i}{i} \right]$		=C2*((1+C3)^C4-1)/C3	
13				
14				

Excel Application 2.3: Annuity of a Future Value (Sinking Fund)

The Excel function for finding an annuity for a given future amount is as follows:

PMT (RATE, NPER, PV, FV, TYPE)

We use the values for the parameters as given in Illustration 2.3. In column C5 we write the formula: *FV* (C5, C4, –C2, –C3, 0). Note that we input both *FV* and *PV* and enter negative sign for PMT. The value of PMT is Rs 5,000.

Instead of the built-in Excel function, we can enter formula or Equation (7) and find the value of the sinking fund (annuity). We will get the same result. You can enter the formula in column C10 and verify the result.

	A	B	C	D	E
1		SINKING FUND			
2	Present value (PV)		0		
3	Future value (FV)		21,873		
4	Years (NPER)		4		
5	Interest Rate (RATE)		6%		
6	Annuity (PMT)	Excel function	5,000		
7					
8	=PMT(RATE,NPER,PV,FV,TYPE)		=PMT(C5,C4,C2,-C3,0)		
9					
10					
11	Annuity (PMT)	Eq. (7)	5,000		
12					
13	$A = FV \times \left[\dfrac{i}{(1+i)^n - 1} \right]$		=C3*(C5/((1+C5)^C4-1))		
14					
15					

fund, which is created out of fixed payments each period to accumulate to a future sum after a specified period. For example, companies generally create sinking funds to retire bonds (debentures) on maturity.

The factor used to calculate the annuity for a given future sum is called the ***sinking fund factor*** (SFF). SFF ranges between zero and 1.0. It is equal to the reciprocal of the compound value factor for an annuity. In Illustration 2.3, the reciprocal of CVFA of 4.3746 is: 1/4.3746 = 0.2286. When we multiply the future sum of Rs 21,875 by SFF of 0.2286, we obtain an annuity of Rs 5,000. The problem can be written as follows:

$$F_n = A \times \text{CVFA}_{n,i}$$
$$A = F_n \times \frac{1}{\text{CVFA}_{n,i}}$$
$$A = F_n \times \text{SFF}_{n,i}$$

The formula for sinking fund can be written as follows as well:

Sinking fund (annuity)

$$= \frac{\text{Future value}}{\text{Compound value factor of an annuity of Re 1}}$$

$$A = F_n \left[\frac{i}{(1+i)^n - 1} \right] \qquad (7)$$

Applying Equation (7) to the above example, we obtain

$$A = 21,875 \times \frac{1}{4.375} = 21,875 \times 0.2286 = \text{Rs } 5,000$$

The sinking fund factor is useful in determining the annual amount to be put in a fund to repay bonds or debentures at the end of a specified period.

PRESENT VALUE

We have so far shown how compounding technique can be used for adjusting for the time value of money. It increases an investor's analytical power to compare cash flows that are separated by more than one period, given her interest rate per period. With the compounding technique, the amount of present cash can be converted into an amount of cash of equivalent value in future. However, it is a common practice to translate future cash flows into their present values. **Present value** of a future cash flow (inflow or outflow) is the amount of current cash that is of equivalent value to the decision maker. Discounting is the process of determining present values of a series of future cash flows. The *compound interest* rate used for discounting cash flows is also called the *discount rate*.

Present Value of a Single Cash Flow

We have shown earlier that an investor with an interest rate, *i* of, say 10 per cent, per year would remain indifferent between Re 1 now and Re 1×1.10^1 = Rs 1.10 one year from now, or Re 1×1.10^2 = Rs 1.21 after two years, or Re 1×1.10^3 = Rs 1.33 after 3 years. We can say that, given 10 per cent interest rate, the present value of Rs 1.10 after one year is: $1.10/1.10^1 = $ Re 1; of Rs 1.21 after two years is: $1.21/1.10^2 = $ Re 1; of Rs 1.331 after three years is: $1.331/1.10^3 = $ Re 1. We can now ask a related question: How much would the investor give up now to get an amount of Re 1 at the end of one year? Assuming a 10 per cent interest rate, we know that an amount sacrificed in the beginning of year will grow to 110 per cent or 1.10 after a year. Thus the amount to be sacrificed today would be: $1/1.10 = $ Rs 0.909. In other words, at a 10 per cent rate, Re 1 to be received after a year is 110 per cent of Re 0.909 sacrificed now. Stated differently, Re 0.909 deposited now at 10 per cent rate of interest will grow to Re 1 after one year. If Re 1 is received after two years, then the amount needed to be sacrificed today would be: $1/1.10^2 = $ Rs 0.826.

How can we express the present value calculations formally? Let i represent the interest rate per period, n the number of periods, F the future value (or cash flow) and P the present value (cash flow). We know the future value after one year, F_1 (viz., present value (principal) plus interest), will be

$$F_1 = P(1+i)$$

The present value, P, will be equal to

$$P = \frac{F_1}{(1+i)^1}$$

The future value after two years is

$$F_2 = P(1+i)^2$$

The present value, P, will be

$$P = \frac{F_2}{(1+i)^2}$$

The present values can be worked out for any combination number of years and interest rate. The following general formula can be employed to calculate the present value of a lump sum to be received after some future periods:

$$P = \frac{F_n}{(1+i)^n} = F_n\left[(1+i)^{-n}\right]$$

$$P = F_n\left[\frac{1}{(1+i)^n}\right] \qquad (8)$$

The term in parentheses is the **discount factor** or **present value factor** (PVF), and it is always less than 1.0 for positive i, indicating that a future amount has a smaller present value. We can rewrite Equation (8) as follows:

Present value = Future value ×

Present value factor of Re 1

$$PV = F_n \times PVF_{n,i} \qquad (9)$$

$PVF_{n,i}$ is the present value factor for n periods at i rate of interest.

When we want to calculate the present value factor, we can use a scientific calculator. Alternatively, we can use a table of pre-calculated present value factors like Table 2.3. You can refer to Table C at the end of this book, which gives the pre-calculated present values of Re 1 after n number of years at i rates of interest. To find out the present value of a future amount, we have simply to find out the present value factor (PVF) for given n and i from Table C and multiply by the future amount.

Illustration 2.4: Present Value of a Lump Sum

Suppose that an investor wants to find out the present value of Rs 50,000 to be received after 15 years. Her interest rate is 9 per cent. First, we will find out the present value factor from Table C. When we read row 15 and 9 per cent column, we get 0.275 as the present value factor. Multiplying 0.275 by Rs 50,000, we obtain Rs 13,750 as the present value:

$$PV = 50,000 \times PVF_{15,0.09} = 50,000 \times 0.275 = Rs\ 13,750$$

What would be the present value if Rs 50,000 were received after 20 years? The present value factor (PVF) for 20 years at 9 per cent rate of interest is 0.178. Thus the present value of Rs 50,000 is $50,000 \times 0.178$ = Rs 8,900.

The present values decline for given interest rate as the time period increases. Similarly given the time period, present values would decline as the interest rate increases. In Figure 2.3 we show the present value of Re 1 (Y-axis) for different rates over a period of time. It can be seen from the figure that the present value declines as interest rates increase and the time lengthens.

Present Value of an Annuity

An investor may have an investment opportunity of receiving an *annuity* – a constant periodic amount – for a certain specified

Table 2.3: Present Value Factor of a Lump Sum of Re 1

Period	1%	2%	3%	4%	5%	10%	15%	20%	25%	30%
					Interest Rate					
1	0.990	0.980	0.971	0.962	0.952	0.909	0.870	0.833	0.800	0.769
2	0.980	0.961	0.943	0.925	0.907	0.826	0.756	0.694	0.640	0.592
3	0.971	0.942	0.915	0.889	0.864	0.751	0.658	0.579	0.512	0.455
4	0.961	0.924	0.888	0.855	0.823	0.683	0.572	0.482	0.410	0.350
5	0.951	0.906	0.863	0.822	0.784	0.621	0.497	0.402	0.328	0.269
6	0.942	0.888	0.837	0.790	0.746	0.564	0.432	0.335	0.262	0.207
7	0.933	0.871	0.813	0.760	0.711	0.513	0.376	0.279	0.210	0.159
8	0.923	0.853	0.789	0.731	0.677	0.467	0.327	0.233	0.168	0.123
9	0.914	0.837	0.766	0.703	0.645	0.424	0.284	0.194	0.134	0.094
10	0.905	0.820	0.744	0.676	0.614	0.386	0.247	0.162	0.107	0.073

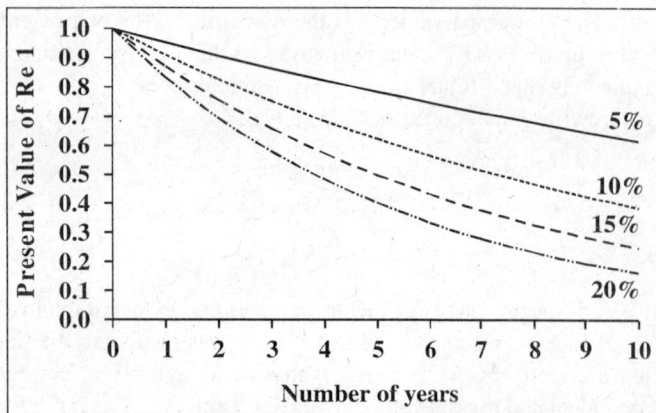

Figure 2.3: Present value of Re 1 in future

number of years. The present value of an annuity cannot be found out by using Equation (8). We will have to find out the present value of the annual amount every year and will have to aggregate all the present values to get the total present value of the annuity. For example, an investor, who has a required interest rate as 10 per cent per year, may have an opportunity to receive an annuity of Re 1 for four years. The present value of Re 1 received after one year is, $P = 1/(1.10) = $ Re 0.909, after two years, $P = 1/(1.10)^2 = $ Re 0.826, after three years, $P = 1/(1.10)^3 = $ Re 0.751 and after four years, $P = 1/(1.10)^4 = $ Re 0.683. Thus the

---

Excel Application 2.4:
Present Value of a Single Cash Flow

We can find the present value of a single cash flow in Excel by using the built-in *PV* function:

PV (RATE, NPER, PMT, FV, TYPE)

The function is similar to *FV* function except the change in places for *PV* and *FV*.

We use the values of parameters as given in Illustration 2.4. We enter in column C5 the formula: *PV* (C4, C3, 0, –C2, 0). We get the same result as in Illustration 2.4. We enter negative sign for *FV*; that is –C2. This is done to avoid getting the negative value for *PV*.

You can also find the present value by directly using Equation (8). You write the formula for Equation (8) as given in column C10 and obtain exactly the same results.

	A	B	C	D
1	PRESENT VALUE OF SINGLE CASH FLOW			
2	Future value (FV)		50,000	
3	Years (NPER)		15	
4	Interest Rate (RATE)		9%	
5	Present value (PV)	Excel function	13,727	
6				
7	=PV(RATE,NPER,PMT,FV,TYPE)		=PV(C4,C3,0,-C2,0)	
8				
9				
10	Present value (PV)	Eq. (8)	13,727	
11				
12	$PV = FV \times \left[\dfrac{1}{(1+i)^n}\right]$		=C2*1/(1+C4)^C3	
13				
14				
15				

---

total present value of an annuity of Re 1 for four years is Rs 3.169 as shown below:

$$P = \frac{1}{(1.10)} + \frac{1}{(1.10)^2} + \frac{1}{(1.10)^3} + \frac{1}{(1.10)^4}$$

$$= 0.909 + 0.826 + 0.751 + 0.683 = \text{Rs } 3.169$$

If Re 1 were received as a lump sum at the end of the fourth year, the present value would be only Re 0.683. Notice that the present value factors of Re 1 after one, two, three and four years can be separately ascertained from Table C given at the end of this book, and when they are aggregated, we obtain the present value of the annuity of Re 1 for four years. The present value of an annuity of Re 1 for four years at 10 per cent interest rate is shown in Figure 2.4. It can be noticed that the present value declines over period for a given discount rate.

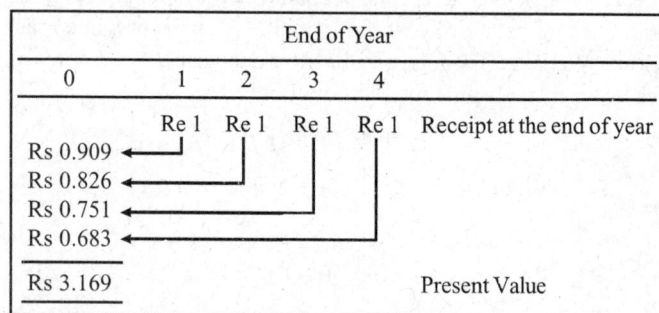

Figure 2.4: Graphic representation of present value of an annuity of Re 1 at 10%

The computation of the present value of an annuity can be written in the following general form:

$$P = \frac{A}{(1+i)} + \frac{A}{(1+i)^2} + \frac{A}{(1+i)^3} + \ldots + \frac{A}{(1+i)^n}$$

$$= A\left[\frac{1}{(1+i)} + \frac{1}{(1+i)^2} + \frac{1}{(1+i)^3} + \ldots + \frac{1}{(1+i)^n}\right]$$

A is a constant cash flow each year. The above equation can be solved and expressed in the following alternate ways:

$$P = A\left[\frac{1 - \dfrac{1}{(1+i)^n}}{i}\right] = A\left[\frac{(1+i)^n - 1}{i(1+i)^n}\right]$$

$$P = A\left[\frac{1}{i} - \frac{1}{i(1+i)^n}\right] \tag{10}$$

The term within parentheses of Equation (10) is the **present value factor of an annuity** of Re 1, which we would call PVFA, and it is a sum of single-payment present value factors.

To illustrate, let us suppose that a person receives an annuity of Rs 5,000 for four years. If the rate of interest is 10 per cent, the present value of Rs 5,000 annuity is

$$P = 5,000\left[\frac{1}{0.10} - \frac{1}{0.10(1.10)^4}\right]$$

$$= 5,000 \times (10 - 6.830) = 5,000 \times 3.170 = \text{Rs } 15,850$$

Table 2.4: Present Value Factor of an Annuity of Re 1

Period	Interest Rate									
	1%	*2%*	*3%*	*4%*	*5%*	*10%*	*15%*	*20%*	*25%*	*30%*
1	0.990	0.980	0.971	0.962	0.952	0.909	0.870	0.833	0.800	0.769
2	1.970	1.942	1.913	1.886	1.859	1.736	1.626	1.528	1.440	1.361
3	2.941	2.884	2.829	2.775	2.723	2.487	2.283	2.106	1.952	1.816
4	3.902	3.808	3.717	3.630	3.546	3.170	2.855	2.589	2.362	2.166
5	4.853	4.713	4.580	4.452	4.329	3.791	3.352	2.991	2.689	2.436
6	5.795	5.601	5.417	5.242	5.076	4.355	3.784	3.326	2.951	2.643
7	6.728	6.742	6.230	6.002	5.786	4.868	4.160	3.605	3.161	2.802
8	7.652	7.325	7.020	6.733	6.463	5.335	4.487	3.837	3.329	2.925
9	8.566	8.162	7.786	7.435	7.108	5.759	4.772	4.031	3.463	3.019
10	9.471	8.983	8.530	8.111	7.722	6.145	5.019	4.192	3.571	3.092

It can be realised that the present value calculations of an annuity for a long period would be extremely cumbersome without a scientific calculator. We can use a table of the pre-calculated present values of an annuity of Re 1 as shown in Table 2.4. Table D at the end of this book gives present values of an annuity of Re 1 for numerous combinations of time periods and rates of interest. To compute the present value of an annuity, we should simply find out the appropriate factor from Table D and multiply it by the annuity value. In our example, the value 3.170, solved by using Equation (10), could be ascertained directly from Table D. Reading fourth year row and 10 per cent column, the value is 3.170. Equation (10) can also be written as follows:

$$\text{Present value} = \text{Annuity} \times \text{Present value of an annuity}$$
$$\text{factor of Re 1}$$
$$P = A \times \text{PVFA}_{n,i} \qquad (11)$$

PVFA$_{n,i}$ is present value factor of an annuity of Re 1 for n periods at i rate of interest. Applying the formula and using Table D, we get:

$$PV = 5,000\, (\text{PVFA}_{4,0.10}) = 5,000 \times 3.170 = \text{Rs } 15,850$$

Capital Recovery and Loan Amortisation

If we make an investment today for a given period of time at a specified rate of interest, we may like to know the annual income. **Capital recovery** is the annuity of an investment made today for a specified period of time at a given rate of interest.

The reciprocal of the present value annuity factor is called the *capital recovery factor* (CRF). From Equation (11) we know:

$$P = A \times \text{PVFA}_{n,i}$$

$$A = P \left[\frac{1}{\text{PVFA}_{n,i}} \right]$$

The tern arithin bracbets may be referred to as. The capital recavery factor (CRF). Thus

$$\text{Sinking fund} = \text{Present value} \times \text{Capital recovery}$$
$$\text{(annuity) recovery factor of Re 1}$$
$$A = P \times \text{CRF}_{n,i} \qquad (12)$$

Suppose that you plan to invest Rs 10,000 today for a period of four years. If your interest rate is 10 per cent, how

---

The Excel *PV* function for an annuity is the same as for a single cash flow. Here we are given value for PMT instead of *FV*. We will set a value with negative sign for PMT (annuity) and a zero value for *FV*. We use the values for the parameters as given in the preceding example. In column C5 we write the formula: *PV* (C3, C4, –C2, 0, 0). *PV* of Rs 21,873 is the same as in the preceding example.

Instead of the built-in Excel function, we can directly use Equation (11) to find the present value. We can enter formula for Equation (11) and find the present value. We will get the same result. You can enter the formula in column C10 and verify the result.

	A	B	C	D
1		**PRESENT VALUE OF ANNUITY**		
2	Payment (PMT)		5,000	
3	Interest Rate (RATE)		10%	
4	Years (NPER)		4	
5	Present value (PV)	Excel function	15,849	
6				
7	=PV(RATE,NPER,PMT,FV,TYPE		=PV(C3,C4,-C2,0,0)	
8				
9				
10	Present value (PV)	Eq. (11)	15,849	
11				
12	$PV_A = A \times \left[\frac{1}{i} - \frac{1}{i(1+i)^n} \right]$		=C2*(1/C3-(1/C3*(1+C3)^C4))	
13				
14				
15				

much income per year should you receive to recover your investment? Using Equation (13), the problem can be solved as follows:

$$A = 10,000 \left[\frac{1}{\dfrac{1}{0.10} - \dfrac{1}{0.10 \times (1.10)^4}} \right]$$

$$= 10,000 \left[\frac{1}{3.170} \right] = 10,000 \times 0.3155 = \text{Rs } 3,155$$

Excel Application 2.6: Capital Recovery

The Excel function for finding an annuity (capital recovery) for a given present value is the same as for finding the sinking fund. *PV* replaces *FV* in the formula.

We use the values for the parameters as given in the example above. In column C5 we write the formula: *FV* (C5, C4, –C2, C3, 0). Note that we input both *FV* and *PV* and enter negative sign for PMT. The value of PMT is Rs 3,155.

Instead of the built-in Excel function, we can enter formula or Equation (13) and find the value of the capital recovery (annuity). We will get the same result. You can enter the formula for Equation (13) in column C10 and verify the result.

	Annuity (PMT)	B	C	D	E
1		CAPITAL RECOVERY			
2	Present value (PV)		10,000.00		
3	Future value (FV)		0.00		
4	Years (NPER)		4		
5	Interest Rate (RATE)		10%		
6	Annuity (PMT)	Excel function	3,155		
7					
8					
9	=PMT(RATE,NPER,PV,FV,TYPE)		=PMT(C5,C4,-C2,C3,0)		
10					
11	Annuity (PMT)	Eq.(13)	3,155		
12					
13	$A = PV\left[\dfrac{i(1+i)^n}{(1+i)^n-1}\right]$		=C2*(C5*(1+C5)^C4)/((1+C5)^C4-1)		
14					
15					
16					

It would be thus clear that the term 0.3155 is the capital recovery factor and it is reciprocal of the present value factor of an annuity of Re 1. The annuity is found out by multiplying the amount of investment by CRF.

Capital recovery factor helps in the preparation of a **loan amortisation schedule** or **loan repayment schedule.** Consider Illustration 2.5.

Illustration 2.5: Loan Amortisation

Suppose you have borrowed a 3-year loan of Rs 10,000 at 9 per cent from your employer to buy a motorcycle. If your employer requires three equal end-of-year repayments, then the annual instalment will be

$$10,000 = A \times \text{PVFA}_{3,0.09}$$

$$10,000 = A \times 2.531$$

$$A = \frac{10,000}{2.531} = \text{Rs } 3,951$$

By paying Rs 3,951 each year for three years, you shall completely pay-off your loan with 9 per cent interest. This can be observed from the loan-amortisation schedule given in Table 2.5.

Table 2.5: Loan Amortisation Schedule

End of Year	Payment	Interest	Principal Repayment	Outstanding Balance
0				10,000
1	3,951	900	3,051	6,949
2	3,951	625	3,326	3,623
3	3,951	326	3,625*	0

* Rounding off error.

You pay Rs 3,951 at the end of each year. At the end of the first year, Rs 900 of this amount is interest (Rs 10,000 × 0.09), and the remaining amount (Rs 3,051) is applied towards the repayment of principal. The balance of loan at the beginning of the second year is Rs 6,949 (Rs 10,000 – Rs 3,051). As for the first year, calculations for interest and principal repayment can be made for the second and third years. At the end of the third year, the loan is completely paid-off.

Present Value of Perpetuity

Perpetuity is an annuity that occurs *indefinitely*. Perpetuities are not very common in financial decision-making. But one can find a few examples. For instance, in the case of **irredeemable preference shares** (i.e. preference shares without a maturity), the company is expected to pay preference dividend perpetually. By definition, in a perpetuity, time period, n, is so large (mathematically n approaches *infinity,* ∞) that the expression $(1 + i)^n$ in Equation (10) tends to become zero, and the formula for a perpetuity simply becomes

$$\text{Present value of a perpetuity} = \frac{\text{Perpetuity}}{\text{Interest rate}}$$

$$P = \frac{A}{i} \tag{13}$$

To take an example, let us assume that an investor expects a perpetual sum of Rs 500 annually from his investment. What is the present value of this perpetuity if his interest rate is 10 per cent? Applying Equation (13), we get

$$P = \frac{500}{0.10} = \text{Rs } 5,000$$

Present Value of an Uneven Cash Flows

Investments made by of a firm do not frequently yield constant periodic cash flows (annuity). In most instances the firm receives a stream of uneven cash flows. Thus the present value factors for an annuity, as given in Table D, cannot be used. The procedure is to calculate the present value of each cash flow (using Table C) and aggregate all present values. Consider the following illustration.

Illustration 2.6: Present Value of Uneven Cash Flows

Consider that an investor has an opportunity of receiving Rs 1,000, Rs 1,500, Rs 800, Rs 1,100 and Rs 400 respectively at the end of one through five years. Find out the present value of this stream of uneven cash flows. The investor's required interest rate is 8 per cent? The present value is calculated as follows:

$$\text{Present value} = \frac{1000}{(1.08)} + \frac{1,500}{(1.08)^2} + \frac{800}{(1.08)^3} + \frac{1,100}{(1.08)^4} + \frac{400}{(1.08)^5}$$

The complication of solving this equation can be resolved by using Table B at the end of the book. We can find out the appropriate present value factors (PVFs) either from Table B (at the end of the book) or by using a calculator and multiply them by the respective amount. The present value calculation is shown below:

$$PV = 1,000 \times \text{PVF}_{1,.08} + 1,500 \times \text{PVF}_{2,.08} + 800 \times$$
$$= \text{PVF}_{3,.08} + 1,100 \times \text{PVF}_{4,.08} + 400 \times \text{PVF}_{5,.08}$$
$$= 1,000 \times .926 + 1,500 \times .857 + 800 \times .794 + 1,100$$
$$\times .735 + 400 \times .681 = \text{Rs } 3,927.60$$

The following equation can be used to calculate the present

Excel Application 2.7:
Present Value of an Uneven Cash Flow

We can set the Excel worksheet to find the present value of an uneven series of cash flows. In the worksheet below, the values for cash flows are entered in column C3 to column C7. Years are entered in column B3 to column B7 and interest rate (10%) in column A3. In column D3 to D7 we have entered formula for the present value factor (PVF) for a single cash flow. For example, you can enter in column D3 the formula: (1/(1+$A$3)^B3 and copy it to other columns. Since the interest rate will be same for all years, we have set it constant by entering $A$3. When you multiply the values in column C by the values in column D, you obtain the present value of each cash flow in column E. The total present value is the sum of all individual present values. You can get the total present value in column E8 by entering the formula: = SUM (E3:E7).

You can also use the built-in Excel function NPV to calculate the present value of uneven cash flows:

NPV(RATE,VALUE1,VALUE2,…)

We enter in column E9 the formula: NPV (A3, C3:C7). We get the same result as above. Note that there is no cash flow in year 0.

	A	B	C	D	E	F
1		PRESENT VALUE OF UNEVEN CASH FLOW				
2	Interest Rate	Year	Cash Flow (CF)	PVF	CF x PVF	
3	10%	1	1,000	0.9091	909.09	
4		2	1,500	0.8264	1,239.67	
5		3	800	0.7513	601.05	
6		4	1,100	0.6830	751.31	
7		5	400	0.6209	248.37	
8	Present value				3,749.50	
9	Excel function		=SUM(E3:E7)		3,749.50	
10						
11	=NPV(RATE,VALUE1,VALUE2,…)				=NPV(A2,C3:C7)	
12						
13						

value of uneven cash flows:

$$P = \frac{A_1}{(1+i)} + \frac{A_2}{(1+i)^2} + \frac{A_3}{(1+i)^3} + ... + \frac{A_n}{(1+i)^n}$$

$$P = \sum_{t=1}^{n} \frac{A_t}{(1+i)^t} \qquad (14)$$

In Equation (14) t indicates number of years, extending from one year to n years. In operational terms, Equation (14) can be written as follows:

$$P = A_1 \times PVF_{1,i} + A_2 \times PVF_{2,i} + A_3 \times PVF_{3,i} + ... + A_n \times PVF_{n,i}$$

Present Value of Growing Annuity

In financial decision-making there are number of situations where cash flows may grow at a constant rate. For example, in the case of companies, dividends are expected to grow at a constant rate. Assume that to finance your post-graduate studies in an evening college, you undertake a part-time job for 5 years. Your employer fixes an annual salary of Rs 1,000 with the provision that you will get annual increment at the rate of 10 per cent. It means that you shall get the following amounts from year 1 through year 5.

End of Year	Amount of Salary (Rs)		
1	1,000	$= 1{,}000 \times 1.10^0$	1,000
2	$1{,}000 \times 1.10 = 1{,}000 \times 1.10^1$		1,100
3	$1{,}100 \times 1.10 = 1{,}000 \times 1.10^2$		1,210
4	$1{,}210 \times 1.10 = 1{,}000 \times 1.10^3$		1,331
5	$1{,}331 \times 1.10 = 1{,}000 \times 1.10^4$		1,464

If your required rate of return is 12 per cent, you can use the following formula to calculate the present value of your salary:

$$P = \frac{1{,}000(1.10)^0}{(1.12)^1} + \frac{1{,}000(1.10)^1}{(1.12)^2} + \frac{1{,}000(1.10)^2}{(1.12)^3}$$

$$+ \frac{1{,}000(1.10)^3}{(1.12)^4} + \frac{1{,}000(1.10)^4}{(1.12)^5}$$

$$= 1{,}000 \times \frac{1}{(1.12)^1} + 1{,}100 \times \frac{1}{(1.12)^2} + 1{,}210 \times \frac{1}{(1.12)^3}$$

$$+ 1{,}331 \times \frac{1}{(1.12)^4} + 1{,}464 \times \frac{1}{(1.12)^5}$$

The calculations of present value is shown in Table 2.6.

Table 2.6: Present Value of a Growing Annuity

Year End	Amount of Salary (Rs)	PVF @ 12%	PV of Salary (Rs)
1	1,000	0.893	893
2	1,100	0.797	877
3	1,210	0.712	862
4	1,331	0.636	847
5	1,464	0.567	830
	6,105		4,309

We can write the formula for calculating the present value of a growing annuity as follows:

$$P = \frac{A}{(1+i)} + \frac{A(1+g)^1}{(1+i)^2} + \frac{A(1+g)^2}{(1+i)^3} + ... + \frac{A(1+g)^{n-1}}{(1+i)^n}$$

$$P = A \left[\frac{1}{(1+i)} + \frac{(1+g)^1}{(1+i)^2} + \frac{(1+g)^2}{(1+i)^3} + ... + \frac{(1+g)^{n-1}}{(1+i)^n} \right] \quad (15)$$

In Equation (15) g is the constant rate of growth of cash flows, and cash flow in year 1 is A, in year two cash flow is $A_2 = A(1+g)^1$, in year 3 cash flow is $A_3 = A(1+g)^2$ and in year n cash flow is $A_n = A(1+g)^{n-1}$. We can simplify Equation (15) to calculate the present value of a constantly growing annuity as given below:

$$P = A\left[\frac{1}{i-g} - \frac{1}{i-g}\left(\frac{1+g}{1+i}\right)^n\right]$$

$$P = \frac{A}{i-g}\left[1 - \left(\frac{1+g}{1+i}\right)^n\right] \quad (16)$$

Let us apply Equation (16) to the above example (you can use a scientific calculator with y^x function):

$$P = \frac{1,000}{0.12-0.10}\left[1 - \left(\frac{1.10}{1.12}\right)^5\right]$$

$$= 50,000 \times (1 - 0.9138) = Rs\ 4,309$$

There is an alternative method of calculating the present value of growing annuities. Let us define

$$\frac{1+g}{1+i} = \frac{1}{1+i*}$$

Solving the above equation, we obtain

$$i* = \frac{i-g}{1+g}$$

When we multiply both sides of Equation (15) by $(1+g)$, substitute $1/(1+i*)$ for $(1+g)/(1+i)$ and define $i* = (i-g)/(1+g)$, we obtain the following equation:

$$P = \frac{A}{(1+g)}\left[\frac{1}{i*} - \frac{1}{i*(1+i*)^n}\right] \quad (17)$$

Illustration 2.7: Value of a Growing Annuity

A company paid a dividend of Rs 60 last year. The dividend stream commencing one year is expected to grow at 10 per cent annum for 15 years and then ends. If the discount rate is 21 per cent, what is the present value of the expected series?

There is a long way to solve this problem. You may first calculate the series of dividends over 15 years. Note that the first annuity (dividend) in year 1 will be: $60 \times 1.10 = Rs\ 66$. Similarly, dividends for other years can be calculated. Once the dividends have been worked out, you can find their present value using the 21 per cent discount rate. This procedure is shown under Excel Application.

There is a short cut to solve the problem. You can use Equation (16) to find the present value of the series of dividend as follows:

$$P = \frac{A}{i-g}\left[1 - \left(\frac{1+g}{1+i}\right)^n\right]$$

$$P = \frac{66}{0.21-0.10}\left[1 - \left(\frac{1.10}{1.21}\right)^{15}\right]$$

$$= 600 \times (1 - 0.909^{15}) = 600 \times 0.7606 = Rs\ 456.36$$

Yet another alternative is to use Equation (17) as shown below.

$$i* = \frac{i-g}{1+g} = \frac{0.11}{1.10} = 0.10$$

$$P = \frac{66}{1.10}\left[\frac{1}{0.10} - \frac{1}{0.10(1.10)^{15}}\right]$$

$$= 60 \times 7.606 = Rs\ 456.36$$

Excel Application 2.8: Constantly Growing Annuity

In Illustration 2.7 the dividend is Rs 60 in the previous year. It will start growing from year 1 at 10 per cent per annum for 15 years. The discount rate is 21 per cent. We need to first compute the stream of dividends from 15 years and then calculate its present value at 21 per cent. We can set up a worksheet for the purpose of making the calculations. Dividend in year 1 is

$$D_1 = D_0(1+g)^1$$

We can enter in column B5 the formula: B$3*(1+B$2)^A5 for calculating dividend in year and copy it up to column B19. Columns B5-B19 show the dividend stream. We can next use the Excel built-in NPV formula and calculate the present value of the dividend stream.

NPV(RATE,VALUE1,VALUE2,…)

The present value of dividends is Rs 456.36.

We can use a short-cut method, Equation (16), for calculating the present value of the dividend stream as shown in the worksheet below. We enter a formula for Equation (16) in column C4:

$$= B5/(B1-B2)*(1-((1+B2)/(1+B1))^{15})$$

The calculated present value, Rs 456.36, is the same.

	A	B	C	D	E
	CONSTANTLY GROWING ANNUITY				
1	Interest rate	21%			
2	Growth rate	10%			
3	Dividend	60.00	456.36		
4	Year	Dividend			
5	1	66.00	=B$3*(1+B$2)^A5		
6	2	72.60			
7	3	79.86			
8	4	87.85			
9	5	96.63			
10	6	106.29			
11	7	116.92			
12	8	128.62			
13	9	141.48			
14	10	155.62			
15	11	171.19			
16	12	188.31			
17	13	207.14			
18	14	227.85			
19	15	250.63			
20	PV	456.36	=NPV(B1,B5:B19)		
21					
22	=NPV(RATE,VALUE1,VALUE2,…)				
23					
24					
25					

The problem in Illustration 2.7 is quite involved. You can easily solve it with a scientific calculator. Alternatively, you can use Excel spreadsheet to solve it (as shown above).

Present Value of Growing Perpetuities

Constantly growing perpetuities are annuities growing indefinitely. How can we value a constantly growing perpetuity? Suppose dividends of Rs 66 after one year in Illustration 2.7 are expected to grow at 10 percent indefinitely. The discount rate is 21 per cent. Hence, the present value of dividends will be as follows:

$$P = \frac{66}{1.21} + \frac{66(1.10)}{(1.21)^2} + \frac{66(1.10)^2}{(1.21)^3} + \ldots + \frac{66(1.10)^{n-1}}{(1.21)^n} + \ldots$$

In mathematical term, we may say that in Equation (17) n – the symbol for the number of years – is not finite and that it extends to infinity (∞). Then the calculation of the present value of a constantly growing perpetuity is given by a simple formula as follows:

$$P = \frac{A}{i-g} \tag{18}$$

Thus, in Illustration 2.7 if the dividend of Rs 66 in year 1 were expected to grow perpetually, the present value would be:

$$P = \frac{66}{0.21 - 0.10} = \frac{\text{Rs } 66}{0.11} = \text{Rs } 600$$

VALUE OF AN ANNUITY DUE

The concepts of compound value and present value of an annuity discussed earlier are based on the assumption that series of cash flows occur at the *end of the period*. In practice, cash flows could take place at the *beginning of the period*. When you buy a fridge on an instalment basis, the dealer requires you to make the first payment *immediately* (viz. in the beginning of the first period) and subsequent instalments in the beginning of each period. It is common in lease or hire purchase contracts that lease or hire purchase payments are required to be made in the beginning of each period. **Lease** is a contract to pay lease rentals (payments) for the use of an asset. **Hire purchase** contract involves regular payments (instalments) for acquiring (owning) an asset. **Annuity due** is a series of fixed receipts or payments *starting at the beginning of each period* for a specified number of periods.

Future Value of an Annuity Due

How can we compute the compound value of an annuity due? Suppose you deposit Re 1 in a savings account at the *beginning* of each year for 4 years to earn 6 per cent interest? How much will be the compound value at the end of 4 years? You may recall that when deposit of Re 1 made at the *end* of each year, the compound value at the end of 4 years is Rs 4.375 (see Figure 2.1). However, Re 1 deposited in the beginning of each of year 1 through year 4 will earn interest respectively for 4 years, 3 years, 2 years and 1 year:

$$F = 1 \times 1.06^4 + 1 \times 1.06^3 + 1 \times 1.06^2 + 1 \times 1.06^1$$
$$= 1.262 + 1.191 + 1 \cdot 124 + 1.06 = \text{Rs } 4.637$$

You can see that the compound value of an annuity due is

more than of an annuity because it earns extra interest for one year. If you multiply the compound value of an annuity by $(1+i)$, you would get the compound value of an annuity due. The formula for the compound value of an annuity due is as follows:

Future value of an annuity due
= Future value of an annuity × $(1 + i)$

$$= A \times \text{CVFA}_{n,i} \times (1+i) \tag{19}$$

$$= A \left[\frac{(1+i)^n - 1}{i} \right] (1+i) \tag{20}$$

Thus the compound value of Re 1 deposited at the beginning of each year for 4 years is

$$1 \times 4.375 \times 1.06 = \text{Rs } 4.637$$

The compound value annuity factors in Table B (at the end of the book) should be multiplied by $(1 + i)$ to obtain relevant factors for an annuity due.

Present Value of an Annuity Due

Let us consider a 4-year annuity of Re 1 each year, the interest rate being 10 per cent. What is the present value of this annuity if each payment is made at the *beginning* of the year? You may recall that when payments of Re 1 are made at the *end* of each year, then the present value of the annuity is Rs 3.169 (see Figure 2.4). Note that if the first payment is made *immediately,* then its present value would be the same (i.e. Re 1) and each year's cash payment will be discounted by one year less. This implies that the present value of an **annuity due** would be higher than the present value of an **annuity.** Thus, the present value of the series of Re 1 payments starting at the *beginning* of a period is

$$PV = \frac{1}{(1.10)^0} + \frac{1}{(1.10)^1} + \frac{1}{(1.10)^2} + \frac{1}{(1.10)^3}$$
$$= 1 + 0.909 + 0.826 + 0.751 = \text{Rs } 3.487$$

The formula for the present value of an annuity due is

Present value of an annuity due =
Present value of an annuity × $(1 + i)$

$$P = A \left[\frac{1}{i} - \frac{1}{i(1+i)^n} \right] (1+i)$$

$$= A \times \text{PVFA}_{n,i} \times (1+i) \tag{21}$$

You can see that the present value of an annuity due is more than of an annuity by the factor of $(1 + i)$. If you multiply the present value of an annuity by $(1 + i)$, you would get the present value of an annuity due.

Applying Equation (21), the present value of Re 1 paid at the beginning of each year for 4 years is

$$1 \times 3.170 \times 1.10 = \text{Rs } 3.487$$

The present value annuity factors in Table D (at the end of the book) should be multiplied by $(1 + i)$ to obtain relevant factors for an annuity due.

MULTI-PERIOD COMPOUNDING

We have assumed in the discussion so far that cash flows occurred once a *year*. In practice, cash flows could occur more than once a year. For example, banks may pay interest on savings account quarterly. On bonds or debentures and public deposits, companies may pay interest semi-annually. Similarly, financial institutions may require corporate borrowers to pay interest quarterly or half-yearly.

The interest rate is usually specified on an annual basis in a loan agreement or security (such as bonds), and is known as the **nominal interest rate.** If compounding is done more than once a year, the actual annualised rate of interest would be higher than the nominal interest rate and it is called the **effective interest rate**. Consider an example.

Suppose you invest Rs 100 now in a bank, interest rate being 10 per cent a year, and that the bank will compound interest semi-annually (i.e., twice a year). How much amount will you get after a year? The bank will calculate interest on your deposit of Rs 100 for first six months at 10 per cent and add this interest to your principal. On this total amount accumulated at the end of first six months, you will again receive interest for next six months at 10 per cent. Thus, the amount of interest for first six months will be

$$\text{Interest} = \text{Rs } 100 \times 10\% \times \tfrac{1}{2} = \text{Rs } 5$$

and the outstanding amount at the beginning of the second six-month period will be: Rs 100 + Rs 5 = Rs 105. Now you will earn interest on Rs 105. The interest on Rs 105 for next six months will be

$$\text{Interest} = \text{Rs } 105 \times 10\% \times \tfrac{1}{2} = \text{Rs } 5.25$$

Thus you will accumulate Rs 100 + Rs 5 + Rs 5.25 = Rs 110.25 at the end of a year. If the interest were compounded annually, you would have received: Rs 100 + 10% × Rs 100 = Rs 110. You received more under semi-annual compounding because you earned interest on interest earned during the first six month. You will get still higher amount if the compounding is done quarterly or monthly.

What effective annual interest rate did you earn on your deposit of Rs 100? On an annual basis, you earned Rs 10.25 on your deposit of Rs 100; so the effective interest rate (EIR) is

$$\text{EIR} = \frac{5 + 5.25}{100} = 10.25\%$$

This implies that Rs 100 compounded annually at 10.25 per cent, or Rs 100 compounded semi-annually at 10 per cent will accumulate to the same amount.

EIR in the above example can also be found out as follows:

$$\text{EIR} = \left[1 + \frac{i}{2}\right]^{1 \times 2} - 1 = \left[1 + \frac{0.10}{2}\right]^2 - 1$$
$$= 1.1025 - 1 = 0.1025 \text{ or } 10.25\%$$

Notice that annual interest rate, i, has been divided by 2 to find our semi-annual interest rate since we want to compound interest twice, and since there are two compounding periods in one year, the term $(1 + i/2)$ has been squared. If the compounding is done quarterly, the annual interest rate, i, will be divided by four and there will be four compounding periods in one year. This logic can be extended further as shown in Illustration 2.7.

Illustration 2.8

You can get an annual rate of interest of 13 per cent on a public deposit with a company. What is the effective rate of interest if the compounding is done (a) half-yearly, (b) quarterly, (c) monthly, and (d) weekly? The calculations are shown in Table 2.6.

The general formula for calculating EIR can be written in the following general form:

$$\text{EIR} = \left[1 + \frac{i}{m}\right]^{n \times m} - 1 \qquad (22)$$

In Equation (22) i is the annual nominal rate of interest, n the number of years and m the number of compounding per year. In annual compounding, $m = 1$, in monthly compounding $m = 12$ and in weekly compounding $m = 52$.

The concept developed above can be used to accomplish the **multiperiod compounding** or **discounting** for any number of years. For example, if a company pays 15 per cent interest, compounded quarterly, on a 3-year public deposit of Rs 1,000, then the total amount compounded after 3 years will be

$$F_3 = 1,000 \times \left[1 + \frac{0.15}{4}\right]^{3 \times 4}$$
$$= 1,000 \times (1.0375)^{12} = 1,000 \times 1.555 = \text{Rs } 1,555$$

We can thus use the Equation (23) for computing the

Table 2.7: Effective Interest Rate (EIR)

Half-Yearly Compounding	*Quarterly Compounding*	*Monthly Compounding*	*Weekly Compounding*
$EIR = \left[1 + \dfrac{i}{2}\right]^{1 \times 2} - 1$	$EIR = \left[1 + \dfrac{i}{4}\right]^{1 \times 4} - 1$	$EIR = \left[1 + \dfrac{i}{12}\right]^{1 \times 12} - 1$	$EIR = \left[1 + \dfrac{i}{52}\right]^{1 \times 52} - 1$
$= \left[1 + \dfrac{0.13}{2}\right]^{1 \times 2} - 1$	$= \left[1 + \dfrac{0.13}{4}\right]^{1 \times 4} - 1$	$= \left[1 + \dfrac{0.13}{12}\right]^{1 \times 12} - 1$	$= \left[1 + \dfrac{0.13}{52}\right]^{1 \times 52} - 1$
$= (1.065)^2 - 1$	$= (1.0325)^4 - 1$	$= (1.01083)^{12} - 1$	$= (1.0025)^{52} - 1$
$= 0.1342 \text{ or } 13.42\%$	$= 0.1365 \text{ or } 13.65\%$	$= 0.1380 \text{ or } 13.80\%$	$= 0.1386 \text{ or } 13.86\%$

compounded value of a sum in case of the multiperiod compounding:

$$F_n = P\left[1 + \frac{i}{m}\right]^{n \times m} \tag{23}$$

F_n is the future value, P the cash flow today, i the annual rate of interest, n is the number of years and m is the number of compounding per year. The compound value of an annuity in case of the multi-period compounding is given as follows:

$$F_n = A\left[\frac{(1 + i/m)^{n \times m} - 1}{i/m}\right] \tag{24}$$

The logic developed above can be extended to compute the present value of a sum or an annuity in case of the multi-period compounding. The discount rate will be i/m and the time horizon will be equal to $n \times m$.

Illustration 2.9: Multiperiod Compounding

Let us find out the compound value of Rs 1,000 interest rate being 12 per cent per annum if compounded annually, semi-annually, quarterly and monthly for 2 years.

(*i*) Annual compounding

$$F_2 = 1,000 \times (1.12)^2 = 1,000 \times 1.254 = \text{Rs } 1,254$$

(*ii*) Half-yearly compounding

$$F_2 = 1,000 \times \left(1 + \frac{0.12}{2}\right)^{2 \times 2} = 1,000 \times (1.06)^4$$
$$= 1,000 \times 1.262 = \text{Rs } 1,262$$

(*iii*) Quarterly compounding

$$F_2 = 1,000 \times \left(1 + \frac{0.12}{4}\right)^{2 \times 4} = 1,000 \times (1.03)^8$$
$$= 1,000 \times 1.267 = \text{Rs } 1,267$$

(*iv*) Monthly compounding

$$F_2 = 1,000 \times \left(1 + \frac{0.12}{12}\right)^{2 \times 12} = 1,000 \times (1.01)^{24}$$
$$= 1,000 \times 1.270 = \text{Rs } 1,270$$

Continuous Compounding

Sometimes compounding may be done continuously. For example, banks may pay interest continuously; they call it *daily* compounding. The **continuous compounding** function takes the form of the following formula:

$$F_n = P \times e^{i \times n} = P \times e^x \tag{25}$$

In Equation (25), $x =$ interest rate i multiplied by the number of years n and e is equal to 2.7183.

In Illustration 2.9 if the compounding is done continuously, then the compound value will be

$$F_2 = 1,000 \times e^{(0.12)(2)} = 1,000 \times e^{0.24}$$
$$= 1,000 \times 1.2713 = \text{Rs } 1,271.30$$

The values of e^x are available in Table F at the end of the book. You can also use of scientific calculator for this purpose.

Equation (25) can be transformed into a formula for calculating present value under continuous compounding.

$$P = \frac{F_n}{e^{in}} = F_n \times e^{-i \times n} \tag{26}$$

Thus, if Rs 1,271.3 is due in 2 years, discount rate being 12 per cent, then the present value of this future sum is

$$P = \frac{1,271.3}{1.2713} = \text{Rs } 1,000$$

NET PRESENT VALUE

We have stated in Chapter 1 that the firm's financial objective should be to maximise the shareholder's wealth. Wealth is defined as net present value. **Net present value** (*NPV*) of a *financial decision is the difference between the present value of cash inflows and the present value of cash outflows.* Suppose you have Rs 200,000. You want to invest this money in land, which can fetch you Rs 245,000 after one year when you sell it. You should undertake this investment if the present value of the expected Rs 245,000 after a year is greater than the investment outlay of Rs 200,000 today. You can put your money to alternate uses. For example, you can invest Rs 200,000 in units (for example, Unit Trust of India sells 'units' and invests money in securities of companies on behalf of investors) and earn, say, 15 per cent dividend a year. How much should you invest in units to obtain Rs 245,000 after a year? In other words, if your opportunity cost of capital is 15 per cent, what is the present value of Rs 245,000 if you invest in land? The present value is

$$PV = 245,000 \times (\text{PVF}_{1,\,0.15})$$
$$= 245,000 \times 0.870 = \text{Rs } 213,150$$

The land is worth Rs 213,150 today, but that does not mean that your wealth will increase by Rs 213,150. You will have to commit Rs 200,000, and therefore, the net increase in your wealth or net present value is: Rs 213,150 – Rs 200,000 = Rs 13,150. It is worth investing in land. The general formula for calculating NPV can be written as follows:

$$NPV = \left[\frac{C_1}{(1+k)} + \frac{C_2}{(1+k)^2} + \dots + \frac{C_n}{(1+k)^n}\right] - C_0$$

$$NPV = \sum_{t=1}^{n} \frac{C_t}{(1+k)^t} - C_0 \tag{27}$$

C_t is cash inflow in period t, C_0 cash outflow today, k the opportunity cost of capital and t the time period. Note that the opportunity cost of capital is 15 per cent because it is the return

---

Excel Application 2.9:
Multiperiod Compounding

We can set up a worksheet as shown below to see the effect of the multiperiod compounding. In column C we calculate the future value of Re 1 at 12 per cent annual rate for different compounding periods. In C6 we enter the formula for calculating the future value:

=B$3*(1+B$4/B6)^B6

Alternatively, you can use the Excel built-in formula *FV*. Since the present value and interest rate are fixed, we insert the dollar sign. We copy the formula up to C11. For contin-uous compoun-ding, we enter the formula in C12 as: =B$3*exp(B$4). The built-in EXP function solves for *e* raised to power of a specified number. We can see that the future value

increases as the frequency of compounding increases. This is also reflected through the higher effective interest rates calculated in column D. You may, however, note that the effective interest rate or future value rises slowly as the compounding frequencies increasing.

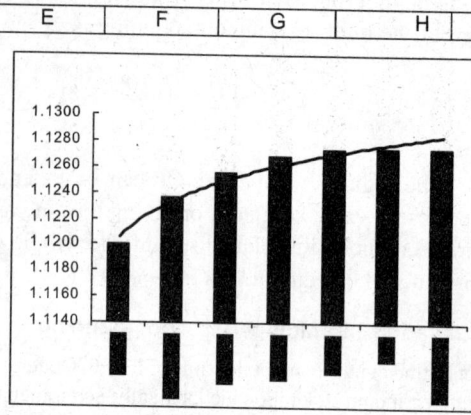

	A	B	C	D	E	F	G	H
1	MULTIPLE COMPOUNDING PERIODS							
2								
3	Present Value	1.00						
4	Annual Value	12%						
5	Compounding periods	Periods/ Year	Future value of Re 1	Effective interest rate				
6	Annual	1	1.12000	12.000%				
7	Semiannual	2	1.12360	12.360%				
8	Quarterly	4	1.12551	12.551%				
9	Monthly	12	1.12683	12.683%				
10	Weekly	52	1.12734	12.734%				
11	Daily	365	1.12747	12.747%				
12	Continuous		1.12750	12.750%				

foregone by investing in land rather than investing in securities (units), assuming risk is the same. The opportunity cost of capital is used as a discount rate.

PRESENT VALUE AND RATE OF RETURN

You may be frequently reading advertisements in newspapers: deposit, say Rs 1,000 today and get twice the amount in 7 years; or pay us Rs 100 a year for 10 years and we will pay you Rs 100 a year thereafter in perpetuity. A company or financial institution may offer you bond or debenture for a current price lower than its face value and repayable in the future at the face value, but without an interest (coupon). A bond that pays some specified amount in future (without periodic interest) in exchange for the current price today is called a **zero-interest bond** or **zero-coupon bond**. In such situations, you would be interested to know what rate of interest the advertiser is offering. You can use the concept of present value to find out the **rate of return** or **yield** of these offers. Let us take some examples.

A bank offers you to deposit Rs 100 and promises to pay Rs 112 after one year. What rate of interest would you earn? The answer is 12 per cent:

$$100 \times (1+i) = 112$$

$$100 = \frac{112}{(1+i)}$$

$$(1+i) = \frac{112}{100}$$

$$i = \frac{112}{100} - 1 = 0.12 \text{ or } 12\%$$

What rate of interest would you earn if you deposit Rs 1,000 today and receive Rs 1,762 at the end of five years? You can set your problem as follows: Rs 1,000 is the present

value of Rs 1,762 due to be received at the end of the fifth year. Thus,

$$1,000 = \frac{1,762}{(1+i)^5} = 1,762 \times (\text{PVF}_{5,i})$$

$$\text{PVF}_{5,i} = \frac{1,000}{1,762} = 0.576$$

Now you refer to Table C, given at the end of the book, that contains the present value of Re 1. Since 0.567 is a PVF at *i* rate of interest for 5 years, look across the row for period 5 and interest rate column until you find this value. You will notice this factor in the 12 per cent column. You will, thus, earn 12 per cent on your Rs 1,000. (*Check:* Rs 1,000 × (1.12)⁵ = Rs 1,000 × 1.762 = Rs 1,762). You can use a scientific calculator to solve for the rate of return:

$$1,000 = \frac{1,762}{(1+i)}$$

$$(1+i)^5 = \frac{1,762}{1,000}$$

$$i = \left(\frac{1,762}{1,000}\right)^{1/5} - 1 = 1.762^{1/5} - 1$$

$$i = 1.12 - 1 = 0.12 \text{ or } 12\%$$

Let us take example of an annuity. Assume you borrow Rs 70,000 from the Housing Development Finance Corporation (HDFC) to buy a flat in Ahmedabad. You are required to mortgage the flat and pay Rs 11,396.93 annually for a period of 15 years. What interest rate would you be paying? You may note that Rs 70,000 is the present value of a fifteen-year annuity of Rs 11,396.93. That is,

$$70,000 = 11,396.93 \times \text{PVAF}_{15,i}$$

$$\text{PVAF}_{15,i} = \frac{70,000}{11,396.93} = 6.142$$

You look across in Table D (at the end of this book) the 15-year row and interest rate columns until you get the value 6.142. You find this value in the 14 per cent column. Thus HDFC is charging 14 per cent interest from you.

Finding the rate of return for an uneven series of cash flows is a bit difficult. By practice and using trial and error method you can find it.[1] Let us consider an example to illustrate the calculation of rate of return for an uneven series of cash flows.

Illustration 2.10: Calculating Rate of Return

Suppose your friend wants to borrow from you Rs 1,600 today and would return to you Rs 700, Rs 600 and Rs 500 in year 1 through year 3 as principal plus interest. What rate to return would you earn?

You should recognise that you earn that rate of return at which the present value of Rs 700, Rs 600 and Rs 500 received, respectively, after one, two and three is Rs 1,600. Suppose (arbitrarily) this rate is 8 per cent. When you calculate the present value of the cash flows at 8 per cent, you get the following amount:

	Cash Flow	*PV of Cash Flow*	
Year	*(Rs)*	*PVF at 8%*	*(Rs)*
1	700	0.926	648.20
2	600	0.857	514.20
3	500	0.794	397.00
			1,559.40

Since the present value at 8 per cent is less than Rs 1,600, it implies that your friend is allowing you a lower rate of return; so you try 6 per cent. You obtain the following results:

Year	*Cash Flow (Rs)*	*PVF at 6%*	*PV of Cash Flow (Rs)*
1	700	0.943	660.00
2	600	0.890	534.00
3	500	0.840	420.00
			1,614.00

The present value at 6 per cent is slightly more than Rs 1,600; it means that your friend is offering you approximately 6 per cent interest. In fact, the actual rate would be a little higher than 6 per cent. At 7 per cent, the present value of cash flows is Rs 1,586. You can interpolate as follows to calculate the actual rate:

$$= 6\% + (7\% - 6\%) \times \frac{(1,614 - 1,600)}{(1,614 - 1,586)}$$

$$= 6\% + 1\% \times \frac{14}{28} = 6\% + 0.5\% = 6.5\%$$

At 6.5 per cent rate of return, present value of Rs 700, Rs 600 and Rs 500 occurring respectively in year one through three is equal to Rs 1,600:

---

1. You can find this by using a scientific calculator and employing Equation (8).

Excel Application 2.10: Yield or IRR Calculation

Excel has built-in functions for calculating the yield or IRR of an annuity and uneven cash flows. The Excel function to find the yield or IRR of an annuity is:

RATE(NPER,PMT,PV,FV,TYPE,GUESS)

GUESS is a first guess rate. It is optional; you can specify your formula without it. In column C6 we enter the formula: = RATE (C5, C4, C2, 0,0,0.10). The last value 0.10 is the guess rate, which you may omit to specify. For investment with an outlay of Rs 20,000 and earning an annuity of Rs 5,000 for 8 years, the yield s 18.62 per cent.

	A	B	C
1	**YIELD OR RATE OF AN ANNUITY**		
2	Present value (PV)		-20,000
3	Future value (FV)		0
4	Annual payment (PMT)		5000
5	Number of years (NPER)		8
6	Yield (RATE)	Excel function	18.62%
7			
8	=RATE(NPER,PMT,PV,FV,TYPE,GUESS)		
9			
10		=RATE(C5,C4,C2,0,0,0.10)	
11			

The Excel built-in function IRR calculates the yield or IRR of uneven cash flows:

IRR(VALUES,GUESS)

The values for the cash flows should be in a sequence, starting from the cash outflow. GUESS is a first guess rate (arbitrary) and it is optional. In the worksheet, we have entered the cash flows of an investment project. In column B4 we enter the formula: =IRR(B3:G3) to find yield (IRR). Note that all cash flows in year 0 to year 5 have been entered in that sequence. The yield (IRR) is 27.43 per cent.

You can also use the built-in function, NPV, in Excel to calculate the net resent value of an investment with uneven cash flows. Assume in the present example that the discount rate is 20 per cent. You can enter in column B5 the NPV formula: NPV(0.20,C3:G3)+B3. The net present value is Rs 8,922. If you do not enter +B3 for the value of the initial cash outflow, you will get the present value of cash inflows (from year 1 through yea 5), and not the net present value.

If you use the internal rate of return (27.43 per cent) to calculate NPV of the cash flows, it would be zero. Why?

	A	B	C	D	E	F	G
1	**IRR OR YIELD OF AN UNEVEN CASH FLOWS**						
2	Year	0	1	2	3	4	5
3	Cash flows	-50,000	10,000	25,000	32,000	18,000	15,000
4	IRR or Yield	27.43%	=IRR(B3:G3)				
5	NPV	8,922					
6		=NPV(0.20,C3:CG3)+B3					
7							

$$= \frac{Rs\ 700}{(1.065)} + \frac{Rs\ 600}{(1.065)^2} + \frac{Rs\ 500}{(1.065)^3}$$

$$= 700 \times 0.939 + Rs\ 600 \times 0.883 + Rs\ 500 \times 0.828$$

$$= Rs\ 1,600$$

The rate of return of an investment is called **internal rate of return** since it depends exclusively on the cash flows of the investment. Once you have understood the logic of the calculation of the internal rate of return, you can use a scientific calculator or Excel to find it.

SUMMARY

❖ Individual investors generally prefer possession of a given amount of cash now, rather than the same amount at some future time. This *time preference for money* may arise because of (*a*) uncertainty of cash flows, (*b*) subjective preference for consumption, and (*c*) availability of investment opportunities. The last reason is the most sensible justification for the *time value of money*.

❖ A *risk premium* may be demanded, over and above the *risk-free rate* as compensation for time, to account for the uncertainty of cash flows.

❖ Interest rate or time preference rate gives money its value, and facilitates the comparison of cash flows occurring at different time periods.

❖ A risk-premium rate is added to the risk-free time preference rate to derive *required interest rate* from risky investments.

❖ Two alternative procedures can be used to find the value of cash flows: compounding and discounting.

❖ In *compounding*, future values of cash flows at a given interest rate at the end of a given period of time are found. The future value (*F*) of a lump sum today (*P*) for *n* periods at *i* rate of interest is given by the following formula:

$$F_n = P(1+i)^n = P(\text{CVF}_{n,i})$$

❖ The compound value factor, $\text{CVF}_{n,i}$ can be found out from Table A given at the end of the book.

❖ The future value of an *annuity* (that is, the same amount of cash each year) for *n* periods at *i* rate of interest is given by the following equation.

$$F_n = P\left[\frac{(1+i)^n - 1}{i}\right] = P(\text{CVFA}_{n,i})$$

❖ The compound value of an annuity factor ($\text{CVFA}_{n,i}$) can be found out from Table B given at the end of the book. The compound value of an annuity formula can be used to calculate an annuity to be deposited to a sinking fund for *n* periods at *i* rate of interest to accumulate to a given sum. The following equation can be used:

$$A = F\left[\frac{1}{\text{CVFA}_{n,i}}\right] = F(\text{SFF}_{n,i})$$

❖ The *sinking fund* factor ($\text{SFF}_{n,i}$) is a reciprocal of $\text{CVFA}_{n,i}$.

❖ In *discounting*, the present value of cash flows at a given interest rate at the beginning of a given period of time is computed. The present value concept is the most important concept in financial decision-making. The present value

(*P*) of a lump sum (*F*) occurring at the end of *n* period at *i* rate of interest is given by the following equation:

$$P = \frac{F_n}{(1+i)^n} = F_n(\text{PVF}_{n,i})$$

❖ The present value factor ($\text{PVF}_{n,i}$) can be obtained from Table C given at the end of the book.

❖ The present value of an annuity (*A*) occurring for *n* periods at *i* rate of interest can be found out as follows:

$$P = A\left[\frac{1 - \frac{1}{(1+i)^n}}{i}\right] = \frac{(1+i)^n - 1}{i(1+i)^n}$$

$$= A\left[\frac{1}{i} - \frac{1}{i(1+i)^n}\right] = A(\text{PVFA}_{n,i})$$

❖ Table D at the end of this book can be used to find out the present value of annuity factor ($\text{PVFA}_{n,i}$).

❖ The present value of an annuity formula can be used to determine annual cash flows to be earned to recover a given investment. The following equation can be used:

$$A = P\left[\frac{1}{\text{PVFA}_{n,i}}\right] = P(\text{CRF}_{n,i})$$

❖ Notice that the capital recovery factor ($\text{CRF}_{n,i}$) is a reciprocal of the present value annuity factor, $\text{PVFA}_{n,i}$.

❖ The present value concept can be easily extended to compute present value of an uneven series of cash flows, cash flows growing at constant rate, or perpetuity.

❖ When interest compounds for more than once in a given period of time, it is called *multiperiod compounding*. If i is the *nominal interest rate* for a period, the *effective interest rate* (EIR) will be more than the nominal rate *i* in multi-period compounding since interest on interest within a year will also be earned, EIR is given as follows:

$$\text{EIR} = \left[1 + \frac{i}{m}\right]^{n \times m} - 1$$

where *m* is the number of compounding in a year and *n* is number of years.

❖ Table 2.8 Gives the summary of the compounding and discounting formulae.

❖ An important corollary of the present value is the *internal rate of return* (IRR). IRR is the rate which equates the present

Table 2.8: Summary of Compounding and Discounting Formulae

Purpose	Given	Calculate	Formula	Purpose	Given	Calculate	Formula
Compound value of a lump sum	P (Present value)	F (Furure value)	$F = P(1+i)^n$	Capital recovery	P (Present value)	A (Annuity)	$A = P\left[\dfrac{i(1+i)^n}{(1+i)^n - 1}\right]$
Compound value of an annuity	A (Annuity)	F (Future value)	$F = A\left[\dfrac{(1+i)^n - 1}{i}\right]$	Present value of a perpetuity	A (Annuity)	P (Present value)	$P = \dfrac{A}{i}$
Sinking fund	F (Future value)	A (Annuity)	$A = F\left[\dfrac{i}{(1+i)^n - 1}\right]$	Present value of a constantly growing perpetuity	A (Annuity)	P (Present value)	$P = \dfrac{A}{i - g}$
Present value of a lump sum	F (Future value)	P (Present value)	$P = F\left[\dfrac{1}{(1+i)^n}\right]$	Compound value of an annuity due	A (Annuity)	F (Future value)	$F = A\left[\dfrac{(1+i)^n - 1}{i}\right](1+i)$
Present value of an annuity	A (Annuity)	P (Present value)	$P = A\left[\dfrac{1}{i} - \dfrac{1}{i(1+i)^n}\right]$	Present value of an annuity due	A (Annuity)	P (Present value)	$P = A\left[\dfrac{(1+i)^n - 1}{i(1+i)^n}\right](1+i)$

value of cash flows to the initial investment. Thus in operational terms, in the present value equation, all variables are known except i; i can be found out by trial and error method as discussed in the chapter.

❖ In view of the logic for the time value of money, the financial criterion is expressed in terms of *wealth maximisation*. As discussed in Chapter 1, the alternate criterion of *profit maximisation* is not only conceptually vague but it also does not take into account the timing and uncertainty of cash flows.

❖ Wealth or net present value of a financial decision is defined as the difference between the present value of cash inflows (benefits) and the present value of cash outflows (costs). Wealth maximisation principle uses interest rate to find out the present value of benefits and costs, and as such, it considers their timing and risk.

KEY CONCEPTS

Annuity	Effective interest rate	Nominal interest rate	Sinking fund
Annuity due	Hire purchase	Opportunity cost of capital	Time preference for money
Capital recovery	Internal rate of return	Perpetuity	Time value of money
Compounding	Lease	Required rate of return	Uncertainty
Continuous compounding	Loan amortisation	Risk	Zero-interest bond
Discount rate	Multi-period compounding	Risk premium	Zero coupon bonds
Discounting	Net present value	Risk-free rate	

ILLUSTRATIVE SOLVED PROBLEMS

Problem 2.1: (*i*) Calculate the present value of Rs 600 (*a*) received one year from now; (*b*) received at the end of five years; (*c*) received at the end of fifteen years. Assume a 5 per cent time preference rate.

(*ii*) Determine the present value of Rs 700 each paid at the end of each of the next six years. Assume an 8 per cent of interest.

(*iii*) Assuming a 10 per cent discount rate, compute the present value of Rs 1,100; Rs 900; Rs 1,500 and Rs 700 received at the end of one through four years. For calculations, use the tables given at the end of the book.

Solution: Table C will be used to compute the present value.

(*i*) Present value of Rs 600·

(*a*) The present value factor at 5 per cent for one year is:

0.952. Therefore, the present value of Rs 600 at the end of one year will be: Rs 600 × 0.952 = Rs 571.20.

(*b*) The present value factor at 5 per cent at the end of five years is: 0.784. Therefore, present value of Rs 600 will be: Rs 600 × 0.784 = Rs 470.40.

(*c*) The present value factor at 5 per cent at the end of fifteen years is 0.481. Therefore, present value of Rs 600 will be: Rs 600 × 0.481 = Rs 288.60.

(*ii*) As the present value of an annuity of Rs 700 has to be computed, Table D will be used. The present value factor of an annuity of Re 1 at 8 per cent for 6 years is 4.623. Therefore, the present value of an annuity of Rs 700 will be: 4 623 × Rs 700 = Rs 3,236.10.

(*iii*) Table C will be used to compute the present value of the uneven series of cash flows. The computation is shown as follows:

$$P = \text{Rs } 1,100 \times 0.909 + \text{Rs } 900 \times 0.826$$
$$+ \text{Rs } 1,500 \times 0.751 + \text{Rs } 700 \times 0.683$$
$$= \text{Rs } 999.90 + \text{Rs } 743.40 + \text{Rs } 1,126.50 + \text{Rs } 478.10$$
$$= \text{Rs } 3,347.90$$

Problem 2.2: Exactly ten years from now Sri Chand will start receiving a pension of Rs 3,000 a year. The payment will continue for sixteen years. How much is the pension worth now, if Sri Chand's interest rate is 10 per cent?

Solution: Sri Chand will receive first payment at the end of 10th year, and last payment at the end of 25th year. That provides him 16 payments of pension money. This can be shown on time scale as follows:

Year end   0————————10————————————25
                    First payment   Last payment

The discounted value of the annuity of Rs 3,000 starting from the end of year 10 until the end of year 25 is the present value of pension received by Sri Chand. Assuming an annuity for 25 years, PVFA is 9.077. But we know that Sri Chand will not receive anything till the end of year 9. Therefore, if we subtract PVAF at ten per cent for 9 years, *viz.*, 5.759 from PVFA at 10 percent for 25 years, 9.077, we shall be left with $9.077 - 5.759 = 3.318$, which is a PVAF for the annuity starting from the end of year 10 and ending at the end of year 25. Thus, the present value of pension will be equal to:

$$(9.077 - 5.759) \times \text{Rs } 3,000 = 3.318 \times \text{Rs } 3,000 = \text{Rs } 9,954$$

Alternatively, the present value of pension can be found in two steps. First, find out present value of the 16-year annuity at 10 per cent interest rate at the end of year 9.

$$P_9 = \text{Rs } 3,000 \times 7.824 = \text{Rs } 23,472$$

Then find out present value now of the lump sum of Rs 23,472:

$$P_0 = \text{Rs } 23,472 \times 0.424 = \text{Rs } 9,954$$

Problem 2.3: Your father has promised to give you Rs 100,000 in cash on your 25th birthday. Today is your 16th birthday. He wants to know two things: (*a*) If he decides to make annual payments into a fund after one year, how much will each have to be if the fund pays 8 per cent? (*b*) If he decides to invest a lump sum in the account after one year and let it compound annually, how much will the lump sum be? (*c*) If in (*a*) the payments are made in the beginning of the year, how much will be the value of annuity?

Solution:

(*a*) $\text{Rs } 100,000 = A(\text{CVFA}_{9,0.08}) = \text{Rs } 100,000 = A(12.488)$

$$A = \frac{\text{Rs } 100,000}{12.488} = \text{Rs } 8007.69$$

(*b*) $\text{Rs } 100,000 = P(\text{CVF}_{9,0.08}) = \text{Rs } 100,000 = P(1.999)$

$$P = \frac{\text{Rs } 100,000}{1.999} = \text{Rs } 50,025$$

(*c*) This is a problem of an annuity due since payment is made at the beginning of the year.

$$\text{Rs } 100,000 = A(\text{CVFA}_{9,0.08}(1.08))$$
$$\text{Rs } 1.00,000 = A(12.487)$$
$$A = \frac{\text{Rs } 100,000}{13.478} = \text{Rs } 7,414.55$$

Problem 2.4: *XYZ* Bank pays 12 per cent and compounds interest quarterly. If Rs 1,000 is deposited initially, how much shall it grow at the end of 5 years?

Solution: The quarterly interest rate will be 3 per cent and the number of periods for which it will be compounded will be 20 (i.e., 5 years × 4). Thus,

$$F_5 = P\left[1 + \frac{i}{m}\right]^{n \times m}$$

$$F_5 = \text{Rs } 1,000\left[1 + \frac{0.12}{4}\right]^{5 \times 4}$$

$$= \text{Rs } 1,000(1.03)^{20} = \text{Rs } 1,000 \times 1.806 = \text{Rs } 1,806$$

Problem 2.5: How long will it take to double your money if it grows at 12 per cent annually?

Solution:
$$F_n = P \times \text{CVF}_{n,i}$$
$$2 = 1 \times \text{CVF}_{n,0.12}$$
$$2 = \text{CVF}_{n.012}$$

From Table A, the factor nearest to 2.00 is $\text{CVF}_{6,0.12} = 1.974$. Therefore, $n = 6$ years.

Problem 2.6: Mohan bought a share 15 years ago for Rs 10. It is now selling for Rs 27.60. What is the compound growth rate in the price of the share?

Solution:
$$F_n = P(\text{CVF}_{n,i})$$
$$27.60 = 10(\text{CVF}_{15,i})$$
$$\text{CVF}_{15,i} = \frac{27.60}{10} = 2,760$$

From Table A, $i = 7\%$.

Problem 2.7: Sadhulal Bhai is borrowing Rs 50,000 to buy a low-income group house. If he pays equal instalments for 25 years and 4 per cent interest on outstanding balance, what is the amount of instalment? What shall be amount of instalment if quarterly payments are required to be made?

Solution: Annual payment:

$$P = A(PVFA_{n,i})$$

$$Rs\ 50,000 = A(PVFA_{25,0.04})$$

$$Rs\ 50,000 = A(15.622)$$

$$A = \frac{Rs\ 50,000}{15.622} = Rs\ 3,200.61$$

Quarterly payment: The quarterly interest rate will be 0.04/4 = 0.01 and number of compounding periods will be 25 × 4 = 100.

$$Rs\ 50,000 = A(PVFA_{100,0.01})$$

$$Rs\ 50,000 = A(63.29)$$

$$A = \frac{Rs\ 50,000}{63.029} = Rs\ 793.28$$

Problem 2.8: A company has issued debentures of Rs 50 lakh to be repaid after 7 years. How much should the company invest in a sinking fund earning 12 per cent in order to be able to repay debentures?

Solution:

$$A\ (PVFA_{0.12,7}) = 50$$

$$A(10.089) = 50$$

$$A = \frac{50}{10.089} = Rs\ 4.96\ lakh$$

Problem 2.9: A bank has offered to you an annuity of Rs 1,800 for 10 years if you invest Rs 12,000 today. What rate of return would you earn?

Solution:

$$12,000 = 1,800(PVFA_{r,10})$$

$$PVFA_{r,10} = \frac{12,000}{1,800} = 6.667$$

When you refer to Table D at the end of the book, you obtain a present value factor of an annuity of Re 1 equal to 6.710 at 8

per cent rate of interest for 10 years. At 9 per cent the factor is 6.418. Thus, the rate of return lies between 8–9 per cent. By interpolation, we can obtain the rate of return as follows:

$$\text{Rate of return} = 8\% + \left[\frac{6.710 - 6.667}{6.710 - 6.418}\right] = 8\% + \frac{0.043}{0.292}$$

$$= 8\% + 0.15\% = 8.15\%$$

Problem 2.10: A firm purchases a machinery for Rs 800,000 by making a down payment of Rs 150,000 and remainder in equal instalments of Rs 150,000 for six years. What is the rate of interest to the firm?

Solution:

$$800,000 - 150,000 = 150,000 \times PVFA_{6,r}$$

$$PVFA_{6,r} = 650,000/150,000 = 4.333$$

For Table B at the end of the book we observe that for 10 per cent rate of interest for 6 years, PVFA is 4.355. Thus the rate of interest, which the firm will be paying, is approximately 10 per cent.

Problem 2.11: *AB* Limited is creating a sinking fund to redeem its preference capital of Rs 5 lakh issued on 6 April 2004 and maturing on 5 April 2015. The first annual payment will be made on 6 April 2004. The company will make equal annual payments and expects that the fund will earn 12 per cent per year. How much will be the amount of sinking fund payment?

Solution: *AB* Co. wants to accumulate a future sum of Rs 500,000. Since the annual payments will be made in the beginning of the year, we can use the formula for the compound value of an annuity due to solve the problem:

$$A(CVFA_{n,i})(1+i) = 500,000$$

$$A(CVFA_{12,0.12})(1.12) = 500,000$$

$$A(24.133)(1.12) = 500,000$$

$$27.029\,A = 500,000$$

$$A = 500,000/27.029$$

$$= Rs\ 18,498.65$$

REVIEW QUESTIONS

1. 'Generally individuals show a time preference for money.' Give reasons for such a preference.
2. 'An individual's time preference for money may be expressed as a rate.' Explain.
3. Why is the consideration of time important in financial decision-making? How can time value be adjusted? Illustrate your answer.
4. Is the adjustment of time relatively more important for financial decisions with short-range implications or for decisions with long-range implications? Explain.
5. Explain the mechanics of calculating the present value of cash flows.
6. What happens to the present value of an annuity when the interest rate rises? Illustrate.
7. What is multi-period compounding? How does it affect the annual rate of interest? Give an example.
8. What is an annuity due? How can you calculate the present and future values of an annuity due? Illustrate.
9. How does discounting and compounding help in determining the sinking fund and capital recovery?
10. Illustrate the concept of the internal rate of return.

PROBLEMS

1. Determine the future values utilising a time preference rate of 9 per cent:
   - (i) The future value of Rs 15,000 invested now for a period of four years.
   - (ii) The future value at the end of five years of an investment of Rs 6,000 now and of an investment of Rs 6,000 one year from now.
   - (iii) The future value at the end of eight years of an annual deposit of Rs 18,000 each year.
   - (iv) The future value at the end of eight years of annual deposit of Rs 18,000 at the beginning of each year.
   - (v) The future values at the end of eight years of a deposit of Rs 18,000 at the end of the first four years and withdrawal of Rs 12,000 per year at the end of year five through seven.

2. Compute the present value of each of the following cash flows using a discount rate of 13 per cent:
   - (i) Rs 2,000 cash outflow immediately.
   - (ii) Rs 6,000 cash inflow one year from now.
   - (iii) Rs 6,000 cash inflow two years from now.
   - (iv) Rs 4,000 cash outflow three years from now.
   - (v) Rs 7,000 cash inflow three years from now.
   - (vi) Rs 3,000 cash inflow four years from now.
   - (vii) Rs 4,000 cash inflow at the end of each of the next five years.
   - (viii) Rs 4,000 cash inflow at the beginning of each of the next five years.

3. Determine the present value of the cash inflows of Rs 3,000 at the end of each year for next 4 years and Rs 7,000 and Rs 1,000 respectively at the end of years 5 and 6. The appropriate discount rate is 14 per cent.

4. Assume an annual rate of interest of 15 per cent. The sum of Rs 100 received immediately is equivalent to what quantity received in ten equal annual payments, the first payment to be received one year from now. What could be the annual amount if the first payment were received immediately?

5. Assume a rate of interest of 10 per cent. We have a debt to pay and are given a choice of paying Rs 1,000 now or some amount X five years from now. What is the maximum amount that X can be for us to be willing to defer payment for five years?

6. We can make an immediate payment now of Rs 13,000 or pay equal amount of A for the next 5 years, first payment being payable after 1 year. (a) With a time value of money of 12 per cent, what is the maximum value of A that we would be willing to accept? (b) What maximum value of A we would be willing to accept if the payments are made in the beginning of the year?

7. Assume that you are given a choice between incurring an immediate outlay of Rs 10,000 and having to pay Rs 2,310 a year for 5 years (first payment due one year from now); the discount rate is 11 per cent. What would be your choice? Will your answer change if Rs 2,310 is paid in the beginning of each year for 5 years?

8. Compute the present value for a bond that promises to pay interest of Rs 150 a year for thirty years and Rs 1,000 at maturity. This first interest payment is paid one year from now. Use a rate of discount of 8 per cent.

9. Exactly twenty years from now Mr. Ahmed will start receiving a pension of Rs 10,000 a year. The payment will continue for twenty years. How much is pension worth now, assuming money is worth 15 per cent per year?

10. Using an interest rate of 10 per cent, determine the present value of the following cash flow series:

End of period		*Cash-flow (Rs)*
0		– 10,000
1–6	(each period)	+ 2,000
7		– 1,500
8		+ 1,600
9–12	(each period)	+ 2,500

11. Find the rate of return in the following cases:
   - (i) You deposit Rs 100 and would receive Rs 114 after one year.
   - (ii) You borrow Rs 100 and promise to pay Rs 112 after one year.
   - (iii) You borrow Rs 1,000 and promise to pay Rs 3,395 at the end of 10 years.
   - (iv) You borrow Rs 10,000 and promise to pay Rs 2,571 each year for 5 years.

12. A bank has offered a deposit scheme, which will triple your money in 9 years; that is, if you deposit Rs 100 today, you can receive Rs 300 at the end of 9 years. What rate of return would you earn from the scheme?

13. You have Rs 6,000 to invest. How much would it take you to double your money if the interest rate is (a) 6%, (b) 10%, (c) 20%, and (d) 30%? Assume annual compounding. Would your answer change if compounding is done half-yearly? Show computations.

14. You had annual earnings of Rs 45,000 in 19X1. By 19X8, your annual earnings have grown to Rs 67,550. What has been the compound annual rate of growth in your earnings?

15. You are planning to buy a 200 square meters of land for Rs 40,000. You will be required to pay twenty equal annual instalments of Rs 8,213. What compound rate of interest will you be paying?

16. Jai Chand is planning for his retirement. He is 45 years old today, and would like to have Rs 3,00,000 when he attains the age of 60. He intends to deposit a constant amount of money at 12 per cent at each year in the public provident fund in the State Bank of India to achieve his objective. How much money should Jai Chand invest at the end of each year for the next 15 years to obtain Rs 3,00,000 at the end of that period?

17. (a) At age 20, how much should one invest at the end of

each year in order to have Rs 10 lakh at age 50, assuming 10 per cent annual growth rate? (*b*) At age 20, how much lump sum should one invest now in order to have 10 lakh at the age of 50, assuming 10 per cent annual growth rate?

18. Your grandfather is 75 years old. He has total savings of Rs 80,000. He expects that he will live for another 10 years, and will like to spend his savings by then. He places his savings into a bank account earning 10 per cent annually. He will draw equal amount each year—the first withdrawal occurring one year from now—in such a way that his account balance becomes zero at the end of 10 years. How much will be his annual withdrawal?

19. You buy a house for Rs 5 lakh and immediately make cash payment of Rs 1 lakh. You finance the balance amount at 12 per cent for 20 years with equal annual instalments. How much are the annual instalments? How much of the each payment goes towards reducing the principal?

20. You plan to buy a flat for Rs 200,000 by making Rs 40,000 down payment. A house financing company offers you a 12-year mortgage requiring end-of-year payments of Rs 28,593. The company also wants you to pay Rs 5,000 as the loan-processing fee, which they will deduct from the amount of loan given to you. What is the rate of interest on loan?

21. An investment promises to pay Rs 2,000 at the end of each year for the next 3 years and Rs 1,000 at the end of each year for years 4 through 7. (*a*) What maximum amount will you pay for such investment if your required rate is 13 per cent? (*b*) If the payments are received at the beginning of each year, what maximum amount will you pay for investment?

22. Mr. Sundaram is planning to retire this year. His company can pay him a lump sum retirement payment of Rs 2,00,000 or Rs 25,000 lifetime annuity—whichever he chooses. Mr. Sundaram is in good health and estimates to live for at least 20 more years. If his interest rate is 12 per cent, which alternative should he choose?

23. Which alternative would you choose: (*a*) an annuity of Rs 5,000 at the end of each year for 30 years; (*b*) an annuity of Rs 6,600 at the end of each year for 20 years; (*c*) Rs 50,000, in cash right now? In each case, the time value of money is 10 per cent.

24. Ms. Punam is interested in a fixed annual income. She is offered three possible annuities. If she could earn 8 per cent on her money elsewhere, which of the following alternatives, if any, would she choose? Why? (*i*) Pay Rs 80,000 now in order to receive Rs 14,000 at the end of each year for the next 10 years. (*ii*) Pay Rs 1,50,000 now in order to receive Rs 14,000 at the end of each year for the next 20 years. (*iii*) Pay Rs 1,20,000 now in order to receive Rs 14,000 at the end of each year for the next 15 years.

25. You have come across the following investment opportunity: Rs 2,000 at the end of each year for the first 5 years plus Rs 3,000 at the end of each year from years 6 through 9 plus Rs 5,000 at the end of each year from years 10 through 15.

(*a*) How much will you be willing to pay for this investment if your required rate of return is 14 per cent?

(*b*) What will be your answer if payments are received at the beginning of each year?

26. You have borrowed a car loan of Rs 50,000 from your employer. The loan requires 10 per cent interest and five equal end-of-year payments. Prepare a loan amortisation schedule.

27. If the nominal rate of interest is 12 per cent per annum, calculate the effective rate of interest when a sum is compounded (*a*) annually, (*b*) semi-annually, (*c*) quarterly, and (*d*) monthly.

28. What amount would an investor be willing to pay for Rs 1,000, ten-year debenture that pays Rs 75 interest half-yearly and is sold to yield 18 per cent?

29. The Madura Bank pays 12 per cent interest and compounds interest quarterly. If one puts Rs 1,000 initially into a savings account, how much will it have grown in 7½ years?

30. An already issued government bond pays Rs 50 interest half-yearly. The bond matures in 7 years. Its face value is Rs 1,000. A newly issued bond, which pays 12 per cent annually, can also be bought. How much would you like to pay for the old bond? How much would you pay for the bond if it is redeemed at a premium of 10 per cent?

31. If you deposit Rs 10,000 in an account paying 8 per cent interest per year compounded quarterly and you withdraw Rs 100 per month, (*a*) How long will the money last? (*b*) How much money will you receive?

32. XY Company is thinking of creating a sinking fund to retire its Rs 800,000 preference share capital that matures on 31 December 19X8. The company plans to put a fixed amount into the fund at the end of each year for eight years. The first payment will be made on 31 December 19X1, and the last on 31 December 19X8. The company expects that the fund will earn 12 per cent a year. What annual contribution must be made to accumulate to Rs 8,00,000 as of 31 December 19X8? What would be your answer if the annual contribution is made in the beginning of the year, the first payment being made on 31 December 19X0?

33. In January 19X1, *X* Ltd. issued Rs 10 crore of five-year bonds to be matured on 1 January 19X6. The interest was payable semi-annually on January 1 and July 1; the interest rate was 14 per cent per annum. Assume that on 1 January 19X2, new four-year bond of equivalent risk could be purchased at face value with an interest rate of 12 per cent and that you had purchased a Rs 1,000 *X* Ltd. bond when the bonds were originally issued. What would be its market value on January 1, 19X2?

34. You want to buy a 285-litre refrigerator of Rs 10,000 on an instalment basis. A distributor of various makes of refrigerators is prepared to do so. He states that the payments will be made in four years, interest rate being 13%. The annual payments would be as follows:

	Rs.
Principal	10,000
Four years of interest at 13%, i.e., Rs 10,000 × 0.13 × 4	5,200
	15,200
Annual payments, Rs 15,200/4	3,800

What rate of return the distributor is earning?

35. You have approached a loan and chit fund company for an eight-year loan of Rs 10,000; payments to the company to be made at the end of year. The loan officer informs you that the current rate of interest on the loan is 12% and that the annual payment will be Rs 2,013. Show that this annual cash flow provides a rate of return of 12% on the bank's investment of Rs 10,000. Is 12% the true interest rate to you? In other words, if you pay interest of 12% on your outstanding balance each year, will the remainder of the Rs 2,013 payments be just sufficient to repay the loan?

36. If a person deposits Rs 1,000 on an account that pays him 10 per cent for the first five years and 13 per cent for the following eight years, what is the annual compound rate of interest for the 13-year period?

CASE

Case 2.1: Divya Handtools Private Limited (DHPL)

DHPL is a small-sized firm manufacturing hand tools. Its manufacturing plant is situated in Faridabad. The company's sales in the year ending on 31 March 2004 were Rs 1,000 million (Rs 100 crore) on an asset base of Rs 650 million. The net profit of the company was Rs 76 million. The management of the company wants to improve profitability further. The required rate of return of the company is 14 per cent. The company is currently considering two investment proposals. One is to expand its manufacturing capacity. The estimated cost of the new equipment is Rs 250 million. It is expected to have an economic life of 10 years. The accountant forecasts that net cash inflows would be Rs 45 million per annum for the first three years, Rs 68 million par annum from year four to year eight and for the remaining two years Rs 30 million per annum. The plant can be sold for Rs 55 million at the end of its economic life.

The second proposal before the management is to replace one of the old machines in the Faridabad plant to reduce the cost of operations. The new machine will involve a net cash outlay of Rs 50 million. The life of the machine is expected to be 10 years without any salvage value. The company will go for the replacement only if it generates sufficient cost savings to justify the investment.

If the company accepts both projects, it would need to raise external funds of Rs 200 million, as about Rs 100 million internal funds are available. The company has the following options of borrowing Rs 200 million:

- The company can borrow funds from the State Bank of India (SBI) at an interest rate of 14 per cent per annum for 10 years. It will be required to pay equal annual instalments of interest and repayment of principal. The managing director of the company was wondering if it were possible to negotiate with SBI to make one single payment of interest and principal at the end of 10 years (instead of annual instalments).

- A large financial institution has offered to lend money to DHPL at a lower rate of interest. The institution will charge 13.5 per cent per annum. The company will have to pay equal quarterly instalments of interest and repayment of principal.

The financial institution has made yet another offer to the company. It can lease the equipments for the capacity expansion and for replacing old equipment to the company at annual lease rental of Rs 52 million payable at the beginning of the year.

Assume that there are no taxes.

Discussion Questions

1. Should the company expand its capacity? Show the computation of NPV.
2. What is the minimum amount of savings from the replacement that would justify the expenditure?
3. What is the annual instalment of the SBI loan?
4. What is the amount of the single payment of interest and principal to SBI after 10 years?
5. Calculate the quarterly instalments of the financial institution loan?
6. Should the company borrow from the SBI or the financial institution? Give reasons for your choice.
7. Would you recommend borrowing from the financial institution or get the equipment on lease? Show necessary calculations.

APPENDIX 2A: COMPOUNDING AND DISCOUNTING FORMULAE[1]

Compound Value of an Annuity

Assuming equal receipts or payments (A) at the end of the year, the compound value of an annuity formula is derived as follows:

$$F_n = A + A(1+i)^1 + A(1+i)^2 + A(1+i)^3 + \ldots + A(1+i)^{n-1}$$
$$F_n = A[1 + (1+i) + (1+i)^2 + (1+i)^3 + \ldots + (1+i)^{n-1}] \qquad \text{(1A)}$$

---

1. For a more rigorous derivation of formulae, see Copeland, T.E., and Weston, J.F., *Financial Theory and Corporate Policy,* Addison-Wesley, 1983, pp. 699–713.

Note that multiplying Equation (1A) by $(1 + i)$, we get

$$F_n(1+i) = A[(1+i)^1 + (1+i)^2 + (1+i)^3 + ... + (1+i)^n] \qquad (2A)$$

Subtracting Equation (1A) from Equation (2A), we obtain

$$F_n(1+i) - F_n = A[(1+i)^n - 1] \qquad (3A)$$

and solving for F_n, we have

$$F_n = A\left[\frac{(1+i)^n - 1}{i}\right] \qquad (4A)$$

Present Value of an Annuity

The present value of an annuity is given by the following formula:

$$P = \frac{A}{(1+i)^1} + \frac{A}{(1+i)^2} + \frac{A}{(1+i)^3} + ... + \frac{A}{(1+i)^n} \qquad (5A)$$

Multiplying both sides of Equation (A5) by $1/1 + i$, we get

$$\frac{P}{(1+i)} = \frac{A}{(1+i)^2} + \frac{A}{(1+i)^3} + ... + \frac{A}{(1+i)^{n+1}} \qquad (6A)$$

Subtracting Equation (6A) from Equation (5A), we obtain

$$P - \frac{P}{(1+i)} = \frac{A}{(1+i)} - \frac{A}{(1+i)^{n+1}} \qquad (7A)$$

and multiplying both sides of Equation (7A) by $(1 + i)$, we have

$$P(1+i) - P = A - \frac{A}{(1+i)^n} \qquad (8A)$$

$$Pi = A\left[1 - \frac{1}{(1+i)^n}\right]$$

$$P = A\left[\frac{1 - \frac{1}{(1+i)^n}}{i}\right] \qquad (9A)$$

$$P = A\left[\frac{1 - (1+i)^{-n}}{i}\right] \qquad (10A)$$

Equation (9A) can be rewritten as follows:

$$P = A\left[\frac{(1+i)^n - 1}{i(1+i)^n}\right] = A\left[\frac{1}{i} - \frac{1}{i(1+i)^n}\right] \qquad (11A)$$

PRESENT VALUE OF CONSTANTLY GROWING ANNUITY

The present value of an amount A (at the end of one year) growing at a constant rate g is given by the following equation:

$$P = \frac{A}{(1+i)^1} + \frac{A(1+g)^1}{(1+i)^2} + \frac{A(1+g)^2}{(1+i)^3} + ... + \frac{A(1+g)^{n-1}}{(1+i)^n} \qquad (12A)$$

When we multiply both sides of Equation (12A) by $(1 + g)$, we get

$$P(1+g) = \frac{A(1+g)^1}{(1+i)^1} + \frac{A(1+g)^2}{(1+i)^2} + \frac{A(1+g)^3}{(1+i)^3} + ... + \frac{A(1+g)^n}{(1+i)^n} \qquad (13A)$$

If we define $(1 + g)/(1 + i) = 1/(1 + i^*)$, Equation (13A) can be rewritten as follows:

$$P(1+g) = \frac{A}{(1+i^*)} + \frac{A}{(1+i^*)^2} + \frac{A}{(1+i^*)^3} + ... + \frac{A}{(1+i^*)^n} \qquad (14A)$$

The right-hand side of Equation (14A) Equation (14A) gives the present value of an annuity of A per period discounted at i^* rate of return. Using the procedures explained in the preceding section to derive Equation (9A), we may rewrite Equation (14A) as follows:

$$P = \frac{A}{1+g}\left[\frac{1 - \frac{1}{(1+i^*)^n}}{i^*}\right]. \qquad (15A)$$

Following Equation (11A), we can express Equation (15A) as follows:

$$P = \frac{A}{1+g}\left[\frac{1}{i^*} - \frac{1}{i^*(1+i^*)^n}\right] \qquad (16A)$$

Since $1/(1 + i^*) = (1 + g)/(1 + i)$, then $i^* = (i - g)/(1 + g)$. Using these relationships, Equation (15A) can be rewritten as follows:

$$P = \frac{A}{i-g}\left[1 - \left(\frac{1+g}{1+i}\right)^n\right] \qquad (17A)$$

Present Value of Constantly Growing Perpetuity

Annuity occurring indefinitely is called perpetuity. Perpetuity may grow at a constant rate. Equation (17A) gives present value of constantly growing annuity where n is a definite time period. In case of perpetuity, n is not definite. In mathematical terms, n extends to infinity (∞). When n extends to infinity, the term $[(1+g)/(1+i)]^n$ becomes equal to zero. Hence the present value of a growing perpetuity is given by:

$$P = \frac{A}{i-g} \qquad (18A)$$

Continuous Compounding and Discounting

The following equation can be used in case of multi-period compounding:

$$F = P\left[1 + \frac{i}{m}\right]^{n \times m} \qquad (19A)$$

Equation (19A) can be modified to allow for continuous compounding. Let us multiply *nm* by *i/i* and rewrite Equation (19A) as follows:

$$F = P\left[1 + \frac{i}{m}\right]^{ni \times \frac{m}{i}} \tag{20A}$$

Defining $x = m/i$ and therefore, $i/m = 1/x$, we can rewrite Equation (20A) as given below:

$$F = P\left[1 + \frac{1}{x}\right]^{ni \times x}$$

It should be clear that as the number of compounding periods, *m*, increases, *x* also increases causing the term in parentheses in Equation (20A) to increase. At the limit, when m and x approach infinity, and compounding is continuous, the term in parenthesis

approaches the value 2.7183. Thus,

$$e = \frac{lim}{m}\left[1 + \frac{1}{x}\right]^{x} = 2.7183 \tag{21A}$$

Substituting *e* for the term in parenthesis, we get

$$F = Pe^{in} \tag{22A}$$

Equation (22A) can be used to find out present value under the assumption of multi-period compounding (discounting). Consider the following:

$$F = Pe^{in}$$

$$P = F\left[\frac{1}{e^{in}}\right] = Fe^{-in} \tag{23A}$$

CHAPTER 3

Valuation of Bonds and Shares

CHAPTER OBJECTIVES

- Explain the fundamental characteristics of ordinary shares, preference shares and bonds (or debentures)
- Show the use of the present value concepts in the valuation of shares and bonds
- Learn about the linkage between the share values, earnings and dividends and the required rate of return on the share
- Focus on the uses and misuses of price-earnings (P/E) ratio

INTRODUCTION

Assets can be real or financial; securities like shares and bonds are called *financial assets* while physical assets like plant and machinery are called real assets. The concepts of return and risk, as the determinants of value, are as fundamental and valid to the valuation of securities as to that of physical assets. We must clarify at the outset that there is no easy way to predict the prices of share and bonds and thus, to become rich by a superior performance in the stock exchange. The unpredictable nature of the security prices is, in fact, a logical and necessary consequence of efficient capital markets. **Efficient capital market** implies a well-informed, properly functioning capital market. We can show why some securities are priced higher than others by using the concept of present value. This will help the financial manager to know the variables, which influence the security prices. He can then design his investment and financing activities in a manner, which exploits the relevant variables to maximise the market value of shares.

It should also be appreciated that ordinary shares are riskier than bonds (or debentures), and also that some shares are more risky than others. It, therefore, naturally follows that investors would commit funds to shares only when they expect that rates of return are commensurate with risk. We know from our earlier discussion in the preceding chapter that the present value formulae are capable of taking into account both time and risk in the evaluation of assets and securities. What they cannot do is: how to measure the degree of risk? For the purpose of our discussion, we shall assume risk as known. A detailed analysis of risk is deferred to the next chapter.

CONCEPTS OF VALUE

How are bonds and shares valued?[1] What is the role of earnings per share (EPS) and price-earnings (P/E) ratios in the valuation of shares? EPS and P/E ratios are the most frequently used concepts by the financial community. Do they really have significance in the valuation of shares? Let us emphasise that *the present value is the most valid and true concept of value*. There are many other concepts of value that are used for different purposes. They are explained below.

---

1. There are a number of excellent investment books and articles dealing with valuation of bonds and shares. We suggest the original work of J.B. Williams, *The Theory of Investment Value,* Harvard University Press, 1938; W.F. Sharpe and Alexander, G.I., *Investments,* Prentice-Hall: 1989 and Francis, J.C., *Investment: Analysis and Management,* McGraw Hill, 1972, for further reading.

Book Value

Book value is an accounting concept. Assets are recorded at historical cost, and they are depreciated over years. Book value may include intangible assets at acquisition cost minus amortised value. The book value of debt is stated at the outstanding amount. The difference between the book values of assets and liabilities is equal to shareholders' funds or net worth. Book value per share is determined as net worth divided by the number of shares outstanding. Book value reflects historical cost, rather than value. Value is what an asset is worth today in terms of its potential benefits.

Replacement Value

Replacement value is the amount that a company would be required to spend if it were to replace its existing assets in the current condition. It is difficult to find cost of assets currently being used by the company. Replacement value is also likely to ignore the benefits of intangibles and the utility of existing assets.

Liquidation Value

Liquidation value is the amount that a company could realise if it sold its assets, after having terminated its business. It would not include the value of intangibles since the operations of the company are assumed to cease. Liquidation value is generally a minimum value, which a company might accept if it sold its business.

Going Concern Value

Going concern value is the amount that a company could realise if it sold its business as an operating business. Going concern value would always be higher than the liquidation value, since it reflects the future value of assets and value of intangibles.

Market Value

Market value of an asset or security is the current price at which the asset or the security is being sold or bought in the market. Market value per share is expected to be higher than the book value per share for profitable, growing firms. A number of factors influence the market value per share, and therefore, it shows wide fluctuations. What is important is the long-term trend in the market value per share. In ideal situation, where the capital markets are efficient and in equilibrium, market value should be equal to present (or intrinsic) value of a share.

FEATURES OF A BOND

A **bond** is a long-term debt instrument or security. Bonds issued by the government do not have any risk of default. The government will always honour obligations on its bonds. Bonds of the public sector companies in India are generally secured, but they are not free from the risk of default. The private sector companies also issue bonds, which are also called **debentures** in India. A company in India can issue secured or unsecured debentures. In the case of a bond or debenture, the rate of interest is generally fixed and known to investors. The principal of a **redeemable bond** or **bond with a maturity** is payable after a specified period, called maturity period.

The main features of a bond or debenture are discussed below.

- **Face value** Face value is called par value. A bond (debenture) is generally issued at a par value of Rs 100 or Rs 1,000, and interest is paid on face value.
- **Interest rate** Interest rate is fixed and known to bondholders (debenture-holders). Interest paid on a bond/debenture is tax deductible. The interest rate is also called **coupon rate.** Coupons are detachable certificates of interest.
- **Maturity** A bond (debenture) is generally issued for a specified period of time. It is repaid on maturity.
- **Redemption value** The value that a bondholder (debenture-holder) will get on maturity is called redemption, or maturity, value. A bond (debenture) may be redeemed at par or at premium (more than par value) or at discount (less than par value).
- **Market value** A bond (debenture) may be traded in a stock exchange. The price at which it is currently sold or bought is called the market value of the bond (debenture). Market value may be different from par value or redemption value.

BONDS VALUES AND YIELDS

It is relatively easy to determine the present value of a bond since its cash flows and the discount rate can be determined without much difficulty. If there is no risk of default, then there is no difficulty in estimating the cash flows associated with a bond. The expected cash flows consist of annual interest payments plus repayment of principal. The appropriate capitalisation, or discount, rate would depend upon the risk of the bond. The risk in holding a government bond is less than the risk associated with a debenture issued by a company. Consequently, a lower discount rate would be applied to the cash flows of the government bond and a higher rate to the cash flows of the company debenture.

Bonds maybe classified into three categories: (*a*) bonds with maturity, (*b*) pure discount bonds and (*c*) perpetual bonds.

Bond with Maturity

The government and companies mostly issue bonds that specify the interest rate (coupon) and the maturity period. The present value of a bond (debenture) is the discounted value of its cash flows; that is, the annual interest payments plus bond's terminal, or maturity, value. The discount rate is the interest rate that investors could earn on bonds with similar characteristics. By comparing the present value of a bond with its current market value, it can be determined whether the bond is *overvalued* or *undervalued*. Let us consider Illustration 3.1.

Illustration 3.1: Value of Bound with Maturity

Suppose an investor is considering the purchase of a five-year, Rs 1,000 par value bond, bearing a nominal rate of interest of 7 per cent per annum. The investor's required rate of return is 8 per cent. What should he be willing to pay now to purchase the bond if it matures at par?

The investor will receive cash Rs 70 as interest each year for 5 years and Rs 1,000 on maturity (i.e., at the end of the fifth year). We can thus determine the present value of the bond (B_0) as follows:

$$B_0 = \frac{70}{(1.08)^1} + \frac{70}{(1.08)^2} + \frac{70}{(1.08)^3} + \frac{70}{(1.08)^4} + \frac{70}{(1.08)^5} + \frac{1000}{(1.08)^5}$$

It may be observed that Rs 70 is an annuity for 5 years and Rs 1,000 is received as a lump sum at the end of the fifth year. Using the present value tables, given at the end of this book, the present value of bond is

$$B_0 = 70 \times 3.993 + 1,000 \times 0.681 = 279.51 + 681 = \text{Rs } 960.51$$

This implies that Rs 1,000 bond is worth Rs 960.51 today if the required rate of return is 8 per cent. The investor would not be willing to pay more than Rs 960.51 for bond today. Note that Rs 960.51 is a composite of the present value of interest payments, Rs 279.51 and the present value of the maturity value, Rs 681.

Since most bonds will involve payment of an annuity (equal interest payments each year) and principal at maturity, we can use the following formula to determine the value of a bond:

Bond value = Present value of interest
+ Present value of maturity value

$$B_0 = \left[\frac{INT_1}{(1+k_d)} + \frac{INT_2}{(1+k_d)^2} + \dots + \frac{INT_n}{(1+k_d)^n} \right] + \frac{B_n}{(1+k_d)^n}$$

$$B_0 = \sum_{t=1}^{n} \frac{INT_t}{(1+k_d)^t} + \frac{B_n}{(1+k_d)^n} \quad (1)$$

Notice that B_0 is the present value of a bond (debenture), INT_t is the amount of interest in period t (from year 1 to n), k_d is the market interest rate or the bond's required rate of return, B_n is bond's terminal or maturity value in period n and n is the number of years to maturity.

In Equation (1), the right-hand side consists of an annuity of interest payments that are constant (i.e., $INT_1 = INT_2 \dots = INT_t$) over the bond's life and a final payment on maturity. Thus, we can use the annuity formula to value interest payments as shown below:

$$B_0 = INT \times \left[\frac{1}{k_d} - \frac{1}{k_d(1+k_d)^n} \right] + \frac{B_n}{(1+k_d)^n} \quad (2)$$

Yield to Maturity

We can calculate a bond's yield or the rate of return when its current price and cash flows are known. Suppose that the market price of a bond is Rs 883.40 (face value being Rs 1,000). The bond will pay interest at 6 per cent per annum for 5 years, after which it will be redeemed at par. What is the bond's rate of return? The **yield-to-maturity** (YTM) is the measure of a bond's rate of return that considers both the interest income and any capital gain or loss. YTM is bond's internal rate of return. The yield-to-maturity of 5-year bond, paying 6 per cent interest on the face value of Rs 1,000 and currently selling for Rs 883.40 is 10 per cent as shown below:

$$883.4 = \frac{60}{(1+YTM)^1} + \frac{60}{(1+YTM)^2} + \frac{60}{(1+YTM)^3}$$
$$+ \frac{60}{(1+YTM)^4} + \frac{60+1,000}{(1+YTM)^5}$$

We obtain YTM = 10 per cent by trial and error.

It is, however, simpler to calculate a perpetual bond's yield-to-maturity. It is equal to interest income divided by the bond's price. For example, if the rate of interest on Rs 1,000 par value perpetual bond is 8 per cent, and its price is Rs 800, its YTM will be

$$B_0 = \sum_{t=1}^{n=\infty} \frac{INT}{(1+k_d)^t} = \frac{INT}{k_d}$$

$$k_d = \frac{INT}{B_0} = \frac{80}{800} = 0.10 \text{ or } 10 \text{ per cent} \quad (3)$$

Excel Application 3.1: Yield to Maturity

Yield-to-maturity is the internal rate of return of the bond given the current market price, interest charges and the maturity value. In the worksheet on the right-hand side, we enter the values of the parameters as given above. Interest is calculated on the face value of the bond in C5 to G5. If we enter IRR formula in B9: IRR(B7:G7), we obtain the yield-to-maturity of 9 per cent.

	A	B	C	D	E	F	G
1	Face Value	1000.00					
2	Interest rate	6%					
3	Year	0	1	2	3	4	5
4	Current price	-883.40					
5	Interest			60	60	60	60	60
6	Maturity value						1000
7	Cash flow	-883.40	60.00	60.00	60.00	60.00	1060.00
8	Yield-to-Maturity	9.0%	←— =IRR(B7:G7)				

Current Yield

Yield-to-maturity is not the same as the current yield. Current yield is the annual interest divided by the bond's current value. In the example, the annual interest is Rs 60 on the *current* investment of Rs 883.40. Therefore, the current rate of return or the **current yield** is: 60/883.40 = 6.8 per cent. Current yield considers only the annual interest (Rs 60 in the example) and does not account for the capital gain or loss. On maturity, the bond price will increase to Rs 1,000 and there would be a capital gain of Rs 116.60 [Rs 1,000 – Rs 883.40]. Thus bond's overall rate of return over 5 years period would be more than the current yield. If the bond's current price were less than its maturity value, its overall rate of return would be less than the current yield.

Yield to Call

A number of companies issue bonds with buy back or call provision. Thus a bond can be redeemed or called before maturity. What is the yield or the rate of return of a bond that may be redeemed before maturity? The procedure for calculating the **yield to call** is the same as for the yield to maturity. The call period would be different from the maturity period and the call (or redemption) value could be different from the maturity value. Consider an example.

Suppose the 10% 10-year Rs 1,000 bond is redeemable (callable) in 5 years at a call price of Rs 1,050. The bond is currently selling for Rs 950. What is bond's yield to call? The bond's yield to call is

$$950 = \sum_{t=1}^{5} \frac{100}{(1+YTC)^t} + \frac{1,050}{(1+YTC)^5}$$

You can solve for YTC through trial and error or use a financial calculator. The yield to call, YTC, is 12.7 per cent. Suppose the bond will be redeemed at Rs 1,050 on maturity. What is the yield to maturity? It is given as follows:

$$950 = \sum_{t=1}^{10} \frac{100}{(1+YTC)^t} + \frac{1,050}{(1+YTC)^{10}}$$

The yield to maturity is 11.3 per cent. If the bond is redeemed at par on maturity, then YTM is 10.9 per cent.

Bond Value and Amortisation of Principal

A bond (debenture) may be amortised every year, i.e., repayment of principal every year rather at maturity. In that case, the principal will decline with annual payments and interest will be calculated on the outstanding amount. The cash flows of the bonds will be uneven. Let us consider Illustration 3.2

Illustration 3.2: Value of a Bond When Principal is Amortised Each Year

The government is proposing to sell a 5-year bond of Rs 1,000 at 8 per cent rate of interest per annum. The bond amount will be amortised (repaid) equally over its life. If an investor has a minimum required rate of return of 7 per cent, what is the bond's present value for him?

The amount of interest will go on reducing because the outstanding amount of bond will be decreasing due to amortisation. The amount of interest for five years will be: Rs 1,000 × 0.08 = Rs 80 for the first year; (Rs 1,000 − Rs 200) × 0.08 = Rs 64 for the second year; (Rs 800 − Rs 200) × 0.08 = Rs 48 for the third year, (Rs 600 − Rs 200) × 0.08 = Rs 32 for the fourth year and (Rs 400 − Rs 200) × 0.08 = Rs 16 for the fifth year. The outstanding amount of bond would be zero at the end of fifth year.

Since the government will have to return Rs 200 every year, the outflows every year will consist of interest payment and repayment of principal: Rs 200 + Rs 80 = Rs 280; Rs 200 + Rs 64 = Rs 264; Rs 200 + Rs 48 = Rs 248; Rs 200 + Rs 32 = Rs 232; and Rs 200 + Rs 16 = Rs 216 respectively from first through five years. Referring to the present value table at the end of the book, the value of the bond is calculated as follows:

$$B_0 = \frac{280}{(1.07)^1} + \frac{264}{(1.07)^2} + \frac{248}{(1.07)^3} + \frac{232}{(1.07)^4} + \frac{216}{(1.07)^5}$$

$$= 280 \times 0.935 + 264 \times 0.873 + 248 \times 0.816 + 232 \times 0.763 + 216 \times 0.713$$

$$= 261.80 + 230.47 + 202.37 + 177.02 + 154.00$$

$$= Rs\ 1025.66$$

The formula for determining the value of a bond or debenture that is amortised every year, can be written as follows:

$$B_0 = \frac{CF_1}{(1+k_d)^1} + \frac{CF_2}{(1+k_d)^2} + ... + \frac{CF_n}{(1+k_d)^n}$$

$$B_0 = \sum_{t=1}^{n} \frac{CF_t}{(1+k_d)^t} \tag{4}$$

Note that cash flow, CF, includes both the interest and repayment of the principal.

Excel Application 3.2: Present Value of a Bond

We can set an Excel worksheet to find the value of a bond. Let us use the values of parameters given in Illustration 3.2. In the worksheet on the right-hand side, we enter in column B3 a formula for interest on the outstanding balance in the beginning: A3*0.08, and copy it down to column A7. The total payment (column D) consists of interest (column B) plus repayment of principal (column C). The outstanding balance is given in column E as the difference between the balance in the beginning (column A) and repayment (column C). The value of the bond is the present value of the total payments (column D). We write in column D8 the formula for NPV: =NPV(0.07,D3:D7) to find the bond value. The value is the same (except for rounding off error) as in Illustration 3.2.

	A	B	C	D	E
1	**PRESENT VALUE OF BOND**				
2	Principal in the beginning	Interest	Repayment	Payment	Principal at the end
3	1000.00	80.00	200.00	280.00	800.00
4	800.00	64.00	200.00	264.00	600.00
5	600.00	48.00	200.00	248.00	400.00
6	400.00	32.00	200.00	232.00	200.00
7	200.00	16.00	200.00	216.00	0.00
8	PV = NPV(0.07, D3:D7) ⟶ *1025.71*				

Bond Values and Semi-annual Interest Payments

It is a practice of many companies in India to pay interest on bonds (or debentures) semi-annually. The formula for bond valuation can be modified in terms of half-yearly interest payments and compounding periods as given below:

$$B_0 = \sum_{t=1}^{2 \times n} \frac{1/2(INT_t)}{\left(1+\frac{k_d}{2}\right)^t} + \frac{B_n}{\left(1+\frac{k_d}{2}\right)^{2 \times n}} \tag{5}$$

Illustration 3.3: Semi-annual Interest Payment and Bond Value

A 10-year bond of Rs 1,000 has an annual rate of interest of 12 per cent. The interest is paid half-yearly. What is the value of the bond if the required rate of return is (*i*) 12 per cent and (*ii*) 16 per cent?

Given the required rate of return of 12 per cent, the value of the bond is

$$B_0 = \sum_{t=1}^{2 \times n} \frac{\frac{1}{2}(INT_t)}{\left(1+\frac{k_d}{2}\right)^t} + \frac{B_n}{\left(1+\frac{k_d}{2}\right)^{2 \times n}}$$

$$= \sum_{t=1}^{2 \times 10} \frac{\frac{1}{2}(120)}{\left(1 + \frac{0.12}{2}\right)^t} + \frac{1,000}{\left(1 + \frac{0.12}{2}\right)^{2 \times 10}}$$

$$= \sum_{t=1}^{20} \frac{60}{(1.06)^t} + \frac{1,000}{(1.06)^{20}}$$

$$= 60 \times \text{Annuity factor } (6\%, 20) + 1,000 \times PV \text{ factor } (6\%, 20)$$

$$= 60 \times 11.4699 + 1,000 \times 0.3118 = 688.20 + 311.80$$

$$= \text{Rs } 1,000$$

If the required rate of return were 16 per cent, then the value of the bond would be

$$B_0 = \sum_{t=1}^{20} \frac{60}{(1.08)^t} + \frac{1,000}{(1.08)^{20}}$$

$$= 60 \times \text{Annuity factor } (8\%, 20) + 1,000 \times PV \text{ factor } (8\%, 20)$$

$$= 60 \times 9.8181 + 1,000 \times 0.2145 = 589.09 + 214.50$$

$$= \text{Rs } 803.59$$

Pure Discount Bonds

Pure discount bond do not carry an explicit rate of interest. It provides for the payment of a lump sum amount at a future date in exchange for the current price of the bond. The difference between the face value of the bond and its purchase price gives the return or YTM to the investor. For example, a company may issue a pure discount bond of Rs 1,000 face value for Rs 520 today for a period of five years. Thus the debenture has (*a*) purchase price of Rs 520, (*b*) maturity value (equal to the face value) of Rs 1,000 and (*c*) maturity period of five years. The rate of interest can be calculated as follows:

$$500 = \frac{1,000}{(1 + \text{YTM})^5}$$

$$(1 + \text{YTM})^5 = \frac{1,000}{520} = 1.9231$$

$$i = 1.9231^{1/5} - 1 = 0.14 \text{ or } 14\%$$

You can also use the trial and error method to obtain YTM, which is 14 per cent.

Pure discount bonds are called **deep-discount bonds** or **zero-interest bonds** or **zero-coupon bonds.** Industrial Development Bank of India (IDBI) was the first to issue a deep-discount bond in India in January 1992. The bond of a face value of Rs 100,000 was sold for Rs 2,700 with a maturity period of 25 years. If an investor holds the IDBI deep-discount bond for 25 years, she would earn an implicit interest rate of: $2,700 = 1,00,000/(1 + i)^{25}$ = 15.54 per cent. IDBI again issued a deep-discount bond in 1998 at a price of Rs 12,750 to be redeemed after 30 years at the face value of Rs 500,000. The implicit interest rate for this bond works out 13 per cent.

It is quite simple to find the value of a pure discount bond as it involves one single payment (face value) at maturity. The **market interest rate,** also called the **market yield,** is used as the discount rate. The present value of this amount is the bond value.

Value of a pure discount bond = PV of the amount on maturity

$$B_0 = \frac{M_n}{(1 + k_d)^n} \qquad (6)$$

Consider the IDBI bond with a face value of Rs 500,000 with a maturity of 30 years. Suppose the current market yield on similar bonds is 9 per cent. The value of the IDBI pure-discount bond today is as follows:

$$B_0 = \frac{500,000}{(1.09)^{30}} = \text{Rs } 37,685.57$$

Perpetual Bonds

Perpetual bonds, also called consols, has an indefinite life and therefore, it has no maturity value. Perpetual bonds or debentures are rarely found in practice. After the Napoleanic War, England issued these types of bonds to pay off many smaller issues that had been floated in prior years to pay for the war.[1] In case of the perpetual bonds, as there is no maturity, or terminal value, the value of the bonds would simply be the discounted value of the infinite stream of interest flows.

Suppose that a 10 per cent Rs 1,000 bond will pay Rs 100 annual interest into perpetuity? What would be its value of the bond if the market yield or interest rate were 15 per cent? The value of the bond is determined as follows:

$$B_0 = \frac{\text{INT}}{k_d} = \frac{100}{0.15} = \text{Rs } 667$$

If the market yield is 10 per cent, the value of the bond will be Rs 1,000 and if it is 20 per cent the value will be Rs 500. Thus the value of the bond will decrease as the interest rate increases and vice-versa. Table 3.1 gives the value of a perpetual bond paying annual interest of Rs 100 at different discount (market interest) rates.

Table 3.1: Value of a Perpetual Bond at Different Bond at Different Discount Rates

Discount Rate (%)	Value of Bond (Rs)
5	2,000
10	1,000
15	667
20	500
25	400
30	333

Bond Values and Changes in Interest Rates

We notice from Illustration 3.3 and calculations in Table 3.1 that the value of the bond declines as the market interest rate (discount rate) increases. Bond values decline with rising interest rates because the bond cash flows (interest and principal repayment) are discounted at higher interest rates. Figure 3.1 shows the value of a 10-year, 12 per cent Rs 1,000 bond for the market interest rates ranging from 0 per cent to 30 per cent. You

---

1. Weston, J.F. and Brigham, E.F., *Managerial Finance,* Dryden, 1975, p. 538.

may notice from the figure that there is a negative relationship between bond values and the market interest rates.

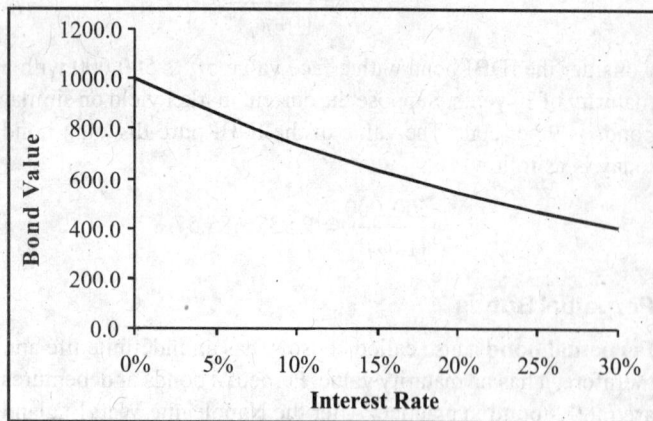

Figure 3.1: Interest rate and bond value

Bond Maturity and Interest Rate Risk

As explained above, the value of a bond depends upon the market interest rate. As interest rate changes, the value of a bond also varies. There is an inverse relationship between the value of a bond and the interest rate. The bond value would decline when the interest rate rises and *vice versa*. For instance, the value of the perpetual bond in Table 3.1 declines to Rs 667 from Rs 1,000 when interest rate rises from 10 per cent to 15 per cent, resulting in a loss of Rs 333 in value to bondholders. Interest rates have the tendency of rising or falling in practice. Thus investors of bonds are exposed to the **interest rate risk;** that is, the risk arising from the fluctuating interest rates.

The intensity of interest rate risk would be higher on *bonds with long maturities* than *bonds with short maturities*. This point can be verified by examining Table 3.2 where values of 10 per cent 5-year and 10-year bonds (maturity value of Rs 1,000) and a perpetual bond are given. These values are also plotted in Figure 3.2. At 10 per cent market interest rate, values of all three bonds are same, *viz.,* Rs 1,000. When the market interest rate rises to, say, 15 per cent, then the value of 5-year bond falls to Rs 832, 10-year bond to Rs 749 and perpetual bond still further to Rs 667. Similarly, the value of long-term bond will fluctuate

Table 3.2: Bond Value at Different Interest Rates

Discount rate (%)	Present Value (Rs)		
	5-Year bond	10-Year bond	Perpetual bond
5	1,216	1,386	2,000
10	1,000	1,000	1,000
15	832	749	667
20	701	581	500
25	597	464	400
30	513	382	333

(increase) more when rates fall below 10 per cent. The differential value response to interest rates changes between short and long term bonds will always be true. Thus, two bonds of same quality (in terms of the risk of default) would have different exposure to interest rate risk—the one with longer maturity is exposed to greater degree of risk from the increasing interest rates.[1]

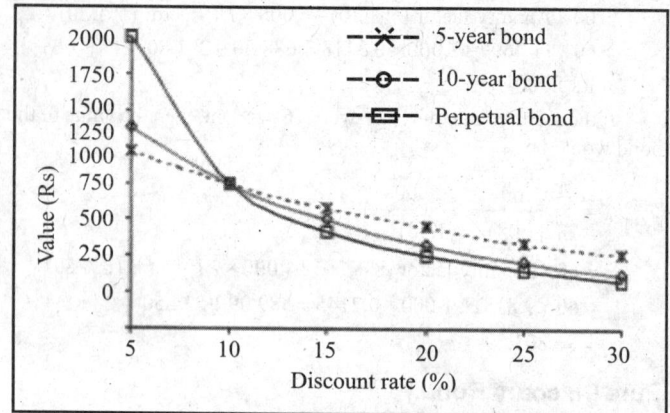

Figure 3.2: Value of bonds at varying interest rates

The reason for this differential responsiveness is not difficult to understand. For example, in the case of 10-year bond, one would get just Rs 100 even if interest rate rises to, say, 15 per cent. In case of 5-year bond, one can, at least, sell the bond after five years, and reinvest money to receive Rs 150 for the next five years.

Bond Duration and Interest Rate Sensitivity

We have discussed that bond prices are sensitive to changes in the interest rates, and they are inversely related to the interest rates. The intensity of the price sensitivity depends on a bond's maturity and the coupon rate of interest. The longer the maturity of a bond, the higher will be its sensitivity to the interest rate changes. Similarly, the price of a bond with low coupon rate will be more sensitive to the interest rate changes.

A bond's maturity and coupon rate provide a general idea of its price sensitivity to interest rate changes. However, the bond's price sensitivity can be more accurately estimated by its duration. A bond's **duration** is measured as the weighted average of times to each cash flow (interest payment or repayment of principal). Duration calculation gives importance to the timing of cash flows; the weight is determined as the present value of cash flow to the bond value. Hence two bonds with similar maturity but different coupon rates and cash flow patterns will have different durations.

Let us consider two bonds with five-year maturity. The 8.5 per cent rate bond of Rs 1,000 face value has a current market value of Rs 954.74 and a YTM of 10 per cent, and the 11.5 per cent rate bond of Rs 1,000 face value has a current market value of Rs 1,044.57 and a yield to maturity of 10.6 per cent. Table 3.3 shows the calculation of duration for the two bonds. Each cash flow is discounted at YTM to calculate its present value.

1. Weston and Brigham, *Ibid.,* p. 545. Also , see Nelson, C.R, *The Term Structure of Interest Rates,* in J.L. Bicksler, Ed., *Handbook of Financial Economics,* North-Holland Publishing Co., 1980, for a review of the interest rate structure theory.

Next we find out the proportion of the present value of each flow to the value of the bond. The duration of the bond is calculated as the weighted average of times to the proportion of the present value of cash flows.

Table 3.3: Duration of Bonds

8.5 Per Cent Bond

Year	Cash Flow	Present Value at 10%	Proportion of Bond Price	Proportion of Bond Price × Time
1	85	77.27	0.082	0.082
2	85	70.25	0.074	0.149
3	85	63.86	0.068	0.203
4	85	58.06	0.062	0.246
5	1,085	673.70	0.714	3.572
		943.14	1.000	4.252

11.5 Per Cent Bond

Year	Cash Flow	Present Value at 10.6 %	Proportion of Bond Price	Proportion of Bond Price × Time
1	115	103.98	0.101	0.101
2	115	94.01	0.091	0.182
3	115	85.00	0.082	0.247
4	115	76.86	0.074	0.297
5	1,115	673.75	0.652	3.259
		1,033.60	1.000	4.086

We can notice from Table 3.3 that 71.4 per cent of the present value of cash flows of the 8.5 per cent bond and 65.2 per cent of the 11.5 per cent bond occur in the last year. The duration of 8.5 per cent bond (the lower coupon bond) is higher than the duration of 11.5 per cent bond (the higher coupon bond).

The **volatility** or the interest rate sensitivity of a bond is given by its duration and YTM. A bond's volatility, referred to as its **modified duration**, is given as follows:

$$\text{Volatility of bond} = \frac{\text{Duration}}{(1 + \text{YTM})} \qquad (7)$$

The volatilities of the 8.5 per cent and 11.5 per cent bonds are as follows:

$$\text{Volatility of } 8.5\% \text{ bond} = \frac{4.252}{(1.100)} = 3.87$$

$$\text{Volatility of } 11.5\% \text{ bond} = \frac{4.086}{(1.106)} = 3.69$$

The 8.5 per cent bond has higher volatility. If YTM increases by 1 per cent, this will result in 3.87 per cent decrease in the price of the 8.5 per cent bond and a 3.69 per cent decrease in the price of the 11.5 per cent bond.

THE TERM STRUCTURE OF INTEREST RATES

So far in our discussion, we did not explicitly mention whether there were one single interest rate or several rates. In fact, there are several interest rates in practice. Both companies and the Government of India offer bonds with different maturities and risk features. Debt in a particular risk class will have its own interest rate. For example, we can notice from Table 3.4 that the market interest rates or yields on the Government bonds of different maturities vary.

Based on the data in Table 3.4, a yield curve for the Government bonds in February 2003 is drawn in Figure 3.4. **Yield curve** shows the relationship between the yields to maturity of bonds and their maturities. It is also called the **term structure of interest rates.** In Figure 3.3, the yield curve has an upward slope. The upward sloping yield curve implies that the long-term yields are higher than the short-term yields. This is the normal shape of the yield curve, which is generally verified by historical evidence. However, many economies in high-inflation periods have witnessed the short-term yields being higher than the long-term yields. The **inverted yield curves** result when the short-term rates are higher than the long-term rates.

Table 3.4: Yields for the Government Bonds, February 2003

Maturity (Years)	Yield (%)
0–1	5.90
1–2	5.91
2–3	5.99
3–4	6.09
4–5	6.10
5–6	6.25
6–7	6.48
7–8	6.42
8–9	6.41
9–10	6.38
>10	7.18

What are the explanations for the shape of the yield curve? There are three theories that explain the yield curve or the term structure of interest rates: (1) the expectation theory, (2) the liquidity premium theory, and (3) the market segmentation theory.

The Expectation Theory

The expectation theory supports the upward sloping yield curve since investors always expect the short-term rates to increase in the future. This implies that the long-term rates will be higher than the short-term rates. But in the present value terms, the return from investing in a long-term security will equal to the return from investing in a series of a short-term security. Let us consider an example.

Suppose you have an investment horizon of three years. You have two choices: either you invest in a three-year bond, or you invest in one-year bond each year for three years. Assume that YTM on a three-year bond is 5.8 per cent. The current YTM on one-year bond is 5.3 per cent. You expect that the interest rate on one-year bond one year from now will be 5.7 per cent and after two years 6.3 per cent. What should you do? The future

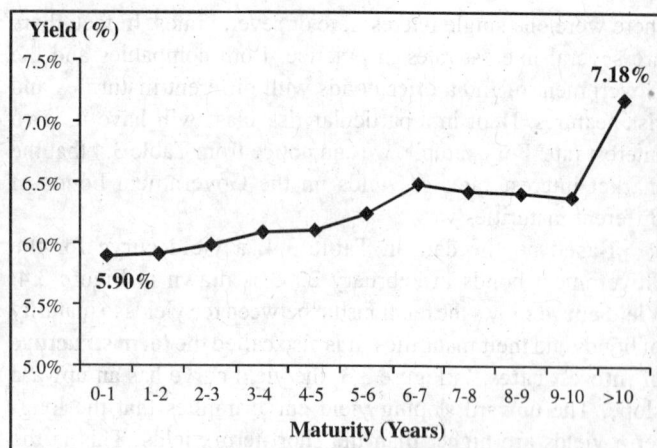

Figure 3.3: Yield Curve (Government of India Bonds)

values of your investment from the three-year bond and the series of one-year bonds are

$$FV, \text{3-year bond} = (1.058)^3 = 1.183$$

$$FV, \text{series of one-year bonds} = (1.053)(1.057)(1.063) = 1.183$$

You may notice that there is no advantage in buying a three-year bond at the current yield of 5.8 per cent as compared to buying one-year bond every year and reinvesting the proceeds. Investing in the three-year bond will be beneficial if you expected one-year rates to remain constant at the current level. Since the future values from the alternative investments are the same, you would be indifferent between them. The expectation theory does assume that capital markets are efficient, there are no transaction costs and investors' sole purpose is to maximize their returns. The long-term rates are geometric average of current and expected short-term rates.

A significant implication of the expectation theory is that given their investment horizon, investors will earn the same average expected returns on all maturity combinations. Hence a firm will not be able to lower its interest cost in the long run by the maturity structure of its debt.

The Liquidity Premium Theory

We have seen that the expectation theory postulates an upward-sloping yield curve. This assumes that investors always expect yields to increase in the future. The theory does not explain reason for this behaviour. The liquidity or risk premium theory provides an explanation for the expectation of the investors. We have explained earlier that the prices of the long-term bonds are more sensitive than the prices of the short-term bonds to the changes in the market rates of interest. Hence investors prefer short-term bonds to the long-term bonds. The investors will be compensated for this risk by offering higher returns on long-term bonds. This extra return, which is called liquidity premium, gives the yield curve its upward bias. However, the yield curve could still be inverted if the declining expectations and other factors have more effect than the liquidity premium.

The liquidity premium theory means that rates on long-term bonds will be higher than on the short-term bonds. From a firm's point of view, the liquidity premium theory suggests that

as the cost of short-term debt is less, the firm could minimise the cost of its borrowings by continuously refinancing its short-term debt rather taking on long-term debt.

The Segmented Markets Theory

The segmented markets theory assumes that the debt market is divided into several segments based on the maturity of debt. In each segment, the yield of debt depends on the demand and supply. Investors' preferences of each segment arise because they want to match the maturities of assets and liabilities to reduce the susceptibility to interest rate changes. For example, the liabilities of pension funds are long-term and they would like to ensure that they have sufficient funds to service these liabilities. Therefore, they will invest their funds in long maturity investments to ensure certainty of returns. On the other hand, the deposits of commercial banks are mostly short-term in nature. Hence, they match their liabilities by lending for short-terms or investing in short-term securities.

The segmented markets theory approach assumes investors do not shift from one maturity to another in their borrowing-lending activities and therefore, the shift in yields are caused by changes in the demand and supply for bonds of different maturities. Overall, it implies that investors strongly prefer to invest in assets with maturities matching their liabilities, and borrowers prefer to issue liabilities that match the maturity of their assets.

Default Risk and Credit Rating

The Central and State Governments, government bodies, and public sector and private sector companies issue bonds. There is a difference between the government bonds and corporate bonds. Generally, the government is not expected to become insolvent. Investors consider their investment safe when they invest in the government bonds; they do not fear that the government will default on its bonds. On the other hand, companies do get into financial problems and may become bankrupt. Hence there are chances that companies may default on their bonds. Bondholders will never get more than the promised payments from companies, but financially distressed companies may not pay full promised amount.

Default risk is the risk that a company will default on its promised obligations to bondholders. Bondholders can avoid the default risk by investing their funds in the government bonds instead of the corporate bonds. However, they may invest in corporate bonds if they are compensated for assuming the default risk. Hence companies, in order to induce investors to invest in their bonds, offer a higher return than the return on the government bonds. This difference, called default premium, is compensation for the default risk. Thus the **default premium** is the *spread* between the promised return on a corporate bond and the return on a government bond with same maturity. The default premium will be higher for bonds with higher chances of default.

How do investors assess the default risk of bonds? In most countries there are credit rating companies that rate bonds according to their safety. In USA, Moody's and Standard and Poor's and others provide bond ratings. In India, the Credit Rating

Table 3.5: CRISIL's Debenture Ratings

High Investment Grades	
AAA (Triple A): *Highest Safety*	Debentures rated 'AAA' are judged to offer highest safety of timely payment of interest and principal. Though the circumstances providing this degree of safety are likely to change, such changes as can be envisaged are most unlikely to affect adversely the fundamentally strong position of such issues.
AA (Double A): *High Safety*	Debentures rated 'AA' are judged to offer high safety of timely payment of interest and principal. They differ in safety from 'AAA' issues only marginally.
Investment Grades	
A: *Adequate Safety*	Debentures rated 'A' are judged to offer adequate safety of timely payment of interest and principal; however, changes in circumstances can adversely affect such issues more than those in the higher rated categories.
BBB (Triple B): *Moderate Safety*	Debentures rated 'BBB' are judged to offer sufficient safety of timely payment of interest and principal for the present; however, changing circumstances are more likely to lead to a weakened capacity to pay interest and repay principal than for debentures in higher rated categories.
Speculative Grades	
BB (Double B): *Inadequate Safety*	Debentures rated 'BB' are judged to carry inadequate safety of timely payment of interest and principal; while they are less susceptible to default than other speculative grade debentures in the immediate future, the uncertainties that the issuer faces could lead to inadequate capacity to make timely interest and principal payments.
B: *High Risk*	Debentures rated 'B' are judged to have greater susceptibility to default; while currently interest and principal payments are met, adverse business or economic conditions would lead to lack of ability or willingness to pay interest or principal.
C: *Substantial Risk*	Debentures rated 'C' are judged to have factors present that make them vulnerable to default; timely payment of interest and principal is possible only if favourable circumstances continue.
D: *In Default*	Debentures rated 'B' are judged to have greater susceptibility to default; while currently interest and principal payments are met, adverse business or economic conditions would lead to lack of ability or willingness to pay interest or principal.

Notes:
1. CRISIL may apply "+" (plus) or "–" (minus) signs for ratings from AA to D to reflect comparative standing within the category.
2. The contents within parenthesis are a guide to the pronunciation of the rating symbols.
3. Preference share rating symbols are identical to debenture rating symbols except that the letters "pf" are prefixed to the debenture rating symbols, e.g. pfAAA ("pf Triple A").

Source: Credit Rating Information Services of India Limited (CRISIL), www.crisil.com

Information Services Limited (CRISIL), Investment Information and Credit Rating Agency (ICRA), and Credit Analysis and Research Limited (CARE) provide bond and other debt ratings. Table 3.7 provide debenture ratings scheme of CRISIL. Debentures (bonds) with highest safety are rated as AAA (triple A). Debentures rated BBB (triple B) and above are **investment grade debentures.** Debentures rated below BBB are speculative grade, and they are also known as **junk bonds** or high yield bonds.

VALUATION OF PREFERENCE SHARES

A company may issue two types of shares: (*a*) ordinary shares and (*b*) preference shares. Owners of shares are called shareholders, and capital contributed by them is called share capital.

Preference shares have preference over ordinary shares in terms of payment of dividend and repayment of capital *if* the company is wound up. They may be issued with or without a maturity period. **Redeemable preference shares** are shares with maturity. **Irredeemable preference shares** are shares without any maturity.[1] The holders of preference shares get dividends at a fixed rate. With regard to dividends, preference shares may be issued with or without cumulative features. In the case of **cumulative preference shares** unpaid dividends accumulate and are payable in the future. Dividends in arrears do not

accumulate in the case of **non-cumulative preference shares.**

Features of Preference and Ordinary Shares

The following are the features of preference and ordinary shares:

- *Claims* Preference shareholders have a claim on assets and income prior to ordinary shareholders. Equity (ordinary) shareholders have a residual claim on a company's income and assets. They are the legal owners of the company.
- *Dividend* The dividend rate is fixed in the case of preference shares. Preference shares may be issued with cumulative rights, i.e. dividend will accumulate until paid-off. In the case of equity shares neither the dividend rate is known, nor does dividend accumulate. Dividends paid on preference and equity shares are not tax deductible.
- *Redemption* Both redeemable and irredeemable preference shares can be issued in India. Redeemable preference shares have a maturity date while irredeemable preference shares are perpetual. Equity shares have no maturity date.
- *Conversion* A company can issue convertible preference shares. That is, after a stated period, such shares can be converted into ordinary shares.

Like bonds, it is relatively easy to estimate cash flows associated with preference shares. The cash flows may include

---

1. In some countries like in India, companies are not allowed to issue irredeemable preference shares.

annual preference dividend and redemption value on maturity in case of redeemable preference shares. The value of the preference share would be the sum of the present values of dividends and the redemption value.

Illustration 3.4: Value of a Preference Share

Suppose an investor is considering the purchase of a 12-year, 10% Rs 100 par value preference share. The redemption value of the preference share on maturity is Rs 120. The investor's required rate of return is 10.5 per cent. What should she be willing to pay for the share now? The investor would expect to receive Rs 10 as preference dividend each year for 12 years and Rs 110 on maturity (i.e., at the end of 12 years). We can use the present value annuity factor to value the constant stream of preference dividends and the present value factor to value the redemption payment.

$$P_0 = 10 \times \left[\frac{1}{0.105} - \frac{1}{0.105 \times (1.105)^{12}} \right] + \frac{120}{(1.105)^{12}}$$

$$= 10 \times 6.506 + 120 \times 0.302 = 65.06 + 36.24 = \text{Rs } 101.30$$

Note that the present value of Rs 101.30 is a composite of the present value of dividends, Rs 65.06 and the present value of the redemption value, Rs 36.24. The Rs 100 preference share is worth Rs 101.3 today at 10.5 per cent required rate of return. The investor would be better off by purchasing the share for Rs 100 today.

A formula similar to the valuation of bond can be used to value preference shares with a maturity period:

Value of preference share = Present value of dividends + Present value of maturity value

$$P_0 = \left[\frac{\text{PDIV}_1}{(1+k_p)^1} + \frac{\text{PDIV}_2}{(1+k_p)^2} + \dots + \frac{\text{PDIV}_n}{(1+k_p)^n} \right] + \frac{P_n}{(1+k_p)^n}$$

$$P_0 = \sum_{t=1}^{n} \frac{\text{PDIV}_1}{(1+k_p)^t} + \frac{P_n}{(1+k_p)^t} \qquad (8)$$

PDIV_t is the preference dividend per share in period t, k_p the required rate of return of preference share and P_n the value of the preference share on maturity. Since PDIV is an annuity, Equation (8) can also be written as follows:

$$P_0 = \text{PDIV} \times \left[\frac{1}{k_p} - \frac{1}{k_p(1+k_p)^n} \right] + \frac{P_n}{(1+k_p)^n} \qquad (9)$$

Note that the term within parentheses on the right-hand side of the equation is the present value factor for an annuity of Re 1.

Valuing Irredeemable preference share: How can we value an irredeemable preference share? Consider that a company has issued Rs 100 irredeemable preference share on which it pays a dividend of Rs 9. Assume that this type of preference share is currently yielding a dividend of 11 per cent. What is the value of the preference share? The preference dividend of Rs 9 is perpetuity. Therefore, the present value of the preference share is

$$P_0 = \frac{\text{PDIV}}{k_p} = \frac{9}{0.11} = \text{Rs } 81.82$$

Yield on preference share: We can ask a different question. If the price of the preference share is Rs 81.82, what return do investors require? In that case, we will have to solve the following equation:

$$81.82 = \frac{9}{k_p}$$

$$k_p = \frac{9}{81.82} = 0.11 \text{ or } 11 \text{ per cent}$$

The rate k_p, is the preference share's yield-to-maturity. For a preference share with maturity (Equation 6), k_p can be found out by trial and error.

VALUATION OF ORDINARY SHARES

The valuation of ordinary or equity shares is relatively more difficult. The difficulty arises because of two factors:[1] First, the rate of dividend on equity shares is not known; also, the payment of equity dividend is *discretionary*. Thus, the estimates of the amount and timing of the cash flows expected by equity shareholders are more uncertain. In the case of debentures and preference shares, the rate of interest and dividend, respectively, are known with certainty. It is, therefore, easy to make the forecasts of cash flows associated with them. Second, the earnings and dividends on equity shares are generally expected to grow, unlike the interest on bonds and preference dividend. This feature of variable dividend on equity shares makes the calculation of share value difficult.

Dividend Capitalisation

The general principle of valuation applies to the share valuation. The value of a share today depends on cash inflows expected by investors and risk associated with those cash inflows. Cash inflows expected from an equity share consist of dividends that the owner expects to receive while holding the share and the price, which he expects to obtain when the share is sold. The price, which the owner is expected to receive when he sells the share, will include the original investment plus a capital gain (or minus a capital loss).

Normally a shareholder does not hold shares in perpetuity. He holds shares for some time, receives the dividends and finally, sells them to a buyer to obtain capital gains. But when he sells the share, the new buyer is also simply purchasing a stream of future dividends and a liquidating price when he also sells the share. The logic can be extended further. The ultimate conclusion is that, for shareholders in general, the expected cash inflows consist only of future dividends and, therefore, the value of an ordinary share is determined by capitalising the future dividend stream at the opportunity cost of capital. The *opportunity cost*

---

1. Weston and Brigham, *op. cit.*

of capital is the return that the shareholder could earn from an investment of equivalent risk in the market. The value of a share is the present value of its future stream of dividends. How can a share be valued?

Single Period Valuation

Let us assume that an investor intends to buy a share and will hold it for one year. Suppose he expects the share to pay a dividend of Rs 2 next year, and would sell the share at an expected price of Rs 21 at the end of the year. If the investor's opportunity cost of capital or the required rate of return (k_e) is 15 per cent, how much should he pay for the share today? The present value of the share today, P_0, will be determined as the present value of the expected dividend per share at the end of the first year, DIV_1, plus the present value of the expected price of the share after a year, P_1.

$$P_0 = \frac{DIV_1 + P_1}{1 + k_e} \qquad (10)$$

$$P_0 = \frac{2 + 21}{1.15} = \text{Rs } 20$$

Equation (9) gives the *'fair'* or *'reasonable'* price of the share since it reflects the present value of the share. The investor would buy the share if the actual price were less than Rs 20. In a *well-functioning capital market,* there ought not to be any difference between the present value and market value of the share. Investors would have full information and it would be reflected in the market price of the share in a well-functioning market. In practice, there could be a difference between the present value and the market value of a share. An **under-valued share** has a market price less than the share's prese . value. On the other hand, an **over-valued share** has a market price higher than the share's present value.

It may be seen in the example that the share value after a year represents an expected growth or capital gain of 5 per cent:

$$g = \frac{21 - 20}{20} = 0.05 \text{ or } 5 \text{ per cent}$$

$$g = \frac{P_1 - P_0}{P_0}$$

An investor can, thus, represent his expectation with regard to the future share price in terms of expected growth. If the share price is expected to grow at g per cent, then we can write P_1 as follows:

$$P_1 = P_0(1 + g)$$

We can rewrite Equation (9) as

$$P_0 = \frac{DIV_1 + P_0(1 + g)}{1 + k_e} \qquad (11)$$

Simplifying Equation (11), we obtain a simple formula for the share valuation as follows:[1]

$$P_0 = \frac{DIV_1}{k_e - g} \qquad (12)$$

In words, the present value of a share is determined by its expected dividend discounted (divided) by the difference of the shareholders capitalisation, or required, rate of return (k_e) and growth rate (g). In the example, if the investor would have expected the share price to grow at 5 per cent, the value of the share today using Equation (12) will be

$$P_0 = \frac{2}{0.15 - 0.05} = \frac{2}{0.10} = \text{Rs } 20$$

Multi-period Valuation

In the preceding section, we discussed a single-period share valuation model, where the investor was expected to hold share for one year and then sell it at the end of the year. The investor will receive dividend for one year, DIV_1, and the share value, P_1, when he sells the share at the end of the year. The value of the share today is given by Equation (9).

Why does the new investor purchase the share at the end of one year? Because he also expects a stream of dividends during the period he holds the share plus the liquidating price of the share. What determines the next year's price (P_1) if the share is held for one year? The price next year (P_1) will depend on expected dividend in year 2 and expected price of the share at the end of year 2. For example, if we consider that $DIV_{12} =$ Rs 2.10 and $P_2 =$ Rs 22.05, then P_1 is

$$P_1 = \frac{2.10 + 22.05}{1.15} = \text{Rs } 21$$

Today's price (P_0) can be calculated as the discounted value of dividends in years 1 and 2 and liquidating price at the end of

---

1.
$$P_0 = \frac{DIV_1 + P_0(1 + g)}{1 + k_e} \qquad (3A)$$

$$P_0 + P_0 k_e = DIV_1 + P_0 + P_0 g \qquad (3B)$$

$$P_0 + P_0 k_e - P_0 - P_0 g = DIV_1 \qquad (3C)$$

$$P_0(k_e - g) = DIV_1 \qquad (3D)$$

$$P_0 = \frac{DIV_1}{k_e - g} \qquad (3E)$$

year 2 as follows:

$$P_0 = \frac{2}{1.15} + \frac{2.10 + 22.05}{(1.15)^2} = Rs\ 20$$

Thus, if Equation (9) holds, P_1 should be given by the following formula:

$$P_1 = \frac{DIV_2 + P_2}{1 + k_e} \tag{13}$$

We can express P_0 as follows:

$$P_0 = \frac{1}{1 + k_e}(DIV_1 + P_1)$$

By substituting the value of P_1 from Equation (13), we obtain the share price today as given below:

$$P_0 = \frac{1}{1 + k_e}\left[DIV_1 + \frac{DIV_2 + P_2}{1 + k_e}\right]$$

$$P_0 = \frac{DIV_1}{1 + k_e} + \frac{DIV_2 + P_2}{(1 + k_e)^2} \tag{14}$$

We can further extend the time horizon. We can, for example, determine the price of the share after 2 years (P_2):

$$P_2 = \frac{DIV_3 + P_3}{1 + k_e} \tag{15}$$

and determine today's price, P_0, in terms of dividends for 3 years and price after 3 years. If the final period is n, we can write the general formula for share value as follows:

$$P_0 = \frac{DIV_1}{(1 + k_e)} + \frac{DIV_2}{(1 + k_e)^2} + \cdots + \frac{DIV_n + P_n}{(1 + k_e)^n} \tag{16}$$

$$P_0 = \sum_{t=1}^{n} \frac{DIV_t}{(1 + k_e)^t} + \frac{P_n}{(1 + k_e)^n} \tag{17}$$

How does Equation (17) work? Consider an example given in Illustration 3.5.

Illustration 3.5: Value of Share Under Constant Growth

Suppose that the price of a share today (P_0) is Rs 20 and it is expected to increase at an annual rate of 5 per cent. Thus, the price after a year will be: Rs 20 (1.05) = Rs 21; after two years: Rs 21 (1.05) = Rs 22.05 and so on. Further, assume that the expected dividend after a year (DIV_1) is Rs 2, and it is also expected to grow at a rate of 5 per cent per annum. Thus, the expected dividend after two years will be: Rs 2 (1.05) = Rs 2.10; after three years: Rs 2.10 (1.05) = Rs 2.21 and so on. Suppose the opportunity cost of capital is 15 per cent, what would be the price of share if it were held for 5 years?

The price would equal the present value of dividends for 5 years plus the present value of the share price at the end of 5 years. That is:

$$P_0 = \left[\frac{2.00}{(1.15)} + \frac{2.10}{(1.15)^2} + \frac{2.21}{(1.15)^3} + \frac{2.32}{(1.15)^4} + \frac{2.43}{(1.15)^5}\right] + \frac{25.53}{(1.15)^5}$$
$$= 7.31 + 12.69 = Rs\ 20$$

The present value of the stream of dividends is Rs 7.31 and of the share price at the and of five years is Rs 12.69. The total present value of the share is Rs 20.

We use the values in Illustration 3.5 to show the present values of dividend stream $[\Sigma PV\,(DIV_t)]$ and the future price $[PV\,(P_n)]$ separately in Table 3.6. You can see from Table 3.6 and Figure 3.4 that as the time horizon lengthens, the proportion of present value contributed by the dividends increases. The present value of future (terminal or liquidating) price declines as the time horizon increases; it is almost zero for 50-year or higher time horizon. You may also notice that after about 50 years the present value contribution of *additional* dividends is insignificant. The total present value of dividends plus terminal price remains the same, i.e. Rs 20, irrespective of the time horizon.[1]

Table 3.6: Present Values of Dividends and Future Price under Various Time Horizons

Year (n)	DIV_t	$\Sigma PV\,(DIV_t)$	P_t	$PV\,(P_t)$	Total PV
1	2.00	1.74	21.00	18.26	20.00
2	2.10	3.33	22.05	16.67	20.00
3	2.21	4.78	23.15	15.22	20.00
4	2.32	6.10	24.31	13.90	20.00
5	2.43	7.31	25.53	12.69	20.00
10	3.10	11.95	32.58	8.05	20.00
20	5.05	16.76	53.07	3.24	20.00
25	6.45	17.94	67.73	2.06	20.00
50	21.84	19.79	229.35	0.21	20.00
75	73.97	19.98	776.65	0.02	20.00
100	250.48	20.00	2,630.03	0.00	20.00

In principle, the time horizon n could be very large; in fact, it can be assumed to approach infinity (∞). *If the time horizon, n, approaches to infinity, then the present value of the future price will approach to zero.* Thus the price of a share today is the present value of an infinite stream of dividends.

$$P_0 = \frac{DIV_1}{(1 + k_e)} + \frac{DIV_2}{(1 + k_e)^2} + \ldots + \frac{DIV_{n=\infty}}{(1 + k_e)^{n=\infty}} \tag{18}$$

$$P_0 = \sum_{t=1}^{n=\infty} \frac{DIV_t}{(1 + k_e)^t} \tag{19}$$

It will be observed that the procedure for calculating the share value is similar to the calculation of an asset's present value; cash flows in terms of dividend stream are discounted by the opportunity cost of capital or the capitalisation rate. It must be remembered that the formula for determining the share price

---

1. The logic of share valuation is given in the original work of Williams, *op. cit.*, and in the work of Gordon, Myron, *The Investment, Financing and Valuation of the Corporation,* Richard D. Irwin, 1962. Also, see Brealey, R. and Myers, S., *Principles of Corporate Finance,* McGraw Hill, 1991, pp. 49–52.

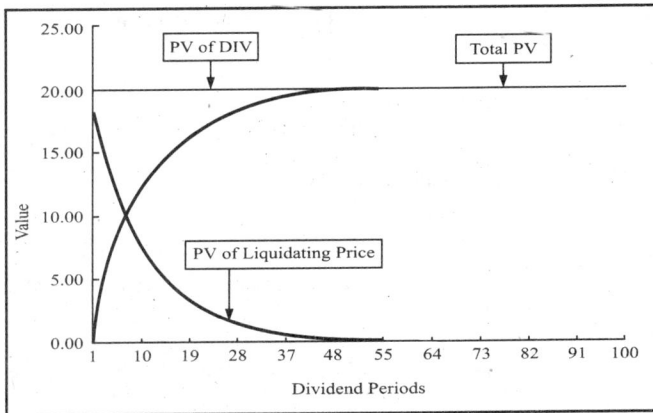

Figure 3.4: Present value of dividends and future share price

[Equations (18) and (19)] does not ignore terminal value of the share and capital gains. The basis of formula was the assumption that value is determined by expected dividends *and* the terminal price, P_n.[1] The term representing terminal price has disappeared from the formula because, as we have shown in Table 3.6 and Figure 3.4, as the holding period approaches infinity, the present value of the terminal price approaches zero.

Dividends, DIV_t, in Equation (17 or 18) represent stream of *expected dividends*. In practice, DIV_t could rise, fall, remain constant, or fluctuate randomly. In the following sections we discuss the cases of rising, falling and constant dividends.

Growth in Dividends

Dividends do not remain constant. Earnings and dividends of most companies grow over time, at least, because of their retention policies. Historical evidence indicates that most companies have been retaining a substantial portion of their earnings (about 50 per cent) for reinvestment in the business. This policy would increase the ordinary shareholder's equity as well as the firm's future earnings. If the number of shares does not change, this policy should tend to increase earnings per share, and consequently, it should produce an expanding stream of dividends per share.

Normal Growth

If a totally equity financed firm retains a constant proportion of its annual earnings (say, b) and reinvests it at its internal rate of return, which is its return on equity (say, ROE), then it can be shown that the dividends will grow at a constant rate equal to the product of retention ratio and return on equity; that is, $g = b \times$ ROE. To illustrate how dividends grow over time, consider a numerical example.

Suppose that the book value of a firm's equity per share today is Rs 100, and its return on equity (ROE) is 10 per cent. He firm's retention ratio is 60 per cent (which implies a payout ratio of 40 per cent). It is expected that the firm will also earn 10 per cent on its retained earnings. Let us also assume that the firm has no debt. The firm's earnings per share after one year will be: $EPS_1 =$ Rs $100 \times 0.10 =$ Rs 10. The firm will retain Rs 6 and distribute Rs 4 as dividends. The book value of equity per share

in the beginning of second year will be: $BV_1 =$ Rs 100 + Rs 6 = Rs 106. The firm's EPS in second year will be: $EPS_2 =$ Rs 106 × 0.10 = Rs 10.6. Again, it will retain 60 per cent of the earnings, *viz.* Rs 6.36 and distribute 40 per cent, *viz.* Rs 4.24. The growth in dividend per share will be

$$\text{Growth in dividends} = \frac{DIV_2 - DIV_1}{DIV_1} = \frac{6.36 - 6}{6}$$

$$= 0.06 \text{ or } 6 \text{ per cent}$$

You can verify that EPS has also grown at 6 per cent. It may be noticed that the increase in dividend per share by Rs 0.36 in the second year has occurred on account of the reinvestment of earnings. The firm had retained Rs 6 per share out of the first year's earnings of Rs 10 per share, and earned additional earnings of Rs 0.60 per share at the rate of 10 per cent. The 40 per cent of the additional income has also gone as dividend to the shareholders in the second year. The example can be extended to verify that dividends in subsequent years will continue growing at a constant rate of 6 per cent.

Table 3.4 shows the growth in book value, earnings per share, dividend per share and retained earnings over a given period of time. It should be noted that 6 per cent growth in dividends is equal to the product of retention rate of 60 per cent and return on equity of 10 per cent: $0.60 \times 0.10 = 0.06$ or 6 per cent:

Growth = Retention ratio × Return on equity

$$g = b \times \text{ROE} \qquad (20)$$

Table 3.7: BV, EPS, DPS and Retained Earnings Under Constant Growth Assumption

Year N	Book value in Beinning, BV_b	Earning Per Share, EPS	Dividend Per Share, DPS	Retained Earnings, RE	Book Value at the End, B_e
1	100.00	10.00	4.00	6.00	106.00
2	106.00	10.60	4.24	6.36	112.36
3	112.36	11.24	4.49	6.74	119.10
4	119.10	11.91	4.76	7.15	126.25
5	126.25	12.62	5.05	7.57	133.82
6	133.82	13.38	5.35	8.03	141.85
7	141.85	14.19	5.67	8.51	150.36
8	150.36	15.04	6.01	9.02	159.38
9	159.38	15.94	6.38	9.56	168.95
10	168.95	16.89	6.76	10.14	179.08
15	226.09	22.61	9.04	13.57	239.66
20	302.56	30.26	12.10	18.15	320.71
25	404.89	40.49	16.20	24.29	429.19

It can be seen that growth will be more if the firm retains higher portion of earnings. The current dividend will, however, be reduced. A share valuation model should explicitly involve growth expectations. Let us assume that dividends grow at a constant rate to infinity. If the firm now pays dividend DIV_0 (that is dividend in year, 0), then dividend at the end of first year will be:

---

1. Brealey and Myers, *op. cit.*, p. 51.

$$DIV_1 = DIV_0(1+g)^1$$

and at the end of the second year, it will be

$$DIV_2 = DIV_1(1+g) = DIV_0(1+g)^2$$

and so on. Thus, when dividends grow constantly the formula for share valuation can be written as follows:

$$P_0 = \frac{DIV_0(1+g)}{(1+k_e)} + \frac{DIV_0(1+g)^2}{(1+k_e)^2} + \ldots + \frac{DIV_0(1+g)^{n=\infty}}{(1+k_e)^{n=\infty}} \quad (21)$$

$$P_0 = \sum_{t=1}^{n=\infty} \frac{DIV_0(1+g)^t}{(1+k_e)^t} \quad (22)$$

After solving Equation (22), we obtain[2]

$$P_0 = \frac{DIV_0(1+g)}{k_e - g}$$

$$P_0 = \frac{DIV_1}{k_e - g} \quad (23)$$

In words, the present value of a share is equal to the dividend after a year, DIV_1, divided by the difference of the capitalisation rate (k_e) and the growth rate (g); that is, ($k_e - g$). Equation (23) is the **perpetual growth model.** It is based on the following assumptions:[2]

- The capitalisation rate or the opportunity cost of capital must be greater than the growth rate, ($k_e > g$), otherwise absurd results will be attained. If $k_e = g$, the equation will yield an infinite price, and if $k_e < g$, the result will be a negative price.
- The initial dividend per share, DIV_1, must be greater than zero (i.e., $DIV_1 > 0$), otherwise Equation (23) will obtain a zero price.
- The relationship between k_e and g is assumed to remain constant and perpetual.

Illustration 3.6: Perpetual Growth

A company paid a dividend of Rs 3.70 in the previous year. The dividends in the future are expected to grow perpetually at a rate of 8 per cent. Find out the share's price today if the market capitalises dividend at 12 per cent?

Using Equation (23), the price of share is

$$P_0 = \frac{DIV_0(1+g)}{k_e - g} = \frac{DIV_1}{k_e - g}$$
$$= \frac{3.70(108)}{0.12 - 0.08} = \frac{4}{0.04} = Rs\ 100$$

Illustration 3.7: Price of a Share Under Perpetual Growth

A company has a book value per share of Rs 137.80. Its return on equity is 15 per cent and it follows a policy of retaining 60 per cent of its earnings. If the opportunity cost of capital were 18 per cent, what would be price of the share today?

1. *Ibid.,* p. 52.
2. Gordon, Myron, *op. cit.*

The company's earnings and dividend per share after a year are expected to be

$$EPS_1 = 137.8 \times 0.15 = Rs\ 2067$$
$$DIV_1 = (1 - 0.60) \times 20.67 = 0.40 \times 20.67 = Rs\ 8.27$$

The growth in dividend would be

$$g = 0.6 \times 0.15 = 0.09$$

Assuming that dividends would grow perpetually, we can use Equation (23) to find out P_0:

$$P_0 = \frac{8.27}{0.18 - 0.09} = Rs\ 91.89$$

Super-normal Growth

The dividends of a company may not grow at the same constant rate indefinitely. It may face a two-stage growth situation. In the first stage, dividends may grow at a **super-normal growth** *rate* when the company is experiencing very high demand for its products and is able to extract premium from customers. Afterwards, the demand for the company's products may normalise and therefore, earnings and dividends may grow at a **normal growth rate.** The share value in a two-stage growth situation can be determined in two parts. First, we can find the present value of constantly growing dividend annuity for a *definite* super-normal growth period. Second, we can calculate the present value of constantly growing dividend indefinitely (in perpetuity) after the super-normal growth period. Let us consider an example in Illustration 3.8.

Illustration 3.8: Super Normal Growth

A company earned Rs 6 per share and paid Rs 3.48 per share as dividend in the previous year. Its earnings and dividends are expected to grow at 15 per cent for six years and then at a rate of 8 per cent indefinitely. The capitalisation rate is 18 per cent. What is the price of the share today?

This is a situation of two-stage growth. You need to first determine the stream of dividends for the super-normal growth period of 6 years. The dividend per share in the first year will be: $DIV_1 = Rs\ 3.48\ (1.15)_1 = Rs\ 4.00$. The second year dividend will be: $DIV_2 = Rs\ 3.48\ (1.15)_2 = Rs\ 4.60$. You can similarly calculate dividends for other years. Figure 3.4 shows the growth in dividends. Dividends grow at compound rate of 15 per cent for the first six years and at 8 per cent thereafter.

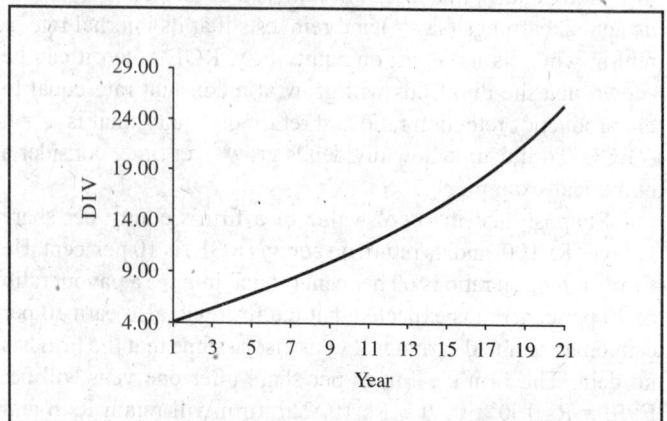

Figure 3.5: Growth in dividends

Once you have calculated dividends for six years, you can calculate the present value as shown below.

(*i*) Present value of the share during the super-normal growth period:

$$P_0 = \sum_{t=1}^{6} \frac{DIV_0(1+g_n)^t}{(1+k_e)^t}$$

$$P_0 = \frac{3.48(1.15)^1}{(1.18)} + \frac{3.48(1.15)^2}{(1.18)^2} + \frac{3.48(1.15)^3}{(1.18)^3}$$

$$+ \frac{3.48(1.15)^4}{(1.18)^4} + \frac{3.48(1.15)^5}{(1.18)^5} + \frac{3.48(1.15)^6}{(1.18)^6}$$

$$= 4 \times 0.8475 + 4.60 \times 0.7182 + 5.29 \times 0.6086$$

$$+ 6.08 \times 0.5158 + 7.00 \times 0.4371 + 8.04 \times 0.3704$$

$$= Rs \ 19.10$$

You may notice that Rs 3.48 is an annuity that is growing at constant rate of 15 per cent per annum for 6 years. Therefore, with the help of a financial calculator, you could also calculate the present value of dividends during the super-normal growth period as follows:

$$P_0 = DIV_1 \times \left[\frac{1}{k_e - g} \times \left\{ 1 - \left(\frac{1+g}{1+k_e}\right)^n \right\} \right]$$

$$= 4.00 \times \left[\frac{1}{0.18 - 0.15} \times \left\{ 1 - \left(\frac{1.15}{1.18}\right)^6 \right\} \right]$$

$$= 4.00 \times 4.7723 = Rs \ 19.10$$

From year 7, dividends grow at a normal rate of 8 per cent indefinitely. This is a case of constantly growing perpetual cash flows. You can obtain the present value of dividends at the end of year 6 if you discount dividends in year 7 by the difference of the capitalisation rate and the normal growth rate. The value so obtained is a single amount at the end of year 6. You will have to discount this amount to find its present value *today* (year 0). The calculations are shown below.

(*ii*) Present value of the share at the end of year 6, growth being 8 per cent:

(*a*) $\quad P_6 = \dfrac{DIV_7}{k_e - g_n} = \dfrac{8.04(1.08)}{0.18 - 0.08} = \dfrac{8.69}{0.10} = Rs \ 86.90$

(*b*) Discount P_6 back to present

$$PV(P_6) = \frac{P_6}{(1+k_e)^6} = \frac{86.83}{(1.18)^6} = 86.90 \times 0.3704 = Rs \ 3219$$

You can add the present values of two stages to get the total present value of the share as follows.

(*iii*) Value of the share today: $P_0 = 19.10 + 32.19 = Rs \ 51.29$

Thus, it is clear that the value of the share is equal to the discounted value of dividends for the first six years, growing at an above-average or super-normal growth rate of 15 per cent plus the discounted value of dividends indefinitely after six years growing at the normal rate of 8 per cent.

We find from Illustration 3.8 that the basic valuation methodology remains the same in two-stage growth situation. The perpetual growth model, as given in Equation (23), should be appropriately modified. By expanding Equation (23) one could incorporate various growth periods in the analysis. If the dividends of a firm are expected to grow at a super normal growth rate, g_s, for n years and then grow at a normal growth rate, g_n, till infinity, the value of the share is given as follows:

Share value = PV of dividends during finite super-
normal growth period + PV of dividends
during indefinite normal growth period

$$P_0 = \sum_{t=1}^{n} \frac{DIV_0(1+g_s)^t}{(1+k_e)^t} + \sum_{t=n+1}^{\infty} \frac{DIV_n(1+g_n)^{t-n}}{(1+k_e)^t} \qquad (24)$$

In Equation (24), the first term gives the value of dividends starting from the first year and growing at a super-normal rate, g_s, for a finite period, $t = n$. It may be noticed that the second term on the right-hand side of Equation (24) gives the share value at the end of the super-normal growth period, n, and equals to the value of a stream of dividends starting from $t = n + 1$ and growing at a constant normal rate *perpetually*. Thus, the second term on the right-hand side of Equation (24) can be written as follows:

$$P_n = \sum_{t=n+1}^{\infty} \frac{DIV_n(1+g_n)^{t-n}}{(1+k_e)^t}$$

$$P_n = \frac{DIV_n(1+g_n)}{k_e - g_n} = \frac{DIV_{n+1}}{k_e - g_n} \qquad (25)$$

You may use the following steps to calculate the value of a share growing at the super-normal rate for some period and then at the normal rate forever:[1]

- Calculate dividend per share for the super-normal growth period and use the common procedure for calculating the present value of the stream of dividends for the super-normal growth period.

- Calculate the present value of the share at the end of the supernormal growth period (P_n) as shown below:

$$P_n = \frac{DIV_n(1+g_n)}{k_e - g_n} = \frac{DIV_{n+1}}{k_e - g_n}$$

- Calculate the present value of P_n at $t = 0$. That is

$$PV(P_n) = \frac{DIV_{n+1}}{k_e - g_n} \left[\frac{1}{(1+k_e)^n} \right]$$

- Calculate the total value of the share by adding values arrived in the first and third steps.

Illustration 3.9: Zero Growth

What would be the price of the share in Illustration 3.8 if (*a*) growth in dividends is zero and (*b*) growth in dividends is 8 per cent per annum forever?

If $g = 0$, then P_0 will be:

$$P_0 = \frac{DIV_0(1+g)}{k_e - g} = \frac{3.48(1.0)}{0.18 - 0} = Rs \ 19.33$$

and when $g = 0.08$, then P_0 will be

---

1. *Ibid.*

$$P_0 = \frac{3.48(1.08)}{0.18 - 0.08} = \frac{3.76}{0.10} = \text{Rs } 37.30$$

It may be noticed from the preceding illustrations that as one moves from zero-growth assumption to supernormal-growth assumption, the price of the share increases from Rs 19.33 to Rs 51.29. Thus, the price of a share increases with growth in earnings and dividends, other things remaining the same.

Firm Paying no Dividends

It sometimes so happens that a company although earns profits but does not declare dividends. How would dividend-capitalisation model explain the share value under such circumstances? In fact, companies paying no dividends do command positive market prices for their shares since the price today depends on the future expectation of dividends. The non-

Excel Application 3.3: Two-stage Growth

We can solve the two-stage growth model in Excel. The following is the worksheet based on the data given in Illustration 3.6. For the first 6 years, the dividend grows at a constant rate of 15 per cent per annum. Given 15 per cent growth rate, 18 per cent required rate of return and the time duration of 6 years, in column B8 of the worksheet we enter the formula for a constantly growing annuity:

= (1/(B7-B4))*(1-((1+B4)/(1+B7))^B5)

To obtain the present value of the dividends over six years, in column B9 we write the formula: = B3*(1+B4)*B8. In this formula the dividend in the first year is given by: DIV_1 = B3*(1+B4). After 6 years, the dividend grows at 8 per cent indefinitely. The value of these dividends is given by: $V_0 = [DIV_7/(0.18 - 0.15)] \times (1/(1.18)^6$. We enter a formula in B10: = ((B3*(1+B6)^B5)*(1+B6))/(B7-B4))*(1/(1+B7)). The formula in B11: =B9+B10 gives the total value of the share.

	A	B	C	D	E	F	G	H	I	J	K
1	**Two Stage Growth Model**										
2	Earnings	6.50									
3	Dividend	3.48				**Supernormal Growth Rate**					
4	Supernormal Growth	0.15		**Duration**	51.30	0.10	0.11	0.12	0.13	0.14	0.15
5	Duration of Supernormal Growth	6			3	39.53	40.53	41.55	42.59	43.64	44.71
6	Estimated Constant Growth	0.08			6	41.11	42.99	44.94	46.98	49.10	51.30
7	Required Return	0.18			9	42.39	45.03	47.84	50.84	54.02	57.41
8	Consantly Growing Annuity Factor	4.77			10	42.76	45.64	48.71	52.01	55.55	59.34
9	PV of Dividends - Supernormal Growth	19.10			15	44.27	48.15	52.45	57.20	62.46	68.29
10	PV of Dividends - Normal Growth	32.20			20	45.33	50.00	55.32	61.37	68.28	76.15
11	Value of Share	51.30			25	46.08	51.37	57.53	64.74	73.17	83.07
					30	46.60	52.37	59.24	67.44	77.29	89.15

Using Excel, we create a two-variable table that explains the sensitivity of the share value with regard to changes in the super-normal growth rate (in row) and its duration (in column). The longer the super-normal growth rate is, the higher the value of the share will be.

payment of dividends may not last forever. Eventually, these companies may start paying dividends one day. Shareholders hold shares of such companies because they *expect* that in the final analysis dividends will be paid, or they will be able to realise capital gains. Thus, the dividend capitalisation model is a valid share valuation model even for those companies that are presently paying no dividends.

Suppose a company is expected to pay dividend for Rs 2 per share on its shares from fifth year to infinity. In present value terms, the share is worth the present value of dividends from year five to infinity, discounted at the opportunity cost of capital or the required rate of return. For example, at a required rate of return of 20 per cent, a perpetual sum of Rs 2 starting from fifth year, is worth Rs 10 at the end of fourth year:

$$P_4 = \frac{2}{0.20} = \text{Rs } 10$$

The Rs 10 may be considered as a lump sum received at the end of fourth year. The worth of the share *today* will be the discounted value of Rs 10:

$$P_0 = \frac{10}{(1.2)^4} = 10 \times 0.483 = \text{Rs } 4.82$$

Alternatively, we assume that Rs 2 flows in from the very beginning, and thus, calculate the worth of the share today as: Rs 10 (P_0 = Rs 2/0.20). But we know that the firm will not pay any dividend for the first four years. If we subtract the present value of dividends *not* received from the calculated price of Rs 10, we obtain the actual present worth of the share; this would again be Rs 4.82; that is, Rs 10 – (Rs 2 × 2.589) = Rs 4.82. (Note that the factor, 2.589, is the present value annuity factor for four years at 20 per cent rate). This procedure can be adopted to incorporate growth in dividends.

Earnings Capitalisation

The dividend capitalisation model, discussed so far, is the basic share valuation model. However, under two cases, the value of the share can be determined by capitalising the expected earnings:[1]

- When the firm pays out 100 per cent dividends; that is, it does not retain any earnings.
- When the firm's return on equity (ROE) is equal to its opportunity cost of capital (k_e).

The first case in which the earnings capitalisation model may be employed is the one when the earnings of the firm are stable. The earnings will not grow if the firm does not retain the

1. Brigham, E.F., *Financial Management: Theory and Practice*, Dryden Press, 1979, p. 84.

earnings (and also does not employ any debt). Thus, if the retention rate, b, is zero, then the growth rate, g, would also be equal to zero and DIV_1 would be equal to EPS_1. Under these conditions, the value of the share will be equal to the expected earnings per share divided by the equity capitalisation rate. Since $DIV_1 = EPS_1 (1 - b)$ and $g = rb$ (where r is equal to ROE), we can write formula for share valuation as follows:

$$P_0 = \frac{EPS_1(1-b)}{k_e - rb} \quad (26)$$

If $b = 0$, then $g = rb$ ought to be zero and the formula simply becomes

$$P_0 = \frac{DIV_1}{k_e} = \frac{EPS_1}{k_e} \quad (27)$$

The second situation, in which the earnings capitalisation will yield the same result as the dividend capital capitalisation, is when the firm lacks real growth opportunities. That is, it earns a rate equal to its cost on its retained earnings. If $r = k_e$, then $g = rb = k_e b$. Substituting the value of g in Equation (26), we obtain

$$P_0 = \frac{EPS_1(1-b)}{k_e - k_e b} = \frac{EPS_1(1-b)}{k_e(1-b)} = \frac{EPS_1}{k_e} \quad (28)$$

Thus, true growth, as opposed to mere expansion, is dependent on the existence of **growth opportunities** to reinvest retained earnings at a rate higher than the capitalisation rate, k_e, thereby creating net present value over and above the investment outlays required.[1]

Illustration 3.10: Earnings Model

Calculate the price of a share if EPS = Rs 2.50, $b = 0.4$, $k_e = 0.10$ and ROE $= r = 0.20$. What shall be the price if $r = k_e = 0.10$?

Employing Equation (26) the price of share, when $r = 0.20$ will be

$$P_0 = \frac{EPS_1(1-b)}{k_e - rb} = \frac{2.5(1-0.4)}{0.1-(0.2)(0.4)} = \frac{1.5}{0.10-0.08} = Rs\ 75$$

where $r = 0.10$, the price will be

$$P_0 = \frac{2.5(1-0.4)}{0.10-(0.1)(0.4)} = \frac{1.5}{0.10-0.4} = \frac{1.5}{0.06} = Rs\ 25$$

However, if $r = k_e$, the price can be determined simply as $P_0 = EPS_1/k_e$. In this illustration using this formula we shall have the same answer as above.

EQUITY CAPITALISATION RATE

So far we have discussed how the present value of a share can be calculated. One must know the expected dividends and the *required rate of return* (the opportunity cost of capital or capitalisation rate). The required rate of return will depend upon the risk of the share. Hence, the required rate of return will be equal to the risk-free rate of interest plus the risk-premium to account for the share's risk. The risk premium would be different for different shares. We shall discuss this method of calculating the required rate of return on equity in a chapter later on.

Suppose the current market price of BHEL's share is Rs 240 and the current dividend per share is Rs 12. You expect dividend per share to grow at 10 per cent per annum forever. How much return do you require investing in the share? We assume that the current price of BHEL's share is a *fair* price. The expected dividend per share next year, DIV_1, is Rs 13.20 (12×1.10). The expected dividend yield is 5.5 per cent (13.20/240) and the expected growth rate is 10 per cent. Therefore, your minimum required rate of return is 15.5 per cent. If you earn less than 15.5 per cent, the current share price cannot be maintained.

In a *well-functioning capital market*, the market price is the *fair* price of a share. Therefore, the shareholders expect the share to earn a minimum return that keeps the current share price intact. For firms for which dividends are expected to grow at a constant rate indefinitely and the current market price is given, we can use modify Equation (23) to estimate the capitalisation or the required rate of return of the share:

$$P_0 = \frac{DIV_1}{k_e - g} \quad (23)$$

$$k_e = \frac{DIV_1}{P_0} + g \quad (29)$$

Illustration 3.11 : Equity Capitalisation Rate

A company's share is currently selling for Rs 50 per share. It is expected that a dividend of Rs 3 per share after one year will grow at 8 per cent indefinitely. What is the equity capitalisation rate? The equity capitalisation rate is given as follows:

$$k_e = \frac{DIV_1}{P_0} + g = \frac{3}{50} + 0.08 = 0.14\ \text{or 14 per cent}$$

CAUTION IN USING CONSTANT-GROWTH FORMULA

The constant growth formula is a useful rule of thumb for calculating the present value of a share and the opportunity cost of capital (or the capitalisation rate).[2] A blind faith in the formula can be misleading. One should be cautious in using the formula.

- *Estimation errors* It is dangerous to estimate the capitalisation rate, k_e, by analysing just one share. A large sample of equivalent risk shares should be employed to estimate k_e. This procedure would help at least to reduce the extent of estimating errors.

- *Unsustainable high current growth* The formula should not be used to those companies which have high current growth rates. The constant-growth formula unrealistically assumes that such growth rates can be sustained indefinitely. Since growth rates slow down with the maturity of firms, the assumption tends to overestimate k_e. It is not realistic to assume that a firm will continue growing forever at 50 per cent, or even 25 per cent? (Imagine the meaninglessness of using the constant-growth formula in case of a 'super-growth' company like Reliance Industries Limited!).

- *Errors in forecasting dividends* The market's estimate of

---

1. Solomon, E., *The Theory of Financial Management*, Columbia University Press, pp. 60–64. Also see Van Horne, J.C., *Financial Management and Policy*, Prentice-Hall of India, 1976, pp. 25–28.

2. Solomon, *op. cit.,* pp. 60–61.

the value of a share may be different from the estimate derived from the constant-growth formula. That does not mean that the formula is incorrect; the reason probably may be that dividend stream has not been correctly forecasted.

LINKAGES BETWEEN SHARE PRICE, EARNINGS AND DIVIDENDS

Why do investors buy shares? Do they buy them for dividends or for capital gain? Investors may choose between growth shares or income shares. **Growth shares** are those, which offer greater opportunities for capital gains. **Dividend yield** (i.e. dividend per shares as a percentage of the market price of the share) on such shares would generally be low since companies would follow a high retention policy in order to have a high growth rate. **Income shares,** on the other hand, are those that pay higher dividends, and offer low prospects for capital gains. Because of the high payout policy followed by companies, their share prices tend to grow at a lower rate. Dividend yield on income shares would generally be high. Those investors who want regular income would prefer to buy income shares, which pay high dividends regularly. On the other hand, if investors desire to earn higher return via capital gains, they would prefer to buy growth shares. They would like a profitable company to retain its earnings in the expectation of higher market price of the share in the future. Is there a linkage between the share price and earnings and dividends?[1] Consider an example.

Suppose a company estimates its earnings per share after a year (EPS_1) at Rs 6.67, it follows a policy of paying 100 per cent dividend (i.e., its retention ratio, b, is zero). Thus, the company's dividend per share (DIV) will equal the earnings per share (EPS), and its earnings and dividends would not grow since it does not reinvest any earnings. What would be the price of the company's share if the opportunity cost of capital were 12 per cent? We can use the following formula:

$$P_0 = \frac{DIV_1}{k_e - g} = \frac{EPS_1(1-b)}{k_e - rb} = \frac{6.67(1-0)}{0.12 - 0} = \frac{6.67}{0.12} = Rs\ 55.58$$

Notice that since retention ratio, b, equals to zero, then DIV_1 = EPS_1 and $g = rb = 0$ and P_0 is given by the earnings per share divided by the opportunity cost of capital, i.e., $P_0 = EPS_1/k_e$.

Suppose that the company would pay a dividend of Rs 4 per share in the first year and reinvest the retained earnings (RE) at a rate of return (r = ROE) of 20 per cent. What is the company's payout ratio, retention ratio and growth rate?

$$Payout\ ratio = \frac{DIV_1}{EPS_1} = \frac{4}{6.67} = 0.6\ or\ 60\%$$

$$Retention\ ratio = 1 - payout = 1 - 0.6 = 0.4\ or\ 40\%$$

$$Growth\ rate = Retention\ ratio \times ROE$$

$$= b \times r = 0.4 \times 0.2 = 0.08\ or\ 8\%$$

If we assume that the company will follow a constant policy of retaining 40 per cent earnings (i.e., payout of 60 per cent) at 20 per cent rate of return, then its earnings and

dividends will grow perpetually at 8 per cent ($g = rb = 0.2 \times 0.4$). What would be the price of the company's share? It is calculated as follows:

$$P_0 = \frac{EPS_1(1-b)}{k_e - rb} = \frac{DIV_1}{k_e - g}$$

$$= \frac{6.67(1-0.4)}{0.12 - 0.2 \times 0.4} = \frac{4.00}{0.12 - 0.08} = Rs\ 100$$

You may note that without retention of earnings ($b = 0$), the company has no growth ($g = 0$) and the price of its share is Rs 55.58. But when 8 per cent growth is expected (from reinvestment of retained earnings), the price of the company's share is Rs 100. Thus the difference: Rs 100 – Rs 55.58 = Rs 44.42 is the **value of growth opportunities.** How is the value of growth opportunities created?

How to Value Growth Opportunities?

Retention of earnings adds value since it generates cash flows. For example, the retained earnings in the first year would be: RE_1 = 0.4 × Rs 6.67 = Rs 2.67 and it would be reinvested at 20 per cent rate of return per year. It would generate a stream of perpetual cash flow (CF) of Rs 0.534 starting from the second year :

$$RE_1 = b \times EPS = 0.40 \times 6.67 = 2.67$$
$$CF = RE_1 \times ROE = 2.67 \times 0.2 = Rs\ 0.534$$

Thus, the earnings per share in the second year (EPS_2) will be enhanced by Rs 0.534, and EPS_2 will be: Rs 6.67 + Rs 0.534 = Rs 7.20. The company will retain Rs 2.88 (i.e. 0.4 × Rs 7.20) and reinvest this amount to earn a perpetual cash flow of Rs 0.576 starting from the third year:

$$RE_2 = b \times EPS_2 = 0.40 \times 7.20 = Rs\ 2.88$$
$$CF = RE_2 \times ROE = 2.88 \times 0.2 = Rs\ 0.576$$

The company's earnings per share in the third year will be: EPS_3 = Rs 6.67 + Rs 0.534 + Rs 0.576 = Rs 7.78. Similar calculations can be made for subsequent years (see Table 3.5). We may note that earnings per share, dividend per share, retained earnings and cash flow from retained earnings are growing at a constant rate of 8 per cent per year.

What is the value of the streams of perpetual cash flows generated through retained earnings? For example, when the company invests Rs 2.67 at the end of the first year, it is expected to receive a perpetual cash flow of Rs 0.534 starting from the second year. Thus the net present value at the end of the first year (NPV_1) will be the present value of perpetual cash flows (Rs 0.534) *minus* investment at the end of the first year (Rs 2.67):

$$NPV_1 = \frac{CF}{k_e} - RE_1$$

$$= \frac{0.534}{0.12} - 2.67 = 4.45 - 2.67 = Rs\ 1.78$$

The company will be able to generate a stream of perpetual cash flows of Rs 0.576 starting from the third year from its

---

1. Brealey, R. and Myers, S., *op. cit.*, p. 54.

reinvestment of Rs 2.88 at the end of the second year. We may note that since the growth rate is 8 per cent, perpetual cash flows from additional reinvestment would grow at this rate. Thus the second stream of cash flows would be: Rs 0.534 × 1.08 = Rs 0.576. The net present value of this stream of cash flows at the end of the second year would be as follows:

$$\text{NPV}_2 = \frac{0.534 \times 1.08}{0.12} - 2.67 \times 1.08$$

$$= \frac{0.576}{0.12} - 2.88 = 4.80 - 2.99 = \text{Rs } 1.92$$

We may note that NPV also grows at 8 per cent. Thus,

$$\text{NPV}_2 = \text{NPV}_1(1 + 0.08) = 1.78(1.08) = \text{Rs } 1.92$$

$$\text{NPV}_3 = \text{NPV}_1(1 + g)^2 = 1.78(1.08)^2 = \text{Rs } 2.08$$

NPV at the end of other years can also be calculated in the similar way (see Table 3.8, Column 6). These NPVs are expected net values of streams of perpetual cash flows resulting from the reinvestment of the company's retained earnings. What is the total value of the company's growth arising from the reinvestment of its earnings?

Table 3.8: EPS, DIV, RE and NPV of Perpetual Cash Flows

Year	Perpetual cash flows from reinvestment, RE × ROE	Earning Per share, EPS	Dividend Per share, DIV	Retained earnings, RE	NPV of perpetual cash flow at the end, NPV
1	—	6.67	4.00	2.67	1.78
2	0.53	7.20	4.32	2.88	1.92
3	0.58	7.78	4.67	3.11	2.07
4	0.62	8.40	5.04	3.36	2.24
5	0.67	9.07	5.44	3.63	2.42
6	0.73	9.80	5.88	3.92	2.61
7	0.78	10.58	6.35	4.23	2.82
8	0.85	11.43	6.86	4.57	3.05
9	0.91	12.35	7.41	4.94	3.29
10	0.99	13.33	8.00	5.33	12.44
20	2.13	28.79	17.27	11.51	7.68
25	3.13	42.30	25.38	16.92	11.28

Assumptions: (a) retention ratio: 40 per cent; (b) ROE: 20 per cent.

The value of growth today, V_g, would be the sum of the discounted values of the stream of NPVs. That is

$$V_g = \frac{\text{NPV}_1}{(1 + k_e)} + \frac{\text{NPV}_2}{(1 + k_e)^2} + \ldots + \frac{\text{NPV}_{n=\infty}}{(1 + k_e)^{n=\infty}} \quad (30)$$

where $\text{NPV}_2 = \text{NPV}_1(1 + g)$, $\text{NPV}_3 = \text{NPV}_1(1 + g)^2$ and so on.

We may note that Equation (30) is similar to the constant dividend-growth model, and therefore, it can be rewritten in the following simplified way:

$$V_g = \frac{\text{NPV}_1}{(k_e - g)} \quad (31)$$

Since $\text{NPV}_1 = \text{Rs } 1.78$, $k = 0.12$ and $g = 0.08$, then V_g will be as follows:

$$V_g = \frac{1.78}{0.12 - 0.08} = \text{Rs } 44.42$$

Thus, the value of a share today, P_0, consists of two components:
- the value of the perpetual stream of earnings under no growth assumption and
- the value of growth resulting from the streams of cash flows from the reinvestment of earnings.

That is

$$P_0 = \frac{\text{EPS}_1}{k_e} + \frac{\text{NPV}_1}{k_e - g} = \frac{6.67}{0.12} + \frac{1.78}{0.12 - 0.08}$$

$$= 55.58 + 44.42 = \text{Rs } 100$$

We know that correct

$$\text{NPV}_1 = \frac{\text{CF}_1}{k_e} - \text{RE}_1$$

and since $\text{CF} = b \times \text{ROE} \times \text{EPS}_1$, and $\text{RE}_1 = b \times \text{EPS}_1$, we can rewrite the above equation as follows:

$$\text{NPV}_1 = \frac{b \times \text{ROE} \times \text{EPS}_1}{k_e} - b \times \text{EPS}_1$$

$$= \frac{b \times \text{ROE} \times \text{EPS}_1 - k_e \times b \times \text{EPS}_1}{k_e}$$

$$= \frac{b \times \text{EPS}_1(\text{ROE} - k_e)}{k_e} \quad (32)$$

Substituting Equation (32) in Equation (31), the formula for the value of growth opportunities can be rewritten as follows:

$$V_g = \frac{\text{NPV}_1}{k_e - g} = \frac{b \times \text{EPS}_1(\text{ROE} - k_e)}{k_e(k_e - g)} \quad (33)$$

We can notice from Equation (33) that the value of the growth opportunities would be positive if the rate of return on reinvested earnings is greater than the capitalisation rate (i.e., $V_g > 0$ if $\text{ROE} > k_e$), and it would be negative if the rate of return is lesser than the capitalisation rate (i.e. $V_g < 0$ if $\text{ROE} < k_e$). In spite of the reinvestment of earnings, the value of growth opportunities would be zero if the rate of return were equal to the capitalisation rate (i.e., $V_g = 0$ if $\text{ROE} = k_e$).

Using Equation (33) in the example, the value of the growth opportunities is calculated as follows:

$$V_g = \frac{0.4 \times 6.67(0.20 - 0.12)}{0.12(0.12 - 0.08)} = \frac{0.21344}{0.0048} = \text{Rs } 44.42$$

PRICE-EARNINGS (P/E) RATIO: HOW SIGNIFICANT?

P/E ratio is calculated as the price of a share divided by earning per share. The reciprocal of P/E ratio is called **earnings-price (E/P) ratio** or **earning yield.** Investors in practice seem to attach a lot of importance to P/E ratios. The financial dailies give information on P/E ratios of a large number of companies, and financial analysts evaluate the performances and prospects of shares in terms of P/E ratios. Some people use P/E multiplier to value the shares of companies. Suppose a company has a P/E multiplier of 14.5 and the company expects its EPS to be Rs 11.67 next year. The expected share value will be: Rs 11.67 × 14.5 = Rs 169.22. Alternatively, you could find the share value by dividing EPS by E/P ratio, which is the reciprocal of P/E ratio: Rs 11.67 ÷ (1/14.5) = Rs 169.22. How is P/E ratio related to the capitalisation rate or opportunity cost of capital? How reliable is P/E ratio as a performance indicator?

How reliable is the reciprocal of P/E ratio (i.e., E/P ratio) as a measure of the opportunity cost of capital? Let us verify. We have discussed in the preceding section that the price of a share is given by the following formula:

$$P_0 = \frac{EPS_1}{k_e} + \left[\frac{b \times EPS_1 (ROE - k_e)}{k_e (k_e - g)} \right] \quad (34)$$

$$P_0 = \frac{EPS_1}{k_e} + V_g \quad (35)$$

From Equation (35) we can derive the following formula for the earnings-price ratio:[1]

$$\frac{EPS_1}{P_0} = k_e \left[1 - \frac{V_g}{P_0} \right] \quad (36)$$

We can observe from Equation (36) that the earning-price (E/P) ratio (i.e., the reciprocal of P/E ratio) is *not* equal to the capitalisation rate, k_e. E/P ratio will be lower than the capitalisation rate, k_e, if the value of growth opportunities, V_g, is positive (i.e., E/P < k_e if V_g > 0), and in the case of negative value of growth opportunities, E/P ratio will be higher than the capitalisation rate, k_e (i.e., E/P > k_e if V_g < 0). *E/P ratio will be equal to the capitalisation rate only if the value of growth opportunities is zero (i.e., E/P = k_e if V_g = 0).* As we have discussed earlier, the value of growth opportunities would be zero under two conditions: First, when a company produces a constant stream of earnings, which are entirely distributed. The dividend per share and the earnings per share would be same and remain constant. Second, when a company earns a rate of

return equal to the capitalisation rate (i.e., $r = k_e$) on the reinvested earnings. The reinvestment of earnings does not make any contribution to the share price in such cases because no net value is created.

Can P/E Ratio Mislead?

P/E ratio can mislead about the performance of a share. A high P/E ratio is considered good but it could be high not because the share price is high but because the earnings per share are quite low. Further, the interpretation of P/E ratio becomes meaningless because of the measurement problems of EPS (see Exhibit 3.4). A number of arbitrary assumptions and choices are made to estimate earnings. Accounting policies may be manipulated and changed which may distort the fair estimation of earnings. (The recent accounting scams involving Enron, WorldCom, Xerox etc. bear this out.) Earnings may also include non-cash items such as depreciation. Thus it is quite difficult to interpret EPS meaningfully and rely on EPS and P/E ratio as measures of performance.

EXHIBIT 3.1: MYTHS ABOUT EPS AND P/E RATIO: A MANAGER'S VIEWS

The following is taken from the Statement of the Chairman, Voltas Limited (39th Annual Report, 1992–93):

- …a little digression on the curious attachment of Indian commentators to EPS (Earnings Per Share) and its counterpart P/E (Price – Earnings) ratio. While every measure of financial performance has its pros and cons so that an ideal, easily understandable and widely acceptable single ratio still eludes us, to me EPS appears to be particularly deficient one. A company's current Earnings Per Share is so dependent on its past policies on dividend distribution, bonus declarations, premia charged on share issues, debt-equity ratio and other factors as to make EPS almost deceptive. Conservative policies on bonus issues, large premia on new issues and the like can inflate EPS and create an illusory impression of the real significance of a high dividend rate. So also since EPS is one element of the Price/Earnings ratios; P/E in India means something very different from its implications in many other countries—such as the US—where earnings are calculated on shareholders funds or Net Worth, of course, excluding revaluation reserves and similar elements.

- …Managements should be accountable for the return on the entirety of shareholders' funds rather than on that portion which is represented by equity [paid-up] capital.

SUMMARY

- ❖ In this chapter we have applied the concept of present value to explain the value of bonds and shares. Like any other assets, the present value of a bond or a share is equal to the discounted value of the stream of cash flows—the discount

rate being the rate of return that investors expect from securities of comparable risk.

- ❖ Bonds or debentures are debt instruments or securities. In case of a bond/debenture the stream of cash flows consists

---

1. *Ibid.,* pp. 56–59.

of annual interest payments and repayment of principal. These flows are fixed and known. The value of the bond can be found by capitalising these flows at a rate of return, which reflects their risk. The market interest rate or yield is used as the discount rate in case of bonds (or debentures). The basic formula for the bond value is as follows:

$$B_0 = \sum_{t=1}^{n} \frac{INT_t}{(1+k_d)^t} + \frac{B_n}{(1+k_d)^n}$$

❖ When the price of a bond is given, a bond's yield to maturity or internal rate of return can be found by equating the present value of the bond's cash outflows with its price.

❖ Zero-interest bonds (called zero-coupon bonds in USA) do not have explicit rate of interest. They are issued for a discounted price; their issue price is much less than the face value. Therefore, they are also called deep-discount bonds. The basic discounting principles apply in determining the value or yield of these bonds.

❖ Preference shares have a preference over ordinary shareholders with regard to dividends. The preference dividend is specified and known. Similarly, in the case of irredeemable preference share the redemption or maturity value is also known. Preference share value can be determined in the same way as the bond value.

❖ Cash flows of an ordinary (or equity) share consist of the stream of dividends and terminal price of the share. Unlike the case of a bond, cash flows of a share are not known. Thus, the risk of holding a share is higher than the risk of a bond. Consequently, equity capitalisation rate will be higher than that of a bond. The general formula for the share valuation is as follows:

$$P_0 = \frac{DIV_1}{(1+k_e)^1} + \frac{DIV_2}{(1+k_e)^2} + \dots + \frac{DIV_1 + P_n}{(1+k_e)^n}$$

❖ As the time horizon, n, becomes very large (say, extends to infinity) the present value of future price approaches zero. Thus the term P_n disappears from the formula, and we can use the following equation to find the value of a share today:

$$P_0 = \sum_{t=1}^{n=\infty} \frac{DIV_1}{(1+k_e)^t}$$

❖ If dividends do not grow, then capitalising earnings can determine the share value. Under no-growth situation, earnings per share (EPS) will be equal to dividends per share (DIV) and the present value is obtained by capitalising earnings per share:

$$P_0 = \frac{DIV_1}{k_e} = \frac{EPS_1}{k_e}$$

❖ In practice, dividends do grow over years. If we assume dividends to grow at a constant rate, g, then $DIV_1 = DIV_0(1+g)$, $DIV_2 = DIV_1(1+g)$, $DIV_3 = DIV_2(1+g)$..., and the share price formula can be written as follows:

$$P_0 = \frac{DIV_1}{k_e - g}$$

❖ This formula is useful in calculating the equity capitalisation rate (k_e) when the price of the share (P_0) is known.

❖ Under the assumption of constant growth, the share value is equal to the capitalized value of earnings plus the value of growth opportunities as shown below:

$$P_0 = \frac{EPS_1}{k_e} + V_g$$

❖ The price of a 'growth stock' is not merely the capitalised value of earnings but it also includes the present value of growth opportunities.

❖ Given a firm's EPS, ROE, the equity capitalisation rate, retention ratio and constant growth, the growth opportunities can be valued as follows:

$$V_g = \frac{NPV_1}{k_e - g} = \frac{b \times EPS_1(ROE - k_e)}{k_e(k_e - g)}$$

❖ We can also rewrite the formula to obtain relationship between the earnings-price ratio and capitalisation rate as follows:

$$E/P \text{ ratio} = \frac{EPS_1}{P_0} = k_e\left[1 - \frac{V_g}{P_0}\right]$$

❖ The E/P ratio will equal the capitalisation rate only when growth opportunities are zero, otherwise it will either over-estimate or under-estimate the capitalisation rate.

KEY CONCEPTS

Bond	Earnings capitalisation	Growth	Preference shares
Book value	Earnings-price (E/P) ratio	Growth shares	Present value
Capital gains	Earnings yield	Income shares	Price-earnings (P/E) ratio
Constant-growth model	Efficient capital markets	Interest rate risk	Real assets
Convertible debentures	Equity shares	Interest rate structure	Redeemable preference share
Convertible preference shares	Equivalent risk shares	Intrinsic value	Replacement value
Coupon rate	Expected rate of return	Irredeemable preference share	Supernormal growth
Debenture	Fair value	Liquidation value	Value of growth opportunities
Dividend capitalisation	Financial assets	Market value	Yield to maturity
Dividend yield	Going concern value	Perpetual bonds	

ILLUSTRATIVE SOLVED PROBLEMS

Problem 3.1: (*a*) A Rs 100 perpetual bond is currently selling for Rs 95. The coupon rate of interest is 13.5 per cent and the appropriate discount rate is 15 per cent. Calculate the value of the bond. Should it be bought? What is its yield at maturity?

(*b*) A company proposes to sell ten-year debentures of Rs 10,000 each. The company would repay Rs 1,000 at the end of every year and will pay interest annually at 15 per cent on the outstanding amount. Determine the present value of the debenture issue if the capitalisation rate is 16 per cent.

Solution:

(*a*) Value of bond $= \dfrac{\text{INT}}{k_d} = \dfrac{13.5}{0.15} = \text{Rs } 90$

The bond is overvalued; therefore, it should not be bought.

$$\text{Yield to maturity} = \frac{\text{Interest}}{\text{Current value of bond}} = \frac{13.5}{95}$$

$$= 0.142 \text{ or } 14.2 \text{ per cent}$$

(*b*) The cash flow of the company every year will be Rs 1,000 plus interest on outstanding amount. The present value is determined as follows:

Year (1)	Interest (Rs) (2)	Repayment (Rs) (3)	Cash flow (Rs) (4) = (2) + (3)	PV factor 16% (5)	Present value (Rs) (6) = (4) × (5)
1	1,500	1,000	2,500	0.862	2,155.00
2	1,350	1,000	2,350	0.743	1,746.05
3	1,200	1,000	2,200	0.641	1,410.20
4	1,050	1,000	2,050	0.552	1,131.60
5	900	1,000	1,900	0.476	904.40
6	750	1,000	1,750	0.410	717.50
7	600	1,000	1,600	0.354	566.40
8	450	1,000	1,450	0.305	442.25
9	300	1,000	1,300	0.263	341.90
10	150	1,000	1,150	0.227	261.05
			Present value of debenture		9,676.35

Problem 3.2: The managing director of a company decides that his company will not pay any dividends till he survives. His current life expectancy is 20 years. After that time it is expected that the company could pay dividends of Rs 30 per share indefinitely. At present the firm could afford to pay Rs 5 per share forever. The required rate of this company's shareholders is 10 per cent. What is the current value of the share? What is the cost to each shareholder of the managing director's policy?

Solution: The value of the share at the end of 20 years is

$$P_{20} = \frac{30}{0.10} = \text{Rs } 300$$

The value today will be

$$P_0 = \frac{300}{(1.1)^{20}} = 300(0.1486) = \text{Rs } 44.58$$

If the company could pay dividends of Rs 5 per share forever from the beginning, the price would be

$$P_0 = \frac{5}{0.10} = \text{Rs } 50$$

Thus, the cost to each shareholder is the lost of the difference of two prices:

$$\text{Rs } 50 - \text{Rs } 44.58 = \text{Rs } 5.42 \text{ per share}$$

Problem 3.3: A company is currently paying a dividend of Rs 2.00 per share. The dividend is expected to grow at a 15 per cent annual rate for three years, then at 10 per cent rate for the next three years, after which it is expected to grow at a 5 per cent, rate forever. (*a*) What is the present value of the share if the capitalisation rate is 9 per cent? (*b*) If the share is held for three years, what shall be its present value?

Solution:

(*a*) PV during super-normal growth period:

Year	Dividend (Rs)	PVF at 9% (Rs)	PVF Dividends (Rs)
1	$2.00 (1.15)^1 = 2.30$	0.917	2.11
2	$2.00 (1.15)^2 = 2.64$	0.842	2.22
3	$2.00 (1.15)^3 = 3.04$	0.772	2.35
4	$3.04 (1.10)^1 = 3.35$	0.708	2.37
5	$3.04 (1.10)^2 = 3.68$	0.650	2.39
6	$3.04 (1.10)^3 = 4.05$	0.596	2.41
			13.85

$$\text{PV at the end of year } 6 = \frac{\text{DIV}_1}{k_e - g} = \frac{4.05(1.05)}{0.09 - 0.05}$$

$$= \frac{4.25}{0.04} = \text{Rs } 106.25$$

PV of Rs 106.25 today at 9 per cent discount rate = Rs 106.25 (0.596) = Rs 63.33

PV of the share today = Rs 13.85 + 63.33 = Rs 77.18

(*b*) Present value of the share at the end of year 3 will be equal to the discounted value of dividends expected after three years. Thus,

$$P_3 = \text{Rs } 2.37 + \text{Rs } 2.39 + \text{Rs } 2.41 + \text{Rs } 63.33 = \text{Rs } 70.50$$

Present value of dividends expected at the end of years 1, 2 and 3

$$= \text{Rs } 2.11 + \text{Rs } 2.22 + \text{Rs } 2.35 = \text{Rs } 6.68$$

The present value of share today, i.e., P_0 = Rs 70.50 + Rs 6.68 = Rs 77.18. Thus, the value is the same if the share is held for three years, instead of indefinitely.

Problem 3.4: A company expects to pay a dividend of Rs 7 next year that is expected to grow at 6 per cent. It retains 30 per cent of earnings. Assume a capitalisation rate of 10 per cent. You are required to (*a*) calculate the expected earnings per share next year (EPS), (*b*) return on equity (ROE), and (*c*) the value of growth opportunities.

Solution: $DIV_1 = (1-b)EPS_1$

(*a*) $$EPS_1 = \frac{DIV}{1-b} = \frac{7}{1-0.3} = Rs\ 10$$

$$g = ROE \times b$$

(*b*) $$ROE = \frac{g}{b} = \frac{0.06}{0.3} = 0.20\ or\ 20\%$$

(*c*) Price of the share with zero-growth:

$$P_0 = \frac{EPS_1}{k_e}$$

$$\frac{10}{0.10} = Rs\ 100$$

Price of the share with 6% growth:

$$P_0 = \frac{DIV_1}{k_e - g} = \frac{7}{0.10 - 0.06} = Rs\ 175$$

Value of growth opportunities: Rs 175 – Rs 100 = Rs 75
Alternatively, the value of growth opportunities can be calculated as follows:

$$V_g = \frac{b\,EPS_1(ROE - k_e)}{k_e(k_e - g)} = \frac{0.3 \times 10(0.2 - 0.1)}{0.10\,(0.10 - 0.06)}$$

$$= \frac{0.3}{0.004} = Rs\ 75$$

Problem 3.5: The price of a company's share is Rs 80, and the value of growth opportunities is Rs 20. If the company's capitalisation rate is 15 per cent, what is the earnings-price ratio? How much is earnings per share?

Solution: $P_0 = \dfrac{EPS_1}{k_e} + V_g$

$$\frac{EPS_1}{P_0} = k_e\left[1 - \frac{V_e}{P_0}\right]$$

$$= 0.15\left[1 - \frac{20}{80}\right]$$

$$= 0.15(1 - 0.25) = 0.1125\ or\ 11.25\%$$

$$\frac{EPS_1}{80} = 0.1125$$

$$EPS_1 = 80 \times 0.1125 = Rs\ 9$$

Problem 3.6: A company's current price of share is Rs 60 and dividend per share is Rs 4. If its capitalisation rate is 12 per cent, what is the dividend growth rate?

Solution: $P_0 = \dfrac{DIV_1}{k_e - g} = \dfrac{DIV(1+g)}{k_e - g}$

$$60 = \frac{4(1+g)}{0.12 - g}$$

$$7.2 - 60g = 4 + 4g$$

$$-64g = -3.2$$

$$g = -3.2/-64 = 0.05\ or\ 5\%$$

REVIEW QUESTIONS

1. Explain the concept of valuation of securities? Why is the valuation concept relevant for financial decision-making purposes?
2. What is a bond? Is it same as a debenture? What are the features of a bond?
3. Illustrate the method of valuing (*i*) bonds in perpetuity and (*ii*) bonds with maturity.
4. What is the interest rate risk? How are values of bonds affected when the market rate of interest changes? Illustrate your answer.
5. Define a yield curve. What are the reasons for an upward sloping yield curve? What is an inverted yield curve?
6. What is default risk and default risk premium? What is the relation between the default risk and credit ratings of bonds (or debentures)?
7. What is the difference between the valuation of a bond and of a preference share? Illustrate.
8. What is the meaning of the term yield to maturity for bonds and preference shares? Is it appropriate to talk of a yield to maturity on a preference share that has no specific maturity date?
9. What is an ordinary share? What are its features? How does it differ from a preference share and a debenture?
10. Explain in detail the method of valuing an ordinary share.
11. What is the perpetual growth model? What are its assumptions? Is this model applicable in a finite case?
12. Why are dividends important in determining the present value of a share? How would you account for the positive market value of a company's share, which currently pays no dividend?
13. What is the difference between the expected and the required rate of return in the context of ordinary shares? When would this difference banish?
14. Illustrate with the help of an example the linkage between share price and earnings. What is the importance of the price-earnings (P/E) ratio? What are its limitations?
15. What is meant by growth opportunities? How are they valued? Illustrate with an example.

PROBLEMS

1. Suppose you buy a one-year government bond that has a maturity value of Rs 1,000. The market interest rate is 8 per cent. (*a*) How much will you pay for the bond? (*b*) If you purchased the bond for Rs 904.98, what interest rate will be you earn on your investment?

2. The Brightways Company has a perpetual bond that pay Rs 140 interest annually. The current yield on this type of bond is 13 per cent. (*a*) At what price will it sell? (*b*) If the required yield rises to 15 per cent, what will be the new price?

3. The Nutmate Limited has a ten-year debenture that pays Rs 140 annual interest. Rs 1,000 will be paid on maturity. What will be the value of the debenture if the required rate of interest is (*a*) 12 per cent, (*b*) 14 per cent and (*c*) 16 per cent?

4. What will be the yield of a 16 per cent perpetual bond with Rs 1,000 par value, when the current price is (*a*) Rs 800, (*b*) Rs 1,300 or (*c*) Rs 1,000?

5. You are considering bonds of two companies. Taxco's bond pays interest at 12 per cent and Maxco's at 6 per cent per year. Both have face value of Rs 1,000 and maturity of three years. (*a*) What will be the values of bonds if the market interest rate is 9 per cent? (*b*) What will be the values of the bonds if the market interest rate increases to 12 per cent? (*c*) Which bond declines more in the value when the interest rate rises? What is the reason? (*d*) If the interest rate falls to 6 per cent, what are the values of bonds? (*e*) If the maturity of two bonds is 8 years (rather than 3 years), what will be the values of two bonds if the market interest rate is (*a*) 9 per cent, (*b*) 6 per cent and (*c*) 12 per cent?

6. Three bonds have face value of Rs 1,000, coupon rate of 12 per cent and maturity of 5 years. One pays interest annually, one pays interest half-yearly, and one pays interest quarterly. Calculate the prices of bonds if the required rate of return is (*a*) 10 per cent, (*b*) 12 per cent and (*c*) 16 per cent.

7. On 31 March 2003, Hind Tobacco Company issued Rs 1,000 face value bonds due 31 March 2013. The company will not pay any interest on the bond until 31 March 2008. The half-yearly interest is payable from 31 December 2008; the annual rate of interest will be 12 per cent. The bonds will be redeemed at 5 per cent premium on maturity. What is the value of the bond if the required rate of return is 14 per cent?

8. Determine the market values of the following bonds, which pay interest semi-annually:

Bond	Interest Rate	Required Rate	Maturity Period (Years)
A	16%	15%	25
B	14%	13%	15
C	12%	8%	20
D	12%	8%	10

9. If the par values of bonds are Rs. 100 and if they are currently selling for Rs 95, Rs 100, Rs 110 and Rs 115, respectively, determine the effective annual yields of the bonds? Also calculate the semi-annual yields?

10. A 20-year 10% Rs 1,000 bond that pays interest half-yearly is redeemable (callable) in twelve years at a buy-back (call) price of Rs 1,150. The bond's current yield to maturity is 9.50% annually. You are required to determine (*i*) the yield to call, (*ii*) the yield to call if the buy-back price is only Rs 1,100, and (*iii*) the yield to call if instead of twelve years the bond can be called in eight years, buy-back price being Rs 1,150.

11. A fertiliser company holds 15-year 15% bond of ICICI Bank Ltd. The interest is payable quarterly. The current market price of the bond is Rs 875. The company is going through a bad patch and has accumulated a substantial amount of losses. It is negotiating with the bank the restructuring of debt. Recently he interest rates have fallen and there is a possibility that the bank will agree for reducing the interest rate to 12 per cent. It is expected that the company will be able service debt t the reduce interest rates. Calculate stated and the expected yields to maturity?

12. You are thinking of buying BISCO's a preference share Rs 100 par value that will pay a dividend of 12 per cent perpetually. (*a*) What price should you pay for the preference share if you are expecting a return of 10 per cent? (*b*) Suppose that BISCO can buy back the share at a price of Rs 110 in seven years. What maximum price should you pay for the preference share?

13. The share of Premier Limited will pay a dividend of Rs 3 per share after a year. It is currently selling at Rs 50, and it is estimated that after a year the price will be Rs 53. What is the present value of the share if the required rate of return is 10 percent? Should the share be bought? Also calculate the return on share if it is bought, and sold after a year.

14. An investor is looking for a four-year investment. The share of Skylark Company is selling for Rs 75. They have plans to pay a dividend of Rs 7.50 per share each at the end of first and second years and Rs 9 and Rs 15 respectively at the end of third and fourth years. If the investor's capitalisation rate is 12 percent and the share's price at the end of fourth year is Rs 70, what is the value of the share? Would it be a desirable investment?

15. A company's share is currently selling at Rs 60. The company in the past paid a constant dividend of Rs 1.50 per share, but it is now expected to grow at 10 per cent compound rate over a very long period. Should the share be purchased if required rate of return is 12 per cent?

16. The earnings of a company have been growing at 15 per cent over the past several years and are expected to increase at this rate for the next seven years and thereafter,

at 9 per cent in perpetuity. It is currently earning Rs 4 per share and paying Rs 2 per share as dividend. What shall be the present value of the share with a discount rate of 12 per cent for the first seven years and 10 per cent thereafter?

17. A company retains 60 per cent of its earnings, which are currently Rs 5 per share. Its investment opportunities promise a return of 15 per cent. What price should be paid for the share if the required rate of return is 13 per cent? What is the value of growth opportunities? What is the expected rate of return from the share if its current market price is Rs 60?

18. The total assets of Rs 80,000 of a company are financed by equity funds only. The internal rate of return on assets is 10 per cent. The company has a policy of retaining 70 per cent of its profits. The capitalisation rate is 12 per cent. The company has 10,000 shares outstanding. Calculate the present value per share.

19. A prospective investor is evaluating the share of Ashoka Automobiles Company. He is considering three scenarios. Under first scenario the company will maintain to pay its current dividend per share without any increase or decrease. Another possibility is that the dividend will grow at an annual (compound) rate of 6 per cent in perpetuity. Yet another scenario is that the dividend will grow at a high rate of 12 per cent per year for the first three years; a medium rate of 7 per cent for the next three years and thereafter, at a constant rate of 4 per cent perpetually. The last year's dividend per share is Rs 3 and the current market price of the share is Rs 80. If the investor's required rate of return is 10 per cent, calculate the value of the share under each of the assumptions. Should the share be purchased?

20. Vikas Engineering Ltd. has current dividend per share of Rs 5, which has been growing at an annual rate of 5 per cent. The company is expecting significant technical improvement and cost reduction in its operations, which would increase growth rate to 10 per cent. Vikas' capitalisation rate is 15 per cent. You are required to calculate (a) the value of the share assuming the current growth rate; and (b) the value of the share if the company achieves technical improvement and cost reduction. Does the price calculated in (b) make a logical sense? Why?

21. Consider the following data of four auto (two / three-wheelers) companies.

Companies	EPS (Rs)	DIV (%)	Share Price (Rs)
1. Bajaj	11.9	50	275.00
2. Hero Honda	10.2	22	135.00
3. Kinetic	12.0	25	177.50
4. Maharashtra Scooters	20.1	25	205.00

The face value of each company's share is Rs 10. Explain the relative performance of the four companies.

22. The dividend per share of Skyjet Company has grown from Rs 3.5 to Rs 10.5 over past 10 years. The share is currently selling for Rs 75. Calculate Skyjet's capitalisation rate.

23. Rama Tours and Travels Limited has current earnings per share of Rs 8.60, which has been growing at 12 per cent. The growth rate is expected to continue in future. Rama has a policy of paying 40 per cent of its earnings as dividend. If its capitalisation rate is 18 per cent, what is the value of the share? Also calculate value of growth opportunities.

24. A company has the following capital in its balance sheet: (a) 12-year 12% secured debentures of Rs 1,000 each; principal amount Rs 50 crore (10 million = crore); the required rate of return (on debentures of similar risk) 10 per cent; (b) 10-year 14% unsecured debentures of Rs 1,000 each; principal amount Rs 30 crore; interest payable half-yearly; the required rate of return 12 per cent; (c) preference share of Rs 100 each; preference dividend rate 15% principal amount Rs 100 crore; required rate of return 13.5 per cent; and (d) ordinary share capital of Rs 200 crore at Rs 100 each share; expected dividend next year, Rs 12; perpetual dividend growth rate 8 per cent; the required rate of return 15 per cent. Calculate the market values of all securities.

25. Satya Systems Company has made net profit of Rs 50 crore. It has announced to distribute 60 per cent of net profit as dividend to shareholders. It has 2 crore ordinary shares outstanding. The company's share is currently selling at Rs 240. In the past, it had earned return on equity of 25 per cent and expects to main this profitability in the future as well. What is the required rate of return on Satya's share?

26. A company has net earnings of Rs 25 million (1 crore = 10 million). Its paid-up share capital is Rs 200 million and the par value of share is Rs 10. If the company makes no new investments, its earnings are expected to grow at 2 per cent per year indefinitely. It does have an investment opportunity of investing Rs 10 million that would generate annual net earnings of Rs 2 million (1 million = 10 lakh) for next 15 years. The company's opportunity cost of capital is 10 per cent. You are required: (a) to find the share value if the company does not make the investment; (b) to calculate the proposed investment's NPV; and (c) to determine the share value if the investment is undertaken?

27. Gujarat Bijali Ltd. has earnings of Rs 80 crore and it has 5 crore shares outstanding. It has a project that will produce net earnings of Rs 20 crore after one year. Thereafter, earnings are expected to grow at 8 per cent per annum indefinitely. The company's required rate of return is 12.5 per cent. Find the P/E ratio.

28. Symphony Limited is an all-equity financed company. It has 10 million shares outstanding, and is expected to earn net cash profits of Rs 80 million. Shareholders of the

company have an opportunity cost of capital of 20 per cent. (*a*) Determine the company share price if it retained 40 per cent of profits and invested these funds to earn 20 per cent return. Will the share price be different if the firm retained 60 per cent profits to earn 20 per cent? (*b*) What will be the share price if investments made by the company earn 24 per cent and it retains 40 per cent of profits? Will share price change if retention is 60 per cent?

29. Sonata Company has no investment opportunities. It expects to earn cash earnings per share of Rs 10 perpetually and distribute entire earnings as dividends to shareholders.(*a*) What is the value of the share if shareholders' opportunity cost of capital is 15 per cent? (*b*) Suppose the company discovers an opportunity to expand its existing business. It estimates that it will need to invest 50 per cent of its earnings annually for ten years to produce 18 per cent return. Management does not foresee any growth after this ten-year period. What will be Sonata's share price if shareholders' opportunity cost of capital is 15 per cent?

CASES

Case 3.1: Shyamulu Rao's Investment Decision

Ashoka Infotech Ltd. is a new company. It has come up with the initial public issue. The issue price of the share is Rs 20 and the par value is Rs 10. Shyamulu Rao, a prospective investor, is considering investing Rs 50,000 in Ashoka Infotech's shares. He is not sure about the returns from his investment. His required rate of return is 15 per cent. Since Ashoka Infotech is a new company, he would like to hold the shares for 10 years before he sells them. As regards the dividend payment by the company, he visualises four possibilities. First, the company may reinvest all its earnings and may not pay any dividend. Second, the company may pay a constant dividend of Rs 3. Third, the company may start with a dividend of Rs 1 per share, which may grow at a constant rate of 10 per cent. Fourth, the company may start paying a dividend of Rs 1.6 per share, which may grow at 15 per cent for the first five years and at 10 per cent thereafter. Shyamulu expects different share prices after 10 years under the four alternatives. The expected earnings per share in year 1 in the normal situation will be Rs 3.

Shyamulu Rao can also invest his money in bonds. A government-owned financial institution is offering Rs 10,000 face value bonds with 10-year maturity at Rs 2,720. He is also considering bonds issued by Reliable Fertiliser Company. These are 15 per cent Rs 1,000 bonds with 10-year maturity. The company will redeem bonds at Rs 1,100 on maturity.

Discussion Questions

1. How much would be Shyamulu's return if he invests his money in Ashoka Infotech's shares?
2. What is his return from the bonds of the (*i*) financial institution and (*ii*) Reliable Fertilise?
3. What should Shyamulu do?

Case 3.2: Hitech Chem Limited

Two IIT graduates founded Hitech Chem Limited as a research and development company in the early eighties as a private limited company. Founders and their family members closely held the company for almost a decade. The fast growth in the business of the company led the founders to convert the company as a public limited company to access capital from the markets.

The initial public issue of the company was at a premium of 30 per cent and the par value was Rs 10 per share. From the inception, the company specialised in the development of speciality chemicals. The rights to manufacture of the two-thirds of products developed by the company are sold to large public and private sectors companies. The remaining one-third products are manufactured and sold by the company itself. The shares of the company are listed on the Bombay Stock Exchange. Hitech Chem has P/E ratio of 18.5:1 as compared to the industry average of 21.75:1. The average P/E ratio of the entire chemical industry is lower at 15:1.

Table 3.1.1 shows the balance sheet of the company as on 31 March 2004.

Table 3.1.1: Hitech Chem Limited: Balance Sheet as at 31 March 2004

(Rs in million)

Assets & Liabilities	*Rs*	*Rs*	*Rs*
Assets			
Fixed assets			
Land, building & plant	3,750		
Goodwill & patents	8,750		12,000
Current assets			
Stock	4,500		
Debtors	1,750		
Bank & cash balance	250	6,500	
Less: Current liabilities			
Trade creditors	600		
15% Bank loan/overdraft	1,400	2,000	
Net current assets			4,500
Net Assets			16,500
Liabilities & Capital			
Shareholders' Funds			
Ordinary shares capital	7,500		
Share premium	2,250		
General reserves	3,750		13,500
12% Long-term loan			3,000
Capital Employed			16,500

---

1. Brealey and Myers, *op. cit.*, p. 57.

The company's annual capital expenditure is Rs 300 million. The average straight-line depreciation rate on fixed tangible assets is 10 per cent. Intangible assets are amortised over a five-year period. The rate of corporate tax is 35 per cent.

Hitech Chem operates in an unstable business environment and its sales fluctuate quite a lot. During the past five years, its average sales were Rs 15,000 million and the standard deviation of sales was 33 per cent. In the current financial year, Hitech Chem's sales were Rs 21,500 million. It earned a PBIT-to-sales ratio of 22 per cent. The company has recently revalued its tangible fixed assets at Rs 6,500 million. Since Hitech Chem is R&D-based company, it has a few patents worth Rs 2,000 million (book value) and about one-fourth of Hitech Chem's sales come from these patents. All these patents would expire within less than a year. The company has been suffering a backlog in its orders. About half of the stocks represent products for which firm has no firm order.

Discussion Questions

1. What is Hitech Chem's value? Show calculations under different methods. Explain the differences in the values.
2. In your opinion, how does stock market value companies like Hitech Chem?

CHAPTER

4 Risk and Return: An Overview of Capital Market Theory

CHAPTER OBJECTIVES

- Discuss the concepts of average and expected rates of return
- Define and measure risk for individual assets
- Show the steps in the calculation of standard deviation and variance of returns
- Explain the concept of normal distribution and the importance of standard deviation
- Compute historical average return of securities and market premium
- Determine the relationship between risk and return
- Highlight the difference between relevant and irrelevant risks

INTRODUCTION

Risk and return are most important concepts in finance. In fact, they are the foundation of the modern finance theory. What is risk? How is it measured? What is return? How is it measured? Other related questions are: how are assets valued in capital markets? How do investors make their investment decisions? We attempt to answer these questions in this chapter.

RETURN ON A SINGLE ASSET

India Cements is a large company with several thousand shareholders. Suppose you bought 100 shares of the company at the beginning of the year at a market price of Rs 225. The par value of each share is Rs 10. Your total investment is cash that you paid out. That is,

Investment: Rs 225 × 100 = Rs 22,500

Rupee returns Suppose during the year, India Cements paid a dividend at 25 per cent. As the dividend rate applies to the par value of the share, your dividend per share would be: Rs 10 × 25% = Rs 2.50, and total dividend would be:

Dividend = (Dividend rate × Par value) × Number of shares
Dividend = Dividend per share × Number of shares
Dividend = Rs 2.50 × 100 = Rs 250

Further, suppose the price of the share at the end of the year turns out to be Rs 267.50. Since the ending share price increased, you have made a capital gain:

Capital gain (loss) = (Selling price − Buying price) × Number of shares
Capital gain (loss) = (Rs 267.50 − Rs 225) × 100 = Rs 4,250

Your total return is:

Total return = Dividend + Capital gain

Total return = Rs 250 + Rs 4,250 = Rs 4,500

If you sold your shares at the end of the year, your cash inflows would be the dividend income plus the proceeds from the sale of shares:

Cash flow at the end of the year

= Dividends + Value of sold shares

= Rs 250 + (Rs 267.50 × 100) = Rs 27,000

This amount equals to your initial investment of Rs 22,500 plus the total return of Rs 4,500: Rs 22,500 + Rs 4,500 = Rs 27,000.

Percentage returns It is more common and convenient to express returns in percentage terms. You earned a total return of Rs 4,500 on an investment of Rs 22,500. You can express your return in percentage term as given below

$$\text{Return in percentage} = \frac{\text{Rs } 4,500}{\text{Rs } 22,500} = 0.20 \text{ or } 20\%$$

Percentage returns are frequently calculated on per share basis. We have seen in the example above that returns from each share have two components: the dividend income and the capital gain. Hence, the rate of return on a share would consist of the **dividend yield** and the **capital gain yield**.[1] The **rate of return** of a share held for one year is as follows:

Rate of return = Dividend yield + Capital gain yield

$$R_1 = \frac{DIV_1}{P_0} + \frac{P_1 - P_0}{P_0} = \frac{DIV_1 + (P_1 - P_0)}{P_0} \quad (1)$$

R_1 is the rate of return in year 1, DIV_1 is dividend per share received in year 1, P_0 is the price of the share in the beginning of the year and P_1 is the price of the share at the end of the year. Dividend yield is the percentage of dividend income, and it is given by dividing the dividend per share at the end the year by the share price in the beginning of the year; that is, DIV_1/P_0. Capital gain is the difference of the share price at the end and the share price in the beginning divided by the share price in the beginning; that is, $(P_1 - P_0)/P_0$. If the ending price were less than the beginning price, there would be a negative capital gain or capital loss.

In the example of India Cements, your rate of return would be as follows:

$$R = \frac{2.5}{225} + \frac{(267.50 - 225)}{225} = 0.011 + 0.189 = 0.20 \text{ or } 20\%$$

The total return of 20 per cent on your investment is made up of 1.1 per cent dividend yield and 18.9 per cent capital gain. What would be your return if the market price of India Cements' share were Rs 200 after a year? The expected rate of return would be:

$$R = \frac{2.5}{225} + \frac{200 - 225}{225} = 0.011 - 0.111 = -0.10 \text{ or } -10\%$$

You would earn a negative rate of return (–10 per cent) because of the capital loss (negative capital gain). The return of a share significantly depends on the change in its share price. The market price of a share shows wide fluctuations. Hence investment in shares is risky. The risk of a security depends on the volatility of its returns.

Unrealised capital gain or loss If an investor holds a share and does not sell it at the end of a period, the difference between the beginning and ending share prices is the unrealised capital gain (or loss). The investor must consider the unrealised capital gain (or loss) as part of her total return. The fact of the matter is that if the investor so wanted, she could have sold the share and *realised* the capital gain (or loss).

Annual Rates of Return: Example of Hindustan Lever Limited (HLL)

The rate of return of a share may be calculated for a period longer than one year. Let us consider HLL's data of the market prices and dividend per share for the 10-year period from 1992 to 2001 to calculate the annual rates of return. Table 4.1 shows calculations.

Table 4.1: HLL's Annual Rates of Return, 1992-2001

Year	Share Price (Rs) P_t	Capital Gain (%) $P_t/P_{t-1}-1$	Dividend Per Share (Rs), DIV_t	Dividend Yield (%) DIV_t/P_{t-1}	Rate of Return (%)
1991	24.75	—	—	—	—
1992	55.50	124.24	6.30	25.46	149.70
1993	86.25	55.41	8.40	15.14	70.54
1994	88.50	2.61	12.00	13.91	16.52
1995	93.60	5.76	15.00	16.95	22.71
1996	121.20	29.49	18.75	20.03	49.52
1997	207.60	71.29	25.50	21.04	92.33
1998	249.60	20.23	33.00	15.90	36.13
1999	337.50	35.22	43.50	17.42	52.64
2000	309.60	–8.27	52.50	15.56	7.29
2001	322.20	4.07	27.50	8.88	12.95
Average	187.16	34.00	24.25	17.03	51.03

* In July 1991 the company issued bonus shares in the ratio of 1:2. Data are adjusted for bonus issues.

Figure 4.1 plots the histogram of the year-to-year total returns on HLL share shown in Table 4.1. The heights of the bars on the horizontal axis indicate the size of returns. The yearly returns show wide variations. During the 10-year period, the highest return of 149.70 per cent was obtained in 1992 and lowest return of 7.29 per cent was obtained in 2000.

Average Rate of Return

Given the yearly returns, we can calculate average or mean return.

---

1. For a simple treatment of return and risk concepts and CAPM, see, Mullins, D.W., *Does the Capital Asset Pricing Model Work? Harvard Business Recent*, Jan-Feb. 1982, and Butters, J.K., *et. al. Case Problems in Finance*, Richard D. Irwin, 1991.

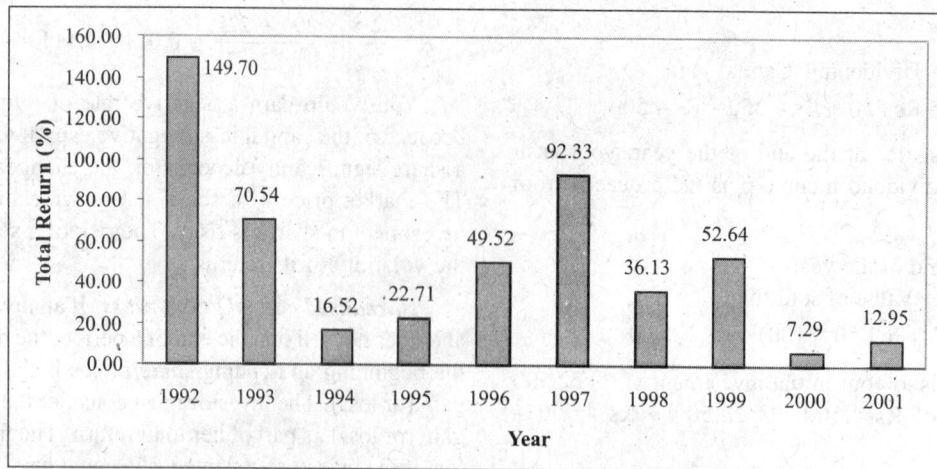

Figure 4.1: Year-to-year total returns on HLL share

The **average rate of return** is the sum of the various one-period rates of return divided by the number of periods. The average rate of return of HLL's shares for ten years can be calculated as the sum of yearly rates divided by the number of years as shown below:

$$\bar{R} = \frac{1}{10}[149.70 + 70.54 + 16.52 + 22.71 + 49.52 + 92.33$$
$$+ 36.13 + 52.64 + 7.29 + 12.95]$$
$$= \frac{1}{10}[5103] = 51.03$$

The **simple arithmetic average** or mean of HLL's 10 annual returns from 1992 to 2001 is about 51 per cent. The formula for the average rate of return is as follows.

$$\bar{R} = \frac{1}{n}[R_1 + R_2 + ... + R_n] = \frac{1}{n}\sum_{t=1}^{n} R_t \qquad (2)$$

$\bar{R}$ is the average rate of return; R_t the observed or realised rates of return in periods 1, 2... t and n the total number of periods.

Rates of Return and Holding Periods

Investors may hold their investment in shares for longer periods than for one year. How do we calculate **holding-period returns**? Suppose you invest Rs 1 today in a company's share for five years. The rates of return are 18 per cent, 9 per cent, 0 per cent, –10 per cent and 14 per cent. What is the worth of your shares? You hold the share for five years; hence, you can calculate the worth of your investment assuming that each year dividends from the previous year are reinvested in shares. The worth of your investment after five years is:

Investment worth after five years
$$= (1 + 0.18) \times (1 + 0.09) \times (1 + 0.0) \times (1 - 0.10) \times (1 + 0.14)$$
$$= 1.18 \times 1.09 \times 1.00 \times 0.90 \times 1.14$$
$$= Rs\ 1.32$$

Your one rupee investment has grown to Rs 1.32 at the end of five years. Thus your total return is: 1.32 – 1 = 0.32 or 32 per cent. Your total return is a five-year holding-period return. How much is the annual compound rate of return? We can calculate the compound annual rate of return as follows:

Compound annual rate of return
$$= \sqrt[5]{1.18 \times 1.09 \times 1.00 \times 0.90 \times 1.14} - 1$$
$$= 1.057 - 1 = 0.057\ or\ 5.7\%$$

This compound rate of return is the **geometric mean return**. You can verify that one rupee invested today at 5.7 per cent compound rate would grow to approximately Rs 1.32 after five years: $(1.057)^5$ = Rs 1.32. Let us take another example. Suppose you invest Rs 1 in the beginning of 1993 in one share of HLL and hold it for two years. From Table 4.1 we see that returns for 1993 and 1994 are 16.52 per cent and 22.71 per cent. The worth of your investment at the end of two years is:

Investment worth after two years $= (1 + 0.1652) \times (1 + 0.2271)$
$$= 1.1652 \times 1.2271 = Rs\ 1.43$$

Your total return is 43 per cent. This is a *two-year holding-period return*. If you hold your one rupee investment in HLL's share at the end of 1991 for 10 years until the end of 2001, it would grow to Rs 41.7 by the end of 2001. Your 10-year holding return is a whopping 407 per cent! You can calculate holding period returns for any number of years.

RISK OF RATES OF RETURN: VARIANCE AND STANDARD DEVIATION

We can observe in Table 4.1 that the annual rates of return of HLL's share show wide fluctuations — ranging from 7.27 per cent in 2000 to 149.70 per cent in 1992. These fluctuations in returns were caused by the volatility of the share prices. The changes in dividends also contributed to the variability of HLL's rates of return. We can think of risk of returns as the variability in rates of return.

How could one measure the variability of rates of return of a share (or an asset)? The variability of rates of return may be defined as the extent of the deviations (or dispersion) of individual rates of return from the average rate of return. There are two measures of this dispersion: **variance** or **standard deviation**. Standard deviation is the square root of variance.

How to Calculate Variance and Standard Deviation

The following steps are involved in calculating variance or

standard deviation of rates of return of assets or securities using historical returns:

- Calculate the average rate of return using Equation (2), i.e.,

$$\overline{R} = \frac{1}{n} \sum_{t=1}^{n} R_t$$

- Calculate the deviation of individual rates of return from the average rate of return and square it, i.e.

$$(R_1 - \overline{R})^2$$

- Calculate the sum of the squares of the deviations as determined in the preceding step and divide it by the number of periods (or observations) less one to obtain variance, i.e.

$$\text{var} = \sigma^2 = \frac{1}{n-1} \sum_{t=1}^{n} (R_t - \overline{R})^2$$

In the case of sample of observations, we divide the sum of squares of the deviations by $n-1$ to account for the degree of freedom. If you were using population data, then the divider will be n.

- Calculate the square root of the variance to determine the standard deviation, i.e.,

$$\text{Standard deviation} = \sqrt{\text{Variance}}$$

$$\sigma = \sqrt{\sigma^2}$$

We can summarise the formulae calculating variance and standard deviation of historical rates of return of a share as follows:

$$\sigma^2 = \frac{1}{n-1} \sum_{t=1}^{n} (R_t - \overline{R})^2 \qquad (3)$$

$$\sigma = \sqrt{\sigma^2} = \sqrt{\frac{1}{n-1} \sum_{t=1}^{n} (R_t - \overline{R})^2} \qquad (4)$$

In Table 4.1 the ten annual rates of return for HLL's share are calculated. The average rate of return is 51.03 per cent. For HLL's rates of return sample of 10 years, you can calculate the variance and the standard deviation using Equations (3) and (4) as follows:

Variance (σ^2)

$$= \frac{1}{10-1} [(149.70 - 51.03)^2 + (70.54 - 51.03)^2$$
$$+ 16.52 - 51.03)^2 + (22.71 - 51.03)^2 + (49.52 - 51.03)^2$$
$$+ (92.33 - 51.03)^2 + (36.13 - 51.03)^2 + (52.64 - 51.03)^2$$
$$+ (7.29 - 51.03)^2 + (12.95 - 51.03)^2]$$

$$= \frac{1}{9} [1740.18] = 1,933.80$$

Standard deviation (σ) $= \sqrt{1,933.80} = 43.97\%$

The annual rates of return of HLL's share show a high degree of variability; they deviate on an average, by about 44 per cent from the average rate of return of 51.03 per cent. Can we use HLL's past returns as a guide for the future returns? It is difficult to say that past returns will help in assessing the future returns since HLL's returns are quite volatile. The actual rate of

---

Excel Application 4.1: Calculation of Variance and Standard Deviation

Columns B and C respectively give Jenson and Nicholson's dividend per share and share price for six years. You can enter a formula for calculating annual return in D3 as shown in the worksheet. Excel has built-in formulae to calculate average, variance and standard deviation. Let us enter formula for average in D8: = Average (D3:D7). We obtain 52 per cent as the 5-year average of Jenson and Nicholson's returns. Similarly, we can write formula for calculating variance in column D9: =Var(D3:D7) and for standard deviation in column D10: Stdev(D3:D7). We find that the standard deviation of returns is 54 per cent.

	A	B	C	D	E
1	Year	DIV	Price	Return	
2	19 x 1	1.53	31.25	-	
3	19 x 2	1.53	20.75	–28.7	=(B3+(C3-C2))/C2*100
4	19 x 3	1.53	30.88	56.2	
5	19 x 4	2.00	67.00	123.4	
6	19 x 5	2.00	100.00	52.2	
7	19 x 6	3.00	154.00	57.0	
8			Average	52.0	=Average(D3:D7)
9			Variance	2915.1	=Var(D3:D7)
10			Standard deviation	54.0	=Stdev(D3:D7)

---

return in any given period may significantly vary from the historical average rate of return.

Let us consider the example of another company, viz. Jenson and Nicholson and show the application of Excel.

HISTORICAL CAPITAL MARKET RETURNS

What rates of returns on shares and other financial instruments have investors in India earned? You can use indices for the share prices and other securities for this purpose. There are several share price indices available in India. The Bombay Stock Exchange and the National Stock Exchange provide a variety of share price indices. We use the Reserve Bank of India (RBI) data that are available from 1971 to 1998. We present year-by-year rates of return for the following financial instruments in India for the years from 1971 to 1998:

1. *Ordinary shares* We use the Reserve Bank of India Share Price Index since price and dividend yield data are available for a long period of time.
2. *Long-term government of India bonds* This is a portfolio of government of India bonds with maturity over 15 years.
3. *Call money market* This is a portfolio of inter-bank transactions.
4. *91-days treasury bills* This is a portfolio of treasury bills of three-month maturity. The return on 91-day treasury bills remained fixed (arbitrarily) at 4.60 per cent until 1993.

In Table 4.2 we present year-by-year rates of return on the

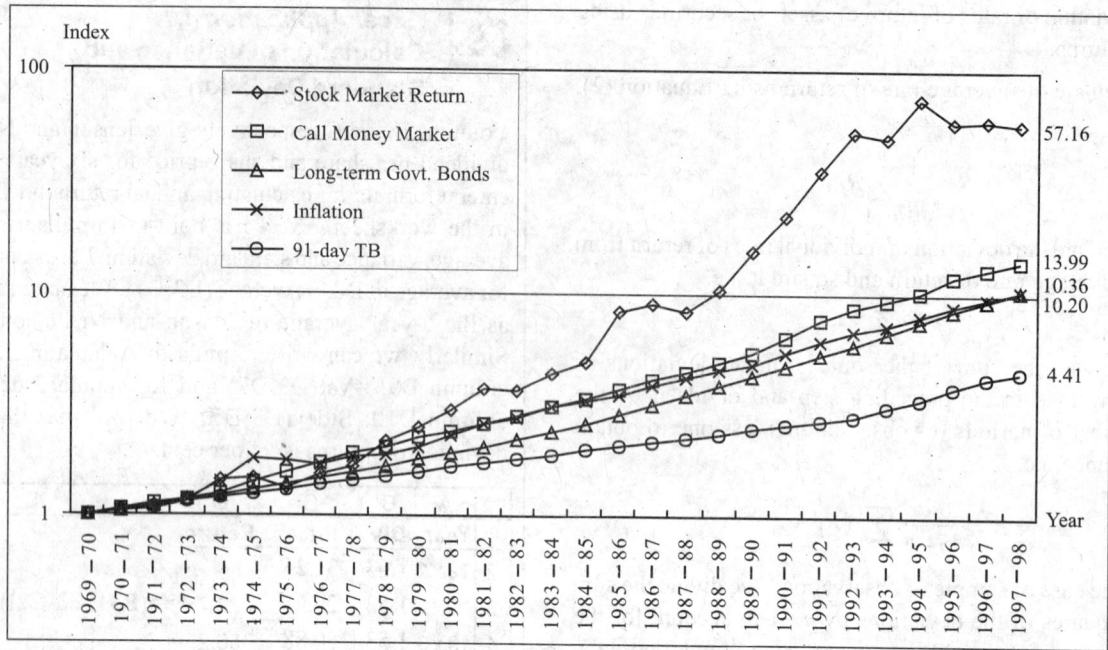

Figure 4.2: Investment worth of different portfolios, 1969–70 to 1997–98

Table 4.2: Year-by-Year Returns, 1970–71 to 1997–98

Year	Stock Market Return	Call Money Market Rate	Long-term Govt. Bonds Yield	91-Day T-bills Yields	Inflation Rate
1970–71	4.04	6.38	5.15	4.60	5.1
1971–72	1.27	5.16	5.37	4.60	3.2
1972–73	8.33	4.15	5.37	4.60	7.8
1973–74	25.53	7.83	5.37	4.60	20.8
1974–75	2.32	12.82	6.16	4.60	26.8
1975–76	−8.81	10.55	6.28	4.60	−1.3
1976–77	13.34	10.84	6.25	4.60	−3.8
1977–78	10.06	9.28	6.25	4.60	7.6
1978–79	28.29	7.57	6.43	4.60	2.2
1979–80	16.22	8.47	6.59	4.60	8.8
1980–81	18.08	7.12	6.97	4.60	11.4
1981–82	25.45	8.96	7.23	4.60	12.5
1982–83	−1.71	8.78	7.73	4.60	7.8
1983–84	19.38	8.63	8.24	4.60	12.6
1984–85	13.49	9.95	9.22	4.60	6.3
1985–86	68.25	10.00	9.94	4.60	6.8
1986–87	7.80	9.99	10.19	4.60	8.7
1987–88	−6.22	9.88	10.34	4.60	8.8
1988–89	23.88	9.77	10.55	4.60	9.4
1989–90	49.83	11.49	10.93	4.60	6.1
1990–91	42.81	15.85	11.45	4.60	11.6
1991–92	58.39	19.57	11.15	4.60	13.5
1992–93	49.63	14.42	10.65	4.60	9.6
1993–94	−5.93	6.99	13.14	8.90	7.5
1994–95	48.85	9.40	12.62	9.11	10.1
1995–96	−20.26	17.73	12.43	12.65	10.2
1996–97	0.44	7.84	11.60	9.67	9.4
1997–98	−2.73	8.69	11.09	6.83	6.8

portfolios of these securities from the year from 1970–71 to 1997–98. It is noticeable that the interest rate structure in India was regulated and controlled by the government until the nineties. The rates of return have become more market determined after deregulation. You may observe from Table 4.2 that the yield on 91-day treasury bills was fixed at 4.60 per cent until 1992–93. It is now market determined and represents a risk-free rate since there is no default risk. From Table 4.2, we can calculate holding period returns for any combination of years. In Figure 4.2 we show the worth of one rupee invested at the end of 1969–70 until 1997-98 for various securities. The figure shows that Re 1 invested in shares at the end of 1969–70 would have grown to Rs 57.16. The long-term government bonds rates and inflation rates have shown similar growth. In the call money market Re 1 investment would have grown to about Rs 14 in 1997–98. Since the yield on 91-day T-bills remained constant at 4.60 per cent until 1992–93, Re 1 investment in T-bills would grow only to Rs 4.41 in 1997–98. Hence the total returns from T-bills have been less than the growth in inflation.

Table 4.3: Returns: Average and Standard Deviations, 1970–71 to 1997–98

Securities	Arithmetic mean	Standard deviation	Risk premium*	Risk premium#
Ordinary shares (RBI Index)	17.50	22.34	12.04	8.76
Call money market	9.93	3.49	4.47	1.19
Long-term government bonds	8.74	2.59	3.28	
91-Day treasury bills	5.46	2.05		
Inflation	8.80	5.82		

* Relative to 91-Days T-bills. # Relative to long-term government bonds.

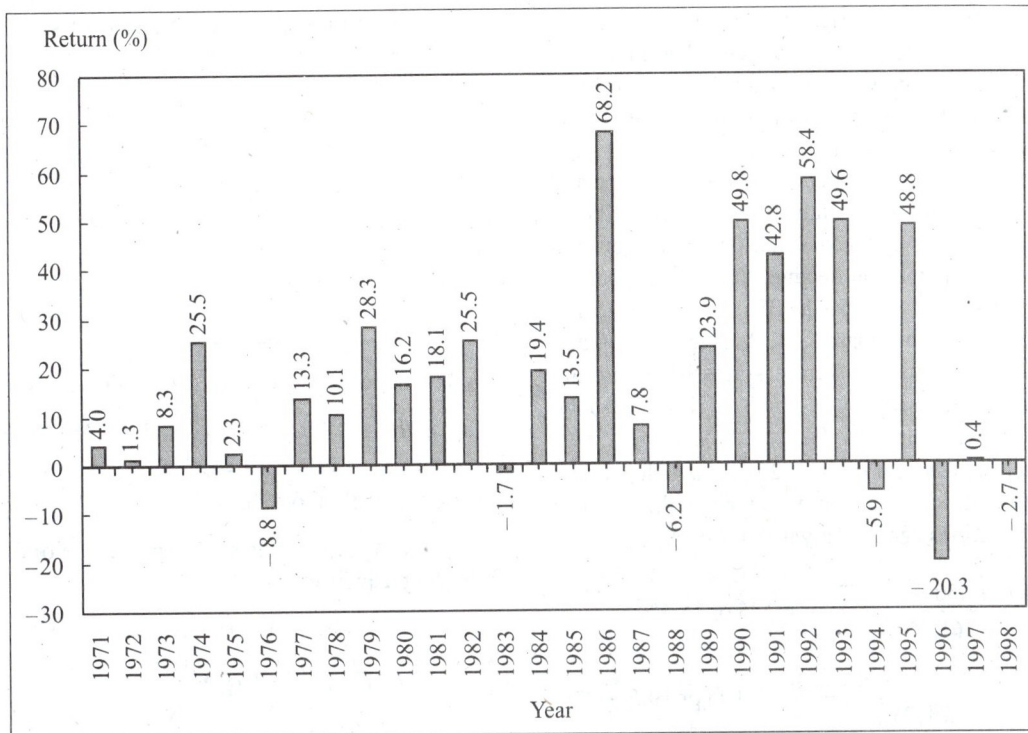

Figure 4.3: Year-to-year market (RBI Index) return, 1970–71 to 1997–98

We can summarise the historical capital-market returns by two numbers: the average return and the standard deviation. As we have explained earlier, standard deviation summarises variability and it is a measure of total risk. Table 4.3 gives these two numbers for different portfolio of securities. The table shows that the average return from stock market (RBI index) is not only highest (17.50%) but its variability is also highest (22.34%). The return from long-term government bonds is 8.74 per cent and its standard deviation is 2.59 per cent. The 91-day T-bills yield a return of 5.46 per cent with a standard deviation of 2.09 per cent.

Historical Risk Premium

We can compare the high-risk average return on the stock market with the low-risk average returns on the government securities. The risk-free government security is T-bills. It is free from risk of default and the variability on its returns is the lowest. The 28-year (from 1970–71 to 1997–98) average return on 91-day T-bills is 5.46 per cent, and the standard deviation of returns is 2.09 per cent. The 28-year average return on the stock market is higher by about 12 per cent in comparison with the average return on 91-day T-bills. However, the historical average return on 91-day T-bills is not very relevant for comparison since the

government artificially kept return on T-bills constant at 4.60 per cent till 1992–93. Since 1993, T-bills rates are based on more active weekly auctions. The 5-year (from 1993–94 to 1997–98) average return on T-bills is 8.13 per cent. Suppose this rate, as a proxy of a very long-term historical average, then the excess return on stock market is 9.37 per cent. An alternative is to consider the average return on the long-term government bonds for comparing with the average return on the stock market. The 28-year average return on the stock market is higher by 8.76 per cent in comparison with the average return on the long-term government bonds. This excess return is a compensation for the higher risk of the return on the stock market; it is commonly referred to as **risk premium.**

EXPECTED RETURN AND RISK: INCORPORATING PROBABILITIES IN ESTIMATES

Instead of using historical data for calculating return and risk, we may use forecasted data. Suppose you are considering buying one share of India Cements, which has a market price of Rs 261.25 today. The company pays a dividend of Rs 2.50 per share. You want to hold the share for one year. What is your expected rate of return? This will depend on the dividend per share you would

Table 4.4: Rates of Returns Under Various Economic Conditions

Economic Conditions (1)	Share Price (2)	Dividend (3)	Dividend Yield (4)	Capital Gain (5)	Return (6) = (4) + (5)
High growth	305.50	4.00	0.015	0.169	0.185
Expansion	285.50	3.25	0.012	0.093	0.105
Stagnation	261.25	2.50	0.010	0.000	0.010
Decline	243.50	2.00	0.008	− 0.068	− 0.060

actually receive and the market price at which you could sell the share. You do not know both the outcomes. The outcomes may depend on the economic conditions, the performance of the company and other factors. You will have to think of the outcomes of dividend and the share price under possible **economic scenarios** to arrive at a judgment about the expected return. You may, for example, assume four (equally likely) possible states of economic conditions and performance: high growth, expansion, stagnation and decline. You also expect the market price of share to be Rs 305.50, Rs 285.50, Rs 261.25 and Rs 243.50 and the dividend per share Rs 4, Rs 3.25, Rs 2.50 and Rs 2 respectively under four different states of economic conditions. Thus the possible outcomes of return can be calculated as follows in Table 4.4.

Note that the current share price is Rs 261.25, and depending on the economic conditions, there are four possibilities. The rates of return calculations can be shown as follows:

$$R_1 = \frac{4 + (305.50 - 261.25)}{261.25} = 0.185 \text{ or } 18.5\%$$

$$R_2 = \frac{3.25 + (285.50 - 261.25)}{261.25} = 0.105 \text{ or } 10.5\%$$

$$R_3 = \frac{2.50 + (261.25 - 261.25)}{261.25} = 0.01 \text{ or } 1\%$$

$$R_4 = \frac{2.00 + (243.50 - 261.25)}{261.25} = -0.060 \text{ or } -6.0\%$$

Your total return is anticipated to vary between – 6 per cent under the unfavourable condition to + 18.5 per cent under the most favourable conditions. What is the chance or likelihood for each outcome anticipated by you to occur? **Probability** is the percentage of the chance or likelihood of an outcome. On the basis of your judgement, you may, for example, say that each outcome is equally likely to occur, i.e., each outcome has a chance of 0.25 or 25 per cent. This is your subjective assessment. The subjective probability is based on the judgement of the investor rather than on an objective assessment of events to occur. The objective probability is based on the appraisal of the occurrence of an event for a very large number of times. The sum of probabilities of the occurrence of outcomes is always equal to 1.

Expected Rate of Return

Table 4.5 summarises the range of returns under the possible states of economic conditions along with probabilities. You can put this information together to calculate the expected rate of return. The **expected rate of return** [E (R)] is the sum of the product of each outcome (return) and its associated probability:

Expected rate of return
= rate of return under scenario 1 × probability of scenario 1 + rate of return under scenario 2 × probability of scenario 2 +… + rate of return under scenario n × probability of scenario n

Table 4.5: Returns and Probabilities

Economic Conditions (1)	Rate of Return (%) (2)	Probability (3)	Expected Rate of Return (%) (4) = (2) × (3)
Growth	18.5	0.25	4.63
Expansion	10.5	0.25	2.62
Stagnation	1.0	0.25	0.25
Decline	– 6.0	0.25	– 1.50
		1.00	6.00

Thus, the expected rate of return is as given below:

$$E(R) = (18.5 \times 0.25) + (10.5 \times 0.25) + (1.00 \times 0.25) + (-6.0 \times 0.25)$$
$$= 0.06 \text{ or } 6\%$$

You can convert this simple procedure of calculation in the following equation:

$$E(R) = R_1 \times P_1 + R_2 \times P_2 + \ldots + R_n P_n$$
$$E(R) = \sum_{i=1}^{n} R_i P_i \tag{5}$$

Note that $E(R)$ is the expected rate of return, R_i the outcome i, P_i is the probability of the occurrence of i and n is the total number of outcomes.

The expected rate of return is the average return. It is 6 per cent in our example. We know that the possible outcomes range between – 6 per cent to + 18.5 per cent. How much is the average dispersion? As stated earlier, this is explained by the **variance** or the **standard deviation**. The steps involved in the calculation of the variance and the standard deviation are the same as already discussed in the preceding section excest that the square of the difference of an outcome (return) from the expected return should be multiplied by its probability. The following formula can be used to calculate the variance of returns:

$$\sigma^2 = [R_1 - E(R)]^2 P_1 + [R_2 - E(R)]^2 P_2 + \ldots + [R_n - E(R)]^2 P_n$$
$$= \sum_{i=1}^{n} [R_n - E(R)]^2 P_n \tag{6}$$

In the above example, the variance of returns is:

$$\sigma^2 = [(18.5 - 6)^2 \times 0.25] + [(10.5 - 6)^2 \times 0.25] + [(1 - 6)^2 \times 0.25)] + [(-6 - 6)^2 \times 0.25] = 86.375$$

and the standard deviation is:

$$\sigma = \sqrt{\sigma^2} = \sqrt{86.375} = 9.29\%$$

Should you invest in the share of India Cement? The returns are expected to fluctuate widely. The expected rate of return is low (6 per cent) and the standard deviation is high (9.29 per cent). You may like to search for an investment with higher expected return and lower standard deviation.

Illustration 4.1: Variance and Standard Calculation

The shares of Hypothetical Company Limited has the following anticipated returns with associated probabilities:

Return (%)	–20	–10	10	15	20	25
Probability	0.05	0.10	0.20	0.25	0.20	0.15

The expected rate of return is:

$$E(R) = -20 \times 0.05 + -10 \times 0.10 + 10 \times 0.20 + 15 \times 0.25$$
$$+ 20 \times 0.20 + 25 \times 0.15 + 30 \times 0.05 = 13\%$$

The risk, measured in terms of variance and standard deviation, is:

$$\sigma^2 = (-20 - 13)^2 \times 0.05 + (-10 - 13)^2 \times 0.10$$
$$+ (10 - 13)^2 \times 0.20 + (15 - 13)^2 \times 0.25$$
$$+ (20 - 13)^2 \times 0.20 + (25 - 13)^2 \times 0.15$$
$$+ (30 - 13)^2 \times 0.05 = 156$$

$$\sigma = \sqrt{156} = 12.49\%$$

Risk Preference

The information about the expected return and standard deviation helps an investor to make decision about investments. This depends on the investor's **risk preference**. Generally investors would prefer investments with higher rates of return and lower standard deviations. According to the economic principle of **diminishing marginal utility**, as a person gets more and more wealth his utility for additional wealth increases at a declining rate. For example, a person obtains less utility from gaining additional Rs 1,000 than she forgoes in losing Rs 1,000. Thus the utility function for risk-averse persons is concave, as shown in Figure 4.4.

A *risk-averse* investor will choose from investments with the equal rates of return, the investment with lowest standard deviation. Similarly, if investments have equal risk (standard deviations), the investor would prefer the one with higher return. A **risk-neutral** investor does not consider risk, and he would always prefer investments with higher returns. A **risk-seeking** investor likes investments with higher risk irrespective of the rates of return. In reality, most (if not all) investors are risk-averse. How would risk-averse investors make their choices if investments have higher returns and higher standard deviations or lower returns and lower standard deviations? We shall provide answer to this question in the next chapter.

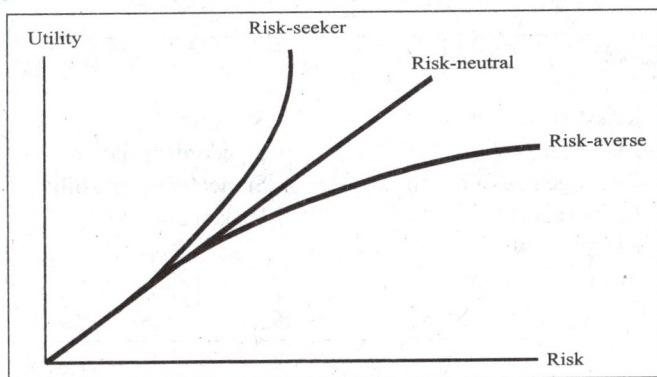

Figure 4.4: Risk preferences

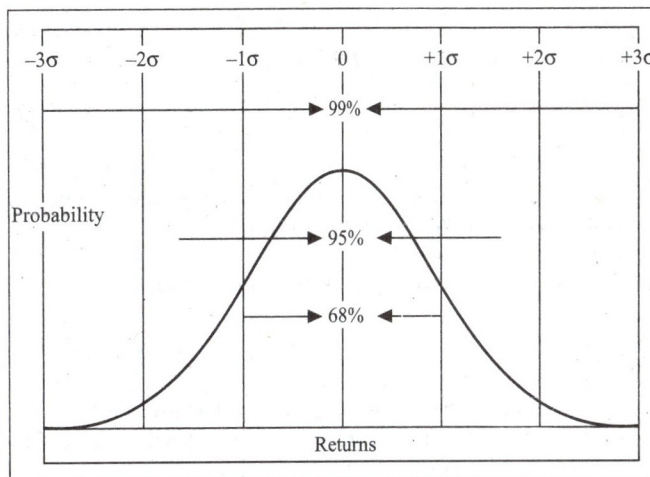

Figure 4.5: Normal distribution

Normal Distribution and Standard Deviation

The **normal distribution** is a smooth, symmetric, continuous, bell-shaped curve as shown in Figure 4.5. The distribution is neither **skewed** nor **peaked**. The spread of the normal distribution is characterised by the standard deviation. What is the probability of obtaining a return exceeding or lower than the expected (mean) return? In case of normally distributed returns, it depends only on the standard deviation. It is useful to notice certain properties of a normal distribution.

- The area under the curve sums to 1.
- The curve reaches its maximum at the expected value (mean) of the distribution and one-half of the area lies on either side of the mean.
- Approximately 50 per cent of the area lies within ± 0.67 standard deviations of the expected value; about 68 per cent of the area lies within ± 1.0 standard deviations of the expected value; 95 per cent of the area lies within ± 1.96 standard deviation of the expected value and 99 per cent of the area lies within ± 3.0 standard deviations of the expected value.

For example, suppose the mean return from shares is 20 per cent with a standard deviation of 25 per cent. Assuming that returns are normally distributed, there is about 67 per cent probability that the return would range between minus 5 per cent [20 per cent – 25 per cent] and plus 45 per cent [20 per cent + 25 per cent]. There are 95 per cent chances that return will be between minus 30 per cent [20 per cent -2×25 per cent] and plus 70 per cent [20 per cent $+ 2 \times 25$ per cent]. The normal probability table, given at the end of this book, can be used to determine the area under the normal curve for various standard deviations. The probability of occurrence can be read from the normal probability table. This table is the 'right tail' of the distribution; that is probabilities of the unknown quantity being greater than X standard deviations from the expected value (mean) are given in the table. The distribution tabulated is a normal distribution with mean zero and standard deviation of 1. Such a distribution is known as a **standard normal distribution**. However, any normal distribution can be standardised and hence the table of normal probabilities will serve for any normal distribution. The formula to standardise is:

$$S = \frac{R - E(R)}{\sigma} \qquad (7)$$

Note that R is the outcome (return) in which we are interested, $E(R)$ is mean or the expected return and S is the number of standard deviations from the expected return.

Illustration 4.2: Probability of Expected Return

An asset has an expected return of 29.32 per cent and the standard deviation of the possible returns is 13.52 per cent. Determine the probability that the return of the asset will be zero or less.

As given in Equation (4.7), we can divide the difference between zero and the expected value of the return by standard deviation of possible net present value as follows:

$$S = \frac{0 - 29.32}{13.52} = -2.17$$

This figure (– 2.17) implies that a return of 0 is positioned 2.17 standard deviations to the left of the expected value of the probability distribution of possible returns. The probability of being less than 2.17 standard deviations from the expected value, according to the normal probability distribution table is 0.015. This means that there is 0.015 or 1.5% probability that the return of the asset will be zero or less.

Normal distribution is a *population-based, theoretical distribution*. In practice, it is difficult to find sample distributions that are normal because of the sampling errors. The actual distributions may be approximately normal or non-normal. Nevertheless, normal distribution is an important concept in statistics and finance. In explaining the risk-return relationship, we assume that returns are normally distributed. If we have returns series for a very long period of time, they would be approximately normally distributed.

SUMMARY

❖ Risk and return concepts are basic to the understanding of the valuation of assets or securities.

❖ Return on a security consists of two parts: the dividend and capital gain. The rate of return for one period is given by the following equation:

Return = Divident yield + Capital gain rate

$$R = \frac{D_1}{P_0} + \frac{(P_1 - P_0)}{P_0}$$

The expected rate of return on a security is the sum of the products of possible rates of return and their probabilities. Thus

$$E(R) = R_1 P_1 + R_2 P_2 + \ldots + R_n P_n = \sum_{i=1}^{n} R_i P_i$$

❖ The expected rate of return is an average rate of return. This average may deviate from the possible outcomes (rates of return). This is referred to as dispersion.

❖ Dispersion can be measured by variance and standard deviation of returns of a security. They can be calculated as follows:

$$\sigma^2 = [R_1 - E(R)]^2 P_i + [R_2 - E(R)]^2 P_2 + \ldots$$
$$+ [(R_n - E(R)]^2 P_n$$

$$= \sum_{i=1}^{n} [R_i - E(R)]^2 P_i$$

$$\sigma = \sqrt{\sigma^2}$$

❖ Variance (σ^2) or standard deviation (σ) is a measure of the risk of returns on a security.

❖ Historically investors have earned different rates of returns. The average return on shares has been more that the average return on government bonds and treasury bills. Also, the variance or standard deviation of returns on shares has been more. Shares are more risky than the government bonds.

❖ Treasury bills offer risk-free rate, as they do not have risk of default. The government guarantees them.

❖ The difference between the average share return and return on government bonds or treasury bills is the risk premium.

❖ Investors have different risk preferences. Investors may be risk-averse, risk seeker or risk neutral. Most of them are, however, risk-averse.

❖ Normal distribution is a smoothed, symmetric curve. It best describes the mean-variance (or standard deviation). We generally assume that returns on shares are normally distributed.

KEY CONCEPTS

Arithmetic mean	Kurtosis	Risk-free security	Skewness
Average return	Normal distribution	Risk-averse	Standard deviation
Capital gains or loss	Objective probability	Risk-free rate of return	Subjective probability
Compound rate of return	Probability	Risk-seeker	Variance
Expected rate of return	Risk	Risk-neutral	
Geometric mean	Risk diversification	Share price index	
Holding period return	Risk premium		

ILLUSTRATIVE SOLVED PROBLEMS

Problem 4.1: The following table gives dividend and share price data for Hind Manufacturing Company.

Year	Dividend Per Share	Closing Share Price
1994	2.50	12.25
1995	2.50	14.20
1996	2.50	17.50
1997	3.00	16.75
1998	3.00	18.45
1999	3.25	22.25
2000	3.50	23.50
2001	3.50	27.75
2002	3.50	25.50
2003	3.75	27.95
2004	3.75	31.30

You are required to calculate: (*i*) the annual rates of return, (*ii*) the expected (average) rate of return, (*iii*) the variance, and (*iv*) the standard deviation of returns.

Solution: (*i*) Annual rates of return

Year	Dividend Per Share	Closing Share Price	Annual Rates of Return (%)
1994	2.50	12.25	
1995	2.50	14.20	$2.50 + (14.20 - 12.25)/12.25 = 36.33$
1996	2.50	17.50	$2.50 + (17.50 - 14.20)/14.20 = 40.85$
1997	3.00	16.75	$3.00 + (16.75 - 17.50)/17.50 = 12.86$
1998	3.00	18.45	$3.00 + (18.45 - 16.75)/16.75 = 28.06$
1999	3.25	22.25	$3.25 + (22.25 - 18.45)/18.45 = 38.21$
2000	3.50	23.50	$3.50 + (23.50 - 22.25)/22.25 = 21.35$
2001	3.50	27.75	$3.50 + (27.75 - 23.50)/23.50 = 32.98$
2002	3.50	25.50	$3.50 + (25.50 - 27.75)/27.75 = 4.50$
2003	3.75	27.95	$3.75 + (27.95 - 25.50)/25.50 = 24.31$
2004	3.75	31.30	$3.75 + (31.30 - 27.95)/27.95 = 25.40$

(*ii*) Average rate of return: We can take the arithmetic average of the annual rates of return.

$(36.33 + 40.85 + 12.86 + 28.06 + 38.21 + 21.35 + 32.98 + 4.50 + 24.31 + 25.40)/10 = 26.48\%$

(*iii*) Variance and (*iv*) standard deviation are calculated as shown below.

Year	Annual Rates of Returns	Annual minus Average Rates of Return	Square of Annual minus Average Rates of Return
1993	36.33	9.84	96.86
1994	40.85	14.36	206.22
1995	12.86	−13.63	185.71
1996	28.06	1.57	2.48
1997	38.21	11.73	137.51
1998	21.35	−5.14	26.38
1999	32.98	6.49	42.17
2000	4.50	−21.98	483.13
2001	24.31	−2.17	4.71
2002	25.40	−1.08	1.17
Sum	264.85		1186.36
Average	26.48		

$$\text{Variance} = \frac{1}{n-1} \sum_{i=1}^{n} (R_i - \overline{R}) = 1186.36/(10 - 1) = 131.82$$

$$\text{Standard deviation} = \sqrt{131.81} = 11.48$$

Problem 4.2: Star Computer System Limited has forecasted returns on its share with the following probability distribution:

Return (%)	Probability
−20	0.05
−10	0.05
−5	0.10
5	0.10
10	0.15
18	0.25
20	0.25
30	0.05

Calculate the expected return, variance and standard deviation of returns for Star.

Solution: Expected Return

$$E(R) = R_1 \times P_1 + R_2 \times P_2 + \dots + R_n \times P_n = \sum_{i=1}^{n} R_i P_n$$

$$(-20 \times .05) + (-10 \times .05) + (-5 \times .10) + (5 \times .10)$$
$$+ (10 \times .15) + (18 \times .25) + (20 \times .25) + (30 \times .05) = 11$$

Variance of Return

$$\sigma^2 = [R_1 - (R)]^2 \times P_1 + [R_2 - E(R)]^2 \times P_2 + \dots + [R_n - E(R)]^2 \times P_n$$
$$= \sum [R_i - E(R)]^2 \times P_i$$
$$= (-20 - 11)^2 \times .05 + (-10 - 11)^2 \times .05 + (-5 - 11)^2 \times .10$$
$$+ (5 - 11)^2 \times .10 + (10 - 11)^2 \times .15 + (18 - 11)^2 \times .25$$
$$+ (20 - 11)^2 \times .25 + (30 - 11)^2 \times .05 = 150$$

$$\sigma = \sqrt{150} = 12.25$$

Problem 4.3: The following are the returns during five years on a market portfolio of shares and 'AAA' corporate bonds:

Year	Portfolio of Shares (%)	'AAA' Bonds (%)
1	29.5	13.4
2	−3.8	12.8
3	26.8	10.5
4	24.6	8.9
5	7.2	9.2

You are require to calculate (*i*) the realised risk premium of shares over the 'AAA' bonds in each year; and (*ii*) the average risk premium of shares over 'AAA' bonds during the period. Can the realised premium be negative? Why?

Solution: The calculations for the premium in each year and the average premium are shown below. The average premium is 4.7 per cent.

The realised premium can be negative as the share prices in practice show wide swings. However, over a long period of time the premium would be positive, as shares are more risky than bonds.

Year	Portfolio of Shares (%)	'AAA' Bonds (%)	Premium (%)
1	29.5	13.4	16.1
2	-3.8	12.8	-16.6
3	26.8	10.5	16.3
4	24.6	12.9	11.7
5	7.2	11.2	-4.0
Avg.	16.9	12.2	4.7

REVIEW QUESTIONS

1. What is a return? Explain the components of (total) return? Should unrealised capital gain (or loss) be included in the calculations of returns?
2. Illustrate the computation of the expected rate of return of an asset.
3. Define holding-period return. How is it calculated?
4. What is risk? How can risk of a security be calculated? Explain your answer with the help of an example.
5. What is a risk-free security? What is risk premium? How can it be estimated from historical data?
6. What is a normal distribution? How does it help to interpret standard deviation?

PROBLEMS

1. On 1 January 2004, Mr. Y.P. Sinha purchased 100 shares of L&T at Rs 212 each. During the year, he received total dividends of Rs 700. Mr. Sinha sold all his shares at Rs 215 each on 31 December 2004. Calculate Mr. Sinha's (*i*) capital gain amount, and (*ii*) total return in (*a*) rupee amount and (*b*) percentage.

2. The closing price of share last year was Rs 50. The dividend per share was Rs 5 during the year. The current year closing price is Rs 57. Calculate the percentage return on the share, showing the dividend yield and the capital gain rate.

3. You acquired Telco's 200 shares at Rs 87 each last year. The par value of a share is Rs 10. Telco paid a dividend of 15 per cent during the year. You sold 200 shares at a total value of Rs 18,500 after one year. What is your (*i*) dividend yield, (*ii*) rate of capital gain, and (*iii*) total rupee and percentage returns.

4. You bought Infosys share for Rs 4,250 two years ago. You held the stock for two years, and received dividend per share of Rs 90 and Rs 125 respectively at the end of the first and the second years. You sold the share for Rs 4,535 after two years. What was your two-year holding period return on Infosys share?

5. You expect to earn a return of 17 per cent on a share. If the inflation rate is 5.5 per cent, what is your real rate of return?

6. Suppose shares of Hind Ltd. and Nirmala Ltd. were selling at Rs 100 two years ago. Hind's price fell in the first year by 12 per cent and rose by 12 per cent in the second year. The reverse was the case for Nirmala's share price — it increased by 12 per cent and then decreased by 12 per cent. Would they have the same price after two years? Why or why not? Show computations.

7. An asset is expected to earn the following rates of return for the period 2004-10:

Year	2004	2005	2006	2007	2008	2009	2010
Return (%)	15.3	-5.6	17.3	25.0	16.8	9.5	28.8

What is the seven-year holding period return from the asset? How much is the annual compound rate of return?

8. The following are the returns on the share of Reliable Company for past five years:

Year	1	2	3	4	5
Return (%)	5.3	15.6	-7.3	15.0	19.8

Calculate the average return for the five years. Also calculate the standard deviation and variance of the returns for the period.

9. The economy of a country may experience rapid growth or moderate growth or recession. There is 0.15 probability of rapid growth and the stock market return is expected to be 19.5 per cent. The probability of moderate growth is 55 per cent with a 14 per cent expectation of the stock market return. There is 0.30 probability of recession and the stock market return is expected to be 7 per cent. Calculate the expected stock market return and the standard deviation of the return.

10. An asset has the following possible returns with associated probabilities:

Possible returns	20%	18%	8%	0	-6%
Probability	0.10	0.45	0.30	0.05	0.10

Calculate the expected rate of return and the standard deviation of that rate of return.

11. Securities X and Y have the following characteristics:

Security X		Security Y	
Return	Probability	Return	Probability
30%	0.10	-20%	0.05
20%	0.20	10%	0.25
10%	0.40	20%	0.30
5%	0.20	30%	0.30
-10%	0.10	40%	0.10

You are required to calculate the expected return and standard deviation of return for each security. Which security would you select for investment and why?

12. The distribution of returns for share P and the market portfolio is given below:

	Returns (%)	
Probability	Share P	Market
0.30	30	-10
0.40	20	20
0.30	0	30

You are required to calculate the expected returns, standard deviation and variance of the returns of share P and the market.

13. The following are the returns during seven years on a market portfolio of shares and 91-day Treasury Bills:

You are required to calculate (i) the realised risk premium of shares over treasury bills in each year and (ii) the average risk premium of shares over treasury bills during the period. Can the realised premium be negative? Why?

Year	Portfolio of Shares (%)	Treasury Bills (%)
1	22.5	11.4
2	-6.8	9.8
3	26.8	10.5
4	24.6	9.9
5	3.2	9.2
6	15.7	8.9
7	12.3	11.2

14. The stock market and treasury bills returns are expected to be as follows:

Economic Conditions	Probability	Market Return (%)	Treasury Bills (%)
Growth	0.20	28.5	9.7
Decline	0.30	-5.0	9.5
Stagnation	0.50	17.9	9.2

You are required to calculate (i) the expected market and treasury bills returns and (ii) the expected risk premium.

15. Suppose that returns of Sunshine Company Limited's share are normally distributed. The mean return is 20 per cent and the standard deviation of returns is 10 per cent. Determine the range of returns in which about 2/3rd of the company's returns fall.

16. Suppose that the rates of return on Maneklal Engineering Ltd.'s share have a normal distribution with a mean of 22 per cent and a standard deviation of 25 per cent. What is the probability of the return being 30 per cent?

CHAPTER 5

Risk and Return: Portfolio Theory and Assets Pricing Models

CHAPTER OBJECTIVES

- Discuss the concepts of portfolio risk and return
- Determine the relationship between risk and return of portfolios
- Highlight the difference between systematic and unsystematic risks
- Examine the logic of portfolio theory
- Show the use of capital asset pricing model (CAPM) in the valuation of securities
- Explain the features and modus operandi of the arbitrage pricing theory (APT)

INTRODUCTION

A **portfolio** is a bundle or a combination of individual assets or securities. The **portfolio theory** provides a normative approach to investors to make decisions to invest their wealth in assets or securities under risk.[1] It is based on the assumption that investors are *risk-averse*. This implies that investors hold **well-diversified portfolios** instead of investing their entire wealth in a single or a few assets. One important conclusion of the portfolio theory, as we explain later, is that if the investors hold a well-diversified portfolio of assets, then their concern should be the expected rate of return and risk of the portfolio rather than individual assets and the contribution of individual asset to the portfolio risk. The second assumption of the portfolio theory is that the returns of assets are normally distributed. This means that the mean (the expected value) and variance (or standard deviation) analysis is the foundation of the portfolio decisions. Further, we can extend the portfolio theory to derive a framework for valuing risky assets. This framework is referred to as the **capital asset pricing model** (CAPM). An alternative model for the valuation of risky assets is the **arbitrage pricing theory** (APT). In this chapter, we discuss the portfolio theory and show how CAPM and APT work in valuing assets.

PORTFOLIO RETURN: TWO-ASSET CASE

The **return of a portfolio** is equal to the weighted average of the returns of individual assets (or securities) in the portfolio with weights being equal to the proportion of investment value in each asset. Suppose you have an opportunity of investing your wealth either in asset X or asset Y. The possible outcomes of two assets in different states of economy are given in Table 5.1.

Table 5.1: Possible Outcomes of two Assets, X and Y

State of Economy	Probability	Return (%)	
		X	Y
A	0.10	−8	14
B	0.20	10	−4
C	0.40	8	6
D	0.20	5	15
E	0.10	−4	20

---

1. For a simple treatment of return and risk concepts and the capital asset pricing model, see Mullins, D. W., Does the Capital Asset Pricing Model Work?, *Harvard Business Review,* Jan–Feb 1982; and Butters, J.K., *et. al., Case Problems in Finance,* Richard D. Irwin, 1991.

The expected rate of return of X is the sum of the product of outcomes and their respective probability. That is:

$$E(R_x) = (-8 \times 0.1) + (10 \times 0.2) + (8 \times 0.4) + (5 \times 0.2) + (-4 \times 0.1) = 5\%$$

Similarly, the expected rate of return of Y is:

$$E(R_y) = (14 \times 0.1) + (-4 \times 0.2) + (6 \times 0.4) + (15 \times 0.2) + (20 \times 0.1) = 8\%$$

We can use the following equation to calculate the expected rate of return of individual asset:

$$E(R_x) = (R_1 \times P_1) + (R_2 \times P)_2 + (R_3 \times P_3) + \ldots + (R_n \times P_n)$$

$$E(R_x) = \sum_{i=1}^{n} R_i P_i \tag{1}$$

Note that $E(R_x)$ is the expected return on asset X, R_i is ith return and P_i is the probability of ith return. Consider an example.

Suppose you decide to invest 50 per cent of your wealth in X and 50 per cent in Y. What is your expected rate of return on a portfolio consisting of both X and Y? This can be done in two steps. First, calculate the combined outcome under each state of economic condition. Second, multiply each combined outcome by its probability. Table 5.2 shows calculations.

There is a direct and simple method of calculating the expected rate of return on a portfolio if we know the expected rates of return on individual assets and their weights. The **expected rate of return on a portfolio** (or simply the **portfolio return**) is the weighted average of the expected rates of return on assets in the portfolio. In our example, the expected portfolio return is as follows:

$$E(R_p) = (0.5 \times 5) + (0.5 \times 8) = 6.5\%$$

In the case of two-asset portfolio, the expected rate of return is given by the following formula:

Expected return on portfolio
= weight of security $X \times$ expected return on security X
+ weight of security $Y \times$ expected return on security Y

$$E(R_p) = w \times E(R_x) + (1 - w) \times E(R_y) \tag{2}$$

Note that w is the proportion of investment in asset X and $(1 - w)$ is the remaining investment in asset Y.

Given the expected returns of individual assets, the portfolio return depends on the weights (investment proportions) of assets. You may be able to change your expected rate of return on the portfolio by changing your proportionate investment in each asset. How much would you earn if you invested 20 per cent of your wealth in X and the remaining wealth in Y? The portfolio rate of return under this changed mix of wealth in X and Y will be:

$$E(R_p) = 0.2 \times 5 + (1 - 0.2) \times 8 = 7.4\%$$

You may notice that this return is higher than what you will earn if you invested equal amounts in X and Y. The expected return would be 5 per cent if you invested entire wealth in X (i.e. $w = 1.0$). On the other hand, the expected return would be 8 per cent if the entire wealth were invested in Y (i.e., $1 - w = 1$, since $w = 0$). Your expected return will increase as you shift your wealth from X to Y. Thus, the expected return on portfolio will depend on the percentage of wealth invested in each asset in the portfolio.

What is the advantage in investing your wealth in both assets X and Y when you could expect highest return of 8 per cent by investing your entire wealth in Y? When you invested your wealth equally in assets X and Y, your expected return is 6.5 per cent. The expected return of Y (8 per cent) is higher than the portfolio return (6.5 per cent). But investing your entire wealth in Y is more risky. Under the unfavourable economic condition, Y may yield a negative return of 4 per cent. The probability of negative return is eliminated when you combine X and Y. Further, the portfolio returns are expected to fluctuate within a narrow range of 3 to 10 per cent (see column 3 of Table 5.2). You may also note that the expected return of X (5 per cent) is not only less than the portfolio return (6.5 per cent), but it also shows greater fluctuations. We discuss the concept of risk in greater detail in the following sections.

PORTFOLIO RISK: TWO-ASSET CASE

We have seen in the previous section that returns on individual assets fluctuate more than the portfolio return. Thus, individual assets are more risky than the portfolio. How is the risk of a portfolio measured? As discussed in the previous chapter, risk of individual assets is measured by their variance or standard deviation. We can use variance or standard deviation to measure the risk of the portfolio of assets as well. Why is a portfolio less risky than individual assets? Let us consider an example.

Suppose you have two investment opportunities A and B as shown in Table 5.3.

Table 5.2: Expected Portfolio Rate of Return

State of Economy (1)	Probability (2)	Combined Returns (%) X(50%) & Y (50%) (3)	Expected Return (%) (4) = (2) × (3)
A	0.10	(−8 × 0.5) + (14 × 0.5) = 3.0	0.10 × 3.0 = 0.3
B	0.20	(10 × 0.5) + (−4 × 0.5) = 3.0	0.20 × 3.0 = 0.6
C	0.40	(8 × 0.5) + (6 × 0.5) = 7.0	0.40 × 7.0 = 2.8
D	0.20	(5 × 0.5) + (15 × 0.5) = 10.0	0.20 × 10.0 = 2.0
E	0.10	(−4 × 0.5) + (20 × 0.5) = 8.0	0.10 × 8.0 = 0.8
Expected return on portfolio			6.5

Table 5.3: Investments in A and B

Economic Condition	Probability	Returns (%) A	Returns (%) B
Good	0.5	40	0
Bad	0.5	0	40

The expected rate of return, variance and standard deviation of A are:

$$E(R_A) = 0.5 \times 40 + 0.5 \times 0 = 20\%$$

$$\sigma_A^2 = 0.5(40-20)^2 + 0.5(0-20)^2 = 400$$

$$\sigma_A = \sqrt{400} = 20\%$$

Similarly, the expected rate of return, variance and standard deviation of B are:

$$E(R_B) = 0.5 \times 0 + 0.5 \times 40 = 20\%$$

$$\sigma_B^2 = 0.5(0-20)^2 + 0.5(40-20)^2 = 400$$

$$\sigma_B = \sqrt{400} = 20\%$$

Both investments A and B have the same expected rate of return (20 per cent) and same variance (400) and standard deviation (20 per cent). Thus, they are equally profitable and equally risky. How does combining investments A and B help an investor? If a portfolio consisting of equal amount of A and B were constructed, the portfolio return would be:

$$E(R_P) = 0.5 \times 20 + 0.5 \times 20 = 20\%$$

This return is the same as the expected return from individual securities, but without any risk. Why? If the economic conditions are good, then A would yield 40 per cent return and B zero and the portfolio return will be:

$$E(R_P) = 0.5 \times 40 + 0.5 \times 0 = 20\%$$

When economic conditions are bad, then A's return will be zero and B's 40 per cent and the portfolio return would still remain the same:

$$E(R_P) = 0.5 \times 0 + 0.5 \times 40 = 20\%$$

Thus, by investing equal amounts in A and B, rather than the entire amount only in A or B, the investor is able to eliminate the risk altogether. She is assured of a return of 20 per cent with a zero standard deviation.

It is not always possible to entirely reduce the risk. It may be difficult in practice to find two assets whose returns move completely in opposite directions like in the above example of securities A and B. It needs emphasis to state that the risk of portfolio would be less than the risk of individual securities, and that the risk of a security should be judged by its contribution to the portfolio risk.

Measuring Portfolio Risk for Two Assets

Like in the case of individual assets, the **risk of a portfolio** could be measured in terms of its variance or standard deviation.

As stated earlier, the portfolio return is the weighted average of returns on individual assets. Is the portfolio variance or standard deviation a weighted average of the individual assets' variances or standard deviations? It is not. The **portfolio variance** or **standard deviation** depends on the co-movement of returns on two assets.

Covariance: When we consider two assets, we are concerned with the co-movement of the assets. **Covariance** of returns on two assets measures their co-movement. How is covariance calculated? Three steps are involved in the calculation of covariance between two assets:

- Determine the expected returns on assets.
- Determine the deviation of possible returns from the expected return for each asset.
- Determine the sum of the product of each deviation of returns of two assets and respective probability.

Let us consider the data of securities of X and Y given in Table 5.4. The expected return on security X is:

$$E(R_x) = (0.1 \times -8) + (0.2 \times 10) + (0.4 \times 8) + (0.2 \times 5)$$
$$+ (0.1 \times -4) = 5\%$$

Security Y's expected return is:

$$E(R_y) = (0.1 \times 14) + (0.2 \times -4) + (0.4 \times 6) + (0.2 \times 15)$$
$$+ (0.1 \times 20) = 8\%$$

If the equal amount is invested in X and Y, the expected return on the portfolio is:

$$E(R_p) = 5 \times 0.5 + 8 \times 0.5 = 6.5\%$$

Table 5.4 shows the calculations of variations from the expected return and covariance, which is the product of deviations of returns of securities X and Y and their associated probabilities:

Table 5.4: Covariance of Returns of Securities X and Y

State of Economy	Probability	Returns X	Returns Y	Deviation from Expected Returns X	Deviation from Expected Returns Y	Product of Deviation & Probability
A	0.1	-8	14	-13	6	-7.8
B	0.2	10	-4	5	-12	-12.0
C	0.4	8	6	3	-2	-2.4
D	0.2	5	15	0	7	0.0
E	0.1	-4	20	-9	12	-10.8
		$E(R_x)$ = 5	$E(R_y)$ = 8			Covar = -33.0

The covariance of returns of securities X and Y is -33.0. The formula for calculating covariance of returns of the two securities X and Y is as follows:

$$\text{Cov}_{xy} = \sum_{i=1}^{n} [R_x - E(R_x)][R_y - E(R_y)] \times P_i \quad (3)$$

Note that Cov_{xy} is the covariance of returns on securities X and

Y, R_x and R_y returns on securities X and Y respectively, $E(R_x)$ and $E(R_y)$ expected returns of X and Y respectively and P_i probability of occurrence of the state of economy i. Using Equation (3), the covariance between the returns of securities X and Y can be calculated as shown below:

$$\begin{aligned}
\text{Cov}_{xy} &= 0.1(-8-5)(-14-8) + 0.2(10-5)(-4-8) \\
&\quad + 0.4(8-5)(6-8) + 0.2(5-5)(15-8) \\
&\quad + 0.1(-4-5)(20-8) \\
&= -7.8 - 12 - 2.4 + 0 - 10.8 = -33.0
\end{aligned}$$

What is the relationship between the returns of securities X and Y? There are following possibilities:

- *Positive covariance* X's and Y's returns could be above their average returns at the same time. Alternatively, X's and Y's returns could be below their average returns at the same time. In either situation, this implies positive relation between two returns. The covariance would be positive.
- *Negative covariance* X's returns could be above its average return while Y's return could be below its average return and vice versa. This denotes a negative relationship between returns of X and Y. The covariance would be negative.
- *Zero covariance* Returns on X and Y could show no pattern; that is, there is no relationship. In this situation, covariance would be zero. In reality, covariance may be non-zero due to randomness and negative and positive terms may not cancel out each other.

In our example covariance between returns on X and Y is negative, that is, -33.0. This is akin to the second situation above; that is, two returns are negatively related. What does the number -33.0 imply? As in the case of variance, covariance also uses squared deviations and therefore, the number cannot be explained. We can, however, compute the correlation to measure the relationship between two returns.

Correlation How can we find relationship between two variables? **Correlation** is a measure of the linear relationship between two variables (say, returns of two securities, X and Y in our case). It may be observed from Equation (3) that covariance of returns of securities X and Y is a measure of both variability of returns of securities and their association. Thus, the formula for covariance of returns on X and Y can also be expressed as follows:

Covariance XY = Standard deviation X × Standard deviation Y
× Correlation XY

$$\text{Cov}_{xy} = \sigma_x \sigma_y \, \text{Cor}_{xy} \tag{4}$$

Note that σ_x and σ_y are standard deviations of returns for securities X and Y and Cor_{xy} is the correlation between returns of X and Y. From Equation (4), we can determine the correlation by dividing covariance by the standard deviations of returns on securities X and Y:

$$\text{Correlation } X, Y = \frac{\text{Covariance } XY}{\text{Standard deviation } X \times \text{Standard deviation } Y}$$

$$\text{Cor}_{xy} = \frac{\text{Cov}_{xy}}{\sigma_x \sigma_y} \tag{5}$$

The value of correlation, called the **correlation coefficient,** could be positive, negative or zero. It depends on the sign of covariance since standard deviations are always positive numbers. The correlation coefficient always ranges between -1.0 and $+1.0$. A correlation coefficient of $+1.0$ implies a **perfectly positive correlation** while a correlation coefficient of -1.0 indicates a **perfectly negative correlation**. The correlation between the two variables will be zero (or not different from zero) if they are not at all related to each other. In a number of situations, returns of any two securities maybe weakly correlated (negatively or positively).

Let us calculate correlation by using data given in Table 5.4. The covariance is -33.0. We need standard deviations of X and Y to compute the correlation. The standard deviation of securities X and Y are as follows:

$$\begin{aligned}
\sigma_x^2 &= 0.1(-8-5)^2 + 0.2(10-5)^2 + 0.4(8-5)^2 \\
&\quad + 0.2(5-5)^2 + 0.1(-4-5)^2 \\
&= 16.9 + 3.6 + 0 + 8.1 = 33.6
\end{aligned}$$

$$\sigma_x = \sqrt{33.6} = 5.80\%$$

$$\begin{aligned}
\sigma_y^2 &= 0.1(14-8)^2 + 0.2(-4-8)^2 + 0.4(6-8)^2 \\
&\quad + 0.2(15-8)^2 + 0.1(20-8)^2 \\
&= 3.6 + 28.8 + 1.6 + 9.8 + 14.4 = 58.2
\end{aligned}$$

$$\sigma_y = \sqrt{58.2} = 7.63\%$$

The correlation of the two securities X and Y is as follows:

$$\text{Cor}_{xy} = \frac{-33.0}{5.80 \times 7.63} = \frac{-33.0}{44.25} = -0.746$$

Securities X and Y are negatively correlated. The correlation coefficient of -0.746 indicates a high negative relationship. If an investor invests her wealth in both instead any one of them, she can reduce the risk. How?

Variance and Standard Deviation of a Two-Asset Portfolio

We know now that the variance of a two-asset portfolio is not the weighted average of the variances of assets since they co-vary as well. The variance of two-security portfolio is given by the following equation:

$$\begin{aligned}
\sigma_p^2 &= \sigma_x^2 w_x^2 + \sigma_y^2 w_y^2 + 2 w_x w_y \, \text{Covar}_{xy} \\
&= \sigma_x^2 w_x^2 + \sigma_y^2 w_y^2 + 2 w_x w_y \sigma_x \sigma_y \, \text{Cor}_{xy}
\end{aligned} \tag{6}$$

It maybe noticed from Equation (6) that the variance of a portfolio includes the proportionate variances of the individual securities and the covariance of the securities. The covariance depends on the correlation between the securities in the portfolio. The risk of the portfolio would be less than the weighted average risk of the securities for low or negative correlation. It is a common practice to use a tabular approach, as given Table 5.5, to calculate the variance of a portfolio:

Table 5.5: Convariance Calculation Matrix

I		II		III	
σ_x^2	Cov_{xy}	w_x^2	$w_x w_y$	$\sigma_x^2 w_x^2$	$w_x w_y Cov_{xy}$
Cov_{xy}	σ_y^2	$w_x w_y$	w_y^2	$w_x w_y Cov_{xy}$	$\sigma_y^2 w_y^2$

The first two parts of Table 5.5 contain the variance, covariance and weights of two securities, X and Y, in the portfolio. The third part gives the cell-by-cell product of the values in the two part. We can obtain Equation (6) when we add all values in the third part.

Using the sequences of Table 5.6, the variance of the portfolio of securities X and Y is given below:
The total of values in the third table: $8.40 - 8.25 - 8.25 + 14.55 = 6.45$ is the variance of the portfolio of securities X and Y.

Applying Equation (6), the variance of portfolio of X and Y will be as follows:

$$\sigma_p^2 = 33.6(0.5)^2 + 58.2(0.5)^2$$
$$+ 2(0.5)(0.5)(5.80)(7.63)(-0.746)$$
$$= 8.4 + 14.55 - 16.51 = 6.45$$

The standard deviation of two-asset portfolio is the square root of variance:

$$\sigma_p = \sqrt{\sigma_x^2 w_x^2 + \sigma_y^2 w_y^2 + 2 w_x w_y \sigma_x \sigma_y Cor_{xy}}$$
$$\sigma_p = \sqrt{6.45} = 2.54\% \tag{7}$$

What does the portfolio standard deviation of 2.54 per cent mean? The implication is the same as in the case of the standard deviation of an individual asset (security). The expected return on the portfolio is 6.5 per cent, and it could vary between 3.96 per cent [i.e., $6.5 - 2.54$] and 9.04 per cent [i.e., $6.5 + 2.54$] within one standard deviation from the mean. There is about 68 per cent probability that the portfolio return would range between 3.96 per cent and 9.04 per cent if we assume that the portfolio return is normally distributed.

Minimum Variance Portfolio

What is the best combination of two securities so that the portfolio variance is minimum? The minimum variance portfolio is also called the **optimum portfolio**. However, investors do not necessarily strive for the minimum variance portfolio. A risk-averse investor will have a trade-off between risk and return. Her choice of a particular portfolio will depend on her risk preference.

We can use the following general formula for estimating optimum weights of two securities X and Y so that the portfolio variance is minimum:

$$w^* = \frac{\sigma_y^2 - Cov_{xy}}{\sigma_x^2 + \sigma_y^2 - 2Cov_{xy}} \tag{8}$$

where w^* is the optimum proportion of investment in security X. Investment in Y will be: $1 - w^*$. In the example above, we find that w^* is:

$$w^* = \frac{58.2 - (-33)}{58.2 + 33.6 - 2(-33)} = 0.578$$

Thus the weight of Y will be: $1 - 0.578 = 0.422$.

The portfolio variance (with 57.8 per cent of investment in X and 42.2 per cent in Y) is:

$$\sigma_p^2 = 33.6(0.578)^2 + 58.2(0.422)^2$$
$$+ 2(0.578)(0.422)(5.80)(7.63)(-0.746)$$
$$= 11.23 + 10.36 - 16.11 = 5.48$$

The standard deviation is:

$$\sigma = \sqrt{5.48} = 2.34$$

Any other combination of X and Y will yield a higher variance or standard deviation.

Portfolio Risk Depends on Correlation between Assets

We emphasise once again that the portfolio standard deviation is not the weighted average of the standard deviations of the individual securities. In our example above, the standard deviation of portfolio of X and Y is 2.54 per cent. Let us see how much is the weighted standard deviation of the individual securities:

Weighted standard deviation of individual securities
$$= 5.8 \times 0.5 + 7.63 \times 0.5 = 6.7\%$$

Thus, the standard deviation of portfolio of X and Y is considerably lower than the weighted standard deviation of these individual securities. This example shows that investing wealth in more than one security reduces portfolio risk. This is attributed to **diversification effect**. However, the extent of the benefits of portfolio diversification depends on the correlation between returns on securities. In our example, returns on securities X and Y are negatively correlated and correlation coefficient is -0.746. This has caused significant reduction in the portfolio risk. Would

Table 5.6: Covariance calculation Matrix: Example

I		II		III	
σ_x^2 33.6	Cov_{xy} −33.0	w_x^2 $(0.5)^2 = 0.25$	$w_x w_y$ $(0.5)(0.5) = 0.25$	$\sigma_x^2 w_x^2$ $(33.6)(0.25) = 8.40$	$w_x w_y Cov_{xy}$ $(0.25)(-33.0) = -8.25$
Cov_{xy} −33.0	σ_y^2 58.20	$w_x w_y$ $(0.5)(0.5) = 0.25$	w_y^2 $(0.5)^2 = 0.25$	$w_x w_y Cov_{xy}$ $(0.25)(-33.0) = -8.25$	$\sigma_y^2 w_y^2$ $(58.2)(0.25) = 14.55$

there be diversification benefit (that is, risk reduction) if the correlation were positive? Let us assume that correlation coefficient in our example is +0.25. How much is the portfolio standard deviation? It is 5.34 as shown below:

$$\sigma_p^2 = 33.6(0.5)^2 + 58.2(0.5)^2 + 2(0.5)(0.5)(5.80)(7.63)(+0.25)$$
$$= 8.4 + 14.55 + 5.53 = 28.48$$
$$\sigma = \sqrt{28.48} = 5.34\%$$

The portfolio risk ($\sigma = 5.34\%$) is still lower than the weighted average standard deviation of individual securities ($\sigma = 6.7\%$). If the returns of securities X and Y are positively perfectly correlated (with the correlation coefficient of 1), then the portfolio standard deviation is as follows:

$$\sigma_p^2 = 33.6(0.5)^2 + 58.2(0.5)^2 + 2(0.5)(0.5)(5.80)(7.63)(+1)$$
$$= 8.4 + 14.55 + 22.13 = 45.08$$
$$\sigma = \sqrt{45.08} = 6.7\%$$

When correlation coefficient of returns on individual securities is perfectly positive (i.e., Cor = 1.0), then there is no advantage of diversification. The weighted standard deviation of returns on individual securities is equal to the standard deviation of the portfolio. We may therefore conclude that diversification always reduces risk provided the correlation coefficient is less than 1.

Illustration 5.1: Risk of Two-Assets Portfolio

Securities M and N are equally risky, but they have different expected returns:

	M	N
Expected return (%)	16.00	24.00
Weight	0.50	0.50
Standard deviation (%)	20.00	20.00

What is the portfolio risk (variance) if (*a*) $\text{Cor}_{mn} = +1.0$, (*b*) $\text{Cor}_{mn} = -1.0$, (*c*) $\text{Cor}_{mn} = 0.0$, (*d*) $\text{Cor}_{mn} = +0.10$, and (*e*) $\text{Cor}_{mn} = -0.10$?

(*a*) When correlation is + 1.0, Equation (7) will reduce to

$$\sigma_p = \sqrt{\sigma_x^2 w_x^2 + \sigma_y^2 w_y^2 + 2w_x w_y \sigma_x \sigma_y}$$
$$= \sigma_x w_x + \sigma_y w_y$$

The standard deviation of portfolio of M and N is as follows:

$$\sigma_p = 20 \times 0.5 + 20 \times 0.5 = 20.0\%$$

(*b*) The portfolio standard deviation is calculated as follows:

$$\sigma_p^2 = \sqrt{20^2 \times 0.5^2 + 20^2 \times 0.5^2 + 2 \times 0.5 \times 0.5 \times 20 \times 20 \times -1.0}$$
$$= \sqrt{100 + 100 - 200} = 0.0\%$$

(*c*) When the correlation is zero, Equation (7) will reduce to

$$\sigma_p = \sqrt{\sigma_x^2 w_x^2 + \sigma_2^2 w_y^2}$$

For the portfolio of M and N, the standard deviation is:

$$\sigma_p = \sqrt{20^2 \times 0.5^2 + 20^2 \times 0.5^2} = \sqrt{200} = 14.14\%$$

(*d*) The portfolio variance under weakly positive correlation (+ 0.10) is given below:

$$\sigma_p^2 = \sqrt{20^2 \times 0.5^2 + 20^2 \times 0.5^2 + 2 \times 0.5 \times 0.5 \times 20 \times 20 \times 0.10}$$
$$= \sqrt{100 + 100 + 20} = \sqrt{220} = 14.83\%$$

(*e*) The portfolio variance under weakly negative correlated (– 0.10) returns of two securities M and N is:

$$\sigma_p^2 = \sqrt{20^2 \times 0.5^2 + 20^2 \times 0.5^2 + 2 \times 0.5 \times 0.5 \times 20 \times 20 \times -0.10}$$
$$= \sqrt{100 + 100 - 20} = \sqrt{180} = 13.42\%$$

It may be observed in the above example that a total reduction of risk is possible if the returns of the two securities are perfectly negatively correlated, though, such a perfect negative correlation will not generally be found in practice. Securities do have a tendency of moving together to some extent, and therefore, risk may not be totally eliminated.

PORTFOLIO RISK – RETURN ANALYSIS: TWO-ASSET CASE

Let us recapitulate that portfolio return depends on the proportion of wealth invested in two assets, and is in no way affected by correlation between asset returns. In contrast, the portfolio risk depends on both correlation and proportions (weights) of assets forming the portfolio. Let us emphasise again that the correlation coefficient will always lie between + 1.0 and – 1.0. Returns on assets or securities vary perfectly together in the same direction when the correlation coefficient is + 1.0 and in perfectly opposite directions when it is – 1.0. A zero correlation coefficient implies that there is no relationship between the returns of securities. In practice, the correlation coefficients of returns of securities may vary between + 1.0 and – 1.0. Let us consider an example to understand the implications of asset correlation and weights for the portfolio risk-return relationship.

Suppose two securities, Logrow and Rapidex have the following characteristics:

	Logrow	*Rapidex*
Expected Return (%)	12.00	18.00
Variance	256.00	576.00
Standard deviation (%)	16.00	24.00

Further, assume four possible correlations between the returns of these securities: perfectly positive correlation (+1.0); perfectly negative correlation (–1.0); no correlation (0.0), positive correlation (0.5) and negative correlation (–0.25). The first three relationships are special situations. They are not rare, but they may not be very common in practice. In the real word, returns of securities have a tendency to move together in the same direction. Sometimes they move in opposite direction. Thus a positive or negative correlation is more likely between two risky securities. Given the characteristics of Logrow and Rapidex and their correlation, what are the interactions between risk and return of portfolios that could be formed by combining them?

Logrow is a low return and low risk security as compared to Rapidex, which has high return and high risk. If you hold 100 per cent investment in Logrow, your expected return is 12 per

Table 5.7: Portfolio Return and Risk for Different Correlation Coefficients

Weight		Portfolio Return (%)	Portfolio Risk, s_p (%) Correlation				
			+1.00	−1.00	0.00	0.50	−0.25
Logrow	Rapidex	R_p	σ_p	σ_p	σ_p	σ_p	σ_p
1.00	0.00	12.00	16.00	16.00	16.00	16.00	16.00
0.90	0.10	12.60	16.80	12.00	14.60	15.74	13.99
0.80	0.20	13.20	17.60	8.00	13.67	15.76	12.50
0.70	0.30	13.80	18.40	4.00	13.31	16.06	11.70
0.60	0.40	14.40	19.20	0.00	13.58	16.63	11.76
0.50	0.50	15.00	20.00	4.00	14.42	17.44	12.65
0.40	0.60	15.60	20.80	8.00	15.76	18.45	14.22
0.30	0.70	16.20	21.60	12.00	17.47	19.64	16.28
0.20	0.80	16.80	22.40	16.00	19.46	20.98	18.66
0.10	0.90	17.40	23.20	20.00	21.66	22.44	21.26
0.00	1.00	18.00	24.00	24.00	24.00	24.00	24.00

Minimum Variance Portfolio

			+1.00	−1.00	0.00	0.50	−0.25
w_L			1.00	0.60	0.692	0.857	0.656
w_R			0.00	0.40	0.308	0.143	0.344
σ^2			256	0.00	177.23	246.86	135.00
σ (%)			16	0.00	13.31	15.71	11.62

cent and standard deviation 16 per cent. On the contrary, if you invest your entire wealth in Rapidex you may expect to earn a higher return of 18 per cent, but the standard deviation, 24 per cent, is also higher. How would the expected return and risk change if you form portfolios of Logrow and Rapidex by combining them in different proportions? In Table 5.7 we show the calculations of the portfolio return and risk for different combinations (weights) of Logrow and Rapidex under different assumptions regarding the correlation between them. We use Equation (2) for calculating the expected return of the portfolio and Equation (7) for the standard deviation of returns of the portfolio. We also show the minimum variance portfolios in the lower part of the table. You can use Equation (8) to calculate the minimum variance portfolio. Later on we show that under certain situations, Equation (8) can be simplified.

Perfect Positive Correlation

Let us first consider the case of perfect positive correlation. It is not unrealistic, though rare, to find two assets or securities that have perfect positive correlation. You can notice from Table 5.7 that as you invest more wealth in Rapidex, your expected return increases, but so does the standard deviation. We draw Figure 5.1 to show the relationship between portfolio return and portfolio risk (standard deviation) under different combinations of two securities, Logrow and Rapidex, when correlation is +1.0. You can see in Figure 5.1 that the expected portfolio return and portfolio risk are linearly related. Higher the expected return, higher the standard deviation and vice-versa. You can choose any portfolio depending on your risk preference. If you are extremely risk-averse, you may choose

to invest all your money in Logrow (point *A*). This is the minimum variance (standard deviation) portfolio. On the other hand, if you do not mind high risk, you could put all your money in Rapidex (point *B*). Others may choose any points on the line *AB*.

When correlation is +1.0, the portfolio risk (standard deviation) is simply given by the following formula:

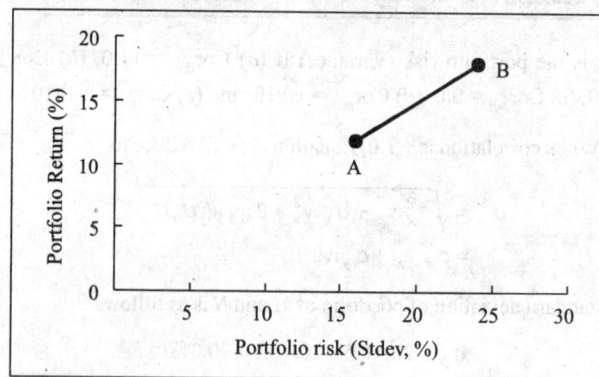

Figure 5.1: Risk-return relationships under perfect positive correlation

$$\sigma_p = \sqrt{\sigma_x^2 w_x^2 + \sigma_y^2 w_y^2 + 2w_x w_y \sigma_x \sigma_y}$$
$$= \sigma_x w_x + \sigma_y w_y \qquad (9)$$

The standard deviation of the returns of the portfolio is just the weighted average of the standard deviations of individual securities. *There is no advantage of diversification when the returns of securities have perfect positive correlation.*

Perfect Negative Correlation

What are the consequence for risk and return of portfolios when securities have perfect negative correlation (– 1.0)? Figure 5.2 shows the return and risk relationships of portfolios of securities Logrow and Rapidex when their returns are perfectly negatively correlated. You may observe that the portfolio return increases and the portfolio risk declines as higher proportion of high-risk security Rapidex is combined with low-risk security Logrow until the combination of 60 per cent of Logrow and 40 per cent of Rapidex is reached. At this combination (point A), the portfolio return is 14.40 per cent and portfolio risk (i.e., standard deviation) is zero. You have been able to diversify (reduce) all risk. This is a **risk-less portfolio** that has resulted from the perfect negative correlation. Notice from Figure 5.2 that you are better off on any point on the line *AC* than on the line *AB*. For example, B_1 on the line *AC* offers higher return with same risk as point *B* on the line *AB*. This is the case with any other point on the line *AC*. Thus, the line *AC dominates* the line *AB*. This implies that any portfolio of Logrow and Rapidex on the line *AC* dominates any portfolio on the line *AB*.

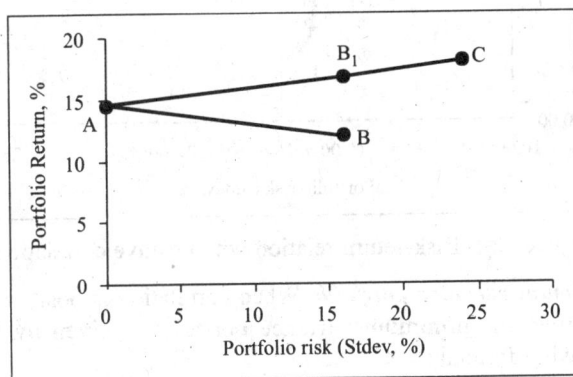

Figure 5.2: Risk-return relationships under perfect negative correlation

Zero-variance portfolio: When correlation is – 1.0, we can simplify Equation (8) and the portfolio risk (standard deviation) is simply given by the following formula:

$$\sigma_p = \sqrt{\sigma_x^2 w_x^2 + \sigma_y^2 w_y^2 - 2 w_x w_y \sigma_x \sigma_y} \qquad (10)$$
$$= ABS \left[\sigma_x w_x - \sigma_y w_y \right]$$

Remember that the standard deviation always has a positive value. Therefore, the solution is an absolute solution (*ABS*). We can use Equation (10) to find the proportions of securities in the portfolio that would result in zero-standard deviation portfolio:

$$\sigma_x w_x - \sigma_y w_y = \sigma_x w_x - \sigma_y \left(1 - w_x\right) = 0$$
$$\sigma_x w_x = \sigma_y \left(1 - w_x\right) = \sigma_y - \sigma_y w_x$$
$$= \sigma_x w_x + \sigma_y w_x = \sigma_y$$
$$w_x = \frac{\sigma_y}{\sigma_x + \sigma_y}$$

For Logrow and Rapidex, the proportions with correlation = – 1.0 are as follows:

$$w_L = \frac{16}{16 + 24} = 0.40 \text{ or } 40\%$$
$$w_R = 1 - w_S = 1 - 0.40 = 0.60 \text{ or } 60\%$$

The portfolio with 40 per cent proportion of Logrow and 60 per cent of Rapidex has zero standard deviation. There is maximum benefit of diversification when the returns of two securities have perfect negative correlation.

Limits to diversification: The risk-return impact of portfolios of Logrow and Rapidex under the assumptions of perfect positive correlation and perfect negative correlation can be combined in Figure 5.3. Since any probable correlation of securities Logrow and Rapidex will range between – 1.0 and + 1.0, the triangle in Figure 5.3 specifies the limits to diversification. The risk-return curves for any correlations within the limits of – 1.0 and + 1.0, will fall within the triangle *ABC*.

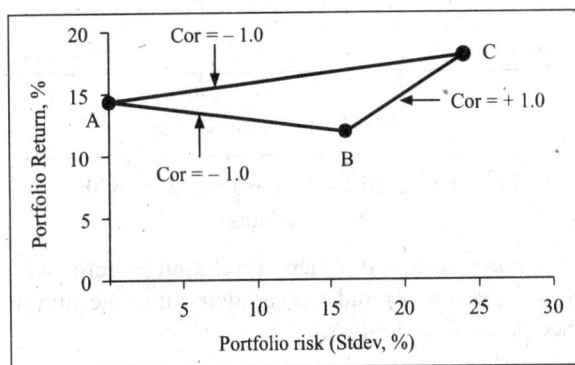

Figure 5.3: Risk-return relationships under perfect negative correlation

Zero Correlation

Zero correlation means that the returns of two securities are independent of each other. Will there be gain from diversification if the correlation were zero? Figure 5.4 shows the risk-return relationship between Logrow and Rapidex securities where correlation is zero. You may notice that point *L* on the curve *LR* represents a portfolio entirely consisting of Logrow. Your expected return is 12 per cent and standard deviation is 16 per cent. You may shift to portfolio B where you divide your investment equally between Logrow and Rapidex. You may see from Table 5.4 that your expected return is 15.0 per cent and standard deviation is 14.42 per cent, which is less than the standard deviation of either security. The benefit of diversification is without any cost; the investor is able to invest in the high-risk security (Rapidex) and improve his expected return while keeping the portfolio risk less than the risk of individual securities. Notice that shifting your investment to more risky security (Rapidex) reduces the portfolio risk. You can appreciate the powerful effect of diversification on risk reduction.

How far can the risk be reduced? You may observe the effect of diversification in Figure 5.4. There is no possibility of the standard deviation reducing to zero and achieving a risk-less portfolio. You may notice in the figure that portfolio *P* is **the minimum variance portfolio.** Portfolio *P* dominates any portfolio on *LP* — the downward sloping part of the curve *LR*.

On *PR* — the upward sloping portion of the curve *LR*, there are portfolios that yield higher return but they have higher risk as well. Notice that portfolio *Q* is outside the curve *LR*. It has lower return than portfolio *R*, but it is equally risky. Thus, portfolio *R* dominates portfolio *Q* and is preferable.

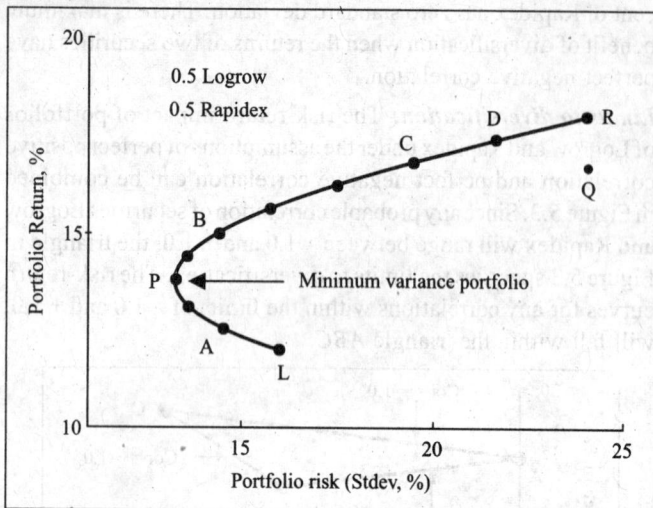

Figure 5.4: Risk-return relationships with zero correlation

Minimum variance When correlation is zero, we can simplify Equation (8) and we can determine the minimum variance portfolio as follows:

$$w_x = \frac{\sigma_y^2}{\sigma_x^2 + \sigma_y^2}$$

Applying this formula in the case of Logrow and Rapidex, we find weights as shown below:

$$w_L = \frac{\sigma_R^2}{\sigma_L^2 + \sigma_R^2} = \frac{24^2}{16^2 + 24^2} = \frac{576}{256 + 576} = 0.308$$

$$w_R = 1 - w_L = 1 - 0.308 = 0.692$$

Your risk (variance or standard deviation) will be minimum if you invest your wealth 30.8 per cent in Logrow and 69.8 per cent in Rapidex. You can verify that the expected return for this portfolio is 13.85 per cent and standard deviation is 13.31 per cent. Would you prefer this portfolio to 50-50 per cent portfolio? This would depend on your risk preference.

Positive Correlation

In reality, returns of most assets have positive but less than 1.0 correlation. Figure 5.5 shows risk and return of various combinations of Logrow and Rapidex when correlation is + 0.50. You may notice that the portfolio risk and return combinations form a curve, which implies the possibility of diversification benefit. The portfolio L in Figure 5.5 represents 100 per cent investment in Logrow. The investor's expected return is 12 per

cent and standard deviation is 16 per cent. Instead, if the investor chooses portfolio A where he invests 60 per cent of his wealth in Logrow and 40 per cent in Rapidex, his expected return is 14.40 per cent and standard deviation 16.63 per cent. He gains an increase of 20 per cent in the return while his risk (standard deviation) increases only by 3.9 per cent. Thus the **incremental return-risk ratio** is: 20 ÷ 3.9 = 5.13. For one unit increase in risk, the return increases by 5.13 times. The investor can consider the possibility of putting all his money in Rapidex. His expected return would be 18 per cent and standard deviation 24 per cent. Now if he invests 60 per cent in Logrow, his risk reduces by 44.3 per cent but the return decreases only by one-fourth.

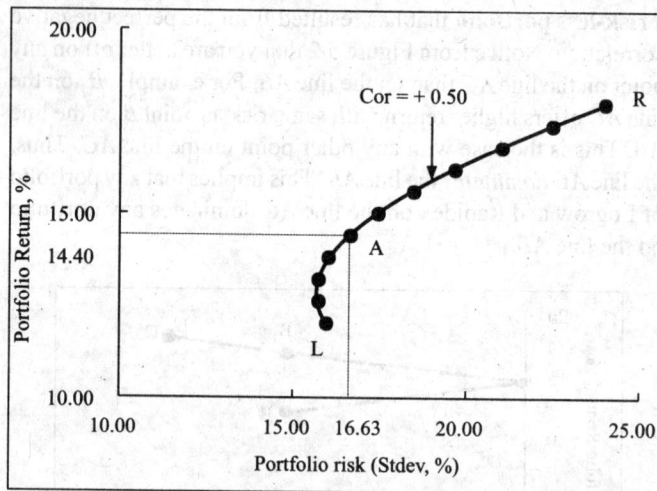

Figure 5.5: Risk-return relation with positive correlation

Minimum variance portfolio When correlation is positive or negative, the minimum variance portfolio is given by the following formula:

$$w_x = \frac{\sigma_y^2 - \sigma_x \sigma_y Cor_{xy}}{\sigma_x^2 + \sigma_y^2 - 2\sigma_x \sigma_y Cor_{xy}} \qquad (11)$$

Applying this formula, you can find that if the investor invests 85.7 per cent in Logrow and 14.3 per cent in Rapidex, the expected return will be 12.86 per cent and standard deviation 15.71 per cent. What should the investor do? The investor's choice of the combination of Logrow and Rapidex will depend on his risk preference. Note that when the variance or standard deviation is lower, the expected return is also low. But the conclusion is quite clear that when correlation is less than + 1.0, it is beneficial to diversify. The incremental return-risk ratio can improve through diversification.

EFFICIENT PORTFOLIO AND MEAN - VARIANCE CRITERION

Investment Opportunity Set: Two-Asset Case

The investor should be aware of the full set of opportunities before she makes her choice of the two-asset portfolio. The

---

We can use the Excel spreadsheet to calculate portfolio return and standard deviation. In the spreadsheet given on the right-hand side, column B2 and B3 and column C2 and C3, respectively, have return and standard deviation for security *X* and security *Y*. Column D4 shows the correlation between returns on *X* and *Y*. The proportions of *X* and *Y* in the portfolio are given, respectively, in column B8 to column B18 for *X* and column C8 to column C18 for *Y*. The calculations of portfolio return and portfolio standard deviation are given in column D and column E.

For calculating the portfolio return, we enter in column D8 the formula: =$B$2*B8+$C$2*C8 and copy it down. For calculating the portfolio standard deviation, we enter in column E8 the formula:

= ($B$3^2*B8^2+$C$3^2*C8^2 + 2*$B$3*$C$3*$D$4)^0.5,

and copy it down. You may notice that the spreadsheet has calculations for the minimum variance portfolio as well. To determine the optimum weight of *X*, in column B19 we enter the formula: = (C3^2 B3*C3* D4)/(B3^2+C3^2- 2B3*C3*D4). The optimum weight of X is 0.857 and of Y: 1 − 0.857 = 0.143. Given these weights for *X* and *Y*, the portfolio standard deviation of 19.64 per cent is given in column E19. This is the minimum standard deviation. The portfolio return,

given in column D19 is 15.71 per cent.

	A	B	C	D	E
1		**X**	**Y**	**XY**	
2	Expected return (%)	15	20		
3	Standard deviation (%)	20	30		
4	Correlation			0.50	
5					
6		**Weight**		**Portfolio**	
7		**X**	**Y**	**Return**	**Stdev.**
8	=$B$2*B8+$C$2*C8	1.00	0.00	15.00	20.00
9		0.90	0.10	15.50	19.67
10		0.80	0.20	16.00	19.70
11	=($B$3^2*B8^2+$C$3^2 *C8^2+2*$B$3*$C$3*$ D$4)^0.5	0.70	0.30	16.50	20.07
12		0.60	0.40	17.00	20.78
13		0.50	0.50	17.50	21.79
14		0.40	0.60	18.00	23.07
15		0.30	0.70	18.50	24.56
16		0.20	0.80	19.00	26.23
17		0.10	0.90	19.50	28.05
18		0.00	1.00	20.00	30.00
19	Minimum variance portfolio	**0.857**	**0.143**	**15.71**	**19.64**
20	=(C3^2- B3*C3*D4)/(B3^2 +C3^2-2B3*C3*D4)				
21					
22					
23					

---

investment or **portfolio opportunity set**[1] represents all possible combinations of risk and return resulting from portfolios formed by varying proportions of individual securities. It presents the investor with the risk-return trade-off. In Figure 5.4 or Figure 5.5 the investment opportunity set is shown by the curve *LR*. The points on the curves show the possible combinations of two securities, Logrow and Rapidex, forming the portfolios. Each point indicates the risk and return of the portfolio. We can form the portfolios by varying the proportions of two securities as shown in Table 5.4. The portfolio return and risk are calculated for different assumptions about correlation.

We have so far discussed that diversification has benefits whenever correlation between returns of assets is less than perfectly correlated. The maximum diversification benefits occur when there is perfect negative correlation between asset returns. Figure 5.6 shows that as correlation decreases from perfect positive correlation, diversification becomes more and more attractive. Figure 5.6 also shows that the investment opportunity sets of all possible combinations for two-asset portfolios depend on correlation. It is important to note that each set has only one value of correlation, and one line specifies all possible combinations of portfolios for each specific case. You can refer

to Table 5.4 for the points on the various opportunity sets in Figure 5.6.

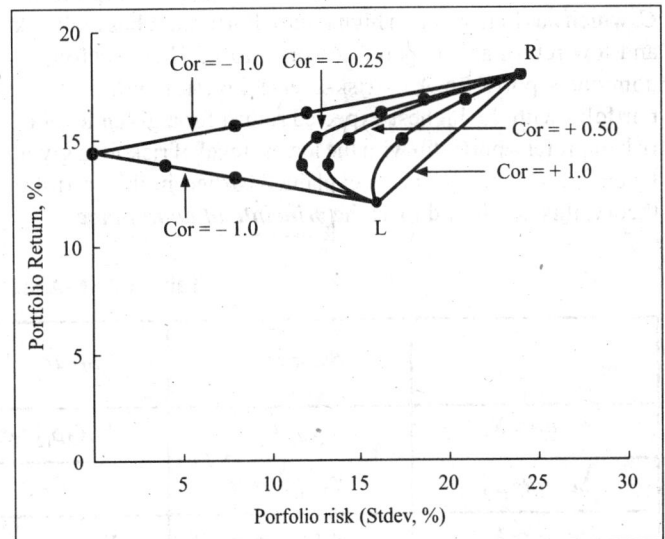

Figure 5.6: Investment opportunity sets given different correlations

---

1. Markovitz first developed the portfolio theory. See H.H. Markoviz, *Portfolio Selection: Efficient Diversification of Investments,* John Wiley, 1959. The concepts discussed here have their origin in Markovitz's landmark work. Others who have contributed to the development of the portfolio theory and the capital asset pricing model include Lintner, J., The Valuation of Risk Assets and the Selection of Risky Investments in Stock Portfolio and Capital Budgets, *Review of Economics and Statistics,* Vol. 47 (Feb. 1965), pp. 13–37; Sharpe, W.F., Capital Asset Prices: A Theory of Market Equilibrium under Conditions of Risk, *Journal of Finance,* Vol. 19 (Sept. 1964), pp. 425–42; and J. Treynor, whose article has not been published.

Mean-variance Criterion

Let us consider Figure 5.4. Note that portfolio P dominates portfolio A. It has higher return and lower risk:

$$E(R_P) \geq E(R_A); \sigma_P \leq \sigma_A$$

Since investors are risk-averse and they behave rationally, they would choose portfolio P rather than A. Portfolio P has minimum variance. The minimum-variance portfolio P and all portfolios above it dominate any portfolio on the downward sloping curve. The portfolios below P are **inefficient portfolios** as they have lower return and higher risk. You may also note in Figure 5.4 that portfolio D dominates C and C dominates P. Similarly, portfolio R dominates portfolios below it as well as Q. Portfolio Q is outside the investment opportunity set, and it has lower return and higher standard deviation than R. Which portfolio should an investor choose on the upward sloping curve? We repeat that it depends on the risk preference of the investor.

Investment Opportunity Set: The N-Asset Case

What will happen to the portfolio opportunity set if an investor holds more than two securities? There are a few thousand shares that are traded on the Bombay Stock Exchange and the National Stock Exchange. We could also construct a large number of portfolios combining these shares in different proportions. Figure 5.7 shows the risk and return of all possible portfolios. The shape of the portfolio opportunity set in case of multiple securities will remain the same as shown in Figure 5.7. However, two-security portfolios are located on a single curve while the multiple securities portfolios lie on much broader area. We may observe that portfolio B has low risk and low return than portfolio C, which has high risk and high return. Portfolio A has high risk and low return as compared to portfolio P. Thus portfolio P dominates portfolio A. A risk-averse investor will prefer a portfolio with the highest expected return for a given level of risk or prefer a portfolio with the lowest level of risk for a given level of expected return. As explained earlier, in the portfolio theory, this is referred to as the *principle of dominance.*

An **efficient portfolio**[1] is one that has the highest expected returns for a given level of risk. The **efficient frontier** is the frontier formed by the set of efficient portfolios. In Figure 5.7, the curve starting from portfolio P, which is the minimum variance portfolio, and extending to the portfolio R is the efficient frontier. All portfolios on the efficient frontier are efficient portfolios. All other portfolios, which lie outside the efficient frontier, are **inefficient portfolios.** For example, portfolio Q has same return as portfolio B but it has higher risk. Similarly, portfolio C has higher return than portfolio Q with same amount of risk. Q is an inefficient portfolio. Portfolios B and C are efficient portfolios —portfolio B has low risk and low return, while portfolio C has high risk and high return. B dominates C. The choice of the portfolio will depend on the investor's risk-return preference.

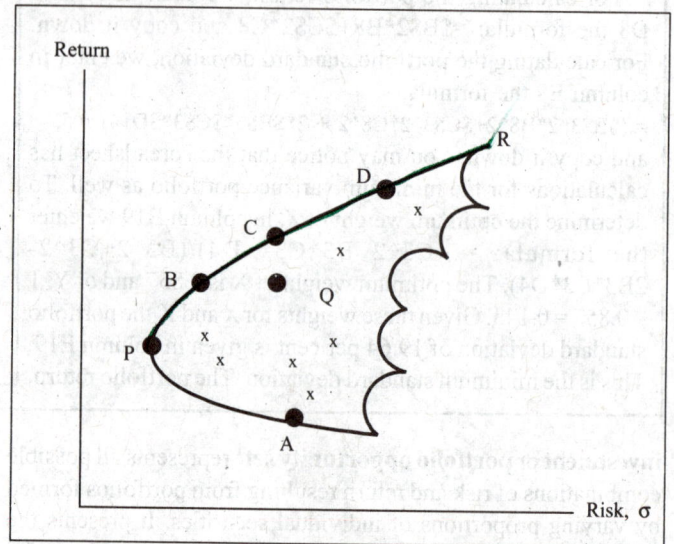

Figure 5.7: Efficient Portfolios of risky securities

PORTFOLIO RISK: THE N-ASSET CASE

We have so far discussed the calculation of risk when a two-asset portfolio is formed. The calculation of risk becomes quite involved when a large number of assets or securities are combined

Table 5.8: N-Asset Portfolio Risk Matrix

	Security X_1	Security X_2	Security X_3	.....	Security X_n
Security X_1	$X_1^2\sigma_1^2$	$X_1X_2\rho_{12}\sigma_1\sigma_2$	$X_1X_3\rho_{12}\sigma_1\sigma_3$	.....	$X_1X_n\rho_{1n}\sigma_1\sigma_n$
Security X_2	$X_2X_1\rho_{21}\sigma_2\sigma_1$	$X_2^2\sigma_2^2$	$X_2X_1\rho_{23}\sigma_2\sigma_3$	.....	$X_2X_n\rho_{2n}\sigma_2\sigma_n$
Security X_3	$X_3X_1\rho_{31}\sigma_3\sigma_1$	$X_3X_2\rho_{32}\sigma_3\sigma_2$	$X_3^2\sigma_3^2$	.....	$X_3X_n\rho_{3n}\sigma_3\sigma_n$
.	.	.			
Security X_n	$X_nX_1\rho_{n1}\sigma_n\sigma_1$	$X_nX_2\rho_{n2}\sigma_n\sigma_2$	$X_nX_3\rho_{n3}\sigma_n\sigma_3$	.....	$X_n^2\sigma_n^2$

1. Markovitz, *op. cit.* Also see Copeland, T. and Weston, J.F., *Financial Theory and Corporate Policy*, Addison-Wesley, 1983, p. 187.

to form a portfolio. The matrix given in Table 5.8 explains the calculation of the portfolio risk in the *N*-security (asset) case. The diagonal terms contain the variances of different securities and the off-diagonal terms contain the covariances. The number of variances will be equal to the number of securities. But the number of covariances will be much more and increase much faster than the number of variances. The portfolio variance will depend on the covariances between the securities.

Based on the logic of the portfolio risk in a two-security case, the portfolio risk in N-security case can be calculated. Let us assume a portfolio where all securities (*n*) have equal weights, they have the same variance and all covariance terms are equal. In this special case, the portfolio variance is given as follows:[1]

$$\text{Portfolio variance} = \sigma_p^2 = n\left[\frac{1}{n^2}\right] \times \text{average variance}$$

$$+ n(n-1)\left[\frac{1}{n^2}\right] \times \text{average covariance}$$

$$\text{Portfolio variance} = \left[\frac{1}{n}\right] \text{average variance}$$

$$+ \left[1 - \frac{1}{n}\right] \times \text{average covariance} \quad (12)$$

$n \to \infty$

We may notice from Equation (12) that the variance of the portfolio is the weighted sum of average variance and the average covariance of securities. Notice that the first term on the right-hand side of Equation (12) will become insignificant when *n* is very large. In fact, when *n* approaches infinity ($n \to \infty$), the weight of the average variance becomes zero and the weight of the average covariance term becomes 1. Thus the variance of the portfolio will be:

$$\text{Portfolio variance (when } n \to \infty) = \text{average covariance} \quad (13)$$

Equation (12) shows that the variance of securities diminishes as the number of securities increases. As the number of securities becomes very large, Equation (13) reveals that the variances of the individual securities disappear, and only the covariance remains. In fact, the portfolio variance becomes equal to the average variance. This is an illustration of risk diversification as the number of securities in a portfolio is increased. We further explain this point in the following section.

RISK DIVERSIFICATION: SYSTEMATIC AND UNSYSTEMATIC RISK

Can diversification reduce all risk of securities? We just explained that when more and more securities are included in a portfolio, the risk of individual securities in the portfolio is reduced. This risk totally vanishes when the number of securities is very large. But the risk represented by covariance remains. Thus, risk has two parts: diversifiable (unsystematic) and non-diversifiable (systematic).[2]

Systematic Risk

Systematic risk arises on account of the economy-wide uncertainties and the tendency of individual securities to move together with changes in the market. This part of risk cannot be reduced through diversification. It is also known as **market risk**. Investors are exposed to market risk even when they hold well-diversified portfolios of securities.[3] The examples of systematic or market risk are given in Table 5.9.

Table 5.9: Examples of Systematic Risk

• The government changes the *interest rate policy*. The *corporate tax* rate is increased.	• The government relaxes the *foreign exchange* controls and announces full *convertibility* of the Indian rupee.
• The government resorts to massive *deficit financing*. • The *inflation* rate increases. • The RBI promulgates a restrictive *credit policy*.	• The government withdraws tax on dividend payments by companies. • The government eliminates reduces the capital gain tax rate.

Unsystematic Risk

Unsystematic risk arises from the unique uncertainties of individual securities. It is also called **unique risk**. These uncertainties are diversifiable if a large numbers of securities are combined to form well-diversified portfolios. Uncertainties of individual securities in a portfolio cancel out each other. Thus unsystematic risk can be totally reduced through diversification. Table 5.10 contains examples of unsystematic risks.

Table 5.10: Examples of Unsystematic Risk

• The company workers declare strike. • The R&D expert leaves the company. • A formidable competitor enters the market. • The company loses a big contract in a bid.	• The company makes a breakthrough in process innovation. • The government increases custom duty on the material used by the company. • The company is unable to obtain adequate quantity of raw material

Total Risk

Total risk of an individual security is the variance (or standard deviation) of its return. It consists of two parts:

$$\text{Total risk of a security} = \text{Systematic risk} + \text{Unsystematic risk} \quad (14)$$

Systematic risk is the covariance of the individual securities in the portfolio. An investor has to suffer the systematic risk, as it cannot be diversified away. The difference between variance and covariance is the diversifiable or unsystematic risk. Thus, Equation (14) can be written as:

$$\text{Variance of security} = \text{covariance of portfolio} + (\text{variance of security} - \text{covariance of portfolio}) \quad (15)$$

---

1. Brealey, R.A. and Myers, S.C., *Principles of Corporate Finance*, McGraw-Hill, 1991, p. 142.
2. Sharpe, *op. cit.*
3. *Ibid.*, p. 441.

Total risk is not relevant for an investor who holds a diversified portfolio. The systematic risk cannot be diversified, and therefore, she will expect a compensation for bearing this risk. She will be more concerned about that portion of the risk of individual securities that she cannot diversify.

Figure 5.8 shows that unsystematic risk can be reduced as more and more securities are added to a portfolio. How many securities should be held by an investor to eliminate unsystematic risk? In USA, it has been found that holding about fifteen shares can eliminate unsystematic risk.[1] In the Indian context, a portfolio of 40 shares can almost totally eliminate unsystematic risk.[2] Diversification is not able to reduce the systematic risk. Thus the source of risk for an investor who holds a well-diversified portfolio is that the market will swing due to economic activities affecting the investor's portfolio. Typically, the diversified portfolios move with the market. The most common well-diversified portfolios in India include the share indices of the Bombay Stock Exchange and the National Stock Exchange. In a study in USA, it is found that market risk contributes about 50 per cent variation in the price of a share.[3] Thus diversification may be able to eliminate only half of the total risk (viz. unsystematic risk). How can we measure systematic (that is, market) risk? What is the relationship between risk and return?

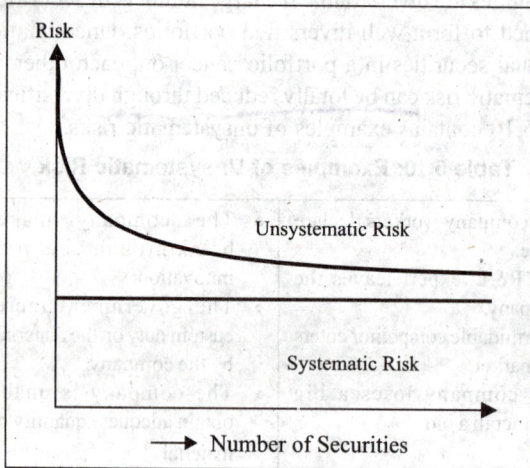

Figure 5.8: Systematic and unsystematic risk and number of securities

COMBINING A RISK-FREE ASSET AND A RISKY ASSET

In the preceding sections, we have discussed the risk-return implications of holding risky securities, and the construction of the portfolio opportunity set. What happens to the choices of investors in the market if they could combine a risk-free security with a single or multiple risky securities? If investors could borrow and lend at the **risk-free rate of interest,** how would the portfolio opportunity set be shaped and how could securities be valued in the market?

A **risk-free asset** or security has a zero variance or standard deviation. The risk-free security has no risk of default. The government treasury bills or bonds are approximate examples of the risk-free security as they have no risk of default.

What happens to return and risk when we combine a risk-free and a risky asset? Let us assume that an investor holds a risk-free security f of which he has an expected return of 5 per cent and a risky security j with an expected return of 15 per cent and a standard deviation of 6 per cent. What is the portfolio return and risk if the investor holds these securities in equal proportion? The portfolio return is:

$$E(R_p) = wE(R_j) + (1-w)R_f \qquad (16)$$
$$= 0.5 \times 0.15 + (1-0.5)0.05$$
$$= 0.075 + 0.025 = 0.10 \text{ or } 10\%$$

Since the risk-free security has zero standard deviation, the covariance between the risk-free security and risky security is also zero. The portfolio risk is simply given as the product of the standard deviation of the risky security and its weight. Thus

$$\sigma_p = w\sigma_j \qquad (17)$$
$$\sigma_p = 0.5 \times 0.06 = 0.03 \text{ or } 3\%$$

Borrowing and Lending

The investor can invest all her wealth in the risk-free security or the risky-security. She may even borrow funds at the risk-free rate of interest and invest more than 100 per cent of her wealth in the risky security. Alternatively, she may invest less than 100 per cent in the risky security and lend the remaining funds at the risk-free rate of interest. Under different combination of the risky security and the risk-free security with borrowing and lending at the risk-free rate of interest, the expected return and risk could be calculated as shown in Table 5.11.

Table 5.11: Risk-return Analysis for a Portfolio of a Risky and a Risk-free Securities

Weights (%)		Expected Return, R_p (%)	Standard Deviation (σ_p) (%)
Risky security	*Risk-free security*		
120	− 20	17	7.2
100	0	15	6.0
80	20	13	4.8
60	40	11	3.6
40	60	9	2.4
20	80	7	1.2
0	100	5	0.0

Figure 5.9 illustrates the risk-return relationship for various combinations of a risk-free security and a risky security, and the resulting portfolio opportunity set. Point *B* represents 100 per cent investment in the risky security expected to yield 15 per cent return and 6 per cent standard deviation. The investor can borrow at the risk-free rate and invest in the risky security. Point

1. Evans, J.L. and Archer, S.H., Diversification and the Reduction of Dispersion: An Empirical Analysis, *Journal of Finance* (December 1968), pp. 761–69.
2. Gupta, L.C., *Rates of Return on Equities: The Indian Experience,* Delhi, Oxford, 1981, pp. 30–35.
3. King, B.F., market and Industry Factors in Stock Price Behaviour, *Journal of Business, 39,* 1 (Jan 1966), pp. 139–90.

C (to the right of Point *B*) shows 120 per cent investment in the risky security after borrowing at the risk-free rate of interest and the investor can expect to earn a return of 17 per cent with a higher risk, *viz.*, a standard deviation of 7.2 per cent. A risk-averse investor may not invest her entire wealth in the risky security, and may like to lend a part of her wealth at the risk-free rate of interest. Point *A* (to the left of Point *B*) illustrates this behaviour. At Point *A* the investor invests 60 per cent of her wealth in the risky security and lends the remaining amount at 5 per cent risk-free rate of interest. She can expect to earn a return of 11 per cent with a standard deviation of 3.6 per cent. A very conservative investor may lend her entire wealth at the risk-free rate of interest. Point *R*f shows that when the investor lends her entire wealth, she could earn 5 per cent return with zero risk. Theoretically, it is possible that an investor may borrow and invest (lend) more than 100 per cent at the risk-free rate of interest. No investor will do this in practice since his or her return will be less for equal or more risk than for a lending-borrowing combination along the line *R*f *D*. Thus line *R*f *D* illustrates the portfolio opportunity set for the possible combinations of a risk-free security and a risky security. Notice that a straight line represents the portfolio opportunity set.

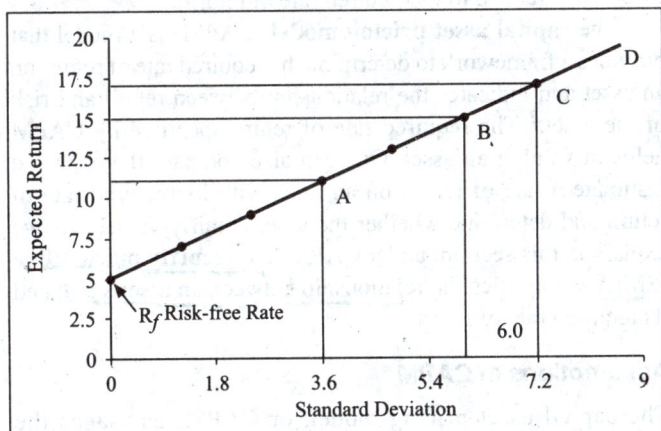

Figure 5.9: Risk-return relationship for portfolio of risky and risk-free securities

MULTIPLE RISKY ASSETS AND A RISK-FREE ASSET

In a market situation, a large number of investors holding portfolios consisting of a risk-free security and multiple risky securities participate. Figure 5.7 shown earlier illustrates all efficient portfolios of risky assets. We can combine Figures 5.7 and 5.9 to draw Figure 5.10 to illustrate the feasible portfolios consisting of the risk-free security and the portfolios of risky securities. We draw three lines from the risk-free rate (5%) to three portfolios. Each line shows the manner in which capital is allocated. This line is called the **capital allocation line** (CAL). The CAL *R*f *PO* is drawn through the minimum variance portfolio *P*. The CAL *R*f *BN* passes through the portfolio *B*. As we know, the risk-averse investors prefer highest return for a given level of risk. Therefore, they will choose portfolios along line *R*f *BN* since those portfolios offer higher return for a given

level of risk than choosing portfolios along the line *R*f *PO*. The investors can continue upwards until the point of tangency with the investment opportunity set is reached. They will choose portfolios along line *R*f *MQ* since those portfolios offer higher return for a given level of risk than choosing portfolios along any other line. For example, portfolios along line *R*f *BN* offer low return for the same level of risk. Thus, in an equilibrium situation, all investors will select portfolios consisting of risk-free security and the risky portfolio *M*. The capital allocation line, *R*f *M*, is called the capital market line. The **capital market line** (CML) is an efficient set of risk-free and risky securities, and it shows the risk-return trade-off in the market equilibrium. Portfolio *M* is the **optimum risky portfolio**, which can be combined with the risk-free asset. The optimum risky portfolio is the **market portfolio** of *all* risky assets where each asset is held in proportion of its market value. It is the best portfolio since it dominates all other portfolios. An investor can thus mix her borrowing and lending with the best portfolio according to her risk preferences. She can invest in two separate investments— a risk free asset and a portfolio of risky securities. This is known as the **separation theorem**.[1]

According to the separation theory, the choice of portfolio involves two separate steps. The first step involves the determination of the optimum risky portfolio. This is a technical task as discussed in the preceding sections. The second step concerns with the investor's decision to form portfolio of the risk-free asset and the optimum risky portfolio depending on her risk preferences.

We may note in Figure 5.10 that *R*f is the intercept of the capital market line (CML) and its slope is given by

$$\text{Slope of CML} = \left[\frac{E(R_m) - R_f}{\sigma_m} \right] \quad (18)$$

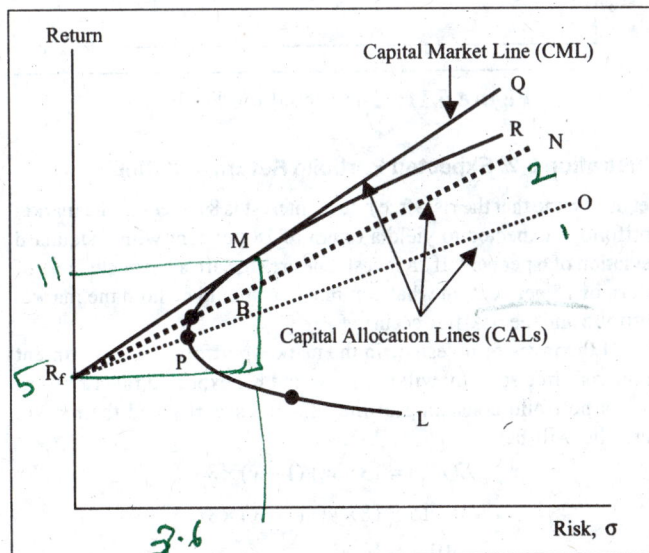

Figure 5.10 : Risk-return relationship for portfolio of risky and risk-free securities

1. Tobin, J., Liquidity Preference as Behaviour toward Risk, *Review of Economic Studies,* Vol. 25 (Feb. 1958), pp. 65–69.

The slope of CML is also referred to as the **reward-to-variability ratio.** Suppose market portfolio M in Figure 5.10 has expected return of 11 per cent and standard deviation of 3.6 per cent. With a risk-free rate of return of 5 per cent, the reward-to-variability ratio or the slope of the capital market line Q is:

$$\text{Slope of CML} = \left[\frac{11.0 - 5.0}{3.6}\right] = 1.67$$

The slope of CML describes the best price of a given level of risk in equilibrium. The expected return on a portfolio on CML is defined by the following equation:[1]

$$E(R_p) = R_f + \left[\frac{E(R_m) - R_f}{\sigma_m}\right]\sigma_p \qquad (19)$$

where $E(R_p)$ is the expected return on portfolios along the capital market line, R_f the risk-free rate of interest (borrowing and lending), $E(R_m)$ the expected market portfolio (M) return, σ_m the market portfolio standard deviation and σ_p the standard deviation of portfolio along the CML.

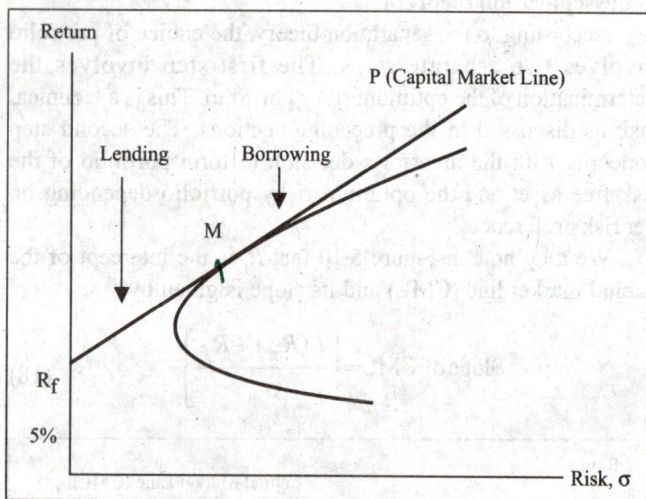

Figure 5.11: The capital market line

Illustration 5.2: Expected Portfolio Return and CML

Let us assume that the risk-free rate of interest is 8 per cent. The market portfolio is expected to yield a return of 18 per cent with a standard deviation of 6 per cent. If an investor desires to earn an expected rate of return of 15 per cent, in what combination should he hold the market portfolio and the risk-free security?

If the investor invests w in the market portfolio, his investment in the risk-free security will be: $1 - w$ and his expected rate of return from a portfolio consisting of the risk-free security and the market portfolio will be:

$$E(R_p) = 18 \times w + (1 - w) \times 8$$
$$15 = 18 \times w + (1 - w) \times 8$$
$$10\,w = 15 - 8$$
$$w = (15 - 8)/10 = 0.7$$

The portfolio risk will be:

$$\sigma_p = w\sigma_m = 0.7(6) = 4.2\%$$

By combining the risk-free security (lending) with the market portfolio, the investor can reduce his risk (from 6 per cent to 4.2 per cent) but his return will be less (15 per cent instead of 18 per cent).

We can also use Equation (17) to calculate the expected portfolio rate of return:

$$E(R_p) = 8\% + \left[\frac{(18\% - 8\%)}{6\%}\right]4.2\% = 8\% + 1.667\,(4.2\%)$$
$$= 8\% + 7\% = 15\%$$

CAPITAL ASSET PRICING MODEL (CAPM)

We have so far discussed the principles of making portfolio choices by investors. We also considered the significance of the risk-free asset in portfolio decisions. In the presence of the risk-free asset, the capital market line (CML) is the relevant efficient frontier, and all investors would choose to remain on CML. This implies that the relevant measure of an asset's risk is its covariance with the market portfolio of risky assets. How do we determine the required rate of return on a risky asset? How is an asset's risk related to its required rate of return?

The **capital asset pricing model** (CAPM) is a model that provides a framework to determine the required rate of return on an asset and indicates the relationship between return and risk of the asset.[2] The required rate of return specified by CAPM helps in valuing an asset. One can also compare the expected (estimated) rate of return on an asset with its required rate of return and determine whether the asset is fairly valued. As we explain in this section, under CAPM, the **security market line** (SML) exemplifies the relationship between an asset's risk and its required rate of return.

Assumptions of CAPM

The capital asset pricing model, or CAPM, envisages the relationship between risk and the expected rate of return on a risky security. It provides a framework to price individual securities and determine the required rate of return for individual securities. It is based on a number of simplifying assumptions. The most important assumptions are:[3]

- *Market efficiency* The capital market efficiency implies that share prices reflect all available information. Also, individual investors are not able to affect the prices of securities. This means that there are large numbers of investors holding small amount of wealth.

- *Risk aversion and mean-variance optimisation* Investors are risk-averse. They evaluate a security's return and risk in terms of the expected return and variance or standard deviation respectively. They prefer the highest expected returns for a given level of risk. This implies that investors are mean-variance optimisers and they form efficient portfolios.

1. Sharpe, *op. cit.*
2. The development of CAPM is mainly attributed to **Sharpe**, *op. cit.*
3. Sharpe, *op. cit.* Also see Fisher, D.E. and Jordan, R.J., *Security Analysis and Portfolio Management,* Prentice-Hall of India, 1990, p. 622.

- *Homogeneous expectations* All investors have the same expectations about the expected returns and risks of securities.
- *Single time period* All investors' decisions are based on a single time period.
- *Risk-free rate* All investors can lend and borrow at a risk-free rate of interest. They form portfolios from publicly traded securities like shares and bonds.

Characteristics Line

We know from the earlier discussion that risk has two parts: unsystematic risk, which can be eliminated through diversification and systematic risk, which cannot be reduced. Since unsystematic risk can be mostly eliminated without any cost, there is no price paid for it. Therefore, it will have no influence on the return of individual securities. Market will pay premium only for systematic risk since it is non-diversifiable. How can we measure the risk of individual securities and their risk-adjusted required rates of return? Let us consider an example.

The following table gives probable rates of return on market portfolio and on Alpha Company's share. There are two possibilities with regard to market conditions, either the market will rise or it will fall. Under each market condition, there are two equally likely outcomes for both the market portfolio and Alpha.

Market Conditions	Market Return (%)	Return on Alpha Co.'s Share (%)
Rising Market	25	30
Rising Market	20	25
Falling Market	−15	−25
Falling Market	−10	−15

Let us examine the behaviour of the market return and return on Alpha's share. The expected return for the market and Alpha are as follows:

Rising market:

Expected market return = 0.5 × 25 + 0.5 × 20 = 22.5%
Expected Alpha return = 0.5 × 30 + 0.5 × 25 = 27.5%

Falling market:

Expected market return = 0.5 × −15 + 0.5 × −10 = −12.5%
Expected Alpha return = 0.5 × −25 + 0.5 × −15 = −20.0%.

The market return in the rising market is 22.5 per cent and it is −12.5 per cent in the falling market. This means that the market return is 35 per cent higher in the rising market *compared* to the market return in the falling market. In case of Alpha, the return in the rising market is 47.5 per cent higher compared to the market return in the falling market. How sensitive is Alpha's return in relation to the market return? Alpha's return increases by 47.5 per cent compared to 35 per cent increase in the market return in the rising market conditions. Alternatively, Alpha's return declines by 47.5 per cent compared to 35 per cent decrease in the market return in the falling market conditions. Thus the

sensitivity of the Alpha's return vis-à-vis the market return is: 47.5%/35% = 1.36. We can refer to this number as the **sensitivity coefficient or index.** The sensitivity coefficient of 1.36 implies that for a unit change (increase or decrease) in the market return, Alpha's return will change by 1.36 times. The sensitivity of the Alpha's return vis-á-vis the market return reflects its risk. The sensitivity coefficient is called **beta.**

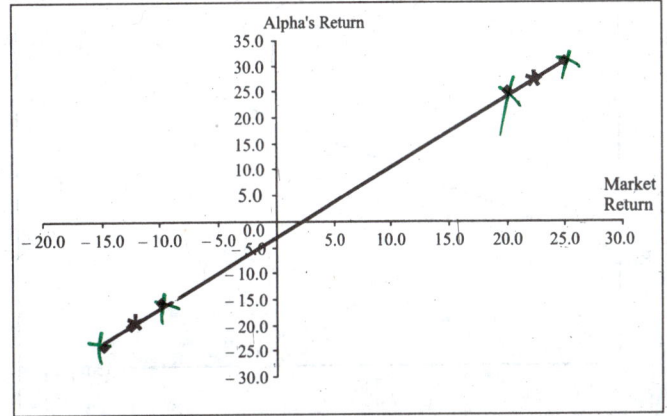

Figure 5.12: Characteristics Line: Market Return vs. Alpha's Return

We plot the combinations of four possible returns of Alpha and market in Figure 5.12. They are shown as four points. The combinations of the expected returns points (22.5%, 27.5% and −12.5%, −20%) are also shown in the figure. We join these two points to form a line. This line is called the **characteristics line.** The slope of the characteristics line is the sensitivity coefficient, which, as stated earlier, is referred to as beta.

Security Market Line (SML)

Under CAPM, risk of an individual risky security is defined as the volatility of the security's return vis-á-vis the return of the market portfolio. This risk of an individual risky security is its systematic risk. Systematic risk is measured as the covariance of an individual risky security with the market portfolio. Figure 5.13 shows the relationship between return and risk as measured by covariance.

The covariance of any asset with itself is represented by its variance (covar$_{j, j}$ = σ^2_j). The return on market portfolio should depend on its own risk, which is given by the variance of the market return (σ^2_M). Therefore, the risk-return relationship equation is as follows:

$$E(R_j) = R_f + \frac{E(R_m) - R_f}{\sigma^2_m}(\text{covar}_{j, m})$$ (20)

The term, covar$_{j, m}/\sigma^2_m$ is called the security beta, β_j. Beta is a standardised measure of a security's systematic risk. The beta of the market portfolio is 1. The market portfolio is the reference for measuring the volatility of individual risky securities. Since a risk-free security has no volatility, it has zero beta. We can rewrite the equation for SML as follows:[1]

---

1. Sharpe, *op. cit.*

$$E(R_j) = R_f + [E(R_m) - R_f]\beta_j \qquad (21)$$

where $E(R_j)$ is the expected return on security j, R_f the risk-free rate of interest, R_m the expected return on the market portfolio and β_j the undiversifiable risk of security j.

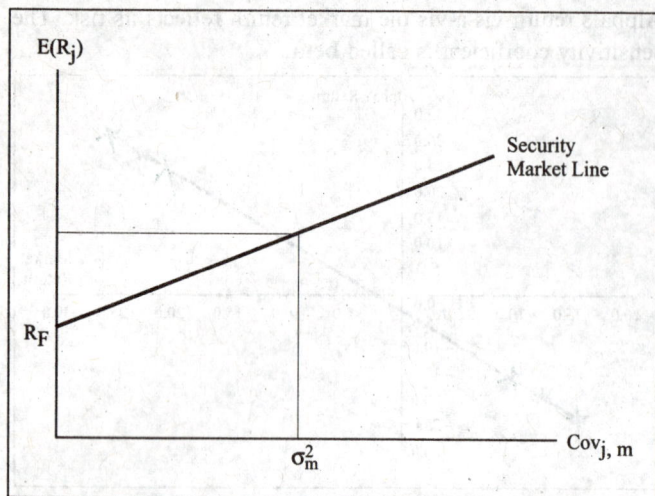

Figure 5.13: Security market line

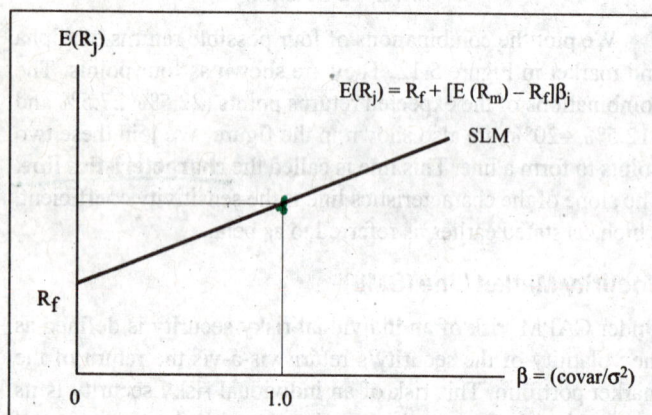

Figure 5.14 : Security market line with normalised systematic risk (β)

Figure 5.14 illustrates SLM with normalised systematic risk as measured by beta. Figure 5.14 and Equation (21) show that the required rate of return on a security is equal to a risk-free rate plus the risk-premium for the risky security. The **risk-premium** on a risky security equals the **market risk premium**, that is, the difference between the expected market return and the risk-free rate. Since the market risk premium is same for all securities, the total risk premium varies directly with systematic risk measured by beta. For a given amount of systematic risk (β), SML shows the required rate of return. A security's beta of 1 indicates systematic risk equal to the aggregate market risk and the required rate of return on the security will be equal to the market rate of return. If the security's beta is greater than 1, then its systematic risk is greater than the aggregate market. This implies that the security's returns fluctuate more than the market returns, and the security's required rate of return will be more than the market rate of return. On the other hand, a security's beta of less than 1 means that the

security's risk is lower than the aggregate market risk. This implies that the security's returns are less sensitive to the changes in the market returns. The security's required rate of return will be less than the market rate of return. Can a security's beta be negative? Theoretically, beta can be negative. A security with negative beta would earn less than the risk-free rate of return.

Illustration 5.3: Required Rate of Return Calculation

The risk free rate of return is 8 per cent and the market rate of return is 17 per cent. Betas for four shares, *P, Q, R* and *S* are respectively 0.60, 1.00, 1.20 and –0.20. What are the required rates of return on these four shares? We can use Equation (21) to calculate the required rates of return.

$$E(R_j) = R_f + [E(R_m) - R_f]\beta_j$$
$$E(R_P) = 0.08 + (0.17 - 0.08) \times 0.60 = 0.134 \text{ or } 13.4\%$$
$$E(R_Q) = 0.08 + (0.17 - 0.08) \times 1.00 = 0.170 \text{ or } 17.0\%$$
$$E(R_R) = 0.08 + (0.17 - 0.08) \times 1.20 = 0.188 \text{ or } 18.8\%$$
$$E(R_S) = 0.08 + (0.17 - 0.08) \times -0.20 = 0.062 \text{ or } 6.2\%$$

Q with beta of 1.00 has a return equal to the market return. *P* has beta lower than 1.00, therefore its required rate of return is lower than the market return. *R* has a return greater than the market return since its beta is greater than 1.00. *S* has a return lower than the risk-free rate since it has a negative beta.

CML vs. SML What is the difference between CML and SML? The CML represents the risk premiums of efficient portfolios as a function of portfolio standard deviation. The SML, on the other hand, depicts individual security risk premium as a function of security risk. The individual security risk is measured by the security's beta. Beta reflects the contribution of the security to the portfolio risk. We can notice from Equation (20) that if a security's return is perfectly positively correlated with the return on the market portfolio, then CML totally coincides with SML with the same slope, viz., σ_j/σ_m.

All fairly valued assets exactly lie on the SML. The required rates of return of such assets are consistent with their risk. The under-priced assets shall lie above the SML and their required rates of return are higher than as implied by the CAPM. On the other hand, overpriced assets lie below the SML and their required rates of return are lower than as implied by the CAPM.

IMPLICATIONS AND RELEVANCE OF CAPM

CAPM is based on a number of assumptions. Given those assumptions, it provides a logical basis for measuring risk and linking risk and return.

Implications

CAPM has the following implications:

- Investors will always combine a risk-free asset with a market portfolio of risky assets. They will invest in risky assets in proportion to their market value.
- Investors will be compensated only for that risk which they cannot diversify. This is the market-related (systematic) risk. Beta, which is a ratio of the covariance between the asset returns and the market returns divided by the market variance, is the most appropriate measure of an asset's risk.

- Investors can expect returns from their investment according to the risk. This implies a linear relationship between the asset's expected return and its beta.

The concepts of risk and return as developed under CAPM have intuitive appeal and they are quite simple to understand. Financial managers use these concepts in a number of financial decision-making such as valuation of securities, cost of capital measurement, investment risk analysis etc. However, in spite of its intuitive appeal and simplicity, CAPM suffers from a number of practical problems.

Limitations of CAPM

CAPM has the following limitations:
- It is based on unrealistic assumptions
- It is difficult to test the validity of CAPM
- Betas do not remain stable over time.

Unrealistic assumptions CAPM is based on a number of assumptions that are far from the reality. For example, it is very difficult to find a risk-free security. A short-term, highly liquid government security is considered as a risk-free security. It is unlikely that the government will default, but inflation causes uncertainty about the real rate of return. The assumption of the equality of the lending and borrowing rates is also not correct. In practice, these rates differ. Further, investors may not hold highly diversified portfolios, or the market indices may not be well diversified. Under these circumstances, CAPM may not accurately explain the investment behaviour of investors and beta may fail to capture the risk of investment.

Testing CAPM Most of the assumptions of CAPM may not be very critical for its practical validity. What we need to know, therefore, is the empirical validity of CAPM. We need to establish that beta is able to measure the risk of a security and that there is a significant correlation between beta and the expected return. The empirical results have given mixed results. The earlier tests showed that there was a positive relation between returns and betas. However, the relationship was not as strong as predicted by CAPM. Further, these results revealed that returns were also related to other measures of risk, including the firm-specific risk. In subsequent research, some studies did not find any relationship between betas and returns. On the other hand, other factors such as size and the market value and book value ratios were found as significantly related to returns.[1]

All empirical studies testing CAPM have a conceptual problem. CAPM is an *ex-ante* model; that is, we need data on expected prices to test CAPM. Unfortunately, in practice the researchers have to work with the actual past (ex-post) data. Thus this will introduce bias in the empirical results.

Stability of beta Beta is a measure of a security's future risk. But investors do not have future data to estimate beta. What they have are past data about the share prices and the market portfolio. Thus, they can only estimate beta based on historical data. Investors can use historical beta as the measure of future

risk only if it is stable over time. Most research has shown that the betas of individual securities are not stable over time. This implies that historical betas are poor indicators of the future risk of securities.

CAPM is a useful device for understanding the risk-return relationship in spite of its limitations. It provides a logical and quantitative approach for estimating risk. It is better than many alternative subjective methods of determining risk and risk premium. One major problem in the use of CAPM is that many times the risk of an asset is not captured by beta alone.

THE ARBITRAGE PRICING THEORY (APT)

The CAPM is not always able to account for the difference in assets' returns using their betas. This paved way for the development of an alternative approach, called the **arbitrage-pricing theory** (APT), for estimating the assets' expected returns.[2] APT, unlike CAPM, does not assume that investors employ mean-variance analysis for their investment decisions. However, like CAPM, APT is founded on the notion that investors are rewarded for assuming non-diversifiable (systematic) risk; diversifiable (unsystematic) risk is not compensated. Beta is considered as the most important single factor in CAPM that captures the systematic risk of an asset. In APT, there are a number of industry-specific and macro-economic factors that affect the security returns. Thus a number of factors may measure the systematic (non-diversifiable) risk of an asset under APT. The fundamental logic of APT is that investors always indulge in arbitrage whenever they find differences in the returns of assets with similar risk characteristics.

Concept of Return Under APT

In APT, the return of an asset is assumed to have two components: predictable (expected) and unpredictable (uncertain) return. Thus, return on asset *j* will be:

$$E(R_j) = R_f + UR \qquad (22)$$

where R_f is the predictable return (risk-free return on a zero-beta asset) and UR is the unanticipated part of the return.

The predictable or expected return depends on the information available to shareholders that has a bearing on the share prices. The unpredictable or uncertain return arises from the future information. This information may be the firm specific and the market-related (macro-economic factors). The firm-specific factors are special to the firm and affect only the firm. The market-related factors affect all firms. Thus the uncertain return may come from the firm specific information and the market related information. We can rewrite Equation (22) as follows:

$$E(R_j) = R_f + UR_s + UR_m \qquad (23)$$

UR_s is the unexpected component of return arising from the specific factors related to the firm. UR_m is that component of the unexpected return that arises from the economy-wide, market-related factors. It is important to notice that the

1. Fama, E.F. and French, R.R., The cross-section of Expected Returns, *Journal of Finance*, No. 47, 1992, pp. 427–66.
2. Ross, R.A., The Arbitrage Theory of Capital Asset Pricing, *Journal of Economic Theory*, Vol. 13, No. 3, 1976.

economy-wide information may be further divided into the expected part and the unexpected or surprise part. For example, the government may announce that inflation rate would be 5 per cent next month. Since this information is already known, market would have already accounted for this and share prices would reflect it. After a month the government announces that the actual inflation rate was 6 per cent. Shareholders know now that the inflation is one per cent higher than the anticipated rate. This is surprise news to them. The expected part of information influences the expected return while the surprise part affects the unexpected part of return.

Concept of Risk under APT

The risk arising from the firm-specific factors is diversifiable. It is *unsystematic risk*. The risk arising from the market-related factors cannot be diversified. This represents *systematic risk*. In CAPM, market risk primarily arises from the sensitivity of an asset's returns to the market returns and this is reflected by the asset's beta. Just one factor – the market returns – affects the firm's return. Hence, CAPM is one-factor model. The betas of the firm would differ depending on their individual sensitivity to market. On the other hand, APT assumes that market risk can be caused by economic factors such as changes in gross domestic product, inflation, and the structure of interest rates and these factors could affects firms differently. For example, different firms may feel the impact of inflation differently. Therefore, under APT, multiple factors may be responsible for the expected return on the share of a firm. Therefore, under APT the sensitivity of the asset's return to each factor is estimated. For each firm, there will be as many betas as the number of factors. Equation (23) can be expressed as follows:

$$E(R_j) = R_f + (\beta_1 F_1 + \beta_2 F_2 + \beta_3 F_3 + \cdots + \beta_n F_n) + UR_s \quad (24)$$

where β_1 is firm j's factor one beta, β_2 is factor two beta and so on. F represents a surprise in factors. Let us consider an example as given in Illustration 5.4.

Illustration 5.4: Total Return Under APT

Suppose that GNP, inflation, interest rate, stock market index and industrial production affect the share return of the firm – Divine Home Company. Further, we have information about the forecasts and actual values of these factors, and the firm's GNP beta, inflation beta, interest rate beta and the stock market beta.

An investor is considering making an investment in the share of Divine Home Company. The following are the attributes of five economic forces that influence the return of Divine's share:

Factor	Beta	Expected Value (%)	Actual Value (%)
GNP	1.95	6.00	6.50
Inflation	0.85	5.00	5.75
Interest rate	1.20	7.00	8.00
Stock market index	2.50	9.50	11.50
Industrial production	2.20	9.00	10.00

The risk-free (anticipated) rate of return on the Divine's share is 9 per cent.

How much is the total return on the share? It is anticipated return plus unanticipated return. The anticipated return includes the effect of known information such as expected inflation and other factors. Therefore we need to determine the surprise part in the systematic factors. The difference in the expected and actual values of the factors is the surprise. Shareholders will be compensated for this. The difference multiplied by a factor beta will compensate shareholders for that factor's systematic risk. The expected value of a factor is the risk-free part. The total return will consist of anticipated (risk-free) return and unanticipated return as follows:

$$E(R) = R_f + \beta_1 (R_{F_1} - R_f) + \beta_2 (R_{F_2} - R_f) + \cdots$$
$$+ \beta_n (R_{F_n} - R_f) \quad (25)$$
$$E(R) = 9 + 1.95(6.5 - 6) + 0.85(5.75 - 5) + 1.20(8 - 7)$$
$$+ 2.5(11.5 - 9.5) + 2.20(10 - 9)$$
$$= 9 + 10 = 19\%$$

Steps in Calculating Expected Return Under APT

From our discussion in the preceding sections, the following three steps are involved in estimating the expected return on an asset under APT:

- searching for the factors that affect the asset's return
- estimation of risk premium for each factor
- estimation of factor beta

Factors What factors are important in explaining the expected return? How are they identified? APT does not indicate the factors that explain assets' returns. The factors are empirically derived from the available data. Different assets will be affected differently by the factors.

The following factors were found important in a research study in the USA:[1]

- industrial production
- changes in default premium
- changes in the structure of interest rates
- inflation rate
- changes in the real rate of return.

Is this an exhaustive list of macro-economic factors? All do not agree. In another study,[2] it has been found that price-to-book-value ratios and size are correlated with the actual returns. These measures have been found as good proxy of the risk.

Risk premium What is the risk premium for each factor? Conceptually, it is the compensation, over and above, the risk-free rate of return that investors require for the risk contributed by the factor. One could use past data on the forecasted and actual values to determine the premium.

Factor beta The beta of the factor is the sensitivity of the asset's return to the changes in the factor. We can use regression approach to calculate the factor beta. For example, a firm's returns could be regressed to inflation rated to determine the inflation beta.

1. Chen, L., Roll, R. and Ross, S.A., Economic Forces and the Stock Market, *Journal of Business*, No. 59, 1986, pp. 383–04.
2. Fama and French, *op. cit.*, pp. 427–66.

SUMMARY

❖ Risk and return concepts are basic to the understanding of the valuation of assets or securities. Return on a security consists of the dividend yield and capital gain. The expected rate of return on a security is the sum of the products of possible rates of return and their probabilities. Thus

$$E(R) = R_1P_1 + R_2P_2 + \cdots + R_nP_n = \sum_{i=1}^{n} R_iP_i$$

❖ The expected rate of return is an average rate of return. This average rate may deviate from the possible outcomes (rates of return). Variance (σ^2) and standard deviation (σ) of returns of a security can be calculated as follows:

$$\sigma^2 = [R_1 - E(R)]^2 P_i + [R_2 - E(R)]^2 P_2 + \cdots$$
$$+ [(R_n - E(R)]^2 P_n = \sum_{i=1}^{n} [R_i - E(R)]^2 P$$
$$\sigma = \sqrt{\sigma^2}$$

❖ Variance or standard deviation is a measure of the risk of returns on a security.

❖ Generally, investors in practice hold multiple securities. Combinations of multiple securities are called portfolios.

❖ The expected return on a portfolio is the sum of the returns on individual securities multiplied by their respective weights (proportionate investment). That is, it is a weighted average rate of return.

❖ In the case of a two-security portfolio, the portfolio return is given by the following equation:

$$E(R_p) = wR_x + (1-w)R_y$$

❖ In the case of n-security portfolio, the portfolio return will be as follows:

$$E(R_p) = w_1R_1 + w_2R_2 + \cdots + w_nR_n = \sum_{i=1}^{n} w_iR_i$$

❖ The portfolio risk is not a weighted average risk. Securities included in a portfolio are associated with each other. Therefore, the portfolio risk also accounts for the covariance between the returns of securities. Covariance is the product of the standard deviations of individual securities times their correlation coefficient.

❖ The portfolio risk in the case of a two-security portfolio can be computed as follows:

$$\sigma_p^2 = w^2\sigma_x^2 + (1-w)^2\sigma_y^2 + 2(w)(1-w)\,\text{Cov}_{xy}$$
$$= w^2\sigma_x^2 + (1-w)^2\sigma_y^2 + 2(w)(1-w)\sigma_x\sigma_y\text{Cor}_{xy}$$
$$\sigma_p = \sqrt{\sigma_p^2}$$

❖ We may observe that the portfolio risk consists of the risk of individual securities plus the covariance between securities. Covariance depends on the standard deviation of individual securities and their correlation.

❖ The magnitude of the portfolio risk will depend on the correlation between the securities. The portfolio risk will be equal to the weighted risk of individual securities if the correlation coefficient is + 1.0. For correlation coefficient of less than 1, the portfolio risk will be less than the weighted average risk. When the two securities are perfectly negatively correlated, i.e., the correlation coefficient is −1.0, the portfolio risk becomes zero.

❖ The minimum variance portfolio is called the optimum portfolio. The following formula can be used to determine the optimum weights of securities in a two-security portfolio:

$$w_x = \frac{\sigma_y^2 - \text{Cov}_{xy}}{\sigma_x^2 + \sigma_y^2 - 2\,\text{Cov}_{xy}}$$

w_x is the optimum weight of security x and $1-w_x$ of security y.

❖ In the case of a n-security portfolio, the portfolio risk can be calculated as follows:

$$\sigma_p^2 = \frac{1}{n} \times \text{average risk} + \left[1 - \frac{1}{n}\right] \times \text{average covariance}$$

❖ As the number of securities in the portfolio increases, the portfolio variance approaches the average covariance. Thus diversification helps in reducing the risk.

❖ The investment or portfolio opportunity set represents all possible combinations of risk and return resulting from portfolios formed by varying proportions of individual securities. It presents the investor with the risk-return trade-off.

❖ For a given risk, an investor would prefer a portfolio with higher expected rate of return. Similarly, when the expected returns are same, she would prefer a portfolio with lower risk. The choice between high risk-high return or low risk-low return portfolios will depend on the investor's risk preference. This is refereed to as the mean-variance criterion.

❖ An efficient portfolio is one that has the highest expected returns for a given level of risk. The efficient frontier is the frontier formed by the set of efficient portfolios.

❖ The capital market line (CML) is an efficient set of risk-free and risky securities, and it shows the risk-return trade-off in the market equilibrium.

❖ The optimum risky portfolio is the market portfolio of all risky assets where each asset is held in proportion of its market value. It is the best portfolio since it dominates all other portfolios. An investor can thus mix her borrowing and lending with the best portfolio according to her risk preferences. She can invest in two separate investments—a risk free asset and a portfolio of risky securities. This is known as the *separation theorem*.

❖ Risk has two parts: unsystematic risk and systematic risk.

❖ Unsystematic risk can be eliminated through diversification. It is a risk unique to a specific security. When individual securities are combined, their unique risks cancel out.

❖ Systematic risk cannot be eliminated through

diversification. It is a market-related risk. It arises because individual securities move with the changes in the market.

❖ Investors are risk-averse. They will take risk only if they are compensated for the risk, which they bear. Since systematic risk can be eliminated through diversification, they will be compensated for assuming systematic risk.

❖ The market prices securities in a manner that they yield higher expected returns than the risk-free securities. The risk-averse investors can be induced to hold risky securities when they are offered risk premium. The capital market line (CML) defines this relationship. The equation for CML is:

$$E(R_p) = R_f + \left[\frac{E(R_m) - R_f}{\sigma_m} \right] \sigma_p$$

where $E(R_p)$ is the portfolio return, R_f the risk-free return, $E(R_m)$ the return on market portfolio, σ_m the standard deviation of market portfolio and σ_p the standard deviation of the portfolio.

❖ The model explaining the risk-return relationship is called the capital asset pricing model (CAPM). It provides that in a well-functioning capital market, the risk premium varies in direct proportion to risk.

❖ CAPM provides a measure of risk and a method of estimating the market's risk-return line. The market (systematic) risk of a security is measured in terms of its sensitivity to the market movements. This sensitivity is referred to the security's beta.

❖ A line that is called the characteristics line can represent the relationship between the security returns and the market returns. The slope of the characteristics line is the sensitivity coefficient, which, as stated earlier, is referred to as *beta*.

❖ Beta reflects the systematic risk, which cannot be reduced. Investors can eliminate unsystematic risk when they invest their wealth in a well-diversified market portfolio. A beta of 1.0 indicates average level of risk while more than 1.0 means that the security's return fluctuates more than that of the market portfolio. A zero beta means no risk.

❖ The expected return on a security is given by the following equation:

$$E(R_j) = R_f + (R_m - R_f)\beta_j$$

where R_f is the risk-free rate, R_m the market return and the measure of the security's systematic risk. This equation gives a line called the *security market line* (SML).

❖ In terms of the security market line, beta is a ratio of the covariance of returns of a security, j, and the market portfolio, m, to the variance of return of the market portfolio:

$$\beta_j = \frac{\text{Cov}_{jm}}{\text{Var}_m} = \frac{\sigma_j \sigma_m \text{Cor}_{jm}}{\sigma_m^2} = \frac{\sigma_j}{\sigma_m} \times \text{Cor}_{jm}$$

where β_j is beta of the security, σ_j the standard deviation of return of security, σ_m the standard deviation of returns of the market portfolio, σ_m^2 the variance of returns of the market portfolio m and Cor_{jm} the correlation coefficient between the returns of the security j and the market portfolio m.

❖ CAPM is based on a number of restrictive assumptions. The most significant assumption being that an investor is compensated for a security's systematic risk that is entirely captured by the security's beta.

❖ The differences of securities' returns may not be fully explained by their betas. The arbitrage pricing theory (APT), resulting from the limitations of CAPM, assumes that many macro-economic factors may affect the system risk of a security (or an asset). Thus, APT is a multi-factor model to explain the return and return of a security. The factors influencing security return may include industrial production, growth in gross domestic product, the interest rate, inflation, default premium, and the real rate of return. Price-to-book-value ratio and size have also been found to explain to the differences in the security returns.

KEY CONCEPTS

Arbitrage	Portfolio opportunity set	Efficient portfolio	Risk-free rate of return
Arbitrage pricing theory	Portfolio return	Expected rate of return	Risk-free security
Beta	Portfolio risk	Lending rate	Security market line
Borrowing rate	Portfolio theory	Limits of diversification	Separation theorem
Capital asset pricing model	Principle of dominance	Market portfolio	Standard deviation
Capital market line	Return	Mean-variance analysis	Subjective probability
Characteristics line	Reward-risk ratio	Minimum portfolio variance	Systematic or market risk
Correlation coefficient	Risk	Objective probability	Unsystematic or unique risk
Covariance	Risk diversification	Portfolio	Variance
Efficient frontier	Risk premium		

ILLUSTRATIVE SOLVED PROBLEMS

Problem 5.1: An investor holds two equity shares x and y in equal proportion with the following risk and return characteristics:

$$E(R_x) = 24\%; \ E(R_y) = 19\%$$

$$\sigma_x = 28\%; \ \sigma_y = 23\%$$

The returns of these securities have a positive correlation of 0.6. You are required to calculate the portfolio return and risk. Further, suppose that the investor wants to reduce the portfolio risk (σ_p) to 15 per cent. How much should the correlation coefficient be to bring the portfolio risk to the desired level?

Solution: The portfolio return is:

$$E(R_p) = 24(0.5) + 19(0.5) = 12 + 9.5 = 21.5\%$$

and the portfolio risk is:

$$\sigma_p = \sqrt{\sigma_p^2}$$

$$\sigma_p^2 = (28)^2 (0.5)^2 + (23)^2 (0.5)^2 + 2(0.5)(0.5)(28)(23)(0.6)$$

$$= 196 + 132.25 + 193.2 = 521.45$$

$$\sigma_p = \sqrt{521.45} = 22.84\%$$

If the investor desires the portfolio standard deviation to be 15 per cent, the correlation coefficient will be as computed below:

$$(15)^2 = (28)^2 (0.5)^2 + (23)^2 (0.5)^2 + 2(0.5)(0.5)(28)(23) \text{Cor}_{xy}$$

$$225 = 196 + 132.25 + 322 \text{Cor}_{xy}$$

$$\text{Cor}_{xy} = \frac{-103.25}{322} = -0.321$$

Problem 5.2: A portfolio consists of three securities P, Q and R with the following parameters:

	P	Q	R	Cor.
Expected return (%)	25	22	20	
Standard deviation (%)	30	26	24	
Correlation:				
PQ				– 0.50
QR				+ 0.40
PR				+ 0.60

If the securities are equally weighted, how much is the risk and return of the portfolio of these three securities?

Solution: The portfolio return is:

$$E(R_p) = (25)(1/3) + 22(1/3) + 20(1/3) = 22.33\%$$

$$\sigma_p^2 = (30)^2 (1/3)^2 + (26)^2 (1/3)^2 + (24)^2 (1/3)^2$$

$$+ 2(1/3)(1/3)(-0.5)(30)(26)$$

$$+ 2(1/3)(1/3)(0.4)(26)(24)$$

$$+ 2(1/3)(1/3)(0.6)(30)(24)$$

$$= 100 + 75.11 + 64 - 86.67 + 55.47 + 96 = 303.91$$

$$\sigma_p = \sqrt{303.91} = 17.43\%$$

Problem 5.3: From the following data compute beta of security j:

$$\sigma_j = 12\%; \ \sigma_m = 9\% \ \text{and} \ \text{Cor}_{jm} = +0.72$$

Solution: $\beta_j = \dfrac{\sigma_j \sigma_m \text{Cor}_{jm}}{\sigma_m^2} = \dfrac{12 \times 9 \times 0.72}{9^2} = \dfrac{77.76}{81} = 0.96$

Problem 5.4: Calculate the expected rate of return for security i from the following information:

$$R_f = 10\%; \ R_m = 18\%; \ \beta_j = 1.35$$

Solution: The expected return of security i will be:

$$E(R_j) = R_f = (R_m - R_f)\beta_j$$

$$= 10\% + (18\% - 10\%)1.35$$

$$= 10\% + 10.8\% = 20.8\%$$

Problem 5.5: An aggressive mutual fund promises an expected return of 16 per cent with a possible volatility (standard deviation) of 20 per cent. On the other hand, a conservative mutual fund promises an expected return of 13 per cent and volatility of 15 per cent. (*a*) Which fund would you like to invest in? (*b*) Would you like to invest in both if you have money? (*c*) Assuming you can borrow money from your provident fund at an opportunity cost of 10 per cent, which fund you would invest your money in? (*d*) Would you consider both funds if you could lend or borrow money at 10 per cent?

Solution:

(*a*) It depends on your preference and risk-taking attitude.
(*b*) You can achieve diversification gains if you invest in both.
(*c*) The slopes of the capital market line for two funds are: aggressive fund = (16 – 10)/20 = 0.30; and conservative fund: (13 – 10)/15 = 0.20. Aggressive fund is preferable.
(*d*) You would receive benefits of diversification if you invest in both funds and also lend and borrow.

Problem 5.6: P Ltd. has an expected return of 22 per cent and standard deviation of 40 per cent. Q Ltd. has an expected return of 24 per cent and standard deviation of 38 per cent. P has a beta of 0.86 and Q 1.24. The correlation between the returns of P and Q is 0.72. The standard deviation of the market return is 20 per cent. (*a*) Is investing in Q better than investing in P? (*b*) If you invest 30 per cent in Q and 70 per cent in P, what is your expected rate of return and the portfolio standard deviation? (*c*) What is the market portfolio's expected rate of return and how much is the risk-free rate? (*d*) What is the beta of portfolio if P's weight is 70 per cent and Q is 30 per cent?

Solution:

(*a*) P has lower return and higher risk than Q. However, investing in both will yield diversification advantage.

(*b*) $r_p = 22 \times 0.7 + 24 \times 0.3 = 22.6\%$

$$\sigma_p^2 = 40^2 \times 0.7^2 + 38^2 \times 0.3^2 + 2 \times 0.7$$

$$\times 0.3 \times 0.72 \times 40 \times 38 = 1374$$

$$\sigma_p = \sqrt{\sigma_p^2} = \sqrt{1374} = 37\%$$

(c) The risk-free rate will be the same for P and Q. Their rates of return are given as follows:

$$r_p = 22 = r_f + (r_m - r_f)0.86$$

$$r_q = 24 = r_f + (r_m - r_f)1.24$$

$$r_p - r_q = -2 - (r_m - r_f)(-0.38)$$

$$r_m - r_f = -2/-0.38 = 5.26\%$$

$$r_p = 22 = r_f + (5.26)0.86$$

$$r_f = 17.5\%$$

$$r_q = 24 = r_f + (5.26)1.24$$

$$r_f = 17.5\%$$

$$r_m - 17.5 = 5.26$$

$$r_m = 22.76\%$$

(d) $\beta_{pq} = \beta_p \times w_p \times \beta_q \times w_q$

$$= 0.86 \times 0.7 + 1.24 \times 0.3 = 0.974$$

REVIEW QUESTIONS

1. Illustrate the computation of the expected rate of return of an asset.
2. What is risk? How can risk of a security be calculated? Explain your answer with the help of an example.
3. What is a portfolio? How is the portfolio return and risk calculated for a two-security portfolio?
4. Does diversification reduce the risk of investment? Explain with an example.
5. Define systematic and unsystematic risks. Give examples of both.
6. Explain the principle of dominance. Define the efficient portfolio and efficient frontier.
7. What is the portfolio theory? Explain the assumptions and principles underlying the portfolio theory?
8. What is the capital asset pricing model? Explain its assumptions and implications.
9. Explain the security market line (SML) with the help of a figure. How does it differ from the capital market line?
10. What is beta? How is it measured? How do you calculate the expected rate of return of a security?
11. Explain the logic of the arbitrage-pricing theory (APT)? How does it compare and contrast with CAPM?

PROBLEMS

1. An asset has the following possible returns with associated probabilities:

Possible returns	20%	18%	8%	0	−6%
Probability	0.10	0.45	0.30	0.05	0.10

Calculate the expected rate of return and the standard deviation of the rate of return.

2. Securities X and Y have the following characteristics:

Security X		Security Y	
Return	Probability	Return	Probability
30%	0.10	−20%	0.05
20%	0.20	10%	0.25
10%	0.40	20%	0.30
5%	0.20	30%	0.30
−10%	0.10	40%	0.10

You are required to calculate (a) the expected return and standard deviation of return for each security and (b) the expected return and standard deviation of the return for the portfolio of X and Y, combined with equal weights.

3. The distribution of returns for share P and the market portfolio M is given below:

Probability	Returns (%)	
	P	M
0.30	30	−10
0.40	20	20
0.30	0	30

You are required to calculate the expected returns of security P and the market portfolio, the covariance between the market portfolio and security P and beta for the security.

4. The standard deviation of return of security Y is 20 per cent and of market portfolio is 15 per cent. Calculate beta of Y if (a) $Cor_{y,m} = 0.70$, (b) $Cor_{y,m} = +0.40$, and (c) $Cor_{y,m} = -0.25$.

5. An investor holds a portfolio, which is expected to yield a rate of return of 18 per cent with a standard deviation of return of 25 per cent. The investor is considering of buying a new share (investment being 5 per cent of the total investment in the new portfolio). The new share has the following distribution of return:

Return	Probability
40%	0.3
30%	0.4
−10%	0.3

If the correlation coefficient between the returns of the new portfolio and the new security is +0.25, calculate the portfolio return and the standard deviation of return of the new portfolio.

6. The Sunrise and Sunset companies have the following probability distribution of returns:

Economic conditions	Probability	Returns (%)	
		Sunrise	*Sunset*
High growth	0.1	32	30
Normal growth	0.2	20	17
Slow growth	0.4	14	6
Stagnation	0.2	−5	−12
Decline	0.1	−10	−16

You are required (*a*) to determine the expected covariance of returns and (*b*) the correlation of returns between the Sunrise and Sunset companies.

7. Two shares, *P* and *Q*, have the following expected returns, standard deviation and correlation:

$E(r_p) = 18\%$	$E(r_Q) = 15\%$
$\sigma_P = 23\%$	$\sigma_Q = 19\%$
Cor $\sigma_Q = 0$	

(*a*) Determine the minimum risk combination for a portfolio of *P* and *Q*.

(*b*) If the correlation of returns of *P* and *Q* is −1.0, then what is the minimum risk portfolio of *P* and *Q*?

6 Beta Estimation and the Cost of Equity

INTRODUCTION

In the earlier chapters, we have discussed two very important concepts: the net present value (NPV) and the return-risk trade-off. NPV of an investment is the discounted value of its future cash flows. The CAPM risk-return framework provides us with a method of determining the discount rate of an investment. In Chapter 5 we have discussed how SML can be used to determine the required rate of return on a firm's equity share. From the firm's point of view, this required rate of return is its cost of equity. The firm's cost of equity can be used as the discount rate to calculate NPV of an investment project that is as risky as the firm. We have discussed in Chapter 5 that we need to know the beta of a firm's share to determine the required rate of return. In this chapter we explain the estimation of beta, determinants of beta and use of beta in calculating a firm's cost of equity.

BETA ESTIMATION

Let us summarise the essence of the concept of risk that we have discussed so far. The risk of a portfolio of securities is measured by its variance or standard deviation. The variance of a portfolio is the sum of:

- the variances of individual securities times (the square of) their respective weights and
- the covariance (that is, the correlation coefficient between

securities times their standard deviations) of securities times twice the product of their respective weights.

In a well-diversified portfolio the weights of individual securities will be very small and therefore, the variances of individual securities will be quite insignificant. But the covariance between the securities will be significant, and its magnitude will depend on the correlation coefficients between securities. The covariance will be negative if all securities in the portfolio are negatively correlated. In practice, securities may have some correlation because they all have a tendency to move with the market. This logic introduces the concepts of **diversifiable risk** and **non-diversifiable risk**. The unique or the **unsystematic risk** of a security can be diversified when it is combined with other securities to form a well-diversified portfolio. On the other hand, the market or the **systematic risk** of the security cannot be diversified because like other securities, it also moves with the market.

Direct Method

How is the systematic risk of a security measured? We have discussed in the previous chapter that beta is the measure of systematic risk and it is the ratio of covariance between market return and the security's return to the market return variance:

$$\beta_j = \frac{\text{Covar}_{j,m}}{\sigma_m^2}$$

$$= \frac{\sigma_j \sigma_m \text{Cor}_{j,m}}{\sigma_m \times \sigma_m} = \frac{\sigma_j}{\sigma_m} \times \text{Cor}_{j,m} \qquad (1)$$

Let us consider an example to show the estimation of beta and intercept.

Illustration 6.1: Estimation of Beta

Table 6.1 shows the percentage returns on the market, represented by the BSE Sensex (Sensitivity Index) and the share of the Jaya Infotech Limited for recent five years:

Table 6.1: Returns on Sensex and Jaya Infotech

Year	Market Return r_m (%)	Jaya Infotech r_j (%)
1	18.60	23.46
2	-16.50	-36.13
3	63.83	52.64
4	-20.65	-7.29
5	-17.87	-12.95

Table 6.2 shows the relevant calculations. The following steps are involved in the calculation of beta:

1. Calculate the average return on market (Sensex) and Jaya's share (columns 2 and 3)
2. Calculate deviations of returns on market from the average return (column 4).
3. Calculate deviations of returns on Jaya's share from the average return (column 5)
4. Multiply deviations of market returns and deviations of Jaya's returns (column 6). Take the sum and divide by 5 (number of observations) to get covariance:

$$\text{Cov}_{m,j} = \frac{4,666.30}{5} = 933.26$$

5. Calculate the squared deviations of the market returns (column 7). Take the sum and divide by 5 to find the variance of market return:

$$\sigma_m^2 = \frac{5,288.23}{5} = 1,057.65$$

6. Divide the covariance of market and Jaya by the market variance to get beta:

$$\beta_j = \frac{\text{Cov}_{j,m}}{\sigma_m^2} = \frac{933.26}{1,057.65} = 0.88$$

7. The intercept term is given by the following formula:

$$\alpha_j = \bar{r}_j - \beta_j \times \bar{r}_m$$
$$= 3.95 - 0.88 \times 5.48 = -0.89$$

8. Thus, the characteristic line of Jaya Infotech is:

$$r_j = -0.89 + 0.88 r_m$$

Table 6.2: Beta Calculation for Jaya Infotech Limited

Year	r_m	r_j	$(r_m - \bar{r}_m)$	$(r_j - \bar{r}_j)$	$(r_m - \bar{r}_m)$ × $(r_j - \bar{r}_j)$	$(r_m - \bar{r}_m)^2$
1	18.60	23.46	13.11	19.51	255.91	171.98
2	-16.50	-36.13	-21.98	-40.08	880.83	483.08
3	63.83	52.64	58.35	48.69	2841.35	3404.85
4	-20.65	-7.29	-26.13	-11.24	293.64	682.96
5	-17.87	-12.95	-23.35	-16.90	394.57	545.35
	$\bar{r}_m$ = 5.48	$\bar{r}_j$ = 3.95			Sum = 4666.30	Sum = 5288.23

The Market Model

Yet another procedure for calculating beta is the use of the market or **index model**. In the market model, we regress returns on a security against returns of the market index.[1] The market model is given by the following regression equation:

$$R_j = \alpha + \beta_j R_m + e_j \qquad (2)$$

where R_j is the expected return on security j, R_m is the expected market return, α is intercept, β_j is slope of the regression and e_j is the error term (with a zero mean and constant standard deviation). The slope, β_j, of the regression measures the variability of the security's returns relative to the market returns and it is the security's beta. As discussed earlier, beta is the ratio of the covariance between the security returns and the market returns to the variance of the market returns. You may note that α indicates the return on the security when the market return is zero. It could be interpreted as return on the security on account of unsystematic risk. Over a long period of time α should be zero given the randomness of unsystematic risks.

We can plot the observed returns on market and Jaya's share and fit a regression line as shown in Figure 6.1. The fitted line is given by Equation (2). As discussed in Chapter 5, the regression line of the market model is called the **characteristics line.**

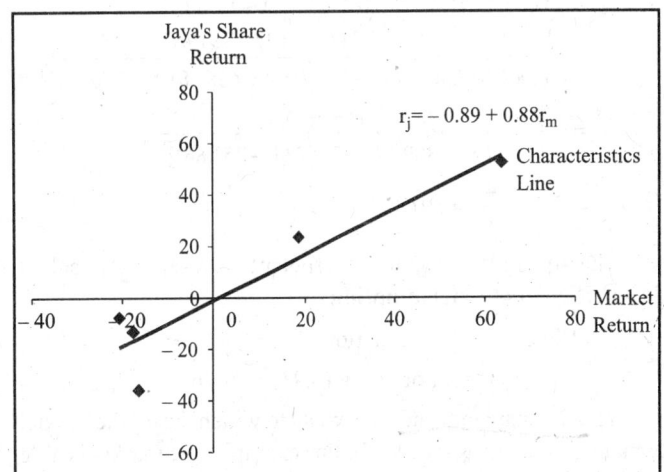

Figure 6.1: The characteristics line

---

1. Shape, W.F., *A Simplified Model for Portfolio Analysis, Management Science*, Jan. 1963, pp. 277–83.

Notice that in Figure 6.1 the estimates of regression equation are also shown. The value of α is -0.89 and the value of β is 0.88. How do we get these estimates? Table 6.3 gives relevant numbers to estimate the regression equation.

The value of β and α in the regression equation are given by the following equations:

$$\beta = \frac{N\Sigma XY - (\Sigma X)(\Sigma Y)}{N\Sigma X^2 - (\Sigma X)^2}$$

$$\beta_j = \frac{(5)(4,774.49) - (27.42)(19.73)}{(5)(5,438.58) - (27.42)^2}$$

$$= \frac{23,872.45 - 541.00}{27,192.90 - 751.86} = \frac{23,331.45}{26,441.04} = 0.88$$

$$\text{Alpha} = \alpha = \overline{Y} - \beta\overline{X}$$

$$\text{Alpha} = \alpha_j = 3.95 - (0.88)(5.48) = -0.89$$

Table 6.3: Estimates for Regression Equation

Year	r_m (X)	r_m (Y)	XY	X^2	Y^2
1	18.60	23.46	436.30	345.88	550.37
2	−16.50	−36.13	595.99	272.10	1305.38
3	63.83	52.64	3360.26	4074.86	2770.97
4	−20.65	−7.29	150.54	426.42	53.14
5	−17.87	−12.95	231.41	319.31	167.70
Sum	$\Sigma X =$ 27.42	$\Sigma Y =$ 19.73	$\Sigma XY =$ 4774.49	$\Sigma X^2 =$ 5438.58	$\Sigma Y^2 =$ 4847.56
Average	$\overline{X} =$ 5.48	$\overline{Y} =$ 3.95			

We can also calculate the correlation between return on market and Jaya's share as follows:

Coefficient of correlation

$$= \frac{N\Sigma XY - (\Sigma X)(\Sigma Y)}{[\{(N\Sigma Y^2) - (\Sigma Y)^2\}\{N\Sigma X^2 - (\Sigma X)^2\}]^{1/2}}$$

$$\text{Cor}_{j,m} = \frac{(5)(4,774.49) - (27.42)(19.73)}{[\{(5)(4,847.56) - (19.73)^2\}\{(5)(5,438.58) - (27.42)^2\}]^{1/2}}$$

$$= \frac{23,872.45 - 541.00}{[(24,237.80 - 389.27)(27,192.90 - 751.86)]^{1/2}}$$

$$= \frac{23,331.45}{25,111.35} = 0.93$$

The squared correlation coefficient or R-square is called the **coefficient of determination.**

Coefficient of determination

$$r^2 = (\text{Cor}_{j,m})^2 = (0.93)^2 = 0.86$$

The R-square indicates the extent to which the market model explains a security's returns. In this example, the market is able to explain 86 per cent of Jaya Infotech's share return.

BETA ESTIMATION IN PRACTICE

In practice, the market portfolio is approximated by a well-diversified share price index. We have several price indices

available in India. For example, these indices are: (*a*) the Bombay Stock Exchange's Sensitivity Index (Sensex), (*b*) the Bombay Stock Exchange's National Index, (*c*) the National Stock Exchange's Nifty, (*e*) the Economic Times Share Price Index, and (*f*) the Financial Express Share Price Index. Notice that these indices include only shares of companies. In theory, the market portfolio should include all risky assets – shares, bonds, gold, silver, real estate, art objects etc.

In computing beta by regression, we need data on returns on market index and the security for which beta is estimated over a period of time. There is no theoretically determined time period and time intervals for calculating beta. The time period and the time interval may vary. The returns maybe measured on a daily, weekly or monthly basis. One should have sufficient number of observations over a reasonable length of time. A number of agencies providing the beta values in developed countries like the USA and the UK use monthly returns for five-year period for estimating beta.

The return on a share and market index may be calculated as **total return**; that is, dividend yield plus capital gain:

$$\text{Rate of return} = \frac{\text{Current Dividend} + \left(\begin{array}{l}\text{Share price in the beginning}\\ - \text{Share price at the end}\end{array}\right)}{\text{Share price in the beginning}}$$

$$= \text{Dividend yield} + \text{Capital gain/loss}$$

$$r = \frac{D_t + (P_t - P_{t-1})}{P_{t-1}} = \frac{D_t}{P_{t-1}} + \left[\frac{P_t}{P_{t-1}} - 1\right] \quad (3)$$

In practice, one may use capital gains/loss or price returns [i.e., $P_t/P_{t-1} - 1$] rather total returns to estimate beta of a company's share. A further modification may be made in calculating the return. One may calculate the compounded rate of return as shown below:

$$r_j = \log[P_t - P_{t-1}] = \log[P_t/P_{t-1}] \quad (4)$$

The advantage of Equation (4) is that it is not influenced by extreme observations.

Examples of Beta Estimation for Companies in India

For illustrative purposes our estimation of the regression equation in Illustration 6.1 is based on just five observations. The sample size is very small to arrive at any definite conclusion. In practice, the sample size would be large which may cover a reasonably long period with frequent time interval. We plot monthly returns on shares of four companies against the monthly returns on Sensex covering a period of five years from April 1997 to March 2002. Thus the total number of observations for each company is 60. The characteristic line of each firm is drawn. The beta for each company is the slope of its characteristic line. You can estimate beta by following the procedure discussed in Table 6.1 or Table 6.2. We have shown R^2, the coefficient of determination as well. You can use Excel to estimate regression (see Excel Application: Beta Estimation box).

There are many important parameters in a regression. In Table 6.4, we summarise statistics of regression parameters for one of the companies, viz. HLL. The parameters are explained below:

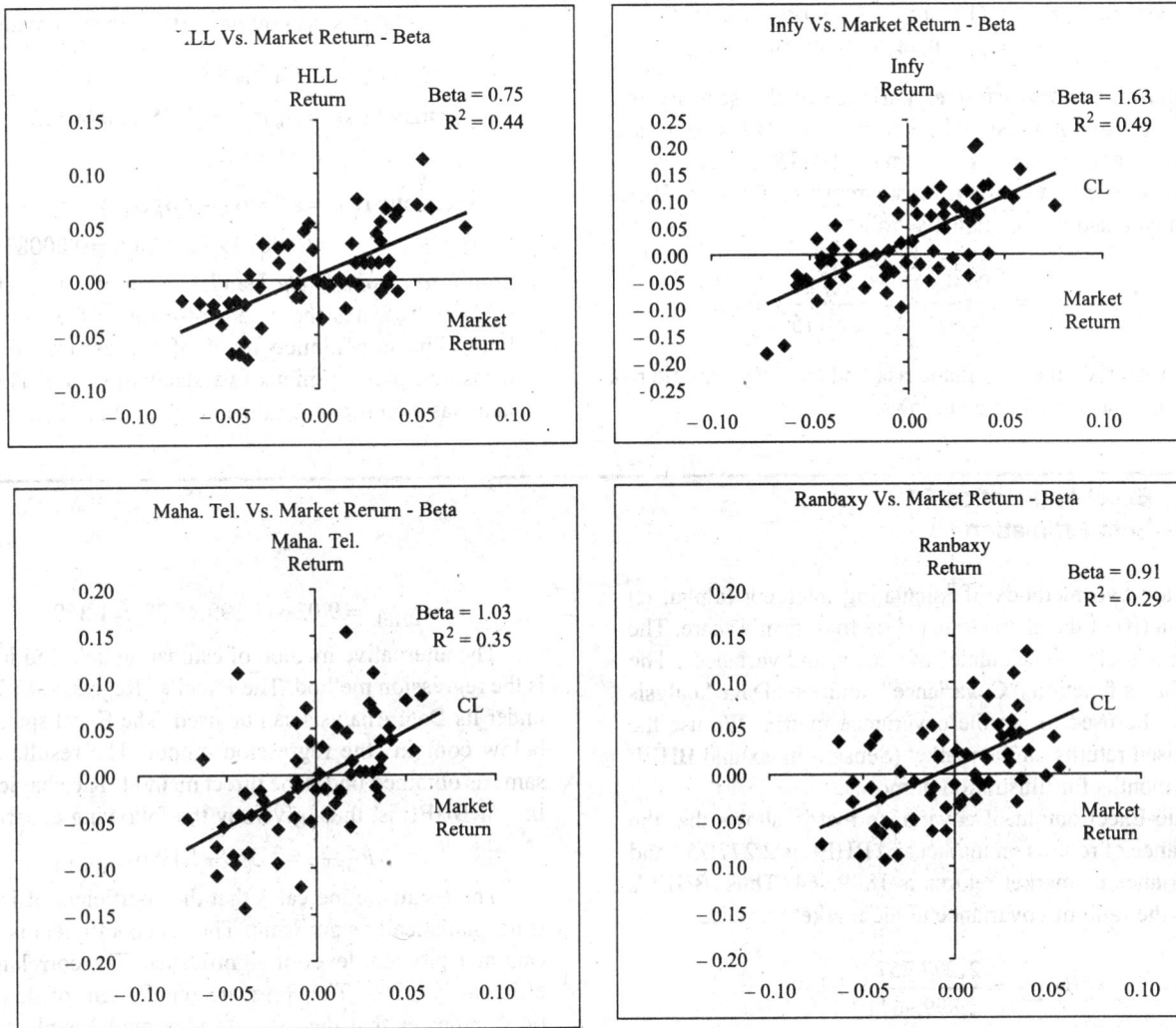

Figure 6.2: Characteristic Lines and Betas for Four Companies (Based on Regression of Monthly Returns of Companies against Returns on Sensex for Five Years, April 1997-March 2002

Table 6.4: Summaries of Regression Parameters for HLL Vs. Market Returns

		Market	HLL
Alpha (intercept)	0.0061		
Standard error of alpha	0.0038		
Beta	0.7479		
Standard error of beta	0.1107		
Correlation	0.6635		
Coefficient of determination	0.4402		
F-statistic	45.6143		
Significance	0.0000		
Average monthly return		0.00046	0.00647
Variance of returns		0.00115	0.00149
Covariance	0.00086		

- **Beta (slope)** HLL has a beta of 0.75 based on the monthly returns during April 1997 to March 2002. A beta of less than 1 means that HLL's returns are less volatile than the market (Sensex) returns.
- **Alpha (intercept)** The intercept is 0.0061 (i.e., 0.6%). This is HLL's return (R_h) when the market return is zero. HLL's

beta (β_h) is 0.75. If the monthly market return (R_m) is expected to be 1 per cent, HLL's expected monthly return is 1.36 per cent:

$$R_h = \alpha + \beta_h R_m = 0.0061 + (0.75)(0.01) = 0.0136$$

- **Coefficient of correlation (Cor)** The coefficient of correlation is 0.66. The positive correlation indicates that when the market return goes up, HLL's return also goes up.
- **Coefficient of determination (Cor²)** The squared coefficient of correlation or the coefficient of determination (Cor²) is 0.44 (or 44%). It indicates the percentage of the variance of HLL's returns explained by the changes in the market returns. Thus, the market explains 44 per cent of HLL's risk (variance of returns). The 56 per cent unexplained variance is the firm-specific variance. Thus, HLL's systematic and non-systematic risks are as follows:

Total risk = Security variance

= Systematic risk + Unsystematic risk

Systematic risk = (Cor²) × (security variance)

= (0.44) × (0.00149) = 0.00066

Unsystematic risk $= (1 - cor^2) \times$ (security variance)

$$= (1 - 0.44) \times (0.00149) = 0.00083$$

- **Variance and covariance:** Variance of the security is a measure of total risk. The variance of HLL's returns is 0.00149 and of the market return is 0.00115. The covariance of the HLL returns and the market returns is 0.00086. HLL's beta can also be calculated as follows:

$$\text{HLL's beta} = \frac{\text{Covar}_{m, h}}{\text{Var}_m} = \frac{0.00086}{0.00115} = 0.75$$

The total risk, the systematic risk and the unsystematic risk can also be estimated as follows:

Total risk = systematic risk + unsystematic risk

$$= \beta_h^2 \sigma_m^2 + e^2$$

Systematic risk $= \beta_h^2 \sigma_m^2 = (0.75)^2 (0.00115)$

$$= 0.00066$$

Unsystematic risk $= e^2 = \sigma_h^2 - (\beta_h^2 \sigma_m^2)$

$$= 0.00149 - 0.00066 = 0.00083$$

- **Standard error of beta** Standard error of beta coefficient is 0.11. It indicates the extent of error in the estimation of beta. The confidence level of the estimated value is measured plus or minus two standard errors. Thus HLL's beta has a confidence range between 0.53 [i.e., 0.75 − (2 ×

⊠ Excel Application 6.1: Beta Estimation

There are two methods of calculating intercept (alpha, α) and beta (β) of the characteristic line for a firm's share. The direct method is to calculate covariance and variances. The Excel has a function, "Covariance", under its Data Analysis that can be used to get the covariance matrix. We use the annualised returns on the market (Sensex) index and BHEL for 12 months for illustration purposes.

The Excel output of covariance matrix shows that the covariance of returns on market and BHEL is 2,277.757 and the variance of market returns is 1899.964. Thus, BHEL's beta is the ratio of covariance to the market variance:

$$\beta_{\text{BHEL}} = \frac{2,277.757}{1,899.964} = 1.199$$

BHEL's intercept is its average return minus the product of its beta and the average market return:

$$\alpha_{\text{BHEL}} = 9.02 - (1.199 \times 6.38) = 1.369$$

The alternative method of estimating beta and intercept is the regression method. The Excel's "Regression" function under its Data Analysis can be used. The Excel spreadsheet below contains the regression output. The results are the same as obtained under the direct method. The characteristic line of BHEL is, thus, given by the following equation:

$$R_{\text{BHEL}} = 1.369 + 1.199 r_{\text{MARKET}}$$

The t-statistic indicates that the coefficient of intercept is not statistically significant. The beta coefficient is significant at 1 per cent level of significance. The correlation coefficient is 0.703. The R-square (coefficient of determination) indicates that the market index model explains about 49 per cent of BHEL's share returns.

$$\alpha_{\text{BHEL}} = 9.02 - (1.199 \times 6.38) = 1.369$$

	A	B	C	D	E	F	G	H
1	**Annualised Return (%)**			**COVARIANCE MATRIX**			**BHEL**	**Market**
2	**Month**	**BHEL**	**Market**	BHEL			5532.628	
3	1	154.58	69.6	Market			2277.757	1899.964
4	2	33.66	-11.8					
5	3	-53.57	65.27					
6	4	62.19	6.05	**SUMMARY OUTPUT OF REGRESSION**				
7	5	-53.66	-54.79					
8	6	-31.38	3.48	*Regression Statistics*				
9	7	18.02	-13.36	Multiple R			0.703	
10	8	-51.03	-34.4	R-square			0.494	
11	9	10.24	14.25	Adjusted R-square			0.443	
12	10	-130.76	-65.9	Standard Error			57.986	
13	11	88.54	60.64	Observations			12	
14	12	61.38	37.54					
15	**Average**	**9.02**	**6.38**		*Coefficient*	*Std. Error*	*t-Stat*	*P-value*
16				Intercept	1.369	16.917	0.081	0.937

0.11)] and 0.97 [i.e., 0.75 + (2 × 0.11)] and there is 95 per cent probability that it would range within these intervals.

Betas for the Sensex Companies

The BSE's sensitivity index includes 30 highly traded shares. In Table 6.5 we provide information on beta and other parameters for these companies. The estimates are based on monthly returns for five years. You may note that HCL has the highest beta of 2.39 and Nestle the lowest beta of 0.39. Twelve companies have negative average monthly returns. The average monthly return on market is positive. You may also notice that the standard deviation of returns on the Sensex (the market portfolio) is the lowest.

Does Beta Remain Stable Over Time?

ACC (the Associated Cement Company) has remained in the cement industry for several years. ACC has a beta of 1.44 when we regress monthly returns on ACC against the monthly market returns for a 5-year period from April 1997 to March 2002. In Figure 6.3 we plot monthly returns on ACC against the monthly market returns for two sub-periods – from April 1997 to September 1999 and from October 1999 to March 2002. We find that ACC's beta for the two periods is different; it has decreased from

1.55 to 1.28. These two estimates are also different from the 5-year estimate of ACC's beta. Betas may not remain stable for a company over time even if a company stays in the same industry. There could be several reasons for this. Over time, a company may witness changes in its product mix, technology, competition or market share. In India, many industrial sectors are witnessing changes in competition and market composition due to the government policy of reforms and deregulation. This is expected to affect the betas of many companies.

DETERMINANTS OF BETA

We have explained that beta is the ratio of covariance between returns on market and a security to variance of the market returns. But what drives the variance and covariance? The variance and covariance and therefore, beta depend on three fundamental factors: the nature of business, the operating leverage and the financial leverage. These factors are discussed below.

Nature of Business

All economies go through business cycles. Firms behave differently with business cycle. The earnings of some companies fluctuate more with the business cycles. Their earnings grow during

Table 6.5: Betas for Sensex Companies (Based on Monthly Returns from April 1997 to March 2002

	Company	Intercept	Beta	Average Return	Stdev. of returns	Cor	Cor²
1	ACC	0.0020	1.44	0.0026	0.0732	0.6730	0.4529
2	BAJAJ	−0.0022	0.62	−0.0019	0.0508	0.4205	0.1769
3	BHEL	−0.0047	1.20	−0.0041	0.0658	0.6249	0.3905
4	BSES	0.0002	0.84	0.0006	0.0552	0.5215	0.2719
5	CASTROL	−0.0013	0.48	−0.0010	0.0472	0.3519	0.1238
6	CIPLA	0.0111	0.66	0.0114	0.0602	0.3757	0.1411
7	COLGATE	−0.0052	0.56	−0.0050	0.0427	0.4499	0.2024
8	DR REDDY'S	0.0174	0.81	0.0178	0.0580	0.4787	0.2291
9	GLAXO	0.0017	0.87	0.0021	0.0566	0.5271	0.2778
10	GRASIM	−0.0017	1.06	−0.0012	0.0740	0.4916	0.2416
11	GUJAMB	0.0023	1.12	0.0028	0.0542	0.7059	0.4983
12	HCL	−0.0087	2.39	−0.0236	0.0928	0.8139	0.6624
13	HEROHONDA	0.0174	0.54	0.0177	0.0591	0.3109	0.0967
14	HINDALCO	−0.0018	0.73	−0.0015	0.0515	0.4868	0.2370
15	HLL	0.0061	0.75	0.0065	0.0386	0.6635	0.4402
16	HPCL	0.0007	0.79	0.0011	0.0581	0.4669	0.2180
17	ICICI	0.0000	1.09	0.0005	0.0647	0.5768	0.3327
18	INFY	0.0231	1.63	0.0239	0.0802	0.6974	0.4864
19	ITC	0.0045	0.70	0.0049	0.0462	0.5222	0.2727
20	L&T	−0.0014	1.54	−0.0007	0.0679	0.7791	0.6070
21	MAHA.TEL	−0.0040	1.03	−0.0035	0.0601	0.5893	0.3472
22	NESTLE	0.0061	0.30	0.0062	0.0459	0.2259	0.0510
23	RANBX	0.0068	0.91	0.0072	0.0578	0.5396	0.2912
24	RELIANCE	0.0056	0.85	0.0060	0.0472	0.6197	0.3841
25	RELPETRO	0.0048	0.80	0.0051	0.0521	0.5270	0.2777
26	SATYAM	0.0276	2.09	0.0286	0.1073	0.6668	0.4446
27	SBI	−0.0020	1.24	−0.0014	0.0566	0.7530	0.5671
28	TELCO	−0.0084	1.59	−0.0077	0.0742	0.7356	0.5411
29	TISCO	−0.0039	1.08	−0.0034	0.0592	0.6233	0.3886
30	ZEE	0.0199	1.55	0.0206	0.1027	0.5157	0.2660
	SENSEX			0.0005	0.0342		

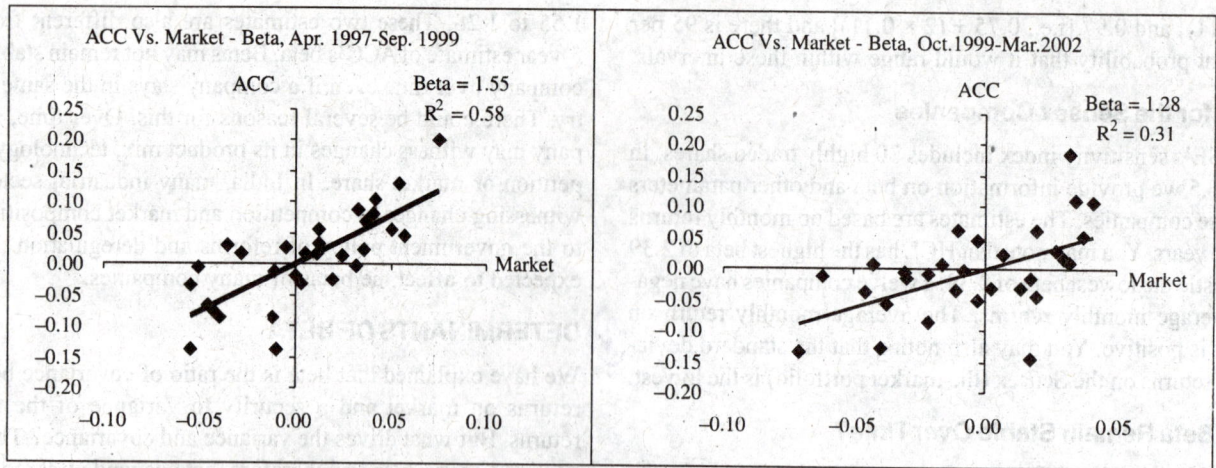

Figure 6.3: ACC's betas for two periods, april 1997–September 1999 and October 1999–March 2002

the growth phase of the business cycle and decline during the contraction phase. For example, the earnings of consumer product firms or the cargo firms are tied with the business cycle and they go up or down with business cycle. On the other hand, the earnings of utility companies remain unaffected by the business cycle. If we regress a company's earnings with the aggregate earnings of all companies in the economy, we would obtain a sensitivity index, which we can call the company's **accounting beta**. The real or the market beta is based on share market returns rather than earnings. The accounting betas are significantly correlated with the market betas. This implies that if a firm's earnings are more sensitive to business conditions, it is likely to have higher beta.

We must distinguish between the **earnings variability** and the **earnings cyclicality**. A company's earnings may be highly variable, but it may not have high beta. The earnings variability is an example of a specific risk that can be diversified. Cyclicality of a company's earnings, on the other hand, is the variability of its earnings vis-à-vis the aggregate earnings of the economy.

Operating Leverage

Operating leverage refers to the use of fixed costs. The **degree of operating leverage** is defined as the change in a company's earnings before interest and tax due to change in sales. Since variable costs change in direct proportion of sales and fixed costs remain constant, the variability in EBIT when sales change is caused by fixed costs. Higher the fixed cost, higher the variability in EBIT for a given change in sales. Other things remaining the same, companies with higher operating leverage (because of higher fixed costs) are more risky. Operating leverage intensifies the effect of cyclicality on a company's earnings. As a consequence, companies with higher degree of operating leverage have high betas.

Financial Leverage

Financial leverage refers to debt in a firm's capital structure. Firms with debt in the capital structure are called **levered firms**. The interest payments on debt are fixed irrespective of the firm's earnings. Hence, interest charges are fixed costs of debt financing. As discussed in the preceding section, the fixed costs of

operations result in operating leverage and cause EBIT to vary with changes in sales. Similarly, the fixed financial costs result in financial leverage and cause profit after tax to vary with changes in EBIT. Hence, the **degree of financial leverage** is defined as the change in a company's profit after tax due to change in its EBIT. Since financial leverage increases the firm's (financial) risk, it will increase the equity beta of the firm.

Asset Beta and Equity Beta

Assets of a levered firm are financed by debt and equity. Therefore, the asset beta should be the weighted average of the equity beta and the debt beta:

$$\begin{pmatrix} \text{Asset} \\ \text{beta} \end{pmatrix} = \begin{pmatrix} \text{Equity} \\ \text{beta} \end{pmatrix} \times \begin{pmatrix} \text{Weight of} \\ \text{equity} \end{pmatrix} + \begin{pmatrix} \text{Debt} \\ \text{beta} \end{pmatrix} \times \begin{pmatrix} \text{Weight of} \\ \text{debt} \end{pmatrix}$$

$$\beta_A = \beta_E \times \frac{\text{Equity}}{\text{Equity} + \text{Debt}} + \beta_D \frac{\text{Debt}}{\text{Equity} + \text{Debt}} \quad (5)$$

You may note that for an unlevered (all-equity) firm, the asset beta and the equity beta would be the same. Debt is less risky than equity. Hence the beta of debt will be lower than the equity beta. In case of the risk-free debt, beta will be zero. If we make the assumption that the beta of debt is zero, then the beta of the assets is given as follows:

$$\beta_A = \beta_E \times \frac{\text{Equity}}{\text{Equity} + \text{Debt}} \quad (6)$$

For a levered firm, the proportion of equity will be less than 1. Therefore, the beta of asset will be less than the beta of equity. The beta of equity for a levered firm is given as follows:

$$\beta_E = \beta_A \left[1 + \frac{\text{Debt}}{\text{Equity}} \right] \quad (7)$$

The second term on the right-hand side of the equation is the measure of financial leverage. You may notice that there is a linear relationship between the equity beta and the financial leverage. As the financial leverage increases, the equity beta also increases. The equity beta is equal to the asset beta if debt is zero.

How would taxes affect the equity beta of a leveraged firm?

Interest on debt is tax deductible, which results into tax savings, called interest tax shield. As we shall explain later on in this book the equity beta of a levered firm, which employs constant amount of debt, is given by the following formula:

$$\beta_E = \beta_A \left[1 + (1 - T) \frac{\text{Debt}}{\text{Equity}} \right] \qquad (8)$$

CAPM AND THE OPPORTUNITY COST OF EQUITY

Shareholders supply capital to a firm. In return, they expect to receive dividends. They can also realise cash by selling their shares. The firm has discretion to retain entire or a part of profits. If dividends were distributed to shareholders, they would have an opportunity to invest cash so received in securities in the capital markets and earn a return. When the firm retains profits, there is loss of opportunity for which shareholders need to be compensated. The expected rate of return from a security of **equivalent risk** in the capital market is the cost of the lost opportunity. Shareholders require the firm to at least earn this rate on their capital invested in projects. From the firm's point of view, the expected rate of return from a security of equivalent risk is the cost of equity.

The expected rate of return or the cost of equity in CAPM is given by the following equation:

$$R_j = k_e = R_f + (R_m - R_f)\beta_j \qquad (9)$$

We need the following information to estimate a firm's cost of equity:

- The risk-free rate,
- The market premium, and
- The beta of the firm's share

Table 6.6: Beta and the Cost of Equity for Companies

Share	Beta β	Risk-free rate r_f	Market premium $(r_m - r_f)$	Expected return $(r_f + (r_m - r_f)\beta$
ACC	0.97	5.8%	9.0%	16.66%
Ashok Leyland	0.89	5.8	9.0	15.77
Dabur India	0.51	5.8	9.0	11.51
HLL	0.82	5.8	9.0	14.98
ICICI Bank	0.97	5.8	9.0	16.66
IFCI	1.44	5.8	9.0	21.93
Infosys	1.79	5.8	9.0	25.85
IOC	0.67	5.8	9.0	13.30
Orient Info. Tech.	2.79	5.8	9.0	37.05
Reliance	1.14	5.8	9.0	18.57
Tata Power	1.11	5.8	9.0	18.23
Telco	1.16	5.8	9.0	18.79
Thermax	1.00	5.8	9.0	17.00

Sources: National Stock Exchange of India (NSE) for beta; RBI for 91-day T-Bill rates; and author's estimate of the market premium.

In Table 6.6 we have given betas for ten companies. The risk-free rate is approximated by 91-day T-Bills. The yield on 91-day T-Bills in October 2002 was 5.8 per cent. In Chapter 4

we showed that the historical risk premium on shares in India was about 9 per cent. We use these numbers to calculate the expected return or cost of equity for various firms in Table 6.6.

You may notice that Dabur India has the lowest beta (0.51) in our sample and its expected rate of return is 11.51 per cent. The expected return of Thermax is equal to the market return (17 per cent) since it has a beta of 1. Orient Information Technology has the highest beta (2.79) and its expected return is 37.05 per cent.

Industry Vs. Company Beta

In Table 6.7 we show the NSE calculated betas of the software companies. You may notice that the betas for the software companies are generally high; a number of companies have betas very close to or more than 2. There is also evidence of wide differences in betas of companies. For example, GTL has the highest beta of 3.23 and Ramco the lowest beta of 1.22. The average beta of all software companies in Table 6.7 is 2.17. For both these companies, the estimates of the required rate of return would show significant differences depending on whether the companies use the industry beta or their individual betas. Suppose the risk-free rate is 5.8 per cent and the risk premium is 9 per cent, the required rates of return for GTL and Ramco with their own betas are:

GTL: $5.8 + 9 \times 3.23 = 34.87\%$

Ramco: $5.8 + 9 \times 1.22 = 16.78\%$

If these companies use the industry beta, then the required rates will be the same for both companies

GTL & Ramco: $5.8 + 9 \times 2.17 = 25.33\%$

What should companies do? Should they use their betas or the industry beta? The use of the industry beta is preferable for those companies whose operations match up with the industry

Table 6.7: Betas for the Software Companies

Company	Beta
CMC	1.32
Digital	2.23
DSQ	2.80
GTL	3.23
HCL	2.65
Hughes	1.88
Infosys	2.09
Mascot	1.61
Mphasis	1.36
NIIT	1.93
Pentasoft	2.18
Polaris	2.74
Ramco	1.22
Rolta	2.47
Satyam	2.65
Silverline	2.87
Sonata	1.84
Tata Info	1.73
Visualsoft	2.49
Wipro	2.10
Industry Average	2.17

Source: www.nseindia.com, National Stock Exchange.

operations. The industry beta is less affected by random variations. Those companies that have operations quite different from a large number of companies in the industry, may stick to the use of their own betas rather than the industry beta. Let us emphasise that there is no theory for the selection of beta. Beta estimation and selection is an art as well, which one learns with experience.

SUMMARY

❖ The market or systematic risk of a security is measured in terms of its sensitivity to the market movements. This sensitivity is referred to the security's beta.

❖ Beta is a ratio of the covariance of returns of a security, j, and the market portfolio, m, to the variance of return of the market portfolio:

$$\beta_j = \frac{\text{Cov}_{jm}}{\text{Var}_m} = \frac{\sigma_j \sigma_m \text{Cor}_{jm}}{\sigma_m^2} = \frac{\sigma_j \text{Cor}_{jm}}{\sigma_m}$$

❖ In practice, the following regression equation is used to estimate beta:

$$R_j = \alpha + \beta_j R_m + e_j$$

❖ The market portfolio may be approximated by a well-diversified share price index such as the Bombay Stock Exchange's National Index or Sensitivity Index (Sensex).

❖ The expected return on the share of a company depends on its beta. The higher the beta, the higher the expected return.

❖ We can use historical data to determine a firm's beta. The estimate of beta would depend on the period of analysis (say, one year, three years or five years) and the frequency of returns (e.g., daily, weekly or monthly). The analyst should be careful in using a reasonable period and time interval.

❖ The beta of a firm depends on a number of factors. The three most important factors are: nature of business, operating leverage and financial leverage. A cyclical firm would have higher beta. If we relate the cyclical firm's earnings with the aggregate earnings, we would obtain accounting beta. Higher the accounting beta, higher the market beta. High operating leverage and financial leverage cause higher beta. As these factors change over time, the firm's beta may also change. Hence, betas of firms may not remain stable.

❖ The calculated beta of a firm is the beta of its equity. In case of a firm that does not employ debt, the equity beta is the same as the firm's asset beta. However, in case of a firm with debt, the asset beta is the weighted average of the equity beta and the debt beta. Since debt is less risky, the debt beta would be less than the equity beta.

❖ If debt is risk free, the debt beta will be zero and the asset beta and the equity beta are given as follows:

$$\beta_A = \beta_E \times \frac{E}{D+E} + \beta_D \times \frac{D}{D+E}$$

$$\beta_A = \beta_E \times \frac{E}{D+E} \qquad (\text{since } \beta_D = 0)$$

$$\beta_E = \beta_A \frac{D+E}{E} = \beta_A \left[1 + \frac{D}{E}\right]$$

❖ The firm uses capital supplied by shareholders. Alternatively, shareholders could invest their funds in securities in the capital market. Thus, they would require firm to earn a return equal to the expected rate of return on security of the equivalent risk. Hence, the cost of equity is equal to the expected rate of return, and can be calculated using SML. The risk-free rate and market premium is common to all firms; betas of firms would be different.

KEY CONCEPTS

Accounting beta	Debt beta	Financial leverage	Risk premium
Asset beta	Earnings cyclicality	Levered firm	Risk-free rate of return
Correlation coefficient	Earnings variability	Market index	Stability of beta
Cost of equity	Equity beta	Market portfolio	Weighted average cost of
Covariance	Expected rate of return	Operating leverage	capital

ILLUSTRATIVE SOLVED PROBLEMS

Problem 6.1: The following are the returns of share S and the market (M) for the last six years:

Year	Return (%) S	M
19X1	18	15
19X2	9	7
19X3	20	16

Year	Return (%) S	M
19X4	−10	−13
19X5	5	4
19X6	12	7

(a) Calculate the covariance and correlation coefficient of returns.

Contd...

(b) Determine the beta coefficient for S.
(c) What is S's total risk? How much is systematic risk?

Year	Return (%)				
	S	M	S^2	M^2	SM
19X1	18	15	324	225	270
19X2	9	7	81	49	63
19X3	20	16	400	256	320
19X4	−10	−13	100	169	130
19X5	5	4	25	16	20
19X6	12	7	144	49	84
Sum	54	36	1,074	764	887
Average	9	6		225	270

Solution: (a)

$$\text{Cov}_{SM} = \frac{1}{N}\sum_{t=1}^{n}(r_S - \bar{r}_S)(r_M - \bar{r}_M)$$

$$= \frac{1}{6}[(18-9)(15-6)+(9-9)(7-6)+(20-9)(16-6)$$

$$+(-10-9)(-13-6)+(5-9)(4-6)+(12-9)(7-6)$$

$$= \frac{1}{6}[563] = 93.83$$

$$\text{Cor}_{SM} = \frac{N(\Sigma SM)-(\Sigma S)(\Sigma M)}{\left\{[(N\Sigma S^2)-(\Sigma S)^2][(N\Sigma M^2)-(\Sigma M)^2]\right\}^{1/2}}$$

$$= \frac{6(887)-(54)(36)}{\left\{[(6)(1074)-(54)^2][(6)(764)-(36)^2]\right\}^{1/2}}$$

$$= \frac{5.322-1.944}{[(6,444-2,916)(4,584-1,296)]^{1/2}}$$

$$= \frac{3,378}{[(3,528)(3,288)]^{1/2}}$$

$$= \frac{3,378}{3,406} = 0.99$$

(b) $$\text{Beta} = \frac{N\Sigma SM - (\Sigma S)(\Sigma M)}{N\Sigma M^2 - (\Sigma M)^2}$$

$$= \frac{(6)(887)-(54)(36)}{(6)(764)-(36)^2}$$

$$= \frac{5,322-1,944}{4,584-1,296}$$

$$= \frac{3,376}{3,288} = 1.03$$

(c) $\text{Var}(r_s) = $ Total risk

$$= \text{Var}(\alpha + \beta_S r_M + e)$$

$$= \text{Var}(\beta_S r_M) + \text{Var}(e) [\because \text{Var}(\alpha) = 0]$$

$$= \beta_S^2 \text{Var}(r_M) + \text{Var}(e)$$

$$= \text{systematic} + \text{unsystematic}$$

Var (e) is the residual variance. Thus, it is systematic risk:
Systematic risk = $(0.99)^2 = 0.98$ or 98% of variance of S's returns
Unsystematic risk = $1 - 0.98$
$$= 0.02 \text{ or } 2\% \text{ of the variance of } S\text{'s returns}$$

REVIEW QUESTIONS

1. What is beta? How is it measured? What are the problems in beta estimation?
2. Do betas remain stable over time? What problem is posed by the instability of the beta?
3. How do you calculate the cost of equity using the CAPM framework?
4. What factors influence the beta of a share? Explain.

PROBLEMS

1. The returns on the share of Delite Industries and the Sensex for the past five years are given below:

Sensex (%)	Delite (%)
− 12.5	− 5.1
1.7	6.7
7.2	7.1
11.5	18.9
6.3	11.9

Calculate the average return on Delite's share and Sensex. What is Delite's beta?

2. Royal Paints Limited is an all-equity firm without any debt. It has a beta of 1.21. The current risk-free rate is 8.5 per cent and the historical market premium is 9.5 per cent. Royal is considering a project that is expected to generate a return of 20 per cent. Assuming that the project has the same risk as the firm, should the firm accept the project?

3. Calculate Excel Company Limited's equity beta given the following information:

Correlation between the returns on Excel's share and Sensex = 0.725
Variance of the returns on Excel's share = 0.006455
Variance of the returns on Sensex = 0.001589

4. The returns from the past 15 months on HLL share and the Sensex (market) are given below:

Month/Year	Return (%)	
	HLL	Sensex
Oct- 02	–1.2	–3.5
Nov- 02	–2.7	–5.1
Dec- 02	–8.6	–4.3
Jan- 02	–3.0	–7.5
Feb- 02	–0.3	–4.8
Mar- 02	–1.9	–1.9
Apr- 02	–0.5	–1.5
May- 02	–0.8	–4.6
Jun- 02	3.3	4.1
Jul- 02	1.3	0.0
Aug- 02	0.3	2.0
Sep- 02	–0.5	–0.2
Oct- 02	6.0	3.9
Nov- 02	–6.0	–10.1
Dec- 02	–2.5	–3.5

What is HLL's beta? Is it higher or lower than the beta of the average share?

5. The following are the regression (characteristics) lines of three assets:

$$\text{Asset } A: r_A = 1.53\% + 0.89 r_M \qquad Cor = 0.78$$
$$\text{Asset } B: r_B = -0.65\% + 1.18 r_M \qquad Cor = 0.83$$
$$\text{Asset } C: r_C = 0.85\% + 1.29 r_M \qquad Cor = 0.65$$

(a) Which asset is the most risky (systematic risk)?
(b) How much is the systematic and unsystematic risk for each asset?

6. Sunlite Soap Limited is an all-equity firm. It has a beta of 1.21. The current risk-free rate is 6.5 per cent and the market premium is 9.0 per cent. Sunlite is considering a project with similar risk, but the project will be financed 30 per cent by debt and 70 per cent by equity. Debt is risk free. What is the expected rate of return on equity that the project should earn to be acceptable by the firm?

7. You have a portfolio of the following four shares:

Share	Beta	Investment (Rs)
A	0.80	100,000
B	1.25	100,000
C	1.00	75,000
D	0.60	125,000

What is the expected rate of return on your portfolio if the risk-free rate of return is 9 per cent and the expected market rate of return is 16 per cent?

CHAPTER 7
Options and Their Valuation

CHAPTER OBJECTIVES

- Explain the meaning of option
- Describe the types of option
- Discuss the implications of combinations of options
- Highlight the factors that have an influence on the valuation of options
- Develop a simple model of valuing options
- Show how the Black-Scholes model of option valuation works

INTRODUCTION

Option means several things to different people.[1] It may refer to choice or alternative or privilege or opportunity or preference or right. To have options is normally regarded good. One is considered unfortunate without any options. Options are valuable since they provide protection against unwanted, uncertain happenings. They provide alternatives to bail out from a difficult situation. Options can be exercised on the happening of certain events.

Options may be explicit or implicit. When you buy insurance on your house, it is an explicit option that will protect you in the event there is a fire or a theft in your house. If you own shares of a company, your liability is limited. Limited liability is an implicit option to default on the payment of debt.

Options have assumed considerable significance in finance. They can be written on any asset, including shares, bonds, portfolios, stock indices, currencies, etc. They are quite useful in risk management. How are options defined in finance? What gives value to options? How are they valued?

OPTIONS

In a broad sense, an **option** is a claim without any liability. It is a claim contingent upon the occurrence of certain conditions. Thus, an option is a **contingent claim.** More specifically, an option is a contract that gives the holder a right, without any obligation, to buy or sell an asset at an agreed price on or before a specified period of time. The option to buy an asset is known as a **call option,** and the option to sell an asset is called a **put option.** The price at which option can be exercised is called an **exercise price** or a **strike price.** The asset on which the put or call option is created is referred to as the **underlying asset.** Depending on when an option can be exercised, it is classified in one of the following two categories:

- **European option** When an option is allowed to be exercised only on the maturity date, it is called a European option.
- **American option** When the option can be exercised any time before its maturity, it is called an American option.

When will an option holder exercise his right? He will exercise his option when doing so provides him a benefit over

---

1. There are a number of books and articles on the subject of option pricing. The two articles that have influenced most writings on the subject are: F. Black and M. Scholes, The Pricing of Options and Corporate Liabilities, *Journal of Political Economy,* 81, pp. 637–54 (May–June 1973); and R.C. Merton, Theory of Rational Option Pricing, *Bell Journal of Economics and Management Science*, 4, pp. 141–81 (Spring 1973). We also suggest the following three books for further reading: (1) J. Cox and M. Rubinstein, *Option Markets*, Prentice-Hall, 1985; (2) J. Hull, *Options, Futures and other Derivatives*, Prentice-Hall, 1993; and (3) R. Jarrow, *Option Pricing,* Dow. Jones-Irwin, 1983.

buying or selling the underlying asset from the market at the prevailing price. There are three possibilities:

- **In-the-money** A put or a call option is said to in-the-money when it is advantageous for the investor to exercise it. In the case of in-the-money call options, the exercise price is less than the current value of the underlying asset, while in the case of the in-the-money put options, the exercise price is higher than the current value of the underlying asset.

- **Out-of-the-money** A put or a call option is out-of-the-money if it is not advantageous for the investor to exercise it. In the case of the out-of-the-money call options, the exercise price is higher than the current value of the underlying asset, while in the case of the out-of-the-money put options, the exercise price is lower than the current value of the underlying asset.

- **At-the-money** When the holder of a put or a call option does not lose or gain whether or not he exercises his option, the option is said to be at-the-money. In the case of the out-of-the-money options the exercise price is equal to the current value of the underlying asset.

Options do not come free. They involve cost. The **option premium** is the price that the holder of an option has to pay for obtaining a call or a put option. The price will have to be paid, generally in advance, whether or not the holder exercises his option.

CALL OPTION

A **call option** on a share (or any asset) is a right to buy the share at an agreed exercise (strike) price. Suppose that the current share price (*S*) of Satyam Computer's share is Rs 130. You expect that price in a 3 month period (S_t) will go up to Rs 150. But you do fear that the price may also fall below Rs 130. To reduce the chance of your risk and at the same time to have an opportunity of making profit, instead of buying the share, you can buy a 3 month call option on Satyam's share at an agreed exercise price (*E*) of, say, Rs 125. Ignoring the option premium, taxes, transaction costs and the time value of money, will you exercise your option if the price of the share is Rs 130 in three months? You will exercise your option since you get a share worth Rs 130 by paying an exercise price of Rs 125. You will gain Rs 5; that is, the pay-off or the value of your call option at expiration (C_t) is Rs 5. Your call option is *in-the-money* at maturity.

What will you do if the price of the share is Rs 120 when the call option on Satyam's share expires? Obviously, you will not exercise the option. You gain nothing. Your call option is worthless, and it is *out-of-the-money* at expiration. You may notice that the value of your call option can never be less than zero. Thus you should exercise call option when:

Share price at expiration > exercise price = $S_t > E$

Do not exercise call option when:

Share price at expiration ≤ exercise price = $S_t \leq E$

The value of the call option at expiration is:

Value of call option at expiration

= Maximum [Share price – Exercise price, 0]

$$C_t = \text{Max} [S_t - E, 0] \qquad (1)$$

The expression above indicates that the value of a call option at expiration is the maximum of the share price minus the exercise price or zero. The call option holder's opportunity to make profits is unlimited. It depends on what the actual market price of the underlying share is when the option is exercised. The greater is the market value of the underlying asset, the larger is the value of the option. Figure 7.1 shows the pay-off or value of a call option.

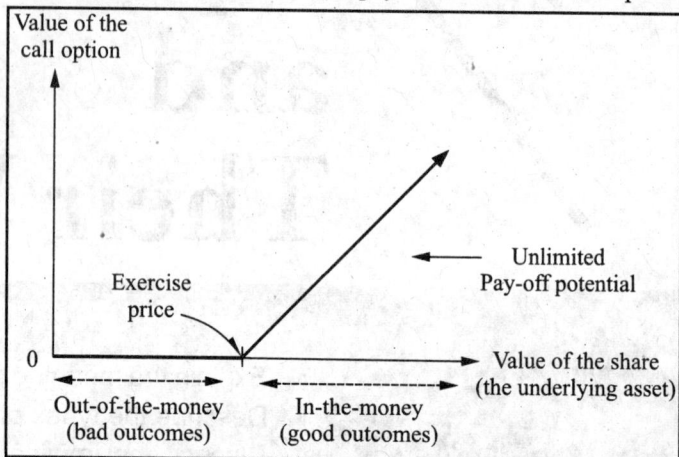

Figure 7.1: Pay-off of a call option buyer

It may be observed from Figure 7.1 that the call buyer's potential pay-off is unlimited once the price of the share (the underlying asset) goes beyond the exercise price. If the share price is on or below the exercise price, the call buyer will not exercise his option. Thus, his pay-off will be zero since the option is worth nothing.

It may also be observed from Figure 7.1 that the possible outcomes can be divided into two parts: one, above the exercise price and other, below the exercise price. The outcomes above the exercise price are said to be in-the-money and are beneficial to the option holder but not the outcomes below the exercise price. It is the exercise price that divides the good and bad outcomes.

How is the seller (or the writer) of a call option affected as the value of the underlying asset changes? Figure 7.2 shows his position as a mirror image of the call buyer's position. The call buyer's gain is call seller's loss. The seller of the call option will

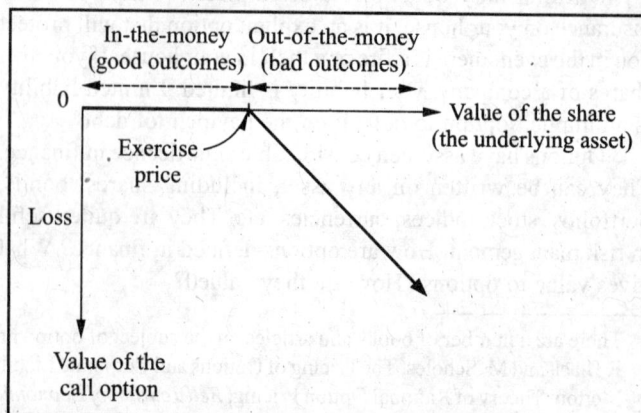

Figure 7.2: Pay-off of a call option writer

not incur any loss when the price of the share (the underlying asset) is less than the exercise price since the buyer will not exercise his option. However, if the share price rises and goes beyond the exercise price, the potential loss of the call seller is very high.

Call Premium

A call buyer exercises his right only when the outcomes are favourable to him. The seller of a call option, being the owner of the asset, gives away the good outcomes in favour of the option buyer. The buyer of a call option must, therefore, pay up-front a price, called **call premium**, to the call seller to buy the option. The call premium is a cost to the option buyer and a gain to the call seller. What is the net pay-off of the buyer and the seller of a call option when the call premium (that the buyer has to pay to the seller) is involved?

Illustration 7.1 : Call Option Pay-off

The share of Telco is selling for Rs 104. Radhey Acharya buys a 3 months call option at a premium of Rs 5. The exercise price is Rs 105. What is Radhey's pay-off if the share price is Rs 100, or Rs 105, or Rs 110, or Rs 115, or Rs 120 at the time the option is exercised? It is calculated in Table 7.1, and also, shown in Figure 7.3. Radhey will exercise his option for any price above the exercise price Rs 105. Since the exercise price is Rs 105 and Radhey (the buyer) has to pay a premium of Rs 5, his pay-off will be zero when the share price rises to Rs 110. Thus, Rs 110 is a break-even price (i.e., the exercise price plus the call premium) for him. The exercise price, Rs 105, separates the good outcomes from the bad outcomes. The seller of the call option (the asset owner) is being paid call premium, Rs 5, for giving up the good outcomes in favour of the buyer of the call option.

Table 7.1: The Call Option Holder's Pay-off at Expiration

	Rs	Rs	Rs	Rs	Rs
Share price (S_t)	100	105	110	115	120
Buyer's inflow :					
Sale of share	—	—	110	115	120
Buyer's outflow :					
Exercise option	—	—	105	105	105
Call premium	5	5	5	5	5
Net pay-off	– 5	– 5	0	+ 5	+ 10

Note: The call option is not exercised when $S_t \leq E$.

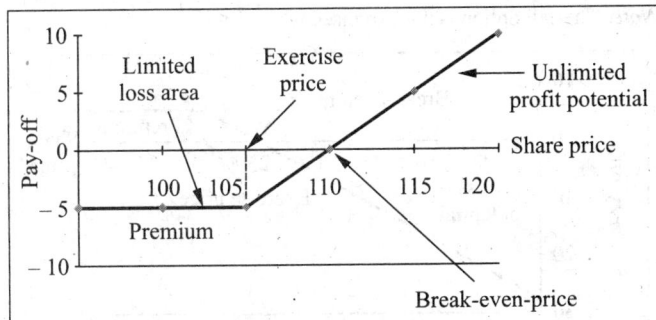

Figure 7.3: Pay-off of the call option buyer

What is the pay-off of the seller of the call option? The position of the call option seller will be opposite to that of the buyer as shown in Table 7.2. If the buyer (Radhey Acharya) exercises his option, the seller

will lose. His (seller's) potential loss is very high, and his profit is limited to Rs 5 (the call premium). If Figure 7.3 is turned up side down, the call seller's position can be depicted graphically in Figure 7.4.

Table 7.2: The Call Option Seller's Pay-off at Expiration

	Rs	Rs	Rs	Rs	Rs
Share price	100	105	110	115	120
Seller's inflow :					
Exercise price	—	—	105	105	105
Call premium	5	5	5	5	5
Seller's outflow :					
Share price	—	—	110	115	120
Net pay-off (profit)	5	5	0	– 5	– 10

Note: The call option is not exercised when $S_t \leq E$.

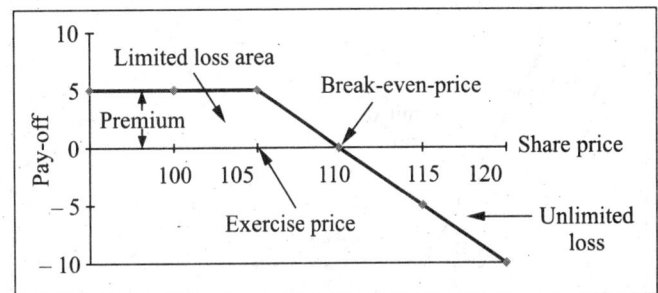

Figure 7.4: Pay-off of the call option seller

PUT OPTION

A **put option** is a contract that gives the holder a right to sell a specified share (or any other asset) at an agreed exercise price on or before a given maturity period. Suppose you expect price of HPCL's share to fall in the near future. Therefore, you buy a 3 month put option at an exercise price (E) of Rs 50. The current market price of HPCL's share (S) is Rs 48. If the price actually falls to (S_t) Rs 35 after three months, you will exercise your option. You will buy the share for Rs 35 from the market and deliver it to the put-option seller (writer) to receive Rs 50. Your gain is Rs 15, ignoring the put option premium, transaction costs and taxes. You will forgo your put option if the share price rises above the exercise price; the put option is worthless for you and its value is zero. A put buyer gains when the share price falls below the exercise price. Ignoring the cost of buying the put option (called put premium), his loss will be zero when the share prices rises above the exercise price since he will not exercise his option. Thus, exercise the put option when:

Exercise price > Share price at expiration = $E > S_t$

Do not exercise the put option when:

Exercise price ≤ Share price at expiration = $E \leq S_t$

The value or pay-off of a put option at expiration will be:

Value of put option at expiration

= Maximum [Exercise price – Share price at expiration, 0]

$$P_t = \text{Max}\left[E - S_t, 0\right] \qquad (2)$$

Figure 7.5 shows that the value of the put option for the option holder depends on the value of the underlying asset. The value of the put option is zero when it is out-of-the-money. You may observe from Figure 7.5 that the potential profit of the put option buyer is limited since share price cannot fall below zero. The exercise price again is the dividing point between the good and bad outcomes. The put option buyer's gain is the seller's loss. The seller insures the buyer from the bad outcomes. Figure 7.6 shows the pay-off of the seller of a put option. It should be clear from Figure 7.6 that the potential loss of the put-option seller is limited to the exercise price. Since the buyer has to pay a premium to the seller for purchasing a put option, the potential profit of the buyer and the potential loss of the seller will reduce by the amount of premium. Let us illustrate this point.

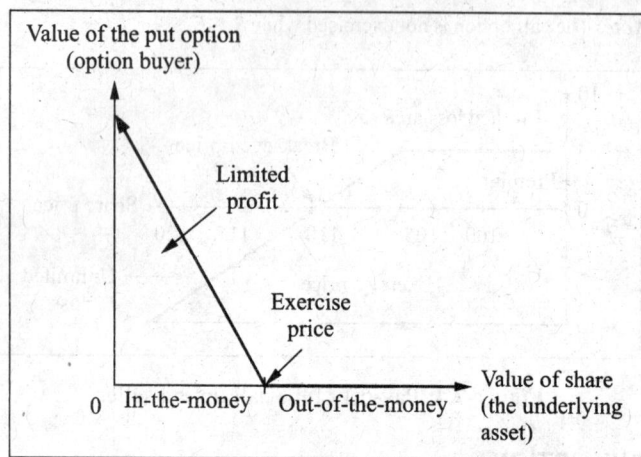

Figure 7.5: Pay-off for a put option buyer

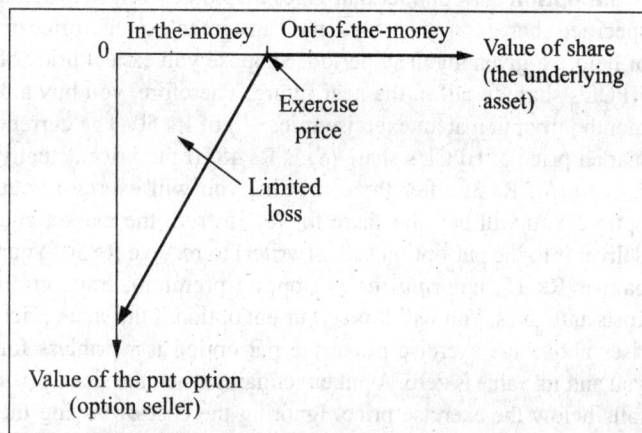

Figure 7.6: Pay-off for a put option seller

Illustration 7.2: Put Option Pay-off

An investor hopes that the price of BHEL's share will fall after three months. Therefore, he purchases a put option on BHEL's share with a maturity of three months at a premium of Rs 5. The exercise price is Rs 30. The current market price of BHEL's share is Rs 28. How much is profit or loss of the put buyer and the put seller if the price of the share at the time of the maturity of the option turns out to be Rs 18, or Rs 25, or Rs 28, or Rs 30, or Rs 40?

The put buyer's net pay-off is shown in Table 7.3 and Figure 7.7. It can be noticed from Figure 7.7 that the buyer's maximum loss is confined to Rs 5; that is, the put premium. His profit is equal to exercise price less the sum of share price and premium. Since the share price cannot fall

below zero, he has a limited profit potential. The put buyer will always exercise his option if the exercise is more than the share price. His break-even share price is Rs 25, that is, the exercise price less premium.

For the seller of a put option, the profit will be limited to Rs 5 – the amount of premium. His loss potential depends on the price of the share (the underlying asset). But it cannot exceed Rs 25, that is, the difference between the exercise price, Rs 30 and the premium, Rs 5. The pay-off for the put seller is shown in Table 7.4 and Figure 7.8.

Table 7.3: The Put Option Holder's Pay-off at Expiration

	Rs	Rs	Rs	Rs	Rs
Share price (S_t)	18	25	28	30	40
Buyer's benefit:					
Exercise option	30	30	30	—	—
Buyer's cost:					
Put premium	5	5	5	5	5
Buy share	18	25	28	—	—
Net pay-off (profit)	7	0	– 3	– 5	– 5

Note: The call option is not exercised when $S_t \leq E$.

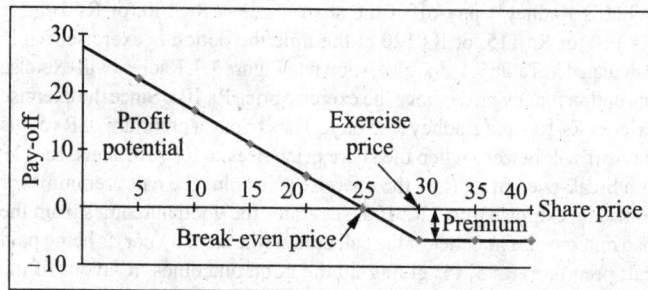

Figure 7.7: Pay-off for a put option buyer

Table 7.4: The Put Option Seller's Pay-off at Expiration

	Rs	Rs	Rs	Rs	Rs
Share price (S_t)	18	25	28	30	40
Seller's benefit:					
Put premium	5	5	5	5	5
Sale share	18	25	28	—	—
Seller's cost:					
Exercise option	30	30	30	—	—
Net pay-off	– 7	0	3	5	5

Note: The call option is not exercised when $S_t \leq E$.

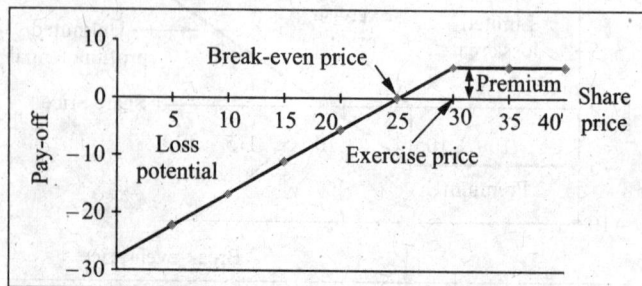

Figure 7.8: Pay-off for the put option seller

OPTIONS TRADING IN INDIA

In the USA, the trading in options was introduced in 1973. The

Table 7.5: Quotations of Listed CALL Options

Underlying Stock	Expiry Date	Strike Price (Rs)	No. of Contracts Traded	Contract Value (Rs lakh)	Last Traded Price (Rs)	Open Interest	Value of Underlying (Rs)
Satyam	28 Nov 02	230.00	295	870.84	16.30	8,11,200	243.90
Satyam	28 Nov 02	240.00	1,093	3,274.54	9.70	10,06,800	243.90
Satyam	28 Nov 02	250.00	1,043	3,197.09	5.35	9,24,000	243.90
Satyam	28 Nov 02	260.00	424	1,337.08	2.65	9,58,800	243.90
Infosys	28 Nov 02	4,000.00	345	1,412.96	99.00	49,000	4,004.90
Infosys	28 Nov 02	4,100.00	216	897.61	57.85	29,500	4,004.90
L&T	28 Nov 02	190.00	471	928.81	7.40	5,65,000	196.00
L&T	28 Nov 02	200.00	435	885.40	3.40	4,65,000	196.00
Reliance	28 Nov 02	260.00	697	1,121.11	7.25	6,82,800	257.80
Nifty	28 Nov 02	960.00	468	907.52	9.95	2,54,200	958.25
Nifty	26 Dec 02	970.00	1		14.00	2,600	
Nifty	30 Jan 03	970.00	2		25.00	200	

Source : The National Stock Exchange of India.

Chicago Board of Trade created the Chicago Board Options Exchange (CBOE) as a centralised market for trading standardised options contracts. The exchange-traded options are a recent phenomenon in India. The Security Exchange Board of India (SEBI) has announced a list of 31 shares for the stock-based option trading from July 2002. SEBI selected these shares for option trading on the basis of the following criteria:

1. Shares must be among the top 200 in terms of market capitalisation and trading volume.
2. Shares must be traded in at least 90 per cent of the trading days.
3. The non-promoter holding should be at least 30 per cent and the market capitalisation of free-float shares should be Rs 750 crore.
4. The six-month average trading volume in the share in the underlying cash market should be a minimum of Rs 5 crore.
5. The ratio of daily volatility of the share vis-à-vis the daily volatility of the index should not be more than four times at any time during the previous six months.

The minimum size of the contract is Rs 2 lakh. For the first six months, there would be cash settlement in options contracts and afterwards, there would be physical settlement. The option sellers will have to pay the margin, but the buyers will have to only pay the premium in advance. The stock exchanges can set limits on exercise price.

Index Options

Index options are call or put options on the stock market indices. In India, there are options on the Bombay Stock Exchange (BSE) Sensex and the National Stock Exchange (NSE) Nifty. The Sensex options are European-type options and expire on last Thursday of the contract month. The put and call index option contracts with 1-month, 2-month and 3-month maturity are available. The settlement is done in cash on a $T + 1$ basis and the prices are based on expiration price as may be decided by the Exchange. Option contracts will have a multiplier of 100. For example, you are

Table 7.6: Detailed Information on Option on Satyam

Contract Specifications

Underlying	Expiry Date	Option Type	Strike Price	Market Lot
Satyam	28 Nov 2002	Call	240.00	1200

Price Information

Prev. Close	Open Price	High Price	Low Price	Avg. Price
11.45	10.00	11.20	8.40	9.66

Last Price	Chg. from Prev. Close	% Change	Underlying Value
9.70	– 1.75	—	243.90

Turnover and Open Interest Information

Number of Contracts Traded	Turnover (Rs lakh)	Open Interest	Change in Open interest	% Change
1,093	3,274.54	10,06,800	94,800	10.39

Order Book

Buy Qty.	Buy Price	Sell Price	Sell Qty.
1200	10.20	10.50	1200
1200	10.15	10.60	1200
1200	10.10	10.70	1200
1200	10.00	10.75	1200
1200	9.20	10.80	1200

Total Buy Qty.		Total Sell Qty.	
2,23,200		88,800	

Source: The National Stock Exchange of India.

bullish on the Sensex and buy one December call option at 3000 for Rs 10 premium. In value terms, it is Rs 300,000 (Rs 3,000 × 100). On expiration, suppose the Sensex closes at 3150, you gain Rs 11,150 [(3150 – 3000) × 100] on an investment of Rs 1,000 (10 × 100). The multiplier for the NSE Nifty Options is 200 with a minimum price change of Rs 10 (200 × 0.05).

Table 7.5 provides quotations of a few listed stock (call) options from the National Stock Exchange (NSE). For example, the third column shows that options on Satyam are traded at strike prices of Rs 230 to Rs 260, in Rs 10 increments. The next three columns indicate, respectively, the number and value of contracts traded and the last traded price for the call. The last column indicates the price of the Satyam share on the stock exchange. The 'open interest' column specifies the number of outstanding contracts.

The stock exchanges provide detailed information about individual stock options. For example, in Table 7.6 we show detailed information on call option on Satyam. As you may notice, there is information on contract specifications, price, turnover and open interest and order book. For example, the price information includes the previous day's closing price and the opening and closing price as well as the high, low and average price for the day.

COMBINATIONS OF PUT, CALL AND SHARE

Theoretically, an investor can form portfolios of options with any assets. In practice, stock options are most popular. A share, a put and a call can be combined together to create several pay-off opportunities. Some of these combinations have significant implications. They are discussed in this section.

Protective Put: Combination of a Share and a Put

A **long position** involves buying and holding shares (or any other assets) to benefit from capital gains and dividend. An investor may create a long position in the shares of a firm. A long position investment strategy is risky. The investor will incur loss if the share price declines. Figure 7.9 shows the investor's long position in the share. He will gain if the share price rises in the future. However, he will incur loss if the price in future turns out to be lower than the current price. An investor can, however, guard himself against the risk of loss in the share value by purchasing a put option that has the exercise price equal to the current market price of the share. Put option *at-the-money* is called a **protective put** (Figure 7.10). The combination of a long position in the share and a protective put helps to avoid the investor's risk when the share price falls. Let consider an example.

Suppose the current share price and the exercise price to be Rs 100, and possible share prices at expiration Rs 90 or Rs 110. The pay-off (value) of a portfolio of a share (long) and a put (long) at expiration is shown in Table 7.7.

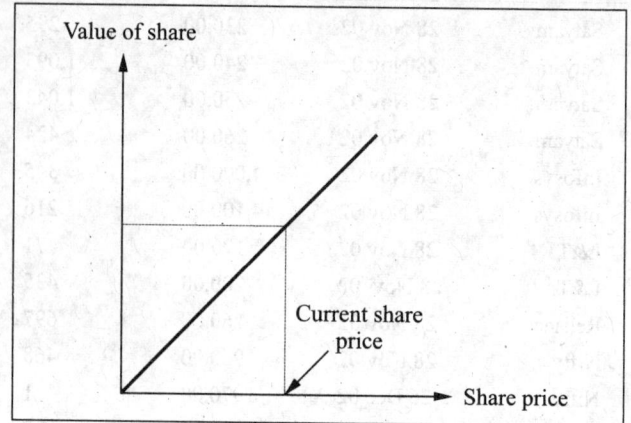

Figure 7.9: Long position in a share

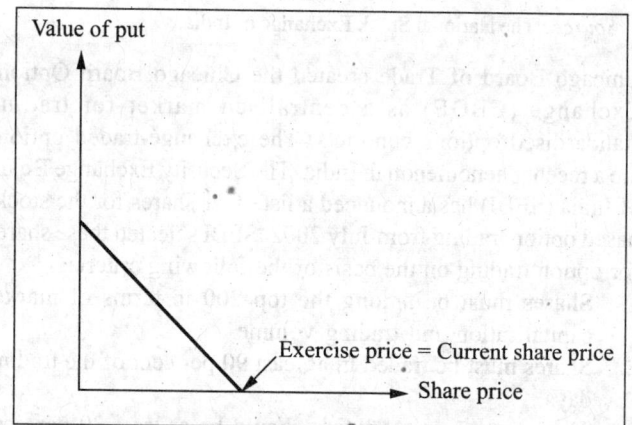

Figure 7.10: Protective put option

If the price of the share increases, the investor gains and the value of his portfolio at expiration will be equal to the share price. The value of put to him will be zero since he will not exercise his option [since $E < S_t$]. On the other hand, if the share price falls, the value of the investor's portfolio will be equal to the share price plus the value of the put option [$E > S_t$]. Since the put was at-the-money when the investor sold it, the value of his portfolio will be at least equal to the share price at that time. In our example, the share price and exercise price were Rs 100 when the investor bought a share and a put. The value of his portfolio will not be less than Rs 100 at expiration whatever happens to the share price. Figure 7.11 shows the value of the combination of the investor's long position in a share and a protective put.

Table 7.7: Pay-off of a Portfolio of a Share and a Put Option

	Situation I: Share price (S_t) Rs 110, Exercise Price (E) Rs 100		Situation II: Share price (S_t) Rs 90, Exercise Price (E) Rs 100	
	$S_t > E$	*Pay-off*	$S_t < E$	*Pay-off*
Value of share at expiration	S_t	110	S_t	90
Plus: Value of put at expiration [Max ($E - S_t$, 0)]	+ 0	+ 0	+ ($E - S_t$)	+ (100 – 90) = 10
Total value (pay-off)	S_t	110 + 0 = 110	$S_t + (E - S_t) = E$	90 + 10 = 100

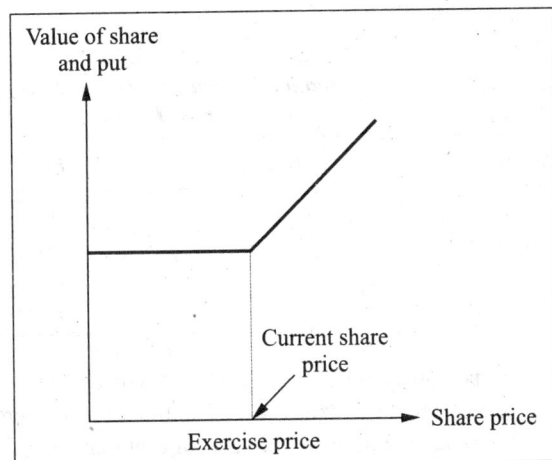

Figure 7.11: Value of portfolio of share and put option

Protective Put vs. Call

Alternatively, suppose you buy a call option on the share with the same exercise price of Rs 100 as in the case of the put option. How would your portfolio of a share and a put (both long) compare with your call option (long) on the share? If the share price moves up to Rs 110, you will exercise the call option and the value of call option at expiration will be: $S_t - E = $ Rs $110 -$ Rs $100 = $ Rs 10. On the other hand, if the price falls to Rs 90, you will not exercise your call option and your call option at expiration will have a zero value. Thus the value of your portfolio of a share and a put at expiration will always be greater than the value of a call at expiration by the exercise price. You can notice this when you compare Figure 7.11 with Figure 7.10. Thus, at expiration, the position will be as follows:

$$\text{Share price at expiration} + \text{Value of put at expiration}$$
$$= \text{Value of call at expiration} + \text{Exercise price}$$
$$S_t + P_t = C_t + E$$

The present value of the portfolio of a share and a put option is equal to the value of a call plus the present value of exercise price:

$$S_0 + P_0 = C_0 + PV(E) \qquad (3)$$

where S_0 is the present value of share, P_0 is the present value of put option, C_0 is the present value of call option and PV (E) is the present value of exercise price. Risk-free rate may be used to

calculate the present value of the exercise price. Thus,

$$S_0 + P_0 = C_0 + \frac{E}{(1 + r_f)^t}$$

and assuming continuous compounding,

$$S_0 + P_0 = C_0 + E\,e^{-r_f t} \qquad (4)$$

Put-call Parity

Suppose you buy a share (long position), buy a put (long position) and sell a call (short). The current share price is Rs 100 and the exercise price of put and call options is the same, that is, Rs 100. Both put and call options are European type options and they will expire after three months. Let us further assume that there are two possible share prices after three months: Rs 110 or Rs 90. What is the value of your portfolio? The value of portfolio at expiration is given in Table 7.8.

You may notice that whether share price rises or falls, the value of the portfolio at expiration is equal to the exercise price (E). It is a **risk-free portfolio** since the outcome will be the same whatever happens to the share price. The present value of the portfolio can be calculated using a risk-free rate of return (r_f). Let us assume that the risk-free rate is 10 per cent. Thus the present value of portfolio is

$$\text{PV of portfolio} = S_0 + P_0 - C_0 = E\,e^{-r_f t} \qquad (5)$$
$$= 100\,e^{-0.1 \times 0.25} = 100 \times 0.9573 = \text{Rs } 97.53$$

We can rewrite Equation (5) as follows :

$$S_0 + P_0 = C_0 + E\,e^{-r_f t} \qquad (6)$$

Equation (6) is the same as Equation (4). This relationship is called **put-call parity**. We can also obtain the following expressions from Equation (6) :

$$C_0 = P_0 + S_0 - E\,e^{-r_f t} \qquad (7)$$
$$P_0 = C_0 - S_0 + E\,e^{-r_f t} \qquad (8)$$

Equations (7) and (8), respectively, give the value of call and put options.

Covered Calls: Buying a Share and Selling a Call

A **naked option** is a position where the option writer does not hold a share in her portfolio that has a counterbalancing effect.

Table 7.8: Value of a Portfolio of a Share and a Put Option

	Situation I: Share price (S_t) Rs 110, Exercise Price (E) Rs 100		Situation II: Share price (S_t) Rs 90, Exercise Price (E) Rs 100	
	$S_t > E$	*Pay-off*	$S_t < E$	*Pay-off*
Value of share (long) at expiration	S_t	110	S_t	90
Plus: Value of put (long) at expiration [*Max.* $(E - S_t, 0)$]	$+ 0$	$+ 0$	$+ (E - S_t)$	$+ (100 - 90) = +10$
Less: Value of Call (short) at expiration [Max $(S_t - E), 0$]	$-(S_t - E)$	$-(110 - 100) = -10$	0	0
Total value (Pay-off)	$S_t - (S_t - E) = E$	100	$S_t + (E - S_t) = E$	$90 + 10 = 100$

Table 7. 9: Pay-off to a Covered Call

	Situation I: Share price (S_t) Rs 110, Exercise Price (E) Rs 100		Situation II: Share price (S_t) Rs 90, Exercise Price (E) Rs 100	
	$S_t > E$	Pay-off	$S_t < E$	Pay-off
Value of share at expiration	S_t	110	S_t	90
Less: Value of call at expiration [Max ($S_t - E$, 0)]	$-(S_t - E)$	$-(110 - 100)$	-0	-0
Total value (pay-off)	$S_t - (S_t - E) = E$ $110 - (110 - 100) = 100$		S_t $90 - 0 = 90$	

The investor can protect herself by taking a covered position. A **covered call** position is an investment in a share plus the sale of a call on that share. The position is covered because the investor holds a share against a possible obligation to deliver the share. The total value or pay-off of a covered call at expiration is the share price minus the value (pay-off) of the call. The value of call is deducted because the investor has taken a short position; that is, he is under an obligation to deliver the share to the buyer of the call option if he chooses to exercise his option. The buyer of the call will do so when the exercise price is lower than the share price. Let us consider an example.

Assume that a call option is at-the-money; that is both the current price of the share and the exercise price is Rs 100. Further, suppose the possible share price at expiration is either Rs 110 or Rs 90. The value of a covered call at expiration is shown in Table 7.9. You may notice from Table 7.9 and Figure 7.12 that in the falling market, when the share price is equal to or less than the exercise price, the investor's pay-off will equal to the share price. The investor's maximum Pay-off to a covered call cannot exceed the exercise price in the rising market. He sacrifices the opportunity of earning capital gains in favour of enhancing the current income by premium. Investors who are in any case planning to sell shares at a price equal to the exercising price will follow this strategy.

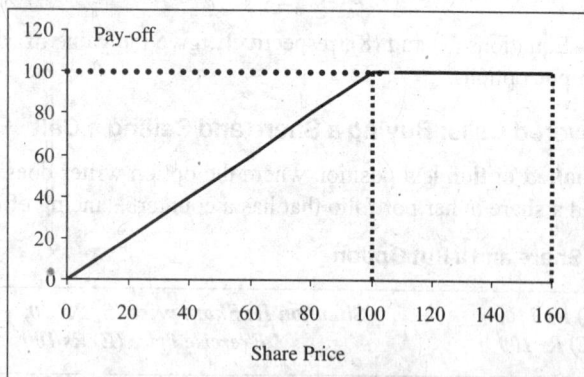

Figure 7.12: Pay-off of a covered call.

Straddle: Combining Call and Put at Same Exercise Price

Suppose Stride Aluminium Company is considering the acquisition of Hind Aluminium Company. It has offered to buy 20 per cent of Hind's shares. The price of Hind's share has started increasing. The price could decline substantially if Stride's attempt fails. How could you take advantage of rising prices and at the same time avoid the risk if the price falls? You can do

so by simultaneously purchasing both put and call options at the same exercise price. A **straddle** is a combined position created by the simultaneous purchase (or sale) of a put and a call with the same expiration date and the same exercise price.

Suppose the exercise price is Rs 105 for both put and call options. What will be your pay-off if the price of Hind's share increases to Rs 120 in three months? You will forgo put option, but you will exercise call option. So your pay-off will be the excess of the share price over the call exercise price: Rs 120 – Rs 105 = Rs 15. On the contrary, suppose that the acquisition attempt fails and Hind's share price falls to Rs 95 in three months. In this situation, you will exercise put option and let the call option lapse. Your pay-off will be the excess of exercise price over the share price: Rs 105 – Rs 95 = Rs 10. Thus, when you invest in a straddle, you will benefit whether the price of the share falls or rises. Figure 7.13 shows the pay-off of the buyer of a straddle.

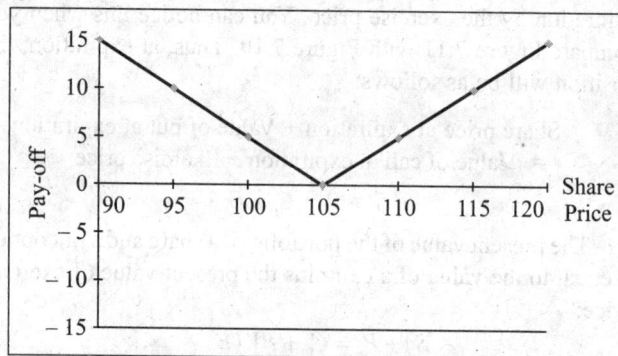

Figure 7.13: Pay-off to a straddle buyer

What will be the position of the seller of a straddle? He will lose whether the price of the share increases or decreases. This is shown in Figure 7.13. But the seller of a straddle will collect put and call premium. Thus, his loss will be reduced or his net pay-off may be even positive.

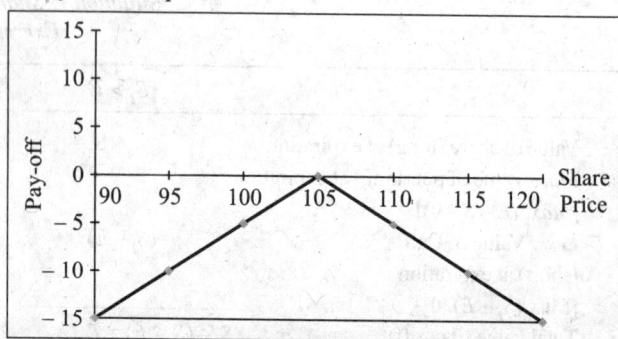

Figure 7.14: Pay-off to a straddle seller

Illustration 7.3: Pay-off of a Straddle

You have set up a straddle position on a M&M's share. You have bought one 3-month call with an exercise price of Rs 75 for a premium of Rs 3 and a 3-month put with same exercise price for a premium of Rs 2. Assume that after three months price goes up to Rs 78 or it comes down to Rs 70. What is your pay-off at expiration of the options?

$$\text{Premium paid} = \text{Rs } 3 + \text{Rs } 2 = \text{Rs } 5$$

Profit or loss at expiration:

Share price Rs 78 : Call : (Rs 78 – Rs 75) +
Put : (0) – Premium : Rs 5 = – Rs 2
Share price Rs 70 : Call : (0) + Put :
(Rs 75 – Rs 70) – Premium : Rs 5 = Rs 0

Strips and Straps

You can design strategies that are variations of a straddle. Strips and straps are two such variations. A **strip** is a combination of two puts and one call with the same exercise price and the expiration date. A **strap**, on the other hand, entails combining two calls and one put. In Figure 7.15 we show the pay-offs to a strip and a strap. We assume that the exercise price for puts and calls is Rs 100 and that share price at expiration is Rs 90, Rs 100 or Rs 110. The investor would have positive pay-off irrespective of the price movement, except when the price equals the exercise price. The potential pay-off would be higher under a strap strategy for share price above the exercise price.

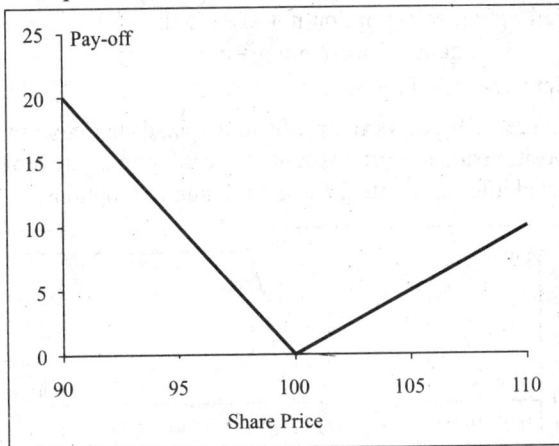

Figure 7.15: (a) Pay-off to a strip

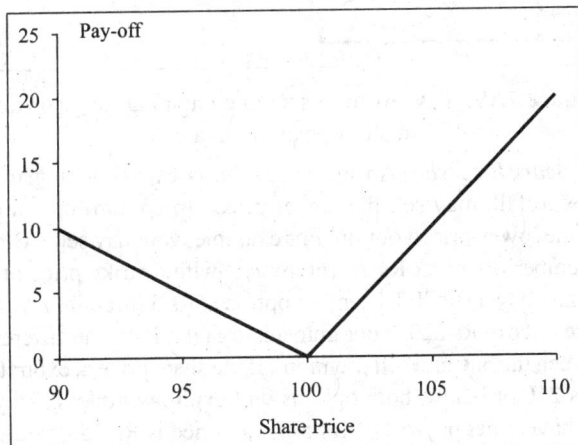

Figure 7.15: (b) Pay-off to a strap

Strangle: Combining Call and Put at Different Exercise Prices

A **strangle** is a portfolio of a put and a call with the same expiration date but with different exercise prices. The investor will combine an out-of-the-money call with an out-of-the-money put. That is, he will buy a call with an exercise price higher than the underlying share's current price and a put with an exercise price lower than the underlying share's current price. The effect of this strategy is similar to the effect of a straddle except that the pay-off range will be larger.

Suppose the Telco share is currently selling for Rs 110. The exercise prices for the Telco put and call are, respectively, Rs 100 and Rs 105. What will be your pay-off if the price of Telco's share increases to Rs 120 in three months? You will forgo put option, but you will exercise call option. So your pay-off will be the excess of the share price over the call exercise price: Rs 120 – Rs 105 = Rs 15. On the contrary, suppose the Telco's share price falls to Rs 95 in three months. In this situation, you will exercise put option and let the call option lapse. Your pay-off will be the excess of exercise price over the share price: Rs 100 – Rs 95 = Rs 5. Your pay-off will be zero when the share price ranges between the two exercise prices – Rs 100 and Rs 105. The pay-off will be outside this range. Figure 7.16 shows the pay-off of the buyer of a strangle. The profit of the strangle strategy is the pay-off adjusted for the premium of options.

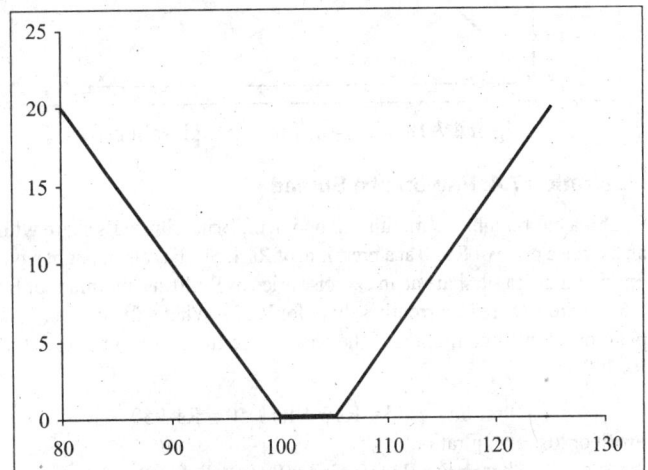

Figure 7.16: Pay-off to a strangle buyer

Spread: Combining Put and Call at Different Exercise Prices

The put and call options on the same share may have different exercise price, and an investor may combine them. A **spread** is a combination of a put and a call with different exercise prices. Suppose that an investor buys simultaneously a 3-month put option at an exercise price of Rs 95 and a call option at an exercise price of Rs 105 on a company's share. What shall be the value (pay-off) of his portfolio at expiration if the share price after three months is Rs 100?

The investor will not exercise call option since the price of the share is less than the exercise price. Put option is also worthless for him because the exercise price is less than the share price. What will be the investor's positions if the share price is Rs 120? He will exercise call option and gain Rs 20. However, he will let put option lapse. How much will be the investor's pay-off if the share price is Rs 90? He will exercise put option and benefit Rs 5, but will not exercise call option. The buyer's gain is the seller's loss. The pay-off for the buyer and the seller of a spread is shown in Figures 7.17 and 7.18.

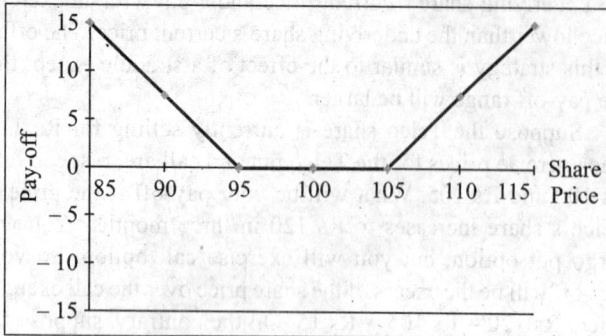

Figure 7.17: Pay-off for a spread buyer

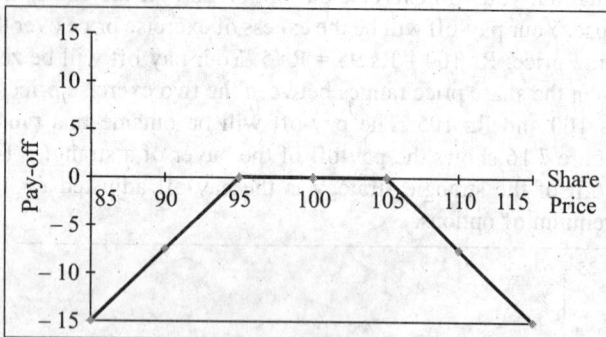

Figure 7.18: Pay-off for a spread seller

Illustration 7.4: Pay-off of a Spread

Radhika has bought a 3-month call option on Brite Limited's share with an exercise price of Rs 50 at a premium of Rs 4. She has also bought a put option on the same share at an exercise price of Rs 40 at a premium of Rs 1.50. Brite's share is currently selling for Rs 45. What will be Radhika's position after three months if the share price turns out to be Rs 50 or Rs 30?

$$\text{Premium paid} = \text{Rs } 3 + \text{Rs } 1.50 = \text{Rs } 4.50$$

Profit or loss at expiration:

Share price Rs 50 : Call : (Rs 0) + Put : (0) – Premium : (Rs 4.50) = – Rs 4.50

Share price Rs 30 : Call : (Rs 0) + Put : (Rs 40 – Rs 30) – Premium : (Rs 4.50) = + Rs 5.50

Spread: Combining the Long and Short Options

A *spread* also involves simultaneously buying and selling call or put options. There are two types of spreads:

1. The **price spread** or the **vertical spread** involves buying and selling options for the same share and expiration date but different strike (exercise) prices. For example, you may buy a BPCL December option at a strike price of Rs 215 and sell a BPCL December option at a strike price of Rs 210.

2. The **calendar spread** or the **horizontal spread** involves buying and selling options for the same share and strike

price but different expiration dates. For example, you may buy a Tata Power December 2002 option at a strike price of Rs 95 and sell a Tata Power January option at a strike price of Rs 90.

Bullish spread An investor maybe expecting the price of an underlying share to rise. But she may not like to take higher risk. Therefore, she would buy the higher-priced (premium) option on the share and sell the lower-priced option on the share. Suppose, you buy a BPCL December option at Rs 10 (premium) with a strike price of Rs 210 and sell a BPCL December option at Rs 5 (premium) with a strike price of Rs 220. You have paid premium of Rs 10 and collected the premium of Rs 5. Hence, your immediate loss is Rs 5. What is your pay-off if the BPCL share price turns out to be Rs 250 at the expiration date?

Your pay-off will be as follows:

Call option bought : gain : share price – exercise price – premium = 250 – 210 –10 = 30

Call option sold : loss : share price – exercise price + premium = 250 – 220 + 5 = 25

Net pay-off: gain – loss = 30 – 25 = + 5

What would the pay-off if the share price were Rs 180 at the expiry date? The pay-off will be :

Call option bought : option not exercised:

loss = 0 – premium = 0 –10 = – 10

Call option sold : option not exercised:

gain = 0 + premium = 0 + 5 = + 5

Net pay-off: – 10 + 5 = – 5

Figure 7.19 shows the profit to a spread that combines a long position and a short position on a call option. The profit is calculated after accounting for the premium on options.

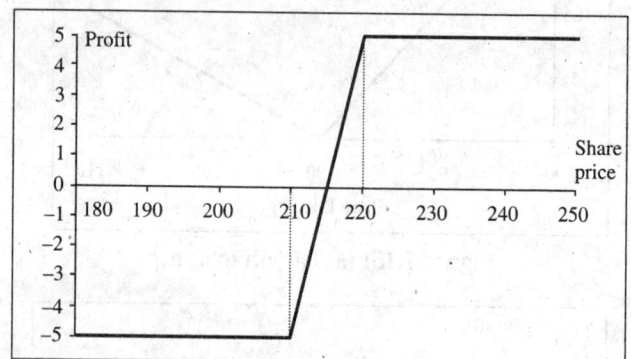

Figure 7.19: Pay-off for a spread combining long position and short position on a call

Bearish spread An investor, who is expecting a share or index to fall, may sell the higher-priced (premium) option and buy the lower-priced option. For example, you may sell a BPCL December option at Rs 10 (premium) with a strike price of Rs 210 and buy a BPCL December option at Rs 5 (premium) with a strike price of Rs 220. Your immediate gain is Rs 5–the difference between the buy and sell premium. If the share price at expiration is Rs 210 or below, both options will expire worthless and you will have a net pay-off of Rs 5. If the price is Rs 250, you will gain : 250 – 220 –5 = Rs 25 and lose : 250 – 210 – 10 = Rs 30; thus, your net loss will be 25 – 30 = – Rs 5.

Butterfly Spread: Buying and Selling Calls

A **long butterfly spread** involves buying a call with a low exercise price, buying a call with a high exercise price and selling two calls with an exercise price in between the two. Thus, there are three call contracts with different strike prices. A **short butterfly spread** involves the opposite position; that is, selling a call with a low exercise price, selling a call with a high exercise price and buying two calls with an exercise price in between the two.

Suppose a share is currently selling at Rs 102 per share. Further, assume that 3-month calls are selling as follows: exercise price Rs 100, premium Rs 12; exercise Rs 105, premium Rs 8 and exercise price Rs 110, premium Rs 6. An investor buys one call with Rs 100 exercise price, one call with Rs 110 exercise price and sells two calls with Rs 105 exercise price. The investor will pay call premium of Rs 12 + Rs 6 = Rs 18 for buying two calls and receive call premium of 2 × Rs 8 = Rs 16. Thus his cost is Rs 2. His net loss will be Rs 2 when the share price stays at Rs 95 or below above Rs 110. Table 7.10 shows calculations. You can make similar calculations for a short butterfly spread.

Table 7.10: Profit to a Butterfly Spread

| Share Price | Pay-off | | | |
	Cost	Long Calls	Short Calls	Profit
95	−2	0	0	−2
100	−2	0	0	−2
105	−2	5	0	3
110	−2	10	−10	−2
115	−2	20	−20	−2

Figure 7.20 shows the pay-off under long and short butterfly spreads. The butterfly spread strategy is appropriate when the share price is unlikely to show high fluctuations. The investor will make profit if the share price is closer to the middle exercise price, but he will incur small losses if price fluctuates up and down.

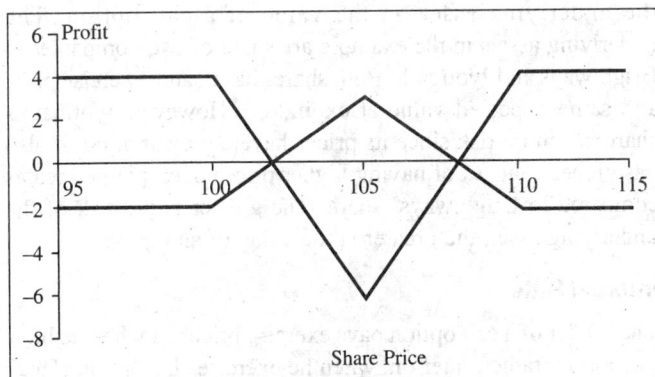

Figure 7.20: Pay-off to a butterfly spread

Collars

A **collar** involves a strategy of limiting a portfolio's value between two bounds. Suppose you are holding a large number

of Infosys shares currently selling at Rs 4,000 per share. You can design a strategy that would let your pay-off to range within a band, irrespective of the price fluctuations in Infosys share. If you do not want your pay-off to go below Rs 3,900, you can buy a protective put with an exercise price of Rs 3,900. Your outlay will be the premium that will be required to pay for buying the put. You can sell a call option with an exercise price of, say, Rs 4,100 at a premium equal to the put premium. Thus, your net outlay would be zero. The short call limits your portfolio's upside potential. Even if the price of Infosys share increases beyond Rs 4,100, your pay-off would not exceed Rs 4,100 because the buyer of the call will exercise his option at the share price higher than the exercise price.

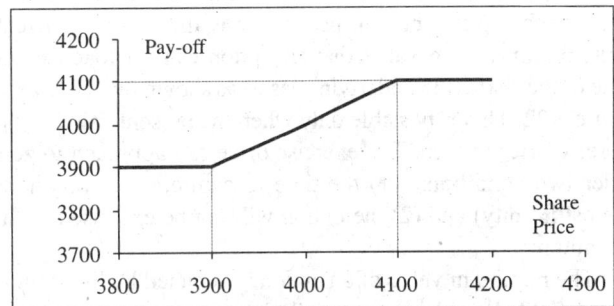

Figure 7.21: Pay-off to a collar

FACTORS DETERMINING OPTION VALUE

The seller of an option gives away the good outcomes of the asset held by him to the option buyer for a price or premium. How is this price or premium determined? As we have discussed earlier, the value of a call option at maturity is either zero or the difference between the price of the share (that is, the underlying asset) and the exercise price. Thus:

$$\text{Value of call option} = \text{Maximum [Share price, } S_t \\ - \text{Exercise price, } E, 0]$$

The option holder will exercise his option only when it is beneficial to do so. The call option will be beneficial to its buyer when the exercise price is less than the price of the share (the underlying asset). When the call option is out-of-the-money (i.e., the exercise price is more than the price of the underlying asset), the minimum value of the call option at expiration will be zero.

How is the value of an option with time to expiration determined? The value of an option depends on the following factors:[1]

1. Exercise price and the share (underlying asset) price
2. Volatility of returns on share
3. Time to expiration
4. Interest rates

Exercise Price and Value of Underlying Asset

Two important determinants of options are the value of the underlying asset and the exercise price. If the underlying asset were a share, the value of a call option would increase as the

1. Hull, *op. cit.*

share price increases. At the expiration date, the holder will know the share price, and he will exercise his option if the exercise price is lower than the share price. The excess of the share price over the exercise price is the value of the option at the expiration of the option. If the share price is more than the exercise price, a call option is said to be in-the-money. The deeper in-the-money is an option, the more is its value.

It is difficult to say what the price of a share at expiration will be. However, we can draw up a probabilistic distribution of the future share prices. What is the maximum value that the buyer of an option on share will pay to the option writer? The call option buyer will be utmost prepared to pay for holding the option a price equal to the value of the share. Instead of paying more for the option, he will prefer to buy the share at present. Thus, the maximum value that an option can approach is the price of the share (the underlying asset) as shown by line Max in Figure 7.22. This is possible only when the present value of the exercise price is zero. The exercise price can approach to zero under two conditions: (1) the time to expiration is very long (almost infinity) and (2) the option will not be exercised in the near future.

The minimum value of an option is depicted by line Min in Figure 7.22. It will be zero until share price rises above the exercise price. At maturity, the value of the option either will be zero or the excess of the share price over the exercise price. Most often, the value of the options will lie between Max and Min lines as portrayed by the convex line in Figure 7.22.

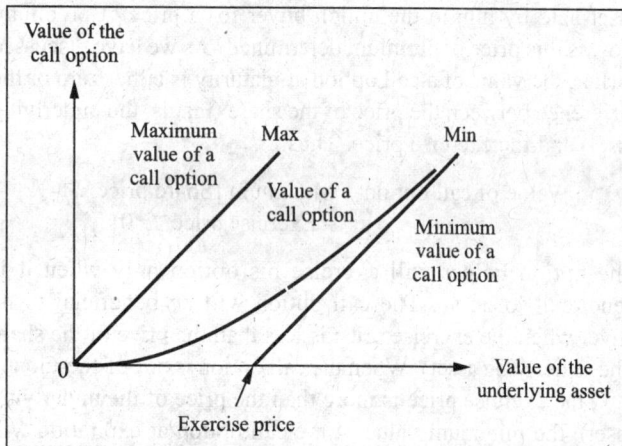

Figure 7.22: Value of a call option

Volatility of Underlying Asset

How is the value of a call option affected by the volatility of the underlying asset (say, a share)? Let us consider an example. Suppose you hold a 2-month option on the share of Brightways Company. The exercise price is Rs 100 and the current market price is Rs 100. The option will be worthless if the share price remains Rs 100 at maturity. But prior to expiration, the option will be valuable if there are chances that the share price may rise above Rs 100. Assume that the probable price of Brightways' share at expiration is as shown in Table 7.11.

You may notice from Table 7.11 that at expiration, the expected value of Brightways' share price is Rs 100, and the expected value of the option is Rs 15.

Table 7.11: Probability Distribution of Brightway's Share Price at Expiration

Share Price (Rs)	Probability	Expected Value of Share at Expiration (Rs)	Value of Call Option at Expiration (Rs)	Expected Value of Call Option at Expiration (Rs)
40	0.25	10	0	0
100	0.50	50	0	0
160	0.25	40	60	15
Expected value		100		15

Let us suppose that you also hold another option on the share of Jyotipath Company Limited with an exercise price of Rs 100 with the distribution as given in Table 7.12. You may notice that the expected price of share of Jyotipath at expiration is the same as that of Brightways' share. However, the expected value of the option on Jyotipath's share is much higher (Rs 25) than on Brightways' share (Rs 15). The reason for this is that Jyotipath's share price has a higher variability; it has a standard deviation of 70.7 as compared to 42.4 of Brightways' share price. As the option value cannot be less than zero, the probability of a higher price of the share causes the option to be worth more.

Table 7.12 : Probability Distribution of Jyotipath's Share Price at Expiration

Share Price (Rs)	Probability	Expected Value of Share Expiration (Rs)	Value of Call Option at Expiration (Rs)	Expected Value of Call Option at Expiration (Rs)
0	0.25	0	0	0
100	0.50	50	0	0
200	0.25	50	100	25
Expected value		100		25

Figure 7.23 shows graphically the effect of the volatility of the underlying asset on the value of a call option. The underlying assets in the example are share of two companies—Brightways and Jyotipath. Both shares have same exercise price and same expected value at expiration. However, Jyotipath's share has more risk since its prices have large variation. It also has higher chances of having higher prices over a large area as compared to Brightways' share. The greater is the risk of the underlying asset, the greater is the value of an option.

Interest Rate

The holder of a call option pays exercise price not when he buys the option, rather, later on, when he exercises his option. Thus, the present value of the exercise price will depend on the interest rate (and the time until the expiration of the option). The value of a call option will increase with the rising interest rate since the present value of the exercise price will fall. The effect is reversed in the case of a put option. The buyer of a put option receives the exercise price and therefore, as the interest rate increases, the value of the put option will decline.

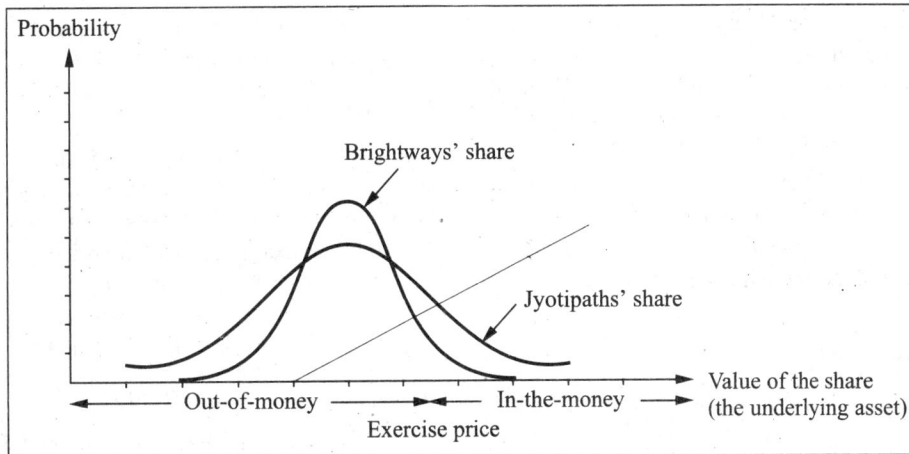

Figure 7.23: Volatility of the share and the value of a call option

Time to Option Expiration

The present value of the exercise price also depends on the time to expiration of the option. The present value of the exercise price will be less if time to expiration is longer and consequently, the value of the option will be higher. Further, the possibility of share price increasing with volatility increases if the time to expiration is longer. Longer is the time to expiration, higher is the possibility of the option to be more in-the-money.

BINOMIAL MODEL FOR OPTION VALUATION

In the previous section, we have enumerated factors that influence the value of an option. Let us now examine the methods of valuing options. We shall illustrate only the valuation of stock (share) options. We shall first discuss simple binomial tree approach to option valuation[1] and later the Black-Scholes option valuation model.

Inadequacy of DCF Analysis

We know that assets are valued using the DCF (discounted cash flow) approach. The value of an asset equals the discounted value of its cash flows. Isn't the value of an option its present value? The DCF approach does not work for options because of the difficulty in determining the required rate of return of an option. Options are **derivative securities.** Their risk is derived from the risk of the underlying security. The market value of a share continuously changes. Consequently, the required rate of return to a stock option is also continuously changing. Therefore, it is not feasible to value options using the DCF technique.

Option gives the holder a right over the favourable outcomes of an asset. These outcomes are, however, highly risky. But a buyer pays much less for an option than the price of the asset. The buyer makes a very small investment in high-risk-outcomes. Options are more risky than the underlying assets.

A Simple Binomial Approach to Option Valuation

Suppose you own a share that has a current price of Rs 150. Its price at the end of one year has two possibilities: either Rs 100 or Rs 300. Assume that you buy a call option on the share with

an exercise price of Rs 200. At the end of the year, you will exercise your option if the share price is Rs 300 and the value of the option will be: Rs 300 – Rs 200 = Rs 100. You will forgo your call option if the share price is Rs 100, and the value of option will be zero. Figure 7.24 shows these two situations.

Share price at the beginning of the year	Share price at the end of the year	Portfolio value of the end of the year
P = Rs 150	Rs 300	Max [Rs 300 – Rs 200, 0] = Rs 100
	Rs 100	Max [Rs 100 – Rs 200, 0] = Rs 0

Figure 7.24: Binomial-tree for option valuation

Share price at the beginning of the year	Value of long position in Δ shares at the end of the year	Value of short position in one call option at the end of the year	Portfolio value end of the year
P = Rs 150	Rs. 300 Δ	– Rs 100	Rs 300Δ – Rs100
	Rs. 100 Δ	Rs 0	Rs 100 Δ

Figure 7.25: Binomial-tree for option valuation

Let us slightly change the example. Instead of buying a call option, you sell a call option on the share. Can you create a portfolio of certain number of shares (let us call it delta, Δ) and one call option in such a way that there is no uncertainty of the value of portfolio at the end of one year? You can do so if you combine a long position (buying) in the share and a short position (selling) in the call option. Let us assume that you create a portfolio of shares and an option by buying Δ (delta)

---

1. Hull, *ibid.* Also see Jarrow, *op.cit.*, and Cox and Rubinstein, *op. cit.*

shares and selling a call option. What is the value of your portfolio if the share prices at expiration increases to Rs 300 or decreases to Rs 100 from its present level of Rs 150? When the price goes up to Rs 300, the buyer of the option will exercise his option and you will lose Rs 100. If the price turns out to be Rs 100 the option buyer will not exercise his option and you do not gain or lose. This situation is shown in Figure 7.24.

Your portfolio will be risk-less if the value of the portfolio is same whether the price of the share increases to Rs 300 or falls to Rs 100. That is

$$300\Delta - 100 = 100\Delta - 0$$

$$\Delta = \frac{100 - 0}{300 - 100} = \frac{100}{200} = 0.5$$

You may notice that the formula for determining the **option delta**, represented by symbol Δ, can be written as follows:

$$\text{Option delta}\,(\Delta) = \frac{\text{Difference in option values}}{\text{Difference in share prices}} \qquad (9)$$

$$= \frac{100 - 0}{300 - 100} = \frac{100}{200} = 0.5$$

The option delta is the measure of the sensitivity of the option value vis-à-vis the change in the share price.

You will have a risk-less portfolio if you combine a long position in 0.5 shares with a short position in one call option. If the price increases to Rs 300, the value of the portfolio is

$$0.5 \times \text{Rs } 300 - \text{Rs } 100 = \text{Rs } 50$$

And if the share price falls to Rs 50, then the value of portfolio is

$$0.5 \times \text{Rs } 100 = \text{Rs } 50$$

The value of portfolio at the end of one year remains Rs 50 irrespective of the increase or decrease in the share price. What is the present value of the portfolio? Since it is a risk-less portfolio, we can use the risk-free rate as the discount rate. Suppose the risk-free rate is 10 per cent, the present value of the portfolio is:

$$\text{PV of portfolio} = \frac{\text{Rs } 50}{(1.10)^1} = \text{Rs } 45.45$$

Since the current price of share is Rs 150, the value of the call option can be found out as follows:

$$\text{Rs } 150\Delta - \text{value of a call option} = \text{Rs } 45.45$$

$$\text{Rs } 150 \times 0.50 - \text{value of a call option} = \text{Rs } 45.45$$

$$\text{Value of a call option} = \text{Rs } 75 - \text{Rs } 45.45 = \text{Rs } 29.55$$

The value of the call option will remain the same irrespective of any probabilities of increase or decrease in the share price. This is so because the option is valued in terms of the price of the underlying share, and the share price already includes the probabilities of its rise or fall.

Risk Neutrality

There is an alternative way to looking at the option valuation. We can assume that investors are risk-neutral. Therefore, for their investment in share, they would simply expect a risk-free rate of return. In our example, the share price could rise by 100 per cent (from Rs 150 to Rs 300) or it could fall by 33.3 per cent (from Rs 150 to Rs 100). Under these situations, a risk-neutral investor's return from the investment in the share is given as follows:

$$\begin{aligned}
\text{Expected return} = &\ (\text{probability of price increase}) \times \\
&\ \text{percentage increase in price} + \\
&\ (1 - \text{probability of price increase}) \times \\
&\ \text{percentage decrease in price} = \text{risk-free rate} \\
= &\ p \times 100 + (1 - p) \times (-33.33) = 10 \\
p = &\ 0.325
\end{aligned}$$

We can utilise this information to determine the value of the call option at the end of the year. The call option is worth Rs 100 when the share price increases to Rs 300, and its worth is zero if the share price declines. We can thus calculate the value of the call option at the end of one year as given below:

Value of call option at the end of the period
$$= 0.325 \times 100 + (1 - 0.352) \times 0 = \text{Rs } 32.50$$

The current (present) value of the call option is:

Current value of the call option = 32.5/1.1 = Rs 29.55

BLACK AND SCHOLES MODEL FOR OPTION VALUATION

The logic of valuing a call option, as discussed in the previous section, is quite simple. The framework can, however, be extended beyond two periods. We can also make the time period and the movement in the share price very small. The computation would be quite complex. Fortunately, we can use the Black and Scholes (B–S) model,[1] which, under certain assumptions, can be used for valuing options as the time period becomes continuous.

Assumptions

The B–S model is based on the following assumptions:
1. The rates of return on a share are log normally distributed.
2. The value of the share (the underlying asset) and the risk-free rate are constant during the life of the option.
3. The market is efficient and there are no transaction costs and taxes.
4. There is no dividend to be paid on the share during the life of the option.

The B–S model is as follows:

$$C_0 = S_0\, N(d_1) - E\, e^{-r_f t}\, N(d_2) \qquad (10)$$

---

1. Black, F. and Scholes, M., The Pricing of Options and Corporate Liabilities, *Journal of Political Economy*, 81, May–June 1973, pp. 637–54.

where

C_0 = the current value of call option
S_0 = the current market value of the share
E = the exercise price
e = 2.7183, the exponential constant
r_f = the risk-free rate of interest
t = the time to expiration (in years)
$N(d1)$ = the cumulative normal probability density function

$$d_1 = \frac{\ln(S_0/E) + \left[r_f + \sigma^2/2\right]t}{\sigma\sqrt{t}} \quad (11)$$

$$d_2 = d_1 - \sigma\sqrt{t} \quad (12)$$

where ln = the natural logarithm; σ = the standard deviation and σ^2 = variance of the continuously compounded annual return on the share.

The Black–Scholes model has two features. First, the parameters of the model, except the share price volatility, are contained in the agreement between the option buyer and seller. Second, in spite of its unrealistic assumptions, the model is able to predict the true price of option reasonably well. The model is applicable to both European and American options with a few adjustments.

We know from put-call parity that the value of put is given by the following relationship:

$$\text{Value of put} = P_0 = C_0 - S_0 + E\,e^{-r_f t} \quad (7)$$

Once we know the value of call option, we can substitute this value in Equation (7) and determine the value of put option.

$$P_0 = S_0 N(d_1) - Ee^{-r_f t} N(d_2) - S_0 + Ee^{-r_f t}$$
$$= S_0\left[N(d_1) - 1\right] + Ee^{-r_f t}\left[1 - N(d_2)\right] \quad (13)$$

Option's Delta or Hedge Ratio

We have earlier explained the concept of the option's delta. The hedge ratio is commonly called the option's delta. The **hedge ratio** is a tool that enables us to summarise the overall exposure of portfolios of options with various exercise prices and maturity periods. An option's hedge ratio is the change in the option price for a rupee one increase in the share price. A call option has a positive hedge ratio and a put option has a negative hedge ratio.

Under the Black-Scholes option valuation formula, the hedge ratio of a call option is $N(d_1)$ and the hedge ratio for a put is $N(d_1) - 1$. Recall that $N(d)$ stands for the area under the standard normal curve up to d. Therefore, the call option hedge ratio must be positive and the put option hedge ratio is negative and of smaller absolute value than 1.0.

Illustration 7.5 : Black-Scholes Formula for Option Valuation

Rakesh Sharma is interested in writing a six-months call option on L&T's share. L&T's share is currently selling for Rs 120. The volatility (standard deviation) of the share returns is estimated as 67 per cent. Rakesh would like the exercise price to be Rs 120. The risk-free rate is assumed to be 10 per cent. How much premium should Rakesh charge for writing the call option?

We assume that the share is not a dividend-paying share. Let us first calculate d_1 and d_2 by Equations (12) and (13) as follows:

$$d_1 = \frac{\ln(120/120) + [0.10 + (0.67)^2/2]\,0.5}{0.67\sqrt{0.5}} = 0.34$$

$$d_2 = \frac{\ln(120/120) + [0.10 - (0.67)^2/2]\,0.5}{0.67\sqrt{0.5}} = -0.14$$

From Table G at the end of this book, we obtain the values of $N(d_1)$ and $N(d_2)$ as follows:

$$N(d_1) = N(0.34) = 0.6331$$
$$N(d_2) = N(-0.14) = 0.4443$$

Using Equation (10), we obtain the call value as given below:

$$C_0 = 120\,(0.6331) - 120\,(0.4443)\,e^{-0.1(0.5)}$$
$$= 75.97 - 120\,(0.4443)(0.9512)$$
$$= 75.97 - 50.71 = \text{Rs } 25.26$$

We can use Equation (7) to calculate the value of put option:

$$P_0 = 25.26 - 120 + 120e^{-0.10 \times 0.50}$$
$$= 25.26 - 120 + 114.15 = \text{Rs } 19.41$$

The hedge ratio of the call option is 0.34, which is the value of $N(d_1)$. The hedge ratio of the put option is: $N(d_1) - 1 = 0.34 - 1 = -0.66$.

Implied Volatility

The Black-Scholes option valuation assumes that the volatility is given. We can ask a different question: What is the volatility (or standard deviation) for the observed option price to be consistent with the Black-Scholes formula? This is implied volatility of the stock. **Implied volatility** is the volatility that the option price implies. An investor can compare the actual and implied volatility. If the actual volatility is higher than the implied volatility, the investor may conclude that the option's fair price is more than the observed price. Hence, she may consider option as potentially a good investment. You can use the Excel spreadsheet to calculate the Black-Scholes option price and implied volatilities (as shown in the box).

Dividend-paying Share Option

We have so far assumed that share on which option has been created does not involve dividend during the life of the option. This may not be so in practice. We can use slightly modified B–S model for this purpose. The share price will go down by an amount reflecting the payment of dividend. As a consequence, the value of a call option will decrease and the value of a put option will increase. The share price is assumed to have a risk-less component and a risky component. The B–S model includes the risky component of the share price. The present value of dividends (from ex-dividend dates to present) can be treated as the risk-less component of the share price. Thus, for valuing a call option, we should adjust downwards the share price for the present value of the dividend payments during the life of the option, and then use the B–S model. We also need to adjust the volatility in case of a dividend-paying share since in the B–S model it is the volatility of the risky part of the share price. This is generally ignored in practice.

Excel Application 7.1:
Black-Scholes Model for Valuing Call and Put Options

In the spreadsheet given below, columns C2 to C6 contain data on Satyam's stock option. We can use excel functions to calculate the value of the call and put options. First we write formulae, as shown in columns D9 and D10, in columns C9 and C10 to calculate values of d_1 and d_2. We can use the Excel NORMSDIST function to find the cumulative normal probability density functions $N(d_1)$ and $N(d_2)$. Next, we can use the values of $N(d_1)$ and $N(d_2)$ in Equation (10) to find the value of the call option. In column C13, we write the formula, as shown in column D13, and determine the value of the call option. We use Equation (7) and write the formula for the value of put option in column C14.

You can use the Excel's Tools menu has the Solver command that can be used to calculate the implied volatility. For example, if the observed call price is Rs 12.03 (column

	A	B	C	D	E
1	*Data*			*Formula*	*Equation*
2	Standard deviation	σ	0.2500		
3	Variance	σ^2_t	0.0625		
4	Maturity in years		0.2500		
5	Risk-free rate (annual)	r_f	0.0850		
6	Share price	S_0	240		
7	Exercise price	E	245		
8	*Results*				
9	d_1		0.067546	LN(C6/C7)+(C5+C3/2)*C4)/(C2*SQRT(C4))	Eq. (11)
10	d_2		-0.057454	C9-(C2*SQRT(C4))	Eq. (12)
11	$N(d_1)$		0.526926	NORMSDIST(C9)	
12	$N(d_2)$		0.477092	NORMSDIST(C10)	
13	Call value	C	12.03	C6*C11-C7*EXP(-C5*C4)*C12	Eq. (10)
14	Put value	P	11.88	C13-C6+C7*EXP(-C5*C4)	Eq. (7)
15					

C13) with other data as shown in the spreadsheet, we can find the implied volatility in column C2 by using Solver. The target cell is C13. If you click "solve", you get a standard deviation in C2 that is consistent with call price in C13.

In Illustration 7.5, let us assume that the ex-dividend date is in three months during the life of the option. The dividend per share is Rs 10. The present value (continuous compounding) of dividend per share is:

$$10e^{-0.25 \times 0.10} = 10 \times 0.9753 = Rs\,9.75$$

The share price of Rs 110.25 (Rs120 – Rs 9.75) will be used in the B–S model to determine the value of the call option. Using the B–S model, we obtain the value of call option as Rs 19. The reduced value of the call option is obtained because of the payment of dividend.

Continuous dividend Instead of assuming that a share pays discrete periodic dividend, we can make a simple assumption that the share pays a continuous dividend. This assumption is not unrealistic in case of an index option since the index consists of large number of shares, which maybe paying dividends in different time periods. Under the assumption of the continuous dividend, the formula for the valuation of the European-type call option is as follows:

$$C_0 = S_0 e^{-\delta t} N(d_1) - E e^{-r_f t} N(d_2) \qquad (14)$$

$N(d_1)$ is determined as follows:

$$d_1 = \frac{\ln(S_0/E) + \left[r_f - \delta + \sigma^2/2 \right] t}{\sigma\sqrt{t}} \qquad (15)$$

The symbol δ is the annual dividend yield.

ORDINARY SHARE AS AN OPTION

One distinguishing feature of ordinary share is that it has limited liability. The *limited liability* feature provides an opportunity to the shareholders to default on a debt. If a firm has incurred a debt, each time a payment is due, the shareholders can decide to make payment or to default. If the firm's value is more than the payment that is due, the shareholders will make payment since

they shall be left with a positive value of their equity and keep the firm. If the payment that is due is more than the value of the firm, the shareholders will default and let the debt-holders keep the firm. Since the shareholders have a hidden right to default on debt without any liability, the debt contract gives them a call option on the firm. The debt-holders are the sellers of call option to the shareholders. The amount of debt to be repaid is the exercise price and the maturity of debt is the time to expiration.

The value of the shareholders equity is the difference between the total value of the firm and the value of the debt. The value of equity cannot be negative. If the value of the firm is less than the value of the debt, the shareholders will not exercise the option of owning the firm. Thus, at the time of exercising the option, the value of equity will be either the excess of the total firm's value over the value of the debt or zero.

There is an alternate way of looking at ordinary share as an option. The shareholders' option can be interpreted as a put option. The shareholders can sell (hand over) the firm to the debt-holders at zero exercise price if they do not want to make the payment that is due.

We can use the Black–Scholes model to value the ordinary share as an option. The following example illustrates this.

Illustration 7.6: Equity as an Option

Excel Corporation is currently valued at Rs 250 crore. It has an outstanding debt of Rs 100 crore with a maturity of 5 years. The volatility (standard deviation) of the Excel share return is 60 per cent. The risk-free rate is 10 per cent. What is the market value of Excel's equity? What is the current market value of its debt?

We can use the B–S model to determine the current market values of equity and debt. The current price of the underlying asset (the firm) is Rs 250 crore and the exercise price (the required amount of debt) is Rs 100 crore. Let us first calculate d_1 and d_2 as follows:

$$d_1 = \frac{\ln(250/100) + [0.10 + (0.60)^2/2]5}{0.60\sqrt{5}} = 1.7090$$

$$d_2 = \frac{\ln(250/100) + [0.10 - (0.60)^2/2]5}{0.60\sqrt{5}} = 0.3673$$

From the table given at the end of this book, we obtain the values $N(d_1)$ and $N(d_2)$ as follows:

$$N(d_1) = N(1.7090) = 0.9563$$
$$N(d_2) = N(0.3673) = 0.6433$$

We obtain the value of equity as

$$C(\text{Value of equity}) = 250(0.9563) - 100(0.6433)e^{-0.1(5)}$$
$$= 239 - 64(0.6065) = 239 - 39$$
$$= \text{Rs } 200 \text{ crore}$$

The market value of debt is

$$\text{Market value of debt} = \text{Value of firm} - \text{value of equity}$$
$$= 250 - 200 = \text{Rs } 50 \text{ crore.}$$

SUMMARY

❖ An option is a contract that gives the holder a right, without any obligation, to buy or sell an underlying asset at a given exercise (or strike) price on or before a specified expiration period. The underlying asset (i.e., asset on which right is written) could be a share or any other asset.

❖ Call option is a right to buy an asset.

❖ Put option is a right to sell an asset.

❖ American option can be exercised at expiration or any time before expiration while European options can be exercised only at expiration.

❖ A buyer of a call option on a share will exercise his right when the actual share price at expiration (S_t) is higher than the exercise price (E), otherwise, he will forgo his right. Similarly, the buyer of a put option will exercise his right if the exercise price is higher than the share price; he will not exercise his option if the share price is equal to or greater than the exercise price. Thus:

Call option		Put option
Exercise if $S_t > E$	In-the-money	Exercise if $E > S_t$
Do not exercise if $S_t < E$	Out-of-the-money	Do not exercise if $E < S_t$
Do not exercise if $S_t = E$	At-the-money	Do not exercise if $S_t = E$

❖ At expiration the maximum value of a call option is:
Value of call option at expiration = Max [($S_t - E$), 0]

❖ The value of put option at expiration is:
Value of put option at expiration = Max [($E - S_t$), 0]

❖ There are several trading strategies that an investor can pursue. He can create a hedged position by combining a long position in the share with a long position in a protective put—a put that is purchased at-the-money (exercise and current share prices being the same).

❖ The investor can also create a portfolio of a call and a put with the same exercise price. This is called a straddle.

❖ If call and put with different exercise price are combined, it is called a spread.

❖ There are five factors that affect the value of a share option: (1) the share price, (2) the exercise price, (3) the volatility (standard deviation) of the share return, (4) the risk-free rate of interest, and (5) the option's time to expiration.

❖ A call option's value will increase with increase in the share price, the rate of interest, volatility and time to expiration.

It will decline with increase in the exercise price.

❖ A put option's value will increase with increase in the exercise price, volatility and time to expiration. It will decrease with increase in the share price, and the rate of interest.

❖ The value of call decreases and the value of put increases in the case of dividend paying shares.

❖ The value of an option can be determined by simple binomial-tree approach in simple situations. In more complex situations where time period and the share price movements can be made very small, we can use the Black and Scholes (B–S) model to value a European call option:

$$C_0 = S_0 N(d_1) - E e^{-r_f t} N(d_2)$$

where C_0 = the value of an option, S = the current market value of the share, E = the exercise price, $e = 2.7183$, the exponential constant, r_f = the risk-free rate on interest, t = the time to expiration (in years), σ = the standard deviation of the continuously compounded annual return on the share and $N(d_1)$, $N(d_2)$ = the cumulative normal probability density function. d_1 and d_2 can be calculated as follows:

$$d_1 = \frac{\ln(S_0/E) + [r_f + \sigma^2/2]t}{\sigma\sqrt{t}}$$
$$d_2 = d_1 - \sigma\sqrt{t}$$

ln = the natural logarithm

❖ The term $N(d_1)$ in the B–S model is interpreted as a hedge ratio, or the call option's delta. The option delta indicates the number of units of a share to be bought for each call sold.

❖ There is a fixed relationship between put and call on the same share with similar exercise price and maturity period. This relationship, called put-call parity, is given as follows:

Value of put + value of share
= value of call + PV of exercise price

$$P_0 + S_0 = C_0 + E e^{-r_f t}$$

❖ There is a hidden option in the case of an ordinary share that arises because of the limited liability of the shareholders. Shareholders have a call option on the firm with an exercise price equal to the required payment for debt. Shareholders will exercise their option to keep the firm (by making required payment to debt-holders) if the value of the firm is higher than the debt payment.

KEY CONCEPTS

American option	Contingent claims	Long position	Short position
At-the-money-option	Covered call	Option	Spread
Bearish spread	Equity as option	Option delta	Straddle
Binomial approach	European option	Option holder or buyer	Strangle
Black-Scholes model	Exercise (strike) price	Option writer or seller	Strap
Bullish spread	Hedge ratio	Out-of-the-money option	Strike (exercise) price
Butterfly	Hedged position	Protective put	Strip
Calendar spread	Horizontal spread	Put option	Underlying asset
Call option	Implied volatility	Put premium	Vertical spread
Call premium	Index option	Put-call parity	
Collar	In-the-money option	Risk-neutrality	

ILLUSTRATIVE SOLVED PROBLEMS

Problem 7.1: A call option with an exercise price of Rs 100 can be bought at a premium of Rs 3. A put option with an exercise price of Rs 95 is available at a premium of Rs 5. How can you combine these options to form a portfolio? What will be your pay-off at expiration?

Solution: You can create a portfolio by buying both options. It is called a straddle. The pay-off will be as follows:

	Share Price	Profit/loss	Option Exercised
Call + Put	$S_t > 100$	$(S_t - 100) - (3 + 5)$	call exercised, put not exercised
Call + Put	$S_t < 95$	$(95 - S_t) - (3 + 5)$	call not exercised, put exercised
Call + Put	$95 < S_t < 100$	$-(3 + 5)$	both call and put not exercised

Problem 7.2: A call option with an exercise price Rs 40 is available at a premium of Rs 3. A put with same maturity and exercise price can be purchased at a premium of Rs 2. If you create a straddle, show the pay-off from it. When would the straddle result in loss?

Solution: The profit from the straddle will be as follows:

	Share Price	Profit/loss	Option Exercised
Call + Put	$S_t > 40$	$[(S_t - 40) - (3 + 2)]$ >0, if $S_t > 45$	call exercised, put not exercised
Call + Put	$S_t < 40$	$[(40 - S_t) - (3 + 2)]$ >0, if $S_t > 35$	call not exercised, put exercised
Call + Put	$35 < S_t < 45$	$-(3 + 2)$	both call and put not exercised

Problem 7.3: A one-year call option with an exercise price of Rs 60 is available at a premium of Rs 6. You can also buy a one-year put with an exercise price of Rs 55 at a premium of Rs 3. If you set up a portfolio of a put and a call, what will be your pay-off if the share price after one year is (*a*) Rs 58, (*b*) Rs 45, or (*c*) Rs 75?

Solution: The pay-off is as follows:

(*a*) Share price Rs 58, you will neither exercise put nor call. Thus,

Profit / loss = – Rs 6 – Rs 3 = –Rs 9

(*b*) Share price Rs 45, you will exercise put, but not call. Thus,

Profit/loss = (Rs 55 – Rs 45) – Rs 9 = + Rs 1

(*c*) Share price Rs 75, you will exercise call, but not put. Thus,

Profit/loss = (Rs 75 – Rs 60) – Rs 9 = + Rs 6

Problem 7.4: The Infosys share is one of the most volatile shares. On 22 September 2002, its put and call options with one-week maturity were selling as follows:

	Strike price (Rs)	Premium (Rs)
Call	4,100	47.30
Put	4,000	88.25
Current share price (Rs)		3,469.00
Lot size		100.00
Volatility (%)		2.97

If you buy a put option and a call option, what would be your profit if the share price ranges between Rs 3,850 to Rs 4,250? Show calculations. Also draw a profit graph.

Solution: Since you have combined a put and a call with different exercise prices but the same maturity, you have created a price spread. The calculations of profit are shown in Table 7.13. You may notice that your minimum profit is Rs 35.55.

In Figure 7.26, we plot the profit graph of your investment strategy.

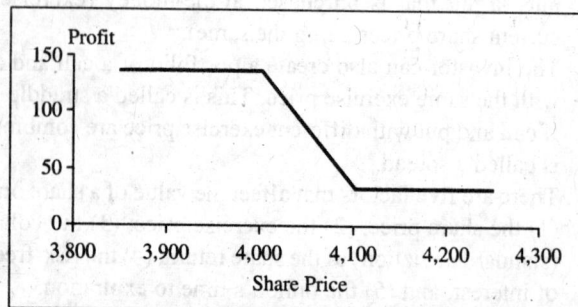

Figure 7.26: Infosys share options: Profit

Table 7.13: Infosys Share Options: Profit/Loss

Pay-off: Long Call 3500 and Short Call 3400

Long call

E	4100	4100	4100	4100	4100	4100	4100	4100	4100
S_t	3850	3900	3950	4000	4050	4100	4150	4200	4250
Pay-off	0	0	0	0	0	0	50	100	150
Premium	47.30	47.30	47.30	47.30	47.30	47.30	47.30	47.30	47.30
Profit (A)	47.3	47.3	47.3	47.3	47.3	47.3	97.3	147.3	197.3

Short Call

E	4000	4000	4000	4000	4000	4000	4000	4000	4000
S_t	3850	3900	3950	4000	4050	4100	4150	4200	4250
Pay-off	0	0	0	0	50	100	150	200	250
Premium	88.25	88.25	88.25	88.25	88.25	88.25	88.25	88.25	88.25
Profit (B)	88.25	88.25	88.25	88.25	38.25	−11.75	−61.75	−111.75	−161.75
Net profit (A - B)	135.55	135.55	135.55	135.55	85.55	35.55	35.55	35.55	35.55

Problem 7.5: A share is currently selling for Rs 120. There are two possible prices of the share after one year: Rs 132 or Rs 105. Assume that risk-free rate of return is 9 per cent per annum. What is the value of a one-year call option (European) with an exercise price of Rs 125?

Solution: Let us set up a portfolio of one call option (short) and Δ shares (long). If the price increases to Rs 132, the value of portfolio after one year will be: Rs 132Δ – (Rs 132 – Rs 125) = Rs 132Δ – Rs 7. If the price falls to Rs 105, then the call option is worth nothing and the portfolio will be worth: Rs 105Δ. The pay-off will be equal if:

$$132\Delta - 105\Delta = 7 - 0$$
$$\Delta = (7 - 0)/(132 - 105) = 7/27 = 0.26$$

The value of portfolio after one year is: $132 \times 0.26 - 7 = 105 \times 0.26 =$ Rs 27.30. The current share price (S) is Rs 120. Therefore, the present value of call option (C) will be:

$$S\Delta - C = PV \text{ of } 27.30$$
$$120 \times 0.26 = \frac{27.30}{1.09}$$
$$C = 120 \times 0.26 - \frac{27.30}{1.09} = 31.20 - 25.05 = \text{Rs } 6.15.$$

Problem 7.6: Calculate the value of a call option using the B–S model given the following information:

Current market price of the share (S): Rs 75

Volatility (standard deviation, S): 0.45

Exercise price (E): Rs 80

Risk-free rate (r_f): 0.12

Time to expiration (t): 6 months = 0.5 years

If an investor wants to buy a put with same exercise price and expiration date as call option, what will be the value of put?

Solution: We shall first determine the value of call option. Let us calculate d_1 and d_2 as follows:

$$d_1 = \frac{\ln(75/80) + [0.12 + (0.45)^2/2]0.5}{0.45\sqrt{0.5}} = 0.1344$$

$$d_2 = \frac{\ln(75/80) + [0.12 - (0.45)^2/2]0.5}{0.45\sqrt{0.5}} = -0.1838$$

From the table at the end of the book, we obtain the value of $N(d_1)$ and $N(d_2)$ as follows:

$$N(d_1) = N(0.1344) = 0.5534$$
$$N(d_2) = N(-0.1838) = 0.4271$$

Using Equation (11), we obtain

$$C_0 = 75(0.5534) - 80(0.421)e^{-0.12(0.5)}$$
$$= 41.50 - 80(0.4271)(0.9418) = 41.50 - 32.18 = \text{Rs } 9.32$$

We can use put-call parity to calculate the value of put;

$$P + S = C + Ee^{-r_f t}$$
$$P = C + Ee^{-r_f t} - S$$
$$= 9.32 + 80e^{-0.12 \times 0.5} - 75$$
$$= 9.32 + 75.34 - 75 = \text{Rs } 9.66.$$

REVIEW QUESTIONS

1. What is an option? What is the difference between a call option and a put option? Illustrate your answer with the help of position diagrams.

2. Show the pay-off graphs of an investor at expiration with the following portfolios:
   (i) One share and a put (long)

   (*ii*) One share and a put (short)
   (*iii*) One share and a call (short)
   (*iv*) One share and two call (short)
   (*v*) Two shares and a call (short)
   (*vi*) A call (long) and a put (short)

3. Explain the difference between selling a call option and buying a put option. Illustrate your answer.

4. Explain when a call option and a put option are in-the-money, at-the-money and out-of-the-money.

5. What are the factors that influence the prices of options on share? Explain how increase in the risk-free rate and decrease in volatility can make an American put attractive if it is exercised early?

6. What will be lower and upper bounds for the price of a call option? Explain the reasons.

7. Why isn't it beneficial to exercise an American call option early? Give reasons.

8. What is a protective put? What position in call option is similar to a protective put?

9. How can a spread be created? What is a straddle? What is a strangle? Draw pay-off graphs to explain the implications of a spread, a straddle and a strangle.

10. How and why a collar is created? What are its implications for an investor?

11. Explain and illustrate a one-step binomial approach to value a European option.

12. What is a risk-neutral valuation approach to valuing a European option. Give an example.

13. What are the assumptions of the Black-Scholes model for option pricing? What are the attributes of the model?

14. Illustrate the concept of put-call parity.

15. What is a hedge ratio or a call option delta? How is it determined?

16. Why is ordinary share an option? Explain.

PROBLEMS

1. Ram Jethabhai has purchased a 3-month call option on a company's share with an exercise price Rs 51. The current price of the share is Rs 50. Determine the value of call option at expiration if the share price turns out to be either Rs 47 or Rs 54. Draw a diagram to illustrate your answer.

2. Sunder Lal has sold a 6-month call option on a company's share with a exercise price of Rs 100. The current share price is Rs 100. Calculate the value of call option to Sunder Lal at maturity if the share price increases to Rs 110 or decreases to Rs 90. Draw a diagram to illustrate your answer.

3. You have bought one 6-month call option on a share with an exercise price of Rs 98 at a premium of Rs 3. The share has a current price of Rs 100. You expect share to either rise to Rs 108 or fall to Rs 95 after six months. What will be your pay-off when option matures? Draw a diagram to explain.

4. Radhika Krishnan has purchased a call option on a share at a premium of Rs 5. The current share price is Rs 44 and the exercise price is Rs 42. At maturity the share price may either increase to Rs 45 or fall to Rs 43. Will Radhika exercise her option? Why?

5. Meena Vasudevan has purchased a 3-month put option on a company's share with an exercise price Rs 101. The current price of the share is Rs 100. Determine the value of put option at expiration if the share price turns out to be either Rs 97 or Rs 104. Draw a diagram to illustrate your answer.

6. S. Rammurthy has sold a 6-month put option on a company's share with an exercise price of Rs 100. The current share price is Rs 100. Calculate the value of put option to Rammurthy at maturity if the share price increases to Rs 110 or decreases to Rs 90. Draw a diagram to illustrate your answer.

7. You have bought one 6-month put option on a share with an exercise price of Rs 96 at a premium of Rs 4. The share has a current price of Rs 100. You expect share to either rise to Rs 108 or fall to Rs 95 after six months. What will be your pay-off when option matures? Draw a diagram to explain.

8. You buy a 3-month European put on a share for Rs 4 with an exercise price of Rs 50. The current share price is Rs 52. when will you exercise your option and when will you make a profit? Draw a diagram to illustrate your answer.

9. Shyam sells a 6-month put with an exercise price of Rs 70 at a premium of Rs 5. Under what situation option will be exercised? When will Shyam make profit? Draw a diagram to illustrate Shyam's profit or loss position with the share prices at maturity.

10. V. Sridharan has purchased a put option on a share at a premium of Rs 5. The current share price is Rs 44 and the exercise price is Rs 42. At maturity the share price may either increase to Rs 45 or fall to Rs 43. Will he exercise his option? Why?

11. Madan Modi holds 50 share of Zeta Zerox Company. He is intending to write calls on Zetas's shares. If he writes a call contract for 50 shares with an exercise price of Rs 50 each share, determine the value of his portfolio when the option expires if (*a*) the current share price of Rs 45 rises to Rs 65, or (*b*) the share price falls to Rs 40.

12. You buy a call option on a share with an exercise price of Rs 100. You also buy a put option on the same share with an exercise price of Rs 97. What profit or loss will you have on maturity from your portfolio of call and put? Explain with the help of a diagram.

13. In Exercise (12) above, assume that you paid a call premium of Rs 3 and a put premium of Rs 5. How would your profit pattern change? Show with the help of a diagram.

14. R.K. Ramachandran has purchased 3-month call on a share with an exercise price of Rs 50 at a premium of Rs 4. He has also bought a 3-month put on the same share with an exercise price of Rs 50 at a premium of Rs 2. Determine Ramachandran's position at maturity if the share price is either Rs 52 or Rs 45.

15. The share of Ashok Enterprises is currently selling for Rs 100. It is known that the share price will either turn to be

Rs 108 or Rs 90. The risk-free rate of return is 12 per cent per annum. If you intend to buy a 3-month call option with an exercise price of Rs 97, how much should you pay for buying the option today? Assume no arbitrage opportunity.

16. A share has a current share price of Rs 100. The share price after six months will be either Rs 115 or Rs 90. The risk-free rate is 10 per cent per annum. Determine the value of a 6-month call option on the share with an exercise price of Rs 100 using the risk-neutral arguement.

17. Zenith Company's share is currently selling for Rs 60. It is expected that after two months the share price may either increase by 15 per cent or fall by 10 per cent. The risk-free rate is 9 per cent per annum. What should be the value of a two-month European call option with an exercise price of Rs 65? What is the value of a two-month European put option with an exercise price of Rs 65?

18. Determine the price of a European call option on a share that does not pay dividend. The current share price is Rs 60, the exercise price Rs 55, the risk-free rate is 10 per cent per annum, the share return volatility is 40 per cent per annum and the time to expiration is six months.

19. Calculate the value of a European put option on a share that does not pay dividend. The current share price is Rs 86, the exercise price Rs 93, the risk-free rate is 12 per cent per annum, the share return volatility is 60 per cent per annum and the time to expiration is four months.

20. A company has a total market value of Rs 230 crore. The face of its debt (assume pure discount debt) is Rs 95 crore. The standard deviation of the firm's share return is 25 per cent and debt has a maturity of 8 years. The risk-free rate is 12 per cent. What is the value of the company's equity?

21. On 26 August 2002, Infosys call option with an exercise of Rs 3,400 is selling at a premium of Rs 186.15 and call option with an exercise of Rs 3,500 is selling at a premium of Rs 38.10. The current share price is Rs 3,469. The lot size is 100. What will be your net profit at share price at expiration ranging from Rs 3200 to Rs 3700 if you buy call with the exercise of Rs 3,500 and sell call with the exercise price of Rs 3,400? Draw a profit graph.

22. VSNL's share price is expected to decline due to non-payment of its dues by the WorldCom, lowering margins and other negative sentiments in the market. The current share price is Rs 123.70 and the daily volatility of the VSNL share is 2.74 percent. Based on the Value at Risk (VaR), the probability of the share price going above Rs 142.5 is quite low. The put on the VSNL share with an exercise price of Rs 150 is selling for Rs 7.50. Should you buy the put? Draw a profit graph.

23. The put on the Infosys share is selling with an exercise price Rs 3,400 at a premium of Rs 37.50 on 22 August 2002. On the same day, the call is selling at a premium of Rs 32.50 with an exercise price of Rs 3,300. The spot price of the share is Rs 3,370. The lot size is 100. What will be your net profit at share price at expiration ranging from Rs 3,200 to Rs 3,700 if you buy call with the exercise price of Rs 3,500 and buy put with the exercise price of Rs 3,300? Draw a profit graph.

PART 2 Investment Decisions

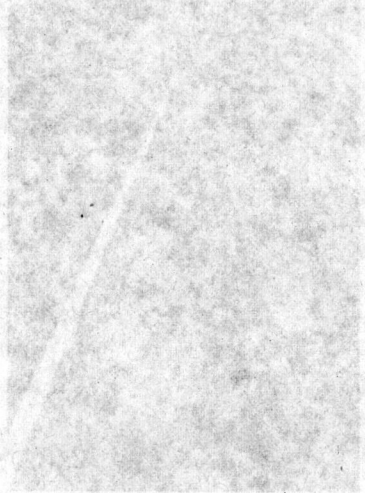

CHAPTER 8

Capital Budgeting Decisions

INTRODUCTION

An efficient allocation of capital is the most important finance function in the modern times. It involves decisions to commit the firm's funds to the long-term assets. Capital budgeting or investment decisions are of considerable importance to the firm since they tend to determine its value by influencing its growth, profitability and risk. In this chapter we focus on the nature and evaluation of capital budgeting decisions.

NATURE OF INVESTMENT DECISIONS

The **investment decisions** of a firm are generally known as the capital budgeting, or capital expenditure decisions. A **capital budgeting decision** may be defined as the firm's decision to invest its current funds most efficiently in the long-term assets in anticipation of an expected flow of benefits over a series of years. The long-term assets are those that affect the firm's operations beyond the one-year period. The firm's investment decisions would generally include expansion, acquisition, modernisation and replacement of the long-term assets. Sale of a division or business (divestment) is also as an investment decision. Decisions like the change in the methods of sales distribution, or an advertisement campaign or a research and development programme have long-term implications for the firm's expenditures and benefits, and therefore, they should also be evaluated as investment decisions. It is important to note that investment in the long-term assets invariably requires large funds to be tied up in the current assets such as inventories and receivables. As such, investment in fixed and current assets is one single activity.

The following are the features of investment decisions:

- The exchange of current funds for future benefits.
- The funds are invested in long-term assets.
- The future benefits will occur to the firm over a series of years.

It is significant to emphasise that expenditures and benefits of an investment should be measured in cash. In the investment analysis, it is cash flow, which is important, not the accounting profit. It may also be pointed out that investment decisions affect the firm's value. The firm's value will increase if investments are profitable and add to the shareholders' wealth. Thus, investments should be evaluated on the basis of a criterion, which is compatible with the objective of the shareholders' wealth maximisation. An investment will add to the shareholders' wealth if it yields benefits in excess of the minimum benefits as per the **opportunity cost of**

capital. In this chapter, we assume that the investment project's opportunity cost of capital is known. We also assume that the expenditures and benefits of the investment are known with certainty. Both these assumptions are relaxed in later chapters.

Importance of Investment Decisions

Investment decisions require special attention because of the following reasons:[1]

- They influence the firm's growth in the long run
- They affect the risk of the firm
- They involve commitment of large amount of funds
- They are irreversible, or reversible at substantial loss
- They are among the most difficult decisions to make.

Growth The effects of investment decisions extend into the future and have to be endured for a longer period than the consequences of the current operating expenditure. A firm's decision to invest in long-term assets has a decisive influence on the rate and direction of its growth. A wrong decision can prove disastrous for the continued survival of the firm; unwanted or unprofitable expansion of assets will result in heavy operating costs to the firm. On the other hand, inadequate investment in assets would make it difficult for the firm to compete successfully and maintain its market share.

Risk A long-term commitment of funds may also change the risk complexity of the firm. If the adoption of an investment increases average gain but causes frequent fluctuations in its earnings, the firm will become more risky. Thus, investment decisions shape the basic character of a firm.

Funding Investment decisions generally involve large amount of funds, which make it imperative for the firm to plan its investment programmes very carefully and make an advance arrangement for procuring finances internally or externally.

Irreversibility Most investment decisions are irreversible. It is difficult to find a market for such capital items once they have been acquired. The firm will incur heavy losses if such assets are scrapped.

Complexity Investment decisions are among the firm's most difficult decisions. They are an assessment of future events, which are difficult to predict. It is really a complex problem to correctly estimate the future cash flows of an investment. Economic, political, social and technological forces cause the uncertainty in cash flow estimation.

TYPES OF INVESTMENT DECISIONS

There are many ways to classify investments. One classification is as follows:

- Expansion of existing business
- Expansion of new business
- Replacement and modernisation.

Expansion and Diversification

A company may add capacity to its existing product lines to expand existing operations. For example, the Gujarat State Fertiliser Company (GSFC) may increase its plant capacity to manufacture more urea. It is an example of **related diversification**. A firm may expand its activities in a new business. Expansion of a new business requires investment in new products and a new kind of production activity within the firm. If a packaging manufacturing company invests in a new plant and machinery to produce ball bearings, which the firm has not manufactured before, this represents expansion of new business or **unrelated diversification**. Sometimes a company acquires existing firms to expand its business. In either case, the firm makes investment in the expectation of additional revenue. Investments in existing or new products may also be called as **revenue-expansion investments**.

Replacement and Modernisation

The main objective of modernisation and replacement is to improve operating efficiency and reduce costs. Cost savings will reflect in the increased profits, but the firm's revenue may remain unchanged. Assets become outdated and obsolete with technological changes. The firm must decide to replace those assets with new assets that operate more economically. If a cement company changes from semi-automatic drying equipment to fully automatic drying equipment, it is an example of modernisation and replacement. **Replacement decisions** help to introduce more efficient and economical assets and therefore, are also called **cost-reduction investments**. However, replacement decisions that involve substantial modernisation and technological improvements expand revenues as well as reduce costs.

Yet another useful way to classify investments is as follows:

- Mutually exclusive investments
- Independent investments
- Contingent investments.

Mutually Exclusive Investments

Mutually exclusive investments serve the same purpose and compete with each other. If one investment is undertaken, others will have to be excluded. A company may, for example, either use a more labour-intensive, semi-automatic machine, or employ a more capital-intensive, highly automatic machine for production. Choosing the semi-automatic machine precludes the acceptance of the highly automatic machine.

Independent Investments

Independent investments serve different purposes and do not compete with each other. For example, a heavy engineering company may be considering expansion of its plant capacity to manufacture additional excavators and addition of new production facilities to manufacture a new product—light commercial vehicles. Depending on their profitability and availability of funds, the company can undertake both investments.

Contingent Investments

Contingent investments are dependent projects; the choice of one investment necessitates undertaking one or more other

---

1. *See* Quirin, G.D., *The Capital Expenditure Decision*, Richard D. Irwin, 1977.

investments. For example, if a company decides to build a factory in a remote, backward area, it may have to invest in houses, roads, hospitals, schools etc. for employees to attract the work force. Thus, building of factory also requires investment in facilities for employees. The total expenditure will be treated as one single investment.

INVESTMENT EVALUATION CRITERIA

Three steps are involved in the evaluation of an investment:

- Estimation of cash flows
- Estimation of the required rate of return (the opportunity cost of capital)
- Application of a decision rule for making the choice.

The first two steps, discussed in the subsequent chapters, are assumed as given. Thus, our discussion in this chapter is confined to the third step. Specifically, we focus on the merits and demerits of various decision rules.

Investment Decision Rule

The investment decision rules may be referred to as capital budgeting techniques, or investment criteria. A sound appraisal technique should be used to measure the economic worth of an investment project. The essential property of a sound technique is that it should maximise the shareholders' wealth. The following other characteristics should also be possessed by a sound investment evaluation criterion:[1]

- It should consider all cash flows to determine the true profitability of the project.
- It should provide for an objective and unambiguous way of separating good projects from bad projects.
- It should help ranking of projects according to their true profitability.
- It should recognise the fact that bigger cash flows are preferable to smaller ones and early cash flows are preferable to later ones.
- It should help to choose among mutually exclusive projects that project which maximises the shareholders' wealth.
- It should be a criterion which is applicable to any conceivable investment project independent of others.

These conditions will be clarified as we discuss the features of various investment criteria in the following pages.

Evaluation Criteria

A number of investment criteria (or capital budgeting techniques) are in use in practice. They may be grouped in the following two categories:

1. *Discounted Cash Flow (DCF) Criteria*
   - Net present value (NPV)
   - Internal rate of return (IRR)
   - Profitability index (PI)
2. *Non-discounted Cash Flow Criteria*
   - Payback period (PB)

- Discounted payback period
- Accounting rate of return (ARR).

Discounted payback is a variation of the payback method. It involves discounted cash flows, but, as we shall see later, it is not a true measure of investment profitability. We will show in the following pages that the net present value criterion is the most valid technique of evaluating an investment project. It is consistent with the objective of maximising the shareholders' wealth.

NET PRESENT VALUE METHOD

The net present value (NPV) method is the classic economic method of evaluating the investment proposals. It is a DCF technique that explicitly recognises the time value of money. It correctly postulates that cash flows arising at different time periods differ in value and are comparable only when their equivalents—present values—are found out. The following steps are involved in the calculation of NPV:

- Cash flows of the investment project should be forecasted based on realistic assumptions.
- Appropriate discount rate should be identified to discount the forecasted cash flows. The appropriate discount rate is the project's opportunity cost of capital, which is equal to the required rate of return expected by investors on investments of equivalent risk.
- Present value of cash flows should be calculated using the opportunity cost of capital as the discount rate.
- Net present value should be found out by subtracting present value of cash outflows from present value of cash inflows. The project should be accepted if NPV is positive (i.e., NPV > 0). Let us consider an example.

Illustration 8.1: Calculating Net Present Value

Assume that Project X costs Rs 2,500 now and is expected to generate year-end cash inflows of Rs 900, Rs 800, Rs 700, Rs 600 and Rs 500 in years 1 through 5. The opportunity cost of the capital may be assumed to be 10 per cent.

The net present value for Project X can be calculated by referring to the present value table (Table C at the end of the book). The calculations are shown below:

$$NPV = \left[\frac{Rs\,900}{(1+0.10)} + \frac{Rs\,800}{(1+0.10)^2} + \frac{Rs\,700}{(1+0.10)^3} + \frac{Rs\,600}{(1+0.10)^4} \right.$$
$$\left. + \frac{Rs\,500}{(1+0.10)^5} \right] - Rs\,2,500$$

$$NPV = [Rs\,900(PVF_{1,\,0.10}) + Rs\,800(PVF_{2,\,0.10}) + Rs\,700(PVF_{3,\,0.10})$$
$$+ Rs\,600(PVF_{4,\,0.10}) + Rs\,500(PVF_{5,\,0.10})] - Rs\,2,500$$

$$NPV = [Rs\,900 \times 0.909 + Rs\,800 \times 0.826 + Rs\,700 \times 0.751$$
$$+ Rs\,600 \times 0.683 + Rs\,500 \times 0.620] - Rs\,2,500$$

$$NPV = Rs\,2,725 - Rs\,2,500 = + Rs\,225$$

Project X's present value of cash inflows (Rs 2,725) is greater than that of cash outflow (Rs 2,500). Thus, it generates a positive net present value (NPV = + Rs 225). Project X adds to the wealth of owners; therefore, it should be accepted.

---

1. See Porterfield, J.T.S., *Investment Decisions and Capital Costs*, Prentice-Hall, 1965.

The formula for the net present value can be written as follows:

$$NPV = \left[\frac{C_1}{(1+k)} + \frac{C_2}{(1+k)^2} + \frac{C_3}{(1+k)^3} + \cdots + \frac{C_n}{(1+k)^n} \right] - C_0$$

$$NPV = \sum_{t=1}^{n} \frac{C_t}{(1+k)^t} - C_0 \tag{1}$$

where C_1, C_2... represent net cash inflows in year 1, 2..., k is the opportunity cost of capital, C_0 is the initial cost of the investment and n is the expected life of the investment. It should be noted that the cost of capital, k, is assumed to be known and is constant.

Why is NPV Important?

A question may be raised: why should a financial manager invest Rs 2,500 in Project X? Project X should be undertaken if it is best for the company's shareholders; they would like their shares to be as valuable as possible. Let us assume that the total market value of a hypothetical company is Rs 10,000, which includes Rs 2,500 cash that can be invested in Project X. Thus the value of the company's other assets must be Rs 7,500. The company has to decide whether it should spend cash and accept Project X or to keep the cash and reject Project X. Clearly Project X is desirable since its *PV* (Rs 2,725) is greater than the Rs 2,500 cash. If Project X is accepted, the total market value of the firm will be: Rs 7,500 + *PV* of Project X = Rs 7,500 + Rs 2,725 = Rs 10,225; that is, an increase by Rs 225. The company's total market value would remain only Rs 10,000 if Project X were rejected.

Why should the *PV* of Project X reflect in the company's market value? To answer this question, let us assume that a new company X with Project X as the only asset is formed. What is the value of the company? We know from our earlier discussion on valuation of shares in Chapter 3 that the market value of a company's shares is equal to the present value of the expected dividends. Since Project X is the only asset of Company X, the expected dividends would be equal to the forecasted cash flows from Project X. Investors would discount the forecasted dividends at a rate of return expected on securities equivalent in risk to company X. The rate used by investors to discount dividends is exactly the rate, which we should use to discount cash flows of Project X. The calculation of the PV of Project X is a replication of the process, which shareholders will be following in valuing the shares of company X. Once we find out the value of Project X, as a separate venture, we can add it to the value of other assets to find out the portfolio value.

The difficult part in the calculation of the PV of an investment project is the precise measurement of the discount rate. Funds available with a company can either be invested in projects or given to shareholders. Shareholders can invest funds distributed to them in financial assets. Therefore, the discount rate is the opportunity cost of investing in projects rather than in capital markets. Obviously, the opportunity cost concept makes sense when financial assets are of equivalent risk as compared to the project.

An alternate interpretation of the positive net present value

Excel Application 8.1: Calculation of NPV

We can easily calculate NPV using the Excel financial function for NPV. The spreadsheet on the right side gives the cash flows of the project. We write the NPV formula in column C8: =NPV(0.10,C3:C7)+C2. You may note that 0.10 (10 per cent) is the discount rate. The project cash flows from year 1 through 5 are contained in column C3 through column C7. The initial cash flow (that is, cash flow in year 0) is added.

	A	B	C	D	E
1	Year	Cash flow		PVF at 10%	PV
2	0	C_0	−2500	1.000	−2500
3	1	C_1	900	0.909	818
4	2	C_2	800	0.826	661
5	3	C_3	700	0.751	526
6	4	C_4	600	0.683	410
7	5.	C_5	500	0.621	310
8		NPV	226	SUM(E2E7) →	226
9	NPV(0.1,C28:C32)+C27				
10					

of an investment is that it represents the maximum amount a firm would be ready to pay for purchasing the opportunity of making investment, or the amount at which the firm would be willing to sell the right to invest without being financially worse-off. The net present value (Rs 225) can also be interpreted to represent the amount the firm could raise at the required rate of return (10%), in addition to the initial cash outlay (Rs 2,500), to distribute immediately to its shareholders and by the end of the projects' life to have paid off all the capital raised and return on it.[1] The point is illustrated by the calculations shown in Table 8.1.

Table 8.1: Interpretation of NPV

Year	Amount outstanding in the beginning	Return on outstanding amount at 10%	Total outstanding flows	Repayment from cash at the end	Balance outstanding
	Rs	Rs	Rs	Rs	Rs
1	2,725.00	272.50	2,997.50	900	2,097.50
2	2,097.50	209.75	2,307.25	800	1,507.25
3	1,507.25	150.73	1,657.98	700	957.98
4	957.98	95.80	1,053.78	600	453.78
5	453.78	45.38	499.16	500	(0.84)*

* Rounding off error.

Calculations in Table 8.1 are based on the assumption that the firm chooses to receive the cash benefit resulting from the investment in the year it is made. Any pattern of cash receipts, such that the net present value is equal to Rs 225, can be selected.

---

1. Bierman, H. and Smidt, S., *The Capital Budgeting Decision*, Macmillan, 1975, p. 73.

Thus, if the firm raises Rs 2,500 (the initial outlay) instead of Rs 2,725 (initial outlay *plus* net present value) at 10 per cent rate of return, at the end of fifth year after having paid the principal sum together with interest, it would be left with Rs 363, whose present value at the beginning of the first year at 10 per cent discount rate is Rs 225. It should be noted that the gain to shareholders would be more if the rate of raising money is less than 10 per cent. (Why?)

Acceptance Rule

It should be clear that the acceptance rule using the NPV method is to accept the investment project if its net present value is positive (NPV > 0) and to reject it if the net present value is negative (NPV < 0). Positive NPV contributes to the net wealth of the shareholders, which should result in the increased price of a firm's share. The positive net present value will result only if the project generates cash inflows at a rate higher than the opportunity cost of capital. A project with zero NPV (NPV = 0) may be accepted. A zero NPV implies that project generates cash flows at a rate just equal to the opportunity cost of capital. The NPV acceptance rules are:

- Accept the project when NPV is positive   NPV > 0
- Reject the project when NPV is negative   NPV < 0
- May accept the project when NPV is zero   NPV = 0

The NPV method can be used to select between mutually exclusive projects; the one with the higher NPV should be selected. Using the NPV method, projects would be ranked in order of net present values; that is, first rank will be given to the project with highest positive net present value and so on.

Evaluation of the NPV Method

NPV is the true measure of an investment's profitability. It provides the most acceptable investment rule for the following reasons:

- *Time value* It recognises the time value of money—a rupee received today is worth more than a rupee received tomorrow.
- *Measure of true profitability* It uses *all* cash flows occurring over the entire life of the project in calculating its worth. Hence, it is a measure of the project's true profitability. The NPV method relies on estimated cash flows and the discount rate rather than any arbitrary assumptions, or subjective considerations.
- *Value-additivity* The discounting process facilitates measuring cash flows in terms of present values; that is, in terms of equivalent, current rupees. Therefore, the NPVs of projects can be added. For example, NPV $(A + B)$ = NPV (A) + NPV (B). This is called the **value-additivity principle.** It implies that if we know the NPVs of individual projects, the value of the firm will increase by the *sum* of their NPVs. We can also say that if we know values of individual assets, the firm's value can simply be found by adding their values. The value-additivity is an important property of an investment criterion because it means that each project can be evaluated, independent of others, on its own merit.
- *Shareholder value* The NPV method is always consistent with the objective of the shareholder value maximisation. This is the greatest virtue of the method.

Are there any limitations in using the NPV rule? The NPV method is a theoretically sound method. In practice, it may pose some computational problems.

- *Cash flow estimation* The NPV method is easy to use *if* forecasted cash flows are known. In practice, it is quite difficult to obtain the estimates of cash flows due to uncertainty.
- *Discount rate* It is also difficult in practice to precisely measure the discount rate.
- *Mutually exclusive projects* Further, caution needs to be applied in using the NPV method when alternative (mutually exclusive) projects with unequal lives, or under funds constraint are evaluated. The NPV rule may not give unambiguous results in these situations. These problems are discussed in detail in a later chapter.
- *Ranking of projects* It should be noted that the ranking of investment projects as per the NPV rule is *not* independent of the discount rates.[1] Let us consider an example. Suppose two projects—A and B—both costing Rs 50 each. Project A returns Rs 100 after one year and Rs 25 after two years. On the other hand, Project B returns Rs 30 after one year and Rs 100 after two years. At discount rates of 5 per cent and 10 per cent, the NPV of projects and their ranking are as follows:

	NPV at 5%	Rank	NPV at 10%	Rank
Project A	67.92	II	61.57	I
Project B	69.27	I	59.91	II

It can be seen that the project ranking is reversed when the discount rate is changed from 5 per cent to 10 per cent. The reason lies in the cash flow patterns. The impact of the discounting becomes more severe for the cash flow occurring later in the life of the project; the higher is the discount rate, the higher would be the discounting impact. In the case of Project B, the larger cash flows come later in the life. Their present value will decline as the discount rate increases.

INTERNAL RATE OF RETURN METHOD

The internal rate of return (IRR) method is another discounted cash flow technique, which takes account of the magnitude and timing of cash flows.[2] Other terms used to describe the IRR method are yield on an investment, marginal efficiency of capital, rate of return over cost, time-adjusted rate of internal return and so on. The concept of internal rate of return is quite simple to understand in the case of a one-period project. Assume that you deposit Rs 10,000 with a bank and would get back Rs 10,800 after

1. Bierman and Smidt, *op. cit.*, p. 31.
2. The use of IRR for appraising capital investment was emphasised in the formal terms, for the first time, by Joel Dean. See, Dean, Joel, *Capital Budgeting*, Columbia University Press, 1951, and his article, Measuring the Productivity of Capital in Solomon, E. (Ed.), *The Management of Corporate Capital*.

one year. The true rate of return on your investment would be:

$$\text{Rate of return} = \frac{10,800 - 10,000}{10,000}$$

$$= \frac{10,800}{10,000} - 10,000 = 1.08 - 1 = 0.08 \text{ or, } 8\%$$

The amount that you would obtain in the future (Rs 10,800) would consist of your investment (Rs 10,000) plus return on your investment (0.08 × Rs 10,000):

$$10,000 \ (1.08) = 10,800$$

$$10,000 = \frac{10,800}{(1.08)}$$

You may observe that the rate of return of your investment (8 per cent) makes the discounted (present) value of your cash inflow (Rs 10,800) equal to your investment (Rs 10,000).

We can now develop a formula for the rate of return (r) on an investment (C_0) that generates a single cash flow after one period (C_1) as follows:

$$r = \frac{C_1 - C_0}{C_0}$$

$$r = \frac{C_1}{C_0} - 1 \qquad (2)$$

Equation (2) can be rewritten as follows:

$$\frac{C_1}{C_0} = 1 + r$$

$$C_0 = \frac{C_1}{(1+r)} \qquad (3)$$

From Equation (3), you may notice that the rate of return, r, depends on the project's cash flows, rather than any outside factor. Therefore, it is referred to as the internal rate of return. The **internal rate of return** (IRR) is the rate that equates the investment outlay with the present value of cash inflow received after one period. This also implies that the rate of return is the discount rate which makes NPV = 0. There is no satisfactory way of defining the true rate of return of a long-term asset. IRR is the best available concept. We shall see that although it is a very frequently used concept in finance, yet at times it can be a misleading measure of investment worth.[1] IRR can be determined by solving the following equation for r:

$$C_0 = \frac{C_1}{(1+r)} + \frac{C_2}{(1+r)^2} + \frac{C_3}{(1+r)^3} + \cdots + \frac{C_n}{(1+r)^n}$$

$$C_0 = \sum_{t=1}^{n} \frac{C_t}{(1+r)^t}$$

$$= \sum_{t=1}^{n} \frac{C_t}{(1+r)^t} - C_0 = 0 \qquad (4)$$

It can be noticed that the IRR equation is the same as the one used for the NPV method. In the NPV method, the required rate of return, k, is known and the net present value is found, while in the IRR method the value of r has to be determined at which the net present value becomes zero.

Uneven Cash Flows: Calculating IRR by Trial and Error

The value of r in Equation (4) can be found out by trial and error. The approach is to select any discount rate to compute the present value of cash inflows. If the calculated present value of the expected cash inflow is lower than the present value of cash outflows, a lower rate should be tried. On the other hand, a higher value should be tried if the present value of inflows is higher than the present value of outflows. This process will be repeated unless the net present value becomes zero. The following illustration explains the procedure of calculating IRR.

Illustration 8.2: Trial and Error Method for Calculating IRR

A project costs Rs 16,000 and is expected to generate cash inflows of Rs 8,000, Rs 7,000 and Rs 6,000 at the end of each year for next 3 years. We know that IRR is the rate at which project will have a zero NPV. As a first step, we try (arbitrarily) a 20 per cent discount rate. The project's NPV at 20 per cent is:

$$\text{NPV} = -\text{Rs} \, 16,000 + \text{Rs} \, 8,000(\text{PVF}_{1,0.20}) + \text{Rs} \, 7,000(\text{PVF}_{2,0.20})$$

$$+ \text{Rs} \, 6,000(\text{PVF}_{3,0.20})$$

$$= -\text{Rs} \, 16,000 + \text{Rs} \, 8,000 \times 0.833 + \text{Rs} \, 7,000 \times 0.694$$

$$+ \text{Rs} \, 6,000 \times 0.579$$

$$= -\text{Rs} \, 16,000 + \text{Rs} \, 14,996 = -\text{Rs} \, 1,004$$

A negative NPV of Rs 1,004 at 20 per cent indicates that the project's true rate of return is lower than 20 per cent. Let us try 16 per cent as the discount rate. At 16 per cent, the project's NPV is:

$$\text{NPV} = -\text{Rs} \, 16,000 + \text{Rs} \, 8,000(\text{PVF}_{1,0.16}) + \text{Rs} \, 7,000(\text{PVF}_{2,0.16})$$

$$+ \text{Rs} \, 6,000(\text{PVF}_{3,0.16})$$

$$= -\text{Rs} \, 16,000 + \text{Rs} \, 8,000 \times 0.862 + \text{Rs} \, 7,000 \times 0.743$$

$$+ \text{Rs} \, 6,000 \times 0.641$$

$$= -\text{Rs} \, 16,000 + \text{Rs} \, 15,943 = -\text{Rs} \, 57$$

Since the project's NPV is still negative at 16 per cent, a rate lower than 16 per cent should be tried. When we select 15 per cent as the trial rate, we find that the project's NPV is Rs 200:

$$\text{NPV} = -\text{Rs} \, 16,000 + \text{Rs} \, 8,000(\text{PVF}_{1,0.15}) + \text{Rs} \, 7,000(\text{PVF}_{2,0.15})$$

$$+ \text{Rs} \, 6,000(\text{PVF}_{3,0.15})$$

$$= -\text{Rs} \, 16,000 + \text{Rs} \, 8,000 \times 0.870 + \text{Rs} \, 7,000 \times 0.756$$

$$+ \text{Rs} \, 6,000 \times 0.658$$

$$= -\text{Rs} \, 16,000 + \text{Rs} \, 16,200 = \text{Rs} \, 200$$

The true rate of return should lie between 15–16 per cent. We can find out a close approximation of the rate of return by the method of linear interpolation as follows:

		Difference
PV required	Rs 16,000	
		200
PV at lower rate, 15%	16,200	
		257
PV at higher rate, 16%	15,943	

$r = 15\% + (16\% - 15\%)200/257$

$\quad = 15\% + 0.80\% = 15.8\%$

---

1. Brealey, R. and Myers, S., *Principles of Corporate Finance*, McGraw Hill, 1991, p. 8.

Level Cash Flows

An easy procedure can be followed to calculate the IRR for a project that produces level or equal cash flows each period. To illustrate, let us assume that an investment would cost Rs 20,000 and provide annual cash inflow of Rs 5,430 for 6 years. If the opportunity cost of capital is 10 per cent, what is the investment's NPV? The Rs 5,430 is an annuity for 6 years. The NPV can be found as follows:

$$NPV = -\, Rs\, 20,000 + Rs\, 5,430(PVFA_{6,0.10})$$
$$= -\, Rs\, 20,000 + Rs\, 5,430 \times 4.355 = Rs\, 3,648$$

How much is the project's IRR? The IRR of the investment can be found out as follows:

$$NPV = -\, Rs\, 20,000 + Rs\, 5,430(PVFA_{6,r}) = 0$$

$$Rs\, 20,000 = Rs\, 5,430(PVFA_{6,r})$$

$$PVFA_{6,r} = \frac{Rs\, 20,000}{Rs\, 5,430} = 3.683$$

The rate, which gives a PVFA of 3.683 for 6 years, is the project's internal rate of return. Looking up PVFA in Table D (given at the end of the book) across the 6-year row, we find it approximately under the 16 per cent column. Thus, 16 per cent is the project's IRR that equates the present value of the initial cash outlay (Rs 20,000) with the constant annual cash inflows (Rs 5,430 per year) for 6 years.

NPV Profile and IRR

We repeat to emphasise that NPV of a project declines as the discount rate increases, and for discount rates higher than the project's IRR, NPV will be negative. NPV profile of the project at various discount rates is shown in Table 8.2 and Figure 8.1. At 16 per cent, the NPV is zero; therefore, it is the IRR of the project. As you may notice, we have used the Excel spreadsheet to make the computations and create the chart using the Excel chart wizard.

Acceptance Rule

The accept-or-reject rule, using the IRR method, is to accept the project if its internal rate of return is higher than the opportunity cost of capital ($r > k$). Note that k is also known as the required rate of return, or the cut-off, or hurdle rate. The project shall be rejected if its internal rate of return is lower than the opportunity cost of capital ($r < k$). The decision maker may remain indifferent if the internal rate of return is equal to the opportunity cost of capital. Thus the IRR acceptance rules are:

- Accept the project when $r > k$
- Reject the project when $r < k$
- May accept the project when $r = k$

The reasoning for the acceptance rule becomes clear if we plot NPVs and discount rates for the project given in Table 8.2 on a graph like Figure 8.1. It can be seen that if the discount rate is less than 16 per cent IRR, then the project has *positive* NPV; if it is equal to IRR, the project has a *zero* NPV; and if it is greater than IRR, the project has negative NPV. Thus, when we compare IRR of the project with the opportunity cost of capital, we are in fact trying to ascertain whether the project's NPV is positive or not. In case of independent projects, IRR and NPV rules will give the same results if the firm has no shortage of funds.

🗙 Excel Application 8.2: Calculation of IRR

We can easily calculate IRR using the Excel function for IRR. The spreadsheet below gives the cash flows of the project. We write the IRR formula in column C7: =IRR(C3:C6). The project cash flows, including the cash outlay in the beginning (C₀ in year 0) are contained in column C3 through column C6. It is optional to include the "guess" rate in the formula.

	A	B	C	D
1	**IRR of An Investment Project**			
2	Year	Cash Flow (Rs)		
3	0	C_0	−16000	
4	1	C_1	8000	
5	2	C_2	7000	
6	3	C_3	6000	
7		IRR	15.8%	IRR(C3:C6)

Table 8.2: NPV Profile

1	**NPV Profile**			
2	**Cash Flow**	**Discount rate**	**NPV**	
3	− 20000	0%	12,580	
4	5430	5%	7,561	
5	5430	10%	3,649	
6	5430	15%	550	
7	5430	16%	0	
8	5430	20%	(1,942)	
9	5430	25%	(3,974)	

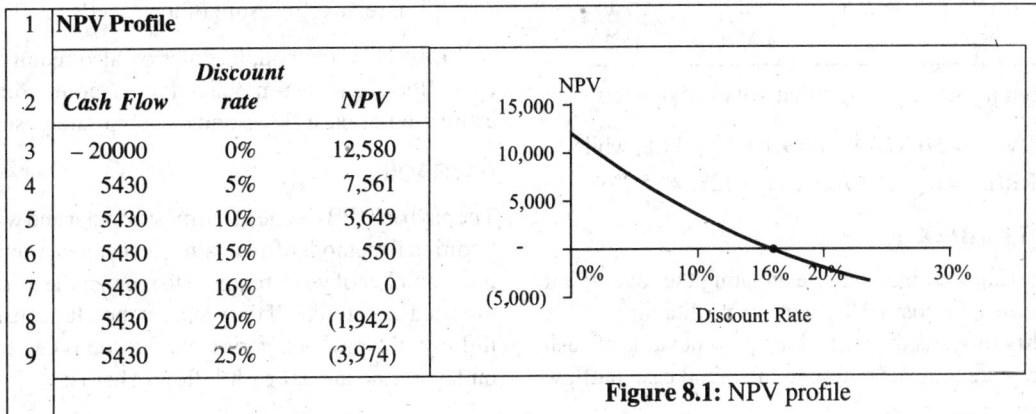

Figure 8.1: NPV profile

Evaluation of IRR Method

IRR method is like the NPV method. It is a popular investment criterion since it measures profitability as a percentage and can be easily compared with the opportunity cost of capital. IRR method has following merits:

- *Time value* The IRR method recognises the time value of money.
- *Profitability measure* It considers *all* cash flows occurring over the entire life of the project to calculate its rate of return.
- *Acceptance rule* It generally gives the same acceptance rule as the NPV method.
- *Shareholder value* It is consistent with the shareholders' wealth maximisation objective. Whenever a project's IRR is greater than the opportunity cost of capital, the shareholders' wealth will be enhanced.

Like the NPV method, the IRR method is also theoretically a sound investment evaluation criterion. However, IRR rule can give misleading and inconsistent results under certain circumstances. Here we briefly mention the problems that IRR method may suffer from.

- *Multiple rates* A project may have multiple rates, or it may not have a unique rate of return. As we explain later on, these problems arise because of the mathematics of IRR computation.
- *Mutually exclusive projects* It may also fail to indicate a correct choice between mutually exclusive projects under certain situations. This pitfall of the IRR method is elaborated later on in this chapter.
- *Value additivity* Unlike in the case of the NPV method, the value additivity principle does not hold when the IRR method is used—IRRs of projects do not add.[1] Thus, for Projects *A* and *B*, IRR(*A*) + IRR(*B*) need not be equal to IRR (*A* + *B*). Consider an example given below.

The NPV and IRR of Projects *A* and *B* are given below:

Project	C_0 (Rs)	C_1 (Rs)	NPV @ 10% (Rs)	IRR (%)
A	– 100	+ 120	+ 9.1	20.0
B	– 150	+ 168	+ 2.7	12.0
A + B	– 250	+ 288	+ 11.8	15.2

It can be seen from the example that NPVs of projects add:

$$\text{NPV}(A) + \text{NPV}(B) = \text{NPV}(A + B) = 9.1 + 2.7 = 11.8, \text{ while}$$
$$\text{IRR}(A) + \text{IRR}(B) \neq \text{IRR}(A + B) = 20\% + 12\% \neq 15.2\%$$

PROFITABILITY INDEX

Yet another time-adjusted method of evaluating the investment proposals is the benefit-cost (B/C) ratio or profitability index (PI). **Profitability index** is the ratio of the present value of cash inflows, at the required rate of return, to the initial cash outflow

of the investment. The formula for calculating **benefit-cost ratio** or profitability index is as follows:

$$\text{PI} = \frac{\text{PV of cash inflows}}{\text{Initial cash outlay}} = \frac{\text{PV}(C_t)}{C_0} = \sum_{t=1}^{n} \frac{C_t}{(1+k)^t} \div C_0 \quad (5)$$

Illustration 8.3: PI of Uneven Cash Flows

The initial cash outlay of a project is Rs 100,000 and it can generate cash inflow of Rs 40,000, Rs 30,000, Rs 50,000 and Rs 20,000 in year 1 through 4. Assume a 10 per cent rate of discount. The PV of cash inflows at 10 per cent discount rate is:

$$\text{PV} = \text{Rs } 40,000(\text{PVF}_{1,\,0.10}) + \text{Rs } 30,000(\text{PVF}_{2,\,0.10})$$
$$+ \text{Rs } 50,000(\text{PVF}_{3,\,0.10}) + \text{Rs } 20,000(\text{PVF}_{4,\,0.10})$$
$$= \text{Rs } 40,000 \times 0.909 + \text{Rs } 30,000 \times 0.826$$
$$+ \text{Rs } 50,000 \times 0.751 + \text{Rs } 20,000 \times 0.68$$
$$\text{NPV} = \text{Rs } 112,350 - \text{Rs } 100,000 = \text{Rs } 12,350$$
$$\text{PI} = \frac{\text{Rs } 112,350}{\text{Rs } 100,000} = 1.1235.$$

Acceptance Rule

The following are the PI acceptance rules:

- Accept the project when PI is greater than one   PI > 1
- Reject the project when PI is less than one   PI < 1
- May accept the project when PI is equal to one   PI = 1

The project with positive NPV will have PI greater than one. PI less than means that the project's NPV is negative.

Evaluation of PI Method

Like the NPV and IRR rules, PI is a conceptually sound method of appraising investment projects. It is a variation of the NPV method, and requires the same computations as the NPV method.

- *Time value* It recognises the time value of money.
- *Value maximisation* It is consistent with the shareholder value maximisation principle. A project with PI greater than one will have positive NPV and if accepted, it will increase share-holders' wealth.
- *Relative profitability* In the PI method, since the present value of cash inflows is divided by the initial cash outflow, it is a relative measure of a project's profitability.

Like NPV method, PI criterion also requires calculation of cash flows and estimate of the discount rate. In practice, estimation of cash flows and discount rate pose problems.

PAYBACK

The payback (PB) is one of the most popular and widely recognised traditional methods of evaluating investment proposals. **Payback** is the number of years required to recover the original cash outlay invested in a project. If the project generates constant annual cash inflows, the payback period can be computed by dividing cash outlay by the annual cash inflow. That is:

---

1. Copeland, T.E. and Weston, J.F., *Financial Theory and Corporate Policy*, Addison-Wesley, 1983, p. 32.

$$\text{Payback} = \frac{\text{Initial Investment}}{\text{Annual Cash Inflow}} = \frac{C_0}{C} \qquad (6)$$

Illustration 8.4: Payback (Constant Cash Flows)

Assume that a project requires an outlay of Rs 50,000 and yields annual cash inflow of Rs 12,500 for 7 years. The payback period for the project is:

$$\text{PB} = \frac{\text{Rs}\,50,000}{\text{Rs}\,12,000} = 4 \text{ years}$$

Unequal cash flows In case of unequal cash inflows, the payback period can be found out by adding up the cash inflows until the total is equal to the initial cash outlay. Consider the following example.

Illustration 8.5: Payback (Uneven Cash Flows)

Suppose that a project requires a cash outlay of Rs 20,000, and generates cash inflows of Rs 8,000; Rs 7,000; Rs 4,000; and Rs 3,000 during the next 4 years. What is the project's payback? When we add up the cash inflows, we find that in the first three years Rs 19,000 of the original outlay is recovered. In the fourth year cash inflow generated is Rs 3,000 and only Rs 1,000 of the original outlay remains to be recovered. Assuming that the cash inflows occur evenly during the year, the time required to recover Rs 1,000 will be (Rs 1,000/Rs 3,000) × 12 months = 4 months. Thus, the payback period is 3 years and 4 months.

Acceptance Rule

Many firms use the payback period as an investment evaluation criterion and a method of ranking projects. They compare the project's payback with a predetermined, standard payback. The project would be accepted if its payback period is less than the maximum or **standard payback** period set by management. As a ranking method, it gives highest ranking to the project, which has the shortest payback period and lowest ranking to the project with highest payback period. Thus, if the firm has to choose between two mutually exclusive projects, the project with shorter payback period will be selected.

Evaluation of Payback

Payback is a popular investment criterion in practice. It is considered to have certain virtues.

- *Simplicity* The most significant merit of payback is that it is simple to understand and easy to calculate. The business executives consider the simplicity of method as a virtue. This is evident from their heavy reliance on it for appraising investment proposals in practice.
- *Cost effective* Payback method costs less than most of the sophisticated techniques that require a lot of the analysts' time and the use of computers.
- *Short-term effects* A company can have more favourable short-run effects on earnings per share by setting up a shorter standard payback period.[1] It should, however, be remembered that this may not be a wise long-term policy as

the company may have to sacrifice its future growth for current earnings.

- *Risk shield* The risk of the project can be tackled by having a shorter standard payback period as it may ensure guarantee against loss. A company has to invest in many projects where the cash inflows and life expectancies are highly uncertain. Under such circumstances, payback may become important, not so much as a measure of profitability but as a means of establishing an upper bound on the acceptable degree of risk.[2]
- *Liquidity* The emphasis in payback is on the early recovery of the investment. Thus, it gives an insight into the liquidity of the project. The funds so released can be put to other uses.

In spite of its simplicity and the so-called virtues, the payback may not be a desirable investment criterion since it suffers from a number of serious limitations:

- *Cash flows after payback* Payback fails to take account of the cash inflows earned after the payback period. For example, consider the following projects X and Y:

Project	C_0	C_1	C_2	C_3	Payback	NPV
			Cash Flows (Rs)			
X	– 4,000	0	4,000	2,000	2 years	+ 806
Y	– 4,000	2,000	2.000	0	3 years	– 530

As per the payback rule, both the projects are equally desirable since both return the investment outlay in two years. If we assume an opportunity cost of 10 per cent, Project X yields a positive net present value of Rs 806 and Project Y yields a negative net present value of Rs 530. As per the NPV rule, Project X should be accepted and Project Y rejected. Payback rule gave wrong results because it failed to consider Rs 2,000 cash flow in third year for Project X.

- *Cash flows ignored* Payback is not an appropriate method of measuring the profitability of an investment project as it does not consider all cash inflows yielded by the project. Considering Project X again, payback rule did not take into account its entire series of cash flows.
- *Cash flow patterns* Payback fails to consider the pattern of cash inflows, i.e., magnitude and timing of cash inflows. In other words, it gives equal weights to returns of equal amounts even though they occur in different time periods. For example, compare the following projects C and D where they involve equal cash outlay and yield equal total cash inflows over equal time periods:

Project	C_0	C_1	C_2	C_3	Payback	NPV
			Cash Flows (Rs)			
C	– 5,000	3,000	2,000	2,000	2 years	+ 881
D	– 5,000	2,000	3,000	2,000	2 years	+ 798

1. Weston, J.F. and Brighane, E.F., *Managerial Finance*, Holt, Rinehart & Winston, 1972, p. 145.
2. Quirin, *op. cit.,* pp. 31–32.

Using payback period, both projects are equally desirable. But Project C *should be* preferable as larger cash inflows' come earlier in its life. This is indicated by the NPV rule; project C has higher NPV (Rs 881) than Project D (Rs 798) at 10 per cent opportunity cost. It should be thus clear that payback is not a measure of profitability. As such, it is dangerous to use it as a decision criterion.

- *Administrative difficulties* A firm may face difficulties in determining the maximum acceptable payback period. There is no rational basis for setting a maximum payback period. It is generally a subjective decision.
- *Inconsistent with shareholder value* Payback is not consistent with the objective of maximising the market value of the firm's shares. Share values do not depend on payback periods of investment projects.[1]

Let us re-emphasise that the payback is not a valid method for evaluating the acceptability of the investment projects. It can, however, be used along with the NPV rule as a first step in roughly screening the projects. In practice, the use of DCF techniques has been increasing but payback continues to remain a popular and primary method of investment evaluation (Exhibit 8.1).

Payback Reciprocal and the Rate of Return

Payback is considered theoretically useful in a few situations. One significant argument in favour of payback is that its reciprocal is a good approximation of the rate of return under certain conditions.[2]

The payback period is defined as follows:

$$\text{Payback} = \frac{\text{Initial investment}}{\text{Annual cash inflow(annuity)}} = \frac{C_0}{C} \quad (7)$$

The formula for the present value of an annuity is given by the following equation as discussed in Chapter 2. (*i* in the original equation is being replaced by *r*, the internal rate of return).

$$C_0 = C \left[\frac{1 - \frac{1}{(1+r)^n}}{r} \right]$$

$$C_0 = \frac{C}{r} - \frac{C}{r} \left[\frac{1}{(1+r)^n} \right]$$

Multiplying both sides by *r*, we get

$$rC_0 = C - C \left[\frac{1}{(1+r)^n} \right]$$

EXHIBIT 8.1: CAPITAL BUDGETING METHODS IN PRACTICE

- In a study of the capital budgeting practices of fourteen medium to large size companies in India, it was found that all companies, except one, used payback. With payback and/or other techniques, about two-thirds of companies used IRR and about two-fifths NPV. IRR was found to be the second most popular method.
- The reasons for the popularity of payback in order of significance were stated to be its *simplicity to use and understand, its emphasis on the early recovery of investment* and *focus on risk.*
- It was also found that one-third of companies always insisted on the computation of payback for all projects, one-third for majority of projects and remaining for some of the projects. For about two-thirds of companies standard payback ranged between 3 and 5 years.
- Reasons for the secondary role of DCF techniques in India included *difficulty in understanding and using these techniques, lack of qualified professionals* and *unwillingness of top management* to use DCF techniques. One large manufacturing and marketing organisation mentioned that conditions of its business were such that DCF techniques were not needed. Yet another company stated that replacement projects were very frequent in the company, and it was not considered necessary to use DCF techniques for evaluating such projects.

Source: Pandey, I.M., Capital Budgeting Practices of Indian Companies, *MDI Management Journal*, Vol. 2, No. 1 (Jan. 1989).

Solving for *r*, we find

$$r = \frac{C}{C_0} - \frac{C}{C_0} \left[\frac{1}{(1+r)^n} \right] \quad (8)$$

where C_0 is the initial investment, *C* is annual cash inflow, *r* is rate of return and *n* is the life of investment.

In Equation (8), the first right-hand term is the reciprocal of the payback period. The second right-hand term is payback reciprocal multiplied by $1/(1 + r)^n$. If *n* is very large or extends to infinity, the second term becomes insignificant (almost equal to zero), and we are left with the term C/C_0. Thus, IRR is equal to the reciprocal of payback.[3]

The reciprocal of payback will be a close approximation of the internal rate of return if the following two conditions are satisfied:

- The life of the project is large or at least twice the payback period.
- The project generates equal annual cash inflows.

---

1. Porterfield, *op. cit.,* p. 22.
2. Gordon, Myron, Payoff Period and Rate of Profit, *Journal of Business*, XXVIII, No. 4, pp. 253–60.

3. In fact, the optimal cut-off for the payback can be computed from the present value of an annuity formula: $\text{Optimal cutoff} = \frac{C_0}{C} = \left[\frac{1}{r} - \frac{1}{r(1+r)^n} \right]$.

The payback reciprocal is a useful technique to quickly estimate the true rate of return. But its major limitation is that every investment project does not satisfy the conditions on which this method is based. When the useful life of the project is not at least twice the payback period, the payback reciprocal will always exceed the rate of return. Similarly, it cannot be used as an approximation of the rate of return if the project yields uneven cash inflows.

L'SCOUNTED PAYBACK PERIOD

One of the serious objections to the payback method is that it does not discount the cash flows for calculating the payback period. We can discount cash flows and then calculate the payback. The **discounted payback period** is the number of periods taken in recovering the investment outlay on the present value basis. The discounted payback period still fails to consider the cash flows occurring after the payback period.

Let us consider an example. Projects *P* and *Q* involve the same outlay of Rs 4,000 each. The opportunity cost of capital may be assumed as 10 per cent. The cash flows of the projects and their discounted payback periods are shown in Table 8.3.

The projects are indicated of same desirability by the simple payback period. When cash flows are discounted to calculate the discounted payback period, Project *P* recovers the investment outlay faster than Project *Q*, and therefore, it would be preferred over Project *Q*. Discounted payback period for a project will be always higher than simple payback period because its calculation is based on the discounted cash flows. Discounted payback rule is better as it discounts the cash flows until the outlay is recovered. But it does not help much. It does not take into consideration the entire series of cash flows. It can be seen in our example that if we use the NPV rule, Project *Q* (with higher discounted payback period) is better.

ACCOUNTING RATE OF RETURN METHOD

The **accounting rate of return** (ARR), also known as the *return on investment* (ROI), uses accounting information, as revealed by financial statements, to measure the profitability of an investment. The accounting rate of return is the ratio of the average after tax profit divided by the average investment. The average investment would be equal to half of the original investment if it were depreciated constantly. Alternatively, it

can be found out by dividing the total of the investment's book values after depreciation by the life of the project. The accounting rate of return, thus, is an average rate and can be determined by the following equation:

$$ARR = \frac{\text{Average income}}{\text{Average investment}} \qquad (9)$$

In Equation (9) average income should be defined in terms of earnings after taxes without an adjustment for interest viz. EBIT $(1 - T)$ or net operating profit after tax. Thus

$$ARR = \frac{\left[\sum_{t=1}^{n} EBIT_t (1-T) \right] / n}{(I_0 + I_n)/2} \qquad (10)$$

where EBIT is earnings before interest and taxes, T tax rate, I_0 book value of investment in the beginning, I_n book value of investment at the end of n number of years.[1]

Illustration 8.6: Accounting Rate of Return

A project will cost Rs 40,000. Its stream of earnings before depreciation, interest and taxes (EBDIT) during first year through five years is expected to be Rs 10,000, Rs 12,000, Rs 14,000, Rs 16,000 and Rs 20,000. Assume a 50 per cent tax rate and depreciation on straight-line basis. Project's ARR is computed in Table 8.4.

$$\text{Accounting Rate of Return} = \frac{3,200}{20,000} \times 100 = 16 \text{ per cent}$$

A variation of the ARR method is to divide average earnings after taxes by the original cost of the project instead of the average cost. Thus, using this version, the ARR in Illustration 8.6 would be: Rs 3,200 ÷ Rs 40,000 × 100 = 8 per cent. This version of the ARR method is less consistent as earnings are averaged but investment is not.[2]

Acceptance Rule

As an accept-or-reject criterion, this method will accept all those projects whose ARR is higher than the minimum rate established by the management and reject those projects which have ARR less than the minimum rate. This method would rank a project as number one if it has highest ARR and lowest rank would be assigned to the project with lowest ARR.

Table 8.3: Discounted Payback Illustrated

	C₀	*C₁*	*C₂*	*C₃*	*C₄*	*Simple PB*	*Discounted PB*	*NPV at 10%*
P	−4,000	3,000	1,000	1,000	1,000	2 yrs	—	—
PV of cash flows	−4,000	2,727	826	751	683		2.6 yrs	987
Q	−4,000	0	4,000	1,000	2,000	2 yrs	—	—
PV of cash flows	−4,000	0	3,304	751	1,366		2.9 yrs	1,421

Column group header: Cash Flows (Rs) spans C₀–C₄

1. We assume straight-line depreciation.
2. Quirin, *op. cit.*, p. 33.

Table 8.4: Calculation of Accounting Rate of Return

						(Rs)
Period	*1*	*2*	*3*	*4*	*5*	*Average*
Earnings before depreciation, interest and taxes (EBDIT)	10,000	12,000	14,000	16,000	20,000	14,400
Depreciation	8,000	8,000	8,000	8,000	8,000	8,000
Earnings before interest and taxes (EBIT)	2,000	4,000	6,000	8,000	12,000	6,400
Taxes at 50%	1,000	2,000	3,000	4,000	6,000	3,200
Earnings before interest and after taxes [EBIT $(1-T)$]	1,000	2,000	3,000	4,000	6,000	3,200
Book value of investment:						
Beginning	40,000	32,000	24,000	16,000	8,000	
Ending	32,000	24,000	16,000	8,000	—	
Average	36,000	28,000	20,000	12,000	4,000	20,000

Evaluation of ARR Method

The ARR method may claim some merits:

- *Simplicity* The ARR method is simple to understand and use. It does not involve complicated computations.
- *Accounting data* The ARR can be readily calculated from the accounting data; unlike in the NPV and IRR methods, no adjustments are required to arrive at cash flows of the project.
- *Accounting profitability* The ARR rule incorporates the entire stream of income in calculating the project's profitability.

The ARR is a method commonly understood by accountants, and frequently used as a performance measure. As a decision criterion, however, it has serious shortcomings.

- *Cash flows ignored* The ARR method uses accounting profits, not cash flows, in appraising the projects. Accounting profits are based on arbitrary assumptions and choices and also include non-cash items. It is, therefore, inappropriate to rely on them for measuring the acceptability of the investment projects.
- *Time value ignored* The averaging of income ignores the time value of money. In fact, this procedure gives more weightage to the distant receipts.
- *Arbitrary cut-off* The firm employing the ARR rule uses an arbitrary cut-off yardstick. Generally, the yardstick is the firm's current return on its assets (book-value). Because of this, the growth companies earning very high rates on their existing assets may reject profitable projects (i.e., with positive NPVs) and the less profitable companies may accept bad projects (i.e., with negative NPVs).

The ARR method continues to be used as a performance evaluation and control measure in practice. But its use as an investment criterion is certainly undesirable. It may lead to unprofitable allocation of capital.

NPV VERSUS IRR

The net present value and the internal rate of return methods are two closely related investment criteria. Both are time-adjusted methods of measuring investment worth. In case of independent projects, two methods lead to same decisions. However, under certain situations (to be discussed later in this section), a conflict arises between them. It is under these cases that a choice between the two criteria has to be made.

Equivalence of NPV and IRR: Case of Conventional Independent Projects

It is important to distinguish between conventional and non-conventional investments in discussing the comparison between NPV and IRR methods. A **conventional investment** can be defined as one whose cash flows take the pattern of an initial cash outlay followed by cash inflows. Conventional projects have only one *change in the sign* of cash flows; for example, the initial outflow followed by inflows, i.e., $- + + +$. A **non-conventional investment**, on the other hand, is one, which has cash outflows mingled with cash inflows throughout the life of the project.[1] Non-conventional investments have more than one change in the signs of cash flows; for example, $- + + +$ $- + + - +$.

In case of conventional investments, which are economically *independent* of each other, NPV and IRR methods result in same accept-or-reject decision *if* the firm is not constrained for funds in accepting *all* profitable projects. Same projects would be indicated profitable by both methods. The logic is simple to understand. As has been explained earlier, all projects with positive net present values would be accepted if the NPV method is used, or projects with internal rates of return higher than the required rate of return would be accepted if the IRR method were followed. The last or **marginal project** acceptable under the NPV method is the one, which has zero net present value; while using the IRR method, this project will have an internal rate of return equal to the required rate of return. Projects with positive net present values would also have internal rates of return higher than the required rate of return and the marginal project will have zero present value only when its internal rate of return is equal to the required rate of return.

---

1. Bierman and Smidt, *op. cit.*, pp. 7–8.

We know that NPV is:

$$NPV = \sum_{t=1}^{n} \frac{C_t}{(1+k)^t} - C_0 \qquad (1)$$

and IRR is that rate r which satisfies the following equation:

$$NPV = \sum_{t=1}^{n} \frac{C_t}{(1+r)^t} - C_0 = 0 \qquad (4)$$

Subtracting Equation (4) from Equation (1), we get

$$NPV = \sum_{t=1}^{n} \left[\frac{C_t}{(1+k)^t} - \frac{C_t}{(1+r)^t} \right] \qquad (11)$$

As we know that C_t, k, r and t are positive, NPV can be positive (NPV > 0) only if $r > k$. NPV would be zero if and only if $r = k$ and it would be negative (NPV < 0) if $r < k$. Thus, we find that NPV and IRR methods are equivalent as regards the acceptance or rejection of independent conventional investments.

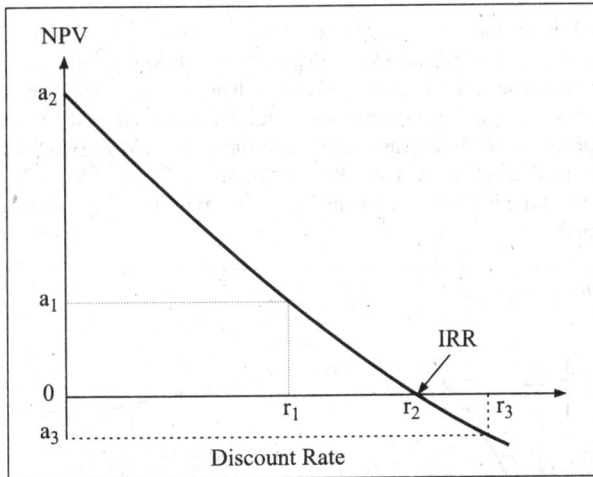

Figure 8.2: Equivalency of NPV and IRR

Figure 8.2 also substantiates this argument where oa_2 represents the highest net present value for the project at zero discount rate; at this point NPV is simply the difference between cash inflows and cash outflows. At r_2, discount rate, the net present value is zero and therefore, by definition, r_2 is the internal rate of return of the project. For discount rate (say r_3) greater than IRR, the net present value would be negative. Conversely, for discount rate (say r_1) lower than IRR, the net present value of the project will be positive. Thus, if the required rate of return is r_1, the project will be accepted under both methods since the net present value, oa_1, is greater than zero and internal rate, r_2, exceeds the required rate, r_1. Project could also be accepted if the required rate is r_2 as net present value is zero and the required rate and internal rate are equal. But the project would be rejected under either method if the required rate is r_3 as the net present value is negative and the internal rate of return is lower than the required rate of return (i.e., $r_2 < r_3$).

Lending and Borrowing-type Projects

Figure 8.3 shows that the NPV of a project declines as the discount rate increases. This may not be true in the case of all projects. Investment projects may have the characteristics of lending or borrowing or both.[1] Consider the following situations:

Project	Cash Flows (Rs)			
	C_0	C_1	IRR	NPV at 10%
X	– 100	120	20%	9
Y	100	– 120	20%	– 9

Figure 8.3 is drawn to show the NPV profiles of projects X and Y. It can be seen in Figure 8.3(a) that for Project X, the NPV declines as the discount rate increases. The NPV is zero at 20 per cent of return; it is positive for rates lower than 20 per cent rate and negative for rates higher than 20 per cent. Project X, a **lending-type project**, is a typical example of a conventional investment in which a series of cash outlays is followed by a series of cash inflows. Interpreted differently, it can be stated that in the case of Project X we are *lending* Rs 100 at a rate of return of 20 per cent. If our opportunity cost of capital is 10 per cent, we shall lend (or invest) Rs 100. The higher the rate we *earn*, the happier we are.

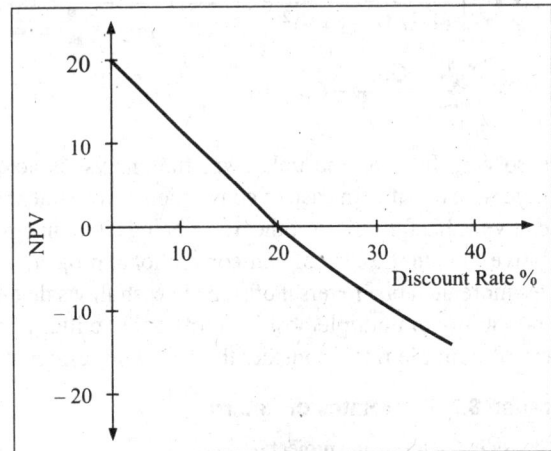

Figure 8.3 (a): Project X

For Project Y, on the other hand, we find that the NPV increases with increase in the discount rate [Figure 8.3(b)]. Like in the case of Project X, the NPV is zero at 20 per cent discount rate. However, it is negative at rates lower than 20 per cent and positive at rates higher than 20 per cent. Project Y is a **borrowing-type project**. In the case of Project Y, we are *borrowing* Rs 100 at a rate of return of 20 per cent. The 20 per cent is a return to the lender; to us it is a cost. We shall be well-off only if we could borrow at a rate less than our opportunity cost of capital (*viz.* 10 per cent in the example). Thus, for us, the borrower, the NPV is negative for rates of discount less than 20 per cent and positive for higher rates of discount. In a borrowing-type project, the lower the rate we *pay*, the happier we are.

---

1. See Bierman and Smidt, *op. cit.*, pp. 218–51, and Brealey and Myers, *op. cit.*, pp. 82–83.

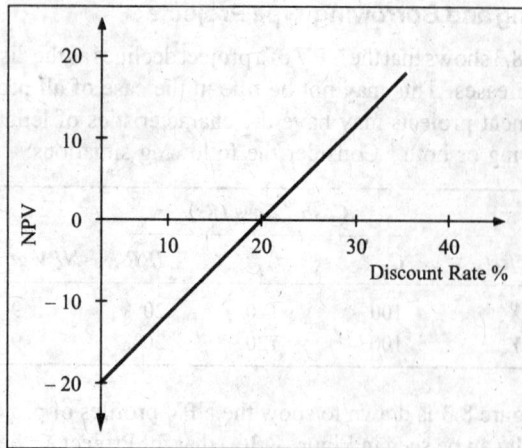

Figure 8.3 (b): Project *Y*

Non-conventional Investments: Problem of Multiple IRRs

A serious shortcoming of the IRR method, when used to evaluate non-conventional investments, is that it can yield multiple internal rates of return.[1] The reason for more than one rate of return solution lies in the *algebra* of the IRR equation. As we know, the formula to calculate IRR is as follows:

$$\text{NPV} = \left[\frac{C_1}{(1+r)} + \frac{C_2}{(1+r)^2} + \cdots + \frac{C_n}{(1+r)^n} \right] - C_0 = 0$$

$$\text{NPV} = \sum_{t=1}^{n} \frac{C_t}{(1+r)^t} - C_0 = 0 \qquad (4)$$

In solving for *r* as the unknown, the analyst is actually solving for *n* roots of *r*. In case of conventional investment only one positive value for *r* exists, other roots being either imaginary or negative. It is in the case of non-conventional project, which involves more than one reversal of signs in cash flows that there is the possibility of multiple positive roots of *r*. To illustrate the problem of multiple rates, consider the following example.

Illustration 8.7: Dual Rates of Return

Let us consider the following project I:

	Cash Flows (Rs)		
Project	*C_0*	*C_1*	*C_2*
I	– 1,000	4,000	– 3,750

We can use the IRR formula to solve the internal rate of return of this project:

$$\frac{4,000}{(1+r)} - \frac{3,750}{(1+r)^2} - 1,000 = 0$$

Assuming $\frac{1}{1+r} = x$, we obtain

$$-3,750x^2 + 4,000x - 1,000 = 0$$

This is a **quadratic equation** of the form: $ax^2 + bx + c = 0$, and we can solve it by using the following formula:

$$x = \frac{-b \pm \sqrt{b^2 - 4ac}}{2a} \qquad (12)$$

Substituting values in Equation (12), we obtain

$$x = \frac{-4,000 \pm \sqrt{(4,000)^2 - 4(-1,000)(-3,750)}}{2(-3,750)}$$

$$x = \frac{-4,000 \pm 1,000}{-7,500} = \frac{2}{5}, \frac{2}{3}$$

Since $x = \frac{1}{1+r}$, therefore

$$\frac{1}{1+r} = \frac{2}{5}, \frac{1}{1+r} = \frac{2}{3}$$

$$r = \frac{3}{2} \text{ or } 150\%, r = \frac{1}{2} = 50\%$$

It is obvious from the above calculation that Project I yields dual rates of return: 50 per cent and 150 per cent. At these two rates of return the net present value of the project is zero. It needs to be emphasised here that this dilemma does not arise when the NPV method is used—we have simply to specify the required rate of return and find NPV. The relationship between discount rates and NPVs are shown in Figure 8.4, where the discount rate is plotted along the horizontal axis and net present value along the vertical axis.

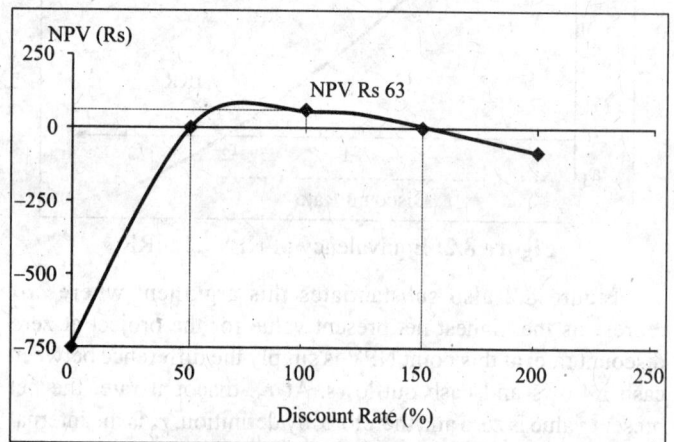

Figure 8.4: Dual rates of return

At zero rate of discount, the net present value of the project is simply the difference of undiscounted cash flows. It is – Rs 750 for Project I (– 1,000 + 4,000 – 3,750 = – 750). As the discount rate increases, the negative net present value diminishes and becomes zero at 50 per cent. The positive net present value increases as the discount rate exceeds 50 per cent, but reaching a maximum it starts decreasing and at 150 per cent it again becomes zero.

It should be clear from Figure 8.4 that Project I combines the features of both lending and borrowing.[2] The first part of the figure has an upward slope typical of a loan; the second part has a downward slope typical of an

---

1. The problem of the multiple rates of return was pointed out by Lorie, J.H. and Savage, L.J., Three Problem in Capital Rationing, *Journal of Business*, 28 (October 1955), pp. 229–39.
2. Bierman and Smidt, *op. cit.*, pp. 48–51.

ordinary investment (lending). Since the NPV curve cuts the horizontal-axis twice, the project has two rates of return, 50 and 150 per cent.

Which of the two rates is correct? None. The project would be worthwhile only when the opportunity cost of the capital falls between these two rates; NPV is positive at the discount rates ranging between 50 and 150 per cent.

The number of rates of return depends on the number of times the sign of the cash flow stream changes. In the case of Project I above, there are two reversals of sign $(- + -)$, and there are two rates of return. Reversal of sign is a necessary but not a sufficient condition for multiple rates of return.

A number of adaptations of the IRR criterion have been suggested to take care of the problem of multiple rates. In our opinion, none of them will work satisfactorily. The simple, straightforward alternative is to use the NPV rule.

Difference: Case of Ranking Mutually Exclusive Projects

We have shown that the NPV and IRR methods yield the same accept-or-reject rule in case of independent conventional investments. However, in real business situations there are alternative ways of achieving an objective and, thus, accepting one alternative will mean excluding the other. As defined earlier, investment projects are said to be **mutually exclusive** when only one investment could be accepted and others would have to be excluded.[1] For example, in order to distribute its products a company may decide either to establish its own sales organisation or engage outside distributors. The more profitable out of the two alternatives shall be selected. This type of exclusiveness may be referred to as technical exclusiveness. On the other hand, two independent projects may also be mutually exclusive if a financial constraint is imposed. If limited funds are available to accept either Project A or Project B, this would be an example of **financial exclusiveness** or **capital rationing**. The NPV and IRR methods can give conflicting ranking to mutually exclusive projects. In the case of independent projects ranking is not important since all profitable projects will be accepted. Ranking of projects, however, becomes crucial in the case of mutually exclusive projects. Since the NPV and IRR rules can give conflicting ranking to projects, one cannot remain indifferent as to the choice of the rule.

The NPV and IRR rules will give conflicting ranking to the projects under the following conditions:[1]

- The cash flow pattern of the projects may differ. That is, the cash flows of one project may increase over time, while those of others may decrease or *vice versa.*
- The cash outlays (initial investments) of the projects may differ.
- The projects may have different expected lives.

Timing of cash flows The most commonly found condition for the conflict between the NPV and IRR methods is the difference in the timing of cash flows. Let us consider the following two Projects, *M* and *N*.

Project	Cash Flows (Rs)				NPV at 9%	IRR
	C_0	C_1	C_2	C_3		
M	− 1,680	1,400	700	140	301	23%
N	− 1,680	140	840	1,510	321	17%

At 9 per cent discount rate, project N has higher NPV of Rs 321 than Project *M*'s NPV of Rs 301. However, Project *N* has a lower IRR of 17 per cent than Project *M*'s IRR of 23 per cent. Why this conflict? Which project should we accept? Let us see how NPVs of Projects *M* and *N* behave with discount rates. The NPV profiles of two projects would be as shown in Table 8.5.

The net present values of Projects *M* and *N*, as a function of discount rates, are plotted in Figure 8.5. It is noticeable from the NPV calculations as well as from Figure 8.5 that the present value of Project *N* falls rapidly as the discount rate increases. The reason is that its largest cash flows come late in life, when the compounding effect of time is most significant. Reverse is true with Project *M* as its largest cash flows come early in the life when compounding effect is not so severe. The internal rates of Projects *M* and *N* respectively are 23 per cent and 17 per cent. The NPV profiles of two projects intersect at 10 per cent discount rate. This is called **Fisher's intersection**.[3]

Table 8.5: NPV Profiles of Projects M and N

Discount Rate (%)	Project M	Project N
0	560	810
5	409	520
10	276	276
15	159	70
20	54	− 106
25	− 40	− 257
30	− 125	− 388

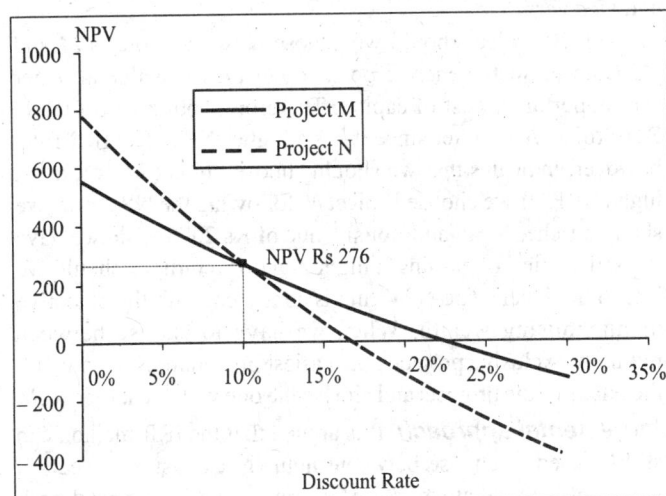

Figure 8.5: NPV versus IRR

1. Bierman and Smidt, *op. cit.*, p. 42.
2. Weston, J.F. and Brigham, E.F., On Capital Budgeting Techniques, in Brigham, E.F. and Johnson, R.E. (Ed.), *Issues in Managerial Finance*, Dryden, 1976, p. 108. Also, see Weston, J.F and Copeland, T.E. *Managerial Finance* Dryden, 1986, pp. 113–20.
3. Fisher, Irwing. *The Rate of Interest*. Macmillan Publishing Co., Inc., 1907.

Fisher's intersection occurs at the discount rate where the NPVs of two projects are equal. We can determine the discount rate at which Fisher's intersection occurs as follows:

$$-1,680 + \frac{1400}{(1+r^*)} + \frac{700}{(1+r^*)^2} + \frac{140}{(1+r^*)^3}$$

$$= -1,680 + \frac{140}{(1+r^*)} + \frac{840}{(1+r^*)^2} + \frac{1,510}{(1+r^*)^3}$$

This equation can be simplified by bringing all terms over the left-hand side.

$$-\frac{1,260}{(1+r^*)} + \frac{140}{(1+r^*)^2} + \frac{1,370}{(1+r^*)^3} = 0$$

Solving for r^*—**Fisher's intersection rate**—by trial and error, we obtain: $r^* = 10\%$.

We can write the following formula for determining the rate at which Fisher's intersection occurs for two Projects M and N:

$$NPV_M = NPV_N$$

$$\sum_{t=1}^{n} \frac{(C_t)_M}{(1+r^*)^t} - (C_0)_M = \sum_{t=1}^{n} \frac{(C_t)_N}{(1+r^*)^t} - (C_0)_N \qquad (13)$$

It is notable from Table 8.5 and Figure 8.5 that at the discount rates less than the intersection rate (10 per cent), Project N has the higher NPV but lower IRR (17 per cent). On the other hand, at the discount rates greater than the intersection rate (10 per cent), Project M has both higher NPV as well as higher IRR (23 per cent). Thus, if the required rate of return is greater than the intersection rate, both NPV and IRR methods will yield consistent results. That is, the project with higher internal rate of return will also have higher net present value. However, if the required rate of return is less than the intersection rate, the two methods will give contradictory results. That is, the project with higher internal rate of return will have lower net present value and *vice versa*.

Which project should we choose between Projects M and N? Both projects generate positive net present value at 9 per cent opportunity cost of capital. Therefore, both are profitable. But Project N is better since it has a higher NPV. The IRR rule, however, indicates that we should choose Project M as it has a higher IRR. If we choose Project N, following the NPV rule, we shall be richer by an additional value of Rs 20. Should we have the satisfaction of earning a higher rate of return, or should we like to be richer? The NPV rule is consistent with the objective of maximising wealth. When we have to choose between mutually exclusive projects, the easiest procedure is to compare the NPVs of the projects and choose the one with the larger NPV.

Incremental approach It is argued that the IRR method can still be used to choose between mutually exclusive projects if we adapt it to calculate rate of return on the incremental cash flows. If we prefer Project N to Project M, there should be *incremental benefits* in doing so. To see this, let us calculate the incremental flows of Project N over Project M. We obtain the following cash flows:

Project	Cash Flows (Rs)				NPV at 9%	IRR
	C_0	C_1	C_2	C_3		
$(N - M)$	0	$-1,260$	140	1,370	20	10%

The IRR on the incremental flows is 10 per cent. It is more than the opportunity cost of 9 per cent. Therefore, Project N should be accepted. Project N is better than Project M despite its lower IRR because it offers all benefits that Project M offers *plus* the opportunity of an incremental investment at 10 per cent—a rate higher than the required rate of return of 9 per cent. It may be noticed that the NPV of the incremental flows is the difference of the NPV of Project N over that of Project M; this is so because of the value-additivity principle.

The incremental approach is a satisfactory way of salvaging the IRR rule. But the series of incremental cash flows may result in negative and positive cash flows (i.e., lending and borrowing type pattern). This would result in multiple rates of return and ultimately the NPV method will have to be used.

Some people find it difficult to appreciate that the IRR rule can mislead.[1] Let us, for instance, assume that we are considering two mutually exclusive Projects M and N, and we are also contemplating an investment opportunity, say Project O, to occur after one year. Project O has the following cash follows:

Project	Cash Flows (Rs)				NPV at 9%	IRR
	C_0	C_1	C_2	C_3		
O	0	$-1,400$	700	948	37	11%

We have established so far that Project N is better than Project M, since it adds more wealth. Still some may argue in favour of Project M. Their reasoning could be that if we accept Project M today, we would also be able to undertake Project O next year that can be financed out of the cash flows generated by Project M in the first year. This reasoning implies a capital shortage next year to undertake Project O if Project M is rejected. In the absence of capital constraint, Project N is definitely better (NPV is higher) than Project M, and Project O can also be accepted next year by raising Rs 1,260 at a rate equal to the cost of capital. It is very unlikely that the large companies would face capital constraint. However, some companies do impose **capital rationing** on their divisions for control purposes. Such impositions are thought to be real constraints by management people at the lower levels. Even if there is a capital constraint, real or self-imposed, the IRR rule cannot be used for ranking projects. The problem under capital rationing is to determine the portfolio of projects, which have the largest net present value satisfying such portfolio. We shall show later on that this problem can be handled through the programming techniques.

---

1. Brealey and Myers, *op. cit.*, pp. 75–77.

Scale of investment Another condition under which the NPV and IRR methods will give contradictory ranking to the projects, is when the cash outlays are of different sizes. Let us consider Projects A and B, involving following cash flows:

Projects	Cash Flow (Rs)		NPV at 10%	IRR
	C_0	C_1		
A	– 1,000	1,500	364	50%
B	– 100,000	120,000	9,091	20%

Project A's NPV at 10 per cent required rate of return of Rs 364 and IRR is 50 per cent. Project B's NPV at 10 per cent required rate of return is Rs 9,091 and internal rate of return is 20 per cent. Thus, the two projects are ranked differently by the NPV and IRR rules.

As we have explained earlier, the NPV method gives unambiguous results. Since the NPV of Project B is high, it should be accepted. The same result will be obtained if we calculate the internal rate of return on the incremental investment:

Project	Cash Flow (Rs)		NPV at 10%	IRR
	C_0	C_1		
(A–B)	– 99,000	118,500	8,727	19.7%

The incremental investment of Rs 99,000 (i.e., Rs 100,000 – Rs 1,000) will generate cash inflow of Rs 118,500 after a year. Thus, the return on the incremental investment is 19.7 per cent, which is in excess of the 10 per cent required rate of return. We should, therefore, prefer Project B to Project A.

Project life span Difference in the life spans of two mutually exclusive projects can also give rise to the conflict between the NPV and IRR rules. To illustrate, let us consider two mutually exclusive Projects, X and Y, of significantly different expected lives:

Projects	Cash Flows (Rs)						NPV at 10%	IRR
	C_0	C_1	C_2	C_3	C_4	C_5		
X	– 10,000	12,000	—	—	—	—	909	20%
Y	– 10,000	0	0	0	0	20,120	2,493	15%

Both the projects require initial cash outlays of Rs 10,000 each. Project X generates a cash flow of Rs 12,000 at the end of one year, while Project Y generated cash flow of Rs 20,120 at the end of fifth year. At 10 per cent required rate of return, Project X's net present value is Rs 908 and internal rate of return is 20 per cent, while Project Y's net present value is Rs 2,495 and internal rate of return is 15 per cent. Thus, the two methods rank the projects differently. The NPV rule can be used to choose between the projects since it is always consistent with the wealth maximisation principle. Thus, Project Y should be preferred since it has higher NPV. The problem of choosing between the short and long-lived assets, which have to be replaced in future, is discussed later on.

REINVESTMENT ASSUMPTION AND MODIFIED INTERNAL RATE OF RETURN (MIRR)

The NPV and IRR rules are sometimes assumed to rest on an underlying *implicit* assumption about reinvestment of the cash flows generated during the lifetime of the project. It is contented that the source of conflict between the two techniques lies in their different **implicit reinvestment rates**.[1] The IRR method is assumed to imply that the cash flows generated by the project can be reinvested at its internal rate of return, whereas the NPV method is thought to assume that the cash flows are reinvested at the opportunity cost of capital. Advocates of the reinvestment assumption calculate **terminal values** of project to prove their point. For example, consider the following projects:

Projects X and Y are equally attractive if the IRR method is used. The terminal value of Project Y is Rs 200. X should also have a terminal value of Rs 200 to have same IRR as Y. Following the IRR method, the terminal value of X would be Rs 200 *only* when its cash flows are assumed to be reinvested at its IRR of 20 per cent. For example, Rs $100 (1 + 20)^2$ + Rs 56 = Rs 200. Given the initial value (Rs 115.74) and terminal value (Rs 200), the compound average annual return should be equal to IRR as shown below:

Projects	Cash Flows (Rs)				NPV at 10%	IRR
	C_0	C_1	C_2	C_3		
X	– 115.74	100	0	56	17.24	20%
Y	– 115.74	0	0	200	34.52	20%

$$\sqrt[3]{\frac{200}{115.74}} - 1 = 0.20 \text{ or } 20\%$$

Some people argue that it is more realistic to use the opportunity cost of capital as the reinvestment rate. If we use 10 per cent as the reinvestment rate, X's terminal value will be Rs 177. Now Project X's compound average annual return would be:

$$\sqrt[3]{\frac{177}{115.74}} - 1 \approx 0.15 \text{ or } 15\%$$

This is a modified internal rate of return. The **modified internal rate of return** (MIRR) is the compound average annual rate that is calculated with a reinvestment rate different than the project's IRR. You can use the Excel function to calculate the MIRR. The Excel built-in function is: MIRR (Values, Finance_Rate Reinvest_Rate), where Values represent the range of cash flows, Finance_Rate is the opportunity cost of capital (the required rate of return) and Reinvest_Rate is the reinvestment rate.

---

1. See Rangarajan, C. and Mampilly, Paul, Net Present Value Versus Internal Rate of Return, *Economic and Political Weekly*, Nov. 27, 1971, pp. M-153–56; and Gupta, L.C., A Comment, *Economic and Political Weekly*, Feb. 27, 1972, and "Further Comment", May 6, 1972.

You may notice that when we use 10 per cent – the opportunity cost of capital – as the reinvestment rate, we get X's terminal value less by Rs 23 than the Project Y's terminal value. The present value of Rs 23 at 10 per cent is equal to the difference between the net present values of Projects X and Y (Rs 34.52 – Rs 17.24) = Rs 23 × 0.751 = Rs 17.28.

Is reinvestment assumption logical? All do not accept the implicit reinvestment assumption vis-à-vis the IRR. They do not consider it valid. According to this view, the source of the implicit reinvestment assumption lies in the use of *compounding* the cash flows to the terminal date of a project, instead of the use of *discounting* to the starting date. Taking the above given example of Project X, let us see whether the IRR and NPV calculations depend in any way on the reinvestment assumption:[1]

Project X	Rs
Initial investment	115.74
Add: 20% return on investment	23.15
	138.89
Less: Recovery in year 1	100.00
Outstanding investment at the beginning of year 2	38.89
Add: 20% return on outstanding investment	7.78
	46.67
Less: Recovery in year 2	nil
Outstanding investment in the beginning of year 3	46.67
Add: 20% return on outstanding investment	9.33
Outstanding investment	56.00
Less: Recovery in year 3	56.00
Balance	nil

Similar calculations can be made for Project Y. What is indicated by these calculations is that 20 per cent return is earned only on the *outstanding balance of investment*. The calculations of IRR and NPV are quite independent of the way in which cash flows are utilised. Let us, for example, consider in the case of Project X that Rs 115.74 is a loan made to a small firm by a bank. The loan is to be repaid Rs 100 after 1 year and Rs 56 after 3 years. This is an investment for the bank. If the bank does not reinvest the cash flows occurring on account of the loan repayment, can it be stated that the bank's return is not 20 per cent? No, the rate of return would still remain 20 per cent. The internal rate of return is a time-adjusted percentage of the principal amount outstanding, and it is independent of how cash flows are received and utilised. We would like to add here that we are not implying that the way in which cash flows are put to use will have no effect on the *overall* profitability of the organisation. What is emphasised is that the profitability of the *project under consideration currently* remains unaffected by such reinvestments of cash flows. We feel that the superficial aspects of the mathematics of the IRR rule should not be focussed at the cost of the economic interpretation of the project's cash flows. Economics provides the logical rationale; mathematics

is just a *tool* in financial decision-making.

The reason for the ranking-conflict between the IRR and NPV rules lies in the different timing of the projects' cash flows, rather than in the wrongly conceived reinvestment assumption. One can see in Figure 8.5 that NPV falls more rapidly in the case of Project N than Project M as the discount rate increases. This is so because the more distant flows from a project show a steeper fall in their present value, as compared to earlier flows, as the discount rate increases. Thus the slopes of the NPV curves for different projects will differ because of the difference in the time-patterns of their cash flows. In Figure 8.5, the ranking changes after the point of intersection of the NPV curves. The change in ranking has nothing to do with any assumptions about reinvestment of cash flows.

VARYING OPPORTUNITY COST OF CAPITAL

We have made a simple assumption that the opportunity cost of capital remains constant over times. This may not be true in reality. If the opportunity cost of capital varies over time, the use of the IRR rule creates problems, as there is not a unique benchmark opportunity cost of capital to compare with IRR.

There is no problem in using NPV method when the opportunity cost of capital varies over time. Each cash flow can be discounted by the relevant opportunity cost of capital as shown below:

$$\text{NPV} = \frac{C_1}{(1+k_1)} + \frac{C_2}{(1+k_2)} + \cdots + \frac{C_n}{(1+k_n)^n} - C_0 \quad (14)$$

It is clear that for each period there is a different opportunity cost of capital. With which of the several opportunity costs do we compare the IRR to accept or reject an investment project? We cannot compare IRR with any of these costs. To get a comparable opportunity cost of capital, we will have to, in fact, compute a weighted average of these opportunity costs, which is a tedious job. It is, however, much easier to calculate the NPV with several opportunity costs.

NPV VERSUS PI

The NPV method and PI yield same accept-or-reject rules, because PI can be greater than one only when the project's net present value is positive. In case of marginal projects, NPV will be zero and PI will be equal to one. But a conflict may arise between the two methods if a choice between mutually exclusive projects has to be made.[2] Consider the following illustration where the two methods give different ranking to the projects.

Illustration 8.8

	Project C	Project D
PV of cash inflows (Rs)	100,000	50,000
Initial cash outflow (Rs)	50,000	20,000
NPV (Rs)	50,000	30,000
PI	2.00	2.50

---

1. Gupta, *op. cit.*
2. Weston and Brigham, *op. cit.*

Project *C* should be accepted if we use the NPV method, but Project *D* is preferable according to the PI. Which method is better?

The NPV method should be preferred, except under capital rationing, because the net present value represents the net increase in the firm's wealth. In our illustration, Project *C* contributes all that Project *D* contributes plus additional net present value of Rs 20,000 (Rs 50,000 – Rs 30,000) at an incremental cost of Rs 50,000 (Rs 1,00,000 – Rs 50,000). As the net present value of Project *C*'s incremental outlay is positive, it should be accepted. Project *C* will also be acceptable if we calculate the incremental profitability index. This is shown as follows:

Because the incremental investment has a positive net present value, Rs 20,000 and a PI greater than one, Project *C* should be accepted.

If we consider a different situation where two mutually exclusive projects return Rs 100,000 each in terms of net present value and one project costs twice as much as another, the profitability index will obviously give a logical answer. The net present value method will indicate that both are equally desirable in absolute terms. However, the profitability index will evaluate these two projects relatively and will give correct answer. Between two mutually exclusive projects with same NPV, the one with lower initial cost (or higher PI) will be selected.

| | *Project C* | *Project D* | *Incremental Flow* |
	Rs	*Rs*	*Rs*
PV of cash inflows (Rs)	100,000	50,000	50,000
Initial cash outlay (Rs)	50,000	20,000	30,000
NPV (Rs)	50,000	30,000	20,000
PI	100,000/50,000 = 2.0	50,000/20,000 = 2.5	50,000/30,000 = 1.67

SUMMARY

❖ Investments involve cash flows. Profitability of an investment project is determined by evaluating its cash flows.

❖ NPV, IRR and PI are the discounted cash flow (DCF) criteria for appraising the worth of an investment project.

❖ The net present value (NPV) method is a process of calculating the present value of the project's cash flows, using the opportunity cost of capital as the discount rate, and finding out the net present value by subtracting the initial investment from the present value of cash flows.

❖ Under the NPV method, the investment project is accepted if its net present value is positive (NPV > 0). The market value of the firm's share is expected to increase by the project's positive NPV. Between the mutually exclusive projects, the one with the highest NPV will be chosen.

❖ The internal rate of return (IRR) is that discount rate at which the project's net present value is zero. Under the IRR rule, the project will be accepted when its internal rate of return is higher than the opportunity cost of capital (IRR > k).

❖ Both IRR and NPV methods account for the time value of money and are generally consistent with the wealth maximisation objective. They give same accept-reject results in case of conventional independent projects.

❖ Under a number of situations, the IRR rule can give a misleading signal for mutually exclusive projects. The IRR rule also yields multiple rates of return for non-conventional projects and fails to work under varying cost of capital conditions. Since the IRR violates the value-additivity principle; since it may fail to maximise wealth under certain conditions; and since it is cumbersome, the use of the NPV rule is recommended.

❖ Profitability index (PI) is the ratio of the present value of cash inflows to initial cash outlay. It is a variation of the NPV rule. PI specifies that the project should be accepted when it has a profitability index greater than one (PI > 1.0) since this implies a positive NPV.

❖ A conflict of ranking can arise between the NPV and PI rules in case of mutually exclusive projects. Under such a situation, the NPV rule should be preferred since it is consistent with the wealth maximisation principle.

❖ In practice, two other methods have found favour with the business executives. They are the payback (PB) and accounting rate of return (ARR) methods.

❖ PB is the number of years required to recoup the initial cash outlay of an investment project. The project would be accepted if its payback is less than the standard payback. The greatest limitations of this method are that it does not consider the time value of money, and does not consider cash flows after the payback period.

❖ The discounted payback considers the time value of money, but like the simple payback it also ignores cash flows after the payback period. Under the conditions of constant cash flows and a long life of the project, the reciprocal of payback can be a good approximation of the project's rate of return.

❖ ARR is found out by dividing the average net operating profit after-tax by the average amount of investment. A project is accepted if its ARR is greater than a cut off rate (arbitrarily selected). This method is based on accounting flows rather than cash flows; therefore, it does not account for the time value of money. Like PB, it is also not consistent with the objective of the shareholders' wealth maximisation.

❖ Table 8.6 provides a summary of the features of various investment criteria.

Table 8.6: Summaries of Investment Criteria

I.   Discounted Cash Flow Methods

1. *Net present value (NPV):* The difference between PV of cash flows and PV of cash outflows is equal to NPV; the firm's opportunity cost of capital being the discount rate.

$$\text{NPV} = \left[\frac{C_1}{(1+k)} + \frac{C_2}{(1+k)^2} + \frac{C_3}{(1+k)^3} + \cdots + \frac{C_n}{(1+k)^n} \right] - C_0$$

$$\text{NPV} = \sum_{t=1}^{n} \frac{C_t}{(1+k)^t} - C_0$$

Acceptance rule
- Accept if NPV > 0 (i.e., NPV is positive)
- Reject if NPV < 0 (i.e., NPV is negative)
- Project may be accepted if NPV = 0

Merits	*Demerits*
• Considers all cash flows	• Requires estimates of cash flows which is a tedious task
• True measure of profitability	• Requires computation of the opportunity cost of capital which poses practical difficulties
• Based on the concept of the time	• Sensitive to discount rates value of money
• Satisfies the value-additivity principle (i.e., NPV's of two or more projects can be added)	
• Consistent with the shareholders' wealth maximisation (SWM) principle.	

2. *Internal rate of return (IRR):* The discount rate which equates the present value of an investment's cash inflows and outflows is its internal rate of return.

$$\left[\frac{C_1}{(1+r)} + \frac{C_2}{(1+r)^2} + \frac{C_3}{(1+r)^3} + \cdots + \frac{C_n}{(1+r)^n}\right] = C_0$$

$$NPV = \sum_{t=1}^{n} \frac{C_t}{(1+r)^t} - C_0 = 0$$

Acceptance rule

- Accept if IRR > k
- Reject if IRR < k
- Project may be accepted if IRR = k

Merits	*Demerits*
• Considers all cash flows	• Requires estimates of cash flows which is a tedious task
• True measure of profitability	• Does not hold the value additivity principle (i.e., IRRs of two or more projects do not add)
• Based on the concept of the time value of money	• At times fails to indicate correct choice between mutually exclusive projects
• Generally, consistent with wealth maximisation principle	• At times yields multiple rates
	• Relatively difficult to compute

3. *Profitability index (PI):* The ratio of the present value of the cash flows to the initial outlay is profitability index or benefit-cost ratio:

$$PI = \frac{PV \text{ of Annual Cash Flows}}{\text{Initial Investment}}$$

$$PI = \frac{\sum_{t=1}^{n} \frac{C_t}{(1+k)^t}}{C_0}$$

Acceptance rule

- Accept if PI > 1.0
- Reject if PI < 1.0
- Project may be accepted if PI = 1.0

Merits	*Demerits*
• Considers all cash flows	• Requires estimates of the cash flows which is a tedious task
• Recognises the time value of money	• At times fails to indicate correct choice between mutually exclusive projects
• Relative measure of profitability	
• Generally consistent with the wealth maximisation principle	

II. Non-Discounted Cash Flow Criteria

4. *Payback (PB):* The number of years required to recover the initial outlay of the investment is called payback.

$$PB = \frac{\text{Initial Investment}}{\text{Annual Cash Flow}} = \frac{C_0}{C}$$

Acceptance rule

- Accept if PB < standard payback
- Reject if PB > standard payback

Merits	*Demerits*
• Easy to understand and compute and inexpensive to use	• Ignores the time value of money
• Emphasises liquidity	• Ignores cash flows occurring after the payback period
• Easy and crude way to cope with risk	• Not a measure of profitability
• Uses cash flows information	• No objective way to determine the standard payback
	• No relation with the wealth maximisation principle

5. *Discount payback:* The number of years required in recovering the cash outlay on the present value basis is the discounted payable period. Except using discounted cash flows in calculating payback, this method has all the demerits of payback method.

6. *Accounting rate of return (ARR):* An average rate of return found by dividing the average net operating profit [EBIT (1 – T)] by the average investment.

$$ARR = \frac{\text{Average Net Operating Profit after Tax}}{\text{Average Investment}}$$

Acceptance rule

- Accept if ARR > minimum rate
- Reject if ARR < minimum rate

Merits	*Demerits*
• Uses accounting data with which executives are familiar	• Ignores the time value of money
• Easy to understand and calculate	• Does not use cash flows
• Gives more weightage to future receipts	• No objective way to determine the minimum acceptable rate of return

Conclusion: Net present value (NPV) method is the most superior investment criterion as it is always consistent with the wealth maximisation principle.

KEY CONCEPTS

Accounting rate of return	Expansion	Marginal investment	Payable reciprocal
Benefit-cost ratio	Fisher's intersection	Modernisation	Profitability index
Borrowing-type projects	Hurdle rate	Multiple rates of return	Reinvestment rate
Capital rationing	Incremental approach	Mutually exclusive	Replacement decisions
Contingent investments	Independent investments	investments	Return on investment
Cost-reduction investments	Internal rate of return	Net present value	Revenue-expansion
Cut-off rate	Investment yield	Non-conventional	investments
Discounted payback	Lending-type projects	investments	Time-adjusted rate of return
Diversification	Marginal efficiency of capital	Opportunity cost of capital	Value-additivity principle

---

ILLUSTRATIVE SOLVED PROBLEMS

Problem 8.1: A company is considering the following investment projects:

		Cash Flows (Rs)		
Projects	C_0	C_1	C_2	C_3
A	– 10,000	+ 10,000		
B	– 10,000	+ 7,500	+ 7,500	
C	– 10,000	+ 2,000	+ 4,000	+ 12,000
D	– 10,000	+ 10,000	+ 3,000	+ 3,000

(a) Rank the project according to each of the following methods: (i) Payback, (ii) ARR, (iii) IRR and (iv) NPV, assuming discount rates of 10 and 30 per cent.

(b) Assuming the projects are independent, which one should be accepted? If the projects are mutually exclusive, which project is the best?

Solution:

(a) (i) **Payback**

Project A : 10,000/10,000 = 1 yr.
Project B : 10,000/7,500 = $1\frac{1}{3}$ yrs.

Project C : $2 \text{ yrs} + \dfrac{10,000 - 6,000}{12,000} = 2\frac{1}{3}$ yrs.

Project D : 1 yr.

(ii) **ARR**

Project A : $\dfrac{(10,000 - 10,000)1/2}{(10,000)1/2} = 0$

Project B : $\dfrac{(15,000 - 10,000)1/2}{(10,000)1/2} = \dfrac{2,500}{5,000} = 50\%$

Project C : $\dfrac{(18,000 - 10,000)1/3}{(10,000)1/2} = \dfrac{2,667}{5,000} = 53\%$

Project D : $\dfrac{(16,000 - 10,000)1/3}{(10,000)1/2} = \dfrac{2,000}{5,000} = 40\%$

Note: The net cash proceeds include recovery of investment also. Therefore, net cash earnings are found by deducting initial investment.

(iii) **IRR**

Project A: The net cash proceeds in year 1 are just equal to investment. Therefore, $r = 0\%$.

Project B: This project produces an annuity of Rs 7,500 for two years. Therefore, the required PVAF is: 10,000/7,500 = 1.33. Looking in Table D across 2 year row, this factor is found under 32% column. Therefore, $r = 32\%$.

Project C: Since cash flows are uneven, the trial and error method will have to be followed. Let us try 20% rate of discount. The NPV is + Rs 1,389. A higher rate should be tried. At 30% rate of discount, the NPV is – Rs 633. The true rate of return should be less than 30%. At 27% rate of discount we find that the NPV is – Rs 86 and at 26% + Rs 105. Through interpolation, we find $r = 26.5\%$.

Project D: In this case also we use the trial and error method, and find that at 37.6% rate of discoutnt NPV becomes almost zero. Therefore, $r = 37.6\%$.

(iv) **NPV**

Project A :
at 10% $-10,000 + 10,000 \times 0.909 = -910$
at 30% $-10,000 + 10,000 \times 0.769 = -2,310$

Project B :
at 10% $-10,000 + 7,500 (0.909 + 0.826) = +3,013$
at 30% $-10,000 + 7,500 (0.769 + 0.592) = +208$

Project C :
at 10% $-10,000 + 2,000 \times 0.909 + 4,000 \times 0.826 + 12,000 \times 0.751 = +4,134$
at 30% $-10,000 + 2,000 \times 0.769 + 4,000 \times 0.592 + 12,000 \times 0.455 = -633$

Project D :
at 10% $-10,000 + 10,000 \times 0.909 + 3,000 \times (0.826 + 0.751) = +3,821$
at 30% $-10,000 + 10,000 \times 0.769 + 3,000 \times (0.592 + 0.4555) = +831$

The projects are ranked as follows according to the various methods:

				Ranks	
Project	PB	ARR	IRR	NPV-10%	NPV-30%
A	1	4	4	4	4
B	2	2	2	3	2
C	3	1	3	1	3
D	1	3	1	2	1

(b) Payback and ARR are theoretically unsound methods for choosing between the investment projects. Between the two time-adjusted (DCF) investment criteria, NPV and IRR, NPV gives consistent results. If the projects are independent (and there is no capital rationing), either IRR or NPV can be used since the same set of projects will be accepted by any of the methods. In the present case, except Project A all the three projects should be accepted if the discount rate is 10%. Only Projects B and D should be undertaken if the discount rate is 30%.

If we assume that the projects are mutually exclusive, then under the assumption of 30% discount rate, the choice is between B and D (A and C are unprofitable). Both criteria IRR and NPV give the same results—D is the best. Under the assumption of 10% discount rate, rankings according to IRR and NPV conflict (except for Project A). If we follow the IRR rule, Project D should be accepted. But the NPV rule tells that Project C is the best. The NPV rule generally gives consistent results in conformity with the wealth maximisation principle. We would, therefore, accept Project C following the NPV rule.

Problem 8.2: The cash flows of Projects C and D in Problem 8.1 are reproduced below:

		Cash Flows (Rs)			NPV	
Projects	C_0	C_1	C_2	C_3	at 10%	IRR
C	– 10,000	+ 2,000	+ 4,000	+ 12,000	+ 4,134	26.5%
D	– 10,000	+ 10,000	+ 3,000	+ 3,000	+ 3,821	37.6%

(a) Why is there a conflict of rankings?

(b) Why should you recommend Project C in spite of a lower rate of return?

Solution: (a) Suppose the discount rate as 0, 10, 15, 30 and 40 per cent. The NPV for each of the projects is given below:

Discount	NPV (Rs)	
Rate (%)	C	D
0	8,000	6,000
10	4,134	3,821
15	2,660	2,942
30	– 634	831
40	– 2,164	– 238

It is noticeable that for Project C, the larger cash flows occur later in its life. At the lower discount rates, Project C's NPV will

be higher than that of Project D. As discount rates start increasing, Project C's NPV will, however, fall at a faster rate simply because its largest cash flows come late in life when the compounding effects of timings are most significant. Till the discount rate reaches 12.5%, Project C has higher NPV than Project D. After this break-even discount rate, Project D has higher NPV as well as higher IRR. Thus the rankings of the projects have differed because of the difference in time-patterns of cash flows.

(b) If the opportunity cost of capital is 10%, Project C should be undertaken because the firm will be richer by additional Rs 313 (i.e., Rs 4,134 – Rs 3,821). This can be better appreciated if we calculate the profitability of the incremental investment (C – D).

		Cash Flows (Rs)			NPV	
Project	C_0	C_1	C_2	C_3	at 10%	IRR
C – D	0	– 8,000	+ 1,000	+ 9,000	+ 313	12.5%

The incremental Project C– D involves an outlay of Rs 8,000 in year 1 and produces cash inflows Rs 1,000 and Rs 9,000 in years 2 and 3. At 10% opportunity cost of capital, the NPV is positive, Rs 313. The IRR is 12.5%. What does this imply? It implies that Project C has all the benefits of Project D as well as gives additional wealth.

Problem 8.3: An investment project has two internal rates of return, 20 and 50 per cent. The investment's NPV at 30 per cent discount rate is + Rs 1,000. Would the project be acceptable if the discount rate is: (a) 40 per cent, (b) 10 per cent, and (c) 60 per cent. Draw NPV graph to justify your answer.

Solution: The investment in question has features of both lending and borrowing. It can be seen from the graph that NPV is positive *if* discount rate lies within 20 per cent and 50 per cent range. Therefore, the investment should be accepted at 40 per cent discount rate ($\therefore$ NPV > 0) and rejected at 10 and 60 per cent ($\therefore$ NPV < 0).

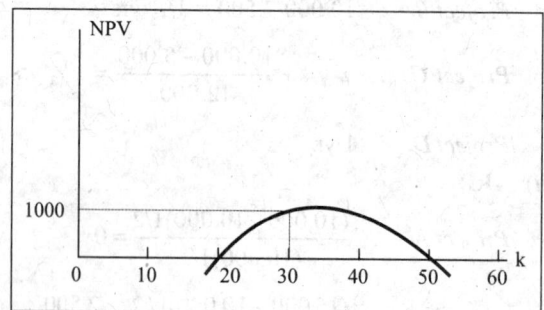

Problem 8.4: A company is considering an investment proposal, involving an initial cash outlay of Rs 45 lakh. The proposal has an expected life of 7 years and zero salvage value. At a required rate of return of 12 per cent, the proposal has a profitability index of 1.182. Calculate the annual cash inflows.

Solution:
$$PI = \frac{\sum_{t=1}^{7} \dfrac{A}{(1+0.12)^t}}{45} = 1.182$$

$$A \times 4,564 = 45 \times 1.182$$

$$A = 53.19 / 4.564 = Rs\, 11.65\, lakh$$

Problem 8.5: Equipment A has a cost of Rs 75,000 and net cash flow of Rs 20,000 per year for six years. A substitute equipment *B* would cost Rs 50,000 and generate net cash flow of Rs 14,000 per year for six years. The required rate of return of both equipments is 11 per cent. Calculate the IRR and NPV for the equipments. Which equipment should be accepted and why?

Solution:

Equipment A:

$$NPV = 20,000 \times PVAF_{6,0.11} - 75,000$$
$$= 20,000 \times 4.231 - 75,000$$
$$= 84,620 - 75,000 = Rs\,9,620$$
$$IRR = 20,000 \times PVAF_{6,r} = 75,000$$
$$PVAF_{6,r} = 75,000/20,000 = 3.75$$

From the present value of an annuity table, we find:

$$PVAF_{6,0.15} = 3.784$$
$$PVAF_{6,0.16} = 3.685$$

Therefore,

$$IRR = r = 0.15 + 0.01 \left[\frac{3.784 - 3.75}{3.784 - 3.685} \right]$$
$$= 0.15 + 0.0034 = 0.1534 \text{ or } 15.34\%$$

Equipment B:

$$NPV = 14,000 \times PVAF_{6,0.11} - 50,000$$
$$= 14,000 \times 4.231 - 50,000$$
$$= 59,234 - 50,000 = Rs\,9,234$$
$$IRR = 14,000 \times PVAF_{6,r} = 75,000$$
$$PVAF_{6,r} = 3.571$$

From the present value of an annuity table, we find:

$$PVAF_{6,0.17} = 3.589$$
$$PVAF_{6,0.18} = 3.498$$

Therefore,

$$IRR = r = 0.17 + 0.01 \left[\frac{3.589 - 3.571}{3.589 - 3.498} \right]$$
$$= 0.17 + 0.002 = 0.172 \text{ or } 17.20\%$$

Equipment *A* has a higher NPV but lower IRR as compared with equipment *B*. Therefore equipment *A* should be preferred since the wealth of the shareholders will be maximised.

REVIEW QUESTIONS

1. What is capital budgeting? Why is it significant for a firm?
2. Despite its weaknesses, the payback period method is popular in practice? What are the reasons for its popularity?
3. How do you calculate the accounting rate of return? What are its limitations?
4. Explain the merits and demerits of the time-adjusted methods of evaluating the investment projects.
5. What is meant by the term value of money? Which capital budgeting methods take into consideration this concept? How is it possible for the capital budgeting methods that do not consider the time value of money to lead to wrong capital budgeting decisions?
6. Under what circumstances do the net present value and internal rate of return methods differ? Which method would you prefer and why?
7. What are the mutually exclusive projects? Explain the conditions when conflicting ranking would be given by the internal rate of return and net present value methods to such projects.
8. What is profitability index? Which is a superior ranking criterion, profitability index or the net present value?
9. Under what conditions would the internal rate of return be a reciprocal of the payback period?
10. "The payback reciprocal has wide applicability as a meaningful approximation of the time adjusted rate of return. But it suffers from certain major limitations." Explain.
11. Comment on the following statements:
    (a) "We use payback primarily as a method of coping with risk."
    (b) "The virtue of the IRR rule is that it does not require the computation of the required rate of return."
    (c) "The average accounting rate of return fails to give weight to the later cash flows."
12. "Discounted payback ensures that you don't accept an investment with negative NPV, but it can't stop you from rejecting projects with a positive NPV." Illustrate why this can happen.

PROBLEMS

1. The following are the net cash flows of an investment project:

Cash Flows (Rs)		
C_0	C_1	C_2
– 5,400	+ 3,600	+ 14,400

Calculate the net present value of the project at discount rates of 0, 10, 40, 50 and 100 per cent.

2. A machine will cost Rs 100,000 and will provide annual net cash inflow of Rs 30,000 for six years. The cost of capital is 15 per cent. Calculate the machine's net present value and the internal rate of return. Should the machine be purchased?

3. A project costs Rs 81,000 and is expected to generate net cash inflow of Rs 40,000, Rs 35,000 and Rs 30,000 over its life of 3 years. Calculate the internal rate of return of the project.

4. The G.K. Company is evaluating a project with following cash inflows:

Cash Flows (Rs)				
C_1	C_2	C_3	C_4	C_5
1,000	800	600	400	200

The cost of capital is 12 per cent. What is the maximum amount the company should pay for the machine?

5. Consider the following three investments:

	Cash Flows (Rs)		
Projects	C_0	C_1	C_2
X	−2,500	0	+3,305
Y	−2,500	+1,540	+1,540
Z	−2,500	+2,875	0

The discount rate is 12 per cent. Compute the net present value and the rate of return for each project.

6. You want to buy a 285 litre refrigerator for Rs 10,000 on an instalment basis. A distributor is prepared to sell the refrigerator on instalments. He states that the payments will be made in four years, interest rate being 12 per cent. The annual payments will be as follows:

	Rs
Principal	10,000
Four year of interest at 12%, i.e., Rs 10,000 × 0.12 × 4	4,800
	14,800
Annual payments (Rs 14,800 ÷ 4)	3,700

What rate of return is the distributor earning? If your opportunity cost of capital is 14 per cent will you accept the offer? Why?

7. Compute the rate of return of the following projects:

	Cash Flows (Rs)			
Projects	C_0	C_1	C_2	C_3
X	−20,000	+8,326	+8,326	+8,326
Q	−20,000	0	0	+24,978

Which project would you recommend? Why?

8. A firm is considering the following two mutually exclusive investments:

	Cash Flows (Rs)			
Projects	C_0	C_1	C_2	C_3
A	−25,000	+5,000	+5,000	+25,640
B	−28,000	+12,672	+12,672	+12,672

The cost of capital is 12 per cent. Compute the NPV and IRR for each project. Which project should be undertaken? Why?

9. You have an opportunity cost of capital of 15 per cent. Will you accept the following investment?

Cash Flows (Rs)	
C_0	C_1
+50,000	−56,000

10. Is the following investment desirable if the opportunity cost of capital is 10 per cent:

Cash Flows (Rs)				
C_0	C_1	C_2	C_3	C_4
+100,000	−33,625	−33,625	−33,625	−33,625

11. Consider the following two mutually exclusive investments:

	Cash Flows (Rs)			
Projects	C_0	C_1	C_2	C_3
A	−10,000	+2,000	+4,000	+11,784
B	−10,000	+10,000	+3,000	+2,830

(a) Calculate the NPV for each project assuming discount rates of 0, 5, 10, 20, 30 and 40 per cent; (b) draw the NPV graph for the projects to determine their IRR, (c) show calculations of IRR for each project confirming results in (b). Also, state which project would you recommend and why?

12. For Projects X and Y, the following cash flows are given:

	Cash Flows (Rs)			
Projects	C_0	C_1	C_2	C_3
X	−750	+350	+350	+159
Y	−750	+250	+250	+460

(a) Calculate the NPV of each project for discount rates 0, 5, 8, 10, 12 and 20 per cent. Plot these on an PV graph.
(b) Read the IRR for each project from the graph in (a).
(c) When and why should Project X be accepted?
(d) Compute the NPV of the incremental investment (Y − X) for discount rates, 0, 5, 8, 10, 12 and 20 per cent. Plot them on graph. Show under what circumstances would you accept X?

13. The following are two mutually exclusive projects.

	Cash Flows (Rs)				
Projects	C_0	C_1	C_2	C_3	C_4
I	−25,000	+30,000			
II	−25,000	0	0	0	43,750

Assume a 10 per cent opportunity cost of capital. Compute the NPV and IRR for each project. Comment on the results.

14. Consider the following projects:

Cash Flows (Rs)

Projects	C_0	C_1	C_2	C_3	C_4
A	– 1,000	+ 600	+ 200	+ 200	+ 1,000
B	– 1,000	+ 200	+ 200	+ 600	+ 1,000
C	– 300	+ 100	+ 100	+ 100	+ 600
D	– 300	0	0	+ 300	+ 600

(a) Calculate the payback period for each project.

(b) If the standard payback period is 2 years, which project will you select? Will your answer be different if the standard payback is 3 years?

(c) If the cost of capital is 10 per cent, compute the discounted payback for each project? Which projects will you recommend if the standard payback is (i) 2 years; (ii) 3 years?

(d) Compute the NPV of each project? Which projects will you recommend?

15. A machine will cost Rs 10,000. It is expected to provide profits before depreciation of Rs 3,000 each in years 1 and 2 and Rs 4,000 each in years 3 and 4. Assuming a straight-line depreciation and no taxes, what is the average accounting rate of return? What will be your answer if the tax rate is 35 per cent?

16. A firm has the following information about a project:

Income Statement (Rs ' 000)

	C_1	C_2	C_3
Cash revenue	16	14	12
Cash expenses	8	7	6
Gross profit	8	7	6
Depreciation	4	4	4
Net profit	4	3	2

The initial investment of the project is estimated as Rs 12,000.

(a) Calculate the project's accounting rate of return.

(b) If it is found that the initial investment will be Rs 9,000 and cash expenses will be more by Rs 1,000 each year,

what will be the project's accounting rate of return. Also, calculate the project's NPV if the cost of capital is 9 per cent.

17. An investment project has the following cash flows:

Cash Flows (Rs)

C_0	C_1	C_2
– 150	+ 450	– 300

What are the rates of return of the investment? Assume a discount rate of 10 per cent. Is the investment acceptable?

18. A firm is considering the following project:

Cash Flows (Rs)

C_0	C_1	C_2	C_3	C_4	C_5
– 50,000	+ 11,300	+ 12,769	+ 14,429	+ 16,305	+ 18,421

(a) Calculate the NPV for the project if the cost of capital is 10 per cent. What is the project's IRR?

(b) Recompute the project's NPV assuming a cost of capital of 10 per cent for C_1 and C_2, of 12 per cent for C_3 and C_4, and 13 per cent for C_5. Should the project be accepted? Can the internal rate of return method be used for accepting or rejecting the project under these conditions of changing cost of capital over time? Why or why not?

19. A finance executive has calculated the profitability index for a new proposal to be 1.12. The proposal's initial cash outlay is Rs 500,000. Find out the proposal's annual cash inflow if it has a life of 5 years and the required rate of return is 8 per cent.

20. Project P has the following cash flows:

Cash Flows (Rs)

C_0	C_1	C_2
– 800	+ 1,200	– 400

Calculate the project's IRRs. If the required rate of return is 25 per cent, would you accept the project. Why?

CASES

Case 8.1: G.S. Petropull Company (GSPC)[1]

GSPC is a fast growing profitable company. The company is situated in Western India. Its sales are expected to grow about three times from Rs 360 million in 2003-04 to Rs 1,100 million in 2004-05. The company is considering of commissioning a 35 km pipeline between two areas to carry gas to a state electricity board. The project will cost Rs 250 million. The pipeline will have a capacity of 2.5 MMSCM. The company will enter into a contract with the state electricity board (SEB) to supply gas. The revenue from the sale to SEB is expected to be Rs 120 million per annum. The pipeline will also be used for transportation of LNG to other users in the area. This is expected to bring additional revenue of Rs 80 million per annum. The company management considers the useful life of the pipeline

---

1. The case is based on published newspaper information. The data and names have been disguished to maintain confidentiality.

to be 20 years. The financial manager estimates cash profit to sales ratio of 20 per cent per annum for the first 12 years of the projects operations and 17 per cent per annum for the remaining life of the project. The project has no salvage value. The project being in a backward area is exempt from paying any taxes. The company requires a rate of return of 15 per cent from the project.

Discussion Questions

1. What is the project's payback and return on investment (ROI)?
2. Compute project's NPV and IRR.
3. Should the project be accepted? Why?

Case 8.2: Calmex Company Ltd.

Calmex is situated in North India. It specializes in manufacturing overhead water tanks. The management of Calmex has identified a niche market in certain Southern cities that need a particular size of water tank, not currently manufactured by the company. The company is therefore thinking of producing a new type of overhead water tank. The survey of the company's marketing department reveals that the company could sell 1,20,000 tanks each year for six years at a price of Rs 1,500 each. The company's current facilities cannot be used to manufacture the new-size tanks. Therefore, it will have to buy new machinery. A manufacturer has offered two options to the company. The first option is that the company could buy four small machines with the capacity of manufacturing 30,000 tanks each at Rs 115 million each. The machine operation and manufacturing cost of each tank will be Rs 535. Alternatively, Calmex can buy a larger machine with a capacity of 120,000 units per annum for Rs 500 million. The machine operation and manufacturing costs of each tank will be Rs 450. The company has a required rate of return of 12 per cent. Assume that the company does not pay any taxes.

Discussion Questions

1. Which option should the company accept? Use the most suitable method of evaluation to give your recommendation and explicitly state your assumptions.
2. Why do you think that the method chosen by you is the most suitable method in evaluating the proposed investment? Give the computation of the alternative methods.

CHAPTER 9

The Cost of Capital

CHAPTER OBJECTIVES

- Explain the general concept of opportunity cost of capital
- Distinguish between the project cost of capital and the firm's cost of capital
- Learn about the methods of calculating component cost of capital and the weighted average cost of capital
- Recognise the need for calculating cost of capital for divisions
- Understand the methodology of determining the divisional beta and divisional cost of capital
- Illustrate the cost of capital calculation for a real company

INTRODUCTION

We have emphasised in Chapter 8 that the use of the DCF techniques for evaluating an investment project requires two basic inputs: (1) the estimates of the project's cash flows and (2) the discount rate. In our discussions of the investment decisions so far we have assumed that the discount rate is known. In this chapter, we focus on the concept of the cost of capital as a discount rate and the procedure of its measurement.

The opportunity cost of capital (or simply, the cost of capital) for a project is the **discount rate** for discounting its cash flows. The **project's cost of capital** is the minimum required rate of return on funds committed to the project, which depends on the riskiness of its cash flows. Since the investment projects undertaken by a firm may differ in risk, each one of them will have its own unique cost of capital. It should be clear at the outset that the cost of capital for a project is defined by its risk, rather than the characteristics of the firm undertaking the project.

The firm represents the aggregate of investment projects undertaken by it. Therefore, **the firm's cost of capital** will be the overall, or average, required rate of return on the aggregate of investment projects. Thus the firm's cost of capital is not the same thing as the project's cost of capital. Can we use the firm's cost of capital for discounting the cash flows of an investment project? The firm's cost of capital can be used for discounting the cash flows of those investment projects, which have risk equivalent to the average risk of the firm. As a first step, however, the firm's cost of capital can be used as a standard for establishing the required rates of return of the individual investment projects. In the absence of a reliable formal procedure of calculating the cost of capital for projects, the firm's cost of capital can be adjusted upward or downward to account for risk differentials of investment projects. That is, an investment project's required rate of return may be equal to the firm's cost of capital plus or minus a risk adjustment factor depending on whether the project's risk is higher or lower than the firm's risk. There does exit a methodology to calculate the cost of capital for projects. The objective method of calculating the risk-adjusted cost of capital for projects is to use the capital asset pricing model (CAPM), as we show later in this chapter.

SIGNIFICANCE OF THE COST OF CAPITAL

We should recognise that the cost of capital is one of the most difficult and disputed topics in the finance theory. Financial experts express conflicting opinions as to the correct way in which the cost of capital can be measured. Irrespective of the measurement problems, it is a concept of vital importance in the financial decision-making. It is useful as a standard for:

- evaluating investment decisions,
- designing a firm's debt policy, and
- appraising the financial performance of top management.

Investment Evaluation

The primary purpose of measuring the cost of capital is its use as a financial standard for evaluating the investment projects. In the NPV method, an investment project is accepted if it has a positive NPV. The project's NPV is calculated by discounting its cash flows by the cost of capital. In this sense, the cost of capital is the discount rate used for evaluating the desirability of an investment project. In the IRR method, the investment project is accepted if it has an internal rate of return greater than the cost of capital. In this context, the cost of capital is the minimum required rate of return on an investment project. It is also known as the **cutoff rate**, or the **hurdle rate**.

An investment project that provides a positive NPV when its cash flows are discounted by the cost of capital makes a *net* contribution to the wealth of shareholders. If the project has zero NPV, it means that its cash flows have yielded a return just equal to the cost of capital, and the acceptance or rejection of the project will not affect the wealth of shareholders. The cost of capital is the minimum required rate of return on the investment project that keeps the present wealth of shareholders unchanged. It may be, thus, noted that the cost of capital represents a financial standard for allocating the firm's funds, supplied by owners and creditors, to the various investment projects in the most efficient manner.

Designing Debt Policy

The debt policy of a firm is significantly influenced by the cost consideration. As we shall learn later on, debt helps to save taxes, as interest on debt is a tax-deductible expense. The interest tax shield reduces the overall cost of capital, though it also increases the financial risk of the firm. In designing the financing policy, that is, the proportion of debt and equity in the capital structure, the firm aims at maximising the firm value by minimising the overall cost of capital.

The cost of capital can also be useful in deciding about the methods of financing at a point of time. For example, cost may be compared in choosing between leasing and borrowing. Of course, equally important considerations are control and risk.[1]

Performance Appraisal

The cost of capital framework can be used to evaluate the financial performance of top management.[2] Such an evaluation will involve a comparison of actual profitability of the investment projects undertaken by the firm with the projected overall cost of capital, and the appraisal of the actual costs incurred by management in raising the required funds.

The cost of capital also plays a useful role in dividend decision and investment in current assets. The chapters dealing with these decisions show their linkages with the cost of capital.

THE CONCEPT OF THE OPPORTUNITY COST OF CAPITAL

Decision-making is a process of choosing among alternatives. In the investment decisions, an individual or a manager encounters innumerable competing investment opportunities to choose from. For example, you may invest your savings of Rs 1,000 either in 7 per cent 3 year postal certificates or in 6.5 per cent 3 year fixed deposit in a nationalised bank. In both the cases, the government assures the payment; so the investment opportunities reflect equivalent risk. You decide to deposit your savings in the bank. By this action, you have foregone the opportunity of investing in the postal certificates. You have, thus, incurred an opportunity cost equal to the return on the foregone investment opportunity. It is 7 per cent in case of your investment. The opportunity cost is the rate of return foregone on the next best alternative investment opportunity of *comparable risk*. Thus, the required rate of return on an investment project is an opportunity cost.

Shareholders' Opportunities and Values

In the case of companies, there is a divorce between management and ownership. In an all-equity financed company, management makes investment decisions, but shareholders supply the capital. Therefore, a question may be raised: whose opportunity cost (or the required rate of return) should be considered in evaluating the investment projects? Since the firm's objective is to maximise the shareholders' wealth, the investment projects should be analysed in terms of their values to shareholders. To appreciate this point, suppose you are the owner-manager of a firm. You make the investment decisions and you supply funds to finance the investment projects. You will use your required rate of return to evaluate the investment projects. Your required rate of return will depend on investment opportunities of equivalent risk available to you in the financial markets. Thus the required rate of return (or the opportunity cost of capital) is market-determined rate.

Suppose you appoint a manager to manage your business. She has the responsibility for the investment decisions. Whose opportunity cost should the manager use? Since you are the supplier of funds and you own the firm and the manager is acting on your behalf, you will require her to use your required rate of return in making investment decisions. If she is unable to earn returns equal to your required rate of return, you can ask her to return the money to you, which you can invest in securities in the financial markets and earn the required rate of return.

Assume that you convert your firm into a joint-stock company where you invite other shareholders to contribute the capital and

1. Quirin, D.G., The Capital Expenditure Decision, Richard D. Irwin, 1967, p. 92.
2. Bhattacharya, S.K., A Cost-of-Capital Framework for Management Control, *Economic and Political Weekly*, Vol. 35, 29 August, 1970.

share ownership with them. Now many shareholders own the firm. The manager should consider *all* owners' (shareholders') required rate of return in evaluating the investment decisions. If the manager is unable to earn the rates on the investment projects, which the shareholders could themselves earn on alternative investment opportunities, they will be within their rights to ask for returning their funds. Thus, management acts as an agent of shareholders. It should evaluate investment opportunities using the shareholders' opportunity cost; that is, the rate the shareholders would use if they were themselves appraising the investment opportunities. Hence, *in an all-equity financed firm, the equity capital of ordinary shareholders is the only source to finance investment projects, the firm's cost of capital is equal to the opportunity cost of equity capital, which will depend only on the business risk of the firm.*

Creditors' Claims and Opportunities

In practice, both shareholders and creditors (debt-holders) supply funds to finance a firm's investment projects. Investors hold different claims on the firm's assets and cash flows, and thus, they are exposed to different degrees of risk. Creditors have a priority claim over the firm's assets and cash flows. The firm is under a legal obligation to pay interest and repay principal. Debt holders are, however, exposed to the risk of default. Since the firm's cash flows are uncertain, there is a probability that it may default on its obligation to pay interest and principal. Preference shareholders hold claim prior to ordinary shareholders but after debt holders. Preference dividend is fixed and known, and the firm will pay it *after* paying interest but before paying any ordinary dividend. Because preference dividend is subordinated to interest, preference capital is more risky than debt. Ordinary shareholders supply capital either in the form of retained earnings or by purchasing new shares. Unlike creditors, they are owners of the firm and retain its control. They delegate powers to management to make investment decisions on their behalf in such a way that their wealth is maximised. However, ordinary shareholders have claim on the residual assets and cash flows. The payment of ordinary dividend is discretionary. Ordinary shareholders may be paid dividends from cash remaining after interest and preference dividends have been paid. Also, the market price of ordinary share fluctuates more widely than that of the preference share and debt. Thus, ordinary share is more risky than both preference share and debt. Various forms of corporate debt can also be distinguished in terms of their differential riskiness. If we compare corporate bonds and government bonds, the later are less risky since it is very unlikely that the government will default in its obligation to pay interest and principal.

Risk Differences in Shareholders' and Creditors' Claims

Investors will require different rates of return on various securities since they have risk differences. Higher the risk of a security, the higher the rate of return demanded by investors. Since ordinary share is most risky, investors will require highest rate of return on their investment in ordinary shares. Preference share is more risky than debt; therefore, its required rate of return will be higher than that of debt. The risk-return relationship for various

securities is shown in Figure 9.1. It may be observed in the figure that the required rate of return of any security is composed of two rates—a risk-free rate and a risk-premium. A risk-free will require compensation for time value and its risk-premium will be zero. Government securities, such as the treasury bills and bonds, are examples of the risk-free securities. Investors expect higher rates of return on risky securities. The higher the risk of a security, the higher will be its risk-premium, and therefore, a higher required rate of return.

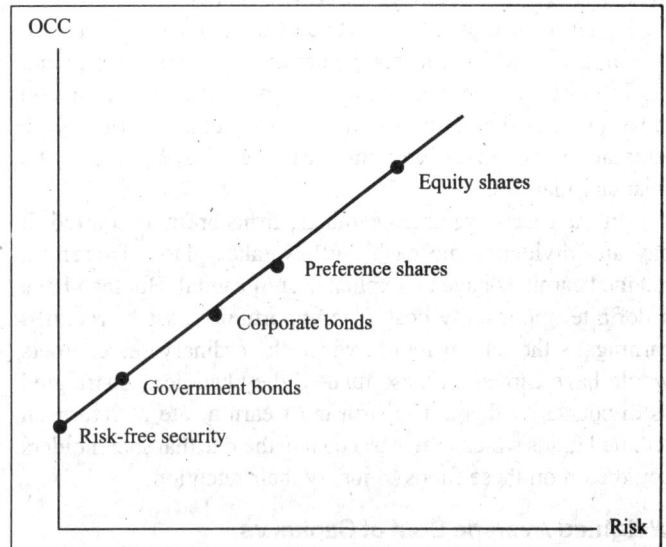

Figure 9.1: Risk-return relationships of various securities

Since the firm sells various securities to investors to raise capital for financing investment projects, it is, therefore, necessary that investment projects to be undertaken by the firm should generate *at least* sufficient net cash flow to pay investors—shareholders and debt holders—their required rates of return. In fact, investment projects should yield more cash flows than to just satisfy the investors' expectations in order to make a net contribution to the wealth of ordinary shareholders. *Viewed from all investors' point of view, the firm's cost of capital is the rate of return required by them for supplying capital for financing the firm's investment projects by purchasing various securities.* It may be emphasised that the rate of return required by all investors will be an *overall rate of return—a weighted rate of return.* Thus, the firm's cost of capital is the 'average' of the opportunity costs (or required rates of return) of various securities, which have claims on the firm's assets. This rate reflects both the business (operating) risk and the financial risk resulting from debt capital. Recall that the cost of capital of an all-equity financed firm is simply equal to the ordinary shareholders' required rate of return, which reflects only the business risk.

General Formula for the Opportunity Cost of Capital

How does a firm know about the required rates of return of investors? The required rates of return are *market-determined.* They are established in the capital markets by the actions of competing investors. The influence of market is direct in the case of new issue of ordinary and preference shares and debt. The market price of securities is a function of the return expected by investors. The demand and supply forces work in such a way that equilibrium rates are established for various securities. Thus, the opportunity cost of capital is given by the following formula:

$$I_0 = \frac{C_1}{(1+k)} + \frac{C_2}{(1+k)^2} + \cdots + \frac{C_n}{(1+k)^n} \qquad (1)$$

where I_0 is the capital supplied by investors in period 0 (it represents a net cash inflow to the firm), C_i are returns expected by investors (they represent cash outflows to the firm) and k is the required rate of return or the cost of capital.

In terms of Equation (1), the cost of capital is the internal rate of return, which equates the present values of inflows and outflows of a financial opportunity.[1] The outflows in Equation (1) represent the returns that investors could earn on the alternative investment opportunities of equivalent risk in the financial markets.

In the case of retained earnings, firms are not required to pay any dividends; no cash outflow takes place. Therefore, retained earnings have no explicit cost of capital. But they have a definite opportunity cost. The opportunity cost of retained earnings is the rate of return, which the ordinary shareholders would have earned on these funds if they had been distributed as dividends to them. The firm must earn a rate of return on retained funds which is at least equal to the rate that shareholders could earn on these funds to justify their retention.

Weighted Average Cost of Capital vs. Specific Costs of Capital

A firm obtains capital from various sources. As explained earlier, because of the risk differences and the contractual agreements between the firm and investors, the cost of capital of each source of capital differs. The cost of capital of each source of capital is known as **component**, or **specific**, **cost of capital**. The combined cost of *all* sources of capital is called *overall*, or *average, cost of capital*. The component costs are combined according to the weight of each component capital to obtain the average costs of capital. Thus, the overall cost is also called the **weighted average cost of capital** (WACC).

Suppose a firm has the cost of equity of 11 per cent and cost of debt of 6 per cent. In the beginning of the year, the firm considers Project *A*, which has an expected rate of return of 10 per cent. The firm decides to finance this project by debt. If the component cost of capital is used to evaluate Project *A*, the firm will accept it since its IRR (10 per cent) is greater than the component cost (6 per cent.). After some time, the company considers Project *B*, which has same risk as Project *A* and also has an expected rate of return of 10 per cent. The firm finds that Project *A* has exhausted borrowings capacity, and hence, it will have to raise equity funds to finance Project *B*. Using the component cost of capital as the cut-off rate, the firm will reject Project *B* since its expected rate of return (10 per cent) is less than the component cost (11 per cent). Thus, out of two projects that are economically identical, the firm accepts one and rejects another simply because it associates the method of financing

with the investment projects. What is wrong with this policy? It fails to consider the relationships between component costs. The various sources of capital are related to each other. The firm's decision to use debt in a given period reduces its future debt capacity as well as increases risk of shareholders. The shareholders will require a higher rate of return to compensate for the increased risk. Similarly, the firm's decision to use equity capital would enlarge its potential for borrowings in the future. Over the long run, the firm is expected to maintain a balance between debt and equity. The mix of debt and equity is called the firm's **capital structure**. Because of the connection between the sources of capital and the firm's desire to have a **target capital structure** in the long run, it is generally agreed that the cost of capital should be used in the composite, overall sense.[2] That is, in terms of the weighted average cost of capital.

The overall cost of capital is the weighted average cost of various sources of capital. For example, if the long-run proportions of debt and equity in the above mentioned example respectively are 60 per cent and 40 per cent, then the combined cost of capital is: $0.06 \times 0.60 + 0.11 \times 0.40 = 0.8$ or 8 per cent. Thus, both Projects *A* and *B* should be accepted since each of them is expected to yield a rate of return higher than the overall cost of capital. Accepting both Projects *A* and *B* will maximise the shareholders' wealth.

In practice, firms do not use the same debt-equity mix to finance their capital expenditures every year. They raise funds in "lumps". They may issue bonds at one time and at another time, they may either issue ordinary shares or may use retained earnings. The target capital structure is a policy decision. Firms may not hold the target capital structure in a particular year. But they maintain it in the long run. Therefore, in spite of "lumpy" financing by firms at different points in time, the overall cost of capital, rather than the component cost of capital, should be used in evaluating investment projects. It is not correct to associate a particular source of financing with a particular investment project.

Like the firm's WACC, we can also calculate the **project's WACC**. The debt capacity of the project may be different from the firm's overall debt capacity. Therefore, the capital structure of the project should be considered in calculating its WACC. In practice, financial managers for convenience may use the firm's capital structure to estimate the project's WACC.

You must remember that the relevant cost in the investment decisions is the **future cost** or the **marginal cost**. Marginal cost is the new or the incremental cost that the firm incurs if it were to raise capital now, or in the near future. The **historical cost** that was incurred in the past in raising capital is not relevant in financial decision-making. Historical costs may be significant to the extent that they help in predicting the future costs and in providing an evaluation of the past performance when compared with standard, or predetermined, costs.

DETERMINING COMPONENT COSTS OF CAPITAL

Generally, the component cost of a specific source of capital is equal to the investors' required rate of return, and it can be

---

1. Porterfield I.T.S., *Investment Decisions and Capital Costs*, Prentice-Hall, 1965, p. 45.
2. Barges, A., The Effect of Capital Structure and the Cost of Capital, Prentice-Hall, 1963, p. 2.

determined by using Equation (1). But the investors' required rate of return should be adjusted for taxes in practice for calculating the cost of a specific source of capital to the firm.[1] In the investment analysis, net cash flows are computed on an after-tax basis, therefore, the component costs, used to determine the discount rate, should also be expressed on an after-tax basis.

COST OF DEBT

A company may raise debt in a variety of ways. It may borrow funds from financial institutions or public either in the form of public deposits or debentures (bonds) for a specified period of time at a certain rate of interest. A debenture or bond may be issued at par or at a discount or premium as compared to its face value. The contractual rate of interest or the coupon rate forms the basis for calculating the cost of debt.

Debt Issued at Par

The before-tax cost of debt is the rate of return required by lenders. It is easy to compute before-tax cost of debt issued and to be redeemed at par; it is simply equal to the *contractual (or coupon rate) of interest*. For example, a company decides to sell a new issue of 7 year 15 per cent bonds of Rs 100 each at par. If the company realises the full face value of Rs 100 bond and will pay Rs 100 principal to bondholders at maturity, the before-tax cost of debt will simply be equal to the rate of interest of 15 per cent. Thus:

$$k_d = i = \frac{INT}{B_0} \qquad (2)$$

where k_d is the before-tax cost of debt, i is the coupon rate of interest, B_0 is the issue price of the bond (debt) and in Equation (2) it is assumed to be equal to the face value (F), and INT is the amount of interest. The amount of interest payable to the lender is always equal to:

Interest = Face value of debt × Interest rate

The before-tax cost of bond in the example is:

$$k_d = \frac{Rs\,15}{Rs\,100} = 0.15 \ \text{ or } \ 15\%$$

We could arrive at same results as above by using Equation (1): cash outflow are Rs 15 interest per year for 7 years and Rs 100 at the end of seventh year in exchange for Rs 100 now. Thus:

$$100 = \frac{15}{(1+k_d)} + \frac{15}{(1+k_d)^2} + \frac{15}{(1+k_d)^3} + \frac{15}{(1+k_d)^4}$$
$$+ \frac{15}{(1+k_d)^5} + \frac{15}{(1+k_d)^6} + \frac{15}{(1+k_d)^7} + \frac{100}{(1+k_d)^7}$$

$$100 = \sum_{t=1}^{n} \frac{15}{(1+k_d)^t} + \frac{100}{(1+k_d)^7}$$

$$100 = 15(PVFA_{7,k_d}) + 100(PVF_{7,k_d})$$

By trial and error, we find that the discount rate (k_d), which solves the equation, is 15 per cent:

$$100 = 15(4.160) + 100(0.376) = 62.40 + 37.60 = 100$$

Clearly, the before-tax cost of bond is the rate, which the investment should yield to meet the outflows to bondholders.

Debt Issued at Discount or Premium

Equations (1) and (2) will give identical results only when debt is issued at par and redeemed at par. Equation (1) can be rewritten as follows to compute the before-tax cost debt:

$$B_0 = \sum_{t=1}^{n} \frac{INT_t}{(1+k_d)^t} + \frac{B_n}{(1+k_d)^n} \qquad (3)$$

where B_n is the repayment of debt on maturity and other variables as defined earlier.[2] Equation (3) can be used to find out the cost of debt whether debt is issued at par or discount or premium, i.e., $B_0 = F$ or $B_0 > F$ or $B_0 < F$. Let us consider an example.

Illustration 9.1: Cost of a Bond Sold at Discount

Assume that in the preceding example of 7-year 15 per cent bonds, each bond is sold below par for Rs 94. Using Equation (3), k_d is calculated as:

$$94 = \sum_{t=1}^{7} \frac{15}{(1+k_d)^t} + \frac{100}{(1+k_d)^7}$$
$$94 = 15(PVFA_{7,k_d}) + 100(PVF_{7,k_d})$$

By trial and error, $k_d = 16.5$ per cent. Let us try 17%:

$$15(3.922) + 100(0.333)$$
$$58.83 + 33.30 = 91.13 < 94$$

Since PV at 17% is less than the required PV (Rs 94), let us try 16%:

---

1. It is argued later in the chapter that flotation costs should not be incorporated in the computation of the cost of capital, rather they should be adjusted in the investment project's cash flows.
2. Financial institutions generally require principal to be amortised periodically. The issue of bond or debenture by a company may also provide for periodical amortisation. When principal is repaid each period instead of a lump sum at maturity, cash outflows each period will include interest and principal, and interest each period will be calculated on the outstanding principal. The following formula can be used to calculate the before-tax cost of debt in this situation:

$$B_0 = \sum_{t=1}^{n} \frac{INT_t + B_t}{(1+k_d)^t} \qquad (1A)$$

where INT_t and B_t are respectively the periodical payment of interest and principal.

$$= 15(4.038) + 100(0.354) = 60.57 + 35.40 = 95.97 > 94$$

The discount rate k_d should lie between $16 - 17\%$. By interpolation, we find:

PV required	94.00
PV at 16%	95.97
PV at 17%	92.13

1.97

3.84

$$k_d = 16\% + (17\% - 16\%)\frac{1.97}{3.84} = 16.5\%$$

$k_d = 16.5$ per cent, Equation (3) is satisfied

$$94 = 15(3.980) + 100(0.343) = 59.70 + 34.30 = 94$$

If the discount or premium is adjusted for computing taxes, the following short-cut method can also be used to calculate the before-tax cost of debt:

$$k_d = \frac{INT + \frac{1}{n}(F - B_0)}{\frac{1}{2}(F + B_0)} \qquad (4)$$

Thus using data of Illustration 9.1, we obtain

$$k_d = \frac{15 + \frac{1}{7}(100 - 94)}{\frac{1}{2}(100 + 94)} = \frac{15.86}{97} = 0.164 \quad \text{or} \quad 16.4\%$$

Note that the short-cut method gives approximately the same result as Equation (3). The principal drawback of the method is that it does not consider the sinking fund payments or the annual compounding.[1]

It should be clear from the preceding discussion that the before-tax cost of bond to the firm is affected by the issue price. The lower the issue price, the higher will be the before-tax cost of debt. The highly successful companies may sell bond or debenture at a premium ($B_0 > F$); this will pull down the before-tax cost of debt.

Tax Adjustment

The interest paid on debt is tax deductible. The higher the interest charges, the lower will be the amount of tax payable by the firm. This implies that the government indirectly pays a part of the lender's required rate of return. As a result of the **interest tax shield**, the after-tax cost of debt to the firm will be substantially less than the investors' required rate of return. The before-tax cost of debt, k_d, should, therefore, be adjusted for the tax effect as follows:

$$\text{After-tax cost of debt} = k_d(1 - T) \qquad (5)$$

where T is the corporate tax rate. If the before-tax cost of bond in our example is 16.5 per cent, and the corporate tax rate is 35 per cent,[2] the after-tax cost of bond will be:

---

1. Quirin, *op. cit.*
2. Currently the corporate tax rate in India is 35 per cent.

$$k_d(1 - T) = 0.1650(1 - 0.35) = 0.1073 \quad \text{or} \quad 10.73\%$$

It should be noted that the tax benefit of interest deductibility would be available only when the firm is profitable and is paying taxes. An unprofitable firm is not required to pay any taxes. It would not gain any tax benefit associated with the payment of interest, and its true cost of debt is the before-tax cost.

It is important to remember that in the calculation of the average cost of capital, the after-tax cost of debt must be used, not the before-tax cost of debt.

Illustration 9.2: Cost of a Bond Sold at Discount and Redeemable at Premmium

A 7-year Rs 100 debenture of a firm can be sold for a net price of Rs 97.75. The rate of interest is 15 per cent per year, and bond will be redeemed at 5 per cent premium on maturity. The firm's tax rate is 35 per cent. Compute the after-tax cost of debenture.

The annual interest will be: $F \times i = $ Rs $100 \times 0.15 = $ Rs 15, and maturity price will be: Rs $100 (1.05) = $ Rs 105. We can use Equation (3) to compute the after-tax cost of debenture:

$$97.75 = \sum_{t=1}^{n} \frac{15}{(1 + k_d)} + \frac{105}{(1 + k_d)^7}$$

By trial and error, we find:

$$k_d = 16\%: \quad 15(4.038) + 105(0.354) = 97.75$$

The after-tax cost of debenture will be:

$$k_d(1 - T) = 0.16(1 - 0.35) = 0.104 \quad \text{or} \quad 10.4\%$$

Cost of the Existing Debt

Sometime a firm may like to compute the "current" cost of its existing debt. In such a case, the cost of debt should be approximated by the current market yield of the debt. Suppose that a firm has 11 per cent debentures of Rs 100,000 (Rs 100 face value) outstanding at 31 December 19X1 to be matured on December 31, 19X6. If a new issue of debentures could be sold at a net realisable price of Rs 80 in the beginning of 19X2, the cost of the existing debt, using short-cut method (Equation 4), will be

$$k_d = \frac{11 + 1/5(100 - 80)}{1/2(100 + 80)} = \frac{15}{90} = 0.167 \quad \text{or} \quad 16.7\%$$

If $T = 0.35$, the after-cost of debt will be:

$$k_d(1 - T) = 0.167(1 - 0.35) = 0.109 \quad \text{or} \quad 10.9\%$$

COST OF PREFERENCE CAPITAL

The measurement of the cost of preference capital poses some conceptual difficulty. In the case of debt, there is a binding legal obligation on the firm to pay interest, and the interest constitutes the basis to calculate the cost of debt. However, in the case of preference capital, payment of dividends is not legally binding on the firm and even if the dividends are paid, it is not a *charge* on earnings; rather it is a distribution or *appropriation* of earnings to preference shareholders. One may, therefore, be tempted to conclude that the dividends on preference capital do not constitute cost. This is not true.

The cost of preference capital is a function of the dividend *expected* by investors. Preference capital is never issued with an intention not to pay dividends. Although it is not legally binding upon the firm to pay dividends on preference capital, yet it is generally paid when the firm makes sufficient profits. The failure to pay dividends, although does not cause bankruptcy, yet it can be a serious matter from the ordinary shareholders' point of view. The non-payment of dividends on preference capital may result in voting rights and control to the preference shareholders. More than this, the firm's credit standing may be damaged. The accumulation of preference dividend arrears may adversely affect the prospects of ordinary shareholders for receiving any dividends, because dividends on preference capital represent a prior claim on profits. As a consequence, the firm may find difficulty in raising funds by issuing preference or equity shares. Also, the market value of the equity shares can be adversely affected if dividends are not paid to the preference shareholders and, therefore, to the equity shareholders. For these reasons, dividends on preference capital should be paid regularly except when the firm does not make profits, or it is in a very tight cash position.

Irredeemable Preference Share

The preference share may be treated as a perpetual security if it is irredeemable.[1] Thus, its cost is given by the following equation:

$$k_p = \frac{\text{PDIV}}{P_0} \quad (6)$$

where k_p is the cost of preference share, PDIV is the expected preference dividend, and P_0 is the issue price of preference share.

Illustration 9.3: Cost of Irredeemable Preference Share

A company issues 10 per cent irredeemable preference shares. The face value per share is Rs 100, but the issue price is Rs 95. What is the cost of a preference share? What is the cost if the issue price is Rs 105?

We can compute cost of a preference share as follows:

Issue price Rs 95:

$$k_p = \frac{\text{PDIV}}{P_0} = \frac{10}{95} = 0.1053 \text{ or } 10.53\%$$

Issue price Rs 105:

$$k_p = \frac{\text{PDIV}}{P_0} = \frac{10}{105} = 0.0952 \text{ or } 9.52\%$$

Redeemable Preference Share

Redeemable preference shares (that is, preference shares with finite maturity) are also issued in practice. A formula similar to Equation (3) can be used to compute the cost of redeemable preference share:

$$P_0 = \sum_{t=1}^{n} \frac{\text{PDIV}_t}{(1+k_p)^t} + \frac{P_n}{(1+k_p)^n} \quad (7)$$

The cost of preference share is not adjusted for taxes because preference dividend is paid after the corporate taxes have been paid. Preference dividends do not save any taxes.[2] Thus, the cost of preference share is automatically computed on an after-tax basis. Since interest is tax deductible and preference dividend is not, the after-tax cost of preference is substantially higher than the after-tax cost of debt.

COST OF EQUITY CAPITAL

Firms may raise equity capital internally by retaining earnings. Alternatively, they could distribute the entire earnings to equity shareholders and raise equity capital externally by issuing new shares. In both cases, shareholders are providing funds to the firms to finance their capital expenditures. Therefore, the equity shareholders' required rate of return would be the same whether they supply funds by purchasing new shares or by foregoing dividends, which could have been distributed to them. There is, however, a difference between retained earnings and issue of equity shares from the firm's point of view. The firm may have to issue new shares at a price lower than the current market price. Also, it may have to incur flotation costs. Thus, **external equity** will cost more to the firm than the **internal equity**.

Is Equity Capital Free of Cost?

It is sometimes argued that the equity capital is free of cost. The reason for such argument is that it is not legally binding for firms to pay dividends to ordinary shareholders. Further, unlike the interest rate or preference dividend rate, the equity dividend rate is not fixed. It is fallacious to assume equity capital to be free of cost. As we have discussed earlier, equity capital involves an *opportunity cost*; ordinary shareholders supply funds to the firm in the expectation of dividends and capital gains commensurate with their risk of investment. The market value of the shares determined by the demand and supply forces in a well functioning capital market reflects the return required by ordinary shareholders. Thus, the shareholders' required rate of return, which equates the present value of the expected dividends with the market value of the share, is the cost of equity. The cost of external equity would, however, be more than the shareholders' required rate of return if the issue price were different from the market price of the share.

In practice, it is a formidable task to measure the cost of equity. The difficulty derives from two factors: First, it is very difficult to estimate the expected dividends. Second, the future earnings and dividends are expected to grow over time. Growth in dividends should be estimated and incorporated in the computation of the cost of equity. The estimation of growth is not an easy task. Keeping these difficulties in mind, the methods of computing the cost of internal and external equity are discussed below.

1. In India, irredeemable preference shares can not be issued.
2. In fact, companies in India now will have to pay tax at 12.5 per cent on the amount of dividend distributed. Thus, the effective cost of preference capital to a company would be more than that shown by Equation (6) or (7). The same argument will be applicable to the equity capital.

Cost of Internal Equity: The Dividend-growth Model

A firm's internal equity consists of its retained earnings. The opportunity cost of the retained earnings is the rate of return foregone by equity shareholders. The shareholders generally expect dividend and capital gain from their investment. The required rate of return of shareholders can be determined from the dividend valuation model.[1]

Normal growth As explained in Chapter 8, the dividend-valuation model for a firm whose dividends are expected to grow at a constant rate of g is as follows:

$$P_0 = \frac{DIV_1}{k_e - g} \qquad (8)$$

where $DIV_1 = DIV_0(1 + g)$.

Equation (8) can be solved for calculating the cost of equity k_e as follows:

$$k_e = \frac{DIV_1}{P_0} + g \qquad (9)$$

The cost of equity is, thus, equal to the expected dividend yield (DIV_1/P_0) plus capital gain rate as reflected by expected growth in dividends (g). It may be noted that Equation (9) is based on the following assumptions:[2]

- The market price of the ordinary share, P_0, is a function of expected dividends.
- The dividend, DIV_1, is positive (i.e., $DIV_1 > 0$).
- The dividends grow at a constant growth rate g, and the growth rate is equal to the return on equity, ROE, times the retention ratio, b (i.e., $g = ROE \times b$).
- The dividend payout ratio [i.e., $(1 - b)$] is constant.

The cost of retained earnings determined by the dividend-valuation model implies that if the firm would have distributed earnings to shareholders, they could have invested it in the shares of the firm or in the shares of other firms of similar risk at the market price (P_0) to earn a rate of return equal to k_e. Thus, the firm should earn a return on retained funds equal to k_e to ensure growth of dividends and share price. If a return less than k_e is earned on retained earnings, the market price of the firm's share will fall. It may be emphasised again that the cost of retained earnings will be equal to the shareholders' required rate of return since no flotation costs are involved.

Illustration 9.4: Constant-Growth Model and the Cost of Equity

Suppose that the current market price of a company's share is Rs 90 and the expected dividend per share next year is Rs 4.50. If the dividends are expected to grow at a constant rate of 8 per cent, the shareholders' required rate of return is:

$$k_e = \frac{DIV_1}{P_0} + g$$

$$k_e = \frac{Rs\,4.50}{Rs\,90} + 0.08 = 0.05 + 0.08 = 0.13 \text{ or } 13\%$$

If the company intends to retain earnings, it should at least earn a return of 13 per cent on retained earnings to keep the current market price unchanged.

Supernormal growth A firm may pass through different phases of growth. Hence, dividends may grow at different rates in the future. The growth rate may be very high for a few years, and afterwards, it may become normal indefinitely in the future. The dividend-valuation model can also be used to calculate the cost of equity under different growth assumptions. For example, if the dividends are expected to grow at a super-normal growth rate, g_s, for n years and thereafter, at a normal, perpetual growth rate of, g_n, beginning in year $n + 1$, then the cost of equity can be determined by the following formula:

$$P_0 = \sum_{t=1}^{n} \frac{DIV_0(1 + g_s)^t}{(1 + k_e)^t} + \frac{P_n}{(1 + k_e)^n} \qquad (10)$$

P_n is the discounted value of the dividend stream, beginning in year $n + 1$ and growing at a constant, perpetual rate g_n, at the end of year n, and therefore it is equal to:

$$P_n = \frac{DIV_{n+1}}{k_e - g_n} \qquad (11)$$

When we multiply P_n by $1/(1 + k_e)^n$ we obtain the present value of P_n in year 0. Substituting Equation (11) in Equation (10), we get

$$P_0 = \sum_{t=1}^{n} \frac{DIV_0(1 + g_s)^t}{(1 + k_e)^t} + \frac{DIV_{n+1}}{k_e - g_n} \times \frac{1}{(1 + k_e)^n} \qquad (12)$$

The cost of equity, k_e, can be computed by solving Equation (12) by trial and error.

Illustration 9.5: Cost of Equity: Two-Stage Growth

Assume that a company's share is currently selling for Rs 134. Current dividends, DIV_0 are Rs 3.50 per share and are expected to grow at 15 per cent over the next 6 years and then at a rate of 8 per cent forever. The company's cost of equity can be found out as follows:

$$134 = \sum_{t=1}^{6} \frac{3.50(1.15)_t}{(1 + k_e)^t} + \frac{DIV_7}{(k_e - 0.08)} \times \frac{1}{(1 + k_e)^6}$$

$$= \frac{4.03}{(1 + k_e)} + \frac{4.63}{(1 + k_e)^2} + \frac{5.33}{(1 + k_e)^3}$$

$$+ \frac{6.13}{(1 + k_e)^4} + \frac{7.05}{(1 + k_e)^5} + \frac{8.11}{(1 + k_e)^6} + \frac{8.11(1.08)}{(k_e - 0.08)} \times \frac{1}{(1 + k_e)^6}$$

$$= 4.03(PV\,A_{1,k_e}) + 4.63(PV\,A_{2,k_e}) + 5.33(PV\,A_{3,k_e})$$

$$+ 6.13(PV\,A_{4,k_e}) + 7.05(PV\,A_{5,k_e}) + 8.11(PV\,A_{6,k_e})$$

$$+ \frac{8.76}{k_e - 0.08}(PV\,A_{6,k_e})$$

By trial and error, we find that $k_e = 0.12$ or 12 per cent:

---

1. The cost of equity can also be determined by using the capital asset pricing model. This is discussed in a later section.
2. Gordon, M., *The Investment, Financing and Valuation of the Corporation*, Richard D. Irwin, 1962.

$$134 = 4.03(0.893) + 4.63(00.797) + 5.33(0.712) + 6.13(0.636)$$

$$+ 7.05(0.567) + 8.11(0.507) + \frac{8.76}{0.12 - 0.08}(0.507)$$

Zero-growth In addition to its use in constant and variable growth situations, the dividend valuation model can also be used to estimate the cost of equity of no-growth companies. The cost of equity of a share on which a constant amount of dividend is expected perpetually is given as follows:

$$k_e = \frac{DIV_1}{P_0} \qquad (13)$$

The growth rate g will be zero if the firm does not retain any of its earnings; that is, the firm follows a policy of 100 per cent payout. Under such case, dividends will be equal to earnings, and therefore Equation (13) can also be written as:

$$k_e = \frac{DIV_1}{P_0} = \frac{EPS_1}{P_0} \quad \text{(since } g = 0) \qquad (14)$$

which implies that in a no-growth situation, the expected earnings–price (E/P) ratio may be used as the measure of the firm's cost of equity.

Cost of External Equity: The Dividend Growth Model

The firm's external equity consists of funds raised externally through public or rights issues. The minimum rate of return, which the equity shareholders require on funds supplied by them by purchasing new shares to prevent a decline in the existing market price of the equity share, is the cost of external equity. The firm can induce the existing or potential shareholders to purchase new shares when it promises to earn a rate of return equal to:

$$k_e = \frac{DIV_1}{P_0} + g$$

Thus, the shareholders' required rate of return from retained earnings and external equity is the same. The cost of external equity is, however, greater than the cost of internal equity for one reason. The selling price of the new shares may be less than the market price. In India, the new issues of ordinary shares are generally sold at a price less than the market price prevailing at the time of the announcement of the share issue. Thus, the formula for the cost of new issue of equity capital may be written as follows:

$$k_e = \frac{DIV_1}{P_I} + g \qquad (15)$$

where P_I is the issue price of new equity. The cost of retained earnings will be less than the cost of new issue of equity if $P_0 > P_I$.

Illustration 9.6: Cost of Internal and External Equity

The share of a company is currently selling for Rs 100. It wants to finance its capital expenditures of Rs 100 million either by retaining earnings or selling new shares. If the company sells new shares, the issue price will be Rs 95. The dividend per share next year, DIV_1, is Rs 4.75 and it is expected to grow at 6 per cent. Calculate (*i*) the cost of internal equity (retained earnings) and (*ii*) the cost of external equity (new issue of shares).

Equation (11) can be used to calculate the cost of internal equity:

$$k_e = \frac{Rs\ 4.75}{Rs\ 100} + 0.06 = 0.0475 + 0.06 = 0.1075 \text{ or } 10.75\%$$

The cost of external equity can be calculated as follow:

$$k_e = \frac{Rs\ 4.75}{Rs\ 95} + 0.06 = 0.05 + 0.06 = 0.11 \text{ or } 11\%$$

It is obvious that the cost of external equity is greater than the cost of internal equity because of the under-pricing (cost of external equity = 11% > cost of internal equity = 10.75%).

Earnings–Price Ratio and the Cost of Equity

As a general rule, it is not theoretically correct to use the ratio of earnings to price as a measure of the cost of equity. The earnings – price (E/P) ratio does not reflect the true expectations of the ordinary shareholders. For example, if the current market price of a share is Rs 500 (face value being Rs 100) and the earning per share is Rs 10, the E/P ratio will be: Rs 10 ÷ Rs 500 = 0.02 or 2 per cent. Does this mean that the expectation of shareholders is 2 per cent? They would, in fact, expect to receive a stream of dividends and a final price of the share that would result in a return significantly greater than the E/P ratio. Thus, the dividend valuation model gives the most of valid measure of the cost of equity.

There are exceptions, however. One exception that we have already pointed out is the no-growth firms. The cost of equity in the case of the no-growth firms is equal to the expected E/P ratio:

$$k_e = \frac{DIV_1}{P_0} + g$$

$$= \frac{EPS_1(1 - b)}{P_0} + br \qquad (\because g = br)$$

$$= \frac{EPS_1}{P_0} \qquad (\because b = 0)$$

where b is the earnings retention rate, EPS_1 is the expected earnings per share and r is the return investment (equity).

Another situation where the expected earnings-price ratio may be used as a measure of the cost of equity is *expansion*, rather than *growth* faced by the firm. A firm is said to be *expanding*, not growing, if the investment opportunities available to it are expected to earn a rate of return equal to the cost of equity.[1] For example, Equation (9) may be written as follows:

$$P_0 = \frac{EPS_1(1 - b)}{(k_e - rb)} \qquad (16)$$

If $r = k_e$, then

---

1. Solomon, E., *The Theory of Financial Management*, Columbia University Press, 1963, p. 64.

$$P_0 = \frac{EPS_1(1-b)}{(k_e - k_e b)} = \frac{EPS_1(1-b)}{k_e(1-b)} = \frac{EPS_1}{k_e}$$

and solving for k_e, we get

$$k_e = \frac{EPS_1}{P_0}$$

Illustration 9.7: Earnings-Price Ratio and the Cost of Equity

A firm is currently earning Rs 100,000 and its share is selling at a market price of Rs 80. The firm has 10,000 shares outstanding and has no debt. The earnings of the firm are expected to remain stable, and it has a payout ratio of 100 per cent. What is the cost of equity? If the firm's payout ratio is assumed to be 60 per cent and that it earns 15 per cent rate of return on its investment opportunities, then, what would be the firm's cost of equity?

In the first case since expected growth rate is zero, we can use expected earnings-price ratio to compute the cost of equity. Thus:

$$k_e = \frac{Rs\,10}{Rs\,80} = 0.125 \text{ or } 12.5\%$$

The earnings per share are Rs 100,000 ÷ 10,000 = Rs 10. If the firm pays out 60 per cent of its earnings, the dividends per share will be: Rs 10 × 0.6 = Rs 6, and the retention ratio will be 40 per cent. If the expected return on interval investment opportunities is 15 per cent, then the firm's expected growth is: 0.40 × 0.15 = 0.06 or 6 per cent. The firm's cost of equity will be:

$$k_e = \frac{Rs\,6}{Rs\,80} + 0.06 = 0.075 + 0.06 = 0.135 \text{ or } 13.5\%$$

COST OF EQUITY AND THE CAPITAL ASSET PRICING MODEL (CAPM)

You may recall from Chapter 6, that the CAPM provides an alternative approach for the calculation of the cost equity. As per the CAPM, the required rate of return on equity is given by the following relationship:

$$k_e = R_f + (R_m - R_f)\beta_j \qquad (17)$$

Equation (17) requires the following three parameters to estimate a firm's cost of equity:

- **The risk-free rate (R_f)** The yields on the government Treasury securities are used as the risk-free rate. You can use returns either on the short-term or the long-term Treasury securities. It is a common practice to use the return on the short-term Treasury bills as the risk-free rate. Since investments are long-term decisions, many analysts prefer to use yields on long-term government bonds as the risk-free rate. You should always use the current risk-free rate rather than the historical average.
- **The market risk premium ($R_m - R_f$)** The market risk premium is measured as the difference between the long-term, historical arithmetic averages of market return and the risk-free rate. Some people use a market risk premium based on returns of the most recent years. This is not a correct procedure since the possibility of measurement errors and variability in the short-term, recent data is high. As we explained in Chapter 4, the variability (standard deviation)

of the estimate of the market risk premium will reduce when you use long series of market returns and risk-free rates. We showed in Chapter 4, that the historical market risk premium on shares in India was about 9 per cent when we use return on the 91-day Treasury bills as the risk-free rate. If you use the current yield on 91-day Treasury bills as the risk-free rate, then the market risk premium should also be based on the historical average return of 91-day Treasury bills. On the other hand, if you use the current yield on 30-year government bonds as the risk-free rate, then the market risk premium should also be based on the historical average yield of 30-year government bonds. You should be consistent; you should match the estimation of the market risk premium with the maturity of the security used as the risk-free rate.

- **The beta of the firm's share (β)** Beta (β) is the systematic risk of an ordinary share in relation to the market. In Chapter 4, we have explained the regression methodology for calculating beta for an ordinary share. The share returns are regressed to the market returns to estimate beta. A broad-based index like the BSE's Sensitivity (Sensex) Index is used as a proxy for the market.

Suppose the risk-free rate is 6 per cent, the market risk premium is 9 per cent and beta of L&T's share is 1.54. The cost of equity for L&T is:

$$k_{L\&T} = 0.06 + 0.09 \times 1.54 = 0.1986 \approx 20\%$$

COST OF EQUITY: CAPM VS. DIVIDEND–GROWTH MODEL

The dividend-growth approach has limited application in practice because of its two assumptions. First, it assumes that the dividend per share will grow at a constant rate, g, forever. Second, the expected dividend growth rate, g, should be less than the cost of equity, k_e, to arrive at the simple growth formula. That is:

$$k_e = \frac{DIV_1}{P_0} + g$$

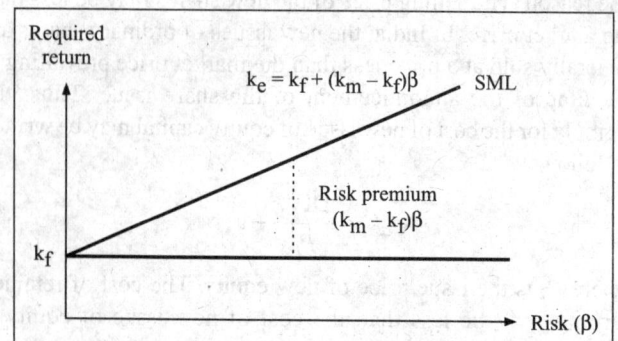

Figure 9.2: Cost of equity under CAPM

These assumptions imply that the dividend-growth approach cannot be applied to those companies, which are not paying any dividends, or whose dividend per share is growing at a rate higher than k_e, or whose dividend policies are highly volatile. The dividend–growth approach also fails to deal with risk directly. In contrast, the CAPM has a wider application although it is based on restrictive assumptions. The only condition for its use is that the company's share is quoted on the stock exchange. Also, all variables in the CAPM are market determined and except the company specific share price data, they are common to all companies. The value of beta is determined in an objective manner by using sound statistical methods. One practical problem with the use of beta, however, is that it does not probably remain stable over time.

THE WEIGHTED AVERAGE COST OF CAPITAL

Once the component costs have been calculated, they are multiplied by the proportions of the respective sources of capital to obtain the weighted average cost of capital (WACC). The proportions of capital must be based on target capital structure. WACC is the composite, or overall cost of capital. You may note that it is the weighted average concept, not the simple average, which is relevant in calculating the overall cost of capital. The simple average cost of capital is not appropriate to use because firms hardly use various sources of funds equally in the capital structure.

The following steps are involved for calculating the firm's WACC:

- Calculate the cost of specific sources of funds
- Multiply the cost of each source by its proportion in the capital structure.
- Add the weighted component costs to get the WACC.

In financial decision-making, the cost of capital should be calculated on an after-tax basis. Therefore, the component costs should be the after-tax costs. If we assume that a firm has only debt and equity in its capital structure, then the WACC (k_0) will be:

$$k_0 = k_d(1-T)w_d + k_e w_e$$
$$k_0 = k_d(1-T)\frac{D}{D+E} + k_e\frac{E}{D+E} \qquad (18)$$

where k_0 is the WACC, $k_d(1-T)$ and k_e are, respectively, the after-tax cost of debt and equity, D is the amount of debt and E is the amount of equity. In a general form, the formula for calculating WACC can be written as follows:

$$k_0 = k_1 w_1 + k_2 w_2 + k_3 w_3 + \cdots \qquad (19)$$

where $k_1, k_2, \ldots$ are component costs and $w_1, w_2, \ldots$ weights of various types of capital employed by the company.

Weighted marginal cost of capital (WMCC) Marginal cost is the new or the incremental cost of new capital (equity and debt) issued by the firm. We assume that new funds are raised at new costs according to the firm's target capital structure. Hence, what is commonly known as the WACC is in fact the weighted marginal cost of capital (WMCC); that is, the *weighted average cost of new capital given the firm's target capital structure*.

Book Value Versus Market Value Weights

You should always use the **market value weights** to calculate WACC. In practice, firms do use the book value weights. Generally, there will be difference between the book value and market value weights, and therefore, WACC will be different. WACC, calculated using the book-value weights, will be understated if the market value of the share is higher than the book value and *vice versa*.

Illustration 9.8: Weighted Average Cost of Capital

Lohia Chemicals Ltd has the following book value capital structure on 31 March, 2004:

Source of Finance	Amount (Rs '000)	Proportion (%)
Share capital	450,000	45
Reserves and surplus	150,000	15
Preference share capital	100,000	10
Debt	300,000	30
	1,000,000	100

The expected after-tax component costs of the various sources of finance for Lohia Chemicals Ltd are as follows:

Source	Cost (%)
Equity	18.0
Reserve and surplus	18.0
Preference share capital	11.0
Debt	8.0

The weighted average cost of capital of Lohia, based on the existing capital structure, is computed in Table 9.1.

Table 9.1: Computation of Weighted Average Cost of Capital

Source	Amount (Rs '000) (1)	Proportion (%) (2)	After-tax Cost (%) (3)	Weighted Cost (%) (4) (5) = (3) × (4)
Equity capital	450,000	45	18	8.1
Reserves & surplus	150,000	15	18	2.7
Preference capital	100,000	10	11	1.1
Debt	300,000	30	8	2.4
	1,000,000	100	WACC	14.3

Suppose Lohia Chemicals Ltd has 45,000,000 equity shares outstanding and that the current market price per share is Rs 20. Assume that the market values and the book values of debt and the preference share capital are the same. If the component costs were the same as before, the market value weighted average cost of capital would be about 15 per cent:

Table 9.2: Computation of Weighted Average Cost of Capital (Market-value Weights)

Amount Source	Proportion (Rs '000) (1)	After-tax (%) (2)	Weighted Cost (%) (3)	Cost (%) (4)	(5) = (3) × (4)
Equity capital	900,000	69.2	18	12.5	
Preference capital	100,000	7.7	11	0.8	
Debt	300,000	23.1	8	1.8	
	1,300,000	100	WACC	15.1	

It should be noticed that the equity capital for Lohia Chemicals Ltd. is the total market value of the ordinary shares outstanding, which includes retained earnings (reserves). It is obvious that the market value weighted cost of capital (15.1%) is higher than the book value weighted cost of capital (14.3%), because the market value of equity share capital (Rs 900,000,000) is higher than its book value (Rs 600,000,000).

Why do managers prefer the book value weights for calculating WACC? Besides the simplicity of the use, managers claim following advantages for the book value weights:

- Firms in practice set their target capital structure in terms of book values.
- The book value information can be easily derived from the published sources.
- The book value debt-equity ratios are analysed by investors to evaluate the risk of the firms in practice.

The use of the book-value weights can be seriously questioned on theoretical grounds. First, the component costs are opportunity rates and are determined in the capital markets. The weights should also be market-determined. Second, the book-value weights are based on arbitrary accounting policies that are used to calculate retained earnings and value of assets. Thus, they do not reflect economic values. It is very difficult to justify the use of the book-value weights in theory.

Market-value weights are theoretically superior to book-value weights. They reflect economic values and are not influenced by accounting policies. They are also consistent with the market-determined component costs. The difficulty in using market-value weights is that the market prices of securities fluctuate widely and frequently. A market value based target capital structure means that the amounts of debt and equity are continuously adjusted as the value of the firm changes.

FLOTATION COSTS, COST OF CAPITAL AND INVESTMENT ANALYSIS

A new issue of debt or shares will invariably involve **flotation costs** in the form of legal fees, administrative expenses, brokerage or underwriting commission. One approach is to adjust the flotation costs in the calculation of the cost of capital. Let us take an example to illustrate the point.

Suppose that a firm is considering an investment project, which involves a net cash outlay of Rs 450,000, and that it is expected to generate an annual net cash inflow of Rs 150,000 for 7 years. The project's target debt ratio is 50 per cent. The flotation costs of debt and share issues are estimated at 10 per cent of the amount raised. To finance the project, the firm will issue 7-year 15 per cent debentures of Rs 250,000 at par (Rs 100 face value), and new shares of Rs 250,000. The issue price of a share is Rs 20 and the expected dividend per share next year is Rs 1.80. Dividends are expected to grow at a compound rate of 7 per cent forever. Assume that corporate tax rate is 50 per cent. What is the NPV of the project?

The project's NPV can be calculated using WACC adjusted for flotation costs as the discount rate. Under this procedure, the before-tax cost of debt is given by the following equation:

$$B_0(1-f) = \sum_{t=1}^{n} \frac{\text{INT}_t + B_t}{(1+k_d)^t} \tag{20}$$

and the cost of equity as follows:

$$k_e = \frac{\text{DIV}_1}{P_0(1-f)} + g \tag{21}$$

where f is the fraction of flotation costs. Thus, the before-tax cost of debt in the example will be:

$$100(1-0.10) = \sum_{t=1}^{7} \frac{15}{(1+k_d)^t} + \frac{100}{(1+k_d)^7}$$

By trial and error, we find $k_d = 17.6$ per cent. If tax rate is 50 per cent, the after-tax cost of debt will be: 0.176 (1 − 0.50) = 0.088 or 8.8 per cent. The cost of equity will be as follows:

$$k_e = \frac{\text{Rs } 1.80}{\text{Rs } 20(1-0.1)} + 0.07 = 0.10 + 0.07 = 0.17 \text{ or } 17\%$$

The 'flotation-costs adjusted' weighted average cost of capital will be:

$$k_o = 0.088 \times 0.50 + 0.17 \times 0.50 = 0.13 \text{ or } 13\%$$

The NPV of the investment project using the discount rate of 13 per cent is

$$\text{NPV} = -450,000 + \sum_{t=1}^{7} \frac{150,000}{(1.13)^t}$$
$$= -450,000 + 150,000 \times 4,423 = \text{Rs } 213,450$$

This is not a correct procedure. Flotation costs are *not* annual costs; they are *one-time costs* incurred when the investment project is undertaken and financed. If the cost of capital is adjusted for the flotation costs and used as the discount rate, the effect of the flotation costs will be compounded over the life of the project.

---

1. Keene, Simon E., The Investment Discount Rate—In Defence of the Market Rate of Interest, *Accounting and Business Research* (Summer 1976); and Ezzell, John R. and Porter, R. Pourr, Floatation costs and the Weighted Average Cost of Capital, *Journal of Financial and Quantitative Analysis*, 11, (Sept. 1976). Also, refer Van Horne, *op. cit.*

Thus, the net present value of the investment project will be biased. The correct procedure is to adjust the investment project's cash flows for the flotation costs and use the weighted average cost of capital, unadjusted for the flotation costs, as the discount rate.[1] Since the flotation costs are incurred at the time the investment project is financed, they can be added to the project's initial cost. The flotation costs in the example are: 0.1 (2,50,000 + 2,50,000) = Rs 50,000. Thus, the net cash outlay of the project will be Rs 500,000. Since the component costs are *not* adjusted for flotation costs, the after-cost of debt will be: 0.15 (1 – 0.5) = 0.075 or 7.5 per cent and the cost of equity will be

$$k_e = \frac{\text{Rs } 1.80}{\text{Rs } 20} + 0.07 = 0.09 + 0.07 = 0.16 \text{ or } 16 \text{ per cent}$$

WACC, without the adjustment of floatation costs, will be

$$k_o = 0.075 \times 0.5 + 0.16 \times 0.5 = 0.12 \text{ or } 12\%$$

The NPV of the investment project will be:

$$\text{NPV} = -500,000 + \sum_{t=1}^{7} \frac{150,000}{(1.12)^t} = -500,000 + 150,000 \times 4.564$$

$$= \text{Rs } 184,600$$

The project's NPV in the example is overstated when we adjust flotation costs in computing the discount rate.

In some situations, it may not be possible to exactly apportion flotation costs to given projects, particularly when the firm raises large amount of capital for unidentified future investments.

CALCULATION OF THE COST OF CAPITAL IN PRACTICE: LARSEN & TOUBRO (L&T) LIMITED

The elegance of a theory lies in its practical application. The theory of measuring cost of capital is not simple. How can we estimate cost of capital in practice? We will use the data of L&T to calculate its cost of capital in the year 2002. L&T was founded in the year 1938. It is a large engineering company with diversified activities. L&T's main activities include dairy equipment, cement and cement equipment, steel, paper, nuclear power and space exploration, hydraulic excavators, switch gears, electronics controls, valves welding alloys, computer peripherals, test and measuring equipment etc. It has total sales of Rs 83,590 million, total gross assets of Rs 156,540 million and net profit of Rs 3,470 million in 2002. The capital structure of the company is given in Table 9.3.

Table 9.3: L&T's Capital Structure, 2001-02

Source of Capital	BV (Rs million)	BV Weights	MV (Rs million)	MV Weights
Short term debt	9,033.8	0.13	9,033.8	0.11
Long term debt	26,420.3	0.39	26,420.3	0.33
Debt	35,454.1	0.52	35,454.1	0.44
Equity	33,074.5	0.48	44,943.5	0.56
Total capital	68,528.6	1.00	80,397.6	1.00

Source: CMIE database.

Note: Equity excludes revaluation reserves

Table 9.4: L&T's Financial Data, 1993–2002

Year	EPS (Rs)	DPS (Rs)	BV (Rs)	MV (Rs)	ROE (%)	EY (%)	DY (%)	Payout (%)
Mar 93	5.64	3.50	64.46	287.50	8.75	2.30	1.43	62.06
Mar 94	9.17	4.00	69.12	240.00	13.27	3.19	1.39	43.62
Mar 95	12.09	5.00	89.74	268.75	13.47	5.04	2.08	41.36
Mar 96	13.44	6.00	110.62	262.00	12.15	5.00	2.23	44.64
Mar 97	16.55	6.00	122.80	253.00	13.48	6.32	2.29	36.25
Mar 98	21.39	6.50	135.88	230.00	15.74	8.45	2.57	30.39
Mar 99	18.94	6.50	147.41	211.25	12.85	8.23	2.83	34.32
Mar 00	13.74	6.50	153.83	397.73	8.93	6.50	3.08	47.31
Mar 01	8.85	6.50	155.10	232.08	5.71	2.23	1.63	73.45
Mar 02	16.51	7.00	163.56	201.28	10.06	7.11	3.02	42.40
Average	13.63	5.75	121.25	258.36	11.44	5.44	2.25	45.58

Source: CMIE database.

The market capitalization (the market value of equity) of L&T in March 2002 is Rs 44,943.5 million. The market value of debt is assumed to be equal to the book value.

Table 9.4 provides data on L&T's EPS, DPS, payout, market value, dividend yield, earnings yield, and ROE for the years 1993 to 2002.

Estimation of L&T's Cost of Equity

There are two approaches for calculating the cost of equity:
- the constant dividend – growth model
- the capital asset pricing model (CAPM)

Dividend–Growth Model The formula for calculating the cost of equity is as follows:

$$k_e = \frac{\text{DIV}_1}{P_0} + g$$

where the first term, DIV_1/P_0, is the expected dividend yield and the second term, g, is the expected (constant) growth in dividends. L&T's dividend yield in 2002 is 3.02 per cent. The dividend yield of the company has varied from 1.39 per cent to 3.08 per cent with an average yield of 2.25 per cent. We assume that the current dividend yield of 3.02 per cent is a fair approximation of L&T's *expected* yield.

Estimation of growth rate In practice, three methods may be used to estimate the growth rate:

(1) ***Internal growth*** Internal growth is the product of retention ratio and return on equity (ROE):

$$g = \text{Retention ratio} \times \text{ROE}$$

This approach may be used when the firm has a stable dividend policy. L&T's payout ratio has fluctuated over years. However, on an average, it has distributed about 45 per cent of its net profit and retained 55 per cent in the past decade. In the most recent year (2002), it retained about 58 per cent of its profit. The company's ROE in 2002 is 10.06 per cent and 10-year average is 11.44 per cent. Assuming that the current retention ratio of 58 per cent and ROE of 10.06 per cent will continue in the future, then L&T's dividend is expected to grow at 6.1 per cent per year:

$$g = \text{Retention ratio} \times \text{ROE} = 0.58 \times 0.106 = 0.061 \text{ or } 6.1\%$$

The constant growth model has its limitations. It is not applicable to those companies, which have highly unstable dividend policy (or retention ratio) and fluctuating ROE. One way to overcome this limitation is to estimate k_e for a large sample of companies of *equivalent risk* in the same industry and use the average k_e as an approximation of the cost of equity of the company under consideration. It is difficult to find similar companies like L&T. It is a diversified company but with a major presence in the engineering industry. One could calculate cost of equity of the industries where L&T has its operations and then, estimate the weighted average cost of equity using the proportion of L&T's investment in each business. In practice, this estimate of L&T's cost of equity may be relatively more reliable that the one based exclusively on its own data.

(2) Past average growth In practice, growth may be based on past EPS rather than DPS since companies do not change their DPS frequently with changes in EPS. Thus, DPS grows at a slower rate. The average of EPS past growth rates may be used as a proxy for the future growth. There are two alternatives available for calculating the average (1) the arithmetic average and (2) the geometric average. These two methods will give different estimates of the average growth rate. The geometric average will give a compounded average and is preferable when there is much variability in EPS data. Table 9.5 shows the calculation of the arithmetic average and the geometric average. The EPS growth in 1993 is calculated as: $g_1 = (\text{EPS}_{93} - \text{EPS}_{92}) \div \text{EPS}_{92}$. Growth for other years is calculated similarly. The arithmetic average growth (for 10-year period from 1993 to 2002) is found as follows:

$$\text{Arithmetic average} = \frac{g_1 + g_2 + \cdots + g_n}{n}$$

The geometric mean is calculated as follows:

$$\text{Geometric mean} = (1 + g_1) \times (1 + g_2) \times \cdots \times (1 + g_n)^{1/n} - 1$$

Table 9.5: EPS Growth of L&T, 1993–2002

Year	EPS	g_{EPS}	$(1 + g_{EPS})$
Mar-92	7.82	—	
Mar-93	5.64	− 0.279	0.721
Mar-94	9.17	0.626	1.626
Mar-95	12.09	0.318	1.318
Mar-96	13.44	0.112	1.112
Mar-97	16.55	0.231	1.231
Mar-98	21.39	0.292	1.292
Mar-99	18.94	− 0.115	0.885
Mar-00	13.74	− 0.275	0.725
Mar-01	8.85	− 0.356	0.644
Mar-02	16.51	0.866	1.866
Average			
Arithmetic		0.142	
Geometric			0.078

An alternative method for calculating the compounded growth rate is as follows:

$$\text{EPS}_n = \text{EPS}_0 (1 + g)^n$$

$$(1 + g)^n = \frac{\text{EPS}_n}{\text{EPS}_0}$$

$$g = \left[\frac{\text{EPS}_n}{\text{EPS}_0} \right]^{1/n} - 1 \tag{22}$$

$$g = \left[\frac{16.51}{7.82} \right]^{1/10} - 1 = 1.078 - 1 = 0.078 \text{ or } 7.8\%$$

(3) Regression approach for estimating growth Both the arithmetic average and the geometric average methods of calculating growth have limitations. Simple average gives equal weight to each year's earnings. Both techniques are quite inadequate to use when earnings are widely fluctuating. The regression technique estimates growth over time (t) incorporating all observations.

The linear regression model is as follows:

$$\text{EPS}_t = a + bt \tag{23}$$

The linear model indicates growth in terms of rupees, rather than in percentage terms.

We know that the following formula explains the compound growth in EPS (or any other variable):

$$\text{EPS}_t = \text{EPS}_0 (1 + g)^t \tag{24}$$

If we take the natural logarithm of EPS_t and EPS_0, Equation (24) can be written as follows:

$$\ln \text{EPS}_t = \ln \text{EPS}_0 + t \ln (1 + g) \tag{25}$$

where $\ln \text{EPS}_t$ is natural logarithm of EPS_t. The regression model can be written as follows:

$$\ln \text{EPS}_t = a + bt \tag{26}$$

where $a = \ln \text{EPS}_0$ and $b = \ln (1 + g)$. The slope of the regression line is $b = \ln (1 + g)$ and it is estimated as follows:

$$\ln (1 + g) = \frac{\sum_{t=1}^{n} (t - \bar{t}) \ln \text{EPS}_t}{\sum_{t=1}^{n} y_t^2} \tag{27}$$

where y_t is $t - \bar{t}$.

Using the data in Table 9.6, we obtain

$$\ln (1 + g) = \frac{5.6717}{82.50} = 0.0687$$

Taking antilog on both sides, we get

$$1 + g = 1.0712$$

$$g = 1.0712 - 1 = 0.0712 \text{ or } 7.12\%$$

Table 9.6: Long-linear Regression Growth Estimate for L&T

Year	t	$y = t - \bar{t}$	EPS	ln (EPS)	y ln (EPS)	y^2
1993	1	−4.50	5.64	1.7299	−7.7845	20.25
1994	2	−3.50	9.17	2.2159	−7.7558	12.25
1995	3	−2.50	12.09	2.4924	−6.2309	6.25
1996	4	−1.50	13.44	2.5982	−3.8974	2.25
1997	5	−0.50	16.55	2.8064	−1.4032	0.25
1998	6	0.50	21.39	3.0629	1.5315	0.25
1999	7	1.50	18.94	2.9413	4.4119	2.25
2000	8	2.50	13.74	2.6203	6.5508	6.25
2001	9	3.50	8.85	2.1804	7.6315	12.25
2002	10	4.50	16.51	2.8040	12.6178	20.25
Sum				25.4517	5.6717	82.50

The growth rate estimated according the different methods are summarised in Table 9.12. The growth rate estimated by log-linear model is the most appropriate since L&T's EPS are highly variable. Thus, for the calculation of the L&T's cost of equity, we shall assume that the future dividend rate will be the same as the current dividend yield (3.02%) is and that the future growth will be 7.1 per cent. According to the dividend – growth model, L&T's cost of equity will be as follows:

$$k_e = \frac{DIV_1}{P_0} + g$$

$$k_e = 3.02\% + 7.12\% = 10.14\%$$

Table 9.7: Estimate of Growth Rates and Cost of Equity

Method	Growth Rate (%)	Cost of Equity (%)
Internal growth	6.30	9.32
Arithmetic average	14.20	17.22
Geometric average	7.80	10.82
Log linear growth	7.12	10.14

For different growth rates, L&T's cost of equity is calculated in Table 9.7. It varies from 9.32 per cent to 17.22 per cent. The geometric average and the log-linear growth methods give almost the same estimates for the growth rate and the cost of capital, i.e., about 10–11 per cent, for L&T.

Capital Asset Pricing Model and L&T's Cost of Equity

A more objective alternative model for calculating L&T's cost of equity is the capital asset pricing model (CAPM). The use of CAPM requires the following information:

- the expected risk-free rate of return
- the expected risk premium
- beta of L&T's returns

Table 9.8: Market and L&T Monthly Returns, April 1997–March 2002

Month/Year	Market Return	L&T Return	Month/Year	Market Return	L&T Return	Month/Year	Market Return	L&T Return
Apr 97	0.0580	0.0536	Dec 98	0.0363	0.0411	Aug 00	0.0196	0.0172
May 97	−0.0098	−0.0262	Jan 99	0.0355	0.0664	Sep 00	−0.0393	−0.0898
Jun 97	0.0544	0.0590	Feb 99	0.0109	0.0094	Oct 00	−0.0423	−0.0486
Jul 97	0.0050	0.0432	Mar 99	0.0414	0.0880	Nov 00	0.0323	0.0876
Aug 97	−0.0457	−0.0784	Apr 99	−0.0510	−0.0971	Dec 00	−0.0028	0.0332
Sep 97	0.0029	−0.0010	May 99	0.0762	0.1162	Jan 01	0.0371	0.1049
Oct 97	−0.0111	−0.0759	Jun 99	0.0190	0.0688	Feb 01	−0.0081	0.0208
Nov 97	−0.0287	−0.0046	Jul 99	0.0402	0.0484	Mar 01	−0.0713	−0.0722
Dec 97	0.0119	0.0363	Aug 99	0.0328	0.0872	Apr 01	−0.0104	−0.0028
Jan 98	−0.0549	−0.0421	Sep 99	−0.0120	−0.0293	May 01	0.0137	0.0531
Feb 98	0.0505	0.0908	Oct 99	−0.0302	0.0365	Jun 01	−0.0215	−0.0534
Mar 98	0.0313	0.0298	Nov 99	0.0170	−0.0067	Jul 01	−0.0163	−0.0132
Apr 98	0.0125	0.0125	Dec 99	0.0346	0.1517	Aug 01	−0.0111	−0.0042
May 98	−0.0358	0.0098	Jan 00	0.0170	−0.1413	Sep 01	−0.0623	−0.1271
Jun 98	−0.0550	−0.0473	Feb 00	0.0197	−0.0544	Oct 01	0.0266	0.0226
Jul 98	−0.0053	−0.0446	Mar 00	−0.0371	−0.0907	Nov 01	0.0413	0.0923
Aug 98	−0.0392	−0.0767	Apr 00	−0.0309	−0.0904	Dec 01	−0.0033	−0.0303
Sep 98	0.0242	0.0258	May 00	−0.0214	−0.0918	Jan 02	0.0064	0.0059
Oct 98	−0.0426	−0.1046	Jun 00	0.0298	0.1157	Feb 02	0.0318	−0.0055
Nov 98	−0.0003	0.0042	Jul 00	−0.0452	−0.1002	Mar 02	0.0023	−0.0233

Source: The CMIE database.

Risk-free rate The risk-free rate is generally approximated by the highly liquid government security. The yield on 91-day T-bills in India in March 2002 is about 6 per cent. This rate could be used as a proxy for the risk-free rate.

Market premium The market premium is the excess of the expected market return over the expected risk-free rate of return. We can use the historical average over a very long period as a proxy for the market premium. There are no estimates of the market premium available in India. In Chapter 4 we showed that the average market premium over a period of 28 years was about 8–9 per cent. We will use 9 per cent as the market premium in our calculations.

L&T's beta We use 5-year monthly data for calculating L&T's beta. Table 9.8 contains monthly returns on market (Sensex) and L&T shares (from April 1997 to March 2002).

We can calculate L&T beta through the following regression equation:

$$R_{L\&T} = \alpha + \beta R_{Market} + \varepsilon$$

We use the regression analysis under the Tools wizard of the Excel to calculate L&T beta. Table 9.9 provides the beta coefficient and other regression statistics.

Table 9.9: Beta for L&T

Regression Statistics

	Alpha	*Beta*
Coefficient	– 0.0014	1.5439
t-stat.	– 0.2543	9.4639
P-value	0.8002	0.0000

Multiple *R*	0.7791
R Square	0.6070
Adjusted *R* Square	0.6002
Standard Error	0.0429
F-value	89.5650
P-value	0.0000
Observations	60

L&T's beta is 1.54. This implies that L&T has above average risk of the market. The correlation coefficient of 0.78 between the market returns and L&T's returns indicates high positive relationship. Given the risk-free rate of return of 6 per cent, risk premium of 9 per cent and beta of 1.54, the cost of equity of L&T is 20 per cent:

$$
\begin{aligned}
\text{L\&T's cost of equity} &= \text{Risk-free rate} + (\text{Market rate} \\
&\quad - \text{Risk-free rate}) \text{ L\&T's beta} \\
&= 0.06 + (0.09 \times 1.54) \\
&= .1986 \approx 0.20 \text{ or } 20\%
\end{aligned}
$$

The CAPM-based cost of equity for L&T (20%) is much higher than the estimates according to the dividend–growth model. CAPM is theoretically superior to the dividend–growth model. We shall use 20 per cent as L&T's cost of equity.

L&T's Cost of Debt

L&T has both short-term (mostly bank borrowing) and long-term debt in its capital structure. It also has current liabilities such as creditors. What is the cost of current liabilities? Should it be included in the computation of the weighted cost of capital? There is no unanimity on this issue. The majority view is that current liabilities do not involve any explicit cost, and therefore, should be excluded from the cost of capital calculation. An alternative view is that they involve implicit cost since creditors build it in the price of their products. How can we compute the implicit cost of current liabilities? Since they involve the same risk as bank borrowings, the before-tax cost of current liabilities can be treated as equal to the cost of bank borrowing. We have ignored current liabilities in the calculation of L&T's cost of capital.

In the year 2002, L&T has debt ratio of 52 per cent comprising 13 per cent short-term debt and 39 per cent long-term debt. This implies that of total debt, short-term debt is 25 per cent (13%/52%) and long-term debt 75 per cent (39%/52%). Over the last five years (from 1998 to 2002), there has been some increase in short-term debt and long-term debt and a decline in L&T's equity. The cost of the short-term debt was about 16 per cent and long-term debt about 14 per cent in 2002. We may assume that L&T will incur these costs in obtaining debt in the future as well. Further, we assume that L&T's short-term debt will continue to be 25 per cent of total debt and long-term debt 75 per cent, and that corporate tax rate will be approximately 35 per cent. The after-tax weighted cost of L&T's debt will be:

$$
\begin{aligned}
\text{After-tax weighted cost of debt} &= 0.16(1-0.35) \times 0.25 \\
&\quad + 0.14(1-0.35) \times 0.75 \\
&= 0.026 + 0.068 \\
&= 0.094 \text{ or approx. } 9.4\%
\end{aligned}
$$

L&T's Weighted Average Cost of Capital

We have estimated L&T's cost of equity and cost of debt. If we know L&T's *target capital structure*, we can estimate L&T's weighted average cost of capital. Theoretically, the target capital structure should be stated in terms of market value. However, target capital structure in practice may be expressed in terms of book value. Let us assume that L&T will maintain its current capital structure in the future. Its weighted average cost of capital will be as follows:

Source of Capital	*Cost of Capital*	*Weights*		*WACC*	
		Book Value	*Market Value*	*Book Value*	*Market Value*
Equity	0.200	0.48	0.56	0.096	0.112
Debt	0.094	0.52	0.44	0.049	0.041
Total				0.145	0.153

L&T's weighted average cost of capital is approximately 14.5 per cent at book value weights and 15.3 per cent at market value weights. Its market value weighted average cost of capital is slightly higher than the book value weighted average cost of capital since the market value of equity is more than the book value. *If L&T is considering an investment project of 'average risk' (that is, similar to L&T's risk) that has the same capital structure as the firm, then it can use 15 per cent as discount rate to compute the project's NPV.* L&T cannot use its WACC for evaluating those projects that have higher or lower risk than the firm.

DIVISIONAL AND PROJECT COST OF CAPITAL

We emphasise again that the required rate of return, or the cost of capital is a market determined rate and it reflects compensation to investors for the time value of money and risk of the investment project. It is, thus, composed of a risk-free rate (compensation for time) *plus* a risk-premium rate (compensation for risk). Investors are generally risk-averse, and demand a premium for bearing risk. The greater the risk of an investment opportunity, the greater the risk-premium required by investors. Therefore, the required rate of return of a division or a project depends on its risk. Since investors are risk-averse, divisions and projects with differing risks should be evaluated using their risk-adjusted required rates of return.

The firm's risk is composed of its overall operating risk and financial risk. **Operating risk** arises due to the uncertainty of cash flows of the firm's investments. **Financial risk** arises on account of the use of debt for financing investments. The firm's risk is also a composite risk of assets financed by the firm. Thus, the firm's cost of capital reflects the rate of return required on its securities commensurate with the perceived 'average' risk. The firm's cost of capital, therefore, cannot be used for evaluating individual divisions or investment projects that have different degree of risk. The firm's cost of capital as a required rate of return for all projects may work well in case of companies that have single line of business or where different businesses are highly correlated. In highly diversified, multiple-business firms like L&T, or Grasim Industries Limited, all projects cannot have same risk. Even Hidustan Lever Limited (HLL), which basically operates in fast moving consumer products markets, has distinct markets for its consumer products. In each market segment, HLL is exposed to different degrees of competition and other environmental forces, which results in different risks for all its market segments. Hence, it is essential to estimate the required rate of return for each market segment or division than using the firm's cost of capital as a single, corporate-wide required rate of return for evaluating projects of divisions. Further, projects within a single division may differ in risk. For example, the risk of introducing a new, innovative product will be higher than the expansion of an existing product. Hence there is need for calculating the required rate of return for projects within a division.

The capital asset pricing model is helpful in determining the required rate of return (or the cost of capital) for a division or a project. The risk-free rate and the market premium for divisions or projects are same as for the firm. What we need is the divisional or project betas. In practice, it is difficult to estimate divisional or project betas. What approach could we follow to estimate the required rate of return of a division or a project?

The Pure-Play Technique

Suppose that Surya Enterprises Limited has three divisions: Pharmaceuticals Division, Financial Services Division and Power Generation Division. The company's cost of capital is 12 per cent. Since the company has three diverse businesses with different operating characteristics, it cannot use its overall cost of capital as the required rate of return for its divisions. It should estimate the required rate of return for each division separately. Suppose Surya is considering an investment in the Pharmaceuticals Division, and therefore, it would like to estimate the required rate of return for the division. A most commonly suggested method for calculating the required rate of return for a division (or project) is the **pure-play technique**. The basic idea is to use the beta of the comparable firms, called **pure-play firms**, in the same industry or line of business as a proxy for the beta of the division or the project. The application of the pure-play approach for calculating the Pharmaceuticals Division's cost of capital will involve the following steps:

Identify comparable firms The critical step is the identification of comparable or pure-play firms. These firms should have business identical to the division or the project. It is rare to find perfectly comparable or pure-play firms in practice, as any two firms in the same line of business cannot have exactly similar features; they would have some differences. However, it is not impossible to identify approximately equivalent matches in terms of product line and product mixes. One or two good matches would suffice as proxy for the division or the project. If good matches cannot be found, the average data of a broader sample of firms should be used to even out the differences. Surya has identified the following three pure-play firms:

Firm	Sales (Rs million)	Assets (Rs million)	Debt (Rs million)	Market value equity (Rs million)
Excel Pharma	1,000	650	325	645
Sunshine Pharma	800	700	180	700
Kiran Pharma	1,400	1,250	625	750

Estimate equity betas for comparable firms Once the comparable or the pure-play firms have been identified, their betas should be calculated using CAPM framework and a market index such as Sensex. Alternatively, we can use betas computed by organizations like the Bombay Stock Exchange or the National Stock Exchange or any other agency. These betas are based on the share price and the market index data. Hence they are the **equity betas** for the pure-play firms. An equity beta (β_e) is also called levered beta ((β_l).

The equity betas for Excel, Sunshine and Kiran, estimated using the CAPM approach, are 1.24, 0.94 and 1.05.

Estimate asset betas for comparable firms The comparable firms also employ debt to finance their assets. The equity betas of these firms are affected by their debt ratios. The firm may have a different target capital structure that the debt ratios of the proxy firms. Therefore, the pure-play technique requires that the levered equity betas of the proxy firms should be changed to unlevered or all-equity beta. Unlevered or all-equity betas are also called asset betas. In Chapter 6, we showed that unlevered (or asset) beta is the weighted average of beta for debt and equity (or levered) beta:

$$\beta_a = \beta_d \left(\frac{D}{V}\right) + \beta_e \left(\frac{E}{V}\right)$$

$$\beta_u = \beta_d \left(\frac{D}{V}\right) + \beta_l \left(\frac{E}{V}\right)$$

If we consider that debt is risk free, then β_d is zero, and we can find unlevered beta as follows:

$$\beta_u = \beta_l \left(\frac{E}{V}\right) = \beta_l \left(1 - \frac{D}{V}\right) \tag{28}$$

where β_u is the beta of the pure-play firm after removing the effect of leverage; β_l is its equity beta with leverage; and E/V is the ratio of the pure-play firm's equity to its total market value. Note Equation (28) is based on two important assumptions. First, that debt is risk free and hence the beta for debt is zero. Second, all pure-play firms maintain target capital structures and therefore, the amounts of debt change with the change in the values of firms.[1] The unlevered or all-equity beta is also called the asset beta as it incorporates only the firm's operating risk and is not influenced by the financial risk arising from the use of debt.

The unlevered or asset betas for Excel, Sunshine and Kiran are as follows:

Asset Beta for Excel

$$\beta_a = 1.24 \times \frac{645}{325 + 645} = 1.24 \times 0.665 = 0.82$$

Asset Beta for Sunshine

$$\beta_a = 0.94 \times \frac{700}{180 + 700} = 0.94 \times 0.795 = 0.75$$

Asset Beta for Kiran

$$\beta_a = 1.05 \times \frac{750}{625 + 750} = 1.05 \times 0.545 = 0.55$$

Calculate the division's beta We can use the average asset beta of the pure-play firms as a proxy for the asset beta of the Pharmaceutical Division of Surya Enterprises Limited. We can use either simple or the weighted average. We can use either sales or assets or the value of the firms as weights. The theory does not tell us whether we should use simple or weighted average and what should be the weights. In practice, financial analysts will have to use their judgment. We think that since there is no theory and since we do not know the nature of measurement error, a simple average will do a good job. For illustration, we calculate the weighted beta using assets as weights:

Weighted asset beta

$$= 0.82 \times \frac{650}{2,600} + 0.75 \times \frac{700}{2,600} + 0.55 \times \frac{1,250}{2,600} = 0.67$$

Calculate the division's all-equity cost of capital Suppose that the risk-free rate is 6 per cent and market risk premium is 9 per cent. The Pharmaceutical Division's all-equity cost of capital is:

$$k_a = r_f + \text{risk} - \text{premium} \times \beta_a$$
$$k_a = 0.06 + 0.09 \times 0.67 = 0.12 \text{ or } 12\%$$

The all-equity cost of capital is without financial risk. As it reflects only the business risk, it is also referred to as the asset or unlevered cost of capital.

Calculate the division's equity cost of capital The asset (or unlevered) beta for the Pharmaceutical Division is 0.67. We need to convert the asset (unlevered) beta into the equity (levered) beta for calculating the cost of equity for the Pharmaceutical Division. To obtain the equity beta, the asset beta should be relevered to reflect the target capital structure of the Pharmaceutical Division. What is the target capital structure of the Pharmaceutical Division? Surya Enterprises Limited may use the firm's target capital structure for the Pharmaceutical Division as well. Alternatively, it may decide the Pharmaceutical Division's target capital structure based on the average debt ratio of the pure-play firms. The average debt ratio (D/V) of the pure-play firms is 0.33. Using this ratio, the equity beta for the Pharmaceutical Division is 1.00:

$$\beta_u = \beta_l \left(\frac{E}{V}\right) = \beta_l \left(1 - \frac{D}{V}\right)$$

$$\beta_{l'} = \beta_u \left(\frac{1}{1 - \dfrac{D}{V}}\right) \tag{29}$$

$$= 0.67 \left(\frac{1}{1 - 0.33}\right) = 0.67 \times 1.49 = 1.00$$

Now we can calculate the cost of equity for the Pharmaceutical Division as follows:

$$k_e = 0.06 + 0.09 \times 1.00 = 0.15 \text{ or } 15\%$$

Calculate the division's cost of capital The cost of capital for the division is the weighted average of the cost of equity and the cost of debt. We have estimated the target debt ratio for the Pharmaceutical Division as 0.33. Suppose the cost of debt (before tax) for the Pharmaceutical Division is 10 per cent and tax rate is 35 per cent, its weighted cost of capital can be calculated as follows:

$$k_0 = k_d (1 - T) \left(\frac{D}{V}\right) + k_e \left(\frac{E}{V}\right) \tag{30}$$

$$= 0.10(1 - 0.35)(0.33) + 0.15(0.67) = 0.12 \text{ or } 12\%$$

---

1. The implication is that the amount of debt, and hence the interest tax shield will fluctuate with the firm's operations. This means that the interest tax shield will be as risky as the operations. Thus, we do not make any adjustment for interest tax shield in unlevering (or levering beta). This point is explained in a subsequent chapter.

It should be clear from the approach discussed here that each division has its own operating risk and debt capacity. Therefore, for calculating the cost of capital for each division, you should determine its operating risk and debt capacity. Assets of the firm are the aggregate of assets of the divisions. Therefore, the beta of assets for the firm should be the weighted average of betas for the divisions:

Firm's asset beta = beta of division 1 × weight of division 1
+ beta of division 2 × weight of division 2 + ···
+ beta of division *n* × weight of division *n* (40)

It seems plausible that weights may be expressed in terms of market value of assets. In practice, the market value of assets of divisions are not available, therefore, weights may be expressed in terms of book value assets or sales.

The calculated average asset beta for the firm may be more than its observed asset beta. This may happen because of the synergy effect. A vertically integrated firm is likely to be more efficient than if the divisions operate as independent, separate firms. The vertically integrated firms are able to reduce operating cost. This premium resulting from diversification should be allocated to the divisions. Management will have to use its judgment in doing so as there is no formula available. Yet another problem that may arise in moving from a single cut-off rate to multiple cut-off rates, relates to the behaviour of managers. Some managers may resist the change. For some divisions (with higher risks), the divisional cut-off rates will be higher than the corporate-wide cut-off rate. These divisions are likely to get fewer funds allocated to them. They may therefore oppose the system of the multiple cut-off rates. Management must take all into confidence and convince them that the use of a single, corporate-wide cut-off rate use is biased in favour of the investment projects of high-risk divisions since their expected returns will be higher. In the long-term, this approach will make the firm highly risky. Ideally, the firm would like to balance risk by having a portfolio of high risk and low risk projects.

Illustration 9.9: Calculation of Beta and Cost of Capital for a Division

Sinhgarh Engineering Company wants to diversify into fertiliser business and organise it as a new division. The company found a comparable fertiliser company of roughly the same characteristics as the proposed division. It has equity beta of 1.35, and debt ratio of 0.72. The corporate tax rate is 35 per cent. Sinhgarh will have a debt ratio of 0.50 for proposed fertiliser business. The risk-free rate is 8 per cent and the risk premium is 10 per cent. Calculate the cost of equity for the proposed new division.

First, we shall 'unlever' the levered equity beta (that is, calculate the asset beta) of the comparable (pure-play) firm:

$$\beta_a = \beta_e \left(1 - \frac{D}{V}\right) = 1.35(1 - 0.72) = 0.38$$

We can use the asset beta of the comparable firm as a proxy for the asset beta of the fertiliser division.

Second, we can now 'lever' the asset beta to obtain the equity beta for the division by incorporating its debt ratio:

$$\beta_e = \beta_a \left(\frac{1}{1 - \frac{D}{V}}\right) = 0.38 \left(\frac{1}{1 - 0.50}\right) = 0.38 \times 2.00 = 0.76$$

The equity beta for the division is lower than that of the comparable firm since it will employ less debt.

Third, we can calculate the division's cost of equity as follows:

$$k_e = 0.08 + 0.10 \times 0.76 = 0.156 \text{ or } 15.6\%$$

The Cost of Capital for Projects

The procedure described for calculating the cost of capital for divisions can be followed in the case of large projects. Many times it may be quite difficult to identify comparable (pure-play) firms. We explained in Chapter 4 that the risk of a project depends on its operating leverage. So you can estimate a project's beta based on its operating leverage. You may also consider the variability of the project's earnings to estimate the beta.

A simple practical approach to incorporate risk differences in projects is to adjust the firm's or division's WACC (upwards or downwards), and use the *adjusted WACC* to evaluate the investment project:

$$\text{Adjusted WACC} = \text{WACC} \pm R \qquad (41)$$

That is, a project's cost of capital is equal to the firm's or division's weighted average cost of capital plus or minus a risk adjustment factor, *R*. The risk adjustment factor would be determined on the basis of the decision maker's past experience and judgment regarding the project's risk. It should be noted that adjusting or division's WACC for risk differences is not theoretically a very sound method; however, this approach is better than simply using the firm's or division WACC for *all* projects without regard for their risk.

Companies in practice may develop policy guidelines for incorporating the project risk differences. One approach is to divide projects into broad risk classes, and use different discount rates based on the decision maker's experience. For example, projects may be classified as:

- Low risk projects
- Medium risk projects
- High risk projects.

Low risk projects include replacement and modernisation projects. The decision maker can estimate the benefits (increase in revenue and/or reduction in costs) of replacement/modernisation projects with relative accuracy. Medium risk projects include investment for expansion of the current business. Although revenue and cost estimates are relatively difficult to make, yet the decision maker is familiar with the nature of businesses. Therefore, using his experience and judgment, he can have a reasonable idea of the variability of cash flows. High-risk projects include diversification into new businesses. As the decision maker has no or little idea of new business, he or she would find greater difficulty in estimating cash flows. Cash flows could show high variability. Within each category, projects could be further sub-divided.

Figure 9.3 illustrates the *risk-adjusted discount rates* for projects classified according to their perceived risk.

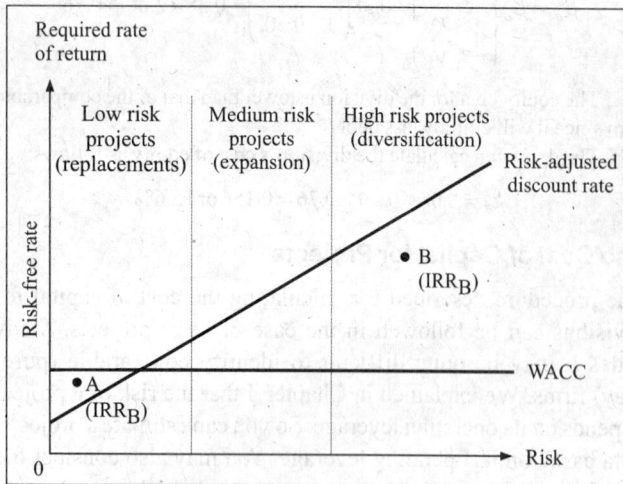

Figure 9.3: Risk-adjusted discount rates for projects

Figure 9.3 indicates that projects' risk differ, and higher the project risk, the higher will be the risk-adjusted discount rate. Replacement projects are discounted at a lower rate than expansion or diversification projects since its risk is the lowest. Diversification projects involve high risk; therefore, their cash flows are discounted at a high discount rate. It may be noted that WACC reflects, "average risk", therefore it is drawn as a horizontal line. It fails to distinguish between projects with different risk characteristics, and can mislead in undertaking profitable projects. For example, consider Projects A and B which respectively have internal rates of return, IRR_A and IRR_B. You can see from Figure 9.3 that if WACC criterion is used, Project A will be rejected (because IRR_A < WACC) and Project B will be accepted (because IRR_B > WACC). However, if risk-adjusted discount rates are used, then Project A should be accepted while Project B rejected. Note that discount rate must reflect risk of the project.

SUMMARY

❖ The cost of capital to a firm is the minimum return, which the suppliers of capital require. In other words, it is a price of obtaining capital; it is a compensation for time and risk.

❖ The cost of capital concept is of vital significance in the financial decision-making. It is used: (*a*) as a discount, or cut-off, rate for evaluating investment projects, (*b*) for designing the firm's debt-equity mix and (*c*) for appraising the top management's financial performance.

❖ Firms obtain capital for financing investments in the form of equity or debt or both. Also, in practice, they maintain a target debt–equity mix. Therefore, the firm's cost of capital means the weighted average cost of debt and equity.

❖ Debt includes all interest-bearing borrowings. Its cost is the yield (return), which lenders expect from their investment. In most cases, return is equal to annual contractual rate of interest (also called coupon rate). Interest charges are tax deductible. Therefore, cost of debt to the firm should be calculated after adjusting for interest tax shield:

$$k_d(1-T)$$

where k_d is before-tax cost of debt and T is the corporate tax rate.

❖ Equity includes paid-up capital and reserve and surplus (retained earnings). Equity has no explicit cost, as payment of dividends is not obligatory. However, it involves an opportunity cost.

❖ The opportunity cost of equity is the rate of return required by shareholders on securities of comparable risk. Thus, it is a price, which the company must pay to attract capital from shareholders.

❖ In practice, shareholders expect to receive dividends and capital gains. Therefore, the cost of equity can be thought to include *expected* dividend yield and percentage capital gain:

$$k_e = \frac{DIV_1}{P_0} + g$$

where DIV_1 is the expected dividend per share, P_0 is the market price today and g is the expected dividend growth (capital gain). The dividend growth rate, g, can be calculated as the product of the firm's retention ratio and rate of return (ROE) in case of a totally equity financed firm. It can also be approximated by the past growth in earnings per share or dividend per share.

❖ When a company issues new share capital, it has to offer shares at a price, which is much less than the prevailing market price. Therefore, the cost of retained earnings will be less than the cost of new issue of equity.

❖ A more objective method for calculating the cost of equity is provided by CAPM:

$$k_e = R_f + \left(R_m - R_f\right)\beta_j$$

where R_f is the risk-free rate equal to current yield on the Treasury bills or government bonds; $(R_m - R_f)$ is the market risk premium measured as average of historical returns of a long series; and β_j is the beta of the firm j.

❖ Three steps are involved in calculating the firm's weighted average cost of capital (WACC). First, the component costs of debt and equity are calculated. Second, weights to each component of capital are assigned according to the target capital structure. Third, the product of component costs and weights is summed up to determine WACC. The weighted average cost of *new* capital is the weighted marginal cost of capital (WMCC). WACC for a firm, which has debt and equity in the capital structure, is given by the following formula:

$$WACC = k_o = k_e\left(\frac{E}{E+D}\right) + k_d(1-T)\left(\frac{D}{E+D}\right)$$

where k_e is the cost of equity, k_d is the cost of debt, T is the tax rate, D is debt and E is equity. The market value weights should be used in calculating WACC.

❖ A firm may have several divisions or product lines with different risks. Therefore, the firm's WACC cannot be used to evaluate divisions or projects. The following procedure can be used to estimate the divisional or the project's cost of capital:

- Identify comparable or pure-play firms and determine their equity beta based on the market data
- Find the average equity beta, and unlever it as follows:

$$\beta_u = \beta_l\left(\frac{E}{V}\right)$$

- Determine the division's target capital structure, and relever the beta as follows:

$$\beta_l = \beta_u\left(\frac{V}{E}\right) = \beta_u\left(1 + \frac{D}{E}\right)$$

- This is division or project's levered or equity beta. Use CAPM to calculate the cost of equity. Calculate the after-tax cost of debt for the division or project.
- Use the target capital structure to calculate the division or project's WACC.

KEY CONCEPTS

Component cost of capital	Explicit cost of capital	Investment opportunity curve	Redeemable preference shares
Cost of debt	Financial risk	Irredeemable	Risk-adjusted discount rates
Cost of equity	Financing policy	Marginal cost of capital	Sinking fund
Cost of preference capital	Firm's cost of capital	Opportunity cost of capital	Supernormal growth
Cost of retained earnings	Flotation cost	Preference shares	Target capital structure
Divisional cost of capital	Implicit cost of capital	Project cost of capital	Weighted average cost of capital
Earnings–price ratio	Interest tax shield		

ILLUSTRATIVE SOLVED PROBLEMS

Problem 9.1: Assuming that a firm pays tax at a 50 per cent rate, compute the after-tax cost of capital in the following cases:

(i) A 8.5 per cent preference share sold at par.

(ii) A perpetual bond sold at par, coupon rate of interest being 7 per cent.

(iii) A ten-year, 8 per cent, Rs 1000 par bond sold at Rs 950 less 4 per cent underwriting commission.

(iv) A preference share sold at Rs 100 with a 9 per cent dividend and a redemption price of Rs 110 if the company redeems it in five years.

(v) An ordinary share selling at a current market price of Rs 120, and paying a current dividend of Rs 9 per share, which is expected to grow at a rate of 8 per cent.

(vi) An ordinary share of a company, which engages no external financing, is selling for Rs 50. The earnings per share are Rs 7.50 of which sixty per cent is paid in dividends. The company reinvests retained earnings at a rate of 10 per cent.

Solution:

(i) The after-tax cost of the preference issue will be 8.5 per cent.

(ii) The after-tax cost of bond is:

$$k_d(1-T) = 0.07(1-0.5) = 0.035 \text{ or } 3.5\%$$

(iii) The after-tax cost of bond is (using approximate method):

$$\frac{(1-T)[\text{INT} + \frac{1}{n}(F - B_0)]}{1/2(F + B_0)}$$

$$= \frac{(1-0.5)[\text{Rs }80 + 1/10(\text{Rs }1000 - \text{Rs }950)]}{1/2(\text{Rs }1000 + \text{Rs }950)}$$

$$= \frac{(1-0.5)[\text{Rs }80 + 1/10(\text{Rs }50)]}{1/2(\text{Rs }1950)}$$

$$= \frac{(1-0.5)(\text{Rs }85)}{\text{Rs }975} = 0.0436 \text{ or } 4.36\%$$

Note: Flotation costs such as underwriting commission should be adjusted to the project's cash flows.

(iv) $$100 = \sum_{t=1}^{5} \frac{9}{(1+k_p)^t} + \frac{110}{(1+k_p)^5}$$

By trial and error, we find $k_p = 0.106$ or 10.6%

(v) $$k_e = \frac{\text{DIV}_1}{P_0} + g = \frac{\text{Rs }9(1.08)}{\text{Rs }120} + 0.08 = \frac{\text{Rs }9.72}{\text{Rs }120} + 0.08$$

$$= 0.081 + 0.08 = 0.161 \text{ or } 16.1\%$$

(vi) $$P_0 = \frac{\text{EPS}(1-b)}{k_e - br}$$

$$k_e = \frac{\text{EPS}(1-b)}{P_0} + br = \frac{\text{Rs }7.50(1-0.4)}{\text{Rs }50} + 0.10 \times 0.4$$

$$= \frac{\text{Rs }4.50}{\text{Rs }50.00} + 0.04 = 0.09 + 0.04 = 0.13 \text{ or } 13 \text{ per cent}$$

Problems 9.2: A firm finances all its investments by 40 per cent debt and 60 per cent equity. The estimated required rate of return on equity is 20 per cent after-taxes and that of the debt is 8 per cent after-taxes. The firm is considering an investment proposal costing Rs 40,000 with an expected return that will last forever. What amount (in rupees) must the proposal yield per year so that the market price of the share does not change? Show calculations to prove your point.

Solution: The minimum overall required rate of return is:

Debt	$0.40 \times 0.08 = 0.032$
Equity	$0.60 \times 0.20 = 0.120$
Weighted average	0.152

Thus, the investment proposal must earn $0.152 \times$ Rs 40,000 = Rs 6,080 per year.

Annual return before taxes	Rs 6,080
Less: interest $0.08 \times 0.40 \times$ Rs 40,000	1,280
Return on equity	Rs 4,800

After-tax rate of return on equity:

Rs $4,800 \div (0.60 \times$ Rs 40,000$)$

Rs $4,800 \div$ Rs 24,000 = 0.20

Problems 9.3: The Servex Company has the following capital structure on 30 June 2004:

	(Rs '000)
Ordinary shares (200,000 shares)	4,000
10% Preference shares	1,000
14% Debentures	3,000
	8,000

The share of the company sells for Rs 20. It is expected that company will pay next year a dividend of Rs 2 per share, which will grow at 7 per cent forever. Assume a 50 per cent tax rate.

You are required to:

(a) Compute a weighted average cost of capital based on the existing capital structure.

(b) Compute the new weighted average cost of capital if the company raises an additional Rs 2,000,000 debt by issuing 15 per cent debenture. This would result in increasing the expected dividend to Rs 3 and leave the growth rate unchanged, but the price of share will fall to Rs 15 per share.

(c) Compute the cost of capital if in (b) above growth rate increases to 10 per cent.

Solution:

(a) WACC: Existing capital structure

	After-tax Cost	Weights	Weighted Cost
Ordinary	0.17	0.500	0.0850
10% Preference	0.10	0.125	0.0125
14% Debenture	0.07	0.375	0.0262
WACC			0.1237

Cost of ordinary share is:

$$k_e = \frac{DIV_1}{P_0} + g = \frac{Rs\,2}{Rs\,20} + 0.07 = 0.10 + 0.07 = 0.17$$

(b) WACC: New capital structure

	Amount (Rs '000)	After-tax Cost	Weights	Weighted Cost
Ordinary	4,000	0.27	0.40	0.108
10% Preference	1,000	0.10	0.10	0.010
14% Debentures	3,000	0.07	0.30	0.021
15% Debentures	2,000	0.075	0.20	0.015
WACC				0.154

Cost of ordinary share is:

$$k_e = \frac{DIV_1}{P_0} + g = \frac{Rs\,3}{Rs\,15} + 0.07 = 0.20 + 0.07 = 0.27$$

(c) WACC: Changed growth rate

	After-tax Cost	Weights	Weighted Cost
Ordinary	0.30	0.40	0.120
10% Preference	0.10	0.10	0.010
14% Debentures	0.07	0.30	0.021
15% Debentures	0.075	0.20	0.015
WACC			0.166

Cost of ordinary share is:

$$k_e = \frac{DIV_1}{P_0} + g = \frac{Rs\,3}{Rs\,15} + 0.10 = 0.20 + 0.10 = 0.30$$

Note: The book value weights have been used to calculate the weighted cost of capital in the above cases.

Problem 9.4: The Kay Company has the following capital structure at 31 March 2003 which is considered to be optimum.

	Rs
14% Debentures	300,000
11% Preference	100,000
Equity (1,00,000 shares)	1,600,000
	2,000,000

The company's share has a current market price of Rs 23.60 per share. The expected dividend per share next year is 50 per cent of the 2003 EPS. The following are the earnings per share figure for the company during the preceding ten years. The past trends are expected to continue.

Year	EPS (Rs)	Year	EPS (Rs)
1994	1.00	1999	1.61
1995	1.10	2000	2000
1996	1.21	2001	1.95
1997	1.33	2002	2.15
1998	1.46	2003	2.36

The company can issue 16 per cent new debentures. The

company's debenture is currently selling at Rs 96. The new preference issue can be sold at a net price of Rs 9.20, paying a dividend of Rs 1.1 per share. The company's marginal tax rate is 50 per cent.

(a) Calculate the after-tax cost (i) of new debt, (ii) of new preference capital and (iii) of ordinary equity, assuming new equity comes from retained earnings.

(b) Find the marginal cost of capital, again assuming no new ordinary shares are sold.

(c) How much can be spent for capital investment before new ordinary shares must be sold? Assume that retained earnings available for next year's investment are 50 per cent of 2003 earnings.

(d) What is the marginal cost of capital (cost of funds raised in excess of the amount calculated in part (c) if the firm can sell new ordinary shares to net Rs 20 a share? The cost of debt and of preference capital is constant.

Solution: The existing capital structure of the firm is assumed to be optimum. Thus, the optimum proportions are:

Type of Capital	Amount (Rs)	Proportions
14% Debentures	300,000	0.15
11% Preference	100,000	0.05
Equity	1,600,000	0.80
	2,000,000	1.00

(a) (i) After-tax cost of debt:

$$k_d = \frac{Rs\,16}{Rs\,96} = 0.1667$$

$$k_d(1-T) = (1-0.5)(0.1667) = 0.0833$$

Note: The above formula is used since the maturity period of the debentures is not given.

(ii) After-tax cost of preference capital:

$$k_p = \frac{Rs\,1.1}{Rs\,9.2} = 0.12$$

Note: Preference shares are assumed to be irredeemable.

(iii) After-tax cost of retained earnings:

$$k_e = \frac{DIV_1}{P_0} + g = \frac{Rs\,1.18}{Rs\,23.60} + 0.10 = 0.05 + 0.10 = 0.15$$

$DIV_1 = 50\%$ of 2003 EPS = 50% of Rs 2.36 = Rs 1.18

Calculation of g: It can be observed from the past trends of EPS that it is growing at an annual compound rate of 10 per cent. For example $E_t = E_0(1+g)^t = Rs\,2.36 = Re\,1(1+g)^9$. Using Table A, we find that the present value factor of 2.36 at the end of 9th year is obtained when the interest rate is 10 per cent. The growth rate is, therefore, 10 per cent.

Type of Capital (1)	Proportion (2)	Specific Cost (3)	Product (2) × (3) = (4)
Debt	0.15	0.0833	0.0125
Preference	0.05	0.1200	0.0060
Equity	0.80	0.1500	0.1200
Marginal cost of capital			0.1385

(b) The marginal cost of capital (MCC) is the weighted average cost of new capital. The firm would maintain its existing capital structure. Therefore, new capital would be raised in proportion to the existing capital structure.

(c) The company can spend the following amount without increasing its MCC and without selling the new shares:

Retained earnings = (0.50)(Rs 2.36×100,000) = Rs 118,000;

The ordinary equity (retained earnings in this case) is 80 per cent of the total capital. Thus

$$\text{Investment before issue of equity} = \frac{\text{Retained earnings}}{\text{Per cent equity}}$$

$$= \frac{Rs\,118,000}{0.80} = Rs\,147,500$$

(d) If the company spends more than Rs 147,500, it will have to issue new shares. The cost of new issue of ordinary shares is:

$$k_e = \frac{Rs\,1.18}{Rs\,20} + 0.10 = 0.059 + 0.10 = 159$$

The marginal cost of capital in excess of Rs 147,500 is:

Type of Capital	Proportion	Specific Costs	Product
Debt	0.15	0.0833	0.0125
Preference	0.05	0.1200	0.0060
Ordinary Equity (new)	0.80	0.1590	0.1272
			0.1457

REVIEW QUESTIONS

1. Define cost of capital? Explain its significance in financial decision-making.
2. What are the various concepts of cost of capital? Why should they be distinguished in financial management?
3. How is the cost of debt computed? How does it differ from the cost of preference capital?
4. 'The equity capital is cost free.' Do you agree? Give reasons.
5. The basic formula to calculate the cost of equity is: $(DIV_1/P_0) + g$. Explain its rationale.
6. Are retained earnings less expensive than the new issue of ordinary shares? Give your views.
7. What is the CAPM approach for calculating the cost of equity? What is the difference between this approach and the constant growth approach? Which one is better? Why?
8. 'Debt is the cheapest source of funds.' Explain.
9. How is the weighted average cost of capital calculated?

What weights should be used in its calculation?

10. Distinguish between the weighted average cost of capital and the marginal cost of capital. Which one should be used in capital budgeting and valuation of the firm? Why?

11. 'Marginal cost of capital is nothing but the average cost of capital.' Explain.

12. How would you apply the cost of capital concept when projects with different risks are evaluated?

PROBLEMS

1. The Ess Kay Refrigerator Company is deciding to issue 2,000,000 of Rs 1,000, 14 per cent 7-year debentures. The debentures will have to be sold at a discount rate of 3 per cent. Further, the firm will pay an underwriting fee of 3 per cent of the face value. Assume a 35% tax rate.
Calculate the after-tax cost of the issue. What would be the after-tax cost if the debenture were sold at a premium of Rs 30?

2. A company issues new debentures of Rs 2 million, at par; the net proceeds being Rs 1.8 million. It has a 13.5 per cent rate of interest and 7 year maturity. The company's tax rate is 52 per cent. What is the cost of debenture issue? What will be the cost in 4 years if the market value of debentures at that time is Rs 2.2 million?

3. A company has 100,000 shares of Rs 100 at par of preference shares outstanding at 9.75 per cent dividend rate. The current market price of the preference share is Rs 80. What is its cost?

4. A firm has 8,000,000 ordinary shares outstanding. The current market price is Rs 25 and the book value is Rs 18 per share. The firm's earnings per share is Rs 3.60 and dividend per share is Rs 1.44. How much is the growth rate assuming that the past performance will continue? Calculate the cost of equity capital.

5. A company has 5,000,000 ordinary shares outstanding. The market price of the share is Rs 96 while the book value is Rs 65. The firm's earnings and dividends per share are Rs 10 and Rs 7 respectively. The company wants to issue 1,000,000 shares with a net proceeds of Rs 80 per share. What is the cost of capital of the new issue?

6. A company has paid a dividend of Rs 3 per share for last 20 years and it is expected to continue so in the future. The company's share had sold for Rs 33 twenty years ago, and its market price is also Rs 33. What is the cost of the share?

7. A firm is thinking of raising funds by the issuance of equity capital. The current market price of the firm's share is Rs 150. The firm is expected to pay a dividend of Rs 3.55 next year. The firm has paid dividend in past years as follows:

Year	Dividend per Share (Rs)
1998	2.00
1999	2.20
2000	2.42
2001	2.66
2002	2.93
2003	3.22

The firm can sell shares for Rs 140 each only. In addition, the flotation cost per share is Rs 10. Calculate the cost of new issue.

8. A company is considering the possibility of raising Rs 100 million by issuing debt, preference capital, and equity and retaining earnings. The book values and the market values of the issues are as follows:

(Rs in millions)

	Book Value	Market Value
Ordinary shares	30	60
Reserves	10	—
Preference shares	20	24
Debt	40	36
	100	120

The following costs are expected to be associated with the above-mentioned issues of capital. (Assume a 35 per cent tax rate.)

(i) The firm can sell a 20-year Rs 1,000 face value debenture with a 16 per cent rate of interest. An underwriting fee of 2 per cent of the market price would be incurred to issue the debentures.

(ii) The 11 per cent Rs 100 face value preference issue fetch Rs 120 per share. However, the firm will have to pay Rs 7.25 per preference share as underwriting commission.

(iii) The firm's ordinary share is currently selling for Rs 150. It is expected that the firm will pay a dividend of Rs 12 per share at the end of the next year, which is expected to grow at a rate of 7 per cent. The new ordinary shares can be sold at a price of Rs 145. The firm should also incur Rs 5 per share flotation cost.

Compute the weighted average cost of capital using (i) book value weights (ii) market value weights.

9. A company has the following long-term capital outstanding as on 31 March 2003: (a) 10 per cent debentures with a face value of Rs 500,000. The debentures were issued in 1999 and are due on 31 March 2008. The current market price of a debenture is Rs 950. (b) Preference shares with a face value of Rs 400,000. The annual dividend is Rs 6 per share. The preference shares are currently selling at Rs 60 per share. (c) Sixty thousand ordinary shares of Rs 10 par value. The share is currently selling at Rs 50 per share. The dividends per share for the past several years are as follow:

Year	Rs	Year	Rs
1996	2.00	2000	2.80
1997	2.16	2001	3.08
1998	2.37	2002	3.38
1999	2.60	2003	3.70

Assuming a tax rate of 35 per cent, compute the firm's weighted average cost of capital.

10. A company is considering distributing additional Rs 80,000 as dividends to its ordinary shareholders. The shareholders are expected to earn 18 per cent on their investment. They are in 30 per cent tax and incur an average brokerage fee of 3 per cent on the reinvestment of dividends received. The firm can earn a return of 12 per cent on the retained earnings. Should the company distribute or retain Rs 80,000?

11. The Keshari Engineering Ltd. has the following capital structure, considered to be optimum, on 31 June 2003.

	Rs in million
14% Debt	93.75
10% Preference	31.25
Ordinary equity	375.00
Total	500.00

The company has 15 million shares outstanding. The share is selling for Rs 25 per share and the expected dividend per share is Rs 1.50, which is expected to grow at 10 per cent. The company is contemplating to raise additional funds of Rs 100 million to finance expansion. It can sell new preference shares at a price of Rs 23, less flotation cost of Rs 3 per share. It is expected that a dividend of Rs 2 per share will be paid on preference. The new debt can be issued at 10 per cent rate of interest. The firm pays taxes at rate of 35 per cent and intends to maintain its capital structure.

You are required (*i*) to calculate the after-tax cost (*a*) of new debt, (*b*) of new preference capital, and (*c*) of ordinary equity, assuming new equity comes only from retained earnings which is just sufficient for the purpose, (*ii*) to calculate the marginal cost of capital, assuming no new shares are sold, (*iii*) to compute the maximum amount which can be spent for capital investments before new ordinary shares can be sold, if the retained earnings are Rs 700,000, and (*iv*) to compute the marginal cost of capital if the firm spends in excess of the amount computed in (*iii*). The firm can sell ordinary shares at a net price of Rs 22 per share.

12. The following is the capital structure of *X* Ltd. as on 31 December 2003.

	Rs in million
Equity capital (paid up)	563.50
Reserves and surplus	485.66
10% Irredeemable Preference shares	56.00
10% Redeemable Preference shares	28.18
15% Term loans	377.71
Total	1,511.05

The share of the company is currently selling for Rs 36. The expected dividend next year is Rs 3.60 per share anticipated to be growing at 8 per cent indefinitely. The redeemable preference shares were issued on 1 January 1997 with twelve-year maturity period. A similar issue today will be at Rs 93.

The market price of 10% irredeemable preference share is Rs 81.81. The company had raised the term loan from IDBI in 1993. A similar loan will cost 10% today.

Assume an average tax rate of 35 per cent. Calculate the weights average cost of capital for the company using book-value weights.

13. The following capital structure is extracted from Delta Ltd.'s balance sheet as on 31 March 2003:

	(Rs '000)
Equity (Rs 25 par)	66,412
Reserves	65,258
Preference (Rs 100 par)	3,000
Debentures	30,000
Long-term loans	5,360
	170,030

The earnings per share of the company over the period 1999–2003 are:

Year	Rs	Year	Rs
1999	2.24	1994	4.40
2000	3.00	1995	5.15
2001	4.21	1996	5.05
2002	3.96	1997	6.00
2003	4.80	1998	6.80

The equity share of the company is selling for Rs 50 and preference for Rs 77.50. The preference dividend rate and interest rate on debenture respectively are 10 per cent and 13 per cent. The long-term loans are raised at an interest rate of 14 per cent from the financial institution. The equity dividend is Rs 4 per share.

Calculate the weighted average cost of capital for Delta Ltd., making necessary assumptions.

14. A company has the following capital structure at the end of 31 March 2003:

	(Rs in million)
Share Capital	6,808
Reserve	34,857
Long-term loans	538,220

The company's EPS, DPS, average market price and ROE for last seven years are given below:

Year	EPS	DPS	AMP	ROE
1997	21.55	5.28	143.04	20.9
1998	22.14	5.76	187.52	18.6
1999	26.40	5.76	312.32	11.7
2000	20.16	6.53	587.52	11.0
2001	20.40	7.68	366.72	9.5
2002	23.09	11.53	416.64	10.3
2003	22.00	7.68	355.20	8.4

Note: EPS, DPS and AMP adjusted for bonus issues.

You are required to calculate: (*a*) growth rate *g*, using alternative methods; (*b*) cost of equity, using dividend – growth model, and (*c*) weighted average cost of capital, using (*i*) book-value weights and (*ii*) market-value weights. Assume that the interest rate on debt is 11 per cent and the corporate income tax rate is 35 per cent.

15. Eskayef Limited manufactures human and veterinary pharmaceuticals, bulk drugs, skin care products, and vaterinary feed supplements and markets bio-analytical and diagnostic instruments. On 31 March 2003, the company has a paid-up share capital of Rs 75 million and reserves of Rs 325.90 million. It does not employ long-term debt. The following are other financial highlights on the company during 1998–2003:

Year	EPS (Rs)	DPS (Rs)	Book Value (Rs)	Market Value
1998	6.21	2.00	26.03	100.00
1999	10.91	2.50	34.44	205.00
2000	11.57	2.50	43.52	209.38
2001	11.47	2.70	37.98	164.00
2002	10.44	3.00	45.42	138.88
2003	11.23	3.20	53.45	155.00

Note: (1) Years 1998, 1999 and 2000 closed on 30 November while years 2001, 2002 and 2003 on 31 March. (2) Market value is the averages of high and low share prices.

You are required to calculate (*a*) ROE, (*b*) dividend payout, (*c*) retention ratio, (*d*) growth rate, (*e*) dividend yield, (*f*) earnings yield and (*g*) cost of equity.

CASES

Case 9.1: Hindustan Lever Limited

Hindustan Lever Limited (HLL) was set up in 1933. It is an important subsidiary of Unilever. Unilever has about 500 subsidiary and associate companies in more than 100 countries. HLL's business areas include home and personal care, foods and beverages, and industrial, agricultural and other products. It is one of the largest producers of soaps and detergents in India. The company has grown organically as well as through acquisitions.

HLL places equal focus on serving both the employees and the shareholders, and it is committed to add value to both. HLL markets more than 100 brands with the help of about 7,000 stockists in over a million outlets. It has more than 50 factories and 70 locations and employs 36,000 persons. In 1997, the company introduced 44 new products and re-launched 20 products.

The company requires the cost of capital estimates for evaluating its acquisitions, investment decisions and the performance of its businesses and for determining the value added to shareholders. It needs to develop a methodology of calculating costs of equity and debt and determine the weighted average cost of capital.

HLL's Performance

Table 9.1.1 contains a summary of HLL's EPS, DPS, share price and market capitalisation. The company's sales and assets have shown significant growth, its profitability has also increased over years. The company has been paying dividends regularly. Its dividend payments have always been more than the retained earnings. HLL's share has enjoyed high price in the stock market. The company's share price has increased from Rs 47.67 in 1987 to Rs 1,383.50 in 1997. The company is conservatively financed. The company's borrowings, both short-term and long-term, for the last three years have shown a declining trend. In 1997, the company had total borrowings of Rs 1,865.80 million and net worth of Rs 12,615 million.

Cost of Capital Assumptions at HLL

The company considers cost of its debt as the effective rate of interest applicable to an "AAA" rated company. It thinks that considering the trends over years, this rate is 14 per cent. The risk-free rate is assumed as the yield on long-tern government bonds, which the company regards as about 12.5 per cent. HLL regards the market-risk premium to be equal to 9 per cent.

Table 9.1.1: Hindustan Lever Limited: EPS, DPS and Share Price

	1987	1988	1989	1990	1991	1992	1993	1994	1995	1996	1997
EPS (Rs)*	3.32	3.48	3.84	4.20	5.73	7.03	9.09	13.02	16.40	20.80	28.14
DPS (Rs)*	1.67	2.13	2.33	2.80	3.85	4.20	5.60	8.00	10.00	12.50	17.00
Share price (Rs)*	47.67	49.33	74.00	96.67	168.00	365.00	575.00	590.00	624.00	807.00	1383.50
Market capitalisation (Rs in Crore)	667	691	1,036	1,353	1,352	5,110	8,049	8,604	9,100	16,073	27,555

* Adjusted for bonus shares (stock dividend).

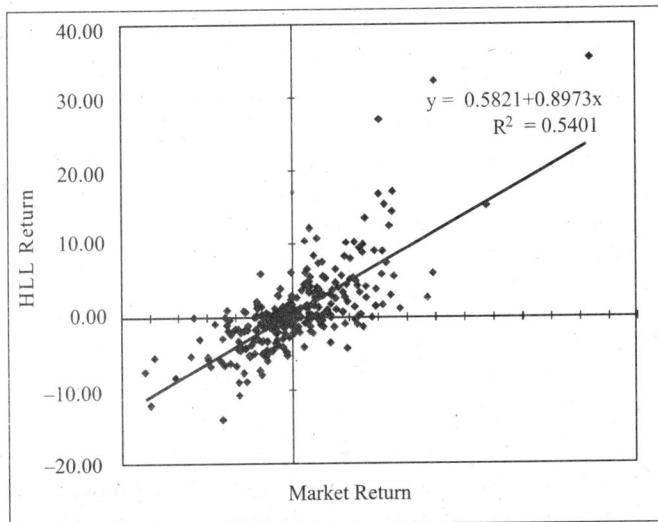

$$y = 0.5821 + 0.8973x$$
$$R^2 = 0.5401$$

Figure 9.1.1: HLL's return Vs. Market return

Figure 9.1.1 charts the weekly rates of return for HLL shares and the stock markets (the BSE's Sensex) for five years (from January 1992 to December 1997). It may be observed that HLL's weekly rates of return have shown a tendency of moving in tandem with the weekly market rates of return (Figure 9.1.1). As shown in the figure, the regression equation is:

$$y = \alpha + \beta x + \varepsilon$$
$$R_{\text{HLL}} = 0.5821 + 0.8973 R_{\text{Market}}$$

Discussion Questions

1. Calculate HLL's cost of equity by using the dividend-growth model.
2. Calculate HLL's cost of equity by using the capital asset pricing model. Do you agree with the company's assumptions regarding the estimates of the risk-free rate and the market premium?
3. Between the dividend-growth model and CAPM, which method do you recommend for HLL and why?
4. What is HLL's weighted average cost of capital (WACC)? What are the uses of WACC for HLL?

Case 9.2: Solidaire Infrastructure Company

Solidaire Infrastructure Company has three businesses organized under three separate divisions. The cement division has its manufacturing plant in Gujarat. It sells about two-thirds of its cement in Gujarat and the remaining quantity in Rajasthan and Madhya Pradesh. The fertilizers division manufactures and markets urea in Gujarat, Maharashtra and Madhya Pradesh. The power generation division, under a long-term agreement, supplies three-fourths of power generated to the government of Gujarat at an agreed price, which is periodically revised with mutual consent of the two parties. All three divisions are profitable and they have plans to expand their activities in the future. Table 9.2.1 gives some financial data for the divisions.

Table 9.2.1: Financial Data for Solidaire Infrastructure Company

(Rs in million)

	Cement Division	Fertiliser Division	Power Division	Solidaire
Sales	700	450	350	1,500
PAT	29	17	24	70
Assets	550	230	420	1,200
Current assets	210	100	20	330
Equity (Market value)				1,000
Debt				1,800

Solidaire has so far used the corporate-wide weighted average cost of capital (WACC) as a cut-off rate for allocating funds to the divisions. The company uses CAPM to determine the cost of equity. Its equity beta, as observed in the market, is 1.5. Investments of the company has long gestation period and lives. Therefore, it uses yield on 30-year government bonds as the risk-free rate, which currently is 5.6 per cent. The company's estimates show that the 30-year simple average of the Sensex stock returns is 17.6 per cent, and 30-year government bonds' yield is 7.8 per cent. The current debt-equity ratio of Solidaire is 1.8 : 1. Being a highly capital intensive company, it has a target debt-equity ratio of 2.5:1. The company after-tax average borrowing rate is 8 per cent.

The power division has strongly opposed the use of the firm's WACC as cut-off rate for allocating funds and evaluating its investment projects. The divisional head of power argues that his division is not exposed to the demand uncertainty, and it has steady flow of earnings. Hence, its operating risk is much less than the risks of other divisions. He also thinks that the power division has a higher debt capacity; as an independent company, it could easily borrow four times of equity. He wondered that because of the low operating risk and high debt capacity, the cut-off rate for his division should be lower. The CEO and some divisional heads thought that the corporate-wide, single cut-off would ensure that only the highly profitable projects will be accepted, and thus, the company will be able to maximize the shareholders wealth. They also thought the average borrowing capacity of the company defines the total amount that it can borrow, and therefore, the debt capacity of a division is not relevant. The target debt-equity ratios for the fertiliser and cement divisions, respectively, are 2 : 1 and 2.5 : 1.

The CFO didn't subscribe to this reasoning. According to him, the cut-off rates of the divisions should reflect their unique risk-return characteristics and debt-bearing capacities. Each division has its own economic sector in which it competes with other firms. According to him, the company's beta is the average of the betas for divisions, and it reflects average risk. He argued that if there are synergy benefits, than there is a possibility that the average beta of divisions will be less than the company's beta.

The CFO proposed that for each division WACC may be

computed as follows: First, identify comparable firm or firms in each sector in which divisions operate, and determine their equity beta based on the market data. Second, adjust the equity betas of comparable firms to remove the effect of their capital structure. Third, estimate the debt and equity proportion of each division and recalculate the betas in steps two to reflect the leverage effect of the divisions. Fourth, use the CAPM and equity betas estimated in step three to estimate the cost of equity of each division. Fifth, calculate the after-tax cost of debt for each division. Last, use the target capital structure to calculate the WACC or cut-off rate for each division.

The CFO asked his assistant to collect relevant information about the comparable firms so that he could estimate the cut-off rates for divisions. The assistant was unable to identify a comparable power generation firm as most firms were under the government control and they did not have market data. The information about two comparable cement and fertilizers firms is given in Table 9.2.2.

Table 9.2.2: Financial Data for Comparable Firms

(Rs in million)

	Kisan Fertilisers Ltd.	*Camel Cement Ltd.*
Sales	550	850
PAT	23	41
Assets	320	700
Current assets	140	300
Market Value of Equity	150	320
Debt	220	650
Equity beta	1.20	1.36

Questions for Discussion

1. Estimate the company's WACC.
2. State your position with regard to the choice between the single company-wide, cut-off rate versus the multiple divisional cut-off rates.
3. Calculate cost of capital for divisions.

APPENDIX 9A: MARGINAL COST OF CAPITAL AND TARGET CAPITAL STRUCTURE

The weighted average cost of capital may be computed for the sources of finances already employed by the firm. One of the purposes in calculating this *historical cost* may be to evaluate the performance of management in raising funds by comparing it with some predetermined standard cost of capital. The most significant role of cost of capital lies in its use as an investment criterion. In the capital budgeting process, the firm is concerned with the selection of new projects. Therefore, the relevant cost is the cost of raising new funds to finance the projects, not the historical cost. Thus, the weighted average cost of incremental capital should be used in capital expenditure decisions. The weighted average cost of new, or incremental, capital is known as the **marginal cost of capital**.

Strictly speaking, the marginal cost of capital may be defined as the cost of raising an additional rupee of capital. Since the capital is raised in lump sum in practice, the marginal cost of capital in finance is referred to the cost incurred in raising the new funds. The marginal cost of capital is the weighted average cost of new capital using the marginal weights. The **marginal weights** represent the proportion of various funds the firm intends to employ. In theory, marginal weights are defined in terms of the firm's target capital structure. The **target capital structure** is one that the firm intends to maintain in the long run given its operating conditions and attitude towards risk.

Let us illustrate the concept of the marginal cost of capital and the relationship between the marginal and average cost of capital.[1] Consider Table 9A.1 which contains the existing capital structure of the Premier Ltd. and the component costs. We can compute the historical weighted average cost of capital (WACC) for Premier using its existing capital structure and the component costs as follows:

$$\text{WACC} = 0.12 \times 0.50 + 0.09 \times 0.10 + 0.04 \times 0.40$$
$$= 0.085 \text{ or } 8.5\%$$

Table 9A.1: Premier's Existing Capital Structure and the Component Costs

Sources of Capital	*Amount (Rs '000)*	*Weight*	*After-tax Cost*
Equity capital	50,000	0.50	0.12
Preference capital	10,000	0.10	0.09
Debt	40,000	0.40	0.04

The 8.5 per cent cost is a historical weighted average cost of capital, and therefore, it is of no use in the capital budgeting decisions. What the firm wants to measure is the cost of raising *new* funds currently, given its target capital structure.

Suppose that Premier has determined its target capital structure same as its existing capital structure: 50 per cent equity, 10 per cent preference capital and 40 per cent debt. Further, the expected after-tax component costs are: 13 per cent cost of equity; 10 per cent cost of preference capital and 8 per cent cost of debt. Premier's weighted average cost of capital, based on the *target capital structure* and the *expected costs* is as follows:

$$\text{WACC} = 0.13 \times 0.50 + 0.10 \times 0.10 + 0.08 \times 0.40$$
$$= 0.107 \text{ or } 10.7 \text{ per cent}$$

Given a firm's target capital structure and same expected component costs for any amount of funds raised, the weighted average cost of capital will equal the marginal cost of capital of the new capital (WACC = MCC), and they can be represented by a horizontal line as shown in Figure 9A.1.

---

1. Also see Brigham, E.F., *Financial Management: Theory and Practice*, Dryden Press, 1979, pp. 567–72.

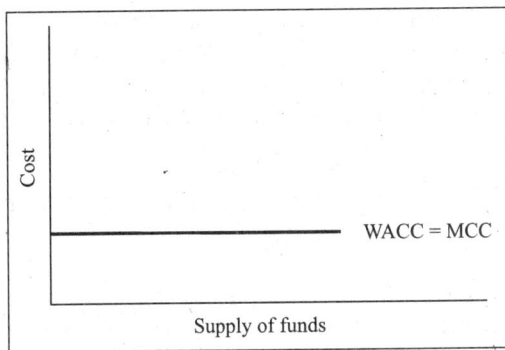

Figure 9A.1: WACC and MCC

In practice, the component costs may change with the amount of funds raised. Then WACC and MCC of new capital will not be same (WACC ≠ MCC). To illustrate this point, let us assume that Premier's expected components costs will be as follows:

Capital	After-tax Cost
1. Retained earnings	13%
2. New issue of equity shares	15%
3. New issue of preference shares	10%
4. Debt: Up to Rs 2 crore	6%
above Rs 2 crore	8%

Further, the company expects to generate retained earnings of Rs 2 crore in the next year. How should Premier raise funds to finance its investment projects? What shall be the cost of funds raised by Premier? What is the optimum capital budget for Premier?

Premier should raise funds in proportion to its target capital structure from its lowest cost sources first. Thus, it should first use the mix of retained earnings, preference capital and lower-cost debt. Once the retained earnings and lower cost debt are exhausted, it can use higher-cost external equity and debt with preference capital for financing its additional funds. The cost of raising funds will depend on the total amount of funds raised.

Premier can determine the total funds that can be raised before Rs 2 crore of internal funds are exhausted. We know that the target equity is 50 per cent; therefore, the total new funds that the internal funds will support is:

$$\text{Internal funds} = \text{Equity weight} \times \text{Total funds}$$

$$\text{Total funds} = \frac{\text{Internal funds}}{\text{Equity weight}} = \frac{\text{Rs 2 crore}}{0.50} = \text{Rs 4 crore}$$

Thus, Premier need not issue any new equity shares if its total financing is limited to Rs 4 crore. Similarly, we can compute the total funds that the lower-cost debt can support:

$$\text{Lower - cost debt} = \text{Debt weight} \times \text{Total funds}$$

$$\text{Total funds} = \frac{\text{Lower - cost debt}}{\text{Debt weight}} = \frac{\text{Rs 2 crore}}{0.40} = \text{Rs 5 crore}$$

This implies that if Premier's total financing ranges between Rs 4 crore to Rs 5 crore, it will have to issue new equity shares but it can still use the lower-cost debt with preference capital.

It should be clear that the cost of raising new funds up to Rs 4 crore will remain the same because retained earnings as well as lower-cost debt support this amount. Thus, the WACC of raising total new funds of Rs 4 crore is:

$$\text{WACC} = 0.13 \times 0.50 + 0.10 \times 0.10 + 0.06 \times 0.40$$
$$= 0.099 \text{ or } 9.9\%$$

The weighted marginal cost of capital (WMCC) to the firm for Rs 4 crore in new financing is also 9.9 per cent. WMCC is the cost of raising *additional* new funds while WACC is the cost of raising *total* new funds in a year. WMCC relates WACC to the total funds raised. Let us emphasise again that if the component costs do not change with additional new funds raised, then WMCC = WACC. But in practice, the component costs do change with the amount of funds raised in a year.

The first *break* in the cost of raising new funds will occur for Premier if it raises new funds in excess of Rs 4 crore. Beyond the total funds of Rs 4 crore but upto Rs 5 crore, Premier will have to issue new equity shares at a higher cost (15 per cent) in place of the lower-cost retained earnings (13 per cent). Thus, WMCC of raising additional new funds (in excess of Rs 4 crore) upto Rs 1 crore is:

$$\text{WMCC} = 0.15 \times 0.50 + 0.10 \times 0.10 + 0.06 \times 0.40$$
$$= 0.109 \text{ or } 10.9\%$$

What is the WACC of total new funds (or the bundle of funds) of Rs 5 crore? We know that Premier will have to issue new equity shares of Rs 50 lakh to maintain the equity weight:

	(Rs in crore)
Equity capital: 0.50 × Rs 5 crore	2.50
Less: Retained earnings	2.00
New equity shares	0.50

Thus, the proportions of various sources for raising the total funds of Rs 5 crore will be as given in Table 9A.2. The WACC of raising the total funds of Rs 5 crore is:

$$\text{WACC} = 0.13 \times 0.40 + 0.15 \times 0.10 + 0.10 \times 0.10 + 0.06 \times 0.40$$
$$= 0.101 \text{ or } 10.1\%$$

Table 9A.2: Proportions of Various Sources for Raising Total Funds of Rs 5 crore

Source of Capital	Amount (Rs '000)	Weight	After-tax Cost
Equity capital:			
Retained earnings	20,000	0.40	0.13
New shares	5,000	0.10	0.15
Preference shares	5,000	0.10	0.10
Debt	20,000	0.40	0.06
	50,000	1.00	

The WACC has increased (from 9.9 per cent to 10.1 per cent) because of the increase in the cost of raising *additional* new funds (from 9.9 per cent to 10.9 per cent). The WACC will always rise as a consequence of increase in marginal cost of raising incremental funds whenever the firm has exhausted its internal funds and is required to issue new shares to maintain its target capital structure.

The second break in the cost of raising new funds will occur if Premier raises the total new funds exceeding Rs 5 crore. Beyond Rs 5 crore of total new funds, Premier will exhaust lower-cost debt also, and therefore, it will have to employ not only the higher-cost external equity but also the higher-cost debt with preference capital. Thus, WMCC of raising additional funds in excess of Rs 5 crore is:

$$WMCC = 0.15 \times 0.50 + 0.10 \times 0.10 + 0.08 \times 0.4$$
$$= 0.117 \text{ or } 11.7\%$$

It may be noted that if no further changes in the component costs are anticipated, WMCC of raising any amount in excess of Rs 5 crore would remain as 11.7 per cent. WACC will rise, and it will depend on the total funds raised. For example, if the firm plans to raise the total funds of Rs 7.50 crore, it will have to issue new shares of Rs 1.75 crore:

	(Rs in crore)
Equity capital: 0.50 × Rs 7.50 crore	3.75
Less: Retained earnings	2.00
New equity shares	1.75

and 8 per cent debt of Rs 1 crore:

	(Rs in crore)
Debt: 0.40 × Rs 7.50 crore	3.00
Less: 6% debt	2.00
8% debt	1.00

For the total financing of Rs 7.5 crore, Premier's sources of capital with their proportions will be as given in Table 9A.3.

WACC of the total new funds of Rs 7.5 crore is:

$$WACC = 0.13 \times 0.267 + 0.15 \times 0.233$$
$$+ 0.10 \times 0.10 + 0.06 \times 0.267 + 0.08 \times 0.133$$
$$= 0.107 \text{ or } 10.7\%$$

Table 9A.3: Proportions of Various Sources for Raising Total Funds of Rs 7.50 crore

Source of Capital	Amount (Rs '000)	Weight	After-tax Cost
Equity capital:			
Retained earnings	20,000	0.267	0.13
New shares	17,500	0.233	0.15
Preference capital	7,500	0.100	0.10
Debt:			
6% debt	20,000	0.267	0.06
8% debt	10,000	0.133	0.08
	75,000	1.000	

Suppose that Premier decides to raise the total new funds of Rs 10 crore. We can determine that the firm will have to issue new shares of Rs 3 crore and 8 per cent debt of Rs 2 crore in addition

to the funds available through lower-cost retained earnings and debt and the preference capital. We can also compute the proportion of each source of financing, and then WACC of the total funds of Rs 10 crore can be determined as follows:

$$WACC = 0.13 \times 0.20 + 0.15 \times 0.30$$
$$+ 0.10 \times 0.10 + 0.06 \times 0.20 + 0.08 \times 0.20$$
$$= 0.109 \text{ or } 10.9\%$$

Notice that the WMCC of raising additional funds is still 11.7 per cent since no changes in the component costs are expected.

For Premier, the WMCC and WACC in relation to the supply of new funds are summarised in Table 13.7. We can observe from the table that the WACC increases with a rise in the WMCC, and that the WMCC increases faster than the WMCC.

Table 9A.4: The WMCC and WACC in Relation to the Supply of New Funds

Total New Funds (Rs '000)	Additional New Funds (Rs '000)	Cost of Additional new Funds: WMCC	Cost of Total New Funds: WACC
Up to – 40,000	40,000	0.099	0.099
40,000 – 50,000	10,000	0.109	0.101
50,000 – 75,000	25,000	0.117	0.107
75,000 – 100,000	25,000	0.117	0.109

Figure 9A.2 is drawn to show WMCC and WACC schedules and the supply of total funds. We can notice from the figure that

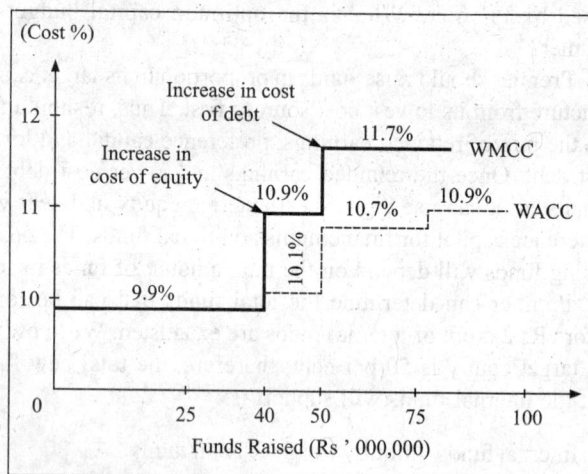

Figure 9A.2: The WMCC and WACC schedules

WMCC and WACC are same for the funds raised up to Rs 4 crore. The first break in WMCC schedule occurs when the firm raises funds in addition to Rs 4 crore after having exhausted the lower-cost internal equity; WMCC increases and so does the WACC. The second break in WMCC occurs when the firm further increases its total financing beyond Rs 5 crore after having exhausted the lower-cost debt also. Whenever there is a change in the component costs, WMCC schedule will show a break, and as a consequence WACC will also increase.

Determining Optimum Capital Budget

Optimum capital budget means the availability of funds to invest in all profitable projects so that the net present value is maximised. WMCC schedule should be used to determine the firm's **optimum capital budget**. The optimum capital budget can be determined by relating the expected returns of the investment projects to the firm's WMCC schedule. First, an **investment opportunity curve** (IOC) is drawn by plotting the expected returns from the proposed investment projects against the cumulative funds required. Next, the marginal cost of capital schedule is drawn. The optimum capital budget is determined at a point at which the investment opportunity curve (IOC) and the marginal cost of capital (MCC) schedule intersect.

To illustrate, let us suppose that Premier has prepared a list of the potential investment projects in the descending order of their internal rates of returns as shown in Table 9A.5.

We assume that all these projects have the same degree of risk as the firm's present business. We can determine the optimum capital budget by drawing the investment opportunity curve (IOC) and by relating it to Premier's marginal cost of capital schedule. The relationship between the IOC and WMCC schedules is shown in Figure 9A.3. Premier's capital budget totals Rs 7.9 crore and includes investment projects *A*, *B*, *C* and *D*. Projects *E* and *F* are excluded because their rates of return are expected to be below weighted marginal cost of capital of 11.7 per cent. Acceptance of Projects *A*, *B*, *C* and *D* will increase the firm's value. It should be noted that the optimum capital budget maximises the value of the firm.

Table 9A.5: Investment Opportunities with their Returns

Investment Project	Capital Expenditure (Rs '000)	Cumulative Capital Expenditure (Rs '000)	Internal Rate of Return (%)
A	15,000	15,000	14.0
B	20,000	35,000	13.7
C	23,000	58,000	13.0
D	21,000	79,000	12.3
E	18,000	97,000	11.0
F	3,000	1,00,000	10.0

Marginal Cost-Marginal Revenue Approach

We emphasise that the (weighted) marginal cost of capital should be used as the cut-off rate in the capital budgeting decisions. Let us redraw Figure 9A.3 to justify the rationale for using the marginal cost-marginal revenue approach.[1] In Figure 9A.4, WMCC and WACC schedules and IOC curves are drawn as smooth curves for simplicity. In the figure, the marginal cost of raising funds is equal to the marginal return of investment at X_1; therefore, OX_1 is the optimum capital budget. The firm will maximise its value by spending funds OX_1 on the investment projects. At X_2 the average cost of capital is equal to the marginal rate of return; but OX_2 *does not* represent the optimum capital budget. Let us illustrate this point.

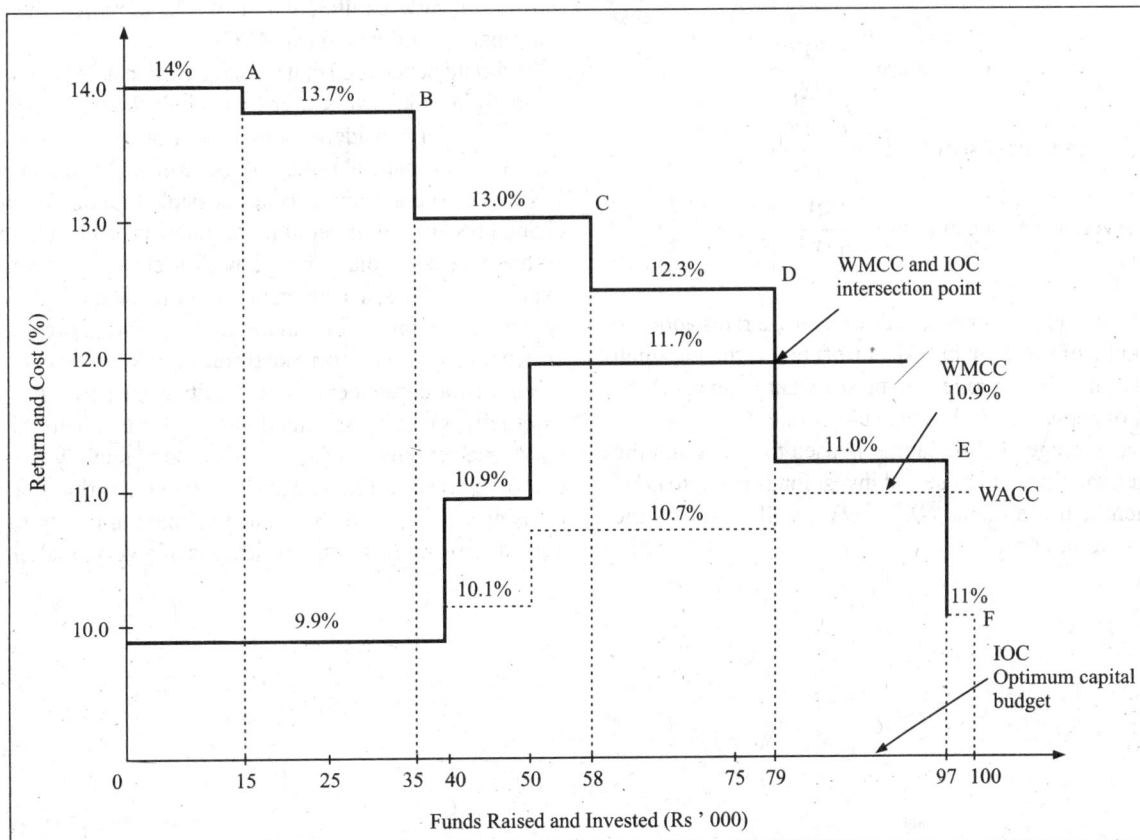

Figure 9A.3: Optimum capital budget

1. Arditti, F.D. and M.S. Tysseland, Three Ways to Present the Marginal Cost of Capital, *Financial Management*, 2, (Summer 1973), pp. 62–67.

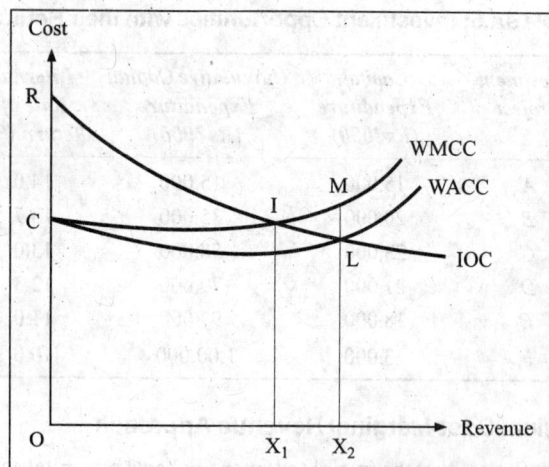

Figure 9A.4: Marginal cost-marginal revenue approach

We can observe the following in Figure 9A.4 when the weighted marginal cost of capital (WMCC) is used as the cut-off rate:

$$\text{Total gross return} = ORIX_1$$
$$\text{Total cost} = OCIX_1$$
$$\text{Total net return} = ORIX_1 - OCIX_1 = CRI$$

Since OX_1 is the total funds employed for the bundle of projects accepted, the average relationship will be as follows:

$$\text{Average rate of return} = \frac{ORIX_1}{OX_1}$$

$$\text{Average cost of funds} = \frac{OCIX_1}{OX_1}$$

$$\text{Average net rate of return} = \frac{CRI_1}{OX_1}$$

Note that in every instance, the three average rates apply to the entire bundle of projects; but the cut-off rate is the marginal cost of capital, not the average. Let us see what happens if the average cost of capital is used as the cut-off rate.

When the average cost of capital is used to determine the capital budget, the firm will raise and invest funds equal to OX_2. The incremental investment, $OX_2 - OX_1$, will result in the following return and cost:

$$\text{Incremental return} = X_1 ILX_2$$
$$\text{Incremental cost} = X_1 IMX_2$$

Since $X_1 ILX_2 < X_1 IMX_2$, the incremental investment will result into a negative net contribution equal to IML—representing a deduction from the total benefits that came in by investing funds equal to OX_1. Since the net return is maximum at X_1 where the WMCC schedule intersects IOC, OX_1 represents the optimum capital budget. When the firm accepts projects involving an investment of OX_1, the value of the firm is expected to increase because the firm is better off by the sum of net present values of cash flows from projects when discounted at the average cost of capital. The total effect on the value of the firm is computed by the use of the average cost of bundle of funds which financed the bundle of projects. But the marginal cost of capital is used as the cut-off rate.[1]

WMCC vs. WACC: A Word of Caution

What is commonly known as the weighted average cost of capital (WACC) in the context of investment and financing decisions in the financial literature is in fact the *weighted average cost of new capital given the firm's target capital structure*. Therefore, WACC is also the weighted marginal cost of capital (WMCC). We have tried to distinguish between the weighted average cost of *total* new funds, which we have called the weighted average cost of capital (WACC) and the weighted average cost of *additional* new capital, which we have called the weighted marginal cost of capital (WMCC).

It should be recalled that we have earlier stated two conditions for defining the firm's cost of capital; that is, the investment projects under consideration will not change the riskiness of the firm and the financial policy of the firm will remain unchanged. Given these conditions, it is not possible for component costs to change because of undertaking the new projects. Of course, the component costs may change with a change in the investors' expectation. Thus, at a given point of time, the weighted average cost of new capital will remain the same for all projects and can be represented by a horizontal line. The only possibility is the change in the component cost of equity when new funds are raised externally. Once the retained earnings are exhausted, the firm may issue new shares whose cost would be slightly more than the cost of retained earnings because of the underpricing. The impact of using external equity in place of internal equity may not be very significant if the underpricing is of a very small magnitude.

1. Arditti and Tysseland, *op. cit.*

10 Determining Cash Flows for Investment Analysis

INTRODUCTION

The important message of the preceding chapter is that sound investment decisions should be based on the net present value (NPV) rule. The first difficult problem to be resolved in applying the NPV rule in practice is: What should be discounted? In theory, the answer is obvious: We should always discount cash flows. In reality, estimating cash flows is the most difficult task. The difficulty in estimating cash flows arises because of uncertainty and accounting ambiguities. Events affecting investment opportunities change rapidly and unexpectedly. There is no easy way to anticipate changes in events. Mostly accounting data forms the basis for estimating cash flows. Accounting data are the result of arbitrary assumptions, choices and allocations. If care is not taken in properly adjusting the accounting data, errors could be made in estimating cash flows.

We consider the cash flow estimation as the most crucial step in investment analysis. A sophisticated technique applied to incorrect cash flows would produce wrong results. The management of a company should devote considerable time, effort and money in obtaining correct estimates of cash flows. The

financial manager prepares the cash flow estimates on the basis of the information supplied by experts in accounting, production, marketing, economics and so on. It is his responsibility to check such information for relevance and accuracy.

The second major problem in applying the NPV rule is: What rate should be used to discount cash flows? In principle, the opportunity cost of capital should be used as the discount rate. The concept of opportunity cost of capital and its measurement is discussed in Chapter 9.

CASH FLOWS VERSUS PROFIT

The use of NPV rule in investment decisions requires information about cash flows. It is the inflow and outflow of cash, which matters in practice. It is cash, which a firm can invest, or pay to creditors to discharge its obligations, or distribute to shareholders as dividends. Cash flow is a simple and objectively defined concept. It is simply the difference between rupees received and rupees paid out.

Cash flow should not be confused with profit. Changes in profits do not necessarily mean changes in cash flows. It is not difficult to find examples of firms in practice that experience cash shortages in spite of increasing profits. Cash flow is not the same thing as profit, at least, for two reasons. *First*, profit, as measured by an accountant, is based on **accrual concept**—revenue (sales) is recognised when it is earned, rather than when cash is received, and expense is recognised when it is incurred rather than when cash is paid. In other words, profit includes cash revenues as well as receivable and excludes cash expenses as well as payable. *Second*, for computing profit, expenditures are arbitrarily divided into revenue and capital expenditures. **Revenue expenditures** are entirely charged to profits while capital expenditures are not. **Capital expenditures** are capitalised as assets (investments), and depreciated over their economic life. Only annual depreciation is charged to profit. **Depreciation** (DEP) is an accounting entry and does not involve any cash flow. Thus, the measurement of profit excludes some cash flows such as capital expenditures and includes some non-cash items such as depreciation.

Let us illustrate the difference between profit and cash flow. Assume that a firm is entirely equity-financed, and it receives its revenues (REV) in cash and pays its expenses (EXP) and capital expenditures (CAPEX) in cash. Also, assume that taxes do not exist. Under these circumstances, profit is equal to:

$$\text{Profit} = \text{Revenues} - \text{Expenses} - \text{Depreciation}$$
$$\text{Profit} = \text{REV} - \text{EXP} - \text{DEP} \tag{1}$$

and cash flow is equal to:

$$\text{Case flow} = \text{Revenues} - \text{Expenses} - \text{Capital Expenditure}$$
$$\text{CF} = \text{REV} - \text{EXP} - \text{CAPEX} \tag{2}$$

It may be noticed from Equations (1) and (2) that profit does not deduct capital expenditures as investment outlays are made. Instead, depreciation is charged on the capitalised value of investments. Cash flow, on the other hand, ignores depreciation since it is a non-cash item and includes cash paid for capital expenditures. In the accountant's book, the net book value of capital expenditures will be equal to their capitalised value minus depreciation.

We can obtain the following definition of cash flows if we adjust Equation (2) for relationships given in Equation (1):

$$\text{CF} = (\text{REV} - \text{EXP} - \text{DEP}) + \text{DEP} - \text{CAPEX}$$
$$\text{CF} = \text{Profit} + \text{DEP} - \text{CAPEX} \tag{3}$$

Equation (3) makes it clear that even if revenues and expenses are expressed in terms of cash flow, still profit will not be equal to cash flows. It overstates cash inflows by excluding capital expenditures and understates them by including depreciation.[1] Thus, profits do not focus on cash flows. Financial managers will be making incorrect decisions if they put emphasis on profits or earnings per share. The objective of a firm is not to maximise profits or earnings per share, rather it is to maximise the shareholders' wealth, which depends on the present value of cash flows available to them. In the absence of taxes and debt, Equation (3) provides the definition of profits available for

distribution as cash dividends to shareholders. Profits fail to provide meaningful guidance for making financial decisions. Profits can be changed by affecting changes in the firm's accounting policy without any effect on cash flows. For example, a change in the method of inventory valuation will change the accounting profit without a corresponding change in cash flows.

In our discussion so far, we have assumed for simplicity an entirely equity-financed firm with no taxes. In the absence of taxes, depreciation is worthless since it has no impact on cash flows. However, it assumes relevance when taxes exist because depreciation is a deductible expense for computing taxes. Thus, it affects cash flows by saving taxes. In the next section, we show the computation of cash flows when taxes exist and the firm also employs debt.

INCREMENTAL CASH FLOWS

It is important to note that all additional cash flows that are directly attributable to the investment project should be considered. A cash flow stream is a series of cash receipts and payments over the life of an investment. The estimates of amounts and timing of cash flows resulting from the investment should be carefully made on an incremental basis.

What do we mean by **incremental cash flows**? Every investment involves a comparison of alternatives. The problem of choice will arise only if there are at least two possibilities. The minimum investment opportunity, which a company will always have, will be either to invest or not to invest in a project. Assume that the question before a company is to introduce a new product. The incremental cash flows in this case will be determined by comparing cash flows resulting with and without the introduction of the new product. If, for example, the company has to spend Rs 50,000 initially to introduce the product, we are implicitly comparing cash outlay for introducing the product with a zero cash outlay of not introducing the product. When the incremental cash flows for an investment are calculated by comparing with a hypothetical zero-cash-flow project, we call them *absolute cash flows*.

Assume now that the question before a company is to invest either in Project *A* or in Project *B*. One way of analysing can be to compute the absolute cash flows for each project and determine their respective NPVs. Then, by comparing their NPVs, a choice can be made. Alternatively, two projects can be compared directly. For example, we can subtract (algebraically) cash flows of Project *B* from that of Project *A* (or vice versa) to find out incremental cash flows (of Project *A minus* Project *B*). The positive difference in a particular period will tell how much more cash flow is generated by Project *A* relative to Project *B*. The incremental cash flows found out by such comparison between two *real* alternatives can be called **relative cash flows**.[2] NPV of this series of relative cash flows will be equal to NPV of the absolute cash flows from Project *A* minus NPV of the absolute cash flows from Project *B*. Thus, NPV $(A - B) = $ NPV $(A) - $ NPV (B). As discussed in the preceding chapter, this is so because of the **principle of value additivity**. The principle of incremental

---

1. Copeland, T.E. and Weston, J.F., *Financial Theory* and *Corporate Policy*, Addison-Wesley, 1983, p. 39.
2. Bierman, H., Jr. and Smidt, S., *The Capital Budgeting Decision*, Macmillan, 1975, p. 115.

cash flows assumes greater importance in the case of **replacement decisions**. Let us consider an example.

Illustration10.1: Incremental Cash Flows

Assume that a firm wants to replace an old equipment, which is capable of generating cash flows of Rs 2,000, Rs 1,000 and Rs 500 during the next 3 years. It has a book value of Rs 5,000 and a market value of Rs 3,000. The firm is considering a new equipment, which will require an initial cash outlay of Rs 10,000, and is estimated to generate cash flows of Rs 8,000, Rs 7,000 and Rs 4,500 for the next 3 years. Both old and new equipments may be assumed to have a zero resale value after 3 years. Further, we assume for the sake of simplicity that taxes do not exist. (Depreciation becomes irrelevant in investment analysis if taxes do not exist).

It should be recognised that the book value of Rs 5,000 of old equipment is not relevant; it is a **sunk cost**. In fact, cash outflow occurred when the equipment was bought. The initial cost of Rs 10,000 of new equipment is an outflow of cash. However, *if* the firm acquires new equipment, *then* the old equipment will be sold. The market value of Rs 3,000 of old equipment is an opportunity cost. Thus, on an incremental basis the net cash outflow of new equipment is: Rs 10,000 – Rs 3,000 = Rs 7,000. Further, if the firm continues with old equipment, it would, in any case, receive cash inflows of Rs 2,000, Rs 1,000 and Rs 500 during the next 3 years. Therefore, the firm should ask the question: What *incremental (additional) cash flows* will occur if a net cash outflow of Rs 7,000 is incurred on the new equipment? The differences of the cash flows of new equipment over the cash flows of old equipment are incremental cash flows. See Table 10.1 for computations.

Table 10.1: Incremental Cash Flows: Replacement Decision

Year	Cash Flows (Rs)			
	0	*1*	*2*	*3*
Cash flows of new equipment	–10,000	8,000	7,000	4,500
Less: Cash flows of old equipment	–3,000	2,000	1,000	500
Incremental cash flows, (New – Old)	–7,000	6,000	6,000	4,000

Let us relax the assumption of no resale value for old and new equipments after 3 years. Assume that the old equipment will realise Rs 500 and new equipment Rs 2,500 as salvage values after 3 years. If the firm goes for the new equipment, the estimated proceeds of Rs 2,500 from its sale after 3 years is an inflow of cash; but then the firm will discard old equipment *today* and forgo the opportunity of realising Rs 500 from its sale after 3 years. As a consequence, the net cash inflow from sale proceeds after 3 years will be Rs 2,500 – Rs 500 = Rs 2,000.

COMPONENTS OF CASH FLOWS

A typical investment will have three components of cash flows:

- Initial investment
- Annual net cash flows
- Terminal cash flows.

Initial Investment

Initial investment is the net cash outlay in the period in which an asset is purchased. A major element of the initial investment is gross outlay or original value (OV) of the asset, which comprises its cost (including accessories and spare parts) and

freight and installation charges. Original value is included in the existing block of assets for computing annual depreciation. Similar types of assets are included in one block of assets. Original value minus depreciation is the asset's book value (BV). When an asset is purchased for expanding revenues, it may require a lump sum investment in net working capital also. Thus initial investment will be equal to: gross investment plus increase in net working capital. Further, in case of replacement decisions, the existing asset will have to be sold if the new asset is acquired. The sale of the existing asset provides cash inflow. The cash proceeds from the sale of the existing assets should be subtracted to arrive at the initial investment. We shall use the term C_0 to represent initial investment.

In practice, a large investment project may comprise of a number of cost components and involve a huge initial net cash outlay. For example, a company is considering the manufacture of wattle extract. The project will require land and site development for constructing a factory building where plant and machinery to be bought by the company will be erected. Its estimated initial investment is shown in Table 10.2.

Table 10.2: Wattle Extract Project: Initial Investment

		(Rs in million)
Land and site development		65
Factory building		500
Plant and machinery:		
Imported	1,320	
Indigenous	460	
Duty and transportation	340	2,120
Erection expenditure	125	
Miscellaneous capital expenditure	290	
Preliminary and pre-operative expenses	250	
Contingency	200	865
Net working capital		600
Total initial investment (C_0)		4,150

Miscellaneous capital expenditure includes expenditure on electrification, water supply, vehicles and fire fighting. Preliminary and pre-operative expenses include legal and promotional expenses and brokerage and commission. These expenses may have to be incurred before the company's actual operations start. Contingencies are *ad hoc* in nature and are provided for any possible delay in, say, land acquisition and development, or in the installation of plant or any other activity. It is important to note that contingencies do *not* account for the uncertainties in the estimates of cash flows; the cash flow uncertainties should be handled differently.

Net Cash Flows

An investment is expected to generate annual cash flows from operations after the initial cash outlay has been made. Cash flows should always be estimated on an after-tax basis. Some people advocate computing of cash flows before taxes and discounting them at the before-tax discount rate to find NPV.

Unfortunately, this will not work in practice since there does not exist an easy and meaningful way for adjusting the discount rate on a before-tax basis.

We shall refer to the after-tax cash flows as net cash flows (NCF) and use the terms $C_1, C_2, C_3, \ldots C_n$ respectively for NCF in period 1, 2, 3, ... n. NCF is simply the difference between cash receipts and cash payments including taxes. NCF will mostly consist of annual cash flows occurring from the operation of an investment, but it is also be affected by changes in net working capital and capital expenditures during the life of the investment. To illustrate, we first take the simple case where cash flows occur only from operations. Let us assume that all revenues (sales) are received in cash and all expenses are paid in cash (obviously cash expenses will exclude depreciation since it is a non-cash expense). Thus, the definition of NCF will be:

$$\text{Net cash flow} = \text{Revenues} - \text{Expenses} - \text{Taxes}$$
$$\text{NCF} = \text{REV} - \text{EXP} - \text{TAX} \tag{4}$$

Notice that in Equation (4) taxes are deducted for calculating the after-tax cash flows. Taxes are computed on the accounting profit, which treats depreciation as a deductible expense.

Depreciation and Taxes

The computation of the after-tax cash flows requires a careful treatment of non-cash expense items such as depreciation. Depreciation is an allocation of cost of an asset. It involves an accounting entry and does not require any cash outflow; the cash outflow occurs when the assets are acquired.

Depreciation, calculated as per the income tax rules, is a deductible expense for computing taxes. In itself, it has no direct impact on cash flows, but it indirectly influences cash flow since it reduces the firm's tax liability. Cash outflow for taxes saved is in fact an inflow of cash. The saving resulting from depreciation is called **depreciation tax shield**. Consider an example.

Table 10.3: Profit and Loss Account for the Investment Project

	Rs
Revenues (cash)	25,000
Less: Expenses (cash)	10,000
Earnings before depreciation, interest and taxes	15,000
Less: Depreciation	5,000
Earnings before interest and taxes (EBIT)	10,000
Less: Taxes (35%)	3,500
Profit after taxes	6,500

Suppose that an investment requires an initial cash outlay of Rs 50,000. It is expected to generate total annual cash sales of Rs 25,000 and to incur total annual cash expenses of Rs 10,000 for the next 10 years. Also, assume that an annual depreciation of Rs 5,000 (i.e., cost recovered equally over the life of the investment) will be charged. If taxes do not exist, depreciation is of no use in computing cash flows, and NCF will simply be: Rs 25,000 – Rs 10,000 = Rs 15,000 per year. In practice, taxes do exist and depreciation is tax deductible. Let us assume a corporate tax rate of 35 per cent. We can recast a profit and loss account for the investment as given in Table 10.3. We see that

the investment yields an annual profit of Rs 6,500. However, this is not equal to the annual cash flow. Depreciation is a noncash item, and should be added to profit to compute actual cash flows. Thus net cash flows will be equal to: Rs 6,500 + Rs 5,000 = Rs 11,500. Now we develop an analytical method for computing the net cash flows from operations.

Taxes are paid on profits and can be calculated as follows:

$$\text{Taxes} = \text{Tax rate} \times \text{profit}$$
$$= \text{Tax rate} \times (\text{Revenues} - \text{Expenses} - \text{Depreciation})$$
$$\text{TAX} = T(\text{REV} - \text{EXP} - \text{DEP}) \tag{5}$$

where T is the corporate tax rate. Notice that the expression within brackets is the taxable income, which in our example is equal to earning before interest and taxes (EBIT), or net operating income (NOI). Thus,

Equation (5) can be rewritten as:

$$\text{TAX} = T\,(\text{EBIT}) \tag{6}$$

In the example (Table 10.3), taxes are equal to:

$$\text{Tax} = 0.35 \times 10,000 = \text{Rs } 3,500$$

and using Equation (4), net cash flow from operations will be

$$\text{NCF} = \text{REV} - \text{EXP} - \text{TAX}$$
$$= \text{Rs } 25,000 - \text{Rs } 10,000 - \text{Rs } 3,500 = \text{Rs } 11,500$$

NCF can also be measured in the following way if we substitute Equation (5) into Equation (4):

$$\text{NCF} = (\text{REV} - \text{EXP}) - T(\text{REV} - \text{EXP} - \text{DEP})$$
$$= (\text{REV} - \text{EXP}) - T(\text{REV} - \text{EXP}) + T(\text{DEP})$$
$$= (\text{REV} - \text{EXP})(1 - T) + T(\text{DEP}) \tag{7}$$
$$= \text{EBDIT}(1 - T) + T(\text{DEP})$$

where EBDIT is earnings before depreciation, interest and taxes. Using Equation (7), NCF is computed as follows:

$$\text{NCF} = (\text{Rs } 25,000 - \text{Rs } 10,000)(1 - 0.35) + 0.35\,(\text{Rs } 5,000)$$
$$= \text{Rs } 9,750 + \text{Rs } 1,750 = \text{Rs } 11.500$$

It may be noted from the above computation that depreciation has provided a tax shield (DTS) equal to tax rate multiplied by the amount of depreciation:

Depreciation tax shield = Tax rate × Depreciation

$$\text{DTS} = T \times \text{DEP} = 0.35 \times \text{Rs } 5,000 = \text{Rs } 1,750$$

After-tax cash flows would have been only Rs 9,750 if the government did not allow depreciation as a tax-deductible expense. Note that for tax computation, depreciation amount must be calculated as per the Income Tax rules. This is explained later on in this section.

We can obtain yet another definition of net cash flows by adjusting Equation (4). Let us add and subtract depreciation (DEP) on the right hand-side of Equation (4):

$$\text{NCF} = \text{REV} - \text{EXP} - \text{DEP} - \text{TAX} + \text{DEP}$$
$$= \text{EBIT} - \text{TAX} + \text{DEP}$$

and if we use the definition of tax as given in Equation (6), then:

$$NCF = EBIT - T(EBIT) + DEP = EBIT(1-T) + DEP \quad (8)$$

Note from Equation (8) that net cash flow from operation is equal to after-tax operating income plus depreciation. In the example, NCF using Equation (9) is given as follows:

$$NCF = (Rs\,25,000 - Rs\,10,000 - Rs\,5,000)(1-0.35) + Rs\,5,000$$
$$= Rs\,10,000(0.65) + Rs\,5,000 = Rs\,6,500 + Rs\,5,000$$
$$= Rs\,11,500$$

Net Working Capital

In computing net cash flows in the above example, we have assumed that all revenues are received in cash and all expenses are paid in cash. In reality, the actual cash receipts and cash payments will differ from revenues (sales) and expenses as given in the profit and loss account. This difference is caused by changes in working capital items, which include trade debtors (accounts receivable), trade creditors (accounts payable) and stock (inventory). Therefore, Equations (7) and (8) may over-or under-state cash flows. Consider the following situations:

- *Change in accounts receivable* The firm's customers may delay payment of bills which will increase receivable. Since revenues (sales) include credit sales, it will overstate cash inflow. Thus, increase (or decrease) in receivable should be subtracted from (or added to) revenues for computing actual cash receipts.
- *Change in inventory* The firm may pay cash for materials and production of unsold output. The unsold output increases inventory. Expenses do not include cash payments for unsold inventory, and therefore, expenses understate actual cash payments. Thus, increase (or decrease) in inventory should be added to (or subtracted from) expenses for computing actual cash payments.
- *Change in accounts payable* The firm may delay payment for materials and production of sold output (sales). This will cause accounts payable (suppliers' credit) to increase. Since accounts payable is included in expenses, they overstate actual cash payments. Thus, increase (or decrease) in accounts payable should be subtracted from (or added to) expenses for computing actual cash payments.

It is, thus, clear that changes in working capital items should be taken into account while computing net cash inflow from the profit and loss account. Instead of adjusting each item of working capital, we can simply adjust the change in net working capital, viz. the difference between change in current assets (e.g., receivable and inventory) and change in current liabilities (e.g., accounts payable) to profit. Increase in net working capital should be subtracted from and decrease added to after-tax operating profit. Thus, we can extend Equation (8) as follows for

computing net cash flow:

$$NCF = EBIT\,(1-T) + DEP - NWC \quad (9)$$

where NWC is net working capital.

Free Cash Flows

In addition to an initial cash outlay, an investment project may require some reinvestment of cash flow (for example, replacement investment) for maintaining its revenue-generating ability during its life. As a consequence, net cash flow will be reduced by cash outflow for additional capital expenditures (CAPEX). Thus, net cash flow will be equal to: after-tax operating income plus depreciation minus (plus) increase (decrease) in net working capital and minus capital expenditure:

$$NCF = EBIT\,(1-T) + DEP - NWC - CAPEX \quad (10)$$

Net cash flows as defined by Equation (10) are called **free cash flow** (FCF). It is the cash flow available to service both lenders and shareholders, who have provided, respectively, debt and equity, funds to finance the firm's investments. It is this cash flow, which should be discounted to find out an investment's NPV.

Notice the difference between Equations (3) and (10); Equation (10) adjusts profits for taxes and net working capital. Equation (10) provides the most valid definition of free cash flows or net cash flow. Since net cash flows are stated on incremental basis in investment analysis, Equation (10) may be rewritten as follows:[1]

$$FCF = \Delta EBIT\,(1-T) + \Delta DEP - \Delta NWC - \Delta CAPEX \quad (11)$$

where Δ (delta) indicates change (increase or decrease).

Terminal Cash Flows

Equation (11) provides a general definition of incremental net cash flow in any period. However, the last or terminal year of an investment may have additional cash flows.

Salvage Value

Salvage value (SV) is the most common example of terminal cash flows. **Salvage value** may be defined as the market price of an investment at the time of its sale. The cash proceeds net of taxes from the sale of the assets will be treated as cash inflow in the terminal (last) year. As per the existing tax laws in India, no *immediate* tax liability (or tax savings) will arise on the sale of an asset because the value of the asset sold is adjusted in the depreciable base of assets.

In the case of a replacement decision, in addition to the salvage value of the new investment at the end of its life, two other salvage values have to be considered: (*a*) the salvage value of the existing asset *now* (at the time of replacement decision) and (*b*) the salvage value of the existing asset at the *end of its life*, if it were not replaced. If the existing asset is replaced, its salvage

---

1. In practice, sales are taken as the basis for computing expected profits and cash flows. If we assume a constant relationship between sales and profit, net working capital and capital expenditure, Equation (11) can be restated as follows:

$$\Delta NCF = \Delta SALES\,(p)\,(1-T) + \Delta EP - (w+f)\,\Delta SALES$$

where p = EBIT as a percentage of sales, w = net working capital as a percentage of sales and f = capital expenditure as a percentage of sales.

value *now* will increase the current cash inflow, or will decrease the initial cash outlay of the new asset. However, the firm will have to forego its end-of-life salvage value. This means reduced cash inflow in the last year of the new investment.

The effects of the salvage values of existing and new assets may be summarised as follows:

- *Salvage value of the new asset* It will increase cash inflow in the terminal (last) period of the new investment.
- *Salvage value of the existing asset now* It will reduce the initial cash outlay of the new asset.
- *Salvage value of the existing asset at the end of its normal life* It will reduce the cash flow of the new investment of in the period in which the existing asset is sold.

Sometimes *removal* costs may have to be incurred to replace an existing asset. Salvage value should be computed after adjusting these costs.

Tax effect of salvage value A company will incur a book loss if an asset is sold for a price less than the asset's book (depreciated) value. On the other hand, the company will make a profit if the asset's salvage value is more than its book value. The profit on the sale of an asset may be divided into ordinary income and capital gain. Capital gain on the sale of an asset is equal to salvage value minus original value of the asset, and ordinary income is equal to original value minus book value (depreciated value) of the asset. Capital gains are generally taxed at a rate lower than the ordinary income. Does a company pay tax on profit or get tax credit on loss on the sale of an asset? In a number of countries, the sale of an asset has tax implications. This was also a practice in India till recently. But as per the current Income Tax rules in India, the depreciable base of the block of assets is adjusted for the sale of the block asset and no taxes are computed when the asset is sold. This point is illustrated later on in this chapter.

The net salvage value (i.e., net proceeds from the sale of the asset) can be calculated as follows assuming tax implications of the sale of assets:

1. SV < BV: Loss

    Net proceeds = Salvage value + Tax credit on loss

    Net proceeds = $SV - T(SV - BV)$

2. SV > BV but SV < OV: Ordinary Profit

    Net proceeds = Salvage value − Tax on profit

    Net proceeds = $SV - T(SV - BV)$

3. SV > OV: Ordinary Profit and Capital Gain

    Net proceeds = Salvage value − Tax on ordinary profit
    − Tax on capital gain

    Net proceeds = $SV - T(OV - BV) - T_c(SV - OV)$

where SV = salvage value; BV = book (depreciated) value; OV = original value; T = ordinary corporate income tax rate, and T_c = capital gain tax rate

Release of Net Working Capital

Besides salvage value, terminal cost flows will also include the release of net working capital. It is reasonable to assume that funds initially tied up in net working capital at the time the investment was undertaken would be released in the last year when the investment is terminated. As discussed earlier, the net working capital in reality may change in every period of the investment's life. Such changes should be considered in computing annual net cash flows. Increase in net working capital is a cash outflow while decrease in net working capital is a cash inflow. In practice, it may not be possible for a firm to recover the entire net working capital at the end of the project's life. The actual amount of net working capital recovered should be considered as the cash inflow in the terminal year.

CALCULATION OF DEPRECIATION FOR TAX PURPOSES

Two most popular methods of charging depreciation are: straight-line and diminishing balance or written-down value (WDV) methods. For reporting to the shareholders, companies in India could charge depreciation either on the straight-line or the written-down value basis. However, no choice of depreciation method and rates for the tax purposes is available to companies in India. In India, depreciation is allowed as deduction every year on the written-down value basis in respect of fixed assets as per the rates prescribed in the Income Tax rules. Depreciation is computed on the written down value of the block of assets. Block of assets means a group of assets falling within a class of assets, being buildings, machinery, plant or furniture, in respect of which some percentage of depreciation is prescribed. Ocean-going ships are also included in the block of assets. For example, plant and machinery has been divided into three blocks with three rates of depreciation: 25 per cent, 50 per cent and 100 per cent. Most of the plants and machineries are covered in the 25 per cent depreciation block. No depreciation is allowed on land.

How is written down value defined? In simple terms, for a single asset, it is the original cost of the asset minus the amount of depreciation charged: OV − DEP. To illustrate, let us consider that an asset of Rs 1,000 which has a three-year life, is acquired on January 1, 19X1. If the prescribed depreciation rate is 25 per cent, the written down value and depreciation of the asset over its life will be as follows:

Year	Initial cost of asset (Rs)	WDV depreciation at 25% (Rs)	Written down value of asset (Rs)
0	1,000	—	1,000
1		$1,000 \times 0.25 = 250$	$1,000 - 250 = 750$
2		$750 \times 0.25 = 188$	$750 - 188 = 562$
3		$562 \times 0.25 = 141$	$562 - 141 = 421$

Depreciation base In the case of block of assets, the written down value is calculated as follows:

The aggregate of the written down value of all assets in the block at the beginning of the year

Plus the actual cost of any asset in the block acquired during the year

Minus the proceeds from the sale of any asset in the block during the year (provided such reduction does not exceed the written down value of the block arrived in the first two items above)

Thus, in a replacement decision, the depreciation base of a new asset (assuming that the new and the old assets belong to the same block of assets) will be equal to:

Cost of new equipment

+ Written down value of old equipment

– Salvage value of old equipment

How do you estimate cash flows of an investment project? We illustrate the cash flow computations for investment projects, involving the treatment of depreciation and salvage value, the following sections.

Cash Flow Estimates for a New Product

A new product may be a slight modification of the firm's existing product or it may be an altogether different, innovative product. The cash flow estimates for a new product will depend on forecasts of sales and operating expenses. Sales forecasts require information on the quantity of sales and the price of the product. The selling price and sales quantity depend on the nature of competition. Anticipating the competitors' reactions when an innovative product is introduced is not easy. Thus the estimation of cash flows for a new product poses considerable difficulty and challenge. The marketing executives developing sales forecasts should be aware with the forecasting techniques as well as they should have the ability of understanding the dynamics of competition. Hence the cash flow estimation for a new product is both an art and a science. We show in Illustration 10.2 the cash flow pattern for a new product.

Illustration 10.2: Cash Flows for a New Product

Bharat Foods Limited is a consumer goods manufacturing company. It is considering a proposal for marketing a new food product. The project will require an investment of Rs 1 million in plant and machinery. It is estimated that the machinery can be sold for Rs 100,000 at the end of its economic life of 6 years. Assume that the loss or profit on the sale of the machine is subject to the corporate tax. The company can charge annual written-down depreciation at 25 per cent for the purpose of tax computation. Assume that the company's tax rate is 35 per cent and the discount rate is 18 per cent. Table 10.4 gives the initial capital investment, annual depreciation and annual working capital for the project. Notice that annual written-down value depreciation is calculated as the depreciation rate 25 per cent times the book value at the end of the previous year (which is also book value at the beginning of the current year). Lines 2–4 show computation of depreciation and book value. Line 5 gives the estimates of net working capital, which may be expected to change with sales.

A simplified profit and loss statement for the project is given in Table 10.5. The first step in estimating the project's cash flows is the forecasts of sales. The marketing executives will have to forecast the units of the product that they could sell as well as the selling price of the product. They will have to keep in mind the competitive pressure and reaction. This makes sales forecasting a tricky job. The estimated sales forecasts in Table 10.5 show that the product demand rises quickly and then starts declining after the fourth year. The estimates of operating expenses and working capital follow the sales forecasts. Table 10.4 and Table 10.5 provide data for determining the project's net cash flows, which are computed in Table 10.6.

Table 10.4: Investment Data for the New Product

	(Rs '000)						
Year	*0*	*1*	*2*	*3*	*4*	*5*	*6*
1. Initial investment	1,000						
2. Depreciation		250	188	141	105	79	59
3. Accumulated depreciation		250	438	579	684	763	822
4. Book value (1 – 2 – 3)	1,000	750	562	421	316	237	178
5. Net working capital	20	30	50	70	70	30	0
6. Total book value (4 + 5)	1,020	780	612	491	386	267	178
7. Salvage value							100

Table 10.5: Summarised Profit & Loss Statement for the New Product

	(Rs '000)					
Year	*1*	*2*	*3*	*4*	*5*	*6*
1. Revenues	550	890	1,840	2,020	1,680	1,300
2. Expenses	–300	–472	–958	–1,075	–890	–680
3. Depreciation	–250	–188	–141	–105	–79	–59
4. Taxable profit (1 – 2 – 3)	0	230	741	840	711	561
5. Tax (.35 × 4)	0	81	259	294	249	196
6. Profit after tax	0	149	482	546	462	365

Table 10.6: Computations of Net Cash Flows for the New Product

	(Rs '000)						
Year	*0*	*1*	*2*	*3*	*4*	*5*	*6*
1. Investment	–1,000						
2. Profit after tax		0	149	482	546	462	365
3. Depreciation		250	188	141	105	79	59
4. Δ NWC	–20	–10	–20	–20	0	40	30
5. Cash flow from operations (2 + 3 + 4)		240	317	603	651	581	581
7. After-tax SV [100 – .35(100 – 178)]							127
8. Net cash flows (1 + 5 + 6)	–1,020	240	317	603	651	581	581
9. Present value factor at 18%	1.000	.847	.718	.609	.516	.437	.370
10. Present value (8 × 9)	–1,020	203	228	367	336	254	215
11. NPV	+ 583						

Cash flows from operations Cash flows with – (minus) signs are outflows and those with + (plus) signs are inflows. Cash flows from operations (line 5 in Table 10.6) are measured as revenues minus expenses and taxes. It would also be computed as earnings after taxes plus depreciation [EBIT $(1 – T)$ + DEP]. Note that depreciation is an operating expense for computing taxes, but it is a non-cash expense. Therefore, depreciation is added back to profit after taxes to arrive at cash flow from operations. The *change* in net working capital is yet another item that affects cash flow from operations. Line 5 in Table 10.4 shows the level of working capital to sustain the forecasted sales. Bharat Foods needs upfront working capital investment of Rs 20,000 before it could sell the new product. This is an outflow of cash. The working capital requirement increases by Rs 10,000 in the first year. This is a use of cash. A decrease in working capital will release cash, which means cash inflow. It may be noticed that net working capital increases (outflows) through year 3, but then gets released (inflows) in the last two years. It is assumed that the working capital is recovered without any diminution in value.

After-tax salvage value The machine has a book value of Rs 178,000 and its salvage value is Rs 100,000 at the end of its useful life of 6 years. Hence the book loss on sale of machine is Rs 78,000. Since in this Illustration it is assumed that *book loss is subject to corporate tax*, the firm will charge loss to its profits and save taxes. Therefore, the after-tax cash proceeds from the sale of machine are Rs 100,000 plus the tax saved; that is: $100,000 - 0.35(100,000 - 178,000) = 100,000 + 27,000 = $ Rs 127,000.

The net cash flows may be summarised as follows:

Year	0	1	2	3	4	5	6
Net Cash flows	−1,020	240	317	603	651	581	581

We may assume that *the project's risk is similar to the company's risk*. Hence the company's opportunity cost of capital of 18 per cent is used to discount the project's cash flows.

$$NPV = -1020 + 240\,(PVF_{0.18,1}) + 317\,(PVF_{0.18,2})$$
$$+ 603\,(PVF_{0.18,3}) + 651\,(PVF_{0.18,4})$$
$$+ 581\,(PVF_{0.18,5}) + 554\,(PVF_{0.18,6})$$
$$= -1020 + 240 \times 0.847 + 317 \times 0.718 + 603 \times 0.609$$
$$+ 651 \times 0.516 + 581 \times 0.437 + 581 \times 0.370$$
$$= -1020 + 203 + 228 + 367 + 336 + 254 + 215$$
$$= Rs\ 583$$

The company obtains a net present value of Rs 583,000 when the cash flows are discounted at 18 per cent. Since NPV is positive, the project should be accepted.

How much is the project's IRR? We can find out IRR by trial and error. (It is easy to calculate IRR using a computer or a financial calculator.) Let us try 30 per cent discount rate: PV = Rs 1,151 and NPV is Rs 131. We should try a higher rate. Let us try 34 per cent. At 34 per cent: PV is Rs 1,043 and NPV is Rs 23. Since NPV is positive at 34 per cent, let us try 35 per cent. At 35 per cent, PV is Rs 1,018 and NPV is minus Rs 2, which is close to zero. Thus, IRR is approximately 35 per cent. In fact, IRR should be between 34 to 35 per cent. We can find IRR as follows:

$$IRR = 34\% + (35\% - 34\%)\left[\frac{1,043 - 1,020}{1,043 - 1,018}\right] = 34\% + 1\%\left(\frac{23}{25}\right)$$
$$= 34\% + 0.92\%$$
$$= 34.92\%$$

Since the project's IRR is greater than the cut-off rate (the opportunity cost of capital), it should be accepted. Note that a project with positive NPV will have IRR greater than the opportunity cost of capital.

Salvage Value and Tax Effects

In Illustration 10.2, we assumed that the firm would get tax credit on the book loss (or unrecovered cost) when the machine

is sold. In India, as per the current tax laws, the remaining book value (i.e., book value minus salvage value) of an asset is included in the block of assets and therefore, the firm continues availing depreciation deduction on the asset's unrecovered cost after its sale. This implies that the tax advantage on unrecovered cost via depreciation tax shield would occur over a long period of time (in fact, an infinite period) rather than at the time the asset is sold.

An asset may be sold for more that its book value (written down). This difference, in excess of the asset's book value, is a book profit on the sale of the asset. According to the Indian tax laws, the balance of the block of assets will reduce by this difference. Hence instead of paying tax on this book profit at the time of sale of the asset, the firm would lose depreciation tax shield in the future. Thus, as per the current tax laws in India, the *after-tax salvage value* should be calculated at follows:

Book value (WDV) > Salvage value (SV):

After-tax salvage value = Salvage value + PV of depreciation tax shield on (BV − SV)

Salvage value (SV) > Book value (BV):

After-tax salvage value = Salvage value − PV of depreciation tax shield lost on (SV − BV)

In Illustration 10.2, book value is greater than salvage value and the remaining balance of the book value is Rs 78,000. Depreciation on this amount will save tax for the firm forever (infinity). We can use the following formula to calculate the present value of the (prepetually decling annuity) depreciation tax shield after the asset is sold at the end of its useful life:[1]

$$PVDTS_n = \left[\frac{T \times d}{k + d}\right] \times \left(BV_n - SV_n\right) \tag{12}$$

Note that $PVDTS_n$ is the present value of depreciation tax shield at the end of n period, T the tax rate, d the depreciation rate, k the discount rate, BV_n is book value at the end of n period and SV_n is salvage value at the end of n period. In Illustration 10.2, PV of depreciation tax shield on the remaining book value of Rs 78,000 is:

$$PVDTS_n = \left[\frac{.35 \times .25}{.18 + .25}\right] \times (178,000 - 100,000)$$
$$= .2035 \times 78,000 = Rs\ 15,873$$

You may notice that this amount is less than the tax saved on book loss allowed at the time of sales of the asset. This is so because the depreciation tax shield occurs over a long period in the future.

Terminal Value for a New Business

In Illustration 10.2, Bharat Foods Limited considered the life of project as six years. The terminal value included the salvage value of the asset and the release of the working capital. In practice, many new products generate new businesses and have the potential of generating revenues and cash flows much

---

1. The formula is derived in Appendix 10.1.

beyond the assumed period of analysis, which is referred to as **horizon period**. Managers make assumption of horizon period because detailed calculations for a long period become quite intricate. The financial analysis of such projects should incorporate an estimate of the value of cash flows after the horizon period without involving detailed calculations.

A simple method of estimating the terminal value at the end of the horizon period is to employ the following formula, which is a variation of the dividend growth model:

$$TV_n = \frac{NCF_n(1+g)}{k-g} = \frac{NCF_{n+1}}{k-g} \qquad (13)$$

where NCF_{n+1} is the project's net cash flow one year after the horizon period, k is the opportunity cost of capital (discount rate) and g is the expected growth in the project's net cash flows. The value of g will be positive if net cash flows are expected to grow; it will be negative if net cash flows are expected to decline; and it will be zero if net cash flows are expected to remain constant. In practice, the financial manager could calculate the effect of a range of values of g on the project's NPV. This will enable him or her to determine the minimum growth rate of cash flows after horizon period that will make the project's NPV positive. The financial manager will be quite confident to accept the project if the minimum growth rate is equal to or greater than the most pessimistic forecast. Let us consider an example.

Illustration 10.3: Effect of Estimated Salvage Value

Suppose that Healthy Drinks Limited is considering introducing a new fruit drink in the market. Sales and cash flows are expected to grow steadily over years. The firm's investment is working capital will not be significant as it expects to finance the accounts receivable (credit given to distributors) by the fruit suppliers' credit. The firm expects to carry small inventory. However, the firm will have to incur significant expenditure on marketing and distribution. Management consider this as a risky project and specifies its discount rate as 25 per cent. The financial manager has made the following estimates of the project's cash flows assuming a horizon period of 7 years:

Year	0	1	2	3	4	5	6	7
Net cash flows (Rs million)	–15	–5.0	2.5	5.0	7.5	9.5	10.5	11.5

The project's NPV is negative:

$$NPV = -15 - \frac{5.0}{(1.25)^1} + \frac{2.5}{(1.25)^2} + \frac{5.0}{(1.25)^3}$$
$$+ \frac{7.5}{(1.25)^4} + \frac{9.5}{(1.25)^5} + \frac{10.5}{(1.25)^6} + \frac{11.5}{(1.25)^7}$$
$$= -Rs\,3.5\ million$$

NPV is still negative if we assume that the entire initial investment is recovered as salvage value at the end of year 7 (tax effect ignored):

$$NPV = -3.5 + \frac{15}{(1.25)^7} = -Rs\,0.4\ million$$

You may notice that the project has initial negative cash flows, but after year 2 its net cash flows become positive and start growing rapidly through year 5. After year 5, net cash flows show a steady growth; the growth rate after 5 years is about 10 per cent. If you assume that the net cash flows will

grow at 10 per cent after year 7, then the present value of terminal value (TV) is

$$PV(TV) = \frac{1}{(1.25)^7} \times \frac{11.5(1.10)}{.25 - .10}$$
$$= 0.210 \times 84.3 = Rs\,17.7\ million$$

The project's NPV is: –3.5 + 17.7 = Rs 14.2 million. What will be project's NPV if net cash flows remain constant after year 7? It will be: –3.5 + (11.5/.25) × .210 = –3.5 + 9.66 = Rs 6.2. It is also likely that due to competitive pressure, sales and cash flows may decline. As a pessimistic forecast, suppose that cash flows will decline at 5 per cent per annum, then the project's NPV will be:

$$NPV = -3.5 + \frac{1}{(1.25)^7} \times \frac{11.5(1 - .05)}{.25 - (-.05)}$$

$$= -3.5 + \frac{1}{(1.25)^7} \times \frac{11.5(0.95)}{.30}$$

$$= -3.5 + 0.210 \times 36.4 = -3.5 + 7.6 = Rs\,4.1\ million$$

The project is profitable even when the cash flow growth rate is negative (–5 per cent). Pure Drinks should accept the project. Note that this analysis ignores any subsequent investment needed to maintain the competitive position of the product. It also ignores the growth opportunities that this product will provide in introducing other new products in the future.

Cash Flow Estimates for Replacement Decisions

Replacement decisions include decisions to replace the existing assets with new assets. Firms undertake replacement decisions either for cost reduction or quality improvement or both. It is relatively easy to estimate cash flow for replacement decision. Generally, these decisions do not involve sales forecasts. They need an assessment of the possible cost savings or improvement in the quality of product, which, to a large extent, depends on the technical specifications of the equipments. In Illustration 10.4, we show the cash flow calculations for a replacement decision.

Illustration 10.4: Replacement Decision

Excel Engineering Company is considering replacement of one of its existing fabrication machines by a new machine, which is expected to cost Rs 160,000. The existing machine has a book value of Rs 40,000, and can be sold for Rs 20,000 now. It is good for the next 5 years and is estimated to generate annual cash revenues of Rs 200,000 and incur annual cash expenses of Rs 140,000. If sold after 5 years, the salvage value of the existing machine can be expected to be Rs 2,000. The new machine will have a life of 5 years. It is expected to save costs and improve the quality of the product that would help to increase sales. The new machine will yield annual cash revenues of Rs 250,000 and incur annual cash expenses of Rs 130,000. The estimated salvage value of the new machine is Rs 8,000.

Excel Company pays tax at 35 per cent, and can write off depreciation at 25 per cent on the written-down value of the asset. The company's opportunity cost of capital is 20 per cent. Should Excel place the existing machine? Assume that there is no inflation.

Given the information, we can compute the incremental cash flows of the replacement decision. Table 10.8 shows the computation of net cash flows and net present value. Cash flows with – (minus) signs are outflows and those with + (plus) signs are inflows.

The following steps are involved in the computation of net cash flows:

Initial investment The initial investment of the new machine will be reduced by the cash proceeds from the sale of the existing machine:

Gross investment in new machine	−160,000
Salvage value of the existing machine	20,000
Net cash outlay	−140,000

On the acquisition of the new machine and sale of old machine, the *incremental* gross block will be: Rs 140,000. Notice that taking the incremental gross block as Rs 140,000 fully adjusts for the lost depreciation tax shield (DTS) on the salvage value and that it is not necessary to make any further adjustments while computing the initial outlay.

Annual cash flows from operations The annual cash flows are found on incremental basis. The new machine will increase gross cash flows by Rs 60,000, which consists of revenues of Rs 50,000 and decrease in expenses of Rs 10,000. Note that the decrease in expenses is an inflow. Net cash flows from operation are found by subtracting payment for taxes after considering incremental depreciation. Table 10.7 shows the depreciation schedule for the incremental block of assets.

Table 10.7: Depreciation Schedule

Year	Differential Depreciation ΔDEP
1	35,000
2	26,250
3	19,687
4	14,765
5	11,074
Total depreciation	106,776
Book value after 5 years	33,224
	140,000

We could use the following formula for computing net cash flows from operations:

$$\Delta NOCF = (\Delta REV - \Delta EXP)(1 - T) + \Delta DEP \times T$$
$$= \Delta EBIT(1 - T) + \Delta DEP \times T$$

Applying the formula to data for year 1 NCF is:

$$NOCF = [(250,000 - 200,000) - (130,000 - 140,000)$$
$$(1 - 0.35) + (45,000 - 10,000) \times 0.35$$
$$= [50,000 - (-10,000)] 0.65 + 35,000 \times 0.35$$
$$= 39,000 + 12,250 = Rs\ 51,250$$

Similar computation can be made for other periods.

Terminal cash flows The firm can charge depreciation forever. Therefore, we need to calculate the value of depreciation tax shield (DTS) at the end of year 5. We can make the calculations of DTS as follows:

Depreciation tax shield at year 5

$$= BV_5 \times \frac{T \times d}{d + k}$$
$$= 140,000 \times (1 - 0.25)^5 \times \frac{0.35 \times 0.25}{0.25 + 0.20}$$
$$= 33.223 \times 0.19444 = Rs\ 6,460$$

The old machine has a salvage value of Rs 20,000 and its book value is Rs 40,000. The firm can avail depreciation of the remaining book value (Rs 40,000 − Rs 20,000) of the old machine forever. Thus, the after-tax salvage value of the *old* machine *now* is more than Rs 20,000. This adjustment is made automatically when we calculate depreciation on the net block of assets (cost of new assets less salvage of the old asset). The net block incorporates adjustment of the old machine's book value and salvage value.

Salvage value of the new and old machines after 5 years will affect cash flows in the last year. If the company decides to go for the new machine, it can expect to obtain a salvage value of Rs 8,000, but then it forgoes the option of receiving Rs 2,000 as the existing machine's salvage value. Thus, the incremental cash proceeds from salvage value are Rs 6,000. In exchange for the salvage value, the firm will lose depreciation tax shield forever. Thus

$$6,000 - [(.35 \times .25)/(.20 + .25)] \times 6,000 = 6,000 - 1,167$$
$$= Rs\ 4,833$$

Table 10.8: Computation of NCF and NPV based on After-Tax Salvage Values

Year	0	1	2	3	4	5
Investment in new machine	−160,000					
Salvage value of old machine	20,000					
Net cash outlay	−140,000					
Cash flows from operations						
EBDIT $(1 - T)$		39,000	39,000	39,000	39,000	39,000
Incremental Depreciation		35,000	26,250	19,687	14,765	11,074
Depreciation tax shield		12,250	9,188	6,890	5,168	3,876
Depreciation tax shield at year end:						
$BV_5 \times [Td/(k + d)] = 33,223 \times [(.35 \times .25)/(.20 + .25)]$						6,460
Year-end incremental salvage value						6,000
Lost depreciation tax shield on incremental salvage value						
$SV_5 \times [Td/(k + d)] = 6,000 \times [(.35 \times .25)/(.20 + .25)]$						−1,167
Net cash flows	−140,000	51,250	48,188	45,890	44,168	54,169
PVF at 20%	1.000	0.8333	0.6944	0.5787	0.4823	0.4019
Present value	−140,000	42,707	33,462	26,557	21,302	21,771
NPV	+5,798					

Table 10.9: Computation of NPV: Alternative Method

	Year 0	Year 10
Incremental investment (Rs 160,000 – Rs 20,000)	–140,000	
PV of after-tax saving: 39,000 × 2.9906 (5-year annuity factor at 20%)	116,634	
PV of perpetual depreciation tax shield (DTS) on incremental block of assets:		
$PVDTS_n = \left[\dfrac{.35 \times .25}{.25 + .20}\right] \times 140,000 = Rs\ 27,222$	27,222	
Incremental salvage value: 6,000 × 0.4019 (PV factor at year 5)	2,411	6,000
PV of lost DTS on incremental salvage value, year 5 : 1,167 × 0.4019 (PVF)	– 469	1,167
$PVDTS_n = \left[\dfrac{.35 \times .25}{.25 + .20}\right] \times 6,000 = Rs\ 1,167$		
Net present value	+5,798	

The net cash flows and NPV of the replacement decision will be as shown in Table 10.8.

There is a simple way of calculating NPV of the replacement decision in Illustration 10.4 as shown in Table 10.9.

ADDITIONAL ASPECTS OF INCREMENTAL CASH FLOW ANALYSIS

The incremental principle should be carefully used in determining an investment's cash flows. All cash flows occurring because of the investment under consideration should be included. Cash flows, which would occur otherwise, whether or not the project is undertaken, should not be taken into account. Similarly, cash flows, which have occurred before the consideration of an investment, are irrelevant in taking the decision now. The following are the examples of some more aspects of incremental cash flow analysis.

Allocated Overheads

Firms generally have a practice of allocating budgeted general overheads to projects, including the new projects under consideration. Since the general overheads will be incurred whether or not the new projects are undertaken, those **allocated overheads** should be ignored in computing the net cash flows of an investment. However, some of the overheads may increase because of the new project; these specific to the project should be charged to the project. The incremental cash flow rule indicates that only incremental overheads are relevant.

The allocation of overheads is a difficult question in practice. One or two investment projects may not cause any change in overhead items such as supervision, rent, employees' welfare or accounting. But the cumulative effect of many investments may ultimately result in an increase in overheads. This creates a problem of cash flow estimation. It is difficult to know when the overheads will change. Efforts should be made to identify such changes so that they may be included in the calculation of net cash flows.

Opportunity Costs of Resources

Sometimes a proposed investment project may use the existing resources of the firm for which explicit, or adequate, cash outlays may not exist. The opportunity costs of such projects should be considered. **Opportunity costs** are the expected benefits, which the company would have derived from those resources if they were not committed to the proposed project. Assume, for example, that a company is considering a project, which requires 7,000 cubic feet of area. Also suppose that the firm has 10,000 cubic feet area available. What is the cost of the area available within the firm if it is used by the project? One answer could be that since no cash outlay is involved, therefore, no charges should be made to the project. But from the point of the alternative investment opportunity foregone by transferring this available area to the project, it seems desirable to charge the opportunity cost of the area to the project. Suppose that the company could rent the area at Rs 18 per cubic feet, and then Rs 126,000 should be considered as the opportunity cost of using the area. The opportunity cost of other resources can also be computed in the same manner. It may be sometimes difficult to estimate opportunity cost. If the resources can be sold, its opportunity cost is equal to the market price. It is important to note that the alternative use rule is a corollary of the incremental cash flow rule.

Incidental Effects

An investment project under consideration may influence the cash flows of other investment opportunities, or the existing projects or products. The incremental cash flow rule applies here; it tells us to identify all cash flows, direct or incidental, occurring as a result of the acceptance of an investment opportunity. It is, therefore, important to note that all incidental effects, in terms of cash flows, should be considered in the evaluation of an investment opportunity. Let us take some examples to illustrate this point.

Contingent costs A company is contemplating setting up of a chemical plant in a remote, backward area of the State of Gujarat. The company can attract the working force for the plant only if it provides basic facilities such as residential houses, approach roads, schools and hospital to the employees. The estimates of cash flows of the chemical plant would include cash outlay to be incurred in creating these basic facilities for the employees.

Cannibalisation A soft-drink manufacturer is considering the introduction of a new soft-drink, a low-calorie drink. The market research has indicated that the total market for soft drinks would be growing at 10 per cent. The company's product, 'Sip-It', is anticipated to capture 20 per cent of the total soft-drink market. It is also revealed that one-sixth of the total volume of the new product would come from erosion of the company's one of the existing products, 'Fresh Cola', a high-calorie drink. The cash flow estimates of 'Sip-It' should include this cannibalisation effect, i.e., the lost contribution of the existing product, 'Fresh Cola.' Let us add some more information to the present example. The managing director of the soft drink company is not convinced that the sale of 'Fresh Cola' will be eroded because of the introduction of the new product, 'Sip-It.' His opinion is that if they do not introduce a low-calorie drink like 'Sip-It', competitors would do so; therefore, sale of 'Fresh Cola' would be eroded, whether 'Sip-It' is introduced or not. If this is a correct information, then the lost contribution of 'Fresh Cola' cannot be considered in the evaluation of 'Sip-It'.

Revenue enhancement Consider yet another example. A state government is considering the construction of a railroad bridge. In itself the construction of the bridge may not be beneficial. However, if the incidental effects, such as the operation of railroad, are considered, the proposal may become enormously profitable. The cash flow estimates of constructing the bridge should include the net benefits of operating the railroad. Similarly, a new project may create opportunities for increasing the sale of existing products. Such benefits should be included in the cash flows of the new project.

Sunk Costs

Sunk costs are cash outlays incurred in the past. They are the results of past decisions, and cannot be changed by future decisions. Since they do not influence future decisions, they are irrelevant costs. They are unavoidable and irrecoverable historical costs; they should simply be ignored in the investment analysis.

To illustrate, let us assume in our preceding example of the soft drink that before deciding to introduce a new product, the company has conducted a market test. The results of the market test were found to be favourable. Should the company include the market test costs in the evaluation of the new product? The answer is no. The costs of the market test have already been incurred and they are sunk costs; the decision to introduce a new product cannot affect them. They are, therefore, irrelevant to the decision of introducing a new product.

Consider another example. A company set up a plant for a cost of Rs 200 million to manufacture ball bearings. The project proved to be bad for the company, and it started accumulating losses. The total outflows to-date is Rs 300 million. The company is thinking of abandoning the plant. Some executives consider it suicidal to abandon a plant on which Rs 300 million have already been spent. Others feel it equally unwise to continue with a plant, which has been incurring losses and offers no possibility of any satisfactory return on that money spent. The arguments of both the groups do not make sense. The Rs 300 million spent by the company is a sunk cost; therefore, it is irrelevant. It is also not correct to discard the plant since it is not earning a satisfactory return on a sunken investment. The company should take the decision to sell or not to sell the plant *today* in light of the *future* cash flows and return.

Tax Incentives

The government provides a number of tax benefits to firms to encourage capital investment. The most significant incentives in India have been investment allowance (withdrawn now) and benefits under Sections 80HH and 80I of the Income Tax Act.

Investment allowance Until a few years ago, a company could charge an amount equal to 25 per cent of the original value of an asset as investment allowance in the period in which it was installed for production. Investment allowance was deductible for tax computation, and thus, it provided tax shield equal to investment allowance times the tax rate. The purpose of investment allowance was to encourage investment in fixed assets by the corporate sector. The government withdrew investment allowance from April 1987. It was however reintroduced only in case of the high tech industries in 1988. The rate was 20 per cent. It has also been withdrawn now.

Investment deposit scheme The government introduced the investment deposit scheme when the investment allowance scheme was withdrawn in 1987. Under this scheme a firm could deposit up to 20 per cent of the profits (before the set off of any unabsorbed business losses of earlier years) with the Industrial Development Bank of India. For this, the firm would be entitled to a deduction equal to the amount of deposit and/or any amount so utilised from the account for the purchase of any new plant and machinery. The scheme has also been withdrawn now.

Other tax incentives There are a number of other tax and non-tax incentives available to a firm when it undertakes a new investment project. For projects in backward areas, the government provides interest free, non-refundable subsidy up to Rs 2.50 million (Rs 25 lakh). Under Section 80 HH of the Income Tax Act, 20 per cent of the profits of business derived from an industrial undertaking set up in a specified backward area is allowed as a deduction for a period of 10 years. Further, under Section 80I of the Income Tax Act, 25 per cent of the profits of any new industrial undertaking are allowed as a deduction for a period of 8 years. In computing the amount of deductions under Sections 80HH and 80I, the relevant profit will be reckoned as if it were the sole source of income of the company. Also, 80I deduction is allowed after deducting 80 HH benefits, if any.

The **sales tax deferral** is also available to a unit set up in a specific backward area. Sales tax equal to 4 per cent of gross sales collected from customers is allowed to be retained, free of interest, for a period of 7 years. Thus, the sales tax collected during a year needs to be remitted to the State Government only in the 8th year. This concession is available for a period of 6 years from commercial production.

INVESTMENT DECISIONS UNDER INFLATION

A common problem, which complicates the practical investment decision-making, is **inflation**. The rule of the game is, as we shall emphasise in the following pages, to be consistent in treating inflation in the cash flows and the discount rate.

Inflation is a fact of life all over the world. A double-digit rate of inflation is a common feature in developing countries.

Because the cash flows of an investment project occur over a long period of time, a firm should usually be concerned about the impact of inflation on the project's profitability. The capital budgeting results will be biased if the impact of inflation is not correctly factored in the analysis.

Business executives do recognise that inflation exists but they do not consider it necessary to incorporate inflation in the analysis of capital investment. They generally estimate cash flows assuming unit costs and selling price prevailing in year zero to remain unchanged. They argue that if there is inflation, prices can be increased to cover increasing costs; therefore, the impact on the project's profitability would be the same if they assume rate of inflation to be zero. This line of argument, although seems to be convincing, is fallacious for two reasons. *First*, the discount rate used for discounting cash flows is generally expressed in *nominal* terms. It would be inappropriate and inconsistent to use a nominal rate to discount constant cash flows. *Second*, selling prices and costs show different degrees of responsiveness to inflation. In the case of certain products, prices may be controlled by the government, or by restrictive competition, or there may exist a long-term contract to supply goods or services at a fixed price. The drugs and pharmaceutical industry is an example of controlled, slow-rising prices in spite of the rising general price level. Costs are usually sensitive to inflation. However, some costs rise faster than others. For example, wages may increase at a rate higher than, say, fuel and power, or even raw materials. There are yet examples of certain items, which are not affected by inflation. The **depreciation tax shield** remains unaffected by inflation since depreciation is allowed on the book value of an asset, irrespective of its replacement or market price, for tax purposes.

The working capital tied up in an investment project may also increase during inflationary conditions. Because of the increasing input prices and manufacturing costs, more funds may have to be tied up in inventories and receivable. The salvage value of the project may also be affected by inflation. In the period of rising prices, the firm may be able to sell an asset at the end of its useful life at a good price. A number of textile and engineering machineries have a good second-hand market in India. They can be sometimes sold at about 50 per cent of **replacement cost** after having been used for a long period of time.

How should the rate of inflation be taken into account in the capital budgeting decisions? We should be consistent in treating inflation. Since the discount rate is market-determined, and it is therefore stated in nominal terms; then the cash flows should also be expressed in nominal terms. In other words, cash flows should reflect effect of inflation, when they are discounted by the inflation affected discount rate. We shall elaborate this point in the following section.

Nominal Vs. Real Rates of Return

Suppose a person—we call him Jose, deposits Rs 100 in the State Bank of India for one year at 10 per cent rate of interest. This means that the bank agrees to return Rs 110 to Jose after a year, irrespective of how much goods or services this money can buy for him. The sum of Rs 110 is stated in nominal terms—the impact of inflation not separated. Thus, 10 per cent is a nominal rate of return on Jose's investment. Let us assume that the rate of inflation is expected to be 7 per cent next year. What does the rate of inflation imply? It means that prices prevailing today will rise by 7 per cent next year. In other words, a 7 per cent rate of inflation implies that what can be bought for Re 1 now can be bought for Rs 1.07 next year. We can thus say that the purchasing power of Rs 1.07 next year is the same as that of Re 1.00 today. What is the purchasing power of Rs 110 received next year? It is Rs 110/1.07 = Rs 102.80; that is, the Rs 110 received next year can buy goods worth Rs 102.80 now. The Rs 110 next year and Rs 102.80 today are equivalent in terms of the purchasing power if the rate of inflation is 7 per cent. The Rs 110 is expressed in nominal terms since they have not been adjusted for the effect of inflation. On the other hand, the Rs 102.80 are in real terms since they have been adjusted for the effect of inflation. Our investor, Jose, thus earns, 10 per cent nominal rate of return, but only 2.8 per cent real rate of return. It should be noted that the rate of inflation is an expected rate; therefore, the real rate of return is also expected. The actual rate of inflation may be different from the expected rate.

The opportunity cost of capital of a firm or project is generally market determined and is based on expected future returns. It is, therefore, usually expressed in nominal terms and reflects the expected rate of inflation. The opportunity cost of capital or the discount rate is a combination of the real rate (say, K) and the expected inflation rate (let us call it, alpha). This relationship, long ago recognised in the economic theory, is called the **Fisher's effect**. It may be stated as follows:

$$\text{Nominal discount rate} = (1 + \text{Real discount rate})$$
$$\times (1 + \text{inflation rate}) - 1$$
$$k = (1 + K)(1 + \alpha) - 1 \qquad (14)$$

If a firm expects a 10 per cent real rate of return from an investment project under consideration and the expected inflation rate is 7 per cent, the nominal required rate of return on the project would be:

$$k = (1.10)(1.07) - 1 = 1.177 - 1 = 0.177 \text{ or } 17.7\%$$

In practice, it is customary to add the real rate and the expected inflation rate to obtain the nominal required rate of return: $k = K + \alpha$.

Equation (14) can be used to derive the real rate of return (K):

$$K = \frac{1.177}{1.07} - 1 = 1.10 - 1 = 0.10 \text{ or } 10\%$$

Let us consider some examples to show how these concepts can be applied in practice to treat inflation in the investment decisions.[1] Suppose a firm is considering a project with the following cash flows, on the assumption that prices and costs increase at the same rate, the firm follows the practice of stating cash flows at the prices of period zero.

Year	0	1	2	3	4
Cash flows	–10,000	3,000	3,000	3,000	3,000

This means that cash flows are expressed in real terms. The firm's opportunity cost of capital, which is market determined and is expressed in nominal terms, is 14 per cent. Can the project's real cash flows be discounted at the 14% nominal rate of discount? Clearly the answer is no! It would be inconsistent to discount the **real cash flows** of the project by the **nominal discount rate**. If we do so, the NVP of the project, as calculated below, will be biased:

$$NPV = \sum_{t=1}^{n} \frac{C_t}{(1+k)} - C_0 = \sum_{t=1}^{n=4} \frac{3,000}{(1.14)^t} - 10,000$$

$$= 3,000(2.914) - 10,000 = -Rs\,1,258$$

The project shows a negative NPV and, therefore, would be rejected. But a bias has entered into the analysis. The cash flows are in real terms while the discount rate is in nominal terms. For a correct analysis, two alternatives are available:

- either the cash flows should be converted into nominal terms and then discounted at the nominal required rate of return, or
- the discount rate should be converted into real terms and used to discount the real cash flows.

Let us assume that in our example the rate of inflation is expected to be 7 per cent. Thus, the cash flows in nominal terms will be:

Cash Flows (Rs)

Year	Real	Inflation adjustment	Nominal
0	– 10,000	– 10,000 (1.07)^0	– 10,000
1	3,000	3,000 (1.07)^1	3,210
2	3,000	3,000 (1.07)^2	3,435
3	3,000	3,000 (1.07)^3	3,675
4	3,000	3,000 (1.07)^4	3,932

If we discount these nominal cash flows at the 14 per cent nominal discount rate, the NPV of the project will be:

$$NPV = 10,000 + \frac{3,210}{(1.14)} + \frac{3,435}{(1.14)^2} + \frac{3,675}{(1.14)^3} + \frac{3,932}{(1.14)^4}$$

$$= -10,000 + 2,815 + 2,642 + 2,481 + 2,328$$

$$= -10,000 + 10,266 = Rs\,266$$

Alternatively, we can find out the **real discount rate** and discount the cash flows without converting them into nominal terms. The real discount rate will be:

$$K = \frac{1.14}{1.07} - 1 = 0.0654$$

The NPV of the Project will be:

$$NPV = \sum_{t=1}^{n=4} \frac{3,000}{(1.0654)^t} - 10,000$$

$$= Rs\,3,000(3.422) - Rs\,10,000 = +Rs\,266$$

Notice that the results under both alternatives are same. The project's NPV is positive, so accept it. Always remember: *Discount nominal cash flows at nominal discount rate; or discount real cash flows at real discount rate.*

The NPV formula can be written as follows when cash flows and discount rates are expressed in nominal terms:

$$NPV = \sum_{t=1}^{n} \frac{C_t(1+\alpha)^t}{(1+K)^t(1+\alpha)^t} - C_0 \qquad (15)$$

where K is the real discount rate, α is the expected inflation rate and C_t is the series of real cash flows, using Equation (15) in the example, we get:

$$NPV = \sum_{t=1}^{4} \frac{Rs\,3,000_t(1.07)^t}{(1.0654)^t(1.07)^t} - 10,000 = Rs\,266$$

Since the inflation factor in the numerator and denominator of Equation (15) is same, the formula becomes:

$$NPV = \sum_{t=1}^{n} \frac{C_t}{(1+K)^t} - C_0$$

Thus it is obvious that when the expected inflation rate is properly reflected in the cash flow estimates and the discount rate, the resulting NPV is stated both in real and nominal terms,[2] and it is free of inflation bias.

Let us now consider a complex example involving multiple inflation rates.

Illustration 10.5: Multiple Inflation Rates

Consider the same example as above. Now we assume that cash inflows are subject to an inflation rate of 7 per cent and cash outflows to 8 per cent. The project provides annual cash inflow of Rs 3,000 in real terms and involves an outlay of Rs 10,000. For simplicity let us assume that depreciation is charged on straight-line basis, and the salvage value of the asset is zero. The nominal discount rate is 14 per cent, reflecting a 7 per cent general inflation. Assume that tax rate is 60 per cent. The details about the net cash inflows (annual) at today's price are as follows:

---

1. The analytical approach discussed here is based on Van Horne, J.C., A Note on Biases in Capital Budgeting Introduced by Inflation, *Journal of Financial and Quantitative Analysis,* 6 (March 1971); and Findlay, M.C. and Frankle, A.W., Capital Budgeting Procedure under Inflation.... *Financial Management,* Autumn, 1976, pp. 83–90. Also see Weston, J.F. and Copeland, T.E., *Managerial Finance,* Dryden Press, 1986, pp. 153–55 for a similar discussion.
2. Findlay and Frankle, *op. cit.,* pp. 83–90.

Cash sales	7,000
Cash expenses	− 3,250
Profit before tax	3,750
Tax at 60%	− 2,250
Profit after tax	1,500
Depreciation tax shield (.60 × 2,500)	1,500
Net cash flows	3,000

The cash inflows and outflows should be subjected to their respective inflation rates to compute unbiased NPV. The nominal cash flows are calculated below:

	Cash Flows (Rs)			
	C_1	C_2	C_3	C_4
Cash inflows ($\alpha = 7\%$)	7,490	8,014	8,575	9,176
Cash outflows ($\alpha = 8\%$)	3,510	3,791	4,094	4,422
Profit before taxes	3,980	4,223	4,481	4,754
Taxes @ 60%	2,388	2,534	2,689	2,852
Profit after taxes	1,592	1,689	1,792	1,902
Depreciation tax shield (Rs 2,500 × 0.60)	1,500	1,500	1,500	1,500
Net cash inflows	3,092	3,189	3,292	3,402

The NPV of the project is:

$$\text{NPV} = -10,000 + \frac{3,092}{(1.14)} + \frac{3,189}{(1.14)^2} + \frac{3,292}{(1.14)^3} + \frac{3,402}{(1.14)^4}$$
$$= -10,000 + 2,712 + 2,452 + 2,222 + 2,014$$
$$= -10,000 + 9,400 = -\text{Rs }600$$

The NPV of the project is negative, so it should be rejected. Clearly, the effects of inflation on the cash outflows were far greater than on the cash inflows.

The computation shown in Illustration 10.6 can be written in the form of an equation as given below:[1]

$$\text{NPV} = \sum_{t=1}^{n} \frac{[(I_t)(1+\alpha_i)^t - (O_t)(1+\alpha_o)^t](1-T) + T(\text{DEP}_t)}{(1+k)^t} - C_0$$

(16)

where I_t is cash inflow, O_t is cash outflow, α_i is the inflation rate for cash inflows and α_0 is the inflation rate for cash outflows.

Let us summarise our discussion on the capital budgeting procedure under inflation. In the first instance when we discounted the real cash flows by the nominal rate (14%), we obtained a negative NPV (−Rs 1,258) of the project. This was a fallacious approach. Since the discount rate was in nominal terms, the cash flows should also have been restated in nominal terms. When we did that, the project yielded a positive net present value (+Rs 266). The same results were obtained when the real cash flows were discounted at the real rate. Thus, a profitable project would have been rejected if inflation were not properly taken into account. When inflation is not consistently treated it introduces a bias in the investment decisions, and leads to unsound allocation of funds. Finally, we assumed the components of the cash flows and the discount rate to be affected differently by inflation. It was assumed that increases in costs (outflows) could not be entirely covered by increases in prices (inflows). As a result, the project, which had a positive NPV under the assumption of same inflation effects for the components of cash flows, showed a negative NPV. How would the NPV of the project be affected by inflation depends on the magnitude of inflation rates affecting various components of the cash flows.

FINANCING EFFECTS IN INVESTMENT EVALUATION

In our discussion so far, we have ignored the question of financing an investment project in the computation of new cash flows. We have implicitly assumed that the firm undertaking the project is a **pure-equity financed firm** and therefore, the project is subject only to business risk. The opportunity cost of capital as the discount rate reflects the business risk of the project. Hence the NPV of the project does not include the financing effect.

A firm in practice may finance an investment project either by debt or partly by debt and partly by equity. How should we treat the financing effect in the investment evaluation? Should the proceeds of debt and equity and payments of interest, dividends and principal be considered in the computation of the investment's net cash flows? According to the conventional capital budgeting approach in which the discount rate is adjusted for financing effects, cash flows should not be adjusted for the financing effects. The firm should not treat the debt and equity proceeds as the investment's inflows nor should it recognize payments of interest, dividends and principal as outflows. Thus, unlike in the computation of the accounting profit, the net cash flows of an investment do not incorporate interest charges and their tax shield. The net cash flows are defined as the free cash flows and calculated as follows:

$$\Delta\text{NCF} = \Delta\text{EBIT}(1-T) + \Delta\text{DEP} - \Delta\text{NWC} - \Delta\text{CAPEX}$$

The adjustment for the financing effect is made in the discount rate. The firm's weighted average cost of capital (WACC) is used as the discount rate.[2] When we discount an investment's free cash flows by the weighted average cost of debt and equity, we are in fact ensuring that the investment yields enough cash flows to make payments of interest and repayment of principal to creditors and dividends to shareholders. Any cash flows remaining after servicing debt and equity capital is an addition to the wealth of shareholders. It is important to note that this approach of adjusting for the finance effect is based on the assumptions that:

- The investment project has the same business risk as the firm.
- The investment project does not cause any change in the firm's target capital structure.

1. Copeland, T.E. and Weston, J.F., *Financial Theory* and *Corporate Policy*, Addison-Wesley, 1983, p. 39.
2. Van Horne, *op. cit.*, pp. 653–58, and Weston and Copeland, *op. cit.*, pp. 153–55.

These assumptions may be valid for small projects, but not in the case of large projects, which may have different business risk and debt capacity. We shall discuss later on the limitations of WACC approach and the alternative approaches of handling the financing effect.

Excel Application 10.1:
Investment Analysis under Inflation

The Excel worksheet makes cash flow analysis very easy. Let us illustrate the use of Excel worksheet in investment analysis. Suppose a firm is considering introducing a new product. The basic assumptions are shown in the worksheet in column A and column B. The equipment will cost Rs 8,00,000 and it will have a life of 8 years. Salvage value is assumed to be zero. The firm will be able to sell 100,000 units of the product at Rs 12 per unit. The variable cost per unit is expected to be Rs 6 and total fixed cost Rs 300,000. Written down value depreciation rate is 25 per cent, tax rate is 45 per cent and the real required rate of return is 8 per cent. The inflation rate is expected to be 5 per cent per annum.

The worksheet shows the calculation of cash flows. Revenues depend on volume, price and inflation. Enter the formula for revenues in cell D18 as: =$B$8*$B$4*(1+$B$9)^D16 and copy it to cell E18 through K18. You can similarly enter formula for variable costs and fixed costs. Depreciation depends on the equipment's book value and the depreciation rate. For depreciation, enter formula in cell D22 as: =(1−$B$7)^C16*$B$2*$B$7 and copy to other cells. Working capital depends on sales and the working capital

ratio. Since sales are adjusted for inflation and working capital is a fixed percentage of sales, the working capital calculation automatically accounts for inflation. Remember to adjust cash flows for the changes in working capital rather than the absolute amount of working capital. Also remember to account for the release for net working capital at the end of the equipment's life. We have ignored the tax effect of the remaining book value of the equipment at the end of its life for simplifying the example.

Once you have estimated the cash flow, you can use the Excel built in formula for calculating NPV and IRR. For calculating NPV, you are the discount rate. Since the cash flows are in nominal terms, you should use the nominal cost of capital as the discount rate. Recall that nominal discount rate is calculated as: $(1 + \text{real cost}) \times (1 + \text{inflation}) - 1$. This formula is used to calculate the nominal cost of capital in cell B13. Now we can enter the NPV formula in cell C30 as: = NPV(B13,D29:K29)+C29. The project has a positive NPV of Rs 926,77; it should be accepted. For calculating IRR, enter the IRR formula in cell C31 as: =IRR(C29:K29). The project's IRR of 15.4 per cent is higher than the required rate of return of 13.4 per cent. The advantage of using the Excel worksheet is that you can change any of the assumptions and see its impact on NPV or IRR.

	A	B	C	D	E	F	G	H	I	J	K
1	*Basic Assumptions*										
2	Equipment cost (Rs)	800,000									
3	Equipment life (years)	8									
4	Selling price (Rs)	12									
5	Variable cost per unit (Rs)	6									
6	Fixed cost (Rs)	300,000									
7	WDV depreciation	25%									
8	Volume (units)	100,000									
9	Inflation	5%									
10	Working capital ratio	30%	=(1+B12)*(1+B9)-1								
11	Tax rate	45%									
12	Real cost of capital	8%									
13	Nominal cost of capital	13.4%									
14			=$B$8*$B$4*(1+$B$9)^D16		=$B$8*$B$5*(1+$B$9)^D16						
15	*Cash Flow Analysis*										(Rs)
16	Year		0	1	2	3	4	5	6	7	8
17	Equipment cost		−800,000								
18	Revenue			1,260,000	1,323,000	1,389,150	1,458,608	1,531,538	1,608,115	1,688,521	1,772,947
19	*Less* : Variable costs			630,000	661,500	694,575	729,304	765,769	804,057	844,260	886,473
20	Contribution	=$B$6*(1+$B$9)^C16		630,000	661,500	694,575	729,304	765,769	804,057	844,260	886,473
21	*Less* : Fixed costs			315,000	330,750	347,288	364,652	382,884	402,029	422,130	443,237
22	*Less* : depreciation	=(1−$B$7)^C16*$B$2*$B$7		200,000	150,000	112,500	84,375	63,281	47,461	35,596	26,697
23	Profit before tax			115,000	180,750	234,788	280,277	319,603	354,568	386,534	416,540
24	Tax			51,750	81,338	105,654	126,125	143,821	159,555	173,940	187,443
25	Profit after tax	=D18*$B$10		63,250	99,413	129,133	154,152	175,782	195,012	212,594	229,097
26	*Add* : depreciation			200,000	150,000	112,500	84,375	63,281	47,461	35,596	26,697
27	Working capital		378,000	396,900	416,745	437,582	459,461	482,434	506,556	531,884	0
28	*Less* : Increase in WC		378,000	18,900	19,845	20,837	21,879	22,973	24,122	25,328	−531,884
29	Net cash flows		−1,178,000	244,350	229,568	220,796	216,648	216,090	218,351	222,862	787,678
30	NPV		96,772	=NPV(A13,D29:K29)+C29							
31	IRR	=IRR(C29:K29)	15.4%								

SUMMARY

❖ The estimation of cash flows, though difficult, is the most crucial step in investment analysis.

❖ *Profits vs. cash flows:* Cash flows are different from profits. Profit is not necessarily a cash flow; it is the difference between revenue earned and expenses incurred rather than cash received and cash paid. Also, in the calculation of profits, an arbitrary distinction between revenue expenditure and capital expenditure is made.

❖ *Incremental cash flows:* Cash flows should be estimated on incremental basis. Incremental cash flows are found out by comparing alternative investment projects. The comparison may simply be between cash flows with and without the investment proposal under consideration when real alternatives do not exist.

❖ *Components of cash flows:* Three components of cash flows can be identified: (1) initial investment, (2) annual cash flows, and (3) terminal cash flows.

❖ *Initial investment:* Initial investment will comprise the original cost (including freight and installation charges) of the project, plus any increase in working capital. In the case of replacement decision, the after-tax salvage value of the old asset should also be adjusted to compute the initial investment.

❖ *Net cash flow:* Annual net cash flow is the difference between cash inflows and cash outflows including taxes. Tax computations are based on accounting profits. Care should be taken in properly adjusting depreciation while computing net cash flows.

❖ *Depreciation* is a non-cash item, but it affects cash flows through tax shield. The following formula can be used to calculate change in net cash flows from operations:

$$\Delta NCF = \Delta EBIT(1 - T) + \Delta DEP$$

❖ *Working capital and capital expenditure*: In practice, changes in working capital items — debtors (receivable), creditors (payable) and stock (inventory) — affect cash flows. Also, the firm may be required to incur capital expenditure during the operation of the investment project. Therefore, the following formula should be used to compute the investment's net cash flows or free cash flows:

$$FCF = \Delta NCF = \Delta EBIT(1 - T) + \Delta DEP - \Delta NWC - \Delta CAPEX$$

❖ *Free cash flows and the discount rate:* Free cash flows are available to service both the shareholders and the debt holders. Therefore, debt flows (interest charges and repayment of principal) are not considered in the computation of free cash flows. The financing effect is captured by the firm's weighted cost of debt and equity, which is used to discount the project's cash flows. This approach is based on two assumptions: (1) the project's risk is the same as the firm's risk, and (2) the firm's debt ratio is constant and the project's debt capacity is the same as the firm's.

❖ *Terminal cash flows* are those, which occur in the project's last year in addition to annual cash flows. They would consist of the after-tax salvage value of the project and working capital released (if any). In case of replacement decision, the foregone salvage value of old asset should also be taken into account.

❖ *Terminal value of a new product* may depend on the cash flows, which could be generated much beyond the assumed analysis or horizon period. The firm may make a reasonable assumption regarding the cash flow growth rate after the horizon period and use the following formula for calculating terminal value:

$$TV_n = \frac{NCF_n(1 + g)}{k - g}$$

❖ The term incremental cash flows should be interpreted carefully. The concept should be extended to include the opportunity cost of the existing facilities used by the proposal. Sunk costs and allocated overheads are irrelevant in computing cash flows. Similarly, a new project may cannibalise sales of the existing products. The project's cash flows should be adjusted for the reduction in cash flows on account of the cannibalisation.

❖ *Inflation*: The NPV rule gives correct answer to choose an investment under inflation if it is treated consistently in cash flows and discount rate. The discount rate is a market-determined rate and therefore, includes the expected inflation rate. It is thus generally stated in nominal terms. The cash flows should also be stated in nominal terms to obtain an unbiased NPV. Alternatively, the real cash flows can be discounted at the real discount rate to calculate unbiased NPV. The following equation gives the relationship between nominal and real cost of capital:

Nominal discount rate
$$= (1 + \text{real discount rate})(1 + \text{inflation rate}) - 1$$

$$\text{Real discount rate} = \frac{1 + \text{nominal discount rate}}{1 + \text{inflation rate}} - 1$$

KEY CONCEPTS

Accrual concept	Depreciation	Nominal discount rate	Salvage value
Block of assets	Depreciation tax shield	Opportunity cost	Sunk cost
Cannibalisation	Free cash flow	Profit	Terminal cash flow
Capital expenditure	Incremental cash flow	Real cash flows	Terminal value
Capitalised expenses	Inflation	Real discount rate	Value additivity
Cash flow from operation	Investment allowance	Revenue expenditure	Written-down value
Contingent costs	Nominal cash flows		

ILLUSTRATIVE SOLVED PROBLEMS

Problem 10.1: A company is considering two mutually exclusive projects. Both require an initial cash outlay of Rs 10,000 each, and have a life of five years. The company's required rate of return is 10 per cent and pays tax at a 50 per cent rate. The projects will be depreciated on a straight-line basis. The before taxes cash flows expected to be generated by the projects are as follows:

			Before-tax Cash Flow (Rs)		
Project	*1*	*2*	*3*	*4*	*5*
A	4,000	4,000	4,000	4,000	4,000
B	6,000	3,000	2,000	5,000	5,000

Calculate for each project: (1) the payback, (2) the average rate of return, (3) the net present value and profitability index, and (4) the internal rate of return. Which project should be accepted and why?

Solution: $NCF = EBDIT(1-T) + T \times DEP$

EBDIT is earnings before depreciation, interest and tax and in the absence of changes in working capital is treated equal to before-tax (operating) cash flows. The annual straight-line depreciation for projects A and B is: Rs $10,000 \div 5 = $ Rs 2,000.

Net cash flow
Project A:

$$NCF = (Rs\,4,000)\,(1-0.5) + 0.5\,(Rs\,2,000)$$
$$= Rs\,2,000 + Rs\,1,000 = Rs\,3,000$$

NCF of Rs 3,000 is an annuity for 5 years.

Project B:

$$Year\,1\;NCF = (Rs\,6,000)(1-0.5) + 0.5\,(Rs\,2,000)$$
$$= Rs\,3,000 + Rs\,1,000 = Rs\,4,000$$
$$Year\,2\;NCF = (Rs\,3,000)(1-0.5) + 0.5\,(Rs\,2,000)$$
$$= Rs\,1,500 + Rs\,1,000 = Rs\,2,500$$
$$Year\,3\;NCF = (Rs\,2,000)(1-0.5) + 0.5\,(Rs\,2,000)$$
$$= Rs\,1,000 + Rs\,1,000 = Rs\,2,000$$
$$Year\,4\,\&\,5\;NCF = (Rs\,5,000)(1-0.5) + 0.5\,(Rs\,2,000)$$
$$= Rs\,2,500 + Rs\,1,000 = Rs\,3,500$$

Payback
Project A:

$$PB = \frac{Rs\,10,000}{Rs\,3,000} = 3\frac{1}{3}\;years\;or\;3\;years\;and\;4\;months$$

Project B:
Rs 4,000 + Rs 2,500 + Rs 2,000 = Rs 8,500 recovered in three years.

The remaining amount of Rs 10,000 – Rs 8,500 = Rs 1,500 to be recovered in the fourth year. Thus,

$$PB = 3\;years + \frac{Rs\,1,500}{Rs\,3,500} = 3\frac{3}{7}\;years\;or\;3\;years\;and\;5\;months$$

Average Rate of Return
Net (accounting) income can be calculated by using the following equation:

$$Net\;income = (EBDIT - DEP)\,(1-T)$$

Project A:

$$Average\;Income = [(4,000 - 2,000)\,(1-.5)$$
$$+ (4,000 - 2,000)\,(1-.5)$$
$$+ (4,000 - 2,000)\,(1-.5)$$
$$+ (4,000 - 2,000)\,(1-.5)$$
$$+ (4,000 - 2,000)\,(1-.5) \div 5$$
$$Average\;Income = (Rs\,1,000 + Rs\,1,000 + Rs\,1,000$$
$$+ Rs\,1,000 + Rs\,1,000) \div 5$$
$$= Rs\,1,000$$
$$Average\;Investment = Rs\,10,000/2 = Rs\,5,000$$
$$ARR = Rs\,1,000/Rs\,5,000 = 0.20\;or\;20\%$$

Project B:

$$Average\;Income = [(6,000 - 2,000)\,(1-.5)$$
$$+ (3,000 - 2,000)\,(1-.5)$$
$$+ (2,000 - 2,000)\,(1-.5)$$
$$+ (5,000 - 2,000)\,(1-.5)$$
$$+ (5,000 - 2,000)\,(1-.5) \div 5$$
$$Average\;Income = (Rs\,2,000 + Rs\,500 + 0$$
$$+ Rs\,1,500 + Rs\,1,500) \div 5$$
$$= Rs\,1,100$$
$$Average\;Investment = Rs\,10,000 \div 2 = Rs\,5,000$$
$$ARR = Rs\,1,100/Rs\,5,000 = 0.22\;or\;22\%$$

Net Present Value and Profitability Index
Project A:

$$NPV = Rs\,3,000\,(PVAF_{5,\,0.10}) - Rs\,10,000$$
$$= Rs\,3,000 \times 3.791 - Rs\,10,000 = Rs\,1,373$$
$$PI = Rs\,11,373 \div Rs\,10,000 = 1.137$$

Project B:

$$NPV = [Rs\,4,000\,(PVF_{1,\,0.10}) + Rs\,2,500\,(PVF_{2,\,0.10}) + Rs\,2,000$$
$$(PVF_{3,\,0.10}) + Rs\,3,500\,(PVF_{4,\,0.10})$$
$$+ Rs\,3,500\,(PVF_{5,\,0.10})] - Rs\,10,000$$
$$= [Rs\,4,000 \times 0.909 + Rs\,2,500 \times 0.826 + Rs\,2,000 \times 0.751$$
$$+ Rs\,3,500 \times 0.683 + Rs\,3,500 \times 0.621] - Rs\,10,000$$
$$= Rs\,1,767$$
$$PI = Rs\,11,767 \div Rs\,10,000 = 1.77$$

You can find NPV using the Excel worksheet and the Excel built in formulae for NPV and IRR:

= NPV (discount rate, cash flows, year 1 to year n)
+ investment (with negative sign)
= IRR (cash flows, year 0 to year n)

Internal Rate of Return

Project A:

$$\text{NPV} = \text{Rs } 3,000\,(\text{PVAF}_{5,\,0.10}) = \text{Rs } 10,000$$

$$(\text{PVAF}_{5,\,0.10}) = \text{Rs } 10,000/\,\text{Rs } 3,000 = 3,333$$

From Table D, we find that the nearest factor is 3.352 at 15 per cent. At 16 per cent, the factor is 3.274. Thus the true rate lies between 15–16 per cent. By interpolation, we find IRR as:

PVAF required	3.333
PVAF at 15%	3.352
PVAF at 16%	3.274

0.019

0.078

$$\text{IRR} = 15\% + 1\%\,\frac{0.019}{0.078} = 15.24\%$$

You can use the Excel worksheet and the Excel built in function to calculate IRR of an annuity. The formula is as follows:

$$= \text{RATE (Nper, Pmt, PV, FV, Type)}$$

Nper is the number of period; Pmt is annuity-payment (receipt) per period; PV is the investment today; FV is the future value which will be taken as zero and Type is beginning of the period (1) or end-of-the-year (0) payment or receipt. Using the numbers in our illustration, IRR is calculated as follows:

$$= \text{RATE (5,3000, }-10,00,000) = 15.24\%$$

Project B:

Since the cash flows of Project *B* are uneven we will have to use trial and error method. Let us try 20 per cent rate of discount. At 20 per cent, NPV = – Rs 684. Since NPV is negative at 20 per cent, we should try a lower rate. At 18 per cent, NPV = – Rs 284. NPV is still negative, therefore, let us try 16 per cent rate of discount. At 16 per cent, NPV = + Rs 186. It is clear that the rate should lie between 16–18 per cent. By interpolation, we get

PV required	Rs 10,000
PV at 16%	10,186
PV at 18%	9,716

186

470

$$\text{IRR} = 16\% + 2\%\,\frac{186}{470} = 16.79\%$$

Which project should be preferred? According to the DCF methods, Project *B* is more profitable. Therefore, it should be preferred over Project *A*. The ARR method also indicates choice of Project *B* while payback shows preference for Project *A*. Both these methods (ARR and payback) are theoretically unsound.

Problem 10.2: A company is faced with the problem of choosing between two mutually exclusive projects. Project *A* requires a cash outlay of Rs 100,000 and cash running expenses of Rs 35,000 per year. On the other hand, Project *B* will cost

Rs 150,000 and require cash running expenses of Rs 20,000 per year. Both the machines have an eight-year life. Project *A* has a Rs 4,000 salvage value and Project *B* has Rs 14,000 salvage value. The company's tax rate is 50 per cent and has a 10 per cent required rate of return. Assume depreciation on straight-line basis and no tax on salvage values of assets. Which project should be accepted?

Solution: We can work with the cash flows of Project (*B–A*).

Net Cash Outlay (B – A)

$$\Delta\text{NCO} = \text{Rs } 150,000 - \text{Rs } 100,000 = \text{Rs } 50,000$$

Incremental depreciation (B – A)

$$\Delta\text{DEP} = \text{Rs } 50,000/8 = \text{Rs } 6,250$$

Net Cash Flows (Annual) (B – A)

$$\Delta\text{NCF} = (\Delta\text{Cash savings})(1-T) + T\,(\text{DEP})$$
$$= (\text{Rs } 35,000 - \text{Rs } 20,000)\,(1-0.5) + 0.5\,(\text{Rs } 6,250)$$
$$= \text{Rs } 7,500 + \text{Rs } 3,125 = \text{Rs } 10,625$$

Terminal Cash Flow (B – A)

Incremental salvage value = Rs 14,000 – Rs 4,000 = Rs 10,000

Net Present Value (B – A)

$$\text{NPV} = -50,000 + 10,625 \times 5.3349 + 10,000 \times 0.4665$$
$$= +\text{Rs } 11,348$$

Note: Book values of both projects are zero after 8 years. Therefore, entire differential salvage value is a gain. No tax on this gain is assumed.

Problem 10.3: A company is considering a proposal of installing a drying equipment. The equipment would involve a cash outlay of Rs 600,000 and working capital of Rs 80,000. The expected life of the project is 6 years without any salvage value. Assume that the company is allowed to charge depreciation on straight-line basis for tax purposes, and that the tax rate is 50 per cent. The estimated before-tax cash flows are given below:

			Before-tax Cash Flows (Rs '000)			
Year	*1*	*2*	*3*	*4*	*5*	*6*
	210	180	160	150	120	100

If the company's opportunity cost of capital is 12 per cent, calculate the equipment's net present value and internal rate of return.

Solution:

(*a*) Equipment's initial cost: Rs 600,000 + Rs 80,000 = Rs 680,000

(*b*) Annual straight line depreciation: Rs 600,000/6 = Rs 100,000

(*c*) Net cash flows can be calculated as follows:

Before-tax cash flows $(1 - T) + \text{Tax} \times$ Depreciation

NPV calculation are given below:

	Cash Flows (Rs '000)						
Year	0	1	2	3	4	5	6
1. Initial cost	− 680						
2. Before-tax cash flows		210	180	160	150	120	100
3. Tax at 50%		105	90	80	75	60	50
4. After-tax cash flows		105	90	80	75	60	50
5. Depreciation tax shield: $T \times DEP$		50	50	50	50	50	50
6. Working capital released							
7. Net cash flows: (4 + 5 + 6)	− 680	155	140	130	125	110	180
8. PVF at 12%	1.000	0.893	0.797	0.712	0.636	0.567	0.507
9. PV (6 × 7)	− 680	138	112	93	80	62	91
10. NPV	− 104						

Since the equipment has a negative NPV, its IRR would be less than the opportunity cost of capital (12 per cent). At 8 per cent trial rate NPV is – Rs 33 and at 6 per cent +Rs 8. Thus the true IRR lies between 6 and 8 per cent:

$$IRR = 6\% + 2\% \left(\frac{688 - 680}{688 - 647} \right) = 6\% + 0.39\% = 6.39\%$$

Problem 10.4: Television Ltd. is a highly profitable firm, it has a proposal for manufacturing car televisions. The project would involve cost of plant of Rs 500 lakh (or Rs 55 million), installation cost of Rs 100 lakh and working capital of Rs 125 lakh. The annual capacity of the plant is to manufacture 20,000 sets. The price per set in the first year would be Rs 12,000. The variable cost to sales ratio is expected to be 65 per cent. The fixed cost per annum would be Rs 300 lakh (excluding depreciation). The company would have to incur promotion expenditure of Rs 120 lakh in the first year. Written-down depreciation rate for tax purposes is 25 per cent. Working capital requirement is estimated to be 25 per cent of sales. The company expects that the plant's capacity utilisation over its economic life of 7 years will be as follows:

Year	1	2	3	4	5	6	7
Capacity utilisation (%)	40	40	50	75	100	100	100

The terminal value of the project is expected to be 20 per cent of its original cost. (1) Calculate the project's NPV assuming a target rate of return of 14 per cent. The corporate tax rate of 35 per cent and profit from the sale of the asset is taxed as ordinary income. (2) How will NPV change if you consider the tax effects on the remaining book value and salvage value as per the current tax laws in India?

Solution:

	Cash Flows (Rs in lakh)							
Year	0	1	2	3	4	5	6	7
Capacity (%)		40	40	50	75	100	100	100
Units ('000)		8	8	10	15	20	20	20
Sales		960	960	1200	1800	2400	2400	2400
Less: Variable cost		624	624	780	1170	1560	1560	1560
Contribution		336	336	420	630	840	840	840
Less: Fixed cost		300	300	300	300	300	300	300
Less: Promotion expd.		120						
PBDIT		−84	36	120	330	540	540	540
Less: Depreciation		150	113	84	63	47	36	27
PBIT		−234	−77	36	267	493	504	513
Less: Tax, 35%		−82*	−27*	12	93	172	177	180
PAT		−152	−50	23	173	320	328	334
Add: Depreciation		150	113	84	63	47	35	27
Funds from operations		−2	63	108	237	368	363	360
Change in NWC	−125	−115	0	−60	−150	−150	0	0
Investment	−600							
After-tax salvage value								93
Release of NWC								600
NCF	−725	−117	63	48	87	218	363	1053
PVF at 14%	1.0000	0.8772	0.7695	0.6750	0.5921	0.5194	0.4556	0.3996
PV of cash flows	−725	−103	48	32	51	113	166	421
NPV	4							
IRR	14.14%							

* Tax credit assumed.

(1) Project's NPV is almost equal to zero. Its IRR is about 14 per cent which is equal to the discount rate.

Assumptions:

(a) The company incurs losses in the first two years. It is assumed that the losses can be set-off against the company's other profitable operations. Thus, tax savings are assumed.

(b) Net working capital is assumed to be released at the end of the project's economic life.

(c) Depreciation has been calculated at 25 per cent on the assets' written-down value. Book value at the end would be: Rs 80 lakh.

(d) Salvage value has been calculated on the cost of plant (excluding installation cost) 0.2 × Rs 500 lakh = 100 lakh. The after-tax salvage value is:

$$SV - T(SV - BV) = 100 - 0.35(100 - 80) = Rs\ 93\ lakh$$

(2) Current tax laws: remaining book value, salvage value and taxes

Remaining book value: $BV_7 = (1 - 0.25)^7 \times 600$
$$= Rs\ 80\ lakh$$

Salvage value: $SV_7 = Rs\ 100\ lakh$

The after-tax salvage value will be: $SV - PVDTS(SV - BV)$
$= 100 - (0.35 \times 0.25)/(0.14 + 0.25) \times (100 - 80) = Rs\ 95.53\ lakh$

If we consider DTS on the remaining book value and salvage value as per the current Indian laws, NPV will increase marginally as after-tax salvage value is higher by Rs 2.53 lakh.

Problem 10.5: A cosmetic company is considering to introduce a new lotion which is useful both in winters and summers. The manufacturing equipment will cost Rs 560,000. The expected life of the equipment is 8 years. The company is thinking of selling the lotion in a single standard pack of 50 grams at Rs 12 each pack. It is estimated that variable cost per pack would be Rs 6 and annual fixed cost, Rs 450,000. Fixed cost includes (straight-line) depreciation of Rs 70,000 and allocated overheads of Rs 30 000 The company expects to sell 100,000 packs of the lotion each year. Assume that the tax rate is 45 per cent and straight-line depreciation is allowed for tax purposes. If the opportunity cost of capital is 12 per cent, should the company manufacture the lotion? Also calculate the time-adjusted break-even point.

Solution: Allocated overheads (Rs 30,000 included in the fixed costs) are irrelevant for the project under consideration since they are not specific to it, and they would be incurred whether or not the project is undertaken.

The annual after-tax cash flows would be:

NCF = [Units (Selling price – Variable cost)
$\qquad$ – Fixed cost] (1 – Tax rate) + Depreciation
$\quad = [100,000(12-6) - 420,000](1 - 0.45) + 70,000$
$\quad = 180,000 \times 0.55 + 70,000 = Rs\ 169,000$

NPV $= -560,000 + 169,000 \times PVFA_{0,12,8}$
$\quad = -560,000 \times 169,000 \times 4,968 = +Rs\ 279,592$

IRR for the project is 25.2 per cent.
B/E point in terms of NPV = 0 is calculated below:

NPV $= [\{Q(12-6) - 420,000\}(1 - 0.45)$
$\qquad + 70,000] \times 4,968 - 560,000$
$\quad = 0$
$\quad = [(6Q - 420,000) \times 0.55 + 70,000]$
$\qquad \times 4,968 - 560,000$
$\quad = 0$
$\quad = 16.3944Q - 1,147,608 + 347,760 - 560,000 = 0$

$$16.3944Q = 1,359,848$$
$$Q = 82,946\ packs.$$

Problem 10.6: *ABC* Company purchased a machine three years ago at a cost of Rs 10,000. The machine had a life of 8 years at the time of its purchase. It is being depreciated on straight-line basis for the purpose of taxes. The company is thinking of replacing it with a new machine costing Rs 20,000 with an expected 5-year life. The profit before depreciation is estimated to increase by Rs 2,440 a year. Assume that the old and new machines will be depreciated on straight-line basis for tax purposes. The salvage value of the new machine is anticipated as Rs 2,500 after 5 years. The market value of the old machine today is Rs 11,500. It is estimated to have zero salvage value after 5 years. The corporate income tax rate may be assumed as 30 per cent. Further, the long-term capital gain tax rate 20 per cent. The amount in excess of the original cost is treated as the long-term capital provided the asset is held, at least, for one year. The short-term capital gains are treated as ordinary income and taxed at 30 per cent. The company's after-tax cost of capital is 12 per cent. Should the new machine be bought?

Solution: The depreciated value of the old machine today is Rs 6,250 as shown below:

Year	Depreciation (15%)	Book-value (balance)
0	—	10,000
1	1,250	8,500
2	1,250	7,500
3	1,250	6,250

The total proceeds from the sale of the old machines Rs 11,500. The total book profit is: $11,500 - 6,250 = Rs\ 5,250$. Of this profit, Rs 1,500 (i.e., Rs 11,500 – 10,000) is long-term capital gain and remaining Rs 3,750 is short-term capital gain (treated as ordinary income). Thus, the after-tax sale proceeds are:

$$= 11,500 - 0.20 \times 1,5000 - 0.30 \times 3,750 = Rs\ 10,075$$

New machine costs Rs 20,000. If it is acquired, the old machine wil be sold. Thus the net cash outlay will be as given below.

Net cash outlay

Cost of new machine	Rs 20,000
Less: Total sale proceeds of old machine	10,075
After tax	Rs 9,925

Differential depreciation The differential (incremental) depreciation base will be: cost of new machine minus the depreciated value of the old machine: Rs 20,000 – Rs 6,250 = Rs 13,750. The differential straight-line depreciation will be:

$$Rs\ 13,750/5 = Rs\ 2,750$$

Annual cash flows Net cash flows

= Profit before depreciation and tax × (1 Tax rate)
+ Tax rate × differential depreciation
= $2,440 × (1 - 0.30) + 0.30 × 2,750 = Rs 2,533$

Terminal cash flows The salvage value of the new machine is Rs 2,500. Since the asset is fully depreciated, the book profit is Rs 2,500. The after-tax salvage value will be:

After-tax salvage value = $SV - T(SV - BV)$
= $Rs 2,500 - 0.30(2,500 - 0)$
= Rs 1,750

Net present value

$$NPV = -Rs\ 9,925 + Rs\ 2,533 × PVA_{5,0.12}$$
$$+ Rs\ 1,750 × PVF_{5,0.12}$$
$$= -Rs\ 9,925 + Rs\ 2,533 × 3.6048$$
$$+ Rs\ 1,750 × 0.5674 = Rs\ 1,990$$

The new machine should be accepted.
IRR of the project is approximately 12,75 per cent.

Problem 10.7: Excel Chemical Ltd. manufactures a special chemical. It is thinking of replacing its existing machine by a new machine, which would cost Rs 24 lakh. The company's current production is 80,000 units, and it is expected to increase to 100,000 units if the new machine is bought. The selling price of the product would remain unchanged at Rs 80 per unit. The following is the cost of producing one unit of product using both the existing and new machines:

The existing machine has an accounting book value of Rs 40,000, and it may practically be treated at fully depreciated for tax purposes. It is estimated that the machine will be useful for 5 years. The supplier of the new machine has offered to accept the old machine in exchange for Rs 100,000. However, the market price of the old machine today is Rs 60,000 and it is

expected to be Rs 14,000 after year 5 year. New machine has a life of 5 years and a salvage value of Rs 100,000 at the end of its economic life. Assume that tax rate is 50 per cent, depreciation is charged on straight-line basis for tax purposes and the after-tax required rate of return is 20 per cent. Further, assume that book profit is treated at ordinary income for tax purposes.

Unit Cost (Rs)

	Existing machine (80,000 units)	New machine (100,000 units)	Difference
Material	30.0	25.5	(4.5)
Wages & salaries	20.5	15.0	(5.5)
Supervision	8.0	10.0	2.0
Repairs	4.5	3.0	(1.5)
Power & fuel	6.2	5.7	(0.5)
Depreciation	0.1	2.0	1.9
Allocated corporate overheads	4.0	5.0	1.0
	73.3	66.2	(7.1)

Solution:

(i) *Net cash outlay of new machine*   *Rs*
   Purchase price   2,400,000
   Less: Exchange value of old
      machine $100,000 - 0.5(1,000,000 - 0)$ 50,000
                                                                    Rs 2,350,000

(ii) *Market value of old machine:* Note that old machine could be sold for Rs 60,000 in the market. Since the exchange value is more than the market value, this option is not attractive. This opportunity will be lost whether the old machine is retained or replaced. Thus, on incremental basis, it has no impact.

Table 10.10: Calculation of Cash Flows and Project Profitability

(Rs '000)

Year	0	1	2	3	4	5	6	7	8
1. After-tax savings		608	608	608	608	608	608	608	608
2. Depreciation		300	300	300	300	300	300	300	300
3. Tax shield on Dep.: Tax rate × Dep.		150	150	150	150	150	150	150	150
4. Net cash flows from operations (1+3)		758	758	758	758	758	758	758	758
5. Initial cost	-2350								
6. Net salvage value									43*
7. NCF (4 + 5 + 6)	-2350	758	758	758	758	758	758	758	801
8. PVF at 20%	1.000	0.833	0.694	0.579	0.482	0.402	0.335	0.279	0.233
9. PV	-2350	632	526	439	366	305	254	212	186
10. NPV	+ 569								
11. IRR	27.8%								

*Salvage value of the old machine will be foregone. Thus, on differential basis, salvage value will be: SV of new – SV of old = 100,000 – 14,000 = Rs 86,000. Since old and new machines are fully depreciated, the book profit is Rs 86,000. The after-tax salvage value is: Rs 86,000 – 0.5 (86,000 – 0) = Rs 43,000.

(iii) Depreciation base: Old machine is fully depreciated for tax purposes; hence, for the purpose of tax depreciation, the book value is zero. Thus, the depreciation base of the new machine will be its original cost, viz., Rs 2,400,000.

(iv) Net cash flows: Unit cost includes depreciation and allocated overheads. Allocated overheads are allocations from corporate office; therefore, they are irrelevant. We can calculate DTS separately. Excluding depreciation and allocated overheats, unit costs can be calculated. The company will obtain additional revenue from 20,000 additional units sold. Thus, after-tax saving, excluding depreciation tax shield, would be:

$$= [100,000(80 - 59.2) - 80,000(80 - 69.2)](1 - 0.5)$$
$$= (2,080,000 - 864,000)0.5 = \text{Rs } 608,000$$

After adjusting depreciation tax shield and salvage value, NCF and NPV are calculated in Table 10.10.

The proposed project will add a new present value of Rs 569,000. Also, it has IRR of 27.8 per cent. It should be accepted.

Problem 10.8: The general manager of the engineering division of Modern Engineering Company is considering the replacement of a six-year old equipment. The company has to incur excessive maintenance cost of the equipment. The equipment has a zero written down value. It can be modernised at a cost of Rs 120,000 enhancing its economic life to 5 years. The equipment could be sold for Rs 20,000 after 5 years. The modernisation of the equipment would help in material handling and in reducing labour and maintenance and remain costs. The company has yet another alternative. It can buy a new machine at a cost of Rs 300,000 with an economic life of 5 years with a terminal value of Rs 60,000. The new machine is expected to be more efficient in reducing costs of material handling, labour and maintenance and repairs etc. The annual costs are as follows:

	Existing Equipment	Modernisation	New Equipment
Wages and salaries	40,000	30,700	11,800
Supervision	20,000	9,500	7,000
Maintenance	28,000	8,000	2,500
Power	20,000	18,000	15,000
Total	108,000	66,200	36,300

The company has a tax rate of 50 per cent and a required rate of return of 10 per cent. Assume straight-line depreciation for tax purposes, and tax on the sale of equipment at the corporate tax rate. Depreciation is calculated net of the expected salvage value. Should the company modernise its equipment or buy new equipment? Make your assumptions explicit.

Solution: We calculate net cash savings of modernisation and new equipment, as compared to the existing equipment.

Incremental Savings (vs. Existing Equipment)			
	Modernisation	New machine	Difference
Wages & salaries	9,300	28,200	18,900
Supervision	10,500	13,000	2,500
Maintenance	20,000	25,500	5,500
Power	2,000	5,000	3,000
Cost savings	41,800	71,700	29,900
Less: Depreciation	20,000	48,000	28,000
Taxable savings	21,800	23,700	1,900
Tax at 50%	10,900	11,850	950
After-tax savings	10,900	11,850	950
Add: Depreciation	20,000	48,000	28,000
Net cash flow	30,900	59,850	28,950

Depreciation = (Cost – Salvage)/No. of years

Existing		Nil
Modernisation (120,000 – 20,000)/5	= Rs 20,000
New (300,000 – 60,000)/5	= Rs 48,000

NPV:

$$\text{Modernisation} = -120,000 + 30,900 \times \text{PVAF}_{0,10.5}$$
$$+ 20,000 \times \text{PVF}_{0,10,5}$$
$$= -120,000 + 30,900 \times 3.791 + 20,000 \times 0.621$$
$$= -120,000 + 117,142 + 12,420 = +9,562$$

$$\text{New machine} = -300,000 + 59,850 \times \text{PVAF}_{0,10.5}$$
$$+ 60,000 \times \text{PVF}_{0,10,5}$$
$$= -300,000 + 59,850 \times 3.791 + 60,000 \times 0.621$$
$$= -300,000 + 226,891 + 37,260 = -35,849$$

New machine minus modernisation:

$$= -180,000 + 28,950 \times 3.791 + 40,000 \times 0.621$$
$$= -180,000 + 109,749 + 24,840 = -45,411$$
$$= \text{NPV, new machine} - \text{NPV, modernisation}$$
$$= (-35,849) - (+9,562) = -45,411$$

The company should modernise its equipment and not buy the new equipment.

Note: The text-book method of calculating straight-line depreciation has been followed. Salvage value at the end has been subtracted from the cost of calculated depreciation. Since at the end book value will be equal to salvage value, no tax adjustments have been made on the sale of the asset.

Problem 10.9: Telestra Company Limited is a growing and highly profitable consumer goods firm. The firm is introducing

Year		0	1	2	3	4	4	6	7
Capacity (%)	100		25	35	50	75	90	100	100
Units (000)	500		125	175	250	375	450	500	500
Selling price (Rs)	140		140	146	153	160	168	175	183
Variable cost (Rs)	85		85	89	93	97	102	106	111
Inflation	4.6%								
									(Rs in lakh)
Sales			175	256	383	601	754	877	917
Less: Variable cost			106	156	232	365	458	532	557
Contribution			69	101	150	236	296	344	360
Less: Fixed cost			150	75	75	75	75	75	75
PBDIT	25%		−81	26	75	161	221	269	285
Less: Depreciation			63	47	35	26	20	15	11
PBIT			−144	−21	40	135	202	255	274
Less: Tax	35%		−50	−7	14	47	71	89	96
PAT			−93	−14	26	88	131	165	178
Add: Depreciation			63	47	35	26	20	15	11
Funds from operations			−31	33	61	114	151	180	189
Change in NWC	15%	−26	−12	−19	−33	−23	−18	−6	138
Investment		−250							
After-tax salvage value									27
Release of NWC									0
Net cash flows		−276	−43	14	29	91	132	174	354
PVF at nominal rate	14%	1.0000	0.8772	0.7695	0.6750	0.5921	0.5194	0.4556	0.3996
PV		−276	−38	11	19	54	69	79	141
NPV		59							
IRR		17.7%							

a new breakfast cereal. The cost of plant is estimated as Rs 250 lakh. The annual capacity of the plant is to manufacture 50,000 packets of 850 grams each. The price per set in the first year would be Rs 140 and the variable cost per packet will be Rs 85. The initial fixed cost would be Rs 150 lakh which includes one-time promotion expenditure of Rs 75 lakh in the first year. Written-down depreciation rate for tax purposes is 25 per cent. Working capital requirement in the beginning of the year is estimated to be 15 per cent of sales. The company expects its revenue and costs to be affected by inflation which is expected to be 4.6 per cent per annum. The company expects that the plant's capacity utilization over its economic life of 7 years will be as follows:

Year	1	2	3	4	5	6	7
Capacity utilisation (%)	25	35	50	75	90	100	100

The terminal value of the project is estimated to be Rs 25 lakh. Calculate the project's NPV assuming a target *real* rate of return of 9 per cent. The corporate tax rate 35 per cent and profit from the sale of the asset is taxed as ordinary income. Assume that depreciation is charged on the block of assets as per the current tax laws in India.

Solution: The NPV and IRR of the projects are given below. You can notice that the price and costs estimated in year 1 are increased in the subsequent years due to inflation of 4.6 per cent per annum. Working capital is estimated as a percentage (15%) of sales with one-year lag (that is, incurred in the beginning of the year). It is assumed that working capital is released in the last year of the project's life. The book value of the asset in year 7 is: $(1 - 0.25)^7 \times 250{,}000 =$ Rs lakh. The after-tax salvage value would be: Rs 25 − PVDTS (Rs 25 − Rs 18) = Rs 25 − $((0.35*0.25)/(0.25 + 0.14)*7) =$ Rs 27 lakh.

The estimated cash flows are in nominal terms. The real discount would be converted into nominal rate as follows:

(1 + nominal rate) = (1 + real rate) × (1 + inflation rate)

Nominal rate = (1.09) × (1.046) − 1 = 0.14 or 14%

Since the project's NPV is positive, it should be accepted. The nominal IRR of 17.7 per cent is higher than the nominal discount rate of 14 per cent. The IRR in real terms is: (1.177) = (1.046) × (1 + real IRR) = (1.177/1.046) − 1 = 0.125 or 12.5 per cent which is higher than the real discount rate of 9 per cent.

Problem 10.10 Ashok Garments Ltd. is considering a new investment proposal of Rs 500,000. The project will provide before-tax cash flows of Rs 300,000 for 5 years. It would be financed by a 5-year loan with the following repayment schedule:

Total Payment	Interest at 15%	Principal	Balance
149,165	75,000	74,165	425,835
149,165	63,875	85,290	340,545
149,165	51,081	98,083	242,462
149,165	36,369	112,796	129,666
149,165	19,450	129,715	(49)*

*Rounding off error.

The income tax rate is 50 per cent. Assume straight-line depreciation for tax purpose. Given the project's business risk and target capital structure, the discount rate is 14 per cent. Calculate the project's NPV.

Solution: The project's discount rate is based on the target capital structure. Hence, we would discount free cash flows (that is, cash flows without adjusting for interest and repayment of debt) to find the project's NPV is:

$$NCF = 300,000 \times (1 - 0.5) + 0.5 \times 100,000$$
$$= 150,000 + 50,000 = Rs\ 200,000$$
$$NPV = -500,000 + 200,000 \times PVAF_{0,14,5}$$
$$= -500,000 + 200,000 \times 3,433$$
$$= + Rs\ 186,600$$

Note that the straight-line depreciation is Rs 100,000 per year, and therefore, depreciation tax shield is: $0.5 \times Rs\ 100,000 = Rs\ 50,000$. Project's IRR is 28.65 per cent.

REVIEW QUESTIONS

1. Distinguish between profits and cash flows. Why are cash flows important in investment decisions?
2. What are incremental cash flows? Briefly explain the effects of the following on the calculation of incremental cash flows: (a) sunk costs, (b) allocated overheads, and (c) opportunity costs.
3. A company has just tested the market for a new product. The test indicates that the product may capture about 40 per cent of the market share. It is also expected that 25 per cent of the new product's share will be at the cost of an existing product. The new product can be manufactured in the existing facilities, which could also be used to meet the expected increase in one of the company's existing products. The company's financial analyst argues that she would include the test costs in the new product's cash flows since they were incurred for testing the new product, but would exclude the lost contribution on an existing product and the value of the existing facilities to be used for the manufacture of the new product because no out-of-pocket cost is incurred. Do you agree with the analyst? Why or why not?
4. How should depreciation be treated in capital budgeting? Do the depreciation methods affect the cash flows differently? How?
5. In an interview with the chief executive of a motorcycle manufacturing company, he commented: "We present our capital budgeting numbers in real terms. Therefore, we have got to anticipate the inflation rate." Discuss the chief executive's comment.
6. The chairman of a rubber company stated, "We don't adjust our capital budgeting calculations for inflation because the price and costs of the product increase by the same rate." Comment.
7. Illustrate the distinction between real and nominal rates of return. Is this distinction important in capital budgeting decisions? Why?
8. Why should investment decisions be separated from financing decisions? Illustrate your answer.

PROBLEMS

1. Following data relate to five independent investment projects:

Projects	Initial (Rs) Outlay	Annual Cash Inflow (Rs)	Life in Years
A	500,000	125,000	8
B	120,000	12,000	15
C	92,000	15,000	20
D	5,750	2,000	5
E	40,000	6,000	10

Assume a 10 per cent required rate of return and a 35 per cent tax rate. Rank these five investment projects according to each of the following criteria: (a) payback period, (b) accounting rate of return, (c) net present value index,

and (d) internal rate of return.

2. A company has to choose one of the following two mutually exclusive projects. Both the projects will be depreciated on a straight-line basis. The firm's cost of capital is 10 per cent and the tax rate is 35 per cent. The before-tax cash flows are:

Project	C_0	C_1	C_2	C_3	C_4	C_5
X	−20,000	4,200	4,800	7,000	8,000	2,000
Y	−15,000	4,200	4,500	4,000	5,000	1,000

Which project should the firm accept if the following criteria are used: (a) payback period, (b) internal rate of return, (c) net present value, and (d) profitability index.

3. From the following data calculate (i) net present value,

(ii) internal rate of return, and (iii) payback period for the following projects. Assume a required rate of return of 10 per cent and a 35 per cent tax rate. Assume straight-line depreciation for tax purpose, and that tax is calculated on book loss or profit on the sale of asset.

Project	M	N
	(Rs)	(Rs)
Initial cash outlay	100,000	140,000
Salvage value	Nil	20,000
Earnings before depreciation and taxes		
Year 1	25,000	40,000
Year 2	25,000	40,000
Year 3	25,000	40,000
Year 4	25,000	40,000
Year 5	25,000	40,000
Expected life	5 years	5 years

4. (a) A company has to choose one of the following three mutually exclusive projects. Which project is the most desirable? Assume a required rate of return of 12 per cent.

Projects		C_0	C_1	C_2	C_3	Rate of Return (%)
O	(Rs)	−50,000	25,270	25,270	25,270	24
P	(Rs)	−25,000	5,000	5,000	25,570	15
Q	(Rs)	−28,000	12,670	12,670	12,670	17

(b) Compute the corresponding incremental cash flow for projects P and Q in problem 4(a). Which project is more desirable?

5. Kemp & Co. is faced with a problem of choosing among two alternative investments. It can invest either in Project A right now or wait for a year and invest in Project B. The following are the cash flows of the two projects:

Projects		C_0	C_1	C_2	C_3
A	(Rs)	−6,000	8,000	2,000	2,000
B	(Rs)	—	−8,000	12,000	4,000

Assume a required rate of return of 10 per cent. Which project should the firm select? Use the present value and internal rate of return methods. Also calculate the rate of return for incremental cash flows.

6. Is the following investment desirable if the firm's cost of capital is 10 per cent?

C_0	C_1	C_2	C_3	C_4
(Rs) 7,000	7,000	7,000	7,000	−25,000

7. The following data relate to a proposed new machine. Should it be acquired? Assume after-tax required rate of return of 10 per cent and a 40 per cent income tax rate. For simplicity assume that machines are depreciated on straight-line basis for tax purposes. Assume no tax on the profit or loss from the rate of asset.

	Rs
Purchase price of the new machine	40,000
Installation cost	8,000
Increase in working capital at the time of purchase of new machine	10,000
Cash salvage value of the new machine in four years	14,000
Annual cash savings (before depreciation and taxes)	16,000
Cash salvage value of the old machine today	20,000
Cash salvage value of the old machine in four years	4,000
Current book value of the old machine	16,000
Service life of both machines is four years	

8. Ram Singh, 45 years of age, has received an inheritance of Rs 300,000 from his father. He is currently working in materials management in a company, and his salary is Rs 36,000 per year, which he does not expect to change if he remains in his present employment till his retirement age of 58. He is considering two alternative investments of his inheritance. The first alternative is to continue in his present employment and to deposit Rs 300,000 in 13-year fixed deposit yielding 15 per cent compound interest. The second would be to purchase and operate a general store. He knows that to own a store, he will have to spend Rs 240,000 including Rs 100,000 for merchandise and the balance for building and fixtures. If he purchases the store, an additional Rs 60,000 will have to be invested for working capital needs. The expected annual receipts of this store are Rs 390,000. Annual out-of-pocket costs are estimated at Rs 300,000. As Ram Singh would manage his own store, he would have to leave his present employment. At the end of 13 years, when he wishes to retire in any event, he estimates the store would be sold for Rs 50,000. The applicable personal income tax rate is 30 per cent.
Which course of action would be more profitable for Ram Singh? Why?

9. The Manekshaw Company is considering the purchase of a new machine. The old machine is in good working condition, and will last for six years. However, the new machine will operate efficiently. It is expected that materials, labour and other direct expenses of the operations will be saved to the extent of Rs 16,000 per year. The new machine will cost Rs 80,000 and will be useful for six years. The old machine has a book value of Rs 64,000. The after-tax minimum required rate of return expected by the company is 10 per cent. Assume a 25 per cent written down depreciation and a 35 per cent tax rate of income. Assume that profit or loss from the sale of the assets are taxed at 35 per cent.
What action should be taken by the company if (a) the salvage value of the old machine is zero; (b) the salvage value of the old machine today is Rs 16,000 and if retained for six years it has zero salvage value; and (c) the salvage value of the old machine today is Rs 16,000, and if retained for six years, its salvage value will be Rs 2,000.

10. X Company is using a fully depreciated machine having a current market value of Rs 20,000. The salvage value of the

machine eight years from now would be zero. The company is considering replacing this machine by a new one costing Rs 102,500, and having an estimated salvage value of Rs 12,500. With the use of the new machine, annual sales are expected to increase from Rs 80,000 to Rs 92,500. Operating efficiencies with the new machine will save Rs 12,500 per year as operating expenses. Depreciation will be charged on written down basis at 25 per cent. The cost of capital is 11 per cent. The new machine has a 8-year life and the company's taxation rate is 35 per cent. Assume that book profit or loss from the sale of the asset are taxable at corporate tax rate. Should the company replace the old machine? Show calculations on incremental cash flow basis. How would your decision be affected if another new machine is available at a cost of Rs 175,000 with a salvage value of Rs 25,000. The machine is expected to increase sales by Rs 12,500 a year and save Rs 30,000 of operating expenses annually over its 8-year life.

11. Alpha Limited is considering replacing its old machine by a new machine. The new machine will cost Rs 360,000. The supplier of the new machine has agreed to accept the old machine at a value of Rs 40,000 in exchange for the new machine. Old machine has been fully depreciated for tax purposes, but it has a book value of Rs 20,000 in the accounting statements meant for external reporting. If the old machine is sold in the market, it cannot fetch more than Rs 30,000. After 10 years, it can be sold for Rs 6,000. The new machine has an expected life of 10 years and a salvage value of Rs 40,000 after 10 years. Alpha uses the old machine for producing a special component used in its main product. The production from old or new machine would be 15,000 units each year.

The following are the projected revenues and costs from the old and new machines:

	Old Machine (Rs)	New Machine (Rs)
Sales	1,080,000	1,080,000
Material cost	240,000	195,000
Direct labour	180,000	120,000
Indirect labour	90,000	100,000
Variable overheads	75,000	50,000
Allocated fixed overheads	120,000	130,000
Depreciation	2,000	36,000
	707,000	631,000
Profit before tax	373,000	449,000
Tax	186,500	224,500
Profit after tax	186,500	224,500

Depreciation is calculated on a straight-line basis. For tax purposes, written down depreciation at 25 per cent per annum is allowed. If Alpha's required rate of return is 12 per cent, should the old machine be replaced? What would be your decision if the component could be bought from outside at a cost of Rs 40 per unit? Assume that as per the current laws in India, depreciation is based on the block of assets.

12. *ABC* Co. is using a five-year old machine, which was bought for a cost of Rs 129,000. The machine is depreciated over its 12-year original life. The current market price of the machine is Rs 40,000. The salvage value of the machine at the end of its life is estimated to be zero.

The company is thinking of replacing this machine by a new machine which will cost Rs 175,000, and would need an installation cost of Rs 25,000. The life of the machine is estimated to be 7 years with a disposal value of Rs 18,000 at the end of its life. Because of the greater capacity of the new machine, it is expected that annual sales will increase from Rs 1,800,000 to Rs 1,870,000. The operating efficiency is not likely to change. The current operating expenses (excluding depreciation) are Rs 1,080,000. The company expects an additional working capital investment of Rs 25,000 if it buys the new machine. The company's cost of capital is 12 per cent.

Assume that the company will be allowed to depreciate the cost of machine on diminishing balance basis at 25 per cent for tax purposes. Assume a corporate tax rate of 35 per cent. You may also assume that no tax is paid on salvage value and it is adjusted for calculating depreciation as per the income tax rules. Would you recommend replacement of the machine? What would be your consideration in arriving at the decision?

13. A company has decided to buy a new machine either by an outright cash purchase at Rs 175,000 or by hiring it at Rs 42,000 per year for the life of the machine. The other relevant data are as follows:

Purchase price of the machine (Rs)	175,000
Estimated life (years)	5
Estimated salvage value if the machine is bought (Rs)	21,000
Annual cost of maintenance (whether hired or purchased) (Rs)	3,500

For simplicity assume that the company depreciates its assets on straight-line basis and pays tax at 50 per cent. Assuming a cost of capital of 10 per cent, which alternative is preferable?

14. A company is considering two mutually exclusive projects. Project *P* will require gross investment of Rs 250,000, and working capital of Rs 50,000. It is expected to have a useful life of ten years and a salvage value of Rs 30,000 at the end of ten years. At the end of five years, an additional investment of Rs 45,000 will have to be made to restore the efficiency of the equipment. The additional investment will be written off to depreciation over the last five years. The project is expected to yield before-tax cash flow (annual) of Rs 90,000. Project *Q* will require an investment of Rs 300,000 and working capital of Rs 60,000. It is expected to have a useful life of ten years with a residual salvage value of Rs 25,000 at the end of ten years. The annual cash flow returns from this project before income tax have been estimated at Rs 80,000 for each of the first five years, and at Rs 160,000 for each of the last five years.

Depreciation is to be charged at 25 per cent on declining balance on the block of assets as per the current tax laws. The corporate income tax rate is 50 per cent, and the opportunity cost of capital is 18 per cent. Calculate the NPV for each project. Which project is better?

15. The Bright Company is evaluating a project, which will cost Rs 100,000 and will have no salvage value at the end of its 5-year life. The project will save costs of Rs 40,000 a year. The company will finance the project by a 14 per cent loan and will repay loan in equal instalments of Rs 20,000 a year. If the firm's tax rate is 50 per cent and the after-tax cost of capital is 18 per cent, what is the NPV of the project? Assume straight-line depreciation for tax purposes.

16. The Vikrant Corporation is considering a new project, which costs Rs 50,000. The project will provide cost savings of Rs 30,000 a year for 5 years. It would be financed by a 5-year loan with the following payment schedule:

Total Payment	Interest at 15%	Principal	Balance
14,916	7,500	7,416	42,584
14,916	6,388	8,528	34,056
14,916	5,108	9,808	24,248
14,916	3,637	11,279	12,969
14,916	1,947	12,969	0

The corporate tax rate is 50 per cent. The project has the same risk as the firm's risk. The firm's cost of capital is 12 per cent. Calculate the project's NPV.

17. A company is considering replacing its existing machine by a more efficient new machine. The cost of production per unit is estimated as follows:

	Cost production per unit (Rs)	
	Old Machine	New Machine
Materials	40	38
Labour	60	40
Variable overheads	30	15
Fixed overheads	20	30
	150	123

For the old machine, fixed overheads include allocations from other departments and the depreciation. In case of the new machine, fixed overheads also include its maintenance cost of Rs 2 per unit.

The old machine was bought 5 years ago for a cost of Rs 300,000, and has a book value of Rs 200,000 now after being depreciated on a straight-line basis for both book as well as tax purposes. It has a remaining life of 10 years. It has a capacity to produce 3,000 units each year, and its capacity is fully utilised.

The new machine would cost Rs 500,000 and would have a salvage value of Rs 50,000 at the end of its life of 10 years. The supplier of the new machine has agreed to buy back the old machine at 50 per cent of its book value in exchange for

the new machine. He has also agreed that the remaining amount could be paid in two instalments: half of the amount now and half, a year later.

The new machine is capable of producing 4,000 units each year. The company is confident of selling the additional units by reducing its current price per unit of Rs 200 by 10 per cent. It is also expected that for operating the new machine, a working capital investment of Rs 25,000 would be required.

Should the new machine be acquired? Assume tax rate of 50 per cent and required rate of return of 15 per cent. Further, assume that depreciation can be charged on straight-line basis for computing tax, and ordinary tax is applicable on the gain or loss from the sale of asset.

18. A firm is considering an investment project involving an initial cost of Rs 200,000. The life of the project is estimated as 5 years. The project will provide annual net cash inflow of Rs 70,000. The cost of capital is 10 per cent. Should the project be accepted?

A subsequent evaluation revealed that firm had not considered price level changes in its estimates of cash flows and the cost of capital. The expected annual rate of inflation is 5 per cent. If inflation is accounted for, what would be the firm's decision?

19. The Indopax Company is considering investment in a machine that produces Product X. The machine will cost Rs 500,000. In the first year 10,000 units of X will be produced and the price will be Rs 20 per unit. The volume is expected to increase by 20 per cent and the price of the product by 10 per cent. The material used to manufacture the product is becoming more expensive. The cost of production is therefore expected to increase by 15 per cent. The production cost in the first year will be Rs 10 per unit. Assume for simplicity that the company will charge straight-line depreciation on the machine for tax purposes. There will be no salvage values of the 5-year life of the machine. The tax rate is 35 per cent, and the discount rate is 20 per cent, based on the expected general inflation rate of 10 per cent. Should the machine be bought?

20. Lodha Chemical Company is considering a project involving a cash outlay of Rs 6 million. Sales are expected to be Rs 1.20 million in year 1 and Rs 2 million in year 2 and thereafter, to grow at 10 per cent due to general rise is price. Operating expenses are estimated to be Rs 600,000 in year 1 and to rise at 10 per cent thereafter. An initial working capital of Rs 500,000 would be needed and afterwards working capital is expected to be 25 per cent of sales. The life of the project is 7 years, and it could be sold for 20 per cent of its original cost adjusted for inflation. Depreciation is charged at 25 per cent on the written down value basis. The company pays tax at 35 per cent. Assume that no tax is payable on the sale of the project at the end of its life. Calculate the project's NPV when the opportunity cost of capital is 21 per cent. Would your answer change if you analyse the project in real terms?

CASES

Case 10.1: Hind Petrochemicals Company

The central government has a refinery in a backward area of Western India. The petrochemical plants of Hind Petrochemicals Company (HPC) are situated in South and East. They want to expand in the West. HPC's existing refinery capacity is 9.5 metric ton. The government refinery has a capacity of 3.5 metric ton. HPC has strategic interest in acquiring the refinery. As a part of its privatisation policy, the central government is willing to sell the refinery for Rs 1,550 million. The company is in touch with the government for the purchase of the refinery for last few months.

According to the company appointed valuers, the refinery would need an additional investment of Rs 5,950 million in machineries and Rs 300 million for working capital before starting the operations. According to the valuer, if the company so desired, the refinery including these facilities (including working capital) could be sold for Rs 3,800 million after the planning horizon of five years. In that case, the company will have to incur Rs 200 million at the end of the economic life of the refinery to clean the site. The initial cost of valuers' work was Rs 25 million. They will be paid an additional amount of Rs 15 million in the first year if the company buys the refinery.

The corporate planning department of the company has estimated the profit from the refinery operation as given in Table 10.1.1:

Table 10.1.1: Profitability Projections

| | | | | | *(Rs in million)* |
| | | | *Year* | | |
	1	*2*	*3*	*4*	*5*
Sales	5730	5930	5870	3790	4500
Wages and salaries	1450	1500	1850	1030	1210
Selling and distribution costs	760	770	1080	530	650
Materials and consumables	180	270	290	200	230
Depreciation	1500	1500	1500	1500	1500
Corporate office costs	400	400	400	400	400
Survey costs	40	—	—	—	—
Interest	750	750	750	750	750
Profit (loss) before-tax	650	740	0	–620	–240
Less: Tax @ 35%	230	260	0	0	0
Profit after-tax	420	480	0	–620	–240

The company has a policy of charging depreciation on straight-line basis. However, for tax purposes, the WDV depreciation on the block of assets applies. The depreciation rate is 25 per cent. Corporate overhead costs include the three-fourths costs as the corporate overhead allocations and one-fourth costs incurred by the corporate office exclusively for the proposed project. The company proposes to finance the projects mostly by raising a 5-year 10 per cent loan from a financial institution. The management of the company feels that the investment in the refinery has the same risk and debt capacity as the current business; it must yield a return of 15 per cent.

The executives of the company are not unanimous on accepting the project. The financial controller's recommendation is to reject the project as it earns profits only in the first two years of the five-year period. The production manager considers the location as a strategic advantage since the company will have a plant in the West and could meet the demand easily. The marketing manager argues that the company should look at the investment's payback period. According to her, the depreciation included in the profit estimates is the recovery of the investment, and in addition, the company also has profit in the first two years.

Discussion Questions

1. Should the project be accepted? Use the most suitable method of evaluation to give your recommendation and explicitly state your assumptions.
2. Does your decision to accept the project change if you use other methods of evaluation? Show computations. Do you agree with the views of the financial controller, the production manager and the marketing manager?
3. Why do you think that the method chosen by you is the most suitable method in evaluating the proposed investment?

Case 10.2: Pure Drinks Company

Pure Drinks is in the business of packaged fruit juices. It already produces and sells orange, apple and pineapple juices. It intends to increase its range of juices. The company engaged a well-known marketing consultant to conduct a market survey to find the scope for guava juice. The market survey indicated tremendous scope for guava juice, and that the company could sell 900,000 sachets of guava juice each year. The Rs 5 million cost of the survey has not been yet paid in cash.

The survey has also shown that for one 1-litre sachet of guava juice, consumers are not prepared to pay more that Rs 65. The management accounting department of the company has estimated that the variable cost per sachet would be Rs 15, which includes material cost of Rs 6.50, labour cost of Rs 3.50 and overhead cost of Rs 5.00. At a capacity of one million sachets, the fixed overhead cost per sachet is estimated at Rs 6.75. The fixed overhead costs are allocations of the corporate general and administrative costs. Because of the project, the corporate marketing expences and some administrative cost are likely to increase by Rs 0.50 million per year. The management accountant feels that the profitability of the project would be affected by inflation. He expects 4 per cent annual consumer price inflation and estimates that the price increases in variable overhead cost and labour cost would be 5 per cent per annum and in material cost 3 per cent per annum. The management is confident that they would be able to increase selling price by the expected consumer price inflation. The company is implementing a computer-based inventory control system that is likely to decrease the project's working capital by about 4 per cent per year by sales volume. In the absence of the new inventory control system the working capital ratio is expected to be 30 per cent. The working capital investment preceds sales by one year.

The company is considering using its existing building for processing the guava juice. The building was fully depreciated for tax purposes and was not in use so far. But a few months ago it received an offer of Rs 100 million (net of taxes) for the purchase of the building from a computer company. If the company does not sell the building immediately, its value is likely to appreciate by Rs 100 million (net of taxes) after five years. The processing facility for guava juice would cost Rs 200 million. It is expected to have an economic life of five years. The estimated savage value

of the processing equipment is Rs 100 million. The company uses straight-line depreciation method for tax purpose and tax is applicable on the profit or loss from the sale of the assets at the corporate income tax rate of 35 per cent.

The company has no debt. The project will be financed from the internally generated funds. The shareholders expect a real rate of 8.65 per cent from the proposed guava project.

Discussion Questions

1. If you ignore inflation, should the projects be accepted? Explicitly state your assumptions and show calculations.

2. What shall be your decision if inflation is considered? Explain how inflation affects business decisions?

APPENDIX 10.1: RPRESENT VALUE OF DEPRECIATION TAX SHIELD

When depreciation is charged on straight-line basis, depreciation tax shield (DTS) will be a constant series over the asset's life. Thus the present value of depreciation tax shield (PVDTS) will be given by the following equation:

PV of depreciation tax shield

= Depreciation tax shield × Present value annuity factor

$$\text{PVDTS} = \text{DTS}\,(\text{PVFA})_{n,k} \qquad (1)$$

Table C given at the end of the book can be used to find out PVFA. It may be recalled that depreciation tax shield (DTS) is equal to:

Depreciation tax shield = Depreciation × Tax rate

$$\text{DTS} = \text{DEP} \times T$$

and depreciation is equal to:

Depreciation = Depreciation rate × Original value of the asset

$$\text{DEP} = d\,(\text{OV})$$

where d is the straight-line depreciation rate and OV is the original value of the asset. Thus, Equation (1) can be written as:

$$\text{PVDTS} = T(d)(\text{OV})[\text{PVFA}_{n,k}] \qquad (2)$$

As we have noted earlier, companies in India are allowed to charge depreciation as per the diminishing balance method (DBM) or written-down value (WDV) method. When DBM (or WDVM) of charging depreciation is followed, depreciation charge each year declines at a constant rate.

Thus, depreciation tax shield (DTS) under WDV is a decreasing series over the asset's life. For example, if Re 1 is the original value of an asset which has to be depreciated at a rate of depreciation (say d) charged on the declining value, the amount of depreciation in the first year (DEP$_1$) will be: $1 \times d = d$, and the asset's written-down value or book value at the end of first year will be: $1 - d$. The amount of depreciation in the second year (DEP$_2$) will be: $d(1 - d)$, and the asset's book value at the end of the second year will be: $(1 - d) - d(1 - d) = (1 - d)(1 - d) = (1 - d)^2$. Similarly, the amount of depreciation in the third year (DEP$_3$) will be: $d(1 - d)^2$, and the asset's book value at the end of

the third year will be: $(1 - d)^2 - d(1 - d)^2 = (1 - d)^2(1 - d) = (1 - d)^3$ and so on. Table 10 A.1 shows the amount of depreciation, book value etc.

Table 10A.1: Depreciation, Depreciation Tax Shield and Book Value

Year	Depreciation	Depreciation Tax Shield	Book Value
1	$\text{DEP}_1 = d$	$T(\text{DEP}) = Td$	$(1 - d)$
2	$\text{DEP}_2 = d(1 - d)$	$T(\text{DEP}_2) = Td(1 - d)$	$(1 - d)^2$
3	$\text{DEP}_3 = d(1 - d)^2$	$T(\text{DEP}_3) = Td(1 - d)^2$	$(1 - d)^3$
.	....	....	....
.	....	....	....
n	$\text{DEP}_n = d(1 - d)^{n-1}$	$T(\text{DEP}_n) = Td(1 - d)^{n-1}$	$(1 - d)^n$

The present value of depreciation tax shield under WDV will be given by the following equation:

$$\text{PVDTS} = T\left[\frac{\text{DEP}_1}{(1+k)} + \frac{\text{DEP}_2}{(1+k)^2} + \frac{\text{DEP}_3}{(1+k)^3} + \cdots + \frac{\text{DEP}_n}{(1+k)^n}\right]$$

$$\text{PVDTS} = T\left[\frac{d}{(1+k)} + \frac{d(1-d)}{(1+k)^2} + \frac{d(1-d)^2}{(1+k)^3} + \cdots + \frac{d(1-d)^{n-1}}{(1+k)^n}\right] \quad (3)$$

If we multiply both sides of Equation (3) by $1 - d$, we get

$$\text{PVDTS}(1 - d)$$

$$= T\left[\frac{d(1-d)}{(1+k)} + \frac{d(1-d)^2}{(1+k)^2} + \frac{d(1-d)^3}{(1+k)^3} + \cdots + \frac{d(1-d)^n}{(1+k)^n}\right] \quad (4)$$

Let us assume that $\dfrac{1}{(1+k^*)} : \dfrac{(1-d)}{1+k}$

Then Equation (4) becomes as follows:

$$\text{PVDTS}(1 - d)$$

$$= T\left[\frac{d}{(1+k^*)} + \frac{d}{(1+k^*)^2} + \frac{d}{(1+k^*)^3} + \cdots + \frac{d}{(1+k^*)^n}\right] \quad (5)$$

Since d is constant, its present value is given by the present value of an annuity formula. Thus, Equation (5) can be written as follows.

$$PVDTS = \frac{Td}{1-d}\left[\frac{1-\left(\dfrac{1}{1+k^*}\right)^n}{k^*}\right] \qquad (6)$$

Substituting $(1-d)/(1+k)$ for $1/(1+k^*)$, we obtain:

$$PVDTS = \frac{Td}{1-d}\left[\frac{1-\left(\dfrac{1-d}{1+k}\right)^n}{\dfrac{k+d}{1-d}}\right] \qquad (7)$$

$$PVDTS = T\left[d\left\{\frac{1-\left(\dfrac{1-d}{1+k}\right)^n}{k+d}\right\}\right] \qquad (8)$$

The term within brackets of the right side of equation is the present value of depreciation tax shield factor (PVDTSF) for given n, k and d when the asset value is Re 1 and WDV method of charging depreciation is followed. Thus PVDTS for the asset's given original value (OV) will be:

$$PVDTS = T\,(PVDTS_{n,d,k}) \times OV \qquad (9)$$

With the use of a scientific calculator, we can calculate PVDTSF for various combinations of n, d and k. It should be noted that Equation (8) or (9) does not include the present value of terminal depreciation tax shield. As discussed earlier, terminal depreciation (or the remaining book value) is adjusted in calculating the net proceeds from the sale of the asset.

In Equation (8), we may assume that n extends to infinity $(n \to \infty)$. In that situation, Equation (8) can be expressed in simple terms as follows:

$$PVDTS = \frac{Td}{k+d} \qquad (10)$$

Let us take an example. The book (depreciated) value of an asset at the end of five years is Rs 2.37 million. The WDV depreciation rate is 25 per cent and the discount rate is 15 per cent. What is the present value of depreciation tax shield at the end of 5 years if the asset is depreciated for ever? We can make the calculations as follows:

$$PVDTS_5 = \frac{Td}{k+d} \times BV = \frac{.35 \times .25}{.15 + .25} \times 2.37$$
$$= .21875 \times 2.37 = Rs\ 0.52$$

The present value of depreciation tax shield today is:

$$PVDTS_0 = \left[\frac{Td}{k+d} \times BV\right] \times \frac{1}{(1+k)^5}$$
$$= \frac{.35 \times .25}{.15 + .25} \times 2.37 \times \frac{1}{(1.15)^5}$$
$$= .21875 \times 2.37 \times .497 = Rs\ 0.26$$

Illustration 10A.1: Present Value of Depreciation Tax Shield

A company is considering the purchase of a machine requiring an immediate cash outlay of Rs 7,500, and it has an expected life of 5 years. The corporate tax rate is 55 per cent and the company's required rate of return is 10 per cent. If WDV depreciation of $33\frac{1}{3}$ per cent is allowed, calculate the present value of depreciation tax shield, using Equation (8). What would be the answer if depreciation rate is 25 per cent and the tax rate is 35 per cent?

We can use Equation (8):

$$PVDTS = 0.55\left[0.333\left\{\frac{1-\left(\dfrac{1-0.333}{1+0.10}\right)^5}{0.10+0.333}\right\}\right] \times 7,500$$

$$= 0.55\left[0.333\left\{\frac{1-\left(\dfrac{0.667}{1.10}\right)^5}{0.433}\right\}\right] \times 7,500$$

$$= 0.55(0.333)(2.120) \times Rs\ 7,500$$
$$= 0.55 \times 0.70596 \times 7,500 = Rs\ 2,912$$

If the depreciation rate is 25 per cent and the tax rate is 35 per cent, then PVDTS will be as follows:

$$= 0.35\left[0.25\left\{\frac{1-\left(\dfrac{1-0.25}{1+0.10}\right)^5}{0.10+0.25}\right\}\right] \times 7,500$$

$$= 0.35\left[0.25\left\{\frac{1-\left(\dfrac{0.75}{1.10}\right)^5}{0.35}\right\}\right] \times 7,500$$

$$= 0.35 \times 0.25 \times 2.436 \times 7,500$$
$$= 0.35 \times 0.609 \times 7,500 = Rs\ 1,599$$

CHAPTER
11 Complex Investment Decisions

CHAPTER OBJECTIVES

- Show the application of the NPV rule in the choice between mutually exclusive projects, replacement decisions, projects with different lives etc.
- Understand the impact of inflation on mutually exclusive projects with unequal lives
- Make choice between investments under capital rationing
- Illustrate the use of linear programming under capital rationing situation

INTRODUCTION

The simple accept-or-reject investment decisions with conventional cash flows may not be quite common in practice. Generally, a firm faces complex investment situations and has to choose among alternatives. The use of the NPV rule can be extended to handle complicated investment decisions.

The choice between mutually exclusive projects is a simple example of project interaction. **Project interactions** occur in numerous other ways. The following are some of the complex investment problems, which we shall discuss in this chapter:[1]

- How shall choice be made between investments with different lives?
- Should a firm make investment now, or should it wait and invest later?
- When should an existing asset be replaced?
- How shall choice be made between investments under capital rationing?

PROJECTS WITH DIFFERENT LIVES

The correct way of choosing between **mutually exclusive projects** with the same lives is to compare their NPVs, and choose the project with a higher NPV. The two mutually exclusive projects being compared, however, may have different lives. The use of the NPV rule without accounting for the difference in the projects' lives may fail to indicate correct choice. In analysing such projects, we should answer the question: What would the firm do after the expiry of the short-lived project if it were acquired instead of the long-lived project? We shall show in the following examples that the choice between projects with *different lives* should be made by evaluating them for *equal periods of time*.

Let us assume that a firm has to choose between two projects *X* and *Y*, which are designed differently, but perform essentially the same function. *X* would involve an initial cash outlay of Rs 120,000 and operating cash expenses of Rs 30,000 per year

---

1. For more details, see Bierman, H., Jr. and Smidt, S., *The Capital Budgeting Decision*, Collier Macmillan, 1975, Chapters 5, 8, 16 and 17; Copeland, T.E. and Weston, J.F., *Financial Theory and Corporate Policy*. Addison-Wesley, 1983, Chapter 3 and Brealey, R. and Myers, S., *Principles of Corporate Finance*, McGraw Hill, 1991, Chapter 6.

for 4 years. On the other hand, *Y* would involve an initial cash outlay of Rs 60,000 and operating cash expenses of Rs 40,000 per year for 2 years. Since the two projects do exactly the same job, we can choose between them on the basis of cost comparison. Cash flows of projects are in real terms and the *real discount rate* is 10 per cent. The present value of costs are shown below

Cash Flows (Rs '000)

	0	1	2	3	4	NPV, 10%
X	120	30	30	30	30	215.10
Y	60	40	40	—	—	129.42

If the difference in the projects' lives is disregarded, one may choose project *Y* since it has a lower present value of costs. But this need not necessarily be the best decision for the firm. *X* will perform the job for 4 years. If *Y* is chosen, it will expire after 2 years and therefore, it will have to be replaced at the end of year 2.

Let us call *Y* undertaken today as Y_1 and *Y* replaced after 2 years as Y_2. The comparison should be between the PV of costs of Y_1 plus Y_2 [i.e., $PV(Y_1 + Y_2)$] and the PV of costs of *X*. Thus, the cash flows of two alternative investments would be as follows:

Cash Flows (Rs '000)

	0	1	2	3	4	NPV, 10%
Y_1	60	40	40	0	0	129.42
Y_2	0	0	60	40	40	106.96
$Y = Y_1 + Y_2$	60	40	100	40	40	236.38
X	120	30	30	30	30	215.10

By the end of year 4, Project *X* wears out while Project *Y* wears out twice. At this point, a decision has to be made to choose between *X* and *Y* (or other versions) regardless of the initial choice of *X* or *Y*. When we compare the PV of costs of *X* with that of the chain of *Y* lasting same period of time as *X*, we would choose *X* since the PV of its costs is lower. Thus, the use of simple NPV rule would give incorrect results in the case of projects with different lives. The correct procedure is to compare NPVs of the projects for *equal periods of time.*

Annual Equivalent Value (AEV) Method

In a choice between machines with different lives, we assume that each machine is replaced in the last year of its life. For the purpose of analysis, the **replacement chains** of the machines can be assumed to extend to the periods of time equal to the *least common multiple* of the lives of the machines. In the above example of Machines *X* and *Y*, we took the time period equal to four years, which is the least common multiple of the lives of these machines.

The method for handling the choice of the mutually exclusive projects with different lives, as discussed above, can become quite cumbersome if the projects' lives are very long. The problem fortunately can be handled by a simpler method. We can calculate the **annual equivalent value** (AEV) of cash flows of each project. We shall select the project that has lower annual equivalent cost. The present value of cash flows of machine *X* is Rs 215,100. Suppose you would like to exchange

this lump sum with a 4-year annuity starting after one year. You can divide Rs 215,100 by a 4-year present value factor for an annuity of Re 1 at 10 per cent. This factor is 3.1699:

$$PVFA_{4, 0.10} = \frac{1}{.10} - \frac{1}{.10(1.10)^4} = 3.1699$$

The annual equivalent value of *X*'s cash flows is:

$$AEV = \frac{NPV}{Annuity\ factor}$$

$$= \frac{215,100}{3.1699} = Rs\ 67,857 \qquad (1)$$

We can make similar calculation for Machine *Y*. For Machine *Y*, the annual equivalent value is: $129,420 \div 1.7355 = Rs\ 74,572$. The annual equivalent cost of Machine *X* is lower than Machine *Y*; therefore, it should be accepted.

AEV for Perpetuities

We could assume that Machine *X* or *Y* would be replaced indefinitely. Then the NPV of costs of machine *X* in perpetuity would be: Rs 67,857/0.10 = Rs 678,570 and of machine *Y* Rs 74,572/0.10 = Rs 745,720. The firm would be better off by Rs 67,150 by always choosing Machine *X*. Same results are provided below in formal terms.

When we assume that projects can be replicated at constant scale indefinitely, we imply that an annuity is paid at the end of every *n* years starting from the first period. This can be written as:

$$NPV_\infty = NPV_n + \frac{NPV_n}{(1+k)^n} + \frac{NPV_n}{(1+k)^{2n}} + \cdots$$

Solving this series, we get

$$NPV_\infty = (NPV_n) + \left[\frac{(1+k)^n}{(1+k)^n - 1} \right] \qquad (2)$$

where NPV_∞ is the present value of the investment indefinitely, NPV_n is the present value of the investment for the original life, *n* and *k* is the opportunity cost of capital.

Using Equation (2) for Machine *X*, we get

$$NPV = (215.10) \left[\frac{(1.10)^4}{(1.10)^4 - 1} \right] = 215.10 \times 3.1547$$

$$= 678.57\ or\ Rs\ 678,570$$

Similarly, for Machine *Y*, we get

$$NPV = (129.42) \left[\frac{(1.10)^2}{(1.10)^2 - 1} \right] = 129.42 \times 5.7619$$

$$= 745.72\ or\ Rs\ 745,720$$

Nominal Cash Flows and Annual Equivalent Value

In the example of Machines *X* and *Y*, we used *real* cash flows (outflows or costs) and *real* discount rate, and calculated present value of cash flows. Using the expected inflation rate, we can convert real cash flows into *nominal* cash flows and real discount rate into *nominal* discount rate. The present value of cash flows will remain the same. However, the annual equivalent value would be different. Suppose the real rate is 10 per cent and the inflation rate is 4 per cent. The nominal discount rate will be: $(1.10) \times (1.04) - 1 = .144$ or 14.4 per cent. For Machine Y, the present value annuity factor will be 1.6382 and the annual equivalent value will be: $129,420 \div 1.6382 = Rs\ 79,000$. Similarly, for Machine X, the annual equivalent value will be: $215,100 \div 2.8900 = Rs\ 74,430$. Still Machine X is preferable since its annual equivalent value (cost) is lower. Let us try a higher inflation rate, say, 15 per cent. As shown in Table 11.1, the annual equivalent value (cost) for Machine X is Rs 93,520 and for Machine Y, it is Rs 91,440. Now Machine X is less attractive than Machine Y. Thus, we find that at higher inflation rates, the ranking of two mutually exclusive projects with unequal lives could change. It is therefore preferable to compare the *real* annual equivalent values (costs) of two mutually exclusive projects and make an appropriate choice.

We can summarise the decision criterion for choosing from mutually exclusive projects with unequal lives as follows: Calculate the *real* annual equivalent value (net operating cost or net operating cash flow) of each project, and go for the project with the least *real* annual equivalent value. This criterion is based on the premise that each asset will be replaced with an *identical* asset. However, if the assets are vulnerable to technological changes, this simple rule will not work, and the decision may not be optimal. In such cases, the analysis should consider the future investment opportunities, and the decision may be made on the basis of the NPV of projects: accept the project with lowest net present value of costs, or in case of revenue-generating projects, the project with the highest NPV.

INVESTMENT TIMING AND DURATION

A firm evaluates a number of investment projects every year. In the absence of a capital constraint, it will undertake all those projects, which have positive NPVs and reject those, which have negative NPVs. Further analysis may, however, indicate that some of the profitable projects may be more valuable (that is, they may have higher NPVs) if undertaken in the future. It may also

be revealed that some of the unprofitable projects may yield positive NPVs if they are accepted later on. These categories of investment projects may have different degrees of postponability; some of them may be postponed at the most to one or two periods, while a few may be undertaken any time in future. Those projects, which are postponable, involve two mutually exclusive alternatives: undertake investments now, or later. The firm should determine the optimum timing of investment.

The timing of investment may be a critical factor in case of those investment projects, which occur once in a while and those, which are of strategic importance to the firm. Such projects cannot be deferred for long. Postponability also creates uncertainty. For example, the NPV analysis may show that a firm should introduce a new product next year. The firm may still decide to introduce the product this year for two reasons: The firm may have a corporate strategy of remaining market leader in introducing new products. If it anticipates that its competitors will introduce the product this year if it does not, it may come up with the product this year to remain the market leader. Also for the reason of unanticipated competition from unknown quarters the firm may decide to introduce the product now.

How do we decide the optimum timing of an investment project, which is postponable? The rule is straightforward: undertake the project at that point of time, which maximizes the NPV. Let us take an example.

Suppose that the Alpha Company is considering an investment opportunity, which can be undertaken now, or after one period, or after two periods. The cash flows of the three mutually exclusive alternatives in terms of timing are as follows:

Project Undertaken at Period	Cash Flows (Rs)			
	C_0	C_1	C_2	C_3
	-100	150		
1		-120	180	
2			-140	205

To decide the optimum timing of investment, we can compare the NPVs of the alternative investment dates. If the opportunity cost of capital is assumed 10 per cent, the NPVs are:

Table 11.1: Inflation and Annual Equivalent Value

Machines	Real Cash Flows (Rs '000)			Nominal Cash Flows (Rs '000)			
	X	Y	X	Y	X	Y	
Year				Inflation 4%		Inflation 15%	
0	120.00	60.00	120.00	60.00	120.00	60.00	
1	30.00	40.00	31.20	41.60	34.50	46.00	
2	30.00	40.00	32.45	43.26	39.68	52.90	
3	30.00		33.75		45.63		
4	30.00		35.10		52.47		
Discount rate	10	.10	.144	.144	.265	.265	
NPV	215.10	129.42	215.10	129.42	215.10	129.42	
PVFA	3.1699	1.7355	2.8900	1.6382	2.2999	1.4154	
AEC	**67.86**	74.57	**74.43**	79.00	93.52	**91.44**	

Project Undertaken at Period	NPV	
0	$-100 + 150 \times 0.909$	$= 36.35$
1	$-120 \times 0.909 + 180 \times 0.826$	$= 39.60$
2	$-140 \times 0.826 + 205 \times 0.751$	$= 38.32$

Since the NPV of the second alternative is highest, the firm should wait and undertake the project after one period.

An alternative way of approaching the timing problem is to ascertain the net value as of each alternative period when the investment can be undertaken and compare the present value of alternative periods. For example, the net value as of each period is:

Year	Project Undertaken at Period	Net Value	% Change in Value
0	$-100 + 150 \times 0.909 =$	Rs 36.35	—
1	$-120 + 180 \times 0.909 =$	Rs 43.62	+ 20.0
2	$-140 + 205 \times 0.909 =$	Rs 46.35	+ 6.3

It is noticeable that the firm will make more money as investment is deferred to one or two periods. But the objective of the firm should be to choose that period for undertaking investment which maximises the NPV. If the net value is divided by $(1 + k)^n$ we will obtain the NPV:

Project Undertaken at Period	NPV (Rs)	
0	$36.35/(1.10)$	$= 36.35$
1	$43.62/(1.10)$	$= 39.60$
2	$46.35/(1.10)$	$= 38.32$

The results are the same as previously calculated. The optimum point to undertake the project is period 1 because this alternative has the maximum NPV.

It should be noticed that the net value increases by 20 per cent, which is greater than the opportunity cost of capital of 10 per cent, when the investment is postponed by one period; obviously the NPV increases. The net value increases by 6.3 per cent if the investment is postponed by two periods; but the gain in value is less than the opportunity cost of capital. Therefore, the NPV drops. It may be thus concluded that the NPV will be maximised at that point of time where the gain in value equals the cost of capital.

Tree Harvesting Problem

The optimum investment timing analysis is of direct relevance in the case of tree harvesting type problems.[1] Suppose that we own a piece of land and are considering growing a crop of trees, we would like to maximise the NPV of investment. The maximisation of the investment's NPV would depend on when we harvest trees. The net future value of trees increases when harvesting is postponed; but the opportunity cost of capital is incurred by not realising the value by harvesting the trees. The NPV will be maximised when the trees are harvested at the point where the percentage increase in value equals the opportunity cost of capital.

Suppose the net future value obtained over the years from harvesting the trees is A_t and if the opportunity cost of capital is k, then the present value (PV) of the net realisable value of trees is given by:

$$PV = \frac{A_t}{(1+k)^t} = A_t(1+k)^{-t}$$

If we assume continuous compounding,[2] the PV will be equal to:

$$PV = A_t e^{-kt} \qquad (3)$$

Assume that A_t is given by the function:

$$A_t = 3{,}000(1+t)^{1/2}$$

and k is equal to 10 per cent. Table 11.2 gives the net future value of the trees over years and the percentage increase in future value, and their present value (continuous compounding assumed):

Table 11.2: Net Future Value etc.

Time t	Net Future Value A_t Rs	Change in Value ΔA_t Rs	Increase in Value $\Delta A_t / A_t$ Rs	PVF e^{-kt}	Present Value $A_t \times e^{-kt}$ Rs
1	4,243	–	–	0.9048	3,839
2	5,196	953	0.225	0.8187	4,254
3	6,000	804	0.155	0.7408	4,445
4	6,708	708	0.118	0.6703	4,497
5	7,348	640	0.095	0.6065	4,457
6	7,937	589	0.080	0.5488	4,356

The present value is maximum when the trees are harvested in period 4. It is noticeable that after 4 years, the rate of increase in the value of trees declines below the opportunity cost of capital of 10 per cent.

We may have to incur initial cost of planting the trees. Assume that the initial cost, C, is Rs 4,000. The NPV will be:

$$NPV = A_t e^{-kt} - C = 3{,}000(1+4)^{1/2}(0.6703) - 4{,}000$$
$$= 4{,}497 - 4{,}000 = Rs\,497$$

The NPV is highest (+ Rs 497) when the trees are harvested in 4 years.

The discussion so far can be put in the formal terms. To determine the optimum harvesting time, which maximises the

---

1. For a more formal treatment, see Copeland and Weston, *op. cit.,* pp. 50–55, and Bierman and Smidt, *op. cit.,* pp. 325–27.

2. Refer to Chapter 2 for continuous compounding.

NPV, we set the derivative of the NPV with respect to t in Equation (3) equal to zero:[1]

$$NPV = A_t e^{-kt} - C$$

$$\frac{d\text{NPV}}{dt} = -kA_t e^{-kt} + \frac{dA_t e^{-kt}}{dt} = 0$$

Solving for k, we obtain

$$k = \frac{dA_t/dt}{A_t}$$

The expression $(dA_t/dt)/A_t$ is the rate at which the obtainable net future values change with time; it is the incremental (marginal) rate of change in value. Thus the NPV will be maximised, when the marginal rate of change in value equals the opportunity cost of capital.

In the example, we can obtain the incremental value as follows:

$$\frac{dA_t}{dt} = \frac{1}{2}(3,000)(1+t)^{-1/2} = 1,500(1+t)^{-1/2}$$

and the incremental rate of gain in value is:

$$\frac{dA_t/dt}{A_t} = \frac{1,500(1+t)^{-1/2}}{(3,000)(1+t)^{-1/2}} = \frac{1}{2(1+t)}$$

To find out the optimum value of t, we set $(dA_t/dt)/A_t$ equal to k:

$$\frac{1}{2(1+t)} = 0.10$$

$$2(1+t)0.10 = 1$$

$$0.2t = 0.8$$

$$t = 0.8/0.2 = 4 \text{ years}$$

The example above assumed that the land has no value after the trees are harvested. In fact, land may have value since the trees can be replanted. Therefore, the correct formulation of the problem will be to assume that once the trees are harvested, the land will be replanted. Thus, if we consider a constant replication of the tree-harvesting investment indefinitely, then the NPV will be:[2]

$$NPV = -C + (A_t - C)e^{-kt} + (A_t - C)e^{-2kt} + \cdots$$

Summing this infinite series, we get

$$NPV = -C + \frac{(A_t - C)}{e^{kt} - 1} \qquad (4)$$

We can apply Equation (4) to find out the optimum duration of the trees, when the land is replanted indefinitely. Table 11.3 gives the calculations.

Table 11.3: Optimum Duration

Time t (1)	A_t Rs (2)	$A_t - C$ Rs (3)	$\dfrac{A_t - C}{e^{kt} - 1}$ (4)	$e^{kt} - 1$ Rs (5)	NPV Rs (6) = (5) − 4,000
1	4,243	243	0.1052	2,310	(1690)
2	5,196	1,196	0.2214	5,402	1,402
3	6,000	2,000	0.3499	5,716	1,716
4	6,708	2,708	0.4918	5,506	1,506
5	7,348	3,348	0.6487	5,161	1,161
6	7,937	3,937	0.8221	4,789	789

We can see from Table 11.3 that the optimum harvesting time is 3 years since at this point the NPV is maximum (+ Rs 1,716).

In general terms, to maximise the NPV, we take derivative of NPV with respect to t in Equation (4) and set it equal to zero:

$$\frac{d\text{NPV}}{dt} = \frac{dA_t}{dt} - \frac{(A_t - C)k}{1 - e^{-kt}} = 0$$

$$= \frac{dA_t}{dt} = \frac{(A_t - C)k}{1 - e^{-kt}} \qquad (5)$$

Using Equation (5), the value of t can be found by trial and error. The NPV will be maximum at the point where incremental value (dA_t/dt) is equal to the present value of the difference between the future value and the initial cost times the opportunity cost of capital.

It may be noticed that under the assumption of simple NPV, the optimum life of the tree-harvesting project was found as 4 years and the NPV was + Rs 497. On the other hand, under the constant scale replication assumption the optimum life was found as 3 years and the NPV was + Rs 1,716. The second formulation of the problem is a correct procedure to handle investment timing situations. Recall that the same logic also applies to the projects with different lives.

REPLACEMENT OF AN EXISTING ASSET

We have discussed in the previous section the method of constant replication or replacement chains to choose between assets with different lives. We assumed in the examples that assets are replaced at the end of their physical lives. In practice, replacement decisions should be governed by the economics and necessity considerations. An equipment or asset should be replaced whenever a more economic alternative is available.

A number of companies follow the practice of approving a new machine only when the existing one can no longer perform its job. These companies follow a simple policy of replacement: replacement is necessary when the machine is beyond repair. They do not decide when to replace, the machine decides for them. This is one of the most expensive wrong policies, which a

---

1. Copeland and Weston, *op. cit.*, p. 52.
2. *Ibid.*, p. 53

company could follow. Such a policy erodes the company's profitability by protecting high operating costs. If the competitors follow cost-reduction policies by following a systematic replacement policy and are able to reduce prices in the future, the high cost company will be squeezed out of the market sooner or later.

Management should follow a replacement policy based on economic considerations and decide when to replace. An economic analysis may indicate to replace machine when it is, say, 5 years old with an improved alternative. If the replacement actually takes place when the machine is, say, 20 years old when it is beyond any repair, the company has been incurring extra costs and losing extra profits for 15 years.

We shall take an example to illustrate how an economic analysis should be made to decide when to replace. Suppose a company is operating equipment, which is expected to produce net cash inflows of Rs 4,000, Rs 3,000 and Rs 2,000 respectively for next 3 years. A design, which is considered to be a technological improvement and more efficient to operate, has appeared in the market. It is expected that the new machine will cost Rs 12,000 and will provide net cash inflow of Rs 6,000 a year for 5 years. What should the company do? One approach can be not to consider replacement at all since the existing equipment can still do the job; it is only after 3 years that the replacement may be considered. This is not a sound policy; the company should make an analysis whenever an alternative is available. It is important to note that the new equipment bought today or later on will also be replaced after sometime. The earlier the company buys the new equipment, the earlier it will need replacement. So the effective choice is between a series of new machines beginning either immediately or later on. The correct method of analysis, therefore, is to compare the annual equivalent value (AEV) of the old and new equipment as given below.

Cash Flows (Rs '000)

Equipment	C_0	C_1	C_2	C_3	C_4	C_5	NPV at 12%
New	–12	6	6	6	6	6	9.63
Old	—	4	3	2	—	—	7.39
AEV, New	—	2.67	2.67	2.67	2.67	2.67	9.63
AEV, Old	—	3.08	3.08	3.08	—	—	7.39

It is indicated that a chain of new machines is equivalent to an annuity of Rs 9,630 ÷ 3.605 = Rs 2,671 a year for the life of the chain. The existing machine is still capable of providing an annuity of: Rs 7,390 ÷ 2.402 = Rs 3,076. So long as the existing machine generates a cash inflow of more than Rs 2,671 there does not seem to be an economic justification for replacing it. The example can be extended to incorporate salvage values.[1] The procedure for analysis would, however, remains the same. Suppose that the new equipment can be sold for Rs 5,000 after 5 years. The present value of this inflow is Rs 5,000 ÷ $(1.12)^5$ = Rs 2,835, and the annuity is: Rs 2,835 ÷ 3.605 = Rs 786. Thus

AEV of the new equipment is Rs 2,671 + Rs 786 = Rs 3,457.

INVESTMENT DECISIONS UNDER CAPITAL RATIONING

Firms may have to choose among profitable investment opportunities because of the limited financial resources. In this section, we shall discuss the methods of solving the capital budgeting problems under **capital rationing**. We shall show that the NPV is the most valid selection rule even under the capital rationing situations.

A firm should accept all investment projects with positive NPV in order to maximise the wealth of shareholders. The NPV rule tells us to spend funds in the projects until the NPV of the last (marginal) project is zero.

Consider the following investment projects:

Projects	Cash Outlay (Rs '000)	NPV at 10% (Rs '000)	IRR	Cumulative Cash Outlay (Rs '000)	Cumulative NPV (Rs '000)
A	200	18.2	20%	200	18.2
B	150	6.8	15%	350	25.0
C	100	0	10%	450	25.0
D	50	(2.3)	5%	500	22.7

The firm will get the highest NPV if it accepts A and B. Any project between B and C should also be accepted by the firm. C is the marginal project; the firm may or may not accept it since it does not increase or decrease NPV. D should be rejected, as its NPV is negative. Thus, the firm may spend Rs 350,000 to obtain the maximum NPV for its shareholders. Suppose the funds available with the firm are limited; it can spend only Rs 200,000. Then it should accept only project A, which yields highest NPV and spends the entire budget. Because of the capital constraint, however, the shareholders' wealth will not be maximised. The IRR rule also indicates the same decisions in the case of independent projects, although it can be misleading in a number of situations. In the example, C earns a rate of return just equal to the cost of capital (C has zero NPV); this is a **marginal project.** Thus, the IRR rule tells us to invest funds in the projects until the marginal rate of return is equal to the cost of capital. Again, because of the limited funds, project B, which yields a return (15%) higher than the cost of capital (10%) will have to be foregone.

Capital rationing refers to a situation where the firm is constrained for external, or self-imposed, reasons to obtain necessary funds to invest in all investment projects with positive NPV. Under capital rationing, the management has not simply to determine the profitable investment opportunities, but it has also to decide to obtain that combination of the profitable projects which yields highest NPV within the available funds.

Why Capital Rationing?

Capital rationing may arise due to external factors or internal constraints imposed by the management. Thus there are two

---

1. Brealey and Myers, *op. cit.,* p. 111.
2. Van Horne, *op. cit.,* pp. 653–58, and Weston and Copeland, *op. cit.,* pp. 153–55.

types of capital rationing:[1]
- External capital rationing
- Internal capital rationing.

External Capital Rationing

External capital rationing mainly occurs on account of the imperfections in capital markets. Imperfections may be caused by deficiencies in market information, or by rigidities of attitude that hamper the free flow of capital. For example, Supreme Electronics Ltd. is a closely held company. It borrows from the financial institutions as much as it can. It still has investment opportunities, which can be financed by issuing equity capital. But it doesn't issue shares. The owner-managers do not approve the idea of the public issue of shares because of the fear of losing control of the business. Consider another case. Tan India Wattle Extracts Ltd. proposes to set up a plant for manufacturing wattle extract. There is expected to be tremendous demand for wattle extract and therefore, the proposed project is likely to be highly profitable. The prospective investors, however, are not convinced of the prospects of the project. For the company, therefore, the capital markets are non-existent. The NPV rule will not work if shareholders do *not* have access to the capital markets. Imperfections in capital markets alone do not invalidate use of the NPV rule. In reality, we will have very few situations where capital markets do not exist for shareholders.

Internal Capital Rationing

Internal capital rationing is caused by self-imposed restrictions by the management. Various types of constraints may be imposed. For example, it may be decided not to obtain additional funds by incurring debt. This may be a part of the firm's conservative financial policy. Management may fix an arbitrary limit to the amount of funds to be invested by the divisional managers. Sometimes management may resort to capital rationing by requiring a minimum rate of return higher than the cost of capital. Whatever may be the type of restrictions, the implication is that some of the profitable projects will have to be foregone because of the lack of funds. However, the NPV rule will work since shareholders can borrow or lend in the capital markets.

It is quite difficult sometimes to justify the internal capital rationing. But generally it is used as a means of financial control. In a divisional set-up, the divisional managers may overstate their investment requirements. One way of forcing them to carefully assess their investment opportunities and set priorities is to put upper limits to their capital expenditures. Similarly, a company may put investment limits if it finds itself incapable of coping with the strains and organisational problems of a fast growth.

Use of Profitability Index in Capital Rationing

Under capital rationing, we need a method of selecting that portfolio of projects which yields highest possible NPV within the available funds. Let us consider a simple situation where a firm has the following investment opportunities and has a 10% cost of capital.

Project	\multicolumn{4}{c}{Cash Flows (Rs '000)}		

Project	C_0	C_1	C_2	C_3	NPV at 10%	Profitability Index
L	− 50	+ 30	+ 25	+ 20	12.94	1.26
M	− 25	+ 10	+ 20	+ 10	8.12	1.32
N	− 25	+ 10	+ 15	+ 15	7.75	1.31

If the firm has no capital constraint, it should undertake all three projects because they all have positive NPVs. Suppose there is a capital constraint and the firm can spend only Rs 50,000 in year zero, what should the firm do? If the firm strictly follows the NPV rule and starts with the highest individual NPV, it will accept the highest NPV Project L, which will exhaust the entire budget. We can, however, see that Projects M and N together have higher NPV (Rs 15,870) than project L (Rs 12,940) and their outlays are within the budget ceiling. The firm should, therefore, undertake M and N rather than L to obtain highest possible NPV. It should be noted that the firm couldn't select projects solely on the basis of individual NPVs when funds are limited. The firm should intend to get the largest benefit for the available funds. That is, those projects should be selected that give the highest ratio of present value to initial outlay. This ratio is the profitability index (PI). In the example, M has the highest PI followed by N and L. If the budget limit is Rs 50,000, we should choose M and N following the PI rule.

The capital budgeting procedure under the simple situation of capital rationing may be summarised as follows: The NPV rule should be modified while choosing among projects under capital constraint. The objective should be to maximise NPV *per rupee of capital* rather than to maximise NPV. Projects should be ranked by their profitability index, and top-ranked projects should be undertaken until funds are exhausted.

Limitations of Profitability Index

The capital budgeting procedure described above does not always work. It fails in two situations:

- Multi-period capital constraints
- Project indivisibility

A serious limitation in using the PI rule is caused by the **multi-period constraints**. In the above example, there is a budget limit of Rs 50,000 in year 1 also and the firm is anticipating an investment opportunity O as in low is year 1. Thus, the decision choices today are as follows:

Project	\multicolumn{4}{c}{Cash Flows (Rs '000)}			

Project	C_0	C_1	C_2	C_3	NPV at 10%	Profitability Index	Rank
L	− 50	+ 30	+ 25	+ 20	12.94	1.26	III
M	− 25	+ 10	+ 20	+ 10	8.12	1.32	I
N	− 25	+ 10	+ 15	+ 15	7.75	1.31	II
O	0	− 80	+ 60	+ 40	6.88	1.09	IV

---

1. Bierman and Smidt, *op. cit.*, p. 147 and p. 152.

Projects M and N have first and second ranks in terms of PI. They together have highest NPV and also exhaust the budget in year 0; so the firm would choose them. Further, projects M and N together are expected to generate Rs 20,000 cash flow next year. This amount with the next year's budget (i.e., Rs 20,000 + Rs 50,000 = Rs 70,000) is not sufficient to accept Project O. Thus, by accepting projects M and N, the firm will obtain a total NPV of Rs 15,870. However, a careful examination of the projects' cash flows reveals that if project L is accepted now it is expected to generate a cash flow of Rs 30,000 after a year, which together with the budget of Rs 50,000 is sufficient to undertake Project O next year. Projects L and O have lower PI ranks than Projects M and N, but they have higher total NPV of Rs 19,820.

The PI rule of selecting projects under capital rationing can also fail because of **project indivisibility**. It may be more desirable to accept many lower ranked smaller projects than a single large project. The acceptance of a single large project, which may be top-ranked, excludes the possibility of accepting small projects, which may have higher total NPV. Consider the following projects:

Project	Outlay (Rs)	NPV (Rs)	PI	Rank
A	500,000	1,10,000	1.22	1
B	150,000	(7,500)	0.95	6
C	350,000	70,000	1.20	2
D	450,000	81,000	1.18	4
E	200,000	38,000	1.19	3
F	400,000	20,000	1.05	5

Suppose that the firm has a budget ceiling of Rs 10 lakh (i.e., Rs 1 million). Following the ranking by PI, the firm would choose A and C. These projects spend Rs 850,000 of the total a budget and have a total NPV of Rs 180,000. The next best project E needs an investment of Rs 200,000, while the firm has only Rs 150,000. If we examine the various combinations of projects satisfying the budget limit, we find the package of C, E and D as the best. They exhaust the entire budget and have a total NPV of Rs 189,000. Thus the firm can choose two lower ranked, small projects, E and D, in place of the high ranked, large project, A. The selection procedure will become very unwieldy if the firm has to choose the best package of projects from a large number of profitable projects.

Our discussion has shown that the profitability index can be used to choose projects under simple, one-period, capital constraint situation. It breaks down in the case of multi-period capital constraints. It will also not work when any other constraint is imposed, or when mutually exclusive projects, or dependent projects are being considered.

Programming Approach to Capital Rationing

The limitations of the profitability index method make it necessary to have a better method for investment decisions under capital rationing. Let us develop a general procedure for solving the capital rationing problem. Reconsider the example in which we had a two-period budget constraint. Our objective is to choose that package of projects, which gives us maximum total net present value subject to the firm's resources. Assume that we can invest in X fraction of each of the four projects. Then NPV from L will be 12.94 X_L, from M 8.12 X_M, and so on. The total NPV will be:

$$NPV = 12.94X_L + 8.12X_M + 7.75X_N + 6.88X_O$$

It should be clear that the values of X's should be such that total NPV is maximum. There are certain conditions for investing in various projects. For example, the total cash outlay in each of the two periods should not exceed Rs 50,000. Thus, the following two constraints should be satisfied while maximising the NPV:

$$50X_L + 25X_M + 25X_N + 0X_O \leq 50$$
$$-30X_L - 10X_M - 10X_N + 80X_O \leq 50$$

It would be obvious to note that the investment in any project cannot be negative and we cannot invest in more than one of each project. Thus we have:

$$0 \leq X_L \leq 1$$
$$0 \leq X_M \leq 1$$
$$0 \leq X_N \leq 1$$
$$0 \leq X_O \leq 1$$

We can summarise the decision problem as follows: Maximise

$$12.94X_L + 8.12X_M + 7.75X_N + 6.88X_O$$

Subject to

$$50X_L + 25X_M + 25X_N + 0X_O \leq 50$$
$$-30X_L - 10X_M - 10X_N + 80X_O \leq 50$$
$$0 \leq X_L \leq 1$$
$$0 \leq X_M \leq 1$$
$$0 \leq X_N \leq 1$$
$$0 \leq X_O \leq 1$$

Linear Programming (LP)

It may be realised that the above situation is a linear programming (LP) problem.[1] It can be easily solved with the help of a computer. (You can use Solver in Excel to solve linear programming problems.) Using the LP model, the computer tells us that we should accept Projects M and N entirely and a fraction equal to 0.875 of Project O; Project L should be rejected. This is the optimal solution, and we shall obtain a maximum NPV equal to:

$$12.94 \times 0 + 8.12 \times 1 + 7.75 \times 1 + 6.88 \times 0.875$$
$$= 21.89 \text{ or Rs } 21,890$$

This answer is quite different from the one, which we obtained earlier. Our earlier answer was that we should accept entire of Projects L and O, generating maximum NPV of Rs 19,820.

---

1. Van Horne, J.C., *Financial Management and Policy*, Prentice-Hall of India, 1985, p. 135.

Integer Programming (IP)

It may be noted in this example that the LP solution requires us to accept a fraction of Project O. Perhaps some projects can be divided. If Project O is divisible, it may be appropriate to undertake a part of it and assume that cash flows will be reduced proportionately. However, a large number of projects in practice are indivisible. When projects are not divisible, we can use **integer programming** (IP) by limiting the X's to be integers of either 0 to 1. Integer programmes are difficult to solve. It may take unwieldy number of iterations for the model to converge on a solution. Also, other restrictions may prove to be redundant on account of integer restriction.

Dual Variable

One important advantage in using the programming models for solving the capital-rationed capital budgeting decisions is the information about '*dual variables.*' **Dual variables** for the budget constraints may be interpreted as '**opportunity costs**' or '**shadow prices.**' In the example, dual variables for the budget constraints in periods 0 and 1 respectively, are 0.344, and 0.086.

The dual variables of 0.344 for period 0 imply that NPV can be increased by Rs 0.344 if the budget in period 0 is increased by Re 1. In other words, the opportunity cost of the budget constraint for period 0 is 34.4 per cent, and for period 1 it is 8.6 per cent. This implies that the NPV could be increased if funds were shifted from period 1 to period 0. Thus, dual variables provide information for deciding the shifting of funds from one period to another.[1]

Extensions of Programming Approach

The use of LP or IP models can be extended to cope with other constraints.[2] A firm may like to provide for the carry over of unspent cash from one period to another. Let C denote funds carried from period 0 to period 1 and let them earn interest at the rate i. Then in the example, we can rewrite budget constraint for the period 0 as:

$$50X_L + 25X_M + 25X_N + 0X_O + C = 50$$

and the constraint for period 1 will become

$$-30X_L - 10X_M - 10X_N + 80X_O \le 50 + (1+i)C$$

We will also add one more restriction limiting $C \le 0$ since carrying forward a negative amount is equal to borrowing.

We can add more requirements (restrictions) in the model. In the example Projects M and N could be assumed mutually exclusive, that is, either M or N be accepted. We can incorporate this condition in an integer programme by specifying that the total investment in M and N cannot be greater than 1 and if M is 1 then N will be zero or if N is 1 then M will be zero:

$$X_M + X_N \le 1, X_M, X_N = 0 \text{ or } 1$$

We can also account for contingent projects in the model. Assume that the acceptance of Project O is contingent on the acceptance of Project L; that is, O can't be accepted unless L is accepted. The following constraint will be added:

$$X_O + X_L \le 0, X_0, X_L = 0 \text{ or } 1$$

In other words, if X_L is 1, X_0 can be 0 or 1; but if X_L is 0, X_0 must be 0.

In addition to financial constraints, non-financial constraints can also be included. For example, four projects in the example may share 1,000 units of a common material. If Project L requires 400 units, Project M 300 units, Project N 250 units, and Project O 250 units, then we need to add the following constraint:

$$400X_L + 300X_M + 250X_N + 250X_O \le 1,000$$

It should be clear that we could go on adding any possible constraint.

Limits to the Use of Programming Approach

LP or IP models seem to be best suited for making investment decisions under limited resources. However, these models are not in common use. There are at least two important reasons for the unpopularity of these models. First, they are costly to use when large, indivisible projects are involved. Second, these models assume that future investment opportunities are known. The discovery of investment opportunities in practice is an unfolding process.

Capital Rationing in Practice

How serious is the problem of capital rationing in practice? Do companies reject projects due to shortage of funds? How do they select projects under capital rationing? Capital rationing does not seem to be a serious problem in practice. It may arise due to the internal constraint or the management's reluctance to raise external funds. When companies face the problem of shortage of funds, they use simple rules of choosing projects rather than the complicated mathematical models (see Exhibit 11.1).

EXHIBIT 11.1: DO COMPANIES FACE CAPITAL RATIONING PROBLEM IN PRACTICE?

- In a study of Indian companies, it is revealed that most companies do not reject projects on account of capital shortage. They face the problem of shortage of funds due to the management's desire to limit capital expenditures to internally generated funds or the reluctance to raise capital from outside.

- Most companies do not use mathematical approach to select projects under capital following. The bases to choose projects under capital rationing are:
  - profitability
  - priorities set by management
  - experience

- Some companies satisfy the criteria of profitability and strategic considerations for allocating limited funds.

- Generally companies do not reject profitable projects under capital rationing; they postpone them till funds become available in future.

Source: I.M. Pandey, Capital Budgeting Practices of Indian Companies, *MDI Management Journal*, Vol. 2, No. 1, Jan. 1989.

---

1. Brealey and Myers, *op. cit.*, pp. 118–19; Van Horne, *op. cit.*, p. 136.

SUMMARY

❖ A firm in practice faces complicated investment decisions. The most common situations include choosing among investments with different lives, deciding about the replacement of an existing asset or timing of an investment and evaluating investments under capital rationing. The NPV rule can be extended to handle such situations.

❖ The choice between projects with unequal lives should be made by comparing their real annual equivalent values (AEVs). AEV is the NPV of an investment divided by the annuity factor given its life and risk-free discount rate:

$$AEV = \frac{NPV}{Annuity\,factor}$$

❖ The procedure of comparing AEVs can be followed while replacing an existing asset by a new asset. The NPV rule also proves handy in resolving the timing problem of an investment.

❖ Capital rationing occurs because of either the external or internal constrain on the supply of funds. In capital rationing situations, the firm cannot accept all profitable projects. Therefore, the firm will aim at maximising NPV subject to the funds constraint.

❖ In simple one-period capital rationing situations, the profitability index (PI) rule can be used. PI rule breaks in the case of multi-period funds constraints and project indivisibility.

❖ A more sophisticated approach—either linear programming or integer programming—can be used to select investment under capital rationing. However, two factors limit the use of these approaches in practice. First, they are costly, and second, they assume investment opportunities as known. Also, large companies in reality hardly face the real capital shortage situations. Mostly it arises on account of the internal constraints imposed by the management for control purposes.

KEY CONCEPTS

Annual equivalent value	External capital	Multi-period capital constraint	Project indivisibility
Capital rationing	rationing	Mutually exclusive projects	Replacement chains
Dual variable	Internal capital rationing	Profitability index	Shadow prices

---

ILLUSTRATIVE SOLVED PROBLEMS

Problem 11.1: A company is evaluating two mutually exclusive projects. Project *X* will cost Rs 10,000 now and will generate cash flows of Rs 5,000 each year over its life of four years. Project *Y* will cost Rs 2,500 and will generate cash flows of Rs 3,000 each year over its life of three years. Which project would you select assuming a risk-free cost of capital of 10 per cent?

Solution Since the projects have different lives, we can compare their annual equivalent value (AEV):

$$AEV = \frac{NPV}{Annuity\,factor}$$

Project *X*:

$$AEV = \frac{-10,000 + (5,000 \times 3,170)}{3,170} = \frac{5,850}{3,170} = Rs\,1,845$$

Project *Y*:

$$AEV = \frac{-2,500 + (3,000 \times 2,487)}{2,487} = \frac{4,961}{2,487} = Rs\,1,995$$

Project *Y* should be selected since it has higher AEV. Note that Project *X* has higher NPV if the differences in the lives of projects are not considered.

Problem 11.2: At a cash outlay of Rs 600,000, a company has kegged its recently found fine wine. Now it expects the value of wine to grow as: A_t = Rs 900,000 ln *t*. If the company has an opportunity cost of capital of 18 per cent, determine the optimum time of bottling for the wine. Assume continuous compounding.

Solution We can use Equation (5) given in the chapter, assuming that the project can be replicated indefinitely:

$$\frac{dA_t}{dt} = \frac{(A_t - C)k}{1 - e^{-kt}}$$

$$\frac{dA_t}{dt} = \frac{d(900,000 \ln t)}{dt} = \frac{900,000}{t}$$

$$\frac{(A_t - C)k}{1 - e^{-kt}} = \frac{(900,000 \ln t - 600,000)^{0.18}}{1 - e^{-0.18t}}$$

t	Da_t/dt	$1 - e^{-kt}$	$(A_t - C)k$	$\dfrac{(A_t - C)k}{1 - e^{-kt}}$
1	900,000	−108,000	0.1647	−655,737
2	450,000	4,290	0.3023	14,191
3	300,000	69,975	0.4173	167,685
4	225,000	116,580	0.5132	227,163
5	180,000	152,729	0.5934	257,380

The optimum kegging time is approximately 4 years as

$$dA_t \,/\, dt = (A_t - C)k\,/\,1 - e^{-kt} \approx 225{,}000$$

Problem 11.3: Kay Bee company is thinking of buying an equipment for Rs 400,000. The equipment is expected to produce each year 10,000 units, 15,000 units, 20,000 units and 8,000 units of product *X* over its estimated life of four years. The price per unit is Rs 30, which is expected to increase by 5 per cent per year after the first year. The cost of production per unit in first year is Rs 20 and is likely to increase by 10 per cent each year. The general rate of inflation is 8 per cent. The market-determined cost of capital is 10 per cent. The company tax rate is 50 per cent. Assume that depreciation can be charged on the straight-line basis for computing taxes. Should the equipment be bought?

Solution:

	Year			
	1	*2*	*3*	*4*
1. Units	10,000	15,000	20,000	8,000
2. Price (5% increase)	30.00	31.50	33.08	34.73
3. Unit cost (10% increase)	20.00	22.00	24.20	26.62
4. Sales (1 × 2)	300,000	472,500	661,600	277,840
5. Costs (1 × 3)	200,000	330,000	484,000	212,960
6. PBDIT	100,000	142,500	177,600	64,880
7. Tax	50,000	71,250	88,800	32,440
8. PAT	50,000	71,250	88,800	32,440
9. Depreciation tax shield	50,000	50,000	50,000	50,000
10. NCF (8 + 9)	100,000	121,250	138,800	82,440
11. PVF at 10%	0.909	0.826	0.751	0.683
12. PV of NCF	90,900	100,153	104,239	56,307
13. NPV (Rs)	351,599 – 400,000 = 48,401			

Since the project has negative NPV, it should not be accepted.

Problem 11.4: A company is considering the following six projects:

Project	Cost (Rs)	NPV (Rs '000)
1	1,000	210
2	6,000	1,560
3	5,000	850
4	2,000	260
5	2,500	500
6	500	95

You are required to calculate the profitability index for each project and rank them. Which projects would you choose if the total available funds are Rs 8,000,000?

Solution:

(*a*)

Project	PV of Inflows (Cost + NPV)	PI (PV/Cost)	Rank
1	1,210	1.21	II
2	7,560	1.26	I
3	5,850	1.17	V
4	2,260	1.13	VI
5	3,000	1.20	III
6	595	1.19	IV

(*b*) Projects 2 and 1 are best in terms of PI. They use Rs 7,000,000 funds and generate NPV of Rs 1,770,000. The company is left with unspent funds of Rs 1,000,000. By trial and error, we can find other combination of projects:

Projects	NPV	Outlay
1, 2	1,770	7,000
2, 4	1,820	8,000
2, 1, 6	1,865	7,500
1, 3, 4	1,320	8,000
3, 4, 6	1,205	7,500
3, 5, 6	1,445	8,000

The best combination is that of Projects 2, 1 and 6. They yield maximum NPV.

REVIEW QUESTIONS

1. Why should you not compare the simple NPV of the mutually exclusive projects with different lives? What is the correct procedure to compare such projects?
2. Show with the help of an illustration that the annual equivalent value and the NPV for infinite period procedures lead to same results in case of the mutually exclusive projects with different lives.
3. How does the NPV rule help in determining the optimum duration of an investment? Illustrate your answer.
4. What are the important considerations in a replacement decision? How would you decide when to replace an equipment?
5. Define capital rationing. How would you select the investment projects under one-period capital constraint? Would capital rationing lead to sub-optimal investment decision?
6. A finance director of a multi-crore engineering company once stated, "We do not face any capital rationing problem. The capital market is big enough to supply us funds in various ways to finance any profitable project. We do, however, impose budget ceiling on the capital expenditures of divisions for control purposes. But that does not imply shortage of funds and therefore, non-acceptance of genuinely profitable projects." What is the finance director talking about?
7. Explain the limitations of the NPV and PI rules in selecting

investment projects under capital rationing.

8. How does mathematical programming help in the optimum choice of projects under capital rationing? Why is not programming approach popular in practice?

PROBLEMS

1. The Damodar Company is considering two mutually exclusive projects with different lives. The costs (cash flows) of the projects are given below:

Project	Cash Flows (Rs '000)				
	C_0	C_1	C_2	C_3	C_4
X	150	30	30	30	30
Y	75	40	40		

The discount rate is 10 per cent. Which project should be selected and why?

2. The K&K Company has two alternative investment projects, A and B. A, short-lived project, will cost Rs 150,000 initially and involve annual operating cash expenses of Rs 40,000 for 4 years. B, on the other hand, will cost Rs 200,000 and involve annual operating expenses of Rs 25,000 for 7 years. Projects have no salvage value. The discount rate is 12 per cent. Which project do you recommend?

3. A firm is evaluating two mutually exclusive machines. Machine P will require an initial investment of Rs 120,000 and provide annual net cash inflows after taxes of Rs 42,000 for 6 years. Machine Q will involve an investment of Rs 300,000 and provide annual net cash inflows after taxes of Rs 80,000 for 8 years. Machine Q is riskier than machine P. The required rate of return of Machine Q is 14 per cent and of Machine P is 12 per cent. Which machine should be selected?

4. A company is thinking of replacing an old machine. The machine was bought 4 years ago for Rs 100,000. It is expected to last for 3 years more and to produce an annual net cash inflow of Rs 60,000. The new alternative machine will cost Rs 150,000 and provide net cash flows of Rs 90,000, Rs 90,000, Rs 80,000, Rs 80,000 and Rs 70,000 from year 1 through year 5. There is no salvage value for machines. The cost of capital is 12 per cent. Should the old machine be replaced?

5. R.K. Company had acquired 5 years ago a machine for Rs 300,000. The current net salvage value of the machine is Rs 60,000. It is expected to last another 3 years and provide net cash inflows of Rs 70,000, Rs 60,000, and Rs 50,000. The salvage value of the machine after 3 years is estimated as Rs 40,000. A technologically superior design is available now. The new machine will cost Rs 300,000 and have a life of 5 years. It will provide annual net cash inflows of Rs 150,000, Rs 130,000, Rs 120,000, Rs 100,000 and Rs 80,000. It is also expected that the new machine will

have a net salvage value of Rs 20,000 after 5 years. The required rate of return is 10 per cent. Should the firm replace old machine now or after 3 years.

6. Radiant Engineers Ltd. has two machines doing the same job. Due to improved processing and manufacturing, the company is in a position to sell one of the machines. Machine X needs repairing costing Rs 10,000 to be operative for next three years. Its annual operating costs are expected to be Rs 12,500 and it could be sold for Rs 8,000 after 3 years. Its market value today is Rs 20,000. Machine Y has a market value of Rs 45,000 today and Rs 10,000 after 8 years. Its annual operating costs are Rs 9,000 and would require repairs costing Rs 12,000 after 3 years. The book values of Machines X and Y are Rs 12,000 and Rs 24,000 respectively. Assume that depreciation is charged on straight-line basis for computing tax. The tax rate is 45 per cent and the required rate of return is 10 per cent. Which machine should be sold?

7. A company manufactures product X by operating two machines, each of which has a capacity of 5,000 units a year. Assume for simplicity that machines have infinite life and no salvage value. The cost of manufacturing one unit of the product is Rs 6. The demand is high between September to February, and machines work full capacity during this period. During March to July, the demand is low and machines work at 50% of capacity. The company is considering whether to replace these machines with available new designed machines. The new machines have the same capacity and therefore, two such machines would be needed to meet peak demand. Each new machine costs Rs 30,000 and lasts indefinitely. The cost of production would be Rs 3 per unit. Should the company buy new machines?

8. The Wangers Ltd. has kegged one of its special wines costing Rs 150,000. Its value is expected to increase over time in the following manner: A_t = Rs 200,000 ln t. The firm's cost of capital is 13 per cent. Determine the optimum time of bottling for the wine. Assume continuous compounding.

9. You have a tract of land on which trees can be grown. The initial cost of planting the trees is Rs 80,000. The net revenue realisable from the harvesting of trees would be as follows:

$$A_t = Rs\,80,000(1+t)^{0.5}$$

The opportunity cost of capital is 10 per cent. What is optimum time for harvesting the trees? Assume continuous compounding.

10. A firm is considering the following two Projects, *M* and *N*:

	Project M	Project N
Investment (Rs)	250,000	250,000
Annual net cash inflow (Rs)	80,000	60,000
Life (years)	6	10
Cost of capital (per cent)	10	10

Because of capital rationing imposed by management, the firm can choose only one project. Which project should be selected? Why?

11. Consider the following investment projects:

	Cash Flows (Rs)		
Project	C_0	C_1	C_3
L	– 3,000	2,250	+ 2,700
M	– 3,950	+ 2,700	+ 3,240

(a) Calculate the NPV and PI for each project assuming a 20 per cent cost of capital.

(b) Which project should be accepted if only one project can be accepted because of capital rationing.

12. A firm has a budget ceiling of Rs 100,000 for capital expenditures. The following proposal with associated profitability index and IRR have been identified:

Proposals	Cash Outlay (Rs)	Profitability Index	Internal Rate of Return (%)
A	100,000	1.22	15
B	50,000	1.17	14
C	40,000	1.46	20
D	30,000	1.72	25
E	20,000	1.13	13
F	10,000	1.04	11

Which project(s) should be undertaken? Which method would you prefer in making your recommendation and why?

13. Zee Company is evaluating the following seven investment proposals. The company has a capital expenditure ceiling of Rs 150 million, and therefore, can accept just enough proposals. You are required to rank proposals according to profitability index and indicate the group of proposals to be accepted.

Project	Cash Outlay (Rs million)	NPV (Rs million)
O	10	1.8
P	50	8.0
Q	20	4.0
S	60	3.6
T	100	25.0
U	80	18.0
V	40	4.0

CASE

Case 11.1: Ritesh Foundaries Limited

Rajesh Bhatt, the production manager of Ritesh Foundries Ltd. (RFL) has just come to know that Indus Engineering Ltd. (IEL) has recently introduced a new fabrication machine for medium-size foundries. This new model is more efficient than the currently available models. Rajesh thought that if the new machine were economically attractive, he could discuss with general manager of the company the possibility of replacing the existing machine, which his company had bought five years ago. He therefore decided to collect the technical and financial information of the machine from IEL.

Jaikumar, the marketing manager of RFL, explained to Rajesh the technical features of the machine, and tried to convince him that his company should go for the new model as it was far superior to their existing machine. Rajesh asked him the financial details of buying the new model. He informed Jaikumar that the existing machine has annual operating cost of Rs 600,000. Jaikumar stated that RFL would incur annual operating cash cost of Rs 250,000, and thus will be able to save cash costs of Rs 350,000 per year. In addition to these savings, RFL would charge straight-line depreciation on the new machine, which will save taxes for the company. He also felt that the new machine would have a salvage value equal to 10 per cent of its original cost at the end of its useful life of 10 years. The machine will cost Rs 1,600,000 plus Rs 200,000 as installation cost.

Rajesh knew that his company had bought the existing machine five years ago for Rs 600,000 and the installation cost was Rs 100,000. The book value of the machine, after charging straight-line depreciation for tax purpose, is Rs 35,000. The machine, if sold today, could fetch a price of Rs. 75,000; if it is not replaced, it could be sold for Rs 125,000 at the end of its original economic life of 10 years.

RFL is a cash rich company. It is entirely equity financed and it has no plans for using long-term debt in the near future to finance its projects. If it decides to replace the old machine, it will utilise internal cash. RFL is a privately held company. It has a practice of measuring its cost of capital by adding premium for inflation and risk to the yield on one-year long-term government bond, which is currently 6 per cent. According to the company management, the expected inflation rate is 5 per cent and the risk premium is 7 per cent. However, for replacement decisions the company considers a risk premium of 4 per cent as reasonable. RFL's corporate income tax is 35 per cent.

Discussion Questions

1. Compute cash flows. Make your assumptions explicit.
2. What is the appropriate discount rate in this case and why?
3. Which alternative should the company choose and why? Explain the logic of the procedure followed by you.

Risk Analysis in Capital Budgeting

INTRODUCTION

In discussing the capital budgeting techniques, we have so far assumed that the proposed investment projects do not involve any risk. This assumption was made simply to facilitate the understanding of the capital budgeting techniques. In real world situation, however, the firm in general and its investment projects in particular are exposed to different degrees of risk. What is risk? How can risk be measured and analysed in the investment decisions?

NATURE OF RISK

Risk exists because of the inability of the decision-maker to make perfect forecasts. Forecasts cannot be made with perfection or certainty since the future events on which they depend are uncertain. An investment is not risky if, we can specify a unique sequence of cash flows for it. But the whole trouble is that cash flows cannot be forecast accurately, and alternative sequences of cash flows can occur depending on the future events. Thus, risk arises in investment evaluation because we cannot anticipate the occurrence of the possible future events with certainty and consequently, cannot make any correct prediction about the cash flow sequence. To illustrate, let us suppose that a firm is considering a proposal to commit its funds in a machine, which will help to produce a new product. The demand for this product may be very sensitive to the general economic conditions. It may be very high under favourable economic conditions and very low under unfavourable economic conditions. Thus, the investment would be profitable in the former situation and unprofitable in the latter case. But, it is quite difficult to predict the future state of economic conditions. Because of the uncertainty of the economic conditions, uncertainty about the cash flows associated with the investment derives.

A large number of events influence forecasts. These events can be grouped in different ways. However, no particular grouping of events will be useful for all purposes. We may, for example, consider three broad categories of the events influencing the investment forecasts:[1]

---

1. Bierman, Harold, Jr. and Seymour, Smidt, *Capital Budgeting Decision*, Macmillan, 1975, p. 162.

- *General economic conditions* This category includes events which influence the general level of business activity. The level of business activity might be affected by such events as internal and external economic and political situations, monetary and fiscal policies, social conditions etc.
- *Industry factors* This category of events may affect all companies in an industry. For example, companies in an industry would be affected by the industrial relations in the industry, by innovations, by change in material cost etc.
- *Company factors* This category of events may affect only a company. The change in management, strike in the company, a natural disaster such as flood or fire may affect directly a particular company.

In formal terms, the risk associated with an investment may be defined as the variability that is likely to occur in the future returns from the investment. For example, if a person invests, say Rs 20,000 in short-term government bonds, which are expected to yield 9 per cent return, he can accurately estimate the return on the investment. Such an investment is relatively risk-free. The reason for this belief is that government *will not* fail and will pay interest regularly and repay the amount invested. It is for this reason that the rate of interest paid on government securities, such as short-term treasury bills, is the *risk-free rate of interest*. Instead of investing Rs 20,000 in government securities, if the investor purchases the shares of a company, then it is not possible to estimate future return accurately. The return could be negative, zero or some extremely large figure. Because of the high degree of the variability associated with the future returns, this investment would be considered risky.

Risk is associated with the variability of future returns of a project. The greater the variability of the expected returns, the riskier the project. Risk can, however, be measured more precisely. The most common measures of risk are **standard deviation** and **coefficient of variations**.

STATISTICAL TECHNIQUES FOR RISK ANALYSIS

Statistical techniques are analytical tools for handling risky investments.[1] These techniques, drawing from the fields of mathematics, logic, economics and psychology, enable the decision-maker to make decisions under risk or **uncertainty**.[2]

The concept of **probability** is fundamental to the use of the risk analysis techniques. How is probability defined? How are probabilities estimated? How are they used in the risk analysis techniques? How do statistical techniques help in resolving the complex problem of analysing risk in capital budgeting? We attempt to answer these questions in this section.

Probability Defined

The most crucial information for the capital budgeting decision is a forecast of future cash flows. A typical forecast is single figure for a period. This is referred to as "best estimate" or "most

likely" forecast. But the questions are: To what extent can one rely on this single figure? How is this figure arrived at? Does it reflect risk? In fact, the decision analysis is limited in two ways by this single figure forecast. Firstly, we do not know the chances of this figure actually occurring, i.e., the uncertainty surrounding this figure. In other words, we do not know the range of the forecast and the chance or the probability estimates associated with figures within this range. Secondly, the meaning of best estimates or most likely is not very clear. It is not known whether it is mean, median or mode. For these reasons, a forecaster should not give just one estimate, but a *range* of associated probability—a probability distribution.

Probability may be described as a measure of someone's opinion about the likelihood that an event will occur. If an event is certain to occur, we say that it has a probability of one of occurring. If an event is certain not to occur, we say that its probability of occurring is zero. Thus, probability of all events to occur lies between zero and one. A probability distribution may consist of a number of estimates. But in the simple form it may consist of only a few estimates. One commonly used form employs only the high, low and best guess estimates, or the optimistic, most likely and pessimistic estimates. For example, the annual cash flows expected from a project could be Rs 200,000 or Rs 170,000 or Rs 80,000:

Assumption	Cash Flow (Rs)
Best guess	200,000
High guess	170,000
Low guess	80,000

It can easily be seen that this is an improvement over the single figure forecast. But still some more information can be disclosed. What does the forecaster feel about the occurrence of these estimates? Are these forecasts likely equal? The forecast should describe more accurately his *degree of confidence* in his forecasts; that is, he should describe his feelings as to the probability of these estimates occurring.[3] For example, he may assign the following probabilities to his estimates:

Assumption	Cash Flows (Rs)	Probability
Best guess	200,000	0.2
High guess	170,000	0.6
Low guess	80,000	0.2

The forecaster considers the chance or probability of the annual cash flows being either Rs 200,000 (maximum) or Rs 80,000 (minimum) 20 per cent each. There is a 60 per cent probability that annual cash flows may be Rs 170,000. The additional information provided by the forecaster is useful in assessing more clearly the impact of a variable, which may assume different values, on the profitability of an investment. A pertinent question is: How to obtain probability distributions?

1. For detailed discussion see Grayson, C. Jackson, The Use of Statistical Techniques in Capital Budgeting, in *Financial Research and Management Decisions*, ed., Alexander A. Robichek, John Wiley, 1967, and Robicheck, A. and Myers, S., *Optimal Financing Decisions*, Prentice-Hall, 1965.
2. Grayson, *op. cit.*, p. 98.
3. *Ibid.*, p. 99.

Assigning probability The classical probability theory assumes that no statement whatsoever can be made about the probability of any single event. In fact, the classical view holds that one can talk about probability in a very long run sense, given that the occurrence or non-occurrence of the event can be repeatedly observed over a very large number of times under independent identical situations. Thus, the probability estimate, which is based on a very large number of observations, is known as an **objective probability**.

The classical concept of objective probability is of little use in analysing investment decisions because these decisions are non-repetitive and hardly made under independent identical conditions over time. As a result, some people opine that it is not very useful to express the forecaster's estimates in terms of probability. However, in recent years another view of probability has revived, that is, the personalistic view, which holds that it makes a great deal of sense to talk about the probability of a single event, without reference to the repeatability, long run frequency concept. It is perfectly valid, therefore, to talk about the probability of rain tomorrow, the probability of sales reaching a certain level next year, or the probability that earnings per share will exceed Rs 2.50 next year, or five years hence.[1] Such probability assignments that reflect the state of belief of a person rather than the objective evidence of a large number of trials are called personal or **subjective probabilities**.

Risk and Uncertainty

Risk is sometimes distinguished from uncertainty. **Risk** is referred to a situation where the probability distribution of the cash flow of an investment proposal is known. On the other hand, if no information is available to formulate a probability distribution of the cash flows the situation is known as **uncertainty**. Most financial authors do not recognise this distinction and use the two terms interchangeably. We too follow this approach.

Expected Net Present Value

Once the probability assignments have been made to the future cash flows, the next step is to find out the **expected net present value**. The expected net present value can be found out by multiplying the monetary values of the possible events (cash flows) by their probabilities. The following equation describes the expected net present value.

Expected net present value = Sum of present values of expected net cash flows

$$\text{ENPV} = \sum_{t=0}^{n} \frac{\text{ENCF}_t}{(1+k)^t} \qquad (1)$$

where ENPV is the expected net present value, ENCF_t expected net cash flows (including both inflows and outflows) in period t and k is the discount rate. The expected net cash flow can be calculated as follows:

$$\text{ENCF}_t = \text{NCF}_{jt} \times P_{jt}$$

where NCF_{jt} is net cash flow for jth event in period t and P_{jt} probability of net cash flow for jth event in period t.

1. Biermand and Smidt, *op. cit.*, p. 164.

Illustration 12.1: Expected Net Cash Flow: Single Period

The following are the possible net cash flows of Projects X and Y and their associated probabilities. Both projects have a discount rate of 10 per cent. Calculate the expected net present value for each project. Which project is preferable?

Possible Event	Project X		Project Y	
	Cash Flow (Rs)	Probability	Cash Flow (Rs)	Probability
A	4,000	0.10	12,000	0.10
B	5,000	0.20	10,000	0.15
C	6,000	0.40	8,000	0.50
D	7,000	0.20	6,000	0.15
E	8,000	0.10	4,000	0.10

Table 12.1 gives the calculations of the expected value for Project X and Project Y.

Table 12.1: Calculation of Expected Value for Project X and Project Y

Possible events	X			Y		
	Net Cash Flow (Rs)	Proba- bility	Expected Value Rs	Net Cash Flow Rs	Proba- bility	Expected Value Rs
A	4,000	0.10	400	2,000	0.10	200
B	5,000	0.20	1,000	10,000	0.15	1,500
C	6,000	0.40	2,400	8,000	0.50	4,000
D	7,000	0.20	1,400	6,000	0.15	900
E	8,000	0.10	800	4,000	0.10	400
ENCF			6,000			8,000

It can be seen from Table 12.1 that Project Y has a higher expected net cash flow, i.e., Rs 8,000 and, therefore, would be preferable to Project X which has an expected net cash flow of Rs 6,000. Project Y will also have a higher net present value when the expected net cash flows of the two projects are discounted at the same rate. If we assume a discount rate of 10 per cent and an equal initial cost of Rs 5,000 for each project, the net present value for Project X is $(0.909 \times \text{Rs } 6,000 - \text{Rs } 5,000) = \text{Rs } 454$. Project Y's NPV is: $(0.909 \times \text{Rs } 8,000 - \text{Rs } 5,000) = \text{Rs } 2,272$.

Instead of one-year cash flow estimates if we have cash flow estimates for several years, the mechanism for calculating the expected value just described can be simply extended.

Illustration 12.2: Expected Net Present Value: Multiple Period

A company has determined the following probabilities for net cash flows for three years generated by a project:

Year 1		Year 2		Year 3	
Cash Flow (Rs)	Probabi- lity	Cash Flow (Rs)	Probabi- lity	Cash Flow (Rs)	Probabi- lity
1,000	0.1	1,000	0.2	1,000	0.3
2,000	0.2	2,000	0.3	2,000	0.4
3,000	0.3	3,000	0.4	3,000	0.2
4,000	0.4	4,000	0.1	4,000	0.1

Calculate the expected net cash flows. Also calculate the present value of the expected cash flow, using 10 per cent discount rate.

Table 12.2 shows the calculation of the expected net present value.

Table 12.2: Calculation of the Expected Value (Three-Year Period)

Year 1			Year 2			Year 3		
Cash Flow (Rs)	Proba-bility	Expec-ted Value (Rs)	Cash Flow (Rs)	Proba-bility	Expec-ted Value (Rs)	Cash Flow (Rs)	Proba-bility	Expec-ted Value (Rs)
1,000	0.1	100	1,000	0.2	200	1,000	0.3	300
2,000	0.2	400	2,000	0.3	600	2,000	0.4	800
3,000	0.3	900	3,000	0.4	1,200	3,000	0.2	600
4,000	0.4	1,600	4,000	0.1	400	4,000	0.1	400
ENCF		3,000			2,400			2.100

The present value of the expected value of cash flow at 10 per cent discount rate has been determined as follows:

$$PV(ENCF) = \frac{ENCF_1}{(1+k)^1} + \frac{ENCF_2}{(1+k)^2} + \frac{ENCF_3}{(1+k)^3}$$

$$= \frac{3,000}{(1.1)^1} + \frac{2.400}{(1.1)^2} + \frac{2,100}{(1.1)^3}$$

$$= 3,000 \times 0.909 + 2,400 \times 0.826 + 2,100 \times 0.751$$

$$= Rs\,6,286.50$$

Illustration 12.3: Eepected NPV

Suppose an investment project has a life of three years, and it would involve an initial cost of Rs 10,000. Based on the possible economic conditions, the expected net cash flows and associated probabilities are given in Table 12.3. If the discount rate is 15 per cent, calculate the expected NPV.

Table 12.3: Expected Cash Flow

Year	Economic Conditions	NCF (Rs)	Probability
0		–10,000	1.0
1	High growth	5,000	0.2
	Average growth	3,000	0.7
	No growth	1,000	0.1
2	High growth	6,000	0.3
	Average growth	4,000	0.5
	No growth	2,000	0.2
3	High growth	8,000	0.4
	Average growth	6,000	0.3
	No growth	3,000	0.3

For each year, ENCF can be calculated as follows:

$$ENCF_1 = (5,000 \times 0.2) + (3,000 \times 0.7) + (1,000 \times 0.1) = 3,200$$

$$ENCF_2 = (6,000 \times 0.3) + (4,000 \times 0.5) + (2,000 \times 0.2) = 4,200$$

$$ENCF_3 = (8,000 \times 0.4) \times (6,000 \times 0.3) + (3,000 \times 0.3) = 5,900$$

Cash outlay of Rs 10,000 in year 0 is expected to remain the same in all economic conditions. The expected NPV can be calculated as follows:

$$ENPV = \frac{3,200}{(1.15)} + \frac{4,200}{(1.15)^2} + \frac{5,900}{(1.15)^3} - 10,000$$

$$= 3,200 \times 0.870 + 4,200 \times 0.756 + 5,900 \times 0.658 - 10,000$$

$$= - Rs\,159$$

Variance or Standard Deviation: Absolute Measure of Risk

Although, through the calculation of the expected net present value, risk is explicitly incorporated into the capital budgeting analysis, yet a better insight into the risk analysis will be obtained if we find out the **dispersion** of cash flows, i.e., the difference between the possible cash flows that can occur and their expected value. The dispersion of cash flow indicates the degree of risk. A commonly used measure of risk is the **standard deviation** or **variance**. Simply stated, variance measures the deviation about expected cash flow of each of the possible cash flows. Standard deviation is the square root of variance. The formulae to calculate variance and standard deviation are as follows:

$$Variance\ of\ NCF = (NCF_1 - ENCF)^2\,Prob_1$$

$$+ (NCF_2 - ENCF)^2\,Prob_2$$

$$+ ... + (NCF_n - ENCF)^2\,Prob_n$$

$$\sigma^2(NCF) = \sum_{j=1}^{n} (NCF_j - ENCF)^2\,P_j \qquad (2)$$

As stated earlier, the square root of variance is standard deviation (σ):

$$\sigma(NCF) = \sqrt{\sigma^2(NCF)} \qquad (3)$$

Given the data for Projects X and Y in Illustration 12.1 and using Equations (2) and (3) we can calculate variance and standard deviation as follows:

Project X:

$$\sigma^2(NCF) = (4,000 - 6,000)^2\,(0.1) + (5,000 + 6,000)^2\,(0.2)$$

$$+ (6,000 - 6,000)^2\,(0.4) + (7,000 - 6,000)^2\,(0.2)$$

$$+ (8,000 - 6,000)^2\,(0.1) = 1,200,000$$

$$\sigma^2(NCF) = \sqrt{1,200,000} = 1095.45$$

Project Y:

$$\sigma^2(NCF) = (12,000 - 8,000)^2\,(0.1) + (10,000 - 8,000)^2\,(0.15)$$

$$+ (8,000 - 8,000)^2\,(0.5) + (6,000 - 8,000)^2\,(0.15)$$

$$+ (4,000 - 8,000)^2\,(0.1) = 4,400,000$$

$$\sigma^2(NCF) = \sqrt{4,400,000} = 2097.62$$

The calculation of standard deviation clearly shows that Project Y is riskier as it has a higher standard deviation. Had the expected net present values of the two projects been same, on the basis of the standard deviation as a measure of risk, Project X would have been favoured. But the decision-maker is in a dilemma because Project Y not only has a larger expected net present value, but also a larger standard deviation as compared to Project X. To resolve such problems, instead of analysing risk in absolute terms, it may be measured in relative terms.

Coefficient of Variation: Relative Measure of Risk

A relative measure of risk is the **coefficient of variation**. It is defined as the standard deviation of the probability distribution divided by its expected value:

$$\text{Coefficient of variation} = CV = \frac{\text{Standard deviation}}{\text{Expected value}} \quad (4)$$

The coefficient of variation is a useful measure of risk when we are comparing the projects which have (*i*) same standard deviations but different expected values, or (*ii*) different standard deviations but same expected values, or (*iii*) different standard deviations and different expected values. In Illustration 12.1, Project X has an expected value of Rs 6,000 and a standard deviation of Rs 1,095.45, while Project Y has an expected value of Rs 8,000 and a standard deviation of Rs 2,097.62. Intuitively, Project Y may be preferred, because of the larger expected net present value. But it is more risky as compared to Project X. This is verified by calculating the coefficients of variation for the two projects. The coefficient of variation for Project X is (1095.45/6,000) = 0.1826, while for Project Y it is (2,097.62/8,000) = 0.2622.

Whether Project X or Project Y should be accepted will depend upon the investor's attitude towards risk. He would prefer Project Y if he is ready to assume more risk in order to obtain a higher expected monetary value. In case he has a great aversion to risk, he would accept Project X, for it is less risky.

CONVENTIONAL TECHNIQUES OF RISK ANALYSIS

A number of techniques to handle risk are used by managers in practice (see Exhibit 12.1). They range from simple rules of thumb to sophisticated statistical techniques.[1] The following are the popular, non-conventional techniques of handling risk in capital budgeting:

- Payback
- Risk-adjusted discount rate
- Certainty equivalent

These methods, as discussed below, are simple, familiar and partially defensible on theoretical grounds. However, they are based on highly simplified and at times, unrealistic assumptions. They fail to take account of the whole range of the effect of risky factors on the investment decision-making.

Payback

Payback is one of the oldest and commonly used methods for explicitly recognising risk associated with an investment project. This method, as applied in practice, is more an attempt to allow for risk in capital budgeting decision rather than a method to measure profitability. Business firms using this method usually

---

EXHIBIT 12.1: RISK ANALYSIS IN PRACTICE

- Most companies in India account for risk while evaluating their capital expenditure decisions. The following factors are considered to influence the riskiness of investment projects:

  price of raw material and other inputs
  price of product
  product demand
  government policies
  technological changes
  project life
  inflation

- Out of these factors, four factors thought to be contributing most to the project riskiness are: selling price, product demand, technical changes and government policies.

- The most commonly used methods of risk analysis in practice are:

  sensitivity analysis
  conservative forecasts

- Sensitivity analysis allows to see the impact of the change in the behaviour of critical variables on the project profitability. Conservative forecasts include using short payback or higher discount rate for discounting cash flows.

- Except a very few companies, most companies do not use the statistical and other sophisticated techniques for analysing risk in investment decisions.

Source: I.M. Pandey, Capital Budgeting Practices of Indian Companies; *MDI Management Journal*, Vol. 2, No. 1 (Jan. 1989).

---

prefer short payback to longer ones, and often establish guidelines that a firm should accept investments with some maximum payback period, say three or five years.

The merit of payback is its simplicity. Also, payback makes an allowance for risk by (*i*) focusing attention on the near term future and thereby emphasising the liquidity of the firm through recovery of capital, and (*ii*) by favouring short term projects over what may be riskier, longer term projects.[2]

It should be realised, however, that the payback period, as a method of risk analysis, is useful only in allowing for a special type of risk — the risk that a project will go exactly as planned for a certain period and will then suddenly cease altogether and be worth nothing. It is essentially suited to the assessment of risks of time nature. Once a payback period has been calculated, the decision-maker would compare it with his own assessment of the projects likely, and if the latter exceeds the former, he would accept the project. This is a useful procedure, economic only if the forecasts of cash flows associated with the project are likely to be unimpaired for a certain period. The risk that a project will suddenly cease altogether after a certain period may arise due to reasons such as civil war in a country, closure of the

---

1. Grayson, *op. cit.*; Robicheck and Myers, *op. cit.*
2. *Ibid.,* p. 93.

business due to an indefinite strike by the workers, introduction of a new product by a competitor which captures the whole market and natural disasters such as flood or fire. Such risks undoubtedly exist but they, by no means, constitute a large proportion of the commonly encountered business risks. The usual risk in business is not that a project will go as forecast for a period and then collapse altogether, rather the normal business risk is that the forecasts of cash flows will go wrong due to lower sales, higher cost etc.[1]

Further, even as a method for allowing risks of time nature, it ignores the time value of cash flows. For example, two projects with, say a four-year payback period are at very different risks if in one case the capital is recovered evenly over the four years, while in the other it is recovered in the last year. Obviously, the second project is more risky. If both cease after three years, the first project would have recovered three-fourths of its capital, while all capital would be lost in the case of second project. Given the uncertainty element, it may well be that a four-year payback period based on fairly certain estimates might be preferred to a three-year payback period, calculated with very uncertain estimates.

Risk-Adjusted Discount Rate

For a long time, economic theorists have assumed that, to allow for risk, the businessman required a premium over and above an alternative, which was risk-free. Accordingly, the more uncertain the returns in the future, the greater the risk and the greater the premium required. Based on this reasoning, it is proposed that the risk premium be incorporated into the capital budgeting analysis through the discount rate. That is, if the time preference for money is to be recognised by discounting estimated future cash flows, at some *risk-free rate*, to their present value, then, to allow for the riskiness, of those future cash flows a *risk premium rate* may be added to risk-free discount rate. Such a composite discount rate, called the **risk-adjusted discount rate**, will allow for both *time preference* and *risk preference* and will be a sum of the risk-free rate and the risk-premium rate reflecting the investor's attitude towards risk. The risk-adjusted discount rate method can be formally expressed as follows:

$$NPV = \sum_{t=0}^{n} \frac{NCF_t}{(1+k)^t} \qquad (5)$$

where k is a risk-adjusted rate. That is:

Risk-adjusted discount rate = Risk-free rate + Risk premium

$$k = k_f + k_r \qquad (6)$$

Under CAPM, the risk-premium is the difference between the market rate of return and the risk-free rate multiplied by the beta of the project.

The risk-adjusted discount rate accounts for risk by varying the discount rate depending on the degree of risk of investment projects. A higher rate will be used for riskier projects and a lower rate for less risky projects. The net present value will decrease with increasing k, indicating that the riskier a project is perceived, the less likely it will be accepted. If the risk-free rate is assumed to be 10 per cent, some rate would be added to it, say 5 per cent, as compensation for the risk of the investment, and the composite 15 per cent rate would be used to discount the cash flows.

Illustration 12.4: Risk-adjusted Discount Rate and NPV

An investment project will cost Rs 50,000 initially and it is expected to generate cash flows in years one through four of Rs 25,000, Rs 20,000, Rs 10,000 and Rs 10,000. What is the project's NPV, if it is expected to generate certain cash flows? Assume a 10 per cent risk-free rate. The net present value for the project, using a 10 per cent risk-free discount rate, is:

$$NPV = -Rs\,50,000 + \frac{Rs\,25,000}{(1+0.10)^1} + \frac{Rs\,20,000}{(1+0.10)^2}$$
$$+ \frac{Rs\,10,000}{(1+0.10)^3} + \frac{Rs\,10,000}{(1+0.10)^2}$$
$$= +Rs\,3,599$$

If the project is risky, than a higher rate should be used to allow for the perceived risk. Assuming this rate to be 15 per cent, the net present value of the project will be:

$$NPV = -Rs\,50,000 + \frac{Rs\,25,000}{(1+0.15)^1} + \frac{Rs\,20,000}{(1+0.15)^2}$$
$$+ \frac{Rs\,10,000}{(1+0.15)^2} + \frac{Rs\,10,000}{(1+0.15)^4}$$
$$= -Rs\,845$$

Thus, we observe that the project would be accepted when no allowance for risk is granted, but it is unacceptable if a risk-premium is added to the discount rate.

In contrast to the net present value method, if a firm uses the internal rate of return method, then to allow for perceived risk of an investment project, the internal rate of return for the project should be compared with the risk-adjusted minimum required rate of return. If the internal rate of return is higher than this adjusted rate, then the project would be accepted; otherwise, it should be rejected.

Evaluation of risk-adjusted discount rate The following are the advantages of risk-adjusted discount rate method:

- It is simple and can be easily understood.
- It has a great deal of intuitive appeal for risk-averse businessman.
- It incorporates an attitude (risk-aversion) towards uncertainty.

This approach, however, suffers from the following limitations:

- There is no easy way of deriving a risk-adjusted discount rate. As discussed earlier, CAPM provides for a basis of calculating the risk-adjusted discount rate. Its use has yet to pick up in practice.

1. Mereret, A. and Allan Sykes, *The Finance and Analysis of Capital Projects,* Longmans, 1966, p. 230.

- It does not make any risk adjustment in the numerator for the cash flows that are forecast over the future years.
- It is based on the assumption that investors are risk-averse. Though it is generally true, there exists a category of risk seekers who do not demand premium for assuming risks; they are willing to pay a premium to take risks. Accordingly, the composite discount rate would be reduced, not increased, as the level of risk increases.[1]

Certainty Equivalent

Yet another common procedure for dealing with risk in capital budgeting is to reduce the forecasts of cash flows to some conservative levels. For example, if an investor, according to his 'best estimate,' expects a cash flow of Rs 60,000 next year, he will apply an intuitive correction factor and may work with Rs 40,000 to be on safe side. There is a **certainty-equivalent** cash flow. In formal way, the certainty equivalent approach may be expressed as:

$$\text{NPV} = \sum_{t=0}^{n} \frac{\alpha_t \, \text{NCF}_t}{(1+k_f)^t} \qquad (7)$$

where NCF_t = the forecasts of net cash flow without risk-adjustment

α_t = the risk-adjustment factor or the certainty-equivalent coefficient

k_f = risk-free rate assumed to be constant for all periods.

The certainty-equivalent coefficient, α_t assumes a value between 0 and 1, and varies inversely with risk. A lower α_t will be used if greater risk is perceived and a higher α_t will be used if lower risk is anticipated. The decision-maker subjectively or objectively establishes the coefficients. These coefficients reflect the decision-maker's confidence in obtaining a particular cash flow in period t. For example, a cash flow of Rs 20,000 may be estimated in the next year, but if the investor feels that only 80 per cent of it is a certain amount, then the certainty-equivalent coefficient will be 0.80. That is, he considers only Rs 16,000 as the certain cash flow. Thus, to obtain certain cash flows, we will multiply estimated cash flows by the certainty-equivalent coefficients.

The certainty-equivalent coefficient can be determined as a relationship between the certain cash flows and the risky cash flows. That is:

$$\alpha_t = \frac{\text{NCF}_t^*}{\text{NCF}_t} = \frac{\text{Certain net cash flow}}{\text{Risky net cash flow}} \qquad (8)$$

For example, if one expected a risky cash flow of Rs 80,000 in period t and considers a certain cash flow of Rs 60,000 equally desirable, then α_t will be 0.75 = 60,000/80,000.

Illustration 12.5: Certainty Equivalent and NPV

A project costs Rs 6,000 and it has cash flows of Rs 4,000, Rs 3,000, Rs 2,000 and Rs 1,000 in years 1 through 4. Assume that the associated

α_t factors are estimated to be: $\alpha_0 = 1.00$, $\alpha_1 = 0.90$, $\alpha_2 = 0.70$, $\alpha_3 = 0.50$ and $\alpha_4 = 0.30$, and the risk-free discount rate is 10 per cent. The net present value will be:

$$\begin{aligned}
\text{NFV} &= 1.0\,(-6,000) + \frac{0.90\,(4,000)}{(1+0.10)^1} + \frac{0.70\,(3,000)}{(1+0.10)^2} \\
&\quad + \frac{0.50\,(2,000)}{(1+0.10)^3} + \frac{0.30\,(1,000)}{(1+0.10)^4} \\
&= -\,\text{Rs}\,36
\end{aligned}$$

The project would be rejected as it has a negative net present value.

If the internal rate of return method is used, we will calculate that rate of discount, which equates the present value of certainty-equivalent cash inflows with the present value of certainty-equivalent cash outflows. The rate so found will be compared with the minimum required risk-free rate. Project will be accepted if the internal rate is higher than the minimum rate; otherwise it will be unacceptable.

Evaluation of certainty equivalent The certainty-equivalent approach explicitly recognises risk, but the procedure for reducing the forecasts of cash flows is implicit and is likely to be inconsistent from one investment to another. Further, this method suffers from many dangers in a large enterprise. First, the forecaster, expecting the reduction that will be made in his forecasts, may inflate them in anticipation. This will no longer give forecasts according to 'best estimate.' Second, if forecasts have to pass through several layers of management, the effect may be to greatly exaggerate the original forecast or to make it ultra conservative. Third, by focusing explicit attention only on the gloomy outcomes, chances are increased for passing by some good investments.

Risk-Adjusted Discount Rate vs. Certainty-Equivalent

The certainty-equivalent approach recognises risk in capital budgeting analysis by adjusting estimated cash flows and employs risk-free rate to discount the adjusted cash flows. On the other hand, the risk-adjusted discount rate adjusts for risk by adjusting the discount rate. It has been suggested that the certainty equivalent approach is theoretically a superior technique over the risk-adjusted discount approach because it can measure risk more accurately.[2]

The risk-adjusted discount rate approach will yield the same result as the certainty-equivalent approach if the risk-free rate is constant and the risk-adjusted discount rate is the same for all future periods. Thus,

$$\frac{\alpha_t \, \text{NCF}_t}{(1+k_f)^t} = \frac{\text{NCF}_t}{(1+k)^t} \qquad (9)$$

To solve for α_t

$$\alpha_t \, \text{NCF}_t \, (1+k)^t = \text{NCF}_t \, (1+k_f)^t$$

$$\alpha_t = \frac{\text{NCF}_t \, (1+k_f)^t}{\text{NCF}_t \, (1+k)^t} = \frac{(1+k_f)^t}{(1+k)^t} \qquad (10)$$

1. Grayson, *op. cit.*, p. 90.
2. Robicheck and Myers, *op. cit.*, pp. 82–86.

For period $t + 1$, Equation (9) will become

$$\alpha_{t+1} = \frac{(1+k_f)^{t+1}}{(1+k)^{t+1}} \quad (11)$$

Earlier, we have stated that the values of α_t will vary between 0 and 1. Thus, if k_f and k are constant for all future periods, then k must be larger than k_f to satisfy the condition that α_t varies between 0 and 1. As a result, α_{t+1} would be less than α_t. To illustrate, let us assume $k = 10$ per cent $k_f = 5$ per cent and $t = 1$, then

$$\alpha_t = \frac{(1.05)^1}{(1.10)^1} = 0.955$$

When $t = 2$, then

$$\alpha_2 = \frac{(1.05)^2}{(1.10)^2} = 0.911$$

Risk over time: It can be observed that α_t will be a decreasing function of time with a constant k. This implies that risk is an increasing function of time. This assumption may or may not be true in the actual investment under consideration. We can think of an investment, which may be more risky during the gestation period, and once established, the risk may reduce. In such a situation, the use of a constant risk-adjusted discount rate is not valid. But the increased or decreased risks over a period of time can easily be accounted for by changing α_t factors when the certainty-equivalent approach is used. Therefore, the certainty-equivalent approach is considered superior to the risk-adjusted discount rate.

Even if the assumption that risk increases with time is valid, the problem with the risk-adjusted discount rate is to select the value of k, which properly measures the degree of increasing risk. It is difficult to specify such a rate. With the certainty-equivalent approach, the α_t factors in each period will specify the different degree of risk.

SENSITIVITY ANALYSIS

In the evaluation of an investment project, we work with the forecasts of cash flows. Forecasted cash flows depend on the expected revenue and costs. Further, expected revenue is a function of sales volume and unit selling price. Similarly, sales volume will depend on the market size and the firm's market share. Costs include variable costs, which depend on sales volume and unit variable cost and fixed costs. The net present value or the internal rate of return of a project is determined by analysing the after-tax cash flows arrived at by combining forecasts of various variables. It is difficult to arrive at an accurate and unbiased forecast of each variable. We can't be certain about the outcome of any of these variables. The reliability of the NPV or IRR of the project will depend on the reliability of the forecasts of variables underlying the estimates of net cash flows. To determine the reliability of the project's NPV or IRR, we can work out how much difference it makes if any of these forecasts goes wrong. We can change each of the forecast, one at a time, to

at least three values: pessimistic, expected, and optimistic. The NPV of the project is recalculated under these different assumptions. This method of recalculating NPV or IRR by changing each forecast is called sensitivity analysis.

Sensitivity analysis is a way of analysing change in the project's NPV (or IRR) for a given change in one of the variables. It indicates how sensitive a project's NPV (or IRR) is to changes in particular variables. The more sensitive the NPV, the more critical is the variable. The following three steps are involved in the use of sensitivity analysis:

- Identification of all those variables, which have an influence on the project's NPV (or IRR).
- Definition of the underlying (mathematical) relationship between the variables.
- Analysis of the impact of the change in each of the variables on the project's NPV.

The decision-maker, while performing sensitivity analysis, computes the project's NPV (or IRR) for each forecast under three assumptions: (a) pessimistic, (b) expected, and (c) optimistic. It allows him to ask "what if" questions. For example, what (is the NPV) if volume increase or decreases? What (is the NPV) if variable cost or fixed cost increases or decreases? What (is the NPV) if the selling price increases or decreases? What (is the NPV) if the project is delayed or outlay escalates or the project's life is more or less than anticipated? A whole range of questions can be answered with the help of sensitivity analysis. It examines the sensitivity of the variables underlying the computation of NPV or IRR, rather than attempting to quantify risk. It can be applied to any variable, which is an input for the after-tax cash flows. Let us consider an example.

Illustration 12.6: Sensitivity Analysis

The financial manager of XL Food Processing Company is considering the installation of a plant costing Rs 10 million to increase its processing capacity. The expected values of the underlying variables are given in Tables 12.4 and 12.5 provides the project's after-tax cash flows over its expected life of 7 years. Salvage value is assumed to be zero.

Table 12.4: Expected Values of Variables

1.	Investment (Rs '000)	10,000
2.	Sales volume (units '000)	1,000
3.	Unit selling price (Rs)	15
4.	Unit variable cost (Rs)	6.75
5.	Annual fixed costs (Rs '000)	4,000
6.	Depreciation (WDV)	25%
7.	Corporate tax rate	35%
8.	Discount rate	12%

The project's NPV at 12 per cent discount rate and IRR are as follows:

$$NPV = +4,973$$
$$IRR = 27.05\%$$

Since NPV is positive (or IRR > discount rate), the project can be undertaken.

Table 12.5: Net Cash Flows of the Project

Cash Flows (Rs '000)

Year	0	1	2	3	4	5	6	7
1. Investment	– 10,000							
2. Revenue		15,000	15,000	15,000	15,000	15,000	15,000	15,000
3. Variable cost		6,750	6,750	6,750	6,750	6,750	6,750	6,750
4. Fixed cost		4,000	4,000	4,000	4,000	4,000	4,000	4,000
5. Depreciation		2,500	1,875	1,406	1,055	791	593	1,347
6. EBIT (2 – 3 – 4 – 5)		1,750	2,375	2,844	3,195	3,459	3,657	2,903
7. Tax		613	831	995	1,118	1,211	1,280	1,016
8. PAT (6 – 7)		1,138	1,544	1,848	2,077	2,248	2,377	1,887
9. NCF (1 + 5 + 8)	– 10,000	3,638	3,419	3,255	3,132	3,039	2,970	3,234

Note: Depreciation in the seventh year includes depreciation of the seventh year, Rs 415 and the present value of depreciation beyond seventh year, Rs 902 = [.25/(.12 + .25)] × Rs 1,335. Rs 1,335 is the book value at the end of seventh year.

How confident is the financial manager about his forecasts of various variables? Before he takes a decision, he may like to know whether the NPV changes, if any, of the forecasts goes wrong. A sensitivity analysis can be conducted with regard to volume, price, costs etc. In order to do so, we must obtain pessimistic and optimistic estimates of the underlying variables. Let us assume the pessimistic and the optimistic values for volume, price and costs as shown in Table 12.6.

Table 12.6: Forecasts Under Different Assumptions

Variable	Pessimistic	Expected	Optimistic
Volume (units '000)	750	1,000	1,250
Units selling price (Rs)	12.75	15.00	16.50
Units variable cost (Rs)	7.425	6.75	6.075
Annual fixed costs (Rs '000)	4,800	4,000	3,200

If we change each variable (others holding constant), the project's NPVs are recalculated in Table 12.7 (detailed calculations not shown).

Table 12.7: Sensitivity Analysis Under Different Assumptions

	Net Present Value (Rs '000)		
Variable	Pessimistic	Expected	Optimistic
Volume	–1,146	4,973	10,091
Units selling price	–1,702	4,973	9,422
Units variable cost	2,970	4,973	6,975
Annual fixed costs	2,599	4,973	7,346

Table 12.7 shows the project's NPV when each variable is set to its pessimistic, expected and optimistic values. The most critical variables are sales volume and unit selling price. If the volume declines by 25 per cent (to 750,000 units), NPV of the project becomes negative (– Rs 1,146,000). Similarly, if the unit selling price falls by 15 per cent (to

Rs 12.75), NPV is minus Rs 1,702,000.

DCF Break-even Analysis

Sensitivity analysis is a variation of the break-even analysis.[1] What you are asking is: what shall be the consequences if volume or price or cost changes? You can ask this question differently: How much lower can the sales volume become before the project becomes unprofitable? What you are asking for is the break-even point. Let us work with the expected values of the variables in Illustration 12.6. We can measure the after-tax cash flows as follows (assuming revenues and expenses are entirely on cash basis):

$$NCF = (REV - EXP)(1 - T) + TDEP$$

In our example, the first part of the right-hand expression is an annuity:

$$[1000 (15 - 6.75) - 4000](1 - 0.35) = Rs\ 2,763$$

and its present value at 12 per cent discount rate is:

$$2,763 \times 4.5638 = 12,610$$

The salvage value is zero. Under the gross block of assets method, the depreciation tax shield is available for ever (until the block of assets is sold). Hence, assuming indefinite period of time, the present value of depreciation tax shield on plant of Rs 10,000 is as follows:

$$PVDTS = \frac{Td}{d + k} \times 0V = \frac{.35 \times .25}{.25 + .12} \times 10,000$$
$$= Rs\ 2,365$$

Here by the break-even point we mean that point where NPV is zero. We can use the following expression to determine break-even point:

1. Reinhardt, U.E., Break-even Analysis for Lockheed's Tristar: An Application of Financial Theory, *Journal of Finance*, 28 (September 1973), pp. 821–38, provides an elaborate exposition of break-even analysis in capital budgeting. Also, see Brealey, R. and Myers, S., *Principles of Corporate Finance*, McGraw-Hill, 1991, pp. 215–23.

$$NPV = PV \text{ of } NCF - Investment = 0$$
$$= [\{V(15 - 6.75) - 4,000\}\, 0.65 \times 4.5638$$
$$+ 2,365] - 10,000 = 0 \quad (12)$$

where V is the sales volume, 4.5638 is the present value factor of a 7-year annuity (at 12 per cent) and Rs 2,365 is the present value of the series of depreciation tax shield. We can solve Equation (12) as follows:

$$NPV = 24.4734V - 11,866 + 2,365 - 10,000 = 0$$
$$24.4734V = 19,501$$
$$V = 797$$

The project will start losing money if the sales volume goes below 797,000 units (i.e., if the sales decline by more than 20 per cent). Let us verify if NPV is zero at this sales volume:

$$NPV = [(797(15 - 6.75) - 4,000)\, 0.65 \times 4.5638 + 2,365]10,000$$
$$= 7,639 + 2,365 - 10,000 \approx 0$$

We can similarly work out the lowest selling price. Given other assumptions, how low the units selling price can go before the project's NPV becomes negative? We can solve the following equations:

$$NPV = [(100(p - 6.75) - 4,000)0.65 \times 4.5638 + 2,365] - 10,000$$
$$= 0$$
$$= 2,966.47p - 20,024 - 11,866 + 2,365 - 10,000 = 0$$
$$= 29,66.47p - 39,525 = 0$$
$$p = 39,525 / 2,966.47 = 13.32$$

Let us verify:

$$NPV = [(1000(13.32 - 6.75) - 4,000)0.65 \times 4.5638 + 2,365]$$
$$- 10,000$$
$$= 7,625 + 2,365 - 10,000 \approx 0$$

You should note that the **DCF break-even point** is different from the accounting break-even point. The **accounting break-even point** is estimated as fixed costs divided by the contribution ratio. It does not account for the opportunity cost of capital, and fixed costs include both cash plus non-cash costs (such as depreciation). Thus, you may be operating above the accounting break-even point but still losing money because you have ignored the opportunity cost of capital.

Pros and Cons of Sensitivity Analysis

Sensitivity analysis has the following advantages:[1]

- It compels the decision maker to identify the variables, which affect the cash flow forecasts. This helps him in understanding the investment project in totality.
- It indicates the critical variables for which additional information may be obtained. The decision maker can consider actions, which may help in strengthening the 'weak spots' in the project.

- It helps to expose inappropriate forecasts, and thus guides the decision-maker to concentrate on relevant variables.

Let us emphasise that sensitivity analysis is not a panacea for a project's all uncertainties. It helps a decision-maker to understand the project better. It has the following limitations:[2]

- It does not provide clear-cut results. The terms 'optimistic' and 'pessimistic' could mean different things to different persons in an organisation. Thus, the range of values suggested may be inconsistent.
- It fails to focus on the interrelationship between variables. For example, sale volume may be related to price and cost. A price cut may lead to high sales and low operating cost.

Scenario Analysis

The simple sensitivity analysis assumes that variables are independent of each other. In practice, the variables will be interrelated and they may change in combination. One way to examine the risk of investment is to analyse the impact of alternative combinations of variables, called **scenarios,** on the project's NPV (or IRR). The decision-maker can develop some plausible scenarios for this purpose. For instance, in our example, we can consider three scenarios: pessimistic, optimistic and expected. In the expected scenario, it may be possible to increase base volume of 1,000,000 units to 1,250,000 units (25 per cent increase) if the company reduces selling price from Rs 15 to Rs 13.50 (10 per cent reduction), resorts to aggressive advertisement campaign, thereby increasing unit variable cost to Rs 7.10 (5 per cent increase) and fixed cost to Rs 4,400,000 (10 per cent increase). Table 12.8 shows that this scenario generates a positive NPV of Rs 2,901,000. NPVs under other scenarios are also shown in Table 12.8. More plausible scenarios could be thought out and analysed to arrive at a final judgement about the project.

Table 12.8: Scenario Analysis: Summary Report

Scenario Summary	Base Values	Pessimistic	Optimistic	Expected
Variables combinations:				
Sales volume (units '000)	1,000	750	1,250	1,250
Selling price/unit (Rs)	15.00	12.75	16.50	13.50
Variable cost/unit (Rs)	6.75	7.43	6.75	7.10
Fixed cost (Rs '000)	4,000	4,800	3,200	4,400
Result:				
NPV (Rs '000)	4,972	−10,038	19,026	3,044

Note: NPV calculation for the expected scenario:

$$NPV = [(1250\,(13.5 - 7.1) - 4400)\, 0.65 \times 4.5638$$
$$+ 2,365] - 10,000$$
$$= 10,679 + 2,222 - 10,000 = Rs\ 3,044$$

1. Hastie, K.L., One Businessman's View of Capital Budgeting, *Financial Management* (Winter 1974), p. 38; and Brealey and Myers, *op. cit.*, p. 198.
2. Brealey and Myers, *op. cit.*

Excel Application 12.1:
Scenario Analysis

Scenario Manager of Excel helps in analyzing the effects of different assumptions or combinations of assumptions on a project's NPV (or IRR). You can use Scenario Manager to view your worksheet under different scenarios, or to create a summary of the effects as shown in Table 12.8. Let us show how you can work with Scenario Manager. Suppose you are considering four possible scenarios given in the upper portion of Table 12.8. The base case illustrates the basic assumptions and NPV calculation as shown in the following worksheet.

Note that depreciation in seventh year also includes present value of depreciation beyond seventh year.

The following steps are involved in creating Scenarios: Select **T**ools **S**cenarios from menus. Press **A**dd and enter the scenario name: *pessimistic*. Click in the Changing Cells,

highlight cells B2:B5 and the press OK. In the dialogue box, you supply the new values for the changing cells. In the box labeled "1" enter 750, in "2" enter 12.75, in "3" 7,435 and in "4" 4,800. Click OK. You can repeat these steps for other scenarios. You may now highlight the scenario of your choice and press **S**how. The worksheet will show all calculations for the scenario that you have highlighted. You can switch another scenario and click **S**how; the worksheet will change to account for the assumption of the chosen scenario.

You can create a summary of all scenarios when you click **S**ummary. The NPV calculation is shown in cell A22. Select cell B22 for **R**esults cells when the Scenario Summary dialog box appears. Table 12.8 is the edited version of the Scenario Summary Report.

	A	B	C	D	E	F	G	H	I
	BASE CASE ASSUMPTIONS								
1	Investment (Rs '000)	10,000							
2	Sales volume (units '000)	1,000							
3	Unit selling price (Rs)	15							
4	Unit variable cost (Rs)	6.75							
5	Annual fixed costs (Rs '000)	4,000							
6	Depreciation (WDV)	25%							
7	Corporate tax rate	35%							
8	Discount rate	12%							
11									
12	Year	0	1	2	3	4	5	6	7
13	Investment	-10,000							
14	Revenue		15,000	15,000	15,000	15,000	15,000	15,000	15,000
15	Variable cost		6,750	6,750	6,750	6,750	6,750	6,750	6,750
16	Fixed cost		4,000	4,000	4,000	4,000	4,000	4,000	4,000
17	Depreciation		2,500	1,875	1,406	1,055	791	593	1,347
18	EBIT		1,750	2,375	2,844	3,195	3,459	3,657	2,903
19	Tax		613	831	995	1118	1211	1280	1,016
20	PAT		1,138	1,544	1,848	2,077	2,248	2,377	1,887
21	NCF	-10,000	3,638	3,419	3,255	3,132	3,039	2,970	3,234
22	NPV	5,041							

The present value of the written-down value depreciation tax shield is Rs 2,365.

SIMULATION ANALYSIS

We have explained in the previous sections that sensitivity and scenario analyses are quite useful to understand the uncertainty of the investment projects. But both approaches suffer from certain weaknesses. As we have discussed, they do not consider the interactions between variables and also, they do not reflect on the probability of the change in variables.

The **Monte Carlo** simulation or simply the **simulation analysis** considers the interactions among variables and probabilities of the change in variables.[1] It does not give the project's NPV as a single number rather it computes the probability distribution of NPV. The simulation analysis is an extension of scenario analysis. In simulation analysis a computer

generates a very large number of scenarios according to the probability distributions of the variables. The simulation analysis involves the following steps:

- First, you should identify variables that influence cash inflows and outflows. For example, when a firm introduces a new product in the market these variables are initial investment, market size, market growth, market share, price, variable costs, fixed costs, product life cycle, and terminal value.
- Second, specify the formulae that relate variables. For example, revenue depends on by sales volume and price; sales volume is given by market size, market share, and market growth. Similarly, operating expenses depend on production, sales and variable and fixed costs.
- Third, indicate the probability distribution for each variable. Some variables will have more uncertainty than others. For

---

1. Hertz was the first author to show the application of Monte Carlo simulation in capital budgeting. See David B. Hertz, "Investment Policies that Pay-off", *Harvard Business Review*, 46, Jan.-Feb. 1968, pp. 96–108.

example, it is quite difficult to predict price or market growth with confidence.

- Fourth, develop a computer programme that randomly selects one value from the probability distribution of each variable and uses these values to calculate the project's NPV. The computer generates a large number of such scenarios, calculates NPVs and stores them. The stored values are printed as a probability distribution of the project's NPVs along with the expected NPV and its standard deviation. The risk-free rate should be used as the discount rate to compute the project's NPV. Since simulation is performed to account for the risk of the project's cash flows, the discount rate should reflect only the time value of money.

Simulation analysis is a very useful technique for risk analysis. Unfortunately, its practical use is limited because of a number of shortcomings. First, the model becomes quite complex to use because the variables are interrelated with each other, and each variable depends on its values in the previous periods as well. Identifying all possible relationships and estimating probability distribution is a difficult task; its time consuming as well as expensive. Second, the model helps in generating a probability distribution of the project's NPVs. But it does not indicate whether or not the project should be accepted. Third, simulation analysis, like sensitivity or scenario analysis, considers the risk of any project in isolation of other projects. We know that if we consider the portfolio of projects, the unsystematic risk can be diversified. A risky project may have a negative correlation with the firm's other projects, and therefore, accepting the project may reduce the overall risk of the firm.

DECISION TREES FOR SEQUENTIAL INVESTMENT DECISIONS

We have so far discussed simple accept-or-reject decisions, which view current investments in isolation of subsequent decisions. But in practice, the present investment decisions may have implications for future investment decisions, and may affect future events and decisions. Such complex investment decisions involve a sequence of decisions over time. It is argued that 'since present choices modify future alternatives, industrial activity cannot be reduced to a single decision and must be viewed as a sequence of decisions extending from the present time into the future.'[1] If this notion of industrial activity as a sequence of decisions is accepted, we must view investment expenditures not as isolated period commitments, but as links in a chain of present and future commitments.[2] An analytical technique to handle the sequential decisions is to employ decision trees.[3] In this section, we shall illustrate the use of **decision trees** in analysing and evaluating the sequential investments.

Steps in Decision Tree Approach

A present decision depends upon future events, and the

alternatives of a whole sequence of decisions in future are affected by the present decision as well as future events. Thus, the consequence of each decision is influenced by the outcome of a chance event. At the time of taking decisions, the outcome of the chance event is not known, but a probability distribution can be assigned to it. A decision tree is a graphic display of the relationship between a present decision and future events, future decisions and their consequences. The sequence of events is mapped out over time in a format similar to the branches of a tree.

While constructing and using a decision tree, some important steps should be considered:

- **Define investment** The investment proposal should be defined. Marketing, production or any other department may sponsor the proposal. It may be either to enter a new market or to produce a new product.
- **Identify decision alternatives** The decision alternatives should be clearly identified. For example, if a company is thinking of building a plant to produce a new product, it may construct a large plant, a medium-sized plant, or a small plant initially and expand it later on or construct no plant. Each alternative will have different conse-quences.
- **Draw a decision tree** The decision tree should be graphed indicating the **decision points**, **chance events** and other data. The relevant data such as the projected cash flows, probability distributions, the expected present value etc., should be located on the decision tree branches.
- **Analyse data** The results should be analysed and the best alternative should be selected.

Illustration 12.7: Decision Tree Analysis: Water Purity Limited

Water Purity Limited has developed a scientifically more effective water filter than the ones currently available in the market. One option before the company is to start production on a large scale by installing a large plant costing Rs 50 lakh. Alternatively, it can initially install a small plant at a cash outlay of Rs 10 lakh and then decide to expand the capacity after a year at a cost of Rs 45 lakh if the initial demand is high. There is a 50–50 chance that the initial demand will be high or low. If it is high, then there is a 70 per cent chance that demand in the subsequent years will be high. If it turns out to be low, it is expected to remain low in subsequent years also.

The large plant is likely to generate net cash flow of Rs 10 lakh in year 1 if demand is high and Rs 7 lakh if demand is low. With a high initial demand, net cash flows are expected to be Rs 16 lakh in perpetuity if the subsequent demand is high and Rs 10 lakh if the subsequent demand is low. The subsequent demand will remain low if the initial demand is low and the expected cash flow in perpetuity will be Rs 7 lakh. The small plant is estimated to yield net cash flows of Rs 4 lakh in year 1 if demand is high and Rs 2 lakh if demand is low. If the initial demand is high, the company will expand its capacity and it is expected to generate net cash flows of Rs 20 lakh in perpetuity if the subsequent demand is high and Rs 8 lakh if the subsequent demand is low. If the initial demand is low, the subsequent demand will be low, and the expected net cash flow is Rs 2 lakh in perpetuity. What should Water Purity Limited do?

1. Masse, Pierre, *Optimal Investment Decisions*. Prentice-Hall, Inc., 1962, p. 250.
2. Mao, James, C.T., *Quantitative Analysis of Financial Decisions,* Macmillan, 1969, p. 307.
3. See Magee, J.F., How to Use Decision Trees in Capital Investment? *Harvard Business Review*, 42 (September-October 1964), pp. 79–96, for a detailed discussion on decision trees.

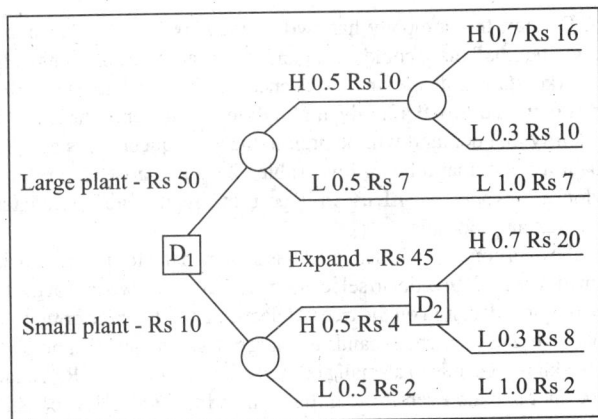

Figure 12.1: Water Purity Ltd.: Decision tree approach

The problem of water filter in Illustration 12.7 is a sequential decision, and can be depicted as a decision tree as shown in Figure 12.1. We may notice the following in Figure 12.1:

- decision points shown by squares
- chance events shown by circles

The decision points faced by the company are represented by squares. The company has to first decide whether a large plant or a small plant should be built. After one year, it has to decide whether the capacity should be expanded if the initial choice was to build a small plant. The chances of initial and subsequent demand being high and low are shown by circles, and are known as chance events. The expected net cash flows with associated probabilities are shown on the branches of tree. The probabilities of demand after year 1 depend on the demand conditions in year 1. For example, there is a 70 per cent probability that the subsequent demand will be high if demand in year 1 is high. What is the probability that demand will be high in the first year as well as the subsequent years? This is given by the joint probability of occurrences of high demand, i.e., $0.5 \times 0.7 = 0.35$.

In order to decide whether the company should build a large plant or a small plant, we should first analyse the problem of plant expansion after the first year. This is called the method of **backward induction** or **rolling back**. If the initial demand is high and the company expands its plant, the expected net cash flow (ENCF) is:

$$ENCF = 0.7 \times 20 + 0.3 \times 8 = Rs\ 16.4\ lakh$$

To calculate the net present value of the expected net cash flow, we need a discount rate. Let us assume that Water Purity Limited has an opportunity cost of capital of 20 per cent. Thus the expected net present value (ENPV) of expansion costing Rs 45 lakh at the end of year 1 is:

$$ENPV = \frac{16.4}{0.2} - 45 = Rs\ 37\ lakh$$

Note that ENCF of Rs 16.4 is perpetuity, and its value is found by simply dividing it by the discount rate. What will be ENPV in year 1 if the company decides not to expand that plant? In our illustration this is possible only if the initial demand is low. The expected net cash flow will remain Rs 2 lakh in perpetuity. Thus ENPV in year 1 is:

$$ENPV = \frac{2}{0.20} - 0 = Rs\ 10$$

and ENPV today is:

$$ENPV = \frac{2 + 10}{1.20} - 0 = 10$$

We may note that when the initial demand is low no future decision is involved since the company will not expand. We could directly calculate ENPV as follows:

$$ENPV = -10 + \frac{2}{0.2} = 0$$

since ENCF of Rs 2 lakh is a perpetuity from the beginning.

Expansion is expected to yield a higher expected net present value if the initial demand is high. What is ENPV today if the company decides in favour of expansion? The company will have to incur an initial cost of Rs 10 lakh. The expected net cash flow in year 1 will be Rs 4 + Rs 37 = Rs 41 lakh if demand is high and Rs 2 + Rs 10 = Rs 12 lakh if demand is low. Thus ENCF today is:

$$ENCF = 0.5 \times 41 + 0.5 \times 12 = Rs\ 26.5\ lakh$$

and ENPV today is:

$$ENPV = -10 + \frac{26.5}{1.2} = Rs\ 12.08\ lakh$$

Instead of building a small plant and then expanding later on, the company has the option of building a large plant today. What is ENPV today if Water Purity Limited decides to build a large plant? The present value of ENCF in year 1 with high initial demand is:

$$NPV = \frac{0.7 \times 16 + 0.3 \times 10}{0.20} = \frac{14.2}{0.20} = Rs\ 71\ lakh$$

and with low initial demand:

$$NPV = \frac{1.0 \times 7}{0.20} = Rs\ 35\ lakh$$

Thus the net cash flow in year 1 is Rs 10 + Rs 71 = Rs 81 lakh if demand is high and Rs 7 + Rs 35 lakh = Rs 42 lakh if demand is low. Thus, ENCF today is:

$$ENCF = 0.5 \times 81 + 0.5 \times 42 = Rs\ 61.5\ lakh$$

and ENPV today is:

$$ENPV = -50 \times \frac{61.5}{1.2} = Rs\ 1.25\ lakh$$

In fact, there is no need to perform backward calculation in case of the large plant since no future decision is involved. We can calculate ENPV today as follows:

$$\begin{aligned}
ENPV &= -50 + \frac{0.5 \times 10 + 0.5 \times 7}{1.2} \\
&+ \frac{0.5\,[0.7 \times 16 + 0.3 \times 10] + 0.5\,(1 \times 7)}{0.2\,(1.2)} \\
&= -50 + \frac{8.5 + (10.6)/0.2}{1.2} + -50 + \frac{8.5 + 53}{1.2} \\
&= +\ Rs\ 1.25\ lakh
\end{aligned}$$

Note that the expected net cash flow in perpetuity after year 1 are Rs 10.6 lakh and their present value today is Rs 53 lakh. Thus the expected net cash flow in year 1 is: 8.5 + Rs 53 = Rs 61.5 and their present value is Rs 51.25 lakh.

Given ENPV calculations, the best alternative for Water Purity Limited seems to build a small plant today and expand it after a year if the initial demand is high. This alternative yields a higher ENPV than the other alternative.

Let us consider another example of sequential investment decision-making.

Illustration 12.8: Decision Tree Analysis: Supreme Engineering Limited

Supreme Engineering Limited (SEL) has developed a new product which has a 10 year expected life. A market study conducted by the company has revealed that a domestic as well as an export market exists for the product. It is also indicated that a small plant will suffice to cater to the domestic demand. However, a large plant will have to be built if export demand also has to be met. The exact magnitude of the export market is not known. The company has the option of building a small plant today, and then, after three years decide to expand. The company may decide to expand if the initial demand consisting of both domestic and export is high. Further, the company has two options *vis-à-vis* its decision to expand: the small plant could be expanded to a large size or a small size. The market study indicates that the chance that the initial demand will be high is 0.60 and low 0.40. Given a high initial demand, there is 0.80 probability that demand will be high in the subsequent years and 0.20 probability of demand being low. Table 12.9 summarises the relevant data for various options. SEL uses a 10 per cent discount rate for evaluating its investment proposals.

The data contained in Table 12.9 is shown in the form of a decision tree in Figure 12.2. In order to select the best alternative, we start at the last chronological decision on the tree. At decision point 2 three options are involved: either the firm expands to a large size and incurs an outlay of Rs 30 lakh or expands to a small size and incurs an outlay of Rs 10 lakh or does not expand even if the initial demand is high. Let us consider expansion to large size first. The annual expected net cash flow for 7 years is:

$$ENCF = 0.8 \times 13 + 0.2 \times 9 = Rs\ 12.2$$

and ENPV is:

$$ENPV = -30 + 12.2 \times PVAF\ at\ 10\%\ for\ 7\ years$$
$$= -30 + 12.2 \times 4.868 = +Rs\ 29.39\ lakh$$

For expansion to a small size, ENCF is:

$$ENCF = 0.8 \times 7 + 0.2 \times 5 = Rs\ 6.6\ lakh$$

and ENPV is:

$$ENPV = -10 + 6.6 \times PVAF\ at\ 10\%\ for\ 7\ years$$
$$= -10 + 6.6 \times 4.868 = +Rs\ 22.13\ lakh$$

What will be ENPV if the initial demand is high and the firm does not want to expand? For this option, ENCF at the end of year 3 is:

Table 12.9: Data for Alternative Investment Options

Plant Size	Cash Outlay	Initial (1-3 years)			Subsequent (4-10 years)		
		Demand	Prob.	NCF	Demand	Prob.	NCF
Large	50	H	0.6	10	H	0.8	12
					L	0.2	10
		L	0.4	8	H	0.2	8
					L	0.8	6
Small	20	H	0.6	4	H	0.8	4
					L	0.2	3
		L	0.4	3	H	0.2	3
					L	0.8	2
Expansion:							
Large	30				H	0.8	13
					L	0.2	9
Small	10				H	0.8	7
					L	0.2	5

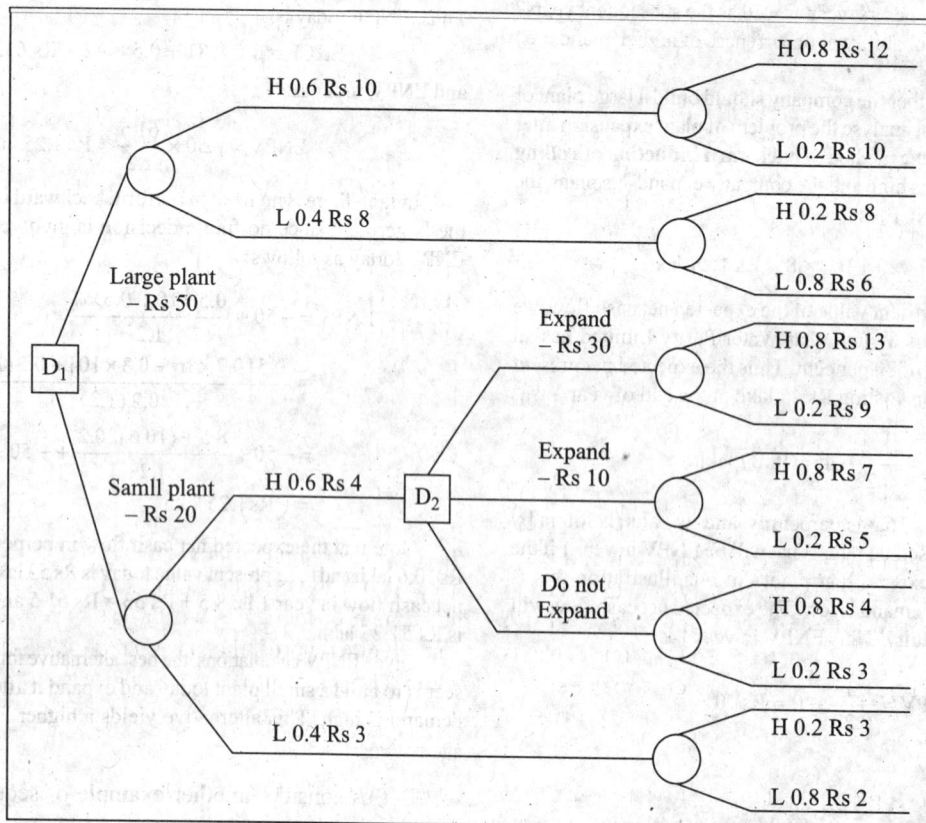

Figure. 12.2: Decision tree

$$ENCF = 0.8 \times 4 + 0.2 \times 3 = Rs\ 3.8\ lakh$$

and ENPV is:

$$ENPV = -0 + 3.8 \times PVAF\ at\ 10\%\ for\ 7\ years$$
$$= -0 + (3.8 \times 4.868) = + Rs\ 18.50\ lakh$$

If the initial demand is low, the firm will not expand. ENCF at the end of year 3 is:

$$ENCF = 0.2 \times 3 + 8 \times 0.2 = Rs\ 2.2\ lakh$$

and ENPV is:

$$ENPV = -0 + 2.2 \times 4.686 = Rs\ 10.71\ lakh$$

The optimum decision at point 2 is to expand the small plant to a large size since ENPV is the highest. All other alternatives at decision point 2 can be eliminated and replaced by ENPV of Rs 29.39 lakh. We can now roll back to decision point 1. If the initial demand is high, the firm is expected to receive net cash flow of Rs 4 lakh each for year 1 and 2 and Rs 4 + Rs 29.39 = Rs 33.39 lakh in year 3. On the other hand if the initial demand is low, net cash flow will be Rs 3 lakh each year for year 1 and 2 and Rs 3 + Rs 10.71 (i.e., present value of ENCF if demand is low and the firm does not expand) = Rs 13.71 lakh in year 3. Thus ENCF will be:

Year 1 & 2	$0.6 \times 4 + 0.4 \times 3 = Rs\ 3.6\ lakh$
Year 3	$0.6 \times 33.39 + 0.4 \times 13.71 = Rs\ 25.52\ lakh$

and ENPV is:

$$ENPV = -20 - \frac{3.6}{(1.1)} + \frac{3.6}{(1.1)^2} + \frac{25.52}{(1.1)^3}$$
$$= -20 + 3.6 \times 0.909 + 3.6 \times 0.826 + 25.52 \times 0.751$$
$$= -20 + 27.75 = Rs\ 5.41\ lakh$$

Usefulness of Decision Tree Approach

The decision tree approach is extremely useful in handling the sequential investments. Working backwards—from future to present—we are able to eliminate unprofitable branches and determine optimum decision at various decision points. The *merits* of the decision tree approach are:[1]

- *Clarity* It clearly brings out the implicit assumptions and calculations for all to see, question and revise.
- *Graphic visualisation* It allows a decision maker to *visualise* assumptions and alternatives in graphic form, which is usually much easier to understand than the more abstract, analytical form.

However, the decision tree diagrams can become more and more complicated as the decision-maker decides to include more alternatives and more variables and to look farther and farther in time. It is complicated even further if the analysis is extended to include interdependent alternatives and variables that are dependent upon one another; for example, sales volume depends on market share which depends on promotion expenses; etc.

The diagram itself quickly becomes cumbersome and calculations become very time-consuming or almost impossible.

UTILITY THEORY AND CAPITAL BUDGETING

We have earlier discussed the use of the concepts of expected value and standard deviation for analysing risk in capital budgeting. On the basis of figures of the expected values and standard deviations, it is difficult to say whether a decision-maker should choose a project with a high expected value and a high standard deviation or a project with a comparatively low expected value and a low standard deviation. The decision-maker's choice would depend upon his **risk preference.** Individuals and firms differ in their attitudes towards risk. In contrast to the approaches for handling risk discussed so far, utility theory aims at incorporation of decision-maker's risk preference explicitly into the decision procedure.[2] In fact, a rational decision-maker would maximise his utility. Thus, he would accept the investment project, which yields maximum utility to him.

Risk Attitude

As regards the attitude of individual investors towards risk, they can be classified in three categories:

- *Risk-averse* investors attach lower utility to increasing wealth. For them the value of the potential increase in wealth is less than the possible loss from the decrease in wealth. In other words, for a given wealth (or return), they prefer less risk to more risk.
- *Risk-neutral* investors attach same utility to increasing or decreasing wealth. They are indifferent to less or more risk for a given wealth (or return).
- *Risk-seeking* investors attach more utility to the potential of additional wealth to the loss from the possible loss from the decrease in wealth. For earning a given wealth (or return), they are prepared to assume higher risk.

It is well established by many empirical studies that individuals are generally risk averters and demonstrate a **decreasing marginal utility** for money function. The utility function for a risk-averse individual may resemble Figure 12.3 in which, the horizontal line represents the potential gain or loss in rupees and the vertical line represents the attitudes of the individual towards such gains and losses, as defined by his utility functions. The utility 'values', measured on relative basis, are called 'utiles' and are measured on an arbitrary scale. The curve in Figure 12.3, which is upward sloping and convex to the origin, indicates that an investor always prefers a higher return to a lower return, and that each successive identical increment of money is worth less to him than the preceding one. In other words, the marginal utility of money is declining, although it is positive.

---

1. Grayson, *op. cit.,* 109.
2. Neumann and Morgenstern developed the utility theory. See Neumann, John Von and Morgenstern, Oskar, *Theory of Games and Economic Behaviour,* Princeton University, 1955. This section draws from their work as well as Grayson *op. cit.*

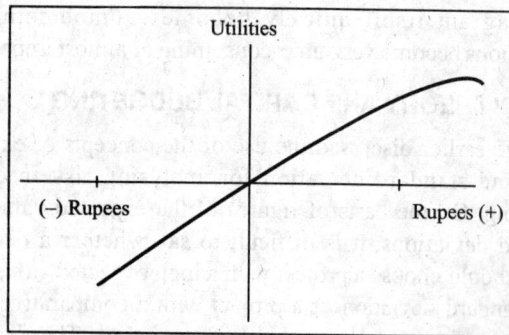

Figure 12.3: Marginal utility of money

The utility theory approach can be applied to investment decisions provided the decision maker's utility functions could be defined.[1] Let us assume that the owner of a firm is considering an investment project, which has 60 per cent of probability of yielding a net present value of Rs 10 lakh and 40 per cent probability of a loss of net present value of Rs 10 lakh. The project's expected net present value is:

$$\text{ENPV} = 10 \times 0.6 + (-10) \times 0.4 = \text{Rs 2 lakh}$$

Should the project be accepted? Without considering the owner's utility function, the answer is affirmative since the project has a positive expected NPV of Rs 2 lakh. However, the owner may be risk averse, and he may consider the gain in utility arising from the positive outcome (positive PV of Rs 10 lakh) less than the loss in utility as a result of the negative outcome (negative PV of Rs 10 lakh). His utility function may be similar to the one shown in Figure 12.3. Because of his risk averseness and given his utility function, the owner may reject the project in spite of its positive ENPV.

Benefits and Limitations of Utility Theory

The utility approach to risk analysis in capital budgeting has certain advantages. First, the risk preferences of the decision-maker are directly incorporated in the capital budgeting analysis. Second, it facilitates the process of delegating the authority for decision. If it is possible to specify the utility function of the superior—the decision maker, the subordinates can be asked to take risks consistent with the risk preferences of the superior.

The use of utility theory in capital budgeting is not common. It suffers from a few limitations. First, in practice, difficulties are encountered in specifying a utility function. Whose utility function should be used as a guide in making decisions? For small firms, the utility function of the owner or one dominant shareholder may be used to guide the decision-making process of the firm.[2] Second, even if the owner's or a dominant shareholder's utility function be used as a guide, the derived utility function at a point of time is valid only for that one point of time. Third, it is quite difficult to specify the utility function if the decision is taken by a group of persons. Individuals differ in their risk preferences. As a result, it is very difficult to derive a consistent utility function for the group.

SUMMARY

❖ Risk arises in the investment evaluation because the forecasts of cash flows can go wrong. Risk can be defined as variability of returns (NPV or IRR) of an investment project. Standard deviation is a commonly used measure of variability.

❖ Statistical techniques are used to measure and incorporate risk in capital budgeting. Two important statistics in this regard are the expected monetary value and standard deviation. The decision-maker instead of working with one single forecast can work with a range of values and their associated probabilities. The expected monetary value is the weighted average of returns where probabilities of possible outcomes are used as weights.

❖ Decision-makers in practice may handle risk in conventional ways. For example, they may use a shorter payback period, or use conservative forecasts of cash flows, or discount net cash flows at the risk-adjusted discount rates.

❖ A more useful technique is the sensitivity analysis. It is a method of analysing change in the project's NPV for a given change in one variable at a time. It helps in asking "what if" questions and calculates NPV under different assumptions.

❖ Scenario analysis is the extension of sensitivity. It considers a few combinations of variables and calculates NPV for each of them. It is a usual practice to calculate NPV under normal, optimistic or pessimistic scenario.

❖ Sensitivity or scenario analysis forces the decision-maker to identify underlying variables, indicates critical variables and helps in strengthening the project by pointing out its weak links. Its limitations are that it cannot handle a large number of interdependent variables and at times, fails to give unambiguous results.

❖ Simulation analysis overcomes the limitations of sensitivity or scenario analysis. The analyst specifies probability distributions for variables and computer generates several hundred scenarios, probability distribution for the project's NPV along with the expected NPV and standard deviation.

❖ Yet another technique of resolving risk in capital budgeting, particularly when the sequential decision-making is involved, is the decision tree analysis. The decision tree provides a way to represent different possibilities so that we can be sure that the decisions we make today, taking proper account of what we can do in the future.

❖ To draw a decision tree, branches from points marked with squares are used to denote different possible decisions, and

---

1. See Van Horne, *op. cit.*, p. 32; and Copeland, T.E. and Weston, J.F., *Financial Theory and Corporate Policy,* Addison-Wesley, 1983, pp. 77–101 for a discussion of axioms and illustration of utility functions.
2. Grayson, *op. cit.,* 109.

branches from points marked with circles denote different possible outcomes. In a decision tree analysis, one has to work out the best decisions at the second stage before one can choose the best first stage decision.

❖ Decision trees are valuable because they display links between today's and tomorrow's decisions. Further, the decision maker explicitly considers various assumptions underlying the decision. The use of decision tree is, however, limited because it can become complicated.

❖ One important theory, which provides insight into risk handling in capital budgeting, is the utility theory. It aims at including a decision-maker's risk preferences explicitly

into the capital expenditure decision. The underlying principle is that an investor prefers a higher return to a lower return, and that each successive identical increment of money is worthless to him than the preceding one. The decision maker's utility function is derived to determine the decision's utility value.

❖ The direct use of the utility theory in capital budgeting is not common. It is very difficult to specify utility function in practice. Even if it is possible to derive utility function, it does not remain constant over time. Problems are also encountered when decision is taken by group of people. Individuals differ in their risk preferences.

KEY CONCEPTS

Backward induction	Expected net present value	Risk neutrals	Subjective probability
Certainty equivalent	Marginal utility of money	Risk seekers	Uncertainty
Chance events	Monte Carlo simulation	Risk-adjusted discount rate	Utility theory
Coefficient of variation	Objective probability	Scenario analysis	Variance
DCF break-even	Payback	Sensitivity analysis	
Decision points	Risk	Simulation analysis	
Decision tree	Risk averters	Standard deviation	

ILLUSTRATIVE SOLVED PROBLEMS

Problem 12.1: A company is considering two mutually exclusive projects. The company uses the certainty equivalent approach. The estimated cash flow and certainty equivalents for each project are as follows:

	Project 1		Project 2	
		Certainty		Certainty
Year	Cash Flow	Equivalents	Cash Flow	Equivalents
0	−30,000	1.00	−40,000	1.00
1	15,000	0.95	25,000	0.90
2	15,000	0.85	20,000	0.80
3	10,000	0.70	15,000	0.70
4	10,000	0.65	10,000	0.60

Which project should be accepted, if the risk-free discount rate is 5 per cent?

Solution:

Project 1

$$NPV = 1.0\,(-30,000) + \frac{0.95\,(15,000)}{(1.05)} + \frac{0.85\,(15,000)}{(1.05)^2}$$
$$+ \frac{0.70\,(10,000)}{(1.05)^3} + \frac{0.65\,(10,000)}{(10.5)^4}$$
$$= Rs\,6,528$$

Project 2

$$NPV = 1.0\,(-40,000) + \frac{0.90\,(25,000)}{(1.05)} + \frac{0.80\,(20,000)}{(1.05)^2}$$
$$+ \frac{0.70\,(15,000)}{(1.05)^3} + \frac{0.60\,(10,000)}{(10.5)^4}$$
$$= Rs\,9,942$$

Project 2 should be preferred since it has higher NPV.

Problem 12.2: *KC* company is considering two mutually exclusive projects. The initial cost of both projects is Rs 5,000, and each has an expected life of five years. Under three possible states of economy, their annual cash flows and associated probabilities are as follows:

		NCF (Rs)	
Economic State	Probability	Project A	Project B
Good	0.3	6,000	5,000
Normal	0.4	4,000	4,000
Bad	0.3	2,000	3,000

If the discount rate is 7 per cent, which project should the company accept?

Solution:

Project A

$$\text{ENCF} = (0.3 \times 6,000) + (0.4 \times 4,000) + (0.3 \times 2,000)$$

$$= \text{Rs } 4,000$$

$$\sigma^2 = (6,000 - 4,000)^2 (0.3) + (4,000 - 4,000)^2 (0.4)$$

$$+ (2,000 - 4,000)^2 (0.3)$$

$$= 2,400,000$$

$$\sigma = \sqrt{24,00,000} \text{ Rs } 1549.2$$

$$\text{ENPV} = -5,000 + 4,000 \times \text{PVAF}_{0.07, 5}$$

$$= -5,000 + 4,000 \times 4.100 = \text{Rs } 11,400$$

Project B

$$\text{ENCF} = (0.3 \times 5,000) + (0.4 \times 4,000) + (0.3 \times 3,000)$$

$$= \text{Rs } 4,000$$

$$\sigma^2 = (5,000 - 4,000)^2 (0.3) + (4,000 - 4,000)^2 (0.4)$$

$$+ (3,000 - 4,000)^2 (0.3)$$

$$= 600,000$$

$$\sigma = \sqrt{600,000} = \text{Rs } 774.6$$

$$\text{ENPV} = -5,000 + 4,000 \times \text{PVAF}_{0.07, 5}$$

$$= -5,000 + 4,000 \times 4.100 = \text{Rs } 11,400$$

Projects *A* and *B* have equal expected net present value of Rs 11,400 but the standard deviation of Project *A*'s cash flow is higher than that of Project *B*. Therefore, *KC* Company should choose Project *B*.

Problem 12.3: A company is considering Projects *X* and *Y* with the following information

	Project	
	X	*Y*
Expected NPV	60,000	227,000
Standard deviation	40,000	135,000

Which project will you recommend? Will your answer change if you use coefficient of variation as a measure of risk instead of standard deviation? Which measure is more appropriate in this situation? Give reasons.

Solution:

(a) Project *Y* has higher standard deviation; therefore, it is more risky than Project *X*. On the basis of standard deviation criterion Project *X* should be accepted.

(b) The coefficients of variations of projects are as follows:

Project X

$$CV = \frac{40,000}{60,000} = 0.67$$

Project Y

$$CV = \frac{135,000}{227,000} = 0.59$$

Project *X* has relatively more risk if we use the coefficient of variation criterion.

(c) In the present situation, it seems more appropriate to consider the coefficient of variation criterion since the expected NPVs of projects are vastly different from each other. Project *Y* is better since it has a much higher expected NPV and lower coefficient of variation.

Problem 12.4: A company is considering a new equipment. The net cash flows of the equipment have been estimated as given below. The equipment's life is estimated to be two years.

	Year 1	Probability	Year 2	Probability
NCF	10,000	0.4	8,000	0.5
			12,000	0.5
NCF	12,000	0.6	16,000	0.4
			20,000	0.6

The cost of equipment is Rs 20,000, and the company's cost of capital is 12 per cent. Use the decision tree approach to recommend whether the equipment should be bought or not.

Solution:

Year					
0	*1*	*2*	*NPV*	*Joint Probability*	*ENPV*
		8,000	−4,694	0.20	−939
	10,000				
	0.4	0.5 — 12,000	−1,506	0.20	−301
−20,000 0.6		0.4 — 16,000	3,468	0.24	832
	12,000				
	0.6	20,000			
			6,656	0.36	2,396
				1.00	1,988

NPV of each path in the decision tree is calculated by discounting NCF at 12 per cent

$$-20,000 + 10,000 \times 0.893 + 8,000 \times 0.797 = -\text{Rs } 4,694$$

$$-20,000 + 10,000 \times 0.893 + 12,000 \times 0.797 = -\text{Rs } 1,506$$

$$-20,000 + 12,000 \times 0.893 + 16,000 \times 0.797 = -\text{Rs } 3,468$$

$$-20,000 + 12,000 \times 0.893 + 20,000 \times 0.797 = -\text{Rs } 6,656$$

REVIEW QUESTIONS

1. Explain the concept of risk? How can risk be measured?
2. What are the advantages of the risk-adjusted discount rate? What is the major problem in using this approach to handle risk in capital budgeting?
3. What are the advantages of using the certainty-equivalent approach? Does it suffer from any limitation?

4. "The certainty equivalent approach is theoretically superior to the risk-adjusted discount rate." Do you agree? Give reasons.
5. What are the limitations of payback method as a risk handling technique? Can it be used as a supplement to more sophisticated techniques?
6. How can you conduct the DCF break-even analysis? Why is the DCF analysis important in risk analysis in capital budgeting?
7. What is sensitivity analysis? What are its advantages and limitations?
8. How can the probability theory be utilised in analysing risk of investment projects? Illustrate.
9. Describe the decision tree approach with the help of an example. How is this technique useful in capital budgeting?
10. How can utility theory be incorporated in the capital budgeting decision to account for the risk preferences of the decision-maker?

PROBLEMS

1. If following is the only available information, which project should be accepted?

   (*i*) Project *A* has ENCF Rs 10,000,
   σ_A = Rs 500; Project *B* has
   ENCF = Rs 10,000, σ_A = Rs 1,000
   (*ii*) Project *A* has ENCF = Rs 10,000
   σ_A = Rs 1,000; Project *B* has
   ENCF = Rs 12,000, σ_B = Rs 500
   (*iii*) Project *A* has ENCF = Rs 500
   σ_A = Rs 500; Project *B* has
   ENCF = Rs 12,000, σ_B = Rs 1,000
   (*iv*) Project *A* has ENCF = Rs 10,000,
   σ_A = Rs 500; Project *B* has
   ENCF = Rs 12,000, σ_B = Rs 600

2. A firm is considering two investment projects, Project *A* requires a net cash outlay of Rs 6,000; *B* requires Rs 5,000. Both projects have an estimated life of 3 years. The net cash inflows have been estimated as: For Project *A*, year 1, a 0.40 chance of Rs 2,000 and a 0.60 chance of Rs 3,000; year 2, a 0.30 chance of Rs 4,000 and a 0.70 chance of Rs 2,000; year 3 a 0.50 chance of Rs 3,000 and a 0.50 chance of Rs 2,200; For Project *B*, year 1, a 0.30 chance of Rs 1,000 and a 0.70 chance of Rs 2,000; year 2, a 0.20 chance of Rs 2,000 and a 0.80 chance of Rs 1,000; year 3, a 0.40 chance of Rs 2,000, and a 0.60 chance of Rs 4,000. Assume a 10 per cent discount rate. Which project should be accepted and why?

3. The Walchand Company is considering two mutually exclusive projects. The expected cash flows and the associated certainty-equivalent coefficients for each project are as follows:

Year	Project A Rs	Certainty Equivalent	Project B Rs	Certainty Equivalent
0	−5,000	1.00	−8,000	1.00
1	1,000	0.90	6,000	0.90
2	2,000	0.80	5,000	0.70
3	3,300	0.70	4,000	0.60
4	4,000	0.60	3,000	0.50
5	1,000	0.30	1,000	0.25

To account for the riskiness of the projects, the company uses the certainty-equivalent approach.

Which of the two projects should be selected if the risk-free discount rate is 6 per cent? If the firm were to use risk-adjusted discount rates instead of certainty-equivalent approach, what rates would be used in order to obtain an equivalent solution?

4. The Lalchand Co. is analysing two mutually exclusive proposals, each costing Rs 30,000 and having a five-year expected life. Each project will have expected cash flows which will increase by Rs 3,000 each year after the first year, and will not have any value after the fifth year. The first year possible net cash inflows for project 1 are Rs 10,000, Rs 14,000 and Rs 16,000 with associated probabilities of 0.25, 0.50 and 0.25, respectively. The first year possible net cash inflows for Project 2 are Rs 4,000, Rs 12,000 and Rs 25,000 with associated probabilities of 0.20, 0.50 and 0.30, respectively. Project 1 is considered less risky and can be evaluated at 8 per cent, while Project 2 is more risky and can be evaluated at 10 per cent rate of discount. Which project should be chosen?

5. The Weston Co. is thinking of building a plant to manufacture a new product recently developed by its R&D department. Several alternatives are available to the firm regarding the size of the plant. The company can construct a large plant, which will cost Rs 500,000. Under different demand conditions the cash flows with associated probabilities are expected to be as follows:

Large Plant		
Demand condition	Probability	Cash inflow (Rs) year 1–10
High	0.50	125,000
Medium	0.40	100,000
Low	0.10	50,000

The alternative to building a large plant is to build a smaller plant for Rs 200,000 now, with an option to build an additional plant after two years, if the product achieves sufficient success. The small plant has a capacity to maintain Rs 80,000 in cash flows. Under high or medium demand the plant will be fully utilised.

The expected cash flows with associated probabilities are as follows:

Small Plant		
Demand condition	Probability	Cash inflow (Rs) year 1–2
High	0.50	80,000
Medium	0.40	80,000
Low	0.10	40,000

After two years, the company can review the situation to expand the smaller plant. If the company experiences a high initial demand for the first two years, a Rs 300,000 addition could be built, increasing yearly revenue potential by Rs 60,000.

The company estimates the net cash flows with associated probabilities under different demand conditions as follows:

High Initial Demand. Additional Plant of Rs 300,000		
Demand condition	Probability	Cash inflow (Rs) year 3–10
High	0.60	140,000
Medium	0.30	110,000
Low	0.10	80,000

If only medium demand was achieved in the first two years then a Rs 150,000 addition would be considered. The expected cash flows and probabilities are as follows:

Medium Initial Demand: Additional Plant of Rs 150,000		
Demand condition	Probability	Cash inflow (Rs) year 3–10
High	0.60	110,000
Medium	0.30	80,000
Low	0.10	25,000

The company also considers the possibility of not building any addition regardless of the level of demand.

Design a decision tree and solve for the most profitable alternative. Assume a 10 per cent discount rate and that the plants do not have any salvage value.

6. A management group of a company has determined its relative utility values for cash flows as follows:

Cash Flow Rs	Utilities
– 20,000	– 100
– 10,000	– 40
– 1,000	– 3
0	0
+ 10,000	+30
+ 9,000	+25
+ 8,000	+18
+ 7,000	+10

Given this utility function, which of the following projects should be accepted? Why?

Project A		Project B	
Cash flow Rs	Prob.	Cash flow (Rs)	Prob.
– 20,000	0.10	–10,000	0.15
10,000	0.20	7,000	0.25
9,000	0.25	8,000	0.40
8,000	0.30	9,000	0.20
7,000	0.15	—	—

7. A company is considering buying an equipment for a new process. The equipment will cost Rs 245,700. The company has made the following estimates of the after-tax cash flows over the equipments possible life of two years:

Year 1		Year 2	
NCF	Prob.	NCF	Prob.
153,500	0.5	122,800	0.7
		184,300	0.3
125,000	0.5	240,500	0.4
		307,000	0.6

The outcome of year 2 is dependent on the outcome of year 1. Use a decision tree approach to answer the following questions (assume 12 per cent discount rate):
(a) What is the equipment's expected net present value?
(b) If the worst outcome occurs, then what would be the project's net present value?
(c) What net present value will be realised if the best outcome occurs? What is its probability?
(d) What is the probability of the company realising a net present value less than zero?

8. The R&D department of a company has developed a new product with an expected life of six years. The manufacturing of the product will require investment of Rs 3 lakh. The following annual profit from the investment is expected:

Selling price		25
Less: Unit variable cost		
Materials	8	
Labour	4	
Overheads	3	15
Contribution		10
Sales revenue (30,000 units)		750,000
Less: Variable costs		450,000
Contribution		300,000
Less: Fixed costs		
(including depreciation Rs 50,000)		120,000
Profit before tax		180,000
Less: Tax at 50%		90,000
Profit after tax		90,000

Assume that the company can charge depreciation on straight-line basis for tax purpose. If the company has a discount rate of 10 per cent, calculate the investment's NPV. Identify the factors which are most critical to the decision. To answer this question, calculate the volume, selling price, unit variable cost, and cash outlay, at which the investment's NPV would be zero, other things remaining the same.

CASES

Case 12.1: Richa Foods Company

Richa Foods Company is a medium-sized firm specializing in packaged food items. The R&D department of the company has developed a new product with an expected life of six years. The manufacturing facilities of the product will require a cash outlay of Rs 6 crore, which the firm would depreciate over six years. The salvage value is assumed to be zero. The company expects to sell 10 lakh units per annum at a price of Rs 60 per unit. The marketing manager has informed that depending on competition and Richa Foods' response to it, both actual volume and price could differ from the expectations. The selling price could decrease as much as by 10 per cent under adverse economic conditions and increase as much as by 15 per cent under favorable economic conditions. Similarly, actual volume could vary from the expected volume between –5 per cent to +10 per cent. The accountant felt that the actual outlay and variable costs could also be different from the forecasts. The actual outlay could increase by 10 per cent and variable costs by 5 per cent to 10 per cent from the expected values. Table 12.1.1 gives financial forecasts based on the most expected assumptions.

Table 12.1.1: Financial Forecasts Based on Expected Sales 10 lakh Units

		Per unit Rs	*Total* *Rs ('000)*
Selling price		60	60,000
Variable costs:			
	Material	16	16,000
	Labour	8	8,000
	Overhead	6	6,000
	Total	30	30,000
Contribution		30	30,000
Fixed costs		20	20,000
Profit before tax		10	10,000
Tax @ 35%		3.5	3,500
Profit after tax		6.5	6,500

Fixed costs include depreciation on straight-line basis. Assume that the company can charge straight-line depreciation for tax purposes. The company has a required rate of return of 12 per cent. Assume zero inflation.

Discussion Questions

1. Identify the factors that are most critical to the decision. Answer this question by calculating the volume, selling price, unit variable cost and cash outlay at which the investment's NPV would be zero, other things remaining the same.
2. What is your recommendation to the company? State any additional information that will be helpful to answer this question.

Case 12.2: Weston Plastics Company

Weston Plastics Company is a medium-size company manufacturing household plastic appliances. The R&D department has come up with the idea of a new product – a plastic shelf to keep utensils. The company is thinking of manufacturing a foldable utensil-shelf. The shelf would have a height of five feet, width of one and a half feet and depth of one foot. It could be fixed on the wall. The shelf could be used to keep cutlery, crockery, dinnerware, cooking utensils etc. The price of the shelf would be Rs 300 each.

The company does not have surplus plant capacity to produce the utensil-shelf. It would have to acquire new equipment. Equipments with different manufacturing capacities are available in the market. The company can acquire large-size equipment, which will cost Rs 50 lakh. The expected demand conditions, their probabilities and cash inflows are given in Table 12.2.1.

Table 12.2.1: Large Equipment (Rs 50 lakh)

Demand Condition	*Probability*	*Cash flow (Rs in lakh) Year 1 – 10*
High	0.50	12.50
Medium	0.40	10.00
Low	0.10	5.00

The company does not know the demand for the product. It may take two years to know the level of demand. Therefore, it may not be wise to go for large capacity equipment right now. The alternative to buying large equipment is to get a smaller plant for Rs 20 lakh now, with an option to acquire additional equipment after two years, if the demand for the product achieves sufficient success. The small plant has a capacity to maintain Rs 8 lakh in cash flows. Under high or medium demand the plant will be fully utilised. Table 12.2.2 gives the expected demand conditions, their probabilities and cash inflows for two years.

Table 12.2.2: Small Equipment (Rs 20 lakh)

Demand Condition	*Probability*	*Cash flow (Rs lakh) Year 1 – 2*
High	0.50	8.00
Medium	0.40	8.00
Low	0.10	4.00

After two years, the company can review the situation to expand its capacity by acquiring additional equipment. If the company experiences a high initial demand for the first two years, an additional equipment of Rs 30 lakh could be acquired, increasing yearly revenue potential by Rs 6 lakh at full capacity utilisation. The company estimates the cash flows with associated probabilities under different demand conditions as follows:

Table 12.2.3: High Initial Demand: Acquire Additional Equipment for Rs 30 lakh

Demand Condition	Probability	Cash inflow (Rs in lakh) Year 3 – 10
High	0.60	14.00
Medium	0.30	11.00
Low	0.10	8.00

If only medium demand was achieved in the first two years then an Rs 15 lakh addition would be considered. The expected cash flows and probabilities are as follows:

Table 12.2.4: Medium Initial Demand: Acquire Additional Equipment for Rs 15 lakh

Demand condition	Probability	Cash inflow (Rs in lakh) Year 3 – 10
High	0.60	11.00
Medium	0.30	8.00
Low	0.10	2.50

The company also considers the possibility of not acquiring any additional equipment regardless of the level of demand.

Discussion Questions

1. Compute the net present values for the various options.
2. Design a decision tree and solve for the most profitable alternative. Assume a 10 per cent discount rate and that the equipments do not have any salvage value.

Appendix 12A: Probability Distribution Approaches to Risk Analysis in Capital Budgeting

We have discussed in this chapter the importance of probability theory in analysing risk in capital budgeting. We have also emphasised that the riskiness of an investment project can be described by calculating the expected net present value and the standard deviation. However, we did not make any explicit assumption regarding the behaviour of the cash flows. In this Appendix, we specifically discuss the use of probability theory in analysing risk in capital budgeting, given various assumptions regarding the independence and dependence of cash flows over time.[1] Once this analysis is completed by developing relevant information about the expected value and dispersion of the probability distribution of possible returns, the decision-maker will make accept-reject decision. This he would do by obtaining a trade-off between risk and return. He would select those projects which yield the highest expected return, but at the same time minimise risk to the firm.

INDEPENDENCE OF CASH FLOWS OVER TIME

The independence of cash flows over time means that the probability distributions for future periods are not dependent on each other. The expected net present value in this situation will be:

$$ENPV = \sum_{t=0}^{n} \frac{ENCF_t}{(1+k_f)^t} \qquad (A1)$$

where $ENCF_t$ is the expected value of net cash flow in the period t and k_f is the risk free rate. It is important to remember that the discount rate should be risk-free when we use probability information for the cash flow distributions. When we use probability information for calculating the expected net present value for a project, we are making explicit adjustment for the risk. The probability of the occurrence of a given set of cash flows will be high or low depending on whether risk is low or high. Thus,

if the cost of capital is used as the discount rate, it would result in double counting for risk.[2] Reason is that the cost of capital incorporates both a risk-free rate as well as a premium for risk.

The standard deviation of net cash flows for each period can be expressed as:

$$\sigma_t = \sqrt{\sum_{t=0}^{n} (NCF_{jt} - ENCF_t)^2 \, P_{jt}} \qquad (A2)$$

where σ_t is the standard deviation of net cash flows in period t, NCF_{jt} is net cash flow, $ENCF_t$ is the expected value of the net cash flow and P_{jt} is the probability associated with each cash flow. Using the standard deviations for the various periods, we can develop a measure of risk for the project i.e., *the standard deviation of the probability distribution of net present values* under assumption of the independence of cash flows over time. It is equal to the discounted sum of annual variances. The following equation can be used to calculate the standard deviation for the project:

$$\sigma = \sqrt{\sum_{t=0}^{n} \frac{\sigma_t^2}{(1+k_f)^{2t}}} \qquad (A3)$$

where σ is the standard deviation of the probability distribution of possible net cash flows and σ_t^2 is the variance of each period. The calculation of the expected value and standard deviation for independent cash flows over time is demonstrated in Illustration 12A.1.

Illustration 12A.1: Project Risk Under Independent Cash Flows

Consider a project which costs Rs 8,000 at $t = 0$ and is expected to yield cash for three years. Table 12A.1 presents the cash flows and probability information for the project. Assume a 10 per cent risk-free discount rate.

---

1. This section draws from the following sources: Van Horne, J.C., *Financial Management and Policy*, Prentice-Hall of India, 1985; pp. 148–56; Hillier, F.S., The Derivation of Probabilistic Information for the Evaluation of Risky Investment, *Management Science*, 9 (April 1963), pp. 443–57, and Hillier, F.S. and Heebink, D.V., 'Evaluating Risk', *Management Science*, 8 (Winter 1965), pp. 71–80.
2. Van Horne, *op. cit.*, p. 148.

The expected cash flows and variance of each period are given in Table 12A.2. Table 12A.3 shows calculations of expected net present value of the project.

Table 12A.1: Projected Cash Flows

Year 1		Year 2		Year 3	
Cash Flow (Rs)	Probability	Cash Flow (Rs)	Probability	Cash Flow (Rs)	Probability
6,000	0.10	3,000	0.15	6,000	0.25
5,000	0.40	4,000	0.50	5,000	0.20
4,000	0.30	5,000	0.25	4,000	0.35
3,000	0.20	6,000	0.10	3,000	0.20

Table 12A.3: Calculation of Expected Net Present Value of Project

PV Factor @ 10%	Expected Value of Cash Flow Rs	PV of Expected Value of Cash Flow Rs
0.909	4,400	4,000
0.826	4,300	3,552
0.751	4,500	3,380
		10,932

Expected net present value = Rs 10,932 – Rs 8,000 = Rs 2,932

Using Equation (A), the standard deviation about the expected value is:

$$\sigma_1 = \sqrt{\sum_{t=0}^{n} \frac{917^2}{(1.10)^2} + \frac{843^2}{(1.10)^4} + \frac{1072^2}{(1.10)^6}}$$

$$= \sqrt{8,40,889 \times 0.826 + 7,10,649 \times 0.6983 + 11,49,184 \times 0.564}$$

$$= \sqrt{18,28,087} = Rs\, 1,352$$

Normal Probability Distribution

The **normal probability distribution** can be used to further analyse the risk element in capital budgeting. The normal probability distribution is a smooth, symmetric, continuous, bell-shaped curve as shown in Figure 12A.1.

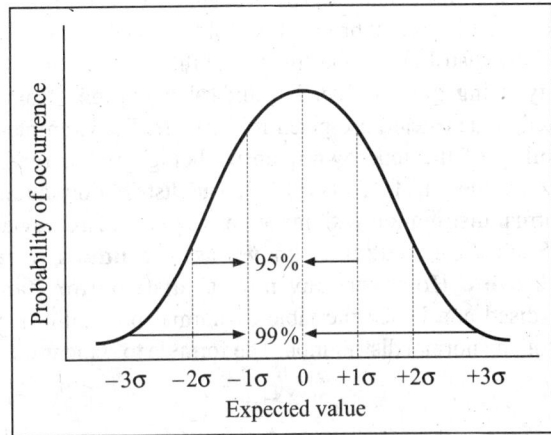

Figure 12A. 1: The normal probability distribution

Table 12A.2: Calculation of Expected Value and Variance for Each Period

	NCF_{jt} Rs	P_{jt}	$NCF_{jt}\, P_{jt}$ Rs	$(NCF_{jt} - ENCF_t)^2$ Rs	$(NCF_{jt} - ENCF_t)^2\, P_{jt}$ Rs
Year 1	6,000	0.10	600	2,560,000	256,000
	5,000	0.40	2,000	360,000	144,000
	4,000	0.30	1,200	160,000	48,000
	3,000	0.20	600	1,960,000	392,000
			$ENCF_1$ = Rs 4,400		σ_1^2 = Rs 840,000
					$\sigma_1 = \sqrt{840,000} = 917$
Year 2	3,000	0.15	450	1,690,000	253,500
	4,000	0.50	2,000	90,000	45,000
	5,000	0.25	1,250	490,000	122,500
	6,000	0.10	600	2,890,000	289,000
			$ENCF_2$ = Rs 4,300		σ_2^2 = Rs 710,000
					$\sigma_1 = \sqrt{710,000} = 843$
Year 3	6,000	0.25	1,500	2,250,000	562,500
	5,000	0.20	1,000	250,000	50,000
	4,000	0.35	1,400	250,000	87,500
	3,000	0.20	600	2,250,000	450,000
			$ENCF_3$ = Rs 4,500		σ_3^2 = Rs 1,150,000
					$\sigma_3 = \sqrt{1,150,000} = 1,072$

It is useful to notice certain properties of such distribution. The area under the curve sums 1, and the curve reaches its maximum at the expected value (mean) of the distribution and one-half of the area lies on either side of the mean. Another important feature of the normal distribution is that approximately 50 per cent of the area lies within ± 0.67 standard deviations of the expected value; about 68 per cent of the area lies within ± 1.0 standard deviations of the expected value; 95 per cent of the area lies within ± 1.96 standard deviation of the expected value and 99 per cent of the area lies within ± 3.0 standard deviations of the expected value. In fact, the normal probability table (given at the end of this book) can be used to determine the area under the normal curve for various standard deviations. The probability of occurrence can be read from the normal probability table. This table is the 'right tail' of the distribution; that is, probabilities of the unknown quantity being greater than X standard deviations from the expected value (mean) are given in the table. For example, the probability of the unknown quantity being greater than the expected value plus 0.85s is 0.1977. The distribution tabulated is a normal distribution with mean zero and standard deviation of 1. Such a distribution is known as a **standard normal distribution**. However, any normal distribution can be standardised and hence the table of normal probabilities will serve for any normal distribution. The formula to standardise is:[1]

$$S = \frac{X - \overline{X}}{\sigma} \qquad (A4)$$

where X is the outcome in which we are interested, $\overline{X}$ is the expected value of the net present value and S is the number of standard deviations from the expected value of the net present value. With the help of Equation (A4) and values of the standard normal distribution functions (see Table E at the end of the book), we can determine the net present value as well as develop the probability distributions for a project's NPVs.

Illustration 12A.2: Probability Distribution

A project has an expected net present value of Rs 2,932 and the standard deviation of the possible net present value is Rs 1,352 (see Illustration 12A.1). Determine the probability that the net present value of the project will be zero or less. Also, show the full range of probability distribution for the project.

As given in Equation (A4), we can divide the difference between zero and the expected value of the net present value by standard deviation of possible net present value as follows:

$$S = \frac{0 - 2,932}{1,352} = -2.17$$

This figure (–2.17) implies that a present value of 0 lies 2.17 standard deviations to the left of the expected value of the probability distribution of possible net present values. The probability of being less than 2.17 standard deviations from the expected value, according to the normal probability distribution table is 0.015. This means that there is 1.5 per cent probability that the net present value of the project will be zero or less.

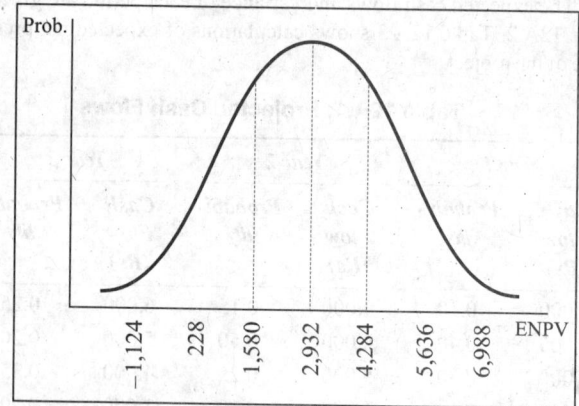

Figure 12A.2: Full range of probability distribution for the project

The probability distribution for the project in Illustration 12A.2 are shown in Figure 12A.2. The data needed to graph the probability distributions are given in Table 12A.4.

Table 12A.4: Data Needed to Construct Horizontal Axis of the Probability Distribution for the Project

Z-value	Expected Net Present Value for the Project
-3σ	$-1,124$
-2σ	228
-1σ	1,580
0	2,932
$+1\sigma$	4,284
$+2\sigma$	5,636
$+3\sigma$	6,988

It is obvious from Table 12A.4 and Figure 12A.2 that the expected value of the net present values is Rs 2,932, and one standard deviation on either side of the mean gives us the net present values of Rs 1,580 and Rs 4,284. This indicates that there is two-thirds probability that the net present value of the project will be between Rs 1,580 and Rs 4,284. Three standard deviations on either side give us net present value between –Rs 1,124 and Rs 6,988. Thus, there is approximately 99 per cent probability that the net present value will fall within the range of minus Rs 1,124 and Rs 6,988. There is 1.5 per cent probability that the net present value will be less than zero and 98.5 per cent (a very high) probability that it will be greater than zero. Thus, with the help of the normal probability distribution, it is possible for us to determine that the net present value of a project will be greater or less than a specified amount.

What is the probability that the project examined in Illustrations 12A.1 and 12A.2 will have the net present value not less than 20 per cent of its cost?

Using the formula $(X - \overline{X})/\sigma$, we find that a net present value of Rs 1,600 (*i.e.*, 20% of Rs 8,000) lies 0.985, *viz.*, [(1,600 – 2,932)/1,352], standard deviations to the left of the expected value. From the normal distribution table, we find that there is approximately 0.17 probability that the net present value will be less than Rs 1,600.

---

1. Van Horne, *ibid.*, p. 150.
2. Van Horne, *ibid.*, p. 154.

DEPENDENCE OF CASH FLOWS OVER TIME

Can a project's cash flows remain independent over time? It is realistic to assume in the case of most investment projects that cash flows are dependent over time. The favourable or unfavourable outcome in the earlier periods is generally accompanied by the favourable or unfavourable outcome in the later periods in the life of an investment project. When cash flows are dependent over time, the standard deviation will be larger than what it would be under the assumption of independence of cash flows. The greater the degree of correlation between cash flows, the larger will be the standard deviation. However, the expected value of net present value remains unchanged irrespective of the dependence or independence of cash flows.

Perfect Correlation

In case the deviation of cash flows for one period implies the same deviation of expected cash flow for the next period, then cash flows are perfectly correlated. The formula for the standard deviation of cash flows in case of perfect correlation is:[1]

$$\sigma = \sum_{t=1}^{n} \frac{\sigma_t}{(1+k_f)^t} \qquad (A5)$$

Using the data for Illustration 12A.1 and applying Equation (A5), the standard deviation about the expected value of net present value for the project is:

$$\sigma = \frac{917}{(1.10)} + \frac{843}{(1.10)^2} + \frac{1,072}{(1.10)^3} = Rs\,2,335$$

It can be noticed that the standard deviation about the expected value is higher (Rs 2,335) when the cash flows are perfectly correlated than the standard deviation under the assumption of independence of the cash flows (Rs 1,352).

Moderate Correlation

In certain cases the cash flows are neither independent nor perfectly correlated over time. They are rather moderately correlated. In case of the moderately correlated cash flows, the methods discussed above do not apply. This problem can be handled by utilising the concepts of **conditional probabilities** and decision trees. The decision tree approach is already discussed in the main text of Chapter 12. Here we take a simple example to illustrate the procedure about conditional and joint probabilities for deriving the measure of risk for moderately correlated cash flows.

Illustration 12A.4: Project's NPV for Moderately Correlated Cash Flows

Let us consider a project costing Rs 8,000 at $t = 0$. The project is expected to generate net cash flows in periods 1, 2 and 3 with the probabilities shown in Table 12A.5. The probabilities are conditional because the cash flows in period 3 are dependent upon what happened in periods 1 and 2. In period 1, the firm may be faced with two levels of demand—high or low. If the demand were high in period 1, the firm would again encounter two possible levels of demand. Similarly, if the demand were low, the firm might again face two possible demand levels. The cash flows of period 3 would also be influenced by the fact whether the demand was high or low in period 2. Thus, as can be seen in Table 12A.5 there are eight possible cash flow series. Had we considered three levels of demand—

Table 12A.5: NCF for a Project (Moderately Correlated Cash Flows)

Period 1			Period 2			Period 3			
D	IP	NCF	D	IP	NCF	D	IP	NCF	JP
						H	0.5	7,000	0.210
			H	0.7	8,000				
						L	0.5	5,000	0.210
H	0.6	6,000							
						H	0.6	5,000	0.108
			L	0.3	6,000				
						L	0.4	4,000	0.072
						H	0.6	6,000	0.192
			H	0.8	5,000				
						L	0.4	4,000	0.128
L	0.4	3,000							
						H	0.7	6,000	0.056
			L	0.2	2,000				
						L	0.3	2,000	0.024

Note: D is level of demand, IP is initial probability, CP is conditional probability, JP is joint probability, NCF is net cash flow, *H* is high and *L* is low.

1. Van Horne, *ibid.*, p. 154.

Table 12A.6: Expected net Present Value (Moderated Correlated Cash Flows)

Period 1 NCF	PVF		Period 2 NCF	PVF		Period 3 NCF	PVF		PV	JP	EPV
6,000 ×	0.909	+	8,000 ×	0.826	+	7,000 ×	0.751	=	17,319	0.210	3,637
6,000 ×	0.909	+	8,000 ×	0.826	+	5,000 ×	0.751	=	15,817	0.210	3,322
6,000 ×	0.909	+	6,000 ×	0.826	+	5,000 ×	0.751	=	14,165	0.108	1,530
6,000 ×	0.909	+	6,000 ×	0.826	+	4,000 ×	0.751	=	13,414	0.072	966
3,000 ×	0.909	+	5,000 ×	0.826	+	6,000 ×	0.751	=	11,363	0.192	2,182
3,000 ×	0.909	+	5,000 ×	0.826	+	4,000 ×	0.751	=	9,861	0.128	1,262
3,000 ×	0.909	+	2,000 ×	0.826	+	6,000 ×	0.751	=	8,885	0.056	498
3,000 ×	0.909	+	2,000 ×	0.826	+	2,000 ×	0.751	=	5,8810	0.024	141
								EPV			13,538
								Cost			8,000
								ENPV			5,538

Note: NCF is net cash flow, PVF is present value factor (at 10% discount rate) PV is present value, EPV is expected present value and JP is joint probability.

high, medium and low—for three periods, the cash flow series would have been 27, and for four years 81 and so on. The last column of the table shows the **joint probability** of occurrence of a particular cash flow series. For series 1, the joint probability of a Rs 6,000 cash flow in period 1, being followed by cash flows of Rs 8,000 and Rs 7,000 in periods 2 and 3, respectively, is 0.6 × 0.7 × 0.5 = 0.210. Similarly, the joint probabilities for the other cash flows series are determined.[1]

The procedure to calculate the net present value is the same as discussed previously. The net present value for the project can be found out by discounting the cash flow of each series, multiplying the sum of the present value for each series by the joint probability to arrive at the expected value of the series, and then subtracting the initial cost of the project from the sum of the expected values for all series. The calculation of the net present value for the project, assuming 10 per cent discount rate, is shown in Table 12A.6.

The following formula is used to determine the standard deviation of the project whose cash flows are moderately correlated over time:[2]

$$\sigma = \sqrt{\sum_{j=1}^{n} (NPV_j - ENPV)^2 \, P_j} \qquad (A6)$$

where NPV_j, is the net present value for series j of net cash flows, covering all periods, ENPV is the expected value of net present value of the project and P_j is the probability of occurrence of that series. The NPV for series j is simply the difference between its expected present value less cost.

It is important to notice that the degree of correlation among cash flows should be correctly determined to measure risk. The risk of a project will be significantly high if cash flows are perfectly correlated over time than they are independent. Thus, if the degree of correlation is wrongly calculated, then a wrong formula would be used to measure risk. This will lead to incorrect accept-reject decision.

ILLUSTRATIVE SOLVED PROBLEMS

Problem 12A.1: The expected value of the probability distribution of the possible net present value for a project is Rs 30,000 and the standard deviation about the expected value is Rs 15,000. Assuming a normal distribution, what is the probability that the net present value will be (*i*) zero or less (*ii*) greater than Rs 45,000 and (*iii*) less than Rs 7,500?

Solution:

The standardised differences for a given amount are:

$$S = \frac{X - \overline{X}}{\sigma}$$

(*i*) For zero or less, $\quad S = \dfrac{0 - 30,000}{15,000} = -2.0$

(*ii*) For Rs 45,000 or more, $S = \dfrac{45,000 - 30,000}{15,000} = +1.0$

(*iii*) For Rs 7,500 or less, $S = \dfrac{7,500 - 30,000}{15,000} = -1.5$

From the normal distribution table, we find that these standardised differences correspond to probabilities of 0.0228, 0.1577 and 0.0668 respectively.

Problem 12A.2: A company is considering investing in a new product with an expected life of three years. It is estimated that if the demand for the product is favourable in the first year, then it is certain to be favourable in the subsequent years. And if it is low in the first year, it would remain low in years 2 and 3. The company feels that cash flows over time are perfectly correlated. The cost of the project is Rs 50,000 and the possible cash flows for three years are:

1. *Ibid.*
2. *Ibid.*, p. 155.

| | Year 1 | | Year 2 | | Year 3 |
Cash flow (Rs)	Probability	Cash flow (Rs)	Probability	Cash flow (Rs)	Probability
0	0.10	5,000	0.15	0	0.15
10,000	0.20	20,000	0.20	7,500	0.20
20,000	0.40	35,000	0.30	15,000	0.30
30,000	0.20	50,000	0.20	22,500	0.20
40,000	0.10	65,000	0.15	30,000	0.15

Assuming a risk-free discount rate of 5 per cent, calculate the expected value and standard deviation of the probability distribution of possible net present values. Assuming a normal distribution, what is the probability of the project providing a net present value of zero or less of Rs 15,000 or more? Is the standard deviation calculated larger or smaller than it would be under an assumption of independence of cash flows over time?

Solution:

The calculation for the expected values of the cash flows for three years are given in the table below:

$$S = [0.10(0 - 20,000) + 0.20(10,000 - 20,000)$$
$$+ 0.40(20,000 - 20,000) + 0.20(30,000 - 20,000)$$
$$+ 0.10(40,000 - 20,000)]$$
$$S = [120,000,000]/1/2 = Rs\ 1,095$$
$$S = [0.15(5,000 - 35,000) + 0.20(20,000 - 35,000)$$
$$+ 0.30(35,000 - 35,000)$$
$$+ 0.20(50,000 - 35,000) + 0.15(65,000 - 35,000)]$$
$$S = [360,000,000]/1/2\ Rs\ 1,879$$
$$S = [0.15(0 - 15,000) + 0.20(7,500 - 15,000)$$
$$+ 0.30(15,000 - 15,000)$$
$$+ 0.20(22,500 - 15,000) + 0.15(30,000 - 15,000)]$$
$$S = [90,000,000]/1/2 = Rs\ 948$$

The standard deviation of the probability distribution of possible net present values under the assumption of perfect correlation of cash flows over time is given by Equation (A5) in the appendix. Thus

$$\sigma = \frac{Rs\ 10,954}{(1.05)} + \frac{Rs\ 18,974}{(1.05)^2} + \frac{Rs\ 9,487}{(1.05)^3}$$
$$= Rs\ 35,834$$

The expected value of net present value of the project is:

$$ENPV = -Rs\ 50,000 + \frac{Rs\ 20,000}{(1.05)} + \frac{Rs\ 35,000}{(1.05)^2} + \frac{Rs\ 15,000}{(1.05)^3}$$
$$= Rs\ 13,745$$

The standardised differences for zero and Rs 15,000 are:

$$\text{for zero or less, } S = \frac{0 - 13,745}{35,834} = 0.384$$

$$\text{for 15,000 or more, } S = \frac{15,000 - 13,745}{35,834} = 0.035$$

From the normal distribution table, we find that these standardised differences correspond to probabilities of approximately 0.32 and 0.48 respectively.

The standard deviation calculated under this assumption is much larger, than it would be under an assumption of independence of cash flows over time as shown below:

$$\sigma = \sqrt{\frac{(Rs\ 10,954)^2}{(1.05)^2} + \frac{(Rs\ 18,974)^2}{(1.05)^4} + \frac{(Rs\ 9,487)^2}{(1.05)^6}}$$
$$= Rs\ 21,730$$

| | Year 1 | | | Year 2 | | | Year 3 | |
Cash Flow (Rs)	Probability	Expected Value	Cash Flow (Rs)	Probability	Expected Value	Cash Flow (Rs)	Probability	Expected Value
0	0.10	0	5,000	0.15	750	0	0.15	0
10,000	0.20	2,000	20,000	0.20	4,000	7,500	0.20	1,500
20,000	0.40	8,000	35,000	0.30	10,500	15,000	0.30	4,500
30,000	0.20	6,000	50,000	0.20	10,000	22,500	0.20	4,500
40,000	0.10	4,000	65,000	0.15	9,750	30,000	0.15	4,500
		20,000			35,000			15,000

PROBLEMS

12A.1. From the following data for Project *M*, calculate the expected value and standard deviation. Assuming a normal distribution, calculate the probability that the net present value will be zero or less; that it will be greater than Rs 20,000 and less than Rs 2,000. Assume further that the cost of the project in period 0 is Rs 20,000 and its life is only one year. Net cash inflows in period 1 are as follows:

Rs	40,000	48,000	24,000	20,000
Probability	0.20	0.40	0.30	0.10

12A.2. The following are the possible net cash flows with associated probabilities for a project:

Assume that the cash flows are independent and the risk-free rate is 6 per cent.

(*a*) Determine the expected net present value, if the project costs Rs 4,000.

(*b*) Calculate the standard deviation about the expected value.

(*c*) If the normal probability distribution is assumed, what is the probability of the net present value being (*i*) zero or less, (*ii*) greater than zero, (*iii*) greater than Rs 2,000 and (*iv*) less than Rs 500?

(*d*) What is probability that the profitability index will be (*a*) 1.00 or less and (*b*) greater than 1.50?

(*e*) Calculate the expected value and the standard deviation if the cash flows are assumed to be perfectly correlated over time.

Period 1		Period 2		Period 3	
Cash Flow (Rs)	Probability	Cash Flow (Rs)	Probability	Cash Flow (Rs)	Probability
4,000	0.30	4,000	0.25	4,000	0.55
5,000	0.40	5,000	0.50	5,000	0.15
6,000	0.30	6,000	0.25	6,000	0.30

CHAPTER 13

Real Options, Investment Strategy and Process

CHAPTER OBJECTIVES

- Understand the capital budgeting process
- Document the policies and practices of companies in India and compare them with that of the companies in developed countries
- Understand the linkage between corporate strategy and investment decisions
- Define strategic real options
- Show the valuation of real options

INTRODUCTION

Capital expenditure or investment planning and control involve a process of facilitating decisions covering expenditures on long-term assets. Since a company's survival and profitability hinges on capital expenditures, especially the major ones, the importance of the capital budgeting or investment process cannot be over-emphasised.[1] A number of managers think that investment projects have strategic elements, and the investment analysis should be conducted within the overall framework of corporate strategy. Some managers feel that the qualitative aspects of investment projects should be given due importance.

In this chapter, we explore the issues relating to the capital budgeting process and practice, and the strategic aspects of capital budgeting. We will answer the following questions. What is the process of capital budgeting that companies employ? What capital budgeting policies and practices do they follow? Is there any link between the corporate strategy and capital budgeting? What are the strategic aspects of capital budgeting? Can the discounted cash flow technique handle the strategic aspects of capital investments? How can we evaluate investment projects that are capable of creating future opportunities and flexibility (options) for companies?

CAPITAL INVESTMENTS

Strictly speaking, **capital investments** should include all those expenditures, which are expected to produce benefits to the firm over a long period of time, and encompass both tangible and intangible assets. Thus R&D (research and development) expenditure is a capital investment. Similarly, the expenditure incurred in acquiring a patent or brand is also a capital investment. In practice, a number of companies follow the traditional definition, covering only expenditures on tangible fixed assets as capital investments (expenditures). The Indian companies are also influenced considerably by accounting conventions and tax regulations in classifying capital expenditures. Large expenditures on R&D, advertisement, or

---

1. This chapter is partially adapted from Pandey, I.M., Capital Budgeting Practices of Indian Companies, *MDI Management Journal,* Vol. 2, No. 1 (Jan. 1989).

employees training, which tend to create valuable intangible assets, may not be included in the definition of capital investments since most of them are allowed to be expensed for tax purposes in the year in which they are incurred. From the point of view of sound decision-making, these expenditures should be treated as capital investments and subjected to proper evaluation.

A number of companies follow the accounting convention to prepare asset wise classification of capital expenditures, which is hardly of much use in decision-making. Some companies classify capital expenditures in a manner, which could provide useful information for decision-making. Their classification is (*i*) replacement, (*ii*) modernisation, (*iii*) expansion, (*iv*) new project, (*v*) research and development, (*vi*) diversification, and (*vii*) cost reduction.

CAPITAL INVESTMENT PLANNING AND CONTROL

At least five phases of capital expenditure planning and control can be identified:

- Identification (or origination) of investment opportunities
- Development of forecasts of benefits and costs
- Evaluation of the net benefits
- Authorisation for progressing and spending capital expenditure
- Control of capital projects.

The available literature puts the maximum emphasises on the evaluation phase. Two reasons may be attributed to this bias. First, this phase is easily amenable to a structured, quantitative analysis. Second, it is considered to be the most important phase by academicians. Practitioners, on the other hand, consider other phases to be more important.[1] The capital investment planning and control phases are discussed below.

Investment Ideas: Who Generates?

Investment opportunities have to be identified or created; they do not occur automatically.[2, 3] Investment proposals of various types may originate at different levels within a firm. Most proposals, in the nature of cost reduction or replacement or process or product improvements take place at plant level. The contribution of top management in generating investment ideas is generally confined to expansion or diversification projects. The proposals may originate systematically or haphazardly in a firm. The proposal for adding a new product may emanate from the marketing department or from the plant manager who thinks of a better way of utilising idle capacity. Suggestions for replacing an old machine or improving the production techniques may arise at the factory level. In view of the fact that

enough investment proposals should be generated to employ the firm's funds fully well and efficiently, a systematic procedure for generating proposals may be evolved by a firm.

In a number of Indian companies, the investment ideas are generated at the plant level. The contribution of the board in idea generation is relatively insignificant. However, some companies depend on the board for certain investment ideas, particularly those that are strategic in nature. Other companies depend on research centres for investment ideas.

Is the investment idea generation primarily a bottom-up process in India? In UK, both bottom-up, as well as top-down processes exist.[4] The Indian practice is more like that in USA. Project initiation is a bottom-up process in USA, with about more than three-fourths of investment proposals coming from divisional management and plant personnel.[5] However, we should note that the small number of ideas generated at the top may represent a high percentage in terms of investment value, so that what looks to be an entirely bottom-up process may not be really so.

Indian companies use a variety of methods to encourage idea generation. The most common methods used are: (*a*) management sponsored studies for project identification, (*b*) formal suggestion schemes, and (*c*) consulting advice. Most companies use a combination of methods. The offer of financial incentives for generating investment idea is not a popular practice. Other efforts employed by companies in searching investment ideas are: (*a*) review of researches done in the country or abroad, (*b*) conducting market surveys, and (*c*) deputing executives to international trade fairs for identifying new products/technology.

Once the investment proposals have been identified, they are be submitted for scrutiny. Many companies specify the time for submitting the proposals for scrutiny.

Developing Cash Flow Estimates

Estimation of cash flows is a difficult task because the future is uncertain. Operating managers with the help of finance executives should develop cash flow estimates. The risk associated with cash flows should also be properly handled and should be taken into account in the decision making process. Estimation of cash flows requires collection and analysis of all qualitative and quantitative data, both financial and non-financial in nature. Large companies would generally have a management information system (MIS) providing such data.

Executives in practice do not always have clarity about estimating cash flows. A large number of companies do not include additional working capital while estimating the investment project cash flows. A number of companies also mix up financial

1. Hastie, K. L., One Businessman's View of Capital Budgeting, *Financial Management,* 3 (Writer 1974), pp. 36, 196.
2. Haynes, W.W. and Solomon, M.B., A Misplaced Emphasis in Capital Budgeting, *Quarterly Review of Economics and Business,* (Jan.-Feb. 1964), pp. 95–106.
3. King, P., Is the Emphasis of Capital Budgeting Theory Misplaced? *Journal of Business Finance and Accounting,* (Spring 1975), pp. 69–82.
4. Rockley, L.E., *Investment for Profitability,* Business Books, 1973.
5. Petty, J.W., and Scott, D.F., Capital Budgeting Practices in large US Firms: A Retrospective Analysis and Update, in Derkindem and Crum (Ed.), *Readings in Strategy for Corporate Investments,* Pitman, 1981.

flows with operating flows. Although companies claim to estimate cash flows on incremental basis, some of them make no adjustment for sale proceeds of existing assets while computing the project's initial cost. The prevalence of such conceptual confusion has been observed even in the developed countries. For example, in the seventies, a number of UK companies were treating depreciation as cash flows.[1]

In the past, most Indian companies chose an arbitrary period of 5 or 10 years for forecasting cash flows. This was so because companies in India largely depended on government-owned financial institutions for financing their projects, and these institutions required 5 to 10 years forecasts of the project cash flows.

Project Evaluation

The evaluation of projects should be performed by a group of experts who have no axe to grind. For example, the production people may be generally interested in having the most modern type of equipments and increased production even if productivity is expected to be low and goods cannot be sold. This attitude can bias their estimates of cash flows of the proposed projects. Similarly, marketing executives may be too optimistic about the sales prospects of goods manufactured, and overestimate the benefits of a proposed new product. It is, therefore, necessary to ensure that projects are scrutinised by an impartial group and that objectivity is maintained in the evaluation process.

A company in practice should take all care in selecting a method or methods of investment evaluation. The criterion selected should be a true measure of the investment's profitability (in terms of cash flows), and it should lead to the net increase in the company's wealth (that is, its benefits should exceed its cost adjusted for time value and risk). It should also be seen that the evaluation criteria do not discriminate between the investment proposals. They should be capable of ranking projects correctly in terms of profitability. The net present value method is theoretically the most desirable criterion as it is a true measure of profitability; it generally ranks projects correctly and is consistent with the wealth maximisation criterion. In practice, however, managers' choice may be governed by other practical considerations also.

A formal financial evaluation of proposed capital expenditures has become a common practice among companies in India. A number of companies have a formal financial evaluation of almost three-fourths of their investment projects. Most companies subject more than 50 per cent of the projects to some kind of formal evaluation. However, projects, such as replacement or worn-out equipment, welfare and statutorily required projects below certain limits, small value items like office equipment or furniture, replacement of assets of immediate requirements, etc., are not often formally evaluated.

Methods of Evaluation As regards the use of evaluation methods, most Indian companies use payback criterion. In addition to payback and/or other methods, companies also use internal rate of return (IRR) and net present (NPV) methods. A few companies use accounting rate of return (ARR) method. IRR is the second most popular technique in India.

The major reason for payback to be more popular than the DCF techniques is the executives' lack of familiarity with DCF techniques. Other factors are lack of technical people and sometimes unwillingness of top management to use the DCF techniques. One large manufacturing and marketing organisation, for example, thinks that conditions of its business are such that the DCF techniques are not needed. By business conditions the company perhaps means its marketing nature, and its products being in seller's markets. Another company feels that replacement projects are very frequent in the company, and therefore, it is not necessary to use the DCF techniques for such projects. Both these companies have fallacious approaches towards investment analysis. They should subject all capital expenditures to formal evaluation.

The practice of companies in India regarding the use of evaluation criteria is similar to that in USA. Almost four-fifths of US firms use either the internal rate of return or net present value models, but only about one-fifth use such discounting techniques without using the payback period or average rate of return methods.[2] The tendency of US firms to use naive techniques as supplementary tools has also been reported in recent studies. However, firms in USA have come to depend increasingly on the DCF techniques, particularly IRR. The British companies use both DCF techniques and return on capital, sometimes in combination sometimes solely, in their investment evaluation; the use of payback is widespread.[3] In recent years the use of the DCF methods has increased in UK, and NPV is more popular than IRR.[4] However, this increase has not reduced the importance of the traditional methods such as payback and return on investment. Payback continues to be employed by almost all companies.

One significant difference between practices in India and USA is that payback is used in India as a 'primary' method and IRR/NPV as a 'secondary' method, while it is just the reverse in USA. Indian managers feel that payback is a convenient method of communicating an investment's desirability, and it best protects the recovery of capital—a scarce commodity in the developing countries.

Cut-off Rate In the implementation of a sophisticated evaluation system, the use of a minimum required rate of return is necessary. The required rate of return or the opportunity cost of capital should be based on the riskiness of cash flows of the investment proposal; it is compensation to investors for bearing the risk in supplying capital to finance investment proposals.

Not all companies in India specify the minimum acceptable

1. Rockley, *op. cit.*
2. Schall, L.D., Sundem, G.L. and Geijsbeak, W.R., Survey and Analysis of Capital Budgeting Methods, *Journal of Finance,* (March 1978), pp. 281–87.
3. Rockley, *op. cit.*
4. Pike, R.H., *Capital Budgeting Survey: An Update,* Bradford University Discussion Paper, 1992.

rate of return. Some of them compute the weighted average cost of capital (WACC) as the discount rate. Unfortunately, all companies do not follow correct methodology of calculating the WACC. Almost all companies use the book value weights.

Business executives in India are becoming increasingly aware of the importance of the cost of capital, but they perhaps lack clarity about its computation. Arbitrary judgment of management also seems to play a role in the assessment of the cost of capital. The fallacious tendency of equating borrowing rate with minimum required rate of return also persists in the case of some companies.[1] In USA, a little more than 50 per cent companies have been found using WACC as cut-off rate.[2] In UK, only a very small percentage of firms were found attempting any calculation of the cost of capital.[3] As in USA and UK, companies in India have a tendency to equate the minimum rate with interest rate or cost of specific source of finance. The phenomenon of depending on management judgement for the assessment of the cost of capital is prevalent as much in USA and UK as in India.

Recognition of Risk

The assessment of risk is an important aspect of an investment evaluation. In theory, a number of techniques are suggested to handle risk. Some of them, such as the computer simulation technique are not only quite involved but are also expensive to use. How do companies handle risk in practice?

Companies in India consider the following as the four most important contributors of investment risk: *selling price*, *product demand*, *technological changes* and *government policies*. India is fast changing from sellers' market to buyers' market as competition is intensifying in a large number of products; hence uncertainty of selling price and product demand are being realised as important risk factors. Uncertain government policies (in areas such as custom and excise duty and import policy, the foreign investment etc.), of course, are a continuous source of investment risk in developing countries like India.

Sensitivity analysis and **conservative forecasts** are two equally important and widely used methods of handling investment risk in India. Each of these techniques is used by a number of Indian companies with other methods while many other companies use either sensitivity analysis or conservative forecasts with other methods. Some companies also use shorter payback and inflated discount rates (risk-adjusted discount rates).

In USA, risk adjusted discount rate is more popular than the use of payback and sensitivity analysis.[4, 5] The British companies hardly use sensitivity analysis.[6] The contrasts in risk evaluation practices in India, on the one hand, and USA and UK, on the other, are sharp and significant. Given the complex nature of risk factors in developing countries, risk evaluation cannot be handled through a single number such as the NPV calculation based on conservative forecasts or risk-adjusted discount rate. Managers must know the impact on project profitability of the full range of critical variables. An American businessman states: "there appear to be more corporations using sensitivity analysis than surveys indicate. In some cases firms may not know that what they are undertaking is called 'sensitivity analysis', and it probably is not in the sophisticated, computer oriented sense... Typically, analysts or middle managers eliminate the alternative assumptions and solutions in order to simplify the decision-making process for higher management."[7]

Capital Rationing

Indian companies, by and large, do not have to reject profitable investment opportunities for lack of funds, despite the capital markets not being so well developed. This may be due to the existence of the government-owned financial system, which is always ready to finance profitable projects. Indian companies do not use any mathematical technique to allocate resources under capital shortage which may sometimes arise on account of internally imposed restrictions or management's reluctance to raise capital from outside. Priorities for allocating resources are determined by management, based on the strategic need for and profitability of projects.

Authorisation

It may not be feasible in practice to specify standard administrative procedures for approving investment proposals. Screening and selection procedures may differ from one company to another. When large sums of capital expenditures are involved, the authority for the final approval may rest with top management. The approval authority may be delegated for certain types of investment projects. Delegation may be affected subject to the amount of outlay, prescribing the selection criteria and holding the authorised person accountable for results.

Funds are appropriated for capital expenditures after the final selection of investment proposals. The formal plan for the appropriation of funds is called the **capital budget**. Generally, the senior management tightly controls the capital expenditures. Budgetary controls may be rigidly exercised, particularly when a company is facing liquidity problem. The expected expenditure should become a part of the annual capital budget, integrated with the overall budgetary system.

Top management should ensure that funds are spent in accordance with appropriations made in the capital budget. Funds for the purpose of project implementation should be spent only after seeking formal permission from the financial manager or any other authorised person.

1. Pandey, I.M., Financing Decision: A Survey of Management Understanding, *Management Review: Economic & Political Weekly,* (Feb. 1984), pp. 27–31.
2. Petty and Scott, *op. cit.*
3. Rockley, *op. cit.*
4. Schall et al., *op. cit.*
5. Petty and Scott, *op. cit.*
6. Rockley, *op. cit.*
7. Hastie, *op. cit.*

In India, as in UK, the power to commit a company to specific capital expenditure and to examine proposals is limited to a few top corporate officials. However, the duties of processing the examination and evaluation of a proposal are somewhat spread throughout the corporate management staff in case of a few companies.

Senior management tightly control capital spending. **Budgetary control** is also exercised rigidly. The expected capital expenditure proposals invariably become a part of the annual capital budget in all companies. Some companies also have formal **long-range plans** covering a period of 3 to 5 years. Some companies feel that long-range plans have a significant influence on the evaluation and funding of capital expenditure proposals.

Control and Monitoring

A **capital investment reporting system** is required to review and monitor the performance of investment projects after completion and during their life. The follow-up comparison of the actual performance with original estimates not only ensures better forecasting but also helps to sharpen the techniques for improving future forecasts. Based on the follow-up feedback, the company may reappraise its projects and take remedial action.

Indian companies practice control of capital expenditure through the use of regular project reports. Some companies require quarterly reporting, others need monthly, half-yearly and yet a few companies require continuous reporting. In most of the companies, the evaluation reports include information on expenditure to date, stage of physical completion, and approved and revised total cost.

Most of the companies in reappraising investment proposals, consider comparison between actual and forecast capital cost, saving and rate of return. They perceive the following advantages of reappraisal: (*i*) improvement in profitability by positioning the project as per the original plan; (*ii*) ascertainment of errors in investment planning which can be avoided in future; (*iii*) guidance for future evaluation of projects; and (*iv*) generation of cost consciousness among the project team. A few companies abandon the project if it becomes uneconomical. The power of review is generally invested with the top executives of the companies in India.

QUALITATIVE FACTORS AND JUDGEMENT IN CAPITAL BUDGETING

In theory, the use of sophisticated techniques is emphasised since they maximise value to shareholders. In practice, however, companies, although tending to shift to the formal methods of evaluation, give considerable importance to qualitative factors. Most companies in India are guided, one time or other, by three qualitative factors: *urgency, strategy*, and *environment*. All companies think that urgency is the most important

consideration while a large number thinks that strategy plays a significant role. Some companies also consider intuition, security and social considerations as important qualitative factors. Companies in USA consider qualitative factors like employees' morals and safety, investor and customer image, or legal matters important in investment analysis.[1]

Due to the significance of qualitative factors, judgement seems to play an important role. Some typical responses of companies about the role of judgement are:

- Vision of judgement of the future plays an important role. Factors like market potential, possibility of technology change, trend of government policies etc., which are judgemental, play important role.
- The opportunities and constraints of selecting a project, its evaluation of qualitative and quantitative factors, and the weightage on every bit of pros and cons, cost-benefit analysis, etc., are essential elements of judgement. Thus, it is inevitable for any management decision.
- Judgement and intuition should definitely be used when a decision of choice has to be made between two or more, closely beneficial projects, or when it involves changing the long-term strategy of the company. For routine matters, liquidity and profits should be preferred over judgement.
- It (judgement) plays a very important role in determining the reliability of figures with the help of qualitative methods as well as other known financial matters affecting the projects.

We feel that what businessmen call intuition or (simply) judgement is in fact *informed judgement* based on experience. A firm growing in a favourable economic environment will be able to identify profitable opportunities without making NPV or IRR computation. Businessmen often act more intelligently than they talk.

INVESTMENT DECISIONS AND CORPORATE STRATEGY

Recently, a lot of emphasis has been placed on the view that a business firm facing a complex and changing environment will benefit immensely in terms of improved quality of decision-making if capital budgeting decisions are taken in the context of its overall corporate strategy.[2, 3] This approach provides the decision-maker with a central theme or a big picture to keep in mind at all times as a guideline for effectively allocating corporate financial resources. As argued by a chief financial officer:[4]

Allocating resources to investments without a sound concept of divisional and corporate strategy is a lot like throwing darts in a dark room.

Similarly, an American businessman argues as follows:[5]

1. Porwal, L.S. *Capital Budgeting in India*, Sultan Chand, 1976.
2. Derkindern, F.G.J. and Crum, R.L., *Capital Budgeting as an Open System*, in Derkindern and Crum, (ed.), *op. cit.*
3. Pandey, I.M., *Financial Policy and Strategic Management*, Working Paper 85–1, Kansas State University, USA, 1985.
4. Hall, W.K., *Changing Perspective on the Capital Budgeting Process*, Long-range Planning, *(Winter 1974)*, pp. 36–44.
5. Hastie, *op. cit.*

We have erred too long by exaggerating the 'improvement in decision-making' that might result from the adoption of DCF or other refined evaluation techniques. What is needed are approximate answers to the precise problems rather than precise answer to the approximate problems. There is little value in refining an analysis that does not consider the most appropriate alternative and does not utilise sound assumptions. *Management should spend its time improving the quality of assumptions and assuring that all the strategic questions have been asked,* rather than implementing and using more refined evaluation techniques. (Emphasis added).

In fact a close linkage between capital expenditures, at least major ones, and strategic positioning exists which has led some researchers to conclude that the set of problems companies refer to as capital budgeting is a task for general management rather than financial analyst.[1] Some recent empirical works amply support the practitioners concern for strategic considerations in capital expenditure planning and control.[2] It is therefore a myopic point of view to ignore strategic dimensions or to assume that they are separable from the problem of efficient resource allocations addressed by capital budgeting theory.[3]

Most companies in India consider strategy as an important factor in investment evaluation. What are the specific experiences of the companies in India in this regard? Examples of six companies showing how they defined their corporate strategy are given as follows:

- To remain market leader by highest quality and remunerative prices. This company undertook the production of a new range of product (which was marginally profitable) for competitive reasons.
- To have moderate growth for saving taxes and to set up plants for forward and backward integration.
- Our strategy is to grow, diversify and expand in related fields of technology only. Any project, which is within the strategy and satisfied profitability yardsticks is accepted. This company found a low-profit chemical production proposal acceptable since it came within its technological capabilities.
- Strategy involves analysis of the company's present position, nature of its relationship with the environmental forces, company's business philosophy and evaluation of company's strong and weak points.
- To take up new projects for expansion in the fields, which are closer to present projects or technology. This company rejected a profitable project (of deep sea fishing and ship building) while it accepted a marginally profitable project (of paint systems) since it was very close to its current heat transfer technology.
- To stay in industrial intermediate and capital goods line, and in the process to achieve three-fold profits in real terms over a 5-year period. This company rejected a highly profitable project (of manufacturing mopeds) since it was a consumer durable and accepted a marginal project (of cold formed structured purlins).

One more example is that of an Indian subsidiary of a giant multinational that looks for projects in high technology, priority sector. This company even sold one of its profitable non-priority sector division to a sister concern to maintain its high-tech priority sector profile.

Strategic management has emerged as a systematic approach in properly positioning companies in the complex environment by balancing multiple objectives. In practice, therefore, a comprehensive capital expenditure planning and control system will not simply focus on profitability, as assumed by modern finance theory, but also on growth, competition, balance of products, total risk diversification, and managerial capability and flexibility. There are umpteen examples in the developing countries like India where unprofitable ventures are not divested even by the private sector companies because of their desirability from the point of view of consumers and employees, in particular and society, in general. Such considerations are not at all less important than profitability since the ultimate survival of companies (and certainly that of management) hinges on them. One must appreciate the dynamics of complex forces influencing resource allocation in practice; it is not simply the use of the most refined DCF techniques.

Certain other practical considerations are as follows:

- Apart from the profitability of the project, other features like its (project's) critical utility in the production of the main product, strategic importance of capturing the new product first, adapting to the changing market environments, have a definite bearing on investment decisions.
- Technological developments play a critical role in guiding investment decisions. Government policies and concessions also have a bearing on these.
- Investment in production equipment is given top priority among the existing products and the new project. Capital investment for expansion in existing lines where market potential is proved is given first priority. Capital investment in new projects is given the next priority. Capital investment for buildings, furniture, cars, office equipments etc., is done on the basis of availability of funds and immediate needs.

These statements reinforce the need for a strategic framework for problem solving under complexities and the relevance of strategic considerations in investment planning. It also implies that resource allocation is not simply a matter of choosing the most profitable new projects as shown by the DCF analysis. What is being stressed is that the strategic framework provides a higher-level screening and an integrating perspective to the whole system of capital expenditure planning and control. Once strategic questions have been answered, investment proposals may be subjected to the DCF evaluation.

1. Bower, J.F., *Managing the Resource Allocation Process,* Richard D. Irwin, 1972.
2. Donaldson, G, *Managing Corporate Wealth,* Praeger, 1984.
3. Petty, D.W., Scott, D.F. and Bird, M.M., Capital Expenditure Decision-Making Process of Large Corporations, *Engineering Economist,* (Spring 1975), pp. 159–72.

MANAGERIAL FLEXIBILITY AND COMMITMENT

Most often we hear managers saying: "Our plans and decisions are always clouded by uncertainty"; "Investment commitments have tremendous competitive value, although you have to pay a cost"; "There is nothing like now or never; we become wiser by waiting for certain decisions"; "Flexibility helps to capture future opportunities"; "Relinquishing an on-going project or liquidating a business may be a good opportunity to bail out a firm". They consider these issues as strategic. In practice, managers consider strategic aspects of investment projects as crucial for making the investment decisions. They will always like to have right to expand; right to exit; right to exchange investments since these rights provide flexibility to managers. Because of uncertainty, managers endeavour to build flexibility into a capital investment. Managers also like to commit doing things in response to competitive, technological, or environmental forces. They like to do things differently from others. These commitments that may be contingent upon certain events taking place, provide managers with flexibility, operating freedom and opportunities to proactively gain an advantage over competition. The discounted cash flow (DCF) method of investment analysis is unable of handling managerial flexibility and commitments and other strategic aspects in investment projects. How do we evaluate strategic investments that incorporate flexibility and commitments?

STRATEGIC REAL OPTIONS

There are a number of investments that may contain elements that could provide valuable opportunities to a firm in the future. Some investments may not be profitable but for the attractive opportunities that they are capable of creating in the future. For example, a chemical company may invest in R&D that may help it to develop new chemical and exploit it to introduce new products in the market. Similarly, a fast-moving-consumer-products company may invest in a brand to leverage sales of its other products. A fertiliser company may install a small plant to manufacture and sell caprolectum to see the reaction of the market, and scale up the plant in future if demand is high. These opportunities are highly valuable and must be identified while evaluating capital investments. Investments with potential future opportunities or flexibility are more valuable than investments without such strategic elements.

Real options are those strategic elements in investments that help creating flexibility of operations, or that have the potential of generating profitable opportunities in the future for the firm. Real options provide discretion to managers to take certain investment decisions, without any obligation, for a given price. We may clarify that real options are not confined to real assets only. Patent, R&D, brands etc. are examples of assets that have a value to the owner. The capital investments should be viewed as strategic investments that incorporate real options. Hence the value of a capital investment will also include the value of the strategic elements in the investment. Valuing real options is real challenge for managers.

The option pricing theory provides a framework for valuing strategic investments. We have discussed the valuation of financial options in Chapter 7. The methods of valuing real options are the same as the financial options although it is difficult to identify the values of certain inputs in case of real options. An investment with real option consists of two values: the value of cash flows from the project's assets plus the value of any future opportunity (option) arising from holding the asset. Like in a financial option, an **exchangeable asset** underlies a real option. For example, the *underlying asset* in the case of an option to expand is the value added through expansion. The cost of expansion is the *exercise price*.

Some capital investments have **embedded options.** Managers must recognise and value these options and exercise them when it is advantageous to do so. A firm can attain flexibility and make commitments by intentionally creating simple options into investment projects. It can obtain flexibility by creating long positions in call or put options. For example, right to expand or right to enter a new venture in the future at a given price is a long position in call option, and right to abandon or right to liquidate in the future at a given price is a long position in put option. Managerial commitments are akin to short positions in call or put options. A firm may agree to disinvest (short call) or invest (short put) contingent upon the action of another party. Some large investment projects may involve **complex options**. There may be options on options, or options may be interdependent or mutually exclusive. Managers must play an active role in identifying or creating options, valuing them, monitoring them and using them appropriately to create values for the company.

Growth Options

In practice, managers may accept investment projects that have negative or insignificant NPV, but may enable companies to find opportunities in the future that add considerable profitability and value. These projects are said to have **growth options.** Examples of growth options include an initial investment in a new (domestic or foreign) market with the intention to expand later on, investment in R&D to develop possible new technology and product, carrying out an expensive advertisement campaign to push sales, acquisition of a patent to have protected returns, acquiring rights over a copper mine, or acquiring a vacant land to develop it in the future. Such investments are called strategic since they define the competitive position of the firm. Options to expand are useful for achieving the future growth. Such options allow the firm to make further investments later on if the business conditions are favourable. The advantage of making investment in stages, rather than at once, is that the firm gains knowledge about the project's true profitability and collects information that may help to unravel uncertainty surrounding the project. Option to expand in the future or make investment in stages provides the manufacturing and marketing flexibility to the firm. Consider an example of an option to expand.

Magic Foods Limited specialises in ready-to-make South Indian dishes. It is toying with an idea of introducing a breakfast cereal. There is a lot of uncertainty about the demand for the breakfast cereal since most Indians like the traditional breakfast foods such as idli, bada, dosa, puri sag, paratha, khaman, dhokala etc. There are indications that the middle and upper class Indians have started going for the Western-type breakfast cereals. Magic

Foods Limited anticipates the demand for such cereals to go up since India has strong middle class buyers. The company will initially introduce the cereal in two cosmopolitan cities, Delhi and Mumbai, to judge the reaction of consumers and the pattern of demand. The estimated cost of this introduction is Rs 30 million and the present value of the estimated cash inflows is Rs 21 million. Thus the project has a negative NPV of Rs 9 million. Management anticipates that if the company does not introduce the cereal, the competitors will do so in the future. Introducing the cereal now will give the company the first mover's advantage, and if the demand picks up, it will have the option to scale up production in the future. The cost of expansion to the company is estimated as Rs 50 million and the present value of the cash flows over the project's anticipated life of five years is expected to be Rs 45 million. This project also has a negative NPV. Thus, on the face of it, the entire investment proposition looks an unattractive investment. But two points may be noticed. First, the second investment is an option, and the company need to exercise it (that is, invest Rs 50 million) if the expected NPV is positive. Second, the demand for the breakfast cereal is highly uncertain, and hence, investment can turn out to be highly beneficial to the company if the market picks up.

Valuing option to expand We should value the second investment as an option. The expansion project is the underlying asset, which has a value of Rs 45 million. The exercise price is the cost of investment, viz., Rs 50 million. The investment is out-of-the-money since the exercise price is higher than the value of the underlying asset. Since the market for cereal is quite uncertain, the value of the project will fluctuate. Let us assume that the expansion project will have average standard deviation of 30 per cent. Based on these assumptions, we have the following parameters to value the option:

S_0 = present value of cash flows = Rs 45 million

E = exercise price = Rs 50 million

t = 5 years

σ = Standard deviation = 0.30

r_f = risk-free rate of return = 8 per cent

Using the Black-Scholes method of option pricing, we obtain the following results:

d_1	0.7746
d_2	0.1038
$N(d_1)$	0.7807
$N(d_2)$	0.5413
Call value	Rs 17 million

The value of call option is found as follows:

$$C_0 = S_0 N(d_1) - E e^{-r_f t} N(d_2)$$
$$= 45 \times 0.7807 - 50 e^{(-0.08 \times (5)} \times 0.5413$$
$$= 35.13 - 18.13 = \text{Rs } 17 \text{ million}$$

The value of the option to expand is Rs 17 million. The project without considering the expansion option has a negative

NPV. The value of the project with the option to expand is:

Value of the project with option to expand

= NPV of the project + Value of option to expand

= (−30 + 21) + 17 = Rs 8 million

Magic Foods Limited should introduce the product, in spite of a negative NPV, since it will acquire much more valuable option.

Valuing a patent Patents give valuable options to firms to achieve growth and create value. Firms, through R&D efforts, can develop technology, products or services and can patent them. A patent allows a firm to have exclusive right for certain number of years to develop and market a product or service. Thus patent may be viewed as a call option. The firm will develop the product only if it creates value; that is, the present value of cash inflows exceeds the cost of introducing the product. Let us consider an example.

Illustration 13.1: The Value of a Patent

Sodrux is a pharmaceutical firm that posses a patent on a drug called Acidex. It is an approved drug, and Sodrux can produce and market it. The firm has the patent on drug for 15 years, and after this period, any pharmaceutical company can produce it. The firm estimates that it will have to incur Rs 125 million (or Rs 12.5 crore) to develop and market the drug. Based on the estimates of potential market and price, the present value of the expected cash flow from the sale of the drug is Rs 167 million. A simulation study shows that the average variance in the value of the project is 0.268. The current yield on 15-year government bonds is 7.8 per cent. What is the value of the patent to the company?

Notice that the life of patent is 15 years. The firm will earn patent-protected returns only during the life of the patent. Delay in introducing the drug will cause the loss of cash flows. The loss of cash flows is like the payment of dividends in the case of a stock option. Assuming that cash flows occur evenly over the life of the project, the cost of initial delay will be 1/15, it will be 1/14 next year and so on.

The following are the inputs for valuing the patent as a call option:

S_0 = the present value of cash flows = Rs 167 million

E = Cost of developing the drug = Rs 125 million

T = life of the patent = 15 years

r_f = 7.8%

σ^2 = Variance = 0.268

Expected cost of delay = y = 1/15 = 6.67%

We can use the Black-Scholes formula to value the patent. We obtain the following output:

d_1	1.2318
d_2	−0.7732
$N(d_1)$	0.8910
$N(d_2)$	0.2197
Call Value	Rs 46.21 million

The value of the patent, which is analogous to a call option, is:

$$C_0 = S_0 e^{-yt} N(d_1) - E e^{-r_f t} N(d_2)$$
$$= 167 e^{(-0.0667)(15)} \times 0.8910 - 125 e^{(-0.078) \times (15)} \times 0.2197$$
$$= 167 \times 0.3680 \times 0.8910 - 125 \times 0.3104 \times 0.2197$$
$$= 54.71 - 8.51 = \text{Rs } 46.20 \text{ million}$$

Abandonment Option

Most investments relating to expansions or diversifications require large amount of funds. Once the decision has been made and funds have been committed, these decisions cannot be reversed without incurring huge losses. When uneconomical investment projects are sold or discarded, it is quite difficult to get a good value. In case of some projects the firm may have to incur substantial dismantling cost. In such projects, which may turn out to be quite unprofitable under adverse economic conditions, the firm may like to have the option to abandon the projects without incurring immense losses. The right to abandon gives flexibility to the firm to exit without much loss. Let us consider an example.

National Chemicals Company (NCC) is considering building a new plant to diversify into the production of urea. The company has two proposals with regard to technology. Proposal *A* is to build a custom-designed, integrated plant using the latest technology that produces urea and by-products in the most economical way. A less expensive and less profitable scheme, Proposal *B*, is to build a standard plant for manufacturing urea. If economic conditions turn out to be unfavourable, and the firm wants to exit from the urea business, it will be difficult for the firm to sell the plant built under Proposal *A*. But it may be able to sell the plant built under Proposal *B* because of its low investment cost. The government policy has a major impact on the company's decision. If the current government policy of imports restrictions and fixing the price of urea equal to the cost plus 12 per cent profit on net worth at 85 per cent capacity continues, Proposal *A* is the better choice. On the contrary, if the current policy changes and the government allows imports and market-determined urea prices, the company may prefer Proposal *B* now so that it has an option to abandon the project by selling it to a larger player in the urea market. Proposal *B* has, in effect, a put option attached to it, giving the flexibility to abandon the proposed operation in favour of some other activity.

Valuing the option to abandon: How do we value the option to abandon? Suppose the present value of Proposal *B* is Rs 100 million without the abandonment option. If the market conditions turn out to be favourable and demand for urea is high, the value of the project at year 1 increases by 30 per cent to Rs 130 million. On the contrary, if the market conditions are unfavourable and demand is low, the project's value declines by 40 per cent to Rs 60 million. Suppose if NCC does not want to continue with the project, it can sell it for Rs 80 million. You can recognise that if demand for urea is low at year 1, then the project value is Rs 60 million, and it is beneficial for NCC to abandon the project and realise Rs 80 million. The value of option when the company exercises it will be Rs 20 million (Rs 80 million minus Rs 60 million). However, NCC will continue with the project if demand is high, as the company will lose value by exercising the option. Figure 13.1 shows the future values and payoff of Proposal *B* with the abandonment value.

What is the present value of the option? We can use the binomial method to value NCC's option to abandon since it involves only two possible outcomes. As discussed in Chapter 7, we assume risk-neutrality for valuing the abandonment option. Under the assumption of risk-neutrality, investors will expect to earn the risk-free rate of return. Let us assume that this rate is 8 per cent. We can calculate the probability of high demand (say, *p*) for urea as follows:

Year 0	Year 1	Pay-off in Year 1
100	130	0
	60	80 − 60 = 20

Figure 13.1: Values of Proposal *B*

$$\text{Expected return} = 8\% = p \times 30\% + (1-p) \times -40\%$$
$$p = 68.8\%$$

The probability of high demand is 0.686 (68.8%) and low demand: $1 - 0.686 = 0.314$ or 31.4 per cent. We know that at the end of the year, the pay-off to the put option will be either Rs 20 million or zero. Therefore, the expected pay-off at year 1 is:

Expected pay-off = $(p \times 0) + [(1 - p) \times 20] = (0.686 \times 0) + (0.313 \times 20) =$ Rs 6.28 million

The expected pay-off occurs at year 1; hence the present value of the expected pay-off is: $6.28/1.08 =$ Rs 5.81 million. This is the value of the abandonment (put) option. Hence, the value of the project with the abandonment option is: $100 + 5.81 =$ Rs 105.81 million.

Let us consider another example and show the application of the Black-Scholes method in valuing the abandonment option.

Illustration 13.2: The Value of Abandonment Option

Suppose that the government of Uttaranchal has asked Jaisurya Hydraulic Power Company (JHPC) to build a hydropower generation plant near Joshimath. The plant will cost Rs 2,000 million. The project will have a life of 25 years. The present value of the project's cash flows is expected to be Rs 1,850 million. Since the project has a negative NPV of Rs 150 million, JHPC is not interested in building the plant. As an incentive to the company, the Uttaranchal government agrees that the company will have option to sell the plant to the government at Rs 1,800 million at the end of ten years. Though this amount is less than the investment (Rs 2,000 million) that JHPC will make, but it will restrict the company's loss. Since the company has the option to sell the plant to the government at a specified price at a specified time—at the end of 10 years, this is a European put option. What is the value of this put (abandonment) option to JHPC? We can use the Balck-Scholes formula to value this European option.

The price of the underlying asset is the project's present value, viz., Rs 1,850 million. The exercise price is the abandonment value of Rs 1,800. The time to maturity is 10 years. We need two more input parameters: the project volatility and the risk-free rate. It is quite difficult to determine the project volatility since it has no traded values. We can simulate the project values under different scenarios and determine the volatility. Suppose the project value is estimated to have a standard deviation of 30 per cent. Let us assume that the risk-free rate is 8 per cent.

We must also note one more factor before we determine the value of the option. An investment project's cash flows have the same effect as dividends on the value of a stock option. A dividend payment before the option matures reduces the ex-dividend price of the underlying asset as well as affects the option payoff at maturity. The option pricing method should account for this effect.

Note that the project has a definite life of 25 years. As the project's life goes on, its present value will decline over time. For simplicity, we may assume that this will be proportional to the time left on the project: 1/ remaining life of the project = 1/25 = 4.0 per cent. This rate is equivalent to dividend yield in case of a stock option. We can now use the Black-Scholes formula to determine the value of abandonment option. We obtain the following results:

d_1	0.9249
d_2	–0.0238
$N(d_1)$	0.8225
$N(d_2)$	0.4905
Black-Scholes Put Value	Rs 191.96 million

The value of the put option is calculated as follows:

$$P = Ee^{-r_f t}\left[1 - N(d_2)\right] - Se^{-yt}\left[1 - N(d_1)\right]$$
$$= 1,800e^{(-0.08)(10)}(1 - 0.4905) - 1,850e^{(-0.04)(10)}(1 - 0.8225)$$
$$= (1,800 \times 0.4493 \times 0.5095) - (1,850 \times 0.6703 \times 0.1775)$$
$$= 412.08 - 220.12 = \text{Rs } 191.96 \text{ million}$$

The value of the project with the abandonment option (Rs 191.46 million) is greater than the negative NPV (Rs 150 million) of the project. JHPC should accept the project with the abandonment option.

Timing Option

Suppose that in the JHPC example, there is no abandonment option. Should the company reject the project as it has a negative NPV? If the company management considers the project as a one time, 'now or never' opportunity, it will be tempted to reject the project. In fact, the company has the option to wait and see how economic conditions turn out to be in the future. If the economic conditions become favourable in the future, the company can undertake the project. The firm creates a call option through its approach of wait and see. Deferring an investment helps the firm to receive useful information about the economics and riskiness of the project. With this information, the firm will be in a much better position to decide about the investment project. The timing options (or options to delay) are highly valuable, particularly those firms that operate in highly dynamic economic and competitive environment. Let us consider an example.

Suppose Som Institute of Management (SIM) is considering installing a solar system for heating water in hostels for students. The system will cost Rs 25 lakh and it is expected to save electricity expenses at the current electricity rates by Rs 2.10 lakh forever. At a cost of capital of 10 per cent, the value of savings is: 2.10/0.10 = Rs 21 lakh and the net present value is: 21 – 25 = – Rs 6 lakh. Since NPV is negative, the project is unattractive for SIM. Suppose the electricity rates will fluctuate and the savings may be either Rs 1.20 lakh or Rs 3.50 lakh. If the savings are Rs 1.20, then the net present value is: 1.20/0.10 – 25 = – Rs 13 lakh. The project is unprofitable. On the other hand, if savings turn out to be Rs 3.50 lakh, then the net present value is: 3.50/0.10 – 25 = Rs 10 lakh. The project looks very attractive now. What should SIM management do? Should it reject the project or should it wait and see how the electricity rates change? You may recognise that delaying the investment gives the SIM

management a chance to see how the electricity rates behave. If the electricity rates increase, SIM's savings will be very high. Delaying the project is like an American call option. What is value of this option to SIM?

Valuing option to delay In case of a stock option, we must note that a dividend payment before the call option matures reduces the ex-dividend price of the stock and the call option's payoff at maturity. In the case of a non-dividend paying American call option, it should not be exercised before maturity since it is always more valuable until the maturity. This is not necessarily true in case of dividend paying stocks. If dividend payments are very large, it may be more advantageous to the call option holder to exercise the option just before the ex-dividend date. An investment project's cash flows have the same effect as the payment of dividends on the value of a stock option. The Black-Scholes formula accurately values non-dividend paying options as they are assumed to be exercised at maturity. We can use the Balck-Scholes method, adjusted for the payment of dividends, to value an American call option, but it will not give value of call option exactly. The Binomial method values the American call option more accurately.

Suppose that SIM accepts the solar project. At year 1, there are two alternative possibilities: either the electricity rates increase or decrease. With increase in the electricity rates, SIM will have total cash flow of Rs 38.50 million, i.e., a cash flow of Rs 3.50 million plus a value of Rs 35 million (3.50/0.10). If the electricity rates decline in the first year, SIM will have total cash flow of Rs 13.20 million, i.e., a cash flow of Rs 1.20 million plus a value of Rs 12 million. This is shown in Figure 13.2.

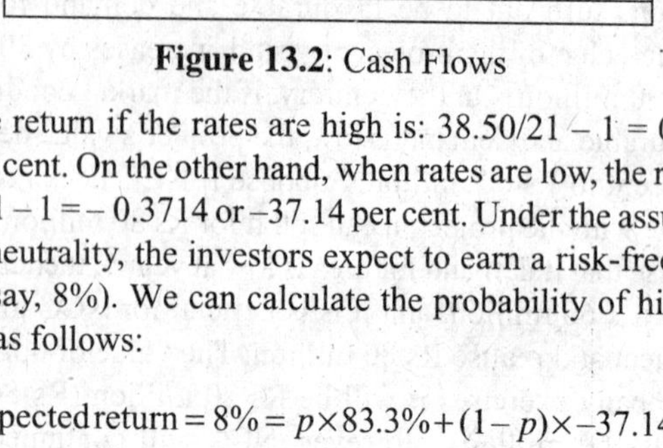

Figure 13.2: Cash Flows

The return if the rates are high is: 38.50/21 – 1 = 0.833 or 83.3 per cent. On the other hand, when rates are low, the return is: 13.20/21 – 1 = – 0.3714 or –37.14 per cent. Under the assumption of risk-neutrality, the investors expect to earn a risk-free rate of return (say, 8%). We can calculate the probability of high rates (say, p) as follows:

$$\text{Expected return} = 8\% = p \times 83.3\% + (1 - p) \times -37.14\%$$
$$p = 37.5\%$$

The probability of high electricity rate is 0.375 (37.5%) and low rate: 1 – 0.375 = 0.625 or 62.5 per cent. We know that at the end of year 1, the pay-off to the put option will be either Rs 10 million or zero. Thus, the expected pay-off is:

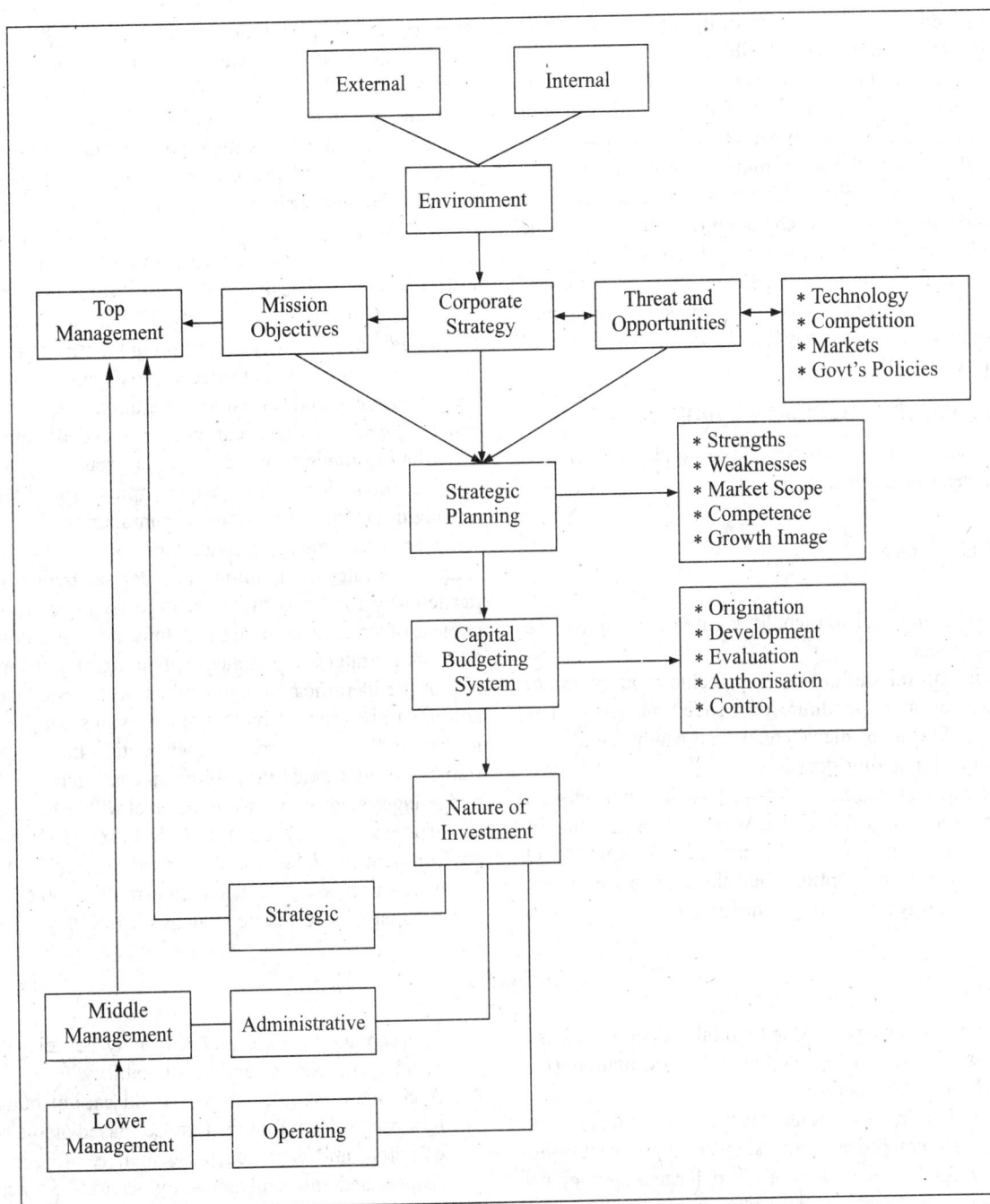

Figure 13.3: Capital investment planning and control model

Expected pay-off $= 0.375 \times 10 + 0.625 \times 0 =$ Rs 3.75 million

The expected pay-off occurs at year 1; hence the present value of the expected pay-off is:

PV of pay-off $= 3.75/1.08 =$ Rs 3.47 million

The option is worth Rs 3.47 million if you keep it open. The project has negative NPV. But it is not sufficient reason for rejecting the project. There is a strategy that is attractive: wait and see.

Flexibility and Operating Options

Most firms would like to build flexibility in their investment projects to be able to do several alternative things in different ways. The flexibility built into the investment projects involves a set of options, called **operating options**. For example, a power-generation company may either build a thermal (coal-based) power plant or a gas power plant or a power plant that could operate on both coal and gas. Building a plant that runs on both coal and gas will be quite expensive, but management will have the flexibility of using either gas or coal depending the fuel prices. The company will gain significantly when the prices of coal and gas are unrelated and vary considerably. The extra cost to create the manufacturing flexibility may be quite valuable to the company.

A company will benefit from the flexibility when it can choose from different raw materials to make the same product or it can use the same material to manufacture different products.

Oil refineries and chemical plants quite often face these situations. Options resulting from flexibility would prove to be very valuable when input or output prices fluctuate enormously. Companies need manufacturing flexibility to maintain their market shares and competitive position in highly fluctuating and unpredictable markets. For example, the quick changes in fashions have made it very difficult for the ready-made garments industry to meet the consumers' changing demand without the flexibility of changing product-mix quickly. To meet the challenge and to have manufacturing flexibility, a large number of companies have invested heavily in sophisticated computer-controlled machines that can easily handle product-mix changes almost instantly.

CAPITAL BUDGETING DECISION-MAKING LEVELS

For planning and control purposes, three levels of decision-making have been identified:

- operating
- administrative, and
- strategic.[1]

Capital budgeting decisions could be categorised into these three decision levels.

Operating capital budgeting may include routine minor expenditures, such as expenditure on office equipment. The lower or the middle level management can easily handle the operating capital budgeting decisions.

Strategic capital budgeting involves large investments such as acquisition of a new business or expansion in a new line of business. Strategic investments are unique and unstructured and involve simple or complex options, and they cast a significant influence on the direction and value of the business. Top management, therefore, generally handles such investments.

Administrative capital budgeting involves medium-size investments such as expenditure on expansion of existing line of business. Administrative capital budgeting decisions are semi-structured in nature, and they may also involve some options, such as option to delay. Generally, the senior management is assigned the responsibility of handling these decisions.

Keeping in view the different decision-making levels, capital expenditures could be classified in a way, which would reflect the appropriate managerial efforts to be placed in planning and controlling them.[2] One useful classification could be: (*i*) strategic projects, (*ii*) expansion in the new line of business, (*iii*) general replacement projects, (*iv*) expansion in the existing line of business, and (*v*) statutory required and welfare projects. Further, each of these categories could be sub-classified according to funds required by the projects.

The model for comprehensive capital expenditure planning and control (Figure 13.3) may be summarised as follows:

Corporate strategy provides the focal point for the firm's long run strategic planning. The capital budgeting system, particularly for large strategic projects, is determined in the context of strategic planning and, thus, it is a top-down process. Corporate strategy and strategic planning play the most crucial role at the identification and evaluation phases. Operating and administrative capital budgeting decisions can be decided at lower/middle level of management within the overall strategic framework and guidelines from top management. The capital budgeting system at lower/middle level will largely be a bottom-up process. It may be noted that external and internal environment provides a context to the company to establish and review its mission's concerns, and multiple objectives, which, in turn, shape its corporate strategy.

SUMMARY

- ❖ The most important aspects of the capital budgeting process are (*i*) identification (*ii*) development, (*iii*) evaluation, (*iv*) authorisation and (*v*) control.

- ❖ Identification of investment ideas is the most critical aspect of the investment process, and should be guided by the overall strategic considerations of a firm. It needs appropriate managerial focus. Each potential idea should be developed into a project.

- ❖ A company should have systems for estimating cash flows of projects. A multi-disciplinary team of managers should be assigned the task of developing cash flow estimates.

- ❖ Once cash flows have been estimated, projects should be evaluated to determine their profitability. Evaluation criteria chosen should correctly rank the projects.

- ❖ Once the projects have been selected they should be monitored and controlled to ensure that they are properly implemented and estimates are realised. Proper authority should exist for capital spending. The top management may supervise critical projects involving large sums of money.

The capital spending authority may be delegated subject to adequate control and accountability.

- ❖ A company should have a sound capital budgeting and reporting system for this purpose. Based on the comparison of actual and expected performance, projects should be reappraised and remedial action should be taken.

- ❖ Companies in practice have a total capital budgeting system including processes for project identification, development, evaluation, authorisation and control. Most companies prepare a capital budget, and integrate it with the overall budgeting system.

- ❖ Companies are increasingly using DCF techniques, but payback remains universally popular for its simplicity and focus on recovery of funds and liquidity.

- ❖ In practice, judgement and qualitative factors also play an important role in investment analysis. A number of companies pay more attention to strategy in the overall selection of projects.

- ❖ Strategic investments are large-scale expansion or diver-

1. Gordon, L. A., Miller D. and Mintzberg M.H., *Normative Models in Decision-Making*, New York: N.A.A., 1985.
2. Ackerman, R. W., *Administrative Science Quarterly*, (September 1970), pp. 341–51.

sification projects, and they involve either by their nature or by managerial actions valuable options. Such options include right to expand, right to abandon, right to delay, right to build new businesses, or right to disinvest or harvest.

❖ Real options create managerial flexibility and commitment. In principle, they can be valued in the same way as financial options are valued. But in practice, it is difficult to get all input parameters for valuing real options. Since large numbers of real assets are not traded in the market, it is quite difficult therefore to get information on the value of the underlying assets and the volatility.

❖ Since real options are valuable, managers must identify them, value them, monitor them and exercise them when it is optimal to do so. Managers generally strive to create flexibility and commitment by building real options into investment projects.

KEY CONCEPTS

Abandonment value	Capital budgeting process	Growth option	Operating options
Administrative capital budgeting	Capital rationing	Long-range planning	Real options
Budgetary control	Conservative forecasts	Managerial flexibility	Sensitivity analysis
Capital budget	Corporate strategy	Operating capital budgeting	Strategic capital budgeting

---

REVIEW QUESTIONS

1. Explain the important steps in the capital budgeting process.
2. Is capital budgeting merely a question of selecting investment projects? Defend your position.
3. What role is played by judgement and qualitative factors in the investment selection? Is it justifiable?
4. Is there any interface between strategy and the capital budgeting system? Why should capital budgeting be seen within a strategic perspective?
5. Briefly discuss the capital budgeting practices of companies in India.
6. What are real options? Give examples of real options. How should real options be evaluated?

PROBLEMS

1. ACC is considering building a cement manufacturing plant in Sri Lanka. The project will cost Rs 800 crore and the present value of the cash flows will be Rs 700 crore. The finance director is not in favour of the proposal since it has a negative NPV. The marketing director, on the other hand, thinks that the potential market for cement in Sri Lanka is enormous. He argues that the company should build the plant now to establish it competitive position and expand after 3 years. The cost of expansion will be Rs 2,000 crore and the present value of cash flows will be Rs 2,100. The demand for cement is expected to fluctuate. The standard deviation of the values of cash flows is estimated to be 32 per cent. The risk-free rate is 7.5 per cent. What is the value of the option to expand?

2. L&T is thinking of entering into a joint venture to build a multi-purpose commercial complex in Dehradun, the capital of Uttaranchal with a local real estate developer. The development is expected to cost Rs 1,200 crore, and have a present value of cash flows of Rs 1,000 crore. The economic life of the project is 30 years. The joint venture will be on 50-50 per cent basis where two partners will share costs and benefits equally. L&T will have a right to sell the complex to the local developer any time over the next seven years for Rs 450 crore. L&T's finance manager finds that the standard deviation in the value of real estate companies is 35 per cent. Assume that the risk-free rate is 7.8 per cent. What is the value of L&T's right to abandon? What should L&T do?

3. A company is analysing an investment project. It will cost Rs 185 crore, and will generate annual cash flows of Rs 24 crore for ever. The company's cost of capital is 10 per cent. A simulation on the project's cash flows shows that the value of the project will have a standard deviation of 25 per cent. Suppose that the company has rights to this project for 25 years. The current yield on 25-year government bond is 5 per cent. What is the project's DCF value? What is the value of the project as an option? Why is there a difference between these two values?

4. A firm is considering a project that is expected to cost Rs 50 crore. The project, on an average, will generate after-tax cash flows of Rs 7.50 crore per annum over its estimated economic life of 15 years. The firm's cost of capital is 15 per cent, and the risk-free rate is 8 per cent. The firm thinks that the cash flows will fluctuate and variance of the value of the cash flows will be 0.0676. As an alternative to taking up the project now, it is thinking of delaying the project. What should the firm do?

5. TechSavvy, a start up, is a high technology company. It has yet to produce and sell products in the market. It has developed an air purifier for residential use, which is technically highly superior as compared to the existing competing products. The company has a patent over the product for 15 years. The cost of introducing the product is estimated to be Rs 250 crore. The current potential market for the product is small since the customers are not very sure about the technical superiority of the product yet. Based on the current demand for the product, the present value of

cash flows is Rs 150 crore. As the customer awareness about the product will increase, the demand is expected to pick up in the future. Assuming different demand scenarios, the standard deviation of the present value of the product is estimated to be 50 per cent. The risk-free rate is 7 per cent. What is the value of the patent?

CASE

Case 13.1: Hind Steel Company Limited (HSCL)

HSCL was formed almost a century ago to carry on steel making business in India. Its manufacturing plants are situated in a state in the Eastern India. The company has a total licensed capacity of 30 million tons.

The vision of the founder of the company was to strengthen India's industrial base through increased productivity and continued application of modern scientific and managerial methods, as well as through systematic growth, in keeping with national aspirations. The company recognizes that profitability provides the main spark for economic activity. The company believes in the protection and safeguarding of the shareholders' investment and ensuring to them a fair return. The policies and objective of the company are also directed towards the effective discharge of its duties and obligations towards employees, customers and community.

Although the company's major objective is to earn higher rates of return on its investments, capital projects have been sometimes undertaken even if return on investment has been less than the cut-off rate. The guiding principle has been the optimization of the system as a whole rather than optimization of a sub-system.

Capital Expenditure Planning and Control

The planning horizon of the company is five years. It has a rolling plan for its capital expenditures. In the rolling plan, the estimates of capital expenditures for the next five years are made every year. A review of expenditure and budget shortfall or excess is made in December-January. On the basis of this information, revised estimates of expenditure are prepared for the ongoing projects.

Capital budget: Annual capital expenditure budget consists of two parts: (1) *Carry over items*: These are the projects, which were started in the past years and are still continuing. The concept of rolling plan is especially applicable to these items. This is so because the revision in capital expenditure is required on account of various environmental factors. (2) *New projects*: These are important because the company makes the crucial decision of committing valuable resources at this point. It is at this point that a cost-benefit analysis is made. These projects go over to the carry over items in the succeeding years. Both for carry over and new projects, phasing of expenditure is worked out on the basis of availability of funds and technical requirements.

Capital projects: The capital expenditure projects of the company have been dividend into two categories: (1) *Minor Schemes*: involving outlays under Rs. 25 lakh. Approximately Rs. 7 crore are allocated to these schemes annually. Schemes undertaken under this heading are: new equipment and modification, prototypes, balancing facilities, replacements, system changes etc. (2) *Major Schemes*: involving outlays of more than Rs. 25 lakh. A total of Rs. 30 to Rs. 35 crore is allocated to these projects annually. The rationale for this classification is that whereas minor schemes involve routine expenditure requiring less intensive managerial attention, major schemes deal with areas that are relatively unknown and the company's commitments are high.

Capital budgeting process: The capital expenditure planning and control at HSCL involves the following process:

Conception stage: The company has a top-down of capital budgeting process. There exists a 'suggestion system' that seeks suggestions mainly with regard to plant operations. The flow of ideas with regard to capital outlays is not frequent. In the suggestions system there exists a system of cash award. The ideas for minor schemes mainly come from departmental heads, possibly because of technical requirements. The ideas for major schemes come from the experiences of steel plants abroad, research and development and top management.

Formalization stage: Departmental head submits the proposals to the Chief Engineer for his consideration. If the proposal is acceptable, it is sent to the project division. Project division provides: (*i*) Estimated life of the project on the basis of the experiences of the respective department. (*ii*) Essentiality of the project—here the factors, which cannot be quantified, are considered. (*iii*) The details of the existing facilities and the description of the proposed projects in terms of technical details. (*iv*) Lists of various alternatives available to achieve the objective and evaluates them. (*v*) The details of the planning of expenditure involved. It also provides information about any further expenditure required and not covered by the estimate. (*vi*) An estimate of the likely date of starting the project and completion time. (*vii*) An estimate of the financial benefits and the operating cost of project. On the basis of these estimates, ROI is calculated.

Project division submits this formalized proposal to the Chief Engineer for his/her reconsideration. The Chief Engineer submits the proposal, if found suitable, to the Controller of Budgets.

Co-ordination: There is a special cell called Projects Division for formalization of the project, which takes into account the impact that a project will have on other departments. To ensure that certain facets of a certain proposal affecting other departments are not missed out, there is a periodical meeting of all the concerned officials. There is a format system for such meeting and the maximum interval between any two such meetings is one week.

Evaluation: The formal proposal is submitted to a study group for studying the viability of the project for the project for the system as a whole. The study group consists of the Chief Engineer, the Controller of Budgets, Controller of Accounts and representatives from works. In case the study group is satisfied, the proposal is put forward to the Capital Expenditure Control

Committee. This committee selects the priority projects in view of the financial constraints spelt out by the head office. Criteria to Assign Priority to a Project

- A simple method of return on investment (book value) is used. Sometimes the payback period is also taken into account. Minimum return on investment is fixed at 15 per cent.
- Apart from the monetary criteria, there are non-monetary factors, which are also considered. These factors are, essentially of the project, government rules and regulation, union contractual requirements and the social objectives of the company.

The company so far did not use the discounted cash flow (DCF) techniques. The reasons for not using DCF techniques are: (*i*) It is thought to be too complicated. (*ii*) Needs a lot of data, which is not available. (*iii*) Most of the capital expenditures are replacement expenditures where the time-tested technique of ROI is preferred, and (*iv*) There is a normal human resistance to change. The company expects that in future large amounts of capital expenditure would be incurred on modernization and expansion. It is actively thinking of using NPV and IRR for the purpose of project evaluation. The top management was wondering how it should implement the system.

Approval and budget finalization stage: All the proposal cleared by the Capital Expenditure Control Committee go into the formal budget. The budget is prepared on an annual basis with phasing over the years. Once in three months the proposals are sent to head office, to be approved by the Board of Directors.

The concerned department head approves the capital expenditure of less than Rs. 1,000, which is charged to the current year's account. Projects up to Rs. 10,000 can be approved, if required, by the Vice-Chairman keeping in view its urgency. A fixed amount of budget is given to the Vice-Chairman for such emergency sanctions. Projects involving expense of Rs. 10,000 to Rs. 25,00,000 (minor schemes) are sent to the board of directors for their approval. Project involving expenditure of more than

Rs. 25 lakh are scrutinized at the head office and only then the approval is given. So long as the total budget for the minor schemes does not exceed the financial constraints, they are sanctioned. Since major projects involve greater commitment of the company resources, they are scrutinized in detail at the head office level. The normal time for proposal to be approved is approximately 10–12 months. However, in the case of urgent expenses, the Controller of Budgets allows the expenditure under intimation to the head office.

Disbursement of sanctioned fund: Immediately after the schemes are approved, the Controller of Budgets is informed by fax of the approval, giving the scheme numbers. The Controller of Budget then disburses the funds to the concerned departments. The Controller of Accounts is also informed about the approval of these schemes so that the necessary funds may be released.

Control of expenses: A check is kept on the way expenses are being incurred in different phases. If deviations are very large, the causes for the deviations are investigated. In case deviations exceed 15 per cent of the original approval, a fresh revised estimate is submitted for approval, along with the reason for deviation.

Performance appraisal: The company has a Make-Good Reports Committee, which goes into the appraisal of projects performance. A kind of ABC analysis is done to analyze the actual performance vis-à-vis the estimated performance. On a random basis, a few projects are picked up for investigations of their performance. In case the actual performance is very poor, it is investigated as to whether the project itself was wrongly conceived or was it due to the wrong operating procedures. It is also investigated as to the grounds on which the project was wrongly formulated. Corrective actions are taken whenever possible; otherwise the project is abandoned in extreme cases.

Discussion Questions

1. What are the objectives of HSCL's capital budgeting system?
2. Critically evaluate the capital budgeting process of HSCL.

PART 3

Financing and Dividend Decisions

14 Financial and Operating Leverage

CHAPTER OBJECTIVES

- Explain the concept of financial leverage
- Discuss the alternative measures of financial leverage
- Understand the risk and return implications of financial leverage
- Analyse the combined effect of financial and operating leverage
- Highlight the difference between operating risk and financial risk

INTRODUCTION

Given the capital budgeting decision of a firm, it has to decide the way in which the capital projects will be financed. Every time the firm makes an investment decision, it is at the same time making a financing decision also. For example, a decision to build a new plant or to buy a new machine implies specific way of financing that project. Should a firm employ equity or debt or both? What are implications of the debt-equity mix? What is an appropriate mix of debt and equity?

CAPITAL STRUCTURE DEFINED

The assets of a company can be financed either by increasing the owners' claims or the creditors' claims. The owners' claims increase when the firm raises funds by issuing ordinary shares or by retaining the earnings; the creditors' claims increase by borrowing. The various means of financing represent the **financial structure** of an enterprise. The left-hand side of the balance sheet (liabilities plus equity) represents the financial structure of a company.[1] Traditionally, short-term borrowings are excluded from the list of methods of financing the firm's capital expenditure, and therefore, the long-term claims are said to form the **capital structure** of the enterprise. The term capital

structure is used to represent the proportionate relationship between debt and equity. Equity includes paid-up share capital, share premium and reserves and surplus (retained earnings).

The financing or capital structure decision is a significant managerial decision. As discussed later in this chapter, it influences the shareholder's return and risk. Consequently, the market value of the share may be affected by the capital structure decision. The company will have to plan its capital structure initially at the time of its promotion. Subsequently, whenever funds have to be raised to finance investments, a capital structure decision is involved. The process of the capital structure decision is shown in Figure 14.1. A demand for raising funds generates a new capital structure since a decision has to be made as to the quantity and forms of financing. This decision will involve an analysis of the existing capital structure and the factors, which will govern the decision at present. The dividend decision, as discussed later on, is, in a way, a financing decision. The company's policy to retain or distribute earnings affects the owners' claims. Shareholders' equity position is strengthened by retention of earnings. Thus, the dividend decision has a bearing on the capital structure of the company. The new financing decision of the company may affect its debt-equity

---

1. In USA the right-hand side of the balance sheet is used to show liabilities and equity.

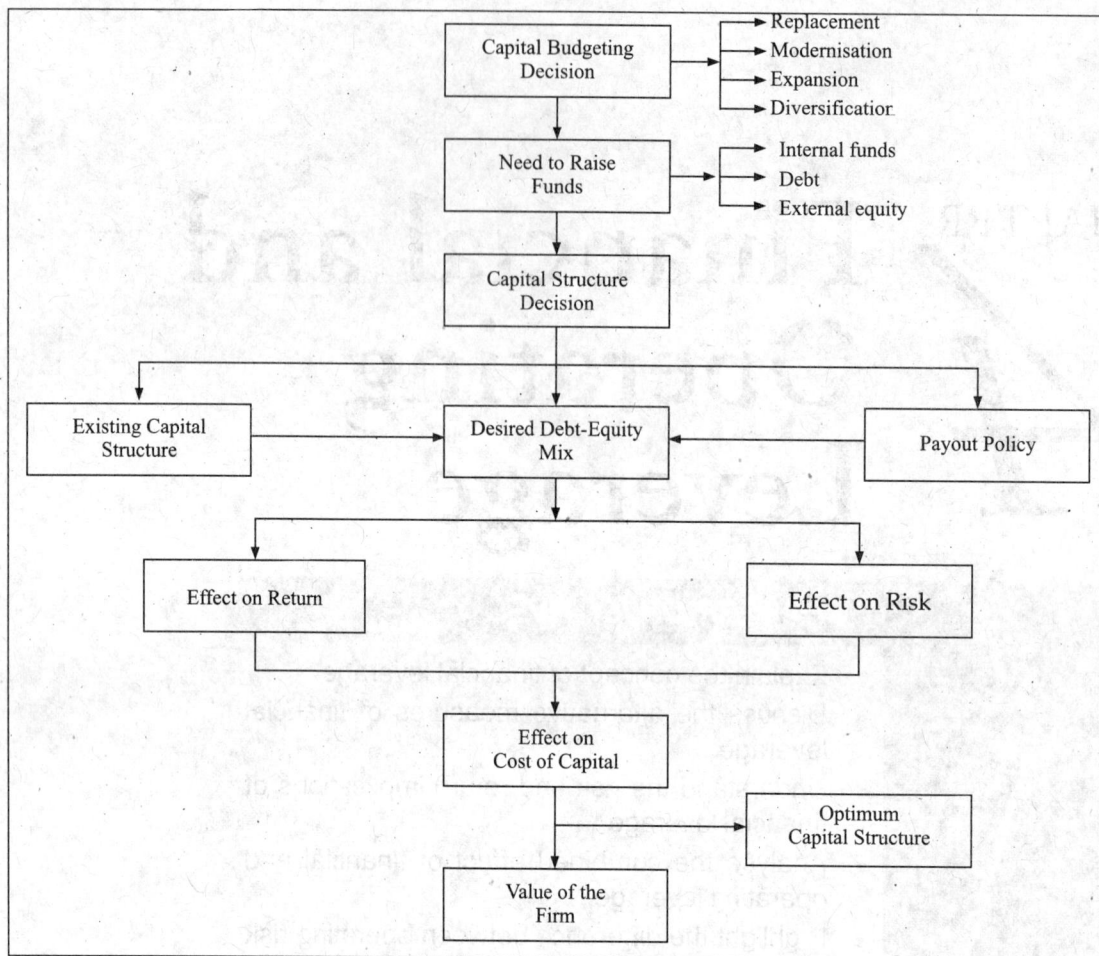

Figure 14.1: The capital structure decision process

mix. The debt-equity mix has implications for the shareholders' earnings and risk, which in turn, will affect the cost of capital and the market value of the firm.

The management of a company should seek answers to the following questions while making the financing decision:

- How should the investment project be financed?
- Does the way in which the investment projects are financed matter?
- How does financing affect the shareholders' risk, return and value?
- Does there exist an optimum financing mix in terms of the maximum value to the firm's shareholders?
- Can the optimum financing mix be determined in practice for a company?
- What factors in practice should a company consider in designing its financing policy?

We will provide answers to these questions in this and next two chapters.

MEANING OF FINANCIAL LEVERAGE

As stated earlier, a company can finance its investments by debt and equity. The company may also use preference capital. The rate of interest on debt is fixed irrespective of the company's rate of return on assets. The company has a legal binding to pay interest on debt. The rate of preference dividend is also fixed; but preference dividends are paid when the company earns profits. The ordinary shareholders are entitled to the residual income. That is, earnings after interest and taxes (less preference dividends) belong to them. The rate of the equity dividend is not fixed and depends on the dividend policy of a company.

The use of the fixed-charges sources of funds, such as debt and preference capital along with the owners' equity in the capital structure, is described as **financial leverage** or **gearing** or **trading on equity**. The use of the term trading on equity is derived from the fact that it is the owner's equity that is used as a basis to raise debt; that is, the equity that is traded upon. The supplier of debt has limited participation in the company's profits and, therefore, he will insist on protection in earnings and protection in values represented by ownership equity.[1]

The financial leverage employed by a company is intended to earn more return on the fixed-charge funds than their costs. The surplus (or deficit) will increase (or decrease) the return on the owners' equity. The rate of return on the owners' equity is

---

1. Waterman, Merwin H., Trading on Equity, in Eitman, W.J. (ed.), *Essays on Business Finance*, Masterco Press, 1953.

levered above or below the rate of return on total assets. For example, if a company borrows Rs 100 at 8 per cent interest (that is, Rs 8 per annum) and invests it to earn 12 per cent return (that is, Rs 12 per annum), the balance of 4 per cent (Rs 4 per annum) after payment of interest will belong to the shareholders, and it constitutes the profit from financial leverage. On the other hand, if the company could earn only a return of 6 per cent on Rs 100 (Rs 6 per annum), the loss to the shareholders would be Rs 2 per annum. Thus, financial leverage at once provides the potentials of increasing the shareholders' earnings as well as creating the risks of loss to them. It is a double-edged sword. The following statement very well summarises the concept of financial leverage:[1]

This role of financial leverage suggests a lesson in physics, and there might be some point in considering the rate of interest paid as the fulcrum used in applying forces through leverage. At least it suggests consideration of pertinent variables; the lower the interest rate, the greater will be the profit, and the less the chance of loss; the less the amount borrowed the lower will be the profit or loss; also, the greater the borrowing, the greater the risk of unprofitable leverage and the greater the chance of gain.

MEASURES OF FINANCIAL LEVERAGE

The most commonly used measures of financial leverage are:[2]

1. **Debt ratio** The ratio of debt to total capital, i.e.,

$$L_1 = \frac{D}{D+E} = \frac{D}{V}$$

where D is value of debt, E is value of shareholders' equity and V is value of total capital (i.e., $D+E$). D and E may be measured in terms of book value. The book value of equity is called net worth. Shareholder's equity may be measured in terms of market value.

2. **Debt-equity ratio** The ratio of debt to equity, i.e.,

$$L_2 = \frac{D}{E} \qquad (1)$$

3. **Interest coverage** The ratio of net operating income (or EBIT) to interest charges, i.e.,[3]

$$L_3 = \frac{EBIT}{Interest} \qquad (2)$$

The first two measures of financial leverage can be expressed either in terms of book values or market values. The market value to financial leverage is theoretically more appropriate because market values reflect the current attitude of investors. But it is difficult to get reliable information on market values in practice. The market values of securities fluctuate quite frequently.

There is no difference between the first two measures of financial leverage in operational terms. They are related to each other in the following manner.[4]

$$L_1 = \frac{L_2}{1+L_2} = \frac{D/E}{1+D/E} = \frac{D}{V} \qquad (3)$$

$$L_2 = \frac{L_1}{1-L_1} = \frac{D/V}{1-D/V} = \frac{D}{E} \qquad (4)$$

These relationships indicate that both these measures of financial leverage will rank companies in the same order. However, the first measure (i.e. D/V) is more specific as its value will range between zero to one. The value of the second measure (i.e. D/E) may vary from zero to any large number. The debt-equity ratio, as a measure of financial leverage, is more popular in practice. There is usually an accepted industry standard to which the company's debt-equity ratio is compared. The company will be considered risky if its debt-equity ratio exceeds the industry standard. Financial institutions and banks in India also focus on debt-equity ratio in their lending decisions.

The first two measures of financial leverage are also measures of **capital gearing**. They are static in nature as they show the borrowing position of the company at a point of time. These measures, thus, fail to reflect the level of financial risk, which is inherent in the possible failure of the company to pay interest and repay debt.

The third measure of financial leverage, commonly known as **coverage ratio**, indicates the capacity of the company to meet fixed financial charges. The reciprocal of interest coverage, that is, interest divided by EBIT, is a measure of the firm's **income gearing**. Again by comparing the company's coverage ratio with an accepted industry standard, investors can get an idea of financial risk. However, this measure suffers from certain limitations.[5] *First*, to determine the company's ability to meet fixed financial obligations, it is the cash flow information, which is relevant, not

---

1. *Ibid.*
2. Bierman, H., Jr., *Financial Policy*, Macmillan, 1970.
3. Fixed charges may also include sinking funds (SF). Then the ratio will be as follows:

$$L_3 = \frac{EBIT}{Interest + (Sinking fund/1 - Tax rate)}$$

Depreciations, being a non-cash item, may be included in the numerator of the equation.

4. Since, $L_1 = \dfrac{D}{D+E} = \dfrac{D}{V}$ then $D = L_1 V$. Similarly, since $L_2 = \dfrac{D}{E}$, then $D = L_2 E$.

Thus, $L_1 V = L_2 E, L_1 = L_2 \dfrac{E}{V} = L_2 \dfrac{V-D}{V}$ or $L_1 = L_2 - L_2 \dfrac{D}{V}$ or $L_1 = L_2 - L_2 L_1$.

Since, $\dfrac{D}{V} = L_1$ or $L_1 = \dfrac{L_2}{(1+L_2)}$ or $L_2 = \dfrac{L_1}{(1-L_1)}$

5. Bierman, *op. cit.*, p. 89.

the reported earnings. During recessionary economic conditions, there can be wide disparity between the earnings and the net cash flows generated from operations. *Second,* this ratio, when calculated on past earnings, does not provide any guide regarding the future riskiness of the company. *Third,* it is only a measure of short-term liquidity rather than of leverage.

Financial Leverage of Companies in India

How much financial leverage do Indian companies employ? Companies differ in the use of financial leverage since it depends on a number of factors such as the size, nature of product, capital intensity, technology, market conditions, management attitude etc. In Table 14.1, we provide the measures of financial leverage for a few largest companies in India for the year ending on 31 March 2004. As you may observe companies show wide variations in the use of financial leverage. Infosys does not use any debt. SAIL's debt ratio is highest and because of its low EBIT, it does not provide much coverage to debt holders.

Table 14.1: Financial Leverage of Largest Indian Companies, 2004

Company	Capital Gearing		Income Gearing	
	Debt ratio	Debt-equity ratio	Interest coverage	Interest to EBIT ratio
1. Indian Oil	0.346	0.530	23.6	0.042
2. HPCL	0.180	0.220	54.6	0.018
3. BPCL	0.315	0.459	26.0	0.038
4. SAIL	0.862	6.247	0.81	1.237
5. ONGC	0.022	0.022	331.00	0.003
6. Tata Motors	0.261	0.353	16.7	0.060
7. TISCO	0.436	0.774	12.1	0.083
8. BHEL	0.101	0.112	15.4	0.065
9. Reliance	0.398	0.660	5.4	0.186
10. L&T	0.329	0.491	11.8	0.085
11. HLL	0.441	0.797	35.1	0.029
12. Infosys	0.000	0.000	NA*	NA*
13. Voltas	0.306	0.440	8.1	0.124

* *NA* = not applicable.

Source: CMIE database.

FINANCIAL LEVERAGE AND THE SHAREHOLDERS' RETURN

The primary motive of a company in using financial leverage is to magnify the shareholders' return under favourable economic conditions. The role of financial leverage in magnifying the return of the shareholders is based on the assumptions that the fixed-charges funds (such as the loan from financial institutions and banks or debentures) can be obtained at a cost lower than the firm's rate of return on net assets (RONA or ROI). Thus, when the difference between the earnings generated by assets financed by the fixed-charges funds and costs of these funds is distributed to the shareholders, the earnings per share (EPS) or return on equity (ROE) increases. However, EPS or ROE will fall if the company obtains the fixed-charges funds at a cost higher than the rate of return on the firm's assets. It should, therefore, be clear that EPS, ROE and ROI are the important figures for analysing the impact of financial leverage.

EPS and ROE Calculations

EPS is calculated by dividing profit after taxes, PAT, (also called net income, NI) by the number of shares outstanding. PAT is found out in two steps. First, the interest on debt, INT, is deducted from the earnings before interest and taxes, EBIT, to obtain the profit before taxes, PBT. Then, taxes are computed on and subtracted from PBT to arrive at the figure of PAT. The formula for calculating EPS is as follows:[1]

$$\text{Earnings per share} = \frac{\text{Profit after tax}}{\text{Number of shares}}$$

$$\text{EPS} = \frac{\text{PAT}}{N} = \frac{(\text{EBIT} - \text{INT})(1 - T)}{N} \quad (5)$$

where T is the corporate tax rate and N is the number of ordinary shares outstanding. If the firm does not employ any debt, then the formula is:

$$\text{EPS} = \frac{\text{EBIT}(1 - T)}{N} \quad (6)$$

ROE is obtained by dividing PAT by equity (E). Thus, the formula for calculating ROE is as follows:[2]

$$\text{Return on equity} = \frac{\text{Profit after tax}}{\text{Value of equity}}$$

$$\text{ROE} = \frac{(\text{EBIT} - \text{INT})(1 - T)}{E} \quad (7)$$

For calculating ROE either the book value or the market value equity may be used.

How does the financial leverage affect EPS and ROE? We shall describe two situations to illustrate the impact of the financial leverage on EPS and ROE. First, we shall analyse the impact of the alternative financial plans on EPS and ROE assuming that EBIT is constant. Second, we shall assume that EBIT varies and shows the effect of the alternative financial plans on EPS and ROE under the conditions of varying EBIT.

Analysing Alternative Financial Plans: Constant EBIT

Suppose a new firm, the Brightways Ltd., is being formed. The management of the firm is expecting a before-tax rate of return of 24 per cent on the estimated total investment of Rs 500,000. This implies EBIT = Rs 500,000 × 0.24 = Rs 120,000. The firm is considering two alternative financial plans: (*i*) either to raise the entire funds by issuing 50,000 ordinary shares at Rs 10 per

---

1. If a company uses preference capital, then EPS may be calculated as follows:

$$\text{EPS} = \frac{(\text{EBIT} - \text{INT})(1 - T) - \text{PDIV}}{N}$$

Notice that PDIV, the preference dividend, is not tax deductible.

2. ROE can also be found out by dividing the earnings per share by the equity capital (book value) per share.

share, or (ii) to raise Rs 250,000 by issuing 25,000 ordinary shares at Rs 10 per share and borrow Rs 250,000 at 15 per cent rate of interest. The tax rate is 50 per cent. What are the effects of the alternative plans for the shareholders' earnings? Table 14.2 shows calculations.

Table 14.2: Effect of Financial Plan on EPS and ROE: Constant EBIT

	Financial Plan	
	Debt-equity (Rs)	All-equity (Rs)
1. Earnings before interest and taxes, EBIT	120,000	120,000
2. *Less:* Interest, INT	0	37,500
3. Profit before taxes, PBT = EBIT – INT	120,000	82,500
4. *Less:* Taxes, T (EBIT – INT)	60,000	41,250
5. Profit after taxes, PAT = (EBIT – INT) (1 – T)	60,000	41,250
6. Total earnings of investors, PAT + INT	60,000	78,750
7. Number of ordinary shares, N	50,000	25,000
8. EPS = (EBIT – INT) (1 – T)/N	1.20	1.65
9. ROE = (EBIT – INT) (1 – T)/E	12.0%	16.5%

From Table 14.2, we see that the impact of the financial leverage is quite significant when 50 per cent debt (debt of Rs 250,000 to total capital of Rs 500,000) is used to finance the investment. The firm earns Rs 1.65 per share, which is 37.5 per cent more than Rs 1.20 per share earned with no leverage. ROE is also greater by the same percentage.

Table 14.3: Gain from Financial Leverage

	Rs
1. EBIT on assets financed by debt, Rs 250,000 × 0.24	60,000
2. *Less:* Interest, Rs 250,000 × 0.15	37,500
3. Surplus earnings to the shareholders, Rs 250,000 × (0.24 – 0.15)	22,500
4. *Less:* Taxes at 50 per cent	11,250
5. After tax surplus earnings accruing to the shareholders (leverage gain)	11,250

EPS is greater under the debt-equity plan for two reasons. First, under this plan, the firm is able to borrow half of its funds requirements at a cost (15 per cent) lower than its rate of return on total investment (24 per cent). Thus, it pays a 15 per cent (or 7.5 per cent after tax) interest on the debt of Rs 250,000 while earns a return of 24 per cent (or 12 per cent after tax) by investing this amount. The difference of 9 per cent (or 4.5 per cent after tax) accrues to the shareholders as owners of the firm without any corresponding investment. The difference in terms of rupees is Rs 22,500 before taxes and Rs 11,250 after taxes. Thus, the gain from the financial leverage is as shown in Table 14.3.

Second, under the debt-equity plan, the firm has only 25,000 shares as against 50,000 shares under the all-equity plan. Consequently, the after-tax favourable leverage of Rs 11,250

dividend by 25,000 shares increases EPS by Re 0.45 from Rs 1.20 to Rs 1.65.

Interest Tax Shield

Another important way of explaining the effect of debt is to see the impact of the interest charges on the firm's tax liability. The interest charges are tax deductible and, therefore, provide tax shield, which increases the earnings of the shareholders. See line 6 in Table 14.2 that compares the total earnings of all investors (shareholders as well debt holders) under two alternative financial plans. The total earnings are more by Rs 18,750 under the debt-equity plan that is exactly the amount of tax saved (i.e. Rs 60,000 – Rs 41,250), on account of the tax deductibility of the interest charges. The **interest tax shield** under the second financial plan could be directly found out as:

$$\text{Interest tax shield} = \text{Tax rate} \times \text{Interest}$$
$$= 0.5 \times 37,500 = \text{Rs} 18,750$$

It is the fact of the tax deductibility of the interest charges, which makes the use of the debt in the capital structure beneficial to a firm.

Instead of following the long procedure discussed in Table 14.2, Equation 5 or 7 can be used to examine the effect of the alternative financial plans on the shareholders' return. Suppose that the management of the firm in the example is considering a third alternative. They want to use 75 per cent debt and 25 per cent equity to finance the assets. Under this financial plan, for raising equity investment of Rs 125,000, the firm will sell 12,500 shares and pay Rs 56,250 interest on a debt of Rs 375,000 at 15 per cent. EPS and ROE will be as follows:

$$EPS = \frac{(EBIT - INT)(1 - T)}{N}$$
$$= \frac{(120,000 - 56,250)(1 - 0.50)}{12,500} = \frac{31,875}{12,500} = \text{Rs} 2.55$$

$$ROE = \frac{(EBIT - INT)(1 - T)}{E} = \frac{31,875}{125,000} = 25.5\%$$

Under the third alternative financial plan of 75 per cent debt, EPS and ROE are more than double as compared with all-equity, no-leverage financial plan.

In the example, we assume that the firm earns EBIT of 24 per cent on its investment (or Rs 500,000 × 0.24 = Rs 120,000). Since the firm pays 15 per cent on debt and earns more (24 per cent) on these funds, the effect of leverage is favourable. The more debt the firm uses, the greater is the EPS or ROE. The 24 per cent overall return is an *expected* figure. Suppose that, for some reason, the firm may not be able to earn 24 per cent before-tax return on its total capital, rather it can earn only 12 per cent return (i.e., EBIT = Rs 60,000). What would be the impact on EPS and ROE? We can use Equations 5 and 7 to calculate EPS and ROE:

No debt plan

$$EPS = \frac{(60,000 - 0)(1 - 0.5)}{50,000} = \frac{30,000}{50,000} = \text{Re} 0.60$$

$$ROE = \frac{30,000}{500,000} = 6\%$$

50% debt plan

$$EPS = \frac{(60,000 - 37,500)(1 - 0.5)}{25,000} = \frac{11,250}{25,000} = Re\ 0.45$$

$$ROE = \frac{11,250}{250,000} = 4.5\%$$

75% debt plan

$$EPS = \frac{(60,000 - 56,250)(1 - 0.5)}{12,500} = \frac{1,875}{12,500} = Re\ 0.15$$

$$ROE = \frac{1,875}{125,000} = 1.5\%$$

We can see from the calculations above that the effect of financial leverage is unfavourable. EPS and ROE decline as more debt is used. Why is the effect of financial leverage unfavourable? It is unfavourable because the firm's rate of return on total funds or assets is less than the cost of debt. The firm is paying 15 per cent on debt and earning a return of 12 per cent on funds employed. The shareholders will have to meet the deficit of 3 per cent. As a result, EPS and ROE decline. If the rate of return on assets were just equal to the cost of debt, it can be seen that financial leverage will have no impact on the shareholders' return. EPS and ROE would be the same under all plans. We are thus led to an important conclusion: *The financial leverage will have a favourable impact on EPS and ROE only when the firm's return on investment (ROI) exceeds the interest cost of debt (i). The impact will be unfavourable if the return on investment is less than the interest cost.* It is in this sense that the financial leverage is said to be a double-edged sword.

Effect of Leverage on ROE and EPS

Favourable	$ROI > i$
Unfavourable	$ROI < i$
Neutral	$ROI = i$

These conclusions become very clear if we rewrite the formula for ROE. Suppose r is the before-tax return on assets or investment i.e. EBIT divided by $V = E + D$, and i is the interest rate on debt. Equation 7 can be written as follows:

$$ROE = \frac{(rV - iD)(1 - T)}{E} = \frac{[r(E + D) - iD](1 - T)}{E}$$

$$ROE = \left[r + (r - i)\frac{D}{E} \right](1 - T) \tag{8}$$

For an all-equity capital structure firm, D/E will be zero. Therefore, ROE for such firm is simply the after-tax return on assets:

$$ROE = r(1 - T) \tag{9}$$

A comparison of Equations (8) and (9) clearly shows that ROE is more by $[(r - i)\ D/E]\ (1 - T)$ factor when the firm uses debt. It is also indicated that if the return on assets exceeds the interest rate $(r > i)$, ROE will increase linearly with increase in the financial leverage (*viz., D/E*). The effect of leverage will depend on both D/E and the spread between the rate of return on assets (r) and interest cost (i). If the return on assets equals the interest rate $(r = i)$, no benefit of the financial leverage will be obtained; that is, $(r - i)\ D/E\ (1 - T) = 0$. The leverage effect will be unfavourable when the return on assets is less than the interest rate (when $r < i$, then $(r - i)\ D/E\ (1 - T)$, would become negative). Equation (8) also shows that for a given level of financial leverage with the interest rate and tax rate being constant, ROE will increase or decline with the increase or decline in the rates of return on assets. The following section illustrates the behaviour of EPS with varying EBIT.

Analysing Alternative Financial Plans: Varying EBIT

In the previous example, we assumed EBIT as constant. In practice, EBIT for any firm is subject to various influences. For example, because of the fluctuations in the economic conditions, sales of a firm change and as a result, EBIT also varies. In a given period, the actual EBIT of the firm may be more or less than the anticipated. It is therefore useful to analyse the impact of the financial leverage on EPS (and ROE) for possible fluctuations in EBIT (or r).

EBIT–EPS analysis Suppose that the Brightways Ltd. may face any of the four possible economic conditions: very poor, poor, normal and good. The firm may have a 5 per cent chance of performing very poorly and earning a negative 5 per cent return on its total assets [EBIT = (0.05) × Rs 500,000 = – Rs 25,000]. If the economic condition is neither very poor nor normal, the firm may be able to manage a return of 10 or 15 per cent. It may have 10 per cent chance of earning 10 per cent return (EBIT = Rs 50,000). Under normal economic conditions, the firm has a 35 per cent chance of earning 24 per cent return (EBIT = Rs 120,000) and a 30 per cent chance of earning 32 per cent return (EBIT = Rs 160,000). If the economic conditions are really favourable, the firm can earn as high as 60 per cent return (EBIT = Rs 300,000). But there is only 5 per cent possibility that the economic conditions will prove to be so good. Brightways' possible levels of sales and operating expenses with their probability of occurrence are given in Table 14.4.

Table 14.4: Expected Sales, EBIT, ROI with Associated Probabilities

(Rs '000)

	Economic Conditions					
	Very poor	*Poor*		*Normal*		*Good*
Probability	0.05	0.10	0.15	0.35	0.30	0.05
Sales (Rs)	510	660	710	800	880	1,160
Costs:						
Variable (Rs)	255	330	355	400	440	580
Fixed (Rs)	280	280	280	280	280	280
Total Costs (Rs)	535	610	635	680	720	860
EBIT (Rs)	– 25	50	75	120	160	300
ROI (*r*)	– 5%	10%	15%	24%	32%	60%

The behaviour of EPS (and ROE) with fluctuating EBIT (or

return on assets) under the alternative financial plans is analysed in Table 14.5. The summary of the effect of the increasing financial leverage on EPS with changing EBIT (see Tables 14.6 and 14.7) provides interesting insights.

Table 14.5: Impact of Financial Leverage: Varying EBIT

(Rs ' 000)

	Economic Conditions					
	Very poor	**Poor**		**Normal**	**Good**	
Plan I: No debt						
EBIT	− 25.00	50.00	75.00	120.00	160.00	300.00
Less: Interest	0.00	0.00	0.00	0.00	0.00	0.00
PBT	− 25.00	50.00	75.00	120.00	160.00	300.00
Less: Tax, 50%	− 12.50*	25.00	37.50	60.00	80.00	150.00
PAT	− 12.50	25.00	37.50	60.00	80.00	150.00
No. of shares ('000)	50.00	50.00	50.00	50.00	50.00	50.00
EPS (Rs)	− 0.25	0.50	0.75	1.20	1.60	3.00
ROE (%)	− 2.50	5.00	7.50	12.00	16.00	30.00
Plan II: 25% debt						
EBIT	− 25.00	50.00	75.00	120.00	160.00	300.00
Less: Interest	18.75	18.75	18.75	18.75	18.75	18.75
PBT	− 43.75	31.25	56.25	101.25	141.25	281.25
Less: Tax, 50%	− 21.88*	15.63	28.13	50.63	70.63	140.63
PAT	− 21.87	15.62	28.12	50.62	70.62	140.62
No. of shares ('000)	37.50	37.50	37.50	37.50	37.50	37.50
EPS (Rs)	− 0.58	0.42	0.75	1.35	1.88	3.75
ROE (%)	− 5.80	4.20	7.50	13.50	18.80	37.50
Plan III: 50% debt						
EBIT	− 25.00	50.00	75.00	120.00	160.00	300.00
Less: Interest	37.50	37.50	37.50	37.50	37.50	37.50
PBT	− 62.50	12.50	37.50	82.50	122.50	262.50
Less: Tax, 50%	− 31.25*	6.25	18.75	41.25	61.25	131.25
PAT	− 31.25	6.25	18.75	41.25	61.25	131.25
No. of shares ('000)	25.00	25.00	25.00	25.00	25.00	25.00
EPS (Rs)	− 1.25	0.25	0.75	1.65	2.45	5.25
ROE (%)	− 12.50	2.50	7.50	16.50	24.50	52.50
Plan IV: 75% debt						
EBIT	− 25.00	50.00	75.00	120.00	160.00	300.00
Less: Interest	56.25	56.25	56.25	56.25	56.25	56.25
PBT	− 81.25	− 6.25	18.75	63.75	103.75	243.75
Less: Tax, 60%	− 40.63*	− 3.13	9.38	31.88	51.88	121.88
PAT	− 40.62	− 3.12	9.37	31.87	51.87	121.87
No. of shares ('000)	12.50	12.50	12.50	12.50	12.50	12.50
EPS (Rs)	− 3.25	− 0.25	0.75	2.55	4.15	9.75
ROE (%)	− 32.50	− 2.50	7.50	25.50	41.50	97.50

* It is assumed that losses will be set off against other profits or tax credit will be available to the firm.

Financial Plan I does not employ any leverage. As EBIT increases, EPS also increases. In fact, EPS increases with improved EBIT under all financial plans (Table 14.6). What is important to note is that as the financial leverage is increased, EPS is further magnified. Take the example of normal and good years. When EBIT increases from Rs 120,000 to Rs 160,000—an increase by 33 per cent, EPS under no financial leverage plan increases proportionately (i.e., by 33 per cent). But EPS increases faster under the high financial leverage plans; it increases by 40 per cent when debt is 25 per cent, by 48 per cent when debt is 50 per cent and by 63 per cent when debt is 75 per cent. Same conclusions can be drawn from Table 14.7 for the behaviour of ROE in relation to return on assets (r). It may be worth repeating that the favourable effect of the increasing financial leverage during normal and good years is on account of the fact that the rates of return on assets (investment) exceed the cost on debt.

Financial leverage works both ways. It accelerates EPS (and ROE) under favourable economic conditions, but depresses EPS (and ROE) when the goings is not good for the firm. It can be seen from Tables 14.6 and 14.7 that EPS or ROE is lower with debt in the capital structure in the poor years. With no leverage plan, if the firm's return on assets is positive, although low, the shareholders do obtain positive EPS or ROE. For example, when the firm's return (r) is 10 per cent, EPS under no leverage plan is Re 0.40 (or ROE is 4 per cent). But it becomes lower with more debt used, and even turns negative under very high leverage plan, such as Financial Plan IV. The unfavourable effect on EPS (and ROE) is more severe with more debt in the capital structure when EBIT (or r) is negative.

Table 14.6: Summary of the Behaviour of EPS with Fluctuating EBIT under Alternative Financial Plans

		Financial Plan			
Economic Conditions	**EBIT**	*No debt* I EPS	*25% debt* II EPS	*50% debt* III EPS	*75% debt* IV EPS
Very poor	− 25,000	− 0.25	− 0.58	− 1.25	− 3.25
Poor	50,000	0.50	0.42	0.25	− 0.25
	75,000	0.75	0.75	0.75	0.75
Normal	1,20,000	1.20	1.35	1.65	2.55
	1,60,000	1.60	1.88	2.45	4.15
Good	3,00,000	3.00	3.75	5.25	9.75

Table 14.7: Summary of the Behaviour of ROE with Fluctuating Return on Assets under Alternative Financial Plans

		Financial Plan			
Economic Conditions	**Return on assets**	*No debt* I	*25% debt* II	*50% debt* III	*75% debt* IV
Very poor	− 5%	− 2.5%	− 5.8%	− 12.5%	− 32.5%
Poor	10%	5.0%	4.2%	2.5%	− 2.5%
	15%	7.5%	7.5%	7.5%	7.5%
Normal	24%	12.0%	13.5%	16.5%	25.5%
	32%	16.0%	18.8%	24.5%	41.5%
Good	60%	30.0%	37.5%	52.5%	97.5%

The reason again lies in the relationship between the return on assets and the cost of debt. If the cost of debt were more than the return on assets, EPS (or ROE) would depress with more leverage. It is indicated from Table 14.6 or Table 14.7 that when the firm earns 15 per cent return on its assets, which is equal to the cost of debt, EPS (or ROE) is the same under all financial plans. Whatever the firm earns on the funds raised through debt is exactly paid to the suppliers of debt as interest charges.

Variability of EPS Yet another significant point to be noted from Table 14.6 is that the higher the financial leverage, the wider the range over which EPS varies with fluctuating EBIT. For example, when no debt is used (Financial Plan I), EPS ranges between a negative Re 0.25 to a positive Rs 3.00—a range of Rs 3.25. Under Financial Plan II, where 25 per cent debt is introduced in the capital structure, EPS ranges from a negative Re 0.58 to a positive Rs 3.75—a range of Rs 4.33. The range of EPS increases to Rs 6.50 and Rs 13.00 when debt is respectively 50 per cent and 75 per cent. The range for ROE shows the similar behaviour (Table 14.7). Thus, for any given level of variability in EBIT (or r), the increased financial leverage increases the degree of variability in EPS (or ROE). The indiscriminate use of financial leverage without taking into account the uncertainty surrounding EBIT (or r) can lead a firm into financial difficulties. More about the risk of the financial leverage is explained in the next section.

EBIT–EPS chart One convenient and useful way of showing the relationship between EBIT and EPS for the alternative financial plans is to prepare the EBIT–EPS chart. The chart is easy to prepare since, for any given level of financial leverage, EPS is linearly related to EBIT.[1] As noted earlier, the formula for calculating EPS is:

$$EPS = \frac{(EBIT - INT)(1 - T)}{N} = \frac{(1 - T)}{N}[EBIT - INT] \quad (10)$$

Equation (10) can also be written as follows:

$$EPS = \frac{(1 - T)}{N}EBIT - \frac{(1 - T)}{N}INT$$

$$= -\frac{(1 - T)}{N}INT + \frac{(1 - T)}{N}EBIT \quad (11)$$

We assume that the level of debt, the cost of debt and the tax rate are constant. Therefore, in Equations (10) and (11), the terms $(1 - T)/N$ and INT (which is equal to interest rate times debt, iD) are constant; EPS will increase if EBIT increases and fall if EBIT declines.

Under the assumptions made, the first part of Equation (11) is a constant and can be represented by a. EBIT is a random variable since it can assume a value more or less than expected. The term $(1 - T)/N$ is also a constant and can be shown as b. Thus, the EPS formula can be rewritten as:

$$EPS = a + b \times EBIT \quad (12)$$

Equation (12) clearly indicates that EPS is a linear function of EBIT.

The EBIT–EPS analysis shown in Table 14.8 could be worked out with the help of Equation (12). As an illustration, we work out Equation (12) for Financial Plan IV: equity Rs 125,000, 15 per cent debt Rs 375,000, number of shares 12,500 and tax rate 50 per cent. The values of a and b ('000 eliminated) are:

$$a = -\frac{(1 - T)}{N}INT = \frac{0.5}{12.5} \times 56.25 = -2.25$$

$$b = \frac{(1 - T)}{N} = \frac{0.5}{12.5} = 0.04$$

EPS for various levels of EBIT will be as shown in Table 14.8.

Table 14.8: EPS Calculations for Financial Plan IV: EPS = a + b EBIT

(1 – T)/N	EBIT	=	b EBIT	+	a	=	EPS = a + b × EBIT
(0.04)	(– 25)	=	– 1.00	+	– 2.25	=	– 3.25
(0.04)	(50)	=	2.00	+	– 2.25	=	– 0.25
(0.04)	(75)	=	3.00	+	– 2.25	=	0.75
(0.04)	(120)	=	4.80	+	– 2.25	=	2.55
(0.04)	(160)	=	6.40	+	– 2.25	=	4.15
(0.04)	(300)	=	12.00	+	– 2.25	=	9.75

Because of the linear relation between EPS and EBIT, the EBIT–EPS chart can be drawn easily. We can use the following information of Financial Plans I and III in our example to draw EBIT– EPS chart in Figure 14.2.

	EPS	
EBIT (Rs '000)	**No debt**	**50% debt**
– 25,000	– 0.25	– 1.25
0	0.00	– 0.75
25,000	0.25	– 0.25
50,000	0.50	0.25
75,000	0.75	0.75
1,00,000	1.00	1.25
1,25,000	1.25	1.75
1,50,000	1.50	2.25
1,75,000	1.75	2.75
2,00,000	2.00	3.25

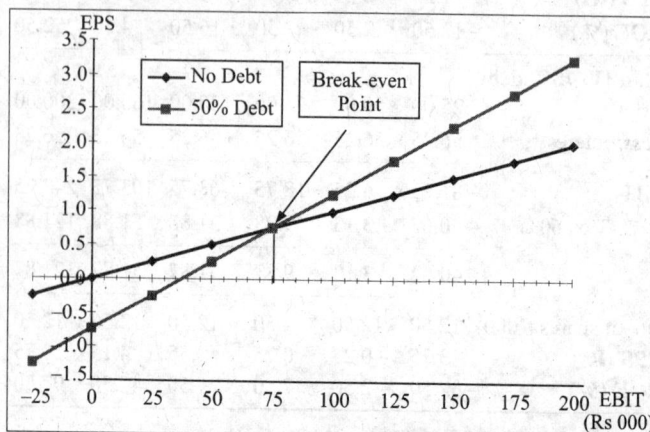

Figure 14.2: EBIT–EPS chart

---

1. Bierman, *op. cit.*

In Figure 14.2 EBIT is shown on a horizontal line and EPS on a vertical line. If we identify any two points of EPS for two given levels of EBIT and join them in a straight line, we obtain EPS-line for a particular financial plan. For example, at EBIT of Rs 50,000 and Rs 75,000, two points of EPS are respectively Re 0.25 and Re 0.75 for Financial Plan III. If we join these two points in a straight line, we get EPS-line for Financial Plan III. The EPS-line can be similarly drawn for 100 per cent equity plan. We can see from Figure 14.2 that EPS-lines for all-equity and 50 per cent debt plans intersect at EBIT Rs 75,000. EPS under both plans are same at this level of EBIT. Figure 14.3, drawn similarly as Figure 14.2, shows four financial plans together.

The steep solid lines in Figure 14.3 show the relation between EBIT and EPS. The line relating EBIT and EPS becomes steeper with more debt in the capital structure, and steeper the line, the more the profit potential to the shareholders with increasing EBIT. If EBIT is declining, the loss to the shareholders will be magnified. The point of intersection of four EBIT–EPS lines in Figure 14.3 indicates the **indifference point** or the **EBIT-EPS break-even point** at which EPS is same regardless of the level of the financial leverage. In the example (see Table 14.6), EPS is same for all financial plans when the firm earns a 15% return on assets or EBIT of Rs 75,000.

		EPS		
EBIT	*No debt*	*25% debt*	*50% debt*	*75% debt*
−25,000	−0.25	−0.583	−1.25	−3.25
0	0.00	−0.250	−0.75	−2.25
25,000	0.25	0.083	−0.25	−1.25
50,000	0.50	0.417	0.25	−0.25
75,000	0.75	0.750	0.75	0.75
1,00,000	1.00	1.083	1.25	1.75
1,25,000	1.25	1.417	1.75	2.75
1,50,000	1.50	1.750	2.25	3.75
1,75,000	1.75	2.083	2.75	4.75
2,00,000	2.00	2.417	3.25	5.75

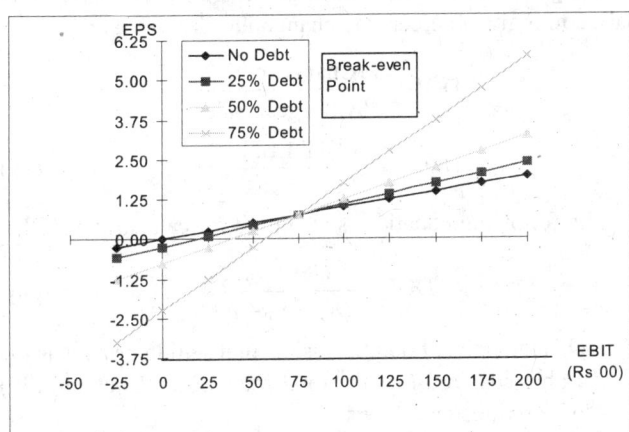

Figure 14.3: EBIT–EPS chart

The 15 per cent return on assets is just equal to the cost of debt. It can also be noticed from Figure 14.3 that below the 'indifference point' the EBIT–EPS lines shift more towards the right when the level of financial leverage increases, indicating unfavourable effect because of a low rate of return on assets than the interest cost. The EBIT–EPS line shifts more towards the left beyond the 'indifference point' when the level of the financial leverage increases. This indicates a favourable effect of leverage because the return on assets exceeds the interest rate. We thus again reach the conclusion that the shareholders will benefit by the use of the financial leverage in terms of the increased EPS if return on assets is higher than the interest cost, and will have reduced EPS if return on assets is lower than the interest cost; the shareholders' earnings will not be affected by the level of leverage if return on assets is just equal to the interest cost.

Calculation of indifference point The break-even, or indifference, point between two alternative methods of financing can be determined by a formula. In the earlier example, suppose the firm is considering only two financial plans—an all-equity plan (Financial Plan I) and a 25 per cent debt and 75 per cent equity plan (Financial Plan II). The firm wants to know the level of EBIT at which EPS would be the same under both the plans. To find out the break-even level of EBIT, we may set the EPS formulae of two plans equal. The EPS formula under **all-equity plan** is

$$EPS = \frac{(1-T)\,EBIT}{N_1}$$

where N_1 is number of ordinary shares under first plan and since the firm has no debt, no interest charges exist. The EPS formula under **debt-equity plan** is:

$$EPS = \frac{(1-T)\,(EBIT - INT)}{N_2}$$

where INT is the interest charges on debt and N_2 is the number of ordinary shares under second plan. Setting the two formulae equal, we have:

$$\frac{(1-T)\,EBIT}{N_1} = \frac{(1-T)\,(EBIT - INT)}{N_2} \tag{13}$$

Using the values for Financial Plans I and II given in the example, we can determine EBIT as follows:

$$\frac{(1-0.5)EBIT}{50,000} = \frac{(1-0.5)(EBIT - 18,750)}{37,500}$$

$$0.5\,EBIT \frac{37,500}{50,000} = 0.5\,EBIT - 9,375$$

$$9,375 = 0.5\,EBIT - 0.375\,EBIT$$

$$EBIT = \frac{9,375}{0.125} = Rs\ 75,000$$

We can simplify Equation (13) as follows:

$$EBIT = \frac{N_1}{N_1 - N_2} \times INT \tag{14}$$

Thus, in the example:

$$\text{EBIT} = \frac{50,000}{50,000 - 37,500} \times 18,750 = 4 \times 18,750 = \text{Rs } 75,000$$

Sometimes a firm may like to make a choice between two levels of debt. Then, the indifference point formula will be:

$$\frac{(1-T)(\text{EBIT} - \text{INT}_1)}{N_1} = \frac{(1-T)(\text{EBIT} - \text{INT}_2)}{N_2} \quad (15)$$

where INT_1 and INT_2 represent the interest charges under the alternative financial plans. After simplifying Equation (15), we obtain:

$$\text{EBIT} = \frac{N_1 \times \text{INT}_2 - N_2 \times \text{INT}_1}{N_1 - N_2} \quad (16)$$

Many other combinations of the methods of financing may be compared. The firm may compare between an all-equity plan and an equity-and-preference share plan. Then the indifference point formula will be:

$$\frac{(1-T)(\text{EBIT})}{N_1} = \frac{(1-T)\text{EBIT} - \text{PDIV}}{N_2} \quad (17)$$

Equation (17) can be simplified as follows:

$$\text{EBIT} = \frac{N_1}{N_1 - N_2} \times \frac{\text{PDIV}}{1-T} \quad (18)$$

Illustration 14.1: Calculation of Indifferent Points

Calculate the level of EBIT at which the indifference point between the following financing alternatives will occur:

(i) Ordinary share capital Rs 10 lakh or 15% debentures of Rs 5 lakh and ordinary share capital of Rs 5 lakh.

(ii) Ordinary share capital of Rs 10 lakh or 13% preference share capital of Rs 5 lakh and ordinary share capital of Rs 5 lakh.

(iii) Ordinary share capital of Rs 10 lakh or ordinary share capital of Rs 5 lakh, 13% preference share capital of Rs 2 lakh and 15% debenture of Rs 3 lakh.

(iv) Ordinary share capital of Rs 6 lakh and 15 debentures of Rs 4 lakh or ordinary share capital of Rs 4 lakh, 13% unit preference share capital of Rs 2 lakh and 15% debentures of Rs 4 lakh.

(v) Ordinary share capital of Rs 8 lakh and 13% preference share capital of Rs 2 lakh or ordinary share capital of Rs 4 lakh, 13% preference share capital of Rs 2 lakh and 15% debentures of Rs 4 lakh.

Assume that the corporate tax rate is 50 per cent and the price of the ordinary share is Rs 10 in each case.

The indifference points for the various combinations of the methods of finance are calculated as follows:

(i) Ordinary shares vs. ordinary shares and debentures:

$$\text{EBIT} = \frac{N_1}{N_1 - N_2} \times \text{INT}$$

$$= \frac{100,000}{100,000 - 50,000} \times 75,000 = \text{Rs } 150,000$$

(ii) Ordinary shares vs. ordinary and preference shares:

$$\text{EBIT} = \frac{N_1}{N_1 - N_2} \times \frac{\text{PDIV}}{1-T} = \frac{100,000}{100,000 - 50,000} \times \frac{65,000}{1 - 0.5}$$

$$= 2 \times 130,000 = \text{Rs } 260,000$$

(iii) Ordinary shares vs. ordinary and preference shares and debentures

$$\text{EBIT} = \frac{N_1}{N_1 - N_2} \times \left[\text{INT} + \frac{\text{PDIV}}{(1-T)} \right]$$

$$= \frac{100,000}{100,000 - 50,000} \times \left[45,000 + \frac{26,000}{(1 - 0.5)} \right]$$

$$= 2 \times (45,000 + 52,000) = \text{Rs } 194,000$$

(iv) Ordinary shares and debentures vs. ordinary and preference shares and debentures:

$$\text{EBIT} = \frac{N_1}{N_1 - N_2} \times \left[\text{INT}_2 + \frac{\text{PDIV}}{(1-T)} \right] - \left[\frac{N_2}{N_1 - N_2} \times \text{INT}_1 \right]$$

$$= \frac{60,000}{60,000 - 40,000} \times \left[60,000 + \frac{26,000}{(1 - 0.5)} \right]$$

$$- \left[\frac{40,000}{60,000 - 40,000} \times 60,000 \right]$$

$$= (3 \times 112,000) - (2 \times 60,000) = \text{Rs } 216,000$$

(v) Ordinary shares and preference shows vs. ordinary and preference shares and debentures:

$$\text{EBIT} = \frac{N_1}{N_1 - N_2} \times \left[\text{INT} + \frac{\text{PDIV}_2}{(1-T)} \right] - \left[\frac{N_2}{N_1 - N_2} \times \frac{\text{PDIV}_1}{(1-T)} \right]$$

$$= \frac{80,000}{80,000 - 40,000} \times \left(60,000 + \frac{26,000}{1 - 0.5} \right)$$

$$- \left(\frac{40,000}{80,000 - 40,000} \times \frac{26,000}{1 - 0.5} \right)$$

$$= 2 \times 112,000 - 1 \times 52,000 = \text{Rs } 172,000$$

COMBINING FINANCIAL AND OPERATING LEVERAGES

Operating leverage affects a firm's operating profit (EBIT), while **financial leverage** affects profit after tax or the earnings per share. The combined effect of two leverages can be quite significant for the earnings available to ordinary shareholders.

Degree of Operating Leverage

The **degree of operating leverage** (DOL) is defined as the percentage change in the earnings before interest and taxes relative to a given percentage change in sales. Thus:

$$\text{DOL} = \frac{\% \text{ Change in EBIT}}{\% \text{ Change in Sales}}$$

$$\text{DOL} = \frac{\Delta \text{ EBIT/EBIT}}{\Delta \text{ Sales/Sales}} \quad (19)$$

The following equation is also used for calculating DOL:

$$\text{DOL} = \frac{Q(s-v)}{Q(s-v) - F} \quad (20)$$

where Q is the units of output, s is the unit selling price, v is the unit variable cost and F is the total fixed costs. Equation (20) can also be written as follows:

$$\text{DOL} = \frac{\text{Contribution}}{\text{EBIT}} \quad (21)$$

Since contribution = EBIT + Fixed cost, Equation (21) can be expressed as follows:

$$DOL = \frac{EBIT + Fixed\,Cost}{EBIT} = 1 + \frac{F}{EBIT} \quad (22)$$

Suppose that in the earlier example of the Brightways Ltd. the management had developed the following income statement based on an expected sales volume of 100,000 units:

	Rs
Sales (100,000 units at Rs 8)	800,000
Less: Variable costs (100,000 at Rs 4)	400,000
Contribution	400,000
Less: Fixed costs	280,000
EBIT	120,000

Applying Equation (20), DOL is:

$$DOL = \frac{100,000\,(Rs\,8 - Rs\,4)}{100,000\,(Rs\,8 - Rs\,4) - Rs\,280,000}$$

$$= \frac{Rs\,400,000}{120,000} = 3.33$$

DOL of 3.33 implies that for a given change in Brightways' sales, EBIT will change by 3.33 times.

Let us suppose in the case of Brightways that a technical expert appointed by the management tells them that they can choose more automated production processes which will reduce unit variable cost to Rs 2 but will increase fixed costs to Rs 480,000. If the management accepts the expert's advice, then the income statement will look as follows:

	Rs
Sales (100,000 at Rs 8)	800,000
Less: Variable costs (100,000 at Rs 2)	200,000
Contribution	600,000
Less: Fixed costs	480,000
EBIT	120,000

With high fixed costs and low variable costs, DOL for Brightways will be:

$$DOL = \frac{Rs\,600,000}{Rs\,120,000} = 5.0$$

If the Brightways Ltd. chooses high-automated technology and if its actual sales happen to be more than expected, its EBIT will increase greatly; an increase of 100 per cent in sales will lead to a 500 per cent increase in EBIT.

Degree of Financial Leverage

We have seen earlier in this chapter that financial leverage affects the earnings per share. When the economic conditions are good and the firm's EBIT is increasing, its EPS increases faster with more debt in the capital structure. The **degree of financial leverage** (DFL) is defined as the percentage change in EPS due to a given percentage change in EBIT:

$$DFL = \frac{\%\,Change\,in\,EPS}{\%\,Change\,in\,EBIT}$$

or

$$DFL = \frac{\Delta\,EPS/EPS}{\Delta\,EBIT/EBIT} \quad (23)$$

In the case of the Brightways Ltd. when EBIT increases from Rs 120,000 to Rs 160,000, EPS increases from Rs 1.65 to Rs 2.45, when it employs 50 per cent debt and pays interest charges of Rs 37,500 (see Table 14.6). Applying Equation (23), DFL at EBIT of Rs 120,000 is:

$$DFL = \frac{(2.45 - 1.65)/1.65}{(160,000 - 120,000)/120,000} = \frac{0.485}{0.333} = 1.456$$

This implies that for a given change in EBIT, EPS will change by 1.456 times.

The following equation can also be used to calculate DFL:

$$DFL = \frac{EBIT}{EBIT - INT} = \frac{EBIT}{PBT} = 1 + \frac{INT}{PBT} \quad (24)$$

We know that EBIT = $Q(p - v) - F$ (and EBIT − INT = PBT). Thus Equation (24) can also be written as follows:

$$DFL = \frac{Q(s - v) - F}{Q(s - v) - F - INT} \quad (25)$$

The numerator of Equation (24) or (25) is earnings before interest and taxes and the denominator is profit before taxes.

In the example, the Brightways Ltd. was considering four alternative debt levels (see Table 14.5). Applying Equation (24), DFL for those alternatives at EBIT of Rs 120,000 is given below:

Table 14.9: Degree of Financial Leverage of Alternative Financial Plans at EBIT of Rs 120,000

Debt Level	*DFL*
0	1.000
25%	1.185
50%	1.456
75%	1.882

It is indicated from Table 14.9 that if the firm does not employ any debt, EPS will increase at the same rate at which EBIT increases. EPS increases faster for a given increase in EBIT when debt is introduced in the capital structure; more the debt in the capital structure, the greater the increase in EPS. The opposite will happen if EBIT declines—the greater will be the fall in EPS with more debt in the capital structure.

Combined Effect of Operating and Financial Leverages

Operating and financial leverages together cause wide fluctuation ir EPS for a given change in sales. If a company employs a high level of operating and financial leverage, even a small change in the level of sales will have dramatic effect on

EPS. A company with cyclical sales will have a fluctuating EPS; but the swings in EPS will be more pronounced if the company also uses a high amount of operating and financial leverage.

The degrees of operating and financial leverages can be combined to see the effect of total leverage on EPS associated with a given change in sales. The **degree of combined leverage (DCL)** is given by the following equation:

$$= \frac{\% \text{Change in EBIT}}{\% \text{Change in sales}} \times \frac{\% \text{Change in EPS}}{\% \text{Change in EBIT}}$$

$$= \frac{\% \text{Change in EPS}}{\% \text{Change in Sales}} \qquad (26)$$

Yet another way of expressing the degree of combined leverage is as follows:

$$DCL = \frac{Q(s-v)}{Q(s-v)-F} \times \frac{Q(s-v)-F}{Q(s-v)-F-INT}$$

$$= \frac{Q(s-v)}{Q(s-v)-F-INT} \qquad (27)$$

Since $Q(s-v)$ is contribution and $Q(s-v) - F - INT$ is the profit after interest but before taxes, Equation (27) can also be written as follows:

$$DCL = \frac{\text{Contribution}}{\text{Profit before taxes}} = \frac{\text{EBIT + Fixed costs}}{\text{PBT}}$$

$$= \frac{PBT + INT + F}{PBT} = 1 + \frac{INT + F}{PBT} \qquad (28)$$

For the Brightways Ltd. when it used less automated production processes, the combined leverage effect at a sales of Rs 8 lakh (100,000 units at Rs 8) and 50 per cent debt level is:

$$DCL = \frac{100,000(8-4)}{100,000(8-4) - 280,000 - 37,500}$$

$$= \frac{400,000}{82,500} = 4.85$$

In the case of the Brightways Ltd. combined effect of leverage is to increase EPS by 4.85 times for one unit increase in sales when it chooses less automated production process and employs 50 per cent debt. Thus, if the Brightways' sales increase by 10 per cent from Rs 8 lakh to Rs 8.80 lakh, then EPS will increase by: 10% × 4.85 = 48.5%. EPS at the sales level of Rs 8 lakh is Rs 1.65 then the new EPS will be:

$$EPS = 1.65 \times 1.485 = Rs\ 2.45$$

The results tally with those worked out in Table 14.5.

Firms can employ operating and financial leverages in various combinations. The Brightways Ltd., for example, can either choose high-automated production processes and high degree of operating leverages or low automated production processes and low degree of operating leverage associated with high or low level of debt. The following are the possible combinations of operating and financial leverages for the Brightways Ltd.:

Table 14.10: Combinations of Operating and Financial Leverage for the Brightways Ltd.

Low Automation			High Automation		
DOL	DFL	DCL	DOL	DFL	DCL
3.33	1.000	3.33	5.00	1.000	5.00
3.33	1.185	3.95	5.00	1.185	5.93
3.33	1.455	4.85	5.00	1.456	7.28
3.33	1.882	6.27	5.00	1.882	9.41

Table 14.10 indicates that the largest effect of leverage (9.41 times) will be obtained when the firm combines higher amount of operating leverage (5.00 times) with the highest level of debt (DFL = 1.882). If the company has this combination, EPS will increase by 9.41 times than the increase in sales. Thus, if Brightways sales increase from Rs 8 lakh to Rs 11.60 lakh—an increase of 45 per cent, EPS increases from Rs 2.55 to Rs 13.35—an increase by 423 per cent (i.e., 45 per cent × 9.41). Detailed calculations are given in Table 14.11.

Table 14.11: Brightways Ltd.: EPS Calculations for Change in Sales

Units sold	100,000	145,000
Sales (at Rs 8)	800,000	1,160,000
Less: Variable costs (at Rs 2)	200,000	290,000
Contribution	600,000	870,000
Less: Fixed costs	480,000	480,000
EBIT	120,000	390,000
Less: Interest	56,250	56,250
PBT	63,750	333,750
Less: Taxes (50%)	31,875	166,875
PAT	31,875	166,875
No. of shares	12,500	12,500
EPS	2.55	13.35
% Change in sales:	$\frac{1,160,000 - 800,000}{800,000} = 45\%$	
% Change in EPS:	$\frac{13.35 - 2.55}{2.55} = 423\%$	

This combination can, however, prove risky for the company. If sales decline, the adverse effect on EPS will be very severe. The right combination of operating and financial leverages will differ among companies. It would generally be governed by the behaviour of sales. Public utilities such as electricity companies can afford to combine high operating leverage with high financial leverage since they generally have stable or rising sales. A company whose sales fluctuate widely and erratically should avoid use of high leverage since it will be exposed to a very high degree of risk.

Alternatives	Equity	Preference	Debentures
1	100%	—	—
2	75%	—	25%
3	75%	25%	—
4	50%	20%	30%
5	50%	—	50%
6	30%	20%	50%

(*i*) Construct an EBIT–EPS chart for the six alternatives over an EBIT range of Rs 10 lakh to Rs 80 lakh.

(*ii*) Determine the indifference points for first and fourth alternatives and for fourth and sixth alternatives.

(*iii*) Is the maximisation of EPS at a specific level of EBIT the only function of a firm's capital structure? If not, are the points determined in (*ii*) truly 'indifference' points?

4. Empire Ltd. needs Rs 1,000,000 to build a new factory which will yield EBIT of Rs 150,000 per year. The company has to choose between two alternative financing plans: 75 per cent equity and 25 per cent debt or 50 per cent equity and 50 per cent debt. Under the first plan shares can be sold at Rs 50 per share, and the interest rate on debt will be 14 per cent. Under the second plan shares can be sold for Rs 40 per share and the interest rate on debt will be 16 per cent. Determine the EPS for each plan assuming a 35 per cent tax rate.

5. Howard Company is considering three financing plans: all equity; 60 per cent equity and 40 per cent debt; and 40 per cent equity and 60 per cent debt. Total funds needed are Rs 300,000. EBIT is expected to be Rs 45,000. Shares can be sold at the rate of Rs 20 per cent share. Funds can be borrowed as follows: up to and including Rs 60,000 at 14 per cent; Rs 60,000 to Rs 150,000 at 16 per cent and over Rs 150,000 at 18 per cent. Compute the EPS of each plan. Assume a tax rate of 35 per cent.

6. *XYZ* Ltd. wishes to raise Rs 1,000,000 to finance the acquisition of new assets. It is considering three alternative ways of financing assets: (*i*) to issue only equity shares at Rs 20 per share, (*ii*) to borrow Rs 500,000 at 14 per cent rate of interest and issue equity shares at Rs 20 per share for the balance or (*iii*) to borrow Rs 750,000 at 14 per cent rate of interest and issue equity shares at Rs 20 per share for the balance. The following are the estimates of the earnings from the assets with their probability distribution:

EBIT (Rs)	Probabilities
80,000	0.10
120,000	0.20
160,000	0.40
200,000	0.20
320,000	0.10

You are required to (*i*) calculate the earnings per share (*ii*) compute the indifference points, and (*iii*) determine the financial risk, for each of the three alternatives. Assume a tax rate of 35 per cent.

7. For *X* Ltd. the following data is available:

EBIT	Rs 200
Contribution	400
Interest	100

If the company's sales are expected to decline by 5 per cent, determine the percentage change in EPS.

8. The expected earnings of firms *A* and *B* are Rs 120,000 with a standard deviation of Rs 30,000. Firm *A* is non-levered. Firm *B* is levered and has to pay annual interest charges of Rs 30,000. Which firm is more risky? Why?

9. Rastogi Ltd. is considering two plans (*a*) 15% debt or (*b*) issue of 100,000 shares of Rs 10 each to finance a proposed expansion at a cost of Rs 1,000,000. The company expects EBIT with associated probabilities as follows:

EBIT (Rs)	Probabilities
100,000	0.05
150,000	0.10
200,000	0.30
250,000	0.40
300,000	0.10
400,000	0.05

Determine the expected EBIT and coefficient of variation of EBIT. Also calculate expected EPS and its variability under two plans. Comment on your results. The company has 100,000 shares outstanding, and the corporate tax rate is 35 per cent.

10. A large chemical company is considering acquiring two small companies. The following is the financial data about two companies:

	(Rs in lakh)	
	Company 1	Company 2
Sales	108.65	108.65
Less: Variable cost	43.46	35.85
Contribution	65.19	72.80
Less: Fixed cost	52.69	61.40
EBIT	12.50	11.40
Less: Interest	9.27	6.95
PBT	3.23	4.45
Less: Tax (35%)	1.13	1.56
PAT	2.10	2.89
Total assets	92.70	92.70
Equity	30.90	46.35
Debt	61.80	46.35

What would be the effect on companies' profitability and risk if sales fluctuate by 10 per cent? If the chemical company intends to acquire a less risky firm, which one should it buy? Give reasons.

11. Indus Engineering Company has gross sales of Rs 137.5 crore and profit after tax of Rs 7.15 crore in the year 2004. The company is considering expanding its capacity by adding 30 per cent more to its existing fixed assets. Sales are likely to increase by Rs 55 crore. For the proposed expansion, PBIT to sales ratio is 18 per cent. The company has never borrowed in the past. The finance director has recommended that the

company should raise 15 per cent interest bearing debt for financing the expansion. In his opinion, given 35 per cent corporate income tax rate, the effective cost of debt will be 9.75 per cent, and considering the current net worth (see balance sheet given below), debt-equity ratio will be only 0.22, which is quite low for an engineering firm. Indus is a highly capital intensive company; its fixed costs are 70 per cent of the total costs. It is notable that the performance of engineering industry is quite susceptible to economic changes. Should the company borrow? Give your analysis by making appropriate assumptions.

Balance Sheet as on 31 December 2004 (Rs in crore)

Share capital			
(4 crore shares at Rs 10)	40.0	Fixed assets	100.0
Reserve	95.0	Current assets:	
Net worth	135.0	Debtors	20.0
Current liabilities	35.5	Inventory	30.0
		Cash	20.5
	170.5		170.5

13. Volga is a large manufacturing and marketing company in the private sector. In 2004, the company had a gross sales of Rs 980.2 crore. The other financial data for the company are given below:

Some Financial Data for Volga, 2004

Items	*Rs in crore*
Net worth	152.31
Borrowing	165.47
EBIT	43.17
Interest	34.39
Fixed costs (excluding interest)	118.23

You are required to calculate (*a*) debt-equity ratio; (*b*) debt ratio; (*c*) interest coverage, (*d*) operating leverage, (*e*) financial leverage and (*f*) combined leverage. Interpret your results and comment on the Volga's debt policy.

CASE

Case 14.1: Central Equipment Company[1]

In the beginning of January 2004, Mr. L.C. Tandon, Director of Finance of Central Equipment Company (CEC), was evaluating the pros and cons of debt and equity financing for the purpose of expansion of CEC's existing production facilities. At a recent meeting of the board of directors, a heated discussion took place on the best method of financing the expansion. Mr. K.C. Soni, Chairman and Managing Director (CMD), had therefore directed Mr. Tandon to critically evaluate the points made by the various members of the board. He also asked him to prepare a report on behalf of the company's management to be presented at the board meeting to be held in the last week of January 2003.

Background of the Company

CEC was started in the late fifties as a government company. It is one of the important engineering companies in the public sector in India, manufacturing a wide range of products. CEC's products include industrial machinery and equipments for chemicals, paper, cement, and fertilizers industries, super heaters, economizers, and solid material handling and conveying equipments.

CEC had started with a paid-up capital of Rs 10 million in 1959. As per the *estimated* balance sheet at the end of the year 2003–04, it has a paid-up capital of Rs 180 million (divided into 1.8 million shares of Rs 100 each) and reserves of Rs 639.60 million. The company's sales have shown a general increasing trend in spite of a number of difficulties such as recessionary conditions, high input cost, frequent power cuts and unremunerative regulated prices of certain products. In the last decade, CEC's sales have increased from Rs 1,804 million in 1994–95 to Rs 3,042 million in 2002–03. The sales for year

Table 14.1.1: Central Equipment Company: Selected Financial Data

Year ending March 31	*Sales (Rs in million)*	*PBIT (Rs in million)*	*PAT (Rs in million)*	*Dividend (Rs in million)*	*EPS (Rs)*
1994–95	1804.0	34.3	17.1	9.0	9.50
1995–96	1707.8	15.5	7.8	9.0	4.33
1996–97	1894.0	41.2	20.6	9.0	11.44
1997–98	2270.8	52.2	26.1	9.0	14.50
1998–99	2520.0	58.0	29.0	10.8	16.11
1999–00	2775.0	66.6	33.3	10.8	18.50
2000–01	2949.2	76.8	38.4	14.4	21.33
2001–02	2433.8	– 5.3	– 5.3	9.0	—
2002–03	3042.3	82.1	43.5	18.0	24.17
2003–2004$	3376.9	94.6	50.3	18.0	27.94
2004–05*	3579.5	85.0	55.2	18.0	30.67
2004–05#	4032.3	125.0	81.3	38.0	21.39

$ Estimates.

* Projections excluding the proposed expansion.

\# Projections include financial impact of proposed expansion and equity financing is assumed.

ending 31 March 2004 are estimated to be Rs 3,377 million. Net profit (profit after tax, PAT) has increased from Rs 17.1 million in 1994–95 to Rs 43.5 million in 2002–03. The company is projecting a profit after tax of Rs 50.3 million in the year 2003–04. Due to the recessionary and other economic factors, sales and profits of the company have shown a cyclical behaviour over the last decade. Table 14.1.1 gives sales and profit data for the ten-year period.

1. Case adapted from, Pandey, I.M. and Bhat, Ramesh, Cases in Financial Management, New Delhi: Tata McGraw, 2nd edition, 2002.

The Expansion Project

The need for expansion was felt because the market was fast growing and the company has at times reached its existing capacity. The project is expected to cost Rs 200 million, and generate an average profit before interest and taxes (PBIT) of Rs 40 million per annum, for a period of eight to ten years. It is expected the new plant will cause significant increase in the firm's fixed costs. The annual total expenses of the company after expansion are expected to consist of 55 per cent of fixed and 45 per cent variable expenses.

The management has already evaluated the financial viability of the project and found it acceptable even under adverse economic conditions. Mr. Soni felt that there would not be any difficulty in getting the proposal approved from the board and relevant government authorities. He also thought that the production could start as early as from April 2004.

Financing of the Project

CEC has so far followed a very conservative financing policy. All these years, the company has financed its growth through budgetary support from the government in the form of equity capital and internally generated funds. The company has also been meeting its requirements for working capital finance from the internal funds. The company has, however, negotiated a standing credit limit of Rs 50 million from a large nationalized bank. In the past, it has hardly used the bank limit because of sufficient internal resources. As may be seen from the estimated balance sheet as on March 31, 2004 in Table 14.1.2, CEC's capital employed included paid-up share capital and reserves without any debt. The CMD feels that given the government's current attitude whereby it would like profitable companies to raise funds from the capital markets for their investments, it may look odd for CEC to obtain budgetary support from the government. However, in his assessment, CEC being a profitable company, government may be willing to provide budgetary support for the project. More significantly, he felt that raising equity capital might dilute equity earnings. Thus, he decided to reconsider the company's policy of avoiding long-term debt. It was thought that the use of debt could be justified by the expected profitable position of the company.

Mr. Tandon has determined that the company could sell Rs 1,000 denomination bonds for an amount of Rs 200 million either to the public or to the financial institutions through private placement. The interest rate on bonds will be 10 per cent per annum, and they could be redeemed after seven years in three equal annual instalments. The bonds and interest thereon will be fully secured against the assets of the company. In Mr. Tandon's view, the company will have to sell a large number of bonds to the financial institutions as CEC being a new company in the capital market, the public may not fully subscribe to the issue. He also felt that from the individual investors' point of view, CEC might have to give an option to the bondholders to sell back to the company bonds up to an amount of Rs 10 million each year. Also, bondholders shall have right to appoint one nominee director on the board of the company which shall however be exercised by the bond trustees only if the company defaults in the payment of interest or repayment on the due date.

Table 14.1.2: CEC: Estimated Balance Sheet as on 31 March 2004

(Rs in million)

Cash and bank balance	89.0
Sundry debtors	180.7
Inventory	41.1
Other current assets	47.1
Current assets	357.9
Gross block	819.9
Less: Accumulated depreciation	234.6
Net block	585.3
Total Assets	943.2
Sundry creditors	151.8
Tax provision	30.3
Other current liabilities	121.5
Current liabilities	303.6
Paid-up share capital	180.0
Reserves and surplus	459.6
Net worth	639.6
Total Liabilities and Capital	943.2

In Mr. Tandon's opinion the bond was a cheaper source of finance, since interest amount was tax deductible. Given the company's tax rate of 35 per cent, the 10 per cent interest rate was equal to 6.5 per cent from the company's point of view. On the other hand, he thought that equity capital would be costly to service, as CEC is currently paying a dividend of 15 per cent on its paid-up capital. Further, as per the current tax laws in India, the company would have to pay 12.5% tax on dividends. Thus, the bond alternative looked attractive to Mr. Tandon on the basis of the comparison of costs.

The expansion proposal was discussed in the January 2004 meeting of the board. As most of the members were convinced about the profitability and desirability of the project, they did not take much time to approve it. Immediately after this decision, Mr. Tandon informed the members about the possibility of raising finance through a bond issue. He then presented his report highlighting the comparison between bond and equity financing. His conclusions clearly showed that bond financing was better for the company. Mr. Tandon was surprised to note that substantial disagreement existed among the members regarding the use of bond.

One director questioned the correctness of Mr. Tandon's calculation of the cost of the bond as he had ignored the implications of the annual requirement arising out of investors exercising the option. According to him, this would mean higher cost of bond as compared to equity capital. Yet another director emphasized that a lot of annual cash outflow will also take place under the bond alternative. He felt that the issue of bond would thus add to the company's risk by pressurizing its liquidity. Most of the directors, however, were in agreement with the estimate of post expansion profit before interest and taxes (PBIT) of Rs 125 million.

One of the directors argued that given the expected higher PBIT, the post-expansion equity return would significantly increase if the funds are raised by issuing bonds. He even emphasized that the job of the management should be to maximize profitability of equity owners by taking reasonable risks. Another director countered this argument by stating that the equity return could be diluted if the company was unable to earn sufficient profit from the existing business and the new project. The discussion on bond versus equity financing was so involved that there did not seem to be any sign of a unanimous agreement being reached. At this juncture, Mr. Tandon suggested that the discussion on financing alternatives might be postponed until January end to allow him sufficient time to come up with a fresh analysis incorporating the various points raised in the current meeting. Mr. Tandon was wondering what he should do so that a unanimous decision could be reached.

Discussion Questions

1. Calculate EPS under the alternatives of employing (*a*) Rs 200 million debt and no fresh equity, (*b*) Rs 100 million debt and Rs 100 million equity and (*c*) Rs 200 million equity and no debt. Also make calculations for uncommitted-EPS. Draw a chart showing PBIT on *x*-axis and EPS and uncommitted-EPS on *y*-axis for debt-equity mix. What inferences do you derive?

2. Debate the issues raised in the case for and against the use of debt. Why do a large number of board members seem to be against the use of debt? What are the real risks involved? How would you measure them?

3. In addition to profitability and risk factors, what are other considerations before CEC to decide about its debt policy? Should it employ debt to finance its expansion?

4. Is there a relationship between debt and value of the firm?

Capital Structure Theory and Policy

INTRODUCTION

In chapter 14, we discussed the effect of leverage on the shareholders' earnings and risk. Under favourable economic conditions, the earnings per share increase with financial leverage. But leverage also increases the financial risk of shareholders. As a result, it cannot be stated definitely whether or not the firm's value will increase with leverage. The objective of a firm should be directed towards the maximisation of the firm's value. The capital structure or financial leverage decision should be examined from the point of its impact on the value of the firm. If capital structure decision can affect a firm's value, then it would like to have a capital structure, which maximises its market value. However, there exist conflicting theories on the relationship between capital structure and the value of a firm. The traditionalists believe that capital structure affects the firm's value while Modigliani and Miller (MM), under the assumptions of perfect capital markets and no taxes, argue that capital structure decision is irrelevant. MM reverse their position when they consider corporate taxes. Tax savings resulting from interest paid on debt creates value for the firm. However, the tax advantage of debt is reduced by personal taxes and financial distress. Hence, the trade-off between costs and benefits of debt can turn capital structure into a relevant decision. There are other views also on the relevance of capital structure. We first discuss the traditional theory of capital structure followed by MM and other views.

RELEVANCE OF CAPITAL STRUCTURE: THE NET INCOME AND THE TRADITIONAL VIEWS

There are several variations of the traditional theory. But the thrust of all views is that capital structure matters. One earlier version of the view that capital structure is relevant is the **net** income (NI) approach.[1] We first discuss the NI approach, followed by other traditional views.

The Net Income Approach

A firm that finances its assets by equity and debt is called a **levered firm**. On the other hand, a firm that uses no debt and finances its assets entirely by equity is called an **unlevered firm**. Suppose firm L is a levered firm and it has financed its assets by equity and debt. It has perpetual expected EBIT or net operating income (NOI) of Rs 1,000 and the interest payment of Rs 300. The firm's cost of equity (or equity capitalisation rate), k_e, is 9.33 per cent and the cost of debt, k_d, is 6 per cent. What is the firm's value? The value of the firm is the sum of the values of all of its securities. In this case, firm L's securities include equity and debt; therefore the sum of the values of equity and debt is the firm's value. The value of a firm's shares (equity), E, is the discounted value of shareholders' earnings, called **net income**, NI. Firm's L's net income is: NOI – interest = 1,000 – 300 = Rs 700, and the cost of equity is 9.33 per cent. Hence the value of L's equity is: 700/0.0933 = Rs 7,500:

Value of equity = discounted value of net income

$$E = \frac{\text{Net Income}}{\text{Cost of equity}} = \frac{\text{NI}}{k_e}$$

$$= \frac{700}{0.0933} = \text{Rs } 7,500 \qquad (1)$$

Similarly the value of a firm's debt is the discounted value of debt-holders' interest income. The value of L's debt is: 300/0.06 = Rs 5,000:

Value of debt = discounted value of interest

$$D = \frac{\text{Interest}}{\text{Cost of debt}} = \frac{\text{INT}}{k_d}$$

$$= \frac{300}{0.06} = \text{Rs } 5,000 \qquad (2)$$

The value of firm L is the sum of the value of equity and the value of debt: 7,500 + 5,000 = Rs 12,500:

Value of the firm = value of equity + value of debt

$$V = E + D$$

$$= 7,500 + 5,000 = \text{Rs } 12,500 \qquad (3)$$

Firm's L's value is Rs 12,500 and its expected net operating income is Rs 1,000. Therefore, the firm's overall expected rate of return or the cost of capital is: 1,000/12,500 = 0.08 or 8 per cent:

$$\text{Firm's cost of capital} = \frac{\text{Net operating income}}{\text{Value of the firm}}$$

$$k_o = \frac{\text{NOI}}{V}$$

$$= \frac{1,000}{12,500} = 0.08 \text{ or } 8\% \qquad (4)$$

The firm's overall cost of capital is the **weighted average cost of capital** (WACC). There is an alternative way of calculating

WACC (k_o). WACC is the weighted average of costs of all of the firm's securities. Firm L's securities include debt and equity. Therefore, firm L's WACC or k_o, is the weighted average of the cost of equity and the cost of debt. Firm L's value is Rs 12,500, value of its equity is Rs 7,500 and value of its debt is Rs 5,000. Hence, the firm's debt ratio (D/V) is: 5,000/12,500 = 0.40 or 40 per cent, and the equity ratio (E/V) is: 7,500/12,500 = 0.60 or 60 per cent. Firm L's weighted average cost of capital is:

WACC = cost of equity × equity weight
$$+ \text{ cost of debt} \times \text{debt weight} \qquad (5)$$

$$k_o = k_e \times \frac{E}{V} + k_d \times \frac{D}{V}$$

$$k_o = 0.0933 \times \frac{7,500}{12,500} + 0.06 \times \frac{5,000}{12,500}$$

$$k_o = 0.0933 \times 0.60 + 0.06 \times 0.40$$

$$= 0.056 + 0.025 = 0.08 \text{ or } 8\%$$

Suppose firm L operates in a *frictionless* world. There are no taxes and transaction costs and debt is risk-free and shareholders perceive no financial risk arising from the use of debt. Under these conditions, the cost of equity, k_e, and the cost of debt, k_d, will remain constant with financial leverage. Since debt is a cheaper source of finance than equity, the firm's weighted average cost of capital will reduce with financial leverage. Suppose firm L's substitutes debt for equity and raises its debt ratio to 90 per cent. Its WACC will be: $0.0933 \times 0.10 + 0.06 \times 0.90 = 0.0633$ or 6.33 per cent. Firm L's WACC will be 6 per cent if it employs 100 per cent debt.

Rearranging Equation (5), we get

$$\text{WACC} = k_o = k_e \times \left(1 - \frac{D}{V}\right) + k_d \times \frac{D}{V}$$

$$\text{WACC} = k_o = k_e - (k_e - k_d)\frac{D}{V} \qquad (6)$$

You may note from Equation (6) that, given constant cost of equity, k_e, and cost of debt, k_d, and k_d less than k_e, the weighted average cost of capital, k_o, will decrease continuously with financial leverage, measured by D/V. You may also notice that k_o equals the cost of equity, k_e, minus the spread between the cost of equity and the cost of debt times D/V. WACC, k_o, will be equal to the cost of equity, k_e, if the firm does not employ any debt (i.e. $D/V = 0$), and k_o, will approach k_d, as D/V approaches one (or 100 per cent).

Under the assumption that k_e and k_d remain constant, the value of the firm will be:

$$V = E + D = \frac{\text{NOI} - \text{INT}}{k_e} + \frac{\text{INT}}{k_d}$$

$$= \frac{\text{NOI} - k_d D}{k_e} + \frac{k_d D}{k_d} = \frac{\text{NOI} - k_d D}{k_e} + D$$

$$= \frac{\text{NOI}}{k_e} + D - \frac{k_d D}{k_e}$$

$$V = \frac{\text{NOI}}{k_e} + D\left(1 - \frac{k_d}{k_e}\right) \qquad (7)$$

---

1. Durand, David, "Costs of Debt and Equity Funds for Business: Trends and Problems of Measurement", reprinted in *The Management of Corporate Capital*, Ezra Solomon (ed.), The Free Press, 1959, pp. 91–16.

You may notice that for an unlevered firm, the second term on the right-hand side of Equation (7) will be zero. The unlevered firm's cost of equity is also its WACC and its expected net operating income is its expected net income. Hence, the value of an unlevered (an all-equity) firm is the discounted value of the net operating income. You may also notice from Equation (7) that as the firm substitutes debt for equity and so long as k_e and k_d are constant, the value of the firm V increases by debt multiplied by a constant rate, $(k_e - k_d)/k_e$.

Illustration 15.1: Firm Value Under Net Income Approach

Suppose that a firm has no debt in its capital structure. It has an expected annual net operating income of Rs 100,000 and the equity capitalisation rate, k_e, of 10 per cent. Since the firm is 100 per cent equity financed firm, its weighted cost of capital equals its cost of equity, *i.e.*, 10 per cent. The value of the firm will be: $100,000 \div 0.10 = Rs\ 1,000,000$.

Let us assume that the firm is able to change its capital structure replacing equity by debt of Rs 300,000. The cost of debt is 5 per cent. Interest payable to debt-holders is: Rs $300,000 \times 0.05 = Rs\ 15,000$. The net income available to equity holders is: Rs 100,000 – Rs 15,000 = Rs 85,000.

The value of the firm is equal to the sum of values of all securities:

$$E = \frac{NOI - interest}{k_e} = \frac{NI}{k_e} = \frac{85,000}{0.10} = Rs\ 850,000$$

$$D = \frac{Interest}{k_d} = \frac{15,000}{0.05} = Rs\ 300,000$$

$$V = E + D = 850,000 + 300,000$$
$$= Rs\ 1,150,000$$

You can also calculate the value of the firm as follows:

$$V = \frac{100,000}{0.10} + 300,000\left(1 - \frac{0.05}{0.10}\right)$$
$$= 1,000,000 + 150,000 = Rs\ 1,150,000$$

The weighted average cost of capital, k_o, is:

$$k_o = \frac{NOI}{V} = \frac{1,00,000}{1,150,000} = 0.087\ or\ 8.7\ per\ cent$$

$$k_o = k_d\frac{D}{V} + k_e\frac{S}{V} = 0.05\left(\frac{300,000}{1,150,000}\right) + 0.10\left(\frac{8,50,000}{1,150,000}\right)$$
$$= 0.013 + 0.074 = 0.087\ or\ 8.7\ per\ cent$$

Table 15.1 shows the calculations of the firm's value and weighted average cost of capital.

Suppose the firm uses more debt in place of equity and increases debt to Rs 900,000. As shown in Table 15.1, the firm's value increases to Rs 1,450,000, and the weighted average cost of capital reduces to 8.1 per cent. Thus, by increasing debt, the firm is able to increase the value of the firm and lower WACC.

Table 15.1: Value of the Firm (NI Approach)

	Zero debt	5% Rs 300,000 debt	5% Rs 900,000 debt
Net operating income, NOI	100,000	100,000	100,000
Total cost of debt, INT = $k_d D$	0	15,000	45,000
Net income, NI: NOI – INT	100,000	85,000	55,000
Market value of equity, E: NI/k_e	1,000,000	850,000	550,000
Market value of debt, D: INT/k_d	0	300,000	900,000
Market value of the firm, V = E + D = NOI/k_o	1,000,000	1,150,000	1,450,000
Debt/Total value, D/V	0.00	0.261	0.62
WACC, NOI $\div$ V = $k_e \times E/V + k_d \times D/V$	0.100	0.087	0.081

We construct Table 15.2 to show the effect of financial leverage on the value of the firm and WACC under the NI approach. It is assumed that the net operating income is Rs 100,000 and the debt-capitalisation rate and the equity-capitalisation rate respectively are 5 per cent and 10 per cent, and they remain constant with debt. It is noticeable from the table that the value of the firm increases steadily as the debt ratio, D/V, increases and WACC declines continuously, ultimately reducing to 5 per cent at 100 per cent debt ratio.

Figure 15.1 plots WACC as a function of financial leverage. Financial leverage, D/V, is plotted along the horizontal axis and WACC, k_o, and the cost of equity, k_e, and the cost of debt, k_d, on the vertical axis. You may notice from Figure 15.1 that, under NI approach, k_e and k_d are constant. As debt is replaced for equity in the capital structure, being less expensive, it causes weighted average cost of capital, k_o, to decrease that ultimately approaches

Table 15.2: Effect of Leverage on Value and Cost of Capital under NI Approach

Leverage (D/V) %	0.00	18.18	33.34	46.15	66.67	94.74	100
NOI	Rs 100	Rs 100	Rs 100	Rs 100	Rs 100	Rs 100	Rs 100
Interest, INT	–	10	20	30	50	90	100
NI = NOI – INT	Rs 100	Rs 90	Rs 80	Rs 70	Rs 50	Rs 10	Rs 0
k_d (%)	5.0	5.0	5.0	5.0	5.0	5.0	5.0
k_e (%)	10.0	10.0	10.0	10.0	10.0	10.0	10.0
k_0 (%)	10.0	9.1	8.3	7.7	6.7	5.3	5.0
$E = (NOI - INT)/k_e$	Rs 1,000	Rs 900	Rs 800	Rs 700	Rs 500	Rs 100	Rs 0
$D = INT/k_d$	0	200	400	600	1,000	1,800	2,000
$V = E + D$	Rs 1,000	Rs 1,100	Rs 1,200	Rs 1,300	Rs 1,500	Rs 1,900	Rs 2,000

the cost of debt with 100 per cent debt ratio (D/V). The optimum capital structure occurs at the point of minimum WACC. Under the NI approach, the firm will have the maximum value and minimum WACC when it is 100 per cent debt-financed.

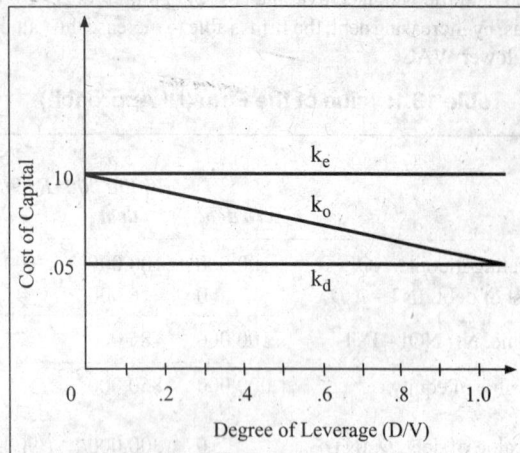

Figure. 15.1: The effect of leverage on the cost of capital under NI approach

The Traditional View

The **traditional view**[1] has emerged as a compromise to the extreme position taken by the NI approach. Like the NI approach, it does not assume constant cost of equity with financial leverage and continuously declining WACC. According to this view, a judicious mix of debt and equity capital can increase the value of the firm by reducing the weighted average cost of capital (WACC or k_0) up to certain level of debt. This approach very clearly implies that WACC decreases only within the reasonable limit of financial leverage and reaching the minimum level, it starts increasing with financial leverage. Hence, a firm has an optimum capital structure that occurs when WACC is minimum, and thereby maximising the value of the firm. Why does WACC decline? WACC declines with moderate level of leverage since low-cost debt is replaced for expensive equity capital. Financial leverage, resulting in risk to shareholders, will cause the cost of equity to increase. But the traditional theory assumes that at moderate level of leverage, the increase in the cost of equity is more than offset by the lower cost of debt. The assertion that debt funds are cheaper than equity funds carries the clear implication that the cost of debt plus the increased cost of equity, together on a weighted basis, will be less than the cost of equity that existed on equity before debt financing.[2] For example, suppose that the cost of capital for totally equity-financed firm is 12 per cent. Since the firm is financed only by equity, 12 per cent is also the firm's cost of equity (k_e). The firm replaces, say, 40 per cent equity by debt bearing 8 per cent rate of interest (cost of debt, k_d). According to the traditional theory, the financial risk caused by the introduction of debt may increase the cost of equity slightly, but not so much that the advantage of cheaper debt is taken off totally. Assume that the cost of equity increases to 13 per cent. The firm's WACC will be:

$$\text{WACC} = \text{cost of equity} \times \text{weight of equity}$$
$$+ \text{cost of debt} \times \text{weight of debt}$$

$$\text{WACC} = k_o = k_e \times w_e + k_d \times w_d$$
$$= 0.13 \times 0.6 + 0.08 \times 0.4 = 0.078 + 0.032 = 0.11 \text{ or } 11\%$$

Thus, WACC will decrease with the use of debt. But as leverage increases further, shareholders start expecting higher risk premium in the form of increasing cost of equity until a point is reached at which the advantage of lower-cost debt is more than offset by more expensive equity. Let us consider an example as given in Illustration 15.2.

Illustration 15.2: The Traditional Theory of Capital Structure

Suppose a firm is expecting a perpetual net operating income of Rs 150 crore on assets of Rs 1,500 crore, which are entirely financed by equity. The firm's equity capitalisation rate (the cost of equity) is 10 per cent. it is considering substituting equity capital by issuing perpetual debentures of Rs 300 crore at 6 per cent interest rate. The cost of equity is expected to increase to 10.56 per cent. The firm is also considering the alternative of raising perpetual debentures of Rs 600 crore and replace equity. The debt-holders will charge interest of 7 per cent, and the cost of equity will rise to 12.5 per cent to compensate shareholders for higher financial risk.

Notice that at higher level of debt (Rs 600 crore), both the cost of equity and cost of debt increase more than at lower level of debt. The calculations for the value of the firm, the value of equity and WACC are shown in Table 15.3.

Table 15.3: Market Value and the Cost of Capital of the Firm (Traditional Approach)

	No Debt (Rs in crore)	6% Debt (Rs in crore)	7% Debt (Rs in crore)
Net operating income, NOI	150	150	150
Total cost of debt, INT = $k_d D$	0	18	42
Net income, NOI– INT	150	132	108
Cost of equity, k_e	0.1000	0.1056	0.1250
Market value of equity, $E = (\text{NOI– INT})/k_e$	1,500	1,250	864
Market value of debt, D	0	300	600
Total value of firm, $V = E + D$	1,500	1,550	1,464
Equity-to-total value, $w_e = E/V$	1.00	0.806	0.590
Debt-to-total value, $w_d = D/V$	0.00	0.194	0.410
WACC, $k_o = \text{NOI}/V$ $= k_e \times w_e + k_d \times w_d$	0.1000	0.0970	0.1030

When the firm has no debt, WACC and the cost of equity are the same (10 per cent). We assume that the expected net operating income, the net income and interest are perpetual flows. We also assume that the expected net income is distributed entirely to shareholders. Therefore, the value of equity is:

$$\text{Value of equity} = \frac{\text{Net income}}{\text{Cost of equity}} = E = \frac{\text{NI}}{k_e}$$

---

1. Solomon, Ezra, *The Theory of Financial Management,* University Press, 1963, p. 92.
2. Barges, A., *The Effect of Capital Structure on the Cost of Capital,* Prentice-Hall, Inc., 1963, p. 11.

Alternatives	Equity	Preference	Debentures
1	100%	—	—
2	75%	—	25%
3	75%	25%	—
4	50%	20%	30%
5	50%	—	50%
6	30%	20%	50%

(i) Construct an EBIT–EPS chart for the six alternatives over an EBIT range of Rs 10 lakh to Rs 80 lakh.

(ii) Determine the indifference points for first and fourth alternatives and for fourth and sixth alternatives.

(iii) Is the maximisation of EPS at a specific level of EBIT the only function of a firm's capital structure? If not, are the points determined in (ii) truly 'indifference' points?

4. Empire Ltd. needs Rs 1,000,000 to build a new factory which will yield EBIT of Rs 150,000 per year. The company has to choose between two alternative financing plans: 75 per cent equity and 25 per cent debt or 50 per cent equity and 50 per cent debt. Under the first plan shares can be sold at Rs 50 per share, and the interest rate on debt will be 14 per cent. Under the second plan shares can be sold for Rs 40 per share and the interest rate on debt will be 16 per cent. Determine the EPS for each plan assuming a 35 per cent tax rate.

5. Howard Company is considering three financing plans: all equity; 60 per cent equity and 40 per cent debt; and 40 per cent equity and 60 per cent debt. Total funds needed are Rs 300,000. EBIT is expected to be Rs 45,000. Shares can be sold at the rate of Rs 20 per cent share. Funds can be borrowed as follows: up to and including Rs 60,000 at 14 per cent; Rs 60,000 to Rs 150,000 at 16 per cent and over Rs 150,000 at 18 per cent. Compute the EPS of each plan. Assume a tax rate of 35 per cent.

6. XYZ Ltd. wishes to raise Rs 1,000,000 to finance the acquisition of new assets. It is considering three alternative ways of financing assets: (i) to issue only equity shares at Rs 20 per share, (ii) to borrow Rs 500,000 at 14 per cent rate of interest and issue equity shares at Rs 20 per share for the balance or (iii) to borrow Rs 750,000 at 14 per cent rate of interest and issue equity shares at Rs 20 per share for the balance. The following are the estimates of the earnings from the assets with their probability distribution:

EBIT (Rs)	Probabilities
80,000	0.10
120,000	0.20
160,000	0.40
200,000	0.20
320,000	0.10

You are required to (i) calculate the earnings per share (ii) compute the indifference points, and (iii) determine the financial risk, for each of the three alternatives. Assume a tax rate of 35 per cent.

7. For X Ltd. the following data is available:

EBIT	Rs 200
Contribution	400
Interest	100

If the company's sales are expected to decline by 5 per cent, determine the percentage change in EPS.

8. The expected earnings of firms A and B are Rs 120,000 with a standard deviation of Rs 30,000. Firm A is non-levered. Firm B is levered and has to pay annual interest charges of Rs 30,000. Which firm is more risky? Why?

9. Rastogi Ltd. is considering two plans (a) 15% debt or (b) issue of 100,000 shares of Rs 10 each to finance a proposed expansion at a cost of Rs 1,000,000. The company expects EBIT with associated probabilities as follows:

EBIT (Rs)	Probabilities
100,000	0.05
150,000	0.10
200,000	0.30
250,000	0.40
300,000	0.10
400,000	0.05

Determine the expected EBIT and coefficient of variation of EBIT. Also calculate expected EPS and its variability under two plans. Comment on your results. The company has 100,000 shares outstanding, and the corporate tax rate is 35 per cent.

10. A large chemical company is considering acquiring two small companies. The following is the financial data about two companies:

		(Rs in lakh)
	Company 1	Company 2
Sales	108.65	108.65
Less: Variable cost	43.46	35.85
Contribution	65.19	72.80
Less: Fixed cost	52.69	61.40
EBIT	12.50	11.40
Less: Interest	9.27	6.95
PBT	3.23	4.45
Less: Tax (35%)	1.13	1.56
PAT	2.10	2.89
Total assets	92.70	92.70
Equity	30.90	46.35
Debt	61.80	46.35

What would be the effect on companies' profitability and risk if sales fluctuate by 10 per cent? If the chemical company intends to acquire a less risky firm, which one should it buy? Give reasons.

11. Indus Engineering Company has gross sales of Rs 137.5 crore and profit after tax of Rs 7.15 crore in the year 2004. The company is considering expanding its capacity by adding 30 per cent more to its existing fixed assets. Sales are likely to increase by Rs 55 crore. For the proposed expansion, PBIT to sales ratio is 18 per cent. The company has never borrowed in the past. The finance director has recommended that the

company should raise 15 per cent interest bearing debt for financing the expansion. In his opinion, given 35 per cent corporate income tax rate, the effective cost of debt will be 9.75 per cent, and considering the current net worth (see balance sheet given below), debt-equity ratio will be only 0.22, which is quite low for an engineering firm. Indus is a highly capital intensive company; its fixed costs are 70 per cent of the total costs. It is notable that the performance of engineering industry is quite susceptible to economic changes. Should the company borrow? Give your analysis by making appropriate assumptions.

Balance Sheet as on 31 December 2004 (Rs in crore)

Share capital			
(4 crore shares at Rs 10)	40.0	Fixed assets	100.0
Reserve	95.0	Current assets:	
Net worth	135.0	Debtors	20.0
Current liabilities	35.5	Inventory	30.0
		Cash	20.5
	170.5		170.5

13. Volga is a large manufacturing and marketing company in the private sector. In 2004, the company had a gross sales of Rs 980.2 crore. The other financial data for the company are given below:

Some Financial Data for Volga, 2004

Items	Rs in crore
Net worth	152.31
Borrowing	165.47
EBIT	43.17
Interest	34.39
Fixed costs (excluding interest)	118.23

You are required to calculate (*a*) debt-equity ratio; (*b*) debt ratio; (*c*) interest coverage, (*d*) operating leverage, (*e*) financial leverage and (*f*) combined leverage. Interpret your results and comment on the Volga's debt policy.

CASE

Case 14.1: Central Equipment Company[1]

In the beginning of January 2004, Mr. L.C. Tandon, Director of Finance of Central Equipment Company (CEC), was evaluating the pros and cons of debt and equity financing for the purpose of expansion of CEC's existing production facilities. At a recent meeting of the board of directors, a heated discussion took place on the best method of financing the expansion. Mr. K.C. Soni, Chairman and Managing Director (CMD), had therefore directed Mr. Tandon to critically evaluate the points made by the various members of the board. He also asked him to prepare a report on behalf of the company's management to be presented at the board meeting to be held in the last week of January 2003.

Background of the Company

CEC was started in the late fifties as a government company. It is one of the important engineering companies in the public sector in India, manufacturing a wide range of products. CEC's products include industrial machinery and equipments for chemicals, paper, cement, and fertilizers industries, super heaters, economizers, and solid material handling and conveying equipments.

CEC had started with a paid-up capital of Rs 10 million in 1959. As per the *estimated* balance sheet at the end of the year 2003–04, it has a paid-up capital of Rs 180 million (divided into 1.8 million shares of Rs 100 each) and reserves of Rs 639.60 million. The company's sales have shown a general increasing trend in spite of a number of difficulties such as recessionary conditions, high input cost, frequent power cuts and unremunerative regulated prices of certain products. In the last decade, CEC's sales have increased from Rs 1,804 million in 1994–95 to Rs 3,042 million in 2002–03. The sales for year

Table 14.1.1: Central Equipment Company: Selected Financial Data

Year ending March 31	Sales (Rs in million)	PBIT (Rs in million)	PAT (Rs in million)	Dividend (Rs in million)	EPS (Rs)
1994–95	1804.0	34.3	17.1	9.0	9.50
1995–96	1707.8	15.5	7.8	9.0	4.33
1996–97	1894.0	41.2	20.6	9.0	11.44
1997–98	2270.8	52.2	26.1	9.0	14.50
1998–99	2520.0	58.0	29.0	10.8	16.11
1999–00	2775.0	66.6	33.3	10.8	18.50
2000–01	2949.2	76.8	38.4	14.4	21.33
2001–02	2433.8	– 5.3	– 5.3	9.0	—
2002–03	3042.3	82.1	43.5	18.0	24.17
2003–2004$	3376.9	94.6	50.3	18.0	27.94
2004–05*	3579.5	85.0	55.2	18.0	30.67
2004–05#	4032.3	125.0	81.3	38.0	21.39

$ Estimates.
* Projections excluding the proposed expansion.
# Projections include financial impact of proposed expansion and equity financing is assumed.

ending 31 March 2004 are estimated to be Rs 3,377 million. Net profit (profit after tax, PAT) has increased from Rs 17.1 million in 1994–95 to Rs 43.5 million in 2002–03. The company is projecting a profit after tax of Rs 50.3 million in the year 2003–04. Due to the recessionary and other economic factors, sales and profits of the company have shown a cyclical behaviour over the last decade. Table 14.1.1 gives sales and profit data for the ten-year period.

---

1. Case adapted from, Pandey, I.M. and Bhat, Ramesh, Cases in Financial Management, New Delhi: Tata McGraw, 2nd edition, 2002.

The Expansion Project

The need for expansion was felt because the market was fast growing and the company has at times reached its existing capacity. The project is expected to cost Rs 200 million, and generate an average profit before interest and taxes (PBIT) of Rs 40 million per annum, for a period of eight to ten years. It is expected the new plant will cause significant increase in the firm's fixed costs. The annual total expenses of the company after expansion are expected to consist of 55 per cent of fixed and 45 per cent variable expenses.

The management has already evaluated the financial viability of the project and found it acceptable even under adverse economic conditions. Mr. Soni felt that there would not be any difficulty in getting the proposal approved from the board and relevant government authorities. He also thought that the production could start as early as from April 2004.

Financing of the Project

CEC has so far followed a very conservative financing policy. All these years, the company has financed its growth through budgetary support from the government in the form of equity capital and internally generated funds. The company has also been meeting its requirements for working capital finance from the internal funds. The company has, however, negotiated a standing credit limit of Rs 50 million from a large nationalized bank. In the past, it has hardly used the bank limit because of sufficient internal resources. As may be seen from the estimated balance sheet as on March 31, 2004 in Table 14.1.2, CEC's capital employed included paid-up share capital and reserves without any debt. The CMD feels that given the government's current attitude whereby it would like profitable companies to raise funds from the capital markets for their investments, it may look odd for CEC to obtain budgetary support from the government. However, in his assessment, CEC being a profitable company, government may be willing to provide budgetary support for the project. More significantly, he felt that raising equity capital might dilute equity earnings. Thus, he decided to reconsider the company's policy of avoiding long-term debt. It was thought that the use of debt could be justified by the expected profitable position of the company.

Mr. Tandon has determined that the company could sell Rs 1,000 denomination bonds for an amount of Rs 200 million either to the public or to the financial institutions through private placement. The interest rate on bonds will be 10 per cent per annum, and they could be redeemed after seven years in three equal annual instalments. The bonds and interest thereon will be fully secured against the assets of the company. In Mr. Tandon's view, the company will have to sell a large number of bonds to the financial institutions as CEC being a new company in the capital market, the public may not fully subscribe to the issue. He also felt that from the individual investors' point of view, CEC might have to give an option to the bondholders to sell back to the company bonds up to an amount of Rs 10 million each year. Also, bondholders shall have right to appoint one nominee director on the board of the company which shall however be exercised by the bond trustees only if the company defaults in the payment of interest or repayment on the due date.

Table 14.1.2: CEC: Estimated Balance Sheet as on 31 March 2004

	(Rs in million)
Cash and bank balance	89.0
Sundry debtors	180.7
Inventory	41.1
Other current assets	47.1
Current assets	**357.9**
Gross block	819.9
Less: Accumulated depreciation	234.6
Net block	**585.3**
Total Assets	**943.2**
Sundry creditors	151.8
Tax provision	30.3
Other current liabilities	121.5
Current liabilities	**303.6**
Paid-up share capital	180.0
Reserves and surplus	459.6
Net worth	**639.6**
Total Liabilities and Capital	**943.2**

In Mr. Tandon's opinion the bond was a cheaper source of finance, since interest amount was tax deductible. Given the company's tax rate of 35 per cent, the 10 per cent interest rate was equal to 6.5 per cent from the company's point of view. On the other hand, he thought that equity capital would be costly to service, as CEC is currently paying a dividend of 15 per cent on its paid-up capital. Further, as per the current tax laws in India, the company would have to pay 12.5% tax on dividends. Thus, the bond alternative looked attractive to Mr. Tandon on the basis of the comparison of costs.

The expansion proposal was discussed in the January 2004 meeting of the board. As most of the members were convinced about the profitability and desirability of the project, they did not take much time to approve it. Immediately after this decision, Mr. Tandon informed the members about the possibility of raising finance through a bond issue. He then presented his report highlighting the comparison between bond and equity financing. His conclusions clearly showed that bond financing was better for the company. Mr. Tandon was surprised to note that substantial disagreement existed among the members regarding the use of bond.

One director questioned the correctness of Mr. Tandon's calculation of the cost of the bond as he had ignored the implications of the annual requirement arising out of investors exercising the option. According to him, this would mean higher cost of bond as compared to equity capital. Yet another director emphasized that a lot of annual cash outflow will also take place under the bond alternative. He felt that the issue of bond would thus add to the company's risk by pressurizing its liquidity. Most of the directors, however, were in agreement with the estimate of post expansion profit before interest and taxes (PBIT) of Rs 125 million.

One of the directors argued that given the expected higher PBIT, the post-expansion equity return would significantly increase if the funds are raised by issuing bonds. He even emphasized that the job of the management should be to maximize profitability of equity owners by taking reasonable risks. Another director countered this argument by stating that the equity return could be diluted if the company was unable to earn sufficient profit from the existing business and the new project. The discussion on bond versus equity financing was so involved that there did not seem to be any sign of a unanimous agreement being reached. At this juncture, Mr. Tandon suggested that the discussion on financing alternatives might be postponed until January end to allow him sufficient time to come up with a fresh analysis incorporating the various points raised in the current meeting. Mr. Tandon was wondering what he should do so that a unanimous decision could be reached.

Discussion Questions

1. Calculate EPS under the alternatives of employing (*a*) Rs 200 million debt and no fresh equity, (*b*) Rs 100 million debt and Rs 100 million equity and (*c*) Rs 200 million equity and no debt. Also make calculations for uncommitted-EPS. Draw a chart showing PBIT on *x*-axis and EPS and uncommitted-EPS on *y*-axis for debt-equity mix. What inferences do you derive?

2. Debate the issues raised in the case for and against the use of debt. Why do a large number of board members seem to be against the use of debt? What are the real risks involved? How would you measure them?

3. In addition to profitability and risk factors, what are other considerations before CEC to decide about its debt policy? Should it employ debt to finance its expansion?

4. Is there a relationship between debt and value of the firm?

Capital Structure Theory and Policy

INTRODUCTION

In chapter 14, we discussed the effect of leverage on the shareholders' earnings and risk. Under favourable economic conditions, the earnings per share increase with financial leverage. But leverage also increases the financial risk of shareholders. As a result, it cannot be stated definitely whether or not the firm's value will increase with leverage. The objective of a firm should be directed towards the maximisation of the firm's value. The capital structure or financial leverage decision should be examined from the point of its impact on the value of the firm. If capital structure decision can affect a firm's value, then it would like to have a capital structure, which maximises its market value. However, there exist conflicting theories on the relationship between capital structure and the value of a firm. The traditionalists believe that capital structure affects the firm's value while Modigliani and Miller (MM), under the assumptions of perfect capital markets and no taxes, argue that capital structure decision is irrelevant. MM reverse their position when they consider corporate taxes. Tax savings resulting from interest paid on debt creates value for the firm. However, the tax advantage of debt is reduced by personal taxes and financial distress. Hence, the trade-off between costs and benefits of debt can turn capital structure into a relevant decision. There are other views also on the relevance of capital structure. We first discuss the traditional theory of capital structure followed by MM and other views.

RELEVANCE OF CAPITAL STRUCTURE: THE NET INCOME AND THE TRADITIONAL VIEWS

There are several variations of the traditional theory. But the thrust of all views is that capital structure matters. One earlier version of the view that capital structure is relevant is the **net**

income (NI) approach.[1] We first discuss the NI approach, followed by other traditional views.

The Net Income Approach

A firm that finances its assets by equity and debt is called a **levered firm**. On the other hand, a firm that uses no debt and finances its assets entirely by equity is called an **unlevered firm**. Suppose firm L is a levered firm and it has financed its assets by equity and debt. It has perpetual expected EBIT or net operating income (NOI) of Rs 1,000 and the interest payment of Rs 300. The firm's cost of equity (or equity capitalisation rate), k_e, is 9.33 per cent and the cost of debt, k_d, is 6 per cent. What is the firm's value? The value of the firm is the sum of the values of all of its securities. In this case, firm L's securities include equity and debt; therefore the sum of the values of equity and debt is the firm's value. The value of a firm's shares (equity), E, is the discounted value of shareholders' earnings, called **net income**, NI. Firm's L's net income is: NOI − interest = 1,000 − 300 = Rs 700, and the cost of equity is 9.33 per cent. Hence the value of L's equity is: 700/0.0933 = Rs 7,500:

Value of equity = discounted value of net income

$$E = \frac{\text{Net Income}}{\text{Cost of equity}} = \frac{\text{NI}}{k_e}$$

$$= \frac{700}{0.0933} = \text{Rs } 7,500 \qquad (1)$$

Similarly the value of a firm's debt is the discounted value of debt-holders' interest income. The value of L's debt is: 300/0.06 = Rs 5,000:

Value of debt = discounted value of interest

$$D = \frac{\text{Interest}}{\text{Cost of debt}} = \frac{\text{INT}}{k_d}$$

$$= \frac{300}{0.06} = \text{Rs } 5,000 \qquad (2)$$

The value of firm L is the sum of the value of equity and the value of debt: 7,500 + 5,000 = Rs 12,500:

Value of the firm = value of equity + value of debt

$$V = E + D$$

$$= 7,500 + 5,000 = \text{Rs } 12,500 \qquad (3)$$

Firm's L's value is Rs 12,500 and its expected net operating income is Rs 1,000. Therefore, the firm's overall expected rate of return or the cost of capital is: 1,000/12,500 = 0.08 or 8 per cent:

$$\text{Firm's cost of capital} = \frac{\text{Net operating income}}{\text{Value of the firm}}$$

$$k_o = \frac{\text{NOI}}{V}$$

$$= \frac{1,000}{12,500} = 0.08 \text{ or } 8\% \qquad (4)$$

The firm's overall cost of capital is the **weighted average cost of capital** (WACC). There is an alternative way of calculating

WACC (k_o). WACC is the weighted average of costs of all of the firm's securities. Firm L's securities include debt and equity. Therefore, firm L's WACC or k_o, is the weighted average of the cost of equity and the cost of debt. Firm L's value is Rs 12,500, value of its equity is Rs 7,500 and value of its debt is Rs 5,000. Hence, the firm's debt ratio (D/V) is: 5,000/12,500 = 0.40 or 40 per cent, and the equity ratio (E/V) is: 7,500/12,500 = 0.60 or 60 per cent. Firm L's weighted average cost of capital is:

WACC = cost of equity × equity weight

$$\qquad + \text{ cost of debt} \times \text{debt weight} \qquad (5)$$

$$k_o = k_e \times \frac{E}{V} + k_d \times \frac{D}{V}$$

$$k_o = 0.0933 \times \frac{7,500}{12,500} + 0.06 \times \frac{5,000}{12,500}$$

$$k_o = 0.0933 \times 0.60 + 0.06 \times 0.40$$

$$= 0.056 + 0.025 = 0.08 \text{ or } 8\%$$

Suppose firm L operates in a *frictionless* world. There are no taxes and transaction costs and debt is risk-free and shareholders perceive no financial risk arising from the use of debt. Under these conditions, the cost of equity, k_e, and the cost of debt, k_d, will remain constant with financial leverage. Since debt is a cheaper source of finance than equity, the firm's weighted average cost of capital will reduce with financial leverage. Suppose firm L's substitutes debt for equity and raises its debt ratio to 90 per cent. Its WACC will be: 0.0933 × 0.10 + 0.06 × 0.90 = 0.0633 or 6.33 per cent. Firm L's WACC will be 6 per cent if it employs 100 per cent debt.

Rearranging Equation (5), we get

$$\text{WACC} = k_o = k_e \times \left(1 - \frac{D}{V}\right) + k_d \times \frac{D}{V}$$

$$\text{WACC} = k_o = k_e - (k_e - k_d)\frac{D}{V} \qquad (6)$$

You may note from Equation (6) that, given constant cost of equity, k_e, and cost of debt, k_d, and k_d less than k_e, the weighted average cost of capital, k_o, will decrease continuously with financial leverage, measured by D/V. You may also notice that k_o equals the cost of equity, k_e, minus the spread between the cost of equity and the cost of debt times D/V. WACC, k_o, will be equal to the cost of equity, k_e, if the firm does not employ any debt (i.e. $D/V = 0$), and k_o, will approach k_d, as D/V approaches one (or 100 per cent).

Under the assumption that k_e and k_d remain constant, the value of the firm will be:

$$V = E + D = \frac{\text{NOI} - \text{INT}}{k_e} + \frac{\text{INT}}{k_d}$$

$$= \frac{\text{NOI} - k_d D}{k_e} + \frac{k_d D}{k_d} = \frac{\text{NOI} - k_d D}{k_e} + D$$

$$= \frac{\text{NOI}}{k_e} + D - \frac{k_d D}{k_e}$$

$$V = \frac{\text{NOI}}{k_e} + D\left(1 - \frac{k_d}{k_e}\right) \qquad (7)$$

1. Durand, David, "Costs of Debt and Equity Funds for Business: Trends and Problems of Measurement", reprinted in *The Management of Corporate Capital*, Ezra Solomon (ed.), The Free Press, 1959, pp.'91–16.

You may notice that for an unlevered firm, the second term on the right-hand side of Equation (7) will be zero. The unlevered firm's cost of equity is also its WACC and its expected net operating income is its expected net income. Hence, the value of an unlevered (an all-equity) firm is the discounted value of the net operating income. You may also notice from Equation (7) that as the firm substitutes debt for equity and so long as k_e and k_d are constant, the value of the firm V increases by debt multiplied by a constant rate, $(k_e - k_d)/k_e$.

Illustration 15.1: Firm Value Under Net Income Approach

Suppose that a firm has no debt in its capital structure. It has an expected annual net operating income of Rs 100,000 and the equity capitalisation rate, k_e, of 10 per cent. Since the firm is 100 per cent equity financed firm, its weighted cost of capital equals its cost of equity, *i.e.*, 10 per cent. The value of the firm will be: $100,000 \div 0.10 = $ Rs 1,000,000.

Let us assume that the firm is able to change its capital structure replacing equity by debt of Rs 300,000. The cost of debt is 5 per cent. Interest payable to debt-holders is: Rs $300,000 \times 0.05 = $ Rs 15,000. The net income available to equity holders is: Rs 100,000 – Rs 15,000 = Rs 85,000.

The value of the firm is equal to the sum of values of all securities:

$$E = \frac{NOI - interest}{k_e} = \frac{NI}{k_e} = \frac{85,000}{0.10} = Rs\ 850,000$$

$$D = \frac{Interest}{k_d} = \frac{15,000}{0.05} = Rs\ 300,000$$

$$V = E + D = 850,000 + 300,000$$
$$= Rs\ 1,150,000$$

You can also calculate the value of the firm as follows:

$$V = \frac{100,000}{0.10} + 300,000\left(1 - \frac{0.05}{0.10}\right)$$
$$= 1,000,000 + 150,000 = Rs\ 1,150,000$$

The weighted average cost of capital, k_o, is:

$$k_o = \frac{NOI}{V} = \frac{1,00,000}{1,150,000} = 0.087\ or\ 8.7\ per\ cent$$

$$k_o = k_d\frac{D}{V} + k_e\frac{S}{V} = 0.05\left(\frac{300,000}{1,150,000}\right) + 0.10\left(\frac{8,50,000}{1,150,000}\right)$$
$$= 0.013 + 0.074 = 0.087\ or\ 8.7\ per\ cent$$

Table 15.1 shows the calculations of the firm's value and weighted average cost of capital.

Suppose the firm uses more debt in place of equity and increases debt to Rs 900,000. As shown in Table 15.1, the firm's value increases to Rs 1,450,000, and the weighted average cost of capital reduces to 8.1 per cent. Thus, by increasing debt, the firm is able to increase the value of the firm and lower WACC.

Table 15.1: Value of the Firm (NI Approach)

	Zero debt	5% Rs 300,000 debt	5% Rs 900,000 debt
Net operating income, NOI	100,000	100,000	100,000
Total cost of debt, INT = $k_d D$	0	15,000	45,000
Net income, NI: NOI – INT	100,000	85,000	55,000
Market value of equity, E: NI/k_e	1,000,000	850,000	550,000
Market value of debt, D: INT/k_d	0	300,000	900,000
Market value of the firm, V = E + D = NOI/k_o	1,000,000	1,150,000	1,450,000
Debt/Total value, D/V	0.00	0.261	0.62
WACC, NOI ÷ V = $k_e \times E/V + k_d \times D/V$	0.100	0.087	0.081

We construct Table 15.2 to show the effect of financial leverage on the value of the firm and WACC under the NI approach. It is assumed that the net operating income is Rs 100,000 and the debt-capitalisation rate and the equity-capitalisation rate respectively are 5 per cent and 10 per cent, and they remain constant with debt. It is noticeable from the table that the value of the firm increases steadily as the debt ratio, D/V, increases and WACC declines continuously, ultimately reducing to 5 per cent at 100 per cent debt ratio.

Figure 15.1 plots WACC as a function of financial leverage. Financial leverage, D/V, is plotted along the horizontal axis and WACC, k_o, and the cost of equity, k_e, and the cost of debt, k_d, on the vertical axis. You may notice from Figure 15.1 that, under NI approach, k_e and k_d are constant. As debt is replaced for equity in the capital structure, being less expensive, it causes weighted average cost of capital, k_o, to decrease that ultimately approaches

Table 15.2: Effect of Leverage on Value and Cost of Capital under NI Approach

Leverage (D/V) %	0.00	18.18	33.34	46.15	66.67	94.74	100
NOI	Rs 100	Rs 100	Rs 100	Rs 100	Rs 100	Rs 100	Rs 100
Interest, INT	–	10	20	30	50	90	100
NI = NOI – INT	Rs 100	Rs 90	Rs 80	Rs 70	Rs 50	Rs 10	Rs 0
k_d (%)	5.0	5.0	5.0	5.0	5.0	5.0	5.0
k_e (%)	10.0	10.0	10.0	10.0	10.0	10.0	10.0
k_0 (%)	10.0	9.1	8.3	7.7	6.7	5.3	5.0
$E = (NOI - INT)/k_e$	Rs 1,000	Rs 900	Rs 800	Rs 700	Rs 500	Rs 100	Rs 0
$D = INT/k_d$	0	200	400	600	1,000	1,800	2,000
$V = E + D$	Rs 1,000	Rs 1,100	Rs 1,200	Rs 1,300	Rs 1,500	Rs 1,900	Rs 2,000

the cost of debt with 100 per cent debt ratio (D/V). The optimum capital structure occurs at the point of minimum WACC. Under the NI approach, the firm will have the maximum value and minimum WACC when it is 100 per cent debt-financed.

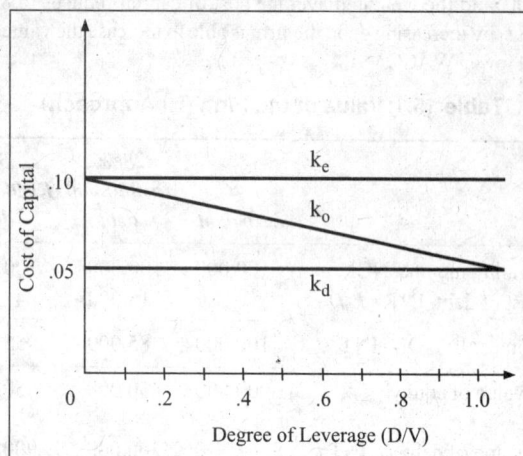

Figure. 15.1: The effect of leverage on the cost of capital under NI approach

The Traditional View

The **traditional view**[1] has emerged as a compromise to the extreme position taken by the NI approach. Like the NI approach, it does not assume constant cost of equity with financial leverage and continuously declining WACC. According to this view, a judicious mix of debt and equity capital can increase the value of the firm by reducing the weighted average cost of capital (WACC or k_0) up to certain level of debt. This approach very clearly implies that WACC decreases only within the reasonable limit of financial leverage and reaching the minimum level, it starts increasing with financial leverage. Hence, a firm has an optimum capital structure that occurs when WACC is minimum, and thereby maximising the value of the firm. Why does WACC decline? WACC declines with moderate level of leverage since low-cost debt is replaced for expensive equity capital. Financial leverage, resulting in risk to shareholders, will cause the cost of equity to increase. But the traditional theory assumes that at moderate level of leverage, the increase in the cost of equity is more than offset by the lower cost of debt. The assertion that debt funds are cheaper than equity funds carries the clear implication that the cost of debt plus the increased cost of equity, together on a weighted basis, will be less than the cost of equity that existed on equity before debt financing.[2] For example, suppose that the cost of capital for totally equity-financed firm is 12 per cent. Since the firm is financed only by equity, 12 per cent is also the firm's cost of equity (k_e). The firm replaces, say, 40 per cent equity by debt bearing 8 per cent rate of interest (cost of debt, k_d). According to the traditional theory, the financial risk caused by the introduction of debt may increase the cost of equity slightly, but not so much that the advantage of cheaper debt is taken off totally. Assume that the cost of equity increases to 13 per cent. The firm's WACC will be:

WACC = cost of equity × weight of equity

+ cost of debt × weight of debt

$$\text{WACC} = k_o = k_e \times w_e + k_d \times w_d$$
$$= 0.13 \times 0.6 + 0.08 \times 0.4 = 0.078 + 0.032 = 0.11 \text{ or } 11\%$$

Thus, WACC will decrease with the use of debt. But as leverage increases further, shareholders start expecting higher risk premium in the form of increasing cost of equity until a point is reached at which the advantage of lower-cost debt is more than offset by more expensive equity. Let us consider an example as given in Illustration 15.2.

Illustration 15.2: The Traditional Theory of Capital Structure

Suppose a firm is expecting a perpetual net operating income of Rs 150 crore on assets of Rs 1,500 crore, which are entirely financed by equity. The firm's equity capitalisation rate (the cost of equity) is 10 per cent. It is considering substituting equity capital by issuing perpetual debentures of Rs 300 crore at 6 per cent interest rate. The cost of equity is expected to increase to 10.56 per cent. The firm is also considering the alternative of raising perpetual debentures of Rs 600 crore and replace equity. The debt-holders will charge interest of 7 per cent, and the cost of equity will rise to 12.5 per cent to compensate shareholders for higher financial risk.

Notice that at higher level of debt (Rs 600 crore), both the cost of equity and cost of debt increase more than at lower level of debt. The calculations for the value of the firm, the value of equity and WACC are shown in Table 15.3.

Table 15.3: Market Value and the Cost of Capital of the Firm (Traditional Approach)

	No Debt	*6% Debt*	*7% Debt*
	(Rs in crore)	*(Rs in crore)*	*(Rs in crore)*
Net operating income, NOI	150	150	150
Total cost of debt, INT = $k_d D$	0	18	42
Net income, NOI– INT	150	132	108
Cost of equity, k_e	0.1000	0.1056	0.1250
Market value of equity, E = (NOI– INT)/ k_e	1,500	1,250	864
Market value of debt, D	0	300	600
Total value of firm, $V = E + D$	1,500	1,550	1,464
Equity-to-total value, $w_e = E/V$	1.00	0.806	0.590
Debt-to-total value, $w_d = D/V$	0.00	0.194	0.410
WACC, $k_o^{\bullet}$ = NOI/V = $k_e \times w_e + k_d \times w_d$	0.1000	0.0970	0.1030

When the firm has no debt, WACC and the cost of equity are the same (10 per cent). We assume that the expected net operating income, the net income and interest are perpetual flows. We also assume that the expected net income is distributed entirely to shareholders. Therefore, the value of equity is:

$$\text{Value of equity} = \frac{\text{Net income}}{\text{Cost of equity}} = E = \frac{\text{NI}}{k_e}$$

---

1. Solomon, Ezra, *The Theory of Financial Management,* University Press, 1963, p. 92.
2. Barges, A., *The Effect of Capital Structure on the Cost of Capital*, Prentice-Hall, Inc., 1963, p. 11.

The value of debt is interest income to debt-holders divided by the cost of debt:

$$\text{Value of debt} = \frac{\text{Interest income}}{\text{Cost of debt}} = D = \frac{INT}{k_d}$$

The sum of values of debt and equity is the firm's total value, and is directly given by net operating income divided by WACC:

$$\text{Value of firm} = \frac{\text{Net operating income}}{WACC} = S + D = \frac{NOI}{k_o}$$

You may notice from the above discussion that, according to the traditional theory, the value of the firm may first increase with moderate leverage, reach the maximum value and then start declining with higher leverage. This is so because WACC first decreases and after reaching the minimum, it starts increasing with leverage. Thus, the traditional theory on the relationship between capital structure and the firm value has three stages.[1]

First Stage: Increasing Value

In the first stage, the cost of equity, k_e, the rate at which the shareholders capitalise their net income, either remains constant or rises slightly with debt. The cost of equity does not increase fast enough to offset the advantage of low-cost debt. During this stage, the cost of debt, k_d, remains constant since the market views the use of debt as a reasonable policy. As a result, the overall cost of capital, WACC or k_o, decreases with increasing leverage, and thus, the total value of the firm, V, also increases.

Second Stage: Optimum Value

Once the firm has reached a certain degree of leverage, increases in leverage have a negligible effect on WACC and hence, on the value of the firm. This is so because the increase in the cost of equity due to the added financial risk just offsets the advantage of low cost debt. Within that range or at the specific point, WACC will be minimum, and the maximum value of the firm will be obtained.

Third Stage: Declining Value

Beyond the acceptable limit of leverage, the value of the firm decreases with leverage as WACC increases with leverage. This happens because investors perceive a high degree of financial risk and demand a higher equity-capitalisation rate, which exceeds the advantage of low-cost debt.

The overall effect of these three stages is to suggest that the cost of capital (WACC) is a function of leverage. It first declines with leverage and after reaching a minimum point or range starts rising. The relation between costs of capital and leverage is graphically shown in Figure 15.2 wherein the overall cost of capital curve, k_o, is saucer-shaped with a horizontal range. This implies that there is a range of capital structures in which the cost of capital is minimised. k_e, is assumed to increase slightly in the beginning and then at a faster rate. In Figure 15.3 the cost of capital curve is shown as U-shaped. The U-shaped cost of capital implies that there is a precise point at which the cost of

capital is minimum. This precise point defines the optimum capital structure.

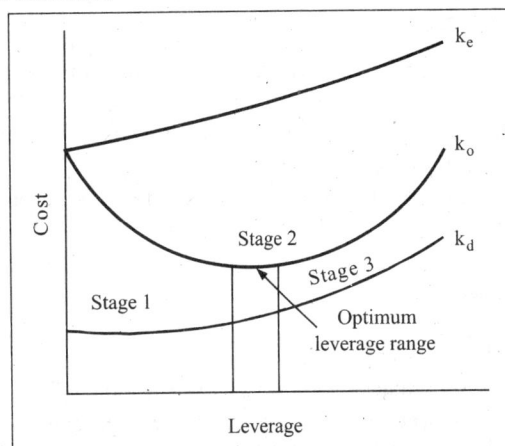

Figure 15.2: The cost of capital (saucer-shaped)

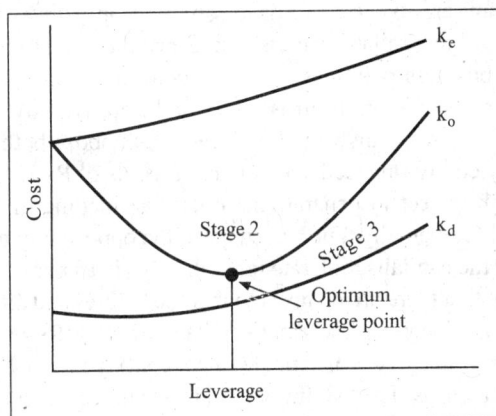

Figure 15.3: The cost of capital (U-shaped)

As stated earlier, many variations of the traditional view exist (Figures 15.2 and 15.3). Whether the cost of equity function is horizontal or rising slightly is not very pertinent from the theoretical point of view, as a number of different costs of equity curves can be consistent with a declining average cost of capital curve. The relevant issue is whether or not the average cost of capital curve declines at all as debt is used.[2] All supporters of the traditional view agree that the cost of capital declines with debt.

Criticism of the Traditional View

The traditional theory implies that investors value levered firms more than unlevered firm. This means that they pay a premium for the shares of levered firms. The contention of the traditional theory that moderate amount of debt in 'sound' firms does not really add very much to the 'riskiness' of the shares is not defensible. There does not exist sufficient justification for the assumption that investors' perception about risk of leverage is different at different levels of leverage. However, as we shall explain later, the existence of an optimum capital structure can be supported on two counts: the tax deductibility of interest charges and other market imperfections.

1. Solomon, *op.cit.*, p. 94, Brigham, Eugene F. and Roman E. Johnson, (eds.), *Issue in Managerial Finance*, Dryden Press, 1976, p. 256.
2. Barges, *op. cit.*, p. 12.

IRRELEVANCE OF CAPITAL STRUCTURE: NOI APPROACH AND THE MM HYPOTHESIS WITHOUT TAXES

Modigliani and Miller (MM) do not agree with the traditional view.[1] They argue that, in perfect capital markets without taxes and transaction costs, a firm's market value and the cost of capital remain invariant to the capital structure changes. The value of the firm depends on the earnings and risk of its assets (business risk) rather than the way in which assets have been financed. The MM hypotheses can be best explained in terms of their two propositions.

Proposition I

Consider two pharmaceutical firms, Ultrafine and Lifeline, which have identical assets, operate in same market segments and have equal market share. These two firms belong to the same industry and they face similar competitive and business conditions. Hence, they are expected to have same net operating income and exposed to similar business risk. Since the two firms have identical business risk, it is logical to conclude that investors' expected rates of return from assets, k_a or the opportunity cost of capital of the two firms would be identical. Suppose both firms are totally equity financed and both have assets of Rs 225 crore each. Both expect to generate net operating income of Rs 45 crore each perpetually. Further, suppose the opportunity cost of capital or the capitalisation rate for both firms is 15 per cent. Let us assume that there are no taxes so that the before- and after-tax net operating income is the same. Capitalising NOI (Rs 45 crore) by the opportunity cost of capital (15 per cent), you can find the value of the firms. The two firms would have the same value: 45/0.15 = Rs 300 crore.

Let us now change the assumption regarding the financing. Suppose Ultrafine is an unlevered firm with 100 per cent equity and Lifeline a levered firm with 50 per cent equity and 50 per cent debt. Should the market values of two firms differ? Debt will not change the earnings potential of Lifeline as it depends on its investment in assets. Debt also cannot affect the business conditions and therefore, the business (operating) risk of Lifeline — the levered firm. You know that the value of a firm depends upon its expected net operating income and the overall capitalisation rate or the opportunity cost of capital. Since the form of financing (debt or equity) can neither change the firm's net operating income nor its operating risk, the values of levered and unlevered firms ought be the same. Financing changes the way in which the net operating income is distributed between equity holders and debt-holders. Firms with identical net operating income and business (operating) risk, but differing capital structure, should have same total value. *MM*'s Proposition I is that, for firms in the same risk class, the total market value is independent of the debt-equity mix and is given by capitalising the expected net operating income by the capitalisation rate (i.e., the opportunity cost of capital) appropriate to that risk class:[2]

Value of levered firm = Value of unleverd firm

$$V_1 = V_u$$

Value of the firm $= \dfrac{\text{Net operating income}}{\text{Firm' s opportunity cost of capital}}$

$$V = V_1 = V_u = \frac{\text{NOI}}{k_a} \qquad (8)$$

where V is the market value of the firm and it is sum of the value of equity, E and the value of debt, D; NOI = EBIT = $\overline{X}$ the expected net operating income; and k_a = the firm's opportunity cost of capital or the capitalisation rate appropriate to the risk class of the firm.

MM's approach is a **net operating income approach** because the value of the firm is the capitalised value of net operating income. Both net operating income and the firm's opportunity cost of capital are assumed to be constant with regard to the level of financial leverage. For a levered firm, the expected net operating income is sum of the income of shareholders and the income of debt-holders. Debt-holders' income is interest and shareholders' income, called net income, is the expected net operating income less interest. The levered firm's value is the sum of the value of equity and value of debt. The levered firm's expected rate of return is the ratio of the expected operating income to the value of all its securities. This is an average expected rate of return that the levered firm's all security-holders would require the firm to earn on total investments. The average rate of return required by all security-holders in a levered firm is the firm's weighted average cost of capital; i.e., WACC $= k_o$ or k_l. Thus

$$V_1 = \frac{\text{NOI}}{k_l = k_a}$$

$$k_o = k_l = \frac{\text{NOI}}{V_l} \qquad (9)$$

In the case of an unlevered firm, the entire net operating income is the shareholders net income. Therefore, the unlevered firm's WACC or k_u is equal to its opportunity cost of capital:

$$k_a = k_u = \frac{\text{NOI}}{V_u} \qquad (10)$$

Since the values of the levered and unlevered firms and the expected net operating income (NOI) do not change with financial leverage, the weighted average cost of capital would also not change with financial leverage. Hence, MM's Proposition I also implies that the weighted average cost of capital for two identical firms, one levered and another unlevered, will be equal to the opportunity cost of capital (Figure 15.1):

Levered firm's cost of capital (k_1) = Unlevered firm's cost of capital (k_u)

$$k_1 = k_o = k_a = k_u$$

---

1. Modigliani, H., and Miller, M.H., The Cost Capital, Corporation Finance and The Theory of Investment, *American Economic Review,* 48 (June 1958), pp. 261–97.
2. *Ibit.,* p. 266.

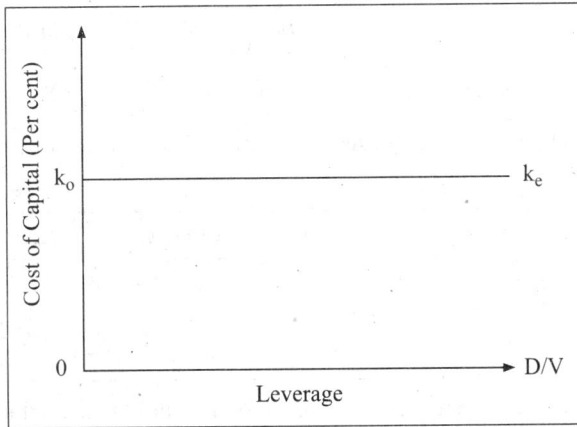

Figure 15.4: The cost of capital under M–M proposition I

Arbitrage Process

Why should MM's Proposition I work? As stated earlier, the simple logic of Proposition I is that two firms with identical assets, irrespective of how these assets have been financed, cannot command different market values. Suppose this were not true and two identical firms, except for their capital structures, have different market values. In this situation, **arbitrage** (or **switching**) will take place to enable investors to engage in the **personal** or **homemade leverage** as against the **corporate leverage** to restore equilibrium in the market. Consider the following example.

Illustration 15.3: The MM Proposition I and Arbitrage

Suppose two firms - Firm U, an unlevered firm and Firm L, a levered firm - have identical assets and expected net operating income (NOI = $\overline{X}$) of Rs 10,000. The value of Firm L is Rs 100,000 assuming the cost of equity of 10 per cent under the traditional view. Since Firm U has no debt, the value of its equity is equal to its total value ($E_u = V_u$). Firm L employs 6 per cent Rs 50,000 debt. Suppose its cost of equity under the traditional view is 11.7 per cent. Thus, the value of Firm L's equity shares (E_1) is Rs 60,000, and its total value (V_l) firm is Rs 110,000 ($V_1 = E_1 + D_1$ = 60,000 + 50,000).

Table 15.4: Value of Levered and Unlevered Firms

	Firm U (Unlevered)	Firm L (Levered)
Net operating income, $\overline{X}$	10,000	10,000
Interest, INT	0	3,000
Net income (dividends), $\overline{X}$ – INT	10,000	7,000
Cost of equity, k_e (traditional view)	0.100	0.117
Market value of equity, E	100,000	60,000
Market value of debt, D	0	50,000
Market value of firm, $V = E + D$	100,000	110,000
WACC, k_o (traditional view)	0.10	0.091

You may notice that Firm L and Firm U have identical assets and NOI, but they have different market prices. The cheaper debt of Rs 50,000 of Firm L has increased shareholders wealth by Rs 10,000. MM argue that this situation cannot continue for long, as **arbitrage** will bring two prices into equilibrium. How does arbitrage work?

Assume that you hold 10 per cent shares of the levered firm L. What is your return from your investment in the shares of firm L? Since you own 10 per cent of L's shares, your equity investment is: $0.10 \times (110,000 - 50,000)$ = Rs 6,000. You also 'own' 10 per cent of L's corporate debt: $0.10 \times 50,000$ = Rs 5,000. You are entitled to 10 per cent of the equity income (dividends):

$$\text{Return} = 0.10(\overline{X} - \text{INT})$$
$$= 0.10(10,000) - 0.06 \times 50,000)$$
$$= 0.10(10,000 - 3,000) = \text{Rs } 700$$

You can earn same return at lesser investment through an alternate investment strategy. This you can do by switching your investment from firm L and firm U as follows:

1. Selling your investment in firm L's shares for Rs 6,000.
2. Borrowing on your *personal account* an amount equal to your share of firm L's corporate debt at 6 per cent rate of interest: $0.10(50,000)$ = Rs 5,000.
3. Buying 10 per cent of the unlevered firm U's shares investing: $0.10 \times 100,000$ = Rs 10,000.

You have Rs 11,000 with you; that is, Rs 6,000 from sale of L's shares and Rs 5,000 borrowed funds. Your investment in U's shares is Rs 10,000. Thus, you have surplus cash of Rs 1,000.

Your return from U is:

Return from investment in U's share = $0.10 \times 10,000$ = Rs 1,000

However, you have borrowed Rs 5,000 at 6 per cent. Therefore, you will have to pay an interest of Rs 300:

Interest payable on borrowed funds = $0.06 \times 5,000$ = Rs 300

Thus your net return is Rs 700 = Rs 1,000 – Rs 300:

	Rs
Equity return from U: $0.10 \times$ Rs 10,000	1,000
Less: Interest on personal borrowing: $0.06 \times$ Rs 5,000	300
Net return	700

You earn the same return from the alternate strategy. But now you also have extra cash of Rs 1,000 that you can invest to enhance your return. Thus, the alternate strategy will yield higher overall return. Your risk is same in both the cases. While shifting your investment from firm U to firm L, you replaced your share of L's debt by personal debt. You have created 'personal' or 'homemade leverage' instead of 'corporate leverage'.

Due to the advantage of the alternate investment strategy, a number of investors will be induced towards it. They will sell their shares in firm L and buy shares and debt of firm U. This arbitrage will tend to increase the price of firm U's shares and to decline that of firm L's shares. It will continue until the equilibrium price for the shares of firm U and firm L is reached.

The arbitrage would work in the opposite direction if we assume that the value of the unlevered firm U is greater than the value of the levered firm L (i.e., $V_u > V_l$). Let us assume that $V_u = E_u$ = Rs 100,000 and $V_1 = E_1 + D_1$ = Rs 40,000 + Rs 50,000 = Rs 90,000. Further, suppose that you still own 10 per cent shares in the unlevered firm U. Your return and investment will be:

$$\text{Return} = 0.10(10,000) = \text{Rs } 1,000$$
$$\text{Investment} = 0.10(100,000) = \text{Rs } 10,000$$

You can design a better investment strategy. You should do the following:

1. Sell your shares in firm U for Rs 10,000.
2. Buy 10 per cent of firm L's shares and debt:

$$\text{Investment} = 0.10(40,000 + 50,000)$$
$$= 4,000 + 5,000 = Rs\,9,000$$

Your investment in firm L is Rs 9,000. You have extra cash of Rs 1,000. Since you own 10 per cent of equity and debt of firm L, your return will include both equity income and interest income. Thus your return is Rs 1,000:

$$\text{Return} = 0.10(10,000) = 0.10(10,000 - 3,000) + 0.10(3,000)$$
$$= Rs\,1,000$$

Note that your alternate investment strategy pays you off the same return but at a lesser investment. Both strategies give the investor same return, but your alternate investment strategy costs you less since $V_1 < V_u$. In such a situation, investors will sell their shares in the unlevered firm and buy the shares and debt of the levered firm. As a result of this switching, the market value of the levered firm's shares will increase and that of the unlevered firm will decline. Ultimately, the price equilibrium will be reached (i.e., $V_1 = V_u$) and there will be no advantage of switching anymore.

We can generalise our discussion in the formal terms.[1] In the first instance, let the value of levered firm L be greater than the value of unlevered firm U (i.e., $V_1 > V_u$). Both firms earn the same expected net operating income, $\overline{X}$. The borrowing and lending rate, k_d, is same for both corporations and individuals. Assume that an investor holds α (alpha) fraction of firm L's shares. His investment and return will be as follows:

	Investment	Return
Investment in L's shares	$\alpha(V_1 - D_1)$	$\alpha(\overline{X} - k_d D_1)$

The investor can also design the following alternate investment strategy:

	Investment	Return
Buy fraction of U's shares	αV_u	$\alpha \overline{X}$
Borrow equal to fraction of L's debt	$- \alpha D_1$	$- \alpha k_d D_1$
	$\alpha(V_u - D_1)$	$\alpha(\overline{X} - k_d D_1)$

The investor obtains the same return, $\alpha(\overline{X} - k_d D_1)$ in both the cases, but his first investment strategy costs more since $V_1 > V_u$. The rational investors at the margin would prefer switching from levered to unlevered firm. The increasing demand for the unlevered firm's shares will increase their market price, while the declining demand for the levered firm's shares will decrease their market price. Ultimately, market values of the two firms will reach equilibrium, and henceforth, arbitrage will not be beneficial.

Let us take the opposite case where $V_u > V_1$. Suppose our investor holds a fraction of firm U's shares. His investment and return will be as follows:

	Investment	Return
Investment in U's shares	αV_u	$\alpha \overline{X}$

The investor can design an alternate investment strategy as follows:

	Investment	Return
Buy fraction of L's shares	$\alpha(V_1 - D_1)$	$\alpha(\overline{X} - k_d D_1)$
Buy equal to fraction of L's debt	$+ \alpha D_1$	$+ \alpha k_d D_1$
	αV_1	$\alpha \overline{X}$

The investor earns the same return from the alternate strategy but by investing less since $V_u > V_1$. Other investors can also benefit similarly by switching their investment. Investors will sell shares of firm U and buy shares of firm L. This arbitrage will cause the price of firm U's shares to decline and that of firm L's shares to increase. It will continue until the value of the levered firm's equals that of the unlevered firm. Thus, in equilibrium the value of levered firm will be equal to the value of unlevered firm, i.e., $V_1 = V_u$.

On the basis of the arbitrage process, MM conclude that the market value of a firm is not affected by leverage. Thus, the financing (or capital structure) decision is irrelevant. It does not help in creating any wealth for shareholders. Hence one capital structure is as much desirable (or undesirable!) as the other.

Key Assumptions

MM's Proposition I is based on certain assumptions. These assumptions relate to the behaviour of investors and capital markets, the actions of the firm and the tax environment.

- *Perfect capital markets* Securities (shares and debt instruments) are traded in the **perfect capital market** situation. This specifically means that (a) investors are free to buy or sell securities; (b) they can borrow without restriction at the same terms as the firms do; and (c) they behave rationally. It is also implied that the transaction costs, i.e., the cost of buying and selling securities, do not exist. The assumption that firms and individual investors can borrow and lend at the same rate of interest is a very critical assumption for the validity of MM Proposition I. The homemade leverage will not be a substitute for the corporate leverage if the borrowing and lending rates for individual investors are different from firms.

- *Homogeneous risk classes* Firms operate in similar business conditions and have similar operating risk. They are considered to have similar operating risk and belong to *homogeneous risk classes* when their expected earnings have identical risk characteristics. It is generally *implied* under the MM hypothesis that firms within same industry constitute a homogeneous class.

- *Risk* The operating risk is defined in terms of the variability

---

1. Modigliani and Miller, Reply to Heins and Sprenkle, *American Economic Review*, 59 (Sept. 1969), pp. 592–95.

of the net operating income (NOI). The risk of investors depends on both the random fluctuations of the expected NOI and the possibility that the actual value of the variable may turn out to be different than their best estimate.[1]

- *No taxes* There do not exist any corporate taxes. This implies that interest payable on debt do not save any taxes.
- *Full payout* Firms distribute all net earnings to shareholders. This means that firms follow a *100 per cent dividend payout*.

Proposition II

We have explained earlier that the value of the firm depends on the expected net operating income and the opportunity cost of capital, k_a, which is same for both levered and unlevered firms. In the absence of corporate taxes, the firm's capital structure (financial leverage) does not affect its net operating income. Hence, for the value of the firm to remain constant with financial leverage, the opportunity cost of capital, k_a, must also stay constant with financial leverage. The opportunity cost of capital, k_a depends on the firm's operating risk. Since financial leverage does not affect the firm's operating risk, there is no reason for the opportunity cost of capital, k_a to change with financial leverage.

Financial leverage does not affect a firm's net operating income, but as we have discussed in Chapter 14, it does affect shareholders' return (EPS and ROE). EPS and ROE increase with leverage when the interest rate is less than the firm's return on assets. Financial leverage also increases shareholders' financial risk by amplifying the variability of EPS and ROE. Thus, financial leverage causes two opposing effects: it increases the shareholders' return but it also increases their financial risk. Shareholders will increase the required rate of return (i.e., the cost of equity) on their investment to compensate for the financial risk. The higher the financial risk, the higher the shareholders' required rate of return or the cost of equity. This is *MM*'s Proposition II.

An all-equity financed or unlevered firm has no debt; its opportunity cost of capital is equal its cost of equity; that is, unlevered firm's $k_e = k_a$. *MM*'s Proposition II provides justification for the levered firm's opportunity cost of capital remaining constant with financial leverage. In simple words, it states that the cost of equity, k_e, will increase enough to offset the advantage of cheaper cost of debt so that the opportunity cost of capital, k_a, does not change. A levered firm has financial risk while an unlevered firm is not exposed to financial risk. Hence, a levered firm will have higher required return on equity as compensation for financial risk. The cost of equity for a levered firm should be higher than the opportunity cost of capital, k_a; that is, the levered firm's $k_e > k_a$. It should be equal to constant k_a, plus a **financial risk premium**. How is this financial risk premium determined? You know that a levered firm's cost of capital is the weighted average of the cost of equity and the cost of debt:

$$k_a = k_e \times \frac{E}{E+D} + k_d \frac{D}{E+D}$$

You can solve this equation to determine the levered firm's cost of equity, k_e:

$$k_e = k_a + \left(k_a - k_d\right)\frac{D}{E} \qquad (11)$$

You may note from the equation that for an unlevered firm, D (debt) is zero; therefore, the second part of the right-hand side of the equation is zero and the opportunity cost of capital, k_a equals the cost of equity, k_e. We can see from the equation that financial risk premium of a levered firm is equal to debt-equity ratio, D/E, times the spread between the constant opportunity cost of capital and the cost of debt, $(k_o - k_d)$. The required return on equity is positively related to financial leverage, because the financial risk of shareholders increases with financial leverage. The cost of equity, k_e, is a linear function of financial leverage, D/E. It is noteworthy that the functional relationship given in Equation (11) is valid irrespective of any particular valuation theory. For example, MM assume the levered firm's opportunity cost of capital or WACC to be constant, while according to the traditional view WACC depends on financial leverage.

Let us consider the following example to understand the implications of MM's Proposition II.

Illustration 15.4: Implications of MM's Proposition II

Suppose Information Technology Limited (ITL) is an all-equity financed company. It has 10,000 shares outstanding. The market value of these shares is Rs 120,000. The expected operating income of the company is Rs 18,000. The expected EPS of the company is: Rs 18,000/10,000 = Rs 1.80. Since ITL is an unlevered company, its opportunity cost of capital will be equal to its cost of equity, k_e:

$$k_a = k_e = \frac{\text{Expected NOI}}{\text{Market value of debt and equity}}$$

$$= \frac{18,000}{120,000} = 0.15 \text{ or } 15\%$$

Let us assume that ITL is considering borrowing Rs 60,000 at 6 per cent rate of interest and buy back 5,000 shares at the market value of Rs 60,000. Now ITL has Rs 60,000 equity and Rs 60,000 debt in its capital structure. Thus, the company's debt-equity ratio is 1. The change in the company's capital structure does not affect its assets and expected net operating income. However, EPS will change. The expected EPS is:

$$\text{EPS} = \frac{\text{Net income}}{\text{Number of shares}} = \frac{18,000 - 3,600}{5,000} = \text{Rs } 2.88$$

ITL's expected EPS increases by 60 per cent due to financial leverage. If ITL's expected NOI fluctuates, its EPS will show greater variability with financial leverage than as an unlevered firm. Since the firm's operating risk does not change, its opportunity cost of capital (or WACC) will still remain 15 per cent. The cost of equity will increase to compensate for the financial risk:

$$k_e = k_a + \left(k_a - \tilde{k}_d\right)\frac{D}{E}$$

$$= 0.15 + \left(0.15 - 0.06\right)\frac{60,000}{60,000} = 0.24 \text{ or } 24\%$$

---

1. Robicheck, A. and Myers, S., *Optimal Financing Decisions*, Prentice-Hall Inc., 1965, pp. 31–34.

The crucial part of Proposition II is that the levered firm's opportunity cost of capital will not rise even if very excessive use of financial leverage is made. The excessive use of debt increases the risk of default. Hence, in practice, the cost of debt, k_d, will increase with high level of financial leverage. *MM* argue that when k_d increases, k_e will increase at a decreasing rate and may even turn down eventually.[1] The reason for this behaviour of k_e, is that debt-holders, in the extreme leveraged situations, own the firm's assets and bear some of the firm's business risk. Since the operating risk of shareholders is transferred to debt-holders, k_e declines. This is illustrated in Figure 15.5.

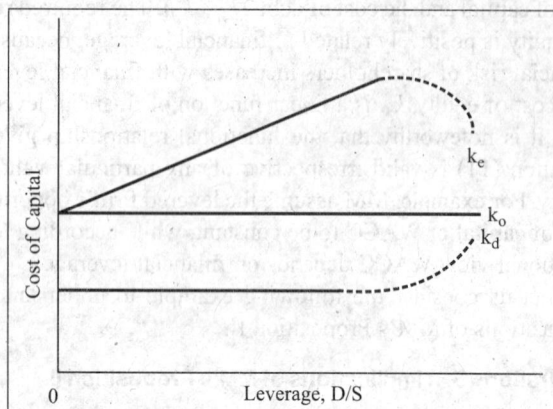

Figure 15.5: Cost of equity under the M–M

Criticism of the MM Hypothesis

The arbitrage process is the behavioural foundation for *MM*'s hypothesis. The shortcomings of this hypothesis lie in the assumption of perfect capital market in which arbitrage is expected to work. Due to the existence of imperfections in the capital market, arbitrage may fail to work and may give rise to discrepancy between the market values of levered and unlevered firms. The arbitrage process may fail to bring equilibrium in the capital market for the following reasons:[2]

Lending and borrowing rates discrepancy The assumption that firms and individuals can borrow and lend at the same rate of interest does not hold in practice. Because of the substantial holding of fixed assets, firms have a higher credit standing. As a result, they are able to borrow at lower rates of interest than individuals. If the cost of borrowing to an investor is more than the firm's borrowing rate, then the equalisation process will fall short of completion.

Non-substitutability of personal and corporate leverages It is incorrect to assume that "personal (home-made) leverage" is a perfect substitute for "corporate leverage." The existence of limited liability of firms in contrast with unlimited liability of individuals clearly places individuals and firms on a different footing in the capital markets. If a levered firm goes bankrupt, all investors stand to lose to the extent of the amount of the purchase price of their shares. But, if an investor creates personal

leverage, then in the event of the firm's insolvency, he would lose not only his principal in the shares of the unlevered company, but will also be liable to return the amount of his personal loan. Thus, it is more risky to create personal leverage and invest in the unlevered firm than investing directly in the levered firm.

Transaction costs The existence of transaction costs also interferes with the working of arbitrage. Because of the costs involved in the buying and selling securities, it would become necessary to invest a greater amount in order to earn the same return. As a result, the levered firm will have a higher market value.

Institutional restrictions Institutional restrictions also impede the working of arbitrage. The "home-made" leverage is not practically feasible as a number of institutional investors would not be able to substitute personal leverage for corporate leverage, simply because they are not allowed to engage in the "home-made" leverage.

Existence of corporate tax The incorporation of the corporate income taxes will also frustrate *MM*'s conclusions. Interest charges are tax deductible. This, in fact, means that the cost of borrowing funds to the firm is less than the contractual rate of interest. The very existence of interest charges gives the firm a tax advantage, which allows it to return to its equity and debt-holders a larger stream of income than it otherwise could have. Consider an example.

Suppose a levered and an unlevered firms have NOI = Rs 10,000. Further, the levered has: $k_d = 0.06$ and $D_1 = $ Rs 20,000. Assume that the corporate income tax exists and the rate is 50 per cent. The unlevered firm's after tax operating income will be: NOI – tax on NOI, i.e., $10,000 - 10,000 \times 0.50 = 10,000 - 5,000 = $ Rs 5000. Interest is tax exempt. Therefore, levered firm's taxes will be less. The after-tax net operating income of the levered firm will be: NOI – tax on NOI minus interest, i.e., $10,000 - (10,000 - 1,200) \times 0.50 = 10,000 - 4,400 = $ Rs 5,600. Thus, the total after-tax operating earnings of debt-holders and equity holders is more in the case of the levered firm. Hence, the total market value of a levered firm should tend to exceed that of the unlevered firm for this very reason. This point is explained further in the following section.

RELEVANCE OF CAPITAL STRUCTURE: THE MM HYPOTHESIS UNDER CORPORATE TAXES

MM's hypothesis that the value of the firm is independent of its debt policy is based on the critical assumption that corporate income taxes do not exist. In reality, corporate income taxes exist, and interest paid to debt-holders is treated as a deductible expense. Thus, interest payable by firms saves taxes. This makes debt financing advantageous. In their 1963 article, *MM* show that the value of the firm will increase with debt due to the deductibility of interest charges for tax computation, and the value of the levered firm will be higher than of the unlevered firm.[3] Consider an example.

1. Modigliani and Miller, *op. cit.*
2. Solomon, *op. cit.,* Durand, *op.cit.* Also see, Pandey, I.M., *Capital Structure and the Cost of Capital,* Vikas, reprint, 1996.
3. Modigliani, F. and M.H. Miller, Corporate Income Taxes and the Cost of Capital : A Correction, *American Economic Review*, 53, June 1966, pp. 433–43.

Illustration 15.5: Debt Advantage: Interest Tax Shields

Suppose two firms L and U are identical in all respects except that firm L is levered and firm U is unlevered. Firm U is an all-equity financed firm while firm L employs equity and Rs 5,000 debt at 10 per cent rate of interest. Both firms have an expected earning before interest and taxes (or net operating income) of Rs 2,500, pay corporate tax at 50 per cent and distribute 100 per cent earnings as dividends to shareholders.

The after-tax income accruing to investors of firm L and firm U are shown in Table 15.5. You may notice that the total income after corporate tax is Rs 1,250 for the unlevered firm U and Rs 1,500 for the levered firm L. Thus, the levered firm L's investors are ahead of the unlevered firm U's investors by Rs 250. You may also note that the tax liability of the levered firm L is Rs 250 less than the tax liability of the unlevered firm U. For firm L the tax savings has occurred on account of payment of interest to debt-holders. Hence, this amount is the *interest tax shield or tax advantage of debt* of firm L: $0.5 \times (0.10 \times 5,000) = 0.5 \times 500 = $ Rs 250. Thus

$$\text{Interst tax shield} = \text{corporate tax rate} \times \text{interest}$$

$$\text{INTS} = T \times \text{INT} = T \times k_d D \tag{12}$$

where T is the corporate tax rate, k_d is the cost of debt, D is the amount of debt and $k_d D$ is the amount of interest (INT). The total after-tax income of investors of firm L is more by the amount of the interest tax shield. The levered firm's after-tax income (Table 15.5) consists of after-tax net operating income and interest tax shield. Note that the unlevered firm is an all-equity firm and its after-tax income is just equal to the after-tax net operating income:

The after-tax income of levered firm
  – the after tax income of unlevered firm
  = interest tax shield

$$= \left[\overline{X}(1-T) + Tk_d D \right] - \left[\overline{X}(1-T) \right] = Tk_d D$$
$$= \left[2,500(1-0.50) + 0.50 \times 0.10 \times 5,000 \right] - \left[2,500(1-0.50) \right]$$
$$= 0.50 \times 0.10 \times 5,000 = 1,250 - 1,000 = \text{Rs } 250$$

Table 15.5: Income of Levered and Unlevered Firms under Corporate Income Tax

Income	*Firm U*	*Firm L*
Net operating income	2,500	2,500
Interest	0	500
Taxable income	2,500	2,000
Tax at 50%	1,250	1,000
Income after tax	1,250	1,000
Total income to investors after corporate tax:		
Dividends to shareholders	1,250	1,000
Interest to debt-holders	0	500
Total income to investors	1,250	1,500
Interest tax shield (tax advantage of debt)	0	250
Relative advantage of debt: 1,500/1,250		1.20

Value of Interest Tax Shield

Interest tax shield is a cash inflow to the firm and therefore, it is valuable. Suppose that firm L will employ debt of Rs 5,000 perpetually (forever). If firm L's debt of Rs 5,000 is permanent,

then the interest tax shield of Rs 250 is a perpetuity. What is the value of this perpetuity? For this, we need a discount rate, which reflects the riskiness of these cash flows.

The cash flows arising on account of interest tax shield are less risky than the firm's operating income that is subject to business risk. Interest tax shield depends on the corporate tax rate and the firm's ability to earn enough profit to cover the interest payments. The corporate tax rates do not change very frequently. Firm L can be assumed to earn at least equal to the interest payable otherwise it would not like to borrow. Thus, the cash inflows from interest tax shield can be considered less risky, and they should be discounted at a lower discount rate. It will be reasonable to assume that the risk of interest tax shield is the same as that of the interest payments generating them. Thus, the discount rate is 10 per cent, which is the rate of return required by debt-holders. The present value of the unlevered firm L's perpetual interest tax shield of Rs 250 is:

$$\text{PV of interest tax shield} = \frac{250}{0.10} = \text{Rs } 2,500$$

Thus, under the assumption of permanent debt, we can determine the present value of the interest tax shield as follows:

$$\text{PV of interest tax shield} = \frac{\text{Corporate tax rate} \times \text{interest}}{\text{Cost of debt}}$$

$$\text{PVINTS} = \frac{T \times k_d D}{k_d} = TD \tag{13}$$

You may note from Equation (13) that the present value of the interest tax shields (PVINTS) is independent of the cost of debt: it is simply the corporate tax rate times the amount of permanent debt (TD). For firm L, the present value of interest tax shield can be determined as: $0.50 \times 5,000 = $ Rs 2,500. Note that the government, through its fiscal policy, assumes 50 per cent (the corporate tax rate) of firm L's Rs 5,000 debt obligation.

Value of the Levered Firm

In our example, the unlevered firm U has the after-tax operating income of Rs 1,250. Suppose the opportunity cost of capital of the unlevered firm U, $k_u = k_a$ is 12.5 per cent. The value of the unlevered firm U will be Rs 10,000:

$$\text{Value of the unlevered firm} = \frac{\text{After-tax net operating income}}{\text{Unlevered firm's cost of capital}}$$

$$V_u = \frac{\text{NOI}(1-T)}{k_a} = \frac{1,250}{0.125} = \text{Rs } 10,000$$

What is the total value of the levered firm L? The after-tax income of the levered firm includes the after-tax operating income, $\text{NOI}(1-T)$ plus the interest tax shield, $Tk_d D$. Therefore, the value of the levered firm is the sum of the present value of the after-tax net operating income and the present value of interest tax shield. The after-tax net operating income, $\text{NOI }(1-T)$, of the levered firm L is equal to the after-tax income of the pure-equity (the unlevered) firm U. Hence, the opportunity cost of capital of a pure-equity firm, k_u or k_a, should be used to discount the stream of the after-tax operating income of the levered firm. Thus, the value of the levered firm L is equal to the value of the unlevered firm U plus the present value of the interest tax shield:

Value of levered firm = Value of unlevered firm
+ PV of tax shield
= 10,000 + 2,500 = Rs 12,500

We can write the formula for determining the value of the levered firm as follows:

$$V_1 = \frac{\overline{X}(1-T)}{k_a} + \frac{Tk_dD}{k_d} \qquad (14)$$

$$V_1 = V_u + TD \qquad (15)$$

Equation (15) implies that when the corporate tax rate, T, is positive ($T > 0$), the value of the levered firm will increase continuously with debt.[1] Thus, theoretically the value of the firm will be maximised when it employs 100 per cent debt. This is shown in Figure 15.6.

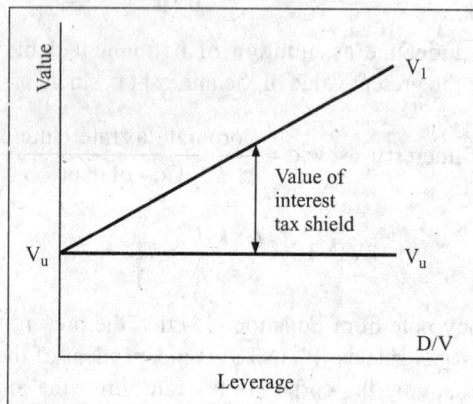

Figure 15.6: Value of the levered firm

One significant implication of the MM hypothesis with the corporate tax in practice is that a firm without debt or with low debt can enhance its value if it exchanges debt for equity. We consider the example of Infosys Technologies Limited to illustrate this point.

Enhancing the Firm Value through Debt: Infosys Technologies Limited

Infosys is a highly regarded computer software company. The company's market value of equity is about ten times of its book value. It does not employ any debt. The summarised book and market value balance sheet of the company for year ending on 31 March 2003 is given in Table 15.6.

1. Equation (13) can also be written as follows:

$$V_l = V_u + TD$$

$$\frac{V_l}{V_l} = \frac{V_u}{V_l} + \frac{TD}{V_l}, \quad 1 = \frac{V_u}{V_l} + TL \quad (\text{setting } (D/V_l) = L)$$

$$V_l = \frac{V_u}{1 - TL}$$

Thus, for $T > 0$, V_l will increase with L, and will be maximum at $L = 1$.

Table 15.6: Infosys Technologies Limited: Balance Sheet as on 31 March 2003

Book Value	Rs in million		Rs in million
Equity	28,607	Net current assets	20,179
Debt	0	Long-term assets	8,427
Total	28,607	Total	28,606
Market Value	Rs in million		Rs in million
Equity	267,108	Net current assets	20,179
Debt	0	Long-term assets	246,929
Total	267,108	Total	267,108

What will happen to Infosys' market value if it decides to replace equity by debt? Suppose the company borrows Rs 14,000 million at 10 per cent rate of interest and uses the money to buy back its shares (at the current market value). The book value total assets and capital will not show any changes; however, the mix of capital will change. Debt will increase by Rs 14,000 million and the book value equity will reduce by this amount. Suppose that debt is permanent and the corporate tax rate is 35 per cent. The company will save taxes on interest paid to debt-holders: $0.35 \times 0.10 \times 14,000 =$ Rs 490 million. The value of the tax saved is: $490/0.10 =$ Rs 4,900 million. The firm is richer by Rs 4,900 million, and its value should increase to Rs 272,008 million. The increase in the firm's value is a gain to its shareholders. How? The value of equity after recapitalisation is Rs 258,008 million. Thus, the value of equity drops by Rs 9,100 million (Rs 267,108 – Rs 258,008 = Rs 9,100 million). But remember that the shareholders received Rs 14,000 million when the company bought back their shares. Hence, the net gain of shareholders is Rs 4,900.

Table 15.7: Infosys Technologies Limited

Book value	Rs in million		Rs in million
Equity	14,606	Net current assets	20,179
Debt	14,000	Long-term assets	8,427
Total	28,606	Total	28,606
Market value	Rs in million		Rs in million
Equity	258,008	Net current assets	20,179
Debt	14,000	Long-term assets	246,929
		Value of tax shield	4,900
Total	272,008	Total	272,008

The value of debt is interest income to debt-holders divided by the cost of debt:

$$\text{Value of debt} = \frac{\text{Interest income}}{\text{Cost of debt}} = D = \frac{\text{INT}}{k_d}.$$

The sum of values of debt and equity is the firm's total value, and is directly given by net operating income divided by WACC:

$$\text{Value of firm} = \frac{\text{Net operating income}}{\text{WACC}} = S + D = \frac{\text{NOI}}{k_o}$$

You may notice from the above discussion that, according to the traditional theory, the value of the firm may first increase with moderate leverage, reach the maximum value and then start declining with higher leverage. This is so because WACC first decreases and after reaching the minimum, it starts increasing with leverage. Thus, the traditional theory on the relationship between capital structure and the firm value has three stages.[1]

First Stage: Increasing Value

In the first stage, the cost of equity, k_e, the rate at which the shareholders capitalise their net income, either remains constant or rises slightly with debt. The cost of equity does not increase fast enough to offset the advantage of low-cost debt. During this stage, the cost of debt, k_d, remains constant since the market views the use of debt as a reasonable policy. As a result, the overall cost of capital, WACC or k_o, decreases with increasing leverage, and thus, the total value of the firm, V, also increases.

Second Stage: Optimum Value

Once the firm has reached a certain degree of leverage, increases in leverage have a negligible effect on WACC and hence, on the value of the firm. This is so because the increase in the cost of equity due to the added financial risk just offsets the advantage of low cost debt. Within that range or at the specific point, WACC will be minimum, and the maximum value of the firm will be obtained.

Third Stage: Declining Value

Beyond the acceptable limit of leverage, the value of the firm decreases with leverage as WACC increases with leverage. This happens because investors perceive a high degree of financial risk and demand a higher equity-capitalisation rate, which exceeds the advantage of low-cost debt.

The overall effect of these three stages is to suggest that the cost of capital (WACC) is a function of leverage. It first declines with leverage and after reaching a minimum point or range starts rising. The relation between costs of capital and leverage is graphically shown in Figure 15.2 wherein the overall cost of capital curve, k_o, is saucer-shaped with a horizontal range. This implies that there is a range of capital structures in which the cost of capital is minimised. k_e, is assumed to increase slightly in the beginning and then at a faster rate. In Figure 15.3 the cost of capital curve is shown as U-shaped. The U-shaped cost of capital implies that there is a precise point at which the cost of

capital is minimum. This precise point defines the optimum capital structure.

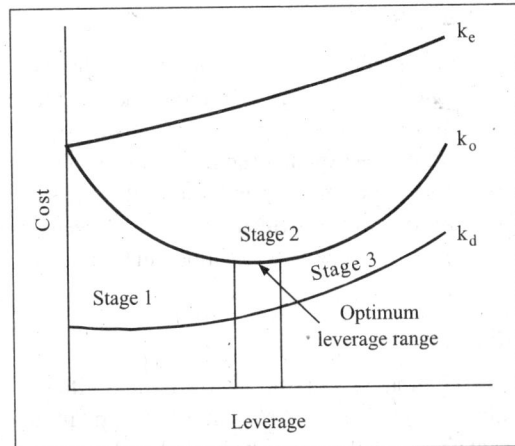

Figure 15.2: The cost of capital (saucer-shaped)

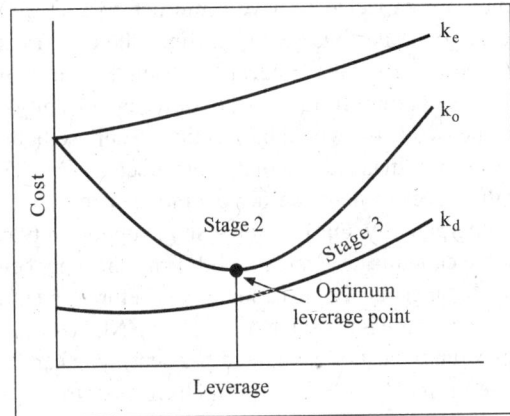

Figure 15.3: The cost of capital (U-shaped)

As stated earlier, many variations of the traditional view exist (Figures 15.2 and 15.3). Whether the cost of equity function is horizontal or rising slightly is not very pertinent from the theoretical point of view, as a number of different costs of equity curves can be consistent with a declining average cost of capital curve. The relevant issue is whether or not the average cost of capital curve declines at all as debt is used.[2] All supporters of the traditional view agree that the cost of capital declines with debt.

Criticism of the Traditional View

The traditional theory implies that investors value levered firms more than unlevered firm. This means that they pay a premium for the shares of levered firms. The contention of the traditional theory that moderate amount of debt in 'sound' firms does not really add very much to the 'riskiness' of the shares is not defensible. There does not exist sufficient justification for the assumption that investors' perception about risk of leverage is different at different levels of leverage. However, as we shall explain later, the existence of an optimum capital structure can be supported on two counts: the tax deductibility of interest charges and other market imperfections.

---

1. Solomon, *op.cit.*, p. 94, Brigham, Eugene F. and Roman E. Johnson, (eds.), *Issue in Managerial Finance,* Dryden Press, 1976, p. 256.
2. Barges, *op. cit.*, p. 12.

IRRELEVANCE OF CAPITAL STRUCTURE: NOI APPROACH AND THE MM HYPOTHESIS WITHOUT TAXES

Modigliani and Miller (MM) do not agree with the traditional view.[1] They argue that, in perfect capital markets without taxes and transaction costs, a firm's market value and the cost of capital remain invariant to the capital structure changes. The value of the firm depends on the earnings and risk of its assets (business risk) rather than the way in which assets have been financed. The MM hypotheses can be best explained in terms of their two propositions.

Proposition I

Consider two pharmaceutical firms, Ultrafine and Lifeline, which have identical assets, operate in same market segments and have equal market share. These two firms belong to the same industry and they face similar competitive and business conditions. Hence, they are expected to have same net operating income and exposed to similar business risk. Since the two firms have identical business risk, it is logical to conclude that investors' expected rates of return from assets, k_a or the opportunity cost of capital of the two firms would be identical. Suppose both firms are totally equity financed and both have assets of Rs 225 crore each. Both expect to generate net operating income of Rs 45 crore each perpetually. Further, suppose the opportunity cost of capital or the capitalisation rate for both firms is 15 per cent. Let us assume that there are no taxes so that the before- and after-tax net operating income is the same. Capitalising NOI (Rs 45 crore) by the opportunity cost of capital (15 per cent), you can find the value of the firms. The two firms would have the same value: 45/0.15 = Rs 300 crore.

Let us now change the assumption regarding the financing. Suppose Ultrafine is an unlevered firm with 100 per cent equity and Lifeline a levered firm with 50 per cent equity and 50 per cent debt. Should the market values of two firms differ? Debt will not change the earnings potential of Lifeline as it depends on its investment in assets. Debt also cannot affect the business conditions and therefore, the business (operating) risk of Lifeline — the levered firm. You know that the value of a firm depends upon its expected net operating income and the overall capitalisation rate or the opportunity cost of capital. Since the form of financing (debt or equity) can neither change the firm's net operating income nor its operating risk, the values of levered and unlevered firms ought be the same. Financing changes the way in which the net operating income is distributed between equity holders and debt-holders. Firms with identical net operating income and business (operating) risk, but differing capital structure, should have same total value. *MM*'s Proposition I is that, for firms in the same risk class, the total market value is independent of the debt-equity mix and is given by capitalising the expected net operating income by the capitalisation rate (i.e., the opportunity cost of capital) appropriate to that risk class:[2]

Value of levered firm = Value of unleverd firm

$$V_1 = V_u$$

Value of the firm $= \dfrac{\text{Net operating income}}{\text{Firm' s opportunity cost of capital}}$

$$V = V_1 = V_u = \frac{\text{NOI}}{k_a} \tag{8}$$

where V is the market value of the firm and it is sum of the value of equity, E and the value of debt, D; NOI = EBIT = $\overline{X}$ the expected net operating income; and k_a = the firm's opportunity cost of capital or the capitalisation rate appropriate to the risk class of the firm.

MM's approach is a **net operating income approach** because the value of the firm is the capitalised value of net operating income. Both net operating income and the firm's opportunity cost of capital are assumed to be constant with regard to the level of financial leverage. For a levered firm, the expected net operating income is sum of the income of shareholders and the income of debt-holders. Debt-holders' income is interest and shareholders' income, called net income, is the expected net operating income less interest. The levered firm's value is the sum of the value of equity and value of debt. The levered firm's expected rate of return is the ratio of the expected operating income to the value of all its securities. This is an average expected rate of return that the levered firm's all security-holders would require the firm to earn on total investments. The average rate of return required by all security-holders in a levered firm is the firm's weighted average cost of capital; i.e., WACC = k_o or k_l. Thus

$$V_1 = \frac{\text{NOI}}{k_l = k_a}$$

$$k_o = k_l = \frac{\text{NOI}}{V_l} \tag{9}$$

In the case of an unlevered firm, the entire net operating income is the shareholders net income. Therefore, the unlevered firm's WACC or k_u is equal to its opportunity cost of capital:

$$k_a = k_u = \frac{\text{NOI}}{V_u} \tag{10}$$

Since the values of the levered and unlevered firms and the expected net operating income (NOI) do not change with financial leverage, the weighted average cost of capital would also not change with financial leverage. Hence, MM's Proposition I also implies that the weighted average cost of capital for two identical firms, one levered and another unlevered, will be equal to the opportunity cost of capital (Figure 15.1):

Levered firm's cost of capital (k_1) = Unlevered firm's cost of

capital (k_u)

$$k_1 = k_o = k_a = k_u$$

1. Modigliani, H., and Miller, M.H., The Cost Capital, Corporation Finance and The Theory of Investment, *American Economic Review,* 48 (June 1958), pp. 261–97.
2. *Ibit.,* p. 266.

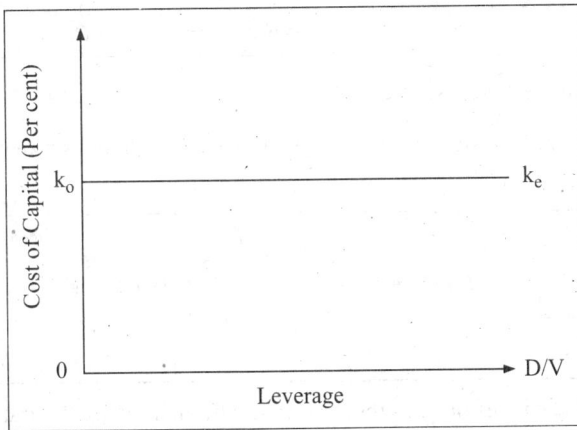

Figure 15.4: The cost of capital under M–M proposition I

Arbitrage Process

Why should MM's Proposition I work? As stated earlier, the simple logic of Proposition I is that two firms with identical assets, irrespective of how these assets have been financed, cannot command different market values. Suppose this were not true and two identical firms, except for their capital structures, have different market values. In this situation, **arbitrage** (or **switching**) will take place to enable investors to engage in the **personal** or **homemade leverage** as against the **corporate leverage** to restore equilibrium in the market. Consider the following example.

Illustration 15.3: The MM Proposition I and Arbitrage

Suppose two firms - Firm U, an unlevered firm and Firm L, a levered firm - have identical assets and expected net operating income (NOI = $\overline{X}$) of Rs 10,000. The value of Firm L is Rs 100,000 assuming the cost of equity of 10 per cent under the traditional view. Since Firm U has no debt, the value of its equity is equal to its total value ($E_u = V_u$). Firm L employs 6 per cent Rs 50,000 debt. Suppose its cost of equity under the traditional view is 11.7 per cent. Thus, the value of Firm L's equity shares (E_1) is Rs 60,000, and its total value (V_1) firm is Rs 110,000 ($V_1 = E_1 + D_1 = 60,000 + 50,000$).

Table 15.4: Value of Levered and Unlevered Firms

	Firm U (Unlevered)	Firm L (Levered)
Net operating income, $\overline{X}$	10,000	10,000
Interest, INT	0	3,000
Net income (dividends), $\overline{X}$ – INT	10,000	7,000
Cost of equity, k_e (traditional view)	0.100	0.117
Market value of equity, E	100,000	60,000
Market value of debt, D	0	50,000
Market value of firm, $V = E + D$	100,000	110,000
WACC, k_o (traditional view)	0.10	0.091

You may notice that Firm L and Firm U have identical assets and NOI, but they have different market prices. The cheaper debt of Rs 50,000 of Firm L has increased shareholders wealth by Rs 10,000. MM argue that this situation cannot continue for long, as **arbitrage** will bring two prices into equilibrium. How does arbitrage work?

Assume that you hold 10 per cent shares of the levered firm L. What is your return from your investment in the shares of firm L? Since you own 10 per cent of L's shares, your equity investment is: $0.10 \times (110,000 – 50,000) =$ Rs 6,000. You also 'own' 10 per cent of L's corporate debt: $0.10 \times 50,000 =$ Rs 5,000. You are entitled to 10 per cent of the equity income (dividends):

$$\begin{aligned} \text{Return} &= 0.10(\overline{X} - \text{INT}) \\ &= 0.10(10,000) - 0.06 \times 50,000) \\ &= 0.10(10,000 - 3,000) = \text{Rs } 700 \end{aligned}$$

You can earn same return at lesser investment through an alternate investment strategy. This you can do by switching your investment from firm L and firm U as follows:

1. Selling your investment in firm L's shares for Rs 6,000.
2. Borrowing on your *personal account* an amount equal to your share of firm L's corporate debt at 6 per cent rate of interest: 0.10 (50,000) = Rs 5,000.
3. Buying 10 per cent of the unlevered firm U's shares investing: $0.10 \times 100,000 =$ Rs 10,000.

You have Rs 11,000 with you; that is, Rs 6,000 from sale of L's shares and Rs 5,000 borrowed funds. Your investment in U's shares is Rs 10,000. Thus, you have surplus cash of Rs 1,000.

Your return from U is:

Return from investment in U's share = $0.10 \times 10,000 =$ Rs 1,000

However, you have borrowed Rs 5,000 at 6 per cent. Therefore, you will have to pay an interest of Rs 300:

Interest payable on borrowed funds = $0.06 \times 5,000 =$ Rs 300

Thus your net return is Rs 700 = Rs 1,000 – Rs 300:

	Rs
Equity return from U: $0.10 \times$ Rs 10,000	1,000
Less: Interest on personal borrowing: $0.06 \times$ Rs 5,000	300
Net return	700

You earn the same return from the alternate strategy. But now you also have extra cash of Rs 1,000 that you can invest to enhance your return. Thus, the alternate strategy will yield higher overall return. Your risk is same in both the cases. While shifting your investment from firm U to firm L, you replaced your share of L's debt by personal debt. You have created 'personal' or 'homemade leverage' instead of 'corporate leverage'.

Due to the advantage of the alternate investment strategy, a number of investors will be induced towards it. They will sell their shares in firm L and buy shares and debt of firm U. This arbitrage will tend to increase the price of firm U's shares and to decline that of firm L's shares. It will continue until the equilibrium price for the shares of firm U and firm L is reached.

The arbitrage would work in the opposite direction if we assume that the value of the unlevered firm U is greater than the value of the levered firm L (i.e., $V_u > V_1$). Let us assume that $V_u = E_u =$ Rs 100,000 and $V_1 = E_1 + D_1 =$ Rs 40,000 + Rs 50,000 = Rs 90,000. Further, suppose that you still own 10 per cent shares in the unlevered firm U. Your return and investment will be:

$$\text{Return} = 0.10(10,000) = \text{Rs } 1,000$$
$$\text{Investment} = 0.10(100,000) = \text{Rs } 10,000$$

You can design a better investment strategy. You should do the following:

1. Sell your shares in firm U for Rs 10,000.
2. Buy 10 per cent of firm L's shares and debt:

$$\text{Investment} = 0.10(40,000 + 50,000)$$
$$= 4,000 + 5,000 = \text{Rs } 9,000$$

Your investment in firm L is Rs 9,000. You have extra cash of Rs 1,000. Since you own 10 per cent of equity and debt of firm L, your return will include both equity income and interest income. Thus your return is Rs 1,000:

$$\text{Return} = 0.10(10,000) = 0.10(10,000 - 3,000) + 0.10(3,000)$$
$$= \text{Rs } 1,000$$

Note that your alternate investment strategy pays you off the same return but at a lesser investment. Both strategies give the investor same return, but your alternate investment strategy costs you less since $V_1 < V_u$. In such a situation, investors will sell their shares in the unlevered firm and buy the shares and debt of the levered firm. As a result of this switching, the market value of the levered firm's shares will increase and that of the unlevered firm will decline. Ultimately, the price equilibrium will be reached (i.e., $V_1 = V_u$) and there will be no advantage of switching anymore.

We can generalise our discussion in the formal terms.[1] In the first instance, let the value of levered firm L be greater than the value of unlevered firm U (i.e., $V_1 > V_u$). Both firms earn the same expected net operating income, $\overline{X}$. The borrowing and lending rate, k_d, is same for both corporations and individuals. Assume that an investor holds α (alpha) fraction of firm L's shares. His investment and return will be as follows:

	Investment	Return
Investment in L's shares	$\alpha(V_1 - D_1)$	$\alpha(\overline{X} - k_dD_1)$

The investor can also design the following alternate investment strategy:

	Investment	Return
Buy fraction of U's shares	αV_u	$\alpha \overline{X}$
Borrow equal to fraction of L's debt	$- \alpha D_1$	$- \alpha k_d D_1$
	$\alpha(V_u - D_1)$	$\alpha(\overline{X} - k_dD_1)$

The investor obtains the same return, $\alpha(\overline{X} - k_d D_1)$ in both the cases, but his first investment strategy costs more since $V_1 > V_u$. The rational investors at the margin would prefer switching from levered to unlevered firm. The increasing demand for the unlevered firm's shares will increase their market price, while the declining demand for the levered firm's shares will decrease their market price. Ultimately, market values of the two firms will reach equilibrium, and henceforth, arbitrage will not be beneficial.

Let us take the opposite case where $V_u > V_1$. Suppose our investor holds a fraction of firm U's shares. His investment and return will be as follows:

	Investment	Return
Investment in U's shares	αV_u	$\alpha \overline{X}$

The investor can design an alternate investment strategy as follows:

	Investment	Return
Buy fraction of L's shares	$\alpha(V_1 - D_1)$	$\alpha(\overline{X} - k_dD_1)$
Buy equal to fraction of L's debt	$+ \alpha D_1$	$+ \alpha k_d D_1$
	αV_1	$\alpha \overline{X}$

The investor earns the same return from the alternate strategy but by investing less since $V_u > V_1$. Other investors can also benefit similarly by switching their investment. Investors will sell shares of firm U and buy shares of firm L. This arbitrage will cause the price of firm U's shares to decline and that of firm L's shares to increase. It will continue until the value of the levered firm's equals that of the unlevered firm. Thus, in equilibrium the value of levered firm will be equal to the value of unlevered firm, i.e., $V_1 = V_u$.

On the basis of the arbitrage process, *MM* conclude that the market value of a firm is not affected by leverage. Thus, the financing (or capital structure) decision is irrelevant. It does not help in creating any wealth for shareholders. Hence one capital structure is as much desirable (or undesirable!) as the other.

Key Assumptions

MM's Proposition I is based on certain assumptions. These assumptions relate to the behaviour of investors and capital markets, the actions of the firm and the tax environment.

- *Perfect capital markets* Securities (shares and debt instruments) are traded in the **perfect capital market** situation. This specifically means that (*a*) investors are free to buy or sell securities; (*b*) they can borrow without restriction at the same terms as the firms do; and (*c*) they behave rationally. It is also implied that the transaction costs, i.e., the cost of buying and selling securities, do not exist. The assumption that firms and individual investors can borrow and lend at the same rate of interest is a very critical assumption for the validity of *MM* Proposition I. The homemade leverage will not be a substitute for the corporate leverage if the borrowing and lending rates for individual investors are different from firms.

- *Homogeneous risk classes* Firms operate in similar business conditions and have similar operating risk. They are considered to have similar operating risk and belong to *homogeneous risk classes* when their expected earnings have identical risk characteristics. It is generally *implied* under the MM hypothesis that firms within same industry constitute a homogeneous class.

- *Risk* The operating risk is defined in terms of the variability

1. Modigliani and Miller, Reply to Heins and Sprenkle, *American Economic Review*, 59 (Sept. 1969), pp. 592–95.

of the net operating income (NOI). The risk of investors depends on both the random fluctuations of the expected NOI and the possibility that the actual value of the variable may turn out to be different than their best estimate.[1]

- *No taxes* There do not exist any corporate taxes. This implies that interest payable on debt do not save any taxes.
- *Full payout* Firms distribute all net earnings to shareholders. This means that firms follow a *100 per cent dividend payout.*

Proposition II

We have explained earlier that the value of the firm depends on the expected net operating income and the opportunity cost of capital, k_a, which is same for both levered and unlevered firms. In the absence of corporate taxes, the firm's capital structure (financial leverage) does not affect its net operating income. Hence, for the value of the firm to remain constant with financial leverage, the opportunity cost of capital, k_a, must also stay constant with financial leverage. The opportunity cost of capital, k_a depends on the firm's operating risk. Since financial leverage does not affect the firm's operating risk, there is no reason for the opportunity cost of capital, k_a to change with financial leverage.

Financial leverage does not affect a firm's net operating income, but as we have discussed in Chapter 14, it does affect shareholders' return (EPS and ROE). EPS and ROE increase with leverage when the interest rate is less than the firm's return on assets. Financial leverage also increases shareholders' financial risk by amplifying the variability of EPS and ROE. Thus, financial leverage causes two opposing effects: it increases the shareholders' return but it also increases their financial risk. Shareholders will increase the required rate of return (i.e., the cost of equity) on their investment to compensate for the financial risk. The higher the financial risk, the higher the shareholders' required rate of return or the cost of equity. This is *MM's Proposition II.*

An all-equity financed or unlevered firm has no debt; its opportunity cost of capital is equal its cost of equity; that is, unlevered firm's $k_e = k_a$. *MM's* Proposition II provides justification for the levered firm's opportunity cost of capital remaining constant with financial leverage. In simple words, it states that the cost of equity, k_e, will increase enough to offset the advantage of cheaper cost of debt so that the opportunity cost of capital, k_a, does not change. A levered firm has financial risk while an unlevered firm is not exposed to financial risk. Hence, a levered firm will have higher required return on equity as compensation for financial risk. The cost of equity for a levered firm should be higher than the opportunity cost of capital, k_a; that is, the levered firm's $k_e > k_a$. It should be equal to constant k_a, plus a **financial risk premium**. How is this financial risk premium determined? You know that a levered firm's cost of capital is the weighted average of the cost of equity and the cost of debt:

$$k_a = k_e \times \frac{E}{E+D} + k_d \frac{D}{E+D}$$

You can solve this equation to determine the levered firm's cost of equity, k_e:

$$k_e = k_a + (k_a - k_d)\frac{D}{E} \qquad (11)$$

You may note from the equation that for an unlevered firm, D (debt) is zero; therefore, the second part of the right-hand side of the equation is zero and the opportunity cost of capital, k_a equals the cost of equity, k_e. We can see from the equation that financial risk premium of a levered firm is equal to debt-equity ratio, D/E, times the spread between the constant opportunity cost of capital and the cost of debt, $(k_o - k_d)$. The required return on equity is positively related to financial leverage, because the financial risk of shareholders increases with financial leverage. The cost of equity, k_e, is a linear function of financial leverage, D/E. It is noteworthy that the functional relationship given in Equation (11) is valid irrespective of any particular valuation theory. For example, MM assume the levered firm's opportunity cost of capital or WACC to be constant, while according to the traditional view WACC depends on financial leverage.

Let us consider the following example to understand the implications of MM's Proposition II.

Illustration 15.4: Implications of MM's Proposition II

Suppose Information Technology Limited (ITL) is an all-equity financed company. It has 10,000 shares outstanding. The market value of these shares is Rs 120,000. The expected operating income of the company is Rs 18,000. The expected EPS of the company is: Rs 18,000/10,000 = Rs 1.80. Since ITL is an unlevered company, its opportunity cost of capital will be equal to its cost of equity, k_e:

$$k_a = k_e = \frac{\text{Expected NOI}}{\text{Market value of debt and equity}}$$
$$= \frac{18,000}{120,000} = 0.15 \text{ or } 15\%$$

Let us assume that ITL is considering borrowing Rs 60,000 at 6 per cent rate of interest and buy back 5,000 shares at the market value of Rs 60,000. Now ITL has Rs 60,000 equity and Rs 60,000 debt in its capital structure. Thus, the company's debt-equity ratio is 1. The change in the company's capital structure does not affect its assets and expected net operating income. However, EPS will change. The expected EPS is:

$$\text{EPS} = \frac{\text{Net income}}{\text{Number of shares}} = \frac{18,000 - 3,600}{5,000} = \text{Rs } 2.88$$

ITL's expected EPS increases by 60 per cent due to financial leverage. If ITL's expected NOI fluctuates, its EPS will show greater variability with financial leverage than as an unlevered firm. Since the firm's operating risk does not change, its opportunity cost of capital (or WACC) will still remain 15 per cent. The cost of equity will increase to compensate for the financial risk:

$$k_e = k_a + (k_a - k_d)\frac{D}{E}$$
$$= 0.15 + (0.15 - 0.06)\frac{60,000}{60,000} = 0.24 \text{ or } 24\%$$

---

1. Robicheck, A. and Myers, S., *Optimal Financing Decisions,* Prentice-Hall Inc., 1965, pp. 31–34.

The crucial part of Proposition II is that the levered firm's opportunity cost of capital will not rise even if very excessive use of financial leverage is made. The excessive use of debt increases the risk of default. Hence, in practice, the cost of debt, k_d, will increase with high level of financial leverage. *MM* argue that when k_d increases, k_e will increase at a decreasing rate and may even turn down eventually.[1] The reason for this behaviour of k_e, is that debt-holders, in the extreme leveraged situations, own the firm's assets and bear some of the firm's business risk. Since the operating risk of shareholders is transferred to debt-holders, k_e declines. This is illustrated in Figure 15.5.

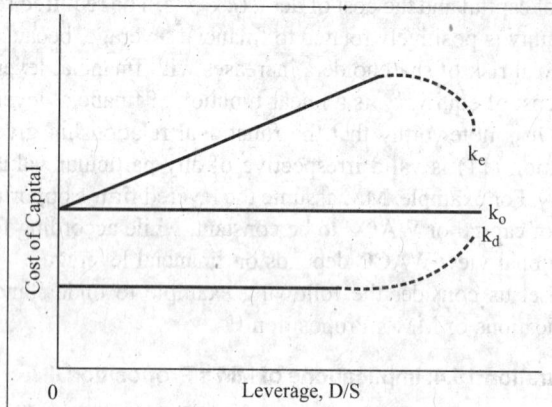

Figure 15.5: Cost of equity under the M–M

Criticism of the MM Hypothesis

The arbitrage process is the behavioural foundation for *MM*'s hypothesis. The shortcomings of this hypothesis lie in the assumption of perfect capital market in which arbitrage is expected to work. Due to the existence of imperfections in the capital market, arbitrage may fail to work and may give rise to discrepancy between the market values of levered and unlevered firms. The arbitrage process may fail to bring equilibrium in the capital market for the following reasons:[2]

Lending and borrowing rates discrepancy The assumption that firms and individuals can borrow and lend at the same rate of interest does not hold in practice. Because of the substantial holding of fixed assets, firms have a higher credit standing. As a result, they are able to borrow at lower rates of interest than individuals. If the cost of borrowing to an investor is more than the firm's borrowing rate, then the equalisation process will fall short of completion.

Non-substitutability of personal and corporate leverages It is incorrect to assume that "personal (home-made) leverage" is a perfect substitute for "corporate leverage." The existence of limited liability of firms in contrast with unlimited liability of individuals clearly places individuals and firms on a different footing in the capital markets. If a levered firm goes bankrupt, all investors stand to lose to the extent of the amount of the purchase price of their shares. But, if an investor creates personal

leverage, then in the event of the firm's insolvency, he would lose not only his principal in the shares of the unlevered company, but will also be liable to return the amount of his personal loan. Thus, it is more risky to create personal leverage and invest in the unlevered firm than investing directly in the levered firm.

Transaction costs The existence of transaction costs also interferes with the working of arbitrage. Because of the costs involved in the buying and selling securities, it would become necessary to invest a greater amount in order to earn the same return. As a result, the levered firm will have a higher market value.

Institutional restrictions Institutional restrictions also impede the working of arbitrage. The "home-made" leverage is not practically feasible as a number of institutional investors would not be able to substitute personal leverage for corporate leverage, simply because they are not allowed to engage in the "home-made" leverage.

Existence of corporate tax The incorporation of the corporate income taxes will also frustrate *MM*'s conclusions. Interest charges are tax deductible. This, in fact, means that the cost of borrowing funds to the firm is less than the contractual rate of interest. The very existence of interest charges gives the firm a tax advantage, which allows it to return to its equity and debt-holders a larger stream of income than it otherwise could have. Consider an example.

Suppose a levered and an unlevered firms have NOI = Rs 10,000. Further, the levered has: $k_d = 0.06$ and D_1 = Rs 20,000. Assume that the corporate income tax exists and the rate is 50 per cent. The unlevered firm's after tax operating income will be: NOI – tax on NOI, i.e., $10,000 – 10,000 \times 0.50 = 10,000 – 5,000 = $ Rs 5000. Interest is tax exempt. Therefore, levered firm's taxes will be less. The after-tax net operating income of the levered firm will be: NOI – tax on NOI minus interest, i.e., $10,000 – (10,000 – 1,200) \times 0.50 = 10,000 – 4,400 = $ Rs 5,600. Thus, the total after-tax operating earnings of debt-holders and equity holders is more in the case of the levered firm. Hence, the total market value of a levered firm should tend to exceed that of the unlevered firm for this very reason. This point is explained further in the following section.

RELEVANCE OF CAPITAL STRUCTURE: THE MM HYPOTHESIS UNDER CORPORATE TAXES

MM's hypothesis that the value of the firm is independent of its debt policy is based on the critical assumption that corporate income taxes do not exist. In reality, corporate income taxes exist, and interest paid to debt-holders is treated as a deductible expense. Thus, interest payable by firms saves taxes. This makes debt financing advantageous. In their 1963 article, *MM* show that the value of the firm will increase with debt due to the deductibility of interest charges for tax computation, and the value of the levered firm will be higher than of the unlevered firm.[3] Consider an example.

1. Modigliani and Miller, *op. cit.*

2. Solomon, *op. cit.,* Durand, *op.cit.* Also see, Pandey, I.M., *Capital Structure and the Cost of Capital,* Vikas, reprint, 1996.

3. Modigliani, F. and M.H. Miller, Corporate Income Taxes and the Cost of Capital : A Correction, *American Economic Review*, 53, June 1966, pp. 433–43.

Illustration 15.5: Debt Advantage: Interest Tax Shields

Suppose two firms L and U are identical in all respects except that firm L is levered and firm U is unlevered. Firm U is an all-equity financed firm while firm L employs equity and Rs 5,000 debt at 10 per cent rate of interest. Both firms have an expected earning before interest and taxes (or net operating income) of Rs 2,500, pay corporate tax at 50 per cent and distribute 100 per cent earnings as dividends to shareholders.

The after-tax income accruing to investors of firm L and firm U are shown in Table 15.5. You may notice that the total income after corporate tax is Rs 1,250 for the unlevered firm U and Rs 1,500 for the levered firm L. Thus, the levered firm L's investors are ahead of the unlevered firm U's investors by Rs 250. You may also note that the tax liability of the levered firm L is Rs 250 less than the tax liability of the unlevered firm U. For firm L the tax savings has occurred on account of payment of interest to debt-holders. Hence, this amount is the *interest tax shield or tax advantage of debt* of firm L: $0.5 \times (0.10 \times 5,000) = 0.5 \times 500 = $ Rs 250. Thus

$$\text{Interst tax shield} = \text{corporate tax rate} \times \text{interest}$$
$$\text{INTS} = T \times \text{INT} = T \times k_d D \qquad (12)$$

where T is the corporate tax rate, k_d is the cost of debt, D is the amount of debt and $k_d D$ is the amount of interest (INT). The total after-tax income of investors of firm L is more by the amount of the interest tax shield. The levered firm's after-tax income (Table 15.5) consists of after-tax net operating income and interest tax shield. Note that the unlevered firm is an all-equity firm and its after-tax income is just equal to the after-tax net operating income:

The after-tax income of levered firm
 – the after tax income of unlevered firm
 = interest tax shield

$$= \left[\overline{X}(1-T) + Tk_d D \right] - \left[\overline{X}(1-T) \right] = Tk_d D$$
$$= \left[2,500(1-0.50) + 0.50 \times 0.10 \times 5,000 \right] - \left[2,500(1-0.50) \right]$$
$$= 0.50 \times 0.10 \times 5,000 = 1,250 - 1,000 = \text{Rs } 250$$

Table 15.5: Income of Levered and Unlevered Firms under Corporate Income Tax

Income	Firm U	Firm L
Net operating income	2,500	2,500
Interest	0	500
Taxable income	2,500	2,000
Tax at 50%	1,250	1,000
Income after tax	1,250	1,000
Total income to investors after corporate tax:		
Dividends to shareholders	1,250	1,000
Interest to debt-holders	0	500
Total income to investors	1,250	1,500
Interest tax shield (tax advantage of debt)	0	250
Relative advantage of debt: 1,500/1,250		1.20

Value of Interest Tax Shield

Interest tax shield is a cash inflow to the firm and therefore, it is valuable. Suppose that firm L will employ debt of Rs 5,000 perpetually (forever). If firm L's debt of Rs 5,000 is permanent,

then the interest tax shield of Rs 250 is a perpetuity. What is the value of this perpetuity? For this, we need a discount rate, which reflects the riskiness of these cash flows.

The cash flows arising on account of interest tax shield are less risky than the firm's operating income that is subject to business risk. Interest tax shield depends on the corporate tax rate and the firm's ability to earn enough profit to cover the interest payments. The corporate tax rates do not change very frequently. Firm L can be assumed to earn at least equal to the interest payable otherwise it would not like to borrow. Thus, the cash inflows from interest tax shield can be considered less risky, and they should be discounted at a lower discount rate. It will be reasonable to assume that the risk of interest tax shield is the same as that of the interest payments generating them. Thus, the discount rate is 10 per cent, which is the rate of return required by debt-holders. The present value of the unlevered firm L's perpetual interest tax shield of Rs 250 is:

$$\text{PV of interest tax shield} = \frac{250}{0.10} = \text{Rs } 2,500$$

Thus, under the assumption of permanent debt, we can determine the present value of the interest tax shield as follows:

$$\text{PV of interest tax shield} = \frac{\text{Corporate tax rate} \times \text{interest}}{\text{Cost of debt}}$$

$$\text{PVINTS} = \frac{T \times k_d D}{k_d} = TD \qquad (13)$$

You may note from Equation (13) that the present value of the interest tax shields (PVINTS) is independent of the cost of debt: it is simply the corporate tax rate times the amount of permanent debt (TD). For firm L, the present value of interest tax shield can be determined as: $0.50 \times 5,000 = $ Rs 2,500. Note that the government, through its fiscal policy, assumes 50 per cent (the corporate tax rate) of firm L's Rs 5,000 debt obligation.

Value of the Levered Firm

In our example, the unlevered firm U has the after-tax operating income of Rs 1,250. Suppose the opportunity cost of capital of the unlevered firm U, $k_u = k_a$ is 12.5 per cent. The value of the unlevered firm U will be Rs 10,000:

$$\text{Value of the unlevered firm} = \frac{\text{After-tax net operating income}}{\text{Unlevered firm's cost of capital}}$$

$$V_u = \frac{\text{NOI}(1-T)}{k_a} = \frac{1,250}{0.125} = \text{Rs } 10,000$$

What is the total value of the levered firm L? The after-tax income of the levered firm includes the after-tax operating income, $\text{NOI}(1-T)$ plus the interest tax shield, $Tk_d D$. Therefore, the value of the levered firm is the sum of the present value of the after-tax net operating income and the present value of interest tax shield. The after-tax net operating income, NOI $(1-T)$, of the levered firm L is equal to the after-tax income of the pure-equity (the unlevered) firm U. Hence, the opportunity cost of capital of a pure-equity firm, k_u or k_a, should be used to discount the stream of the after-tax operating income of the levered firm. Thus, the value of the levered firm L is equal to the value of the unlevered firm U plus the present value of the interest tax shield:

Value of levered firm = Value of unlevered firm

+ PV of tax shield

= 10,000 + 2,500 = Rs 12,500

We can write the formula for determining the value of the levered firm as follows:

$$V_1 = \frac{\overline{X}(1-T)}{k_a} + \frac{Tk_dD}{k_d} \tag{14}$$

$$V_1 = V_u + TD \tag{15}$$

Equation (15) implies that when the corporate tax rate, T, is positive $(T > 0)$, the value of the levered firm will increase continuously with debt.[1] Thus, theoretically the value of the firm will be maximised when it employs 100 per cent debt. This is shown in Figure 15.6.

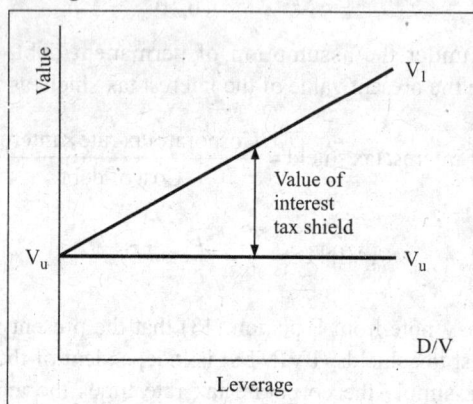

Figure 15.6: Value of the levered firm

One significant implication of the MM hypothesis with the corporate tax in practice is that a firm without debt or with low debt can enhance its value if it exchanges debt for equity. We consider the example of Infosys Technologies Limited to illustrate this point.

Enhancing the Firm Value through Debt: Infosys Technologies Limited

Infosys is a highly regarded computer software company. The company's market value of equity is about ten times of its book value. It does not employ any debt. The summarised book and market value balance sheet of the company for year ending on 31 March 2003 is given in Table 15.6.

---

1. Equation (13) can also be written as follows:

$$V_l = V_u + TD$$

$$\frac{V_l}{V_l} = \frac{V_u}{V_l} + \frac{TD}{V_l}, \quad 1 = \frac{V_u}{V_l} + TL \quad (\text{setting } (D/V_l) = L$$

$$V_l = \frac{V_u}{1 - TL}$$

Thus, for $T > 0$, V_l will increase with L, and will be maximum at $L = 1$.

Table 15.6: Infosys Technologies Limited: Balance Sheet as on 31 March 2003

Book Value	Rs in million		Rs in million
Equity	28,607	Net current assets	20,179
Debt	0	Long-term assets	8,427
Total	28,607	Total	28,606
Market Value	Rs in million		Rs in million
Equity	267,108	Net current assets	20,179
Debt	0	Long-term assets	246,929
Total	267,108	Total	267,108

What will happen to Infosys' market value if it decides to replace equity by debt? Suppose the company borrows Rs 14,000 million at 10 per cent rate of interest and uses the money to buy back its shares (at the current market value). The book value total assets and capital will not show any changes; however, the mix of capital will change. Debt will increase by Rs 14,000 million and the book value equity will reduce by this amount. Suppose that debt is permanent and the corporate tax rate is 35 per cent. The company will save taxes on interest paid to debt-holders: $0.35 \times 0.10 \times 14,000 = $ Rs 490 million. The value of the tax saved is: $490/0.10 = $ Rs 4,900 million. The firm is richer by Rs 4,900 million, and its value should increase to Rs 272,008 million. The increase in the firm's value is a gain to its shareholders. How? The value of equity after recapitalisation is Rs 258,008 million. Thus, the value of equity drops by Rs 9,100 million (Rs 267,108 − Rs 258,008 = Rs 9,100 million). But remember that the shareholders received Rs 14,000 million when the company bought back their shares. Hence, the net gain of shareholders is Rs 4,900.

Table 15.7: Infosys Technologies Limited

Book value	Rs in million		Rs in million
Equity	14,606	Net current assets	20,179
Debt	14,000	Long-term assets	8,427
Total	28,606	Total	28,606
Market value	Rs in million		Rs in million
Equity	258,008	Net current assets	20,179
Debt	14,000	Long-term assets	246,929
		Value of tax shield	4,900
Total	272,008	Total	272,008

Consequently, it is being increasingly realised that a company should plan its capital structure to maximise the use of the funds and to be able to adapt more easily to the changing conditions.

Theoretically, the financial manager should plan an **optimum capital structure** for his company. The optimum capital structure is one that maximises the market value of the firm. So far our discussion of the optimum capital structure has been theoretical. In practice, the determination of an optimum capital structure is a formidable task, and one has to go beyond the theory. There are significant variations among industries and among companies within an industry in terms of capital structure. Since a number of factors influence the capital structure decision of a company, the judgment of the person making the capital structure decision plays a crucial part. Two similar companies may have different capital structures if the decision-makers differ in their judgment of the significance of various factors. A totally theoretical model perhaps cannot adequately handle all those factors, which affect the capital structure decision in practice. These factors are highly psychological, complex and qualitative and do not always follow accepted theory, since capital markets are not perfect and the decision has to be taken under imperfect knowledge and risk.

The board of directors or the chief financial officer (CFO) of a company should develop an appropriate or **target capital structure**, which is most advantageous to the company. This can be done only when all those factors, which are relevant to the company's capital structure decision, are properly analysed and balanced. The capital structure should be planned generally keeping in view the interests of the equity shareholders and the financial requirements of a company. The equity shareholders, being the owners of the company and the providers of risk capital (equity), would be concerned about the ways of financing a company's operations. However, the interests of other groups, such as employees, customers, creditors, society and government, should also be given reasonable consideration. As stated in Chapter 1, when the company lays down its objective in terms of the shareholder wealth maximisation (SWM), it is generally compatible with the interests of other groups. Thus, while developing an appropriate capital structure for its company, the financial manager should *inter alia* aim at maximising the long-term market price per share. Theoretically, there may be a precise point or range within which the market value per share is maximum. In practice, for most companies within an industry there may be a range of an appropriate capital structure within which there would not be great differences in the market value per share. One way to get an idea of this range is to observe the capital structure patterns of companies vis-à-vis their market prices of shares. It may be found empirically that there are not significant differences in the share values within a given range. The management of a company may fix its capital structure near the top of this range in order to make maximum use of favourable leverage, subject to other requirements such as flexibility, solvency, control and norms set by the financial institutions, the Security Exchange Board of India (SEBI) and stock exchanges.

Elements of Capital Structure

A company formulating its long-term financial policy should, first of all, analyse its current financial structure. The following are the important elements of the company's financial structure that need proper scrutiny and analysis:[1]

Capital Mix Firms have to decide about the mix of debt and equity capital. Debt capital can be mobilised from a variety of sources. How heavily does the company depend on debt? What is the mix of debt instruments? Given the company's risks, is the reliance on the level and instruments of debt reasonable? Does the firm's debt policy allow it flexibility to undertake strategic investments in adverse financial conditions? The firms and analysts use debt ratios, debt-service coverage ratios, and the funds flow statement to analyse the capital mix.

Maturity and Priority The maturity of securities used in the capital mix may differ. Equity is the most permanent capital. Within debt, commercial paper has the shortest maturity and public debt longest. Similarly, the priorities of securities also differ. **Capitalised debt** like lease or hire purchase finance is quite safe from the lender's point of view and the value of assets backing the debt provides the protection to the lender. Collateralised or secured debts are relatively safe and have priority over unsecured debt in the event of insolvency. Do maturities of the firm's assets and liabilities match? If not, what trade-off is the firm making? A firm may obtain a risk-neutral position by matching the maturity of assets and liabilities; that is, it may use current liabilities to finance current assets and short-medium and long-term debt for financing the fixed assets in that order of maturities. In practice, firms do not perfectly match the sources and uses of funds. They may show preference for retained earnings. Within debt, they may use long-term funds to finance current assets and assets with shorter life. Some firms are more aggressive, and they use short-term funds to finance long-term assets.

Terms and Conditions Firms have choices with regard to the basis of interest payments. They may obtain loans either at fixed or floating rates of interest. In case of equity, the firm may like to return income either in the form of large dividends or large capital gains. What is the firm's preference with regard to the basis of payments of interest and dividend? How do the firm's interest and dividend payments match with its earnings and operating cash flows? The firm's choice of the basis of payments indicates the management's assessment about the future interest rates and the firm's earnings. Does the firm have protection against interest rates fluctuations? The financial manager can protect the firm against interest rates fluctuations through the **interest rates derivatives.**[2] There are other important terms and conditions that the firm should consider. Most loan agreements include what the firm can do and

---

1. Piper, Thomas R. and Weinhol, Wolf A., "How Much Debt is Right for Your Company?" *Harward Business Review,* 1982; and Bruner, Robert F., "Structuring Corporate Financial Policy: Diagnosis of Problems and Evaluation of Strategies", in Bruner, Robert F., *Cases Studies in Finance: Managing for Value Creation,* Illinois: Irwin/McGraw, 1999, pp. 832–49.
2. Derivatives are explained in Chapter 33.

what it can't do. They may also state the schemes of payments, pre-payments, renegotiations etc. What are the lending criteria used by the suppliers of capital? How do negative and positive conditions affect the operations of the firm? Do they constraint and compromise the firm's operating strategy? Do they limit or enhance the firm's competitive position? Is the company level to comply with the terms and conditions in good time and bad time?

Currency Firms in a number of countries have the choice of raising funds from the overseas markets. Overseas financial markets provide opportunities to raise large amounts of funds. Accessing capital internationally also helps company to globalise its operations fast. Because international financial markets may not be perfect and may not be fully integrated, firms may be able to issue capital overseas at lower costs than in the domestic markets. The exchange rates fluctuations can create risk for the firm in servicing it foreign debt and equity. The financial manager will have to ensure a system of risk hedging. Does the firm borrow from the overseas markets? At what terms and conditions? How has firm benefited – operationally and/or financially in raising funds overseas? Is there a consistency between the firm's foreign currency obligations and operating inflows?

Financial innovations Firms may raise capital either through the issues of simple securities or through the issues innovative securities. Financial innovations are intended to make the security issue attractive to investors and reduce cost of capital. For example, a company may issue convertible debentures at a lower interest rate rather than non-convertible debentures at a relatively higher interest rate. A further innovation could be that the company may offer higher simple interest rate on debentures and offer to convert interest amount into equity. The company will be able to conserve cash outflows. A firm can issue varieties of option-linked securities; it can also issue tailor-made securities to large suppliers of capital. The financial manager will have to continuously design innovative securities to be able to reduce the cost. An innovation introduced once does not attract investors any more. What is the firm's history in terms of issuing innovative securities? What were the motivations in issuing innovative securities and did the company achieve intended benefits?

Financial market segments There are several segments of financial markets from where the firm can tap capital. For example, a firm can tap the private or the public debt market for raising long-term debt. The firm can raise short-term debt either from banks or by issuing commercial papers or certificate deposits in the money market. The firm also has the alternative of raising short-term funds by public deposits. What segments of financial markets have the firm tapped for raising funds and why? How did the firm tap and approach these segments?

Framework for Capital Structure: The FRICT Analysis

A financial structure may be evaluated from various perspectives. From the owners' point of view, return, risk and value are important considerations. From the strategic point of view, flexibility is an important concern. Issues of control, flexibility and feasibility assume great significance. A sound capital structure will be achieved by balancing all these considerations:

- *Flexibility* The capital structure should be determined within the debt capacity of the company, and this capacity should not be exceeded. The debt capacity of a company depends on its ability to generate future cash flows. It should have enough cash to pay creditors' fixed charges and principal sum and leave some excess cash to meet future contingency. The capital structure should be flexible. It should be possible for a company to adapt its capital structure with a minimum cost and delay if warranted by a changed situation. It should also be possible for the company to provide funds whenever needed to finance its profitable activities.

- *Risk* The risk depends on the variability in the firm's operations. It may be caused by the macroeconomic factors and industry and firm specific factors. The excessive use of debt magnifies the variability of shareholders' earnings, and threatens the solvency of the company.

- *Income* The capital structure of the company should be most advantageous to the owners (shareholders) of the firm. It should create value; subject to other considerations, it should generate maximum returns to the shareholders with minimum additional cost.

- *Control* The capital structure should involve minimum risk of loss of control of the company. The owners of closely held companies are particularly concerned about dilution of control.

- *Timing* The capital structure should be feasible to implement given the current and future conditions of the capital market. The sequencing of sources of financing is important. The current decision influences the future options of raising capital.

The FRICT (flexibility, risk, income, control and timing) analysis provides the general framework for evaluating a firm's capital structure.[1] The particular characteristics of a company may reflect some additional specific features. Further, the emphasis given to each of these features will differ from company to company. For example, a company may give more importance to flexibility than control, while another company may be more concerned about solvency than any other requirement. Furthermore, the relative importance of these requirements may change with shifting conditions. The company's capital structure should, therefore, be easily adaptable.

APPROACHES TO ESTABLISH TARGET CAPITAL STRUCTURE

The capital structure will be planned initially when a company is incorporated. The initial capital structure should be designed very carefully. The management of the company should set a **target capital structure** and the subsequent financing decisions should be made with a view to achieve the target capital structure. The financial manager has also to deal with an existing capital structure. The company needs funds to finance its activities continuously. Every time when funds have to be procured, the financial manager weighs the pros and cons of various sources of finance and selects the most advantageous sources keeping in view the target capital

---

1. Bruner, Robert, F., *op. cit.*

structure. Thus, the capital structure decision is a continuous one and has to be taken whenever a firm needs additional finances.

As discussed in the previous chapter and this chapter earlier, the following are the three most common approaches to decide about a firm's capital structure:

- **EBIT-EPS approach** for analysing the impact of debt on shareholders' return and risk.
- **Valuation approach** for determining the impact of debt on the shareholders' value.
- **Cash flow approach** for analysing the firm's ability to service debt and avoid financial distress.

EBIT-EPS Analysis

We have discussed the EBIT-EPS analysis in Chapter 14. Let us summarise the most important points here. The EBIT-EPS analysis is an important tool to analyse the impact of alternative financial plans on the shareholders' income and its variability. The firm should consider the possible fluctuations in EBIT and examine their impact on EPS (or ROE) under different financial plans. If the probability of the rate of return on the firm's assets falling below the cost of debt is low, the firm can employ high debt to increase EPS. Other things remaining the same, this may also have a favourable effect on the market value the firm's share. On the other hand, if the probability of the rate of return on the firm's assets falling below the cost of debt is very high, the firm should refrain from employing too much debt capital. Thus, the greater the level of EBIT and lower the probability of downward fluctuations, the more beneficial it is to employ debt. However, it should be realised that the EBIT-EPS analysis is a first step in deciding about a firm's capital structure. It suffers from certain limitations and does not provide unambiguous guide in determining the level of debt in practice.

EPS is one of the most widely used measures of a company's performance in practice. Hence, in choosing between debt and equity, sometimes too much attention is paid on EPS, which, however, has serious limitations as a financing-decision criterion. As discussed in Chapter 1, the major shortcomings of the EPS as a financing-decision criterion are:

- It is based on arbitrary accounting assumptions and does not reflect the economic profits.
- It does not consider the time value of money.
- It ignores the variability about the expected value of EPS, and hence, ignores risk.

The belief that investors would be just concerned with the expected EPS is not well founded. Investors in valuing the shares of the company consider both expected value and risk (variability).[1]

EPS variability and financial risk We know that the EPS variability, resulting from the use of leverage, causes financial risk. The extreme variability in earnings can threaten the firm's solvency. A firm can avoid financial risk altogether if it does not employ any debt. But then the shareholders will be deprived of the benefit of the expected increases in EPS. Therefore, a company may employ debt to take advantage of the increase in earnings provided shareholders do not perceive the financial risk exceeding the benefit of increased EPS. As we have discussed earlier in this chapter, as a firm increases the use of debt, the expected EPS may continue to increase, but the value of the company may fall because of the greater exposure of shareholders to financial risk in the form of financial distress. Shareholders expect higher compensation for taking the additional financial risk.

The EPS criterion does not consider the long-term perspectives of financing decisions. It fails to deal with the risk-return trade-off. A long-term view of the effects of financing decisions will lead one to a criterion of wealth maximisation rather than EPS maximisation. *The EPS criterion is an important performance measure but not a decision criterion.*[2]

Given its limitations, should the EPS criterion be ignored in making financing decisions? Remember that it is an important index of the firm's performance and that investors rely heavily on it for their investment decisions. Investors also do not have information on the projected earnings and cash flows and they base their evaluation on historical data. In choosing between alternative financial plans, management should start with the evaluation of the impact of each alternative on near-term EPS. But the best interests of shareholders should guide management's ultimate decision making. Therefore, a long-term view of the effect of the alternative financial plans on the value of the shares should be taken. If management opts for a financial plan, which will maximise value in the long run but has an adverse impact on near-term EPS, the reasons must be communicated to investors. A careful communication to market will be helpful in reducing the misunderstanding between management and investors.[3]

Operating conditions and business risk The level and variability of EPS depends is the *growth* and *stability of sales*. As you may recall from Chapter 14, EPS will fluctuate with fluctuations in sales. The magnitude of the EPS variability with sales will depend on the degrees of operating and financial leverages employed by the company. A firm with stable sales and favourable cost and price structure and well-focused operating strategy will have stable earnings and cash flows and thus, it can employ a high degree of financial leverage; it will not face difficulty in meeting the fixed charges commitments of debt. The likely fluctuations in sales increase the business risk. A small change in sales can lead to a dramatic change in the earnings of a company when its fixed costs are high. The fixed interest charges shift the break-even point upward. Hence, shareholders perceive a high degree of financial risk if companies with high operating leverage employ high amount of debt. A company will get into a debt trap if operating conditions become unfavourable and if it lacks a well articulated, focussed strategy (see Exhibit 15.1 for an example of a company in a debt trap).

1. Modigliani and Miller, *op. cit.*

2. Solomon, E. and Pringle, *An Introduction to Financial Management,* Prentice-Hall of India, 1978, p. 449.

3. *Ibid.*, 451.

Sales of the consumer goods industries show wide fluctuations; therefore, they do not employ a large amount of debt. On the other hand, the sales of public utilities are quite stable and predictable. Public utilities, therefore, employ a large amount of debt to finance their assets. The expected growth in sales also affects the degree of leverage. The greater the expectation of growth, the greater the amount of external financing needed since it may not be possible for the firm to cope up with growth through internally generated funds. A number of managers consider debt to be cheaper and easy to raise. The growth firms, therefore, may usually employ a high degree of leverage. Companies with declining sales should not employ debt, as they would find difficulty in meeting their fixed obligations. Non-payment of fixed charges can force a company into liquidation. It may be noted that sales growth and stability is just one factor in the leverage decision; many other factors would dictate the final decision. There are instances of a large number of high growth firms employing no or small amount of debt.

Valuation Approach

We have discussed that shareholders assume a high degree of risk than debt-holders. Hence debt is a cheaper source of funds than equity. But debt causes financial risk, which increases the cost of equity. Higher debt increases the costs of financial distress and the agency costs also increase. The tax deductibility of interest charges, however, adds value to shareholders. Thus, there is a trade-off between the tax benefits and the costs of financial distress and agency problems. The firm should employ debt to the point where the marginal benefits and costs are equal. This will be the point of maximum value of the firm and minimum weighted average cost of capital.

The difficulty with the valuation framework is that managers find it difficult to put into practice. It is not possible for them to quantify the effect of debt on the value of the firm. Also, the operations of the financial markets are so complicated that it is not easy for the financial managers to understand them. But the analysis of the impact of debt on the value is crucial and it must be carried out. A financial manager should think and act like investors. He or she must determine the contribution of alternative financial policies in creating value for shareholders. The most desirable capital structure is the one that creates the maximum value.

Cash Flow Analysis

One practical method of assessing the firm's ability to carry debt without getting into serious financial distress is to carry out a comprehensive cash flow analysis over a long period of time. A sound capital structure is expected to be conservative. Conservatism does not mean employing no debt or small amount of debt. Conservatism is related to the firm's ability to generate cash to meet the fixed charges created by the use of debt in the capital structure under adverse conditions. Hence, in practice, the question of the optimum debt-equity mix boils down to the firm's ability to service debt without any threat of insolvency and operating inflexibility. A firm is considered prudently financed if it is able to service its fixed charges under any reasonably predictable adverse conditions.

The fixed charges of a company include payment of interest and principal, and they depend on both the amount of loan, interest rates and the terms of payment. The amount of fixed charges may be high if the company employs a large amount of debt with short-term maturity. Whenever a company thinks of raising additional debt, it should analyse its expected future cash flows to meet the fixed charges. It is mandatory to pay interest and repay the principal amount of debt. If a company is not able to generate enough cash to meet its fixed obligation, it may face financial distress leading to insolvency. The companies expecting larger and stable cash inflows in the future can employ a large amount of debt in their capital structure. It is quite risky to employ high amount of debt by those companies whose cash inflows are unstable and unpredictable. It is possible for a high growth, profitable company to suffer from cash shortage if its liquidity (working capital) management is poor. We have examples of Indian companies like BHEL and NTPC, whose debtors are very sticky and they continuously face liquidity problem in spite of being profitable and high growth companies. Servicing debt proves burdensome for these companies.

Debt-servicing coverage ratio One important ratio, which should be examined at the time of planning the capital structure, is the ratio of expected net operating cash flows to fixed charges or the **debt-servicing coverage ratio**. This ratio indicates the number of times the fixed financial obligations are covered by the net operating cash flows generated by the company. The greater is the expected coverage ratio, the greater is the amount of debt a company could use. However, a company with a small coverage can also employ high amount of debt if there are not significant yearly variations in its operating cash flows and if there is a low probability of these cash flows being considerably less to meet fixed charges in a given period. Thus, it is not the average cash flows but the yearly cash flows, which are important to determine the debt capacity of a company. Fixed financial obligations must be met when due, not on an average or in most years, but always.[1] This requires a full cash flow analysis showing the impact of different capital structures under different economic conditions.[2]

Debt capacity The technique of cash flow analysis is helpful in determining a firm's debt capacity. **Debt capacity** is the amount, which a firm can service easily even under adverse conditions; it is the amount that the firm *should* employ. There may be lenders who are prepared to lend to the firm at higher interest rates. But the firm should borrow only if it can service debt without any problem. A firm can avoid the risk of financial distress if it can maintain its ability to meet contractual obligation of interest and principal payments. Debt capacity, therefore, should be thought in terms of the operating cash flows servicing debt rather than debt ratios. A high debt ratio is not necessarily bad. If a firm can service high amount of debt without much financial risk, it will increase shareholders' wealth. On the other hand, a low debt ratio can prove to be burdensome for a firm, which has liquidity problem. A firm faces financial distress (or even insolvency) when it has cash flow problem. It is dangerous to finance a capital-intensive project out of borrowings, which has built in uncertainty about the earnings and cash flows. National Aluminium Company is an example of a wrong initial choice of capital structure, which was inconsistent with its operating conditions (see Exhibit 15.2).

Some companies define their target capital structure or debt capacity in terms of the debt rating they desire. They choose the debt-equity ratio consistent with the debt rating. They work out the financial consequences of this choice and adjust their operations and other sources of finance ensuring the feasibility of the chosen capital structure.

Components of cash flows The cash flows should be analysed over a long period of time, which can cover the various adverse phases, for determining the firm's debt policy.[3] The cash flow analysis involves preparing *proforma* cash flow statements showing the firm's financial conditions under adverse conditions such as a recession. The expected cash flows can be categorised into three groups:[4]

- Operating cash flows
- Non-operating cash flows
- Financial flows

EXHIBIT 15.2: DEBT BURDEN UNDER CASH CRUNCH SITUATION: CASE OF NALCO

- National Aluminium Company (NALCO), started in 1981, is the largest integrated aluminium complex in Asia of total investment of Rs 2,408 crore, borrowings from a consortium of European banks financed to the extent of $ 830 million or Rs 1,119 crore (46.5 per cent). The loan was repayable by 1995. Aluminium is an electricity-intensive business; each tonne of aluminium needs over 15,000 kw of electricity. Since its commissioning in 1988, Nalco has exported substantial portion of its production since the domestic demand has been very low than what the company had projected at its inception. The falling international prices in last few years have eroded the company's profitability. The net profit of Rs 172 crore in 1989 dropped to Rs 14 crore in 1991–92. The Rs 1,119 crore Eurodollar loan has appreciated to Rs 2,667 crore inspite of having repaid Rs 644 crore. Due to profitability and liquidity problem and hit by the depreciating rupee and the liberalised exchange mechanism, the company is forced to reschedule repayments of its debt by the year 2003 instead of 1995. Nalco's debt-equity ratio has increased from 1:1 to 2.7:1.

- The reasons for Nalco's plight is its decision to go for the production of aluminium which consumes heavy electricity in addition to alumina. The problem of power shortage led to the setting up of power plant, which is proving very costly to the company. The overcapacities of aluminium production worldwide and highly competitive prices have added to Nalco's woes. Nalco is trying to get out of its problems by attempting to diversify into value-added products.

- Nalco's fate can change if the domestic demand for aluminium picks up and international prices rise. The mounting debt of the company poses a question: Should you use heavy dose of debt (since it is available from certain sources) to finance investments in a business like aluminium which has worldwide overcapacity, fluctuating international prices and expensive and short supply of electricity in the country in which it is set up? Debt would accentuate the financial crises when a company has built-in operating uncertainties.

Source: Based on an article by Sudipt Dutta, "NALCO: Under a Debt Mountain", *Business India*, August 17–30, 1992, pp. 77–78.

Operating cash flows relate to the operations of the firm and can be determined from the projected profit and loss statements. The behaviour of sales volume, output price and input price over the period of analysis should be examined and predicted.

Non-operating cash flows generally include capital

---

1. Johnson, R.L., *Financial Decision Making,* Goodyear, 1973.
2. Donaldson, G., *Corporate Debt Capacity,* Harvard Business School, 1961.
3. *Ibid.*
4. *Ibid.*, Solomon and Pringle, p. 489.

expenditures and working capital changes. During a recessionary period, the firm may have to specially spend on advertising etc. for the promotion of the product. Such expenditures should be included in the non-operating cash flows. Certain types of capital expenditures cannot be avoided even during most adverse conditions. They are necessary to maintain the minimum operating efficiency of the firm's resources. Such irreducible, minimum capital expenditures should be clearly identified.

Financial flows include interest, dividends, lease rentals, repayment of debt etc. They are further divided into: contractual obligations and policy obligations. **Contractual obligations** include those financial obligations, like interest, lease rentals and principal payments that are matters of contract, and should not be defaulted. **Policy obligations** consist of those financial obligations, like dividends, that are at the discretion of the board of directors. Policy obligations are also called **discretionary obligations**.

The cash flow analysis may indicate that a decline in sales, resulting in profit decline or losses, may not necessarily cause cash inadequacy. This may be so because cash may be realised from permanent inventory and receivable. Also, some of the permanent current liabilities may decline with fall in sales and profits. On the other hand, when sales and profits are growing, the firm may face cash inadequacy, as large amount of cash is needed to finance growing inventory and receivable. If the profits decline due to increase in expenses or falling output prices, instead of the decline in the number of units sold, the firm may face cash inadequacy because its funds in inventory and receivable will not be released. The point to be emphasised is that a firm should carry out cash flow analysis to get a clear picture of its ability to service debt obligations even under the adverse conditions, and thus, decide about the proper amount of debt. The firm must examine the impact of alternative debt policies on the firm's cash flow ability. The firm should then choose the debt policy, which it can implement.

Utility of cash flow analysis Is cash flow analysis superior to EBIT-EPS analysis? How does it incorporate the insights of the finance theory? The cash flow analysis has the following advantages:[1]

- It focuses on the *liquidity* and *solvency* of the firm over a long period of time, even encompassing adverse circumstances. Thus, it evaluates the firm's ability to meet fixed obligations.
- It is more *comprehensive* and goes beyond the analysis of profit and loss statement and also considers changes in the balance sheet items.
- It identifies *discretionary cash flows*. The firm can thus prepare an action plan to face adverse situations.
- It provides a list of *potential financial flows*, which can be utilised under emergency.
- It is a long-term *dynamic analysis* and does not remain confined to a single period analysis.

The most significant advantage of the cash flow analysis is that it provides a practical way of incorporating the insights of the finance theory. As per the theory, debt financing has tax advantage. But it also involves risk of financial distress. Therefore, the optimum amount of debt depends on the trade-off between tax advantage of debt and risk of financial distress. Financial distress occurs when the firm is not in a position to meet its contractual obligations. The cash flow analysis indicates when the firm will find it difficult to service its debt. Therefore, it is useful in providing good insights to determine the debt capacity, which helps to maximise the market value of the firm.

Cash flow analysis versus debt-equity ratio The cash flow analysis might reveal that a higher debt–equity ratio is not risky if the company has the ability of generating substantial cash inflows in the future to meet its fixed financial obligations. Financial risk in this sense is indicated by the company's cash-flow ability, not by the debt-equity ratio. To quote Van Horne:[2]

> …the analysis of debt-to-equity ratios alone can be deceiving, and analysis of the magnitude and stability of cash-flows relative to fixed charges is extremely important in determining the appropriate capital structure for the firm. To the extent that creditors and investors analyse a firm's cash-flow ability to service debt, and management's risk preferences correspond to those of investors, capital structure decisions made in this basis should tend to maximise share price.

The cash-flow analysis does have its limitations. It is difficult to predict all possible factors, which may influence the firm's cash flows. Therefore, it is not a foolproof technique to determine the firm's debt policy.

PRACTICAL CONSIDERATIONS IN DETERMINING CAPITAL STRUCTURE

The determination of capital structure in practice involves additional considerations in addition to the concerns about EPS, value and cash flow. A firm may have enough debt servicing ability but it may not have assets to offer as collateral. Attitudes of firms with regard to financing decisions may also be quite often influenced by their desire of not losing control, maintaining operating flexibility and have convenient timing and cheaper means of raising funds. Some of the most important considerations are discussed below.

Assets

The forms of assets held by a company are important determinants of its capital structure. Tangible fixed assets serve as collateral to debt. In the event of financial distress, the lenders can access these assets and liquidate them to realise funds lent by them. Companies with higher tangible fixed assets will have less expected costs of financial distress and hence, higher debt ratios. On the other hand, those companies, whose primary assets are intangible assets, will not have much to offer by way of collateral and will have higher costs of financial distress.

1. Donaldson, *op.cit.*; Solomon and Pringle, *op.cit.*, p. 489.
2. Van Horne, James C., *Financial Management and Policy,* Prentice-Hall of India, 195, p. 290.

Companies have intangible assets in the form of human capital, relations with stakeholders, brands, reputation etc., and their values start eroding as the firm faces financial difficulties and its financial risk increases.

Growth Opportunities

The nature of growth opportunities has an important influence on a firm's financial leverage. Firms with high market-to-book value ratios have high growth opportunities. A substantial part of the value for these companies comes from organisational or intangible assets. These firms have a lot of investment opportunities. There is also higher threat of bankruptcy and high costs of financial distress associated with high growth firms once they start facing financial problems. These firms employ lower debt ratios to avoid the problem of under-investment and costs of financial distress. But bankruptcy is not the only time when debt-financed high-growth firms let go of the valuable investment opportunities. When faced with the possibility of interest default, managers tend to be risk averse and either put off major capital projects or cut down on R&D expenses or both. Therefore, firms with growth opportunities will probably find debt financing quite expensive in terms of high interest to be paid due to lack of good collateral and investment opportunities to be lost. High growth firms would prefer to take debts with lower maturities to keep interest rates down and to retain the financial flexibility since their performance can change unexpectedly any time. They would also prefer unsecured debt to have operating flexibility.

Mature firms with low market-to-book value ratio and limited growth opportunities face the risk of managers spending free cash flow either in unprofitable maturing business or diversifying into risky businesses. Both these decisions are undesirable. This behaviour of managers can be controlled by high leverage that makes them more careful in utilising surplus cash. Mature firms have tangible assets and stable profits. They have low costs of financial distress. Hence these firms would raise debt with longer maturities as the interest rates will not be high for them and they have a lesser need of financial flexibility since their fortunes are not expected to shift suddenly. They can avail high interest tax shields by having high leverage ratios.

Debt- and Non-debt Tax Shields

We know that debt, due to interest deductibility, reduces the tax liability and increases the firm's after-tax free cash flows. In the absence of personal taxes, the interest tax shields increase the value of the firm. Generally, investors pay taxes on interest income but not on equity income. Hence, personal taxes reduce the tax advantage of debt over equity. The tax advantage of debt implies that firms will employ more debt to reduce tax liabilities and increase value. In practice, this is not always true as is evidenced from many empirical studies. Firms also have non-debt tax shields available to them. For example, firms can use depreciation, carry forward losses etc. to shield taxes. This implies that those firms that have larger non-debt tax shields would employ low debt, as they may not have sufficient taxable profit available to have the benefit of interest deductibility.

However, there is a link between the non-debt tax shields and the debt tax shields since companies with higher depreciation would tend to have higher fixed assets, which serve as collateral against debt.

Financial Flexibility and Operating Strategy

A cash flow analysis might indicate that a firm could carry high level of debt without much threat of insolvency. But in practice, the firm may still make conservative use of debt since the future is uncertain and it is difficult to be able to consider all possible scenarios of adversity. It is, therefore, prudent to maintain **financial flexibility** that enables the firm to adjust to any change in the future events or forecasting error.

As discussed earlier, financial flexibility is a serious consideration in setting up the capital structure policy. Financial flexibility means a company's ability to adapt its capital structure to the needs of the changing conditions. The company should be able to raise funds, without undue delay and cost, whenever needed, to finance the profitable investments. It should also be in a position to redeem its debt whenever warranted by the future conditions. The financial plan of the company should be flexible enough to change the composition of the capital structure as warranted by the company's operating strategy and needs. It should also be able to substitute one form of financing for another to economise the use of funds. Flexibility depends on loan covenants, option to early retirement of loans and the financial slack, viz., excess resources at the command of the firm.

Loan Covenants

Restrictive covenants are commonly included in the long-term loan agreements and debentures. These restrictions curtail the company's freedom in dealing with the financial matters and put it in an inflexible position. Covenants in loan agreements may include restrictions to distribute cash dividends, to incur capital expenditure, to raise additional external finances or to maintain working capital at a particular level. The types of covenants restricting the firm's investment, financing and dividend policies vary depending on the source of debt. While private debt contains both affirmative and negative covenants, public debt has a lot of negative covenants and commercial paper does not entail much restrictions. Loan covenants may look quite reasonable from the lenders' point of view as they are meant to protect their interests, but they reduce the flexibility of the borrowing company to operate freely and it may become burdensome if conditions change. Growth firms prefer to take private rather than public debt since it is much easier to renegotiate terms in time of crisis with few private lenders than several debenture-holders. Generally, a company while issuing debentures or accepting other forms of debt should ensure to have minimum of restrictive clauses that circumscribe its financial actions in the future in debt agreements. This is a tough task for the financial manager. A highly levered firm is subject to many constraints under debt covenants that restrict its choice of decisions, policies and programmes. Violation of covenants can have serious adverse consequences. The firm's ability to respond quickly to changing conditions also reduces. The operating inflexibility could prove to he very costly for the firms that are operating in unstable environment. These companies are likely to have low debt ratios and maintain high financial flexibility to remain competitive and not allow compromising their competitive posture. Thus, financial flexibility is essential to maintain the operating flexibility and face unanticipated contingencies.

Financial Slack

The financial flexibility of a firm depends on the **financial slack** it maintains. The financial slack includes unused debt capacity, excess liquid assets, unutilised lines of credit and access to various untapped sources of funds. The financial flexibility depends a lot on the company's debt capacity and **unused debt capacity**. The higher is the debt capacity of a firm and the higher is the unused debt capacity, the higher will be the degree of flexibility enjoyed by the firm. If a company borrows to the limit of its debt capacity, it will not be in a position to borrow additional funds to finance unforeseen and unpredictable demands except at restrictive and unfavourable terms. Therefore, a company should not borrow to the limit of its capacity, but keep available some unused capacity to raise funds in the future to meet some sudden demand for finances.[1]

Early repayment A considerable degree of flexibility will be introduced if a company has the discretion of early repaying its debt. This will enable management to retire or replace cheaper source of finance for the expensive one whenever warranted by the circumstances. When a company has excess cash and does not have profitable investment opportunities, it becomes desirable to retire debt. Similarly, a company can take advantage of declining rates of interest if it has a right to repay debt at its option. Suppose that funds are available at 12 per cent rate of interest presently. The company has outstanding debt at 16 per cent rate of interest. It can save in terms of interest cost if it can retire the 'old' debt and replace it by the 'new' debt.

Limits of financial flexibility Financial flexibility is useful, but the firm must understand its limit. It can help a profitable firm to seize opportunities, and it can provide temporary help in adverse situation, but it cannot save a firm, which is basically unhealthy. No doubt that financial flexibility is desirable, but the firm should have basic financial strength. Also, it is achieved at a cost. A company trying to obtain loans on easy terms will have to pay interest at a higher rate. Also, to obtain the right of refunding, it may have to compensate lenders by paying a higher interest or may have to allow them to participate in the equity. Therefore, the company should compare the benefits and costs of attaining the desired degree of flexibility and balance them properly.

Sustainability and Feasibility

The financing policy of a firm should be sustainable and feasible in the long run. Most firms want to maintain the sustainability of their financing policy over a long period of time. The **sustainable growth model** helps to analyse the sustainability and the feasibility of the long-term financial plans in achieving growth. This model is based on the assumption that the firm uses the internal financing and debt, consistent with the target debt-equity ratio and payout ratio and does not issue shares during the planning horizon. Given the firm's financing and payout policies and operating efficiency, this model implies that its assets and sales will grow in tandem with growth in equity (internal). Thus, the sustainable growth depends on return on equity (ROE) and retention ratio:

$$\text{Sustainable growth} = \text{ROE} \times (1 - \text{payout}) \qquad (30)$$

ROE depends on assets turnover, net margin, and financial leverage:

$$\text{ROE} = \text{asset turnover} \times \text{net margin} \times \text{leverage}$$
$$\text{ROE} = \text{assets/sales} \times \text{net profit/sales} \times \text{assets/equity} \qquad (31)$$

Alternatively, ROE depends on the firm's before-tax return on capital employed (ROCE), the financial leverage premium and the tax rate:

$$\text{ROE} = [\text{ROCE} + (\text{ROCE} - k_d)\,D/E](1 - T) \qquad (32)$$

The sustainable growth model indicates the growth rate that the firm should target. Any other growth rate will not be consistent with the financial policies set by the management. If the firm intends to achieve a different growth rate than that implied by the sustainable growth model, it will have to change its financial policy, either the debt-equity ratio, or the payout ratio or both. In fact, the model also indicates the trade-offs between the financing and operating policies. Instead of changing its financial policies for achieving higher growth, the firm can examine its operating policies vis-à-vis price, cost, assets utilisation etc. The firm must realise that growth does not ensure value creation. If the firm does not account for the investment duration and the cost of capital, growth may destroy value. The firm should also examine the impact of alternative financial policy on the value of the firm.

Control

In designing the capital structure, sometimes the existing management is governed by its desire to continue control over the company. This is particularly so in the case of the firms promoted by entrepreneurs. The existing management team not only wants control and ownership but also to manage the company, without any outside interference.

Widely held companies The ordinary shareholders elect the directors of the company. If the company issues new shares, there is risk of dilution of control. The company can issue rights shares to avoid dilution of ownership. But the existing shareholders may not be willing to fully subscribe to the issue. Dilution is not a very important consideration in the case of widely held companies. Most shareholders are not interested in taking active part in a company's management. Nor do they have time and money to attend the meetings. They are interested in dividends and capital gains. If they are not satisfied, they will sell their shares. Thus, the best way to ensure control and to have the

---

1. Solomon, E. and Pringle, *op.cit.,* p.490.

confidence of the shareholders is to manage the company most efficiently and compensate shareholders in the form of dividends and capital gains. The risk of loss of control can be reduced by distribution of shares widely and in small lots.

Closely held companies The consideration of maintaining control may be significant in case of closely held and small companies. A shareholder or a group of shareholders can purchase all or most of the new shares of a small or closely held company and control it. Even if the owner-managers hold the majority shares, their freedom to manage the company will be curtailed when they go for initial public offerings (IPOs). Fear of sharing control and being interfered by others often delays the decision of the closely held small companies to go public. To avoid the risk of loss of control, small companies may slow their rate of growth or issue preference shares or raise debt capital. If the closely held companies can ensure a wide distribution of shares, they need not worry about the loss of control so much.

The holders of debt do not have voting rights. Therefore, it is suggested that a company should use debt to avoid the loss of control. However, when a company uses large amount of debt, a lot of restrictions are put by the debt-holders, specifically the financial institutions in India, since they are the major providers of loan capital to the companies. These restrictions curtail the freedom of the management to run the business. A very excessive amount of debt can also cause serious liquidity problem and ultimately render the company sick, which means a complete loss of control.

Marketability and Timing

Marketability means the readiness of investors to purchase a security in a given period of time and to demand reasonable return. Marketability does not influence the initial capital structure, but it is an important consideration to decide about the appropriate timing of security issues. The capital markets are changing continuously. At one time, the market favours debenture issues, and, at another time, it may readily accept share issues. Due to the changing market sentiments, the company has to decide whether to raise funds with an equity issue or a debt issue. The alternative methods of financing should, therefore, be evaluated in the light of general market conditions and the internal conditions of the company.

Capital market conditions If the capital market is depressed, a company will not issue equity shares, but it may issue debt and wait to issue equity shares till the share market revives. During boom period in the share market, it may be advantageous for the company to issue shares at high premium. This will help to keep its debt capacity unutilised. The internal conditions of a company may also dictate the marketability of securities. For example, a highly levered company may find it difficult to raise additional debt. Similarly, when restrictive covenants in existing debt-agreements preclude payment of dividends on equity shares, convertible debt may be the only source to raise additional funds. A small company may find difficulty in issuing any security in the market merely because of its small size. The heavy indebtedness, low payout, small size, low profitability, high degree of competition etc. cause low rating of the company,

which would make it difficult for the company to raise external finance at favourable terms.

Issue Costs

Issue or **flotation costs** are incurred when the funds are externally raised. Generally, the cost of floating a debt is less than the cost of floating an equity issue. This may encourage companies to use debt than issue equity shares. Retained earnings do not involve flotation costs. The source of debt also influences the issue costs with fixed costs being much higher for issue of commercial paper and public debt (debenture) than the private debt. This also means that economies of scale are high for the debt instruments having high fixed costs. Hence these instruments should be used when large amounts of funds are needed. Issue costs as a percentage of funds raised will decline with larger amount of funds. Large firms require large amounts of funds, and they may plan large issues of securities to economise on the issue costs. These firms are more likely than others to resort to commercial paper or public debt for raising capital. A large issue of securities can, however, curtail a company's financial flexibility. The company should raise only that much of funds, which it can employ profitably. Many other more important factors have to be considered when deciding about the methods of financing and the size of a security issue.

Capacity of Raising Funds

The size of a company may influence its capital and availability of funds from different sources. A small company finds great difficulties in raising long-term loans. If it is able to obtain some long-term loan, it will be available at a higher rate of interest and inconvenient terms. The highly restrictive covenants in loan agreements in case of small companies make their capital structures very inflexible and management cannot run business freely without interference. Small companies, therefore, depend on share capital and retained earnings for their long-term funds requirements. It is quite difficult for small companies to raise share capital in the capital markets. Also, the capital base of most small companies is so small that they can not be listed on the stock exchanges. For those small companies, which are able to approach the capital markets, the cost of issuing shares is generally more than the large ones. Further, resorting frequently to ordinary share issues to raise long-term funds carries a greater risk of the possible loss of control for a small company. The shares of small companies are not widely scattered and the dissident group of shareholders can be easily organised to get control of the company. The small companies, therefore, sometimes limit the growth of their business to what can easily be financed by retaining the earnings.

A large company has relative flexibility in designing its capital structure. It can obtain loans on easy terms and sell ordinary shares, preference shares and debentures to the public. Because of the large size of issues, its cost of distributing a security is less than that for a small company. A large issue of ordinary shares can be widely distributed and thus, making the loss of control difficult. The size of the firm has an influence on the amount and the cost of funds, but it does not necessarily determine the pattern of financing. In practice, the debt-equity ratios of the firms do not have a definite relationship with their size.

MANAGER'S ATTITUDE TOWARDS DEBT

We know now the factors, which are theoretically important in determining the capital structure policy of a company. They are interest tax shield (adjusted for personal taxes) and costs of financial distress. We also know the additional factors in practice such as sales growth and stability, cash flow, market conditions, transaction costs etc. which may have influence on the choice of capital structure. How do managers really view the question of borrowing? There seems to be a mixed feeling. Some would prefer borrowing while others would like to decide after considering a variety of factors. They also feel that they can borrow only when lenders are prepared to lend. They think that

lenders evaluate a number of factors before deciding to lend, and these factors go beyond the theoretical considerations of risk return and value. Exhibit 15.3 summarises the perceptions of managers vis-à-vis borrowing.

CAPITAL STRUCTURE ANALYSIS OF L&T LIMITED

In this section, we shall analyse the capital structure of L&T. We introduced L&T in Chapter 9. L&T is a large diversified company in the private sector. In 2003, it had a total sales of Rs 8,783 crore and gross fixed assets of Rs 6,305 crore. Table 15.11 provides data about L&T's debt-equity ratio, interest coverage, interest as a percentage of sales and average share price for the period from 1990 to 2003. L&T's debt-equity ratio shows a fluctuating pattern during this period. From a high level of 2.5 in 1990, it has significantly reduced to a very low level of 0.20 in 1993. The ratio started increasing gradually and was close to 1 in 2003 (Fig. 15.9).

L&T's interest coverage ratio has been more than 3.0 times except during 1990-92 and 2000-2002. (Figure 15.10). Thus, the company has been maintaining a good debt-servicing ability and has also been employing debt to take advantage of interest tax shield. Interest, as a percentage of sales, was quite high in the beginning of the nineties and during 2000-02 but it has reduced to about 3 per cent of sales in 2003.

Table 15.11: L&T's Debt-Equity Ratio and Other Financial Data

Year	D/E ratio	D/E index	Interest Coverage	Interest to Sales Ratio	AMP	AMP Index
1990	2.46	100.00	1.81	7.92	71.00	100.00
1991	1.53	100.62	1.82	7.73	122.50	172.54
1992	0.70	145.52	2.63	6.43	245.00	345.07
1993	0.20	287.62	5.19	2.26	287.50	404.93
1994	0.34	288.35	5.21	2.15	240.00	338.03
1995	0.32	325.12	5.87	2.35	268.75	378.52
1996	0.40	305.01	5.51	2.58	262.00	369.01
1997	0.65	242.48	4.38	3.16	253.00	356.34
1998	0.84	274.36	4.96	2.35	230.00	323.94
1999	0.92	167.18	3.02	3.39	211.25	297.54
2000	1.05	109.81	1.98	5.37	397.73	560.18
2001	1.09	93.86	1.70	6.14	232.08	326.87
2002	1.07	119.26	2.15	4.62	201.28	283.49
2003	0.92	213.23	3.85	2.56	182.80	257.46

How have L&T's share price and debt-equity ratio moved? From 1990 to 1998, L&T's share price and debt-equity ratio have moved in tandem and have shown increasing trend. However, they seem to have moved in opposite direction during 1998-2003. (Figure15.11 and columns 6 and 7 in Table 15.11). Figure 15.11 shows that in the recent years, L&T's debt-equity ratio has been increasing while the share price has been declining.

L&T has borrowed funds from various sources. Long-term sources provide more than 70 per cent of total debt. Its long-terms sources include debentures, borrowings from banks and financial institutions and other sources such as public deposits

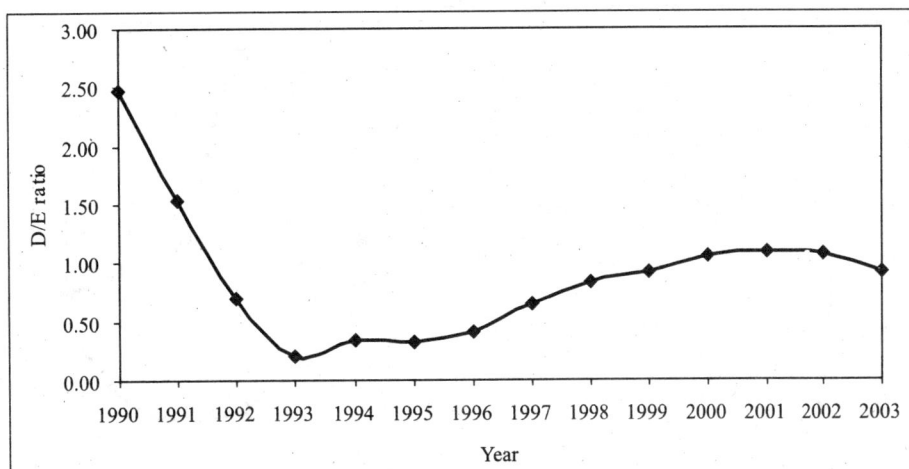

Figure 15.9: L&T's debt-equity ratio, 1990–2003

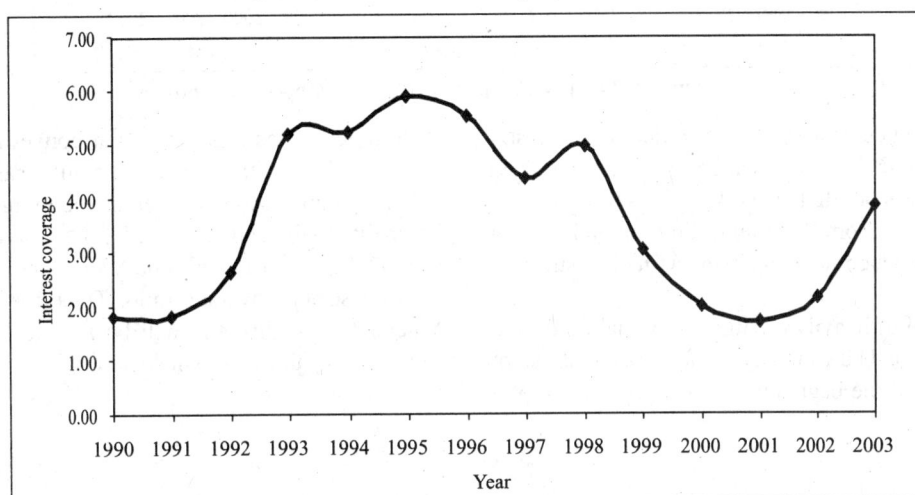

Figure 15.10: L&T's interest coverage ratio, 1990–2003

Table 15.12: L&T's Sources and Uses of Funds%

| Year | Debt | LTD | STD | STD | | | LTD | | |
				STBB	CP	LTBB	FIB	Deb.	OLTB
1990	100	84.28	15.72	100.00	0.00	4.91	4.38	78.61	12.10
1991	100	95.21	4.79	100.00	0.00	9.17	2.83	77.90	10.10
1992	100	89.70	10.30	100.00	0.00	11.13	2.24	75.58	11.04
1993	100	47.28	52.72	100.00	0.00	44.90	5.04	13.45	36.60
1994	100	60.93	39.07	100.00	0.00	32.40	38.56	2.80	26.23
1995	100	51.48	48.52	100.00	0.00	55.78	21.52	0.39	22.31
1996	100	61.58	38.42	100.00	0.00	62.88	18.76	0.14	18.22
1997	100	77.11	22.89	93.50	6.50	34.85	19.78	33.28	12.08
1998	100	79.85	20.15	82.56	17.44	30.30	14.99	41.20	13.52
1999	100	78.19	21.81	42.48	57.52	26.15	10.20	48.10	15.55
2000	100	70.62	29.38	69.57	30.43	21.20	9.46	57.73	11.61
2001	100	67.80	32.20	60.47	39.53	21.67	6.57	63.35	8.41
2002	100	75.86	24.14	62.39	37.61	30.65	2.88	53.35	13.12
2003	100	72.80	27.20	88.46	11.54	30.07	2.27	52.63	15.04

Note: LTD = long-term debt; STD = short-term debt; STBB = short-term bank borrowings; CP = commercial paper; LTBB = long-term bank borrowings; FIB = borrowings from financial institutions; Deb. = debentures; OLTB = other long-term borrowings.
Source: CMIE Database.

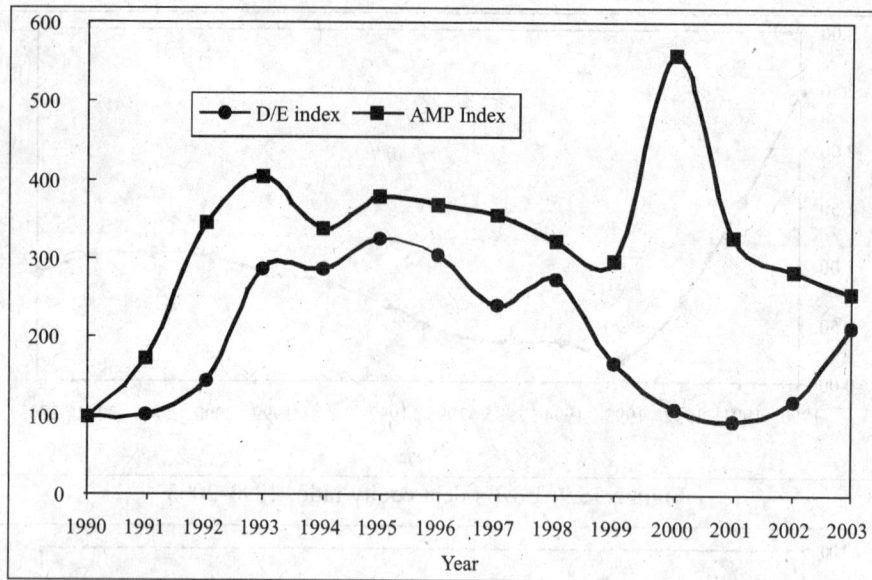

Figure 15.11: L&T's share price and debt-equity indices

etc. For financing its net current assets, the company has mostly used bank borrowing. L&T's short-term borrowings come from banks and commercial paper. In the last few years the company has reduced its borrowing from financial institutions and is using banks borrowings and debentures for financing its investments. (Table 15.12).

L&T has a history of heavily relying on internal funds and equity issues until 1980. The company made substantial use of debt during eighties and the beginning of nineties. A large part of long-term was raised through convertible debentures. The company has strengthened its equity base by converting its debentures into equity as well as retaining about 60 per cent of its profit. At the end of 2003, L&T has a total debt-equity ratio of 0.92. The debt includes both short-term and long-term debt. It has a strong coverage ratio. Thus, the company has strong financial capability and will be able to raise debt and equity funds for its future growth.

SUMMARY

❖ The capital structure decision of the firm can be characterised as a choice of that combination of debt and equity, which maximises the market value of the firm.

❖ According to Modigliani and Miller's (MM's) Proposition I, the firm's market value is not affected by capital structure; that is, any combination of debt and equity is as good as any other.

❖ Firms borrow by offering investors various types of securities. In MM's world of perfect capital market, because of same borrowing and lending rates for all investors and no taxes, investors can borrow at their own. Why should they pay a premium for a firm's borrowing?

❖ MM accept that borrowing increases shareholders return, but they argue, it also increases financial risk. They show that increased financial risk via increased cost of equity exactly offsets the increased return; thus leaving the position of shareholders unchanged. This is MM's Proposition II.

❖ As against MM's hypothesis, the traditionalists argue that market imperfections make borrowing by individual investors costly, risky and inconvenient.

❖ The arbitrage envisaged by MM will not work because of market imperfections, and investors may be willing to pay a premium for shares of levered firms. But thousands of the levered firms would have already satisfied the demand of investors who like their shares. Therefore, a firm changing its debt policy is unlikely to influence the market value of the firm.

❖ One unrealistic assumption of MM's hypothesis is that, they assume no existence of taxes. When corporate taxes are assumed, firms can increase earnings of all investors through borrowing which results in interest tax shield. The value of perpetual interest tax shield (PVINTS) is equal to TD:

$$\text{PVINTS} = \frac{T(k_d D)}{k_d} = TD$$

where T is the corporate tax rate, k_d is the cost of debt and D is the amount of debt.

❖ Thus the market value of the levered firm will be equal to the market value of an all-equity or unlevered firm (V_u) plus the present value of interest tax shield (TD);

$$V_l = V_u + TD$$

This equation implies that a firm can continuously increase its value by borrowing more debt. Thus firms should have 100 per cent debt in their capital structures.

In practice, we do not find all firms using high amounts of debt. One explanation for this behaviour could be personal income taxes.

❖ Miller has propounded a theory incorporating both corporate and personal income taxes. According to him, the advantage of interest tax shield is offset by the personal taxes paid by debt-holders on interest income.

❖ Interest income is tax-exempt at corporate level while dividend income is not. Interest income is taxed at personal level while dividend income may largely escape personal taxes.

❖ Thus companies can induce tax-paying investors to buy debt securities if they are offered high rate of interest. But after a stage it will not be possible to attract investors in the high-tax brackets. This point establishes the optimum debt ratio for the individual firms.

❖ It is difficult to believe that corporate borrowing is not at all beneficial to the firms. In reality, personal taxes on dividend income may not be zero in all countries. Also, there are always investors in different tax brackets. Thus, the tax advantage of corporate borrowing is partly taken away by the lost personal taxes.

❖ There is another factor, which reduces the tax advantage of borrowing. It is financial distress, which is costly. It includes cost of inflexibility, inconvenience and insolvency. Thus the value of a levered firm is:

$$V_l = V_u + TD - PV \text{ of financial distress}$$

❖ The value will reach optimum value where advantage of corporate borrowing, *TD*, equals present value of costs of financial distress (PVFD).

❖ The capital structure is also affected by the agency costs. Agency costs arise because of the conflict between managers and shareholders interests, on the one hand and shareholders and debt holders interests, on the other hand.

❖ The advantage of debt is that it saves taxes since interest is a deductible expense. On the other hand, its disadvantage is that it can cause financial distress. Therefore, the capital structure decision of the firm in practice should be governed by the trade-off between tax advantage and costs of financial distress and agency costs.

❖ Many firms in practice follow a pecking order—they first use retain earnings then how risk debt followed by high risk debt and lastly new equity to finance their assets.

❖ Financial distress becomes costly when the firm finds it difficult to pay interest and principal. From this point of view, both debt ratio and EBIT-EPS analysis have their limitations. They do not reflect the debt-servicing ability of the firm.

❖ A full cash flow analysis over a long period, which covers the adverse situation also, helps to determine the firm's debt capacity.

❖ Debt capacity means the amount of debt, which a firm should use given its cash flows. Cash flow analysis indicates how much debt a firm can service without any difficulty.

❖ A firm does not exhaust its debt capacity at once. It keeps reserve debt capacity to meet financial emergencies.

❖ The actual amount of debt also depends on flexibility, control and size of the firm in terms of its assets.

❖ Other factors, which are important when capital is actually raised, include timing (marketability) and flotation costs.

KEY CONCEPTS

Agency costs	Discretionary obligations	Interest tax shield	Personal leverage
Arbitrage	Financial distress	Net income approach	Policy obligations
Capitalisation rate	Financial flexibility	Net operating income approach	Signalling
Cash inadequacy	Flotation costs	Non-operating cash flows	Target capital structure
Corporate leverage	Growth opportunities	Optimum capital structure	Trade-off theory
Cost of debt	Homemade leverage	Over-investment	Traditional approach
Cost of equity	Homogeneous risk class	Pecking order hypothesis	Under-investment
Debt capacity	Information asymmetry	Perfect capital markets	Weighted average cost of captial

---

ILLUSTRATIVE SOLVED PROBLEMS

Problem 15.1: Kelley Manufacturing Co. has a total capitalisation of Rs 1,000,000, and it normally earns Rs 100,000 (before interest and taxes). The financial manager of the firm wants to take a decision regarding the capital structure. After a study of the capital market, he gathers the following data:

(*a*) What amount of debt should be employed by the firm if the traditional approach is held valid?

(*b*) If the Modigliani-Miller approach is followed, what should be the equity capitalisation rate?

Assume that corporate taxes do not exist, and that the firm always maintains its capital structure at book values.

Amount of Debt Rs	Interest Rate %	Equity Capitalisation Rate % (at given level of debt)
0	—	10.00
100,000	4.0	10.50
200,000	4.0	11.00
300,000	4.5	11.60
400,000	5.0	12.40
500,000	5.5	13.50
600,000	6.0	16.00
700,000	8.0	20.00

Solution:

(a) As per the traditional approach, optimum capital structure exists when the weighted average cost of capital is minimum. The weighted average cost of capital calculations at book value weights are as follows:

The firm should employ debt of Rs 400,000 as the weighted average cost of capital is minimum at this level of debt.

(b) According to the M-M approach, the cost of capital is a constant, and the cost of equity increases linearly with debt. The equilibrium cost of capital is assumed to be equal to pure equity capitalisation rate, which is 10 per cent in the present problem. The equity capitalisation rate is given by the following formula:

k_e (1)	w_e (2)	k_d (3)	w_d (4)	$k_e w_e$ (5)	$k_d w_d$ (6)	k_o (7) = (5) + (6)
0.100	1.0	—	—	0.1000	—	0.1000
0.105	0.9	0.040	0.1	0.0945	0.0040	0.0985
0.110	0.8	0.040	0.2	0.0880	0.0080	0.0960
0.116	0.7	0.045	0.3	0.0812	0.0135	0.0947
0.124	0.6	0.050	0.4	0.0744	0.0200	0.0944
0.135	0.5	0.055	0.5	0.0675	0.0275	0.0950
0.160	0.4	0.060	0.6	0.0640	0.0360	0.1000
0.200	0.3	0.080	0.7	0.0600	0.0560	0.1160

The equity capitalisation rates are shown in the following table.

Problem 15.2: The Levered Company and the Unlevered Company are indentical in every respect except that the Levered Company has 6 per cent Rs 200,000 debt outstanding. As per the NI approach, the valuation of the two firms is as follows:

	Unlevered Co. Rs	Levered Co. Rs
Net operating income $\overline{X}$	60,000	60,000
Total cost of debt, $k_d D$	0	12,000
Net earnings, NI	60,000	48,000
Equity capitalisation rate, k_e	0.100	0.111
Market value of shares, E	600,000	432,000
Market value of debt, D	0	200,000
Total value of the firm, V	600,000	632,000

Mr X holds Rs 2,000 worth of the Levered Company's shares. Is it possible for Mr X to reduce his outlay to earn same return through the use of arbitrage? Illustrate.

Solution: Through arbitrage it is possible for Mr X to reduce his outlay and earn the same return.

1. Mr X would sell his shares in the Levered Company for Rs 2,000.
2. He would create a personal leverage equal to his share of debt in the Levered Company by borrowing Rs 926 (= Rs 2,000 × Rs 200,000/Rs 432,000).
3. He would buy Rs 2,778 (= Rs 600,000 × Rs 2,000/Rs 432,000) of the Unlevered Company's shares.

His return is:

Return on the Unlevered Co.'s shares: Rs 2,778 ×10%	Rs 277.80
Less: Interest, Rs 926 × 6%	55.56
Net return	Rs 222.24

His return from the Levered Co. is Rs 2,000 × 11.1% = Rs 222.22, same as in the Unlevered Co. However, the funds involved in the Unlevered Co. are Rs 2,778 – Rs 926 = Rs 1,852 which is less than Rs 2,000 cash outlay involved in the Levered Company.

Problem 15.3: Firms A and B are similar except that A is unlevered, while B has Rs 200,000 of 5 per cent debentures outstanding. Assume that the tax rate is 40 per cent; NOI is Rs 40,000 and the cost of equity is 10 per cent. (i) Calculate the value of the firms, if the M-M assumptions are met. (ii) Suppose V_B = Rs 360,000. According to M-M, do these represent equilibrium values? How will equilibrium be set? Explain.

Solution: (i) The value of the unlevered firm is:

$$V_A = \frac{(1-T)\overline{X}}{k} = \frac{(1-0.4)\,\text{Rs }40,000}{0.10} = \text{Rs }240,000$$

The value of the levered firm is:

$$V_B = V_A + TD = \text{Rs }240,000 + 0.4 \text{ of Rs }200,000$$
$$= \text{Rs }240,000 + \text{Rs }80,000 = \text{Rs }320,000$$

(ii) These do not represent the equilibrium values. Firm B is overvalued by Rs 40,000 (= Rs 360,000 – Rs 320,000). The

Table 15.13: Equity Capitalisation Rates

Debt (Rs)	k_d	k_o		$(k_o - k_d)$	Debt/Equity		k_e
0	—	0.10	+	(0.10 – 0.000)	0	=	0.1000
100,000	0.040	0.10	+	(0.10 – 0.040)	100,000 / 900,000	=	0.1067
200,000	0.040	0.10	+	(0.10 – 0.040)	200,000 / 800,000	=	0.1150
300,000	0.040	0.10	+	(0.10 – 0.045)	300,000 / 700,000	=	0.1236
400,000	0.050	0.10	+	(0.10 – 0.050)	400,000 / 600,000	=	0.1333
500,000	0.050	0.10	+	(0.10 – 0.055)	500,000 / 500,000	=	0.1450
600,000	0.060	0.10	+	(0.10 – 0.060)	600,000 / 400,000	=	0.1600
700,000	0.080	0.10	+	(0.10 – 0.080)	700,000 / 300,000	=	0.1467

arbitrage process with taxes will work as follows to restore equilibrium.

Assume an investor owns 10 per cent of B Co.'s shares. His investment is:

$$0.10 \times (Rs\ 360,000 - Rs\ 200,000) = 0.10 \times Rs\ 160,000$$
$$= Rs\ 16,000$$

and return is

$$0.10 \times [(Rs\ 40,000 - Rs\ 10,000)(1 - 0.4)] = 0.10 \times Rs\ 18,000$$
$$= Rs\ 1,800$$

The investor can get the same income by shifting his investment to A Co. He would sell his holdings in B Co. for Rs 16,000 and borrow on personal account Rs 12,000, which is his percentage holdings in B Co.'s debt i.e., 0.10 (1 − 0.4) Rs 200,000 = Rs 12,000. He would, then, purchase 10 per cent of A Co.'s shares: 0.10 × Rs 2,40,000 = 24,000. His return and outlay would be

	Rs
Return 0.10[(1 − 0.4) Rs 40,000]	2,400
Less: Cost of personal debt 0.05 × Rs 12,000	600
Net return	1,800
Total funds available at his disposal:	
From sale of B Co.'s shares	16,000
Borrowed funds	12,000
	28,000
Total cash outlay in A Co.'s shares	24,000
Uncommitted funds	4,000

Through arbitrage and the substitution of personal for corporate leverage, the investor can switch from B Company to A Company, earn the same total return of Rs 1,800, and have funds left over to invest elsewhere. This process would continue till the equilibrium is restored.

Problem 15.4: The following are the costs and values for the firms A and B according to the traditional approach:

	A Rs	B Rs
Total value of firm, V	50,000	60,000
Market value of debt, D	0	30,000
Market value of equity, E	50,000	30,000
Expected net operating income	5,000	5,000
Cost of debt, INT $= k_d D$	0	1,800
Net income, NOI $- k_d D$	5,000	3,200
Cost of equity, $k_e = (- k_d D)/E$	10.00%	10.70%
Debt-equity ratio, D/E	0	0.5
Average cost of capital, k_o	10.00%	8.33%

Compute the equilibrium value for Firms A and B in accordance with the M-M thesis. Assume that (i) taxes do not exist and (ii) the equilibrium value of k_o is 9.09 per cent.

Solution: The equilibrium values are shown below:

	A Rs	B Rs
Expected net operating income, $\overline{X}$	5,000	5,000
Total cost of debt, INT $= k_d D$	0	1,800
Net income, $\overline{X} - k_d D$	5,000	3,200
Average cost of capital, k_o	0.909	0.909
Total value of firm, $V = \overline{X}/k_o$	55,000	55,000
Market value of debt, D	0	30,000
Market value of shares, $S = V - D$	55,000	25,000
Cost of equity, $k_e = (\overline{X} - k_d D)/S$	0.909	0.128

REVIEW QUESTIONS

1. Explain the assumptions and implications of the NI approach and the NOI approach. Illustrate your answer with hypothetical examples.
2. Describe the traditional view on the optimum capital structure. Compare and contrast this view with the NOI approach and the NI approach.
3. Explain the position of M-M on the issue of an optimum capital structure, ignoring the corporate income taxes. Use an illustration to show how home-made leverage by an individual investor can replicate the same risk and return as provided by the levered firm.
4. Assuming the existence of the corporate income taxes, describe M–M's position on the issue of an optimum capital structure.
5. 'The M-M thesis is based on unrealistic assumptions.' Evaluate the reality of the assumptions made by M-M.
6. How does the cost of the equity behave with leverage under the traditional view and the M–M position?
7. Consider two firms, L and U, that are identical except that L is levered whereas U is unlevered. Let V_l and V_u stand respectively, for the market values of L and U. In a perfect market, would one expect V_u to be less than, greater than, or equal to V_l? Explain.
8. "When the corporate income taxes are assumed to exist, Modigliani and Miller and the traditional theorists agree that capital structure does affect value, so the basic point of dispute disappears." Do you agree? Why or why not?
9. Explain the effect of capital structure on the value of the firm when both corporate and personal income taxes are considered?
10. What is financial distress? How does it affect the value of the firm?
12. Define the capital structure. What are the elements of a capital structure? What do you mean by an appropriate capital structure? What are the features of an appropriate capital structure?
13. Briefly explain the factors that influence the planning of

the capital structure in practice.

14. Explain the features and limitations of three approaches of determining a firm's capital structure: (a) EBIT – EPS approach, (b) valuation approach, and (c) cash flow approach.

15. "...the analysis of debt-to-equity ratios alone can be deceiving, and an analysis of the magnitude and stability of cash-flows relative to fixed changes is extremely important in determining the appropriate capital structure—

." Give your opinion.

16. What are the implications of growth opportunities for the financial leverage?

17. What is meant by financial flexibility? Is a flexible capital structure costly?

18. What is the importance of marketability and floatation costs in the capital structure decision of a company?

19. How do the considerations of control and size affect the capital structure decision of the firm?

PROBLEMS

1. X Co. has a net operating income of Rs 200,000 on an investment of Rs 1,000,000 in assets. It can raise debt at a 16 per cent rate of interest. Assume that taxes do not exist.

   (a) Using the NI approach and an equity-capitalisation rate of 18 per cent, compute the total value of the firm and the weighted average cost of capital if the firm has (i) no debt, (ii) Rs 300,000 debt, (iii) Rs 600,000 debt.

   (b) Using the NOI approach and an overall capitalisation rate of 12 per cent, compute the total value of the firm, value of shares and the cost of equity if the firm has (i) no debt, (ii) Rs 300,000 debt, (iii) Rs 600,000 debt.

2. Firm L and Firm U are in the same risk class and are identical in every respect except that Firm L is levered and Firm U is unlevered. Firm L has 12 per cent Rs 400,000 debentures outstanding. Both firms earn 18 per cent before interest and taxes on their total assets of Rs 800,000. Assume a corporate tax rate of 50 per cent and a pure equity capitalisation rate of 15 per cent.

   (a) Compute the total value of the firms using (i) the NI approach, (ii) the NOI approach.

   (b) Using the NOI approach, calculate the after-tax weighted average cost of capital for both the firms. Which of the two firms has an optimum capital structure and why?

   (c) According to the NOI approach, the values for Firms A and B computed in part (a) using the NI approach are not in equilibrium. Under such a situation, an investor can secure same return at lower cash outlay through the arbitrage process. Assume that an investor owns 5 per cent of L's shares, show the arbitrage process. When would this arbitrage process stop?

3. The values for two firms X — an unlevered firm and Y—a levered firm with Rs 600,000 debt at 6 per cent rate of interest are given as below. An investor holds Rs 20,000 worth of Y's shares. Show the process by which he can earn same return at a lesser cost.

	X Rs	Y Rs
Net operating income $\overline{X}$,	200,000	200,000
Cost of debt, INT $= k_d D$	—	36,000
Net income, NI	200,000	164,000

	X Rs	Y Rs
Equity-capitalisation rate, k_e	0.111	0.125
Market value of equity, E	1,800,000	1,312,000
Market value of debt, D	—	600,000
Total value of firm, $V = E + D$	1,800,000	1,912,000
Overall capitalisation rate, k_o	0.1111	0.1046

4. Two firms A and B are identical in all respect except that B has Rs 500,000 debt outstanding at a 6 per cent rate of interest. The values of the two

	A Rs	B Rs
Net operating income $\overline{X}$	150,000	150,000
Cost of debt, k_d	—	30,000
Net income NI	150,000	120,000
Equity-capitalisation rate, k_e	0.10	0.15
Market value of equity, E	1,500,000	800,000
Market value of debt, D	—	500,000
Total value of firm, $V = E + D$	1,500,000	1,300,000
Overall capitalisation rate, k_e	0.10	0.1154

Assume that an investor owns 10 per cent of A's shares. How can the investor obtain same return at a lower cost?

5. Sppose X = Rs 50,000, k_d = 0.06, $E_u = V_u$ = Rs 500,000, E_1 = Rs 280,000. D_l = Rs 250,000 and $V_l = D_l + E_l$ = Rs 530,000. Calculate the cost of equity and the weighted average cost of capital for two firms. If an investor owns 5 per cent of the levered firm's shares, how can he be benefited by resorting to the arbitrage process?

6. A new company proposes to invest Rs 10 lakh in assets and will maintain its capital structure at book value. It is expected to earn a net operating income of Rs 160,000. The company wants to have an optimum mix of debt and equity. The cost of debt and the equity-capitalisation rate at different debt-equity ratio are as follows:

   (a) What is the optimum capital structure for this company?

   (b) If the M-M hypothesis is valid, what should be the equity-capitalisation rate at different debt-equity ratios?

Contd...

Debt-Equity Ratio	Cost of Debt	Equity-capitalisation Rate
—	—	0.125
10: 90	0.05	0.130
20: 80	0.05	0.136
30: 70	0.06	0.143
40: 60	0.07	0.160
50: 50	0.08	0.180
60: 40	0.10	0.200

7. The values for the two firms X and Y in accordance with the traditional theory are given below:

	X Rs	Y Rs
Expected net operating income, $\overline{X}$	50,000	50,000
Total cost of debt, $k_d D = INT$	0	10,000
Net income, $\overline{X} - INT$	50,000	40,000
Cost of equity, k_e	0.10	0.11
Market value of shares, E	500,000	360,000
Market value of debt, D	0	200,000
Total value of firm, $V = E + D$	500,000	560,000
Average cost of capital, $k_o = X/V$	0.10	0.09
Debt–equity ratio	0	0.556

Compute the values for firms X and Y as per the M-M thesis. Assume that (i) corporate income taxes do not exist and (ii) the equilibrium value of k_o is 12.5 per cent.

8. The following are the equilibrium value for two firms M and N as per the Modigliani-Miller approach:

	M Rs	N Rs
Net operating income $\overline{X}$,	12,000	12,000
Total cost of debt, $INT = k_d D$	0	2,000
Net income, $\overline{X} - INT$	12,000	10,000
Overall capitalisation rate, k_o	0.08	0.08

Contd...

	M Rs	N Rs
Total value of firm, $V = X/k_o$	1,50,000	1,50,000
Market value of debt, D	0	40,000
Market value of shares, $E = V - D$	1,50,000	1,10,000
Cost of debt, $k_d = INT/D$	0	0.05
Cost of equity, $k_e = (\overline{X} - INT)/E$	0.08	0.091

Recompute the values for firms M and N in accordance with the traditional theory. Assume that the cost of equity of firm M is 10 per cent and for firm N it is 10.5 per cent.

9. Firm L and U have same expected earnings before interest and taxes of Rs 25,000. Firm U has employed 100 per cent equity of Rs 100,000 while firm L has employed Rs 50,000 equity and Rs 50,000 debt at an expected rate of return (cost of debt) of 15 per cent. You are required to calculate for each firm: (a) earnings of all investors and (b) value of interest tax shield under the following alternatives: (i) no corporate and personal taxes; (ii) 50 per cent corporate taxes and zero personal taxes; (iii) 50 per cent corporate taxes and 30 per cent personal taxes; and (iv) 50 per cent corporate taxes, 20 per cent personal taxes on dividend income and 40 per cent personal taxes on interest income.

10. A company has set its target debt-equity ratio at 1:1 and target payout ratio at 40 per cent. The company wants to achieve a growth rate of 20 per cent per annum. The company is expecting before tax return on assets of 21 per cent. Its sales-to-assets ratio is 1.8 times. The current interest rate is 12 per cent. The corporate tax rate for the company is 35 per cent. Can the company sustain its intended growth? What should it do to achieve the growth rate?

11. *Hindustan Lever Limited (HLL):* From the following financial data for years from 1992 to 2002 (year ending 31 December) for HLL in Table 15.14, critically review the company's financing practice.

12. *Philips India Limited*: Table 15.15 gives data for Philips India Limited for the years from 1990 to 2002. The Company changed its accounting period from March to December in 1993, thus, data for the year 1993 are for 9 months. Comment on the company's investment and financing policy.

Table 15.14: Hindustan Lever Limited

(Rs in crore)

Year	GFA	NCA	INVST	NW	Debt	NS	PBIT	INT	PAT
1992	330.5	323.1	12.3	333.3	200.3	1221.1	197.0	32.2	60.0
1993	365.6	285.8	51.0	385.7	115.2	1505.0	244.9	27.2	79.8
1994	491.8	299.7	191.5	538.3	146.5	1721.3	327.4	29.5	97.3
1995	563.8	193.0	122.8	638.3	160.2	2039.4	385.2	20.2	122.1
1996	953.6	168.9	328.8	937.5	260.1	2798.8	654.2	57.0	185.2
1997	1035.2	567.2	544.6	1260.8	186.6	3337.8	874.2	33.9	232.0
1998	1273.4	895.3	729.5	1712.4	264.3	6560.7	1130.5	29.3	404.7
1999	1349.7	1151.8	1068.1	2102.6	177.3	7736.8	1420.1	22.4	570.3
2000	1539.4	1087.1	1832.2	2487.6	111.6	9426.1	1668.4	13.2	808.2
2001	1778.3	1349.7	1668.9	3043.0	83.7	10116.5	1865.6	7.7	1079.8
2002	1836.9	1639.0	2397.7	3658.2	58.3	10588.2	2154.4	9.2	1300.3

Table 15.14: Philips India Limited

(Rs in crore)

Year	GFA	NCA	INVST	NW	TD	STBB	LTB	DEBN	NS	PAT
1990	154.7	82.1	2.1	41.3	116.5	12.1	104.4	56.7	391.2	-8.2
1991	162.1	97.1	7.6	63.6	101.8	16.0	85.8	48.3	523.1	26.7
1992	181.8	122.9	12.2	76.5	114.6	31.1	83.6	41.2	689.5	21.5
1993	232.1	112.8	13.8	129.3	69.3	6.4	52.9	22.8	672.0	9.0
1994	253.1	141.3	13.2	175.9	62.5	12.8	39.6	3.2	1092.7	33.7
1995	319.2	223.4	14.7	187.4	169.7	91.3	63.4	3.0	1454.4	22.1
1996	376.1	194.3	19.6	190.9	186.9	71.5	100.3	32.7	1438.8	11.8
1997	386.0	175.8	16.7	171.7	168.3	47.6	80.7	32.7	1509.4	44.6
1998	414.8	217.8	15.5	176.2	195.7	44.8	110.9	72.2	1620.1	39.2
1999	330.4	213.1	14.0	191.6	159.9	35.4	104.5	50.0	1662.9	41.4
2000	363.3	134.1	14.0	167.8	127.3	25.8	86.5	53.8	1444.4	-3.1
2001	334.7	40.0	17.3	147.3	66.1	45.9	20.2	0.0	1459.5	40.4
2002	605.4	67.6	1.9	306.4	48.0	5.5	42.5	8.3	1492.8	85.5

GFA = gross fixed assets; NCA = net current assets; INVST = investment; NW = net worth; TD = total debt borrowings; STBB = short-term bank borrowings; LTB = long-term borrowings including debentures; DEBN = debentures; NS = net sales; PAT = profit after tax.

CASE

Case 15.1: Samrudh Company Limited[1]

Samrudh Company Limited (SCL) is a public limited company, whose shares are listed on the Ahmedabad Stock Exchange. The company produces and markets a wide range of well-known home-use products. Because of the fragmented market shares of its products and high competition from small and medium size firms, the sales of the company have grown moderately. The company finances its activities employing both debt and equity. It follows an implicit policy of not allowing its debt level to exceed the industry average. The company's current debt ratio is not high in comparison with the industry average. However, the company is constrained by the terms and conditions of debt.

At the end of March 2004, the management is worried as it is near violating the terms and conditions of debt that it had borrowed from the Industrial Development Bank of India (IDBI) in 1998. The interest rates when the company borrowed from IDBI in 1998 were high. It had raised the loan amount at 14 per cent from IDBI to buy plant and machinery for expanding its business. The loan was secured against the plant and machinery. The loan is repayable in equal instalments at par during 2005–08. There are three covenants attaching to the loan from IDBI. These covenants are: (1) The company's book value debt-equity ratio should not exceed 1:1; (2) the current ratio, defined as sum

of stock, debtors and cash divided by the sum of creditors, provisions and bank credit, shall be at least 1; and (3) the interest coverage ratio should be at least 3 times.

The current interest rates are very low. Banks and financial institutions have a lot of liquidity and long-term loans are available at about 9.0 per cent rate of interest. The finance director argues that SCL should take advantage of low interest rates. The company should refinance its existing debt by borrowing funds at about 9 per cent from the banks. IDBI may not agree to the company's proposal of pre-payment unless it is given some incentives. It will ask for redemption of principal at a premium of 11 per cent. The finance director proposes to pay this premium by drawing down the company's surplus cash and negotiate more flexible debt covenants with the new lender. He argues that since the interest rate comes down by five percentage points, the 11% redemption premium will be recovered in a little over two years. He also claims that the improved profitability and EPS will lead to a rise in the share price. SCL's share is currently selling for Rs 35.25. The average P/E ratio of the companies in the same industry is 8.5.

Assume that for income tax purposes, SCL will be able to charge the premium paid as expense in equal annual instalments from 2003–04 to 2007–08.

---

1. The author is thankful to Professor Jayanth R. Varma, IIMA, Ahmedabad for his useful suggestions.

Table 15.1.1: Estimated Summarized Balance Sheet for Samrudh for Year Ending 31 March 2004

(Rs in crore)

Assets and Liabilities	Rs	Rs	Rs
Fixed Assets (net):			
Land			167.39
Buildings			186.91
Machinery and equipments			468.26
			822.56
Current Assets:			
Stocks	83.70		
Debtors	83.91		
Cash	66.74	234.35	
Current liabilities:			
Creditors	133.91		
Provisions	100.44	234.35	
Net current assets			0.00
Net Assets			822.56
Financed by:			
Ordinary shares (Rs 10 par value)			217.00
Reserves			185.56
Shareholders' funds			402.56
Borrowings:			
14% IDBI Loan			420.00
			822.56

Table 15.1.2: Estimated Profit and Loss Account for the Year Ended 31 March 2004

	Rs crore
Sales	771.75
Less: Variable cost	355.96
Less: Fixed cost	170.60
Profit before interest and taxes	235.19
Less: Interest	58.80
Profit before tax	176.39
Less: Tax @35%	61.74
Profit after tax	114.65

Discussion Questions

1. How close is SCL to violating the loan covenants?
2. If SCL wants to refinance, which loan covenants will it have to renegotiate with the new lender? Would the new lender agree?
3. Should SCL refinance its existing debt?
4. Assuming that the market was not expecting a refinancing, estimate the impact on SCL's share price if it decides to refinance?

CHAPTER 16

Valuation and Financing

CHAPTER OBJECTIVES

- Understand the relationship between leverage, beta and the cost of capital
- Explain the unlevering and levering of beta for calculating the cost of capital
- Discuss the utility and limitations of WACC in evaluating an investment project
- Compare the free cash flow (FCF) approach and the capital cash flow (CCF) approach of investment evaluation
- Focus on the advantages of using the adjusted present value (APV) approach in project evaluation
- Explain the methodology for determining the value of the firm and the value of equity

INTRODUCTION

In Chapter 15 we have explained the relationship between the firm's value and cost of capital and its capital structure. The use of debt results in tax savings on interest, which creates additional value for the firm. It also increases the financial risk of the firm's shareholders. Thus, the capital structure of the firm also affects its cost of capital. The firm's cost of capital will change with change in its capital structure.

We have discussed so far that evaluation of a project requires estimates of free cash flows and the cost of capital that reflects the risk of the project and its target capital structure. We made the simplifying assumption that the project's and firm's risk and target capital structure are equivalent. Hence the firm's weighted average cost of capital (WACC) was used to discount the project's cash flows. WACC is based on the assumption that the target capital structure remains unchanged over time. In practice, all projects do not necessarily have same risk and capital structure as the firm. Also, some projects support fixed amount of debt instead of a constant capital structure. In this chapter, we focus

on these issues and discuss alternative approaches of valuation and dealing with the financing effects.

BETA, COST OF CAPITAL AND CAPITAL STRUCTURE

The Modigliani-Miller (MM) capital structure models are based on the assumption that the levered and the unlevered firms belong to the same 'homogeneous risk-class'. This assumption is necessary to control the operating or the business risk of the firms and isolate the effects of the financial leverage and risk. The opportunity cost of capital of a firm depends on its business risk. Hence, the opportunity cost of capital of a levered firm and an unlevered firm belonging to the same homogeneous (business) risk class will be the same. You may recall that under CAPM, the observed equity beta captures both the business and financial risk. The equity beta may, thus, be referred to as the **levered equity beta**. Financial leverage causes variability in the return of shareholders. This adds financial risk. As a consequence, beta of a levered firm's equity will increase as debt is introduced in the firm's capital structure. The **unlevered beta** is a measure of the business risk of the firm. It is not directly observed in the market place. However, it can be derived from the equity and debt betas of the firm. How can we do this?

We know that a portfolio consists of individual securities. Each security has its beta, and the beta of the portfolio is the weighted average beta of individual securities in the portfolio. Similarly, a firm has a portfolio of assets, and therefore, the asset beta of a firm, β_a is the weighted average of betas of individual assets. Thus, **asset beta** is given by the following equation:

Asset beta = beta of asset 1 × weight of asset 1
+ beta of asset 2 × weight of asset 2
+ ... + beta of asset n × weight of asset n

$$\beta_a = \beta_1 w_1 + \beta_2 w_2 + \cdots + \beta_n w_n$$
$$= \sum_{i=1}^{n} \beta_i w_i \qquad (1)$$

where β_a is the weighted average beta of assets, β_i is the beta of ith asset and w_i is the weight of ith asset.

A firm's assets are generally financed by debt and equity. Therefore, a firm's asset beta is also equal to the weighted average of the firm's equity beta and debt beta. Assuming no corporate tax, the beta of assets will be as follows:

Asset beta = equity beta × equity weight
+ debt beta × debt weight

$$\beta_a = \beta_e \frac{E}{V} + \beta_d \frac{D}{V} \qquad (2)$$

where β_e is equity beta, β_d is debt beta, E is the market value of shareholders' equity, D is the market value of debt and V is the total value of the firm ($V = E + D$). You can observe equity beta and debt beta for a company from the market place, but not its asset beta. Based on the observed equity and debt betas, you can calculate the asset beta using Equation (2). A risky debt will have a positive debt beta (greater than zero), but generally much less than the equity beta.

We can rewrite Equation (2) to obtain the following equation for the equity beta of a levered firm:

$$\beta_e = \beta_a + (\beta_a - \beta_d)\frac{D}{E} \qquad (3)$$

You can see from Equation (3) that the equity beta increases linearly with leverage (debt-to-equity, D/E, ratio) since it adds financial risk to shareholders.

Under the CAPM, the asset or opportunity cost of capital of a pure-equity (unlevered) firm is given as follows:

$$\begin{matrix} \text{Opportunity} \\ \text{cost of capital} \end{matrix} = \begin{matrix} \text{Risk-free} \\ \text{rate} \end{matrix} + \begin{matrix} \text{risk} \\ \text{premimu} \end{matrix} \times \begin{matrix} \text{Asset} \\ \text{beta} \end{matrix}$$

$$k_a = r_f + r_p \beta_a \qquad (4)$$

The cost of debt and the cost of equity of a levered firm are given as follows:

$$\text{Pre-tax cost of debt} = k_d = r_f + r_p \beta_d \qquad (5)$$

$$\text{Cost of equity} = k_e = r_f + r_p \beta_e \qquad (6)$$

You can calculate the pre-tax weighted average cost of capital (WACC) as follows:

$$\text{Pre-tax WACC} = k_e \frac{E}{V} + k_d \frac{D}{V} \qquad (7)$$

Substituting the values for k_d and k_e, respectively, from Equation (5) and Equation (6) in Equation (7), we obtain:

$$\text{Pre-tax WACC} = \left(r_f + r_p \beta_e\right)\frac{E}{V} + \left(r_f + r_p \beta_d\right)\frac{D}{V}$$
$$= r_f\left(\frac{E}{V} + \frac{D}{V}\right) + r_p\left(\beta_e \frac{E}{V} + \beta_d \frac{D}{V}\right)$$
$$= r_f + r_p\left(\beta_e \frac{E}{V} + \beta_d \frac{D}{V}\right) \qquad (8)$$

You may notice that the term within parentheses on the right hand side of Equation (8) represents the asset beta. Hence, we can conclude that the asset or opportunity cost of capital is the same as the pre-tax WACC. Hence,

$$\text{Pre-tax WACC} = k_e \frac{E}{V} + k_d \frac{D}{V} = k_a$$
$$= r_f + r_p \beta_a \qquad (9)$$

What is the cost of equity of a levered firm? You can substitute Equation (3) for the equity beta in Equation (6) for calculating the cost of equity of a levered firm with risky debt as follows:

$$k_e = r_f + r_p\left[\beta_a + (\beta_a - \beta_d)\frac{D}{E}\right] \qquad (10)$$

The shareholders of a levered firm require compensation for both business risk and financial risk. Hence,

$$\begin{matrix} \text{Cost of} \\ \text{equity} \end{matrix} = \begin{matrix} \text{Risk-free} \\ \text{rate} \end{matrix} + \begin{matrix} \text{Business risk} \\ \text{premium} \end{matrix} + \begin{matrix} \text{Financial risk} \\ \text{premium} \end{matrix}$$

We can rewrite Equation (10) as follows to decompose risk premium into business risk and financial risk:

$$k_e = r_f + r_p \beta_a + r_p(\beta_a - \beta_d)\frac{D}{E} \qquad (11)$$

You may notice that shareholders of the levered firm demand premium equal to $r_p \beta_a$ for assuming the business risk and additional premium equal to $r_p(\beta_a - \beta_d)$ D/E for assuming the financial risk. In the case of an unlevered firm, financial risk premium is zero and shareholders are compensated only for the business risk.

Risk-free Debt, Equity Beta and Cost of Equity

Debt may be risk-free. The debt beta of the risk-free debt will be zero ($\beta_d = 0$). If $\beta_d = 0$, then the second-term on the right-hand side of Equation (2) will disappear and asset beta, β_a is given as follows:

$$\beta_a = \beta_e \frac{E}{V} \qquad (12)$$

When the beta of debt is zero, the equation for equity beta can be written as follows:

$$\beta_e = \beta_a \frac{V}{E} = \beta_a \left(1 + \frac{D}{E}\right) \qquad (13)$$

You can rewrite Equation (11) for calculating the cost of equity of a levered firm with risk-less debt as follows:

$$k_e = r_f + r_p \beta_a \left(1 + \frac{D}{E}\right)$$
$$= r_f + r_p \beta_a + r_p \beta_a \frac{D}{E} \qquad (14)$$

Illustration 16.1: Calculating Asset Beta and Costs of Capital

The observed beta on the equity of levered Firm L is 1.20. The beta of debt is 0.20. The company has a debt-equity ratio of 0.40. The risk-free rate of return is 10 per cent and the market risk premium is 9 per cent. What is Firm L's cost of debt, the cost of equity and the opportunity cost of capital? How will these estimates change if debt was risk free and the equity beta still is 1.20?

The cost of debt is as follows:

$$k_d = r_f + r_p \beta_d$$
$$= 0.10 + 0.09 \times 0.20 = 0.118 \text{ or } 11.8\%$$

The cost of equity is as follows:

$$k_e = r_f + r_p \beta_e$$
$$= 0.10 + 0.09 \times 1.20 = 0.208 \text{ or } 20.8\%$$

The firm has debt-equity ratio of 0.40. Hence, debt to value and equity to value ratios will he as follows:

$$\frac{D}{V} = \frac{D/E}{1 + D/E} = \frac{0.40}{1.40} = 0.286$$
$$\frac{E}{V} = 1 - \frac{D}{V} = 1 - 0.286 = 0.714$$

You can now calculate Firm L's asset beta to estimate its opportunity or asset cost of capital. The asset beta is given as follows:

$$\beta_a = \beta_e \frac{E}{V} + \beta_d \frac{D}{V}$$
$$= 1.20 \times 0.714 + 0.20 \times 0.286 = 0.914$$

The opportunity cost of capital is:

$$k_a = r_f + r_p \beta_a$$
$$= 0.10 + 0.09 \times 0.914 = 0.182 \text{ or } 18.2\%$$

The alternative way of calculating the asset or the opportunity cost of capital is to calculate the pre-tax WACC:

$$\text{Pre-tax WACC} = k_e \frac{E}{V} + k_d \frac{D}{V}$$
$$= 0.208 \times 0.714 + 0.118 \times 0.276$$
$$= 0.182 \text{ or } 18.2\%$$

Now let us assume that Firm L's debt is risk-free and beta of debt is zero. What is L's asset beta? How much is its opportunity cost of capital? The asset beta will be as follows:

$$\beta_a = \beta_e \frac{E}{V} = 1.20 \times 0.714 = 0.86$$

The opportunity cost of capital is:

$$k_a = r_f + r_p \beta_a$$
$$= 0.10 + 0.09 \times 0.86 = 0.177 \text{ or } 17.7\%$$

Alternatively, the opportunity cost of capital can be calculated as follows:

$$\text{Pre-tax WACC} = k_e \frac{E}{V} + k_d \frac{D}{V}$$
$$= 0.208 \times 0.714 + 0.10 \times 0.276$$
$$= 0.177 \text{ or } 17.7\%$$

Capital Structure Changes: Unlevering and Relevering Beta

Suppose a levered firm has an equity beta of 1.15, debt beta of 0.30, and market value debt ratio equal to 0.40. You can calculate the firm's asset beta as: $1.15 \times 0.60 + 0.30 \times 0.40 = 0.81$. What happens to the equity beta of the firm if it changes its capital structure? Suppose the firm is contemplating to increase market value debt ratio to 0.60. The equity beta of the firm will change since its financial risk has changed. Two steps are involved in estimating the new equity beta of the firm:

- First, you should **unlever** the firm's equity beta. This means that you should estimate the firm's asset beta:

$$\beta_a = \beta_e \times \frac{E}{V} + \beta_d \times \frac{D}{V}$$

- In our example the asset or unlevered beta is 0.81. In practice, we generally assume debt beta is zero. The asset beta is given as follows:

$$\beta_a = \beta_e \times \frac{E}{V}$$

- Second, you should now **relever** the equity beta to reflect the new debt-equity ratio:

$$\beta_e = \beta_a + (\beta_a - \beta_d) \times \frac{D}{E}$$

- In the example, the relevered equity beta will be: $0.81 + (0.81 - 0.30) \times 1.50 = 1.575$. We assume that the debt beta remains 0.30.

In case the debt beta is zero, the equity beta is relevered as follows:

$$\beta_e = \frac{\beta_a}{E/V} = \beta_a \left[1 + \frac{D}{E}\right]$$

Illustration 16.2: Unlevering and Levering Beta

A large engineering company wants to diversify into fertiliser business and organise it as a new division. The company found a comparable fertiliser company that has an equity beta of 1.20, and debt-to-market value ratio of 0.72. The debt beta is zero. The engineering company will have a debt-to-value ratio of 0.60 for proposed fertiliser business. Calculate the beta for the proposed new division.

The capital structure of the project is different from the comparable firm's capital structure. Hence its equity beta will be different. First, we shall unlever the equity beta of the comparable firm to calculate its asset beta:

$$\beta_a = \beta_e \times \frac{E}{V} = 1.20 \times 0.28 = 0.336$$

The proposed debt ratio for the division is 0.60; therefore, we shall now relever beta for the division by incorporating its debt ratio:

$$\beta_e = \frac{\beta_a}{E/V} = \frac{\beta_a}{1 - D/V}$$

$$\beta_e = 0.336/(1 - 0.60) = 0.84$$

Corporate Taxes, Interest Tax Shields and Beta

Firms in practice pay taxes, and interest paid on debt is tax deductible. Interest tax shields add value. According to the MM tax-corrected hypotheses, the values of levered and unlevered firms would differ by the value of interest tax shield. Do the interest tax shields reduce a firm's business risk? It depends on whether the interest tax shields are less risky than the operating income of the firm. We shall discuss two situations: First, we shall assume that debt-to-value ratio is fixed; that is, debt is a fixed proportion of the value. In the second situation, we shall assume that the amount of debt is fixed.

Fixed debt-to-value ratio Most firms have target capital structures. The target capital structure is expressed in terms of debt-to-value ratio. Value means market value of a firm. In case of a new investment, value will be present value of the expected cash flows. If we assume that debt-to-value ratio is fixed, then the debt *levels* will change whenever the value changes. In this situation, the interest tax shields are tied to the firm's operations and value, and therefore, they are as risky as the firm's operations are. Under the assumption of the fixed debt ratio, the beta of the interest tax shields will be equal to the asset beta.[1] This implies that interest tax shield will not reduce the risk of the firm. Hence, there is no case for adjusting the asset beta for the effect of interest tax shields. The asset beta of the levered firm (β_l) will be equal to the asset beta of the unlevered firm (β_u). The equity beta of the levered firm will be given by Equation (3) in case of risky debt

$$\beta_e = \beta_a + (\beta_a - \beta_d) \times \frac{D}{E}$$

and by Equation (13) in case of risk-free debt

$$\beta_e = \frac{\beta_a}{E/V} = \beta_a \left[1 + \frac{D}{E} \right]$$

Illustration 16.3: Calculating Cost of Equity

Desai Chemicals has asset beta of 1.25. The company has a target capital structure with a fixed debt-to- market value ratio of 0.4. The risk-free rate of return is 9 per cent and the expected market premium is 12 per cent. The corporate tax rate is 35 per cent. What is Desai Chemical's required rate of return on equity?

Since the company has a fixed debt ratio, the interest tax shields beta will be equal to the asset beta. Hence there is no need of any adjustment

for the tax effects. Assuming that debt is risk free, the equity beta will be as follows:

$$\beta_e = \frac{\beta_a}{E/V} = \beta_a \left[1 + \frac{D}{E} \right] = 1.25 \times (1 + 0.4/0.6) = 2.083$$

Since debt ratio is 0.4, equity ratio will be 0.6 and debt-equity (D/E) ratio will be $0.4/0.6 = 0.67$. Desai Chemicals' cost of equity will be as follows:

$$k_e = 0.09 + 0.12 \times 2.083 = 0.34 \text{ or } 34\%$$

Fixed Amount of Debt

When a firm (or project) employs fixed amount of debt, it will not fluctuate with the value. The interest flows and tax savings are known, and they will remain tied to debt. They remain insulated from fluctuations in the value. The interest tax shields are as safe or risky as debt is. If debt is risk free, the interest tax shields will also be risk free. The interest tax shields will be risky if debt is risky. Hence the beta of the interest tax shields will be equal to the beta of debt.[2] When debt is a fixed amount, and interest tax shields have same risk as debt, it is quite plausible to discount the interest tax shields by the cost of debt.

The equality of the betas of the interest tax shields and debt under the fixed debt assumption means that a levered firm (or project) will have lower systematic risk. Therefore, the asset beta should be adjusted for the tax effects of debt. Hamada[3] showed that the adjustment factors would include the corporate tax rate and the firm's leverage (debt ratio). The adjusted asset beta of the levered firm will be as follows:

$$\beta_a = \beta_e \frac{E}{V - TD} + \beta_d \frac{D}{V - TD} \qquad (15)$$

We can rewrite Equation (15) as follows:

$$\beta_a = \left[\beta_e \frac{E}{V} + \beta_d \frac{D}{V} \right] \left(\frac{1}{1 - T(D/V)} \right) \qquad (16)$$

We can derive the equity beta from Equation (15) and simplify it as follows:

$$\beta_e = \beta_a \left[1 + \frac{D}{E}(1 - T) \right] - \beta_d \frac{D}{E} \qquad (17)$$

If debt is risk-free, debt-holders will earn risk-free rate and the beta of debt (β_d) will be zero. Thus, in case of the risk-free debt, Equation (17) can be expressed as follows:

$$\beta_e = \beta_a \left[1 + \frac{D}{E}(1 - T) \right] \qquad (18)$$

Equation (13) defines the equity beta without tax effects. When we consider taxes, you may notice from Equation (17) that the equity beta of a levered firm is reduced by the tax effect. From Equation (18), we obtain the asset beta as follows:[4]

---

1. Ruback, R.S., "A Note on Capital Cash Flow Valuation", Harvard Business School, 1995.

2. *Ibid.*

3. Hamada, R.S., "Portfolio Analysis: Market Equilibrium and Corporate Finance", *Journal of Finance*, March 1969.

4. The equity beta is also given as follows: $\beta_e = \beta_a \left[\frac{1 - LT}{1 - L} \right]$ L is D/V and T is the corporate tax rate.

$$\beta_a = \frac{\beta_e}{\left[1 + \dfrac{D}{E}(1-T)\right]} \qquad (19)$$

Using Equation (18), we can write the following formula for calculating the cost of equity:

$$k_e = r_f + r_p \beta_a \left[1 + \frac{D}{E}(1-T)\right] \qquad (20)$$

We can rearrange Equation (20) as follows:

$$k_e = r_f + r_p \beta_a + r_p \beta_a \left[\frac{D}{E}(1-T)\right] \qquad (21)$$

You may notice from Equation (21) that shareholders of a levered firm demand premium for assuming the business risk, $r_p \beta_a$ and premium for assuming the financial risk, $r_p \beta_a [D/E(1-T)]$. In the case of an unlevered firm, shareholders are compensated only for the business risk.

When debt is risk-free and the debt amount is fixed, Equations (18) and (19) are the appropriate equations for unlevering and relevering beta.[1] However, in practice, even with risk-free fixed debt, interest tax shields may be considered risky. Interest tax shields are tied to the uncertain earnings of the firm and to the tax rate that government may change. Further, those companies that have non-interest tax shields like depreciation and carry forward losses may not be able to take advantage of interest tax shields. Further, in case of risky debt, the information on the debt beta may not be available or it may be small. Hence, in practice, the debt beta may be assumed to be zero and the effect of interest tax shield may be ignored in unlevering or relevering beta. Thus, for practical purpose, Equations (12) and (13) may be used for unlevering and relevering beta.

Illustration 16.4: Tax Effects, Asset Beta and Cost of Equity

Nicole Publishing Company's market value of shares and debt is Rs 50 crore and Rs 15 crore respectively. The company's equity beta is 1.32. The risk-free rate of return is 10 per cent and the market risk premium is 9 per cent. The expected corporate tax rate for the company is 35 per cent. Calculate Nicole's cost of equity.

Let us first calculate the asset beta:

$$\beta_a = \frac{\beta_e}{\left[1 + \dfrac{D}{E}(1-T)\right]}$$

$$\beta_a = \left[\frac{1.32}{\left[1 + \dfrac{15}{50}(1-0.35)\right]}\right] = \frac{1.32}{1.195} = 1.105$$

We can use the following alternative formula for calculating the asset beta:

$$\beta_a = \beta_e \left[\frac{1-D/V}{1-D/VT}\right] = 1.32 \times \frac{1-15/65}{1-(15/65)\times 0.35}$$

$$= 1.32 \times \frac{1-0.23}{1-0.23\times 0.35} = 1.32 \times 0.837 = 1.105$$

Nicole's cost of equity is given as follows:

$$k_e = r_f + r_p \beta_a + r_p \beta_a \left(\frac{D}{E}(1-T)\right)$$

$$= 0.10 + (0.09 \times 1.105) + \left(0.09 \times 1.105 \times \frac{15}{50} \times (1-0.35)\right)$$

$$= 0.10 + 0.10 + 0.019 = 0.219 \text{ or } 21.9\%$$

You may notice that the premium for the business risk is 10 per cent, and there is additional premium of 1.9 per cent for the financial risk. If the firm were unlevered, then the cost of equity, which is also the unlevered (or all-equity financing) cost of capital, is 20 per cent and it includes only the premium for the business risk.

You may have noticed that the calculation of betas for the levered and unlevered firms depends on the assumption with regard to whether debt is a fixed proportion or a fixed amount. The various approaches to the calculations of asset beta and equity beta for levered and unlevered firms are summarised in Table 16.1.

Table 16.1: Summary of Methods of Calculating Asset Beta and Equity Beta for Levered and Unlevered Firms under Different Capital Structure Assumption

	Fixed Debt Ratio		Fixed Amount of Debt	
	Risky Debt	Risk-free Debt	Risky Debt	Risk-free Debt
No Corporate Taxes				
Asset beta	$\beta_a = \beta_e \dfrac{E}{V} + \beta_d \dfrac{D}{V}$	$\beta_a = \beta_e \dfrac{E}{V}$	$\beta_a = \beta_e \dfrac{E}{V} + \beta_d \dfrac{D}{V}$	$\beta_a = \beta_e \dfrac{E}{V}$
Equity beta	$\beta_e = \beta_a + (\beta_a - \beta_d)\dfrac{D}{E}$	$\beta_e = \beta_a \left(1 + \dfrac{D}{E}\right)$	$\beta_e = \beta_a + (\beta_a - \beta_d)\dfrac{D}{E}$	$\beta_e = \beta_a \left(1 + \dfrac{D}{E}\right)$
Corporate Taxes				
Asset beta	$\beta_a = \beta_e \dfrac{E}{V} + \beta_d \dfrac{D}{V}$	$\beta_a = \beta_e \dfrac{E}{V}$	$\beta_a = \left[\beta_e \dfrac{E}{V} + \beta_d \dfrac{D}{V}\right]\left(\dfrac{1}{1-T(D/V)}\right)$	$\beta_a = \dfrac{\beta_e}{\left[1 + \dfrac{D}{E}(1-T)\right]}$
Equity beta	$\beta_e = \beta_a + (\beta_a - \beta_d)\times\dfrac{D}{E}$	$\beta_e = \beta_a \left[1 + \dfrac{D}{E}\right]$	$\beta_e = \beta_a \left[1 + \dfrac{D}{E}(1-T)\right] - \beta_d \dfrac{D}{E}$	$\beta_e = \beta_a \left[1 + \dfrac{D}{E}(1-T)\right]$

---

1. Here the implicit assumption is that the amount of debt is fixed during the investment horizon period.

FREE CASH FLOW AND WACC

How can you handle the effect of interest tax shield in the investment evaluation? The traditional approach of investment evaluation is to use free cash flows (FCF) and WACC. WACC is the weighted average of the after-tax costs of equity and debt; the after-tax cost of debt includes the effect of the interest tax shield. This is the approach that we have explained in the previous chapters so far for evaluating investment projects. Let us examine the assumptions and merits and demerits of this approach again. As we shall see, unfortunately, WACC breaks down in many practical situations.

You may recollect that free cash flows (FCFs) exclude debt flows (interest and debt repayment). As discussed earlier, FCF is calculated as follows:

$$FCF = EBIT(1 - T) + DEP - \Delta NWC - CAPEX$$

A more elaborate way of calculating FCF is as follows:

Earnings before interest and tax (EBIT)	xxx
Less: Tax	xxx
Add: Depreciation	xxx
Less: Increase in working capital	xxx
Less: Capital expenditure	xxx
Free cash flow	xxx

FCFs are **unlevered cash flows**, which are available for serving both equity shareholders and debt holders. How do we account for the financing effect of the interest tax shields? This is accounted for through WACC as the discount rate. WACC uses after tax cost of debt since interest saves taxes; thus, it includes the effect of interest tax shields. WACC is calculated as the average of the cost of equity multiplied by the weight of shareholders' equity plus the after-tax cost of debt multiplied by the weight of debt. Remember that WACC assumes a **target capital structure** based on the market values of equity and debt. WACC is given as follows:

$$WACC = k_e \frac{E}{V} + k_d(1 - T)\frac{D}{V}$$

You may recall that k_e can be determined either using the CAPM or the constant dividend growth model. WACC is the **'levered' cost of capital**. How can you determine the 'unlevered' cost of capital? The opportunity or the asset cost of capital of a pure-equity firm is the unlevered cost of capital. As discussed earlier, under CAPM, the opportunity cost of capital, k_a, is given as follows:

$$k_a = risk-free\ rate + risk\ premium \times asset\ beta$$

$$k_a = r_f + r_p \times \beta_a$$

We have shown earlier that the opportunity cost of capital, k_a, is also equal to the pre-tax WACC:

$$Pre\text{-}tax\ WACC = k_a = k_e \frac{E}{V} + k_d \frac{D}{V}$$

You may recall from Chapter 15 that the concept of pre-tax

WACC as the opportunity (or unlevered) cost of capital is based on the MM Proposition I. It assumes that financing (capital structure) does not affect the firm's opportunity cost of capital, k_a (pre-tax WACC). The opportunity (or unlevered) cost of capital of two identical firms – one levered and another unlevered — is the same. In practice, we do not observe a firm's opportunity cost of capital, k_a. But we can easily estimate k_e and k_d and then compute k_a. Let us consider an example.

Illustration 16.5: Opportunity Cost of Capital, WACC and Free Cash Flow

Gujarat Engineering Company (GEC) has book value equity of Rs 166 crore; the market value of equity is Rs 208 crore. The company has debt of Rs 312 crore. Let us assume that the book and the market values of debt are same. The firm's cost of equity is 20 per cent and the cost of debt is 15 per cent. The corporate tax rate is 35 per cent. What is the company's opportunity cost of capital? What is its WACC?

We use the MM Proposition I to estimate the opportunity cost of capital (OCC) as follows:

$$OCC = Pre\text{-}tax\ WACC = 0.20 \times \frac{208}{520} + 0.15 \times \frac{312}{520}$$

$$= 0.20 \times 0.40 + 0.15 \times 0.60$$

$$= 0.17\ or\ 17\%$$

The firm's after-tax WACC is given as follows:

$$WACC = 0.20 \times \frac{208}{520} + 0.15(1 - 0.35)\frac{312}{520}$$

$$= 0.20 \times 0.40 + 0.15 \times 0.65 \times 0.60$$

$$= 0.1385\ or\ 13.85\%$$

Further, suppose that the company is considering an expansion project to manufacture steel tubes. The estimated project outlay is Rs 64 crore. Let us assume that the project has the same risk as the firm, and its debt capacity also equals the firm's existing debt capacity. The project is expected to generate PBIT (or EBIT) of Rs 11.5 crore annually over its eight-year life. Assume straight-line depreciation for tax purposes, and Rs 1 crore for capital charges (increase in net working capital, NWC and capital expenditure, Capex) annually. For simplicity assume that the terminal value of the project is zero. Should the company make investment to manufacture steel tube?

The relevant cash flows are free-cash flows (or unlevered cash flows). Since the project is a replica of the firm, we can use the firm's WACC as the appropriate discount rate. The annual after-tax unlevered or free cash flow of the project, as shown below, is Rs 14.5 crore:

	Rs in crore
PBIT	11.5
Less: Tax at 35%	4.0
PAT	7.5
Add: Straight-line depreciation	8.0
Less: Capital charges*	1.0
Free cash flow	14.5

* Increase in net working capital (NWC) and capital expenditure (Capex).

The project is expected to generate an after-tax annuity of Rs 14.5 crore for 8 years. As per the FCF and WACC approach, the NPV of the project is as follows:

$$NPV = -64 + \sum_{t=1}^{8} \frac{14.5_t}{(1.1385)^t}$$

$$= -64 + 14.5 \times 4.6623 = -64 + 67.60 = Rs\ 3.60$$

The project's value is Rs 67.60 crore and it generates positive NPV of Rs 3.60 crore; the firm should accept it.

Constant Capital Structure and Debt Rebalancing

WACC is based on the assumption that debt is a constant proportion of value. This means that as value changes, the firm adjusts the amount of debt to maintain the proportionality of debt. For example, the debt capacity of GEC's project is 60 per cent. This implies that GEC can borrow 60 per cent of the project's value every year. Since the project value will change each year, the amount of debt will change every year, maintaining debt proportionality at 60 per cent of the project's value. We will have to calculate the project value at the start of each year to determine the amount of debt. The value at the start of the project in year 1 (or end of year 0) is the value of free cash flows over 8 years. This value is Rs 67.6 crore. GEC will borrow 60 per cent of this value, viz., Rs 40.60 crore. The value at the start of year 2 (or end of year 1) will be the value of cash flows for remaining 7 years. This value is Rs 62.5 crore. GEC debt will be Rs 62.5 × 60% = Rs 37.5 crore. It is implied that Rs 3.1 crore (Rs 40.6 crore – Rs 37.5 crore) debt is repaid to rebalance capital structure, and keep debt ratio at 60 per cent. Similar calculations can be made for other years (see Table 16.2). WACC remains constant during the life of the project since capital structure does not change.

Table 16.2: Calculations of Value and Debt

Year	Value (Rs cr.)	Debt (Rs cr.)	D/V	S/V	WACC	Interest	Interest tax shield (Rs cr.)
1	67.6	40.6	0.6	0.4	0.1385	6.1	2.1
2	62.5	37.5	0.6	0.4	0.1385	5.6	2.0
3	56.6	34.0	0.6	0.4	0.1385	5.1	1.8
4	50.0	30.0	0.6	0.4	0.1385	4.5	1.6
5	42.4	25.4	0.6	0.4	0.1385	3.8	1.3
6	33.7	20.2	0.6	0.4	0.1385	3.0	1.1
7	23.9	14.4	0.6	0.4	0.1385	2.2	0.8
8	12.7	7.6	0.6	0.4	0.1385	1.1	0.4

Note that in practice there is no need for calculating the amount of debt, interest and interest tax shields under the FCF approach of project evaluation because the capital structure is assumed to be constant and WACC is adjusted for the interest tax shields. WACC assumes that debt is rebalanced to maintain the constant capital structure.

GEC's expansion project is an 'average-risk' project. The firm's risk is the average risk of all projects (assets). What if the project's risk is higher or lower than the 'average' risk, and/or its debt capacity is different than the firm's debt capacity? You cannot use the firm's WACC for discounting the project's FCFs. You will have to calculate the project's cost of capital commensurate with its operating risk and capital structure. Can we ad-

just the firm's WACC to arrive at an estimate of the project's cost of capital if its capital structure is different from the firm's capital structure? We show below how you can do this.

Adjusting the Firm's WACC for the Project's Risk and Debt Capacity

We just stated that we could use the firm's WACC as discount rate only for those projects that are carbon copies of the firm. We should calculate the project's cost of capital if its risk or debt capacity is different. Let us assume that in the example above, GEC's expansion project has the same business risk as the firm, but it can support 40 per cent debt rather than 60 per cent. Let us assume that the cost of debt remains 15 per cent. What is the project's cost of capital? The following steps are involved in calculating the project's cost of capital:

First, calculate the firm's opportunity cost of capital (assuming that *MM* Proposition I works) as follows:

$$OCC = Pre\text{-}tax\ WACC = 0.20 \times \frac{208}{520} + 0.15 \times \frac{312}{520}$$

$$= 0.20 \times 0.40 + 0.15 \times 0.60$$

$$= 0.17\ or\ 17\%$$

You can use 17 per cent as the project's opportunity cost of capital provided the project's business risk is the same as the firm's. If the project's risk is different, you will have to make adjustment to the firm's opportunity cost of capital to approximate the project's opportunity cost of capital. As we have discussed in an earlier chapter, you might consider the project's operating leverage or earnings variability vis-à-vis the firm's operating leverage or earnings variability to make the adjustment.

Second, calculate the new cost of debt. The cost of debt may change if the capital structure of the project changes. In the present example, we assume that the cost of debt does not change.

Third, calculate the project's cost of equity, as given by MM's Proposition II, using the opportunity cost of capital and the project's debt-equity ratio:

$$k_e = k_a + (k_a - k_d)D/E$$

$$= 0.17 + (0.17 - 0.15) \times 0.667$$

$$= 0.1833\ or\ 18.33\%$$

Note that debt ratio of 40 per cent translates into debt-equity ratio of 0.667. The project's cost of equity is less than the firm's cost of equity because the financial risk of the project is less due to lower debt-equity ratio.

Fourth, calculate the project's cost of capital as the after-tax weighted average cost of debt and the cost of equity:

$$Project's\ WACC = 0.1833 \times 0.60 + 0.15 \times (1 - 0.35) \times 0.40$$

$$= 0.1833 \times 0.60 + 0.0975 \times 0.40$$

$$= 0.149\ or\ 14.9\%$$

The project's cost of capital, 14.9 per cent, is more than the firm's WACC, 13.85 per cent. You may notice that the project has less financial risk; therefore, its cost of equity is less than the firm's cost of equity. But its interest tax shields are also less, which reflect in its weighted cost of capital. Overall, we find that the project's loss of tax shields (because of lower debt capacity) is more than the gain in the cost of equity, and as a consequence, it has higher cost of capital than the firm's WACC.

It is important to note that the firm's WACC or the project's WACC as the 'adjusted WACC' assumes that the debt ratio (debt as a proportion of value) remains constant. This implies that the firm continuously adjusts the amount of debt as the value of the firm or project changes to maintain the debt ratio. Thus, a constant debt ratio means rebalancing capital structure. In practice, the financing of large projects involves fixed amount of debt rather than fixed debt ratio. Hence you cannot use WACC (firm's or project's) as the discount rate.

Equity Cash Flows and the Cost of Equity

A variation of the FCF approach is the **equity cash flow** (ECF) approach. In this approach, ECFs are calculated net of debt flows (i.e., interest, interest tax shield and debt repayments). Since these **residual cash flows** include the effect of debt, they are also called **levered cash flows.** This approach discounts ECFs—the cash flows available to shareholders—at the levered cost of equity, k_e. Like the FCF (and WACC) approach, this approach also assumes that the capital structure is constant and hence, the cost of equity, k_e does not change over time. You need to know the amount of debt and interest to calculate ECFs. Given the constant debt ratio, the amount of debt will change as the value of the firm changes. For the GEC project the debt flows are calculated in Table 16.2. Table 16.3 shows the calculation of ECFs for GEC's project. Notice that unlike FCFs, ECFs are adjusted for interest, interest tax shields and incremental debt flows. Like in FCF approach, we assume that capital structure is con-

stant (i.e., debt is 60 per cent of value) and the cost of equity, 18.33 per cent, remains constant. Interest is calculated as 15 per cent of the debt outstanding. We assume that the interest rate and the cost of debt are the same. The initial investment is net of initial debt flow, and it is the equity capital contributed by shareholders. Like in the FCF approach, NPV is Rs 3.6 crore. Conceptually, both the FCF approach and the ECF approach are the same and give the same results under the assumption that debt is a constant proportion of value. Hence it is easier to use FCF and WACC approach when debt proportion is fixed since it avoids the need of calculating the debt flows.

Limitations of the WACC

The FCF approach using WACC as discount rate cannot be used to evaluate all projects. This approach has the following limitations:

1. *Cash flow patterns* The original form of WACC assumes that free cash flows are level and perpetual. In practice, we rarely witness projects with perpetual cash flow. However, it has been shown that WACC works for any patterns of cash flows.[1]

2. *Business risk* WACC application assumes that the project under evaluation has the same business risk as the existing assets of the firm. This may be a tenable assumption for replacement and minor expansion projects in the same line of business. However, the project evaluation will be distorted if the project has different business risk profile. Projects belonging to different businesses of a company will not have the same business risk. In such cases, you need to work out the divisional costs of capital. As we have shown

Table 16.3: ECF Approach

(Rs in crore)

					Year				
	0	**1**	**2**	**3**	**4**	**5**	**6**	**7**	**8**
PBIT		11.5	11.5	11.5	11.5	11.5	11.5	11.5	11.5
Less: Interest		6.1	5.6	5.1	4.5	3.8	3.0	2.2	1.2
PBT		5.5	5.9	6.4	7.0	7.7	8.5	9.4	10.4
Less: Tax		1.9	2.1	2.3	2.5	2.7	3.0	3.3	3.6
PAT		3.5	3.8	4.2	4.6	5.0	5.5	6.1	6.8
Add: Depreciation		8.0	8.0	8.0	8.0	8.0	8.0	8.0	8.0
Less: Capital charges		1.0	1.0	1.0	1.0	1.0	1.0	1.0	1.0
Net cash flows		10.5	10.8	11.2	11.6	12.0	12.5	13.1	13.8
Investment	−64.0								
Incremental debt	40.6	−3.1	−3.5	−4.0	−4.5	−5.2	−5.9	−6.7	−7.6
Equity cash flows (ECF)	−23.4	7.5	7.3	7.2	7.0	6.8	6.6	6.4	6.1
Discount factor at 18.33%	1.000	0.833	0.694	0.579	0.482	0.402	0.335	0.279	0.233
PV	−23.4	6.2	5.1	4.2	3.4	2.7	2.2	1.8	1.4
NPV	3.6								

1. Miles, J. and Ezzell, R., "The Weighted Average Cost of Capital, Perfect Capital Markets, and Project Life: A Clarification," *Journal of Financial and Quantitative Analysis*, 15 (September 1980), 719–30.

in an earlier chapter, the CAPM methodology is quite useful in calculating the divisional costs of capital.

3. ***Debt capacity*** The application of the firm's WACC as discount rate assumes that the project under evaluation contributes debt capacity equal to the firm's debt capacity and like the firm, it has a fixed capital structure (debt ratio). Except for a few average projects, this might not be true in reality for all projects. Projects have finite life, and firms are able to raise funds from financial institutions or public, which are tied to specific projects. This is more so under **project financing**. Thus, the amounts of interest and principal repayments are predetermined, and they are accounted for within the life of the project. Such projects have their unique capital structures, which change as the amount of debt is repaid.

4. ***Issue costs*** WACC does not provide a sound basis for treating the costs of issuing securities. These are one time costs; therefore, they cannot be adjusted in the calculation of WACC which is used as a discount rate for free cash flows occurring over a long period of time.

5. ***Financing effects*** WACC accounts for the interest tax shields on debt financing. But there are several other effects that it is unable to incorporate. For example, it is quite common in many countries, particularly the developing countries, to grant **subsidised loans** (loans at interest rates lower than the cost of borrowing) and provide **guarantees** to certain categories of projects, or projects located in economically backward areas. In India, the government also makes available non-returnable **capital subsidy** for certain categories of businesses located in the backward areas. Certain **special tax benefits** and investment incentives are also available for these businesses. It is quite difficult to estimate WACC for such projects.

We need alternative methodologies than the WACC approach to evaluate projects that do not have constant debt ratio, have different cash flow patterns and have several financing effects. We discuss two alternative approaches – the capital cash flows (CCF) and the adjusted present value (APV) – below.

CAPITAL CASH FLOWS AND THE OPPORTUNITY COST OF CAPITAL

In the FCF approach, we adjust the effect of the interest tax shields in the discount rate (WACC) rather than the cash flows. We can use an alternative approach — the **capital cash flow approach** — where we may adjust the interest tax shields in the cash flows instead of the discount rate. In this approach capital cash flows are discounted at the project's opportunity cost of capital. **Capital cash flows** are the free-cash flows plus the interest tax shields:

Capital cash flows (CCF)

$$= \text{Free cash flows} + \text{Interest tax shield}$$
$$= (EBIT - k_d D)(1-T) + k_d D + DEP - \Delta NWC - \text{Capex}$$
$$= \underbrace{[EBIT(1-T) + DEP - \Delta NWC - \text{Capex}]}_{\text{Free Cash Flows}} + \underbrace{Tk_d D}_{\substack{\text{Interest} \\ \text{Tax Shield}}}$$

In practice, CCF may be calculated as follows:

EBIT	xxx
Less: Interest	xxx
PBT	xxx
Less: Tax	xxx
Profit after tax	xxx
Plus: Interest	xxx
Plus: Depreciation	xxx
Less: Increase in working capital	xxx
Less: Capital expenditure	xxx
Capital cash flows (CCF)	xxx

In the CCF approach, the discount rate—the opportunity cost of capital—does not depend on the project's capital structure, and given the project's business risk, it remains constant during the project's life. The CCF approach gives the same results as the FCF approach. However, this approach is simpler to use when the project has fixed debt (rather than fixed debt ratio). How does the CCF approach work? We shall assume two situations with regard to capital structure: the fixed amount of debt and the fixed proportion of debt.

Fixed Debt

In project financing, the debt amount may be fixed. Suppose that the debt financing of the GEC project will support fixed amount of debt equal to 60 per cent of the *project cost* (initial book value). Let us assume that the company will borrow Rs 38.40 crore for eight years at 15 per cent rate of interest from a financial institution. The financial institution requires GEC to repay loan in three equal instalments at the end of years 6, 7 and 8. You will notice that the amount of loan, Rs 38.40 crore, is fixed and the repayment schedule is indicated. There is no fixed debt ratio; the capital structure will change with change in the project's value. Hence we cannot use the FCF approach with constant WACC to value the project. You can, of course, find the debt ratio each year and estimate WACC each year. You can determine the value of the project discounting FCFs by the varying WACC. These will be highly involved calculations. The much easier way is to use the CCF approach discounting CCFs by the opportunity cost of capital, which is independent of the capital structure. Table 16.4 shows the calculations where CCFs have been discounted by the project's unlevered or opportunity cost of capital, 17 per cent. The NPV of the project is Rs 4.8 crore.

Fixed Debt Ratio

How does the CCF approach work when the project has a constant capital structure? Let us consider the GEC project again. Suppose capital structure is constant and debt ratio (debt as a proportion of value) is fixed at 60 per cent. We need to determine the value of the project each year to determine the amount of debt and interest tax shields; the value in turn will depend on the amount of interest tax shield. Thus, we need a dynamic approach to determine value. For simplicity and convenience, let us use the values already calculated under the FCF approach and use this information to estimate debt, interest, interest tax

Table 16.4: Capital Cash Flow Approach—Fixed Debt

Year	0	1	2	3	4	5	6	7	8
Debt outstanding	38.40	38.40	38.40	38.40	38.40	38.40	25.60	12.80	0.00
Interest at 15%		5.76	5.76	5.76	5.76	5.76	5.76	3.84	1.92
PBIT		11.50	11.50	11.50	11.50	11.50	11.50	11.50	11.50
Less: Interest		5.76	5.76	5.76	5.76	5.76	5.76	3.84	1.92
PBT		5.74	5.74	5.74	5.74	5.74	5.74	7.66	9.58
Less: Tax		2.01	2.01	2.01	2.01	2.01	2.01	2.68	3.35
PAT		3.73	3.73	3.73	3.73	3.73	3.73	4.98	6.23
Add: Interest		5.76	5.76	5.76	5.76	5.76	5.76	3.48	1.92
Add: Depreciation		8.00	8.00	8.00	8.00	8.00	8.00	8.00	8.00
Less: Capital charges		1.00	1.00	1.00	1.00	1.00	1.00	1.00	1.00
CCF	−64.00	16.49	16.49	16.49	16.49	16.49	16.49	15.82	15.15
Discount factor	1.000	0.855	0.731	0.624	0.534	0.456	0.390	0.333	0.285
PV	−64.00	14.10	12.05	10.29	8.81	7.52	6.43	5.27	4.32
NPV	4.79								

shields and CCFs. Table 16.5 shows calculations of CCFs. When we discount CCFs by the project's opportunity cost of capital, we obtain NPV of Rs 3.6 crore, same amount as in the case of the FCF approach. Both the FCF approach and the CCF approach yield the same results.[1] You might have realised that when debt ratio is fixed (constant capital structure), it is easier to use the FCF (and WACC) approach as the CCF approach involves additional calculations of the project value each year, debt and interest tax shields. It is much easier to use the CCF approach when the amount of debt is fixed.

ADJUSTED PRESENT VALUE (APV)

We have seen that the FCF approach and the CCF approach of project evaluation are equivalent. The FCF approach is very convenient to use when debt ratio is fixed and the CCF approach is more expedient to use when the debt level is fixed and known and the capital structure changes in each period. These approaches handle the interest tax shields differently — one in the discount rate and another in the cash flows- but they arrive at the same value. In addition to the interest tax shield, the financing effects of a project may involve issues costs, subsidised financing, backward area subsidies, guarantees or tax concessions. Each of these effects may have different risk, and hence, it may require a different discount rate. We need an approach that unbundles the various sources of value of an investment project.

---

1. Let us assume that cash flows are constant and perpetual. Under the free cash flow approach, the value is given by the following equation:

$$V = \frac{FCF}{WACC} \quad \text{(i)}$$

WACC is given as follows:

$$WACC = k_e\, E/V + k_d(1-T)\, D/V \quad \text{(ii)}$$

We can express the formula for WACC as follows:

$$WACC = \left(k_e\, E/V + k_d\, D/V\right) - T k_d\, D/V \quad \text{(iii)}$$

The expression within parenthesis on the left-hand side is the pre-tax WACC and equal to the opportunity cost of capital, k_a as per the MM Proposition I. Using Equation (iii), we can rewrite Equation (i) as follows:

$$V = \frac{FCF}{k_a - T k_d\, D/V} \quad \text{(iv)}$$

Dividing both sides of Equation (iv) by V and rearranging the equation, we get the following expression:

$$V = \frac{FCF + T k_d D}{k_a} = \frac{CCF}{k_a} \quad \text{(v)}$$

You may notice that on the right-hand side of Equation (v), the numerator is capital cash flow (free cash flow plus interest tax shields) and denominator is the opportunity cost of capital. Thus, CCF and FCF methods give same value.

Table 16.5: Capital Cash Flow Approach

(Rs in crore)

	Year								
	0	**1**	**2**	**3**	**4**	**5**	**6**	**7**	**8**
PBIT		11.5	11.5	11.5	11.5	11.5	11.5	11.5	11.5
Less: Interest		6.1	5.6	5.1	4.5	3.8	3.0	2.2	1.2
PBT		5.5	5.9	6.4	7.0	7.7	8.5	9.4	10.4
Less: Tax		1.9	2.1	2.3	2.5	2.7	3.0	3.3	3.6
PAT		3.5	3.8	4.2	4.6	5.0	5.5	6.1	6.8
Add: Interest		6.1	5.6	5.1	4.5	3.8	3.0	2.2	1.2
Add: Depreciation		8.0	8.0	8.0	8.0	8.0	8.0	8.0	8.0
Less: Capital charges		1.0	1.0	1.0	1.0	1.0	1.0	1.0	1.0
CCF	−64.0*	16.6	16.5	16.3	16.1	15.8	15.6	15.3	14.9
Discount factor	1.000	0.855	0.731	0.624	0.534	0.456	0.390	0.333	0.285
PV	−64.0	14.2	12.0	10.2	8.6	7.2	6.1	5.1	4.2
NPV	3.6								

* Initial investment.

The **adjusted present value** (APV) approach[1] is the most appropriate approach for evaluating projects, which have several financing side effects. This logic of APV approach is based on the MM model about the value of a levered firm:

Value of the levered firm = Value of the unlevered firm + Value of interest tax shields

$$V_l = V_u + TD \qquad (22)$$

The value of the levered firm is an **adjusted value**; it is the value of the unlevered – all-equity firm plus the value of the financing effect, that is, the interest tax shields resulting from the use of debt financing. The MM model assumes that the interest tax shields are a perpetuity and they are as risky as debt flows are. Hence, under the MM model, the interest tax shields are discounted at the market cost of borrowing.[2]

The APV approach can handle any patterns of cash flows (perpetuity or uneven cash flows) and it can be extended to calculate the adjusted present value of an investment project incorporating several financing effects. It divides the net present value of a project into two main parts: the first part consists of the **all-equity NPV** or the **base-case NPV** assuming that the project is entirely equity financed and the second part consists of the value of the interest tax shields and other financing effects:

APV = All-equity NPV + Value of financing effects (23)

The application of the APV approach involves the following three steps:

1. First, find the 'all-equity NPV', or the "base-case NPV". The base case assumes that the project is entirely financed by equity and that there are no financing effects. Thus, the firm is exposed to operating risk only. The after-tax cash flows, which are free cash flows, are discounted by the project's opportunity cost of capital. The project's opportunity cost of capital is what shareholders would require on an entirely equity financed project. Hence, this is also referred to as "all-equity cost of capital".

2. Second, find the present value of cash flows resulting from the financing of the project. Each cash flows are discounted by the discount rate appropriate to the risk of each cash flow. For example, in MM tax-corrected model the debt amount is fixed and perpetual and the interest tax shields are considered as risky as debt. Therefore, the interest tax shields are discounted by the **market cost of debt**. But, as we shall discuss below, there may be situations where interest tax shields may be considered as risky as the operating cash flows. In such situation, a higher discount rate is used to determine the value of the interest tax shields. In addition to the interest tax shields, the project may involve other financing effects like the issue costs, special tax benefits, capital subsidy, subsidized interest etc. All these flows are discounted at their risk-adjusted rates.

3. Third, sum the 'all-equity NPV' and the present value of financing effects to arrive at the project's NPV.

Accept the positive APV projects and reject the ones with negative APV. Consider the example of GEC's project in Illustration 16.6 to see the application of the APV approach.

Illustration 16.6: Application of APV

Let us assume that GEC will borrow fixed loan amount of Rs 38.4 crore for eight years at 15 per cent rate of interest from a financial institution, and repay the loan in three equal instalments at the end of years 6, 7 and 8.

The first step in the APV approach is to value the project as an all-equity financed (unlevered) project. The relevant cash flows are free-cash flows (unlevered cash flows) and the appropriate discount rate is the opportunity cost of capital, k_a. The project is expected to generate the after-tax FCF annuity of Rs 14.5 crore for 8 years. The opportunity cost of capital is 17 per cent. The all-equity or base-case NPV of the project is as follows:

$$\text{All-equity NPV} = -64 + \sum_{t=1}^{8} \frac{14.5_t}{(1.17)^t}$$
$$= -64 + 14.5 \times 4.2072 = -\text{Rs } 3$$

The Rs 3 crore negative NPV implies that the project is not viable, and it will destroy the shareholder value. However, the project can support fixed debt of Rs 38.4 crore. The use of debt will create value, as the interest paid on debt will save taxes. The interest tax shield each year will be interest paid times the corporate tax rate.[3] At what rate should the interest tax shields be discounted? The amount of loan is fixed and known. Therefore, the interest tax shields are as risky as debt and less risky than

---

1. Myers suggested this approach. See Myers, S.C., "Interactions of Corporate Financing and Investment Decisions – Implications for Capital Budgeting," *Journal of Finance*, 29 (March 1974), pp.1–25.
2. The before-tax cost of debt rather than the after-tax cost of debt is used on the assumption that interest tax shields are not used to enhance the debt capacity.
3. Personal taxes on interest income of debt holders and other non-tax shields may reduce the actual tax savings.

Table 16.6: Value of Interest Tax Shield

Year	0	1	2	3	4	5	6	7	8	Sum
Loan at the Beginning		38.40	38.40	38.40	38.40	38.40	38.40	25.60	12.80	
Interest paid	—	5.76	5.76	5.76	5.76	5.76	5.76	3.84	1.92	
Principal Repayment	—	—	—	—	—	—	12.80	12.80	12.80	
Loan at the End	38.40	38.40	38.40	38.40	38.40	38.40	25.60	12.80	0.00	
Interest Tax Shield (ITS)	—	2.02	2.02	2.02	2.02	2.02	2.02	1.34	0.67	
Value of ITS at 15%	—	1.75	1.52	1.33	1.15	1.00	0.87	0.51	0.22	8.35
Value of ITS at 17%	—	1.72	1.47	1.26	1.08	0.92	0.79	0.45	0.19	7.87

the cash flows from operations. Hence the appropriate discount rate is the market rate of interest (cost of debt), which, in the present case, is 15 per cent. Discounting the interest tax shields at the cost of debt will give the present value of the interest tax shields. Calculations of the interest tax shields and their value are given in Table 16.6. The present value of the interest tax shields is Rs 8.4 crore. Adding the value of interest tax shield to the all-equity NPV gives APV of the project as follows:

$$APV = -3 + 8.4 = + Rs\ 5.4\ crore$$

After considering the value created by debt, the project becomes valuable to the firm. GEC should accept the project. Notice that we have considered only the interest tax shields in calculating APV and ignored the cash flows arising from loan amount, repayments and the before-tax interest flows. If you discount these flows at the rate of interest, the present value will be zero. Try it out yourself.

Issue Costs

When a firm raises equity or debt capital for financing a project, it incurs costs of issuing securities. These are onetime costs. There is no way to adjust these costs in the calculation of WACC or the opportunity cost of capital. The APV method can easily handle the issue costs. These costs are incurred at the start of the project and hence they reduce the project's APV. In case of the GEC project, let us assume that the firm has to incur Rs 1.10 crore costs of issuing equity and debt securities. The project's APV will be:

APV = All-equity NPV + PV of interest tax shields – Issue costs
APV = –3.0 + 8.4 – 1.10 = + Rs 4.30 crore

You may notice from the example in Illustration 16.6 that APV calculation is based on the assumption that debt amounts are fixed and repayments are as per specified payment schedule. The initial amount of debt equals 60 per cent of the initial book value of the project. Like the CCF approach, the APV approach is easy to use when the debt is attached to the project's book value or when debt repayment schedule is known. Both approaches use the opportunity cost of capital to discount the free cash flows. However, the interest tax shields are discounted by different rates under the two approaches. In the CCF approach, the interest tax shields are discounted by the opportunity cost of capital while in the APV approach by the cost of debt. Since the cost of debt is always less than the opportunity cost of capital, the NPV of a project under the CCF approach will always be less than its APV.

Fixed Debt Ratio

In the above example, we assumed that the amount of debt is fixed with a known schedule of payments. As stated earlier, in many situations it might be more plausible to assume that the project debt capacity is related to the project value as a constant percentage. Suppose the debt capacity of GEC's project is 60 per cent of the value. We will have to calculate the project value at the start of each year to determine the amount of debt. The value at the start of the project in year 1 (or end of year 0) is the value of cash flows over 8 years. The value at the start of year 2 (or end of year 1) will be the value of cash flows for the remaining 7 years. Similar calculations can be made for other years.

At what discount rate should the interest tax shields be discounted when the debt ratio is fixed? The risk of these savings is different from the savings under the assumption of fixed debt. Here the amounts of debt are not known. They are tied to the value of the project. As the project value fluctuates, they also fluctuate. To maintain the proportionality of debt, the firm will have to rebalance debt as the project value changes. The interest tax shields under the assumption of debt rebalancing (i.e., constant debt-to-value ratio) are as risky as the project's operations. Therefore, it is more appropriate to discount these flows at the project's opportunity cost of capital instead of the cost of debt as under the fixed debt assumption.[1]

In the case of the GEC project, we have seen under the CCF approach that at 17 per cent discount rate (the opportunity cost of capital), the present value of interest tax shields is Rs 6.6 crore. Thus, the project's APV is: – Rs 3 crore + Rs 6.6 crore = Rs 3.6 crore. This value is the same as NPV under the CCF approach or the FCF approach. But it is different from the value that we obtained under the assumption of fixed debt. There are two reasons for this. First, the amounts of debt differ. Second, the interest tax shields are discounted now at a higher rate (the opportunity cost of capital rather than the cost of debt).

---

1. Theoretically, a further adjustment is needed since for some interest tax shields uncertainty resolution takes place over time. For example, the interest tax shield in year 1 is *known* in year 0 as the amount of debt is known at the start of the project. The appropriate discount rate for year 1's interest tax shield is the cost of debt. Year 2's interest tax shield is not known in year 0. But in year 1, once the debt has been rebalanced, the interest tax shield is known. Hence at year 2, interest tax shield should be discounted one year at the opportunity cost of capital and one year at the cost of debt. This procedure will continue until the investment horizon period. See Brealey and Myers, *Principles of Corporate Finance*, McGraw Hill, sixth edition, 2000, pp. 561–62.

When you use the APV approach under the assumption of constant capital structure, you should calculate the value of cash flows including the interest tax shields each year to estimate the amount of debt. But you would need to know the amount of debt to determine the interest tax shields. Thus the determination of the value each year requires a dynamic approach. In practice, you may calculate base present value of the free cash flows each year and determine the amount of debt. For the GEC project, these calculations are shown in Table 16.7. Notice that the amounts of debt and the interest tax shields are less than what they ought to be and consequently, you get slightly lower present value of the interest tax shields; that is, Rs 6.1 crore instead Rs 6.3 crore.

Table 16.7: Value of Interest Tax Shield: Debt Rebalanced

Year	Base PV (Rs cr.)	Debt Outstanding (Rs cr.)	Interest @ 15% (Rs cr.)	INTS (Rs cr.)	PVF @ 17% (Rs cr.)	PV (INTS) (Rs cr.)
0	61.00	36.6				
1	56.9	34.1	5.5	1.9	0.855	1.6
2	52.0	31.2	5.1	1.8	0.731	1.3
3	46.4	27.8	4.7	1.6	0.624	1.0
4	39.8	23.9	4.2	1.5	0.534	0.8
5	32.0	19.2	3.6	1.3	0.456	0.6
6	22.3	13.8	2.9	1.0	0.390	0.4
7	12.4	7.4	2.1	0.7	0.333	0.2
8	0.00	0.00	1.1	0.4	0.285	0.1
Value of interest tax shield						6.1

You may notice that under the assumption of fixed debt ratio and debt rebalancing, both free cash flows and interest tax shields are discounted at the project's opportunity cost of capital to determine the APV. Hence, you can combine these two flows and then discount them by the project's opportunity cost of capital. We know that the free-cash flows plus the interest tax shields are equal to the capital cash flows. Thus, the CCF approach and the APV approach under the assumption of constant capital structure and debt rebalancing are the same. The CCF approach is, therefore, referred to as the **"compressed" APV approach**. You may recall that the CCF approach is equal to the FCF approach. Hence, under the assumption of the constant capital structure (fixed debt ratio), the CCF approach, the modified (compressed) APV approach and the FCF will give the same value for the project. The FCF approach with WACC as the discount rate is easier to use under this situation because it does not require calculations of the project value, debt amounts and the interest tax shields.

The CCF and the APV approaches differ when debt is fixed and payment schedules are known. The CCF approach still discounts the interest tax shields at the project's opportunity cost of capital while the APV approach considers them less risky and discounts at the cost of debt (the market interest rate). One could argue that the CCF approach is more realistic in discounting the interest tax shields by the opportunity cost of capital. Even when the debt amount is fixed, the interest tax shields are tied to

the project's (or the firm's) operations. The project's operations fluctuate randomly. It can avail the interest tax shields only when the operations are profitable. If the project (or the firm) gets into problems over a long period of time, the interest tax shields may be totally lost. The personal taxes on the income of lenders also take away the advantage of the interest tax shields. Thus, the interest tax shields may not really be less risky.

The APV approach is more flexible and can handle many financing side effects. Let us show how you can use the APV approach for evaluating subsidised financing.

APV and Subsidised Financing

In many countries, particularly the developing countries, governments provide a number of financing incentives to the companies for undertaking new projects to achieve economic growth and efficiency. The APV approach is quite flexible to determine the value of the various incentives. Let us consider the case of subsidised financing.

Assuming that GEC can borrow 60 per cent of the project's cost (book value in the beginning) and it will repay principal in three equal instalments in the last three years. What will happen to the APV of GEC's project if the company is able to negotiate loan of Rs 24 crore at subsidised interest rate of 10 per cent from the Government of Gujarat? The market interest rate is 15 per cent; hence the project gets 'interest subsidy' of 5 per cent. The firm saves paying interest at 5 per cent p.a. It will get tax shield on interest paid at 10 per cent p.a. But it will lose the interest tax shield on the amount of interest subsidy. The after-tax interest subsidy and interest tax shields are calculated as follows (assuming that loan is repaid in equal instalments at the end of years 6, 7 and 8):

Year	Interest Tax Shield	After-tax Interest Subsidy
1	$0.35 \times 0.10 \times 38.40 = 1.34$	$(0.15 - 0.10) \times 38.40 \times 0.65 = 1.25$
2	$0.35 \times 0.10 \times 38.40 = 1.34$	$(0.15 - 0.10) \times 38.40 \times 0.65 = 1.25$
3	$0.35 \times 0.10 \times 38.40 = 1.34$	$(0.15 - 0.10) \times 38.40 \times 0.65 = 1.25$
4	$0.35 \times 0.10 \times 38.40 = 1.34$	$(0.15 - 0.10) \times 38.40 \times 0.65 = 1.25$
5	$0.35 \times 0.10 \times 38.40 = 1.34$	$(0.15 - 0.10) \times 38.40 \times 0.65 = 1.25$
6	$0.35 \times 0.10 \times 38.40 = 1.34$	$(0.15 - 0.10) \times 38.40 \times 0.65 = 1.25$
7	$0.35 \times 0.10 \times 25.60 = 0.90$	$(0.15 - 0.10) \times 25.60 \times 0.65 = 0.83$
8	$0.35 \times 0.10 \times 12.80 = 0.45$	$(0.15 - 0.10) \times 12.80 \times 0.65 = 0.42$

The interest tax shields are discounted at the pre-tax cost of debt, and the after-tax interest subsidies are discounted at the after-tax cost of debt. The project's APV will be as shown below:

APV = −Investment + All-equity PV + PV of interest tax shields + PV of interest subsidies

$$\text{APV} = -64 + \sum_{t=1}^{8} \frac{14.5}{(1.17)^8} + \left[\sum_{t=1}^{6} \frac{1.34_t}{(1.15)^t} + \frac{0.90}{(1.15)^7} + \frac{0.45}{(1.15)^8} \right]$$

$$+ \left[\sum_{t=1}^{6} \frac{1.25_t}{(1.0975)^t} + \frac{0.83}{(1.0975)^7} + \frac{0.42}{(1.0975)^8} \right]$$

$$= -64 + 61 + 5.57 + 6.11 = \text{Rs } 8.68$$

The project's APV is positive. The interest tax shields together with the interest subsidy have added more value to the project. Notice that the APV approach has unbundled the value created by the project into three parts: the value created from operations (which is negative Rs 3 crore in the present case); the value created by the interest tax shields (Rs 5.6 crore); and the value created by the interest subsidy (Rs 6.1 crore). But for the financing effects, the project is not economically profitable.

Value of the Subsidised Financing

GEC has the opportunity of borrowing Rs 38.4 crore at 10 per cent rate of interest instead of 15 per cent market rate of return. What is the value of this loan? The value of the loan is the present value of after-tax cash flows. If the value of the loan is less than Rs 38.4 crore, the borrower – in this case GEC – will be happy. GEC will commit to make fixed payments once it agrees to take the loan. Inflation will not change cash flows since the debt flows are fixed. Thus, these are **nominal cash flows** and they are quite safe. The appropriate discount rate for discounting nominal after-tax cash flows of debt is the after-tax borrowing rate. In this case, it is: $0.15 \times (1 - 0.35) = 0.097$ or 9.75 per cent. The value of GEC's Rs 38.4 crore loan is calculated in Table 16.8.

Table 16.8: Value of Subsidised Financing

Year	Cash outflows	Interest Tax shield	After-tax cash outflows	Discount factor at 9.75%	Present value
1	3.84	1.34	2.50	0.91	2.28
2	3.84	1.34	2.50	0.83	2.08
3	3.84	1.34	2.50	0.76	1.89
4	3.84	1.34	2.50	0.69	1.72
5	3.84	1.34	2.50	0.63	1.57
6	16.64	1.34	15.30	0.57	8.76
7	15.36	0.90	14.46	0.52	7.54
8	14.08	0.45	13.63	0.48	6.48
Present value of subsidised loan					32.30

The value of GEC's after-tax cash outflows is Rs 32.30 crore. In other words, the after-tax cash flows can service a loan of Rs 32.31 crore *if* the borrowing rate is 15 per cent. For GEC, the same cash flows are serving a higher amount of debt, viz., Rs 38.4 crore. GEC benefits from the subsidised loan to the extent of Rs 38.4 crore – Rs 32.3 crore = Rs 6.1 crore. As we have shown above, this amount is equal to the present value of the interest subsidy.

THE ADJUSTED COST OF CAPITAL: PERPETUAL CASH FLOWS

Suppose a firm is evaluating a project that will require investment, Rs 10,000 and generate annual after-tax free cash flows, Rs 1,500 in perpetuity. The project's opportunity cost of capital (all-equity financing cost) is 15 per cent. The all-equity NPV of the project will be:

$$\text{All-equity NPV} = -10,000 + \frac{1,500}{0.15} = -10,000 + 10,000 = 0$$

The project has zero NPV. Can it be more attractive? Let us assume that it will support the perpetual fixed amount of debt, Rs 5,000 at the cost of debt, 10 per cent. The corporate tax rate is 35 per cent. The perpetual interest tax shields on debt will be: $0.35 \times 0.10 \times \text{Rs } 5,000 = \text{Rs } 175$. The present value of the interest tax shields will be:

$$\text{PV(INTS)} = \frac{175}{0.10} = \text{Rs } 1,750$$

Thus, the project's APV will be as follows:
Project's APV = –Investment + PV with all-equity financing + PV of interest tax shield

$$\begin{aligned}
\text{APV} &= -10,000 + \frac{1,500}{0.15} + \frac{175}{0.10} \\
&= -10,000 + 10,000 + 1,750 \\
&= \text{Rs } 1,750
\end{aligned}$$

The APV of the project is Rs 1,750. The total value of the project is Rs 11,750. The fixed amount of debt is Rs 5,000. Given the perpetual cash flows and the expected value of cash flows each year of Rs 1,500, the value each year will remain at Rs 11,750. Therefore, debt as a proportion of value is: 5,000/11,750 = 0.4255. The after-tax return of the project is: (1,500 + 175)/11,750 = 0.1426 or 14.26 per cent. What is the minimum rate of return that the project should yield to be acceptable to the firm? It is that rate of return at which the project's APV is zero. At zero APV, the value of the project will be equal to the investment.

$$\begin{aligned}
\text{Project's APV} &= -I_0 + \frac{C}{k_a} + \frac{Tk_dD}{k_d} = 0 \\
&= -I_0 + \frac{C}{k_a} + TD = 0 \quad (24)
\end{aligned}$$

where I_0 is investment, C is after-tax free cash flows, k_a is the asset or the opportunity cost of capital, T is the corporate tax rate, k_d is the cost of debt and D the amount of debt. Rearranging the equation, we get the minimum rate of return as follows:

$$\text{Minimum rate of return} = \frac{C}{I_0} = k_a - k_a T \frac{D}{I_0} \quad (25)$$

The ratio of (after-tax) cash flows to investment, C/I_0 is the minimum required rate of return from the project. Notice that the project's investment is Rs 10,000 and it supports debt equal to 42.55 per cent of the value. Since at zero APV, value will be equal to Rs 10,000 (investment), the amount of debt will be Rs 4,255. The interest tax shields on debt will be: $0.35 \times 0.10 \times 4,255 = \text{Rs } 148.93$. We can plug these numbers in the equation to obtain minimum rate of return and the minimum cash flows as follows:

$$\text{Minimum rate of return} = \frac{C}{10,000} = 0.15 - 0.15 \times 0.35 \times \frac{4,255}{10,000}$$

$$\text{Minimum rate of return} = \frac{C}{10,000} = 0.15 - 0.0223 = 0.1277$$

$$\text{Minimum cash flow} = C = 10,000 \times 0.1277 = \text{Rs } 1,277$$

On an investment of Rs 10,000, the minimum perpetual cash flow is Rs 1,277, or the minimum rate of return is 12.77 per cent. This minimum rate is the **adjusted cost of capital**, k^*. The project's NPV will be zero at this rate. The adjusted cost of capital is equal to the opportunity cost of capital (15% in the example) less the value created by the project by adding to the firm's debt capacity (2.23% in the example). This adjusted cost of capital, 12.77 per cent, can be used as a discount rate to any other project with similar business risk (and therefore, same opportunity cost of capital, 15 per cent) and similar debt capacity (42.55 debt ratio). Instead of using APV approach, we can discount a project's free cash flows at the adjusted cost of capital. In our example, we can calculate the project's NPV using the adjusted cost of capital approach as follows:

$$\text{Project's NPV} = -\text{Investment} + \frac{\text{Free Cash Flow}}{k^*}$$

$$\text{Project's NPV} = -I_0 + \frac{C}{k^*}$$

$$\text{Project's NPV} = -10,000 + \frac{1,500}{0.1277}$$

$$= -10,000 + 11,750 = \text{Rs } 1,750$$

You get the same answer as under the APV approach. The adjusted cost of capital is the MM formula for the cost of capital of a levered firm (project). The opportunity cost of capital is reduced by the value created by the interest tax shields. In general terms, the adjusted cost of capital for a levered firm is as follows:

$$\frac{\text{Adjusted}}{\text{cost of capital}} = \frac{\text{Opportunity}}{\text{Cost of capital}} \times (1 - \text{tax rate} \times \text{leverage})$$

$$k^* = k_a \left(1 - T\frac{D}{V}\right) \qquad (26)$$

We can also express Equation (26) as follows:

$$k^* = (r_f + r_p \beta_a)\left(1 - T\frac{D}{V}\right) \qquad (27)$$

Equations (26) and (27) imply that the cost of capital of a levered firm is equal to the cost of capital of an unlevered firm less the debt advantage equal to the product of tax rate (T), financial leverage (D/V) and the pure-equity capitalisation rate, k_a. It should be clear from Equation (26) or Equation (27) that the levered firm's cost of capital declines with financial leverage. When we use the levered firm's cost of capital to evaluate the project, we assume that the project's risk is equivalent to the

firm's risk and both have same debt capacity.

The levered firm's cost of capital under MM "tax-corrected" hypothesis is strictly based on two critical assumptions:

- The firm's cash flows are perpetual.
- The amount of debt is fixed and permanent. Thus, the firm's capital structure determined initially does not change; the debt ratio remains the same.

If the APV approach is also based on these assumptions, then it will give the same results as the adjusted cost of capital (ACC) approach. However, the APV approach is quite versatile and more general than the ACC approach. It works for projects with different cash flow patterns and changing amounts of debt.

WACC and Miles and Ezzell's Formula for Adjusted Cost of Capital

Can we use MM's adjusted cost of capital when the cash flows are perpetual but debt is proportional to value? In case of the proportional debt, the amount of debt will rebalance whenever value changes. MM's adjusted cost of capital does not allow for rebalancing of debt. But there is an alternative. We can use the Miles-Ezzell formula when debt ratio is fixed and the amount of debt rebalances:[1]

$$k^* = k_a - Tk_d \frac{D}{V}\left[\frac{1 + k_a}{1 + k_d}\right] \qquad (28)$$

Plugging numbers from our example, we get adjusted cost of capital using the Miles-Ezzell formula as follows:

$$k^* = 0.15 - 0.35 \times 0.10 \times 0.4255\left[\frac{1.15}{1.10}\right]$$

$$= 0.15 - 0.0156 = 0.1344 \text{ or } 13.44\%$$

You may recognise that WACC is also an adjusted cost of capital. Like the Miles-Ezzell's formula, it assumes that debt is rebalanced. We can rewrite WACC formula as follows:

$$WACC = k_e \frac{S}{V} + k_d(1 - T)\frac{D}{V} = k_e \frac{S}{V} + k_d \frac{D}{V} - Tk_d \frac{D}{V}$$

$$= k_a - Tk_d \frac{D}{V} \qquad (29)$$

Look at Equations (28) and (29). You can observe that the Miles-Ezzell's formula will give a slightly lower estimate of the adjusted cost of capital than WACC. Using the numbers from the example, WACC works out 13.51 per cent. The Miles-Ezzell adjusted cost of capital of 13.44 per cent does not differ significantly from the WACC of 13.51 per cent.

MM's adjusted opportunity cost of capital is based on the assumptions of permanent debt and constant cash flows. Hence it has highly restricted application. It will give distorted values for projects with uneven cash flows and finite life. WACC and the Miles-Ezzell formula, on the other hand, work for projects with even or uneven cash flows with finite or infinite life. Both

---

1. As discussed in footnote 1 on page 363, the Miles-Ezzell formula is based on the assumption that some interest tax shields are uncertain and for some uncertainty resolves over time. The term $(1 + k_a)/(1 + k_d)$ makes the correction for the resolved uncertainty.

are based on the assumption that debt-to-market value ratio remains constant. The implication of the fixed debt ratio is that in case of uncertain cash flows, the market value will go up or down, and debt levels will be adjusted each time. You can easily guess that for those projects for which the amount of debt is fixed, the debt ratio will not remain constant. Hence, for such projects, the constant WACC will not work. But if you calculate WACC for each period as the debt ratio changes, you could still use free cash flow and WACC approach. But it will become an involved exercise. The APV approach (and the CCF approach as well) is an easier method to handle the situation of changing amounts of debt.

CHOICE OF THE APPROPRIATE VALUATION APPROACH

The choice among the APV, the FCF and the CCF approaches rests more on the convenience of calculation rather than on the theoretical grounds. The ease of the use depends on whether debt ratio is a fixed or the debt amount is fixed. In case of those investment projects where the debt amounts are fixed for the future periods, or the debt repayment schedule is given, it is much easier to use the APV approach or the CCF approach – known as the compressed APV approach. Both these methods can easily handle the value the interest tax shields consequent upon the changing amount of debt over the life of the project.

In case of those projects where the debt policy is specified in terms of the fixed proportion of debt in relation to the value of the project, the WACC method is much easier to apply. Given the constant capital structure, the interest tax shields are easily incorporated in the calculation of the WACC. The APV or the CCF approach requires highly involved calculations of the project's value for each period in order to calculate the implied debt flows.

Apart from the interest tax shields, an investment project may have other financing effects. The APV approach (or its variant the compressed APV approach) is more versatile as it allows for the incorporation of the impact of several side effects on the project's NPV.

VALUATION OF A FIRM

Valuing a firm involves the same basic principles that are applied in valuing an investment project. The discounted cash flow (DCF) approach is theoretically the most appropriate valuation approach. The value of a firm depends on the expected cash flows and the discount rate. The expected cash flows of the firm depend on the operating efficiencies and market conditions. The discount rate depends on the risk of the expected cash flows. Firms generally specify target capital structures in terms of fixed debt-to-value ratio. Hence, WACC is the appropriate discount rate for valuing a firm. A firm in operations is assumed to be a going concern with an infinite life. Therefore, the value of the firm is given as follows:

$$V = \sum_{t=1}^{n=\infty} \frac{FCF_t}{(1+k_0)^t} \tag{30}$$

where FCF is the free cash flow and k_0 is the weighted average cost of capital (WACC). FCF can follow any growth pattern in practice. If FCF remains constant forever (i.e., FCF is a perpetuity), then the value of the firm is given by the following simple equation:

$$V = \frac{FCF}{k_0} \tag{31}$$

Earnings are the basis for estimating free cash flows of a firm. Cash flows include adjustments for depreciation, capital expenditure and working capital. Earnings depend on sales. If we assume constant relations of earnings, working capital and capital expenditure to sales, we can write the equation for the free cash flows as follows:

$$NCF = FCF$$
$$= SALES \times p \times (1-T) + DEP - (w+f)SALES \tag{32}$$

where p = EBIT as a percentage of sales, T = corporate tax rate, DEP = depreciation, w = net working capital as a percentage of sales and f = capital expenditure as a percentage of sales.

The following steps are involved in estimating free cash flows of the firm:

Sales projections The first step in the estimation of cash flows is the projection of sales. The financial analyst evaluating the firm must consider the drivers of sales. Sales growth will depend on the firm's market share and the market growth rate. Market share of the firm will be determined by its competitive advantage and its ability to sustain that advantage. A firm cannot continuously maintain its competitive superiority. It goes through super-normal, normal and declining growth phases. The financial analyst should estimate the time horizon of super-normal growth and other growth periods to estimate the firm's sales and cash flows.

Estimate of expenses The second step is to estimate expenses. Two major categories of expenses are cost of goods sold and selling and administrative expenses. The most important component of the cost of goods sold in the case of manufacturing companies is raw material followed by wages and salaries and power and fuel. If the firm has control over the supply of raw material or it has a better bargaining power vis-à-vis its suppliers, it can reduce the cost of raw material. The firm can also reduce the effective cost of wages and salaries and power and fuel by improving labour and machine productivity through innovations and better management practices.

Estimate of depreciation Depreciation is a non-cash item, but it is a deductible expense for calculating taxes. Hence it affects the after-tax cash flows of the firm. Depreciation amount will depend on fixed assets and the prescribed depreciation method and rates. In India, the written down value method of depreciation at specified rates is applicable for calculating the amount of deductible depreciation expense. Assets are categorised into different blocks and different depreciation rates apply to the different blocks of assets. The anticipated capital expenditure should be considered to estimate the amount of depreciation.

Capital expenditure In order to maintain the firm's operating efficiency and sales growth, the firm may be required to continuously incur capital expenditure each year. However, constant-growth firms may not need high capital expenditure; they may invest an amount equal to depreciation as capital expenditure to maintain their current operations. Capital expenditure is an outflow of cash and it reduces the after-tax cash flows of the firm.

Estimates of increase in net working capital In estimating free cash flows, the financial analyst should also account for changes in net working capital (NWC) due to expansion of sales. If the sales of the firm are constant, there will be no change in the working capital (except for the effect of change in prices). Increase in NWC is outflow of cash and decrease an inflow.

Treatment of interest expenses In calculating free cash flows, we ignore interest expenses. The free cash flow approach determines the **value of the firm**—representing the value of both equity and debt. Therefore, our concern is to determine the after-tax cash flows available to service *all investors* of the firm. The weighed cost of capital, which includes after-tax cost of debt, is used as the discount rate. Hence interest expenses are not subtracted in calculating free flows. We repeat that the free cash flow approach assumes that the debt ratio remains constant through out the period of analysis.

Tax rate Free cash flows should always be determined after taxes. The marginal corporate tax rate should be used to calculate the free cash flows.

Inflation We have explained in Chapter 10 that to avoid any bias in your computation of value, you should treat inflation consistently in estimating cash flows and the discount rate. Generally the firm's all cash flows should be estimated in nominal terms. Discount rate is market determined and therefore, it is always given in the nominal terms.

Horizon Period and Terminal Value

In the evaluation of an investment project, the financial analyst estimates the project's economic life based on the technology and other economic factors. In the terminal year, the project's cash flows also include the realisable value of the asset and the release of the working capital. In the case of a firm, it continuously makes investments that generate revenues and cash flows, theoretically, forever. Therefore, the financial analyst assumes a **horizon period** (H) for detailed calculations of cash flows. Financial analysts or managers make assumption of horizon period because detailed calculations for a long period become quite intricate. The financial analysis of such projects should incorporate an estimate of the value of cash flows after the horizon period without involving detailed calculations. Thus, the value of the firm is given as follows:

$$V = \sum_{t=1}^{H} \frac{FCF_t}{(1+k_0)^t} + \frac{TV_H}{(1+k_0)^H} \tag{33}$$

What happens to the cash flows after the horizon period? Since the firm is a going concern; it will continue making investments so long the investment return is higher than the cost of capital and earn revenues. Generally, the horizon period is the period of superior growth. It is assumed that during this period the company has superior advantage over its competitors. But after this period, the competitors may imitate the company and its competitive advantage may be eroded.

Constant perpetual cash flows There are various possibilities

vis-à-vis the competitive advantage after the initial phase (horizon period). One possibility is that after the horizon period, the competitors will dominate and the firm will totally lose its competitive advantage. Under this scenario, the firm's revenues will stop growing, and hence, no additional working capital will be needed. The firm will not incur any new capital expenditure and the capital expenditure equal to depreciation amount may be sufficient to maintain the constant level of operations. Thus, the firm will obtain constant perpetual cash flows after the horizon period. The value of these perpetual cash flows in the terminal year (end of the horizon period) is given as follows:

$$TV_H = \frac{FCF_{n+1}}{k_0} \tag{34}$$

Growing perpetual cash flows There is another possibility. The growth of the firm may slow down and it may grow at normal or lower rate to infinity. A simple method of estimating the terminal value at the end of the horizon period is to employ the following formula, which is the same as the dividend growth model:

$$TV_H = \frac{FCF_H(1+g)}{k_0 - g} = \frac{FCF_{n+1}}{k_0 - g} \tag{35}$$

where NCF_{n+1} is the project's net cash flow one year after the horizon period, k_0 (WACC) is the opportunity cost of capital (discount rate) and g is the expected growth in the project's net cash flows. The value of g will be positive if net cash flows are expected to grow; it will be negative if net cash flows are expected to decline; and it will be zero if net cash flows are expected to remain constant. In practice, the financial manager or analyst could calculate the effect of a range of values of g on the firm's value.

Other methods of valuing terminal value There are many other ad hoc methods used in practice to determine terminal value.

- ***Price-earnings (P/E) ratio*** Terminal value at horizon period could be determined as the product of the estimated after-tax earnings in the year after the horizon period and the expected P/E ratio:

  TV_H = Profit after tax in year $n + 1 \times$ Expected P/E ratio

  This approach suffers from several limitations: (a) Earnings depend on arbitrary accounting policies and choices. Hence they do not provide an objective measurement of the firm's profitability. (b) Value depends on cash flows; earnings are not cash flows. (c) It is quite difficult to determine the expected P/E ratio.

- ***Market-to-book value (M/B) ratio*** In this approach, the terminal value is calculated as the estimated book value of equity in the year after the horizon period multiplied by expected M/B ratio:

  TV_H = Book value of equity in year n
  $+ 1 \times$ Expected M/B ratio

  This approach is similar to P/E ratio approach. It also suffers from certain limitations; (a) Book value of equity depends on accounting earnings. Hence it is not an objectively determined number to rely upon. (b) Value does not depend on book value. (*c*) There is a problem in estimating the expected M/B ratio.

- *Replacement cost of assets* Under this method, the terminal value is equal to the replacement cost of the firm's assets at the end of the horizon period. In practice, it is difficult to get information of replacement cost of all assets. Some assets may be worthless or some may be more valuable than their replacement costs. This method also ignores the value of intangible assets such as the brand value and the value of the human capital.

Value of the Firm's Equity

The free cash flows and WACC approach gives the value of the firm's assets. In a number of situations like merger or acquisition, the firm may be interested in finding the value of the equity. The value of the equity can be obtained as the value of the firm minus the value of the firm's debt:

$$\text{Value of the equity} = \text{Value of the firm} - \text{Value of the debt}$$

Value of the equity per share

$$= \frac{\text{Value of the firm} - \text{Value of the debt}}{\text{Number of outstanding equity shares}}$$

As we have discussed earlier, you can follow the equity cash flows (ECF) approach to directly determine the value of equity. The ECFs account for debt flows (interest, interest tax shields and debt repayments) and are discounted at the equity cost of capital. Like WACC, the cost of equity capital assumes that the capital structure is constant and therefore, it will remain constant in the future periods. The cost of equity will change if the leverage changes. In practice, it is difficult to use the EFC approach since it requires calculation of the firm's value to determine the expected debt flows.

In summary, the following steps are involved in the valuation of a firm:

- Identify sales growth and profitability assumptions
- Consider depreciation, change in net working capital, capital expenditure and taxes in estimating the free cash flows
- Estimate the amounts of free cash flows for the horizon period
- Estimate the cash flow patterns beyond the horizon period and determine the terminal value
- Estimate the firm's weighted average cost of capital
- Be consistent in treating inflation in the estimation of free cash flows and WACC

- Compute present value cash flows using WACC as the discount rate
- Subtract the value of the outstanding debt from the value of the firm to find out the value of its equity. The value of the equity divided by the outstanding number of shares gives the equity value per share.

Illustration 16.7: Valuing a Firm

Sahitya Printing Press Limited is thinking of acquiring the Royal Paper Company. For Sahitya, it is a backward integration and the acquisition would help in stabilising its operations. Sahitya is less profitable than Royal, but it is less risky. Sahitya's P/E ratio is 12 and it has a weighted average cost of capital of 14 per cent. The financial manager of Sahitya has prepared the forecasts for Royal's operations for the next 10 years (Table 16.9). She was not sure about the value of Royal's assets after 10 years. She thought that most of the growth of the business would take place in the first 10 years and thereafter the business might not grow or grow at a very low rate. Royal does not employ any debt, and it has 2.5 million outstanding equity shares. Its current P/E ratio is 8 and the equity beta is 1.28. The financial manager argued that the acquisition of Royal would contribute to the firm's debt capacity equal to 30 per cent of its value. Sahitya will be able to borrow at risk-free rate of 8.5 per cent. The risk premium is 9 per cent. The corporate tax rate is 35 per cent. What is the value of Royal?

To value Royal, we need estimates of its free cash flows, value at horizon period and WACC. Currently, Royal does not employ any debt; hence its equity beta of 1.28 is the unlevered beta. The equity beta will change with the addition of debt equal to 30 per cent of the value. Thus the levered equity beta will be: unlevered beta/proportion of equity = 1.28/ 0.70 = 1.83. Royal's cost of equity and WACC will be as follows:

$$\text{Royal's cost of equity} = 0.085 + 0.09 \times 1.83 = 0.25 \text{ or } 25\%$$
$$\text{Royal's WACC} = 0.25 \times 0.70 + 0.085 \times (1 - 0.35) \times 0.30$$
$$= 0.19 \text{ or } 19\%$$

Table 16.10 gives estimates of the free cash flows. We have adjusted depreciation, working capital changes and capital expenditure to profits after tax to estimate the free cash flows. Our next step is to calculate the terminal or horizon value. The free cash flows at the end of 2013 are Rs 72.18 million. We may assume that these cash flows would remain constant forever. Thus, the terminal value will be:

$$TV_{13} = \frac{FCF_{13}}{WACC} = \frac{72.18}{0.19} = \text{Rs} \, 379.89 \text{ million}$$

Another alternative to calculate terminal value is to use P/E multiplier to profit after tax (PAT) at the end of the horizon period. As shown below, Royal's PAT in 2013 is Rs 42.77 million (and EPS Rs 17.11). Its current P/E ratio is 8. One conservative assumption is that P/E ratio will stay at 8 in the future. Using this ratio, the terminal value at the end of 2013 is: Rs 42.77 × 8 = Rs 340.16 million. In fact, if Royal performs as forecasted, it is likely that its P/E ratio would improve. The

Table 16.9: Forecasts for Royal

(Rs in million)

	2004	2005	2006	2007	2008	2009	2010	2011	2012	2013
PBDIT	71.21	101.26	140.84	126.25	132.51	121.60	131.40	136.31	109.75	105.33
Capex	43.07	70.76	97.33	21.32	21.32	13.69	10.91	10.91	5.17	4.62
Depreciation	32.66	44.22	54.69	61.41	64.53	61.41	53.59	42.34	41.09	39.53
Change in NWC	20.19	37.12	23.34	10.45	8.36	8.35	8.80	7.04	7.38	5.50

Table 16.10: Earning Per Share

	2004	2005	2006	2007	2008	2009	2010	2011	2012	2013
PAT	25.06	37.08	56.00	42.15	44.18	39.13	50.58	61.08	44.63	42.77
Number of shares	2.5	2.5	2.5	2.5	2.5	2.5	2.5	2.5	2.5	2.5
EPS	10.02	14.83	22.40	16.86	17.67	15.65	20.23	24.43	17.85	17.11

Table 16.11: Estimates of Free Cash Flows

(Rs in million)

	2003	2004	2005	2006	2007	2008	2009	2010	2011	2012	2013
PBDIT		71.21	101.26	140.84	126.25	132.51	121.60	131.40	136.31	109.75	105.33
Less: Depreciation		32.66	44.22	54.69	61.41	64.53	61.41	53.59	42.34	41.09	39.53
PBIT		38.55	57.04	86.16	64.84	67.98	60.20	77.81	93.96	68.66	65.79
Tax		13.49	19.97	30.15	22.69	23.79	21.07	27.23	32.89	24.03	23.03
PAT		25.06	37.08	56.00	42.15	44.18	39.13	50.58	61.08	44.63	42.77
Add: Depreciation		32.66	44.22	54.69	61.41	64.53	61.41	53.59	42.34	41.09	39.53
Less: Change in NWC		20.19	37.12	23.34	10.45	8.36	8.35	8.80	7.04	7.38	5.50
Less: Capex		43.07	70.76	97.33	21.32	21.32	13.69	10.91	10.91	5.17	4.62
Free Cash Flows		−5.54	−26.58	−9.98	71.78	79.04	78.49	84.46	85.47	73.17	72.18
Terminal Value											379.89
Net Cash Flows		−5.54	−26.58	−9.98	71.78	79.04	78.49	84.46	85.47	73.17	452.07
PVF at 19%		0.8403	0.7062	0.5934	0.4987	0.4190	0.3521	0.2959	0.2487	0.2090	0.1756
Present value		−4.65	−18.77	−5.92	35.80	33.12	27.64	24.99	21.25	15.29	79.38
Value of the Firm	208.13										

two estimates of the terminal values are not significantly different. However, we prefer the value based on cash flows rather than earnings.

As shown in Table 16.11, the value of Royal is Rs 208.13 million – the present value of free cash flows is Rs 151.42 million and the present value of the terminal value is Rs 66.70. The firm's debt ratio is 30 per cent; hence the value of equity will be: Rs 208.13 million (1 – 0.30) = Rs 145.69 million and the value per share: Rs 145.69/2.5 = Rs 58.28.

Growth Patterns and the Firm Value

Firms in practice might go through different stages of growth. For example, a firm may experience two-stage growth – a high growth followed by a normal growth. Some firm might experience high growth followed by the medium growth and they might finally revert to normal or no growth. The DCF valuation of a firm makes assumptions about the growth patterns of the firm during the horizon period and beyond. Generally, there are the following four possibilities:

- *No growth* The firm has reached maturity and its earnings show no growth.
- *Constant growth* The firm is in a stable growth stage and there is no high growth period for the firm. It will grow at a constant rate forever.
- *Two-stage growth* The firm will grow at a high rate for a period followed by constant growth rate for infinity.
- *Three-stage growth* The firm will grow at a high rate for a period followed by a period of declining growth before

growing at a constant growth rate forever. In the third stage, it is possible that the firm reaches maturity stage and its growth rate becomes zero.

The growth pattern of a firm depends on the market growth rate, the size of market, the firm's market share, the barriers to entry and the firm's competitive advantages. Because of the competitive forces, it is very difficult for a firm to sustain high growth for a very long period of time.

Illustration 16.8: Two-stage Growth

Sangma Corporation has 100 million outstanding shares. The market value of equity is Rs 4,500 million and the market value of debt is Rs 1,500 million. The firm will maintain the market value debt ratio forever. The expected interest rate on debt is 12.3 per cent. The firm's equity beta is 1.15. The 30-year government bonds yield is 5.65 per cent. The historical market premium is estimated as 9 per cent. The marginal corporate tax rate of the company is 35 per cent. The company's current free cash flows are Rs 225 million. The company expects its cash flows to grow at 12 per cent for 7 years and thereafter, at 6 per cent forever. Determine the value of the firm? What is the value of the firm's equity? How much is the value per share?

We should calculate the cost of equity and the cost of debt to determine the firm's WACC. We can use CAPM to calculate the cost of equity:

$$k_e = 0.0565 + 0.09 \times 1.15 = 0.16 \text{ or } 16\%$$

The after-tax cost of debt is:

$$k_d(1 - T) = 0.123(1 - 0.35) = 0.08 \text{ or } 8\%$$

The firm's WACC is as follows:

$$WACC = 0.16 \times \frac{4,500}{4,500+1,500} + 0.08 \times \frac{1,500}{4,500+1,500}$$

$$= 0.14 \text{ or } 14\%$$

The first scenario anticipates two-stage growth. The value of the firm is given by the following equation:

$$V = \sum_{t=1}^{H} \frac{FCF(1+g_h)_t}{(1+k_0)^t} + \frac{FCF_h(1+g_n)}{k_0 - g_n} \qquad (36)$$

$$\underbrace{\qquad}_{\substack{\text{Value of FCF} \\ \text{during horizon period}}} \qquad \underbrace{\qquad}_{\substack{\text{Value of FCF} \\ \text{after horizon period}}}$$

where g_h is high growth rate during the horizon period and g_n is the stable growth rate for infinity. The first part on the right-hand side of Equation (36) is the present value of a constantly growing annuity during the horizon period. We can simplify this part as follows (refer to Chapter 2 for explanation):

$$V = \frac{FCF}{k_0 - g_h}\left[1 - \left(\frac{1+g_h}{1+k_0}\right)^H\right]$$

$$+ \frac{FCF(1+g_h)^H(1+g_n)}{k_0 - g_n} \times \frac{1}{(1+k_0)^H} \qquad (37)$$

Substituting the given values in the above equation, we obtain the value of Sangma Corporation as follows:

$$V = \frac{225}{0.14 - 0.12}\left[1 - \left(\frac{1.12}{1.14}\right)^7\right] + \frac{225(1.12)^7(1.06)}{0.14 - 0.06} \times \frac{1}{1.14^7}$$

$$V = 11,250 \times 0.1165 + \frac{527.25}{0.08} \times 0.400 = 1,311 + 2,634$$

$$= \text{Rs } 3,945 \text{ million}$$

The value of equity shares is:

Value of equity shares = value of the firm - value of debt

$$= 3,945 - 1,500 = \text{Rs } 2,445 \text{ million}$$

Value per share = 2,445/100 = Rs 24.45

Comparative Firms Valuation Approach

In the comparable companies or comparable transactions approach, key relationships are calculated for a group of similar companies or similar transactions as a basis for the valuation of a firm. This approach is based on the premise that similar companies should sell for similar prices. This is a straight-forward approach that appeals to managers and financial analysts in practice.

The following steps are involved in applying the comparative firms approach:

- Identify the comparable firms based on the criteria of similar products, size, age, growth and profitability trends.
- For the comparable firms, calculate the firm value as a ratio of sales, EBIT, free cash flows and market value-to-book value of assets. Sales, EBIT, free cash flow and book value of assets are assumed as value drivers. Notice that firm value to EBIT ratio is equivalent of price-earnings (P/E) ratio.
- Average the ratios of the comparable firms, and apply them to the sales, EBIT and free cash flow data of the firm.

Let us illustrate the application of the comparable firms approach. Suppose you are interested in valuing firm Z. You have identified P, Q, R and S as four comparable firms which are approximately similar to Z. The four ratios and their averages for these firms are given in Table 16.12, Part A. You may notice that there are not significant differences in the ratios of the four comparable firms. In case of significant differences, the use of average ratio is not very meaningful. In Part B of the table we apply the average ratios of the comparable firms to Z. We get four estimates of value based on sales, EBIT, FCF and book value of assets. The four calculated values are quite close to each other, and therefore, you can be confident to rely on them. The average of the four values is Rs 784 crore.

Table 16.12: Comparative Firms Data

Comparable firms	Firm market value/sales	Firm market value/EBIT	Firm market value/FCF	Firm market value to book value
Part A: Ratios for Comparable Firms				
P	1.52	16.50	19.00	1.27
Q	1.45	18.50	24.50	1.54
R	1.43	22.00	28.00	1.22
S	1.39	20.50	21.50	1.40
Average	1.45	19.38	23.25	1.36

Part B: Value of Firm Z	Rs crore	Average ratio	Estimated value Rs crore
Sales	500	1.45	725
EBIT	43	19.38	833
FCC	35	23.25	814
Book value of assets	562	1.36	764
Average			784

The virtue of the comparable firms approach is its simplicity. It does not require involved computations and assumptions. Most managers and financial analysts favour this approach since it is based on the ratios that they easily understand. This approach is quite useful in case of those firms which do not publicly available share values. The limitation of this approach is that it is not very scientific. It assumes that value is driven by a factor like sales or EBIT. True or fair value depends on cash flows and discount rate which are driven by many factors.

Balance Sheet Approach to Firm Valuation

Balance sheet or adjusted book value uses assets and liabilities information to determine the value of the firm. Without any adjustment, the book value of equity funds and debt funds represent the claims of investors over the firm's assets. Hence, the value of the firm is at least equal to the book value of its assets. However, assets are not worth the amounts shown in the balance sheet. They are worth more or less than the book values because of change in technology, inflation and earnings capacity. For example, non-operating assets are worthless or worth much less than their book values. On the other hand, some other assets are still quite useful and their replacement cost is much higher than the current book value. Therefore, assets should be revalued to determine the value of the firm. One approach to estimate the adjusted book values of assets is to determine their current or replacement costs. It is relatively easy to find out the current costs of current assets. For example, stated amount of debtors may be adjusted for bad and doubtful debts and inventories may be valued at the current costs after adjusting for redundant in-ventories. Fixed assets like land and buildings are also rela-tively easy to value as some benchmark prices are available. It is hard to find the replacement value of plant and machinery, par-ticularly when the technology has changed significantly and there is no active secondary market for these assets. In this re-gard, the firm can use the services of valuers.

A firm is not worth the current or replacement costs of its assets only. The value of the intangible assets like brand equity, customer loyalty, or human capital drives the value of the firm. In practice, both tangible and intangible assets should be valued to determine the value of the firm.

SUMMARY

❖ We need estimate of the discount rate to determine the net present value of a project. The discount rate depends on the project's business risk and financial risk. Under CAPM, the equity beta captures both the business risk and the finan-cial risk. Financial risk arises when the firm uses debt.

❖ The asset beta, β_a reflects the business risk of the firm or the project. Thus, under CAPM the firm's or the project's op-portunity cost of capital is given by the risk-free rate plus the product of the risk premium and the asset beta.

❖ Following the MM Proposition I, the opportunity cost of capital can be calculated as the pre-tax weighted average cost of capital.

❖ The asset beta is not observable in practice. You can estimate the equity beta and the debt beta from the market data and then estimate the asset beta. Assuming the debt is risk-free and the debt beta is zero, the asset beta and the equity beta are given as follows:

$$\beta_a = \beta_e \frac{E}{V}$$

$$\beta_e = \beta_a \frac{V}{E} = \beta_a \left[1 + \frac{D}{E}\right]$$

❖ In case of fixed amount of debt, the interest tax shields reduce the systematic risk. If debt is risk-free, the asset beta is given as follows:

$$\beta_a = \beta_e \left[\frac{E}{E + D(1-T)}\right]$$

❖ The equity beta and the asset beta of an all-equity (unlevered) firm will be same. But the equity beta of a levered firm (assuming fixed amount of debt) will be as follows:

$$\beta_e = \beta_a \left[1 + \frac{D}{E}(1-T)\right]$$

❖ In practice, the interest tax shields depend on the firm's profitability, which fluctuates randomly. Therefore, the interest tax shields may not reduce the systematic risk. Under this assumption, the levered firm's cost of equity shown below includes compensation for financial risk as well:

$$k_e = r_f + (r_m - r_f)\beta_a + (r_m - r_f)\beta_a \frac{D}{E}$$

❖ Following MM's Proposition II, the levered firm's cost of equity can also be calculated as follows:

$$k_e = k_a + (k_a - k_d)\frac{D}{E}$$

❖ There are four methods of investment evaluation. The most popular method of the project evaluation is to discount the free cash flows at the firm's weighted average cost of capital (WACC):

$$V = \sum_{t=1}^{n} \frac{FCF_t}{(1+WACC)^t} + \frac{TV_n}{(1+WACC)^n}$$

WACC is calculated as follows:

$$WACC = k_e \frac{E}{V} + k_d(1-T)\frac{D}{V}$$

❖ The free cash flow approach adjusts the effect of the interest tax shields in the discount rate (WACC) rather than the project's cash follows. This approach is based on the as-sumption that the capital structure (debt ratio) is constant over time. It also assumes that the project's and the firm's risk and capital structures are the same. Hence, this approach will not work if the project's and the firm's risk and capital structure are different, and where the project's capital struc-ture is not constant.

❖ The equity cash flow (ECF) approach is similar to the FCF approach and it is based on the same assumptions. In the ECF approach the equity cash flows, which are residual cash flows available to the equity shareholders, are dis-counted by the levered cost of equity.

❖ An alternative approach, the capital cash flow (CCF) ap-proach, is much easier to use when the project's debt amount is fixed and the capital structure does not remain constant. CCFs are calculated as the free cash flows plus the interest tax shields, and they are discounted by the project's all-equity or opportunity cost of capital. The project's oppor-tunity cost of capital depends on its business risk and is not affected by the capital structure. In the CCF approach the effect of the interest tax shields are adjusted in the cash flows rather than the discount rate.

❖ The adjusted present value (APV) approach is an alternative approach for the project's evaluation. It is a flexible approach that unbundles the project's value into several parts. It separates the operational part from the financing effects. The base-case NPV is calculated by discounting the free cash flows at the project's opportunity cost of capital. The present values of the financing effects are calculated separately using the discount rates appropriate to the risk of these effects. For example, the interest tax shields are treated as risky as debt. Hence, the interest tax shields are discounted at the cost of debt. APV is the sum of the base-case NPV and the value of financing effects:

APV = Base-NPV + value of interest tax shields
                + value of other financing effects

❖ APV is a useful approach in the project financing where the debt is fixed and there are several other financing effects like issue costs, investment incentives and special tax benefits.

❖ The APV formula under the assumption of the perpetual cash flows and the perpetual fixed amount of debt and without other financing effects is as follows:

$$APV = \frac{FCF}{k_a} + \frac{Tk_d D}{k_d}$$

❖ An alternative to the above approach is to estimate the adjusted cost of capital (or discount rate) and use it to discount the free cash flows:

$$ACC = k^* = k_a \left[1 - T D/V\right]$$

$$NPV = \frac{FCF}{k^*}$$

❖ The concept of the adjusted cost of capital is based on the MM tax-corrected hypothesis. Two critical assumptions are that that the cash flows are perpetual and the amount of debt is fixed. In case of the fixed debt ratio, which implies rebalancing of debt, the adjusted cost of capital can be estimated using the Miles-Ezzell formula as given below:

$$ACC = k^* = k_a - Tk_d \, D/V \left[\frac{1+k_a}{1+k_d}\right]$$

This formula is same as WACC except for the last term, $(1 + k_a)/(1 + k_d)$. Both WACC and the Miles-Ezzell formula assume the fixed debt ratio and debt rebalancing.

❖ The use of the DCF techniques can be extended to value a business firm. In the valuation of a firm a financial analyst usually assumes a constant debt ratio.

❖ The firm can be valued using FCFs and WACC. Further, the analyst assumes a horizon period for analysis and calculates the horizon value at the end of the horizon period. Horizon value depends on the growth prospects of the firm after the horizon period. Thus, the value of he firm is given as follows:

$$V = \sum_{t=1}^{H} \frac{FCF_t}{(1 + WACC)^t} + \frac{TV_H}{(1 + WACC)^H}$$

❖ The value of equity is obtained by subtracting the outstanding amount of debt from the value of the firm. The value of equity divided by the number of outstanding shares gives the equity value per share.

KEY CONCEPTS

Adjusted cost of capital	Capital cash flows	Levered beta	Project financing
Adjusted present value	Compressed APV	Levering beta	Unlevered beta
Assets cost of capital	Free cash flows	Opportunity cost of	Unlevering beta
Base-NPV	Horizon value	capital	WACC

ILLUSTRATIVE PROBLEMS

Problem 16.1: Brightways Diversified Limited has multiple products. The company's debt capacity is 50 per cent of the market value of its assets. The company's equity beta is 1.20. The risk-free rate is 10 per cent and the average market premium is 9 per cent. The corporate tax rate is 30 per cent. Brightways so far has the practice of using WACC in evaluating the investment projects. The company is currently considering an electronic project requiring an investment of Rs 50 crore. The project is expected to generate the after-tax free cash flows of Rs 8.85 crore in perpetuity. According to the finance manager, this project will add only 30 per cent debt capacity. She also feels that electronics business is more risky than the average risk of the firm. In her opinion, the fluctuations in electronics business will

be 1.30 times of the fluctuations in the overall business of the company. What is Brightways WACC? Should the project be evaluated using the firm's WACC? In your opinion how should the project be evaluated? Show calculations.

Solution:

(1) Brightways' WACC:

Brightways' cost of equity = 0.10 + 0.09 × 1.20
                     = 0.208 or 20.8%

Brightways' after-tax cost of debt = 0.10 × (1–0.30)
                       = 0.07 or 7%

Brightways' WACC = 0.208 × 0.50 + 0.07 × 0.50
                     = 0.139 or 13.9%

(2) The electronic project has higher risk and lower debt

capacity than the firm. Therefore, it is inappropriate to use the firm's WACC to evaluate it. We should calculate the project's opportunity cost of capital and WACC. Let us first unlever the firm's equity beta and estimate the asset beta:

Firm's asset beta, $\beta_a = \beta_e (E/V) = 1.20 (0.50) = 0.60$

This is the firm's asset beta. The project has 1.30 higher business risk than the firm. Hence the project's asset beta is:

Project's asset beta, $\beta_a = 0.60 \times 1.30 = 0.78$

Project's equity beta, $\beta_e = \beta_a (V/E) = 0.78 \times (1/0.7) = 1.114$

The project's opportunity cost of capital and cost of equity are:

Project's opportunity cost of capital,

$$k_a = 0.10 + 0.09 \times 0.78 = 0.1702 \text{ or approx. } 17\%$$

Project's cost of equity,

$$k_e = 0.10 + 0.09 \times 1.114 = 0.2002 \text{ or approx. } 20\%$$

We can also estimate the project's cost of equity using *MM*'s Proposition II as follows:

Project's cost of equity,

$$k_e = 0.17 + (0.17 - 0.10)(0.3/0.7) = 0.20 \text{ or approx. } 20\%$$

The project's WACC is as follows:

Project's WACC = $0.20 \times 0.7 + 0.07 \times 0.3 = 0.161$

(3) The project has a fixed debt ratio. Hence we can use WACC approach to evaluate the project as follows:

$$NPV = -50 + \frac{8.85}{0.161} = \text{Rs 5 crore}$$

Problem 16.2: Star Engineering Company has cost of equity of 17 per cent, cost of debt of 12 per cent and debt ratio of 40 per cent. The company is considering an investment project in its existing line of business. The project will need a cash outlay of Rs 120 crore. It is expected to generate annual EBDIT of Rs 35 crore for 8 years. The project will require Rs 3 crore each year for net working capital and capital expenditure. Star will be able to borrow 50 per cent of the project's cost from a financial institution. The interest rate is 12 per cent p.a., and the loan will be repaid in five equal instalments after three years. The corporate tax rate is 30 per cent. Assume straight-line depreciation for computing taxes and zero terminal value of the project. Should Star accept the project? What shall happen to the project's NPV if Star is able to negotiate loan from the financial institution at

lower interest rate of 10 per cent p.a.?

Solution: In this situation, the project has fixed amount of debt, therefore, the WACC approach will be difficult to use. The APV approach will be more appropriate. First, we shall discount the free cash flows by the project's opportunity cost of capital to determine the base-case NPV. Since the risk of the firm and the project is same, we can use the firm's opportunity cost of capital as the project's opportunity cost of capital. MM proposition I gives the firm's opportunity cost of capital as follows:

$$k_a = 0.17 \times 0.6 + 0.12 \times 0.4 = 0.15 \text{ or } 15\%$$

The free cash flows are as follows:

FCF = (EBDIT − depreciation) $(1 - T)$ + depreciation − (NWC + Capex)

FCF = $(35 - 15)(1 - 0.30) + 15 - 3 = $ Rs 26 crore

The base-case NPV of the project is as follows:

$$\text{Base-case NPV} = -120 + \sum_{t=1}^{8} \frac{26_t}{(1.15)^t}$$

$$= -120 + 26 \times 4.487 = -\text{Rs } 3.34$$

Without considering the financing effect, the project is unattractive as it has negative base-case NPV.

Let us now calculate the present value of the interest tax shields. The calculations are shown below:

Year	Loan Outstanding (Rs in cr.)	Interest @12% (Rs in cr.)	Interest tax shield (ITS) (Rs in cr.)	Discount factor	PV of ITS (Rs in cr.)
0	60	—	—	—	—
1	60	7.20	2.16	0.893	1.93
2	60	7.20	2.16	0.797	1.72
3	60	7.20	2.16	0.712	1.54
4	48	7.20	2.16	0.636	1.37
5	36	5.76	1.73	0.567	0.98
6	24	4.32	1.30	0.506	0.66
7	12	2.99	0.90	0.452	0.41
8	0	1.44	0.43	0.404	0.17
Present value of interest tax shields					8.78

Table 16.13: Present Value of Interest Tax Shield and Interest Tax Subsidy

Year	Loan Outstand. (Rs in cr.)	INT @10% (Rs in cr.)	ITS (Rs in cr.)	Discount Factor @ 12% (Rs in cr.)	PV (ITS) (Rs in cr.)	INTSUB @ 2% (Rs in cr.)	AT INTSUB @ 1.4% (Rs in cr.)	Discount factor @ 8.4%	PV (AT INTSUB) (Rs in cr.)
0	60	—	—	—	—				
1	60	6.0	1.80	0.893	1.61	1.20	0.84	0.923	0.77
2	60	6.0	1.80	0.797	1.43	1.20	0.84	0.851	0.71
3	60	6.0	1.80	0.712	1.28	1.20	0.84	0.785	0.66
4	48	6.0	1.80	0.636	1.14	1.20	0.84	0.724	0.61
5	36	4.8	1.44	0.567	0.82	0.96	0.67	0.668	0.45
6	24	3.6	1.08	0.506	0.55	0.72	0.50	0.616	0.31
7	12	2.4	0.72	0.452	0.33	0.48	0.34	0.569	0.19
8	0	1.2	0.36	0.404	0.15	0.24	0.17	0.525	0.09
					7.30				3.80

The adjusted present value of the project is:

Project's APV = Base-case NPV + PV of INTS

$$= -3.34 + 8.78 = \text{Rs } 5.44 \text{ crore}$$

The project has positive APV, Rs 5.44 crore. The financing effect has turned the project profitable. The company should accept it.

If the company is able to negotiate a subsidised loan, it shall save taxes on interest paid at the rate of 10 per cent and obtain after-tax interest subsidy at the rate of 1.40 per cent p.a.; that is, (12% – 10%) (1 – 0.30) = 1.40 per cent. The calculations

of the present value of interest tax shields and the interest tax subsidy are shown below:

The project's APV is:

Project's APV = Base-case NPV + PV of interest tax shields
+ PV of after-tax interest subsidy

Project's NPV = –3.34 + 7.30 + 3.80 = Rs 7.76 crore

If you discount the outflows of the subsidised loan at the after-tax cost of debt (8.4 per cent), you will get the value of the subsidised loan as Rs 56.20 crore. The actual borrowing is Rs 60 crore. The difference is the value of the subsidy for the company.

REVIEW QUESTIONS

1. What is an asset beta? How is it calculated? Assume no taxes.
2. Do the interest tax shields reduce the systematic risk? If yes, how is the asset's beta affected by the interest tax shields?
3. How is the equity beta determined? How is it affected by the capital structure?
4. What is the asset cost of capital? How is it calculated? Is the asset cost of capital same as the opportunity cost of capital?
5. Using CAPM, how would you calculate the cost of equity? Show that the levered firm's cost of equity requires compensation for both the business risk and the financial risk?
6. How is the levered firm's cost of equity determined according to the MM Proposition II? Is it equivalent to the cost of equity under CAPM?
7. What is the logic of the MM adjusted cost of capital? Can you use it as a discount rate for evaluating an investment project?
8. How do you calculate WACC? What are its assumptions? Can you use it to evaluate an investment proposal? Is it same as the MM adjusted cost of capital?
9. How will you calculate a project's WACC with its unique capital structure given the firm's cost of capital and capital structure data?
10. How does the free cash flow and WACC approach work in the project evaluation? What are the limitations of this approach?
11. Does the equity cash flow approach give the same results as the free cash flow approach in evaluating a project? Why?
12. What are the capital cash flows? How does the capital cash flow approach work? How does it differ from the FCF approach?
13. What is the adjusted present value (APV) of a project? How is it calculated? What is the difference between the CCF approach and the APV approach?
14. What principles govern the valuation of a firm? How will you calculate the value of the firm's equity?
15. Why is the calculation of the terminal value critical in determining the value of the firm? How is the terminal value calculated?
16. What is the comparative firm valuation approach? How does it work?
17. What is the balance sheet approach to the valuation of a firm? What are its merits and limitations?

PROBLEMS

1. A company's equity beta is 1.84. The risk free rate is 9 per cent and the average market premium is 8.5 per cent. The company is considering a project that has a beta of 1.20 and the expected rate of return of 18 per cent. The company is thinking of issuing equity shares to finance the project. Should the company accept the project?
2. A power company has 85 per cent debt-to-assets ratio and an equity beta of 0.90. The risk-free rate is 6.5 per cent and the expected market rate of return is 12.5 per cent. The corporate taxes are 35 per cent. What is the opportunity cost of capital of the company? How is the required return on the equity?
3. A software company has no debt. Its equity beta is 1.15. Assume that the corporate tax rate is 40 per cent. If the company wants its beta to increase to 2.50, how much leverage should it take?
4. A firm's cost of equity is 20 per cent. The risk-free rate is 8

per cent and the expected market return is 14 per cent. The asset beta of the company is 1.10. How much is the business risk premium and the financial risk premium for the firm's equity?
5. Suppose the risk-free rate is 8 per cent, the market risk premium is 9 per cent and the tax rate is 30 per cent. A firm has the following market values and beta based on the market data and the company's own analysis for various sources of financing:

Source of Capital	Market value (Rs in crore)	Beta
Ordinary share capital	500	1.45
Debentures	400	0.30
Public deposits	100	0.15

You are required to calculate (i) the required rate of return for each source of finance; (*ii*) the weighted average cost of capital; (*iii*) the asset beta; and (*iv*) the opportunity cost of capital on the firm's assets.

6. An engineering company has a debt-to-market value ratio of 40 per cent. The company can raise new debt at 12 per cent. The corporate tax rate for the company is 35 per cent. The company has estimated the required return on equity as 22 per cent. What is the company's weighted average cost of capital? The company is thinking of raising its bet-to-market value ratio to 60 per cent. What will be the company's new weighted cost of capital?

7. Torrent Automotive Company's debt capacity is 50 per cent of the market value of its assets. The company's equity beta is 1.40. The risk-free rate is 9 per cent and the average market premium is 12 per cent. The corporate tax rate is 30 per cent. The company is considering an investment project in the existing line of business requiring an investment of Rs 100 crore. The project is expected to generate the after-tax free cash flows of Rs 15 crore in perpetuity. What is the project's NPV if it has the same debt capacity as the firm? Suppose that the company can borrow 30 per cent of the cost of the project, how will you evaluate the project? Show calculations.

8. Indo Software Company has cost of equity of 20 per cent, cost of debt of 10 per cent and debt-to-total assets ratio of 20 per cent. The company is considering an expansion project. The project will need a cash outlay of Rs 80 crore. It is expected to generate annual EBDIT of Rs 20 crore for 8 years. The project will require Rs 1 crore each year for net working capital and capital expenditure. IndoSoftware will be able to borrow 40 per cent of the project's cost from a financial institution. The interest rate is 10 per cent p.a.,

and the loan amount will be repaid in equal annual instalments over eight years. The corporate tax rate 40 per cent. Assume straight-line depreciation for computing taxes and zero terminal value of the project. Should the company accept the project?

9. Dhatu Industries Limited is a manufacturer of iron and steel. It has an equity beta of 1.10. The target debt-equity ratio of the company is 2:1. The company is intending to diversify into different lines of businesses. It is considering a cement project requiring an investment of Rs 105 crore. The company will be able to raise Rs 70 crore loan from a financial institution at 10 per cent p.a. The loan is repayable at the end of 5 years. The project is expected to generate annual profit before interest and taxes of Rs 22 crore for 7 years. Assume that the project's cost can be depreciated over its life of 7 years on the straight-line basis. The company has identified one public limited cement company as a proxy for the project. This company has an equity beta of 1.3 and debt-equity ratio of 1.5:1. The risk-free rate is 7 per cent and the market risk premium is 8 per cent. The corporate tax rate is 30 per cent. Should Dhatu undertake the cement project?

10. Suppose that Dhatu Industries Limited in (9) above decides to locate the cement project in an economically backward area. As a consequence, it is able to negotiate the loan amount from the financial institution at 8 per cent instead of the market rate of interest of 10 per cent. Evaluate the viability of the project showing the sources of value for the project.

11. Suppose that Dhatu Industries Limited in (9) above does not have to pay any taxes on the income of the cement project since it is located in the backward area. How does this affect the profitability of the project?

CASES

Case 16.1: Supreme Buildings Products Limited

Supreme Buildings Products Limited manufactures building products. The company's profitability in the last five years has been low as the construction industry was under recession. It has just come out of the recession, and its sales and profits have shown improvement. The company is thinking of adding a new product – the designer ceramic tiles – to its product portfolio. This product is meant for home improvement and beautification. Therefore, the company thinks that the demand will be less susceptible to the economic conditions of the construction industry. The company will organise the new business as a separate division. The project has an estimated cost of Rs 70 crore, including Rs 3.33 crore for initial working capital. The details of the costs are as follows:

The project will be located in a backward area of Maharashtra. The company will be entitled to receive an interest free non-refundable subsidy of Rs 25 lakh, of which the company expects to receive Rs 10 lakh immediately and the remaining amount after a year. Also, the company will be able to avail certain tax benefits. Under Section 80HH of the Income Tax Act, Supreme will be exempt 20 per cent of the project's

taxable profits from taxes for a period of 10 years. Further, under Section 80I of the Income Tax Act, 25 per cent of the project's taxable profits, after computing the benefits from Section 80 HH, will be exempt from taxes for 8 years. In computing the amount of deductions under Sections 80HH and 80I, the relevant profit will be reckoned as if it were the sole source of income of the company. However, the company can set off unabsorbed depreciation and a normal loss from the project against the company's other profits.

	Rs in lakh
Land and site development	68
Buildings	285
Plant and machinery	5,549
Miscellaneous fixed asset	57
Engineering fees	120
Preliminary and pre-operative expenses	284
Provision for contingency	305
Margin money for working capital	332
Total cost	7,000

Table 16.1.1: Summarised Profit and Loss Statement of the Project (*Rs in lakh*)

Year	1	2	3	4	5	6	7	8	9	10
Gross sales	2,370	3,950	5,925	7,110	7,900	7,900	7,900	7,900	7,900	7,900
Excise duty	395	658	987	1,210	1,317	1,317	1,317	1,317	1,317	1,317
Net sales	1,975	3,292	4,937	5,900	6,583	6,583	6,583	6,583	6,583	6,583
Variable expenses	1,024	1,696	2,544	3,053	3,392	3,392	3,392	3,392	3,392	3,392
Fixed expenses	193	242	287	300	302	327	341	357	373	389
Total expenses	1,217	1,938	2,831	3,353	3,694	3,719	3,733	3,749	3,765	3,780
EBDIT	757	1,354	2,106	2,547	2,889	2,864	2,850	2,834	2,818	2,803
Change in WC	−600	−312	-392	−235	−157	0	0	0	52	1,642

Table 16.1.2: Depreciation on Assets (*Rs in lakh*)

	Dep. Rate (%)	0	1	2	3	4	5	6	7	8	9	10
Land	0.00	75	0	0	0	0	0	0	0	0	0	0
Building	10.00	312	31	28	25	23	20	18	17	15	13	12
Machinery	33.33	6,087	2,029	1,352	902	601	401	267	178	119	79	53
Misc. assets	10.00	62	6	6	5	5	4	4	3	3	3	2
Eng. Fees	16.67	131	22	22	22	22	22	22	0	0	0	0
		6,667	2,088	1,408	954	650	447	312	198	137	95	67

Note: (1) Preliminary and pre-operating expenses have been proportionately allocated to other assets. (2) Engineering fees have been amortised equally over 6 years. (3) Depreciation rates are as per the rules existing at the time project was considered. The block of assets concept is followed for charging depreciation.

The estimated sales, expenses and changes in working capital of the company over a period of 10 years are given in Table 16.1.1. Table 16.1.2 shows computation of depreciation for tax purposes. Further, it is expected that the project will have a salvage value of 20 per cent of the original cost of the project. The corporate tax rate is 35 per cent tax rate.

Supreme's market capitalisation is Rs 500 crore and it has total borrowings of Rs 300 crore. It has always paid dividend to its shareholders. However, its share prices have fluctuated more than the stock market prices. The company's estimated cost of equity is 20 per cent. The finance director states that the company can avail borrowings up to Rs 42 crore for financing the project at a subsidised interest rate of 10 per cent p.a. The company can start repaying the loan amount after two years in equal instalments during the life of the project. The market rate of interest is 12 per cent. He suggests that the company should borrow since it will pay interest at the subsidised rate and the interest paid will be allowed as deductible expenses for computing taxes on profits. The marketing director is not in favour of borrowing. According to her the increased debt ratio of the company will make its operations more vulnerable to the economic fluctuations. She also argues that the cash outlay for servicing debt will be much more than the payment of dividend if the project is financed by the issue of shares. The managing director suggested that let the staff of the finance director work out the profitability of the project under both borrowing and no borrowing options.

Discussion Questions

1. Do you agree with the views of the marketing director? Explain.
2. Work out the cash flows of the project assuming: (i) no borrowing, and (ii) borrowing Rs 30 crore.
3. What is the company's levered and unlevered cost of capital?
4. Can the company use its WACC to evaluate the proposed project? Why?
5. Evaluate the project's profitability under both no borrowing and Rs 30 crore borrowing options. Clearly show the values created from the operations, special tax benefits and financing effects.

Case 16.2: Sunlight Paints Limited

Sunlight Paints Limited is one of the six large paints manufacturers in India. The company was established as a private limited company in 1959 to manufacture decorative paints. Over the years, Sunlight diversified into industrial paints, and has very recently added marine paints also in its portfolio of products. It was converted to a public limited company in 1987. Sunlight's business has grown steadily and has been consistently profitable. From 1996 to 2000, its sales and profits have grown about 9–10 per cent each year, but its performance was adversely affected in 2002 and 2003 due to an industry downturn. In 2003, Sunlight's share price fell to a record low in last 10 years. The company addressed its low performance by cost reduction, downsizing its workforce and consolidating its marketing efforts by focusing on high margin marine and industrial paints businesses. These efforts helped the company to improve its sales and profits and its share price increased substantially in 2004 and it ranged between Rs 50–62. The managing director of the company was very optimistic about the future prospects of the company as the economy was fast recovering, and the company has strong product lines and investment plans to expand sales, improve productivity and cut costs. The company's book value equity is Rs 250 crore (divided into 25 crore outstanding shares) and it has Rs 100 crore AAA-rated debt. The current yield on the AAA-rated bonds is 8.1 per cent. The market value of the company's equity is Rs 500 crore. The company has an equity beta of 1.05. Sunshine has an estimated cost of equity of 18 per cent. The market risk premium is 10 per cent.

Sunlight's business has confined mostly to major cities in the Northern India. The company has plans to expand its business to the Western India. This will require substantial capital expenditure to enhance production capacity. The managing director is aware that the company will take one or two years to build the customer base, and hence, the profitability will suffer temporarily.

The managing director felt that at the current debt-equity ratio of 1:5, his company was conservatively financed. He thought he could create more value for his shareholders by adding more debt. He felt his company could easily have a debt-equity ratio of 2:5. He was interested to know the worth of his company's shares today based on his future plans of expansion, profitability improvement and enhanced debt capacity. He asked the finance department staff to make estimates and work out the value of the company's shares. The finance department estimated that the company would require about Rs 125 crore to expand

and modernise its facilities. This amount will be spent in two years on plant and machinery, but it will improve sales and profits after two years.

Table 16.2.1 shows estimates of sales and profits prepared by Sunlight's finance department. These forecasts are based on capital expenditures to expand facilities, modernise the plants, to improve their efficiency and to maintain the existing facilities. The company would also invest in working capital for financing inventory and debtors (Table 16.2.2). The company's sales and profits in 2004 were Rs 191 crore and Rs 9.6 crore. The company did not incur any capital expenditure, but the net working capital was Rs 67 crore. The company has planned major capital expenditures in the beginning of 2005 and 2006.

Sunlight's finance staff assumed that after 2014 the capital expenditure would equal the depreciation amount, and the company's sales might grow at about 3-5 per cent and it may earn about 10 per cent after-tax cash flows on sales indefinitely. But the finance staff also considered a more conservative scenario, which acknowledged increased competition and as a consequence, the company might be just able to maintain its sales without much growth.

Discussion Questions

1. Calculate free cash flows. Assume tax rate of 35 per cent.
2. Determine the appropriate discount rate to find the present value of the free cash flows.
3. What value will you assign to the company's operations after 2014? Justify your answer.
4. What is the value of the firm? What is the value per equity share? Why do you think there is a difference between this value and the current market value of the firm's share?

Table 16.2.1: Sales and Profits Forecasts

(Rs in crore)

Year	2005	2006	2007	2008	2009	2010	2011	2012	2013	2014
Sales	202.30	224.91	281.14	334.55	386.07	443.99	497.26	546.99	601.69	649.83
Cash expenses	161.27	173.70	204.63	234.00	262.34	294.19	323.50	350.84	380.93	407.40
Depreciation	135.92	105.20	77.72	59.63	44.72	34.29	26.05	20.10	15.52	12.15

Table 16.2.2: Capital Expenditure and NWC

(Rs in crore)

Year	2005	2006	2007	2008	2009	2010	2011	2012	2013	2014
Capex	75.00	50.00	20.60	18.80	18.00	16.60	15.00	16.20	13.20	13.50
NWC	70.81	78.72	98.40	117.09	130.18	144.28	151.50	159.07	167.03	175.38

CHAPTER 17

Dividend Theory

CHAPTER OBJECTIVES

- Highlight the issues of dividend policy
- Critically evaluate why some experts feel that dividend policy matters
- Discuss the bird-in-the-hand argument for paying current dividends
- Explain the logic of the dividend irrelevance
- Identify the market imperfections that make dividend policy relevant

INTRODUCTION

Dividend decision of the firm is yet another crucial area of financial management. The important aspect of dividend policy is to determine the amount of earnings to be distributed to shareholders and the amount to be retained in the firm. Retained earnings are the most significant internal sources of financing the growth of the firm. On the other hand, dividends may be considered desirable from shareholders' point of view as they tend to increase their current return. Dividends, however, constitute the use of the firm's funds.

ISSUES IN DIVIDEND POLICY

In theory, the objective of a dividend policy should be to maximise a shareholder's return so that the value of his investment is maximised. Shareholders' return consists of two components: dividends and capital gains. Dividend policy has a direct influence on these two components of return.

Let us consider an example to highlight the issues underlying the dividend policy. **Payout ratio**—which is dividend as a percentage of earnings—is an important concept vis-à-vis the dividend policy. 100 per cent minus payout percentage is called **retention ratio**. Suppose two companies, Low Payout Company and High Payout Company, both have a return on equity (ROE) of 20 per cent. Assume that both companies' equity consists of one share each of Rs 100. High Payout Company distributes 80 per cent while Low Payout Company distributes 20 per cent of its earnings as dividends. As

you may recall, growth rate is the product of return on equity (ROE) times retention ratio (b):

$$\text{Growth} = \text{ROE} \times \text{Retention ratio}$$
$$g = \text{ROE} \times b$$

For Low Payout Company, the growth rate is:

$$g = 0.20 \times 0.80 = 0.16 \text{ or } 16\%$$

For High Payout Company the growth rate will be:

$$g = 0.20 \times 0.20 = 0.04 \text{ or } 4\%$$

It may be seen from Table 17.1 that High Payout's dividend is initially four times that of Low Payout's. However, over a long period of time, Low Payout overtakes High Payout's dividend payments. As shown in Figure 17.1, in our example, fourteenth year onwards Low Payout's dividend exceeds that of High Payout. Note that Low Payout retains much more than High Payout, and as a consequence, High Payout's earnings, dividends and equity investment are growing at 16 per cent while that of Low Payout's at 4 per cent only.

A low payout policy might produce a higher share price because it accelerates earnings growth. Investors of growth companies will realise their return mostly in the form of **capital gains. Dividend yield**—dividend per share divided by the market price per share—will be low for such companies. The impact of dividend policy on future capital gains is, however, complex.

Table 17.1: Consequences of High and Low Payout Policies

Year	Equity Rs	Earnings at 20% Rs	Dividends Rs	Retained Earnings Rs
High Payout Company				
1	100.00	20.00	16.00	4.00
2	104.00	20.80	16.64	4.16
3	108.16	21.63	17.31	4.32
4	112.48	22.50	18.00	4.50
5	116.98	23.40	18.72	4.68
10	142.33	28.47	22.77	5.69
15	173.17	34.63	27.71	6.92
20	210.68	42.14	33.71	8.43
Low Payout Company				
1	100.00	20.00	4.00	16.00
2	116.00	23.20	4.64	18.56
3	134.56	26.91	5.38	21.53
4	156.09	31.22	6.24	24.98
5	181.07	36.21	7.24	28.97
10	380.30	76.06	15.21	60.85
15	798.75	159.75	31.95	127.80
20	1,677.65	335.53	67.11	268.42

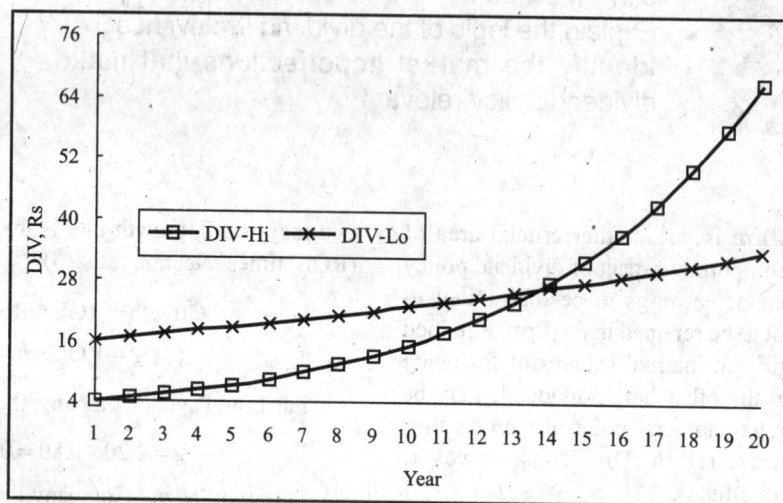

Figure 17.1: Dividend per share under high and low payout policies

Capital gains occur in distant future, and therefore, many people consider them uncertain. It is not sure that low-payout policy will necessarily lead to higher prices in reality. It is quite difficult to clearly identify the effect of payout on share price. Share price is a reflection of so many factors that the long-run effect of payout is quite difficult to isolate.

A high payout policy means more current dividends and less retained earnings, which may consequently result in slower growth and *perhaps* lower market price per share. As stated earlier, low payout policy means less current dividends, more retained earnings and higher capital gains and *perhaps* higher market price per share. Capital gains are future earnings while dividends are current earnings. Dividends in most countries are taxed more than capital gains.[1] Therefore, it is quite plausible that some investors would prefer high-payout companies while others may prefer low-payout companies.

What does dividend policy imply? Paying dividends involves outflow of cash. The cash available for the payment of dividends is affected by the firm's investment and financing decisions. A decision to incur capital expenditure implies that less cash will be available for the payment of dividends. Thus, investment decision affects dividend decision. If the firm's value is affected, is it because of the investment decision or the dividend decision? Given the firm's capital expenditure, and that it does not have sufficient internal funds to pay dividends, it can raise funds by issuing new shares. In this case, the dividend

---

1. In India, there is no personal tax on dividends and short-term capital gains while the long-term capital gains as taxed at 10 per cent.

decision is not separable from the firm's financing decision.

The firm will have a given amount of cash available for paying dividends given its investment and financing decisions. Thus, a dividend decision involves a trade-off between the retained earnings and issuing new shares. It is essential to separate the effect of dividend changes from the effects of investment and financing decisions. Do changes in dividend policy alone affect the value of the firm? What factors are important in formulating a dividend policy in practice?

On the relationship between dividend policy and the value of the firm, different theories have been advanced. These theories can be grouped into two categories: (*a*) theories that consider dividend decision to be irrelevant and (*b*) theories that consider dividend decision to be an active variable influencing the value of the firm. In the latter, there are two extreme views, that is: (*i*) dividends are good as they increase the shareholder value; (*ii*) dividends are bad since they reduce the shareholder value. The following is the critical evaluation of some important theories representing these points of views.

DIVIDEND RELEVANCE: WALTER'S MODEL

Professor James E. Walter argues that the choice of dividend policies almost always affect the value of the firm.[1] His model, one of the earlier theoretical works, shows the importance of the relationship between the firm's rate of return, r, and its cost of capital, k, in determining the dividend policy that will maximise the wealth of shareholders. Walter's model is based on the following assumptions:[2]

- **Internal financing** The firm finances all investment through retained earnings; that is, debt or new equity is not issued.
- **Constant return and cost of capital** The firm's rate of return, r, and its cost of capital, k, are constant.
- **100 per cent payout or retention** All earnings are either distributed as dividends or reinvested internally immediately.
- **Constant EPS and DIV** Beginning earnings and dividends never change. The values of the earnings per share, EPS, and the dividend per share, DIV, may be changed in the model to determine results, but any given values of EPS or DIV are assumed to remain constant forever in determining a given value.
- **Infinite time** The firm has a very long or infinite life.

Walter's formula to determine the market price per share is as follows:

$$P = \frac{DIV}{k} + \frac{r(EPS - DIV)/k}{k} \qquad (1)$$

where
P = market price per share
DIV = dividend per share
EPS = earnings per share
r = firm's rate of return (average)
k = firm's cost of capital or capitalisation rate

Equation (1) reveals that the market price per share is the sum of the present value of two sources of income: (*i*) the present value of the infinite stream of constant dividends, DIV/k and (*ii*) the present value of the infinite stream of capital gains, [r (EPS – DIV)/k]/k. When the firm retains a perpetual sum of (EPS – DIV) at r rate of return, its present value will be: r (EPS – DIV)/k. This quantity can be known as a capital gain which occurs when earnings are retained within the firm. If this retained earnings occur every year, the present value of an infinite number of capital gains, r (EPS – DIV)/k, will be equal to: [r (EPS – DIV)/k]/k. Thus, the value of a share is the present value of all dividends plus the present value of all capital gains as shown in Equation (1) which can be rewritten as follows:

$$P = \frac{DIV + (r/k)(EPS - DIV)}{k} \qquad (2)$$

Illustration 17.1: Dividend Policy: Application of Walter's Model

To illustrate the effect of different dividend policies on the value of share respectively for the growth firm, normal firm and declining firm Table 17.2 is constructed.

Table 17.2 shows that, in Walter's model, the optimum dividend policy depends on the relationship between the firm's rate of return, r and its cost of capital, k. Walter's view on the optimum dividend–payout ratio is explained in the next section.[3]

Growth Firm: Internal Rate More Than Opportunity Cost of Capital ($r > k$)

Growth firms are those firms which expand rapidly because of ample investment opportunities yielding returns higher than the opportunity cost of capital. These firms are able to reinvest earnings at a rate (r) which is higher than the rate expected by shareholders (k). They will maximise the value per share if they follow a policy of retaining all earnings for internal investment. It can be seen from Table 17.2 that the market value per share for the growth firm is maximum (i.e., Rs 150) when it retains 100 per cent earnings and minimum (i.e., Rs 100) if it distributes all earnings. Thus, the optimum payout ratio for a growth firm is zero. The market value per share P, increases as payout ratio declines when $r > k$.

Normal Firms: Internal Rate Equals Opportunity Cost of Capital ($r = k$)

Most of the firms do not have unlimited surplus-generating investment opportunities, yielding returns higher than the opportunity cost of capital. After exhausting super profitable opportunities, these firms earn on their investments rate of return equal to the cost of capital, $r = k$. For **normal firms** with $r = k$, the dividend policy has no effect on the market value per share in Walter's model. It can be noticed from Table 17.2 that the market value per share for the normal firm is same (i.e., Rs 100) for different dividend-payout ratios. Thus, there is no unique optimum payout ratio for a normal firm. One dividend policy is as good as the other. The market value per share is not affected by the payout ratio when $r = k$.

1. Walter, James E., Dividend Policy: Its Influence on the Value of the Enterprise, *Journal of Finance*, 18 May, 1963, p. 280–91.
2. Francis, Jack Clark, *Investments: Analysis and Management*, McGraw Hill, 1972, p. 344.
3. Walter, *op. cit.*, also, see Francis, *op. cit.*

Table 17.2: Dividend Policy and the Value of Share (Walter's Model)

Growth Firm, r > k	Normal Firm, r = k	Declining Firm, r < k
	Basic Data	
$r = 0.15$	$r = 0.10$	$r = 0.08$
$k = 0.10$	$k = 0.10$	$k = 0.10$
EPS = Rs 10	EPS = Rs 10	EPS = Rs 10
Payout Ratio 0%		
DIV = Re 0	DIV = Re 0	DIV = Re 0
$P = 0 + (0.15/0.10)(10-0)/0.10$	$P = 0 + [(0.10/0.10)(10-0)]/0.10$	$P = 0 + [(0.08/0.10)(10-0)]/0.10$
$= Rs\ 150$	$= Rs\ 100$	$= Rs\ 80$
Payout Ratio 40%		
DIV = Rs 4	DIV = Rs 4	DIV = Rs 4
$P = [4 + (0.15/0.10)(10-4)]/0.10$	$P = [4 + (0.10/0.10)(10-4)]/0.10$	$P = [4 + (0.08/0.10)(10-4)]/0.10$
$= Rs\ 130$	$= Rs\ 100$	$= Rs\ 88$
Payout Ratio 80%		
DIV = Rs 8	DIV = Rs 8	DIV = Rs 8
$P = [8 + (0.15/0.10)(10-8)]/0.10$	$P = [8 + (0.10/0.10)(10-8)]/0.10$	$P = [8 + (0.08/0.10)(10-8)]/0.10$
$= Rs\ 110$	$= Rs\ 100$	$= Rs\ 96$
Payout Ratio 100%		
DIV = Rs 10	DIV = Rs 10	DIV = Rs 10
$P = [10 + (0.15/0.10)(10-10)]/0.10$	$P = [10 + (0.10/0.10)(10-10)]/0.10$	$P = [10 + (0.08/0.10)(10-10)]/0.10$
$= Rs\ 100$	$= Rs\ 100$	$= Rs\ 100$

Declining Firms: Internal Rate Less Than Opportunity Cost of Capital ($r < k$)

Declining firms do not have any profitable investment opportunities to invest the earnings. These firms would earn on their investments rates of return less than the minimum rate required by investors. Investors of such firm would like earnings to be distributed to them so that they may either spend it or invest elsewhere to get a rate higher than earned by the declining firms. The market value per share of a declining firm with $r < k$ will be maximum when it does not retain earnings at all. It can be observed from Table 17.2 that, when the declining firm's payout ratio is 100 per cent (i.e., zero retained earnings) the market value per share is Rs 100 and it is Rs 80 when payout ratio is zero. Thus, the optimum payout ratio for a declining firm is 100 per cent. The market value per share, P, increases as payout ratio increases when $r < k$.

Thus, in Walter's model, the dividend policy of the firm depends on the availability of investment opportunities and the relationship between the firm's internal rate of return, r and its cost of capital, k. Thus:

- Retain all earnings when $r > k$
- Distribute all earnings when $r < k$
- Dividend (or retention) policy has no effect when $r = k$.

Thus, dividend policy in Walter's model is a financing decision. When dividend policy is treated as a financing decision, the payment of cash dividends is a **passive residual**.[1]

Criticism of Walter's Model

Walter's model is quite useful to show the effects of dividend policy on all equity firms under different assumptions about the rate of return. However, the simplified nature of the model can lead to conclusions that are not true in general, though true for the model. The following is a critical evaluation of some of the assumptions underlying the model.

No external financing Walter's model of share valuation *mixes* dividend policy with investment policy of the firm. The model assumes that retained earnings finance the investment opportunities of the firm and no external financing—debt or equity—is used for the purpose. When such a situation exists, either the firm's investment or its dividend policy or both will be sub-optimum. This is shown graphically in Figure 17.2.[2] The horizontal axis represents the amount of earnings, investment and new financing in rupees. The vertical axis shows the rates of return and the cost of capital. It is assumed that the cost of capital, k, remains constant regardless of the amount of new capital raised.

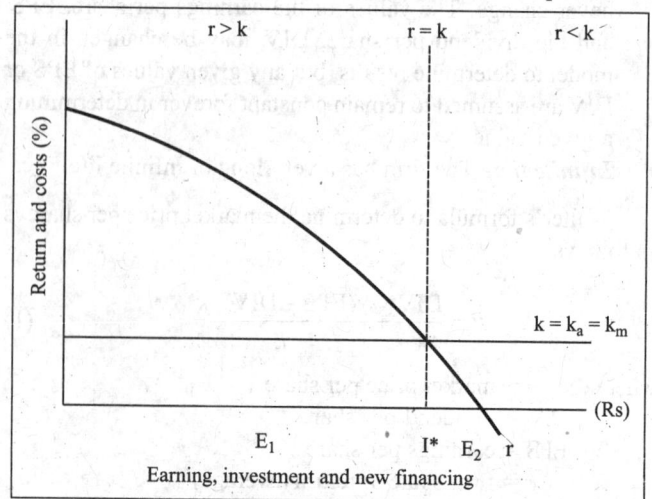

Figure 17.2

1. Solomon, Ezra, *The Theory of Financial Management*, Columbia Press, 1963, pp. 139–40.
2. Francis, *op. cit.*, p. 347.

Thus, the average cost of capital k_a is equal to the marginal cost of capital, k_m. The rates of return on investment opportunities available to the firm are assumed to be decreasing. This implies that the most profitable investments will be made first and the poorer investments made last. In Figure 17.2, I^* rupees of investment occurs where $r = k$. I^* is the optimum investment regardless of whether the capital to finance this investment is raised by selling shares, debentures, retaining earnings or obtaining a loan. If the firm's earnings are E_1, then $(I^* - E_1)$ amount should be raised to finance the investments. However, external financing is not included in Walter's simplified model. Thus, for this situation Walter's model would show that the owner's wealth is maximised by retaining and investing firm's total earnings of E_1 and paying no dividends. In a more comprehensive model allowing for outside financing, the firm should raise new funds to finance I^* investment. The wealth of the owners will be maximised only when this optimum investment is made.

Constant return, r Walter's model is based on the assumption that r is constant. In fact, r decreases as more and more investment is made. This reflects the assumption that the most profitable investments are made first and then the poorer investments are made. The firm should stop at a point where $r = k$. In Figure 17.2, the optimum point of investment occurs at I^* where $r = k$; if the firm's earnings are E_2 it should pay dividends equal to $(E_2 - I)^*$; on the other hand, Walter's model indicates that, if the firm's earnings are E_2, they should be distributed because $r < k$ at E_2. This is clearly an erroneous policy and will fail to optimise the wealth of the owners.

Constant opportunity cost of capital, k A firm's cost of capital or discount rate, k, does not remain constant; it changes directly with the firm's risk. Thus, the present value of the firm's income moves inversely with the cost of capital. By assuming that the discount rate, k, is constant, Walter's model abstracts from the effect of risk on the value of the firm.

DIVIDEND RELEVANCE: GORDON'S MODEL

Myron Gordon develops one very popular model explicitly relating the market value of the firm to dividend policy.[1] Gordon's model is based on the following assumptions:[2]

- **All-equity firm** The firm is an all-equity firm, and it has no debt.
- **No external financing** No external financing is available. Consequently, retained earnings would be used to finance any expansion. Thus, just as Walter's model Gordon's model too confounds dividend and investment policies.
- **Constant return** The internal rate of return, r, of the firm is constant. This ignores the diminishing marginal efficiency of investment as represented in Figure 17.2.
- **Constant cost of capital** The appropriate discount rate k for the firm remains constant. Thus, Gordon's model also

ignores the effect of a change in the firm's risk-class and its effect on k.
- **Perpetual earnings** The firm and its stream of earnings are perpetual.
- **No taxes** Corporate taxes do not exist.
- **Constant retention** The retention ratio, b, once decided upon, is constant. Thus, the growth rate, $g = br$, is constant forever.
- **Cost of capital greater than growth rate** The discount rate is greater than growth rate, $k > br = g$. If this condition is not fulfilled, we cannot get a meaningful value for the share.

According to Gordon's dividend-capitalisation model, the market value of a share is equal to the present value of an infinite stream of dividends received by the shareholders as explained earlier in Chapter 3. Thus:

$$P_0 = \frac{DIV_1}{(1+k)} + \frac{DIV_2}{(1+k)^2} + \cdots + \frac{DIV_\infty}{(1+k)^\infty} = \sum_{t=1}^{\infty} \frac{DIV_t}{(1+k)^t} \qquad (3)$$

However, the dividend per share is expected to grow when earnings are retained. The dividend per share is equal to the payout ratio, $(1 - b)$ times earnings per share, EPS; that is, $DIV_t = (1 - b) EPS_t$ where b is the fraction of retained earnings. It is assumed that the retained earnings are reinvested within the all-equity firm at the firm's internal rate of return, r. This allows earnings to grow at $g = br$ per period. When we incorporate growth in earnings and dividends, resulting from the retained earnings, in the dividend-capitalisation model, the present value of a share is determined by the following formula:

$$P_0 = \frac{DIV(1+g)}{(1+k)} + \frac{DIV(1+g)^2}{(1+k)^2} + \frac{DIV(1+g)^3}{(1+k)^3}$$
$$+ \cdots + \frac{DIV(1+g)^\infty}{(1+k)^\infty}$$
$$= \sum_{t=1}^{\infty} \frac{DIV(1+g)^t}{(1+k)^t} \qquad (4)$$

When Equation (4) is solved it becomes:

$$P_0 = \frac{DIV_1}{k - g} \qquad (5)$$

Substituting $EPS_1 (1 - b)$ for DIV_1 and br for g, Equation (5) can be rewritten as

$$P_0 = \frac{EPS_1(1 - b)}{k - br} \qquad (6)$$

Equation (6) explicitly shows the relationship of expected earnings per share, EPS_1, dividend policy as reflected by retention ratio, b, internal profitability, r, and the all-equity firm's cost of capital, k, in the determination of the value of the share. Equation (6) is particularly useful for studying the effects of dividend policy on the value of the share.

1. Gordon, Myron J., *The Investment, Financing and Valuation of Corporation*, Richard D. Irwin, 1962.
2. Francis, op. *cit.*, p. 352.

Let us consider the case of a normal firm where the internal rate of return of the firm equals its cost of capital, i.e., $r = k$. Under this situation, Equation (6) may be expressed as follows:

$$P_0 = \frac{EPS_1(1-b)}{k-br} = \frac{rA(1-b)}{k-br} \qquad (7)$$

(since $EPS = rA$, A = assets per share)

If $r = k$, then

$$P_0 = \frac{EPS_1(1-b)}{k-br} = \frac{rA(1-b)}{k-br} = \frac{EPS}{k} = \frac{rA}{r} = A \qquad (8)$$

Equation (8) shows that regardless of the firm's earnings per share, EPS_1, or risk (which determines k), the firm's value is not affected by dividend policy and is equal to the book value of assets per share. That is, when $r = k$, dividend policy is irrelevant since b, completely cancels out of Equation (8). Interpreted in economic sense, this finding implies that, under competitive conditions, the opportunity cost of capital, k, must be equal to the rate of return generally available to investors in comparable shares. This means that any funds distributed as dividends may be invested in the market at the rate equal to the firm's internal rate of return. Consequently, shareholders can neither lose nor gain by any change in the company's dividend policy, and the market value of their shares must remain unchanged.[1]

Considering the case of the declining firm where $r < k$, Equation (8) indicates that, if the retention ratio, b, is zero or payout ratio, $(1-b)$, is 100 per cent the value of the share is equal to:

$$P_0 = \frac{rA}{k} \qquad (b = 0) \qquad (9)$$

If $r < k$ then $r/k < 1$ and from Equation (9) it follows that P_0 is smaller than the firm's investment per share in assets, A. It can be shown that if the value of b increases, the value of the share continuously falls.[2] These results may be interpreted as follows:

If the internal rate of return is smaller than k, which is equal to the rate available in the market, profit retention clearly becomes undesirable from the shareholders' standpoint. Each additional rupee (sic) retained reduces the amount of funds that shareholders could invest at a higher rate elsewhere and thus further depresses the value of the company's share. Under such conditions, the company should adopt a policy of contraction and disinvestment, which would allow the owner to transfer not only the net profit but also paid in capital (or a part of it) to some other, more remunerative enterprise.[3]

Finally, let us consider the case of a growth firm where $r > k$. The value of a share will increase as the retention ratio, b, increases under the condition of $r > k$. However, it is not clear as to what the value of b should be to maximise the value of the

share, P_0. For example, if $b = k/r$, Equation (6) reveals that denominator, $k - br = 0$, thus making P_0 infinitely large, and if $b = 1$, $k - br$ becomes negative, thus making P_0 negative. These absurd results are obtained because of the assumption that r and k are constant, which underlie the model. Thus, to get the meaningful value of the share, according to Equation (6), the value of b should be less than k/r. Gordon's model is illustrated in Illustration 17.2.

Illustration 17.2 : Application of Gordon's Dividend Model

Let us consider the data in Table 17.3 on the next page. The implications of dividend policy, according to Gordon's model, are shown respectively for the growth, the normal and the declining firms.

It is revealed that under Gordon's model:

- The market value of the share, P_0, increases with the retention ratio, b, for firms with growth opportunities, i.e. when $r > k$.
- The market value of the share, P_0, increases with the payout ratio, $(1-b)$, for declining firms with $r < k$.
- The market value of the share is not affected by dividend policy when $r = k$.

Gordon's model's conclusions about dividend policy are similar to that of Walter's model. This similarity is due to the similarities of assumptions that underlie both the models. Thus the Gordon model suffers from the same limitations as the Walter model.

DIVIDENDS AND UNCERTAINTY: THE BIRD-IN-THE-HAND ARGUMENT

According to Gordon's model, dividend policy is irrelevant where $r = k$, when all other assumptions are held valid. But when the simplifying assumptions are modified to conform more closely to reality, Gordon concludes that dividend policy *does affect* the value of a share even when $r = k$. This view is based on the assumption that under conditions of uncertainty, investors tend to discount distant dividends (capital gains) at a higher rate than they discount near dividends. Investors, behaving rationally, are risk-averse and, therefore, have a preference for near dividends to future dividends. The logic underlying the *dividend effect* on the share value can be described as the **bird-in-the-hand argument**. Kirshman, first of all, put forward the bird-in-the-hand argument in the following words:

Of two stocks with identical earnings record, and prospects but the one paying a larger dividend than the other, the former will undoubtedly command a higher price merely because stockholders prefer present to future values. Myopic vision plays a part in the price-making process. Stockholders often act upon the principle that a bird in the hand is worth two in the bush and for this reason are willing to pay a premium for the stock with the higher dividend rate, just as they discount the one with the lower rate.[4]

1. Dobrovolsky, Sergie P., *The Economics of Corporation Finance,* McGraw Hill, 1971, p. 55.
2. *Ibid.*, p. 56.
3. *Ibid.*
4. Krishman, John, E., *Principles of Investment.* McGraw Hill, 1933, p. 737; cf. in Mao, J.C.T., *Quantitative Analysis of Financial Decision,* Macmillan, 1969.

Table 17.3: Dividend Policy and the Value of the Firm

Growth Firm, r > k	*Normal Firm, r = k*	*Declining Firm, r < k*
	Basic Data	
$r = 0.15$	$r = 0.10$	$r = 0.08$
$k = 0.10$	$k = 0.10$	$k = 0.10$
$EPS_1 = Rs\ 10$	$EPS_1 = Rs\ 10$	$EPS_1 = Rs\ 10$

Payout Ratio 40%

$g = br = 0.6 \times 0.15 = 0.09$	$g = br = 0.6 \times 0.10 = 0.06$	$g = br = 0.6 \times 0.08 = 0.048$
$P = \dfrac{10(1 - 0.6)}{0.10 - 0.09}$	$P = \dfrac{10(1 - 0.6)}{0.10 - 0.06}$	$P = \dfrac{10(1 - 0.6)}{0.10 - 0.048}$
$= \dfrac{4}{0.01} = Rs\ 400$	$= \dfrac{4}{0.04} = Rs\ 100$	$= \dfrac{4}{0.052} = Rs\ 77$

Payout Ratio 60%

$g = br = 0.4 \times 0.15 = 0.06$	$g = br = 0.4 \times 0.10 = 0.04$	$g = br = 0.4 \times 0.08 = 0.032$
$P = \dfrac{10(1 - 0.4)}{0.10 - 0.06}$	$P = \dfrac{10(1 - 0.4)}{0.10 - 0.04}$	$P = \dfrac{10(1 - 0.4)}{0.10 - 0.032}$
$= \dfrac{6}{0.04} = Rs\ 150$	$= \dfrac{6}{0.06} = Rs\ 100$	$= \dfrac{6}{0.068} = Rs\ 88$

Payout Ratio 90%

$g = br = 0.10 \times 0.15 = 0.015$	$g = br = 0.10 \times 0.10 = 0.01$	$g = br = 0.10 \times 0.08 = 0.008$
$P = \dfrac{10(1 - 0.1)}{0.10 - 0.015}$	$P = \dfrac{10(1 - 0.1)}{0.10 - 0.01}$	$P = \dfrac{10(1 - 0.1)}{0.10 - 0.008}$
$= \dfrac{9}{0.085} = Rs\ 106$	$= \dfrac{9}{0.09} = Rs\ 100$	$= \dfrac{9}{0.092} = Rs\ 98$

Graham and Dodd also hold a similar view when they state:

The typical investor would most certainly prefer to have his dividend today and let tomorrow take care of itself. No instances are on record in which the withholding of dividends for the sake of future profits has been hailed with such enthusiasm as to advance the price of the stock. The direct opposite has invariably been true. *Given two companies in the same general position and with the same earning power, the one paying the larger dividend will always sell at a higher price.*[1] (Emphasis added)

Myron Gordon has expressed the bird-in-the-hand argument more convincingly and in formal terms. According to him, uncertainty increases with futurity; that is, the further one looks into the future, the more uncertain dividends become. Accordingly, when dividend policy is considered in the context of uncertainty, the appropriate discount rate, k, cannot be assumed to be constant. In fact, it increases with uncertainty; investors prefer to avoid uncertainty and would be willing to pay higher price for the share that pays the greater current dividend, all other things held constant. In other words, the appropriate discount rate would increase with the retention rate as shown in Figure 17.2. Thus, distant dividends would be discounted at a higher rate than near dividends. Symbolically, $k_t > k_{t-1}$ for $t = 1, 2, 3, \ldots$ because of increasing uncertainty in the future. As the discount rate increases with the length of time, a low dividend payment in the beginning will tend to lower the value of share in future.

When the discount rate is assumed to be increasing, Equation (3) can be rewritten as follows:

$$P_0 = \frac{DIV_1}{(1 + k_1)} + \frac{DIV_2}{(1 + k_2)^2} + \frac{DIV_3}{(1 + k_3)^3} + \cdots + \frac{DIV_n}{(1 + k_n)^n}$$

$$= \sum_{t=1}^{\infty} \frac{DIV_t}{(1 + k_t)^t} \tag{10}$$

where P_0 is the price of the share when the retention rate, b, is zero and $k_t > k_{t-1}$. If the firm is assumed to retain a fraction b of earnings, dividend per share will be equal to $(1 - b)\,EPS_1$ in the first year. Thus, the dividend per share is expected to grow at rate $g = br$, when retained earnings are reinvested at r rate of return. The dividend in the second year will be $DIV_0(1 + g)^2 = (1 - b)\,EPS_1(1 + br)^2$, in the third year $DIV_0(1 + g)^3 = (1 + b)\,EPS_2(1 + br)^3$ and so on. Discounting this stream of dividends at the corresponding discount rates of $k_1, k_2 \ldots$ we obtain the following equation:

$$P_b = \frac{DIV_0(1 + g)^1}{(1 + k_1)^1} + \frac{DIV_0(1 + g)^2}{(1 + k_2)^2} + \cdots + \frac{DIV_0(1 + g)^n}{(1 + k_n)^n} \tag{11}$$

where P_b is the price of the share when the retention rate b is positive i.e., $b > 0$. The value of P_b calculated in this way can be determined by discounting this dividend stream at the uniform

---

1. Graham, Benjamin and David L. Dodd, *Security Analysis.*; McGraw Hill, Inc., 1st ed., 1934, p. 327.

rate, k', which is the weighted average of k_i:[1]

$$P_b = \frac{DIV_0(1+g)}{(1+k')} + \frac{DIV_0(1+g)^2}{(1+k')^2} + \cdots + \frac{DIV_0(1+g)^n}{(1+k')^n}$$

$$= \frac{DIV_1}{k'-g} = \frac{(1-b)EPS_1}{k'-br} \qquad (12)$$

Assuming that the firm's rate of return equals the discount rate, will P_b be higher or lower than P_0? Gordon's view, as explained above, is that the *increase* in earnings retention will result in a lower value of share. To emphasise, he reached this conclusion through two assumptions regarding investors' behaviour: (*i*) investors are risk averters and (*ii*) they consider distant dividends as less certain than near dividends. On the basis of these assumptions, Gordon concludes that the rate at which an investor discounts dividend stream increases with the futurity of this dividend stream. If investors discount distant dividend at a higher rate than near dividends, increasing the retention ratio has the effect of raising the average discount rate, k', or equivalently lowering share prices.

Thus, incorporating uncertainty into his model, Gordon concludes that dividend policy affects the value of the share. His reformulation of the model justifies the behaviour of investors who value a rupee of dividend income more than a rupee of capital gains income. These investors prefer dividend above capital gains because dividends are easier to predict, are less uncertain and less risky, and are therefore, discounted with a lower discount rate.[2] However, all do not agree with this view.

DIVIDEND IRRELEVANCE: THE MILLER-MODIGLIANI (MM) HYPOTHESIS

According to Miller and Modigliani (MM), under a perfect market situation, the dividend policy of a firm is irrelevant, as it does not affect the value of the firm.[3] They argue that the value of the firm depends on the firm's earnings that result from its investment policy. Thus, when investment decision of the firm is given, dividend decision—the split of earnings between dividends and retained earnings—is of no significance in determining the value of the firm.

A firm, operating in perfect capital market conditions, may face one of the following three situations regarding the payment of dividends:

- The firm has sufficient cash to pay dividends.
- The firm does not have sufficient cash to pay dividends, and therefore, it issues new shares to finance the payment of dividends.
- The firm does not pay dividends, but a shareholder needs cash.

In the first situation, when the firm pays dividends, shareholders get cash in their hands, but the firm's assets reduce (its cash balance declines). What shareholders gain in the form of cash dividends, they lose in the form of their claims on the (reduced) assets. Thus, there is a transfer of wealth from shareholders' one pocket to their another pocket. There is no net gain or loss. Since it is a fair transaction under perfect capital market conditions, the value of the firm will remain unaffected.

In the second situation, when the firm issues new shares to finance the payment of dividends, two transactions take place. First, the existing shareholders get cash in the form of dividends, but they suffer an equal amount of capital loss since the value of their claim on assets reduces. Thus, the wealth of shareholders does not change. Second, the new shareholders part with their cash to the company in exchange for new shares at a **fair price per share**. The fair price per share is share price before the payment of dividends less dividend per share to the existing shareholders. The existing shareholders transfer a part of their claim (in the form of new shares) to the new shareholders in exchange for cash. There is no net gain or loss. Both transactions are fair, and thus, the value of the firm will remain unaltered after these transactions.

In the third situation, if the firm does not pay any dividend a shareholder can create a "**home-made dividend**" by selling a part of his/her shares at the market (fair) price in the capital market for obtaining cash. The shareholder will have less number of shares. He or she has exchanged a part of his claim on the firm to a new shareholder for cash. The net effect is the same as in the case of the second situation. The transaction is a fair transaction, and no one loses or gains. The value of the firm remains the same, before or after these transactions. Consider an example.

Illustration 17.3: Dividend Irrelevance: The Miller-Modigliani Hypothesis

The Himgir Company Limited currently has 2 crore outstanding shares selling at a market price of Rs 100 per share. The firm has no borrowing. It has internal funds available to make a capital expenditure (capex) of Rs 30 crore. The capex is expected to yield a positive net present value of Rs 20 crore. The firm also wants to pay a dividend per share of Rs 15. Given the firm's capex plan and its policy of zero borrowing, the firm will have to issue new shares to finance payment of dividends to its shareholders. How will the firm's value be affected (i) if it does not pay any dividend; (ii) if it pays dividend per share Rs 15?

The firm's current value is: $2 \times 100 = $ Rs 200 crore. After the capex, the value will increase to: $200 + 20 = $ Rs 220 crore. If the firm does not pay dividends, the value per share will be: $220/2 = $ Rs 110.

If the firm pays a dividend of Rs 15 per share, it will entirely utilise its internal funds ($15 \times 2 = $ Rs 30 crore), and it will have to raise Rs 30 crore by issuing new shares to undertake capex. The value of a share after paying dividend will be: $110 - 15 = $ Rs 95. Thus, the existing shareholders get cash of Rs 15 per share in the form of dividends, but incur a capital loss of Rs 15 in the form of reduced share value. They neither gain nor lose. The firm will have to issue: 30 crore/95 = 31,57,895 (about 31.6 lakh) shares to raise Rs 30 crore. The firm now has 2.316 crore shares at Rs 95 each share. Thus, the value of the firm remains as: $2.316 \times 95 = $ Rs 220 crore.

The crux of the MM dividend hypothesis, as explained above,

---

1. Mao, James C.T., *Quantitative Analysis of Financial Decision*, Macmillan, 1969, p. 482.

2. Francis, *op. cit.*, p. 354.

3. Miller, Merton H. and Modigliani, France, Dividend Policy, Growth and Valuation of the Shares, *Journal of Business*, XXIV (October 1961), pp. 411–33.

is that shareholders do not necessarily depend on dividends for obtaining cash. In the absence of taxes, flotation costs and difficulties in selling shares, they can get cash by devising "homemade dividend" without any dilution in their wealth. Therefore, firms paying high dividends (i.e. high-payout firms), need not command higher prices for their shares. A formal explanation of the MM hypothesis is given in the following pages.

MM's hypothesis of irrelevance is based on the following assumptions:[1]

- *Perfect capital markets* The firm operates in perfect capital markets where investors behave rationally, information is freely available to all and transactions and flotation costs do not exist. Perfect capital markets also imply that no investor is large enough to affect the market price of a share.
- *No taxes* Taxes do not exist; or there are no differences in the tax rates applicable to capital gains and dividends. This means that investors value a rupee of dividend as much as a rupee of capital gains.
- *Investment policy* The firm has a fixed investment policy.
- *No risk* Risk of uncertainty does not exist. That is, investors are able to forecast future prices and dividends with certainty, and one discount rate is appropriate for all securities and all time periods. Thus, $r = k = k_t$ for all t.

Under the MM assumptions, r will be equal to the discount rate, k and identical for all shares. As a result, the price of each share must adjust so that the rate of return, which is composed of the rate of dividends and capital gains, on every share will be equal to the discount rate and be identical for all shares. Thus, the rate of return for a share held for one year may be calculated as follows:

$$r = \frac{\text{Dividends} + \text{Capital gains (or loss)}}{\text{Share price}}$$

$$r = \frac{\text{DIV} + (P_1 - P_0)}{P_0} \tag{13}$$

where P_0 is the market or purchase price per share at time 0, P_1 is the market price per share at time 1 and DIV_1 is dividend per share at time 1. As hypothesised by MM, r should be equal for all shares. If it is not so, the low-return yielding shares will be sold by investors who will purchase the high-return yielding shares. This process will tend to reduce the price of the low-return shares and increase the prices of the high-return shares. This **switching or arbitrage** will continue until the differentials in rates of return are eliminated. The discount rate will also be equal for all firms under the MM assumptions since there are no risk differences.

From MM's fundamental principle of valuation described by Equation (13), we can derive their valuation model as follows:

$$r = \frac{\text{DIV}_1 + (P_1 - P_0)}{P_0}$$

$$P_0 = \frac{\text{DIV}_1 + P_1}{(1+r)} = \frac{\text{DIV}_1 + P_1}{(1+k)} \tag{14}$$

since $r = k$ in the assumed world of certainty and perfect markets. Multiplying both sides of Equation (14) by the number of shares outstanding, n, we obtain the total value of the firm if no new financing exists:

$$V = nP_0 = \frac{n(\text{DIV}_1 + P_1)}{(1+k)} \tag{15}$$

If the firm sells m number of new shares at time 1 at a price of P_1, the value of the firm at time 0 will be:

$$nP_0 = \frac{n(\text{DIV}_1 + P_1) + mP_1 - mP_1}{(1+k)}$$

$$= \frac{n\text{DIV}_1 + nP_1 + mP_1 - mP_1}{(1+k)}$$

$$= \frac{n\text{DIV}_1 + (n+m)P_1 - mP_1}{(1+k)} \tag{16}$$

MM's valuation Equation (16) allows for the issue of new shares, unlike Walter's and Gordon's models. Consequently, a firm can pay dividends and raise funds to undertake the optimum investment policy (as explained in Figure 17.1). Thus, dividend and investment policies are not confounded in the MM model, like Walter's and Gordon's models. As such, MM's model yields more general conclusions.

The investment programmes of a firm, in a given period of time, can be financed either by retained earnings or the issue of new shares or both. Thus, the amount of new shares issued will be:

$$mP_1 = I_1 - (X_1 - n\text{DIV}_1) = I_1 - X_1 + n\text{DIV}_1 \tag{17}$$

where I_1 represents the total amount of investment during first period and X_1 is the total net profit of the firm during first period.

By substituting Equation (17) into Equation (16), MM showed that the value of the firm is unaffected by its dividend policy, Thus,

$$nP_0 = \frac{n\text{DIV}_1 + (n+m)P_1 - mP_1}{(1+k)}$$

$$= \frac{n\text{DIV}_1 + (n+m)P_1 - (I_1 - X_1 + n\text{DIV}_1)}{(1+k)}$$

$$= \frac{(n+m)P_1 - I_1 + X_1}{(1+k)}$$

A firm which pays dividends will have to raise funds externally to finance its investment plans. MM's argument, that dividend policy does not affect the wealth of the shareholders, implies that when the firm pays dividends, its advantage is offset by external financing. This means that the terminal value of the share (say, price of the share at first period if the holding period is one year) declines when dividends are paid. Thus, the wealth of the shareholders—dividends plus terminal price—remains unchanged. As a result, the present value per share after dividends and external financing is equal to the present value per share before the payment of dividends. Thus, the shareholders are indifferent between payment of dividends and retention of earnings.

---

1. Francis, *op. cit.*

Illustration 17.4 : Dividend Policy with and without Issue of Shares

The Vikas Engineering Co. Ltd., currently has one lakh outstanding shares selling at Rs 100 each. The firm has net profits of Rs 10 lakh and wants to make new investments of Rs 20 lakh during the period. The firm is also thinking of declaring a dividend of Rs 5 per share at the end of the current fiscal year. The firm's opportunity cost of capital is 10 per cent. What will be the price of the share at the end of the year if (*i*) a dividend is not declared; (*ii*) a dividend is declared. (*iii*) How many new shares must be issued?

The price of the share at the end of the current fiscal year is determined as follows:

$$P_0 = \frac{DIV_1 + P_1}{(1+k)}$$

$$P_1 = P_0(1+k) - DIV_1$$

The value of P_1 when dividend is not paid is:

$$P_1 = Rs\,100(1.10) - 0 = Rs\,110$$

The value of P_1 when dividend is paid is:

$$P_1 = Rs\,100(1.10) - Rs\,5 = Rs\,105$$

It can be observed that whether dividend is paid or not the wealth of shareholders remains the same. When the dividend is not paid the shareholder will get Rs 110 by way of the price per share at the end of the current fiscal year. On the other hand, when dividend is paid, the shareholder will realise Rs 105 by way of the price per share at the end of the current fiscal year *plus* Rs 5 as dividend.

The number of new shares to be issued by the company to finance its investments is determined as follows:

$$mP_1 = I - (X - nDIV_1)$$
$$105m = 2,000,000 - (1,000,000 - 500,000)$$
$$105m = 1,500,000$$
$$m = 1,500,000/105 = 14,285\,shares.$$

RELEVANCE OF DIVIDEND POLICY UNDER MARKET IMPERFECTIONS

The MM hypothesis of dividend irrelevance is based on simplifying assumptions as discussed in the preceding section. Under these assumptions, the conclusion derived by them is logically consistent and intuitively appealing. But the assumptions underlying MM's hypothesis may not always be found valid in practice. For example, we may not find capital markets to be perfect in reality; there may exist issue costs; dividends may be taxed differently than capital gains; investors may encounter difficulties in selling their shares. Because of the unrealistic nature of the assumptions, MM's hypothesis is alleged to lack practical relevance. This suggests that internal financing and external financing are not equivalent. Dividend policy of the firm may affect the perception of shareholders and, therefore, they may not remain indifferent between dividends and capital gains. The following are the situations where the MM hypothesis may go wrong.

Uncertainty and Shareholders' Preference for Dividends

Many believe that dividends are relevant under conditions of **uncertainty**. It is suggested that dividends resolve uncertainty in the minds of investors and, therefore, they prefer dividends than capital gains. As explained earlier, Gordon and others have referred to the argument that dividends are relevant under uncertainty as the bird-in-the-hand argument. Gordon asserts that uncertainty increases with the length of time period. Investors are risk-averters and, therefore, prefer near dividends to future dividends. Thus, future dividends are discounted at a higher rate than near dividends. This implies that the discount rate increases with uncertainty. As a result, a firm paying dividends earlier will command a higher value than a firm which follows a policy of retention. This view implies that there exists a **high-payout clientele** who value shares of dividend paying more than those which do not pay dividends.

The uncertainty argument is not very convincing. MM argue that, even if the assumption of perfect certainty is dropped from their hypothesis, dividend policy continues to be irrelevant. They contend that the market prices of two firms with identical investment and capital structure policies and risk, cannot be different because they follow different dividend policies. These firms will have the same cash flows from their investments despite the differences in dividend policies. The risk (uncertainty) of the firms' shareholders is alike, given the similarities of their risk and investment and capital structure policies. Dividend policy does not change the amount and risk of cash flows from investments; it simply splits these cash flows into dividend payments and retained earnings.

The current receipt of money in the form of dividends is considered safer than the uncertain potential gain in the future. The reason for this safety is that it is cash in hand rather than that it is dividend income and not a capital gain. The shareholders can sell some of their shares to obtain current cash if a firm does not distribute dividends. The risk-return trade-off will make shareholders to expect lower returns from those firms that have high-payout ratios. Let us emphasise again that given a firm's investment and capital structure policies, paying dividends does not affect the firm's or shareholders' risk. Thus the difference between current dividends and the future capital gains does not alter the firm's value under the efficient market conditions. However, there may still exist a high-payout clientele, not because current dividends safer, but because some shareholders need a **steady source of income**, or because some will prefer to receive dividends as early as possible since some firms do not provide reliable information about their investments and earnings.

Yet another reason for shareholders preferring current dividends maybe their desire to diversify their portfolios according to their risk preferences. Hence, they would like firms to distribute earnings. They will be able to invest dividends received in other assets keeping in mind their need for **diversification**. Under these circumstances, investors may discount the value of the firms that use internal financing.

Transaction Costs and the Case against Dividend Payments

MM argue that internal financing (retained earnings) and external financing (issue of shares) are equivalent. This implies that when firms pay dividends, they can finance their investment plans by issuing shares. Whether the firm retains earnings or issues new shares, the wealth of shareholders would remain unaffected. This cannot be true since the issue of shares involve **flotation** or **issue costs**, including costs of preparing and issuing prospectus, underwriting fee, brokers' commission etc. No flotation costs are involved if the earnings are retained. The presence of flotation or **transaction costs** makes the external financing costlier than the internal financing via retained earnings. Thus, if flotation costs are considered, the equivalence between retained earnings and new share capital is disturbed and the retention of earnings would be favoured over the payment of dividends. In practice, dividend decisions seem to be sticky for whatever reasons. Companies continue paying same dividends, rather increasing it, unless earnings decline, in spite of need for funds.

Under the MM hypothesis, the wealth of a shareholder will be same whether the firm pays dividends or not. If a shareholder is not paid dividends and she desires to have current income, she can sell the shares held by her. When the shareholder sells her shares to satisfy her desire for current income, she will have to pay brokerage fee. This fee is more for small sales. Further, it is inconvenient to sell the shares, particularly for investors with small share holdings. Some emerging markets are not very liquid, and many shares are not frequently traded. Because of the transactions costs and inconvenience associated with the sale of shares to realise capital gains, shareholders may prefer dividends to capital gains.

Information Asymmetry and Agency Costs and the Case for Dividend Payments

Managers in practice may not share complete information with shareholders. This gap between information available with managers and what is actually shared with shareholders is called **information asymmetry**. This leads to several agency problems, viz., conflicts between managers and shareholders. Managers may not have enough incentive to disclose full information to shareholders. They may act in their own self-interest and take away the firm's wealth in the form of non-pecuniary benefits. Shareholders incur agency costs to obtain full information about a company's investment plans, future earnings, expected dividend payments etc. The shareholders-managers conflict can be reduced through monitoring which includes bonding contracts and limiting the power of managers vis-à-vis allocation of wealth and managerial compensation.[1] However, monitoring involves costs that are referred to as agency costs. Payment of dividend allocates resources to shareholders, and thus, alleviates the need for monitoring and incurring agency costs.

The high-payout policy of a company helps to reduce the conflict arising out of information asymmetry.[2] It is argued that companies which pay high dividends regularly may be raising capital more frequently from the primary markets. Therefore, the actors in primary markets like the financial institutions and banks would be monitoring the performance of these companies. If the professionals in the banks and financial institutions

continuously do such monitoring, shareholders need not incur monitoring (agency) costs.

Dividend payout also allocates financial resources in favour of shareholders as against lenders. Lenders have prior claims over a company's cash flows generated internally. The payment of dividend changes this priority in favour of shareholders as they receive cash flows before the loan principals of lenders are redeemed. Thus, we observe that from the point of view of agency costs, shareholders would generally prefer payment of dividend.

Tax Differential: Low-Payout and High-Payout Clientele

MM's assumption that taxes do not exist is far from reality. Investors have to pay taxes on dividends and capital gains. But different tax rates are applicable to dividends and capital gains. Dividend income is generally treated as the ordinary income, while capital gains are specially treated for tax purposes. In most countries, the capital gains tax rate is lower than the marginal tax rate for ordinary income. From the tax point of view, a shareholder in high tax bracket should prefer capital gains over current dividends for two reasons: (*i*) the capital gains tax is less than the tax on dividends, and (*ii*) the capital gains tax is payable only when the shares are actually sold. The effect of the favourable tax differential in case of capital gains will result in tax savings. As a consequence, the value of the share should be higher in the internal financing case than in the external financing one. Thus, the tax advantage of capital gains over dividends strongly favours a low-dividend payout policy. This implies that investors will pay more for low-dividend yield shares. Tax differential should attract **tax clienteles**. Investors in high-tax brackets should own low-payout shares, and those in low-tax bracket should own high-payout shares. In reality, most investors may have marginal income tax rate higher than the capital gains tax rate. Thus, dividends, on an average, are considered bad since they will result in higher taxes and reduction in the wealth of shareholders. Tax differential generally favour **low-payout clientele.**

Consider an example. Two identical firms X and Y have different dividend policy. Both have after tax profit, P of Rs 100. X pays 100 per cent dividend. Y does not pay any dividend and shareholders get capital gains. Assume further that capital gains from shares held at least for one year are taxed at 20 per cent and marginal income tax rate is 40 per cent. Suppose Y's shareholders are in highest tax bracket and pay tax on dividend income at 40 per cent. X's shareholders will receive dividends of Rs 100 and their after tax dividend income will be: $100 \times (1 - 0.40) =$ Rs 60. Y's shareholders will realize capital gains of Rs 100 and their after tax capital gains will be: $100 \times (1 - 0.20) =$ Rs 80. Y's shareholders are better off as they have tax advantage. Since the after tax equity income of Y's shareholders is higher than X's shareholders and since both firms are identical in all other respects, Y's equity price will be higher. To match capital gain of Re 1 of Y's shareholders, X's shareholders should receive dividend of Rs 1.33:

1. Jensen, M.C. and Meckling, W.H., Theory of the Firm: Managerial Behaviour, Agency Costs and Ownership Structure, *Journal of Financial Economics*, October 1976.
2. Rozeff, M., Growth, Beta and Agency Cost as Determinants of Dividend Payout Ratios, *Journal of Financial Research*, Fall 1982, pp. 249–59.

After-tax dividend = After-tax capital gain

$$(1 - 0.40)\,DIV = (1 - 0.20)$$

$$DIV = 0.80/0.60 = 1.33$$

If X's shareholders get dividend of Rs 1.33 and Y's shareholders get capital gain of Rs 1, both will have after tax income of Rs 0.80.

If a tax system favours capital gains to dividend income, there may still be several investors who are in lower tax brackets. These investors investing in shares will prefer dividend income rather capital gains. Thus, there may exit **high-payout clientele**. In a tax system that treats dividends more favourably than capital gains, shareholders in high tax brackets will also prefer receiving dividends rather than capital gains. Under this tax system, dividends will be considered good and it will generally attract **high-payout clientele**. This situation prevails currently in India. There is no tax on dividend income in the hands of shareholders (both individuals and companies), but companies are required to pay tax at 12.5 per cent on dividends paid to shareholders. Capital gains are taxed at 20 per cent. As a result of this system, shareholders in India will prefer to receive current dividends rather than capital gains. Since companies paying dividends are required to pay additional tax, this taxation system may create a conflict between shareholders and companies. Companies would like to pay no or low dividends to save additional tax while shareholders would like to have more dividends as they have no tax liability on the dividend income. If the objective of the companies is to maximise the wealth of shareholders, the tax system augurs for paying higher dividends.

India is an exception where dividends are not taxed but capital gains are. In most countries, tax systems favour capital gains with no or low tax rates as compared to dividends. Thus, the preference for low-payout or high-payout shares will depend on the tax status of the individual investors. (See Exhibit 17.1 for the different tax systems regarding dividends and capital gains.)

Neutrality of Dividend Policy: The Black-Scholes Hypothesis

We have just explained that the benefits of dividends for shareholders are that they satisfy their desire for current income, avoid the need to sell shares and incur transaction costs and signal the firm's prospects and risk allowing them to make choices with regard to their investment portfolios. The cost of dividends is the higher tax on dividend. Black and Scholes argue that shareholders trade off the benefits of dividends against the tax loss. Based on the trade offs that shareholders make, they could be classified into three clienteles: (*i*) a clientele that considers dividends are always good; (*ii*) a clientele that considers dividends are always bad; and (*iii*) a clientele that is indifferent to dividends. Shareholders in high tax brackets may belong to high-payout clientele since in their case the tax disadvantage may outweigh the benefits of dividends. On the other hand, shareholders in low tax brackets may fit in to low-payout clientele as they may suffer marginal tax disadvantage of dividends. Tax-exempt investors are indifferent between dividends and capital gains, as they pay no taxes on their income.

In a real world situation, all three clienteles exist as tax status and need for current incomes of investors differ. There are several hundreds of companies that 'supply' dividends to meet the demand of the three types of clienteles. Black and Scholes argue that since the supply of dividends and demand for dividends match, there will be no gains if a firm changes its

---

EXHIBIT 17.1: TAXES AND DIVIDENDS

Shareholders' earnings are taxed differently in different countries. We can identify the following four tax systems regarding the taxation of shareholders' earnings:

- **Double taxation:** Under this system, shareholders' earnings are taxed twice; first the corporate tax is levied on profits at the level of the company, and then, the after-tax profits distributed as dividends are taxed as ordinary income in the hands of shareholders. Most countries have a higher marginal tax rate for dividend income than capital gains. The wealthy shareholders with high personal tax rates will prefer capital gains to dividends. A number of countries such as USA follow the double (or two-tier) taxation system. India practised this system until the change in the tax laws in 1997.

- **Single taxation:** Under this system, shareholders' earnings are taxed only once at the corporate level. Dividends received by shareholders are exempt from tax. India currently follows this system. Companies in India pay tax on their profits at 35 per cent, and they will have to pay additional tax at 12.5 per cent on the after-tax profits distributed as dividends to shareholders. Shareholders, both individuals and corporate, do not pay taxes on the dividend income. However, they do pay tax on short-term capital gains. The marginal personal rate is 30 per cent and short-term capital gain tax rate is 10 per cent. Under this system, all investors will prefer dividends and long-term capital gains

- **Split-rate taxation:** Under this system, corporate profits are divided into retained earnings and dividends for the purpose of taxation. A higher tax rate is applied to retained earnings and a lower rate to earnings distributed as dividends. Shareholders pay tax on dividends and capital gains. This system, but for a lower tax rate on dividend, is similar to double taxation system. Tax-exempt and low-tax paying shareholders would prefer dividends while shareholders in high tax brackets will prefer capital gains.

- **Imputation taxation:** Under this system, shareholders' earnings are not subjected to double taxation. A company pays corporate tax on its earnings. Shareholders pay personal taxes on dividends but get full or partial tax relief for the tax paid by the company. In Australia, shareholders get full tax relief while in Canada they get partial relief. Under full tax relief, a tax-exempt shareholder or a shareholder, who has a personal tax rate lower than the corporate tax rate, will get a tax refund.

dividend policy; the investors have already made their choices or there already exist opportunities for shareholders to shift from one firm to another. How will companies determine whether change in dividend policy will affect their share prices? This is an empirical question and a difficult question to answer, given the problems with statistical techniques. However, the Black-Scholes hypothesis shows that the tax disadvantage of dividends is not so great as made out by some academicians.

INFORMATIONAL CONTENT OF DIVIDENDS

It is contended that dividends are relevant because they have **informational value**. A company can make statements about its expected earnings growth to inform shareholders in order to create a favourable impression on them. However, these statements would be paid better attention if they follow with a dividend action – a disbursement of cash. The cash payment for dividends conveys to shareholders that the company is profitable and financially strong. When a firm changes its dividend policy in a significant manner, investors assume that it is in response to an expected change in the firm's profitability which will last long. An increase in payout ratio signals to shareholders a permanent or long-term increase in firm's expected earnings. It is, therefore, argued that the announcement of changes in dividend policy influences shares prices, and that managers use the dividend changes to convey information about the future earnings of their companies. They may also influence the perceptions of the investors about the risk of the company which follows a stable dividend policy. This sort of argument is also known as the **dividend-signalling hypothesis**.[1] Solomon contends that dividends may offer tangible evidence of the firm's ability to generate cash, and as a result, the dividend policy of the firm may affect the share price. He states,

> ...in an uncertain world in which verbal statements can be ignored or misinterpreted, dividend action does provide a clearcut means of 'making a statement' that 'speaks louder than a thousand words.[2]

The dividend-signalling hypothesis implies that the most valuable dividend policy is the one that provides information that cannot be effectively communicated through other means. The most dividend policies are likely to be those that very closely reflect the firm's long-term performance. Let us consider some examples. Suppose that a company has been following a dividend policy of paying Rs 2 per share for quite sometime. Assume that the company's current earnings of, say, Rs 4 per share increases to, say, Rs 7 per share. If the company does not increase dividend from Rs 2 per share, the message conveyed to the shareholders will be that the increase in earnings is only a temporary, cyclical occurrence. Therefore, the market price of the share may not be affected very significantly. On the other hand, if the dividends were raised from, say, Rs 2 per share to Rs 3 per share, the shareholders would imply that management is expecting a long-term increase in the earning levels. This

thinking of shareholders might have a favourable impact on the market value of the share. The market value of the share is affected not because of the change in dividends, but because of the information about change in the future expected earnings conveyed through the payment of higher dividends. Dividends per share do not affect the share value.

The reaction of market to the information conveyed by the dividend action depends upon the established dividend policy of the company. If the long-established policy of the firm is to pay, say, 50 per cent of earnings to shareholders and has increased dividends in the past only when earnings increased to new levels on a permanent basis, an increase in dividends will communicate convincing information that the earnings of the company have grown. As a result, the market price of the share may be significantly influenced. On the other hand, if a company follows a dividend policy of changing dividends with every cyclical change in earnings, the market price may not be affected or may be affected little because shareholders had the information.

The payout ratios of the companies may depend on the fact whether they are mature or growth companies. Mature companies may characterise high payout ratios as they may have few profitable investment opportunities. Shareholders of such companies are more concerned with dividend income. Therefore, any change in the amount of dividend is immediately reflected in the market price of the share. Growth companies, on the other hand, have a low payout ratio as they have enough internal investment opportunities to employ retained earnings. The shareholders of growth companies are interested in capital gains than dividends. A steady increase in both earnings and dividends coupled with a continuing low payout ratio gives the message that the firm expects to keep growing. A greater increase in the dividends than the earnings may convey to the shareholders that profitable investment opportunities of the firm are diminishing. This understanding of shareholders may depress the market price of the share in spite of an increase in the dividends.

MM accept the informational content of dividends. They contend that the price of the share is determined by the expected future earnings and the firm's investment policy and not by the dividends. They argue that the informational value of dividends indicates that they are merely a reflection of the firm's investment policy and the expected earnings and do not have any impact on the value in their own accord.

Do dividends matter? The above discussion of market imperfections indicates that shareholders may not be indifferent as to how the earnings of the firms are divided between dividends and retained earnings. The tax differential effect and the presence of flotation costs favour the capital gains resulting from the retention of earnings, while the existence of transactions costs, agency costs, information asymmetry and desire for current income and diversification favour the payment of dividends. The dividend policy may also become relevant because of the informational content of dividend.

---

1. Ross, S., The Determinant of Financial Structure: The Incentive-Signalling Approach, *Bell Journal of Economics,* spring 1977, pp. 23–40.
2. Solomon, Ezra, *The Theory of Financial Management*, Colombia University Press, 1963, p. 142.

SUMMARY

❖ Earnings distributed to shareholders are called dividends. The percentage of earnings paid as dividends is called payout ratio.

❖ A high payout ratio means more dividends and less funds for expansion and growth. A low payout, on the other hand, results in a higher growth.

❖ Does dividend policy affect the market value of the firm? Whether dividend will increase value or not may depend on the profitable investment opportunities available to the firm.

❖ In Walter's view it depends on the profitability of investment opportunities available to the firm and the cost of capital. If the firm has profitable opportunities, its value will be maximum when 100 per cent of earnings are retained.

❖ Walter's formula for the market price of shares is:

$$P = \frac{DIV}{k} + \frac{r(EPS - DIV)/k}{k}$$

where r is return on investment opportunities and k is the cost of capital.

❖ Gordon also arrives at the same conclusion with the help of the following formula:

$$P_0 = \frac{DIV_1}{k - rb}$$

where b is the retention ratio and $rb = g$ is growth in dividends.

❖ Yet another view is that because of the uncertainty of capital gains, investors like more dividends. This implies that, the market price of shares of high-payout companies will command premium.

❖ Miller and Modigliani do not agree with the view that dividends affect the market value of shares. According to them if the investment policy of the firm is given, then dividend policy is a trade-off between cash dividends and issue of ordinary shares. The share price will be adjusted by the amount of dividend distributed. Thus, the existing shareholder is neither better off nor worse off. His wealth remains unchanged. For their view, M–M assume perfect capital market, no transaction costs and no taxes.

❖ The practical world is not simple; there exist transaction costs as well as taxes. In such a world, one view is that investors like cash dividends. Thus there is a clientele for high-payout shares.

❖ Except tax-exempt investors, there does not seem to be a strong reason for investors to prefer high-payout shares. In fact, in a tax-differential world, where capital gains are taxed at low rate, investors in high-tax brackets would prefer low-payout shares.

❖ In an extreme situation like the one currently prevailing in India, where dividends are not taxed while capital gains are taxed, investors will prefer dividends.

❖ Thus, there does not seem to be a consensus on whether dividends matter or not. In practice, a number of factors will have to be considered before deciding about the appropriate dividend policy of the firm.

KEY CONCEPTS

Agency costs	Growth firm	Low-payout clientele	Single taxation
Declining firm	High-payout clientele	Payout ratio	Split-rate taxation
Dividend signalling	Imputation taxation	Perferct capital markets	The bird-in-the-hand
Dividend yield	Information asymmetry	Retention ratio	argument
Double taxation	Information content of dividends		

ILLUSTRATIVE SOLVED PROBLEMS

Problem 17.1: The earnings per share of a company are Rs 10. It has an internal rate of return of 15 per cent and the capitalisation rate of its risk class is 12.5 per cent. If Walter's model is used: (*i*) What should be the optimum payout ratio of the firm? (*ii*) What would be the price of the share at this payout? (*iii*) How shall the price of the share be affected if a different payout were employed?

Solution Walter's model to determine share value is:

$$P = \frac{DIV + (r/k)(EPS - DIV)}{k}$$

(*i*) If $r/k > 1$, the value of the share will increase as EPS has increased. The price of the share would be maximum when

the firm retains all the earnings. Thus, the optimum payout ratio in this case is zero.

(*ii*) When the optimum payout is zero, the price of the share is:

$$P = \frac{0 + (0.15/0.125)(10 - 0)}{0.125} = \frac{12}{0.125} = Rs\ 96$$

(*iii*) If the firm, under the condition of $r/k > 1$, chooses a payout other than zero, the price of the share will fall. Suppose the firm has a payout of 20 per cent, the price of the share will be:

$$P = \frac{2 + (0.15/0.125)(10 - 2)}{0.125} = \frac{11.60}{0.125} = Rs\ 92.80$$

Problem 17.2: A company has a total investment of Rs 500,000 in assets, and 50,000 outstanding ordinary shares at Rs 10 per share (par value). It earns a rate of 15 per cent on its investment, and has a policy of retaining 50 per cent of the earnings. If the appropriate discount rate of the firm is 10 per cent, determine the price of its share using Gordon's model. What shall happen to the price of the share if the company has a payout of 80 per cent or 20 per cent?

Solution The share valuation model of Gordon is:

$$P_0 = \frac{DIV_1}{k - g} = \frac{(1-b)EPS_1}{k - br} = \frac{(1-b)rA}{k - br}$$

where A represents investment per share, which is Rs 10 in this case.

(*i*)   At a payout of 50 per cent, the price of the share is:

$$P_0 = \frac{(1-0.5)0.15 \times 10}{0.10 - 0.15 \times 0.5} = \frac{0.75}{0.025} = Rs\,30$$

(*ii*)   At a payout of 80 per cent, the price of the share is:

$$P_0 = \frac{(1-0.2)0.15 \times 10}{0.10 - 0.15 \times 0.2} = \frac{1.20}{0.07} = Rs\,17$$

(*iii*)   When the payout is 20 per cent, the price of the share is determined as follows:

$$P_0 = \frac{(1-0.8)0.15 \times 10}{0.10 - 0.15 \times 0.8} = \frac{0.30}{(-)0.02} = Rs\,15$$

The price is negative. This is an absurd result and is due to some simplifying assumptions of Gordon's model. For example, it is assumed that k and r constant and do not change with retention and uncertainty. If these factors are allowed in the model, we will not get negative price of the share.

REVIEW QUESTIONS

1. What are the essentials of Walter's dividend model? Explain its shortcomings.
2. What are the assumptions which underlie Gordon's model of dividend effect? Does dividend policy affect the value of the firm under Gordon's model?
3. "Walter's and Gordan's models are essentially based on the same assumptions. Thus, there is no basic difference between the two models." Do you agree or not? Why?
4. "According to Walter's model the optimum payout ratio can be either zero or 100 per cent." Explain the circumstances, when this is true.
5. "The contention that dividends have an impact on the share price has been characterised as the bird-in-the-hand argument." Explain the essentials of this argument. Why is this argument considered fallacious?
6. What is Miller-Modigliani's dividend irrelevance hypothesis? Critically evaluate its assumptions.
7. "The assumptions underlying the MM dividend irrelevance hypothesis are unrealistic." Explain and illustrate.
8. Give arguments to support the view that dividends are relevant.
9. What is the informational content of dividend payments? How does it affect the share value?
10. What is the relationship between taxes and dividend policy? Explain by citing the impact of different tax systems.

PROBLEMS

1. A company earns Rs 10 per share at an internal rate of 15 per cent. The firm has a policy of paying 40 per cent of earnings as dividends. If the required rate of return is 10 per cent, determine the price of the share under (*i*) Walter's model, (*ii*) Gordon's model.
2. Saraswati Glass Works has an investment of Rs 30 crore divided into 30 lakh ordinary shares. The profitability rate of the firm is 20 per cent and the capitalisation rate is 12.5 per cent. What is the optimum dividend payout for the firm if Walter's model is used? What shall be the price of the share at optimum payout? Shall your answer change if the profitability rate is assumed to be 15 per cent? What would happen if profitability rate is 10 per cent? Show computations.
3. The following data relate to a firm: earnings per share Rs 10, capitalisation rate 10 per cent, retention ratio 40 per cent. Determine the price per share under Walter's and Gordon's models if the internal rate of return is 15 per cent, 10 per cent and 5 per cent.
4. Manex Company has outstanding 50 lakh shares selling at Rs 120 per share. The company is thinking of paying a dividend of Rs 10 per share at the end of current year. The capitalisation rate for the risk class of this firm is 10 per cent. Using Modigliani and Miller's model you are required: (*i*) to calculate the price of the share at the end of the current year if dividends are paid and if they are not paid; (*ii*) to determine the number of shares to be issued if the company earns Rs 9 crore, pays dividends and makes new investments of Rs 6.60 crore?
5. A company has outstanding 10 lakh shares. The company needs Rs 5 crore to finance its investments, for which Rs 1 crore is available out of profits. The market price of per share at the end of current year is expected to be Rs 120. If the discount rate is 10 per cent, determine the present value of a share using the MM model.
6. The current market price of a company's shares is Rs 125 per share. The expected earnings per share and dividend per share are Rs 10 and Rs 5 respectively. The shareholders' expected rate of return is 15 per cent. Suppose the company declares that it will switch to 100 per cent payout policy, issuing shares as necessary to finance growth. Use the perpetual-growth model to show that current price of share is unchanged.

7. The following data relate to a firm in the cotton textile industry:

	Rs in crore
Share capital (at Rs 10 per share)	12.50
Reserve	7.50
Profit after tax	1.85
Dividends paid	1.50
P/E ratio	13.33

You are required (a) to comment on the firm's dividend policy using Walter's model; (b) to determine the optimum payout ratio using Walter's model; (c) to determine the price – earnings ratio at which dividend payout will have no effect on share price.

8. Turant Pharma is thinking of diversifying its business in the field of energy. The firm has decided to make a capital expenditure of Rs 35 crore in an energy project. The project is expected to yield a positive net present value of Rs 25 crore. The firm is also considering a payment of dividends of Rs 20 crore. The internal funds available with the firm are Rs 10 crore. It has a paid-up share capital of Rs 50 crore divided into 5 crore shares of Rs 10 each. The current price of the firm's share is Rs 25. The firm has not borrowed funds in the past, and would continue with this policy in the future. Given the firm's capital expenditure and the policy of zero borrowing, show the implications of the payment of dividends for the shareholder value. Will your answer be different if Turant decides not to pay any dividends? Assume no taxes and no issue costs.

9. The share of X Company is selling for Rs 100. It is a no-tax paying company. The price of X's share is expected to be Rs 115 after one year. Company Y is identical to company X in terms of risk and the future earnings potential. It is a dividend paying company, and is expected to pay a dividend of Rs 10 per share after one year. Assume dividend income is taxed at 35 per cent and there is no tax on capital gains. What should be the current price of B's share and how much should be its before-tax expected return?

10. The shares of Firm A and Firm B have identical risk. Both have an after-tax required rate of return of 15 per cent. Firm A pays no dividend, while Firm B is a high dividend paying firm. The price of Firm A's share is expected to be Rs 60 after one year and the price of Firm B Rs 50 with Rs 10 dividend per share. Assume that the income tax rate is 40 per cent and capital gain tax rate is 20 per cent. Determine the current prices of Firm A's and Firm B's shares.

11. The expected before-tax incomes (consisting of dividend and capital gains) on shares of firms X, Y and Z are given below:

Share	Dividend income (Rs)	Capital gain (Rs)
X	0	10
Y	5	5
Z	10	0

Suppose that the current price of each share is Rs 60. Further, an investor is in 50 per cent tax bracket and capital gain tax rate is 20 per cent. Which share will give highest after-tax return to the investor? Now suppose that the each share was expected to have expected after-tax yield of 12 per cent for the investor. Determine the price of each share.

CASE

Case 17.1: The Great Eastern Shipping Co. Ltd. (GESC)

GESC was started in 1948, and today, it is the largest shipping company in the private sector. The chairman of the company in his statement in 1993 focused on the future dividend policy of the company.[1] His statement is given below:

"I wish to concentrate on a specific issue germane to the future growth of your company. The matter I wish to address is the question of how best to balance the dividend payments on your Company's fleet.

Shipping, as we all know, is very capital intensive business in which freight rates and value of ships can move quickly. In the wake of this, I believe, a shipping company should always be cash rich and should limit its overall borrowings to match its equity. Secondly, the industry is dominated by private ship-owners who, due to the nature of their ownership structure, look at ship investments with a medium to long term approach. (They are not influenced by short term considerations). Being independent they neither need to concern themselves about dividend payment nor do they need to ensure immediate returns on equity. They can, and do, retain all their earnings in the company for future growth….

There are four sources of funds for investment. First there is retained earnings; second there is the raising of fresh capital from existing shareholders through a rights issue; third the raising of the capital from investors outside the existing shareholders; and fourth there is borrowings from banks and institutions.

Of all these four methods of raising resources, the first and fourth, i.e, retained earnings and borrowings are the least disturbing. The other two methods involve issuing fresh capital which means permanent change in the structure of the Company.

The issuance of shares to the existing shareholders has the advantage of eliminating the risk of mispricing since the market price of the share adjusts to the new rights so issued. Here, your company would like to continue its hitherto policy of pricing its rights at the cheapest possible value i.e., at par. In pursuing this policy, your Company's equity capital would increase quite substantially. This in my opinion should not matter if you remove

---

1. For a full understanding of GESC's dividend policy, refer to Professor S. Sinha's case on *Great Eastern Shipping*, Indian Institute of Management, Ahmedabad.

the misconception that dividends are recognised in per centage terms. Managements all over the world distribute dividends in relation to the Company's profit. Moreover, dividend paid out is always a certain amount per share held by the shareholder and, therefore, so long as the Company's earning's grow the total dividend received by a shareholder will increase. All companies follow this rule as a broad dividend policy. However, the dividend distribution per share varies from company to company because some managements prefer to issue rights at premium whereas some managements, like yours, prefer to issue rights at par. As I have said earlier, the pricing of the share issued as rights is not important because of the price adjustment of the share after issuance of rights. What does vary, due to the difference in the pricing of the rights, is the dividend payment per share. When a company increases its capital through rights issue at par it is obviously difficult to maintain the same dividend per share so issued although the total amount of dividend that the shareholder will receive would be higher in quantum. Although, as I have explained before, shareholders should be quite indifferent to any reduction in the dividend per share that they receive so long as the total amount of dividend received in their hands is increasing since that is a clear sign of their company's earnings increasing.

There are two principal disadvantages, however, in the payment of dividends. Firstly, in the case of Indian companies, the dividend receipt is taxed in the hands of the shareholder.[1] Thus, for example if we pay a divided of Rs 100, you, the shareholder, may receive only Rs 70, if there is a 30% average tax on dividend. Now supposing we give you Rs 100 as dividend and simultaneously ask you to subscribe to Rs 100 in a right issue, we will all lose because (*a*) on the dividend you will pay Rs 30 in tax and (*b*) on the rights issue your company will have to bear substantial expenses which amount to at least 5% of the issue. So, for every Rs 100 the Company pays in dividend, the shareholder receives Rs 95. So, between the company and its shareholders, there is a total loss of resources from transferring money from and to the company. The total loss is not insubstantial.

The payment of dividends has another rather subtle deleterious effects on the shareholder. This is a consequence of the modern method that value shares on price/earning multiples. Let me try to explain. I am told that most institutions tend to appraise shares at many times the earnings of a company. Thus, if the earnings per share is Rs. 10 and the multiple they apply to the company is 15*X*, then the fair value of the share is considered to be Rs 150. Now take a company that pays out Rs. 3 per share as dividend. If the company does not pay this money out but invests in business, earning a return, of let us say, 30%, then its permanent income should rise by Re 0.90 per share than what it would

have been paying out a dividend. The result is that if shares are valued at 15 times multiple of earnings than for every Re 0.90 per share increase in earnings the share value will go up by Re 13.5. Thus, for a sacrifice of Rs 3 in dividends the worth of shares should go up by Rs 13.5.

Many of you will find this argument too theoretical and therefore, somewhat unpersuasive. I sympathise with those of you who are unconvinced. However, I must tell you that the example I have given is quite realistic. It is a fact that the return on your equity in shipping has, over time, been, well in excess of 30%. Further the shares of your company have been valued at anywhere between twelve and fifteen times earnings. Although the past is no guide to the future, it would be unreasonable to deny the fact that the growth of your company would be faster if we took less out of it in dividends.

In partial pursuit of these policies, we have repeatedly tried to tell you that we intend to restrict our dividends. We recognise that there must be some formula for a dividend policy and we have chosen to restrict it to a percentage of net profits after tax. Unfortunately, this message has not got home. Let me therefore repeat what we have already said. We do not intend to maintain dividends as a percentage of the face value of your shares, nor do we intend to maintain the dividend at a fixed rupee value. Subject to your approval it is our intention to retain as much profit as we possibly can, ideally we should like to retain all our earnings, we certainly believe that to be in shareholders interest, but we also have to recognise that dividend policies can only be modified gradually. I do hope you will take note of these policy statements because otherwise you will be disappointed by misconceived notions.

Let me now summarise the main thrust of my argument. I have attempted to show that payment of dividends is an inefficient way of increasing the shareholders' wealth. That had we been a new company the most sensible policy may well have been to pay no dividends and accumulate our profits. This is a policy followed by some of the most successful companies in the world. We have been inhabited in doing so by tradition and conventional wisdom. Perhaps we have no escape from following a system which you are familiar, but I have to put these issues before you so that you can consider for yourselves whether we should adopt a different course."

Discussion Questions

1. Identify and critically evaluate the issues raised by GESC's chairman in his above statement regarding the financing of the company's growth and the role of dividend policy.
2. How would you justify GESC's chairman's views on theoretical grounds?
3. Do you think the issues raised in the case are still relevant in 2003?

---

1. This is not true now. Shareholders are not required to pay tax on their dividend income in India.

18 Dividend Policy

CHAPTER OBJECTIVES

- Explain the objectives of dividend policy
- Understand the factors that influence a firm's dividend policy
- Focus on the importance of the stability of dividend
- Discuss the significance and implications of bonus shares and stock splits and the share buyback
- Explain the corporate behaviour of dividends

INTRODUCTION

We have discussed in Chapter 17 whether dividends affect the value of a share. The theoretical views differ on this issue. On the one hand, we have the view that dividends increase the value of the share. On the other hand, there is the view that dividends are bad as they result into the payment of higher taxes (because of the difference in the ordinary income and capital gains tax rates), and thus, they reduce the shareholders' wealth. We also have a moderate view, which asserts that because of the information value of dividends, some dividends should be always paid to maintain the value of the share. Given these theoretical differences, how do companies set their dividend policies in practice? What factors do they consider in setting their policies?

OBJECTIVES OF DIVIDEND POLICY

As discussed in the previous chapter, a firm's **dividend policy** has the effect of dividing its net earnings into two parts: retained earnings and dividends. The retained earnings provide funds to finance the firm's long-term growth. It is the most significant source of financing a firm's investments in practice. Dividends are paid in cash. Thus, the distribution of earnings uses the available cash of the firm. A firm which intends to pay dividends

and also needs funds to finance its investment opportunities will have to use external sources of financing, such as the issue of debt or equity. Dividend policy of the firm, thus, has its effect on both the long-term financing and the wealth of shareholders. As a result, the firm's decision to pay dividends may be shaped by the following two possible viewpoints.

Firm's Need for Funds

When dividend decision is treated as a financing decision, the net earnings of the firm may be considered as a source of long-term funds. With this approach, dividends will be paid only when the firm does not have profitable investment opportunities. The firm grows at a faster rate when it accepts highly profitable investment projects. External equity could be raised to finance investments. But retained earnings are preferred because, unlike external equity, they do not involve any flotation costs. The distribution of cash dividends causes a reduction in internal funds available to finance profitable investment opportunities and consequently, either constrains growth or requires the firm to find other costly sources of financing.[1] Thus, firms may retain their earnings as a part of long-term financing decision. The dividends will be paid to shareholders when a firm cannot profitably reinvest earnings. With this approach, dividend

---

1. Rozeff, M.S., Growth, Beta and Agency Costs as Determinants of Dividends Payout Ratios. *Journal of Financial Research*, 5 (fall 1982), pp. 249–59; Weston, J.F. and Copeland, T.E., *Managerial Finance*, Dryden Press, 1986, p. 659.

decision is viewed merely as a **residual decision**.

Shareholders' Need for Income

One may argue that capital markets are not perfect; therefore, shareholders are not indifferent between dividends and retained earnings. Because of the market imperfections and uncertainty, shareholders may prefer the near dividends to the future dividends and capital gains. Thus, the payment of dividends may significantly affect the market price of the share. Higher dividends may increase the value of the shares and low dividends may reduce the value. It is believed by some that, in order to maximise wealth under uncertainty, the firm must pay enough dividends to satisfy investors.[1] Investors in high tax brackets, on the other hand, may prefer to receive capital gains rather than dividends. Their wealth will be maximised if firms retain earnings rather than distributing them.

The management of a firm, while evolving a dividend policy, must strike a proper balance between the above-mentioned two approaches. When the firm increases the retained portion of the net earnings, shareholders' current income in the form of dividends decreases. But the use of retained earnings to finance profitable investments will increase the future earnings. On the other hand, when dividends are increased, shareholders' current income will increase, but the firm may have to forego some investment opportunities for want of funds and consequently, the future earnings may decrease. Management should develop a dividend policy, which divides the net earnings into dividends and retained earnings in an optimum way to achieve the objective of maximising the wealth of shareholders. The development of such policy will be greatly influenced by investment opportunities available to the firm and the value of dividends as against capital gains to the shareholders. The other possible aspects of the dividend policy relate to the stability of dividends, the constraints on paying dividends and the forms of dividends.

PRACTICAL CONSIDERATIONS IN DIVIDEND POLICY

The view that dividends are irrelevant is not entirely correct, once we modify the assumptions underlying this view to consider the realities of the world. In practice, every firm follows some kind of dividend policy. The typical dividend policy of most firms is to retain between one-third to half of the net earnings and distribute the remaining amount to shareholders. Companies in India specify dividends in terms of a **dividend rate** (a percentage of the paid-up capital per share). Most of them also tend to increase dividend rate particularly when their profits increase substantially.

There are a very few exceptions to the practice of paying high dividends and continuously increasing dividends. The Chairman and Managing Director of the Great Eastern Shipping Company Limited, is in favour of not paying any dividends. Deliberating on the company's dividend policy in his 1992–93 Chairman's Statement, he stated:

... We do not intend to maintain dividends as a percentage of the face value of your share, nor do we intend to maintain dividend at a fixed rupee value.... it is our intention to retain as much profit as we possibly can, ideally we should like to retain all our earnings, we certainly believe that to be in the shareholders' interest, ... payment of dividends is an inefficient way of increasing shareholders' wealth. That, had we been a new company the most sensible policy may well have been to pay no dividends and accumulate our profits. This is a policy followed by the most successful companies in the world. We have been inhibited in doing so by tradition and conventional wisdom. ...

The following questions relate to the dividend policy of a firm:

- What are the firm's financial needs given its growth plans and investment opportunities?
- Who are the firm's shareholders and what are their preferences with regard to dividend payments?
- What are the firm's business risks?
- What are the firm's constraints–financial and legal–in paying dividends?
- Is control a consideration for the firm?
- Should the firm follow a stable dividend policy?
- How should the firm pay dividends—cash dividend or bonus shares or shares buyback?

It is not easy to answer these questions. A number of factors will have to be evaluated to analyse each of these questions to evolve a long-term dividend policy for the firm. Broadly speaking, to develop a long-term dividend policy, the directors of a company should aim at bringing a balance between the desires of shareholders and the needs of the company. The factors that generally influence the dividend policy of the firm are discussed below.[2]

Firm's Investment Opportunities and Financial Needs

Firms should tailor their dividend policies to their long-term investment opportunities to have maximum financial flexibility and avoid financial frictions and costs of raising external funds. Growth firms have a large number of investment opportunities requiring substantial amount of funds. Hence they will give precedence to the retention of earnings over the payment of dividends in order to finance its expanding activities. For matured firms, investment opportunities occur infrequently. These firms may distribute most of their earnings. The retained earnings of these firms during periods, when they do not have investment opportunities, may be invested in short-term securities yielding nominal returns. Some of these firms may follow the policy of paying 100 per cent dividends and raise external funds when investment opportunities occur.

---

1. This is the bird-in-the-hand argument expounded by Gordon, M.J., *The Investment, Financing and Valuation of Corporation*, Richard D. Irwin, 1962. Also, see Ch. 17 of this book.
2. A variety of factors are indicated to influence a firm's dividend policy. See Hastings, P.G., *The Management of Business Finance*, Von Nostrand Co., 1966; Weston, J.F. and Brigham, E.F., *Managerial Finance*, Dryden Press, 1972, pp. 346–49; Brandt, L.K., *Analysis* for *Financial Management*,, Prentice-Hall, 1972; Van Horne, J.C., *Finance Management and Policy*, Prentice-Hall of India, 1976, pp. 287–90.

Generally, retained earnings should be used as a source of internal financing only when a company has profitable investment opportunities. If shareholders themselves have better investment opportunities, the earnings should be distributed to them so that they may be able to maximise their wealth. Theoretically, when the company has an internal rate of return greater than the return required by shareholders, it would be to the advantage of shareholders to allow the reinvestment of earnings by the company. When the company does not have highly profitable opportunities and earns a rate on investment, which is lower than the rate required by shareholders, it is not in the interest of shareholders to retain earnings.

It is sometimes argued that, even if the company has highly profitable investment opportunities, earnings should be distributed and funds should be raised externally to finance the investment. This will exert a discipline on the company's management in proper deployment of funds. But companies in practice prefer to retain earnings because issuing new share capital is inconvenient as well as involves flotation costs. If the company raises debt, the financial obligations and risk will increase. As a matter of fact, directors may neither follow a practice of paying 100 per cent dividends, nor a practice of retaining 100 per cent earnings. The company may have a **target payout ratio** consistent with its investment opportunities and may like to achieve it slowly and steadily. In the absence of profitable investment opportunities, it can pay some 'extra' dividend, but still retaining some earnings for the continued existence of the enterprise. Though shareholders are the owners of the company and directors should follow a policy desired by them, yet they cannot sacrifice the interests of other groups, such as debt-holders, employees, society and customers. Shareholders are the residual claimants to the earnings of the company. Directors must retain some earnings, whether or not profitable investment opportunities exist, to *maintain* the company as a sound and solvent enterprise and to have financial flexibility. Only a financially sound and flexible company can discharge its debt obligations, provide monetary benefits to its employees, produce quality products for its customers and make social contributions by paying taxes and making donations.[1]

Thus, depending on the needs to finance their long-term investment opportunities, companies may follow different dividend policies. **Mature companies** that have fewer investment opportunities may generally have high payout ratios. Shareholders of these companies would be more interested in dividends, as they obtain higher return on their investments outside the company. The share prices of such companies are very sensitive to dividend changes. The directors of these companies retain only a small portion of the earnings to meet emergent financial needs and to finance the occasional investment opportunities and distribute the rest. **Growth companies**, on the other hand, have plenty of investment opportunities and hence, they may have low payout ratios. They are continuously in need of funds to finance their fast growing fixed assets. The distribution of earnings will reduce the funds of the company. Therefore, sometimes growth companies retain most of their earnings and issue bonus shares, regularly or from time to time, to satisfy the dividend needs of shareholders. These companies would slowly increase the amount of dividends as the profitable investment opportunities start fading.

Shareholders' Expectations

Legally, the board of directors has discretion to decide the distribution of the earnings of a company. Shareholders are the legal owners of the company, and directors, appointed by them, are their agents. Therefore, directors should give due importance to the expectations of shareholders in the matter of dividend decision Shareholders' preference for dividends or capital gains may depend on their economic status and the effect of tax differential on dividends and capital gains. In most countries, dividend income is taxed at a rate higher than the capital gains. A wealthy shareholder, in a high income-tax bracket, may be interested in capital gains than current dividends. On the other hand, a retired person with small means, whose main source of income is dividend, would like to get regular dividend and may not be interested in capital gains.[2] The ownership concentration in a firm may define the shareholders' expectations.

In case of a **closely held company**, the body of the shareholders is small and homogeneous and management usually knows the expectations of shareholders. Therefore, they can easily adopt a dividend policy, which satisfies most shareholders. If most of the shareholders are in high tax brackets and have a preference for capital gains to current dividend incomes, the company can establish a dividend policy of paying sufficient dividends and retaining the earnings within the company, subject to its growth opportunities.

It is a formidable task to ascertain the preferences of shareholders in a **widely held company**. The number of shareholders is very large, they are dispersed and they may have diverse desires regarding dividends and capital gains. Hence it is not possible in case of widely held company to follow a dividend policy, which equally satisfies all shareholders. The firm may follow a dividend policy, which serves the purpose of the dominating group, but does not completely neglect the desires of others. Shareholders of a widely held company may be divided, for example, into four groups: small, retired, wealthy and institutional shareholders.[3]

Small shareholders are not the frequent purchasers of the shares. They hold a small number of shares in a few companies with the purpose of receiving dividend income, or sometimes making capital gains. They may not have a definite investment policy. They purchase shares only when their savings permit. **Retired and old persons** generally invest in shares to get a regular

---

1. Hasting, *op. cit.*
2. Dividend income in India has been completely exempted from tax while on capital gains, the tax rate is 20 per cent. Thus, the Indian shareholders may prefer dividend over capital gains. The companies, on the other hand, will have to pay tax at 12.5 per cent on the dividends distributed to shareholders. Thus, the effective corporate tax rate would be higher (than 35 per cent) for the dividend distributing companies.
3. Hasting's, *op. cit.*, p. 378.

income. They use their savings or provident or pension funds to purchase shares. These persons may, therefore, select shares of the companies that have a history of paying regular and liberal dividends. However, a retired person who has some source of income and is in a high tax bracket may be interested in capital gains as well. **Wealthy investors** are very much concerned with the dividend policy followed by a company. They have a definite investment policy of increasing their wealth and minimising taxes. These persons are in high tax brackets and the dividends received in cash by them would be taxed at a high rate. Therefore, they generally prefer a dividend policy of retaining earnings and distributing bonus shares. The wealthy shareholders' group is quite dominating in many companies as they hold relatively large blocks of shares and are able to influence the composition of the board of directors by their significant voting rights. On the dividend policies of these companies, this group will have a considerable influence. **Institutional investors** purchase large blocks of shares to hold them for relatively long periods of time. Institutional investors, unlike wealthy shareholders, are not concerned with personal income taxes but with profitable investments. Most institutional investors avoid speculative issues, seek diversification in their investment portfolio and favour a policy of regular cash dividend payments.

It should be obvious from the above discussion that, in the case of a widely held company, the interests of the various shareholders' groups are in conflict. It is not easy to reconcile these conflicting interests of the different types of shareholders. However, the board of directors should consider two points.[1] First, the board should adopt a dividend policy, which gives some consideration to the interests of each of the groups comprising a substantial proportion of shareholders. Second, the dividend policy, once established, should be continued as long as it does not interfere with the financing needs of the company. A definite dividend policy, followed for a long period in the past, tends to create a particular kind of **clientele** for the company. That is, it attracts those investors who consider the dividend policy in accord with their investment requirements. If the company suddenly changes its dividend policy, it may work to the detriment of these shareholders, as they may have to switch to other companies to fulfil their investment needs. Thus, an established dividend policy should be changed slowly and only after having analysed its probable effects on the existing shareholders.

Constraints on Paying Dividends

Most companies recognise that the shareholders have some desire to receive dividends, although shareholders are also interested in the capital gains. How much dividend should a company pay? The company's decision regarding the amount of earnings to be distributed as dividends depends on legal and financial constraints.

Legal restrictions The dividend policy of the firm has to evolve within the legal framework and restrictions. The directors are not legally compelled to declare dividends. For example, the Indian Companies Act provides that dividend shall be declared or paid only out of the current profits or past profits after providing for depreciation. However, the Central Government is empowered to allow any company to pay dividend for any financial year out of the profits of the company without providing for depreciation. The Central Government shall give such relief only when it is in the public interest. The dividend should be paid in cash, but a company is not prohibited to capitalise profits or reserves (retained earnings) for the purpose of issuing fully paid bonus shares (stock dividend). It has been held in some legal cases that **capital profits** should not be distributed as dividends unless (*i*) the distribution is permitted by the company's Articles of Association and (*ii*) the profits have been actually realised.

The legal rules act as boundaries within which a company can operate in terms of paying dividends. Acting within these boundaries, a company will have to consider many financial variables and constraints in deciding the amount of earnings to be distributed as dividends.

Liquidity The payment of dividends means cash outflow. Although a firm may have adequate earnings to declare dividend, it may not have sufficient cash to pay dividends. Thus, the cash position of the firm is an important consideration in paying dividends; the greater the cash position and overall liquidity of a company, the greater will be its ability to pay dividends. A mature company is generally liquid and is able to pay large amount of dividends. It does not have much investment opportunities; much of its funds are not tied up in permanent working capital and, therefore, it has a sound cash position. On the other hand, growing firms face the problem of liquidity. Even though they make good profits, they continuously need funds for financing growing fixed assets and working capital. Because of the insufficient cash or pressures on liquidity, in case of growth firms, management may follow a conservative dividend policy.

Financial condition and borrowing capacity The financial condition or capability of a firm depends on its use of borrowings and interest charges payable. A high degree of financial leverage makes a company quite vulnerable to changes in earnings, and also, it becomes quite difficult to raise funds externally for financing its growth. A highly levered firm is, therefore, expected to retain more to strengthen its equity base. However, a company with steady growing earnings and cash flows and without much investment opportunities, may follow a high dividend payment policy in spite of high amount of debt in its capital structure. A growth firm lacking liquidity may borrow to pay dividends. But this is not a sound policy. This will adversely affect the firm's financial flexibility. Financial flexibility includes the firm's ability to access external funds at a later date. The firm may lose the flexibility and capacity of raising external funds to finance growth opportunities in the future.

Access to the capital market A company that is not sufficiently liquid can still pay dividends if it is able to raise debt or equity in the capital markets. If it is well established and has a record of profitability, it will not find much difficulty in raising funds in the capital markets. Easy accessibility to the capital markets provides flexibility to the management in paying

---

1. Hasting's, *ibid.,* p. 380.

dividends as well as in meeting the corporate obligations. A fast growing firm, which has a tight liquidity position, will not face any difficulty in paying dividends if it has access to the capital markets. A company that does not have sound cash position and it is also unable to raise funds, will not be able to pay dividends. Thus, the greater is the ability of the firm to raise funds in the capital markets, greater will be its ability to pay dividends even if it is not liquid.

Restrictions in loan agreements Lenders may generally put restrictions on dividend payments to protect their interests when the firm is experiencing low liquidity or low profitability. As such, the firm agrees as part of a contract with a lender to restrict dividend payments. For example, a loan agreement may prohibit payment of dividends as long as the firm's debt-equity ratio is in excess of, say, 1.5:1 or when the liquidity ratio is less than, say, 2:1 or may require the firm to pay dividends only when some amount of current earnings has been transferred to a sinking fund established to retire debt. These are some of the examples of the restrictions put by lenders on the payment of dividends. When these restrictions are put, the company is forced to retain earnings and have a low payout.

Inflation Inflation can act as a constraint on paying dividends. Our accounting system is based on historical costs. Depreciation is charged on the basis of original costs at which assets were acquired. As a result, when prices rise, funds equal to depreciation set aside would not be adequate to replace assets or to maintain the capital intact. Consequently, to maintain the capital intact and preserve their earnings power, firms earnings may avoid paying dividends. On the contrary, some companies may follow a policy of paying more dividends during high inflation in order to protect the shareholders from the erosion of the real value of dividends. Companies with falling or constant profits may not be able to follow this policy.

Control

The objective of maintaining control over the company by the existing management group or the body of shareholders can be an important variable in influencing the company's dividend policy. When a company pays large dividends, its cash position is affected. As a result, the company will have to issue new shares to raise funds to finance its investment programmes. The control of the existing shareholders will be diluted if they do not want or cannot buy additional shares. Under these circumstances, the payment of dividends may be withheld and earnings may be retained to finance the firm's investment opportunities.

STABILITY OF DIVIDENDS

Stability of dividends is considered a desirable policy by the management of most companies in practice. Shareholders also seem generally to favour this policy and value stable dividends higher than the fluctuating ones. All other things being the same, the stable dividend policy may have a positive impact on the market price of the share.

Stability of dividends also means regularity in paying some dividend annually, even though the amount of dividend may fluctuate over years, and may not be related with earnings. There are a number of companies, which have records of paying dividend for a long, unbroken period. More precisely, stability of dividends refers to the amounts paid out regularly. Three forms of such stability may be distinguished:

- Constant dividend per share or dividend rate
- Constant payout
- Constant dividend per share plus extra dividend

Constant Dividend Per Share or Dividend Rate

In India, companies announce dividend as a per cent of the paid-up capital per share. This can be converted into dividend per share. A number of companies follow the policy of paying a fixed amount per share or a fixed rate on paid-up capital as dividend every year, irrespective of the fluctuations in the earnings. This policy does not imply that the dividend per share or dividend rate will never be increased. When the company reaches new levels of earnings and expects to maintain them, the annual dividend per share or dividend rate may be increased. The earnings per share and the dividend per share relationship under this policy is shown in Figure 18.1.

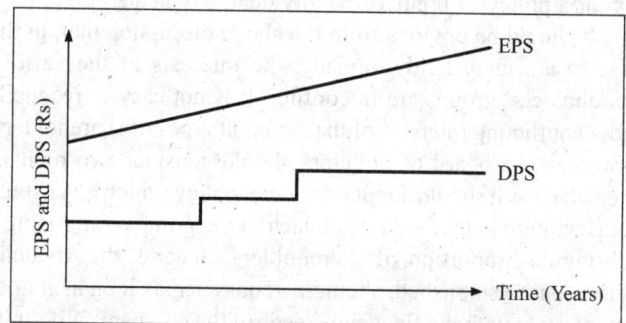

Figure 18.1: Constant dividend per share policy

It is easy to follow this policy when earnings are stable. However, if the earnings pattern of a company shows wide fluctuations, it is difficult to maintain such a policy. With earnings fluctuating from year to year, it is essential for a company, which wants to follow this policy to build up surpluses in years of higher than average earnings to maintain dividends in years of below average earnings. In practice, when a company retains earnings in good years for this purpose, it earmarks this surplus as **dividend equalisation reserve**. These funds are invested in current assets like tradable (marketable) securities, so that they may easily be converted into cash at the time of paying dividends in bad years.

A constant dividend per share policy puts ordinary shareholders at per with preference shareholders irrespective of the firm's investment opportunities or the preferences of shareholders.[1] Those investors who have dividends as the only source of their income may prefer the constant dividend policy. They do not accord much importance to the changes in share prices. In the long run, this may help to stabilise the market price of the share.[2]

1. Brandt, *op. cit.*, p. 447.
2. *Ibid.*

Constant Payout

The ratio of dividend to earnings is known as **payout ratio**. Some companies may follow a policy of constant payout ratio, i.e., paying a fixed per centage of net earnings every year. With this policy the amount of dividend will fluctuate in direct proportion to earnings. If a company adopts a 40 per cent payout ratio, then 40 per cent of every rupee of net earnings will be paid out. For example, if the company earns Rs 2 per share, the dividend per share will be Re 0.80 and if it earns Rs 1.50 per share the dividend per share will be Re 0.60. The relation between the earnings per share and the dividend per share under this policy is exhibited in Figure 18.2.

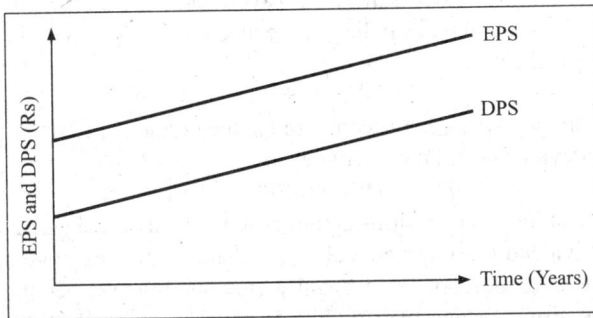

Figure 18.2: Dividend policy of constant payout ratio

This policy is related to a company's ability to pay dividends. If the company incurs losses, no dividends shall be paid regardless of the desires of shareholders. Internal financing with retained earnings is automatic when this policy is followed. At any given payout ratio, the amount of dividends and the additions to retained earnings increase with increasing earnings and decrease with decreasing earnings. This policy does not put any pressure on a company's liquidity since dividends are distributed only when the company has profits.[1]

Constant Dividend Per Share Plus Extra Dividend

For companies with fluctuating earnings, the policy to pay a minimum dividend per share with a step-up feature is desirable. The small amount of dividend per share is fixed to reduce the possibility of ever missing a dividend payment. By paying extra dividend (a number of companies in India pay an **interim dividend** followed by a regular, **final dividend**) in periods of prosperity, an attempt is made to prevent investors from expecting that the dividend represents an increase in the established dividend amount. This type of policy enables a company to pay constant amount of dividend regularly without a default and allows a great deal of flexibility for supplementing the income of shareholders only when the company's earnings are higher than the usual, without committing itself to make larger payments as a part of the future fixed dividend. Certain shareholders like this policy because of the certain cash flow in the form of regular dividend and the option of earning extra dividend occasionally.

We have discussed three forms of stability of dividends. Generally, when we refer to a stable dividend policy, we refer to the first form of paying constant dividend per share. A firm pursuing a policy of stable dividend, as shown in Figure 18.1, may command a higher price for its shares than a firm, which varies dividend amount with cyclical fluctuations in the earnings as depicted in Figure 18.2.

Merits of Stability of Dividends

The stability of dividends has several advantages as discussed below:

- Resolution of investors' uncertainty.
- Investors' desire for current income.
- Institutional investors' requirements.
- Raising additional finances.

Resolution of investors' uncertainty We have argued in the previous chapter that dividends have informational value, and resolve uncertainty in the minds of investors. When a company follows a policy of stable dividends, it will not change the amount of dividends if there are temporary changes in its earnings. Thus, when the earnings of a company fall and it continues to pay same amount of dividend as in the past, it conveys to investors that the future of the company is brighter than suggested by the drop in earnings. Similarly, the amount of dividends is increased with increased earnings level only when it is possible to maintain it in future. On the other hand, if a company follows a policy of changing dividends with cyclical changes in the earnings, shareholders would not be certain about the amount of dividends.

Investors' desire for current income There are many investors, such as old and retired persons, women etc., who desire to receive regular periodic income. They invest their savings in the shares with a view to use dividends as a source of income to meet their living expenses. Dividends are like wages and salaries for them. These investors will prefer a company with stable dividends to the one with fluctuating dividends.

Institutional investors' requirements Financial, educational and social institutions and unit trusts also invest funds in shares of companies. In India, financial institutions such as IFCI, IDBI, LIC, and UTI are some of the largest investors in corporate securities. Every company is interested to have these financial institutions in the list of their investors. These institutions may generally invest in the shares of those companies, which have a record of paying regular dividends. These institutional investors may not prefer a company, which has a history of adopting an erratic dividend policy. Thus, to cater the requirement of institutional investors, a company prefers to follow a stable dividend policy.

Raising additional finances: A stable dividend policy is also advantageous to the company in its efforts to raise external finances. Stable and regular dividend policy tends to make the share of a company as quality investment rather than a speculation. Investors purchasing these shares intend to hold them for long periods of time. The loyalty and goodwill of shareholders towards a company increases with stable dividend policy. They would be more receptive to an offer by the company for further issues of shares. A history of stable dividends serves to spread ownership of outstanding shares more widely among small investors, and

---

1. *Ibid.*, pp. 448–49.

thereby reduces the chance of loss of control. The persons with small means, in the hope of supplementing their income, usually purchase shares of the companies with a history of paying regular dividends. A stable dividend policy also helps the sale of debentures and preference shares. The fact that the company has been paying dividend regularly in the past is a sufficient assurance to the purchasers of these securities that no default will be made by the company in paying their interest or preference dividend and returning the principal sum. The financial institutions are the largest purchasers of these securities. They purchase debentures and preference shares of those companies, which have a history of paying stable dividends.

Danger of Stability of Dividends

The greatest danger in adopting a stable dividend policy is that once it is established, it cannot be changed without seriously affecting investors' attitude and the financial standing of the company. If a company, with a pattern of stable dividends, misses dividend payment in a year, this break will have an effect on investors more severe than the failure to pay dividend by a company with unstable dividend policy. The companies with stable dividend policy create a 'clientele' that depends on dividend income to meet their living and operating expenses. A cut in dividend is considered as a cut in 'salary.' Because of the serious depressing effect on investors due to a dividend cut, directors have to maintain stability of dividends during lean years even though financial prudence would indicate elimination of dividends or a cut in it. Consequently, to be on the safe side, the dividend rate should be fixed at a conservative figure so that it may be possible to maintain it even in lean periods of several years. To give the benefit of the company's prosperity, extra or interim dividend, can be declared. When a company fails to pay extra dividend, it does not have a depressing effect on investors as the failure to pay a regular dividend does.

TARGET PAYOUT AND DIVIDEND SMOOTHING: LINTNER'S MODEL OF CORPORATE DIVIDEND BEHAVIOUR

We have discussed stability of dividends in terms of stable dividends per share (or dividend rate) and stable payout ratio. A stable payout ratio results into fluctuating dividend per share pattern, which could be a cause of uncertainty for investors. In practice, firms express their dividend policy either in terms of dividend per share or dividend rate. Does this mean that payout ratio is not considered important by firms while determining their dividend policies? Lintner,[1] in his study of the USA companies, found that firms generally think in terms of proportion of earnings to be paid out. Investment requirements are not considered for modifying the pattern of dividend behaviour. Thus firms generally have target payout ratios in view while determining change in dividend per share (or dividend rate).

What are the perceptions of managers of companies in India about the payment of dividends? A study[2] shows that managers are strongly in favour of companies regularly paying dividends and striving to move towards a target payout. The dividend policy should be stable, and should be changed only when it can be maintained in the future. Managers feel that current dividends depend on current earnings, the future earnings potential as well as on dividends paid in the previous year. Dividends must be paid even when a company needs funds for undertaking profitable investment projects.

How can Lintner's model be expressed in formal terms? Let us assume that a firm has EPS_1, as the expected earnings per share in year 1, and p as the target payout ratio. If the firm strictly follows stable payout policy, the expected dividend per share, DIV_1 will be:

$$DIV_1 = pEPS_1 \qquad (1)$$

and dividend *change* (as compared to the dividend per share for the previous year, DIV_0) will be:

$$DIV_1 - DIV_0 = pEPS_1 - DIV_0 \qquad (2)$$

But, in practice, firms do not change the dividend per share (or dividend rate) immediately with change in the earnings per share. Shareholders like a steadily growing dividend per share. Thus, firms change their dividends slowly and gradually even when there are large increases in earnings. This implies that firms have standards regarding the *speed* with which they attempt to move towards the full adjustment of payout to earnings. Lintner has, therefore, suggested the following formula to explain the change in dividends of firms in practice:

$$DIV_1 - DIV_0 = b\,(pEPS_1 - DIV_0) \qquad (3)$$

where b is the **speed of adjustment**. A conservative company will move slowly towards its **target payout**.

The implications of Equation (3) are (*i*) that firms establish their dividends in accordance with the level of current earnings, and (*ii*) that the changes in dividends over time do not correspond exactly with changes in earnings in the immediate time period. In other words, the expected dividend per share (DIV_1) depends on the firm's current earnings (EPS_1) as well as the dividend per share of the previous year (DIV_0); the previous year's dividend per share (DIV_0) depends on that year's earnings per share (EPS_0) and the dividend per share in the year before (DIV_{-1}).

Lintner's model can be expressed in the form of the following regression equation:

$$DIV_t - DIV_{t-1} = a + b\,(pEPS_t - DIV_{t-1}) + e_t$$

$$DIV_t = a + bpEPS_t - bDIV_{t-1} + DIV_{t-1} + e_t$$

$$DIV_t = a + bDIV_{t-1}^* + (1-b)\,DIV_{t-1} + e_t \qquad (4)$$

where DIV_t is the dividend per share in year t, b is the adjustment factor, $DIV_t^* = pEPS_t$ is desired dividend per share, p is the target payout ratio; DIV_{t-1} is dividend per share in year $t-1$ and e is the error term.[3]

---

1. Lintner, J., Distribution of Incomes of Corporations Among Dividends, Retained Earning, and Taxes, *American Economic Review,* 46 (May 1956), pp. 97–133.
2. Bhat, Ramesh and Pandey, I.M., Dividend Decisions: A Study of Managers' Perception, *Decision,* Vol. 21, Nos. 1&2, January–June 1994.
3. In practice, the target payout may not be known. Hence, Equation (4) can be written as follows:
$$DIV_t = a + b_1\,EPS_t + b_2\,DIV_{t-1} + e_t$$
where $b_1 = bp$ (adjustment factor multiplied by target payout), and $b_2 = 1 - b$ (one minus adjustment factor).

We can interpret the term $(1 - b)$ as a **safety factor** that the management observes by not increasing the dividend payment to the levels where it cannot be maintained. Together coefficients a and b can be used to test the hypothesis that management is more likely to increase dividend over time rather than cut them.

FORMS OF DIVIDENDS

The usual practice is to pay dividends in cash. Other options are payment of the **bonus shares** (referred to as **stock dividend** in USA) and **shares buyback**. In this section, we shall also discuss **share split**. The share (stock) split is not a form of dividend; but its effects are similar to the effects of the bonus shares.

Cash Dividend

Companies mostly pay dividends in cash. A company should have enough cash in its bank account when cash dividends are declared. If it does not have enough bank balance, arrangement should be made to borrow funds. When the company follows a stable dividend policy, it should prepare a cash budget for the coming period to indicate the necessary funds, which would be needed to meet the regular dividend payments of the company. It is relatively difficult to make cash planning in anticipation of dividend needs when an unstable policy is followed.

The cash account and the reserves account of a company will be reduced when the cash dividend is paid. Thus, both the total assets and the net worth of the company are reduced when the cash dividend is distributed. The market price of the share drops in most cases by the amount of the cash dividend distributed.[1]

Bonus Shares

An issue of **bonus shares** is the distribution of shares free of cost to the existing shareholders. In India, bonus shares are issued in addition to the cash dividend and not in lieu of cash dividend. Hence companies in India may supplement cash dividend by bonus issues. Issuing bonus shares increases the number of outstanding shares of the company. The bonus shares are distributed proportionately to the existing shareholder. Hence there is no dilution of ownership. For example, if a shareholder owns 100 shares at the time when a 10 per cent (i.e., 1:10) bonus issue is made, she will receive 10 additional shares. The declaration of the bonus shares will increase the paid-up share capital and reduce the reserves and surplus (retained earnings) of the company. The total net worth (paid-up capital plus reserves and surplus) is not affected by the bonus issue. In fact, a bonus issue represents a recapitalisation of reserves and surplus. It is merely an accounting transfer from reserves and surplus to paid-up capital. The following example illustrates this point.

Illustration 18.1: The Effect of Bonus Share

The following is the capital structure of Walchand Sons & Company

Walchand pays bonus shares in 1:10 ratio. At the time of the issue of bonus shares, the market price per share is Rs 30. The bonus shares are issued at the market price - a premium of Rs 20 over the face value of Rs 10 each share.

	Rs in crore
Paid-up share capital (1 crore shares, Rs 10 par)	10
Share premium	15
Reserves and surpluses	8
Total net worth	33

A 1:10 bonus issue implies an issue of 10 lakh new shares to the existing shareholders. Thus, a shareholder holding 10 shares shall get one additional share. At a price of Rs 30 per share, the total value of new shares issued will be Rs 3 crore. This amount would be transferred from the reserves and surplus account into the paid-up share capital account and the share premium account. The share capital account will be increased by Rs 1 crore (10 lakh × Rs 10) and the remaining Rs 2 crore will be transferred to the share premium account. The new capitalisation will be as follows:

	Rs in crore
Paid-up share capital (1.10 crore shares, Rs 10 par)	11
Share premium	17
Reserves and surpluses	5
Total net worth	33

Notice that the total net worth of the company does not change by the bonus shares; only the balance of the paid-up share capital is readjusted.

Does the issue of bonus shares increase the wealth of shareholders? Normatively speaking, the issue of bonus shares does not affect the wealth of shareholders. The earnings per share and market price per share will fall proportionately to the bonus issue. For example, as a result of increasing the number of shares by 10 per cent, the earnings per share of Walchand Company will decrease by 10 per cent. The market price per share will also fall by 10 per cent, all other things being equal. Suppose the net earnings of the company are Rs 2.20 crore. The earnings per share before the declaration of the bonus issue is Rs 2.20 (Rs 2.20 crore/1.00 crore) and after the bonus shares, the earnings per share are Rs 2 (Rs 2.20 crore/1.10 crore). However, the proportional earnings of shareholders will remain unchanged. Thus, the total earnings of a shareholder holding 100 shares before the bonus shares is Rs 220 (Rs 2.20 × 100) and his total earning will still be Rs 220 after the bonus issue (Rs 2.00 × 110). Similarly, the market price per share will drop by Rs 2.73; that is, Rs 30 $(1 - 1.00/1.10)$. The total market value of the shareholder's holdings after the bonus shares is Rs 3,000 (Rs 27.27 × 110), same as the total value before the bonus shares. Thus, the bonus shares have no impact on the wealth of shareholders. In practice, it is observed that, immediately after the announcement of bonus issue, the market price of a company's share changes depending on the investor's expectations. Sometimes a sharp decline in the share price may be observed if the bonus issue falls short of the investors' expectation.

It may be emphasised here that the market value of the share may improve as a result of the bonus issue if it is followed by increased dividends in the immediate future. If the dividends do not increase, it is likely that the market price may fall. This is confirmed by an empirical study conducted under the Indian context.[2]

Advantages of Bonus Shares

Prima facie the bonus shares do not affect the wealth of the shareholders. In practice, however, it carries certain advantages both for shareholders and the company.[3]

---

1. Hastings, *op.cit.*, p.370.
2. Gupta, L.C., *Bonus Shares*, Macmillan Co. of India Ltd.
3. For a discussion of pros and cons of bonus shares (stock dividend), see Gupta, *op. cit.*, Porterfield, J.T.S., Dividends, Dilution and Delusion, *Harvard Business Review*, 37 (Nov.–Dec. 1959), pp. 156–57; Barker, C.A., Evaluation of Stock Dividends, *Harvard Business Review*, 36 (July–August 1958); Eismann, P.C. and Moser, E.A., Stock Dividends: Management's View, *Financial Analysis Journal*, (July–Aug. 1978), pp. 77–80.

Shareholders The following are advantages of the bonus shares to shareholders:

Tax benefit One of the advantages to shareholders in the receipt of bonus shares is the beneficial treatment of such dividends with regard to income taxes. When a shareholder receives cash dividend from company, this is included in his ordinary income and taxed at ordinary income tax rate. But the receipt of bonus shares by the shareholder is not taxable as income. Further, the shareholder can sell the new shares received by way of the bonus issue to satisfy his desire for income and pay capital gain taxes, which are usually less than the income taxes on the cash dividends. The shareholder could sell a few shares of his original holding to derive capital gains. But selling the original shares are considered as a sale of asset by some shareholders. They do not mind selling the shares received by way of the bonus shares as they consider it a windfall gain and not a part of the principal. Note that in India as per the current law investors do not pay any taxes on dividends but they have to pay tax on capital gains. Hence, the Indian law makes bonus shares less attractive than dividends.

Indication of higher future profits The issue of bonus shares is normally interpreted by shareholders as an indication of higher profitability. When the profits of a company do not rise, and it declares a bonus issue, the company will experience a dilution of earnings as a result of the additional shares outstanding. Since a dilution of earnings is not desirable, directors usually declare bonus shares only when they expect rise in earnings to offset the additional outstanding shares. Bonus shares, thus, may convey some information that may have a favourable impact on value of the shares. But it should be noticed that the impact on value is that of the growth expectation and not the bonus shares per se.

Future dividends may increase If a company has been following a policy of paying a fixed amount of dividend per share and continues it after the declaration of the bonus issue, the total cash dividends of the shareholders will increase in the future. For example, a company may be paying a Re 1 dividend per share and pays 1:1 bonus shares with the announcement that the cash dividend per share will remain unchanged. If a shareholder originally held 100 shares, he will receive additional 100 shares. His total cash dividend in future will be Rs 200 (Rs 1 × 200) instead of Rs 100 (Re 1 × 100) received in the past. The increase in the shareholders' cash dividend may have a favourable effect on the value of the share. It should be, however, realised that the bonus issue per se has no effect on the value of the share; it is the increase in earnings from the company's invests that affects the value.

Psychological value The declaration of the bonus issue may have a favourable psychological effect on shareholders. The receipt of bonus shares gives them a chance to sell the shares to make capital gains without impairing their principal investment. They also associate it with the prosperity of the company. Because of these positive aspects of the bonus issue, the market usually receives it positively. The sale of the shares, received by way of the bonus shares, by some shareholders widens the distribution of the company's shares. This tends to increase the market interest in the company's shares; thus supporting or raising its market price.

Company The bonus share is also advantageous to the company. The advantages are:

Conservation of cash The declaration of a bonus issue allows the company to declare a dividend without using up cash that may be needed to finance the profitable investment opportunities within the company. The company is, thus, able to retain earnings and at the same time satisfy the desires of shareholders to receive dividend. We have stated earlier that directors of a company must consider the financial needs of the company and the desires of shareholders while making the dividend decision. These two objectives are often in conflict. The use of bonus issue represents a compromise which enables directors to achieve both these objectives of a dividend policy. The company could retain earnings without declaring bonus shares issue. But the receipt of bonus shares satisfies shareholders psychologically. Also, their total cash dividend can increase in future, when cash dividend per share remains the same. Note that in India, bonus shares cannot be issued in lieu of dividends; hence the cash conservation argument for issuing bonus shares is not a strong argument.

Only means to pay dividend under financial difficulty and contractual restrictions In some situations, even if the company's intention is not to retain earnings, the bonus issue (with a small amount of dividend) is the only means to pay dividends and satisfy the desires of shareholders. When a company is facing a stringent cash situation, the only way to replace or reduce cash dividend is the issue of bonus shares. The declaration of the bonus issue under such a situation should not convey a message of the company's profitability, but financial difficulty. The declaration of the bonus issue is also necessitated when the restrictions to pay the cash dividend are put under loan agreements. Thus, under the situations of financial stringency or contractual constrain in paying cash dividend, the bonus issue is meant to maintain the confidence of shareholders in the company.

More attractive share price Sometimes the intention of a company in issuing bonus shares is to reduce the market price of the share and make it more attractive to investors. If the market price of a company's share is very high, it may not appeal to small investors. If the price could be brought down to a desired range, the trading activity would increase. Therefore, the bonus issue is used as a means to keep the market price of the share within a desired trading range. As we shall discuss below, this objective can also be achieved by share split.

Limitations of Bonus Shares

Bonus shares have the following limitations:

- Shareholders' wealth remains unaffected
- Costly to administer
- Problem of adjusting EPS and P/E ratio

Bonus shares are considered valuable by most shareholders. But they fail to realise that the bonus shares do not affect their wealth and therefore, in itself it has no value for them. The declaration of bonus shares is a method of capitalising the past earnings of the shareholders. Thus, it is a formal way of recognising something (earnings), which the shareholders already own. It merely divides the ownership of the company into a large number of share certificates. Bonus shares represent simply a division of corporate pie into a large number of pieces.[1] In fact, the bonus issue does not give any extra or special benefit to a shareholder. His proportionate ownership in the company does not change. The chief advantage of the bonus share issue is that it has a favourable psychological impact on shareholders. The issue of bonus shares gives an indication of the company's growth to shareholders. Shareholders welcome the distribution of bonus shares since it has informational value.

The disadvantage of bonus issues from the company's point of view is that they are *more costly to administer* than cash dividend.[2] The company has to now print certificates and post them to thousands of shareholders. The bonus issue can be disadvantageous if the company declares periodic small bonus shares. The investment analysts do not adjust the earnings per share for small issues of bonus shares. They adjust only the significant issues of bonus shares. When the earnings per share are not adjusted, the measured growth in the earnings per share will be less than the true growth based on the adjusted earnings per share. As a result the price–earnings ratio would be distorted downwards.

Conditions for the Issue of Bonus Shares

In India, bonus shares are issued in addition to, and not in lieu of, cash dividends. A company is not allowed to declare bonus shares unless partly paid-up shares have been converted into fully paid-up shares. Bonus shares are made out of share premium and free reserve, which includes investment allowance reserve but excludes capital reserve on account of assets revaluation. In no time the amount of bonus issue should exceed the paid-up capital. A company can declare bonus shares once in a year. The company's shareholders should pass a resolution approving the proposal of the bonus issue, clearly indicating the rate of dividend is payable on the increased capital. Company intending to issue bonus shares should not be in default of payments of statutory dues to employees and term loans to financial institutions.

The maximum bonus shares ratio is 1:1; that is, one bonus share for one fully paid-up share held by the existing shareholders. However, two criteria are required to be satisfied within the limit of the maximum ratio. They are:

- Residual reserve criterion
- Profitability criterion.

Residual reserve criterion It requires that reserve remaining after the amount capitalised for bonus issue should be at least equal to 40 per cent of the increased paid-up capital. Redemption reserve and capital reserve on account of assets revaluation are excluded while investment allowance reserve is included in computing the minimum residual reserve. This criterion can be expressed as follows:

$$(\text{Pre-bonus reserve}) - \text{Pre-bonus paid-up capital}$$
$$\times \text{Bonus ratio} \geq 0.4\,(1 + \text{Bonus ratio})$$
$$\times \text{Pre-bonus paid-up capital} \qquad (5)$$

Profitability criterion It requires that 30 per cent of the previous three years' average pre-tax profit (PBT) should be at least equal to 10 per cent of the *increased* paid-up capital. This criterion can be expressed as follows:

$$0.3 \times \text{three year average PBT} \geq 0.1(1 + \text{bonus ratio})$$
$$\times \text{pre–bonus paid-up capital}$$

Consider an example. A company has the following data:

	Rs
Paid-up share capital	80
Reserves	100
Net worth	180
Average PBT of previous three years	50

We can plug these data respectively in Equations (1) and (2) as follows to determine the maximum bonus ratio:

Residual reserve criterion

$$100 - (80 \times \text{Bonus ratio}) \geq 0.4(1 + \text{Bonus ratio}) \times 80$$
$$100 - (80 \times \text{Bonus ratio}) \geq 32 + 32 \times \text{Bonus ratio})$$
$$68 \geq 112 \times \text{Bonus ratio}$$
$$68/112 \geq \text{Bonus ratio or } 17 : 28 \text{ Bonus ratio}$$

Profitability criterion

$$0.3 \times 50 \geq 0.1(1 + \text{Bonus ratio}) \times 80$$
$$15 \geq 8 + 8 \times \text{Bonus share}$$
$$7 \geq 8 \times \text{Bonus ratio}$$
$$7/8 \geq \text{Bonus ratio or } 7 : 8 \text{ Bonus ratio}$$

Note that 68/112 is less than 7/8. Therefore, the company will be allowed to declare bonus issue in the ratio of 68:112 (or 17:28). The increased paid-up capital and residual reserve will be as follows:

	Rs
Paid-up share capital (80 + 80 × 17/28)	128.57
Reserve (100 – 80 × 17/28)	51.43
	180.00

You may notice that residual reserve (Rs 51.43) is 40 per cent of the increased paid-up capital (Rs 128.57).

SHARE SPLIT

A **share split** is a method to increase the number of outstanding shares through a proportional reduction in the par value of the share. A share split affects only the par value and the number of

---

1. Porterfield, James, T.S., Dividend, Dilution and Delusion, *Harvard Business Review*, November–December 1959, pp. 156–61.
2. Van Horne, James, C., *Financial Management and Policy,* Prentice-Hall of India, 1971, p. 277.

outstanding shares; the shareholders' total funds remain unaltered. Consider an example. The following is the capital structure of Walchand Sons & Company

	Rs
Paid-up share capital (1 crore Rs 10 par)	10
Share premium	15
Reserves and surplus	8
Total net worth	33

Walchand Company split their shares two-for-one. The capitalisation of the company after the split is as follows:

	Rs
Paid-up share capital (2 crore Rs 5 par)	10
Share premium	15
Reserves and surplus	8
Total net worth	33

Bonus Share vs. Share Split

As with the bonus share the total net worth does not change and the number of outstanding shares increases substantially with the share split. The bonus issue and the share split are similar except for the difference in their accounting treatment. In the case of bonus shares, the balance of the reserves and surpluses account decreases due to a transfer to the paid-up capital and the share premium accounts. The par value per share remains unaffected. With a share split, the balance of the equity accounts does not change, but the par value per share changes. The earnings per share will be diluted and the market price per share will fall proportionately with a share split. But the total value of the holdings of a shareholder remains unaffected with a share split.

Reasons for Share Split

The following are reasons for splitting of a firm's ordinary shares:[1]

- To make trading in shares attractive
- To signal the possibility of higher profits in the future
- To give higher dividends to shareholders

To make shares attractive The main purpose of a stock split is to reduce the market price of the share in order to make it attractive to investors. With reduction in the market price of the share, the shares of the company are placed in a more popular trading range. For example, if the shares of a company are sold in the lots of 100 shares, it requires Rs 10,000 to buy 100 shares selling for Rs 100 per share. A five-for-one split would lower the price to Rs 20 per share and the total cost of 100 shares to Rs 2,000. The wealthy investor can still purchase shares of Rs 10,000 by acquiring a larger number of shares (500 share at Rs 20). But a small investor can also afford to buy 100 shares for Rs 2,000 for which she otherwise needed Rs 10,000 before the split. Thus, the reduction in the market price, caused by the

share split, motivates more investors, particularly those with small savings, to purchase the shares. This helps in increasing the marketability and liquidity of a company's shares.

Indication of higher future profits The share splits are used by the company management to communicate to investors that the company is expected to earn higher profits in future. The market price of high-growth firm's shares increases very fast. If the shares are not split periodically, they fall outside the popular trading range. Therefore, these companies resort to share splits from time to time. The share split like bonus shares, thus, has an informational value that the firm is expected to perform efficiently and profitably and that the shares have been split to avoid future high price per share.

Increased dividend When the share is split, seldom does a company reduce or increase the cash dividend per share proportionately. However, the total dividends of a shareholder increase after a share split. For example, a company may be paying a cash dividend of Rs 3 per share before the share split. But after a split of three-of-one, the company may pay a cash dividend of Rs 1.50 per share. A shareholder holding 100 shares before the split will receive a total cash dividend of Rs 300. The number of shares owned by the shareholder will increase to 300 after the split and his total cash dividend will be Rs 450. The increased dividends may favourably affect the after-split market price of the share. It should be noted that the share split per se has no effect on the market price of share.

Reverse Split

Under the situation of falling price of a company's share, the company may want to reduce the number of outstanding shares to prop up the market price per share. The reduction of the number of outstanding shares by increasing per share par value is known as a **reverse split**. For example, a company has 20 lakh outstanding shares of Rs 5 par value per share. Suppose it declares a reverse split of one-for-four. After the split, it will have 5 lakh shares of Rs 20 par value per share. The reverse split is sometimes used to stop the market price per share below a certain level, say, Rs 10 per share which is par value of most shares in India. The reverse split is generally an indication of financial difficulty, and is, therefore, intended to increase the market price per share.[2]

BUYBACK OF SHARES

The **buyback of shares** is the repurchase of its own shares by a company. Until recently, the buyback of shares by companies in India was prohibited under Section 77 of the Indian Companies Act. As a result of the Companies (Amendment) Act 1999, a company in India can now buyback its own shares. A number of companies, such as Reliance Industries and Ashok Leyland, took advantage of this change immediately and offered to buy back the equity shares.

In India the following conditions apply in case of the buyback shares:

---

1. Hausman, W.H., *et. al.,* Stock Splits, Price Changes and Trading Profit: A Synthesis, *Journal of Business,* 44 (Jan. 1971), pp. 69–77. Also see Barker, C.A., Effective Stock Splits, *Harvard Business Review,* 34 (Jan.–Feb. 1956) pp. 101–06.
2. West, R.R. and Brouilette, A.B., Reverse Stock Splits, *Financial Executives,* 38 (Jan. 1970), pp. 12–17.

- A company buying back its shares will not issue fresh capital, except bonus issue, for the next 12 months.
- The company will state the amount to be used for the buyback of shares and seek prior approval of shareholders.
- The buyback of shares can be affected only utilizing the free reserves, viz., reserves not specifically earmarked for some purpose.
- The company will not borrow funds to buy back shares.
- The shares bought under the buyback schemes will be extinguished and they cannot be reissued.

Methods of Shares Buyback

There are two methods of the share buyback in India. First, a company can buy its shares through **authorized brokers** on the open market. For example, Reliance Industries announced buyback of shares in the year 2000 at a price of Rs 303 per share. The total amount for the buyback was Rs 11 billion (or Rs 1,100 crore). The reason for the buyback was that the company wanted to signal to the shareholders that it would reward its shareholders by returning surplus cash to them. Second, the company can make a **tender offer**, which will specify the purchase price, the total amount and the period within which shares will be bought back. For example, Kirloskar Oil Engines Limited made a tender offer to buy back 40 lakh shares at Rs 75 for Rs 30 crore or Rs 300 million). This was about 21 per cent of the existing equity capital of the company. The stated purpose of the buyback was to return surplus cash to shareholders resulting in improvement in earnings and enhance shareholder value. Similarly, India Nippon Electricals Limited offered to buyback through the tender offer 395,600 shares of the face value of Rs 10 each aggregating 7.68 per cent of the paid-up share capital at a price not exceeding Rs 230 per share. The total amount for the buyback was Rs 9.10 crore. Yet another company going via the tender route was India Forge and Drop Stampings Limited. The offer was for 3.75 lakh shares at Rs 12. The face value is Rs 10. There is a third method of the share buyback. The firm can buy block of shares from a single buyer at negotiated price. This route is not available in India for normal buyback activity since it involves takeover code.

Effects of the Shares Buyback

Are there financial reasons for the buyback of shares? It is believed that the buyback will be financially beneficial to the company, the buying shareholders and the remaining shareholders. As we have explained, the bought up shares will be extinguished and will not be reissued. This will permanently reduce the amount of equity capital and the number of outstanding shares. If the company distributed surplus cash and it maintains its operating efficiency, EPS will increase. The share price will increase as P/E ratio is expected to remain the same after the buyback. Yet another consequence will be the increase in the company's debt-equity ratio due to reduced equity capital. Companies with exiting low debt-equity ratio will be able to move to their target capital structure. Let us consider an example.

Illustration 18.2: Financial Consequences of the Buyback of Shares

XYZ Company has equity capital (net worth) of Rs 800 crore – paid-up share capital Rs 200 crore and reserve and surplus of Rs 600 crore. The par value of fully paid-up shares is Rs 10. Thus, the company has 20 crore outstanding shares, and the book value per share is Rs 40. *XYZ* has profit after tax of Rs 250 crore. The company's EPS is: 250/20 = Rs 12.50. The current market price of the share is Rs 100 giving a P/E ratio of Rs 100/Rs 12.50 = 8 times. The company's current dividend rate is 60 per cent, which translates into DPS of Rs $10 \times 60\%$ = Rs 6 and current dividend yield of Rs 6/Rs 100 = 0.06 or 6 per cent. The company's debt is Rs 1,200 crore, which implies a book value debt-equity ratio of 1.50. The market value debt-equity ratio is Rs 1,200/(Rs 100×20) = 0.60. Suppose the company decides to buyback shares amounting to Rs 120 crore at the rate of Rs 120 each share (20 per cent premium over the current market price). What are the consequences? The buying shareholders gain as the offered price is higher than the current market price. The other financial effects of the share buyback are shown below:

Equity capital	Rs 800 – Rs 120 = Rs 680 crore
Number of shares	20 – 1 = 19 crore
EPS	250/19 = Rs 13.15
Percentage increase in EPS	Rs 13.15/Rs 12.50 – 1 = 0.052 or 5.2%
P/E ratio	8 times (assumed to remain constant)
Market price	Rs 13.15×8 = Rs 105.20
Percentage increase in share price	Rs 105.20/Rs 100 – 1 = 0.052 or 5.2%
DPS	Rs 6
Dividend yield	Rs 6/Rs 105.20 = 0.057 or 5.7%
Debt-equity ratio (book value)	Rs 1,200/Rs 680 = 1.76
Debt-equity ratio (market value)	Rs 1,200/(Rs 105.20×19) = 0.60

Now assume that the share price is Rs 40 instead of Rs 100, and the company buys back each share at Rs 48. What are the effects of buying back shares? The current P/E ratio is Rs 40/Rs 12.5 = 3.2, and dividend yield is Rs 6/Rs 40 = 0.15 or 15%. The book value debt-equity ratio is 1.50, and the market value debt-equity ratio is also Rs 1,200/(Rs 40×20)= 1.50. The company will be able to reduce the number of shares by Rs 120 crore/Rs 48 = 2.5 crore. The other effects are as follows:

Equity capital	Rs 800 – Rs 120 = Rs 680 crore
Number of shares	20 – 2.5 = 17.5 crore
EPS	250/17.5 = Rs 14.30
Percentage increase in EPS	Rs 14.30/Rs 12.50 – 1 = 0.144 or 14.4%
P/E ratio	3.2 times (assumed to remain constant)
Market price	Rs 14.30×3.2 = Rs 45.76
Percentage increase in share price	Rs 45.76/Rs 40 – 1 = 0.144 or 14.4%
DPS	Rs 6
Dividend yield	Rs 6/ Rs 45.76 = 0.1311 or 13.11%
Debt-equity ratio (book value)	Rs 1,200/Rs 680 = 1.76
Debt-equity ratio (market value)	Rs 1,200/(Rs 45.76×17.5) = 1.50

You may notice that the remaining shareholders' expected benefit is more when the company's share is quoted below its book value. Both EPS and share price increase by a higher percentage. You may also notice that the book value debt-equity ratio increases after the shares buyback. However, there is no change in the market value debt-equity ratio. Remember that we have assumed that the P/E ratio remains constant.

Illustration 18.2 shows that the effect of the buyback on share prices is higher for those companies whose shares sell at lower prices or are undervalued before the buyback programmes. In India, the share prices of a number of the Sensex companies are quite high. These companies will require huge amount of cash to buyback even a small fraction of their equity. Also, a number of these companies have high book value debt-equity ratio, which is likely to increase after the buyback of shares. This may affect the credit ratings of debt instruments of these companies. Further, these companies, as per the existing law, cannot issue fresh capital until one year after the buyback. Thus, only those high capitalisation companies that have huge surplus cash and who do not require cash in the near future will go for the shares buyback.

Evaluation of the Share Buyback

The most plausible reason for the buyback seems to be that a company may like to return surplus cash, which it cannot put to any profitable investment, to shareholders. Companies may also like to use surplus cash to buy back shares rather than pay large dividends, which they cannot maintain in the future years. In those countries, where dividends are taxed at a higher rate than the capital gains, companies may like to resort to shares buyback from time to time to reduce shareholders tax burden. However, it is inconceivable that a profitable, growing company will like to distribute cash to shareholders through the buyback route. There might be other reasons for the buyback programmes of the companies. A company, which has very low debt-equity ratio, may like to reduce equity capital through the buyback mechanism to achieve a higher target debt-equity mix. The only reason for doing so may to reduce the chances of takeover. Yet another reason may be the need to buy back shares from the employees who hold shares after exercising stock options, and they are unable to sell or are restricted to sell shares to the outsiders.

We can summarise the advantages of the buyback as follows:

- *Return of surplus cash to shareholders* The buying shareholders will benefit since the company generally offer a price higher than the current market price of the share.
- *Increase in the share value* When the company distributes the surplus cash, its operating efficiency and P/E ratio remains intact. With reduced number of shares, EPS increases and share price also increases.
- *Increase in the temporarily undervalued share price* The share price of a number of companies may be undervalued. This maybe especially true for the developing capital markets. Companies may buyback shares at higher prices to move up the current share prices.
- *Achieving the target capital structure* If a company has high proportion of equity in its capital structure, it can reduce equity capital by buying back its shares.
- *Consolidating control* The promoters of the company benefit by consolidating their ownership and control over companies through the buyback arrangement. They do not sell their shares to the company rather make the buyback attractive for others. Their proportionate ownership increases.
- *Tax savings by companies* Dividend payments are taxable in the hands of companies at 12.5 per cent. They will avoid paying dividend taxes if they compensate shareholders through the share buyback. This game will be played only if the tax authorities disregard it.
- *Protection against hostile takeovers* In a hostile takeover, a company may buyback its shares to reduce the availability of shares and make takeover difficult.

Thus the buyback of shares provides a flexible financial mechanism to adjust the capital structure and financial position of a company when warranted. It is a tool to enhance the shareholder value. It can also be used to defend the company from the hostile takeovers.

All do not think that the share buyback is a virtuous tool in the hands of the company. The following are the drawbacks of the buyback:

- *Not an effective defence against takeover* The buyback of shares may be useful as a defence against hostile takeover only in case of the cash rich companies. In India, companies are not allowed to borrow to buy back their shares. Therefore, the buyback is not effective in protecting those companies that do not have cash.
- *Shareholders do not like the buyback* Most companies will not offer the buyback schemes frequently; they will buyback shares once in a while. Shareholders may not, therefore, like the buyback of shares; they might prefer increasing dividends over the years, They consider dividends more dependable than the share buyback.
- *Loss to the remaining shareholders* The remaining shareholders may lose if the company pays excessive price for the shares under the buyback scheme.
- *Signal of low growth opportunities* The buyback of shares utilises the firm's cash. It may signal to investors that the company does not have long-term growth opportunities to utilise the cash. It may also weak competitive position.

DIVIDEND POLICY ANALYSIS: CASE OF (L&T) LIMITED

We have already analysed in earlier chapters L&T's cost of capital and capital structure, respectively. In this section, we shall analyse L&T's dividend policy. Table 18.1 provides financial data for L&T from the year 1990 to the year 2003.

Table 18.1: L&T's EPS, DPS and other financial data

Year	EPS Rs	DPS Rs	Payout %	P/E times	DY %	EY %	Price Rs
Mar–90	6.3	2.3	37.2	13.0	3.1	7.7	82.0
Mar–91	9.4	3.0	31.8	12.0	2.7	8.3	112.5
Mar–92	7.8	2.4	30.8	49.9	0.9	2.0	390.1
Mar–93	5.6	3.3	57.6	31.5	2.0	3.2	177.7
Mar–94	9.2	4.0	44.0	29.4	1.5	3.4	269.9
Mar–95	12.1	4.8	39.5	21.5	1.9	4.7	259.9
Mar–96	13.4	5.6	41.4	18.0	2.5	5.6	242.1
Mar–97	16.6	6.0	36.3	12.1	3.0	8.3	199.9
Mar–98	21.4	6.5	30.4	11.4	2.7	8.8	243.0
Mar–99	18.9	6.5	34.4	12.4	2.8	8.1	233.9
Mar–00	13.7	6.5	47.4	20.9	2.3	4.8	287.4
Mar–01	8.9	6.5	73.5	25.0	2.9	4.0	221.2
Mar–02	16.5	7.0	42.5	11.0	3.9	9.1	180.8
Mar–03	17.4	7.5	43.1	10.6	4.1	9.4	184.7
Average	12.7	5.1	42.2	19.9	2.6	6.2	220.4

Behaviour of EPS, DPS and payout L&T's EPS has grown faster than its DPS. EPS has shown wide fluctuations, while DPS has been slowly and steadily growing (Figure 18.3). Consequently,

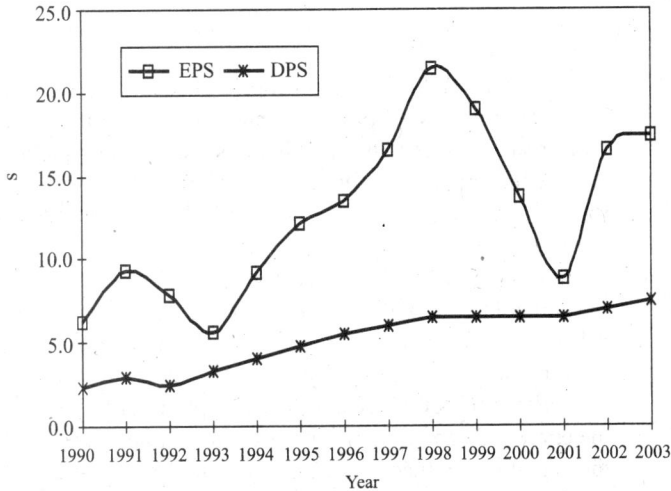

Figure 18.3: L&T's EPS and DPS during 1990–2003

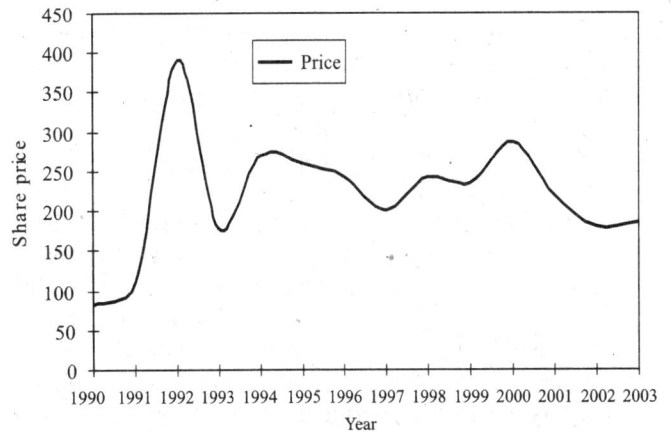

Figure 18.5: L&T's Share Price Behaviour, 1990–2003

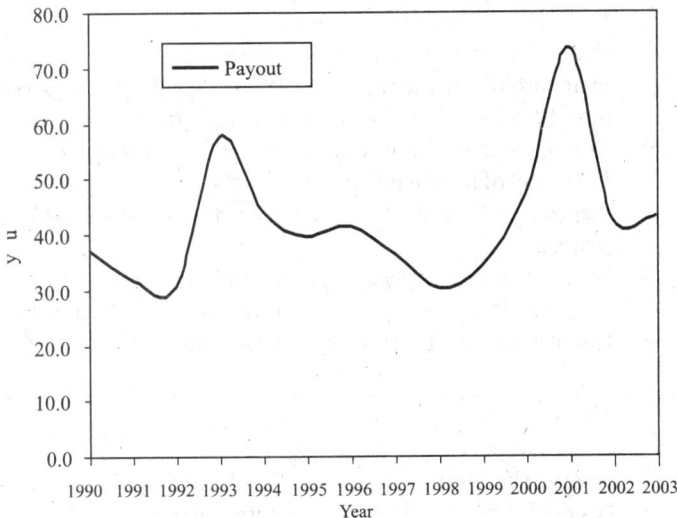

Figure 18.4: L&T's Payout Ratio, 1990–2003

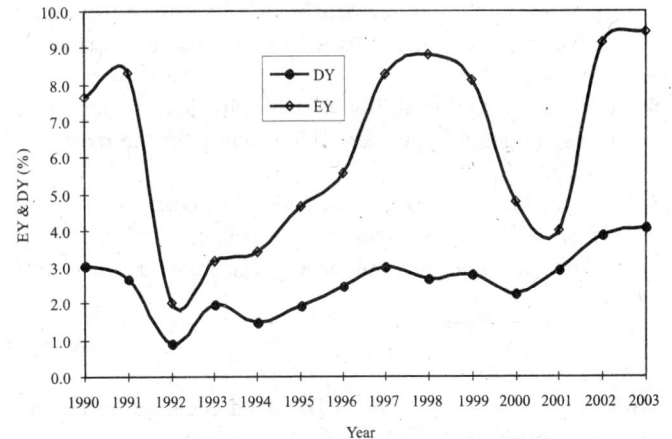

Figure 18.6: L&T's Earnings and dividend yield

dividend payout ratio shows wide variations—ranging between 30 per cent in 1992 to 74 per cent in 2001 (Figure 18.4). The average payout during 1990 to 2003 is 42 per cent.

Behaviour of share price Figure 18.5 shows that L&T's share price after reaching peak in 1992 (the year of stock scam in india), has been fluctuating within a narrow range. There does seem to be significant correlation between L&T's share price and EPS or DPS or payout ratio.

Earnings and dividend yields L&T's dividend yield declined from 1990 to 1993, and after that , it has been increasing except in 1994 and 2000. It has, however, remained below 3 per cent. The average dividend yield from 1990 to 2003 is 2.6 per cent. L&T's earnings yield showed a high degree of variability (Figure 18.6). It peaked to 9.4 per cent in 2003. The average earnings yield during 1990 to 2003 was 6.2 per cent.

Target payout We can use Lintner's model to explain L&T's dividend behaviour. We obtained the following results when we regressed DIV_t.(we use the term DIV for DPS) with EPS_t and DIV_{t-1}.

$$DIV_t = a + b_1\,EPS_t + b_2\,DIV_{t-1} + e_t$$

$$DIV_t = 0.620 + 0.039\,EPS_t + 0.851\,DIV_{t-1}$$

It may be seen from the results that L&T's dividend decision is influenced much more by the past dividend than by current EPS. Assuming that L&T's expected EPS in 2004 is Rs 20, then, the expected dividend per share will be:

$$DIV_{2004} = 0.620 + 0.039 \times 20 + 0.851 \times 7.5 = Rs\ 7.8$$

We may recall that the target payout ratio, $DIV^* = pEPS$. Therefore, the coefficient $b_1 = 0.039 = bp$ (where p is the target payout and b is the speed of adjustment factor) and the coefficient $b_2 = 0.851 = 1 - b$. Thus the value of b (adjustment factor) and p (target payout) is given as follows:

$$bp = 0.039$$

$$1 - b = 0.851$$

$$b = 1 - 0.851 = 0.149$$

$$0.149p = 0.039$$

$$p = 0.039 / 0.149 = 0.26$$

L&T's empirically determined target payout is 26 per cent. However, Its actual average payout during 1990-2003 is 42 per cent.

SUMMARY

- Dividends may take two forms: cash dividend and bonus shares (stock dividend). In India, bonus shares cannot be issued in lieu of cash dividends. They are paid with cash dividends.
- Bonus shares have a psychological appeal. They do not increase the value of shares.
- Companies generally prefer to pay cash dividends. They finance their expansion and growth by issuing new shares or borrowing. This behaviour is based on the belief that shareholders are entitled to some return on their investment.
- Most companies have long-term payment ratio targets. But they do not apply target payout ratios to each year's earnings. They try to stabilise dividend payments by moving slowly towards the target payout each year.
- Also, they consider past dividends and current as well as future earnings in determining dividend payment. Investors recognise this. Any extreme changes are read as signals of management's expectations about the company's performance in future. Thus dividends have information contents.
- Companies like to follow a stable dividend policy since investors generally prefer such a policy for the reason of certainty.
- A stable dividend policy does not mean constant dividend per share. It means reasonably predictable dividend policy. Companies determine dividend per share or dividend rate keeping in mind their long-term payout ratio.
- The firm's ability to pay dividend depends on its funds requirements for growth, shareholders' desire and liquidity. A growth firm should set its dividend rate at a low level (because of its high needs for funds) and move towards its target slowly.
- In addition to cash dividends, companies issue bonus shares to shareholders. Bonus shares have no real economic gain; it has psychological value and information content.
- Shareholders expect that the company in the future will improve its performance and it will apply dividend rate to the enhanced capital. In this hope the price may increase. If the actual experience is poor performance and no increase in dividends, share will decline. Share split has the same effect as the bonus shares.
- In India now companies are authorised to buy back their shares. But they cannot do so by raising debt. They will use their surplus cash for doing so. Also, after the buyback for next 12 months they can issue share capital.
- The purpose of the buyback is to provide companies the flexibility of improving their EPS and share price, to defend themselves from hostile takeovers and adjust their capital structure.
- In practice, share prices may fall if the buyback results into slow growth. It may not be effective in countering the takeover if it does not have enough surplus cash.

KEY CONCEPTS

Bonus	Dividend equalisation reserve	Reserve share split	Stock dividend
Buyback of shares	Dividend safety factor	Residual dividend theory	Target payout
Clientele effect	Dividend smoothing	Speed of adjustment factor	
Dividend	Dividend stability		

ILLUSTRATIVE SOLVED PROBLEMS

Problem 18.1: Two companies—Alpha Ltd. and Beta Ltd. are in the same industry with identical earnings per share for the last five years. The Alpha Ltd. has a policy of paying 40 per cent of earnings as dividends, while the Beta Ltd. pays a constant amount of dividend per share. There is disparity between the market prices of the shares of the two companies. The price of Alpha's share is generally lower than that of Beta, even though in some years Alpha paid more dividends than Beta. The data on earnings, dividends and market price for the two companies are as under:

Alpha Ltd.

Year	EPS Rs	DPS Rs	Market Price Rs
2000	4.00	1.60	12.00
2001	1.50	0.60	8.50
2002	5.00	2.00	13.50
2003	4.00	1.60	11.50
2004	8.00	3.20	14.50

Beta Ltd.

Year	EPS Rs	DPS Rs	Market Price Rs
2000	4.00	1.80	13.50
2001	1.50	1.80	12.50
2002	5.00	1.80	12.50
2003	4.00	1.80	12.50
2004	8.00	1.80	15.00

(*i*) Calculate (*a*) payout ratio, (*b*) dividend yield and (*c*) earning yield for both the companies.

(*ii*) What are the reasons for the differences in the market prices of the two companies' shares?

(*iii*) What can be done by Alpha Limited to increase the market price of its shares?

Solution:

(i) The following table shows payout, dividend yield and earnings yield for Alpha and Beta.

Year	Payout Alpha	Payout Beta	Dividend Yield Alpha	Dividend Yield Beta	Earnings Yield Alpha	Earnings Yield Beta
2000	0.40	0.45	0.13	0.13	0.33	0.30
2001	0.40	1.20	0.07	0.14	0.18	0.12
2002	0.40	0.36	0.15	0.14	0.37	0.40
2003	0.40	0.45	0.14	0.44	0.35	0.32
2004	0.40	0.23	0.22	0.12	0.55	0.53

(ii) It seems that investors evaluate the shares of these two companies in terms of dividend payments. The average dividend per share over a period of five years for both the firms is Rs 1.80. But the average market price for Beta Ltd. (Rs 13.20) has been 10 per cent higher than the average market price for Alpha Ltd. (Rs 12). The market has used a higher capitalisation rate to discount the fluctuating dividend per share of Alpha Ltd., thus valuing the shares of Alpha Ltd. at a lower price than that of the Beta Ltd.

(iii) It is obvious that the market evaluates these firms in terms of dividends. A higher market price might be obtained for the shares of Alpha Ltd., if it increases its dividend payout ratio. The company should evaluate this option in light of funds requirements.

Problem 18.2: The Sisodia Ltd. is a fast growing manufacturing firm. It earns above industry return on its investment. It has been earning a rate in excess of 25 per cent on its investments in the past and has good prospects of earnings at the same rate in future as well. The Sisodia Ltd. has been following a dividend policy of paying 70 per cent of the earnings to shareholders and retaining 30 per cent. This dividend policy is justified on the grounds that the sole objective of a company is to pay dividends and that dividends have a positive impact upon the price of the share.

If most of the company's shareholders are young wealthy persons in high tax brackets, is the current dividend policy of the company justified?

Solution: The current dividend policy of the company is not justified on two grounds: (i) the company is earning a high rate of return on its investment, which shareholders are unlikely to earn themselves, and (ii) shareholders are wealthy persons in high tax brackets; therefore, they would prefer greater retention (which should result in future capital gains) than is being presently done by the company. The current dividend policy results into a growth of $0.25 \times 0.3 = 0.075$ or 7.5 per cent only. If the company retains more, say 70 per cent, its growth rate would be $0.25 \times 0.7 = 0.175$ or 17.5 per cent which would reflect in high share price. Thus, shareholders can earn high capital gains on which tax rate is lower than the ordinary income. Though a company may exist for the purpose of paying dividends in the long-run, if it can currently earn more than shareholders, the retention ratio should be quite high. Since the company is growing at an above-average rate, it is likely that the market price of the company's shares is lower than it might be with higher retention.

REVIEW QUESTIONS

1. Explain the nature of the factors which influence the dividend policy of a firm.
2. 'The primary purpose for which a firm exists is the payment of dividend. Therefore, irrespective of the firm's needs and the desires of shareholders, a firm should follow a policy of very high dividend payout.' Do you agree? Why or why not?
3. What are the factors that influence management's decision to pay dividend of a certain amount?
4. What is a stable dividend policy? Why should it be followed? What can be the consequences of changing a stable dividend policy?
5. How is the corporate dividend behaviour determined? Explain Lintner's model in this regard.
6. What are the different payout methods? How do shareholders react to these methods?
7. What is a bonus issue or stock dividend? What are its advantages and disadvantages?
8. Explain a stock split? Why is it used? How does it differ from a bonus shares?
9. 'Bonus shares represent simply a division of corporate pie into a large number of pieces.' Explain.
10. What are the effects of bonus issue and share split on the earnings per share and the market price of the share?
11. What is meant by the buyback of shares? What are its effects? Is it really beneficial to the company and shareholders?

PROBLEMS

1. B. Das Co. has been a fast-growing firm and has been earning very high return on its investment in the past. Because of the availability of highly profitable investment internally, the company has been following a policy of retaining 70 per cent of earnings and paying 30 per cent of earnings as dividends. The company has now grown matured and does not have enough profitable internal opportunities to reinvest its earnings. But it does not want to deviate from its past dividend policy on the ground that investors have been accustomed to it and any change may not be welcome by them. The company, thus, invests retained earnings in the short-term government securities. Is the company justified in following the current dividend policy? Give reasons to support your answer.

2. D. Damodar Co. is a fast-growing firm in the engineering industry. In the past, the firm has earned a return of 25 per cent on its investments and this trend is likely to continue. The firm has been retaining 25 per cent of its earnings and

paying 75 per cent of earnings as dividends. This policy has been justified on the grounds that dividends are generally preferred over retained earnings by shareholders.

Is the current dividend policy justified if most of the shareholders are wealthy persons in high tax brackets? Will your answer change if most of the shareholders of the company were (a) retired persons with no other source of income and (b) the financial institutions?

3. The following data relate to the Brown Limited and the Crown Limited which belong to the same industry and sell the same product:

Brown Ltd.

Year Rs	EPS Rs	DPS Rs	Market Price High	Market Price Low Rs	Book value Rs*
2000	3.60	2.00	48	52	37.20
2001	3.90	2.00	53	34	38.80
2002	3.70	2.00	51	30	40.60
2003	3.20	2.00	59	31	42.30
2004	3.80	2.00	60	35	43.20

*The face value per share is Rs 10.

Crown Ltd.

Year Rs	EPS Rs	DPS Rs	Market Price High	Market Price Low Rs	Book value Rs*
2000	3.50	1.75	38	34	30.50
2001	3.00	1.50	42	32	32.50
2002	2.50	1.25	42	28	33.75
2003	6.00	3.00	50	30	36.50
2004	5.00	2.50	48	27	38.50

*The face value per share is Rs 10.

Calculate payout ratio, dividend yield, earnings yield and price–earning ratio. Which company is more profitable? Explain the reason for the difference in the market prices of the two companies' shares.

4. A multinational pharmaceutical company in India has following information about its EPS and dividends payment from 1987 to 2004.

You are required to answer the following questions: (a) What minimum annual percentage dividend increase the company intends to give to its shareholders? (b) Is there any relationship between the earnings increase and the rise in dividends? (c) Do you think that the company has a long-term target payout ratio? (d) The company's payout in 2003 was 150 per cent. How will you explain this? (e) What clientele does the company have?

Year	EPS Rs	Change in EPS (%)	DPS Rs	Change in DPS (%)	Payout (%)
1987	13.9	−7.2	5.3	11.7	37.9
1988	15.9	14.2	5.9	11.7	37.0
1989	16.4	3.1	6.5	10.5	39.7
1990	18.4	12.8	7.4	14.3	40.2
1991	19.8	7.4	8.3	11.7	41.8
1992	23.6	19.3	9.4	13.4	39.7
1993	24.7	4.7	10.5	11.8	42.4
1994	25.9	4.5	11.5	9.4	44.4
1995	27.8	7.6	13.0	12.9	46.6
1996	30.7	10.2	14.2	9.5	46.3
1997	30.1	−2.0	15.1	6.1	50.1
1998	31.2	3.7	15.9	5.7	51.1
1999	33.9	8.7	17.2	7.7	50.7
2000	34.9	2.9	19.1	11.5	54.9
2001	81.8	134.5	21.6	12.9	26.4
2002	44.9	−45.1	23.5	8.6	52.3
2003	53.6	19.5	80.5	243.1	150.1
2004	36.5	−32.0	28.2	−65.0	77.2

5. Ashoka Ltd. has a capital structure shown below:

	Rs (crore)
Equity share capital (Rs 10 par, 5 crore shares)	50
Preference share capital (Rs 100 par, 50 lakh shares)	50
Share premium	50
Reserves and surpluses	80
Net worth	230

Show the changed capital structure if the company declares a bonus issue of shares in the ratio of 1:5 to ordinary shareholders when the issue price per share is Rs 100. How would the capital structure be affected if the company had split its stock five-for-one instead of declaring bonus issue?

6. Polychem Co.'s current capital structure as on 31 March, 2004 is as follows:

	Rs (crore)
Share capital (Rs 100 par, 2 crore shares)	200
Share premium	100
Reserves and surpluses	190
	490

The current market price of the company's shares is Rs 140 per share. The earnings per share for the year 2003 was Rs 17. The company has been paying a constant dividend of Rs 6.50 per share for the last ten years.

What shall be the effect on earnings per share, dividend, share price and the capital structure if the company (*i*) splits its shares two-for-one or (*ii*) declares a bonus issue of one-for-twenty?

7. Surendra Auto Limited is considering a bonus shares issue. The following data are available:

		Rs (crore)
Paid up share capital		12
Reserves		16
Previous three years' pre-tax profit	Year 1	8.0
	Year 2	8.6
	Year 3	8.3

Recommend the maximum bonus ratio. Give reasons.

CASE

Case 18.1: A.C. Company Ltd.

A.C. Company Ltd. has improved its profitability in 2003–04, and is on a growth path after poor performance in the preceding two years. The following is the summary of the company's operations during preceding three years:

The company's focus in 2003–04 was on cost reduction and funds management rather than growth in sales. Operating and interest costs fell by 3.3 per cent and 60 per cent respectively. According to the company's managing director, "The turnover in 2003–04 dipped because of a drop in volumes. However, the sales are not strictly comparable because in the previous year, there was a large order worth Rs 15 crore from a public sector oil company. On the other hand, the net profit growth was higher because of better asset management. This resulted into reduced borrowings and lowered the financial charges." The company was able to bring down its inventory holding period to 46 days from 81 days and debtors holding period to 95 days from 119 days. The company is changing its debt policy to a conservative policy. The debt-equity ratio of 1.8:1 in 2001–02 has been brought down to 0.5:1 in 2003–04.

Table 18.1.1: A.C. Company Ltd.: Operating Performance

		(Rs in crore)	
	2001–02	*2002–03*	*2003–04*
Sales	53.4	75.6	69.5
Gross profit	3.4	4.5	12.3
Net profit	1.3	1.3	5.9
EPS (Rs)	1.8	1.8	8.1

The prospects of the company for increased business in 2004–05 are estimated to be good. According to the managing director, "The general industrial activity as such has picked up which should result in a better demand for the company's products from sectors such as automobiles, mining and chemicals." Experts think that compressor industry will grow at 10 per cent in 2004–05. The company is anticipating a sales growth of 15–20 per cent in 2004–05. The company's strategy of cost reduction and improving marketing efficiency will continue.

The company operates in the compressor industry and drilling and mining equipment industry. It is number two in the compressor industry after Inger Soll Rand. The product profile of the company in the years has shifted in favour of the compressor sector.

In 2003–04 the company's gross block increased to Rs 22 crore from Rs 20 crore. The company has planned for an investment of Rs 5 crore in its Poona factory. The company's share enjoys good liquidity and its P/E ratio is 32. In the expectation of good performance, the company's share price started rising since January 2004, and sharply increased to Rs 285 just before the budget from Rs 190 in January. The current price (after technical correction) is around Rs 225–35.

In the last two years, the company paid a dividend of 10 per cent. The company was wondering if it should declare a higher dividend in 2003–04?

Discussion Questions

1. Evaluate the company's financial condition.
2. Recommend the dividends to be paid by A.C. Company Ltd. Justify your advice.

PART 4

Long-Term Financing

Capital Market Efficiency and Capital Markets in India

INTRODUCTION

Companies raise long-term funds in the forms of equity and debt from the capital markets. Finance managers should, therefore, know the ways in which securities are traded and priced in the capital markets. They should also know the procedures followed in issuing securities. Securities will be fairly priced in the capital markets if they are efficient. In this chapter we shall explain the meaning of the capital market efficiency and the developments in capital markets in India.

CAPITAL MARKET EFFICIENCY

Capital markets facilitate the buying and selling of securities, such as shares and bonds or debentures. They perform two valuable functions: liquidity and pricing securities.

Liquidity

Liquidity means the convenience and speed of transforming assets into cash, or transferring assets from one person to another without any loss of value. Cash is the most liquid asset as it can be readily converted into any other asset, or transferred to another person without any decline in value.

Capital markets make securities liquid. They facilitate the buying and selling of securities by a large number of investors continuously and instantaneously without incurring significant costs. They help to reduce, if not eliminate, transaction costs. For ensuring the liquidity, capital markets do require certain investors who are always ready to buy or sell securities. These **market makers** enhance liquidity and reduce transaction costs.

Fair Price of Securities

How are the prices of securities determined? Are these fair prices? In the capital markets hundred of investors make several deals a day. The screen-based trading makes these deals known to all in the capital markets. Thus, a large number of buyers and sellers interact in the capital markets. The demand and supply forces help in determining the prices. Since all information is publicly available, and since no single investor is large enough to influence the security prices, the capital markets provide a measure of fair price of securities.

A financial manager borrows and lends (invests) funds in the capital markets. Capital markets facilitate the allocation of funds between savers and borrowers. This allocation will be optimum if the capital markets have efficient pricing mechanism. What does capital market efficiency mean? Are capital markets efficient?

Weekly Index

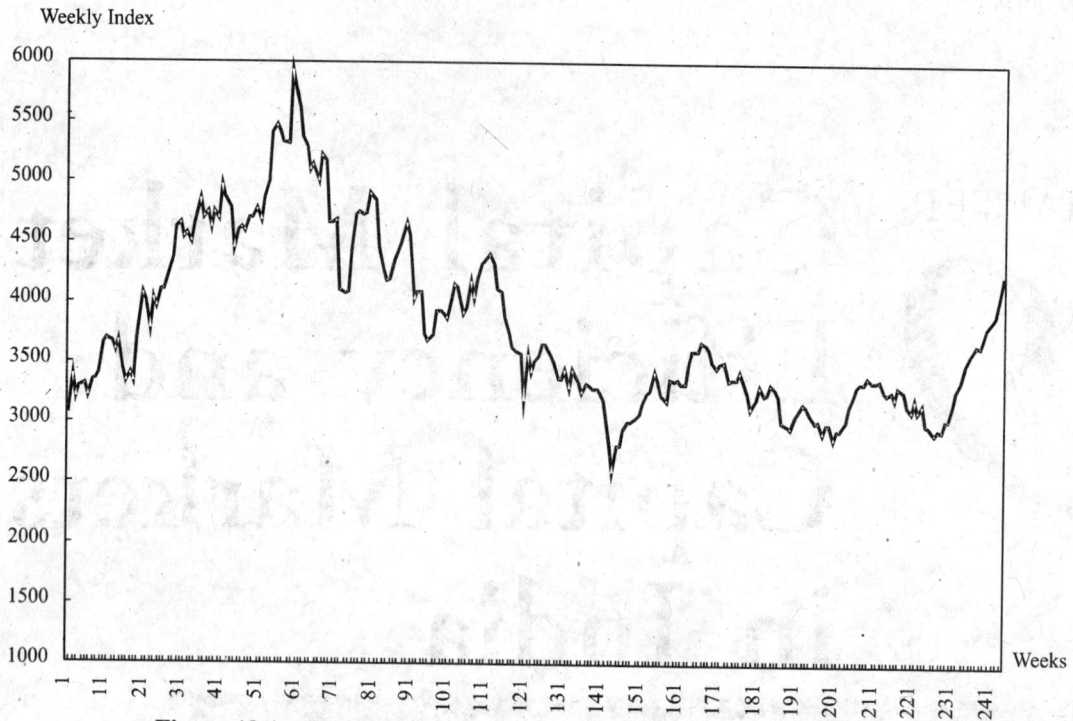

Figure 19.1: Weekly Share Price Index, 2 Jan. 1999 to 31 August 2003

Weekly Returns

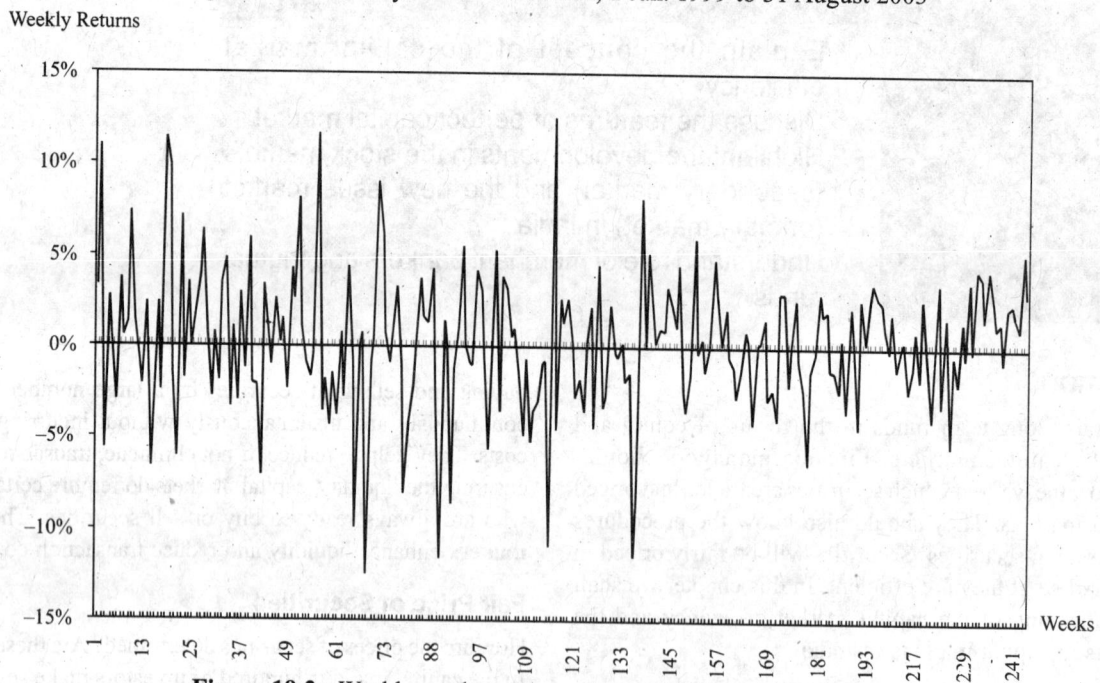

Figure 19.2: Weekly market returns, 2 Jan. 1999 to 31 August 2003

The security prices have been observed to move randomly and unpredictably. We can see the randomness of share prices in Figure 19.1 and of the market returns in Figure 19.2. In Figure 19.1 the weekly prices of the Bombay Stock Exchange's Sensitivity Index (Sensex) are plotted from 2 January 1999 to 31 August 2003. Figure 19.2 plots the *changes* in the weekly prices; that is, raw weekly returns. This randomness of security prices (and returns) may be interpreted to imply that investors in the capital markets

take a quick cognisance of all information relating to security prices, and that the security prices quickly adjust to such information. Thus, the efficiency of security prices depends on the speed of price adjustment to any available information. The more is the speed of adjustment, the more efficient will be the security prices. The **capital market efficiency** may, therefore, be defined as the ability of securities to reflect and incorporate all relevant information, almost instantaneously, in their prices.

Forms of Capital Market Efficiency

The finance theory refers to three forms of capital market efficiency:[1]

- Weak-form of efficiency
- Semi-strong form of efficiency
- Strong-form of efficiency.

Weak form of market efficiency The security prices reflect all past information about the price movements in the **weak form of efficiency**. It is, therefore, not possible for an investor to predict future security price by analysing historical prices, and achieve a performance (return) better than the stock market index such as the Bombay Stock Exchange Share Price Index or the Economic Times Share Price Index. It is so because the capital market has no memory, and the stock market index has already incorporated past information about the security prices in the current market price.

How does one know that the capital market is efficient in its weak form? To answer this question, we can find out the correlation between the 'security prices over time.' In an efficient capital market, there should not exist a significant correlation between the security prices over time.[2] Most empirical tests have shown that there exists serial independence between the security prices over time. In other words, share prices behave randomly. Hence the weak form of efficiency is referred to as the **random walk hypothesis**. An alternative method of testing the weakly efficient market hypothesis is to formulate the **trading strategies** using the security prices and compare their performance with the stock market performance. The capital market will be inefficient if the investor's trading strategy could beat the market. Researchers have studied a large number of trading rules, and have concluded that it is not possible for investors to outperform the market.

Semi-strong form of market efficiency In the **semi-strong form of efficiency**, the security prices reflect all publicly available information. This implies that an investor will not be able to outperform the market by analysing the existing company-related or other relevant information available in, say, the annual accounts, or financial dailies/magazines (e.g. the *Economic Times* or *Business India*). In fact, such publicly available information is already impounded in the current security prices.

How can we establish that capital market is semi-strong efficient? Researchers have employed **event studies** to study the semi-strong form of the market efficiency.[3] One can study the effect of events such as the earnings/dividends announcements, bonus issues, rights issues, changes in accounting policies etc. For example, if a company increases its dividend rate, one can study the speed with which the price of the company share is adjusted to this information. The semi-strong efficient market hypothesis implies that the share price reflects an event or information very

quickly, and therefore, it is not possible for an investor to beat the market using such information.

How can event studies be conducted? Fama, Fisher, Jensen and Roll have developed a methodology for event studies. The following steps are involved:[4]

- Calculate the expected and actual return before and after the event using the market model or the capital asset price model.
- Calculate the abnormal return (AR) as the difference between the expected return and the actual return.
- Calculate the cumulative abnormal return (CAR).

For the capital market to be efficient in its semi-strong form, the value of CAR should be equal to zero before event, rise to a positive number just after the event and then stay. In an inefficient capital market, the value of CAR will continue rising for several weeks after the event. Let us consider an example to illustrate how event studies can be used to discern whether the capital market is efficient or not.

Illustration 19.1: Event Study

You are employed by a finance company, and you have been assigned the responsibility of analysing the effect of an unannounced bonus issue of 1:1 for Maxima India Limited. You think that the market is efficient. The first thing which you do is to determine the equation for the expected return for Maxima's shares. You choose weekly returns for a three-year period up to six weeks before the unannounced bonus issue. Using the market model, you obtain the following characteristic line for Maxima:

$$r_{MAX} = 0.022 + 1.3r_m$$

where r_{MAX} is Maxima's return and r_m is the market return. If the market return is zero, Maxima's return will be 2.2 per cent. You found that six months before the event, the market return was 12.6 per cent. You can calculate Maxima's expected return as follows:

$$r_{MAX} = 0.022 + 1.3(0.126) = 0.186 \text{ or } 18.6\%$$

Maxima's actual return was also 18.6 per cent. Thus, there was no abnormal return:

$$\text{Abnormal return} = \text{Expected return} - \text{Actual return}$$
$$= 18.6\% - 18.6\% = 0$$

Similar calculations, shown in Table 19.1, can be made for weekly periods before and after the event (bonus issue). The cumulative addition of abnormal returns will give CAR. Data in Table 19.1 are plotted in Figure 19.3. You can see from Table 19.1 and Figure 19.3 that CAR was 2.3 per cent until the bonus announcement (in time 0). After the bonus issue was announced, CAR increased to about 4 per cent and remained unchanged for each week during next six weeks. Maxima's CARs increased in anticipation of the bonus issue at time 0. Once this information was incorporated in the share prices, there was no more changes in the prices. For any other new information, the share price may adjust again.

---

1. Roberts, H.V., Statistical versus Clinical Prediction of the Stock Market, (unpublished paper) quoted in Brealey, R.A. and Mayers, S.C., *Principles of Corporate Finance*, McGraw-Hill, 1991, p. 295.

2. Fama, E.F., Random Walks in Stock Market Prices, *Financial Analysts Journal*, (Sept.–Oct. 1965) pp. 55–59; and Fama, E.F., Efficient Capital Markets: A Review of Theory and Empirical Work, *Journal of Finance* (May 1970), pp. 383–417.

3. Fama, E.F. *et. al.*, The Adjustment of Stock Price to New Information, *International Economic Review*, Feb. 1969, pp. 1–21.

4. Fama *et. al.*, *ibid*.

This behaviour is consistent with the capital market efficiency in the semi-strong form.

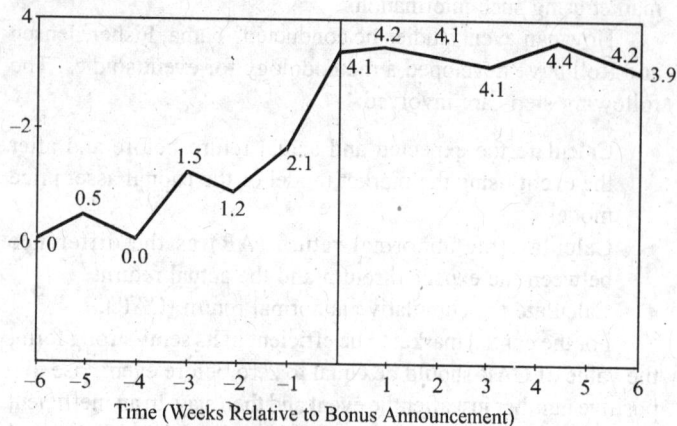

Figure 19.3: Effect of unannounced bonus issue on market efficiency

Table 19.1: Effect of Announced Bonus Issue on Market Efficiency

Market Return r_m (%)	Maxima's Exp. Return $E(r_{MAX})$ (%)	Maxima's Act. Return r_a (%)	Abnormal Return, AR $r_a - E(r_{MAX})$ (%)	Cumulative Abnormal Return, CAR (%)	Time (weeks before & after bonus announcement)
12.6	18.6	18.6	0.0	0.0	−6
13.4	19.6	20.1	0.5	0.5	−5
−6.8	−6.6	−7.1	−0.5	0.0	−4
16.2	23.3	24.7	1.4	1.5	−3
18.9	26.8	26.5	−0.3	1.2	−2
−8.0	−8.2	−7.3	0.9	2.1	−1
9.6	14.7	16.7	2.0	4.1	0
−5.3	−4.7	−4.6	0.1	4.2	1
8.2	12.9	12.8	−0.1	4.1	2
9.9	15.1	15.0	−0.1	4.1	3
−5.4	−4.8	−4.5	0.3	4.4	4
4.0	7.4	7.2	−0.2	4.2	5
6.0	10.0	10.3	−0.3	3.9	6

Strong form of efficiency In the **strong form of efficiency**, the security prices reflect all published and unpublished, public and private information. This is a significantly strong assertion, and empirical studies have not borne out the validity of the efficient market hypothesis in the strong form of efficiency. People with private or inside information have been able to outperform the market.

Are Capital Markets Perfect?

We have seen that market efficiency refers to the **information efficiency**. The degree of efficiency depends on the level of information disclosure and the speed with which information is processed by the market and incorporated in the share prices. Capital markets have been found to be fairly efficient in the advanced economies as well as in a number of emerging capital markets. Are these markets perfect as well? A **perfect capital market** envisions more stringent conditions. The following are the attributes of a perfect capital market:

- *No entry barriers* Anyone can participate in the market. Thus the suppliers or users of funds can enter the market and deal with each other.
- *Large number of buyers and sellers* Perfect competition in the market is ensured by the presence of a large number of buyers and sellers of securities. no single market participant should be large enough to be able to affect security prices.
- *Divisibility of financial assets* Financial assets are divisible and therefore, affordable investments are made by all participants.
- *Absence of transaction costs* There are no transaction costs. Participants can buy and sell securities with ease and without much cost.
- *No tax differences* Ideally, there are no taxes. There should not be any tax distortions. One set of investors should not be favoured over others.
- *Free trading* Any one is free to trade in securities in the capital market. There should not be government restrictions on trading.

An efficient capital market is perfect if the above-mentioned conditions are fully satisfied. A capital market which is otherwise reasonably efficient will have imperfections to the extent it does not satisfy the conditions of the perfect capital market. There are three significant imperfections that may be found in most capital markets in different degrees:

- *Tax asymmetries* Most economies have varieties of taxes and tax incentives which cause tax asymmetries. Tax asymmetries make security transactions more beneficial to some. A number of financial transactions may create additional wealth because of tax differences.
- *Information asymmetries* Most financial information is published and is publicly available. But, sometimes, certain persons may have superior information than others. These persons may earn abnormal returns for some time. In certain economies, the quality of the disclosure of information is low. All information is not easily and timely available and it involves cost. Certain kinds of information provide signals to the market participants. In an efficient capital market, all information is speedily incorporated in the prices.
- *Transaction costs* Transaction costs do not affect the prices. But they can cause one transaction to be more profitable than the other. Transaction costs of two similar financial transactions may be different. Thus, investors would prefer one transaction over the other. Similarly, transaction costs of two persons to a transaction may be different.

In practice, capital markets have imperfections. Efficient markets may not be perfect. For developing frameworks for analysing financial decisions, a good starting point is to assume that capital markets are perfect. Once a framework is obtained, the practical implications of market imperfections can be analysed.

**Table 19.2: Resources Mobilised through Public Issues by
Non-Government Public Companies**

Years	1990–91	1991–92	1992–93	1993–94	1994–95	1995–96	1996–97	1997–98	1998–99	1999–00	2000–01	2001–02	2002–03
Funds mobilised	4,312	6,193	19,803	19,330	26,417	16,075	10,410	3,138	5,013	5,153	4,949	5,692	1,878
% GDS	3.3	4.4	12.8	10.0	10.5	5.3	3.3	0.8	1.3	1.1	1.0	1.2	0.7

Source: National Stock Exchange of *India, Indian Securities Market*: A Review, Mumbai: NSE, 2002, p. 15.

CAPITAL MARKETS IN INDIA[1]

Capital market facilitates the free trading (buy and sell) in all securities. It has two mutually supporting and indivisible segments: the **primary market** and the **secondary market**. In the primary market companies issue new securities to raise funds. Hence it is also referred to the **new issues market**. The secondary market deals with the second-hand securities; viz., securities that have already been issued by companies that are listed in a stock exchange. Since the securities are listed and traded in the stock exchange, the secondary market is also called the **stock market.** In the primary market, companies interact with investors directly while in the secondary market investors interact with themselves. In both cases, the capital market intermediaries (the investment or merchant bankers, stock brokers etc.) play an important role. The secondary market, based on all-available information, determines the price and risk of the issued securities. It provides useful signals to both listed companies and investors to act in the primary markets.

The secondary market may also include the **over-the-counter** (OTC) **market** and the **derivatives market**. In the stock market share prices are determined by the demand and supply forces. On the other hand, in the OTC market prices are negotiated between the buyer and the seller. The derivatives market deals in futures and options. In the derivatives markets, securities or portfolios of securities (for example, a market index) are traded for future delivery. In case of options, the future delivery is conditional as the option buyer has a right to exercise or not to exercise the option.

PRIMARY CAPITAL MARKET IN INDIA

Primary capital market is a conduit for the sale of new securities. New or listed companies may make the public issues of shares. The **initial public offerings** (IPOs) are the public issues of securities by new companies for the first time. In the IPOs or public offerings by the established companies, securities are sold to the public - all individuals and institutional investors. Private corporate sector did not show much enthusiasm to offer capital to the public till 1980, because of the following factors:

- Small size of the operations and narrow capital base
- Availability of loan capital on easy terms from the term-lending institutions
- Fear of losing control over the company
- Highly regulated environment

The decade of eighties, however, witnessed a sea change in the funds mobilisation efforts of companies through public issues of equity and debt, encouraged by the deregulation of capital markets and other economic reforms. As a result, the annual funds mobilisation in the new issues market, which was only to the tune of about Rs 70 crore in sixties and Rs 90 crore in seventies, increased substantially during the 80s.[2] The funds raised through the public issues of corporate securities by the non-government companies amounted to Rs 4,312 crore in 1990–91 which increased to a phenomenal level of Rs 26,417 crore in 1994–95. The funds mobilised in 1990–91 was 3.3 per cent of gross domestic savings (GDS) and 10.5 per cent in 1994–95. However, there was significant drop in the funds mobilised through public issues after 1996–97. Table 19.2 shows the trend.

Financial Instruments

Equity and debt are the two basic instruments of raising capital from the primary markets. Equity was more important source of capital until 1995–96. The share of equity in funds mobilisation through public issues was 72 per cent in 1995–96 which declined to 15 per cent in 1998–99. After showing an increase in 1999–00 and 2000–01, the share of equity has dropped to about 17 per cent (Table 19.3). Hence once again debt has dominated the public issues.

**Table 19.3: Resources Mobilised through
Debt and Equity (%)**

	1995–96	1996–97	1997–98	1998–99	1999–00	2000–01	2001–02	2002–03
Equity	72.4	56.0	41.2	15.3	58.4	52.8	16.9	18.0
Debt	27.6	44.0	58.8	84.7	41.6	47.2	83.1	82.0

Companies in practice offer a number of variations of equity and debt securities. They include:

- *Ordinary shares* Ordinary (equity) shares represent the ownership position in a company. The holders of the equity shares are the owners of the company, and they provide permanent capital. They have voting rights and receive dividends at the discretion of the board of directors.
- *Preference shares* The holders of the preference shares have a preference over the equity in the event of the liquidation of the company. The preference dividend rate is fixed and

---

1. The discussion of Indian capital markets in this chapter draws a lot of data and information from National Stock Exchange, *Indian Securities Market: A Review*, Mumbai: National Stock Exchange, 2002. Other references, which provide useful historical perspective on Indian capital markets, include M.R. Mayya, *Indian Stock Markets* (talk delivered in Hong Kong, 12 April, 1990), and *Indian Stock Markets: Prospects, Problems and Prescriptions* (talk delivered at IIM, Ahmedabad).
2. National Stock Exchange, *Indian Securities Market: A Review*, Mumbai: National Stock Exchange, 2002, p. 15.

known and is payable before paying dividend on the ordinary share capital. Companies in India can issue redeemable preference shares; but they can't issue irrredeemable preference shares. A preference share may also provide for the accumulation of dividend. It is called cumulative preference share. Companies in India now hardly issue preference shares.

- *Debentures* Debentures represent long-term debt given by the holders of debentures to the company. Debentures maybe secured or unsecured. Secured debentures are also known as **bonds**. The rate of interest on debentures is specified and interest charges are treated deductible expenses in the hands of the company. Straight debentures, without a conversion feature, are called **non-convertible debentures** (NCDs). Debentures may be issued without an interest rate. They are called **zero-interest debentures**. Such debentures are issued at a price much lower than their face value. Hence they are also called **deep-discount debentures/bonds**.
- *Convertible debentures* A debenture may be issued with the feature of being convertible into equity shares after a specified period of time at a given price. Thus a convertible debenture (CDs) will have features of a debenture as well as equity.
- *Warrants* A company may issue equity shares or debentures attached with warrants. Warrants entitle an investor to buy equity shares after a specified time period at a given price.
- *Cumulative convertible preference shares* (CCPS) CCPS is an instrument giving regular returns at, say, 10 per cent during the gestation period from three years to five years and equity benefit thereafter. In India, Government introduced CCPS in 1984. However, it has failed to catch the investors' interest mainly because the rate of return was considered too low in the initial years and the provision for conversion into equity was also unattractive if the company failed to perform well.
- *Derivative securities* Securities with options to buy or sell are called derivative securities. CDs, CCPSs and warrants are examples of **derivative securities**.
- *Borrowings from financial institutions* In India, besides issuing debentures, companies raise debt capital through borrowings from the financial institutions and banks. Banks are the important source of working capital for companies.

Table 19.4: Resource Mobilisation from IPOs and Rights Issues

Issue	2001–02 Number	2001–02 Amount (Rs in crore)	2002–03 Number	2002–03 Amount (Rs in crore)
IPOs	7	1,202	6	1,039
Issues by Listed Companies	28	6,341	20	3,032
Public issues	(13)	(5,300)	(8)	(2,600)
Rights issues	(15)	(1,041)	(12)	(431)
Total	35	7,543	26	4,072

Source: SEBI, cf., NSE, *Indian Securities Market: A Review*, Mumbai: NSE, 2002, p. 57.
Note: Number are rounded off.

The offerings of securities maybe made only to the existing shareholders. When the securities are offered only to the company's existing shareholders, it is called a **rights issue**. Table 19.4 gives data of resource mobilisation from public issues, IPOs and rights issues for the years 2001–02 and 2002–03. It is clear from Table 19.4 that public issues are preferred routes of mobilising capital than the rights issues.

Private Placement

Instead of a public issue of securities, a company may offer them privately only to a few investors; that is, less than 50 in number. This is referred to as **private placement** of securities. It maybe noticed that private placement has become the most significant method of mobilising funds by the Indian companies recently. About 30 per cent of total funds mobilised by the public and private companies in 1990–91 was through private placement, and this increased to 87 per cent in 2002–03 (Table 19.5). The reasons for this development are:

- Private placement of securities is subject to much less compliance than the public issues
- Private placement is cost effective as compared to public issues
- Private placement is time effective as deals can be easily and directly negotiated with a few investors
- Private placement helps to tailoring the issues according to the needs of the companies

The private placement market, however, has several limitations for the efficient functioning of the capital markets. There is little information available about this market and there is little transparency.

Euro Issues

The increasing use of euro issues by the Indian companies also indicates that Indian capital market is integrating with the international capital markets. Companies in India have also started raising funds via **euro issues** in the foreign capital markets. Euro issues include **foreign currency convertible bonds** (FCCBs), **global depository receipts** (GDRs) and **American depository receipts** (ADRs). ADRs and GDRs are like shares and they are traded in the overseas stock exchanges. Indian companies raised significant amount of funds by way of euro issues in nineties. Euro issues contributed Rs 3,426 crore in 2002–03 as against Rs 4,197 crore in 2000–01 in the total resource mobilisation (Table 19.5).

Government Securities

Both the central and state governments borrow large sums of money from the primary market by issuing **dated securities** (long-term securities) and **Treasury bills** (T-Bills). T-Bills in India are issued for short duration. The total issue of government securities has increased over years. The central government's mobilisation of funds from the primary market increased 15 times from Rs 8,989 crore in 1990–91 to Rs 151,126 crore in 2002–03 (Table 19.5). The state governments' mobilisation of funds from the primary market increased almost fifteen times from 1990–91 to 2001–02.

A large part of the central government's borrowings goes in financing the fiscal deficit. In 2001–02, the net borrowings (gross borrowings less repayments) financed 69.4 per cent of the central government's gross fiscal deficit. In case of the states, the net borrowing financed about 15 per cent of the gross fiscal deficit.

The largest holders of the government securities are commercial banks followed by the Life Insurance Corporation (LIC) of India. They are, in fact, captive investors for the government due to various investment restrictions. The Reserve Bank of India (RBI) has created a primary auction market with authorised primary dealers. More auctions have started taking place on market basis. But still the government securities are not issued at entirely market interest rates.

Pricing of New Issues

Until 1992, the Controller of Capital Issues (CCI) decided the prices of securities to be offered to the public. CCI does not exist now. Companies in India can freely price share issues, subject to the SEBI guidelines. In the case of the listed companies the current market price provides a basis for pricing the new issue of securities. Companies generally fix the issue price 10 to 15 per cent below the current market price to account for the effect of the supply pressure. It is relatively difficult to price an IPO. Companies use the services of merchant or investment bankers, who act as issue managers, to determine the issue price and manage the issue of securities.

A company is required to issue a **prospectus** when it issues shares to the public. The prospectus should disclose full information, including the risk factors in the issue, to the investors to be able to appraise the pricing and form a judgement. New companies should give the justification for the pricing to the prospective investors. Generally, the price of the issue is fixed well before the actual issue. The price is not changed at any stage. This price is generally kept on the lower side so that the issue is fully subscribed and there is no devolvement on underwriters. However, **book building** is an alternative to the fixed-pricing method.

Book-Building and Price Discovery

In the case of normal public issue, the price is fixed and known in advance. At the close of subscription, the company knows the number of shares applied for. **Book-building** is an alternative to the traditional fixed-price method of security issue. In book building the issue price is not fixed. Book building is a process of offering securities at various bid prices from investors. The demand for the security is assessed and the price is discovered based on bids made by investors. **Price discovery**, therefore, depends on the demand for the shares at different prices. In book building, the issuing company indicates the floor price but not the ceiling price. Book building involves the following steps:

- The company plans an IPO via the book-building route
- The company appoints an issue manager (usually a merchant banker) as book-runner
- The company issues a draft prospectus containing all required disclosure
- The draft prospectus is filed with SEBI
- The issue manager (book-runner) appoints syndicates members and other registered intermediaries to garner subscription
- Price discovery begins through the bidding process
- At the close of bidding, book-runner and company decide upon the allocation and allotments.

Bids should be submitted electronically through the syndicate members. The bids should remain open for at least five days and the demand should be displayed at the end of every day. The issue manager determines the issue price in consultation with the issuing company. The book building enables faster issue of securities at lesser cost and trading can commence quite early, viz., within 15 days from the closure of the issue.

Table 19.5: New Issues in Primary Markets, 1990–91—2002–03

(Rs in crore)

Year	Total Corporate Securities	Domestic Issues	Non-Govt. Public Cos.	PSU Bonds	Govt. Cos.	Banks & FIs	Private Placement	Euro Issues	Central Govt.	State Govt.
1990–91	14,219	14,219	4,312	5,663	—	—	4,244	—	8,989	2,569
1991–92	16,366	16,366	6,193	5,710	430	—	4,463	—	8,919	3,364
1992–93	23,537	23,286	19,803	1,062	819	356	1,635	702	13,885	3,805
1993–94	44,498	37,044	19,330	5,586	888	3,843	7,466	7,898	50,388	4,145
1994–95	48,084	41,974	26,417	3,070	1,000	425	11,174	6,743	38,108	5,123
1995–96	36,689	36,193	16,075	2,292	650	3,465	13,361	1,297	40,509	6,274
1996–97	37,147	33,872	10,410	3,394	43	4,352	15,066	5,594	36,152	6,536
1997–98	42,125	37,738	3,138	2,982	—	1,476	30,099	4,009	59,637	7,749
1998–99	60,192	59,044	5,013	—	—	4,352	49,679	1,148	93,953	12,114
1999–00	72,450	68,963	5,153	—	—	2,551	61,259	3,487	99,630	13,706
2000–01	78,396	74,199	4,890	—	350	1,472	67,836	4,197	115,183	13,300
2001–02	74,403	72,061	5,692	—	—	1,070	64,950	2,342	133,801	18,707
2002–03	70,039	66,613	1,878	—	—	2,989	61,746	3,426	151,126	30,853

Source: RBI, cf., NSE, Indian Securities Market: A Review, Mumbai, NSE, 2002, p. 16.

The price under book building is the price that the market can bear, and it is usually higher than the price under the fixed-pricing method. It is believed that the book-building route of pricing is in favour of issuers, and that this method has made IPOs less attractive and risky for the ordinary investors.[1]

SECONDARY MARKETS IN INDIA

Secondary capital market deals in the second-hand issued securities. Stock exchanges are secondary markets where buyers and sellers trade in already issued securities. A stock exchange provides the following useful economic functions:

- Help determining **fair prices** based on demand and supply forces and all-available information
- Provide easy **marketability** and **liquidity** for investors
- Facilitate in **capital allocations** in primary markets through price signalling
- Enable investors to **adjusting portfolios** of securities

India has one of the oldest stock markets in Asia, viz., the Bombay Stock Exchange (**BSE**). BSE was established in 1875. Later on, many more stock exchanges were established in other Indian cities like Ahmedabad, Calcutta, Madras, Kanpur etc. Until eighties, there were eight stock exchanges in India; the number has now increased to 23. However, in terms of business activities, the two most prominent all-India stock exchanges are the Bombay Stock Exchange (BSE) and the National Stock Exchange (**NSE**). NSE was set up in June 1994. It started the **screen-based trading** in India which has been now adopted by BSE and other stock exchanges as well.

The relatively high level of issued capital required for a company to be eligible to be listed in a stock exchange prompted the Government of India to grant recognition to the **Over-the-Counter Exchange of India** (OTCEI), which was promoted by Unit Trust of India, Industrial Credit and Investment Corporation of India Ltd. and others. OTCEI is also a screen-based market.

The Securities Contracts (Regulation) Act 1956 was the first all-India legislation regulating the stock exchanges in the country. Now the **Security Exchange Board of India** (SEBI) regulates the operations of the primary and secondary markets in India.

Securities and Exchange Board of India (SEBI)

The establishment of the Securities and Exchange Board of India (SEBI), on the lines of the Securities and Investment Board of the UK, is a major development in the Indian capital market. SEBI which was established on the 12 April 1988 is required to take a holistic view of the Indian securities markets. SEBI is required to regulate and promote the securities market by:

- Providing fair dealings in the issues of securities and ensuring a market place where funds can be raised at a relatively low cost;
- Providing a degree of protection to the investors and safeguard their rights and interests so that there is a steady

flow of savings into the market;
- Regulating and developing a code of conduct and fair practices by intermediaries in the capital market like brokers and merchant banks with a view to making them competitive and professional.

Developments in Stock Market[2]

There has been impressive growth in the number of shareholders, number of listed companies, market capitalisation and stock turnover in India over last two decades. The number of shareholders is estimated to be about 40 million; twenty years ago it was estimated to be one million. Thus India, after USA, has the second largest population of shareholders.

Table 19.6 contains selected indicators of the stock market operations. In 1990–91, there were 6,229 companies listed on the Indian stock exchange. This number has increased to 9,413 in 2002–03. India thus occupies the second position in the world next to USA in terms of the number of listed companies. The number of share brokers has also increased from 6,711 in 1995–96 to 9,519 in 2002–03.

The turnover in the Indian stock exchanges has shown significant increase until 2001 and then it declined in 2002. The turnover in 1993–94 was Rs 203,703 crore which increased to Rs 2,880,990 crore in 2001 and then declined to Rs 895,826 crore in 2002 and increased slightly to Rs 968,910 crore in 2003. Table 19.6 shows the trend since 1994. The average daily turnover increased from Rs 150 crore in 1990 to Rs 12,000 crore in 2000. As shown in Table 19.6, the turnover ratio was 50.9 per cent in 1993–94 which increased to 374.7 per cent in 2000–01 and then declining to 119.6 per cent in 2001–02 and increasing to 153.3 per cent in 2003.

The market capitalisation growth was quite low until mid-eighties. During 1990–91 to 1999–2000, the market capitalisation showed more than 10 times growth. The market capitalisation dropped from Rs 1,192,630 crore in 1999–00 to Rs 631,921 crore in 2003. The market capitalisation ratio, which is an indicator of the market size, increased to 85 per cent by 2000 from 20.6 per cent in 1990-91. The ratio, however, dropped sharply to 29 per cent in 2003.

NSE's S&P CNX Nifty and BSE's Sensex are two widely used stock exchange indices. Table 19.6 shows the trend in two indices. The indices have generally shown an increasing trend until 1999–2000. Sensex touched 5,000 mark and S&P CNX Nifty 1,500 mark in 1999–2000. In the next three years, the stock indices showed decline in the market.

Government Securities Market

The private corporate debt market is not well developed in India. The government debt market constitutes about three-fourths of the debt market in India. Commercial banks and financial institutions in India own a large proportion of the government debt securities due to statutory liquidity and other investment requirements.

1. Gupta, L.C., "Asymmetric Information, Book Building and Investor Protection", *NSENEWS*, February 2002.
2. For a detailed analysis of the stock market developments, refer to NSE, *Indian Securities Markets: A Review*, Mumbai, NSE, Vol. 2, 2002.

Table 19.6: Secondary Market — Selected Indicators

End of Financial Year	No. of Brokers	No. of Listed Companies	S&P CNX Nifty (Index)	Sensex (Index)	Market Capitalisation (Rs crore)	Market Capitalisation Ratio (%)	Turnover (Rs crore)	Turnover Ratio (%)
1990–91	NA	6,229	366.45	1167.97	110,279	20.6	NA	NA
1991–92	NA	6,480	1261.65	4285.00	354,106	57.4	NA	NA
1992–93	NA	6,925	660.51	2280.52	228,780	32.4	NA	NA
1993–94	NA	7,811	1177.11	3778.99	400,077	45.6	203,703	50.9
1994–95	6,711	9,077	990.24	3260.96	437,349	45.6	162,905	34.4
1995–96	8,476	9,100	985.30	3366.61	572,257	47.0	227,368	39.7
1996–97	8,867	9,890	968.85	3360.89	488,332	34.6	646,116	132.3
1997–98	9,005	9,833	1116.65	3892.75	589,816	37.7	908,681	154.1
1998–99	9,069	9,877	1078.05	3739.96	574,064	34.1	1,023,382	178.3
1999–00	9,192	9,871	1528.45	5001.28	1,192,630	84.7	2,067,031	173.3
2000–01	9,782	9,954	1148.20	3604.38	768,863	54.5	2,880,990	374.7
2001–02	9,687	9,644	1129.55	3469.35	749,248	36.4	895,826	119.6
2002–03	4,519	9,413	978.20	3048.72	631,921	28.5	968,910	153.3

Note: Turnover figures for the respective year. NA. *Not Available.*
Source: NSE, *Indian Securities Market: A Review,* Mumbai, NSE, 2002.

In 2001–02, for the first time, turnover in the government securities was higher than the turnover of equities in all stock exchanges in India. The turnover of government securities increased from Rs 56,229 crore in 1994–95 to Rs 2,988,560 crore – more than 30 times increase in 2002–03. NSE has developed the wholesale debt market (WDM) for government securities. The share of the NSE WDM segment has increased to about 60 per cent in the total turnover of the government securities. The government debt securities have high level of liquidity. The turnover of the dated securities has been higher in the recent years. The primary dealers offer two-way quotes for the active government securities.

Table 19.7: Turnover of Government Securities and Derivatives

(Rs crore)

Year	NSE WDM Segment	SGL	Total Turnover Govt. Securities	Derivatives Market
1994–95	5,660	50,569	56,229	
1995–96	9,988	127,179	137,167	
1996–97	38,308	122,941	161,249	
1997–98	103,585	185,708	289,293	
1998–99	95,280	227,228	322,508	
1999–00	293,887	539,232	833,119	
2000–01	414,096	698,121	1,112,217	4,018
2001–02	927,604	1,573,893	2,501,497	103,848
2002–03	1,032,829	1,955,731	2,988,560	442,333

Source: NSE, *Indian Securities Market: A Review*, Mumbai, NSE, 2002.

Derivatives Market

Derivatives are securities *derived* from other securities (called underlying securities) like equity, debt, or any other type of

security. It also includes contracts that derive their values from prices or index of prices. In India, the OTC derivatives are not allowed; the legal derivatives must trade on recognised stock exchanges only. Derivatives trading in India started in June 2000 with SEBI approving trading in **index future contracts** based on BSE's Sensex index and NSE's S&P CNX Nifty index. Immediately after this, approval for trading in options in these two indices and some individual shares followed in July 2001.

Trading in derivatives mostly takes place in NSE accounting for 98 per cent of the total volume. The derivative turnover was only Rs 4,018 crore during 2000–01 which increased to Rs 442,333 crore in 2002–03 (Table 19.7).

Trading and Settlement

Investors can carry out their operations (buying and selling of securities through brokers and sub-brokers. A **broker** is an enrolled member of a stock exchange who is authorised to the stock exchange trade. He or she is registered with SEBI. **Sub-brokers** are affiliated to the members (brokers) of the stock exchange and registered with SEBI as sub-brokers. Investors can hold and trade in securities in dematerialised form.

Dematerialisation of shares Dematerialisation is a process of changing paper certificates of securities into electronic form and recording in computers by a depository. A **depository** holds shares in dematerialised (demat) form, and maintains ownership records and also facilitates transfer of ownership. All transactions take place through computers without paper work. An investor may hold shares in physical or demat form, but he or she can trade and settle deals in most shares easily in demat form. In India, there are two depositories – NSDL and CDSL and they compete with each other. Dematerialisation of shares in India was introduced in 1998. Within three years, a very high level of dematerialisation was achieved. Now almost 100 per cent trades are settled in demat form. The growth of dematerialisation in

India has been the fastest in emerging capital markets and most developed markets. The following features maybe observed about dematerialisation:[1]

- Fall in settlement and other charges
- No stamp duty
- Depository facility has effected changes in the stock market microstructure
- Breadth and depth of investment culture has further got extended to interior areas of the country faster
- Explicit transaction cost has been falling
- Increased growth in turnover

Trading Buying and selling of shares is an agreement between the broker/sub-broker and the client (investor) once he or she has filled in a client registration. The broker charges a fee, which is between 0.50 per cent and 1 per cent of the value of transaction, for executing the transaction in the stock exchanges. Sub-brokers cannot charge commission more than 1 per cent. Stock exchanges have scheduled pay-in day and pay-out day. The **pay-in day** is the day when the broker makes payment or delivery of securities to the exchange. The **pay-out** day is the day when the exchange makes payment or delivery of securities to the broker.

Rolling settlement In **rolling settlement** system, the trading period (T) is one day. With effect from 1 April 2003, the obligations have to be netted and settled on the 2nd working day on a $T + 2$ rolling settlement scheme. For example, the trade done on Monday will be settled on Tuesday. Every day is a settlement day in the rolling settlement scheme. Hence it is necessary that securities are held in demat form.

SEBI introduced **rolling settlement** cycle of five days for most active securities with effect from 2nd July 2001 and for remaining securities with effect from 31st December 2001. Before this change, trade settlement was inefficient; the trades carried out from Mondays to Fridays were settled by payment of monies and delivery of securities in the following week. Under this system, trades done on a Monday would get settled Thursday next week. The rolling settlement cycle of 5 days was subsequently brought down to three days and finally to two days.

Circuit breaker Extreme volatility in the stock market is not considered healthy. The **circuit breaker** or **price bands** system helps to control the extreme volatility. From 2nd July 2001 SEBI has moved to a system of index-based circuit breaker system market-wide. The system applies when the market moves in either direction by specified circuit breakers (limits). The three stages of the market movement are 10 per cent, 15 per cent and 20 per cent. Whenever these limits are breached, depending on the extent of breach, the stock exchange authorities will halt the market for the specified period. These circuit breakers bring about a co-ordinated trading halt in all equity and equity derivatives market across the country, and the movement of either BSE Sensex or the NSE S&P CNX Nifty, whichever is breached earlier, triggers the market-wide circuit breakers.[2]

MERCHANT BANKING: ROLE IN CAPITAL MARKETS

Merchant banks, also called **investment banks**, are most significant institutions in the financial markets of the developed countries. They help in promoting and sustaining capital markets, and they provide a variety of financial services to the corporate sector. In Europe, they perform these functions along with the commercial banking functions. Investment banks in the USA perform merchant banking functions, and they are prohibited from carrying on the commercial banking activities.

Merchant banks are needed in developing countries for developing and activating the capital markets. With the deregulation and liberalisation of financial sectors in a number of developing countries, merchant banking activities are assuming a very important role. The scope of merchant banking activities has been expanding in India over the years. The recent changes in the Indian economy and financial markets are expected to provide a further impetus to the faster development of the merchant banking.

Merchant banks, contrary to what is suggested by the name, are, in fact, neither merchants nor necessarily banks. The term came into usage after merchants in London started financing foreign trade through acceptance of **bills of exchange**. Since merchants were the first to provide this "banking service", they came to be known as merchant banks. Over years, they expanded and diversified scope of their operations. Merchant banks started assisting the governments of developing countries in raising long term funds through flotation of bonds on the London Stock Exchange; for syndication of short-term finance for domestic business; underwriting of securities; managing security issues and transfers; acting as debenture trustees; providing advice in investment and portfolio management, mergers and take-overs, capital restructuring, liquidity management and other corporate services; arranging finances including new sources such as leasing, venture capital etc.

Merchant bankers benefit corporate clients in a number of ways. First, they help in releasing valuable management time by looking into the legal and procedural complications involved in the securities issues and raising of loans. Second, they provide professionally competent advice to corporate clients in matters of investment, capital restructuring, mergers and acquisitions, valuation, etc. Third, merchant bankers help in cultivating investment attitude and climate as well as financial innovativeness in the individual investors as well as corporate clients.

Status of Merchant Banking in India

The Grindlays Bank was the first bank which formally initiated merchant banking activities in India by setting up a Merchant Banking Division in 1967. Citibank was next to start merchant banking in 1970. After two years, the State Bank of India entered the field in 1972. The erstwhile Industrial Credit and Investment Corporation of India (ICICI) was the first development financial

---

1. SEBI, "Dematerialisation: A Silent Revolution in the Indian Capital Market", Working Paper, April 2001; cf., NSE, *Indian Securities Market: A Review*, Mumbai, NSE, 2002, p. 120.
2. NSE, *Indian Securities Market: A Review, op. cit.*

institution to offer merchant banking services in 1974. Today, there are a large number of banks, financial institutions and private sector organisations providing merchant banking services. Some of the services provided by merchant banks today as underwriting of securities, bill discounting, project finance, technical advice etc. were offered by commercial banks, development banks, insurance and investment companies and other organisations in India long before the appearance of formal merchant banking organisations.

A large number of nationalised banks have set up divisions or subsidiaries for offering merchant banking services. **Issue management** is the dominant activity of most of them, while a few provide numerous other services also. Amongst the nationalised banks, the State Bank of India has the largest share of merchant banking business on account of its large network of branches and customer base.

In the private sector in India, merchant banking services are provided by financial consultancy firms and stock brokers. On a small scale, they carry on a wide range of merchant banking activities. Some of them are quite active in acting as advisor/ managers of fixed deposits attracted by companies. A few firms, representing foreign banks, assist companies in the area of international finance.

Today the number of merchant banking organisations as well as the scope of services offered by them have increased significantly. Service provided by merchant banking organisations in India include corporate counselling: project counselling and pre-investment studies; capital restructuring; credit syndication and project finance; issue management and underwriting; portfolio management; non-resident investment; working capital finance; acceptance credit and bill discounting; mergers, amalgamations and take-overs; venture capital; leasing finance; foreign currency finance; fixed deposit broking; mutual funds; relief to sick industries.[1]

The merchant banking activity in India is governed by SEBI under the SEBI (Merchant Bankers) Regulations 1992. Each merchant banker is required to have capital adequacy with prescribed net worth. The SEBI regulations specify the code of conduct, lead managers' duties, payment of fees and disclosures. The new regulations make a clear distinction between the merchant banker and the non-banking financial company (NBFC). The merchant bankers are not allowed to engage in the fund-based activates except those that relate the capital market operations like underwriting.

MUTUAL FUNDS AND CAPITAL MARKETS

Indian investors started investing through **mutual funds** since 1964 when the government set up the Unit Trust of India (UTI). UTI's objective was to mobilise the savings of the public, and invest them in securities and other assets enabling the investors to earn good returns. Government provided several fiscal incentives to UTI to make its schemes attractive for investors. UTI remained a monopoly until 1987 after which government controlled banks established mutual funds followed by the insurance companies. Now the mutual funds industry is highly

competitive and investors have a variety of schemes to choose from. SEBI (Mutual Fund) Regulation 1993 has also provided for the fair functioning of mutual funds by prescribing disclosure and advertising norms and that the fund sponsor, trustees, custodian and asset management company (AMC) must have an arm's length relationship. During 1964–1987, when UTI was the only mutual fund in India, it mobilised Rs. 45.63 billion. As shown in Table 19.8, mutual funds mobilised substantial funds after more funds entered the market and the industry became competitive. Table 19.9 provides data on assets under management as on 31 August 2003.

Table 19.8: Funds Mobilised by Mutual Funds

Period	*Funds Mobilised (Rs in billion)*
1964–1987	45.63
1987–1992	329.77
1992–1997	458.45
1997–2002	833.85
2002–2003	45.80

Table 19.9: Assets under Management as on 31 August 2003

Schemes	*Number*	*Amount (Rs in billion)*
Bank Sponsored	2,219	230.25
Institutions	1,867	63.08
Private sector:		
Indian	11,866	173.12
Predominantly Indian	10,829	285.37
Predominantly Foreign	17,205	433.50
Total	43,986	1185.32

Mutual funds mobilize savings from a large number of investors and invest these funds in shares and other securities. The return obtained from the mutual funds investments is shared among the investors, called shareholders or unit holders, in proportion to their investment. Mutual funds employ a professional team to carry out the investment activities on behalf of unit holders. The main feature of a mutual fund is that it makes diversification of portfolio a possibility for the small investors who otherwise may not be able to do so with their limited resources. These investors are also able to get professional investment management services and are relieved of the attendant worries that are normally involved in investing in securities like book-keeping and transaction. Mutual fund is really a financial innovation of this century that provides a novel way of mobilising savings from small investors and allowing them to participate in the equity and other securities of the companies and other commercial organization with less risk. Mutual funds are *sine qua non* for the development of the capital markets and the creation of the equity cult in an economy.

---

1. Verma, J.C., *Merchant Banking: Organisation and Management*, Tata McGraw-Hill, p. 6.

Mutual funds issue shares or units to investors. Mutual funds have two broad categories:

- *Closed-ended mutual funds* Close-ended mutual funds are created for a specific duration which is specified at the start of the fund. It has fixed number of shares or units outstanding. After the initial issue of shares/units, they trade on the stock exchanges or over-the-counter-markets. The price of the shares/units is determined by the supply of and demand for the shares/units. Because of the volatility of prices, timing is an important consideration for buying a closed-end fund. The **repurchase price**, also called **bid price**, is the price at which a close-ended fund repurchases its units and it may include a charge called the **back-end load.**

- *Open-ended fund* Open-end mutual funds continue to operate for unlimited period of time; investors can join and leave the funds any time. Thus, there is no fixed number of shares or units; it changes everyday depending on purchases and sales. The price per share/unit is determined by the **net asset value** (NAV) of the open-end fund. The NAV of each share/unit is the total asset value minus liabilities of a mutual fund divided by the number of shares/units outstanding. Mutual funds are obligated to buy and sell shares at the current NAV. The price at which they repurchase the shares/units is called **redemption price**.

Various kinds of funds are possible within these two categories:

  - *Income funds* Income funds have the primary objective of a high current return, and investment is made in portfolios of high yielding shares.
  - *Growth funds* aim for capital gains and hence invest large proportion of their funds in equity shares with high growth potential.
  - *Balanced funds* Balanced funds combine the objectives of earning current income and capital appreciation. So, their portfolio consists of both equities and bonds.
  - *Taxes saving funds* Tax saving funds are targeted to investors in high tax brackets. Income for these funds is tax-exempt.
  - *Sector-based funds* Mutual funds may offer opportunities to investors to invest in the securities of specific sectors. For example, mutual funds have made available several sector-based funds like Infrastructure, Technology, and Pharmaceutical to *investors.*

Benefits of Mutual Funds

Mutual funds are financial intermediaries, facilitating the process of savings and investment. They mobilise savings form investors by selling their units or shares. The savings so collected are invested in the shares and other securities of a large number of companies and institutions. Mutual fund is a convenient and hassle-free method of investing in securities. It allows an investor to pool her investment with other investors with common financial objectives. Mutual funds offer the following advantages to investors:

- *Simplicity* Mutual funds are the simplest means of investing in the stock market securities for small investors and those investors who have no understanding of stock market or who do not have time or liking to actively trade stocks. These investors can simply identify mutual funds that meet their financial goals, and let the fund managers manage their investments at a reasonable fee.

- *Diversification* Small investors may not be able to invest in many securities as they may have limited savings. They may confine their investment to single or a very few securities. Hence, they are unable to diversify their investment risk. Mutual funds invest in large number of shares and/or other types of securities like government bonds, corporate bonds etc. This helps to spread out the investor's investment risk.

- *Professional management* Mutual funds employ expert managers to manage investors' investments. Thus, small investors are able to avail services of professional fund managers without a heavy cost. Fund managers invest investors' money according to their financial goals. From time to time, they disclose to investors whether they are able to meet their goals.

- *Affordability* Most mutual funds offer a variety of investment schemes with different investment goals and they specify low amounts as the minimum investments. Thus, small and all other investors have plenty of investment opportunities.

- *Flexibility* Investors do not want waste time visiting the mutual funds for buying and selling shares. These days, most mutual funds facilitate buying, selling, and transfer of shares by phone. In case of a number of mutual funds, investors can transact with them online. Some times mutual funds provide opportunities to investors to shift their investment from one scheme to another without any additional cost.

Drawbacks of Mutual Funds

The biggest drawback of mutual funds is the high fees and expenses, which can adversely affect investors' returns.

- *High fees and expenses* The high fee and expenses of mutual funds include sales fee, management fee and funds expenses. The loaded funds have initial charges called sales load or **front-end load** when they sell units/shares to investors. They charge a fee, called back-end load when they repurchase units/shares from investors. Some funds may charge penalty for early redemption of investment. Management fees include charges for managerial services and typically range from 0.25 to 2 per cent. Fund expenses also include charges for legal and administrative expenses.

- *Brokerage fees* Investors are required to pay brokerage fees in addition to the high fees and expenses of mutual funds. The mutual fund's expense ratio does not include the brokerage fees of buying and selling shares. **Expense ratio** is the per centage of a mutual fund's profits that holders must pay for management fees, operating costs, administrative fees, and any other costs.

- *Hidden costs* There is soft money or hidden brokerage fees that the mutual funds use for research. Usually, this money may be used for giving incentives to the fund managers like vacations for them and their families. Investors must examine the mutual fund's turnover rate or ratio. **Turnover**

rate or ratio is the percentage of a mutual fund's holdings that have been sold over in the past year. The higher the turnover rate, the higher the likelihood of the large hidden brokerage costs.

- *Cost of diversification* The diversification advantage provided by the mutual funds might become a disadvantage as they curb the possibility for large gains of individual shares. For example, if an investor owned Infosys share for a decade, she could have a large capital gain from her investment. But a mutual fund that owned Infosys share might report small gain since the fund usually hold a small percentage of an individual share.
- *Risks of ownership* The mutual funds investors suffer the usual ownership risks. When the market falls, the worth of investors' investment reduces, and in a stock market crash, their investment value may be totally eroded.

Investors must collect information about a mutual fund before deciding to make an investment. They should analyse the fund's prospectus that describes its goals, portfolio, prior performance, managers, fees, and other information. The annual or half-yearly report will list the securities the fund currently holds. The important considerations for an investor in choosing a fund are: consistent past performance, tolerable risk, low expense ratio, and manageable assets size and tax efficiency. The managers of fast growing funds may make hasty and risk investment as they have large pools of cash. It is preferable for small investors to invest in the mutual funds that have manageable assets.

Index Fund

Investors sometimes want to take advantages of growth in certain industrial sectors, or the market as a whole. Hence they might be interested in investing their money in shares of specific sectors. They can do so by putting their money in **sector funds**. These funds buy all of the shares in a particular sector in proportion to the weights of the sector stock index. If an investor likes shares of the fast moving consumer goods (FMCG) companies, he can buy sector funds that invest in FMCG shares. Investing in sector funds adds diversification to the investor's portfolio. For example, if an investor wants to invest on the basis of the popularity of, say, computer software shares, she does not have to invest in just the Infosys share. Sector funds will allow her to own shares of many other software companies. Sector funds allow an investor to earn higher returns with less risk than an actively managed index fund. The **actively managed funds** are the portfolios created by mutual funds managers for investors, which they change every day depending on the market swings, and attempt to beat the market.

In an **index fund**, the funds manager creates the fund by buying shares included in a stock market index such as the BSE Sensex or the NSE Nifty or a sector specific stock index. Sector funds are index funds as they are based on stock market indices. Stock market indices keep track of all types of companies. The BSE Sensex includes 30 most liquid and actively traded shares. The BSE 100 Index covers large companies. The NSE's S&P CNX 500 is a broad-based index representing about 94 per cent

of total market capitalisation and about 98 per cent of the total turnover on the NSE. The S&P CNX 500 companies are disaggregated into 74 industry indices. Industry weightages in the index reflect the industry weightages in the market. The CNX Midcap 200 Index includes medium-size companies. Similarly, both BSE and NSE have many sector specific stock market indices. The examples of index funds in India include UTI Master Index Fund, Franklin India Index Fund, Pioneer ITI Index Fund Nifty Plan, or HDFC Index Fund Nifty Plan.

The concept of index funds is based on the notion that the capital markets are efficient. In an efficient capital market, it is not possible for the funds managers to beat the market. Instead, the market may beat the actively managed funds as they may not be efficiently diversified. Hence many investors do not want to take risk and they prefer to invest in index funds desiring to obtain steady returns with less risk.

An index fund offers several advantages:

- *Less expenses* Index funds have lower expenses since they do not need to buy and sell as many shares as actively managed funds do.
- *Low research cost* Index funds is based on the market index; therefore, there is no need to do research to determine or change the composition of funds portfolios.
- *Regular follow-up* Since index funds are market based, it is easy for investors to follow their funds daily. In the actively managed funds, the investors have to wait for the periodic reports –monthly or quarterly.

Index funds are not without problems. They have the following limitations:

- Index funds can never outperform the market. They may do as good or as bad as the market does. When market crashes, they do not provide any protection to investors.
- The small investors may not be able to invest in index funds as several funds require a large initial investment.

Hedge Fund

A **hedge fund** does varieties of things than merely buying and selling securities. It takes both long and short positions, uses arbitrage, buys and sells undervalued securities, trades options or bonds, and invest in almost any opportunity in any market where it foresees impressive gains at reduced risk. Most hedge funds aim at reducing volatility and risk, while offering high returns under different market conditions. However, strategies of hedge funds may differ offering different combinations of volatility, risk and return. For example, some funds may hedge only against the equity market downturns. On the other hand, a global hedge fund may invest in shares, bonds, options, and foreign currencies. Note that global funds are not very common. Only about 5 per cent of hedge funds are global funds.

- *Positive returns* Many hedge funds strategies have the ability to generate positive returns in both rising and falling equity and bond markets.
- *Risk reduction* Inclusion of hedge funds in a balanced portfolio reduces overall portfolio risk and volatility and increases returns.

- ***Wide choices*** Huge variety of hedge fund investment styles – many uncorrelated with each other – provides investors with a wide choice of hedge fund strategies to meet their investment objectives.
- ***High returns*** Academic research proves hedge funds have higher returns and lower overall risk than traditional investment funds.

- ***Ideal investment*** Hedge funds provide an ideal long-term investment solution, eliminating the need to correctly time entry and exit from markets.
- ***Better diversification*** Adding hedge funds to an investment portfolio provide diversification not otherwise available in traditional investing.

SUMMARY

❖ Since financial managers raise funds from the capital markets, they must be familiar with their operations and requirements and procedures for raising capital.

❖ Capital markets deal with financial assets or securities. Securities will be fairly priced in the capital markets if they are efficient.

❖ Capital markets are considered to be efficient if the prices of securities reflect the available information. Depending on the extent of the information being impounded in the security prices, capital markets may be efficient in weak, semi-strong or strong form.

❖ Capital market consists of two components: the primary capital market and the secondary capital market. Companies raise new capital in the primary markets either through public issues, rights issues or private placement. Secondary market deals with securities that have been previously issued.

❖ The over-the-counter market and the derivatives market are other two forms of the secondary market. The OTC market is an informal market where negotiated deals take place. Derivatives market deals in future and options; it is basically a market for future delivery and payment.

❖ Options provide right, but not obligations to buy or sell securities. Therefore, in option market delivery is conditional. In the derivatives market options and future may include individual securities or index.

❖ India's capital market includes primary, secondary, OTC and derivatives segments. As a consequence of the growing economy and the government's policy of liberalisation and deregulation, the various segments of capital market in India have grown at phenomenal rates.

❖ The first stock exchange—the Bombay Stock Exchange—was established in 1875. Now there are 23 stock exchanges in India. The number of shareholders has increased to about 30–40 million. There are about 9000 listed companies. Both the market capitalisation and volume of trades have shown general growth, although they have fluctuated over years.

❖ Stock exchanges in India have well-developed procedures for listing, trading, settlement etc. The recent changes include shortening of the trading and settlement period, rolling settlement, index-based price bands, dematerialised share etc.

❖ A number of systems and rules exist for the regulation of the stock exchanges. The Securities and Exchange Board of India (SEBI) is the central regulatory authority regulating capital markets in India.

❖ The new issues market has also shown phenomenal growth after the eighties. A number of companies are able to raise substantial amount from the capital market. The corporate sector's dependence on the financial institutions for their funds requirements is declining with the development of the new issues market.

❖ We can also witness new financial instruments such as convertible securities, derivatives, warrants, etc. being issued by companies for raising capital.

❖ Yet another significant development is the free pricing of the new issues by companies. Within the norms prescribed by SEBI, a company can decide the issue price of its securities.

❖ Now companies are also allowed book building. In book building investors make price bids for shares. This leads to price discovery and the issuing company can assess the demand based on different prices.

❖ Merchant bankers play the role of intermediaries in the capital market in India. They help companies in the total management of issues of securities. Therefore, they are called issue managers. As members of stock exchange, underwriters of new issues and book builders, they help to make market, and hence, are known as market makers also. Merchant bankers cannot undertake the pure fund-based activities.

❖ Mutual funds provide a mechanism for collective investment. Generally they mobilise funds from individual investors and invest the collected funds in portfolios of securities. There are two basic types of mutual funds: open-ended and close-ended. An investor can buy and sell units or shares of open-ended funds at the market price continuously. In close-ended funds, the net asset value per share or unit is determined based on the total value of investment.

❖ Within these two broad categories, mutual funds may offer income funds, growth funds, balanced funds, tax-savings funds etc.

❖ Mutual funds companies also offer index funds and hedged funds to investors. Index funds invest investors' money in combination of securities in a general index like Sensex or in some sector index. Hedged funds are broad based and may include foreign exchange market also. They combine several investment strategies and try to maximise investors' returns.

❖ Mutual funds have several advantages to investors: simplicity, diversification, professional expertise, affordability and flexibility. They do have certain limitations: high brokerage, ownership risk, or no opportunity of making extra-ordinary profit.

KEY CONCEPTS

Capital market efficiency	Derivatives market	Perfect capital market	Serial independent
Circuit breaker	Event studies	Price bands	Strong-form of efficiency
Convertible securities	Hedge funds	Primary markets	Tax asymmetries
Cumulative abnormal return (CAR)	Index funds	Random walk hypothesis	Transaction costs
	Information asymmetries	Rolling settlement	Warrants
Cumulative convertible preference shares (CCPS)	Market capitalisation	Secondary markets	Weak form of efficiency
	Market makers	Semi-strong form of efficiency	Zero-coupon bonds
Deep-discount debentures	Mutual funds		
Derivatives	OTC market		

REVIEW QUESTIONS

1. Explain the concept of the capital market efficiency. What are the different forms of the capital market efficiency?

2. What is the difference between the primary market and the secondary market? Briefly describe some significant developments in the stock markets in India.

3. Briefly discuss the procedures for trading and settlement on the stock exchanges in India.

4. What developments have taken place in the capital markets in India? What are their implications for financial managers?

5. Explain the role of merchant banking in capital markets. What is the status of merchant banking in India?

6. What are mutual funds? What are their characteristics? What are the advantages and limitations of mutual funds?

7. What are index funds and hedged funds? Explain their merits and demerits.

20 Long-Term Finance: Shares, Debentures and Term Loans

CHAPTER OBJECTIVES

- Explain the features of ordinary shares
- Focus on the benefits and valuation of rights shares
- Discuss the pros and cons of debentures and preference shares
- Highlights the features of term loans

Two long-term securities available to a company for raising capital are—shares and debentures. Shares include ordinary (common) shares and preference shares. Ordinary shares provide ownership rights to investors. Debentures or bonds provide loan capital to the company, and investors get the status of lenders. Loan capital is also directly available from the financial institutions to the companies. What are the characteristics of loan capital and equity capital? What are their merits and demerits?

ORDINARY SHARES

Ordinary shares (referred to as common shares in USA) represent the ownership position in a company. The holders of ordinary shares, called **shareholders** (or stockholders in USA), are the legal owners of the company. Ordinary shares are the source of permanent capital since they do not have a maturity date. For the capital contributed by shareholders by purchasing ordinary shares, they are entitled for dividends. The amount or rate of dividend is not fixed; the company's board of directors decides it. An ordinary share is, therefore, known as a **variable income security**. Being the owners of the company, shareholders bear the risk of ownership; they are entitled to dividends after the income claims of others have been satisfied. Similarly, when the company is wound up, they can exercise their claims on assets after the claims of other suppliers of capital have been met.

Reporting of Ordinary Shares

The capital represented by ordinary shares is called share capital or equity capital. It appears on the left-hand side of a firm's account-form balance sheet or on the top of sources of capital in the step-form balance sheet. Details about share capital are generally contained in schedules attached to the balance sheet. Table 20.1 shows the details of share capital for the Gujarat Narmada Valley Fertilisers Company Limited (GNFC).

Table 20.1: GNFC's Share Capital as on 31 March, 2003

		(Rs in lakh)
(a)	Authorised 250,000,000 equity shares of Rs 10 each	25,000.00
(b)	Issued 148,565,000 equity shares of Rs 10 each	14,865.00
(c)	Subscribed and paid up 146,476,214 equity shares of Rs 10 each fully paid up	14,647.62
(d)	Reserves and Surplus	58,377.39
(e)	Net Worth (*c* + *d*)	73,025.01

Shareholder's equity includes both ordinary shares and preference shares (if any). Therefore, the capital attributable to ordinary shares excludes preference shares capital. In GNFC's case, the ordinary shareholders' equity capital is: Rs 73,025.01 lakh. **Authorised share capital** represents the maximum amount of capital, which a company can raise from shareholders. A company can, however, change its authorised share capital by altering its memorandum of association (a charter of the company). The alteration of memorandum involves somewhat complicated legal procedures. The portion of the authorised share capital, which has been offered to shareholders, is called **issued share capital**. **Subscribed share capital** represents that part of the issued share capital, which has been accepted by shareholders. The amount of subscribed share capital actually paid up by shareholders to the company is called **paid-up share capital**. Often, subscribed and paid-up share capital may be the same.

The total paid-up share capital is equal to the issue price of an ordinary share multiplied by the number of ordinary shares. The *issue price* may include two components: the **par value** and the **share premium**. The par value is the price per ordinary share stated in the memorandum of association. Generally, the par value of a ordinary share is in the denomination of Rs 100 or Rs 10. Any amount in excess of the par value is called the share premium. In the case of new companies the par value and the issue price may be the same. The existing, highly profitable companies may issue ordinary shares at a premium. The paid-up share capital is stated at the par value. The excess amount is separately shown as the share premium. The company's earnings, which have not been distributed to shareholders and have been retained in the business, are called reserves and surplus. They belong to owners—ordinary shareholders. Thus, the total shareholders' equity is the sum of: (*i*) paid-up share capital, (*ii*) share premium, and (*iii*) reserves and surplus. The total shareholders' equity or share capital is also called **net worth**.

The book value per ordinary share is calculated as follows:

$$\text{Book value per share} = \frac{\text{Net worth}}{\text{Number of ordinary shares}} \qquad (1)$$

For GNFC, the book value per share as on 31 March 2003 is:

$$= \frac{73,025.01}{1,464.76} = \text{Rs } 49.85$$

Note that the book value is based on historical figures in the balance sheet. It is in no way related with the **market value** of an ordinary share. The market value of a share is the price at which it trades in the stock market. It is generally based on expectations about the performance of the economy, in general and the company, in particular. GNFC's highest market price per share on Bombay Stock Exchange on 31 March 2003 was Rs 31.10 and lowest Rs 27.40. Thus, GNFC's market price is performing much below the book value. Ordinary shares of all companies may not be traded on stock markets. Therefore, the market value of ordinary shares of all companies may not be available.

Features of Ordinary Shares

Ordinary share has a number of special features which distinguish it from other securities. These features generally relate to the rights and claims of ordinary shareholders.

Claim on income Ordinary shareholders have a **residual ownership** claim. They have a claim to the residual income, which is, earnings available for ordinary shareholders, after paying expenses, interest charges, taxes and preference dividend, if any. This income may be split into two parts: dividends and retained earnings. Dividends are immediate cash flows to shareholders. Retained earnings are reinvested in the business, and shareholders stand to benefit in future in the form of the firm's enhanced value and earnings power and ultimately enhanced dividend and capital gain. Thus, residual income is either directly distributed to shareholders in the form of dividend or indirectly in the form of capital gains on the ordinary shares held by them.

Dividends payable depend on the discretion of the company's board of directors. A company is not under a legal obligation to distribute dividends out of the available earnings. Capital gains depend on future market value of ordinary shares. Thus, an ordinary share is a risky security from the investor's point of view. Dividends paid on ordinary shares are not tax deductible in the hands of the company.

Claim on assets Ordinary shareholders also have a residual claim on the company's assets in the case of liquidation. Liquidation can occur on account of business failure or sale of business. Out of the realised value of assets, first the claims of debt-holders and then preference shareholders are satisfied, and the remaining balance, if any, is paid to ordinary shareholders. In case of liquidation, the claims of ordinary shareholders may generally remain unpaid.

Right to control Control in the context of a company means the power to determine its policies. The board of directors approves the company's major policies and decisions while managers appointed by the board carry out the day-to-day operations. Thus, control may be defined as the power to appoint directors. Ordinary shareholders have the *legal* power to elect directors on the board. If the board fails to protect their interests, they can replace directors. Ordinary shareholders are able to control management of the company through their voting rights and right to maintain proportionate ownership.

Voting rights Ordinary shareholders are required to vote on a number of important matters. The most significant proposals include: election of directors and change in the memorandum of association. For example, if the company wants to change its authorised share capital or objectives of business, it requires ordinary shareholders' approval. Directors are elected at the annual general meeting (AGM) by the majority votes. Each ordinary share carries one vote. Thus, an ordinary shareholder has votes equal to the number of shares held by him. Shareholders may vote in person or by *proxy*. A proxy gives a designated person right to vote on behalf of a shareholder at the company's annual general meeting. When management takeovers are threatened, **proxy fights**—battles between rival groups for proxy votes—occur. An earlier example in this regard was that of Gamon India where both existing management and the Chhabrias fought for the control of the company and put all efforts to collect proxy votes. The existing management could continue its hold on the company with the help of majority shareholders including the financial institutions.

Pre-emptive rights The **pre-emptive right** entitles a shareholder to maintain his proportionate share of ownership in the company. The law grants shareholders the right to purchase new shares in the same proportion as their current ownership. Thus, if a shareholder owns 1 per cent of the company's ordinary shares, he has pre-emptive right to buy 1 per cent of new shares issued. A shareholder may decline to exercise this right. The shareholders' option to purchase a stated number of new shares at a specified price during a given period is called **rights**. These rights can be exercised at a subscription price, which is generally much below the share's current market price, or they can be allowed to expire, or they can be sold in the stock market.[1]

Limited liability Ordinary shareholders are the true owners of the company, but their liability is limited to the amount of their investment in shares. If a shareholder has already fully paid the issue price of shares purchased, he has nothing more to contribute in the event of a financial distress or liquidation. This position of shareholders is different from the owners in the case of sole proprietary businesses or partnership firms where they have unlimited liability. In the event of the insolvency of these firms, owners are required to bring in additional capital from their personal savings to pay claims of creditors. The limited liability feature of ordinary share encourages otherwise unwilling investors to invest their funds in the company. Thus, it helps companies to raise funds.

Pros and Cons of Equity Financing

Equity capital is the most important long-term source of financing. It offers the following advantages to the company:

- *Permanent capital* Since ordinary shares are not redeemable, the company has no liability for cash outflow associated with its redemption. It is a permanent capital, and is available for use as long as the company goes.
- *Borrowing base* The equity capital increases the company's financial base, and thus its borrowing limit. Lenders generally lend in proportion to the company's equity capital. By issuing ordinary shares, the company increases its financial capability. It can borrow when it needs additional funds.
- *Dividend payment discretion* A company is not legally obliged to pay dividend. In times of financial difficulties, it can reduce or suspend payment of dividend. Thus, it can avoid cash outflow associated with ordinary shares. In practice, dividend cuts are not very common and frequent. A company tries to pay dividend regularly. It cuts dividend only when it cannot manage cash to pay dividends. For example, in 1986 the Reliance Industries Limited experienced a sharp drop in its profits and had a severe liquidity problem; as a consequence, it had to cut its dividend rate from 50 per cent to 25 per cent. The company, however, increased the dividend rate next year when its performance improved.

Equity capital has some disadvantages to the firm compared to other sources of finance. They are as follows:

- *Cost* Shares have a higher cost at least for two reasons: Dividends are not tax deductible as are interest payments, and flotation costs on ordinary shares are higher than those on debt.
- *Risk* Ordinary shares are riskier from investors' point of view as there is uncertainty regarding dividend and capital gains. Therefore, they require a relatively higher rate of return. This makes equity capital as the highest cost source of finance.
- *Earnings dilution* The issue of new ordinary shares dilutes the existing shareholders' earnings per share if the profits do not increase immediately in proportion to the increase in the number of ordinary shares.
- *Ownership dilution* The issuance of new ordinary shares may dilute the ownership and control of the existing shareholders. While the shareholders have a pre-emptive right to retain their proportionate ownership, they may not have funds to invest in additional shares. Dilution of ownership assumes great significance in the case of closely held companies. The issuance of ordinary shares can change the ownership.

Public Issue of Equity

Public issue of equity means raising of share capital directly from the public. For example, Riga Sugar Company Limited (RSIL), a subsidiary of Belsund Sugar Limited made a public issue of equity shares of Rs 10 crore on 12 July 1994. The issue price per share is Rs 50—representing a premium of Rs 40 over its par value. The issue price is also higher than its book value of Rs 26.35 per share. The company needs funds for expansion and modernisation of its plant as well as for diversification into the manufacture of ethyl alcohol. The company expects to pay a dividend of 20 per cent in 1993–94 and 1994–95 and 25 per cent in 1995–96.

Consider another case. N.R. Agarwal Industries Limited is approaching the public for the first time to raise Rs 3.20 crore on 7 July 1994. Incorporated as a public limited company in December 1993, the maiden issue of equity shares is intended to part-finance its project for manufacturing industrial paper in Vapi, Gujarat. The share is issued at par at Rs 10.

As per the existing norms, a company with a track record is free to determine the issue price for its shares. Thus, it can issue shares at a premium. However, a new company has to issue its shares at par.

Underwriting of issues It is legally obligatory to underwrite a public and a rights issue. In an underwriting, the underwriters—generally banks, financial institution, brokers etc.—guarantee to buy the shares if the issue is not fully subscribed by the public. The agreement may provide for a firm buying by the underwriters. The company has to pay an underwriting commission to the underwriter for their services.

Private Placement

Private placement involves sale of shares (or other securities) by

---

1. Gupta, L.C., *Rates of Return on Equities: The Indian Experience*, Oxford University Press, 1981, pp. 9–11.

a company to few selected investors, particularly the institutional investors like the Unit Trust of India (UTI), the Life Insurance Corporation of India (LIC), the Industrial Development Bank of India (IDBI), etc. Private placement has the following advantages:

- **Size** It is helpful to issue small amount of funds.
- **Cost** It is less expensive. In the case of public issue of securities, the issue costs, including both statutory and other costs, are quite high, ranging between 10 to 20 per cent of the size of issue. A substantial part of these costs can be avoided through private placement.
- **Speed** It takes less time to raise funds through private placement, say, less than 3 months. Public issues involve a number of requirements to be fulfilled, and this requires a lot of time to raise capital.

RIGHTS ISSUE OF EQUITY SHARES

A **rights issue** involves selling of ordinary shares to the existing shareholders of the company. The law in India requires that the new ordinary shares must be first issued to the existing shareholders on a *pro rata* basis. Shareholders through a special resolution can forfeit this pre-emptive right. Obviously, this will dilute their ownership.

Terms and Procedures

A company can make rights offering to its shareholders after meeting the requirements specified by the Securities and Exchange Board of India (SEBI). Those shareholders who renounce their rights are not entitled for additional shares. Shares becoming available on account of non-exercise of rights are allotted to shareholders who have applied for additional shares on *pro rata* basis. Any balance of shares left after issuing the additional shares can be sold in the open market.

Let us assume that a company announces on 2nd January 2004 that all shareholders whose names are in the register of members as on 25th February 2004 will be issued rights, which will expire on 10th March 2004. The company will mail the "letter of rights" on 5th April 2004. In the example, 2nd January 2004 is the announcement date, 25th February 2004 is the *holder-of-the-register-of-members date*, 5th April 2004 is the *offer-of-rights date* and 10th March 2004 is the *expiration-of-rights date*. It may be possible that the share may be traded (bought and sold) a few days before the holder-of-the-register-of-members date (5th April 2004 in the example), and it may not be transferred and registered in the new name. The rights might then be wrongly sent to the old shareholder. If the share is traded within the *ex-rights date*, it will be duly registered in the name of purchaser. The ex-rights date occurs a few days prior to the holder-of-the-register-of-member date. This implies that after the ex-rights date the share sells without the rights. The price of the share before the ex-rights date is called as **right-on** or **cum-rights** while the price after this date is referred to as the **ex-rights** price.

In India along with the letter of rights, four forms may be sent. Form A is intended for accepting the rights and applying for additional shares. Form B is meant for the purpose of foregoing the rights in favour of other person. Form C has to be used by the person in whose favour the rights have been renounced for making application. Form D is for the purpose of requesting for the split forms.

When the rights are offered for raising funds, three issues are involved: (*i*) the number of rights needed to buy a new share, (*ii*) the theoretical value of a right, and (*iii*) the effect of rights offerings on the value of the ordinary shares outstanding. We shall consider an example to discuss these issues.

The Sunshine Industries Limited has 900,000 shares outstanding at current market price of Rs 130 per share. The company needs Rs 22.50 million (or Rs 2.25 crore) to finance its proposed modernisation-cum-expansion project. The board of the company has decided to issue rights for raising the required money. The subscription (issue) price (P_s) has been fixed at Rs 75 per share. The subscription price has been set below the market price to ensure that the rights issue is fully subscribed. How many rights required purchasing a new share? What is the value of a right?

Value of a Right

We can first determine the number of new shares to be issued to raise Rs 22.50 million at Rs 75 per share:

$$\text{No. of new shares}(s) = \frac{\text{Desired funds}}{\text{Subscription price } (P_s)}$$

$$= \frac{22,500,000}{75} = 300,000 \text{ shares} \quad (2)$$

We know that each ordinary share will get one right; therefore, there are a total number of 900,00 rights. The company wants to sell 300,000 new shares. The number of rights required to buy on new share will be equal to the number of existing shares outstanding (S_o) divided by new share (s) to be sold:

$$\text{No. of rights} = \frac{\text{Existing shares}}{\text{New shares}}$$

$$N = \frac{S_o}{s} \quad (3)$$

In our example, the number of rights required are:

$$= \frac{900,000}{300,000} = 3 \text{ rights}$$

This implies that to purchase a new share, an existing shareholder should have 3 rights and Rs 75. What is the price of one share after rights offering? The price of the share after the rights issue is called *ex-rights price* (P_x). It is equal to the value of 3 rights plus Rs 75.

Price of a share
after rights issue (P_x) = Value of 3 rights + Rs 75

The formula for the ex-rights issue (P_x) can be written as follows:

$$P_x = N \times R + P_s \quad (4)$$

where N is the number of rights needed to buy one share, R is the value of a right and P_s is the subscription price. In fact, this price can be found out directly. The price of a share after rights issue is equal to the sum of value of existing shares (900,000) at the current market-price (Rs 130) and the value of new shares (300,000) at subscription price (Rs 75) divided by total number of shares after the rights issue (900,000 + 300,000 = 1,200,000):

Price of share after rights issue

= (Existing shares × Current market price + New shares

    × Subscription price) ÷ (Existing shares + New shares)

$$P_x = \frac{S_o \times P_o + s \times P_s}{S_o + s} = \frac{S_o P_o + s P_s}{S} \quad (5)$$

where $S = S_o + s$. In the example, the price is:

$$= \frac{900,000 \times 130 + 300,000 \times 75}{900,000 + 300,000} = \frac{1,170,000 + 22,500,000}{1,200,000}$$

$$= \text{Rs} 116.25$$

In the case of the Sunshine rights issue, we know that a shareholder can buy one new share for Rs 75 plus 3 rights. The company's share after the ex-rights date is theoretically worth Rs 116.25. Therefore, the total value of 3 rights together is Rs 41.25. (Rs 116.25 – Rs 75), and the value of each right is Rs 13.75 (Rs 41.25/3). Thus the share price on the ex-right date drops by Rs 13.75 from the cum-rights (rights-on) price of Rs 130 to the ex-rights price of Rs 116.25. This drop is the value of one right. In fact, what has happened is that the cum-rights (rights-on) price (P_o = Rs 130) has divided into the ex-rights price (P_x = Rs 116.25) and the value of a right (R = Rs 13.75). Thus, $P_o = P_x + R$.

We can also use other formulae to determine the value of a right. We can combine Equations (4) and (5) to find out value of a right as follows:

$$P_x = \frac{S_o P_o + s P_s}{S} = NR + P_s$$

$$NR = P_x - P_s$$

$$R = \frac{P_x - P_s}{N} \quad (6)$$

where R is the value of a right, P_x is the ex-rights price which is given by Equation (4) and P_s is the subscription price. Applying Equation (6) to our example, R is equal to:

$$R = \frac{116.25 - 75}{3} = \frac{41.25}{3} = \text{Rs} 13.75$$

Notice that Equation (6) gives the value of a right when the share is selling ex-rights. What is the value of a right when the share is selling cum-rights (rights-on)? We know that the cum-rights price (P_o) is:

$$P_o = P_x + R \quad (7)$$

and the ex-rights price (P_x) is:

$$P_x = P_o - R \quad (8)$$

The price of a right when share is selling ex-rights is:

$$R = \frac{P_x - P_s}{N} \quad (9)$$

Substituting $P_o - R$ for P_x from Equation (8) into Equation (6), we obtain:

$$R = \frac{P_o - R - P_s}{N}$$

$$NR = P_o - R - P_s$$

$$NR + R = P_o - P_s$$

$$R(N+1) = P_o - P_s$$

$$R = \frac{P_o - P_s}{N+1}$$

For the Sunshine Limited the value of a right is:

$$R = \frac{130 - 75}{3 + 1} = \frac{55}{4} = \text{Rs} 13.75$$

This is the same value as found by Equation (6) under the assumption that the share was selling ex-rights.

Effect on Shareholders' Wealth

From the calculations of the value of a right when the share is selling ex-rights, or cum-rights, it should be clear that the existing shareholder does not benefit or lose from rights issue. What he receives in the form of the value of a right, he loses in the form of decline in share price. His wealth remains unaffected when he exercises his rights. Of course, he will lose if he does not exercise his rights or sells them. Thus, the shareholder has three options: (1) he exercises his rights, (2) he sells his rights, or (3) he does not exercise or sell his rights. He will lose under the third option. Let us illustrate.[1]

Suppose a shareholder in Sunshine owns 3 shares. At a current market price of Rs 130, his total wealth is Rs 390. Let us assume that he exercises his rights as offered by the company. After the exercise of his rights, he will own 4 shares at the ex-rights price of Rs 116.25. Therefore, his total wealth is: Rs 116.25 × 4 = Rs 465. But he has spent Rs 75 to obtain the additional share. So his net wealth is: Rs 465 – Rs 75 = Rs 390—same as before the rights issue. Now assume that he does not exercise his rights rather sells them at Rs 13.75 per right. He still own 3 shares but at a price of Rs 116.25 per share (ex-rights price). So his total value of shares is: Rs 116.25 × 3 = Rs 348.75. But he also obtains: Rs 13.75 × 3 = Rs 41.25 by selling his rights. Therefore, his net wealth is: Rs 348.75 + Rs 41.25 = Rs 390—once again same as before the rights issue. Let us now assume that he does nothing.

---

1. Gupta, *ibid.*

This means that he would simply own 3 shares at a price of Rs 116.25 after the expiry of rights issue. Thus his wealth would decline to Rs 348.75 from Rs 390.

Is Subscription Price of Any Significance?

Is the subscription price (P_s) significant? It is irrelevant in terms of the impact on the shareholders' wealth. It can be fixed at any level below the current market price. What the shareholder gains in terms of the value of rights, he will lose in terms of decline in the share price. The primary objective in setting the subscription price low is that after the rights offering the market price should not fall below it.

Will the theoretical value of a right always equal its actual market value? The theoretical value could differ from the actual value for three reasons.[1] *First*, the high transaction costs can limit the investor arbitrage that would otherwise push the market price of the right to its theoretical value. *Second*, speculation over the subscription period can push the market price above or below the theoretical value. *Third*, large flotation costs can also affect these two values.

Pros and Cons of Rights Issue

There are three main advantages of the rights issue. *First*, the existing shareholders' control is maintained through the *pro rata* issue of shares. This is significant in the case of closely held company or when a company is going into financial difficulties or is under a takeover threat. *Second*, raising funds through the sale of rights issue rather than the public issue involves less flotation costs as the company can avoid underwriting commission. *Third*, in the case of profitable companies, the issue is more likely to be successful since the subscription price is set much below the current market price.

The main disadvantage is to the shareholders who fail to exercise their rights. They lose in terms of decline in their wealth. Yet another disadvantage is for those companies whose shareholding is concentrated in the hands of financial institutions because of the conversion of loan into equity. They would prefer public issue of shares rather than the rights issue.

PREFERENCE SHARES

Preference share is often considered to be a **hybrid security** since it has many features of both ordinary shares and debenture. It is similar to ordinary share in that (*a*) the non-payment of dividends does not force the company to insolvency, (*b*) dividends are not deductible for tax purposes, and (*c*) in some cases, it has no fixed maturity date. On the other hand, it is similar to debenture in that (*a*) dividend rate is fixed, (*b*) preference shareholders do not share in the residual earnings, (*c*) preference shareholders have claims on income and assets prior to ordinary shareholders, and (*d*) they usually do not have voting rights.

Features

Preference share has several features. Some of them are common to all types of preference shares while others are specific to some.[2]

Claims on income and assets Preference share is a **senior security** as compared to ordinary share. It has a prior claim on the company's income in the sense that the company must first pay preference dividend before paying ordinary dividend. It also has a prior claim on the company's assets in the event of liquidation. The preference share claim is honoured after that of a debenture and before that of ordinary share. Thus, in terms of risk, preference share is less risky than ordinary share. There is a cost involved for the relative safety of preference investment. Preference shareholders generally do not have voting rights and they cannot participate in extraordinary profits earned by the company. However, a company can issue preference share with voting rights (called **participative preference shares**).

Fixed dividend The dividend rate is fixed in the case of preference share, and preference dividends are not tax deductible. The preference dividend rate is expressed as a percentage of the par value. The amount of preference dividend will thus be equal to the dividend rate multiplied by the par value. Preference share is called **fixed-income security** because it provides a constant income to investors. The payment of preference dividend is not a legal obligation. Usually, a profitable company will honour its commitment of paying preference dividend.

Cumulative dividends Most preference shares in India carry a cumulative dividend feature, requiring that all past unpaid preference dividend be paid before any ordinary dividends are paid. This feature is a protective device for preference shareholders. The preference dividends could be omitted or passed without the cumulative feature. Preference shareholders do not have power to force company to pay dividends; non-payment of preference dividend also does not result into insolvency. Since preference share does not have the dividend enforcement power, the cumulative feature is necessary to protect the rights of preference shareholders.

Redemption Theoretically both redeemable and perpetual (irredeemable) preference shares can be issued.[3] Perpetual or irredeemable preference share does not have a maturity date. Redeemable preference share has a specified maturity. In practice, redeemable preference shares in India are not often retired in accordance with the stipulation since there are not serious penalties for violation of redemption feature.

Sinking fund Like in the case of debenture, a sinking fund provision may be created to redeem preference share. The money set aside for this purpose may be used either to purchase preference share in the open market or to buy back (call) the preference share. Sinking funds for preference shares are not common.

Call feature The call feature permits the company to buy back preference shares at a stipulated **buy-back** or **call price**. Call price may be higher than the par value. Usually, it decreases with the passage of time. The difference between call price and par value of the preference share is called *call premium.*

Participation feature Preference shares may in some cases have participation feature which entitles preference shareholders to participate in extraordinary profit earned by the company. This means that a preference shareholder may get dividend amount in

1. For a simple treatment of the issues refer to Keown, A.J., *et. al.*, *Basic Financial Management*, Prentice-Hall, 1985, p. 649.
2. See Keown *et. al. ibid.*, p. 637–38.
3. In India, companies cannot issue irredeemable preference shares.

excess of the fixed dividend. The formula for determining extra dividend would differ. A company may provide for extra dividend to preference shareholders equal to the amount of ordinary dividend that is in excess of the regular preference dividend. Thus if the preference dividend rate is 10 per cent and the company pays an ordinary dividend of 16 per cent, then preference shareholders will receive extra dividend at 6 per cent (16 per cent–10 per cent). Preference shareholders may also be entitled to participate in the residual assets in the event of liquidation.

Voting rights Preference shareholders ordinarily do not have any voting rights. They may be entitled to **contingent** or **conditional voting rights**. In India, if a preference dividend is outstanding for two or more years in the case of cumulative preference shares, or the preference dividend is outstanding for two or more consecutive preceding years or for a period of three or more years in the preceding six years, preference shareholders can nominate a member on the board of the company.

Convertibility Preference shares may be convertible or non-convertible. A convertible preference share allows preference shareholders to convert their preference shares, fully or partly, into ordinary shares at a specified price during a given period of time. Preference shares, particularly when the preference dividend rate is low, may sometimes be converted into debentures. For example, the Andhra Cement converted its preference shares of Re 0.33 crore into debentures in 1985. To make preference share attractive, the government of India has introduced **convertible cumulative preference share** (CCPS). Unfortunately, companies in India have hardly used this security to raise funds.

Pros and Cons

Preference share has a number of advantages to the company, which ultimately occur to ordinary shareholders.[1]

- *Riskless leverage advantage* Preference share provides financial leverage advantages since preference dividend is a fixed obligation. This advantage occurs without a serious risk of default. The non-payment of preference dividends does not force the company into insolvency.
- *Dividend postponability* Preference share provides some financial flexibility to the company since it can postpone payment of dividend.
- *Fixed dividend* The preference dividend payments are restricted to the stated amount. Thus preference shareholders do not participate in excess profits as do the ordinary shareholders.
- *Limited voting rights* Preference shareholders do not have voting rights except in case dividend arrears exist. Thus the control of ordinary shareholders is preserved.

The following are the limitations of preference shares:

- *Non-deductibility of dividends* The primary disadvantage of preference share is that preference dividend is not tax deductible. Thus it is costlier than debenture.
- *Commitment to pay dividend* Although preference dividend can be omitted, they may have to be paid because of their cumulative nature. Non-payment of preference dividends can adversely affect the image of a company, since equity holders cannot be paid any dividends unless preference shareholders are paid dividends.

Preference shares provide more flexibility and lesser burden to a company. The dividend rate is less than on equity and it is fixed. Also, the company can redeem it when it does not require the capital. In practice, when a company reorganises its capital, it may convert preference capital into equity. Some time equity may be converted into preference capital. For example, IDBI in 1994 proposed to convert its equity capital as preference capital.

DEBENTURES

A **debenture** is a long-term promissory note for raising loan capital. The firm promises to pay interest and principal as stipulated. The purchasers of debentures are called debenture holders. An alternative form of debenture in India is **bond**. Mostly public sector companies in India issue bonds. In USA, the term debenture is generally understood to mean unsecured bond.

Features

A debenture is a long-term, fixed-income, financial security. Debenture holders are the creditors of the firm. The *par value* of a debenture is the face value appearing on the debenture certificate. Corporate debentures in India are issued in different denominations. The large public sector companies issue bonds in the denominations of Rs 1,000. Some of the important features of debentures are discussed below.

Interest rate The interest rate on a debenture is fixed and known. It is called the **contractual rate of interest**. It indicates the percentage of the par value of the debenture that will be paid out annually (or semi-annually or quarterly) in the form of interest. Thus, regardless of what happens to the market price of a debenture, say, with a 15 per cent interest rate, and a Rs 1,000 par value, it will pay out Rs 150 annually in interest until maturity. Payment of interest is legally binding on a company. Debenture interest is tax deductible for computing the company's corporate tax. However, it is taxable in the hands of a debenture holder as per the income tax rules. However, public sector companies in India are sometimes allowed by the government to issue bonds with tax-free interest. That is, the bondholder is not required to pay tax on his bond interest income.

Maturity Debentures are issued for a specific period of time. The *maturity* of a debenture indicates the length of time until the company redeems (returns) the par value to debenture-holders and terminates the debentures. In India, a debenture is typically redeemed after 7 to 10 years in instalments.

Redemption As indicated earlier, debentures are mostly redeemable; they are generally redeemed on maturity. Redemption of debentures can be accomplished either through a **sinking fund** or **buy-back (call) provision**.

Sinking fund A sinking fund is cash set aside periodically for retiring debentures. The fund is under the control of the trustee who redeems the debentures either by purchasing them in the

---

1. For a detailed discussion of the characteristics, merits and demerits of preference shares in India, see Gupta, L.C., *Preference Shares and Company Finance,* IFMR, 1975. Also refer to Keown, *op. cit.,* pp. 638–43.

market or calling them in an acceptable manner. In some cases, the company itself may handle the retirement of debentures using the sinking funds. The advantage is that the periodic retirement of debt through the sinking funds reduces the amount required to redeem the remaining debt at maturity. Particularly when the firm faces temporary financial difficulty at the time of debt maturity, the repayment of huge amount of principal could endanger the firm's financial viability. The use of the sinking fund eliminates this potential danger.

Buy-back (call) provision Debenture issues include buy-back provision. Buy-back provisions enable the company to redeem debentures at a specified price before the maturity date. The **buy-back (call) price** may be more than the par value of the debenture. This difference is called *call or buy-back premium*. In India, it is generally 5 per cent of the par value.

Indenture An **indenture** or **debenture trust deed** is a legal agreement between the company issuing debentures and the debenture trustee who represents the debenture holders. It is the responsibility of the trustee to protect the interests of debenture holders by ensuring that the company fulfils the contractual obligations. Generally, a financial institution, or a bank, or an insurance company or a firm of attorneys is appointed as a trustee. The debenture trust deed (indenture) provides the specific terms of the agreement, including a description of debentures, rights of debenture holders, rights of the issuing company and responsibilities of trustee.

Security Debentures are either *secured* or *unsecured*. A secured debenture is secured by a lien on the company's specific assets. If the company defaults, the trustee can seize the security on behalf of the debenture holders. In India, debentures are usually secured by a charge on the present and future immovable assets of the company. This is called **equitable mortgage**. When debentures are not protected by any security, they are known as unsecured or naked debentures. As stated earlier, in USA the term debenture always means unsecured bond while bond could be secured or unsecured. If the debentures are unsecured, it will generally be difficult for the firm to attract investors to subscribe to them. Security, however, does not necessarily ensure the safety of a debenture/bond from the investor's point of view. Professional bodies rate bonds/debentures to indicate the degree of their safety. Credit rating of a bond/debenture shows the chances of timely payment of interest and principal by a borrower.

In India, the Credit Rating and Information Services of India Limited (CRISIL) provides rating for bonds/debentures, fixed deposits and commercial papers. Other rating companies include CARE and ICRA. Exhibit 20.1 explains the nature of debenture ratings given by CRISIL.

Yield The **yield** on a debenture is related to its market price; therefore, it could be different from the coupon rate of interest. Two types of yield could be distinguished. The **current yield** on a debenture is the ratio of the annual interest payment to the debenture's market price. For example, the current yield of a 14 per cent Rs 1,000 debenture currently selling at Rs 750 is:

$$\text{Current yield} = \frac{\text{Annual interest}}{\text{Market price}} = \frac{140}{750}$$
$$= 0.187 \text{ or } 18.7\%$$

EXHIBIT 20.1: CREDIT RATING OF DEBENTURES IN INDIA

CRISIL provides the following ratings to bonds/debentures.

- *AAA (highest safety)* Triple A (AAA) rated debentures imply highest safety in the timely payment of interest and principal even if changes take place in the circumstances subsequently.

- *AA (high safety)* Double A (AA) rated debentures ensure high safety—marginally less than the safety provided by triple A debentures.

- *A (adequate safety)* Single A rated debentures provide for timely payment of interest and principal, but the changed circumstances in future may affect such debentures as compared to the higher rated debentures.

- *BBB (low safety)* Triple B (BBB) debentures ensure sufficient safety with regard to the payment of interest and principal. But the changed circumstances later on are more likely to weaken the capacity of the issuing company to pay interest and principal.

- *BB (inadequate safety)* Double B (BB) rated debentures do not provide adequate safety of timely payment of interest and principal. The uncertainties of future can lead to inadequate capacity to make timely payment of interest and principal.

- *B (high risk)* Single B rated debentures are likely to default. Adverse circumstances can render the ability or willingness of a borrower quite weak to pay interest or principal.

- *C (substantial risk)* C rated debentures have current factors that make them vulnerable to default. For no default of payment of interest or principal, favourable circumstances must continue.

- *D (in default)* D rated debentures are in default or are expected to be in default.

Source: Information published by CRISIL.

The **yield to maturity** takes into account the payments of interest and principal over the life of the debenture. Thus, it is the internal rate of return of the debenture. Mathematically, the yield to maturity is the discount rate that equates the present value of the interest and principal payments with the current market price of the debentures. You may recall that we have discussed the formula for the calculation of the yield to maturity in Chapter 3.

Claims on assets and income Debenture holders have a claim on the company's earnings prior to that of the shareholders. Debentures interest has to be paid before paying any dividends to preference and ordinary shareholders. A company can be forced into bankruptcy if it fails to pay interest to debenture holders. Therefore, in practice, the debenture holders' claim on income is generally honoured except in the case of extreme financial difficulties faced by the company.

In liquidation, the debenture holders have a claim on assets prior to that of shareholders. However, secured debenture holders will have priority over the unsecured debenture holders. Thus, different types of debt may have a hierarchy among themselves as their order of claim on the company's assets.

Types of Debentures

Debentures may be straight debentures or convertible debentures. A convertible debenture (CD) is one which can be converted, fully or partly, into shares after a specified period of time. Thus on the basis of convertibility, debentures may be classified into three categories.

- Non-convertible debentures (NCDs)
- Fully convertible debentures (FCDs)
- Partly convertible debentures (PCDs).

Non-convertible debentures (*NCDs*) NCDs are pure debentures without a feature of conversion. They are repayable on maturity. The investor is entitled for interest and repayment of principal. The erstwhile Industrial Credit and Investment Corporation of India (ICICI) issued debentures for Rs 200 crores fully non-convertible bonds of Rs 1,000 each at 16 per cent rate of interest, payable half-yearly. The maturity period was five years. However, the investors had the option to be repaid fully or partly the principal after 3 years after giving due notice to ICICI.

As we have discussed in Chapter 3, companies in practice also issue **zero-interest debentures** (ZID). These debentures are issued at a highly discounted issue price. The difference between the issue price and the maturity value is the implicit amount of interest. Zero-interest debentures are also called **deep-discount debentures** (bonds).

Fully-convertible debentures (*FCDs*) FCDs are converted into shares as per the terms of the issue with regard to price and time of conversion. The pure FCDs carry interest rates, generally less than the interest rates on NCDs since they have the attraction feature of being converted into equity shares. Recently, companies in India are issuing FCDs with zero rate of interest. For example, Jindal Iron and Steel Company Limited raised Rs 111.2 each. After 12 months of allotment, each FCD was convertible into one share of Rs 100—Rs 90 being the premium.

Partly-convertible debentures (*PCDs*) A number of debentures issued by companies in India have two parts: a convertible part and a non-convertible part. Such debentures are known as partly-convertible debentures (PCDs). The investor has the advantages of both convertible and non-convertible debentures blended into one debenture. For example, Proctor and Gamble Limited (P&G) issued 400,960 PCDs of Rs 200 each to its existing shareholders in July 1991. Each PCD has two parts: convertible portion of Rs 65 each to be converted into one equity share of Rs 10 each at a premium of Rs 55 per share at the end of 18 months from the date of allotment and non-convertible portion of Rs 135 payable in three equal instalments on the expiry of 6th, 7th and 8th years from the date of allotment.

Pros and Cons

Debenture has a number of advantages as long-term source of finance:

- *Less costly* It involves less cost to the firm than the equity financing because (a) investors consider debentures as a relatively less risky investment alternative and therefore, require a lower rate of return and (b) interest payments are tax deductible.
- *No ownership dilution* Debenture-holders do not have voting rights; therefore, debenture issue does not cause dilution of ownership.
- *Fixed payment of interest* Debenture holders do not participate in extraordinary earnings of the company. Thus the payments are limited to interest.
- *Reduced real obligation* During periods of high inflation, debenture issue benefits the company. Its obligation of paying interest and principal which are fixed decline in real terms.

Debenture has some limitations also:

- *Obligatory payments* Debenture results in legal obligation of paying interest and principal, which, if not paid, can force the company into liquidation.
- *Financial risk* It increases the firm's financial leverage, which may be particularly disadvantageous to those firms which have fluctuating sales and earnings.
- *Cash outflows* Debentures must be paid on maturity, and therefore, at some points, it involves substantial cash outflows.
- *Restricted covenants* Debenture indenture may contain restrictive covenants which may limit the company's operating flexibility in future.

TERM LOANS

Debt capital of a company may consist of either debentures or bonds which are issued to public for subscription or term loans which are obtained directly from the banks and financial institutions. Term loans are sources of long-term debt. In India, they are generally obtained for financing large expansion, modernisation or diversification projects. Therefore, this method of financing is also called **project financing**.

Features of Term Loans

Term loans represent long-term debt with a maturity of more than one year. They are obtained from banks and specially created financial institutions (FIs) in India by private placement rather than a public subscription, as is the case with most debenture issues. The purpose of term loans is mostly to finance the company's capital expenditures. Term loans have a number of basic features. They include the following: (1) maturity, (2) direct negotiation, (3) security, (4) restrictive covenants, (5) convertibility, and (6) repayment schedule.

Maturity Banks and specially created financial institutions (FIs) are the main sources of term loans in India. FIs provide term loans generally for a period of 6 to 10 years. In some cases, a grace period (moratorium) of 1 to 2 years is also granted: this is the period during which the company has not to make any payment. Commercial banks advance term loans for a period of 3 to 5 years.

Direct negotiation A firm negotiates term loans for project finance directly with a bank or FI. Thus term loan is a private placement. Sometimes debentures *may* also be privately placed to FIs, but most debenture issues are placed for public subscription. The advantages of private placement are the ease of negotiation and low cost of raising loan. Unlike in the case of public issue, the firm need not underwrite term loans. Thus it avoids underwriting commission and other flotation costs.

Security Term loans are always secured. Specifically the assets acquired using term loan funds secure them. This is called **primary security**. The company's current and future assets also generally secure term loans. This is called **secondary** or **collateral security**. Also, the lender may create either fixed or floating charge against the firm's assets. **Fixed charges** means **legal mortgage** of specific assets. For creating a fixed charge, the firm has to pay a heavy stamp duty which may be equal to 2 1/2 per cent of the amount of loan. **Floating charge** is a **general mortgage** (equitable mortgage) covering all assets. In this case, stamp duty is only 1/2 per cent. Floating charge provides the firm with relative flexibility as it can deal with its assets in the normal course of business without obtaining lender's approval.

Restrictive covenants In addition to the asset security, lender would like to protect itself further. Therefore, FIs add a number of restrictive covenants. A financially weak firm attracts stringent terms of loan from lenders. The borrowing firm has generally to keep the lender informed by furnishing financial statements and other information periodically. The restrictive covenants may be categorised as follows:

Asset-related covenants Lender would like the firm to maintain its minimum asset base. Therefore, restrictions may include to maintain minimum working capital position in terms of a minimum current ratio and not to sell fixed assets without the lender's approval. The firm may also be required to refrain from creating any additional charge on its assets.

Liability-related covenants The firm may be restrained from incurring additional debt or repay existing loan. It may be allowed to do so with the concurrence of the lender. The firm may also be required to reduce its debt-equity ratio by issuing additional equity and preference capital. The freedom of promoters to dispose of their shareholding may also be limited.

Cash flow-related covenants Lenders my restrain the firm's cash outflow by restricting cash dividends, capital expenditures, salaries and perks of managerial staff etc.

Control-related covenants Lenders expect that the firm's management will be competent enough to manage its operations. They may therefore provide for the effective organisational set-up and appointment of suitable staff and the broad-base Board of Directors. One special feature of term loans in this regard could be the provision for the appointment of **nominee director** by FIs. Nominee director may be appointed in case of those firms, which have been granted substantial financial help by FIs. His role is to safeguard the interests of FIs. He should keep himself well acquainted with the operations of the company without undue interference. He should contribute to the company's policies and sound financial management.

Convertibility FIs in India provide huge amount of loan assistance to the companies. Because of the substantial financial stake of these institutions, in the past they had the option to convert a part of the rupee loan into equity. FIs would state the terms and conditions of the conversion. FIs in India insist on the option of converting loans into equity.

Repayment Schedule

The repayment schedule or **loan amortisation** specifies the time schedule for paying interest and principal. Payment of loan is a legal obligation. Interest charges are tax deductible in the hands of the borrowing firm. The general rate of interest on term loans in India is above 14 or 15 per cent. For companies undertaking their projects in specified backward areas, loans at concessional interest rate (usually 1½ per cent lower) are available.

The common practice in India to amortise loan is to require repayment of principal in equal instalments (semi-annual or annual) and pay interest on the unpaid (outstanding) loan. Thus, interest payment will decline over the years, and the total loan payment (interest plus principal) will not be equal in each period. Repayment of loan in instalments saves the company from repaying huge amount at the end of loan maturity. Such payments are called **balloon payments.**

Consider an example. Suppose a company negotiates a Rs 3 crore loan for eight years from FIs. The interest rate will be 14 per cent per annum on the outstanding balance. The principal will be repaid in eight equal year-end instalments. What is the payment schedule?

The payment schedule will include both interest and principal payment. Interest will be calculated on the outstanding balance on loan. Note that Rs 3 crore was borrowed in the beginning of first year; therefore, the interest charges at the end of the year will be: 0.14×3 = Rs 0.42 crore. The instalments of principal will be: 3/8 = Rs 0.375 crore. Thus, loan balance at the end of first year will be: $3.0 - 0.375$ = Rs 2.62. This balance will be the basis for calculating interest next year. Calculations are shown in Table 20.2.

Table 20.2: Loan Amortisation Schedule (Equal Principal Repayment) (Rs '000)

(Rs '000)

Year (1)	Loan in the Beginning (2)	Principal Repayment (3)	Interest (4)	Loan Payment (3 + 4) (5)	Loan at the end (2 – 5) (6)
1	30,000	3,750	4,200	7,950	26,250
2	26,250	3,750	3,675	7,425	22,500
3	22,500	3,750	3,150	6,900	18,750
4	18,750	3,750	2,625	6,375	15,000
5	15,000	3,750	2,100	5,850	11,250
6	11,250	3,750	1,575	5,325	7,500
7	7,500	3,750	1,050	4,800	3,750
8	3,750	3,750	525	4,275	0

An alternative way for amortising loan is to require to pay equal loan instalments including both interest and principal payments. If this is done, then we find out the amount of instalment by using the concept of **capital recovery** (as discussed in chapter 7). In our example, we want to find out answer to the following question: What should be the annuity for eight years at 14 per cent rate of return to obtain a present value of Rs 3 crore? We can write it in the form of following equation:

$$3 = \text{Annuity} \times \text{Present value annuity factor}, 8 \text{ yrs}, 14\%$$

$$3 = A \times \text{PVFA}_{8, 0.14}$$

$$A = 3\left[\frac{1}{4.6389}\right] = 3 \times 0.21556$$

$$= \text{Rs } 0.6467 \text{ crore}$$

From the present value table at the back of the book, we can find $\text{PVAF}_{8, 0.14}$ equal to 4.6389. Reciprocal of this factor, 0.21556, is the capital recovery factor. The repayment schedule is as given in Table 20.3.

Table 20.3: Loan Amortisation Schedule (Equal Loan Payment)

(Rs in thousand)

Year (1)	Loan in the Beginning (2)	Loan Payment (3)	Interest (4)	Principal Repayment (3 – 4) (5)	Loan at the end (2 – 5) (6)
1	30,000	6,467	4,200	2,267	27,7333
2	27,733	6,467	3,883	2,584	25,149
3	25,149	6,467	3,521	2,946	22,203
4	22,203	6,467	3,108	3,359	18,844
5	18,844	6,467	2,638	3,829	15,015
6	15,015	6,467	2,102	4,365	10,650
7	10,650	6,467	1,491	4,976	5,674
8	5,674	6,467	794	5,673	0

SUMMARY

❖ Ordinary share, preference share and debentures are three important securities used by the firms to raise funds to finance their activities.

❖ Ordinary shares provide ownership rights to ordinary shareholders. They are the legal owners of the company. As a result, they have residual claims on income and assets of the company. They have the right to elect the board of directors and maintain their proportionate ownership in the company, called the pre-emptive right.

❖ The pre-emptive right of the ordinary shareholders is maintained by raising new equity funds through rights offerings. Rights issue does not affect the wealth of a shareholder.

❖ The price of the share with rights-on gets divided into ex-rights price and the value of a right. So what the shareholder gains in terms of the value of right he loses in terms of the low ex-rights price. However, he will lose if he does not exercise his rights.

❖ Debenture or bond is a long-term promissory note. The debenture trust deed or indenture defines the legal relationship between the issuing company and the debenture trustee who represents the debenture holders.

❖ Debenture holders have a prior claim on the company's income and assets. They will be paid before shareholders are paid anything.

❖ Debentures could be secured and unsecured and convertible and non-convertible. Debentures are issued with a maturity date. In India, they are generally retired after 7 to 10 years by instalments.

❖ Preference share is a hybrid security as it includes some features of both an ordinary share and a debenture. In regard to claims on income and assets, it stands before an ordinary share but after a debenture.

❖ Most preference shares in India have a cumulative feature, requiring that all past outstanding preference dividends be paid before any dividend to ordinary shareholders is announced.

❖ Preference shares could be redeemable, i.e., with a maturity date or irredeemable i.e. perpetual, without maturity date. Like debentures, a firm can issue convertible or non-convertible preference shares.

❖ Term loans are loans for more than a year maturity. Generally, in India, they are available for a period of 6 to 10 years. In some cases, the maturity could be as long as 25 years. Interest on term loans is tax deductible.

❖ Mostly, term loans are secured through an equitable mortgage on immovable assets. To protect their interest, lending institutions impose a number of restrictions on the borrowing firm.

KEY CONCEPTS

Convertible debenture	Hybrid security	Project financing	Yield
Credit rating	Loan amortisation	Rights Issue	Yield-to-maturity
Current yield	Ordinary shares	Sinking fund	Zero-interest
Debentures	Pre-emptive rights	Straight debenture	debentures
Deep-discount debentures	Preference shares	Underwriting	

REVIEW QUESTIONS

1. What is an ordinary share? How does it differ from a preference share and a debenture? Explain its most important features.

2. What are the advantages and disadvantages of ordinary shares to the company? What are the merits and demerits of the shareholders' residual claim on income from the investors' point of view?

3. What is the significance of voting rights to the ordinary shareholders? What is a proxy? Why do proxy fights occur?
4. What is a rights issue? What are its advantages and disadvantages from the company's and shareholders' points of views?
5. Since the rights issue allows the ordinary shareholders to purchase the shares at a price much lower than the current market price, why does not shareholders' wealth increase? Illustrate your answer.
6. What is a debenture? Explain the features of a debenture.
7. What are the *pros* and *cons* of debentures from the company's

and investors' point of views?
8. Why is a preference share called a hybrid security? Do you agree that it combines the worst features of ordinary shares and bonds?
9. Explain the advantages and disadvantages of preference shares to the company.
10. What are term loans? What are their features?
11. How does a term loan differ from a non-convertible debenture?
12. What is common between term loans and debentures in India? Explain the comparative merits and demerits of both.

PROBLEMS

1. A firm is thinking of a rights issue to raise Rs 5 crore. It has a 5 lakh shares outstanding and the current market price of the share is Rs 170. The subscription price on the new share will be Rs 125 per share. (*ii*) How many shares should be sold to raise the required funds? (*ii*) How many rights are needed to purchase one new share? (*iii*) What is the value of one right?

2. A company is considering a rights offering to raise funds to finance new projects, which require Rs 4.5 crore. The flotation cost will be 10 per cent of funds raised. The company currently has 20 lakh shares outstanding and the current market price of its share is Rs 100. The subscription price has been fixed at Rs 50 per share. (*i*) How many shares should be sold to raise the funds required for financing the new projects? (*ii*) How many rights are required to buy one new share? (*iii*) What is the value of one right? (*iv*) Show the impact on a shareholder's wealth who holds required rights to buy one new share if (*a*) he exercises rights, or (*b*) sells his rights, or (*c*) does not exercise rights.

3. The Greaves Company, started in 1922, is a diversified company. Having commenced operation as trading and servicing of engineering equipments, it diversified into manufacturing and marketing. The company's proposed capital expenditures include (*a*) expansion of the capacity of diesel engine from 22,500 units to 32,500 units in 1992–93, 40,000 units in 1993-94 and 55,000 units in 1994–95 at a cost of Rs 37.9 crore, (*b*) manufacture of 3-wheeler diesel unit, a forward integration project, at a cost of Rs 18.8 crore, with installed capacity of 8,000 units in 1993–94, 10,000 units in 1994–95 and 20,000 units in 1995–96, (*c*) manufacture of vibratory compactors at a cost of Rs 2.06 crore, (*d*) R&D capital expenditure of Rs 3.62 crore for developing a portable diesel low noise, smaller HP engines, (*e*) investment of Rs 49.4 crore in the equity of three

companies, (*f*) investment of Rs 73.0 crore in a subsidiary for the manufacture of engineering plastics and (*g*) normal capital expenditure of Rs 35 crore for the enhancement of long-term resources. Of the first project only cost equal to Rs 30.1 crore will be met of the present issue.

The company has proposed to issue 144 lakh equity shares of Rs 10 each at a premium of Rs 70 each totalling to Rs 115.21 crore in the ratio of 1 : 1 on rights basis. The Rs 10 paid-up share of the company has a market price of Rs 102.50 and a net asset value (NAV) of Rs 44.80. The company has made the following projections:

	1993–94	1994–95	1995–96
Revenues (Rs crore)	360.00	420.00	563.00
Net profit (Rs crore)	17.10	18.10	25.30
EPS (Rs)	11.78	7.38	9.00
NAV (Rs)	62.96	71.87	78.86

The following are a few indicators of the company's performance during last two years:

	1991–92	1992–93
Revenues (Rs crore)	250.0	285.0
Pre-tax profits (Rs)	10.7	12.0
Equity dividend (%)	20.0	23.0
Borrowing (Rs crore)	57.0	74.0
Interest (Rs crore)	7.0	12.0
EPS (Rs)	–	7.2

Source: The Economic Times, 14 December 1992.
Critically evaluate Greaves' rights issue.

CASES

Case 20.1: German Remedies[1]

German Remedies, established in 1949, is a well-known pharmaceutical company. It is a fast growing company. In the last decade, its gross fixed assets have grown from Rs 6.60 crore

to Rs 31.60 crore. Except in 1986, the company has regularly paid dividend during the last 10 years. It has also been issuing bonus share to its shareholders. It has issued bonus shares in the ratio of 1:2 in 1976, 3:5 in 1979 and 1982 and 1:1 in 1991. The

1. *Source: The Economic Times,* 4 January 1993.

company had made its first public issue of shares in 1973 when it diluted its foreign equity by issuing 3.30 lakh equity shares of Rs 10 each at a premium of Re 1. The issue was over-subscribed by 47 times. An investor who held one share in 1973 now holds 7.86 shares on account of issue of bonus shares.

The company has come up with an offer of 10.83 lakh 15% secured redeemable partly convertible debentures of Rs 100 each, totalling to Rs 10.83 crore on rights basis in the ratio of one debenture for every four equity shares held by the existing shareholders and employees. The issue has been given a rating of "*BBB +*" by CRISIL India (a credit rating organisation), which implies sufficient protection to investors. The issue is intended to finance fixed investment of Rs 3 crore for modernisation of two units in the state of Maharashtra and long-term working capital requirements of Rs 8.50 crore.

The following is the performance of the company during last two years:

	1990–91	*1991–92*
Sales (Rs in crore)	67.80	72.63
Net Profit (Rs in crore)	2.34	1.11
EPS (Rs)	3.56	1.69
Dividend (%)	11.00	9.00
Book value (Rs)	—	22.40
Market price (Rs)	—	90.00
Borrowing (Rs in crore)	24.50	32.50
Interest (Rs in crore)	2.82	4.22

In spite of growth in sales, net profits declined because of the increases in the cost of inputs.

In the proposed issue, each debenture of Rs 100 will have a convertible portion of Rs 55 to be converted into one equity share on December 1, 1993. The non-convertible portion of Rs 45 will be redeemed at par.

The company has made the following projections for the next three years:

	1992–93	*1993–94*	*1994–95*
Sales (Rs crore)	93.85	105.10	118.77
Net profit (Rs crore)	0.74	1.95	2.52
EPS (Rs)	1.14	2.56*	3.31*

* On equity capital of Rs 7.61 crore after conversion of debentures.

It may be noted that for the six-month period ended September 30 1992, the company's sales were Rs 40.37 crore with a net loss of Rs 0.19 crore.

Discussion Questions

1. Explain the features of the proposed debenture.
2. Evaluate the proposed debenture issue from the points of views of investors and company.

Case 20.2: Delite Furniture Company Limited

Delite Furniture Company Limited (DFCL), situated in North of India, manufactures a range of home and office furniture and sells its product under the 'Delite' brand name, all over India. It is currently facing serious problems of maintaining high quality in its office furniture division, which operates an old plant. These problems endanger the company's standing as producer of high-quality furniture. It has been approached, through a common banker, by a competing furniture manufacturing company in the East of India to become its trade partner and distribute its office furniture under its own brand name – Delite. The competitor's product is of good quality and is well known in Eastern India, but its products are not known in the rest of the country. If DFCL agrees to the competitor's offer, it will have to close the manufacturing set-up of the office furniture division and restructure the division as a marketing division. The cost of restructuring the division is estimated to be Rs 60 crore.

DFCL's evaluation of the proposal indicates that it will be quite profitable to use its brand name to sell the quality product of the competitor. Because of the relatively lower costs in the East of India, the competitor's range of office furniture is about 5 to 10 per cent less costly. DFCL will be able to sell more than what it was able to sell its own manufactured furniture. DFCL could enter into a five-year agreement with its competitor for selling its office furniture. It is estimated that DFCL will have PBIT of Rs 24 crore p.a. for five years from this arrangement.

DFCL's worry is how to finance the restructuring of the office furniture division. The management was faced with three alternative means of financing: (1) internal financing by reducing the dividend, (2) a rights issue and (3) long-term loan from a bank at a fixed rate of 10 per cent p.a.

The company's latest annual report shows that it has paid up share capital of Rs 400 crore (par value each share Rs 100) and reserves and surplus of Rs 260 crore. It has a high debt ratio. The current profit after tax is Rs 80 crore and the proposed dividends of Rs 50 crore. There is 20 per cent tax on dividends paid to shareholders and the corporate tax is 36.5 per cent. DFCL's required rate of return is 18 per cent. The company's share is selling in the range of Rs 170–Rs 195. The company's investment banker suggests an issue price of Rs 170 if it goes for a rights issue. The finance director thinks that the issue price in the case of the rights issue should be fixed at Rs 190.

Discussion Questions

1. Should the company restructure its business? What are the important financial and non-financial considerations?
2. Which financial alternative do you suggest for the company and why?
3. Analyse the option of issuing the rights issue in detail.

CHAPTER 21 Convertible Debentures and Warrants

CHAPTER OBJECTIVES

- Explain the features and valuation of convertible debentures.
- Focus on the characteristics and valuations of warrants.
- Discuss the features of new capital market instruments like the zero-interest debentures or deep-discount bonds

INTRODUCTION

There are two ways of making fixed-income securities attractive to the investors. A company can issue convertible securities and warrants to ensure the success of its debt issue. Convertible securities, particularly convertible debentures, are quite popular in India. Warrants are also becoming popular in the Indian capital market now. There have been many issues of warrants in the recent years. We shall discuss the features of these securities and their valuation in this chapter.[1]

CONVERTIBLE DEBENTURES

A **convertible debenture** is a debenture that can be changed into a specified number of ordinary shares at the option of the owner. A company is, in fact, issuing equity shares in future whenever it offers convertible debentures. The most notable feature of this debenture is that it promises a fixed income associated with debenture as well as chance of capital gains associated with equity share after the owner has exercised his conversion option. Because of this combination of fixed income and capital gains in the convertible debenture, it has been called

a **hybrid security**. A company can also issue convertible preference share. In our discussion in this section, we will consider only examples of convertible debentures.

Suppose a company issues 8 lakh 15 per cent convertible debentures of Rs 125 each that are convertible into two equity shares of Rs 62.50 each after two years from the date of allotment but within three months after this period. At the time of issue, the company will receive a cash inflow of: 8 lakh × Rs 125 = Rs 1000 lakh (less flotation cost). Owners of the convertible debentures will get a fixed income in the form of interest of: Rs 1000 × 15 per cent = Rs 150 lakh for two years. After two years, the owner can exchange one debenture for two equity shares at Rs 62.50 each. Assuming that all debentureholders have exercised their option, the company would have actually issued: Rs 1000 lakh ÷ Rs 62.5 = 16 lakh equity shares, and convertible debentures would have fully redeemed and disappeared from the company's balance sheet. The company does not get any cash at the time of conversion. The debentureholders now become shareholders, and they will be entitled to dividends and capital gains on their holdings.

---

1. Some useful references on convertible debentures and warrants include Walter, J.E. and Que, A.V., The Valuation of Convertible Bonds, *Journal & Finance*, 28 (June 1973), pp. 713–32; Shelton, J.P., The Relation of the Price of a Warrant to the Price of its Associated Stock, *Financial Analysts Journal* (May–June 1967); pp. 143–51; (July–Aug. 1967), pp. 88–99; Brigham, E.F., Analysis of Convertible Debentures: Theory and Some Empirical Evidence, *Journal of Finance* 27 (May 1972); pp. 399–417. For a simple exposition of the features and valuation of convertible securities and warrants, see Moyer, R.C. *et. al.*, *Contemporary Financial Management*, West Publishing Company, 1984 and Keown, A.J., *et. al.*, *Basic Financial Management*, Prentice-Hall, 1985.

Characteristics of Convertible Debentures

When a company issues a convertible debenture, it clearly specifies conversion terms, which indicate the number of equity shares in exchange for the convertible debenture, the price at which conversion will take place and the time when the conversion option can be exercised.

Conversion ratio and conversion price The **conversion ratio** is the number of ordinary shares that an investor can receive when he exchanges his convertible debenture. In other words, the number of ordinary shares per one convertible security is called the conversion ratio. The **conversion price** is the price paid for the ordinary share at the time of conversion. If you know the *par value* of the convertible security and its conversion price, you can easily find out the conversion ratio:

$$\text{Conversion ratio} = \frac{\text{Par value of convertible debenture}}{\text{Conversion price}} \quad (1)$$

In our earlier example of the convertible debenture, the conversion ratio is:

$$\text{Rs } 125/\text{Rs } 62.5 = 2$$

You can also find conversion price if the par value of the debenture and conversion ratio are known. In India, companies generally specify both conversion ratio as well as conversion price. For example, in May 1989, Tata Steel announced two types of convertible debentures. First, it issued 32.54 lakh 12 per cent fully convertible debentures of Rs 600 each at par on rights basis to its existing shareholders. Each convertible debenture was fully convertible into one share of Rs 600 (i.e., Rs 100 par plus a premium of Rs 500) within six months from the date of allotment of debentures. Thus, the company stated both conversion ratio of one share for each convertible and conversion price of Rs 600 each share. Tata Steel also announced a public issue of 30 lakh 12 per cent partly convertible debentures of Rs 1,200 each. Like the rights issue, Rs 600 of the debenture's face value was convertible. The non-convertible portion of the debenture was to be redeemed at the end of 8 years from the date of allotment.

There is a peculiar difference between the ways conversion price is set in a developed capital market like USA and in a developing capital market like India. In USA, the conversion price is set about 20 per cent *above* the equity share's market price prevailing at the time of issue. In India, the conversion price is set much below the equity share's prevailing market price. For example, in May 1989, Tata Steel's market price of each equity share was around Rs 1,265. Thus, the conversion price (Rs 600) was set at a discount of Rs 665 per share (i.e., 52.6 per cent) in contrast to the prevailing market price.

The purchasers of convertible securities are generally safeguarded against dilution arising on account of bonus shares issue or share split. For example, if Tata Steel were to issue bonus shares in the ratio of 3:5, the conversion price and conversion ratio will be adjusted. The new conversion price will be: Rs 600 × 5/8 = Rs 375 and the new conversion ratio will be: 8/5 = 1.6.

Valuation of Convertible Debentures

The valuation of convertible debentures[1] is more complex than the valuation of non-convertible (straight) securities since they combine features of both ordinary shares and fixed-income securities. The market value of a convertible debenture will thus depend on: market price of ordinary share, conversion value, and the value of the non-convertible or straight debenture, called investment value.

Conversion value The **conversion value** of a convertible debenture is equal to the conversion ratio multiplied by the ordinary share's market price. Thus:

$$\text{Conversion value} = \text{Conversion ratio} \times \text{Share price} \quad (2)$$

In other words, the conversion value is simply the money worth of the convertible debenture if it is converted into shares *now*. In the Tata Steel example, the conversion ratio is 1 and the market price now is Rs 1,265, therefore, the conversion value is: $1 \times \text{Rs } 1,265 = \text{Rs } 1,265$.

Value of non-convertible debenture The non-convertible debenture (NCD) is also known as a straight-debenture. The value of NCD may be referred to as the value of convertible debenture (CD) without the feature of conversion. This value of the convertible is also called the **investment value** or the **security value**. It is equal to the sum of the present value of future interest payments and principal redemption at the required rate of return. The methodology of calculating the value of a straight-debt is discussed in Chapter 3.

In the Tata Steel example, the company also has a non-convertible portion of the proposed debenture issue. The interest rate on non-convertible portion is 12 per cent. Assuming that the required rate of return is also 12 per cent, and the debenture will be redeemed at the end of 8 years, the investment value of the debenture will be:

$$\text{Value of NCD} = \sum_{t=1}^{8} \frac{72}{(1.12)^t} + \frac{600}{(1.12)^8}$$

$$= 72(\text{PVFA}_{0.12,\,8}) + 600(\text{PVF}_{0.12,\,8})$$

$$= 72 \times 4.9676 + 600 \times 0.4039$$

$$= 357.67 + 242.33 = \text{Rs } 600$$

The investment value is equal to the face value of the debenture since we have assumed the interest rate and required rate to be the same and the redemption of the debenture at par. If we assume that the current yield on similar type of non-convertible debenture is 15 per cent, then the investment value of the Tata Steel's straight-debenture or NCD will be:

$$= \sum_{t=1}^{8} \frac{72}{(1.15)^t} + \frac{600}{(1.15)^8}$$

$$= 72 \times 4.4873 + 600 \times 0.3269$$

$$= 323.09 + 196.14 = \text{Rs } 519.23$$

As the required rate changes, the investment value changes. Thus, regardless of what happens to the Tata Steel's share price, the *lowest value* that the convertible debenture can drop to is its

---

1. Also see Moyer, R.C., *et. al.*, *op. cit.*, pp. 656–67, and Walter and Que, *op. cit.*, pp. 713–32.

value as a straight-debenture, which is Rs 600 (or Rs 519.23 if we assume 15 per cent as the required rate of return).

Market value of convertible debenture The convertible securities are traded (bought and sold) in the stock market until they are converted into equity shares. The price at which the convertible security sells is called its market value. In India, the secondary market for debentures—including both convertible and non-convertible—is still in a developing stage.

What is the relationship between a convertible debenture's market value, its investment value and its conversion value?[1] A convertible debenture' market value depends on both investment and conversion value. More importantly, its market value cannot be less than its investment value or its conversion value. The difference between the convertible debenture's market value and the higher of the conversion or the NCD value (investment value) is called the **conversion premium**. Thus:

Conversion premium

$$\left[\frac{\text{Market value} - \text{Conversion or investment value}}{\text{Conversion or investment value}}\right] \quad (3)$$

In our example of the Tata Steel convertible debenture, we determined that if it were selling as a straight-debenture, its price would be Rs 519.23 (at a required rate of return of 15 per cent). Thus, irrespective of its ordinary share price, the minimum value of the convertible debenture would be Rs 519.23. Why? Because investment value is the price which the investors would pay for the convertible debenture even without the convertible feature. If Tata Steel's share price is Rs 1,265 and conversion ratio is 1, then the conversion value is Rs 1,265. Thus, its convertible debenture is worth much more as an ordinary share than if it were a non-convertible debenture. The market value of the convertible debenture should not fall below its conversion value. If it were so, **arbitrage** – purchase and sell of the same securities in different markets—will take place, and will ultimately force the market value to be at least equal to the conversion value.

Figure 21.1 shows the relationship between the convertible debenture's market, investment and conversion value and the ordinary share price. The investment value is independent of the ordinary share price; therefore, it is shown as a horizontal line. The conversion value, on the other hand, is related to the ordinary share price. It increases as the ordinary share price increases. Since the market value of the convertible debenture should not be less than the investment and conversion values, the market value line in Figure 21.1 cannot be below them. Typically, the market value is higher than both the investment and conversion value; therefore, the market value line in Figure 21.1 is shown above both the investment and conversion value lines. The difference is the conversion premium. The premium results because the convertible debenture offers fixed income at a low risk of price decline while assuring the chances of capital gains when the share price increases. Thus, the upside variability of share price is not affected while the downside variability is well protected.

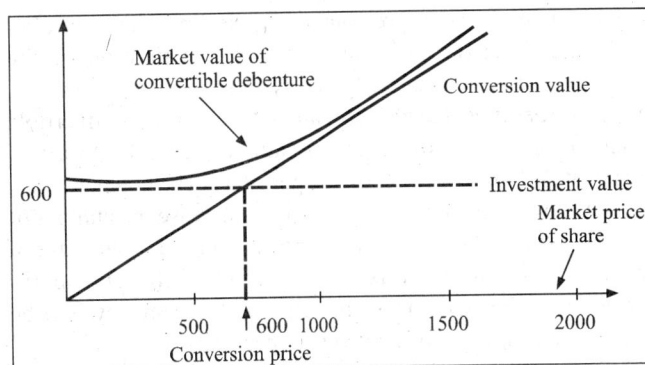

Figure 21.1: Value of a Convertible Debenture

Why Issue Convertible Debentures?

At least four reasons can be cited for issuing the convertible debentures. They are: (*a*) 'sweetening' debentures to make them attractive, (*b*) selling ordinary shares in the future at a higher price, (*c*) avoiding immediate dilution of earnings, and (*d*) using low cost capital initially.

Sweetening fixed-income securities The primary purpose of issuing convertible debenture is to make the issue attractive enough so that it is fully subscribed. Investors generally prefer fixed interest convertible debentures to non-convertible because this enables them to earn a definite, fixed income with the chance of making capital gains. Hence, the convertibility feature 'sweetens' the issue. Also, the company may offer relatively low interest rate on convertible debenture because of the value of the conversion feature as compared to a non-convertible debenture. In our example of Tata Steel, the company is proposing raising large amount of capital by issuing fixed-interest debentures on rights basis to the public. The company is offering only 12 per cent interest rate while the current yield on a similar non-convertible debenture would be around 15 per cent. By adding the convertibility feature, the company has 'sweetened' the issue and ensured its success. Also, it has been able to save on interest cost.

Deferred equity financing By issuing a convertible debenture, the firm is in effect selling ordinary shares in future. A company would do so when it considers the current market price of its share to be low, but wants to issue shares at a higher price. This can be achieved by setting the conversion price to be higher than the ordinary share's prevailing market price. In USA, as we have stated earlier, conversion price is set 10 to 20 per cent higher than the prevailing market price. "Selling Ordinary shares in future at a premium" does not seem to be an argument for convertible debentures in India where the conversion price in most cases is much below the prevailing market price. Tata Steel's market price in May 1989 was around Rs 1,265 and it announced an issue of convertible debenture at a conversion price of Rs 600. Also, the conversion option is applicable after six months of the allotment of the convertible debentures. What will Tata Steel gain by deferring equity issue just by six months? This was an indirect

---

1. See Brealey, R. and Myers, S., *Principles of Corporate Finance*, McGraw Hill, 1984, pp. 529–31; Walter and Que, *op. cit.*, pp. 713–32; and Moyer, *et. al., op. cit.,* p. 542–43.

way of obtaining higher premium on equity since the Controller of Capital Issue (CCI)[1] in existence at that time was quite conservative in allowing direct equity issue at a high premium.

Avoiding earnings dilution Yet another reason for convertible debenture as a deferred equity financing could be to avoid immediate dilution of the earnings per share. The company may like to use fixed-income security and not increase the number of issued shares until its investment starts paying off. In the case of Tata Steel, since the conversion will take place after six months of the debenture issue, it is unlikely that the company will be able to avoid dilution of its earnings per share.

Raising low cost capital A company may raise funds to finance a large expansion or modernisation or diversification. It may like to finance such needs through equity financing, but it may instead choose a convertible debenture. By doing so, the company is able to use the lower cost of capital (interest on debt is tax deductible) during the initial stage of investment when its effects are not fully reflected in the earnings. When the project is complete, the company's earnings will rise, increasing the share prices. The holders of the convertible debentures, who initially provided cheap funds to the company, can now convert their debentures into ordinary shares and participate in the prosperity of the company.

WARRANTS

A **warrant** entitles the purchaser to buy a fixed number of ordinary shares at a particular price during a specified time period. Warrants are generally issued along with debentures as 'sweeteners.' In USA, warrants have been used in the past mainly by financially weaker firms to attract investors. Now, of course, large, profitable companies use warrants as a part of a major financing package. Warrants may also be used in conjunction with ordinary or preference shares. The purpose is the same; that is, to improve the marketability of the issue.

Deepak Fertilisers and Petrochemicals Corporation Limited (DFPC) was the first company issuing warrants in conjunction with its offering of 14 per cent Rs 100 debenture of Rs 190 crore in January 1987. Each debenture had three parts: Part A of Rs 20 which will compulsorily and automatically be converted into one equity share with face value of Rs 10 at a premium of Rs 10 on 1st January 1990; Part B of Rs 30 which will compulsorily and automatically convert into one equity share of face value of Rs 10 at a premium of Rs 20 on 1st January 1991, and Part C of Rs 50 which will have a detachable warrant attached to it. The warrant will entitle the holder to apply for one equity share of Rs 10 between 1993 and 1995 at a price to be approved by the Controller of Capital Issues (CCI) but not exceeding Rs 50. The warrant will be separately listed and traded on the stock exchanges.

Characteristics of Warrants

Warrants have a number of features. We shall use the DFPC's warrants issue as an example to illustrate features of warrants.[2]

Exercise price The **exercise price** of a warrant is the price at which its holder can purchase the issuing firm's ordinary shares.

In USA, the exercise price normally remains constant over the life of the warrant and is set 10–30 per cent above the ordinary share's market price prevailing at the time of issue. The exercise price of DFPC's warrant is not known; what is known is that it cannot exceed Rs 50. In 1987, the average market price of the DFPC ordinary share was Rs 37 per share. If it were allowed an exercise price of Rs 50, then it would be 35 per cent above the market price prevailing at the time of issue.

Exercise ratio The **exercise ratio** states the number of ordinary shares that can be purchased at the exercise price per warrant. This is same as the conversion ratio in the case of the convertible securities. If the exercise ratio were 2 to 1, this implies that the holder of warrants is entitled to buy two ordinary shares in exchange for one warrant at the exercise price. Usually, the exercise ratio is 1:1. In the DFPC case, the exercise ratio is 1:1.

Expiration date The **expiration date** is the date when the option to buy ordinary shares in exchange for warrants expires. The expiration date of the DFPC warrants is the end of 1995, which means that the life of these warrants is 8 years. Also, the option cannot be used before 1993. In USA, the typical life of warrants is between 5 and 10 years. Some warrants are perpetual—they do not have any expiration date.

The management of DFPC expects that the market price of ordinary shares will increase above the exercise price and remain so until after the warrants expire in 1995. One advantage in the case of the DFPC warrant is that exercise price will be determined before the option becomes exercisable in 1993. The exercise price can be determined below the ordinary share's market price prevailing at that time. This will encourage some investors to exercise their option. Some may wait until the expiry date in the expectation that the market price may go up further. If the ordinary share price is more than the exercise price between 1993 and 1995, then the holders of warrants will exercise their options. Assuming an exercise price of Rs 50, DFPC will receive funds totalling Rs 95 crore (1.9 crore warrants times Rs 50 per warrant) before the warrant expires. Thus, the company will be raising additional capital at the time of exercise. In this respect, warrants differ from convertible securities; the company does not obtain any funds at the time of conversion of convertible securities.

Detachability A warrant can be either detachable or non-detachable. If a warrant can be sold separately from the debenture (or preference share) to which it was originally attached, it is called a **detachable warrant**. A debentureholder may sell his warrant when its price increases but continue holding the debenture. The DFPC warrant is a detachable warrant. The company will list it separately, and it will be traded on the stock exchanges. A **non-detachable warrant** cannot be sold separately from the debenture to which it was originally attached.

Right Warrants entitle to purchase ordinary shares. Therefore, the holders of warrants are not the shareholders of the company until they exercise their options. Therefore, they do not have rights of ordinary shareholders, such as the right to vote or receive dividends. Once they exercise their warrants and buy ordinary shares, they become the company's ordinary shareholders.

---

1. CCI has been abolished now.
2. A number of books explain features of warrant. A simple exposition is given in Moyer, *et. al., op. cit;* pp. 544–45 and Keown, *et. al., op. cit.,* p. 664.

Valuation of Warrants[1]

A **warrant** is an *option* to buy a stated number of a company's ordinary shares at a given exercise price on or before a specified maturity date. Thus, it is similar to an American call option. As a call option, its market value will be dependent on the market price of the ordinary share and the exercise price. The market price of a company's ordinary share is a function of its expected performance and that of the economy as a whole. Thus, a warrant's market price will in general depend on the issuing company's performance and the general economic conditions.

Theoretical value The theoretical value of a warrant can be found out if we know the ordinary share's market price and warrant's exercise price

Warrant's theoretical value
$$= \text{(Share price} - \text{Exercise price)} \times \text{Exercise ratio} \quad (4)$$

Suppose that the market price of DFPC's ordinary share in December 1992 is expected to be Rs 65 while the exercise price is fixed at Rs 50, then the theoretical value of its warrants is:

Warrant's theoretical value $= (65 - 50) \times 1 = \text{Rs } 15$

This is a straight, ordinary sense solution. If you want to obtain one share of DFPC, you can either buy one share for Rs 65 or buy a warrant and exercise the option by paying Rs 50 and acquire a share. Thus, the market price of the DFPC share can be written as follows:

Share price = Rs 65 = Rs 50 + 1 warrant

1 warrant = Rs 65 − Rs 50 = Rs 15

When the share price is less than the exercise price, the warrant's theoretical value will be *negative* [Equation (4)]. A warrant cannot sell for negative price. Therefore, the warrant's theoretical value in this case is defined as zero. If share price is less than exercise price, then warrant's theoretical value will be zero.

At the end of May 1989, the DFPC's share was selling for Rs 27.75. With an exercise price of Rs 50, the theoretical value of the warrant will be considered zero.

Premium The difference between the warrant's market value and its theoretical value is called the premium. It can be found as follows:

Premium

$$= \left[\frac{\text{Warrant's market value} - \text{Warrant's theoretical value}}{\text{Warrant's theoretical value}} \right] \quad (5)$$

Suppose during December 1992, the DFPC warrant sells for Rs 20, then the premium is:

$$\text{Premium} = \left[\frac{20 - 15}{15} \right] = 0.333 \text{ or } 33.3 \text{ per cent.}$$

Investors generally consider a warrant to be worth more than its theoretical value. This is on account of the **leverage** effect (Figure 21.2).[2] Investors pay a premium because the possible loss is small and the warrant's market price is a small fraction of the market price of the ordinary share. As the market price of the ordinary share increases, the market value of warrant also rises. It may be seen in Figure 21.2 that, the premium is greatest when the share price is near the exercise price. The reason is that at low share prices, the chance of investors exercising their warrants is quite low. When the exercise price is equal to the share price, investors have the potential of large gains if the share price increases. At the same time, their potential losses are limited to the price paid for the warrant. The potential to gain substantially but have limited loss, when share price changes, is referred to the leverage effect.

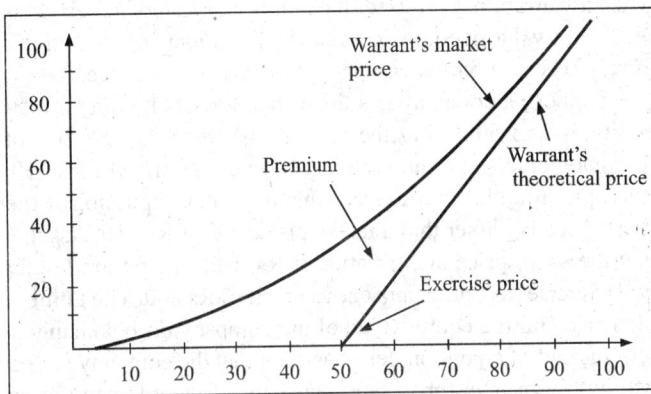

Figure 21.2: Market Value of a Warrant

Can a warrant's market price fall below its theoretical value? If this happens, it will be immediately corrected by arbitrage. Suppose that the exercise price is Rs 50, the share price is Rs 65, and the exercise ratio is 1, then the warrant's theoretical value will be Rs 15. Let us assume that the warrant's market value is Rs 10. An arbitrageur will purchase the warrant for Rs 10, exercise it for Rs 50 to buy one share and sell the share for Rs 65. He would have made a profit of Rs 5: [Rs 65 − (Rs 10 + Rs 50)] = Rs 5. Arbitrageurs at the margin will compete for this profit, and would cause the market price of the warrant to increase until it becomes equal to the warrant's theoretical value. The arbitrage will stop at this point.

Using the Black-Scholes Model for the Valuation of Warrants

We have explained the use of the B-S model in the valuation of options in Chapter 10. To recapitulate, the B-S model is as follows:

$$C_0 = S_0 N(d_1) - E e^{-r_f t} N(d_2)$$

where C_0 is the value of a call option, S_0 is the current market value of the share, E is the exercise price, e is the exponential constant and equals 2.7183, r_f is the risk-free rate of interest, t is the time to expiration (in years), ln is the natural logarithm and σ is the standard deviation of the continuously compounded

---

1. Shelton, *op. cit.* provides a basic framework for valuation of warrants. Also see Moyer, *et. al., op. cit.* and Keown *et. al., op cit.* for a simple exposition.
2. *Ibid.* Also see Brigham, *op. cit.;* Breley and Myers, *op. cit.*

annual return on the share, and $N(d_1)$ is the cumulative normal probability density function. d_1 and d_2 are calculated as follows:

$$d_1 = \frac{\ln(S_0/E) + \left[r_f + \sigma^2/2\right]t}{\sigma\sqrt{t}}$$

$$d_2 = \frac{\ln(S_0/E) + \left[r_f - \sigma^2/2\right]t}{\sigma\sqrt{t}}$$

$$d_2 = d_1 - \sigma\sqrt{t}$$

A warrant is similar to a call option; but there are significant differences as well. Investors issue options, while companies issue warrants. The number of shares and the value of equity do not change when an option is exercised. On the other hand, when a warrant is exercised, the number of shares increases as well as the value of equity increases by the amount of the exercise money received by the company. Consider an example.

Suppose a company has three shareholders holding a total equity of Rs 1,500. Thus the value per share is Rs 500. One of the shareholders sells an option at an exercise price of Rs 750. The option holder will exercise his option at expiration if the share price is higher than the exercise price of Rs 750. Assume that the share price at expiration is Rs 950. The option holder will exercise his option and earn a profit of Rs 200. The number of shares and the equity value of the company do not change.

Instead of an option, let us assume that the company sells a warrant to an investor to buy one share of the company at an exercise price of Rs 750 at a specified period of time. Suppose the share price increases to Rs 950 and the warrant is exercised. The company will issue an additional share and receive Rs 750, i.e., the warrant's exercise price. Thus, after the exercise of warrant, the company will have four shares and the equity value of Rs 3,600 (Rs 950 × 3 + Rs 750). The value per share will be Rs 900 (Rs 3,600/4 = Rs 900). Thus, there is a dilution in the value of equity per share (it reduces from Rs 950 to Rs 900). The earnings per share will also be diluted. The investor pays Rs 750 to obtain one-fourth share holding worth Rs 900. His gain is Rs 150. The warrant holder acquires one-fourth ownership in the company before the exercise of warrant which is worth Rs 712.5 (Rs 2,850/4). The one-fourth of the exercise price paid by him belongs to him. Thus, in effect, he parts away only three-fourths: Rs 562.5 (Rs 750 × 3/4). His gain is still Rs 150 (Rs 712.5 – Rs 562.5).

It should be clear from the above example that the exercise of warrant has dilution effect. If the proportion of warrants to the existing shares is, say, w, then the dilution factor will be: $1/(1 + w)$. This fact should be considered when the B-S model is used to value warrants. In the example above, we assumed that warrants were issued free of cost. If warrants are issued at a cost, then the value of equity per share after the issue will be the total market price of the equity plus the warrant money divided by the number of outstanding shares. That is:

Value of per share after the warrant issue $= S^*$

$$= \frac{\begin{array}{c}(\text{Current share price} \times \text{Number of existing shares}) \\ + \text{Warrant money}\end{array}}{\text{Number of existing shares}} \quad (6)$$

It is this value, S^* (and not S) that shall be used in applying the B-S model for valuing warrants. The risk (standard deviation) of this value will be higher than the risk (standard deviation) of the share price itself. Therefore, the standard deviation of the share price will be modified (see Illustration 21.1 below). Given the dilution effect, the value of warrant at expiration will be:

Warrant value at expiration

$$= \frac{1}{1 + w}\left[\text{Maximum}(S^* - E, 0)\right] \quad (7)$$

Illustration 21.1: Valuing a Warrant

Damani Industries Limited has total assets worth Rs 100 crore. Its equity, divided in 2.5 crore outstanding shares, has market value of Rs 60 crore. Currently the company has debt of Rs 40 crore. The company has just made an issue of debentures (Rs 100 each) of the total amount of Rs 25 crore plus one warrant of Re 1 for each debenture. A warrant will entitle the debenture holders to apply for one equity share at an exercise price of Rs 25 at the end of two years. The annual standard deviation of the share price variability before the debenture issue is: $\sigma = 1.58$. Assume that the interest rate is 12 per cent. What is the value of a warrant?

Damani issues 0.25 crore warrants with debentures for Re 1 each warrant. Thus, the current value per share is Rs 24.1 (i.e., $(60 + 0.25)/2.5$ = Rs 24.1). Damani's warrant is a 2-year call option with an equity value per share of Rs 24.1 and an exercise price of Rs 25. Since the assets of the company have changed after the debentures and warrants issue, the standard deviation of the share price variability will change. Assuming debt as risk free, the standard deviation of the existing assets of the company will be:

Standard deviation of existing assets

= standard deviation of equity × weight of equity

+ standard deviation of debt × weight of debt

= $1.58 \times (60/100) + 0 \times (40/100) = 0.948$

After the issue of debentures and warrants, Damani's assets are Rs 125.25 crore; the value of equity is Rs 60.25 crore and debt Rs 65 crore. If we assume that the assets' risk remains the same after the issue, then the standard deviation of the equity will be:

Standard deviation of existing assets

= standard deviation of equity

× weight of equity

+ standard deviation of debt

× weight of debt

0.948 = standard deviation of equity

× $(60.25/125.25) + 0$

Revised standard deviation of equity = $0.948 \times (125.25/60.25)$

$= 1.97$

We can now use the B-S model to calculate the value of a call where the value per share is Rs 24.1, exercise price is Rs 25, interest rate is 12 per cent, standard deviation is 1.97 and the time to expiration is 2 years. The values of $d_1 = 1.4612$; $d_2 = -1.3248$; $N(d_1) = 0.9286$ and $N(d_2) = 0.0926$. The value of call is: Rs 20.52. Since warrant has a dilution effect, the value of warrant will be:

Value of warrant $= \frac{1}{1 + w} \times 20.52$

$= \frac{1}{1.1} \times 20.52 = \text{Rs } 18.65.$

Why Issue Warrants?

Why do companies issue warrants? Generally, three reasons are cited for issuing warrants. They include 'sweetening' of debt security, issuing ordinary shares in future and obtaining capital in future.[1]

Sweetening debt Warrants help to make the issue of equity and debentures attractive. If the company is doubtful about the full subscription of the debenture issue, warrants are used to 'sweeten' the issue by giving the investors an opportunity to participate in capital gains when the share price appreciates. A company may also offer relatively low interest rate to the investors if the warrants are attached to the debenture. It may be recalled that the convertible debentures perform the same function. DFPC seems to have the objective of making its debentures issue attractive upper most in its mind. Its financing package includes both conversion as well as warrant. Also, it offered the maximum allowed interest rate at the time, i.e., 14 per cent.

Deferred equity financing Warrants provide a company an opportunity for deferred equity financing. What is the advantage of deferred equity financing? The company sells its ordinary shares in future at a premium by setting exercise price higher than the prevailing share price. What is important, however, is the future share price. If the market price in future does not rise higher than the exercise price, investors may not exercise the warrants.

Cash inflow in future The company obtains cash when investors exercise their warrants. The warrant holder exchanges the warrant plus cash for the new ordinary shares. In contrast, in the case of the convertible debentures, no cash inflow takes place at the time of conversion; the company received cash when the convertible debentures were offered.

Many other advantages of warrants are also claimed in practice:[2]

- Issue of warrants keeps the share price high because it keeps equity at a lower level and thereby causes earnings per share to increase.
- The investor is enabled to have access to the shares without investing the full amount in the share now. The issue of non-convertible debentures (NCDs) with attached warrants allows investor to strip the warrant and sell NCD at a very small discount. Thus his investment today is almost zero. He pays for share after some time in future.
- Issue of warrants enables promoters to increase their holdings. An issue of partly convertible debentures (PCDs) is almost same as an issue of NCDs with warrants attached. NCDs with warrants attached are not well understood by public. Therefore, they are under-subscribed. This helps the promoters to subscribe to NCDs with warrants attached by putting extra money and increase their holdings.

CONVERTIBLE ZERO-INTEREST DEBENTURES

We know from discussion in Chapter 3 that **zero-interest debentures** (ZID) or **zero-coupon bonds** do not carry an explicit rate of interest. The difference between the face value of the bond and its purchase price is the return of the investor. A firm may issue **convertible zero-interest debentures** (CZID). Mahindra and Mahindra (M&M) was the first company in India to issue convertible zero-interest bonds in January 1990. The bonds were offered on rights basis to the company's shareholders and employees. A shareholder owing 4 shares could get a bond of Rs 90. The bond had two parts. Part A of the bond had face value of Rs 45 and was compulsorily and automatically convertible into one equity share at a premium of Rs 35 on 1 April 1991, and Part B of the bond issued at Rs 45 will also be simultaneously converted into one share after 18 months from the date of allotment. M&M also provided an option of 12.5% fully convertible debentures (FCDs) to investors if they were not interested in the zero-interest fully convertible bonds (ZCBs). Assuming that the company was able to raise, say, Rs 43 crore in the form of ZCBs, it will not have to pay any interest over 18 month period, and after the conversion, equity dividend will be paid on paid-up share capital of Rs 9.60 crore only.

The purely zero-interest debenture was issued by Best and Crompton Engineering Company in December 1990. The company issued 46.86 lakh zero-interest debentures of Rs 70 each on a rights basis to its existing shareholders in the ratio of 10:17. The shareholders had an option to covert their debentures into equity after 3 years at a price to be decided by the (now defunct) Controller of Capital Issues.

SECURED PREMIUM NOTES (SPN) WITH WARRANTS

Secured premium note (SPN) is a secured debenture redeemable at a premium, i.e., at a price higher than the purchase (or face) price. It is a medium to long-term debenture. TISCO issued SPNs with warrants attached in India for the first time to raise Rs 346.5 crore. TISCO's SPN issue was a part of Rs 1,200 crore rights issue. The company offered 20 SPNs to each shareholder and 10 SPNs to each employee/director. The face value of each SPN was Rs 300. The features of TISCO's SPNs are as follows:

- No interest was payable for the first three years after the allotment.
- Between four to seven years, principal will be repaid in instalments of Rs 75 each year.
- Between four and seven years, an amount of Rs 75 each year will be paid as interest and redemption premium. The investors can choose any one of the following options at the end of the third year:

Option I:	Interest Rs 37.5, premium Rs 37.5
Option II:	Interest Rs 25.0, premium Rs 50.0
Option III:	Interest Rs 50.0, premium Rs 25.0

- The warrant attached to each SPN will entitle the holder to buy one equity share for Rs 100 between first year and one-and-a-half year after allotment.

TISCO's SPN is in fact a zero interest bond (ZIB) with an equity warrant attached to it. Yet another difference is in terms of the interest payment and capital repayment, which is spread over four

---

1. *Ibid.*
2. Vijay, P.N., Useful Warrants, *The Economics Times*, 23 February 1994.

years unlike ZIB where capital and interest payments are bundled together and paid once at the end of the ZIB's maturity. How much will be an investor's return if he buys one SPN?

Let us assume that: (*a*) Rs 300 are paid now, (*b*) warrant is not exercised, and (*c*) there was no tax implications. We can use DCF technique to calculate the rate of return:

$$300 = \frac{0}{(1+r)} + \frac{0}{(1+r)^2} + \frac{0}{(1+r)^3} + \frac{150}{(1+r)^4} + \frac{150}{(1+r)^5}$$
$$+ \frac{150}{(1+r)^6} + \frac{150}{(1+r)^7}$$

By trial and error, we obtain a rate of return (*r*) equal to 13.64 per cent.

How much will be return if the investor exercises warrant acquiring one equity share after one year? We know that exercise price is Rs 100. The average market price of TISCO's share at the time of announcement of issue was about Rs 195. If we assume the price of the share to remain at this level after one year (unrealistic assumption!), then the value of the value of warrant will be:

= (Market price – Exercise price) × No. shares per warrant
= (195 – 100) × 1 = Rs 95

Thus the rate of return will be:

$$300 = \frac{95}{(1+r)} + \frac{0}{(1+r)^2} + \frac{0}{(1+r)^3} + \frac{150}{(1+r)^4} + \frac{150}{(1+r)^5}$$
$$+ \frac{150}{(1+r)^6} + \frac{150}{(1+r)^7}$$

We obtain a rate of return of 20.37 per cent by trial and error.

The market price after a year could be more or less than what it is today, and accordingly the value of warrant will change.

How much will be the rate of return if tax implications for the investor are considered? Let us make the following assumptions: (*a*) redemption premium will be allowed as capital gains,

(*b*) interest income will be taxed as ordinary income in the hands of the investor, (*c*) investors' marginal income-tax rate is 51.75 per cent, (*d*) investor sells the warrant at Rs 95 after one year and it is treated as capital gain and (*e*) investor has sufficient deduction available under the Income Tax Act to take care of capital gains, which implies that investor pays no capital gain tax. Thus he would choose option II with regard to the division of Rs 75 into interest and premium. Investor will get after-tax interest income of Rs 12. The cash flows will be as follows:

Year	0	1	2	3	4	5	6	7
Cash flows	300	95	0	0	137	137	137	137

By trial and error, the rate of return is 18.45 per cent. The rate of return will be less if the investor has to pay tax on capital gains at 20 per cent, or if the entire premium and the gain on the sale of warrant is not allowed as capital gains by the tax authorities. Investors may be in different tax brackets as regards their ordinary incomes. These adjustments can be made and the rate of return can be recalculated.

From TISCO's point of view, the cost of SPN is less than the prevailing rates of interest on bank/financial institution borrowings or non-convertible debenture. Further, no cash outflow is involved for the first three years on account of interest payments. The company will also be able to mobilise about Rs 115 crore if investors exercise warrants. This will add only Rs 12 crore to paid-up capital, which the company can service in terms of dividends quite comfortably. SPN is a convenient and relatively less expensive financial instrument for TISCO given its high degree of financial leverage and need for substantial funds for undertaking large investment projects.

It may be pointed out that TISCO's SPN issue faced difficulties as the Central Board of Direct Taxes and the Department of Company Affairs objected to their proposal of treating returns as capital gains rather than income. Since capital gains tax rate is much lower than the income-tax rate, there will be loss of revenue to the government.

SUMMARY

❖ Convertible security is either a debenture or a preference share that can be exchanged for a stated number of ordinary shares at the option of the investor.

❖ Companies offer convertible securities to sweeten debt and thereby make it attractive. It is a form of deferred equity financing, and provides low cost funds during the early stage of investment project.

❖ The valuation of convertible securities depends on its value as a straight, non-convertible security (investment value) and its value if converted into ordinary shares. It generally sells for a premium; that is, its market price exceeds the higher of its investment or conversion value.

❖ A warrant is an option to buy a specified number of ordinary shares at an indicated price during a specified period.

❖ A detachable warrant is bought and sold independent of the

debenture to which it is associated.

❖ Warrants are generally used to sweeten a debt to make it marketable and lower the interest costs. When warrants are exercised, the firm obtains additional cash.

❖ The market value of warrants depends primarily on the ordinary share price. Warrants generally sell above their minimum, theoretical value. The difference between the market price and theoretical value of warrants is the premium.

❖ A company may also issue zero-interest or deep-discount bonds or debentures with conversion option. Such debentures are issued at a price much lower than their face value. Thus, there is an implicit rate of interest.

❖ A company may also issue debentures redeemable at premium and/or with warrants attached. These features are added to make the issue of debentures attractive to the investors.

KEY CONCEPTS

Arbitrage	Convertible zero-interest	Exercise ratio	debentures (NCDs)
Conversion premium	debentures	Fully convertible	Non-detachable warrants
Conversion price	Deferred equity	debentures (FCDs)	Partially convertible
Conversion ratio	Detachable warrants	Hybrid security	debentures (PCDs)
Conversion value	Equity sweetener	Leverage effect	Special premium notes
Convertible debenture	Exercise price	Non-convertible	Warrants

REVIEW QUESTIONS

1. Define the following terms: (a) conversion price, (b) conversion value, and (c) conversion premium.
2. What are the important features of a convertible security? What reasons are generally given for issuing convertible securities?
3. Convertible debentures generally carry lower rates of interest than the non-convertible debentures. If this is true, does it mean that the cost of capital on convertible debentures is lower than on non-convertibles? Why or why not?
4. How is a convertible security valued? Explain your answer with the help of a graph.
5. What is a warrant? What are its characteristic features? Why are warrants issued?
6. Explain the difference between a convertible security and a warrant.
7. Explain the valuation of warrants with the help of a graph.
8. What is meant by zero-interest debentures and deep-discount debentures? How is their cost determined? Illustrate your answer.

PROBLEMS

1. In January 2004, a company announced two types of convertible debentures. First, it issued 50 lakh 10 per cent fully convertible debentures of Rs 1000 each at par. Each convertible debenture was fully convertible into 5 shares of Rs 200 (i.e., Rs 100 par plus a premium of Rs 100) after two years from the date of allotment of debentures. The company also announced a public issue of 50 lakh 10 per cent partly convertible debentures of Rs 2000 each. Like the first issue, Rs 1000 of the debenture's face value was convertible into 5 shares. The non-convertible portion of the debenture was to be redeemed at the end of 10 years from the date of allotment. At the time of these issues, the company's share was selling for Rs 120. Analyse both types of debentures by making appropriate assumptions.

2. Kamani Limited has total assets Rs 1000 crore. Its equity, divided in 25 crore outstanding shares, has market value of Rs 800 crore. Currently the company has debt of Rs 400 crore. The company has just made an issue of debentures (Rs 100 each) of the total amount of Rs 400 crore plus one warrant of Re 10 for each debenture. A warrant will entitle the debenture holders to apply for one equity share at an exercise price of Rs 15 at the end of two years. The annual standard deviation of the share price variability before the debenture issue is: $\sigma = 4.5$. Assume that the interest rate is 10 per cent. What is the value of a warrant?

CASES

Case 21.1: Tata Steel[1]

Tata Iron and Steel Company Limited (Tata Steel) opened its debentures issue on June 5 1989. The purpose of the issue was to partly finance its modernisation and expansion programme costing about Rs 1,500 crore spread over 5 years. Of this, about Rs 850 crore is expected to be raised from internal cash generation and term loans. It is estimated that the balance of Rs 650 crore will be required during the next three years when capital expenditure will be at its peak. The purpose of the convertible debenture issue is to meet this requirement.

Each debenture has a face value of Rs 1,200 consisting of two parts, namely, Part A—a convertible part of Rs 600 and Part B—a non-convertible part of Rs 600. The convertible part of Rs 600 will be automatically converted into one fully paid up ordinary share of Rs 100 each at a premium of Rs 500 per share on expiry of six months from the deemed date of allotment, namely on February 1, 1990. The debentures will carry interest rate of 12 per cent per annum and will be payable half-yearly. The non-convertible part of the debentures of Rs 600 each will be redeemed at par on the expiry of eight years from the date of allotment of the debentures.

The working results of the company for the year ended March 1988 are encouraging. While the sales increased from Rs 1,224 crore in 1985–86 to Rs 1,348 crore in 1987–88 and to Rs 1,450

---

1. *Source:* The newspaper reporting and the company prospectus.

crore in 1987–88, net profits declined from Rs 107.8 crore to Rs 75.4 crore but rose to Rs 83.6 crore. The company has paid a dividend of 25 per cent per year for last three years. The company issued bonus shares in the ratio of 2:5 in 1987 and subsequently rights shares in the ratio of 1:3. For 10 months ended January 31 1989, turnover stood at Rs 1,405 crore with net profits of Rs 129 crore. As on March 31 1988, total assets amounted to Rs 2,042 crore. Gross fixed assets stood at Rs 1,686 crore. As against an equity capital of Rs 156 crore, reserves and surplus stood at Rs 667.3 crore. Total loans amounted to Rs 610.9 crore. The Rs 100 paid-up equity shares are currently quoted at Rs 1,265 against the book value per share of Rs 535.

Discussion Questions

1. Analyse the features of the Tata Steel convertible debenture issue.
2. Show its impact on shareholders' earnings and wealth.
3. With the help of a graph and whatever reasonable assumptions you wish to make, show how the market value of the convertible debenture will be determined.

Case 21.2: Western Hatcheries Limited[1]

The company announced on 29th May 1989 a 14 per cent 1,06,250 fully convertible debenture issue for Rs 250 each debenture for cash at par. The purpose of the issue is to finance its expansion project costing Rs 10 crore. The financing package for the project is: Rs 3.13 crore convertible debentures, Rs 1.25 crore unsecured loans, Rs 4.93 crore term loans and Rs 0.70 crore internal funds.

The convertible debentures will have a face value of Rs 250 each and each debenture will be converted into two stages; Rs 80 per debenture will be converted into five equity shares of Rs 10 each at a premium of Rs 6 per share on allotment. The balance of Rs 170 will be converted into equity shares of Rs 10 each at the end of two years from the date of allotment at a price (including premium, if any) to be decided by the Controller of Capital Issue. The offer of convertible debentures opens on 29th May 1989 and closes earliest on 1st June 1989.

Western Hatcheries was incorporated in 1978 in Maharashtra. The working results of the company are very encouraging. Sales income went up from Rs 42.8 lakh in 1983–84 to Rs 217.3 lakh in 1986–87 and to Rs 246.9 lakh in 1987–88. Net profits went up from Rs 2.6 lakh to Rs 20.9 lakh and to Rs 43.7 lakh during the same period. The sales income for the six-month period ended December 1988 amounted to Rs 121.1 lakh with net profits of Rs 13.6 lakh. The company issued bonus shares in the ratio of 2 : 1 by capitalising Rs 50 lakh in April 1989. Thus the paid-up capital has increased to Rs 75 lakh. The company has paid a dividend of 25 per cent per annum for the last three years. The total net worth of the company is Rs 134.94 lakh (Rs 75 lakh equity capital plus Rs 59.94 lakh reserves).

During the nine month period ending March 1989, sales income amounted to Rs 2 crore with net profits of Rs 0.25 crore. The sales income is projected to rise to Rs 11.63 crore in 1989–90 and to Rs 20.44 crore in 1990–91 yielding net profits of Rs 1.15 crore and Rs 2.15 crore respectively. No quotation for the company's share is available so far. The book value per share is Rs 17.59.

Discussion Question

1. Evaluate Western Hatcheries' debenture issue in all its aspects from the viewpoints of both the company and investors.

---

1. *Source:* The newspaper reporting and the company prospectus.

22 Asset-Based Financing: Lease, Hire Purchase and Project Financing

CHAPTER OBJECTIVES

- Define lease and highlight its true advantages
- Explain methods for evaluating a lease
- Discuss the concept of a leveraged lease
- Highlight the difference between hire purchase financing and lease financing
- Focus on project financing as a special mechanism for financing large projects in infrastructure and other sectors

The traditional financing is related to the liability side of the balance sheet. The firm issues long-term debt or equity to meet its financing needs, and in the process, expands its capitalisation. The dangers of traditional financing are that equity becomes an expensive method of financing because of decreasing corporate earnings and low price-earning ratios. The high rate of inflation causes long-term debt to be an expensive source of financing as interest rates rise. The corporate finance managers, therefore, are developing financing alternatives related to the asset side of the balance sheet. These alternatives may lower the cost and redistribute the risk. Asset-based financing uses assets as direct security. There are many possibilities. We shall discuss three most popular asset-based financing: (*i*) lease; (*ii*) hire purchase, and (*iii*) project financing.[1]

LEASE FINANCING

Leasing is widely used in Western countries to finance investments. In USA, which has the largest leasing industry in the world, lease financing contributes approximately one-third of total business investments. In the changing economic and financial environment of India, it has assumed an important role. What is lease financing? What are its advantages and disadvantages? How can a lease be evaluated?

Lease Defined

Lease is a contract between a lessor, the owner of the asset, and a lessee, the user of the asset. Under the contract, the owner gives the right to use the asset to the user over an agreed period of time for a consideration called the **lease rental**. The lessee pays the rental to the lessor as regular fixed payments over a period of time at the beginning or at the end of a month, quarter, half-year, or year. Although generally fixed, the amount and timing of payment of lease rentals can be tailored to the lessee's profits or cash flows. In **up-fronted leases**, more rentals are charged in the initial years and less in the later years of the contract. The opposite happens in **back-ended leases**. At the end of the lease contract, the asset reverts to the lessor, who is the legal owner of the asset. As the legal owner, it is the lessor not lessee, who is entitled to claim depreciation on the leased asset. In long-term lease contracts, the lessee is generally given

---

1. The topic of leasing is an adaptation of article by I.M. Pandey, Myths and Realities about Leasing, *Vikalpa,* Vol. II, No. 4, Oct.–Dec. 1986, and the topic of project financing is adapted from S. Sinha, "Return to Equity, Financial Structure, and Risk Contracting in Infrastructure Projects", *Vikalpa,* Vol. 20, No. 4, Oct.–Dec. 1995.

an option to buy or renew the lease. Sometimes, the lease contract is divided into two parts—primary lease and secondary lease for the purposes of lease rentals. **Primary lease** provides for the recovery of the cost of the asset and profit through lease rentals during a period of about four or five years. A perpetual, secondary lease may follow it on nominal lease rentals. Various other combinations are possible.

Although the lessor is the legal owner of a leased asset, the lessee bears the risk and enjoys the returns. The lessee benefits if the leased assets operates profitably, and suffers if the asset fails to perform. Leasing separates ownership and use as two economic activities, and facilitates asset use without ownership.[1]

A lessee can be individual or a firm interested in the use of an asset without owning. Lessors may be equipment manufacturers or leasing companies who bring together the manufacturers and the users. In USA, equipment manufacturers are the largest group of lessors followed by banks. In India, independent leasing companies form the major group in number in the leasing industry. Banks together with financial institutions are the largest group in terms of the volume of business.

Types of Leases

Two types of leases can be distinguished:
- Operating lease
- Financial lease
- Sale-and-lease-back

Operating lease Short-term, cancellable lease agreements are called **operating leases**. Convenience and instant services are the hallmarks of operating leases. Examples are: a tourist renting a car, lease contracts for computers, office equipment, car, trucks and hotel rooms. For assets such as computers or office equipment, an operating lease may run for 3 to 5 years. The lessor is generally responsible for maintenance and insurance. He may also provide other services. A single operating lease contract may not fully amortise the original cost of the asset; it covers a period considerably shorter than the useful life of the asset. Because of the short duration and the lessee's option to cancel the lease, the risk of obsolescence remains with the lessor. Naturally, the shorter the lease period and/or higher the risk of obsolescence, the higher will be the lease rentals.

Financial lease Long-term, non-cancellable lease contracts are known as **financial leases**. Examples are plant, machinery, land, building, ships, and aircraft. In India, financial leases are very popular with high-cost and high technology equipment. Financial leases amortise the cost of the asset over the term of lease; they are, therefore, also called **capital** or **full-payout leases**. Most financial leases are **direct leases**. The lessor buys the asset identified by the lessee from the manufacturer and signs a contract to lease it out to the lessee.

Sale-and-lease-back Sale-and-lease-back is a special financial lease arrangement. Sometimes, a user may sell an (existing) asset owned by him to the lessor (leasing company) and lease it back from him. Such **sale-and-lease-back** arrangements may provide substantial tax benefits. For example, in April 1989, Shipping Credit and Investment Corporation of India (SCICI) purchased Great Eastern Shipping Company's bulk carrier, Jag Lata, for Rs 12.5 crore and then leased it back to Great Eastern on a five-year lease, the rentals being Rs 28.13 lakh per month. The ship's written-down book value was Rs 2.5 crore.

In financial lease, the maintenance and insurance are normally the responsibility of the lessee. The lessee also bears the risk of obsolescence. A financial lease agreement may provide for renewal of contract or purchase of the asset by the lessee after the contract expires. The option of purchasing the leased asset by the lessee is not incorporated in the lease contract in India, because if such an option is provided the lease is legally construed to be a hire purchase agreement.

There are a large number of lease terminologies used in practice. Exhibit 22.1 explains some of the commonly used lease terms.

Cash Flow Consequences of a Financial Lease

A financial lease has cash flow consequences. It is a way of normal financing for a company. Suppose a company has found it financially worthwhile to acquire an equipment costing Rs 800 lakh. The equipment is estimated to last eight years. Instead of buying, the company can lease the equipment for eight years at an annual (end-of-the period) lease rental of Rs 160 lakh from the manufacturer. Suppose that the company will have to provide for the maintenance, insurance, and other operating expenses associated with the use of the asset in both alternatives—leasing or buying. Assume a straight-line depreciation for tax purposes, a borrowing rate of 14 per cent, and a marginal tax rate of 35 per cent for the company. The cash flow consequences of the lease (as compared to the buy option) are shown in Table 22.1. They would be:

- *Avoidance of the purchase price (P_0)* The company can acquire the asset without immediately paying for it. Cash outflow saved is equivalent to a cash inflow; there is a cash inflow of Rs 800 lakh.
- *Loss of depreciation tax shield (DTS)* Depreciation is a deductible expense and saves taxes. Depreciation tax shield is equal to the amount of depreciation each year multiplied by the tax rate. The company will lose a series of depreciation tax shields when it takes the lease. The straight-line depreciation will be: Rs 800/8 = Rs 100 lakh, and the lost DTS will be: Rs 100 × 0.35 = Rs 35 lakh.
- *After-tax payment of lease rentals (L_t)* There is a cash outflow of Rs 160 lakh per year as lease payment. But these payments will yield tax shield of Rs 160 × 0.35 = Rs 56 lakh per year. Thus, the after-tax lease payments would be Rs 160 lakh – Rs 56 lakh = Rs 104 lakh per year.

The cash flow consequences of leasing depend on the tax status of a company; tax shields are available only when the company pays taxes. In case it does not, then depreciation is worth nothing to it. Also, tax shields would vary with the marginal tax rate for the company.

---

1. Miller, M.H. and C.W. Upton, Leasing, Buying and the Cost of Capital, *Journal of Finance*, 1976, 31, pp. 761–86.

EXHIBIT 22.1: COMMONLY USED LEASE TERMINOLOGY

Two basic types of lease are: (*a*) financial lease and (*b*) operating lease. Finance lease in further divided into (*i*) leveraged lease, (*ii*) sale-and-lease-back, (*iii*) cross-border lease.

- *Leveraged lease* Leveraged lease involves lessor, lessee and financier. Lessor (leasing company) provides equity equal to about 25 per cent of the asset's cost while the remaining amount is provided by the financier (a bank or a financial institution), mainly as loan. Leveraged lease is a popular method of financing expensive assets.
- *Sale-and-lease-back* As discussed in the main text, the lessee first sells asset owned by him to the lessor and then leases it back from the lessor. This provides liquidity as well as possible tax gains to the lessee.
- *Cross-border lease* In case of cross-border or international lease, the lessor and the lessee are situated in two different countries. Because the lease transaction takes place between parties of two or more countries, it is called cross-border lease. It involves relationships and tax implications more complex than the domestic lease. When the lease transaction takes place between three parties manufacturer/vendor, lessor and lessee in three different countries, it is called *foreign-to-foreign lease*.

  There many other terms used by the leasing industry. Some of them are defined below.
- *Closed and open ended lease* In the close ended lease, the asset gets transferred to the lessor at the end, and the risk of obsolescence, residual value etc. remain with the lessor being the legal owner of the asset. In the open ended lease, the lessee has the option of purchasing the asset at the end of lease.
- *Direct lease* It is a mix of operating and finance lease on a full payout basis and provides for the purchase option to the lessee.
- *Master lease* Master lease provides for a period longer than the asset's life and holds the lessor responsible for providing equipment in good operating condition during the lease period.
- *Percentage lease* Percentage lease provide for a fixed rent plus some per cent of the previous year's gross revenue to be paid to the lessor. This ensures protection against inflation.
- *Wet and dry lease* In the aircraft industry, when the lease involves financing as well as servicing and fuel, it is called wet lease. Dry lease provides only for financing.
- *Net net net lease* In the triple net (net net net) lease, the lessee is obliged to take care of maintenance, taxes and insurance of the equipment.
- *Update lease* Update lease is intended to protect the lessee against the risk of obsolescence. The lessor agrees to replace obsolete asset with new one at specified rent.

Table 22.1: Cash Flow Consequences of a Lease

(Rs in lakh)

Year (1)	Purchase Price Avoided (P_0) (2)	Depreciation (D) (3)	Depreciation Tax Shield (DTS) (4) = (3) × 0.35	Before-tax Lease Rentals (BTLR) (5)	After-tax Lease (ALR) (6) = .65 × (5)	Net Cash Flow (NCF) (7) = (1) + 4 + (5)
0	800					800
1		−100	−35	−160	−104	−139
2		−100	−35	−160	−104	−139
3		−100	−35	−160	−104	−139
4		−100	−35	−160	−104	−139
5		−100	−35	−160	−104	−139
6		−100	−35	−160	−104	−139
7		−100	−35	−160	−104	−139
8		−100	−35	−160	−104	−139

Myths About Leasing

We can now examine the truth about some myths on leasing.[1]

Leasing provides 100 per cent financing One misconception about leasing is that it provides 100 per cent financing for the asset as the lessee can avoid payment for acquiring the asset. The lessee, it is assumed, can preserve his liquid resources for other purposes. When a firm borrows to buy an asset, cash increases with borrowing and decreases by the same amount with the purchase of the asset. It has the asset to use but a liability to repay the loan and interest. In leasing also, the firm acquires the asset and incurs the liability to make fixed payments in future. In practice, therefore, leasing, like borrowing, commits the company for a stream of payments in future.

Leasing provides off-the-balance-sheet financing As the lessee may not be obliged to disclose his lease liability on the balance sheet, it is believed that leasing does not affect the debt-equity ratio while borrowing increases his debt-equity ratio. The myth goes, therefore, that leasing provides off-the-balance-sheet financing leaving the firm's debt raising ability intact. This is a fallacious argument. First, a debt-equity norm puts a limit on the firm's total borrowings. Its **debt capacity** depends on its debt servicing ability rather than the balance sheet ratios. Contractual obligations of any form through a lease or loan, reduce debt servicing ability and add to financial risk. Lenders recognise the lessee's cash flow burden arising from lease payments. As a lease uses the firm's debt capacity, it displaces debt.

Leasing can certainly help companies which have enough debt servicing ability but cannot borrow from banks or financial institutions on account of institutional norms on debt-equity or regulations. Under no circumstances can a lease enhance the firm's debt capacity.

---

1. A variety of views exist on the merits and demerits of leasing. For example, see Brealey, R. and Myers S., *Principles of Corporate Finance*, McGraw Hill, 1991, pp. 654–58.

Leasing improves performance Another myth is that the return on investment (profits divided by investment) will increase since a lease does not appear as an investment on the books or the balance sheet. Besides, back-ended leases enable showing higher profits in the initial years of the lease. Such performance ratios are illusory.

A firm's value is affected by the value of its assets and liabilities rather than book profits created through accounting adjustments. A lease will create value to the firm only if the benefits from it are more than its costs.

Leasing avoids control of capital spending Another misconception is that leasing does not need capital expenditure screening as no investments are involved. Since a long-term lease involves long-term financial commitments, it ought to be screened accordingly in any good capital expenditure planning and control system. If leasing is not screened and is used to circumvent capital expenditure screening and approval, it may add to the firm's risk, make it vulnerable to business fluctuations, and endanger its survival.

Advantages of Leasing

If all these myths are exploded, why then should a company lease instead of following the straightforward alternative of a secured loan and purchase of the asset? The primary consideration is the cost of lease *vs.* cost of buying. They can be different. For, if a firm is incurring losses or making low profits, it cannot take full advantage of the depreciation tax shield on purchase of assets. It is, therefore, sensible for it to let the leasing company (lessor) own the assets, take full advantage of tax benefits, and expect that the lessor passes on at least some part of the benefits in the form of reduced lease rentals. Both the lessor and the lessee may stand to gain financially.

Apart from these tangible financial implications, there are other real advantages to leasing.

Convenience and flexibility If an asset is needed for a short period, leasing makes sense. Buying an asset and arranging to resell it after use is time consuming, inconvenient and costly.

Long-term financial leases also offer flexibility to the user. In India, borrowing from banks and financial institutions involve long, complicated procedures. Institutions often put restrictions on borrowers, stipulate conversion of loan into equity, and appoint nominee directors on the board.[1] Financial leases are less restrictive and can be negotiated faster, especially if the leasing industry is well developed. Yet another advantage of a lease is the flexibility it provides to tailor lease payments to the lessee's cash flows. Such tailored payment schedules are helpful to a lessee who has fluctuating cash flows.

New or small companies in non-priority sectors such as confectioneries, bottlers and distilleries find it difficult to raise funds from banks and financial institutions in India.

Shifting of risk of obsolescence When the technology embedded in assets, as in a computer, is subject to rapid and unpredictable changes, a lessee can, through a short-term cancellable lease, shift the risk of obsolescence to the lessor. A manufacturer-lessor, or a specialised leasing company, is usually in a better position than the user to assume the risk of obsolescence and manage the fast advancing technology. Specialised leasing companies are emerging in India. In fact, in such situations, the lessee is buying an insurance against obsolescence, paying a premium in terms of higher lease rentals.

Maintenance and specialised services With a full-service lease, a lessee can look for advantages in maintenance and specialised services. For example, computer manufacturers who lease out computers are better equipped than the user to provide effective maintenance and specialised services. Their cost too may be less than what the lessee would have to incur if he were to maintain the leased asset. The lessor is able to provide maintenance and other services cheaply because of his larger volume and specialisation. He may pass on a part of that advantage to the lessee. We do not yet have in India many integrated specialised leasing companies.

In the face of such myths and realities, how does one evaluate a lease?

EVALUATING A FINANCIAL LEASE

Leasing is a two-step decision for the lessee firm. First, it has to evaluate the economic viability of the asset as an investment. If the asset has a positive net present value, the company should proceed to acquire the asset. Once it has decided to do so, the firm can compare the costs of financing the asset through leasing with that of normal sources of financing.

When the firm finances the asset by normal financing, it takes the following two steps.[2]

- Purchases the asset for cash, for say, X.
- Purchases the necessary cash by selling a package of financing instruments (debt and/equity), taking into account its long-term target capital structure, for say, Y.

When the asset is leased, the following two transactions take place simultaneously:

- Purchase of the asset for cash, for say, A.
- Purchase of necessary cash, for say, B, by (i) giving up the asset's depreciation tax shield, and salvage value and (ii) by agreeing to make a stream of cash payments as lease rentals to the lessor.

It is to the firm's advantage to finance the asset by leasing if there is a positive difference, in net present value terms, of B over Y. Thus, in evaluating a lease, a firm should be concerned about how the value of the firm is affected if the lease is used as a 'substitute' for normal finance.[3] The net present value of an asset (investment project) is found by discounting the cash flows associated with the use of the asset by the firm's cost of capital, given its target debt-equity structure.

---

1. The stipulations of mandatory conversion of loan into equity and appointment of nominee directors have been removed now.

2. Schall, L., The Lease-or-Buy and Asset Acquisition Decision, *Journal of Finance,* September 1974, pp. 1203–14; and S.C. Myers *et. al.,* Valuation of Financial Lease Contracts, *Journal of Finance,* June 1976, pp. 799–820.

3. Bower, *op. cit.*; Myers *et. al., op. cit.*

In evaluating the lease, a key question is: at what rate should the cash flows be discounted to arrive to net present values? Should it be cost of capital of the firm or its after-tax borrowing rate? There is much debate on this question. The weight of the arguments, however, is in favour of using the after-tax borrowing rate since leasing is functionally equivalent to a secured debt. Leasing affects the firm's capital structure exactly the same way as debt does; lease displaces the firm's debt capacity.

Leasing can be evaluated using either the equivalent loan method or the net advantage of lease method. These are described next.

Equivalent Loan Method

The equivalent loan method of evaluating a financial lease consists of the following steps:[1]

- Find out the *incremental* cash flows from leasing.
- Determine the amount of equivalent loan such incremental cash flows can service (explained below).
- Compare the equivalent loan so found with lease finance. If the lease finance is more than equivalent loan, the firm should finance the asset by leasing (provided, as explained earlier, the asset is worth having).

Equivalent loan is that amount of loan, which commits a firm to exactly the same stream of fixed obligations, as does the lease liability. In our example, the net cash flows from leasing are as given in column 7 of Table 22.1. These cash flows can be said to "service" the loan. We can determine the amount of loan that they can service as follows.

The lease contract was completed with the last year's payment of Rs 139 lakh. This amount serviced a principal amount at the beginning of the eighth year and the after-tax interest for the eighth year. Let the outstanding amount at the beginning of the eighth year be P. If the interest rate is 14 per cent and tax rate, T, is 35 per cent, then the after-tax interest rate will be: $k_d(1-T)$ = 0.14 (1 − 0.35) = 0.091 or 9.1 per cent. We can write the following equation:

$$1.091P = 139$$

$$P = \frac{139}{1.091} = Rs\,127.41\,lakh$$

Thus, the cash flow of Rs 139 lakh in the eighth year is apportioned as: principal repayment of Rs 127.41 lakh and an after-tax interest (ATI) for the eighth year of: Rs 139 − Rs 127.41 = Rs 11.59 lakh. The before-tax interest (BTI) paid will be:

$$ATI/(1-T) = Rs\,11.59/0.65 = Rs\,17.84\,lakh$$

The equivalent outstanding loan at the beginning of seventh year would be equal to principal repayments in seventh and eighth years. The principal repaid in the eighth year was Rs 127.41 lakh. The after-tax interest in seventh year would be:

$$0.091\,(P + 127.41) = 0.091P + 11.59$$

The total amount paid in the seventh year was Rs 139 lakh. This was for repayment of principal, P, and the after-tax interest

in the seventh year. We can write the equation as follows:

$$1.091P + 11.59 = 139$$

$$1.091P = 139 - 11.59 = P = 127.41/1.091 = Rs\,116.78\,lakh$$

Thus, in the seventh year, the principal repaid is Rs 116.78 lakh. The after-tax interest is: Rs 139 − Rs 116.78 = Rs 22.22 lakh, and the before-tax interest paid is: Rs 22.22 ÷ 0.65 = Rs 34.19 lakh.

Similarly, we can work backwards to calculate the equivalent loan in the year 0. The calculations are shown in Table 22.2. As can be seen from column (6) row 1 of Table 22.2, an initial equivalent loan of Rs 766.49 lakh could be serviced by the cash outflows of lease financing at 14 per cent before-tax interest rate.

Table 22.2: Equivalent Loan Calculations

(Rs in lakh)

Year (1)	Net Cash Flows (2)	Before-tax Interest (3)	After-tax Interest (4)	Principal Repaid (5)	Loan Outstand-ing (6)
0					766.49
1	139	107.31	69.75	69.25	697.24
2	139	97.61	63.45	75.55	621.69
3	139	87.04	56.57	82.43	539.26
4	139	75.50	49.07	89.93	449.33
5	139	62.91	40.89	98.11	351.22
6	139	49.17	31.96	107.04	244.19
7	139	34.19	22.22	116.78	127.41
8	139	17.84	11.59	127.41	0

Should the firm accept lease financing? The lease cash flows can service an equivalent loan of Rs 766.49 lakh while the available lease finance for the same cash flows, is Rs 800 lakh. Thus, the lease finance is advantageous, and the firm should accept the decision to lease the equipment. The equivalent loan is, in fact, the present value of lease cash flows discounted at the after-tax cost of borrowing and is given by following equation:

Equivalent loan = PV of cash flows of a lease

$$EL = \sum_{t=1}^{n} \frac{(1-T)L_t + DTS_t}{[1+k_d(1-T)]^t} \qquad (1)$$

Equation (1) can be modified to include other lease cash flows such as the operating expenses incurred by the lessor (or the lessee) on maintaining the leased asset and the salvage value of the asset forgone by the lessee.

Net Advantage of a Lease

Another method of evaluating a lease is by finding its net advantage. As discussed earlier, the direct cash flow consequences are:

- The purchase price of the asset, A_0, is avoided.
- The depreciation tax shield, DTS_t, is lost.

---

1. See Brealey, R. and Myers, S., *op. cit.*, pp. 661–63 for discussion of the equivalent loan method.

- The after-tax lease rentals, $(1-T)L_t$, are paid.
- Lease financing also has an indirect effect; it displaces debt. Thus, the interest tax shield on the displaced debt, $Tk_d D_t$, is lost.

The present value of these flows can be calculated by discounting each flow by a rate that reflects its risk. The lease cash flows, including after-tax lease rentals and lost DTS are safe cash flows since the after-tax rentals and DTS are fixed and known. Hence, lease being equivalent to a loan, the after-tax lease cash flows can be discounted by the after-tax cost of borrowing, i.e., $k_d(1-T)$. There is, however, controversy in the literature as to the appropriate discount rate to be applied to the lease cash flows.[1]

Appropriate discount rate One may argue[2] that the risk characteristics of the lease payments and tax shields are similar respectively to interest and principal payments of debt. Lease payments can thus be discounted at the firm's after-tax borrowing rate. The position is not very clear with respect to tax shields. They encompass some of the firm's business risks as they can be availed only when profits are made. But because of the carry forward provisions, the firm can use tax shields in the long run when it earns sufficient profits. If so, tax shields are relatively safe and their risk characteristics are not similar to the firm's risk.

The problem of handling the indirect effect due to interest tax shield is related to the question of debt displaced by the lease. This is the difficult part in lease evaluation. The amount of debt displaced by the lease depends on the value of the lease liability, and lease liability depends on the amount of debt displaced. It is well established in literature that debt is valuable because of the tax deductibility of interest.[3] The optimum debt capacity of the firm, therefore, can be said to depend on the firm's business risk (variability of operating cash flows) and the value of its assets and tax shields. Tax shields generated by depreciation and interest are the firm's assets since they create economic value. The tax shields generated by the lease rentals can, therefore, be treated essentially the same way as those generated by depreciation and interest.

It is then possible to discount the after-tax rentals and depreciation tax shields at the after-tax borrowing rate. The after-tax borrowing rate implicitly recognises the lost interest tax shield on displaced debt.[4] Table 22.3 provides the present value of the lease cash flows discounted at the after-tax borrowing rate $(1-T)k_d = (1-0.35)0.14 = 0.091$ or 9.1 per cent. It may be seen that the present value of lease is equal to Rs 766.49 lakh. It is the same as the equivalent loan determined using the first method because the discount rate used for the lease cash flows was the same as the borrowing rate in both cases. Under the net advantage of lease method, it is possible to use a different rate for each stream, in which case, the present value of the lease would differ from the equivalent loan.

When the present value of lease is subtracted from the purchase price avoided, A_0, (Rs 800 lakh), we get the net advantage of leasing, which is:

Net advantage of leasing $= A_0$ − Present value of lease cash flows

$$= 800 - 766.49 = + \text{Rs } 33.51 \text{ lakh}$$

Summary of present values shown in Table 22.3 is as follows:

(Rs in lakh)

Purchase price avoided, (P_0)	+ 800.00
Present value of depreciation tax shield, PV (DTS)	− 193.00
Present value of after-tax lease payments, PV $[(1-T)L_t]$	− 573.49
Net advantage of leasing, NAL	+ 33.51

Table 22.3: Depreciation Shield and Cash Flows Under a Lease

(Rs in lakh)

Year (1)	Purchase price avoided (2)	Lost depreciation tax shield (3)	After-tax lease rentals (4)	Net Cash Flows (5)	PV factor @ 9.1% (6)	Present Value (7)
0	+800.00			800.00	1.0000	+800.00
1		−35.00	−104.00	−139.00	0.9166	−127.41
2		−35.00	−104.00	−139.00	0.8401	−116.78
3		−35.00	−104.00	−139.00	0.7701	−107.04
4		−35.00	−104.00	−139.00	0.7058	−98.11
5		−35.00	−104.00	−139.00	0.6470	−89.93
6		−35.00	−104.00	−139.00	0.5930	−82.43
7		−35.00	−104.00	−139.00	0.5435	−75.55
8		−35.00	−104.00	−139.00	0.4982	−69.25
Present value	+800.00	−193.00	−573.49	−766.49		+33.51

Net Present Value and Net Advantage of Leasing

The net advantage of leasing denotes the incremental advantage over the net present value of buying the asset through normal financing channels. A positive net advantage of leasing implies that leasing has an advantage over the net present value of the asset as an investment, which may itself be either positive or negative. A positive net advantage of leasing does not by itself imply that the asset should be acquired. The net present value of the asset should first be assessed as an investment. A positive net advantage of leasing implies advantage to leasing. It is possible that leasing may make a financially unattractive asset investment worthwhile. Suppose the net present value of an asset is negative Rs 40,000, and the lessor offers it under lease terms that have a positive net advantage to the buyer of, say, Rs 60,000. Then he can acquire the asset by leasing. His overall position would be a net present value of: Rs 60,000 − Rs 40,000 = Rs 20,000.

The lessee's overall gain will be enhanced by the positive net advantage of leasing in situation 1, that is, positive net present value (investment) and positive net advantage of leasing

---

1. Bower, *op. cit.*
2. Myers, *et. al., op. cit.*
3. Modigliani, F. and M.H. Miller, Corporate Income Taxes and the Cost of Capital, *American Economic Review*, June 1963, pp. 433–43.
4. Bower, *op. cit.* and Myers *et. al., op. cit.*

will add (Table 22.4). In situation 2, the lessee should not lease because it has a negative net advantage of leasing; he should buy the asset through normal financing. One should not set off negative advantage of leasing from positive net present value, since leasing is ruled out. Interpretation of situation 4 also needs caution. The option of buying the asset through normal financing is undesirable, since its net present value itself is negative. The lessee may acquire the asset by leasing if its net advantage more than compensates the negative net present value of investment.

Table 22.4: Combination of Net Present Value of Investment and Net Advantage of Leasing

Situation	Net Present Value of Investment	Net Advantage of Leasing	Decision
1	Positive	Positive	Lease
2	Positive	Negative	Buy
3	Negative	Negative	Reject
4	Negative	Positive	Lease if sum of net present value and net leasing advantage is positive, otherwise reject

CAN A LEASE BENEFIT BOTH LESSOR AND LESSEE?

What is the present value of a lease to the lessor? The present value of the lease cash flows to the lessor is given in Table 22.5. We assume that the lessor's tax rate is 35 per cent and the lending rate is 14 per cent. Note that the lease cash flows are the same as for lessee except for the change in signs; what the lessee loses the lessor gains and vice versa. There is a loss to the lessor. He will like to charge more lease rental from the lessee.

Table 22.5: Present Value of Lessor's Cash Flows

Cash flows	Present Value (Rs in lakh)
Purchase price	− 800.00
Depreciation tax shield (35 × 5.5143)*	+ 193.00
After-tax lease rental (104 × 5.5143)*	+ 573.49
Net present value	−33.51

*After-tax lease payment $(1 - 0.35)L_t$; 5.5143 is the present value factor of an annuity for 8 years at 9.1 per cent.

A lease will be taken when it benefits both the lessor and the lessee. It can benefit both when their tax rates differ. The lessor and the lessee determine the attractiveness of the lease rentals given their tax rates. Given the lessor's tax rate of 35 per cent, he can take full advantage of tax shields. The minimum lease payments for the lessor to break-even would be:

Net present value $= -800 + 193 + 5.5143 \times 0.65L_t$

$$3.5843L_t = 607$$

$$L_t = 607/3.5843 = Rs\,169.34\,lakh$$

The minimum lease rentals, which the lessor should charge to earn 9.1 per cent after-tax required rate of return is Rs 169.34 lakh. The monthly rate per Rs 1,000 worth of asset works out at Rs 17.16.[1]

Let us assume that the tax rate of the lessee is 0. Hence, there is no loss of depreciation tax shields foregone by him. The present value to the lessee of the lease is given in Table 22.6.

Table 22.6: Present Value of Lessee's Cash Flows (T = 0)

Cash Flows	Present Value (Rs in lakh)
Purchase price avoided	+ 800.00
Present value of lease rentals 4.6389* × 160	−742.22
Net advantage of lease	+ 57.78

*The 4.6389 is present value annuity factor for 8 years at 14 percent. If cash flows are compounded monthly, the factor for 96 months at 1.667 per cent is 57.5655.

The break-even lease payments to the lessee would be as follows:

Net advantage of leasing $= 800 - 4.6389L_t = 0$

$$L_t = 800/4.6389 = Rs\,172.45\,lakh$$

The maximum lease rental that the lessee will be prepared to pay would be Rs 172.45 lakh per annum. The monthly rental per Rs 1,000 of the asset is Rs 17.37 (at 14 per cent interest rate).

The break-even levels of lease payments of the lessor and the lessee give them adequate room for negotiations. Note that the break-even lease payments for both lessor and lessee would be the same if their tax rates are the same.

Suppose the actual lease rental in the example is Rs 170 lakh (instead of Rs 160 lakh), then both the lessor (with 35 per cent tax rate) and the lessee (with zero tax rate) will benefit from leasing. The lessor's gain is: Rs 170 – 169.34 = Rs 0.66 lakh per annum and the lessee's gain is Rs 172.45 – 170 = Rs 2.45 lakh per annum. The present value of the lessor's gain (at 9.1 per cent discount rate) is: (1 – 0.35) 0.66 × 5.5143 = Rs 2.37 lakh. The present value of the lessee's gain should be calculated at 14 per cent discount rate, since we have assumed that his tax rate is 0. Thus, the present value of the lessee's gain would be: Rs 2.45 × 4.6389 = Rs 11.37 lakh.

The lessee has benefitted because the lessor has passed on to him a part of the tax shield he got in the form of reduced rentals. The difference in the lessor's tax rate and the lessee's

---

1. The present value factor of an annuity for 96 months (8 years × 12) at the monthly rate of 0.007583 per cent (i.e., 0.091/12) will be calculated to find out the monthly lease rentals. Thus

$$NPV = -800 + 193 + 0.65 \times 68.0173\,L_t = 0$$
$$L_t = 607/44.2113 = Rs\,13.73\,lakh$$

Rs 13.73 lakh per month is the break-even rental for asset worth Rs 800 lakh. Therefore, monthly rental for an asset worth Rs 1,000 is: Rs (13.73/800) × 1,000 = Rs 17.16.

rate provides the opportunity that the lease would be mutually beneficial to both the lessor and the lessee. In the absence of taxes, it is hard to believe that leasing would be advantageous if the capital markets are reasonably well functioning.

Where from do leasing Benefits Come?

How can both the lessee and the lessor benefit from a lease? Both gain at government's expense because of the difference in their tax rates. The government gains from the tax on lease rentals while it loses on depreciation and interest tax shields. The implicit principal payments in a lease rental are shielded by depreciation, while interest deductions provide for implicit return on the lessee's capital. With a positive interest rate and accelerated depreciation, the government's receipts of tax on lease rentals will fall short, in present value terms, of depreciation and interest tax shields.

Consider the example given. The gain to the lessor was Rs 2.37 lakh and to the lessee Rs 11.37 lakh adding up to Rs 13.74 lakh. This is exactly the net loss to the government as shown in Table 22.7.[1]

Table 22.7 Lessee's and Lessor's Benefits Equal Government Loss

(Rs in lakh)

Loss: Present Value of:	
Depreciation tax shield (1)	− 193.00
Interest tax shield on displaced debt (2)	− 148.82
Gain: Present Value of:	
Tax on lease rentals (3)	+ 328.10
Net loss to the government	− 13.72

Notes:

(1) Depreciation tax shield is taken from Table 22.3. It is assumed that the lessor can avail them and borrow against them.

(2) The lessor's rentals are similar to the fixed obligations under debt. Thus, under an equivalent loan situation, the government would have received tax on interest. The present value of the tax is the difference between present value of rentals at the 9.1 per cent adjusted cost and present value of rentals at the 14 per cent cost of capital. Thus $(5.5143 - 4.6389) \times 170 =$ Rs 148.82 lakh.

(3) The present value of tax on lease rentals received by the government equals: $0.35 \times 170 \times 5.5143 =$ Rs 328.10 lakh.

Net Advantage of a Lease (NAL) Including Operating Costs and Salvage Value

How do we incorporate analysis of operating cost and salvage value in the lease evaluation?

The following equation can be used to find out NAL:

$$NAL = A_0 - \sum_{t=1}^{n} \frac{(1-T)L_t + DTS_t}{[1 + k_d(1-T)]^t} \qquad (2)$$

where A_0 is purchase price of the asset, T is the tax rate of the company, L_t is the lease rental paid in year t, DTS_t is the depreciation tax shield in year t and k_d is the cost of borrowings.

We have so far assumed that the asset has no salvage value at the end of its life and that the lessee firm might incur the maintenance, insurance and other operating costs associated with the leased asset. Under a full-service lease, the lessor may bear the maintenance, insurance and operating costs. If so, the present value of the lease to the lessee will increase by the present value of the stream of after-tax operating costs. On salvage value, the value of the lease to the lessee will decline by the after-tax proceeds from the sale of assets at the end of its economic life. Both operating costs and salvage value are difficult to predict. Therefore, they should be discounted at a rate higher than the firm's borrowing rate. There is a fair degree of unanimity among academicians about using the firm's cost of capital for discounting operating costs and salvage value.[2] We can modify Equation (2) as follows to calculate the net advantage of leasing:

$$NAL = A_0 - \sum_{t=1}^{n} \frac{(1-T)L_t + DTS_t}{[1 + k_d(1-T)]^t} + \sum_{t=1}^{n} \frac{(1-T)OC_t}{(1+k)^t} - \frac{ATSV_n}{(1+k)^n} \qquad (3)$$

where k is the after-tax cost of capital of the firm, OC_t is the operating cost in year t and $ATSV_n$ is the after-tax salvage value of the leased asset at the end of the life, n. As per the latest tax rule in India, salvage value is not taxed rather the depreciable value of the asset is adjusted. This point is illustrated later on.

Table 22.8: Cash Flows Under a Lease

(Rs in lakh)

Year (1)	Asset Price Avoided (P_0) (2)	Deprecia-tion Tax-shield lost (DTS) (3)	After-tax lease rentals (ATLR) (4)	After-tax operating expenses (ATOE) (5)	After-tax salvage value (SV) (6)	Net cash Flows (NCF) (7)
0	800.00					800.00
1		−35	−104.00	0.39		−138.61
2		−35	−104.00	0.39		−138.61
3		−35	−104.00	0.39		−138.61
4		−35	−104.00	0.39		−138.61
5		−35	−104.00	0.39		−138.61
6		−35	−104.00	0.39		−138.61
7		−35	−104.00	0.39		−138.61
8		−35	−104.00	0.39	−18.00	−156.61
PV		−193*	−573.49*	+1.81**	− 6.31**	+29.01

* Depreciation tax shield (DTS) and after-tax lease rentals (ATLR) are discounted at the after-tax cost of borrowing 9.1 per cent.

** After-tax operating expenses (ATOE) and salvage value (SV) are discounted at after-tax cost of capital, 14 per cent. SV is assumed on after-tax basis.

In the example used so far, suppose the equipment manufacturer agrees to maintain the asset that would have cost the lessee firm about Rs 0.60 lakh per annum. Also, let the estimated after-tax salvage value of the equipment be Rs 18 lakh. Assume a 14 per cent after-tax cost of capital for the lessee firm. The present value (PV) of the lease will increase by:

---

1. Myers, op. cit.
2. Bower, op. cit.

PV of after-tax operating cost $= \sum_{t=1}^{8} \frac{(1-0.35)0.60_t}{(1.14)_t}$

$$= 0.39 \times 4.6389 = Rs\,1.81\,lakh$$

and decrease by

PV of after tax salvage value $= \dfrac{18}{(1.14)^8}$

$$= 18 \times 0.3506 = Rs\,6.31\,lakh$$

Thus, the net advantage of the lease will be:

$$NAL = +33.51 + 1.81 - 6.31 = Rs\,29.01$$

You may note that cash flows given in Table 22.8 include the after-tax operating expenses saved by the lessee and the salvage value foregone by him. The lease with the positive net advantage of Rs 29.01 lakh is still advantageous.

Internal Rate of Return Approach for Evaluating a Lease

Besides the net present value (viz., NAL) or equivalent approach, a lease can also be evaluated in terms of its internal rate of return (IRR). IRR approach finds favour with many leasing companies in practice. We can recast Equation (3) to calculate IRR of a lease:

$$NAL = A_0 - \sum_{t=1}^{n} \frac{(1-T)(L_t - OC_t) + DTS_t}{(1+r)^t} - \frac{ATSV_n}{(1+r)^n} = 0 \quad (4)$$

IRR of a lease is that rate which makes NAL equal to zero. Using net cash flows as given in Table 22.8, we can calculate IRR of the lease in our example as follows:

$$NAL = 800 - \frac{138.61}{(1+r)^1} + \frac{138.61}{(1+r)^2} + \frac{138.61}{(1+r)^3} + \frac{138.61}{(1+r)^4}$$
$$+ \frac{138.61}{(1+r)^5} + \frac{138.61}{(1+r)^6} + \frac{138.61}{(1+r)^7} + \frac{156.61}{(1+r)^8}$$
$$= 0$$

By trial and error, we find IRR, $r = 8.2$ per cent. This represents after-cost of lease financing to the lessee. It comprises after-tax lease rentals, depreciation tax lost and salvage value foregone. It also implicitly includes the loss of interest tax shield on debt displaced by leasing. Since the after-tax cost of borrowing (9.1 per cent) of the lessee in our example is more than the after-tax cost of lease financing (8.2 per cent), the lessee should go for leasing the asset rather than buying it.

DEPRECIATION TAX SHIELD AND SALVAGE VALUE UNDER INDIAN TAX LAWS

We have discussed earlier in this book that in India WDV depreciation on the block of assets is allowed for the purpose of tax. When an asset is sold from the block of assets, the firm obtains salvage value but loses depreciation tax shield on the amount of salvage value forever. Recall that depreciation tax shields are safe cash nominal flows. Hence they are discounted at the after-tax borrowing cost. On the other hand, salvage value is an uncertain cash flow; therefore, it is discounted at the firm's cost of capital. Once the firm sells an asset, it will know the

salvage value on which it will lose the depreciation tax shield. Thus, lost depreciation tax shield on salvage value should be treated as safe cash flows and would be discounted at the after-tax cost of borrowing. Let us illustrate this point.

Illustration 22.1: Lease Evaluation: Indian Tax System

Surana Fasteners Limited wants to lease an equipment costing Rs 1,000 lakh for a period of seven years. The end of the year annual lease rental is Rs 240 lakh. As compared to the buy option, the company will have to provide for the maintenance, insurance, and other operating expenses associated with the use of the leased asset. The company will take a maintenance service contract for a period of seven years at a fixed annual cost of Rs 10 lakh payable in the beginning of the year. Under the buy option, the company could charge WDV depreciation at 25 per cent on the block of assets including the equipment. Under the lease option, it will have to forgo the salvage value of the equipment estimated as Rs 100 lakh at the end of seven years. Surana's cost of capital is 15 per cent and the cost of borrowing is 10 per cent. The corporate tax rate is 35 per cent.

In this case the incremental lease cash flows are as follows:

1. The company will avoid paying the purchase price of Rs 1,000 lakh in year 0.
2. The company will lose DTS forever. DTS are safe cash flows; hence, they will be discounted at the after-tax cost of borrowing. You may recall that the discounted value of a constantly declining DTS perpetuity is given as follows (T is tax rate, d depreciation rate and k_d cost of borrowing):

$$\frac{T \times d}{k_d(1-T) + d}$$

3. The company will pay each year after-tax lease rentals of Rs 156 lakh [$(1-0.35) \times Rs\,240\,lakh$]. These are fixed obligations and will be discounted at the after-tax cost of borrowing of 6.50 per cent.
4. The company will incur in the beginning of each year after-tax annual operating cost of Rs 6.50 lakh [$(1-0.35) \times Rs\,10\,lakh$]. This amount is known and it is fixed by the contract. Hence it is a safe nominal cash flow, and it should be discounted at the after-tax cost of borrowing.

Table 22.9: Lease Evaluation: Indian Tax Laws *(Rs in lakh)*

	Cash Flows	Discount rate	Present Value
Purchase price avoided, P_0	Year 0		+1,000.00
Lost DTS on equipment cost, $1000 \times \dfrac{0.35 \times 0.25}{0.25 + 0.065}$	Year 1 to infinity	0.065	−277.78
After-tax lease rentals, 156×5.4845	Year 1–7 annuity	0.065	−855.58
After-tax operating cost, $6.50 \times 5.4845 \times 1.065$	Year 0–6 annuity due	0.065	−37.97
Salvage value, $100 \times \dfrac{1}{1.15^7} = 100 \times 0.3759$	Year 7	0.15	−37.59
DTS on salvage value, $100 \times \dfrac{0.35 \times 0.25}{0.25 + 0.065} \times \dfrac{1}{1.15^7}$	Year 7	0.065; 0.15	+10.44
Net advantage of leasing			−198.48

5. The company will have to forgo the equipment's salvage value of Rs 100 lakh. This amount is uncertain; therefore, it should be discounted at the company's cost of capital.

6. The loss of the salvage value will be adjusted for the present value of depreciation tax shield on the salvage value. This amount is known at the end of the seventh year. Hence the series of DTS on the salvage value *after* seventh year is known and it is a safe cash flow. Its present value at the end of the seventh year should be calculated at the after-tax cost of borrowing. Salvage value is uncertain *until the end* of the seventh year, and so is the case with DTS on salvage value. To determine the present value of DTS on salvage value occurring at the end of seventh year, it will be discounted at the firm's cost of capital.

The values of cash flows of leasing are calculated in Table 22.9.

LEVERAGED LEASE

Under a **leveraged lease**, four parties are involved: the manufacturer of the asset, the lessor, the lender from whom the lessor borrows a substantial portion of the asset's purchase price, and the lessee. In a direct lease, the lessor buys the asset and becomes the owner by making the full payment of the asset. In a leveraged lease, the lessor makes substantial borrowing, even up to 80 per cent of the asset's purchase price. He provides the remaining amount—about 20 per cent or so—as equity to become the owner (Figure 22.1). The lessor claims all tax benefits related to the ownership of the asset. Lenders, generally the large financial institutions, provide loans on a **non-recourse** basis to the lessor. Their debt is serviced exclusively out of the lease proceeds. To secure the loan provided by lenders, the lessor also agrees to give them a mortgage on the asset. Thus, lenders have the first claim on the lease payments together with the collateral on the asset. Lenders will take charge of the asset if the lessee is unable to make lease payments.

Leveraged lease are called so because the high non-recourse debt creates a high degree of leverage. The effect is to amplify the return of the equity-holder (that is, the lessor). But the risk is also quite high if the lease payments are not received. Leveraged lease is quite useful for large capital equipment with long economic life, say, 20 years or more. It is one of the popular means of financing large infrastructure projects.

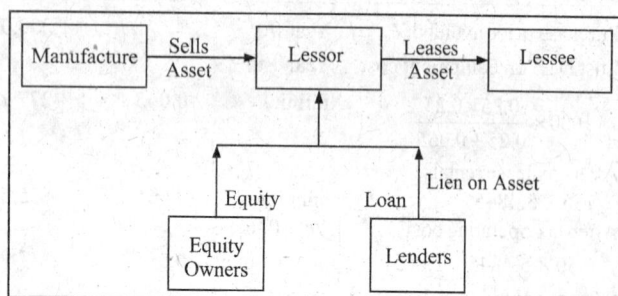

Figure 22.1: Leveraged lease

HIRE PURCHASE FINANCING

Hire purchase financing is a popular financing mechanism especially in certain sectors of Indian business such as the automobile sector. In **hire purchase financing**, there are three parties: the manufacturer, the hiree and the hirer. The hiree may be a manufacturer or a finance company. The manufacturer sells asset to the hiree who sells it to the hirer in exchange for the payment to be made over a specified period of time (Figure 22.2).

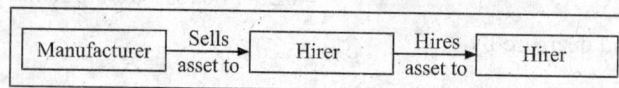

Figure 22.2: Hire purchase financing

A hire purchase agreement between the hirer and the hiree involves the following three conditions:

- The owner of the asset (the hiree or the manufacturer) gives the possession of the asset to the hirer with an understanding that the hirer will pay agreed instalments over a specified period of time.
- The ownership of the asset will transfer to the hirer on the payment of all instalments.
- The hirer will have the option of terminating the agreement any time before the transfer of ownership of the asset.

Thus, for the hirer, the hire purchase agreement is like a cancellable lease with a right to buy the asset. The hirer is required to show the hired asset on his balance sheet and is entitled to claim depreciation, although he does not own the asset until full payment has been made. The payment made by the hirer is divided into two parts: interest charges and repayment of principal. The hirer, thus, gets tax relief on interest paid and not the entire payment.

Hire Purchase Financing vs. Lease Financing

Both hire purchase financing and lease financing are a form of secured loan. Both displace the debt capacity of the firm since they involve fixed payments. However, they differ in terms of the ownership of the asset. The hirer becomes the owner of the assets as soon as he pays the last instalment. In case of lease, the asset reverts back to the lessor at the end of lease period. In practice, the lessee may be able to keep the asset after the expiry of the primary lease period for nominal lease rentals. The following are the differences between hire purchase financing and lease financing:

Table 22.10: Difference between Leasing and Hire Purchase Financing

Hire Purchase Financing	*Lease Financing*
• *Depreciation* Hire is entitled to claim depreciation tax shield.	• *Depreciation* Lessee is not entitled to claim depreciation tax shield.
• *Hire purchase payments* Hire purchase payments include interest and repayment of principal. Hirer gets tax benefits only on the interest.	• *Lease payments* Lessee can charge the entire lease payments for tax purposes. Thus, he/she saves taxes on the lease payments.
• *Salvage value* Once the hirer has paid all instalments, he becomes the owner of the asset and can claim salvage value.	• *Salvage value* Lessee does not become owner of the asset. Therefore, he has no claim over the asset's salvage value.

Instalment Sale

In contrast to the acquisition of an asset on the hire purchase basis, a customer can buy and own it out rightly on instalment basis. **Instalment sale** is a credit sale and the legal ownership of the asset passes immediately to the buyer as soon as the agreement is made between the buyer and the seller. The outstanding instalments are treated as secured loan. As the owner of the asset, the buyer is entitled to depreciation and interest as deductible expenses and can claim salvage value on the sale of the asset. Except for the timing of the transfer of ownership, instalment sale and hire purchase are similar in nature.

Evaluation of Hire Purchase Financing

The hiree charges interest at a flat rate, and he requires hirer to pay equal instalments each period. Let us assume that a corporate customer wants to acquire an equipment of Rs 80,000. Kuber Finance Company offers a hire purchase financing to the customer. The hire purchase instalments will be paid annually for eight years and Kuber will calculate interest at a flat rate of 14 per cent. The calculations of interest and instalments are given below:

$$\text{Interest} = \text{Rs } 80,000 \times 14\% \times 8 = \text{Rs } 89,600$$

$$\text{Instalment} = (\text{Rs } 80,000 + \text{Rs } 89,600)/8 = \text{Rs } 21,200$$

How will be the total interest of Rs 89,600 distributed over eight years? One of the most commonly used methods is to follow the **sum-of-years-digit (SYD) method**. In our example, the sum of years' digit is: $1 + 2 + 3 + 4 + 5 + 6 + 7 + 8 = 36$. Thus, the amount of interest each year will be as follows:

Year 1: $89,600 \times (8/36)$ = Rs 19,911
Year 2: $89,600 \times (7/36)$ = Rs 17,422
Year 3: $89,600 \times (6/36)$ = Rs 14,933
Year 4: $89,600 \times (5/36)$ = Rs 12,444
Year 5: $89,600 \times (4/36)$ = Rs 9,956
Year 6: $89,600 \times (3/36)$ = Rs 7,467
Year 7: $89,600 \times (2/36)$ = Rs 4,978
Year 8: $89,600 \times (1/36)$ = Rs 2,489

Table 22.11: Interest and Instalment Calculation under Hire Purchase

Year	Principal (Rs)	Instal-ment (Rs)	Interest (Rs)	Principal Repaid (Rs)	Out-standing (Rs)	Implied Interest Rate (%)
0	80,000				80,000	–
1		21,200	19,911	1,289	78,711	24.89
2		21,200	17,422	3,778	74,933	22.13
3		21,200	14,933	6,267	68,666	19.93
4		21,200	12,444	8,756	59,910	18.12
5		21,200	9,956	11,244	48,666	16.62
6		21,200	7,467	13,733	34,933	15.34
7		21,200	4,978	16,222	18,711	14.25
8		21,200	2,489	18,711	0	13.30
	Total	169,600	89,600	80,000	–	–

Table 22.10 shows the division of the annual instalment into interest and principal repayment. It may be noticed from the table that interest rate of 14 per cent is a flat rate and the total

amount of interest has been allocated over eight year period according to SYD method. Considering the principal payment and outstanding balance each year, the yearly implied rates of interest are different from the stated flat rate of 14 per cent (as shown in Table 22.11).

Is Kuber earning 14 per cent return? Kuber is earning much more; it is earning a compound rate of return (before-tax) of 20.6 percent as shown below:

$$80,000 = \frac{21,200}{(1+r)^1} + \frac{21,200}{(1+r)^2} + \frac{21,200}{(1+r)^3} + \frac{21,200}{(1+r)^4} + \frac{21,200}{(1+r)^5}$$
$$+ \frac{21,200}{(1+r)^6} + \frac{21,200}{(1+r)^7} + \frac{21,200}{(1+r)^8}$$

By trial and error, we find $r = 0.206$ or 20.6 per cent.

Let us assume that the customer in our example agrees for the hire purchase financing from Kuber Finance Company. The customer will be able to avoid the purchase price now. He will be entitled to claim the depreciation tax shield. His payments will include interest and principal repayment. Since interest is tax deductible, he will save taxes on interest payments. Assume that tax rate is 35 per cent and the asset has no salvage value. Cash flows under hire purchase financing are shown in Table 22.12. The after-tax cost of the hire purchase financing to the customer is about 7.53 per cent.

Let us assume that Kuber Finance Company can also offer the asset on lease to the customer. Given the after-tax cost of 7.53 per cent of the hire purchase financing, how much lease rentals will the customer be prepared to pay? Under lease, the customer will lose tax shield on depreciation and will have to pay lease rentals on which he will save taxes. The lease payments at 7.53 per cent are calculated as follows:

$$80,000 = \sum_{t=1}^{8} \frac{(1-T)L_t}{(1.0753)^t}$$

$$5.8506\,(1-0.35)L_t = 80,000$$

$$3.8029\,L_t = 80,000$$

$$L_t = \frac{80,000}{3.8029} = \text{Rs } 21,037$$

The before-tax lease rentals are Rs 21,037. The customer will be indifferent between the lease financing and hire purchase financing if the lease rentals are Rs 21,037 per year. For lease rentals higher than Rs 21,037, hire purchase will be preferable.

In practice, finance companies require lease or hire purchase payments to be made on monthly or quarterly basis. They also require the lessee or the hirer to pay management fee or service and administration charges. In case of hire purchase, some finance companies require hirer to make a deposit on which he gets interest. In certain states, the lease payments are treated 'sales' and the lessee is required to pay sales tax on lease payments. The cash flow calculations under a lease or hire purchase will include their effects as well.

Illustration 22.2: Leasing Decision in Practice

Ananthshyam Leasing and Finance Company has been approached by Diehard Chemicals Limited for leasing an equipment costing Rs one crore

Table 22.12: Cash Flows under Hire Purchase Financing

(Rs)

Year (1)	Purchase Price Avoided (2)	Instalment (3)	Interest (4)	Principal Repaid (5)	After-tax Interest (6)	Depreciation (7)	DTS (8)	Net Cash Flow 2 − 5 − 6 + 8 (9)
0	80,000							80,000
1		−21,200	−19,911	− 1,289	−12,942	20,000	7,000	−7,231
2		−21,200	−17,422	− 3,778	−11,324	15,000	5,250	−9,852
3		−21,200	−14,933	− 6,267	−9,707	11,250	3,938	−12,036
4		−21,200	−12,444	− 8,756	−8,089	8,438	2,953	−13,891
5		−21,200	−9,956	− 11,244	−6,471	6,328	2,215	−15,501
6		−21,200	−7,467	− 13,733	−4,853	4,746	1,661	−16,926
7		−21,200	−4,978	− 16,222	−3,236	3,560	1,246	−18,212
8		−21,200	−2,489	− 18,711	−1,618	4,725 *	1,654 *	−19,395
	IRR	20.6%						7.53%

* Includes present value of depreciation (Rs 2,055) beyond eight years. After-tax cost of borrowing, 0.14 × (1 − 0.35) = 0.091 or 9.1 per cent is used as the discount rate.

(A_0). Ananthshyam offers Diehard Chemicals a lease for 5 years starting from March 1998. Lease payments (LR_t) will be Rs 8,00,000 per quarter payable at the beginning of the quarter. Ananthshyam will charge upfront a management fee (MF_0) equal to 1 per cent of the cost of the equipment. The salvage value (SV_n) of the equipment is expected to be about 10 per

Table 22.13: Evaluation of Diehard's Lease Decision

(Rs '0000)

t	Quarter	P_0	DEP_t	$TDEP_t$	LR_t	MF_0	TAX_t	$ATLR_t$	SV_n	$ATCF_t$
0	Mar	1000	−37.50	−13.13	−80	−10	17.33	−72.68		914.20
1	Jun		−75.00	−26.25	−80		34.65	−45.35		−71.60
2	Sept		−75.00	−26.25	−80		34.65	−45.35		−71.60
3	Dec		−62.50	−21.88	−80		28.88	−51.13		−73.00
4	Mar		−28.13	−9.84	−80		16.80	−63.20		−73.04
5	Jun		−56.25	−19.69	−80		33.60	−46.40		−66.09
6	Sept		−56.25	−19.69	−80		33.60	−46.40		−66.09
7	Dec		−46.88	−16.41	−80		28.00	−52.00		−68.41
8	Mar		−21.09	−7.38	−80		16.80	−63.20		−70.58
9	Jun		−42.19	−14.77	−80		33.60	−46.40		−61.17
10	Sept		−42.19	−14.77	−80		33.60	−46.40		−61.17
11	Dec		−35.16	−12.30	−80		28.00	−52.00		−64.30
12	Mar		−15.82	−5.54	−80		16.80	−63.20		−68.74
13	Jun		−31.64	−11.07	−80		33.60	−46.40		−57.47
14	Sept		−31.64	−11.07	−80		33.60	−46.40		−57.47
15	Dec		−26.37	−9.23	−80		28.00	−52.00		−61.23
16	Mar		−11.87	−4.15	−80		16.80	−63.20		−67.35
17	Jun		−23.73	−8.31	−80		33.60	−46.40		−54.71
18	Sept		−23.73	−8.31	−80		33.60	−46.40		−54.71
19	Dec		−19.78	−6.92	−80		28.00	−52.00		−58.92
20	Mar								−100	−100.00
NPV at 3%										−77.87
IRR (quarterly)										3.92%

cent of the cost of the equipment. Diehard is a profitable company. It can borrow funds at 18.65 per cent per year. Taxes are payable in advance every quarter as follows: 15 per cent in March, 30 per cent each in June and September and remaining 25 per cent in December. The corporate tax rate is 35 per cent (T). Should Diehard lease the equipment?

Cash flows of Diehard's lease decision are given in Table 22.13 Diehard's after-tax cost of borrowing is: (1 − 0.35) × 0.1865 = 0.12 or 12 per cent a year. Thus the quarterly rate is 3 per cent. Diehard will have to pay lease rentals of Rs 32,00,000 each year at the rate of Rs 8,00,000 each quarter. The total tax of Rs 1,12,000 each year is paid over four quarters (each quarter, respectively, 15 per cent, 30 per cent, 30 per cent and 25 per cent). Depreciation tax shield is similarly treated. Management fee to be paid by Diehard will save taxes. The net advantage of the lease to Diehard is negative (NAL = − Rs 7,87,700). IRR per quarter is 3.92 per cent or per year 15.68 per cent. The cost of leasing is more than the cost of borrowing. Thus, Diehard should not accept the lease.

INFRASTRUCTURE PROJECT FINANCING[1]

There is a growing realisation in many developing countries of the limitations of governments in managing and financing economic activities, particularly large infrastructure projects. Provision of infrastructure facilities, traditionally in the government domain, is now being offered for private sector investments and management. This trend has been reinforced by the resource crunch faced by many governments. Infrastructure projects are usually characterised by large investments, long gestation periods, and very specific domestic markets.

In evaluating these projects, an important question is the appropriate rate of return on the equity investment. Tolls and tariffs are set so as to recover operating costs and to provide a return to capital—interest and repayment of debt and return on equity. Therefore, the decision on the appropriate return to equity has implications for the overall viability and acceptability of the project. While most elements of costs can be determined

1. This section is an adapted version of the article, Sinha, Sidharth, "Return to Equity, Financial Structure, and Risk Contracting in Infrastructure Projects", *Vikalpa*, Vol. 20, No. 4, October–December 1995, pp.11–19. The article is used with some modifications with the permission of the author and the editor of *Vikalpa*.

with reference to market prices, return to equity cannot be determined in the same way since most of the equity is provided by the sponsor or by a small number of investors. This leaves room for disagreement on the appropriate return to equity. In the case of the Indian power projects, this has been one of the contentious issues.[1]

This section draws on finance theory to develop an understanding of the problem of appropriate return to equity investment in an infrastructure project. Return to equity will depend upon the risk of cash flows from the project and the financial structure, i.e., the relative proportion of debt and equity. Since infrastructure projects employ a number of risk mitigation contracts, it is important to understand these arrangements before addressing the question of return to equity and financial structure.

What is Project Financing?

In **project financing**, the project, its assets, contracts, inherent economics and cash flows are separated from their promoters or sponsors in order to permit credit appraisal and loan to the project, independent of the sponsors. The assets of the specific project serve as a collateral for the loan, and all loan repayments are made out of the cash flows of the project. In this sense, the loan is said to be of non-recourse or limited recourse to the sponsor. Thus, project financing may be defined as that scheme of 'financing of a particular economic unit in which a lender is satisfied in looking at the cash flows and the earnings of that economic unit as a source of funds, from which a loan can be repaid, and to the assets of the economic unit as a collateral for the loan.'[2] In the past, project financing was mostly used in oil exploration and other mineral extraction through joint ventures with foreign firms. The most recent use of project financing can be found in infrastructure projects, particularly in power and telecommunication projects.

Project financing is made possible by combining undertakings and various kinds of guarantees by parties who are interested in a project. It is built in such a way that no one party alone has to assume the full credit responsibility of the project. When all the undertakings are combined and reviewed together, it results in an equivalent of the satisfactory credit risk for the lenders. It is often suggested that project financing enables a parent company to obtain inexpensive loans without having to bear all the risks of the project. This is not true. In practice, the parent company is affected by the actual plight of the project, and the interest on the project loan depends on the parents stake in the project.[3]

The traditional form of financing is the **corporate financing** or the **balance sheet financing**. In this case, although financing is apparently for a project, the lender looks at the cash flows and assets of the whole company in order to service the debt and provide security. Figure 22.3 shows the basic differences between balance sheet financing and project financing.

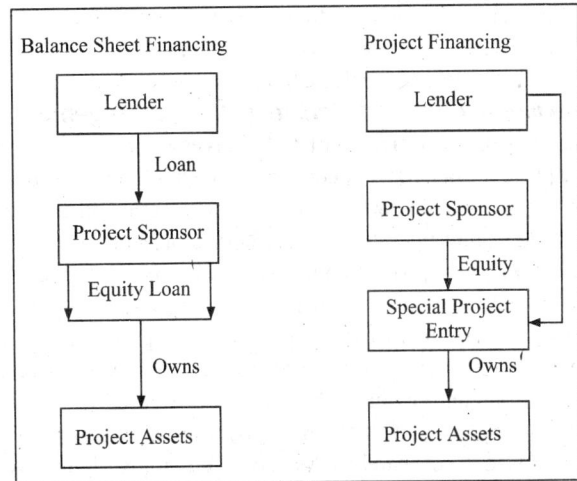

Figure 22.3: Balance sheet financing vs. Project financing

The following are the characteristics of project financing:

- *Separate project entity* A separate project entity is created that receives loans from lenders and equity from sponsors. This entity is called **special purpose vehicle/enterprise** (SPV or SPE).
- *Leveraged financing* The component of debt is very high in project financing. Thus, project financing is a **highly leveraged financing**.
- *Cash flows separated* The project funding and all its other cash flows are separated from the parent company's balance sheet.
- *Collateral* Debt services and repayments entirely depend on the project's cash flows. Project assets are used as collateral for loan repayments.
- *Sponsor's guarantees* Project financiers' risks are not entirely covered by the *sponsor's guarantees*.
- *Risk sharing* Third parties like suppliers, customers, government and sponsors commit to share the risk of the project.

Project financing is most appropriate for those projects which require large amount of capital expenditure and involve high risk. It is used by companies to reduce their own risk by allocating the risk to a number of parties. It allows sponsors to:
- finance large projects than the company's credit and financial capability would permit,
- insulate the company's balance sheet from the impact of the project,
- use high degree of leverage to benefit the equity owners.

Financing Arrangements for Infrastructure Projects

The project financing arrangements may range from simple conventional type of loans to more complex arrangements like the build-own-operate-transfer (BOOT). The typical arrangements, particularly in the power sector, include:

---

1. Indian power projects provide for a 16 per cent return on equity (ROE) in foreign currency at 68.5 per cent plant load factor (PLF) with additional 0.7 per cent ROE for each 1 per cent rise in PLF.
2. Nevitt, P.K., *Project Financing,* Euromoney Publications, 1983.
3. Brealey, R.A. and Myers, S.C., *Principles of Corporate Finance,* Fourth Ed., McGraw Hill, 1991, pp. 608–12.

1. The build-own-operate-transfer (BOOT) structure
2. The build-own-operate (BOO) structure
3. The build-lease-transfer (BLT) structure.

The build-own-operate-transfer (BOOT) arrangement The **build-own-operate-transfer** (**BOOT**) is essentially an extension of the project financing concept. It is a special financing scheme, which is designed to attract private participation in financing, constructing and operating infrastructure projects. In a BOOT scheme, a private project company builds a project, operates it for a sufficient period of time to earn an adequate return on investment, and then transfers it to the host government or its agency. Quite often, the value of efficiency gain from private participation can outweigh the extra cost of borrowing through a BOOT project, relative to direct government borrowing.[1]

BOOT projects can be either solicited or unsolicited. When proposals are solicited, the project is identified and formulated by the government and the private sector is invited to submit offers for participation. Private companies or a group of companies can also submit unsolicited proposals on their own accord.

The private group usually consists of international construction contractors, heavy equipment suppliers, and plant and system operators along with local partners.

BOOT projects have been implemented or are in the process of being implemented in many developing countries. Power and roads are the two sectors with the largest number of projects. BOOT projects have also been implemented for ports and mass transit and rail. There have been only a few BOOT projects in the telecommunication sector in Thailand and Indonesia. According to a recent World Bank study, the reason why BOOT schemes have not been popular in the telecommunication sector is the potential complexity associated with co-ordinating the BOOT operator's distribution networks with those of the state-owned incumbent. Issues involving interconnections, sharing of ducts, maintenance procedures and trade-offs between maintenance and new investments, all must be resolved. These factors tend to increase risks for investors, make management co-ordination harder, and raise the questions for investors as to whether they will have adequate control over the facilities in which they have invested to achieve appropriate levels of productivity.[2]

The build-own-operate (BOO) arrangement The issue of "transfer" (the T in BOOT projects) is ambiguous because most of the BOOT projects under operation or consideration have the transfer dates quite far away and, therefore, they are not a real concern as yet. One problem with the transfer provision is the likelihood of the capital stock of the project being run down as the date of transfer draws nearer.

This may take place in spite of legal agreements, which includes inspection plans and other such measures. In any case, there does not seem to be any rationale for such a transfer if the very basis of the projects was to run it outside the public sector. One alternative to transfer that has been suggested is for the foreign shareholders to divest themselves of their equity either entirely or up to some negotiated percentage at the end of the

stipulated time period. Such an arrangement is generally referred to as the **build-operate-own** (**BOO**) arrangement.

In BOO arrangement, projects are funded without any direct sovereign guarantee. Thus, it implies limited recourse financing. Unlike in BOOT arrangements, in BOO structure, the project is not transferred to the host government, rather the owner will divest his stake and seek investments from investors in the capital markets. This facilitates the availability of finances. BOOT and BOO arrangements are essentially similar except that in BOO arrangement the sponsor preserves the ownership. Figure 22.4 shows the BOOT and BOO arrangements in a power project.

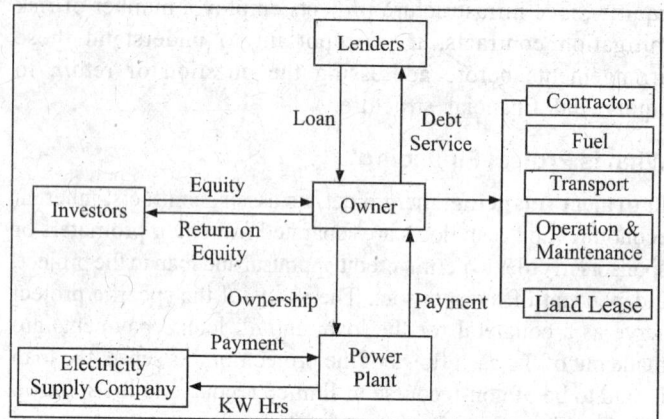

Figure 22.4: BOOT/BOO Structure of a Power Plant (Adapted from the World Bank, Industry & Energy Depeartment Occasional Paper, 1994)

The build-lease-transfer (BLT) arrangement In the **build-lease-transfer** (**BLT**) arrangement, the control of the project is transferred from the project owners (shareholders) to a lessee. The shareholders retain the full ownership of the project, but, for operation purposes, they lease it to a lessee. The host government agrees with the lessee to buy the output (for example, electricity in the case of a power project) or service of the project. The lessor (special purpose entity) receives the lease rental guaranteed by the host government. Figure 22.5 illustrates the BLT structure for a power project.

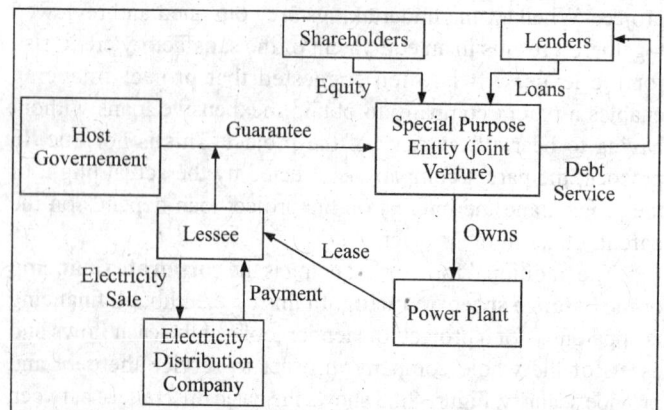

Figure 22.5: The Built-Lease-Transfer (BLT) Structure (*Source:* Adapted from Independent Energy, October 1994)

---

1. World Bank, *World Development Report*, 1994.
2. Smith, P.L. and Staple, G., *Telecommunication Sector Reform in Asia: Towards a New Pragmatism*, World Bank Discussion Paper No. 232, the World Bank, 1994.

Risks Allocation in Project Financing

From the perspective of potential investors, the main risks relate to project completion, market, foreign currency, and supply of inputs. The objective is to allocate these risks to those parties who are in the best position to control particular risk factors. This reduces the '*moral hazard*' problem and minimises the cost of bearing risks.

Project completion risk This is the major risk factor in most infrastructure projects. It is usually covered by a fixed price, firm date, turnkey construction contract with liquidated damages for delay supported by performance bonds. The contract specifies performance parameters and warranty periods for defects. Lenders require sponsors of the project company to provide a guarantee to fund cost overruns. In addition, a standby credit facility may also be employed.

Market risk Having long-term quantity and price agreements covers the **market risk**. In the case of power projects where the electricity is likely to be sold to a government controlled distribution company, this is achieved through a 'take or pay' power purchase agreement (PPA). Under this contract, certain payments have to be made irrespective of the actual off-take as long as the company makes available the capacity. The tariff is determined on a cost plus basis using standard costs. For power projects in India, the government has evolved a system of two part tariffs. The first part ensures recovery of fixed costs based on performance at normative parameters. Fixed costs include depreciation, operating and maintenance expenses, tax on income, interest on loans, and working capital and a return on equity. This part of the tariff is paid irrespective of the amount of power actually taken. The second part covers variable expenses based on the units of electricity actually supplied. Variable costs are the costs of primary and secondary fuel based on set norms for fuel consumption. Apart from the PPA, payments may be made to a trustee, usually an international bank, as additional security, in an escrow account which then directly makes payments to creditors and suppliers.

These arrangements effectively transfer the market risk to the power purchaser. In more sophisticated and privatised regulatory environments, independent power producers may take more market risk. For example, in a Chilean BOO power project, the company is developing the project without having a single-purchaser PPA. Instead, it has signed several long-term contracts with different private purchasers.[1]

In the case of transport projects, tolls have to be collected from the public and not from a government agency. This can give rise to problems while enforcing toll agreements. Competition from alternative roads or transit systems can also affect the traffic flow. Therefore, unlike power projects which have power purchase agreements, in transport projects, lenders cannot rely on a fixed revenue over the life of the project. Hence the project continues to carry market risk. This is sought to be mitigated by several other arrangements. If traffic flows are below

expectations, the project has recourse to such measures as an adjustment in the revenue sharing proportion; an increase in tolls on the system; and an extension of the concession periods. In many cases, there are automatic escalation clauses in the toll agreement to account for inflation.

Foreign exchange risk Foreign exchange risks are perhaps the single largest concern of foreign financiers investing in developing countries. In the case of infrastructure projects the risk is greater since most of these projects with the exception of some telecommunication and port projects, generate local currency revenues. The risk is at two levels:

- ***macro-economic convertibility,*** i.e., whether the project will have access to foreign exchange to cover debt service and equity payments; and

- ***tariff adjustment for currency depreciation,*** i.e., whether the foreign exchange equivalent of the project's local revenues will be adequate to service foreign debts and equity.

The risk of macro-economic convertibility will generally require a few government guarantees. In many BOOT projects, there is provision for tariff escalation to account for currency depreciation and protect returns to investors in foreign currency terms. For Indian power projects, the return on foreign equity included in the tariff can be provided in the respective foreign currency.

Supply of inputs This is important for power projects that require a reliable supply of quality fuel. The risk is covered through a contract with a fuel supply agency. The price risk is usually covered through a provision to pass on increases in the price of inputs through higher tariffs. Such an arrangement, i.e., transferring the risk of increases in fuel prices from the project to the power purchaser, may have an adverse impact on the incentives of the project sponsor to control price increases. As a corollary, it increases the responsibility of the power purchaser to monitor the increase in input prices.

Government Guarantees and Risk Mitigation

Most BOOT projects have guarantees by the government or government agencies in various forms. As pointed out by the *World Development Report,* 1994, government guarantees for infrastructure projects have historical precedents in India, like the setting up of the railways during the British rule. "In India, if a railway company did not attain a minimum rate of return of, for example, 5 per cent, the government made up the difference under the terms of a guarantee backed by its full power of taxation. ...But guarantees removed incentives for investors to monitor management performance while opening the way for promoters to negotiate the so called "sweetheart" deals with construction and supply companies. Because many infrastructure projects were one of a kind, the practice could be readily disguised."[2]

1. Bond, G. and Carter, L., *Financing Private Infrastructure Projects: Emerging Trends from IFC's* Experience, Discussion Paper No. 23, International Finance Corporation, 1994.
2. World Bank, *World Development Report,* 1994, p. 94.

Government guarantees relate to:

- country risk,
- sector policy risk, and
- commercial risk.

Country risk includes risks of currency transfer, expropriation, war and civil disturbances, and breach of contract by the host government. The Multilateral Investment Guarantee Agency (MIGA) of the World Bank provides guarantee against country risk for an appropriate premium. Export credit agencies also provide such guarantees but they usually seek counter-guarantees from the host government.

Sector risk refers to the risk in certain sectors because of the role of government agencies in those sectors. For example, in the power sector, the buyer is usually a government utility agency that transmits and distributes power. The solvency of the utility is critical for the 'take or pay' power purchase agreement to have any value. For selected power projects, the Indian government has agreed in principle to give counter guarantees to back up state government guarantees for the State Electricity Boards (SEBs), payment obligations to private generating companies, on a specific request to the state government concerned and subject to the state government agreeing to certain terms and conditions.

The Turkish government for its power projects and the Philippine government for the Metro Manila gas turbine project have offered similar guarantees. If fuel is supplied by a government agency, guarantees may be required that the agency will honour its commitments under its supply agreements with the project company.

For toll roads, government support may be necessary to enforce toll collections. Similarly, in the case of municipal services such as water supply and solid waste disposal, the support of municipal authorities is important. In each case, the government may guarantee contract compliance of the respective agencies.

Commercial risk refers to the risk to profitability arising from market demand and price; availability of inputs and prices; and variations in operating efficiency. These risks, except to the extent they are induced by country risk and sector policy risk, should ideally be borne by the investors. However, as noted in the *World Development Report*, 1994, "in such projects, the market risk or the risk arising from fluctuation in demand is effectively transferred to the government through the 'take or pay' formula. This becomes necessary because the market risk is intermingled with the danger that financially troubled power purchasers (transmission utilities) or water users may not honour their commitments. Overall sector reform is required to eliminate policy induced risk and thus reveal the market risk."[1]

Government guarantees are likely to be more important for transport projects where there are no assured revenues. For example, in the case of Second Tagus Crossing, Lisbon project,

the government is obliged to re-establish financial equilibrium of the project company in the event of *force majeure* and changes to construction or operating regime required by the government.[2] There is also a clear commitment from the government that financial equilibrium will be restored if it is unable to impose agreed tolls. This is significant in view of the recent disturbances on the bridge arising from the government attempts to impose higher tolls. In the case of Shah Alam Expressway, Malaysia, in case of a default by the concessionaire, the lenders will be repaid all outstanding amounts by the government.[3] In an IFC assisted Mexico toll road project, the government agency awarding the toll concession guaranteed a minimum level of traffic.[4] If this was not achieved, the concessionaire was allowed to extend the life of the concession.

Financial Structure of Infrastructure Projects

Infrastructure projects in developing countries usually have a financing pattern of 20–30 per cent equity and 70–80 per cent debt. One set of comprehensive information of the financial structure of infrastructure projects is provided by IFC's infrastructure approvals. Generally power projects have a higher debt-equity ratio of about 70:30 and telecommunication projects with low ratio of 50:50. According to the IFC, "this reflects the lower risk associated with power project markets which are usually contractually determined. The high equity share in telecom projects also reflects the significant part played by internal cash generation, particularly for expansion of existing main telephone operators—but also, to a lesser extent, for cellular projects".[5]

Debt The debt component is usually provided by commercial banks, international financial institutions, domestic financial institutions, and export credit agencies such as the Japan EXIM and US EXIM banks. Loans are on a limited recourse basis. Recourse will be limited to the project company and its assets including any insurance or government guarantee the project company has been able to obtain. The main problem with commercial bank lending is the limited number of banks world wide which provide project financing. Moreover, each bank has exposure limits to individual clients, sectors and countries so that in many cases loans have to be syndicated. Commercial banks are also not in a position to provide long maturity loans, e.g., over 10 years, usually required by infrastructure projects. Long-term international loans usually do not exceed 7–12 years. In response to this problem, a number of infrastructure funds have been established for equity participation in infrastructure projects in developing countries.

Bonds Share and bond issue, especially in the international capital markets, are rare. Enron, a US power producer, issued bonds through private placement in the US market under the US Securities and Exchange Commission Rule No. 144A for the

---

1. World Bank, *World Development Report,* 1994, p. 94
2. Schroders, *Transport Case Study,* presentation at the Seminar on Private Sector Investment in Infrastructure organised by SCICL India and ADB, Manila, August 1994.
3. *Ibid.*
4. Bond and Carter, *op. cit.*
5. International Finance Corporation.

Subic power station in the Philippines. Its plan for a similar issue for a Dabhol power project in India was later scrapped.

Equity The major portion of equity is provided by project sponsors. In the case of IFC approved projects, which by definition have some foreign financing, foreign sponsors played an important part especially in **Greenfield projects**. Of the 30 Greenfield projects approved during 1966–93, foreign sponsors had significant equity stakes in 22 of the companies. All of the cellular projects included a foreign partner, often holding a controlling stake, and virtually all of the BOOT/BOO projects involved foreign partners as either equity holders or as participants in Operation and Maintenance (O&M) agreement.

In many cases, the construction company and the equipment supplier also control the management and equity of the project company. This gives rise to the possibility of inflated project costs. In the case of the Shah Alam Expressway where the contractor is also a shareholder, an independent consulting engineer had been hired to ensure fairness between the contractor and concession company.[1]

The host government may also provide some equity. Among the projects with IFC involvement, only in four of the projects had there been a significant government stake.

Appropriate Return to Equity and Financial Structure in Infrastructure Project Financing

The appropriate return to equity and financial structures are both functions of the risk of cash flows from a project. Risk of cash flows are affected by various guarantees and risk mitigation arrangements and to this extent, appropriate return to equity and financial structures are also affected.

Return of equity It is important to distinguish between the accounting concept of return on equity (ROE) and the internal rate of return (IRR), which investors use to evaluate investments. ROE is given by profit after-tax (PAT) as a percentage of the average book value of equity for a specified period of time. ROE does not take into account the construction period and the timing of investor's cash flows. In contrast, IRR is based on all cash inflows and outflows over the entire life of the project. It is the rate of return, which makes the present value of inflows equal to the present value of outflows.

Risk measurement In standard finance theory, return to equity in any investment project should be commensurate with the risk of cash flows to equity. Cash flow to equity is PAT adjusted for depreciation, capital expenditure, and changes in current assets. Risk or uncertainty of equity cash flows will depend upon the uncertainty of revenues and the operating and financial leverage of the firm or project. *Operating leverage* is determined by the proportion of fixed and variable costs—the higher the proportion of fixed costs, the higher is the operating leverage. With higher operating leverage, a given uncertainty in revenue translates into a higher uncertainty in profits before interest and tax (PBIT). The proportion of debt in the financial structure determines financial leverage. Higher the financial leverage, higher is the uncertainty in PAT, and, therefore, in equity cash flows, given the uncertainty in PBIT.

In practice, the required return to equity is rarely estimated by directly analysing the uncertainty of revenues and the degree of operating leverage. Usually, it is measured by estimating the required or expected return to the equity of another existing firm or project with the same business risk. Since required return is measured from the perspective of the investor, what is relevant is the risk of equity of the investor. If the investor holds a portfolio of securities, then the relevant risk of a security is the risk that it contributes to that portfolio. This will be different from the risk of holding the security in isolation because of the benefits of diversification. Thus, a security with a high risk, if held in isolation, could have a low risk as a part of a portfolio if it has low correlation with other securities in the portfolio. Under a certain set of assumptions, the relevant risk of a security is the risk that it contributes to the market portfolio, i.e., the portfolio of all securities in the market held in proportion to their outstanding market value. This risk is measured by *beta* and is referred to as the *systematic* or *beta risk* as opposed to the *total risk* as measured by the standard deviation of returns. The expected or required return is then given by the Capital Asset Pricing Model (CAPM) as the sum of the risk free rate and a risk premium which is beta times the risk premium on the market portfolio. The resulting estimate can then be adjusted for the financial structure of a specific project.

In order to implement the above methodology, it is essential to find comparable firms whose equity trade in financial markets. This is possible for standard products or industries but is difficult to implement for infrastructure projects since comparable firms may not be available. Additionally, in most infrastructure projects, foreign investors provide a significant proportion of equity. In this case, the systematic risk should be measured with respect to the foreign investor's market portfolio rather than the domestic market portfolio of the country in which the infrastructure project is being implemented. This is especially relevant if capital markets are segmented and investment in infrastructure projects also provide an avenue for international diversification.

Impact of guarantees Equity risk measurement is further complicated by the impact of numerous guarantees. It is important to distinguish the role of guarantees in ensuring continuity of operations as opposed to ensuring shareholder returns. The fixed price, firm date, turnkey construction contract for ensuring project completion on time and within budget; price and quantity agreements including adjustment clauses for input prices, exchange rates etc.; and input supply agreements directly reduce the risk of cash flows to equity investors. Guarantees by the governments or export credit agencies for the repayment of principal and interest on debt enable the firm to raise loans at a cheaper rate and, therefore, are a form of subsidy to the firm. The value of the subsidy is the present value of the interest savings. These guarantees do not directly affect the risk to equity holders since they come into effect only if the project fails to generate enough cash flows to service the debt. However, if the guarantors, e.g., governments or international agencies, can influence cash flows through appropriate policies, the debt

---

1. Schroders, *op. cit.*

guarantees provide them with the incentive to take such actions in order to avoid making payments under the guarantees. This in turn can affect the risk of cash flows to equity holders.

Return expectations Information on equity investor's return expectations is limited. According to General Electric, for projects in the US, equity investors expect at least a 20 per cent IRR after taxes, on equity based on a 20-year contract.[1] At the time of project preparation, when there are greater uncertainties about project terms, investors look for higher rates to reflect the higher risks. On international projects, the IRR expectation is between 25–35 per cent. According to ABB in the US, at the time of financial close, i.e., before construction, a return of 20 per cent is acceptable. However, at the conceptual stage, i.e., when the project terms etc. have still to be finalised, the expected rate of return is higher at 25–30 per cent. Once the construction is over and the plant has cleared the performance tests, the investment is like a high risk bond and a return of 13–14 per cent is considered adequate. With changes in the risk return scenario in both the US and other countries, these rates cannot be directly transferred to projects currently under consideration in emerging markets.

Financial structure From a risk-return perspective, apart from the effect of taxes, the pattern of financing is irrelevant to the value of the firm and the value of equity. The risk and return of a project is determined by the pattern of cash flows, without taking into account, the financial structure. Financial structure merely determines the distribution of overall risk and return between the two classes of investors. In this framework, increasing debt in the capital structure increases risk and return to equity in such a way that the value of equity remains unchanged. Simultaneously, the risk and return to debt also increases to account for the increase in bankruptcy risk. However, changes in financial structure leave risk and return, and, therefore, value for the firm as a whole remains unchanged. An alternative interpretation is that the firm's cost of capital is not affected by its financial structure. Even if the debt is cheaper than equity, increasing the proportion of debt increases the risk and the cost of equity so that the overall cost of capital remains unchanged. From the perspective of the appropriate return to equity, the major implication is that as the debt-equity ratio increases, the risk, and, therefore, the appropriate return to equity also increases.

Taxes The above conclusion has to be modified for the effect of corporate and personal taxes. At the corporate level, while interest on debt is tax deductible, return to equity is not. This provides a tax shield benefit for debt financing. At the personal level, interest is taxed as income increases but the large portion of returns from equity in the form of capital gains can be deferred with lower effective taxes. Therefore, while corporate taxes favour debt, personal taxes favour equity. To the extent that income from infrastructure projects enjoy tax concessions or exemptions at the corporate level, the advantage to debt is reduced. For example, in the last Union Budget for India, a five-year tax holiday was allowed to any industrial undertaking engaged in the generation or generation and distribution of power; any enterprise which builds, maintains and operates any infrastructure

facility such as roads, highways or expressways or new bridges, airports, ports and rapid rail transport systems on BOT or BOOT or similar other basis (where there is an ultimate transfer of the facility to a government or public authority). Section 36(1)(viii) of the Income Tax Act has also been amended to extend the benefit of deduction up to 40 per cent of the income credited to a special reserve account to approved financial corporations providing long-term finance for development of infrastructure facilities in India.

Financial distress Financial structure also has implications for **financial distress**. Interest and principal repayments on debt have to be made as per the schedule but there is no fixed commitment for dividend payments. Therefore, a project with a lower level of debt has greater flexibility in managing its cash flows and capable of dealing with cash flow fluctuations without being pushed into a situation of financial distress. Costs of financial distress may not be an important consideration for infrastructure projects in the presence of guarantees covering debt servicing and repayments. Such debt guarantees may also reduce the overall risk of the project because of the involvement of various governments. Moreover, risk mitigation arrangements, e.g., power purchase and fuel supply arrangements, reduce the risk of project cash flows in the post development and construction phase. This raises the level of debt which the project can take on without significantly increasing the risk of financial distress.

Government restrictions Several governments have placed restrictions on the extent of debt financing in infrastructure projects. In India, a maximum debt-equity ratio of 4:1 is permissible. Pakistan also has a maximum of 4:1 debt-equity ratio. From the government's perspective, the rationale for these restrictions appears to be to limit the extent of external commercial borrowings for the country as a whole. An additional consideration may be to ensure minimum equity participation by the project sponsors.

Conclusion

Return to equity in infrastructure projects will be determined by the risk of specific projects, sectors and countries taking into account specific guarantees. In the case of power projects where most of the market risk is removed through power purchase agreements and foreign exchange guarantees (which in turn have sovereign guarantees of one form or another), the only remaining risk in country risk. Therefore, it would seem that the return to equity should not be much higher than the cost of debt in foreign currency not guaranteed for country risk. While this is true for the operating period, when the plant is up and running, the required return may be higher for development, construction and commissioning periods. The development period has the highest risk with the promoter running the risk of the project being aborted before financial close or the development period taking longer time and requiring more resources than was expected. The construction and commissioning periods are also periods of high risk with the investors taking the risk of cost overruns, delays, or plant commissioning deficiencies falling

1. World Bank, Private Sector Participation in Power through BOOT Schemes, Industry and Energy Department, Working Paper, *Energy Series Paper No. 33*, 1990.

outside the scope and penalties of the construction contract. The overall return to equity will be an average of the return to equity for various phases. One implication of this for governments is that they can work to reduce the risks of the development and construction phases by creating a suitable legal and regulatory environment, which reduces delays and uncertainties in finalising and implementing projects. This, in turn, will reduce the investors' risk and the required rates of return from such projects.

Similar considerations would apply in the case of transport projects except that there are no revenue guarantees in the form of power purchase agreements. However, in most cases, the government provides some kind of revenue support or other considerations, which effectively eliminate market risk.

Competitive bidding for infrastructure projects on the basis of final price for power or other infrastructure service eliminates the need to directly estimate the appropriate return to equity. Of course, competitive tendering requires a substantial amount of work on the part of the government agency in defining details of the project and other terms and conditions such as power purchase agreements, guarantees, etc. Only then would the various offers be comparable. Moreover, it assumes that there are a sufficient number of bidders interested in taking part. Bidding on the basis of final price will be preferable to bidding on the basis of return to equity because of the possibility of passing on some of the return to equity as operating costs or inflated equipment prices an showing a lower return to equity.

SUMMARY

- A lease is an agreement for the use of the asset for a specified rental. The owner of the asset is called the lessor and the user the lessee.

- Two important categories of leases are: operating leases and financial leases. Operating leases are short-term, cancellable leases where the risk of obsolescence is borne by the lessor. Financial leases are long-term non-cancellable leases where any risk in the use of the asset is borne by the lessee and he enjoys the returns too.

- The most compelling reason for leasing an equipment rather than buying it is the tax advantage of depreciation that can mutually benefit both the lessee and the lessor. Other advantages include convenience and flexibility as well as specialised services to the lessee.

- In India, lease proves handy to those firms, which cannot obtain loan capital from normal sources.

- Financial lease involves fixed obligations in the form of lease rentals. Thus it is like a debt and can be evaluated that way.

- Given the lease rentals and tax shields, one can find the amount of debt which these cash flows can service. This is equivalent loan. If equivalent loan is more than the cost of the asset, it is not worth leasing the equipment.

- You can also approach lease evaluation by calculating the net advantage of lease (NAL). After-tax lease rentals and tax shields may be discounted at the after-tax borrowing rate while operating costs and salvage value at the firm's cost of capital to find out NAL:

$$\text{NAL} = A_o - \sum_{t=1}^{n} \frac{(1-T)L_t + \text{TDEP}_t}{[1+i(1-T)]^t} + \frac{(1-T)\text{OC}_t}{(1+k)^t} - \frac{\text{ATSV}_n}{(1+k)^n}$$

- Under a hire purchase arrangement, like in a lease, the hire purchaser is able to avoid the payment for the purchase of the asset now, and instead pays hire purchase instalments (either monthly or quarterly or any other agreed period) over a specified period and time. The hire purchaser becomes the owner of the asset once he had paid all instalments. Unlike the leasee, he is entitled to claim depreciation as well as the salvage value of the acquired asset.

- Hire purchase arrangement differs from instalment sale arrangement in terms of the ownership. Under hire purchase, ownership passes to the hire purchaser on the payment of the last instalment, while under instalment sale ownership is transferred once the agreement has been made between the buyer and the seller.

- Project financing is yet another asset-based financing arrangement. It is the financing of a project as an independent economic unit, where the project itself forms a direct security, and its cash flows are used to service the debt or equity provided by the project sponsor. Project financing is the most common method of financing large infrastructure projects.

- A project finance may take the form of a simple loan, or may involve a more complex arrangement such as the build-own-operate-transfer (BOOT).

- In a BOOT arrangement, the project sponsor builds a project, operates it for a long period of time to earn a reasonable return, and then transfers it to the host government or its agency.

- Alternatively, in a build-own-operate (BOO) arrangement, the project is not transferred to the host government, rather the owner divests its stake in the capital markets. In a build-lease-transfer arrangement, the owner transfers the project to a lessee for operational purposes, but keeping ownership intact.

- Project financing involves considerable risk in the form of completion risk, market risk, foreign exchange risk, political risk etc. Therefore, generally the project sponsors seek guarantees from the host governments and use various risk mitigation arrangements. Usually, the risk will be distributed among owners, contractors, suppliers of inputs, customers, government etc.

KEY CONCEPTS

Back-ended lease	Cross-border lease	Full-payout lease	Operating leverage
Balance sheet financing	Dry lease	Hire purchase	Primary lease
Build-lease-transfer (BLT)	Equivalent loan	Instalment sale	Project financing
Build-own-operate (BOO)	Financial distress	Lease	Sale-and-lease-back
Build-own-operate-transfer	Financial lease	Leveraged lease	Secondary lease
(BOOT)	Financial leverage	Moral hazard	Up-fronted lease
Capital lease	Force majeure	Operating lease	Wet lease

ILLUSTRATIVE SOLVED PROBLEM

Problem 22.1: A company is considering the lease of an equipment which has a purchase price of Rs 350,000. The equipment has an estimated economic life of 5 years. As per the Income Tax Rule a written down depreciation at 25 per cent is allowed. The lease rentals per year are Rs 120,000. Assume that the company's marginal corporate tax rate is 50 per cent. If the before-tax borrowing rate for the company is 16 per cent, should the company lease the equipment? Ignore tax shield on depreciation after 5 years.

Solution: The table 22.14 shows the cash flow consequences of the lease and NAL (net advantage or present value of lease).
Notes:

1. Depreciation is calculated at 25 per cent (WDV) as follows:

Year	1	2	3	4	5
Dep.	87,500	65,625	49,219	36,914	27,685

2. Lost tax shield on depreciation is depreciation multiplied by tax rate.
3. Salvage value is assumed to be zero.

Table 22.14: Net Present Value of Lease

Year	0	1	2	3	4	5
Purchase price avoided	350,000					
Lost depreciation tax shield		−43,750	−32,813	−24,610	−18,457	−13,843
After-tax lease rentals		−60,000	−60,000	−60,000	−60,000	−60,000
Net cash flows	350,000	−103,750	−92,813	−84,610	−78,457	−73,843
PV at 8%	350,000	−96,073	−79,541	−67,180	−57,666	−50,287
NPV	−747					

The net present value of lease is negative. The company may like to purchase the equipment. The purchase option would still be better if the equipment has a salvage value at the end of its economic life.

REVIEW QUESTIONS

1. Define a lease. How does it differ from a hire purchase and instalment sale? What are the cash flow consequences of a lease? Illustrate.
2. What are the myths and advantages of a lease?
3. Explain and illustrate the equipment loan method of lease evaluation.
4. What is net advantage of a lease? How is it calculated?

5. What is the difference between equivalent loan and net advantage of lease methods of the lease evaluation?
6. "It makes sense for companies that pay no taxes to lease from companies that do." Explain.
7. What is a leveraged lease? What are its merits and demerits?
8. What is the hire purchase financing? How does it differ from the lease financing?

PROBLEMS

1. A company wants to lease a Rs 10 lakh equipment. The lessor requires eight annual end-of-the-year lease payments of Rs 1,75,000. The company's marginal tax rate is 35 per cent. If it buys the equipment, it can write-off the written-down cost of asset at 25 per cent. The company's borrowing rate is 15 per cent. Should the company lease the equipment? Use equivalent loan method to answer the question.
2. A cement manufacturer is considering to lease a drying equipment which is worth Rs 75 lakh. It will have to pay five annual beginning-of-the-year lease rentals of Rs 20 lakh. The tax rate is 35 per cent and the manufacturer can write-off the cost of equipment at 25 per cent written down

basis for 5 years. The manufacturer's effective borrowing rate is 16 per cent. Should the equipment be leased? Show that equivalent loan method and net advantage of lease method will lead to the same answer.
3. Readymade Garments Limited wants to lease a computer system for the purpose of colour matching. The system will cost Rs 30 lakh, and if bought can be depreciated over its life of 5 years. The annual rentals, payable at the end of year for 5 years, will be Rs 8.4 lakh. The applicable written-down depreciation rate is 25 per cent. The lessor will maintain the computer system at its cost which works out to be Rs 50,000 per year. At the end of its useful life, the system can

be sold for 50 per cent of its depreciated value. The company's borrowing rate is 14 per cent and tax rate is 35 per cent. Should the system be leased? Show your calculations.

4. A firm proposes to lease an asset of Rs 20 lakh. The annual, end of the year, lease rentals will be Rs 5 lakh for 5 years. The firm is not in a position to pay tax for next 5 years. The depreciation rate (WDV) is 25 per cent per annum. The lessor's marginal tax rate is 35 per cent. Calculate the net present value of lease to the lessee and the lessor. What are the break-even rentals to the lessee and the lessor? How can both benefit from the deal? Show your computations. Assume that the lessee's post-tax borrowing rate is 14 per cent.

5. You are planning to buy or lease an IBM notebook. It will cost you Rs 1,50,000. You can lease it for 8 years for Rs 2,500 per month payable in the beginning of the month. As per the tax rules, you can neither claim depreciation nor deduct interest on your personal borrowings from your income. Your friend is willing to lend you Rs 1,50,000 at 10 per cent per annum. Should you lease the notebook or borrow from your friend and buy it?

6. A company is considering whether it should buy or lease an equipment that costs Rs 80 lakh. A finance company has offered to lease the equipment for 5 years at annual lease payments Rs 20 lakh at the beginning of each year. The owner of the equipment can claim depreciation on written-down basis at 25 per cent each year. The company's (lessee's) tax rate is 35 per cent, and its cost of borrowing is 14 per cent, and the cost of capital is 16 per cent.

   (a) Should the company buy the asset or lease it?
   (b) What would your answer be if (a) we assume that the equipment has a salvage value of Rs 10 lakh at the end of its life, and that the lessor will maintain the equipment which would otherwise cost the lessee Rs 1 lakh each year? (b) Instead of lease the company goes for a hire purchase, how much maximum hire-purchase instalment should it be prepared to pay each year?

CASE

Case 22.1: Vishal Engineering Enterprises

Vishal Engineering Enterprises is a medium-sized engineering company. It had total assets of Rs 270 crore and sales of Rs 256 crore in 1998. The company has been growing at an annual rate of 23 per cent during the last five years, and the management expects to maintain this trend for the next couple of years. The growing operations of the company led the management to consider the possibility of acquiring a medium size, specially designed computer for its CAD/CAM functions. The management of the company therefore invited representatives of some leading computer firms to help them in designing a useful and cost-effective system. After an evaluation of various available alternatives, the company fixed up its mind on TECH 2005 computer supplied by a leading computer manufacturing company, which would best meet its current and expected future needs.

The finance department evaluated the profitability of buying TECH 2005 computer using its normal capital budgeting procedures. The company has a policy of using 12 per cent after-tax cut-off rate for modernisation, upgradation or automation projects. For higher risk projects, a higher cut-off rate is used. It was found that computer has a positive expected NPV.

The chief finance manager has been recently reading a lot about leasing and hire purchase business in India. The subsidiaries of a number of banks, private firms as well as manufacturers have been offering lease and hire purchase finance. He thought that there should be some merit in these options. He therefore decided to talk to the management of the computer manufacturing company if they could sell the computer on lease or hire purchase basis. He found that the manufacturer was ready to consider supplying the computer on lease or hire purchase.

The purchase price of the computer is Rs 75 lakh. It has an expected life of eight years. The company expects to receive a pre-tax benefit of Rs 18 lakh per year from the use of computer. The company's tax consultant had indicated that if the computer is purchased, the company can depreciate the computer on written down value basis at 25 per cent per annum. On the other hand, if the company decides to take the computer on lease, it will have to forego tax benefit on depreciation. The company will be required to pay lease rentals of Rs 14 lakh at the beginning of each year for eight years. If Vishal Engineering Enterprises buys the computer, it will be serviced and maintained by the computer company for no extra cost, but in the case of lease, Vishal Engineering Enterprises is expected to incur a maintenance cost of about Rs.1.75 lakh per annum.

The chief financial manager is not sure whether there would be any salvage value. However, he thought that if the technology does not change drastically, it may be sold for Rs 6 lakh. He knew that if the computer was taken on lease, he will have to forego the salvage value. He believed that the company's after-tax cost of borrowing estimated to be 9.5 per cent is the appropriate rate to use to evaluate the cash flows of leasing. The company's marginal tax rate is 35 per cent.

As regards the hire purchase option, the manufacturer quoted a hire purchase instalment of Rs.18.375 lakh per annum payable in the beginning of the year. He had calculated the annual instalment as shown in the table here.

	Rs in lakh
Cost of computer	75
Interest: 75 × 8 × 12%	72
	147
Annual instalment: 147/8	18.375

The finance manager was surprised to find a higher quotation for the hire purchase instalment than the lease rental. But he did realise that under hire purchase, his company will be entitled to claim tax benefit on depreciation and receive salvage value. Therefore, he thought it appropriate to systematically analyse the economics of both options.

Discussion Questions

1. Determine cash flows under the lease.
2. Why does the chief financial manager believe that the company's after-tax borrowing rate is the appropriate discount rate for evaluating the lease alternative? Should he use this rate to discount the depreciation also? Why should he use WACC for discounting the salvage value?
3. Is leasing the computer attractive for Vishal? What is the net advantage of lease to the company? How much equivalent loan could the company borrow given the lease cash flows?
4. What is the effective rate of interest on hire purchase? Is the hire purchase better option for the company? Show calculations. Assume that the sum-of-years-digit method is used for allocating interest over the hire purchase period for tax purposes.

23

Venture Capital Financing

Venture capital plays a strategic role in financing small-scale enterprises and high technology and risky ventures. The venture capital activity is quite advanced in the developed countries. It has also taken root in a number of developing countries. Venture capital has potential to become an important source for financing of small-scale enterprises (SSEs).[1] What is venture capital? How does it differ from the traditional financing? What are its potential benefits? What is the status of venture capital in India? We discuss these and other issues in the chapter.

NOTION OF VENTURE CAPITAL

Venture capital (VC) is a significant innovation of the twentieth century. It is generally considered as a synonym of **risky capital**. Venture capital finance is often thought of as "the early stage financing of new and young enterprises seeking to grow rapidly."[2] It usually implies an involvement by the venture capitalist in the management of the client enterprises. It has also come to be associated with the financing of high and new technology based enterprises. The conventional financiers generally support proven technologies with established markets. Venture capital focuses on high technology, but it is not a necessary condition for venture financing. According to Pratt:[3]

There is a popular misconception that high technology is the principal driving factor behind the investment decision of US venture capitalist. Only a small minority of venture capital investments are in new concepts of technology where potential technical problems add a significant amount of risk to the new business development.

There is, however, no doubt that young, high tech companies would look forward to the venture capitalists for making risky capital available to them. In broad terms, venture capital is the investment of long-term equity finance where the venture capitalist earns his return primarily in the form of capital gains. The underlying assumption is that the entrepreneur and the venture capitalist would act together in the interest of the enterprise as 'partners'. The true venture capital finances any risky idea. In fact, venture capital can prove to be a powerful mechanism to institutionalise innovative entrepreneurship. It is a commitment of capital for the formation and setting up of small-scale enterprises specialising in new ideas or new technologies. The venture capitalist focuses on growth; he would like to see small business growing into larger ones.

---

1. This chapter is based on I.M. Pandey, *Venture Capital and Entrepreneurial Development: The Indian Experience,* Working Paper No. 1032, Indian Institute of Management, Ahmedabad, June 1992.
2. Pratt, *Pratt's Guide on Venture Capital,* 1983, USA.
3. *Ibid.*

Features of Venture Capital

The main attributes of venture capital can be summarised as follows:[1]

- *Equity participation* Venture financing is actual or potential equity participation through direct purchase of shares, options or convertible securities. The objective is to make capital gains by selling-off the investment once the enterprise becomes profitable.

- *Long-term investment* Venture financing is a long-term illiquid investment; it is not repayable on demand. It requires long-term investment attitude that necessitates the venture capital firms (VCFs) to wait for a long period, say 5–10 years, to make large profits.

- *Participation in management* Venture financing ensures continuing participation of the venture capitalist in the management of the entrepreneur's business. This hands-on management approach helps him to protect and enhance his investment by actively involving and supporting the entrepreneur. More than finance, venture capitalist gives his marketing, technology, planning and management skills to the new firm.

The venture capitalist's management approach differs significantly from that of a conventional banker or a lender. The banker does not directly get involved in the operation and management of the company. He plays safe, keeps off management, remains passive and insists on security (collateral). Of course, when the banker's stake is very high, he may get his nominee appointed on the board of the company to safeguard his interests. The venture capitalist is also not exactly like the stock market investor who merely trades in the shares of a company without any relations with or knowledge of its management. In fact, venture capitalist combines the qualities of banker, stock market investor and entrepreneur in one.

In India, the Securities and Exchange Board of India (SEBI) guidelines govern the operations of venture capital funds (VCFs). **Venture capital fund** may be structured as a company or trust to raise finances through loans, donations, issue of securities or units, and to make investments in new ventures in accordance with the SEBI regulations.

Stages in Venture Financing

Historically venture capital evolved as a method of early-stage financing, but the notion of venture capital recognises different stages of financing. It also includes development, expansion and buyout financing for those enterprises which are unable to raise funds from the normal financing channels. VCFs also provide turnaround finance to revitalise and revive sick enterprises (Table 23.1).[2]

The focus of venture capital in India is on providing seed capital and financing for high technology. In fact, the venture capital mechanism in India should be used for fostering the growth and development of enterprise, and need not be confined only to technology financing. Business enterprises in various sectors need venture capital for financing various stages of development. This broad approach would even help the venture capital firms to diversify their investment across various enterprises—some high tech, some low tech, and thus spread their risks. It does not make a business sense to expect venture capital firms to invest in high tech, high-risk start-ups only.

Table 23.1: Stages in Venture Financing

1. Early stage financing	• Seed financing for supporting a concept or idea • R&D financing for product development • Start-up capital for initial production and marketing • First stage financing for full-scale production and marketing
2. Expansion financing	• Second stage financing for working capital and initial expansion • Development financing for facilitating public issue • Bridge financing for facilitating public issue
3. Acquisition/buyout financing growth	• Acquisition financing for acquiring another firm for further growth • Management buyout financing for enabling operating group to acquire firm or part of its business • Turnaround financing for turning around a sick unit

THE BUSINESS PLAN[3]

The first step for a company (or an entrepreneur) proposing a new venture in obtaining venture capital is to prepare a business plan for the consideration of a venture capitalist. A venture capitalist receives hundreds of business plans every year. The business plan must therefore convince the venture capitalist that the company (entrepreneur) and the management team have the ability to achieve the stated goals within the specified time.

The business plan should explain the nature of the proposed venture's business, what it wants to achieve and how it is going to do it. The venture's management should prepare the plan setting challenging but achievable goals.

The length of the business plan depends on the particular circumstances but, as a general rule, it should not be very long (not longer than 10 pages). It should use simple language and technical details should be explained without jargons.

Essential Elements of a Business plan

1. *Executive summary* This is the most important aspect of a business plan and it is often best written last. It summarises the business plan and is placed at the front of the document.

1. Lorenz, T., *Venture Capital Today,* Woodhead-Faulkner, Cambridge, 1985.
2. Pratt, *op. cit.*
3. This section is adopted, with suitable modifications, from IVCA, www.ivca.com. The author is thankful to Mr. Saurabh Srivastava, President, IVCA for granting the permission.

It is vital to give this summary significant thought and time, as it may well determine the amount of consideration the venture capital investor will give to the detailed proposal. It should be clearly written and powerfully persuasive, yet balance "sales talk" with realism in order to be convincing. It should be limited to no more than two pages and include the key elements of the business plan.

2. *Background on the venture* The business plan should provide a summary of the fundamental nature of the proposed venture and its activities, and an outline of its objectives. If an existing company proposes the venture, a brief history of the company should be included.

3. *The product or service* The plan should explain the venture's product or service in plain English. This is especially important if the product or service is technically orientated. A non-specialist must be able to understand the plan. The plan should emphasise the product's, or service's competitive edge or unique selling point. It should describe the stage of development of the product or service (seed, early stage, expansion). It should explain, wherever applicable, the legal protection such as patents obtained, pending or required, that the proposer of the business plan has on the product, and should provide an assessment of the impact of legal protection on the marketability of the product.

4. *Market analysis* The plan should convince the venture capital firm that there is a real commercial opportunity for the business and its products and services. It should offer the reader a combination of clear description and analysis, including a realistic "SWOT" (strengths, weaknesses, opportunities and threats) analysis. It should define the market for the product/service and explain in what industry sector the venture will operate. What is the size of the whole market? What are the prospects for this market? How developed is the market as a whole, i.e., developing, growing, mature, declining? How does the company fit within this market? Who are the competitors? For what proportion of the market do they account for? What is their strategic positioning? What are their strengths and weaknesses? What are the barriers to new entrants? The plan should also describe the distribution channels. Who are customers for the proposed product/service? The plan should comment on the price sensitivity of the market. In the case of the existing company, the plan should explain the historic problems faced by the business and its products or services in the market. Have these problems been overcome, and if so, how? The plan should address to the current issues, concerns and risks affecting the business and the industry in which it operates. What are the projections for the company and the market? The plan should assess future potential problems and how they will be tackled, minimized or avoided.

5. *Marketing* Having defined the relevant market and its opportunities, it is necessary to address how the prospective business will exploit these opportunities. The plan should outline the company's sales and distribution strategy. What is the company's planned sales force? What are its strategies for different markets? What distribution channels is the company planning to use and how do these compare with the competitors'? The plan should identify overseas market access issues and how these will be resolved. What is the company's pricing strategy? How does this compare with the competitors'? What are the company's advertising, public relations and promotion plans?

6. *Business operations* The plan should explain how the business operates. It should explain how the company makes the products or provide the service, first in brief and then in more detail. What are the sources of raw materials? Who are the suppliers? What are the labour requirements? What is the company's approach to industrial relations? The plan should outline the company's approach to research and development.

7. *The management team* The plan should demonstrate that the company has the quality of management to be able to turn the business plan into reality. The senior management team ideally should be experienced in complementary areas, such as management strategy, finance and marketing, and their roles should be specified. The special abilities each member brings to the venture should be explained. A concise curriculum vita should be included for each team member, highlighting the individual's previous track record in running, or being involved with, successful businesses. The plan should identify the current and potential skills gaps and explain the method to fill them. Venture capital firms will sometimes assist in locating experienced managers where an important post is unfilled, provided they are convinced about the other aspects of the plan. The plan should explain controls, performance measures and remuneration for management, employees and others. The plan should list auditors and other advisers and include organization chart.

8. *Financial projections* The proposer should consider using an external accountant to verify and act as "devil's advocate" for this part of the plan. The plan should realistically assess sales, costs (fixed and variable), cash flow and working capital. It should produce a proforma profit and loss statement and balance sheet and ensure that these are easy to update and adjust. It should assess the company's present and prospective future margins in detail, bearing in mind the potential impact of competition and explain the research undertaken to support these assumptions. The plan should demonstrate the company's growth prospects over, for example, a three to five year period. What is the value attributed to the company's net tangible assets? What is the level of gearing (i.e., debt to shareholders' funds ratio)? How much debt is secured on what assets and what is the current value of those assets? What are the costs associated with the business? The plan should split sales costs (e.g., communications to potential and current customers) and marketing costs (e.g., research into potential sales areas). What are the sale prices or fee charging structures? What are the budgets for each area of the company's activities? What is the proposer doing to ensure that he/she and his/her management team keeps within these or improve on these budgets? The plan should

present different scenarios for the financial projections of sales, costs and cash flow for the short and long term. It should ask "what if?" questions to ensure that key factors and their impact on the financings required are carefully and realistically assessed. For example, what if sales decline by 20 per cent, or supplier costs increase by 30 per cent, or both? How does this affect the profit and cash flow projections? The plan should be feasible and not overly optimistic. It should highlight challenges and show how they will be met. Relevant historical financial performance should also be presented. The company's historical achievements can help give meaning, context and credibility to future projections.

9   *Amount and use of finance required and exit opportunities* The business plan should state how much finance is required by the business and from what sources (i.e., management, venture capital, banks and others) and explain the purpose for which it will be applied. It should outline the capital structure and ownership before and after financing. It should also consider how the venture capital investors will exit the investment and make a return. Possible exit strategies for the investors may include floating the company on a stock exchange or selling the company to a trade buyer.

What does a Venture Capitalist Look for in a Venture?[1]

Venture capitalists are high-risk investors and, in accepting these risks, they desire a higher return on their investment. The venture capitalist manages the **risk-return ratio** by only investing in businesses that fit their investment criteria and after having completed extensive **due diligence**.

Venture capitalists have differing operating approaches. These differences may relate to the location of the business, the size of the investment, the stage of the company, industry specialization, structure of the investment and involvement of the venture capitalists in the company's activities. The entrepreneur should not be discouraged if one venture capitalist does not wish to proceed with an investment in the company. The rejection may not be a reflection of the quality of the business, but rather a matter of the business not fitting with the venture capitalist's particular investment criteria.

Venture capital is not suitable for all businesses, as a venture capitalist typically seeks:

- *Superior businesses* Venture capitalists look for companies with superior products or services targeted at fast-growing or untapped markets with a defensible strategic position. Alternatively, for **leveraged management buyouts**, they are seeking companies with high borrowing capacity, stability of earnings and an ability to generate surplus cash to quickly repay debt.
- *Quality and depth of management* Venture capitalists must be confident that the firm has the quality and depth in the management team to achieve its aspirations. Venture capitalists seldom seek managerial control; rather, they want

to add value to the investment where they have particular skills including fundraising, mergers and acquisitions, international marketing and networks.

- *Corporate governance and structure* In many ways the introduction of a venture capitalist is preparatory to a public listing. The venture capitalist will want to ensure that the investee company has the willingness to adopt modern corporate governance standards, such as non-executive directors, including a representative of the venture capitalist. Venture capitalists are put off by complex corporate structures without a clear ownership and where personal and business assets are merged.
- *Appropriate investment structure* As well as the requirement of being an attractive business opportunity, the venture capitalist will also be seeking to structure a satisfactory deal to produce the anticipated financial returns to investors.
- *Exit plan* Lastly, venture capitalists look for clear exit routes for their investment such as public listing or a third-party acquisition of the investee company.

THE PROCESS OF VENTURE CAPITAL FINANCING

The venture capital activity is a sequential process involving the following six steps:[2]

- Deal origination
- Screening
- Evaluation (due diligence)
- Deal structuring
- Post-investment activity
- Exist plan

Deal Origination

A continuous flow of deal is essential for the venture capital business. Deals may originate in various ways: (*i*) referral system, (*ii*) active search and (*iii*) intermediaries. Referral system is an important source of deals. Deals may be referred to VCFs by their parent organisations, trade partners, industry associations, friends etc. Yet another important source of deal flow is the active search through networks, trade fairs, conferences, seminars, foreign visits etc. A third source, used by venture capitalists in developed countries like USA, is certain intermediaries who match VCFs and the potential entrepreneurs.

Screening

Venture capital is a service industry, and VCFs generally operate with a small staff. In order to save on time and to select the best ventures, before going for an in-dept analysis, VCFs carry out initial screening of all projects on the basis of some broad criteria. For example, the screening process may limit projects to areas in which the venture capitalist is familiar in terms of technology, or product, or market scope. The size of investment, geographical location and stage of financing could also be used as the broad screening criteria.

---

1. This section is adopted, with suitable modifications, from IVCA, www.ivca.com. The author is thankful to Mr. Saurabh Srivastava, President, IVCA for granting the permission.

2. Tyebjee, T.T. and Bruno, A.A., A Model for Venture Capital Investment Activity, *Management Science*, 30, 1981, pp. 1051–66.

Due Diligence

Once a proposal has passed through initial screening, it is subjected to a detailed evaluation or **due diligence** process. Most ventures are new and the entrepreneurs may lack operating experience. Hence, a sophisticated, formal evaluation is neither possible nor desirable. The venture capitalists, thus, may rely on a subjective, but comprehensive, evaluation. They evaluate the quality of entrepreneur before appraising the characteristics of the product, market or technology. Most venture capitalists ask for a *business plan* to make an assessment of the possible risk and return on the venture. Business plan contains detailed information about the proposed venture.

The evaluation of ventures by VCFs in India includes the following steps:

- *Preliminary evaluation* The applicant is required to provide a brief profile of the proposed venture to establish prima facie eligibility. Promoters are also encouraged to have a face-to-face discussion to clarify issues.
- *Detailed evaluation* Once the project has crossed the qualifying hurdle through initial evaluation, the proposal is evaluated in greater detail. A lot of stress is placed on techno-economic evaluation. Most of the VCFs involve experts for the technical appraisal, whenever necessary.

The venture evaluation in India, after receipt of the business plan, starts with a detailed evaluation of the entrepreneur's background. VCFs in India expect the entrepreneur to have:

- integrity
- long-term vision
- urge to grow
- managerial skills
- commercial orientation.

They also focus on the entrepreneur's technical abilities, entrepreneurial skills, manufacturing and marketing capabilities and experience. After ascertaining the commitment of the entrepreneur, the project itself is evaluated in terms of its technological, manufacturing and marketing viability.

Risk analysis VCFs in India also make a through analysis of the risk of the proposed venture.[1] They generally analyse product, market, technology and entrepreneurial risks of the venture before they decide to finance it:

- *Product risk* In the case of new or untried ideas, there is a risk whether the product can be produced and commercialised. Technically sound products may fail on commercial basis.
- *Market risk* Market risk may result from several factors such as unexpected competition, problems of marketing channels, non-acceptance by customers, quality, price, etc.
- *Technological risk* Technological risk arises when technology is too complex to implement. It may be an imported technology, and there may be problems of assimilation and management.
- *Entrepreneurial risk* Entrepreneurial risk could arise when the entrepreneur lacks managerial capabilities, and/or when

he is too optimistic or too pessimistic. Young, innovative entrepreneurs may have bright ideas, but due to lack of experience, may fail to implement their ideas successfully.

VCFs take final decision with regard to financing new ventures in terms of the expected risk-return trade-off as shown in Figure 23.1.

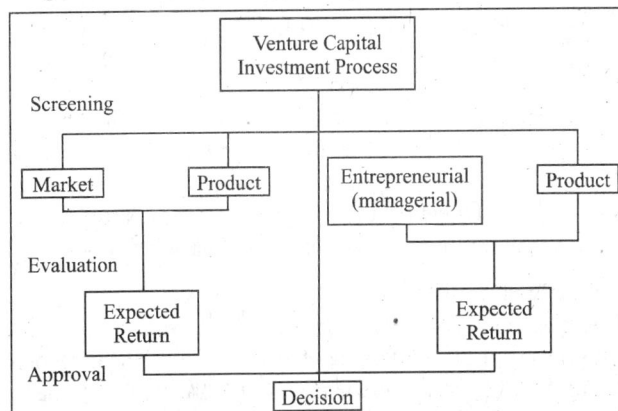

Figure 23.1: Venture Capital Investment Process [Adapted from Tyebjee & Bruno (1984)]

Deal Structuring

Once the venture has been evaluated as viable, the venture capitalist and the venture company negotiate the terms of the deal, viz., the amount, form and price of the investment. This process is termed as **deal structuring**. The agreement also includes the protective covenants and **earn-out arrangements**. Covenants include the venture capitalist's right to control the venture company and to change its management if needed, buyback arrangements, acquisition, making initial public offerings (IPOs), etc. Earned-out arrangements specify the entrepreneur's equity share and the objectives to be achieved.

Venture capitalists generally negotiate deals to ensure protection of their interests. They would like a deal to provide for a return commensurate with the risk, influence over the firm through board membership, minimum taxes, investment liquidity, right to replace management in case of consistent poor managerial performance, etc.

The venture companies like deal to be structured in such a way that their interests are protected. They would like to earn reasonable return, minimise taxes, have enough liquidity to operate their businesses and remain in commanding position of their business.

There are number of common concerns shared by both the venture capitalists and the venture companies. They should be flexible, and have a structure that protects their interests and provides enough incentives to both to co-operate with each other.

Post-investment Activities

Once the deal has been structured and agreement finalised, the venture capitalist generally assumes the role of a partner and collaborator. He also gets involved in shaping the direction of

---

1. Pandey, I.M., Venture Capital Development Process in India, *Technovation,* Vol. 18, No. 4, 1998.

the venture. This may be done via a formal representation on the board of directors, or informal influence in improving the quality of marketing, finance and other managerial functions. The degree of the venture capitalist's involvement depends on his policy. It may not, however, be desirable for a venture capitalist to get involved in the day-to-day operations of the venture. If a financial or managerial crisis occurs, the venture capitalist may intervene, and even install a new management team.

Exit Plan

Venture capitalists typically aim at making medium to long-term capital gains. They generally want to cash-out their gains in five to ten years after the initial investment. They play a positive role in directing the company towards particular exit routes. A venture may exit in one of the following ways:

1. Initial public offerings (IPOs)
2. Acquisition by another company
3. Purchase of the venture capitalist's share by the promoter
4. Purchase of the venture capitalist's share by an outsider.

The secondary, over-the-counter (OTC), market which specialises in the trading of shares of small companies plays a critical role in exit through IPOs and acquisitions. More details about the divestment mechanism follow in a later section.

METHODS OF VENTURE FINANCING

A pre-requisite for the development of an active venture capital industry is the availability of a variety of financial instruments which cater to the different risk-return needs of investors. They should be acceptable to entrepreneurs as well. In developed countries, innovation of financial instruments is a distinct feature of venture capital.

Venture finance, conceptually being risk finance, should be available in the form of equity or **quasi-equity** (conditional or convertible loans). A straight or conventional loan, involving fixed payments, would be unsuitable form of providing assistance to a new, risky venture. New ventures have the problem of cash flows in the initial years of their development; hence they are not able to service debt. However, the requirement for this kind of assistance could still arise in a few cases, particularly during the second stage of financing after the venture has taken off. Venture capital financing in India in the past took three forms: equity, conditional loans and income notes. Conventional loan has also been a quite popular source of funds made available by VCFs in India in the past.

Equity

All VCFs in India provide equity. Generally, their contribution may not exceed 49 per cent of the total equity capital. Thus, the effective control and majority ownership of the firm may remain with the entrepreneur. When a venture capitalist contributes equity capital, he acquires the status of an owner, and becomes entitled to a share in the firm's profits as much as he is liable for losses. VCFs buy shares of an enterprise with an intention to ultimately sell them off to make capital gains. The advantage of the equity financing for the company seeking venture finance is that it does not have the burden of serving the capital, as

dividends will not be paid if the company has no cash flows. The advantage to the VCF is that it can share in the high value of the venture and make capital gains if the venture succeeds. But the flip side is that the VCF will lose if the venture is unsuccessful. Venture financing is a risky business.

Conditional Loan

A **conditional loan** is repayable in the form of a royalty after the venture is able to generate sales. No interest is paid on such loans. In India, VCFs charged royalty ranging between 2 and 15 per cent; actual rate depended on other factors of the venture such as gestation period, cost-flow patterns, risk and other factors of the enterprise. Some VCFs gave a choice to the enterprise of paying a high rate of interest (which could be well above 20 per cent) instead of royalty on sales once it becomes commercially sound. Some funds recovered only half of the loan if the venture failed.

Income Note

A unique way of venture financing in India was **income note**. It was a hybrid security which combined the features of both conventional loan and conditional loan. The entrepreneur had to pay both interest and royalty on sales, but at substantially low rates. Some venture funds provided funding equal to about 80 per cent of a project's cost for commercial application of indigenous technology or adapting imported technology to wider domestic applications. Funds were made available in the form of unsecured loans at a lower rate of interest during development phase and at a higher rate after development. In addition to interest charges, royalty on sales could also be charged.

Other Financing Methods

A few venture capitalists, particularly in the private sector, introduced innovative financial securities. The '**participating debenture**' is an example of innovative venture financial. Such security carries charges in three phases: In the start-up phase, before the venture attains operations to a minimum level, no interest is charged. After this, a low rate of interest is charged up to a particular level of operation. Once the venture starts operating on full commercial basis, a high rate of interest is required to be paid. A variation could be in terms of paying a certain share of the post-tax profits instead of royalty.

VCFs in India provide venture finance through **partially** or **fully convertible debentures** and **cumulative convertible preference shares** (CPP). CPP could be particularly attractive in the Indian context since CPP shareholders do not have a right to vote. They are, however, entitled to voting if they do not receive dividend consecutively for two years. Both convertible debenture and convertible preference share require an active secondary market to be attractive securities from the investors' point of view.

In the Indian context, both VCFs and entrepreneurs earlier favoured a financial package which has a higher component of loan. This was so because of the promoter's fear of loss of ownership and control to the financier and because of the traditional reluctance and conservatism of financier to share in the risk inherent in the use of equity. The venture financing mechanisms like conditional loan and income notes are quite expensive as compared to conventional loans once a project becomes successful. They involve substantial cash outflows from the entrepreneurs' point of view. What he needs is a financing method that does not burden him with cash flow problems.

In developed countries, like the USA and the UK, the venture capital firms are accustomed to using a wide range of financial instruments. They include:

1. **Deferred shares** where ordinary share rights are deferred for a certain number of years.
2. **Convertible loan stock** which is unsecured long-term loan convertible into ordinary shares and subordinated to all creditors.
3. **Special ordinary shares** with voting rights but without a commitment towards dividends.
4. **Preferred ordinary shares** with voting rights and a modest fixed dividend right and a right to share in profits.

Venture capital funds abroad also provide conventional loans, hire-purchase finance, lease finance and even overdraft finance, but the overall financial package is always tilted in favour of equity component.

DISINVESTMENTS MECHANISMS

The objective of a true venture capitalist is to sell off his investment at substantial capital gains. But most venture funds in India aim to operate on commercial lines along with satisfying their developmental objectives. Public sector venture funds invariably have some developmental objectives as well and they would also like to disinvest their holdings at adequate return with a view to recycle funds. A venture capital is generally not in a position to realise his investment before five to seven years.

What are the disinvestments options available to Indian venture funds? As discussed earlier, the disinvestments options generally available to venture capitalists in developed countries are the promoter's buyback, public issue, sale to other VCFs, sale in the over-the-counter (OTC) stock market, management buyouts etc. Some of these are feasible options in India. In USA, the venture capital industry, since its inception, had access to well-developed, efficiently functioning capital markets, and later on, to well-developed OTC stock market. The stock markets and OTC markets in a number of European countries and a few developing countries including India are recent phenomena. So far, they have been using other avenues for disinvestments. These avenues, although help to produce significant profits to investors, yet they are considered second best in comparison to the stock market disinvestments. In India, the OTC stock exchange has been in operation for quite some time but it has not been very successful.

Buyback by Promoters

The most popular disinvestments route in India is shares buyback by promoters. This route is suited to the Indian condition because it keeps the ownership and control of the promoter intact. The obvious limitation, however, is that in a majority of cases the market value of the shares of the venture firm would have appreciated so much after some years that the promoter would not be in a financial position to buy them back. In India, the promoters are invariably given the first option to buyback equity

of their enterprises. If the promoter fails to buyback the shares within the stipulated period, the VCF reserves the discretion to divest them in any manner deemed appropriate. VCFs generally make disinvestments, in consultation with the promoter, usually after the project has settled down to a profitable level and the entrepreneur was in a position to avail of finance under conventional schemes of assistance from banks or other financial institutions.

Initial Public Offerings (IPOs)

The benefits of disinvestments via **initial public offerings** (IPOs) route are improved marketability and liquidity, better prospects for capital gains and widely known status of the venture as well as market control through public share participation. This option has certain limitations in the Indian context. The promotion of the public issues would be difficult and expensive since the first generation entrepreneurs are not known in the capital markets. Further, difficulties will be caused if the entrepreneur's business is perceived to be unattractive investment proposition by investors. Also, the emphasis by the Indian investors on short-term profits and dividends may tend to make market price unattractive. Yet another difficulty in India until recently was that the Controller of Capital Issues (CCI) guidelines for determining premium on shares took into account the book value and the cumulative average EPS till the date of the new issue. This formula failed to give due weightage to the expected stream of earnings of the venture firm. Thus the formula would underestimate the premium. The Government has now abolished the Capital Issues Control Act, 1947 and consequently, the office of the Controller of Capital Issues.[1] The existing companies are now free to fix the share prices. The public issue form of investment can involve high transaction costs because of the inefficiency of the secondary market in a country like India. Also, this option has been rendered far less feasible for small ventures on account of the higher listing requirement of the stock exchanges.

Secondary Stock Market

An active secondary capital market provides the necessary impetus to the success of venture capital. VCFs should be able to sell their holdings, and investors should be able to trade shares conveniently and freely. In USA, there exists a well-developed OTC market where dealers trade in shares on telephone/terminal. Such mechanism enables new, small companies to enlist on the OTC markets which are not otherwise eligible to be listed on the stock exchanges, and provides liquidity to investors. The National Association of Securities Dealers Automated Quotation System (NASDAQ) in USA daily quotes over 8,000 stock prices of companies backed by venture capital.

The OTC Exchange in India (OTCEI) was established in June 1992. It opened a new avenue for disinvestments for small and medium size companies.

Management Buyouts

The promoter of a new venture, which has taken off, may sell it to its managers. The managers will generally raise venture capital to buyout the venture. This transaction is called management buyouts. When the buyers (managers or outsiders) incur heavy debt to buy the venture, the deal is called **leveraged buyout**. Management buyouts will take place in the case of those ventures which have high growth potential. Managers are very familiar with the venture, therefore, they can make a good assessment of its prospects. After acquiring the venture, if they are able to convert the high growth of the business in high profitability and value, they could make substantial gains. But there is high risk as the potential growth may not be realised later on. Management buyouts are not very popular in India yet.

DEVELOPMENT OF VENTURE CAPITAL IN INDIA

The venture capital industry in India is about two decades old. But it is still not in a developed stage, and requires promotional efforts as well as policy initiatives for a fast growth. The concept of venture capital was formally introduced in India in 1987 when the government announced the creation of a venture fund to be operated by the Industrial Development Bank of India (IDBI). The government levied a 5 per cent cess on all know-how import payments to create the venture fund. The Industrial Credit and Investment Corporation of India (ICICI)[1] also started venture capital activity in the same year. Later on, ICICI floated a separate venture capital company - Technology Development and Information Corporation (TDICI).

VCFs in India can be categorised into the following four groups:[2]

1. VCFs promoted by the central (federal) government-controlled development finance institutions such as Risk Capital and Technology Finance Corporation Limited (RCTFC) by the Industrial Finance Corporation of India (IFCI) and Risk Capital Fund by IDBI.
2. VCFs promoted by the state government-controlled developmental finance institutions such as Gujarat Venture Finance Company Limited (GVCFL) by Gujarat Industrial Investment Corporation (GIIC) and Andhra Pradesh Venture Capital Limited (APVCL) by Andhra Pradesh State Finance Corporation (APSFC).
3. VCFs promoted by the public sector banks such as Canfina by Canara Bank and SBI-Cap by State Bank of India.
4. VCFs promoted by the foreign banks and private sector companies and financial institutions such as Indus Venture Fund, Credit Capital Venture Fund and Grindlay's India Development Fund.

There has been a steady increase in the numbers of projects (ventures) as well as in the amount invested by VCFs. The VCFs' average investment in each venture has also increased over the years. This steady increase reflects the general trend in the venture capital industry in the country, with investors (VCFs) focusing on high tech, small-and medium-sized ventures. The total venture capital funds available for investment have also increased. In the early years of the venture capital in India, the bulk of the funding for VCFs came from the central (federal) government-controlled financial institutions. Other investors included the multilateral development agencies, such as the World Bank; the private sector; non-resident Indians and the nationalised banks. Further, there are state government-controlled financial institutions, foreign institutional investors, the public sector, insurance companies, mutual funds, other banks and even members of the public that also contribute to the capital pool of VCFs.

The total venture investment in 2003 was estimated to be equal to US$ 800 million, which is likely to increase to US$ 1 billion in 2004. India has number three position in 2003 in the world in terms the level of investment. As regards the investment by the stages of business development, very little investment goes into the start-up stage ventures. Almost half of the venture capital investment in India is in the IT sector.[3]

Banks and financial institutions that have wide experience in lending promoted most of the venture capital funds in India in the initial stage. In spite of this, their risk taking behaviour varies from each other. Risk taking behaviour of VCFs may be influenced by the size of the fund and the nature of venture capital organisation. It is expected that funds promoted by the financial institutions and nationalised banks are likely to take more risks because of their missions of development and social responsibility. Private funds are likely to emphasise commercial operations and profit. Thus, they may follow a prudently cautious approach towards risk-taking. As regards private venture funds, many entrepreneurs feel that their enterprises may be acquired once they become successful. Besides, they are also apprehensive of the representation of the venture capital firms' personnel on their boards of directors, leading to close supervision and control of their operations.

VCFs in India provide different services such as managerial consultancy, technical support and information, equity participation, etc. Some of them, particularly those associated with the central or state-level financial institutions and nationalised banks, assist the entrepreneurs in obtaining terms loans and working capital. This gives them an edge over new entrants in private sector. The support provided by VCFs in India, in varying degree, include preparation of a business and financial plan, formulation of marketing plan and strategy, technical advice, assistance in resource identification, recruitment, organisation structuring etc.

For obtaining venture capital, entrepreneurs are required to submit business plans. Also, VCFs do not finance all businesses; they look for certain factors in the proposed ventures before they consider them for venture capital financing.

FISCAL INCENTIVES

Fiscal incentives have been found to play a central role in the growth of venture capital in the developed countries. For example, in USA the reduction of the capital gains tax rate from 49 per cent to 28 per cent and later on to 20 per cent gave an

---

1. ICICI after several structural changes is now a fully private sector company known as ICICI Bank.
2. Pandey, I.M., Venture Capital Development Process in India, *Technovation,* Vol. 18, No. 4, 1998.
3. *The Economic Times*, 13 December 2003, p. 3.

unprecedented boost to the development of venture capital. Tax incentives could be provided to the venture capital companies, new and small businesses, or investors investing in equity shares. VCFs need preferential tax treatment for the fast development of venture capital in developing countries like India. There is need to give tax incentives both to the institutions and individuals investing in venture capital firms. This would encourage establishment of more venture capital firms in the private sector. Investors investing in SMEs can be provided additional tax incentives. In a number of developed countries, investors can deduct from their taxable income part of the cost of investment in the equity shares of specified VCFs. In some countries, such as UK, investors are provided income tax relief if they invest in qualifying, unquoted companies or in new companies. Investors are also charged capital gains tax at lower rate, and are allowed to set off losses on sale of shares against income tax. Some countries, like Australia, have removed double taxation on dividends. A number of countries also provide tax incentives to SMEs in the forms of capital cost allowance, deduction of R&D expenditure, tax relief on profits etc. Most countries also make government finance available to VCFs.

FUTURE PROSPECTS OF VENTURE FINANCING

Venture capital can play a more innovative and developmental role in a developing country like India. It could help the rehabilitation of sick units through people with ideas and turnaround management skills. A large number of small enterprises in India become sick even before the commencement of production. Venture capitalists could also assist small ancillary units to upgrade their technologies so that they could be in line with the developments taking place in their parent companies. Yet another area where VCFs can play a significant role in developing countries is the service sector including tourism, publishing, health care etc. They could also provide financial assistance to people coming out of the universities, technical institutes etc. who wish to start their own venture with or without high-tech content, but involving high risk. This would encourage entrepreneurial spirit. It is not only the initial funding which is needed from the venture capitalists, but they should also simultaneously provide management and marketing expertise— a real critical aspect of venture capital in developing countries. VCFs can improve their effectiveness by setting up venture capital cells in R&D and other scientific organisations, providing syndicated or consortium financing and acting as **business incubators**.

In sum, venture capital, by combining risk financing with management and marketing assistance, could become an effective instrument in fostering development of entrepreneurship and transfer of technology in developing countries. The experiences of developed countries and the detailed case study of venture capital in India, however, indicate that the following elements are needed for the success of venture capital in any country:

- *Entrepreneurial tradition* A broad-based (and less family based) entrepreneurial tradition and societal and government encouragement for innovations, creativity and enterprise.
- *Unregulated economic environment* A less regulated and controlled business and economic environment where attractive customer opportunities exist or could be created for high-tech and quality products.
- *Disinvestments avenues* Existence of disinvestments mechanisms, particularly, over-the-counter stocks exchange catering to the needs of SMEs.
- *Fiscal incentives* Fiscal incentives which render the equity investment more attractive and develop 'equity cult' in investors.
- *Broad-based education* A more general, business and entrepreneurship oriented education system where scientists and engineers have knowledge of accounting, finance and economics and accountants understand engineering or physical sciences.
- *Venture capital managers* An effective management education and training programme for developing professionally competent and committed venture capital managers; they should be trained to evaluate and manage high tech, high risk ventures.
- *Promotion efforts* A vigorous marketing thrust, promotional efforts and development strategy, employing new concepts such as venture fairs, venture clubs, venture networks, business incubators etc. for the growth of venture capital.
- *Institute-industry linkage* Linkage between universities/ technology institutions, R&D organisations, industry and financial institutions including venture capital firms.
- *R&D activities* Encouragement and funding of R&D by private and public sector companies and the government for ensuring technological competitiveness.

SUMMARY

- ❖ Venture capital is risk financing available in the form of equity or quasi-equity. A venture capitalist also provides management support and acts as a partner and adviser to the entrepreneur. Thus, he is different from a banker and an investor of the shares of an enterprise.
- ❖ Venture capital is available as early stage financing, expansion financing and acquisition financing.
- ❖ Venture capital activity in developed countries has been encouraged because of a large number of tax incentives available to venture capital firms and investors, well- developed avenues for buying and selling shares of the small scale enterprises and favourable social climate and government policy for encouraging entrepreneurial activities.
- ❖ Venture capital activity has just begun in India. There are about a dozen venture capital organisations in India, mainly started by central and state-level financial institutions and commercial banks. A few private sector venture capital funds have also been established.
- ❖ Venture capital is available in three forms in India : equity, conditional loans and income notes. Conventional loans

are also made available by venture capital firms. Income notes are hybrid securities, combining the features of both conventional and conditional loans.

❖ Overall, in India the focus in venture capital is still on debt financing.

❖ India has yet to develop reasonable mechanisms of disinvestment. The OTC market has started functioning, and hopefully, it would provide an impetus to venture capital activity.

❖ India lacks sufficient tax incentives to encourage venture capital activity. There is need for separate tax concessions for developing venture capital in India.

KEY CONCEPTS

Business incubators	Convertible loan	Early-stage financing	Preferred ordinary shares
Business plan	Convertible loan stock	Income notes	Turnaround financing
Buyout financing	Deferred shares	Initial public offerings (IOPs)	Venture capital
Conditional loan	Due diligence	Over-the-counter-market	

REVIEW QUESTIONS

1. Define venture capital. Explain its characteristics.
2. What are the steps involved in a venture capital investment process? Explain them briefly.
3. What is the strategic role of venture capital in developing entrepreneurship in a country?
4. What is the need of venture capital in India? What is the status of venture capital in India?
5. What are the possible disinvestments avenues available to venture capital firm in India? Explain their merits and demerits.
6. Do you think tax incentives are necessary to encourage venture capital activity in a company? Why? Make recommendations in the Indian context.

PART 5

Financial and Profit Analysis

CHAPTER 24
Financial Statements and Cash Flow Analysis

CHAPTER OBJECTIVES

- Introduce financial statements—balance sheet and profit and loss account
- Distinguish between accounting profit and economic profit
- Discuss the meaning of funds flow and working capital flow
- Highlight the need for analysing the changes in a firm's funds and cash flow position
- Explain the mechanism of preparing funds flow and cash flow statements
- Emphasise the need and utility of preparing a comprehensive statements of financial position that explains changes in cash flow from operations, investment activities and financing activities

INTRODUCTION

The basis for financial planning, analysis and decision-making is the financial information. Financial information is needed to predict, compare and evaluate the firm's earning ability. It is also required to aid in economic decision-making—investment and financing decision-making. The financial information of an enterprise is contained in the **financial statements** or **accounting reports**. Three basic financial statements of great significance to owners, management and investors are balance sheet, profit and loss account and cash flow statement.

BALANCE SHEET

Balance sheet is the most significant financial statement. It indicates the financial condition or the state of affairs of a business at a particular moment of time. More specifically, balance sheet contains information about resources and obligations of a business entity and about its owners' interests in the business at a particular point of time. Thus, the balance sheet of a firm prepared on 31 March 2004 reveals the firm's financial position on this specific date. In the language of accounting, balance sheet communicates information about **assets, liabilities** and **owner's equity** for a business firm as on a specific date. It provides a snapshot of the financial position of the firm at the close of the firm's accounting period.

Assets are valuable economic resources owned by the firm. They embody future benefits and are measured in monetary terms. Assets represent: (*a*) stored purchasing power (*e.g.*, cash), (*b*) money claims (*e.g.*, receivables, stock) and (*c*) tangible and intangible items that can be sold or used in business to generate earnings. Tangible items include land, building, plant, equipment or stocks of materials and finished goods and all such other items which have physical substance. Intangible items do not have any physical existence, but they have value to a firm. They include patents, copyrights, trade name or goodwill.

Assets are classified as: (1) current assets and (2) fixed (long-term) assets. **Current assets**, sometimes called **liquid assets**, are those resources of a firm which are either held in the form of cash or are expected to be converted in cash within the accounting period or the operating cycle of the business. The accounting period is of one-year duration. The **operating cycle** is the time taken to convert the raw materials into finished goods, sell finished goods, and convert receivables (goods sold on credit) into cash. Mostly, operating cycle is equal to or less than the accounting period. Current assets include cash, tradable (marketable) securities, debtors (account receivables) and stock of raw material, work-in-process and finished goods.

Fixed assets are long-term in nature; they are held for periods longer than the accounting period. They include **tangible fixed assets** like land, building, machinery, equipment, furniture etc. These assets are normally recorded at cost. Costs of tangible fixed assets are allocated over their useful lives. The amount so allocated each year is called **depreciation**. Costs of tangible fixed assets are reduced every year by the amount of depreciation. Depreciating an asset is a process of allocating cost and does not involve any cash outlay. **Intangible fixed assets** represent the firm's rights and include patents, copyrights, franchises, trademarks, trade names and goodwill. Costs of intangible fixed assets are **amortised** over their useful lives. In India, the term **gross block** is used for the original cost of total fixed assets. When accumulated depreciation is subtracted from the gross block, the difference is called the **net block**.

Firm's obligations are called **liabilities.** Liabilities represent debts payable in the future by the firm to its lenders and creditors. They represent economic obligations to pay cash or to provide goods or services in some future period. Generally, borrowing money or purchasing goods or services on credit creates liabilities. Examples of liabilities are creditors, bills payable, wages and salaries payable, interest payable, taxes payable, bonds, debentures, borrowing from banks and financial institutions, public deposits etc.

Liabilities are of two types: (1) current liabilities; and (2) long-term (fixed) liabilities. **Current liabilities** are debts payable within an accounting period. Current assets are converted into cash to pay current liabilities. Sometimes new current liabilities may be incurred to liquidate the existing ones. The typical examples of current liabilities are creditors, bills payable, bank overdraft, tax provision (payable), provision for dividends, outstanding expenses and incomes received in advance. **Long-term liabilities** are the obligations or debts payable in a period of time greater than the accounting period. Long-term liabilities usually represent borrowing for a long period of time. They include debentures, bonds, and secured long-term loans from financial institutions.

The financial interests of the owners are called **owners' equity** or simply equity. The owners' interest is *residual* in nature, reflecting the excess of the firm's assets over its liabilities. As liabilities are the claims of outside parties, equity represents owners' claim against the business entity as of the balance sheet date. But the nature of the owners' claim is not the same as that of the creditors. Creditors' claims are defined and have to be met within a specified period. The claim of owners change and the amount payable to them can be determined only when the firm

is liquidated. Since assets are recorded at cost, there can be considerable difference between the owners' book claim and the real claim.

Initially, owners' equity arises on account of the funds invested by them. But it changes due to the earnings of the firm and their distribution. The firm's earnings (or losses) do not affect the creditors' claims. Owners' equity will increase when the firm makes earnings and retains whole or part. If the firm incurs losses, owners' claim will be reduced. In case of joint stock companies, owners are called **shareholders** (or stockholders in USA). Therefore, owners' equity is referred to as **shareholders' equity** or **shareholders' funds**. Shareholders' equity has two parts (i) paid-up share capital and (ii) reserves and surplus. (retained earnings)—representing undistributed profits. **Paid-up share capital** is the amount of funds directly contributed by the shareholders through purchase of shares. **Reserves and surplus** or **retained earnings** are undistributed (book) profits. Paid-up share capital and reserve and surplus together are called **net worth**.

Summarised Balance Sheet in Practice: Example of GNFC

How do companies present their balance sheet in the published annual report? Table 24.1 gives summarised balance sheet of Gujarat Narmada Valley Fertilisers Company Limited (GNFC) as on 31 March 2000 and 2001.

The following significant points may be noted in GNFC's balance sheet for the year 2001:

- GNFC's sources of funds include shareholders' funds (equity or net worth)–Rs 844.51 crore and loan funds crore (borrowings, both long- and short-term)–Rs 845.16. GNFC's capital employed (CE) is Rs 1,689.67 crore:

$$CE = \text{Net worth} + \text{Borrowings}$$
$$= 844.51 + 845.16$$
$$= \text{Rs } 1,689.67 \text{ crore}$$

- GNFC's sources of funds do not include current liabilities – Rs 347.21 crore. It has shown net current assets (NCA) – the difference between current assets (CA) and current liabilities (CL)—as application of funds. GNFC's net current assets are Rs 503.97 crore:

$$NCA = CA - CL$$
$$= 851.18 - 347.21$$
$$= \text{Rs } 503.97 \text{ crore}$$

- GNFC's application of funds includes net fixed assets (NFA), investments, (INVT), net current assets (NCA) and other assets (OA). The total application of funds represents GNFC's net assets of Rs 1,689.67 crore:

$$NA = NFA + INVT + NCA + OA$$
$$= 954.82 + 227.07 + 503.97 + 3.81$$
$$= \text{Rs } 1,689.67 \text{ crore}$$

- GNFC's sources of funds are equal to application of funds. In other words, GNFC's capital employed finances its net assets.

Note that GNFC has contingent liabilities of Rs 186.20 crore. They appear as a note to the balance sheet. Contingent liabilities are not actual liabilities now; they are liabilities contingent upon the occurrence of some future event.

Table 24.1: Gujarat Narmada Valley Fertilisers Company
Balance Sheet as on 31 March

(Rs in crore)

	2001	2000
SOURCES OF FUNDS		
Shareholders' Funds		
Share Capital	146.48	146.48
Reserves and Surplus	698.03	636.07
Total Shareholders Funds	844.51	782.55
Loan Funds		
Secured Loans	558.22	524.64
Unsecured Loans	286.94	343.52
Total Debt	845.16	868.16
Total Funds	1689.67	1650.71
APPLICATION OF FUNDS		
Fixed Assets		
Gross Block	1724.33	1660.18
Less: Accumulated Depreciation	903.92	842.71
Net Block	820.41	817.47
Capital Work in Progress	134.41	62.43
Total Net Fixed Assets	954.82	879.90
Investments	227.07	229.72
Current Assets, Loans & Advances		
Inventories	243.10	226.51
Sundry Debtors	235.87	248.25
Cash and Bank Balance	17.50	18.16
Loans and Advances	354.71	338.82
	851.18	831.74
Less: **Current Liabilities & Provisions**		
Current Liabilities	204.87	167.34
Provisions	142.34	128.29
	347.21	295.63
Net Current Assets	503.97	536.11
Miscellaneous Expenditure	3.81	4.98
Total Assets	1689.67	1650.71
Contingent Liabilities	*186.20*	*220.82*

PROFIT AND LOSS ACCOUNT

Balance sheet is considered as a very significant statement by bankers and other lenders because it indicates the firm's financial solvency and liquidity, as measured by its resources and obligations. However, creditors, particularly bankers and financial analysts in India have recently started paying more attention to the firm's earning capacity as a measure of its financial strength. The earning capacity and potential of a firm are reflected by its **profit and loss account**. The profit and loss account is a "score-board" of the firm's performance during a period of time. The generally accepted convention is to show one year's events in the profit and loss account. Since the profit and loss account reflects the results of operations *for a period of time*, it is a *flow* statement. In contrast, the balance sheet is a *stock*, or *status* statement as it shows assets, liabilities and owners' equity *at a point of time*.

Profit and loss account presents the summary of revenues, expenses and net income (or net loss) of a firm. It serves as a measure of the firm's profitability. **Revenues** are amounts that the customers pay to the firm for providing them goods and services. The firm uses economic resources in providing goods and services to customers. The cost of the economic resources used to earn revenues during a period of time is called **expenses**. Thus, to determine **net profit**, the accounting system *matches* expenses incurred during the accounting period against revenues earned during that period. This matching of expenses with revenue is called **matching concept**. The time period for which matching is done is called the *accounting period*. Normally, the accounting period for the business firms is of one year's duration. *Net profit or net income*, which is an indicator of the firm's profitable operations, is the amount by which revenues earned during a period exceed expenses incurred during that period. If the firm's operations prove to be unprofitable, total expenses will exceed total revenues and the difference is referred to as *net loss*.

Revenues and expenses are sometimes categorised as operating and non-operating. Revenues (expenses) arising from the main operations or business of the firm are called **operating revenues** (**operating expenses**). For example, gross proceeds from the sale of products manufactured by a firm are operating revenues. Revenues (expenses) which are incidental or indirect to the main operations of the firm are called **non-operating revenues** (*expenses*). For example, the gross proceeds from the sale of old equipment is non-operating revenue. Similarly, dividend and interest income from temporary investments are examples of non-operating revenues. Expenses incurred in generating non-operating revenues are called non-operating expense.

Concepts of profit There are several useful concepts of profit as given below:

- *Gross profit* (GP) is the difference between sales and cost of goods sold (CGS). CGS includes manufacturing costs. Cost of goods sold is the manufacturing costs of the goods that have been sold. Unsold goods are assets.
- *Profit before depreciation, interest and taxes* (PBDIT) is equal to revenue minus all operating expenses except depreciation, interest and taxes. Some companies call PBDIT the gross profit. An alternative expression for PBDIT is EBITDA – earnings before interest, taxes, depreciation and amortisation.
- *Operating profit* (OP) is the difference between gross profit and operating expenses consisting of general and administrative and selling expenses and depreciation, (OP = GP – OEXP – DEP). Note that interest charges (INT) on borrowed funds are not subtracted. Thus operating profit

may also be known as profit or earnings before interest and taxes (PBIT or EBIT). PBIT measures the performance of the firm's operations without regard to the sources of financing (i.e., debt or equity), and may include other incomes.

- *Profit before taxes* (PBT) is the difference between profit before interest and taxes and interest charges (PBT = PBIT − INT). PBT may also include non-operating profit (viz., non-operating revenue minus non-operating expenses).

- *Profit after taxes* (*PAT*) or *net profit* (*NP*) is the difference between profit before tax and taxes (NP = PBT − TAX).

- *Net operating profit after tax* (*NOPAT*) is PBIT minus tax on PBIT. That is, PBIT × (1 − Tax rate). Alternatively, it is equal to profit after tax plus after tax interest.

Summarised Profit and Loss Account: Example of GNFC

The usual practice is to prepare the profit and loss account in the summary form and details regarding expenses and revenue are given in separate schedules. Also, the cost of goods sold figure is not generally given in the published annual accounts. Table 24.2 shows the summarised profit and loss statement of the Gujarat Narmada Valley Fertiliser Company Limited for the years ending on 31 March 2000 and 2001.

Table 24.2: Gujarat Narmada Valley Fertilisers Company
Profit & Loss Account for the year ended on 31 March

(Rs in crore)

	2001	2000
Income		
Sales Turnover	1422.25	1213.48
Other Income	68.23	43.54
Stock Adjustments (Change)	8.76	24.39
Total Income	1499.24	1281.41
Expenditure		
Raw Materials	615.24	496.04
Excise Duty	82.86	60.42
Power and Fuel Cost	227.65	201.05
Other Manufacturing Expenses	80.83	95.04
Employee Cost	91.85	82.28
Selling and Administration Expenses	103.75	97.33
Miscellaneous Expenses	14.02	12.74
Depreciation	68.91	63.41
Interest and Financial Charges	101.18	97.44
	1386.29	1205.75
Less: Preoperative Expenditure Capitalised	0.00	0.00
Total Expenditure	1386.29	1205.75
Profit for the Year	112.95	75.66
Provision for tax	7.40	9.55
Profit After Tax	105.55	66.11
Adjustment	0.00	0.00
P&L Balance brought forward	94.34	83.10
Appropriations	66.41	54.87
P&L Balance brought forward	133.48	94.34

The following are some significant points in GNFC's profit and loss account for the year 2001:

- GNFC's net sales are: sales turnover minus excise duty, i.e., Rs 1422.25 crore − Rs 82.86 crore = Rs 1339.39 crore. Stock adjustment should be considered in the calculation of cost of goods sold.

- GNFC's earnings before interest, tax and depreciation (and amortisation), called EBITDA (or profit before depreciation, interest and tax, PBDIT) is:

$$PBDIT = EBITDA = PBT + Depreciation + Interest$$
$$= 112.95 + 69.91 + 101.18 = Rs\ 283.04$$

- GNFC's profit before interest and tax (PBIT) is Rs 112.95 crore and profit after tax (PAT) is Rs 105.55 crore.

DEFINITION OF PROFIT: ECONOMIC VERSUS ACCOUNTING

The measurement of profit is one of the difficult problems faced by the accounting profession. Accountant's concept of profit differs from that of the economist's. The figure of **accounting profit** is the result of the application of **generally accepted accounting principles** (GAAP). The accountant has to use his judgement, which at times is based on arbitrary assumptions for measuring profit. The *recognition* of revenue and expenses during the accounting period poses a basic measurement problem. Most firms use **accrual concept** to allocate receipts and expenditures to accounting periods as revenue and expenses. For example, a transaction is treated as sale and recorded as revenue when title to goods is transferred to the buyer, irrespective of the period in which cash is received. Similarly, expense is recognised in the period in which it is *incurred*, not when cash is paid.

The figure of accounting profit is also distorted because of the optional ways of treating depreciation, research and development expenditures, goodwill and patents and inventory valuation. The price-level changes further complicate the measurement of profit. Because of inflation, the accounting profit fails to reveal the true profitability of the firm. During inflation, profits are earned on inventories held by the firm, and depreciation allowance based on historical cost fails to maintain the firm's earning power.

In economic sense, profit would mean net increase in the wealth, viz., cash flow plus change in the value of the firm's assets. This definition incorporates the time dimension, and therefore, implies the discounted value (or present value) of the stream of benefits. The accounting definition of profit is based on accrual principle and includes non-cash items. Even if we assume that all items of revenue and expense are on cash basis still there would be difference between accounting profit and cash profit; the accountant charges depreciation, which is a non-cash item, to compute accounting profit. Thus, the operating cash flow (i.e., cash from operations) or cash profit can be found out by adding depreciation to the accounting profit. The *total* cash flow of the firm, however, is also affected by the balance sheet changes. An investment outlay made during a period affects the total cash flow, but not the operating cash flow. For calculating the net increase in wealth, the economist uses the figure of total cash flow.

The focus of the finance managers should be on the cash flow in decision-making. They will be misled and would fail to achieve the objective of maximising shareholders' wealth if they base their decision-making on accounting profit or earnings per share. The accounting profit (or earning per share) provides the basis for computing the cash flow. It is an important performance-criterion, but not a decision-criterion.

CHANGES IN FINANCIAL POSITION

Balance sheet gives a summary of the firm's resources (assets) and obligations (liabilities and owners' equity) at a point of time; the profit and loss account reflects the results of the business operations by summarising revenues and expenses during a period of time. Both these statements fail to explain the *changes* in assets, liabilities and owners' equity. The balance sheet gives a 'static' view of the *sources* and *uses* of finances. But it does not indicate the causes of changes or the movement of finances between two periods. The change in owners' equity is partly reflected through the profit and loss account, but besides profits, owners' equity may change due to other factors such as additional investment or withdrawal of profits. Therefore, an additional statement is needed to show the changes in assets, liabilities and owners' equity between dates of two balance sheets. Such a statement is referred to as **the statement of changes in financial position**. This statement summarises:[1]

€ changes in assets and liabilities resulting from *financial* and *investment* transactions during the period, as well as those changes which resulted due to change in owners' equity; and

€ the way in which the firm used its financial resources during the period (for example to acquire fixed assets, to pay debts, to pay dividends to shareholders and so on).

The most commonly used forms of the statement of changes in financial position are called the **funds flow statement** and the **cash flow statement**. The cash flow statement is now regarded as an important part of financial reporting by companies. It is mandatory for listed company to include cash flow statement in their annual accounts.

Nature of Changes in the Financial Position

The analysis of changes in the financial position begins with an analysis of balance sheet changes over a desired period of time. The *ABC* Company's balance sheets on March 31, 19X1 and March 31, 19X2 and changes over these years are given in Table 24.3.

How do we interpret the balance sheet changes given in Table 24.3? During the period 19X1 and 19X2 the company's total assets increased by Rs 18,171. This increased requirement of funds was met from increase in net worth (via increase in retained earnings, i.e., reserves and surplus; paid-up share capital did not change during the period), Rs 7,185 and increase in

outsiders' liability, Rs 10,986. Increase in assets is use of funds, and increase in liabilities and net worth shareholders' equity is source of funds. However, assets can decrease when it is sold; liability can decrease when payment to creditors is made and net worth can decrease when the company's reserves are depleted because of losses. Therefore, sources of funds also include decrease in assets and uses of funds include decrease in liabilities and retained earnings.

Data in Table 24.3 can be recast in a simple format of sources and uses of funds. We can see from Table 24.2 that inventory has utilised largest funds. Is the expansion of inventory due to growth in sales or inefficiency of inventory management? Why have the fixed assets increased? The increase in cash is quite low. Is the liquidity position of the company sound? In the sources we find that retained earnings, followed by bank borrowings and creditors, contribute largest funds. Why is not the company using long-term debt? Has it reached its debt limit? Is the company depending excessively on trade credit as a source of funds? Is it prompt in making payment to creditors? Many more questions can be raised about the operation of the company. The sources and uses of funds analysis helps to identify the problem areas that can be further investigated.

Table 24.3: ABC Co.

Balance Sheet Changes March 31, 19X1 and March 31, 19X2

(Rs '000)

	19X1	*19X2*		*Change*
Assets				
Cash	54	135	(+)	81
Debtors	6,750	8,235	(+)	1,485
Stock	10,125	22,680	(+)	12,555
Total current assets	16,929	31,050	(+)	14,121
Fixed assets (net)	2,970	6,075	(+)	3,105
Other assets	945	1,890	(+)	945
Total Assets	20,844	39,015	(+)	18,171
Liabilities and Capital				
Bank borrowing	3,510	8,664	(+)	5,154
Creditors	2,835	6,615	(+)	3,780
Provision for taxes	270	972	(+)	702
Accrued expenses	810	2,700	(+)	1,890
Total current liabilities	7,425	18,951	(+)	11,526
Long-term debt	1,944	1,404	(−)	540
Total Liabilities	9,369	20,355	(+)	10,986
Paid-up share capital	8,370	8,370		−
Reserves and surplus	3,105	10,290	(+)	7,185
Total Funds	20,844	39,015	(+)	18,171

We have presented a simple analysis of funds changes in Table 24.3. In practice, a number of refinements can be made. For example, we have shown increase in fixed assets *net of*

---

1. Woelfel, C.J., *Accounting: An Introduction,* Goodyear, 1977, p. 515.

depreciation. The actual expenditure on fixed assets would be the change in *gross* fixed assets between March 31, 19X1 and March 31, 19X2. The increase in reserves (retained earnings) may be net of dividends, provisions and other non-fund items. Thus, change in reserve may not show true picture of funds from operations. Dividends may consume substantial funds; therefore, it may be separately shown as a use of funds. These and many other refinements are discussed in the following sections.

Definition of Funds

A question can be raised as to the definition of 'funds.' From Table 24.4 we can observe that the net effect of all changes in sources and uses has been an increase of Rs 81,000 in cash; that is the net inflow of funds in terms of cash during March 31, 19X1 and March 31, 19X2. Why has cash increased? Has this increase been caused by retention of earnings, by increase in bank borrowing or by extra credit extended by ABC's suppliers (creditors) or others (provision on taxes and accrued expenses)? The correct answer is that all of these as well as other activities have caused the *change* in cash. What we can say is that *sources* of cash exceeded *uses* by Rs 81,000. Instead of change in cash, one may be interested in knowing the flow of net working capital which is the difference between current assets and current liabilities. From Table 24.5 we can find that there is net increase of Rs 2,595,000 in working capital (Rs 14,121,000 – Rs 11,526,000), that is:

Table 24.4: ABC Co. Sources and Uses of Funds

(Rs '000)

	Amount	*%*
Sources		
Increase in current liabilities:		
Bank borrowing	5,154	27.5
Creditors	3,780	20.2
Provision for taxes	702	3.8
Accrued expenses	1,890	10.1
Total	11,526	61.6
Increase in shareholders' equity:		
Reserves (retained earnings)	7,185	38.4
Total Sources	18,711	100.0
Uses		
Increase in current assets:		
Cash	81	0.4
Debtors	1,485	7.9
Stock (inventory)	12,555	67.1
Total	14,121	75.4
Increase in fixed assets	3,105	16.6
Increase in other assets	945	5.1
Decrease in long-term debt	540	2.9
Total Uses	18,711	100.0

Table 24.5: ABC Co. Change in Working Capital

	Current Assets	*Less*	*Current Liabilities*	*Equals*	*Net Working Capital*
Year-end 19X1	16,929	–	7,425	=	9,504
Year-end 19X2	31,050	–	18,951	=	12,099
Change	14,121	–	11,526	=	2,595

Thus:

* funds may mean change in *cash* only;
* funds may mean change in *working capital* (the difference between current assets and current liabilities) only.

A more comprehensive definition of funds may be given as follows:

* funds may mean change in *financial resources*, arising from changes in *working capital* items and from *financing* and *investing* activities of the enterprise, which may involve only non-current items.

The funds flow statement analyses only the causes of changes in the firm's working capital position. The cash flow statement is prepared to analyse changes in the flow of cash only. These statements fail to consider the changes in the firm's *total* financial resources. They do not reveal some significant items that do not affect the firm's cash or working capital position, but considerably influence the financing position and asset mix of the firm. For example, ordinary shares issued to acquire some asset, say land, affect the financing and asset mix of the firm. But funds or cash flow statement will not include this transaction, as it does not involve any change in cash or working capital. A comprehensive statement of changes in financial position would disclose this information along with information on cash or working capital changes.

The statement of changes in financial position is an extension of the funds flow statement or the cash flow statement. It is more informative and comprehensive in indicating the changes in the firm's financial position. However, the analysis of changes in the firm's cash position or working capital is still very significant. Therefore, to get better insights, a firm may prepare a comprehensive, all-inclusive, statement of changes in financial position incorporating changes in the firm's cash and working capital positions. In the following sections, we illustrate the preparation and use of the statement of changes in financial position involving:

* changes in the firm's working capital position,
* changes in the firm's cash position, and
* changes in the firm's total financial resources.

FUNDS FLOW STATEMENT

The statement of changes in financial position, prepared to determine only the sources and uses of working capital between dates of two balance sheets, is known as the funds flow statement. **Working capital** is defined as the difference between current assets and current liabilities. Working capital determines the liquidity position of the firm.

As a historical analysis, the statement of changes in working capital reveals to management the way in which working capital was obtained and used. With this insight, management can prepare the estimates of the working capital flows. A statement reporting the changes in working capital is useful in addition to the financial statements. A projected statement of changes in working capital is immensely useful in the firm's long-range planning. Management, for example, wants to anticipate the working capital flows in order to plan the repayment schedules of its long-term debt. For a fast growth and expansion, a firm needs larger amount of working capital. Therefore, estimates of working capital on a long-term basis are also required to determine whether or not adequate working capital will be generated to meet the firm's expansion. If not, the firm can make arrangements in advance to procure funds from outside to meet its needs.

Concept of Working Capital Flow

The working capital flow or fund arises when the net effect of a transaction is to increase or decrease the amount of working capital. Normally, a firm will have some transactions that will change net working capital and some that will cause no change in net working capital. Transactions that change net working capital include most of the items of the profit and loss account and those business events that simultaneously affect both current and non-current balance sheet items. On the other hand, transactions that do not increase or decrease working capital include those that affect only current accounts or only non-current accounts. Let us take examples to illustrate the concept of the flow of working capital.

Suppose that a company issues ordinary shares for cash. Two accounts are involved in this case—the cash account, which is a current (asset) account and the share capital account, which is a non-current account. The company receives cash against the owners' increased claims. Thus, there occurs a net increase in working capital.

A company purchases machinery for cash; again two accounts—the cash account, which is a current (asset) account and the machinery account, which is a non-current (asset) account—are affected. The company acquires a fixed asset by paying cash. This has the effect of decreasing working capital.

Some transactions do not change working capital. For example, if a company receives cash from its debtors, it represents increase of cash—a current asset account and decrease of debtors—again a current asset account. Thus, there will be no net change in the amount of working capital, although the composition of working capital will be affected.

If the company pays cash to its creditors, two current accounts will be affected. The cash account, being a current asset account, decreases and the creditors account, being a current liability account, also decreases. The net effect will be no net change in the working capital, although the composition of working capital will change.

Working capital will also not be affected if both the accounts involved are non-current. Suppose that the company purchases land and makes payment by issuing shares to the landowner. Both accounts are non-current in nature and do not at all affect current asset or current liability. Therefore, working capital will remain unaffected. Similarly, if the company converts loan or debentures into equity, it will have no effect on working capital.

In the profit and loss account the revenue items increase cash or receivables and, therefore, increase working capital; the expense items reduce cash or create current liabilities and, therefore, decrease working capital. But there are certain items in the profit and loss account that are non-current, and, thus they have no effect on the net flow of working capital. Depreciation is an example. It reduces fixed assets but does not increase or decrease working capital. Therefore, in determining the net flow of working capital from operations, the amount of depreciation is added to net profit to set right the effect of depreciation deduction.

We may conclude that a transaction will cause net flow of working capital only when one of the accounts affected is a current account (current asset or current liability) and another account is a non-current account (long-term assets or long-term liability). The concept of working capital flow may be summarised as follows:

- The net working capital increases or decreases when a transaction involves a current account and a non-current account.
- The net working capital remains unaffected when a transaction involves *only* current accounts.
- The net working capital remains unaffected when a transaction involves *only* non-current accounts.

The concept of the flow of working capital is further illustrated in Fig. 24.1.

Decrease → Increase →	Current Account	Non-current Account
Current Account	No Impact	Impact
Non-current Account	Impact	No Impact

Figure 24.1: Effect of Changes in Accounts on Working Capital

Sources of Working Capital

The typical *sources* of working capital are summarised below:
1. Funds from operations (adjusted net income)
2. Sale of non-current assets:
   - sale of long-term investments (shares, bonds/debentures etc.)
   - sale of tangible fixed assets like land, building, plant, or equipments
   - sale of intangible fixed assets like goodwill, patents, or copyrights.
3. Long-term financing:
   - long-term borrowings (institutional loans, debentures, bonds etc.)
   - issuance of equity and preference shares.
4. Short-term financing such as bank borrowings.

In the following paragraphs we explain the measurement of funds from operations, since it usually involves a number of adjustments.

Funds from operations The major source of working capital is the firm's net profit from operations. The ultimate success of a company depends upon its ability to earn profits. However, the profit and loss account contains certain items that do not affect working capital. Therefore, in determining the amount of working capital from operations, the figure of net profit, as shown in the profit and loss account, should be adjusted. The expense items that do not involve working capital should be added to net profit. Let us take example of depreciation to illustrate the point.

Depreciation The most common example of the expense which does not affect working capital is depreciation. All expenses reduce owners' equity, so does depreciation. While most of other expenses also reduce current assets (cash) or create current liabilities (expense payable), it reduces non-current assets (plant, machinery, or equipment) without affecting cash. Because the combination of accounts influenced by it is only non-current, it does not affect working capital. It should, therefore, be added to net profit. If it is not added to net profit, the amount of working capital generated from operations would be understated. Same logic applies to *amortised expenses* such as goodwill written off. **Myth about depreciation** The adding-back of depreciation to determine the funds from operations is misunderstood by some people; they think that depreciation is a source of working capital (or cash). It must be realised very well that depreciation is not a source of funds. Revenue is the source of funds (working capital or cash), not depreciation. Unlike other operating expenses, depreciation does not use cash or working capital. However, like most expenses, it can indirectly influence the flow of funds by affecting the firm's tax liability. Depreciation, calculated as per the income-tax rules, is tax deductible; thus the tax liability of the firm will be reduced. There will be less outflow of cash to the income tax authority. Except through its impact on tax liability, depreciation expense has no effect on working capital. It must, therefore, be remembered that 'depreciation is the accountant's way of *matching* costs of fixed assets with the benefits derived from those assets; *depreciation is not a source of funds*. The funds flow occurs when fixed assets are acquired; moreover at that time the flow is a *use* (investment) of funds, not a source. Depreciation simply spreads that outflow over the life of the assets for purposes of measuring results of operations'.[1]

Gain or loss from sale of a non-current asset The net profit figure should also be adjusted for any gain or loss from the sale of a non-current asset. The loss should be added to, while the gain should be subtracted from, the net profit. This is done because the sale of non-current assets is listed separately as a source of working capital. The total inflow of cash on the sale of non-current assets is shown as a source of working capital. If the gain or loss is not adjusted in the net profit, this will amount to double counting as the cash realisation from the sale of a non-current asset includes gain or loss.

Firms also meet their working capital requirements by raising funds externally. They can issue shares or borrow from capital markets on short or long-term basis.

Uses of Working Capital

The typical uses of working capital are as follows:

1. Adjusted net loss from operations
2. Purchase of non-current assets:
    - purchase of long-term investments like shares, bonds/debentures etc.
    - purchase of tangible fixed assets, like land, building, plant, machinery, equipment etc.
    - purchase of intangible fixed assets, like goodwill, patents, copyrights etc.
3. Repayment of long-term debt (debentures or bonds) and short-term debt (bank borrowing)
4. Redemption of redeemable preference shares
5. Payment of cash dividend.

Adjusted net loss The loss from operations consumes the firm's working capital. Loss arises when expenses, that involve application of working capital, exceed revenues, that generate working capital. As with net profit, the expense and revenue items involving no working capital should be adjusted to net loss. The non-fund expense items like depreciation when added to net loss (shown with negative sign) will reduce its magnitude. The gain or loss on the sale of non-current assets should also be adjusted to net loss.

A firm applies its working capital funds for acquiring non-current assets such as land and building, plant and machinery, or equipment. Working capital will also be applied when the firm retires its borrowings and *redeemable preference shares,* i.e., preference shares payable on maturity. A profitable firm usually pays cash dividend to its equity and preference shareholders. This is also a use of working capital.

Forms of Funds Flow Statement

The statement of changes in working capital or funds flow is the summary of the sources and uses of working capital. This statement may be presented in two parts as shown in Table 24.6. The first part explains the causes of the change in the amount of working capital from the end of one period to another. It gives a list of sources which provided working capital and uses to which working capital was applied. The second part of the statement contains an analysis of the changes in the working capital items. This part of the statement shows items of current assets and current liabilities at the beginning and at the end of the accounting period and the effect of their changes between two periods on the working capital.

---

1. AICPA, Accounting Principles Board, Opinion No. 19, *Reporting Changes in Financial Position*, American Institute of Certified Public Accountants, New York, 1971, para 7.

Table 24.6: XY Company

Statement of Changes in Working Capital for the year ended December 31, 19X1

(a) Sources and Uses of Working Capital

Sources	Rs
Funds from operations	120,000
Sale of machine	30,000
Issuance of debentures	100,000
Issuance of equity shares	100,000
Funds Provided	**350,000**
Uses	
Purchase of long-term investments	80,000
Payment of long-term loans	90,000
Payment of cash dividend	60,000
Increase in working capital	120,000
Funds Applied	**350,000**

(b) Schedule of Changes in Working Capital

	31 Dec. 19X1 Rs	31 Dec. 19X2 Rs	Increase Rs	Decrease Rs
Current Assets				
Cash	80,000	125,000	45,000	
Debtors	50,000	45,000		5,000
Inventory	115,000	165,000	50,000	
Total	245,000	335,000	95,000	5,000
Current Liabilities				
Bills payable	20,000	8,000	12,000	
Creditors	45,000	47,000		2,000
Other current liabilities	25,000	5,000	20,000	
Total	90,000	60,000	32,000	2,000
Working Capital	155,000	275,000	127,000	7,000
Increase in working capital				120,000
Total			127,000	127,000

Table 24.7: XY Company

Funds Flow Statement

Sources and Uses of Working Capital

Sources	Rs
Funds from operations	120,000
Sale of machine	30,000
Issuance of debentures	100,000
Issuance of ordinary shares	100,000
Funds Provided	**350,000**
Uses	
Purchase of long-term investments	80,000
Payment of long-term loans	90,000
Payment of cash dividend	60,000
Funds Applied	**230,000**
Increase in Working Capital	**120,000**

Let us consider a comprehensive example (Illustration 24.1) to illustrate the mechanics of preparing a funds flow statement.

Illustration 24.1: Funds Flow Statement

The comparative balance sheets as on December 31, 19X1, and December 31, 19X2 and a profit and loss account for the year ended on December 31, 19X2 for the ACME Company are given in Table 24.8 (A) and (B). The additional information is given below:

1. During the year plant costing Rs 50,000 (accumulated depreciation Rs 20,000) was sold.
2. The debentures of Rs 30,000 were converted to share capital at par.
3. The company declared a cash dividend of Rs 40,000 and bonus shares of Rs 20,000 during the year.
4. The company issued 5,000 additional shares, par value Rs 10 per share, at a premium of Re 1 per share during the year.

Table 24.8: (A) ACME Company

Comparative Balance Sheets
for the year ended 31 December, 19X2 and 19X1   (Rs)

	19X1	19X2	Change
Current Assets			
Cash	70,000	50,000	(+) 20,000
Debtors	40,000	45,000	(−) 5,000
Inventory	125,000	90,000	(+) 35,000
Total current assets	235,000	185,000	(+) 50,000
Fixed Assets			
Land & building	150,000	100,000	(+) 50,000
Plant & machinery	220,000	200,000	(+) 20,000
Less: Accumulated depreciation	(82,000)	(80,000)	(−) 2,000
Total net fixed assets	288,000	220,000	(+) 68,000
Total Assets	523,000	405,000	(+)118,000
Current Liabilities			
Creditors	25,000	30,000	(−) 5,000
Salaries payable	15,000	10,000	(+) 5,000
Provision for tax	50,000	60,000	(−) 10,000
Provision for dividend	40,000	40,000	—
Total Current Liabilities	130,000	140,000	(−) 10,000
Long-term Liabilities			
Institutional loan	23,000	15,000	(+) 8,000
Debentures	120,000	150,000	(−) 30,000
Total long-term liabilities	143,000	165,000	(−) 22,000
Total Liabilities	273,000	305,000	(−) 32,000
Shareholders' Equity			
Share capital	175,000	75,000	(+)100,000
Share premium	12,500	7,500	(+) 5,000
Reserve and surplus	62,500	17,500	(+) 45,000
Net Worth	250,000	100,000	(+)150,000
Total Funds	523,000	405,000	(+)118,000

Table 24.8: (B) ACME Company

Profit and Loss Account
for the year ended December 31, 19X2   *(Rs)*

Sales		500,000
Less: Cost of goods sold		210,000
		290,000
Less: Operating expenses		
Office & administrative	45,000	
Selling & distribution	25,000	
Interest	12,000	
Depreciation	22,000	104,000
Operation profit		186,000
Add: Gain on sale of plant		6,000
Profit before tax		192,000
Less: Income-tax		87,000
Net Profit		105,000

Working Capital from Operations

As stated earlier, the major source of working capital is a firm's profitable operations. Working capital from operations is not necessarily equal to net profit. The items of the income statement, which do not involve working capital, should be adjusted to the net profit figure. The net profit for 19X2 of Rs 105,000 includes the effect of a depreciation deduction of Rs 22,000. As depreciation does not reduce working capital, it should be added back to net profit. The gain on the sale of plant, Rs 6,000, will be deducted from net profit because the total amount received from the sale of plant will be shown as a separate source of working capital. This amount includes both the recovery of the net book value (original cost *less* accumulated depreciation) and the gain. If the amount of gain is not deducted from net income, it would amount to double counting. Thus, the working capital from operations will be as given below:

	Rs
Net profit	1,05,000
Add: Depreciation	22,000
	1,27,000
Less: Gain on the sale of plant	6,000
Working capital from operations	1,21,000

The comparative balance sheets of the ACME Company can be recast to get a broad idea of the causes of changes in working capital during the period ended December 31, 19X2 (Table 24.9). The comparative picture presented in Table 24.9 reveals that the working capital increased by Rs 60,000. The working capital was provided from the shareholders' equity (Rs 150,000) and institutional loan (Rs 8,000). The working capital was applied to the purchase of fixed assets (land and building Rs 50,000 and plant and machinery Rs 20,000) and the payment of debentures (Rs 30,000). However, the comparative balance sheet approach does not give accurate information about the

causes of the changes in the working capital. For example, in case of the ACME Company, a cash dividend of Rs 40,000 was paid, the repayment of debentures of Rs 30,000 did not involve working capital as they were converted into equity: the company sold plant; working capital was also obtained from operations (remember depreciation is not a source of working capital) and so on. All this information can be revealed when we prepare funds flow statement involving a comprehensive analysis of the changes in working capital position. The procedure to prepare such a statement is explained in the next section.

Working Capital Flow from Non-current Accounts

The non-current items of balance sheet should be analysed to determine the inflow and outflow of working capital. In case of the ACME Company, the working capital will increase from the following sources:

Table 24.9: ACME Company

Comparative Balance Sheets
for the year ended 31 December 19X2 and 19X1   *(Rs)*

	31 Dec. 19X1	31 Dec. 19X2	Change
Change in Working Capital:			
Current Assets			
Cash	70,000	50,000	(+) 20,000
Debtors	40,000	45,000	(−) 5,000
Stock	125,000	90,000	(+) 35,000
Total Current Assets (A)	235,000	185,000	(+) 50,000
Current Liabilities			
Creditors	25,000	30,000	(−) 5,000
Salaries payable	15,000	10,000	(+) 5,000
Provision for tax	15,000	10,000	(+) 5,000
Provision for dividend	40,000	40,000	–
Total Current Liabilities (B)	130,000	140,000	(−) 10,000
Working Capital (C) = (A − B)	105,000	45,000	60,000
Fixed Assets			
Land & building	150,000	100,000	(+) 50,000
Plant & machinery	220,000	200,000	(+) 20,000
Less: Accumulated depreciation	(82,000)	(80,000)	(−) 2,000
Net Fixed Assets (D)	288,000	220,000	68,000
Net Assets (E) = (C + D)	393,000	265,000	(+) 128,00
Shareholder's Equity			
Share capital	175,000	75,000	(+) 100,000
Share premium	12,500	7,500	(+) 5,000
Reserve & surplus	62,500	17,500	(+) 45,000
Net Worth (F)	250,000	100,000	(+) 150,000
Long-term Liabilities			
Institution loan	23,000	15,000	(+) 8,000
Debentures	120,000	150,000	(−) 30,000
Total Debt (G)	143,000	165,000	(−) 22,000
Capital Employed (H) = (F+G)	393,000	265,000	(+) 128,000

1. *Sale of plant:* The plant sold by the company had an original cost of Rs 50,000. As the accumulated depreciation on it was Rs 20,000, its net book value was Rs 30,000. The plant was sold for a gain of Rs 6,000. Therefore, the sale proceeds of the plant must be Rs 36,000 (Rs 30,000 + Rs 6,000).

2. *Increase in institutional loan:* The institutional loan was Rs 15,000 on December 31, 19X1 and Rs 23,000 on December 31, 19X2. This implies an additional loan of Rs 8,000 is obtained. As the cash resources of the firm will increase by this additional loan, it is a source of working capital.

3. *Issuance of shares:* The shareholder's equity has increased by Rs 150,000 between December 31, 19X1 and December 31, 19X2. This increase includes Rs 45,000 of retained earnings (increase in reserves and surplus), which has already been taken into account in working capital from operations (via adjusted net income). Out of the remaining increase of Rs 105,000, Rs 30,000 represent conversion of debentures and Rs 20,000 represent issuance of bonus shares to shareholders. Both these items do not involve working capital. Therefore, the net increase in working capital due to the issuance of shares is of Rs 55,000. (Rs 55,000 is cash received by the company by issuing 5,000 shares, Rs 10 par value, at a premium of Re 1 per share. Conversion of debentures into equity and issue of bonus shares were merely the book entries).

The following non-current items involved the use of working capital:

1. *Purchase of land and building:* Land and building registered an increase of Rs 50,000 between dates of two balance sheets. In the absence of any information about depreciation and sale of land and building, this amount represents the net purchases. The acquisition of land and building reduces working capital.

2. *Purchase of plant and machinery:* If we consider the sale of the plant of Rs 50,000, the plant and machinery should have been reduced to Rs 150,000 (Rs 200,000 – Rs 50,000) on December 31, 19X2. But it has increased to Rs 220,000. This implies that the company must have acquired additional plant and machinery of Rs 70,000 (Rs 220,000 – Rs 150,000).

3. *Conversion of debentures:* The company converted debentures of Rs 30,000 into equity shares. This is a book entry, where both the accounts involved are non-current accounts. Therefore, no working capital is involved.

4. *Payment of dividend:* The company paid a cash dividend of Rs 40,000. This is use of working capital. However, the issuance of bonus shares of Rs 20,000 did not reduce working capital. Bonus shares represent conversion of a portion of net profit into share capital. It is a book entry and does not involve use of funds.

We can now prepare a statement of changes in financial position on the basis of the above analysis (see Table 24.10).

Table 24.10: ACME Company

Funds Flow Statement
for the year ended 31 December 19X2 (Rs)

Sources and Uses of Working Capital

Sources		
Working capital from operations	1,21,000	
Sale of plant	36,000	
Institutional loan	8,000	
Issuance of ordinary shares	55,000	
Funds Provided		2,20,000
Uses		
Purchase of land and building	50,000	
Purchase of plant and machinery	70,000	
Payment of cash dividend	40,000	
Funds Applied		1,60,000
Increase in Working Capital		60,000

Schedule of Changes in Working Capital

	31 Dec. 19X1	31 Dec. 19X2	Increse	Decrease
Current Assets				
Cash	50,000	70,000	20,000	
Debtors	45,000	40,000		5,000
Stock	90,000	1,25,000	35,000	
Total (A)	1,85,000	2,35,000	55,000	5,000
Current Liabilities				
Creditors	30,000	25,000	5,000	
Salaries payable	10,000	15,000		5,000
Provision for tax	60,000	50,000	10,000	
Provision for dividend	40,000	40,000		
Total (B)	1,40,000	1,30,000	15,000	5,000
Working Capital (A – B)	45,000	1,05,000	70,000	10,000
Increase in Working Capital				60,000
			70,000	70,000

Comprehensive Funds Flow Statement: Financial Resources Basis

The statement of funds flow can be expanded also to disclose all those transactions which significantly influence the firm's financial position, but do not increase or decrease working capital.[1] In Illustration 24.1, the ACME Company converted its debentures of Rs 30,000 into equity shares. This is a significant event as it changes the company's debt-equity position. This transaction should be disclosed in the statement. Similarly, the issuance of bonus shares (stock dividend) does not involve working capital, but increases the paid-up share capital. The funds flow statement for ACME is recast to incorporate changes in all financial resources (Table 24.11).

---

1. Anthony, Robert N. and James S. Reece, *Management Accounting Principles,* Taraporewala, 1977, p. 227.

Table 24.11: ACME Company

Statement of Funds Flow (Total Financial Resources Basis)
for the year ended December 31, 19X2   **(Rs)**

Source	
Financial resources from operations	1,21,000
Sale of plant	36,000
Institutional loan	8,000
Issuance of ordinary shares for cash	55,000
Financial resources not affecting working capital	
Issuance of ordinary shares to convert debentures	30,000
Issuance of ordinary shares as bonus shares	20,000
Financial Resources Provided	2,70,000
Uses	
Purchase of land building	50,000
Purchase of plant and machinery	70,000
Payment of cash dividend	40,000
Financial resources not affecting working capital	
Payment of debentures through conversion into equity	30,000
Payment as bonus shares	20,000
Financial Resources Applied	2,10,000
Increase in Working Capital	60,000

A comparison of Tables 24.10 and 24.11 reveals that the comprehensive statement of changes in financial position listing all changes is more useful as it discloses more information. The transactions not affecting working capital are also shown. The conversion of debentures into equity is a source of financial resources because shareholder's equity increases. But at the same time, it is an application of the financial resources towards the retirement of a long-term liability, i.e., debentures. Thus, the working capital is not changed by these transactions, but the overall financial position is affected.

CASH FLOW STATEMENT

An analysis of cash flows is useful for short-run planning. A firm needs sufficient cash to pay debts maturing in the near future, to pay interest and other expenses and to pay dividends to shareholders. The firm can make projections of cash inflows and outflows for the near future to determine the availability of cash. This cash balance can be matched with the firm's need for cash during the period, and accordingly, arrangements can be made to meet the deficit or invest the surplus cash temporarily. A historical analysis of cash flows provides insight to prepare reliable cash flow projections for the immediate future.

A statement of changes in financial position on *cash basis*, commonly known as the cash flow statement, summarises the causes of changes in cash position between dates of the two balance sheets. It indicates the sources and uses of cash. The cash flow statement is similar to the funds flow statement except that it focuses attention on cash (immediate or near term liquidity) instead of working capital or funds (potential or medium term liquidity). Thus, this statement analyses changes in non-current accounts as well as current accounts (other than cash) to determine the flow of cash.

Sources and Uses of Cash

The following are the *sources* of cash:
- the profitable operations of the firm,
- decrease in assets (except cash),
- increase in liabilities (including debentures or bonds), and
- sale proceeds from an ordinary or preference share issue.

The *uses* of cash are:
- the loss from operations,
- increase in assets (except cash),
- decrease in liabilities (including redemption of debentures or bonds),
- redemption of redeemable preference shares, and
- cash dividends.

The easiest and the direct method of preparing a statement of changes in cash position is to only record inflows and outflows of cash, and find out the net change during a given period. The rupees (or any other unit of currency) received minus the rupees paid during a period is the cash balance at the end of the period. If the net change in the cash position has to be found out from the income statement and comparative balance sheets, adjustments for the non-cash items are made. These adjustments are made in the same way as in preparing funds flow statement. For example, cash from operations can be found out by adding depreciation to net profit. Gain on sale of a non-current asset should be deducted while loss should be added to net profit. In addition, changes in current assets and current liabilities also affect flow of cash from operations. This is discussed below.

Change in current assets Increases in current assets (that is, end of the year balance exceeding the beginning balance) reduce cash flow from operations while decreases in current assets (that is, beginning balance exceeding end of the year balance) increase cash flow. Consider the following examples. (*i*) Increase in debtors implies that cash collections from customers are less than sales figure (shown in the profit and loss statement), while decrease in debtors indicates that cash collections are greater than sales figure. (*ii*) Increase or decrease in inventory is adjusted to the cost of goods sold. Increase in inventory implies that cash outflow is greater than the cost of goods sold figure (shown in the profit and loss statement), while decrease in inventory means that cash outflow is less than the cost of goods sold figure. (*iii*) Increase in prepaid expenses implies that cash outflow is more than the amount of actual expenses (shown in the profit and loss statement), while decrease in prepaid expenses means that cash outflow is less than the amount of actual expenses.

Change in current liabilities Increase in current liabilities increases cash flow from operation while decrease in current liabilities reduces it. Consider the following examples: (*i*) Increase in creditors implies that cash payments to creditors are less than the purchase figure (as shown in the profit and loss statement), while decrease in creditors indicates that cash payments to creditors are greater than purchases figure. (*ii*) Increase in 'income in advance' implies greater cash inflow than shown in the profit and loss statement as income, while decrease in 'income in advance' means less cash inflow than shown as income.

We may thus conclude that (in addition to the adjustments for depreciation and gain or loss from the sale of non-current assets) cash flow from operation should be arrived at by adding decreases in current assets and increases in current liabilities to net profit and subtracting increases in current assets and decreases in current liabilities from net profit.

Illustration 24.2: Cash Flow Statement

The data of Illustration 24.1 are used to prepare a cash flow statement. From the comparative balance sheets presented in Table 24.8, we find that cash balance had increased by Rs 20,000. The columns for change in Table 24.8 broadly indicate the way in which current and non-current accounts have brought a change in cash balance. But more meaningful and useful information is revealed when we prepare a statement analysing changes in cash systematically. Such a statement is presented in Tables 24.12 and 24.13.

Table 24.12: ACME Company

Cash Flow Statement
for the year ended December 31, 19X2 **(Rs)**

Sources		
Cash from operations	81,000	
Sale of plant	36,000	
Institutional loan	8,000	
Issuance of equity shares	55,000	
Cash Provided		180,000
Uses		
Purchase of land & building	50,000	
Purchase of plant & machinery	70,000	
Payment of cash dividend	40,000	
Cash Applied		160,000
Increase in Cash		20,000

The net increase in cash from operations is Rs 81,000. The figure has been found out after adjusting net profit for non-cash items and for increases and decreases in current accounts (other than cash). The cash from operations is determined as follows:

	Rs	*Rs*
Net Profit	105,000	
Add: Depreciation	22,000	
Decrease in debtors	5,000	
Increase in salaries payable	5,000	137,000
Less: Gain from the sale of plant	6,000	
Increase in inventory	35,000	
Decrease in creditors	5,000	
Decrease in tax provision	10,000	56,000
Cash from operations		81,000

The items of non-current accounts are analysed exactly in the same way as in the case of working capital analysis. The cash flow statement can be shown in an alternate way. The alternative form of the statement is presented in Table 24.13.

Table 24.13: ACME Company

Cash Flow Statement
for the year ended December 31, 19X2 **(Rs)**

Cash balance, 31 December 19X1		50,000
Add: Increase from the following sources		
Cash from operations	81,000	
Sale of plant	36,000	
Institutional loan	8,000	
Issuance of equity shares	55,000	1,80,000
		2,30,000
Less: Decrease from the following uses		
Purchase of land & building	50,000	
Purchase of plant & machinery	70,000	
Payment of cash dividend	40,000	1,60,000
Cash balance, 31 December 19X2		70,000

Comprehensive Cash Flow Statement: Financial Resources Basis

As stated earlier, the statement of changes in the financial position must reveal all changes, whether it is prepared on cash basis or working capital basis. The cash flow statement can be easily adapted to reflect all changes in financial resources. Table 24.14 shows a statement summarising the effect of changes in cash along with other significant investment and financing activities which do not involve cash.

Table 24.14: ACME Company

Cash Flow Statement (Total Financial Basis)
for the year ended 31 December, 19X2

	Rs	*Rs*
Sources		
Cash from operations	81,000	
Sale of plant	36,000	
Additional institutional loan	8,000	
Issuance of equity shares	55,000	
Financial resources not affecting cash		
Issuance of ordinary shares to convert debentures	30,000	
Issuance of ordinary shares as bonus shares	20,000	
Financial Resources Provided		230,000
Uses		
Purchase of land & building	50,000	
Purchase of plant & machinery	70,000	
Payment of cash dividend	40,000	
Financial resources not affecting cash		
Payment of debentures through conversion debentures	30,000	
Payment of bonus shares	20,000	
Financial Resources Applied		210,000
Increase in Cash		20,000

Table 24.15: Gujarat Narmada Valley Fertilisers Company

Cash Flow Statement
for the year ended on 31 March

	(Rs in crore)	
	2001	**2000**
A. Cash Flow from Operating Activities		
Net Profit before Tax & Extraordinary Items	112.95	75.66
Adjustment for		
Depreciation	68.91	63.41
Interest (Net)	75.24	80.14
Dividend Received	−10.18	−10.71
P/L on Sales of Assets	−0.63	0.1
Provisions & W/O (Net)	1.17	1.2
P/L in Foreign Exchange	0.31	1.74
	134.82	135.88
Operating Profit before Working Capital Changes	247.77	211.54
Adjustment for		
Trade and other receivables	7.65	−44.85
Inventories	−16.59	−27.35
Trade Payables	41.76	−32.43
	32.82	−104.63
Cash Generated from/(used in) Operations	280.59	106.91
Interest Paid (Net)	0	0
Direct Taxes Paid	−11.33	−14.77
	−11.33	−14.77
Cash Flow before Extraordinary Items	269.26	92.14
Extraordinary Items	0	0
Net Cash from Operating Activities	269.26	92.14
B. Cash Flow from Investing Activities		
Investment in Assets:		
Purchased of Fixed Assets	−144.51	−167.62
Sale of Fixed Assets	1.32	0.08
Sale of Investments	2.65	2.35
Interest Received	23.11	14.43
Dividend Received	10.19	10.72
Net Cash Used in Investing Activities	−107.24	−140.04
C. Cash Flow from Financing Activities		
Proceeds:		
Proceed from other Long Term Borrowings	192.5	139.53
Proceed from Bank Borrowings	0	0
Proceed from Short Term Borrowings	0	154.13
Payments:		
Of other Long Term Borrowings	−87.72	−100.25
Of Short Term Borrowings	−127.78	0
Dividend Paid	−38.24	−38.99
Others	−101.44	−94.31
Net Cash Used in Financing Activities	−162.68	60.11
Cash Flow Summary		
Cash and Cash Equivalents at Beginning of the year	18.16	5.95
Net Cash from Operating Activities	269.26	92.14
Net Cash Used in Investing Activities	−107.24	−140.04
Net Cash Used in Financing Activities	−162.68	60.11
Net Inc./(Dec.) in Cash and Cash	−0.66	12.21
Cash and Cash Equivalents at End of the year	17.5	18.16

Cash Flow Statement of Gujarat Narmada Valley Fertilisers Company

Most listed public limited companies in India now prepare a comprehensive cash flow statement. Such a statement shows changes in cash flows from operating activities, investment activities and financing activities. Table 24.15 provides cash flow statement of Gujarat Narmada Fertilisers Valley Company (GNFC) for the years 2000 and 2001. The following points may be observed from the GNFC's cash flow statement for the year 2001:

- GNFC utilised Rs 144.51 crore in acquiring fixed assets. After adjusting for investment income and sale of assets, the net outflow on account of investment activities was Rs 107.24 crore.

- GNFC generated Rs 269.26 crore cash flow from its operating activities.

- GNFC raised Rs 192.50 crore from long-term borrowings. Its repayments were far more than this amount resulting in net negative financing flow of Rs 162.68 crore. The company did not issue any shares.

- GNFC's net cash flow from its operating, investment and financing activities was a negative figure of Rs 0.66 crore. Hence, the company cash balance was by this amount. The previous year had a positive net cash flow of Rs 12.21 crore.

USES OF THE STATEMENT OF CHANGES IN FINANCIAL POSITION

The statement of changes in financial position has an analytical value as well as it is an important planning tool. It gives a clear picture of the causes of changes in the company's working capital or cash flow position. It indicates the financing and investment policies followed by the company in the past. The statement reveals the non-current assets acquired by the company, and the manner in which they have been financed from the internal and external sources. The statement is useful as a tool of historical analysis as it helps to answer questions such as given below:[1]

1. What is the liquidity position of the firm?
2. What are the causes of changes in the firm's working capital or cash position?
3. What fixed assets are acquired by the firm?
4. Did the firm pay dividends to its shareholders or not? If not, was it due to shortage of funds?
5. How much of the firm's working capital needs were met by the funds generated from current operations?
6. Did the firm use external sources of finances to meet its needs of funds?
7. If the external financing was used, what ratio of debt and equity was maintained?
8. Did the firm sell any of its non-current assets? If so, what were the proceeds from such sales?
9. Could the firm pay its long-term debt as per the schedules?
10. What were the significant investment and financing activities of the firm that did not involve working capital?

Realising the importance of the cash (and fund) flow statement, the stock exchange requires listed companies in India to include cash flow statement in their annual reports.

A projected statement of changes in financial position is an important planning tool. The estimates of working capital for a long-term period, say, for five to ten years, help management to plan the repayment of long-term debt and interest, acquisition of fixed assets and payment of cash dividends. If the firm needs working capital for expansion, which cannot be ordinarily provided from operations, it can plan on the basis of the estimate—how much, and from what sources the required working capital will be procured in the future.

A projected statement of changes in the financial position is also useful in obtaining loans from banks and other financial institutions. Nowadays lenders invariably ask for such projected statement. These statements indicate to them the liquidity position of the firm and its ability to pay interest regularly and repay the principal.

The statement prepared to analyse the cash flows is an important tool of the short-term financial planning. In the long run, the firm is interested in working capital because the items of working capital will ultimately change into cash. But to make payments in the immediate future the firm needs cash. Cash is needed to pay maturing debts, interest, dividend and various expenses in the near future. Therefore, the firm would like to estimate its cash balances on monthly or quarterly basis.

SUMMARY

- Balance sheet is a statement of a firm's assets, liabilities and equity on a specific date. Assets are economic resources that help generating revenues. Liabilities are the firm's obligations to creditors. Equity is the investment made by owners in the firm.

- Both the balance sheet and the profit and loss statement do not explain the changes in assets, liabilities and owner's equity. The statement of changes in financial position is prepared to show these changes. Two common forms of such statement are: (*a*) the funds flow statement, and (*b*) the cash flow statement.

- The term "fund" can be defined at least in three ways: It may mean (*i*) cash, (*ii*) working capital (the difference between current assets and current liabilities), or (*iii*) financial resources (arising from both current and non-current items). The funds flow statement provides an analysis of changes in the firm's working capital position. The cash flow statement is prepared to analyse changes in the firm's cash position. Both these statements can be recast to incorporate additional financial information that does not affect cash or working capital but influences the financing and asset mix of the firm.

---

1. Woelfel, *op. cit.*

❖ The main source of funds—working capital or cash—is the firm's operations. Funds from operations are calculated by adjusting the figure of net profit for non-fund or non-cash items such as depreciation. Depreciation is added to net profits to arrive at funds from operation. To determine cash from operations, changes in current assets and current liabilities are also adjusted in net profits. Increase in current assets and decrease in current liabilities reduce cash while decrease in current assets and increase in current liabilities increase cash. Other sources of working capital or cash include sale of fixed assets, issue of share capital and borrowings. The typical examples of uses of funds are: acquisition of fixed assets, repayment of debt and payment of cash dividend.

❖ Funds flow and cash flow statement are important managerial tools for financial analysis. They help the firm to know its liquidity position, capital expenditures incurred, dividend paid and extent of external financing. A projected funds or cash flow statement guides the firm to plan the matching of inflow and outflow of funds or cash.

KEY CONCEPTS

Assets	Equity	Funds from operation	Statement of changes in
Balance sheet	Financial resources	Liabilities	financial position
Cash flow statement	Fixed assets	Profit and loss statement	Working capital flow
Current assets	Funds flow	Redeemable preference shares	Working capital from
Current liabilities	Funds flow statement	Retained earnings	operation

---

ILLUSTRATIVE SOLVED PROBLEMS

Problem 24.1: From the following data of Jalan Company, prepare (a) a statement of sources and uses of working capital (funds), (b) a schedule of changes in working capital, and (c) a statement of sources and uses of cash:

Table 24.16: Jalan Company

Balance Sheet
for the year ended on 31 December **(Rs)**

Assets	19X2	19X1
Cash	126,000	114,000
Short-term investment	42,400	20,000
Debtors	60,000	50,000
Stock	38,000	28,000
Long-term investment	28,000	44,000
Machinery	200,000	140,000
Buildings	240,000	80,000
Land	14,000	14,000
Total	748,400	490,000
Liabilities and Equity		
Accumulated depreciation	110,000	60,000
Creditors	40,000	30,000
Bills payable	20,000	10,000
Secured	200,000	100,000
Share capital	220,000	160,000
Share premium	24,000	–
Reserve and surplus	134,000	130,000
Total	748,000	490,000

Table 24.17: Jalan Company

Income Statement
for the year ended on 31 December, 19X2 **(Rs)**

Sales		240,000
Cost of goods sold		134,800
Gross profit		105,200
Less: Operating expenses:		
Depreciation—Machinery	20,000	
Depreciation—Buildings	32,000	
Other expenses	40,000	92,000
Net profit from operations		13,200
Gain on sale of long-term investment		4,800
Total		18,000
Loss on sale of machinery		2,000
Net Profit		16,000

Note: The proceeds from the sale of machinery were Rs 6,000.

(*M.Com., D.U., adapted*)

Solution: Tables 24.18 to 24.20 respectively show Jalan's statement of sources and uses of working capital, schedule of working capital changes and the statement of sources and uses of cash.

Table 24.18: Jalan Company

Statement of Sources and Uses of Working Capital
for the year ended on 31 December, 19X2 **(Rs)**

Sources

Working capital from operations	65,200	
Sale of long-term investment	20,800	
Sale of machinery	6,000	
Secured loan	1,00,000	
Share capital	60,000	
Share premium	24,000	2,76,000

Uses

Purchase of machinery	70,000	
Purchase of building	1,60,000	
Payment of dividend	11,600	2,41,600
Increase in Working Capital		34,400

Notes: (*i*) Working capital from operations is found as follows:

	Rs	Rs
Net profit	16,000	
Add: Depreciation		
Machinery	20,000	
Buildings	32,000	
Loss on sale of machinery	2,000	70,000
Less: Gain on sale of long-term investment		4,800
Working capital from operations		65,200

(*ii*) The comparative balance sheet indicates that long-term investments have decreased by Rs 16,000, which is due to the sale of investments. On sale, a gain of Rs 4,800 is made. This means that the long-term investment must have been sold for cash of Rs 20,800 (Rs 16,000 + Rs 4,800).

(*iii*) The proceeds from the sale of machine, Rs 6,000, have been reported as source of working capital.

Table 24.19: Jalan Company: Schedule of Working Capital Changes

	(Rs)	
	Increase	*Decrease*
Current Assets		
Cash	12,000	
Short-term investments	22,400	
Debtors	10,000	
Stocks	10,000	
Current Liabilities		
Creditors		10,000
Bill payable		10,000
Increase in Working Capital		34,400
	54,400	54,400

Table 24.20: Jalan Company

Statement of Sources and Uses of Cash
for the year ended 31 December, 19X2 **(Rs)**

Sources

Cash from operations	65,200	
Sale of long-term investments	20,800	
Sale of machinery	6,000	
Secured loan	100,000	
Share capital	60,000	
Share premium	24,000	276,000

Uses

Purchase of machinery	70,000	
Purchase of buildings	160,000	
Payment of dividend	11,600	
Purchase of marketable securities	22,400	264,000
Increase in cash		12,000

Cash from operations is found as follows:

	Rs	Rs
Net profit	16,000	
Add: Depreciation—Machinery	20,000	
Depreciation—Building	32,000	
Loss on sale of machinery	2,000	
Increase in creditors	10,000	
Increase in bills payable	10,000	90,000
Less: Gain on sale of long-term investments	4,800	
Increase in debtors	10,000	
Increase in stock	10,000	24,800
Cash from operations		65,200

(*iv*) Secured loan increased by Rs 1,00,000; thus providing working capital. Share capital together with share premium has contributed a working capital of Rs 84,000 (Rs 60,000 + Rs 24,000).

(*v*) During the year working capital was utilised to acquire machinery of Rs 70,000. The opening balance of machinery account is Rs 1,40,000. After the sale of machinery costing Rs 10,000, this balance at the close of the year should have been Rs 1,30,000. But the closing balance is Rs 2,00,000, which implies that machinery worth Rs 70,000 is acquired.

(*vi*) The cost of machinery sold has been as follows: The accumulated depreciation has increased by Rs 50,000 (Rs 1,10,000 − Rs 60,000). If we subtract depreciation on buildings, Rs 32,000, we are left with the closing balance of accumulated depreciation of Rs 18,000 for machinery. But during the year depreciation provided on machinery is Rs 20,000. This means that the accumulated depreciation on machinery sold was Rs 2,000 (Rs 20,000 − Rs 18,000) which must have been written off at the time of the sale of machinery. Thus, the cost of machinery sold is: sale proceeds, Rs 6,000 plus accumulated depreciation, Rs 2,000, plus loss, Rs 2,000, i.e., Rs 10,000.

(*vii*) The increase in buildings by Rs 1,60,000 is a purchase, using working capital funds.

(*viii*) The net profits are Rs 16,000, but the reserve has increased by

Rs 4,400 only. This means that the difference, Rs 11,600 (Rs 16,000 – Rs 4,400) must have been paid as cash dividends to the shareholders.

Problem 24.2: The following are the financial statements of X Ltd.:

Table 24.21: X Ltd.

Balance Sheets

		Rs
	31 March 19X2	31 March 19X1
Assets		
Cash	349,600	483,600
Trade investments	160,000	420,000
Debtors	305,400	308,600
Stock	235,200	184,600
Prepaid expenses	7,600	9,200
Investment in A Ltd.	300,000	–
Land	14,400	14,400
Buildings, net of depreciation	2,407,200	713,600
Machinery, net of depreciation	443,400	428,200
Total Assets	4,222,800	2,562,200
Liabilities		
Creditors	115,200	108,400
Bank overdraft	30,000	25,000
Accrued expenses	17,400	18,400
Income-tax payable	193,000	67,400
Current installment due on long-term loans	40,000	–
Long-term loans	160,000	200,000
Debentures, net of discount	960,000	–
Share capital, Rs 10 par value	670,000	600,000
Share premium	1,340,000	950,000
Reserves and surplus	697,200	493,000
Total Liabilities	4,222,800	2,562,200

Table 24.22: X LTD.

Income Statement
for the year ended 31 March, 19X2 (*Rs*)

Sales	1,692,400
Cost of goods sold and operating expenses including depreciation on buildings of Rs 26,400 and depreciation on machinery of Rs 45,600	1,191,200
Operating profit	501,200
Gain on sale of trade investments	25,600
Gain on sale of machinery	7,400
Profit before taxes	534,200
Income taxes	209,400
Net profit	324,800

Additional information: (*i*) Machinery with a net book value of Rs 36,600 was sold during the year. (*ii*) The shares of A Ltd. were acquired upon a payment of Rs 120,000 in cash and the issuance of 3,000 shares of X Ltd. The share of X Ltd. was selling for Rs 60 a share at that time. (*iii*) A new building was purchased at a cost of Rs 1,720,000. (*iv*) Debentures having a face value of Rs 100 each were issued in January 19X2, at 96. (*v*) The cost of trade investments sold was Rs 260,000. (*vi*) The company issued 4,000 shares for Rs 280,000. (*vii*) Cash dividends of Rs 1.80 a share were paid on 67,000 outstanding shares.

Prepare a statement of changes in financial position on working capital basis as well as cash basis of X Ltd. for the year ended 31 March, 19X2. (*C.A., adapted*)

Solution:

Table 24.23: X Ltd.

Statement of Changes in Financial Position
(Working Capital Basis)
for the year ended 31 March, 19X2 (*Rs*)

Sources	
Working capital from operations:	
Net income after tax	324,800
Add: Depreciation	72,000
	396,800
Less: Gain on sale of machinery	7,400
	389,400
Sale of machinery (Rs 36,600 + Rs 7,400)	44,000
Debentures issued	960,000
Share capital issued for cash (including share premium)	280,000
Financial transaction not affecting working capital	
Shares issued in partial payment for investments in A Ltd.	180,000
Financial Resources Provided	1,853,400
Uses	
Purchase of buildings	1,720,000
Purchase of machinery	97,400
Instalment currently due on long-term loans	40,000
Payment of cash dividends	120,600
Purchase of investments in A Ltd. for cash	120,000
Financial transaction not affecting working capital	
Purchase of investments in A Ltd. in exchange of issue of 3000 shares @ Rs 60 each	180,000
Financial Resources Applied	2,278,000
Net Decrease in Working Capital	424,600

The amount of machinery sold is found out as follows:

Machinery

	Rs		Rs
Opening balance (given)	428,200	Sale of machinery (given)	36,600
Purchases (plug)	97,400	Depreciation (given)	45,600
		Closing balance (given)	443,400
	525,600		525,600

Table 24.24: X Ltd.

Statement of Changes in Financial Position (Cash Basis)
for the year ended 31 March, 19X2   **(Rs)**

Sources

Cash from operations:		
Net income after tax	324,800	
Add: Depreciation	72,000	
Decrease in debtors	3,200	
Decrease in prepaid expenses	1,600	
Increase in creditors	6,800	
Increase in income tax payable	25,600	434,000
Less: Gain on sale of machinery	7,400	
Increase in stock	50,600	
Decrease in accrued expenses	1,000	59,000
	375,000	
Sale of trade investment		260,000
Increase in bank overdraft		5,000
Sale of machinery		44,000
Debentures issued		960,000
Shares issued		280,000
Financial transaction not affecting cash		
Share issued in partial payment for investments in A Ltd.		180,000
Instalment currently due on long-term loans		40,000
Financial Resources Provided		**2,144,000**
Uses		
Purchase of buildings		1,720,000
Purchase of machinery		97,400
Payment of cash dividend		120,600
Purchase of investments in A Ltd. for cash		120,000
Financial transaction not affecting cash		
Purchase of investments in A Ltd. in exchange of issue of		
3,000 shares @ Rs 60 each		180,000
Instalment currently due on long-term loans		40,000
Financial Resources Applied		**2,278,000**
Net Decrease in Cash		**134,000**

Notes:

1. Funds from operations are shown in net of taxes. Alternatively, payment of tax may be separately treated as use of funds. In that case, tax would be added to net profit.
2. If tax shown in Profit and Loss Account is assumed to be a provision, then the amount of cash paid for tax has to be calculated. In the present problem if this procedure is followed, then cash paid for tax is: Rs 167,400 + Rs 209,400 – Rs 193,000 = Rs 183,800.
3. Gain on the sale of trade investments is considered an operating income.

Problem 24.3. The following are the balance sheets of Mega Company for the years ending 31 July, 19X1 and 31 July, 19X2.

Table 24.25: Mega Company

Balance Sheet
for the year ending on 31 July   **(Rs)**

	19X1	*19X2*
Capital and Liabilities		
Share capital	300,000	350,000
General reserve	100,000	125,000
Capital reserve (profit on sale of investment)	–	5,000
Profit and loss account	50,000	100,000
15% Debentures	150,000	100,000
Accrued expenses	5,000	6,000
Creditors	80,000	125,000
Provision for dividend	15,000	17,000
Provision for taxation	35,000	38,000
Total	735,000	866,000
Assets		
Fixed assets	500,000	600,000
Less: Accumulated depreciation	100,000	125,000
Net fixed assets	400,000	475,000
Long-term investments (at cost)	90,000	90,000
Stock (at cost)	100,000	135,000
Debtors (net of provisions for doubtful debts of Rs 20,000 and Rs 25,000 respectively for 19X1 and 19X2)	112,500	122,500
Bills receivables	20,000	32,500
Prepaid expenses	5,000	6,000
Miscellaneous expenditure	7,500	5,000
Total	735,000	866,000

Additional information: (*i*) During the year 19X2, fixed asset with a net book value of Rs 5,000 (accumulated depreciation Rs 15,000) was sold for Rs 4,000. (*ii*) During the year 19X2, investments costing Rs 40,000 were sold, and also investments costing Rs 40,000 were purchased. (*iii*) Debentures were retired at a premium of 10 per cent. (*iv*) Tax of Rs 27,500 was paid for 19X1. (*v*) During 19X2, bad debts of Rs 7,000 were written off against the provision for doubtful debt account. (*vi*) The proposed dividend for 19X1 was paid in 19X2.

You are required to prepare a funds flow statement (i.e., statement of changes in financial position on working capital basis) for the year ended 31 July 19X2. (*C.A., adapted*)

Solution:

Table 24.26: Mega Company

Funds Flow Statement
for the year ended 31 July, 19X2 **(Rs)**

Sources

Working capital from operations	171,000	
Sale of fixed asset	4,000	
Sale of investments	45,000	
Share capital issued	50,000	
Total Funds Provided		270,000

Uses

Purchase of fixed assets	120,000	
Purchase of investments	40,000	
Payment of debentures (at a premium of 10%)	55,000	
Payment of dividend	15,000	
Payment of taxes	27,500	
Total Funds Applied		257,500
Increase in Working Capital		12,500

Notes:

1. Funds from operations:

	Rs
Profit and loss balance on 31 July, 19X2	100,000
Add: Depreciation	40,000
Loss on sale of asset	1,000
Misc. expenditure written off	2,500
Transfer to reserve	25,000
Premium on redemption of debentures	5,000
Provision for dividend	17,000
Provision for taxation	30,500
	221,000
Less: Profit and loss balance on 31 July, 19X1	50,000
Funds from operations	171,000

2. Depreciation for the year 19X2 was Rs 40,000. The accumulated depreciation on 31 July, 19X1 was Rs 100,000 of which Rs 15,000 was written off during the year on account of sale of asset. Thus the balance on 31 July, 19X2 should have been Rs 85,000. Since the balance is Rs 125,000, the company would have provided a depreciation of Rs 40,000 (i.e., Rs 125,000 – Rs 85,000) during the year 19X2.
3. Fixed assets were of Rs 500,000 in 19X1. With the sale of a fixed asset costing Rs 20,000 (i.e., Rs 5,000 + Rs 15,000), this balance should have been Rs 480,000. But the balance on 3 July, 19X2 is Rs 600,000. This means fixed assets of Rs 1,20,000 were acquired during the year.
4. Profit on the sale of investment, Rs 5,000 has been credited to capital reserve account. It implies that investments were sold for Rs 45,000 (i.e., Rs 40,000 + Rs 5,000).
5. The provision for taxation during the year 19X2 is Rs 30,500 (i.e., Rs 38,000 – (Rs 35,000 – Rs 27,500)).
6. Bad debts written off against the provision account have no significance for funds flow statement, as they do not affect working capital.

Problem 24.4: From the following balance sheet of Rupa Company Limited, a wholly owned subsidiary of Sadhana Manufacturing Limited, prepare a statement of sources and application of funds and a schedule of changes in working capital (with the column for changes in other assets):

Table 24.27: Rupa Company Limited

Balance Sheet

Liabilities	Jan. 1	Dec. 31	Assets	Jan. 1	Dec. 31
Current liabilities	200,000	250,000	Current Assets	400,000	5,01,000
Capital surplus	300,000	—	Net fixed Assets	1,000,000	1,016,000
Earned surplus	700,000	—	Deferred charges	50,000	40,000
Equity capital	800,000	—	Goodwill	650,000	60,000
Inter-company account	100,000	1,367,000			
	2,100,000	1,617,000		2,100,000	1,617,000

On March 31, Rs 600,000 of goodwill was charged off Rs 300,000 to capital surplus and Rs 300,000 to earned surplus. In the first half of the year the subsidiary bought the assets of a business, consisting of some fixed assets and goodwill and Rs 50,000 for inventory and accounts receivable. The total amount paid was Rs 170,000. Old machinery was sold for Rs 1,000; it had a book value of Rs 12,000, and Rs 8,000 depreciation has been provided. On June 30, the subsidiary company was dissolved and was made a division of the parent company. Its accounts continued in a separate divisional ledger. A net profit of Rs 317,000, after providing Rs 80,000 for depreciation and Rs 10,000 for amortisation of goodwill, has been made and was credited to inter-company account. The deferred charges consist of unexpired insurance and prepaid current expenses. *(C.A., adapted)*

Solution:

Table 24.28: Rupa Company Limited

Statement of Sources and Uses of Funds **(Rs)**

Sources

Funds from operations	420,000	
Sale of plant	1,000	
Loan from holding company	950,000	
Total Funds Raised		1,371,000

Uses

Purchase of fixed assets	100,000	
Purchase of goodwill	20,000	
Payment of dividend	400,000	
Payment of capital	800,000	
Total Funds Applied		1,320,000
Increase in Working Capital		51,000

Table 24.29: Rupa Company Limited

Schedule of Changes in Working Capital (Rs)

	Change in working capital		Change in other assets		
Assets					
Current assets	400,000	501,000	(+)101,000		—
Net fixed assets	1,000,000	1,016,000	—	(+)	16,000
Deferred changes	50,000	40,000	—	(−)	10,000
Goodwill	650,000	60,000	—	(−)	590,000
	2,100,000	1,617,000	(+)101,000	(−)	584,000
Liabilities					
Current liabilities	200,000	250,000	(+) 50,000		—
Capital surplus	300,000	—	—	(−)	300,000
Earned surplus	700,000	—	—	(−)	700,000
Equity capital	800,000	—	—	(−)	800,000
Inter-company account	100,000	1,367,000	—	(+)	1,267,000
	2,100,000	1,617,000			
Increase in Working Capital			(+) 51,000	(−)	51,000
			101,000	(−)	584,000

Notes:

1. Funds from operations are calculated as follows:

	Rs
Net profit during the year	317,000
Add: Depreciation written off	80,000
Loss on sale of machinery	3,000
Deferred charges written off	10,000
Goodwill written off	10,000
Funds from operations	420,000

2. *Loss on sale of machinery:* The depreciated value of machine sold is Rs 4,000 (i.e., original book value of Rs 12,000 minus accumulated depreciation of Rs 8,000). Since it is sold for Rs 1,000, a loss of Rs 3,000 is incurred.

3. *Purchase of fixed assets:* The opening balance is Rs 1,000,000; depreciation provided during the year is Rs 80,000 and old machine of Rs 4,000 (depreciated value) is sold. Thus, the balance left should have been Rs 916,000. Since the balance at the end of the year is Rs 1,016,000, additions of Rs 100,000 must have been made.

4. *Deferred charges written off:* The opening balance is Rs 50,000 while the balance at the end is Rs 40,000. This implies that Rs 10,000 have been written off to profit and loss account during the year.

5. *Goodwill written off:* It is given in the problem that subsidiary bought asset of Rs 170,000. Out of this Rs 50,000 are invested in inventory and accounts receivable. As explained in (3) above, fixed assets of Rs 1,00,000 are also acquired. Thus, the difference, Rs 170,000 − Rs 150,000 = Rs 20,000 must have been paid for goodwill. The opening balance of goodwill is Rs 650,000. Adding Rs 20,000, its balance should be Rs 670,000. Out of this Rs 600,000 have been written off, Rs 300,000 each respectively from earned surplus and capital surplus. Thus the balance at the end should have been Rs 70,000. As the balance at the end is Rs 60,000, goodwill of Rs 10,000 must have been written off during the year.

6. *Inter-company account:* The opening balance in this head is Rs 100,000; Rs 317,000 are transferred from net profits. Thus the total should be Rs 417,000. Since the ending balance is Rs 1,367,000, Rs 950,000 must have been provided as loan by the holding company.

7. *Payment of dividend:* The beginning balance of earned surplus account is Rs 700,000, out of which Rs 300,000 are written off for goodwill. The unaccounted amount of Rs 400,000 has been assumed to be paid as dividend.

8. *Payment of capital:* No ending balance of equity capital implies its payment on dissolution.

REVIEW QUESTIONS

1. Explain the concept of 'working capital flow'. Give examples of transactions that affect working capital, and that do not affect working capital.

2. "Depreciation is an important source of working capital (funds)." Do you agree? Defend your answer.

3. Explain the major sources and uses of working capital.

4. Explain and illustrate the preparation of a statement of changes in working capital.

5. What is the utility of funds flow statement in which 'funds' refer to 'all financial resources'?

6. How can a statement of changes in cash flows be prepared? How does it differ from the statement prepared on working capital basis?

7. Explain why transactions such as depreciation expense, amortisation of debenture discount and similar internal items are neither sources nor applications of financial resources, yet are treated as adjustments to net profit.

8. How can a statement of changes in working capital or cash position be converted into a statement of changes in financial position on 'all financial resources' basis? Illustrate your answer.

9. Is it possible for a company, with sizeable net profit, not to be in a position to pay dividends to shareholders? Illustrate your answer.

10. What is a statement of changes in financial position? How does it differ from funds flow or cash flow statement?

11. What are the uses of a statement of sources and uses of working capital? When is it more appropriate to prepare a statement of cash flow?

PROBLEMS

1. The comparative balance sheets of Doba Company showed the following changes in balance sheet items from 19X1 to 19X2:

	Rs
Working capital	127,500 increase
Long-term investments	45,000 increase
Land	48,000 increase
Machinery (less accumulated depreciation)	90,000 increase
15% Debentures	240,000 increase
Share capital	60,000 increase
Reserves and surplus	10,500 decrease

The following additional data are provided: (i) Net profit for the year was Rs 157,500 (ii) Accumulated depreciation for 19X1 was Rs 67,500 and for 19X2 Rs 90,000. (iii) A machine of Rs 112,500 was purchased during the year; depreciation expenses for the year was Rs 22,500. (iv) A bonus issue of shares of Rs 60,000 was made during the year. (v) A cash dividend of Rs 87,000 was declared and paid during the year.

Prepare a statement of changes in financial position for Doba Company.

2. The comparative balance sheets for Soma Pvt. Ltd. are given below:

Table 24.30: Soma Pvt. Ltd.

Comparative Balance Sheets
for the year ended on 31 December (Rs)

	19X2	19X1
Assets		
Cash	82,000	22,000
Debtors	104,000	24,000
Stock	112,000	60,000
Prepaid expenses	22,000	14,000
Plant and machinery	380,000	360,000
Goodwill	36,000	40,000
Total	736,000	520,000
Equities		
Creditors	30,000	14,000
Provision for depreciation	100,000	60,000
Debentures	102,000	102,000
Premium on debentures issue	12,000	18,000
Share capital	190,000	90,000
Share premium	30,000	–
Reserves and surplus	272,000	236,000
Total	736,000	520,000

The company made a net profit of Rs 66,000 during the year. Prepare a statement of changes in financial position on (a) working capital basis, (b) cash basis. Also prepare a schedule of working capital changes.

3. From the following data of Kamdhenu Company, prepare a statement of changes in financial position.

Table 24.31: Kamdhenu Company

Balance Sheets
for the year ended on 31 March (Rs)

	19X2	19X1
Assets		
Cash	30,000	22,500
Debtors	45,000	40,000
Stock	20,000	16,000
Long-term investments	15,000	25,000
Machinery	20,000	12,500
Buildings	45,000	37,500
Land	10,000	10,000
Total	185,000	163,500
Liabilities and Equity		
Provision for depreciation:		
Machinery	3,750	1,500
Buildings	9,000	6,000
Provision for doubtful debts	1,500	1,000
Creditors	20,000	16,500
Outstanding expenses	2,250	1,750
Loan (adjust security of machinery)	22,500	25,000
Share capital	100,000	100,000
Reserves and surplus	26,000	11,750
Total	185,000	163,500

Additional data:

(i) Net profit for the year 19X2 is Rs 27,500.
(ii) Machinery costing Rs 2,500, on which depreciation of Rs 500 has accumulated, was sold for Rs 3,000. The gain is included in net profit.
(iii) Investments costing Rs 10,000 were sold during the year for Rs 12,500. The gain is included in net profit.
(iv) Cash dividends paid during the year, Rs 13,250.

4. Prepare (a) a statement of changes in financial position on (i) working capital basis, (ii) cash basis, and (b) a schedule of changes in working capital from the following data:

Table 24.32: M Company

Balance Sheet
for the year ended on 30 June (Rs)

Assets	19X1	19X2	Equities	19X1	19X2
Cash	15,000	9,000	Creditors	60,000	0
Marketable			Bills payable	15,000	24,000
securities	21,000	15,000	Accrued expenses	6,000	6,000
Debtors	30,000	45,000	Tax payable	9,000	15,000
Stock	36,000	45,000	Long-term debt	0	45,000
Fixed assets, net	150,000	1,65,000	Share capital		
Other non-			including		
current assets	24,000	15,000	reserve	180,000	210,000
	270,000	3,00,000		270,000	300,000

Table 24.33: M Company

Profit and Loss Account
for the year ended 30 June **(Rs)**

Sale		150,000
Expenses:		
Cost of goods sold	75,000	
Selling, general and administrative expenses	15,000	
Depreciation	15,000	
Interest	3,000	108,000
Profit before tax		42,000
Less: Tax		21,000
Profit after tax		21,000
Reserve, 30 June 19X1		120,000
		141,000
Less: Cash dividends		9,000
Reserve, 30 June 19X2		132,000

5. Balance sheet and profit and loss account of JB Sons Company Limited as on December 31, 19X1 and 19X2 are as follows:

Table 24.34: JB Sons

Balance Sheet
as on 31 December **(Rs)**

Liabilities	19X1	19X2	Assets	19X1	19X2
Accounts payable	15,000	25,000	Cash balance	5,000	2,000
Cash credit	13,000	10,000	Accounts		
Outstanding			receivable	10,000	8,000
expenses	2,000	3,000	Loan and		
Long-term loan	30,000	20,000	advances	5,000	–
Capital	30,000	30,000	Inventories	20,000	25,000
Surplus	10,000	12,000	Fixed assets (net)	60,000	65,000
	100,000	1,00,000		100,000	100,000

Table 24.35: JB Sons Company

Profit and Loss Account
for the year 19X2 **(Rs)**

Sales	200,000
Less: Cost of goods sold (including depreciation of Rs 10,000)	170,000
Gross profit	30,000
Less: Other expenses	20,000
Income before tax	10,000
Less: Income-tax provision	5,000
Income after tax	5,000

Prepare a statement of sources and uses of funds.

(*C.A., adapted*)

6. A company finds on 1 January, 19X3, that it is short of funds with which to implement its programme of expansion. On 1 January, 19X1, it had a cash credit balance of Rs 180,000. From the following information, prepare a statement for the board of directors to show how the overdraft of Rs 68,750 as at the 31 December, 19X2 has arisen:

	19X1 Rs	19X2 Rs		19X1 Rs	19X2 Rs
Fixed assets	750,000	11,20,000	Trade creditors	270,000	350,000
Stock and stores	190,000	3,30,000	Share capital		
Debtors	380,000	3,35,000	(in shares of	250,000	300,000
Bank balance	180,000	–	Rs 10 each)		
Bank overdraft	–	68,750	Bills receivables	87,500	95,000

The profit for the year ended December 31, 19X2 before charging depreciation and taxation amounted to Rs 240,000. The 5,000 shares were issued on 1 January 19X2 at a premium of Rs 5 per share, and Rs 137,500 was paid in March 19X2 by way of income tax. Dividend was paid as follows: on the capital on 31 December, 19X1 at 10% less tax at 25%; 19X2 (interim) 5 per cent free of tax.

(*C.A., adapted*)

7. From the following data of Pandit Sons Limited, prepare a statement of sources and uses of funds:

Table 24.36: Pandit Sons Limited

Balance Sheet
as on 31 December **(Rs '000)**

Liabilities	19X2	19X1	Assets	19X2	19X1
Accumulated			Cash	315	285
depreciation	275	150	Marketable securities	106	50
Creditors	100	75	Debtors	150	125
Bills payable	50	25	Inventories	95	70
Debentures	500	250	Investments	70	110
Equity capital	550	400	Machinery	500	350
Premium on shares	60	–	Buildings	600	200
Retained earning	336	325	Land	35	35
	1,871	1,225		1,871	1,225

Table 24.37: Pandit Sons Limited

Income Statement
for the year ended December 31, 19X2 **(Rs '000)**

Sales		600
Cost of goods sold		337
Gross margin on sales		263
Operating expenses:		
Depreciation — machinery	50	
— buildings	80	
Other expenses	100	230
Net margin from operations		33
Gain on sales on long-term investments		12
Total		45
Loss on sales of machinery (proceeds from sales Rs 15,000)		5
Net income		40

8. From the following balance sheet of Alpha Ltd. make out (1) statement of changes in the working capital, and (2) funds flow statement:

Table 24.38: Alpha Co.

Balance Sheet

(Rs)

Liabilities	19X1	19X2	Assets	19X1	19X2
Equity share			Goodwill	100,000	80,000
capital	300,000	400,000	Land and		
8% Redeemable			building	200,000	170,000
Preference			Plant	80,000	200,000
capital	150,000	100,000	Investments	20,000	30,000
Capital reserve	–	20,000	Sundry		
General reserve	40,000	50,000	debtors	140,000	170,000
Profit and loss			Stock	77,000	109,000
account	30,000	48,000	Bills receivable	20,000	30,000
Proposed dividend	42,000	50,000	Cash in hand	15,000	10,000
Sundry creditors	25,000	47,000	Cash at bank	10,000	8,000
Bills payable	20,000	16,000	Preliminary		
Liabilities for			expenses	15,000	10,000
expenses	30,000	36,000			
Provision for					
taxation	40,000	50,000			
	677,000	817,000		677,000	817,000

Additional data: (*i*) A piece of land has been sold out in 19X2 and the profit on sale has been carried to capital reserve. (*ii*) A machine has been sold for Rs 10,000. The written down value of the machine was Rs 12,000. Depreciation of Rs 10,000 is charged on plant account in 19X2. (*iii*) The investments are trade investments; Rs 3,000 by way of dividend is received including Rs 1,000 from pre-acquisition profit which has been credited to investment account. (*iv*) An interim dividend of Rs 20,000 has been paid in 19X2. (*C.A., adapted*)

9. The following are the summaries of the balance sheets of C Victory Limited as on 31 December, 19X1 and 31 December 19X2:

Table 24.39: C Victory Ltd.

Balance Sheet

(Rs)

Liabilities	19X1	19X2	Assets	19X1	19X2
Sundry creditors	39,500	41,135	Cash at bank	2,500	2,700
Bills payable	33,780	11,525	Sundry debtors	87,490	73,360
Bank overdraft	59,510	–	Stock	111,040	97,370
Provision for			Land and		
taxation	40,000	50,000	building	148,500	144,250
Reserves	50,000	50,000	Plant and		
Profit and loss			machinery	112,950	116,200
account	39,690	41,220	Goodwill	–	20,000
Share capital	200,000	260,000			
	462,480	453,880		462,480	453,880

The following additional information is obtained from the general ledger: (*a*) During the year ended December 19X2 an interim dividend of Rs 26,000 was paid. (*b*) The assets of another company were purchased for Rs 60,000 payable in fully paid shares of the company. These assets consisted of stock Rs 22,000, machinery Rs 18,000, and goodwill Rs 20,000. In addition sundry purchases of plant were made totalling Rs 5,600. (*c*) Income-tax paid during the year amounted to Rs. 25,000. (*d*) The net profit for the year before tax was Rs 65,530.

You are required to prepare a statement showing the sources and application of funds for the year 19X2 and a schedule setting out changes in working capital. (*C.A., adapted*)

10. The comparative balance sheets of Bombay Industries Ltd. as on 31 December, 19X1 and 19X2 are as under:

Table 24.40: Bombay Industries Ltd.

Balance Sheet

(Rs)

Liabilities	19X1	19X2	Assets	19X1	19X2
Current Liabilities			**Current Assets**		
Sundry creditors	40.40	43.20	Cash at bank	44.60	47.80
Provision for			Debtors	10.80	17.00
taxation	10.80	12.20	Stock-in-trade	44.00	67.20
Liabilities for			Miscellaneous	30.20	8.00
expenses	2.60	1.00	Total current		
Total current			assets	129.60	140.00
liabilities	53.80	56.40			
Long-term Loans	22.00	21.00	**Fixed Assets**		
Total liabilities	75.80	77.40	Plant, mach.		
			& bldng.	283.40	368.00
Owner's Equity			*Less:* Total		
Paid-up capital	280.00	320.00	depreciation	25.80	34.20
				257.60	333.80
Reserves and			Land	50.00	50.00
surplus	140.60	163.60	Total fixed		
Total equity	420.60	483.60	assets	307.60	383.80
			Investments	42.40	25.20
			Intangible Assets	16.80	12.00
			Total non-current		
			assets	366.80	421.00
Total Capital	496.40	561.00	**Total Assets**	496.40	561.00

The income for the year amounted to Rs 57.80 lakh after charging depreciation of Rs 8.40 lakh but before making the following adjustments: (*i*) profit on land purchased and sold in 19X2, Rs 15.60 lakh; (*ii*) loss on sale of marketable securities Rs 2.80 lakh, included under miscellaneous current assets; (*iii*) write off intangible assets Rs. 4.80 lakh; (*iv*) write off long-term investments Rs 17.20 lakh.

The dividend declared and paid during the year amounted to Rs 25.60 lakh. From the above particulars prepare. (*i*) statement of sources and application of funds, and (*ii*) statement of changes in working capital. (*C.A., adapted*)

11. Following are the summarised balances of PQ Limited on 30 June, 19X1 and 19X2:

Table 24.41: PQ Limited

Balances as on 30 June				(Rs)
	19X1		**19X2**	
	Dr.	Cr.	Dr.	Cr.
Equity share capital:				
30,000 shares of Rs. 10 each issued and fully paid	–	300,000	–	300,000
Capital reserve	–	–	–	49,200
14% Debentures	–	–	–	50,000
Debenture discount	–	–	1,000	–
Freehold property at cost	122,000	–	–	–
Freehold property at valuation	–	–	165,000	–
Plant and machinery at cost	223,000	–	283,000	–
Depreciation on plant and machinery	–	107,600	–	122,000
Debtors	104,600	–	154,600	–
Stock and work-in-progress	124,000	–	162,500	–
Creditors	–	37,400	–	49,200
Profit and loss account	–	112,000	–	112,000
Net profit for the year	–	–	–	76,500
Dividend in respect of 19X1	–	–	30,000	–
Provision for doubtful debts	–	3,100	–	6,400
Trade investment at cost	–	–	47,000	–
Bank	–	13,500	–	77,800
	573,600	573,600	843,100	843,100

You are informed that: (*i*) The capital reserve on 30 June, 19X2 represented the realised profit on the sale of one freehold property together with the surplus arising on revaluation. (*ii*) During the year ended 30 June, 19X2, plant costing Rs 18,000 against which a depreciation provision of Rs 13,500 had been made was sold for Rs 7,000. (*iii*) On 1 July, 19X1, Rs 50,000 debentures were issued for cash at a discount of Rs 1,000. (*iv*) The net profit for the year is arrived at after crediting the profit on the sale of machinery and charging debenture interest. You are required to prepare a statement which will explain why bank borrowing has increased by Rs 64,300 during the year ended 30 June 19X2. Taxation is to be ignored. (*C.A., adapted*)

12. From the information provided, you are required to prepare a "Source and Disposition of Funds" statement explaining how CD Limited has improved cash position in the year ended 31 December 19X2. The summarised balance sheets of CD Limited as on 31 December 19X1 and 31 December 19X2 were as follows:

Table 24.42: CD Ltd.

	Balance Sheet				(Rs)
Liabilities	**19X1**	**19X2**	*Assets*	**19X1**	**19X2**
Issued share capital	100,000	1,50,000	Freehold property	110,000	130,000
Share premium	15,000	35,000	Plant and machinery	120,000	151,000
Profit and loss	28,000	70,000	Fixtures and fittings, at cost	24,000	29,000
Debentures	70,000	30,000			
Bank overdraft	14,000	–	Stocks	37,000	51,000
Creditors	34,000	48,000			
Proposed dividends	15,000	20,000	Debtors	43,000	44,000
Depreciation:			Bank balance	–	16,000
Plant	45,000	54,000	Premium on redeemed debentures		
Fixtures	13,000	15,000		–	1,000
	334,000	422,000		334,000	422,000

The following additional information is relevant: (*i*) There had been no disposal of freehold property in the year. (*ii*) A machine tool which has cost Rs 8,000 and in respect of which Rs 6,000 depreciation has been provided was sold for Rs 3,000 and fixtures, which had cost Rs 5,000 in respect of which depreciation of Rs 2,000 had been provided, were sold for Rs 1,000. The profits and losses on these transactions had been dealt with through the profit and loss account. (*iii*) The actual premium on the redemption of debentures was Rs 2,000 of which Rs 1,000 has been written off to the profit and loss account. (*iv*) No interim dividend has been paid. (*C.A., adapted*)

13. *GNFC* In Chapter 2, the comparative balance sheets and profit and loss accounts for the years 2000 and 2001 for Gujarat Naramada Valley Fertilisers Company are given in Tables 2.3 and 2.8. Prepare funds flow statements for the year 2001. Explain its implications.

CASES

Case 24.1: Continental Equipment Company

The managing director of Continental Equipment Company was not happy to find a decline in working capital for the year 2004, when he reviewed the financial statements for the year. He had a plan to acquire a new machine by issuing equity shares and by utilising the profit for the year. He had expected working capital to remain at the 2003 level. The managing director was wondering why his plans could not succeed. He was perplexed to find that in spite of profits, Continental's working capital had declined.

The financial statements of the company are given as under:

Table 24.1.1 Continental Equipment Company

Balance Sheet
for the year ended on 31 March **(Rs in lakh)**

	2004	2003
Assets		
Current assets		
Cash	525	750
Debtors	310	375
Stock	785	692
Prepaid expenses	15	18
Total current assets	1,635	1,835
Investments	400	280
Net block of assets	1,800	800
Total assets	3,835	2,915
Liabilities		
Current liabilities:		
Creditors	210	229
Bank borrowing	120	112
Accrued expenses	50	36
Provision for tax	300	180
Total current liabilities	680	557
Debentures	750	900
Shareholder's equity:		
Share capital, Rs 10 par value	1,000	420
Share premium	400	280
Reserves and surplus	1,005	758
Total liabilities	3,835	2,915

Table 24.1.2: Continental Equipment Company

Profit and Loss Account
for the year ended 31 March, 2004 **(Rs in lakh)**

Sales	3,400
Less: Cost of goods sold	1,920
Gross profit	1,480
Less: Operating expenses	780
Add: Profit on sale of asset	3
Profit before interest and tax	703
Less: Interest expenses	60
Profit before taxes	643
Less: Provision for taxes	296
Net profit	347

Operating expenses include depreciation on machinery Rs 140 lakh. The book value of the asset sold was Rs 4 lakh and its original cost was Rs 10 lakh six years ago.

Discussion Questions

1. Explain to the managing director why his plans could not succeed.
2. In spite of profits, why did continental's working capital decline? Show computations.

Case 24.2: Bharat Chemicals Limited

The managing director of Bharat Chemicals Ltd. is surprised to find that though his company incurred a loss during the year ended 31 March, 2004, the cash balance had shown an increase. He was puzzled further when he found that stock of unsold goods had increased, and the collections from the customers had slowed down. He was keen to know how cash could increase when her company was selling less and delaying in collections.

The financial statements for the company are given below:

Table 24.2.1: Bharat Chemicals Ltd.

Profit and Loss Account
for the year ended 31 March, 2004 **(Rs in lakh)**

Sales		560
Cost of goods sold (depreciation on equipment Rs 60 lakh)		385
Gross profit		175
Operating expenses:		
Office and administrative	170	
Selling and distribution	55	
Amortisation of goodwill	25	250
Net loss		(75)

Table 24.2.2: Bharat Chemicals Ltd.

Comparative Balance Sheet
for the year ended 31 March **(Rs in lakh)**

	2004	2003
Assets		
Cash	140	95
Debtors	80	55
Stock	100	80
Insurance in advance	10	12
Land	150	150
Plant, net of depreciation	440	600
Goodwill	75	100
Total assets	995	1,092
Capital & Liabilities		
Creditors	60	90
Bills payable	10	5
Interest payable	10	9
Accrued wages	20	18
Debentures	245	245
Share capital	600	600
Reserve and surplus	50	125
Total funds	995	1,092

Discussion Questions

1. How could cash balance increase in spite of unfavourable operations? Explain to the chief manager by calculating cash flow from the operations. Also prepare a statement of the sources and uses of cash.
2. Prepare funds flow statement and explain the difference

between cash and funds flow of Bharat Chemicals Ltd.? How are these statements useful to the management?

Case 24.3: Bajaj Auto Limited

Bajaj Auto Limited is the largest scooters manufacturer in India. Tables 24.3.1 and 24.3.2 contain comparative balance sheets and profit and loss accounts for the year 2000 and 2001 for the company. As per the requirement of the stock exchange for the listed companies, Bajaj also includes a cash flow statement in its annual accounts. The cash flow statement of the company is given in Table 24.3.3.

Table 24.3.1: Bajaj Auto Limited
Balance Sheet as on 31st March

(Rs in crore)

	2000	2001
I. SOURCES OF FUNDS		
1. Shareholders' Funds		
Share Capital	119.39	101.18
Reserves & Surplus	3084.69	2535.35
Total	3204.08	2636.53
2. Loan Funds		
Secured Loans	101.58	55.97
Unsecured Loans	394.09	457.74
Total	495.67	513.71
Total Funds	3699.75	3150.24
II. APPLICATION OF FUNDS		
1. Fixed assets		
Gross Block	2041.15	2467.82
Less: Accumulated Depreciation	1007.34	1127.89
Net Block	1033.81	1339.93
Capital Work in Progress	80.44	22.42
Net Fixed assets	1114.25	1362.35
2. Investments	1952.36	1184.58
Total non-current assets	3066.61	2546.93
3. Current Assets, Loans & Advances		
Inventories	261.13	253.44
Sundry Debtors	185.80	120.72
Cash and Bank Balance	35.98	21.34
Loans and Advances	1890.46	1666.12
Total Current Assets	2373.37	2061.62
Less: **Current Liabilities & Provisions**		
Current Liabilities	540.35	467.55
Provisions	1200.32	1006.79
Total Current Liabilities	1740.67	1474.34
Net Current Assets	632.70	587.28
4. Misc. Exp. not w/o	0.44	16.03
Total Assets	3699.75	3150.24
Contingent Liabilities	*451.80*	*359.56*

Table 24.3.2: Bajaj Auto Limited
Profit and Loss Account for the Year Ended 31st March

(Rs in crore)

	2002	2001
Income		
Sales Turnover	3705.15	3597.95
Less: Excise Duty	615.82	574.83
Net Sales	3089.33	3023.12
Other Income	510.40	365.99
Total Income	3599.73	3389.11
Expenditure		
Raw Materials	1902.22	2026.03
Power & Fuel Cost	753.01	913.71
Interest	3.17	7.39
Depreciation	145.31	177.29
Less: Capitalised	28.90	27.58
Total Expenses	2774.81	3096.84
Profit before tax	824.92	292.27
Provision for taxation	211.19	26.64
Profit for the year	613.73	265.63
Adjustments	21.13	−12.61
Profit after Adjustment	634.86	253.02
Proposed dividend	119.39	80.95
Corporate dividend tax	13.13	8.26
Transferred to reserves	502.34	163.81

Table 24.3.3: Bajaj Auto Limited
Cash Flow Statement for the Year

(Rs in crore)

	2001	2000
I. Cash Flow from Operating Activities		
(A) Net Profit before Tax & Extraordinary Items	289.56	825.23
(B) Adjustment for		
Depreciation	177.29	145.31
Interest (Net)	−108.12	−133.18
Dividend Received	−34.18	−37.84
P/L on Sales of Assets	1.53	−2.63
P/L on Sales of Invest	−24.96	−143.34
Prov. & W/O (Net)	6.57	13.38
P/L in Forex	0.00	0.00
Fin. Lease & Rental Chrgs	−42.83	−46.51
Others	−63.32	−289.24
	−88.02	−494.05
Operating Profit before Working Capital Changes	201.54	331.18
(C) Change in Working Capital		
Trade & 0th receivables	65.09	28.66
Inventories	7.69	−83.63

Contd...

	2001	*2000*
Trade Payables	0.00	0.00
Loans & Advances	4.96	−105.10
Change in Deposits	0.00	0.00
Others	−73.26	118.55
	4.48	−41.52
Cash Generated from/(used in) Operations	206.02	289.66
Less: Extraordinary items	0.00	0.00
Net Cash from Operating Activities	206.02	289.66

II. Cash Flow from Investing Activities

Investment in Assets:

	2001	*2000*
Sale of Fixed Assets	7.16	7.63
Capital WIP	−397.93	−335.53
Sale of Investments	786.08	−358.13
Interest Received	113.25	133.96
Dividend Received	34.18	37.84
Others	70.90	156.20
Net Cash Used in Investing Activities	613.64	−358.03

III. Cash Flow From Financing Activities

Proceeds:

	2001	*2000*
Proceed from Short Term Borrowing	65.29	86.70
Payments:		
Dividend Paid	−118.92	−94.92
Others	−780.67	58.49
Net Cash Flow from Financing Activities	−834.30	50.27

Cash Flow Summary

	2001	*2000*
Cash & Cash Equivalents at Beginning of the year	35.98	54.08
Net Cash from Operating Activities	206.02	289.66
Net Cash Used in Investing Activities	613.64	−358.03
Net Cash Used in Financing Activities	−834.30	50.27
Net Inc/(Dec) in Cash and Cash	−14.64	−18.10
Cash and Cash Equivalents at End of the year	21.34	35.98

Discussion Questions

1. How has company managed its funds? Explain by preparing funds flow statement from the information given in Tables 24.1.1 and 24.1.2.

2. Read Table 24.3.3 carefully and critically evaluate Bajaj's cash flow position.

Financial Statements Analysis

INTRODUCTION

In Chapter 24, we highlighted the contents and importance of the statements of changes in financial position (funds and cash flow statements). Management, creditors, investors and others to form judgement about the operating performance and financial position of the firm use the information contained in these statements. Users of financial statements can get further insight about financial strengths and weaknesses of the firm if they properly analyse information reported in these statements. Management should be particularly interested in knowing financial strengths of the firm to make their best use and to be able to spot out financial weaknesses of the firm to take suitable corrective actions. The future plans of the firm should be laid down in view of the firm's financial strengths and weaknesses. Thus, financial analysis is the starting point for making plans, before using any sophisticated forecasting and planning procedures. Understanding the past is a prerequisite for anticipating the future.

USERS OF FINANCIAL ANALYSIS

Financial analysis is the process of identifying the financial strengths and weaknesses of the firm by properly establishing relationships between the items of the balance sheet and the profit and loss account. Financial analysis can be undertaken by management of the firm, or by parties outside the firm, *viz.*

owners, creditors, investors and others.[1] The nature of analysis will differ depending on the purpose of the analyst.

- *Trade creditors* are interested in firm's ability to meet their claims over a very short period of time. Their analysis will, therefore, confine to the evaluation of the firm's liquidity position.

- *Suppliers of long-term debt*, on the other hand, are concerned with the firm's long-term solvency and survival. They analyse the firm's profitability over time, its ability to generate cash to be able to pay interest and repay principal and the relationship between various sources of funds (capital structure relationships). Long-term creditors do analyse the historical financial statements, but they place more emphasis on the firm's projected, or *proforma*, financial statements to make analysis about its future solvency and profitability.

- *Investors*, who have invested their money in the firm's shares, are most concerned about the firm's earnings. They restore more confidence in those firms that show steady growth in earnings. As such, they concentrate on the analysis of the firm's present and future profitability. They are also interested in the firm's financial structure to the extent it influences the firm's earnings ability and risk.

- *Management* of the firm would be interested in every aspect of the financial analysis. It is their overall responsibility to see that the resources of the firm are used most effectively and efficiently, and that the firm's financial condition is sound.

---

1. For a detailed discussion, see Foster, G., *Financial Statement Analysis*, Prentice-Hall, 1986, pp. 2–7.

NATURE OF RATIO ANALYSIS

Ratio analysis is a powerful tool of financial analysis. A **ratio** is defined as "the indicated quotient of two mathematical expressions" and as "the relationship between two or more things."[1] In financial analysis, a ratio is used as a benchmark for evaluating the financial position and performance of a firm. The absolute accounting figures reported in the financial statements do not provide a meaningful understanding of the performance and financial position of a firm. An accounting figure conveys meaning when it is related to some other relevant information. For example, a Rs 5 crore net profit may look impressive, but the firm's performance can be said to be good or bad only when the net profit figure is related to the firm's investment. The relationship between two accounting figures, expressed mathematically, is known as a financial ratio (or simply as a ratio). Ratios help to summarise large quantities of financial data and to make *qualitative judgement* about the firm's financial performance. For example, consider current ratio (discussed in detail later on). It is calculated by dividing current assets by current liabilities; the ratio indicates *a relationship*—a quantified relationship between current assets and current liabilities. This relationship is an index or yardstick, which permits a qualitative judgement to be formed about the firm's ability to meet its current obligations. It measures the firm's liquidity. The greater the ratio, the greater the firm's liquidity and *vice versa*. The point to note is that a ratio reflecting a *quantitative* relationship helps to form a *qualitative judgement*. Such is the nature of all financial ratios.

Standards of Comparison

The ratio analysis involves comparison for a useful interpretation of the financial statements. A single ratio in itself does not indicate favourable or unfavourable condition. It should be compared with some standard. Standards of comparison may consist of:[2]

- *past ratios*, i.e., ratios calculated from the past financial statements of the same firm;
- *competitors' ratios*, i.e., ratios of some selected firms, especially the most progressive and successful competitor, at the same point in time;
- *industry ratios*, i.e., ratios of the industry to which the firm belongs; and
- *projected ratios*, i.e., ratios developed using the projected, or *proforma*, financial statements of the same firm.

Time series analysis The easiest way to evaluate the performance of a firm is to compare its present ratios with the past ratios. When financial ratios over a period of time are compared, it is known as the **time series analysis**. It gives an indication of the direction of change and reflects whether the firm's financial performance has improved, deteriorated or remained constant over time. The analyst should not simply determine the change, but, more importantly, he/she should understand why ratios have changed. The change, for example, may be affected by changes in the accounting policies without a material change in the firm's performance.

Cross-sectional analysis Another way of comparison is to compare ratios of one firm with some selected firms in the same industry at the same point in time. This kind of comparison is known as the **cross-sectional analysis** or **inter-firm analysis**. In most cases, it is more useful to compare the firm's ratios with ratios of a few carefully selected competitors, who have similar operations. This kind of a comparison indicates the relative financial position and performance of the firm. A firm can easily resort to such a comparison, as it is not difficult to get the published financial statements of the similar firms.

Industry analysis To determine the financial condition and performance of a firm, its ratios may be compared with average ratios of the industry of which the firm is a member. This sort of analysis, known as the **industry analysis**, helps to ascertain the financial standing and capability of the firm *vis-à-vis* other firms in the industry. Industry ratios are important standards in view of the fact that each industry has its characteristics, which influence the financial, and operating relationships. But there are certain practical difficulties in using the industry ratios. *First*, it is difficult to get average ratios for the industry. *Second*, even if industry ratios are available, they are averages—averages of the ratios of strong and weak firms. Sometimes differences may be so wide that the average may be of little utility. *Third*, averages will be meaningless and the comparison futile if firms within the same industry widely differ in their accounting policies and practices. If it is possible to standardise the accounting data for companies in the industry and eliminate extremely strong and extremely weak firms, the industry ratios will prove to be very useful in evaluating the relative financial condition and performance of a firm.

Proforma analysis Sometimes future ratios are used as the standard of comparison. Future ratios can be developed from the projected, or **proforma financial statements**. The comparison of current or past ratios with future ratios shows the firm's relative strengths and weaknesses in the past and the future. If the future ratios indicate weak financial position, corrective actions should be initiated.

Types of Ratios

Several ratios, calculated from the accounting data, can be grouped into various classes according to financial activity or function to be evaluated. As stated earlier, the parties interested in financial analysis are short- and long-term creditors, owners and management. Short-term creditors' main interest is in the liquidity position or the short-term solvency of the firm. Long-term creditors, on the other hand, are more interested in the long-term solvency and profitability of the firm. Similarly, owners concentrate on the firm's profitability and financial condition. Management is interested in evaluating every aspect of the firm's performance. They have to protect the interests of all parties and see that the firm grows profitably. In view of the requirements of the various users of ratios, we may classify them

1. Webster's *New Coolegiate Dictionary*, 8th Ed., Springfiled, Mass, G & C, Merriam, 1975, p. 958.
2. Anthony, R.N. and Reece, J.S., *Management Accounting Principles*, Taraporewala, 1975, pp. 260–63.

into the following four important categories:[1]

- Liquidity ratios
- Leverage ratios
- Activity ratios
- Profitability ratios.

Liquidity ratios measure the firm's ability to meet current obligations; **leverage ratios** show the proportions of debt and equity in financing the firm's assets; **activity ratios** reflect the firm's efficiency in utilising its assets, and **profitability ratios** measure overall performance and effectiveness of the firm. Each of these ratios is discussed below. The accounting data are taken from the financial statements for the Hindustan Manufacturing Company (the real name of the company has been disguised) to illustrate calculation and use of ratios.

Illustration 25.1: Assessing Financial Health of a Firm with Ratio Analysis

The Hindustan Manufacturing Company is a leading producer and exporter of engineering items such as steel pipes, ingots, billets etc. It has also recently added a chemical plant and a paper plant as a part of its diversification strategy. The company started with a share capital of Rs 25 lakh in the early sixties, which has now increased to Rs 225 lakh. The number of shares outstanding is 22.50 lakh. The average market price (AMP) of the company's share during 19X1–19X3 has been: Rs 26.38 in 19X1, Rs 34.50 in 19X2 and Rs 29.25 in 19X3. The financial data for the company are given in Tables 25.1 to 25.3. For illustrative purpose, calculations of ratios have been shown only for the year 19X3. However, tables indicating trend in ratios during 19X1–19X3 are also given.

Table 25.1: Hindustan Manufacturing Company

Profit and Loss Account
for the year ending on 31 March (Rs in lakh)

	19X1	19X2	19X3
A. Net sales*	2,338.90	2,825.69	3,717.23
B. Cost of goods sold**	1,929.04	2,322.80	3,053.66
C. Gross profit (A – B)	409.86	502.89	663.57
D. *Less:* Selling and administrative expenses	239.72	262.10	357.87
E. Operating income (C – D)	170.14	240.79	305.70
F. *Add:* Other income	15.24	25.38	36.91
G. Earning before interest and tax (EBIT) (E + F)	185.38	266.17	342.61
H. *Less:* Interest	59.84	124.98	143.46
I. Profit before tax (PBT) (G – H)	125.54	141.19	199.15
J. Provision for tax	41.79	30.00	64.29
K. Profit after tax (PAT) (I – J)	83.75	111.19	134.86
L. Effective tax rate***	33%	21%	32%
M. Dividend distributed	33.75	39.38	45.00
N. Retained earnings	50.00	71.81	89.86

* Net of excise duty.
** Depreciation included.
*** Provision for tax divided by profit before tax.

Table 25.2: Hindustan Manufacturing Company

Statement of Cost of Goods Sold
for the year ending on March 31 (Rs in lakh)

	19X1	19X2	19X3
Raw material	1,587.34	2,019.54	2,751.52
Direct labour	138.13	170.86	228.94
Depreciation	23.07	38.64	41.59
Other mfg. expenses	205.34	255.72	329.44
	1,953.88	2,484.76	3,351.49
Add: Opening stock in process	57.09	85.74	150.55
	2,010.97	2,570.50	3,502.04
Less: Closing stock in process	85.74	150.55	230.83
Cost of Production	1,925.23	2,419.95	3,271.21
Add: Opening finished stock	150.93	147.12	244.26
	2,076.16	2,567.07	3,515.47
Less: Closing finished stock	147.12	244.26	461.81
Cost of Goods Sold	1,929.04	2,322.81	3,053.66

Table 25.3: Hindustan Manufacturing Company

Balance Sheet
as on 31 March (Rs in lakh)

	19X1	19X2	19X3
A. Net Worth			
Share capital	225.00	225.00	225.00
Reserve	286.13	357.95	447.81
Net worth	511.13	582.95	672.81
B. Borrowings			
Long-term: Debentures	–	75.75	76.46
Others	199.87	285.90	312.73
Long-term debt	199.87	361.65	389.19
Short-term: Bank borrowings	442.92	641.39	839.87
Borrowings	642.79	1,003.04	1229.06
C. Capital Employed (A + B)	1,153.92	1,585.99	1,901.87
D. Fixed Assets			
Gross block	653.49	841.64	921.55
Less: Depreciation	159.55	194.46	235.44
Net block	493.94	647.18	686.11
Other non-current assets	52.76	16.44	60.72
Net fixed assets	546.70	663.62	746.83
E. Current Assets			
Inventories:			
Raw material	243.42	384.06	457.74
Stock in process	85.74	150.55	230.84
Finished goods	147.12	244.28	461.81

(Contd.)

---

1. This is the most common, traditional classification of ratios. However, empirical evidence indicates that ratios can be classified in a variety of ways. Also, depending on their beliefs and objectives, different authors have classified ratios differently. For a comprehensive treatment of the financial statement analysis, see Foster, *op. cit.*

	19X1	*19X2*	*19X3*
Inventories	476.28	778.89	1,150.39
Debtors	253.16	340.61	483.18
Cash and bank balance	8.37	98.84	26.08
Others	128.27	186.21	211.27
Current assets	866.08	1,404.55	1,870.92
F. *Less:* **Current Liabilities***			
Trade creditors	35.99	211.21	339.35
Provision and others	222.87	270.97	376.53
Current liabilities	258.86	482.18	715.88
G. **Net Current Assets** (E – F)	607.22	922.37	1,155.04
H. **Net Assets** (D + G)	1,153.92	1,585.99	1,901.87

* If bank borrowings are considered, then the current liabilities for 19X1 through 19X3 will be: Rs 701.78 lakh; Rs 1123.57 lakh; and Rs 1555.75 lakh.

LIQUIDITY RATIOS

It is extremely essential for a firm to be able to meet its obligations as they become due. **Liquidity ratios** measure the ability of the firm to meet its current obligations (liabilities). In fact, analysis of liquidity needs the preparation of cash budgets and cash and fund flow statements; but liquidity ratios, by establishing a relationship between cash and other current assets to current obligations, provide a quick measure of liquidity. A firm should ensure that it does not suffer from lack of liquidity, and also that it does not have excess liquidity. The failure of a company to meet its obligations due to lack of sufficient liquidity, will result in a poor credit worthiness, loss of creditors' confidence, or even in legal tangles resulting in the closure of the company. A very high degree of liquidity is also bad; idle assets earn nothing. The firm's funds will be unnecessarily tied up in current assets. Therefore, it is necessary to strike a proper balance between high liquidity and lack of liquidity.

The most common ratios, which indicate the extent of liquidity or lack of it, are: (*i*) current ratio and (*ii*) quick ratio. Other ratios include cash ratio, interval measure and net working capital ratio.

Current Ratio

Current ratio is calculated by dividing current assets by current liabilities:

$$\text{Current ratio} = \frac{\text{Current assets}}{\text{Current liabilities}} \qquad (1)$$

Current assets include cash and those assets that can be converted into cash within a year, such as marketable securities, debtors and inventories. Prepaid expenses are also included in current assets as they represent the payments that will not be made by the firm in the future. All obligations maturing within a year are included in current liabilities. Current liabilities include creditors, bills payable, accrued expenses, short-term bank loan, income-tax liability and long-term debt maturing in the current year.

The current ratio is a measure of the firm's **short-term solvency**. It indicates the availability of current assets in rupees for every one rupee of current liability. A ratio of greater than one means that the firm has more current assets than current claims against them.

For HMC, the current ratio is:

$$\text{Current ratio} = \frac{\text{Rs } 1870.92}{\text{Rs } 1555.75} = 1.20 : 1$$

How to interpret current ratio? As a conventional rule, a current ratio of 2 to 1 or more is considered satisfactory. The Hindustan Manufacturing Co. has a current ratio of 1.20:1; therefore, it may be interpreted to be insufficiently liquid. This rule is based on the logic that in a worse situation, even if the value of current assets becomes half, the firm will be able to meet its obligation. The current ratio represents a **margin of safety** for creditors. The higher the current ratio, the greater the margin of safety; the larger the amount of current assets in relation to current liabilities, the more the firm's ability to meet its current obligations. However, an arbitrary standard of 2 to 1 should not be blindly followed. Firms with less than 2 to 1 current ratio may be doing well, while firms with 2 to 1 or even higher current ratios may be struggling to meet their obligations. This is so because the current ratio is a *test of quantity*, not quality. The current ratio measures only total rupees' worth of current assets and total rupees' worth of current liabilities. It does not measure the *quality* of assets. Liabilities are not subject to any fall in value; they have to be paid. But current assets can decline in value. If the firm's current assets consist of doubtful and slow-paying debtors or slow moving and obsolete stock of goods, then the firm's ability to pay bills is impaired; its short-term solvency is threatened. Thus, too much reliance should not be placed on the current ratio; a further investigation about the quality of the items of current assets is necessary. However, the current ratio is a *crude-and-quick* measure of the firm's liquidity.

Quick Ratio

Quick ratio, also called **acid-test ratio,** establishes a relationship between *quick*, or *liquid, assets* and current liabilities. An asset is liquid if it can be converted into cash immediately or reasonably soon without a loss of value. Cash is the most liquid asset. Other assets that are considered to be relatively liquid and included in quick assets are debtors and bills receivables and marketable securities (temporary quoted investments). Inventories are considered to be less liquid. Inventories normally require some time for realising into cash; their value also has a tendency to fluctuate. The quick ratio is found out by dividing quick assets by current liabilities.

$$\text{Quick ratio} = \frac{\text{Current assets} - \text{Inventories}}{\text{Current liabilities}} \qquad (2)$$

For the Hindustan Manufacturing Company, the ratio is:

$$\text{Quick ratio} = \frac{\text{Rs } 720.53}{\text{Rs } 1555.75} = 0.46 : 1$$

Thus, if the HMC's inventories do not sell, and it has to pay all its current liabilities, it may find it difficult to meet its obligations because its quick assets are 0.46 times of current liabilities.

Is quick ratio a better measure of liquidity? Generally, a quick ratio of 1 to 1 is considered to represent a satisfactory current financial condition. Although quick ratio is a more penetrating test of liquidity than the current ratio, yet it should be used cautiously. A quick ratio of 1 to 1 or more does not necessarily imply sound liquidity position. It should be remembered that all debtors may not be liquid, and cash may be immediately needed to pay operating expenses. It should also be noted that inventories are not absolutely non-liquid. To a measurable extent, inventories are available to meet current obligations. Thus, a company with a high value of quick ratio can suffer from the shortage of funds if it has slow paying, doubtful and long-duration outstanding debtors. On the other hand, a company with a low value of quick ratio may really be prospering and paying its current obligation in time if it has been turning over its inventories efficiently. Nevertheless, the quick ratio remains an important index of the firm's liquidity.

Cash Ratio

Since cash is the most liquid asset, a financial analyst may examine **cash ratio** and its equivalent to current liabilities. Trade investment or marketable securities are equivalent of cash; therefore, they may be included in the computation of cash ratio:

$$\text{Cash ratio} = \frac{\text{Cash} + \text{Marketable securities}}{\text{Current liabilities}} \qquad (3)$$

For the Hindustan Manufacturing Company, cash ratio is as follows:

$$= \frac{\text{Rs } 26.08}{\text{Rs } 1555.75} = 0.017 \text{ or } 2\% \text{ approx.}$$

The company in our example carries a small amount of cash. There is nothing to be worried about the lack of cash if the company has reserve borrowing power. In India, firms have credit limits sanctioned from banks, and can easily draw cash.

Interval Measure

Yet another ratio, which assesses a firm's ability to meet its regular cash expenses, is the **interval measure**. Interval measure relates liquid assets to average daily operating cash outflows. The daily operating expenses will be equal to cost of goods sold plus selling, administrative and general expenses *less* depreciation (and other non-cash expenditures) divided by number of days in the year (say 360)

$$\text{Interval measure} = \frac{\text{Current assets} - \text{Inventory}}{\text{Average daily operating expenses}} \qquad (4)$$

For HMC, the interval measure is:

$$= \frac{\text{Rs } 1,870.92 - \text{Rs } 1,150.39}{\text{Rs } 3,369.94 \div 360} = 77 \text{ days}$$

For HMC, interval measure indicates that it has sufficient liquid assets to finance its operations for 77 days, even if it does not receive any cash.

Interval measure may be refined further. Instead of calculating only the daily operating expenditures, one may also include expenditures required for paying interest, acquiring assets and repaying debt.

Net Working Capital Ratio

The difference between current assets and current liabilities excluding short-term bank borrowing is called net working capital (NWC) or net current assets (NCA). NWC is sometimes used as a measure of a firm's liquidity. It is considered that, between two firms, the one having the larger NWC has the greater ability to meet its current obligations. This is not necessarily so; the measure of liquidity is a *relationship*, rather than the difference between current assets and current liabilities. NWC, however, measures the firm's potential reservoir of funds. It can be related to net assets (or capital employed):

$$\text{NWC ratio} = \frac{\text{Net working capital (NWC)}}{\text{Net assets (NA)}} \qquad (5)$$

For HMC, NWC ratio is:

$$= \frac{\text{Rs } 1,154.04}{\text{Rs } 1901.87} = 0.61$$

Table 25.4 presents the three-year trend of HMC's liquidity ratios.

Table 25.4: Hindustan Manufacturing Company Liquidity Ratios

	19X1	19X2	19X3
Current ratio	1.24	1.25	1.20
Quick ratio	0.56	0.56	0.46
Cash ratio	0.01	0.09	0.02
Interval measure (days)	65.00	87.00	77.00
Net working capital ratio	0.53	0.58	0.61

Ratios in Table 25.4 indicate that HMC's liquidity is deteriorating. A note of caution may be sounded : liquidity ratio can mislead since current assets and current liabilities can change quickly. Their utility becomes more doubtful for firms with seasonal business. In the case of seasonal businesses, liquidity ratios from quarterly or monthly financial data would be more appropriate.

LEVERAGE RATIOS

The short-term creditors, like bankers and suppliers of raw material, are more concerned with the firm's current debt-paying ability. On the other hand, long-term creditors, like debenture holders, financial institutions etc. are more concerned with the firm's long-term financial strength. In fact, a firm should have a strong short-as well as long-term financial position. To judge the long-term financial position of the firm, **financial leverage,** or **capital structure ratios** are calculated. These ratios indicate mix of funds provided by owners and lenders. As a general rule, there should be an appropriate mix of debt and owners' equity in financing the firm's assets.

The manner in which assets are financed has a number of implications. *First*, between debt and equity, debt is more risky from the firm's point of view. The firm has a legal obligation to pay interest to debt holders, irrespective of the profits made or losses incurred by the firm. If the firm fails to pay to debt holders in time, they can take legal action against it to get payments and in extreme cases, can force the firm into liquidation. *Second*, use of debt is advantageous for shareholders in two ways: (*a*) they can retain control of the firm with a limited stake and (*b*) their earning will be magnified, when the firm earns a rate of return on the total capital employed higher than the interest rate on the borrowed funds. The process of magnifying the shareholders' return through the use of debt is called "**financial leverage**" or "**financial gearing**" or "**trading on equity**." However, leverage can work in opposite direction as well. If the cost of debt is higher than the firm's overall rate of return, the earnings of shareholders will be reduced. In addition, there is threat of insolvency. If the firm is actually liquidated for non-payment of debt-holders' dues, the worst sufferers will be shareholders—the residual owners. Thus, use of debt magnifies the shareholders' earnings as well as increases their risk. *Third*, a highly debt-burdened firm will find difficulty in raising funds from creditors and owners in future. Creditors treat the owners' equity as a margin of safety; if the equity base is thin, the creditors risk will be high. Thus, leverage ratios are calculated to measure the financial risk and the firm's ability of using debt to shareholders' advantage.

Leverage ratios may be calculated from the balance sheet items to determine the proportion of debt in total financing. Many variations of these ratios exist; but all these ratios indicate the same thing—the extent to which the firm has relied on debt in financing assets. Leverage ratios are also computed from the profit and loss items by determining the extent to which operating profits are sufficient to cover the fixed charges.

Debt Ratio

Several debt ratios may be used to analyse the long-term solvency of a firm. The firm may be interested in knowing the proportion of the interest-bearing debt (also called funded debt) in the capital structure. It may, therefore, compute **debt ratio** by dividing total debt (TD) by capital employed (CE) or net assets (NA). Total debt will include short and long-term borrowings from financial institutions, debentures/bonds, deferred payment arrangements for buying capital equipments, bank borrowings, public deposits and any other interest-bearing loan. Capital employed will include total debt and net worth (NW).

$$\text{Debt ratio} = \frac{\text{Total debt (TD)}}{\text{Total debt (TD)} + \text{Net worth (NW)}}$$

$$= \frac{\text{Total debt (TD)}}{\text{Capital employed (CE)}} \qquad (6)$$

Note that capital employed (CE) equals net assets (NA) that consist of net fixed assets (NFA) and net current assets (NCA). Net current assets are current assets (CA) minus current liabilities (CL) *excluding interest-bearing short-term debt for working capital*. These relationships are:

$$NFA + CA = NW + TD + CL$$

$$NFA + CA - CL = NW + TD$$

$$NFA + NCA = NW + TD$$

$$NA = CE$$

Because of the equality of capital employed and net assets, debt ratio can also be defined as total debt divided by net assets:

$$\text{Debt ratio} = \frac{\text{Total debt (TD)}}{\text{Net Assets (NA)}} \qquad (7)$$

For HMC, the ratio is:

$$\text{Debt ratio} = \frac{\text{Rs } 389.19 + \text{Rs } 839.87}{\text{Rs } 389.19 + \text{Rs } 839.87 + \text{Rs } 672.81}$$

$$= \frac{\text{Rs } 1229.06}{\text{Rs } 1901.87} = 0.646$$

The debt ratio of 0.646 means that lenders have financed 64.6 per cent or about two-thirds of HMC's net assets (capital employed). It obviously implies that owners have provided the remaining finances. They have financed: $1 - 0.646 = 0.354 = 35.4$ per cent or about one-third of net assets.

Debt-Equity Ratio

It is clear that from the total debt ratio that HMC's lenders have contributed more funds than owners; lenders' contribution is 1.83 times of owners' contribution, *viz.*, 0.646/0.354 = 1.83. This relationship describing the lenders' contribution for each rupee of the owners' contribution is called **debt-equity ratio**. Debt-equity (DE) ratio is directly computed by dividing total debt by net worth:

$$\text{Debt-Equity ratio} = \frac{\text{Total debt (TD)}}{\text{Net worth (NW)}} \qquad (8)$$

For Hindustan, the ratio is:

$$\text{D / E ratio} = \frac{\text{Rs } 1229.06}{\text{Rs } 672.81} = 1.83$$

Capital employed to net worth ratio There is yet another alternative way of expressing the basic relationship between debt and equity. One may want to know: How much funds are being contributed together by lenders and owners for each rupee of the owners' contribution? Calculating the ratio of capital employed or net assets to net worth can find this out:

$$\text{CE-to-NW ratio} = \frac{\text{Capital employed (CE)}}{\text{Net worth (NW)}}$$

or $$\text{NA-to-NW ratio} = \frac{\text{Net assets (NA)}}{\text{Net worth (NW)}} \qquad (9)$$

For HMC, the ratio is:

$$\frac{\text{CE}}{\text{NW}} = \frac{\text{Rs } 1901.87}{\text{Rs } 672.81} = 2.83$$

Note that CE/NW ratio is simply one plus debt-equity ratio:

$$\frac{CE}{NW} = \frac{NW+TD}{NW} = 1 + \frac{TD}{NW} \qquad (10)$$

Other Debt Ratios

Current liabilities (non-interest bearing current obligations) are generally excluded from the computation of leverage ratios. One may like to include them on the ground that they are important determinants of the firm's financial risk since they represent obligations and exert pressure on the firm and restrict its activities. Thus, to assess the proportion of total funds— short and long-term—provided by outsiders to finance total assets, the following ratio may be calculated:

$$\text{TL-to-LF ratio} = \frac{\text{Total liabilities (TL)}}{\text{Total assets (TA)}} \qquad (11)$$

For HMC, the TL/TA ratio is:

$$\frac{TL}{TA} = \frac{Rs\,1944.93}{Rs\,2617.75} = 0.743$$

In addition to debt ratios explained so far, a firm may wish to calculate leverage ratios in terms of the long-term capitalisation or funds (LTF) alone. Long-term funds or capitalisation will include long-term debt and net worth. Thus, the firm may calculate the following long-term debt ratios:

$$\text{LT-to-LF ratio} = \frac{\text{Long-term debt (LD)}}{\text{Long-term debt (LD)} + \text{Net worth (NW)}} \qquad (12)$$

$$\text{LT-to-NW ratio} = \frac{\text{Long-term debt (LD)}}{\text{Net worth (NW)}} \qquad (13)$$

For HMC, the long-term debt ratios are:

$$\frac{LD}{LD+NW} = \frac{Rs\,389.19}{Rs\,389.19 + Rs\,672.81} = \frac{Rs\,389.19}{Rs\,1062.00} = 0.366$$

$$\frac{LD}{NW} = \frac{Rs\,389.19}{Rs\,672.81} = 0.581$$

How to treat preference capital? Some firms have **preference share capital** in their capital structure. How should it be treated in computing leverage ratios? Whether the preference capital will be included in debt or net worth will depend on the purpose for which the leverage ratio is being calculated. If it is calculated to show the effect of leverage on the ordinary (or common) shareholders' earnings, the preference capital should be included in debt. The preference dividend is fixed like the interest cost and the ordinary shareholders' earnings will be magnified if the rate of preference dividend is less than the firm's overall rate of return. But if the leverage ratio is calculated to reflect the **financial risk**, the preference capital should be included in net worth. "The treatment of preference share capital as debt ignores

the fact that debt and preference share capital present different risk to shareholders. In one case failure to meet payments means bankruptcy and possible elimination of the common shareholders, while in the other case failure to meet payments presents no such risk."[1] In the financial analysis, leverage is seen to reflect the financial risk; therefore, preference capital should be included in net worth.

How to treat lease payments? When a company obtains the use of fixed assets under long-term lease agreements, it commits itself to a series of fixed payments (*viz.*, lease rentals). The value of lease obligations is thus equivalent to debt. It is, therefore, natural to include the capitalised value of lease obligation in debt while measuring the firm's financial leverage:

$$\text{Debt ratio} = \frac{\text{Total debt} + \text{Value of lease}}{\text{Total debt} + \text{Value of lease} + \text{Net worth}} \qquad (14)$$

$$\text{Debt-Equity ratio} = \frac{\text{Total debt} + \text{Value of lease}}{\text{Net worth}} \qquad (15)$$

What do debt ratios imply? Whatever way the debt ratio is calculated, it shows the extent to which debt financing has been used in the business. A high ratio means that claims of creditors are greater than those of owners. A high level of debt introduces inflexibility in the firm's operations due to the increasing interference and pressures from creditors. A high-debt company is able to borrow funds on very restrictive terms and conditions. The loan agreements may require a firm to maintain a certain level of working capital, or a minimum current ratio, or restrict the payment of dividends, or fix limits to the officers' and employees' salaries and so on. Heavy indebtedness leads to creditors' pressures and constraints on the management's independent functioning and energies.[2] During the periods of low profits, a highly debt-financed company suffers great strains: it cannot even pay the interest charges of creditors. As a result, their pressure and control are further tightened. To meet their working capital needs, the firm finds difficulty in getting credit. It may have to borrow on highly unfavourable terms. Thus, it gets entangled in a **debt-trap**.

A low debt-equity ratio implies a greater claim of owners than creditors. From the point of view of creditors, it represents a satisfactory situation since a high proportion of equity provides a larger margin of safety for them. During the periods of low profits, the debt servicing will prove to be less burdensome for a company with low debt-equity ratio. However, from the shareholders' point of view, there is a disadvantage during the periods of good economic activities if the firm employs a low amount of debt. The higher the debt-equity ratio, the larger the shareholders' earnings when the cost of debt is less than the firm's overall rate of return on investment. Thus, there is a need to strike a proper balance between the use of debt and equity. The most appropriate debt-equity combination would involve a trade-off between return and risk.

1. Barges, Alexander, *The Effect of Capital Structure on the Cost of Capital*, Prentice-Hall Inc., 1963, p. 35.
2. Miller, D.E., *The Meaningful Interpretation of Financial Statement*, AMA, 1966.

Interpretation of debt-ratio needs caution. Companies do not show some fixed obligations in the balance sheet but state them in the notes to the annual accounts. Liability arising out of the possible payment of pension benefits is an example. Similarly, some of the **contingent liabilities** may become real liabilities. They should not be ignored while analysing financial leverage and risk of the firm.

The three-year trend of the HMC's leverage ratios is shown in Table 25.5.

Table 25.5: Hindustan Manufacturing Company: Leverage Ratios

	19X1	19X2	19X3
Total debt ratio	0.56	0.63	0.65
Debt-equity ratio	1.26	1.72	1.83
Equity ratio	2.26	2.72	2.83
Total liabilities ratio	0.64	0.71	0.74
Long-term debt ratio	0.28	0.38	0.37

HMC seems to depend more on outsiders' funds to finance its expanding activities. The level of long-term debt is not very excessive, but the proportion of other liabilities is increasing. As much as three-fourths of the company's assets are financed by outsiders' money; the stake of owners is quite low in the total capital employed by the company. From the creditors' point of view, the trend is risky and undesirable.

Coverage Ratios

Debt ratios described above are static in nature, and fail to indicate the firm's ability to meet interest (and other fixed-charges) obligations. The **interest coverage ratio** or the **times-interest-earned** is used to test the firm's debt-servicing capacity. The interest coverage ratio is computed by dividing earnings before interest and taxes (EBIT) by interest charges:

$$\text{Interest coverage} = \frac{\text{EBIT}}{\text{Interest}} \qquad (16)$$

For HMC, the interest coverage is:

$$\text{Interest coverage} = \frac{\text{Rs}\,115.50}{\text{Rs}\,1.10} = \text{Rs}\,105$$

The interest coverage ratio shows the number of times the interest charges are covered by funds that are ordinarily available for their payment. Since taxes are computed after interest, interest coverage is calculated in relation to before tax earnings. Depreciation is a non-cash item. Therefore, funds equal to depreciation are also available to pay interest charges. We can thus calculate the interest average ratio as earnings before interest taxes, depreciation and amortisation (EBITDA) divided by interest:

$$\text{Interest coverage} = \frac{\text{EBITDA}}{\text{Interest}} = \frac{\text{Rs}\,342.61 + \text{Rs}\,41.59}{\text{Rs}\,143.46} = 2.7 \ (17)$$

This ratio indicates the extent to which earnings may fall without causing any embarrassment to the firm regarding the payment of the interest charges. A higher ratio is desirable; but

too high a ratio indicates that the firm is very conservative in using debt, and that it is not using credit to the best advantage of shareholders. A lower ratio indicates excessive use of debt, or inefficient operations. The firm should make efforts to improve the operating efficiency, or to retire debt to have a comfortable coverage ratio.

The limitation of the interest coverage ratio is that it does not consider repayment of loan. Therefore, a more inclusive ratio—the **fixed-charges coverage**—is calculated. This ratio is calculated by dividing EBITDA by interest plus principal repayment:

$$\begin{matrix}\text{Fixed-charges}\\ \text{coverage ratio}\end{matrix} = \frac{\text{EBITDA}}{\text{Interest} + \dfrac{\text{Loan repayment}}{1 - \text{Tax rate}}} \qquad (18)$$

In Equation (18) all variables are on before-tax basis. Since only the after-tax earnings are available to repay principal, the principal repayment is converted to a before-tax basis by dividing it by 1 – tax rate. Depreciation and other non-cash charges are added to the numerator to provide a coverage measure in terms of cash flow rather than earnings. Equation (18) can be extended to include other fixed obligations such as preference dividends and lease rentals. Thus, the fixed-charges coverage ratio will be:

$$= \frac{\text{EBITDA}}{\text{Interest} + \text{Lease rentals} + \dfrac{\text{PDIV} + \text{Loan repay}}{1 - \text{Tax rate}}} \qquad (19)$$

It should be obvious that a high level of debt is a problem for a company only if its future cash flows (earnings being a large component) are uncertain. An analyst, therefore, may analyse the variability of the company's cash flows (or earnings) over time. This may be done by calculating the standard deviation of yearly changes in cash flows (or earnings) relative to the average level of cash flows (or earnings).

ACTIVITY RATIOS

Funds of creditors and owners are invested in various assets to generate sales and profits. The better the management of assets, the larger the amount of sales. **Activity ratios** are employed to evaluate the efficiency with which the firm manages and utilises its assets. These ratios are also called **turnover ratios** because they indicate the speed with which assets are being converted or turned over into sales. Activity ratios, thus, involve a relationship between sales and assets. A proper balance between sales and assets generally reflects that assets are managed well. Several activity ratios can be calculated to judge the effectiveness of asset utilisation.

Inventory Turnover

Inventory turnover indicates the efficiency of the firm in producing and selling its product. It is calculated by dividing the cost of goods sold by the average inventory:

$$\text{Inventory turnover} = \frac{\text{Cost of goods sold}}{\text{Average inventory}} \qquad (20)$$

The average inventory is the average of opening and closing balances of inventory. In a manufacturing company inventory of finished goods is used to calculate inventory turnover.

For HMC, the inventory turnover ratio is:

$$\text{Inventory turnover} = \frac{\text{Rs } 3053.66}{(\text{Rs } 244.26 + \text{Rs } 461.81)/2}$$

$$= \frac{\text{Rs } 3053.66}{\text{Rs } 353.03} = 8.6 \text{ times}$$

HMC is turning its inventory of finished goods into sales (at cost) 8.6 times in a year. In other words, it holds average inventory of: 12 months/8.6 = 1.4 months, or 360 days/8.6 = 42 days. The reciprocal of inventory turnover gives average inventory holdings in percentage term. When the numbers of days in a year (say, 360) are divided by inventory turnover, we obtain **days of inventory holdings** (DIH):

$$\text{DIH} = \frac{\text{Average inventory}}{\text{Cost of goods sold}} \times 360 = \frac{360}{\text{Inventory turnover}} \quad (21)$$

For HMC, DIH is:

$$\text{DIH} = \frac{360}{8.6} = 42 \text{ days}$$

The cost of goods sold figure may not be available to an outside analyst from the published annual accounts. He/she may therefore compute inventory turnover as sales divided by the average inventory or the year-end inventory.

$$\text{Inventory turnover} = \frac{\text{Sales}}{\text{Inventory}} \quad (22)$$

$$\text{DIH} = \frac{\text{Inventory}}{\text{Sales}} \times 360 \quad (23)$$

For HMC, the inventory turnover and DIH in terms of sales and year-end inventory are:

$$\text{Inventory turnover} = \frac{\text{Rs } 3717.23}{\text{Rs } 461.81} = 8.0$$

$$\text{DIH} = \frac{\text{Rs } 461.82}{\text{Rs } 3717.23} \times 360 = 0.214 \times 360 = 45 \text{ days}$$

It should be noticed that Equation (20) is more logical than Equation (22) in calculating the inventory turnover. In Equation (20) both the numerator—the cost of goods sold and the denominator—the average inventory, are valued at cost and are comparable. While in Equation (22) the numerator—sales—is valued at *market price* and the denominator is valued at *cost* and is non-comparable. Further, the average inventory figure is more appropriate to use than the year-end inventory figure because the levels of inventories fluctuate over the year. The average inventory figure smoothes out the fluctuations. If the firm has a strong seasonal character, it is more desirable to take the average of the monthly inventory levels.

Components of inventory The manufacturing firm's inventory consists of two more components: (*i*) raw materials and (*ii*) work-in-process. An analyst may also be interested in examining the efficiency with which the firm converts raw materials into work-in-process and work-in-process into finished

goods. That is, the analyst would like to know the levels of raw materials inventory and work in process inventory held by the firm on an average. The raw material inventory should be related to materials consumed, and work-in-process to the cost of production. Thus:

Raw material inventory turnover:

$$= \frac{\text{Material consumed}}{\text{Average raw material inventory}} \quad (24)$$

Work-in-process inventory turnover:

$$= \frac{\text{Cost of prduction}}{\text{Average work-in-process inventory}} \quad (25)$$

Material consumed can be found out as opening balance of raw material plus purchases minus closing balance of raw material. Cost of production is determined as material consumed plus other manufacturing expenses plus opening balance minus closing balance of work-in-process. In the absence of information of material consumed or cost of production, raw material and work-in-process inventories may be related to sales.

For HMC, the raw material and the work-in-process inventory turnovers are:

Raw material inventory turnover

$$= \frac{\text{Rs } 2751.52}{(\text{Rs } 384.06 + \text{Rs } 457.74)/2} = \frac{\text{Rs } 2751.52}{\text{Rs } 420.90} = 6.5 \text{ times}$$

Work-in-process inventory turnover

$$= \frac{\text{Rs } 3271.21}{(\text{Rs } 150.55 + \text{Rs } 230.84)/2} = \frac{\text{Rs } 3271.21}{\text{Rs } 190.70} = 17 \text{ times}$$

HMC's inventories of raw material and work-in-process on an average turn respectively 6.5 times and 17 times in a year. Interpreted differently, the company holds 55 days' (i.e., 360/6.5) inventory of raw material and 21 days' (i.e., 360/17) inventory of work-in-process.

What does inventory turnover indicate? The inventory turnover shows how rapidly the inventory is turning into receivable through sales. Generally, a high inventory turnover is indicative of good inventory management. A low inventory turnover implies excessive inventory levels than warranted by production and sales activities, or a slow-moving or obsolete inventory. A high level of sluggish inventory amounts to unnecessary tie-up of funds, reduced profit and increased costs. If the obsolete inventories have to be written off, this will adversely affect the working capital and liquidity position of the firm. However, a relatively high inventory turnover should be carefully analysed. A high inventory turnover may be the result of a very low level of inventory, which results in frequent stock outs; the firm may be living from hand-to-mouth. The turnover will also be high if the firm replenishes its inventory in too many small lot sizes. The situations of frequent stock outs and too many small inventory replacements are costly for the firm. Thus, too high and too low inventory turnover ratios should be investigated further. The computation of inventory turnovers for individual components of inventory may help to detect the imbalanced investments in the various inventory components.

To judge whether HMC's inventory turnover is good or not, it should be compared with the past and the expected ratios as well as with inventory turnover ratios of similar firms and industry average. The HMC's trend in inventory turnover ratios is given in Table 25.6.

Table 25.6: Hindustan Manufacturing Company: Inventory Turnover Ratio

	19X1		19X2		19X3	
Finished goods turnover	12.9	(28)	11.9	(30)	8.6	(42)
Work-in-process turnover	27.0	(13)	20.5	(18)	17.1	(21)
Materials turnover	6.5*	(55)	6.4	(56)	6.5	(55)
Sales to total inventory	4.9**	(73)	3.6**	(100)	3.2**	(113)
Inventory to sales	20.4%		27.8%		31.3%	

Notes: Numbers within parenthesis give number of days inventory holdings.
* Year-end inventory is used for calculating 19X1 ratio.
** Total of year-end inventory of raw material, work-in-process and finished goods is used.

HMC's efficiency in turning its inventories is continuously deteriorating. The company's utilisation of inventories in generating sales is poor; the yearly holding of all types of inventories is increasing.

Debtors (Accounts Receivable) Turnover

A firm sells goods for cash and credit. Credit is used as a marketing tool by a number of companies. When the firm extends credits to its customers, debtors (accounts receivables) are created in the firm's accounts. Debtors are convertible into cash over a short period and, therefore, are included in current assets. The liquidity position of the firm depends on the quality of debtors to a great extent. Financial analysts apply three ratios to judge the quality or liquidity of debtors: (*a*) debtors turnover, (*b*) collection period, and (*c*) aging schedule of debtors.

Debtors turnover: **Debtors turnover** is found out by dividing credit sales by average debtors:

$$\text{Debtors turnover} = \frac{\text{Credit sales}}{\text{Average debtors}} \qquad (26)$$

Debtors turnover indicates the number of times debtors turnover each year. Generally, the higher the value of debtors turnover, the more efficient is the management of credit.

To outside analyst, information about credit sales and opening and closing balances of debtors may not be available. Therefore, debtors turnover can be calculated by dividing total sales by the year-end balance of debtors:

$$\text{Debtors turnover} = \frac{\text{Sales}}{\text{Debtors}} \qquad (27)$$

For HMC, the ratio is:

$$\text{Debtors turnover} = \frac{\text{Rs } 3717.23}{\text{Rs } 483.18} = 7.7 \text{ times}$$

Collection period HMC is able to turnover its debtors 7.7 times in a year. In other words, its debtors remain outstanding for: 12 months/7.7 = 1.56 months or 360 days/7.7 = 47 days. The average number of days for which debtors remain outstanding is called the **average collection period** (ACP) and can be computed as follows:

$$\text{ACP} = \frac{360}{\text{Debtors turnover}} = \frac{\text{Debtors}}{\text{Sales}} \times 360 \qquad (28)$$

For HMC, ACP is:

$$\text{ACP} = \frac{360}{7.7} = 47 \text{ days}$$

or

$$= \frac{\text{Rs } 483.18}{\text{Rs } 3717.23} \times 360 = 0.13 \times 360 = 47 \text{ days}.$$

Note that HMC's debtors are 13 per cent of its sales. For making calculation of ACP, we have used sales for the year. It would be consistent to do so when the firm has constant sales rate throughout the year. ACP calculated on the basis of sales for the year will give a distorted and misleading picture of the firm's collection rate if sales are seasonal or rapidly growing. ACP calculated at different points of time will vary on account of varying sales rate although there may not be any change in collection rate. Therefore, ACP in the case of seasonal or growing firms should be interpreted cautiously.

What does collection period measure? The average collection period measures the quality of debtors since it indicates the speed of their collection. The shorter the average collection period, the better the quality of debtors, since a short collection period implies the prompt payments by debtors. The average collection period should be compared against the firm's credit terms and policy to judge its credit and collection efficiency. For example, if the credit period granted by a firm is 35 days, and its average collection period is 50 days, the comparison reveals that the firm's debtors are outstanding for a longer period than warranted by the credit period of 35 days. An excessively long collection period implies a very liberal and inefficient credit and collection performance. This certainly delays the collection of cash and impairs the firm's liquidity. The chances of bad debt losses are also increased. On the other hand, a low collection period is not necessarily favourable. Rather, it may indicate a very restrictive credit and collection policy. Because of the fear of bad debt losses, the firm sells only to those customers whose financial conditions are undoubtedly sound, and who are very prompt in making the payment. Such a policy succeeds in avoiding the bad debt losses, but it so severely curtails sales that overall profits are reduced. The firm should consider relaxing its credit and collection policy to enhance the sales level and improve profitability. In addition to measuring the firm's credit-and-collection efficiency with its own credit terms, the analyst must compare the firm's average collection period with the industry average. If there is a great divergence between the industry average and the firm's average collection period, the analyst must investigate the causes. The investigation may reveal that the firm manages its debtors more efficiently or inefficiently than the industry, or its credit policy is too liberal or too restrictive. This may warrant a change in the credit policy. The effect of the changes in the firm's existing credit policy on sales, profits and liquidity should be analysed.

The collection period ratio thus helps an analyst in two respects:[1]

- in determining the collectibility of debtors and thus, the efficiency of collection efforts, and
- in ascertaining the firm's comparative strength and advantage relative to its credit policy and performance *vis-à-vis* the competitors' credit policies and performance.

It is useful to examine trend in ACP to know the firm's collection experience. HMC's debtors turnover, ACP and debtors to sales ratio for three years are given in Table 25.7.

Table 25.7: Hindustan Manufacturing Company: Days of Sales Outstanding

	19X1	*19X2*	*19X3*
Debtors turnover (times)	9.2	8.3	7.7
Average collection period (days)	39	43	47
Debtors/sales ratio (per cent)	10.9	12.1	13.0

HMC's average collection period has been increasing; it has increased from 39 days in 19X1 to 47 days in 19X3. This increase may be due to change in the economic conditions and/or laxity in managing receivables.

Aging schedule The average collection period measures the quality of debtors in an aggregative way. We can have a detailed idea of the quality of debtors through the **aging schedule**. The aging schedule breaks down debtors according to the length of time for which they have been outstanding. A hypothetical example of the aging schedule is given in Table 25.8.

The aging schedule given in Table 25.8 shows that, within the collection period ranging between zero to 25 days, 50 per cent of its debtors are overdue. It also reveals that some of the accounts of the firm have serious problems of collection. The aging schedule gives more information than the collection period, and very clearly spots out the slow-paying debtors.

Table 25.8: Example of Debtors Aging Schedule

Outstanding Period (days)	*Outstanding Amount of Debtors Rs*	*Percentage of Total Debtors*
0–25	2,00,000	50.0
26–35	1,00,000	25.0
36–45	50,000	12.5
46–60	30,000	7.5
Over 60	20,000	5.0
	4,00,000	100.0

Assets Turnover Ratios

Assets are used to generate sales. Therefore, a firm should manage its assets efficiently to maximise sales. The relationship between sales and assets is called **assets turnover**. Several assets turnover ratios can be calculated.

Net assets turnover The firm can compute **net assets turnover** simply by dividing sales by net assets (NA).

$$\text{Net assets turnover} = \frac{\text{Sales}}{\text{Net assets}} \qquad (29)$$

It may be recalled that net assets (NA) include net fixed assets (NFA) and net current assets (NCA), that is, current assets (CA) minus current liabilities (CL). Since net assets equal capital employed, net assets turnover may also be called **capital employed turnover**. For Hindustan, the ratio is

$$\text{Net assets turnover} = \frac{\text{Rs } 3717.23}{\text{Rs } 1901.87} = 1.95 \text{ times}$$

The net assets turnover of 1.95 times implies that Hindustan is producing Rs 1.95 of sales for one rupee of capital employed in net assets.

A firm's ability to produce a large volume of sales for a given amount of net assets is the most important aspect of its operating performance. Unutilised or under-utilised assets increase the firm's need for costly financing as well as expenses for maintenance and upkeep. The net assets turnover should be interpreted cautiously. The net assets in the denominator of the ratio include fixed assets net of depreciation. Thus old assets with lower book (depreciated) values may create a misleading impression of high turnover without any improvement in sales.

Some analysts exclude intangible assets like goodwill, patents etc., while computing the net assets turnover. Similarly, fictitious assets, accumulated losses or deferred expenditures may also be excluded for calculating the net assets turnover ratio.

Total assets turnover Some analysts like to compute the **total assets turnover** in addition to or instead of the net assets turnover. This ratio shows the firm's ability in generating sales from *all* financial resources committed to total assets. Thus:

$$\text{Total assets turnover} = \frac{\text{Sales}}{\text{Total assets}} \qquad (30)$$

Total assets (TA) include net fixed assets (NFA) and current assets (CA) (TA = NFA + CA). For Hindustan, the ratio is:

$$\text{Total assets turnover} = \frac{\text{Rs } 3717.23}{\text{Rs } 2617.75} = 1.42 \text{ times}$$

The total assets turnover of 1.42 times implies that Hindustan generates a sale of Rs 1.42 for one rupee investment in fixed and current assets together.

Fixed and current assets turnover The firm may wish to know its efficiency of utilising fixed assets and current assets separately. For HMC, the fixed assets turnover is:

$$\text{Fixed assets turnover} = \frac{\text{Sales}}{\text{Net fixed assets}}$$

$$= \frac{\text{Rs } 3717.23}{\text{Rs } 746.83} = 4.98 \text{ times} \qquad (31)$$

---

1. Miller, *op. cit.*, p. 67.

The current assets turnover is:

$$\text{Current assets turnover} = \frac{\text{Sales}}{\text{Current assets}}$$
$$= \frac{\text{Rs } 3717.23}{\text{Rs } 1870.92} = 1.99 \text{ times} \qquad (32)$$

HMC turns over its fixed assets faster than current assets. Interpreting the reciprocals of these ratios, one may say that for generating a sale of one rupee, the company needs respectively Rs 0.20 investment in fixed assets and Rs 0.50 investment in current assets.

As explained previously, the use of depreciated value of fixed assets in computing the fixed assets turnover may render comparison of firm's performance over period or with other firms meaningless. Therefore, gross fixed assets (GFA) may be used to calculate the fixed assets turnover for a meaningful comparison.

Working capital turnover A firm may also like to relate net current assets (or net working capital gap) to sales. It may thus compute net working capital turnover by dividing sales by net working capital. For HMC, the ratio is:

$$\text{Net current assets turnover} = \frac{\text{Sales}}{\text{Net current assets}}$$
$$= \frac{\text{Rs } 3717.23}{\text{Rs } 1155.04} = 3.2 \text{ times} \qquad (33)$$

The reciprocal of the ratios is 0.31. Thus it is indicated that for one rupee of sales, the company needs Rs 0.31 of net current assets. This gap will be met from bank borrowings and long-term sources of funds.

Table 25.9 gives the three-year summary of assets turnover ratios for the HMC's turnover ratios do not show much improvement. The company has marginally improved its utilisation of fixed assets, but its current assets turnover is declining.

Table 25.9: Hindustan Manufacturing Company: Assets Turnover Ratios

	19X1	19X2	19X3
Current assets turnover (sales/CA)	2.70 (37.0)	2.01 (49.8)	1.99 (50.3)
Net current assets turnover (sales/NCA)	3.85 (26.0)	3.06 (32.7)	3.22 (31.1)
Fixed assets turnover (sales/NFA)	4.28 (23.4)	4.26 (23.5)	4.98 (20.1)
Total assets turnover (sales/TA)	1.66 (60.4)	1.37 (73.2)	1.42 (70.4)
Net assets or capital employed turnover (sales/NA)	2.03 (49.3)	1.78 (56.1)	1.95 (51.3)

Note: Numbers in parentheses represent assets as percentage of sales.

PROFITABILITY RATIOS

A company should earn profits to survive and grow over a long

period of time. Profits are essential, but it would be wrong to assume that every action initiated by management of a company should be aimed at maximising profits, irrespective of concerns for customers, employees, suppliers or social consequences. It is unfortunate that the word 'profit' is looked upon as a term of abuse since some firms always want to maximise profits at the cost of employees, customers and society. Except such infrequent cases, it is a fact that sufficient profits must be earned to sustain the operations of the business to be able to obtain funds from investors for expansion and growth and to contribute towards the social overheads for the welfare of the society.[1]

Profit is the difference between revenues and expenses over a period of time (usually one year). Profit is the ultimate 'output' of a company, and it will have no future if it fails to make sufficient profits. Therefore, the financial manager should continuously evaluate the efficiency of the company in term of profits. The **profitability ratios** are calculated to measure the operating efficiency of the company. Besides management of the company, creditors and owners are also interested in the profitability of the firm. Creditors want to get interest and repayment of principal regularly. Owners want to get a required rate of return on their investment. This is possible only when the company earns enough profits.

Generally, two major types of profitability ratios are calculated:

- profitability in relation to sales
- profitability in relation to investment.

How is Profit Measured?

As already discussed in Chapter 2, profit can be measured in various ways. **Gross profit** (GP) is the difference between sales and the manufacturing cost of goods sold. A number of companies in India define gross profit differently. They define it as earnings profit before depreciation, interest and taxes (PBDIT or EBDIT). A number of multinational companies call this profit or earnings measure as earnings before interest, taxes and depreciation and amortisation or EBITDA. The most common measure of profit is **profit after taxes** (PAT), or net income (NI), which is a result of the impact of all factors on the firm's earnings. Taxes are not controllable by management. To separate the influence of taxes, therefore, **profit before taxes** (PBT) may be computed. If the firm's profit has to be examined from the point of view of *all* investors (lenders and owners), the appropriate measure of profit is **operating profit**. Operating profit is equivalent of **earnings before interest and taxes** (EBIT). This measure of profit shows earnings arising directly from the commercial operations of the business without the effect of financing. The concept of EBIT may be broadened to include non-operating income if they exist. On an after-tax basis, profit to investors is equal to: EBIT $(1 - T)$, where T is the corporate tax rate. This profit measure is called net operating profit after tax or NOPAT.

Gross Profit Margin

The first profitability ratio in relation to sales is the **gross profit**

---

1. Drucker, P.F., *The Practice of Management*, Pan, 1968, pp. 99–100.

margin (or simply *gross margin* ratio[1]). It is calculated by dividing the gross profit by sales:

$$\text{Gross profit margin} = \frac{\text{Sales} - \text{Cost of goods sold}}{\text{Sales}}$$

$$= \frac{\text{Gross profit}}{\text{Sales}} \qquad (34)$$

For HMC, the ratio is:

$$\text{Gross profit margin} = \frac{\text{Rs}\,663.57}{\text{Rs}\,3717.23} = 0.179 \text{ or } 17.9\%$$

The gross profit margin reflects the efficiency with which management produces each unit of product. This ratio indicates the average spread between the cost of goods sold and the sales revenue. When we subtract the gross profit margin from 100 per cent, we obtain the ratio of cost of goods sold to sales. Both these ratios show profits relative to sales after the deduction of production costs, and indicate the relation between production costs and selling price. A high gross profit margin relative to the industry average implies that the firm is able to produce at relatively lower cost.

A high gross profit margin ratio is a sign of good management. A gross margin ratio may increase due to any of the following factors;[2] (*i*) higher sales prices, cost of goods sold remaining constant, (*ii*) lower cost of goods sold, sales prices remaining constant, (*iii*) a combination of variations in sales prices and costs, the margin widening, and (*iv*) an increase in the proportionate volume of higher margin items. The analysis of these factors will reveal to the management how a depressed gross profit margin can be improved.

A low gross profit margin may reflect higher cost of goods sold due to the firm's inability to purchase raw materials at favourable terms, inefficient utilisation of plant and machinery, or over-investment in plant and machinery, resulting in higher cost of production. The ratio will also be low due to a fall in prices in the market, or marked reduction in selling price by the firm in an attempt to obtain large sales volume, the cost of goods sold remaining unchanged. The financial manager must be able to detect the causes of a falling gross margin and initiate action to improve the situation.

Net Profit Margin

Net profit is obtained when operating expenses, interest and taxes are subtracted from the gross profit. The **net profit margin** ratio is measured by dividing profit after tax by sales:

$$\text{Net profit margin} = \frac{\text{Profit after tax}}{\text{Sales}} \qquad (35)$$

For HMC, the ratio is:

$$\text{Net profit margin} = \frac{\text{Rs}\,134.86}{\text{Rs}\,3717.23} = 0.036 \text{ or } 3.6\%$$

If the non-operating income figure is substantial, it may be excluded from PAT to see profitability arising directly from sales. For HMC, operating profit after taxes to sales ratio is 3.6 per cent.

Net profit margin ratio establishes a relationship between net profit and sales and indicates management's efficiency in manufacturing, administering and selling the products. This ratio is the overall measure of the firm's ability to turn each rupee sales into net profit. If the net margin is inadequate, the firm will fail to achieve satisfactory return on shareholders' funds.

This ratio also indicates the firm's capacity to withstand adverse economic conditions. A firm with a high net margin ratio would be in an advantageous position to survive in the face of falling selling prices, rising costs of production or declining demand for the product. It would really be difficult for a low net margin firm to withstand these adversities. Similarly, a firm with high net profit margin can make better use of favourable conditions, such as rising selling prices, falling costs of production or increasing demand for the product. Such a firm will be able to accelerate its profits at a faster rate than a firm with a low net profit margin.

An analyst will be able to interpret the firm's profitability more meaningfully if he/she evaluates both the ratios—gross margin and net margin—jointly. To illustrate, if the gross profit margin has increased over years, but the net profit margin has either remained constant or declined, or has not increased as fast as the gross margin, this implies that the operating expenses relative to sales have been increasing. The increasing expenses should be identified and controlled. Gross profit margin may decline due to fall in sales price or increase in the cost of production. As a consequence, net profit margin will decline unless operating expenses decrease significantly. The crux of the argument is that both the ratios should be jointly analysed and each item of expense should be thoroughly investigated to find out the causes of decline in any or both the ratios.

Net Margin Based on NOPAT

The profit after tax (PAT) figure excludes interest on borrowing. Interest is tax deductible, and therefore, a firm that pays more interest pays less tax. Tax saved on account of payment of

---

1. If a firm categorises its expenses into fixed and variable components, it can calculate contribution to sales ratio (also called profit/volume or P/V ratio):

$$\text{Contribution ratio} = \frac{\text{Sales} - \text{Variable expenses}}{\text{Sales}} = \frac{\text{Contribution}}{\text{Sales}} \qquad (34A)$$

Equation (34A) can also be written as follows:

$$\text{Contribution ratio} = 1 - \frac{\text{Variable expenses}}{\text{Sales}} \qquad (34B)$$

2. Kennedy, R.D. and McMuller, S.Y., *Financial Statements*, Richard D. Irwin, 1968, p. 404.

interest is called *interest tax shield*. Thus the conventional measure of net profit margin—PAT to sales ratio—is affected by the firm's financing policy. It can mislead if we compare two firms with different debt ratios. For a true comparison of the **operating performance** of firms, we must ignore the effect of financial leverage, *viz.*, the measure of profit should ignore interest and its tax effect. Thus net profit margin (for evaluating operating performance) may be computed in the following way:[1]

$$\text{Net profit margin} = \frac{\text{EBIT}(1-T)}{\text{Sales}} = \frac{\text{NOPAT}}{\text{Sales}} \qquad (36)$$

where T is the corporate tax rate. EBIT $(1-T)$ is the after-tax operating profit, assuming that the firm has no debt.

We can see in Table 25.1 that the effective tax rate for the HMC in 19X3 is 32 per cent. Therefore, the net margin (modified) ratio is:

$$= \frac{342.61(1-0.32)}{3717.23} = \frac{232.97}{3717.23} = 0.063 \text{ or } 6.3\%$$

Taxes are not controllable by a firm, and also, one may not know the marginal corporate tax rate while analysing the published data. Therefore, the margin ratio may be calculated on before tax basis:[2, 3]

$$\text{Profit margin} = \frac{\text{EBIT}}{\text{Sales}} \qquad (37)$$

For HMC, the EBIT/Sales ratio is:

$$= \frac{\text{Rs } 342.61}{\text{Rs } 3717.23} = 0.092 \text{ or } 9.2\%$$

Operating Expense Ratio

The **operating expense ratio** explains the changes in the profit margin (EBIT to sales) ratio. This ratio is computed by dividing operating expenses *viz.*, cost of goods sold plus selling expenses and general and administrative expenses (excluding interest) by sales:

$$\text{Operating expenses ratio} = \frac{\text{Operating expenses}}{\text{Sales}} \qquad (38)$$

For HMC, the ratio is:

$$\text{Operating expenses ratio} = \frac{\text{Rs } 3411.53}{\text{Rs } 3717.23} = 0.918 \text{ or } 91.8\%$$

The operating ratio for HMC indicated that 91.8 per cent of sales have been consumed together by the cost of goods sold and other operating expenses. This implies that 8.2 per cent of sales is left to cover interest, taxes, and earnings to owners. Other incomes contribute about 1 per cent of sales. In practice, a firm may decompose the operating expense ratio into: (*a*) cost of goods sold ratio and (*b*) other operating expense ratio. For HMC, these ratios are calculated as follows:

$$\text{Cost of goods sold ratio} = \frac{\text{Cost of goods sold}}{\text{Sales}}$$

$$= \frac{3053.66}{3717.23} = 0.822 \text{ or } 82.2\%$$

$$\text{Other operating expense ratio} = \frac{\text{Other operating expenses}}{\text{Sales}}$$

$$= \frac{357.87}{3717.23} = 0.096 \text{ or } 9.6\%$$

What does operating expense ratio reveal? A higher operating expenses ratio is unfavourable since it will leave a small amount of operating income to meet interest, dividends, etc. To get a comprehensive idea of the behaviour of operating expenses, variations in the ratio over a number of years should be studied. Certain expenses are within the managerial discretion; therefore, it should be seen whether change in **discretionary expenses** is due to changes in the management policy. Detailed analysis may reveal that the year-to-year variations in the operating expense ratio are temporary in nature arising due to some temporary conditions. The variations in the ratio, temporary or long-lived, can occur due to several factors such as: (*a*) changes in the sales prices, (*b*) changes in the demand for the product, (*c*) changes in the administrative or selling expenses, or (*d*) changes in the proportionate shares of sales of different products with varying gross margins. These and other causes of variations in the operating ratio should be thoroughly examined.

The operating expense ratio is a yardstick of operating efficiency, but it should be used cautiously. It is affected by a number of factors, such as external uncontrollable factors, internal factors, employees and managerial efficiency (or inefficiency), all of which are difficult to analyse. Further, the ratio cannot be used as a test of financial condition in the case of those firms where non-operating revenue and expenses form a *substantial* part of the total income.

---

1. Note that PAT = (EBIT – INT) $(1 – T)$ = EBIT $(1 – T)$ – INT + TINT or EBIT $(1 – T)$ = PAT + INT – TINT = PAT + INT $(1 – T)$. TINT is tax shield on interest.

2. Sometimes the following ratio is suggested:

$$\text{Net profit margin} = \frac{\text{PAT} + \text{Interest}}{\text{Sales}}$$

Note that this measure is still biased by financial leverage. Since numerator has not eliminated the effect of interest tax shield (see footnote 1).

3. When fixed and variable expenses data are available, the firm can calculate EBIT to contribution ratio. Since EBIT = contribution – fixed expenses, this ratio indicates the effect of fixed expenses on profitability. The product of contribution ratio and EBIT to contribution ratio is equal to EBIT to sales ratio:

$$\frac{\text{Contribution}}{\text{Sales}} \times \frac{\text{EBIT}}{\text{Contribution}} = \frac{\text{EBIT}}{\text{Sales}}$$

The operating expense ratio indicates the average aggregate variations in expenses, where some of the expenses may be increasing while others may be falling. Thus, to know the behaviour of specific expense items, the ratio of each individual operating expense to sales should be calculated. These ratios when compared from year to year for the firm will throw light on managerial policies and programmes. For example, the increasing selling expenses, without a sufficient increase in sales, can imply uncontrolled sales promotional expenditure, inefficiency of the marketing department, general rise in selling expenses, or introduction of better substitutes by competitors. The expenses ratios of the firm should be compared with the ratios of the similar firms and the industry average. This will reveal whether the firm is paying higher or lower salaries to its employees as compared to other firms; whether its capacity utilisation is high or low; whether the salesmen are given enough commission; whether it is unnecessarily spending on advertisement and other sales promotional activities; whether its cost of production is high or low and so on.

Return on Investment (ROI)

The term investment may refer to total assets or net assets. The funds employed in net assets in known as capital employed. Net assets equal net fixed assets plus current assets minus current liabilities excluding bank loans. Alternatively, capital employed is equal to net worth plus total debt.

The conventional approach of calculating **return on investment** (ROI) is to divide PAT by investment. Investment represents pool of funds supplied by shareholders and lenders, while PAT represent residue income of shareholders; therefore, it is conceptually unsound to use PAT in the calculation of ROI. Also, as discussed earlier, PAT is affected by capital structure. It is, therefore more appropriate to use one of the following measures of ROI for comparing the operating efficiency of firms:

$$ROI = ROTA = \frac{EBIT(1-T)}{Total\ assets} = \frac{EBIT(1-T)}{TA} \qquad (39)$$

$$ROI = RONA = \frac{EBIT(1-T)}{Net\ assets} = \frac{EBIT(1-T)}{NA} \qquad (40)$$

where ROTA and RONA are respectively **return on total assets** and **return on net assets**. RONA is equivalent of **return on capital employed**, i.e., ROCE. The after tax ROTA and RONA for HMC are:

$$ROI = ROTA = \frac{Rs\,342.61(1-0.32)}{Rs\,2617.75} = 0.089\ or\ 8.9\%$$

$$ROI = RONA = \frac{Rs\,342.61(1-0.32)}{Rs\,1901.87} = 0.122\ or\ 12.2\%$$

Since taxes are not controllable by management, and since firm's opportunities for availing tax incentives differ, it may be more prudent to use before-tax measure of ROI. Thus, the before-tax ratios are:[1]

$$ROI = ROTA = \frac{EBIT}{TA} \qquad (41)$$

$$ROI = RONA = \frac{EBIT}{NA} \qquad (42)$$

For HMC, the before-tax ROI is:

$$ROI = ROTA = \frac{Rs\,342.61}{Rs\,2615.75} = 0.131\ or\ 13.1\%$$

$$ROI = RONA = \frac{Rs\,342.61}{Rs\,1901.87} = 0.180\ or\ 18.0\%$$

Many companies use EBIDTA (instead of EBIT) to calculate ROI. For HMC, the ratio is:

$$ROI = \frac{EBITDA}{TA} = \frac{382.20}{2615.75} = 0.147\ or\ 14.7\%$$

Return on Equity (ROE)

Common or ordinary shareholders are entitled to the residual profits. The rate of dividend is not fixed; the earnings may be distributed to shareholders or retained in the business. Nevertheless, the net profits after taxes represent their return. A return on shareholders' equity is calculated to see the profitability of owners' investment. The shareholders' equity or net worth will include paid-up share capital, share premium and reserves and surplus *less* accumulated losses. Net worth can also be found by subtracting total liabilities from total assets.

The **return on equity** is net profit after taxes divided by shareholders' equity which is given by net worth:[2]

$$ROE = \frac{Profit\ after\ taxes}{Net\ worth\ (Equity)} = \frac{PAT}{NW} \qquad (43)$$

For HMC, the ratio is:

$$= \frac{Rs\,134.86}{Rs\,672.81} = 0.20\ or\ 20\%$$

---

1. Depreciation policy of a firm may change over years. Similarly, the pattern of fixed assets acquisition (capital expenditures) may vary over years. This can distort the computation of ROI. Therefore ROI calculation may be modified as follows:

$$ROI = \frac{EBITDA}{GFA + NCA}$$

where EBITDA is earnings before interest, tax and depreciation and amortisation, GFA is gross fixed assets and NCA is net current assets. This ratio is quite useful in cross-sectional comparison of firms since their depreciation policies may differ significantly.

2. If a company has both preference and ordinary share capital, ROE should be calculated after deducting preference dividend from PAT, and using only the ordinary shareholders' capital.

ROE indicates how well the firm has used the resources of owners. In fact, this ratio is one of the most important relationships in financial analysis. The earning of a satisfactory return is the most desirable objective of a business. The ratio of net profit to owners' equity reflects the extent to which this objective has been accomplished. This ratio is, thus, of great interest to the present as well as the prospective shareholders and also of great concern to management, which has the responsibility of maximising the owners' welfare.

The returns on owners' equity of the company should be compared with the ratios for other similar companies and the industry average. This will reveal the relative performance and strength of the company in attracting future investments.

Earning Per Share (EPS)

The profitability of the shareholders' investment can also be measured in many other ways. One such measure is to calculate the earnings per share. The **earnings per share** (EPS) is calculated by dividing the profit after taxes by the total number of ordinary shares outstanding.

$$\text{EPS} = \frac{\text{Profit after tax}}{\text{Number of share outstanding}} \qquad (44)$$

For HMC, the earnings per share is:

$$\text{EPS} = \frac{\text{Rs}\,134.86}{22.50} = \text{Rs}\,6.00$$

EPS calculations made over years indicate whether or not the firm's earnings power on per-share basis has changed over that period. The EPS of the company should be compared with the industry average and the earnings per share of other firms. EPS simply shows the profitability of the firm on a per-share basis; it does not reflect how much is paid as dividend and how much is retained in the business. But as a profitability index, it is a valuable and widely used ratio.

Bonus and rights issues adjustment Adjustments for bonus or rights issues should be made while comparing EPS over a period of time. **Bonus shares** are free additional shares issued (through a transfer from reserves and surplus to the share capital) to the shareholders. The total wealth of a shareholder before or after bonus issue remains the same. Suppose the share price before bonus issue is Rs 100, and a bonus issue of 1:3 is made. A shareholder holding 3 shares before bonus issue has a wealth of: Rs 100 × 3 = Rs 300. Since no cash flow takes place when bonus shares are issued his/her total wealth remains same but is now divided into 4 shares. Thus, the share price after bonus is diluted to: Rs 300/4 = Rs 75 (**ex-bonus price**).

For a proper comparison of EPS, DPS (**dividend per share**), book value and share price for the periods before bonus issue, the data for the periods after bonus issue should be adjusted. For example, if a bonus issue in the proportion of 1:3 is made, then the adjustment factor 4/3 should be applied to adjust EPS of the year in which bonus issue is made as well as the subsequent years. Further, if the bonus issue, say, of 1:5 is made once again after some years, then the adjustment factor will become: $4/3 \times 6/5 = 24/15 = 1.68$, for the bonus year and subsequent years.

Rights issues are the shares issued to the existing shareholders of a company at a subscription price that may be different (generally lower) from the current share price. Suppose the market price of a company's share is Rs 100, and the subscription price per share under a rights issue is Rs 60. The share price of Rs 100 with the rights is called **cum-rights price**. Further, assume that 3 rights are needed to subscribe to one share (i.e., 1:3 rights issue). What is the implication of this for the shareholder's wealth? Before the rights issue, the wealth of the shareholder holding 3 shares is: Rs 100 × 3 = Rs 300. After subscribing to the rights issue, he/she owns one additional share by paying Rs 60. Thus, the shareholder now has a wealth of: Rs 300 + Rs 60 = Rs 360 divided into 4 shares. Thus, the price per share after exercising the rights (**ex-rights price**) will be: Rs 360/4 = Rs 90. The shareholder's existing wealth remains unchanged; he/she has paid Rs 60 to increase his/her wealth by this amount. However, the shareholder's proportionate ownership remains the same when he/she exercises the rights. When the rights shares have been issued, EPS, DPS, book value and share price are diluted (as the number of shares increase). To make them comparable with the data of earlier periods (before the issue of rights), they should be adjusted for the effect of the rights issue. In the example, the rights adjustment factor will be in proportion to cum-right and ex-right prices: 100/90 = 1.11.

Dividends Per Share (DPS or DIV)

The net profits after taxes belong to shareholders. But the income, which they really receive, is the amount of earnings distributed as cash dividends. Therefore, a large number of present and potential investors may be interested in DPS, rather than EPS. DPS is the earnings distributed to ordinary shareholders divided by the number of ordinary shares outstanding:

$$\text{DPS} = \frac{\text{Earnings paid to shareholders (dividends)}}{\text{Number of ordinary shares outstanding}} \qquad (45)$$

For HMC, DPS is:

$$\text{DPS} = \frac{\text{Rs}\,45.00}{22.50} = \text{Rs}\,2.00$$

The company distributed Rs 2.00 per share as dividend out of Rs 6.00 earned per share. The difference per share is retained in the business. Like in the case of EPS, adjustments for bonus or rights issues should be made while calculating DPS over years.

Dividend-Payout Ratio

The **dividend-payout ratio** or simply **payout ratio** is DPS (or total equity dividends) divided by the EPS (or profit after tax):

$$\text{Payout ratio} = \frac{\text{Equity dividends}}{\text{Profit after tax}}$$

$$= \frac{\text{Dividends per share}}{\text{Earnings per share}} = \frac{\text{DPS}}{\text{EPS}} \qquad (46)$$

For HMC, the payout ratio is:

$$\text{Payout ratio} = \frac{\text{Rs}\,2.00}{\text{Rs}\,6.00} = 0.33 \text{ or } 33.3\%$$

Earnings not distributed to shareholders are retained in the business. Thus retention ratio is: 1 – Payout ratio. If this figure is multiplied by the return on equity (ROE), we can know the growth in the owners' equity as a result of retention policy. Thus, HMC, the growth in equity is:[1]

$$\text{Growth in equity} = \text{Retention ratio} \times \text{ROE}$$

$$g = b \times \text{ROE} \qquad (47)$$

For HMC, growth in equity is as follows:

$$g = 0.667 \times 0.20 = 0.133 \text{ or } 13.3\%$$

Dividends and Earnings Yields

The **dividend yield** is the dividends per share divided by the market value per share, and the **earnings yield** is the earnings per share divided by the market value per share. That is:

$$\text{Dividend yield} = \frac{\text{Dividend per share}}{\text{Market value per share}} = \frac{\text{DPS}}{\text{MV}} \qquad (48)$$

$$\text{Earnings yield} = \frac{\text{Earnings per share}}{\text{Market value per share}} = \frac{\text{EPS}}{\text{MV}} \qquad (49)$$

For HMC, these ratios are as follows:

$$\text{Dividend yield} = \frac{\text{Rs } 2.00}{\text{Rs } 29.25} = 0.068 \text{ or } 6.8\%$$

$$\text{Earnings yield} = \frac{\text{Rs } 6.00}{\text{Rs } 29.25} = 0.205 \text{ or } 20.5\%$$

The dividend yield and earnings yield evaluate the shareholders' return in relation to the market value of the share. The earnings yield is also called the **earnings-price** (E/P) **ratio.** The information on the market value per share is not generally available from the financial statements; it has to be collected from external sources, such as the stock exchanges or the financial newspapers.

Price-Earnings Ratio

The reciprocal of the earnings yield is called the **price-earnings** (**P/E**) **ratio.** Thus:

$$\text{Price - earnings ratio} = \frac{\text{Market value per share}}{\text{Earnings per share}} = \frac{\text{MV}}{\text{EPS}} \qquad (50)$$

For HMC, the P/E ratio is:

$$\text{P/E ratio} = \frac{\text{Rs } 29.25}{\text{Rs } 6.00} = 4.88 \text{ times}$$

The price earnings ratio is widely used by the security analysts to value the firm's performance as expected by investors. It indicates investors' judgement or expectations about the firm's performance. Management is also interested in this market appraisal of the firm's performance and will like to find the causes if the P/E ratio declines.

P/E ratio reflects investors' expectations about the growth in the firm's earnings. Industries differ in their growth prospects; accordingly, the P/E ratios for industries vary widely.

Market Value-to-Book Value (MV/BV) Ratio

Market value-to-book value (M/B) ratio is the ratio of share price to book value per share: HMC:

$$\text{M/B ratio} = \frac{\text{Market value per share}}{\text{Book value per share}} \qquad (51)$$

For HMC, the ratio is calculated as given below:

$$\text{M/B ratio} = \frac{\text{Rs } 29.25}{\text{Rs } 29.90} = 0.98$$

Note that book value per share is net worth divided by the number of shares outstanding. HMC's M/B ratio of 0.98 means that the company is worth 2 per cent less than the funds, which shareholders have put into it.

Tobin's *q*

Tobin's *q* is the ratio of the market value of a firm's assets (or equity and debt) to its assets' replacement costs. Thus

$$\text{Tobin's } = \frac{\text{Market value of assets}}{\text{Replacement cost of assets}} \qquad (52)$$

This ratio differs from the market value-to-book value ratio in two respects: it includes both debt and equity in the numerator, and all assets in the denominator, not just the book value of equity. It is argued that firms will have incentive to invest when *q* is greater than 1. They will be reluctant to invest once *q* becomes equal to 1.[2]

---

1. $\text{Growth in equity} (g) = \dfrac{\Delta \text{ Net worth per share}}{\text{Net worth per share}} = \dfrac{\Delta \text{NWPS}}{\text{NWPS}}$

$$g = \frac{(\text{EPS} - \text{DPS})}{\text{EPS}} \times \frac{\text{EPS}}{\text{NWPS}} = \text{Retention ratio} \times \text{ROE}$$

(EPS – DPS) indicates the change in equity as a result of retention policy.

$$g = \left[1 - \frac{\text{DPS}}{\text{EPS}}\right] \times \frac{\text{EPS}}{\text{NWPS}} = \frac{\text{EPS} - \text{DPS}}{\text{NWPS}} = \frac{\text{REPS}}{\text{NWPS}}$$

where the difference between EPS and DPS is REPS—retained earnings per share.
2. Brealey, R. and Myers, S., *Principles of Corporate Finance*, McGraw Hill, 1984, p. 578.

The trend in profitability ratios for HMC is given below:

Table 25.10: Hindustan Manufacturing Company: Profitability Ratios

	19X1	*19X2*	*19X3*
Gross Margin	0.175	0.178	0.179
Net Margin	0.036	0.039	0.036
EBIT/Sales	0.079	0.094	0.092
PAT/Total Assets	0.059	0.054	0.052
EBIT/Total Assets	0.131	0.129	0.131
PAT/Net Assets	0.072	0.070	0.071
EBIT/Net Assets	0.161	0.168	0.180
Return on Equity	0.164	0.191	0.200

It can be seen from Table 25.10 that sales as well as investment related ratios of the company have remained more or less constant. Return on equity has shown an increase. This is perhaps due to the use of more debt over years by the company.

Table 25.11 gives trend in the company's EPS, DPS and Market-related profitability ratios.

Table 25.11: Hindustan Manufacturing Company: EPS, DPS and Market-related Profitability Ratios

	19X1	*19X2*	*19X3*
EPS (Rs)	3.72	4.94	5.99
DPS (Rs)	1.50	1.75	2.00
Market value (average) (Rs)	26.38	34.50	29.25
Book value (Rs)	22.72	25.91	29.90
Dividend payout	0.40	0.35	0.33
Earnings yield	0.141	0.143	0.205
Dividend yield	0.057	0.051	0.068
P/E Ratio (times)	7.09	7.00	4.88
M/B ratio (times)	1.16	1.33	0.98

It is indicated that the company's EPS and DPS are increasing; but the proportionate increase in DPS is less than that in EPS and therefore, dividend payout ratio is declining. EPS may be increasing more as a result of increasing use of debt than due to improved operations. Because of increase in the financial risk, the market price of share may come down. In spite of the increase in EPS and DPS, the market price of Hindustan's share has declined to Rs 29.25 in 19X3. As a result, the P/E ratio has substantially reduced to 4.88 in 19X3. The market value-to-book value ratio has also declined to 0.98. Thus, in terms of market performance, the company is showing deterioration.

EVALUATION OF A FIRM'S EARNING POWER: DuPont Analysis

RONA (or ROCE) is the measure of the firm's operating performance. It indicates the firm's earning power. It is a product of the asset turnover, gross profit margin and **operating leverage**.[1] Thus, RONA can be computed as follows:

$$RONA = \frac{EBIT}{NA} = \frac{Sales}{NA} \times \frac{GP}{Sales} \times \frac{EBIT}{GP} \qquad (53)$$

For HMC, the ratio is:

$$\frac{342.61}{1901.87} = \frac{3717.23}{1901.87} \times \frac{663.57}{3717.23} \times \frac{342.61}{663.57}$$

$$0.180 = 1.95 \times 0.179 \times 0.516 = 0.180$$

$$RONA = 18\%$$

It may be seen from Table 25.12 that HMC's RONA has shown improvement over years in spite of a constant gross margin and slightly declining assets turnover. RONA has increased on account of a higher operating leverage, as measured by EBIT/GP ratio, employed by the company.

All firms would like to improve their RONA. In practice, however, competition puts a limit on RONA. Also, firms may have to trade-off between asset turnover and gross profit margin. To improve profit margin, some firms resort to vertical integration for cost reduction and synergistic benefits.

A firm can convert its RONA into an impressive ROE through financial efficiency. Financial leverage and debt-equity ratios affect ROE and reflect financial efficiency. ROE is thus a product of RONA (reflecting operating efficiency) and financial leverage ratios (reflecting financing efficiency):

$$ROE = \text{Operating performance} \times \text{Leverage factor}$$

$$ROE = \frac{PAT}{NW} = \frac{EBIT}{NA} \times \frac{PAT}{EBIT} \times \frac{NA}{NW} \qquad (54)$$

For HMC, the ratio is:

$$\frac{134.86}{672.81} = \frac{342.61}{1901.87} \times \frac{134.86}{342.61} \times \frac{1901.87}{672.81}$$

$$0.200 = 0.180 \times (0.394 \times 2.83)$$

$$ROE = 0.18 \times 1.12 = 0.20 \text{ or } 20.0\%$$

HMC's PAT/EBIT has deteriorated, while the net assets/equity (NA/NW) ratio has increased over period. The combined effect (1.12), however, has been favourable; Hindustan's ROE has increased from 16.4 per cent to 20.0 per cent. The product of PAT/EBIT and NA/NW is referred to as the **leverage factor.**

A firm can convert its ROE into a growth in equity through retention. Equity growth as a result of retention policy is a product of ROE and retention ratio:

$$\text{Equity growth} = ROE \times \text{Retention ratio}$$

$$\frac{\Delta NW}{NW} = \frac{RE}{NW} = \frac{PAT}{NW} \times \frac{RE}{PAT} \qquad (55)$$

For HMC, the ratio is:

$$\frac{89.86}{672.81} = \frac{134.86}{672.81} \times \frac{89.86}{134.86}$$

$$0.134 = 0.200 \times 0.67 = 0.134$$

HMC's retention ratio has increased over years. With an increasing ROE this has resulted in higher growth in equity over years.

---

1. Operating leverage may be defined as change in EBIT for a given change in sales. EBIT changes more or less than change in sales depending on the proportion of fixed costs. Alternatively, operating leverage may be defined as earnings before interest and taxes (EBIT) to gross profit (GP). More discussion on operating leverage follows later on.

The combined effect of three aspects—operating efficiency, financing efficiency and retention—shows that HMC has a steadily improving performance (Table 25.12). The computations of ratios in Table 25.12 clearly show the interaction between operating (turnover) ratios, profitability ratios and leverage ratios for obtaining return on the shareholders' earnings. Thus:

$$\text{ROE} = \frac{\text{Sales}}{\text{NA}} \times \frac{\text{GP}}{\text{Sales}} \times \frac{\text{EBIT}}{\text{GP}} \times \frac{\text{PAT}}{\text{EBIT}} \times \frac{\text{NA}}{\text{NW}} \quad (56)$$

As shown earlier, ROE multiplied by retention ratio gives growth. A chart (sometimes known as a DuPont chart) can also be used to depict Hindustan's performance in terms of shareholders' return (see Figure 25.1).

Table 25.12: Hindustan Manufacturing Company Analysis of Earning Power

		19X1	*19X2*	*19X3*
A. Sales/NA	**Turnover**	**2.03**	**1.78**	**1.95**
B. GP/Sales	Gross margin	0.175	0.178	0.179
C. EBIT/GP	Operating leverage	0.452	0.529	0.516
D. EBIT/NA				
(A × B × C)	RONA	**0.161**	**0.168**	**0.180**
E. PAT/EBIT	Financial leverage	0.452	0.418	0.394
F. NA/NW	Financial leverage	2.26	2.72	2.83
G. PAT/NW				
(D × E × F)	ROE	**0.164**	**0.191**	**0.200**
H. RE/PAT	Retention	0.60	0.65	0.67
I. **RE/NW** (G × H)	Equity growth	**0.098**	**0.123**	**0.134**

COMPARATIVE STATEMENTS ANALYSIS

A simple method of tracing periodic changes in the financial performance of a company is to prepare comparative statements. Comparative financial statements will contain items at least for two periods. Changes—increases and decreases—in income statement and balance sheet over period can be shown in two ways: (1) aggregate changes and (2) proportional changes.

Drawing special columns for aggregate amount or percentage, or both, of increases and decreases, can indicate aggregate changes. Recording percentage calculated in relation to a common base in special columns, on the other hand, shows relative, or proportional, changes. For example, in the case of profit and loss statement, sales figure is assumed to be common base (and therefore, equal to 100) and all other items are expressed as percentage of sales. Similarly, the balance sheet items are expressed as percentage of total assets or total funds. The financial statements prepared in terms of common base percentages are called **common-size statements**. This kind of analysis is called **vertical analysis** and it indicates static relationships since relative changes are studied at a specific date.

Table 25.13 shows comparative balance sheets and corresponding changes in balance sheet data for the Hindustan Manufacturing Company.

Table 25.13: Hindustan Manufacturing Company: Comparative Balance Sheet

(Rs in lakh)

	19X2	*19X3*	Change	Percent-age Change
Liabilities and Capital				
Current liabilities	1123.57	1555.74	(+) 432.17	(+) 38.5%
Long-term liabilities	361.65	389.19	(+) 27.54	(+) 7.6%
Share capital	225.00	225.00	0	0
Reserves	357.95	447.81	(+) 89.86	(+) 25.1%
Total	2068.17	2617.74	(+) 549.57	(+) 26.6%
Assets				
Current assets	1404.55	1870.92	(+) 466.37	(+) 33.2%
Net fixed assets	647.18	686.11	(+) 38.93	(+) 6.0%
Other assets	16.44	60.72	(+) 44.28	(+) 269.3%
Total	2068.17	2617.75	(+) 549.58	(+) 26.6%

An investigation of the comparative financial statements helps to highlight the significant facts and points out the items which need further analysis. The published balance sheets and profit and loss accounts of joint-stock companies in India are presented in two-year comparative form. Some of the companies also report to shareholders condensed comparative statements

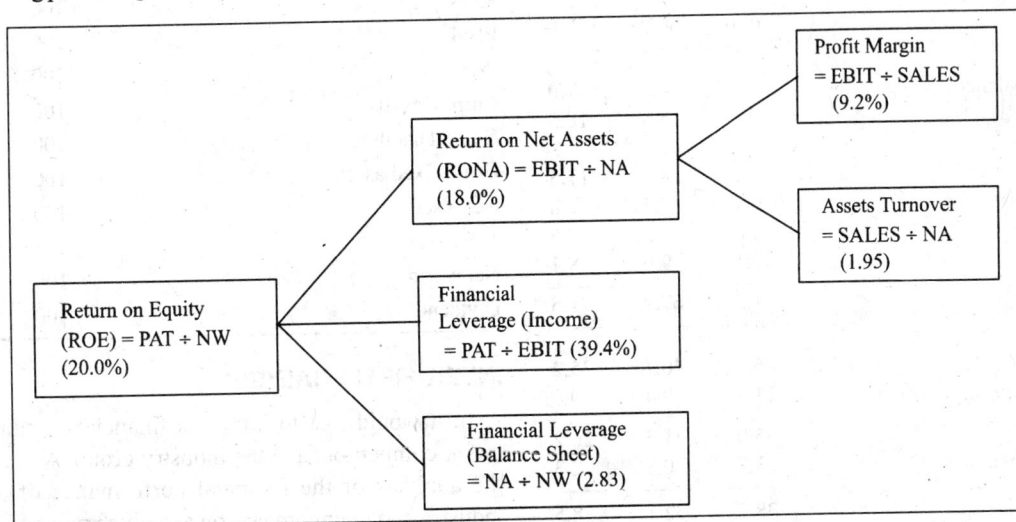

Figure 25.1: DuPont Chart: Hindustan Manufacturing Company's Financial Performance, 19X3

covering an extended period of years. From analytical point of view, such statements are quite useful to investors.

For HMC, the common-size statements are given in Tables 25.14 and 25.15.

Table 25.14: Hindustan Manufacturing Company

Common-size Profit and Loss Statement

	19X1	19X2	19X3
Net Sales	100.0	100.0	100.0
Cost of goods sold	82.5	82.2	82.1
Gross profit	17.5	17.8	17.9
Less: Selling and administrative expenses	10.2	9.3	9.6
Operating income	7.3	8.5	8.3
Add: Other income	0.7	0.9	1.0
EBIT	8.0	9.4	9.3
Less: Interest	2.6	4.4	3.9
PBT	5.4	5.0	5.4
Taxes	1.8	1.1	1.7
PAT	3.6	3.9	3.7

Table 25.15: Hindustan Manufacturing Company

Common-size Balance Sheet

	19X1	19X2	19X3
Current Liabilities			
Bank borrowing	31.4	31.0	32.1
Trade creditors	2.5	10.2	13.0
Provision etc.	15.8	13.1	14.3
Total	49.7	54.3	59.4
Long-term Liabilities			
Debentures	0.0	3.7	2.9
Others	14.1	13.8	12.0
Total	14.1	17.5	14.9
Total Liabilities	63.8	71.8	74.3
Net Worth			
Share capital	15.9	10.9	8.6
Reserve	20.3	17.3	17.1
Total	36.2	28.2	25.7
Total Funds	100.0	100.0	100.0
Current Assets			
Cash and bank balance	0.6	4.8	1.0
Trade debtors	17.9	16.5	18.5
Inventory:			
Raw material	17.2	18.5	17.5
Work-in-process	6.1	7.3	8.8
Finished goods	10.4	11.8	17.6
Others	9.1	9.0	8.1
Total	61.3	67.9	71.5
Fixed Assets			
Gross block	46.3	40.7	35.2
Less: Accumulated depreciation	11.3	9.4	9.0
Net block	35.0	31.3	26.2
Other non-current assets	3.7	0.8	2.3
Total	38.7	32.1	28.5
Total Assets	100.0	100.0	100.0

TREND ANALYSIS

In financial analysis the direction of changes over a period of years is of crucial importance. **Time series** or **trend analysis** of ratios indicates the direction of change. This kind of analysis is particularly applicable to the items of profit and loss account. It is advisable that trends of sales and net income may be studied in the light of two factors: the rate of fixed expansion or secular trend in the growth of the business and the general price level. It might be found in practice that a number of firms would show a persistent growth over a period of years. But to get a true trend of growth, the sales figures should be adjusted by a suitable index of general prices. In other words, sales figures should be deflated for rising price level. When the resulting figures are shown on a graph, we will get trend of growth devoid of price changes. Another method of securing trend of growth and one, which can be used instead of the adjusted sales figures or as check on them is to tabulate and plot the output or physical volume of sales expressed in suitable units of measure. If the general price level is not considered while analysing trend of growth, it can mislead management. They may become unduly optimistic in periods of prosperity and pessimistic in dull periods.

For trend analysis, the use of index numbers is generally advocated. The procedure followed is to assign the number 100 to items of the base year and to calculate percentage changes in each items of other years in relation to the base year. This procedure may be called as "**trend-percentage method.**"

Table 25.16 gives trend percentages for profit and loss statement and balance sheet items. Hindustan's EBIT has increased faster than the growth in sales, while PAT has shown slightly better performance than sales. Current assets and current liabilities have moved together. Total assets have grown faster than net worth, which implies the greater reliance on outsiders' money by HMC.

Table 25.16: Hindustan Manufacturing Company

Trend Analysis

	19X1	19X2	19X3
Sales	100	120.8	158.9
EBIT	100	143.6	184.8
PAT	100	132.8	161.0
Current assets	100	162.2	216.0
Current liabilities	100	160.1	221.7
Gross fixed assets	100	128.8	141.0
Net assets	100	137.5	164.8
Total assets	100	146.4	185.3
Net worth	100	114.0	131.6
Dividend	100	116.7	133.3

INTER-FIRM ANALYSIS

A firm would like to know its financial standing *vis-à-vis* its major competitors and the industry group. As explained earlier, the analysis of the financial performance of all firms in an industry and their comparison at a given point of time is referred to the **cross-section analysis** or the **inter-firm analysis**. To ascertain the relative financial standing of a firm, its financial ratios are compared either with its immediate competitors or with the industry average. We have used the data of construction firms to illustrate the inter-firm comparison.

Table 25.17 contains the financial data of eleven construction firms. Table 25.18 shows six important ratios for each firm. These ratios are also shown in Figures 25.2 to 25.7.

Table 25.17: Financial Data for Construction Companies

Company Name	CE	NW	NS	PBIT	PBT	PAT	DIV
Jaiprakash	89801	15614	36139	8825	3812	3812	1050
Continental	36601	11850	5203	2791	419	279	330
Hind. Const.	19779	2450	9134	1410	161	161	113
Unitech.	14264	2662	5880	762	639	464	173
Gammon	10498	1553	6383	348	59	43	43
ATV Projects	8818	3173	7433	1287	702	667	183
Dorroliver	5683	2809	4648	674	648	350	143
Ansal Housing	5445	598	2625	431	261	173	236
Cemindia	2252	1024	2264	174	140	75	38
V.M. Jog	1843	539	1419	162	60	38	24
Acrow	781	309	1073	67	25	18	10
Total (annualised)	203861	43658	84212	16519	6482	5636	2305

CE = capital employed; NW = net worth; NS = net sales; PBIT = profit before interest and tax; PBT = profit before-tax; PAT = profit after-tax; DIV = dividend.

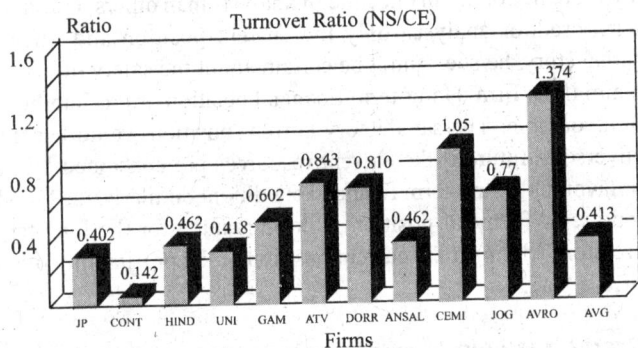

Figure 25.2: Turnover ratio (NS/CE)

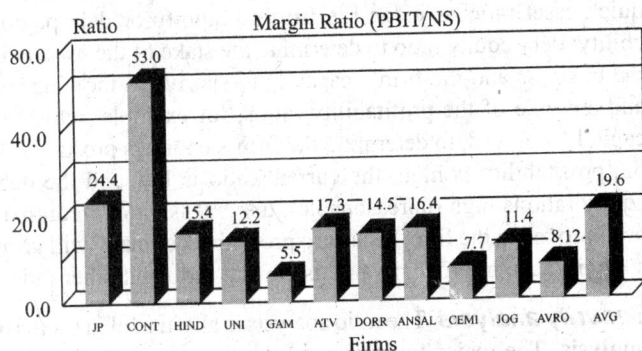

Figure 25.3: Margin Ratio (PBIT/NS)

9 per cent. The market shares of next three companies range between 6 to 8 per cent. The last three companies' market shares vary between 1 to 3 per cent.

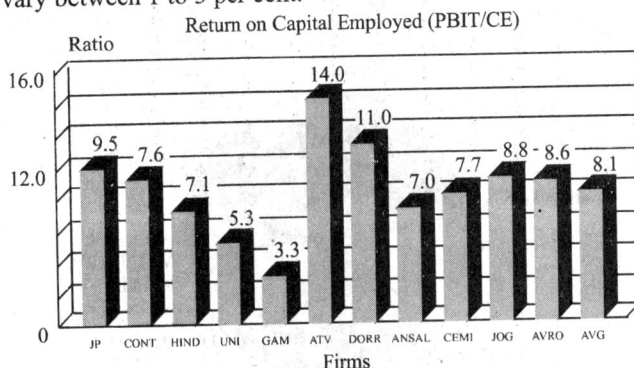

Figure 25.4: Return on Capital Employed (PBIT/CE)

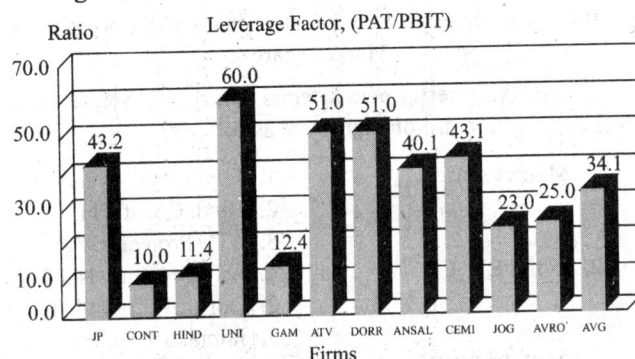

Figure 25.5: Tax Leverage (PAT/PBIT)

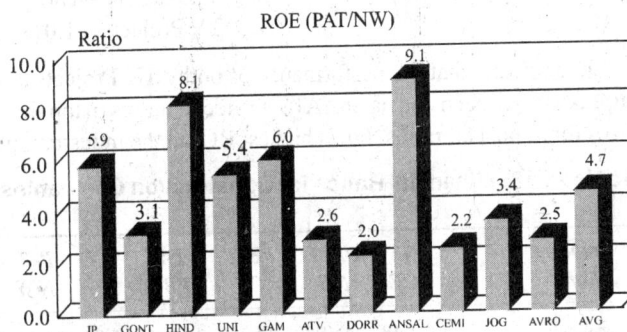

Figure 25.6: ROE (PAT/NW)

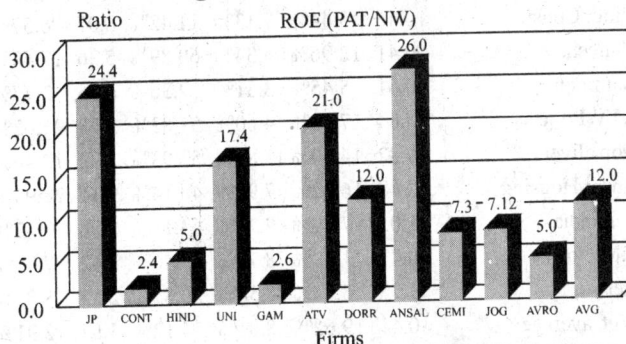

Figure 25.7: Financial Leverage (CE/NW)

Figure 25.8 shows the proportionate market share of the eleven companies. In terms of the market share, Jaiprakash is the largest company, holding 44 per cent market share, followed by Hindustan Construction with 11 per cent and ATV Projects with

Figures 25.2 to 25.7 show the relative position of companies regarding various financial dimensions. The industry shows significant variation across firms in terms of all ratios. Although Jaiprakash is the largest company, it is Ansal, which has the highest ROE of 28.9 per cent; Jaiprakash comes at the second place with ROE of 24.4 per cent. Both companies' ROE is almost double than the industry average. Other ratios can also be interpreted in the similar way.

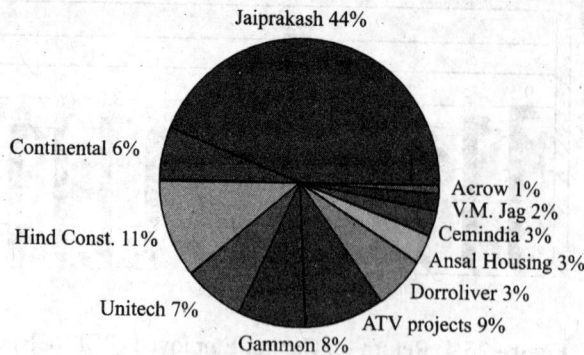

Figure 25.8: Construction industry: Inter-firm Comparison Market Share

The top three performers in terms of market share, return on investment and return on equity are as follows.

1. Market share	1. Jaiprakash (44%)
	2. Hind. Const. (11%)
	3. ATV Projects (9%)
2. ROI: PBIT/CE	1. ATV Projects (14.6%)
	2. Dorroliver (11.9%)
	3. Jaiprakash (9.8%)
3. ROE: PAT/NW	1. Ansal (28.9%)
	2. Jaiprakash (24.4%)
	3. ATV Projects (21.0%)

It is notable that the performance of both ATV Projects and Jaiprakash has been consistent. ATV Projects figures in top three firms for almost all ratios. It has highest ROI in the industry, but,

Table 25.18: Financial Ratios for Construction Companies

Company Name	NS CE	PBIT NS	PBIT CE	PAT PBIT	CE NW	PAT NW
Jaiprakash	0.48	24.42%	9.83%	43.20%	5.75	24.41%
Continental	0.41	53.64%	7.63%	10.00%	3.09	2.35%
Hind. Const.	0.46	15.44%	7.13%	11.42%	8.07	6.57%
Unitech.	0.41	12.96%	5.34%	60.89%	5.36	17.43%
Gammon	0.61	5.45%	3.31%	12.36%	6.76	2.77%
ATV Projects	0.84	17.31%	14.60%	51.83%	2.78	21.02%
Dorroliver	0.82	14.50%	11.86%	51.93%	2.02	12.46%
Ansal Housing	0.48	16.42%	7.92%	40.14%	9.11	28.93%
Cemindia	1.01	7.69%	7.73%	43.10%	2.20	7.32%
V.M. Jog	0.77	11.42%	8.79%	23.46%	3.42	7.05%
Acrow	1.37	6.24%	8.58%	26.87%	2.53	5.83%
Wgt. average	0.41	19.62%	8.01%	34.12%	4.67	12.91%

because of a low leverage ratio, its ROE is lower than Jaiprakash and Ansal, both highly geared companies. Jaiprakash has highest market share, but low ROI because of the poor utilisation of assets in turning over sales. Ansal has been able to obtain highest ROE because of the highest gearing (CE/NW = 1 + debt-equity)

of 9.11 in the industry.

UTILITY OF RATIO ANALYSIS

The ratio analysis is the most powerful tool of the financial analysis. As stated in the beginning of the chapter, many diverse groups of people are interested in analysing the financial information to indicate the operating and financial efficiency, and growth of the firm. These people use ratios to determine those financial characteristics of the firm in which they are interested. With the help of ratios, one can determine:

- the ability of the firm to meet its current obligations;
- the extent to which the firm has used its long-term solvency by borrowing funds;
- the efficiency with which the firm is utilising its assets in generating sales revenue, and
- the overall operating efficiency and performance of the firm.

Performance analysis As stated previously, a short-term creditor will be interested in the current financial position of the firm, while a long-term creditor will pay more attention to the solvency of the firm. The long-term creditor will also be interested in the profitability of the firm. The equity shareholders are generally concerned with their return and may bother about the firm's financial condition only when their earnings are depressed. In fact, it has to be realised that the short- and long-term financial position and the profitability of the firm are tested in every kind of financial analysis, but the emphasis would differ. Some ratios are more important in one kind of analysis than others. If a short-term creditor analyses only the current position and finds it satisfactory, he/she cannot be certain about the safety of his/her claim if the firm's long-term financial position or profitability is unfavourable. The satisfactory current position would become adverse in future if the current resources are consumed by the unfavourable long-term financial condition. Similarly, the 'good' long-term financial position is no guarantee for the long-term creditors' claims if the current position or the profitability of the firm is 'bad.'

Credit analysis In **credit analysis**, the analyst will usually select a few important ratios. He may use the current ratio or quick-asset ratio to judge the firm's liquidity or debt-paying ability; debt-equity ratio to determine the stake of the owners in the business and the firm's capacity to survive in the long run and any one of the profitability ratios, for example, return on capital employed, to determine the firm's earnings prospects. If the profitability is high, the current ratio is low and the debt equity ratio is high (unreasonable), the extension of credit may be approved to the firm, because a profitable company will grow and will have improvement in its current ratio and other ratios.

Security analysis The ratio analysis is also useful in **security analysis**. The major focus in security analysis is on the long-term profitability. Profitability is dependent on a number of factors and, therefore, the security analyst also analyses other ratios. He would certainly be concerned with the efficiency with which the firm utilises its assets and the financial risk to which the firm is exposed. Therefore, besides analysing the profitability ratios meticulously, he will also analyse activity ratios and leverage ratios. The detailed analysis of the earning power is important for security analysis.

Competitive analysis The ratios of a firm by themselves do not reveal anything. For meaningful interpretation, the ratios of a firm should be compared with the ratios of similar firms and industry. This comparison will reveal whether the firm is significantly out of line with its competitors. If it is significantly out of line, the firm should undertake a detailed analysis to spot out the trouble areas.

Trend analysis The ratio analysis will reveal the financial condition of the firm more reliably when trends in ratios over time are analysed. Ratios at a point of time can mislead the analyst, because they may be high or low for some exceptional circumstances at that point of time. An impressive present financial position may really be eroding over time, while a weak position may be improving at a rapid rate over time. Thus, the trend analysis of the ratios adds considerable significance to the financial analysis because it studies ratios of several years and isolates the exceptional instances occurring in one or two periods. Although the trend analysis of the company's ratios itself is informative, but it is more informative to compare the trends in the company's ratios with the trends in industry ratios. This comparison indicates how well the company has been operating over time relative to its competitors and may also help to explain the trends in the company's ratios. For example, if the company's return on capital employed (net assets) shows a declining trend, the comparison can reveal whether this decline is characteristic of the firm only or there is a general declining trend in the industry.

Management has to protect the interests of all concerned parties, creditors, owners and others. They have to ensure some minimum operating efficiency and keep the risk of the firm at a minimum level. Their survival depends upon their operating performance. From time to time, management uses ratio analysis to determine the firm's financial strengths and weaknesses, and accordingly takes actions to improve the firm's position. Management is in a better position to analyse the firm's financial position as it has access to internal information, which is not available to the credit analyst or the security analyst.

Diagnostic Role of Ratios

The essence of the financial soundness of a company lies in balancing its goals, commercial strategy, product-market choices and resultant financial needs. The company should have financial capability and flexibility to pursue its commercial strategy. Ratio analysis is a very useful analytical technique to raise pertinent questions on a number of managerial issues. It provides bases or clues to investigate such issues in detail. While assessing the financial health of the company with the help of ratio analysis, answers to the following questions relating to the company's profitability, assets utilisation, liquidity, financing and strategies capabilities may be sought:[1]

Profitability analysis

1. How profitable is the company? What accounting policies and practices are followed by the company? Are they stable?
2. Is the profitability (RONA) of the company high/low/average? Is it due to:

   - profit margin
   - assets utilisation
   - non-operating income
   - window dressing
   - change in accounting policy
   - inflationary conditions?

3. Is the return on equity (ROE) high/low/average? Is it due to:

   - return on investment
   - financing mix
   - capitalisation of reserves?

4. What is the trend in profitability? Is it improving because of better utilisation of resources or curtailment of expenses of strategic importance? What is the impact of cyclical factors on profitability trend?
5. Can the company sustain its impressive profitability or improve its profitability given the competitive and other environmental situations?

Assets utilisation

1. How effectively does a company utilise its assets in generating sales?
2. Are the levels of debtors and inventories relative to sales reasonable, given the firm's competitive and operating characteristics?
3. What are the trends in collection period, inventory turnover and fixed assets turnover?
4. Is the improvement in the fixed assets turnover due to:

   - depreciated book value of fixed assets?
   - sale of some fixed assets?

Liquidity analysis

1. What is the level of current assets relative to current liabilities? Is it reasonable given the nature of the company's business?
2. What is the mix of current assets? Is the proportion of slow moving inventories high?
3. How promptly does the company pay its creditors?
4. How far can it stretch payment to creditors without jeopardising its relations with them?
5. How efficiently and frequently does the company convert its current assets into cash?
6. Given the company's riskiness and future financial needs, how soundly is it financed?

   - What is the mix of debt and equity?
   - What is the maturity structure of debt? Is the company faced with large debt repayments in the near future?

---

1. This section draws from Butters, K.J., *et. al.*, *Case Problems in Finance*, Richard D. Irwin, 1981, pp. 3–7.

- Does the company generate enough cash flows to service debt adequately?
- Is the company close to its borrowing limits of restrictive convenants?

7. Does the company have lease commitments not disclosed in the balance sheet?
8. Does it have large contingent liabilities?
9. What potential does the company have to raise debt on acceptable terms? From whom? On what conditions? How quickly?
10. Can the company raise equity funds? Would market respond favourably? To whom and at what price shares would be sold? Is management willing for dilution of control if shares are issued?

Strategic Analysis

A number of other questions go beyond the scope of ratio analysis. They however need to be answered while assessing the financial health of the company. These questions are:[1]

1. What are the goals and strategies of the company?
2. How successfully has the company pursued its goals and strategies? Is change in them warranted?
3. Are the company's goals, strategies, product-market choices, investment requirements, financing needs, and financing capabilities in balance?
4. What would happen to the above-referred balance if the company will have to face an adversity?
5. If the company is struck by adversity:

- What kinds of competitive, operating and environmental risks would occur?
- How would management respond in strategic and operating terms?
- What kinds of financial pressures would be faced?
- Would it be able to raise necessary funds on acceptable terms?
- Would the company be able to use its reserve resources? In what sequence would these resources be used?

CAUTIONS IN USING RATIO ANALYSIS

The ratio analysis is a widely used technique to evaluate the financial position and performance of a business. But there are certain problems in using ratios. The analyst should be aware of these problems. The following are some of the limitations of the ratio analysis:[2]

- It is difficult to decide on the proper basis of comparison.
- The comparison is rendered difficult because of differences in situations of two companies or of one company over years.
- The price level changes make the interpretations of ratios invalid.
- The differences in the definitions of items in the balance sheet and the profit and loss statement make the interpretation of ratios difficult.

- The ratios calculated at a point of time are less informative and defective as they suffer from short-term changes.
- The ratios are generally calculated from past financial statements and, thus are no indicators of future.

Standards for comparison Ratios of a company have meaning only when they are compared with some standards. It is difficult to find out a proper basis of comparison. Usually, it is recommended that ratios should be compared with industry averages. But the industry averages are not easily available. In India, industry data on financial ratios are available from company finance studies conducted by the Reserve Bank of India. CMIE (Center for Monitoring Indian Economy) provides large database of companies as well as ratios.

Company differences Situations of two companies are never same. Similarly, the factors influencing the performance of a company in one year may change in another year. Thus, the comparison of the ratios of two companies becomes difficult and meaningless when they are operating in different situations.

Price level changes The interpretation and comparison of ratios are also rendered invalid by the changing value of money. The accounting figures, presented in the financial statements, are expressed in the monetary unit, which is assumed to remain constant. In fact, prices change over years, which affects accounting earnings. At least three effects of inflation can be identified. *First*, the nominal value of inventory increases on account of rising prices. This results into '*inventory profit.*' A firm will lose in real terms if the general price level increases faster than appreciation in the value of inventory. *Second*, assets are stated at original cost (less depreciation) in the balance sheet. Because of inflation, their current value or replacement cost will be much higher than book value. Thus depreciation calculated on book value will be very low. *Third*, inflation affects accounting profits of the firms, which borrow. If the interest rate is fixed, shareholders gain at the cost of lenders. The real value of the lenders' obligation is reduced by inflation. The accounting profits do not recognise the gain from borrowing arising due to inflation. Since firms will differ in terms of the nature of their inventory, age and type of assets and debt policy, inflation will affect them differently.

Different definitions of variables In practice, differences exist as to the meaning of certain terms. Diversity of views exists as to what should be included in net worth or shareholders' equity, current assets or current liabilities. Whether preference share capital and current liabilities should be included in debt in calculating the debt-equity ratio? Should intangible assets be excluded to calculate the rate of return on investment? If intangible assets have to be included, how will they be valued? Similarly, profit means different things to different people.

Changing situations The ratios do not have much use if they are not analysed over years. The ratios at a moment of time may suffer from temporary changes. This problem can be resolved by analysing trends of ratios over years. Although trend analysis is

---

1. *Ibid.,* pp. 6–7.
2. See Anthony and Reece, *op. cit.*, pp. 257–64, for a detailed discussion.

more useful but still the analysis is static to an extent. The balance sheets, prepared at different points of time are static in nature. They do not reveal the changes, which have taken place between dates of two balance sheets. The statements of changes in financial position reveal this information.

Historical data The basis to calculate ratios are historical financial statements. The financial analyst is more interested in what happens in future, while the ratios indicate what happened in the past. Management of the company has information about the company's future plans and policies and, therefore, is able to predict future happening to a certain extent. But the outside analyst has to rely on the past ratios, which may not necessarily reflect the firm's financial position and performance in the future.

FINANCIAL RATIOS AS PREDICTORS OF FAILURE

In the finance literature a lot of importance has been attached to financial ratios for assessing the financial health of a firm. The financial institutions and commercial banks are interested to know whether a particular company will be in a position to repay its debts. Which ratios are important to predict the firm's ability to repay its debts?

Non-parametric Analysis

William Beaver compared the financial ratios of 79 manufacturing firms that subsequently failed with the ratios of 79 that remained solvent.[1] His study revealed five ratios, which could discriminate between failed and non-failed firms. These ratios are: (*i*) cash flow to total debt, (*ii*) net income to total assets, (*iii*) total debt to total assets, (*iv*) working capital to total assets, and (*v*) current ratios. As expected, failed firms had more debt and lower return on assets. They had less cash but more receivables as well as low current ratios. They also had less inventory.

In the Indian context, L.C. Gupta[2] attempted a refinement of Beaver's method with the objective of building a forewarning system of corporate sickness. A simple non-parametric test for measuring the relative differentiating power of the various financial ratios was used. The test is based on taking a sample of sick and non-sick companies, arraying them by the magnitude of each ratio to be tested, selecting a cut-off point which will divide the array into two classes with a minimum possible number of misclassifications, and then computing the percentage classification error.[3] The cut-off point is determined by visual inspection. The percentage classification error is determined as

number of misclassifications divided by the number in the sample. The ratio, which results into the lowest percentage classification error, is the most efficient ratio.[4]

Gupta's study, unlike that of Beaver, is *not* based on the technique of 'paired sample' but on broadly 'matching groups' of sick and non-sick companies. In all 56 ratios for the 13-year period, 1962–74, for the textile and non-textile groups of industries were selected for testing. The number of arrays for the textile sample was 728 (i.e. the number of ratios multiplied by the number of years). In the case of the textile sample the two best ratios were:

- earnings before depreciation, interest and taxes (EBDIT) to sales.
- operating cash flow (OCF) to sales.

The next best were the following three ratios:

- EBDIT/Total assets including accumulated depreciation.
- OCF/Total assets including accumulated depreciation.
- EBDIT/(Interest + 0.25 Debt). This ratio measures the extent of the firm's estimated debt servicing ability.

These five ratios have a high degree of predictive power, as reflected in low percentage classification error, at least 2–3 years before a near-bankruptcy by the sample sick textile companies. The EBIT ratios were found to be inferior to both EBDIT' and OCF measures. The worst performers were those related to net worth, i.e., PBT/Net worth and PAT/Net worth.

Among the balance sheet ratios, only two ratios were found to have some power of predicting possible sickness. They were:

- Net worth/debt, including both short- and long-term debt
- All outside liabilities/tangible assets.

It is thus indicated that incidence of sickness and inadequacy of equity base are associated. Surprisingly, all liquidity ratios give very poor results.

Combining the ratios can reduce the percentage error of classification. A combination of four of the five profitability ratios minimises misclassification of sick companies. "... in order to be classed as healthy, a company should earn a satisfactory *gross profit* (i.e., profit *before* depreciation, interest and taxation) on sales as well as on its total *gross* assets; and at the same time, it must also earn a satisfactory *cash profit* (i.e., profit after interest and taxation with depreciation added back) again on both sales and total gross assets. The combination seems to automatically

---

1. Beaver, W.H., Financial Ratios and Predictors of Failure, *Empirical Research in According: Selected Studies Supplement to Journal of Accounting Research,* 1966, pp. 77–111.
2. Gupta, L.C., *Financial Ratios as Forewarning Indicators of Corporate Sickness*, Bombay, ICICI, 1999.
3. *Ibid.*, p. 5.
4. The methodology may be discussed as follows: Assume that the ratio, *R* for a sample of 16 companies – 8 being sick (S) and 8 being non-sick (N)— is computed. The companies are arranged according to the ratio in the descending order:

	N	N	N	Ⓢ	N	N	Ⓢ	N	N	↑	S	S	S	S	Ⓝ	S	S
Rank	1	2	3	4	5	6	7	8	9	cut-off point	10	11	12	13	14	15	16

The number of misclassification is 3, which is, 18.75 per cent of the sample. The number of misclassification would have been greater for any other cut-off point chosen. See Gupta, *op. cit.*

take care, under most circumstances, of vulnerability arising from unduly high debt, making it unnecessary to test separately for debt servicing ability."[1]

In case of the non-textile sample, all profitability ratios did equally well; none emerged as the best. Also, profit ratios did better than the balance sheet ratios. Thus, the conclusion based on the textile sample is vindicated.

Multiple Discriminant Analysis

The studies referred above provide for looking at a number of separate clues (ratios to sickness or failure). It would be more useful to combine the different ratios into a single measure of the probability of sickness or failure (bankruptcy). The technique of **multiple discriminant analysis** (MDA) helps to do so. MDA can be used to classify companies, on the basis of their characteristics as measured by financial ratios, into two groups: those, which are likely to fail (and go bankrupt) and those not likely to fail. In the literature, the likelihood of bankruptcy is associated with financial ratios. For instance, it is assumed that the probability of bankruptcy is higher for a firm with a low current ratio, high debt ratio and low rate of return. The empirical studies of Beaver (in the USA) and Gupta (in India) identified ratios, which have discriminating power. What is, however, required from practical point of view is the understanding of seriousness posed by low performing ratios and the combined effect of favourable and unfavourable ratios. The use of MDA helps to consolidate the effects of all ratios. MDA constructs a boundary line—a **discriminant function**—using historical data of the bankrupt and non-bankrupt firms. Edward Altman was the first person to apply discriminant analysis in finance for studying bankruptcy.[2] His study helped in identifying five ratios that were efficient in predicting bankruptcy. The model was developed from a sample

of 66 firms—half of which went bankrupt. He derived the following discriminant function:

$$Z = 0.012X_1 + 0.014X_2 + 0.033X_3 + 0.006X_4 + 0.010X_5$$

where

Z = discriminant function score of a firm
X_1 = net working capital/total assets (%)
X_2 = retained earning/total assets (%)
X_3 = EBIT/total assets (%)
X_4 = market value of total equity/book value of debt (%)
X_5 = sales/total assets (times)

Altman, established a guideline Z score which can be used to classify firms as either financially sound—a score above 2.675—or headed towards bankruptcy—a score below 2.675. The lower the score, the greater the likelihood of bankruptcy and *vice versa.*

Illustration 25.2: Z-Score

Let us assume that Zeta Company has the following ratios:

X_1 = 15%, X_2 = 31.5%, X_3 = 14.5%, X_4 = 110% and X_5 = 1.2.

Zeta's Z score will be as follows:

$$Z = 0.012 (15\%) + 0.014 (31.5\%) + 0.033 (14.5\%)$$
$$+ 0.06 (110\%) + 0.010 (1.2) = 1.772$$

Since Zeta's Z-score of 1.772 is below 2.675, there is a chance that it will go bankrupt in the near future, since its financial condition is not very good.

Altman's original bankruptcy forecasting model has been refined and broadened in the recent years.[3] The new model can be applied to retailing firms as well. This model is about 70% accurate as much as 5 years prior to bankruptcy.

SUMMARY

❖ A financial ratio is a relationship between two financial variables. It helps to ascertain the financial condition of a firm.

❖ Ratio analysis is a process of identifying the financial strengths and weaknesses of the firm. This may be accomplished either through a trend analysis of the firm's ratios over a period of time or through a comparison of the firm's ratios with its nearest competitors and with the industry averages.

❖ The four most important financial dimensions, which a firm would like to analyse, are: liquidity, leverage, activity and profitability.

❖ Liquidity ratios measure the firm's ability to meet current obligations, and are, calculated by establishing relationships between current assets and current liabilities.

❖ Leverage ratios measure the proportion of outsiders' capital in financing the firm's assets, and are calculated by establishing relationships between borrowed capital and equity capital.

❖ Activity ratios reflect the firm's efficiency in utilising its assets in generating sales, and are calculated by establishing relationships between sales and assets.

❖ Profitability ratios measure the overall performance of the firm by determining the effectiveness of the firm in generating profit, and are calculated by establishing relationships between profit figures on the one hand, and sales and assets on the other.

❖ The following is the summary of the most important financial ratios:

1. Gupta, *op. cit.,* p.20.
2. Altman, E.I., *Financial Ratios, Discriminant Analysis,* and *The Prediction* of *Corporate Bankruptcy, Journal of Finance* Sept. 1968, pp. 589–609.
3. Altman, E.I., Haldeman, R.G. and Narayan, P., *Zeta* Analysis: A New Model to Identify Bankruptcy Risk of Companies, *Journal of Banking and Finance,* June 1977, pp. 29–54.

❖ Ratio analysis is a very useful tool to raise relevant questions on a number of managerial issues. It provides clues to investigate those issues in detail.

❖ However, caution needs to be applied while interpreting ratios as they are calculated from the accounting numbers. Accounting numbers suffer from accounting policy changes, arbitrary allocation procedures and inflation.

Table 25.19: Summary of Ratios

Liquidity Ratios:

- Current ratio $= \dfrac{\text{Current assets}}{\text{Current liabilities}}$

- Quick ratio $= \dfrac{\text{Current assets} - \text{Inventory}}{\text{Current liabilities}}$

- Interval measure $= \dfrac{\text{Current assets} - \text{Inventory}}{\text{Average daily cash operating expenses}}$

Leverage Ratios:

- Total debt ratio $= \dfrac{\text{Total debt}}{\text{Capital employed}}$

- Debt-equity ratio $= \dfrac{\text{Net worth}}{\text{Total debt}}$

- Capital-equity ratio $= \dfrac{\text{Capital employed or net assets}}{\text{Net worth}}$

- Interest coverage $= \dfrac{\text{EBIDTA}}{\text{Interest}}$

Activity Ratios:

- Inventory turnover $= \dfrac{\text{Cost of goods sold or sales}}{\text{Inventory}}$

- No. of days, inventory $= \dfrac{360}{\text{Inventory turnover}}$

- Debtors turnover $= \dfrac{\text{Credit sales or sales}}{\text{Debtors}}$

- Collection period $= \dfrac{360}{\text{Debtors turnover}}$

- Assets turnover $= \dfrac{\text{Sales}}{\text{Net assets or capital employed}}$

- Working capital turnover $= \dfrac{\text{Sales}}{\text{Net working capital}}$

Profitability Ratios:

- Gross margin $= \dfrac{\text{Gross profit}}{\text{Sales}}$ or $= \dfrac{\text{EBIT}}{\text{Sales}}$

- Net margin $= \dfrac{\text{Profit after tax}}{\text{Sales}}$ or $= \dfrac{\text{EBIT}(1-T)}{\text{Sales}}$

- PAT to EBIT ratio $= \dfrac{\text{PAT}}{\text{EBIT}}$

- Return on investment (ROI) before tax $= \dfrac{\text{EBIT}}{\text{Net assets or capital employed}}$

- Return on investment (ROI) after tax $= \dfrac{\text{EBIT }(1 - \text{Tax rate})}{\text{Net assets or capital employed}}$

- Return on investment (ROI) before-tax $= \dfrac{\text{EBIDTA}}{\text{Total assets or Net assets}}$

- Return on equity (ROE) $= \dfrac{\text{Profit after-tax}}{\text{Net worth}}$

There exists a relationship between various ratios. For example, ROE can be expressed as follows:

- ROE $= \dfrac{\text{Sales}}{\text{Net assets}} \times \dfrac{\text{EBIT}}{\text{Sales}} \times \dfrac{\text{PAT}}{\text{EBIT}}$
$\times \dfrac{\text{Net assets}}{\text{Net worth}}$

In practice, companies calculate many other ratios. Most important ratios include:

- EPS $= \dfrac{\text{PAT}}{\text{No. of shares}}$

- DPS $= \dfrac{\text{Profit distributed}}{\text{No. of shares}}$

- Payout $= \dfrac{\text{DPS}}{\text{EPS}}$

- Price-earnings ratio $= \dfrac{\text{Market value of share}}{\text{EPS}}$

- Market value - book value ratio $= \dfrac{\text{Market value of share}}{\text{Book value of share}}$

KEY CONCEPTS

Activity ratios	DuPont analysis	Interval measure	Replacement costs
Aging schedule	Earnings power	Inventory holding period	Retention ratio
Assets turnover	Earnings yield	Inventory profit	Return on capital
Bonus shares	Earnings-price ratio	Inventory turnover	employed (ROCE)
Cash ratio	Ex-bonus price	Lease	Return on equity (ROE)
Collection period	Ex-rights price	Leverage factor	Return on investment (ROI)
Common-size statement	Financial analysis	Leverage ratios	Return on net assets
Contingent liabilities	Financial gearing or	Liquidity ratios	(RONA)
Cross-sectional ratio	leverage	Long-term solvency	Rights shares
analysis	Financial risk	Net profit margin	Short-term solvency
Current ratio	Fixed-charges	Net working capital ratio	Time series ratio
Debt ratio	coverage	Operating leverage	analysis
Debt-equity ratio	Gross profit margin	Payout ratio	Tobin's q
Debtors turnover	Industry analysis	Price-earnings ratio	Trading on equity
Debt-trap	Interest coverage	Proforma analysis	Vertical analysis
Discriminant analysis	Interest tax shield	Profitability ratios	Z-score
Dividend yield	Inter-firm analysis	Quick ratio	

ILLUSTRATIVE SOLVED PROBLEMS

Problem 25.1: X Co. has made plans for the next year. It is estimated that the company will employ total assets of Rs 800,000; 50 per cent of the assets being financed by borrowed capital at an interest cost of 8 per cent per year. The direct costs for the year are estimated at Rs 480,000 and all other operating expenses are estimated at Rs 80,000. The goods will be sold to customers at 150 per cent of the direct costs. Tax rate is assumed to be 50 per cent.

You are required to calculate: (*i*) net profit margin; (*ii*) return on assets; (*iii*) assets turnover and (*iv*) return on owners' equity.

Solution:

The net profit is calculated as follows:

	Rs	Rs
Sales (150% of Rs 480,000)		720,000
Direct costs		480,000
Gross profit		240,000
Operating expenses	80,000	
Interest charges (8% of Rs 400,000)	32,000	112,000
Profit before taxes		128,000
Taxes (@ 50%)		64,000
Net profit after taxes		64,000

(*i*)

$$\text{Net profit margin} = \frac{\text{Rs } 64,000}{\text{Rs } 720,000} = 0.089 \text{ or } 8.9\%$$

$$\text{Net profit margin} = \frac{\text{EBIT}(1-T)}{\text{Sales}} = \frac{160,000(1-0.5)}{720,000}$$
$$= 0.111 \text{ or } 11.1\%$$

(*ii*)

$$\text{Return on assets} = \frac{\text{EBIT}(1-T)}{\text{Assets}} = \frac{160,000(1-0.5)}{800,000}$$
$$= 0.10 \text{ or } 10\%$$

(*iii*)

$$\text{Assets turnover} = \frac{\text{Sales}}{\text{Assets}} = \frac{\text{Rs } 720,00}{\text{Rs } 800,000} = 0.9 \text{ times}$$

(*iv*)

$$\text{Return on equity} = \frac{\text{Net profit after taxes}}{\text{Owner's equity}}$$
$$= \frac{\text{Rs } 64,000}{50\% \text{ of Rs } 800,000} = \frac{\text{Rs } 64,000}{\text{Rs } 400,000}$$
$$= 0.16 \text{ or } 16\%$$

Problem 25.2: The total sales (all credit) of a firm is Rs 640,000. It has a gross profit margin of 15 per cent and a current ratio of 2.5. The firm's current liabilities are Rs 96,000; inventories Rs 48,000 and cash Rs 16,000. (*a*) Determine the average inventory to be carried by the firm, if an inventory turnover of 5 times is expected? (Assume a 360-day year), (*b*) Determine the average collection period if the opening balance of debtors is intended to be of Rs 80,000? (Assume a 360-day year).

Solution:

(*a*) Inventory turnover : $\dfrac{\text{Cost of goods sold}}{\text{Average inventory}}$

Since gross profit margin is 15 per cent, the cost of goods sold should be 85 per cent of the sales.

Cost of goods sold $= 0.85 \times$ Rs $640,000 =$ Rs $544,000$

$$= \frac{\text{Rs } 544,000}{\text{Average inventory}} = 5$$

Thus Average inventory $= \dfrac{\text{Rs } 544,000}{5} =$ Rs $108,800$

(b) Average collection period:

$$\frac{\text{Average debtors}}{\text{Credit sales}} \times 360$$

Average debtors = (op. debtors + cl. debtors)/2

Closing balance of debtors is found as follows:

Current assets (2.5 of current liabilities)		Rs 240,000
Less: Inventories	Rs 48,000	
Cash	16,000	64,000
∴ Debtors		Rs 176,000

Average debtors = (Rs 176,000 + Rs 80,000)/2
= Rs 128,000

Average collection period $= \dfrac{\text{Rs } 128,000}{\text{Rs } 640,000} \times 360 = 72$ days

Problem 25.3: The following figures relate to the trading activities of Hind Traders Limited for the year ended 30th June, 19X1:

Table 25.20: Hind Traders Limited

	Rs		Rs
Sales	1,500,000	*Administrative expenses*	
Purchases	966,750	Salaries	81,000
Opening stock	228,750	Rent	8,100
Closing stock	295,500	Stationery, postage, etc.	7,500
Sales returns	60,000	Depreciation	27,900
Selling and distribution expenses		Other charges	49,500
Salaries	45,900	Provision for taxation	120,000
Advertising	14,100	*Non-operating income*	
Travelling	6,000	Dividend on shares	27,000
Non-operating expenses		Profit on sale of shares	9,000
Loss on sale of assets	12,000		

You are required (1) rearrange the above figures in a form suitable for analysis, and (2) show separately the following ratios: (i) gross profit ratio; (ii) operating stock (iii) stock turnover ratio.

Solution:

(a) Gross profit ratio:

$$= \frac{\text{Rs } 600,000}{\text{Rs } 1,500,000} = 0.40 \text{ or } 40\%$$

(b) Operating ratio:

$$= \frac{\text{Cost of goods} + \text{Operating expenses}}{\text{Sales}}$$

$$= \frac{\text{Rs } 1,140,000}{\text{Rs } 1,500,000} = 0.76 \text{ or } 76\%$$

(c) Stock turnover ratio:

$$= \frac{\text{Cost of goods sold}}{\text{Average stock}} = \frac{\text{Rs } 900,000}{\text{Rs } 262,125} = 3.43 \text{ times}$$

Table 25.21: Hind Traders Ltd.

Profit and Loss Statement

		Rs
Sales (less returns)		1,500,000
Less: Cost of goods sold:		
Opening Stock	228,750	
Purchases	966,750	
	1,195,500	
Less: Closing stock	295,500	900,000
Gross profit		600,000
Operating expenses		
Selling and distribution expenses	66,000	
Administrative expenses	174,000	240,000
Operating net profit		360,000
Non-operating income	36,000	
Non-operating expenses	12,000	24,000
Profit before-tax		384,000
Provision for taxes		120,000
		264,000

Problem 25.4: Towards the end of 19X1 the directors of Wholesale Merchants Ltd. decided to expand their business. The annual accounts of the company for 19X1 and 19X2 may be summarised as follows:

You are informed that: (a) All sales were from stocks in the company's warehouse. (b) The range of merchandise was not changed and buying prices remained steady throughout the two years. (c) Budgeted total sales for 19X2 were Rs 390,000. (d) The debenture loan was received on 1st January, 19X2, and additional fixed assets were purchased on that date.

Table 25.22: Wholesale Merchants Ltd

	Financial Statements	(Rs)
	Year 19X1	Year 19X2
Sales:		
Cash	42,000	44,800
Credit	378,000	478,800
	420,000	523,600
Cost of sales	330,400	417,200
Gross margin	89,600	106,400
Expenses:		
Warehousing	18,200	19,600
Transport	8,400	14,000
Administration	26,600	26,600
Selling	15,400	19,600
Debenture interest		2,800
	68,600	82,600
Net profit	21,000	23,800

You are required to state the internal accounting ratios that you would use in this type of business to assist the management of the company in measuring the efficiency of its operation, including its use of capital.

Your answer should name the ratios and give the figures (calculated to one decimal place) for 19X1 and 19X2, together with possible reasons for changes in the ratios for the two years. Ratios relating to capital employed should be based on the capital at the end. Ignore taxation.   (*C.A., adapted*)

	on 31st Dec. 19X1		on 31st Dec. 19X2	
Fixed assets				
(*Less:* Depreciation)		42,000		56,000
Current assets				
Stock	84,000		131,600	
Debtors	70,000		114,800	
Cash	14,000	168,000	9,800	256,200
Less: Current liabilities		70,000		106,400
Net current assets		98,000		149,800
Net assets		140,000		205,800
Share capital		105,000		105,000
Reserves and undistributed profit		35,000		58,000
Debenture loan		—		42,000
Capital employed		140,000		205,800

Solution:

The following ratios are calculated for Wholesale Merchants Ltd.:

Comments. The return on capital employed has fallen from 15% in 19X1 to 12.9% in 19X2. The reason lies in the sales to capital ratio which has also fallen in 19X2. The increase in capital employed has not been profitably utilised. The increased capital seems to have been blocked in stock and debtors.

It will be noticed that the gross margin ratio decreased from 21.3% in 19X1 to 20.3% in 19X2. This may be attributed to

reduced selling price or granting of trade discounts on bulk orders. The operating ratio (expense to sales ratio) has fallen in 19X1 by 1% and this had a slight impact on net profit ratio which has increased by 0.1%.

The short-term solvency of the company, reflected by current ratio and quick ratio, is more or less constant. However, there has been deterioration in the stock turnover and debtors turnover ratios. This implies the company is holding stocks for longer periods and allowing longer credit periods to customers.

There is no threat to the long-term solvency of the company. It did not use any long-term debt in 19X1. A debenture loan of Rs 42,000 is taken in 19X2 and is about 0.26 of the equity funds. By a normal criterion, the company could have a debt equity ratio of 2:1.

Problem 25.5: Assume that a firm has owners' equity of Rs 100,000. The ratios for the firm are:

Current debt to total debt	0.40
Total debt to owners' equity	0.60
Fixed assets to owners' equity	0.60
Total assets turnover	2 times
Inventory turnover	8 times

Complete the following balance sheet, given the information above.

Liabilities	*Rs*	*Assets*	*Rs*
Current debt	.....	Cash	......
Long-term debt	......	Inventory	......
Total debt	......	Total current assets	......
Owners' equity	......	Fixed assets	......
Total capital	......	Total assets	......

Solution:

(*i*)   Total debt $= 0.60 \times$ owners' equity
                  $= 0.60 \times$ Rs 100,000 = Rs 60,000

(*ii*) Fixed assets $= 0.60 \times$ owners' equity
                  $= 0.60 \times$ Rs 100,000 = Rs 60,000

Table 25.23: Ratios for Whole Sale Merchant Ltd.

	Ratios	(Rs'000)	Year 19X1	(Rs'000)	Year 19X2
1.	Net margin: EBIT/Sales	21,000/420,000	5.0%	26,600/523,600	5.1%
2.	Sales to capital employed	420,000/140,000	3.0 times	523,600/205,800	2.5 times
3.	Return on capital employed: EBIT/CE	21,000/140,000	15.0%	26,600/205,800	12.9%
4.	Gross margin: gross profit/sales	89,600/420,000	21.2%	106,400/523,600	20.3%
5.	Expenses (excluding interest) to sales	68,600/420,000	16.3%	79,800/523,600	15.2%
6.	Stock turnover: CGS/Stock	330,400/84,000	3.9 times	417,200/131,600	3.2 times
7.	Debtors turnover: credit sales/debtors	378,000/70,000	5.4 times	478,800/114,800	4.2 times
8.	Current ratio: CA/CL	168,000/70,000	2.4 times	256,200/106,400	2.4 times
9.	Quick ratio: CA-Stock/CL	84,000/70,000	1.2 times	124,600/106,400	1.2 times
10.	Long-term debt-equity		0	42,000/163,800	0.3

Note: EBIT for 19X1 and 19X2 respectively is: Rs 21,000 + 0 = Rs 21,000 and Rs 23,800 + 2,800 = Rs 26,600.

(*iii*) Total Capital = Total debt + Owners' equity

$$= Rs\ 60,000 + Rs\ 100,000 = Rs\ 160,000$$

(*iv*) Total assets consisting of current assets and fixed assets must be equal to Rs 160,000 (Assets = Liabilities + Owners' equity). Fixed assets are Rs 60,000, therefore, current assets should be Rs 160,000 – Rs 60,000 = Rs 100,000.

(*v*) Sales are found as follows:

$$\text{Assets turnover} = \frac{\text{Sales}}{\text{Assets}} = 2 = \frac{\text{Sales}}{Rs\ 160,000} = 2$$

$$\therefore \qquad \text{Sales} = Rs\ 160,000 \times 2 = Rs\ 320,000$$

$$\therefore \quad \text{Sales} = Rs\ 160,0002 = Rs\ 320,000$$

(*vi*) Inventories are found as follows:

$$\text{Inventory tornover} = \frac{\text{Sales}}{\text{Inventory}} = \frac{Rs\ 320,000}{\text{Inventory}} = 8$$

$$\text{Inventory} = \frac{320,000}{8} = Rs\ 40,000$$

(*vii*) Cash = Current assets – Inventory

$$= Rs\ 100,000 - Rs\ 40,000 = Rs\ 60,000$$

(*viii*) Current debt = 0.40 × Total debts = 0.40 × Rs 60,000

$$= Rs\ 24,000$$

(*ix*) Long-term debt = Total debt – Current debt

$$= Rs\ 60,000 - Rs\ 24,000 = Rs\ 36,000.$$

With all this information, the balance sheet can be prepared as follows:

Equities	Rs	Assets	Rs
Current debt	24,000	Cash	60,000
Long-term debt	36,000	Inventory	40,000
Total debt	60,000	Total current assets	100,000
Owners' equity	100,000	Fixed assets	60,000
Total equity	160,000	Total assets	160,000

Problem 25.6: The following are the financial statements for *XYZ* Co., for 19X4:

Table 25.24: XYZ Company

Balance Sheet
as on 31 December, 19X3

Liabilities & Capital	Rs	Assets	Rs
Creditors	280,000	Cash	70,000
Bills payable	140,000	Debtors	350,000
Outstanding exps.	40,000	Stock	490,000
Provision for tax	100,000	Fixed assets, net	1,050,000
Long-term debt	840,000	Goodwill	140,000
Preference share capital	280,000		
Equity share capital	140,000		
Reserves	280,000		
	2,100,000		2,100,000

Table 25.25: XYZ Company

Profit and Loss A/c
for the year ended 31 December, 19X3   **(Rs)**

Sales:		
Cash		2,80,000
Credit		1,120,000
		1,400,000
Less: Expenses:		
Cost of goods sold	840,000	
Selling, administrative and general expenses	140,000	
Depreciation	98,000	
Interest on long-term debt	42,000	1,120,000
Profit before taxes		280,000
Taxes		140,000
Profit after taxes		140,000
Less: Preference dividend		17,000
Net profit for ordinary shareholders		123,000
Add: Reserve at 1 January, 19X3		182,000
		305,000
Less: Dividend paid to equity shareholders		25,000
Reserve at 31 December, 19X3		280,000

The ratios for the years 19X1 and 19X2 for *XYZ* company and their industry ratios are given below:

	19X1	19X2	Industry
Current ratio	2.54	2.10	2.30
Acid-test ratio	1.10	0.96	1.20
Debtors turnover	6.00	4.80	7.00
Stock turnover	3.80	3.05	3.85
Long-term debt to total capital	37%	42%	34%
Gross profit margin	38%	41%	40%
Net profit margin	18%	16%	15%
Return on equity	24%	29%	19%
Return on total assets	7%	6.8%	8%
Tangible assets turnover	0.80	0.70	1.00
Interest coverage	10	9	10

(*a*) Calculate ratios for 19X3 and evaluate the company's financial position.

(*b*) Using relevant ratios, indicate what decision would be taken in the following situations: (*i*) *XYZ* Co. wants to buy material of Rs 70,000 on a three months credit from A. (*ii*) *XYZ* Co. offers to sell 70,000 additional shares for Rs 112 per shares to a financial institution. (*iii*) *XYZ* Co. wants to issue 16% debentures of Rs 300,000 with a ten-year maturity.

Solution:

(a) The ratios for 19X3 for *XYZ* Co. are as follows:

Ratio	19X3
1. Current ratio	910,000/560,000 = 1.63
2. Acid-test ratio	420,000/560,000 = 0.75
3. Debtors turnover	1,120,000/350,000 = 3.20
4. Stock turnover	840,000/490,000 = 1.71
5. Debt-to-total capital ratio	840,000/1,400,000* = 60%
6. Gross profit margin	560,000/1,400,000 = 40%
7. Net profit margin	140,000/1,400,000 = 10%
8. Return on equity	123,200/280,000* = 44%
9. Return on total assets	(280,000 + 42,000) (1 – 0.5)/1,960,000 * = 8.2%
10. Tangible assets turnover	1,400,000/1,960,000 * = 0.71
11. Interest coverage	322,000/42,000 = 7.67

* Intangible asset of Rs 140,000 is excluded.

Evaluation of the company's position:

(*a*) (*i*) The liquidity position of the firm is falling, which is evident from the Ratios 1 to 4.

(*ii*) The gross profit margin is constant and matches with the industry average, but the net profit margin ratio is declining. The two ratios together imply that the firm's selling and administrative expenses, depreciation and interest charges are rising.

(*iii*) The decline in the net margin is partly due to rapid increase in debt (Ratio 5). This increase also explains why the return on equity (Ratio 8) has been rising while the return on assets is declining (Ratio 9). The decline in the net margin and the return on assets can also be attributed to the decline in assets turnover (Ratio 10). The impact of the increase in debt and overall decline in profitability are also shown by reduction in the interest coverage (Ratio 11).

(*b*) (*i*) The primary focus of the analyst here will be on the liquidity of current assets. He/she would, therefore, concern himself/herself with Ratios 1 to 4. The credit may not be granted to *XYZ* Co. because of its deteriorating liquidity and lengthy terms of payment.

(*ii*) The analysis for the purpose of investing in shares generally concentrates on the return on equity and leverage ratios. The return on equity of *XYZ* Co. is increasing, therefore, the shares *may* be purchased. But the company has a high degree of leverage (Ratio 5) and its profitability (Ratios 8, 9, 10) is declining. This will go against the buying of shares. The decision will depend upon the financial institution's assessment about the company's future profitability and long-term financial conditions.

(*iii*) The company may find difficulty in selling the debentures. Already, it has a high leverage ratio. If the debentures are issued its leverage ratio will increase to 67 per cent (Rs 11,40,000 ÷ Rs 17,00,000) and the coverage ratio at the same level of earning will decline to 5.2. The liquidity and the profitability

of the firm are also declining.

Problem 25.7: The following financial data relate to Lakme, a cosmetic and toiletries company in the Tata Group of companies for the period ending on March 31, 19X1 and 19X2:

Table 25.26: Lakme

Financial Data
for the year ending on March 31   (*Rs in lakh*)

	19X1	19X2
Revenue (REV)	6561	9773
Operating profit (PBITDA)	625	839
Depreciation	88	115
PBIT	537	724
Interest	216	376
Tax	0	65
Profit after tax (PAT)	321	283
Share capital	316	316
Reserve and surplus	1130	1264
Borrowings	1473	1530
Capital employed	2919	3110
Gross fixed assets	1336	1589
EPS	10.17	8.97
DPS	5.00	5.00

Comment on Lakme's performance. Show computations to support your answer.

Solution:

Table 25.27: Lakme

Financial Analysis

Ratio	Financial dimension	19X1	19X2	Change
REV/CE	Turnover	2.25	3.14	increase
PBIT/REV	Margin	8.2%	7.4%	decrease
PBIT/CE	ROI	18.4%	23.3%	increase
PAT/PBIT	Tax leverage	59.8%	39.1%	decrease
CE/NW	Finance leverage	2.02	1.97	decrease
PAT/NW	ROE	22.2%	17.9%	decrease
RE/PAT	Retention	50.8%	44.2%	decrease
RE/NW	Growth	11.3%	7.9%	decrease

Lakme registered an impressive growth in revenue. Although revenue increased by 49%, operating profit increased by 34% and PBIT increased by 35%. However, PAT declined by 12% due to 74% increase in interest and 31% increase in depreciation. As a result, EPS reduced to Rs 8.97 in 19X2 from Rs 10.17 in 19X1. The company maintained DPS at Rs 5, which tended to increase payout ratio to 50.8% from 44.3% in 19X1.

Lakme's margin reduced in 19X2, but was more than compensated by improved utilisation of capital; its turnover increased to 3.14 in 19X2 from 2.25 in 19X1. This resulted in an impressive improvement in before-tax return on investment. However, the company paid more interest and tax in 19X2, while maintaining its debt equity ratio. This resulted in about 4% drop in its ROE in 19X2. Lower ROE and lower retention (or higher payout) in 19X2, reduced the company's equity growth.

Problem 25.8: Tata Unisys is an integrated information technology company. Its products include mini and micro-processor based systems, software sets, serial printers and handlers. Table 25.28 contains financial highlights of the company for the year 19X1–X2 and 19X2–X3. You are required to provide a critical evaluation of the company's performance. Calculate required ratios to support your evaluation.

Table 25.28: Tata Unisys

Financial Data

for year ended 31 March   (*Rs in lakh*)

	19X1–X2	19X2–X3
Profit and Loss Items		
Net sales	6,448	8,994
Raw material	1,318	2,011
Salaries and wages	814	1,043
Power and fuel	50	75
Operating profit (PBDIT)	1,597	2,226
Interest	73	91
Depreciation	308	488
Profit before tax	1,216	1,647
Provision for tax	465	635
Profit after tax	751	1,012
Balance Sheet Items		
Share capital	438	613
Reserves and surplus	2,097	2,813
Borrowings	553	998
Gross fixed assets	1,819	2,836
Additional Information		
Dividend rate (%)	25	25
Bonus issue	–	2:5
Market price of share:		
High (Rs)	–	550
Low (Rs)	–	200
No. of shares (lakh)	43.8	61.3
NW (Net worth)	2535	3426
CE (Capital employed)	3088	4424
PBIT (Profit before interest and tax)	1289	1738

Solution:

Table 25.29: Tata Unisys

Ratio	*Financial dimension*	*19X1*	*19X2*	*Change*
REV/CE	Turnover	2.25	3.14	increase
Sales/CE	Turnover	2.09	2.03	decrease
PBIT/Sales	Margin	20.00%	19.32%	decrease
PBIT/CE	ROI	41.74%	39.29%	decrease
PAT/PBIT	Tax leverage	58.26%	58.23%	no change
CE/NW	Fin. leverage	1.22	1.29	no change
PAT/NW	ROE	29.63%	29.54%	no change
RE/PAT	Retention	85.35%	84.88%	decrease
RE/NW	Growth	25.29%	25.07%	decrease
Equity Performance				
EPS (Rs)		17.15	23.11	increase
DPS (Rs)		2.50	3.50	increase
Payout		14.65%	15.12%	increase
Dividend yield		–	6.67%	
P/E ratio		–	22.72	

The company sales grew by 39.5% while its PBIT registered a growth of 34.8% (from Rs 1,289 lakh in 19X1–X2 to Rs 1,738 lakh in 19X2–X3). PAT also increased by 34.8%. Tata Unisys did not increase dividend rate but issued bonus shares in the ratio of 2:5. Thus, in effect, dividend increased by 40%, while EPS by 34.8%, causing a slight increase in payout. Dividend yield in 19X2–X3 at the average market price is 6.67% and P/E ratio 22.72 (adjusted for bonus issue).

In spite of an impressive growth in sales, the company's profitability both in terms of sales as well as capital employed (i.e., net worth plus borrowings) showed a slight decline. The company retains about 85% of its profits and earns an ROI of about 29.5% which gives it an impressive growth rate of about 25%.

REVIEW QUESTIONS

1. Explain the need for the financial analysis. How does the use of ratios help in financial analysis?
2. What do you mean by the liquidity of a firm? How can the liquidity of a firm be assessed?
3. Is it possible for a firm to have a high current ratio and still find difficulties in paying its current debt? Explain with illustration.
4. What are the leverage, or capital-structure, ratios? Explain the significance and limitations of the debt-equity ratio as a measure of the firm's solvency?
5. Why are the activity ratios calculated? Do calculations of current asset turnover ratios indicate their quality? Explain.
6. How would you calculate the fixed assets turnover and the capital-employed turnover ratios? What do they imply?
7. Why is it necessary to calculate the profitability ratios in relation to sales? Illustrate your answer.

8. Explain the calculation and significance of the various measures of rate of return on investment.
9. Explain the ratios which you, as an analyst, will focus your attention to in the following cases:
   (*i*) A bank is approached by a company for a loan of Rs 50 lakh for working-capital purposes.
   (*ii*) A company requests a financial institution to grant a 10-year loan of Rs 5 crore.
10. Which of the financial ratios of a company would you most likely refer to in each of the following situations? Give reasons.
   (*i*) The company asks you to sell material on credit.
   (*ii*) You are thinking of investing Rs 25,000 in the company's debentures.
   (*iii*) You are thinking of investing Rs 25,000 in the company's shares.

11. What is the firm's earning power? How are the net profit margin and the assets turnover related?
12. What is a DuPont analysis? Explain with the help of a chart.
13. "A higher rate of return on capital employed implies that the firm is managed efficiently." Is this true in every situation? What or why not?
14. Ratios are generally calculated from historical data. Of what use are they in assessing the firm's future financial condition?
15. Explain the significance and limitations of the ratio analysis.

PROBLEMS

1. - (a) A firm's sales are Rs 450,000, cost of goods sold is Rs 240,000 and inventory is Rs 90,000. What is its turnover? Also, calculate the firm's gross margin.
   (b) The only current assets possessed by a firm are: cash Rs 105,000, inventories Rs 560,000 and debtors Rs 420,000. If the current ratio for the firm is 2-to-1, determine its current liabilities. Also, calculate the firm's quick ratio.
   (c) At the close of the year, a company has an inventory of Rs 150,000 and cost of goods sold for Rs 975,000. If the company's turnover ratio is 5, determine the opening balance of inventory.

2. (a) The total sales of a firm are Rs 400,000. It has a gross profit margin of 20 per cent. If the company has an average inventory of Rs 50,000, determine the inventory turnover.
   (b) A company has an inventory of Rs 180,000, debtors of Rs 115,000 and an inventory turnover of 6. The gross profit margin of the company is 10 per cent, and its credit sales are 20 per cent of the total sales. Calculate the average collection period. (Assume a 360-day year).
   (c) A company has the shareholders' equity of Rs 200,000. Total assets are 160 per cent of the shareholders' equity, while the assets turnover is 4. If the company has an inventory turnover of 5, determine the amount of inventory.

3. (a) A firm has cost of Rs 200,000, sales of Rs 250,000 and an asset turnover of 4. What is the rate of return on asset?
   (b) A firm has profit before interest and taxes of Rs 80,000, interest charges of Rs 8,000, taxes of Rs 30,000, total assets of Rs 500,000 and total liabilities Rs 300,000? What is its (i) return of equity, and (ii) interest coverage?
   (c) Determine the P/E ratio of a firm that has a net profit after taxes of Rs 150,000 and 30,000 shares outstanding, selling at a market price of Rs 10 per share. What rate of return do shareholders expect?
   (d) A company has a net profit after taxes of Rs 1,20,000 and pays a cash dividend of Rs 48,000 on its 36,000 shares outstanding at a time when the share is selling for Rs 12. What is the yield and the dividend payout?

4. The balance sheets and trading and profit and loss accounts for the year ended 30 June, 19X2 of S Ltd. and T Ltd. are given in Tables 4.30 and 4.31. You may assume that stocks have increased evenly throughout the year. You are required to:
   (a) Calculate three of the following ratios separately for each company:
   (i) net profit for the year as a percentage of net assets employed at 30 June, 19X2;
   (ii) net profit for the year as a percentage of sales;
   (iii) gross profit for the year as a percentage of sales;
   (iv) current assets to current liabilities at 30 June, 19X2;
   (v) liquid ratio at 30 June, 19X2; and
   (vi) stock turnover during the year.
   (b) Describe briefly the main conclusions which you draw from a comparison of the ratios which you have calculated for each company.   (*C.A., adapted*)

Table 25.30: S Ltd. and T Ltd.

Balance Sheet as on 30 June, 19X2			(Rs)
	S Ltd.		T Ltd.
Fixed assets at cost	60,000		30,000
Less: Provision for depreciation	20,000		10,000
		40,000	20,000
Current assets			
Stock	57,000		30,000
Debtors	22,000		20,000
Cash	11,000		10,000
	90,000		60,000
Less: Current liabilities	30,000		30,000
Net current assets		60,000	30,000
Net assets		100,000	50,000
Paid-up share capital		95,000	45,000
Revenue reserve		5,000	5,000
		100,000	50,000

Table 25.31: S Ltd. and T Ltd.

Trading and Profit and Loss Account for the year ended 30 June, 19X2		(Rs)
	S Ltd.	T Ltd.
Sales	160,000	120,000
Stock at July 1, 19X1	39,000	20,000
Add: Purchases	114,000	85,000
	153,000	105,000
Less: Stock at June 30, 19X2	57,000	30,000
Cost of goods sold	96,000	75,000
Gross profit	64,000	45,000
Less: General expenses	56,000	39,000
Net profit for the year	8,000	6,000
Add: Balance brought forward	3,000	1,000
	11,000	7,000
Less: Dividend paid	6,000	2,000
Balance carried forward	5,000	5,000

5. Extracts from financial accounts of *XYZ* Ltd. are given below:

Table 25.32: XYZ Ltd.

	Year I		Year II	
	Assets	Liabilities	Assets	Liabilities
Stock	10,000	–	20,000	–
Debtors	30,000	–	30,000	–
Payment in advance	2,000	–	–	–
Cash in hand	20,000	–	15,000	–
Sundry creditors	–	25,000	–	30,000
Acceptances	–	15,000	–	12,000
Bank overdraft	–	–	–	5,000
	62,000	40,000	65,000	47,000

Sales amounted to Rs 350,000 in the first year and Rs 300,000 in the second year. You are required to comment on the solvency position of the concern with the help of accounting ratios.

6. From the following information you are required to (*a*) analyse the relative position of *ABC* Ltd. in the industry and (*b*) point out the deficiencies and suggest improvements.

Table 25.33: ABC Ltd.

Balance Sheet
as on 31 December, 19X1 (*Rs*)

Share capital	1,278,000	Fixed assets:		
Current liabilities:		Equipment	600,000	
Creditors	150,000	*Less:* Depreciation	80,000	520,000
Bank loan	300,000	Current assets:		
		Cash		180,000
		Debtors		240,000
		Stock		660,000
		Prepaid expenses		128,000
Total capital	1,728,000	Total assets		1,728,000

Table 25.34: ABC Ltd.

Profit and Loss
for the year ended 31 December, 19X1 (*Rs*)

Sales	345,000
Cost of goods sold	150,000
Gross profit	195,000
Operating expenses	90,000
Profit before interest and taxes	105,000
Interest	24,000
Profit before taxes	81,000
Tax	27,000
Profit after taxes	54,000

Table 25.35: ABC Ltd.

Industry Averages

Current ratio	2.95
Quick ratio	1.05
Debt-equity ratio	50%
Times interest earned	2.60%
Inventory turnover	0.35
Fixed-assets turnover	0.80
Total assets turnover	0.50
Net profit margin	16%
Return on assets	15%
Return on equity	21%

7. The two firms, *M* and *N*, have the following data:

	N Rs	M Rs
Sales	800,000	200,000
Total assets	4,000,000	600,000
Net profit	750,000	420,000

Compute return on investment for both firms. Explain how the figures are similar and how they are different.

8. The summary of the balance sheets and the profit and loss accounts from 19X1 to 19X5 for Jagan Limited is given in Tables 25.36 and 25.37. During this period, the company undertook a major expansion programme. You are required to calculate important ratios for the five years and assess the financial health of the company. Also, explain the implications of the development of the financial health of the company for the shareholders. (*C.A. Engg., adapted*)

Table 25.36: Jagan Ltd.

Balance Sheets (*Rs '000*)

	19X1	19X2	19X3	19X4	19X5
Liabilities and Equity					
Creditors	25	25	25	25	25
Debentures	250	1,000	1,750	2,500	3,250
Share capital	1,000	1,000	1,000	1,000	1,000
Reserves	225	225	225	2,25	2,25
Total	1,500	2,250	3,000	37,50	45,00
Asset					
Cash	50	50	50	50	50
Debtors	50	50	50	50	50
Stock	400	650	900	11,50	1,400
Fixed assets, net	1,000	1,500	2,000	2,500	3,000
Total	1,500	2,250	3,000	3,750	4,500

Table 25.37: Jagan Ltd.

Profit and Loss Accounts (Summary)   (Rs '000)

	19X1	19X2	19X3	19X4	19X5
Sales	300	450	600	750	900
Cost of goods sold	100	150	200	250	300
Gross profit	200	300	400	500	600
Operating expenses	25	50	100	150	200
EBIT	175	250	300	350	400
Interest	15	67.5	127.5	195	270
Profit before tax	160	182.5	172.5	155	130
Tax	67.55	75.35	73.55	65.15	53.1
Net profit	92.45	107.15	98.95	89.85	76.9
No. of shares	100	100	100	100	100
P/E ratio	5	5	4	3.5	3.5

9. Using the following data, complete the balance sheet given below:

Gross profit (Rs)	54,000
Shareholders' equity (Rs)	600,000
Gross profit margin	20%
Credit-sales to total-sales	80%
Total assets turnover	0.3 times
Inventory turnover	4 times
Average collection period (a 360-day year)	20 days
Current ratio	1.8
Long-term debt to equity	40%

Balance Sheet

Creditors	....	Cash	....
Long-term debt	....	Debtors	....
Shareholders' equity	....	Inventory	....
	....	Fixed assets	....
	....		....

10. Surendra Mohan and Sons are wholesale distributors of electric goods. Tables 25.38 and 25.39 contain their balance sheets and profit and loss statements during the period 19X1 to 19X3. You are required to critically evaluate the firm's financial performance.

Table 25.38: Surendra Mohan and Sons

Comparative Balance Sheets   (Rs)

	19X3	19X2	19X1
Liabilities and Capital			
Creditors	65,994	62,229	55,065
Accrued expenses	2,645	1,920	1,168
Total current liabilities	68,639	64,149	56,233
Owner's capital	208,812	181,341	163,394
Total	277,451	245,490	219,627

	19X3	19X2	19X1
Assets			
Cash	19,550	14,376	9,542
Debtors	86,784	61,601	40,217
Stock	61,661	63,167	68,086
Prepaid expenses	2,667	1,433	863
Total current assets	170,662	140,577	118,708
Fixed assets	99,285	97,878	96,229
Investments	7,504	7,035	4,690
Total non-current assets	106,789	104,913	100,919
Total	277,451	245,490	219,627

Table 25.39: Surendra Mohan and Sons

Summarised Profit and Loss Statements   (Rs)

	19X3	19X2	19X1
Sales	481,053	457,172	399,291
Cost of goods sold	310,720	275,514	229,878
Gross profit	170,333	181,658	169,413
Operating expenses	141,377	137,984	120,593
Net profit	28,956	43,674	48,820

11. The following are the comparative financial statements for three years for Plastic Works Limited. You are required to comment on the firm's financial condition and indicate the areas which require management's attention.

Table 25.40: Plastic Works Limited

Comparative Balance Sheets   (Rs)

	19X3	19X2	19X1
Liabilities and Capital			
Bank borrowing	30,525	10,175	–
Creditors	331,127	147,725	113,980
Accrued expenses	21,510	14,361	20,350
Provision for dividend	20,350	20,350	20,350
Provision for taxes	56,367	88,435	86,111
Total current liabilities	459,879	281,046	240,791
Long-term loan	71,225	Nil	Nil
Total liabilities	531,104	281,046	240,791
Share capital	407,000	407,000	407,000
Reserves and surplus	80,983	88,826	67,067
Net worth	487,983	495,826	474,067
Total Funds	1019,087	776,872	714,858
Assets			
Cash	99,164	35,922	13,930
Debtors	215,356	207,780	211,196
Stock:			
Raw material	133,577	107,409	98,411
Work in process	47,882	50,179	42,230
Finished goods	266,534	177,788	174,892
Prepaid expenses	17,350	13,726	12,697
Total current assets	779,863	592,804	553,356

Contd...

	19X3	19X2	19X1
Buildings, plant and equipment	229,314	177,047	161,502
Misc. fixed assets	9,910	7,021	–
Total non-current assets	239,224	184,068	161,502
Total Assets	1,019,087	776,872	714,858

Table 25.41: Plastic Works Limited

Summarised Profit & Loss Statements
for the year ended 31 December   (*Rs*)

	19X3	19X2	19X1
Sales	1,872,937	1,599,315	1,429,818
Cost of goods sold	896,953	767,673	683,597
Gross profit	975,984	831,642	746,221

	19X3	19X2	19X1
Operating expenses	846,059	640,048	545,750
Profit before taxes	129,925	191,594	200,471
Taxes	56,367	88,435	93,050
Net profit	73,558	103,159	107,421
Dividends	81,400	81,400	81,400

12. *Tata Iron & Steel Company Limited (TISCO).* TISCO was established in 1907 at Jamshedpur. It is the largest private sector company. Tables 25.42 and 25.43 give the profit and loss statements and balance sheets for the last seven years for the company. You are required to provide an analysis of the company's financial performance.

Table 25.42: Tata Iron and Steel Company Limited

Summarised Balance Sheet as on 31 March   (*Rs in crore*)

	1995	1996	1997	1998	1999	2000	2001
ASEETS							
Gross fixed assets	6,962.89	7,408.46	7,850.82	8,948.52	10,032.17	10,668.33	11,258.17
Less: Cumulative depreciation	1,749.41	2,014.90	2,324.42	2,648.48	2,973.59	3,241.95	3,720.08
Net fixed assets	5,213.48	5,393.56	5,526.40	6,300.04	7,058.58	7,426.38	7,538.09
Investments	220.65	410.94	664.90	626.08	588.84	818.89	850.83
Current Assets							
Inventories	865.34	1,076.57	1,021.11	1,039.70	1,016.51	944.85	921.77
Receivables	1,341.87	1,723.63	2,178.76	1,948.40	1,874.18	1,868.77	2,060.70
Marketable investment	175.51	365.75	479.77	453.03	399.51	342.35	381.38
Cash and bank balance	162.44	437.09	251.38	462.96	336.19	232.87	239.78
	2,545.16	3,603.04	3,931.02	3,904.09	3,626.39	3,388.84	3,603.63
Misc. expenses not written off	31.33	167.99	278.32	896.98	1,118.53	828.12	920.29
Total Assets	7,835.11	9,209.78	9,920.87	11,274.16	11,992.83	12,119.88	12,531.46
CAPITAL & LIABILITIES							
Net worth	2,688.04	3,742.40	3,974.02	4,064.88	4,164.42	4,558.40	4,888.43
Share capital	336.87	367.23	367.38	367.55	367.77	517.77	507.77
Equity capital	336.87	367.23	367.38	367.55	367.77	367.77	367.77
Preference capital	0.00	0.00	0.00	0.00	0.00	150.00	140.00
Reserves & surplus	2,351.17	3,375.17	3,606.64	3,697.33	3,796.65	4,040.63	4,380.66
Total borrowings	3,582.73	3,842.07	4,082.49	5,212.44	5,503.26	4,946.52	4,672.56
Current liabilities & provisions	1,564.34	1,625.31	1,864.36	1,996.84	2,325.15	2,614.96	2,970.47
Current liabilities	1,421.51	1,326.82	1,385.47	1,414.66	1,463.35	1,492.55	1,696.38
Sundry creditors	1,256.72	1,203.97	1,251.00	1,296.61	1,340.17	1,345.65	1,574.35
Others	164.79	122.85	134.47	118.05	123.18	146.90	122.03
Provisions	142.83	298.49	478.89	582.18	861.80	1,122.41	1,274.09
Tax provision	21.24	18.96	111.40	150.58	185.53	167.04	180.20
Dividend provision	118.24	156.97	165.66	147.25	147.11	147.11	183.89
Other provisions	3.35	122.56	201.83	284.35	529.16	808.26	910.00
Total Liabilities	7,835.11	9,209.78	9,920.87	11,274.16	11,992.83	12,119.88	12,531.46

Table 25.43: Tata Iron and Steel Company Limited

Summarised Profit & Loss Account for the Year Ending on 31 March

(Rs in crore)

	1995	1996	1997	1998	1999	2000	2001
Income							
Sales	4993.39	6349.35	6919.4	7012.35	6885.12	7015.16	7822.58
Less: Excise	440.77	592.61	696.49	724.34	710.09	796.86	920.83
Net sales	4552.62	5756.74	6222.91	6288.01	6175.03	6218.3	6901.75
Other income	44.58	76.18	150.52	117.16	96.73	68.51	86.53
Change in stocks	–17.35	66.24	42.12	4.8	46.18	–33.19	–56.74
Non-recurring income	16.03	0.35	11.2	27.59	139.84	152.44	13.15
Total Income	4595.88	5899.51	6426.75	6437.56	6457.78	6406.06	6944.69
PBDIT (EBITDA)	808.1	1212.74	1260.45	1030.38	1058.26	1291.98	1507.68
Less: Depreciation	262.26	297.61	326.83	343.23	382.18	426.54	492.25
PBIT	545.84	915.13	933.62	687.15	676.08	865.44	1015.43
Less: Interest	281.4	348.91	390.66	323.42	360.35	388.35	412.39
PBT	264.44	566.22	542.96	363.73	315.73	477.09	603.04
Less: Tax provision	0.25	0.43	73.75	41.65	33.5	54.5	49.6
PAT	264.19	565.79	469.21	322.08	282.23	422.59	553.44
Appropriation of Profit							
Equity Dividends	118.24	156.97	165.66	147.25	147.11	154.86	196.09
Dividend Tax	0	0	16.57	14.73	16.18	17.04	21.52
Retained earnings	145.95	408.82	286.98	160.1	118.94	250.69	335.83
Other Financial Items							
Cash profit	530.35	867.3	801.69	665.31	664.41	849.13	1045.69
Cash flow from business activities	681.14	638.86	881.3	880.44	1007.98	1323.94	1718.7
Value of output	4504.29	5795.26	6238.2	6257.51	6189.62	6154.84	6812.71
Gross value added	1501.19	2174.54	2205.36	2055.3	1998.68	2273.55	2732.1
Net value added	1238.93	1876.93	1878.53	1712.07	1616.5	1847.01	2239.85

13. *Agro-Chemical & Pesticides Industry.* The financial data in Table 25.44 related to ten agro-chemicals and pesticides companies for the year ending on March 31, 19X2. Provide a detailed analysis of the profitability and the market performance of the companies. How have these companies performed in relation to the industry performance? Show computations.

14. *Glass Manufacturing Companies.* The financial data in Table 25.45 are for the glass manufacturing companies for the year 19X1 and 19X2. Comment on the profitability and the market performance of the companies. How do they compare with the industry average?

Table 25.44: Agro-Chemicals and Pesticides Companies

Financial Data

for the year ending on 31 March, 19X2

(Rs in crore)

	Buyer	Cynamide	Excel	Khaitau	Monsanto	Montari	Paushak	Searle	UP straw	United
Sales	218.43	100.46	175.31	26.85	14.32	59.69	12.30	74.36	1600	101.17
PBDIT	33.69	15.15	39.83	5.12	1.72	7.61	1.50	9.71	1.77	22.75
Dep.	5.33	1.91	4.12	1.30	0.04	1.22	0.20	1.14	0.50	1.34
PBIT	28.36	13.24	35.71	3.82	1.68	6.39	1.30	8.57	1.27	21.41
Int.	17.07	11.17	28.12	1.18	1.32	1.95	0.61	5.99	0.96	18.21
PBT	17.07	11.17	28.12	1.18	1.32	1.95	0.61	5.99	0.96	18.21
Tax	8.25	5.09	9.50	0.00	0.70	0.00	0.08	1.80	0.00	4.00
PAT	8.82	6.08	18.62	1.18	0.62	1.95	0.53	4.19	0.96	14.21
EPS	54.38	11.56	26.87	2.34	6.20	3.18	6.24	8.03	3.54	20.01
DPS	24.00	3.50	10.10	2.50	2.30	2.20	1.70	2.50	0.00	5.00
Book value	268.5	52.23	62.37	19.21	25.40	14.67	27.18	57.85	15.72	33.72
Market value	2100.00	280.00	630.00	47.50	250.00	120.00	130.00	280.00	58.00	590.00

Source: The Economics Times.

Table 25.45: Glass Manufacturing Companies

Financial Data

(Rs in crore)

		Alembic	Ashi	Borosil	Excel	Fgp.	Hind.	Indo.	Maha	Triveni	Victory	Industry
Sales	19X1	19.8	19.3	24.7	9.7	29.4	66.2	54.3	9.7	31.5	7.8	271.5
	19X2	28.2	26.4	31.1	13.5	30.8	76.7	83.0	12.4	48.2	8.2	338.5
PBIT	19X1	1.6	1.9	3.8	0.7	4.7	6.3	12.3	1.0	6.2	1.0	39.6
	19X2	2.7	4.2	5.9	1.2	4.0	8.2	12.6	1.5	14.9	1.4	56.5
Interest	19X1	1.3	1.5	1.9	8.4	1.4	3.0	1.6	0.5	0.8	0.6	13.0
	19X2	1.7	2.1	2.1	0.6	1.6	3.0	1.3	0.6	0.7	0.0	15.3
Tax	19X1	0.0	0.1	0.7	0.1	1.2	0.0	1.7	0.0	2.0	0.0	5.7
	19X2	0.0	0.0	1.8	0.1	0.4	0.0	6.0	0.4	6.3	0.0	15.1
PAT	19X1	0.3	0.3	1.2	0.2	2.1	3.3	9.0	0.5	3.4	0.4	20.9
	19X2	1.0	2.1	2.0	0.5	2.0	4.4	5.3	0.5	7.9	0.6	26.1
Per Share Data												
EPS	19X1	11.3	1.7	3.1	1.5	3.5	22.8	27.8	3.7	29.2	3.5	
	19X2	38.5	11.2	5.6	3.7	3.1	30.5	8.2	3.7	67.7	4.9	
DPS	19X1	0.0	1.0	2.5	1.4	2.2	1.0	4.0	1.4	3.0	1.5	
	19X2	0.0	1.5	0.25	1.8	2.2	1.0	23.0	1.4	3.6	2.0	
BV	19X1	93.8	12.3	45.4	20.4	31.4	96.5	63.0	17.7	115.0	17.1	
	19X2	129.6	22.5	48.6	22.2	32.3	126.9	45.6	20.0	180.3	20.0	
MV	19X2	575.0	227.5	85.0	75.0	85.0	35.0	145.0	6.0	675.0	45.0	

CASES

Case 25.1: Patel Computers System

Hanshmukh Patel and Sadhuram Patel established Patel Computers System as a private limited company in 1986 to provide computer software services to small and medium enterprises in high technology areas. The business picked up fast and the firm has grown at a high rate. The founders converted the firm into a public limited company in 1992 to access external capital. In spite of being a public limited company, it still continues to be closely controlled by the founders and their families. The business is still growing, except for some slowing down in 1998-99. The company is strong in technical and marketing functions, but the founders who do not have formal knowledge of the intricacies of finance controlled the finance function. It is recently that they realised the need of a finance expert to manage the financial activities of the company. The company has now appointed a chief financial officer (CFO). The first task of the chief financial officer was to evaluate the company's most recent balance sheet and profit and loss account and find out if the financial operations were all right. When the CFO looked at the financial statements of the company she got an impression that the company was overtrading.

The financial statements of company are given in Table 25.1.1.

Table 25.1.1: Patel Computers System

(Rs in lakh)

Balance Sheet as at 31st March, 2004

Assets		
Property	6,750	
Less: Accumulated depreciation	500	6,250
Systems equipments	5,500	
Less: Accumulated depreciation	1,350	4,150
Fixed assets		10,400
Current assets		
Stock	3,300	
Trade debtors	7,550	
	10,850	
Less: Current liabilities		
Trade creditors	11,450	
Proposed dividend	130	
Taxation	780	
Bank overdraft	1,300	13,660
Net current assets		(2,810)
Net Assets		7,590
Capital and Liabilities		
Ordinary shares, Rs 10 par		3,000
Reserve & surplus		2,090
Net worth		5,090
Secured loan (15%)		2,500
Total Funds		7,590

Table 25.1.2: Patel Computers System

Profit and Loss Account for the year ended 31 March, 2004

(*Rs in lakh*)

Revenue		82,000
Less: Cost of sales		
Opening stock	2,700	
Purchases	52,800	
	55,500	
Less: Closing stock	3,200	52,300
Gross profit		29,700
Less: Selling and distribution expenses	2,1710	
Administration expenses	4,700	
Finance expenses	390	26,800

Contd...

Profit and Loss Account for the year ended 31 March, 2004

(*Rs in lakh*)

Net profit before taxation	2,900
Corporation tax	1,000
Net profit after taxation	1,900
Proposed dividend	1,000
Profit transferred to reserve & surplus for the year	900

Discussion Questions

1. Critically evaluate Patel Computers System's profitability? Show relevant ratios.
2. Do you think the company is overtrading? Calculate the ratios that support your contention.
3. What are the causes of overtrading in Patel Computers System and what are your suggestions to remedy it?

Case 25.2: Reliance Industries Limited

Data in Tables 25.2.1 and 25.2.2 relate to the Reliance Industries Ltd. Calculate relevant ratios and indicate the company's performance over years.

Table 25.2.1: Reliance Industries Ltd.

Summarised Profit & Loss Account during the Year Ending at 31 March

(*Rs in crore*)

	2001	2000	1999	1998	1997	1996	1995
EARNINGS							
Sales	23,024.17	15,847.16	10,624.15	9,719.18	6,441.65	5,726.66	5,388.15
Less: Excise	2,578.91	2,451.53	1,929.46	1,893.13	1,283.85	1,507.83	1,517.13
Net Sales	20,445.26	13,395.63	8,694.69	7,826.05	5,157.80	4,218.83	3,871.02
Other Income	976.79	976.56	629.19	363.09	318.78	271.85	312.59
Total Income	21,422.05	14,372.19	9,323.88	8,189.14	5,476.58	4,490.68	4,183.61
PBDIT	5,561.72	4,746.61	3,317.54	2,886.54	1,947.81	1,751.91	1,622.60
Depreciation	1,565.11	1,278.36	855.04	667.32	410.14	336.51	278.24
PBIT	3,996.61	3,468.25	2,462.50	2,219.22	1,537.67	1,415.40	1,344.36
Interest	1,215.99	1,008.00	728.81	503.55	169.97	110.13	279.51
PBT	2,780.62	2,460.25	1,733.69	1,715.67	1,367.70	1,305.27	1,064.85
Tax	135.00	57.00	30.00	63.00	45.00	0.00	0.00
PAT	2,645.62	2,403.25	1,703.69	1,652.67	1,322.70	1,305.27	1,064.85
Additional Information							
Equity Dividend	447.85	384.65	350.16	326.81	299.24	276.22	199.34
Preference Dividend	4.77	35.57	23.39	10.33	0.00	28.00	0.83
Corporate Dividend Tax	46.20	46.22	40.86	63.64	0.00	0.00	0.00
EPS (Rs)	24.63	22.04	17.56	16.94	28.85	27.87	23.34
Book Value (Rs)	113.86	103.65	100.12	96.83	184.77	179.07	157.66

Table 25.2.2: Reliance Industries Ltd

Summarised Profit & Loss Account during the Year Ending at 31 March

(Rs in crore)

	2001	2000	1999	1998	1997	1996	1995
CAPITAL & LIABILITIES							
Total Shareholders Funds							
Equity Share Capital	1,053.49	1,053.45	933.39	931.90	458.45	458.23	455.86
Preference Capital Paid Up	0.00	292.95	252.95	187.95	0.00	200.00	5.50
Reserves & Surplus	13,711.88	12,636.35	11,183.00	10,862.75	8,012.49	7,747.07	6,731.29
	14,765.37	13,982.75	12,369.34	11,982.60	8,470.94	8,405.30	7,192.65
Borrowings							
Term Loans—Institutions	68.66	158.51	46.24	57.41	859.70	411.95	284.79
Term Loans—Banks	0.00	1,400.94	1,527.00	200.53	950.48	607.19	160.27
Non Convertible Debentures	3,761.98	3,779.85	3,578.04	2,413.54	2,012.98	1,780.95	1,273.04
Working Capital Advances	237.76	648.81	327.03	65.98	425.92	591.88	405.63
Other Loans	6,067.39	5,532.13	5,206.98	5,509.87	3,376.40	1,329.48	816.19
Total Borrowings	10,135.79	11,520.24	10,685.29	8,247.33	7,625.48	4,721.45	2,939.92
Current Liabilities & Provisions							
Creditors	3,859.22	2,953.96	3,338.73	3,095.04	2,386.23	1,305.32	1,118.23
Provisions	863.50	265.80	544.37	475.99	352.23	282.02	201.57
Other	251.58	646.07	1,218.27	586.97	701.26	324.29	76.67
Total Current Liabilities	4,974.30	3,865.83	5,101.37	4,158.00	3,439.72	1,911.63	1,396.47
Total Liabilities	29,875.46	29,368.82	28,156.00	24,387.93	19,536.14	15,038.38	11,529.04
ASSETS							
Fixed assets							
Gross Block	25,355.99	24,330.95	18,650.33	17,848.33	10,955.92	6,885.50	5,315.40
Less: Accum. Depreciation	11,841.53	9,214.06	6,691.93	4,944.47	3,491.20	2,141.34	1,805.78
Net Block	13,514.46	15,116.89	11,958.40	12,903.86	7,464.72	4,744.16	3,509.62
Capital Work in Progress	512.38	331.42	3,437.83	2,069.43	3,708.63	4,488.71	3,075.09
Total Fixed assets	14,026.84	15,448.31	15,396.23	14,973.29	11,173.35	9,232.87	6,584.71
Investments	6,726.11	6,066.56	4,294.59	4,282.33	4,455.68	1,952.91	1,993.41
Current Assets	9,122.51	7,853.95	8,465.18	5,132.31	3,907.11	3,852.60	2,950.92
Total Assets	29,875.46	29,368.82	28,156.00	24,387.93	19,536.14	15,038.38	11,529.04

Discussion Questions

1. How effectively has Reliance used its assets in generating sales? Show relevant ratios.
2. How has Reliance financed its assets? Do you think there is appropriate balance between equity and borrowed funds?
3. Critically evaluate Reliance's profitability. Show the ratios that contribute to the company profitability.
4. Does Reliance have sufficient liquidity? Compute appropriate ratios in support of our view.

Case 25.3: Bajaj Auto Ltd.

The Bachraj Trading Corporation incorporated in 1945 was renamed as Bajaj Auto Private Limited in 1960. The company manufactures Bajaj brand of scooters, motorcycles and spare parts. Table 25.3.1 gives a summary of company's financial items during the years from 1997 to 2001.

Table 25.3.1: Bajaj Auto Limited
Summary of Financial Items

(Rs in crore)

	2001	2000	1999	1998	1997
Net Sales	3023.12	3089.33	2961.98	2643.22	2638.47
PBDIT	473.88	973.4	895.57	840.94	802.23
Depreciation	177.29	145.31	132.7	143.62	117.87
Interest	7.39	3.17	4.67	8.47	7.41
Other Income	365.99	510.4	380.29	355.57	296.89
PBT	289.2	824.92	758.2	688.85	676.95

(Contd.)

	2001	2000	1999	1998	1997
Tax Provision	26.64	211.19	217.68	224.7	236.38
Net Profit	262.56	613.73	540.52	464.15	440.57
Equity Dividend	80.95	119.39	95.51	95.51	79.59
Retained Profit	181.61	494.34	445.01	368.64	360.98
Current Assets	2061.62	2373.37	2197.01	1809.38	1363.55
Net Fixed Assets	1362.35	1114.25	921.81	682.91	603.95
Current Liabilities	1474.34	1740.67	1527.18	1259.83	988.27
Secured Loans	55.97	101.58	41.08	27.54	22.04
Unsecured Loans	457.74	394.09	308.61	230.67	191.83
Total Liabilities	4624.58	5440.42	4578.61	3636.26	2962.84
Net Worth	2636.53	3204.08	2701.74	2118.22	1760.7
Bonus Ratio	–	–	–	–	1.02
EPS	25.13	50.31	44.39	38.08	54.35
DPS	8.00	10.00	8.00	8.00	10.00
Book Value Per Share	260.58	268.37	226.3	177.42	221.22
Market Value Per Share*	257.70	384.00	615.80	594.30	601.70

* Closing price in March.

Discussion Questions

1. Assume you are the chairman & managing director (CMD) of Bajaj Auto, how would you rate the company's performance? Support your arguments with relevant ratios.
2. Instead of the CMD, if you were a shareholder in Bajaj Auto, what would be your comments on the company's performance?
3. What is DuPont analysis? Show this analysis for Bajaj Auto.

26 Financial Planning and Strategy

CHAPTER OBJECTIVES

- Understand the difference between financial forecasting and financial planning
- Explain the components of a financial plan
- Discuss the technique of financial forecasting
- Develop an approach to construct a financial model
- Examine the features and implications of sustainable growth model
- Show the linkage between strategic planning and financial planning

INTRODUCTION

A firm should be managed effectively and efficiently. This implies that the firm should be able to achieve its objectives by minimising the use of resources. Thus managing implies coordination and control of the efforts of the firm for achieving the organisational objectives. The process of managing is facilitated when management charts its future course of action in advance, and takes decisions in a professional manner, utilising the individual and group efforts in a coordinated and rational manner. One systematic approach for attaining effective management performance is financial planning and budgeting. **Financial planning** indicates a firm's growth, performance, investments and requirements of funds during a given period of time, usually three to five years. It involves the preparation of projected or *proforma* profit and loss account, balance sheet and funds flow statement. Financial planning and profit planning help a firm's financial manager to regulate flows of funds which is his primary concern.

STRATEGIC DECISION-MAKING AND PLANNING

Strategy provides foundation for any system of planning. It provides the basis for operational planning and financial planning. Strategy is a central theme that establishes an effective and efficient match between the firm's resources, competences and opportunities and risks created by environmental changes. It is a link between the multiple goals and objectives pursued by the firm to satisfy its various stakeholders and the plans and policies used by it to guide its daily operations. Hofer and Schendel[1] provide a comprehensive definition of the **content of strategy** as:

> ...fundamental pattern of present and planned resource developments and environmental interactions and indicates how the organisation will achieve its objectives.

The definition highlights distinctive competences (resource deployments) as an important component of strategy and emphasises that competitive advantage can stem not only from product/market positioning but also from *unique resource deployments*. Thus, the ultimate success of the firm may not simply depend on scope but it can also be greatly influenced by competitive advantage and resource deployments. The four components of strategy can be seen as influences on the firm's effectiveness and efficiency. The firm's effectiveness is determined by the combined influence of scope, distinctive competences and competitive advantages, while synergies among distinctive competences and product/market segments determine its efficiency.

1. Hofer, C.W. and Schendel, D., *Strategy Formulation: Analytical Concepts*, St. Paul, West Publishing Company, 1978.

A financial planning involving financial policy has direct interaction with scope and resource deployment. Financial policies – investment and financing choices — should therefore be considered at the corporate level, and should not be treated as functional area policy decisions to be decided at lower levels. Business-level strategy involves operational planning and focuses on how to compete in a particular product/market segment or industry. Competitive advantages and distinctive competences thus become dominant strategic concerns at this level. At the functional-level, the primary focus of strategy is on effeciency.

Strategic Choices and Planning

The business portfolio models are most popular and useful to understand the firm's strategic concerns and choices and plan for the future. They define the firm's scope or domain by highlighting the inter-relatedness of diverse factors such as market growth, market share, cost and cash flow patterns, capital intensity, product maturity and so on. They also focus on combined effect of those factors on the firm's long-term success and survival.

The **market growth-market share model** (Figure 26.1), popularised by the Boston Consulting Group (BCG),[1] is the simplest model to put the firm's strategic posture at corporate level in proper perspective. As can be seen in Figure 26.1, businesses are grouped in a two-cell matrix according to market growth rates and relative market shares: '*Stars*' are best performers representing super profit and growth opportunities in a rapidly growing market. They are generally self-sustaining in terms of cash flows, although some of 'stars' may be net users of cash because of their very high growth rate. '*Cash cows*' are declining stars and they are providers of cash to be utilised elsewhere in the firm. '*Dogs*' will have a weak competitive position and little chance of improvement because of low growth and low share. Being unprofitable, they are hardly in a position to generate cash to sustain their existing positions. The firm would attempt to extract its investment in 'dogs' by liquidating or selling them. '*Wild cats*' or '*question marks*' (also called 'problem children') are opportunities either to be developed into 'stars' if the firm can capture a larger share in the rapidly growing markets, or to be divested if they remain unprofitable on account of the firm's inability to increase its share in those businesses. Wild cat businesses, which the firm is attempting to develop into 'stars', will need more cash because of high growth rates than what they can generate due to low market share.

In **strategic finance** terms, the BCG model implies that cash surplus from 'cash cows' should be transferred to 'wild cats' in the hope of growing them into 'stars' and to those existing 'stars' which are still growing rapidly to sustain them so that they ultimately start generating surplus cash (that is, they become 'cash cows'). The model also indicates that 'dogs' have no chance of improvement, and therefore, they should be divested to extract any cash.

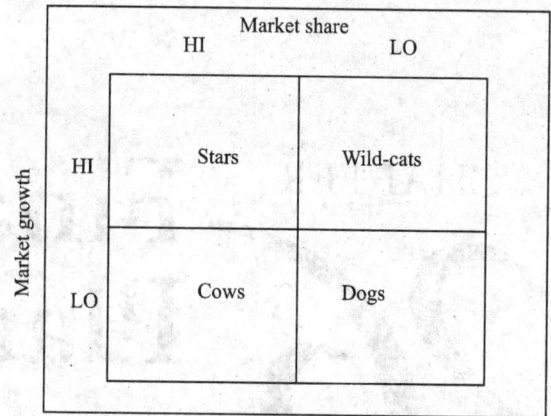

Figure 26.1: Market growth-market share model

The foundation of the BCG model is the concept of **experience curve**, which assumes that unit cost is a declining function of accumulated experience.[2] Accumulated experience depends on sales volume, which is a function of market share. Thus, the firm with highest market share or relative competitive dominance will have lowest costs, resulting in highest, stable profits and net cash flows. It is a most desirable strategy to gain and maintain a dominant market position as compared to competitors. The dominant market position should be achieved during the growth phase since the firm can capture a larger market share by obtaining a small share of market growth. It is generally difficult and expensive to seize market share from competitors when markets are matured. The firm should hold its dominant market position by reducing prices and thus keeping away the high cost competitors. Cash flows are likely to be negative during the growth phase in a dominant market since the firm will have to keep on investing to maintain its competitive edge. Dominant position generates positive cash flows during the mature stage of the life-cycle.

The **BCG model** makes it very clear that a firm for its ultimate success needs a balanced portfolio of products or businesses. The individual businesses are analysed to form a corporate portfolio, which should act as a guide to commit the firm's resources. **Strategic planning** ensures that portfolio of businesses are balanced in terms of profits, cash flows, and overall corporate risk.

The strategic position of a complex business can be analysed by using a more elaborate portfolio model such as the nine-cell matrix model developed by the General Electric Company.[3] The relationships predicted by the portfolio models are substantiated by the **PIMS (profit impact on market share)** data analysis, that is, profitability is determined by market share, and cash flow by both market share and market growth rate.[4]

The main points of the strategic decision-making framework may be summarised as follows:

* A firm operates in a complex environment.
* Strategy is a central theme that establishes a match between the firm's competences and opportunities created by

1. Boston Consulting Group (BCG) Staff, *Perspectives on Experience*, Boston Consulting Group, 1968.
2. *Ibid.*
3. Hofer and Schendel, *op. cit.*
4. Schoeffler, S., Buzzel, R.D. and Heavy, D.F., Impact of Strategic Planning on Profit Performance, *Harvard Business Review*, March–April 1974.

environment changes.

- A firm is multi-directed; strategy is a link between the multiple goals of the firm and its plans and policies.
- Product-market scope, competitive advantages, distinctive competences and synergy are the most important components of strategy.
- Market dominance (particularly, during the growth stage) is the most desirable strategy.
- A firm should have a balanced portfolio of businesses.

STRATEGIC FINANCIAL PLANNING

Two important tasks of the financial manager are:

- Allocation of funds (*viz.*, investment decision)
- Generation of funds (*viz.*, financial decision).

The theory of finance makes two crucial assumptions to provide guidance to the financial manager in making these decisions. First, the objective of the firm is to maximise the wealth of shareholders. It is argued that shareholders are the ultimate owners of the firm and the role of the manager is that of an agent acting on their behalf. It is therefore imperative on the part of the financial manager to make decisions that will increase the value of the shareholders' stake in the firm. Second, capital markets are efficient. An efficient capital market implies that investors have free access to the market with full knowledge, zero transaction costs and that individual investors are unable to influence prices. The efficient capital markets enable investors to lend or borrow funds. This helps them to make choice between consumption and investments. Lending helps to postpone consumption and borrowing helps to bring it forward. The separation of investment and consumption, known as the **Fisher separation theorem**,[1] implies that financial decisions can be delegated to managers.

The corporate finance theory thus implies that:

- Owners have the primary interest in the firm, and therefore, the main objective of the firm should be to maximise owner's (shareholders') wealth.
- The current value of the share is the measure of the shareholders' wealth.
- The firm should accept only those investments that generate positive net present values (NPVs) and thus, increase the current value of the firm's share.
- NPVs of the individual projects simply add; therefore, the firm's diversification policy does not create any 'extra' value. It is not desirable from investors' point of view.
- The firm's capital structure and dividend decisions become important only because of imperfections.

It is well-known in the economics literature that product and labour markets are no perfect. Empirical studies also do not universally and unequivocally support the efficient capital market hypothesis. The financial economists do recognise market imperfections such as transaction cost, bankruptcy costs, taxes, information gap, agency costs, signalling effects etc. However, each of those imperfections is looked at within the context of a theoretical system in which markets are otherwise perfectly competitive.[2] Strategic planning considers all markets, including product, labour and capital, as imperfect and changing. Strategies are developed to manage the business firm in uncertain and imperfect market conditions and environment and exploit opportunities. It is an important management task to analyse changing market conditions and environment to make forecasts, and plan generation and allocation of resources. Firms develop financial plan within the overall framework of strategic plan.

FINANCIAL PLANNING

Growth in sales is an important objective of most firms. An increase in a firm's market share will lead to higher growth. The firm would need assets to sustain the higher growth in sales. It may have to invest in additional plant and machinery to increase its production capacity. Also, it would need additional current assets to produce and sell more goods or services. The firm would have to acquire raw materials and convert them into finished goods after incurring manufacturing expenses. It may have to sell goods on credit because of the industry norms or to push up sales. This gives rise to debtors or accounts receivables. The suppliers of raw materials may extend credit to the firm. The firm may use its internally generated funds to finance current and fixed assets. When the firm grows at a high rate, internal funds may not be sufficient. Thus the firm would have to raise external funds either by issuing equity or debt or both. Financial planning is the process of analysing a firm's investment options and estimating the funds requirement and deciding the sources of funds.

In summary, the financing planning process involves the following facets:

- Evaluating the current financial condition of the firm
- Analying the future growth prospects and options
- Appraising the investment options to achieve the stated growth objective
- Projecting the future growth and profitability
- Estimating funds requirement and considering alternative financing options
- Comparing and choosing from alternative growth plans and financing options
- Measuring actual performance with the planned performance

Financial Forecasting and Modelling

Financial forecasting is an integral part of financial planning. It uses past data to estimate the future financial requirements. A financial planning model establishes the relationship between financial variables and targets, and facilitates the financial forecasting and planning process. A model makes it easy for the financial managers to prepare financial forecasts. It makes financial forecasting automatic and saves the financial managers' time and efforts performing a tedious activity. Financial planning models help in examining the consequences of alternative financial strategies.

---

1. Fisher, I., *The Theory of Interest*, New York, Macmillan, 1965.
2. Gordon, M.J., Interest in a Corporation of its Management, Workers and Country, in Derkinderm and Crum (ed.), *Readings in Strategy for Corporate Investment*, Pitman, 1981.

A financial planning model has the following three components:

- **Inputs** The model builder starts with the firm's current financial statements and the future growth prospects. The firm's growth prospects depend on the market growth rate, firm's market share and intensity of competition. The growth objective is determined by the management team consisting of marketing, manufacturing and finance executives.
- **Model** The model defines the relations between financial variables and develops appropriate equations. For example, net working capital and fixed assets investment may be related to sales. As sales change, they may change in direct proportion to sales. Hence the model will specify working capital and fixed assets as ratio of sales. Similarly, given the payout policy of the firm, dividend may be specified as a ratio of profit after tax.
- **Output** Applying the model equations to the inputs, output in the form of projected or proforma financial statements are obtained. The output shows the investment and funds requirement given the sales growth objective and relationships between the financial variables.

Constructing Financial Model

How can we construct a financial model? Let us consider an example. Suppose for the year 2004, profit and loss statement and balance sheet for Indus Furniture Company are given in Table 26.1. The managing director of the company forecasts that sales volume will grow at 10 per cent next year. He also thinks that inflation rate will be 4.55 per cent and that his company will be able to adjust sales price for inflation.

Table 26.1: Indus Furniture Company: Financial Statements

Profit and Loss Statement for the year ending 31 March, 2004

	(Rs in lakh)
Sales	100,000
Variable cost	60,000
Fixed cost	10,000
Depreciation	2,500
EBIT	27,500
Interest	2,800
PBT	24,700
Tax	8,645
PAT	16,055
Dividend	12,844
Retained earnings	3,211

Balance Sheet as on 31 March, 2004

	(Rs in lakh)
Assets	
Net working capital	45,000
Fixed assets	25,000
Total assets	70,000
Liabilities & Equity	
Debt	28,000
Equity	42,000
Total liabilities	70,000

The managing director asked his planning team to prepare the next year's *proforma* profit and loss statement, balance sheet and funds flow statement. The planning team through a consultative process in the company, made several assumptions about the relationships between financial variables. These assumptions and model equations are shown in Table 26.2. There are significant financial policy variables included in Table 26.2. For example, the company's payout ratio is 80 per cent and debt ratio is 40 per cent. It is assumed that the company will maintain these policies in the future as well.

Table 26.2: Model Inputs and Assumptions

Model inputs and assumptions		
Current year's sales, S_0	given, (Rs in lakh)	100,000
Growth – volume, v		10.0%
Growth – inflation, η		4.6%
Overall growth, g	$(1 + v) * (1 + \eta) - 1$	15.0%
Variable cost ratio, vc	ratio of sales	60.0%
Fixed cost, F_0	given, (Rs in lakh)	10,000
Annual increase in fixed cost, fc		12.0%
Depreciation rate, dep	ratio of fixed assets	10.0%
Interest rate, i		10.0%
Tax rate, T		35.0%
Net working capital ratio, w	ratio of sales	45.0%
Fixed assets investment ratio, fa	ratio of sales	25.0%
Payout ratio, p	ratio of PAT	80.0%
Debt ratio, d	ratio of total assets	40.0%

Based on the model inputs and assumptions, the planning team developed the model equations for proforma profit and loss statement, funds flow statement and balance sheet as shown in Table 26.3. You may observe from Table 26.3 that we have developed 28 equations covering proforma profit and loss statement, statement of sources and uses of funds and balance sheet.

Table 26.3: Model Equations

Profit & Loss Statement	Equation	Output
1. Sales	$S = S_0(1 + g)$	S
2. Variable cost	$S * vc$	VC
3. Fixed cost	$(1 + fc) * F_0$	FC
4. Depreciation	$dep * FA$	DEP
5. Earnings before interest & tax	$S - VC - FC - DEP$	EBIT
6. Interest	$i * D$	INT
7. Profit before tax	$EBIT - INT$	PBT
8. Tax	$T * (EBIT - INT)$	TAX
9. Profit after tax	$PBT - TAX$	PAT
10. Dividend	$p * PAT$	DIV
11. Retained earnings	$PAT - DIV$	RE
Sources & Uses of Funds		
12. Profit after tax	Source: Profit & Loss Statement	PAT
13. Depreciation	Source: Profit & Loss Statement	DEP
14. Operating cash flows	$PAT + DEP$	OCF
15. *Less:* Dividend	$p * PAT$	DIV

(Contd.)

Profit & Loss Statement	Equation	Output
16. Internal funds	OCF – DIV	IF
17. External funds:	TSF – IF	EF
(a) Borrowing	EF – EI	ΔD
(b) Equity Issue	$E - E_0 - RE$	EI
18. Total Sources of Funds (TSF)	TSF = TUF	TSF
19. Change in Net working capital	$NWC - NWC_0$	ΔNWC
20. Fixed assets investment	$FA - FA_0$	ΔFA
21. Total Uses of Funds (TUF)	$\Delta NWC + \Delta FA$	
Balance Sheet		
Assets		
22. Net working capital	$w*S = NWC_0 + \Delta NWC$	NWC
23. Fixed assets	$fa*S = FA_0 + \Delta FA$	FA
24. Total assets	NWC + FA	TA
Liabilities & Equity		
25. Debt	$d*TA = D_0 + \Delta D$	D
26. Equity	$(1 - d)*TA$	
	$= E_0 + EI + RE$	E
27. Total liabilities & equity	D + E = TA	TL

We can use the information given in Tables 26.1–26.3 to prepare proforma financial statements as shown in Tables 26.4–26.6. Given its expected growth and profit margin, Indus will be able to earn a net profit of Rs 18,733 lakh the year in 2005. The company follows a liberal payout policy. After distributing 80 per cent of profits, Indus will be able to retain profit equal to Rs 3,746 lakh.

Table 26.4: Proforma Profit and Loss Statement

Profit & Loss Statement	Year 2004 (Actual)	Equation	Year 2005 (Projected)
Sales (S)	100,000	100,000 × 1.15	115,000.00
Variable cost (VC)	60,000	0.60 × 115,000	69,000.00
Fixed cost (FC)	10,000	1.12 × 10,000	11,200.00
Depreciation (DEP)	2,500	0.10 × 28,750	2,875.00
Earnings before interest & tax (EBIT)	27,500	115,000 – 69,000 –11,200 –2,875	31,925.00
Interest (INT)	2,800	0.10 × 31,050	3,105.00
Profit before tax (PBT)	24,700	31,925 – 3,105	28,820.00
Tax (TAX)	8,645	0.35 × 28,820	10,087.00
Profit after tax (PAT)	16,055	28,820 – 10,087	18,733.00
Dividend (DIV)	12,844	0.80 × 18,733	14,986.40
Retained earnings (RE)	3,211	18,733 – 14,986	3,746.60

Adding depreciation (which is a non-cash expense) to retained earnings, the company has Rs 6,621.60 lakh internal funds available to meet its funds requirement. It is assumed that increase in sales will require more funds for net working capital (current assets minus current liabilities) and fixed assets. Given the working capital ratio and fixed assets ratio as percentages of sales, Indus' investment needs are Rs 10,500 lakh. The company has internal funds of Rs 6,621 lakh. Hence the company needs to raise: 10,500 – 6,621.60 = Rs 3,878.40 lakh externally. If the company maintains its debt ratio, of the total external funds

debt will be Rs 3,050 lakh and equity issue will be Rs 828.40. Notice that retained earnings are Rs 3,746.60 lakh. Hence equity contribution is: 828.40 + 3,746.60 = Rs 4,575 lakh.

Table 26.5: Proforma Funds Flow Statement

Statement of Sources & Uses of Funds	Equation	Year 2005 (Projected)
Profit after tax (PAT)		18,733.00
Depreciation (DEP)		2,875.00
Operating cash flows (OCF)	18,733 + 2,875	21,608.00
Less: Dividend		14,986.40
Internal funds	21,608 – 14,986	6,621.60
External funds (EF):	10,500 – 6,621.60	3,878.40
Borrowing (ΔD)	3,878.40 – 828.40	3,050.00
Equity Issue (EI)	46,575 – 42,000 – 3,746.60	828.40
Total Sources of Funds (TSF)	TUF = 10,500	10,500.00
Change in NWC (ΔNWC)	51,750 – 45,000	6,750.00
Net fixed assets investment (ΔFA)	28,750 – 25,000	3,750.00
Total Uses of Funds (TUF)		10,500.00

To support sales of Rs 115,000 lakh, Indus needs total working capital of Rs 51,750 lakh and gross fixed assets of Rs 28,750 lakh. After providing for depreciation, the net fixed assets are Rs 25,875 lakh. The company maintains the debt ratio as percentage of total assets. Hence its total equity in 2005 will be Rs 46,575 lakh. This includes retained earnings (Rs 3,746.60 lakh) and fresh equity issue (Rs 828.40 lakh).

Table 26.6: Proforma Balance Sheet

Balance Sheet	Year 2004 (Actual)		Year 2005 (Projected)
Assets	*(Rs in lakh)*		*(Rs in lakh)*
Net working capital	45,000	0.45 × 115,000	51,750.00
Gross fixed assets	25,000	0.25 × 115,000	28,750.00
Less: Depreciation	2,500	0.10 × 28,750	2,875.00
Net fixed assets	22,500	28,750 – 2,875	25,875.00
Total assets	67,500		77,625.00
Liabilities & Equity			
Debt	28,000	0.40 × 77,625	31,050.00
Equity	42,000	(1 – 0.40) × 77,625	46,575.00
Total liabilities & equity	67,500	31,050 + 46,575	77,625.00

What will happen to Indus' investment and funds requirements if sales grow at, say, 20 per cent? What are the consequences if the company wants to change its payout and/or debt policy? What happens to internal funds if variable costs ratio is higher? If you set up your equations correctly in the Excel worksheet, it will take a few seconds to make necessary calculations. You can change your assumptions and see the consequences. In the Excel Application: Constructing Financial Model given below, we show how you can develop a financial

Excel Application: 26.1:
Constructing Financial Model

Here we show how you can write formulae in Excel to develop a financial plan. The basic assumptions are given in A3 to A16. The formulae entered in column D are shown in column B.

	A	B	C	D
1	**FINANCIAL MODEL**			
2	**Model Inputs**			
3	Current year's sales, S_0 (Rs lakh)	100,000		
4	Growth rate - volume	10.0%		
5	Growth rate - inflation	4.55%		
6	Overall growth, g	15.00%		
7	Variable cost ratio, vc	60.0%		
8	Fixed cost, F (Rs lakh)	10,000		
9	Annual increase in fixed cost, fc	12.0%		
10	Depreciation rate, dep	10.0%		
11	Interest rate, i	10.0%		
12	Tax rate, T	35.0%		
13	Net working capital ratio, w	45.0%		
14	Fixed assets investment, fa	25.0%		
15	Payout ratio, p	80.0%		
16	Debt ratio, d	40.0%		*(Rs in lakh)*
17	**Profit & Loss Statement**	*Formula (in D)*	*Actual*	*Projected*
18	Sales	=B3 *(1+B6)	100,000	115,000
19	Variable cost	=D18*(1+B7)	60,000	69,000
20	Fixed cost	=B8*(1+B9)	10,000	11,200
21	Depreciation	=B10*D46	2,500	2,875
22	Earnings before interest & tax	=D18–D19–D20–D21	27,500	31,925
23	Interest	=B11*D51	2,800	3,105
24	Profit before-tax	=D22–D23	24,700	28,820
25	Tax	=B12*D24	8,645	10,087
26	Profit after-tax	=D24–D25	16,055	18,733
27	Dividends	=B15*D26	12,844	14,986
28	Retained earnings	=D26–D27	3,211	3,747
29	**Sources & Uses of Funds**			*Projected*
30	Profit after-tax	=D26		18,733
31	Depreciation	=D21		2,875
32	Operating cash flows	=D30+D31		21,608
33	*Less:* Dividends	=D27		14,986
34	Internal Funds	=D32–D33		6,622
35	External funds:	=D38–D34		3,878
36	Borrowing	=D35–D37		3,050
37	Equity Issue	=D52–C52–D28		828
38	Total Sources of Funds	=D42		10,500
39				
40	Change in Net working capital	=D45–C45		6,750
41	Fixed assets investment	=D46–C46		3,750
42	Total Uses of Funds	=D40+D41		10,500
43	**Balance Sheet**			
44	**Assets**		*Actual*	*Projected*
45	Net working capital	=B13*D18	45,000	51,750
46	Gross fixed assets	=B14*D18	25,000	28,750
47	*Less:* depreciaion	=D21	2,500	2,875
48	Net fixed assets	=D46–D47	22,500	25,875
49	Total assets	=D45+D48	67,500	77,625
50	**Liabilities & Equity**			
51	Debt	=B16*D49	28,000	31,050
52	Equity	=(1–B16)*D49	42,000	46,575
53	Total liabilities	=D51+D52	67,500	77,625

model using Excel. You can change the assumptions and see the consequences for profitability, investments and funds requirements.

You may notice that we developed 28 equations to prepare a financial model for Indus Fertilisers Company. It can be further improved by including many more financial variables. For example, variable and fixed costs could be divided into various important components. We can separately show current assets and current liabilities. Borrowings could be bifurcated into short-term and long-term components. You could make your model as detailed as you like. However, in practice, financial managers keep their financial model simpler so that they do not lose sight of critical parameters and decisions. A complicated model may distract attention from real, strategic issues.

Long-term Financial Plan

Large companies generally prepare financial plan for a long period, say, five years. Small companies may choose a shorter period, say, one year. The financial plan of large companies maybe highly detailed document containing financial plans for different strategic business units (SBUs) and divisions. In practice, long-term financial forecasts are prepared by relating the items of profit and loss account and balance sheet to sales. This is called the **percentage to sales method**. We shall consider case of Bharat Machinery Limited to illustrate the technique of long-tern financial forecasting.

Bharat Machinery Limited (BML) is a large machine tools and machinery manufacturing company. The company has been growing at a high rate. Because of the long production cycles of a number of its products, it carries large inventory. BML has its customers both in the public and private sectors. It faces a problem of realising its credit sales on time from the public sector customers. In the past, the company has generally resorted to borrowings to meet its funds requirements. Tables 26.7 and 26.8 contain BML's profit and loss statements and balance sheets for the years 2000 to 2004.

Table 26.7: Bharat Machinery Limited: Profit & Loss Statement for the Year Ending 31 March

				(Rs in crore)	
	2000	*2001*	*2002*	*2003*	*2004*
Net sales	139.0	152.0	183.0	206.2	238.3
Cost of goods sold	81.2	87.7	104.5	123.7	138.7
Gross profit	57.8	64.3	78.5	82.7	99.6
Administrative expenses	10.3	11.6	12.9	16.8	19.3
Selling expenses	20.1	21.1	23.2	25.0	27.1
Other expenses	11.6	12.9	13.4	15.5	19.1
Non-manufacturing expenses	42.0	45.6	49.5	57.3	65.5
PBIT	15.8	18.7	28.8	25.4	34.1
Interest	9.8	11.1	16.0	17.8	18.6
PBT	6.0	7.6	12.8	7.6	15.5
Tax	2.8	3.6	6.2	3.9	8.2
PAT	3.2	4.0	6.6	3.7	7.3
Dividends	1.5	1.5	3.0	3.0	3.0
Retained earnings	1.7	2.5	3.3	0.7	4.3

				(Rs in crore)	
	2000	2001	2002	2003	2004
SOURCES OF FUNDS					
Net Worth					
Share capital	40.0	40.0	40.0	40.0	40.0
Reserves	12.1	14.6	17.9	18.6	22.9
Net worth	52.1	54.6	57.9	58.6	62.9
Borrowings	67.0	71.8	96.0	110.8	114.8
Capital employed	119.1	126.4	153.9	169.4	177.7
USES OF FUNDS					
Net Fixed Assets					
Gross block	86.1	92.3	99.3	115.8	141.5
Less: Accumulated depreciation	30.2	34.3	38.7	45.9	54.1
Net block	55.9	58.0	60.6	69.9	87.4
Capital works-in-progress	3.4	4.6	10.3	17.3	7.0
Net fixed assets	59.3	62.6	70.9	87.2	94.4
Current Assets					
Inventory	97.4	110.3	122.5	119.4	122.7
Debtors	47.4	67.8	108.3	126.3	127.9
Cash and bank	5.4	2.8	3.9	6.4	11.6
Others	17.0	14.4	17.0	22.2	23.5
Current assets	167.2	195.3	251.7	274.3	285.7
Less: Current liabilities	107.4	133.5	168.7	192.1	202.4
Net Current Assets	59.8	61.8	83.0	82.2	83.3
Net Assets	119.1	124.4	153.9	169.4	177.7

How has BML financed its operations in the past? How has it performed? If BML grows as in the past, what would be its funds requirements?

We can prepare funds flow statement for the company to see how it financed its activities in the year ending on 31 March, 2004 (see Table 26.9).

We can calculate BML's financial ratios to analyse its past performance. Table 26.10 shows relationships of a number of profit and loss account and balance sheet items to sales and also provides an analysis of BML's profitability during the year 2000 to 2004.

BML's sales have been growing at about 15 per cent. The company improved its assets utilisation from 1.17 times in 2000 to 1.34 times in 2004. Its profit margin (PBIT/NS) ranged between 11.4 per cent (in 2000) and 15.7 per cent (2002). The company's net margin (PAT/NS) showed more fluctuation because of a high proportion of interest. BML earned an average net margin of 2.7 percent during 2000 to 2004. On an average, the company distributed a little more than fifty per cent of its profits as dividend to the shareholders. BML's net worth did not increase rapidly because of low margin and high payout. As a consequence, the company depended on borrowings to meet its requirement of funds, and debt-equity ratio increased from 1.29 in 2000 to 1.83 in 2004. BML has high levels of inventory and debtors. It improved its utilisation of current assets in the year 2004. Because of the better utilisation of fixed assets and

improvement in the turnover of current assets, net assets as a percentage of sales declined to about 75 per cent (from 86 per cent in 2000) in 2004. The company can improve its assets turnover and profitability by bringing down the collection period and inventory holding period.

Table 26.9: Bharat Machinery Limited : Funds Flow Statement for Year Ending on 31 March, 2004

	(Rs in crore)
SOURCES OF FUNDS	
Profit after-tax	7.3
Depreciation	8.2
Funds from operations	15.5
Borrowings	4.0
	19.5
USES OF FUNDS	
Gross block (fixed assets)	25.7
Capital works-in-progress	(10.3)
Dividends	3.0
Increase in net current assets (NCA)	1.1
	19.5
CHANGES IN NET CURRENT ASSETS	
Current Assets	
Inventory	3.3
Debtors	1.6
Cash and bank balance	5.2
Other assets	1.3
Change in current assets	11.4
Less: **Current Liabilities**	10.3
Change in NCA	1.1

Can we estimate BML's future requirement of funds if we assume the past performance to continue? We may notice that net margin, except in 2003, showed a gradual improvement. The company's performance improved in 2004 because it could affect cost control and better management of assets. Sales grew at 15.6 per cent in 2004, while the average growth rate has been 14.5 per cent. If the company is able to maintain its operating efficiency and financial policies, we can make the following assumptions:

- Sales growth 15 per cent
- Net profit margin 3 per cent
- Net assets to sales ratio 75 per cent (i.e., NFA to sales 40 per cent and NCA to sales 35 per cent)
- Tax rate 50 per cent
- Dividend 10 per cent of paid-up capital.

Table 26.11 provides financial forecasts for BML during the next five years on the basis of assumptions made above. Taking the 2004 sales of Rs 238.3 crore as the basis, sales for 2005 is calculated as: Rs 238.3 × 1.15 = Rs 274 crore. Similar calculations have been made for other years. It may be noted that projected sales have been used for estimating items of profit and loss account and balance sheet.

Table 26.10: Bharat Machinery Limited Financial Ratios

	2000	2001	2002	2003	2004	Average
PERCENTAGE OF SALES						
Profit and Loss Items						
Cost of goods sold	58.4	57.7	57.2	60.0	58.2	58.3
Administrative expenses	7.4	7.6	7.0	8.1	8.1	7.7
Selling expenses	14.5	13.9	12.7	12.1	11.4	12.9
Other expenses	8.3	8.5	7.3	7.5	8.0	7.9
Interest	7.1	7.3	8.7	8.6	7.8	7.9
PAT	2.3	2.6	3.6	1.8	3.1	2.7
Balance Sheet Items						
Net fixed assets	42.7	41.2	38.7	42.3	39.6	40.9
Inventory	70.1	72.6	66.9	57.9	51.5	63.8
Debtors	34.1	44.6	59.2	61.3	53.7	50.6
Cash and bank balance	3.9	1.8	2.1	3.1	4.9	3.2
Other current assets	12.2	9.5	9.3	10.8	9.9	10.3
Current assets	120.3	128.5	137.5	133.0	119.9	127.8
Current liabilities	77.3	87.8	92.2	93.2	84.9	87.1
Net current assets	43.0	40.7	45.4	39.9	35.0	70.8
Net assets	85.7	81.8	84.1	82.2	74.6	81.7
PROFITABILITY ANALYSIS						
Assets turnover: NS/NA	1.17	1.22	1.19	1.22	1.34	1.23
Profit margin: PBIT/NS (%)	11.4	12.3	15.7	12.3	14.3	13.2
Return on investment: PBIT/NA (%)	13.3	15.0	18.7	15.0	19.2	16.2
Leverage factor: PAT/PBIT (%)	20.3	21.4	22.9	14.6	21.4	20.1
Debt ratio: NA/NW (i.e., 1+D/F)	2.29	2.28	2.66	2.89	2.83	2.59
Return on equity: PAT/NW (%)	6.1	7.3	11.4	6.3	11.6	8.5
Retention ratio: RE/PAT (%)	53.1	62.5	54.5	18.9	58.9	49.6
Growth in equity: RE/NW (%)	3.3	4.6	6.2	1.2	6.8	4.4
Growth in sales (%)	—	9.4	20.4	12.7	15.6	14.5

The funds flow statement in Table 26.11 shows the differences in the balance sheet items. For simplicity, adjustment of depreciation is not made. We may note that as BML's sales increase, its requirement for funds increases. Total funds required for financing net fixed assets and net current assets during 2005 to 2009 are: Rs 181.8 crore. Given BML's policy of paying 10 per cent dividend (Rs 4 crore each year), retained earnings provide Rs 35.5 crore. The company will have to raise the balance amount, Rs 146.3 crore, either by issuing equity or debt. If BML does not want to finance its assets by issue of equity, it will have to borrow funds. BML's forecasted ROE and debt-equity ratio will be as follows:

	2005	2006	2007	2008	2009
ROE %	12.2	13.1	13.7	14.1	14.6
D/E ratio	2.06	2.26	2.42	2.55	2.65

Table 26.11: Bharat Machinery Limited: Financial Forecasts

(Rs in crore)

	2005	2006	2007	2008	2009
PROFIT AND LOSS ACCOUNT					
Net sales	274.0	315.2	362.4	416.8	479.3
Cost of goods sold	159.5	183.4	210.9	242.6	279.0
Gross profit	114.5	131.8	151.5	174.2	200.3
Non-manufacturing exps.	75.1	86.4	49.3	114.2	131.3
PBIT	39.4	45.4	52.2	60.0	69.0
Interest	23.0	26.4	30.4	35.1	40.1
PBT	16.4	19.0	21.8	24.9	28.9
Tax	8.2	9.5	10.9	12.4	14.5
PAT	8.2	9.5	10.9	12.5	14.4
Dividend	4.0	4.0	4.0	4.0	4.0
Retained earnings	4.2	5.5	6.9	8.5	10.4
BALANCE SHEET					
Share capital	40.0	40.0	40.0	40.0	40.0
Reserves	27.1	32.6	39.5	48.0	58.4
Net worth	67.1	72.6	79.5	88.0	98.4
Borrowings	138.4	163.8	192.3	224.7	261.1
Capital employed	205.5	236.4	271.8	312.7	359.5
Net fixed assets	109.6	126.1	145.0	166.7	191.7
Net current assets	95.9	110.3	126.8	146.0	167.8
Net assets	205.5	236.4	271.8	312.7	359.5
FUNDS FLOW STATEMENT					
Retained earnings (RE)	4.2	5.5	6.9	8.5	10.4
Funds needed	23.6	25.4	28.5	32.4	36.4
Sources	27.8	30.9	35.4	40.9	46.8
Net fixed assets (NFA)	15.2	16.5	18.9	21.7	25.0
Net current assets (NCA)	12.6	14.4	16.5	19.2	21.8
Uses	27.8	30.9	35.4	40.9	46.8

Sensitivity Analysis

What will happen to BML's financial plan if all or some of the assumptions do not hold? It is assumed that sales will grow at 15 per cent per annum. Historically, the company has grown in some years at a rate less than 15 per cent. Can BML maintain its profit margin at 3 per cent? The 5-year average is 2.7 per cent. The margin has been as low as 1.8 per cent in 2003. One could also doubt the assumption of asset ratio of 75 per cent. Except in the most recent year (2004), net assets to sales ratio has varied from 82 per cent to 87 per cent. If BML cannot improve its profitability and assets utilisation, should it continue paying dividend? If it cuts or discontinues payment of dividend, what will be the reaction of shareholders?

The financial manager of BML can answer these and similar questions, if he/she performs a sensitivity analysis to examine the effect of changing assumptions on the firm's funds requirement. He/she can vary one variable at a time, and see its effect. For example, the effect of the following possibilities may be analysed: (*a*) sales growth 12 per cent, (*b*) profit margin 2.5 per cent and (*c*) net assets to sales ratio 82 per cent (net fixed assets to sales 41 per cent and net current assets to sales 41 per cent.) The financial manager can as well think of possible scenarios where the effect of combinations of variables may be analysed. For example, two possible scenarios could be (*i*) sale growth 15%, profit margin 2.5 per cent, and assets ratio 82 per cent, and (*ii*) sales growth 12 per cent, profit margin 2.5 per cent and assets ratio 82 per cent. Table 26.12 shows the results of changes in individual variables and possible scenarios.

**Table 26.12: Bharat Machinery Limited:
Financial Forecasts: Sensitivity Analysis**

(Rs in crore)

				Scenarios	
	Growth 12%	Margin 2.5%	Asset ratio 82%	Growth 15% Margin 2.5% Asset ratio 82%	Growth 15% Margin 2.5% Asset ratio 82%
NFA	73.6	97.3	102.1	102.1	77.8
NCA	63.7	84.5	113.2	113.2	88.9
Total	137.3	181.8	215.3	215.3	166.7
RE	36.9	26.2	35.4	26.2	22.4
Funds needed	106.4	155.6	179.9	189.1	144.3
Total	143.3	181.8	215.3	215.3	166.7

It may be observed from Table 26.12 that BML's funds requirement is quite sensitive to sales growth and assets utilisation. The burden of raising external funds is maximum when the company grows at 15 per cent, margin is 2.5% and asset ratio is 82%. If BML is not in a position to raise large amounts of external funds, it may have to slow down its growth and considerably improve the efficiency of assets utilisation. The company may also have to reconsider its decision of paying 10 per cent dividend. Financial *planning* starts where financial *forecasting* ends. Forecasting provides a basis for planning; it is not planning.

Steps in Financial Planning

We emphasise again that financial forecasting is the basis for financial planning. Forecasts are merely estimates based on the past data. Historical performance may not occur in the future. Planning means what a company would like to happen in the future, and includes necessary action plans for realising the predetermined intensions. After analysing the historical performance of BML, the management can ask the following questions: (1) Should BML remain satisfied with a 3 per cent profit margin? (2) How can it reduce its costs? (3) How can the company reduce its inventory holding and collect period? (4)

What are the steps necessary to improve the efficiency in the use of fixed assets? (5) How much dividend should BML pay? (6) How much should it borrow? (7) What is the prudent debt-equity mix for the company? (8) Should it raise funds by using equity capital? (9) If funds are not available, should the company slow down its growth? (10) What would be the implications of the slowing down of growth? Financial planning helps to answer these and many other questions.

The following steps are involved in financial planning:

- *Past performance* Analysis of the firm's past performance to ascertain the relationships between financial variables, and the firm's financial strengths and weaknesses.
- *Operating characteristics* Analysis of the firm's operating characteristics—product, market, competition, production and marketing policies, control systems, operating risk etc. to decide about its growth objective.
- *Corporate strategy and investment needs* Determining the firm's investment needs and choices, given its growth objective and overall strategy.
- *Cash flow from operations* Forecasting the firm's revenues and expenses and need for funds based on its investment and dividend policies.
- *Financing alternatives* Analysing financial alternatives within its financial policy and deciding the appropriate means of raising funds.
- *Consequences of financial plans* Analysing the consequences of its financial plans for the long-term health and survival to firm.
- *Consistency* Evaluating the consistency of financial policies with each other and with the corporate strategy.

Financial planning involves the questions of a firm's long-term growth and profitability and investment and financing decisions. It focuses on aggregative capital expenditure programmes and debt-equity mix rather than the individual projects and sources of finance. Financial planning also involves an interface between the corporate policy and financial planning and the trade off between financial policy variables.

PLANNING FOR SUSTAINABLE GROWTH

Strategic financial planning stresses a balanced relationship between financial goals. It asks the question: What growth rate is sustainable given a company's established financial policies? Financial planning model involves considerations of growth, investment and financing. A simple way of ascertaining the growth potential of a company, given its current financial conditions, is to examine the interaction between four financial policy goals expressed as ratios:

- target sales growth
- target return on investment (net assets)
- target dividend payout and
- target debt-equity (capital structure)

Thus, there are **demand-related financial goals** – driven by the company's strategic goal of sales growth (requiring funds for investment in fixed and current assets) and **supply–related**

financial goals – driven by the company's desire to earn superior return, pay dividends to shareholders and enhance funds by incurring debt supported by its internal funds.[1]

Growth Potential of a Single-product Company

A simple way of ascertaining the growth potential of a company is to model the interaction between four financial goals expressed as ratios—two operating ratios: net assets to sales (NA/S) and net margin, i.e., net profit to sales (PAT/S) and two financial policy ratios: retention ratio, i.e., retained profits/PAT and leverage or debt-equity ratio, i.e., D/E. **Sustainable growth** may be defined as the annual percentage growth in sales that is consistent with the firm's financial policies (assuming no issue of fresh equity).[2] The following model can be used to determine the sustainable growth (g_s) in sales:

Sustainable growth

$$= \frac{\text{Net margin} \times \text{retention} \times \text{leverage}}{\text{Assets-to-sales} - (\text{net margin} \times \text{retention} \times \text{leverage})}$$

$$g_s = \frac{\text{PAT/S} \times \text{RE/PAT} \times (1 + \text{D/E})}{\text{NA/S} - [\text{PAT/S} \times \text{RE/PAT} \times (1 + (\text{D/E}))]}$$

$$g_s = \frac{p \times b \times l}{a - (p \times b \times l)} \qquad (1)$$

where p = net margin = PAT/sales, b = retention ratio = retained earnings (RE)/net profit (PAT) or one minus payout ratio, i.e., (1– payout), l = leverage = net assets (or capital employed) to equity (net worth) = (1 + D/E), and a = asset-sales ratio = net assets sales.

The net assets to sales ratio determines the requirement of funds for investing in assets to support a given level of sales. The requirement for funds would increase with expanding sales. The net profit minus the dividends is an internal source of funds. Thus, the product of net profit to sales ratio and retained profit to net profit (net margin × retention ratio) gives an idea of the funds available internally to support the growth of the firm. Retained earnings increase the debt raising capacity of the firm. Thus, given the target capital structure, the total funds would be equal to retained earnings plus debt supported by the retained earnings [*viz. pb (1 + l)*]. Net assets or capital employed (*viz.* debt plus equity) to equity is a leverage measure, and is equal to one plus debt-equity ratio.

Illustration 26.1: Sustainable Growth Calculations

Consider the financial data of East & West Hotel for the current year given in Table 26.13 to understand the concept of substantial growth as shown in Equation (1).

Applying Equation (1), the sustainable growth for East & West Hotel is:

$$g_s = \frac{21.04/80.85 \times 13.90/21.04 \times 154.13/142.17}{154.13/80.85 - [21.04/80.85 \times 13.90/21.04 \times 154.13/142.17]}$$

$$= \frac{0.2602 \times 0.6606 \times 1.0841}{1.9064 - [0.2602 \times 0.6606 \times 1.0841]}$$

$$= \frac{0.1863}{1.9064 - 0.1863} = 0.108 \text{ or } 10.8\%$$

Table 26.13: East & West Financial Data

Financial Data	*(Rs in crore)*
Revenues	80.85
PBIT	27.84
Net profit	21.04
Net assets	154.13
Net worth	142.17
Debt	11.96
Dividends	7.14
Retained earnings	13.90
Ratios	
Net profit to revenues	0.2602
PBIT to Net assets	0.1806
Retained earnings to net profit	0.6606
(1 + D/E) or net assets to net worth	1.0841
Net assets to revenues	1.9064

Thus, if East & West maintains its operating efficiency (*viz.*, net profit margin, 26.0%) at the current year level and given its retention policy (retention ratio, 66.1%) and debt-equity policy (debt-equity ratio, 0.08:1), it can grow only at 10.8% without raising external equity.

East & West has achieved only 10.8 per cent growth rate in spite of a high net margin of 26.0 per cent, before-tax RONA of 18 per cent and ROE of 15 per cent because it has hardly used any debt; its D/E ratio is 0.08:1. Assume that East & West wants to grow at 15 per cent in the future but without changing its retention and debt-equity ratios. How much should be its profit margin to obtain a 15 per cent growth? It is calculated as follows:

$$0.15 = \frac{p \times 0.66 \times 1.08}{1.91 - [p \times 0.66 \times 1.08]}$$

$$0.15 = \frac{0.713p}{1.91 - 0.713p}$$

$$0.82p = 0.2865$$

$$p = 0.2865/0.82 = 0.349 \text{ or say, } 35\%$$

East & West's margin (net profit to sales) will have to jump to 35 per cent to obtain a growth rate of 15 per cent. Alternatively, it can change its financial policy; for example, it can increase the use of debt to achieve 15 per cent growth without affecting any change in the profit margin:

$$0.15 = \frac{0.262 \times 0.66 \times l}{1.91 - [0.262 \times 0.66 \times l]}$$

$$l = 1.45$$

The debt-equity ratio will have to increase to 0.45:1. The company can think other possible trade-offs between its financial goals to achieve its desired growth rate.

In the above analysis, we assume that the relation between assets and sales is constant, i.e., inflation does not exist. The sustainable growth model as given by Equation (1) can be modified to incorporate impact of inflation and other factors.[3] It

---

1. *Ibid.*
2. Boston Consulting Group Staff, *Perspectives on Experiences*, Boston Consulting Group, 1968.
3. See R.C. Higgins, Sustainable Growth Under Inflation, *Financial Management*, Autumn 1981, pp. 36–40, and D.A. Johnson, The Behaviour of Financial Structure and Sustainable Growth in an Inflationary Environment, Financial Management, Autumn, 1981, pp. 30–35.

can be easily seen that the company can affect a change in the sustainable growth rate if it changes its retention policy or debt policy or both. A cost reduction strategy resulting into higher net profits would also lead to higher growth.

Sustainable Growth Model for a Multi-product Company

The sustainable growth approach as expressed in Equation (1) is generally applicable to a single-product or single division company. A more general method of determining the sustainable growth rate in the case of multi-product or multi-division company is to calculate the sustainable growth rate at the corporate level in terms of growth in assets.[1]

A firm sets its growth objective in terms of sales growth rate. Sales growth demands funds for investment in assets. If the firm does not want to raise external equity, the funds will be supplied from internal generation and debt supported by internal funds. Thus the assets of the firm will grow by an amount equal to retained earnings plus retained earning multiplied by debt-equity ratio. The assets growth rate can be calculated by dividing this amount by the current amount of net assets:

$$\text{Growth} = \frac{\text{Retained earnings}}{\text{Net assets}}(1 + \text{Debt/equity ratio})$$

$$g_s = \frac{\text{RE}}{\text{NA}}(1 + D/E) \qquad (2)$$

Assuming that the assets turnover remains constant, sales will also grow at the same rate as assets. Thus, the firm's growth is critically based on its ability and willingness to retain profits. How much profits the firm would be able to retain depends on its operating efficiency, financial leverage and dividend policy. Operating efficiency, reflected by PBIT to net assets ratio, is the product of assets productivity in generating sales (sales to net assets ratio) and profit margin (PBIT to sales ratio):

$$\text{RONA} = \text{Asset} \times \text{Profit margin}$$

$$\frac{\text{PBIT}}{\text{NA}} = \frac{S}{\text{NA}} \times \frac{\text{PBIT}}{S} \qquad (3)$$

Profits so generated are constrained by payment of interest and taxes and dividends. Thus, the retained earnings available to support growth are given by the product of RONA, leverage factor (as reflected by PAT/PBIT ratio) and retention ratio:

$$\frac{\text{RE}}{\text{NA}} = \frac{\text{PBIT}}{\text{NA}} \times \frac{\text{PAT}}{\text{PBIT}} \times \frac{\text{RE}}{\text{PAT}} \qquad (4)$$

The growth can be enhanced by additional borrowing equal to the target debt-equity ratio times the retained earnings. Thus the growth that a firm can sustain, given its financial goals and policies, can be found out as follows:

$$\text{Sustainable Growth} = \text{Assets turnover} \times \text{Profit margin}$$
$$\times \text{Leverage factor}$$
$$\times \text{Retention ratio} (1 + D/E)$$

$$g_s = \frac{S}{\text{NA}} \times \frac{\text{PBIT}}{S} \times \frac{\text{PAT}}{\text{PBIT}} \times \frac{\text{RE}}{\text{PAT}}(1 + D/E) \qquad (5)$$

Notice that Equation (5) includes all elements of a firm's financial goals system. It is composed of:

- The firm's return on net assets (a product of assets turnover and profit margin).
- The firm's degree of financial and tax leverage (reflected by PAT/PBIT and debt-equity ratio).
- The firm's retention ratio (the reverse of the dividend payout).

The elements of the financial goals system, as reflected in Equation (5), are **financial policy targets**. Given these targets and without resorting to the external equity financing, a firm can determine the growth rate that it can sustain.

Equation (5) can be presented differently by rearranging its terms. Note that net assets equal debt and equity (net worth), NA $= D + E$. Therefore, NA/E $= (D + E)/E$. Thus,

$$g_s = \frac{\text{PBIT}}{\text{NA}} \times \frac{\text{PAT}}{\text{PBIT}} \times \frac{\text{NA}}{E} \times \frac{\text{RE}}{\text{PAT}}$$

$$= \frac{\text{PAT}}{E} \times \frac{\text{RE}}{\text{PAT}} = \text{ROE} \times \text{Retention ratio} \qquad (6)$$

Thus, growth can also be defined as the product of retention ratio and return on equity. We can also use the following alternative formula for calculating the sustainable growth rate (see Exhibit 26.1):

$$g_s = b[(r + (r - i)D/E](1 - T) \qquad (7)$$

where b is retention ratio, RE/PAT, r is RONA (before-tax), i is the interest rate, D/E is debt-equity ratio and T is the corporate tax rate.

EXHIBIT 26.1: SUSTAINABLE GROWTH EQUATION

Let us assume that net assets equal debt plus equity (net worth), NA $= D + E$, r is the (before-tax) return on net assets, PBIT/NA, i is the interest rate on debt, b is the retention ratio, i.e., RE/PAT and T is the corporate tax rate. ROE can be calculated as follows:

$$\text{ROE} = \frac{\text{PAT}}{E} = \left[\frac{r\text{NA} - i\text{D}}{E}\right](1 - T) = \left[\frac{r(D + E) - i\text{D}}{E}\right](1 - T)$$

$$= \left[\frac{r\text{D} + r\text{E} - i\text{D}}{E}\right](1 - T) = [r + (r - i)D/E](1 - T)$$

Notice that in the absence of debt (D = 0), ROE is equal to the after-tax return on net assets. ROE $= r (1 - T)$. Thus $[(r - i) D/E] (1 - T)$ is the leverage gain to the equity-holders. The product of ROE and retention ratio gives the sustainable growth rate ($g_s = \text{ROE} \times b$). Thus,

$$g_s = b[r + (r - i)D/E](1 - T)$$

Illustration 26.2:

Greaves Limited was started in 1922 as a trading company. In 1992, Greaves branched out to manufacturing and now it is a well diversified manufacturing company. Table 26.12 gives the summary of the financial data for the company for 5-year period immediately after the diversification.

---

1. P. Varadarajan, The Sustainable Growth Model: A Tool for Evaluating the Financial Feasibility of Market Share Strategies, *Strategic Management Journal*, 1983, pp. 353–367.

Table 26.14: Greaves Limited's Financial Data

(Rs in crore)

	Year 1	Year 2	Year 3	Year 4	Year 5	Average
Sales (S)	311.14	354.25	521.56	728.15	801.11	543.24
PBIT	34.51	39.64	42.98	65.67	82.64	53.09
Interest (INT)	19.62	17.17	21.48	28.25	27.54	22.81
Tax (T)	0.00	4.00	7.00	8.60	15.80	7.08
PAT	14.89	8.47	14.50	28.82	39.30	23.20
Dividend (DIV)	4.06	7.29	8.58	12.85	14.18	9.39
Ratained earnings (RE)	10.83	11.18	5.92	15.97	25.12	13.80
Net worth (NW)	119.39	200.60	206.52	219.81	243.19	197.90
Debt (D)	84.61	130.82	158.73	183.94	203.66	152.3
Net asset (NA)	204.00	331.42	365.25	403.75	446.85	350.25
Interest rate (i)	0.232	0.131	0.135	0.154	0.135	0.16
Tax rate (T)	0.000	0.178	0.320	0.230	0.287	0.200

Table 26.14 provides the computations of Greaves' financial policy variable and its growth performance. The company has generally performed well during 5-years period. The company's (before-tax) RONA and ROE have been generally increasing over the years and are 18.5 per cent and 16.2 per cent, respectively, in the last year. Greaves' debt-equity ratio has shown some increase in the recent years. The company's retention ratio has been high, except for the third year. It has been able to sustain an average growth of 7 per cent during past five years. Yearly growth rates have shown significant variation. For example, it was lowest 2.9 per cent in the third year and highest 10.3 per cent in fifth year.

Table 26.15: Greaves' Financial Performance and Growth

	Year 1	Year 2	Year 3	Year 4	Year 5	Average
Asset turnover: S/NA	1.530	1.070	1.430	1.800	1.790	1.520
Margin: PBIT/S	0.111	0.112	0.082	0.090	0.103	0.100
RONA: PBIT/NA	0.169	0.120	0.118	0.163	0.185	0.150
Leverage factor:						
PAT/PBIT	0.431	0.466	0.337	0.439	0.476	0.043
Debt ratio: NA/NW	1.710	1.650	1.770	1.840	1.840	1.760
ROE: PAT/NW	0.125	0.092	0.070	0.131	0.162	0.120
Retention: RE/PAT	0.727	0.605	0.408	0.554	0.639	0.590
Sustainable Growth:						
RE/NW	0.091	0.056	0.029	0.073	0.103	0.070

It is evident that Greaves was able to achieve a growth rate of 10.3 per cent in fifth year, given its financial policies (D/E of 0.84:1 and retention 64 per cent) and effective tax rate of 28.5 per cent. Equation (7) can also be used to calculate Greaves' growth rate:

$$g = b\,[\{r + (r - i)\mathrm{D/E}\}(1 - T)]$$
$$g = 0.639\,[\{0.185 + (0.185 - 0.135)0.84\}(1 - 0.285)]$$
$$g = 0.639\,[0.1322 + 0.030] = 0.103 \text{ or } 10.3\%$$

Can Greaves sustain a higher growth rate, say, 15 per cent? Let us assume that Greaves in the future would like to continue with its current financial policies; that is, it will retain about two-thirds (65 per cent) of its profits and maintain a debt equity-ratio of 0.85:1. Further, the company's marginal tax rate will be 35 per cent, and it could borrow funds at 15 per cent rate of interest. Given its financial policy and desire to grow at 15 per cent, Greaves' RONA is calculated as follows:

$$g = b\,[\{r + (r - i)\mathrm{D/E}\}(1 - T)]$$
$$0.15 = 0.65\,[\{r + (r - 0.15)0.85\}(1 - 0.35)]$$
$$0.15 = 0.65\,[0.65r + 0.5525r - 0.0829]$$
$$0.15 = 0.7816r - 0.0539$$
$$r = 0.2039/\,0.7816 = 0.261 = 26.1\%$$

Greaves' RONA will have to substantially increase to 26.1 per cent before-tax or 17 per cent after-tax. Table 34.4 gives before-tax and after-tax RONA to be earned for achieving a desired growth rate, given the company's financial policies. The growth-return relationship is also shown in Figure 26.2.

Greaves' given financial goals systems will be self-sustaining only if its growth and after-tax RONA targets are represented by a single point on the diagonal in Fig. 26.2. If Greaves did not have any debt and retained entire profits, it could grow at a rate equal to after-tax RONA. In such situation, the graph is divided equally by the diagonal having a 45° slope. The area to the left of the diagonal represents a deficit, as the company is unable to meet funds requirement, within its policy constraints, to support high growth rate. Similarly, the area to the right of the diagonal depicts a surplus since the company has more funds available than warranted by its growth rate. The utility of such graph lies in top management communicating the meaning and discipline of an integrated set of financial goals to subordinates and to track performance against goals. The graph shows the impact of the trade-offs constantly necessitated by competing goals and objectives.[1]

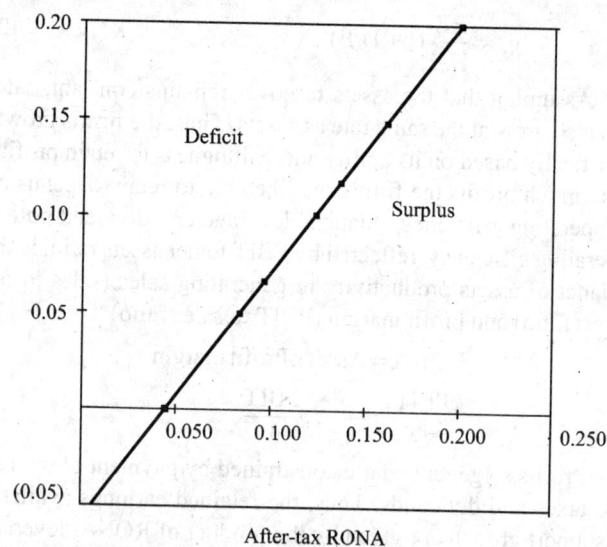

Figure 26.2: Sustainable growth given Greaves' financial policy

Table 26.16: RONA and Sustainable Growth: Greaves' Financial Policies

Growth Rate (g)	Before-tax RONA (r)	After-tax RONA [(1 – T) r]
(0.05)	0.005	0.003
0.00	0.069	0.045
0.05	0.133	0.086
0.07	0.158	0.103
0.10	0.197	0.128
0.12	0.222	0.145
0.15	0.261	0.170
0.20	0.325	0.211

---

1. Donaldson, *op. cit.*

The highest RONA for Greaves in the last five year is 18.5 per cent in Year 5. Assuming that it cannot earn a RONA of more than 18.5 per cent and it still wants to grow at 15 per cent. The company does not see much scope for changing its dividend policy. Under the circumstances, the company can achieve its growth if it changes its debt policy. The company's debt-equity ratio will have to be 4.86:1 as shown below:

$$g = b\,[\{r + (r - i)\,D/E\}(1 - T)]$$
$$0.15 = 0.65\,[\{0.185 + (0.185 - 0.15)\,D/E\}\,(1 - 0.35)]$$
$$0.15 = 0.65\,[0.12025 + 0.2275\,D/E]$$
$$0.15 = 0.078163 + 0.014788\,D/E$$
$$D/E = 0.071837/\,0.014788 = 4.86$$

A more aggressive debt-equity goals combined with a lower dividend payout would raise the growth potential for any given rate of return (RONA) higher than the cost of debt. Thus, the factors governing the maximum, sustainable long-term sales growth rate are mainly financial in character. The sustainable growth model indicates the sales growth that can be supported by, and is consistent with, the firm's financial policies. The firm will have to revise its financial policies or resort to external equity if it intends to achieve a growth rate higher than the maximum sustainable growth. The firm, on the other hand, can consider the alternatives of increasing payout, or reducing debt, or building up liquid assets when its achievable growth rate is lower.

SUMMARY

❖ Financial planning of a company has close links with strategic planning. The company's strategy establishes an effective and efficient match between its resources, opportunities and risks. It provides a mechanism of integrating goals of multiple stakeholders. Financial plan should be developed within the overall context of the strategic planning.

❖ Financial forecasting is an integral part of financial planning. Forecasting uses past data to estimate the future financial requirements. A simple approach to financial forecasting is to relate the items of profit and loss account and balance sheet to sales. Financial planning is more than forecasting. It is a process of identifying a firm's investments and financing needs, given its growth objectives. It involves trade-off between various investment and financing options. A financial plan may be prepared for a period of three or five years.

❖ Financial modelling facilitates financial forecasting. It makes forecasting easy. A financial model has three components: input – current financial statement and growth forecasts; model – a system of equations based on the relations between financial variables; output – projected financial statements.

❖ Financial models a large company can be very complicated when more details are considered. In practice, companies focus on the most crucial decisions and variables and keep the model simple.

❖ Sometimes companies will like to achieve growth that their current financial policies could sustain. Sustainable growth is the annual percentage growth in sales that is consistent with the firm's financial policies (assuming no issue of fresh equity).

KEY CONCEPTS

BCG Matrix	Financial modelling	PIMS	Strategic planning
Experience curve	Financial plan	Sensitivity analysis	Strategy
Financial forecasting	Financial planning	Separation theorem	Sustainable growth

REVIEW QUESTIONS

1. What is a financing planning? How does it differ from financial forecasting?

2. Explain the steps involved in preparing a financial plan. What are the merits of financial planning?

3. Is there a relationship between strategic planning and financial planning? Explain.

4. What is a financial model? Illustrate the development of a simple financial model. What are the advantages and limitations of a financial model?

5. What is meant by sustainable growth? Explain sustainable growth models with illustrations.

PROBLEMS

1. Table 26.17 gives a summary of Bajaj's financial items during the years from 1997 to 2001.

Table 26.17: Bajaj Auto Limited: Summary of Financial Items

(Rs in crore)

	2001	2000	1999	1998	1997
Net Sales	3023.12	3089.33	2961.98	2643.22	2638.47
PBDIT	473.88	973.4	895.57	840.94	802.23
Depreciation	177.29	145.31	132.7	143.62	117.87
Interest	7.39	3.17	4.67	8.47	7.41
Other Income	365.99	510.4	380.29	355.57	296.89
PBT	289.2	824.92	758.2	688.85	676.95
Tax Provision	26.64	211.19	217.68	224.7	236.38
Net Profit	262.56	613.73	540.52	464.15	440.57
Equity Dividend	80.95	119.39	95.51	95.51	79.59
Retained Profit	181.61	494.34	445.01	368.64	360.98
Current Assets	2061.62	2373.37	2197.01	1809.38	1363.55
Net Fixed Assets	1362.35	1114.25	921.81	682.91	603.95
Current Liabilities	1474.34	1740.67	1527.18	1259.83	988.27
Secured Loans	55.97	101.58	41.08	27.54	22.04

Contd...

	2001	2000	1999	1998	1997
Unsecured Loans	457.74	394.09	308.61	230.67	191.83
Total Liabilities	4624.58	5440.42	4578.61	3636.26	2962.84
Net Worth	2636.53	3204.08	2701.74	2118.22	1760.7
Bonus Ratio	–	–	–	–	1.02
EPS	25.13	50.31	44.39	38.08	54.35
DPS	8.00	10.00	8.00	8.00	10.00
Book Value Per Share	260.58	268.37	226.3	177.42	221.22
Market Value Per Share*	257.70	384.00	615.80	594.30	601.70

* Closing price in March.

Based on the company's past performance and appropriate assumptions that you may like to make, develop a financial forecast for five years. Show the impact if your assumptions go wrong.

2. Tables 26.18 and 26.19 contain Reliance Industries Limited's profit and loss account and balance sheet for seven years. You are required to identify the trends in Reliance's financial performance and policies. Using this information, prepare a financial plan for Reliance. Discuss the implications of your plan.

Table 26.18: Reliance Industrie Ltd.
Summarised Profit & Loss Account during the Year Ending at 31 March

(Rs in crore)

	2001	2000	1999	1998	1997	1996	1995
EARNINGS							
Sales	23,024.17	15,847.16	10,624.15	9,719.18	6,441.65	5,726.66	5,388.15
Less: Excise	2,578.91	2,451.53	1,929.46	1,893.13	1,283.85	1,507.83	1,517.13
Net Sales	20,445.26	13,395.63	8,694.69	7,826.05	5,157.80	4,218.83	3,871.02
Other Income	976.79	976.56	629.19	363.09	318.78	271.85	312.59
Total Income	21,422.05	14,372.19	9,323.88	8,189.14	5,476.58	4,490.68	4,183.61
PBDIT	5,561.72	4,746.61	3,317.54	2,886.54	1,947.81	1,751.91	1,622.60
Depreciation	1,565.11	1,278.36	855.04	667.32	410.14	336.51	278.24
PBIT	3,996.61	3,468.25	2,462.50	2,219.22	1,537.67	1,415.40	1,344.36
Interest	1,215.99	1,008.00	728.81	503.55	169.97	110.13	279.51
PBT	2,780.62	2,460.25	1,733.69	1,715.67	1,367.70	1,305.27	1,064.85
Tax	135.00	57.00	30.00	63.00	45.00	0.00	0.00
PAT	2,645.62	2,403.25	1,703.69	1,652.67	1,322.70	1,305.27	1,064.85
Additional Information							
Equity Dividend	447.85	384.65	350.16	326.81	299.24	276.22	199.34
Preference Dividend	4.77	35.57	23.39	10.33	0.00	28.00	0.83
Corporate Dividend Tax	46.20	46.22	40.86	63.64	0.00	0.00	0.00
EPS (Rs)	24.63	22.04	17.56	16.94	28.85	27.87	23.34
Book Value (Rs)	113.86	103.65	100.12	96.83	184.77	179.07	157.66

Table 26.19: Reliance Industries Ltd: Balance Sheet as at 31 March

(Rs in crore)

	2001	2000	1999	1998	1997	1996	1995
CAPITAL & LIABILITIES							
Total Shareholders Funds							
Equity Share Capital	1,053.49	1,053.45	933.39	931.90	458.45	458.23	455.86
Preference Capital Paid Up	0.00	292.95	252.95	187.95	0.00	200.00	5.50
Reserves & Surplus	13,711.88	12,636.35	11,183.00	10,862.75	8,012.49	7,747.07	6,731.29
	14,765.37	13,982.75	12,369.34	11,982.60	8,470.94	8,405.30	7,192.65
Borrowings							
Term Loans – Institutions	68.66	158.51	46.24	57.41	859.70	411.95	284.79
Term Loans – Banks	0.00	1,400.94	1,527.00	200.53	950.48	607.19	160.27
Non-Convertible Debentures	3,761.98	3,779.85	3,578.04	2,413.54	2,012.98	1,780.95	1,273.04
Working Capital Advances	237.76	648.81	327.03	65.98	425.92	591.88	405.63
Other Loans	6,067.39	5,532.13	5,206.98	5,509.87	3,376.40	1,329.48	816.19
Total Borrowings	10,135.79	11,520.24	10,685.29	8,247.33	7,625.48	4,721.45	2,939.92
Current Liabilities & Provisions							
Creditors	3,859.22	2,953.96	3,338.73	3,095.04	2,386.23	1,305.32	1,118.23
Provisions	863.50	265.80	544.37	475.99	352.23	282.02	201.57
Other	251.58	646.07	1,218.27	586.97	701.26	324.29	76.67
Total Current Liabilities	4,974.30	3,865.83	5,101.37	4,158.00	3,439.72	1,911.63	1,396.47
Total Liabilities	29,875.46	29,368.82	28,156.00	24,387.93	19,536.14	15,038.38	11,529.04
ASSETS							
Fixed assets							
Gross Block	25,355.99	24,330.95	18,650.33	17,848.33	10,955.92	6,885.50	5,315.40
Less: Accum. Depreciation	11,841.53	9,214.06	6,691.93	4,944.47	3,491.20	2,141.34	1,805.78
Net Block	13,514.46	15,116.89	11,958.40	12,903.86	7,464.72	4,744.16	3,509.62
Capital Work in Progress	512.38	331.42	3,437.83	2,069.43	3,708.63	4,488.71	3,075.09
Total Fixed assets	14,026.84	15,448.31	15,396.23	14,973.29	11,173.35	9,232.87	6,584.71
Investments	6,726.11	6,066.56	4,294.59	4,282.33	4,455.68	1,952.91	1,993.41
Current Assets	9,122.51	7,853.95	8,465.18	5,132.31	3,907.11	3,852.60	2,950.92
Total Assets	29,875.46	29,368.82	28,156.00	24,387.93	19,536.14	15,038.38	11,529.04

3. Tables 26.20 and 26.21 give balance sheet and profit and loss account of Mason Industries Limited. What is the sustainable growth rate for the company?

Table 26.20: Mason Industries Limited Balance Sheet, 31 December 2004

	Rs ' 000		Rs ' 000
Creditors	6,725	Cash	4,035
Borrowings	40,350	Debtors	9,415
Share capital	40,000	Inventory	20,175
Reserve & surplus	27,250	Gross block	107,700
		Less: Accumulated depreciation	27,000
	114,325		114,325

Table 26.21: Mason Industries Limited: Profit & Loss Account, 31 December 2003

Sales	40,935
Less: Cost of sales	10,916
Gross profit	30,019
Less: Selling & admin. Expenses	15,010
Profit before interest and tax	15,010
Less: Interest (at 12%)	4,776
Profit before tax	10,234

4. Fine Toys Limited has a capital structure comprising 45 per cent debt and 55 per cent equity at book values. The company's payout ratio is 60 per cent. Management wants a growth rate of 20 per cent per annum in the future. Is this rate sustainable? After-tax interest rate is 5 per cent.

CASES

Case 26.1: Express Foods Limited

Express Foods Limited (EFL) was incorporated in 1958. It is the largest food processing company in India with a sales turnover of Rs 428 crore in 2003. The company is a market leader in bakery products with over 30 well-known brands of biscuits, bread and cakes. In the recent years, the company has been on the forefront of exports; its exports have totalled over Rs 200 crore during the last three years. For its excellent exports performance, the government of India has awarded a Star Trading House status to the company.

Table 26.1.1: Express Foods Limited

Five-year Summary of Financial Data *(Rs in lakh)*

	1999	2000	2001	2002	2003
Net fixed assets	214.6	329.0	374.5	403.6	355.4
Investments	47.6	0.5	0.5	1.3	103.2
Net current assets	242.1	264.4	374.5	570.9	450.0
Net assets	504.3	593.9	749.5	975.8	908.6
Equity Capital	123.8	123.9	185.7	185.7	185.7
Reserves	230.1	211.1	272.6	319.3	367.6
Loan funds	150.4	258.9	291.2	470.8	355.3
Capital employed	504.3	593.9	749.5	975.8	908.6
Sales	1921.5	2666.1	3142.8	3606.2	4278.5
Depreciation	16.9	18.5	23.4	26.9	23.3
PBT	96.0	135.6	150.2	165.0	195.8
Tax	33.6	47.5	52.6	64.5	88.0
PAT	62.4	88.1	95.6	100.5	107.8
Dividends	31.4	39.1	44.6	53.8	59.4

The company is in the process of diversifying its export operations in computer software, biscuits and other value-added products. EFL has entered into partnership with the BSN group (the European giant with over 100 world famous food brands). The company is investing in the equity capital of Britco Foods Company, a joint venture with JMRPCO Ltd. of Hong Kong to manufacture beverage bases and essence of Coca-Cola, Fanta and Sprint and to export processed snack foods. Table 26.1.1 gives the summary of important financial data for five years, and Tables 26.1.2 and 26.1.3 give profit and loss statements and balance sheets for the years 2002 and 2004.

During the year 2004, the company's bakery division performed satisfactorily in spite of high inflation, high raw material costs and increased competition. Biscuit sales recorded a growth of 7.7 per cent and bread sales 5.7 per cent. The company launched two special breads that were well received in the market. Export sales of Rs 75 crore registered a growth rate of 30 per cent over the previous year. The company also continued its R&D efforts to make significant contributions in the areas of new products and packaging development.

Table 26.1.2: Express Foods Ltd.

Profit and Loss Statement
year ending 31 March *(Rs in lakh)*

	2003	2004
Income:		
Sales	3606.2	4278.5
Other income	74.0	65.3
Total	3680.2	4343.8
Expenditure:		
Raw material	1944.6	2351.1
Excise duty	113.0	142.5
Salaries and Wages	256.8	294.8
Depreciation	26.9	23.3
R&D expenses	144.8	170.6
Other expenses	1029.8	1165.7
Total	3515.2	4148.0
PBT	165.0	195.8
Tax	64.5	88.0
PAT	100.5	107.8

Table 26.1.3: Express Foods Ltd.

Balance Sheet
as on 31 March 1993 *(Rs in lakh)*

	2003	2004
Sources of Funds:		
Share capital	185.7	185.7
Reserves	319.3	367.6
	505.0	553.3
Loan funds (secured)	407.8	355.3
Total	975.8	908.6
Application of Funds:		
Gross Block	557.2	460.8
Less: Depreciation	181.4	153.5
Net block	375.7	307.3
Capital work-in-progress	27.8	48.1
Net fixed assets	403.5	355.4
Investments	1.3	103.3
Current assets:		
Inventories	476.7	427.4
Debtors	264.7	113.8
Cash	9.6	6.2
Loans and advances	273.3	377.8
Total	1024.4	925.2
Less: Current liabilities	453.6	475.2
Net current assets	570.8	450.0
Total	975.8	908.6

Discussion Questions

1. Evaluate the performance of Express Foods Limited.
2. Prepare a five-year financial plan for the company. Explain the logic of your assumptions.

Case 26.2: State Bank of India[1]

State Bank of India (SBI) is the largest bank in India. It has the most widespread branch network and the largest deposits. It controls about one-third of foreign exchange business and a high proportion of the government business. The deposits of the bank consist of 25 per cent saving, 15 per cent current and 60 per cent time deposits. It has a focus on retail banking. In order to improve its performance, the bank has adopted two-prong strategy of focusing on technology and cost reduction. SBI has invested Rs 500 crore in technology. It has planned 1000 ATMs, of which more than half are already operational. It has introduced corporate Internet banking in some branches. It has diversified into credit cards and insurance and therefore, expects increase in its fee-based income. SBI in collaboration with GE Capital has issued 9 lakh credit cards. The bank is facing competition due to the deregulation of the banking industry. It is reported that 'it expects to stabilise its margins with the help of competitive pricing, high resource availability, well-diversified loan book, deposit repricing and CRR cut'.

SBI is making all efforts to improve the quality of its operations. It is noted that 'the credit rating of its loan portfolio is improving and 87% of the portfolio has high credit rating. Its gross non-performing assets (NPAs) to total assets are merely 5 per cent, the lowest in the country. Its net NPAs to total assets is 2.17% against a norm of 2.51% for the banking industry'. Further, 'to leverage its large customer base of high net worth individuals, SBI is opening personal banking branches (PBBs) with 50 regular branches being converted into PBBs. To get into high value housing and car finance, SBI has initiated aggressive pricing and marketing. It hopes to hike the share of personal loans in total advances from 15% now to about 20% in three years'.

Table 26.2.1 State Bank of India: Operating Performance

(Rs in crore)

	2001-02	2000-01
Interest income	29810.09	26138.59
Other income	4174.48	3883.04
Interest expanded	20728.84	17756.02
Operating expenses	7210.90	8298.83
Operating profit	6044.83	3966.78

Contd...

	2001-02	2000-01
Provisions	2010.19	1391.1
Tax	1603.02	971.36
Net profit	2431.62	1604.25
Equity	526.30	526.30
Reserves	15224.38	12935.24
EPS (Rs.)	46.20	30.48
Book Value (Rs.)	299.27	255.78

The *Economic Times* article reports the following as regards SBI's prospects in the next year:

- 'SBI has projected advances growth of more than 16% and growth in non-interest income of more than 20% in the current fiscal. SBI expects margins to remain steady on account of deposits repricing with an endeavour to keep NPAs below 5%, resulting in reduced provisioning and costs-to-income ratio at 53%. Cost saving benefits on account of VRS is expected to begin accruing from this financial year.
- To maintain stability in its income, SBI is targeting net interest spread of 3% and non-interest income at 40% of total income. In the next three-year time frame, SBI aims to bring down expenses to income ratio at 51%. It has embarked on a Rs. 500 crore tech upgradation to serve as backbone for universal banking.
- Return on equity (RoE) is expected to be maintained at over 18%. SBI has witnessed its RoE growing from 11.79% in FY-99 to 16.66% in the last fiscal'.

The article further states: 'In short, SBI has all the trappings of any new private sector banks with its technology initiatives. While just a couple of new private sector banks have attained critical mass, advantages accruing to SBI as a result of cost saving would result in manifold growth in returns. At Rs 240, the scrip comes at a PE of 5.2 to FY02 earnings and much lower than its book value. Greater market attention on banking sector, expected easing of FII holding norms and fundamental growth story would be key drivers of the stock. A 25% return could be expected in the medium term'.

Discussion Questions

1. Critically evaluate SBI's strategy to enhance its income?
2. How has SBI performed during the past two years? Do you agree with the contention that SBI has a bright future? Why or why not?
3. Similar to Table 26.2.1 financial items, prepare a financial plan for SBI for the next year? Make appropriate assumptions. Is it a feasible plan?

---

1. This case draws from the article by Goel, Rajeev, "A Giant Gets Agile", ET Investor's Guide, *The Economic Times*, 24 June 2002, p. 3.

27 Principles of Working Capital Management

CHAPTER OBJECTIVES

- Underline the need for investing in current assets, and elaborate the concept of operating cycle
- Highlight the necessity of managing current assets and current liabilities
- Explain the principles of current asset investment and financing
- Focus on the proper mix of short-term and long-term financing for current assets

INTRODUCTION

So far we have discussed the management of fixed assets and long-term financing. In this part, issues relating to the management of current assets will be discussed. The management of current assets is similar to that of fixed assets in the sense that in both cases a firm analyses their effects on its return and risk. The management of fixed and current assets, however, differs in three important ways: *First,* in managing fixed assets, time is a very important factor; consequently, discounting and compounding techniques play a significant role in capital budgeting and a minor one in the management of current assets. *Second,* the large holding of current assets, especially cash, strengthens the firm's liquidity position (and reduces riskiness), but also reduces the overall profitability. Thus, a risk-return trade off is involved in holding current assets. *Third,* levels of fixed as well as current assets depend upon *expected sales,* but it is only current assets which can be adjusted with sales fluctuations in the short run. Thus, the firm has a greater degree of flexibility in managing current assets.

CONCEPTS OF WORKING CAPITAL

There are two concepts of working capital—gross and net.

- *Gross working capital* refers to the firm's investment in current assets. **Current assets** are the assets which can be converted into cash within an accounting year and include cash, short-term securities, debtors, (accounts receivable or book debts) bills receivable and stock (inventory).

- *Net working capital* refers to the difference between current assets and current liabilities. **Current liabilities** are those claims of outsiders which are expected to mature for payment within an accounting year and include creditors (accounts payable), bills payable, and outstanding expenses. Net working capital can be positive or negative. A positive net working capital will arise when current assets exceed current liabilities. A negative net working capital occurs when current liabilities are in excess of current assets.

The two concepts of working capital—gross and net—are not exclusive; rather, they have equal significance from the management viewpoint.

Focusing on Management of Current Assets

The gross working capital concept focuses attention on two aspects of current assets management: (1) How to optimise investment in current assets? (2) How should current assets be financed?

The consideration of the level of investment in current assets should avoid two danger points—*excessive* or *inadequate* investment in current assets. Investment in current assets should be just adequate to the needs of the business firm. Excessive investment in current assets should be avoided because it impairs the firm's profitability, as idle investment earns nothing. On the other hand, inadequate amount of working capital can threaten solvency of the firm because of its inability to meet its current obligations. It should be realised that the working capital needs of the firm may be fluctuating with changing business activity. This may cause excess or shortage of working capital frequently. The management should be prompt to initiate an action and correct imbalances.

Another aspect of the gross working capital points to the need of arranging funds to finance current assets. Whenever a need for working capital funds arises due to the increasing level of business activity or for any other reason, financing arrangement should be made quickly. Similarly, if suddenly, some surplus funds arise they should not be allowed to remain idle, but should be invested in short-term securities. Thus, the financial manager should have knowledge of the sources of working capital funds as well as investment avenues where idle funds may be temporarily invested.

Focusing on Liquidity Management

Net working capital is a qualitative concept. It indicates the liquidity position of the firm and suggests the extent to which working capital needs may be financed by permanent sources of funds. Current assets should be sufficiently in excess of current liabilities to constitute a margin or buffer for maturing obligations within the ordinary operating cycle of a business. In order to protect their interests, short-term creditors always like a company to maintain current assets at a higher level than current liabilities. It is a conventional rule to maintain the level of current assets twice the level of current liabilities. However, the quality of current assets should be considered in determining the level of current assets *vis-à-vis* current liabilities. A weak liquidity position poses a threat to the solvency of the company and makes it unsafe and unsound. A negative working capital means a negative liquidity, and may prove to be harmful for the company's reputation. Excessive liquidity is also bad. It may be due to mismanagement of current assets. Therefore, prompt and timely action should be taken by management to improve and correct the imbalances in the liquidity position of the firm.

Net working capital concept also covers the question of judicious mix of long-term and short-term funds for financing current assets. For every firm, there is a minimum amount of net working capital which is permanent. Therefore, a portion of the working capital should be financed with the permanent sources of funds such as equity share capital, debentures, long-term debt, preference share capital or retained earnings. Management must, therefore, decide the extent to which current assets should be financed with equity capital and/or borrowed capital.

In summary, it may be emphasised that both gross and net concepts of working capital are equally important for the efficient management of working capital. There is no precise way to determine the exact amount of gross, or net working capital for any firm. The data and problems of each company should be analysed to determine the amount of working capital. There is no specific rule as to how current assets should be financed. It is not feasible in practice to finance current assets by short-term sources only. Keeping in view the constraints of the individual company, a judicious mix of long and short-term finances should be invested in current assets. Since current assets involve cost of funds, they should be put to productive use.

OPERATING AND CASH CONVERSION CYCLE

The need for working capital to run the day-to-day business activities cannot be overemphasised. We will hardly find a business firm which does not require any amount of working capital. Indeed, firms differ in their requirements of the working capital.

We know that a firm should aim at maximising the wealth of its shareholders. In its endeavour to do so, a firm should earn sufficient return from its operations. Earning a steady amount of profit requires successful sales activity. The firm has to invest enough funds in current assets for generating sales. Current assets are needed because sales do not convert into cash instantaneously. There is always an **operating cycle** involved in the conversion of sales into cash.

There is a difference between current and fixed assets in terms of their liquidity. A firm requires many years to recover the initial investment in fixed assets such as plant and machinery or land and buildings. On the contrary, investment in current assets is turned over many times in a year. Investment in current assets such as inventories and debtors (accounts receivable) is realised during the firm's operating cycle that is usually less than a year.[1] What is an operating cycle?

Operating cycle is the time duration required to convert sales, after the conversion of resources into inventories, into cash. The operating cycle of a manufacturing company involves three phases:

- *Acquisition of resources* such as raw material, labour, power and fuel etc.
- *Manufacture of the product* which includes conversion of raw material into work-in-progress into finished goods.
- *Sale of the product* either for cash or on credit. Credit sales create account receivable for collection.

These phases affect cash flows, which most of the time, are neither synchronised nor certain. They are not synchronised because cash outflows usually occur before cash inflows. Cash inflows are not certain because sales and collections which give rise to cash inflows are difficult to forecast accurately. Cash outflows, on the other hand, are relatively certain. The firm is, therefore, required to invest in current assets for a smooth, uninterrupted functioning. It needs to maintain liquidity to purchase raw materials and pay expenses such as wages and salaries, other manufacturing, administrative and selling expenses and taxes as there is hardly a matching between cash inflows and outflows. Cash is also held to meet any future exigencies. Stocks of raw material and work-in-process are kept to ensure smooth production and to guard against non-availability of raw material and other components. The firm

---

1. Moyer, R.C. *et. al., Contemporary Finance Management,* West Publishing Co., 1984, p. 562.

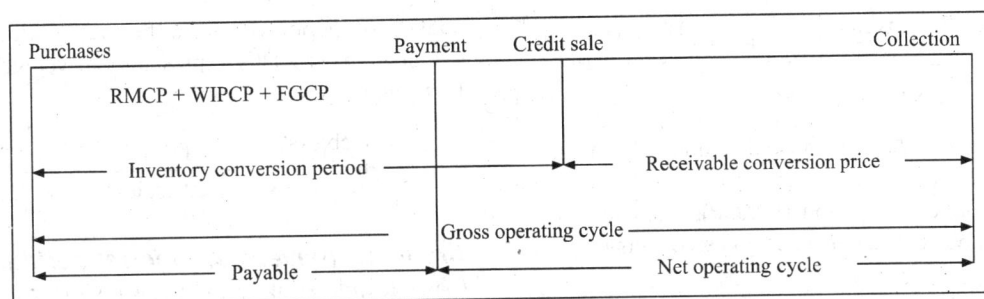

Figure 27.1: Operating cycle of a manufacturing firm

holds stock of finished goods to meet the demands of customers on continuous basis and sudden demand from some customers. Debtors (accounts receivable) are created because goods are sold on credit for marketing and competitive reasons. Thus, a firm makes adequate investment in inventories, and debtors, for smooth, uninterrupted production and sale.

How is the length of operating cycle determined? Figure 27.1 illustrates this.[1] The length of the operating cycle of a manufacturing firm is the sum of: (*i*) **inventory conversion period** (ICP) and (*ii*) **debtors (receivable) conversion period** (DCP). The inventory conversion period is the total time needed for producing and selling the product. Typically, it includes: (*a*) **raw material conversion period** (RMCP), (*b*) **work-in-process conversion period** (WIPCP), and (*c*) **finished goods conversion period** (FGCP). The debtors conversion period is the time required to collect the outstanding amount from the customers. The total of inventory conversion period and debtors conversion period is referred to as **gross operating cycle** (GOC).

In practice, a firm may acquire resources (such as raw materials) on credit and temporarily postpone payment of certain expenses. Payables, which the firm can defer, are **spontaneous sources of capital** to finance investment in current assets. The **creditors (payables) deferral period** (CDP) is the length of time the firm is able to defer payments on various resource purchases. The difference between (gross) operating cycle and payables deferral period is **net operating cycle** (NOC). If depreciation is excluded from expenses in the computation of operating cycle, the net operating cycle also represents the **cash conversion cycle** (CCC). It is net time interval between cash collections from sale of the product and cash payments for resources acquired by the firm. It also represents the time interval over which additional funds, called working capital, should be obtained in order to carry out the firm's operations. The firm has to negotiate working capital from sources such as commercial banks. The negotiated sources of working capital financing are called **non-spontaneous sources**. If net operating cycle of a firm increases, it means further need for negotiated working capital.

Let us illustrate the computation of the length of operating cycle. Consider the statement of costs of sales for a firm given in Table 27.1.

Table 27.1: Statement of Cost of Sales

(Rs in lakh)

Items	Actual 19X1	Projected 19X2
1. Purchase of raw material (credit)	4,653	6,091
2. Opening raw material inventory	523	827
3. Closing raw material inventory	827	986
4. Raw material consumed (1 + 2 – 3)	4,349	5,932
5. Direct labour	368	498
6. Depreciation	82	90
7. Other mfg. expenses	553	704
8. Total cost (4 + 5 + 6 + 7)	5,352	7,224
9. Opening work-in-process inventory	185	325
10. Closing work-in-process inventory	325	498
11. Cost of production (8 + 9 – 10)	5,212	7,051
12. Opening finished goods inventory	317	526
13. Closing finished goods inventory	526	995
14. Cost of goods sold (11 + 12 – 13)	5,003	6,582
15. Selling, administrative and general expenses	304	457
16. Cost of sales (14 + 15)	5,307	7,039

The firm's data for sales and debtors and creditors are given in Table 27.2.

Table 27.2: Sales and Debtors

(Rs in lakh)

	19X1	19X2
Sales (credit)	6,087	8,006
Opening balance of debtors	545	735
Closing balance of debtors	735	1,040
Opening balance of creditors	300	454
Closing balance of creditors	454	642

Gross Operating Cycle (GOC)

The firm's gross operating cycle (GOC) can be determined as inventory conversion period (ICP) plus debtors conversion period (DCP). Thus, GOC is given as follows:

---

1. Richards, V.D. and Laughlin, E.J., A Cash-Conversion Cycle Approach to Liquidity Analysis, *Financial Management,* (Spring, 1980), pp. 32–38. Also see Moyer *et. al., op. cit.,* pp. 562–63.

$$\text{Gross operating} \atop \text{cycle} = \text{Inventory} \atop \text{conversion period} + \text{Debtors} \atop \text{conversion period}$$

$$GOC = ICP + DCP \qquad (1)$$

Inventory conversion period What determines the inventory conversion period? The inventory conversion (ICP) is the sum of raw material conversion period (RMCP), work-in-process conversion period (WIPCP) and finished goods conversion period (FGCP):

$$ICP = RMCP + WIPCP + FGCP \qquad (2)$$

- **Ram material conversion period (RMCP)** The raw material conversion period (RMCP) is the average time period taken to convert material in to work-in-process. RMCP depends on: (*a*) raw material consumption per day, and (*b*) raw material inventory. Raw material consumption per day is given by the total raw material consumption divided by the number of days in the year (say, 360). The raw material conversion period is obtained when raw material inventory is divided by raw material consumption per day. Similar calculations can be made for other inventories, debtors and creditors. The following formula can be used:

$$\text{Raw material} \atop \text{conversion} \atop \text{period} = \frac{\text{Raw material} \atop \text{inventory}}{[\text{Raw material consumption}]/360}$$

$$RMCP = RMI \div \frac{RMC}{360} = \frac{RMI \times 360}{RMC} \qquad (3)$$

- **Work-in-process conversion period (WIPCP)**: Work-in-process conversion period (WIPCP) is the average time taken to complete the semi-finished or work-in-process. It is given by the following formula:

$$\text{Work-in-process} \atop \text{conversion} \atop \text{period} = \frac{\text{Work-in-process} \atop \text{inventory}}{[\text{Cost of production}]/360}$$

$$WIPCP = WIPI \div \frac{COP}{360} = \frac{WIPI \times 360}{COP} \qquad (4)$$

- **Finished goods conversion period (FGCP)**: Finished goods conversion period (FGCP) is the average time taken to sell the finished goods. FGCP can be calculated as follows:

$$\text{Finished goods} \atop \text{conversion} \atop \text{period} = \frac{\text{Finished goods} \atop \text{inventory}}{[\text{Cost of goods sold}]/360}$$

$$FGCP = FGI \div \frac{CGI}{360} = \frac{FGI \times 360}{CGS} \qquad (5)$$

Debtors (receivable) conversion period (DCP) Debtors conversion period (DCP) is the average time taken to convert debtors into cash. DCP represents the average **collection period**. It is calculated as follows:

$$\text{Debtors} \atop \text{conversion} \atop \text{period (DCP)} = \frac{\text{Debtors}}{\text{Credit sales}/360} = \frac{\text{Debtors} \times 360}{\text{Credit sales}} \qquad (6)$$

Creditors (payables) deferral period (CDP) Creditors (payables) deferral period (CDP) is the average time taken by the firm in paying its suppliers (creditors). CDP is given as follows:

$$\text{Creditors} \atop \text{deferral} \atop \text{period (CDP)} = \frac{\text{Creditors}}{\text{Credit purchases}/360} = \frac{\text{Creditors} \times 360}{\text{Credit purchases}} \qquad (7)$$

Cash Conversion or Net Operating Cycle

Net operating cycle (NOC) is the difference between gross operating cycle and payables deferral period.

$$\text{Net operating} \atop \text{cycle} = \text{Gross} \atop \text{operating} \atop \text{cycle} - \text{Creditors} \atop \text{deferral} \atop \text{period}$$

$$NOC = GOC - CDP \qquad (8)$$

Net operating cycle is also referred to as **cash conversion cycle**. Some people argue that depreciation and profit should be excluded in the computation of cash conversion cycle since the firm's concern is with cash flows associated with conversion *at cost*; depreciation is a non-cash item and profits are not costs. A contrary view is that a firm has to ultimately recover total costs and make profits; therefore, the calculation of operating cycle should include depreciation, and even the profits. Also, in using the above-mentioned formulae, average figures for the period may be used.

For our example, Table 27.3 shows detained calculations of the components of a firm's operating cycle. Table 27.4 provides the summary of calculations.

During 19X1 the daily raw material consumption was Rs 12.1 lakh and the company held an ending raw material inventory of Rs 827 lakh. If we assume that this is the average inventory held by the company, the raw material consumption period works out to be 68 days. You may notice that for 19X2, the projected raw material conversion period is 60 days. This has happened because both consumption (Rs 16.5 lakh per day) and level of inventory (Rs 986 lakh) have increased, but the consumption rate has increased (by 36.4 per cent) much more than the increase in inventory holding (by 19.2 per cent). Thus, the raw material conversion period has declined by 8 days. Raw material is the result of daily raw material consumption and total raw material consumption during a period given the company's production targets. Thus, raw material inventory is controlled through control over purchases and production. We can similarly interpret other calculations in Table 27.3.

Table 27.3: Operating Cycle Calculation

(Rs in lakh)

Items	Actual 19X1	Projected 19X2
1. Raw Material Conversion Period		
(a) Raw material consumption	4,349	5,932
(b) Raw material consumption per day	12.1	16.5
(c) Raw material inventory	827	986
(d) Raw material inventory holding days	68d	60d
2. Work-in-Process Conversion Period		
(a) Cost of production*	5,212	7,051
(b) Cost of production per day	14.5	19.6
(c) Work-in-process inventory	325	498
(d) Work-in-process inventory holding days	22d	25d
3. Finished Goods Conversion Period		
(a) Cost of goods sold*	5,003	6,582
(b) Cost of goods sold per day	13.9	18.3
(c) Finished goods inventory	526	995
(d) Finished goods inventory holding days	38d	54d
4. Collection Period		
(a) Credit sales (at cost)**	6,087	8,006
(b) Sales per day	16.9	22.2
(c) Debtors	735	1,040
(d) Debtors outstanding days	43d	47d
5. Creditors Deferral Period		
(a) Credit purchases	4,653	6,091
(b) Purchase per day	12.9	16.9
(c) Creditors	454	642
(d) Creditors outstanding days	35d	38d

*   Depreciation is included.

** All sales are assumed on credit.

Table 27.4: Summary of Operating Cycle Calculations (Number of Days)

	Actual		Projected	
GROSS OPERATING CYCLE				
1. Inventory Conversion Period				
(i) Raw material	68		60	
(ii) Work-in-process	22		25	
(iii) Finished goods	38	128	54	139
2. Debtors Conversion Period		43		47
3. Gross Operating Cycle (1 + 2)		171		186
4. Payment Deferral Period		35		38
NET OPERATING CYCLE (3 – 4)		136		148

We note a significant change in the company's policy for 19X2 with regard to finished goods inventory. It is expected to increase to 54 days holding from 38 days in the previous year. One reason could be a conscious policy decision to avoid stock-out situations and carry more finished goods inventory to expand sales. But this policy has a cost; the company, in the absence of a significant increase in payables (creditors) deferral period, will have to negotiate higher working capital funds. In the case of the firm in our example, its net operating cycle is expected to increase from 136 days to 148 days (Table 27.4). How does a company manage its inventories, debtors and suppliers' credit? How can it reduce its operating cycle? We shall attempt to answer these questions in the next four chapters.

The operating cycle concept as shown in Figure 27.1 relates to a manufacturing firm. Non-manufacturing firms such as wholesalers and retailers will not have the manufacturing phase. They will acquire stock of finished goods and convert them into debtors (receivable) and debtors into cash. Further, service and financial enterprises will not have inventory of goods (cash will be their inventory). Their operating cycles will be the shortest. They need to acquire cash, then lend (create debtors) and again convert lending into cash.

PERMANENT AND VARIABLE WORKING CAPITAL

We know that the need for current assets arises because of the operating cycle. The operating cycle is a continuous process and, therefore, the need for current assets is felt constantly. But the magnitude of current assets needed is not always the same; it increases and decreases over time. However, there is always a minimum level of current assets which is continuously required by a firm to carry on its business operations. **Permanent** or **fixed, working capital** is the minimum level of current assets. It is permanent in the same way as the firm's fixed assets are. Depending upon the changes in production and sales, the need for working capital, over and above permanent working capital, will fluctuate. For example, extra inventory of finished goods will have to be maintained to support the peak periods of sale, and investment in debtors (receivable) may also increase during such periods. On the other hand, investment in raw material, work-in-process and finished goods will fall if the market is slack.

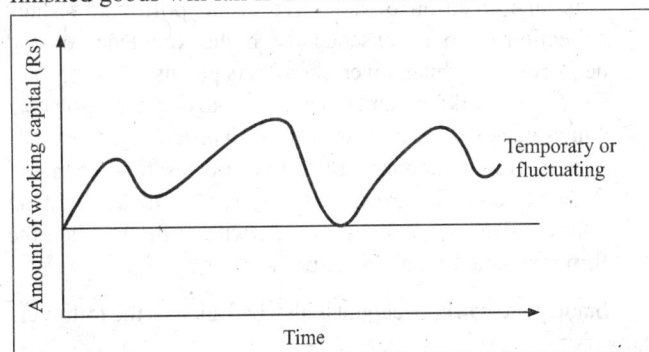

Figure 27.2: Permanent and temporary working capital

Fluctuating or **variable working capital** is the extra working capital needed to support the changing production and sales activities of the firm. Both kinds of working capital—permanent and fluctuating (temporary)—are necessary to facilitate production and sale through the operating cycle. But the firm to meet liquidity requirements that will last only temporarily creates the temporary working capital. Figure 27.2 illustrates differences between permanent and temporary working capital. It is shown that permanent working capital is stable over time, while temporary working capital is fluctuating—sometimes increasing and sometimes decreasing.

However, the permanent working capital line need not be horizontal if the firm's requirement for permanent capital is increasing (or decreasing) over a period. For a growing firm, the difference between permanent and temporary working capital can be depicted through Figure 27.3.

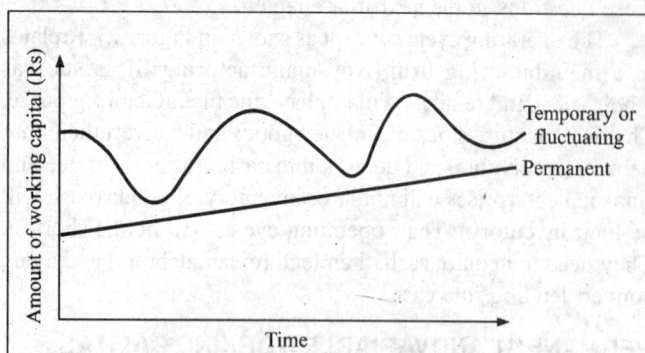

Figure 27.3: Permanent and temporary working capital

BALANCED WORKING CAPITAL POSITION

The firm should maintain a sound working capital position. It should have adequate working capital to run its business operations. Both excessive as well as inadequate working capital positions are dangerous from the firm's point of view. Excessive working capital means holding costs and idle funds which earn no profits for the firm. Paucity of working capital not only impairs the firm's profitability but also results in production interruptions and inefficiencies and sales disruptions.

The dangers of excessive working capital are as follows:[1]

- It results in unnecessary accumulation of inventories. Thus, chances of inventory mishandling, waste, theft and losses increase.
- It is an indication of defective credit policy and slack collection period. Consequently, higher incidence of bad debts results, which adversely affects profits.
- Excessive working capital makes management complacent which degenerates into managerial inefficiency.
- Tendencies of accumulating inventories tend to make speculative profits grow. This may tend to make dividend policy liberal and difficult to cope with in future when the firm is unable to make speculative profits.

Inadequate working capital is also bad and has the following dangers:[2]
- It stagnates growth. It becomes difficult for the firm to undertake profitable projects for non-availability of working capital funds.
- It becomes difficult to implement operating plans and achieve the firm's profit target.
- Operating inefficiencies creep in when it becomes difficult even to meet day-to-day commitments.
- Fixed assets are not efficiently utilised for the lack of

working capital funds. Thus, the firm's profitability would deteriorate.
- Paucity of working capital funds render the firm unable to avail attractive credit opportunities etc.
- The firm loses its reputation when it is not in a position to honour its short-term obligations. As a result, the firm faces tight credit terms.

An enlightened management should, therefore, maintain the right amount of working capital on a continuous basis. Only then a proper functioning of business operations will be ensured. Sound financial and statistical techniques, supported by judgement, should be used to predict the quantum of working capital needed at different time periods.

A firm's net working capital position is not only important as an index of liquidity but it is also used as a measure of the firm's risk. Risk in this regard means chances of the firm being unable to meet its obligations on due date. The lender considers a positive net working as a measure of safety. All other things being equal, the more the net working capital a firm has, the less likely that it will default in meeting its current financial obligations. Lenders such as commercial banks insist that the firm should maintain a minimum net working capital position.

DETERMINANTS OF WORKING CAPITAL

There are no set rules or formulae to determine the working capital requirements of firms. A large number of factors, each having a different importance, influence working capital needs of firms. The importance of factors also changes for a firm over time. Therefore, an analysis of relevant factors should be made in order to determine total investment in working capital. The following is the description of factors which generally influence the working capital requirements of firms.[3]

Nature of Business

Working capital requirements of a firm are basically influenced by the nature of its business. Trading and financial firms have a very small investment in fixed assets, but require a large sum of money to be invested in working capital. Retail stores, for example, must carry large stocks of a variety of goods to satisfy varied and continuous demands of their customers. A large departmental store like Wal-Mart may carry, say, over 20,000 items. Some manufacturing businesses, such as tobacco manufacturers and construction firms, also have to invest substantially in working capital and a nominal amount in fixed assets. In contrast, public utilities may have limited need for working capital and have to invest abundantly in fixed assets. Their working capital requirements are nominal because they may have only cash sales and supply services, not products. Thus, no funds will be tied up in debtors and stock (inventories). For the working capital requirements most of the manufacturing companies will fall between the two extreme requirements of trading firms and public utilities. Such concerns have to make

---

1. Also see, Ramamoorthy, V.E., *Working Capital Management,* IFMR, Chennai, 1976, p. 11.
2. *Ibid.,* p. 11.
3. *Ibid.,* pp. 51–63.

adequate investment in current assets depending upon the total assets structure and other variables.

Market and Demand Conditions

The working capital needs of a firm are related to its sales. However, it is difficult to precisely determine the relationship between volume of sales and working capital needs. In practice, current assets will have to be employed before growth takes place. It is, therefore, necessary to make advance planning of working capital for a growing firm on a continuous basis.

Growing firms may need to invest funds in fixed assets in order to sustain growing production and sales. This will, in turn, increase investment in current assets to support enlarged scale of operations. Growing firms need funds continuously. They use external sources as well as internal sources to meet increasing needs of funds. These firms face further problems when they retain substantial portion of profits, as they will not be able to pay dividends to shareholders. It is, therefore, imperative that such firms do proper planning to finance their increasing needs for working capital.

Sales depend on demand conditions. Large number of firms experience seasonal and cyclical fluctuations in the demand for their products and services. These business variations affect the working capital requirement, specially the temporary working capital requirement of the firm. When there is an upward swing in the economy, sales will increase; correspondingly, the firm's investment in inventories and debtors will also increase. Under boom, additional investment in fixed assets may be made by some firms to increase their productive capacity. This act of firms will require further additions of working capital. To meet their requirements of funds for fixed assets and current assets under boom period, firms generally resort to substantial borrowing. On the other hand, when there is a decline in the economy, sales will fall and consequently, levels of inventories and debtors will also fall. Under recession, firms try to reduce their short-term borrowings.

Seasonal fluctuations not only affect working capital requirement but also create production problems for the firm. During periods of peak demand, increasing production may be expensive for the firm. Similarly, it will be more expensive during slack periods when the firm has to sustain its working force and physical facilities without adequate production and sales. A firm may, thus, follow a policy of **level production**, irrespective of seasonal changes in order to utilise its resources to the fullest extent. Such a policy will mean accumulation of inventories during off-season and their quick disposal during the peak season.

The increasing level of inventories during the slack season will require increasing funds to be tied up in the working capital for some months. Unlike cyclical fluctuations, seasonal fluctuations generally conform to a steady pattern. Therefore, financial arrangements for seasonal working capital requirements can be made in advance. However, the financial plan or arrangement should be flexible enough to take care of some abrupt seasonal fluctuations.

Technology and Manufacturing Policy

The **manufacturing cycle** (or the inventory conversion cycle) comprises of the purchase and use of raw materials and the production of finished goods. Longer the manufacturing cycle, larger will be the firm's working capital requirements. For example, the manufacturing cycle in the case of a boiler, depending on its size, may range between six to twenty-four months. On the other hand, the manufacturing cycle of products such as detergent powder, soaps, chocolate etc. may be a few hours. An extended manufacturing time span means a larger tie-up of funds in inventories. Thus, if there are alternative technologies of manufacturing a product, the technological process with the shortest manufacturing cycle may be chosen. Once a manufacturing technology has been selected, it should be ensured that manufacturing cycle is completed within the specified period. This needs proper planning and coordination at all levels of activity. Any delay in manufacturing process will result in accumulation of work-in-process and waste of time. In order to minimise their investment in working capital, some firms, specifically those manufacturing industrial products, have a policy of asking for advance payments from their customers. Non-manufacturing firms, service and financial enterprises do not have a manufacturing cycle.

A strategy of level or steady production may be maintained in order to resolve the working capital problems arising due to seasonal changes in the demand for the firm's product. A **steady or level production policy** will cause inventories to accumulate during the off-season periods and the firm will be exposed to greater inventory costs and risks. Thus, if costs and risks of maintaining a constant production schedule are high, the firm may adopt a **variable production policy**, varying its production schedules in accordance with changing demand. Those firms, whose productive capacities can be utilised for manufacturing varied products, can have the advantage of diversified activities and solve their working capital problems. They will manufacture the original product line during its increasing demand and when it has an off-season, other products may be manufactured to utilise physical resources and working force. Thus, production policies will differ from firm to firm, depending on the circumstances of individual firm.

Credit Policy

The credit policy of the firm affects the working capital by influencing the level of debtors. The credit terms to be granted to customers may depend upon the norms of the industry to which the firm belongs. But a firm has the flexibility of shaping its credit policy within the constraint of industry norms and practices. The firm should use discretion in granting credit terms to its customers. Depending upon the individual case, different terms may be given to different customers. A **liberal credit policy**, without rating the credit-worthiness of customers, will be detrimental to the firm and will create a problem of collection later on. The firm should be prompt in making collections. A high collection period will mean tie-up of large funds in debtors. Slack collection procedures can increase the chance of bad debts.

In order to ensure that unnecessary funds are not tied up in debtors, the firm should follow a rationalised credit policy based on the credit standing of customers and other relevant factors. The firm should evaluate the credit standing of new customers and periodically review the credit-worthiness of the existing customers. The case of delayed payments should be thoroughly investigated.

Availability of Credit from Suppliers

The working capital requirements of a firm are also affected by credit terms granted by its suppliers. A firm will needless working capital if liberal credit terms are available to it from suppliers. Suppliers' credit finances the firm's inventories and reduces the cash conversion cycle. In the absence of suppliers' credit the firm will have to borrow funds for bank. The availability of credit at reasonable cost from banks is crucial. It influences the working capital policy of a firm. A firm without the suppliers' credit, but which can get bank credit easily on favourable conditions, will be able to finance its inventories and debtors without much difficulty.

Operating Efficiency

The operating efficiency of the firm relates to the optimum utilisation of all its resources at minimum costs. The efficiency in controlling operating costs and utilising fixed and current assets leads to operating efficiency. The use of working capital is improved and pace of cash conversion cycle is accelerated with operating efficiency. Better utilisation of resources improves profitability and, thus, helps in releasing the pressure on working capital. Although it may not be possible for a firm to control prices of materials or wages of labour, it can certainly ensure efficient and effective use of its materials, labour and other resources.

Price Level Changes

The increasing shifts in price level make functions of financial manager difficult. She should anticipate the effect of price level changes on working capital requirements of the firm. Generally, rising price levels will require a firm to maintain higher amount of working capital. Same levels of current assets will need increased investment when prices are increasing. However, companies that can immediately revise their product prices with rising price levels will not face a severe working capital problem. Further, firms will feel effects of increasing general price level differently as prices of individual products move differently. Thus, it is possible that some companies may not be affected by rising prices while others may be badly hit.

ISSUES IN WORKING CAPITAL MANAGEMENT

Working capital management refers to the administration of all components of working capital–cash, marketable securities, debtors (receivable) and stock (inventories) and creditors (payables). The financial manager must determine *levels* and *composition* of current assets. He must see that right sources are tapped to finance current assets, and that current liabilities are paid in time.

There are many aspects of working capital management which make it an important function of the financial manager:[1]

- **Time** Working capital management requires much of the financial manager's time.
- **Investment** Working capital represents a large portion of the total investment in assets.
- **Criticality** Working capital management has great significance for all firms but it is very critical for small firms.
- **Growth** The need for working capital is directly related to the firm's growth.

Empirical observations show that the financial managers have to spend much of their time to the daily internal operations, relating to current assets and current liabilities of the firms. As the largest portion of the financial manager's valuable time is devoted to working capital problems, it is necessary to manage working capital in the best possible way to get the maximum benefit.

Investment in current assets represents a very significant portion of the total investment in assets. For example, in the case of the large and medium public limited companies in India, current assets constitute about 60 per cent of total assets or total capital employed.[2] In a large company such as Bharat Heavy Electricals Limited (BHEL) current assets as a percentage of total assets may be as high as, say, 90 per cent. (See Exhibit 22.1 for examples of other companies). This clearly indicates that the financial manager should pay special attention to the management of current assets on a continuing basis. Actions should be taken to curtail unnecessary investment in current assets.

Working capital management is critical for all firms, but particularly for small firms. A small firm may not have much investment in fixed assets, but it has to invest in current assets. Small firms in India face a severe problem of collecting their debtors (book debts or receivables). Further, the role of current liabilities in financing current assets is far more significant in case of small firms, as, unlike large firms, they face difficulties in raising long-term finances.

There is a direct relationship between a firm's growth and its working capital needs. As sales grow, the firm needs to invest more in inventories and debtors. These needs become very frequent and fast when sales grow continuously. The financial manager should be aware of such needs and finance them quickly. Continuous growth in sales may also require additional investment in fixed assets.

It may, thus, be concluded that all precautions should be taken for the effective and efficient management of working capital. The finance manager should pay particular attention to the levels of current assets and the financing of current assets. To decide the levels and financing of current assets, the risk–return implications must be evaluated.

1. Weston, J. Fred and Eugene F. Brigham, *Managerial Finance,* Illinois: Dryden Press, 1975, pp. 123–24.
2. Reserve Bank of India, Finance of Medium and Large Public Limited Companies, various issues of *Reserve Bank of India Bulletin.*

EXHIBIT 27.1: LEVELS OF CURRENT ASSETS: SOME EXAMPLES OF INDIAN COMPANIES

Current assets form a significant portion of total assets of many Indian companies. Consider the following examples:

	BHEL	**GNFC**	**L&T**	**Voltas**
Sales	7651.1	1476.7	8782.5	1232.3
Total assets (TA)	9600.4	1991.9	17095.9	862.9
Current assets (CA)	8601.0	882.9	11398.4	658.4
CA/TA	89.6	44.3	66.7	76.3
CA/Sales	112.4	59.8	129.8	53.4

Note: Data for the year 2003 except in case of BHEL.

- *Voltas* Voltas is a large, well-diversified, private sector marketing-cum-manufacturing organisation. In 2003, the company's current assets are three-fourths of total assets and more than half of sales.
- *L&T Limited* L&T is also a diversified company in the private sector. In 2003, its current assets are two-thirds of total assets and about one and a third times of sales.
- *GNFC* GNFC is a joint sector (joint venture between state of Gujarat and private sector) company manufacturing fertilizers, industrial products (methanol, formic acid, nitric acid, amonium nitrate, liquid nitrogen etc.) and electronic products. Its current assets in the year 2003 are less than half of total assets and 60 per cent of sales.
- *BHEL* BHEL was started as a large public sector company. Its shares have been partly divested now. It has a dominant position in the power sector. Its manufacturing operations are spread into industrial and transportation sectors also. A large number of its products are long production cycle products. The company's main customers are State Electricity Boards who fail to pay their due on time. BHEL's current assets in 2002 are 90 per cent of total assets and 112 per cent of sales.

Current Assets to Fixed Assets Ratio

The financial manager should determine the optimum level of current assets so that the wealth of shareholders is maximised.[1] A firm needs fixed and current assets to support a particular level of output. However, to support the same level of output, the firm can have different levels of current assets. As the firm's output and sales increase, the need for current assets increases. Generally, current assets do not increase in direct proportion to output; current assets may increase at a decreasing rate with output. This relationship is based upon the notion that it takes a greater proportional investment in current assets when only a few units of output are produced than it does later on when the firm can use its current assets more efficiently.[2]

The level of the current assets can be measured by relating current assets to fixed assets.[3] Dividing current assets by fixed assets gives CA/FA ratio. Assuming a constant level of fixed assets, a higher CA/FA ratio indicates a **conservative current assets policy** and a lower CA/FA ratio means an **aggressive current assets policy** assuming other factors to be constant. A conservative policy implies greater liquidity and lower risk; while an aggressive policy indicates higher risk and poor liquidity. **Moderate current assets policy** fall in the middle of conservative and aggressive policies. The current assets policy of the most firms may fall between these two extreme policies. The alternative current assets policies may be shown with the help of Figure 27.4.

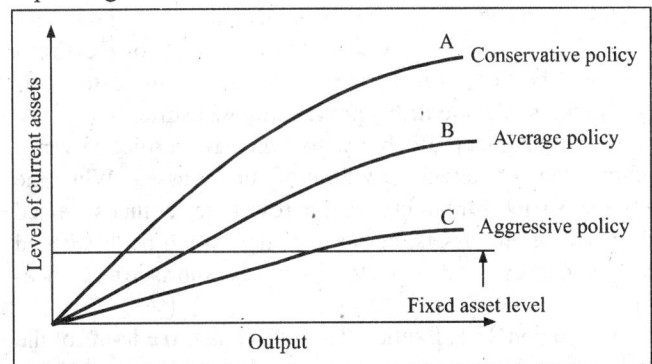

Figure 27.4: Alternative current asset policies

In Figure 27.4 alternative A indicates the most conservative policy, where CA/FA ratio is greatest at every level of output. Alternative C is the most aggressive policy, as CA/FA ratio is lowest at all levels of output. Alternative B lies between the conservative and aggressive policies and is an average policy.

Liquidity vs. Profitability: Risk–Return Trade-off

The firm would make just enough investment in current assets if it were possible to estimate working capital needs exactly. Under perfect certainty, current assets holdings would be at the minimum level. A larger investment in current assets under certainty would mean a low rate of return on investment for the firm, as excess investment in current assets will not earn enough return. A smaller investment in current assets, on the other hand, would mean interrupted production and sales, because of frequent stock-outs and inability to pay to creditors in time due to restrictive policy.

As it is not possible to estimate working capital needs accurately, the firm must decide about levels of current assets to be carried. Given a firm's technology and production policy, sales and demand conditions, operating efficiency etc., its current assets holdings will depend upon its working capital policy. It may follow a conservative or an aggressive policy. These policies involve risk–return trade-offs.[4] A conservative

---

1. The basic principles applicable to working capital management are discussed in Walker, E.W., Towards a Theory of Working Capital, *Engineering Economist,* (Jan.–Feb. 1964), pp. 21–35. Also, see Mehta, Dilip, *Working Capital Management,* Prentice-Hall, 1966.
2. Van Horne, James, C., *Financial Management and Policy,* Prentice-Hall of India Pvt. Ltd., 1975, p. 906.
3. Van Horne, *op. cit.,* Weston, J.F. and Brigham, E.F., *Management Financial,* Holt, Rinehart and Winston, 1972, pp. 516–18.
4. The risk-return analysis of working capital policies are discussed in detail in Van Horne, J.C., A Risk-Return Analysis of a Firm's Working-Capital Position, *Engineering Economist,* (Oct. 1970), pp. 50–58.

policy means lower return and risk, while an aggressive policy produces higher return and risk.

The two important aims of the working capital management are: *profitability* and *solvency*. **Solvency**, used in the technical sense, refers to the firm's continuous ability to meet maturing obligations. Lenders and creditors expect prompt settlements of their claims as and when due. To ensure solvency, the firm should be very liquid, which means larger current assets holdings. If the firm maintains a relatively large investment in current assets, it will have no difficulty in paying claims of creditors when they become due and will be able to fill all sales orders and ensure smooth production. Thus, a liquid firm has less risk of insolvency; that is, it will hardly experience a cash shortage or a stock-out situation. However, there is a cost associated with maintaining a sound liquidity position. A considerable amount of the firm's funds will be tied up in current assets, and to the extent this investment is idle, the firm's profitability will suffer.

To have higher profitability, the firm may sacrifice solvency and maintain a relatively low level of current assets. When the firm does so, its profitability will improve as fewer funds are tied up in idle current assets, but its solvency would be threatened and would be exposed to greater risk of cash shortage and stock-outs.

Illustration 27.1: Explians the **risk-return trade-off** of the working capital management.

Illustration 27.1: Working Capital Risk-return Trade-off

Suppose, a firm has the following data for some future year:

	Rs
Sales (100,000 units @ Rs 15)	1,500,000
Earnings before interest and taxes	150,000
Fixed assets	500,000

The three possible current assets holdings of the firm are: Rs 500,000, Rs 400,000 and Rs 300,000. It is assumed that fixed assets level is constant and profits do not vary with current assets levels. The effect of the three alternative current assets policies is shown in Table 27.5.

Table 27.5: Effect of Alternative Working Capital Policies

Working Capital Policy	Conservative A Rs	Moderate B Rs	Aggressive B Rs
Sales	1,500,000	15,00,000	1,500,000
Earnings before interest & taxes (EBIT)	150,000	150,000	150,000
Current assets	500,000	400,000	300,000
Fixed assets	500,000	500,000	500,000
Total assets	1,000,000	900,000	800,000
Return on total assets (EBIT/Total assets)	15%	16.67%	18.75%
Current assets/Fixed assets	1.00	0.80	0.60

The calculations in Table 27.5 indicate that alternative. A, the most conservative policy, provides greatest liquidity (solvency) to the firm, but

also the lowest return on total assets. On the other hand, alternative C, the most aggressive policy, yields highest return but provides lowest liquidity and thus, is very risky to the firm. Alternative B demonstrates a moderate policy and generates a return higher than alternative A but lower than alternative C and is less risky than alternative C but more risky than alternative A.

Illustration 27.1 is a simple example of risk–return trade-off.[1] The calculation of risk-return trade-off is difficult in practice. Risk and returns are affected differently by different assets, and generalisation is not possible. The level of each current asset and the risk–return trade-off is discussed in Chapters 23 to 25.

The Cost Trade-off

A different way of looking into the risk-return trade-off is in terms of the cost of maintaining a particular level of current assets. There are two types of costs involved: **cost of liquidity** and **cost of illiquidity**. If the firm's level of current assets is very high, it has excessive liquidity. Its return on assets will be low, as funds tied up in idle cash and stocks earn nothing and high levels of debtors reduce profitability. Thus, the cost of liquidity (through low rates of return) increases with the level of current assets.

The cost of illiquidity is the cost of holding insufficient current assets. The firm will not be in a position to honour its obligations if it carries too little cash. This may force the firm to borrow at high rates of interest. This will also adversely affect the credit-worthiness of the firm and it will face difficulties in obtaining funds in the future. All this may force the firm into insolvency. Similarly, the low level of stocks will result in loss of sales and customers may shift to competitors. Also, low level of debtors may be due to tight credit policy, which would impair sales further. Thus, the low level of current assets involves costs that increase as this level falls.

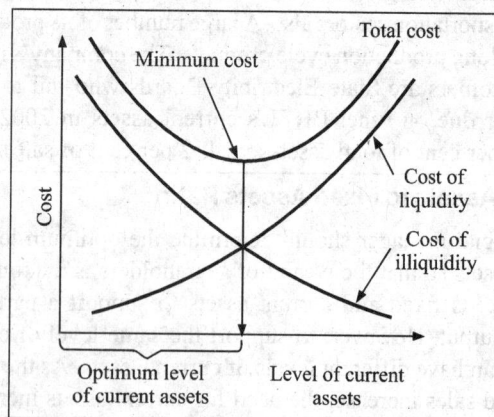

Figure 27.5: Cost Trade-off

In determining the optimum level of current assets, the firm should balance the profitability-solvency tangle by minimising total costs—cost of liquidity and cost of illiquidity. This is illustrated in Figure 27.5. It is indicated in the figure that with the level of current assets the cost of liquidity increases while the cost of illiquidity decreases and vice versa. The firm should maintain its current assets at that level where the sum of these two costs is minimised. The minimum cost point indicates the optimum level of current assets in Figure 27.5.

---

1. See Weston and Brigham, *op. cit.*, pp. 517–18.

ESTIMATING WORKING CAPITAL NEEDS

The most appropriate method of calculating the working capital needs of a firm is the concept of operating cycle. However, a number of other methods may be used to determine working capital needs in practice. We shall illustrate here three approaches which have been successfully applied in practice:

- *Current assets holding period* To estimate working capital requirements on the basis of average holding period of current assets and relating them to costs based on the company's experience in the previous years. This method is essentially based on the operating cycle concept.
- *Ratio of sales* To estimate working capital requirements as a ratio of sales on the assumption that current assets change with sales.
- *Ratio of fixed investment* To estimate working capital requirements as a percentage of fixed investment.

To illustrate the above methods of estimating working capital requirements and their impact on rate of return we shall take examples of two hypothetical firms (as given in Table 27.6).

Table 27.6: Data for Two Firms

	Firm A Rs	Firm B Rs
Material cost:		
Raw material consumed	248,000	248,000
Less: By-product	68,800	68,800
Net material cost	179,200	179,200
Manufacturing cost		
Labour	171,200	171,200
Maintenance	160,000	160,000
Power and fuel	57,600	57,600
Factory overheads	240,000	240,000
Depreciation	160,000	320,000
Total manufacturing cost	788,800	948,800
Total product cost	968,000	1,128,000
Annual sales	1,448,000	1,448,000
PBIT	480,000	320,000
Investment	1,600,000	3,200,000
Period	1 year	1 year
Plant life	10 year	10 year
PBDIT	640,000	640,000
ROI [PBIT/(investment – depreciation)]	33.3%	11.1%

The calculations are based on the following assumptions regarding each of the three methods:

Method 1: Inventory: one month's supply of each of raw material, semifinished goods and finished material. Debtors: one month's sales. Operating cash: one month's total cost.

Method 2: 25–35% of annual sales.

Method 3: 10–20% of fixed capital investment.

The following calculations based on data of firm A are made to show how three methods work. You may complete calculations for firm B.

Method 1: *Current Assets Holding Period*

Let us first compute inventory requirements as shown below:

Raw material: one month's supply:

$$\text{Rs } 248,000 \div 12 = \text{Rs } 20,667$$

Semi-finished material: one month's supply (based on raw material plus assume one-half of normal conversion cost):

$$\text{Rs } 20,667 + (\text{Rs } 171,200 + \text{Rs } 160,000 + \text{Rs } 57,600)\, 1/2 \div 12$$
$$= \text{Rs } 20,667 + 16,200 = \text{Rs } 36,867$$

Finished material: one month's supply:

$$\text{Rs } 968,000 \div 12 = \text{Rs } 80,666$$

The total inventory needs are:

$$\text{Rs } 20,667 + \text{Rs } 36,867 + \text{Rs } 80,666 = \text{Rs } 138,200$$

After determining the inventory requirements, projection for debtors and operating cash should be made.

Debtors: One month's sales:

$$\text{Rs } 1,448,000 \div 12 = \text{Rs } 120,667$$

Operating cash: One month's total cost:

$$\text{Rs } 968,000 \div 12 = \text{Rs } 80,667$$

Thus the total working capital required is:

$$\text{Rs } 138,200 + \text{Rs } 120,667 + \text{Rs } 80,666 = \text{Rs } 339,533$$

Method 2: *Ratio of Sales*

The average ratio is 30 per cent. Therefore, 30 per cent of annual sales, Rs 1,448,000 is Rs 434,400.

Method 3: *Ratio of Fixed Investment*

The ratio of current assets to fixed investment ranges between 10 to 20 per cent. We shall use the average rate of 15 per centages. The 15 per cent of fixed investment, Rs 1,600,000 is Rs 240,000.

The first method gives details of the working capital items. This approach is subject to error if markets are seasonal. As per the first method the working capital requirement is Rs 339,533. If this figure is considered in calculating the rate of return, it is lowered from 33.3 per cent to 27 per cent. On the other hand, the return of Firm B drops from 11.1 per cent to 9.9 per cent. The estimated working capital for firm B as per the first method is Rs 366,200. Rates of return are calculated as follows:

$$\text{Rate of return} = \frac{\text{PBIT}}{\text{Net fixed investment} + \text{Working capital}}$$

$$\text{Firm A} = \frac{480,000}{[(1,600,000 - 160,000) + 339,533]} = 27\%$$

$$\text{Firm B} = \frac{320,000}{[(3,200,000 - 320,000) + 366,200]} = 9.9\%$$

You may notice that investments have been taken net of depreciation.

The second method has a limited reliability. Its accuracy is dependent upon the accuracy of sales estimates. The rate of return of Firm A drops to 25.6 per cent and that of Firm B to 9.7 per cent when the working capital computed by this method is incorporated.

Third method relates working capital to investment. If estimate of investment is inaccurate, this method cannot be relied upon. This method is not generally used in practice to estimate working capital needs. The rates of return from Firms A and B are respectively 28.6 per cent and 9.5 per cent when the working capital computed by this method is considered.

A number of factors will govern the choice of methods of estimating working capital. Factors such as seasonal variations in operations, accuracy of sales forecasts, investment cost and variability in sales price would generally be considered. The production cycle and credit and collection policy of the firm would have an impact on working capital requirements. Therefore, they should be given due weightage in projecting working capital requirements.

POLICIES FOR FINANCING CURRENT ASSETS

A firm can adopt different financing policies vis-à-vis current assets. Three types of financing may be distinguished:

- *Long-term financing* The sources of long-term financing include ordinary share capital, preference share capital, debentures, long-term borrowings from financial institutions and reserves and surplus (retained earnings).
- *Short-term financing* The short-term financing is obtained for a period less than one year. It is arranged in advance from banks and other suppliers of short-term finance in the money market. Short-term finances include working capital funds from banks, public deposits, commercial paper, factoring of receivable etc.
- *Spontaneous financing* Spontaneous financing refers to the *automatic* sources of short-term funds arising in the normal course of a business. Trade (suppliers') credit and outstanding expenses are examples of spontaneous financing. There is no explicit cost of spontaneous financing. A firm is expected to utilise these sources of finances to the fullest extent. The real choice of financing current assets, once the spontaneous sources of financing have been fully utilised, is between the long-term and short-term sources of finances.

What should be the mix of short-and long-term sources in financing current assets?

Depending on the mix of short- and long-term financing, the approach followed by a company may be referred to as:

- matching approach
- conservative approach
- aggressive approach

Matching Approach

The firm can adopt a financial plan which matches the expected life of assets with the expected life of the source of funds raised to finance assets. Thus, a ten-year loan may be raised to finance a plant with an expected life of ten years; stock of goods to be sold in thirty days may be financed with a thirty-day commercial

paper or a bank loan. The justification for the exact matching is that, since the purpose of financing is to pay for assets, the source of financing and the asset should be relinquished simultaneously. Using long-term financing for short-term assets is expensive as funds will not be utilised for the full period. Similarly, financing long-term assets with short-term financing is costly as well as inconvenient as arrangement for the new short-term financing will have to be made on a continuing basis.

When the firm follows **matching approach** (also known as **hedging approach**), long-term financing will be used to finance fixed assets and permanent current assets and short-term financing to finance temporary or variable current assets. However, it should be realised that exact matching is not possible because of the uncertainty about the expected lives of assets.

Figure 27.6 is used to illustrate the matching plan over time.[1] The firm's fixed assets and permanent current assets are financed with long-term funds and as the level of these assets increases, the long-term financing level also increases. The temporary or variable current assets are financed with short-term funds and as their level increases, the level of short-term financing also increases. Under matching plan, no short-term financing will be used if the firm has a fixed current assets need only.

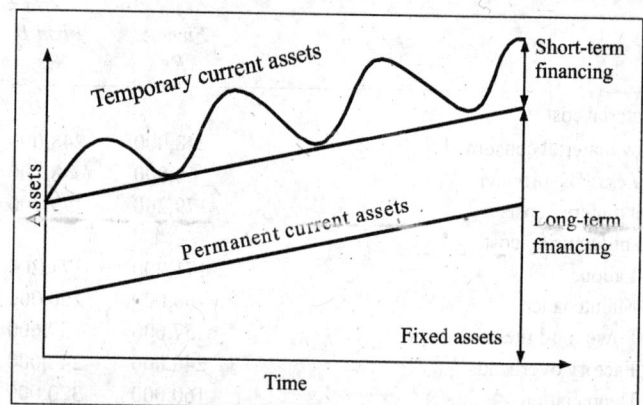

Figure 27.6: Financing under matching plan

Conservative Approach

A firm in practice may adopt a **conservative approach** in financing its current and fixed assets. The financing policy of the firm is said to be conservative when it depends more on long-term funds for financing needs. Under a conservative plan, the firm finances its permanent assets and also a part of temporary current assets with long-term financing. In the periods when the firm has no need for temporary current assets, the idle long-term funds can be invested in the tradable securities to conserve liquidity. The conservative plan relies heavily on long-term financing and, therefore, the firm has less risk of facing the problem of shortage of funds. The conservative financing policy is shown in Figure 27.7.[2] Note that when the firm has no temporary current assets [e.g., at (a) and (b)]; the long-term funds released can be invested in marketable securities to build up the liquidity position of the firm.

1. Weston and Brigham, *op. cit.*, p. 510.
2. *Ibid.*, p. 511.

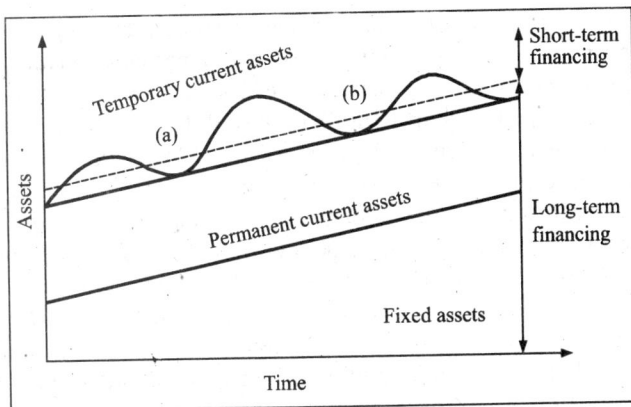

Figure 27.7: Conservative financing

Aggressive Approach

A firm may be aggressive in financing its assets. An **aggressive policy** is said to be followed by the firm when it uses more short-term financing than warranted by the matching plan. Under an aggressive policy, the firm finances a part of its permanent current assets with short-term financing. Some extremely aggressive firms may even finance a part of their fixed assets with short-term financing. The relatively more use of short-term financing makes the firm more risky. The aggressive financing is illustrated in Figure 27.8.[1]

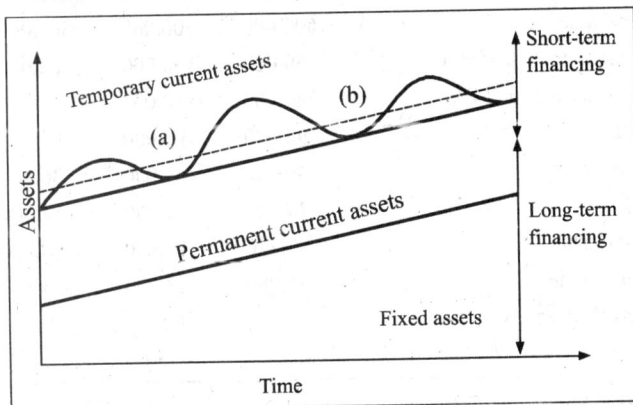

Figure 27.8: Aggressive financing

Short-term Vs. Long-term Financing: A Risk-Return Trade-off

A firm should decide whether or not it should use short-term financing. If short-term financing has to be used, the firm must determine its portion in total financing. This decision of the firm will be guided by the risk-return trade-off. Short-term financing may be preferred over long-term financing for two reasons: (*i*) the cost advantage and (*ii*) flexibility.[2] But short-term financing is more risky than long-term financing.

Cost: Short-term financing should generally be less costly than long-term financing. It has been found in developed countries, like USA, that the rate of interest is related to the maturity of debt. The relationship between the maturity of debt and its cost is called the **term structure of interest rates**. The curve, relating

to the maturity of debt and interest rates, is called the **yield curve**. The yield curve may assume any shape, but it is generally *upward sloping*. Figure 27.9 shows the yield curve. The figure indicates that more the maturity greater the interest rate.

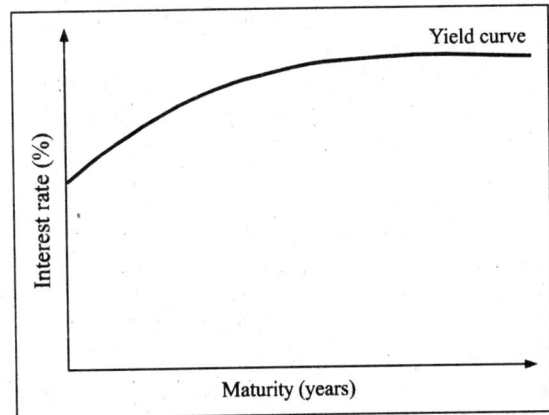

Figure 27.9: Yield curve

As discussed earlier in this book, the justification for the higher cost of long-term financing can be found in the **liquidity preference theory**. This theory says that since lenders are risk averse, and risk generally increases with the length of lending time (because it is more difficult to forecast the more distant future), most lenders would prefer to make short-term loans. The only way to induce these lenders to lend for longer periods is to offer them higher rates of interest.

The cost of financing has an impact on the firm's return. Both short and long-term financing have a leveraging effect on shareholders' return. But the short-term financing ought to cost less than the long-term financing; therefore, it gives relatively higher return to shareholders.

It is noticeable that in India short-term loans cost more than long-term loans. Banks are the major suppliers of the working capital finance in India. Their rates of interest on working capital finance are quite high. The main source of long-term loans are financial institutions which till recently were not charging interest at differential rates. The prime rate of interest charged by financial institutions is lower than the rate charged by banks.

Flexibility It is relatively easy to refund short-term funds when the need for funds diminishes. Long-term funds such as debenture loan or preference capital cannot be refunded before time. Thus, if a firm anticipates that its requirements for funds will diminish in near future, it would choose short-term funds.

Risk Although short-term financing may involve less cost, it is more risky than long-term financing. If the firm uses short-term financing to finance its current assets, it runs the risk of renewing borrowings again and again. This is particularly so in the case of permanent assets. As discussed earlier, permanent current assets refer to the minimum level of current assets which a firm should always maintain. If the firm finances its permanent current assets with short-term debt, it will have to raise new short-term funds as debt matures. This continued financing exposes the firm to certain risks. It may be difficult for the firm to borrow during

---

1. *Ibid.*
2. Also see Western and Brigham, *op. cit.*, pp. 512–13.

stringent credit periods. At times, the firm may be unable to raise any funds and consequently, its operating activities may be disrupted. In order to avoid failure, the firm may have to borrow at most inconvenient terms. These problems are much less when the firm finances with long-term funds. There is less risk of failure when the long-term financing is used.

Risk-return trade-off Thus, there is a conflict between long-term and short-term financing. Short-term financing is less expensive than long-term financing, but, at the same time, short-term financing involves greater risk than long-term financing. The choice between long-term and short-term financing involves a trade-off between risk and return. This trade-off may be further explained with the help of an example in Illustration 27.2.

Illustration 27.2: Working Capital Financing: Risk-return Trade-off

Suppose that a firm has an investment of Rs 50 crore in assets, Rs 30 crore invested in fixed assets and Rs 20 crore in current assets. It is expected that assets will yield a return of 18 per cent before interest and taxes. Tax rate is assumed to be 35 per cent. The firm maintains a debt ratio of 60 per cent. Thus, the firm's assets are financed by 40 per cent equity that is Rs 20 crore equity funds are invested in its total assets. The firm has to decide whether it should use a 12 per cent short-term debt or a 14 per cent long-term debt to finance its current assets. The financing plans would affect the return on equity funds differently. The calculations of return on equity are shown in Table 27.7.

It is shown in Table 27.7 that return on equity is highest under the aggressive plan and lowest under the conservative plan. The results of moderate plan are in between these two extremes. However, the aggressive plan is the most risky as short-term financing as a ratio of total financing is maximum in this case. The short-term financing to total financing ratio is minimum in case of the conservative plan and, therefore, it is less risky.

Let us summarise our discussion on the structure and financing of current assets. The relative liquidity of the firms assets structure is measured by current assets to fixed assets (or current assets to total assets) ratio. The greater this ratio, the less risky as well as less profitable will be the firm and *vice versa*. Similarly, the relative liquidity of the firm's financial structure can be measured by the short-term financing to total financing ratio. The lower this ratio, the less risky as well as profitable will

be the firm and *vice versa*. In shaping its working capital policy, the firm should keep in mind these two dimensions—*relative asset liquidity* (level of current assets) and *relative financing liquidity* (level of short-term financing) of the working capital management. A firm will be following a very conservative working capital policy if it combines a high level of current assets with a high level of long-term financing (or low level of short-term financing). Such a policy will not be risky at all but would be less profitable. An aggressive firm, on the other hand, would combine low level of current assets with a low level of long-term financing (or high level of short-term financing). This firm will have high profitability and high risk. In fact, the firm may follow a conservative financing policy to counter its relatively liquid assets structure in practice. The conclusion of all this is that the considerations of assets and financing mix are crucial to the working capital management.

Table 27.7: Effect of Long-Term and Short-Term Financing

| | Financing Plan | | |
	Conservative	Moderate	Aggressive
	Rs '000	*Rs '000*	*Rs '000*
Fixed assets	300,000	300,000	300,000
Current assets	200,000	200,000	200,000
Total assets	500,000	500,000	500,000
Short-term debt (12%)	60,000	150,000	300,000
Long-term debt (14%)	240,000	150,000	0
PBIT	90,000	90,000	90,000
Interest	40,800	39,000	36,000
EBT	49,200	51,000	54,000
Tax (35%)	17,220	17,850	18,900
Net income	31,980	33,150	35,100
Return on equity	16.00%	16.58%	17.55%
SF/TF	12%	30%	60%

* SF = Short-term financing, TF = Total financing.

SUMMARY

❖ Gross working capital refers to the firm's investment in current assets.

❖ Net working capital means the difference between current assets and current liabilities, and therefore, represents that position of current assets which the firm has to finance either from long-term funds or bank borrowings.

❖ A firm is required to invest in current assets for a smooth, uninterrupted production and sale. How much a firm will invest in current assets will depend on its operating cycle.

❖ Operating cycle is defined as the time duration which the firm requires to manufacture and sell the product and collect cash. Thus operating cycle refers to the acquisition of resources, conversion of raw materials into work-in-process into finished goods, conversion of finished goods into sales and collection of sales. Larger is the operating cycle, larger

will be the investment in current assets.

❖ In practice, firms acquire resources on credit. To that extent, firm's need to raise working finance is reduced.

❖ The term net operating cycle is used for the difference between operating cycle (or gross operating cycle) and the payment deferral period (or the period for which creditors remain outstanding).

❖ The manufacturing cycle (that is conversion of raw material into work-in-process into finished goods) is a component of operating cycle, and therefore, it is a major determinant of working capital requirement. Manufacturing cycle depends on the firm's choice of technology and production policy.

❖ The firm's credit policy is another factor which influences the working capital requirement. It depends on the nature and norms of business, competition and the firm's desire to use it as a marketing tool.

❖ The requirement for working capital finance will be reduced to the extent the firm is able to exploit the credit extended by suppliers. Depending on the possible availability of working capital finance and its own profitability, a firm may carry more or less investment in current assets than warranted by technical factors.

❖ The firm's decision about the level of investment in current assets involves a trade-off between risk and return. When the firm invests more in current assets it reduces the risk of illiquidity, but loses in terms of profitability since the opportunity of earning from the excess investment in current assets is lost. The firm therefore is required to strike a right balance.

❖ The financing of current assets also involves a trade-off between risk and return. A firm can choose from short- or long-term sources of finance.

❖ If the firm uses more of short-term funds for financing both current and fixed assets, its financing policy is considered aggressive and risky.

❖ Its financing policy will be considered conservative if it makes relatively more use in financing its assets.

❖ A balanced approach is to finance permanent current assets by long-term sources and 'temporary' current assets by short-term sources of finance. Theoretically, short-term debt is considered to be risky and costly to finance permanent current assets.

KEY CONCEPTS

Cash conversion cycle	Liquidity-profitability trade-off	Permanent working capital	Term structure of interest rates
Financing policy	Manufacturing cycle	Variable working capital	Working capital policy
Gross working capital	Net working capital	Spontaneous financing	Yield curve
Liquidity preference theory	Operating cycle		

ILLUSTRATIVE SOLVED PROBLEMS

Problem 27.1: A proforma cost sheet of a company provides the following data:

	Rs
Costs (per unit):	
Raw materials	52.0
Direct labour	19.5
Overheads	39.0
Total cost (per unit)	110.5
Profit	19.5
Selling price	130.0

The following is the additional information available:

Average raw material in stock: one month; average materials in process : half a month. Credit allowed by suppliers: one month; credit allowed to debtors: two months. Time lag in payment of wages: one and a half weeks. Overheads: one month. One-fourth of sales are on cash basis. Cash balance is expected to be Rs 120,000.

You are required to prepare a statement showing the working capital needed to finance a level of activity of 70,000 units of output. You may assume that production is carried on evenly throughout the year and wages and overheads accrue similarly.

Solution:

Table 27.8: Calculation of Working Capital Needs

	Rs
A. Investment in inventory	
1. Raw material inventory: one month (30 days)	
(RMC/360) × RMCP = {(70,000 × 52)/360} × 30	303,333.33

(Contd.)

	Rs
2. Work-in-process inventory: half-a-month (15 days)	
(COP/360) × WIPCP = {(70,000 × 110.5)/360} × 15	322,291.67
3. Finished goods inventory: one month (30 days)	
(COS/360) × FGCP = {(70,000 × 110.5)/360} × 30	644,583.33
	1,270,208.33
B. Investment in debtors: two months (60 days)	
(Credit sale (cost)/360) × BDCP	
= {(52,500 × 110.5)/360} × 60	966,875.00
C. Cash balance	120,000.00
D. Investment in current assets (A + B + C)	2,357,708.33
E. Current liabilities: deferred payment	
1. Creditors: one month (30 days)	
(Purchases of raw material/360) × PDP	
= {(70,000 × 52)/360} × 30	303,333.33
2. Deferred wages: 1 1/2 weeks (10 days)	
= {(70,000 × 19.5)/360} × 10	37,916.67
3. Deferred overheads: one month (30 days)	
= {(70,000 × 39)/360} × 30	227,500.00
F. Total deferred payment (spontaneous sources of working capital [E (1 + 2 + 3)]	568,750.00
G. Net working capital (D – F)	1,788,958.33

Problem 27.2: A firm has applied for working capital finance from a commercial bank. You are requested by the bank to prepare an estimate of the working capital requirements of the firm. You may add 10 per cent to your estimated figure to account for exigencies. The following is the firm's projected profit and loss account:

	Rs
1. Sales	2,247,000
2. Cost of goods sold	1,637,100
3. Gross profit (1 – 2)	609,900
4. Administrative expenses	149,800
5. Selling expenses	139,100
6. Profit before tax [3 – (4 + 5)]	321,000
7. Tax provision	107,000
8. Profit after tax (6 – 7)	214,000

The cost of goods sold (COGS) is calculated as follows:

	Rs
Materials used	898,800
Wages and other mfg. expenses	668,750
Depreciation	251,450
	1,819,000
Less: Stock of finished goods	
(10% product not yet sold)	181,900
Cost of goods sold	1,637,100

The figures given above relate only to the goods that have been finished, and not to work in progress; goods equal to 15 per cent of the year's production (in terms of physical units) are in progress on an average requiring full material but only 40 per cent of other expenses. The firm has a policy of keeping two months consumption of material in stock.

All expenses are paid one month in arrear. Suppliers of material grant one and a half months credit; sales are 20 per cent cash while remaining sold on two months credit. 70 per cent of the income tax has to be paid in advance in quarterly instalments.

Solution:

Table 27.9: Estimation of Working Capital

	Rs
A. Investment in inventories	
1. Raw material: 2 months	
(RMC/12) × 2 = (8,98,800/12) × 2	149,800.00
2. Work-in-process: 15% of COP (adjusted)	
= COP × 15% = (898,800 + 40% of 668,750)	
× 15% = 11,66,300 × 15%	174,945.00
3. Finished goods : given	
181,900 – non-cash depreciation	
= 181,900 – 10% of 251,450	156,755.00
	481,500.00
B. Investment in debtors: 2 months	
(Credit sale (cost)/12) × 2	
= (80% cost of sales/12) × 2	
= 80% (1,637,100 – 251,450	
+ 149,800 + 139,100) 2/12	223,273.33
C. Cash balance	0.00
D. Investment in current assets (A + B + C)	704,773.33
E. Current liabilities: deferred payments:	

(Contd.)

	Rs
1. Creditors: 1½ months (Purchases/12) × 1½	
= (898,800/24) × 3	112,350.00
2. Deferred wages and other manufacturing, selling and administration expenses: one month	
(668,750 + 149,800 + 139,100/12) × 1	79,804.17
F. Total current liabilities	192,154.17
G. Net working capital (*D – F*)	512,619.16

Notes:

1. Depreciation is a non-cash item. Therefore, it has been ignored in calculations.
2. Cost of production does not include selling and administrative expenses.
3. Profit has been ignored in calculating net working capital. Since taxes can be paid out of profits, they have also been ignored. Alternatively, advance payment taxes require additional working capital, and profits are sources of working capital.

Problem 27.3: An engineering company is considering its working capital investment for the next year. Estimated fixed assets and current liabilities for the next year are respectively Rs 2.60 crore and Rs 2.34 crore. Sales and profit before interest and taxes (PBIT) depend on current assets investment—particularly inventories and book debts. The company is examining the following alternative working capital policies:

Working Capital Policy	Investment in Current Assets (Rs in crore)	Estimated Sales (Rs in crore)	EBIT (Rs in crore)
Conservative	4.50	12.30	1.23
Moderate	3.90	11.50	1.15
Aggressive	2.60	10.00	1.00

You are required to calculate the following for each policy (*a*) rate of return on total assets, (*b*) net working capital position, (*c*) current ratio, and (*d*) current asset to fixed asset ratio. Also discuss the return-risk trade offs of the three policies.

Solution:

Return-risk trade-off: Rate of return on total assets is the measure of return while CA/CL ratio or net working capital position can be taken as the measure of risk. Expected return and risk are minimum under conservative policy and highest under the aggressive policy. This implies that if the firm wants to increase its profitability by reducing investment in working capital, it has to be ready to bear more risk of being unable to meet its financial obligations.

(Rs in crore)

	Working Capital Investment Policies		
	Conservative	Moderate	Aggressive
A. Current assets (CA)	4.50	3.90	2.60
B. Fixed assets (FA)	2.60	2.60	2.60
C. Total assets (TA)	7.10	6.50	5.20
D. Current liabilities (CL)	2.34	2.34	2.34
E. Forecasted sales	12.30	11.50	10.00

(Contd.)

	Working Capital Investment Policies		
	Conservative	*Moderate*	*Aggressive*
F. Expected PBIT	1.23	1.15	1.00
(*i*) Rate of return (F ÷ C)	17.3%	17.7%	19.2%
(*ii*) Net working capital			
(A – D)	2.16	1.56	0.26
(*iii*) Current ratio (A ÷ D)	1.92	1.67	1.11
(*iv*) CA/FA	1.73	1.50	1.00

Problem 27.4: Assume that the engineering firm in Problem 27.3 has chosen the moderate working capital policy (that is, investment of Rs 3.90 crore in current assets). The company is now examining the use of long-term and short-term borrowing for financing its assets. The company will use Rs 2.50 crore of equity funds. The corporate tax rate is 35 per cent. The company is considering the following debt alternatives:

Financing policy	*Short-term Debt (Rs in cr.)*	*Long-term Debt (Rs in cr.)*
Conservative	0.54	1.12
Moderate	1.00	0.66
Aggressive	1.50	0.16

The average effective interest rate on short-term debt is 12 per cent while on long-term debt it is 16 per cent. Determine the following for each of the financing policies: (*a*) rate of return on shareholders' equity, (*b*) net working capital position, and (*c*) current ratio. Also, evaluate the return-risk trade offs of these policies.

Expected return and risk are lowest under the conservative policy and highest under the aggressive policy. It implies that if the company wants more return it will have to incur more risk via its financing policy.

Solution:

Table 27.10: Effects of Alternative Financial Policies

		Financing Policies		
		Conservative (Rs in cr.)	*Moderate (Rs in cr.)*	*Aggressive (Rs in cr.)*
1.	Current assets (CA)	3.90	3.90	3.90
2.	Fixed assets (FA)	2.60	2.60	2.60
3.	Total assets (TA)	6.50	6.50	6.50
4.	Current liabilities	2.34	2.34	2.34
5.	Short-term debt	0.54	1.00	1.50
6.	Long-term debt	1.12	0.66	0.16
7.	Equity capital	2.50	2.50	2.50
8.	Total capital (4 + 5 + 6 + 7)	6.50	6.50	6.50
9.	Forecasted sales	11.50	11.50	11.50
10.	Expected EBIT	1.15	1.15	1.15
11.	Interest: STD	0.06	0.12	0.18
	LTD	0.18	0.11	0.03
12.	Profit before tax (10 – 11)	0.91	0.92	0.94
13.	Taxes, 35%	0.32	0.32	0.33
14.	Profit after tax (12 – 13)	0.59	0.60	0.61
	(*a*) Return on equity (14 ÷ 7)	23.7%	23.9%	24.4%
	(*b*) Net working capital position [1 – (4 + 5)]	1.02	0.56	0.06
	(*c*) Current ratio [1 ÷ (4 + 5)]	1.35	1.17	1.02

REVIEW QUESTIONS

1. Explain the concept of working capital. Are gross and net concepts of working capital exclusive? Discuss.
2. What is the importance of working capital for a manufacturing firm? What shall be the repercussions if a firm has (*a*) paucity of working capital, (*b*) excess working capital?
3. What is the concept of working capital cycle? What is meant by cash conversion cycle? Why are these concepts important in working capital management? Give an example to illustrate.
4. Briefly explain factors that determine the working capital needs of a firm.
5. How is working capital affected by (*a*) sales, (*b*) technology and production policy, and (*c*) inflation? Explain.
6. Define the working capital management. Why is it important to study the management of working capital as a separate area in financial management?
7. Illustrate the profitability-solvency tangle in the current assets holding.
8. How would you determine the optimum level of current assets? Illustrate your answer.
9. Explain the costs of liquidity and illiquidity. What is the impact of these costs on the level of current assets?
10. "Merely increasing the level of current asset holding does not necessarily reduce the riskiness of the firm. Rather, the composition of current assets, whether highly liquid or highly illiquid, is the important factor to consider." Explain your position.
11. Explain the merit of a matching financing plan relative to a financing plan that extensively uses (*a*) long-term financing, or (*b*) short-term financing.
12. Explain the risk-return trade-off of current assets financing.
13. Do you recommend that a firm should finance its current assets entirely with short-term financing? Explain your answer.
14. What methods do you suggest for estimating working capital needs? Illustrate your answer.

PROBLEMS

1. The following cost of sales statements are available for D.D. manufacturers:

Statement of Cost of Sales   (Rs in crore)

Items	19X1	19X2	19X3
1. Opening raw material inventory	5.2	6.8	7.6
2. Purchases	25.6	33.5	45.6
3. Closing raw material inventory	6.8	7.6	9.2
4. Raw material consumed (1 + 2 – 3)	24.0	32.7	44.0
5. Wages and salaries	8.1	11.2	15.3
6. Other mfg. expenses	3.2	4.4	5.8
7. Depreciation	1.8	2.0	2.6
8. Total cost (4 + 5 + 6 + 7)	37.1	50.3	67.7
9. Opening work-in-process inventory	1.8	2.0	3.1
10. Closing work-in-process inventory	2.0	3.1	4.6
11. Cost of production	36.9	49.2	66.2
12. Opening finished goods inventory	3.2	2.8	3.6
13. Closing finished goods inventory	2.8	3.6	2.9
14. Cost of goods sold	37.3	48.4	66.9
15. Selling, administrative and other expenses	1.3	1.9	2.1
16. Cost of sales (14 + 15)	38.6	50.3	69.0

The following are the additional data available:

		19X1	19X2	19X3
Sales		45.9	60.1	82.7
PBIT		7.3	9.8	13.7
Debtors:	Opening	8.3	10.8	14.9
	Closing	10.8	14.9	20.5
Creditors:	Opening	3.7	4.6	8.0
	Closing	4.6	8.0	12.0

You are required to calculate (*i*) operating cycle, (*ii*) net operating cycle, and (*iii*) cash conversion cycle for each of the three years.

2. X & Co. is desirous to purchase a business and has consulted you, and one point on which you are asked to advise them is the average amount of working capital which will be required in the first year's working.

You are given the following estimates and are instructed to add 10 per cent to your computed figure to allow for contingencies:

	Figures for the Year Rs
Average amount backed up for stocks:	
Stocks of finished product	5,000
Stocks of stores, materials, etc.	8,000
Average credit given:	

(Contd.)

		Figures for the Year Rs
Inland sales	6 weeks' credit	3,12,000
Export sales	1½ weeks' credit	78,000
Lag in payment of wages and other outgoings:		
Wages	1½ weeks	260,000
Stocks, materials, etc.	1½ weeks	48,000
Rent, royalties, etc.	6 months	10,000
Clerical staff	½ month	62,000
Manager	½ month	4,800
Miscellaneous expenses	1½ months	48,000
Payment in advance:		
Sundry expenses (paid quarterly in advance)		8,000
Undrawn profits on the average throughout the year.		11,000

Set up your calculations for the average amount of working capital required.   (*C.A., adapted*)

3. A *proforma* cost sheet of a company provides the following particulars:

	Amount per unit Rs
Raw material	80
Direct labour	30
Overheads	60
Total cost	170
Profit	30
Selling price	200

The following further particulars are available:

(*a*) Raw material in stock, on an average one month; materials in process, on average half a month; finished goods in stock, on an average one month.

(*b*) Credit allowed by suppliers is one month; credit allowed to debtors is two months; lag in payment of wages is one and a half weeks; lag in payment of overhead expenses is one month; one-fourth of the output is sold against cash; cash in hand and at bank is expected to be Rs 25,000.

You are required to prepare a statement showing working capital needed to finance a level of activity of 104,000 units of production. You may assume that production is carried on evenly throughout the year, and wages and overheads accrue similarly.   (*C.A., adapted*)

4. While preparing a project report on behalf of a client you have collected the following facts. Estimate the net working capital required for that project. Add 10 per cent to your computed figure to allow for contingencies.

	Amount per unit Rs
Estimated cost per unit of production is:	
Raw material	42.4
Direct labour	15.9
Overheads (exclusive of depreciation)	31.8
Total cost	90.1

Additional information:

Selling price	Rs 106 per unit, 100,000 units
Level of activity	of production per annum
Raw material in stock	average 4 weeks
Work-in-progress (assume 50% completion stage)	average 2 weeks
Finished goods in stock	average 4 weeks
Credit allowed by suppliers	average 4 weeks
Credit allowed to debtors	average 8 weeks
Lag in payment of wages	average 1½ weeks

Cash at bank is expected to be Rs 125,000.

You may assume that production is carried on evenly throughout the year (52 weeks) and wages and overheads accrue similarly. All sales are on credit basis only.

(M.Com., D.U., adapted)

5. The following are the given cost of liquidity and illiquidity for different ratios of current assets to fixed assets of a firm. Determine the optimum ratio of current assets to fixed assets. Also show your answer on a graph.

CA/FA	Cost of Liquidity	Cost of Liquidity
0.10	138,000	2,200,000
0.25	275,000	1,650,000
0.40	550,000	1,100,000
0.70	1,100,000	830,000
1.00	2,200,000	690,000
1.50	4,140,000	550,000
2.50	6,890,000	276,000

6. GG Industries have estimated its monthly needs of net working capital for 19X1 as follows:

The firm is rated to have average risk; therefore, working capital finance from a bank will cost the firm 16 per cent per annum. Long-term borrowing will be available at 14 per cent. The firm can invest excess funds in the form of inter-corporate lending at 12 per cent per annum.

(i) Assume the firm finances the maximum amount of its working capital requirements for the next year with long-term borrowing and investing any excess funds in the form of inter-corporate lending. Calculate GG Industries net interest cost during 19X1.

Month	Amount Rs lakh	Month	Amount Rs lakh
January	72.65	July	58.12
February	58.13	August	72.66
March	29.06	September	82.30
April	24.22	October	87.19
May	33.90	November	92.02
June	43.60	December	87.17

(ii) Assume the firm finance all its working capital requirements for the next year with short-term borrowing. Determine GG Industries interest cost during 19X1.

(iii) Discuss the return-risk trade-offs associated with the above two policies.

7. A company wants to analyse the effect of its working capital investment and financing policies on shareholders' return and risk. Assume that the firm has Rs 180 crore in fixed assets and Rs 150 crore in current liabilities. The company has a policy of maintaining a debt to total assets ratio of 60 per cent, where debt consists of both short-term debt from banks and long-term debt. The following data relate to three alternative policies:

Working Capital Policies	Investment in Current Assets (Rs crore)	Bank Borrowings (Rs crore)	Projected Sales (Rs crore)	EBIT (Rs crore)
Aggressive	252	216	531	53
Moderate	270	162	540	54
Conservative	288	108	549	55

Assume that bank borrowing will cost 16 per cent while the effective interest cost of long-term borrowing will be 18 per cent per annum. You are required to determine: (a) return on shareholders equity, (b) net working capital position, (c) current ratio, and (d) current assets to total assets ratio. Also evaluate the return-risk trade offs associated with these three policies.

CASE

Case 27.1: Reliable Texamill Limited[1]

In the beginning of 2003, Mr Shyam Lal, Chairman and Managing Director of The Reliable Texamill Limited (RTL) was concerned about the company's working capital management.

As the company was expecting its net sales to increase from Rs 1,208.61 lakh in 2002 to Rs 2,185.94 lakh in 2003, the management of working capital components would assume greater importance. The company would need more working

---

1. This case is an adapted version of the original case written by the author and published in Pandey, I.M. and Bhat, Ramesh, *Cases in Financial Management*, Tata McGraw Hill, 2002.

capital funds to support the expanding sales. Mr. Shyam Lal knew that it may not be easy to get funds from banks. He was wondering how he could reduce the working capital funds requirement of his company without affecting sales.

Background

RTL commenced commercial production in 1999. It manufactures synthetic blended yarn which is a raw material for other textile weaving mills and also for handloom and power looms. The company's mills are situated in an industrially less developed area in a northern State. The company has a licensed capacity of 80,000 spindles and existing installed capacity of 26,390 spindles (this includes 6,210 spindles added during 2001–02). The average capacity utilization of the company was 81 per cent during 2000-01 and 85 per cent during 2001–02. It expects to use 87 per cent of the installed capacity during 2002–03.

In the year 1999-00, the company could generate net sales of Rs 191.13 lakh, and incurred a net loss of Rs 57.11 lakh. The acute power shortage was the dominant reason, besides the initial teething troubles, for the poor beginning of the company. RTL has since been able to increase its sales to Rs 973.32 lakh in 2000-01, and to Rs 1,203.61 lakh in 2001-02 as against the estimated sales of Rs 1,767.55 lakh. It produced 1,315 tonnes of yarn in 2001-02 against 1,182 tonnes during the previous year. The management of RTL has attributed the lower actual sales to the sluggish market conditions that prevailed during the second half of the year 2001-02, forcing the company to keep its production at a low level, and also to a certain extent due to the company manufacturing substantial quantity of yarn of lesser counts and blends of lower value to suit the market conditions. After incurring a loss in the first year (the company operated for seven months only), the company made a net profit of Rs 24.48 lakh in 2000-01. The company showed a net profit before depreciation of Rs 32.42 lakh in 2001-02. Power cuts, high input costs and increased administrative expenses on account of expansion resulted in poor profitability.

RTL has not so far paid any tax and dividends. Its tax liability is expected to be nil for quite some time as it enjoys tax benefits being a new unit located in an industrially less developed area. The actual and estimated balance sheets and the profit and loss account of the company are given in Tables 27.1.1, 27.1.2 and 27.1.3.

PRODUCTION FACILITIES

The company's existing production facilities are considered adequate for operating the spinning mills at the enhanced installed capacity. The production process for obtaining the main product, viz. the synthetic yarn, originates with the mixing up of the different fibres, i.e., acrylic, polyester and viscose as per the blend proposed to be manufactured. The annual consumption of these fibres generally depends on the product mix manufactured during the particular year; the actual consumption during the years 2000-01 and 2001-02 being about 1,973 tonnes and 2,303 tonnes valued respectively at Rs 713.11 lakh and Rs 902.30 lakh. The company generally does not encounter any significant difficulties in procuring its full requirements of raw materials and stores at the current market prices from suppliers.

Because of the frequent power cuts, the company built up adequate captive power generating capacity by installing one more set of 860 kVA diesel power generator. RTL is now planning to replace two sets of 250 kVA by the purchase of one imported SKODA set of 869 kVA at a cost of Rs 47.70. The new set is expected to be more economical from the point of view of diesel consumption and usage for longer period.

COMPETITION AND SELLING ARRANGEMENTS

The company's end products cater to the needs of large and medium scale manufacturers of fabrics and also handlooms and power looms. The major buyers, accounting for 80 to 85 per cent of sales, include reputed firms. The remaining 15–20 per cent is sold to small dealers and traders.

RTL faces a fair amount of competition from a number of companies. In spite of the stiff competition, the synthetic blended yarn manufactured by RTL is well received in the market and is supposed to enjoy a premium over the yarn manufactured by other leading manufacturers in the country. Its four branches located in different parts of the country manage the selling operations of the company. The full-fledged sales depots recently opened are situated far away from the company's factory. As a result, a good part of the finished goods remains in transit at any point of time. About 65 per cent of the company's sales are being affected on credit terms ranging from 45 to 60 days depending on the market conditions. The company has been finding it difficult to realize its dues within the normal credit period allowed to customers. The management attributed this to its being new to the competitive textile market. Till 2001–02, the company had a practice of selling a part of its production through selling agents to small buyers. This practice has been discontinued, and now the company directly sells to these buyers. The company, however, allows a discount ranging between two to two-and-half per cent for sales on demand/cash basis.

EXPANSION

Soon after starting commercial production in 1999, RTL planned to undertake an expansion programme for installation of another 20,000 additional spindles. Since the company incurred a loss in the very first year, the company attempted a modest expansion programme involving installation of additional 6,210 spindles only during 2001-02. The company felt that this increase in its installed capacity was absolutely necessary in order to bring about a better economy in its operations. The expansion programme was completed with a capital expenditure of about Rs 276 lakh against the estimated cost of Rs 253 lakh. The additional spindles would be put to commercial production from April 2004.

FUTURE PROSPECTS

The prices of the basic raw material viz. viscose/polyester fibres, are lower in the international market than in India. While the prices of viscose/polyester fibres have increased substantially during the last two years, 2000-01 and 2001-02, the prices of RTL's end products have, more or less, remained at the same level. The company has not been able to absorb in the selling prices the increased costs of inputs. The power supply in the

State, where the company is situated, is presently showing signs of improvement, and it is expected to be satisfactory in the coming months. With the consumer preference during the recent years having shifted to blended fabrics and the company's products being of good quality and well accepted in the market, RTL can hope to fare well in the coming years.

Table 27.11: Reliable Texamill Limited: Balance Sheet as on March 31

(Rs in lakh)

	Actual		Projected
	2001	**2002**	**2003**
LIABILITIES			
Current Liabilities	625.95	805.78	866.16
Bank borrowings	366.74	490.02	622.91
Trade creditors	200.94	239.16	70.79
Term loans payable	10.56	5.89	98.74
Misc. liabilities and provisions	47.71	70.71	73.72
Term liabilities	531.22	801.14	802.37
Term loans payable	479.68	641.88	613.73
Deferred credit	29.95	24.06	17.21
Term deposits	10.27	20.54	56.77
Others	11.32	114.66	114.66
Total liabilities	1,157.17	1,606.92	1,668.53
Net Worth	191.07	223.49	288.74
Share capital	199.44	199.44	199.44
Reserves	24.26	24.26	24.26
P&L surplus (deficit)	−32.63	−0.21	65.04
Total funds	1,348.24	1.830.41	1.957.27
ASSETS			
Current Assets	580.03	757.47	913.59
Cash and bank balance	4.35	6.06	7.44
Receivables	293.25	269.48	303.19
Inventory:			
Raw materials	162.00	202.13	275.22
Stock-in process	51.02	64.96	80.85
Finished goods	22.94	160.44	177.87
Consumable spares	16.80	27.20	32.34
Others	29.67	27.20	36.68
Fixed Assets	760.46	1,056.61	1,027.35
Gross Block	820.04	1,121.13	1,146.19
Acc. Depreciation	73.66	73.66	127.34
Net block	746.38	1.047.47	1,018.85
Other non-0current assets	14.08	9.14	8.50
Intangible Assets	7.75	16.33	16.33
Total assets	1,348.24	1,830.41	1,957.27

RTL produced 1,182 tonnes and 1,315 tonnes of yarn during the years 2000-01 and 2001-02 respectively. In 2002-03, it has planned production of 1,758 tonnes. RTL normally plans its production schedule on the basis of the market trend, i.e. as per the counts/blends of synthetic yarn acceptable in the market so as to sell the end products with ease. RTL's production plan for 2002-03 has been devised keeping in view the changes in the market conditions and other factors. RTL has planned to manufacture more quantities of yarn in blends of higher value during the period 2002-03. Those blends are expected to be more acceptable in the market.

The company has projected its energy costs at about 3.4 per cent of the total cost of production. The other expenses have been estimated in line with the past experience. Also, the assets and liabilities of the company have been estimated in accordance with the past trends.

RTL had depended quite substantially on trade credit for meeting its working capital needs. Trade credit forms about one-third of the current liabilities. The normal credit period allowed by the suppliers is 45 days; however, a discount of 2 per cent for payments made within 15 days of the purchase date is allowed. In the past, creditors did not object to RTL's stretching of payments to them. In view of the credit squeeze, they are likely to pressurize hard for early payment of dues.

Table 27.12: Reliable Texamill Limited
Profit and Loss Account for the year ended March 31

(Rs in lakh)

	Actual		Projection
	2001	**2002**	**2003**
Net Sales	973.32	1,208.61	2,185.94
Cost of goods sold	775.98	921.96	1,850.33
Gross profit	197.34	286.65	335.61
Operating expenses:			
Selling and administration	97.26	123.30	127.74
Interest	81.68	137.83	140.68
Operating profit	18.40	25.52	67.19
Other income (loss)	6.08	6.90	−1.94
Profit before tax	24.48	32.42	65.25
Provision	0.00	0.00	0.00
Profit after tax	24.48	32.42	65.25

Table 27.13: Reliable Texamill Limited: Statement of Costs of Sales

(Rs in lakh)

	Actual		Projection
	2001	**2002**	**2003**
Raw material	685.94	933.67	1,649.36
Power and fuel	36.67	55.37	64.68
Direct labour	40.00	57.14	79.41
Other manufacturing expenses	12.87	27.21	36.52
Depreciation	41.57	–	53.68
Total	817.05	1,073.39	1,883.65
Add: Opening stock-in-progress	24.92	51.02	64.96
Total	841.97	1,124.41	1,948.61
Less: Closing stock-in-progress	51.02	64.96	80.85
Cost of production	790.95	1,059.45	1,867.76

Contd...

| | Actual | Projection | |
	2001	2002	2003
Add: Opening finished goods	7.97	22.95	160.44
Total	798.92	1,082.40	2,028.20
Less: Closing finished goods	22.94	160.44	177.87
Cost of Sales	775.98	921.96	1,850.30

Discussion Questions

1. Critically evaluate RTL's performance and financing of its operations.
2. How has the company managed its working capital in the past? Illustrate with appropriate calculations.
3. What are RTL's plans to improve its working capital management? Show calculation of operating cycle to justify your answer.
4. Do you accept the financial plan prepared by RTL? What modifications would you suggest in the plan and why?

28 Receivables Management and Factoring

INTRODUCTION

Trade credit arises when a firm sells its products or services on credit and does not receive cash immediately. It is an essential marketing tool, acting as a bridge for the movement of goods through production and distribution stages to customers. A firm grants trade credit to protect its sales from the competitors and to attract the potential customers to buy its products at favourable terms. Trade credit creates **accounts receivable** or **trade debtors** (also referred to *book debts* in India) that the firm is expected to collect in the near future. The customers from whom receivable or book debts have to be collected in the future are called *trade debtors* or simply as debtors and represent the firm's claim or asset. A credit sale has three characteristics:[1] *First*, it involves an element of risk that should be carefully analysed. Cash sales are totally riskless, but not the credit sales as the cash payment are yet to be received. *Second*, it is based on economic value. To the buyer, the economic value in goods or services passes immediately at the time of sale, while the seller expects an equivalent value to be received later on. *Third*, it implies futurity. The buyer will make the cash payment for goods or services received by him in a future period.

Debtors constitute a substantial portion of current assets of several firms. For example in India, trade debtors, after inventories, are the major components of current assets. They form about one-third of current assets in India. Granting credit and creating debtors amount to the blocking of the firm's funds. The interval between the date of sale and the date of payment has to be financed out of working capital. This necessitates the firm to get funds from banks or other sources. Thus, trade debtors represent investment. As substantial amounts are tied-up in trade debtors, it needs careful analysis and proper management.

CREDIT POLICY: NATURE AND GOALS

A firm's *investment in accounts receivable* depends on: (a) the volume of credit sales, and (b) the collection period. For example, if a firm's credit sales are Rs 30 lakh per day and customers, on an average, take 45 days to make payment, then the firm's average investment in accounts receivable is:

Daily credit sales × Average collection period

$$\text{Rs } 30 \text{ lakh} \times 45 = \text{Rs } 1,350 \text{ lakh}$$

The investment in receivable may be expressed in terms of costs of sales instead of sales value.

The volume of credit sales is a function of the firm's total sales and the percentage of credit sales to total sales. Total sales depend on market size, firm's market share, product quality,

---

1. Ramamoorthy, V.E., *Working Capital Management,* Chennai: Institute for Financial Management and Research, 1976, p. 183.

intensity of competition, economic conditions etc. The financial manager hardly has any control over these variables. The percentage of credit sales to total sales is mostly influenced by the nature of business and industry norms. For example, car manufacturers in India, until recently, were not selling cars on credit. They required the customers to make payment at the time of delivery; some of them even asked for the payment to be made in advance. This was so because of the absence of genuine competition and a wide gap between demand for and supply of cars in India. This position changed after economic liberalisation which led to intense competition. In contrast, the textile manufacturers sold two-thirds of their total sales on credit to the wholesale dealers. The textile industry is still going through a difficult phase.

There is one way in which the financial manager can affect the volume of credit sales and collection period and consequently, investment in accounts receivable. That is through the changes in credit policy. The term credit policy is used to refer to the combination of three decision variables: (*i*) credit standards, (*ii*) credit terms, and (*iii*) collection efforts, on which the financial manager has influence.

- *Credit standards* are criteria to decide the types of customers to whom goods could be sold on credit. If a firm has more slow-paying customers, its investment in accounts receivable will increase. The firm will also be exposed to higher risk of default.
- *Credit terms* specify duration of credit and terms of payment by customers. Investment in accounts receivable will be high if customers are allowed extended time period for making payments.
- *Collection efforts* determine the actual collection period. The lower the collection period, the lower the investment in accounts receivable and *vice versa*.

Goals of Credit Policy

A firm may follow a lenient or a stringent credit policy. The firm following a **lenient credit policy** tends to sell on credit to customers on very liberal terms and standards; credits are granted for longer periods even to those customers whose creditworthiness is not fully known or whose financial position is doubtful. In contrast, a firm following a **stringent credit policy** sells on credit on a highly selective basis only to those customers who have proven creditworthiness and who are financially strong. In practice, firms follow credit policies ranging between stringent to lenient.

Marketing Tool

Why at all do firms sell on credit? Firms use credit policy as a *marketing tool* for expanding sales. In a declining market, it may be used to maintain the market share. Credit policy helps to retain old customers and create new customers by weaning them away from competitors. In a growing market, it is used to increase the firm's market share. Under a highly competitive situation or recessionary economic conditions, a firm may loosen its credit policy to maintain sales or to minimise erosion of sales.

In practice, companies may grant credit for several other reasons such as the company position, buyer's status and requirement, dealer relationship, transit delays, industrial practice etc. (see Exhibit 28.1)

EXHIBIT 28.1: WHY DO COMPANIES IN INDIA GRANT CREDIT?

Companies in practice feel the necessity of granting credit for several reasons:

- *Competition* Generally the higher the degree of competition, the more the credit granted by a firm. However, there are exceptions such as firms in the electronics industry in India.
- *Company's bargaining power* If a company has a higher bargaining power *vis-á-vis* its buyers, it may grant no or less credit. The company will have a strong bargaining power if it has a strong product, monopoly power, brand image, large size or strong financial position.
- *Buyer's requirements* In a number of business sectors buyers/dealers are not able to operate without extended credit. This is particularly so in the case of industrial products.
- *Buyer's status* Large buyers demand easy credit terms because of bulk purchases and higher bargaining power. Some companies follow a policy of not giving much credit to small retailers since it is quite difficult to collect dues from them.
- *Relationship with dealers* Companies sometimes extend credit to dealers to build long-term relationships with them or to reward them for their loyalty.
- *Marketing tool* Credit is used as a marketing tool, particularly when a new product is launched or when a company wants to push its weak product.
- *Industry practice* Small companies have been found guided by industry practice or norm more than the large companies. Sometimes companies continue giving credit because of past practice rather than industry practice.
- *Transit delays* This is a forced reason for extended credit in the case of a number of companies in India. Most companies have evolved systems to minimise the impact of such delays. Some of them take the help of banks to control cash flows in such situation.

Source: Pandey, I.M. and Bhat, R., *Managing Corporate Funds*, Ch. 8 (unpublished monograph).

Maximisation of sales vs. incremental profit Is sales maximisation the goal of the firm's credit policy? If it was so, the firm would follow a very lenient credit policy, and would sell on credit to everyone. Firms in practice do not follow very loose credit policy just to maximise sales. Sales do not expand without costs. The firm will have to evaluate its credit policy in terms of both return and costs of additional sales. Additional sales should add to the firm's operating profit. There are three types of costs involved:

Production and selling costs These costs increase with expansion in sales. If sales expand within the existing production capacity, then only the variable production and selling costs will increase. If capacity is added for sales expansion resulting from loosening of credit policy, then the incremental production and selling costs will include both variable and fixed costs.

The difference between incremental sales revenue (Δ SALES) and the incremental production and selling costs (Δ COST) is the incremental contribution (Δ CONT) of the change in the credit policy. Note that a tight credit policy means rejection of certain types of accounts whose creditworthiness is doubtful. This results into loss of sales and consequently, loss of contribution. This is an **opportunity loss** to the firm. As the firm starts loosening its credit policy, it accepts all or some of those accounts which the firm had earlier rejected. Thus, the firm will recapture lost sales and thus, lost contribution. The opportunity cost of lost contribution declines with the loosening of credit policy.

Administration costs Two types of administration costs are involved when the firm loosens its credit policy: (*a*) credit investigation and supervision costs and (*b*) collection costs. The firm is required to analyse and supervise large number of accounts when it loosens its credit policy. Similarly, the firm will have to intensify its collection efforts to collect outstanding bills from financially less sound customers. The incremental costs of credit administration will be nil if the existing credit department without any additional costs can implement the new credit policy. This will be the case when the credit department has idle capacity.

Bad-debt losses Bad-debt losses arise when the firm is unable to collect its accounts receivable. The size of bad-debt losses depends on the quality of accounts accepted by the firm. This firm tends to sell to customers with relatively less credit standing when it loosens its credit policy. Some of these customers delay payments, and some of them do not pay at all. As a result, bad-debt losses increase. The firm can certainly avoid or minimise these losses by adopting a very tight credit policy. Is minimisation of bad-debt losses a goal of credit factoring? If it was so, no firm will ever sell on credit to anyone. If this happens, then the firm is not availing the opportunity of using credit policy as a marketing tool for expanding sales, and will incur opportunity cost in terms of lost contribution.

Thus, the evaluation of a *change* in a firm's credit policy involves analysis of:[1]

- opportunity cost of lost contribution
- credit administration costs and bad-debt losses.

These two costs behave contrary to each other. Consider Figure 28.1. You can see that as the firm moves from tight to loose credit policy, the opportunity cost declines (that is, the firm recaptures lost sales and thus, lost contribution), but the credit administration costs and bad-debt losses increase (that is, more accounts have to be handled which also include bad accounts which ultimately fail to pay). How should the firm determine its credit policy? The firm's credit policy will be determined by the trade-off between opportunity cost and credit administration

costs and bad debts losses. In the Figure 28.1, this trade-off occurs at point *A* where the total of opportunity costs of lost contribution and credit administration costs and bad-debts losses is minimum. Does point *A* represent *optimum credit policy?* How can a firm establish an optimum credit policy?

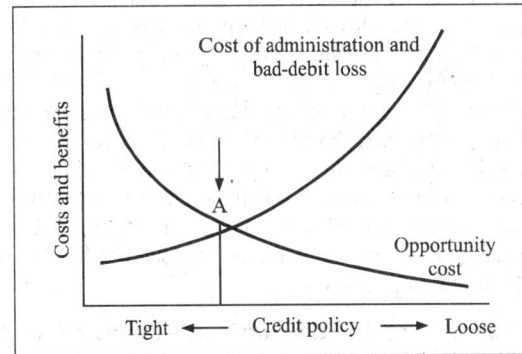

Figure 28.1: Costs of Credit Policy

OPTIMUM CREDIT POLICY: A MARGINAL COST-BENEFIT ANALYSIS

The firm's operating profit is maximised when total cost is minimised for a given level of revenue. Credit policy at point *A* in Figure 28.1 represents the *maximum operating profit* (since total cost is minimum). But it is not necessarily the **optimum credit policy**. Optimum credit policy is one which maximises the firm's value. The value of the firm is maximised when the **incremental** or **marginal rate of return** of an investment is equal to the **incremental** or **marginal cost of funds** used to finance the investment. The incremental rate of return can be calculated as incremental operating profit divided by the incremental investment in receivable. The incremental cost of funds is the rate of return required by the suppliers of funds, given the risk of investment in accounts receivable. Note that the required rate of return is *not* equal to the borrowing rate. Higher the risk of investment, higher the required rate of return. As the firm loosens its credit policy, its investment in accounts receivable becomes more risky because of increase in slow-paying and defaulting accounts. Thus the required rate of return is an upward sloping curve.

In sum, we may state that the goal of the firm's credit policy is to maximise the value of the firm. To achieve this goal, the evaluation of investment in accounts receivable[2] should involve the following four steps:

- Estimation of incremental operating profit
- Estimation of incremental investment in accounts receivable
- Estimation of the incremental rate of return of investment
- Comparison of the incremental rate of return with the required rate of return.

Consider an example.[3]

1. Solomon, E. and Pringle, J.J., *An Introduction to Financial Management,* Prentice-Hall of India, 1977, pp. 200–01.
2. The analytical approach discussed in this next section is based on J.S., "Opportunity Cost in the Evaluation of Investment in Accounts Receivables", *Financial Management,* Summer 1976; and Dyle, E.A., "Another Look at the Evaluation of Investments in Account Receivables", *Financial Management,* Winter 1977.
3. See the case titled, Allen Distribution Company in Butters, *et. al., Case Problems in Finance,* Richard D. Irwin, 1981, for a detailed practical situation.

Illustration 28.1: Marginal Cost-Benefit Analysis of Credit Policy

In 19X1, the Standard Furniture Mart has total sales of Rs 600 lakh and after-tax profit of Rs 69 lakh. Standard's profit margins have been declining over last two-three years. The proprietor of the company thought that this could be due to about 10 per cent of total sales to customers who are not financially very strong. He thought that perhaps the cost of maintaining these accounts is high which may be causing a decline in the firm's profit margin. He therefore asked his financial manager to analyse the impact of tightening the credit policy by discontinuing sales to these customers.

The financial manager should first calculate the incremental operating profit to be foregone by changing the credit policy. He should ascertain the behaviour of costs. Assume that after analysing past data, he has determined cost behaviour as given in Table 28.1. The financial manager, on investigation, found that bad-debt losses and collection costs are entirely attributable to the marginal accounts.

Table 28.1: Standard Furniture Mart's Behaviour of Cost (Percentage)

	Fixed Cost	*Variables Cost*	*Total Cost*
Cost of goods sold	–	82.00	82.00
Administrative costs	2.50	4.00	6.50
Selling costs	2.80	5.70	8.50
Bad-debt losses	–	0.05	0.05
Collection costs	–	0.02	0.02
	5.30	91.77	97.07

Standard's *variable* production, administrative and selling costs are 91.7 per cent of sales (bad-debt losses and collection costs excluded). Thus contribution is 8.3 per cent of sales: $100 - 91.7 = 8.3$ per cent. By tightening its credit policy, Standard can expect to lose sales of Rs 60 lakh (10 per cent of total sales of Rs 600 lakh). Thus, the lost contribution will be Rs 4.98 lakh:

Change in contribution = Change in sales × Contribution ratios

$$\Delta\,\text{CONT} = \text{SALES} \times c = -60 \times 0.083 = \text{Rs} - 4.98 \text{ lakh} \qquad (1)$$

Since bad-debt losses and collection costs were entirely attributable to the marginal accounts, with the discontinuance of sales to those customers, these costs will be avoided. We should subtract these avoidable costs from contribution to find lost operating profit, which is equal to Rs 4.56 lakh:

$$\frac{\text{Change in}}{\text{operating profit}} = \frac{\text{Change in}}{\text{contribution}} - \frac{\text{Additional}}{\text{cost}}$$

$$\begin{aligned}\Delta\text{OP} &= \Delta\text{CONT} - \text{SALES}\,(b + d) \\ &= -4.98 - [-60\,(0.0005 + 0.0002)] \\ &= -4.98 + 0.04 = -\text{Rs}\ 4.94 \text{ lakh}\end{aligned} \qquad (2)$$

where b is bad-debt losses ratio and d is collection expense ratio.

The next step is to determine the investment in accounts receivable (arising on account of marginal accounts). The financial manager found out that the average collection period of marginal accounts was 60 days against 45 days of all other accounts, and 80 per cent of sales to marginal accounts are on credit. Thus the sales value tied down in accounts receivable is Rs 8 lakh:

---

1. Solomon and Pringle, *op. cit.,* p. 204.

$$\frac{\text{Investment in}}{\text{accounts receivable}} = \frac{\text{Credit sales}}{\text{per day}} \times \frac{\text{Average}}{\text{collection period}}$$

$$\text{INVST} = \frac{\text{SALES} \times f}{360} \times \text{ACP} = \frac{60(0.8)}{360} \times 60 = \text{Rs}\ 8 \text{ lakh} \qquad (3)$$

In Equation (3), f is the fraction of credit sales in total sales. Note that not all of Rs 8 lakh represent *out-of-pocket cash investment*; it includes profit margin. Therefore, one view is that investment in accounts receivable should be measured in terms of cost either variable cost or total cost. Considering only the variable costs, Standard's average investment in accounts receivable (including bad-debt losses and collection charges) is: Rs 7.34 lakh.

$$8 \times 0.9177 = \text{Rs}\ 7.34 \text{ lakh}$$

We can now calculate the rate of return which the marginal accounts generate:

$$\text{Rate of return} = \frac{\text{Operating profit after tax}}{\text{Investment in accounts receivable}}$$

$$r = \frac{\Delta\text{OPAT}}{\Delta\text{INVST}} = \frac{\Delta\text{OP}\,(1-T)}{\Delta\text{INVST}} \qquad (4)$$

In our example, assuming tax rate (T) of 35 per cent, the rate of return is 43.8 per cent

$$r = \frac{4.94\,(1-0.35)}{7.34} = 0.438 \text{ or } 43.8 \text{ per cent}$$

If the sales value is used in determining the investment in accounts receivable, the rate of return works out as 40.1 per cent.

Given the risk of marginal accounts, is this an adequate return? Standard's required rate of return for average risk project is 20 per cent. The financial manager thought it appropriate to add additional 5 per cent for risk premium since marginal accounts are highly risky. Comparing the expected rate of return 40.1 per cent (or 43.8 per cent) with the required rate of return of 25 per cent, Standard should continue with its policy of selling to the marginal accounts. Marginal accounts make a net contribution to operating profits:

$$= \left(\begin{matrix}\text{Expected} \\ \text{return}\end{matrix} - \begin{matrix}\text{Required} \\ \text{return}\end{matrix}\right) \times \begin{matrix}\text{Investment in} \\ \text{receivable}\end{matrix}$$

$$= (0.401 - 0.25) \times 8 = \text{Rs}\ 1.21 \text{ lakh}$$

In fact, there is a case to further loosening the credit policy. If Standard does so, its administrative costs, bad debt losses and collection costs will increase. The expected rate of return will fall. Thus, loosening of credit policy causes return to fall. Where should Standard stop? The firm will obtain the maximum value for the credit policy when the incremental rate of return on investment in receivable is equal to the opportunity cost of capital (the incremental cost of funds).[1]

As the investment in accounts receivable is increased two things happen: *First,* marginal expected rate of return falls. *Second,* risk increases, so the required rate of return increases. This is shown in Figure 28.2. The optimum investment lies at a level of investment below that which maximises operating profit. In the figure operating profit is maximum at the point at which incremental rate of return is zero.

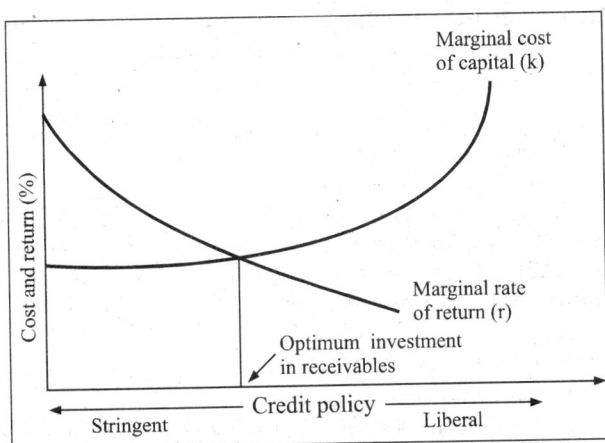

Figure 28.2: Optimum Level of Receivables

CREDIT POLICY VARIABLES

In establishing an optimum credit policy, the financial manager must consider the important decision variables which influence the level of receivables. As stated in the preceding section, the major controllable decision variables include the following:

- Credit standards and analysis
- Credit terms
- Collection policy and procedures

The financial manager or the credit manager may administer the credit policy of a firm. It should, however, be appreciated that credit policy has important implications for the firm's production, marketing and finance functions. Therefore, it is advisable that a committee that consists of executives of production, marketing and finance departments formulates the firm's credit policy. Within the framework of the credit policy, as laid down by this committee, the financial or credit manager should ensure that the firm's value of share is maximised. He does so by answering the following questions:

- What will be the *change* in sales when a decision variable is altered?
- What will be the *cost* of altering the decision variable?
- How would the level of receivable be affected by changing the decision variable?
- How are expected rate of return and cost of funds related?

The most difficult part of the analysis of impact of change in the credit policy variables is the estimation of sales and costs. Even if sales and costs can be estimated, it would be difficult to establish an optimum credit policy, as the best combination of the variables of credit policy is quite difficult to obtain. For these reasons, the establishment of credit policy is a slow process in practice. A firm will change one or two variables at a time and observe the effect. Based on the actual experience, variables may be changed further, or change may be reversed. It should also be noted that the firm's credit policy is greatly influenced by economic conditions. As economic conditions change, the credit policy of the firm may also change. Thus, the credit policy decision is not one time static decision. The impacts of changes in the major decision variables of credit policy are discussed below.[1]

Credit Standards

Credit standards are the criteria which a firm follows in selecting customers for the purpose of credit extension. The firm may have tight credit standards; that is, it may sell mostly on cash basis, and may extend credit only to the most reliable and financially strong customers. Such standards will result in no bad-debt losses, and less cost of credit administration. But the firm may not be able to expand sales. The profit sacrificed on lost sales may be more than the costs saved by the firm. On the contrary, if credit standards are loose, the firm may have larger sales. But the firm will have to carry larger receivable. The costs of administering credit and bad-debt losses will also increase. Thus, the choice of optimum credit standards involves a trade-off between incremental return and incremental costs.

Credit analysis Credit standards influence the quality of the firm's customers. There are two aspects of the quality of customers: (*i*) the time taken by customers to repay credit obligation and (*ii*) the default rate. The **average collection period** (ACP) determines the speed of payment by customers. It measures the number of days for which credit sales remain outstanding. The longer the average collection period, the higher the firm's investment in accounts receivable. **Default rate** can be measured in terms of bad-debt losses ratio—the proportion of uncollected receivable. Bad-debt losses ratio indicates default risk. **Default risk** is the likelihood that a customer will fail to repay the credit obligation. On the basis of past practice and experience, the financial or credit manager should be able to form a reasonable judgment regarding the chances of default. To estimate the probability of default, the financial or credit manager should consider three *C*'s: (*a*) character, (*b*) capacity, and (*c*) condition.[2]

- *Character* refers to the customer's willingness to pay. The financial or credit manager should judge whether the customers will make honest efforts to honour their credit obligations. The moral factor is of considerable importance in credit evaluation in practice.

- *Capacity* refers to the customer's ability to pay. Ability to pay can be judged by assessing the customer's capital and assets which he may offer as security. Capacity is evaluated by the financial position of the firm as indicated by analysis of ratios and trends in firm's cash and working capital position. The financial or credit manager should determine the real worth of assets offered as collateral (security).

- *Condition* refers to the prevailing economic and other conditions which may affect the customers' ability to pay. Adverse economic conditions can affect the ability or

1. See Oh, *op. cit.,* and Dyle, *op. cit.,* for the approach adopted here.
2. Two more *C's* may be added to this: *capital* and *collateral.* See, Weide, J.V. and Maier, S.E., *Managing Corporate Liquidity: An Introduction to Working Capital Management,* John Wiley, 1985, p. 258. Also, see Weston, J.F. and Copeland, T.E., *Managerial Finance,* Dryden Press, 1986, pp. 341–42.

willingness of a customer to pay. An experienced financial or credit manager will be able to judge the extent and genuineness to which the customer's ability to pay is affected by the economic conditions.

Information on these variables may be collected from the customers themselves, their published financial statements and outside agencies which may be keeping credit information about customers. A firm should use this information in preparing *categories of customers* according to their creditworthiness and default risk. This would be an important input for the financial or credit manager in formulating its credit standards. The firm may categorise its customers, at least, in the following three categories:

- *Good accounts*; that is, financially strong customers.
- *Bad accounts*; that is, financially very weak, high risk customers.
- *Marginal accounts*; that is, customers with moderate financial health and risk (falling between good and bad accounts).

The firm will have no difficulty in quickly deciding about the extension of credit to *good accounts* and rejecting the credit request of *bad accounts*. Most of the firm's time will be taken in evaluating *marginal accounts*; that is, customers who are not financially very strong but are also not so bad to be outrightly rejected. A firm can expand its sales by extending credit to marginal accounts. But the firm's costs and bad-debt losses may also increase. Therefore, credit standards should be relaxed upon the point where incremental return equals incremental cost. Consider an example given in Illustration 28.2.

Illustration 28.2: Analysing Change in Credit Standards

The Peacock Silk Company is contemplating to alter its credit standards. On the basis of the financial position and probabilities of default, the company has divided its customers into four risk categories. The company's potential sales to each category, starting from low to high risk, is Rs 1.2 crore, Rs 1.0 crore, Rs 0.55 crore and Rs 0.40 crore, and the average collection period is 30 days, 35 days, 45 days and 60 days. The bad-debt ratio is negligible in case of first two categories while it is 2.0 per cent and 5.0 per cent respectively in case of third and fourth categories. Currently, the company extends unlimited credit to the first three categories of customers and none to the last category. The company's variable cost ratio is approximately 80 per cent, and after-tax required rate of return is 15 per cent. The corporate tax rate is 35 per cent. The company wants to extend full credit to category four customers. It is expected that 5 per cent collection costs will have to be spent for this category of customers. The analysis is shown in Table 28.2.

Since the marginal rate of return, 39 per cent, is more than the marginal cost of funds, 15 per cent (or there is net increase in after-tax operating profits by Rs 1 lakh), the firm can relax its credit standards and extend credit to high-risk customers.

Table 28.2: Peacock Silk Company: Analysis of Decision to Relax Credit Standards

(Rs in lakh)

1.	Incremental sales, Δ SALES	40.0
2.	Incremental contribution, Δ CONT $= \Delta \text{ SALES} \times c = 40\,(1 - 0.80)$	8.0
3.	Incremental bad-debt loss and collection costs, $\Delta \text{ SALES}\,(b + d) = 40 \times (0.05 + 0.05)$	4.0
4.	Incremental after-tax operating profit, $\Delta \text{ OPAT} = [\Delta \text{ CONT} - \Delta \text{ SALES}\,(b + d)]\,(1 - T)$ $= (8.0 - 4.0)\,(1 - 0.35)$	2.6
5.	Incremental investment in receivables $\Delta \text{INVST} : (\Delta \text{SALE} \times \text{ACP}/360) = 40/360 \times 60$	6.7
6.	Marginal rate of return, Δ OPAT $/ \Delta$ INVST	39%
7.	Net increase in operating profits, $\Delta \text{ OPAT} - k\,\Delta \text{ INVEST} = 2.6 - 0.15 \times 6.7$	1.6

Numerical credit scoring A variety of factors influence a customer's creditworthiness. This makes credit investigation a difficult task. A firm can use numerical credit scoring to appraise credit applications when it is dealing with a large number of small customers. The firm, based on its past experience or empirical study, may identify both financial and non-financial attributes that measure the credit standing of a customer. The numerical credit scoring models may include:

- *Ad hoc* approach
- Simple discriminant analysis
- Multiple discriminant analysis

Ad hoc approach A firm may develop its own *ad hoc* approach of numerical credit scoring to determine the creditworthiness of customers. The attributes identified by the firm may be assigned weights depending on their importance and be combined to create an overall (simple or weighted) score or index. For example, a bank may consider the attributes given in Table 28.3 while considering a car loan to a customer.

Suppose you are 23 years of age and unmarried, and have just graduated from one of the IIMs and got a job of Rs. 7.5 lakh per annum. You have taken a flat on rent connected with a telephone. Your integrity is assessed to be excellent. What is your credit score if you apply for the bank loan for buying a car? Your score is 16 points; that is, telephone-1 point; employment-2 points; income-4 points; bank account-1 point; residence-1 point; marital status-2 points; age-2 points; integrity-3 points. If the cut-off score is 12, bank may grant you loan.

Simple discriminant analysis A firm can use more objective methods of differentiating between good and bad customers. For example, empirical analysis may show that the ratio of earnings before depreciation, interest and taxes (EBDIT) to sales is a significant factor in discriminating good

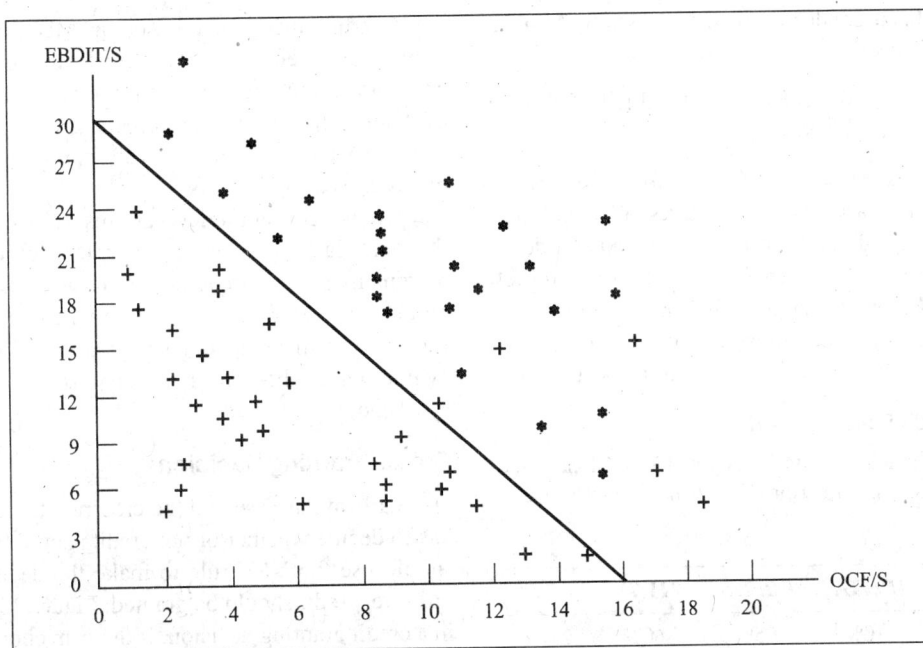

Figure 28.3: Discriminant analysis based on EBDIT/S and OCF/S ratios

Table 28.3: Ad Hoc Approach: Car Loan Decision

Attribute	Feature	Points
• Telephone	Yes	1
	No	0
• Employment	Employed	2
	Self-employed	1
	Unemployed	0
• Income	More than Rs 5 lakh	4
	Rs 2.5 lakh to Rs 5 lakh	3
	Rs 1.0 lakh to Rs 2.5 lakh	2
	Less than Rs 1.0 lakh	1
• Bank accounts	More than one	2
	One	1
	None	0
• Residence	Own	3
	Rented: house	2
	Flat	1
• Marital status	Married	3
	Unmarried	2
	Divorced	1
• Age	Under 25	2
	25 to 35	3
	Over 35	1
• Integrity	Excellent	3
	Good	2
	Fair	1
	Bad	0

customers from bad customers.[1] How can the firm determine the cut-off EBDIT to sales ratio? The following steps are involved. First, arrange the paying (good) and non-paying (bad) customers by the magnitude of EBDIT to sales ratio. Second, select a cut-off point to divide the array into two parts with a minimum number of misclassification. The cut-off point is selected by visual inspection. The firm can consider granting credit to those customers who have EBDIT to sales ratio above the cut-off point.

It may still be better if the firm uses two factors to distinguish between good and bad customers. Two ratios—EBDIT to sales and operating cash flows to sales—together are better indicator of a customer's financial health than one ratio alone.[2] A combination of these ratios may be plotted on a graph for paying and non-paying customers as shown in Figure 28.3. A straight line in the graph should separate the two groups of customers in a manner that there are minimum mis-classifications. This line will tell us how much importance should be given to each ratio. In our example, the **discriminant index** is:

$$Z = 30 \text{ EBDIT/S ratio} + 16 \text{ OCF/S ratio}$$
$$= 1.88 \text{ EBDIT/S ratio} + 1 \text{ OCF/S ratio}$$

A customer will be considered creditworthy if his Z score is 30 or more.

Multiple-discriminant analysis In practice, the credit worthiness of a customer will depend on many factors that may interact with each other. The technique of multiple-discriminant analysis combines many factors according to the importance (weight) to be given to each factor and determines a composite score to differentiate good customers from bad customers. Altman, focusing on the financial attributes of firms in the USA, used **multiple-discriminant analysis** to predict bankruptcy of firms.[3]

---

1. Gupta, L.C., *Financial Ratios as Forewarning Indicators of Corporate Sickness.* Bombay, ICICI, 1979.
2. *Ibid.*
3. Altman, E.I., Financial Ratios, Discriminant Analysis and the Prediction of Corporate Bankruptcy, *Journal of Finance*, 23, pp. 589–609 (September 1968).

Similar studies have been conducted in India as well. Altman derived the following discriminant function:

$$Z = 0.012 \, (NWC/TA) + 0.014 \, (RE/TA) + 0.033 \, (EBIT/S)$$
$$+ 0.006 \, (MV/D) + 0.010 \, (S/TA)$$

where NWC = net working capital; TA = total assets; RE = retained earnings; EBIT = earnings before interest and taxes; S = sales; MV = market value of equity and D = book value of debt.

On the basis of statistical analysis, Altman's model established a cut-off Z score of 2.675; firms with a score above 2.675 are financially strong while those that have score below 2.675 have a very high likelihood of becoming bankrupt.

Illustration 28.2: Credit Scorring Model

You are considering extending credit to firms X and Y which have the following financial ratios. What are their Z scores if you use Altman's model?

Firm	NWC/TA	RE/TA	EBIT/S	MV/D	S/TA
X	20%	10%	7.5%	360%	2.8
Y	16%	12%	6.5%	210%	2.5

Z Score for the firms are calculated as given below:

Z Score for firm X: $0.012 \times 20 + 0.014 \times 10 + 0.033 \times 7.5$
$+ 0.006 \times 360 + 0.010 \times 2.8 = 2.8155$

Z Score for firm Y: $0.012 \times 16 + 0.014 \times 12 + 0.033 \times 6.5$
$+ 0.006 \times 210 + 0.010 \times 2.5 = 1.8595$

Since the cut-off score (in Altman's model) is 2.675, firm X with a higher score (2.8155) may be extended credit while firm Y (with a lower score of 1.8595) should be denied credit.

Credit scoring models, such as MDA, are based on objective factors, and help a firm to quickly distinguish between good and bad customers. The firm can devote enough time in evaluating the marginal customers. A credit appraiser in the firm can consistently and objectively apply credit standards based on credit scoring models.

Credit scoring models can mislead since they are based on the past data. The firm may refuse credit to a number of marginally good customers. Similarly, a customer who has been regular in paying the dues in the past may fail to do so in the future. A firm need to go beyond credit scoring models in evaluating credit-granting decisions; it may have to rely on good judgement also.

Credit-granting Decision

Once a firm has assessed the creditworthiness of a customer, it has to decide whether or not credit should be granted. The firm should use the NPV rule to make the decision. If the NPV is positive, credit should be granted. Figure 28.4 shows the choice in a credit granting decision. If the firm chooses not to grant any credit, the firm avoids the possibility of any loss but loses the opportunity of increasing its profitability. On the other hand, if it grants credit, then it will benefit if the customer pays. There is some probability that the customer will default, and then the firm may lose its investment. The expected net payoff of the firm is the difference between the present value of net benefit and present value of the expected loss.

Suppose a customer wants to purchase goods of Rs 20,000 on 4-month credit from Karima Wholesale Dry-fruits Merchants & Company. There is 90 per cent probability that the customer will pay in four months and 10 per cent probability that he will

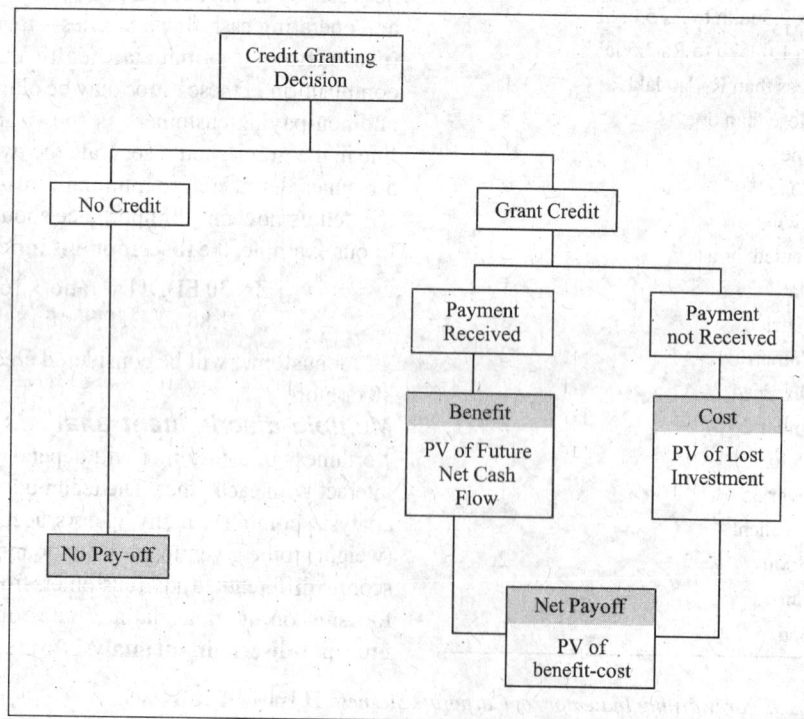

Figure 28.4: Credit-granting Decision

not pay anything. The firm's investment (say, equal to the cost of goods sold) is Rs 14,000. The firm's required rate of return is 18 per cent. Should credit be granted? If the firm does not give any credit, it loses a possibility of making any profits. On the other hand, if it offers credit, its expected payoff is as follows:

$$NPV = \left[\frac{p(REV)}{(1+k)^t} - COST\right] - \left[\frac{(1-p)COST}{(1+k)^t}\right] = 0$$

$$NPV = \left[\frac{0.9(20,000)}{(1.18)^{1/3}} - 14,000\right] - \left[\frac{(1-0.9)14,000}{(1.18)^{1/3}}\right]$$

$$NPV = 3,034 - 1,325 = Rs\,1,709 \qquad (5)$$

Since the expected net pay-off is a positive NPV, Karima should extend credit to the customer. Let us ask a different question. What should be the probability of collection that the firm incurs no loss? We can find out the probability of collection at which NPV is zero. That is:

$$NPV = \left[\frac{p(20,000)}{(1.18)^{1/3}} - 14,000\right] - \left[\frac{(1-p)14,000}{(1.18)^{1/3}}\right] = 0$$

$$18,926p - 14,000 = 13,248 - 13,248p$$

$$32,174p = 27,248$$

$$p = 0.85$$

If the chances that the customer will make payment are better than 85 per cent, Karima Company should extend credit of Rs 20,000 for four months to the customer.

Let us take another example. Suppose a new customer has asked for a credit of Rs 11,000 for three months. There is 85 per cent probability that he will make payment after the stipulated time and 15 per cent probability that he will not pay. The firm's cost of the credit (investment) is Rs 8,000, and it has a required rate of return of 15 per cent. If the firm grants credit, the expected net pay-off is:

$$NPV = \left[\frac{0.85(11,000)}{(1.15)^{1/4}} - 8,000\right] - \left[\frac{(1-0.85)8,000}{(1.15)^{1/4}}\right]$$

$$NPV = 1,029 - 1,159 = -Rs\,130$$

The firm will decide not to extend credit since NPV is negative. But, what if the customer actually pays and places a repeat order with the firm? If the customer has paid once, there is a high probability, say 95 per cent, that he will pay in the second period. The firm's pay-off in the second period is:

$$NPV = \left[\frac{0.95(11,000)}{(1.15)^{1/4}} - 8,000\right] - \left[\frac{(1-0.95)8,000}{(1.15)^{1/4}}\right]$$

$$NPV = 2,091 - 386 = Rs\,1,705$$

The pay-off from the second period is a positive NPV of Rs. 1,705. The present value this pay-off is:

$$PV\ of\ second\ period\ pay\text{-}off = 1.705/(1.15)^{1/4} = 1,646$$

The firm has an expected loss of Rs 130 from the initial order. But it has an 85 per cent chance that the customer will pay for the initial order and repeat the order that will give the firm a net benefit of Rs 1,646 today. Therefore, the total expected pay-off is: $-130 + 0.85 \times 1,646 = Rs\,1,269$. The firm should decide to grant credit in spite of the possibility of a loss on the initial order because if the customer proves trustworthy, the firm will get repeat orders and ultimately, its benefits will far exceed the expected loss. Thus, in their credit granting decisions, firms should have a long-term perspective and should think in terms of securing dependable customers who will stay with the firm for long period.

Credit terms The stipulations under which the firm sells on credit to customers are called **credit terms**. These stipulations include: (*a*) the credit period, and (*b*) the cash discount.

Credit period The length of time for which credit is extended to customers is called the **credit period**. It is generally stated in terms of a net date. For example, if the firm's credit terms are 'net 35', it is expected that customers will repay credit obligation not later than 35 days. A firm's credit period may be governed by the industry norms. But depending on its objective, the firm can lengthen the credit period. On the other hand, the firm may tighten its credit period if customers are defaulting too frequently and bad-debt losses are building up.

A firm lengthens credit period to increase its operating profit through expanded sales. However, there will be net increase in operating profit only when the cost of extended credit period is less than the incremental operating profit. With increased sales and extended credit period, investment in receivable would increase. Two factors cause this increase: (*a*) incremental sales result in incremental receivable and (*b*) existing customers will take more time to repay credit obligation (*i.e.,* the average collection period will increase), thus increasing the level of receivable. Let us consider an example.

Illustration 28.4: Change in Credit Period Policy

Sudarsan Trading Limited is considering to increase its credit period from 'net 35' to 'net 50.' The firm's expected sales to increase from Rs 120 lakh to Rs 180 lakh and average collection period to increase from 35 days to 50 days. The bad-debt loss ratio and collection costs ratio are expected to remain at 5 per cent and 6 per cent respectively. The firm's variable costs ratio is 85 per cent, corporate tax rate is 35 per cent and the after-tax required rate of return is 20 per cent.

Table 28.4 contains the analysis of the impact of changing the credit period. Note that incremental investment in receivables is calculated assuming that credit period will increase from 35 days to 50 days for all customers.

The firm's decision to relax credit period is not beneficial; the expected return of 11.7 per cent is much less than the cost of funds of 20 per cent. If the firm goes ahead with its decision, it will decrease its operating profit by Rs 1.11 lakh.

You may notice in Table 28.4 the way in which the incremental investment in receivable has been calculated. Incremental investment in receivable can be calculated by using the following formula:

Table 28.4: Sundarsan Trading Limited: Analysis of the Impact of Change in Credit Period

	(Rs in lakh)
1. Incremental sales, Δ SALES	60.0
2. Incremental contribution, Δ CONT $= \Delta$ SALES $\times c$, 60×0.15	9.0
3. Incremental bad-debt and collection costs, Δ COST $= \Delta$ SALES $(b + d) = 60.0 \times (0.05 + 0.06)$	6.6
4. Incremental operating profit, Δ OP $= \Delta$ CONT $- \Delta$ COST, $9.0 - 6.6$	2.4
5. Incremental after-tax operating profit, Δ OPAT $= \Delta$ OP $(1 - T)$, $2.4\ (1 - 0.35)$	1.56
6. Incremental investment in receivable, Δ INVST $= (\text{SALES}_n/360) \times \text{ACP}_n$ $\quad - (\text{SALES}_0/360) \times \text{ACP}_0$ $= (180/360 \times 50) - (120/360 \times 35)$	13.33
7. Marginal rate of return, Δ OPAT/Δ INVST, $1.56 \div 13.33$	11.7%
8. Net increase in operating profits, Δ OPAT $- k\, \Delta$ INVST, $1.56 - 0.2 \times 13.33$	–1.11

New level of receivable – old level of receivable

$= $ (New sales/360)$\times$ (New average collection period)

$\quad - $ (Old sales/360)$\times$ (Old average collection period)

$$= \frac{\text{SALES}_n}{360} \times \text{ACP}_n - \frac{\text{SALES}_0}{360} \times \text{ACP}_0 \qquad (6)$$

where SALES_n is new sales, SALES_0 is present sales, ACP_n is new average collection period and ACP_0 is old collection period.

For a quick calculation, we can use the following equation to determine the net increase in operating profit:

$$= [\Delta \text{SALES} \times c - \Delta \text{SALES}(b + d)](1 - T) - k \times \text{INVST}$$
$$= \Delta \text{SALES}(c - b - d)(1 - T) - k \times \text{INVST} \qquad (7)$$

where (INVST) is equal to:

$$\Delta \text{INVST} = (\text{SALES}_n \times \text{ACP}_n - \text{SALES}_0 \times \text{ACP}_0)/360 \qquad (8)$$

Similarly, the expected rate of return can be calculated as follows:

$$r = \frac{\Delta \text{SALES}(c - b - d)(1 - T)}{\Delta \text{INVST}}$$

Note that c is contribution ratio, b bad-debt ratio, d collection cost, ACP collection period and T tax rate.

Illustration 28.5: Collection Period Analysis

An analysis of Delite Plastics Private Limited's credit policy reveals that it is very loose, and as a result, the firm's collection period is very long as well as bad-debt losses are building up. The firm, therefore, is considering tightening up its credit standards by shortening credit period from 45 days to 30 days. The expected result of this policy would be to reduce sales from Rs 600,000 to Rs 500,000 and bad-debt losses ratio from 4

per cent to 2 per cent and collection expenses from 2 per cent to 1 per cent of total sales. The firm's variable cost ratio is 80 per cent, tax rate is 40 per cent and the after-tax cost of funds is 12 per cent.

The first step is to determine the change in the after-tax operating profit. Sales are expected to decline by Rs 100,000. Contribution ratio is: $1 - 0.8 = 0.2$; therefore, decline in total contribution is:

$$\Delta \text{CONT} = \Delta \text{SALES} \times c = (100,000) \times 0.2 = \text{Rs } (20,000)$$

Because of the tightening of the credit policy, both bad-debt losses and collection costs will decline. The decline will be equal to the difference between current losses minus new loss. The decline in these two costs will be:

$$\Delta \text{COST} = \text{Bad-debt losses} + \text{Collection costs}$$
$$= (\text{SALES}_n \times b_n - \text{SALES}_0 \times b_0)$$
$$\quad + (\text{SALES}_n \times d_n - \text{SALES}_0 \times d_0)$$
$$= \text{SALES}_n (b_n + d_n) - \text{SALES}_0 (b_0 + d_0)$$

In our example, the cost will decline by:

$$\Delta \text{COST} = 500,000(0.02 + 0.01) - 600,000(0.04 + 0.02)$$
$$= 15,000 - 36,000 = \text{Rs } (21,000)$$

Thus, the change in operating profit is:

$$\Delta \text{OP} = \Delta \text{CONT} - \Delta \text{COST}$$
$$= -20,000 - (-21,000) = +\text{Rs } 1,000$$

and the change in after-tax operating profit is:

$$\Delta \text{OPAT} = \Delta \text{OP}\ (1 - T) = 1,000\ (1 - 0.4) = \text{Rs } 600$$

Next step is to calculate investment in receivable; since both sales and average collection period decline, investment in receivable will also decline. It is given by the difference between new level of receivable minus current level of receivable:

$$\Delta \text{INVST} = \frac{\text{SALES}_n}{360} \times \text{ACP}_n - \frac{\text{SALES}_0}{360} \times \text{ACP}_0$$
$$= \frac{500,000}{360} \times 30 - \frac{600,000}{360} \times 45$$
$$= 41,667 - 75,000 = \text{Rs}(33,333)$$

Since investment declines, the opportunity cost of funds tied in receivables will also reduce:

$$k \times \Delta \text{INVST} = 0.12 \times (33,333) = \text{Rs } (4,000)$$

The net increase in the after-tax operating profit is:

$$\Delta \text{OPAT} - k \times \Delta \text{INVST} = 600 - (-4,000) = \text{Rs } 4,600$$

The firm should introduce the change. Alternatively, to arrive at the decision, the expected rate to return (r) could be compared with the cost of funds (k). The expected rate of return in the example is:

$$r = \frac{\Delta \text{OPAT}}{\Delta \text{INVST}} = \frac{4,600}{33,333} = 0.138 \text{ or } 13.8\%$$

Since $r = 13.8$ per cent is greater than $k = 12$ per cent, the policy change is beneficial to the firm. One could have arrived at the results by using the following equation:

$$= [\Delta \text{SALES} \times c - \{\text{SALES}_n (b_n + d_n) - \text{SALES}_0 (b_0 + d_0)\}](1 - T)$$
$$\quad - [k\{(\text{SALES}_n \times \text{ACP}_n - \text{SALES}_0 \times \text{ACP}_0)\}/360] \quad (11)$$

Using data in example, we obtain:

$$= [-100,000 \times 0.2 - \{500,000\,(0.02 + 0.001) - 600,000\,(0.04 + 0.02)\}]$$
$$(1 - 0.4) - [0.12\{500,000 \times 30 - 600,000 \times 45)/360\}]$$
$$= [-20,000 - (-21,000)]\,(1 - 0.4) - 0.12\,(-33,333)$$
$$= 1,000\,(1 - 0.4) - (-4,000)$$
$$= 600 + 4,000 = \text{Rs } 4,600$$

Cash discounts A **cash discount** is a reduction in payment offered to customers to induce them to repay credit obligations within a specified period of time, which will be less than the normal credit period. It is usually expressed as a percentage of sales. Cash discount terms indicate the rate of discount and the period for which it is available. If the customer does not avail the offer, he must make payment within the normal credit period.

In practice, credit terms would include: (*a*) the rate of cash discount, (*b*) the cash discount period, and (*c*) the net credit period. For example, credit terms may be expressed as '2/10, net 30.' This means that a 2 per cent discount will be granted if the customer pays within 10 days; if he does not avail the offer he must make payment within 30 days.

A firm uses cash discount as a tool to increase sales and accelerate collections from customers. Thus, the level of receivable and associated costs may be reduced. The cost involved is the discounts taken by customers.

Illustration 28.6: Analysing Cash Discount Decision

The Swan Fabric Limited is considering of introducing a cash discount. The company's credit terms are 'net 40', and would like to change to '1/15, net 40.' The current average collection period is 60 days and is expected to decrease to 30 days with the new credit terms. It is expected that 50 per cent of customers will take advantage of the changed credit terms. Swan's annual sales are Rs 6,000,000, and required rate of return is 15 per cent. Assume corporate tax rate of 50 per cent.

Note that Swan is not expecting any change in sales. The decision under consideration will be analysed in terms of cost of cash discount and saving of opportunity cost of reduced investment in receivable. The cost of cash discount is:

$$\text{Cost of cash discount} = \text{Sales} \times \text{Percentage of taking discount}$$
$$\times \text{Percentage discount}$$
$$= 6,000,000 \times 0.5 \times 0.01 = \text{Rs } 30,000$$

Since the firm can deduct cash discount of Rs 30,000 for taxes, its after tax cost will be: $30,000 \times 0.5 = \text{Rs } 15,000$.

Next step is to determine the change in investment in receivable. It can be found out as the difference between new level of receivable minus current level of receivable:

$$\Delta \text{INVST} = \frac{\text{SALES}}{360} \times \text{ACP}_n - \frac{\text{SALES}}{360} \times \text{ACP}_0$$
$$= [\text{SALES}(\text{ACP}_n - \text{ACP}_0)]/360$$

Thus in our example, it is:

$$= [6,000,000\,(30 - 60)]/360 = \text{Rs } 500,000$$

The net change in the firm's operating profit is:

$$\Delta \text{OPAT} = -15,000 + 0.15 \times 500,000$$
$$= -15,000 + 75,000 = \text{Rs } 60,000$$

The new credit terms are expected to be beneficial to the firm.

Collection Policy and Procedures

A collection policy is needed because all customers do not pay the firm's bills in time. Some customers are slow-payers while some are non-payers. The collection efforts should, therefore, aim at accelerating collections from slow-payers and reducing bad-debt losses. A collection policy should ensure prompt and regular collection. Prompt collection is needed for fast turnover of working capital, keeping collection costs and bad-debts within limits and maintaining collection efficiency. Regularity in collections keeps debtors alert, and they tend to pay their dues promptly.

The collection policy should lay down clear-cut collection procedures. The collection procedures for past dues or delinquent accounts should also be established in unambiguous terms. The slow-paying customers should be handled very tactfully. Some of them may be permanent customers. The collection process initiated quickly, without giving any chance to them, may antagonise them, and the firm may lose them to competitors.

The responsibility for collection and follow-up should be explicitly fixed. It may be entrusted to the accounts or sales department, or to a separate credit department. The co-ordination between accounts and sales departments is necessary and must be ensured formally. The accounting department maintains the credit records and information. If it is responsible for collection, it should consult the sales department before initiating an action against non-paying customers. Similarly, the sales department must obtain past information about a customer from the accounting department before granting credit to him.

Though collection procedures should be firmly established, individual cases should be dealt with on their merits. Some customers may be temporarily in tight financial position and in spite of their best intentions may not be able to pay on due date. This may be due to recessionary conditions, or other factors beyond the control of the customers. Such cases need special considerations. The collection procedure against them should be initiated only after they have overcome their financial difficulties and do not intend to pay promptly.

The firm should decide about offering cash discount for prompt payment. Cash discount is a cost to the firm for ensuring faster recovery of cash. Some customers fail to pay within the specified discount period, yet they may make payment after deducting the amount of cash discount. Such cases must be promptly identified and necessary action should be initiated against them to recover the full amount.

In practice, companies may take certain precautions *vis-à-vis* collections. Some companies require their customers to give *pre-signed cheques*. **Bills discounting** is another practice in India. Unfortunately, it is not very popular with a number of companies. Some companies provide for penal rate of interest for debtors who fail to pay in time. Exhibit 28.2 gives a brief account of the credit policy and practices at Siemens (India).

CREDIT EVALUATION OF INDIVIDUAL ACCOUNTS

For effective management of credit, the firm should lay down clear cut guidelines and procedures for granting credit to individual customers and collecting individual accounts. The firm need not follow the policy of treating all customers equal

---

EXHIBIT 23.2: CREDIT POLICY AND PRACTICES AT SIEMENS INDIA

Siemens (India) is a large, heavy engineering company. The following is the summary of the company's credit policy and practices (in the beginning of nineties).

- The company sells about 85 per cent of its products through dealers, and the remaining 15 per cent is sold directly to large corporate customers. Generally, a 45-day credit is extended to dealers, but a lot of variation exists for different dealers.

- The company grants credit to dealers for three reasons: (a) It is an industry norm in this sector to grant credit. (b) The time lag between delivery of goods and the receipt of payments by the company's customers are large. Therefore, they expect company to extend credit to them. (c) The company wants its dealers to make about 5 per cent profits, and credit is extended to enable them to achieve this goal.

- The company has a system of centralised control and decentralised collections. The control office receives a statement of sales and outstandings daily from all branches to initiate appropriate actions, if any. The company also requires its dealers to give a 3 monthly forecast of their requirements. No large changes are permitted in orders, and dealers' requirements are shipped regularly, without their enquiries. Branch managers are authorised to decide credit for both dealers and corporate clients.

- The company sells to corporate clients only through a bank guarantee. Initially new dealers are given no credit. After dealing with the company for some time, they are granted credit.

- The company follows a rigorous system of credit evaluation for both corporate clients as well as dealers. Branches involve corporate office in the evaluation of dealers. The customers are required to make payments by demand drafts. Local customers could pay by cheques.

- It is the responsibility of salesmen to collect dues if they are delayed. For delayed payments, the company charges a penalty interest rate of 22 per cent. However, if a dealer has no defaults, he gets a quarter of percentage of sales as bonus. The company hardly faces the problem of bad debts. Also, cheques received from customers have hardly bounced.

Source: Based on information collected by Amardeep Singh and Varun Kapur.

---

for the purpose of extending credit. Each case may be fully examined before offering any credit terms. Similarly, collection procedure will differ from customer to customer. With the permanent, but temporarily defaulting, customers, the firm may not be very strict in following the collection procedures.

The credit evaluation procedure of the individual accounts should involve the following steps: (1) credit information, (2) credit investigation, (3) credit limits, and (4) collection procedures.[1]

Credit Information

In extending credit to customers, the firm would ensure that receivables will be collected in full and on due date. Credit should be granted to those customers who have the ability to make the payment on time. To ensure this, the firm should have credit information concerning each customer to whom the credit will be granted.

Little progress has been made in India in the matter of developing the sources of credit information in the name of secrecy and confidentiality. The sources of credit information in advanced countries include independent information service companies, banks, fellow business firms and associates, competitors, suppliers etc. In India, banks are sometimes used to collect information about potential customers.

Collecting credit information involves cost. The cost of collecting information should, therefore, be less than the potential profitability. For small accounts, comprehensive information may not be collected; the decision to grant credit may be made on the basis of limited information. In addition to cost, the time required to collect information should also be considered. The decision to grant credit cannot be delayed for long because of the time involved in collecting the credit information. Depending on these two factors of time and cost, any, or a combination of the following sources may be employed to collect the information.

Financial statement One of the easiest ways to obtain information regarding the financial condition and performance of the prospective customer is to scrutinise his financial statements—balance sheet and the profit and loss account. The published financial statements of public limited companies are easily available. The real difficulty arises in obtaining the financial statements from partnership firms or individuals, particularly the audited accounts since they do not have legal obligation to audit their accounts. The credit granting firm must insist on the audited financial statements. In case of firms that have seasonal sales, data on monthly sales, inventory and cash flows ought to be sought and analysed.

Bank references Another source of collecting credit information is the bank where the customer maintains his account. In advanced countries like USA, many banks have large credit departments which can provide detailed credit information. The firm should seek to obtain the information through its bank. A customer can also be requested to instruct his banker to provide information required by the firm. In India, banks as a source of information are not very useful because of their indifference in providing information. A bank does not provide unambiguous answers to the enquiries made by the firm. Even if it provides information to the firm about the conduct of the customer's account, it can not be taken as a complete basis for believing that the customer will be able to settle his dues in time. More information from other sources may be collected to supplement it.

Trade references A firm can ask the prospective customer to give trade references. It may insist to give the names of such

---

1. See Van Horne, J.C., *Financial Management and Policy,* Prentice-Hall of India, 1985, pp. 398–405; and Ramamoorthy, *op. cit.,* pp. 188–202.

persons or firms with whom the customer has current dealings. This is a useful source to obtain credit information at no cost. The trade referees may be contacted personally to obtain all relevant information required by the firm. A customer can furnish misleading references. To guard against this, the honesty and seriousness of the referees should be examined. The firm can insist on furnishing the references of people or firms of repute.

Other sources A firm can also obtain information about the prospective customer from the credit rating organisations (such as CRISIL, CARE or ICRA) and trade and industry associations. In advanced countries like the USA, credit bureau reports are an important source of information about a customer.

Credit Investigation and Analysis

After having obtained the credit information, the firm will get an idea regarding the matters which should be further investigated. The factors that affect the extent and nature of credit investigation of an individual customer are:[1]

- The type of customer, whether new or existing.
- The customer's business line, background and the related trade risks.
- The nature of the product—perishable or seasonal.
- Size of customer's order and expected further volumes of business with him.
- Company's credit policies and practices.

Analysis of credit file The firm should maintain a credit file for each customer. It should be updated with the information about the customer collected from the reports of salesmen, bankers and directly from the customer. The firm's trade experiences with the customer and his performance report based on financial statements submitted by him should also be recorded in his credit file. A regular examination of the customer's credit file will reveal to the firm the credit standing of the customer. Whenever the firm experiences a change in the customer's paying habit or receives a request for extended credit terms or large order on credit, his credit file should be thoroughly scrutinised. The intensity and depth of credit review on investigation will depend upon the quality of the customer's account and the amount of credit involved. A little review will be required in case of the customers who have had clear deals with the firm in the past. But a comprehensive investigation will be required in case of the customers whose quality of accounts is falling and who have not been able to honour the firm's credit terms regularly in the past.

Analysis of financial ratios The evaluation of the customer's financial conditions should be done very carefully. The financial statements submitted by the prospective customer will form a basis to analyse the performance and trends of his business activities. Ratios should be calculated to determine the customer's liquidity position and ability to repay debts. The performance of the customer should be compared with industry average and his nearest competitors. This will be helpful in determining whether his relatively poor performance is due to some general economic condition affecting the whole industry, or it is due to the internal inefficiencies of the applicant.

Analysis of business and its management Besides appraising the financial strength of the applicant, the firm should also consider the quality of management and the nature of the customer's business. The firm should conduct a **management audit** to identify the management weaknesses of the customer's business. An over-centralised structure of the customer's business without proper management systems can degenerate into mismanagement, over-trading and business failure.

If the nature of the customer's business is highly fluctuating or he has financially weak buyers or his business depends on a few buyers, then it is relatively risky to extend credit to him. The implications of these aspects should be fully understood before extending credit to customers.

Credit Limit

A **credit limit** is a maximum amount of credit which the firm will extend at a point of time. It indicates the extent of risk taken by the firm by supplying goods on credit to a customer.[2] Once the firm has taken a decision to extend credit to the applicant, the amount and duration of the credit have to be decided. The decision on the magnitude of credit will depend upon the amount of contemplated sale and the customer's financial strength. In case of customers who are frequent buyers of the firm's goods, a credit limit can be established. This would avoid the need to investigate each order from the customers. Depending on the regularity of payment, the line of credit for a customer can be fixed on the basis of his normal buying pattern. For example, if a customer normally buys goods of Rs 25,000 per month on an average, for him the line of credit can be fixed at this level. In case of a customer who is not fairly regular in settling the dues, the credit limit may be fixed with reference to the outstanding amount.

The credit limit must be reviewed periodically. If tendencies of slow paying are found, the credit can be revised downward. At times, a customer may ask for the amount of credit in excess of his credit limit. The firm may at such times agrees to his request if the product has a high margin or if additional sales help to use the unutilised capacity of the firm, and the cost of expected delayed payment or bad-debt loss is less than the expected incremental profit.

The firm has not only to determine the amount of credit but also the duration of credit. Keeping in view the industry norm, the normal collection period should be determined. Some customers can seek relaxation in the collection period. As has been discussed earlier, a longer collection period involves costs—the opportunity costs of funds being tied-up for a longer period and the cost of possible bad-debt losses. But if the extended credit period motivates sales, a comparison between the cost of extended credit period and the additional profit resulting from the increased sale should be made. If profits exceed costs, the collection period may be extended, otherwise not.

---

1. Ramamoorthy, *op. cit.*, p. 195.
2. Van Horne, *op. cit.*, p. 402.

Collection Efforts

The firm should follow a well laid down collection policy and procedure to collect dues from its customers. When the normal credit period granted to a customer is over, and he has not made the payment, the firm should send a polite letter to him reminding that the account is overdue. If the customer does not respond, the firm may send progressively strong-worded letters. If receivable still remains uncollected, letters may be followed by telephone, telegram, and personal visit of the firm's representative. If the payment is still not made, the firm may initiate a legal action against the customer. Before taking the legal action, the firm must examine the customer's financial condition. If it is weak, legal action against him will simply hasten his insolvency. The firm will not be able to get anything from the customer. Under such situation, it is better to be patient and wait, or accept reduced payment in the settlement of the account.

MONITORING RECEIVABLE

A firm needs to continuously monitor and control its receivable to ensure the success of collection efforts. Two traditional methods of evaluating the management of receivable are: (1) **average collection period** (ACP) and (2) **aging schedule**. These methods have certain limitations to be useful in monitoring receivable. A better approach is the **collection experience matrix**.

Average Collection Period

We have earlier defined average collection period as:

$$ACP = \frac{Debtors \times 360}{Credit\ sales}$$

The average collection period so calculated is compared with the firm's stated credit period to judge the collection efficiency. For example, if a firm's stated credit period is 25 days and the actual collection period is 40 days, then one may conclude that the firm has a lax system of collection. An extended collection period delays cash inflows, impairs the firm's liquidity position and increases the chances of bad-debt losses. The average collection period measures the quality of receivable since it indicates the speed of their collectability.

There are two limitations of this method. *First*, it provides an average picture of collection experience and is based on aggregate data. For control purposes, one needs specific information about the age of outstanding receivables. *Second*, it is susceptible to sales variations and the period over which sales and receivables have been aggregated. Thus, average collection period cannot provide a very meaningful information about the quality of outstanding receivable.[1]

Aging Schedule

The aging schedule removes one of the limitations of the average collection period. It breaks down receivables according to the length of time for which they have been outstanding. We can repeat our example in Chapter 25 to illustrate aging schedule of receivables:

If the firm's stated credit period is 25 days, the aging schedule indicates that 50 per cent of receivables remain outstanding beyond this period. A significant amount of receivables remains uncollected much longer than the firm's credit period. Thus, aging schedule provides more information about the collection experience. It helps to spot out the slow-paying debtors. However, it also suffers from the problem of aggregation, and does not relate receivables to sales of the same period.

Outstanding	Outstanding (Rs)	Percentage
0–25	200,000	50.0
26–35	100,000	25.0
36–45	50,000	12.5
46–60	30,000	7.5
Over 60	20,000	5.0
	400,000	100.0

Collection Experience Matrix

The major limitations of the traditional methods is that they are based on aggregated data and fail to relate outstanding receivables of a period with the credit sales of the same period. Thus, using the traditional methods, two analysts can come up with entirely different signals about the status of receivables if they aggregate sales and receivables data differently. Using disaggregated data for analysing collection experience can eliminate this problem. The key is to relate receivables to sales of the same period. When sales over a period of time are shown horizontally and associated receivables vertically in a tabular form, a matrix is constructed. Therefore, this method of evaluating receivables is called **collection experience matrix**. Consider an example.[2]

Suppose that the financial manager of a firm is analysing its receivables from the credit sales of past six months starting from July to December. The credit sales of the company are as follows:

	Rs in lakh		Rs in lakh
July	400	October	220
August	410	November	205
September	370	December	350

From the sales ledger, the financial manager gathered outstanding receivables data for each month's sales. For example, he found that for July, there was a sale for Rs 400 lakh, the outstanding receivables during July, August and September were Rs 330 lakh, Rs 242 lakh and Rs 80 lakh. Similarly, he ascertained receivables for sales of other months. This information is shown in Table 28.5.

How do we interpret information contained in Table 28.5? We can convert the table to a collection experience matrix by dividing the outstanding receivables in each column by sales

1. For a discussion of the limitations of average collection period and aging schedule, see Lewellen, W.G. and Johnson, R.W., Better Way to Monitor Accounts Receivables, *Harvard Business Review*, (May–June, 1972), pp. 101–19.
2. See Lewellen and Johnson, *op. cit.*, for a detailed discussion of the logic and example of collection experience matrix.

amount in that column. This is shown in Table 28.6, which contains information on the percentage of receivables to the credit sales from which those receivables have originated. For example, for the sales of July, 82.5 per cent receivables (i.e., 330/400) were outstanding at the end of July, 60.5 per cent (i.e., 242/400) at the end of August and 20 per cent (i.e., 80/400) at the end of September. In other words, 17.5 per cent receivables were paid by the end of July, 39.5 per cent by the end of August (viz., 39.5 – 17.5 = 22 per cent additional receivables were paid in August), 80 per cent by the end of September (viz., 80 – 39.5 = 41.5 per cent additional receivables were paid during September) and remaining receivables were collected during October so that the balance of book debts became nil at the end of October. Receivables of other months can also be analysed in the same way. Thus, when we read a column top-down, we get an idea of the manner in which the firm collects a given month's sales. How well does the firm collect current month's sales? This can be ascertained by reading the diagonals drawn in Table 28.6. For example, the top diagonal shows the manner in which current month's sales are collected. The next diagonal shows receivables one month older and so on. For the firm in our example, we find in Table 28.6 that about 80 per cent of sales in a given month remain uncollected by the end of that month. In other words, about 20 per cent of sales in a given month are collected in the same month. If the percentages increase as we move down any diagonal, it implies that the firm is unable to collect its receivables faster. This requires an investigation for appropriate remedial action.

Table 28.5: Sales and Receivables from July to December

(Rs in lakh)

Month	July	Aug.	Sept.	Oct.	Nov.	Dec.
Sales	400	410	370	220	205	350
Receivables						
July	330					
Aug.	242	320				
Sept.	80	245	320			
Oct.	0	76	210	162		
Nov.	0	0	72	120	160	
Dec.	0	0	0	40	130	285

Table 28.6: Collection Experience Matrix

(Rs in lakh)

Month	July	Aug.	Sept.	Oct.	Nov.	Dec.
Sales	400	410	370	220	205	350
Receivables (%)						
July	82.5					
Aug.	60.5	78.0				
Sept.	20.0	59.8	86.5			
Oct.	0	18.5	56.8	73.6		
Nov.	0	0	19.5	54.5	78.0	
Dec.	0	0	0	18.2	63.0	81.4

FACTORING

Credit management is a specialised activity, and involves a lot of time and effort of a company. Collection of receivables poses a problem, particularly for small-scale enterprises. Banks have the policy of financing receivables. However, this support is available for a limited period and the seller of goods and services has to bear the risk of default by debtors. A company can assign its credit management and collection to specialist organisations, called factoring organisations. **Factoring** is a popular mechanism of managing, financing and collecting receivables in developed countries like USA and UK, and has extended to a number of other countries in the recent past, including India. Subsidiaries of four Indian banks provide factoring services. In this section, we explain the nature and types of factoring services and its costs and benefits.

Nature of Factoring

Factoring is a unique financial innovation. It is both a financial as well as a management support to a client. It is a method of converting a non-productive, inactive asset (i.e., receivable) into a productive asset (viz., cash) by selling receivables to a company that specialises in their collection and administration.[1] For a number of companies, cash may become a scarce resource if it takes a long time to receive payment for goods and services supplied by them. Such a current asset in the balance sheet is, in fact, illiquid and serves no business purpose; it is much better to sell that asset for cash which can be immediately employed in the business. A 'factor' makes the conversion of receivables into cash possible.

One can define factoring as "a business involving a continuing legal relationship between a financial institution (the factor) and a business concern (the client) selling goods or providing services to trade customers (the customers) whereby the factor purchases the client's accounts receivable and in relation thereto, controls the credit, extended to customers and administers the sales ledger."[2] Factoring may also be defined as "a contract between the suppliers of goods/services and the factor under which (a) the supplier and its customers (debtors) other than those for the sale of goods bought primarily for their personal, family or household use; (b) the factor is to perform at least two of the following functions—(i) finance for the supplier, including loans and advance payments; (ii) maintenance of accounts (ledgering relating to the receivables); (iii) collection of accounts (ledgering relating to the receivables) and (iv) protection against default in payment by debtors; (c) notice of assignment of the receivables is to be given to debtors".[3] The agreement between the supplier and the factor specifies the factoring procedure. Usually, the firm sends the customer's order to the factor for evaluating the customer's creditworthiness and approval. Once the factor is satisfied about the customer's creditworthiness and agrees to buy receivables, the firm despatches goods to the customer. The customer will be informed

1. Westlake, M., *Factoring,* Pitman, 1975, p. 1.

2. Biscoe, P.N., *Law and Practice of Credit Factoring,* Butterworth & Company, 1975, p. 5.

3. Definition given by the Unidroit Convention on International Factoring held in Ottawa, Canada, May 1988, quoted in the Reserve Bank of India, *Report of the Study Group for Examining Introduction of Factoring Services in India,* Reserve Bank of India, December 1988, pp. 44–45.

that his account has been sold to the factor, and he is instructed to make payment directly to the factor. To perform his functions of credit evaluation and collection for a large number of clients, a factor may maintain a credit department with specialised staff. Once the factor has purchased a firm's receivables and if he agrees to *own* them, he will have to provide protection against any bad-debt losses to the firm.

Factoring Services

While purchase of receivables is fundamental to the functioning of factoring, the factor provides the following three basic services to clients:[1]

- Sales ledger administration and credit management.
- Credit collection and protection against default and bad-debt losses.
- Financial accommodation against the assigned book debts (receivables).

Credit administration A factor provides full credit administration services to his clients. He helps and advises them from the stage of deciding credit extension to customers to the final stage of book debt collection. The factor maintains an account for all customers of all items owing to them, so that collections could be made on due date or before. He helps clients to decide whether or not and how much credit to extend to customers. He provides clients with information about market trends, competition and customers and helps them to determine the creditworthiness of customers. He makes a systematic analysis of the information regarding credit for its proper monitoring and management. He prepares a number of reports regarding credit and collection, and supplies them to clients for their perusal and action.

Credit collection and protection When individual book debts become due from the customer, the factor undertakes all collection activity that is necessary. He also provides full or partial protection against bad-debts. Because of his dealings with a variety of customers and defaults with different paying habits, he is in a better position to develop appropriate strategy to guard against possible defaults.

Financial assistance Often factors provide financial assistance to the client by extending advance cash against book debts. Customers of "clients" become debtors of a factor and have to pay to him directly in order to settle their obligations. Factoring thus involves an outright purchase of debts, allowing full credit protection against any bad debts and providing financial accommodation against the firm's book debts. In USA, the maximum advance a factor provides is equal to the amount of factored receivables *less* the sum of (*i*) the factoring commission, (*ii*) interest on advance, and (*iii*) reserve that the factor requires to cover bad-debts losses. The amount of reserve depends on the quality of factored receivables and usually ranges between 5 to 20 per cent in the USA.

In view of the services provided by a factor, factoring involves the purchase of a client's book debts with the purpose of facilitating credit administration, collection and protection. It is also a means of short-term financing. It provides protection against the default in payment for book debts. For these services, the factor, however, charges a fee from the client. Thus, factoring has a cost.

Other services In developed countries like the USA, factors provide many other services. They include: (*i*) providing information on prospective buyers; (*ii*) providing financial counselling; (*iii*) assisting the client in managing its liquidity and preventing sickness; (*iv*) financing acquisition of inventories; (*v*) providing facilities for opening letters of credit by the client etc.[2]

Factoring and Short-term Financing

Although factoring provides short-term financial accommodation to the client, it differs from other types of short-term credit in the following manner:[3]

- Factoring involves 'sale' of book debts. Thus, the client obtains advance cash against the expected debt collection and does not incur a bad-debt.
- Factoring provides flexibility as regards credit facility to the client. He can obtain cash either immediately or on due date or from time to time, as and when he needs cash. Such flexibility is not available from formal sources of credit.
- Factoring is a unique mechanism which not only provides credit to the client but also undertakes the total management of client's book debts.

Factoring and Bills Discounting

Factoring should be distinguished from bill discounting. Bill discounting or invoice discounting consists of the client drawing bills of exchange for goods and services on buyers, and then discounting it with bank for a charge. Thus, like factoring, bill discounting is a method of financing. However, it falls short of factoring in many respects. Factoring is all of bills discounting plus much more. Bills discounting has the following limitations in comparison to factoring:

- Bills discounting is a sort of borrowing while factoring is the efficient and specialised management of book debts along with enhancing the client's liquidity.
- The client has to undertake the collection of book debt. Bill discounting is always 'with recourse', and as such the client is not protected from bad-debts.
- Bills discounting is not a convenient method for companies having large number of buyers with small amounts since it is quite inconvenient to draw a large number of bills.

1. For a detailed discussion, see Phelps, C.W., *The Role of Factoring,* Commercial Credit Company, 1956, pp. 17–47.
2. Reserve Bank of India (R.B.I.), *Report of the Study Group for Examining the Introduction of Factoring Services in India,* Bombay, Reserve Bank of India, 1988, p. 17.
3. Gupta, G.P., *et. al., Factoring—An Innovative Financial Service for Small Scale Sector,* (Internal Document), Industrial Development Bank of India, August 1985.

Types of Factoring

The factoring facilities available worldwide can be broadly classified into four main groups:[1]

1. Full service non-recourse (old line)
2. Full service recourse factoring
3. Bulk/agency factoring
4. Non-notification factoring

Full service non-recourse Under this method, book debts are purchased by the factor, assuming 100 per cent credit risk. The full amount of invoices have to be paid to clients in the event of debt becoming bad. He also advances cash upto 80–90 per cent of the book debts immediately to the client. Customers are required to make payment directly to the factor. The factor maintains the sales ledger and accounts and prepares age-wise reports of outstanding book debts.

Non-recourse factoring is most suited to the following situations where[2]

- amounts involved per customer are relatively substantial and financial failure can jeopardise client's business severely;
- there are a large number of customers of whom the client cannot have personal knowledge; and
- the client prefers to obtain 100 per cent cover under factoring rather than take insurance policy which provides only 70–80 per cent cover.

Non-recourse factoring is very popular in the USA, where it is also known as **'old-line' factoring.** Old-line factors are true factors and they differ from those who merely finance receivables.

Full service recourse factoring In this method of factoring, the client is not protected against the risk of bad-debts. He has no indemnity against unsettled or uncollected debts. If the factor has advanced funds against book debts on which a customer subsequently defaults, the client will have to refund the money.

Most countries practice recourse factoring since it is not easy to obtain credit information, and the cost of bad-debt protection is very high. This type of factoring is often used as a method of short-term financing, rather than pure credit management and protection service. It is less risky from the factor's point of view, and thus, it is less expensive to the client than non-recourse factoring. This type of factoring is also preferred when large spread of customers with relatively low amount per customer is involved, or the client is selling to high-risk customers.[3]

Advance factoring and maturity factoring The non-recourse and recourse factoring can be further classified into:

- Advance factoring
- Maturity factoring

As discussed above, under the **advance factoring**, the factor advances cash against book debts due to the client immediately. **Maturity factoring** implies that payment will be made to the client on maturity. In the case of non-recourse maturity factoring, payment is on maturity or when the book debts are collected, or on the insolvency of the customers. In the case of recourse maturity factoring, the factor pays to the client when the books debts have been collected. The client with sound financial condition and liquidity may prefer maturity factoring.

Bulk/agency factoring This type of factoring is basically used as a method of financing book debts. Under this the client continues to administer credit and operate sales ledger. The factor finances the book debts against bulk either on recourse or without recourse. This sort of factoring became popular with the development of mini-computers market where marketing and credit management was not a problem but the firms needed temporary financial accommodation. Those companies which have good systems of credit administration, but need finances, prefer this form of factoring.

Non-notification factoring In this type of factoring, customers are not informed about the factoring agreement. It involves the factor keeping the accounts ledger in the name of a sales company to which the client sells his book debts. It is through this company that the factor deals with the client's customers. The factor performs all his usual functions without a disclosure to customers that he owns the book debts. This type of factoring is available in the UK to financially strong companies.

Costs and Benefits of Factoring

There are two types of costs involved:

- the factoring commission or service fee
- the interest on advance granted by the factor to the firm.

Factoring commission is paid for credit evaluation and collection and other services and to cover bad-debt losses. It is usually expressed as a percentage of full net face value of receivables factored, and in developed countries like USA, it ranges between 1 to 3 per cent.[4] In India, a charge of around 2.5 to 3 per cent is envisaged. In fact, factoring commission will depend on the total volume of receivables, the size of individual receivables, and the quality of receivables. The commission is expected to be higher for 'without recourse' factoring since the factor assumes the entire credit risk.

The interest on advance would be higher than the prevailing prime rate of interest or the bank overdraft rate. In USA, factors charge a premium ranging between 2 to 5 per cent over and above the prime rate of interest. If this rule is applied to India where the prime rate of interest on the working capital finance is about 16 per cent, then the interest rate on advances by factors may range between 18 to 23 per cent. However, in the opinion of experts, factors should not charge more than what the banks are

1. See Phelps, *op. cit.,* R.B.I., *op. cit.,* Gupta, *et. al., op. cit.*
2. Gupta, *et. al., op. cit.,* p. 10.
3. Gupta, *et. al., op. cit.,* p. 11.
4. R.B.I., *op. cit.,* p. 111.

charging since they would be in competition with them as regards the financing of receivables.[1]

If factoring is so expensive, why should firms go for it? There are certain benefits which result from factoring receivables, and they more than offset the costs of factoring. Factoring has the following benefits:

- Factoring provides specialised service in credit management, and thus, helps the firm's management to concentrate on manufacturing and marketing.
- Factoring helps the firm to save cost of credit administration due to the scale of economics and specialisation.

Technical or marketing entrepreneurs often start many firms, and they may fail or may lack expertise to provide adequate attention to credit control and financial management. This leads to inefficient management of working capital and the undertaking of unwarranted risks. By utilising a factoring facility, companies are able to access specialist management service in the highly specialised field of credit management, covering efficient credit control and protection, sales ledger accounting and credit collection. As a company grows, the factor will involve more professionals to handle these problems. Thus the management time is released to focus on technology, production, marketing, personnel and other managerial functions.

A factor is in a position to employ specialists for the credit control and management since he has to cater to a larger number of firms and has substantial funds to invest, whereas for a small growing company its level of business operations deter the use of expensive functional specialists. The credit management specialisation by the factor and his employment of highly skilled personnel for many clients, allows enormous benefits for his individual clients. Thus, the firm can save costs of credit administration. It does not require a credit department; it does not have to incur costs of credit investigation, evaluation and collection and the bad-debt losses. A factor, who specialises in credit administration, is better placed to control bad debt losses than the credit department or the financial manager of a small or medium size firm due to its experience and specialisation in handling receivables of a variety of firms.

Once the business of a factor grows, he can develop such a degree of specialisation in certain areas that his services are also demanded by large firms who are not in a position to perform similar services as diligently and efficiently. Large firms can particularly use the services of factors for the purpose of preventing defaults and bad debts. In this area the factor has the advantage of dealing with certain industries and a large number of customers with different profiles and habits. Thus, he is able to inculcate distinct skills of analysing the debt paying habits of customers.

A firm should evaluate costs and benefits of factoring to arrive at a decision regarding the employment of a factor. Let us consider an example to illustrate the trade-off between costs and benefits of factoring.

Illustration 28.8: Analysis of Factoring Decision

A small firm has credit sales of Rs 80 lakh and its average collection period is 80 days. The past experience indicates that bad-debt losses are around 1 per cent of credit sales. The firm spends about Rs 120,000 per annum on administering its credit sales. This cost includes salaries of one officer and two clerks who handle credit checking, collection, etc., and telephone and telex charges. These are avoidable costs. A factor is prepared to buy the firm's receivables. He will charge 2 per cent commission. He will also pay advance against receivables to the firm at an interest rate of 18 per cent after withholding 10 per cent as reserve. What should the firm do?

Let us first calculate the average level of receivables. The collection period is 80 days and credit sales are Rs 80 lakh; therefore, the average level of receivables is (assuming 360 days in a year):

$$\text{Average level of receivables} = \frac{8,000,000}{360} \times 80 = \text{Rs } 1,777,778$$

The advance, which the factor will pay, will be the average level of receivables less factoring commission, reserve and interest on advance. The factoring commission is 2 per cent of average receivables (80 days):

$$\text{Factoring commission} = 0.02 \times 1,777,778 = \text{Rs } 35,556$$

and reserve is:

$$\text{Reserve} = 0.10 \times 1,777,778 = \text{Rs } 177,778$$

Thus, the amount available for advance is:

$$\text{Advance available} = 1,777,778 - 35,556 - 177,778$$
$$= \text{Rs } 1,564,444$$

However, the factor will also deduct 18 per cent interest before paying the advance for 80 days. Therefore, the amount of advance to be paid by the factor is:

$$\text{Advance to be paid} = 1,564,444 - (0.18 \times 1,564,444 \times 80/360)$$
$$= 1,564,444 - 62,578 = \text{Rs } 1,501,866$$

What is the annual cost of factoring to the firm? The annual costs include the following:

Factoring commission:	$35,556 \times 360/80$	160,002
Interest charges:	$62,578 \times 360/80$	281,601
		Rs 441,603

The firm saves the following costs:

Cost of credit administration	120,000
Cost of bad-debt loss, $0.01 \times 8,000,000$	80,000
	Rs 200,000

The net cost of factoring to the firm is:

$$\text{Net cost of factoring} = 441,603 - 200,000 = \text{Rs } 241,603$$

The effective rate of interest of firm is:

$$\text{Effective rate of annual cost} = \frac{241,603}{1,501,866}$$
$$= 0.161 \text{ or } 16.1 \text{ per cent}$$

The annual percentage cost of 16.1 per cent of factoring receivables can be compared with the cost of other possible sources of short-term financing.

Ideally, factoring should benefit all—client, customer and factor. This may not happen because of the lack of clarity as regards the roles of the client and the factor, inept handling of

---

1. R.B.I., *ibid.*

credit and other functions by the client and the factor, overestimation of benefits or underestimation of costs etc. The client should understand that the factor can function efficiently with his full cooperation. For example, it is not possible for a factor to resolve all disputes arising between the client and the factor, particularly those which are technical in nature. Similarly, a conflict may arise between the client and the factor as regards the question of credit-risk. The factor may like to reduce or enhance credit limit to customers depending on his assessment of the credit risk which the client may not agree with. Factoring benefits the client, but the overall benefits in the long-run occur from the good management of production and marketing operations. Factoring, by ensuring the credit collection, helps the firm to concentrate on production and marketing.

SUMMARY

❖ Trade credit creates debtors (book debts) or accounts receivable. It is used as a marketing tool to maintain or expand the firm's sales.

❖ A firm's investment in accounts receivable depends on volume of credit sales and collection period.

❖ The financial manager can influence volume of credit sales and collection period through credit policy. Credit policy includes credit standards, credit terms, and collection efforts.

❖ Credit standards are criteria to decide to whom credit sales can be made and how much. If the firm has soft standards and sells to almost all customers, its sales may increase but its costs in the form of bad-debt losses and credit administration will also increase. Therefore, the firm will have to consider the impact in terms of increase in profits and increase in costs of a change in credit standards or any other policy variable.

❖ The incremental return that a firm may gain by changing its credit policy should be compared with the cost of funds invested in receivables. The firm's credit policy will be considered optimum at the point where incremental rate of return equals the cost of funds.

❖ The cost of funds is related to risk; it increases with risk. Thus, the goal of credit policy is to maximise the shareholders wealth; it is neither maximisation of sales nor minimisation of bad-debt losses.

❖ The conditions for extending credit sales are called credit terms and they include the credit period and cash discount.

❖ Cash discounts are given for receiving payments before than the normal credit period. All customers do not pay within the credit period. Therefore, a firm has to make efforts to collect payments from customers.

❖ Collection efforts of the firm aim at accelerating collections from slow-payers and reducing bad-debt losses. The firm should in fact thoroughly investigate each account before extending credit. It should gather information about each customer, analyse it and then determine the credit limit. Depending on the financial condition and past experience with a customer, the firm should decide about its collection tactics and procedures.

❖ There are three methods to monitor receivables. The average collection period and aging schedule are based on aggregate data for showing the payment patterns, and therefore, do not provide meaningful information for controlling receivables. The third approach that uses disaggregated data is the collection experience matrix. Receivables outstanding for a period are related to credit sales of the same period. This approach is better than the two traditional methods of monitoring receivables.

❖ Factoring involves sale of receivables to specialised firms, called factors. Factors collect receivables and also advance cash against receivables to solve the client firms' liquidity problem. For providing their services, they charge interest on advance and commission for other services.

KEY CONCEPTS

Advance factoring	Credit limit	Discriminant analysis	Maturity factoring
Aging schedule	Credit period	Factoring	Non-notification factoring
Bills discounting	Credit standards	Full service non-recourse	Numerical credit scoring
Bulk or agency factoring	Credit terms	factoring	Optimum credit policy
Collection experience matrix	Default risk	Full service recourse factoring	Trade credit

ILLUSTRATIVE SOLVED PROBLEMS

Problem 28.1: A company is currently selling 100,000 units of its product at Rs 50 each unit. At the current level of production, the cost per unit is Rs 45, variable cost per unit being Rs 40. The company is currently extending one month's credit to its customers. It is thinking of extending credit period to two months in the expectation that sales will increase by 25 per cent. If the required rate of return (before-tax) on the firm's investment is 30 per cent, is the new credit policy desirable?

Solution:

The incremental sales units are 25,000 units and contribution per unit is Rs 10. Therefore, the incremental contribution (Δ CONT) is:

$$\Delta \text{CONT} = 25,000 \times \text{Rs } 10 = \text{Rs } 250,000$$

If the credit is increased to 60 days, it may be assumed that it will be availed by all customers. Therefore, the new level of receivables given increased sales of Rs 6,250,000 (i.e., 125,000 × Rs 50) will be:

$$\text{New level of receivables} = \frac{6,250,000 \times 60}{360} = \text{Rs } 1,041,667$$

$$\text{Old level of receivables} = \frac{5,000,000 \times 30}{360} = \text{Rs } 416,667$$

The incremental investment in receivables is:

New level of receivables – Old level of receivables

$$= 1,041,667 - 416,667 = \text{Rs } 625,000$$

The incremental rate of return is:

$$r = \frac{250,000}{625,500} = 0.4 \text{ or } 40 \text{ per cent}$$

Since the expected incremental rate of return, 40 per cent, is greater than the required rate of return, 30 per cent, the firm should change its credit period. In fact, the net gain to the firm is:

Increment profit – Increment cost

$$= 250,000 - 0.30 \times 625,000$$

$$= 250,000 - 187,500 = \text{Rs } 62,500$$

The result is based on the following assumptions: (i) all sales are credit sales, (ii) fixed costs do not change and (iii) investment in receivables is represented by sales value. If we drop the third assumption and calculate investment in receivables at cost, the profitability would increase. The calculations for investment in receivables at cost are as follows:

$$\text{Old level of receivables (at cost)} = 5,000,000 \times \frac{45}{50} \times \frac{30}{360}$$

$$= \text{Rs } 375,000 \; .$$

Since fixed costs will remain constant and they have been absorbed by existing sales, the level of receivables in additional sales will be calculated at variable cost. Thus:

New level of receivables (at cost)

$$= 5,000,000 \times \frac{45}{50} \times \frac{60}{360} + 1,250,000 \times \frac{40}{50} \times \frac{60}{360}$$

$$= 750,000 + 166,667 = \text{Rs } 916,667$$

Thus, the incremental level of receivables at cost is:

$$916,667 - 375,000 = \text{Rs } 541,667$$

The required profit on incremental investment (Δ INVST) is:

$$0.3 \times 541,667 = \text{Rs } 162,500$$

Thus the net gain to the firm is:

$$250,000 - 162,500 = \text{Rs } 87,500$$

Problem 28.2: A company currently has annual sales of Rs 500,000 and an average collection period of 30 days. It is considering a more liberal credit policy. If the credit period is extended, the company expects sales and bad-debt losses to increase in the following manner:

Credit Policy	Increase in Credit Period	Increase in Sales Rs	Bad-debt % of Total Sales
A	10 days	25,000	1.2
B	15 days	35,000	1.5
C	30 days	40,000	1.8
D	42 days	50,000	2.2

The selling price per unit is Rs 2. Average cost per unit at the current level of operation is Rs 1.50 and variable cost per unit is Rs 1.20. If the current bad-debt loss is 1 per cent of sales and the required rate of return investment is 20 per cent, which credit policy should be undertaken? Ignore taxes, and assume 360 days in a year.

Solution:

The firm will maximize the shareholders value if it extends its period by additional 30 days (since expected return is higher than required return). In fact, it can further relax credit period until its expected return becomes 20% or net gain becomes zero.

The investment in receivables could be calculated at cost. At current level of sales, the firm's average unit cost is Rs 1.50. Since variable cost per unit is Rs 1.20, we can find total fixed costs:

Fixed cost = Total cost – Variable cost

$$= \frac{\text{Rs } 500,000 \times \text{Rs } 1.50}{\text{Rs } 2}$$

$$- \frac{\text{Rs } 500,000 \times \text{Rs } 1.20}{\text{Rs } 2}$$

$$= \text{Rs } 375,000 - \text{Rs } 300,000 = \text{Rs } 75,000$$

		Increase in Credit Period			
	Existing	10 days	15 days	30 days	42 days
A. Credit period (days)	30	40	45	60	72
B. Annual sales	500,000	525,000	535,000	540,000	550,000
C. Level of receivables (at sales value) $(A \times B)/360$	41,667	58,333	66,875	90,000	110,000
D. Incremental investment in receivables, $C - 41,667$	–	16,667	25,208	48,333	68,333
E. Required incremental profit at 20%, $0.2 \times D$	–	3,333	5,042	9,667	13,667
F. Incremental contribution on additional sales @ 40%	–	10,000	14,000	16,000	20,000
G. Bad-debt losses, $B \times \%$ bad-debt	5,000	6,300	8,025	9,720	12,100
H. Incremental bad-debt losses, $G - 5,000$	–	1,300	3,025	4,720	7,100
I. Incremental expected profit, $F - H$	–	8,700	10,975	11,280	12,900
J. Net gain, $I - E$	–	5,367	5,933	1,613	(767)
K. Expected return, I/D	–	52.2%	43.5%	23.3%	18.9%

Thus the total cost of different level of sales is (assuming unit price and fixed costs do not change):

Sales		Cost
525,000	$(525,000) \times (1.20)/2 + 75,000$	= Rs 390,000
535,000	$(535,000) \times (1.20)/2 + 75,000$	= Rs 396,000
540,000	$(540,000) \times (1.20)/2 + 75,000$	= Rs 399,000
550,000	$(550,000) \times (1.20)/2 + 75,000$	= Rs 405,000

and level of account receivables will be:

Level of Receivables		Δ INVST
$(375,000) \times (30)/360$	= Rs 31,250	–
$(390,000) \times (40)/360$	= Rs 43,333	12,083
$(396,000) \times (45)/360$	= Rs 49,500	18,250
$(399,000) \times (60)/360$	= Rs 66,500	35,250
$(405,000) \times (72)/360$	= Rs 81,000	49,750

The net gain from the credit policy can be recalculated using incremental investment in accounts receivables at cost. It would be higher now.

REVIEW QUESTIONS

1. Explain the objective of credit policy? What is an optimum credit policy? Discuss.
2. Is the credit policy that maximises expected operating profit an optimum credit policy? Explain.
3. What benefits and costs are associated with the extension of credit? How should they be combined to obtain an appropriate credit policy?
4. What is the role of credit terms and credit standards in the credit policy of a firm?
5. What are the objectives of the collection policy? How should it be established?
6. What shall be the effect of the following changes on the level of the firm's receivables:
   (a) Interest rate increases
   (b) Recession

   (c) Production and selling costs increase.
   (d) The firm changes its credit terms from "2/10, net 30" to "3/10, net 30."
7. 'The credit policy of a company is criticised because the bad-debt losses have increased considerably and the collection period has also increased.' Discuss under what conditions this criticism may not be justified.
8. What credit and collection procedures should be adopted in case of individual accounts? Discuss.
9. How would you monitor receivables? Explain the pros and cons of various methods.
10. What is factoring? What functions does it perform?
11. Explain the features of various types of factoring.
12. How does factoring differ from bills discounting and short-term financing?

PROBLEMS

1. Delta Company has current sales of Rs 30 crore. To push up sales, the company is considering a more liberal credit policy. The current average collection period of the company is 25 days. If the collection period is extended, sales increase in the following manner.

Credit Policy	Increase in Collection Period	Increase in Sales (Rs in lakh)
X	15 days	12
Y	25 days	27
Z	35 days	47

The company is selling its product at Rs 10 each. Average cost per unit at the current level is Rs 8 and variable cost per unit Rs 6. If the company required a return of 12 per cent on its investment, which credit policy is desirable? State your assumptions. (Assume a 360-day year).

2. The credit terms of a firm currently is "net 30." It is considering changing it to "net 60." This will have the effect of increasing the firm's sales. As the firm will not relax credit standards, the bad-debt losses are expected to remain at the same percentage, i.e., 3 per cent of sales. Incremental production, selling and collection costs are 80 per cent of sales and expected to remain constant over the range of

anticipated sales increases. The relevant opportunity cost for receivables is 15 per cent. Current credit sales are Rs 300 crore and current level of receivables is Rs 30 crore. If the credit terms are changed, the current sale is expected to change to Rs 360 crore and the firm's receivables level will also increase. The firm's financial manager estimates that the new credit terms will cause the firm's collection period to increase by 30 days.

   (a) Determine the present collection period and the collection period after the proposed change in credit terms.
   (b) What level of receivables is implied by the new collection period?
   (c) Determine the increased investment in receivables if the new credit terms are adopted.
   (d) Are the new credit terms desirable?

3. The Syntex Company is planning to relax its credit policy to motivate customers to buy on credit terms of net 30. It is expected that the variable costs will remain 75 per cent of sales. The incremental sales are expected to be on credit basis. For the perceived increase in risk in liberalising the credit terms, the company requires higher required return. If the following is the projected information, which credit policy should the company pursue?

Credit Policy	Required Return	Collection Period	New Sales (Rs)
A	20%	40	600,000
B	25%	45	500,000
C	32%	55	400,000
D	40%	70	300,000

4. X Ltd. has current annual sales of Rs 60 crore and an average collection period of 30 days. The company is considering of liberalising its credit policy. If the collection period is extended, sales and bad debt are expected to increase in the following way:

Credit Policy	Increase in Collection Period	Increase in Sales Rs (crore)	Per cent Bad Debt Losses
I	15 days	4.0	1.5
II	30 days	4.5	1.7
III	45 days	5.3	2.0
IV	60 days	6.5	2.5

The firm sells its product for Rs 10 per unit. Average cost at current level of sales is 90 per cent for sales and variable cost is 80 per cent of sales. If the current bad debt loss is 1.5 per cent of sales and the required return is 18 per cent, which credit policy should be pursued? (Assume a 360-day year). State your assumptions.

5. A company has a 15 per cent required rate of return. It is currently selling on terms of net 10. The credit sales of the company are Rs 120 crore a year. The company's collection period currently is 60 days. If company offered terms of 2/10, net 30, 60 per cent of its customers will take the discount and the collection period will be reduced to 40 days. Should the terms be changed?

6. A firm has current sales of Rs 7,200,000. The firm has unutilised capacity; therefore, with a view to boost its sales, it is considering lengthening its credit period from 30 days to 45 days. The average collection period will also increase from 30 to 45 days. Bad-debt losses are estimated to remain constant at 3 per cent of sales. The firm's sales are expected to increase by Rs 360,000. The variable production, administrative and selling costs are 70 per cent of sales. The firm's corporate tax rate is 35 per cent, and it requires an after-tax return of 15 per cent on its investment. Should the firm change its credit period?

7. A firm has current sales of Rs 720,000. It is considering offering the credit terms '2, 10, net 30' instead of 'net 30.' It is expected that sales will increase by Rs 20,000 and the average collection period will reduce from 30 days to 20 days. It is also expected that 50 per cent of the customers will take discounts and pay on 10th day and remaining 50 per cent will pay on 30th day. Bad-debt losses will remain at 2 per cent of sales. The firm's variable cost ratio is 70 per cent, corporate tax rate is 50 per cent and opportunity cost of investment in receivables is 10 per cent. Should the company change its credit terms?

8. The Electro Limited is a distributor of electric equipments. Its sales in 2004 amounted to Rs 22 crore and after tax profit Rs 1.10 crore.

The company has been experiencing a declining profit margin for the last three years. It is felt that this is due to the loose credit policy. On investigation, a group of slow paying customers was identified. It is recommended that the credit policy should be tightened to eliminate them. Sales to this group amounted to about 20 per cent of the company's total sales.

Table 28.8 gives information about the company's cost structure. It is expected that if the slow-paying accounts are eliminated only variable costs would decline. It is also believed that bad-debt and collection expenses are entirely attributable to these accounts. Using this information, you are required to allocate Electro's income and expenses between "slow-paying" accounts and "good" accounts.

Table 28.8: The Electro Limited: Fixed and Variable Costs (Per cent of Sales)

	Total	Fixed	Variable
Cost of goods sold	85.0	–	85.0
Selling	4.6	2.0	2.6
Administration	2.4	0.8	1.6
Warehousing	2.4	1.0	1.4
Bad-debts	0.4	–	0.4
Collection	0.2	–	0.2

A study of credit files indicated that the collection period on 'slow-paying' accounts average to 50 days versus 35 days for all accounts. The balance of debtors for these accounts averaged Rs 885,000 during 2004.

Should the Electro Limited tighten its credit policy? Make suitable assumptions.

9. The PQR Company's annual credit sales are Rs 60 crore. The company's existing credit terms are 1/15, net 40. Generally 60 per cent of the customers avail the cash discount facility. The average collection period is 45 days. The percentage default rate is 0.5 per cent. The company is thinking of two alternative changes in credit terms:

Credit Terms	Percentage Taking Discount	Collection Period	Default Percentage
2/10, net 35	80	20	1.0
3/10, net 25	95	14	1.5

What strategy should be followed by PQR if sales are expected to remain stable and the required rate of return is 18 per cent?

10. Bansali Textiles Limited has annual sales of Rs 200 crore. It sells 80 per cent of its products on a 60-day credit. Its average collection period is 80 days. The company's bad debts, based on the past experience, could be estimated as 0.9 per cent of credit sales. The company's annual cost of administering credit sales is Rs 0.75 crore. It is possible to avoid Rs 0.20 crore of these costs

if the company transfers credit administration to a factor. The factor will charge 1.75 per cent commission for his services. He can also extend advance against receivables to the company at an interest rate of 16.5 per cent after withholding 10 per cent as reserve. Should the company hire services of the factor?

CASE

Case 28.1: Relax Pharmaceuticals Limited

Relax Pharmaceuticals Limited is medium-size pharmaceutical company. Its annual sales are Rs 1,200 million. Relax has been facing tough competition from multinational and domestic pharmaceutical companies over last few years, particularly because of deregulation of the industry. Relax's profit margins have been declining during three years. The managing director of the company thought that this could be due to about 15 per cent of total sales to financially weak customers. He thought that perhaps the cost of maintaining these marginal accounts is high which may be causing a decline in the firm's profit margin. He therefore asked his financial manager to analyse the impact of tightening the credit policy by discontinuing sales to these customers. After analysing past data, the financial manager has determined cost behaviour, given Rs 1,200 million sales, as given in Table 28.1.1. On further investigation, he found that bad-debt losses are entirely attributable to the marginal accounts, while 25 per cent of the collection costs are for the good customers and remaining for the marginal accounts.

Table 28.1.1: Standard Furniture Mart's Behaviour of Cost (Percentage)

	Fixed	*Variables*	*Total*
Cost of goods sold	–	80.00	80.00
Administrative costs	3.50	3.00	6.50
Selling costs	4.50	3.73	8.23
Bad-debt losses	–	0.15	0.15
Collection costs	–	0.12	0.12
	8.00	87.00	95.00

The company's cash sales are about 10 per cent. The financial manager found out that the average collection period of marginal accounts was 70 days against 60 days of all other accounts, and 100 per cent of sales to marginal accounts are on credit. The company has a policy of extending 50 days' credit to all customers. Relax's required rate of return for average risk project is 15 per cent.

It was the view of the marketing manager that the company was facing competition, and it could increase its sales by relaxing the credit policy rather making it restrictive. He discussed this with the finance manager. According to the marketing managers if the customers are allowed a credit period of 70 days, instead of the current policy of 50 days, sales could increase by 20 per cent. It is expected that the increased sales will be on credit and the three-fourths of this sales will come from the marginal customers. It is also expected that the average collection period of the marginal accounts will increase to 90 days and 75 days for the good customers. In case of the sales to the marginal customers the bad-debt losses are expected to increase to 5.5 per cent. The collection charges mostly attributable to the marginal accounts will increase by Rs 50,000. Along with relaxing the credit terms, the financial manager also thought of introducing the scheme of discount for the prompt payment. Customers could avail 2 per cent cash discount if they pay within 30 days; they should otherwise pay within 70 days. A quick analysis of accounts indicated that 30 per cent of the good customers might avail cash discount, and the remaining good customers might, on average, take 75 days to make payment. There is no possibility of the marginal accounts availing the discount.

Discussion Questions

1. What is Relax's investment in accounts receivable (debtors)? Is it high?
2. What are marginal accounts? Should Relax discontinue its sales to marginal accounts? Why or why not? Show calculations.
3. Discuss the features of Relax's proposed credit policy? What are its financial implications? Show calculations.
4. Do you think that average collection period is a relevant criterion for monitoring Relax's debtors? What alternative do you suggest and why?

CHAPTER 29 Inventory Management

CHAPTER OBJECTIVES

- Highlight the need for and nature of inventory
- Explain the techniques of inventory management
- Focus on the need for analysing inventory problem as an investment decision
- Discuss the process for managing inventory

INTRODUCTION

Inventories constitute the most significant part of current assets of a large majority of companies in India. On an average, inventories are approximately 60 per cent of current assets in public limited companies in India. Because of the large size of inventories maintained by firms, a considerable amount of funds is required to be committed to them. It is, therefore, absolutely imperative to manage inventories efficiently and effectively in order to avoid unnecessary investment. A firm neglecting the management of inventories will be jeopardising its long-run profitability and may fail ultimately. It is possible for a company to reduce its levels of inventories to a considerable degree, e.g., 10 to 20 per cent, without any adverse effect on production and sales, by using simple inventory planning and control techniques. The reduction in 'excessive' inventories carries a favourable impact on a company's profitability.

NATURE OF INVENTORIES

Inventories are stock of the product a company is manufacturing for sale and components that make up the product. The various forms in which inventories exist in a manufacturing company are: raw materials, work-in-process and finished goods.

- **Raw materials** are those basic inputs that are converted into finished product through the manufacturing process. Raw materials inventories are those units which have been purchased and stored for future productions.
- **Work-in-process** inventories are semi-manufactured products. They represent products that need more work before they become finished products for sale.

- **Finished goods** inventories are those completely manufactured products which are ready for sale. Stocks of raw materials and work-in-process facilitate production, while stock of finished goods is required for smooth marketing operations. Thus, inventories serve as a link between the production and consumption of goods.

The levels of three kinds of inventories for a firm depend on the nature of its business. A manufacturing firm will have substantially high levels of all three kinds of inventories, while a retail or wholesale firm will have a very high level of finished goods inventories and no raw material and work-in-process inventories. Within manufacturing firms, there will be differences. Large heavy engineering companies produce long production cycle products; therefore, they carry large inventories. On the other hand, inventories of a consumer product company will not be large because of short production cycle and fast turnover.

Firms also maintain a fourth kind of inventory, **supplies or stores and spares**. Supplies include office and plant cleaning materials like soap, brooms, oil, fuel, light bulbs etc. These materials do not directly enter production, but are necessary for production process. Usually, these supplies are small part of the total inventory and do not involve significant investment. Therefore, a sophisticated system of inventory control may not be maintained for them.

NEED TO HOLD INVENTORIES

The question of managing inventories arises only when the company holds inventories. Maintaining inventories involves tying up of the company's funds and incurrence of storage and handling costs. If it is expensive to maintain inventories, why do companies hold inventories? There are three general motives for holding inventories.[1]

- *Transactions motive* emphasises the need to maintain inventories to facilitate smooth production and sales operations.
- *Precautionary motive* necessitates holding of inventories to guard against the risk of unpredictable changes in demand and supply forces and other factors.
- *Speculative motive* influences the decision to increase or reduce inventory levels to take advantage of price fluctuations.

A company should maintain adequate stock of materials for a continuous supply to the factory for an uninterrupted production. It is not possible for a company to procure raw materials whenever it is needed. A time lag exists between demand for materials and its supply. Also, there exists uncertainty in procuring raw materials in time on many occasions. The procurement of materials may be delayed because of such factors as strike, transport disruption or short supply. Therefore, the firm should maintain sufficient stock of raw materials at a given time to streamline production. Other factors which may necessitate purchasing and holding of raw material inventories are quantity discounts and anticipated price increase. The firm may purchase large quantities of raw materials than needed for the desired production and sales levels to obtain quantity discounts of bulk purchasing. At times, the firm would like to accumulate raw materials in anticipation of price rise.

Work-in-process inventory builds up because of the *production cycle*. Production cycle is the time span between introduction of raw material into production and emergence of finished product at the completion of production cycle. Till production cycle completes, stock of work-in-process has to be maintained. Efficient firms constantly try to make production cycle smaller by improving their production techniques.

Stock of finished goods has to be held because production and sales are not instantaneous. A firm cannot produce immediately when customers demand goods. Therefore, to supply finished goods on a regular basis, their stock has to be maintained. Stock of finished goods has also to be maintained for sudden demands from customers. In case the firm's sales are seasonal in nature, substantial finished goods inventories should be kept to meet the peak demand. Failure to supply products to customers, when demanded, would mean loss of the firm's sales to competitors. The level of finished goods inventories would depend upon the coordination between sales and production as well as on production time.

OBJECTIVE OF INVENTORY MANAGEMENT

In the context of inventory management, the firm is faced with the problem of meeting two conflicting needs:

- To maintain a large size of inventories of raw material and work-in-process for *efficient and smooth production* and of finished goods for uninterrupted sales operations.

- To maintain a minimum investment in inventories to maximise profitability.

Both *excessive* and *inadequate* inventories are not desirable. These are two danger points within which the firm should avoid. The objective of inventory management should be to determine and maintain optimum level of inventory investment. The optimum level of inventory will lie between the two danger points of excessive and inadequate inventories.

The firm should always avoid a situation of over investment or under-investment in inventories. The major dangers of over investment are: (*a*) unnecessary tie-up of the firm's funds and loss of profit, (*b*) excessive carrying costs, and (*c*) risk of liquidity. The excessive level of inventories consumes funds of the firm, which cannot be used for any other purpose, and thus, it involves an opportunity cost. The carrying costs, such as the costs of storage, handling, insurance, recording and inspection, also increase in proportion to the volume of inventory. These costs will impair the firm's profitability further. Excessive inventories carried for long-period increase chances of loss of liquidity. It may not be possible to sell inventories in time and at full value. Raw materials are generally difficult to sell as the holding period increases. There are exceptional circumstances where it may pay to the company to hold stocks of raw materials. This is possible under conditions of inflation and scarcity. Work-in-process is far more difficult to sell. Similarly, difficulties may be faced to dispose off finished goods inventories as time lengthens. The downward shifts in market and the seasonal factors may cause finished goods to be sold at low prices. Another danger of carrying excessive inventory is the physical deterioration of inventories while in storage. In case of certain goods or raw materials deterioration occurs with the passage of time, or it may be due to mishandling and improper storage facilities. These factors are within the control of management; unnecessary investment in inventories can, thus, be cut down.

Maintaining an inadequate level of inventories is also dangerous. The consequences of under-investment in inventories are: (*a*) production hold-ups and (*b*) failure to meet delivery commitments. Inadequate raw materials and work-in-process inventories will result in frequent production interruptions. Similarly, if finished goods inventories are not sufficient to meet the demand of customers regularly, they may shift to competitors, which will amount to a permanent loss to the firm.

The aim of inventory management, thus, should be to avoid excessive and inadequate levels of inventories and to maintain sufficient inventory for the smooth production and sales operations. Efforts should be made to place an order at the right time with the right source to acquire the right quantity at the right price and quality. An effective inventory management should

- ensure a continuous supply of raw materials to facilitate uninterrupted production,
- maintain sufficient stocks of raw materials in periods of short supply and anticipate price changes.
- maintain sufficient finished goods inventory for smooth sales operation, and efficient customer service.

---

1. Starr, Martin, K. and David W. Miller, *Inventory Control: Theory and Practice*. Englewood Cliffs, N.J., Prentice-Hall, 1962, p. 17.

- minimise the carrying cost and time, and
- control investment in inventories and keep it at an optimum level.

INVENTORY MANAGEMENT TECHNIQUES

In managing inventories, the firm's objective should be in consonance with the shareholder wealth maximisation principle. To achieve this, the firm should determine the optimum level of inventory. Efficiently controlled inventories make the firm flexible. Inefficient inventory control results in unbalanced inventory and inflexibility—the firm may sometimes run out of stock and sometimes may pile up unnecessary stocks. This increases the level of investment and makes the firm unprofitable.

To manage inventories efficiency, answers should be sought to the following two questions:

- How much should be ordered?
- When should it be ordered?

The first question, how much to order, relates to the problem of determining **economic order quantity** (EOQ), and is answered with an analysis of costs of maintaining certain level of inventories. The second question, when to order, arises because of uncertainty and is a problem of determining the re-order point.[1]

Economic Order Quantity (EOQ)

One of the major inventory management problems to be resolved is how much inventory should be added when inventory is replenished. If the firm is buying raw materials, it has to decide lots in which it has to be purchased on replenishment. If the firm is planning a production run, the issue is how much production to schedule (or how much to make). These problems are called **order quantity problems**, and the task of the firm is to determine the optimum or economic order quantity (*or* **economic lot size**). Determining an optimum inventory level involves two types of costs: (*a*) *ordering costs* and (*b*) *carrying costs*. The economic order quantity is that inventory level that minimises the total of ordering and carrying costs.

Ordering costs The term ordering costs is used in case of raw materials (or supplies) and includes the entire costs of acquiring raw materials. They include costs incurred in the following activities: requisitioning, purchase ordering, transporting, receiving, inspecting and storing (store placement). Ordering costs increase in proportion to the number of orders placed. The clerical and staff costs, however, do not have to vary in proportion to the number of orders placed, and one view is that so long as they are committed costs, they need not be reckoned in computing ordering cost. Alternatively, it may be argued that as the number of orders increases, the clerical and staff costs tend to increase. If the number of orders are drastically reduced, the clerical and staff force released now can be used in other departments. Thus, these costs may be included in the ordering costs. It is more appropriate to include clerical and staff costs on a *pro rata* basis.

Ordering costs increase with the number of orders; thus the more frequently inventory is acquired, the higher the firm's ordering costs. On the other hand, if the firm maintains large inventory levels, there will be few orders placed and ordering costs will be relatively small. Thus, ordering costs decrease with increasing size of inventory.

Carrying costs Costs incurred for maintaining a given level of inventory are called carrying costs. They include storage, insurance, taxes, deterioration and obsolescence. The storage costs comprise cost of storage space (warehousing cost), stores handling costs and clerical and staff service costs (administrative costs) incurred in recording and providing special facilities such as fencing, lines, racks etc. Table 29.1 provides summary of ordering and carrying costs.

Table 29.1: Ordering and Carrying Costs

Ordering Costs	*Carrying Costs*
• Requisitioning	• Warehousing
• Order placing	• Handling
• Transportation	• Clerical and staff
• Receiving, inspecting and storing	• Insurance
• Clerical and staff	• Deterioration and obsolescence

Carrying costs vary with inventory size. This behaviour is contrary to that of ordering costs which decline with increase in inventory size. The economic size of inventory would thus depend on trade-off between carrying costs and ordering costs.

Ordering and carrying costs trade-off The optimum inventory size is commonly referred to as **economic order quantity.** It is that order size at which annual total costs of ordering and holding are the minimum. We can follow three approaches—the trial and error approach, the formula approach and the graphic approach—to determine the economic order quantity (EOQ). We assume that total annual demand is known with certainty and usage of materials is steady. Also, ordering cost per order and carrying cost per unit are assumed to be constant.

Trial and error approach The trial and error, or analytical, approach to resolve the order quantity problem can be illustrated with the help of a simple example. Let us assume the following data for a firm:

Estimated annual requirements, *A*	1,200 units
Purchasing cost per unit, *P* (Rs)	50
Ordering cost (per order), *O* (Rs)	37.50
Carrying cost per unit, *c* (Re)	1

A number of alternatives are available to the firm. It may purchase its entire requirement of 1,200 units in the beginning of the year in one single lot or in 12 monthly lots of 100 units each and so on. If only one order of 1,200 units is placed, the

---

1. Extensive standard writings exist on inventory management models. For example, see Martin and Miller, *op. cit.,* and well known series of articles by Magee, J.F. "Guides of Inventory Policy" I–III, *Harvard Business Review,* 34 (January–February 1956), pp. 49–60 (March–April 1956), pp. 103–16 and (May–June 1956), pp. 57–70.

firm will have a starting inventory of 1,200 units. With the constant consumption, the inventory size will reduce in a systematic way and will reach zero level at the end of the year. As the firm will hold 1,200 units in the beginning and zero unit at the end of the year, the average inventory held during the year will be 600 units, (i.e., (1200 + 0)/2 = 600 units), representing an average value of Rs 30,000 (600 × Rs 50). On the other hand, if the monthly purchases are made, 12 orders of 100 units each will be placed during the year. Thus, the firm will have 100 units at the start of a month and zero unit at the end of the month and the average inventory held will be 50 units (i.e., (100 + 0)/2 = 50 units), representing an average value of Rs 2,500 (50 × Rs 50). Many other possibilities can be worked out in the same manner. If the objective is to minimise the inventory investment, then monthly orders or even less than that, if possible, may be favoured. However, this may not be most economical. To determine the economical order size, implications of both carrying and order costs should be studied.[1]

If we assume known annual requirements and steady usage, the inventory levels under different lot size alternatives are shown in Figure 29.1. For illustrative purposes, we have depicted only two alternatives—placing one order in the beginning or 12 monthly orders. The single order plan (say, Plan 1) involves an average inventory level of 600 units, starting with the highest level of 1,200 units and ending with zero level. On the other hand, the multiple order plan entailing 12 orders results in an average inventory level of 50 units.

The multiple order plan (say, Plan II) involves less investment in inventories; but it is not necessarily the most economic plan. To determine optimum order quantity, a comparison of total costs at different lot sizes should be made. The computations are shown in Table 29.2.

In terms of the total annual costs, Plan II is preferable, as it has a total annual cost of Rs 500 as against the total annual cost of Rs 637.5 of Plan I. But for an economic solution, other alternatives should also be considered. Computations in Table 29.2 show that the total annual cost is minimum, i.e., Rs 300 when the number of orders in the year is 4. The economic order quantity, therefore, is 300 units.

Table 29.2: Total Costs of Various Orders

Annual requirements (A): 1,200 units
Carrying cost per unit (c): Re 1
Ordering cost per order (O): Rs 37.50

Order size (Q)	1,200	600	400	300	240	200	150	120	100
Average Inventory (Q/2)	600	300	200	150	120	100	75	60	50
Number of orders (A/Q)	1	2	3	4	5	6	8	10	12
Annual carrying cost (Rs) (cQ/2)	600	300	200	150	120	100	75	60	50
Annual ordering costs (Rs) (OA/Q)	37.5	75	112.5	150	187.5	225	300	375	450
Total annual costs (Rs)	637.5	375	312.5	300	307.5	325	375	435	500

Order-formula approach The trial and error, or analytical, approach is somewhat tedious to calculate the EOQ. An easy way to determine EOQ is to use the order-formula approach. Let us illustrate this approach.[2]

Suppose the ordering cost per order, O, is fixed. The total order costs will be number of orders during the year multiplied by ordering cost per order. If A represents total annual requirements and Q the order size, the number of orders will be A/Q and total order costs will be:

$$\text{Total ordering cost} = \frac{(\text{Annual requirement} \times \text{Per order cost})}{\text{Order size}}$$

$$\text{TOC} = \frac{AO}{Q} \qquad (1)$$

Let us further assume that carrying cost per unit, c, is constant.

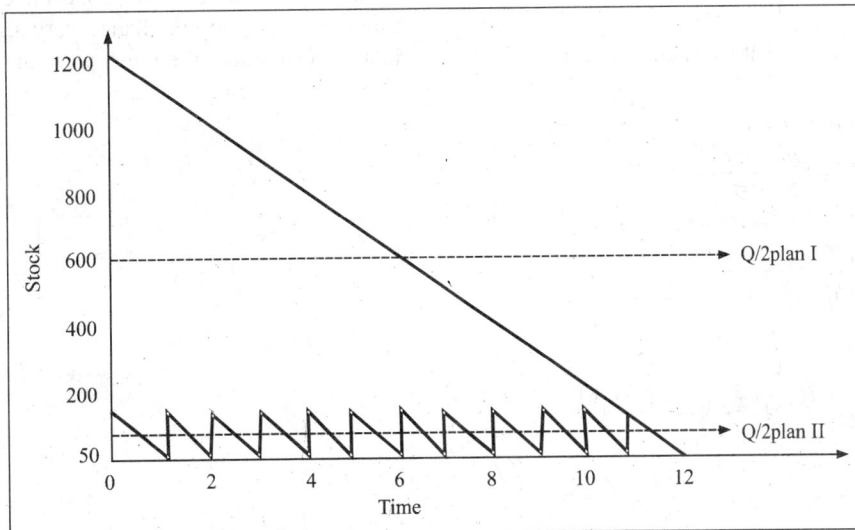

Figure 29.1: Inventory Level Over Time

1. Ramamoorthy, *op. cit.,* pp. 156–57.
2. Also see Van Horne, J.C., *Financial Management and Policy,* Prentice-Hall of India, 1985, pp. 416–19.

The total carrying costs will be the product of the average inventory units and the carrying cost per unit. If Q is the order size and usage is assumed to be steady, the average inventory will be:

$$\text{Average inventory} = \frac{\text{Order size}}{2} = \frac{Q}{2} \tag{2}$$

and total carrying costs will be:

$$\text{Total carrying cost} = \text{Average inventory}$$
$$\times \text{Per unit carrying cost}$$
$$\text{TCC} = \frac{Qc}{2} \tag{3}$$

The total inventory cost, then, is the sum of total carrying and ordering costs:

$$\text{Total cost} = \text{Total carrying cost} + \text{Total order cost}$$
$$\text{TC} = \frac{Qc}{2} + \frac{AO}{Q} \tag{4}$$

Equation (4) reveals that for a large order quantity, Q, the carrying cost will increase, but the ordering costs will decrease. On the other hand, the carrying costs will be lower and ordering cost will be higher with the lower order quantity. Thus, the total cost function represents a trade-off between the carrying costs and ordering costs for determining the EOQ.

To obtain the formula for EOQ, Equation (4) is differentiated with respect to Q and setting the derivative equal to zero, we obtain:[1]

Economic order quantity

$$= \sqrt{\frac{2 \times \text{quantity required} \times \text{ordering cost}}{\text{carrying cost}}}$$

$$\text{EOQ} = \sqrt{\frac{2AO}{c}} \tag{5}$$

We note from Equation (5) that EOQ changes directly with

total requirements, A, and order cost O, and has an inverse relationship with the carrying cost, c. However, the square-root sign restrains the relationship in both cases. Thus, if the usage is double, the economic order quantity is not doubled; it will increase by, or about 1.4 times.[2]

To illustrate the use of EOQ formula, let us assume data of the example taken to illustrate the trial and error approach. As assumed earlier, if the total requirement is 1,200 units, ordering cost per order is Rs 37.50 and carrying cost per unit is Re 1, the economic order quantity will be:

$$\text{EOQ} = \sqrt{\frac{2 \times 1,200 \times 37.5}{1}} = 300 \text{ units}$$

This corresponds with the answer found out by trial and error approach.

Graphic approach The economic order quantity can also be found out graphically. Figure 29.2 illustrates the EOQ function. In the figure, costs—carrying, ordering and total—are plotted on vertical axis and horizontal axis is used to represent the order size. We note that total carrying costs increase as the order size increases, because, on an average, a larger inventory level will be maintained, and ordering costs decline with increase in order size because larger order size means less number of orders. The behaviour of total costs line is noticeable since it is a sum of two types of costs which behave differently with order size. The total costs decline in the first instance, but they start rising when the decrease in average ordering cost is more than offset by the increase in carrying costs.[3] The economic order quantity occurs at the point Q^* where the total cost is minimum. Thus, the firm's operating profit is maximised at point Q^*.

It should be noted that the total costs of inventory are fairly insensitive to moderate changes in order size. It may, therefore, be appropriate to say that there is an economic order range, not a point. To determine this range, the order size may be changed by some percentage and the impact on total costs may be studied. If the total costs do not change very significantly, the firm can change EOQ within the range without any loss.[4]

---

1. See Van Horne, *op. cit.*, pp. 156–57.

$$\text{TC} = \frac{Qc}{2} + \frac{AO}{Q} \tag{5A}$$

Differentiating Equation (5A) with respect to Q

$$\frac{d\text{TC}}{dQ} = \frac{c}{2} + \frac{AO}{Q^2} \tag{5B}$$

Setting Equation (5B) to zero: $\dfrac{c}{2} - \dfrac{AO}{Q^2} = 0$

$$cQ^2 = 2AO$$
$$Q^2 = \frac{2AO}{c}$$
$$Q = \sqrt{\frac{2AO}{c}} \tag{5C}$$

2. *Ibid.*, p. 419.
3. *Ibid.*
4. Synder, Arthur, Principles of Inventory Management, *Financial Executive*, XXXII (April 1964).

Optimum production run The use of the EOQ approach can be extended to production runs to determine the optimum size of manufacture. Two costs involved are set-up costs and carrying costs. Set-up costs include costs on the following activities: preparing and processing the stock orders, preparing drawings and specifications, tooling machines set-up, handling machines, tools, equipments and materials, over time etc. Production costs or set-up costs will reduce with bulk production runs, but carrying costs will increase as large stocks of manufactured inventories will be held. The **economic production size** will be the one where the total of set-up and carrying costs is minimum.

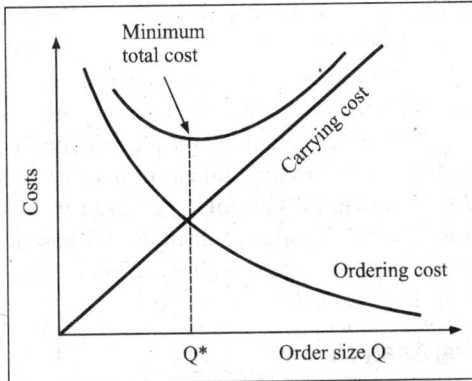

Figure 29.2: Economic Order Quantity

Equation (5) can be used to determine economic lot (or production) size (ELS), simply by replacing order costs O by set-up costs S. That is:

$$\text{ELS} = \sqrt{\frac{2AS}{c}} \qquad (6)$$

where A is the total estimated production, S is the set-up cost and c is the carrying cost. Suppose the estimated production for the next year is 90,000 units, set-up cost per production run is Rs 50 and the carrying cost is Re 1 per unit, the economic lot size will be:

$$\text{ELS} = \sqrt{\frac{2 \times 90,000 \times 50}{1}} = 3,000 \text{ units per production run}$$

Quantity discount Many suppliers encourage their customers to place large orders by offering them quantity discount. With **quantity discount**, the firm will save on the per unit purchase price. However, the firm will have to increase its order size more than the EOQ level to avail the quantity discount. This will reduce the number of orders and increase the average inventory holding. Thus, in addition to discount savings, the firm will save on ordering costs, but will incur additional carrying costs. The net return is the difference between the resultant savings and additional carrying costs. If the net return is positive, the firm's order size should equal the quantity necessary to avail the discount; if negative its order size should equal EOQ level.

Let us assume in the illustration in the preceding section that the firm is offered 0.5 per cent (0.005) or Re 0.05 per unit quantity discount on orders of 400 units or more. The net return should be calculated for deciding whether the order size should be increased from 300 to 400 units.

The discount savings will be:

Discount rate × Purchase price × Annual quantity

$$= d \times P \times A = 0.005 \times 50 \times 1200 = \text{Rs } 300 \qquad (7)$$

The savings on ordering costs will be:

$$= O\frac{A}{Q^*} - O\frac{A}{Q'} = O\left[\frac{A}{Q^*} - \frac{A}{Q'}\right] \qquad (8)$$

where O is per order cost, A is the annual requirement (units), Q^* is the EOQ and Q' is the discount quantity. We obtain savings as follows:

$$= 37.50\left[\frac{1200}{300} - \frac{1200}{400}\right] = 37.50(4-3) = \text{Rs } 37.50$$

The additional carrying costs will be:

$$= c\frac{Q'}{2} - C\frac{Q^*}{2} = \frac{c}{2}(Q' - Q^*) \qquad (9)$$

Using values for c = Re 1, Q' = 400 units and Q^* = 300 units, we obtain additional carrying costs as follows:

$$= 1/2(400 - 300) = \text{Rs } 50$$

The net return is given by the following equation:

$$= d\text{PA} + O\left[\frac{A}{Q^*} - \frac{A}{Q'}\right] - \frac{c}{2}(Q' - Q^*)$$

$$= 300 + 37.50 - 50 = \text{Rs } 287.50 \qquad (10)$$

Since the net return is positive, the firm should have an order quantity of 400 units.

Reorder Point

The problem, how much to order, is solved by determining the economic order quantity, yet the answer should be sought to the second problem, when to order. This is a problem of determining the reorder point. The **reorder point** is that inventory level at which an order should be placed to replenish the inventory. To determine the reorder point under certainty, we should know: (a) lead time, (b) average usage, and (c) economic order quantity. **Lead time** is the time normally taken in replenishing inventory after the order has been placed. By certainty we mean that usage and lead time do not fluctuate. Under such a situation, reorder point is simply that inventory level which will be maintained for consumption during the lead time. That is:

$$\text{Reorder point} = \text{Lead} \times \text{Average usage} \qquad (11)$$

To illustrate, let us assume that the economic order quantity is 500 units, lead time is three weeks and average usage is 50 units per week. If there is no lead time, that is, delivery of inventory is instantaneous, the new order will be placed at the end of tenth week, as soon as EOQ reaches zero level. But, as the lead time is three weeks, the new order should be placed at the end of seventh week, when there are 150 units left to consume during the lead time. As soon as the lead time ends and inventory level reaches zero, the new stock of 500 units will arrive. Thus, the reorder point is 150 units (50 units × 3 weeks). This is illustrated in Figure 29.3. which shows that the order will be placed at the end of seventh week, where 150 units are left for consumption during the lead time. At the end of tenth week, the firm will get a supply of 500 units. If the lead time is nil, the re-order point will be the zero level of inventory.

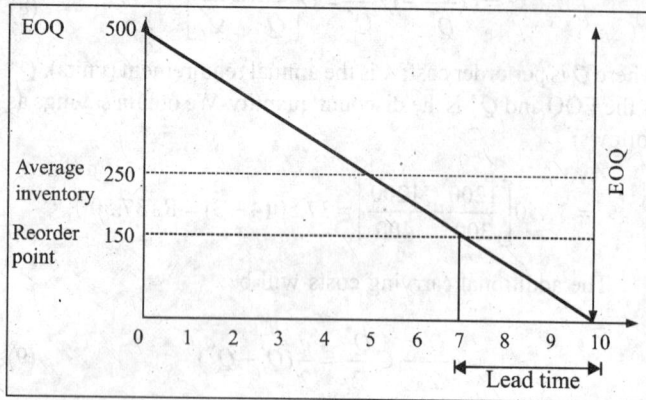

Figure 29.3: Reorder Point under Certainty

Safety stock In our example, the reorder point was computed under the assumption of certainty. It is difficult to predict usage and lead time accurately. The demand for material may fluctuate from day-to-day or from week-to-week. Similarly, the actual delivery time may be different from the normal lead time. If the actual usage increases or the delivery of inventory is delayed, the firm can face a problem of stock-out which can prove to be costly for the firm. Therefore, in order to guard against the stock-out, the firm may maintain a safety-stock—some minimum or buffer inventory as cushion against expected increased usage and/or delay in delivery time. Assume in the previous example, the reasonable expected stock-out is 25 units per week. The firm should maintain a safety stock of 75 units (25 units × 3 weeks). Thus, the reorder point will be 150 units + 75 units = 225 units. The maximum inventory will be equal to the economic order

quantity plus the safety stock, *i.e.*, 500 units + 75 units = 575 units. Thus, the formula to determine the reorder point when safety stock is maintained is as follows:

Re-order point = Lead × Average usage + Safety stock (12)

Figure 29.4 shows the reorder point under the assumption of the safety stock.

ANALYSIS OF INVESTMENT IN INVENTORY

It is a major responsibility of the financial manager to oversee the management of inventory since inventories represent investment of the firms' large funds in practice. A decision to determine or change the level of inventory is an investment decision. The analysis should therefore involve an evaluation of the profitability of investment in inventory. The goal of the inventory policy should be maximisation of the firm's value. The inventory policy will maximise the firm's value at a point at which **incremental** or **marginal return** from the investment in inventory equals the **incremental** or **marginal cost** of funds used to finance the investment in inventory. You may recall that the cost of funds is the required rate of return to the suppliers of funds, and it depends on the risk of the investment opportunity.

Incremental Analysis

Like the investment in receivable, the investment in inventory should be analysed involving the following four steps:

- Estimation of operating profit
- Estimation of investment in inventory
- Estimation of the rate of return on investment in inventory
- Comparison of the rate of return on investment with the cost of funds.

The **incremental analysis** should be used to compute the values of operating profit, investment in inventory, rate of return and cost of funds. A change in the inventory policy is desirable if the incremental rate of return exceeds the required rate of return. The following example illustrates the process of analysing investment in inventory.[1]

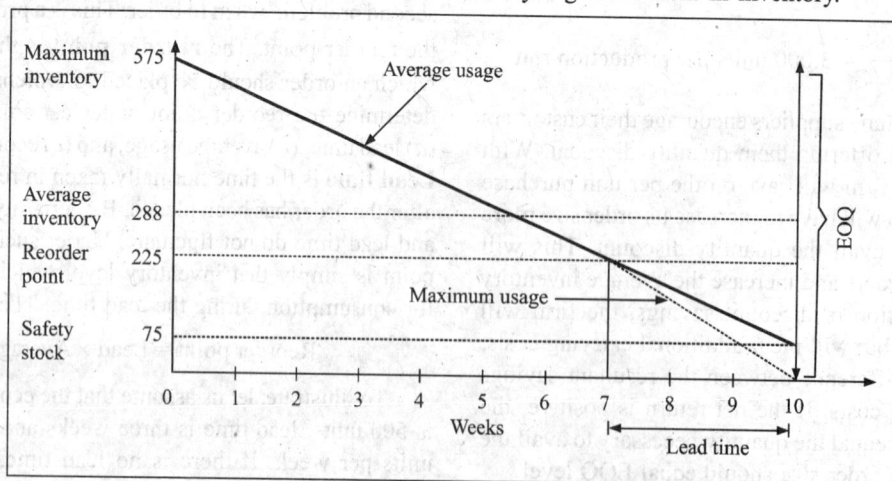

Figure 29.4: Reorder Point under Unertainty

---

1. See case titled Electricircuit, Inc., in Andrews, V.L., *et. al.*, *Financial Management: Cases and Readings*, Richard D. Irwin, 1982, for a similar, but comprehensive example. For a similar analysis also see Solomon, E. and Pringle, J.J., *An Introduction to Financial Management*, Prentice-Hall of India, 1978, pp. 218–21.

Illustration 29.1: Analysis of Investment in Inventory

Bansal Engineering Limited (BEL) produces many products. The managing director has estimated sales for the next year as Rs 176 crore and gross profit Rs 70 crore, after deducting cost of goods sold of Rs 106 crore. The average working capital requirements to support the forecast sales are estimated as follows:

	(Rs in lakh)	Percentage of Forecast Sales
Current Assets		
Cash	175	1.0
Receivable	3,520	20.0
Inventories		
Raw Materials	704	4.0
Work-in-process	816	4.6
Finished goods	490	2.8
Total	5,705	32.4
Less: Current liabilities	1,305	7.4
Working capital	4,400	25.0

The company uses sales forecasts as the basis for production and inventory of finished goods. The shortage of funds forced the company to tightly control inventories and maintain finished goods inventory below the target levels as desired by the sales forecasts. The company has been losing orders to competitors because of stock-outs resulting from the tight inventory control.

The problem of lost sales forced management to reconsider its inventory policy. The company is therefore considering adopting a system of safety stocks to avoid stock-out problem. It will like to estimate the costs and benefits of all new options. It was, therefore, thought necessary to compile data on possible inventory levels, lost sales on account of stock-outs and annual cost of maintaining higher levels of finished goods inventory. Table 29.3 provides these estimates.

Table 29.3: Bansal Engineering Limited: Impact of Alternative Inventory Policies

Inventory Policy Options	*Inventory Level (Rs in lakh)*	*Lost Sales (Rs in lakh)*	*Carrying Cost (Rs in lakh)*
Current	490	772	27
A	610	550	34
B	770	350	42
C	1013	190	56
D	1276	90	70
E	1406	50	77

It can be seen from Table 29.3 that the company can affect reduction in stock-outs and thus increase sales by increasing levels of finished goods inventory. To do so, however, the company will incur additional carrying costs including warehousing, handling, administration, set up, insurance etc. Notice that interest cost is not considered because the rate of return on investment is compared with the cost of funds which includes interest cost. The *expected operating profit* of each inventory policy will depend on the contribution from increased sales minus the additional carrying costs. The aim of the firm should be to maximise operating profit in relation to investment, *viz. expected return on investment.* This will take account of risk and cost of funds used to finance investment in inventory of finished goods. Let us calculate the rate of return on investment.

Incremental operating profit The first step in computing the rate of return, *r*, is to estimate *incremental operating profit*, ΔOP. In case of BEL, we know the amount of sales which the company can gain by shifting to higher levels of inventory. We also know that cost of goods sold (CGS) is about 60 per cent (Rs 106 crore CGS in relation to Rs 176 crore sales), and therefore, contribution ratio is 40 per cent. In the absence of information, we can make the assumption that cost of goods sold is in terms of variable cost and other costs do not increase with increase in sales. Given 40 per cent contribution ratio, we can calculate incremental contribution, $\Delta CONT$, from increased sales, $\Delta SALES$, resulting from moving to higher levels of inventory. We obtain incremental operating profit when we subtract the incremental carrying costs, $\Delta COST$, from incremental contribution. In the present example,

$$\Delta OP = \Delta CONT - \Delta COST \tag{13}$$

where OP is operating profit, CONT contribution and COST carrying cost and Δ (delta) change or increment in variable. We have assumed that carrying costs are 5.5 per cent of the finished goods inventory (Table 29.3). Table 29.4 shows calculation of incremental operating profits before tax (OPBT) and after tax (OPAT).

Table 29.4: Bansal Engineering Limited: Calculation of Incremental Operating Profit, DOP

Change in Inventory Policy (Rs in lakh)	Δ Sales (Rs in lakh)	CONT (Rs in lakh)	Δ COST (Rs in lakh)	Δ OPBT (Rs in lakh)	Δ OPAT (Rs in lakh)
Current to A	222	89	7	82	41
A to B	200	80	8	72	36
B to C	160	64	14	50	25
C to D	100	40	14	26	13
D to E	40	16	7	9	5

Incremental investment The next step in analysis is to estimate the incremental inventory investment, ΔINV, required to move from one inventory policy to next. We notice from Table 29.5 that if the company moves from current policy to policy A, investment in finished goods inventory increases by Rs 120 lakh (from Rs 490 lakh to Rs 610 lakh) and so on. Ideally, the investment in inventory should be measured in terms of out-of-pocket costs. It should also be noticed that to support increase in sales resulting from higher levels of inventory, the company will also require investment in other current assets which will partially be financed by current liabilities. Thus, **incremental investment**, Δ INVEST will be the sum of (*i*) increased finished goods inventories, ΔINV, and (*ii*) corresponding increase in other net working capital, ΔNWC, to support higher level of sales resulting from the increased level of finished goods inventory:

$$\Delta INVST = \Delta INV + \Delta NWC \tag{14}$$

Excluding finished goods inventory, net working capital for

BEL works out to be 22.2 per cent of increased sales based on the forecasts of next year. The incremental investment is calculated in Table 29.5 using this percentage for net working capital.

Table 29.5: Bansal Engineering Limited: Calculation of Incremental Investment,
Δ **INVST = Δ INV + Δ NWC**

Change in Inventory Policy (Rs in lakh)	Δ INV (Rs in lakh)	Δ NWC (Rs in lakh)	Δ INVST (Rs in lakh)	Cumulative Investment (Rs in lakh)
Current to A	120	49	169	169
A to B	160	44	204	373
B to C	243	36	279	652
C to D	263	22	285	937
D to E	130	9	139	1076

Return on investment Once we have calculated incremental operating profit and incremental investment, we can relate them to compute rate of return on investment (r) as follows:

$$r = \frac{\Delta OP}{\Delta INVST} \qquad (15)$$

Table 29.6 shows calculations for before-tax and after-tax expected rate of return. We notice that the company yields an attractive expected rate of return of 48.5 per cent, before-tax or 24.3 per cent, after-tax when it increases its investment in inventories by Rs 1,69,000. But the successive increments of investment in finished goods inventories regain less lost sales and therefore, less lost operating profit. As a result, incremental expected rate of return declines. The incremental return from policy E is only 6.5 per cent before tax or 3.2 per cent after tax.

Table 29.6: Bansal Electricals Limited: Calculations for Before-tax and After-tax Expected Rate of Return

Change in Inventory Policy	Before-tax Expected Rate of Return, Δ (OPBT/INVST)	After-tax Expected Rate of Return, Δ (OPAT/INVST)
Current to A	48.5%	24.3%
A to B	35.3%	17.6%
B to C	17.9%	9.0%
C to D	9.1%	4.6%
D to E	6.5%	3.2%

Choice of policy The choice of the inventory policy by the management of BEL will depend on the required rate of return on incremental (or marginal) investment in inventories. The concept of the required rate of return, k, has been discussed earlier in this book. At this stage, we shall emphasise that the required rate of return is not the borrowing rate. It depends on the risk of investment. Higher the risk, higher the required rate of return. If BEL increases its investment in inventories, its risk

increases. For example, the company may not be able to realise receivables, or inventory may become obsolete if it cannot sell goods because of recession or other unfavourable market conditions.

Thus the choice of inventory policy will depend on a comparison of the expected rate of return and the required rate of return. The firm should invest in higher level of inventory if $r \geq k$.

Assuming that BEL'S after-tax required rate of return is 9 per cent, it can adopt policy C since the marginal rate is just equal to the required rate of return. In Figure 29.5 this is shown at point X. At point X, the inventory policy is optimum as the value of the firm is maximised; at any other point the net wealth of the firm will be less. Note that the incremental rate of return declines as the firm invests more in inventory. The loosening of the inventory policy will increase risk, and therefore, the required rate of return increases. If risk is zero, the required rate of return will be equal to risk-free rate of return.[1]

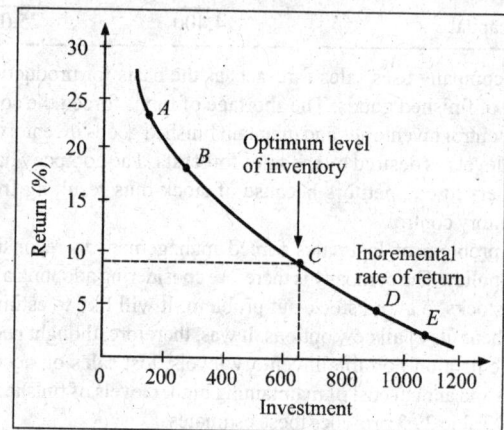

Figure 29.5: Optimal Inventory Policy

In the example, both return and cost are estimates; there can be some error of estimation. Therefore, if the firm is conservative and wants to play safe, it may choose policy B where the expected rate of return is much higher than the required rate of return. Another factor that merits consideration in the present case is the funds availability. BEL is currently facing the problem of shortage of funds. It will need to invest total additional funds of Rs 652 lakh if it chooses policy C. If the firm finds it difficult to raise enough funds to finance higher level of finished goods inventory, it may settle for an inventory policy which requires maintaining lower level of finished goods inventory. But by doing so, the firm will fail to maximise its value. Thus there is an opportunity cost of the shortage of funds.

We take another example to further explain the analysis of investment in inventories.

Illustration 29.2: Investment in Inventories

Divya Paints Limited is a medium-size company, manufacturing about 30 varieties of industrial paints. The company is known for its quality of products and prompt service. The demand of Divya's paints is much more than what the company can supply. Sunil Baluja, the managing

---

1. Solomon and Pringle, *op. cit.*, p. 222.

director of the company, is a chartered account, and he plans his sales and investment in inventories in such a way that he is able to maximise his gross margin. The following are Divya's current year data for sales, gross margin, profit before tax, inventory and net assets employed. Profit before tax is arrived at after deducting selling, general and administrative expenses from gross margin. The variable part of these expenses is about 9 per cent of sales. The managing director considers delivery time, usage rate and price while determining its order size and inventory level. He considers an inventory turnover of 5.0 as minimum for his business. The firm's current inventory turnover is 5.55. He has been adjusting his order size for anticipated price rise. Because of high inflation, prices are generally expected to rise.

	Rs
Sales	13,558,625
Gross margin	2,684,608
Profit before tax	540,232
Inventory	2,443,932
Net assets	4,978,808
Net working capital	3,528,622

Sunil Baluja has a policy of taking advantage of this price fluctuation. He has invested about Rs 180,000 in inventories in anticipation of price increase and expects to make a profit of about Rs 50,000 on this investment. Is this 'speculative' investment in inventory profitable to the firm?

The firm earns a return of about 28 per cent on this investment:

$$= \frac{\text{Speculative profit before-tax}}{\text{Speculative investment}} = \frac{50,000}{180,000} = 0.278 \text{ or } 27.8\%$$

On the other hand, the firm's return on net assets (RONA) employed is only 10.9 per cent (and if we exclude speculative inventory and its profit, firm's ROI is 10 per cent):

$$\frac{\text{Profit before-tax}}{\text{Net assets}} = \frac{540,232}{4,978,808} = 0109 \text{ or } 10.9\%$$

The speculative investment seems attractive even if we calculate the firm's return on 'operating' inventory:

Inventories excluding speculative investment (operating inventory) (Rs)	2,263,932
Before-tax profit excluding speculative profit (Rs)	490,232
Before-tax rate of return on inventory excluding speculative investment	21.7%

What we should consider, in fact, is the alternative use of funds if they are released from 'speculative' inventory investment. The firm can use these funds in 'operating' inventory to generate additional sales, Δ SALES. Since demand exceeds supply, the firm will not find any difficulty in expanding its sales (assuming capacity is available). The inventory turnover, excluding speculative inventory, is:

$$\text{Inventory turnover} = \frac{13,558,625}{2,443,932 - 180,000} = 6$$

Thus if the firm used Rs 180,000 worth inventory for operation, it could generate additional sales, Δ SALES, equal to the following amount:

$$\Delta \text{SALES} = 180,000 \times 6 = \text{Rs } 1,080,000$$

and since the firm's gross margin ratio is 19.8 per cent,

$$\text{Gross margin ratio} = \frac{2,684,608}{13,558,625} = 0.198 \text{ or } 19.8\%$$

it will be able to generate additional gross margin, Δ GMAR, calculated as follows:

$$\Delta \text{GMAR} = 1,080,000 \times 0.198 = \text{Rs } 213,840$$

Deducting other variable costs at the rate of 9 per cent of additional sales, the firm will gain an incremental before tax operating profit, Δ OPBT, of:

$$\Delta \text{OPBT} = 2,13,840 - (1,080,000 \times 0.09) = 213,840 - 97,200$$
$$= \text{Rs } 116,640$$

It should be recognised that incremental sales, Δ SALES, will require additional investment in other working capital, such as receivables etc. In case of Divya, it is 8 per cent of sales as shown below:

$$\text{NWC (excluding inventories) to sales} = \frac{3,528,622 - 2,443,932}{13,558,625}$$
$$= 0.08 \text{ or } 8\%$$

Thus, the incremental investment, Δ INVST, is:

$$\Delta \text{INVST} = \Delta \text{INV} + \Delta \text{NWC} = 180,000 + (1,080,000 \times 0.08)$$
$$= \text{Rs } 266,400$$

and the incremental before-tax rate of return on incremental is as follows:

$$r \text{ (before tax)} = \frac{\Delta \text{OPBT}}{\Delta \text{INVST}} = \frac{116,640}{266,400} = 0.438 \text{ or } 43.8\%$$

We find that the incremental return on investment on 'operating' inventory (43.8 per cent) is much higher than the return on 'speculative' investment (28 per cent). The firm should stop price speculation and use the funds so released in 'operating' inventory to generate additional sales. This will help the firm to increase its value.

INVENTORY CONTROL SYSTEMS

A firm needs an **inventory control system** to effectively manage its inventory. There are several inventory control systems in vogue in practice. They range from simple systems to very complicated systems. The nature of business and the size dictate the choice of an inventory control system. For example, a small firm may operate a **two-bin system**. Under this system, the company maintains two bins. Once inventory in one bin is used, an order is placed, and meanwhile the firm uses inventory in the second bin. For a large departmental store that sells hundreds of items, this system is quite unsatisfactory. The departmental store will have to maintain a self-operating, automatic computer system for tracking the inventory position of various items and placing order.

ABC Inventory Control System

Large numbers of firms have to maintain several types of inventories. It is not desirable to keep the same degree of control on all the items. The firm should pay maximum attention to those items whose value is the highest. The firm should, therefore, classify inventories to identify which items should receive the most effort in controlling. The firm should be *selective* in its approach to control investment in various types of inventories. This analytical approach is called the **ABC analysis** and tends to measure the significance of each item of inventories in terms of its value. The high-value items are classified as 'A items' and would be under the tightest control. 'C items' represent relatively least value and would be under simple control. 'B items' fall in between these two categories and require reasonable attention of management. The ABC analysis concentrates on important items and is also known as **control by importance and exception** (CIE).[1] As the items are classified in the importance of their relative value, this approach is also known as **proportional value analysis** (PVA).

The following steps are involved in implementing the ABC analysis:

- Classify the items of inventories, determining the expected use in units and the price per unit for each item.
- Determine the total value of each item by multiplying the expected units by its units price.
- Rank the items in accordance with the total value, giving first rank to the item with highest total value and so on.
- Compute the ratios (percentage) of number of units of each item to total units of all items and the ratio of total value of each item to total value of all items.
- Combine items on the basis of their relative value to form three categories—A, B and C.

The data in Table 29.7 and Figure 29.6 illustrate the ABC analysis.

Table 29.7: ABC Analysis

Item	Units	% of Total	Cumu- lative %	Unit Price (Rs)	Total Cost (Rs)	% of Total	Cumu- lative %
1	10,000	10	15	30.40	304,000	38.00	70
2	5,000	5		51.20	256,000	32.00	
3	16,000	16	45	5.50	88,000	11.00	90
4	14,000	14		5.14	72,000	9.00	
5	30,000	30	100	1.70	51,000	6.38	100
6	15,000	15		1.50	22,500	2.81	
7	10,000	10		0.65	6,500	0.81	
Total	100,000				800,000		

The tabular and graphic presentation indicate that 'Item A' forms a minimum proportion, 15 per cent of total units of all items, but represents the highest value, 70 per cent. On the other hand, 'Item C' represents 55 per cent of the total units and only 10 per cent of the total value. 'Item B' occupies the middle place. Items A and B jointly represent 45 per cent of the total units and 90 per cent of the investment. More than half of the total units are item C, representing merely 10 per cent of the investment. Thus, a tightest control should be exercised on 'Item A' in order to maximise profitability on its investment. In case of 'Item C', simple controls will be sufficient.

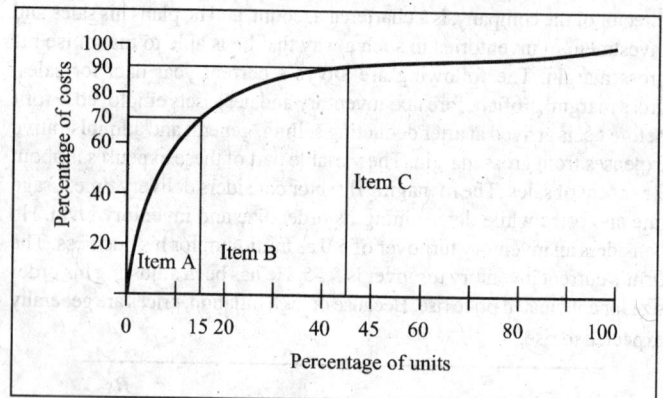

Figure 29.6: Graphic Presentation of ABC Analysis

Just-in-Time (JIT) Systems

Japanese firms popularised the **just-in-time (JIT) system** in the world. In a JIT system material or the manufactured components and parts arrive to the manufacturing sites or stores just few hours before they are put to use. The delivery of material is synchronised with the manufacturing cycle and speed. JIT system eliminates the necessity of carrying large inventories, and thus, saves carrying and other related costs to the manufacturer. The system requires perfect understanding and coordination between the manufacturer and suppliers in terms of the timing of delivery and quality of the material. Poor quality material or components could halt the production. The JIT inventory system complements the **total quality management (TQM)**. The success of the system depends on how well a company manages its suppliers. The system puts tremendous pressure on suppliers. They will have to develop adequate systems and procedures to satisfactory meet the needs of manufacturers.

Out-Sourcing

A few years ago there was a tendency on the parts of many companies to manufacture all components in-house. Now more and more companies are adopting the practice out-sourcing. **Out-sourcing** is a system of buying parts and components from outside rather than manufacturing them internally. Many companies develop a single source of supply, and many others help developing small and middle size suppliers of components that they require. Tata Motors has, for example, developed number of ancillary units around its manufacturing sites that supply parts and components to its manufacturing plants. With the help of Tata Motors the, ancillaries are able to maintain the high quality of the manufactured components. The car manufacturing company, Maruti, which is now controlled by Suzuki of Japan has the similar system of supply.

Computerised Inventory Control Systems

More and more companies, small or large size, are adopting the computerised system of controlling inventories A **computerised inventory control system** enables a company to easily track large items of inventories. It is an automatic system of counting

---

1. Richmond, Herbert J., Effective Inventory Management—Fact or Fiction? *Financial Executive*, March 1969, pp. 74–78.

inventories, recording withdrawals and revising the balance. There is an in-built system of placing order as the computer notices that the reorder point has been reached. The computerised inventory system is inevitable for large retail stores, which carry thousands of items. The computer information systems of the buyers and suppliers are linked to each other. As soon as the supplier's computer receives an order from the buyer's system, the supply process is activated.

THE INVENTORY MANAGEMENT PROCESS

The techniques of inventory management, discussed above, are very useful in determining the optimum level of inventory and finding answers to the problems of the economic order quantity, the re-order point and the safety stock. These techniques are very essential to economise the use of resources by minimising the total inventory cost. Our discussion of inventory management indicates the broad framework for managing inventories. More sophisticated techniques may be used to handle inventory management problems more efficiently and effectively. It should, however, be realised that inventory management, more than the use of techniques, is a managerial process of continuous planning, coordination, control and monitoring, motivation etc. It involves a number of steps in these areas. See Exhibit 29.1 for the inventory management process at BHEL.

EXHIBIT 29.2: LEVELS OF INVENTORY: SOME EXAMPLES

(Rs in crore)

	Voltas	L&T	GNFC	BHEL
Raw material	37.7	44.3	4.8	655.6
Stores & spares	0.9	234.3	13.0	90.3
Semi-finished goods	56.1	268.2	1.5	1,050.7
Finished goods	32.3	258.0	3.9	197.7
Total inventory	127.1	804.8	23.2	1,994.3
Inventory percentage of:				
Sales	10.3	9.2	16.0	26.1
Current assets	19.3	7.1	31.0	23.2
Total assets	14.7	4.7	12.0	20.8

Note: Figures are for the year 2003 except that BHEL's figures are for 2002.

Source: CMIE Database

For a number of companies, inventory represents a substantial investment (see Exhibit 29.2). The goal of the wealth maximisation is affected by the efficiency with which inventory is managed. The task of managing inventory primarily rests with the operating managers—purchase manager, materials control manager, production manager and marketing manager. Financial manager has no operating responsibility to control inventory. He has a role to analyse the behaviour of inventory and report its implications to operating managers. The financial manager should see that an optimum amount of funds is invested in inventory. He should be familiar with the inventory control techniques. He should introduce the policies which reduce the

EXHIBIT 29.1: THE INVENTORY MANAGEMENT PROCESS: CASE OF BHEL

- BHEL produces long production cycle items against the firm orders from customers. Because of this as well as sizeable imported raw materials and compulsory bulk purchases of items like steel and copper in line with availability from SAIL and MMTC, the company has to carry high level of inventories.

- As shown below, the company, because of lack of focussed inventory management policy and proper controls, carried very high inventories in seventies and eighties. It carried inventories of 375 days in 1978 and almost 300 days in 1981.

Year	Inventory	Sales	Inventory-to-sales (%)	Inventory Holding Period (days)
1978	512.9	498.6	102.9	375
1981	640.5	787.0	81.4	297
1990	1,080.3	3,035.6	35.6	130
1991	1,155.0	3,279.3	35.2	129
1992	1,149.1	3,487.4	32.9	120
1993	1,230.5	3,650.5	33.7	123
1994	1,304.4	3,708.1	35.2	128
1995	1,495.2	4,234.1	35.3	129
1996	1,809.6	4,974.3	36.4	133
1997	1,876.6	5,893.9	31.8	116
1998	1,713.3	6,647.0	25.8	94
1999	1,818.7	7,057.1	25.8	94
2000	1,793.9	6,991.3	25.7	94
2001	2,034.8	6,753.9	30.1	110
2002	1,994.2	7,651.1	26.1	95

- After taking a series of steps, BHEL has been able to substantially reduce the inventory-holding period to 94 days in 2002. How did this happen? BHEL took the following steps in the beginning of eighties to control its inventory:

  - An inventory monitoring cell was constituted at the corporate office.
  - The purchases were controlled by the materials management group reporting to the Director of Finance.
  - The company provided for weekly meetings between material planning, production control and purchase departments for better matched material availability.
  - Monthly review of total inventory at the level of chief executives of plants and corporate management was introduced.
  - Inventory control was dovetailed with the budgeting system.
  - Top 100 inventory items were identified for closer scrutiny and control.

lead time, regulate usage and thus, minimise safety stock.[1] The net effect would be to reduce inventory investment and increase the firm's prospects of making more profits.

---

1. Van Horne, *op. cit.*, p. 426.

SUMMARY

* Inventories constitute about 60 per cent of current assets of public limited companies in India. The manufacturing companies hold inventories in the form of raw materials, work-in-process and finished goods. There are at least three motives for holding inventories.
  * To facilitate smooth production and sales operation (transaction motive).
  * To guard against the risk of unpredictable changes in usage rate and delivery time (precautionary motive).
  * To take advantage of price fluctuations (speculative motive).
* Inventories represent investment of a firm's funds. The objective of the inventory management should be the maximisation of the value of the firm. The firm should therefore consider: (a) costs, (b) return, and (c) risk factors in establishing its inventory policy.
* Two types of costs are involved in the inventory maintenance:
  * *Ordering costs*: requisition, placing of order, transportation, receiving, inspecting and storing and clerical and staff services. Ordering costs are fixed per order. Therefore, they decline as the order size increases.
  * *Carrying costs*: warehousing, handling, clerical and staff services, insurance and taxes. Carrying costs vary with inventory holding. As order size increases, average inventory holding increases and therefore, the carrying costs increase.
* The firm should minimise the total cost (ordering plus carrying). The economic order quantity (EOQ) of inventory will occur at a point where the total cost is minimum. The following formula can be used to determine EOQ:

$$EOQ = Q^* = \sqrt{\frac{2AO}{c}}$$

where A is the annual requirement, O is the per order cost, and c is the per unit carrying cost.

* The economic order level of inventory, Q^*, represents maximum operating profit, but it is not optimum inventory policy. The value of the firm will be maximised when the marginal rate of return of investment in inventory is equal to the marginal cost of funds. The marginal rate of return (r) is calculated by dividing the incremental operating profit by the incremental investment in inventories, and the cost of funds is the required rate of return of suppliers of funds.
* When should the firm place an order to replenish inventory? The inventory level at which the firm places order to replenish inventory is called the reorder point. It depends on (a) the lead time and (b) the usage rate. Under perfect certainty about the usage rate, and instantaneous delivery (i.e., zero lead time), the reorder point will be equal to: Lead time × usage rate.
* In practice, there is uncertainty about the lead time and/or usage rate. Therefore, firms maintain safety stock which serves as a buffer or cushion to meet contingencies. In that case, the reorder point will be equal to: Lead time × Usage rate + Safety stock. The firm should strike a trade-off between the marginal rate of return and marginal cost of funds to determine the level of safety stock.
* A firm, which carries a number of items in inventory that differ in value, can follow a selective control system. A selective control system, such as the A-B-C analysis, classifies inventories into three categories according to the value of items: A-category consists of highest value items, B-category consists of high value items and C-category consists of lowest value items. More categories of inventories can also be created. Tight control may be applied for high-value items and relatively loose control for low-value items.
* Large number of companies these days follow the total quality management (TQM) system which requires companies to adopt JIT and computerised system of inventory management.

KEY CONCEPTS

ABC analysis	Economic order quantity	Ordering costs	Safety stock
Carrying cost	(EOQ)	Precautionary motive	Set-up cost
Control by importance	Lead time	Proportional value	Spectulative inventory
and exception (CIE)	Operating inventory	analysis (PVA)	Speculative motive
Economic lot size (ELS)	Optimum production run	Reorder point	Transaction motive

---

ILLUSTRATIVE SOLVED PROBLEMS

Problem 29.1: A manufacturing company has an expected usage of 50,000 units of certain product during the next year. The cost of processing an order is Rs 20 and the carrying cost per unit is Re 0.50 for one year. Lead time on an order is five days and the company will keep a reserve supply of two days' usage. You are required to calculate (a) the economic order quantity and (b) the reorder point. (Assume 250-day year).

Solution:

(a) The economic order quantity is:

$$EOQ = \sqrt{\frac{2AO}{c}} = \sqrt{\frac{2 \times 50,000 \times 20}{0.50}} = \sqrt{40,00,000} = 2,000 \text{ units}$$

(b) The reorder point is:

Daily usuage $= 50{,}000 \div 250 = 200$ units

Reorder point $=$ Safety stock $+$ Lead time $\times$ Usuage

$$= 2(200) + 5(200) = 400 + 1{,}000 = 1{,}400$$

Problem 29.2: A customer has been ordering 5,000 units at the rate of 1,000 units per order during last year. The production cost is Rs 12 per unit—Rs 8 for materials and labour and Rs 4 overhead cost. It costs Rs 1,500 to set up for one run of 1,000 units and inventory carrying cost is 20% of the production cost. Since this customer may buy at least 5,000 units this year, the company would like to avoid making five different production runs. Determine the most economic production run.

Solution:

The most economic run is:

$$= \sqrt{\frac{2 \times 5{,}000 \times 1{,}500}{12 \times 20\%}}$$

$$= \sqrt{\frac{2 \times 5{,}000 \times 1{,}500}{2.40}} = \sqrt{\frac{1{,}500{,}000}{2.40}}$$

$$= \sqrt{6{,}250{,}000} = 2{,}500 \text{ units}$$

Problem 29.3: A company's requirements for ten days are 6,300 units. The ordering cost per order is Rs 10 and the carrying cost per unit is Re 0.26. The following is the discount schedule applicable to the company:

Lot size	Discount per unit (Rs)
1 – 999	0
1,000 – 1,499	0.010
1,500 – 2,499	0.015
2,500 – 4,999	0.030
5,000 – and above	0.050

Determine the economic order quantity.

Solution:

The economic order quantity without considering the discount is:

$$\text{EOQ} = \sqrt{\frac{2 \times 6{,}300 \times 10}{0.26}}$$

$$= \sqrt{\frac{126{,}000}{0.26}} = 700 \text{ units (approx)}.$$

The following table is constructed to take account of the discount.

When the quantity discounts are available, the company should place four orders of 1,575 units each, as the total cost is minimum Rs 150.

No. of orders	1	2	3	4	5	6	7	8	9	10
Order size	6,300	3,150	2,100	1,575	1,260	1,050	900	787.5	700	630
Av. inventory	3,150	1,575	1,050	787.5	630	525	450	393.7	350	315
Carrying cost (Rs)	819	410	273	205	164	137	117	102	91	82
Order cost (Rs)	10	20	30	40	50	60	70	80	90	100
Total cost (Rs)	829	430	303	245	214	297	187	182	181	182
Less discount	315	189	95	95	63	63	–	–	–	–
Total cost after discount (Rs)	514	241	208	150	151	234	187	182	181	182

Note: Discount will be available on the total quantity, 6,300 units. However, discount per unit increases as order size increases.

Problem 29.4: A company is considering a selective inventory control using the following data:

Item	Units	Unit Cost (Rs)
1	6,000	4.00
2	61,200	0.05
3	16,800	2.10
4	3,000	6.00
5	55,800	0.20
6	22,680	0.50
7	26,640	0.65
8	14,760	0.40
9	20,520	0.40
10	90,000	0.10
11	29,940	0.30
12	24,660	0.50

Assuming the ABC analysis of selective control is indicated, arrange the data for presentation to the management.

Solution:

	Item	Units	% of Total Units	Unit Cost Rs	Total Cost Rs	% of Total Cost
A	3	16,800	4.52	2.10	35,280	21.43
	1	6,000	1.61	4.00	24,000	14.58
	4	3,000	0.81	6.00	18,000	10.94
	7	26,640	7.16	0.65	17,316	10.52
			14.10%			57.47%
B	12	24,660	6.63	0.50	12,330	7.49
	6	22,680	6.10	0.50	11,340	6.89
	5	55,800	15.00	0.20	11,160	6.78
	10	90,000	24.19	0.10	9,000	5.47
	11	29,940	8.05	0.30	8,982	5.46
	9	20,520	5.51	0.40	8,208	4.99
			65.48%			37.08%
C	8	14,760	3.97	0.40	5,904	3.59
	2	61,200	16.45	0.05	3,060	1.86
			20.42%			5.45%

REVIEW QUESTIONS

1. Why should inventory be held? Why is inventory management important? Explain the objectives of inventory management?

2. "There are two dangerous situations that management should usually avoid in controlling inventories." Identify the danger points and Explain.

3. Define the economic order quantity. How is it computed?

4. "The management of inventory must meet two opposing needs." What are they? How is a balance brought in these two opposing needs?

5. "The practical approach in determining economic order quantity is concerned with locating a minimum cost *range* rather than a minimum cost point." Explain.

6. What are ordering and carrying costs? What is their role in inventory control?

7. Define safety stock? How can safety stock be computed?

8. What are the cost of stock-outs? How should the costs of stock-out and the carrying costs be balanced to obtain the optimum safety stock?

9. How is the re-order point determined? Illustrate with an example and graphically.

10. What is lead time? How does it affect the computation of re-order point under certainty and uncertainty?

11. What is a selective control of inventory? Why is it needed? Illustrate with an example and graph the ABC analysis.

12. Explain the steps involved in analysing investment in inventories? Illustrate with an example.

PROBLEMS

1. A company has Rs 4 per year carrying cost on each unit of inventory, an annual usage of 50,000 units and an ordering cost of Rs 100 per order. Calculate the economic order quantity. What shall be the total annual cost of EOQ? If a quantity discount of Re 0.25 per unit is offered to the company when it purchases in lots of 1,000 units, should the discount be accepted?

2. A firm's estimated demand for a material during the next year is 2,500 units. Acquisition costs are Rs 400 per order and carrying cost is Rs 50 per unit. The safety stock is set at 25 per cent of the EOQ. The daily usage is 10 units and lead time is 10 days. Determine (*a*) the EOQ, (*b*) the safety stock, and (*c*) the reorder point.

3. A firm's requirement of materials is 3,000 units (price Rs 20 per unit) for 6 days. The ordering cost per order is Rs 30 and the carrying cost is Re 0.50. If the schedule of discount given below is applicable to the firm, determine the most economical order quantity.

Lot Size	Discount Rate
1 – 499	none
500 – 699	1%
700 – 999	2%
1000 – 2,499	4%
2500 and above	7%

4. AB Co. is considering a selective control for its inventories using the following data:
You are required to prepare the ABC plan and also show the ABC plan on a chart.

Units	Units Cost
7,000	10.00
8,000	9.00
10,000	2.00
6,000	8.00
8,000	1.00
2,000	60.00
5,000	0.40
4,000	40.00

5. Paul's Sales India, a large retailer situated in the Western India, has been losing sales because of non-availability of stock many times. The company's average inventory is Rs 200 lakh. Its contribution ratio is 30 per cent. The inventory carrying cost is 3.5 per cent per annum. In a study carried out by the financial manager of the company, it was found that the company will lose sales if it carried an inventory less than Rs 450 lakh per annum. The range of inventories carried and expected lost sales is given below:

Expected inventory level (Rs in lakh)	200	250	300	350	400	450
Expected lost sales (Rs in lakh)	250	180	120	50	20	0

The company's working capital (excluding inventory) to sales ratio is 18 per cent. Assuming a tax rate of 35 per cent and an after-tax opportunity cost of 12 per cent, show which inventory policy the company should adopt.

CASE

Case 29.1: Indus Engineering Limited

Indus Engineering Limited (IEL) is a well-known manufacturer of engineering products. The company's product line includes about 100 models of various products. Table 29.1.1 gives items of the profit and loss statement and balance sheet for the company for the current year. As compared to the last year, sales have grown by 15 per cent. The managing director is expecting sales to grow at this rate next year as well. She also thinks that there will be no change in the gross margin and working capital ratios.

Table 29.1.1: Summarised Profit and Loss Statement and Balance Sheet

Items	Rs (crore)
Profit and Loss Statement	
Sales	876
Less: Cost of goods sold	673
Gross profit	203
Less: Other expenses, including interest	117
Profit before tax	86
Less: Tax	32
Profit after tax	54
Balance Sheet	
Share capital	100
Reserve and surplus	204
Shareholders' Funds	304
Borrowings	458
Total Funds	762
Net fixed assets	504
Current Assets:	
Cash	9
Receivable	195
Inventories	
Raw Materials	44
Work-in-process	32
Finished goods	50
Total	330
Less: Current liabilities	72
Net current assets	258
Total Assets	762

The company produces and stocks goods according to the sales forecasts for each item. Given sales forecasts, goods are produced in quantities that raise levels of stocks to estimated sales requirements. Recently, the company has introduced a tight inventory control system because of the shortage of financial resources, and it has been maintaining inventories below the target levels. It was thought by many company executives that the policy of tight inventory control has resulted in substantial loss of sales. It was noticed that the company has been frequently losing orders to competitors because of stock-outs.

The problem of lost sales forced management to reconsider its inventory policy. The company therefore appointed a committee, consisting of general managers of finance, marketing and production, to determine whether finished goods inventory levels should be increased. The committee reported that more than the tightness of the current inventory control system; it was based on inaccurate sales forecasts. It was noted that it was very difficult to make prediction of new demand since customers erratically placed orders.

The committee recommended that the company should adopt a system of safety stocks to avoid stock-out problem. It was suggested that safety stocks should be determined after a careful consideration of (*i*) costs, (*ii*) return, and (*iii*) risks associated with inventory maintenance. It was, therefore, thought necessary to compile data on possible inventory levels, lost sales on account of stock-outs and annual cost of maintaining higher levels of finished goods inventory. Table 29.1.2 provides such estimates. The company's after-tax required rate of return is 12 percent. Assume 35 per cent tax rate.

Table 29.1.2: Alternative Inventory Policies

Inventory Options Policy	Inventory Level (Rs in crore)	Lost Sales (Rs in crore)	Carrying Cost (Rs in crore)
Current	50	75	2.2
A	60	55	3.0
B	80	40	4.1
C	100	20	5.9
D	130	10	7.1
E	140	5	7.7

Discussion Questions

1. What are Indus' problems in managing inventories?
2. Which inventory policy is the optimum for Indus? Why? Show calculations.

CHAPTER 30 Cash Management

CHAPTER OBJECTIVES

- Explain the reasons for holding cash
- Underline the need for cash management
- Discuss the techniques of preparing cash budget
- Focus on the management of cash collection and disbursement
- Emphasise the need for investing surplus cash in marketable securities

INTRODUCTION

Cash is the important current asset for the operations of the business. Cash is the basic input needed to keep the business running on a continuous basis; it is also the ultimate output expected to be realised by selling the service or product manufactured by the firm. The firm should keep sufficient cash, neither more nor less. Cash shortage will disrupt the firm's manufacturing operations while excessive cash will simply remain idle, without contributing anything towards the firm's profitability. Thus, a major function of the financial manager is to maintain a sound cash position.

Cash is the money which a firm can disburse immediately without any restriction. The term cash includes coins, currency and cheques held by the firm, and balances in its bank accounts. Sometimes near-cash items, such as marketable securities or bank times deposits, are also included in cash. The basic characteristic of near-cash assets is that they can readily be converted into cash. Generally, when a firm has excess cash, it invests it in marketable securities. This kind of investment contributes some profit to the firm.

FACETS OF CASH MANAGEMENT

Cash management is concerned with the managing of: (*i*) cash flows into and out of the firm, (*ii*) cash flows within the firm, and (*iii*) cash balances held by the firm at a point of time by financing deficit or investing surplus cash. It can be represented by a **cash management cycle** as shown in Figure 30.1. Sales generate cash which has to be disbursed out. The surplus cash has to be invested while deficit has to be borrowed. Cash management seeks to accomplish this cycle at a minimum cost. At the same time, it also seeks to achieve liquidity and control. Cash management assumes more importance than other current assets because cash is the most significant and the least productive asset that a firm holds. It is significant because it is used to pay the firm's obligations. However, cash is unproductive. Unlike fixed assets or inventories, it does not produce goods for sale. Therefore, the aim of cash management is to maintain adequate control over cash position to keep the firm sufficiently liquid and to use excess cash in some profitable way.

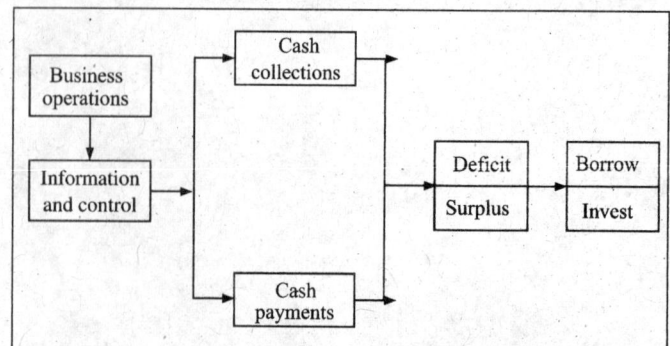

Figure 30.1: Cash management cycle

Cash management is also important because it is difficult to predict cash flows accurately, particularly the inflows, and there is no perfect coincidence between the inflows and outflows of cash. During some periods, cash outflows will exceed cash inflows, because payments for taxes, dividends, or seasonal inventory build up. At other times, cash inflow will be more than cash payments because there may be large cash sales and debtors may be realised in large sums promptly. Further, cash management is significant because cash constitutes the smallest portion of the total current assets, yet management's considerable time is devoted in managing it. In recent past, a number of innovations have been done in cash management techniques. An obvious aim of the firm these days is to manage its cash affairs in such a way as to keep cash balance at a minimum level and to invest the surplus cash in profitable investment opportunities.

In order to resolve the uncertainty about cash flow prediction and lack of synchronisation between cash receipts and payments, the firm should develop appropriate strategies for cash management. The firm should evolve strategies regarding the following four facets of cash management:

- *Cash planning* Cash inflows and outflows should be planned to project cash surplus or deficit for each period of the planning period. **Cash budget** should be prepared for this purpose.
- *Managing the cash flows* The flow of cash should be properly managed. The cash inflows should be accelerated while, as far as possible, the cash outflows should be decelerated.
- *Optimum cash level* The firm should decide about the appropriate level of cash balances. The cost of excess cash and danger of cash deficiency should be matched to determine the optimum level of cash balances.
- *Investing surplus cash* The surplus cash balances should be properly invested to earn profits. The firm should decide about the division of such cash balance between alternative short-term investment opportunities such as bank deposits, marketable securities, or inter-corporate lending.

The ideal cash management system will depend on the firm's products, organisation structure, competition, culture and options available. The task is complex, and decisions taken can affect important areas of the firm. For example, to improve collections if the credit period is reduced, it may affect sales. However, in certain cases, even without fundamental changes, it is possible to significantly reduce cost of cash management system by choosing a right bank and controlling the collections properly.

MOTIVES FOR HOLDING CASH

The firm's need to hold cash may be attributed to the following three motives:[1]

- The transactions motive
- The precautionary motive
- The speculative motive

Transaction Motive

The **transactions motive** requires a firm to hold cash to conduct its business in the ordinary course. The firm needs cash primarily to make payments for purchases, wages and salaries, other operating expenses, taxes, dividends etc. The need to hold cash would not arise if there were perfect synchronisation between cash receipts and cash payments, i.e., enough cash is received when the payment has to be made. But cash receipts and payments are not perfectly synchronised. For those periods, when cash payments exceed cash receipts, the firm should maintain some cash balance to be able to make required payments. For transactions purpose, a firm may invest its cash in marketable securities. Usually, the firm will purchase securities whose maturity corresponds with some anticipated payments, such as dividends, or taxes in the future. Notice that the transactions motive mainly refers to holding cash to meet anticipated payments whose timing is not perfectly matched with cash receipts.

Precautionary Motive

The **precautionary motive** is the need to hold cash to meet contingencies in the future. It provides a cushion or buffer to withstand some unexpected emergency. The precautionary amount of cash depends upon the predictability of cash flows. If cash flows can be predicted with accuracy, less cash will be maintained for an emergency. The amount of precautionary cash is also influenced by the firm's ability to borrow at short notice when the need arises. Stronger the ability of the firm to borrow at short notice, less the need for precautionary balance. The precautionary balance may be kept in cash and marketable securities. Marketable securities play an important role here. The amount of cash set aside for precautionary reasons is not expected to earn anything; therefore, the firm should attempt to earn some profit on it. Such funds should be invested in high-liquid and low-risk marketable securities. Precautionary balance should, thus, be held more in marketable securities and relatively less in cash.

Speculative Motive

The **speculative motive** relates to the holding of cash for investing in profit-making opportunities as and when they arise. The opportunity to make profit may arise when the security prices change. The firm will hold cash, when it is expected that interest rates will rise and security prices will fall. Securities can be purchased when the interest rate is expected to fall; the firm will benefit by the subsequent fall in interest rates and increase in security prices. The firm may also speculate on materials' prices. If it is expected that materials' prices will fall, the firm can postpone materials' purchasing and make purchases in future when price actually falls. Some firms may hold cash for speculative purposes. By and large, business firms do not engage in speculations. Thus, the primary motives to hold cash and marketable securities are: the transactions and the precautionary motives.

CASH PLANNING

Cash flows are inseparable parts of the business operations of firms. A firm needs cash to invest in inventory, receivable and

---

1. Pogue, G.A., Faucett, R.B. and Bussard, R.N., Cash Management: A Systems Approach, *Industrial Management Review*, (Feb. 1970), pp. 35–74.

fixed assets and to make payment for operating expenses in order to maintain growth in sales and earnings. It is possible that firm may be making adequate profits, but may suffer from the shortage of cash as its growing needs may be consuming cash very fast. The 'cash poor' position of the firm can be corrected if its cash needs are planned in advance. At times, a firm can have excess cash with it if its cash inflows exceed cash outflows. Such excess cash may remain idle. Again, such excess cash flows can be anticipated and properly invested if cash planning is resorted to. **Cash planning** is a technique to plan and control the use of cash. It helps to anticipate the future cash flows and needs of the firm and reduces the possibility of idle cash balances (which lowers firm's profitability) and cash deficits (which can cause the firm's failure).

Cash planning protects the financial condition of the firm by developing a projected cash statement from a forecast of expected cash inflows and outflows for a given period. The forecasts may be based on the present operations or the anticipated future operations. Cash plans are very crucial in developing the overall operating plans of the firm.

Cash planning may be done on daily, weekly or monthly basis. The period and frequency of cash planning generally depends upon the size of the firm and philosophy of management. Large firms prepare daily and weekly forecasts. Medium-size firms usually prepare weekly and monthly forecasts. Small firms may not prepare formal cash forecasts because of the non-availability of information and small-scale operations. But, if the small firms prepare cash projections, it is done on monthly basis. As a firm grows and business operations become complex, cash planning becomes inevitable for its continuing success.

Cash Forecasting and Budgeting

Cash budget is the most significant device to plan for and control cash receipts and payments. A cash budget is a summary statement of the firm's expected cash inflows and outflows over a projected time period. It gives information on the timing and magnitude of expected cash flows and cash balances over the projected period. This information helps the financial manager to determine the future cash needs of the firm, plan for the financing of these needs and exercise control over the cash and liquidity of the firm.[1]

The time horizon of a cash budget may differ from firm to firm. A firm whose business is affected by seasonal variations may prepare monthly cash budgets. Daily or weekly cash budgets should be prepared for determining cash requirements if cash flows show extreme fluctuations. Cash budgets for a longer intervals may be prepared if cash flows are relatively stable.

Cash forecasts are needed to prepare cash budgets. Cash forecasting may be done on short or long-term basis. Generally, forecasts covering periods of one year or less are considered short-term; those extending beyond one year are considered long-term.

Short-term Cash Forecasts

It is comparatively easy to make short-term cash forecasts. The important functions of carefully developed short-term cash forecasts are:

- To determine operating cash requirements
- To anticipate short-term financing
- To manage investment of surplus cash.

The short-term forecast helps in determining the cash requirements for a predetermined period to run a business. If the cash requirements are not determined, it would not be possible for the management to know-how much cash balance is to be kept in hand, to what extent bank financing be depended upon and whether surplus funds would be available to invest in marketable securities.

To know the operating cash requirements, cash flow projections have to be made by a firm. As stated earlier, there is hardly a perfect matching between cash inflows and outflows. With the short-term cash forecasts, however, the financial manager is enabled to adjust these differences in favour of the firm.

It is well-known that, for their temporary financing needs, most companies depend upon banks. One of the significant roles of the short-term forecasts is to pinpoint when the money will be needed and when it can be repaid. With such forecasts in hand, it will not be difficult for the financial manager to negotiate short-term financing arrangements with banks. This in fact convinces bankers about the ability of the management to run its business.

The third function of the short-term cash forecasts is to help in managing the investment of surplus cash in marketable securities. Carefully and skilfully designed cash forecast helps a firm to: (*i*) select securities with appropriate maturities and reasonable risk, (*ii*) avoid over and under-investing and (*iii*) maximise profits by investing idle money.

Short-run cash forecasts serve many other purposes. For example, multi-divisional firms use them as a tool to coordinate the flow of funds between their various divisions as well as to make financing arrangements for these operations. These forecasts may also be useful in determining the margins or minimum balances to be maintained with banks. Still other uses of these forecasts are:[2]

- Planning reductions of short and long-term debt
- Scheduling payments in connection with capital expenditures programmes
- Planning forward purchases of inventories
- Checking accuracy of long-range cash forecasts
- Taking advantage of cash discounts offered by suppliers
- Guiding credit policies.

Short-term Forecasting Methods

Two most commonly used methods of short-term cash forecasting are:

- The receipt and disbursements method
- The adjusted net income method.

The receipts and disbursements method is generally employed to forecast for limited periods, such as a week or a month. The

1. Van Horne, J.C. *Financial Management and Policy,* Prentice-Hall of India, p. 422. Also see Weston, J.F. and Copeland, T.E., *Managerial Finance*, Dryden Press, 1986, pp. 223–26 for an illustrative discussion on cash budgeting.
2. Conference Board, *Cash Management*, New York: The Conference Board Inc., 1973, p. 5.

adjusted net income method, on the other hand, is preferred for longer durations ranging between a few months to a year. Both methods have their *pros* and *cons*. The cash flows can be compared with budgeted income and expense items if the receipts and disbursements approach is followed. On the other hand, the adjusted income approach is appropriate in showing a company's working capital and future financing needs.

Receipts and disbursements method Cash flows in and out in most companies on a continuous basis. The prime aim of receipts and disbursements forecasts is to summarise these flows during a predetermined period. In case of those companies where each item of income and expense involves flow of cash, this method is favoured to keep a close control over cash.

Three broad sources of cash inflows can be identified: (*i*) operating, (*ii*) non-operating, and (*iii*) financial. Cash sales and collections from customers form the most important part of the operating cash inflows. Developing a sales forecast is the first step in preparing a cash forecast. All precautions should be taken to forecast sales as accurately as possible. In case of cash sales, cash is received at the time of sale. On the other hand, cash is realised after sometime if sale is on credit. The time in realising cash on credit sales depends upon the firm's credit policy reflected in the average collection period. Consider an example.[1]

Illustration 30.1: Short-term Cash Forecasting

Suppose that a firm makes 80 percent of its sales on a 30-day credit. Its actual experience shows that 80 percent of debtors are realised after one month and 20 percent after two months after goods are sold. With this information, the expected cash receipts from sales can be calculated if sales forecast are available. For example, sale receipts for January, February, March and April are calculated in Table 30.1 on the basis of assumed sales forecasts.

Table 30.1: Estimated Sales Receipts

(Rs. '000)

	Actual		Forecast			
	Nov.	*Dec.*	*Jan.*	*Feb.*	*Mar.*	*Apr.*
Total sales	500	600	550	660	700	1,000
Credit sales (80%)	400	480	440	528	560	800
Collections						
One month	–	320	384	352	422	448
Two months	–	–	80	96	88	106
Total collections			464	448	510	554
Cash sales			110	132	140	200
Total sales receipts			574	580	650	754

It can be seen from Table 30.1 that total sales for January are estimated to be Rs 550,000, of which 80 percent (i.e., Rs 440,000) are credit sales and 20 percent (i.e., Rs 110,000) are cash sales. The 80 percent of credit sales or Rs 352,000 are expected to be received in February and 20 percent or Rs 88,000 is expected to be realised in March. Sales of other months are also shown in the same way.

It can easily be noted that cash receipts from sales will be affected by changes in sales volume and the firm's credit policy. To develop a realistic cash budget, these changes should be accounted for. If the demand for the firm's products slackens, sales will fall and the average collection period is likely to be longer which increases the chances of bad debts. In preparing cash budget, account should be taken of sales discounts, returns and allowances and bad debts as they reduce the amount of cash collections from debtors.

Non-operating cash inflows include sale of old assets and dividend and interest income. The magnitude of these items is generally small. When internally generated cash flows are not sufficient, the firm resorts to external sources. Borrowings and issuance of securities are external financial sources. These constitute financial cash inflows.

The next step in the preparation of a cash budget is the estimate of cash outflows. Cash outflows include: (*i*) operating outflows: cash purchases, payments of payables, advances to suppliers, wages and salaries and other operating expenses, (*ii*) capital expenditures, (*iii*) contractual payments: repayment of loan and interest and tax payments; and (*iv*) discretionary payments: ordinary and preference dividend. In case of credit purchases, a time lag will exist for cash payments. This will depend on the credit terms offered by the suppliers.

It is relatively easy to predict the expenses of the firm over short run. Firms usually prepare capital expenditure budgets, therefore, capital expenditures are predictable for the purposes of cash budget. Similarly, payments of dividend do not fluctuate widely and are paid on specific dates. Cash outflow can also occur when the firm repays its long-term debt. Such payments are generally planned and, therefore, there is no difficulty in predicting them.

Once the forecasts for cash receipts and payments have been developed, they can be combined to obtain the net cash inflow or outflow for each month. The net balance for each month would indicate whether the firm has excess cash or deficit. The peak cash requirements would also be indicated. If the firm has a policy of maintaining some minimum cash balance, arrangements must be made to maintain this minimum balance in periods of deficit. The cash deficit can be met by borrowing from banks. Alternatively, the firm can delay its capital expenditures or payments to creditors or postpone payment of dividends.

One of the significant advantages of cash budget is to determine the net cash inflow or outflow so that the firm is enabled to arrange finances. However, the firm's decision for appropriate sources of financing should depend upon factors such as cost and risk. Cash budget helps a firm to manage its cash position. It also helps to utilise ideal funds in better ways. On the basis of cash budget, the firm can decide to invest surplus cash in marketable securities and earn profits.

The preparation of a cash budget is explained in Illustration 30.2.

---

1. See Van Horne, *op. cit.*, p. 425, and Weston, and Copeland, *op. cit.*, pp. 223–28, for a detailed illustration and discussion on the receipts and disbursements method.

Illustration 30.2: Preparing Cash Budget

On the basis of the following information, prepare a cash budget for Marshall Manufacturing Company for the first six months of 2004:

1. Prices and costs are assumed to remain unchanged.
2. Credit sales are 75 per cent of total sales.
3. The 60 percent of credit sales are collected after one month, 30 percent after two months and 10 per cent after three months.
4. Actual and forecast sales are as follows:

Actual	Rs ('000)	Forecast	Rs ('000)
Oct. 2003	120,000	Jan. 2004	60,000
Nov. 2003	140,000	Feb. 2004	80,000
Dec. 2003	160,000	Mar. 2004	80,000
		Apr. 2004	120,000
		May 2004	100,000
		June 2004	80,000
		July 2004	120,000

5. The company expects a profit margin of 20 per cent.
6. Anticipated sales of each month are purchased and paid in the preceding month.
7. The anticipated operating expenses are as below:

	Rs ('000)		Rs ('000)
Jan.	12,000	Apr.	20,000
Feb.	16,000	May	16,000
Mar.	20,000	June	14,000

8. Interest on 12 per cent debenture Rs 100 million is to be paid in each quarter.
9. An advance tax of Rs 20 million is due in April.
10. A purchase of equipment of Rs 12 million is to be made in June.
11. The company has a cash balance of Rs 40 million at 31 December 2004, which is the minimum balance to be maintained. Funds can be borrowed in multiples of Rs 2 million on a monthly basis at 18 per cent annum.
12. Interest is payable on the first of the month after the borrowing.
13. Rent is Rs 0.80 million per month.

In Table 30.2, cash inflows are estimated in accordance with the company's total sales and collection policy. For example, of the total sales of Rs 60 million for January, 25 per cent (Rs 15 million) are collected as cash sales in January: 60 per cent of credit sales (60% of Rs 45 million = Rs 27 million) are collected in February, 30% (Rs 135 million) in March and remaining 10 per cent (Rs 4.5 million) in April. Similarly, the sales of other months are broken.

Table 30.2: Cash Budget

	Actual 2003			Forecast 2004					
	Oct.	Nov.	Dec.	Jan.	Feb.	Mar.	Apr.	May	June
A. Cash Receipts (Rs '000)									
Total sales	120,000	140,000	160,000	60,000	80,000	80,000	120,000	100,000	80,000
Credit sales	90,000	105,000	120,000	45,000	60,000	60,000	90,000	75,000	60,000
Cash sales collection	30,000	35,000	40,000	15,000	20,000	20,000	30,000	25,000	20,000
1 month 60%	–	54,000	63,000	72,000	27,000	36,000	36,000	54,000	45,000
2 months 30%	–	–	27,000	31,500	36,000	13,500	18,000	18,000	27,000
3 months 10%	–	–	–	9,000	10,500	12,000	4,500	6,000	6,000
Total receipt (A)				**127,500**	**93,500**	**81,500**	**88,500**	**103,000**	**98,000**
B. Cash Payments (Rs '000)									
Purchases				64,000	64,000	96,000	80,000	64,000	96,000
Rent				800	800	800	800	800	800
Operating exps.				12,000	16,000	20,000	20,000	16,000	14,000
Equipment				–	–	–	–	–	12,000
Interest				–	–	3,000	–	–	3,000
Advance tax				–	–	–	20,000	–	–
Total payment (B)				**76,800**	**80,800**	**119,800**	**120,800**	**80,800**	**125,800**
C. Cash Balance (Rs '000)									
Net cash balance (A) – (B)				50,700	12,700	(38,300)	(32,300)	22,200	(27,800)
Total cash				90,700	103,400	65,100	32,800	63,000	27,080
Beginning of month borrowings*				–	–	–	8,000	–	14,000
Interest on borrowings				–	–	–	–	(120)	–
Repayment of borrowings				–	–	–	–	(8,000)	–
Total end of month cash balance				**90,700**	**103,400**	**65,100**	**40,800**	**54,880**	**41,080**

* To maintain minimum cash balance of Rs 40,000, the company will borrow.

Section B of Table 30.2 shows all anticipated cash payments. Anticipated sales for each month are purchased and paid in the preceding month. As the profit margin is 20 percent, the cost of purchases will be 80 percent of sales. Thus, for the month of February, purchases equal to 80 percent of its anticipated sales of Rs 80 million (i.e., Rs 64 million purchases) will be made and paid in January. Other items of cash outflows shown are rent, wages and salaries, taxes, capital expenditures and interest on debt. The quarterly payment of interest will be made in March and June. In order to maintain a minimum cash balance of Rs 40 million, Rs 8 million will have to be borrowed in the month of April. Interest at 18 percent on this amount will be paid only in May.

The difference between total receipts and total payments gives us the net cash flow. To this is added the beginning of month's balance to get the total cash balance in a particular month. In April the total balance is Rs 32.8 million; therefore, to maintain the minimum requirements of Rs 40 million a borrowing of Rs 8 million will be made. In May there is a cash balance of Rs 62.88 million after paying interest of Rs 0.12 million; therefore, Rs 8 million can be repaid without impairing the minimum cash balance requirement. Again, Rs 14 million will have to be borrowed in June to maintain cash balance at Rs 40 million.

The virtues of the receipt and payment methods are:
- It gives a complete picture of all the items of expected cash flows.
- It is a sound tool of managing daily cash operations.

This method, however, suffers from the following limitations:
- Its reliability is reduced because of the uncertainty of cash forecasts. For example, collections may be delayed, or unanticipated demands may cause large disbursements.
- It fails to highlight the significant movements in the working capital items.

Adjusted net income method This method of cash forecasting involves the tracing of working capital flows. It is sometimes called the **sources** and **uses approach.** Two objectives of the adjusted net income approach are: (*i*) to project the company's need for cash at a future date and (*ii*) to show whether the company can generate the required funds internally, and if not, how much will have to be borrowed or raised in the capital market.

As regards the form and content of the adjusted net income forecast, it resembles the cash flow statement discussed previously. It is, in fact, a **projected cash flow statement** based on **proforma financial statements.** It generally has three sections: sources of cash, uses of cash and the adjusted cash balance. This procedure helps in adjusting estimated earnings on an accrual basis to a cash basis. It also helps in anticipating the working capital movements.

In preparing the adjusted net income forecasts items such as net income, depreciation, taxes, dividends etc., can easily be determined from the company's annual operating budget. Normally, difficulty is faced in estimating working capital changes; especially the estimates of accounts receivable (debtors) and inventory pose problem because they are influenced by factors such as fluctuations in raw material costs, changing demand for the company's products and possible delays in collections. Any error in predicting these items can make the reliability of forecast doubtful.

One popularly used method of projecting working capital is to use ratios relating accounts receivable and inventory to sales. For example, if the past experience tells that accounts receivable of a company range between 32 per cent to 36 per cent of sales, an average rate of 34 per cent can be used. The difference between the projected figure and that on the books will indicate the expected increase or decrease in cash attributable to receivable.

The benefits of the adjusted net income method are:
- It highlights the movements in the working capital items, and thus helps to keep a control on a firm's working capital.
- It helps in anticipating a firm's financial requirements.

The major limitation of this method is:
- It fails to trace cash flows, and therefore, its utility in controlling daily cash operations is limited.

Sensitivity Analysis

The example on cash budget in Table 30.2 is not entirely meaningful since it is based on only one set of assumptions about cash flows. The estimates of cash flows in the example may be considered based on expected or most probable values. In practice, many alternatives are possible because of uncertainty. One useful method of getting insights about the variability of cash flows is **sensitivity analysis.** A firm can, for example, prepare cash budget based on three forecasts; *optimistic, most probable* and *pessimistic*. On the basis of its experience, the firm would know that sales could decrease at the most by 20 per cent under unfavourable conditions as compared to the most probable estimate. Thus, cash budget can be prepared under three sales conditions. Knowledge of the outcome of extreme expectations will help the firm to be prepared with contingency plans. A cash budget prepared under worst conditions will prove to be useful to the management to face those circumstances.

Long-term Cash Forecasting

Long-term cash forecasts are prepared to give an idea of the company's financial requirements in the distant future. They are not as detailed as the short-term forecasts are. Once a company has developed long-term cash forecast, it can be used to evaluate the impact of, say, new product developments or plant acquisitions on the firm's financial condition three, five, or more years in the future. The major uses of the long-term cash forecasts are:[1]
- It indicates as company's future financial needs, especially for its working capital requirements.
- It helps to evaluate proposed capital projects. It pinpoints the cash required to finance these projects as well as the cash to be generated by the company to support them.
- It helps to improve corporate planning. Long-term cash forecasts compel each division to plan for future and to formulate projects carefully.

Long-term cash forecasts may be made for two, three or five years. As with the short-term forecasts, company's practices may differ on the duration of long-term forecasts to suit their particular needs.

---

1. Conference Board, *op. cit.*, p. 13.

The short-term forecasting methods, i.e., the receipts and disbursements method and the adjusted net income method, can also be used in long-term cash forecasting. Long-term cash forecasting reflects the impact of growth, expansion or acquisitions; it also indicates financing problems arising from these developments.

MANAGING CASH COLLECTIONS AND DISBURSEMENTS

Once the cash budget has been prepared and appropriate net cash flow established, the financial manager should ensure that there does not exist a significant deviation between projected cash flows and actual cash flows. To achieve this, cash management efficiency will have to be improved through a proper control of cash collection and disbursement. The twin objectives in managing the cash flows should be to accelerate cash collections as much as possible and to decelerate or delay cash disbursements as much as possible.

Accelerating Cash Collections

A firm can conserve cash and reduce its requirements for cash balances if it can speed up its cash collections. The first hurdle in accelerating the cash collection could be the firm itself. It may take a long time to process the invoice. Days taken to get the invoice to buyers adds to order processing delay. In India, yet another problem is with regard to the extra time enjoyed by the buyers in clearing of bills; particularly, the government agencies take time beyond what is allowed by sellers in paying bills. Cash collections can be accelerated by reducing the lag or gap between the time a customer pays bill and the time the cheque is collected and funds become available for the firm's use.

The amount of cheques sent by customer which are not yet collected is called *collection* or **deposit float**. Within this time gap, the delay is caused by the mailing time, i.e. the time taken by cheque in transit and the *processing time*, i.e., the time taken by the firm in processing cheque for internal accounting purposes. This also depends on the processing time taken by the bank as well as the inter bank system to get credit in the desired account. The greater the firm's deposit float, the longer the time taken in converting cheques into usable funds. In India, these floats can assume sizeable proportions as cheques normally take a longer time to get realised than in most countries.[1] An efficient financial manager will attempt to reduce the firm's deposit float by speeding up the mailing, processing and collection times. How can this be achieved? A firm can use decentralised collection system and lock-box system to speed up cash collections and reduce deposit float.

Illustration 30.3

XY Ltd. has a Rs. 1.20 lakh balance available in its bank account as well as this is the balance shown in its ledger. XY Ltd. receives a cheque of Rs 50,000 that it records in its books and deposits in the bank. It will take 3 days for the amount to be credited to XY Ltd's bank account. How much is the deposit (collection) float today?

XY Ltd.'s book balance increases, but its bank balance remains unaltered until Rs 50,000 get credited. Thus, the float is a negative float of Rs 50,000:

$$\text{Deposit float} = \text{Balance available in bank} - \text{Balance in books}$$
$$= 120,000 - 170,000 = -50,000.$$

Decentralised Collections

A large firm operating over wide geographical areas can speed up its collections by following a decentralised collection procedure. A decentralised collection procedure, called **concentration banking** in USA, is a system of operating through a number of collection centres, instead of a single collection centre centralised at the firm's head office. The basic purpose of the decentralised collections is to minimise the lag between the mailing time from customers to the firm and the time when the firm can make use of the funds. Under decentralised collections, the firm will have a large number of bank accounts operated in the areas where the firm has its branches. All branches may not have the collection centres. The selection of the collection centre will depend upon the volume of billing. The collection centres will be required to collect cheques from customers and deposit in their local bank accounts. The collection centre will transfer funds above some predetermined minimum to a central or **concentration bank account**, generally at the firm's head office, each day. A concentration bank is one where the firm has a major account—usually disbursement account.[2] Funds can be transferred to a central or concentration bank by wire transfer or telex or fax or electronic mail. Decentralised collection procedure is, thus, a useful way to reduce float.

Decentralised collection system saves mailing and processing time and, thus, reduces the deposit float, and consequently, the financing requirements. For example, suppose a company has credit sales of Rs 146 crore per year. Its collections will average Rs 40 lakh per day (146 crore ÷ 365). If the company could reduce its mailing and processing time from five days to three days and deposit cheques into the bank two days earlier, outstanding balance would be reduced by Rs 80 lakh. If the annual borrowing rate was 18 percent, the company has saved an opportunity cost of Rs 14.40 lakh on annual basis. Thus, a decentralised collection system results in potential savings which should be compared with the cost of maintaining the system. The system should be adopted only when savings are greater than cost.

Lock-box System

Another technique of speeding up the mailing, processing and collection time which is quite popular in USA and European countries, and has been now introduced in the developing countries, is the **lock-box system**. Some foreign and Indian banks in India have started providing this service to individuals and firms in India. In case of the concentration banking, cheques are received by a collection centre and after processing, are deposited in the bank. Lock-box system helps the firm to eliminate the

1. Ramamoorthy, V.E., *op. cit.*, p. 136.
2. Van Horne, *op. cit.*, p. 423.

time between the receipt of cheques and their deposit in the bank. In a lock-box system, the firm establishes a number of collection centres, considering customer locations and volume of remittances. At each centre, the firm hires a post office box and instructs its customers to mail their remittances to the box. The firm's local bank is given the authority to pick up the remittances directly from the local-box. The bank picks up the mail several times a day and deposits the cheques in the firm's account. For the internal accounting purposes of the firm, the bank prepares detailed records of the cheques picked up.

Two main advantages of the lock-box system are:[1] *First,* the bank handles the remittances prior to deposit at a lower cost. *Second,* the cheques are deposited immediately upon receipt of remittances and their collection process starts sooner than if the firm would have processed them for internal accounting purposes prior to their deposit. The firm can still process the cheques on the basis of the records supplied by the bank without delaying the collection. Thus, lock-box system eliminates the period between the time cheques are received by the firm and the time they are deposited in the bank for collection.

The lock-box system involves cost. For the services provided under a lock-box arrangement, banks charge a fee or require a minimum balance to be maintained. Whether a lock-box system should be used or not will depend upon the comparison between its cost and benefits. Generally the benefits will exceed if the average remittances are very large and the firm's cost of financing is high.

Cash Collection Instruments in India[2]

The main instruments of collection used in India are: (*i*) cheques, (*ii*) drafts, (*iii*) documentary bills, (*iv*) trade bills, and (*v*) letter of credit (see Table 30.3).

Clearing

The instruments of exchange (e.g. cheques, drafts, etc.) are used to receive or pay claims. Before the amount is credited or debited to any account, it has to pass through the clearing system. The **clearing process** refers to the exchange of instruments by banks drawn on them through a **clearing house**. Instruments like cheques, demand drafts, interest and dividend warrants and refund orders can go through clearing. Documentary bills, or promissory notes do not go through clearing.

The clearing process has been highly automated in a number of countries. Electronic data is used instead of paper. Banks in India have started using MICR to automate the clearing process. They maintain an account with the Reserve Bank of India (RBI) which is debited for inward clearing (items drawn on plus outward returns) and credited for outward clearing (items drawn on other banks plus inward returns).

The clearing house covers banks located within a defined geographical area. Thus, when we say a cheque is payable in local clearing in Bombay then it must be drawn on a bank located within the geographical area covered by the Bombay clearing house. Clearing operations are based on time limits. There is a time by which the cheques have to be given to the clearing house and a time by which returned cheques have to be given back. A cheque that is not returned is treated as paid.

Credit is given to the customer as soon as the banks get credit through the clearing. This credit is with a hold for the time it takes to get returns back and debit them. Thus, the

Table 30.3: Features of Instruments of Collection in India

Instrument	Pros	Cons
1. Cheques	• No charge • Payable through clearing • Can be discounted after receipt • Low discounting charge • Requires customer limits which are inter changeable with overdraft limits	• Can bounce • Collection times can be long • Collection charge
2. Drafts	• Payable in local clearing • Chances of bouncing are less	• Cost of collection • Buyers account debited on day one
3. Documentary bills	• Low discounting charge • Theoretically, goods are not released till payments are made or the bill is accepted	• Not payable through clearing • High collection cost • Long delays
4. Trade bills	• No charge except stamp duty • Can be discounted. • Discipline of payment on due date	• Procedure is relatively cumbersome • Buyers are reluctant to accept the due date discipline
5. Letters of credit	• Good credit control as goods are released on payment or acceptance of bill • Seller forced to meet delivery schedule because of expiry date.	• Opening charges • Transit period interest • Negotiation charges • Need bank lines to open LC • Stamp duty on usance bills

---

1. Solomon, E. and Pringle, J.J., *An Introduction to Financial Management*, Prentice-Hall of India, 1977, p. 182.
2. Based on a handout prepared by Mr. Sanjeev Sirpal.

customer cannot draw on these funds till the hold is removed. Some banks credit customers only after funds are cleared. This creates a problem for customers with advances accounts as they continue paying interest for the clearing period.

Cheques deposited by customers drawn on other banks go for outward clearing. In the manual process that applies for non-MICR cheques, the cheques have to be sorted by bank, listed and tallied before presenting them to the clearinghouse. For MICR cheques, the cheques have to be encoded and then presented to the clearinghouse. Physical sorting of cheques is avoided. The MICR code line on the cheques has information on the city, bank, branch, cheque number, type of cheque (transaction code), the account number and amount. Using this, the clearinghouse is able to sort the cheques by city, bank, and branch and deliver the cheques to the drawee bank. RBI now operates national clearing between a few major cities.

In inward clearing the banks receive instruments that have been issued by them. In case a customer does not have funds in his account or his lines are exceeded, the cheque is returned unless appropriate approvals are obtained. The cheques have also to be scrutinised for signature, forgery or other defects (post dated, unauthorised alterations, etc.).

Cheques must be returned within a tight deadline; so quick processing is essential. Returned cheques can be divided into two categories: (*a*) inward returns (cheques presented by other banks and returned), and (*b*) outward returns (cheques returned by other banks). Return cheques have to be processed independently from the people handling clearing. In the case of outward returns, it is essential that the presenting department is stamped on the cheque as otherwise the clearing department will not know the area to debit.

To conclude this section on collections, it may be stated that the major advantage of accelerating collections is to reduce the firm's total financing requirements. Other advantages also follow. By transferring clerical function to the bank, the firm may reduce its costs, improve internal control and reduce the possibility of fraud.

Controlling Disbursements

The effective control of disbursement can also help the firm in conserving cash and reducing the financial requirements. Disbursements arise due to trade credit, which is a (spontaneous) source of funds. The firm should make payments using credit terms to the fullest extent. There is no advantage in paying sooner than agreed. By delaying payments as much as possible, the firm makes maximum use of trade credit as a source of funds—a source which is interest free. To illustrate the point, suppose that a company purchased raw materials worth Rs 730 million in 2004 and followed the policy of paying within credit terms offered by the supplier. If the company paid one day earlier, creditors' balance would decline by one day's purchase. Trade credit would decrease by Rs 2 million (Rs 730 million ÷ 365) and financing requirement from other sources will increase by this amount. If the interest rate is 18 percent, the company's interest costs will increase by Rs 360,000 on an annual basis.

Delaying disbursements results in maximum availability of funds. However, the firms that delay in making payments may endanger its credit standing. This can put the firm in difficulties in obtaining enough trade credit. Also, the suppliers may build implicit costs in the prices of goods supplied, and may also reduce the quality. On the other hand, paying early may not result in any substantial advantage to the firm unless cash discounts are offered. Thus, keeping in view the norms of the industry, the firm should pay within the terms offered by the suppliers.

While, for accelerated collections a decentralised collection procedure may be followed, for a proper control of disbursements, a centralised system may be advantageous. The payments of bills will be made from a single central account. For the local payees, who are far from the central account, the transit time will increase and the firm will gain by this delay.

Disbursement or Payment Float

Some firms use the technique of '**playing the float**' to maximise the availability of funds. When the firm's actual bank balance is greater than the balance shown in the firm's books, the difference is called **disbursement** or **payment float**. The difference between the total amount of cheques drawn on a bank account and the balance shown on the bank's books is caused by transit and processing delays. If the financial manager can accurately estimate when the cheques issued will be deposited and collected, he or she can invest the 'float' during the float period to earn a return. However, it is a risky game and should be played very cautiously.

Illustration 30.4: Payment Float

AB Ltd. has a balance of Rs 20 lakh in its books as well as in its bank account. AB Ltd. issues an outstation cheque for Rs 2 lakh that will take 7 days to clear. AB Ltd.'s book balance will reduce to Rs 18 lakh immediately when the cheque is written. But its bank will not charge until 7 days. Thus, it has a payment float of Rs 2 lakh available for 7 days.

Determining the Optimum Cash Balance

One of the primary responsibilities of the financial manager is to maintain a sound liquidity position of the firm so that the dues are settled in time. The firm needs cash to purchase raw materials and pay wages and other expenses as well as for paying dividend, interest and taxes. The test of liquidity is the availability of cash to meet the firm's obligations when they become due.

A firm maintains the operating cash balance for transaction purposes. It may also carry additional cash as a buffer or safety stock. The amount of cash balance will depend on the risk-return trade-off. If the firm maintains small cash balance, its liquidity position weakens, but its profitability improves as the released funds can be invested in profitable opportunities (marketable securities). When the firm needs cash, it can sell its marketable securities (or borrow). On the other hand, if the firm keeps high cash balance, it will have a strong liquidity position but its profitability will be low. The potential profit foregone on holding large cash balance is an opportunity cost to the firm. The firm should maintain optimum – just enough, neither too much nor too little—cash balance. How to determine the optimum cash balance if cash flows are predictable and if they are not predictable?

Optimum Cash Balance under Certainty: Baumol's Model

The **Baumol model** of cash management provides a formal approach for determining a firm's optimum cash balance under certainty.[1] It considers cash management similar to an inventory management problem. As such, the firm attempts to minimise the sum of the cost of holding cash (inventory of cash) and the cost of converting marketable securities to cash.

The Baumol's model makes the following assumptions:

- The firm is able to forecast its cash needs with certainty.
- The firm's cash payments occur uniformly over a period of time.
- The opportunity cost of holding cash is known and it does not change over time.
- The firm will incur the same transaction cost whenever it converts securities to cash.

Let us assume that the firm sells securities and starts with a cash balance of C rupees. As the firm spends cash, its cash balance decreases steadily and reaches to zero. The firm replenishes its cash balance to C rupees by selling marketable securities. This pattern continues over time. Since the cash balance decreases steadily, the average cash balance will be: $C/2$. This pattern is shown in Fig. 30.2.

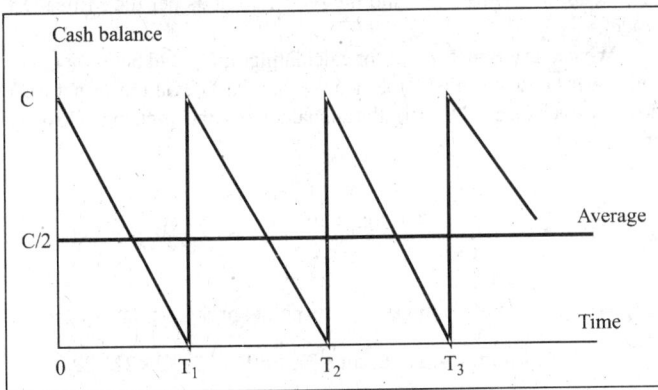

Figure 30.2: Baumol's model for cash balance

The firm incurs a **holding cost** for keeping the cash balance. It is an opportunity cost; that is, the return foregone on the marketable securities. If the opportunity cost is k, then the firm's holding cost for maintaining an average cash balance is as follows:

$$\text{Holding cost} = k(C/2) \tag{1}$$

The firm incurs a **transaction cost** whenever it converts its marketable securities to cash. Total number of transactions during the year will be total funds requirement, T, divided by the cash balance, C, i.e. T/C. The per transaction cost is assumed to be constant. If per transaction cost is c, then the total transaction cost will be:

$$\text{Transaction cost} = c(T/C) \tag{2}$$

The total annual cost of the demand for cash will be:

$$\text{Total cost} = k(C/2) + c(T/C) \tag{3}$$

What is the optimum level of cash balance, C^*? We know that the holding cost increases as demand for cash, C, increases. However, the transaction cost reduces because with increasing C the number of transactions will decline. Thus, there is a trade-off between the holding cost and the transaction cost. Fig. 30.3 depicts this trade-off.

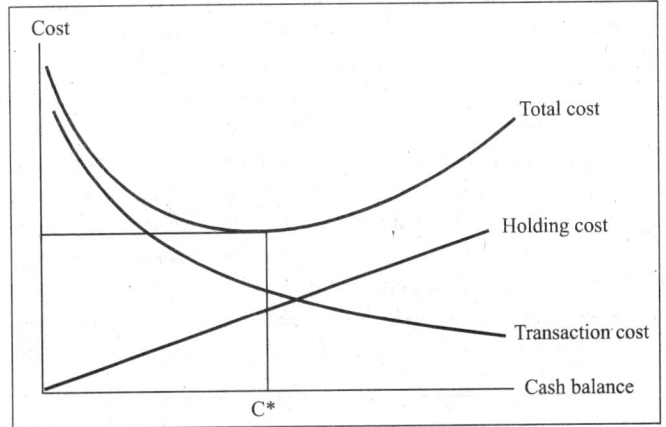

Figure 30.3: Cost trade-off: Baumol's model

The optimum cash balance, C^*, is obtained when the total cost is minimum. The formula for the optimum cash balance is as follows:

$$C^* = \sqrt{\frac{2cT}{k}} \tag{4}$$

where C^* is the optimum cash balance, c is the cost per transaction, T is the total cash needed during the year and k is the opportunity cost of holding cash balance. The optimum cash balance will increase with increase in the per transaction cost and total funds required and decrease with the opportunity cost.

Illustration 30.5: Baumol's Model

Advani Chemical Limited estimates its total cash requirement as Rs 2 crore next year. The company's opportunity cost of funds is 15 per cent per annum. The company will have to incur Rs 150 per transaction when it converts its short-term securities to cash. Determine the optimum cash balance. How much is the total annual cost of the demand for the optimum cash balance? How many deposits will have to be made during the year?

$$C^* = \sqrt{2cT/k}$$
$$C^* = \sqrt{\frac{2(150)(20,000,000)}{0.15}} = \text{Rs } 200,000$$

The annual cost will be:

$$\begin{aligned}
\text{Total cost} &= 150\,(20,000,000/200,000) + 0.15\,(200,000/2) \\
&= 150\,(100) + 0.15\,(100,000) = 15,000 + 15,000 \\
&= \text{Rs } 30,000
\end{aligned}$$

During the year, the company will have to make 100 deposits, i.e. converting marketable securities to cash.

---

1. Baumol, W.J., The Transaction Demand for Cash: An Inventory Theoretical Approach, *Quarterly Journal of Economics*, No. 66, November 1952, pp. 545–56.

Optimum Cash Balance under Uncertainty: The Miller-Orr Model

The limitation of the Baumol model is that it does not allow the cash flows to fluctuate. Firms in practice do not use their cash balance uniformly nor are they able to predict daily cash inflows and outflows. The **Miller-Orr (MO) model** overcomes this shortcoming and allows for daily cash flow variation.[1] It assumes that net cash flows are normally distributed with a zero value of mean and a standard deviation. As shown in Figure 30.4, the MO model provides for two control limits—the upper control limit and the lower control limit as well as a return point. If the firm's cash flows fluctuate randomly and hit the upper limit, then it buys sufficient marketable securities to come back to a normal level of cash balance (the return point). Similarly, when the firm's cash flows wander and hit the lower limit, it sells sufficient marketable securities to bring the cash balance back to the normal level (the return point).

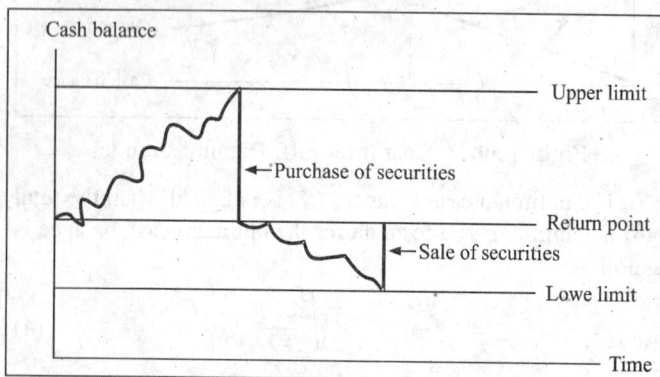

Figure 30.4: Miller-Orr model

The firm sets the lower control limit as per its requirement of maintaining minimum cash balance. At what distance the upper control limit will be set? The difference between the upper limit and the lower limit depends on the following factors:

- the transaction cost (*c*)
- the interest rate, (*i*)
- the standard deviation (σ) of net cash flows.

The formula for determining the distance between upper and lower control limits (called *Z*) is as follows:

$$(\text{Upper Limit} - \text{Lower Limit}) = (3/4 \times \text{Transaction Cost} \times \text{Cash Flow Variance}/ \text{Interest per day})^{1/3} \quad (5)$$

$$Z = \left(3/4 \times c\sigma^2 / i\right)^{1/3} \quad (6)$$

We can notice from Equation (6) that the upper and lower limits will be far off from each other (i.e. *Z* will be larger) if transaction cost is higher or cash flows show greater fluctuations. The limits will come closer as the interest increases. *Z* is inversely related to the interest rate. It is noticeable that the upper control limit is three times above the lower control limit and the return point lies between the upper and the lower

limits. Thus,

$$\text{Upper Limit} = \text{Lower Limit} + 3Z \quad (7)$$

$$\text{Return Point} = \text{Lower Limit} + Z \quad (8)$$

The net effect is that the firms hold the average cash balance equal to:

$$\text{Average Cash Balance} = \text{Lower Limit} + 4/3\ Z \quad (9)$$

The MO model is more realistic since it allows variation in cash balance within lower and upper limits. The financial manager can set the lower limit according to the firm's liquidity requirement. The past data of the cash flow behaviour can be used to determine the standard deviation of net cash flows. Once the upper and lower limits are set, managerial attention is needed only if the cash balance deviates from the limits. The action under these situations are anticipated and planned in the beginning.

Illustration 30.6: The Miller-Orr Model

PKG Company has a policy of maintaining a minimum cash balance of Rs 500,000. The standard deviation of the company's daily cash flows is Rs 200,000. The annual interest rate is 14 per cent. The transaction cost of buying or selling securities is Rs 150 per transaction. Determine PKG's upper control limit and the return point as per the Miller-Orr model.

We can use Equation (6) for calculating the spread between upper and lower control limits (*Z*). Since the standard deviation of net cash flows is given on a daily basis, the annual interest rate is changed to daily basis.

$$\text{or} \quad Z = \left[\frac{3}{4} \times \frac{150 \times 200,000^2}{0.14/365}\right]^{\frac{1}{3}} = \text{Rs } 227,227$$

The upper control limit and return point are as follows:

$$\text{Upper Limit} = \text{Lower Limit} + 3Z = 500,000 + (3 \times 227,227)$$
$$= \text{Rs } 1,181,680$$
$$\text{Return Point} = \text{Lower Limit} + Z = 500,000 + 227,227$$
$$= \text{Rs } 727,227$$
$$\text{Av. Cash Balance} = \text{Lower Limit} + 4/3Z = 500,000 + 4/3(227,227)$$
$$= \text{Rs } 802,969$$

PKG will not allow the lower limit of cash balance of Rs 500,000. If the firm's cash balance touches this limit, it will sell marketable securities worth (*Z*) Rs 227,227 and restore return point to Rs 727,227 cash balance level. On the other hand, if PKG's cash balance touches the upper limit of Rs 1,181,680, it will spend cash buying marketable securities worth (2*Z*) Rs 454,454 and bring cash balance to the return point: Rs 1,181,680 – Rs 454,454 = Rs 727,227.

INVESTING SURPLUS CASH IN MARKETABLE SECURITIES

There is a close relationship between cash and money market securities or other short-term investment alternatives. Investment in these alternatives should be properly managed. Excess cash should normally be invested in those alternatives that can be

---

1. Miller, M.H. and Orr, D., A Model for the Demand for Money by Firms. *Quarterly Journal of Economics*, No. 80, August 1966, pp. 413–35.

conveniently and promptly converted into cash. Cash in excess of the requirement of operating cash balance may be held for two reasons. *First*, the working capital requirements of the firm fluctuate because of the elements of seasonality and business cycles. The excess cash may build up during slack seasons but it would be needed when the demand picks up. Thus, excess cash during slack season is idle temporarily, but has a predictable requirement later on. *Second*, excess cash may be held as a buffer to meet unpredictable financial needs. A firm holds extra cash because cash flows cannot be predicted with certainty. Cash balance held to cover the future exigencies is called the precautionary balance and is usually invested in the short-term money market investments until needed.

Instead of holding excess cash for the above-mentioned purpose, the firm may meet its precautionary requirements as and when they arise by making short-term borrowings. The choice between the short-term borrowings and liquid assets holding will depend upon the firm's policy regarding the mix of short-term financing.

The excess amount of cash held by the firm to meet its variable cash requirements and future contingencies should be temporarily invested in **marketable securities**, which can be regarded as near moneys. A number of marketable securities may be available in the market. The financial manager must decide about the portfolio of marketable securities in which the firm's surplus cash should be invested.

Selecting Investment Opportunities

A firm can invest its excess cash in many types of securities or short-term investment opportunities. As the firm invests its temporary cash balance, its primary criterion in selecting a security or investment opportunities will be its quickest convertibility into cash, when the need for cash arises. Besides this, the firm would also be interested in the fact that when it sells the security or liquidates investment, it, at least, gets the amount of cash equal to the investment outlay. Thus, in choosing among alternative investment, the firm should examine three basic features of security: *safety, maturity and marketability*.[1]

Safety   Usually, a firm would be interested in receiving as high a return on its investment as is possible. But the higher returns yielding securities or investment alternatives are relatively more risky. The firm would invest in very safe securities as the cash balance invested in them is needed in near future. Thus, the firm would tend to invest in the highest yielding marketable securities subject to the constraint that the securities have acceptable level of risk. The risk referred here is the default risk. The **default risk** means the possibility of default in the payment of interest or principal on time and in the amount promised. The default in payment may mean more than one thing. In an extreme case, the security may not be redeemed at all. In a less severe case, the security may be sold at a loss, when the firm needs cash. To minimise the chances of default risk and ensure safety of principal or interest, the firm should invest in safe securities. Other things remaining constant, higher the

default risks, higher the return from security. Low-risk securities will earn low return.

Maturity   Maturity refers to the time period over which interest and principal are to be made. The price of long-term security fluctuates more widely with the interest rate changes than the price of short-term security. Over time, interest rates have a tendency to change. Because of these two factors, the long-term securities are relatively more risky. For safety reasons, therefore, the firms for the purpose of investing excess cash prefer short-term securities.

Marketability   Marketability refers to convenience and speed with which a security or an investment can be converted into cash. The two important aspects of marketability are price and time. If the security can be sold quickly without loss of price, it is highly liquid or marketable. The government treasury bills fall under this category. If the security needs time to sell without loss, it is considered illiquid. As the funds invested in marketable securities will be needed by the firm in near future, it would invest in the securities that are readily marketable. The securities that have low marketability usually have higher yields in order to attract investment. Thus, differences in marketability also cause differences in the security yields.

Types of Short-term Investment Opportunities

The following short-term investment opportunities are available to companies in India to invest their temporary cash surplus:

- *Treasury bills*   Treasury bills (TBs) are short-term government securities. The usual practice in India is to sell treasury bills at a discount and redeem them at par on maturity. The difference between the issue price and the redemption price, adjusted for the time value of money, is return on treasury bills. They can be bought and sold any time; thus, they have liquidity. Also, they do not have the default risk.
- *Commercial papers*   Commercial papers (CPs) are short-term, unsecured securities issued by highly creditworthy large companies. They are issued with a maturity of three months to one year. CPs are marketable securities, and therefore, liquidity is not a problem.
- *Certificates of deposits*   Certificates of deposits (CDs) are papers issued by banks acknowledging fixed deposits for a specified period of time. CPs are negotiable instruments that make them marketable securities.
- *Bank deposits*   A firm can deposit its temporary cash in a bank for a fixed period of time. The interest rate depends on the maturity period. For example, the current interest rate for a 30 to 45 days deposit is about 3 per cent and for 180 days to one year is about 6–7 per cent. The default risk of the bank deposits is quite low since the government owns most banks in India.
- *Inter-corporate deposits*   Inter-corporate lending borrowing or deposits (ICDs) is a popular short-term investment alternative for companies in India. Generally a cash surplus company will deposit (lend) its funds in a

---

1. Also see Van Horne, *op. cit.*, pp. 441–44.

sister or associate companies or with outside companies with high credit standing. In practice, companies can negotiate inter-corporate borrowing or lending for very short periods. The risk of default is high, but returns are quite attractive.

● *Money market mutual funds* Money market mutual funds (MMMFs) focus on short-term marketable securities such as TBs, CPs, CDs or call money. They have a minimum lock-in period of 30 days, and after this period, an investor can withdraw his or her money any time at a short notice or even across the counter in some cases. They offer attractive yields; yields are usually 2 per cent above than on bank deposits of same maturity. MMMFs are of recent origin in India, and they have become quite popular with institutional investors and some companies.

SUMMARY

❖ Cash is required to meet a firm's transactions and precautionary needs. A firm needs cash to make payments for acquisition of resources and services for the normal conduct of business. It keeps additional funds to meet any emergency situation. Some firms may also maintain cash for taking advantages of speculative changes in prices of input and output.

❖ Management of cash involves three things: (*a*) managing cash flows into and out of the firm, (*b*) managing cash flows within the firm, and (*c*) financing deficit or investing surplus cash and thus, controlling cash balance at a point of time. It is an important function in practice because it is difficult to predict cash flows and there is hardly any synchronisation between inflows and outflows.

❖ Firms prepare cash budget to plan for and control cash flows. Cash budget is generally prepared for short periods such as weekly, monthly, quarterly, half-yearly or yearly.

❖ For making forecasts of cash receipts and payments, two approaches are used in practice: (*i*) the receipts and disbursements method, and (*ii*) the adjusted income method.

❖ The receipts and disbursements method is employed to forecast for shorter periods. The individual items of receipts and payments are identified and analysed. Cash inflows could be categorised as: (*i*) operating, (*ii*) non-operating, and (*iii*) financial. Cash outflows could be categorised as: (*i*) operating, (*ii*) capital expenditure, (*iii*) contractual, and (*iv*) discretionary. Such categorisation helps in determining avoidable or postponable expenditures.

❖ The adjusted income method uses proforma income statement (profit and loss statement) and balance sheet to work out cash flows (by deriving proforma cash flow statement). As cash flows are difficult to predict, a financial manager does not base his forecasts only on one set of assumptions. He or she considers possible scenarios and performs a sensitivity analysis. At least, forecasts under optimistic, most probable and pessimistic scenarios can be worked out.

❖ Cash budget will serve its purpose only if the firm can accelerate its collections and postpone its payments within allowed limits. The main concerns in collections are: (*a*) to obtain payment from customers within the credit period, and (*b*) to minimise the lag between the time a customer pays the bill and the time cheques etc. are collected.

❖ A number of methods such as concentration banking and lock-box system can be followed to expedite conversion of an instrument (e.g. cheque, draft, bills, etc.) into cash.

❖ The financial manager should be aware of the instruments of payments, and choose the most convenient and least costly mode of receiving payment. Disbursements or payments can be delayed to solve a firm's working capital problem. But this involves cost that, in the long run, may prove to be highly detrimental. Therefore, a firm should follow the norms of the business.

❖ A firm should hold an optimum balance of cash, and invest any temporary excess amount in short-term (marketable) securities. In choosing these securities, the firm must keep in mind safety, maturity and marketability of its investment.

KEY CONCEPTS

Adjusted net income method	Concentration banking	Marketable securities	Receipts & disbursements
Cash budgeting	Deposit float	Money market mutual	method
Cash forecasting	Documentary bills	funds (MMMF)	Speculative motive
Cash management cycle	Inter-corporate deposits (ICD)	Optimum cash balance	Trade bills
Cash planning	Inward clearing	Outward clearing	Transaction motive
Certificate of deposit (CD)	Letter of credit (L/C)	Payment float	Treasury bills
Commercial paper (CP)	Lock-box system	Precautionary motive	

ILLUSTRATIVE SOLVED PROBLEMS

Problem 30.1: From the information and the assumption that the cash balance in hand on 1 January 19X1 is Rs 72,500, prepare a cash budget.

Assume that 50 per cent of total sales are cash sales. Assets are to be acquired in the months of February and April. Therefore, provisions should be made for the payment of Rs 8,000 and Rs 25,000 for the same. An application has been made to the bank for the grant of a loan of Rs 30,000 and it is hoped that the loan amount will be received in the month of May.

It is anticipated that a dividend of Rs 35,000 will be paid in June. Debtors are allowed one month's credit. Creditors for materials purchased and overheads grant one month's credit. Sales commission at 3 per cent on sales is paid to the salesman each month.

Month	Sales Rs	Materials Purchases Rs	Salaries & Wages Rs	Production Overheads Rs	Office and Selling Overheads Rs
January	72,000	25,000	10,000	6,000	5,500
February	97,000	31,000	12,100	6,300	6,700
March	86,000	25,500	10,600	6,000	7,500
April	88,600	30,600	25,000	6,500	8,900
May	102,500	37,000	22,000	8,000	11,000
June	108,700	38,800	23,000	8,200	11,500

Problem 30.2: The Divya Paints Ltd. is currently following a centralised collection system. Most of its customers are located in the cities of Northern India. The remittances mailed by customers to the central location take four days to reach. Before depositing the remittances in the bank, the firm loses two days in processing them. The daily average collection of the firm is Rs 100,000.

The company is thinking of establishing a lock-box system. It is expected that such a system will reduce mailing time by one day and processing time by one day.

(i)   Find out the reduction in cash balances expected to result from the adoption of the lock-box system.

(ii) Determine the opportunity cost of the present centralised collection system if the interest rate is assumed to be 18 per cent.

(iii) Should the lock-box system be established if its annual cost is Rs 24,500?

Solution:

(1) The total time saved by the firm by establishing the lock-box system is 2 days

Reduction in cash balances = Times saved × daily average collection

$$2 \times Rs\ 100,000 = Rs\ 200,000$$

(2) Opportunity cost = 18% × Rs 200,000 = Rs 36,000

(3) The lock-box system should be established because the opportunity cost of the present system (Rs 36,000) is higher than the cost of the lock-box system (Rs 24,500).

Solution:

Table 30.4: Cash Budget

	Jan. Rs	Feb. Rs	Mar. Rs	Apr. Rs	May Rs	June Rs	Total Rs
Receipts							
Cash sales	36,000	48,500	43,000	44,300	51,250	54,350	277,400
Collections from debtors	–	36,000	48,500	43,000	44,300	51,250	223,050
Bank loan	–	–	–	–	30,000	–	30,000
Total	36,000	84,500	91,500	87,300	125,550	105,600	530,450
Payments							
Materials	–	25,000	31,000	25,500	30,600	37,000	149,100
Salaries and wages	10,000	12,100	10,600	25,000	22,000	23,000	102,700
Production Overheads	–	6,000	6,300	6,000	6,500	8,000	32,800
Office and selling overheads	–	5,500	6,700	7,500	8,900	11,000	39,600
Sales commission	2,160	2,910	2,580	2,658	3,075	3,261	16,644
Capital expenditure	–	8,000	–	25,000	-	-	33,000
Dividend	–	–	–	–	–	35,000	35,000
Total	12,160	59,510	57,180	91,658	71,075	117,261	408,844
Net cash flow	23,840	24,990	34,320	(4,358)	54,475	(11,661)	121,606
Balance, beginning of month	72,500	96,340	121,330	155,650	151,292	205,767	194,106
Balance, end of month	96,340	121,330	155,650	151,292	205,767	194,106	315,712

Problem 30.3: Bharat Engineering Company undertakes large turnkey projects. It is situated in Lucknow and receives large payments on contracts as and when work progresses. The cheques received from customers are deposited in a local branch of a nationalised bank and the money becomes available after 10 days. The cheques are mostly drawn on a bank in Mumbai. The company is thinking of collecting the funds sooner by sending an accounts executive to Mumbai. A visit to Mumbai may cost Rs 10,000. If Bharat Engineering Company's opportunity cost of capital is 18 per cent, what minimum amount of cheque will justify sending a person to Mumbai?

Solution: The company will be able to save interest for 10 days at 18 per cent. Thus, the amount of cheque should be:

$$0.18 \times 10/360 \times \text{Amount} = 10,000$$
$$\text{Amount} = (10,000) \div (0.18 \times 10/360)$$
$$= 10,000/0.005 = \text{Rs } 2,000,000$$

Problem 30.4: Hansa Steel Tube Limited is considering whether or not to go for a lock-box system. The cost of the system is expected to be Rs 1.25 per cheque. The average cheque size will be Rs 5,000. The firm can invest the funds received earlier by using the lock-box system in the money market instruments earning a return of 8 per cent per annum. How much should be the reduction in the cheque collection time for Hansa to be able to accept the decision about the lock-box?

Solution: The company needs to balance the cost of lock-box (Rs 1.25 per cheque) with its benefits (return on investment of Rs 5,000 at 8 per cent for certain number of days). We assume there are 360 days in a year. Thus:

$$1.25 = \text{Days} \times \text{Rs } 5,000 \times 0.08/360$$
$$1.25 = \text{Days} \times 1.111$$
$$\text{Days} = 1.25/1.111 = 1.13 \text{ days}$$

Problem 30.5: Sonal Hand Tools Limited has annual sales of Rs 2.65 crore. The company has investment opportunities in the money market to earn a return of 16 per cent per annum. If the company could reduce its float by 2 days, what would be the company's total return?

Solution:

$$\text{Sales per day} = \frac{\text{Rs } 2.65 \text{ crore}}{365}$$
$$= \text{Rs } 72,603 \text{ (Assuming 365 days/years)}$$

Total returns $= 72,603 \times 0.16 \times \text{days} = \text{Rs } 23,233$

REVIEW QUESTIONS

1. Explain the three principal motives for holding cash.
2. What are the advantages of cash planning? How does cash budget help in planning the firm's cash flows?
3. Explain and illustrate the utility of a cash budget.
4. Illustrate with example the *modus operandi* of preparing a cash budget.
5. Explain the techniques that can be used to accelerate the firm's collections?
6. What are the advantages of decentralised collection over a centralised collection?
7. What is a lock-box system? How does it help to reduce the cash balances?
8. Distinguish between a deposit float and a payment float. What are the advantages and dangers of "playing the float?" Explain the techniques for managing float.
9. What are the objectives of a firm in controlling its disbursements? How can the disbursements be slowed down?
10. How can the appropriate level of operating cash balance be determined? How does uncertainty affect this problem?
11. Explain the criteria that a firm should use in choosing the short-term investment alternatives in order to invest surplus cash.
12. Other things remaining constant, what effect would the following events have on the average cash balance that a firm keeps for transaction purposes? Explain your answer.
    (*a*) Increase in interest rates.
    (*b*) It becomes more expensive to transfer funds from cash to securities and vice versa.
    (*c*) The variability of net cash flows increase.

PROBLEMS

1. Kashiram & Co. is a manufacturer of children's garments. The sales vary seasonally, and are highest in the month of May. The management of the company wishes to prepare a cash budget from the period January through June. The financial manager starts with the balance sheet of 1 January as shown in Table 30.5 and prepares a cash budget. Table 30.6 gives the sales for seven months.

   To prepare the cash budget, the following additional information is given:

Table 30.5: Kashiram & Co's Balance Sheet, 1 January

Liabilities & Capital	Amount (Rs '000)	Assets	Amount (Rs '000)
Current liabilities	3,000	Cash	84,480
Other liabilities	10,800	Debtors	42,000
Share capital	317,280	Inventory	123,000
		Fixed assets	81,600
Total funds	331,080	Total assets	331,080

Table 30.6: Sales Estimates

	(Rs '000)		(Rs '000)
December	60,000	April	228,000
January	84,000	May	288,000
February	156,000	June	108,000
March	132,000	July	108,000

(a) Sales for the month of December were Rs 60,000,000.

(b) Credit sales are 70 per cent and cash sales 30 per cent of the total sales.

(c) Sales are collected after one month.

(d) Gross profit margin on sales is expected to be 25 per cent.

(i) Payments for the purchases are made one month in advance.

(f) A minimum inventory of Rs 60,000,000 at cost is always maintained. The company purchases sufficient inventory each month to take care of sales of the subsequent month.

(g) Other monthly expenses are:

	(Rs '000)
Salary	9,600
Rent	2,400
Depreciation	720
Other	1% of sales

(h) A 16 per cent interest on borrowed funds is payable in the next month of every quarter on the outstanding balance. Borrowing is possible each month in the multiples of Rs 1,000,000.

2. Kay Co. always prepares a cash budget for the months of January, February and March. Estimated sales for these months are Rs 500,000, Rs 600,000 and Rs 750,000 respectively. Actual sales for the month of December were Rs 520,000. About 80 per cent of Kay Co.'s total sales are on cash basis and 20 per cent credit sales collectible after one month. Kay Co. pays its creditors, which are usually about 40 per cent of sales, one month after the sale month. The forecasts of salary expenses for the coming three months are expected to be Rs 280,000 per month. Kay Co. is expected to spend about Rs 80,000 in February and Rs 190,000 in March on capital expenditures. A previously declared dividend of Rs 75,000 is to be paid in January and miscellaneous expenses are estimated to be Rs 15,000 per month. The company also has Rs 36,000 bills payable in February.

(a) Prepare a statement showing the sale receipts.

(b) Assuming that the 1 January cash balance is Rs 500,000 and that the minimum cash balance requirement of the company is Rs 500,000, prepare a cash budget for the next three months.

(c) Explain the reason for estimated cash shortage that appears imminent.

(d) Suppose that Kay Co. lends any surplus at 15 per cent

per year for one month and borrows for three months at 18 per cent year when there is a cash shortage. Make the necessary changes in your cash budget prepared in (b) to make it balance. Assume that interest is paid at the end of any borrowing or lending period.

3. Prepare a cash budget for the Kamp Manufacturing Company for three months of May, June and July. The company has a policy of maintaining a minimum cash balance of Rs 30,000. The company's cash balance as on 30 April is Rs 30,000.

Actual Sales (Rs)		Estimated Sales (Rs)	
January	75,500	May	105,000
February	75,000	June	120,000
March	90,000	July	150,000
April	90,000	August	150,000

Consider the following additional information:

(a) Cash sales are 60 per cent of the total sales. The remaining sales are collected equally during the following two months.

(b) Cost of goods manufactured is 75 per cent of sales. 80 per cent of this cost is paid after one month and the balance is paid after two months of the cost incurrence.

(c) Fixed operating expenses are Rs 15,000 per month. Variable operating expenses are 10 per cent of sales each month.

(d) Half yearly interest on 12% Rs 450,000 debentures is paid during July.

(e) Rs 60,000 are expected to be invested in fixed assets during June.

(f) An advance tax of Rs 15,000 will be paid in July.

You are also required to determine whether or not borrowing will be necessary during the period and if yes, when and for how much.

4. X Co. has average credit sales of Rs 1,500,000 per year. The working days per year are 300. If the company could reduce its bill processing time by two days, what would be the annual savings, assuming an interest rate of 18 per cent?

5. The Sirsa Company is a large wholesale distributor of consumer goods that sells mostly on credit. Collections from a particular location average Rs 200,000 per day. The total float averages 6 days for customers in this location. The opportunity cost of funds is 15 per cent.

(a) The company has an offer from a bank to set up a lock-box system that will reduce float by 4 days, but the company will have to maintain a minimum balance of Rs 400,000 with the bank. Should the offer be accepted?

(b) The bank also offers an option of a fixed fee of Rs 20,000 per year. What should the company do?

6. A company has a central billing system. Its daily collections on an average are Rs 500,000. The total time for administering the collection is 6 days.

(a) If a firm's required rate of return is 10 per cent, what is the cost of the system to the firm?

(b) If the management designs a lock-box system that reduces lag by 3 days, what is the reduction in cash balances?

7. Garima Detergents has discovered that it takes about 10 days to collect the funds for use in the company once the cheques are received from the customers. The company's annual turnover is Rs 9.70 crore. How much funds is to be freed if the company could reduce the collection time from 10 days to 8 days? If the freed funds could be used to reduce bank borrowings which costs 18 per cent per annum, what would be the net savings to the company? Assume a 360-day year and 35 per cent corporate tax rate.

8. A company located in Ahmedabad wants to transfer Rs 15 lakh to its branch in Chennai. It will cost the company Rs 10 to mail the draft by a registered post. It will take 10 days for money to be finally transferred in Chennai. During these 10 days, the company is losing an opportunity of earning 12 per cent p.a. Alternatively, the company can instantaneously transfer the money telegraphically that will cost the company Rs 1,000. What should the company do?

CASES

Case 30.1: Bright Paints Limited

Bright Paints Limited, situated in Punjab, is a large whole-seller of industrial paints. The company sells paints mostly to small retailers in cities and towns of Northern states. About 10 per cent of sales are made directly to the public on cash basis. For meeting its working capital requirement, the company has a cash credit limit from State Bank of India. However, it has been recently facing a liquidity problem. In its cash credit account, the company has an overdraft balance of Rs 24 lakh at the end of March 2004. The managing director of the company is quite concerned about its adverse cash position. He discussed the matter with his finance manager, and asked him to make an assessment of the company's cash situation for the next six months. The finance manager's staff made the following estimates of revenues and expenditures for the next six months:

The company has a plan to buy two delivery vans in June for Rs 8 lakh. It will pay taxes in June and September. The corporate tax rate is 35 per cent. The company sells to retailers on two months' credit terms. Debtors at the end of March are Rs 500 lakh. The company makes more purchases in the months of April, May and June for high demands in the next three months. Suppliers extend one month's credit to the company. At the beginning of March, creditors were Rs 630 lakh.

(Rs in lakh)

	April	May	June	July	Aug.	Sep.
Expected sales	1000	1400	1750	2180	2400	2700
Purchases	1250	1700	2000	1800	1700	1700
Advertising	170	190	220	250	350	380
Rent	50	50	50	50	50	50
Depreciation	12	12	12	12	12	12
Wages	180	180	180	180	190	190
Sundry expenses	260	260	260	270	280	280

Discussion Questions

1. Prepare a cash flow forecast for Bright Paints Limited for the six months. What are the benefits of preparing a cash flow forecast to the company?

2. What do you think are the problems for the company during the next six months? What remedies do you suggest?

Case 30.2: Payal Plastics Company

Payal Plastics Company (PPC) is engaged in the manufacture of plastic-based products for home use. The company is located in Faridabad in Haryana. It is one of the leading suppliers of plastic products in the markets of Haryana, Punjab and Delhi. In recent years, the competition has intensified and many small manufacturers have entered the market. PPC has been able to face the competition on the strength of the quality and price of its products. In spite of high competition, it has grown rapidly.

PPC is a profitable company, but it has been facing liquidity problem for a couple of years. The company has defaulted in paying its obligations and has stretched payment to its creditors. This has affected company's creditworthiness. The company management is worried that the frequent stretching of credit payments might cause suppliers to demand cash payments for purchases. The managing director, therefore, wants the finance manager to prepare a cash budget and make a plan for meeting a deficit situation.

The finance manager set to develop a monthly cash budget for the period starting from April 2004 to September 2004. She obtained the actual sales figures from the records of the last three months, and based on the past trends and future market prospects, developed the sales forecasts as shown below:

Actual sales	(Rs in lakh)	Sales forecasts	(Rs in lakh)
January	240	April	260
February	280	May	210
March	320	June	160
		July	240
		August	200
		September	160
		October	200

Of the total sales, PPC's cash sales are 20 per cent and credit sales 80 per cent. The company's credit terms are 30 days. But it is able to collect only about fifty per cent of the accounts receivables in the first month after sales. About 30 per cent collections take place in the second month after the sales and the remaining in the third month of sales.

PPC's products require a very heavy use of material. The average consumption of raw material is 70 per cent of sales. The company buys 60 per cent of the materials required for the next month in the previous month. Suppliers' credit terms are 30 days. But the records show that the company pays for 60 per cent of purchases in a month, 20 per cent in two months and the remaining in three months. The following payments are expected for wages and salaries:

Month	(Rs in lakh)	Month	(Rs in lakh)
April	42	July	40
May	39	August	32
June	32	September	28

The fixed and variable general administrative and marketing expenses are estimated to be about Rs 2.5 lakh per month and 5 per cent of sales, respectively. Power and fuel expenses are expected to be 4 per cent of sales and depreciation Rs 12 lakh per month. The company has planned a capital expenditure of Rs 70 lakh, of which 50 per cent will be paid in May and the remaining in June. On a Rs 20 lakh borrowing, half-yearly interest at 16 per cent annual rate is to be paid in the month of June. A tax payment on the previous year's profit of Rs 2.5 lakh is due in April. The financial manager estimated that PPC's tax liability for the next year is expected to be Rs 24 lakh, which is payable in equal instalments in March, June, September and December. The company is expected to have cash and bank balance of Rs 140,000 in the beginning of April.

After collecting the information about cash flows, the finance manager created an Excel file by classifying each item of cash flows systematically into cash receipts and payments. His concern was that as and when any change in sales or collection experience is made the cash flow forecasts should automatically get updated.

Discussion Questions

1. Prepare a cash budget for PPC, and provide an explanation for the results.
2. Assume that sales forecasts are off by ± 10 per cent. What are the implications? Show calculations?

CHAPTER 31
Working Capital Finance

INTRODUCTION

External funds available for a period of one year or less are called short-term finance. In India, short-term funds are used to finance working capital. Two most significant short-term sources of finance for working capital are: trade credit and bank borrowing. The use of trade credit has been increasing over years in India. Trade credit as a ratio of current assets is about 40 per cent. Bank borrowing is the next important source of working capital finance. Before seventies, bank credit was liberally available to firms. It became a restricted resource in eighties and nineties because of the change in the government policy; banks were required to follow the government prescribed norms in financing working capital requirements of firms. Now there are no government norms, and banks are free to take business decisions in granting finance for working capital.

Two other short-term sources of working capital finance which have recently developed in India are: (i) factoring of receivables and (ii) commercial paper. We have already discussed factoring in an earlier chapter.

TRADE CREDIT

Trade credit refers to the credit that a customer gets from suppliers of goods in the normal course of business. In practice, the buying firms do not have to pay cash immediately for the purchases made. This deferral of payments is a short-term financing called trade credit. It is a major source of financing for firms. In India, it contributes to about one-third of the short-term financing. Particularly, small firms are heavily dependent on trade credit as a source of finance since they find it difficult to raise funds from banks or other sources in the capital markets.

Trade credit is mostly an informal arrangement, and is granted on an **open account** basis. A supplier sends goods to the buyer on credit which the buyer accepts, and thus, in effect, agrees to pay the amount due as per sales terms in the invoice. However, he does not formally acknowledge it as a debt; he does not sign any legal instrument. Once the trade links have been established between the buyer and the seller, they have each other's mutual confidence, and trade credit becomes a routine activity which may be periodically reviewed by the supplier. Open account trade credit appears as **sundry creditors** (known as **accounts payable** in USA) on the buyer's balance sheet.

Trade credit may also take the form of **bills payable**. When the buyer signs a bill—a negotiable instrument—to obtain trade credit, it appears on the buyer's balance sheet as bills payable. The bill has a specified future date, and is usually used when the supplier is less sure about the buyer's willingness and ability to pay, or when the supplier wants cash by discounting the bill from a bank. A bill is formal acknowledgement of an obligation to repay the outstanding amount. In USA, **promissory notes**—a formal acknowledgement of an obligation with a promise to pay on a specified date—are used as an alternative to the open account, and they appear as **notes payable** in the buyer's balance sheet.

Credit Terms

Credit terms refer to the conditions under which the supplier sells on credit to the buyer, and the buyer is required to repay the credit. These conditions include the *due date* and the *cash discount* (if any) given for prompt payment. *Due date* (also called net date) is the date by which the supplier expects payment. Credit terms indicate the length and beginning date of the credit period. *Cash discount* is the concession offered to the buyer by the supplier to encourage him to make payment promptly. The cash discount can be availed by the buyer if he pays by a certain date which is quite earlier than the due date. The typical way of expressing credit terms is, for example, as follows: '3/15, net 45'. This implies that a 3 per cent discount is available if the credit is repaid on the 15th day, and in case the discount is not taken, the payment is due by the 45th day.

Benefits and Costs of Trade Credit

As stated earlier, trade credit is normally available to a firm; therefore, it is a **spontaneous source of financing.** As the volume of the firm's purchase increases, trade credit also expands. Suppose that a firm increases its purchases from Rs 50,000 per day to Rs 60,000 per day. Assume that these purchases are made on credit terms of 'net 45', and the firm makes payment on the 45th day. The average accounts payable outstanding (trade credit finance) will expand to Rs 27 lakh (Rs 60,000 × 45) from Rs 22.50 lakh (Rs 50,000 × 45).

The major advantages of trade credit are as follows:[1]

*   *Easy availability* Unlike other sources of finance, trade credit is relatively easy to obtain. Except in the case of financially very unsound firms, it is almost automatic and does not require any negotiations. The easy availability is particularly important to small firms which generally face difficulty in raising funds from the capital markets.
*   *Flexibility* Flexibility is another advantage of trade credit. Trade credit grows with the growth in firm's sales. The expansion in the firm's sales causes its purchases of goods and services to increase which is automatically financed by trade credit. In contrast, if the firm's sales contract, purchases will decline and consequently trade credit will also decline.
*   *Informality* Trade credit is an informal, spontaneous source of finance. It does not require any negotiations and formal agreement. It does not have the restrictions which are usually parts of negotiated sources of finance.

Is trade credit a cost free source of finance? It appears to be cost free since it does not involve explicit interest charges. But in practice, it involves *implicit cost*. The cost of credit may be transferred to the buyer via the increased price of goods supplied to him. The user of trade credit, therefore, should be aware of the costs of trade credit to make use of it intelligently. The reasoning that it is cost free can lead to incorrect financing decisions.

The supplier extending trade credit incurs costs in the form of the opportunity cost of funds invested in accounts receivable and cost of any cash discount taken by the buyer. Does the supplier bear these costs? Most of the time he passes on all or part of these costs to the buyer implicitly in the form of higher purchase price of goods and services supplied. How much of the costs can he really pass on depends on the market supply and demand conditions. Thus if the buyer is in a position to pay cash immediately, he should try to avoid implicit costs of trade credit by negotiating lower purchase price with the supplier.

Credit terms sometimes include cash discount if the payment

is made within a specified period. The buyer should take a decision whether or not to avail it. A trade-off is involved. If the buyer takes discount, he benefits in terms of less cash outflow, but then he foregoes the credit granted by the supplier beyond the discount period. In contrast, if he does not take discount, he avails credit for the extended period but pays more. The buyer incurs an opportunity cost when he does not avail cash discount. Suppose that the Nirmal Company is extended Rs 100,000 credit on terms of '2/15, net 45'. As shown in Figure 31.1, Nirmal can either pay less amount (100,000 – 0.02 × 100,000 = Rs 98,000) by the end of the discount period i.e. the 15th day or the full amount (Rs 100,000) by the end of the credit period i.e. the 45th day. If the firm foregoes cash discount and does not pay on the 15th day, it can use Rs 98,000 for an additional period of 30 days, and implicitly paying Rs 2,000 in interest. If a credit of Rs 98,000 is available for 30 days by paying Rs 2,000 as interest, how much is the annual rate of interest? It can be found as follows:

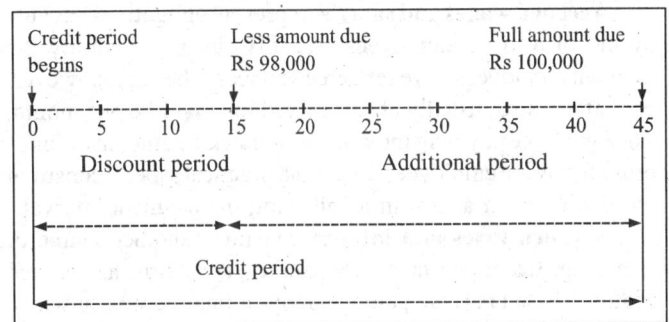

Figure 31.1: Cost of cash discount

$$\text{Implicit interest rate} = \frac{2,000}{98,000} \times \frac{360}{30} = 0.245 \text{ or } 24.5\%$$

We can also use the following formula to calculate the implicit rate of interest:

Implicit interest rate:

$$\frac{\% \text{ Discount}}{100 - \% \text{ Discount}} \times \frac{360}{\text{Credit period} - \text{Discount period}} \quad (1)$$

Using data of our example, we obtain:

$$= \frac{2}{100 - 2} \times \frac{360}{45 - 15} = \frac{2}{98} \times \frac{360}{30} = 0.245 \text{ or } 24.5\%$$

As the example above indicates, the annual opportunity cost of foregoing cash discount can be very high. Therefore, a firm should compare the opportunity cost of trade credit with the costs of other sources of credit while making its financing decisions.

For meeting its financing needs, should a company stretch its accounts payable? When a firm delays the payment of credit beyond the due date, it is called **stretching accounts payable.** Stretching accounts payable does generate additional short-term finances, but it can prove to be a very costly source. The firm will have to forgo the cash discount and may also be required to pay penalty interest charges. Thus the firm will not only be charged higher implicit costs, but its creditworthiness will also be adversely affected. If the firm stretches accounts payable

---

1. Moyer, R.C., *et. al., Contemporary Financial Management*, West Publishing Co., 1980, p. 666.

frequently, it may not be able to obtain any credit in future. It may also find it difficult to obtain finances from other sources once its creditworthiness is seriously damaged.

ACCRUED EXPENSES AND DEFERRED INCOME

In addition to trade credit, accrued expenses and deferred income are other spontaneous sources of short-term financing.[1] Accrued expenses are more automatic source since, by definition, they permit the firm to receive services before paying for them.

Accrued Expenses

Accrued expenses represent a liability that a firm has to pay for the services which it has already received. Thus they represent a spontaneous, interest-free sources of financing. The most important component of accruals are wages and salaries, taxes and interest.

Accrued wages and salaries represent obligations payable by the firm to its employees. The firm incurs a liability the moment employees have rendered services. They are, however, paid afterwards, usually at some fixed interval like one month. The longer the payment interval, the greater the amount of funds provided by the employees. Legal and practical aspects constrain the flexibility of a firm in lengthening the payment interval.

Accrued taxes and interest constitute another source of financing. Corporate taxes are paid after the firm has earned profits. These taxes are paid quarterly during the year in which profits are earned. This is a deferred payment of the firm's obligation and thus, is a source of finance. Like taxes, interest is paid periodically during a year while the firm continuously uses the borrowed funds. Thus accrued interest on borrowed funds requiring semi-annual interest payments can be used as a source of financing for a period as long as six months. Note that these expenses are not postponable for long and a firm does not have much control over their frequency and magnitude. It is a limited source of short-term financing.

Deferred Income

Deferred income represents funds received by the firm for goods and services which it has agreed to supply in future. These receipts increase the firm's liquidity in the form of cash; therefore, they constitute an important source of financing.

Advance payments made by customers constitute the main item of deferred income. These payments are common in case of expensive products like boilers, turnkey projects, large contracts or where the product is in short supply and the seller has a strong bargaining power as compared to the buyer. These payments are not recorded as revenue until goods and services have been delivered to the customers. They are, therefore, shown as a liability in the firm's balance sheet.

BANK FINANCE FOR WORKING CAPITAL

Banks are the main institutional sources of working capital finance in India. After trade credit, bank credit is the most important source of financing working capital requirements. A

bank considers a firm's sales and production plans and the desirable levels of current assets in determining its working capital requirements. The amount approved by the bank for the firm's working capital is called **credit limit.** Credit limit is the maximum funds which a firm can obtain from the banking system. In the case of firms with seasonal businesses, banks may fix separate limits for the **peak level credit** requirement and normal, **non-peak level credit** requirement indicating the periods during which the separate limits will be utilised by the borrower. In practice, banks do not lend 100 per cent of the credit limit; they deduct **margin money.** Margin requirement is based on the principle of conservatism and is meant to ensure security. If the margin requirement is 30 per cent, bank will lend only up to 70 per cent of the value of the asset. This implies that the security of bank's lending should be maintained even if the asset's value falls by 30 per cent.

Forms of Bank Finance

A firm can draw funds from its bank within the maximum credit limit sanctioned. It can draw funds in the following forms: (*a*) overdraft, (*b*) cash credit, (*c*) bills purchasing or discounting, and (*d*) working capital loan.

Overdraft Under the overdraft facility, the borrower is allowed to withdraw funds in excess of the balance in his current account up to a certain specified limit during a stipulated period. Though overdrawn amount is repayable on demand, they generally continue for a long period by annual renewals of the limits. It is a very flexible arrangement from the borrower's point of view since he can withdraw and repay funds whenever he desires within the overall stipulations. Interest is charged on daily balances—on the amount actually withdrawn—subject to some minimum charges. The borrower operates the account through cheques.

Cash credit The cash credit facility is similar to the overdraft arrangement. It is the most popular method of bank finance for working capital in India. Under the cash credit facility, a borrower is allowed to withdraw funds from the bank upto the sanctioned credit limit. He is not required to borrow the entire sanctioned credit once, rather, he can draw periodically to the extent of his requirements and repay by depositing surplus funds in his cash credit account. There is no commitment charge; therefore, interest is payable on the amount actually utilised by the borrower. Cash credit limits are sanctioned against the security of current assets. Though funds borrowed are repayable on demand, banks usually do not recall such advances unless they are compelled by adverse circumstances. Cash credit is a most flexible arrangement from the borrower's point of view.

Purchase or discounting of bills Under the purchase or discounting of bills, a borrower can obtain credit from a bank against its bills. The bank purchases or discounts the borrower's bills. The amount provided under this agreement is covered within the overall cash credit or overdraft limit. Before purchasing or discounting the bills, the bank satisfies itself as to the creditworthiness of the drawer. Though the term 'bills purchased' implies that the bank becomes owner of the bills, in practice,

---

1. Moyer, *et. al., op. cit.,* p. 667.

bank holds bills as security for the credit. When a bill is discounted, the borrower is paid the discounted amount of the bill (viz., full amount of bill minus the discount charged by the bank). The bank collects the full amount on maturity.

To encourage bills as instruments of credit, the Reserve Bank of India introduced the new bill market scheme in 1970. The scheme was intended to reduce the borrowers' reliance on the cash credit system which is susceptible to misuse. It was also envisaged that the scheme will facilitate banks to deploy their surpluses or deficits by rediscounting or selling the bills purchased or discounted by them. Banks with surplus funds could repurchase or rediscount bills in the possession of banks with deficits. There can be situation where every bank wants to sell its bills. Therefore, the Reserve Bank of India plays the role of the lender of last resort under the new bill market scheme. Unfortunately, the scheme has not worked successfully so far.

Letter of credit Suppliers, particularly the foreign suppliers, insist that the buyer should ensure that his bank will make the payment if he fails to honour its obligation. This is ensured through a letter of credit (L/C) arrangement. A bank opens an L/C in favour of a customer to facilitate his purchase of goods. If the customer does not pay to the supplier within the credit period, the bank makes the payment under the L/C arrangement. This arrangement passes the risk of the supplier to the bank. Bank charges the customer for opening the L/C. It will extend such facility to financially sound customers. Unlike cash credit or overdraft facility, the L/C arrangement is an indirect financing; the bank will make payment to the supplier on behalf of the customer only when he fails to meet the obligation.

Working capital loan A borrower may sometimes require *ad hoc* or temporary accommodation in excess of sanctioned credit limit to meet unforeseen contingencies. Banks provide such accommodation through a **demand loan** account or a separate **non-operable cash credit account**. The borrower is required to pay a higher rate of interest above the normal rate of interest on such additional credit.

Security Required in Bank Finance

Banks generally do not provide working capital finance without adequate security. The following are the modes of security which a bank may require.

Hypothecation Under hypothecation, the borrower is provided with working capital finance by the bank against the security of movable property, generally inventories. The borrower does not transfer the property to the bank; he remains in the possession of property made available as security for the debt. Thus hypothecation is a charge against property for an amount of debt where neither ownership nor possession is passed to the creditor. Banks generally grant credit hypothecation only to first class customers with highest integrity. They do not usually grant hypothecation facility to new borrowers.

Pledge Under this arrangement, the borrower is required to transfer the physical possession of the property offered as a security to the bank to obtain credit. The bank has a right of lien and can retain possession of the goods pledged unless payment of the principal, interest and any other expenses is made. In case of default, the bank may either (*a*) sue the borrower for the amount due, or (*b*) sue for the sale of goods pledged, or (*c*) after giving due notice, sell the goods.

Mortgage Mortgage is the transfer of a legal or equitable interest in a specific immovable property for the payment of a debt. In case of mortgage, the possession of the property may remain with the borrower, with the lender getting the full legal title. The transferor of interest (borrower) is called the mortgagor, the transferee (bank) is called the mortgagee, and the instrument of transfer is called the mortgage deed.

The credit granted against immovable property has some difficulties. They are not self-liquidating. Also, there are difficulties in ascertaining the title and assessing the value of the property. There is limited marketability, and therefore, security may often be difficult to realise. Also, without the court's decree, the property cannot be sold. Usually, for working capital finance, the mode of security is either hypothecation or pledge. Mortgages may be taken as additional security.

Lien Lien means right of the lender to retain property belonging to the borrower until he repays credit. It can be either a particular lien or general lien. Particular lien is a right to retain property until the claim associated with the property is fully paid. General lien, on the other hand, is applicable till all dues of the lender are paid. Banks usually enjoy general lien.

REGULATION OF BANK FINANCE

Banks have been following certain norms in granting working capital finance to companies. These norms have been greatly influenced by the recommendations of various committees appointed by the Reserve Bank of India from time to time. The norms of working capital finance followed by bank since mid-70's were mainly based on the recommendations of the Tandon Committee. The Chore Committee made further recommendations to strengthen the procedures and norms for working capital finance by banks. The norms based on the recommendations of these committees are discussed below. In the deregulated economic environment in India recently, banks have considerably relaxed their criteria of lending. In fact, each bank can develop its own criteria for the working capital finance.

Guidelines for Bank Finance: Historical Perspective

A study group, popularly known as the Tandon Committee, was appointed by the Reserve Bank of India in July 1974 to suggest guidelines for the rational allocation and optimum use of bank credit.[1] This was done on the presumption that the existing system of bank lending had a number of weaknesses.

The existing system has served its primary objective of financing trade quite efficiently in the past, when the industrial structure was simple. Industries in India, however, grew rapidly in the last three decades and, as a result, the industrial system became very complex. One can also witness a shift in the bank's

---

1. Discussion in this section is based on Reserve Bank of India, *Report of the Study Group to Frame Guidelines for Follow-up of Bank Credit*, Bombay: Reserve Bank of India, 1975, and Gupta, L.C., ed., *Banking and Working Capital Finance*, Macmillan.

role from trade financing to industrial financing during this period. But the commercial bank's lending practices and style remained almost the same.

Because of the easy availability of bank credit, industries in the past did not use it properly and efficiently. Still today industries are not using banks funds skilfully and for appropriate purposes. A majority of the companies in India are not cash, or resource, conscious; their techniques of managing funds at times, are unscientific and non-professional. A number of companies, even among the largest industrial units, have yet to learn the methods of reducing costs, optimising use of inputs per unit of output, conserving resources, improving and developing product, orienting their marketing practices and policies to customers and so on. If they fail in using these techniques of modern management, industries in the country may become a national burden. Already a number of units have become sick and the number of such units is on the increase. To an extent, the abnormal conditions are the cause for this, but, perhaps, mismanagement of resources is far more responsible for the present state of industries.

Background   Bank credit is a scare resource; hence it should be optimally utilised under all circumstances. For industrial units, it has become scarcer. There are many other contenders for bank credit: agriculture, small-scale industry, farmers, small man and many others. Public enterprises also approach commercial bank for their working capital requirements.

In view of the growing demand on bank funds from all sectors, industrial companies have no option but to use bank funds in the most efficient way. In the past, they misused or mismanaged the bank funds. Bank credit primarily meant for working capital finance was found to be used for long-term purposes and to finance subsidiaries and associated companies. Not only this, cheap credit available from banks has been used to build-up disproportionate stocks of materials to realise trading profits.

In fact, the misuse of bank funds was made possible by the existing system of bank lending, based on **cash credit system**. The practice was to lend generally to the extent of 75 per cent of the value of inventory and receivables, the remaining 25 per cent being the margin. The value of inventory included purchases of materials on credit. Thus, this amounted to double financing—from creditors as well as banks. Bank lending, under the cash credit system, was directly related to security in the form of inventory and receivables, irrespective of borrower's operations. So long as the borrower continued to provide the required margin, the banker considered his advance to be safe and liquid, and did not bother about the way in which advance was being utilised. The borrower's limit was generally increased, without much questioning about his operations, whenever inventory and receivable levels went up. The banker never took a closer look into the affairs of the customer.

One important drawback of the system was that the banker sanctioned a maximum limit within which the borrower could draw at his will. Under this procedure, the level of advances in a bank is determined not by how much a banker can lend at a particular point of time but the borrower's decision to borrow at that time. Under a tight situation, such a system would put banks to considerable strain. The cash credit system makes credit planning by banks very difficult.

The existing practice in fixing limit was to value inventory at the market prices for fixing limit. For this reason and because of the availability of credit from creditors, a borrower was able to borrow more than his current assets requirements. Accordingly, it was possible for the borrower to divert banks' funds to acquire fixed assets, including investments and make advances to subsidiaries and associated concerns.

The Dehejia committee   The above-mentioned deficiencies of the existing system of bank lending, based on cash credit system, were formally highlighted by the Dehejia Committee in 1968. The committee concluded that the diversion of bank finance for the acquisition of fixed and other non-current assets was made possible by the banker's fixation on security under the cash credit lending system. The committee felt that, while theoretically commercial bank lending was for short-term purposes, in actual practice, it was not so. According to their report, a large part of bank lending was really long-term in character, and was repayable on demand only in name.

The major weaknesses in the existing system of working finance to industry, as pointed out by the Dehejia Committee and again identified by the Tandon Committee, are summarised below:
1.   It is the borrower who decides how much he would borrow; the banker does not decide how much he would lend and is, therefore, not in a position to do credit planning.
2.   The bank credit is treated as the first source of finance and not as supplementary to other sources of finance.
3.   The amount of credit extended is based on the amount of security available, not on the level of operations of borrower.
4.   Security does not by itself ensure safety of bank funds since all bad and sticky advances are secured advances; safety essentially lies in the efficient follow-up of the industrial operations of the borrower.

Although the monetary authorities were aware of this faulty system of bank lending, yet it was only in 1973, when the demand for bank credit rose sharply in spite of stagnant production and when a number of banks had to freeze credit limits abruptly, that a serious consideration was given to the matter. Following this and the background of the unprecedented price rise in 1974, the Reserve Bank constituted the Tandon Committee to frame guidelines for follow-up of bank credit.

The Tandon committee recommendations   The recommendations of the Tandon Committee are based on the following notions:
1.   *Operating plan*   The borrower should indicate the likely demand for credit. For this purpose, he should draw operating plans for the ensuing year and supply them to the banker. This procedure will facilitate credit planning at the banks' level. It will also help the bankers in evaluating the borrower's credit needs in a realistic manner and in the periodic follow-up during the ensuing year.
2.   *Production-based financing*   The banker should finance only the genuine production needs of the borrower. The borrower should maintain reasonable levels of inventory and receivable; he should hold just enough to carry on his target production. Efficient management of resources

should, therefore, be ensured to eliminate slow moving and flabby inventories.

3. *Partial bank financing*   The working capital needs of the borrower cannot be entirely financed by the banker. The banker will finance only a reasonable part of it; for the remaining the borrower should depend upon his own funds, generated internally and externally.

The following are the major recommendations of the Tandon Committee:

Inventory and receivable norms   The Tandon Committee made a number of important recommendations regarding the bank lending practices. But it is the recommendation regarding the inventory and receivable norms which have been debated and criticised mostly.

The Committee pointed out that the borrower should be allowed to hold only a reasonable level of current assets, particularly inventory and receivable. Only the normal inventory, based on a production plan, lead time of supplies, economic ordering levels and reasonable factor of safety, should be financed by the banker. Flabby, profit-making or excessive inventory should not be permitted under any circumstance. Similarly, the banker should finance only those receivables which are in tune with the practices of the borrower's firm and industry.

The norms for reasonable levels of inventory and receivable are needed to ensure rational allocation of resources and to avoid the undesirable holding and financing of current assets. The norms should also be specified to bring uniformity in the banks' approach in assessing the working capital requirements, which was lacking in the past. Further, in view of an inflationary situation, the need for defining norms is all the more necessary.

The Tandon Committee, in its final report, suggested norms for fifteen industries excluding heavy engineering and highly seasonal industries, like, sugar. The norms were applied to all industrial borrowers, including small-scale industries, with aggregate limits from the banking system in excess of Rs 10 lakh. The Committee expected that the norms could be extended to smaller borrowers progressively as early as possible. Although the Committee defined norms in the case of fifteen industries only, yet it emphasised, and rightly so, that industries not covered should not be exempt from the discipline of norms. In such cases, banks should keep in view the purpose and spirit behind the norms when considering the extension of credit facilities.

It should be appreciated that the norms suggested by the Tandon Committee were not merely meant for banks to follow in financing the borrower's working capital needs, rather they represented the maximum limit which should not be exceeded in the normal circumstances. The norms did not suggest entitlement to hold inventories and receivables up to the prescribed level. If a borrower was efficient and could manage with less in the past, he should continue to do so.

The Committee admitted that the norms cannot be followed rigidly. It allowed for flexibility in the application of norms when a major change in the environment justifies. The Committee visualised the circumstances, such as power cuts, strikes, transport delays etc., under which a deviation from norms could be permitted. Deviations should generally be allowed for short periods and should be agreed upon in advance between the borrower and the banker. There should be a return to the norms when conditions revert to normal. The Committee also felt that the norms should be kept under constant review. If circumstances justified modification of the norms, it could be effected.

Lending norms   Another important recommendation of the Committee related to the approach to be followed by commercial banks in lending credit to borrowers. The Committee felt that the main function of a banker as a lender was to supplement the borrower's resources to carry an acceptable level of current assets. This implied: (*a*) the level of current assets must be reasonable and based on norms, (*b*) a part of the fund requirements for carrying current assets must be financed from long-term funds comprising owned funds and term borrowings including other non-current liabilities.

The banker was required to finance only a part of the working capital gap; the other part was to be financed by the borrower from the long-term sources. **Working capital gap** is defined as current assets minus current liabilities excluding bank borrowings. Current assets will be taken at estimated values or values as per the Tandon Committee norms, whichever is lower. Current assets will consist of inventory and receivables, referred as **chargeable current assets** (CCA) and other current assets (OCA).

Maximum Permissible Bank Finance (MPBF) In view of the above approach to bank lending, the Committee suggested the following three methods of determining the permissible level of bank borrowings:

• *First method*   In the first method, the borrower will contribute 25 per cent of the working capital gap; the remaining 75 per cent can be financed from bank borrowings. This method will give a minimum current ratio of 1:1.

• *Second method*   In the second method, the borrower will contribute 25 per cent of the total current assets. The remaining of the working capital gap (i.e. the working capital gap less the borrower's contribution) can be bridged from the bank borrowings. This method will give a current ratio of 1.3:1.

• *Third method*   In the third method, borrower will contribute 100 per cent of **core assets**, as defined and 25 per cent of the balance of current assets. The remaining of the working capital gap can be met from the borrowings. This method will further strengthen the current ratio.

The first two methods, immediately accepted for implementation by the Reserve Bank, are illustrated in Table 31.1.

Table 31.1: Methods for Determining Permissible Bank Borrowing

	1st Method (Rs)		2nd Method (Rs)	
(*a*) Current assets, *CA*	100		100	
(*b*) Current liabilities, excluding bank borrowing, *CL*	20		20	
(*c*) Working capital gap *CA – CL*, (*a – b*)	80		80	
(*d*) Borrower's contribution	20	[25% of (*c*)]	25	[25% of (*a*)]
(*e*) Permissible bank finance, (*c – d*)	60		55	

The Committee recommended the first method and advocated it mainly as a stop-gap method till borrowers got used to the new approach of lending and moved towards the ideal third method. The borrowers who were already in the second stage were not allowed to revert to the first stage. The aim should be to move forward. The recommendation was applied to all borrowers having credit limits in excess of Rs 20 lakh from the banking system.

At the time the new system of lending was introduced, in some cases the net working capital was negative while in others it was equal to 25 per cent of working capital gap. The Committee allowed this deficiency to be financed, in addition to the permissible bank finance, by banks. It was, however, to be regularised over a period of time depending upon the funds generating capacity and ability of the borrower. This kind of credit facility was called **working capital term loan.** The working capital term loan was not allowed to be raised in the subsequent years. For additional credit requirement arising in subsequent years, the borrower's long-term sources were required to provide 25 per cent of the additional working capital gap. The banks could grant regular term loans against fixed assets.

Style of credit In view of the deficiencies of the cash credit system of lending, the Committee also suggested a change in the style of bank lending. The Committee recommended the bifurcation of total credit limit into fixed and fluctuating parts. The fixed component was to be treated as a demand loan for the year representing the minimum level of borrowings which the borrower expected to use throughout the year. The fluctuating component was to be taken care of by a demand cash credit. The cash credit portion could be partly used by way of bills. It was also suggested by the Committee that the new cash credit limit should be placed on a quarterly budgeting – reporting system.

The Committee also recommended the interest differentials. As an incentive to switch over to the new style of credit, the Committee recommended that interest rate on the loan component be charged lower than the cash credit account. The Reserve Bank stipulated the differential at 1 per cent.

Information   system Yet   another   important recommendation of the Tandon Committee related to the flow of information from the borrower to the bank. The Committee advocated for the greater flow of information both for operational purposes and for the purpose of supervision and follow-up credit. Information was sought to be provided in three loans—operating statement, quarterly budget and funds flow statement. The statements prepared will give estimates and actuals. Projected annual figures would facilitate a genuine credit appraisal, while quarterly figures, furnished continuously, would enable a systematic and regular follow-up. As a first step, borrowers with credit limits of more than Rs 1 crore were required to supply the quarterly information. The Committee also suggested some modifications in the form of periodical stock statements submitted by the borrowers to their bankers for more effective follow up.

The information supplied by the borrower was required to be properly used by bank to follow up and supervise the use of credit. The bank must ensure that the bank credit was used for the purposes for which it was granted, keeping in view the borrower's operation and environment. From the periodical data supplied, the bank should ascertain whether the actual results were in conformity with the expected results or there was a variance calling for remedial action. A ± 10 per cent variance was considered as normal. The variance beyond this limit was, however, required to be investigated and discussed by the banker and the borrower.

The main thrust of the Tandon Committee's recommendation regarding the information flow was that the banker should be treated as a partner in the business with whom information was to be shared freely and frankly, so that he would be in constant touch with the operations of the borrower to whom the bank credit has been allocated.

The Tandon Committee Report has been widely debated and criticised. It is true that bankers found difficulties in implementing the committee's recommendations. But it must be admitted that the Tandon Committee report has brought about a perceptible change in the outlook and attitude of both the bankers and their customers. They have become quite aware in the matter of making best use of a scarce resource like bank credit. The report has helped in bringing a financial discipline through a balanced and integrated scheme for bank lending.

The Chore Committee Recommendations

In April 1979, the Reserve Bank of India constituted a working group to review the system of cash credit under the chairmanship of Mr. K.B. Chore. The main terms of reference for the group were to review the cash credit system and suggest modifications and/or alternate types of credit facilities to promote greater credit discipline and relate credit limits to production. The major recommendations having a bearing on bank credit to firms of the Group are as follows:[1]

Reduced dependence on bank credit Borrowers should contribute more funds to finance their working capital requirements, and reduce dependence on bank credit. Therefore, the group recommended firms to be placed in the second method of lending as explained by the Tandon Committee. In case the borrower was unable to comply with this requirement immediately, he would be granted excess borrowing in the form of working capital term loan (WCTL). WCTL should be repaid in semi-annual instalments for a period not exceeding five years and a higher rate of interest than under the cash credit system would be charged.

Credit limit to be separated into 'peak level' and 'normal peak level' limits Banks should appraise and fix separate limits for the 'peak level' and 'normal non-peak level' credit requirements for all borrowers in excess of Rs 10 lakh, indicating the relevant periods. Within the sanctioned limits for these two periods the borrower should indicate in advance his need for funds during a quarter. Any deviation in utilisation beyond 10 per cent tolerance limit should be treated, as an irregularity and

---

1. Reserve Bank of India, *Report of the Working Group to Review the System of Cash Credit*, Bombay, Reserve Bank of India, 1979.

appropriate action should be taken. *Banks should discourage ad hoc or temporary credit limits.* If sanctioned under exceptional circumstances, additional interest of 1 per cent per annum should be charged for such limits.

Existing lending system to continue The existing system of three types of lending: *Cash credit*, loans and bills should continue. Cash credit system should, however, be replaced by loan and bills wherever possible. Cash credit accounts in case of large borrowers should be scrutinised once in a year. Bifurcation of cash credit account into demand loan and fluctuating cash credit component practised as per the Tandon Committee recommendation should discontinue. Advances against book debts should be converted to bills wherever possible and atleast 50 per cent of the cash credit limit utilised for financing purchase of raw material inventory should also be changed to this bill system.

Information system The discipline relating to the submission of quarterly statements to be obtained from the borrowers under the existing system should be strictly adhered to in respect of all borrowers having working capital limits of Rs 50 lakhs and over from the banking system.

The Chore Committee made many other recommendations. A summary of the Committee's recommendations is contained in Appendix 31A.

COMMERCIAL PAPER

Commercial paper (CP) is an important money market instrument in advanced countries like USA to raise short-term funds. In India, on the recommendation of the Vaghul Working Group, the Reserve Bank of India (RBI) introduced the commercial paper scheme in the Indian money market in 1989. Commercial paper, as it is known in the advanced countries, is a form of unsecured promissory note issued by firms to raise short-term funds. The commercial paper market in the USA is a blue-chip market where financially sound and highest rated companies are able to issue commercial papers. The buyers of commercial papers include banks, insurance companies, unit trusts and firms with surplus funds to invest for a short period with minimum of risk. Given this investment objective of the investors in the commercial paper market, there would exist demand for commercial papers of highly creditworthy companies.

Use and Maturity

In India, the Reserve Bank of India regulates the issue of commercial papers. Those companies are allowed to issue commercial papers which have a net worth of Rs 10 crore, i.e., Rs 100 million, maximum permissible bank finance of not less than Rs 25 crore, and are listed on the stock exchange. The Vaghul Working Group recommended that the size of a single issue should be at least Rs 1 crore and the size of each commercial paper should not be less than Rs 5 lakh. The RBI has provided for the minimum issue of Rs 25 lakh (rather than Rs 5 lakh recommended by the Vaghul Committee). These norms imply that only the large, highly rated companies are able to operate in the commercial paper market in India. In fact, in USA it is mostly the largest companies that raise

funds from the commercial paper market. However, recently some smaller companies and large foreign companies have been able to tap the commercial paper market in USA. A company can issue CPs amounting to 75 per cent of the permitted bank credit.

What is the maturity of commercial papers? In the USA it runs from 1 to 270 days. In India, on the other hand, the maturity runs between 91 to 180 days. In USA, the commercial paper market existed for long period, but the use of commercial paper started since the World War II and increased in a significant way during 1960s and 1970s because of the tight money conditions. In recent years, some US companies have made aggressive use of commercial papers and have used them even for the partial financing of the long-term assets. In India, it is expected that commercial paper will be used only for short-term financing and as an alternative source of finance to bank credit and other short-term sources. Since the beginning of 1993, the volume of CPs has significantly increased because of the large surplus funds available from the banking sector as well as limited availability of other assets. On 31 August 2003, the commercial paper total amount outstanding was Rs 7,646 crore. The low and high interest rates were, respectively, 5 per cent and 6.65 per cent, showing a spread of 165 basis points.

Cost

Though the Reserve Bank of India regulates the issue of commercial paper, the market determines the interest rate. In advanced countries like USA, the interest rate on a commercial paper is a function of prime lending rate, maturity, credit-worthiness of the issuer and the rating of the paper provided by the rating agency. In the USA two main rating agencies— Standard and Poor and Moody—have three-point rating schemes with the safest paper rated 1 and the riskiest 3. In India, there are three rating companies – CRISIL, CARE and ICRA that provide ratings for CPs. CRISIL awards P1 plus, P1, P2 plus, and P2 ratings for CPs, and ICRA awards five ratings: A1 plus, A2, A3, A4 and A5. Rating depends on debt obligations, cash accruals, unused cash credit limits and tradable securities like units.

Interest rate on commercial paper is generally less than the bank borrowing rate. A firm does not pay interest on commercial paper rather sells it at a discount rate from face value. The yield calculated on this basis is referred to as interest yield. The interest yield can be found as follows:

$$\text{Interest yield} = \frac{\left[\begin{array}{c}\text{Face}\\\text{value}\end{array}\right] - \left[\begin{array}{c}\text{Sale}\\\text{price}\end{array}\right]}{\text{Sale price}} \times \frac{360}{\text{Days of maturity}} \quad (2)$$

Sales price will be net of flotation costs associated with the issue of commercial paper. Suppose a firm sells 120-day commercial paper (Rs 100 face value) for Rs 96 net, the interest yield will be 12.5 per cent:

$$\text{Interest yield} = \left[\frac{100 - 96}{96}\right]\left[\frac{360}{120}\right] = 0.125 \text{ or } 12.5 \text{ per cent}$$

Interest on CP is tax deductible: therefore, the after-tax

interest will be less. Assuming that the firm's marginal tax rate is 35 per cent, the after-tax interest yield is 8.13 per cent:

$$0.125 (1 - 0.35) = 0.0813 \text{ or } 8.13 \text{ per cent.}$$

In India, the cost of a CP will include the following components:

- discount
- rating charges
- stamp duty
- issuing and paying agent (IPA) charges

Illustration 31.1: Cost of Commercial Paper

Suppose a company issues a 90-day CP of a face value of Rs 1,000 at Rs 985. The credit rating expenses are 0.5 per cent of the size of issue, IPA charges being 0.35 per cent and stamp duty 0.5 per cent. What is the cost of CP?

The discount is Rs 15 and rating and IPA charges and stamp duty amounts to: 1.35 per cent × Rs 1,000 = Rs 13.5. Thus, the cost of CP is:

$$\text{Cost of CP} = \frac{15+13.5}{985} \times \frac{360}{90} = 0.1157 \text{ or } 11.6\%$$

Merits and Demerits

There are two important advantages of commercial paper from the issuing firm's point of view:

- It is an alternative source of raising short-term finance, and proves to be handy during periods of tight bank credit.
- It is a cheaper source of finance in comparison to the bank credit. Usually, interest yield on commercial paper is less than the prime rate of interest.

From an investor's point of view, it provides an opportunity to make a safe, short-term investment of surplus funds.

The following are the limitations of this source of financing:

- It is an *impersonal* method of financing. If a firm is unable to redeem its paper due to financial difficulties, it may not be possible for it to get the maturity of paper extended.
- It is always available to the financially sound and highest rated companies. A firm facing temporary liquidity problems may not be able to raise funds by issuing new paper.
- The amount of loanable funds available in the commercial paper market is limited to the amount of excess liquidity of the various purchasers of commercial paper.
- It cannot be redeemed until maturity. Thus if a firm doesn't need the funds any more, it cannot repay it until maturity and will have to incur interest costs.

SUMMARY

❖ Most important short-term sources of financing current assets are: (*a*) trade credit, (*b*) deferred income and accrued expenses, and (*c*) bank finance. The first two sources are available in the normal course of business, and therefore, they are called spontaneous sources of working capital finance. They do not involve any explicit costs. Bank finances have to be negotiated and involve explicit costs. They are called non-spontaneous or negotiated sources of working capital finance. Two alternative ways of raising short-term finances in India are: factoring and commercial paper.

❖ Trade credit refers to the credit that a buyer obtains from the suppliers of goods and services. Payment is required to be made within a specified period. Suppliers sometimes offer cash discount to buyers for making prompt payment. Buyer should calculate the cost of foregoing cash discount to decide whether or not cash discount should be availed. The following formula can be used:

$$\frac{\% \text{ Discount}}{100 - \% \text{ Discount}} \times \frac{360}{\text{Credit period} - \text{Discount period}}$$

❖ A buyer should also consider the implicit costs of trade credit, and particularly, that of stretching accounts payable. These implicit costs may be built into the prices of goods and services. Buyer can negotiate for lower prices for making payment in cash.

❖ Accrued expenses and deferred income also provide some funds for financing working capital. However, it is a limited source as payment of accrued expenses cannot be postponed for a long period. Similarly, advance income will be received only when there is a demand–supply gap or the firm is a monopoly.

❖ Bank finance is the most commonly negotiated source of the working capital finance. It can be availed in the forms of overdraft, cash credit, purchase/discount of bills and loan. Each company's working capital need is determined as per the norms. These norms are based on the recommendation of the Tandon Committee and later on, the Chore Committee. The policy is to require firms to finance more and more of their capital needs from sources other than bank. Banks are the largest providers of working capital finance to firms.

❖ Commercial paper is an important money market instrument for raising short-term finances. Firms, banks, insurance companies, individuals etc. with short-term surplus funds invest in commercial papers. Investors would generally invest in commercial paper of a financially sound and creditworthy firm. In India, commercial papers of 91 to 180 days maturity are being floated. The interest rate will be determined in the market. The yield on commercial paper can be calculated as follows:

$$\text{CP yield} = [\text{Face value} - \text{Sale price} / \text{Sale price}] \times [360 / \text{Days to maturity}]$$

KEY CONCEPTS

Cash credit system	Hypothecation	Bank Finance (MPBF)	Peak level credit
Chargeable current assets	Letter of credit (L/C)	Mortgage	Pledge
Commercial paper	Lien	Non-peak level credit	Stretching accounts payable
Core current assets	Margin money	Open account credit	Trade credit
Credit limit	Maximum Permissible	Overdraft financing	Working capital gap

REVIEW QUESTIONS

1. Explain the importance of trade credit and accruals as sources of working capital. What is the cost of these sources?
2. Explain the rationale of the Tandon Committee's recommendations.
3. Describe the important features of the Tandon Committee's recommendations.
4. What are the implications of the recommendations suggested by the Tandon Committee?
5. Define commercial paper. Explain its *pros* and *cons*.

PROBLEMS

1. The following is the balance sheet and production plan of Neo-Pharma Ltd.

Table 31.2: Neo-Pharma Limited Balance Sheet as on June 30, 20X2

(Rs in lakh)

Liabilities			Assets		
Share capital		54	Fixed assets		31
Reserves		8	Investments		5
Long-term loans		4	Current assets:		
Current liabilities:			Raw materials	64	
Sundry creditors	41		Work-in-progress	7	
Other current liabilities	10		Finished goods	49	
Bank borrowings	135		Sundry debtors	91	
Provisions for tax and dividends	14	200	Outstanding exports sales 15		
			Cash and bank balances	6	
			Misc. current assets	11	
			Advance tax payment	2	230
		266			266

Notes: (*i*) Bills discounted with banks and outstanding as on June 30, 20X2 is Rs 500,000.

(*ii*) An instalment of Rs 100,000 falls due on December 31, 20X2 as a part repayment of long-term loan.

Table 31.3: Production Plan for The Year 20X2–03

(Rs in lakh)

	20X1 (Actuals)		20X2 (Projects)	
Sales of which export sales	50	266	75	291
Cost of production of which:		211		238
(a) Raw materials	151		173	
(b) Wages and salaries	50		55	

(Contd.)

	20X2 (Actuals)	20X2 (Projects)
(c) Direct manufacturing expenses	10	10
Gross profit	55	53
Operating expenses	44	42
Cost of sales	255	280
Non-operating income	4	3
Provision for taxation	8	8
Net profit	7	6

Table 31.4: Projected Balance Sheet as on June 30, 20X3

(Rs in lakh)

Liabilities			Assets		
Share capital		54	Fixed assets		25
Reserves		13	Investments		1
Long-term loans		3	Current assets of which:		
Current liabilities of which:					
			Raw materials	60	
Sundry creditors	44		Work-in-progress	17	
Other current liabilities	6		Finished goods	52	
Bank borrowings	139		Sundry debtors	98	
Provisions for tax and dividends	15	204	Outstanding exports sales 27		
			Cash and bank balances	7	
			Misc. current assets	8	
			Advance tax payment	6	248
		274			274

Notes: (*i*) Bills discounted with banks and outstanding as on June 30, 20X3, Rs 1,000,000.

(*ii*) An instalment of Rs 250,000 falls due on December 31, 20X3 as a part repayment of long-term loan.

Table 31.5: Working Capital Norms for Pharmaceutical Industry

Raw materials and others	2 ¾ months consumption
Work-in-progress	½ month's cost of production
Finished goods	2 months cost of sales
Receivables and bills purchased and discounted.	1 ¼ months of sale

You are required to calculate the maximum permissible bank finance (MPBF) as per the Tandon Committee recommendations regarding Method 1 and Method 2.

2. Ananta Chemicals Limited is considering raising of Rs 15 crore by issuing CPs for 120 days. CPs will be sold at a discount of 11.25 per cent. Stamp duty charges will be 0.5 per cent of the size of the issue. The issuing and other charges will amount to Rs 3.75 lakh and rating charges to 0.40 per cent of the issue size. Calculate the effective cost of CP.

3. XY Ltd. is planning to sell a 90-day CP of Rs 100 for Rs 94.75. The company will have to incur expenses as follows: (*a*) rating of issue: 0.35 per cent, (*b*) stamp duty 0.5 per cent, (*c*) issuing charges 0.2 per cent and (*d*) dealer's fee 0.15 per cent. What is the cost of CP?

CHAPTER 32

Corporate Restructuring, Mergers and Acquisitions

CHAPTER OBJECTIVES

- Discuss the form of mergers and acquisitions
- Highlight the real motives of mergers and acquisitions
- Show how mergers and acquisitions could help creating value
- Illustrate the methodology for valuing mergers and acquisitions
- Focus on the considerations that are important in the mergers and acquisitions negotiations
- Consider the issues involved in post-merger integration
- Understand the implications and valuation of the leveraged buy-outs and disinvestment
- Explain the legal framework for mergers and acquisition in India

INTRODUCTION

Corporate restructuring includes mergers and acquisitions (M&A), amalgamation, take-overs, spin-offs, leveraged buy-outs, buy-back of shares, capital reorganisation, sale of business units and assets etc. M&A are the most popular means of corporate restructuring or business combinations. They have played an important role in the external growth of a number of leading companies the world over. In the United States, the first merger wave occurred between 1890 and 1904 and the second began at the end of the World War I and continued through the 1920s. The third merger wave commenced in the latter part of World War II and continues to the present day.[1] About two-thirds of the large public corporations in the USA have merger or amalgamation in their history. In India, about 1180 proposals for amalgamation of corporate bodies involving about 2,400 companies were filed with the High Courts during 1976–86. These formed 6 per cent of the 40,600 companies at work at the beginning of 1976.[2] In the year 2003–04, 834 mergers and acquisitions deals involved Rs 35,980 crore. Mergers and acquisitions, the way in which they are understood in the Western

1. Arthur, R., Waya, H., A Critical Study of Accounting for Business Combinations, *Accounting Research Study*, New York, American Institute of Certified Public Accountants, 1963, p. 7.
2. Bhattacharyya, H.K., Amalgamation and Takeovers, *Company News and Notes*, 1988, pp. 1–11.

countries, have started taking place in India in the recent years. A number of mega mergers and hostile takeovers could be witnessed in India now.

There are several aspects relating to mergers and acquisitions that are worthy of study. Some important questions are:

1. What are the basic economic forces that lead to mergers and acquisitions? How do these interact with one another?
2. What are the manager's true motives for mergers and acquisitions?
3. Why do mergers and acquisitions occur more frequently at some times than at other times? Which are the segments of the economy that stand to gain or lose?
4. How could merger and acquisition decisions be evaluated?
5. What managerial process is involved in merger and acquisition decisions?
6. What process is followed in integrating merging and merged firms post-merger?

In this chapter, we shall also discuss other forms of corporate restructuring like takeovers, leveraged buy-outs and spin-offs.

CORPORATE RESTRUCTURING

Corporate restructuring refers to the changes in ownership, business mix, assets mix and alliances with a view to enhance the shareholder value. Hence, corporate restructuring may involve ownership restructuring, business restructuring and assets restructuring. A company can affect **ownership restructuring** through mergers and acquisitions, leveraged buy-outs, buyback of shares, spin-offs, joint ventures and strategic alliances. **Business restructuring** involves the reorganization of business units or divisions. It includes diversification into new businesses, out-sourcing, divestment, brand acquisitions etc. **Asset restructuring** involves the acquisition or sale of assets and their ownership structure. The examples of asset restructuring are sale and leaseback of assets, securitization of debt, receivable factoring, etc.

The basic purpose of corporate restructuring is to enhance the shareholder value. A company should continuously evaluate its portfolio of businesses, capital mix and ownership and assets arrangements to find opportunities for increasing the shareholder value. It should focus on assets utilization and profitable investment opportunities, and reorganize or divest less profitable or loss making businesses/products. The company can also enhance value through capital restructuring; it can design innovative securities that help to reduce cost of capital.

Our focus here is on mergers and acquisitions, leveraged buy-outs and divestment. We have discussed many other aspects of restructuring like buyback of shares, capital structuring etc. earlier in this book.

TYPES OF BUSINESS COMBINATION

There is a great deal of confusion and disagreement regarding the precise meaning of terms relating to the business combination, *viz.*, merger, acquisition, takeover, amalgamation and consolidation. Sometimes, these terms are used in broad sense, encompassing most dimensions of business combination, while sometimes they are defined in a restricted legal sense. We shall define these terms keeping in mind the relevant legal framework in India.

Merger or Amalgamation

A **merger** is said to occur when two or more companies combine into one company. One or more companies may merge with an existing company or they may merge to form a new company. In merger, there is complete amalgamation of the assets and liabilities as well as shareholders' interests and businesses of the merging companies. There is yet another mode of merger. Here one company may purchase another company without giving proportionate ownership to the shareholders' of the acquired company or without continuing the business of the acquired company.[1] Laws in India use the term **amalgamation** for merger. For example, Section 2(1A) of the Income Tax Act, 1961 defines amalgamation as the merger of one or more companies (called **amalgamating company** or companies) with another company (called **amalgamated company**) or the merger of two or more companies to form a new company in such a way that all assets and liabilities of the amalgamating company or companies become assets and liabilities of the amalgamated company and shareholders holding not less than nine-tenths in value of the shares in the amalgamating company or companies become shareholders of the amalgamated company. We shall use the terms merger and amalgamation interchangeably.

Merger or amalgamation may take two forms:
- Merger through absorption
- Merger through consolidation

Absorption Absorption is a combination of two or more companies into an existing company. All companies except one lose their identity in a merger through absorption. An example of this type of merger is the absorption of Tata Fertilisers Ltd. (TFL) by Tata Chemicals Ltd. (TCL). TCL, an acquiring company (a buyer), survived after merger while TFL, an acquired company (a seller), ceased to exist. TFL transferred its assets, liabilities and shares to TCL. Under the scheme of merger, TFL shareholders were offered 17 shares of TCL (market value per share being Rs 114) for every 100 shares of TFL held by them.

Consolidation Consolidation is a combination of two or more companies into a new company. In this form of merger, all companies are legally dissolved and a new entity is created. In a consolidation, the acquired company transfers its assets, liabilities and shares to the new company for cash or exchange of shares. In a narrow sense, the terms amalgamation and consolidation are sometimes used interchangeably. An example of consolidation is the merger or amalgamation of Hindustan Computers Ltd., Hindustan Instruments Ltd., Indian Software Company Ltd., and Indian Reprographics Ltd. in 1986 to an entirely new company called HCL Ltd.

Acquisition

A fundamental characteristic of merger (either through absorption or consolidation) is that the acquiring or amalgamated

---

1. ICAI, Statements of Accounting Standards (AS 14): Accounting for Amalgamation, New Delhi: ICAI. http://www.icai.org/resource/as14_defin.html

company (existing or new) takes over the ownership of other company and combines its operations with its own operations. **Acquisition** may be defined as an act of acquiring effective control over assets or management of a company by another company without any combination of businesses or companies. A **substantial acquisition** occurs when an acquiring firm acquires substantial quantity of shares or voting rights of the target company. Thus, in an acquisition, two or more companies may remain independent, separate legal entity, but there may be change in control of companies. An acquirer may be a company or persons acting in concert that act together for the purpose of substantial acquisition of shares or voting rights or gaining control over the target company.

Takeover Generally speaking **takeover** means acquisition. A takeover occurs when the acquiring firm takes over the control of the target firm. An acquisition or take-over does not necessarily entail full, legal control. A company can have effective control over another company by holding minority ownership. Under the Monopolies and Restrictive Trade Practices Act, takeover means acquisition of not less than 25 per cent of the voting power in a company. Section 372 of the Companies Act defines the limit of a company's investment in the shares of another company. If a company wants to invest in more than 10 per cent of the subscribed capital of another company, it has to be approved in the shareholders general meeting and also by the central government. The investment in shares of other companies in excess of 10 per cent of the subscribed capital can result into their takeovers.

Takeover vs. acquisition Sometimes, a distinction between takeover and acquisition is made. The term takeover is understood to connote hostility. When an acquisition is a 'forced' or 'unwilling' acquisition, it is called a takeover. In an unwilling acquisition, the management of "target" company would oppose a move of being taken over. When managements of acquiring and target companies mutually and willingly agree for the takeover, it is called acquisition or friendly takeover. An example of acquisition is the acquisition of controlling interest (45 per cent shares) of Universal Luggage Manufacturing Company Ltd. by Blow Plast Ltd. Similarly, Mahindra and Mahindra Ltd., a leading manufacturer of jeeps and tractors acquired a 26 per cent equity stake in Allwyn Nissan Ltd. Yet another example is the acquisition of 28 per cent equity of International Data Management (IDM) by HCL Ltd. In recent years, due to the liberalisation of financial sector as well as opening up of the economy for foreign investors, a number of hostile take-overs could be witnessed in India. Examples include takeover of Shaw Wallace, Dunlop, Mather and Platt and Hindustan Dorr Oliver by Chhabrias, Ashok Leyland by Hindujas and ICIM, Harrison Malayalam and Spencers by Goenkas. Both Hindujas and Chhabrias are non-resident Indian (NRIs).

Holding company A company can obtain the status of a **holding company** by acquiring shares of other companies. A holding company is a company that holds more than half of the nominal value of the equity capital of another company, called a **subsidiary company**, or controls the composition of its Board of Directors. Both holding and subsidiary companies retain their separate legal entities and maintain their separate books of accounts. Unlike some countries, like the USA, or the UK, India it is not legally required to consolidate accounts of holding and subsidiary companies.

Forms of Merger

There are three major types of mergers:

Horizontal merger This is a combination of two or more firms in similar type of production, distribution or area of business. Examples would be combining of two book publishers or two luggage manufacturing companies to gain dominant market share.

Vertical merger This is a combination of two or more firms involved in different stages of production or distribution. For example, joining of a TV manufacturing (assembling) company and a TV marketing company or the joining of a spinning company and a weaving company. Vertical merger may take the form of forward or backward merger. When a company combines with the supplier of material, it is called backward merger and when it combines with the customer, it is known as forward merger.

Conglomerate merger This is a combination of firms engaged in unrelated lines of business activity. A typical example is merging of different businesses like manufacturing of cement products, fertilizers products, electronic products, insurance investment and advertising agencies. Voltas Ltd. is an example of a conglomerate company.

MERGERS AND ACQUISITION TRENDS IN INDIA

Economic reforms and deregulation of the Indian economy has brought in more domestic as well as international players in Indian industries. This has caused increased competitive pressure leading to structural changes of Indian industries. M&A is a part of the restructuring strategy of Indian industries. The first M&A wave in India took place towards the end of 1990s. The data presented in the Table 32.1 reveal that substantial growth in the M&A activities in India occurred in 2000–01. The total number of M&A deals in 2000–01 was estimated at 1,177 which is 54 per cent higher than the total number of deals in the previous year. The amount involved in deals has shown variation; after falling to Rs 23,106 crore in 2002–03 the amount increased to Rs 35,980 crore in 2003–04.

Table 32.1: M&A in India

Year	Deals	
	Number	*Amount (Rs in crore)*
1998–99	292	16,071
1999–00	765	36,963
2000–01	1,177	32,130
2001–02	1,045	34,322
2002–03	838	23,106
2003–04	834	35,980

The total number of mergers in 2003–04 was 284, down from 381 mergers in the previous period. From data in Table 32.2, it appears that mergers account for around one-third of total M&A

deals in India. It implies that takeovers or acquisitions are the dominant feature of M&A activity in India, similar to the trend in most of the developed countries. Along with the rise in M&A, there has also an increase in the number of open offers, *albeit* at a lower pace. The number of open offers rose to 109 in 2002–03 from 58 in 1998–99. In 2003–04, 72 open offers involved Rs 1,122 crore – much less than as compared to the previous year.

Table 32.2: Share of Mergers in M&A in India

Year	M&A	Merger	%
1998–99	292	80	27.4%
1999–00	765	193	25.2%
2000–01	1177	327	27.8%
2001–02	1045	323	30.9%
2002–03	838	381	45.5%
2003–04	834	284	34.1%

MOTIVES AND BENEFITS OF MERGERS AND ACQUISITIONS

Why do mergers take place? It is believed that mergers and acquisitions are strategic decisions leading to the maximisation of a company's growth by enhancing its production and marketing operations. They have become popular in the recent times because of the enhanced competition, breaking of trade barriers, free flow of capital across countries and globalisation of business as a number of economies are being deregulated and integrated with other economies. A number of reasons are attributed for the occurrence of mergers and acquisitions. For example, it is suggested that mergers and acquisition are intended to:[1]

- Limit competition
- Utilise under-utilised market power
- Overcome the Problem of slow growth and profitability in one's own industry
- Achieve diversification
- Gain economies of scale and increase income with proportionately less investment
- Establish a transnational bridgehead without excessive start-up costs to gain access to a foreign market
- Utilise under-utilised resources—human and physical and managerial skills
- Displace existing management
- Circumvent government regulations
- Reap speculative gains attendant upon new security issue or change in P/E ratio
- Create an image of aggressiveness and strategic opportunism, empire building and to amass vast economic powers of the company.

Are there any real benefits of merger? A number of benefits of mergers are claimed.[2] All of them are not real benefits. Based on the empirical evidence and the experiences of certain companies, the most common motives and advantages of mergers and acquisitions are explained below:

- Maintaining or accelerating a company's growth, particularly when the internal growth is constrained due to paucity of resources;
- Enhancing profitability, through cost reduction resulting from economies of scale, operating efficiency and synergy;
- Diversifying the risk of the company, particularly when it acquires those businesses whose income streams are not correlated;
- Reducing tax liability because of the provision of setting-off accumulated losses and unabsorbed depreciation of one company against the profits of another;
- Limiting the severity of competition by increasing the company's market power.

Accelerated Growth

Growth is essential for sustaining the viability, dynamism and value-enhancing capability of a company. A growth-oriented company is not only able to attract the most talented executives but it would also be able to retain them. Growing operations provide challenges and excitement to the executives as well as opportunities for their job enrichment and rapid career development. This helps to increase managerial efficiency. Other things remaining the same, growth leads to higher profits and increase in the shareholders' value. A company can achieve its growth objective by:

- Expanding its existing markets
- Entering in new markets.

A company may expand and/or diversify its markets internally or externally. If the company cannot grow internally due to lack of physical and managerial resources, it can grow externally by combining its operations with other companies through mergers and acquisitions. Mergers and acquisitions may help to accelerate the pace of a company's growth in a convenient and inexpensive manner.

Internal growth requires that the company should develop its operating facilities—manufacturing, research, marketing etc. Internal development of facilities for growth also requires time. Thus, lack or inadequacy of resources and time needed for internal development constrains a company's pace of growth. The company can acquire production facilities as well as other resources from outside through mergers and acquisitions. Specially, for entering in new products/markets, the company may lack technical skills and may require special marketing skills and/or a wide distribution network to access different segments of markets. The company can acquire existing company or companies with requisite infrastructure and skills and grow quickly.

Mergers and acquisitions, however, involve cost. External growth could be expensive if the company pays an excessive price for merger. Benefits should exceed the cost of acquisition

1. Ansoff H.L. *et. al.*, *Acquisitive Behaviour of U.S. Manufacturing Firms* 1946–65, Vanderbilt University Press, 1971.
2. For example, see Van Horne, J.C., *Financial Management and Policy*, Prentice-Hall of India, 1985, pp. 610–13; and Brealey, R.A. and Myers, S.C., *Principles of Corporate Finance*, McGraw Hill, 1991, pp. 820–28.

for realising a growth which adds value to shareholders. In practice, it has been found that the management of a number of acquiring companies paid an excessive price for acquisition to satisfy their urge for high growth and large size of their companies. It is necessary that price may be carefully determined and negotiated so that merger enhances the value of shareholders.

Enhanced Profitability

The combination of two or more companies may result in more than the average profitability due to cost reduction and efficient utilisation of resources. This may happen because of the following reasons:

- Economies of scale
- Operating economies
- Synergy.

Economies of scale Economies of scale arise when increase in the volume of production leads to a reduction in the cost of production per unit. Merger may help to expand volume of production without a corresponding increase in fixed costs. Thus, fixed costs are distributed over a large volume of production causing the unit cost of production to decline. Economies of scale may also arise from other indivisibilities such as production facilities, management functions and management resources and systems. This happens because a given function, facility or resource is utilised for a larger scale of operation. For example, a given mix of plant and machinery can produce scale economies when its capacity utilisation is increased. Economies will be maximised when it is optimally utilised. Similarly, economies in the use of the marketing function can be achieved by covering wider markets and customers using a given sales force and promotion and advertising efforts. Economies of scale may also be obtained from the optimum utilisation of management resource and systems of planning, budgeting, reporting and control. A company establishes management systems by employing enough qualified professionals irrespective of its size. A combined firm with a large size can make the optimum use of the management resource and systems resulting in economies of scale.

Operating economies In addition to economies of scale, a combination of two or more firms may result into cost reduction due to operating economies. A combined firm may avoid or reduce overlapping functions and facilities. It can consolidate its management functions such as manufacturing, marketing, R&D and reduce operating costs. For example, a combined firm may eliminate duplicate channels of distribution, or create a centralised training centre, or introduce an integrated planning and control system.

In a vertical merger, a firm may either combine with its suppliers of input (**backward integration**) and/or with its customers (**forward integration**). Such merger facilitates better coordination and administration of the different stages of business operations—purchasing, manufacturing, and marketing—eliminates the need for bargaining (with suppliers and/or customers), and minimises uncertainty of supply of inputs and demand for product and saves costs of communication.

An example of a merger resulting in operating economies is the merger of Sundaram Clayton Ltd (SCL) with TVS-Suzuki Ltd (TSL). By this merger, TSL became the second largest producer of two-wheelers after Bajaj. The main motivation for the takeover was TSL's need to tide over its different market situation through increased volume of production. It needed a large manufacturing base to reduce its production costs. Large amount of funds would have been required for creating additional production capacity. SCL also needed to upgrade its technology and increase its production. SCL's and TSL's plants were closely located which added to their advantages. The combined company has also been enabled to share the common R&D facilities. Yet another example of a horizontal merger motivated by the desire for rationalisation of operations is the takeover of Universal Luggage by Blow Plast. The intended objectives were elimination of fierce price war and reduction of marketing staff.

Synergy Synergy implies a situation where the combined firm is more valuable than the sum of the individual combining firms. It is defined as 'two plus two equal to five' $(2+2=5)$ phenomenon. Synergy refers to benefits other than those related to economies of scale. Operating economies are one form of synergy benefits.[1] But apart from operating economies, synergy may also arise from enhanced managerial capabilities, creativity, innovativeness, R&D and market coverage capacity due to the complementarities of resources and skills and a widened horizon of opportunities.

Diversification of Risk

Diversification implies growth through the combination of firms in unrelated businesses. Such mergers are called conglomerate mergers. It is difficult to justify conglomerate merger on the ground of economies, as it does not help to strengthen horizontal or vertical linkages. It is argued that it can result into reduction of total risk through substantial reduction of cyclicality of operations. Total risk will be reduced if the operations of the combining firms are negatively correlated.

In practice, investors can reduce **non-systematic risk** (the company related risk) by diversifying their investment in shares of a large number of companies. **Systematic risk**[2] (the market related risk) is not diversifiable. Therefore, investors do not pay any premium for diversifying total risk via reduction in non-systematic risk that they can do on their own, cheaply and quickly. For example, an investor who holds one per cent of shares of Company X and one per cent of shares of Company Y could achieve the same share of earnings and assets if Companies X and Y merged and he held one per cent of shares of the merged company. The risk from his point of view has been diversified by his acquiring shares of the two companies. Of course, the merger of two companies may reduce the variability of earnings, but it would not necessarily reduce the variability of earnings *vis-à-vis* the market-related variables. What advantage can result from conglomerate mergers for shareholders who can diversify their portfolios to reduce non-

---

1. Van Horne, *op. cit.*, p. 611.
2. Refer to Chapter 5 for a detailed explanation of systematic (non-diversifiable) and non-systematic (diversifiable) risk.

systematic risk? The reduction of total risk, however, is advantageous from the combined company's point of view, since the combination of management and other systems strengthen the capacity of the combined firm to withstand the severity of the unforeseen economic factors that could otherwise endanger the survival of individual companies. Conglomerate mergers can also prove to be beneficial in the case of shareholders of unquoted companies since they do not have opportunity for trading in their company's shares.

An example of diversification through mergers to reduce total risk and improve profitability is that of RPG Enterprises (Goenka Group). The group started its takeover activity in 1979. It comprises a large number of companies, most of which have been takeover. The strategy has been to look out for any foreign disinvestment, or any cases of sick companies, which could prove right targets at low takeover prices. In 1988, RPG took over ICIM and Harrisons Malayalam Limited. In the case of ICIM, the parent company, ICL, continued to hold 40 per cent of the equity stake with the Goenkas acquiring 10 per cent of the equity by private placement of shares. For the Goenkas, this has provided an easy access to the electronics industry.

Reduction in Tax Liability

In a number of countries, a company is allowed to carry forward its accumulated loss to set-off against its future earnings for calculating its tax liability. A loss-making or sick company may not be in a position to earn sufficient profits in future to take advantage of the carry forward provision. If it combines with a profitable company, the combined company can utilise the carry forward loss and save taxes. In India, a profitable company is allowed to merge with a sick company to set-off against its profits the accumulated loss and unutilised depreciation of that company. A number of companies in India have merged to take advantage of this provision.

An example of a merger to reduce tax liability is the absorption of Ahmedabad Cotton Mills Limited (ACML) by Arbind Mills in 1979. ACML was closed in August 1977 on account of labour Problem. At the time of merger in April 1979, ACML had an accumulated loss of Rs 3.34 crore. Arbind Mills saved about Rs 2 crore in tax liability for the next two years after the merger because it could set-off ACML's accumulated loss against its profits. Yet another example of a merger induced by tax saving is the takeover of Sidhpur Mills by Reliance in 1979. The carry-forward losses and unabsorbed depreciation of Sidhpur amounted to Rs 2.47 crores. In addition to tax savings, the merger provided Reliance with an opportunity for vertical integration (Sidhpur would supply grey cloth to Reliance) and capacity expansion (Sidhpur had 490 looms and 50,000 spindles and 40 acres of land).

When two companies merge through an exchange of shares, the shareholders of selling company can save tax. The profit arising from the exchange of shares are not taxable until the shares are actually sold. When the shares are sold, they are subject to capital gains tax rate which is much lower than the ordinary

income tax rate. For example, in India capital gains tax rate is 20 per cent while the personal tax rate is 30 per cent.

A strong urge to reduce tax liability, particularly when the marginal tax rate is high (as has been the case in India) is a strong motivation for the combination of companies. For example, the high tax rate was the main reason for the post-war merger activity in the USA. Also, tax benefits are responsible for one-third of mergers in the USA.[1]

Financial Benefits

There are many ways in which a merger can result into financial synergy and benefits. A merger may help in:

- Eliminating the financial constraint
- Deploying surplus cash
- Enhancing debt capacity
- Lowering the financing costs.

Financing constraint A company may be constrained to grow through internal development due to shortage of funds. The company can grow externally by acquiring another company by the exchange of shares and thus, release the financing constraint.

Surplus cash A cash-rich company may face a different situation. It may not have enough internal opportunities to invest its surplus cash. It may either distribute its surplus cash to its shareholders or use it to acquire some other company. The shareholders may not really benefit much if surplus cash is returned to them since they would have to pay tax at ordinary income tax rate. Their wealth may increase through an increase in the market value of their shares if surplus cash is used to acquire another company. If they sell their shares, they would pay tax at a lower, capital gains tax rate. The company would also be enabled to keep surplus funds and grow through acquisition.

Debt capacity A merger of two companies, with fluctuating, but negatively correlated, cash flows, can bring stability of cash flows of the combined company. The stability of cash flows reduces the risk of insolvency and enhances the capacity of the new entity to service a larger amount of debt. The increased borrowing allows a higher interest tax shield which adds to the shareholders wealth.

Financing cost Does the enhanced debt capacity of the merged firm reduce its cost of capital? Since the probability of insolvency is reduced due to financial stability and increased protection to lenders, the merged firm should be able to borrow at a lower rate of interest. This advantage may, however, be taken off partially or completely by increase in the shareholders' risk on account of providing better protection to lenders.

Another aspect of the financing costs is issue costs. A merged firm is able to realize economies of scale in flotation and transaction costs related to an issue of capital. Issue costs are saved when the merged firm makes a larger security issue.

Increased Market Power

A merger can increase the market share of the merged firm. As discussed earlier, the increased concentration or market share

---

1. Weston, J.F. and Brigham, E.F., *Essentials of Managerial Finance*, Dryden Press, 1977, p. 515.

improves the profitability of the firm due to economies of scale. The bargaining power of the firm *vis-à-vis* labour, suppliers and buyers is also enhanced. The merged firm can also exploit technological breakthroughs against obsolescence and price wars. Thus, by limiting competition, the merged firm can earn super-normal profit and strategically employ the surplus funds to further consolidate its position and improve its market power.

We can once again refer to the acquisition of Universal Luggage by Blow Plast as an example of limiting competition to increase market power. Before the merger, the two companies were competing fiercely with each other leading to a severe price war and increased marketing costs. As a result of the merger, Blow Plast has obtained a strong hold on the market and now operates under near monopoly situation. Yet another example is the acquisition of Tomco by Hindustan Lever. Hindustan Lever at the time of merger was expected to control one-third of three million-tonne soaps and detergents markets and thus, substantially reduce the threat of competition (see Exhibit 32.1).

Merger or acquisition is not the only route to obtain market power. A firm can increase its market share through internal growth or joint ventures or strategic alliances. Also, it is not necessary that the increased market power of the merged firm will lead to efficiency and optimum allocation of resources. Market power means undue concentration that could limit the choice of buyers as well as exploit suppliers and labour.

VALUE CREATION THROUGH MERGERS AND ACQUISITIONS

A merger will make economic sense to the acquiring firm if its shareholders benefit. Merger will create an economic advantage (EA) when the combined present value of the merged firms is greater than the sum of their individual present values as separate entities. For example, if firm *P* and firm *Q* merge, and they are separately worth V_P and V_Q, respectively, and worth V_{PQ} in combination, then the economic advantage will occur if:

$$V_{PQ} > (V_P + V_Q)$$

The economic advantage is equal to:

$$EA = V_{PQ} - (V_P + V_Q)$$

Acquisition or merger involves costs. Suppose that firm *P* acquires firm *Q*. After acquisition *P* will gain the present value of *Q*, i.e., V_Q, but it will also have to pay a price (say in cash) to *Q*. Thus, the cost of merging to *P* is: Cash paid – V_Q. For *P*, the net economic advantage of merger (NEA) is positive if the economic advantage exceeds the cost of merging. Thus

$$\begin{aligned}\text{Net economic} \\ \text{advantage}\end{aligned} = \begin{aligned}\text{Economic} \\ \text{advantage}\end{aligned} - \begin{aligned}\text{Cost of} \\ \text{merger}\end{aligned}$$

$$NEA = [V_{PQ} - (V_P + V_Q)]$$
$$- (\text{cash paid} - V_Q)$$

The economic advantage, i.e., $[V_{PQ} - (V_P + V_Q)]$, represents the benefits resulting from operating efficiencies and synergy when two firms merge. If the acquiring firm pays cash equal to the value of the acquired firm, i.e., cash paid – V_Q = 0, then the entire advantage of merger will accrue to the shareholders of the

acquiring firm. In practice, the acquiring and the acquired firm may share the economic advantage between themselves.

EXHIBIT 32.1: THE TOMCO–LEVER MEGA MERGER

- On the afternoon of 9 March, 1993 Tata Oils Mills Company Limited (Tomco) informed the Bombay Stock Exchange about its intention to merge with the Hindustan Lever Ltd (Levers). The board of directors of the two companies approved the merger on 19 March, 1993. Tomco is a Rs 4,460 million turnover (1992) company and Lever a Rs 20,000 million.

- Lever would control one-third of three million-tonne soaps and detergents markets by this merger. Some competitors of Levers think that it will eliminate competition. The management of Lever, however, feels that the merger would result into a strategic fit in many areas such as brand positioning, manufacturing locations, geographical reach and distribution network. Tomco has four manufacturing plants and a large distributor network covering 2,400 stockists and nine million outlets. It is quite strong in South.

- Merger would have many benefits for Tomco which is reported to have incurred a loss of Rs 66 millions the first six months of 1992–93. It was Lever's nearest rival, but lagged much behind in the eighties. A number of attempts by management to revive Tomco through diversification did not succeed.

- The acquisition of Tomco by Levers to gain the market leadership and dominance is seen strategically important in view of the intensifying competition and the strategic alliance of competition such as the one between Godrej Soaps and the American multinational Proctor and Gamble. A number of people think that it is a land-mark merger. But to obtain the full advantages of the merger a number of issues will have to be resolved:
  - rationalisation of the duplicate brands
  - effective deployment and productivity improvement of Tomco's 5,500 employees
  - bridging the gap between two cultures.

Source: Karmali, "Tomco-Levers: A Short-term Marriage", *Business India*, March 15–28, 1993, p. 77.

Illustration 32.1: Sharing Economic Advantage

Firm *P* has a total market value of Rs 18 crore (12 lakh shares of Rs 150 market value per share). Firm *Q* has a total market value of Rs 3 crore (5 lakh of Rs 60 market value per share). Firm *P* is considering the acquisition of Firm *Q*. The value of P after merger (that is, the combined value of the merged firms) is expected to be Rs 25 crore due to the operating efficiencies. Firm *P* is required to pay Rs 4.5 crore to acquire Firm *Q*. What is the net economic advantage to Firm *P* if it acquires Firm *Q*?

The net economic advantage is the difference between the economic advantage and the cost of merger to *P*:

$$NEA = [25 - (18 + 3)] - (4.5 - 3)$$
$$= 4 - 1.5 = Rs\ 2.5\ crore$$

The economic advantage of Rs 4 crore is divided between the acquiring firm Rs 2.5 crore and the target firm, Rs 1.5 crore.

The acquiring firm can issue shares to the target firm instead of paying cash. The effect will be the same if the shares are exchanged in the ratio of cash-to-be-paid to combined value of the merged firms. In Illustration 32.1, Firm *P* may issue 4.5/25 = 0.18 or 18 per cent shares to *Q*'s shareholders in the combined firm. Then the total number of shares (*X*) in the combined firm will be as follows:

$$X = 12 + 0.18X$$
$$X - 0.18X = 12$$
$$X = 12/0.82 = 14.63 \text{ lakh shares}$$

The new share price will be: 25/0.1463 = Rs 170.9. Firm *Q* will get 2.63 lakh shares of Rs 170.9 each. Thus, the cost of acquisition to Firm *P* remains the same: (2.63 lakh × Rs 170.9) − Rs 3 crore = Rs 1.5 crore.

In practice, the number of shares to be exchanged may be based on the current market value of the acquiring firm. Thus, in Illustration 32.1, Firm *Q* may require 300,000 shares (i.e., Rs 4.5 crore/Rs 150) of the acquiring Firm *P*. Now Firm *P* after merger will have 15 lakh shares of total value of Rs 25 crore. The new share price will be: Rs 25/0.15 = Rs 166.67. The worth of shares given to the shareholders of Firm *Q* will be Rs 5 crore (i.e., Rs 166.67 × 3 lakh). The cost of merger to Firm *P* is Rs 2 crore (i.e., the value of share exchanged, Rs 5 crore less the value of the acquired firm, Rs 3 crore). Thus, the effective cost of merger may be more when issuing shares rather than paying cash finances the merger.

VALUATION UNDER MERGERS AND ACQUISITIONS: DCF APPROACH

In a merger or acquisition, the acquiring firm is buying the business of the target firm, rather than a specific asset. Thus, merger is a special type of capital budgeting decision. What is the value of the target firm to the acquiring firm? This value should include the effect of operating efficiencies and synergy. The acquiring firm should appraise merger as a capital budgeting decision, following the discounted cash flow (DCF) approach. The acquiring firm incurs a cost (in buying the business of the target firm) in the expectation of a stream of benefits (in the form of cash flows) in the future. The merger will be advantageous to the acquiring company if the present value of the target merger is greater than the cost of acquisition.

Mergers and acquisitions involve complex set of managerial problems than the purchase of an asset. Nevertheless, DCF approach is an important tool in analyzing mergers and acquisitions. In order to apply DCF technique, the following information is required:

- estimation of free cash flows over the horizon period
- estimation of the value of cash flows beyond the horizon period
- discount rate

Earnings are the basis for estimating free cash flows. As discussed in previous chapters, free cash flows include adjustments for depreciation, capital expenditure and working capital. The appropriate discount rate depends on the risk of the expected cash flows of the target company. Given the target firm's target capital structure, its WACC is used as the discount rate. The following steps are involved in the valuation of a merger (or acquisition):[1]

- Identify growth and profitability assumptions
- Estimate cash flows and terminal value
- Estimate the cost of capital
- Compute present value of cash flows
- Decide if the acquisition is attractive on the basis of present value
- Decide if the acquisition should be financed through cash or exchange of shares
- Evaluate the impact of the merger on EPS and price-earnings ratio.

Consider the case of SFC and Excel in Illustration 32.2 for an approach for the financial evaluation of a merger.

Illustration 32.2: DCF Valuation of an Acquisition

The management of Sangam Fertilisers Company (SFC) is concerned about the fluctuating sales and earnings. The variability of the company's earnings has caused its P/E ratio at about 22 to be much lower than the industry average of about 45. Tables 32.1 and 32.2 contain SFC's most recent summarised profit and loss account and balance sheet. Currently, SFC's share is selling for Rs 57.60 in the market. To boost its sales and bring stability to its earnings, SFC's management has identified Excel Chemicals Company as a possible target for acquisition. Excel is known for its quality of products and its nation-wide markets. The company has not been performing well in the recent past due to poor management (see Tables 32.3 and 32.4 for Excel's summarised financial performance). Its sales have grown at 4 per cent per year during the 2000–04 against the industry growth rate of 8 per cent per year. The current price of Excel's share is Rs 24.90.

Table 32.3: SFC: Summarised Profit and Loss Account during the Year Ending on 31 March, 2004

	(Rs in crore)
Profit and Loss Items	
Net Sales	8,205
Cost of goods sold	5,975
Depreciation	143
Selling & administrative	1,020
Total expenses	7,138
PBIT	1,067
Interest	284
PBT	783
Tax	380
PAT	403
Per Share Data	
EPS (Rs)	2.56
DPS (Rs)	1.80
Book value (Rs)	27.49
Market Value (Rs):	
High	75.05
Low	38.00
Average	56.53
P/E ratio:	
High	29.32
Low	14.84
Average	22.08

1. Rappapport, A., "Strategic Analysis for More Profitable Acquisitions, *Harvard Business Review*, July-August 1979, pp. 99–110.

The management of SFC is confident that after acquisition, they could turn around Excel. They could increase Excel's growth rate to 8 per cent within two-three years and reduce cost of goods sold to 66 per cent of sales and selling and administrative expenses to 15 per cent. SFC anticipates that to support the growth in Excel's sales, capital expenditure (CAPEX) equal to 5 per cent of sales may be needed each year. The capital will maintain its capital structure in the market value terms at the current level. The market borrowing rate is 15 per cent. The corporate tax rate is 35 per cent.

What is the value of Excel if SFC acquires it? At what price should SFC pay for each share of Excel?

Table 32.4: SFC: Summarised Balance Sheet as on 31 March, 2004

	(Rs in crore)	
Source of Funds		
Shareholders' Funds		
Paid up capital (157.50 crore shares @ Rs 10)	1,575	
Reserves and Surplus	2,755	4,330
Borrowed Funds:		
Secured	1,203	
Unsecured	967	2,170
Capital Employed		6,500
Uses of Funds		
Gross Block	6,231	
Less: Depreciation	1,626	
Net Block	4,605	
Investment	29	4,634
Current Assets	3,726	
Less: Current Liabilities	1,860	
Net Current Assets		1,866
Net Assets		6,500

Table 32.5: Excel Chemicals Company: Summarised Profit and Loss Statement and Per Share Data

					(Rs in crore)
	2000	2001	2002	2003	2004
Profit and Loss Items					
Net Sales	1,442	1,477	1,580	1,642	1,695
Cost of goods sold	995	1,042	1,125	1,165	1,195
Depreciation	37	40	45	45	40
Selling and admin. expenses	260	275	280	292	302
Total expenses	1,292	1,357	1,450	1,502	1,537
PBIT	150	120	130	140	158
Interest	19	15	23	25	30
PBT	131	105	107	115	128
Tax	45	34	35	40	45
PAT	86	71	72	75	83

(Contd.)

					(Rs in crore)
	2000	2001	2002	2003	2004
Per Share Data					
EPS (Rs)	3.44	2.84	2.88	3.00	3.32
DPS (Rs)	1.70	1.50	1.50	1.70	2.20
Book value (Rs)	23.76	25.00	26.28	27.68	29.20
Market Value (Rs):					
High	30.84	44.04	42.25	35.48	28.16
Low	22.12	25.80	24.38	16.28	13.14
Average	26.48	34.92	33.32	25.88	20.65
P/E ratio:					
High	8.97	15.51	14.67	11.83	8.48
Low	6.43	9.08	8.47	5.43	3.96
Average	7.70	12.30	11.57	8.27	6.22

Table 32.6: Excel Chemicals Company: Summarized Balance Sheet as on 31 March, 2004

Balance Sheet Items	*(Rs in crore)*	
Source of Funds		
Shareholders' Funds		
Paid up capital (25,000 shares of Rs 10 each)	250	
Reserves and Surplus	425	675
Borrowed Funds:		
Secured	200	
Unsecured	95	295
Capital Employed		970
Uses of Funds		
Gross Block	657	
Less: Depreciation	285	
Net Block		372
Investment		23
Current Assets	753	
Less: Current Liabilities	178	
Net Current Assets		575
Net Assets	970	

We can use the DCF approach to determine the value of Excel to SFC. The economic gain from the merger of Excel with SFC would basically come from the higher sales growth and improved profitability due to reduction in the cost of goods sold and the selling and administrative expenses. It is expected that if SFC acquires Excel, it would be able to improve Excel's overall management, use its strong distribution system for increasing sales, and consolidate its operations, systems and functions to facilitate operating economies and cost reduction.

Estimating Free Cash Flows

Revenues and expenses The first step in the estimation of cash flows is the projection of sales. Excel in the past has grown at an average annual rate of 4 per cent. After acquisition, sales are expected to grow at 8 per cent per year. We assume that SFC would need a few years to achieve this growth rate. Thus sales may be assumed to grow at 5 per cent in 2005, 6 per cent in 2006, 7 per cent in 2007 and thereafter, at 8 per cent per annum. The second step is to estimate expenses. Due to operating efficiency and consolidation of operations, costs are expected to decline. Excel's cost of goods sold has averaged around 70–71 per cent of sales and is now anticipated to be brought down to 66 per cent of sales. We may assume that SFC would take about two-three years to reduce the cost of goods sold. Selling and administrative expenses can also be estimated in the similar way.

Capex and depreciation Depreciation can be estimated keeping in mind the anticipated capital expenditure in each year (*viz.*, 5 per cent of sales) and average annual depreciation rate (*viz.*, about 11 per cent for Excel during the past five years). We have assumed a diminishing balance method for depreciation.[1] Thus, depreciation for 2005 and 2006 would be as follows:

$$DEP_{05} = 0.11(372 + CAPEX_{04})$$
$$= 0.11(372 + 0.05 \times 1780)$$
$$= 0.11(372 + 89) = 0.11(461) = 51$$
$$DEP_{06} = 0.11(461 - 50 + 0.05 \times 1887)$$
$$= 0.11(411 + 94) = 56$$

CAPEX and depreciation for other years can be similarly calculated as shown in Table 32.5.

Working capital changes In the calculation of the cash flows, we should also account for increase in net working capital (NWC) due to expansion of sales. Excel's net working capital to sales ratio in 2004 is 34 per cent. If assume that working capital is managed as in the past, we can

expect NWC to sales ratio to remain as 34 per cent. Note that since we shall be calculating the value of Excel (representing the value of both shareholders and lenders), using the weighed cost of capital as the discount rate, interest charges would not be subtracted in calculating free flows. Excel has been paying an average tax of 34 per cent. This might be due to tax incentives available to the company. The company will pay tax at current marginal tax rate of 35 per cent. Table 32.7 provides the estimation of net cash flows.

Estimating the Cost of Capital

Since we are determining Excel's value, the discount rate should be Excel's average cost of capital. In the year 2004, the outstanding debt of the company is Rs 295 crore and interest paid is Rs 30 crore. Thus, the interest rate works out to 10.2 per cent. The current rate of borrowing is 15 per cent. On the after-tax basis, the cost of debt would be: 0.15 (1 − 0.35) = 0.975 or 9.75 per cent.

We can calculate the company's cost of equity using the dividend–growth model. Excel's current share price is Rs 24.90, and it paid a dividend of Rs 2.20 in 2004. Thus, its dividend yield is: 2.20/24.90 = 0.088 or 8.8 per cent. The company has been paying about 55 per cent of its earnings as dividend and retaining 45 per cent. The average return (over last five years) on equity has been about 12 per cent. Thus, the company's growth rate is: 0.45 × 0.12 = 0.054 or 5.4 per cent. Excel's

Table 32.7: Excel Chemicals Company

Estimation of Cash Flows

(Rs in crore)

| Year | Actual | Estimates | | | | | | | | | |
	2004	2005	2006	2007	2008	2009	2010	2011	2012	2013	2014
Net sales	1695	1780	1887	2019	2180	2354	2543	2746	2966	3203	3460
Cost of goods sold	1195	1246	1302	1360	1439	1554	1678	1813	1958	2114	2283
S&A expenses	302	302	302	302	327	353	381	412	445	480	519
Depreciation	40	51	56	61	66	72	78	84	91	99	107
Total expenses	1537	1599	1660	1723	1832	1979	2137	2309	2494	2693	2909
PBIT	158	181	227	296	348	376	405	438	472	510	550
Tax @ 35%	55	63	79	104	122	132	142	153	165	178	193
NOPAT	103	118	148	192	226	244	264	284	307	331	358
Plus: Depreciation	40	51	56	61	66	72	78	84	91	99	107
Funds from operations	143	168	203	253	292	316	341	369	398	430	465
Less: Increase NWC*		30	36	45	55	59	64	69	75	81	87
Cash from operations		138	167	208	237	257	277	299	324	350	378
Less: Capex		89	94	101	109	118	127	137	148	160	173
Free cash flows		49	72	107	128	139	150	162	175	189	205
Add: Salvage value											2369
NCF		49	72	107	128	139	150	162	175	189	2574
PVF at 13%		.885	.783	.693	.613	.543	.480	.425	.376	.333	.295
Present value	1355	43	56	74	78	75	72	69	66	63	759
* NWC (34% of sales)	575	605	641	686	741	801	865	934	1008	1089	.1176

---

1. It is assumed that 11 per cent represent the average of the WDV depreciation rates for the various blocks of assets, as prescribed under the Indian tax rules.

cost of equity is: $0.088 + 0.054 = 0.142$ or 14.20 per cent. The company has outstanding debt of Rs 295 crore and the market value of equity is Rs 622.50 crore (25 crore × Rs 24.90). Thus debt ratio is: $295/622.50 = 0.32$ or 32 per cent. Given its capital structure in the year 2004, its weighted average cost of capital is about 13 per cent (see Table 32.8).

Table 32.8: Excel's Weighted Average Cost of Capital

	Amount (Rs in crore)	Weighted	Cost	Weight Cost
Equity	622.50	0.68	0.1420	0.097
Debt	295.00	0.32	0.0975	0.031
	917.50	1.000		0.128

Terminal Value

Terminal value is the value of cash flows after the horizon period. It is difficult to estimate the terminal value of the firm. One approach is to capitalise the net operating profit after tax (NOPAT) at the end of the *horizon period* at WACC. NOPAT at the end of horizon period (tenth year) is Rs 358 crore and the discount rate is 13 per cent. Thus, the salvage value is:

$$\text{Salvage value} = \frac{\text{NOPAT}}{\text{Cost of capital}} = \frac{358}{0.13} = \text{Rs } 2,754$$

The conceptually more appropriate approach is to consider net cash flows (not earnings) for calculating the salvage value. We may take a conservative approach and assume that after horizon period, cash flows will not grow. Thus the terminal value will be as follows:

$$\text{Salvage value} = \frac{\text{NCF}}{\text{Cost of capital}} = \frac{205}{0.13} = \text{Rs } 1,577$$

The alternative assumption is that net cash flows would grow at a constant normal rate of 4 per cent. Then, the salvage value can be calculated using a method similar to the dividend-growth model as follows:

$$SV_n = \frac{\text{NCF}_n(1+g)}{k-g}$$
$$= \frac{205(1.04)}{0.13-0.04} = \frac{213.20}{0.09} \text{ Rs } 2,369$$

We have used this value, (Rs 2,369 crore) in our calculations in Table 32.7.

Value of Excel's Shares

We can discount the net cash flows in Table 32.5 to calculate Excel's value. It is Rs 1,300 crore. Since EXCEL has Rs 295 crore outstanding debt in the year 2004, the value of its shares is:

	(Rs in crore)
Excel's Value	1355
Less: Debt	295
Value of Excel's Shares	1060

$$\text{Value per share} = \frac{1060}{25} = \text{Rs } 42.40$$

The maximum price per share that SFC may be prepared to pay for Excel's share is Rs 42.40. The current market price of the share is Rs 24.90. Thus, SFC may have to pay a premium of about 70 per cent over the current market price. How should SFC finance acquisition of Excel? Should it exchange shares or pay in cash?

FINANCING A MERGER

Cash or exchange of shares or a combination of cash, shares and debt can finance a merger or an acquisition. The means of financing may change the debt-equity mix of the combined or the acquiring firm after the merger. When a large merger takes place, the desired capital structure is difficult to be maintained, and it makes the calculation of the cost of capital a formidable task. Thus, the choice of the means of financing a merger may be influenced by its impact on the acquiring firm's capital structure. The other important factors are the financial condition and liquidity position of the acquiring firm, the capital market conditions, the availability of long-term debt etc.

Cash Offer

A cash offer is a straightforward means of financing a merger. It does not cause any dilution in the earnings per share and the ownership of the existing shareholders of the acquiring company. It is also unlikely to cause wide fluctuations in the share prices of the merging companies. The shareholders of the target company get cash for selling their shares to the acquiring company. This may involve tax liability for them.

Let us assume that SFC decided to offer a price of Rs 42.40 per share to acquire Excel's shares. If SFC wants to pay cash for the shares, it would need Rs 1,060 crore in cash. It can borrow funds as well as use its tradable (temporary) investment and surplus cash for acquiring Excel. SFC's current debt is Rs 2,170 crore, which is 50 per cent of its book value equity. After merger, the combined firm's debt would be Rs 2,465 crore (Rs 2,170 crore of SFC and Rs 295 crore of Excel). The debt capacity of the combined firm would depend on its target debt-equity ratio. Assuming that it is 1:1, then it can have a total debt of Rs 4,330 crore (i.e., equal to the combined firm's equity, which is, pre-merger equity of SFC). Thus, unutilised debt capacity is Rs 1,865, crore (i.e., Rs 4,330 crore minus the combined debt of SFC and Excel, Rs 2,465 crore). Further, both companies have marketable investments of Rs 52 crore, which may also be available for acquisition. Given SFC has unutilised debt capacity (Rs 1,865 crore), it can borrow Rs 1,060 crore to acquire Excel.

Share Exchange

A share exchange offer will result into the sharing of ownership of the acquiring company between its existing shareholders and new shareholders (that is, shareholders of the acquired company). The earnings and benefits would also be shared between these two groups of shareholders. The precise extent of net benefits that accrue to each group depends on the **exchange ratio** in terms of the market prices of the shares of the acquiring and the acquired companies. In an exchange of shares, the receiving shareholders would not pay any ordinary income tax immediately. They would pay capital gains tax when they sell their shares after holding them for the required period.

SFC, instead of paying cash, could acquire Excel through the exchange of shares. For simplicity, let us assume that SFC's share price is fairly valued in the market. If the company feels that its shares are either under-valued or over-valued in the market, it can follow a similar procedure as in the case of Excel to calculate the value of its shares. SFC's current price per share is Rs 57.80 and it has 157.50 crore outstanding shares. At its current share price, the company must exchange: Rs 1,060 crore/ Rs 57.80 = 18.34 crore shares to pay Rs 1,060 crore to Excel. After acquisition, SFC would have 175.84 crore (157.50 crore + 18.34 crore) shares outstanding. Thus, in the combined firm, Excel's shareholders would hold about 10.4 per cent of shares (i.e., 18.34/175.84). Excel's shares are valued at Rs 1,060 crore and the value of SFC's shares at the current market price is Rs 9,104 crore (157.5 crore × Rs 57.80). Thus the post-merger value of the combined firm is Rs 10,164 crore, and per share value is: Rs 10,164/175.84 = Rs 57.80. Thus there is no loss, no gain to SFC's shareholders.

Table 32.8: Impact of SFC and Excel Merger on EPS

SFC's (the acquiring firm) PAT before merger, PAT$_a$ (Rs in crore)	403.00
Excel's (the acquired firm) PAT if merged with SFC, PAT$_b$ (Rs in crore)	83.00
PAT of the combined firms after merger, PAT$_a$ + PAT$_b$ = PAT$_c$ (Rs in crore)	486.00
SFC's EPS before merger (EPS$_a$) (Rs)	2.56
Maximum number of SFC's shares maintaining EPS of Rs 2.56: (486/2.56) (crore)	189.84
SFC's (the acquiring firm) outstanding shares before merger (N_a) (crore)	157.50
Maximum number of shares to be exchanged without diluting EPS: (189.84–157.50) (crore)	32.34

SFC would be offering 18.34 crore shares for 25 crore outstanding shares of Excel, which means 0.734 shares of SFC for one share of Excel or a **swap ratio** of 0.734:1. The book value of SFC's share in 2004 is Rs 27.49 while that of Excel is Rs 29.20. Thus, SFC alternatively could offer 0.94 shares for each outstanding share of Excel without diluting its present book value. Since it is exchanging only 0.734 shares, its book value of equity should increase.

Impact on Earnings per Share Would SFC's EPS be diluted if it exchanged 18.34 crore shares to Excel? Or, what is the maximum number of shares, which SFC could exchange without diluting its EPS? Let us assume the earnings of both firms at 2004 level. We can calculate the maximum number of SFC's shares to be exchanged for Excel's shares without diluting the former company's EPS after merger as shown in Table 32.8.

We can also directly calculate the maximum number of shares as follows:

Maximum number of share to be exchanged without EPS dilutio

$$= \frac{\text{Acquiring firm's post-merger earnings}}{\text{Acquiring firm's pre-merger EPS}} - \text{Acquiring firm's pre-merger shares}$$

$$= \frac{\text{PAT}_a + \text{PAT}_b}{\text{EPS}_a} - N_a$$

$$= \frac{403 + 83}{2.56} - 157.5 = 32.34 \text{ crore}$$

Thus SFC (the acquiring firm) could exchange 1.294 (i.e., 32.34/25) of its shares for one share of Excel (the acquired firm) without diluting its EPS after merger. Since it is exchanging only 0.734 shares, its EPS after merger would be as shown below:

SFC's PAT after merger (Rs 403 crore + Rs 83 crore)	486.00
Number of shares after merger (157.50 + 18.34)	175.84
SFC's EPS after merger: 486/175.84	2.76

Table 32.9 summarizes the effect of the merger of Excel with SFC on EPS, market value and price-earning ratio with an exchange ratio of 0.734.

Table 32.9: Merger of Excel with SFC: Impact on EPS, Book Value, Market Value and P/E Ratio

	SFC (before merger)	Excel	SFC (after merger)
1. Profit after tax (Rs in crore)	403.00	83.00	486.00
2. Number of shares (crore)	157.50	25.00	175.84
3. EPS (Rs)	2.56	3.32	2.76
4. Market value per share (Rs)	57.80	24.90	57.80
5. Price-earnings ratio (times)	22.60	7.50	20.94
6. Total market capitalisation (Rs in crore)	9,104	1,060	10,164

Notes:

(a) In line 2 SFC's number of shares after merger would be: 157.5 + (0.734 × 25) = 175.84 crore.

(b) In line 6, the value of Excel's share is based on its evaluation by SFC reflecting future growth and cost savings. At the current market value of Rs 24.90, the market capitalisation in Rs 622.50 crore.

(c) Market value per share after merger would be: Rs 10,164/175.84 = Rs 57.80.

You may observe that for Excel's (the acquired firm) pre-merger EPS of Rs 3.32, the price paid is Rs 42.40. Thus, the price-earnings ratio *paid* to Excel is: Rs 42.40/3.32 = 12.2 times. Since the price-earnings ratio exchanged is less than SFC's (the acquiring firm) price-earnings ratio of 22.6, SFC's EPS after merger increases. However, in terms of value, there is no change. In fact, the post merger price-earnings ratio falls to: Rs 57.8/ Rs 2.76 = 20.94 times.

We can notice from Table 32.9 that after merger the market value per share is Rs 57.80 and total capitalisation increases to Rs 10,164 crore, more by Rs 437.50 crore of the sum of the capitalization of individuals firms (Rs 57.80 × 157.50 crore plus Rs 24.90 × 25 crore) = Rs 9,104 crore + Rs 622.50 crore = Rs 9,726.50 crore. This increased wealth, however, does not benefit the shareholders of SFC since it is entirely transferred to Excel's shareholders as shown below:

Total capitalisation of Excel's shareholders after merger (Rs in crore)	1,060.00
Total capitalisation of Excel's shareholders before merger (Rs in crore)	622.50
Net gain (Rs in crore)	437.50

Would the shareholders of SFC gain if there was no economic gain from the merger and the exchange ratio was in terms of the current market price of the two companies' shares? The market price **share exchange ratio** (SER) would be:

$$SER = \frac{\text{Share price of acquired firm}}{\text{Share price of the acquiring firm}} = \frac{P_b}{P_a} = \frac{24.90}{57.80} = 0.431 \quad (2)$$

Bootstrapping: SFC would issue 10.77 (i.e., 25 × 0.431) shares to Excel in terms of current prices SER. Does the acquiring firm benefit if shares are exchanged in proportion of the current share prices? Let us assume that there are no benefits of acquisition. Table 32.10 summaries the impact of the share exchange in terms of the current market prices (without any gain from merger/acquisition). SER at current share prices implies that the acquiring company (SFC) pays no premium to the acquired company (Excel).

Table 32.10: Impact of the Acquisition of Excel by SFC: SER 0.431

	SFC (before merger)	*Excel*	*SFC (after merger)*
1. Profit after tax (Rs in crore)	403.00	83.00	486.00
2. Number of shares (crore)	157.50	25.00	168.30
3. EPS (Rs)	2.56	3.32	2.89
4. Market value per share (Rs)	57.80	24.90	57.80
5. Price-earnings ratio (times)	22.60	7.50	20.00
6. Total market capitalisation (Rs in crore)	9,104.00	622.50	9,726.50

Notes:

(*a*) In line 2 SFC's number of shares after merger would be: 157.50 + (0.431 × 25) = 168.30 crore.

(*b*) In line 6, the value of Excel's share is taken as the current market price.

(*c*) Market value per share after merger would be: Rs 9,726.50/168.30 = Rs 57.80.

There is no gain from the merger and the market value after acquisition of Excel remains the same. However, SFC is able to increase its EPS from Rs 2.56 to Rs 2.89 after acquisition. The reason is that its profit after tax increases by 20.6 per cent after acquisition while the number of shares increases by 6.9 per cent only. The price-earnings ratio declines to 20 (P/E = Rs 57.8/2.89 = 20) as there is no change in the market value per share and EPS increases after merger. This is known as the **bootstrapping phenomenon**, and it creates an illusion of benefits from the merger.[1] Once again, it may be noticed that the price-earnings

ratio exchanged by the acquiring firm (SFC), Rs 24.9/Rs 3.32 = 7.50 is less than its price-earnings ratio, and this resulted in higher EPS for the acquiring firm.

In case of Excel's acquisition by SFC, there is expected to be increase in Excel's capitalisation due to improvement in profit margin and operating efficiencies. We have seen earlier that if the exchange ratio is 0.734, the entire gain is transferred to the shareholders of Excel. Possibly, Excel's shares would remain 'under valued', if SFC does not acquire it. Can a negotiation take place so that the shareholders of SFC also gain from the increased wealth from merger? Let us assume economic gain (Rs 1,060 – Rs 622.5 = Rs 437.5 crore) and SER in terms of the current market value of two companies, i.e., 0.431. The effect is shown in Table 32.11.

Table 32.11: Impact of the Acquisition of Excel by SFC: SER 0.431

	SFC (before merger)	*Excel*	*SFC (after merger)*
1. Profit after tax (Rs in crore)	403.00	83.00	486.00
2. Number of shares (crore)	157.50	25.00	168.30
3. EPS (Rs)	2.56	3.32	2.89
4. Market value per share (Rs)	57.80	24.90	60.39
5. Price-earnings ratio (times)	22.50	7.50	21.40
6. Total market capitalisation (Rs in crore)	9,104.00	1,060.00	10,164.00

Notes:

(*a*) In line 2, SFC's number of shares after merger would be: 157.50 + (0.431 × 25) = 168.30 crore.

(*b*) In line 6, the value of Excel's share is taken as Rs 1,060 crore, which is based on its evaluation by SFC reflecting future growth and cost savings.

(*c*) Market value per share after merger would be: Rs 10,164/168.30 = Rs 60.39.

We may observe from Table 32.12 that the market value of SFC's share is expected to be higher (Rs 60.39) after merger as compared to the before-merger value (Rs 57.80). Shareholders of both Excel and SFC, as shown below, share the net increase in wealth:

(Rs in crore)

Gain to SFC's (the acquiring firm) shareholders:

$$(P_{ab} - P_a)N_a = (60.39 - 57.80) \times 157.50 \qquad 409.00$$

Gain to Excel's (the acquired firm shareholders):

$$P_{ab} \times (SER) N_b - P_a \times N_b = 60.39 \times 10.78 - 24.90 \times 25 \qquad 28.50$$

Total gain:

$$P_{ab} \times (N_a + (SER) N_b) - (P_a \times N_a + P_b \times N_b)$$
$$= 60.39 (157.5 + 0.431 \times 25) - (57.8 \times 157.5 + 24.9 \times 25) \qquad 437.50$$

Thus, the distribution of the merger gain between the shareholders of the acquiring and target companies can be calculated as follows:

---

1. Myers, S.C., A Framework for Evaluating Mergers, *Modern Developments in Financial Management*, S.C. Myers (ed.), Praeger, 1976. Also see Brealey and Myers, *op. cit.*, p. 825.

Merger gain = Gain to the acquiring company's
                   shareholders + Gain to the acquired
                   company's shareholders

$$= (P_{ab} - P_a) N_a + P_{ab} (N_a + \text{SER} (N_b)) - P_b \times N_b \quad (3)$$

where P_{ab} is the price per share after merger, P_a before-merger share price of the acquiring company, P_b before-merger share price of the target company, N_a before-merger number of shares of the acquiring company, N_b before-merger number of shares of the target company and SER is the share exchange ratio. Using Equation (3), the merger gain for the shareholders of SFC and Excel in Illustration 32.2 can be computed as follows:

$$1,060 - 622.50 = (60.4 - 57.8)\ 157.5$$
$$+ [60.4 \times (24.9/57.8)\ (25) - 24.9 \times 25]$$
$$437.50 = 2.60 \times 157.5 + [60.4 \times (0.431)\ 25 - 24.9 \times 25]$$
$$= 409.0 + 28.5 = \text{Rs } 437.50 \text{ crore}$$

We may observe that the market value per share of the combined firm (P_{ab}) is higher than that of the acquiring or the acquired firm because of the operating economies and improved margin in the operation of the acquired firm. Thus the total gain is also equal to the fair value of Excel's shares (Rs 1,060 crore) minus the current market capitalization (Rs 622.5), i.e., Rs 437.50.

MERGER NEGOTIATIONS: SIGNIFICANCE OF P/E RATIO AND EPS ANALYSIS

In practice, investors attach a lot of importance to the earnings per share (EPS) and the price-earnings (P/E) ratio. The product of EPS and P/E ratio is the market price per share. In an efficient capital market, the market price of a share should be equal to the value arrived by the DCF technique. In reality, a number of factors may cause a divergence between these two values. Thus, in addition to the market price and the discount value of shares, the mergers and acquisitions decisions are also evaluated in terms of EPS, P/E ratio, book value etc. We have already discussed the impact of merger on these variables in the case of the merger of SFC and Excel (Illustration 32.2). In this section, we extend the discussion in a more formal manner in the context of the negotiations in terms of exchange of shares.

Share Exchange Ratio

In practice, in a number of deals, the current market values of the acquiring and the acquired firms are taken as the basis for exchange of shares. As discussed earlier, the share exchange ratio (SER) would be as follows:

$$\text{Share exchange ratio} = \frac{\text{Share price of the acquired firm}}{\text{Share price of the acquiring firm}}$$
$$= \frac{P_b}{P_a}$$

The exchange ratio in terms of the market value of shares will keep the position of the shareholders in value terms unchanged after the merger since their proportionate wealth would remain at the pre-merger level. There is no incentive for

the shareholders of the acquired firm, and they would require a premium to be paid by the acquiring company. Could the acquiring company pay a premium and be better off in terms of the additional value of its shareholders? In the absence of net economic gain, the shareholders of the acquiring company would become worse-off unless the price-earnings ratio of the acquiring company remains the same as before the merger. For the shareholders of the acquiring firm to be better-off after the merger without any net economic gain either the price-earnings ratio will have to increase sufficiently higher or the share exchange ratio is low, the price-earnings ratio remaining the same. Let us consider an example.

Suppose Shyama Enterprise is considering the acquisition of Rama Enterprise. The following are the financial data of two companies:

	Shyama Enterprise	*Rama Enterprise*
Profit after tax (Rs)	40,000	8,000
Number of shares	10,000	4,000
EPS (Rs)	4	2
Market value per share (Rs)	60	15
Price earnings ratio (times)	15	7.5
Total market capitalisation (Rs)	600,000	60,000

Shyama Enterprise is thinking of acquiring Rama Enterprises through exchange of shares in proportion of the market value per share. If the price-earnings ratio is expected to be (a) pre-merger P/E ratio of Rama, i.e., 7.5, (b) pre-merger P/E ratio of Shyama, i.e., 15, (c) weighted average of pre-merger P/E ratio of Shyama and Rama, i.e., 13.75, what would be the impact on the wealth of shareholders after merger?

Since the basis of the exchange of shares is the market value per share of the acquiring (Shyama Enterprise) and the acquired (Rama Enterprise) firms, then Shyama would offer 0.25 of its shares to the shareholders of Rama:

$$\text{SER} = \frac{P_b}{P_a} = \frac{15}{60} = 0.25$$

In terms of the market value per share of the combined firm after the merger, the position of Rama's shareholders would remain the same; that is, their per-share value would be: Rs 60 × 0.25 = Rs 15. The total number of shares offered by Shyama (the acquiring firm) to Rama's (the acquired firm) shareholders would be:

No. of shares exchanged = SER × Pre-merger number of
                                          shares of the acquired firm
$$= (P_b / P_a)N_b = 0.25 \times 4,000$$
$$= 1,000$$

The total number of shares after the merger would be: N_a + (SER) N_b = 10,000 + 1,000 = 11,000. The combined earnings (PAT$_c$) after the merger would be: Rs 40,000 + Rs 8,000 = Rs 48,000 and EPS after the merger would be:

Post-merger combined EPS

$$= \frac{\text{Post-merger combined PAT}}{\text{Post-merger combined shares}}$$

$$= \frac{\text{PAT}_a + \text{PAT}_b}{N_a + (\text{SER})N_b} \qquad (4)$$

$$= \frac{40,000 + 8,000}{10,000 + (0.25)\,4,000}$$

$$= \frac{48,000}{11,000} = \text{Rs } 4.36$$

The earnings per share of Shyama (the acquiring firm) increased from Rs 4 to Rs 4.36, but for Rama's (the acquired firm) shareholders, it declined from Rs 2 to Rs 1.09; that is, Rs 4.36 × 0.25 = Rs 1.09.

Given the earnings per share after the merger, the post-merger market value per share would depend on the price-earnings ratio of the combined firm. How would P/E ratio affect the wealth of shareholders of the individual companies after the merger? Table 32.12 shows the impact.

Table 32.12: Rama and Shyama Enterprises: P/E Ratio and Effect on Value

P/E Ratio	EPS After Merger	Combined Firm's Market Value After Merger	Market value: Shyama		Market value: Rama	
			Before merger	After merger	Before merger	After merger
7.50	4.36	32.70	60.00	32.70	15.00	8.18
15.00	4.36	65.40	60.00	65.40	15.00	16.35
13.75	4.36	60.00	60.00	60.00	15.00	15.00

Notes:

(a) Shyama's share price after merger is equal to its EPS of Rs 4.36 times the P/E ratio.

(b) Rama's share price after merger is equal to its share of EPS, Rs 1.09 times P/E ratio.

Note that Rama's shareholders' value in terms of their shareholding in Shyama is: MV after merger × 0.25. We can observe from Table 32.12 that the shareholders of both the acquiring and the acquired firms neither gain nor lose in value terms if post-merger P/E ratio is merely a weighted average of pre-merger P/E ratios of the individual firms. The post-merger weighted P/E ratio is calculated as follows:

Post-merger weighted P/E ratio:

(Pre-merger P/E ratio of the acquiring firm) × (Acquiring firm's pre-merger earnings × Post-merger combined earnings) + (Pre-merger P/E ratio of the acquired firm) × (Acquired firm's pre-merger earnings × Post-merger combined earnings)

$$\text{P/E}_w = (\text{P/E}_a)(\text{PAT}_a / \text{PAT}_c) + (\text{P/E}_b) \times (\text{PAT}_b / \text{PAT}_c) \qquad (5)$$

---

1. Van Horne, *op cit.*, p. 615.

Using Equation (5) in our example, we obtain

$$= (15)\,(40,000/48,000) + (7.5)\,(8,000/48,000)$$
$$= 12.5 + 1.25 = 13.75$$

The acquiring company would lose in value if post-merger P/E ratio is less than the weighted P/E ratio. Any P/E ratio above the weighted P/E ratio would benefit both the acquiring as well as the acquired firms in value terms. An acquiring firm would always be able to improve its earnings per share after the merger whenever it acquires a company with a P/E ratio lower than its own P/E ratio. The higher EPS need not necessarily increase the share price. It is the quality of EPS rather than the quantity that would influence the price.

An acquiring firm would lose in value if its post-merger P/E ratio is less than the weighted P/E ratio. Shyama Enterprise would lose Rs 27.30 value per share if P/E ratio after merger was 7.5 Any P/E ratio above the weighted P/E ratio would benefit both the acquiring as well as the acquired firm in value terms. When the post-merger P/E ratio is 15, Shyama gains Rs 5.40 value per share and Rama Rs 1.35.

Why does Shyama Enterprise's EPS increase after merger? It increases because it has a current P/E ratio of 15, and it is required to exchange a lower P/E ratio:

$$\text{P/E exchanged} = \frac{\text{SER} \times P_a}{\text{EPS}_b} = \frac{0.25 \times 60}{2} = 7.5 \qquad (6)$$

Shyama Enterprise's EPS after merger would be exactly equal to its pre-merger EPS if P/E ratio paid is equal to its pre-merger P/E ratio of 15. In that case, given Rama's EPS of Rs 2, the price paid would be Rs 30 or a share exchange ratio of 0.5. Thus, Shyama Enterprise would issue 0.5 × 4,000 = 2,000 shares to Rama Enterprise. The acquiring firm's EPS after merger would be: Rs 48,000/12,000 = Rs 4. It may be noticed that at this P/E ratio, Shyama's shareholders would have the same EPS as before the merger: 0.5 × Rs 4 = Rs 2. It can be shown that if the acquiring firm takes over another firm by exchanging a P/E ratio higher than its P/E ratio, its EPS will fall and that of the acquired firm would increase after the merger.[1]

Let us assume in our illustration that Shyama exchanges a P/E ratio of 22.5 to acquire Rama. This implies a price of Rs 45 per share and a share exchange ratio of 0.75. The earnings per share after acquisition would be as follows:

$$\text{Post-merger EPS} = \frac{40,000 + 8,000}{10,000 + 0.75 \times 4,000} = \frac{48,000}{13,000} = \text{Rs } 3.69$$

Thus, the acquiring firm's EPS falls (from Rs 4 to Rs 3.69) and the acquired firm's EPS increases (from Rs 2 to Rs 3.69 × 0.75 = Rs 2.77).

Earnings Growth

At share exchange ratio, based on the current market values, Shyama's (the acquiring firm) EPS falls. Should it acquire Rama? It can acquire Rama if its (Rama's) future earnings are expected to grow at a higher rate. After acquisition, Shyama's EPS would increase faster than before since the future growth rate would be the weighted average of the growth rates of the merging firms.

Let us assume that Shyama's EPS is expected to grow at 6 per cent and Rama's at 15 per cent. The weighted EPS growth for Shyama would be:

$$g_w = 0.06 \times \frac{40,000}{48,000} + 0.15 \times \frac{8,000}{48,000} = 0.075 \text{ or } 7.5 \text{ per cent}$$

Thus, the formula for weighted growth in EPS can be expressed as follows:

Weighted Growth in EPS = Acquiring firm's growth × (Acquiring firm's pre-merger PAT/combined firm's PAT) + Acquired firm's growth × (Acquired firm's pre-merger PAT/combined firm's PAT)

$$g_w = g_a \times \frac{PAT_a}{PAT_c} + g_b \times \frac{PAT_b}{PAT_c} \qquad (7)$$

where g_w is the weighted average growth rate after the merger, g_a and EPS_a are growth rate and earnings per share respectively of the acquiring firm before the merger, g_b and EPS_b are growth rate and the earnings per share of the acquired firm before the merger, EPS_c earnings per share of the combined firm after merger.

Table 32.13 shows the future EPS of Shyama with and without merger.

We can see from Table 32.13 and Figure 32.1 that without merger, Shyama's current EPS of Rs 4.00 would grow at 6 per cent per year and with merger the diluted EPS of Rs 3.69 would grow at 7.5 per cent (the weighted average growth rate). Shyama's EPS with merger would remain depressed until five years after merger. Its EPS, however, would start growing faster after five years.

Table 32.13: Shyama's EPS with and without Merger (Rs)

Year	Without Merger (g = 6%)	With Merger (g = 7.5%)
0	4.00	3.69
1	4.24	3.97
2	4.49	4.26
3	4.76	4.58
4	5.05	4.93
5	5.35	5.30
6	5.67	5.69
7	6.01	6.12
8	6.38	6.58
9	6.76	7.07
10	7.16	7.60
15	9.59	10.92
20	12.83	15.67

In fact, Shyama has a higher P/E ratio that is an indication of the investors' expectation of high future growth. Therefore, it is more likely that it would grow rapidly. Under such situation, it would not pay any premium to Rama. At a share exchange ratio of 0.25, Shyama's EPS after merger would be Rs 4.36. Assume that its earnings are expected to grow at 24 per cent and Rama's at 15

per cent. How would Shyama's EPS behave with or without merger? This is shown in Table 32.14 and Figure 32.2. It may be observed that merger would help the acquiring company to grow rapidly (than without merger) for seven years after merger. After seven years, the position would reverse. Thus, the company would either acquire other companies with lower P/E ratios, or improve its operating efficiency and continue growing.

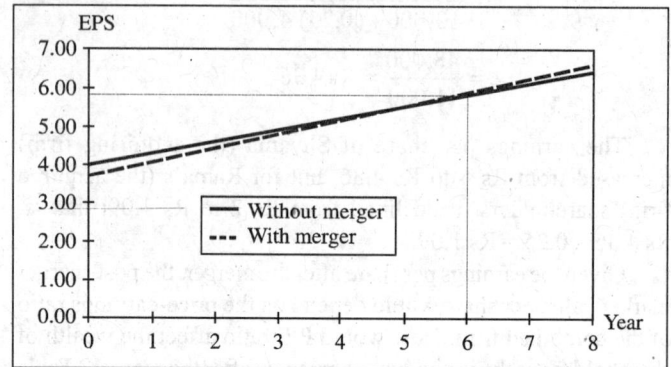

Figure 32.1: EPS with and without merger

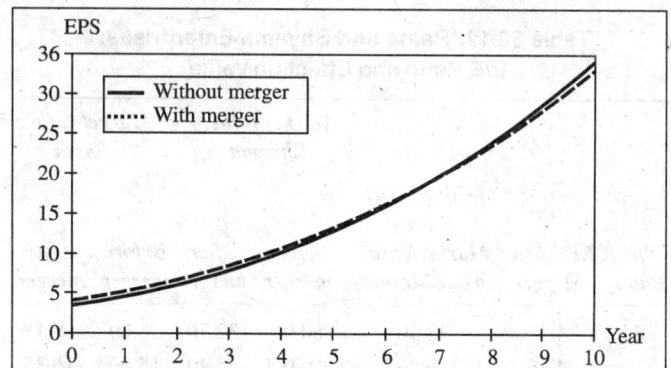

Figure 32.2: EPS with and without merger

Table 32.14: Shyama's EPS with and without Merger

Year	Without merger (g = 24%)	With merger (g = 22.5%)
0	4.00	4.36
1	4.96	5.34
2	6.15	6.54
3	7.63	8.01
4	9.46	9.82
5	11.73	12.03
6	14.54	14.73
7	18.03	18.05
8	22.36	22.11
9	27.72	27.08
10	34.37	33.18
15	100.78	91.52
20	295.46	252.47

It should be obvious from calculation in Tables 32.13 and 32.14 as well as from Figures 32.1 and 32.2 that the important factors influencing the earnings growth of the acquiring firm in future are:[1]

---

1. Weston, J.F. and Copeland, T.E., *Managerial Finance*, Dryden, 1986, p. 918.

- The price-earnings ratios of the acquiring and the acquired companies
- The ratio of share exchanged by the acquiring company for one share of the acquired company
- The pre-merger earnings growth rates of acquiring and the acquired companies
- The level of profit after-tax of the merging companies
- The weighted average of the earnings growth rates of the merging companies.

TENDER OFFER AND HOSTILE TAKEOVER

A **tender offer** is a formal offer to purchase a given number of a company's shares at a specific price. The acquiring company asks the shareholders of the target company to "tender" their shares in exchange for a specific price. The price is generally quoted at a premium in order to induce the shareholders to tender their shares. Tender offer can be used in two situations.[1] First, the acquiring company may directly approach the target company for its takeover. If the target company does not agree, then the acquiring company may directly approach the shareholders by means of a tender offer. Second, the tender offer may be used without any negotiations, and it may be tantamount to a **hostile takeover**. The shareholders are generally approached through announcement in the financial press or through direct communication individually. They may or may not react to a tender offer. Their reaction exclusively depends upon their attitude and sentiment and the difference between the market price and the offered price. The tender offer may or may not be acceptable to the management of the target company. In the USA, the tender offers have been used for a number of years. In India, one may see only one or two instances of tender offer in the recent years.

In September 1989, Tata Tea Ltd. (TTL), the largest integrated tea company in India, made an open offer for controlling interest to the shareholders of the Consolidated Coffee Ltd. (CCL). TTL's Chairman, Darbari Seth, offered one share in TTL and Rs 100 in cash (which is equivalent of Rs 140) for a CCL share that was then quoting at Rs 88 on the Madras Stock Exchange. TTL's decision is not only novel in the Indian corporate sector but also a trendsetter. TTL had notified in the financial press about its intention to buyout some tea estates and solicited offers from the shareholders concerned.

The management of the target company generally do not approve of tender offers. The major reason is the fear of being replaced. The acquiring company's plans may not be compatible with the best interests of the shareholders of the target company.

The management of the target company can try to convince its shareholders that they should not tender their shares since the offer value is not enough in the light of the real value of shares, i.e., the offer is too low comparative to its real value. The management may use techniques to dissuade its shareholders from accepting tender offer. For example, it may lure them by announcing higher dividends. If this helps to raise the share price due to psychological impact or information content, then the shareholders may not consider the offer price tempting enough. The company may issue bonus shares and/or rights shares and make it difficult for the acquirer to acquire controlling shares.

The target company may also launch a counter-publicity programme by informing that the tender is not in the interest of the shareholders. If the shareholders are convinced, then the tender offer may fail. The target company can follow delay tactics and try to get help from the regulatory authorities such as the Securities and Exchange Board of India (SEBI), or the Stock Exchanges of India.

Defensive Tactics

A target company in practice adopts a number of tactics to defend itself from hostile takeover through a tender offer. These tactics include a divestiture or spin-off, poison pill, greenmail, white knight, crown jewels, golden parachutes, etc.[2]

- *Divestiture* In a *divestiture* the target company divests or spins off some of its businesses in the form of an independent, subsidiary company. Thus, it reduces the attractiveness of the existing business to the acquirer.
- *Crown jewels* When a target company uses the tactic of divestiture it is said to sell the *crown jewels*. In some countries such as the UK, such tactic is not allowed once the deal becomes known and is unavoidable.
- *Poison pill* An acquiring company itself could become a target when it is bidding for another company. The tactics used by the acquiring company to make itself unattractive to a potential bidder is called *poison pills*. For example, the acquiring company may issue substantial amount of convertible debentures to its existing shareholders to be converted at a future date when it faces a takeover threat. The task of the bidder would become difficult since the number of shares to have voting control of the company will increase substantially.
- *Greenmail* Greenmail refers to an incentive offered by management of the target company to the potential bidder for not pursuing the takeover. The management of the target company may offer the acquirer for its shares a price higher than the market price.
- *White knight* A target company is said to use a *white knight* when its management offers to be acquired by a friendly company to escape from a hostile takeover. The possible motive for the management of the target company to do so is not to lose the management of the company. The hostile acquirer may replace the management.
- *Golden parachutes* When a company offers hefty compensations to its managers if they get ousted due to takeover, the company is said to offer *golden parachutes*. This reduces their resistance to takeover.

---

1. Weston and Copeland, *op. cit.*, pp. 901–03.
2. For a detailed explanation of the takeover defences, see Weston, J.I., Chung, K.S., and Hoag, S.E., *Mergers, Restructuring, and Corporate Control*, Prentice-Hall, New Delhi, 1996, pp. 481–529.

CORPORATE STRATEGY AND ACQUISITIONS

In our earlier discussion, we made distinctions between merger and acquisition or takeover. However, they generally involve similar analyses and evaluations. A merger or acquisition might be considered successful if it increases the shareholder value. Though it is quite difficult to say how the firm would have performed without merger or acquisition, but the post-merger poor performance would be attributed as a failure of merger or acquisition. What are the chances that mergers or acquisitions would succeed? Empirical evidence shows that there is more than fifty per cent chance that they would succeed.

There are several reasons responsible for the failure of a merger or acquisition. They include :

- *Excessive premium* An acquirer may pay high premium for acquiring its target company. The value paid may far exceed the benefits. This happens when acquirer becomes to eager to acquire the target for prestige or increasing the size of its empire.
- *Faulty evaluation* At times acquirers do not carry out the detailed diligence of the target company. They make a wrong assessment of the benefits from the acquisition and land up paying a higher price.
- *Lack of research* Acquisition requires gathering a lot of data and information and analyzing it. It requires extensive research. A shoddily carried out research about the acquisition causes the destruction of the acquirer's wealth.
- *Failure to manage post-merger integration* Many times acquirers are unable to integrate the acquired companies in their businesses. They overlook the organisational and cultural issues. They do not have adequate understanding of the culture of the acquired companies which creates problem of integration and synergy.

To avoid these problems, the acquiring company needs to have an acquisition and merger strategy. All acquisitions must be seen as strategic. The acquisition should be well planned; target companies should be carefully selected after adequate screening. The acquiring company must understand the organisational climate and culture of the target company while performing the due diligence.

There are four important steps involved in a decision regarding merger or acquisition[1]

- Planning
- Search and screening
- Financial evaluation
- Integration

Planning

A merger or acquisition should be seen in the over-all strategic perspective of the acquiring company. It should fit with the strategy and must contribute in the growth of the company and in creating value for shareholders and other stakeholders. The acquiring company must assess its strengths and weaknesses and likely opportunities arising from the acquisitions in order to identify the target companies. The acquiring firm should review its objective of acquisition in the context of its strengths and weaknesses, and corporate goals. This will help in indicating the product–market strategies that are appropriate for the company. It will also force the firm to identify business units that should be dropped and those that should be added or strengthened.

The following two steps are involved in the planning process:

- *Acquisition strategy* The company should have a well articulated acquisition strategy. It should be growth-oriented. It should spell out the objectives of acquisition and other growth options. The acquisition strategy should be formulated after an assessment of the company's own strengths and weaknesses.
- *Assessment approaches and criteria* The company should spell out its approach to acquisitions and the criteria to be applied to acquisitions.

The planning of acquisition will require the analysis of industry-specific and the firm-specific information. The acquiring firm will need industry data on market growth, nature of competition, ease of entry, capital and labour intensity, degree of regulation etc. About the target firm the information needed will include the quality of management, market share, size, capital structure, profitability, production and marketing capabilities etc.

Search and Screening

Search focuses on how and where to look for suitable candidates for acquisition. Screening process shortlists a few candidates from many available. Detailed information about each of these candidates is obtained. Merger objectives would be the basis for search and screening. The objectives may include attaining faster growth, improving profitability, improving managerial effectiveness, gaining market power and leadership, achieving cost reduction etc. These objectives can be achieved in various ways rather than through mergers alone. The alternatives to merger include joint ventures, strategic alliances, elimination of inefficient operations, cost reduction and productivity improvement, hiring capable managers etc. If merger is considered as the best alternative, the acquiring firm must satisfy itself that it is the best available option in terms of its own screening criteria and economically most attractive.

Financial Evaluation

Financial evaluation is the most important part of **due diligence**. Due diligence would also include evaluation of the target company's organisational climate and culture, competencies and skills of employees etc. Financial evaluation of a merger is needed to determine the earnings and cash flows, areas of risk, the maximum price payable to the target company and the best way to finance the merger. The acquiring firm must pay a fair consideration to the target firm for acquiring its business. In a competitive market situation with capital market efficiency, the current market value is the correct and fair value of the share of

---

1. In Rappaport, A., *op. cit.*, pp. 99–110, the first three steps are focused.

the target firm. The target firm will not accept any offer below the current market value of its share. The target firm may, in fact, expect the offer price to be more than the current market value of its share since it may expect that merger benefits will accrue to the acquiring firm. A merger is said to be at a premium when the offer price is higher than the target firm's pre-merger market value. The acquiring firm may pay the premium if it thinks that it can increase the target firm's profits after merger by improving its operations and due to synergy. It may have to pay premium as an incentive to the target firm's shareholders to induce them to sell their shares so that the acquiring firm is enabled to obtain the control of the target firm.

Integration

The most difficult part of the merger or acquisition is the integration of the acquired company into the acquiring company. In the case of a hostile takeover, the acquiring company may get disappointed to find the inferior quality of the acquired firm's assets and employees. The difficulty of integration also depends on the degree of control desired by the acquirer. The acquirer may simply desire financial consolidation leaving the entire management to the existing managers. On the other hand, if the intention is total integration of manufacturing, marketing, finance, personnel etc., integration becomes quite complex.

A horizontal merger or acquisition requires a detailed planning for integration.

- *Integration plan* After the merger or acquisition, the acquiring company should prepare a detailed strategic plan for integration based on its own and the acquired company's strengths and weaknesses. The plan should highlight the objectives and the process of integration.
- *Communication* The integration plan should be communicated to all employees. The management should also inform the employees about their involvement in making the integration smooth and easy and remove any ambiguity and fears in the minds of the staff.
- *Authority and responsibility* The first step that the acquiring company should take is to take all employees into confidence and decide the authority and responsibility relationships. The detailed organisational structure can be decided upon later on. This is essential to avoid any confusion and indecisiveness.
- *Cultural integration* People management is the most critical step in integration. A number of mergers and acquisitions fail because of the failure of management to integrate people from two different organisations. Management should focus the culture integration of the employees. A proper understanding of the cultures of two organisations, clear communication and training can help to bridge the cultural gaps.
- *Skill and competencies up-gradation* If there is difference in the skills and competencies of employees of the merging companies, management should prepare a plan for skill and competencies up-gradation through training and implement it immediately. To make an assessment of the gaps in the skills and competencies, the acquiring company can conduct a survey of employees.

- *Structural adjustments* After affecting the cultural integration and skills up-gradation, management may design the new organization structure and redefine the roles, authorities and responsibilities. Management should be prepared to make adjustments to accommodate the aspirations of the employees of the acquired company.
- *Control systems* Management must ensure that it is in control of all resources and activities of the merged firms. It must put proper financial control in place so that resources are optimally utilized and wastage is avoided.

Peter Drucker provides the following five rules for the integration process:[1]

- Ensure that the acquired firm has a "common core of unity" with the parent. They should have overlapping characteristics like shared technology or markets to exploit synergies.
- The acquirer should think through what potential skill contribution it can make to the acquiree.
- The acquirer must respect the products, markets and customers of the acquired firm.
- The acquirer should provide appropriately skilled top management for the acquiree with in a year.
- The acquirer should make several cross-company promotions within a year.

Post-merger Integration: Integrating VSNL with Tata Group[2]

Tata Group acquired VSNL in February 2002. Tata Group is the most respected group of companies in private sector. VSNL is a public sector company. These two companies belonged to two different environments, systems and culture. Both had committed people but with capabilities and expectations. Hence the task of integration was quite difficult and demanding. Tata Group's primary focus to protect its 'market position in the ILD business, get the national long-distance business launched as soon as possible, and work on making the operations of the company more market/customer focused and efficient'. The integration process involved the following steps :

- The Tata Group constituted multiple task forces for the purpose prioritising tasks and achieving objectives.
- The Group simultaneously focused on the integration of operations, processes and technology and people.
- The people issue was considered as important as the integration of operations, processes and technology.
- A special programme called 'Confluence' was conducted for the senior management team from VSNL. They were informed about Tata Group's the mission, value systems and practices. Similar programmes were organised for more than 500 employees.

1. Drucket, P.F., "Five Rules for Successful Acquisition", *Wall Street Journal*, 15 October, 1981.
2. This section draws from "The Integrated Approach", Mr. *N. Srinath, Director (Operations), VSNL, as spoke to Christabelle Noronha:* http://www.tata.com/vsnl/articles/20030526_the_integrated_approach.htm May 27, 2003.

- A people driven organisational restructuring was undertaken at headquarters simultaneously as the employees were being trained. Employees from different backgrounds, disciplines and levels discussed about the organisational roles, structure and responsibility relationship. After the headquarters, the focus was to the regional and branch offices for the similar initiatives.
- Several new functions were created. Weak were strengthened and supplemented by sales and marketing people brought in from other Tata Group companies. These areas included carrier relations to work with domestic and international telecom carriers, OSP or outside plant to implement the countrywide fibre optic backbone for NLD, and customer services.
- The employees were trained to take up the new roles and challenges, and to strengthen their marketing skills to focus on customer. Training programmes were organised on functional areas.
- A management development programme was conducting focusing on critical commercial skills like business management, people and performance management, negotiating skills, and planning and budgeting skills. A key part of this exercise was that Tata Group executives, who are operating managers, were invited to share their experiences as managers with the VSNL teams.
- Information about initiatives or changes was communicated through new processes. The house magazine, _Patrika_, was supplemented with a monthly wallpaper called _VSNL Buzz_, which shared information about important developments within the company — new customer wins, major milestones achieved, new technical and product developments, etc.— to make the employee feel proud to be part of the VSNL and Tata family.
- Periodic briefing sessions, at which members of the management spoke on the recent performance and achievements in the company, were also started.
- The existing processes could not give the company the competitive edge in the marketplace. Hence, VSNL is restructuring a few of internal processes, ranging from product development to service delivery. It has also begun leveraging the experience and processes available in the Tata Group telecom companies in marketing, customer acquisition and customer services. Many of these are applicable to VSNL, though with fine-tuning to meet specific requirements.
- The first areas to be re-engineered will be those that impact the customer. A structure is planned that is aligned with the industry best practices in customer care.
- Customer service is being broken down into four functions. The first is the customer access point, the call centre or the public office. The second is the backend that handles the issues, queries or complaints received by the front office. The third function is credit and collection; the fourth is that of order management.

Mr. Srinath, Director (Operations), VSNL says: "We realise that our most valuable asset, across all our businesses, is people.

They are the repository of business experience and culture, and the outward face of the company to the client. This combination of structures, skills and processes, supported by the right tools, should provide our employees a healthy work environment to enable them to reach their full potential, while facilitating the company's drive to achieve all its objectives in the marketplace".

ACCOUNTING FOR MERGERS AND ACQUISITIONS

Mergers and acquisitions involve complex accounting treatment. A merger, defined as amalgamation in India, involves the absorption of the target company by the acquiring company, which results in the uniting of the interests of the two companies. The merger should be structured as pooling of interest. In the case of acquisition, where the acquiring company purchases the shares of the target company, the acquisition should be structured as a purchase.

Pooling of Interests Method

In the **pooling of interests method** of accounting, the balance sheet items and the profit and loss items of the merged firms are combined without recording the effects of merger. This implies that asset, liabilities and other items of the acquiring and the acquired firms are simply added at the book values without making any adjustments. Thus, there is no revaluation of assets or creation of goodwill. Let us consider an example as given in Illustration 32.3.

Illustration 32.3: Pooling of Interest

Firm _T_ merges with Firm _S_. Firm _S_ issues shares worth Rs 15 crore to Firm _T_'s shareholders. The balance sheets of both companies at the time of merger are shown in Table 32.15. The balance sheet of Firm _S_ after merger is constructed as the addition of the book values of the assets and liabilities of the merged firms. It may be noticed that the shareholders funds are recorded at the book value, although _T_'s shareholders received shares worth Rs 15 crore in Firm _S_. They now own Firm _S_ along with its existing shareholders.

Table 32.15: Pooling of Interests Method: Merger of Firms S and T

(Rs in crore)

	Firm T	Firm S	Combined Firm
Assets			
Net fixed assets	24	37	61
Current assets	8	13	21
Total	32	50	82
Liabilities			
Shareholders Fund	10	18	28
Borrowings	16	20	36
Current liabilities	6	12	18
Total	32	50	82

Purchase Method

Under the **purchase method**, the assets and liabilities of the acquiring firm after the acquisition of the target firm may be stated at their exiting carrying amounts or at the amounts adjusted for the purchase price paid to the target company. The assets and liabilities after merger are generally revalued under the purchase method. If the acquirer pays a price greater than the fair market value of assets and liabilities, the excess amount is shown as goodwill in the acquiring company's books. On the contrary, if the fair value of assets and liabilities is less than the purchase price paid, then this difference is recorded as capital reserve. Let us consider an example as given in Illustration 32.4.

Illustration 32.4: Purchase Method

Firm *S* acquires Firm *T* by assuming all its assets and liabilities. The fair value of Firm *T*'s fixed assets and current assets is Rs 26 crore and Rs 7 crore. Current liabilities are valued at book value while the fair value of debt is estimated to be Rs 15 crore. Firm *S* raises cash of Rs 15 crore to pay to *T*'s shareholders by issuing shares worth Rs 15 crore to its own shareholders. The balance sheets of the firms before acquisition and the effect of acquisition are shown in Table 32.16. The balance sheet of Firm *S* (the acquirer) after acquisition is constructed after adjusting assets, liabilities and equity.

Table 32.16: Purchase Method: Merger of Firms S and T

(Rs in crore)

	Firm T	Firm S	Firm S after Merger
Assets			
Net fixed assets	24	37	63
Current assets	8	13	20
Goodwill	—	—	3
Total	32	50	86
Liabilities			
Shareholders fund	10	18	33
Borrowings	16	20	35
Current liabilities	6	12	18
Total	32	50	86

The goodwill is calculated as follows:

Payment to *T*'s shareholders		Rs 15
Fair value of fixed assets	26	
Fair value of current assets	7	
Less: Fair value of borrowings	15	
Less: Fair value of current liabilities	6	
Fair value of net assets		12
Goodwill		Rs 3

LEVERAGED BUY-OUTS

A **leveraged buy-out** (LBO) is an acquisition of a company in which the acquisition is substantially financed through debt. When the managers buy their company from its owners employing debt, the leveraged buy-out is called **management buy-out** (MBO). Debt typically forms 70–90 per cent of the purchase price and it may have a low credit rating. In the USA, the LBO shares are not bought and sold in the stock market, and the equity is concentrated in the hands of a few investors.[1] Debt

is obtained on the basis of the company's future earnings potential. LBOs generally involve payment by cash to the seller.

LBOs are very popular in the USA. It has been found there that in LBOs, the sellers require very high premium, ranging from 50 to 100 per cent. The main motivation in LBOs is to increase wealth rapidly in a short span of time. A buyer would typically go public after four or five years, and make substantial capital gains.

LBO Targets

Which companies are targets for the leveraged buy-outs? The following firms are generally the targets for LBOs:
* High growth, high market share firms
* High profit potential firms
* High liquidity and high debt capacity firms
* Low operating risk firms

In LBOs, a buyer generally looks for a company that is operating in a high growth market with a high market share. It should have a high potential to grow fast, and be capable to earning superior profits.[2] The demand for the company's product should be known so that its earnings can be easily forecasted. A typical company for a leveraged buy-out would be one that has high profit potential, high liquidity and low or no debt. Low operating risk of such companies allows the acquiring firm or the management team to assume a high degree of financial leverage and risk.

Risk and Rewards

Why is a lender prepared to assume high risk in a leveraged buy-out? A lender provides high leverage in a leveraged buy-out because he may have full confidence in the abilities of the managers-buyers to fully utilise the potential of the business and convert it into enormous value. His perceived risk is low because of the soundness of the company and its assumed, predictable performance. He would also guard himself against loss by taking ownership position in the future and retaining the right to change the ownership of the buyers if they fail to manage the company. The lender also expects a high return on his investment in a leveraged buy-out since the risk is high. He may, therefore, stipulate that the acquired company will go public after four or five years. A major portion of his return comes from capital gains.

MBOs/LBOs can create a conflict between the (acquiring) managers and shareholders of the firm. The shareholders' benefits will reduce if the deal is very attractive for the managers. This gives rise to *agency costs*. It is the responsibility of the board to protect the interests of the shareholders, and ensure that the deal offers a fair value of their shares.

Another Problem of LBOs could be the fall in the price of the LBO target company's debt instruments (bonds/debentures). This implies a transfer of wealth from debentureholders to shareholders since their claim gets diluted. Debentureholders may, thus, demand a protection in the event of a LBO/MBO. They may insist for the redemption of their claims at par if the ownership/control of the firm changes.

---

1. Brealey and Myers, *op. cit.*, p. 842.
2. Weston and Copeland, *op. cit.*, p. 925.

LBO Evaluation

The evaluation of LBO transactions involves the same analysis as for mergers and acquisitions. The DCF approach is used to value an LBO. As LBO transactions are heavily financed by debt, the risk of lender is very high. Therefore, in most deals they require a stake in the ownership of the acquired firm. Illustration 32.5 provides an example of a leverage buy-out and also explains the methodology for estimating the return and the share of ownership of the lender in such deals.

Illustration 32.5: Evaluation of LBO

Hindustan Chemicals is a small size private limited company. The company manufactures a specialized industrial chemical. The large and medium size industrial companies are its buyers, and it commands about three-fourths of the market due to its excellent quality, prompt delivery and reasonable price. Suraj Bhan Gupta and Mahesh Chand Goyal own the company, both are chemical engineers and are college-days friends. The current sales of the company are Rs 99.8 lakh, and the annual sales growth rate in the past years has been 12–13 per cent. The company has been showing good profits. It has been retaining profits and financing its activities internally without resorting to any external funding. Its earnings before interest and tax (EBIT) are Rs 18.41 lakh for the current year, giving a profit margin of 18.5 per cent and a 25 per cent return on assets. Tables 32.17 and 32.18 give summary of the company's profit and loss statements and balance sheet.

Table 32.17: Hindustan Chemical Private Limited

Summary Profit and Loss Statement for the Year Ending on 31 March

(Rs in lakh)

	2000	2001	2002	2003	2004
Net sales	62.80	65.32	76.49	92.15	99.76
Less: Cost of goods sold	38.76	40.18	47.72	60.43	64.32
Gross profit	24.04	25.14	28.77	31.72	35.44
Selling and admin. expenses	(10.35)	(11.78)	(13.97)	(16.78)	(18.05)
Non-operating surplus	0.36	0.97	0.65	1.10	1.02
Profit before tax	14.05	14.33	15.45	16.04	18.41
Less: Tax	7.25	7.65	7.60	8.00	9.10
Profit after tax	6.80	6.68	7.85	8.04	9.31

Both Suraj and Mahesh have decided to retire from business. Their general manager, Brij Mohan Varsheny, has agreed to buy the entire business for Rs 100 lakh. Brij has only Rs 10 lakh of his savings, and he will have to raise the remaining amount externally. He is confident that on the basis of the strong profitability of the company, he would be able to raise funds from a private finance company, if it is offered an attractive return on its investment. The finance company may grant to him a loan of Rs 90 lakh at 10 per cent rate of interest per year plus warrants to buy enough equity shares when the company goes public to earn at least a return of 25 per cent. Brij knows that the finance company would expect him to go public after about four or five years, and would also require him to repay the principal between six to ten years in equal instalments.

Table 32.18: Hindustan Chemical Private Limited

Summary Balance Sheet

as on 31 March 2004   (Rs in lakh)

Capital and Liabilities			Asset		
Capital	8.50		Net fixed assets	41.28	
Reserve	59.50		Other non-current		
Net worth		68.00	assets	2.13	
					43.41
Current Liabilities:			Current Assets:		
Creditors	4.35		Inventory	4.12	
Outstanding					
expenses	2.36		Debtors	9.15	
Tax provision	1.79	8.50	Cash	18.50	
			Others	1.32	33.09
Total Funds		76.50	Total Assets		76.50

Brij expects that for next ten years sales would grow at 25 per cent, and afterwards the growth rate may slow down. He expects EBIT as a percentage of sales to be 25 per cent. In order to maintain the sales growth, he would have to incur some capital expenditure that is likely to increase from fourth year onwards. The tax depreciation and capital expenditures are estimated as given in Table 32.20. He also expects net working capital to sales ratio to remain approximately at its present level, say, at about 24 per cent. Should Brij Mohan borrow Rs 90 lakh to buy-out Hindustan Chemicals?

Let us analyse the performance of Hindustan Chemical in the year 2004. Most important ratios are as follows:

Table 32.19: Hindustan Chemicals: Financial Performance, 2004

Net sales/Total assets	1.30
EBIT/Net sales (%)	18.45
EBIT/Total assets (%)	24.07
PAT/EBIT (%)	50.57
Total assets/Net worth (%)	1.13
PAT/Net worth (%)	13.70
CA/CL (%)	3.89
NWC/Net sales (%)	24.65

The company is highly profitable and liquid. It employs no debt. The only liabilities are current liabilities. Net worth is 89 per cent of the total funds. Net working capital to sales ratio is 24.7 per cent, and is quite high. The company can reduce level of its current assets, and release funds to finance its future growth. It is certainly an attractive company to buy. The purchase price of Rs 100 lakh seems to be quite reasonable. At the 2004 profit after tax, it gives a price multiplier of 5.43 only.

The company would have equity of Rs 10 lakh against loan of Rs 90 lakh, giving a debt-equity ratio of 9:1. In a conventional sense, this is a very high leverage, and therefore, the traditional financiers would not provide any funds to the company. However, the company is very sound, and it has the capacity to service a high level of debt. It is a market leader with three-fourths of the market share, its products have excellent quality, and it has an assured market. Thus, the company's earnings are predictable as well as the performance is expected to improve due to cost reduction and operating efficiency. Table 32.20 shows the company's expected earnings and cash flows, and reveals that it would be in a very comfortable position to service its debt.

One important consideration in this deal is that the financier expected a return of 25 per cent and issue of shares to him in the year 2009, when the company is likely to go public. The value of business should be sufficiently high so that Brij Mohan's ownership is not diluted below 50 per cent. How much should be the value of shares to the finance company so that it could earn 25 per cent rate of return?

The finance company invests Rs 90 lakh, and its cash inflows are interest received, repayments of principal and the value of shares in Hindustan Chemical in the year 2009. Its return would be 25 per cent if the present value of its investment at 25 per cent were equal to the present value of its inflows (i.e., NPV = 0).

$$NPV = PV \text{ of interest} + PV \text{ of repayment}$$
$$+ PV \text{ of shares} - \text{Investment} = 0$$

We know that the finance company is expected to receive Rs 9 lakh interest per year for eight years and Rs 6 lakh and Rs 3 lakh in ninth and tenth years. Also, it would get Rs 30 lakh each in the last three years. Using the present value table given at the end of the book, we can calculate the present value of interest and repayment of principal. NPV at 25 per cent discount rate is as follows:

$$NPV = 31.1 + 12.2 + 0.328 \times \text{Value of shares} - 90.0 = 0$$
$$\text{Value of shares} = 46.7/0.328 = Rs \ 142.4 \text{ lakh}$$

How much is the value of Hindustan Chemicals shares expected after five years? It is a growing company. Therefore, it would not be unreasonable to assume a price-earnings ratio of 15 after five years. The value of the company's shares in 2009 could be expected as: Rs 33.5 × 15 = Rs 502.5 lakh. Thus, the company should be prepared to give about 28 per cent ownership (142.4/502.5) to the finance company. If the price-earnings is expected to be low, say 10, Hindustan Chemical may have to sacrifice about 43 per cent of its ownership.

Illustration 32.4 shows that Hindustan Chemical was a highly successful company. It has a much brighter future because of its high potential to grow at a much higher rate, save costs and improve its profit margin. It is being considered to be bought out by its managers. Since they have so well managed the company in the past, the lender has confidence in them and is prepared to provide a high leverage. Lender is also expecting a high return. Therefore, he would have to be given '**equity**

sweetener' by the buyer. He would lend funds to the manager-buyers of Hindustan chemicals at concessional rate of interest but he would also like to have a stake in the company's equity. He is expecting a return of 25 per cent. The manager-buyers should estimate the value of the company after five years when the lender may like to use his option to buy the company's shares and accordingly decide how much ownership they should be prepared to share with the lender. They should use the discounted cash flow approach, as shown in the illustration, for this purpose.

Divestment

A **divestment** involves the sale of a company's assets, or product lines, or divisions or brand to the outsiders. It is reverse of acquisition. Companies use divestment as a means of restructuring and consolidating their businesses for creating more value for shareholders. In divestment, the selling company intends to create more value for shareholders. It sells the part of business for a higher price than its current worth. The remaining business might also find it true value. Thus, divestment creates reverse synergy.

The following are some of the common motives for divestment:

- **Strategic change** Due to the economic and competitive changes, a company may change its product-market strategy. It might like to concentrate its energy to certain types of businesses where it has competencies and competitive advantage. Hence it may sell businesses that more fit with the new strategy.
- **Selling cash cows** Some of the company's businesses might have reached saturation. The company might sell these businesses which are now 'cash cows'. It might realise high cash flows that it can invest in 'stars' that have high growth potential in the future.
- **Disposal of unprofitable businesses** Unprofitable businesses are a drain on the company's resources. The company would be better of discarding such businesses.
- **Consolidation** A company might have become highly diversified due to unplanned acquisitions in the past. It

Table 32.20: Hindustan Chemical: Estimation of Cash Flows

(Rs in lakh)

	2005	2006	2007	2008	2009	2010	2011	2012	2013	2014
Net sales	124.7	155.9	194.8	243.6	304.6	380.6	475.7	594.7	743.4	929.2
EBIT	31.2	39.0	48.7	60.9	76.1	95.2	118.9	148.7	185.8	232.3
Interest	9.0	9.0	9.0	9.0	9.0	9.0	9.0	9.0	6.0	3.0
PBT	22.2	30.0	39.7	51.9	67.1	86.2	109.9	139.7	179.8	229.3
Tax	11.1	15.0	19.9	26.0	33.6	43.1	55.0	69.9	90.0	114.7
PAT	11.1	15.0	19.8	25.9	33.5	43.1	54.9	69.8	89.9	114.6
Plus: Depreciation	1.6	1.7	1.8	1.9	2.1	2.5	2.9	3.6	4.4	5.4
CFO	12.7	16.7	21.6	27.8	35.6	45.6	57.8	73.4	94.3	120.0
Less: Change in NWC	5.3	7.5	9.4	11.8	14.5	18.2	22.9	28.6	35.7	44.6
Less: Change CAPEX	0.8	0.8	1.0	1.3	2.1	3.5	4.6	6.2	8.0	10.2
NCF	6.6	8.4	11.2	14.7	19.0	23.9	30.3	38.6	50.6	65.2
Repayment								30.0	30.0	30.0
Cash flow available to owners	6.6	8.4	11.2	14.7	19.0	23.9	30.3	8.6	20.6	35.2

might sell its unrelated businesses, and consolidate its remaining businesses as a balanced portfolio.

- *Unlocking value* Sometimes stock market is not able to value a diversified company properly since it does not have full disclosure of information for the businesses separately. Once the businesses are separated, the stock market correct values the businesses.

Sell-off

There are two types of divestment: sell-off and spin-off. When a company sells part of its business to a third party, it is called sell-off. It is a usual practice of a large number of companies to sell-off is to divest unprofitable or less profitable businesses to avoid further drain on its resources. Sometimes the company might sell its profitable, but non-core businesses to ease its liquidity problems.

Spin-offs

When a company creates a new from the existing single entity, it is called spin-off. The spin-off company would usually be created as a subsidiary. Hence, there is no change in ownership. After the spin-off, shareholders hold shares in two different companies.

Spin-off may have the following advantages:

1. When the businesses are legally and physically separated, shareholders would have information about separate businesses. They would be able to value separate businesses more easily. Management would now know which business is a poor-performing business. Quick managerial action could be initiated to improve the performance.
2. There may be improvement in the operating efficiency of the separate businesses as they would receive concentrated attention of the respective managements.
3. Spin-offs could reduce the attractiveness for acquisition when the new company is clearly an under performer. As a part of a single entity, it might be obvious that the business unit is an under-performer.
4. Spin-off (and sell-off as well) makes it possible for companies to allocate their resources to growth opportunities that have the potential of creating high values for shareholders in the future.

REGULATIONS OF MERGERS AND TAKEOVERS IN INDIA

Mergers and acquisitions may degenerate into the exploitation of shareholders, particularly minority shareholders. They may also stifle competition and encourage monopoly and monopolistic corporate behaviour. Therefore, most countries have legal framework to regulate the merger and acquisition activities. In India, mergers and acquisitions are regulated through the provision of the Companies Act, 1956, the Monopolies and Restrictive Trade Practice (MRTP) Act, 1969, the Foreign Exchange Regulation Act (FERA), 1973, the Income Tax Act, 1961, and the Securities and Controls (Regulations) Act, 1956.[1] The Securities and Exchange Board of India (SEBI) has issued guidelines to regulate mergers, acquisitions and takeovers.

Legal Measures against Takeovers

The Companies Act restricts an individual or a company or a group of individuals from acquiring shares, together with the shares held earlier, in a public company to 25 per cent of the total paid-up capital. Also, the Central Government needs to be intimated whenever such holding exceeds 10 per cent of the subscribed capital. The Companies Act also provides for the approval of shareholders and the Central Government when a company, by itself or in association of an individual or individuals purchases shares of another company in excess of its specified limit. The approval of the Central Government is necessary if such investment exceeds 10 per cent of the subscribed capital of another company. These are precautionary measures against the takeover of public limited companies.

Refusal to Register the Transfer of Shares

In order to defuse situation of hostile takeover attempts, companies have been given power to refuse to register the transfer of shares. If this is done, a company must inform the transferee and the transferor within 60 days. A refusal to register transfer is permitted if:

- a legal requirement relating to the transfer of shares have not be complied with; or
- the transfer is in contravention of the law; or
- the transfer is prohibited by a court order; or
- the transfer is not in the interests of the company and the public.

Protection of Minority Shareholders' Interests

In a takeover bid, the interests of all shareholders should be protected without a prejudice to genuine takeovers. It would be unfair if the same high price is not offered to all the shareholders of prospective acquired company. The large shareholders (including financial institutions, banks and individuals) may get most of the benefits because of their accessibility to the brokers and the takeover dealmakers. Before the small shareholders know about the proposal, it may be too late for them. The Companies Act provides that a purchaser can force the minority shareholder to sell their shares if:

- the offer has been made to the shareholders of the company;
- the offer has been approved by at least 90 per cent of the shareholders of the company whose transfer is involved, within 4 months of making the offer; and
- the minority shareholders have been intimated within 2 months from the expiry of 4 months referred above.

If the purchaser is already in possession of more than 90 per cent of the aggregate value of all the shares of the company, the transfer of the shares of minority shareholders is possible if:

- the purchaser offers the same terms to all shareholders and
- the tenders who approve the transfer, besides holding at least 90 per cent of the value of shares, should also form at least 75 per cent of the total holders of shares.

---

1. Bhattacharyya, *op. cit.*

SEBI Guidelines for Takeovers

The salient features of some of the important guidelines as follows:[1]

Disclosure of share acquisition/holding Any person who acquires 5% or 10% or 14% shares or voting rights of the target company, should disclose of his holdings at every stage to the target company and the Stock Exchanges within 2 days of acquisition or receipt of intimation of allotment of shares.

Any person who holds more than 15% but less than 75% shares or voting rights of target company, and who purchases or sells shares aggregating to 2% or more shall within 2 days disclose such purchase or sale along with the aggregate of his shareholding to the target company and the Stock Exchanges.

Any person who holds more than 15% shares or voting rights of target company and a promoter and person having control over the target company, shall within 21 days from the financial year ending March 31 as well as the record date fixed for the purpose of dividend declaration, disclose every year his aggregate shareholding to the target company.

Public announcement and open offer An acquirer who intends to acquire shares which along with his existing shareholding would entitle him to exercise 15% or more voting rights, can acquire such additional shares only after making a public announcement to acquire at least additional 20% of the voting capital of target company from the shareholders through an open offer.

An acquirer who holds 15% or more but less than 75% of shares or voting rights of a target company, can acquire such additional shares as would entitle him to exercise more than 5% of the voting rights in any financial year ending March 31 only after making a public announcement to acquire at least additional 20% shares of target company from the shareholders through an open offer.

An acquirer, who holds 75% shares or voting rights of a target company, can acquire further shares or voting rights only after making a public announcement to acquire at least additional 20% shares of target company from the shareholders through an open offer.

Offer price The acquirer is required to ensure that all the relevant parameters are taken into consideration while determining the offer price and that justification for the same is disclosed in the letter of offer. The relevant parameters are:

- negotiated price under the agreement which triggered the open offer.
- price paid by the acquirer for acquisition, if any, including by way of allotment in a public or rights or preferential issue during the twenty six week period prior to the date of public announcement, whichever is higher;
- the average of the weekly high and low of the closing prices of the shares of the target company as quoted on the stock exchange where the shares of the company are most frequently traded during the twenty six weeks or the average

of the daily high and low prices of the shares as quoted on the stock exchange where the shares of the company are most frequently traded during the two weeks preceding the date of public announcement, whichever is higher.

In case the shares of Target Company are not frequently traded then parameters based on the fundamentals of the company such as return on net worth of the company, book value per share, EPS etc. are required to be considered and disclosed.

Disclosure The offer should disclose the detailed terms of the offer, identity of the offerer, details of the offerer's existing holdings in the offeree company etc. and the information should be made available to all the shareholders at the same time and in the same manner.

Offer document The offer document should contain the offer's financial information, its intention to continue the offeree company's business and to make major change and long-term commercial justification for the offer.

The objectives of the Companies Act and the guidelines for takeover are to ensure full disclosure about the mergers and takeovers and to protect the interests of the shareholders, particularly the small shareholders. The main thrust is that public authorities should be notified within two days.

In a nutshell, an individual or company can continue to purchase the shares without making an offer to other shareholders until the shareholding exceeds 10 per cent. Once the offer is made to other shareholders, the offer price should not be less than the weekly average price in the past 6 months or the negotiated price.

Legal Procedures

The following is the summary of legal procedures for merger or acquisition laid down in the Companies Act, 1956:

- *Permission for merger* Two or more companies can amalgamate only when amalgamation is permitted under their memorandum of association. Also, the acquiring company should have the permission in its object clause to carry on the business of the acquired company. In the absence of these provisions in the memorandum of association, it is necessary to seek the permission of the shareholders, board of directors and the Company Law Board before affecting the merger.
- *Information to the stock exchange* The acquiring and the acquired companies should inform the stock exchanges where they are listed about the merger.
- *Approval of board of directors* The boards of the directors of the individual companies should approve the draft proposal for amalgamation and authorize the managements of companies to further pursue the proposal.
- *Application in the High Court* An application for approving the draft amalgamation proposal duly approved by the boards of directors of the individual companies

---

1. Based on the Securities and Exchange Board of India (Substantial Acquisition of Shares and Takeovers) Regulation, 1977. *New Takeover Code*, The Report of the Committee Appointed by SEBI on Takeover under the chairmanship of Justice P.N. Bhagwati was the basis of SEBI guidelines for takeovers.

should be made to the High Court. The High Court would convene a meeting of the shareholders and creditors to approve the amalgamation proposal. The notice of meeting should be sent to them at least 21 days in advance.

- *Shareholders' and creditors' meetings* The individual companies should hold separate meetings of their shareholders and creditors for approving the amalgamation scheme. At least, 75 per cent of shareholders and creditors in separate meeting, voting in person or by proxy, must accord their approval to the scheme.
- *Sanction by the High Court* After the approval of shareholders and creditors, on the petitions of the companies, the High Court will pass order sanctioning the amalgamation scheme after it is satisfied that the scheme is fair and

reasonable. If it deems so, it can modify the scheme. The date of the court's hearing will be published in two newspapers, and also, the Regional Director of the Company Law Board will be intimated.

- *Filing of the Court order* After the Court order, its certified true copies will be filed with the Registrar of Companies.
- *Transfer of assets and liabilities* The assets and liabilities of the acquired company will be transferred to the acquiring company in accordance with the approved scheme, with effect from the specified date.
- *Payment by cash or securities* As per the proposal, the acquiring company will exchange shares and debentures and/or pay cash for the shares and debentures of the acquired company. These securities will be listed on the stock exchange.

SUMMARY

❖ A merger is the combination of two or more firms into one of the firms. Merger could be horizontal, vertical or conglomerate.

❖ Horizontal merger is the combination of two or more firms in the same stage of production/distribution/area of business.

❖ Vertical integration is combination of two or more firms involved in different stages of production or distribution.

❖ Conglomerate merger is the combination of firms engaged in unrelated lines of business. Acquisition or takeover means a combination in which the acquiring company acquires all or part of assets (shares) of the target company. In acquisition, there exists willingness of the management of the target company to be acquired while this may not be so under takeover.

❖ A merger results into an economic advantage when the combined firms are worth more together than as separate entities. Merger benefits may result from economies of scale, economies of vertical integration, increased efficiency, tax shields or shared resources.

❖ Merger should be undertaken when the acquiring company's gain exceeds the cost. Cost is the premium that the buyer (acquiring company) pays for the selling company (target company) over its value as a separate entity.

❖ Discounted cash flow technique can be used to determine the value of the target company to the acquiring company. However, the mechanics of buying a company is very complex than those of buying an equipment or machine. Integrating an acquired company successfully to the buying company's operation is quite difficult and challenging task.

❖ The assets and liabilities of the post-merger firm can be

combined later using either the pooling of interest method or the purchase method. In the pooling of interest method, assets and liabilities are combined at book values. In the purchase method, the assets and liabilities are revalued and then combined. The difference between book values of assets and liabilities and their revaluation is shown as goodwill or capital reserve.

❖ In a leveraged buy-out (LBO), a company is bought by raising most funds through borrowings. When the company is bought-out by its own managers, it is called management buy-out (MBO). After acquisition, the LBO generates lot of profits and creates high value. Lenders get high return by converting their loans into equity or using warrants buying the company's shares.

❖ Companies undertake corporate restructuring to enhance the shareholder value. Corporate restructuring make take the forms of ownership restructuring, business restructuring and assets restructuring. Mergers and acquisitions and leveraged buy-outs results in change in ownership. Divestment of a business unit is an example of business restructuring. Sale of asset amounts to asset restructuring.

❖ A business restructuring may take place through sale-off or spin-off. Sale-off involves transfer of the business or asset to an outside part. Spin-off usually takes the form of a subsidiary company and does amount to change in shareholding. Shareholders of the erstwhile entity hold shares of the separate companies.

❖ Merger and acquisition activities are regulated under various laws in India. The objectives of the laws as well as the stock exchange requirements are to make merger deals transparent and protect the interest of all shareholders.

KEY CONCEPTS

Absorption	Crown jewels	Hostile acquisition	Share exchange ratio
Acquisition	Debt capacity	Leveraged buy-out	Synergy
Agency costs	Divestiture	Management buy-out	Systematic risk
Backward integration	Forward integration	Merger	Takeover
Boot-strapping	Golden parachutes	Non-systematic risk	Tender offer
Combination	Greenmail	Poison pills	Vertical merger
Conglomerate merger	Holding company	Pooling of interest	· White knight
Consolidation	Horizontal merger	Purchase method	

ILLUSTRATIVE SOLVED PROBLEMS

Problem 32.1: Gama Fertilisers Company is taking over Theta Petrochemical Company. The shareholders of Theta would receive 0.8 shares of Gama for each shares held by them. The merger is not expected to yield in economies of scale and operating synergy. The relevant data for the two companies are as follows:

	Gama	Theta
Net sales (Rs in crore)	335.00	118.00
Profit after-tax (Rs in crore)	58.00	12.00
Number of share (crore)	12.00	3.00
Earnings per share (Rs)	4.83	4.00
Market value per share (Rs)	30.00	20.00
Price-earnings ratio	6.21	5.00

For the combined company (after merger), you are required to calculate (a) EPS, (b) P/E ratio, (c) market value per share, (d) number of shares, and (e) total market capitalisation. Also calculate the premium paid by Gama to the shareholders of Theta.

Solution

Premium paid to Theta's shareholders:

Value of each share in Gama: 0.8 × Rs 30	= Rs 24
Value of Theta's share before merger	= Rs 20
Premium	= Rs 4

Premium percentage = 4/20 = 20 per cent

Number of shares paid to Theta's shareholders: 3 × 0.8 = 2.4 crore

Number of shares of the combined company: 12 + 2.4 = 14.4 crore

Combined profit after tax: Rs 58 + Rs 12 = Rs 70 crore

Combined EPS = 70/14.4 = Rs 4.86

Combined price-earnings ratio:

$$6.21 \times (58/70) + 5 \times (12/70) = 6.00$$

Combined firm's market capitalization:

Market value per share = P/E ratio × EPS = 6.00 × 4.86
$$= Rs\ 29.16$$

Capitalisation: MVPS × No. of shares = Rs 29.16 × 14.4
$$= Rs\ 419.9\ crore$$

Problem 32.2: Pee Company has decided to acquire Kay company. The following are the relevant financial data for the two companies:

	Pee Co.	Kay Co.
Net sales (Rs in lakh)	350.00	45.00
Profit after-tax (Rs in lakh)	28.13	3.75
Number of shares (lakh)	7.50	1.50
Earnings per share (Rs)	3.75	2.5
Dividend per share (Rs)	1.30.	0.60
Total market capitalisation (Rs in lakh)	420.00	45.00

Calculate: (a) pre-merger market value per share for both companies, (b) post-merger EPS, market value per share and price-earnings ratio if Kay's shareholders are offered a share of (i) Rs 30, or (ii) Rs 56, or (iii) Rs 20 in a share exchange for merger, (c) Pee's EPS if Kay's shareholders are offered Rs 100, 15 per cent convertible debenture for each 3 shares held in Kay, and (d) post-merger dividend or interest available to Kay's shareholders with exchanges referred in (b) and (c) Assume 50 per cent tax rate.

Solution:

(a) Pre-merger market value per share = $\dfrac{\text{Market capitalisation}}{\text{Number of shares}}$

Pee: 420/7.50 = Rs 56; Kay: 45/1.50 = Rs 30

(b) Share exchange ratio:

(i) 30/56 = 0.536 (ii) 56/56 = 1 (iii) 20/56 = 0.357

Number of shares of the surviving company:

(i) 7.5 + (0.536 × 1.5) = 8.30 (ii) 7.5 + (1 × 1.5) = 9.00

(iii) 7.5 + (0.357 × 1.5) = 8.04

Combined EPS: Combined PAT/Combined number of shares

(i) (28.13 + 3.75)/8.30 = Rs 3.84

(ii) (28.13 + 3.75)/9.00 = Rs 3.5

(iii) (28.13 + 3.75/8.04 = Rs 3.97

Combined firm's P/E ratio = weighted average of the individual firm's pre-merger P/E ratio

$$\{(420/28.13) \times \{(28.13/(28.13 + 3.75)\}$$
$$+ \{(45/3.75) \times \{3.75/(28.13 + 13.75)\}$$
$$= 14.93 \times 0.882 + 12 \times 0.118 = 14.58$$

Market value per share of the surviving firm:

(i) (3.84 × 14.58) = Rs 56 (ii) (3.54 × 14.58) = Rs 51.61

(iii) (3.97 × 14.58) = Rs 57.88

(c)   Number of convertible debentures; 1.50/3 = 0.50 lakh
Interest on debenture 1.50 × Rs 100 × 15% = Rs 7.5 lakh
Combined profit after-tax = 28.13 + 3.75 – 7.5 + 0.5 × 7.5
Pee's EPS after merger = 28.13/7.50 = Rs 3.75

Note: Interest will be deducted from the combined profit but is will save tax at 50 per cent tax rate.

(d) Dividend to Kay's shareholders after merger:
Exchange of shares:
(i) 0.804 × 1.30 = Rs 1.05 lakh
(ii) 1.50 × 1.30 = Rs 1.95 lakh
(iii) 0.536 × 1.30 = Rs 0.70 lakh

Interest 0.50 × 100 × 0.15 = Rs 7.50 lakh
Post-merger dividend: 1.50 × 0.6 = Rs 0.90 lakh.

Problem 32.3: Small Company is being acquired by Large Company on a share exchange basis. Their selected data are as follows:

	Large	*Small*
Profit after-tax (Rs in lakh)	56	21
Number of shares (lakh)	10	8.4
Earnings per share (Rs)	5.6	2.5
Price-earnings ratio	12.5	7.5

Determine (a) pre-merger, market value per share, and (b) the maximum exchange ratio Large Company should offer without the dilution of (i) EPS (ii) market value per share.

Solution:

(a)   Pre-merger market-value per share: P/E ratio × EPS
Large: 12.5 × 5.6 = Rs 70
Small: 7.5 × 2.5 = Rs 18.75

(b) (i) Maximum exchange ratio without dilution of EPS:

Pre-merger PAT of Large (Rs in lakh)	56
Pre-merger PAT of Small (Rs in lakh)	21
Combined PAT without Synergy (Rs in lakh)	77
Large's EPS	5.6
Maximum number of shares of Large after merger (77/5.6) (lakh)	13.75
Existing number of shares (lakh)	10.00
Maximum number of shares to be exchanged (lakh)	3.75
Maximum share exchange ratio: 3.75/8.4	0.446

(ii) Maximum exchange ratio without dilution of market value per share:

Pre-merger market capitalisation of Large: MV × No. of shares = Rs 70 × 10 lakh	700
Pre-merger market capitalisation of Small: MV × No. of shares = Rs 18.75 × 8.4 lakh	157.5
Combined market capitalisation (Rs in lakh)	857.5
Current market value per share for Large shareholders (Rs)	70
Maximum number of shares of Large (surviving company) (857.5/70) (lakh)	12.25
Current number of shares of Large (lakh)	10.00
Maximum number of shares to be exchanged (lakh)	2.25
Maximum shares exchanged ratio: 2.25/8.4	0.268

Note: In a share exchange, there would not be a dilution of EPS if the acquiring company offers to pay a P/E ratio for the acquired firm's shares equal to its pre-merger P/E ratio. Large has a P/E ratio of 12.5 and the acquired firm's pre-merger EPS is Rs 2.5. Thus it could offer upto 12.5 × 2.5 = Rs 31.25 for Small's shares. The maximum exchange ratio is: 31.25/70 = 0.446.

Problem 32.4: *XYZ* Company is acquiring *PQR* Company. *XYZ* will pay 0.5 of it shares to the shareholders of *PQR* for each share held by them. The data for the two companies are as given below:

	XYZ	*PQR*
Profit after-tax (Rs in lakh)	150	30
Number of shares (lakh)	25	8
Earnings per share (Rs)	6.00	3.75
Market price of share (Rs)	78.00	33.75
Price-earnings ratio	13	9

Calculate the earnings per share of the surviving firm after merger. If the price-earnings ratio falls to 12 after the merger, what is the premium received by the shareholders of *PQR* (using the surviving firm's new price)? Is the merger beneficial for *XYZ*'s shareholders?

Solution:

Combined profit after-tax = 150 + 30 = Rs 180 lakh
Combined shares = 25 + 0.5(8) = 29 lakh
EPS = 180/29 = Rs 6.21
Market price after merger = P/E × EPS = 12 × 6.21 = Rs 74.52
Premium = {0.5 (74.52) – 33.75}/33.75
= (37.26 – 33.75)/33.75 = 0.104 or 10.4%

The merger is not beneficial to *XYZ*'s shareholders because their price falls from Rs 78 to Rs 74.52—a loss of 4.5 per cent.

Problem 32.5: The chief executive of a company thinks that shareholders always look for the earnings per share. Therefore, he considers maximisation of the earnings per share as his company's objective. His company's current net profits are Rs 80 lakh and EPS is Rs 4. The current market price is Rs 42. He wants to buy another firm which has current income of Rs 15.75 lakh, EPS of Rs 10.50 and the market price per share of Rs 85.

What is the maximum exchange ratio which the chief executive should offer so that he could keep EPS at the current level? If the chief executive borrows funds at 15 per cent rate of interest and buys-out another company by paying cash, how much should he offer to maintain his EPS? Assume a tax rate to 52 per cent.

Solution:

(a) Combined net profit/No. of shares = 4.00
(80 + 15.75)/(20 + x) = 4
80 + 15.75 = 80 + 4x
x = 3.9375 lakh

Thus the share exchange ratio is 3.9375/1.5 = 2.625

Note: Number of shares = PAT/EPS

(b) Combined net profit/No. of shares = 4.00
{80 + 15.75 – 0.15 (Debt) (1 – 0.52)}/20 = 4.00
(95.75 – 0.072 Debt)/20 = 4

Debt = 0.7875/0.0036 = Rs 218.75 lakh

The chief executive should offer Rs 218.75/1.5 = Rs 145.83 cash per share.

Problem 32.6: Rama International is investigating the acquisition of Shivani International Company. Shivani's balance sheet is given below:

Table 32.21: Shivani International Company: Balance Sheet

	(Rs in crore)
10% cumulative preference capital	100
Ordinary share capital	
(30 crore shares at Rs 10 per share)	300
Reserves and surplus	150
14% Debentures	80
Current liabilities	100
Total	730
Net fixed assets	275
Investments	50
Current Assets:	
Stock	190
Book debts	150
Cash and bank balance	65 405
Total	730

Rama proposed to offer the following to Shivani:

(a) 10% convertible preference shares of Rs 100 crore in Rama for paying 10% cumulative preference capital of Shivani;

(b) 12% convertible debentures of Rs 84 crore in Rama to redeem 14% debentures of Shivani;

(c) One ordinary share of Rama for every three shares held by Shivani's shareholders, the market price per share being Rs 42 for Rama's shares and Rs 20 for Shivani's shares.

After acquisition, Rama is expected to dispose off Shivani's stock (inventory) for Rs 150 crore, book debts for Rs 102 crore and investments for Rs 55 crore. It would pay entire current liabilities. What is the cost of acquisition to Rama? If Rama's required rate of return is 20 per cent, how much should be the annual after-tax cash flows from Shivani's acquisition assuming a time horizon of eight years and a zero salvage value? Would your answer change if there is a salvage value of Rs 30 crore after 8 years?

Solution:

(a) Cost of acquisition

		(Rs in crore)
10% convertible preference share		100
12% convertible debentures		84
Ordinary share capital: (30/3) × Rs 42		420
Payment of current liabilities		100
Gross payment		704
Less: Realisation from:		
Investments	55	
Stock	150	
Book debts	102	
Cash	65	372
Net Cost		332

(b) (i) $332 = A \times PVAF_{0.20, 8}$

$332 = A \times 3.837$

$A = 332/3.837 = $ Rs 86.53 crore

(ii) $332 = A \times PVAF_{0.20, 8} + 30\ PVF_{0.20, 8}$

$332 = 3.837A + 0.233 \times 30$

$332 = 3.837A + 6.99$

$A = (332 - 6.99)/3.837 = $ Rs 84.70 crore.

REVIEW QUESTIONS

1. Define and distinguish between the concepts of merger, takeover and amalgamation. Illustrate your answer with suitable examples in the Indian context.

2. Explain the concepts of horizontal, vertical and conglomerate merger with examples.

3. What are the advantages and disadvantages of mergers and takeovers?

4. What are the important reasons for mergers and takeovers?

5. Discuss in brief the legislation applicable to mergers and takeovers in India. What are the objectives of such legislation?

6. Explain and illustrate the impact of mergers on earnings per share, market price per share and book value per share of the acquiring company.

7. When do mergers make economic sense? Explain.

8. What do you mean by "tender offer"? What tactics are used by a target company to defend itself from a hostile takeover?

9. What do you understand by leveraged buy-out and management buy-out? Explain the steps involved in the evaluation of LBO?

10. What leads to the failure of a merger or acquisition? How should a company ensure that merger or acquisition is successful?

11. What are the problems of post-merger integration? How can integration be achieved?

12. What is the difference between the pooling of interest and purchase methods of accounting for mergers? Illustrate your answer.

PROBLEMS

1. X Company Ltd. intends to take over Y Company Ltd. by offering two of its shares for every five shares in Y Company Ltd. Relevant financial data are as follows:

	X Co. Ltd.	Y Co. Ltd.
Earnings per share (Rs)	2	2
Market price per share (Rs)	100	40
Price-earnings ratio	50	20
Number of shares ('000)	100	250
Profit after tax (Rs '000)	200	500
Total market value (Rs '000)	10,000	10,000

What is the combined earnings per share? Calculate the P/E ratio of the combined firm. Has any wealth been created for shareholders?

2. Alpha Ltd. is considering the acquisition of Beta Ltd. By making an offer of shares at 5 times of Beta's present earnings. Alternatively, a reverse takeover is possible whereby Beta could offer to buy Alpha's shares at 20 times its present earnings. What are the implications of these proposals? The relevant data are as follows:

	Alpha	Beta
Earnings per share (Rs)	2	2
Market price per share (Rs)	40	20
Price-earnings ratio	20	10
Number of shares ('000)	400	400
Profit after tax (Rs '000)	800	800
Total market value (Rs '000)	16,000	8,000

Calculate the effect on EPS. Would your answer be different if there are merger benefits of Rs 200,000 and Rs 100,000 in the first proposal and second proposals, respectively?

3. Rama Company is considering the acquisition of Krishna Company with exchange of its shares. The financial data for the companies are as follows:

	Rama Co.	Krishna Co.
Profit after-tax (Rs '000)	800	600
No. of equity shares ('000)	200	300
Earnings per share (Rs)	4	2
Price-earnings ratio	15	10
Market price per share (Rs)	60	20

Krishna Company expects an offer of 125 per cent of its current market price from Rama Company.

(a) What is the exchange ratio of shares? How many new shares will be issued?

(b) What is the acquiring company's EPS after the merger? Assume 15 per cent synergy benefits accrue due to the merger.

(c) If the price/earnings ratio after merger is at 20 times, what is the market price per share of the surviving company?

4. The following data relate to Companies A and B:

	Company A	Company B
Profit after-tax (Rs '000)	100	20
Equity shares ('000)	50	5
Price-earnings ratio	20	10

(a) If A and B merge by exchanging one share of Company A for each share of Company B, how would earnings per share of the two companies be affected? What is the market value exchange ratio?

(b) If the exchange ratio were 3 shares of A for two shares of B, what would be the impact of earnings per share after merger. Assume that there would be synergy benefits equal to 20 per cent increase in the present earnings due to merger.

(c) What exchange ratio would you suggest for the above merger?

5. X Company wants to acquire Y Company. If the merger were effected through an exchange of shares, X Company would be willing to pay 40 per cent premium for Y Company's shares. The following data are pertinent to Companies X and Y:

	X Company	Y Company
Net Profit (Rs '000)	1000	200
Number of shares ('000)	500	250
Market price per share (Rs)	120	30

(a) Compute the combined earnings per share.

(b) What exchange ratio would you suggest?

(c) If the exchange ratio were 1 share of Company X for each share of Company Y, what would happen?

6. Sholapur Shoes Limited is evaluating the possibility of acquiring Kohalapur Shoes Limited. The following are data for the two companies:

	Sholapur	Kohalapur
Profit after-tax (Rs in lakh)	54.75	9.90
Earnings per shares (Rs)	7.30	2.20
Dividend per share (Rs)	4.20	1.20
Number of shares (lakh)	7.50	4.50
Total market capitalization (Rs in lakh)	1,000.00	135.00

(a) Calculate the price-earnings ratio of both the companies before merger.

(b) Kohalapur's earnings and dividends are expected to grow at 7.5 per cent without merger and at 10 per cent with merger. You are required to determine: (i) gain from the merger, (ii) the cost of merger if Kohalapur is paid cash of Rs 40 per share, and (iii) the cost of merger if the share exchange ratio is 0.25.

7. Varun Chemicals Limited is proposing a takeover of Siddharth Pharm Limited. Varun's main objective of the takeover is to increase its size as well as diversify its operations. Varun's after-tax profits in the recent past have grown at 18 per cent per year and of Siddharth at 15 per cent per year. Both companies pay dividends regularly. Varun retains about 70 per cent of its profits and Siddharth 50 per cent.

The summarised financial information for the two companies are given in the following.

Summarised Profit and Loss Account *(Rs in crore)*

	Varun	*Siddharth*
Net sales	4545	3500
PBIT	1590	480
Interest	750	25
PBT	1440	455
Provision for tax	650	205
PAT	790	250
Dividends	235	125
Undistributed profit	555	125

Varun's share is currently selling for Rs 52 and Siddharth's Rs 75. The par value of both companies' share is Rs 10. Varun's land and building are stated at recent price. Siddharth's land and buildings were revalued three years ago. There has been 30 per cent per year increase in the value of land and building.

Summarised Balance Sheet *(Rs in crore)*

	Varun		*Siddharth*	
Fixed Assets:				
Land and building, net	720		190	
Plant and machinery, net	900		350	
Furniture and fixtures, net	30	1650	10	550
Current Assets:				
Inventory	400		280	
Debtors	350		250	
Cash and bank balance	25	775	50	580
Less: Current Liabilities				
Creditors	230		130	
Overdrafts	35		10	
Provision for tax	145		50	
Provision for dividends	60	470	50	240
Net assets		1955		890
Paid up share capital	250		125	
Reserves and surplus	1050	1300	660	785
Borrowing		655		105
Capital employed		1955		890

Varun's management wants to determine the premium over the current market price of the shares which should be paid for the acquisition of Siddharth. Varun's financial analyst is considering two options. The price should be determined using: (*a*) the dividend-growth formula, or (*b*) the balance sheet net worth adjusted for the current value of land and buildings plus the estimated average after tax profits for the next five years. After merger, Siddharth's growth is expected to be 18 per cent each year.

8. Grewal Industries Ltd. is a diversified company with multiple businesses, and it also owns several subsidiary companies. Richa Foods Ltd. is one of its subsidiaries that sell packaged food items. Grewal is in the process of consolidating its businesses and therefore, it is changing its strategic focus. In light of its new strategic focus, it has decided to sell Richa Foods Ltd. A number of companies, some from the reputed business houses, have shown considerable interest in buying Richa Foods.

Table 32.22 and Table 32.23 contain the most recent Balance Sheet and Profit and Loss statement of Richa Foods Ltd.

32.22: Balance Sheet as at 31 December, 2004

			Rs in crore
Buildings		930	
Less: Accumulated depreciation		155	775
Plant & Machinery		124	
Less: Accumulated depreciation		81	43
Furniture & Fixtures		39	
Less: Accumulated depreciation		8	31
			849
Current assets			
Stock at cost		132	
Debtors		85	
Cash at bank		78	
		295	
Less: Creditors			
Trade creditors	202		
Acquired expenses	54	256	39
Net assets			888
13% Long-term Loan			388
			500
Shareholders' Funds			
Ordinary share capital (Rs 10 share)			233
General reserve			54
Profit and Loss			213
			500

Table 32.23: Profit and Loss Account for the Year Ended 31 May, 1995

	(Rs in crore)
Sales turnover	1365
Profit before interest and taxation	135
Interest charges	47
Profit before taxation	88
Corporation tax	25
Profit after taxation	63
Dividend proposed and paid	16
Transfer to general reserve	12
Profit and Loss	35

Richa Foods' sales and profits have shown steady growth. The following are the possible realizable value of assets:

	(Rs in crore)
Buildings	911
Plant & machinery	31
Furniture & Fixtures	19
Stock	140

The book values of other assets are close approximation of their realisable value. A close competitor of Richa Foods has a price-earnings ratio of 12.5 and dividend yield of 5.4 per cent. The corporate income tax rate is 35 per cent.

Calculate the value of Richa Foods using alternative methods. Which method do you suggest as most appropriate? Why should Grewal Industries Ltd. sell its subsidiary?

CASE

Case 32.1: Sarangi Engineering Company

Sarangi Engineering Company (SEC) was established in 1953 to manufacture industrial equipments for cement, fertiliser and textile industries. The company's management is concerned about the instability of its earnings due to the cyclical nature of its business. During the past five years, SEC's sales have grown at about 11 per cent per annum. The fluctuating profits of the company have caused its P/E ratio of 27 to be much lower than the industry average of 45 (see Tables 32.1.1 and 32.2.2 for SEC's summarised financial performance). Currently, SEC's share is selling for Rs 88.83 in the market.

SEC's top management has chalked out a plan of acquisition to reduce its earnings instability. The company laid down three criteria for acquisition. First, the target company should broadly belong to the related business. Second, it should be a well-known company in its field, but should be smaller than SEC in size. Third, it should have a wide range of products in growth markets with a high degree of stability. Applying these criteria, SEC has identified *XL* Equipment Company as a possible target company for acquisition. *XL* is known for its quality of products and strong distribution. Due to poor management, the company's performance in the past few years has not been good. Its sales have grown at an average rate of 6 per cent per year during 2000–04 against the industry growth rate of 12 per cent per year. The company's earnings have been low, and the average

market price of company's shares in recent times has been lower than its book value (see Tables 32.1.3 and 32.1.4 for *XL*'s summarised financial performance). The current price of *XL*'s share is Rs 38.94.

SEC intends to totally merge *XL*'s business with its operations after acquisition to gain the advantage of synergy. Hence, it would like to acquire substantial number of *XL*'s shares. *XL*'s shares are held by the promoters (23.5 per cent), financial institutions (22.7 per cent), mutual funds (12.3 per cent) and individuals (41.5 per cent). Promoters will be willing to sell their shares if the offer price is attractive. *XL* has borrowed funds from the financial institutions that also hold *XL*'s shares. It is estimated that about 25 per cent individual shareholders have short-term investment objectives and would always look for profitable opportunities to sell their holdings.

The management of SEC thinks that they could turnaround *XL* after its acquisition. SEC could increase *XL*'s growth rate to 12 per cent. The company may be able to maintain the high sales growth rate (12 per cent) for about seven years followed by normal growth rate of 6 per cent for five years, and eventually the sales growth may drop to zero under competitive pressures. SEC also hopes to reduce *XL*'s cost of goods sold to 65 per cent of sales and selling and administrative expenses to 10 per cent. SEC does not anticipate major capital expenditures for *XL*; amounts equal to depreciation would be

Table 32.1.1: Sarangi Engineering Company: Summarised Profit and Loss Statement and Per Share Data

(Rs in lakh)	*2000*	*2001*	*2002*	*2003*	*2004*
Net Sales	8,335.72	9,378.06	11,057.40	11,464.28	12,805.60
Cost of goods sold	5,943.20	6,857.54	8,315.91	8,349.43	9,105.28
Depreciation	167.63	236.20	211.82	190.49	217.92
Selling & admin. expenses	1,021.01	1,200.83	1,497.99	1,528.47	1,554.37
Total expenses	7,131.84	8,294.57	10,025.72	10,068.39	10,877.58
PBIT	1,203.88	1,083.49	1,031.68	1,395.89	1,928.02
Interest	198.11	230.11	263.63	291.06	432.79
PBT	1,005.77	853.38	768.04	1,104.83	1,495.23
Tax	307.77	266.26	256.53	385.58	518.85
PAT	698.01	587.13	511.52	719.24	976.39
EPS	4.65	3.91	3.41	4.79	5.19
DPS	2.00	2.00	2.00	2.75	3.25
P/E	26.54	33.27	34.59	28.79	27.16

sufficient for minor capital expenditures. The corporate tax rate is 35 per cent. Assume average WDV depreciation rate of 20 per cent for block of assets.

SEC's weighted average cost of capital is 18 per cent. *XL* has equity beta of 1.20. Its debt is rated 'BBB'. The current yield on BBB-rated corporate bonds is 9.38 per cent that is about 3.15 per cent higher than the long-term government bonds. The historical average of return from the share market exceeds the average yield on the long-term government bonds has by about 9 per cent.

Questions for Discussions:

1. What is *XL*'s value to SEC? Explicitly state all assumptions.
2. How much price should SEC pay for *XL*'s share?
3. What are the consequences of acquisition for SEC's shareholders? Should SEC acquire *XL*?

Table 32.1.2: Sarangi Engineering Company:
Summarised Balance Sheet as on 31 March 2003

		(Rs in lakh)
Source of Funds		
Shareholders' Funds		
Paid up capital (150 lakh shares of Rs 10 each)	1,500.00	
Reserves and Surplus	8,442.90	10,942.54
Borrowed Funds:		
Secured	3,040.16	
Unsecured	2,443.75	5,483.91
Capital Employed		16,426.45
Uses of Funds		
Gross Block	15,746.65	
Less: Depreciation	4,109.14	
Net Block	11,637.51	
Investment	73.29	11,710.80
Current Assets	9,416.15	
Less: Current Liabilities	4,700.49	
Net Current Assets		4,715.65
Net Assets		16,426.45

Table 32.1.3: XL Equipment Company:
Summarized Balance Sheet as on 31 March 2004

Balance Sheet Items		(Rs in lakh)
Source of Funds		
Shareholders' Funds		
Paid up capital (50 lakh shares of Rs 10 each)	500.00	
Reserves and Surplus	940.80	1,440.80
Borrowed Funds:		
Secured	282.24	
Unsecured	188.16	470.40
Capital Employed		1,911.20
Uses of Funds		
Gross Block	1,287.72	
Less: Depreciation	558.60	
Net Block		729.12
Investment		45.08
Current Assets	1,475.88	
Less: Current Liabilities	338.88	
Net Current Assets		1,137.00
Net Assets		1,911.20

Table 32.1.4: XL Equipment Company:
Summarised Profit and Loss Statement and Per Share Data

(Rs in lakh)	2000	2001	2002	2003	2004
Net Sales	2,579.74	2,726.78	2,895.84	3,060.04	3,247.31
Cost of goods sold	1,780.06	1,923.70	2,061.91	2,171.10	2,289.40
Depreciation	66.19	73.85	82.48	83.86	76.63
Selling and admin. expenses	465.14	507.69	513.19	544.17	578.58
Total expenses	2,311.39	2,505.24	2,657.58	2,799.13	2,944.61
PBIT	268.35	221.54	238.27	260.90	302.70
Interest	33.99	27.69	42.15	46.59	57.47
PBT	234.36	193.85	196.11	214.31	245.22
Tax	70.78	67.85	67.07	74.41	86.32
PAT	163.58	126.00	129.04	139.90	158.91
EPS	3.27	2.52	2.58	2.80	3.18
DPS	1.20	1.20	1.20	1.30	1.50
P/E	8.7	11.8	11.5	9.27	7.5

CHAPTER 33

Derivatives for Managing Financial Risk

CHAPTER OBJECTIVES

- Understand the reasons for hedging
- Show how options can be used to hedge risk
- Explain forward and futures contracting
- Illustrate use of future and forward contracts for hedging risk
- Discuss use of swaps to change the risk of interest rates and currencies

INTRODUCTION

A firm faces several kinds of risk. Its profitability fluctuates due to unanticipated changes in demand, selling price, costs, taxes, interest rates, technology, exchange rate and host of other factors. Managers may not be able to fully control these risks, but, to some degree, they can decide the risks that the firm should take. They adopt many strategies to reduce their firms' risks. They keep several options open; they create operating flexibility that might bail them out in difficulties.

Managers can reduce their risk exposure by entering into **financial contracts**. We have explained in an earlier chapter how firms could use real options to increase their flexibility and reduce their exposure to risk. In this chapter, we shall discuss many more financial contracts that managers can use to hedge various kinds of risks.

DERIVATIVES AND RISK HEDGING

The term derivatives can simply be understood as those items that do not have their own independent values, rather they have derived values. Derivatives have a significant place in finance and risk management. A **derivative** is a financial instrument whose pay-off is derived from some other asset which is called **an underlying** asset. You may recall that in Chapter 7 we discussed options. An option is a derivative. For example, in case of a stock option, the underlying asset is share (stock) of a company. The value of the stock option depends on the value of

the share. Options are more complicated derivatives. There are a large number of simple derivatives like futures or forward contracts or swaps.

Firms do not like risk; they do not consider it desirable. Firms will take risks only when they are appropriately compensated for the risk. By reducing risk, they can avoid cash flow fluctuations and thus, increase value of their assets or investments. Not surprisingly, firms always look for ways and means of reducing their risk. As we shall discuss later in this chapter, derivatives are tools to reduce a firm's risk exposure. A firm can do away with unnecessary parts of risk exposure and even convert exposures into quite different forms by using derivatives. **Hedging** is the term used for reducing risk by using derivatives.

There are several advantages of better risk management through hedging:

1. *Debt capacity enhancement* Financial risk management helps to understand and manage investment and financing risk. It reduces a firm's costs of financial distress. Hence, the firm can increase debt capacity and interest tax shield.

2. *Increased focus on operations* Financial risk management requires managers to hedge against possible movements in interest rates and exchange rates. These factors are not under the control of managers nor can they predict their behaviour. Hedging against such risks encourages managers to concentrate their efforts on improving operations rather than worrying about factors that are not in their control.

3. *Isolating managerial performance* Hedging helps to separate out the effects of fluctuating external factors (interest or exchange rate) and good or bad management on the firm's profitability. If a company that always hedges its risk suffers a loss or its profits drop, then it means bad management.

In the following sections, we shall discuss how risk can be hedged by using options, futures and forward contracts and swaps.

RISK HEDGING WITH OPTIONS

You may recall from Chapter 7 that an **option** is a right to buy or sell an asset at a specified exercise price at a specified period of time. Option is a right and does not constitute any obligation on the part of the buyer or seller of the option to buy or sell the underlying asset.

A foreign currency option is a handy method of reducing foreign exchange risk. Similarly, options on interest rates and commodities are quite popular with managers to reduce risk. Many options trade on option exchanges. However, in practice, banks and companies strike private option deals.

How does option help reducing risk of a company? Consider an example. Suppose Indian Oil Company (IOC) imports thousands of barrels of oil. The company is expecting increase in the price of oil. The company can lock in the price of oil by purchasing an option to buy oil at a predetermined future date at a specified exercise price. For example, it could acquire 3-month option to buy 3,000 barrels of oil at an exercise price of $50. There is no free lunch; IOC will have to pay **option premium** to the seller of the option. Assume that this premium is $0.60 per barrel. By incurring a small cost (option premium), IOC has bought an insurance against increase in the oil price.

Suppose the oil price at the time of option expiry is $52 per barrel. Since the oil price is higher than the exercise price of $50, IOC will gain by exercising the option. It will be able to buy oil at $50 while the actual price (called spot price) is $52. In practice, firms may collect the difference between the exercise price and the oil price. Since IOC paid a premium to acquire the option, its net payoff is:

$$\text{Net pay-off} = (52 - 50) \times 3,000 - 0.60 \times 3,000$$
$$= 6,000 - 1,800 = \$4,200$$

The cost of oil to IOC is: $52 \times 3,000 = \$156,000$. Thus, the net cost to the company is: $156,000 - 4,200 = \$145,800$.

On the other hand, if the oil price is below the exercise price, IOC will let the option expire as it is worthless for the company. If the oil price is $49, it is in IOC's interest to buy oil from the market at $49 spot price rather than pay an exercise price of $50. Thus, the cost of oil to the company is: $49 \times 3,000 = \$147,000$. IOC has a net loss from option in the form of option premium: $0.60 \times 3,000 = \$1,800$. The net cost to the company is: $147,000 + 1,800 = \$148,800$.

We may observe from this example that buying an option shields a company from increases in the prices while the company can continue benefiting from the decease in the prices. Thus, option creates an opportunity to guard against risk and benefit from changes in the prices. The cost of this opportunity is option premium.

Let us consider another example. Suppose ONGC sells oil to Indian Petrochemical Limited (IPCL). ONGC wants to protect itself from a potential fall in oil prices. What should it do? It should buy a put option – a right to sell oil at a specified exercise price at a specified time. ONGC will be able to protect itself from falling prices and at the same time benefit from increase in the oil prices. Suppose ONGC buys the put option with the Rs 25,000 exercise price at a premium of Rs 50 per barrel. If the price of oil on the day option expires is less than the exercise price, ONGC will exercise the option since it will fetch the locked in price of Rs 25,000 per barrel. On the other hand, if the oil price is more than the exercise price, it will allow the option to lapse as it can get sell the oil at a higher price. In both situations there is a cost in the form of option premium involved.

Illustration 33.1: Hedging with Options

A goldsmith from Surat plans to import 1,000 troy ounces of gold in three months. He suspects fluctuations in the gold prices. The price could be $320, $340 or $360 an ounce. The goldsmith is thinking of buying a 3-month call option on 1,000 ounces of gold with an exercise price of $340. The option will cost $4 per ounce. What is the total cost to the goldsmith under different gold prices?

The gold smith would exercise the call option when the gold price is more than the exercise price, otherwise he would allow it to lapse. When the gold price is higher than the exercise price, the goldsmith's payoff will be the difference between the gold price and the exercise price. The total cost to the gold smith is as follows:

	Gold Price, Dollar per ounce		
	$320	$340	$360
Cost of 1,000 ounces	320,000	340,000	360,000
Less: Pay-off on call option	0	0	20,000
Plus: option premium	4,000	4,000	4,000
	324,000	344,000	344,000

FORWARD CONTRACTS

We do frequently enter into arrangements or understanding now for buying or selling items in the future. These arrangements, when formalised, are referred to as **forward contracts**. Let us clarify further with the help of an example. Suppose you have been admitted to a post-graduate management programme of one of the prestigious management institutes in India. To cope with the academic workload and particularly, to do assignments in finance and quantitative courses, you intend to buy a desktop computer. You approach a computer dealer on 1 July. When you go to the computer shop, you find that the computer make of your choice is not available for immediate delivery. The shopkeeper offers to deliver computer of your choice to you after 15 days (15 July) for Rs 30,000. He also states that if you don't accept the offer, and if you want to buy computer after 15 days, you will have to pay the actual or the **spot price** on that day which could be more than Rs 30,000. You agree to the shopkeeper's offer. In fact, you have entered into a forward contract with the shopkeeper. You are under an obligation to buy the computer and pay to the shopkeeper Rs 30,000 after 15 days and the shopkeeper is obliged to deliver computer to you. As you agree to buy the computer, you are buying a forward contract. You will be **taking delivery** of the computer, called **deliverable instrument**, on due date. The shopkeeper, by handing over the computer to you, will be **making delivery** to you. Table 33.1 illustrates the forward contract vis-à-vis your computer deal.

Table 33.1: Example of Forward Contract for Computer Purchase

1 July 2004	*15 July 2004*
Buyer of Forward Contract	**Buyer of Forward Contract**
1. Agrees to pay price of Rs 30,000	1. Makes payment of Rs 30,000
2. Agrees to take delivery of computer on agreed due date (15 July)	2. Takes delivery of computer
Seller of Forward Contract	**Seller of Forward Contract**
1. Agrees to make delivery of computer on agreed due date (15 July)	1. Makes delivery of computer
2. Agrees to receive purchase price of Rs 30,000 on agreed due date (15 July)	2. Receives payment of Rs 30,000

After 15 days, when you take delivery of computer, you discover that the actual price of computer, called **spot price**, is Rs 31,000. You have a gain of Rs 1,000 since you shall pay Rs 1,000 less than the current price. Forward contract is a very simple tool of hedging risk. A **forward contract** is an agreement between two parties to exchange an asset for cash at a predetermined future date for a price that is specified today.

Suppose that when you approach the shopkeeper for buying the computer, he has it for immediate delivery. You will pay him cash and take the delivery. This is a **cash transaction** where the exchange takes place immediately. Forward contracts must be differentiated from the cash transactions.

You would notice that a forward contract is similar to an option in hedging risk, but there is a significant difference. In case of a forward contract, both the buyer and the seller are bound by the contract; the buyer must take the delivery and the seller must make the delivery at the agreed price on the specified due date. Under an option, the buyer has a right to decide whether or not she would exercise the option.

Forward contracts are flexible. They are tailor-made to suit the needs of the buyers and sellers. You can enter into a forward contract for any goods, commodities or assets. You can choose your delivery date for any quantity of goods or commodities. For example, you need a small quantity of gold, say, two troy ounce, after 45 days. You can fix the price of two troy ounce of gold today by an agreement with a gold supplier forward. After 45 days, you will take the delivery of gold by paying the agreed price. There should always be willing buyers and sellers for entering into a forward contract. Though forward contracts are entered into for different goods, commodities or assets etc., but the foreign currencies forwards have the largest trading.

Illustration 33.2: Hedging through Forward Contract

An Indian company has ordered machinery from USA. The price of $500,000 is payable after six months. The current exchange rate is Rs 45.75/$. At the current exchange rate, the company would need: 45.75 × 500,000 = Rs 22,875,000. But the company anticipates depreciation of Indian rupee over time. The cost to the company in Indian rupees will increase if rupee depreciates when payment is made after six months. What should the company do? The company can lock in the exchange rate by entering into a forward contract and forget about any fluctuation in the exchange rate. Suppose the six-month forward exchange rate is Rs 45.95. The company can buy dollars forward. At the time of making payment, it will exchange Rs 22,975,000 for buying $500,000.

FUTURES CONTRACTS

Suppose a farmer produces barley. He is expecting to have an excellent yield of barley; but he is worried. He is concerned about the future prices of barley. The farmer fears fall in the barley prices in the future. How can he protect himself from the potential of falling price of barley? The farmer supplies barley to a breakfast cereal manufacturer. The farmer can reduce his risk exposure and worries if he could lock in the barley price today. He can do so by entering into a contract today with the manufacturer who wants to buy barley for delivery in the future. The farmer agrees today to sell barley to the manufacturer at a specified future date at a price agreed upon today. The manufacturer is in a different position than the farmer; he is worried that the barley price might increase in the future. He can fix the barley price ahead of time, and take delivery in the future. He would agree to buy barley at a predetermined price on a specified due date.

In fact, the manufacturer and the farmer have entered into a **futures contract**. The farmer will deliver barley to the manufacturer in the future and receive the agreed price and the manufacturer will take delivery of barley and pay to the farmer. What are the consequences of doing so? First, there is no exchange of money when the contract is entered. The barley farmer agrees to sell barley on a specified future date at a price agreed upon today. The miller agrees to buy at the same price and on the same due date. Second, the contract is binding on both the parties. The barley farmer must sell the barley and the miller must buy irrespective to the actual price in the future.

You may be wondering that futures contracts are like forward contracts. It is true that future contracts are no different from forward contracts as they serve the same purpose and operate through a contract between counterparties. The difference is in terms of standardisation and method of operation. Futures contracts have standardised contract size and they trade only on the organised exchanges. Thus, future contracts are forwards contracts traded on organised exchanges in standardised contract size. For example, the standard contract size for barley in the barley international exchange is 20 metric ton. You can enter into barley futures contracts for 20 metric ton or its multiples. If your requirement is less than 20 metric ton, then you should enter into a forward contract as it can be custom made for your specific requirement.

Both the farmer and the manufacturer have hedged risk and both have less risk than before. The farmer has protected himself against risk by selling barley futures; his action is called a **short hedge**. The short hedge is a common occurrence in business, and it takes place whenever a firm or an individual is holding goods or commodities (or any other asset) or is expecting to receive goods or commodities. Farmers anticipate receiving commodities from harvesting agriculture commodities. A producer of petrochemical products may carry inventory of oil. In our example, the manufacturer has protected himself against risk by buying barley futures; his action is referred to as a **long hedge**. Generally, a long hedge occurs when a person or the firm is committed to sell at a fixed price.

Like options, one could use futures contracts to hedge risk. But, as with forward contract and option, there is a difference between these two instruments as well. Unlike options but like forward contracts, future contracts are obligations; on the due date the seller (farmer) has to deliver barley to the buyer (miller) and the buyer will pay the seller the agreed price.

In the futures contracts, like in the forward contracts, one party would lose and another will gain. The profit and the loss will depend on the agreed futures price and the actual price at the time of contract maturity. Suppose the futures price of barley is Rs 20,000 per metric ton and the market price turns out to be Rs 21,500 per metric ton on due date. The barley farmer will receive Rs 1,500 per metric ton less. His loss is the miller's gain; he will pay Rs 1,500 per metric ton less. Thus, the seller of the contract gains when the contracted price is more than the actual market price later on. The buyer of the contract will gain when the contracted price is less than the actual market price.

Both the barley farmer and the miller are able to hedge their risk. The farmer has locked in the selling price and the miller has locked in the buying price. Both, instead of worrying about the fluctuations in the barley price, can concentrate on their operations.

Illustration 33.3: Hedging with Futures

A coal mining company is concerned about short-term volatility in its revenues. Coal currently sells for Rs 7,000 per ton. But the price could fall as low as Rs 6,500 per ton or as high as Rs 7,400 per ton. The company will supply about 5,000 tons to the market next month. What are the consequences if the company does not hedge? What is the cost to the company if it enters into a futures contract to deliver 5,000 tons of coal at an agreed price of Rs 7,050 per ton next month?

If the company does not hedge risk, it will not know what the selling price will be after one month and its revenues will depend on the actual price after one month. If the company hedges through the coal futures, it will lock in the selling price which in the present case is Rs 7,050 per ton. Thus, the company's position will be as shown below:

Hedging Risk:			
Futures price	7,050	7,050	7,050
Spot price	7,400	7,000	6,500
Profit/loss	−350	+50	+550

Financial Futures

Futures are traded in a wide variety of commodities: wheat, sugar, gold, silver, copper, oranges, coco, oil soybean etc. Commodity prices fluctuate far and wide. For large buyers of a commodity whose prices swing downward and upward, there are significant cost implications. These companies reduce their risk of upward movements in prices by hedging with commodity futures.

There are firms which do not have commodity prices exposure but they have significant exposure of interest rates and exchange rates fluctuations. These firms can hedge their exposure through financial futures. **Financial futures**, like the commodity futures, are contracts to buy or sell financial assets at a future date at a specified price. Financial futures, introduced for the first time in 1972 in USA, have become very popular. Now the trading in financial futures far exceeds trading in commodity futures.

Futures Contracts vs. Forward Contracts

Futures contracts originated for hedging risk of agricultural commodities and later on many more commodities were covered under futures contracts. In terms of the basic nature, forward contracts and futures contracts are same. But in the operating terms there are the following differences.

Table 33.2: Examples of Listed Futures Contracts

Contract	*Contract size*	*Exchange*
Corn	5,000 bushels	CBT
Soybeans	5,000 bushels	CBT
Wheat	5,000 bushels	KC
Barley	20 metric ton	WPG
Rye	21 metric ton	WPG
Pork bellies	40,000 lbs	CME
Cotton	50,000 lbs	CTN
Orange juice	15,000 lbs.	CTN
Sugar (world)	112,000 lbs.	CSCE
Coffee	37,500 lbs.	CSCE
Gold	100 troy oz.	CMX
Crude oil (light sweet)	1,000 barrels	NYM
Eurodollar	$1 million	LIFFE
German Mark	125,000 marks	IMM
Treasury bonds	$100,000	CBT
Treasury notes	$100,000	CBT
S&P Index	500 times Index	CME
NYSE Composite	501 times Index	NYFE
Major Market Index	250 times Index	CBT

CBT = Chicago Board of Trade
KC = Kansas City
WPG = Winnipeg
CME = Chicago Mercantile Exchange
CTN = New Cotton Exchange
CSCE = Coffee, Sugar, and Cocoa Exchange
CMX = Commodity Exchange in New York
NYM = New York Mercantile
IMM = International Monetary Market in Chicago
LIFFE = London International Financial Futures Exchange
NYFE = New York Futures Exchange

Organised futures exchanges Forward contracts are contracts between two parties, called the **counterparties** and they are not traded on any exchange. Future contracts are traded in the organised future exchanges. As stated earlier, futures contracts are forward contracts traded on the futures exchanges. The Chicago

Board of Trade is the largest futures exchange. Other exchanges include Commodity Exchange in New York, International Monetary Market in Chicago, London International Financial Futures Exchange etc. In a futures exchange the delivery dates are specified, but there is choice of delivery dates. The futures prices would be higher as the delivery date extends. For example, the December 2004 futures contract will have a higher price than, say, the October 2004 futures contract.

Standardised contracts Futures contracts are standardised contracts in terms of the amount or quantity as well as the quality of the product. The seller of the futures contract will have to deliver goods or commodities of a specified quality. Forward contracts are non-standard. They are custom-made depending on the requirements of the counterparties. Table 33.2 gives examples of futures contracts in certain commodities, products and financial instruments, contract size and the exchange where these futures contracts are traded. For example, you may notice that if you want to enter into a barley futures contract, the minimum size of the contract 20 metric ton.

Margin The buyers and sellers of the futures contracts are required to deposit some cash or securities as margin. This is done to ensure that the buyers and sellers honour the deal. In case of forward contracts, there is no formal requirement of margin.

Marked to market This is a significant difference between forward contracts and futures contracts. Forward contracts are settled on the due date. But in the case of futures contracts, there is daily closing and reopening of the position which is called **marked to market**. Consider an example to understand the meaning of marked to market. Suppose you have a futures contract to deliver 1,000 troy ounces of gold at $300 per troy ounce. Assume that the price of the gold futures next day is $305 per troy ounce of gold. You have a loss on your sales of 1,000 troy ounces of gold: $1,000 (305 - 300) = \$5,000$. You will be required to pay this amount to the futures exchange. After the first day your loss is $5 per troy ounce and now your obligation is to deliver gold at $305 per troy ounce. This is like buying back your future position each day and then entering into a new futures contract. The buyer of the gold has a reverse position. He makes a profit of $5 due to increase in the futures price. He will receive this profit from the exchange. On the part of the buyer of gold, this is like selling back the futures position each day and then entering into a new futures contract. This is referred to marked to market. Marked to market means that profit and loss on a futures contract are calculated each day, and if there is a profit, you receive profit from the exchange but if there is a loss, you pay loss to the exchange.

Delivery A seller of the futures contract may wait for the contract to mature and then make the delivery. In practice, the seller of the futures contracts buys back the futures just before delivery. Most forward contracts are made to give and take delivery.

Futures and Spot Prices of Financial Futures

The price of a commodity or financial asset for immediate delivery is known as the **spot price**. The futures price and spot price today will not be the same. Let us first explain the futures and spot prices of a financial asset. The difference in the prices will be on account of the financial cost and dividend or interest associated with a financial security. Suppose a person owns a share that he can sell immediately for cash or sell at a later date at the futures price. If he sells the financial asset at the spot price immediately instead of selling share futures, he will earn interest on the amount received, but he will have to forgo any dividend on the share that he would have received by holding the asset. Let us consider another example where a person wants to buy a share. He can buy it immediately at spot price, or enter into a futures contract and take delivery in the future at futures price. Under the futures contract, there will be no outgo of cash and the buyer has an opportunity of earning interest on the purchase price. But, since the buyer will not hold the share, he will lose the opportunity of earning dividends (or interest in case of a debt security). Thus, the relationship between the spot and the future prices will be as follows:

$$\text{Futures price} = \text{Spot price} \, (1 + r_f)^t - \text{dividend foregone}$$

$$\text{Spot price} = \frac{\text{Future price}}{(1 + r_f)^t} + \frac{\text{Dividend foregone}}{(1 + r_f)^t} \tag{1}$$

Alternatively, we can write the following equation:

$$\text{Spot price} - \frac{\text{Dividend foregone}}{(1 + r_f)^t} = \frac{\text{Future price}}{(1 + r_f)^t} \tag{2}$$

Note that r_f is the risk-free rate of interest. Let us consider an example of the stock index futures.

Stock Index Futures Stock index futures are futures contracts on stock market indices. For example, stock index futures are available on New York Stock Exchange, S&P500, S&P100, and the Major market Index etc. What is the relationship between the stock index futures and spot prices?

Suppose the stock index is at 2,500. The risk-free interest rate is 6 per cent per annum. The average annul dividend yield is 2 per cent. How much would be the one-year stock index futures?

$$\text{Futures price} = 2,500 \, (1.06)^1 - 2,500 \, (0.02)^1 = 2,600$$

Stock index futures, like other futures contracts are traded in organised exchanges and have standardised size. For example, the S&P500 index has a contract size of $500 times the index.

On 20 November, 2004, a broker is anticipating rise in S&P500 when the December S&P500 futures is at 1,200. The broker purchases one December contract for $1,200 \times \$500 = \$600,000$. The S&P500 index increases to 1,250 by 20 December, 2004. The broker decides to sell his contract. How much profit does the broker make?

The broker's profit is: $(1,250 - 1,200) \times \$500 = \$125,000$.

Spot and Future Prices of Commodity Futures: There is a difference between the spot and futures prices of financial assets and commodities. In case of commodity futures, there is no dividend forgone. Further, the buyer of commodity futures does not need to store commodity as delivery will be in the future. Therefore, he avoids storage cost. Also, the buyer does not have commodity on hand which does not give him a comfort or convenience of meeting sudden requirements. Thus, the buyer saves storage cost but loses in terms of **convenience yield**.[1] The spot and futures prices relationship in case of commodities futures is given as follows:

$$\text{Spot price} = \frac{\text{Future price}}{(1+r_f)^t} - \frac{\text{Storage costs}}{(1+r_f)^t}$$
$$+ \frac{\text{Convenience yield}}{(1+r_f)^t} \qquad (3)$$

$$\frac{\text{Future price}}{(1+r_f)^t} = \text{Spot price}$$
$$+ \left(\frac{\text{Storage costs}}{(1+r_f)^t} - \frac{\text{Convenience yield}}{(1+r_f)^t} \right) \qquad (4)$$

The difference between the present value storage costs and convenience yield is **net convenience yield** (NCY). In practice, it can be inferred as the difference between the present value of futures price and spot price.

Illustration 33.4: Convenience Yield

Suppose the spot price for wheat was $2.85 per bushel in September 2004. The one-year futures price was $3.38 per bushel. The interest rate is 6 per cent. What is the net convenience yield?

$$\frac{3.38}{(1.06)^1} = 2.85 + \text{PV (storage costs − convenience yield)}$$

$$\text{PV (NCY)} = 3.19 - 2.85 = \$\,0.34$$

Trading in the futures contracts runs into billions of dollars each day. Since the futures contracts are traded on the organised exchanges, there is high degree of liquidity. But the futures contracts may not suit the needs of all. The contract size is standardised and the delivery dates are specified in each year. If the futures contracts are not suitable for the needs of a company, it can buy or sell forward contracts.

SWAPS

Swaps are similar to futures and forwards contracts in providing hedge against financial risk. A **swap** is an agreement between two parties, called counterparties, to trade cash flows over a period of time. Swaps arrangements are quite flexible and are useful in many financial situations. Two most popular swaps are **currency swaps** and **interest-rate swaps**. These two swaps can be combined when interest on loans in two currencies are swapped. The development of the swaps in the eighties is a significant development. The interest rate and currency swap markets enable firms to arbitrage the differences between capital markets. They make use of their comparative advantage of borrowing in their domestic market and arranging swaps for interest rates or currencies that they cannot easily access.

Currency Swaps

Currency swap involves an exchange of cash payments in one currency for cash payments in another currency. Most international companies require foreign currency for making investments abroad. These firms find difficulties in entering new markets and raising capital at convenient terms. Currency swap is an easy alternative for these companies to overcome this problem.

Suppose Ranbosche, an Indian pharmaceutical company, has a subsidiary in Malaysia. It wants to expand its operations in Malaysia which will cost the company 50 million ringits. The ringit interest rate is 8 per cent per annum. The company is well known in India; therefore, it is in a much better position to raise rupee loan in India than ringit loan in Malaysia. The financial manager decides to issue 10 per cent bonds of Rs 600 million to Indian investors. As a result, Ranbosch will receive cash flow of Rs 600 million now and will undertake to pay Rs 60 million interest each year for five years and repay Rs 600 million after five years. The financial manager simultaneously enters into a swap deal with National Bank of India to exchange its future rupee liability for ringits. Suppose the spot exchange rate is 1 Malaysian ringit = 12 Indian rupees. The bank will pay Ranbosche rupees to service its rupee loan; and the company will make annual payments in ringits to the bank. The cash flow consequences of the deal are shown in Table 33.3. Column 1 shows cash flows of the rupee loan – Ranbosche will receives Rs 600 million in year 0 and will pay Rs 60 million annual interest for five years and repay Rs 600 million principal amount after five years. The company will trade Rs 600 million for Ringit 50 million at the spot exchange rate with National Bank in year 0. Ranbosche will receive sufficient rupees from the bank to service the rupee loan and will undertake to pay the bank Malaysian ringits. The net effect of these transactions is to swap Ranbosche's 10 per cent rupee loan into 8 per cent Malaysian ringit loan.

Table 33.3: Cash Flows under Currency Swap

Year	Currency	Issue rupee loan	Swap rupees for ringits	Net cash flow on swap
Year 0	Rupees	+600	-600	0
	Ringits		+50	+50
Year 1	Rupees	−60	+60	0
	Ringits		−4	−4
Year 2	Rupees	−60	+60	0
	Ringits		−4	−4
Year 3	Rupees	−60	+60	0
	Ringits		−4	−4
Year 4	Rupees	−60	+60	0
	Ringits		−4	−4
Year 5	Rupees	−660	+660	0
	Ringits		−54	−54

Currency swaps are a form of **back-to-back loan**. For example, an Indian company wants to invest in Singapore. Suppose the government regulations restrict the purchase of Singapore dollars for investing abroad but the company is allowed to lend rupees abroad and borrow Singapore dollars. The company could find a Singapore company that needs Indian rupees to invest in India. The Indian company would borrow Singapore dollars and simultaneously lend rupees to the

1. Brealey, Richard A. and Myers, Stewart C., *Principles of Corporate Finance*, New York, Irwin McGraw-Hill, sixth edition, 2000, pp. 767–68.

Singapore company. Currency swaps have replaced the back-to-back loans. Back-to-back loans developed in UK when there were restrictions on companies to buy foreign currency for investing outside the country.

Interest Rate Swaps

The **interest rate swap** allows a company to borrow capital at fixed (or floating rate) and exchange its interest payments with interest payments at floating rate (or fixed rate). Suppose Company X is AAA-rated company located in USA. The company has borrowed $10 million floating-rate loan to finance a capital expenditure investment. The five-year floating-rate loan is indexed to LIBOR (London Interbank Offer Rate). LIBOR is the market-determined interest rate for banks to borrow from each other in the Eurodollar market. When the company issued floating-rate loan the interest rates were low. Now the interest rates are showing great volatility. Under the floating-rate loan, the company's interest payments will depend on LIBOR rate. The interest amount each year will be: LIBOR rate × $10 million. Suppose LIBOR rate is either 5.75 per cent, or 6.25 per cent or 6.75 per cent. The company's floating-rate interest payments will be:

	LIBOR Rate		
	5.75%	6.25%	6.75%
Floating-rate loan interest (LIBOR rate × $10 million)	575,000	625,000	675,000

Suppose Company X expected to have a steady flow of revenue from its investment. The company, instead of a floating-rate loan, could have taken five-year fixed-rate loan to finance the capital expenditure. The fixed-rate loan would have made sense for Company X since it would be using a fixed-rate liability (loan) to finance a fixed-rate asset (capital expenditure). Under its floating-rate loan, the company will have to pay higher amount of interest when the interest rate rises while it is earning a steady profit from its investment. With the fixed-rate loan, the company would pay constant amount of interest and could avoid the interest rate risk associated with a floating-rate loan. What should Company X do?

The company could buy back the floating-rate loan and instead take fixed-rate loan. This is a costly alternative. The company has to incur transaction costs and might suffer trading loss. However, there is a convenient alternative available to the company. It can enter into an interest rate swap. The company can swap the fixed-rate loan for the floating-rate loan. It would pay fixed payments for payments indexed to floating interest rates. If the interests rise, it will increase the company's interest amount on the floating-rate loan but, under swap, its receipts will also increase. Thus, swap will offset the company's exposure.

Company X finds that currently the floating-rate loan based on LIBOR can be exchanged for 6.25 per cent fixed-rate loan. If the company decides to enter into a swap arrangement, it can agree to pay 6.25 per cent on notional amount of $10 million to a swap dealer and receive payment for the LIBOR rate on the same amount of the notional capital.

	LIBOR Rate		
	5.75%	6.25%	6.75%
Swap cash payment (LIBOR rate × $10 million)	575,000	625,000	675,000
Swap cash receipts (0.0625 × $10 million)	625,000	625,000	625,000
Net cash flow on swap	+50,000	0	−50,000

The net cash flow consequences of swap agreement and the floating-rate loan for the company under three different LIBOR rates will be as shown below:

	LIBOR Rate		
	5.75%	6.25%	6.75%
Floating-rate loan interest payment (LIBOR rate × $10 million)	575,000	625,000	675,000
+ Net cash flow on swap [(0.0625 − LIBOR)]	50,000	—	−50,000
Net payment	625,000	625,000	625,000

You may note that Company X's total payment on the floating-rate loan with swap is equal to $625,000 irrespective of what happens to LIBOR rate. The company has been able to hedge its interest rate risk without buying back its floating-rate loan and issuing fixed-rate loan. Through the swap arrangement, the company converted the floating-rate loan into 6.25 per cent synthetic fixed-rate loan.

The interest rate swaps can be used by portfolio managers and pension fund managers to convert their bond or money market portfolios from floating rate (or fixed rate) to synthetic fixed rate (or synthetic floating rate). There are many other possible applications of the interest rate swaps.

Illustration 33.5: Interest Rate Swaps

Mr. John is the portfolio manager in Osram Mutual Fund Company. He has a debt fund that has invested Rs 200 million in long-term corporate debentures. He wants to convert the holding into a synthetic floating-rate portfolio. The portfolio pays 9 per cent fixed return. Assume that a swap dealer offers 9 per cent fixed for MIBOR (Mumbai Inter Borrowing Rate). What should Mr. John do?

Mr. John should swap receiving MIBOR on a notional principal of Rs 200 million in exchange for payment at 9 per cent fixed rate. The cash flows of portfolio will change with MIBOR as shown below:

	MIBOR Rate		
(Rs in million)	8.50%	9.00%	9.50%
Fixed-rate portfolio return (9% × Rs 200 million)	18	18	18
+ Net cash flow on swap [(MIBOR − 0.09) × Rs 200 million]	−1	—	1
Net payment	17	18	19

RISK MANAGEMENT STRATEGY: CASE OF BHP LIMITED[1]

BHP is a global company with its headquarters in Australia. Its operations are confined to natural resources and it has three main lines of business: minerals exploration, production, and processing the main minerals under consideration being coal, copper, iron ore, diamonds, silver, lead, and zinc; hydrocarbon exploration and production primarily petroleum; and steel production. In the year 2000, 35 per cent of its revenues came from Australia and the remaining from USA (17 per cent), Japan (13 per cent) and Asia and Europe (35 per cent). Thus, the company's revenue streams are geographically diversified.

In spite of being diversified – productwise and geographically, BHP's businesses are influenced by external factors. It is exposed to selling and purchasing price risks, credit risks and interest rates and foreign exchange rates risks. In minerals business, the company is exposed to volatile prices of items like copper, gold, silver, lead, and zinc. It also purchases large quantity of diesel and natural gas. Its purchases relating to steel business include zinc, aluminium, tin, and electricity. In the petroleum business, it is exposed to risk of selling prices all kinds of petroleum products.

The basic consideration in the traditional risk management policy has been the reduction of the variability of the firm's future cash flows. Under this policy, derivatives are used as the major tools of reducing the cash flow variability. It is assumed that cash flow variability mitigation is good from the shareholders point of view and this will cause the shareholder value to increase. One effect is to reduce the chances of financial distress and thus, improve the firm's debt capacity and increased interest tax shields. However, these are not unique advantages as, according to the portfolio theory, shareholders can diversify their portfolios and mitigate their risks arising from cash flow variability of a particular business. A firm's financial policies – investment and financing – have an impact on the variability of its cash flows and financial distress. Thus, the risk management policy should be seen as an integrated risk management system incorporating the investment and financing choices.

Like many companies, BHP, in the past, had been using derivatives to hedge its risks. Also, there was no integrated policy for the entire company rather each business was individually managing risk exposures to specific commodities and exposures arising from interest rates and exchange rates. The BHP's risk management policy had the following problems:

1. BHP used financial derivatives, generally with a maximum period of 60 months, as main tools of hedging risks. Financial derivatives, with a limited time horizon as the main risk mitigating instruments cannot reduce all kinds of risks.
2. It did not consider its worldwide operations, locations, investments and financing choices as tools of natural hedge.
3. Each business was left to itself to hedge its risks. There was

no coordination. At times, there was duplication of efforts and risk policies of businesses would contradict each other.

New Policy

Under the new management policy, BHP introduced a new risk management policy. The following are the features of the new policy:

1. The company considers the **natural hedge** created from its diversified operations as the effective risk mitigation tool. It will reduce the residual risks, which are not expected to be very high.
2. It considers **integrated risk management** from the entire firm's point of view rather than allowing each business to have its own risk programme.
3. The company focuses on **cash flow at risk** (CFaR) for the firm. CFaR is a concept that estimates cash flows and their probabilities. Assuming a normal distribution, CFaR is estimated. (See Illustration 33.6 for an example of CFaR).
4. The firm recognises **financial structure** as a tool to reduce risk. In fact, the company had a very high debt ratio, which it has reduced now as a substitute for the unhedged position. The maturity of debt has also been reduced.
5. The company's approach of encouraging **structured non-recourse financing** for projects helps the company to pass on risks to financiers.
6. The company considers both direct and indirect **costs of risk reduction** under its new risk management policy.
7. To improve the overall performance and the effectiveness of risk management, the company has affected **organisational restructuring**. The new structures and systems enable the company to operate in a coordinated manner.

Illustration 33.6: Cash Flow at Risk (CFaR)

Suppose a wheat farmer will produce 50,000 bushels of wheat next year. He is expecting a price of $3.50 per bushel. Hence his expected cash flows are $50,000 \times 3.50 = \$175,000$. Since wheat prices fluctuate, there is uncertainty about the farmer's cash flows. The price could fall to $2.75 per bushel or could rise to $ 4.25 per bushel. The farmer needs to estimate the range of prices (and hence cash flows) with associated probabilities. The farmer may choose, say 95 per cent level of confidence at which the expected cash flows are given. Suppose the expected cash flows are $150,000 and $200,000. The farmer can say that he has $50,000 cash flow at risk with a 5 per cent probability.

USE OF DERIVATIVES

The opportunities to use derivatives to hedge risks are not available to all companies. In many countries, particularly the developing countries, no derivatives or very few types of derivatives are available. Even in developed economies where derivatives markets are well developed, all companies do not make full use of derivatives. Most surveys on the use of derivatives reveal that derivatives are popular among the large listed companies in US.

1. This section draws from the following articles: (i) Sinha, Siddarth, BHP Limited: Risk Management Strategy, *Vikalpa*, Vol. 27, No. 2, April-June 2002; (ii) Pandey, Ajay, Diagnosis–BHP Limited: Risk Management Strategy, *Vikalpa*, Oct.-Dec. 2002; and (iii) Basu, Sankarshan, Diagnosis – BHP Limited: Risk Management Strategy, *Vikalpa*, Oct.-Dec. 2002.

About the half of publicly traded firms uses one or the other form of derivatives. Among the companies using derivatives, the most widely used derivatives are the interest rate derivatives and the foreign exchange rate derivatives.[1]

The objective of firms using derivatives is to reduce the cash flow volatility and thus, to diminish the financial distress costs. This is consistent with the theory of risk management through derivatives. Some firms use derivatives not for the purpose of hedging risk rather to speculate about futures prices.[2]

There are a number of examples of companies who made substantial losses using derivatives. Perhaps the largest loss was incurred by German firm Metallgesellschaft (MGAG) and its American subsidiary MG Refining and Marketing (MGRRM).[3] The reported derivatives trading loss of MGRM was $1 billion. MRGM sold gasoline, heating oil and diesel fuel at fixed prices for up to 10 years. Unfortunately, the prices of most of these products increased and MRGM lost lots of money. MRGM could have hedged its position by buying forwards to acquire heating oil etc. for delivery in 10 years. Alternatively, it could have bought 10-year futures oil. The problem was that 10-year futures were not available. Of course, there were many more problems with MRGM's derivatives policies.

The other companies with large derivatives losses include Procter and Gamble and Gibson Greetings Card. The Barings Bank was brought down by the derivatives trading by Nicholas Leeson. It will take long to settle the question whether these losses occurred because of the misuse of derivatives. One lesson is clear that derivatives may not serve their purpose of hedging risk, rather may enhance the risk, if they are not used judiciously. If a firm sells futures without creating an offsetting position, it wll be said to be speculating rather than hedging the risk. Derivatives markets do require professional speculators to provide liquidity and protection to firms who trade in derivatives for risk reduction. But speculation by companies can lend them into deep problems.

Should firms continue using derivatives? Of course, companies must use derivatives to hedge risk, but with great care and caution. They must use derivatives just for reducing risk and not for speculation. They may make money sometime speculating in derivatives, but one day it may so happen that they may lose everything like Barings or the Japanese company, Sumitomo Corporation.

SUMMARY

❖ Investors, including firms, are risk averse. They aim at reducing risk by hedging through derivatives.

❖ Derivatives are instruments that derive their value and payoff from another asset, called underlying asset.

❖ Hedging helps to (i) reduce costs of financial distress, (ii) isolate the effects of changes in external factor like interest rates and foreign exchange rates on profitability, and (iii) allow managers to focus on improving operating efficiency rather worrying about changes in factors on which they have no control.

❖ Derivatives include options, forward contracts, futures contracts and swaps.

❖ A forward contract is an agreement between two parties, called counterparties, to buy and sell an asset at a future date at a price agreed upon today. There is no immediate flow of cash. Cash is paid or received on the due date. Forward contracts are obligations. They are not traded on organised exchanges.

❖ A futures contract is like a forward contract. But, unlike forward contracts, futures contracts are traded on organised exchanges. Thus, they are liquid. Yet another feature of futures contract is that they are marked to market. Prices differences every day are settled through the exchange clearing house. The clearinghouse pays to the buyer if the price of a futures contract increases on a particular day. The seller pays money to the clearing house. The reverse will happen if the prices decrease.

❖ Swaps are arrangements to exchange cash flows over time. In a currency swap, the agreement provides for exchanging payments denominated in one currency for payments in another currency over a period of time. In an interest rate swap, one type of interest payments, say, fixed-rate payments, is exchanged for another, interest payments, say, floating-rate payments. The floating interest rates may be tied to LIBOR.

KEY CONCEPTS

Cash flow at risk (CFaR)	Forward contracts	Interest rate swaps	Spot price
Cash transaction	Futures contracts	Long hedge	Swaps
Currency swaps	Futures price	Natural hedge	Synthetic fixed-rate loan
Deliverable instrument	Hedging	Options	Synthetic floating-rate loan
Derivatives	Integrated risk management	Short hedge	Taking delivery

1. Howton, Shwan D. and Perfect, Steven B., "Currency and Interest Rates Derivatives use in US Firms", *Financial Management*, winter, 1998.
2. Dolde, Walter, "The Trajectory of Corporate Financial Risk Management," *Journal of Applied Corporate*, Finance, fall, 1993.
3. Culp, C. and Miller, M., "Metallgesellschaft and the Economics of Synthetic Storage," *Journal of Applied Corporate Finance*, winter 1995.

REVIEW QUESTIONS

1. What are derivatives? Why do companies hedge risk using derivatives?
2. How can options be used to hedge risk? Illustrate your answer.
3. Define forward and future contracts? What are the differences between forward and future contracts?
4. What is the difference between commodity futures and financial futures? What is the relationship between spot and future prices of the financial futures?
5. Consider the following two strategies. Strategy 1: Buy gold at spot price today and hold it for six months. Strategy 2: Take a long position on the gold futures contract expiring in six months. Lend money at risk-free interest rate that will be equal to the futures price in six months. Show the relationship between the spot price and the futures price.
6. Define a swap. Illustrate how interest rate swap helps to reduce risk exposure?
7. What is a currency swap? How does currency swap reduce exposure to risk? Give an example.

ILLUSTRATIVE SOLVED PROBLEMS

Problem 33.1: A farmer in Punjab expects to harvest 20,000 bushels of wheat in late July. On 10 June, the price of wheat is Rs 160 per bushel. The farmer is worried as he suspects that price will fall below Rs 160 before his July delivery date. He can hedge his position by selling July wheat futures. The July wheat futures price is Rs 157 per bushel. The farmer sold the July wheat futures. When July end approached, the price had fallen to Rs 150 per bushel. What is the value of the hedged position?

Solution: The gain on the futures contract is:

Gain = $(157 - 150) \times 20,000$ = Rs 140,000

Revenue from the sale of wheat = $150 \times 20,000$

           = Rs 3,000,000

Total cash flow = 140,000 + 3,000,000 = Rs 3,140,000

Cash flow per bushel of wheat = 3,140,000/20,000

           = Rs 157

You may notice that the farmer's cash flow per bushel is equal to the futures price, his loss from the physical sale of wheat is compensated from gain from the futures contract. This is an example of perfect hedge.

Problem 33.2: Jhaveri Brothers generally buys 1,000 troy ounces of gold every quarter. The firm is anticipating that the price of gold will rise to $450 per ounce from the current level of $405 per ounce before its quarterly purchase. The price of 3-month gold futures is $415 per ounce. What should the firm do? If the price after three months rises to $440, what are the consequences for Jhaveri Brothers?

Solution: Jhaveri Brothers should hedge its position by buying the gold futures contract. The firm should buy 3-month gold futures contracts at $415 per ounce. If the price really increases as anticipated by the firm, the loss from the high purchase price will be compensated by gain from the futures contract. For example, if the price is $440, the firm will have to pay: 440 × 1,000 = $440,000 in the cash market, but the firm will gain: (440 – 415) × 1,000 = $25,000. The total cash flow will be: 440,000 – 25,000 = $415,000, which is' equal to $415 per troy ounce of gold.

Problem 33.3: A prospective investor is expecting an increase in interest rate in next three months. The March T-Bills futures contracts are selling for 92 on 20 December. What should the investor do?

Solution: The investor should sell March T-Bills futures contracts short. If the investor's anticipation proves correct and interest rates rise, the investor should buy same number of contract that he sold and thus make money.

Problem 33.4: In the beginning of December 2004, Sunil – a broker on Bombay stock exchange is bullish about Sensex. The January Sensex futures is at 5,400. Suppose the contract size is Rs 5,000 times the index. Sunil buys one contract for Rs 270,000 (5,400 × 5,000). By the beginning of January, the January Sensex index rises to 5,500. What should Sunil do?

Solution: Sunil should sell his contract for Rs 275,000. His gain is: Rs 275,000 – Rs 270,000 = Rs 5,000.

PROBLEMS

1. Gold is currently selling $340 an ounce. The price is likely to fluctuate. It could increase to $360 or could decrease to $320 an ounce after three months. A gold mine company will supply 3,000 ounces in the market after three months. The company is considering hedging its risk. It has two alternatives available. It can enter a futures contract to deliver gold after three months at a futures price of $342. Alternatively, the company can buy 3-month put option at an exercise price of $340 an ounce at a premium of $3 per ounce. What should company do? What will be the consequences if the company does not hedge?

2. A flour mill plans to purchase 100 quintals of wheat in three months. The wheat prices can be Rs 7,000 or Rs 7,500 or Rs 8,000 per quintal. The owner of the flour mill is worried about the possible change in price. How can he protect himself against the price risk? Show the consequences of your suggestion to him.

3. Suppose wheat futures price is $3.40 per bushel for 3-month contract. The spot price today is $3.00. The risk-free interest rate is 12 per cent per year. The present value of storage cost is $0.23. What is the present value of wheat?

4. In March 2004, three-month future on Sensex stock index traded at 5,686.4. The dividend yield was 1.4 per cent and interest rate 8 per cent per annum. What should be the spot index?

5. Company *X* and company *Y* need funds to finance expansion of their operations. *X* is a AAA-rated company while *Y* is a BBB-rated company. *X* can borrow funds at 11 per cent or LIBOR + 0.03 per cent floating rate. *Y* can borrow funds at 14 per cent or LIBOR + 1.5 per cent. Can *X* and *Y* benefit from swap? How can you structure a swap arrangement between Company *X* and Company *Y*?

6. Firm *P* can get a 5-year fixed-rate dollar loan at 9 per cent and Euro loan at 7 per cent. Firm *Q*, on the other hand, can get 5-year fixed-rate dollar loan at 11 per cent and Euro loan at 8 per cent. Suppose *P* wants to take Euro loan and *Q* dollar loan. Can you structure a swap so that the borrowing cost to each company is less? Assume that spot exchange rate is 1.2 dollar to one Euro.

CHAPTER 34

International Financial Management

CHAPTER OBJECTIVES

- Understand how the foreign exchange market operates
- Explain the relationship between interest rates, inflation rates and exchange rates
- Focus on the techniques that can be used to hedge the foreign exchange risk
- Illustrate how the international capital budgeting decisions are made
- Highlight the methods of financing international operations

INTRODUCTION

The basis objectives of financial management in international (or multinational) firms remain the same as in domestic firms.[1] Like a domestic firm, a multinational firm's goal is to maximise the shareholder value on a global basis. It acquires assets that have present value more than their initial investment and it creates claims against them by issuing liabilities that are worth as much as or less than the funds raised. Multinational firms, however, operate in more than one country and their operations involve multiple foreign currencies. Their operations are influenced by politics and the laws of the countries where they operate. Thus, they face higher degree of risk as compared to domestic firms. A matter of great concern for the international firms is to analyse the implications of the changes in interest rates, inflation rates and exchange rates on their decisions and minimise the foreign exchange risk.

THE FOREIGN EXCHANGE MARKET

Consider an example of how and when a foreign exchange (forex) is involved. Suppose that Reliance Industries Limited (RIL) has entered into a contract with a French firm to import a machine for two crore French franc (FF). As per the contract, RIL (importing firm) is required to make the payment to the French firm (exporting firm) in French francs. RIL will need French francs to honour its payment obligation for which it will approach a commercial bank dealing in the foreign exchange market to purchase French francs by exchanging Indian rupees (INR). Take another example. Hindustan Lever Limited (HLL) has exported goods to a German importer. The importing German company will make payment to HLL in its currency–Duesch Mark (DM). HLL will convert German marks in Indian rupees in the foreign exchange market.

The **foreign exchange market** is the market where the currency of one country is exchanged for the currency of another country. Most currency transactions are channelled through the worldwide interbank market. **Interbank market** is the wholesale market in which major banks trade with each other. Forex market is a worldwide market of an informal network of telephone, telex, satellite, facsimile, and computer communications between the forex market participants which include banks, foreign exchange

---

1. There are a number of excellent textbooks on international finance. Two very popular text books are: Eitman, D.K. and Stonehill, A.F., Multinational Business Finance, Addison-Wesley, 1995; and Shapiro, A.C., Multinational Financial Management, Prentice-Hall International, 1996.

dealers, arbitrageurs, and speculators. The foreign market operators are guided by different motives when they deal in the foreign exchange market. The following is a typical classification of the participants in the foreign exchange market:

- *Arbitrageurs* Arbitrageurs seek to earn risk-less profits by taking advantage of differences in exchange rates among countries.
- *Traders* Traders engage in the export or import of goods to a number of countries. They operate in the foreign exchange market because exporters receive foreign currencies which they have to convert into local currencies, and importers make payments in foreign currencies which they purchase by exchanging the local currency. They also operate in the foreign exchange market to hedge their risk.
- *Hedgers* Multinational firms have their operations in a number of countries and their assets and liabilities are designated in foreign currencies. The foreign exchange rates fluctuations can cause diminution in the home currency value of their assets and liabilities. They operate in the foreign exchange market as hedgers to protect themselves against the risk of fluctuations in the foreign exchange rates.
- *Speculators* Speculators are guided purely by the profit motive. They trade in foreign currencies to benefit from the exchange rate fluctuations. They take risks in the hope of making profits.

Foreign Exchange Rates

A **foreign exchange rate** is the price of one currency quoted in terms of another currency. For example, an exchange rate of US dollar (US$) 0.02538 per Indian rupee (INR) means that the price of one INR is $ 0.02538. When the rate is quoted per unit of the domestic currency, it is referred to as **direct quote**. Thus, the US$ and INR exchange rate would be written as US$ 0.02538/INR. The rate can be expressed differently. We can say that the price of one US dollar in INR 39.40, that is, INR 39.40/US$. When the rate is quoted as units of domestic currency per unit of the foreign currency, it is referred to as **indirect quote**. The exchange rate between the US dollar and Indian rupee can be expressed in either Indian rupees per US dollar or in US dollar per Indian rupee.

Cross Rates

Given the exchange rates of two currencies, we can find the exchange rate for the third currency. For example, the US dollar-Thai baht exchange rate is: US$ 0.02339/Baht, and the US dollar-Indian rupee exchange rate is: US$ 0.02538/INR. Suppose that INR is not quoted against Thai baht. What is the Baht/INR exchange rate? One Indian rupee costs US$ 0.02538 while one baht costs US$ 0.02339. Thus one Indian rupee should cost: 0.02539/0.02339 = Baht1.085. That is:

$$\frac{US\$\,0.02538}{INR} \div \frac{US\$\,0.02339}{Baht} = \frac{US\$\,0.02538}{US\$\,0.02339} \times \frac{Baht}{INR}$$

$$= \frac{Baht\,1.085}{INR}$$

A **cross rate** is an exchange rate between the currencies of two countries that are not quoted against each other, but are quoted against one common currency. Currencies of many countries are not freely traded in the forex market. Therefore, all currencies are not quoted against each other. Most currencies are, however, quoted against the US dollar. The cross rates of currencies that are not quoted against each other can be quoted in terms of the US dollar.

Illustration 34.1: Cross-rate Calculation

Suppose that German DM is selling for $ 0.62 and the buying rate for the French franc (FF) is $ 0.17, what is the FF/DM cross-rate? It is

$$\frac{US\$\,0.62}{DM} \times \frac{FF}{US\$\,0.17} = \frac{FF\,3.65}{DM}$$

Spot exchange rates The **spot exchange rate** is the rate at which a currency can be bought or sold for immediate delivery which is within two business days after the day of the trade. In the spot market, currencies are traded for immediate delivery (within two days). Financial newspapers generally provide information on exchange rates. Table 34.1 shows the foreign exchange rates quotes from the Internet. For example, if you want to buy pound sterling, a bank will sell one British pound for INR 82.5861. These rates are wholesale rates for trades among dealers in the interbank market. Financial dailies also quote cross rates.

Table 34.1: Exchange Rates: Indian Rupee (INR) vis-à-vis Foreign Currencies

Currency	INR per	per INR
Australian dollar	32.2037	0.0311
Brazilian real	15.7864	0.0633
British pound	82.5861	0.0121
Canadian dollar	35.5573	0.0281
Chinese yuan	5.5505	0.1802
Euro	56.2879	0.0178
Hong Kong dollar	5.8908	0.1698
Japanese yen	0.4191	2.3863
Mexican peso	3.9605	0.2525
New Zealand dollar	30.3453	0.0330
Norwegian krone	6.7187	0.1488
Singapore dollar	27.1633	0.0368
South African rand	7.0637	0.1416
South Korean won	0.0401	24.9271
Swedish krona	6.1937	0.1615
Swiss franc	36.4473	0.0274
Thai baht	1.1117	0.8996
US dollar	45.9400	0.0218

Indian rupee as of Tuesday, September 14, 2004, 19:05 EDT
Source: http://www.uta.fi/~ktmatu/rate-inr.html

Bid-ask Spread

The foreign exchange dealers are always ready to buy or sell foreign currencies. The quotations are given as a **bid-ask price**. The difference between the buying (bid) and selling (ask) rates is the forex operator's (say, a bank) spread. **Bid-ask spread** is the difference between the bid and ask rates of a currency. It is based on the breadth and depth of the market for that currency and its volatility. This spread is a cost of transacting in the foreign exchange market. It is computed as given below:

$$\text{Spread} = \frac{\text{Ask price} - \text{Bid price}}{\text{Ask price}} \quad (1)$$

Forward Exchange Rates

The **forward exchange** rate is the rate that is currently paid for the delivery of a currency at some future date. In the forward market, currencies are traded for future delivery. In terms of the volume of currency transactions, the spot exchange market is much larger than the forward exchange market.

Forward rates (for example, 30-day, 90-day, or 180-day forward rates) for a few currencies are quoted in the forex market. Most banks will, however, quote currency forward rates to the traders.

Forward premium or discount The forward rate may be at a premium or at a discount. Forward rate premium or discount may be shown as an annualised percentage deviation from the spot rate. Suppose that US$-INR spot exchange rate is US$ 0.025063/INR. You can purchase US dollars at this exchange rate for immediate delivery (within two business days). Instead of buying US dollars immediately, you can enter into an agreement with a bank to deliver US dollars to you after six months. The bank has quoted a 6-month forward rate of US$ 0.024390/INR. Is the 6-month forward rate of US dollar at a premium or at discount? You may observe that the forward rate of dollar is lower than the spot rate. If you purchased US dollars for a 6-month delivery, you will get fewer dollars for your rupees than in a spot purchase. Since forward dollars are more expensive than spot dollars, the dollar is said to be trading at a premium relative to the Indian rupee. For a direct quote, the annualised forward discount or premium can be calculated as follows:

$$\begin{array}{l}\text{Forward premium} \\ \text{or discount}\end{array} \left[\dfrac{\dfrac{\text{Spot}}{\text{rate}} - \dfrac{\text{Forward}}{\text{rate}}}{\text{Spot rate}}\right] \times \dfrac{360}{\text{Days}} \quad (2)$$

For a 6-month forward, the annualised premium is as follows:

$$\begin{array}{l}\text{6-month forward} \\ \text{discount or premium}\end{array} = \left[\dfrac{0.025063 - 0.02439}{0.02439}\right] \times \dfrac{360}{180} = 5.5\%$$

Thus, the forward dollar is at a premium of 5.5 per cent relative to the Indian rupee. We can also say that the forward rupee is selling at a discount of 5.5 per cent relative to the dollar. In terms of indirect quote, the INR/$ spot exchange rate is INR 39.90/$ and forward rate is INR 41.00/$. For an indirect quote, the forward premium or discount can be calculated as follows:

$$\begin{array}{l}\text{Forward premium} \\ \text{or discount}\end{array} \left[\dfrac{\dfrac{\text{Forward}}{\text{rate}} - \dfrac{\text{Spot}}{\text{rate}}}{\text{Spot rate}}\right] \times \dfrac{360}{\text{Days}}$$

$$= \frac{41.00 - 39.90}{39.90} \times 2 = 5.5\%$$

Forward contracts are tailor-made according to the firm's needs. Two parties to a forward contract can negotiate the terms in accordance with the currency, amount, premium/discount or any other issue.

INTERNATIONAL PARITY RELATIONSHIPS

The forex markets are considered efficient when exchange rates impound all available information and adapt expeditiously to new information. It is not possible for investors to earn abnormal profits in an **efficient forex markets**. Speculators or arbitrageurs will have opportunities to consistently earn large profits without any increase in risk only when the forex markets are inefficient. In an efficient forex market, comprising of large number of traders having access to information without much cost, the **arbitrage** activity will ensure that the disparities in the exchange rates are eliminated. It will also ensure that the exchange-adjusted prices of similar goods and financial assets will be equal in all the countries. This economic behaviour is referred to as the **law of one price**.

In a highly competitive forex market, free from government intervention, both spot and the forward exchange rates should be affected significantly by the current expectation of future events. They should change in expectation of a change in interest rates. In an efficient market, the change in the interest differential will get reflected quickly in both spot and forward exchange rates. Interest rates are influenced by inflation rates. If we assume that the forex markets are efficient, then interest rates, inflation rates and exchange rates will have equilibrium relationships. There are the following four international parity relationships:

1. Interest rate parity (IRP)
2. Purchasing power parity (PPP)
3. Forward rates and future spot rates parity
4. International Fisher effect (IFE)

Interest Rate Parity

Suppose that the interest rate on a one-year bond (rupee-denominated) in India is 14 per cent while a similar bond (franc-denominated) in France pays 9 per cent interest. The spot rate for French franc is FF 0.1522/INR and the 1-year forward rate is FF 0.1455/INR. If you have a choice of investment, which one should you choose?

You may notice that INR is trading at a forward discount. (Alternatively, FF is trading at a forward premium relative to INR). Let us assume that you have FF 1,000. If you invest FF 1,000 in France, at the end of one year, you will receive: FF 1,000 × 1.09 = FF 1,090. Alternatively, you can exchange FF 1,000 for the Indian rupees at the spot rate; you will receive: 1,000/0.1522 = INR 6,570.30. You can invest INR 6,570.30 at 14 per cent for one year. At maturity, you will receive: INR 6,570.30 × 1.14 = INR 7,490.14. You can sell the Indian rupees forward and immediately receive French franc: INR 7,490.14 × 0.1455 = FF 1,090. Both investments are of equal value. What you gain on the interest rate differential, you lose on the exchange rate differential. In other words, there is a parity between the interest rates and exchange rates, or simply interest rate parity. Thus:

$$\frac{1.09}{1.14} = \frac{0.1455}{0.1522} = 0.956$$

Interest rate parity characterises the relationship between interest rates and exchange rates of two countries. It states that the exchange rate of two countries will be affected by their interest rate differential. In other words, the currency of a high-interest-rate-country will be at a forward discount relative to the currency of a low-interest-rate-country, and vice versa. This implies that the exchange rate (forward and spot) differential will be equal to the interest rate differential between the two countries. That is:[1]

Interest differential = Exchange rate (forward and spot)
differential

$$\frac{(1+r_F)}{(1+r_D)} = \frac{f_{F/D}}{s_{F/D}} \qquad (3)$$

where r_F is interest rate of country F (say, the foreign country), r_D is interest rate of country D (say, domestic country), $s_{F/D}$ is the spot exchange rate between the countries F and D and $f_{F/D}$ is the forward rate between the countries F and D.

Interest rate parity states that the high interest rate on a currency is offset by the forward discount and that low interest rate is offset by forward premium. Arbitrage will ensure that this happens.

Suppose that in the example above, the 1-year forward exchange rate is FF 0.1512 (instead of FF 0.1455). Then, on selling the Indian rupees forward, you will get French franc: INR 7,490.14 × 0.1512 = FF 1,132.51. Thus, it is more profitable for you to invest in India. You can also borrow French franc, convert them in the Indian rupees at the spot rate and invest in India. Suppose you borrowed FF 100,000 for one year and invested in India, the following are the consequences:

1. You borrow FF 100,000 at 9 per cent for one year. After one year, you will have to pay: FF 100,000 × 1.09 = FF 109,000.
2. You convert FF 100,000 into INR at the spot rate. You will receive: FF 100,000/0.1522 = INR 657,030.
3. You invest INR7 657,030 at 14 per cent interest for one year. At the end of one year, you will receive: INR 657,030 × 1.14 = INR 749,015.
4. You sell INR 749,015 at 1-year forward rate of FF 0.1512 to receive after one year an assured amount of French franc: INR 749,015 × 0.1512 = FF 113,251.
5. After returning (principal plus interest) FF 109,000, you will be left with a profit of: FF 113,251 − FF 109,000 = FF 4,251. This is the **arbitrage profit.**

If you can make a riskless arbitrage profit, others will also. The arbitrage activity should result in the following effects:

1. The French interest rate will increase as arbitrageurs borrow francs.

2. The spot rate of the Indian rupees against the French franc will appreciate as arbitrageurs demand rupees against francs.
3. The interest rate in India will tend to fall as arbitrageurs invest rupees.
4. The forward rate of rupees against franc will depreciate as arbitrageurs sell rupees against francs.

The opportunity to make arbitrage profit will be, thus, eliminated soon. The equilibrium will be reached in terms of interest rate parity, and the interest rate differential will become equal to the exchange rate differential.

Interest rate parity works fairly well in the international capital markets where no restrictions exist for the flow of funds from one country to another and no tax asymmetries exist. **Eurocurrency markets** are such international capital markets where there are minimum restrictions and controls, and the market forces determine interest rates.

Purchasing Power Parity

Suppose the price of 10-gram standard gold in France is FF 761, how much should it cost in India? If the law of one price prevails, then the 10-gram standard gold in India should exactly cost FF 761 equivalent in the Indian rupees. Suppose it costs INR 5,000. For the prices to be equal, the current spot exchange rate between the French franc and the Indian rupee should be: FF 761/INR 5,000 = FF 0.1522/INR. In other words, FF 761/0.1522 = INR 5,000. This is referred to as the purchasing power parity in its absolute version. Now suppose that the inflation rate in India is expected to be 8 per cent and in France 5 per cent, the price of the 10-gram standard gold in France is expected to rise to FF 799. Will FF 799 also buy the 10-gram standard gold in India? The Indian inflation rate of 8 per cent is higher than the French interest rate of 5 per cent. The Indian price will increase to INR 5,400. The exchange rate will have to adjust for the gold's equivalent price in the French franc to be same in India. The Indian rupee relative to the French franc will have to depreciate by:

$$(1.08)/(1.05) - 1 = 0.02857 \quad \text{or} \quad 2.86 \text{ per cent}$$

to account for the difference in the inflation rates in the two countries. The expected exchange rate will be:

$$FF/INR = 0.1522 \times (1 - 0.02857) = FF\ 0.1479/INR$$

Thus, INR 5,400 × 0.1479 = FF 799. This is referred to as the purchasing power parity.

In absolute terms, **purchasing power parity** states that the exchange rate between the currencies of two countries equals the ratio between the prices of goods in these countries. Further, the exchange rate must change to adjust to the change in the prices of goods in the two countries. In relative terms, purchasing power states that the exchange rate between the currencies of the two countries will adjust to reflect changes in the inflation

---

1. The interest rate parity condition can be alternatively written as follows

$$\frac{(1+r_D)}{(1+r_F)} = \frac{f_{D/F}}{r_{D/F}} .$$

rates of the two countries. In formal terms, it implies that the expected inflation differential equals to the current spot rate and the expected spot rate differential. Thus:[1]

$$\begin{matrix} \text{Inflation rate} \\ \text{differential} \end{matrix} = \begin{matrix} \text{Current spot and expected spot} \\ \text{rate differential} \end{matrix}$$

$$\frac{(1+i_F)}{(1+i_D)} = \frac{E(s_{F/D})}{s_{F/D}} \qquad (4)$$

where i_D the rate of inflation in country D, i_F is the rate of inflation in country F, $s_{D/F}$ is the spot exchange rate between countries D and F, and $E(s_{D/F})$ is the expected spot rate between countries D and F, in future.

Illustration 34.2: Purchasing Power Parity and Spot Exchange Rate

Thailand and South Korea are running annual inflation rates of 5 per cent and 7 per cent, respectively. The current spot exchange rate is Won 18.50/Baht. What should be the value of the Thai baht in one year?

If purchasing power parity holds, then:

$$\frac{1.07}{1.05} = \frac{E(s_{W/B})}{18.5}$$

$$E(s_{W/B}) = 18.5 \times \frac{1.07}{1.05} = 18.85$$

The expected spot rate after one year will be: Won 18.85/Baht.

Expectation Theory of Forward Rates

What is the relationship between the forward rates and the expected spot rates in the future? Suppose you are an exporter who is expecting to receive the US dollars in the future. You have two choices. You can either wait until you receive your dollars and then convert them into rupees. You are exposed to the risk of drop in the value of dollar in the future. The second alternative is that you fix the price of the dollar today and sell the US dollars forward. You are thus able to avoid risk of a possible fall in the value of dollar. On the other hand, suppose you happen to be an importer who is required to make payment in the US dollars in the future. You will do the opposite. You will buy the US dollars forward to avoid the risk of a possible appreciation in the value of dollar in the future. If both the exporters and the importers are in large numbers, the forward rate of US dollar relative to the Indian rupee will be very close to the expected future spot rate. This is the **expectation theory of exchange rates.**

The expected future spot rate depends on the expectations of the forex market participants. If they can hedge their forex risk or if they are risk neutral, then the forward rate must be equal to the expected future spot rate.

In general, when the forward rate for any currency is higher than the market participants' prediction of the expected future spot rate, they will tend to sell the foreign currency forward. This should cause a fall in the forward rate until it equals the expected future spot rate. Similarly, when the forward rate is lower than the expected future spot rate, the market participants will purchase the foreign currency forward. As a consequence, the forward rate will rise until it reaches the expected future spot rate. The expectation theory of forward exchange rates states that the forward rate provides the best and unbiased forecast of the expected future spot rate. In formal terms, it means that the forward rate and the current rate differential must be equal to the expected spot rate and the current spot rate differential. Thus[2]:

$$\begin{matrix} \text{Forward and current} \\ \text{spot rates differential} \end{matrix} = \begin{matrix} \text{Expected and current} \\ \text{spot rate differential} \end{matrix}$$

$$\frac{f_{F/D}}{s_{F/D}} = \frac{E(s_{F/D})}{s_{F/D}} \qquad (5)$$

where $E(s_{F/D})$ is the expected future exchange rate (unit of foreign currency per unit of domestic currency) and $f_{F/D}$ is the forward rate.

In simple terms, the forward rate must be equal to the expected future spot rate. Thus:

Forward rate = Expected future spot rate

$$f_{F/D} = E(s_{F/D}) \qquad (6)$$

Does the expectation theory of exchange rates work in practice? The expectation theory works on an average. The actual future spot rates have been found to differ from the earlier forward rates. It is very difficult to predict accurately the exchange rates. However, the forward rate is the best possible forecaster of the expected future spot rate than any other alternative.

International Fisher Effect

We know that the **nominal interest rate** comprises of a **real interest rate** and an **expected rate of inflation**. The nominal rate of interest adjusts when the inflation rate is expected to change. The nominal interest rate will be higher when a higher inflation rate is expected and it will be lower when a lower inflation rate is expected. This is referred to as the **Fisher effect.** It is formally expressed as follows:

$$\left(1 + \begin{matrix} \text{nominal} \\ \text{interest rates} \end{matrix}\right) = \left(1 + \begin{matrix} \text{real interest} \\ \text{rate} \end{matrix}\right)\left(1 + \begin{matrix} \text{inflation} \\ \text{rate} \end{matrix}\right)$$

$$(1 + r_n) = (1 + r_r)(1 + i)$$

$$r_n = r_r + i + r_r i \qquad (7)$$

where r_n is nominal rate of interest, r_r is real rate on interest, and i is the inflation rate.

Note that the nominal rate of interest also includes a cross-

---

1. The purchasing power parity condition can be alternatively written as follows:

$$\frac{(1+i_D)}{(1+i_F)} = \frac{E(s_{D/F})}{s_{D/F}}$$

2. The alternative formula is:

$$\frac{f_{D/F}}{s_{D/F}} = \frac{E(s_{D/F})}{s_{D/F}}$$

product term, $r_r i$. In practice, this term is ignored.

If the international capital markets are perfect, then the equivalent risk investments in two countries should offer the same expected real rate of return. This is ensured by arbitrage. If the **expected real rate of return** is higher in one country than in another, capital would flow from the second to the first country, and investors will have opportunities to make riskless arbitrage profit. The arbitrage activity will persist until equilibrium is established in the expected real returns in the two countries. If the real rates of return are the same in two countries, then, as per the Fisher effect, the nominal rates of interest in the two countries will adjust exactly for the change in the inflation rates. In formal terms, the **international Fisher effect** states that the nominal interest rate differential must equal to the expected inflation rate differential in two countries. Thus[1]:

$$\frac{\text{Nominal interest}}{\text{rate differential}} = \frac{\text{Expected inflation}}{\text{rate differential}}$$

$$\frac{(1+r_F)}{(1+r_D)} = \frac{E(1+i_F)}{E(1+i_D)} \qquad (8)$$

Illustration 34.3: Purchasing Power Parity and Inflation

Suppose that the interest rate in Germany is 11 per cent and the expected inflation rate is 5 per cent. The British interest rate is 9 per cent. How much is the expected inflation rate in Britain?

If purchasing power parity holds, then the British inflation rate will be:

$$\frac{1.11}{1.09} = \frac{1.05}{1+i_B}$$

$$i_B = \frac{1.09 \times 1.05}{1.11} - 1 = 0.031 \text{ or } 3.1\%$$

You can verify that:

$$\frac{1.11}{1.09} = \frac{1.05}{1.031} = 1.018$$

In effect, the international Fisher effect implies that the expected future spot rate of a currency with a higher interest rate will tend to fall in value in the long run and the expected future spot rate of a currency with a lower interest rate will tend to rise in value in the long run. Thus, the interest differential between two countries should provide an unbiased forecast of the future change in the spot rate:

$$\frac{1+r_F}{1+r_D} = \frac{E(s_{F/D})}{s_{F/D}} \qquad (9)$$

Since the forward rate is an unbiased predictor of the future spot rate, Equation (9) converts into interest rate parity. The international Fisher effect follows from interest rate parity,

purchasing power parity and the expectation theory of forward exchange rate. Thus:[2]

$$\frac{(1+r_F)}{(1+r_D)} = \frac{(1+i_F)}{(1+i_D)} = \frac{E(s_{F/D})}{s_{F/D}} = \frac{f_{F/D}}{s_{F/D}} \qquad (10)$$

Illustration 34.4: International Fisher Effect

Suppose the one-year interest rate is 5 per cent on Swedish krona (SK) and the expected inflation rate is 2 per cent. The expected inflation rate on French franc (FF) is 6 per cent. The current spot exchange rate is FF 1.063/SK (which is equal to FF 1 = SK 0.9407). How much is the spot rate expected in one year? What will be the one-year forward rate?

According to the international Fisher effect, the interest rate differential must be equal to the inflation rate differential, and the interest rate differential provides a forecast of the expected future spot rate. If the expectation theory of exchange rate holds, then the forward rate should be equal to the expected future spot rate. Thus:

$$\frac{1+r_{FF}}{1.05} = \frac{1.06}{1.02} = \frac{E(s_{FF/SK})}{1.063} = \frac{f_{FF/SK}}{1.063}$$

$$\frac{1.091}{1.05} = \frac{1.06}{1.02} = \frac{1.1047}{1.063} = \frac{1.1047}{1.063} = 1.0392$$

The interest rate on French franc is 9.1 per cent; the expected future spot rate and the forward rate are FF 1.1047/SK (SK 0.9052/FF).

FOREIGN EXCHANGE RISK AND HEDGING

An international firm deals in foreign currency. It expects to receive or make payment in the foreign currency. The exchange rate between the firm's domestic currency and the foreign currency may rise or fall by the time the firm receives or pays the cash flows in the foreign currency. This exposes the firm to what is called the foreign exchange risk. **Foreign exchange risk** is the risk that the domestic currency value of cash flows, denominated in foreign currency, may change because of the variation in the foreign exchange rate. There would not be any foreign exchange risk if the exchange rates were fixed. We can distinguish between three types of foreign exchange exposures:

- Transaction exposure
- Economic exposure
- Translation exposure

Transaction Exposure

Suppose Air India Limited enters into an agreement with Airbus Industries to buy A-340 planes. The price of the planes is fixed in French franc. Air India will receive the planes immediately but will make payment of the total value of FF 1,000 million after six months. The current spot exchange rate is INR 6.60/FF. At the current exchange rate, the value of the contract is: FF 1,000 million × 6.60 = INR 6,600 million. The exchange rate

---

1. The alternative formula is:

$$\frac{(1+r_D)}{(1+r_F)} = \frac{E(1+i_D)}{E(1+i_F)}$$

2. The alternate formula is:

$$\frac{(1+r_D)}{(1+r_F)} = \frac{(1+i_D)}{(1+i_F)} = \frac{E(s_{D/F})}{s_{D/F}} = \frac{f_{D/F}}{s_{D/F}}$$

can change in the six months. Suppose the exchange rate at the end of six months is INR 6.95/FF, now Air India will have to spend: FF 1,000 million × 6.95 = INR 6,950 million; that is, INR 350 million more to buy FF 1,000 million and make payment to Airbus Industries. Of course, Air India will gain and pay less than the expected value at the time of the contract if the Indian rupee appreciates against the French franc. The problem lies in the fact that Air India cannot predict what the exchange rate would be after six months. It cannot be sure if the rupee will appreciate or depreciate. Air India is exposed to transaction risk. **Transaction exposure** involves the possible exchange loss or gain on existing foreign currency-denominated transactions. Let us consider another example.

Advani Exporters Limited has exported cotton fabrics to a firm in Malaysia at a total value of INR 5 million, or 421,940 ringits at the current exchange rate of 11.85 Indian rupee per Malaysian ringit. The change in the exchange rate will have no effect on Advani Exporters if the value of exports is fixed in terms of Indian rupees. However, Advani Exporters will face the exchange risk if they were to receive payment in Malaysian ringit. For example, if, at the time the payment is received, the exchange rate is 12.05 Indian rupees per ringit, Advani Exporters will receive 414,938. The actual loss of cash flows is: 421,940 – 414,938 = 7,002 ringits. This is a foreign currency transaction loss.

Economic Exposure

The changes in the foreign exchange rate affect the cash flows from operations. The value of the firm is affected by the unexpected changes in the expected cash flows. **Economic exposure** refers to the change in the value of the firm caused by the unexpected changes in the exchange rate. It is also referred to as **operating exposure** or the long-term cash flow exposure. Thus, the exchange risk may be defined as the variability of the firm's value resulting from the unanticipated exchange rate changes. Suppose an Indian company operates internationally; it buys goods and services from abroad, say, USA and sells goods and services, whose price is denominated in US dollars, in the foreign markets. If the exchange rate between Indian rupee and the US dollar changes, then the values of the cash flows in Indian rupees will change affecting the operating profitability. If the foreign exchange rate changes are unexpected, the value of the Indian firm would also be affected. The expected cash flows can change due to various factors. The input costs, prices of goods or investments can cause the cash flows to change. The cash flows are also affected by the pricing policy changes. Let us consider an example.

Suppose US company exported its goods of $ 100,000 at an exchange rate of 0.022 dollars per Indian rupee. To the importing Indian company the cost is: $ 100,000/0.022 = Rs 4,545,455. If the Indian rupee suddenly depreciates and the exchange rate shifts to $ 0.0218 per rupee, then the cost to the Indian importer would be: $ 100,000/0.0218 = Rs 4,587,156. The importer might increase the price of the products sold to the domestic buyers to cover the higher costs. If he does not increase price, his profit margins would fall. But he might lose the market share because of the increase in the price. This would

also have effect on the exporter's future sales which may shrink as the demand from the importer falls. The exporter may reduce the price to keep the cost of import same to the importer. The exporter's price would be: Rs 4,545,455 × 0.0218 = $ 99,091. But this would cause exporter's revenue to fall and profit to shrink. However, he would be able to maintain his market share and volumes. This example shows that a shift in the exchange rate could affect the immediate cash flows and as well as the cash flows in the future. The future cash flows are affected because a change in the exchange rate could also affect the price, volume, market share, and ultimately, a firm's competitiveness.

The example above reveals that economic exposure has two components: the transaction exposure and the real operating exposure. Transaction exposure involves the possible exchange loss or gain on existing foreign currency-denominated transactions. Real operating exposure takes into account the impact of both the exchange rate changes and the inflation rate changes. The exchange rate and inflation rate changes together could have serious effect on the magnitude of cash flows. The value of the firm would be affected if the cash flows change in real terms. We must note that the competitiveness of the firm will be affected if the real exchange rate changes. You may recall that under the international purchasing power parity condition, the real returns do not alter; the exchange rate changes are offset by the inflation differential between two countries. Thus, the real exchange rate will remain constant, and the firm's competitive position will not be affected by changes in the nominal exchange rate. In this sense, the firm does not face real operating exposure.

A firm's economic exposure, in fact, depends on the structures of the input and the output markets. The firm can manage the effects of exchange rate changes on its competitiveness by adjusting markets, product mix and input sourcing. Since, ultimately it is the firm's competitive position that gets affected, the exchange rate exposure should be dealt with strategically and it should be a concern of marketing, production and finance managers who should develop effective production, marketing and financial strategies. The objective should be to smooth the flow of cash under the variable exchange rates situations. The firm can locate its manufacturing to low cost production sites, maintain flexible manufacturing and pricing, explore new markets etc.

Translation Exposure

Ranbaxy, an Indian pharmaceutical company, has subsidiaries in USA, Malaysia, China, Vietnam and many other countries. The financial statements of these subsidiaries will be stated in the local currencies. When Ranbaxy consolidates financial statements of its subsidiaries with its financial statement, it will have to translate local currencies to the home currency, that is, Indian rupees. The exchange rate at the end of the accounting period may differ from the rate in the beginning of the accounting period. **Translation exposure** refers the exchange gain or loss occurring from the difference in the exchange rates at the beginning and the end of the accounting period. Notice that translation gain or loss is an accounting gain or loss, and it may not be related to economic gain or loss.

A firm is exposed to translation loss if it uses current exchange rate to translate its assets and liabilities. There are four methods in use in translating assets and liabilities:[1]

Current/Non-Current Method

Under this method, current assets and current liabilities are translated at the current rate and non-current assets and non-current liabilities at the historical rate. Profit and loss statement items are translated at the average exchange rate of the period. However, revenues and expenses related to non-current assets and non-current liabilities are translated at historic rate.

Monetary/Non-Monetary Method

Under this method, monetary balance sheet accounts such as cash, accounts receivables, payables, and long-term debt are translated at the current rate. Non-monetary accounts such as inventory, fixed assets, and long-term investments are translated at the historic rate. The profit and loss statement items are translated at the average exchange rate during the period. However, revenues and expense accounts related to non-monetary balance sheet accounts are translated at the historic rate.

Temporal Method

This method is similar to the monetary/non-monetary method with the only difference that the inventory may be translated at the current rate when it is shown at the market value.

Current Rate Method

Under this method, all balance sheet and income statement items are translated at the current rate.

Hedging Foreign Exchange Risk

If the Air India management thinks that the rupee will appreciate against the French franc in six months, it may not cover its foreign exchange exposure. This is a high-risk approach. It can benefit Air India significantly, if later on the rupee actually appreciates. But the potential cost is also very high. If subsequently the rupee depreciates, instead of appreciating as predicted by the Air India management, the company's cost can be very high. Some companies have a policy of partially covering their exposure. This policy suffers from subjectivism as there is no sound method of deciding how much to cover and how much to keep uncovered. The firm's risk remains unlimited in the partially covered exposure. In fact, keeping the foreign exchange exposure totally or partially uncovered tantamount to **speculation.**

There are three alternatives available to companies to hedge against the foreign exchange exposure:

- Forward contract
- Foreign currency option
- Money market operations

The hedging techniques of foreign currency option and money operations may not be available to companies in many countries, particularly developing countries. However, a large majority of companies can cover their foreign exchange exposure through forward contracts.

Forward contract Air India may like to eliminate fully its currency risk. Hence it can take a **full forward cover** against its foreign exchange exposure and entirely hedge its risk. It can contract with a bank to buy French franc forward at an agreed exchange rate. Suppose the six-month forward rate is INR 6.70/FF 1.00. This means that Air India has a definite cost of INR 6,700 million. Irrespective of the actual exchange rate at the end of six months, its cost will remain INR 6,700 million. The advantage of this approach is that the Air India management can concentrate on its operations rather than worrying about the foreign exchange loss (or gain). Most international companies have the policy of covering hundred per cent of their foreign exchange risk.

Suppose the Air India management is expecting the French franc to fall. It may therefore leave its exposure uncovered since it would benefit the company. But the management is not sure that the French franc will fall *definitely*. Hence, instead of going for a full forward cover or keeping the exposure fully uncovered, the Air India management may decide to go for partial forward cover. Suppose it covers 50 per cent of its exposure, keeping 50 per cent exposure uncovered. This is a subjective policy as there is no objective way to determine the appropriate ratio of covered and uncovered exposure. Further, this policy implies that Air India would buy INR 3,300 million with forward contracts of INR 6.70/FF 1.00 and INR 3,300 million at the spot exchange rate at the end of six months. Air India's total potential exposure is still unlimited since INR 3,300 million exposure is uncovered. If the French franc appreciates, Air India would incur a heavy loss. The partial cover policy is never a win-win situation.

In Figure 34.1, we show the cost of uncovered, 50 per cent covered and 100 per cent covered strategies for Air India for different spot rates at the end of six months. The cost of uncovered position depends on the spot rate. If French franc falls and is below the current spot rate (INR 6.60/INR 1.00), Air India would benefit. But the loss would be very high if the French franc appreciates. The uncovered position line in Figure 34.1 has the steepest slope. On the other hand, the cost remains the same, irrespective of the spot rate, in the full covered strategy. The partial covered position line is less steep than the uncovered position line, but the exposure is clearly unlimited if the French franc appreciates.

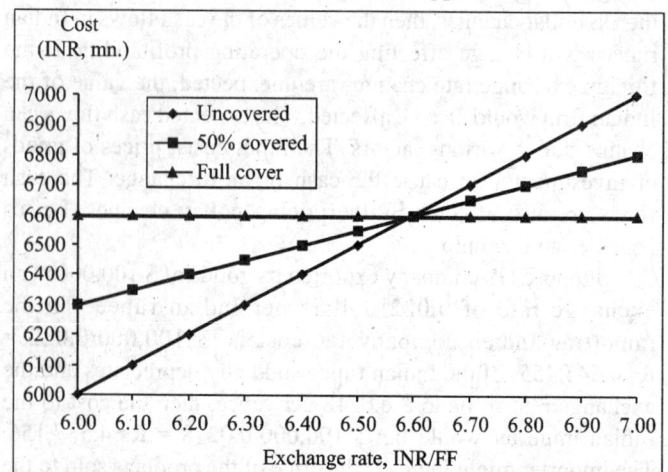

Figure 34.1: Cost of alternative hedging strategies

Cost of forward contract What is the cost of the forward contract? It is the difference between the forward rate and the expected spot rate (*not* the current spot rate) at the time cash flows are paid or received. Thus the cost of the forward contract in case of direct quote (units of foreign currency per unit of domestic currency) is:

$$\text{Cost of forward contract (annual)} = \left[\frac{f_{F/D} - E(s_{F/D})}{f_{F/D}}\right] \times \frac{360}{\text{Days}}$$

In case of indirect quote (units of domestic currency per unit of foreign currency), the cost of forward contract is:

$$\text{Cost of forward contract (annual)} = \left[\frac{E(s_{D/F}) - f_{D/F}}{E(s_{D/F})}\right] \times \frac{360}{\text{Days}}$$

Suppose Air India (the domestic company) takes full forward cover and the 6-month forward exchange rate is INR 6.70/FF 1.00. After six months, the expected spot rate is INR 6.95. The cost of forward contract to Air India is:

$$\text{Cost of forward contract (annual)} = \left[\frac{6.95 - 6.70}{6.95}\right] \times \left(\frac{360}{180}\right)$$
$$= 0.072 \text{ or } 7.2\%$$

Foreign Currency Option

The **foreign currency option** is the right (not an obligation) to buy or sell a currency at an agreed exchange rate (exercise price) on or before an agreed maturity period. The right to buy is called a **call option** and right to sell a **put option**. A foreign currency option holder will exercise his right only if it is advantageous to do so. Let us suppose that it is possible for Air India to purchase a 6-month put option on rupees. The put option exercise rate is INR 6.70. Since two currencies – INR and FF – are involved, Air India's put option on rupees can also be referred to as its call option on French franc. Air India will be required to pay a premium for purchasing the option. Let us assume that it is 5 per cent of the value of put option; that is: INR 6,700 million × 0.05 = INR 335 million. Thus, the maximum final cost: 1,000 × 6.70 + 335 = INR 7,035 million is known to Air India. Suppose at the end of six months, the exchange rate is INR 6.80/FF, Air India should exercise its put option since it will sell (pay) INR 6.70 (the exercise price) to obtain one French franc. In the open market, it will be required to pay INR 6.80. What will happen if the rupee appreciates and the exchange rate at the end of six months is: INR 6.35/FF? Air India should not exercise its option. In the open market, it needs to pay only INR 6.35 (instead of INR 6.70 exercise price) to buy one French franc. However, it has already paid the option premium. If it does not exercise the option, its total cost will be: 1,000 × 6.35 + 335 = INR 6,685. Except for the cost of option premium, the foreign currency option provides a unique hedging alternative; you can avoid the loss by exercising your option and gain from the favourable change in the exchange rate by not exercising the option.

Figure 34.2 shows the cost of buying a put option on Indian rupees. Air India avoids the potential loss as it will not exercise the put option if French franc appreciates and the spot rate is higher than INR 6.70/FF 1.00. Thus Air India would wish the French franc to fall (or INR to appreciate), so that it does not exercise the put option. However, the company will have to incur a cost of INR 335 million (or FF 50.76 million) whether or not it exercises the put option. The two lines indicate the cost with and without the premium.

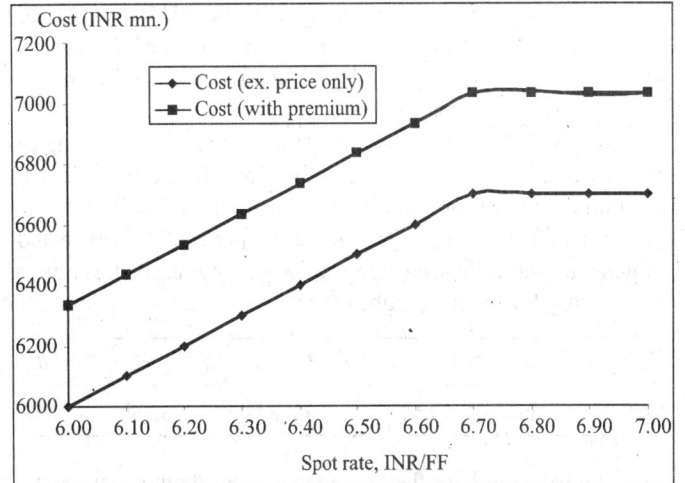

Figure 34.2: Cost of put option

Money Market Operations

Another hedging technique is the **money market operations.** Let us continue with the Air India example. Suppose Air India has no surplus funds available. It could borrow enough Indian rupees today and convert into French franc and invest for six months in French money market. It will have enough French francs to pay to Airbus Industries. It would also repay its Indian borrowings from its domestic resources. If interest rate parity holds, the difference in the forward rate and the spot rate is the reflection of the differences in the interest rates in two countries. Thus, Air India will be able to hedge against the change in the exchange rate.

Suppose the current spot rate is FF 6.80/INR, the rupee interest rate is 9.6 per cent and the French franc interest rate is 6 per cent. To obtain FF 1,000 million after six months, Air India needs to invest today: FF 1,000 million/1.03 = FF 970.87 million in French franc. In Indian rupees, this amount at the current spot rate is: 970.87 × 6.80 = INR 6,602 million. Thus, Air India could borrow INR 6,602 million in India at 9.6 per cent per annum for six months. It would use these funds to purchase French franc at the current spot rate: 6.602/6.80 = FF 970.87. It would invest these funds in French money market at 6 per cent per annum. After six months, Air India would have: 970.87 × 1.03 = FF 1,000 million to pay to Airbus. It would use its domestic funds to return its Indian borrowings with interest: INR 6,602 × 1.048 = INR 6,919 million.

The problem with the money market alternative is that all markets are not open and all currencies are not fully convertible. The Indian rupee is not fully convertible and there are restrictions on the free flow of funds outside the country.

INTERNATIONAL CAPITAL INVESTMENT ANALYSIS

The basic principles applicable to an international investment decision are similar to a domestic investment decision. The incremental cash flow of the investment should be discounted at an opportunity cost of capital appropriate to the risk of the investment. The investment should be accepted if the net present value is positive. One factor that distinguishes the international investment decisions from the domestic investment decisions is that cash flows are earned in foreign currency. This fact should be considered while estimating the incremental cash flows. Let us consider an example to illustrate the evaluation of an international investment project.

Suppose a Taiwanese toy manufacturing firm is thinking of an investment for making toys in Thailand. It is estimated that the initial project cost will be 12.5 million in Thai baht. The project will have a target debt ratio of 40 per cent. It is expected to generate the following free cash flows (net cash flows after tax) in baht for the next eight years:

Year	1	2	3	4	5	6	7	8
NCF (baht in million)	2.50	2.73	2.97	3.24	3.53	3.85	4.19	4.57

The following are the key assumptions about the project:

Table 34.2: Key Assumptions about the Project in Thailand

	Taiwan (T$)	Thailand (baht)
Inflation rate	9%	6.1%
Government bond yield	12.3%	9.4%
Risk premium	11.0%	8.0%
Interest rate	15.5%	12.4%
Tax rate	35.0%	30%
Spot exchange rate	1 baht equal to 0.8160 Taiwanese dollar (T$)	

How should the project be evaluated? Should it be undertaken? As we stated earlier, we can discount the free cash flows of the project by its WACC to determine its NPV. We should accept the project if NPV is positive.

There are two alternatives ways to state the free cash flows and the discount rate. We can either use the Taiwanese dollar cost of capital to discount free cash flows in Taiwanese dollars or the Thai baht cost of capital to discount free cash flows in Thai baht.

Cash Flows in Taiwanese Dollars

The project will operate in Thailand and the initial cash flows are estimated in Thai baht. The estimated baht cash flows should be converted into Taiwanese dollars at the expected future or forward exchange rates. These cash flows should be discounted at the Taiwanese dollar opportunity cost of capital. The firm should not worry about the currency risk as it can hedge the currency risk. Therefore, there is no need to *forecast* the exchange rates; the firm should simply estimate the forward exchange rate based on the inflation rates or interest rates in the two countries. We assume that international parity conditions will hold. A firm making an investment in a foreign country should separate its

investment decision from its feelings about the future exchange rates. The firm should accept a profitable project and hedge the currency risk. A firm's decision to consider a foreign project on the basis of management's outlook about the future exchange rates rather than its inherent viability will amount to speculation. Speculation is always risky.

The following steps are involved in evaluating the project in Taiwanese dollars:

- Convert the initial cost of 12.50 million baht into Taiwanese dollars at the *current spot rate* of T$ 0.816/baht 1.00: 12.50 million × 0.8160 = T$ 10.20 million.
- Forecast the forward exchange rate assuming that the international parity condition would hold. For example, the forward exchange rate at the end of one year will be:

$$E(s_{B/T\$}) = s_{B/T\$} \times \frac{(1+i_B)}{(1+i_{T\$})} = s_{B/T\$} \times \frac{(1+r_B)}{(1+r_{T\$})}$$

where i_B and r_B are Thai inflation rate and interest rate and $i_{T\$}$ and $r_{T\$}$ are Taiwanese inflation rate and interest rate.

- Since the Taiwanese inflation rate is expected to be 9 per cent and the Thai inflation rate 6.1 per cent, the Thai baht should appreciate in value. The expected spot rate (or forward exchange rate) after one year should be:

$$E(s_{B/T\$}) = 0.816 \times \frac{1.090}{1.061} = 0.816 \times 1.027 = 0.838$$

Similarly, the expected spot rate (forward exchange rate) after two years should be

$$E(s_{B/T\$}) = 0.816 \times \left[\frac{1.090}{1.061}\right]^2 = 0.816 \times 1.055 = 0.861$$

- Convert annual net cash flows into Taiwanese dollars at the expected spot rates. For example, net cash flow of 2.50 million baht at the end of the first year will be equal to: 2.50 × 0.838 = T$2.10 million.
- Discount all cash flows converted into Taiwanese dollars at the **Taiwanese dollar cost of capital** ($k_{T\$}$).

Taiwanese Dollar Cost of Capital

Since we have estimated the Taiwanese dollar free cash flows, we should use the Taiwanese dollar weighted average cost of capital as the discount rate. The after cost of debt is: $0.155 \times (1 - 0.35) = 0.101$ or 10.1 per cent. We can use the CAPM methodology to calculate the Taiwanese dollar cost of equity. The government bond yield can be used as the risk-free rate of interest which is 12.3 per cent. The risk premium is 11 per cent. Suppose the Taiwanese firm considers investment in Thailand more risky than the similar investment domestically, and estimates beta of the Thai investment as 1.16. Thus the Taiwanese dollar cost of equity will be:

$$\text{Tiawanese cost of equity} = \text{Nominal risk-free interest rate} + \text{Risk premium} \times \beta \quad (12)$$

$$k_{T\$} = 0.123 + 0.11 \times 1.16 = 0.25 \text{ or } 25\%$$

The Taiwanese dollar WACC is:
$$WACC = k_0 = 0.25 \times 0.60 + 0.101 \times 0.40$$
$$= 0.19 \text{ or } 19 \text{ per cent}$$

Estimating Beta

Beta of a foreign investment can be calculated by regressing the project's return to a benchmark market index. What is the appropriate benchmark market index? The answer to this question will depend on whether the international financial markets are integrated or segmented. In fully **integrated international financial markets**, both firms and the individual investors are free to invest anywhere in the world. In this case, the project's cost of capital does not depend on any country. Investors could diversify internationally and obtain the international diversification benefits themselves. In this case, beta is calculated relative the **world market index**. In practice, international markets may be segmented. A number of countries, particularly in emerging markets, allow firms to invest internationally, but not individual investors. Further, investors typically invest in their home markets even if they are allowed to invest in foreign markets. Hence, they would expect to earn the risk-free rate of home markets plus risk premium in home markets multiplied by the foreign investment's beta relative to the home market index.

In our example, we assume that the Taiwanese investors mostly invest in the home market. Therefore, the beta of the project in Thailand should reflect the Taiwanese firm's risk of investing in a project in Thailand. We can take an indirect approach to estimate the beta of the toys manufacturing project in Thailand. We can first estimate the betas for a sample of Thai toys firms relative to the Taiwanese market index. Then we can find the average (simple or weighted) of these betas and use the average beta as a proxy for the beta of investment in Thailand.

Table 34.3 shows the NPV calculation of the project in terms of Taiwanese dollars. The project has a positive NPV of T\$ 1.30 million. The firm should accept it.

Table 34.3: NPV Calculation of the Project (Taiwanese Dollar)

Year	Net Cash Flows (baht)	Estimated Exchange Rate	Net Cash Flows (T\$)	PV Factor at 19%	Present Value
0	−12.50	0.8160	−10.20	1.0000	−10.20
1	2.50	0.8383	2.10	0.8403	1.76
2	2.73	0.8612	2.35	0.7062	1.66
3	2.97	0.8848	2.63	0.5934	1.56
4	3.24	0.9089	2.94	0.4987	1.47
5	3.53	0.9338	3.30	0.4190	1.38
6	3.85	0.9593	3.69	0.3521	1.30
7	4.19	0.9855	4.13	0.2959	1.22
8	4.57	1.0125	4.63	0.2487	1.15
Net Present Value (T\$, million)					1.30

Thai Baht Cost of Capital and Cash Flows

The second approach is to discount the project's baht cash flows at the baht cost of capital and estimate NPV in terms of Thai baht. The NPV in baht can be converted into the Taiwanese dollars at the current spot exchange rate. The baht cost of capital can be estimated from the Taiwanese dollar cost of capital. The Thai interest rate is 12.4 per cent, which is lower than the Taiwanese interest rate of 15.5 per cent. Therefore, the Thai cost of capital should be lower than the Taiwanese cost of capital. We can use the following formula for converting the Taiwanese dollar cost of capital to the Thai baht cost of capital:

$$\left(1 + \frac{\text{Baht cost}}{\text{of capital}}\right) = \left(1 + \frac{\text{Taiwanese dollar}}{\text{cost of capital}}\right) \times \frac{1 + r_{baht}}{1 + r_{T\$}} \quad (13)$$

$$k_{baht} = 1.19 \times \frac{1.124}{1.155} - 1 = 0.158 \text{ or } 15.8\%$$

The project's net cash flows in baht will be discounted at the baht cost of capital. The NPV calculations are shown in Table 34.4. The project has a positive NPV of Baht 1.61 million. Converting baht into Taiwanese dollars at the current spot exchange rate, NPV in Taiwanese dollars is:

$$\text{NPV in Taiwanese dollars} = 1.61 \times 0.816 = T\$ 1.30$$

Table 34.4: NPV Calculation of the Project (Thai Baht)

Year	Net Cash Flow (baht)	PV Factor at 15.8%	Present Value
0	−10.00	1.000	−12.50
1	2.50	0.864	2.16
2	2.73	0.746	2.04
3	2.97	0.644	1.91
4	3.24	0.556	1.80
5	3.53	0.480	1.70
6	3.85	0.415	1.60
7	4.19	0.358	1.50
8	4.57	0.309	1.41
Net Present Value (baht, million)			1.61

Investment Evaluation: Parent versus Project

Should the foreign investment be evaluated from the parent's point of view? Generally, the parent will have control over cash flows of the foreign project that are the basis for remittance of dividends, reinvestment of cash flows anywhere, or repayment of debt by the parent. In this case, the project's cash flows are also parent's cash flows, and there is no need for separate valuations of the investment project.

In many situations, there may be significant difference in the parent's and project's cash flows. These differences may arise because of the host country's current and future policy of exchange controls and taxes on the foreign profits of the parent company.

Restrictions on Remittances

The parent may not be allowed by the host country to appropriate the project's cash flows; there may be restrictions on the dividend repatriation; the reinvestment of cash flows may be restricted;

the project's cash flows may not be allowed to service the firm's debt taken outside the host country.

Differences in Taxes

There may be differences in the tax rates in the parent's country and the country where the subsidiary operates. The earnings may be taxed in the host country, but not in the parent's country. Alternatively, if the tax rate in the parent's country is higher, on the remitted earnings the parent may have to pay differential tax. In some cases, there is no tax treaty between two countries and earnings of the subsidiaries are taxed twice – once by the host government and then by the parent's government if these are remitted to the parent.

Cash Flows to Parent

There are many ways in which a parent company could obtain cash flows from its foreign project. There may be restriction on dividend repatriation, but the host government may allow payment of royalty or license and management fees to the parent. The parent may supply material or components to the project at a profit to 'recover' cash flows when there are restrictions on transfer of cash flows from the host country.

When the cash flows of the project are different from the parent's cash flows, the parent will be interested in evaluating project from both parent and project viewpoints. You should follow the principle of relevant cash flows to the project and the parent in performing the investment analysis.

POLITICAL RISK OF FOREIGN INVESTMENTS

Investment in a foreign country is not only exposed to the exchange rate, but also to the political risk. A firm, which is deciding to make investment in another country, must vouch for the political risk in the host country. A firm's exposure to political risk depends on the host country's political system, its economic conditions and the government's policies and actions towards foreign direct investment (FDI) that affect the firm's investment cash flows. A country with large deficit relative to the gross domestic product (GDP), high growth of money expansion, fully or partially controlled exchange rate, enormous public sector firms, huge low-yielding government expenditures, controlled prices and interest rates and trade restrictions would have potentially high political risk. A country with poor economic performance, low degree of economic integration with the world system and controlled political regime poses high degree of political risk. The most important, but less frequent now, political risk is the **risk of expropriation**. The most frequent political risks arise on account of the host government's regulations that constraint the efficient operations of the foreign firms. There is conflict of goals between the host government and the foreign firms that lead to regulatory constrains on the foreign firms' activities. The host government may restrict repatriation of dividends, may impose additional taxes on the income of the foreign firm or may control price of its output after the firm has made investment in the host country.

The total avoidance of the political risk is not possible as all countries do have some degree of political risk. A firm should have a strategy of managing the political risk. It can insure its foreign investment with international insurance companies. But the insurance against political risk is not a guarantee against the economic value as it only guarantees the initial investment. The most appropriate strategy for the firm is to increase its bargaining power. If expropriation is a threat, the firm can increase the cost of expropriation and benefits of not expropriating to the host country. It can enter into contracts, which interlocks the interests of the host government, customers and major international suppliers of funds and the host country's financial institutions.

Suppose a French company wants to make an investment in a power-generation plant in China. The company can take several steps to protect itself from expropriation and uneconomic government policies. It can ask the Chinese government to make equity investment and provide guarantees for the minimum return. It can borrow funds from the Chinese financial institutions. The company can finance equipment purchases with non-recourse loans from the World Bank and from other developed countries. It can have **'pay or take' agreements** with the government buyers of power. Under this agreement, the government will have to pay to the company for the generated power, whether or not it is taken off. The French company can raise funds from the private sector power distribution companies against the future supply of power. It can provide for in the contract with the Chinese government that any dispute will be settled in the International Court or a court in France. The French firm can bring most funds in the form debt. Similarly, it can also provide to receive income in the form of license fees or royalty. The host governments generally do not put restrictions on debt service or payment of license fees and royalty while they tend to restrict payment of dividends.

Foreign Political Risks and Investment Evaluation

How should political risk be handled in the evaluation of a foreign investment? There are two ways in which a firm can handle the political risks in the investment evaluation. The firm may increase the cost of capital (discount rate) to allow for the political risks. In practice, it is very difficult to adjust the cost of capital for the political risks. Hence, an alternative available to the firm is to adjust the investment's cash flows to account for political risk. It is relatively easy to adjust cash flows by making conservative forecasts of cash flows when political risks are high.

FINANCING INTERNATIONAL OPERATIONS

Financial markets help to shift funds from the savers (lenders) to the investors (borrowers) in exchange for a return. They allocate funds among the potential users on the basis of the risk-return trade-off. International financial markets transfer funds across countries. The government regulations in many countries do not allow foreigners to access funds from those domestic financial markets.

The most important sources of international finance are: Eurocurrency loans, Eurobonds, and American or Global Depository Receipts (ADRs or GDRs).

Eurocurrency Loans

Most international firms can raise funds from the **Eurocurrency markets**. **Eurocurrency** is any freely convertible currency deposited in banks outside the country of its origin. Depositors put their savings in banks for short periods. Thus they hold short-term claims on banks. Banks that make Eurocurrency loans to international companies for a long period of time use these deposits. Thus the short-term deposits are transformed into long-term claims on borrowers. Banks act as intermediaries between the depositors and the borrowers. Usually, the size of the Eurocurrency loans is very large, and therefore, these loans are syndicated by more than one bank. These loans are made mostly on the basis of floating rates of interest. Interest rates are fixed as **LIBOR** (London Interbank Offering Rate) plus a premium (margin), based on the default risk. A borrower can borrow in multiple currencies from the Eurocurrency market and may choose to make payment of interest and principal in one or more currencies. The Eurocurrency market is a very large market.

Eurobonds and Foreign Bonds

A company can also raise funds by issuing Eurobonds and foreign bonds to investors in other countries. **Eurobonds** are bonds sold outside the country in whose currency they are denominated. They are issued directly by borrowers to investors. For example, an Indian company may issue US dollar-denominated bonds to investors in Switzerland. Eurobonds may be issued in different currencies. They are known by the currency in which they are denominated. For example, borrowers all over the world may issue US dollar Eurobonds (Eurodollars bonds), Japanese yen Eurobonds (Euroyen bonds), French franc Eurobonds (Eurofranc bonds) or bonds in any other currency. Eurobond market is a free market without any regulation. It is a self-regulated market.

Eurobonds are generally issued as **bearer bonds**. The bearer is the owner of the bond. When a bearer bond is sold, it is transferred to the buyer and he or she becomes the owner of the bond. Thus, the bearer Eurobonds offer the ease of transfer. On the other hand, **a registered bond** will have the name of the owner on the bond certificate. When a registered bond is sold, a new certificate is issued to the buyer with his or her name on the certificate.

A **foreign bond** is denominated in the currency of the country where it is issued, and is subjected to the laws and regulations of that country. For example, a Mexican company may issue US dollar-denominated bonds in the USA. Foreign bonds have fancy names. For example, yen-denominated foreign bonds issued in Japan are known as **Samurai bonds**. The dollar-denominated foreign bonds issued in the USA are called **Yankee bonds**. Similarly, pound sterling denominated bonds issued to investors in the UK are known as **Bulldog bonds**. In developed markets such as the USA, Europe or Japan, markets for Eurobonds, foreign bonds and the domestic bonds operate together and compete with each other. The size of Eurobonds market is larger than the foreign bonds.

The international bond market has witnessed a number of innovations. Borrowers have issued bonds with different features. **A straight fixed-rate bond** offers a fixed rate of interest as a percentage of the face value and promises to repay the principal at designated maturity. In case of the fixed-rate Eurobonds, which are mostly bearer bonds, the interest is payable annually. A **floating-rate note** (FRNs) offers to pay a rate of interest that is indexed to a benchmark rate. The benchmark rate is either three-month or six-month US dollar LIBOR. Depending on the risk of default, the rate of interest will be: LIBOR + default risk premium. The interest is payable either quarterly or semi-annually. FRNs are not issued for very long periods; they are medium-term bonds.

Eurobonds may be issued with the conversion feature or with warrants. A **convertible Eurobond** is a bond where the investor has an option to convert his or her bond to equity shares in a given proportion. Because of the conversion feature, convertible Eurobonds usually have lower rate of interest than the straight fixed rate bond. The minimum value of a convertible Eurobond will equal to the value of a straight fixed rate bond. Eurobonds may be issued with warrants attached to them. **Eurobonds with warrants** are straight fixed rate bonds with sweeteners in the form of warrants. A warrant is a call option and it gives the bondholder right to buy equity shares at a given price over a given time period.

More and more companies across the world are raising funds by issuing Eurobonds – straight or convertible and/or with equity warrants. A number of developing countries have tapped large funds from the Eurobond market. The size of the Eurobond market has grown considerably over years. However, the Eurocurrency loan market is still larger than the Eurobond market.

Depository Receipts

It is difficult for companies from developing countries to raise equity capital from developed capital markets. The country risk of these companies is high and the listing and disclosure requirements of the developed capital markets, like the US market, are very stringent. An indirect method of raising equity capital from foreign markets is to issue **depository receipts.** A **depository receipt** represents number of foreign shares that are deposited in a bank in the foreign country. For example, an Indian company can issue **American Depository Receipts** (ADRs) in the USA and raise capital there. How are ADRs issued? A company issues its shares to a reputed international financial institution in the USA that acts as a depository or the transfer agent. The depository bundles a specified number of shares as a depository receipt and issues them to investors in the USA. ADRs can be listed and traded on the USA stock exchanges. The depository receives dividends from the issuing Indian firm and then pays it to the depository receipt holders in the USA. ADRs are denominated in US dollars and ADR investors receive dollar equivalent dividends.

The Indian firms can also issue **Global Depository Receipts** (GDRs) in many other countries. For example, GDRs allow an Indian firm (or any other foreign firm) to raise funds from the UK, and list and trade GDRs on the London Stock Exchange. A number of foreign countries also list their GDRs on the Luxembourg Stock Exchange. Reliance and Grasim were the first companies to issue GDRs in May and November 1992, respectively. The Reliance issue was for US$ 150 million; the issue price of one GDR, representing two shares of Reliance, was US$ 16.2. This represented a 15 per cent discount relative to the market price of two Reliance shares.

After 1992, a number of Indian companies have raised funds from the international capital market by issuing ADRs/GDRs and convertible and non-convertible Eurobonds.

Cost and Risk of International Financing

An international firm will be governed by relative cost and risk in raising funds from various sources in the international capital markets. The firm will strive to minimise the cost of funds, keeping risk at the lowest level. It should try to raise funds below the market rate. In a competitive international capital market, it is not possible to raise funds at a cost lower than the market rate. A firm may be capable of raising funds below market rate due to government subsidies, tax asymmetries, and government regulations. **Tax asymmetries** can make one source of funds attractive or unattractive relative to another on after tax basis. If a government allows some corporations to issue tax-exempt bonds and refuses to others, then the later category corporations may have to offer higher yields on their bonds to attract tax-paying investors.

Borrowing in local currency to finance a foreign investment can expose a company to foreign exchange risks. A Taiwanese company may invest in Thailand by borrowing Taiwanese dollars in the domestic market and may convert them into baht. Later on, baht may depreciate or appreciate against the Taiwanese dollar. The Thai operations will earn less Taiwanese dollars if baht depreciates, and servicing of the Taiwanese dollar loan will become difficult. The company will have more Taiwanese dollars and will be comfortable in servicing the Taiwanese dollar loan if baht appreciates. The Taiwanese firm has two alternatives to avoid the risk of change in the exchange rate. It may borrow in the Taiwanese dollars and simultaneously, sell baht forward. Alternatively, it can borrow in baht. Since its Thailand operations have assets in baht, creating a liability in baht will provide an automatic or **natural hedging**. If the Taiwanese company uses its Thai operations to manufacture goods whose prices are fixed in Taiwanese dollars, then there is no foreign exchange risk.

SUMMARY

- The guiding principle for international financial management, like domestic financial management, is the shareholder wealth maximisation. International financial management, however, differs from domestic financial management, as it has to deal with multiple currencies, interest rates, inflation rates and foreign exchange and political risks.

- The foreign exchange rate is the price of one currency in terms of the other currency.

- Spot rate is the current exchange rate, and is used for immediate delivery of currency (which is two business days). Forward rate is the price determined today for delivery in the future.

- There exists a definite relationship between interest rates, inflation rates and exchange rates. These relationships are called international parity conditions:

$$\frac{(1+r_F)}{(1+r_D)} = \frac{(1+i_F)}{(1+i_D)} = \frac{E(s_{F/D})}{s_{F/D}} = \frac{f_{F/D}}{s_{F/D}}$$

- The difference between the current exchange rate and the forward rate results from the differences in the interest rates of two countries. This is referred to as the interest rate parity.

- A forward exchange rate should be what the foreign exchange market participants expect the future spot rate to be. This is the expectation theory of exchange rates.

- The expected future spot rate deviates from the current spot rate because of the difference in the expected inflation rates in two countries. This notion is based on the law of one price. The price of similar goods should be same in foreign currency equivalent. This is known as purchasing power parity. Nominal interest rates reflect the expected inflation rates.

- In a perfect capital market, real rates will be same in all countries. This is the international Fisher effect.

- An international company expecting to receive or pay cash flows in future in foreign currency is exposed to foreign exchange risk.

- We can distinguish between three types of foreign exchange risk: transaction exposure; economic exposure and translation exposure.

- Transaction exposure involves the possible exchange loss (or gain) on existing foreign currency-denominated transactions due to change in the exchange rate.

- Economic exposure refers to change in the value of the firm caused by the unexpected changes in the exchange rate.

- Translation exposure is caused when for translating the assets and liabilities of subsidiaries of a multinational company, the exchange rate at the end of the accounting period is different from the exchange rate at the beginning.

- There are three alternatives available to hedge the foreign exchange risk: forward contract; currency options; money market operations.

- A company can take a forward contract. It can either buy or sell a currency forward at a known forward rate.

- The company can buy a currency option. A call option is the right to buy and a put option is the right to sell currency at a predetermined exchange rate. The company will exercise its option only when it is advantageous to do so. Currency options allow the company to hedge against risk and gain from favourable change in the exchange rate.

- The company can also hedge its foreign exchange exposure through money market operations; that is, borrowing and investing in the money markets.

- International capital budgeting decisions, like domestic capital budgeting decisions, require estimates of cash flows and an appropriate discount rate. The cash flows can be estimated either in the domestic currency or in the foreign currency. The financial managers should forecast the foreign exchange rates assuming the parity conditions. The opportunity costs should be appropriately modified, reflecting the interest rate of the country in whose currency cash flows are estimated.

- There are a number of ways in which an international company can finance its foreign operations. It should strive to reduce its risk and minimise cost. It should take advantages of government subsidies and tax asymmetries. To avoid the foreign exchange risk of borrowing, a company can borrow a mix of currencies – local as well as foreign. It can also hedge against the risk of its liabilities if it creates assets in those currencies.

❖ A number of companies access funds in the Eurocurrency markets either through borrowing from banks or by issuing Eurobonds. Eurocurrency loans or Eurobonds are issued in countries other than the country in whose currency they are denominated. Eurocurrency markets are free from government regulations. Some companies also issue foreign bonds in foreign domestic capital markets.

❖ A number of companies, particularly developing countries, also raise funds through depository receipts. Depository receipts, representing claims on the shares of a company, are issued by a depository, usually an international finance firm to investors in developed countries. Depository is an intermediary between the company and depository receipt holders. He receives dividends from the company and then converts it into receipt holders' currency and distributes to them. Depository receipts issued to investors in the US are called American Depository Receipts (ADRs). Global Depository Receipts (GDRs) are issued in many countries.

KEY CONCEPTS

American depository receipts (ADRs)	Eurocurrency	Forward discount	LIBOR
Arbitrage	Eurocurrency loans	Forward exchange rate	Money market operations
Bid-ask price	Exchange rate	Forward premium	Natural hedging
Cross rates	Expectation theory	Global depository receipts (GDRs)	Nominal interest rate
Default-risk premium	Fisher effect		Purchasing power parity
Depository receipts	Floating-rate Notes (FRNs)	Hedging	Real interest rate
Direct quotes	Foreign bonds	Indirect quote	Spot exchange rate
Economic exposure	Foreign currency options	Interest rate parity	Straight-fixed rate bonds
Eurobonds	Foreign exchange risk	International Fisher effect	Translation exposure
	Forward contract	Law of one price	Transaction exposure

ILLUSTRATIVE SOLVED PROBLEMS

Problem 34.1: A financial manager of a French company has FF 25 million that she can invest for one year. She is considering the possibility of either investing in France where a 1-year investment yields an interest rate of 9 per cent, or in Germany where a 1-year investment produces an interest rate of 12 per cent. The current exchange rate is: DM 3.35/FF. Calculate the 1-year forward exchange rate that will make the financial manager indifferent between investing in France or Germany.

Solution: According to international parity conditions, the interest rate differential equals the inflation differential that equals the expected changes in spot rates which is equal to the forward and the spot rate differential. Thus:

$$\frac{1+r_{DM}}{1+r_{FF}} = \frac{f_{DM/FF}}{s_{DM/FF}} = \frac{1.12}{1.09} = 1.0275 = \frac{f_{DM/FF}}{3.35}$$

$$f_{DM/FF} = 3.4421$$

Problem 34.2: In India the interest rate on a 1-year loan is 14.5 per cent and inflation is expected to be 6.5 per cent. The expected inflation rate in Thailand is 8.5 per cent. What should be the interest rate of a 1-year loan in Thailand?

Solution: The differences in the expected inflation rates should be equal to the differences in the interest rates. Thus:

$$\frac{(1+i_I)}{(1+i_T)} = \frac{(1+r_I)}{(1+r_T)} = \frac{1.065}{1.085} = \frac{1.145}{(1+r_T)}$$

$$= r_T = \frac{1.085 \times 1.145}{1.065} - 1 = 0.1665 \text{ or } 16.65\%$$

Problem 34.3: The current spot exchange rate between US dollar and Indian rupees is: INR 40.11/US\$, and the 1-year forward rate is: INR 43.52/US\$. The expected inflation rate in India is 8.5 per cent. What is the expected inflation rate in US?

Solution: The expected difference between the forward and the spot rates should be equal to the difference in the expected inflation rates. Thus:

$$\frac{f_{INR/\$}}{s_{INR/\$}} = \frac{(1+i_{INR})}{(1+i_\$)} = \frac{43.52}{40.11} = \frac{(1.085)}{(1+i_\$)}$$

$$i_\$ = \frac{40.11 \times 1.085}{43.52} - 1 = 0.0 \text{ or } 0\%$$

Probelm 34.4: Suppose French franc interest rate is 12 per cent and DM interest rate is 14.5 per cent, how much is the forward discount on DM?

Solution: The interest rate parity theory provides the answer to this problem. Thus:

$$(1.145)(1 - \text{discount}) = 1.12; \text{ discount} = 0.0218 \text{ or } 2.18\%$$

Problem 34.5: The 6-month interest rates (annualised) in Italy and France are 13 per cent and 11 per cent, respectively. The current exchange rate is Lira 296.10/FF and the 6-month forward rate is Lira 326.50/FF. (*a*) Where should a French investor invest? (*b*) Where should he borrow from? (*c*) Is there any arbitrage opportunity for the investor?

Solution:

(*a*) The French investor can convert his Franc into Lira at the current exchange rate and invest in Italy for six months at 6.50 per cent (13 per cent/2). He can simultaneously sell the Lira proceeds forward for Francs. His Franc return will be:

$$6.5 \times (296.10/326.50) = 5.89\%$$

This return is higher than what the investor can get by investing in France: $11/2 = 5.5\%$.

(*b*) The cost of borrowing in France is lower (since the return is lower).

(*c*) In the absence of any transaction cost, the investor can borrow in France at 5.50% and invest in Italy at 5.89% to make the arbitrage profit.

REVIEW QUESTIONS

1. How does financial management of an international firm differ from that of a domestic firm?

2. What is a foreign exchange market? Who are the participants in a foreign exchange market? What are their motivations?

3. What is a spot exchange rate? How is it different from a forward rate? How will you calculate forward premium or discount?

4. You know the exchange rates of two countries. A third country's exchange rate is quoted against only the first of these countries. How can you determine the exchange for this third country against the second country? Illustrate your answer.

5. Name the four international parity conditions. Explain each one briefly.

6. What is interest rate parity? How does it work? Give an example to illustrate your answer.

7. What is the Fisher effect? How is this principle extended to international finance?

8. Why should forward rate be the possible forecast of an expected future spot rate?

9. What is the law of one price? How is it applied to international finance? Give an example.

10. Explain with the help of an example how the international Fisher effect reflects interest parity, purchasing power parity and the expectation theory of forward rates.

11. What is foreign exchange risk? What are the implications when foreign exchange exposure is not covered or covered partially?

12. What is a forward cover? How does it provide a hedge against the foreign exchange risk?

13. Explain the foreign exchange option as a hedging technique. What are its pros and cons?

14. How do money market operations provide hedging against the foreign exchange risk?

15. How do international capital investment decisions differ from domestic capital investment decisions? Explain the methods of evaluating international investment decisions.

16. What are the various alternatives available to a firm to finance its international investments? Explain two major methods of financing international operations.

17. What is Eurocurrency market? How do Eurocurrency loans differ from Eurobonds?

18. How does the depository receipts methods of raising funds operate? What is an American Depository Receipt? How is it different from a Global Depository Receipt?

PROBLEMS

1. The current spot rate of British pound against the US dollar is UK£ 1.5763/US$. The 90-day forward rate is UK£ 1.5436. Calculate the annual forward discount or premium for the US dollar.

2. The 60-day forward rate of Indian rupee relative to the US dollar is: INR 40.85/US$. The spot rate is INR 38.95/US$. Is Indian rupee at a premium or discount? What is the annual percentage?

3. Suppose you have INR 10 million that you can invest for one year anywhere in the world without any restriction. You are considering to either invest in the US or in India. The interest rate on one-year bonds in India is 15 per cent and on one-year bonds in the US is 10 per cent. The current exchange rate is INR 39.80/US$. What should be the one-year forward rate so that you earn the same return whether you invest in India or in the US?

4. The expected inflation rate in France is 5 per cent and in Italy 7 per cent. The one-year loan in France returns 8 per cent. What should be the return on one-year loan in Italy?

5. One-year Thai baht and US dollar forward rate is Baht 46.75/US$. The expected inflation rate in Thailand is 9 per cent and in the US 4 per cent. What is the current spot rate of exchange?

6. The expected inflation rate in India is 5 per cent. The current spot rate between Indian rupee and South Korean Won is: Won 1.2345/INR and one-year forward rate is Won 1.2567. How much is the expected inflation rate in South Korea?

7. The French franc-Japanese yen exchange rate is: ¥105.20/FF. The French franc-Indian rupee exchange rate is: INR 6.50/FF. What is the Japanese yen-Indian rupee exchange rate?

8. A Thai company is expecting to receive US$ 5 million from an importer in the US after three months. The current spot exchange rate is Baht 43.75/US$ and 90-day forward rate is Baht 45.35/US$. What will be the consequences if the Thai firm (*a*) does not cover its exposure, (*b*) covers 60 per cent and keeps 40 per cent exposure uncovered, and (*c*) covers 100 per cent of its exposure by entering into a forward contract? Suppose the spot exchange rate at the time the

Thai company receives payment is Baht 44.10 US$. What is the cost of the forward contract (partial and full)?

9. An Indian firm is considering the possibility of building a plant to manufacture an industrial chemical in Thailand. The cost of investment is estimated to be Baht 25 million. The life of the investment is expected to be 12 years. It is expected the annual net cash flow in real terms will be Baht 4 million. The current spot exchange rate is Baht 1.105/INR. The risk-free interest rate in Thailand and India are 12 per cent and 10 per cent, respectively. The expected inflation rate in Thailand is 8 per cent. The Indian firm considers the opportunity cost of capital to be 7.25 per cent above the risk-free rate. Should the Indian firm make investment in Thailand? Show NPV calculations in Indian rupees using cash flows in (*a*) baht and (*b*) rupees.

CASE

34.1: Premier Computers, Inc.[1]

Premier Computers, Inc. of USA is considering a project for manufacturing computers in India. It plans to sell 20,000 units of desktop computers in the first year and the company expects volume growth at 10 per cent per annum. If Premier USA makes the investment in India, it will operate the plant for five years and then sell the plant to Indian investors at the depreciated value at the time of sale plus working capital. The Indian government will allow Premier to repatriate all net cash flows to the USA each year.

Premier will have to invest $10 million in plant and $5 million for the initial working capital. Working capital is expected to remain constant through the life of the project. Plant will be depreciated over five years on a straight-line basis for tax purpose. Over the next five years, the selling price of computers will remain at $500 per computer converted into Indian rupees at the prevailing exchange rate each year. Similarly, operating expenses in India are expected to be rupees equivalent of $250 per computer. Premier USA will finance the project with a debt equity ratio of 0.50. The debt will be raised in rupees and the company will pay interest at market borrowing rate of 10 per cent for five years; principal is repayable in four equal instalments starting from year two. Premier USA uses the CAPM to calculate cost of capital. The market risk premium is 8 per cent and the asset beta for computer manufacturers is 1.25. The corporate tax rate is 35% in India and because of a double taxation treaty no further taxes will be payable in the US. Assume that investment is made now, and cash flows occur from year one through five. The current exchange rate is Rs 45/$1. The risk free rates of interest in the USA and India, respectively, are 6 per cent and 9 per cent.

Discussion Questions

1. Calculate the rupees cash flows of the project.
2. Calculate the Indian rupee cost of capital and the US dollar cost of capital. State your assumptions
3. What is its NPV in rupees? (Round the discount rate to the nearest per cent for calculating NPV).

---

1. The author is thankful to Professor Jayant Varma for his suggestions.

CHAPTER 35

Shareholder Value and Corporate Governance

CHAPTER OBJECTIVES

- Review the implications of financial theory for the corporate finance policies
- Emphasise the need for a linkage between the financial policies and strategic management
- Focus on the shareholder value creation
- Develop a framework for the shareholder value analysis
- Discuss the concept of economic value added (EVA) and market value added (MVA)
- Highlight the features of good corporate governance

INTRODUCTION

The theory of finance has undergone fundamental changes over the past three decades or so. Finance is no more a descriptive discipline; it is now viewed as a specialised branch of applied micro-economics, and the emphasis now is on the development of formal models, using sophisticated mathematical and econometrics tools. This approach seems to have created some gap between theory and practice. It is also felt that the finance theory is not complete and meaningful without its linkage with the strategic management. Therefore, there is a need for interdisciplinary interactions.

How can the finance theory and practice be used for designing of the corporate policies? How to establish a close link between the financial policies and strategic management? Strategy is an integrating mechanism, and that the corporate finance policy should be developed in the context of the strategic decision-making framework. How can the financial policies and strategy be directed towards the shareholder value creation?

FINANCIAL GOALS AND STRATEGY

Financial goals are the quantitative expressions of a company's

mission and strategy, and are set by its long-term planning system as a trade-off among conflicting and competing interests. In a study of twelve large American corporations, Donaldson has identified several characteristics of a company's financial goals system:[1]

- Companies are not always governed by the maximum profit criterion.
- Financial priorities change according to the changes in the economic and competitive environment.
- Competition sets the constraints within which a company can attain its goals.
- Managing a company's financial goals system is a continuous process of balancing different priorities in a manner that the demand for and supply of funds is reconciled.
- A change in any goal cannot be effected without considering the effect on other goals.
- Financial goals are changeable and unstable, and therefore, managers find it difficult to understand and accept the financial goals system.

In practice, the financial goals system boils down to the management of flow of funds. The objectives of growth and

---

1. Donaldson G, Financial Goals and Strategic Consequences, *Harvard Business Review*, May–June 1985, pp. 57–66.

return can assume different priorities during the life cycle of a company. For fulfilling its desire of attaining high growth, a company may have to sacrifice superior return. Similarly, it may be able to achieve maximum return by constraining its growth. For supporting its growth target, a company needs to ensure adequate supply of funds which require trade-offs among the company's dividend or debt policies or various sources of funds. A financial goals system of low payout and high debt will provide a profitable firm an opportunity to sustain a high level of sales growth. You may recall the discussion of financial policy trade-off and sustainable growth model in Chapter 26.

Corporate managers in India consider the following four financial goals as the most important (Exhibit 35.1):

- ensuring fund availability
- maximising growth
- operating profit before interest and taxes
- return on investment

It is notable that in the recent times more and more companies in India are focusing on shareholder value creation. These companies have adopted different methods of measuring shareholder value. A number of then measure and report economic value added (EVA), market value added (MVA), and the shareholder return based on the market value of shares.

SHAREHOLDER VALUE CREATION

The value of a firm is the market value of its assets which is reflected in the capital markets through the market values of equity and debt. Thus, shareholder value is:

Shareholder value = Market value of the firm
– Market value of debt

The market value of the shareholders' equity is directly observable from the capital markets. In theory, the market value should be equal the warranted economic value of the firm. The true economic value of a firm or business or division or project or any strategy depends on the cash flows and the appropriate discount rate (commensurate with the risk of cash flows). In the earlier chapters, we have discussed methods for calculating the present or economic value of a firm or a business/division or a project. Here we shall discuss briefly three most commonly advocated methods of shareholder value.

The first method, called the free cash flow method, uses the weighted average cost of debt and equity (WACC) to discount free cash flows. You may recall that free cash flows are calculated as follows:

$$FCF = PBIT(1-T) + DEP \pm ONCI \pm \Delta NWC - \Delta CAPEX \quad (1)$$

Notice that PBIT = profit before interest and tax, T = corporate tax rate, DEP = tax depreciation, ONCI = other non-cash items, ΔNWC = change in net working capital (i.e., stocks plus trade debtors minus trade creditors), and $\Delta CAPEX$ = incremental investment. When the value of a firm or a business over a planning horizon is calculated, then an estimate of the terminal cash flows or value (TV) will also be made. The firm or the business is expected to grow at a high rate during the planning horizon and then, competition may force cash flows to remain constant or grow at a low rate. Terminal or residual value reflects the value of post-planning cash flows. Thus, the economic value or simply value of a firm or a business is:

Economic value = PV of net operating cash flows (NOCF)
                    + PV of terminal value

$$V = \sum_{t=1}^{n} \frac{FCF_t}{(1+WACC)^t} + \frac{TV_n}{(1+WACC)^n} \qquad (2)$$

The value of a firm or a business generating perpetual FCF will be as follows:

$$V = \frac{FCF}{WACC} \qquad (3)$$

You may recall that FCF estimates do not make any adjustment for interest charges. Thus, FCF do not include financing (leverage) effect, and therefore, they are **unlevered** or **ungeared cash flows.** The weighted average cost of capital (WACC) includes after-tax cost of debt. Hence the financing effect is incorporated in WACC rather than cash flows. WACC, you may, recall, is calculated as follows:

$$WACC = k_e \left(\frac{E}{V} \right) + k_d (1-T) \left(\frac{D}{V} \right) \qquad (4)$$

You may recall that WACC is based on the assumptions that the firm has an optimum (or target) capital structure and that debt is perpetual. These assumptions may not hold in practice and therefore, the use of WACC may not be appropriate for determining the economic value of a firm or a business or a project.

The second method calculates the economic value of a firm or business into two parts: the economic value of unlevered firm and the economic value of the financing effects. The value of an unlevered firm over its planning period is given as follows:

$$V_u = \sum_{t=1}^{n} \frac{FCF_t}{(1+k_u)^t} + \frac{TV_n}{(1+k_u)^n} \qquad (5)$$

Notice that k_u is the cost of capital of an unlevered firm. For the levered firm, the second part includes the value of interest tax shield (V_{ITS}):

$$V_{ITS} = \sum_{t=1}^{n} \frac{ITS_t}{(1+k_d)} \qquad (6)$$

Thus, the value of a levered firm or business is:

Value of a   Value of   Value of
levered firm = unlevered firm + interest fax shield

We can obtain the warranted value of shareholders' equity as the difference between the economic value of the firm and the claims of debt-holders. The value per share (VPS) can be obtained by dividing the value of shares (E) by the number of shares (N):

$$VPS = \frac{E}{N} \qquad (7)$$

We can summarise the steps involved in the second method of estimation of the firm's total value and the shareholder value as follows:

1. Estimate the firm's unlevered cash flows and terminal value.
2. Determine the unlevered cost of capital (k_u).
3. Discount the unlevered cash flows and the terminal value by the unlevered cost of capital.
4. Calculate the present value of the interest tax shield discounting at the cost of debt.
5. Add these two values to obtain the levered firm's total value.
6. Subtract the value of debt from the total value to obtain the value of the firm's shares.
7. Divide the value of shares by the number of shares to obtain the economic value per share.

The third method for determining the shareholder economic value is to calculate the value of equity by discounting cash flows available to shareholders by the cost of equity. The equity cash (ECF) flows are adjusted of cash flows related to debt.

Equity cash flows are net of interest charges and investments, and, therefore, at the corporate level they coincide with dividends. Equity cash flows reflect the expected growth in future cash flows. At the end of the planning period (the term of investment), the terminal or residual value of investment will have to be estimated. The economic value of equity is given by the discounted value of equity cash flows plus the present value of terminal value.

Market Value Added

Does higher growth and accounting profitability lead to increased value to shareholders? Modern financial management posits that a firm must seek to maximise the shareholder value. As stated earlier, market value of the firm's shares is a measurement of the shareholder wealth. It is the shareholders' appraisal of the firm's efficiency in employing their capital. The capital contributed by shareholders is reflected by the book value of the firm's shares. In terms of market and book values of shareholder investment, **shareholder value creation** (SVC) may be defined as the excess of market value over book value. SVC is also referred to as the **market value added** (MVA):

Market value   Market   Invested
added   =   value   −   capital   (8)

Market value is also referred to as the "**enterprise value**". It is the total of the firm's market value (MV) of debt and market value of equity. Invested capital (IC) or capital employed (CE) is the amount equity capital and debt capital supplied by the firm's shareholders and debt-holders to finance assets. The firm is said to have created value if MVA is positive; that is, the firm's MV is in excess of IC (or CE). MVA accrues to shareholders since subtracting IC sets off debt-holders' claims from MV. Hence MVA may also be calculated as the difference between market value of equity and invested equity capital. Managers must aim at earning higher MVA for shareholders. You may recall from our earlier discussion on valuation that MV increases only when the firm earns a return in excess of the cost of capital on invested capital. MVA would be reduced if the firm invests capital in negative NPV projects.

There is conceptual problem with MVA. Invested capital is at historical value. Considering the alternative opportunities of equivalent risk, the **economic value** of the invested capital would be much higher today. Suppose the market value of an entirely equity-financed firm, which was incorporated 10 years ago, is Rs 500 crore. The shareholders' investment remains Rs 200 crore. The firm's MVA = Rs 500 crore – Rs 200 crore = Rs 300 crore. Suppose the firm's cost of equity is 10 per cent (through out the 10-year period). This implies that the shareholders' investment after 10 years would have grown to: Rs 200 $(1.10)^{10}$ = Rs 519 crore. The amount of Rs 519 crore is the economic value of invested capital. The market value of the equity is Rs 500 crore. Thus, in effect, the firm has destroyed value of about Rs 19 crore. Thus,

$$\text{MVA} = \text{Market value} - \text{Economic value} \qquad (9)$$
$$= 500 - 519 = - \text{Rs } 19$$

Yet another problem with MVA is that it ignores cash flows received by shareholders in the form of dividends and share buyback and cash contributed by them as additional share capital. We can easily incorporate these factors into the calculation of MVA. The economic value of invested equity capital would be equal the future value of dividends, share buyback and additional capital invested. You can use the firm's cost of equity to calculate the economic value.

Market-to-Book Value (M/B)

An alternative measure of shareholder value creation is the market-to-book value (M/B) approach. As you know, the market value of equity is given as follows:

$$\text{Market value of equity} = \text{Market value of the firm}$$
$$- \text{Market value of debt} \qquad (10)$$

We obtain market value per share (M) when we divide the market value of equity by the number of shares outstanding. Similarly, the book value per share (B) can be calculated by dividing invested equity capital by the number of shares outstanding. A firm is said to create shareholder value when its market value per share is greater than its book value per share; that is, $M > B$. The market-to-book value (M/B) analysis implies the following:

- **Value creation**   If $M/B > 1$, the firm is creating value of shareholders.
- **Value maintenance**   If $M/B = 1$, the firm is not creating value of shareholders.
- **Value destruction**   If $M/B < 1$, the firm is destroying value of shareholders.

As explained in Chapter 3, the market value of a firm's share is the present value of the expected stream of dividend per share (DIV). DIV depends on the firm's payout ratio $(1 - b)$ and the earnings growth (g). Earnings growth depends on the retention ratio (b) and the return on equity (ROE):

$$g = b \times \text{ROE}$$

The stream of DIV is discounted at the cost of equity (k_e). The market value per share is given as follows equation:

$$M = \sum_{t=1}^{\infty} \frac{\text{DIV}_t}{(1+k_e)^t} = \sum_{t=1}^{\infty} \frac{\text{EPS}_t(1-b)}{(1+k_e)^t} \qquad (11)$$

In Equation (11), DIV (dividend per share) is expected to grow at a constant rate, g. That is,

$$\text{DIV}_t = \text{DIV}_{t-1}(1+g) = \text{DIV}_0(1+g)^t$$

If we assume an infinite time period ($n = \infty$), then Equation (11) can be simplified as follows:

$$M = \frac{\text{DIV}_1}{k_e - g} = \frac{\text{EPS}_1(1-b)}{k_e - g} \qquad (12)$$

Since EPS_1 is the product of the book value of firm's share and its return on equity (i.e., $\text{EPS}_1 = \text{ROE} \times B$), Equation (12) can be written as follows:

$$M = \frac{\text{ROE}(1-b)B}{k_e - g} \qquad (13)$$

Dividing both sides of Equation (13) by B (book value per share), we obtain M/B equation as follows:

$$\frac{M}{B} = \frac{\text{ROE} - g}{k_e - g} \qquad (14)$$

The time horizon, n may be assumed to be finite. Then Equation (14) becomes as follows:[1]

$$\frac{M}{B} = \left[\frac{\text{ROE} - g}{k_e - g}\right]\left[1 - \left(\frac{1+g}{1+k_e}\right)^n\right] + \left[\frac{1+g}{1+k_e}\right]^n \qquad (15)$$

We can notice from Equation (14) or Equation (15) that the following are the determinants of the M/B ratio:

- *Economic profitability or spread* The magnitude of the spread between return on equity and the cost of equity, i.e., $\text{ROE} - k_e$ determines the M/B ratio. The spread, sometimes referred to as the **economic profitability**, must be positive to create the shareholder value. The higher the positive spread, the higher the M/B ratio.
- *Growth* Growth depends on the firm's retention ratio (b) and the return on equity, (ROE). Given the firm's ROE, higher the retention ratio, higher will be the growth rate. However, a higher growth rate does not necessarily increase the shareholder value. It will accelerate the M/B ratio only when the return on equity is greater than the firm's cost of equity (ROE > k_e). Growth will have a negative effect on value if the cost of equity is more than the return on equity (k_e > ROE). Thus, a firm should be economically profitable (i.e., ROE > k_e) for growth to be of value to the shareholders.[2] Growth is detrimental from the value perspective when the firm is economically unprofitable (i.e., ROE < k_e).

1. W.E., *Financial Strategy,* Illinois' Richard D. Irwin, 1979, pp. 65–68.
2. *Ibid.*

- ***Investment period*** The number of years over which the future investment will grow also determines the market value. In Equation (14), the time horizon, *n* is assumed infinite while Equation (15) assumes a finite time period.

Figure 35.1 shows the interaction between variables that leads to growth and the value of the firm's share. It can be seen from the figure that the connecting link between the sustainable growth model and the shareholder (market) value is the spread between the return on equity and the cost of equity. The firm's growth objective will be consistent with the shareholder value when this spread is positive.

Economic Value Added (EVA)

Increasing MVA should be the objective of managers of firms. In large, publicly listed companies, the incentive compensations of top managers are linked to the share performance of their companies. In managers-owned or promoters-managed companies, the wealth of promoters and managers is directly

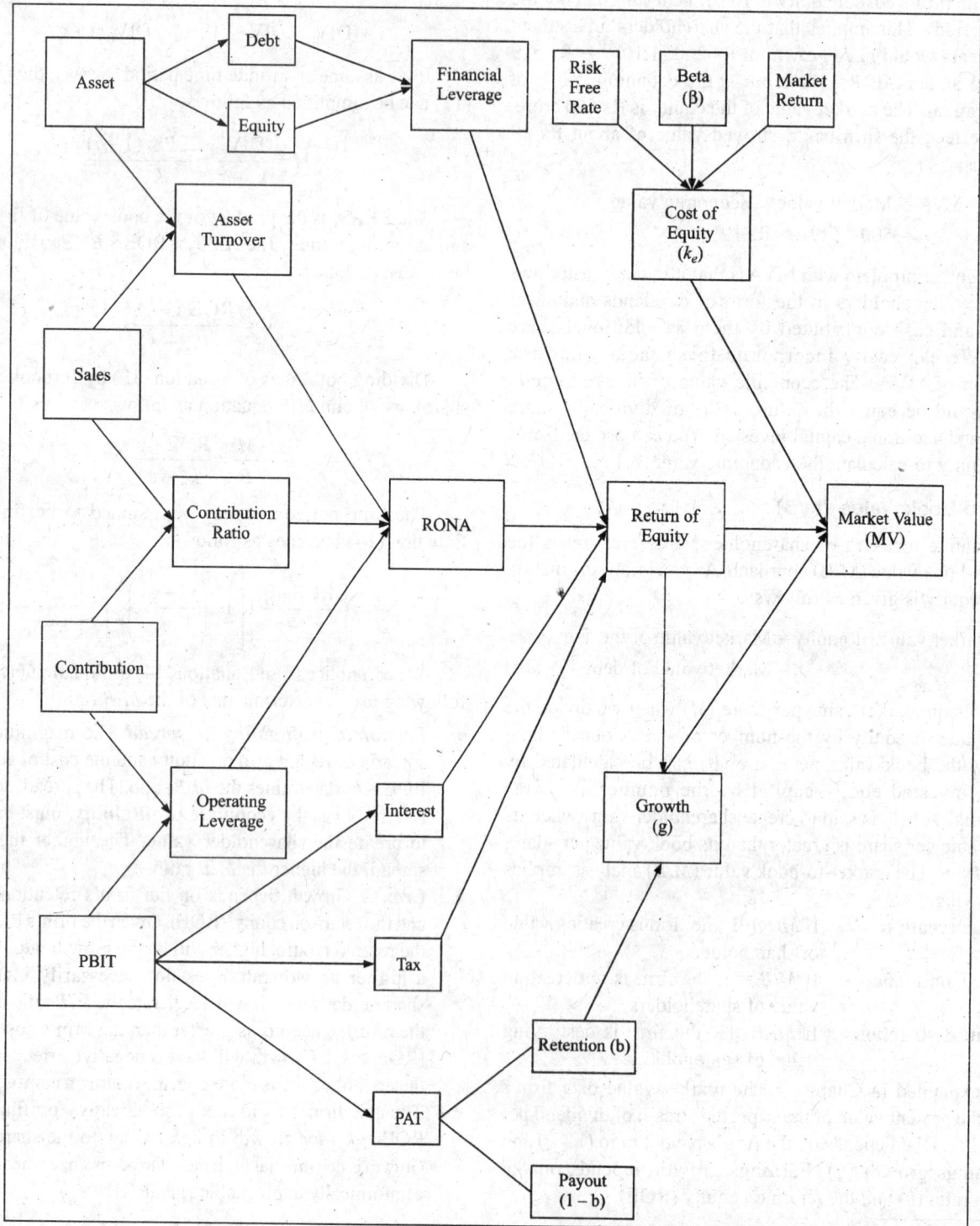

Figure 35.1: Growth and Value

related to the share performance. The incentives of top and other senior managers also depend on profits or related measures. Managers at operating and divisional levels do not have a direct control over market value. Their incentive compensations are mostly dependent on accounting measures like sales growth, cost reduction, profits or relative profitability measured return on investment, return on equity or earnings per share. Hence MVA or share performance-based measure cannot be used as a system of evaluating, motivating and incentivising managers at all management levels. Accounting-based measures can be directly related to the absolute performance and actions of managers and other employees. Accounting measures can be implemented at operating levels.

Accounting measures, like earnings or return on investment, however, have several problems:

1. They are based on arbitrary assumptions and policies and have scope for easy manipulability. Profits can be affected by changing depreciation methods, inventory valuations methods or allocating costs as revenue or capital expenditures without any change in true profitability.

2. They could motivate managers to take short-term decisions at the cost of long-term profitability of the company. Managers could reduce R&D expenditure or expenditure of building the staff capability to bolster short-term profitability. This would happen more in those companies where the compensations of managers are based on short-term earnings.

3. They do not reflect true profitability of the firm. Earnings are not cash flows. No distinction is made for the timing of earnings. Thus, earnings measures ignore time value of money and risk.

4. The most serious problem with accounting measures is that they might destroy shareholders' wealth. A manager can increase earnings by undertaking investment projects that have positive returns but negative net present value. In other words, these projects earn returns less than the cost of capital. They would increase earnings but destroy shareholders' wealth. Shareholders are not interested in growth in earnings rather they would like their wealth to increase through positive NPV projects.

We must recognise that although managers do not have a direct control over market value, but their actions influence the drivers of market value. Therefore, there is a need to identify a measure of performance that is related to value and that managers can directly observe and can see the influence of their actions over it. Even when accounting-based rates of return are used for performance evaluation, managers must consider the cost of capital. They must earn rates of return higher than the cost of capital. Suppose a firm's after-tax return on investment is 15 per cent. Its cost of capital is 12 per cent. The firm is earning a net return of 3 per cent. This is a value enhancing performance. On the other hand, if the firm could earn only 9 per cent return, its net return is negative 3 per cent and hence it is destroying value.

Economic value added (EVA[TM])[1] is a measure which goes beyond the rate of return and considers the cost of capital as well. In its simple form, it measures earnings *after* the cost of capital. EVA calculation is based on the firm's financial statements with which managers are quite familiar. Let us consider an example.

Suppose a firm has total assets of Rs 55 crore. The shareholders' equity is Rs 30 crore and the cost of equity is 13 per cent. The firm's net earnings are given below:

	(Rs in crore)
Sales	103.0
Less:	
Material costs	52.0
Wages and salaries	13.5
Depreciation	4.5
Power	7.0
Other manufacturing expenses	6.5
Administrative expenses	3.5
Selling and distribution expenses	6.0
Total expenses	93.0
Profit before interest and taxes (PBIT)	10.0
Less: Interest	2.5
Profit before taxes (PBT)	7.5
Less: Taxes	2.6
Profit after taxes (PAT)	4.9

The after-tax earnings available to shareholders are Rs 4.9 crore. This gives ROE of 4.9/30 = 16.3 per cent. The total rupee cost of the shareholders' equity is: Rs 30 crore × 0.13 = Rs 3.9 crore. There is a net gain of Rs 4.9 − Rs 3.9 = Rs 1.0 crore to shareholders when we consider the cost of their funds. The firm has been able to earn more than the minimum rate of return required by the shareholder; management has created the shareholder value. Shareholders have gained since the firm had earned more than Rs 3.9 crore. This is the cost of the shareholders' equity. If the cost of equity were, say, 18 per cent, shareholders' loss would have been Rs 4.9 − Rs 30 × 0.18 = − Rs 0.5 crore.

Economic value added, economic profit or **residual income** is defined as net earnings (PAT) in excess of the charges (cost) for shareholders' invested capital (equity):

$$\begin{aligned} \text{Economic value added} &= \text{PAT} - \frac{\text{Charges for}}{\text{equity}} \\ &= \text{PAT} - \frac{\text{Cost of}}{\text{equity}} \times \frac{\text{Equity}}{\text{capital}} \end{aligned} \qquad (16)$$

The firm is said to have earned **economic return** (ER) if its return on equity (ROE) exceeds the cost of equity (COE):

$$\text{Economic return} = \text{ROE} - \text{COE} \qquad (17)$$

In case of our example, ER is

$$\text{ER} = 0.163 - 0.13 = -0.033 \text{ or } 3.3\%$$

The economic return translates into EVA of: $(0.163 - 0.13) \times 30 = \text{Rs } 1.0$ crore

---

1. EVA[TM] is trade marked by the Stern-Steward consulting firm.

EVA approach is founded on the same logic as the *M/B* approach. Both are based on the concept of economic profit as different from the accounting profit. In a divisionalised company, the separate information about the debt and equity may not be available. Hence there is a popular alternative way of calculating EVA in such situations as given below:

$$\text{Economic value added} = \frac{\text{Net operating}}{\text{profit after tax}} - \frac{\text{Charges for}}{\text{capital employed}}$$

$$\text{EVA} = \text{NOPAT} - \text{COCE}$$

NOPAT is profit after depreciation and taxes disregarding interest on debt. In other words, NOPAT is profit before interest and taxes (PBIT) minus tax without any adjustment for interest. It can also be calculated as profit after tax (PAT) plus after-tax interest. Thus:

$$\text{NOPAT} = \text{PBIT}(1-T) = \text{PAT} + \text{INT}(1-T) \quad (18)$$

As stated earlier, NOPAT is **ungeared** or **unlevered profit after tax** to service both lenders and shareholders.

For our example, NOPAT is as follows:

	(Rs in crore)
PBIT	10.0
Less: Tax, 10 × 0.35	3.5
NOPAT, 10 (1 – 0.35)	6.5
Alternate Method:	
PAT	4.9
Plus: Interest	2.5
Less: Interest tax shield, 0.35 × Rs 2.5	–0.9
NOPAT, 4.9 + 2.5 (1 – 0.35)	6.5

Post-tax ROCE is the ratio of the net operating after tax (NOPAT) to invested capital (IC) or capital employed (CE):

$$\text{ROCE} = \frac{\text{NOPAT}}{\text{CE}} = \frac{\text{PBIT}(1-T)}{\text{CE}}$$

For our example, ROCE is:

$$\text{ROCE} = \frac{6.5}{55} = 0.118 \text{ or } 11.8\%$$

As we have already explained in earlier chapters, WACC is calculated as follows:

$$\text{WACC} = k_o = k_e\left(\frac{E}{V}\right) + k_d(1-T)\left(\frac{D}{V}\right)$$

The cost of equity in our example is 13 per cent. Suppose the cost of debt is 10 per cent. WACC in our example would be:

$$\text{WACC} = k_0 = 0.13\left(\frac{30}{55}\right) + 0.10\,(1-0.35)\left(\frac{25}{55}\right) = 0.10 \text{ or } 10\%$$

EVA can be calculated as the difference between ROCE and WACC multiplied by invested capital or capital employed:

$$\text{EVA} = (\text{ROCE} - \text{WACC}) \times \text{CE} \quad (19)$$

In our example, the EVA is: $(0.118 - 0.100) \times 55 = $ Rs 1.00 crore.

The economic value is added to shareholders whenever ROCE is higher than WACC (i.e., ROCE > WACC). The economic value will be destroyed if WACC exceeds ROCE (i.e., WACC > ROCE). EVA is net earnings in excess of the cost of capital supplied by lenders and shareholders. It represents the excess return (over and above the minimum required return) to shareholders; it is the net value added to shareholders.

EVA can be calculated for the firm as well as for the firm's divisions. We require calculation of the divisional cost of capital to determine divisional EVA. We have discussed earlier in this book the methodology for calculating the divisional cost of capital.

The advantages of EVA over the market-based and accounting-based measures of value creation are as follows:

1. EVA can be calculated for divisions and even projects.
2. EVA is a measure that gauges performance over a period of time rather than at a point of time. EVA is a **flow variable** and depends on the ongoing and future operations of the firm or divisions. MVA, on the other hand, is a **stock variable.**
3. EVA is not bound by the Generally Accepted Accounting Principles (GAAP). As we discuss below, appropriate adjustment are made to calculate EVA. This removes arbitrariness and scope for manipulations that is quite common in the accounting-based measures.
4. EVA is a measure of the firm's economic profit. Hence, it influences and is related to the firm's value.

EVA Adjustments

EVA measures economic profit since it accounts for the cost of capital. However, it is still based on accounting information. Hence, to become a true measure of economic profit, the calculation of EVA needs refinements. The EVA approach assumes a refined standardised accounting system. Calculation of EVA requires appropriate changes in accounting policies and practices. A company might be required to make as many as over 150 adjustments in its reported profits to estimate EVA. However, there are only few critical adjustments, say 10 – 15, that are necessary for estimating EVA; others have minor effect. Some typical examples of the EVA accounting adjustments include the following:[1]

Impaired or non-performing assets Non-performing assets, (NPAs) as the name indicates, do not generate any earnings. Future value can be created only from the performing assets. Hence NPAs should be written off. If the asset's value is significantly impaired, and so too is the company's ability to extract economic business from it, the asset should be accordingly written down.

Research and development According to the US GAAP, companies can expense R&D expenditure as incurred. In India also, in some cases the capital expenditure on R&D is allowed to be expensed as incurred for tax purposes. R&D expenditure is

1. Yound, S. David and O'Byrne, Stephen F., *EVA® and Value-based Management: A Practical Guide to Implementation*, McGraw Hills, 2001, pp. 206–68.

an investment that is supposed to benefit the company in the future over long run. Hence it is more appropriate to capitalise R&D and other expenditures on intangibles like brands. There is yet another dimension to this. If R&D is expensed immediately, managers might tend to under-invest in R&D as it would show up as as costs without any immediate corresponding benefits.

Deferred tax The timing differences between taxable income and book income causes deferred taxes. Accounting and tax depreciation causes deferred tax in most companies. Most companies in India use straight-line depreciation for reporting profit but they are required to use written down value method of depreciation for tax purposes. This difference normally results in more book profit than the taxable profit and hence a deferred tax liability. Deferred tax assets arise when companies make provisions for future costs that reduce current book profit. These assets are not tax deductible until companies spend the cash in a later period. Deferred taxes are non-cash costs; hence they should be ignored in calculating EVA.

Provisions Accounting is based on the concept of conservatism. Following GAAP, accountants make provisions for all future liabilities. The most common provisions include provision for bad and doubtful debts, guarantees, revaluation or restructuring. Provisions are non-cash items and a source of manipulating accounting profits. EVA calculation requires to profits to adjust for provisions and bring accounting profit closer to cash profit.

LIFO valuation of inventory In rising prices LIFO produces cost of goods sold figures that reflect current costs inventory. This is consistent with the matching of revenues and expenses. LIFO valuation under rising prices also saves tax as the cost of goods sold is higher than under alternative inventory valuation approaches. However, inventory value is understated and when this inventory is liquidated, profit and EVA are overstated.

Goodwill Goodwill is the difference between actual price paid for acquiring a company and the fair price of its assets and liabilities. This item is treated differently in different countries. The immediate write off of goodwill to reserves distorts true operating profit and invested capital. Any write-offs in the current year should be added to NOPAT. In India, the general practice is to write-off goodwill over a period of time, say, six years. This process also understates invested capital (although slowly) and true operating profits. Goodwill written off should be added to capital and profits.

Leases A lease is equivalent to secured borrowing. For accounting purposes the lease payments are treated as a rental expense, while the asset and debt might not appear on the balance sheet, particularly in the case of operating leases. This approach would understate the capital employed as lease is a substitute for debt. The capitalised value of lease should appear in the balance sheet. The borrowing rate should be applied to capitalised value of lease and necessary adjustment made in the interest income.

Restructuring charges Restructuring charges are investments for improving the future prospects of the business. Hence the EVA supporters argue that restructuring and other special charges should be capitalized.

Evaluation of M/B and EVA

Both *M/B* and EVA approaches focus on economic profitability rather than on accounting profitability. The *M/B* approach defines economic profitability as the spread between the return on equity and the cost of equity while in the popular version of EVA, it is the spread between the return on total capital and the cost of total capital. The spread in both approaches is same and it is value added to shareholders. From the accounting perspective, a firm is profitable if its return on equity is positive. However, from an economic perspective, the firm is profitable if the return on equity exceeds the cost of equity, or return on capital employed exceeds the over-all cost of the total capital employed. Hax and Majluf emphasise that:[1]

It is economic and not accounting profitability, that determines the capability of wealth creation on the part of the firm. It is perfectly possible that a company is in the black, and yet its market values is way below its book value, which means that, from economic point of view, its resources would be more profitable if deployed in an alternative investment of similar risk.

Both the approaches are an improvement over the traditional accounting measures of performance. But both do suffer from the limitation that they are partially based on accounting numbers. In the *M/B* approach, return on equity is an accounting number (profit after tax and book value of shareholders' investment) while the cost of equity is market determined. Similarly, the EVA approach uses the accounting-based net operating profit after tax while the cost of capital is market determined. Both return on equity and EVA are biased because they use accounting earnings (NOPAT or PAT) which are based on arbitrary assumptions, allocations and accounting policy changes. They also do not include changes in working capital and capital expenditures. Therefore, the measure of EVA is not equivalent to cash flow from operation, although with adjustments to accounting profit it comes closer to cash flows.

Value Drivers

What are the drivers of EVA or value based on the discounted cash flow approach? What generic strategies can be pursued by a firm to create shareholder value? EVA depends on revenue, costs, taxes and cost of capital. Similarly, cash flows under the DCF valuation depend on these same factors plus changes in working capital and capital expenditure over a given time horizon. Thus, the following are the financial value drivers or generic strategies to enhance value:[2]

- **Revenue enhancement** The firm can increase its revenue by improving its market share and/or increasing the price of the product. The strategies needed to do so include creating barriers like patents, product differentiation, monopoly power etc.
- **Cost reduction** The firm can become a cost leader by

1. Hax, A.C. and Majluf, N.S., *Strategic Management,* New Jersey, Prentice-Hall, Inc., pp. 214–15.
2. Hax and Majluf, *op. cit.,* Fruhan, *op. cit.*

lowering its costs beneath that of its competitors through economies of scale, vertical integration, or captive sources of material.

- *Asset utilisation* The firm can improve its profitability by reducing its capital intensity through improved utilisation of its assets.

- *Cost of capital reduction* The firm can design debt and equity securities that appeal to special niche of capital markets and thereby attract cheaper funds. It can reduce its business risk and design a capital structure that minimises the overall cost of capital by increasing interest tax shield without much increase in financial risk.

SHAREHOLDER VALUE ANALYSIS: CASE OF CADILA HEALTHCARE COMPANY

CHL is the flagship company of Zydus group in Ahmedabad. It is a leading integrated pharmaceutical company in India. In the domestic formulations market, it is ranked as number five with a market share of 3.85 per cent. It is one of the principal players of complex bulk drugs. One-fourth of the company's revenue comes from exports and 80 per cent from the domestic business. It aims to be a leading global generic player by the end of this decade.

CHL has stated its vision as follows:[1]

- One of India's leading healthcare players, we aim to be global-research driven by 2020.

- We shall achieve sales of $ 400 million by 2006.

- We shall be top ten global generics company with a strong R&D pipeline and sales in excess of $ 1 billion by 2010.

The company has expressed its vision in terms of competitive excellence through R&D and sales growth and size. The mission of the company is articulated in the following words: "We are dedicated to life…in all its dimensions. Our world is shaped by a passion for innovation, commitment to partners and concern for people in an effort to create healthier communities, globally." Table 35.1 provides the company's 5-year performance.

Table 35.1: Cadila Healthcare Company's Performance

	2000	2001	2002	2003	2004
Sales (Rs cr.)	4,778	5,088	5,888	10,282	11,723
Assets turnover	0.57	0.74	0.61	0.86	0.92
PBDIT/sales	15.2%	16.6%	17.0%	18.7%	21.2%
ROCE	8.7%	12.2%	10.4%	16.1%	19.5%
D/E	0.47	0.10	0.49	1.01	0.77
ROE	7.7%	12.1%	12.2%	17.4%	27.2%
EPS	6.28	10.97	11.27	12.2	22.75
DPS	2.32	3.00	3.50	3.50	6.00
Payout	36.9%	27.3%	31.1%	28.7%	26.4%
Book value per share	82.70	91.20	92.60	69.90	83.50
Market value per share	130.00	127.95	130.05	123.50	454.20
M/B	1.57	1.40	1.40	1.77	5.44

Source: Annual report 2003-04

1. Annual Report 2003–04.

How has CHC performed? The company's sales have increased from Rs 4,778 crore in 2000 to Rs 11,723 at a compound growth rate of 25 per cent per annum. The company's ROCE and ROE have increased over the years. It retains almost three-fourths of its profits and debt-equity ratio is less than 1, which implies higher capital stake of shareholders. In spite of low payout, earnings per share and dividend per share are increasing as the company's profits are growing.

Has CHC been able to convert its high profitability and growth into higher value for shareholders? The company believes in adding value to shareholders. CHC's market value of equity and debt showed tremendous increase in 2004 and the market value added increased from Rs 3,196 crore to Rs 23,278 crore (Table 35 .2). As a per cent of invested capital or capital employed market value added increased from 36 per cent in 2003 to 250 per cent in 2004 – almost seven fold increase.

Table 35.2: CHC's Market Value Added

(Rs in crore)	2003	2004
Market value of equity (*E*)	7,586	28,525
Market value of debt (*D*)	4,429	4,057
Value of equity & debt (*V*)	12,015	32,582
Less: Capital employed (*CE*)	8,819	9,304
Market value added (MVA)	3,196	23,278
MVA/V	26.6%	71.4%
MVA/CE	36.2%	250.2%

Table 35.3 shows CHC's EVA for 2003 and 2004. The after-tax cost of debt was 8.3 per cent in 2003 and 5.7 per cent in 2004. The cost of equity is calculated using the capital asset price model (CAPM). The risk-free rate is taken as the yield on 10-year long-term government bonds. The risk-premium is 7 per cent and beta of 0.70. The weighted average cost of capital was 10.4 per cent in 2003 and 9.70 per cent in 2004. CHC uses market value weights in calculating WACC. The reduction in WACC occurred because of the decrease in the post-tax cost of debt.

Table 35.3: CHC's EVA

(Rs in crore)	2003	2004
Cost of Capital		
Equity (E)	4,390	5,247
Debt (D)	4,429	4,057
Capital employed (CE)	8,819	9,304
Post-tax cost of debt	8.30%	5.70%
Cost of equity	11.60%	10.60%
WACC (market value weights)	10.40%	9.70%
Economic Value Added		
EBIT	1,489	1,837
Less: Taxes (adjusted for interest tax shield)	116	100
NOPAT	1,372	1,737
Cost of capital employed	948	883
Economic value added (EVA)	424	854
EVA/CE (%)	4.8%	9.2%

CHC's EVA performance 2004 doubled as compared to 2003; it increased from Rs 424 crore to Rs 854 crore. EVA as a per cent of capital employed was 4.8 per cent in 2003 which increased to 9.2 per cent in 2004. The enhanced EVA performance of the company is reflected in the high market value of the company's share that has increased from Rs 123 per share in 2003 to Rs 454 per share in 2004. The market value-to-book value ratio increased from 1.54 in 2003 to 5.44 in 2004 (Table 35.2).

Table 35.4: CHC: Drivers of EVA

		2003	2004
Sales/assets	Assets turnover	0.86	0.92
PBIT/sales	Margin	15.0%	16.7%
PBIT/assets	ROI	12.9%	15.3%
Assets/net worth	Capital Leverage	2.72	2.43
PAT/PBIT	Income Leverage	49.7%	73.0%
(A/NW) × (PAT/PBIT)	Leverage factor	1.35	1.78
PAT/NW	ROE	17.4%	27.2%
$R_f + R_p \times \beta$	Cost of equity	11.6%	10.6%
ER = ROE − COE	Economic return or EVA%	5.8%	16.6%

Table 35.4 shows EVA analysis in terms of return on equity and cost of equity, and traces the financial drivers of CHC's higher EVA in 2004. The higher EVA in 2004 was caused by increase in assets productivity (assets turnover ratio), better margin, resulting from cost reduction, increased leverage factor and lower cost of equity. The company used less borrowing but was able to save on interest payment and taxes which enhanced the leverage factor. The reduction in financial risk and reduced interest rates caused the cost of equity to fall.

MANAGERIAL IMPLICATIONS OF SHAREHOLDER VALUE

The shareholder value approach is based on the assumption that a principal-agent relationship exists between the shareholders and the management. As shareholders' agent, management is charged with the responsibility of creating wealth for shareholders. Therefore, all management actions and strategies should be guided by SVC. The foundation of SVC is the notion that the shareholder value depends on future cash flows and their risk. The cost of capital, accounting for the timing and risk of future cash flows, is used to determine the present value of cash flows. We should note that SVC emphasises the present value of future cash flows rather than earnings. Earnings suffer from accounting policy biases and subjectivism. They are not directly linked to value.

SVC takes a long-term perspective and focuses on valuation. A number of companies in India use the DCF analysis to evaluate projects. They accept those projects which are expected to generate internal rate of return higher than the cost of capital, or a positive net present value of future cash flows when discounted at the cost of capital. More and more corporate managers now realise the strong need for the extensive adoption of SVC in evaluating all management actions, projects, business strategies and overall strategic planning. SVC can be used to evaluate the consequences of strategies pursued by the company. At the business unit or division level, it is used to evaluate the alternative competitive strategies, to identify the key business factors that impact SVC and to set performance targets that are consistent with value creation. At the corporate level, it is used to evaluate the contribution of the strategies followed by business units/divisions, to form strategic combinations of businesses that will create maximum value, to identify products or businesses for divestiture and to mergers and acquisition activities.

The following steps are involved in using SVC based on DCF approach for strategic analysis and planning:

- Evaluate the current position of each division assuming that there will not be any significant changes from the current strategy.
- Estimate the business unit's net operating cash flows from the current strategy over the planning horizon; make explicit assumptions about sales growth, operating profit margin, tax rate, changes in working capital and additional capital expenditure needed to sustain the existing strategies.
- Estimate the unlevered cost of capital (k_u) of the business unit. The unlevered beta of an independent company similar to the business unit can be used for calculating the business unit's cost of capital.
- Estimate the terminal or the residual value of post-planning period. Make appropriate assumption about the post-planning growth of cash flows keeping in mind the nature of competition.
- Calculate the present value of net operating cash flows and terminal value at the cost of capital.
- Calculate the present value of interest tax shield at the cost of debt. If the amount of debt is not directly observable, then use the debt ratio of similar independent firms to determine the business unit's amount of debt.
- Add the present values of net operating cash flows, terminal value and interest tax shield to obtain the total value of the business.
- Subtract the value of debt from the total value to calculate the shareholder value.
- Repeat the above mentioned steps to calculate the shareholder value if the business unit follows a new strategy.
- The difference between the shareholder value of the current strategy and the new strategy is the value created (or destroyed). Go for new strategy if a positive value is created for the shareholder.
- Strategic plans of all business units should be integrated into the corporate strategic plan. SVC approach should be utilised to exploit the synergy between various units. The focus should be on maximising the overall shareholder value rather than treating business units as absolutely autonomous and working at cross purposes.

DCF approach is easily amenable for evaluating long-term projects and business strategies. However, tracking the operating performance more frequently, EVA approach is operationally more feasible. EVA, after making appropriate adjustments, is closer to cash flows. It is the experience of a large number of adopters of EVA that higher EVA leads to higher market value of shares.

The SVC approach helps to strengthen the competitive position of the firm by focusing on wealth creation. It provides an objective and consistent framework of evaluation and decision-making across all functions, departments and units of the firm. It can be easily implemented since cash flow data can be obtained by suitably adapting the firm's existing system of financial projection and planning. The only additional input needed is the cost of capital. The adoption of the SVC approach does require a change of the mind-set and educating managers about the shareholder value approach and its implementation.

CORPORATE GOVERNANCE

Corporate governance implies that the company would manage its affairs with diligence, transparency, responsibility and accountability, and would maximise shareholder wealth. Hence it is required to design systems, processes, procedures, structures and take decisions to augment its financial performance and stakeholder value in the long run. Good corporate governance requires companies to adopt practices and policies which comprise performance accountability, effective management control by the Board of Directors, constitution of Board Committees as a part of the internal control system, fair representation of professionally qualified, non-executive and independent Directors on the Board, the adequate timely disclosure of information and the prompt discharge of statutory duties. In fact, companies are needed to at least have policies and practices in conformity with the requirements stipulated under Clause 49 of the Listing Agreement.

Board of Directors

The Board of Directors constitute the top and strategic decision making body of a company. The Board of Directors should be composed of Executive and Non-Executive Directors meeting the requirement of the Code of Corporate Governance. The Board should represent an optimum mix of professionalism, knowledge and expertise. The Board should meet frequently and all pertinent information affecting or relating to the functioning of the company should be placed before the Board. Some of the significant matters generally placed before the Board include:[1]

- Review of annual operating plans of business, capital expenditure budget and updates, if any.
- Quarterly results of the Company.
- Minutes of the meeting of the Audit Committee and other committees.
- Information on the recruitment and remuneration of senior officers just below the Board level including the appointment and removal of the Chief Financial Officer and the Company Secretary.
- Materially important show causes, demands, prosecutions and penalty notices.

- Fatal or serious accidents or dangerous occurrences.
- Any materially significant effluent or pollution issues.
- Any materially relevant default in financial obligations to and by the Company or any substantial non-payment for goods sold by the Company.
- Any issue which involves possible public or product liability claims of a substantial nature.
- Details of any joint venture or collaboration agreement.
- Transactions that involve substantial payments towards goodwill, brand equity and intellectual property, if any.
- Significant labour problems and development in human resources/industrial relations.
- Material sale of investments, subsidiaries and assets not in the normal course of business.
- Quarterly details of foreign exchange exposure and the steps taken by the management to limit the risk of adverse exchange rate movement.
- Non-compliance of any regulatory provision or listing requirements as well as shareholder service such as the non-payment of dividend and delays in share transfer.
- Working of the subsidiary companies.

Almost half the Directors on the Board should be independent Directors. The independent Directors are expected to act independently, without any prejudice to anyone, and should play a significant role in Board Meetings. They make critical assessment of all issues discussed in the Board meetings and make significant contribution drawing from their wide experience and expertise in various fields.

The meetings of the Board of Directors should be held at regular intervals of not more than four months. The provisions under the Companies Act, 1956 and those under Clause 49 of the Listing Agreement should be strictly followed in this regard. The Board should meet at least once a quarter to review the performance and financial results. The statutory auditors and senior executives of the Company maybe invited to the Board Meeting for discussion and to provide inputs whenever required.

Audit Committee

The appointment of the Audit Committee is mandatory, and it's a very powerful instrument of ensuring good governance in the financial matters. The Audit Committee should have independent directors as its members. The members should have experience in the areas of finance, accounts, taxation, company law etc. The Company could derive significant advantage from the discussions in the Audit committee meetings.

The Audit Committee carries out the functions in accordance with the terms of reference set out under Clause 49(II) of the Listing Agreement read together with Section 292A of the Companies Act, 1956, and additional responsibilities assigned to the Committee by the Board of Directors. The Committee also reviews reports of the internal auditors and statutory auditors along with the comments and action taken. Senior executives are invited to the meetings of the Audit

---

1. This is a typical list of information placed before the Board. The information here is taken from the Annual Report 2004 of Cadila Healthcare Company.

Committee as and when considered appropriate. The head of the management audit, the head of the finance function, statutory auditors and cost auditor regularly attend the meetings of the Audit Committee; the Company Secretary acts as the Secretary of the Committee.

The functions of the Audit Committee inter alia include the following:[1]

- Overseeing the Company's financial reporting process and ensuring the correct, adequate and credible disclosure of financial statements,
- Reviewing with management, the annual financial statements before their submission to the Board with a special emphasis on accounting policies and practices, internal control requirements, compliance with the accounting standards and other legal requirements concerning financial statements,
- Reviewing the adequacy of the audit and compliance function, including their policies, procedures, techniques and other regulatory requirements,
- Recommending the appointment of statutory auditors,
- To review the observations of internal and statutory auditors about the findings during the audit of the Company.

Shareholders'/Investors' Grievance Committee

As a part of corporate governance, companies should form a Shareholders'/Investors' Grievance Committee under the Chairmanship of a non-executive independent director. The Committee monitors investors' grievances. The committee is responsible for attending to shareholders and investors grievances relating to transfer of shares and non-receipt of dividend.

Remuneration Committee

The company may appoint a Remuneration Committee to decide the remuneration and other perks etc. of the CEO and other senior management officials as the Companies Act and other relevant provisions.

Management Analysis

Management is required to make full disclosure of all material information to investors. It should give detailed discussion and analysis of the company's operations and financial information. There should be enough information given about the share prices and movement during the period under review.

Communication

The quarterly, half-yearly and annual financial results of the Company must be sent to the Stock Exchanges immediately after they have been taken on record by the Board. Some companies simultaneously post them on their web site. Companies may also provide periodic event-based information to investors and the public at large by way of press releases/ intimation to the Stock Exchanges where the shares of the companies are listed.[2]

The Company also makes the presentation to the Institutional Investors and the copy of presentation are also filed with the Stock Exchange and also uploaded on the Company's website for the information of the investors at large.

Auditors' Certificate on Corporate Governance

The external auditors are required to give a certificate on the compliance of corporate governance requirements. The following is an example of the auditors' certificate on Cadila Healthcare Company's corporate governance (Annual Report 2004):

We have examined the compliance of the conditions of Corporate Governance by Cadila Healthcare Limited, for the year ended on 31st March, 2004 as stipulated in Clause 49 of the Listing Agreement of the said Company with the concerned Stock Exchanges in India.

The compliance of the conditions of corporate governance is the responsibility of the management. Our examination was limited to the procedures and implementation thereof, adopted by the Company for ensuring the compliance of the conditions of Corporate Governance. It is neither an audit nor an expression of an opinion on the financial statements of the Company.

In our opinion and to the best of our information and explanations given to us, we certify that the company has complied with the conditions of Corporate Governance as stipulated in the above mentioned listing agreements.

We state that in respect of the investor grievances received during the year ended 31st March, 2004, no such investor grievances remained unattended/pending for more than 30 days.

We further state that such compliance is neither an assurance as to the future viability of the Company nor the efficiency or effectiveness with which the management has conducted the affairs of the Company.

BALANCED SCORECARD

We have discussed the measurement and implications of EVA and its link to the shareholder value creation. EVA provides a financial perspective; it is a performance measurement as well as a management system. In practice, most organisations balance financial perspective with other (non-financial) perspectives. The most successful organisations do not exclusively rely either on financial or non-financial performance measures. They know that financial performance measures reflect the results of the past actions. No doubt, these measures are important for shareholders as well as all other stakeholders. They must be monitored continuously by managers. Non-financial performance measures focus on current activities that would drive the future financial performance. Thus, an organisation needs a balanced view on various perspectives of performance. This viewpoint is referred to the balanced scorecard. The **balanced scorecard** aims at improving the performance measurement systems which focus dominantly on past financial performance and did not consider other perspectives and areas for strategic change and improvement.

---

1. Annual Report 2004 of Cadila Healthcare Company.
2. For example, this is the practice followed by Cadila Healthcare Company. See Annual Report 2004.

The balanced scorecard integrates multiple perspectives and enables organisations to clarify their vision and strategy and translate them into operational objectives and action. It provides feedback about the internal business processes and external factors that helps in strategic improvement and performance. According to Kaplan and Norton[1]: "The balanced scorecard retains traditional financial measures. But financial measures tell the story of past events, an adequate story for industrial age companies for which investments in long-term capabilities and customer relationships were not critical for success. These financial measures are inadequate, however, for guiding and evaluating the journey that information age companies must make to create future value through investment in customers, suppliers, employees, processes, technology, and innovation."

The balanced scorecard looks at organisational performance from four perspectives, and requires developing appropriate measures for all perspectives:

- The learning and growth perspective
- The business process perspective
- The customer perspective
- The financial perspective

Figure 35.2 shows the balanced scorecard integrating four perspectives to each other and the vision and strategy of the organisation.

The Learning and Growth Perspective

This perspective focuses on people – their attitude, culture, knowledge, development etc. and their ability to learn and grow for managing and sustaining change and improvement. In any organisation, and particularly, a knowledge-based organisation, human resource is the most critical resource. In the current environment of rapid technological changes, employees need to continuously learn. The learning and growth perspective, thus, emphasises employee training and building a corporate cultural that facilitates individual self-improvement and corporate development and growth. An organisation must provide funds for the training and development of employees, and managers should ensure that they pay adequate attention to employees' learning and development.

It is important to recognise that 'learning' is more than 'training'. Mangers should act as coach who should continuously guide and mentor the employees. The organisational communication system should allow for easy interaction to learn from and get help from each other in understanding and solving problems. The technological tools like the Intranet should also form the part of the learning and growth perspective. The key performance indicators are: employee satisfaction, employee retention and employee productivity.

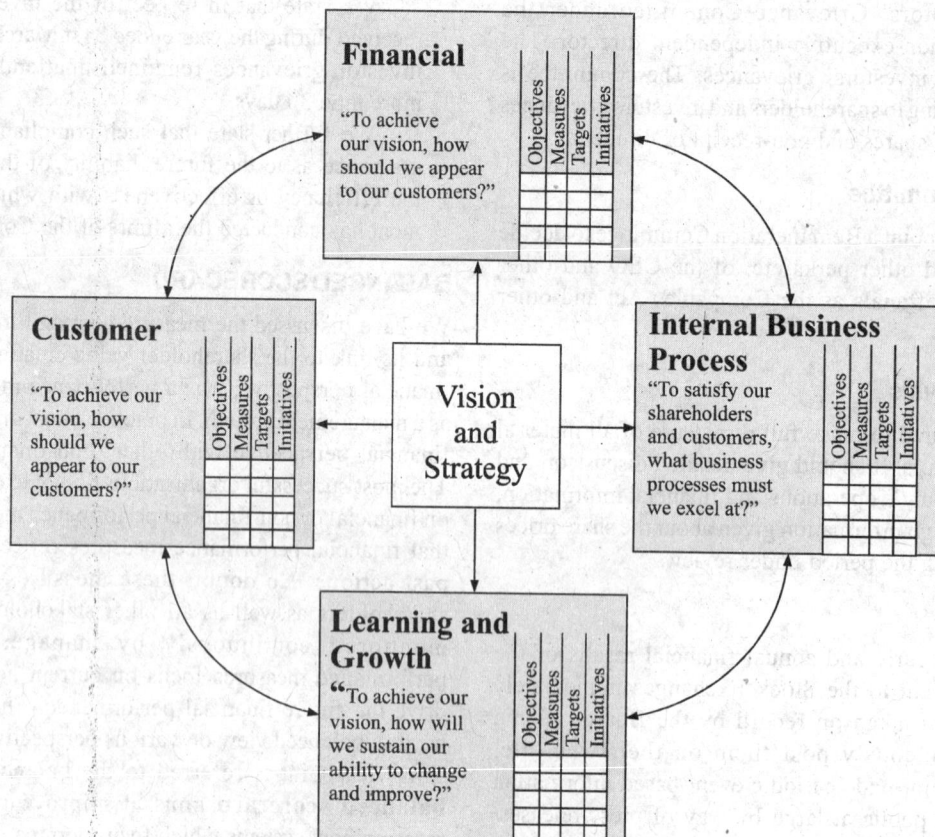

Figure 35.2: The balanced scorecard (adapted from Kaplan and Norton, The Balanced Scorecard: Translating Strategy into Action, Boston: Harvard Business School Publishing, 1996.)

---

1. Kaplan, R. S. and Norton, D. P. *The Balanced Scorecard: Translating Strategy into Action*, Boston: Harvard Business School Publishing, 1996.

The Business Process Perspective

This perspective includes internal business processes which ensure highest quality of products and services. The managers should ensure that their business is running well, and the firm's products and services meet customer requirements. The key performance indicators are: process improvement, and suppliers' relations.

The Customer Perspective

Each organisation must know: How do our customers see us? A large customer base means more revenue, which, other things remaining same, leads to improved financial performance. The customer perspective requires an organization to know how it should look to its customers if it is to succeed. Organisations have learnt the importance of customer focus and customer satisfaction in a sustained financial performance. Poor performance in terms of customer satisfaction is thus a leading indicator of future decline in spite of a good current financial performance. The key performance indicators under this perspective are: customer satisfaction, customer retention, market share and customer profitability.

The Financial Perspective

Balanced scorecard puts equal importance to the financial perspective. It does not disregard the need of financial data and financial performance measures. Financial measures provide a common language for analysing and comparing companies. Note that financial measures alone are not sufficient to guide performance in creating value, and non-financial measures are not sufficient for providing the bottom line score. There is a need for a proper balance. The key financial performance indicators include: return on investment and economic value added.

SUMMARY

- ❖ In practice, financial policy of a company is closely linked with its corporate strategy. A firm's strategy establishes an effective and efficient match between its competences and opportunities and environmental risks. It provides a mechanism integrating the goals of its multiple consistencies. Financial policies of the firms should be developed in context of its corporate strategy.
- ❖ Within the overall framework of the firm's strategy, there should be consistency between financial policies—investment, debt and dividend. For example, a firm can sustain a high-growth strategy only when its investment projects generate high profits and it follows a policy of low payout and high debt.
- ❖ Growth should lead to the enhancement of the shareholder value. This will happen when the firm is economically profitable; that is, when the firm's return on equity (ROE) is higher than its cost of equity (k_e). Value is created when ROE > k_e; value is maintained when ROE = k_e; and value is destroyed when ROE < k_e. Alternatively, ROCE can be compared with WACC. Value is created when ROCE > WACC.
- ❖ The amount of EVA is the difference between after-tax PBIT and the charges for capital employed or invested capital:

$$EVA = PBIT\,(1 - T) - WACC \times CE$$

KEY CONCEPTS

Agency theory	Economic value added (EVA)	Residual income	Strategy
Corporate governance	Fisher's separation theorem	Shareholder value	Sustainable growth
Economic return	Information signalling	Strategic planning	Ungeared earnings
Economic profit			

REVIEW QUESTIONS

1. Describe the interface between financial policies and corporate strategy.
2. What is sustainable growth rate? What factors determine it?
3. What is shareholder value analysis? What relationship exists between growth, economic profitability and the shareholder value?
4. Define MVA? How is it calculated? What are its pros and cons?
5. What is economic value added? How is it calculated?
6. What are the advantages and disadvantages of economic value added? Is it a superior method of performance evaluation than return on capital employed? How?
7. Define corporate governance. Describe the attributes of a good corporate governance system.

PROBLEMS

1. The following are the financial statements of Macro Company Limited for the year 2004:

Capital & Liabilities	Rs (lakh)	Assets	Rs (lakh)
Creditors	7,500	Cash	15,000
Borrowings	35,000	Inventory	18,000
Paid-up share capital	25,000	Debtors	6,000
Reserve & surplus	26,500	Net fixed assets	55,000
	94,000		94,000

Profit & Loss	
Sales	43,000
Gross profit	31,000
PBIT	3,500
PBT	27,500
PAT	24,875

Calculate sustainable growth rate for Macro Company

Limited. Dividend payout is 70 per cent.

2. A firm has grown at 15 per cent in the past few years. Its after-tax ROI and after-tax interest rate have been, respectively, 16 per cent and 7 per cent. It now has a target growth rate of 18 per cent. The company expects its profitability and interest cost to remain constant and maintain its payout ratio at 60 per cent. How can the firm achieve its target growth? Show calculations.

3. A manufacturing company earned PAT of Rs 123 crore in 2004 paying interest of Rs 24 crore. The company's invested capital is Rs 1,340 crore and WACC 15 per cent. Calculate the company's EVA. Tax rate is 35 per cent.

4. *Infosys* Table 35.5 provides certain financial data for Infosys from year 1999 to year 2003. The company uses CAPM to calculate cost of equity. You are required to calculate the following: (*i*) MVA, (*ii*) EVA, (*iii*) M/B and (*iv*) Economic Return. Comment on the company's market performance.

Table 35.5: Infosys: Economic Value Added Analysis

	2003	2002	2001	2000	1999
Average capital employed (Rs in crore)	2,470.48	1,734.97	1,111.47	703.87	245.42
Average debt/total capital (%)	—	—	—	—	—
Beta variant	1.57	1.41	1.54	1.48	1.48
Risk-free debt cost (%)	6.00	7.30	10.30	10.45	12.00
Market premium	7.00	7.00	7.00	8.00	9.00
PBT (excluding extraordinary income)	1,158.93	943.39	696.03	325.65	155.86
Tax	201.00	135.43	72.71	39.70	22.94
Enterprise value					(Rs in crore)
Market value of equity	26,847.33	24,654.33	26,926.35	59,338.17	9,672.80
Less: Cash and cash equivalents	1,638.51	1,026.96	577.74	508.37	416.66
Add: Debt	—	—	—	—	—
Enterprise value	25,208.82	23,627.37	26,348.61	58,829.80	9,256.14

CASE

Case 35.1: Hindustan Lever Limited*

Hindustan Lever Limited (HLL) was set up in 1933. It is an important subsidiary of Unilever. Unilever has about 500 subsidiary and associate companies in more than 100 countries. Its revenue was $48,353 million and operating profit $ 7,625 million in 2003. HLL's business areas include home and personal care, foods and beverages, and industrial, agricultural and other products. It is one of the largest producers of soaps and detergents in India. In 1983, the company reorganised its business and transferred some of its units to Lipton India Limited. In 1993, Tata Oil Mills Company was amalgamated with HLL, making the merged company the most dominant player in the domestic

soap and detergent industry. The Brooke Bond Lipton India Ltd. merged with HLL in 1996. Many more mergers and acquisitions have taken place in the recent years.

HLL places equal focus on serving both the employees and the shareholders, and it is committed to add value to them. The company markets about 100 brands with the help of about 7,000 stockists in over a million outlets. It has more than 50 factories and 70 locations and employs 36,000 persons. HLL has been regularly introducing has been introducing new products and rationalising its product portfolio. It is a highly profitable company and it follows a liberal policy of dividend payment. The market value of its share has shown significant appreciation

---

* This is an abridged version of the case prepared by Professor I.M. Pandey on the basis of information given in Hindustan Lever Limited's annual reports and other publicly available sources.

over years. The company has significantly expanded its operations through internal development and acquisitions. The company needs estimate of the cost of capital for evaluating its acquisitions, investment decisions and the performance of its businesses and for determining the value added to shareholders.

The HLL management uses the concept of economic value added (EVA)[1] in its decision-making and performance evaluation since it believes that shareholder value creation (SVC) is directly linked to EVA. How does HLL measure EVA and use it for performance evaluation? How is it superior to other measures of performance evaluation? Does it really lead to SVC?

Corporate Purpose

The company has stated its corporate purpose in the following words:

Our purpose is to meet the everyday needs of people everywhere – to anticipate the aspirations of our consumers and customers and to respond creatively and competitively with products and services which raise the quality of life.

Our deep roots in local cultures and markets are our unparalleled inheritance and the foundation of our future growth. We will bring our wealth of knowledge and international expertise to the service of our consumers.

Our long-term success requires a total commitment to exceptional standards of performance and productivity, to working together effectively and to a willingness to embrace new ideas and learn continuously.

We believe that to succeed requires the highest standards of corporate behaviour towards our employees, consumers and societies and world in which we live.

This is our road to sustainable, profitable growth for our business and long-term value creation for our shareholders and employees.

Our approach to Corporate Social Responsibility (CSR) is rooted in the belief that "to succeed requires the highest standards of corporate behaviour towards our employees, consumers and the societies and word in which we live"

Our CSR philosophy is embedded in our commitment to all stakeholders – our consumers, our employees, the environment and the society that we operate in. It is

this commitment we believe, that will deliver sustainable profitable growth.

The HLL management claims:

In Hindustan Lever, the goal of sustainable long-term value creation for our shareholders is well understood by all the business groups. Measures to evaluate business performance and to set targets take into account this concept of value creation.

In operational terms, the company focuses on the measurement and maximisation of EVA for shareholder value creation.

EVA Approach at HLL

HLL has grown very fast and its profitability has also increased over years. It pays dividend liberally. The company's share has enjoyed high price in the stock market. The company's market capitalisation has shown an impressive growth; it has increased from Rs 8,048 crore in 1993 to 40,008 crore in 2002. The company is very conservatively financed as it employs low amount of debt in relation to its equity funds.

HLL's philosophy is to add value to shareholders. It considers that the concept of EVA is more relevant in creating shareholder value rather than the conventional measures such as earnings capitalisation, market capitalisation and present value of estimated future cash flows.[2] It uses EVA concept in evaluating projects, business performance and setting targets. It has defined EVA as the difference between net operating profit after tax (NOPAT) and cost of capital employed (COCE). NOPAT is profit after depreciation and taxes but before interest cost and COCE is the weighted average cost of the company's debt and equity.

HLL's Cost of Capital[3]

The company considers cost of its debt as the effective rate of interest applicable to an "AAA" rated company. It thinks that considering the trends over years, this rate was 10.2 per cent in 2002 and 12 per cent in 2001. According to the company the cost of equity is the return expected by the investors to compensate them for the variability in returns caused by fluctuating earnings and share price. The risk-free rate is taken as the yield on long-term government bonds, which the company regards as about 7.2 percent in 2002. HLL takes the market-risk premium to be equal to 9 per cent for calculating the cost of equity. The cost of equity is calculated using the capital asset price model (CAPM). HLL has estimated its beta (a measure of the sensitivity of HLL's returns on share *vis-à-vis* the stock market returns) as 0.80.

The company's computations of NOPAT, COCE and EVA during the period from 1993 to 2002 are given in Table 35.1.1. HLL's EVA has been increasing over years.

---

1. EVA[TM] is trade marked by Stern Stewart Company.
2. HLL's Annual Report, 2002.
3. HLL Annual Report, 2002, p. F33.

Shareholder Value, Investment and Return

Table 35.1.2 provides information about HLL's shareholders' return and investment as well as the market performance of its shares. The market value of the shareholders investment has increased much faster than the book value·investment. ROE has shown increasing trend, and similar growth could be witnessed in EPS, DPS and P/E ratio.

Table 35.1.1: HLL's EVA Performance, 1993-2002

EVA Trends: 1993–2002

(Rs in crores)

	1993	1994	1995	1996	1997	1998	1999	2000	2001	2002
Cost of Capital Employed (COCE)										
1. Average Debt	135	97	110	156	160	165	162	93	50	45
2. Average Equity	359	462	588	815	1,127	1,487	1,908	2,296	2,766	3,351
3. Average Capital Employed: (1)+(2)	494	559	698	971	1,287	1,652	2,070	2,389	2,816	3,396
4. Cost of Debt, post-tax %	6.76	7.36	7.56	7.88	8.82	9.10	8.61	8.46	7.72	6.45
5. Cost of Equity %	19.70	19.70	19.70	19.70	19.70	19.70	19.70	19.70	16.70	14.4
6. Weighted Average Cost of Capital % (WACC)	16.17	17.57	17.79	17.80	18.34	18.64	18.83	19.27	16.54	14.3
7. Coce: (3) × (6)	80	98	124	173	236	308	390	460	466	486
Economic Value Added (EVA)										
8. Profit after tax, before exceptional items	127	190	239	413	580	837	1,070	1,310	1,541	1,716
9. *Add:* Interest, after taxes	13	15	11	32	21	19	14	8	5	6
10. Net Operating Profits After Taxes (NOPAT)	140	205	250	445	601	856	1,084	1,318	1,546	1,722
11. COCE, as per (7) above	− 80	− 98	− 124	− 173	− 236	− 308	− 390	− 460	− 466	− 486
12. EVA: (19) − (11)	60	107	126	272	365	548	694	858	1,080	1,236

Source: HLL's Reports and Accounts 2002.

Table 35.1.2: Share Price Data

	1993	1994	1995	1996	1997	1998	1999	2000	2001	2002
HLL Share Price on BSE (Rs. Per Share of Re. 1)	57.50	59.00	62.40	80.70	138.35	166.35	225.00	206.35	223.65	181.75
Market Capitalisation (Rs. in crores)	8049	8604	9100	16073	27555	36525	49513	45409	49231	40008
EPS	0.91	1.30	1.64	2.08	2.81	3.67	4.86	5.95	7.46	7.98
DPS	0.56	0.80	1.00	1.25	1.70	2.20	2.90	3.50	5.00	5.50

Discussion Questions

1. Why does HLL calculate EVA?
2. How does HLL calculate cost of capital?
3. Comment on HLL's methodology of calculating EVA?

What modifications would you suggest?

4. Comment on HLL's performance using earnings per share, dividend per share and share price data?

CHAPTER
36

Financial Management in Government Companies*

CHAPTER OBJECTIVES

- Understand the nature and the scope of finance function in government (or public sector) companies
- Discuss the features of investment, financing, working capital and dividend decisions in government companies
- Review the concept, structure and significance of memorandum of understanding (MoU)
- Explain the meaning and application of zero-base budgeting and performance budgeting to government companies

INTRODUCTION

The basic principles of financial management equally apply to the government companies or public sector undertakings (PSUs). In this chapter, we discuss finance objectives, outline organisation for financial management, explain key components of finance function, critically examine financial controls and functioning of Memorandum of Understanding (MoU), indicate distinctive features of financial management and provide an overview of changing shape of finance function in PSUs.

SCOPE AND ORGANISATION OF FINANCE FUNCTION

PSUs have come of age, and have to function like other business systems. They must ensure that they have an effective bottom line. Globalisation of Indian economy necessitates these enterprises to be sound in terms of profitability and earnings per share. PSUs have to be self-sustaining organisations, and financial management assumes significance in this context.

Finance objectives constitute the core of overall business objectives of private or public sector companies. There is a view that PSUs need not have any finance objective as they are not expected to generate profits since their losses could be made good by the State. However, though these enterprises have chosen to explicitly indicate the sub-financial objectives, they face the dilemma of evolving a full-fledged financial objective. Some PSUs point out stepping up the rate of internal resource generation as their finance objective. By being "public", these enterprises lend themselves to the ownership and control of the Government and management by it. The "enterprise" dimension makes it obligatory on them to produce goods and render services at a price which should result into profits to be recorded in the profit and loss account and balance sheet. A trade-off would have to be achieved by giving due credit to the nature and activities of the enterprise. While PSUs having a larger public dimension would lay stress on profitability, those dominated by

---

* This chapter is contributed by Dr. R.K. Mishra, Dean, Institute of Public Enterprises, Hyderabad and Dr. P.L. Joshi, Professor of Accounting, University of Bahrain, Kingdom of Bahrain. Dr. Joshi has contributed the section on Performance and Zero-Base Budgeting.

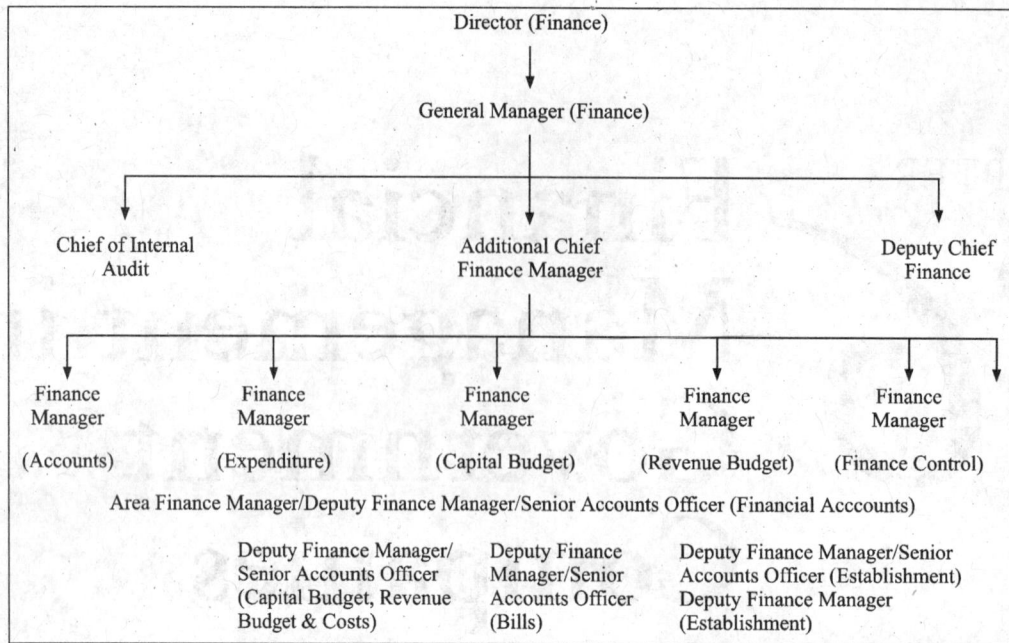

Figure 36.1: Organisation for finance function in Coal India

the enterprise dimension would make efforts to maximize their profitability. Relating the profitability to net worth, PSUs in India can have a scale of financial objectives, from "keeping the net worth intact to its maximization of return on net worth".

The consolidated profit and loss accounts and balance sheets of PSUs owned by the Central Government show an increase in the profit from Rs 909 crore in 1984–85 to Rs 32141 crore in 2002–03. Though the profits multiplied by over 15 times during this period, they never exceeded 5 per cent of the capital employed in these enterprises, which was much lower than the cost of their capital. The net economic value added was negative, destroying their capital base.

The organization for finance is shaped, among other things, by the structure of the enterprise. If it has a simple structure in terms of products and location, the organization would be functional. The organization for finance would be complex, in the case of multi-product, multi-unit and multi-locational undertakings. In the initial years when public sector units were coming up, the finance function was looked after by executives functioning at the middle or junior levels in the organisation. The finance departments were inadequately staffed. The background of the finance personnel was considered to be immaterial, and so were their training and education. Though finance was a staff function, the variegated expertise was missing, and the line relationships within the finance department dominated the staff requirements. Over the years, the organisation for finance has been undergoing a shift from a pure functional and centralised type to decentralised and divisionalised type organisation. For example, in Coal India Limited, the finance function at the corporate level is organized as shown in Figure 36.1.

The finance function has rapidly evolved in terms of the sub-functional areas. The staffers include functionaries such as the Assistant Accounts Officer, Accounts Officer, Finance Manager, Senior Finance Manager, Deputy General Manager (Accounts), General Manager (Finance), Executive Director

(Finance), and Director (Finance). The Director (Finance) is accountable to the Board and not to the Finance Ministry as was the practice the 1960s, In the enterprises owned by the State Governments, the finance function is normally headed by an executive of the rank of General Manager or below that level.

The finance function in PSUs is becoming more and more inclusive. Figure 36.2 shows that it has grown beyond the traditional boundaries to take cognizance of newly emerging elements such as restructuring and corporate governance. This evolution also underlines the importance of cash flow, growth and cost of capital as the nerve centre of the finance function in PSUs.

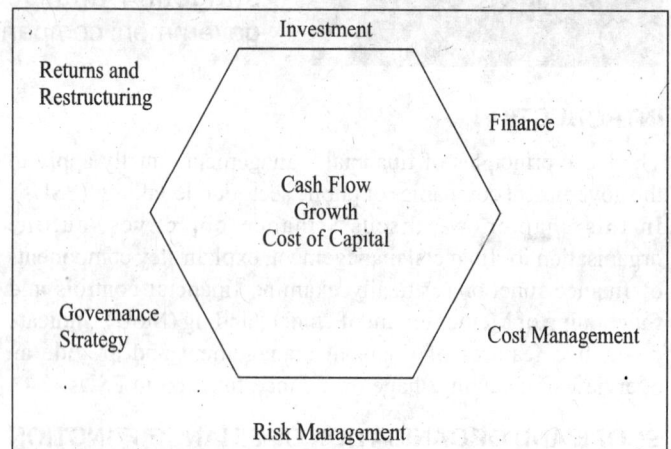

Figure 36.2: Scope of finance function

The scope of the finance function has undergone a great transformation. Earlier, when these enterprises had a Financial Adviser, most of his activities were confined to this control aspect. With the replacement of the Financial Adviser by the Finance Director, who now happens to be an integral part of the Management Board, the area of focus of the finance function has widened to include other functions having a bearing upon the management of investments and financing.

Most of the decisions in business enterprises have an indirect or direct bearing on finance. The responsibilities of Finance Function in PSUs are:

- Projecting cash flows by providing for risks.
- Determining the financial resources required to meet the company's operating programme.
- Forecasting how much of the requirements would be met by internal generation of funds and how much would have to be obtained from outside.
- Developing the best plans to obtain external funds.
- Establishing and maintaining a system of financial control governing the allocation and use of funds.
- Formulating programmes to provide the most effective profit-volume cost relationship.
- Analysing the financial results of all operations, reporting the facts to the top management, and making recommendations concerning future operations.
- Carrying out special studies with a view to reduce costs, and improve efficiency and profitability.
- Carrying out feasibility studies and preparing project reports.
- Budgeting.

The Finance Department is the principal coordinating office for carrying out the following activities:

- Preparation of long-term operating budget.
- Preparation of long-term capital expenditure budget and reporting on capital expenditure in regard to the expenditure likely to be incurred during the year.
- Preparation of the annual operating budget.
- Preparing the budget returns that flow out of the comprehensive budgetary system in operation.
- Analysing variations between budget figures and the expenditure incurred, and comment on the causes that have led to such variations to facilitate the management to control expenditure.
- Preparation of cash flow statement.
- Assessment of the total working capital requirements for the fiscal year.
- Assisting in all matters relating to purchase of equipment, raw material, and laying down suitable procedures for purchase.
- Advising the Chief Executive on the policies to be followed in regard to the prices of products, inter-departmental issues. charging of material to jobs, etc.
- Advise the management on all service matters having financial implications.
- Organising an Internal Audit Department and processing the reports submitted by the Internal Auditor, and placing them before the Board.
- Ensuring that the annual accounts are prepared in time according to the law on all matters relating to the statutory audit and the audit by the Comptroller and Auditor General.
- Acting as custodian of the cash of the company, and in discharging the duty, the department has to ensure that adequate financial control is exercised.

- Furnishing the management with prospective costs of the products to enable them to determine the optimum product etc.
- Preparation of quarterly reports on resources employed Cash-flows, Capital Expenditure, Profit and Loss Accounts and Ratio Analysis.
- Ensuring sound finance, non-finance interface.

INVESTMENT MANAGEMENT

Like in the private sector, Investment Management is an important segment of the finance function in PSUs. In 2002–03, the net block of PSUs was Rs 262,535 crore. The capital works in progress amounted to Rs 64,081 crore. The fixed assets, which also include investments under the heads "unallocated expenditure" and "other fixed assets", totaled Rs 48,304 crore during 2002–03. The total investment in fixed assets of all kinds was about Rs 461,222 crore in the case of PSUs.

Investment proposals are examined by various agencies of the Government, including the Project Appraisal Division of the Planning Commission, the Department of Public Enterprises, the Public Investment Board, and the Cabinet Committee on Economic Affairs (CCEA). At present, the Board of Directors of PSUs can sanction capital expenditure of Rs 5 crore without prior approval of the Government. The limits on capital expenditure and the approvals required are:

Up to Rs 5 crore	By the enterprise
Up to 5–20 crore	By the enterprise having integrated finance system for sanctioning project schemes.
Rs. 20–50 crore	Proposal to come from (lie enterprise, to be approved by the Administrative Ministry and finally to be sanctioned by the Expenditure Finance Committee chaired by Secretary of the Ministry of the Department.
Proposals above Rs. 50 crore	By the Public Appraisal Division, Public Investment Board, and Cabinet Committee on Economic Affairs. However, if they spend more than Rs. 100 crore, then they have to follow the same procedure as the non-MoU-signing companies permitted to spend Rs 50 crore and above on capital expenditure programme.

As part of public enterprise reforms, the government announced new autonomy accountability package called '**Navratanas**' and '**Miniratanas**' delegations vast financial powers with regard to capital expenditure to such companies. Investment proposals are made either from the PSUs or from the Administrative Ministries of the Departments. Their acceptance is guided by the priorities indicated in the National Plan. The proposals are expected to step up the rate of growth of the country, find wherewithal for their financing, increase employment potential, lead to import indigenisation and contribute to the growth of the export potential. The Public Appraisal Division, the Public Investment Board, and the CCEA assess both the financial and economic returns from the proposed projects.

Studies on financial management in PSUs reveal that fixed assets have been acquired disproportionate to their requirement, the utilisation of which is very low. Proper capital budgeting methods have not been introduced for clearing the replacement, modification, modernization and new acquisition of capital equipment proposals. Some externalities have also contributed to the excess build up of plant and equipment in PSUs. These include the nature of foreign aid—tied or untied—enterprises and consultancy and lack of foresight in assessing the requirements of plant and equipment and absence of drawings of vital parts and components related to plans.

WORKING CAPITAL MANAGEMENT

The management of working capital is a vital element in PSUs. The assets of the Central PSUs were of the order of Rs 461,221 crore in 2002–03. The liabilities and provisions amounted to Rs 47,466 crore (inclusive of cash-credit and short-term advances). These enterprises had a net working capital of Rs 156,202 crore to support their day-to-day operations. The management of working capital poses problems both in respect of individual components of assets and the volume and maturity of liabilities. A number of enterprises do not have a well-defined policy in regard to working capital management.

The Board of Directors in the case of each PSU is expected to determine the reasonable level of working capital, and review the position from time to time to ensure that the total investment in working capital is kept as low as possible. PSUs could approach the State Bank of India, or any other nationalised bank to finance their working" capital requirements. The bank should be requested to provide for the entire working capital needs. If necessary, the excess over the margin money could be covered by a guarantee from the Central Government. The margin money should be arranged by these PSUs on their own. Whenever the total requirements of the working capital cannot be met by cash credit arrangements with the banks, the PSUs may approach the Government for short-term loans. Such requests are examined *vis-á-vis* the position of the internal resources of the undertaking. The use of the depreciation fund for working capital needs is categorically prohibited. If a PSU wishes to transfer its entire amount from one public sector bank to another, or make a change in the membership of the consortium of banks financing it, it is open to it to settle the matter in consultation with the banks concerned.

The working capital requirements of PSUs are generally met through cash credits and advances arranged with the State Bank of India and other nationalised banks. The amount of outstanding cash credit/advances drawn by the Central Public Enterprises (CPSUs) from banks and others as on March 31, 2003 was Rs 69,294 crore.

In special cases, non-plan loans are also advanced by the Central Government to some enterprises for meeting their working capital requirements. As on March 31, 2003, a total of Rs 1,815 crore was outstanding from 51 enterprises as working capital loan from the Central Government. The principal

beneficiaries of this facility, having outstanding balances of working capital loans from the Central Government of more than Rs 100 crore, as on March 31, 2003, were National Manufacturers Corporation Limited, Delhi Transport Corporation, Hindustan Steel Works Construction Corporation Limited, Hindustan Shipyard Limited, Scooters India Limited, and Cycle Corporation of India Limited.

Over the years, PSUs have evolved systems and procedures to manage investments in inventories, sundry debtors, loans and advances, and cash and shot-term securities on the lines similar to private sector companies. Similarly, current liabilities, as a components of sources of funds, have started receiving comparatively greater attention. Despite these welcome changes, there has been no perceptible change in the locking up of funds in working capital. On an average, current assets, exceed about six months' turnover. Some of the contributory factors to the excess build-up of working capital include its slow transmutation, unfavourable credit management, absence of motivation to reduce investment in different components of working capital, and lack of awareness concerning the current techniques to working capital management.

In 2002–03, the inventory build-up was Rs 58,333 crore. The money locked up in cash was about Rs 34,967crore, the sundry debtors amounted to Rs 53,552 crore and the loans and advances totaled to Rs 40,013 crore. Such huge investments were not in the nature of capital formation.

FINANCING AND CAPITALIZATION

Financing decisions occupy a key place in the financial management of PSUs. At the end of March 1994, the Governments investment stood at Rs 55,683 crore which was about 20 per cent of the total investment in PSUs. Some State Governments, financing institutions and banks, both Indian and Foreign, have also contributed to the investment in these enterprises.

The sources of financing in PSUs have many salient features. The Government has been the main provider of both equity and long term debt in PSUs. Internal financing plays an insignificant role as a source of financing. The financial institutions have provided about 2 per cent of the total long-term investment needs. Foreign equity/loans account for more than 10 per cent of the long-term investment needs. Deferred credits took a lion's share of the foreign finance. Private participation from Indian business and investors is about 11 per cent of their total long-term resources. A major chunk of this amount has come in the form of bonds and public deposits.

The capital structure in PSUs is formulated on the basis of 1:1 debt equity mix suggested by the Government of India in 1961. Such a mix has been vehemently opposed by the PSU managers. The Committee on Public Undertakings and the Administrative Reforms Commission lent their support to the contention of managers. Those who support the Government policy argue that differentiating between equity and loans is immaterial in the case of PSUs, as both the dividend and interest are a transfer entry. This argument does not stand good when PSUs approach the capital and financial markets for raising bonds and public deposits. Moreover, this argument is against the basic principle of financial motivation to optimise the capital structure. The dependence of most PSUs on Government finance is substantial. In the face of challenges placed before PSUs, it is not a matter of time that they would be required to considerably reduce their dependence on the Government. As a result, they would have to approach the capital markets in future constantly.

The issue of public participation in the equity of PSUs received the attention of the Estimates Committee of Parliament as early as 1955. The Committee recommended that at least 25 per cent of the capital of PSUs be made available for the public to secure their interest and cooperation in the management.

The Krishna Menon Committee (1959) also vehemently advocated public participation in the equity. The reasons given by the Committee for permitting private investments were (*i*) it is a way of finding capital; (*ii*) it is a way of mopping up additional earnings of lower income groups; (*iii*) it is an anti-inflationary measure; and (*iv*) it enables members of (the community to participate in the profits of public enterprises. The matter was also examined in detail by two official committees which favoured public participation. The Administrative Reforms Commission in its Report on Public Sector Undertakings in 1967 strongly pleaded for public participation.

Public enterprises for a long-time were not permitted to approach the capital market to raise money through the flotation of debentures, public deposits and other securities. Scooters India Limited was permitted to offer in 1975 a part of its equity to the public at large. In 1981, PSUs were allowed to approach the capital market to mobilise money through public deposits. On March 31, 2003, PSUs had raised Rs 21,017 crore through this source. Between 1984–85 and 1988–89 they were permitted to raise long-term funds through the flotation of non-convertible 7-year redeemable debentures which formed a part of the funds raised through capital market.

During the Sixth Plan period, some public enterprises were given permission to approach the foreign bond markets and to raise borrowings with limits provided under the category of external commercial borrowings. In 1978, Hindustan Machine Tools Limited had offered its debentures to finance 50 per cent of its loan requirements for the Lamp Project. Other PSUs, however, did not emulate this example. Many PSUs have raised short-term finance through Commercial Papers in the post-1990 period.

DIVIDENDS PAYMENTS IN PSUs

Table 36.1 shows that PSUs pay normal dividends. In 1988–89, the dividends declared were less than 1 per cent of the paid up capital. Due to a revised stipulation announced as a part of the new economic policy, these enterprises have to now declare 50 per cent of their profits as dividends. However, in 1997–98, the dividends declared were a mere 30 per cent of the net profit earned by these enterprises. This percentage increased in the years to follow and 70 per cent of profits are now required to be declared as dividends.

In 2002–03, the dividends declared measured up to 32 per cent of the net profits earned by the PSUs. The dividend performance of the PSUs was very heartening which could be seen from Table 36.1 which shows that not only number of dividend declaring PSUs increased but also the quantum of dividends declared attained a new high in 2002–03.

FINANCIAL CONTROLS

Financial controls include internal audit, budgeting and financial reporting systems. Internal audit is a weak link in the chain of financial controls in PSUs. According to Section 619 of the Companies Act, 1956, a Government company should make available its accounts to the Comptroller and Auditor General of India (C&AG) for his review. In his audit reports on PSUs, C&AG always held the view that PSUs should strengthen their internal audit. However, the progress in this regard has been inadequate. Among other things, the absence of internal audit manuals, inadequate staffing and lack of expertise have hampered the quality of internal audit in PSUs. In large enterprises, internal audit is often not commensurate with their size. The Steel Authority of India Limited, Maruti Udyog Limited, Indian Rare Earths Limited, Stale Trading Corporation, Heavy Engineering Corporation, and Indian Tourism Corporation could be cited as cases in point.

Table 36.1: Aggregate Profit and Dividend Declared by PSUs for the Period from 1984–85 to 2002-03

Year	No. of PSUs Earning Profit	Aggregate Profit After Tax of PSUs in (2) (Rs in crores)	No of Dividend Paying PSUs	Aggregate Dividend Declared by PSUs (Rs in crores)	Average Payout
(1)	(2)	(3)	(4)	(5)	(6)
1984–85	113	2,021	58	177	8.76
1985–86	119	2,857	60	191	6.69
1986–87	108	3,470	64	213	6.14
1987–88	114	3,775	58	314	8.32
1988–89	117	4,917	57	353	7.18
1989–90	131	5,751	55	323	5.62
1990–91	123	5,394	56	413	7.66
1991–92	133	6,079	62	687	11.30
1992–93	131	7,384	64	792	10.73
1993–94	120	9,722	61	1,015	10.44
1994–95	126	7,186	67	1,436	19.98
1995–96	142	9,878	79	2,205	22.32
1996–97	132	9,991	81	3,084	30.87
1997–98	134	13,725	95	4,050	29.51
2002–03	118	43,085	81	13,735	31.88

Source: Mishra, C.S. and Narender V., "Corporate Dividend Policy: A Study of PSUs", **The Journal of Institute of Public Enterprise**, Vol. 18 (3&4), p. 119 (1995). Public Enterprises Survey: Vol. I (1994–95 to 1997–98 and 2002–03), Govt. of India, New Delhi.

Internal Audit

Internal audit is an important component of financial controls. This element has not received its due attention at the hands of PSUs managements in terms of its location, organisation, empowerment, resource allocation, staffing and performance. Mostly, this element is headed by an executive at the middle or senior level. The internal audit staff is not equipped adequately in terms of talents and no attention is paid to their capacity building. The techniques adopted are perfunctory in nature and limited to test check. The internal audit department is not organised in a way as to enable it to render a service to management and look beyond accounting function. Internal controls are not put in place and the internal audit is considered as a statutory requirement in many PSUs. The internal audit manual is conspicuous by its absence in many PSUs. There is a suggestion that the quality of internal audit could improve in PSUs if it is outsourced to an external organisation. The Administrative Reforms Commission in its report submitted in 1966 to the Government of India had recommended the setting up of strong internal audit departments in PSUs. The Committee on Public Undertakings has reiterated this recommendation time and again in many of its vertical and horizontal reports. Internal audit is not achieving its objectives in the organisation due to the fact that it is placed under the charge of a functionary who is not a part of the top rung of the hierarchy. When the status of the Head of the Department is not being enjoyed by this functionary, it does not allow a smooth flow of information and undermines the importance of the function. It is, therefore, suggested that in the first stage, internal audit is given the status of an independent function reporting to Member, Accounts. In the second stage, the internal audit department may report to the Chairman and, finally, only to a Committee appointed by the Board, or the Board itself. The elevation of the internal audit function to such a status would increase its coverage and effectiveness and bring all activities within its gamut.

Budget and Budgetary Control

The budget and budgetary control form the backbone of any control system. Till 1960, PSUs were characterised as entities devoid of budgeting and budgetary control systems. It was only on the renewed insistence of the Estimates Committee, Public Accounts Committee, Committee on Public Undertakings, and Administrative Reforms Commission that these enterprises introduced budgeting.

PSUs prepare a master budget which is supported by budgets classified partly under three heads, *viz.*, revenue, capital expenditure and cash budgets. While enterprises such as Steel Authority of India Limited and Bharat Heavy Electricals Limited have earned the distinction of being good planners and executors of the area of budgeting and budgetary control, there are scores of other PSUs which are yet to accept the budget philosophy. The budget targets are evolved not by consensus but from top down to bottom. The incremental approach to budgeting overshadows the zero-base and programme-cum-performance approaches. The budgeting system is not supported by a proper backup of the management information system.

Costing and Cost Control

Costing and cost control have received scant attention in a large number of PSUs. It is interesting to note that many PSUs either do not have cost manuals or have not developed proper systems and procedures to put the cost manuals into practice. The costs have not been standardised. The cost audits conducted are few

and far between. Cost reduction drives are seldom undertaken. The concept of just-in-time inventory is still uncommon to PSUs. Variance analysis is not a regular feature, and the information resulting from such an analysis is not effectively utilised. Raw material consumption norms and optimum inventory limits have not been developed by many PSUs Computerisation of inventory has not been attempted Indigenisation and import substitution are rare phenomena. The best way to come out of this muddle is to introduce extensive costing systems and install appropriate procedures for their operationalisation.

PERFORMANCE AND ZERO BASE BUDGETING*

Developing and adopting a budget is perhaps the single most important and time-consuming activity of any organisation whether in a government department, PSUs or private sector company. However, developing countries, like India, have been facing severe fiscal constraints due to rising demands for more and better public services. Over the years, the governments at every level have been discussing, experimenting with, and implementing new ways of budgeting. The budget is increasingly being talked about as a tool to promote accountability and effectiveness, rather than simply as a vehicle for allocating resources and controlling expenditures. Similarly, since the 'liberalisation' of Indian economy, the environment of PSUs has undergone substantial changes. PSUs have been trying to respond to these changes in some manner specially by reforming their budgetary practices. Performance Budgeting (PB) and Zero Base Budgeting. (ZBB) are special budgeting techniques used by government departments and companies.

Line-Item Budgeting

Despite several budgetary innovations and experimentations, the **line-item** or **incremental budget** represents the most commonly used budgeting method. In a line-item budget, each category of activity is afforded its separate appearance. It facilitates very less detail for both planning and cost control purposes. It assumes the continuation of present programmes. The proposed line-item amounts are generally based on a predetermined increase from last year's amounts. In other words, previous year's actual spending is extrapolated for next year by adding a growth factor (generally for inflation).

Table 36.2: Line-Item Budget

Expenditure Items	Last Year #	Current Year	Next Year
Salaries			
Materials			
Other expenses			
Total			

The main advantage of line-item budget is the ease of its preparation; it makes a simple comparison of performance from one fiscal period to another fiscal period. The main problem with this approach is the difficulty of relating the line budget to the goals of the parent organisation. Without much reviews, past

---

* This section is contributed by Dr. P.L. Joshi, Professor of Accounting, University of Bahrain, Kingdom of Bahrain.

inefficient activities are carried forward, making some resources wasteful. An example of line budget is shown in Table 36.2.

Performance Budgeting

Originated from the US, performance-based budgeting has been widely applied in government and other public sector entities around the world. Indeed, it is a system that the World Bank and the International Monetary Fund (IMF) recommend to countries seeking to reform their budgetary systems.

Performance budgeting (PB) is a system wherein managers are provided with the flexibility to utilize department or organisation's resources as required, in return for their commitment to achieve certain performance results. PB is a system of planning, budgeting, and evaluation that emphasises the relationship between money budgeted and results expected. Common characteristics of a performance budget include:

- Organisation's identification of mission, goals, and objectives.
- Linkage of strategic planning information with the budget.
- Development and integration of performance measures into the budget, and
- Disaggregation of expenditures into very broad areas (such as personnel, operating expenses, and capital outlays) rather than more specific line-items.

Some of the positive aspects or advantages of PB are follows:

- PB has more of a policy-making orientation. It connects plans, measures, and budgets.
- PB forces departments and policy-makers to think about the big picture.
- PB provides better information about the impact of budget decisions on people.
- PB gives department's increased budgetary flexibility and incentives for generating budget savings.
- PB allows for ongoing monitoring to see if agencies are moving in the right direction.
- PB helps in developing unit costs for the activities. Activity-based costing may be applied under this approach.
- PB strengthens legislative decision-making and oversight.
- PB enhances financial accountability to citizens, decision makers, and governmental monitoring agencies, and
- PB supports better management and evaluation.
- Performance information can increase public accountability and public services.[1] Furthermore, performance information provide decision makers information they need for evidence-based policy-making.

The primary disadvantage associated with a PB is the emphasis on quantity, not quality, of the activity being monitored. Beside, the link between performance measures and resource allocations are subject to political choices. There may also be lack of credible and useful performance information. In addition, difficulties may arise in achieving consensus on goals and measures. There could also be dissimilarities in programme and fund reporting structure as well as the limitations of information and accounting system. Tables 36.3 and 36.4 illustrate PB system.

Table 36.3: Performance Budget

Expenditure Items	Function #1	Function #2	Function #3	Totals
Salaries				
Materials				
Other expenses				
Total				
per cent				100 per cent

Tale 36.4: An Example of PB for a Health Department

Major head (Function)	Health Department
Minor head (Programme)	Control of communicable diseases
Sub-head (activity)	Leprosy eradication
Objectives (Physical targets)	(a) To detect 110,000 cases
	(b) To cure 80,000 leprosy patients
Detailed head (Financial targets or expenditures)	Total Budget Rs. 57,000,000

Salary
Wages
Office expenses
Rent
Stationery
Supplies
Diet
Medicines
Grants
Vehicles
Others

Categories of manpower:	Gazetted	28
	Non-gazetted	132
	Class IV	58

Budget (Rs in crore)

2001–02	2002–03	2003–04	2004–05
Actuals	Revised	Budget	Forecast
4.62	4.95	5.70	6.39

Under PB, the selection of a good set of performance indicators should be based on the concept of CREAM as was used by Andhra Pradesh (AP) government in its PB exercise.

CREAM

C = Clear	Precise and unambiguous
R = Relevance	Appropriate to goal
E = Economic	Available with reasonable cost
A = Adequate	Provides sufficient basis to assess performance
M = Measurable	Quantifiable

In setting measurable performance, the concept of SMART can be used.

SMART

S = Specific
M = Measurable
A = Attainable
R = Realistic
T = Time-bound

---

1. Premchand, A., *Appraisal of Recent Effort to Improve Financial Management*, World Bank, 1997.

Some of the examples of performance measurement indicators as used by the AP government for its Land Administration were: 1. Collection of water tax 2. Collection of non-agricultural tax 3. Assignment of government land for agriculture 4. Distribution of pattadar passbooks 5. Distribution of title deeds 6. Distribution of surplus land.

Programme Budgeting

Under a **programme budgeting system**, department or agency budget requests not only include the funding that it would like to receive, but also the outputs and outcomes they expect to produce as a result of that funding. The legislature then establishes performance targets for outcomes and outputs in the implementing act to the appropriations act. Departments or agencies then report their actual performance in their long range programme plans and budget requests for the following fiscal year. Agencies may be given incentives for performance that exceeds standards or disincentives for performance that falls below standards. These incentives and disincentives can be monetary or non-monetary. An example of a monetary incentive would be performance bonuses for employees and managers. An example of a non-monetary incentive would be an increase in budget flexibility.

Therefore, by its nature, a programme budget focuses on the output services that the programme provides to its users. It also more readily relates to overall organisational goals and objectives.

Zero-base Budgeting (ZBB)

Zero-base budgeting (ZBB) is a budgeting method for a corporation or government in which all expenditures must be justified afresh each year and not just amounts in excess of the previous year. Under ZBB, nothing is considered as sacrosanct. Every time, the managers are supposed to start from scratch or writing on a 'clean slate'.

ZBB is claimed to be a new technique of planning and decision-making. It reverses the working process of traditional budgeting. In traditional budgeting, departmental managers need to justify only increases over the previous year budget. This means what has been already spent is automatically sanctioned. While in ZBB, no reference is made to the previous level of expenditure. Every department function is reviewed comprehensively and all expenditures rather then only increases, are approved. ZBB is a technique, by which the budget request has to be justified in complete detail by each division manager starting from the zero-base. The zero-base is indifferent to whether the total budget is increasing or decreasing.

ZBB was first developed and introduced for business by Peter A. Pyhrr while working as a Manager, Staff Control, at Texas Instruments, Inc.' Dallas.[1] From this beginning, ZBB has been explored and adopted by many other businesses. Later, Jimmy Carter, then the Governor of Gerogia State, implemented ZBB in the Government environment with the help of Mr. Pyhrr. This was followed by some other state and federal government departments and put into practice the management concepts of ZBB. Also, various school districts have chosen to use the ZBB model for managing their educational operations. The results were mixed.

Process of ZBB

The development and implementation of the ZBB model requires managers and others in the organisation to engage in several major planning, analytic and decision-making processes. These major processes of ZBB include the following:

1. Identification or redefining the mission and goals of the organisation.
2. Identification of the organisation's Decision Units and Decision Packages.
3. Ranking of decision packages based on cost-benefit or qualitative criteria.
4. Fixing a cut-off point for funding.
5. Acceptance and allocation of resources.
6. Budget execution.
7. Monitoring and evaluation.

Decision Units and Decision Packages

A ZBB **decision unit** is an activity/programme or department for which decision packages are to be developed and analysed. It can also be described as a cost or a budget centre. Managers of each decision unit are responsible for developing a description of each programme to be operated in the next fiscal year or years. In ZBB, these programmes are referred to as **decision packages** and each decision package usually will have three or more alternative ways of achieving the decision package's objectives. These are called funding levels and generally include: a minimum level, a current level and an incremental level/s.

Under ZBB, while preparing and reviewing budgets for programmes and activities, the following certain hard and critical questions are asked:

1. Is this programme/activity considered redundant?
2. Is this programme/activity legally required?
3. Is there any measurable evidence of the value of the programme/activity under review?
4. Are these goals and objectives of the programme/activity important enough to warrant the expenditures being made?
5. What would happen if the funding for the programme/activity was not provided at all?
6. Are there other less costly and more effect ways of achieving these objects?
7. Where would the programme fit in if all programmes were displayed in order of importance?

---

1. Phyrr, P.A., *Zero-Base Budgeting: A Practical Guide*, New York, John Willey, 1973.

An important element of this budgeting procedure is that it forces prioritisation of programmes and activities. With the prospect of insufficient revenue to match the demand for spending, it is useful for a government or a PSU to have a ranking of programmes and activities based on proven effectiveness, as well as suggested alternatives to expensive or ineffective programmes.

Ranking of Decision Packages

Once decisions packages have been completed, they are ranked in order of priority within the organisation. The managers and their staff analyze each of the several decision package alternatives. The analysis allows the manager to select that one alternative that has the greatest potential for achieving the objective(s) of the decision package. Ranking is a way of evaluating all decision packages in relation to each other. Ranking may be undertaken on a cost-benefit basis or on an agreed qualitative basis. The main point is that the ranking of decision packages is an important process of ZBB.

Managers, following a review and analysis of all decision packages, will determine the level of resources to be allocated to each decision package. Managers at different levels of responsibility in the organisation usually perform the review and analysis. There is always a possibility that the executive levels of management may require the managers of the decision packages to revise and resubmit their decision packages for additional review and analysis. This often happens when the resource position is extremely scare.

Applications of ZBB

ZBB may be virtually applied to all government departments, programmes, schemes and activities. For example, Maharashtra Government applied it on the review of fees and levies; review of subsidies; review of redundant and low priority schemes; review of staff norms; review of work procedures and financial delegation, and review of objectives and priorities of various programmes.

In case of PSUs and private sector companies, ZBB is generally applied in the overhead area on which management has discretionary options or judgement. For example, research and development costs, advertising, repair and maintenance, internal audit function, training, transportation, printing and publications etc. However, ZBB is not applicable to direct production area which is better controlled through standard costing and industrial engineering techniques.

It is to be noted that a complete methodology of ZBB may not be applicable in certain situations and departments. As such, a **Zero Base Review** (ZBR) may be substituted for ZBB. ZBR is not so detailed as ZBB. It focuses on the review of the most critical activities.

Benefits of ZBB

1. Elimination of obsolete, non-relevant decision packages
2. Increased or decreased levels of funding for some decision packages and addition of new decision packages.
3. ZBB encourages budget participation at the operating level. As a result, managers and employees become more focused.

4. The comprehensive resource cost analysis process is a strong internal planning characteristic of ZBB.
5. ZBB, when properly implemented, holds great promise for assisting personnel of an organisation to plan and make decisions about the most efficient and effective ways to use their available resources to achieve their defined mission, goals and objectives.
6. Results in efficient allocation of resources as it is based on needs and benefits.
7. Forces and derives managers to think critically in order to find out cost effective ways to improve operations.
8. Useful for service department where the output is difficult to identify.
9. Increases communication and coordination within the organisation.
10. Managers and employees learn more about the organisation's activities and problems.

Possible Problems

1. Increase in paper work and time consuming.
2. In certain areas of the organisation, it is difficult to define decision units and decision packages.
3. It forces the managers to justify every related to expenditure. Sometimes, certain departments like R&D may be threatened while production department would benefit.
4. In the first year, cost of training, paper work and implementation of ZBB may go up because without its proper understanding, it cannot be successfully implemented.
5. Organisation may face some resistance from the employees and their unions.
6. Difficult to administer and communicate the budgeting because more managers are involved in the process. Since ZBB threatens certain positions of the managers and executives, they may play games and politics.

Modified Version of ZBB

In a few countries, a modified version of ZBB called **service level budgeting** (SLB) have been attempted. This modified model matches spending levels with services to be performed. In a ZBB exercise, a great deal of effort is generally devoted on documenting personnel and expense requirements that are readily accepted as necessary. The modified version of ZBB, avoids this by starting at a base that is higher than zero. An appropriate starting point for a jurisdiction level might be, say, 70 or 80 per cent of current spending levels. Higher priority requirements above this level could be identified to restore part or all of the current year's service levels. Then desirable new programmes could also be considered for funding. Consequently, a legislative body might be presented the choice of reducing some current operations in favour of adopting a new programme. Therefore, a new programme might be funded out of savings incurred reduction of an existing programme.

MEMORANDUM OF UNDERSTANDING (MoU) IN PSUs

The PSUs dominate the public enterprise system in India in terms of investment and their presence in the various sectors of the economy. These enterprises registered a phenomenal growth between 1960s and 1980s. However, as noted earlier they were more focused on 'social dimension' of their performance as compared to its 'economic dimension'. This resulted in their under performance in terms of indicators concerning the bottom line leading to questions about their retention in the portfolio of the government. The Krishna Menon Committee (1959), the Administrative Reforms Committee (1967), the M.S. Pathak Committee (1971), the Mohammed Fazal Committee (1980) and the Jha Commission (1983) commented at length on the performance of the PSUs. These committees expressed their deep concern about the low performance of these enterprises and offered a number of suggestions to improve their functioning. The Government of India appointed the Arjun Sen Gupta Committee (1984) to look into the performance of these enterprises intensively. This Committee observed that the unhealthy interface between the government and public enterprises was the key reason for the unsatisfactory performance of the PSUs. The Committee, therefore, recommended the adoption of the Memorandum of Understanding (MoU) as an instrument to rectify the sub-optimal interface between the PSUs and the government.

In pursuance of the Arjun Sen Committee's recommendations, the Government introduced the MoU in PSUs in 1987–88 during which year four enterprises signed the MoU. The number of MoUs signing enterprises increased to 99 in 2003–04. During the first few years of the introduction of MoU in the PSUs, the Government was guided by the French model of MoU which did not relate the performance to rewards. But, later on the Government of India switched over to the Korean Model of MoU which linked performance to incentives.

The MoU Philosophy

The basic philosophy guiding the MoU is to create an understanding between the government and the PSUs about the accountability of the latter to the former and the autonomy the former would provide to the latter in the task of achieving the objectives for which the PSUs were set up. It was expected that such an agreement would minimise the references that the PSUs were expected to make to the Government, on the one hand, and control that the Government would exercise on the PSUs to ensure their effective performance, on the other. To quote Suresh Kumar:

> Performance Contracts for Public Sector Units are known as MOUs (Memorandum of Understanding) in India. The MOU is rooted in an evaluation system which not only looks at performance comprehensively, i.e., at both commercial and non-commercial criteria of performance in their static and dynamic aspects, but also ensures and forces improvement of performance of managements and industries by making the autonomy and accountability

aspects clearer and more transparent. It is an annual document which is an intrinsic part of a long-term corporate plan in which the government (represented by the Secretary in the line ministry) and the public enterprise (represented by its CEO) lay down their mutual obligations and responsibilities, based on the missions and objectives of public investment, and after mutual negotiations. The idea is to choose appropriate criteria, assign mutually acceptable priorities to them and decide at the beginning of the year how the achievement of targets (and deviations there from) are to be evaluated. The crux of the evaluation systems is to set the evaluation parameters in advance and before the actual performance is delivered. Further, the process of negotiation is assisted by an objective third body which finally evaluates the performance also importing complete objectivity into the system.[1]

The Public Enterprises Survey, 1988-89, presented to the Parliament on 15 March, 1990, spelt out the purpose and mechanism of MoU in the following words: "In order to improve the performance of the public sector, government took a policy initiative by introducing the concept of Memorandum of Understanding. MoU is an instrument, which defines clearly the relationship of the PSUs with the government, to achieve better performance. The MoU is also an attempt to bring a proper balance between accountability and autonomy. The emphasis is on achieving the negotiated and agreed objectives rather than interfering in the day-to-day affairs".

The main objective of introducing the MoU was to reduce the quantity of controls by the government and substitute the same by the quality of controls by linking managers with ministers.[2] In the budget presentation for the fiscal 1996–97, the government reiterated this concept and allocated sincere involvement of PSUs in the formulation and implementation of MoU to thwart unnecessary public criticism, on the count of public accountability, conferment of greater autonomy to these enterprises gradually over a period of time with regard to matters concerning capital expenditure, mobilisation of funds, formulation of incentive schemes, joint ventures, etc.[3]

The Public Enterprise Policy pronounced by the Government of India on 24 July 1999 as a part of the 'Statement on Industrial Policy suggested a greater thrust on autonomy through MoU systems through which managers were to be granted greater autonomy and were to be held accountable.[4]

The investment decisions to create public sector units were based on social cost benefit analysis. A number of public sector enterprises came to be set up because the social internal rate of return and social cost benefit ratio were positive, even when their private profitability was negative. Moreover, most of the public sector enterprises were not expected to maximise profit These investment decisions by themselves do not create any problem for evaluation and performance. However, the

1. Suresh Kumar, *Performance Contracts: An Indian Case Study*, prepared for the Commonwealth Secretariat, London 1994, p. 2.
2. Prajapati Trivedi (ed.), Memorandum of Understanding : An Approach to Improving *Public Enterprise Performance*, International Management Publishers, New Delhi, 1990, p. 1, 2).
3. R.K. Mishra and Gerard de Bernis, *Privatisation of Public Enterprises: Indo-French Perspectives and Global Relevance*, Manak, New Delhi, 2002.
4. R.K. Mishra, et al., *The Role of Memorandum of Understanding in Public Enterprise Reform*, Vikas Publication, New Delhi, 2002.

instrument (i.e., the accounting system) that was chosen to evaluate the performance was borrowed from the private sector. And this accounting system judges performance ,on a single criteria on, which is, profit. The public sector enterprises performance therefore, came to be evaluated based on their financial profit. There was clearly a lack of an instrument that could measure the performance of PSUs taking into account the complexity of fusing social and financial objectives and translating them into measurable parameters.

Though the importance of the need for both autonomy as well as accountability was well understood, putting it into practice proved to be difficult. For ensuring autonomy as well as accountability, greater reliance was placed on setting out rules and procedures, through government directives, circulars, memorandum etc. these directives would be followed up by prescribing elaborate forms and returns that the enterprises must submit periodically to the line Ministry so that the line Ministry could monitor compliance of these directives. With the passage of time the number of these forms and returns increased manifold and ultimately the line Ministry ends up controlling more and more of day-to-day functions of the enterprises. The manager, hence, finds that most of the decisions for running the enterprises are taken by other people and therefore he sees no reason why he should be held accountable for results.

With the above background, the Government policy towards PSUs has been reviewed from time to time and in 1984, the Government appointed Arjun Sengupta Committee to review the policy in respect of Public Sector Enterprises. Following the recommendations of the committee report, the Government of India introduced the concept of the Memorandum of Understanding in 1988 to improve the performance of the PSUs and to introduce an objective system of evaluation of the performance of the managements of the PSUs.

Concept and Objectives of MoU

The concept of Memorandum of Understanding is very simple. It is supposed to be a freely negotiated document between the Government, acting as the owner, and a specific PSU. Second, it is supposed to clearly specify the intentions obligations and mutual responsibilities of both parties to the Memorandum of Understanding (MoU).

If either of the above two conditions is violated, the effectiveness of the MoU as an instrument of performance improvement is bound to be affected. Further, MoU makes an attempt to move the management of PSUs from management by controls and procedures to management by results and objectives. Another way of saying the same thing is that MoU makes an attempt to move the management of PSUs from reliance on ex-ante controls to a system of ex-post controls

The objectives of the MoU system are to:

- Measure the performance of PSUs taking into account the complexity effusing social and financial objectives and translating them into measurable parameters;
- Ensure simultaneous increase in autonomy as well as accountability;
- Set up new institutions and administrative and personnel systems;

- Replace 'multiply' principles with multiple objectives' with clarity in goals and objectives.

Structure of MoU

The MoU is not merely a document, it is a way of life or a management system. This tool for performance improvement incorporates within its fold three sub-system, namely, performance information system, performance evaluation system and performance incentive system.

Performance evaluation in MoU involves five steps. First three steps are taken at the beginning of the year and the last two steps are taken at the end of the year.

Beginning of the Year
Step 1: Criteria Selection
Step 2: Criteria Weight Selection
Step 3: Criteria Value Selection

At the End of the Year
Step 4: Performance Valuation
Step 5: Performance Reward

Step 1: Criteria Selection In the first step, one has to choose appropriate set of criteria to be included in the MoU. This raises the question: what constitutes an appropriate set of criteria? According to the MoU philosophy only those criteria should be included in the MoU which are "fair" to the manager, as well as "fair" to the country and have been negotiated freely. Fairness to managers implies that the criteria included in the MoU should measure only those aspects of managerial performance which are under manager's control.

Performance criteria must be selected carefully and not arbitrarily. These should be based on the enterprises' corporate plan that looks at three to five years in the future. They must also be consistent with plan and budgetary goals of the government. In the MoUs for the central public sector enterprises, therefore, the MoU target and budgetary goals are kept identical. Very often, no distinction is made between managerial performance and enterprises performance. MoU is an instrument that measures the performance of the manager and not that of the enterprises. While selecting performance criteria this must be kept in mind and only those parameters that judge managerial performance should be selected.

Step 2: Criteria Weight Selection Next step deals with criteria weight selection. For running an enterprise successfully a Chief Executive has to undertake a number of tasks. However, not all the tasks are of equal importance. A smart Chief Executive therefore, priorities his tasks based on his perception of the relative importance of different activities in hand. The perception of the Chief Executive and that of the owner may not coincide in this case. In the interest of clarity of purpose it is necessary that from the long list of things to do, the manager must be told what are the relative priorities so that he can allocate his time more effectively in achieving those priorities.

This is not an academic issue. Rather, it represents a key difference between the Action Plan type of monitoring instrument and the MoU system. At the end of 1989–90, the Government of India found it difficult to evaluate the performance of PSUs based on their MoU commitments. Thus, after a careful examination of how this problem had been overcome in other countries, it was decided to introduce this system of relative weights.

Step 3: Criterion Value Selection The third step in the performance evaluation system relates to criteria value selection. To understand one needs to distinguish between "criteria" and "criteria value". Now, kilometers per liter is a criterion to measure efficiency of motor vehicles: like cars, scooters, trucks and so on. However, 10 kilometers/liter may be excellent for a truck but it is terrible for a scooter. This value of 10 kilometers/liter is the criteria value. It is a value, which distinguishes various levels of performance. The MoU is rated on a 5-point scale, where "1" represents "excellent" performance and "5" represents "poor" performance.

Once decided on the relevant set of criteria to be included in the MoU, their relative priorities and the criteria values, there is nothing to be done till the end of the year. This indeed, is the very heart of the MoU philosophy. Once you have specified the objectives for the managers you should not interfere in the operation and wait till the end of the year for them to deliver the goods.

The selection of criterion values should be carried out through a participative process. Experience suggests that without a participative approach, targets tend to take the form of formal directives which are often overtly accepted and covertly resisted. These targets should be easy to understand and well defined. It is desirable at this stage to also agree upon definitions of various criteria and methodology for measuring them. The sources of information which could assist in setting criterion values include:

- The original objectives at the project formulation stage.
- Comparisons with similar undertakings of other selected developed and developing countries.
- Comparisons with the performance of the same firm in the previous years.
- Professional judgement by third parties.
- Professional judgement at the Ministry level.
- Professional judgement at the enterprise level.

Step 4: Performance Evaluation The fourth step is taken at the end of year, when we look at the achievements of the PSUs and compare them with the criteria values and determine the scores. The value of the composite score will also lie between "1" and "5". If the management has done excellent in all fronts included in the MoU, they will get a score of "1". But, suppose, they have done terrible job on all fronts included in the MoU, they will get a score of "5". A mixed performance results in a score somewhere between "1" and "5".

This concept of composite score is a very key concept in the MoU exercise. It measures the ability of the enterprise to meet its own commitments. It also allows us to compare and rank various enterprise, according to the composite scores, while the commitments of the enterprises may be different. For example, the commitments of Air India and Steel Authority of India are very different. Yet, through this exercise we are able to compare their ability to meet their respective commitments. This final step in the performance evaluation exercise cannot be a mechanical procedure. Everything in life does not always of according to plans and hence there has to be some opportunity to deal with such exigencies in any credible system. In the MoU system the review factors which were genuinely unanticipated by both parties to the MoU, i.e., factors which were not predicted and could not have been predicted by either party, such natural disaster, wars etc. This is essential to keep the system 'fair'.

Step 5: Performance Reward While performance evaluation of PSUs provides a measures of the degree of achievement of the objectives set out, evaluation by itself does not lead to improvement of performance. Unless performance evaluation is coupled with a system of rewards and penalties and utilised as a means for that purpose, it provides no motivation to the PSUs for improving their performance. A transparent system of rewards and punishment is thus a corollary to the introduction of an objective performance evaluation system of the PSUs. Thus a performance reward scheme constitutes an essential complement of the MoU system.

The MoU system is in operation in the PSUs for more than 15 years. The Institute of Public Enterprise in its survey of 76 MoU signing PSUs in 1998–99 noted the following:

- 60 enterprises were organisationally prepared for the MoU;
- 30 enterprises held the view the MoUs helped them in obtaining greater autonomy;
- 30 enterprises felt that the MoU ensured accountability;
- 44 enterprises indicated that MoU was an improvement on the previous evaluation methods;
- 46 enterprises suggested to make the MoU a permanent feature of performance evaluation;
- 21 enterprises thought that MoU was relevant in the present context of liberalisation and globalisation;
- 36 enterprises were of the view that the preparation of the MoU should be increased;
- 34 enterprises thought that MoU score reflected their related performances; and
- 46 enterprises concluded that MoU helped them in their overall performance.

It is clear from the survey that whereas there are strong proponents of MoU within the PE system, there are formidable opponents also not seeing the so called virtues in the system. It is alleged that the MoU is an agreement between two unequals, suffers from information asymmetry and is characterised by soft targeting. The MoU has been compared as wrong end of the stick containing more memorandum than understanding.[1]

FEATURES OF THE PSU FINANCIAL MANAGEMENT

Often a question is asked as to how financial management in PSUs is different from its counterparts in the private sector. The distinctions are numerous. Whereas in private enterprises the financing is done on long and short-term considerations, in PSUs this needs to be done keeping in view their stage of operation. The sources side of the balance sheet of PSUs reveals that these

1. Murthy K.S. MoU. More Memorandum than Understanding, in R.K. Mishra, *et. al.*, The Role of Memorandum of Understanding in Public Enterprise Reform, Vikas Chennai, 2002, pp 53–74.

entities depend more on external resources, whereas their counterparts in the private sector have a tendency to depend more on internal resources.

The use of current liabilities as a source of finance is less in PSUs as compared to the enterprises in the private sector. The cost of capital is at the back of every move in a private sector enterprise, whereas in PSUs it does not hold the position of that strength. The control mechanisms in PSUs are still evolving and have yet to take firm root.

There are five main drivers for change in the shape of the finance functions in PSUs

- Intense competition.
- New opportunities, but also new risks.
- Increasingly onerous regulatory and environmental pressure
- shareholders and stakeholder activism with social pressure often running a head of strictly legal requirements, influencing corporate governance.
- An entirely new attitude to quality and service regarded as an act of faith and often even transcending all financial calculations.

The corporate world has reacted predictably by altering their organisation structures and the way they do business. It is no wonder that in many companies the business re-engineering programme's are being led by finance. Members and the financial staff are regarded as business partners by their colleagues who insist that finance can no longer stand and watch them from the sidelines but must play a full part in management. The finance directors role has moved subtly from managing the financial staff to representing the financial view at top management level: it is an ambassadorial nature than a purely technical role. The three key elements: the factory, the counting house, and the power house are still there but there has been a significant change in focus. Finance is now intimately involved in strategy and planning. The importance of the management of risk has been recognised.

PSUs in India have to provide a face-lift to their finance functions to make it useful to 'top management' therein. The present 'mindset' in finance has to give way to appreciate the new sensitivities. PSUs are discerning the trend to develop suitable organisation for their finance function. Financial management in PSUs shows that they have to go a long way to shore up their financial functioning. There is an immense scope to economies on fixed assets and working capital. There is a need to strengthen the financial control mechanisms. The trends in the global financial management show that 'risk assessment' and 'controlling cost' are the greatest financial challenges faced by business enterprises and new initiatives to strengthen financial management in public enterprises need to be focused on these areas. The chief executives are increasingly relying on their finance professionals to help them navigate through the maze of new economic legislative and commercial risks. The effective use of financial information is regarded as a doorway to success with well trained finance specialists holding the key to unlocking its potential. Public enterprises may quite well respond to this challenge by designing and implementing suitable training programme's for their finance executives. The approach to financing and capitalisation needs a new orientation, providing for emphasis on asset liabilities management capital adequacy ratio, change from the existing control bias to support service and domestic to global financial management. The finance, non-finance interface requires to be placed on better footing. The new portends in financial management in PSUs indicate signs of this transformation. The changing shape of finance functions emphasises the need for paradigm shift in the present roles and responsibilities of the financial management in PSUs.

SUMMARY

- ❖ Like the private sector companies, the government companies also aim at profitability and value creation. However, they also focus much more on non-financial and social objectives.

- ❖ The organisation of finance function of the government companies is evolving over the years, and it has become now a specialised function with a decentralised structure in care of multi-divisional and multi-product companies.

- ❖ The scope of finance function in the government companies is as extended as in the case of the private sector companies. It includes the funds management, budgeting, cost control, assets management and security etc.

- ❖ The basic principle of value creation governs the investment decisions of the government companies. But these company also use economic return and the social impact criteria in choosing projects.

- ❖ The authority for investment expenditure goes beyond the management of the company. Government departments and ministries play important role in authorising investment expenditures beyond certain specified limits.

- ❖ Government companies have huge investment in current assets. Hence, working capital management assumes for greater importance. A number of companies (e.g., BHEL, NTPC) have well-established policies and practices of managing working capital. However, a large number of companies have inadequate working capital management. The Boards of the companies hardly discuss the working capital management issues and lay down policies and procedures.

- ❖ Most government companies are dependent on the government funding for financing their expansion and growth. The government funding is available either as equity or debt. Hence, the issue of capital structure is considered redundant as the source of the debt and equity is the same, that is, the taxpayers money allocated by the government.

- ❖ A very few government companies make profits and declare dividend. In 2002–03, 81 companies, out of 118 profit making companies paid about 36 per cent of their net profits as dividends.

- ❖ Financial controls in government companies are more

stringent in the private sector companies. They are subjected to internal audit, statutory audit and audit by controller and Auditor General.

❖ An additional feature of performance evaluation and control in government companies is Memorandum of Under-standing (MoU).

❖ MoU is a performance contract between the government and the company management. It specifies the performance targets as well as explicitly states the autonomy and accountability of management in meeting financial and non-financial objectives and targets. The emphasis is only reducing the close control of the government and the day-to-day interference in the management of companies.

❖ Performance budgeting and zero-base-budgeting (ZBB) are special budgeting control tools used by government companies.

❖ Performance budgeting is a flexible system of aligning organisational mission, goals and objectives with budgeted funds and expected results. It takes a comprehensive, policy oriented approach, rather than a short term mechanical approach of preparing budgets.

❖ Performance budgeting may be extended to each specific programmes, and it is referred to programme budgeting.

❖ Zero-base budgeting is based on the notion that each activity or programme and its funding must be justified each time afresh.

KEY CONCEPTS

C&AG audit	Internal audit	Navratanas	Public sector companies
Decision points	Line-item budgeting	Performance budgeting	Service level budgeting
Decisions packages	Memorandum of understanding	Performance contract	Zero-base-budgeting
Government companies	Mini-navratanas	Programme budgeting	Zero-base review
Incremental budgeting			

REVIEW QUESTIONS

1. What is the nature and scope of finance function in government companies? What are the special features of financial functions in government companies?

2. How are investment, financing and dividend decisions organised in government companies?

3. What is the nature of working capital in government companies? What steps should be taken to improve the effectiveness of working capital management in government companies?

4. What is zero-base budgeting? How is it different from the traditional budgeting? What are its merits and demerits?

5. Explain the steps in the process of zero-base budgeting.

6. What is performance budgeting? What is programme budgeting? What are their pros and cons.

7. What is a Memorandum of Understanding (MoU)? How is it structured? How does it help the performance improvement and measurement?

Table A: Compound Value Factor of a Lump Sum (CVF) of Re 1

Year							Interest Rate							
	1%	2%	3%	4%	5%	6%	7%	8%	9%	10%	11%	12%	13%	14%
1	1.010	1.020	1.030	1.040	1.050	1.060	1.070	1.080	1.090	1.100	1.110	1.120	1.130	1.140
2	1.020	1.040	1.061	1.082	1.103	1.124	1.145	1.166	1.188	1.210	1.232	1.254	1.277	1.300
3	1.030	1.061	1.093	1.125	1.158	1.191	1.225	1.260	1.295	1.331	1.368	1.405	1.443	1.482
4	1.041	1.082	1.126	1.170	1.216	1.262	1.311	1.360	1.412	1.464	1.518	1.574	1.630	1.689
5	1.051	1.104	1.159	1.217	1.276	1.338	1.403	1.469	1.539	1.611	1.685	1.762	1.842	1.925
6	1.062	1.126	1.194	1.265	1.340	1.419	1.501	1.587	1.677	1.772	1.870	1.974	2.082	2.195
7	1.072	1.149	1.230	1.316	1.407	1.504	1.606	1.714	1.828	1.949	2.076	2.211	2.353	2.502
8	1.083	1.172	1.267	1.369	1.477	1.594	1.718	1.851	1.993	2.144	2.305	2.476	2.658	2.853
9	1.094	1.195	1.305	1.423	1.551	1.689	1.838	1.999	2.172	2.358	2.558	2.773	3.004	3.252
10	1.105	1.219	1.344	1.480	1.629	1.791	1.967	2.159	2.367	2.594	2.839	3.106	3.395	3.707
11	1.116	1.243	1.384	1.539	1.710	1.898	2.105	2.332	2.580	2.853	3.152	3.479	3.836	4.226
12	1.127	1.268	1.426	1.601	1.796	2.012	2.252	2.518	2.813	3.138	3.498	3.896	4.335	4.818
13	1.138	1.294	1.469	1.665	1.886	2.133	2.410	2.720	3.066	3.452	3.883	4.363	4.898	5.492
14	1.149	1.319	1.513	1.732	1.980	2.261	2.579	2.937	3.342	3.797	4.310	4.887	5.535	6.261
15	1.161	1.346	1.558	1.801	2.079	2.397	2.759	3.172	3.642	4.177	4.785	5.474	6.254	7.138
16	1.173	1.373	1.605	1.873	2.183	2.540	2.952	3.426	3.970	4.595	5.311	6.130	7.067	8.137
17	1.184	1.400	1.653	1.948	2.292	2.693	3.159	3.700	4.328	5.054	5.895	6.866	7.986	9.276
18	1.196	1.428	1.702	2.026	2.407	2.854	3.380	3.996	4.717	5.560	6.544	7.690	9.024	10.575
19	1.208	1.457	1.754	2.107	2.527	3.026	3.617	4.316	5.142	6.116	7.263	8.613	10.197	12.056
20	1.220	1.486	1.806	2.191	2.653	3.207	3.870	4.661	5.604	6.727	8.062	9.646	11.523	13.743
25	1.282	1.641	2.094	2.666	3.386	4.292	5.427	6.848	8.623	10.835	13.585	17.000	21.231	26.462
30	1.348	1.811	2.427	3.243	4.322	5.743	7.612	10.063	13.268	17.449	22.892	29.960	39.116	50.950
40	1.489	2.208	3.262	4.801	7.040	10.286	14.974	21.725	31.409	45.259	65.001	93.051	132.782	188.884
50	1.645	2.692	4.384	7.107	11.467	18.420	29.457	46.902	74.358	117.391	184.565	289.002	450.736	700.233

(Contd..)

Table A Contd.

Year							Interest Rate						
	15%	16%	17%	18%	19%	20%	21%	22%	23%	24%	25%	30%	40%
1	1.150	1.160	1.170	1.180	1.190	1.200	1.210	1.220	1.230	1.240	1.250	1.300	1.400
2	1.323	1.346	1.369	1.392	1.416	1.440	1.464	1.488	1.513	1.538	1.563	1.690	1.960
3	1.521	1.561	1.602	1.643	1.685	1.728	1.772	1.816	1.861	1.907	1.953	2.197	2.744
4	1.749	1.811	1.874	1.939	2.005	2.074	2.144	2.215	2.289	2.364	2.441	2.856	3.842
5	2.011	2.100	2.192	2.288	2.386	2.488	2.594	2.703	2.815	2.932	3.052	3.713	5.378
6	2.313	2.436	2.565	2.700	2.840	2.986	3.138	3.297	3.463	3.635	3.815	4.827	7.530
7	2.660	2.826	3.001	3.185	3.379	3.583	3.797	4.023	4.259	4.508	4.768	6.275	10.541
8	3.059	3.278	3.511	3.759	4.021	4.300	4.595	4.908	5.239	5.590	5.960	8.157	14.758
9	3.518	3.803	4.108	4.435	4.785	5.160	5.560	5.987	6.444	6.931	7.451	10.604	20.661
10	4.046	4.411	4.807	5.234	5.695	6.192	6.727	7.305	7.926	8.594	9.313	13.786	28.925
11	4.652	5.117	5.624	6.176	6.777	7.430	8.140	8.912	9.749	10.657	11.642	17.922	40.496
12	5.350	5.936	6.580	7.288	8.064	8.916	9.850	10.872	11.991	13.215	14.552	23.298	56.694
13	6.153	6.886	7.699	8.599	9.596	10.699	11.918	13.264	14.749	16.386	18.190	30.288	79.371
14	7.076	7.988	9.007	10.147	11.420	12.839	14.421	16.182	18.141	20.319	22.737	39.374	111.120
15	8.137	9.266	10.539	11.974	13.590	15.407	17.449	19.742	22.314	25.196	28.422	51.186	155.568
16	9.358	10.748	12.330	14.129	16.172	18.488	21.114	24.086	27.446	31.243	35.527	66.542	217.795
17	10.761	12.468	14.426	16.672	19.244	22.186	25.548	29.384	33.759	38.741	44.409	86.504	304.913
18	12.375	14.463	16.879	19.673	22.901	26.623	30.913	35.849	41.523	48.039	55.511	112.455	426.879
19	14.232	16.777	19.748	23.214	27.252	31.948	37.404	43.736	51.074	59.568	69.389	146.192	597.630
20	16.367	19.461	23.106	27.393	32.429	38.338	45.259	53.358	62.821	73.864	86.736	190.050	836.683
25	32.919	40.874	50.658	62.669	77.388	95.396	117.391	144.210	176.859	216.542	264.698	705.641	4499.880
30	66.212	85.850	111.065	143.371	184.675	237.376	304.482	389.758	497.913	634.820	807.794	2619.996	24201.432
40	267.864	378.721	533.869	750.378	1051.668	1469.772	2048.400	2847.038	3946.430	5455.913	7523.164	36118.865	700037.697
50	1083.657	1670.704	2566.215	3927.357	5988.914	9100.438	13780.612	20796.561	31279.195	46890.435	70064.923	497929.223	20248916.240

Table B: Compound Value Factor of an Annuity (CVFA) of Re 1

Year	1%	2%	3%	4%	5%	6%	7%	8%	9%	10%	11%	12%	13%	14%
1	1.000	1.000	1.000	1.000	1.000	1.000	1.000	1.000	1.000	1.000	1.000	1.000	1.000	1.000
2	2.010	2.020	2.030	2.040	2.050	2.060	2.070	2.080	2.090	2.100	2.110	2.120	2.130	2.140
3	3.030	3.060	3.091	3.122	3.153	3.184	3.215	3.246	3.278	3.310	3.342	3.374	3.407	3.440
4	4.060	4.122	4.184	4.246	4.310	4.375	4.440	4.506	4.573	4.641	4.710	4.779	4.850	4.921
5	5.101	5.204	5.309	5.416	5.526	5.637	5.751	5.867	5.985	6.105	6.228	6.353	6.480	6.610
6	6.152	6.308	6.468	6.633	6.802	6.975	7.153	7.336	7.523	7.716	7.913	8.115	8.323	8.536
7	7.214	7.434	7.662	7.898	8.142	8.394	8.654	8.923	9.200	9.487	9.783	10.089	10.405	10.730
8	8.286	8.583	8.892	9.214	9.549	9.897	10.260	10.637	11.028	11.436	11.859	12.300	12.757	13.233
9	9.369	9.755	10.159	10.583	11.027	11.491	11.978	12.488	13.021	13.579	14.164	14.776	15.416	16.085
10	10.462	10.950	11.464	12.006	12.578	13.181	13.816	14.487	15.193	15.937	16.722	17.549	18.420	19.337
11	11.567	12.169	12.808	13.486	14.207	14.972	15.784	16.645	17.560	18.531	19.561	20.655	21.814	23.045
12	12.683	13.412	14.192	15.026	15.917	16.870	17.888	18.977	20.141	21.384	22.713	24.133	25.650	27.271
13	13.809	14.680	15.618	16.627	17.713	18.882	20.141	21.495	22.953	24.523	26.212	28.029	29.985	32.089
14	14.947	15.974	17.086	18.292	19.599	21.015	22.550	24.215	26.019	27.975	30.095	32.393	34.883	37.581
15	16.097	17.293	18.599	20.024	21.579	23.276	25.129	27.152	29.361	31.772	34.405	37.280	40.417	43.842
16	17.258	18.639	20.157	21.825	23.657	25.673	27.888	30.324	33.003	35.950	39.190	42.753	46.672	50.980
17	18.430	20.012	21.762	23.698	25.840	28.213	30.840	33.750	36.974	40.545	44.501	48.884	53.739	59.118
18	19.615	21.412	23.414	25.645	28.132	30.906	33.999	37.450	41.301	45.599	50.396	55.750	61.725	68.394
19	20.811	22.841	25.117	27.671	30.539	33.760	37.379	41.446	46.018	51.159	56.939	63.440	70.749	78.969
20	22.019	24.297	26.870	29.778	33.066	36.786	40.995	45.762	51.160	57.275	64.203	72.052	80.947	91.025
25	28.243	32.030	36.459	41.646	47.727	54.865	63.249	73.106	84.701	98.347	114.413	133.334	155.620	181.871
30	34.785	40.568	47.575	56.085	66.439	79.058	94.461	113.283	136.308	164.494	199.021	241.333	293.199	356.787
40	48.886	60.402	75.401	95.026	120.800	154.762	199.635	259.057	337.882	442.593	581.826	767.091	1013.704	1342.025
50	64.463	84.579	112.797	152.667	209.348	290.336	406.529	573.770	815.084	1163.909	1668.771	2400.018	3459.507	4994.521

Interest Rate

(Contd..)

Table B Contd.

Interest Rate

Year	15%	16%	17%	18%	19%	20%	21%	22%	23%	24%	25%	30%	40%
1	1.000	1.000	1.000	1.000	1.000	1.000	1.000	1.000	1.000	1.000	1.000	1.000	1.000
2	2.150	2.160	2.170	2.180	2.190	2.200	2.210	2.220	2.230	2.240	2.250	2.300	2.400
3	3.473	3.506	3.539	3.572	3.606	3.640	3.674	3.708	3.743	3.778	3.813	3.990	4.360
4	4.993	5.066	5.141	5.215	5.291	5.368	5.446	5.524	5.604	5.684	5.766	6.187	7.104
5	6.742	6.877	7.014	7.154	7.297	7.442	7.589	7.740	7.893	8.048	8.207	9.043	10.946
6	8.754	8.977	9.207	9.442	9.683	9.930	10.183	10.442	10.708	10.980	11.259	12.756	16.324
7	11.067	11.414	11.772	12.142	12.523	12.916	13.321	13.740	14.171	14.615	15.073	17.583	23.853
8	13.727	14.240	14.773	15.327	15.902	16.499	17.119	17.762	18.430	19.123	19.842	23.858	34.395
9	16.786	17.519	18.285	19.086	19.923	20.799	21.714	22.670	23.669	24.712	25.802	32.015	49.153
10	20.304	21.321	22.393	23.521	24.709	25.959	27.274	28.657	30.113	31.643	33.253	42.619	69.814
11	24.349	25.733	27.200	28.755	30.404	32.150	34.001	35.962	38.039	40.238	42.566	56.405	98.739
12	29.002	30.850	32.824	34.931	37.180	39.581	42.142	44.874	47.788	50.895	54.208	74.327	139.235
13	34.352	36.786	39.404	42.219	45.244	48.497	51.991	55.746	59.779	64.110	68.760	97.625	195.929
14	40.505	43.672	47.103	50.818	54.841	59.196	63.909	69.010	74.528	80.496	86.949	127.913	275.300
15	47.580	51.660	56.110	60.965	66.261	72.035	78.330	85.192	92.669	100.815	109.687	167.286	386.420
16	55.717	60.925	66.649	72.939	79.850	87.442	95.780	104.935	114.983	126.011	138.109	218.472	541.988
17	65.075	71.673	78.979	87.068	96.022	105.931	116.894	129.020	142.430	157.253	173.636	285.014	759.784
18	75.836	84.141	93.406	103.740	115.266	128.117	142.441	158.405	176.188	195.994	218.045	371.518	1064.697
19	88.212	98.603	110.285	123.414	138.166	154.740	173.354	194.254	217.712	244.033	273.556	483.973	1491.576
20	102.444	115.380	130.033	146.628	165.418	186.688	210.758	237.989	268.785	303.601	342.945	630.165	2089.206
25	212.793	249.214	292.105	342.603	402.042	471.981	554.242	650.955	764.605	898.092	1054.791	2348.803	11247.199
30	434.745	530.312	647.439	790.948	966.712	1181.882	1445.151	1767.081	2160.491	2640.916	3227.174	8729.985	60501.081
40	1779.090	2360.757	3134.522	4163.213	5529.829	7343.858	9749.525	12936.535	17154.046	22728.803	30088.655	120392.883	1750091.741
50	7217.716	10435.649	15089.502	21813.094	31515.336	45497.191	65617.202	94525.279	135992.154	195372.644	280255.693	1659760.743	50622288.099

Table C: Present Value Factor of a Lump Sum (PVF) of Re 1

Year	1%	2%	3%	4%	5%	6%	7%	8%	9%	10%	11%	12%	13%	14%
1	0.990	0.980	0.971	0.962	0.952	0.943	0.935	0.926	0.917	0.909	0.901	0.893	0.885	0.877
2	0.980	0.961	0.943	0.925	0.907	0.890	0.873	0.857	0.842	0.826	0.812	0.797	0.783	0.769
3	0.971	0.942	0.915	0.889	0.864	0.840	0.816	0.794	0.772	0.751	0.731	0.712	0.693	0.675
4	0.961	0.924	0.888	0.855	0.823	0.792	0.763	0.735	0.708	0.683	0.659	0.636	0.613	0.592
5	0.951	0.906	0.863	0.822	0.784	0.747	0.713	0.681	0.650	0.621	0.593	0.567	0.543	0.519
6	0.942	0.888	0.837	0.790	0.746	0.705	0.666	0.630	0.596	0.564	0.535	0.507	0.480	0.456
7	0.933	0.871	0.813	0.760	0.711	0.665	0.623	0.583	0.547	0.513	0.482	0.452	0.425	0.400
8	0.923	0.853	0.789	0.731	0.677	0.627	0.582	0.540	0.502	0.467	0.434	0.404	0.376	0.351
9	0.914	0.837	0.766	0.703	0.645	0.592	0.544	0.500	0.460	0.424	0.391	0.361	0.333	0.308
10	0.905	0.820	0.744	0.676	0.614	0.558	0.508	0.463	0.422	0.386	0.352	0.322	0.295	0.270
11	0.896	0.804	0.722	0.650	0.585	0.527	0.475	0.429	0.388	0.350	0.317	0.287	0.261	0.237
12	0.887	0.788	0.701	0.625	0.557	0.497	0.444	0.397	0.356	0.319	0.286	0.257	0.231	0.208
13	0.879	0.773	0.681	0.601	0.530	0.469	0.415	0.368	0.326	0.290	0.258	0.229	0.204	0.182
14	0.870	0.758	0.661	0.577	0.505	0.442	0.388	0.340	0.299	0.263	0.232	0.205	0.181	0.160
15	0.861	0.743	0.642	0.555	0.481	0.417	0.362	0.315	0.275	0.239	0.209	0.183	0.160	0.140
16	0.853	0.728	0.623	0.534	0.458	0.394	0.339	0.292	0.252	0.218	0.188	0.163	0.141	0.123
17	0.844	0.714	0.605	0.513	0.436	0.371	0.317	0.270	0.231	0.198	0.170	0.146	0.125	0.108
18	0.836	0.700	0.587	0.494	0.416	0.350	0.296	0.250	0.212	0.180	0.153	0.130	0.111	0.095
19	0.828	0.686	0.570	0.475	0.396	0.331	0.277	0.232	0.194	0.164	0.138	0.116	0.098	0.083
20	0.820	0.673	0.554	0.456	0.377	0.312	0.258	0.215	0.178	0.149	0.124	0.104	0.087	0.073
25	0.780	0.610	0.478	0.375	0.295	0.233	0.184	0.146	0.116	0.092	0.074	0.059	0.047	0.038
30	0.742	0.552	0.412	0.308	0.231	0.174	0.131	0.099	0.075	0.057	0.044	0.033	0.026	0.020
40	0.672	0.453	0.307	0.208	0.142	0.097	0.067	0.046	0.032	0.022	0.015	0.011	0.008	0.005
50	0.608	0.372	0.228	0.141	0.087	0.054	0.034	0.021	0.013	0.009	0.005	0.003	0.002	0.001

Interest Rate

(Contd..)

Table C Contd.

Interest Rate

Year	15%	16%	17%	18%	19%	20%	21%	22%	23%	24%	25%	30%	40%
1	0.870	0.862	0.855	0.847	0.840	0.833	0.826	0.820	0.813	0.806	0.800	0.769	0.714
2	0.756	0.743	0.731	0.718	0.706	0.694	0.683	0.672	0.661	0.650	0.640	0.592	0.510
3	0.658	0.641	0.624	0.609	0.593	0.579	0.564	0.551	0.537	0.524	0.512	0.455	0.364
4	0.572	0.552	0.534	0.516	0.499	0.482	0.467	0.451	0.437	0.423	0.410	0.350	0.260
5	0.497	0.476	0.456	0.437	0.419	0.402	0.386	0.370	0.355	0.341	0.328	0.269	0.186
6	0.432	0.410	0.390	0.370	0.352	0.335	0.319	0.303	0.289	0.275	0.262	0.207	0.133
7	0.376	0.354	0.333	0.314	0.296	0.279	0.263	0.249	0.235	0.222	0.210	0.159	0.095
8	0.327	0.305	0.285	0.266	0.249	0.233	0.218	0.204	0.191	0.179	0.168	0.123	0.068
9	0.284	0.263	0.243	0.225	0.209	0.194	0.180	0.167	0.155	0.144	0.134	0.094	0.048
10	0.247	0.227	0.208	0.191	0.176	0.162	0.149	0.137	0.126	0.116	0.107	0.073	0.035
11	0.215	0.195	0.178	0.162	0.148	0.135	0.123	0.112	0.103	0.094	0.086	0.056	0.025
12	0.187	0.168	0.152	0.137	0.124	0.112	0.102	0.092	0.083	0.076	0.069	0.043	0.018
13	0.163	0.145	0.130	0.116	0.104	0.093	0.084	0.075	0.068	0.061	0.055	0.033	0.013
14	0.141	0.125	0.111	0.099	0.088	0.078	0.069	0.062	0.055	0.049	0.044	0.025	0.009
15	0.123	0.108	0.095	0.084	0.074	0.065	0.057	0.051	0.045	0.040	0.035	0.020	0.006
16	0.107	0.093	0.081	0.071	0.062	0.054	0.047	0.042	0.036	0.032	0.028	0.015	0.005
17	0.093	0.080	0.069	0.060	0.052	0.045	0.039	0.034	0.030	0.026	0.023	0.012	0.003
18	0.081	0.069	0.059	0.051	0.044	0.038	0.032	0.028	0.024	0.021	0.018	0.009	0.002
19	0.070	0.060	0.051	0.043	0.037	0.031	0.027	0.023	0.020	0.017	0.014	0.007	0.002
20	0.061	0.051	0.043	0.037	0.031	0.026	0.022	0.019	0.016	0.014	0.012	0.005	0.001
25	0.030	0.024	0.020	0.016	0.013	0.010	0.009	0.007	0.006	0.005	0.004	0.001	0.000
30	0.015	0.012	0.009	0.007	0.005	0.004	0.003	0.003	0.002	0.002	0.001	0.000	0.000
40	0.004	0.003	0.002	0.001	0.001	0.001	0.000	0.000	0.000	0.000	0.000	0.000	0.000
50	0.001	0.001	0.000	0.000	0.000	0.000	0.000	0.000	0.000	0.000	0.000	0.000	0.000

Table D: Present Value Factor of an Annuity (PVFA) of Re 1

Interest Rate

Year	1%	2%	3%	4%	5%	6%	7%	8%	9%	10%	11%	12%	13%	14%
1	0.990	0.980	0.971	0.962	0.952	0.943	0.935	0.926	0.917	0.909	0.901	0.893	0.885	0.877
2	1.970	1.942	1.913	1.886	1.859	1.833	1.808	1.783	1.759	1.736	1.713	1.690	1.668	1.647
3	2.941	2.884	2.829	2.775	2.723	2.673	2.624	2.577	2.531	2.487	2.444	2.402	2.361	2.322
4	3.902	3.808	3.717	3.630	3.546	3.465	3.387	3.312	3.240	3.170	3.102	3.037	2.974	2.914
5	4.853	4.713	4.580	4.452	4.329	4.212	4.100	3.993	3.890	3.791	3.696	3.605	3.517	3.433
6	5.795	5.601	5.417	5.242	5.076	4.917	4.767	4.623	4.486	4.355	4.231	4.111	3.998	3.889
7	6.728	6.472	6.230	6.002	5.786	5.582	5.389	5.206	5.033	4.868	4.712	4.564	4.423	4.288
8	7.652	7.325	7.020	6.733	6.463	6.210	5.971	5.747	5.535	5.335	5.146	4.968	4.799	4.639
9	8.566	8.162	7.786	7.435	7.108	6.802	6.515	6.247	5.995	5.759	5.537	5.328	5.132	4.946
10	9.471	8.983	8.530	8.111	7.722	7.360	7.024	6.710	6.418	6.145	5.889	5.650	5.426	5.216
11	10.368	9.787	9.253	8.760	8.306	7.887	7.499	7.139	6.805	6.495	6.207	5.938	5.687	5.453
12	11.255	10.575	9.954	9.385	8.863	8.384	7.943	7.536	7.161	6.814	6.492	6.194	5.918	5.660
13	12.134	11.348	10.635	9.986	9.394	8.853	8.358	7.904	7.487	7.103	6.750	6.424	6.122	5.842
14	13.004	12.106	11.296	10.563	9.899	9.295	8.745	8.244	7.786	7.367	6.982	6.628	6.302	6.002
15	13.865	12.849	11.938	11.118	10.380	9.712	9.108	8.559	8.061	7.606	7.191	6.811	6.462	6.142
16	14.718	13.578	12.561	11.652	10.838	10.106	9.447	8.851	8.313	7.824	7.379	6.974	6.604	6.265
17	15.562	14.292	13.166	12.166	11.274	10.477	9.763	9.122	8.544	8.022	7.549	7.120	6.729	6.373
18	16.398	14.992	13.754	12.659	11.690	10.828	10.059	9.372	8.756	8.201	7.702	7.250	6.840	6.467
19	17.226	15.678	14.324	13.134	12.085	11.158	10.336	9.604	8.950	8.365	7.839	7.366	6.938	6.550
20	18.046	16.351	14.877	13.590	12.462	11.470	10.594	9.818	9.129	8.514	7.963	7.469	7.025	6.623
25	22.023	19.523	17.413	15.622	14.094	12.783	11.654	10.675	9.823	9.077	8.422	7.843	7.330	6.873
30	25.808	22.396	19.600	17.292	15.372	13.765	12.409	11.258	10.274	9.427	8.694	8.055	7.496	7.003
40	32.835	27.355	23.115	19.793	17.159	15.046	13.332	11.925	10.757	9.779	8.951	8.244	7.634	7.105
50	39.196	31.424	25.730	21.482	18.256	15.762	13.801	12.233	10.962	9.915	9.042	8.304	7.675	7.133

(Contd..)

Table D Contd.

Year	15%	16%	17%	18%	19%	20%	21%	22%	23%	24%	25%	30%	40%
						Interest Rate							
1	0.870	0.862	0.855	0.847	0.840	0.833	0.826	0.820	0.813	0.806	0.800	0.769	0.714
2	1.626	1.605	1.585	1.566	1.547	1.528	1.509	1.492	1.474	1.457	1.440	1.361	1.224
3	2.283	2.246	2.210	2.174	2.140	2.106	2.074	2.042	2.011	1.981	1.952	1.816	1.589
4	2.855	2.798	2.743	2.690	2.639	2.589	2.540	2.494	2.448	2.404	2.362	2.166	1.849
5	3.352	3.274	3.199	3.127	3.058	2.991	2.926	2.864	2.803	2.745	2.689	2.436	2.035
6	3.784	3.685	3.589	3.498	3.410	3.326	3.245	3.167	3.092	3.020	2.951	2.643	2.168
7	4.1o0	4.039	3.922	3.812	3.706	3.605	3.508	3.416	3.327	3.242	3.161	2.802	2.263
8	4.487	4.344	4.207	4.078	3.954	3.837	3.726	3.619	3.518	3.421	3.329	2.925	2.331
9	4.772	4.607	4.451	4.303	4.163	4.031	3.905	3.786	3.673	3.566	3.463	3.019	2.379
10	5.019	4.833	4.659	4.494	4.339	4.192	4.054	3.923	3.799	3.682	3.571	3.092	2.414
11	5.234	5.029	4.836	4.656	4.486	4.327	4.177	4.035	3.902	3.776	3.656	3.147	2.438
12	5.421	5.197	4.988	4.793	4.611	4.439	4.278	4.127	3.985	3.851	3.725	3.190	2.456
13	5.583	5.342	5.118	4.910	4.715	4.533	4.362	4.203	4.053	3.912	3.780	3.223	2.469
14	5.724	5.468	5.229	5.008	4.802	4.611	4.432	4.265	4.108	3.962	3.824	3.249	2.478
15	5.847	5.575	5.324	5.092	4.876	4.675	4.489	4.315	4.153	4.001	3.859	3.268	2.484
16	5.954	5.668	5.405	5.162	4.938	4.730	4.536	4.357	4.189	4.033	3.887	3.283	2.489
17	6.047	5.749	5.475	5.222	4.990	4.775	4.576	4.391	4.219	4.059	3.910	3.295	2.492
18	6.128	5.818	5.534	5.273	5.033	4.812	4.608	4.419	4.243	4.080	3.928	3.304	2.494
19	6.198	5.877	5.584	5.316	5.070	4.843	4.635	4.442	4.263	4.097	3.942	3.311	2.496
20	6.259	5.929	5.628	5.353	5.101	4.870	4.657	4.460	4.279	4.110	3.954	3.316	2.497
25	6.464	6.097	5.766	5.467	5.195	4.948	4.721	4.514	4.323	4.147	3.985	3.329	2.499
30	6.566	6.177	5.829	5.517	5.235	4.979	4.746	4.534	4.339	4.160	3.995	3.332	2.500
40	6.642	6.233	5.871	5.548	5.258	4.997	4.760	4.544	4.347	4.166	3.999	3.333	2.500
50	6.661	6.246	5.880	5.554	5.262	4.999	4.762	4.545	4.348	4.167	4.000	3.333	2.500

Table E: Continuous Compounding of Re 1 e^x and Continuous Discounting of Re 1

$$(e^x): \lim_{m \to \infty} \left(1+\frac{i}{m}\right)^{(nm)} \quad \text{or} \quad e^{(i)(n)}$$

x	e^x Value	e^{-x} Value	x	e^x Value	e^{-x} Value	x	e^x Value	e^{-x} Value
0.00	1.0000	1.00000	0.45	1.5683	.63763	0.90	2.4596	.40657
0.01	1.0110	0.99005	0.46	1.5841	.63128	0.91	2.4843	.40252
0.02	1.0202	.98020	0.47	1.6000	.62500	0.92	2.5093	.39852
0.03	1.0305	.97045	0.48	1.6161	.61878	0.93	2.5345	.39455
0.04	1.0408	.96079	0.49	1.6323	.61263	0.94	2.5600	.39063
0.05	1.0513	.95123	0.50	1.6487	.60653	0.95	2.5857	.38674
0.06	1.0618	.94176	0.51	1.6653	.60050	0.96	2.6117	.38298
0.07	1.0725	.93239	0.52	1.6820	.59452	0.97	2.6379	.37908
0.08	1.0833	.92312	0.53	1.6989	.58860	0.98	2.6645	.37531
0.09	1.0942	.91393	0.54	1.7160	.58275	0.99	2.6912	.37158
0.10	1.1052	.90484	0.55	1.7333	.57695	1.00	2.7183	.36788
0.11	1.1163	.89583	0.56	1.7307	.57121	1.20	3.3201	.30119
0.12	1.1275	.88692	0.57	1.7683	.56553	1.30	3.6693	.27253
0.13	1.1388	.87809	0.58	1.7860	.55990	1.40	4.0552	.24660
0.14	1.1503	.86936	0.59	1.8040	.55433	1.50	4.4817	.22313
0.15	1.1618	.86071	0.60	1.8221	.54881	1.60	4.9530	.20190
0.16	1.1735	.85214	0.61	1.8404	.54335	1.70	5.4739	.18268
0.17	1.1853	.84366	0.62	1.8589	.53794	1.80	6.0496	.16530
0.18	1.1972	.83527	0.63	1.8776	.53259	1.90	6.6859	.14957
0.19	1.2092	.82696	0.64	1.9865	.52729	2.00	7.3891	.13534
0.20	1.2214	.81873	0.65	1.9155	.52205	3.00	20.086	.04979
0.21	1.2337	.81058	0.66	1.9348	.51885	4.00	54.598	.01832
0.22	1.2461	.80252	0.67	1.9542	.51171	5.00	148.41	.00674
0.23	1.2586	.79453	0.68	1.9739	.50662	6.00	403.43	.00248
0.24	1.2712	.78663	0.69	1.9937	.50158	7.00	1096.6	.00091
0.25	1.2840	.77880	0.70	2.0138	.49659	8.00	2981.0	.00034
0.26	1.2969	.77105	0.71	2.0340	.49164	9.00	8103.1	.00012
0.27	1.3100	.76338	0.72	2.0544	.48675	10.00	22026.5	.00005
0.28	1.3231	.75578	0.73	2.0751	.48191			
0.29	1.3364	.74826	0.74	2.0959	.47711			
0.30	1.3499	.74082	0.75	2.1170	.47237			
0.31	1.3634	.73345	0.76	2.1383	.46767			
0.32	1.3771	.72615	0.77	2.1598	.46301			
0.33	1.3910	.71892	0.78	2.1815	.45841			
0.34	1.4049	.71177	0.79	2.2034	.45384			
0.35	1.4191	.70569	0.80	2.2255	.44933			
0.36	1.4333	.69768	0.81	2.2479	.44486			
0.37	1.4477	.69073	0.82	2.2705	.44043			
0.38	1.4623	.68386	0.83	2.2933	.43605			
0.39	1.4770	.67707	0.84	2.3164	.43171			
0.40	1.4918	.67032	0.85	2.3396	.42741			
0.41	1.5068	.66365	0.86	2.3632	.42316			
0.42	1.5220	.65705	0.87	2.3869	.41895			
0.43	1.5373	.65051	0.88	2.4109	.41478			
0.44	1.5527	.64404	0.89	2.4351	.41066			

Table F: Value of the Standard Normal Distribution Function

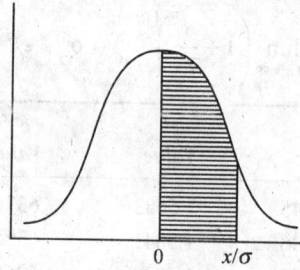

d	.00	.01	.02	.03	.04	.05	.06	.07	.08	.09
0.0	.0000	.0040	.0080	.0120	.0160	.0199	.0239	.0279	.0319	.0359
0.1	.0398	.0438	.0478	.0517	.0557	.0596	.0636	.0675	.0714	.0753
0.2	.0793	.0832	.0871	.0910	.0948	.0987	.1026	.1064	.1103	.1141
0.3	.1179	.1217	.1255	.1293	.1331	.1368	.1406	.1443	.1480	.1517
0.4	.1554	.1591	.1688	.1664	.1700	.1736	.1772	.1808	.1844	.1879
0.5	.1915	.1950	.1985	.2019	.2054	.2088	.2123	.2157	.2190	.2224
0.6	.2257	.2291	.2324	.2357	.2389	.2422	.2454	.2486	.2517	.2549
0.7	.2580	.2611	.2642	.2673	.2704	.2734	.2764	.2794	.2823	.2852
0.8	.2818	.2910	.2939	.2967	.2995	.3023	.3051	.3078	.3106	.3133
0.9	.3159	.3186	.3212	.3238	.3264	.3289	.3315	.3340	.3365	.3389
1.0	.3413	.3438	.3461	.3485	.3508	.3531	.3554	.3577	.3599	.3621
1.1	.3643	.3665	.3686	.3708	.3729	.3749	.3770	.3790	.3810	.3830
1.2	.3849	.3869	.3888	.3907	.3925	.3944	.3962	.3980	.3997	.4015
1.3	.4032	.4049	.4066	.4082	.4099	.4115	.4131	.4147	.4162	.4177
1.4	.4192	.4207	.4222	.4236	.4251	.4265	.4279	.4292	.4306	.4319
1.5	.4332	.4345	.4357	.4370	.4382	.4394	.4406	.4418	.4429	.4441
1.6	.4452	.4463	.4474	.4484	.4495	.4505	.4515	.4525	.4535	.4545
1.7	.4554	.4564	.4573	.4582	.4591	.4599	.4608	.4616	.4625	.4633
1.8	.4641	.4649	.4656	.4664	.4671	.4678	.4686	.4693	.4699	.4706
1.9	.4713	.4719	.4726	.4732	.4738	.4744	.4750	.4756	.4761	.4767
2.0	.4772	.4778	.4783	.4788	.4793	.4798	.4803	.4808	.4812	.4817
2.1	.4821	.4826	.4830	.4834	.4838	.4842	.4846	.4850	.4854	.4857
2.2	.4861	.4864	.4868	.4871	.4875	.4878	.4881	.4884	.4887	.4890
2.3	.4893	.4896	.4898	.4901	.4904	.4906	.4909	.4911	.4913	.4916
2.4	.4918	.4920	.4922	.4925	.4927	.4929	.4931	.4932	.4934	.4936
2.5	.4938	.4940	.4941	.4943	.4945	.4946	.4948	.4949	.4951	.4952
2.6	.4953	.4955	.4956	.4957	.4959	.4960	.4961	.4962	.4963	.4964
2.7	.4965	.4966	.4967	.4968	.4969	.4970	.4971	.4972	.4973	.4974
2.8	.4974	.4975	.4976	.4977	.4977	.4978	.4979	.4979	.4980	.4981
2.9	.4981	.4982	.4982	.4983	.4984	.4984	.4985	.4985	.4986	.4986
3.0	.4987	.4987	.4987	.4988	.4988	.4989	.4989	.4989	.4990	.4990

Table G: Comulative Distribution Function for the Standard Normal Random Variable

d	.00	.01	.02	.03	.04	.05	.06	.07	.08	.09
−0.0	0.5000	0.4960	0.4920	0.4880	0.4840	0.4801	0.4761	0.4721	0.4681	0.4641
−0.1	0.4602	0.4562	0.4522	0.4483	0.4443	0.4404	0.4364	0.4325	0.4286	0.4247
−0.2	0.4207	0.4168	0.4129	0.4090	0.4052	0.4013	0.3974	0.3936	0.3897	0.3859
−0.3	0.3821	0.3783	0.3745	0.3707	0.3669	0.3632	0.3594	0.3557	0.3520	0.3483
−0.4	0.3446	0.3409	0.3372	0.3336	0.3300	0.3264	0.3228	0.3192	0.3156	0.3121
−0.5	0.3085	0.3050	0.3015	0.2981	0.2946	0.2912	0.2877	0.2843	0.2810	0.2776
−0.6	0.2743	0.2709	0.2676	0.2643	0.2611	0.2578	0.2546	0.2514	0.2483	0.2451
−0.7	0.2420	0.2389	0.2358	0.2327	0.2296	0.2266	0.2236	0.2206	0.2177	0.2148
−0.8	0.2119	0.2090	0.2061	0.2033	0.2005	0.1977	0.1949	0.1922	0.1894	0.1867
−0.9	0.1841	0.1814	0.1788	0.1762	0.1736	0.1711	0.1685	0.1660	0.1635	0.1611
−1.0	0.1587	0.1562	0.1539	0.1515	0.1492	0.1469	0.1446	0.1423	0.1401	0.1379
−1.1	0.1357	0.1335	0.1314	0.1292	0.1271	0.1251	0.1230	0.1210	0.1190	0.1170
−1.2	0.1151	0.1131	0.1112	0.1093	0.1075	0.1056	0.1038	0.1020	0.1003	0.0985
−1.3	0.0968	0.0951	0.0934	0.0918	0.0901	0.0885	0.0869	0.0853	0.0838	0.0823
−1.4	0.0808	0.0793	0.0778	0.0764	0.0749	0.0735	0.0721	0.0708	0.0694	0.0681
−1.5	0.0668	0.0655	0.0643	0.0630	0.0618	0.0606	0.0594	0.0582	0.0571	0.0559
−1.6	0.0548	0.0537	0.0526	0.0516	0.0505	0.0495	0.0485	0.0475	0.0465	0.0455
−1.7	0.0446	0.0436	0.0427	0.0418	0.0409	0.0401	0.0392	0.0384	0.0375	0.0367
−1.8	0.0359	0.0351	0.0344	0.0336	0.0329	0.0322	0.0314	0.0307	0.0301	0.0294
−1.9	0.0287	0.0281	0.0274	0.0268	0.0262	0.0202	0.0250	0.0244	0.0239	0.0233
−2.0	0.0228	0.0222	0.0217	0.0212	0.0207	0.0158	0.0197	0.0192	0.0188	0.0183
−2.1	0.0179	0.0174	0.0170	0.0166	0.0162	0.0122	0.0154	0.0150	0.0146	0.0143
−2.2	0.0139	0.0136	0.0132	0.0129	0.0125	0.0094	0.0119	0.0116	0.0113	0.0110
−2.3	0.0107	0.0104	0.0102	0.0099	0.0096	0.0071	0.0091	0.0089	0.0087	0.0084
−2.4	0.0082	0.0080	0.0078	0.0075	0.0073	0.0054	0.0069	0.0068	0.0066	0.0064
−2.5	0.0062	0.0060	0.0059	0.0057	0.0055	0.0040	0.0092	0.0051	0.0049	0.0048
−2.6	0.0047	0.0045	0.0044	0.0043	0.0041	0.0030	0.0039	0.0038	0.0037	0.0036
−2.7	0.0035	0.0034	0.0033	0.0032	0.0031	0.0022	0.0029	0.0028	0.0027	0.0026
−2.8	0.0026	0.0025	0.0024	0.0023	0.0023	0.0016	0.0021	0.0021	0.0020	0.0019
−2.9	0.0019	0.0018	0.0018	0.0017	0.0016	0.0011	0.0015	0.0015	0.0014	0.0014
−3.0	0.0014	0.0013	0.0013	0.0012	0.0012	0.0008	0.0011	0.0011	0.0010	0.0010
−3.1	0.0010	0.0009	0.0009	0.0009	0.0008	0.0006	0.0008	0.0008	0.0007	0.0007
−3.2	0.0007	0.0007	0.0006	0.0006	0.0006	0.0004	0.0006	0.0005	0.0005	0.0005
−3.3	0.0005	0.0005	0.0005	0.0004	0.0004	0.0003	0.0004	0.0004	0.0004	0.0004
−3.4	0.0003	0.0003	0.0003	0.0003	0.0003	0.0002	0.0003	0.0003	0.0003	0.0003
−3.5	0.0002	0.0002	0.0002	0.0002	0.0002	0.0001	0.0002	0.0002	0.0002	0.0002
−3.6	0.0002	0.0001	0.0001	0.0001	0.0001	0.0001	0.0001	0.0001	0.0001	0.0001
−3.7	0.0001	0.0001	0.0001	0.0001	0.0001	0.0001	0.0001	0.0001	0.0001	0.0001
−3.8	0.0001	0.0001	0.0001	0.0001	0.0001	0.0001	0.0001	0.0001	0.0001	0.0001
−3.9	0.0000	0.0000	0.0000	0.0000	0.0000	0.0000	0.0000	0.0000	0.0000	0.0000
−4.0	0.0000	0.0000	0.0000	0.0000	0.0000	0.0000	0.0000	0.0000	0.0000	0.0000

(Contd..)

Table G Contd.

d	.00	.01	.02	.03	.04	.05	.06	.07	.08	.09
0.0	0.5000	0.5040	0.5080	0.5120	0.5160	0.5199	0.5239	0.9279	0.5319	0.5359
0.1	0.5398	0.5438	0.5478	0.5517	0.5557	0.5596	0.5636	0.5675	0.5714	0.5753
0.2	0.5793	0.5832	0.5871	0.5910	0.5948	0.5987	0.6026	0.6064	0.6103	0.6141
0.3	0.6179	0.6217	0.6255	0.6293	0.6331	0.6368	0.6406	0.6443	0.6480	0.6517
0.4	0.6554	0.6591	0.6628	0.6664	0.6700	0.6736	0.6772	0.6808	0.6844	0.6879
0.5	0.6915	0.6950	0.6985	0.7019	0.7054	0.7088	0.7123	0.7157	0.7190	0.7224
0.6	0.7257	0.7291	0.7324	0.7357	0.7389	0.7422	0.7454	0.7486	0.7517	0.7549
0.7	0.7580	0.7611	0.7642	0.7673	0.7704	0.7734	0.7764	0.7794	0.7823	0.7852
0.8	0.7881	0.7910	0.7939	0.7967	0.7995	0.8023	0.8051	0.8078	0.8106	0.8133
0.9	0.8159	0.8186	0.8212	0.8238	0.8264	0.8289	0.8315	0.8340	0.8365	0.8389
1.0	0.8413	0.8438	0.8461	0.8485	0.8508	0.8531	0.8554	0.8577	0.8599	0.8621
1.1	0.8643	0.8665	0.8686	0.8708	0.8729	0.8749	0.8770	0.8790	0.8810	0.8830
1.2	0.8849	0.8869	0.8888	0.8907	0.8925	0.8944	0.8962	0.8980	0.8997	0.9015
1.3	0.9032	0.9049	0.9066	0.9082	0.9099	0.9115	0.9131	0.9147	0.9162	0.9177
1.4	0.9192	0.9207	0.9222	0.9236	0.9251	0.9265	0.9279	0.9292	0.9306	0.9319
1.5	0.9332	0.9345	0.9357	0.9370	0.9382	0.9394	0.9406	0.9418	0.9429	0.9441
1.6	0.9452	0.9463	0.9474	0.9484	0.9495	0.9505	0.9515	0.9525	0.9535	0.9595
1.7	0.9554	0.9564	0.9573	0.9582	0.9591	0.9599	0.9608	0.9616	0.9625	0.9633
1.8	0.9641	0.9649	0.9656	0.9664	0.9671	0.9678	0.9686	0.9693	0.9699	0.9706
1.9	0.9713	0.9719	0.9726	0.9732	0.9738	0.9744	0.9750	0.9756	0.9761	0.9767
2.0	0.9772	0.9778	0.9783	0.9788	0.9793	0.9798	0.9803	0.9808	0.9812	0.9817
2.1	0.9821	0.9826	0.9830	0.9834	0.9838	0.9842	0.9846	0.9850	0.9854	0.9857
2.2	0.9861	0.9864	0.9868	0.9871	0.9875	0.9878	0.9881	0.9884	0.9887	0.9890
2.3	0.9893	0.9896	0.9898	0.9901	0.9904	0.9906	0.9909	0.9911	0.9913	0.9916
2.4	0.9918	0.9920	0.9922	0.9925	0.9927	0.9929	0.9931	0.9932	0.9934	0.9936
2.5	0.9938	0.9940	0.9941	0.9943	0.9945	0.9946	0.9948	0.9949	0.9991	0.9952
2.6	0.9953	0.9955	0.9956	0.9957	0.9959	0.9960	0.9961	0.9962	0.9963	0.9964
2.7	0.9965	0.9966	0.9967	0.9968	0.9969	0.9970	0.9971	0.9972	0.9973	0.9974
2.8	0.9974	0.9975	0.9976	0.9977	0.9977	0.9978	0.9979	0.9979	0.9980	0.9981
2.9	0.9981	0.9982	0.9982	0.9983	0.9984	0.9984	0.9985	0.9985	0.9986	0.9986
3.0	0.9986	0.9987	0.9987	0.9988	0.9988	0.9989	0.9989	0.9989	0.9990	0.9990
3.1	0.9990	0.9991	0.9991	0.9991	0.9992	0.9992	0.9992	0.9992	0.9993	0.9993
3.2	0.9993	0.9993	0.9994	0.9994	0.9994	0.9994	0.9994	0.9995	0.9995	0.9995
3.3	0.9995	0.9995	0.9995	0.9996	0.9996	0.9996	0.9996	0.9996	0.9996	0.9997
3.4	0.9997	0.9997	0.9997	0.9997	0.9997	0.9997	0.9997	0.9997	0.9997	0.9998
3.5	0.9998	0.9998	0.9998	0.9998	0.9998	0.9998	0.9998	0.9998	0.9998	0.9998
3.6	0.9998	0.9998	0.9999	0.9999	0.9999	0.9999	0.9999	0.9999	0.9999	0.9999
3.7	0.9999	0.9999	0.9999	0.9999	0.9999	0.9999	0.9999	0.9999	0.9999	0.9999
3.8	0.9999	0.9999	0.9999	0.9999	0.9999	0.9999	0.9999	0.9999	0.9999	0.9999
3.9	1.0000	1.0000	1.0000	1.0000	1.0000	1.0000	1.0000	1.0000	1.0000	1.0000
4.0	1.0000	1.0000	1.0000	1.0000	1.0000	1.0000	1.0000	1.0000	1.0000	1.0000

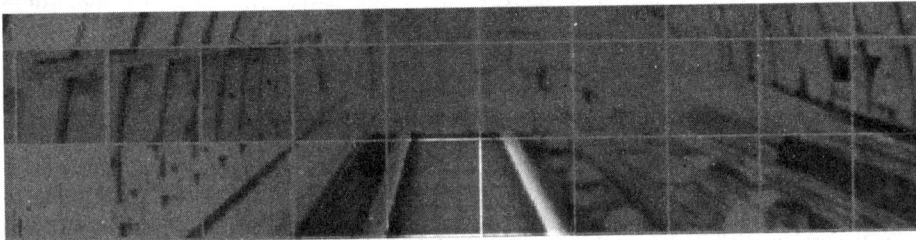

Author Index

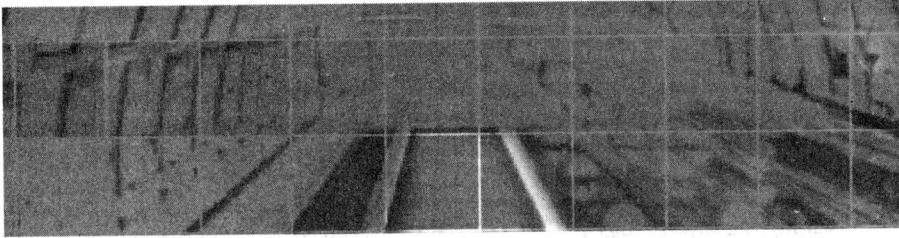

Subject Index